ORIGINAL VERSION

ETHIOPIAN BIBLE

In English

The Complete Encyclopedia, Including The Missing Deuterocanonical Apocrypha Enoch, Jubilees, Meqabyan And The Lost Writings.

88

Books

Edward Jones

Copyright Notice:

Disclaimer:

This book presents a unique selection of sacred texts from the Ethiopian Bible, carefully translated and curated from original manuscripts written in Ge'ez, Hebrew, and other ancient languages. The texts have been organized to provide a comprehensive and accessible resource for readers interested in exploring the rich biblical tradition of the Ethiopian Orthodox Tewahedo Church. The author has introduced and commented on the material to offer context and facilitate reflection.

Limitation of Liability:

GO TO THE END OF THE BOOK AND SCAN THE QR CODE, TO ACCESS YOUR PRIVATE AREA

INSIDE THE APP YOU WILL FIND:

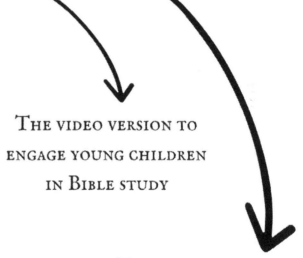

THE DIGITAL VERSION OF THE BIBLE SO YOU CAN READ IT ANYTIME.

THE VIDEO VERSION TO ENGAGE YOUNG CHILDREN IN BIBLE STUDY

A DEDICATED FORUM TO EXCHANGE OPINIONS AND THOUGHTS WITH OTHER READERS

THE FULL AUDIO VERSION OF THE BIBLE SO YOU CAN LISTEN TO IT QUIETLY DURING A TRIP.

TABLE OF CONTENT

Introduction

The Ethiopian Bible, known as one of the oldest and most complete collections of sacred texts, is a spiritual and cultural heritage that dates back to the early history of Christianity. Written in the revered Ge'ez language, an ancient Semitic language of the Horn of Africa, it is much more than a simple religious text: it represents the heart of the faith and identity of the Ethiopian people. Its 88 books differ significantly from Western versions, such as the King James Version (KJV), which contains only 66 books.

The origins of the Ethiopian Bible are closely linked to the spread of Christianity in Ethiopia, one of the first nations in the world to adopt Christianity as the state religion in the 4th century AD, during the reign of King Ezana of Axum. The translation of the Bible into Ge'ez, which probably took place around the 5th century, allowed the Ethiopian people to access the Holy Scriptures directly, contributing to the establishment of a unique religious tradition distinct from other Eastern and Western Christian currents.

This Bible is distinguished by its richness and variety, offering a view of early Christianity that includes universally recognized canonical texts and a vast array of deuterocanonical and apocryphal writings. The **Old Testament** of the Ethiopian Bible includes the books of the **Pentateuch**—Genesis, Exodus, Leviticus, Numbers, and Deuteronomy—that form the basis of the Mosaic law. These are followed by the **Historical Books**, which narrate the people's events of Israel, from the conquest of the Promised Land under Joshua to the post-exilic period. This section also features texts exclusive to the Ethiopian tradition, such as the Additions to Esther, 1 and 2 Esdras, and the two books of Baruch, enriching the biblical narrative with unique perspectives and details.

The **Wisdom Books** provide philosophical and moral reflections through works such as the **Wisdom of Solomon** and **Sirach**, along with the Psalms and the additional Psalm 151, a text not included in the Hebrew and Western Christian canon. The **Prophetic Books**, which include Isaiah, Jeremiah, Ezekiel, and the twelve minor prophets, are complemented by additional writings such as the **Prayer of Azariah**, **Susanna**, and **Bel and the Dragon**, offering a broader prophetic and apocalyptic picture compared to other biblical traditions.

The **New Testament** opens with the four canonical Gospels and continues with the **Acts of the Apostles** and the Pauline epistles, including the rare addition of 1 Clement, an apostolic letter that attests to the authority and influence of the early Church. Moreover, the apocalyptic section is vibrant, including the **Book of Revelation** and texts such as the two books of Enoch and the **Jubilees**, which provide essential prophetic and cosmological visions for Ethiopian theology.

A distinctive and fascinating feature of the Ethiopian Bible is the inclusion of the Books of Meqabyan I-III, a set of texts unrelated to the Maccabees found in other traditions but dealing with themes of faith and resistance. These texts, along with the Prayer of Manasseh, complete a collection that, with its 88 books, represents the most extensive and inclusive biblical tradition.

The Ethiopian Bible is not just a sacred text for the Ethiopian Orthodox Tewahedo Church but also a source of identity and unity for the Ethiopian people. The Bible provided strength and hope during centuries of challenges, invasions, and oppressions, serving as a spiritual and cultural guide. Today, it represents a treasure for the world, offering a glimpse into an ancient Christianity whose roots intertwine with the earliest Christian communities in the Middle East and Africa.

For scholars, believers, and the curious, the Ethiopian Bible invites exploration into a rich and diverse tradition that challenges the boundaries of the conventional biblical canon and opens up new perspectives on the meaning of faith and revelation. Its extraordinary preservation and the dedication with which it has been passed down through the centuries testify to its importance for Ethiopia and all humanity.

The Pentateuch (Torah or Law)

Genesis

Genesis Chapter 1

1 In the beginning, when God created the heavens and the earth,2 the earth was a formless wasteland, and darkness covered the abyss, while a mighty wind swept over the waters. 3 Then God said, "Let there be light," and there was light. 4 God saw how good the light was. God then separated the light from the darkness. 5 God called the light "day," and the darkness he called "night." Thus evening came, and morning followed - the first day.6 Then God said, "Let there be a dome in the middle of the waters, to separate one body of water from the other." And so it happened: 7 God made the dome, and it separated the water above the dome from the water below it. 8 God called the dome "the sky." Evening came, and morning followed - the second day. 9 Then God said, "Let the water under the sky be gathered into a single basin, so that the dry land may appear." And so it happened: the water under the sky was gathered into its basin, and the dry land appeared. 10 God called the dry land "the earth," and the basin of the water he called "the sea." God saw how good it was. 11 Then God said, "Let the earth bring forth vegetation: every kind of plant that bears seed and every kind of fruit tree on earth that bears fruit with its seed in it." And so it happened: 12 the earth brought forth every kind of plant that bears seed and every kind of fruit tree on earth that bears fruit with its seed in it. God saw how good it was. 13 Evening came, and morning followed - the third day.14 Then God said: "Let there be lights in the dome of the sky, to separate day from night. Let them mark the fixed times, the days and the years,15 and serve as luminaries in the dome of the sky, to shed light upon the earth." And so it happened: 16 God made the two great lights, the greater one to govern the day, and the lesser one to govern the night; and he made the stars. 17 God set them in the dome of the sky, to shed light upon the earth, 18 to govern the day and the night, and to separate the light from the darkness. God saw how good it was. 19 Evening came, and morning followed - the fourth day. 20 Then God said, "Let the water teem with an abundance of living creatures, and on the earth let birds fly beneath the dome of the sky." And so it happened: 21 God created the great sea monsters and all kinds of swimming creatures with which the water teems, and all kinds of winged birds. 22 God saw how good it was, and God blessed them, saying, "Be fertile, multiply, and fill the water of the seas; and let the birds multiply on the earth." 23 Evening came, and morning followed - the fifth day. 24 Then God said, "Let the earth bring forth all kinds of living creatures: cattle, creeping things, and wild animals of all kinds." And so it happened: 25 God made all kinds of wild animals, all kinds of cattle, and all kinds of creeping things of the earth. God saw how good it was. 26 Then God said: "Let us make man in our image, after our likeness. Let them have dominion over the fish of the sea, the birds of the air, and the cattle, and over all the wild animals and all the creatures that crawl on the ground." 27 God created man in his image; in the divine image he created him; male and female he created them. 28 God blessed them, saying: "Be fertile and multiply; fill the earth and subdue it. Have dominion over the fish of the sea, the birds of the air, and all the living things that move on the earth." 29 God also said: "See, I give you every seed-bearing plant all over the earth and every tree that has seed-bearing fruit on it to be your food; 30 and to all the animals of the land, all the birds of the air, and all the living creatures that crawl on the ground, I give all the green plants for food." And so it happened. 31 God looked at everything he had made, and he found it very good. Evening came, and morning followed - the sixth day.

Genesis Chapter 2

1 Thus the heavens and the earth and all their array were completed. 2 Since on the seventh day God was finished with the work he had been doing, he rested on the seventh day from all the work he had undertaken. 3 So God blessed the seventh day and made it holy, because on it he rested from all the work he had done in creation. 4 Such is the story of the heavens and the earth at their creation. At the time when the LORD God made the earth and the heavens - 5 while as yet there was no field shrub on earth and no grass of the field had sprouted, for the LORD God had sent no rain upon the earth and there was no man to till the soil, 6 but a stream was welling up out of the earth and was watering all the surface of the ground - 7 The LORD God formed man out of the clay of the ground and blew into his nostrils the breath of life, and so man became a living being. 8 Then the LORD God planted a garden in Eden, in the east, and he placed there the man whom he had formed. 9 Out of the ground the LORD God made various trees grow that were delightful to look at and good for food, with the tree of life in the middle of the garden and the tree of the knowledge of good and bad. 10 A river rises in Eden to water the garden; beyond there it divides and becomes four branches. 11 The name of the first is the Pishon; it is the one that winds through the whole land of Havilah, where there is gold. 12 The gold of that land is excellent; bdellium and lapis lazuli are also there. 13 The name of the second river is the Gihon; it is the one that winds all through the land of Cush. 14The name of the third river is the Tigris; it is the one that flows east of Asshur. The fourth river is the Euphrates. 15 The LORD God then took the man and settled him in the garden of Eden, to cultivate and care for it. 16 The LORD God gave man this order: "You are free to eat from any of the trees of the garden 17 Except the tree of knowledge of good and bad. From that tree you shall not eat; the moment you eat from it you are surely doomed to die." 18 The LORD God said: "It is not good for the man to be alone. I will make a suitable partner for him." 19 So the LORD God formed out of the ground various wild animals and various birds of the air, and he brought them to the man to see what he would call them; whatever the man called each of them would be its name. 20 The man gave names to all the cattle, all the birds of the air, and all the wild animals; but none proved to be the suitable partner for the man. 21 So the LORD God cast a deep sleep on the man, and while he was asleep, he took out one of his ribs and closed up its place with flesh. 22 The LORD God then built up into a woman the rib that he had taken from the man. When he brought her to the man, 23 The man said: "This one, at last, is bone of my bones and flesh of my flesh; This one shall be called 'woman,' for out of 'her man' this one has been taken." 24 That is why a man leaves his father and mother and clings to his wife, and the two of them become one body. 25The man and his wife were both naked, yet they felt no shame.

Genesis Chapter 3

1 Now the serpent was the most cunning of all the animals that the LORD God had made. The serpent asked the woman, "Did God really tell you not to eat from any of the trees in the garden?" 2 The woman answered the serpent: "We may eat of the fruit of the trees in the garden; 3 it is only about the fruit of the tree in the middle of the garden that God said, 'You shall not eat it or even touch it, lest you die.'" 4 But the serpent said to the woman: "You certainly will not die! 5 No, God knows well that the moment you eat of it your eyes will be opened and you will be like gods who know what is good and what is bad." 6 The woman saw that the tree was good for food, pleasing to the eyes, and desirable for gaining wisdom. So, she took some of its fruit and ate it; and she also gave some to her husband, who was with her, and he ate it. 7 Then the eyes of both of them were opened, and they realized that they were naked; so, they sewed fig leaves together and made loincloths for themselves. 8 When they heard the sound of the LORD God moving about in the garden at the breezy time of the day, the man and his wife hid themselves from the LORD God among the trees of the garden. 9 The LORD God then called to the man and asked him, "Where are you?" 10 He answered, "I heard you in the garden; but I was afraid, because I was naked, so I hid myself." 11 Then he asked, "Who told you that you were naked? You have eaten, then, from the tree of which I had forbidden you to eat!" 12 The man replied, "The woman whom you put here with me - she gave me fruit from the tree, so I ate it." 13 The LORD God then asked the woman, "Why did you do such a thing?" The woman answered, "The serpent tricked me into it, so I ate it." 14 Then the LORD God said to the serpent: "Because you have done this, you shall be banned from all the animals and from all the wild creatures; On your belly shall you crawl, and dirt shall you eat all the days of your life. 15 I will put enmity between you and the woman, and between your offspring and hers; He will strike at your head, while you strike at his heel." 16 The woman he said: "I will intensify the pangs of your childbearing; in pain shall you bring forth children. Yet your urge shall be for your husband, and he shall be your master." 17 To the man he said: "Because you listened to your wife and ate from the tree of which I had forbidden you to eat, "Cursed be the ground because of you! In toil shall you eat its yield all the days of your life. 18 Thorns and thistles shall it bring forth to you, as you eat of the plants of the field. 19 By the sweat of your face shall you get bread to eat, Until you return to the ground, from which you were taken; For you are dirt, and to dirt you shall return." 20 The man called his wife Eve, because she became the mother of all the living. 21 For the man and his wife the LORD God made leather garments, with which he clothed them. 22 Then the LORD God said: "See! The man has become like one of us, knowing what is good and what is bad! Therefore, he must not be allowed to put out his hand to take fruit from the tree of life also, and thus eat of it and live forever."

23 The LORD God therefore banished him from the garden of Eden, to till the ground from which he had been taken. 24 When he expelled the man, he settled him east of the garden of Eden; and he stationed the cherubim and the fiery revolving sword, to guard the way to the tree of life.

Genesis Chapter 4

1 The man had relations with his wife Eve, and she conceived and bore Cain, saying, "I have produced a man with the help of the LORD." 2 Next, she bore his brother Abel. Abel became a keeper of flocks, and Cain a tiller of the soil. 3 In the course of time Cain brought an offering to the LORD from the fruit of the soil, 4 While Abel, for his part, brought one of the best firstlings of his flock. The LORD looked with favor on Abel and his offering, 5 But on Cain and his offering he did not. Cain greatly resented this and was crestfallen. 6 So the LORD said to Cain: "Why are you so resentful and crestfallen? 7 If you do well, you can hold up your head; but if not, sin is a demon lurking at the door: his urge is toward you, yet you can be his master." 8 Cain said to his brother Abel, "Let us go out in the field." When they were in the field, Cain attacked his brother Abel and killed him. 9 Then the LORD asked Cain, "Where is your brother Abel?" He answered, "I do not know. Am I my brother's keeper?" 10 The LORD then said: "What have you done! Listen: your brother's blood cries out to me from the soil! 11 Therefore you shall be banned from the soil that opened its mouth to receive your brother's blood from your hand. 12 If you till the soil, it shall no longer give you its produce. You shall become a restless wanderer on the earth." 13 Cain said to the LORD: "My punishment is too great to bear. 14 Since you have now banished me from the soil, and I must avoid your presence and become a restless wanderer on the earth, anyone may kill me at sight." 15 Not so!" the LORD said to him. "If anyone kills Cain, Cain shall be avenged sevenfold." So, the LORD put a mark on Cain, lest anyone should kill him at sight. 16 Cain then left the LORD'S presence and settled in the land of Nod, east of Eden. 17 Cain had relations with his wife, and she conceived and bore Enoch. Cain also became the founder of a city, which he named after his son Enoch. 18 To Enoch was born Irad, and Irad became the father of Mehujael; Mehujael became the father of Methusael, and Methusael became the father of Lamech. 19 Lamech took two wives; the name of the first was Adah, and the name of the second Zillah. 20 Adah gave birth to Jabal, the ancestor of all who dwell in tents and keep cattle. 21 His brother's name was Jubal; he was the ancestor of all who play the lyre and the pipe. 22 Zillah, on her part, gave birth to Tubalcain, the ancestor of all who forge instruments of bronze and iron. The sister of Tubalcain was Naamah. 23 Lamech said to his wives: "Adah and Zillah, hear my voice; wives of Lamech, listen to my utterance: I have killed a man for wounding me, a boy for bruising me. 24 If Cain is avenged sevenfold, then Lamech seventy-sevenfold." 25 Adam again had relations with his wife, and she gave birth to a son whom she called Seth. "God has granted me more offspring in place of Abel," she said, "because Cain slew him." 26 To Seth, in turn, a son was born, and he named him Enosh. At that time men began to invoke the LORD by name.

Genesis Chapter 5

1 This is the record of the descendants of Adam. When God created man, he made him in the likeness of God; 2 He created them male and female. When they were created, he blessed them and named them "man." 3 Adam was one hundred and thirty years old when he begot a son in his likeness, after his image; and he named him Seth. 4 Adam lived eight hundred years after the birth of Seth, and he had other sons and daughters. 5 The whole lifetime of Adam was nine hundred and thirty years; then he died. 6 When Seth was one hundred and five years old, he became the father of Enosh. 7 Seth lived eight hundred and seven years after the birth of Enosh, and he had other sons and daughters. 8 The whole lifetime of Seth was nine hundred and twelve years; then he died. 9 When Enosh was ninety years old, he became the father of Kenan. 10 Enosh lived eight hundred and fifteen years after the birth of Kenan, and he had other sons and daughters. 11 The whole lifetime of Enosh was nine hundred and five years; then he died. 12 When Kenan was seventy years old, he became the father of Mahalalel. 13 Kenan lived eight hundred and forty years after the birth of Mahalalel, and he had other sons and daughters. 14 The whole lifetime of Kenan was nine hundred and ten years; then he died. 15 When Mahalalel was sixty-five years old, he became the father of Jared. 16 Mahalalel lived eight hundred and thirty years after the birth of Jared, and he had other sons and daughters. 17 The whole lifetime of Mahalalel was eight hundred and ninety-five years; then he died. 18 When Jared was one hundred and sixty-two years old, he became the father of Enoch. 19 Jared lived eight hundred years after the birth of Enoch, and he had other sons and daughters. 20 The whole lifetime of Jared was nine hundred and sixty-

two years; then he died. 21 When Enoch was sixty-five years old, he became the father of Methuselah. 22 Enoch lived three hundred years after the birth of Methuselah, and he had other sons and daughters. 23 The whole lifetime of Enoch was three hundred and sixty-five years. 24 Then Enoch walked with God, and he was no longer here, for God took him. 25 When Methuselah was one hundred and eighty-seven years old, he became the father of Lamech. 26 Methuselah lived seven hundred and eighty-two years after the birth of Lamech, and he had other sons and daughters. 27 The whole lifetime of Methuselah was nine hundred and sixty-nine years; then he died. 28 When Lamech was one hundred and eighty-two years old, he begot a son 29 and named him Noah, saying, "Out of the very ground that the LORD has put under a curse, this one shall bring us relief from our work and the toil of our hands." 30 Lamech lived five hundred and ninety-five years after the birth of Noah, and he had other sons and daughters. 31 The whole lifetime of Lamech was seven hundred and seventy-seven years; then he died. 32 When Noah was five hundred years old, he became the father of Shem, Ham, and Japheth.

Genesis Chapter 6

1 When men began to multiply on earth and daughters were born to them, 2 The sons of heaven saw how beautiful the daughters of man were, and so they took for their wives as many of them as they chose. 3 Then the LORD said: "My spirit shall not remain in man forever, since he is but flesh. His days shall comprise one hundred and twenty years." 4 At that time the Nephilim appeared on earth (as well as later), after the sons of heaven had intercourse with the daughters of man, who bore them sons. They were the heroes of old, the men of renown. 5 When the LORD saw how great was man's wickedness on earth, and how no desire that his heart conceived was ever anything but evil, 6 He regretted that he had made man on the earth, and his heart was grieved. 7 So the LORD said: "I will wipe out from the earth the men whom I have created, and not only the men, but also the beasts and the creeping things and the birds of the air, for I am sorry that I made them." 8 But Noah found favor with the LORD. 9 These are the descendants of Noah. Noah, a good man and blameless in that age, 10 For he walked with God, begot three sons: Shem, Ham, and Japheth. 11 In the eyes of God the earth was corrupt and full of lawlessness. 12 When God saw how corrupt the earth had become, since all mortals led depraved lives on earth, 13 He said to Noah: "I have decided to put an end to all mortals on earth; the earth is full of lawlessness because of them. So I will destroy them and all life on earth. 14 Make yourself an ark of gopherwood, put various compartments in it, and cover it inside and out with pitch. 15 This is how you shall build it: the length of the ark shall be three hundred cubits, its width fifty cubits, and its height thirty cubits. 16 Make an opening for daylight in the ark, and finish the ark a cubit above it. Put an entrance in the side of the ark, which you shall make with bottom, second and third decks. 17 I, on my part, am about to bring the flood (waters) on the earth, to destroy everywhere all creatures in which there is the breath of life; everything on earth shall perish. 18 But with you I will establish my covenant; you and your sons, your wife and your sons' wives, shall go into the ark. 19 Of all other living creatures you shall bring two into the ark, one male and one female, that you may keep them alive with you. 20 Of all kinds of birds, of all kinds of beasts, and of all kinds of creeping things, two of each shall come into the ark with you, to stay alive. 21 Moreover, you are to provide yourself with all the food that is to be eaten, and store it away, that it may serve as provisions for you and for them." 22 This Noah did; he carried out all the commands that God gave him.

Genesis Chapter 7

1 Then the LORD said to Noah: "Go into the ark, you and all your household, for you alone in this age have I found to be truly just. 2 Of every clean animal, take with you seven pairs, a male and its mate; and of the unclean animals, one pair, a male and its mate; 3 Likewise, of every clean bird of the air, seven pairs, a male and a female, and of all the unclean birds, one pair, a male and a female. Thus, you will keep their issue alive over all the earth. 4 Seven days from now I will bring rain down on the earth for forty days and forty nights, and so I will wipe out from the surface of the earth every moving creature that I have made." 5 Noah did just as the LORD had commanded him. 6 Noah was six hundred years old when the flood waters came upon the earth. 7 Together with his sons, his wife, and his sons' wives, Noah went into the ark because of the waters of the flood. 8 Of the clean animals and the unclean, of the birds, and of everything that creeps on the ground, 9 (two by two) male and female entered the ark with Noah, just as the LORD had commanded him. 10 As soon as the seven days were over, the waters of the flood came upon the earth. 11 In the six hundredth year of Noah's life, in the second month, on the seventeenth day of the month: it was

on that day that all the fountains of the great abyss burst forth, and the floodgates of the sky were opened. 12 For forty days and forty nights heavy rain poured down on the earth. 13 On the precise day named, Noah and his sons Shem, Ham, and Japheth, and Noah's wife, and the three wives of Noah's sons had entered the ark, 14 Together with every kind of wild beast, every kind of domestic animal, every kind of creeping thing of the earth, and every kind of bird. 15 Pairs of all creatures in which there was the breath of life entered the ark with Noah. 16 Those that entered were male and female, and of all species they came, as God had commanded Noah. Then the LORD shut him in. 17 The flood continued upon the earth for forty days. As the waters increased, they lifted the ark, so that it rose above the earth. 18 The swelling waters increased greatly, but the ark floated on the surface of the waters. 19 Higher and higher above the earth rose the waters, until all the highest mountains everywhere were submerged, 20 The crest rising fifteen cubits higher than the submerged mountains. 21 All creatures that stirred on earth perished: birds, cattle, wild animals, and all that swarmed on the earth, as well as all mankind. 22 Everything on dry land with the faintest breath of life in its nostrils died out. 23 The LORD wiped out every living thing on earth: man, and cattle, the creeping things and the birds of the air; all were wiped out from the earth. Only Noah and those with him in the ark were left. 24 The waters maintained their crest over the earth for one hundred and fifty days,

Genesis Chapter 8

1 And then God remembered Noah and all the animals, wild and tame, that were with him in the ark. So God made a wind sweep over the earth, and the waters began to subside. 2 The fountains of the abyss and the floodgates of the sky were closed, and the downpour from the sky was held back. 3 Gradually the waters receded from the earth. At the end of one hundred and fifty days, the waters had so diminished 4 That, in the seventh month, on the seventeenth day of the month, the ark came to rest on the mountains of Ararat. 5 The waters continued to diminish until the tenth month, and on the first day of the tenth month the tops of the mountains appeared. 6 At the end of forty days Noah opened the hatch he had made in the ark, 7 And he sent out a raven, to see if the waters had lessened on the earth. It flew back and forth until the waters dried off from the earth. 8 Then he sent out a dove, to see if the waters had lessened on the earth. 9 But the dove could find no place to alight and perch, and it returned to him in the ark, for there was water all over the earth. Putting out his hand, he caught the dove and drew it back to him inside the ark. 10 He waited seven days more and again sent the dove out from the ark. 11 In the evening the dove came back to him, and there in its bill was a plucked-off olive leaf! So Noah knew that the waters had lessened on the earth. 12 He waited still another seven days and then released the dove once more; and this time it did not come back. 13 In the six hundred and first year of Noah's life, in the first month, on the first day of the month, the water began to dry up on the earth. Noah then removed the covering of the ark and saw that the surface of the ground was drying up. 14 In the second month, on the twenty-seventh day of the month, the earth was dry. 15 Then God said to Noah: 16 "Go out of the ark, together with your wife and your sons and your sons' wives. 17 Bring out with you every living thing that is with you - all bodily creatures, be they birds or animals or creeping things of the earth - and let them abound on the earth, breeding and multiplying on it." 18 So Noah came out, together with his wife and his sons and his sons' wives. 19 And all the animals, wild and tame, all the birds, and all the creeping creatures of the earth left the ark, one kind after another. 20 Then Noah built an altar to the LORD and choosing from every clean animal and every clean bird, he offered holocausts on the altar. 21 When the LORD smelled the sweet odor, he said to himself: "Never again will I doom the earth because of man, since the desires of man's heart are evil from the start; nor will I ever again strike down all living beings, as I have done. 22 As long as the earth lasts, seedtime and harvest, cold and heat, Summer and winter, and day and night shall not cease."

Genesis Chapter 9

1 God blessed Noah and his sons and said to them: "Be fertile and multiply and fill the earth. 2 Dread fear of you shall come upon all the animals of the earth and all the birds of the air, upon all the creatures that move about on the ground and all the fishes of the sea; into your power they are delivered. 3 Every creature that is alive shall be yours to eat; I give them all to you as I did the green plants. 4 Only flesh with its lifeblood still in it you shall not eat. 5 For your own lifeblood, too, I will demand an accounting: from every animal I will demand it, and from man in regard to his fellow man I will demand an accounting for human life. 6 If anyone sheds the blood of man, by man shall his blood be shed; For in the image of God has man been made. 7 Be fertile, then, and multiply; abound on earth and subdue it." 8 God said to Noah and to his sons with him: 9 "See, I am now establishing my covenant with you and your descendants after you 10 And with every living creature that was with you: all the birds, and the various tame and wild animals that were with you and came out of the ark. 11 I will establish my covenant with you, that never again shall all bodily creatures be destroyed by the waters of a flood; there shall not be another flood to devastate the earth." 12 God added: "This is the sign that I am giving for all ages to come, of the covenant between me and you and every living creature with you: 13 I set my bow in the clouds to serve as a sign of the covenant between me and the earth. 14 When I bring clouds over the earth, and the bow appears in the clouds, 15 I will recall the covenant I have made between me and you and all living beings, so that the waters shall never again become a flood to destroy all mortal beings. 16 As the bow appears in the clouds, I will see it and recall the everlasting covenant that I have established between God and all living beings - all mortal creatures that are on earth." 17 God told Noah: "This is the sign of the covenant I have established between me and all mortal creatures that are on earth." 18 The sons of Noah who came out of the ark were Shem, Ham and Japheth. (Ham was the father of Canaan.) 19 These three were the sons of Noah, and from them the whole earth was peopled. 20 Now Noah, a man of the soil, was the first to plant a vineyard. 21 When he drank some of the wine, he became drunk and lay naked inside his tent. 22 Ham, the father of Canaan, saw his father's nakedness, and he told his two brothers outside about it. 23 Shem and Japheth, however, took a robe, and holding it on their backs, they walked backward and covered their father's nakedness; since their faces were turned the other way, they did not see their father's nakedness. 24 When Noah woke up from his drunkenness and learned what his youngest son had done to him, 25 He said: "Cursed be Caanan! The lowest of slaves shall he be to his brothers." 26 He also said: "Blessed be the LORD, the God of Shem! Let Canaan be his slave. 27 May God expand Japheth, so that he dwells among the tents of Shem; and let Canaan be his slave." 28 Noah lived three hundred and fifty years after the flood. 29 The whole lifetime of Noah was nine hundred and fifty years; then he died.

Genesis Chapter 10

1 These are the descendants of Noah's sons, Shem, Ham, and Japheth, to whom sons were born after the flood. 2 The descendants of Japheth: Gomer, Magog, Madai, Javan, Tubal, Meshech, and Tiras. 3 The descendants of Gomer: Ashkenaz, Riphath, and Togarmah. 4 The descendants of Javan: Elishah, Tarshish, the Kittim, and the Rodanim. 5 These are the descendants of Japheth, and from them sprang the maritime nations, in their respective lands - each with its own language - by their clans within their nations. 6 The descendants of Ham: Cush, Mizraim, Put, and Canaan. 7 The descendants of Cush: Seba, Havilah, Sabtah, Raamah, and Sabteca. The descendants of Raamah: Sheba and Dedan. 8 Cush became the father of Nimrod, who was the first potentate on earth. 9 He was a mighty hunter by the grace of the LORD; hence the saying, "Like Nimrod, a mighty hunter by the grace of the LORD." 10 The chief cities of his kingdom were Babylon, Erech, and Accad, all of them in the land of Shinar. 11 From that land he went forth to Asshur, where he built Nineveh, Rehoboth-Ir, and Calah, 12 As well as Resen, between Nineveh and Calah, the latter being the principal city. 13 Mizraim became the father of the Ludim, the Anamim, the Lehabim, the Naphtuhim, 14 The Pathrusim, the Casluhim, and the Caphtorim from whom the Philistines sprang. 15 Canaan became the father of Sidon, his first-born, and of Heth; 16 Also of the Jebusites, the Amorites, the Girgashites, 17 The Hivites, the Arkites, the Sinites, 18 The Arvadites, the Zemarites, and the Hamathites. Afterward, the clans of the Canaanites spread out, 19 So that the Canaanite borders extended from Sidon all the way to Gerar, near Gaza, and all the way to Sodom, Gomorrah, Admah and Zeboiim, near Lasha. 20 These are the descendants of Ham, according to their clans and languages, by their lands and nations. 21 To Shem also, Japheth's oldest brother and the ancestor of all the children of Eber, sons were born. 22 The descendants of Shem: Elam, Asshur, Arpachshad, Lud, and Aram. 23 The descendants of Aram: Uz, Hul, Gether, and Mash. 24 Arpachshad became the father of Shelah, and Shelah became the father of Eber. 25 To Eber two sons were born: the name of the first was Peleg, for in his time the world was divided; and the name of his brother was Joktan. 26 Joktan became the father of Almodad, Sheleph, Hazarmaveth, Jerah, 27 Hadoram, Uzal, Diklah, 28 Obal, Abimael, Sheba, 29 Ophir, Havilah, and Jobab. All these were descendants of Joktan. 30 Their settlements extended all the way to Sephar, the eastern hill country. 31 These are the descendants of Shem, according to their clans and languages by their lands and nations. 32 These are the groupings of Noah's sons, according to their origins and by their nations. From these the other nations of the earth branched out after the flood.

Genesis Chapter 11

¹ The whole world spoke the same language, using the same words. ² While men were migrating in the east, they came upon a valley in the land of Shinar and settled there. ³ They said to one another, "Come, let us mold bricks and harden them with fire." They used bricks for stone, and bitumen for mortar. ⁴ Then they said, "Come, let us build ourselves a city and a tower with its top in the sky, and so make a name for ourselves; otherwise we shall be scattered all over the earth." ⁵ LORD came down to see the city and the tower that the men had built. ⁶ Then the LORD said: "If now, while they are one people, all speaking the same language, they have started to do this, nothing will later stop them from doing whatever they presume to do. ⁷ Let us then go down and there confuse their language, so that one will not understand what another says." ⁸ Thus the LORD scattered them from there all over the earth, and they stopped building the city. ⁹ That is why it was called Babel, because there the LORD confused the speech of all the world. It was from that place that he scattered them all over the earth. ¹⁰ This is the record of the descendants of Shem. When Shem was one hundred years old, he became the father of Arpachshad, two years after the flood. ¹¹ Shem lived five hundred years after the birth of Arpachshad, and he had other sons and daughters. ¹² When Arpachshad was thirty-five years old, he became the father of Shelah. ¹³ Arpachshad lived four hundred and three years after the birth of Shelah, and he had other sons and daughters. ¹⁴ When Shelah was thirty years old, he became the father of Eber. ¹⁵ Shelah lived four hundred and three years after the birth of Eber, and he had other sons and daughters. ¹⁶ When Eber was thirty-four years old, he became the father of Peleg. ¹⁷ Eber lived four hundred and thirty years after the birth of Peleg, and he had other sons and daughters. ¹⁸ When Peleg was thirty years old, he became the father of Reu. ¹⁹ Peleg lived two hundred and nine years after the birth of Reu, and he had other sons and daughters. ²⁰ When Reu was thirty-two years old, he became the father of Serug. ²¹ Reu lived two hundred and seven years after the birth of Serug, and he had other sons and daughters. ²² When Serug was thirty years old, he became the father of Nahor. ²³ Serug lived two hundred years after the birth of Nahor, and he had other sons and daughters. ²⁴ When Nahor was twenty-nine years old, he became the father of Terah. ²⁵ Nahor lived one hundred and nineteen years after the birth of Terah, and he had other sons and daughters. ²⁶ When Terah was seventy years old, he became the father of Abram, Nahor and Haran. ²⁷ This is the record of the descendants of Terah. Terah became the father of Abram, Nahor, and Haran, and Haran became the father of Lot. ²⁸ Haran died before his father Terah, in his native land, in Ur of the Chaldeans. ²⁹ Abram and Nahor took wives; the name of Abram's wife was Sarai, and the name of Nahor's wife was Milcah, daughter of Haran, the father of Milcah and Iscah. ³⁰ Sarai was barren; she had no child. ³¹ Terah took his son Abram, his grandson Lot, son of Haran, and his daughter-in-law Sarai, the wife of his son Abram, and brought them out of Ur of the Chaldeans, to go to the land of Canaan. But when they reached Haran, they settled there. ³² The lifetime of Terah was two hundred and five years; then Terah died in Haran.

Genesis Chapter 12

¹ The LORD said to Abram: "Go forth from the land of your kinsfolk and from your father's house to a land that I will show you. ² "I will make of you a great nation, and I will bless you; I will make your name great, so that you will be a blessing. ³ I will bless those who bless you and curse those who curse you. All the communities of the earth shall find blessing in you." ⁴ Abram went as the LORD directed him, and Lot went with him. Abram was seventy-five years old when he left Haran. ⁵ Abram took his wife Sarai, his brother's son Lot, all the possessions that they had accumulated, and the persons they had acquired in Haran, and they set out for the land of Canaan. When they came to the land of Canaan, ⁶ Abram passed through the land as far as the sacred place at Shechem, by the terebinth of Moreh. (The Canaanites were then in the land.) ⁷ The LORD appeared to Abram and said, "To your descendants I will give this land." So Abram built an altar there to the LORD who had appeared to him. ⁸ From there he moved on to the hill country east of Bethel, pitching his tent with Bethel to the west and Ai to the east. He built an altar there to the LORD and invoked the LORD by name. ⁹ Then Abram journeyed on by stages to the Negeb. ¹⁰ There was famine in the land; so, Abram went down to Egypt to sojourn there, since the famine in the land was severe. ¹¹ When he was about to enter Egypt, he said to his wife Sarai: "I know well how beautiful a woman you are. ¹² When the Egyptians see you, they will say, 'She is his wife'; then they will kill me, but let you live. ¹³ Please say, therefore, that you are my sister, so that it may go well with me on your account and my life may be spared for your sake." ¹⁴ When Abram came to Egypt, the Egyptians saw how beautiful the woman was; and when Pharaoh's courtiers saw her, ¹⁵ They praised her to Pharaoh. So, she was taken into Pharaoh's palace. ¹⁶ On her account it went very well with Abram, and he received flocks and herds, male and female slaves, male and female asses, and camels. ¹⁷ But the LORD struck Pharaoh and his household with severe plagues because of Abram's wife Sarai. ¹⁸ Then Pharaoh summoned Abram and said to him: "How could you do this to me! Why didn't you tell me she was your wife? ¹⁹ Why did you say, 'She is my sister,' so that I took her for my wife? Here, then, is your wife. Take her and be gone!" ²⁰ Then Pharaoh gave men orders concerning him, and they sent him on his way, with his wife and all that belonged to him.

Genesis Chapter 13

¹ From Egypt Abram went up to the Negeb with his wife and all that belonged to him, and Lot accompanied him. ² Now Abram was very rich in livestock, silver, and gold. ³ From the Negeb he traveled by stages toward Bethel, to the place between Bethel and Ai where his tent had formerly stood, ⁴ The site where he had first built the altar; and there he invoked the LORD by name. ⁵ Lot, who went with Abram, also had flocks and herds and tents, ⁶ So that the land could not support them if they stayed together; their possessions were so great that they could not dwell together. ⁷ There were quarrels between the herdsmen of Abram's livestock and those of Lot's. (At this time the Canaanites and the Perizzites were occupying the land.) ⁸ So Abram said to Lot: "Let there be no strife between you and me, or between your herdsmen and mine, for we are kinsmen. ⁹ Is not the whole land at your disposal? Please separate from me. If you prefer the left, I will go to the right; if you prefer the right, I will go to the left." ¹⁰ Lot looked about and saw how well watered the whole Jordan Plain was as far as Zoar, like the LORD'S own garden, or like Egypt. (This was before the LORD had destroyed Sodom and Gomorrah.) ¹¹ Lot, therefore, chose for himself the whole Jordan Plain and set out eastward. Thus they separated from each other; ¹² Abram stayed in the land of Canaan, while Lot settled among the cities of the Plain, pitching his tents near Sodom. ¹³ Now the inhabitants of Sodom were very wicked in the sins they committed against the LORD. ¹⁴ Lot had left, the LORD said to Abram: "Look about you, and from where you are, gaze to the north and south, east and west. ¹⁵ All the land that you see I will give to you and your descendants forever. ¹⁶ I will make your descendants like the dust of the earth; if anyone could count the dust of the earth, your descendants too might be counted. ¹⁷ Set forth and walk about in the land, through its length and breadth, for to you I will give it." ¹⁸ Abram moved his tents and went on to settle near the terebinth of Mamre, which is at Hebron. There he built an altar to the LORD.

Genesis Chapter 14

¹ In the days of. . . , Amraphel king of Shinar, Arioch king of Ellasar, Chedorlaomer king of Elam, and Tidal king of Goiim ² Made war on Bera king of Sodom, Birsha king of Gomorrah, Shinab king of Admah, Shemeber king of Zeboiim, and the king of Bela (that is, Zoar).ᵛ³ All the latter kings joined forces in the Valley of Siddim (that is, the Salt Sea). ⁴ For twelve years they had been subject to Chedorlaomer, but in the thirteenth year they r ebelled. ⁵ In the fourteenth year Chedorlaomer and the kings allied with him came and defeated the Rephaim in Ashteroth-karnaim, the Zuzim in Ham, the Emim in Shaveh-kiriathaim, ⁶ And the Horites in the hill country of Seir, as far as Elparan, close by the wilderness. ⁷ They then turned back and came to Enmishpat (that is, Kadesh), and they subdued the whole country both of the Amalekites and of the Amorites who dwelt in Hazazon-tamar. ⁸ Thereupon the king of Sodom, the king of Gomorrah, the king of Admah, the king of Zeboiim, and the king of Bela (that is, Zoar) marched out, and in the Valley of Siddim they went into battle against them: ⁹ Against Chedorlaomer king of Elam, Tidal king of Goiim, Amraphel king of Shinar, and Arioch king of Ellasar-four kings against five. ¹⁰ Now the Valley of Siddim was full of bitumen pits; and as the kings of Sodom and Gomorrah fled, they fell into these, while the rest fled to the mountains. ¹¹ The victors seized all the possessions and food supplies of Sodom and Gomorrah and then went their way, ¹² taking with them Abram's nephew Lot, who had been living in Sodom, as well as his possessions. ¹³ A fugitive came and brought the news to Abram the Hebrew, who was camping at the terebinth of Mamre the Amorite, a kinsman of Eshcol and Aner; these were in league with Abram. ¹⁴ When Abram heard that his nephew had been captured, he mustered three hundred and eighteen of his retainers, born in his house, and went in pursuit as far as Dan. ¹⁵ He and his party deployed against them at night, defeated them, and pursued them as far as Hobah, which is north of Damascus. ¹⁶ He recovered all the possessions, besides bringing back his kinsman Lot and his possessions, along with the women and the other captives. ¹⁷ When Abram returned from his victory over

Chedorlaomer and the kings who were allied with him, the king of Sodom went out to greet him in the Valley of Shaveh (that is, the King's Valley). ¹⁸ Melchizedek, king of Salem, brought out bread and wine, and being a priest of God Most High, he blessed Abram with these words: ¹⁹ Blessed be Abram by God Most High, the creator of heaven and earth; ²⁰ And blessed be God Most High, who delivered your foes into your hand." Then Abram gave him a tenth of everything. ²¹ The king of Sodom said to Abram, "Give me the people; the goods you may keep." ²² But Abram replied to the king of Sodom: "I have sworn to the LORD, God Most High, the creator of heaven and earth, ²³ that I would not take so much as a thread or a sandal strap from anything that is yours, lest you should say, 'I made Abram rich.' ²⁴ Nothing for me except what my servants have used up and the share that is due to the men who joined me - Aner, Eshcol and Mamre; let them take their share."

Genesis Chapter 15

¹ Sometime after these events, this word of the LORD came to Abram in a vision: "Fear not, Abram! I am your shield; I will make your reward very great." ² But Abram said, "O Lord GOD, what good will your gifts be, if I keep on being childless and have as my heir the steward of my house, Eliezer?" ³ Abram continued, "See, you have given me no offspring, and so one of my servants will be my heir." ⁴ Then the word of the LORD came to him: "No, that one shall not be your heir; your own issue shall be your heir." ⁵ He took him outside and said: "Look up at the sky and count the stars, if you can. Just so," he added, "shall your descendants be." ⁶ Abram put his faith in the LORD, who credited it to him as an act of righteousness. ⁷ He then said to him, "I am the LORD who brought you from Ur of the Chaldeans to give you this land as a possession." ⁸ "O Lord GOD," he asked, "How am I to know that I shall possess it?" ⁹ He answered him, "Bring me a three-year-old heifer, a three-year-old she-goat, a three-year-old ram, a turtle-dove, and a young pigeon." ¹⁰ He brought him all these, split them in two, and placed each half opposite the other; but the birds he did not cut up. ¹¹ Birds of prey swooped down on the carcasses, but Abram stayed with them. ¹² As the sun was about to set, a trance fell upon Abram, and a deep, terrifying darkness enveloped him. ¹³ Then the LORD said to Abram: "Know for certain that your descendants shall be aliens in a land not their own, where they shall be enslaved and oppressed for four hundred years. ¹⁴ But I will bring judgment on the nation they must serve, and in the end they will depart with great wealth. ¹⁵ You, however, shall join your forefathers in peace; you shall be buried at a contented old age. ¹⁶ In the fourth time-span the others shall come back here; the wickedness of the Amorites will not have reached its full measure until then." ¹⁷ When the sun had set and it was dark, there appeared a smoking brazier and a flaming torch, which passed between those pieces. ¹⁸ It was on that occasion that the LORD made a covenant with Abram, saying: "To your descendants I give this land, from the Wadi of Egypt to the Great River (the Euphrates), ¹⁹ the land of the Kenites, the Kenizzites, the Kadmonites, ²⁰ the Hittites, the Perizzites, the Rephaim, ²¹ the Amorites, the Canaanites, the Girgashites, and the Jebusites."

Genesis Chapter 16

¹ Abram's wife Sarai had borne him no children. She had, however, an Egyptian maidservant named Hagar. ² Sarai said to Abram: "The LORD has kept me from bearing children. Have intercourse, then, with my maid; perhaps I shall have sons through her." Abram heeded Sarai's request. ³ Thus, after Abram had lived ten years in the land of Canaan, his wife Sarai took her maid, Hagar the Egyptian, and gave her to her husband Abram to be his concubine. ⁴ He had intercourse with her, and she became pregnant. When she became aware of her pregnancy, she looked on her mistress with disdain. ⁵ So Sarai said to Abram: "You are responsible for this outrage against me. I myself gave my maid to your embrace; but ever since she became aware of her pregnancy, she has been looking on me with disdain. May the LORD decide between you and me!" ⁶ Abram told Sarai: "Your maid is in your power. Do to her whatever you please." Sarai then abused her so much that Hagar ran away from her. ⁷ The LORD'S messenger found her by a spring in the wilderness, the spring on the road to Shur, ⁸ and he asked, "Hagar, maid of Sarai, where have you come from and where are you going?" She answered, "I am running away from my mistress, Sarai." ⁹ But the LORD'S messenger told her: "Go back to your mistress and submit to her abusive treatment. ¹⁰ I will make your descendants so numerous," added the LORD'S messenger, "that they will be too many to count. ¹¹ Besides," the LORD'S messenger said to her: "You are now pregnant and shall bear a son; you shall name him Ishmael, For the LORD has heard you, God has answered you. ¹² He shall be a wild ass of a man, his hand against everyone, and everyone's hand against him; In opposition to all his kin shall he encamp." ¹³ To the LORD who spoke to her she gave a name, saying, "You are the God of Vision"; she meant, "Have I really seen God and remained alive after my vision?" ¹⁴ That is why the well is called Beer-lahai-roi. It is between Kadesh and Bered. ¹⁵ Hagar bore Abram a son, and Abram named the son whom Hagar bore him Ishmael. ¹⁶ Abram was eighty-six years old when Hagar bore him Ishmael.

Genesis Chapter 17

¹ When Abram was ninety-nine years old, the LORD appeared to him and said: "I am God the Almighty. Walk in my presence and be blameless. ² Between you and me I will establish my covenant, and I will multiply you exceedingly." ³ When Abram prostrated himself, God continued to speak to him: ⁴ "My covenant with you is this: you are to become the father of a host of nations. ⁵ No longer shall you be called Abram; your name shall be Abraham, for I am making you the father of a host of nations. ⁶ I will render you exceedingly fertile; I will make nations of you; kings shall stem from you. ⁷ I will maintain my covenant with you and your descendants after you throughout the ages as an everlasting pact, to be your God and the God of your descendants after you. ⁸ I will give to you and to your descendants after you the land in which you are now staying, the whole land of Canaan, as a permanent possession; and I will be their God." ⁹ God also said to Abraham: "On your part, you and your descendants after you must keep my covenant throughout the ages. ¹⁰ This is my covenant with you and your descendants after you that you must keep: every male among you shall be circumcised. ¹¹ Circumcise the flesh of your foreskin, and that shall be the mark of the covenant between you and me. ¹² Throughout the ages, every male among you, when he is eight days old, shall be circumcised, including houseborn slaves and those acquired with money from any foreigner who is not of your blood. ¹³ Yes, both the houseborn slaves and those acquired with money must be circumcised. Thus, my covenant shall be in your flesh as an everlasting pact. ¹⁴ If a male is uncircumcised, that is, if the flesh of his foreskin has not been cut away, such a one shall be cut off from his people; he has broken my covenant." ¹⁵ God further said to Abraham: "As for your wife Sarai, do not call her Sarai; her name shall be Sarah. ¹⁶ I will bless her, and I will give you a son by her. Him also will I bless; he shall give rise to nations, and rulers of peoples shall issue from him." ¹⁷ Abraham prostrated himself and laughed as he said to himself, "Can a child be born to a man who is a hundred years old? Or can Sarah give birth at ninety?" ¹⁸ Then Abraham said to God, "Let but Ishmael live on by your favor!" ¹⁹ God replied: "Nevertheless, your wife Sarah is to bear you a son, and you shall call him Isaac. I will maintain my covenant with him as an everlasting pact, to be his God and the God of his descendants after him. ²⁰ As for Ishmael, I am heeding you: I hereby bless him. I will make him fertile and will multiply him exceedingly. He shall become the father of twelve chieftains, and I will make of him a great nation. ²¹ But my covenant I will maintain with Isaac, whom Sarah shall bear to you by this time next year." ²² When he had finished speaking with him, God departed from Abraham. ²³ Then Abraham took his son Ishmael and all his slaves, whether born in his house or acquired with his money - every male among the members of Abraham's household - and he circumcised the flesh of their foreskins on that same day, as God had told him to do. ²⁴ Abraham was ninety-nine years old when the flesh of his foreskin was circumcised, ²⁵ and his son Ishmael was thirteen years old when the flesh of his foreskin was circumcised. ²⁶ Thus, on that same day Abraham and his son Ishmael were circumcised; ²⁷ and all the male members of his household, including the slaves born in his house or acquired with his money from foreigners, were circumcised with him.

Genesis Chapter 18

¹ The LORD appeared to Abraham by the terebinth of Mamre, as he sat in the entrance of his tent, while the day was growing hot. ² Looking up, he saw three men standing nearby. When he saw them, he ran from the entrance of the tent to greet them; and bowing to the ground, ³ he said: "Sir, if I may ask you this favor, please do not go on past your servant. ⁴ Let some water be brought, that you may bathe your feet, and then rest yourselves under the tree. ⁵ Now that you have come this close to your servant, let me bring you a little food, that you may refresh yourselves; and afterward you may go on your way." "Very well," they replied, "do as you have said." ⁶ Abraham hastened into the tent and told Sarah, "Quick, three seahs of fine flour! Knead it and make rolls." ⁷ He ran to the herd, picked out a tender, choice steer, and gave it to a servant, who quickly prepared it. ⁸ Then he got some curds and milk, as well as the steer that had been prepared, and set these before them; and he waited on them under the tree while they ate. ⁹ "Where is your wife Sarah?" they asked him. "There in the tent," he replied. ¹⁰ One of them said, "I will surely return to you about this time next year, and Sarah will then have a son." Sarah was listening at the entrance of the tent, just behind him. ¹¹ Now Abraham and Sarah were old, advanced in years, and Sarah

had stopped having her womanly periods. 12 So Sarah laughed to herself and said, "Now that I am so withered and my husband is so old, am I still to have sexual pleasure?" 13 But the LORD said to Abraham: "Why did Sarah laugh and say, 'Shall I really bear a child, old as I am?' 14 Is anything too marvelous for the LORD to do? At the appointed time, about this time next year, I will return to you, and Sarah will have a son." 15 Because she was afraid, Sarah dissembled, saying, "I didn't laugh." But he said, "Yes you did." 16 The men set out from there and looked down toward Sodom; Abraham was walking with them, to see them on their way. 17 The LORD reflected: "Shall I hide from Abraham what I am about to do, 18 now that he is to become a great and populous nation, and all the nations of the earth are to find blessing in him? 19 Indeed, I have singled him out that he may direct his sons and his posterity to keep the way of the LORD by doing what is right and just, so that the LORD may carry into effect for Abraham the promises he made about him." 20 Then the LORD said: "The outcry against Sodom and Gomorrah is so great, and their sin so grave, 21 that I must go down and see whether or not their actions fully correspond to the cry against them that comes to me. I mean to find out." 22 While the two men walked on farther toward Sodom, the LORD remained standing before Abraham. 23 Then Abraham drew nearer to him and said: "Will you sweep away the innocent with the guilty? 24 Suppose there were fifty innocent people in the city; would you wipe out the place, rather than spare it for the sake of the fifty innocent people within it? 25 Far be it from you to do such a thing, to make the innocent die with the guilty, so that the innocent and the guilty would be treated alike! Should not the judge of all the world act with justice?" 26 The LORD replied, "If I find fifty innocent people in the city of Sodom, I will spare the whole place for their sake." 27 Abraham spoke up again: "See how I am presuming to speak to my Lord, though I am but dust and ashes! 28 What if there are five less than fifty innocent people? Will you destroy the whole city because of those five?" "I will not destroy it," he answered, "if I find forty-five there." 29 But Abraham persisted, saying, "What if only forty are found there?" He replied, "I will forebear doing it for the sake of the forty." 30 Then he said, "Let not my Lord grow impatient if I go on. What if only thirty are found there?" He replied, "I will forebear doing it if I can find but thirty there." 31 Still he went on, "Since I have thus dared to speak to my Lord, what if there are no more than twenty?" "I will not destroy it," he answered, "for the sake of the twenty." 32 But he still persisted: "Please, let not my Lord grow angry if I speak up this last time. What if there are at least ten there?" "For the sake of those ten," he replied, "I will not destroy it." 33 The LORD departed as soon as he had finished speaking with Abraham, and Abraham returned home.

Genesis Chapter 19

1 The two angels reached Sodom in the evening, as Lot was sitting at the gate of Sodom. When Lot saw them, he got up to greet them; and bowing down with his face to the ground, 2 he said, "Please, gentlemen, come aside into your servant's house for the night, and bathe your feet; you can get up early to continue your journey." But they replied, "No, we shall pass the night in the town square." 3 He urged them so strongly, however, that they turned aside to his place and entered his house. He prepared a meal for them, baking cakes without leaven, and they dined. 4 Before they went to bed, all the townsmen of Sodom, both young and old - all the people to the last man - closed in on the house. 5 They called to Lot and said to him, "Where are the men who came to your house tonight? Bring them out to us that we may have intimacies with them." 6 Lot went out to meet them at the entrance. When he had shut the door behind him, 7 he said, "I beg you, my brothers, not to do this wicked thing. 8 I have two daughters who have never had intercourse with men. Let me bring them out to you, and you may do to them as you please. But don't do anything to these men, for you know they have come under the shelter of my roof." 9 They replied, "Stand back! This fellow," they sneered, "came here as an immigrant, and now he dares to give orders! We'll treat you worse than them!" With that, they pressed hard against Lot, moving in closer to break down the door. 10 But his guests put out their hands, pulled Lot inside with them, and closed the door; 11 at the same time they struck the men at the entrance of the house, one and all, with such a blinding light that they were utterly unable to reach the doorway. 12 Then the angels said to Lot: "Who else belongs to you here? Your sons (sons-in-law) and your daughters and all who belong to you in the city - take them away from it! 13 We are about to destroy this place, for the outcry reaching the LORD against those in the city is so great that he has sent us to destroy it." 14 So Lot went out and spoke to his sons-in-law, who had contracted marriage with his daughters. "Get up and leave this place," he told them; "the LORD is about to destroy the city." But his sons-in-law thought he was joking. 15 As dawn was breaking, the angels urged Lot on, saying, "On your way! Take with you your wife and your two daughters who are here, or you will be swept away in the punishment of the city." 16 When he hesitated, the men, by the LORD'S mercy, seized his hand and the hands of his wife and his two daughters and led them to safety outside the city. 17 As soon as they had been brought outside, he was told: "Flee for your life! Don't look back or stop anywhere on the Plain. Get off to the hills at once, or you will be swept away." 18 "Oh, no, my lord!" replied Lot. 19 "You have already thought enough of your servant to do me the great kindness of intervening to save my life. But I cannot flee to the hills to keep the disaster from overtaking me, and so I shall die. 20 Look, this town ahead is near enough to escape to. It's only a small place. Let me flee there - it's a small place, isn't it? - that my life may be saved." 21 "Well, then," he replied, "I will also grant you the favor you now ask. I will not overthrow the town you speak of. 22 Hurry, escape there! I cannot do anything until you arrive there." That is why the town is called Zoar. 23 The sun was just rising over the earth as Lot arrived in Zoar; 24 at the same time the LORD rained down sulphurous fire upon Sodom and Gomorrah (from the LORD out of heaven). 25 He overthrew those cities and the whole Plain, together with the inhabitants of the cities and the produce of the soil. 26 But Lot's wife looked back, and she was turned into a pillar of salt. 27 Early the next morning Abraham went to the place where he had stood in the LORD'S presence. 28 As he looked down toward Sodom and Gomorrah and the whole region of the Plain, he saw dense smoke over the land rising like fumes from a furnace. 29 Thus it came to pass: when God destroyed the Cities of the Plain, he was mindful of Abraham by sending Lot away from the upheaval by which God overthrew the cities where Lot had been living. 30 Since Lot was afraid to stay in Zoar, he and his two daughters went up from Zoar and settled in the hill country, where he lived with his two daughters in a cave. 31 The older one said to the younger: "Our father is getting old, and there is not a man on earth to unite with us as was the custom everywhere. 32 Come, let us ply our father with wine and then lie with him, that we may have offspring by our father." 33 So that night they plied their father with wine, and the older one went in and lay with her father; but he was not aware of her lying down or her getting up. 34 Next day the older one said to the younger: "Last night it was I who lay with my father. Let us ply him with wine again tonight, and then you go in and lie with him, that we may both have offspring by our father." 35 So that night, too, they plied their father with wine, and then the younger one went in and lay with him; but again he was not aware of her lying down or her getting up. 36 Thus both of Lot's daughters became pregnant by their father. 37 The older one gave birth to a son whom she named Moab, saying, "From my father." He is the ancestor of the Moabites of today. 38 The younger one, too, gave birth to a son, and she named him Ammon, saying, "The son of my kin." He is the ancestor of the Ammonites of today.

Genesis Chapter 20

1 Abraham journeyed on to the region of the Negeb, where he settled between Kadesh and Shur. While he stayed in Gerar, 2 he said of his wife Sarah, "She is my sister." So Abimelech, king of Gerar, sent and took Sarah. 3 But God came to Abimelech in a dream one night and said to him, "You are about to die because of the woman you have taken, for she has a husband." 4 Abimelech, who had not approached her, said: "O Lord, would you slay a man even though he is innocent? 5 He himself told me, 'She is my sister,' and she herself also stated, 'He is my brother.' I did it in good faith and with clean hands." 6 God answered him in the dream: "Yes, I know you did it in good faith. In fact, it was I who kept you from sinning against me; that is why I did not let you touch her. 7 Therefore, return the man's wife - as a spokesman he will intercede for you - that your life may be saved. If you do not return her, you can be sure that you and all who are yours will certainly die." 8 Early the next morning Abimelech called all his court officials and informed them of everything that had happened, and the men were horrified. 9 Then Abimelech summoned Abraham and said to him: "How could you do this to us! What wrong did I do to you that you should have brought such monstrous guilt on me and my kingdom? You have treated me in an intolerable way. 10 What were you afraid of," he asked him, "that you should have done such a thing?" 11 "I was afraid," answered Abraham, "because I thought there would surely be no fear of God in this place, and so they would kill me on account of my wife. 12 Besides, she is in truth my sister, but only my father's daughter, not my mother's; and so she became my wife. 13 When God sent me wandering from my father's house, I asked her: 'Would you do me this favor? In whatever place we come to, say that I am your brother.'" 14 Then Abimelech took flocks and herds and male and female slaves and gave them to Abraham; and after he restored his wife Sarah to him, 15 he said, "Here, my land lies at your disposal; settle wherever you please." 16 To Sarah he said: "See, I have given your brother a thousand shekels of silver. Let that serve you as a vindication before all who are with you; your honor has been preserved

with everyone." 17 Abraham then interceded with God, and God restored health to Abimelech, that is, to his wife and his maidservants, so that they could bear children; 18 for God had tightly closed every womb in Abimelech's household on account of Abraham's wife Sarah.

Genesis Chapter 21

1 The LORD took note of Sarah as he had said he would; he did for her as he had promised. 2 Sarah became pregnant and bore Abraham a son in his old age, at the set time that God had stated. 3 Abraham gave the name Isaac to this son of his whom Sarah bore him. 4 When his son Isaac was eight days old, Abraham circumcised him, as God had commanded. 5 Abraham was a hundred years old when his son Isaac was born to him. 6 Sarah then said, "God has given me cause to laugh, and all who hear of it will laugh with me. 7 Who would have told Abraham," she added, "that Sarah would nurse children! Yet I have borne him a son in his old age." 8 Isaac grew, and on the day of the child's weaning, Abraham held a great feast. 9 Sarah noticed the son whom Hagar the Egyptian had borne to Abraham playing with her son Isaac; 10 so she demanded of Abraham: "Drive out that slave and her son! No son of that slave is going to share the inheritance with my son Isaac!" 11 Abraham was greatly distressed, especially on account of his son Ishmael. 12 But God said to Abraham: "Do not be distressed about the boy or about your slave woman. Heed the demands of Sarah, no matter what she is asking of you; for it is through Isaac that descendants shall bear your name. 13 As for the son of the slave woman, I will make a great nation of him also, since he too is your offspring." 14 Early the next morning Abraham got some bread and a skin of water and gave them to Hagar. Then, placing the child on her back, he sent her away. As she roamed aimlessly in the wilderness of Beer-sheba, 15 the water in the skin was used up. So she put the child down under a shrub, 16 and then went and sat down opposite him, about a bowshot away; for she said to herself, "Let me not watch to see the child die." As she sat opposite him, he began to cry. 17 God heard the boy's cry, and God's messenger called to Hagar from heaven: "What is the matter, Hagar? Don't be afraid; God has heard the boy's cry in this plight of his. 18 Arise, lift up the boy and hold him by the hand; for I will make of him a great nation." 19 Then God opened her eyes, and she saw a well of water. She went and filled the skin with water, and then let the boy drink. 20 God was with the boy as he grew up. He lived in the wilderness and became an expert bowman, 21 with his home in the wilderness of Paran. His mother got a wife for him from the land of Egypt. 22 About that time Abimelech, accompanied by Phicol, the commander of his army, said to Abraham: "God is with you in everything you do. 23 Therefore, swear to me by God at this place that you will not deal falsely with me or with my progeny and posterity, but will act as loyally toward me and the land in which you stay as I have acted toward you." 24 To this Abraham replied, "I so swear." 25 Abraham, however, reproached Abimelech about a well that Abimelech's men had seized by force. 26 "I have no idea who did that," Abimelech replied. "In fact, you never told me about it, nor did I ever hear of it until now." 27 Then Abraham took sheep and cattle and gave them to Abimelech and the two made a pact. 28 Abraham also set apart seven ewe lambs of the flock, 29 and Abimelech asked him, "What is the purpose of these seven ewe lambs that you have set apart?" 30 Abraham answered, "The seven ewe lambs you shall accept from me that thus I may have your acknowledgment that the well was dug by me." 31 This is why the place is called Beer-sheba; the two took an oath there. 32 When they had thus made the pact in Beer-sheba, Abimelech, along with Phicol, the commander of his army, left and returned to the land of the Philistines. 33 Abraham planted a tamarisk at Beer-sheba, and there he invoked by name the LORD, God the Eternal. 34 Abraham resided in the land of the Philistines for many years.

Genesis Chapter 22

1 Some time after these events, God put Abraham to the test. He called to him, "Abraham!" "Ready!" he replied. 2 Then God said: "Take your son Isaac, your only one, whom you love, and go to the land of Moriah. There you shall offer him up as a holocaust on a height that I will point out to you." 3 Early the next morning Abraham saddled his donkey, took with him his son Isaac, and two of his servants as well, and with the wood that he had cut for the holocaust, set out for the place of which God had told him. 4 On the third day Abraham got sight of the place from afar. 5 Then he said to his servants: "Both of you stay here with the donkey, while the boy and I go on over yonder. We will worship and then come back to you." 6 Thereupon Abraham took the wood for the holocaust and laid it on his son Isaac's shoulders, while he himself carried the fire and the knife. 7 As the two walked on together, Isaac spoke to his father Abraham. "Father!" he said. "Yes, son," he replied. Isaac continued, "Here are the fire and the wood, but where is the sheep for the holocaust?" 8 "Son," Abraham answered, "God himself will provide the sheep for the holocaust." Then the two continued going forward. 9 When they came to the place of which God had told him, Abraham built an altar there and arranged the wood on it. Next he tied up his son Isaac, and put him on top of the wood on the altar. 10 Then he reached out and took the knife to slaughter his son. 11 But the LORD'S messenger called to him from heaven, "Abraham, Abraham!" "Yes, Lord," he answered. 12 "Do not lay your hand on the boy," said the messenger. "Do not do the least thing to him. I know now how devoted you are to God, since you did not withhold from me your own beloved son." 13 As Abraham looked about, he spied a ram caught by its horns in the thicket. So he went and took the ram and offered it up as a holocaust in place of his son. 14 Abraham named the site Yahweh-yireh; hence people now say, "On the mountain the LORD will see." 15 Again the LORD'S messenger called to Abraham from heaven 16 and said: "I swear by myself, declares the LORD, that because you acted as you did in not withholding from me your beloved son, 17 I will bless you abundantly and make your descendants as countless as the stars of the sky and the sands of the seashore; your descendants shall take possession of the gates of their enemies, 18 and in your descendants all the nations of the earth shall find blessing - all this because you obeyed my command." 19 Abraham then returned to his servants, and they set out together for Beer-sheba, where Abraham made his home. 20 Sometime afterward, the news came to Abraham: "Milcah too has borne sons, to your brother Nahor: 21 Uz, his first-born, his brother Buz, Kemuel (the father of Aram), 22 Chesed, Hazo, Pildash, Jidlaph, and Bethuel." 23 Bethuel became the father of Rebekah. These eight Milcah bore to Abraham's brother Nahor. 24 His concubine, whose name was Reumah, also bore children: Tebah, Gaham, Tahash, and Maacah.

Genesis Chapter 23

1 The span of Sarah's life was one hundred and twenty-seven years. 2 She died in Kiriatharba (that is, Hebron) in the land of Canaan, and Abraham performed the customary mourning rites for her. 3 Then he left the side of his dead one and addressed the Hittites: 4 "Although I am a resident alien among you, sell me from your holdings a piece of property for a burial ground, that I may bury my dead wife." 5 The Hittites answered Abraham: "Please, sir, 6 listen to us! You are an elect of God among us. Bury your dead in the choicest of our burial sites. None of us would deny you his burial ground for the burial of your dead." 7 Abraham, however, began to bow low before the local citizens, the Hittites, 8 while he appealed to them: "If you will allow me room for burial of my dead, listen to me! Intercede for me with Ephron, son of Zohar, asking him 9 to sell me the cave of Machpelah that he owns; it is at the edge of his field. Let him sell it to me in your presence, at its full price, for a burial place." 10 Now Ephron was present with the Hittites. So Ephron the Hittite replied to Abraham in the hearing of the Hittites who sat on his town council: 11 "Please, sir, listen to me! I give you both the field and the cave in it; in the presence of my kinsmen I make this gift. Bury your dead!" 12 But Abraham, after bowing low before the local citizens, addressed Ephron in the hearing of these men: 13 "Ah, if only you would please listen to me! I will pay you the price of the field. Accept it from me, that I may bury my dead there." 14 Ephron replied to Abraham, "Please, 15 sir, listen to me! A piece of land worth four hundred shekels of silver - what is that between you and me, as long as you can bury your dead?" 16 Abraham accepted Ephron's terms; he weighed out to him the silver that Ephron had stipulated in the hearing of the Hittites, four hundred shekels of silver at the current market value. 17 Thus Ephron's field in Machpelah, facing Mamre, together with its cave and all the trees anywhere within its limits, was conveyed 18 to Abraham by purchase in the presence of all the Hittites who sat on Ephron's town council. 19 After this transaction, Abraham buried his wife Sarah in the cave of the field of Machpelah, facing Mamre (that is, Hebron) in the land of Canaan. 20 Thus the field with its cave was transferred from the Hittites to Abraham as a burial place.

Genesis Chapter 24

1 Abraham had now reached a ripe old age, and the LORD had blessed him in every way. 2 Abraham said to the senior servant of his household, who had charge of all his possessions: "Put your hand under my thigh, 3 and I will make you swear by the LORD, the God of heaven and the God of earth, that you will not procure a wife for my son from the daughters of the Canaanites among whom I live, 4 but that you will go to my own land and to my kindred to get a wife for my son Isaac." 5 The servant asked him: "What if the woman is unwilling to follow me to this land? Should I then take your son back to the land from which you migrated?" 6 "Never take my son back there for any reason," Abraham told him. 7 "The LORD, the God of heaven, who took me from my father's house and the land of my kin, and who confirmed by oath the promise he then made to me, 'I will give this land to your descendants'

- he will send his messenger before you, and you will obtain a wife for my son there. 8 If the woman is unwilling to follow you, you will be released from this oath. But never take my son back there!" 9 So the servant put his hand under the thigh of his master Abraham and swore to him in this undertaking. 10 The servant then took ten of his master's camels, and bearing all kinds of gifts from his master, he made his way to the city of Nahor in Aram Naharaim. 11 Near evening, at the time when women go out to draw water, he made the camels kneel by the well outside the city. 12 Then he prayed: "LORD, God of my master Abraham, let it turn out favorably for me today and thus deal graciously with my master Abraham. 13 While I stand here at the spring and the daughters of the townsmen are coming out to draw water, 14 if I say to a girl, 'Please lower your jug, that I may drink,' and she answers, 'Take a drink, and let me give water to your camels, too,' let her be the one whom you have decided upon for your servant Isaac. In this way I shall know that you have dealt graciously with my master." 15 He had scarcely finished these words when Rebekah (who was born to Bethuel, son of Milcah, the wife of Abraham's brother Nahor) came out with a jug on her shoulder. 16 The girl was very beautiful, a virgin, untouched by man. She went down to the spring and filled her jug. As she came up, 17 the servant ran toward her and said, "Please give me a sip of water from your jug." 18 "Take a drink, sir," she replied, and quickly lowering the jug onto her hand, she gave him a drink. 19 When she had let him drink his fill, she said, "I will draw water for your camels, too, until they have drunk their fill." 20 With that, she quickly emptied her jug into the drinking trough and ran back to the well to draw more water, until she had drawn enough for all the camels. 21 The man watched her the whole time, silently waiting to learn whether or not the LORD had made his errand successful. 22 When the camels had finished drinking, the man took out a gold ring weighing half a shekel, which he fastened on her nose, and two gold bracelets weighing ten shekels, which he put on her wrists. 23 Then he asked her: "Whose daughter are you? Tell me, please. And is there room in your father's house for us to spend the night?" 24 She answered: "I am the daughter of Bethuel the son of Milcah, whom she bore to Nahor. 25 There is plenty of straw and fodder at our place," she added, "and room to spend the night." 26 The man then bowed down in worship to the LORD, 27 saying: "Blessed be the LORD, the God of my master Abraham, who has not let his constant kindness toward my master fail. As for myself also, the LORD has led me straight to the house of my master's brother." 28 Then the girl ran off and told her mother's household about it. 29 Now Rebekah had a brother named Laban. 30 As soon as he saw the ring and the bracelets on his sister Rebekah and heard her words about what the man had said to her, Laban rushed outside to the man at the spring. When he reached him, he was still standing by the camels at the spring. 31 So he said to him: "Come, blessed of the LORD! Why are you staying outside when I have made the house ready for you, as well as a place for the camels?" 32 The man then went inside; and while the camels were being unloaded and provided with straw and fodder, water was brought to bathe his feet and the feet of the men who were with him. 33 But when the table was set for him, he said, "I will not eat until I have told my tale." "Do so," they replied. 34 "I am Abraham's servant," he began. 35 "The LORD has blessed my master so abundantly that he has become a wealthy man; he has given him flocks and herds, silver and gold, male and female slaves, and camels and asses. 36 My master's wife Sarah bore a son to my master in her old age, and he has given him everything he owns. 37 My master put me under oath, saying: 'You shall not procure a wife for my son among the daughters of the Canaanites in whose land I live; 38 instead, you shall go to my father's house, to my own relatives, to get a wife for my son.' 39 When I asked my master, 'What if the woman will not follow me?,' 40 he replied: 'The LORD, in whose presence I have always walked, will send his messenger with you and make your errand successful, and so you will get a wife for my son from my own kindred of my father's house. 41 Then you shall be released from my ban. If you visit my kindred and they refuse you, then, too, you shall be released from my ban.' 42 "When I came to the spring today, I prayed: 'LORD, God of my master Abraham, may it be your will to make successful the errand I am engaged on! 43 While I stand here at the spring, if I say to a young woman who comes out to draw water, Please give me a little water from your jug, 44 and she answers, Not only may you have a drink, but I will give water to your camels, too - let her be the woman whom the LORD has decided upon for my master's son.' 45 "I had scarcely finished saying this prayer to myself when Rebekah came out with a jug on her shoulder. After she went down to the spring and drew water, I said to her, 'Please let me have a drink.' 46 She quickly lowered the jug she was carrying and said, 'Take a drink, and let me bring water for your camels, too.' So I drank, and she watered the camels also. 47 When I asked her, 'Whose daughter are you?' she answered, 'The daughter of Bethuel, son of Nahor, borne to Nahor by Milcah.' So I put the ring on her nose and the bracelets on her wrists. 48 Then I bowed down in worship to the LORD, blessing the LORD, the God of my master Abraham, who had led me on the right road to obtain the daughter of my master's kinsman for his son. 49 If, therefore, you have in mind to show true loyalty to my master, let me know; but if not, let me know that, too. I can then proceed accordingly." 50 Laban and his household said in reply: "This thing comes from the LORD; we can say nothing to you either for or against it. 51 Here is Rebekah, ready for you; take her with you, that she may become the wife of your master's son, as the LORD has said." 52 When Abraham's servant heard their answer, he bowed to the ground before the LORD. 53 Then he brought out objects of silver and gold and articles of clothing and presented them to Rebekah; he also gave costly presents to her brother and mother. 54 After he and the men with him had eaten and drunk, they spent the night there. When they were up the next morning, he said, "Give me leave to return to my master." 55 Her brother and mother replied, "Let the girl stay with us a short while, say ten days; after that she may go." 56 But he said to them, "Do not detain me, now that the LORD has made my errand successful; let me go back to my master." 57 They answered, "Let us call the girl and see what she herself has to say about it." 58 So they called Rebekah and asked her, "Do you wish to go with this man?" She answered, "I do." 59 At this they allowed their sister Rebekah and her nurse to take leave, along with Abraham's servant and his men. 60 Invoking a blessing on Rebekah, they said: "Sister, may you grow into thousands of myriads; And may your descendants gain possession of the gates of their enemies!" 61 Then Rebekah and her maids started out; they mounted their camels and followed the man. So the servant took Rebekah and went on his way. 62 Meanwhile Isaac had gone from Beer-lahai-roi and was living in the region of the Negeb. 63 One day toward evening he went out. . . in the field, and as he looked around, he noticed that camels were approaching. 64 Rebekah, too, was looking about, and when she saw him, she alighted from her camel 65 and asked the servant, "Who is the man out there, walking through the fields toward us?" "That is my master," replied the servant. Then she covered herself with her veil. 66 The servant recounted to Isaac all the things he had done. 67 Then Isaac took Rebekah into his tent; he married her, and thus she became his wife. In his love for her Isaac found solace after the death of his mother Sarah.

Genesis Chapter 25

1 Abraham married another wife, whose name was Keturah. 2 She bore him Zimran, Jokshan, Medan, Midian, Ishbak, and Shuah. 3 Jokshan became the father of Sheba and Dedan. The descendants of Dedan were the Asshurim, the Letushim, and the Leummim. 4 The descendants of Midian were Ephah, Epher, Hanoch, Abida, and Eldaah. All of these were descendants of Keturah. 5 Abraham deeded everything that he owned to his son Isaac. 6 To his sons by concubinage, however, he made grants while he was still living, as he sent them away eastward, to the land of Kedem, away from his son Isaac. 7 The whole span of Abraham's life was one hundred and seventy-five years. 8 Then he breathed his last, dying at a ripe old age, grown old after a full life; and he was taken to his kinsmen. 9 His sons Isaac and Ishmael buried him in the cave of Machpelah, in the field of Ephron, son of Zohar the Hittite, which faces Mamre, 10 the field that Abraham had bought from the Hittites; there he was buried next to his wife Sarah. 11 After the death of Abraham, God blessed his son Isaac, who made his home near Beer-lahai-roi. 12 These are the descendants of Abraham's son Ishmael, whom Hagar the Egyptian, Sarah's slave, bore to Abraham. 13 These are the names of Ishmael's sons, listed in the order of their birth: Nebaioth (Ishmael's firstborn), Kedar, Adbeel, Mibsam, 14 Mishma, Dumah, Massa, 15 Hadad, Tema, Jetur, Naphish, and Kedemah. 16 These are the sons of Ishmael, their names by their villages and encampments; twelve chieftains of as many tribal groups. 17 The span of Ishmael's life was one hundred and thirty-seven years. After he had breathed his last and died, he was taken to his kinsmen. 18 The Ishmaelites ranged from Havilah-by-Shur, which is on the border of Egypt, all the way to Asshur; and each of them pitched camp in opposition to his various kinsmen. 19 This is the family history of Isaac, son of Abraham; Abraham had begotten Isaac. 20 Isaac was forty years old when he married Rebekah, the daughter of Bethuel the Aramean of Paddan-aram and the sister of Laban the Aramean. 21 Isaac entreated the LORD on behalf of his wife, since she was sterile. The LORD heard his entreaty, and Rebekah became pregnant. 22 But the children in her womb jostled each other so much that she exclaimed, "If this is to be so, what good will it do me!" She went to consult the LORD, 23 and he answered her: "Two nations are in your womb, two peoples are quarreling while still within you; But one shall surpass the other, and the older shall serve the younger." 24 When the time of her delivery came, there were twins in her womb.

25 The first to emerge was reddish, and his whole body was like a hairy mantle; so, they named him Esau. 26 His brother came out next, gripping Esau's heel; so, they named him Jacob. Isaac was sixty years old when they were born. 27 As the boys grew up, Esau became a skillful hunter, a man who lived in the open; whereas Jacob was a simple man, who kept to his tents. 28 Isaac preferred Esau, because he was fond of game; but Rebekah preferred Jacob. 29 Once, when Jacob was cooking a stew, Esau came in from the open, famished. 30 He said to Jacob, "Let me gulp down some of that red stuff; I'm starving." (That is why he was called Edom.) 31 But Jacob replied, "First give me your birthright in exchange for it." 32 "Look," said Esau, "I'm on the point of dying. What good will any birthright do me?" 33 But Jacob insisted, "Swear to me first!" So, he sold Jacob his birthright under oath. 34 Jacob then gave him some bread and the lentil stew; and Esau ate, drank, got up, and went his way. Esau cared little for his birthright.

Genesis Chapter 26

1 There was a famine in the land (distinct from the earlier one that had occurred in the days of Abraham), and Isaac went down to Abimelech, king of the Philistines in Gerar. 2 The LORD appeared to him and said: "Do not go down to Egypt but continue to camp wherever in this land I tell you. 3 Stay in this land, and I will be with you and bless you; for to you and your descendants I will give all these lands, in fulfillment of the oath that I swore to your father Abraham. 4 I will make your descendants as numerous as the stars in the sky and give them all these lands, and in your descendants all the nations of the earth shall find blessing - 5 this because Abraham obeyed me, keeping my mandate (my commandments, my ordinances, and my instructions)." 6 So Isaac settled in Gerar. 7 When the men of the place asked questions about his wife, he answered, "She is my sister." He was afraid, if he called her his wife, the men of the place would kill him on account of Rebekah, since she was very beautiful. 8 But when he had been there for a long time, Abimelech, king of the Philistines, happened to look out of a window and was surprised to see Isaac fondling his wife, Rebekah. 9 He called for Isaac and said: "She must certainly be your wife! How could you have said, 'She is my sister'?" Isaac replied, "I thought I might lose my life on her account." 10 "How could you do this to us!" exclaimed Abimelech. "It would have taken very little for one of the men to lie with your wife, and you would have thus brought guilt upon us!" 11 Abimelech therefore gave this warning to all his men: "Anyone who molests this man or his wife shall forthwith be put to death." 12 Isaac sowed a crop in that region and reaped a hundredfold the same year. Since the LORD blessed him, 13 he became richer and richer all the time, until he was very wealthy indeed. 14 He acquired such flocks and herds, and so many work animals, that the Philistines became envious of him. 15 (The Philistines had stopped up and filled with dirt all the wells that his father's servants had dug back in the days of his father Abraham.) 16 So Abimelech said to Isaac, "Go away from us; you have become far too numerous for us." 17 Isaac left there and made the Wadi Gerar his regular campsite. 18 (Isaac reopened the wells which his father's servants had dug back in the days of his father Abraham and which the Philistines had stopped up after Abraham's death; he gave them the same names that his father had given them.) 19 But when Isaac's servants dug in the wadi and reached spring water in their well, 20 the shepherds of Gerar quarreled with Isaac's servants, saying, "The water belongs to us!" So, the well was called Esek, because they had challenged him there. 21 Then they dug another well, and they quarreled over that one too; so, it was called Sitnah. 22 When he had moved on from there, he dug still another well; but over this one they did not quarrel. It was called Rehoboth, because he said, "The LORD has now given us ample room, and we shall flourish in the land." 23 From there Isaac went up to Beer-sheba. 24 The same night the LORD appeared to him and said: "I am the God of your father Abraham. You have no need to fear, since I am with you. I will bless you and multiply your descendants for the sake of my servant Abraham." 25 So he built an altar there and invoked the LORD by name. After he had pitched his tent there, his servants began to dig a well nearby. 26 Abimelech had meanwhile come to him from Gerar, accompanied by Ahuzzath, his councilor, and Phicol, the general of his army. 27 Isaac asked them, "Why have you come to me, seeing that you hate me and have driven me away from you?" 28 They answered: "We are convinced that the LORD is with you, so we propose that there be a sworn agreement between our two sides - between you and us. Let us make a pact with you: 29 you shall not act unkindly toward us, just as we have not molested you, but have always acted kindly toward you and have let you depart in peace. Henceforth, 'The LORD'S blessing be upon you!'" 30 Isaac then made a feast for them, and they ate and drank. 31 Early the next morning they exchanged oaths. Then Isaac bade them farewell, and they departed from him in peace. 32 That same day Isaac's servants came and brought him news about the well they had been digging; they told him, "We have reached water!" 33 He called it Shibah; hence the name of the city, Beer-sheba, to this day. 34 When Esau was forty years old, he married Judith, daughter of Beeri the Hittite, and Basemath, daughter of Elon the Hivite. 35 But they became a source of embitterment to Isaac and Rebekah.

Genesis Chapter 27

1 When Isaac was so old that his eyesight had failed him, he called his older son Esau and said to him, "Son!" "Yes, father!" he replied. 2 Isaac then said, "As you can see, I am so old that I may now die at any time. 3 Take your gear, therefore - your quiver and bow - and go out into the country to hunt some game for me. 4 With your catch prepare an appetizing dish for me, such as I like, and bring it to me to eat, so that I may give you my special blessing before I die." 5 Rebekah had been listening while Isaac was speaking to his son Esau. So when Esau went out into the country to hunt some game for his father, 6 Rebekah said to her son Jacob, "Listen! I overheard your father tell your brother Esau, 7 'Bring me some game and with it prepare an appetizing dish for me to eat, that I may give you my blessing with the LORD'S approval before I die.' 8 Now, son, listen carefully to what I tell you. 9 Go to the flock and get me two choice kids. With these I will prepare an appetizing dish for your father, such as he likes. 10 Then bring it to your father to eat, that he may bless you before he dies." 11 "But my brother Esau is a hairy man," said Jacob to his mother Rebekah, "and I am smooth-skinned! 12 Suppose my father feels me? He will think I am making sport of him, and I shall bring on myself a curse instead of a blessing." 13 His mother, however, replied: "Let any curse against you, son, fall on me! Just do as I say. Go and get me the kids." 14 So Jacob went and got them and brought them to his mother; and with them she prepared an appetizing dish, such as his father liked. 15 Rebekah then took the best clothes of her older son Esau that she had in the house, and gave them to her younger son Jacob to wear; 16 and with the skins of the kids she covered up his hands and the hairless parts of his neck. 17 Then she handed her son Jacob the appetizing dish and the bread she had prepared. 18 Bringing them to his father, Jacob said, "Father!" "Yes?" replied Isaac. "Which of my sons are you?" 19 Jacob answered his father: "I am Esau, your first-born. I did as you told me. Please sit up and eat some of my game, so that you may give me your special blessing." 20 But Isaac asked, "How did you succeed so quickly, son?" He answered, "The LORD, your God, let things turn out well with me." 21 Isaac then said to Jacob, "Come closer, son, that I may feel you, to learn whether you really are my son Esau or not." 22 So Jacob moved up closer to his father. When Isaac felt him, he said, "Although the voice is Jacob's, the hands are Esau's." 23 (He failed to identify him because his hands were hairy, like those of his brother Esau; so in the end he gave him his blessing.) 24 Again he asked him, "Are you really my son Esau?" "Certainly," he replied. 25 Then Isaac said, "Serve me your game, son, that I may eat of it and then give you my blessing." Jacob served it to him, and Isaac ate; he brought him wine, and he drank. 26 Finally his father Isaac said to him, "Come closer, son, and kiss me." 27 As Jacob went up and kissed him, Isaac smelled the fragrance of his clothes. With that, he blessed him, saying, "Ah, the fragrance of my son is like the fragrance of a field that the LORD has blessed! 28 "May God give to you of the dew of the heavens And of the fertility of the earth abundance of grain and wine. 29 "Let peoples serve you, and nations pay you homage; Be master of your brothers, and may your mother's sons bow down to you. Cursed be those who curse you, and blessed be those who bless you." 30 Jacob had scarcely left his father, just after Isaac had finished blessing him, when his brother Esau came back from his hunt. 31 Then he too prepared an appetizing dish with his game, and bringing it to his father, he said, "Please, father, eat some of your son's game, that you may then give me your special blessing." 32 "Who are you?" his father Isaac asked him. "I am Esau," he replied, "your first-born son." 33 With that, Isaac was seized with a fit of uncontrollable trembling. "Who was it, then," he asked, "that hunted game and brought it to me? I finished eating it just before you came, and I blessed him. Now he must remain blessed!" 34 On hearing his father's words, Esau burst into loud, bitter sobbing. "Father, bless me too!" he begged. 35 When Isaac explained, "Your brother came here by a ruse and carried off your blessing," 36 Esau exclaimed, "He has been well named Jacob! He has now supplanted me twice! First he took away my birthright, and now he has taken away my blessing." Then he pleaded, "Haven't you saved a blessing for me?" 37 Isaac replied: "I have already appointed him your master, and I have assigned to him all his kinsmen as his slaves; besides, I have enriched him with grain and wine. What then can I do for you, son?" 38 But Esau urged his father, "Have you only that one blessing, father? Bless me too!" Isaac, however, made no reply; and Esau wept aloud. 39 Finally Isaac spoke again and said to him: "Ah, far from the fertile earth shall be your dwelling; far from the dew of the

heavens above! 40 "By your sword you shall live, and your brother you shall serve; But when you become restive, you shall throw off his yoke from your neck." 41 Esau bore Jacob a grudge because of the blessing his father had given him. He said to himself, "When the time of mourning for my father comes, I will kill my brother Jacob." 42 When Rebekah got news of what her older son Esau had in mind, she called her younger son Jacob and said to him: "Listen! Your brother Esau intends to settle accounts with you by killing you. 43 Therefore, son, do what I tell you: flee at once to my brother Laban in Haran, 44 and stay with him a while until your brother's fury subsides 45 (until your brother's anger against you subsides) and he forgets what you did to him. Then I will send for you and bring you back. Must I lose both of you in a single day?" 46 Rebekah said to Isaac: "I am disgusted with life because of the Hittite women. If Jacob also should marry a Hittite woman, a native of the land, like these women, what good would life be to me?"

Genesis Chapter 28

1 Isaac therefore called Jacob, greeted him with a blessing, and charged him: "You shall not marry a Canaanite woman! 2 Go now to Paddan-aram, to the home of your mother's father Bethuel, and there choose a wife for yourself from among the daughters of your uncle Laban. 3 May God Almighty bless you and make you fertile, multiply you that you may become an assembly of peoples. 4 May he extend to you and your descendants the blessing he gave to Abraham, so that you may gain possession of the land where you are staying, which he assigned to Abraham." 5 Then Isaac sent Jacob on his way; he went to Paddan-aram, to Laban, son of Bethuel the Aramean, and brother of Rebekah, the mother of Jacob and Esau. 6 Esau noted that Isaac had blessed Jacob when he sent him to Paddan-aram to get himself a wife there, charging him, as he gave him his blessing, not to marry a Canaanite woman, 7 and that Jacob had obeyed his father and mother and gone to Paddan-aram. 8 Esau realized how displeasing the Canaanite women were to his father Isaac, 9 so he went to Ishmael, and in addition to the wives he had, married Mahalath, the daughter of Abraham's son Ishmael and sister of Nebaioth. 10 Jacob departed from Beer-sheba and proceeded toward Haran. 11 When he came upon a certain shrine, as the sun had already set, he stopped there for the night. Taking one of the stones at the shrine, he put it under his head and lay down to sleep at that spot. 12 Then he had a dream: a stairway rested on the ground, with its top reaching to the heavens; and God's messengers were going up and down on it. 13 And there was the LORD standing beside him and saying: "I, the LORD, am the God of your forefather Abraham and the God of Isaac; the land on which you are lying I will give to you and your descendants. 14 These shall be as plentiful as the dust of the earth, and through them you shall spread out east and west, north and south. In you and your descendants all the nations of the earth shall find blessing. 15 Know that I am with you; I will protect you wherever you go, and bring you back to this land. I will never leave you until I have done what I promised you." 16 When Jacob awoke from his sleep, he exclaimed, "Truly, the LORD is in this spot, although I did not know it!" 17 In solemn wonder he cried out: "How awesome is this shrine! This is nothing else but an abode of God, and that is the gateway to heaven!" 18 Early the next morning Jacob took the stone that he had put under his head, set it up as a memorial stone, and poured oil on top of it. 19 He called that site Bethel, whereas the former name of the town had been Luz. 20 Jacob then made this vow: "If God remains with me, to protect me on this journey I am making and to give me enough bread to eat and clothing to wear, 21 and I come back safe to my father's house, the LORD shall be my God. 22 This stone that I have set up as a memorial stone shall be God's abode. Of everything you give me, I will faithfully return a tenth part to you."

Genesis Chapter 29

1 After Jacob resumed his journey, he came to the land of the Easterners. 2 Looking about, he saw a well in the open country, with three droves of sheep huddled near it, for droves were watered from that well. A large stone covered the mouth of the well. 3 Only when all the shepherds were assembled there could they roll the stone away from the mouth of the well and water the flocks. Then they would put the stone back again over the mouth of the well. 4 Jacob said to them, "Friends, where are you from?" "We are from Haran," they replied. 5 Then he asked them, "Do you know Laban, son of Nahor?" "We do," they answered. 6 He inquired further, "Is he well?" "He is," they answered, "and here comes his daughter Rachel with his flock." 7 Then he said: "There is still much daylight left; it is hardly the time to bring the animals home. Why don't you water the flocks now, and then continue pasturing them?" 8 "We cannot," they replied, "until all the shepherds are here to roll the stone away from the mouth of the well; only then can we water the flocks." 9 While he was still talking with them, Rachel arrived with her father's sheep; she was the one who tended them. 10 As soon as Jacob saw Rachel, the daughter of his uncle Laban, with the sheep of his uncle Laban, he went up, rolled the stone away from the mouth of the well, and watered his uncle's sheep. 11 Then Jacob kissed Rachel and burst into tears. 12 He told her that he was her father's relative, Rebekah's son, and she ran to tell her father. 13 When Laban heard the news about his sister's son Jacob, he hurried out to meet him. After embracing and kissing him, he brought him to his house. Jacob then recounted to Laban all that had happened, 14 and Laban said to him, "You are indeed my flesh and blood." After Jacob had stayed with him a full month, 15 Laban said to him: "Should you serve me for nothing just because you are a relative of mine? Tell me what your wages should be." 16 Now Laban had two daughters; the older was called Leah, the younger Rachel. 17 Leah had lovely eyes, but Rachel was well formed and beautiful. 18 Since Jacob had fallen in love with Rachel, he answered Laban, "I will serve you seven years for your younger daughter Rachel." 19 Laban replied, "I prefer to give her to you rather than to an outsider. Stay with me." 20 So Jacob served seven years for Rachel, yet they seemed to him but a few days because of his love for her. 21 Then Jacob said to Laban, "Give me my wife, that I may consummate my marriage with her, for my term is now completed." 22 So Laban invited all the local inhabitants and gave a feast. 23 At nightfall he took his daughter Leah and brought her to Jacob, and Jacob consummated the marriage with her. 24 (Laban assigned his slave girl Zilpah to his daughter Leah as her maidservant.) 25 In the morning Jacob was amazed: it was Leah! So, he cried out to Laban: "How could you do this to me! Was it not for Rachel that I served you? Why did you dupe me?" 26 "It is not the custom in our country," Laban replied, "to marry off a younger daughter before an older one. 27 Finish the bridal week for this one, and then I will give you the other too, in return for another seven years of service with me." 28 Jacob agreed. He finished the bridal week for Leah, and then Laban gave him his daughter Rachel in marriage. 29 (Laban assigned his slave girl Bilhah to his daughter Rachel as her maidservant.) 30 Jacob then consummated his marriage with Rachel also, and he loved her more than Leah. he remained in Laban's service another seven years. 31 When the LORD saw that Leah was unloved, he made her fruitful, while Rachel remained barren. 32 Leah conceived and bore a son, and she named him Reuben; for she said, "It means, 'The LORD saw my misery; now my husband will love me.'" 33 She conceived again and bore a son, and said, "It means, 'The LORD heard that I was unloved,' and therefore he has given me this one also"; so, she named him Simeon. 34 Again she conceived and bore a son, and she said, "Now at last my husband will become attached to me, since I have now borne him three sons"; that is why she named him Levi. 35 Once more she conceived and bore a son, and she said, "This time I will give grateful praise to the LORD"; therefore, she named him Judah. Then she stopped bearing children.

Genesis Chapter 30

1 When Rachel saw that she failed to bear children to Jacob, she became envious of her sister. She said to Jacob, "Give me children or I shall die!" 2 In anger Jacob retorted, "Can I take the place of God, who has denied you the fruit of the womb?" 3 She replied, "Here is my maidservant Bilhah. Have intercourse with her, and let her give birth on my knees, so that I too may have offspring, at least through her." 4 So she gave him her maidservant Bilhah as a consort, and Jacob had intercourse with her. 5 When Bilhah conceived and bore a son, 6 Rachel said, "God has vindicated me; indeed, he has heeded my plea and given me a son." Therefore, she named him Dan. 7 Rachel's maidservant Bilhah conceived again and bore a second son, 8 and Rachel said, "I engaged in a fateful struggle with my sister, and I prevailed." So, she named him Naphtali. 9 When Leah saw that she had ceased to bear children, she gave her maidservant Zilpah to Jacob as a consort. 10 So Jacob had intercourse with Zilpah, and she conceived and bore a son. 11 Leah then said, "What good luck!" So, she named him Gad. 12 Then Leah's maidservant Zilpah bore a second son to Jacob; 13 and Leah said, "What good fortune!" - meaning, "Women call me fortunate." So, she named him Asher. 14 One day, during the wheat harvest, when Reuben was out in the field, he came upon some mandrakes which he brought home to his mother Leah. Rachel asked Leah, "Please let me have some of your son's mandrakes." 15 Leah replied, "Was it not enough for you to take away my husband, that you must now take my son's mandrakes too?" "Very well, then!" Rachel answered. "In exchange for your son's mandrakes, Jacob may lie with you tonight." 16 That evening, when Jacob came home from the fields, Leah went out to meet him. "You are now to come in with me," she told him, "Because I have paid for you with my son's mandrakes." So that night he slept with her, 17 and God heard her prayer; she conceived and bore a fifth son to Jacob. 18 Leah then said, "God has given me my reward for having let my husband have

my maidservant"; so, she named him Issachar. ¹⁹ Leah conceived again and bore a sixth son to Jacob; ²⁰ and she said, "God has brought me a precious gift. This time my husband will offer me presents, now that I have borne him six sons"; so, she named him Zebulun. ²¹ Finally, she gave birth to a daughter, and she named her Dinah. ²² Then God remembered Rachel; he heard her prayer and made her fruitful. ²³ She conceived and bore a son, and she said, "God has removed my disgrace." ²⁴ So she named him Joseph, meaning, "May the LORD add another son to this one for me!" ²⁵ After Rachel gave birth to Joseph, Jacob said to Laban: "Give me leave to go to my homeland. ²⁶ Let me have my wives, for whom I served you, and my children, too, that I may depart. You know very well the service that I have rendered you." ²⁷ Laban answered him: "If you will please..."I have learned through divination that it is because of you that God has blessed me. ²⁸ So," he continued, "state what wages you want from me, and I will pay them." ²⁹ Jacob replied: "You know what work I did for you and how well your livestock fared under my care; ³⁰ the little you had before I came has grown into very much, since the LORD'S blessings came upon you in my company. Therefore, I should now do something for my own household as well." ³¹ "What should I pay you?" Laban asked. Jacob answered: "You do not have to pay me anything outright. I will again pasture and tend your flock, if you do this one thing for me: ³² go through your whole flock today and remove from it every dark animal among the sheep and every spotted or speckled one among the goats. Only such animals shall be my wages. ³³ In the future, whenever you check on these wages of mine, let my honesty testify against me: any animal in my possession that is not a speckled or spotted goat, or a dark sheep, got there by theft!" ³⁴ "Very well," agreed Laban. "Let it be as you say." ³⁵ That same day Laban removed the streaked and spotted he-goats and all the speckled and spotted she-goats, all those with some white on them, as well as the fully dark-colored sheep; these he left. . . in charge of his sons. ³⁶ Then he put a three days' journey between himself and Jacob, while Jacob continued to pasture the rest of Laban's flock. ³⁷ Jacob, however, got some fresh shoots of poplar, almond and plane trees, and he made white stripes in them by peeling off the bark down to the white core of the shoots. ³⁸ The rods that he had thus peeled he then set upright in the watering troughs, so that they would be in front of the animals that drank from the troughs. When the animals were in heat as they came to drink, ³⁹ the goats mated by the rods, and so they brought forth streaked, speckled and spotted kids. ⁴⁰ The sheep, on the other hand, Jacob kept apart, and he set these animals to face the streaked or fully dark-colored animals of Laban. Thus, he produced special flocks of his own, which he did not put with Laban's flock. ⁴¹ Moreover, whenever the hardier animals were in heat, Jacob would set the rods in the troughs in full view of these animals, so that they mated by the rods; ⁴² but with the weaker animals he would not put the rods there. So, the feeble animals would go to Laban, but the sturdy ones to Jacob. ⁴³ Thus the man grew increasingly prosperous, and he came to own not only large flocks but also male and female servants and camels and asses.

Genesis Chapter 31

¹ Jacob learned that Laban's sons were saying, "Jacob has taken everything that belonged to our father, and he has accumulated all this wealth of his by using our father's property." ² Jacob perceived, too, that Laban's attitude toward him was not what it had previously been. ³ Then the LORD said to Jacob, "Return to the land of your fathers, where you were born, and I will be with you." ⁴ So Jacob sent for Rachel and Leah to meet him where he was in the field with his flock. ⁵ There he said to them: "I have noticed that your father's attitude toward me is not as it was in the past; but the God of my father has been with me. ⁶ You well know what effort I put into serving your father; ⁷ yet your father cheated me and changed my wages time after time. God, however, did not let him do me any harm. ⁸ Whenever your father said, 'The speckled animals shall be your wages,' the entire flock would bear speckled young; whenever he said, 'The streaked animals shall be your wages,' the entire flock would bear streaked young. ⁹ Thus God reclaimed your father's livestock and gave it to me. ¹⁰ Once, in the breeding season, I had a dream in which I saw mating he-goats that were streaked, speckled and mottled. ¹¹ In the dream God's messenger called to me, 'Jacob!' 'Here!' I replied. ¹² Then he said: 'Note well. All the he-goats in the flock, as they mate, are streaked, speckled and mottled, for I have seen all the things that Laban has been doing to you. ¹³ I am the God who appeared to you in Bethel, where you anointed a memorial stone and made a vow to me. Up, then! Leave this land and return to the land of your birth.'" ¹⁴ Rachel and Leah answered him: "Have we still an heir's portion in our father's house? ¹⁵ Are we not regarded by him as outsiders? He not only sold us; he has even used up the money that he got for us! ¹⁶ All the wealth that God reclaimed from our father really belongs to us and our children. Therefore, do just as God has told you."

¹⁷ Jacob proceeded to put his children and wives on camels, ¹⁸ and he drove off with all his livestock and all the property he had acquired in Paddan-aram, to go to his father Isaac in the land of Canaan. ¹⁹ Now Laban had gone away to shear his sheep, and Rachel had meanwhile appropriated her father's household idols. ²⁰ Jacob had hoodwinked Laban the Aramean by not telling him of his intended flight. ²¹ Thus he made his escape with all that he had. Once he was across the Euphrates, he headed for the highlands of Gilead. ²² On the third day, word came to Laban that Jacob had fled. ²³ Taking his kinsmen with him, he pursued him for seven days until he caught up with him in the hill country of Gilead. ²⁴ But that night God appeared to Laban the Aramean in a dream and warned him, "Take care not to threaten Jacob with any harm!" ²⁵ When Laban overtook Jacob, Jacob's tents were pitched in the highlands; Laban also pitched his tents there, on Mount Gilead. ²⁶ "What do you mean," Laban demanded of Jacob, "by hoodwinking me and carrying off my daughters like war captives? ²⁷ Why did you dupe me by stealing away secretly? You should have told me, and I would have sent you off with merry singing to the sound of tambourines and harps. ²⁸ You did not even allow me a parting kiss to my daughters and grandchildren! What you have now done is a senseless thing. ²⁹ I have it in my power to harm all of you; but last night the God of your father said to me, 'Take care not to threaten Jacob with any harm!' ³⁰ Granted that you had to leave because you were desperately homesick for your father's house, why did you steal my gods?" ³¹ "I was frightened," Jacob replied to Laban, "at the thought that you might take your daughters away from me by force. ³² But as for your gods, the one you find them with shall not remain alive! If, with my kinsmen looking on, you identify anything here as belonging to you, take it." Jacob, of course, had no idea that Rachel had stolen the idols. ³³ Laban then went in and searched Jacob's tent and Leah's tent, as well as the tents of the two maidservants; but he did not find the idols. Leaving Leah's tent, he went into Rachel's. ³⁴ Now Rachel had taken the idols, put them inside a camel cushion, and seated herself upon them. When Laban had rummaged through the rest of her tent without finding them, ³⁵ Rachel said to her father, "Let not my lord feel offended that I cannot rise in your presence; a woman's period is upon me." So, despite his search, he did not find his idols. ³⁶ Jacob, now enraged, upbraided Laban. "What crime or offense have I committed," he demanded, "that you should hound me so fiercely? ³⁷ Now that you have ransacked all my things, have you found a single object taken from your belongings? If so, produce it here before your kinsmen and mine, and let them decide between us two. ³⁸ "In the twenty years that I was under you, no ewe or she-goat of yours ever miscarried, and I have never feasted on a ram of your flock. ³⁹ I never brought you an animal torn by wild beasts; I made good the loss myself. You held me responsible for anything stolen by day or night. ⁴⁰ How often the scorching heat ravaged me by day, and the frost by night, while sleep fled from my eyes! ⁴¹ Of the twenty years that I have now spent in your household, I slaved fourteen years for your two daughters and six years for your flock, while you changed my wages time after time. ⁴² If my ancestral God, the God of Abraham and the Awesome One of Isaac, had not been on my side, you would now have sent me away empty-handed. But God saw my plight and the fruits of my toil, and last night he gave judgment." ⁴³ Laban replied to Jacob: "The women are mine, their children are mine, and the flocks are mine; everything you see belongs to me. But since these women are my daughters, I will now do something for them and for the children they have borne. ⁴⁴ Come, then, we will make a pact, you and I; the LORD shall be a witness between us." ⁴⁵ Then Jacob took a stone and set it up as a memorial stone. ⁴⁶ Jacob said to his kinsmen, "Gather some stones." So, they got some stones and made a mound; and they had a meal there at the mound. ⁴⁷ Laban called it Jegar-sahadutha, but Jacob named it Galeed. ⁴⁸ "This mound," said Laban, "shall be a witness from now on between you and me." That is why it was named Galeed - ⁴⁹ and also Mizpah, for he said: "May the LORD keep watch between you and me when we are out of each other's sight. ᵇ⁵⁰ If you mistreat my daughters, or take other wives besides my daughters, remember that even though no one else is about, God will be witness between you and me." ⁵¹ Laban said further to Jacob: "Here is this mound, and here is the memorial stone that I have set up between you and me. ⁵² This mound shall be witness, and this memorial stone shall be witness, that, with hostile intent, neither may I pass beyond this mound into your territory, nor may you pass beyond it into mine. ⁵³ May the God of Abraham and the god of Nahor (their ancestral deities) maintain justice between us!" Jacob took the oath by the Awesome One of Isaac. ⁵⁴ He then offered a sacrifice on the mountain and invited his kinsmen to share in the meal. When they had eaten, they passed the night on the mountain.

Genesis Chapter 32

1 Early the next morning, Laban kissed his grandchildren and his daughters goodbye; then he set out on his journey back home, 2 while Jacob continued on his own way. Then God's messengers encountered Jacob. 3 When he saw them he said, "This is God's encampment." So he named that place Mahanaim. 4 Jacob sent messengers ahead to his brother Esau in the land of Seir, the country of Edom, 5 with this message: "Thus shall you say to my lord Esau: 'Your servant Jacob speaks as follows: I have been staying with Laban and have been detained there until now. 6 I own cattle, asses and sheep, as well as male and female servants. I am sending my lord this information in the hope of gaining your favor.'" 7 When the messengers returned to Jacob, they said, "We reached your brother Esau. He is now coming to meet you, accompanied by four hundred men." 8 Jacob was very much frightened. In his anxiety, he divided the people who were with him, as well as his flocks, herds and camels, into two camps. 9 "If Esau should attack and overwhelm one camp," he reasoned, "the remaining camp may still survive." 10 Then he prayed: "O God of my father Abraham and God of my father Isaac! You told me, O LORD, 'Go back to the land of your birth, and I will be good to you.' 11 I am unworthy of all the acts of kindness that you have loyally performed for your servant: although I crossed the Jordan here with nothing but my staff, I have now grown into two companies. 12 Save me, I pray, from the hand of my brother Esau! Otherwise I fear that when he comes he will strike me down and slay the mothers and children. 13 You yourself said, 'I will be very good to you, and I will make your descendants like the sands of the sea, which are too numerous to count.'" 14 After passing the night there, Jacob selected from what he had with him the following presents for his brother Esau: 15 two hundred she-goats and twenty he-goats; two hundred ewes and twenty rams; 16 thirty milch camels and their young; forty cows and ten bulls; twenty she-asses and ten he-asses. 17 He put these animals in charge of his servants, in separate droves, and he told the servants, "Go on ahead of me, but keep a space between one drove and the next." 18 To the servant in the lead he gave this instruction: "When my brother Esau meets you, he may ask you, 'Whose man are you? Where are you going? To whom do these animals ahead of you belong?' 19 Then you shall answer, 'They belong to your brother Jacob, but they have been sent as a gift to my lord Esau; and Jacob himself is right behind us.'" 20 He gave similar instructions to the second servant and the third and to all the others who followed behind the droves, namely: "Thus and thus shall you say to Esau, when you reach him; 21 and be sure to add, 'Your servant Jacob is right behind us.'" For Jacob reasoned, "If I first appease him with gifts that precede me, then later, when I face him, perhaps he will forgive me." 22 So the gifts went on ahead of him, while he stayed that night in the camp. 23 In the course of that night, however, Jacob arose, took his two wives, with the two maidservants and his eleven children, and crossed the ford of the Jabbok. 24 After he had taken them across the stream and had brought over all his possessions, 25 Jacob was left there alone. Then some man wrestled with him until the break of dawn. 26 When the man saw that he could not prevail over him, he struck Jacob's hip at its socket, so that the hip socket was wrenched as they wrestled. 27 The man then said, "Let me go, for it is daybreak." But Jacob said, "I will not let you go until you bless me." 28 "What is your name?" the man asked. He answered, "Jacob." 29 Then the man said, "You shall no longer be spoken of as Jacob, but as Israel, because you have contended with divine and human beings and have prevailed." 30 Jacob then asked him, "Do tell me your name, please." He answered, "Why should you want to know my name?" With that, he bade him farewell. 31 Jacob named the place Peniel, "Because I have seen God face to face," he said, "yet my life has been spared." 32 At sunrise, as he left Penuel, Jacob limped along because of his hip. 33 That is why, to this day, the Israelites do not eat the sciatic muscle that is on the hip socket, inasmuch as Jacob's hip socket was struck at the sciatic muscle.

Genesis Chapter 33

1 Jacob looked up and saw Esau coming, accompanied by four hundred men. So, he divided his children among Leah, Rachel and the two maidservants, 2 putting the maids and their children first, Leah and her children next, and Rachel and Joseph last. 3 He himself went on ahead of them, bowing to the ground seven times, until he reached his brother. 4 Esau ran to meet him, embraced him, and flinging himself on his neck, kissed him as he wept. 5 When Esau looked about, he saw the women and children. "Who are these with you?" he asked. Jacob answered, "They are the children whom God has graciously bestowed on your servant." 6 Then the maidservants and their children came forward and bowed low; 7 next, Leah and her children came forward and bowed low; lastly, Rachel and her children came forward and bowed low. 8 Then

Esau asked, "What did you intend with all those droves that I encountered?" Jacob answered, "It was to gain my lord's favor." 9 "I have plenty," replied Esau; "you should keep what is yours, brother." 10 "No, I beg you!" said Jacob. "If you will do me the favor, please accept this gift from me, since to come into your presence is for me like coming into the presence of God, now that you have received me so kindly. 11 Do accept the present I have brought you; God has been generous toward me, and I have an abundance." Since he so urged him, Esau accepted. 12 Then Esau said, "Let us break camp and be on our way; I will travel alongside you." 13 But Jacob replied: "As my lord can see, the children are frail. Besides, I am encumbered with the flocks and herds, which now have sucklings; if overdriven for a single day, the whole flock will die. 14 Let my lord, then, go on ahead of me, while I proceed more slowly at the pace of the livestock before me and at the pace of my children, until I join my lord in Seir." 15 Esau replied, "Let me at least put at your disposal some of the men who are with me." But Jacob said, "For what reason? Please indulge me in this, my lord." 16 So on the same day that Esau began his journey back to Seir, 17 Jacob journeyed to Succoth. There he built a home for himself and made booths for his livestock. That is why the place was called Succoth. 18 Having thus come from Paddan-aram, Jacob arrived safely at the city of Shechem, which is in the land of Canaan, and he encamped in sight of the city. 19 The plot of ground on which he had pitched his tent he bought for a hundred pieces of bullion from the descendants of Hamor, the founder of Shechem. 20 He set up a memorial stone there and invoked "El, the God of Israel."

Genesis Chapter 34

1 Dinah, the daughter whom Leah had borne to Jacob, went out to visit some of the women of the land. 2 When Shechem, son of Hamor the Hivite, who was chief of the region, saw her, he seized her and lay with her by force. 3 Since he was strongly attracted to Dinah, daughter of Jacob, indeed was really in love with the girl, he endeavored to win her affection. 4 Shechem also asked his father Hamor, "Get me this girl for a wife." 5 Meanwhile, Jacob heard that Shechem had defiled his daughter Dinah; but since his sons were out in the fields with his livestock, he held his peace until they came home. 6 Now Hamor, the father of Shechem, went out to discuss the matter with Jacob, 7 just as Jacob's sons were coming in from the fields. When they heard the news, the men were shocked and seethed with indignation. What Shechem had done was an outrage in Israel; such a thing could not be tolerated. 8 Hamor appealed to them, saying: "My son Shechem has his heart set on your daughter. Please give her to him in marriage. 9 Intermarry with us; give your daughters to us and take our daughters for yourselves. 10 Thus you can live among us. The land is open before you; you can settle and move about freely in it and acquire landed property here." 11 Then Shechem, too, appealed to Dinah's father and brothers: "Do me this favour, and I will pay whatever you demand of me. 12 No matter how high you set the bridal price; I will pay you whatever you ask; only give me the maiden in marriage." 13 Jacob's sons replied to Shechem and his father Hamor with guile, speaking as they did because their sister Dinah had been defiled. 14 "We could not do such a thing," they said, "as to give our sister to an uncircumcised man; that would be a disgrace for us. 15 We will agree with you only on this condition, that you become like us by having every male among you circumcised. 16 Then we will give you our daughters and take yours in marriage; we will settle among you and become one kindred people with you. 17 But if you do not comply with our terms regarding circumcision, we will take our daughter and go away." 18 Their proposal seemed fair to Hamor and his son Shechem. 19 The young man lost no time in acting in the matter, since he was deeply in love with Jacob's daughter. Moreover, he was more highly respected than anyone else in his clan. 20 So Hamor and his son Shechem went to their town council and thus presented the matter to their fellow townsmen: 21 "These men are friendly toward us. Let them settle in the land and move about in it freely; there is ample room in the country for them. We can marry their daughters and give our daughters to them in marriage. 22 But the men will agree to live with us and form one kindred people with us only on this condition, that every male among us be circumcised as they themselves are. 23 Would not the livestock they have acquired - all their animals - then be ours? Let us, therefore, give in to them, so that they may settle among us." 24 All the able-bodied men of the town agreed with Hamor and his son Shechem, and all the males, including every able-bodied man in the community, were circumcised. 25 On the third day, while they were still in pain, Dinah's full brothers Simeon and Levi, two of Jacob's sons, took their swords, advanced against the city without any trouble, and massacred all the males. 26 After they had put Hamor and his son Shechem to the sword, they took Dinah from Shechem's house and left. 27 Then the other sons of Jacob followed up the slaughter and sacked the city in reprisal for their sister Dinah's defilement. 28 They seized their flocks, herds and asses,

whatever was in the city and in the country around. 29 They carried off all their wealth, their women, and their children, and took for loot whatever was in the houses. 30 Jacob said to Simeon and Levi: "You have brought trouble upon me by making me loathsome to the inhabitants of the land, the Canaanites and the Perizzites. I have so few men that, if these people unite against me and attack me, I and my family will be wiped out." 31 But they retorted, "Should our sister have been treated like a harlot?"

Genesis Chapter 35

1 God said to Jacob: "Go up now to Bethel. Settle there and build an altar there to the God who appeared to you while you were fleeing from your brother Esau." 2 So Jacob told his family and all the others who were with him: "Get rid of the foreign gods that you have among you; then purify yourselves and put on fresh clothes. 3 We are now to go up to Bethel, and I will build an altar there to the God who answered me in my hour of distress and who has been with me wherever I have gone." 4 They therefore handed over to Jacob all the foreign gods in their possession and also the rings they had in their ears. 5 Then, as they set out, a terror from God fell upon the towns round about, so that no one pursued the sons of Jacob. 6 Thus Jacob and all the people who were with him arrived in Luz (that is, Bethel) in the land of Canaan. 7 There he built an altar and named the place Bethel, for it was there that God had revealed himself to him when he was fleeing from his brother. 8 Death came to Rebekah's nurse Deborah; she was buried under the oak below Bethel, and so it was called Allonbacuth. 9 On Jacob's arrival from Paddan-aram, God appeared to him again and blessed him. 10 God said to him: "You whose name is Jacob shall no longer be called Jacob, but Israel shall be your name." Thus, he was named Israel. 11 God also said to him: "I am God Almighty; be fruitful and multiply. A nation, indeed, an assembly of nations, shall issue from you, and kings shall issue from your loins. 12 The land I once gave to Abraham and Isaac I now give to you; And to your descendants after you will I give this land." 13 Then God departed from him. 14 On the site where God had spoken with him, Jacob set up a memorial stone, and upon it he made a libation and poured out oil. 15 Jacob named the site Bethel, because God had spoken with him there. 16 Then they departed from Bethel; but while they still had some distance to go on the way to Ephrath, Rachel began to be in labor and to suffer great distress. 17 When her pangs were most severe, her midwife said to her, "Have no fear! This time, too, you have a son." 18 With her last breath - for she was at the point of death-she called him Ben-oni; his father, however, named him Benjamin. 19 Thus Rachel died; and she was buried on the road to Ephrath (that is, Bethlehem). 20 Jacob set up a memorial stone on her grave, and the same monument marks Rachel's grave to this day. 21 Israel moved on and pitched his tent beyond Migdal-eder. 22 While Israel was encamped in that region, Reuben went and lay with Bilhah, his father's concubine. When Israel heard of it, he was greatly offended. The sons of Jacob were now twelve. 23 The sons of Leah: Reuben, Jacob's first-born, Simeon, Levi, Judah, Issachar, and Zebulun; 24 the sons of Rachel: Joseph and Benjamin; 25 the sons of Rachel's maid Bilhah: Dan and Naphtali; 26 the sons of Leah's maid Zilpah: Gad and Asher. These are the sons of Jacob who were born to him in Paddan-aram. 27 Jacob went home to his father Isaac at Mamre, in Kiriath-arba (that is, Hebron), where Abraham and Isaac had stayed. 28 The lifetime of Isaac was one hundred and eighty years. 29 then he breathed his last. After a full life, he died as an old man and was taken to his kinsmen. His sons Esau and Jacob buried him.

Genesis Chapter 36

1 These are the descendants of Esau (that is, Edom). 2 Esau took his wives from among the Canaanite women: Adah, daughter of Elon the Hittite; Oholibamah, granddaughter through Anah of Zibeon the Hivite; 3 and Basemath, daughter of Ishmael and sister of Nebaioth. 4 Adah bore Eliphaz to Esau; Basemath bore Reuel; 5 and Oholibamah bore Jeush, Jalam and Korah. These are the sons of Esau who were born to him in the land of Canaan. 6 Esau took his wives, his sons, his daughters, and all the members of his household, as well as his livestock comprising various animals and all the property he had acquired in the land of Canaan, and went to the land of Seir, out of the way of his brother Jacob. 7 Their possessions had become too great for them to dwell together, and the land in which they were staying could not support them because of their livestock. 8 So Esau settled in the highlands of Seir. (Esau is Edom.) 9 These are the descendants of Esau, ancestor of the Edomites, in the highlands of Seir. 10 These are the names of Esau's sons: Eliphaz, son of Esau's wife Adah; and Reuel, son of Esau's wife Basemath. 11 The sons of Eliphaz were Teman, Omar, Zepho, Gatam, and Kenaz. 12 (Esau's son Eliphaz had a concubine Timna, and she bore Amalek to Eliphaz.) These are the descendants of Esau's wife Adah. 13 The sons of Reuel were Nahath, Zerah, Shammah,

and Mizzah. These are the descendants of Esau's wife Basemath. 14 The descendants of Esau's wife Oholibamah - granddaughter through Anah of Zibeon - whom she bore to Esau were Jeush, Jalam, and Korah. 15 The following are the clans of Esau's descendants. The descendants of Eliphaz, Esau's first-born: the clans of Teman, Omar, Zepho, Kenaz, 16 Korah, Gatam, and Amalek. These are the clans of Eliphaz in the land of Edom; they are descended from Adah. 17 The descendants of Esau's son Reuel: the clans of Nahath, Zerah, Shammah, and Mizzah. These are the clans of Reuel in the land of Edom; they are descended from Esau's wife Basemath. 18 The descendants of Esau's wife Oholibamah: the clans of Jeush, Jalam, and Korah. These are the clans of Esau's wife Oholibamah, daughter of Anah. 19 Such are the descendants of Esau (that is, Edom) according to their clans. 20 The following are the descendants of Seir the Horite, the original settlers in the land: Lotan, Shobal, Zibeon, Anah, 21 Dishon, Ezer, and Dishan; they are the Horite clans descended from Seir, in the land of Edom. 22 Lotan's descendants were Hori and Hemam, and Lotan's sister was Timna. 23 Shobal's descendants were Alvan, Mahanath, Ebal, Shepho, and Onam. 24 Zibeon's descendants were Aiah and Anah. (He is the Anah who found water in the desert while he was pasturing the asses of his father Zibeon.) 25 The descendants of Anah were Dishon and Oholibamah, daughter of Anah. 26 The descendants of Dishon were Hemdan, Eshban, Ithran, and Cheran. 27 The descendants of Ezer were Bilhan, Zaavan, and Akan. 28 The descendants of Dishan were Uz and Aran. 29 These are the Horite clans: the clans of Lotan, Shobal, Zibeon, Anah, 30 Dishon, Ezer, and Dishan; they were the clans of the Horites, clan by clan, in the land of Seir. 31 The following are the kings who reigned in the land of Edom before any king reigned over the Israelites. 32 Bela, son of Beor, became king in Edom; the name of his city was Dinhabah. 33 When Bela died, Jobab, son of Zerah, from Bozrah, succeeded him as king. 34 When Jobab died, Husham, from the land of the Temanites, succeeded him as king. He defeated the Midianites in the country of Moab; the name of his city was Avith. 35 When Husham died, Hadad, son of Bedad, succeeded him as king. 36 When Hadad died, Samlah, from Masrekah, succeeded him as king. 37 When Samlah died, Shaul, from Rehoboth-on-the-River, succeeded him as king. 38 When Shaul died, Baal-hanan, son of Achbor, succeeded him as king. 39 When Baal-hanan died, Hadar succeeded him as king; the name of his city was Pau. (His wife's name was Mehetabel; she was the daughter of Matred, son of Mezahab.) 40 The following are the names of the clans of Esau individually according to their subdivisions and localities: the clans of Timna, Alvah, Jetheth, 41 Oholibamah, Elah, Pinon, 42 Kenaz, Teman, Mibzar, 43 Magdiel, and Iram. These are the clans of the Edomites, according to their settlements in their territorial holdings. (Esau was the father of the Edomites.)

Genesis Chapter 37

1 Jacob settled in the land where his father had stayed, the land of Canaan. 2 This is his family history. When Joseph was seventeen years old, he was tending the flocks with his brothers; he was an assistant to the sons of his father's wives Bilhah and Zilpah, and he brought his father bad reports about them. 3 Israel loved Joseph best of all his sons, for he was the child of his old age; and he had made him a long tunic. 4 When his brothers saw that their father loved him best of all his sons, they hated him so much that they would not even greet him. 5 Once Joseph had a dream, which he told to his brothers: 6 "Listen to this dream I had. 7 There we were, binding sheaves in the field, when suddenly my sheaf rose to an upright position, and your sheaves formed a ring around my sheaf and bowed down to it." 8 "Are you really going to make yourself king over us?" his brothers asked him. "Or impose your rule on us?" So, they hated him all the more because of his talk about his dreams. 9 Then he had another dream, and this one, too, he told to his brothers. "I had another dream," he said; "this time, the sun and the moon and eleven stars were bowing down to me." 10 When he also told it to his father, his father reproved him. "What is the meaning of this dream of yours?" he asked. "Can it be that I and your mother and your brothers are to come and bow to the ground before you?" 11 So, his brothers were wrought up against him, but his father pondered the matter. 12 One day, when his brothers had gone to pasture their father's flocks at Shechem, 13 Israel said to Joseph, "Your brothers, you know, are tending our flocks at Shechem. Get ready; I will send you to them." "I am ready," Joseph answered. 14 "Go then," he replied, "see if all is well with your brothers and the flocks and bring back word." So, he sent him off from the valley of Hebron. When Joseph reached Shechem, 15 a man met him as he was wandering about in the fields. "What are you looking for?" the man asked him. 16 "I am looking for my brothers," he answered. "Could you please tell me where they are tending the flocks?" 17 The man told him, "They have moved on from here; in fact, I heard them say, 'Let us go on to Dothan.'" So, Joseph went after his brothers

and caught up with them in Dothan. ¹⁸ They noticed him from a distance, and before he came up to them, they plotted to kill him. ¹⁹ They said to one another: "Here comes that master dreamer! ²⁰ Come on, let us kill him and throw him into one of the cisterns here; we could say that a wild beast devoured him. We shall then see what comes of his dreams." ²¹ When Reuben heard this, he tried to save him from their hands, saying: "We must not take his life. ²² Instead of shedding blood," he continued, "just throw him into that cistern there in the desert; but don't kill him outright." His purpose was to rescue him from their hands and restore him to his father. ²³ So when Joseph came up to them, they stripped him of the long tunic he had on; ²⁴ then they took him and threw him into the cistern, which was empty and dry. ²⁵ They then sat down to their meal. Looking up, they saw a caravan of Ishmaelites coming from Gilead, their camels laden with gum, balm and resin to be taken down to Egypt. ²⁶ Judah said to his brothers: "What is to be gained by killing our brother and concealing his blood? ²⁷ Rather, let us sell him to these Ishmaelites, instead of doing away with him ourselves. After all, he is our brother, our own flesh." His brothers agreed. ²⁸ They sold Joseph to the Ishmaelites for twenty pieces of silver. Some Midianite traders passed by, and they pulled Joseph up out of the cistern and took him to Egypt. ²⁹ When Reuben went back to the cistern and saw that Joseph was not in it, he tore his clothes, ³⁰ and returning to his brothers, he exclaimed: "The boy is gone! And I - where can I turn?" ³¹ They took Joseph's tunic, and after slaughtering a goat, dipped the tunic in its blood. ³² Then they sent someone to bring the long tunic to their father, with the message: "We found this. See whether it is your son's tunic or not." ³³ He recognized it and exclaimed: "My son's tunic! A wild beast has devoured him! Joseph has been torn to pieces!" ³⁴ Then Jacob rent his clothes, put sackcloth on his loins, and mourned his son many days. ³⁵ Though his sons and daughters tried to console him, he refused all consolation, saying, "No, I will go down mourning to my son in the nether world." Thus did his father lament him. ³⁶ The Midianites, meanwhile, sold Joseph in Egypt to Potiphar, a courtier of Pharaoh and his chief steward.

Genesis Chapter 38

¹ About that time Judah parted from his brothers and pitched his tent near a certain Adullamite named Hirah. ² There he met the daughter of a Canaanite named Shua, married her, and had relations with her. ³ She conceived and bore a son, whom she named Er. ⁴ Again she conceived and bore a son, whom she named Onan. ⁵ Then she bore still another son, whom she named Shelah. They were in Chezib when he was born. ⁶ Judah got a wife named Tamar for his first-born, Er. ⁷ But Er, Judah's first-born, greatly offended the LORD; so the LORD took his life. ⁸ Then Judah said to Onan, "Unite with your brother's widow, in fulfillment of your duty as brother-in-law, and thus preserve your brother's line." ⁹ Onan, however, knew that the descendants would not be counted as his; so whenever he had relations with his brother's widow, he wasted his seed on the ground, to avoid contributing offspring for his brother. ¹⁰ What he did greatly offended the LORD, and the LORD took his life too. ¹¹ Thereupon Judah said to his daughter-in-law Tamar, "Stay as a widow in your father's house until my son Shelah grows up" - for he feared that Shelah also might die like his brothers. So Tamar went to live in her father's house. ¹² Years passed, and Judah's wife, the daughter of Shua, died. After Judah completed the period of mourning, he went up to Timnah for the shearing of his sheep, in company with his friend Hirah the Adullamite. ¹³ When Tamar was told that her father-in-law was on his way up to Timnah to shear his sheep, ¹⁴ she took off her widow's garb, veiled her face by covering herself with a shawl, and sat down at the entrance to Enaim, which is on the way to Timnah; for she was aware that, although Shelah was now grown up, she had not been given to him in marriage. ¹⁵ When Judah saw her, he mistook her for a harlot, since she had covered her face. ¹⁶ So he went over to her at the roadside, and not realizing that she was his daughter-in-law, he said, "Come, let me have intercourse with you." She replied, "What will you pay me for letting you have intercourse with me?" ¹⁷ He answered, "I will send you a kid from the flock." "Very well," she said, "provided you leave a pledge until you send it." ¹⁸ Judah asked, "What pledge am I to give to you?" She answered, "Your seal and cord, and the staff you carry." So he gave them to her and had intercourse with her, and she conceived by him. ¹⁹ When she went away, she took off her shawl and put on her widow's garb again. ²⁰ Judah sent the kid by his friend the Adullamite to recover the pledge from the woman; but he could not find her. ²¹ So he asked the men of the place, "Where is the temple prostitute, the one by the roadside in Enaim?" But they answered, "There has never been a temple prostitute here." ²² He went back to Judah and told him, "I could not find her; and besides, the men of the place said there was no temple prostitute there." ²³ "Let her keep the things," Judah replied; "otherwise we shall become a laughingstock. After all, I did send her the kid, even

though you were unable to find her." ²⁴ About three months later, Judah was told that his daughter-in-law Tamar had played the harlot and was then with child from her harlotry. "Bring her out," cried Judah; "she shall be burned." ²⁵ But as they were bringing her out, she sent word to her father-in-law, "It is by the man to whom these things belong that I am with child. Please verify," she added, "whose seal and cord and whose staff these are." ²⁶ Judah recognized them and said, "She is more in the right than I am, since I did not give her to my son Shelah." But he had no further relations with her. ²⁷ When the time of her delivery came, she was found to have twins in her womb. ²⁸ While she was giving birth, one infant put out his hand; and the midwife, taking a crimson thread, tied it on his hand, to note that this one came out first. ²⁹ But as he withdrew his hand, his brother came out; and she said, "What a breach you have made for yourself!" So, he was called Perez. ³⁰ Afterward his brother came out; he was called Zerah.

Genesis Chapter 39

¹ When Joseph was taken down to Egypt, a certain Egyptian (Potiphar, a courtier of Pharaoh and his chief steward) bought him from the Ishmaelites who had brought him there. ² But since the LORD was with him, Joseph got on very well and was assigned to the household of his Egyptian master. ³ When his master saw that the LORD was with him and brought him success in whatever he did, ⁴ he took a liking to Joseph and made him his personal attendant; he put him in charge of his household and entrusted to him all his possessions. ⁵ From the moment that he put him in charge of his household and all his possessions, the LORD blessed the Egyptian's house for Joseph's sake; in fact, the LORD'S blessing was on everything he owned, both inside the house and out. ⁶ Having left everything he owned in Joseph's charge, he gave no thought, with Joseph there, to anything but the food he ate. Now Joseph was strikingly handsome in countenance and body. ⁷ After a time, his master's wife began to look fondly at him and said, "Lie with me." ⁸ But he refused. "As long as I am here," he told her, "my master does not concern himself with anything in the house, but has entrusted to me all he owns. ⁹ He wields no more authority in this house than I do, and he has withheld from me nothing but yourself, since you are his wife. How, then, could I commit so great a wrong and thus stand condemned before God?" ¹⁰ Although she tried to entice him day after day, he would not agree to lie beside her, or even stay near her. ¹¹ One such day, when Joseph came into the house to do his work, and none of the household servants were then in the house, ¹² she laid hold of him by his cloak, saying, "Lie with me!" But leaving the cloak in her hand, he got away from her and ran outside. ¹³ When she saw that he had left his cloak in her hand as he fled outside, ¹⁴ she screamed for her household servants and told them, "Look! my husband has brought in a Hebrew slave to make sport of us! He came in here to lie with me, but I cried out as loud as I could. ¹⁵ When he heard me scream for help, he left his cloak beside me and ran away outside." ¹⁶ She kept the cloak with her until his master came home. ¹⁷ Then she told him the same story: "The Hebrew slave whom you brought here broke in on me, to make sport of me. ¹⁸ But when I screamed for help, he left his cloak beside me and fled outside." ¹⁹ As soon as the master heard his wife's story about how his slave had treated her, he became enraged. ²⁰ He seized Joseph and threw him into the jail where the royal prisoners were confined. But even while he was in prison, ²¹ the LORD remained with Joseph; he showed him kindness by making the chief jailer well-disposed toward him. ²² The chief jailer put Joseph in charge of all the prisoners in the jail, and everything that had to be done there was done under his management. ²³ The chief jailer did not concern himself with anything at all that was in Joseph's charge, since the LORD was with him and brought success to all he did.

Genesis Chapter 40

¹ Sometime afterward, the royal cupbearer and baker gave offense to their lord, the king of Egypt. ² Pharaoh was angry with his two courtiers, the chief cupbearer and the chief baker, ³ and he put them in custody in the house of the chief steward (the same jail where Joseph was confined). ⁴ The chief steward assigned Joseph to them, and he became their attendant. After they had been in custody for some time, ⁵ the cupbearer and the baker of the king of Egypt who were confined in the jail both had dreams on the same night, each dream with its own meaning. ⁶ When Joseph came to them in the morning, he noticed they looked disturbed. ⁷ So he asked Pharaoh's courtiers who were with him in custody in his master's house, "Why do you look so sad today?" ⁸ They answered him, "We have had dreams, but there is no one to interpret them for us." Joseph said to them, "Surely, interpretations come from God. Please tell the dreams to me." ⁹ Then the chief cupbearer told Joseph his dream. "In my dream," he said, "I saw a vine in front of me, ¹⁰ and on the vine were three branches. It had barely

budded when its blossoms came out, and its clusters ripened into grapes. ¹¹ Pharaoh's cup was in my hand; so I took the grapes, pressed them out into his cup, and put it in Pharaoh's hand." ¹² Joseph said to him: "This is what it means. The three branches are three days; ¹³ within three days Pharaoh will lift up your head and restore you to your post. You will be handing Pharaoh his cup as you formerly used to do when you were his cupbearer. ¹⁴ So if you will still remember, when all is well with you, that I was here with you, please do me the favor of mentioning me to Pharaoh, to get me out of this place. ¹⁵ The truth is that I was kidnaped from the land of the Hebrews, and here I have not done anything for which I should have been put into a dungeon." ¹⁶ When the chief baker saw that Joseph had given this favorable interpretation, he said to him: "I too had a dream. In it I had three wicker baskets on my head; ¹⁷ in the top one were all kinds of bakery products for Pharaoh, but the birds were pecking at them out of the basket on my head." ¹⁸ Joseph said to him in reply: "This is what it means. The three baskets are three days; ¹⁹ within three days Pharaoh will lift up your head and have you impaled on a stake, and the birds will be pecking the flesh from your body." ²⁰ And in fact, on the third day, which was Pharaoh's birthday, when he gave a banquet to all his staff, with his courtiers around him, he lifted up the heads of the chief cupbearer and chief baker. ²¹ He restored the chief cupbearer to his office, so that he again handed the cup to Pharaoh; ²² but the chief baker he impaled-just as Joseph had told them in his interpretation. ²³ Yet the chief cupbearer gave no thought to Joseph; he had forgotten him.

Genesis Chapter 41

¹ After a lapse of two years, Pharaoh had a dream. He saw himself standing by the Nile, ² when up out of the Nile came seven cows, handsome and fat; they grazed in the reed grass. ³ Behind them seven other cows, ugly and gaunt, came up out of the Nile; and standing on the bank of the Nile beside the others, ⁴ the ugly, gaunt cows ate up the seven handsome, fat cows. Then Pharaoh woke up. ⁵ He fell asleep again and had another dream. He saw seven ears of grain, fat and healthy, growing on a single stalk. ⁶ Behind them sprouted seven ears of grain, thin and blasted by the east wind; ⁷ and the seven thin ears swallowed up the seven fat, healthy ears. Then Pharaoh woke up, to find it was only a dream. ⁸ Next morning his spirit was agitated. So he summoned all the magicians and sages of Egypt and recounted his dreams to them; but no one could interpret his dreams for him. ⁹ Then the chief cupbearer spoke up and said to Pharaoh: "On this occasion I am reminded of my negligence. ¹⁰ Once, when Pharaoh was angry, he put me and the chief baker in custody in the house of the chief steward. ¹¹ Later, we both had dreams on the same night, and each of our dreams had its own meaning. ¹² There with us was a Hebrew youth, a slave of the chief steward; and when we told him our dreams, he interpreted them for us and explained for each of us the meaning of his dream. ¹³ And it turned out just as he had told us: I was restored to my post, but the other man was impaled." ¹⁴ Pharaoh therefore had Joseph summoned, and they hurriedly brought him from the dungeon. After he shaved and changed his clothes, he came into Pharaoh's presence. ¹⁵ Pharaoh then said to him: "I had certain dreams that no one can interpret. But I hear it said of you that the moment you are told a dream you can interpret it." ¹⁶ "It is not I," Joseph replied to Pharaoh, "but God who will give Pharaoh the right answer." ¹⁷ Then Pharaoh said to Joseph: "In my dream, I was standing on the bank of the Nile, ¹⁸ when up from the Nile came seven cows, fat and well-formed; they grazed in the reed grass. ¹⁹ Behind them came seven other cows, scrawny, most ill-formed and gaunt. Never have I seen such ugly specimens as these in all the land of Egypt! ²⁰ The gaunt, ugly cows ate up the first seven fat cows. ²¹ But when they had consumed them, no one could tell that they had done so, because they looked as ugly as before. Then I woke up. ²² In another dream I saw seven ears of grain, fat and healthy, growing on a single stalk. ²³ Behind them sprouted seven ears of grain, shriveled and thin and blasted by the east wind; ²⁴ and the seven thin ears swallowed up the seven healthy ears. I have spoken to the magicians, but none of them can give me an explanation." ²⁵ Joseph said to Pharaoh: "Both of Pharaoh's dreams have the same meaning. God has thus foretold to Pharaoh what he is about to do. ²⁶ The seven healthy cows are seven years, and the seven healthy ears are seven years - the same in each dream. ²⁷ So also, the seven thin, ugly cows that came up after them are seven years, as are the seven thin, wind-blasted ears; they are seven years of famine. ²⁸ It is just as I told Pharaoh: God has revealed to Pharaoh what he is about to do. ²⁹ Seven years of great abundance are now coming throughout the land of Egypt; ³⁰ but these will be followed by seven years of famine, when all the abundance in the land of Egypt will be forgotten. When the famine has ravaged the land, ³¹ no trace of the abundance will be found in the land because of the famine that follows it - so utterly severe will that famine be. ³² That

Pharaoh had the same dream twice means that the matter has been reaffirmed by God and that God will soon bring it about. ³³ "Therefore, let Pharaoh seek out a wise and discerning man and put him in charge of the land of Egypt. ³⁴ Pharaoh should also take action to appoint overseers, so as to regiment the land during the seven years of abundance. ³⁵ They should husband all the food of the coming good years, collecting the grain under Pharaoh's authority, to be stored in the towns for food. ³⁶ This food will serve as a reserve for the country against the seven years of famine that are to follow in the land of Egypt, so that the land may not perish in the famine." ³⁷ This advice pleased Pharaoh and all his officials. ³⁸ "Could we find another like him," Pharaoh asked his officials, "a man so endowed with the spirit of God?" ³⁹ So Pharaoh said to Joseph: "Since God has made all this known to you, no one can be as wise and discerning as you are. ⁴⁰ You shall be in charge of my palace, and all my people shall dart at your command. Only in respect to the throne shall I outrank you. ⁴¹ Herewith," Pharaoh told Joseph, "I place you in charge of the whole land of Egypt." ⁴² With that, Pharaoh took off his signet ring and put it on Joseph's finger. He had him dressed in robes of fine linen and put a gold chain about his neck. ⁴³ He then had him ride in the chariot of his vizier, and they shouted "Abrek!" before him. Thus was Joseph installed over the whole land of Egypt. ⁴⁴ "I, Pharaoh, proclaim," he told Joseph, "That without your approval no one shall move hand or foot in all the land of Egypt." ⁴⁵ Pharaoh also bestowed the name of Zaphnath-paneah on Joseph, and he gave him in marriage Asenath, the daughter of Potiphera, priest of Heliopolis. ⁴⁶ Joseph was thirty years old when he entered the service of Pharaoh, king of Egypt. After Joseph left Pharaoh's presence, he traveled throughout the land of Egypt. ⁴⁷ During the seven years of plenty, when the land produced abundant crops, ⁴⁸ he husbanded all the food of these years of plenty that the land of Egypt was enjoying and stored it in the towns, placing in each town the crops of the fields around it. ⁴⁹ Joseph garnered grain in quantities like the sands of the sea, so vast that at last he stopped measuring it, for it was beyond measure. ⁵⁰ Before the famine years set in, Joseph became the father of two sons, borne to him by Asenath, daughter of Potiphera, priest of Heliopolis. ⁵¹ He named his first-born Manasseh, meaning, "God has made me forget entirely the sufferings I endured at the hands of my family". ⁵² and the second he named Ephraim, meaning, "God has made me fruitful in the land of my affliction." ⁵³ When the seven years of abundance enjoyed by the land of Egypt came to an end, ⁵⁴ the seven years of famine set in, just as Joseph had predicted. Although there was famine in all the other countries, food was available throughout the land of Egypt. ⁵⁵ When hunger came to be felt throughout the land of Egypt and the people cried to Pharaoh for bread, Pharaoh directed all the Egyptians to go to Joseph and do whatever he told them. ⁵⁶ When the famine had spread throughout the land, Joseph opened all the cities that had grain and rationed it to the Egyptians, since the famine had gripped the land of Egypt. ⁵⁷ In fact, all the world came to Joseph to obtain rations of grain, for famine had gripped the whole world.

Genesis Chapter 42

¹ When Jacob learned that grain rations were available in Egypt, he said to his sons: "Why do you keep gaping at one another? ² I hear," he went on, "that rations of grain are available in Egypt. Go down there and buy some for us, that we may stay alive rather than die of hunger." ³ So ten of Joseph's brothers went down to buy an emergency supply of grain from Egypt. ⁴ It was only Joseph's full brother Benjamin that Jacob did not send with the rest, for he thought some disaster might befall him. ⁵ Thus, since there was famine in the land of Canaan also, the sons of Israel were among those who came to procure rations. ⁶ It was Joseph, as governor of the country, who dispensed the rations to all the people. When Joseph's brothers came and knelt down before him with their faces to the ground, ⁷ he recognized them as soon as he saw them. But he concealed his own identity from them and spoke sternly to them. "Where do you come from?" he asked them. They answered, "From the land of Canaan, to procure food." ⁸ When Joseph recognized his brothers, although they did not recognize him, ⁹ he was reminded of the dreams he had about them. He said to them: "You are spies. You have come to see the nakedness of the land." ¹⁰ "No, my lord," they replied. "On the contrary, your servants have come to procure food. ¹¹ All of us are sons of the same man. We are honest men; your servants have never been spies." ¹² But he answered them: "Not so! You have come to see the nakedness of the land." ¹³ "We your servants," they said, "were twelve brothers, sons of a certain man in Canaan; but the youngest one is at present with our father, and the other one is gone." ¹⁴ "It is just as I said," Joseph persisted; "you are spies. ¹⁵ This is how you shall be tested: unless your youngest brother comes here, I swear by the life of Pharaoh that you shall not leave here. ¹⁶ So send one of your number to get your brother, while the rest of you stay here under arrest. Thus shall your

words be tested for their truth; if they are untrue, as Pharaoh lives, you are spies!" 17 With that, he locked them up in the guardhouse for three days. 18 On the third day Joseph said to them: "Do this, and you shall live; for I am a God-fearing man. 19 If you have been honest, only one of your brothers need be confined in this prison, while the rest of you may go and take home provisions for your starving families. 20 But you must come back to me with your youngest brother. Your words will thus be verified, and you will not die." To this they agreed. 21 To one another, however, they said: "Alas, we are being punished because of our brother. We saw the anguish of his heart when he pleaded with us, yet we paid no heed; that is why this anguish has now come upon us."22 "Didn't I tell you," Broke in Reuben, "not to do wrong to the boy? But you wouldn't listen! Now comes the reckoning for his blood." 23 They did not know, of course, that Joseph understood what they said, since he spoke with them through an interpreter. 24 But turning away from them, he wept. When he was able to speak to them again, he had Simeon taken from them and bound before their eyes. 25 Then Joseph gave orders to have their containers filled with grain, their money replaced in each one's sack, and provisions given them for their journey. After this had been done for them,26 they loaded their donkeys with the rations and departed. 27 At the night encampment, when one of them opened his bag to give his donkey some fodder, he was surprised to see his money in the mouth of his bag. 28 "My money has been returned!" he cried out to his brothers. "Here it is in my bag!" At that their hearts sank. Trembling, they asked one another, "What is this that God has done to us?" 29 When they got back to their father Jacob in the land of Canaan, they told him all that had happened to them. 30 "The man who is lord of the country," they said, "spoke to us sternly and put us in custody as if we were spying on the land. 31 But we said to him: 'We are honest men; we have never been spies. 32 There were twelve of us brothers, sons of the same father; but one is gone, and the youngest one is at present with our father in the land of Canaan.' 33 Then the man who is lord of the country said to us: 'This is how I shall know if you are honest men: leave one of your brothers with me, while the rest of you go home with rations for your starving families. 34When you come back to me with your youngest brother, and I know that you are honest men and not spies, I will restore your brother to you, and you may move about freely in the land.'" 35 When they were emptying their sacks, there in each one's sack was his moneybag! At the sight of their moneybags, they and their father were dismayed.36 Their father Jacob said to them: "Must you make me childless? Joseph is gone, and Simeon is gone, and now you would take away Benjamin! Why must such things always happen to me?" 37 Then Reuben told his father: "Put him in my care, and I will bring him back to you. You may kill my own two sons if I do not return him to you." 38 But Jacob replied: "My son shall not go down with you. Now that his full brother is dead, he is the only one left. If some disaster should befall him on the journey you must make, you would send my white head down to the nether world in grief."

Genesis Chapter 43

1 Now the famine in the land grew more severe. 2 So when they had used up all the rations they had brought from Egypt, their father said to them, "Go back and procure us a little more food." 3 But Judah replied: "The man strictly warned us, 'You shall not appear in my presence unless your brother is with you.' 4 If you are willing to let our brother go with us, we will go down to procure food for you. 5 But if you are not willing, we will not go down, because the man told us, 'You shall not appear in my presence unless your brother is with you.'" 6 Israel demanded, "Why did you bring this trouble on me by telling the man that you had another brother?" 7 They answered: "The man kept asking about ourselves and our family: 'Is your father still living? Do you have another brother?' We had to answer his questions. How could we know that he would say, 'Bring your brother down here'?" 8 Then Judah urged his father Israel: "Let the boy go with me, that we may be off and, on our way, if you and we and our children are to keep from starving to death. 9 I myself will stand surety for him. You can hold me responsible for him. If I fail to bring him back, to set him in your presence, you can hold it against me forever. 10 Had we not dilly-dallied, we could have been there and back twice by now!"11 Their father Israel then told them: "If it must be so, then do this: Put some of the land's best products in your baggage and take them down to the man as gifts: some balm and honey, gum and resin, and pistachios and almonds. 12 Also take extra money along, for you must return the amount that was put back in the mouths of your bags; it may have been a mistake. 13 Take your brother, too, and be off on your way back to the man. 14 May God Almighty dispose the man to be merciful toward you, so that he may let your other brother go, as well as Benjamin. As for me, if I am to suffer bereavement, I shall suffer it." 15 So the men got the gifts, took double the amount of money with them, and, accompanied by Benjamin, were

off on their way down to Egypt to present themselves to Joseph. 16 When Joseph saw Benjamin with them, he told his head steward, "Take these men into the house, and have an animal slaughtered and prepared, for they are to dine with me at noon." 17 Doing as Joseph had ordered, the steward conducted the men to Joseph's house. 18 But on being led to his house, they became apprehensive. "It must be," they thought, "on account of the money put back in our bags the first time, that we are taken inside; they want to use it as a pretext to attack us and take our donkeys and seize us as slaves." 19 So they went up to Joseph's head steward and talked to him at the entrance of the house. 20 "If you please, sir," they said, "we came down here once before to procure food. 21 But when we arrived at a night's encampment and opened our bags, there was each man's money in the mouth of his bag - our money in the full amount! We have now brought it back. 22 We have brought other money to procure food with. We do not know who put the first money in our bags." 23 "Be at ease," he replied; "you have no need to fear. Your God and the God of your father must have put treasures in your bags for you. As for your money, I received it." With that, he led Simeon out to them. 24 The steward then brought the men inside Joseph's house. He gave them water to bathe their feet and got fodder for their donkeys. 25 Then they set out their gifts to await Joseph's arrival at noon, for they had heard that they were to dine there. 26 When Joseph came home, they presented him with the gifts they had brought inside, while they bowed down before him to the ground. 27 After inquiring how they were, he asked them, "And how is your aged father, of whom you spoke? Is he still in good health?" 28 "Your servant our father is thriving and still in good health," they said, as they bowed respectfully. 29 When Joseph's eye fell on his full brother Benjamin, he asked, "Is this your youngest brother, of whom you told me?" Then he said to him, "May God be gracious to you, my boy!" 30 With that, Joseph had to hurry out, for he was so overcome with affection for his brother that he was on the verge of tears. He went into a private room and wept there. 31 After washing his face, he reappeared and, now in control of himself, gave the order, "Serve the meal." 32 It was served separately to him, to the brothers, and to the Egyptians who partook of his board. (Egyptians may not eat with Hebrews; that is abhorrent to them.) 33 When they were seated by his directions according to their age, from the oldest to the youngest, they looked at one another in amazement; 34 and as portions were brought to them from Joseph's table, Benjamin's portion was five times as large as anyone else's. So, they drank freely and made merry with him.

Genesis Chapter 44

1 Then Joseph gave his head steward these instructions: "Fill the men's bags with as much food as they can carry and put each man's money in the mouth of his bag. 2 In the mouth of the youngest one's bag put also my silver goblet, together with the money for his rations." The steward carried out Joseph's instructions. 3 At daybreak the men and their donkeys were sent off. 4 They had not gone far out of the city when Joseph said to his head steward: "Go at once after the men! When you overtake them, say to them, 'Why did you repay good with evil? Why did you steal the silver goblet from me? 5 It is the very one from which my master drinks and which he uses for divination. What you have done is wrong.'" 6 When the steward overtook them and repeated these words to them, 7 they remonstrated with him: "How can my lord say such things? Far be it from your servants to do such a thing! 8 We even brought back to you from the land of Canaan the money that we found in the mouths of our bags. Why, then, would we steal silver or gold from your master's house? 9 If any of your servants is found to have the goblet, he shall die, and as for the rest of us, we shall become my lord's slaves." 10 But he replied, "Even though it ought to be as you propose, only the one who is found to have it shall become my slave, and the rest of you shall be exonerated." 11 Then each of them eagerly lowered his bag to the ground and opened it; 12 and when a search was made, starting with the oldest and ending with the youngest, the goblet turned up in Benjamin's bag. 13 At this, they tore their clothes. Then, when each man had reloaded his donkey, they returned to the city. 14 As Judah and his brothers reentered Joseph's house, he was still there; so they flung themselves on the ground before him. 15 "How could you do such a thing?" Joseph asked them. "You should have known that such a man as I could discover by divination what happened." 16 Judah replied: "What can we say to my lord? How can we plead or how try to prove our innocence? God has uncovered your servants' guilt. Here we are, then, the slaves of my lord - the rest of us no less than the one in whose possession the goblet was found." 17 "Far be it from me to act thus!" said Joseph. "Only the one in whose possession the goblet was found shall become my slave; the rest of you may go back safe and sound to your father." 18 Judah then stepped up to him and said: "I beg you, my lord, let your servant speak earnestly to my lord, and do not become angry with your servant, for you are the equal of Pharaoh. 19 My lord asked

your servants, 'Have you a father, or another brother?' 20 So we said to my lord, 'We have an aged father, and a young brother, the child of his old age. This one's full brother is dead, and since he is the only one by that mother who is left, his father dotes on him.' 21 Then you told your servants, 'Bring him down to me that my eyes may look on him.' 22 We replied to my lord, 'The boy cannot leave his father; his father would die if he were to leave him.' 23 But you told your servants, 'Unless your youngest brother comes back with you, you shall not come into my presence again.' 24 When we returned to your servant our father, we reported to him the words of my lord. 25 "Later, our father told us to come back and buy some food for the family. 26 So we reminded him, 'We cannot go down there; only if our youngest brother is with us can we go, for we may not see the man if our youngest brother is not with us.' 27 Then your servant our father said to us, 'As you know, my wife bore me two sons. 28 One of them, however, disappeared, and I had to conclude that he must have been torn to pieces by wild beasts; I have not seen him since. 29 If you now take this one away from me too, and some disaster befalls him, you will send my white head down to the nether world in grief.' 30 "If then the boy is not with us when I go back to your servant my father, whose very life is bound up with his, he will die as soon as he sees that the boy is missing; 31 and your servants will thus send the white head of our father down to the nether world in grief. 32 Besides, I, your servant, got the boy from his father by going surety for him, saying, 'If I fail to bring him back to you, father, you can hold it against me forever.' 33 Let me, your servant, therefore, remain in place of the boy as the slave of my lord, and let the boy go back with his brothers. 34 How could I go back to my father if the boy were not with me? I could not bear to see the anguish that would overcome my father."

Genesis Chapter 45

1 Joseph could no longer control himself in the presence of all his attendants, so he cried out, "Have everyone withdraw from me!" Thus no one else was about when he made himself known to his brothers. 2 But his sobs were so loud that the Egyptians heard him, and so the news reached Pharaoh's palace. 3 "I am Joseph," he said to his brothers. "Is my father still in good health?" But his brothers could give him no answer, so dumbfounded were they at him. 4 "Come closer to me," he told his brothers. When they had done so, he said: "I am your brother Joseph, whom you once sold into Egypt. 5 But now do not be distressed, and do not reproach yourselves for having sold me here. It was really for the sake of saving lives that God sent me here ahead of you. 6 For two years now the famine has been in the land, and for five more years tillage will yield no harvest. 7 God, therefore, sent me on ahead of you to ensure for you a remnant on earth and to save your lives in an extraordinary deliverance. 8 So it was not really you but God who had me come here; and he has made of me a father to Pharaoh, lord of all his household, and ruler over the whole land of Egypt. 9 "Hurry back, then, to my father and tell him: 'Thus says your son Joseph: God has made me lord of all Egypt; come to me without delay. 10 You will settle in the region of Goshen, where you will be near me - you and your children and grandchildren, your flocks and herds, and everything that you own. 11 Since five years of famine still lie ahead, I will provide for you there, so that you and your family and all that are yours may not suffer want.' 12 Surely, you can see for yourselves, and Benjamin can see for himself, that it is I, Joseph, who am speaking to you. 13 Tell my father all about my high position in Egypt and what you have seen. But hurry and bring my father down here." 14 Thereupon he flung himself on the neck of his brother Benjamin and wept, and Benjamin wept in his arms. 15 Joseph then kissed all his brothers, crying over each of them; and only then were his brothers able to talk with him. 16 When the news reached Pharaoh's palace that Joseph's brothers had come, Pharaoh and his courtiers were pleased. 17 So Pharaoh told Joseph: "Say to your brothers: 'This is what you shall do: Load up your animals and go without delay to the land of Canaan. 18 There get your father and your families, and then come back here to me; I will assign you the best land in Egypt, where you will live off the fat of the land.' 19 Instruct them further: 'Do this. Take wagons from the land of Egypt for your children and your wives and to transport your father on your way back here. 20 Do not be concerned about your belongings, for the best in the whole land of Egypt shall be yours.'" 21 The sons of Israel acted accordingly. Joseph gave them the wagons, as Pharaoh had ordered, and he supplied them with provisions for the journey. 22 He also gave to each of them fresh clothing, but to Benjamin he gave three hundred shekels of silver and five sets of garments. 23 Moreover, what he sent to his father was ten jackasses loaded with the finest products of Egypt and ten jennies loaded with grain and bread and other provisions for his journey. 24 As he sent his brothers on their way, he told them, "Let there be no recriminations on the way." 25 So they left Egypt and made their way to their father Jacob in the land of Canaan. 26 When they told him, "Joseph

is still alive - in fact, it is he who is ruler of all the land of Egypt," he was dumbfounded; he could not believe them. 27 But when they recounted to him all that Joseph had told them, and when he saw the wagons that Joseph had sent for his transport, the spirit of their father Jacob revived. 28 "It is enough," said Israel. "My son Joseph is still alive! I must go and see him before I die."

Genesis Chapter 46

1 Israel set out with all that was his. When he arrived at Beer-sheba, he offered sacrifices to the God of his father Isaac. 2 Their God, speaking to Israel in a vision by night, called, "Jacob! Jacob!" "Here I am," he answered. 3 Then he said: "I am God, the God of your father. Do not be afraid to go down to Egypt, for there I will make you a great nation. 4 Not only will I go down to Egypt with you; I will also bring you back here, after Joseph has closed your eyes." 5 So Jacob departed from Beer-sheba, and the sons of Israel put their father and their wives and children on the wagons that Pharaoh had sent for his transport. 6 They took with them their livestock and the possessions they had acquired in the land of Canaan. Thus, Jacob and all his descendants migrated to Egypt. 7 His sons and his grandsons, his daughters and his granddaughters - all his descendants - he took with him to Egypt. 8 These are the names of the Israelites, Jacob and his descendants, who migrated to Egypt. Reuben, Jacob's first-born, 9 and the sons of Reuben: Hanoch, Pallu, Hezron, and Carmi. 10 The sons of Simeon: Nemuel, Jamin, Ohad, Jachin, Zohar, and Shaul, son of a Canaanite woman. 11 The sons of Levi: Gershon, Kohath, and Merari. 12 The sons of Judah: Er, Onan, Shelah, Perez, and Zerah - but Er and Onan had died in the land of Canaan; and the sons of Perez were Hezron and Hamul. 13 The sons of Issachar: Tola, Puah, Jashub, and Shimron. 14 The sons of Zebulun: Sered, Elon, and Jahleel. 15 These were the sons whom Leah bore to Jacob in Paddan-aram, along with his daughter Dinah - thirty-three persons in all, male and female. 16 The sons of Gad: Zephon, Haggi, Shuni, Ezbon, Eri, Arod, and Areli. 17 The sons of Asher: Imnah, Ishvah, Ishvi, and Beriah, with their sister Serah; and the sons of Beriah: Heber and Malchiel. 18 These were the descendants of Zilpah, whom Laban had given to his daughter Leah; these she bore to Jacob - sixteen persons in all. 19 The sons of Jacob's wife Rachel: Joseph and Benjamin. 20 In the land of Egypt Joseph became the father of Manasseh and Ephraim, whom Asenath, daughter of Potiphera, priest of Heliopolis, bore to him. 21 The sons of Benjamin: Bela, Becher, Ashbel, Gera, Naaman, Ahiram, Shupham, Hupham, and Ard. 22 These were the sons whom Rachel bore to Jacob - fourteen persons in all. 23 The sons of Dan: Hushim. 24 The sons of Naphtali: Jahzeel, Guni, Jezer, and Shillem. 25 These were the sons of Bilhah, whom Laban had given to his daughter Rachel; these she bore to Jacob - seven persons in all. 26 Jacob's people who migrated to Egypt - his direct descendants, not counting the wives of Jacob's sons - numbered sixty-six persons in all. 27 Together with Joseph's sons who were born to him in Egypt - two persons - all the people comprising Jacob's family who had come to Egypt amounted to seventy persons in all. 28 Israel had sent Judah ahead to Joseph, so that he might meet him in Goshen. On his arrival in the region of Goshen, 29 Joseph hitched the horses to his chariot and rode to meet his father Israel in Goshen. As soon as he saw him, he flung himself on his neck and wept a long time in his arms. 30 And Israel said to Joseph, "At last I can die, now that I have seen for myself that Joseph is still alive." 31 Joseph then said to his brothers and his father's household: "I will go and inform Pharaoh, telling him: 'My brothers and my father's household, whose home is in the land of Canaan, have come to me. 32 The men are shepherds, having long been keepers of livestock; and they have brought with them their flocks and herds, as well as everything else they own.' 33 So when Pharaoh summons you and asks what your occupation is, 34 you must answer, 'We your servants, like our ancestors, have been keepers of livestock from the beginning until now,' in order that you may stay in the region of Goshen, since all shepherds are abhorrent to the Egyptians."

Genesis Chapter 47

1 Joseph went and told Pharaoh, "My father and my brothers have come from the land of Canaan, with their flocks and herds and everything else they own; and they are now in the region of Goshen." 2 He then presented to Pharaoh five of his brothers whom he had selected from their full number. 3 When Pharaoh asked them what their occupation was, they answered, "We, your servants, like our ancestors, are shepherds. 4 We have come," they continued, "in order to stay in this country, for there is no pasture for your servants' flocks in the land of Canaan, so severe has the famine been there. Please, therefore, let your servants settle in the region of Goshen." 5 Pharaoh said to Joseph, "They may settle in the region of Goshen; and if you know any of them to be qualified, you may put them in charge of my own livestock." Thus, when

Jacob and his sons came to Joseph in Egypt, and Pharaoh, king of Egypt, heard about it, Pharaoh said to Joseph, "Now that your father and brothers have come to you, 6 the land of Egypt is at your disposal; settle your father and brothers in the pick of the land." 7 Then Joseph brought his father Jacob and presented him to Pharaoh. After Jacob had paid his respects to Pharaoh, 8 Pharaoh asked him, "How many years have you lived?" 9 Jacob replied: "The years I have lived as a wayfarer amount to a hundred and thirty. Few and hard have been these years of my life, and they do not compare with the years that my ancestors lived as wayfarers." 10 Then Jacob bade Pharaoh farewell and withdrew from his presence. 11 As Pharaoh had ordered, Joseph settled his father and brothers and gave them holdings in Egypt on the pick of the land, in the region of Rameses. 12 And Joseph sustained his father and brothers and his father's whole household, down to the youngest, with food. 13 Since there was no food in any country because of the extreme severity of the famine, and the lands of Egypt and Canaan were languishing from hunger, 14 Joseph gathered in, as payment for the rations that were being dispensed, all the money that was to be found in Egypt and Canaan, and he put it in Pharaoh's palace. 15 When all the money in Egypt and Canaan was spent, all the Egyptians came to Joseph, pleading, "Give us food or we shall perish under your eyes; for our money is gone." 16 "Since your money is gone," replied Joseph, "give me your livestock, and I will sell you bread in return for your livestock." 17 So they brought their livestock to Joseph, and he sold them food in return for their horses, their flocks of sheep and herds of cattle, and their donkeys. Thus he got them through that year with bread in exchange for all their livestock. 18 When that year ended, they came to him in the following one and said: "We cannot hide from my lord that, with our money spent and our livestock made over to my lord, there is nothing left to put at my lord's disposal except our bodies and our farm land. 19 Why should we and our land perish before your very eyes? Take us and our land in exchange for food, and we will become Pharaoh's slaves and our land his property; only give us seed, that we may survive and not perish, and that our land may not turn into a waste." 20 Thus Joseph acquired all the farm land of Egypt for Pharaoh, since with the famine too much for them to bear, every Egyptian sold his field; so the land passed over to Pharaoh, 21 and the people were reduced to slavery, from one end of Egypt's territory to the other. 22 Only the priests' lands Joseph did not take over. Since the priests had a fixed allowance from Pharaoh and lived off the allowance Pharaoh had granted them, they did not have to sell their land. 23 Joseph told the people: "Now that I have acquired you and your land for Pharaoh, here is your seed for sowing the land. 24 But when the harvest is in, you must give a fifth of it to Pharaoh, while you keep four-fifths as seed for your fields and as food for yourselves and your families (and as food for your children)." 25 "You have saved our lives!" they answered. "We are grateful to my lord that we can be Pharaoh's slaves." 26 Thus Joseph made it a law for the land in Egypt, which is still in force, that a fifth of its produce should go to Pharaoh. Only the land of the priests did not pass over to Pharaoh. 27 Thus Israel settled in the land of Egypt, in the region of Goshen. There they acquired property, were fertile, and increased greatly. 28 Jacob lived in the land of Egypt for seventeen years; the span of his life came to a hundred and forty-seven years. 29 When the time approached for Israel to die, he called his son Joseph and said to him: "If you really wish to please me, put your hand under my thigh as a sign of your constant loyalty to me; do not let me be buried in Egypt. 30 When I lie down with my ancestors, have me taken out of Egypt and buried in their burial place." 31 "I will do as you say," he replied. But his father demanded, "Swear it to me!" So, Joseph swore to him. Then Israel bowed at the head of the bed.

Genesis Chapter 48

1 Sometime afterward, Joseph was informed, "Your father is failing." So he took along with him his two sons, Manasseh and Ephraim. 2 When Jacob was told, "Your son Joseph has come to you," he rallied his strength and sat up in bed. 3 Jacob then said to Joseph: "God Almighty appeared to me at Luz in the land of Canaan, and blessing me, 4 he said, 'I will make you fertile and numerous and raise you into an assembly of tribes, and I will give this land to your descendants after you as a permanent possession.' 5 Your two sons, therefore, who were born to you in the land of Egypt before I joined you here, shall be mine; Ephraim and Manasseh shall be mine as much as Reuben and Simeon are mine. 6 Progeny born to you after them shall remain yours; but their heritage shall be recorded in the names of their two brothers. 7 I do this because, when I was returning from Paddan, your mother Rachel died, to my sorrow, during the journey in Canaan, while we were still a short distance from Ephrath; and I buried her there on the way to Ephrath (that is, Bethlehem)." 8 When Israel saw Joseph's sons, he asked, "Who are these?" 9 "They are my sons," Joseph answered his father, "whom

God has given me here." "Bring them to me," said his father, "that I may bless them." 10 (Now Israel's eyes were dim from age, and he could not see well.) When Joseph brought his sons close to him, he kissed and embraced them. 11 Then Israel said to Joseph, "I never expected to see your face again, and now God has allowed me to see your descendants as well!" 12 Joseph removed them from his father's knees and bowed down before him with his face to the ground. 13 Then Joseph took the two, Ephraim with his right hand, to Israel's left, and Manasseh with his left hand, to Israel's right, and led them to him. 14 But Israel, crossing his hands, put out his right hand and laid it on the head of Ephraim, although he was the younger, and his left hand on the head of Manasseh, although he was the first-born. 15 Then he blessed them with these words: "May the God in whose ways my father's Abraham and Isaac walked, The God who has been my shepherd from my birth to this day, 16 The Angel who has delivered me from all harm, bless these boys That in them my name be recalled, and the names of my fathers, Abraham and Isaac, And they may become teeming multitudes upon the earth!" 17 When Joseph saw that his father had laid his right hand on Ephraim's head, this seemed wrong to him; so, he took hold of his father's hand, to remove it from Ephraim's head to Manasseh's, 18 saying, "That is not right, father; the other one is the first-born; lay your right hand on his head!" 19 But his father resisted. "I know it, son," he said, "I know. That one too shall become a tribe, and he too shall be great. Nevertheless, his younger brother shall surpass him, and his descendants shall become a multitude of nations." 20 So when he blessed them that day and said, "By you shall the people of Israel pronounce blessings; may they say, 'God make you like Ephraim and Manasseh,'" he placed Ephraim before Manasseh. 21 Then Israel said to Joseph: "I am about to die. But God will be with you and will restore you to the land of your fathers. 22 As for me, I give to you, as to the one above his brothers, Shechem, which I captured from the Amorites with my sword and bow."

Genesis Chapter 49

1 Jacob called his sons and said: "Gather around, that I may tell you what is to happen to you in days to come. 2 "Assemble and listen, sons of Jacob, listen to Israel, your father. 3 "You, Reuben, my first-born, my strength and the first fruit of my manhood, excelling in rank and excelling in power! 4 Unruly as water, you shall no longer excel, for you climbed into your father's bed and defiled my couch to my sorrow. 5 "Simeon and Levi, brothers indeed, weapons of violence are their knives. 6 Let not my soul enter their council, or my spirit be joined with their company; For in their fury they slew men, in their willfulness they maimed oxen. 7 Cursed be their fury so fierce, and their rage so cruel! I will scatter them in Jacob, disperse them throughout Israel. 8 "You, Judah, shall your brothers praise - your hand on the neck of your enemies; the sons of your father shall bow down to you. 9 Judah, like a lion's whelp, you have grown up on prey, my son. He crouches like a lion recumbent, the king of beasts - who would dare rouse him? 10 The scepter shall never depart from Judah, or the mace from between his legs, while tribute is brought to him, and he receives the people's homage. 11 He tethers his donkey to the vine, his purebred ass to the choicest stem. In wine he washes his garments his robe in the blood of grapes. 12 His eyes are darker than wine, and his teeth are whiter than milk. 13 "Zebulun shall dwell by the seashore (This means a shore for ships), and his flank shall be based on Sidon. 14 "Issachar is a rawboned ass, crouching between the saddlebags. 15 When he saw how good a settled life was, and how pleasant the country, He bent his shoulder to the burden and became a toiling serf. 16 "Dan shall achieve justice for his kindred like any other tribe of Israel. 17 Let Dan be a serpent by the roadside, a horned viper by the path, that bites the horse's heel, so that the rider tumbles backward. 18 "(I long for your deliverance, O LORD!) 19 "Gad shall be raided by raiders, but he shall raid at their heels. 20 "Asher's produce is rich, and he shall furnish dainties for kings. 21 "Naphtali is a hind let loose which brings forth lovely fawns. 22 "Joseph is a wild colt, a wild colt by a spring, a wild ass on a hillside. 23 Harrying and attacking, the archers opposed him; 24 But each one's bow remained stiff, as their arms were unsteady, By the power of the Mighty One of Jacob, because of the Shepherd, the Rock of Israel, 25 The God of your father, who helps you, God Almighty, who blesses you, With the blessings of the heavens above, the blessings of the abyss that crouches below, The blessings of breasts and womb, 26 the blessings of fresh grain and blossoms, The blessings of the everlasting mountains, the delights of the eternal hills. May they rest on the head of Joseph, on the brow of the prince among his brothers. 27 "Benjamin is a ravenous wolf; mornings he devours the prey, and evenings he distributes the spoils." 28 All these are the twelve tribes of Israel, and this is what their father said about them, as he bade them farewell and gave to each of them an appropriate message. 29 Then he gave them this charge: "Since I am

about to be taken to my kindred, bury me with my fathers in the cave that lies in the field of Ephron the Hittite, 30 the cave in the field of Machpelah, facing on Mamre, in the land of Canaan, the field that Abraham bought from Ephron the Hittite for a burial ground. 31 There Abraham and his wife Sarah are buried, and so are Isaac and his wife Rebekah, and there, too, I buried Leah - 32 the field and the cave in it that had been purchased from the Hittites." 33 When Jacob had finished giving these instructions to his sons, he drew his feet into the bed, breathed his last, and was taken to his kindred.

Genesis Chapter 50

1 Joseph threw himself on his father's face and wept over him as he kissed him. 2 Then he ordered the physicians in his service to embalm his father. When they embalmed Israel, 3 they spent forty days at it, for that is the full period of embalming; and the Egyptians mourned him for seventy days. 4 When that period of mourning was over, Joseph spoke to Pharaoh's courtiers. "Please do me this favor," he said, "and convey to Pharaoh this request of mine. 5 Since my father, at the point of death, made me promise on oath to bury him in the tomb that he had prepared for himself in the land of Canaan, may I go up there to bury my father and then come back?" 6 Pharaoh replied, "Go and bury your father, as he made you promise on oath." 7 So Joseph left to bury his father; and with him went all of Pharaoh's officials who were senior members of his court and all the other dignitaries of Egypt, 8 as well as Joseph's whole household, his brothers, and his father's household; only their children and their flocks and herds were left in the region of Goshen. 9 Chariots, too, and charioteers went up with him; it was a very large retinue. 10 When they arrived at Goren-ha-atad, which is beyond the Jordan, they held there a very great and solemn memorial service; and Joseph observed seven days of mourning for his father. 11 When the Canaanites who inhabited the land saw the mourning at Goren-ha-atad, they said, "This is a solemn funeral the Egyptians are having." That is why the place was named Abel-mizraim. It is beyond the Jordan. 12 Thus Jacob's sons did for him as he had instructed them. 13 They carried him to the land of Canaan and buried him in the cave in the field of Machpelah, facing on Mamre, the field that Abraham had bought for a burial ground from Ephron the Hittite. 14 After Joseph had buried his father he returned to Egypt, together with his brothers and all who had gone up with him for the burial of his father. 15 Now that their father was dead, Joseph's brothers became fearful and thought, "Suppose Joseph has been nursing a grudge against us and now plans to pay us back in full for all the wrong we did him!" 16 So they approached Joseph and said: "Before your father died, he gave us these instructions: 17 'You shall say to Joseph, Jacob begs you to forgive the criminal wrongdoing of your brothers, who treated you so cruelly.' Please, therefore, forgive the crime that we, the servants of your father's God, committed." When they spoke these words to him, Joseph broke into tears. 18 Then his brothers proceeded to fling themselves down before him and said, "Let us be your slaves!" 19 But Joseph replied to them: "Have no fear. Can I take the place of God? 20 Even though you meant harm to me, God meant it for good, to achieve his present end, the survival of many people. 21 Therefore have no fear. I will provide for you and for your children." By thus speaking kindly to them, he reassured them. 22 Joseph remained in Egypt, together with his father's family. He lived a hundred and ten years. 23 He saw Ephraim's children to the third generation, and the children of Manasseh's son Machir were also born on Joseph's knees. 24 Joseph said to his brothers: "I am about to die. God will surely take care of you and lead you out of this land to the land that he promised on oath to Abraham, Isaac and Jacob." 25 Then, putting the sons of Israel under oath, he continued, "When God thus takes care of you, you must bring my bones up with you from this place." 26 Joseph died at the age of a hundred and ten. He was embalmed and laid to rest in a coffin in Egypt.

Exodus

Exodus Chapter 1

1 These are the names of the sons of Israel who, accompanied by their households, migrated with Jacob into Egypt: 2 Reuben, Simeon, Levi and Judah; 3 Issachar, Zebulun and Benjamin; 4 Dan and Naphtali; Gad and Asher. 5 The total number of the direct descendants of Jacob was seventy. Joseph was already in Egypt. 6 Now Joseph and all his brothers and that whole generation died. 7 But the Israelites were fruitful and prolific. They became so numerous and strong that the land was filled with them. 8 Then a new king, who knew nothing of Joseph 4 , came to power in Egypt. 9 He said to his subjects, "Look how numerous and powerful the Israelite people are growing, more so than we ourselves! 10 Come, let us deal shrewdly with them to stop their increase; otherwise, in time of war they too may join our enemies to fight against us, and so

leave our country." 11 Accordingly, taskmasters were set over the Israelites to oppress them with forced labor. Thus they had to build for Pharaoh the supply cities of Pithom and Raamses. 12 Yet the more they were oppressed, the more they multiplied and spread. The Egyptians, then, dreaded the Israelites 13 and reduced them to cruel slavery, 14 making life bitter for them with hard work in mortar and brick and all kinds of field work - the whole cruel fate of slaves. 15 The king of Egypt told the Hebrew midwives, one of whom was called Shiphrah and the other Puah, 16 When you act as midwives for the Hebrew women and see them giving birth, if it is a boy, kill him; but if it is a girl, she may live." 17 The midwives, however, feared God; they did not do as the king of Egypt had ordered them, but let the boys live. 18 So the king summoned the midwives and asked them, "Why have you acted thus, allowing the boys to live?" 19 The midwives answered Pharaoh, "The Hebrew women are not like the Egyptian women. They are robust and give birth before the midwife arrives." 20 Therefore God dealt well with the midwives. The people, too, increased and grew strong. 21 And because the midwives feared God, he built up families for them. 22 Pharaoh then commanded all his subjects, "Throw into the river every boy that is born to the Hebrews, but you may let all the girls live."

Exodus Chapter 2

1 Now a certain man of the house of Levi married a Levite woman, 2 who conceived and bore a son. Seeing that he was a goodly child, she hid him for three months. 3 When she could hide him no longer, she took a papyrus basket, daubed it with bitumen and pitch, and putting the child in it, placed it among the reeds on the riverbank. 4 His sister stationed herself at a distance to find out what would happen to him. 5 Pharaoh's daughter came down to the river to bathe, while her maids walked along the riverbank. Noticing the basket among the reeds, she sent her handmaid to fetch it. 6 On opening it, she looked, and lo, there was a baby boy, crying! She was moved with pity for him and said, "It is one of the Hebrews' children." 7 Then his sister asked Pharaoh's daughter, "Shall I go and call one of the Hebrew women to nurse the child for you?" 8 "Yes, do so," she answered. So, the maiden went and called the child's own mother. 9 Pharaoh's daughter said to her, "Take this child and nurse it for me, and I will repay you." The woman therefore took the child and nursed it. 10 When the child grew, she brought him to Pharaoh's daughter, who adopted him as her son and called him Moses; for she said, "I drew him out of the water." 11 On one occasion, after Moses had grown up, when he visited his kinsmen and witnessed their forced labor, he saw an Egyptian striking a Hebrew, one of his own kinsmen. 12 Looking about and seeing no one, he slew the Egyptian and hid him in the sand. 13 The next day he went out again, and now two Hebrews were fighting! So he asked the culprit, "Why are you striking your fellow Hebrew?" 14 But he replied, "Who has appointed you ruler and judge over us? Are you thinking of killing me as you killed the Egyptian?" Then Moses became afraid and thought, "The affair must certainly be known." 15 Pharaoh, too, heard of the affair and sought to put him to death. But Moses fled from him and stayed in the land of Midian. As he was seated there by a well, 16 seven daughters of a priest of Midian came to draw water and fill the troughs to water their father's flock. 17 But some shepherds came and drove them away. Then Moses got up and defended them and watered their flock. 18 When they returned to their father Reuel, he said to them, "How is it you have returned so soon today?" 19 They answered, "An Egyptian saved us from the interference of the shepherds. He even drew water for us and watered the flock!" 20 "Where is the man?" he asked his daughters. "Why did you leave him there? Invite him to have something to eat." 21 Moses agreed to live with him, and the man gave him his daughter Zipporah in marriage. 22 She bore him a son, whom he named Gershom; for he said, "I am a stranger in a foreign land." 23 A long time passed, during which the king of Egypt died. Still the Israelites groaned and cried out because of their slavery. As their cry for release went up to God, 24 he heard their groaning and was mindful of his covenant with Abraham, Isaac and Jacob. 25 He saw the Israelites and knew...

Exodus Chapter 3

1 Meanwhile Moses was tending the flock of his father-in-law Jethro, the priest of Midian. Leading the flock across the desert, he came to Horeb, the mountain of God. 2 There an angel of the LORD appeared to him in fire flaming out of a bush. As he looked on, he was surprised to see that the bush, though on fire, was not consumed. 3 So Moses decided, "I must go over to look at this remarkable sight and see why the bush is not burned." 4 When the LORD saw him coming over to look at it more closely, God called out to him from the bush, "Moses! Moses!" He answered, "Here I am." 5 God said, "Come no nearer! Remove the sandals from your feet, for the place where you stand is holy ground. 6 I am the God of your father," he continued, "the God of Abraham, the

God of Isaac, the God of Jacob." Moses hid his face, for he was afraid to look at God. 7 But the LORD said, "I have witnessed the affliction of my people in Egypt and have heard their cry of complaint against their slave drivers, so I know well what they are suffering. 8 Therefore I have come down to rescue them from the hands of the Egyptians and lead them out of that land into a good and spacious land, a land flowing with milk and honey, the country of the Canaanites, Hittites, Amorites, Perizzites, Hivites and Jebusites. 9 So indeed the cry of the Israelites has reached me, and I have truly noted that the Egyptians are oppressing them. 10 Come, now! I will send you to Pharaoh to lead my people, the Israelites, out of Egypt." 11 But Moses said to God, "Who am I that I should go to Pharaoh and lead the Israelites out of Egypt?" 12 He answered, "I will be with you; and this shall be your proof that it is I who have sent you: when you bring my people out of Egypt, you will worship God on this very mountain." 13 "But," said Moses to God, "when I go to the Israelites and say to them, 'The God of your fathers has sent me to you,' if they ask me, 'What is his name?' what am I to tell them?" 14 God replied, "I am who am." Then he added, "This is what you shall tell the Israelites: I AM sent me to you." 15 God spoke further to Moses, "Thus shall you say to the Israelites: The LORD, the God of your fathers, the God of Abraham, the God of Isaac, the God of Jacob, has sent me to you. "This is my name forever; this is my title for all generations. 16 "Go and assemble the elders of the Israelites, and tell them: The LORD, the God of your fathers, the God of Abraham, Isaac and Jacob, has appeared to me and said: I am concerned about you and about the way you are being treated in Egypt; 17 so I have decided to lead you up out of the misery of Egypt into the land of the Canaanites, Hittites, Amorites, Perizzites, Hivites and Jebusites, a land flowing with milk and honey. 18 "Thus, they will heed your message. Then you and the elders of Israel shall go to the king of Egypt and say to him: The LORD, the God of the Hebrews, has sent us word. Permit us, then, to go a three days' journey in the desert, that we may offer sacrifice to the LORD, our God. 19 Yet I know that the king of Egypt will not allow you to go unless he is forced.20 I will stretch out my hand, therefore, and smite Egypt by doing all kinds of wondrous deeds there. After that he will send you away. 21 I will even make the Egyptians so well-disposed toward this people that, when you leave, you will not go empty-handed. 22 Every woman shall ask her neighbour and her house guest for silver and gold articles and for clothing to put on your sons and daughters. Thus, you will despoil the Egyptians."

Exodus Chapter 4

1 "But" objected Moses, "suppose they will not believe me, nor listen to my plea? For they may say, 'The LORD did not appear to you.'" 2 The LORD therefore asked him, "What is that in your hand?" "A staff," he answered. 3 The LORD then said, "Throw it on the ground." When he threw it on the ground it was changed into a serpent, and Moses shied away from it. 4 "Now, put out your hand," the LORD said to him, "and take hold of its tail." So he put out his hand and laid hold of it, and it became a staff in his hand. 5 "This will take place so that they may believe," he continued, "that the LORD, the God of their fathers, the God of Abraham, the God of Isaac, the God of Jacob, did appear to you." 6 Again the LORD said to him, "Put your hand in your bosom." He put it in his bosom, and when he withdrew it, to his surprise his hand was leprous, like snow. 7 The LORD then said, "Now, put your hand back in your bosom." Moses put his hand back in his bosom, and when he withdrew it, to his surprise it was again like the rest of his body. 8 "If they will not believe you, nor heed the message of the first sign, they should believe the message of the second. 9 And if they will not believe even these two signs, nor heed your plea, take some water from the river and pour it on the dry land. The water you take from the river will become blood on the dry land." 10 Moses, however, said to the LORD, "If you please, LORD, I have never been eloquent, neither in the past, nor recently, nor now that you have spoken to your servant; but I am slow of speech and tongue." 11 The LORD said to him, "Who gives one man speech and makes another deaf and dumb? Or who gives sight to one and makes another blind? Is it not I, the LORD? 12 Go, then! It is I who will assist you in speaking and will teach you what you are to say." 13 Yet he insisted, "If you please, Lord, send someone else!" 14 Then the LORD became angry with Moses and said, "Have you not your brother, Aaron the Levite? I know that he is an eloquent speaker. Besides, he is now on his way to meet you. 15 When he sees you, his heart will be glad. You are to speak to him, then, and put the words in his mouth. I will assist both you and him in speaking and will teach the two of you what you are to do. 16 He shall speak to the people for you: he shall be your spokesman, and you shall be as God to him. 17 Take this staff in your hand; with it you are to perform the signs." 18 After this Moses returned to his father-in-law Jethro and said to him, "Let me go back, please, to my kinsmen in Egypt, to see whether they are still living." Jethro replied, "Go in peace." 19 In Midian the LORD said to Moses, "Go back

to Egypt, for all the men who sought your life are dead." 20 So Moses took his wife and his sons, and started back to the land of Egypt, with them riding the ass. The staff of God he carried with him. 21 The LORD said to him, "On your return to Egypt, see that you perform before Pharaoh all the wonders I have put in your power. I will make him obstinate, however, so that he will not let the people go. 22 So you shall say to Pharaoh: Thus says the LORD: Israel is my son, my first-born. 23 Hence I tell you: Let my son go, that he may serve me. If you refuse to let him go, I warn you, I will kill your son, your first-born." 24 On the journey, at a place where they spent the night, the Lord came upon Moses and would have killed him. 25 But Zipporah took a piece of flint and cut off her son's foreskin and, touching his person, she said, "You are a spouse of blood to me." 26 Then God let Moses go. At that time, she said, "A spouse of blood," in regard to the circumcision. 27 The LORD said to Aaron, "Go into the desert to meet Moses." So he went, and when they met at the mountain of God, Aaron kissed him. 28 Moses informed him of all the LORD had said in sending him, and of the various signs he had enjoined upon him. 29 Then Moses and Aaron went and assembled all the elders of the Israelites. 30 Aaron told them everything the LORD had said to Moses, and he performed the signs before the people. 31 The people believed, and when they heard that the LORD was concerned about them and had seen their affliction, they bowed down in worship.

Exodus Chapter 5

1 After that, Moses and Aaron went to Pharaoh and said, "Thus says the LORD, the God of Israel: Let my people go, that they may celebrate a feast to me in the desert." 2 Pharaoh answered, "Who is the LORD, that I should heed his plea to let Israel go? I do not know the LORD; even if I did, I would not let Israel go." 3 They replied, "The God of the Hebrews has sent us word. Let us go a three days' journey in the desert, that we may offer sacrifice to the LORD, our God; otherwise he will punish us with pestilence or the sword." 4 The king of Egypt answered them, "What do you mean, Moses and Aaron, by taking the people away from their work? Off to your labor! 5 Look how numerous the people of the land are already," continued Pharaoh, "and yet you would give them rest from their labor!" 6 That very day Pharaoh gave the taskmasters and foremen of the people this order: 7 "You shall no longer supply the people with straw for their brickmaking as you have previously done. Let them go and gather straw themselves. 8 Yet you shall levy upon them the same quota of bricks as they have previously made. Do not reduce it. They are lazy; that is why they are crying, 'Let us go to offer sacrifice to our God.' 9 Increase the work for the men, so that they keep their mind on it and pay no attention to lying words." 10 So the taskmasters and foremen of the people went out and told them, "Thus says Pharaoh: I will not provide you with straw. 11 Go and gather the straw yourselves, wherever you can find it. Yet there must not be the slightest reduction in your work." 12 The people, then, scattered throughout the land of Egypt to gather stubble for straw, 13 while the taskmasters kept driving them on, saying, "Finish your work, the same daily amount as when your straw was supplied." 14 The foremen of the Israelites, whom the taskmasters of Pharaoh had placed over them, were beaten, and were asked, "Why have you not completed your prescribed amount of bricks yesterday and today, as before?" 15 Then the Israelite foremen came and made this appeal to Pharaoh: "Why do you treat your servants in this manner? 16 No straw is supplied to your servants, and still we are told to make bricks. Look how your servants are beaten! It is you who are at fault." 17 Pharaoh answered, "It is just because you are lazy that you keep saying, 'Let us go and offer sacrifice to the LORD.' 18 Off to work, then! Straw shall not be provided for you, but you must still deliver your quota of bricks." 19 The Israelite foremen knew they were in a sorry plight, having been told not to reduce the daily amount of bricks. 20 When, therefore, they left Pharaoh and came upon Moses and Aaron, who were waiting to meet them, 21 they said to them, "The LORD look upon you and judge! You have brought us into bad odor with Pharaoh and his servants and have put a sword in their hands to slay us." 22 Moses again had recourse to the LORD and said, "Lord, why do you treat this people so badly? And why did you send me on such a mission? 23 Ever since I went to Pharaoh to speak in your name, he has maltreated this people of yours, and you have done nothing to rescue them."

Exodus Chapter 6

1 Then the LORD answered Moses, "Now you shall see what I will do to Pharaoh. Forced by my mighty hand, he will send them away; compelled by my outstretched arm, he will drive them from his land." 2 God also said to Moses, "I am the LORD. 3 As God the Almighty I appeared to Abraham, Isaac and Jacob, but my name, LORD, I did not make known to them. 4 I also established my covenant with them, to

give them the land of Canaan, the land in which they were living as aliens. 5 And now that I have heard the groaning of the Israelites, whom the Egyptians are treating as slaves, I am mindful of my covenant. 6 Therefore, say to the Israelites: I am the LORD. I will free you from the forced labor of the Egyptians and will deliver you from their slavery. I will rescue you by my outstretched arm and with mighty acts of judgment. 7 I will take you as my own people, and you shall have me as your God. You will know that I, the LORD, am your God when I free you from the labor of the Egyptians 8 and bring you into the land which I swore to give to Abraham, Isaac and Jacob. I will give it to you as your own possession - I, the LORD!" 9 But when Moses told this to the Israelites, they would not listen to him because of their dejection and hard slavery. 10 Then the LORD said to Moses, 11 "Go and tell Pharaoh, king of Egypt, to let the Israelites leave his land."12 But Moses protested to the LORD, "If the Israelites would not listen to me, how can it be that Pharaoh will listen to me, poor speaker that I am!" 13 Still, the LORD, to bring the Israelites out of Egypt, spoke to Moses and Aaron and gave them his orders regarding both the Israelites and Pharaoh, king of Egypt. 14 These are the heads of the ancestral houses. The sons of Reuben, the first-born of Israel, were Hanoch, Pallu, Hezron and Carmi; these are the clans of Reuben. 15 The sons of Simeon were Jenuel, Jamin, Ohad, Jachin, Zohar and Shaul, who was the son of a Canaanite woman; these are the clans of Simeon. 16 The names of the sons of Levi, in their genealogical order, are Gershon, Kohath and Merari. Levi lived one hundred and thirty-seven years. 17 The sons of Gershon, as heads of clans, were Libni and Shimei. 18 The sons of Kohath were Amram, Izhar, Hebron and Uzziel. Kohath lived one hundred and thirty-three years. 19 The sons of Merari were Mahli and Mushi. These are the clans of Levi in their genealogical order. 20 Amram married his aunt Jochebed, who bore him Aaron, Moses and Miriam. Amram lived one hundred and thirty-seven years. 21 The sons of Izhar were Korah, Nepheg and Zichri. 22 The sons of Uzziel were Mishael, Elzaphan and Sithri. 23 Aaron married Amminadab's daughter, Elisheba, the sister of Nahshon; she bore him Nadab, Abihu, Eleazar and Ithamar. 24 The sons of Korah were Assir, Elkanah and Abiasaph. These are the clans of the Korahites. 25 Aaron's son, Eleazar, married one of Putiel's daughters, who bore him Phinehas. These are the heads of the ancestral clans of the Levites. 26 This is the Aaron and this the Moses to whom the LORD said, "Lead the Israelites from the land of Egypt, company by company." 27 These are the ones who spoke to Pharaoh, king of Egypt, to bring the Israelites out of Egypt - the same Moses and Aaron. 28 On the day the LORD spoke to Moses in Egypt 29 he said, "I am the LORD. Repeat to Pharaoh, king of Egypt, all that I tell you." 30 But Moses protested to the LORD, "Since I am a poor speaker, how can it be that Pharaoh will listen to me?"

Exodus Chapter 7

1 The LORD answered him, "See! I have made you as God to Pharaoh, and Aaron your brother shall act as your prophet. 2 You shall tell him all that I command you. In turn, your brother Aaron shall tell Pharaoh to let the Israelites leave his land. 3 Yet I will make Pharaoh so obstinate that, despite the many signs and wonders that I will work in the land of Egypt, 4 he will not listen to you. Therefore I will lay my hand on Egypt and by great acts of judgment I will bring the hosts of my people, the Israelites, out of the land of Egypt, 5 so that the Egyptians may learn that I am the LORD, as I stretch out my hand against Egypt and lead the Israelites out of their midst." 6 Moses and Aaron did as the LORD had commanded them. 7 Moses was eighty years old and Aaron eighty-three when they spoke to Pharaoh. 8 The LORD told Moses and Aaron, 9 "If Pharaoh demands that you work a sign or wonder, you shall say to Aaron: Take your staff and throw it down before Pharaoh, and it will be changed into a snake." 10 Then Moses and Aaron went to Pharaoh and did as the LORD had commanded. Aaron threw his staff down before Pharaoh and his servants, and it was changed into a snake. 11 Pharaoh, in turn, summoned wise men and sorcerers, and they also, the magicians of Egypt, did likewise by their magic arts. 12 Each one threw down his staff, and it was changed into a snake. But Aaron's staff swallowed their staffs. 13 Pharaoh, however, was obstinate and would not listen to them, just as the LORD had foretold. 14 Then the LORD said to Moses, "Pharaoh is obdurate in refusing to let the people go. 15 Tomorrow morning, when he sets out for the water, go and present yourself by the river bank, holding in your hand the staff that turned into a serpent. 16 Say to him: The LORD, the God of the Hebrews, sent me to you with the message: Let my people go to worship me in the desert. But as yet you have not listened. 17 The LORD now says: This is how you shall know that I am the LORD. I will strike the water of the river with the staff I hold, and it shall be changed into blood. 18 The fish in the river shall die, and the river itself shall become so polluted that the Egyptians will be unable to drink its water." 19 The LORD then said to Moses, "Say to Aaron: Take your staff and stretch out your hand over the waters of Egypt - their streams and canals and pools, all their supplies of water - that they may become blood. Throughout the land of Egypt there shall be blood, even in the wooden pails and stone jars." 20 Moses and Aaron did as the LORD had commanded. Aaron raised his staff and struck the waters of the river in full view of Pharaoh and his servants, and all the water of the river was changed into blood. 21 The fish in the river died, and the river itself became so polluted that the Egyptians could not drink its water. There was blood throughout the land of Egypt. 22 But the Egyptian magicians did the same by their magic arts. So, Pharaoh remained obstinate and would not listen to Moses and Aaron, just as the LORD had foretold. 23 He turned away and went into his house, with no concern even for this. 24 All the Egyptians had to dig in the neighborhood of the river for drinking water, since they could not drink the river water. 25 Seven days passed after the LORD had struck the river. 26 Then the LORD said to Moses, "Go to Pharaoh and tell him: Thus says the LORD: Let my people go to worship me. 27 If you refuse to let them go, I warn you, I will send a plague of frogs over all your territory. 28 The river will teem with frogs. They will come up into your palace and into your bedroom and onto your bed, into the houses of your servants, too, and your subjects, even into your ovens and your kneading bowls. 29 The frogs will swarm all over you and your subjects and your servants."

Exodus Chapter 8

1 The LORD then told Moses, "Say to Aaron: Stretch out your hand and your staff over the streams and canals and pools, to make frogs overrun the land of Egypt." 2 Aaron stretched out his hand over the waters of Egypt, and the frogs came up and covered the land of Egypt. 3 But the magicians did the same by their magic arts. They, too, made frogs overrun the land of Egypt. 4 Then Pharaoh summoned Moses and Aaron and said, "Pray the LORD to remove the frogs from me and my subjects, and I will let the people go to offer sacrifice to the LORD." 5 Moses answered Pharaoh, "Do me the favor of appointing the time when I am to pray for you and your servants and your subjects, that the frogs may be taken away from you and your houses and be left only in the river." 6 "Tomorrow," said Pharaoh. Then Moses replied, "It shall be as you have said, so that you may learn that there is none like the LORD, our God. 7 The frogs shall leave you and your houses, your servants and your subjects; only in the river shall they be left." 8 After Moses and Aaron left Pharaoh's presence, Moses implored the LORD to fulfill the promise he had made to Pharaoh about the frogs; 9 and the LORD did as Moses had asked. The frogs in the houses and courtyards and fields died off. 10 Heaps and heaps of them were gathered up, and there was a stench in the land. 11 But when Pharaoh saw that there was a respite, he became obdurate and would not listen to them, just as the LORD had foretold. 12 Thereupon the LORD said to Moses, "Tell Aaron to stretch out his staff and strike the dust of the earth, that it may be turned into gnats throughout the land of Egypt." 13 They did so. Aaron stretched out his hand, and with his staff he struck the dust of the earth, and gnats came upon man and beast. The dust of the earth was turned into gnats throughout the land of Egypt. 14 Though the magicians tried to bring forth gnats by their magic arts, they could not do so. As the gnats infested man and beast, 15 the magicians said to Pharaoh, "This is the finger of God." Yet Pharaoh remained obstinate and would not listen to them, just as the LORD had foretold. 16 Again the LORD told Moses, "Early tomorrow morning present yourself to Pharaoh when he goes forth to the water and say to him: Thus says the LORD: Let my people go to worship me. 17 If you will not let my people go, I warn you, I will loose swarms of flies upon you and your servants and your subjects and your houses. The houses of the Egyptians and the very ground on which they stand shall be filled with swarms of flies. 18 But on that day, I will make an exception of the land of Goshen: there shall be no flies where my people dwell, that you may know that I am the LORD in the midst of the earth. 19 I will make this distinction between my people and your people. This sign shall take place tomorrow." 20 This the LORD did. Thick swarms of flies entered the house of Pharaoh and the houses of his servants; throughout Egypt the land was infested with flies. 21 Then Pharaoh summoned Moses and Aaron and said to them, "Go and offer sacrifice to your God in this land." 22 But Moses replied, "It is not right to do so, for the sacrifices we offer to the LORD, our God, are an abomination to the Egyptians. If before their very eyes we offer sacrifices which are an abomination to them, will not the Egyptians stone us? 23 We must go a three days' journey in the desert to offer sacrifice to the LORD, our God, as he commands us." 24 "Well, then," said Pharaoh, "I will let you go to offer sacrifice to the LORD, your God, in the desert, provided that you do not go too far away and that you pray for me." 25 Moses answered, "As soon as I leave your presence I will pray to the LORD that the flies may depart tomorrow from Pharaoh and his servants and his subjects. Pharaoh, however, must not play false again

by refusing to let the people go to offer sacrifice to the LORD." 26 When Moses left Pharaoh's presence, he prayed to the LORD; 27 and the LORD did as Moses had asked. He removed the flies from Pharaoh and his servants and subjects. Not one remained. 28 But once more Pharaoh became obdurate and would not let the people go.

Exodus Chapter 9

1 Then the LORD said to Moses, "Go to Pharaoh and tell him: Thus says the LORD, the God of the Hebrews: Let my people go to worship me. 2 If you refuse to let them go and persist in holding them, 3 I warn you; the LORD will afflict all your livestock in the field - your horses, asses, camels, herds and flocks - with a very severe pestilence. 4 But the LORD will distinguish between the livestock of Israel and that of Egypt, so that none belonging to the Israelites will die." 5 And setting a definite time, the LORD added, "Tomorrow the LORD shall do this in the land." 6 And on the next day the LORD did so. All the livestock of the Egyptians died, but not one beast belonging to the Israelites. 7 But though Pharaoh's messengers informed him that not even one beast belonging to the Israelites had died, he still remained obdurate and would not let the people go. 8 Then the LORD said to Moses and Aaron, "Take a double handful of soot from a furnace, and in the presence of Pharaoh let Moses scatter it toward the sky. 9 It will then turn into fine dust over the whole land of Egypt and cause festering boils on man and beast throughout the land." 10 So they took soot from a furnace and stood in the presence of Pharaoh. Moses scattered it toward the sky, and it caused festering boils on man and beast. 11 The magicians could not stand in Moses' presence, for there were boils on the magicians no less than on the rest of the Egyptians. 12 But the LORD made Pharaoh obstinate, and he would not listen to them, just as the LORD had foretold to Moses. 13 Then the LORD told Moses, "Early tomorrow morning present yourself to Pharaoh and say to him: Thus says the LORD, the God of the Hebrews: Let my people go to worship me, 14 or this time I will hurl all my blows upon you and your servants and your subjects, that you may know that there is none like me anywhere on earth. 15 For by now I would have stretched out my hand and struck you and your subjects with such pestilence as would wipe you from the earth. 16 But this is why I have spared you: to show you my power and to make my name resound throughout the earth! 17 Will you still block the way for my people by refusing to let them go? 18 I warn you, then, tomorrow at this hour I will rain down such fierce hail as there has never been in Egypt from the day the nation was founded up to the present. 19 Therefore, order all your livestock and whatever else you have in the open fields to be brought to a place of safety. Whatever man or beast remains in the fields and is not brought to shelter shall die when the hail comes upon them." 20 Some of Pharaoh's servants feared the warning of the LORD and hurried their servants and livestock off to shelter. 21 Others, however, did not take the warning of the LORD to heart and left their servants and livestock in the fields. 22 The LORD then said to Moses, "Stretch out your hand toward the sky, that hail may fall upon the entire land of Egypt, on man and beast and every growing thing in the land of Egypt." 23 When Moses stretched out his staff toward the sky, the LORD sent forth hail and peals of thunder. Lightning flashed toward the earth, and the LORD rained down hail upon the land of Egypt; 24 and lightning constantly flashed through the hail, such fierce hail as had never been seen in the land since Egypt became a nation. 25 It struck down every man and beast that was in the open throughout the land of Egypt; it beat down every growing thing and splintered every tree in the fields. 26 Only in the land of Goshen, where the Israelites dwelt, was there no hail. 27 Then Pharaoh summoned Moses and Aaron and said to them, "I have sinned again! The LORD is just; it is I and my subjects who are at fault. 28 Pray to the LORD, for we have had enough of God's thunder and hail. Then I will let you go; you need stay no longer." 29 Moses replied, "As soon as I leave the city I will extend my hands to the LORD; the thunder will cease, and there will be no more hail. Thus you shall learn that the earth is the LORD'S. 30 But you and your servants, I know, do not yet fear the LORD God." 31 Now the flax and the barley were ruined, because the barley was in ear and the flax in bud. 32 But the wheat and the spelt were not ruined, for they grow later. 33 When Moses had left Pharaoh's presence and had gone out of the city, he extended his hands to the LORD. Then the thunder and the hail ceased, and the rain no longer poured down upon the earth. 34 But Pharaoh, seeing that the rain and hail and thunder had ceased, sinned again: he with his servants became obdurate, 35 and in his obstinacy, he would not let the Israelites go, as the LORD had foretold through Moses.

Exodus Chapter 10

1 Then the LORD said to Moses, "Go to Pharaoh, for I have made him and his servants obdurate in order that I may perform these signs of mine among them 2 and that you may recount to your son and grandson how ruthlessly I dealt with the Egyptians and what signs I wrought among them, so that you may know that I am the LORD." 3 So Moses and Aaron went to Pharaoh and told him, "Thus says the LORD, the God of the Hebrews: How long will you refuse to submit to me? Let my people go to worship me. 4 If you refuse to let my people go, I warn you, tomorrow I will bring locusts into your country. 5 They shall cover the ground, so that the ground itself will not be visible. They shall eat up the remnant you saved unhurt from the hail, as well as all the foliage that has since sprouted in your fields. 6 They shall fill your houses and the houses of your servants and of all the Egyptians; such a sight your fathers or grandfathers have not seen from the day they first settled on this soil up to the present day." With that he turned and left Pharaoh. 7 But Pharaoh's servants said to him, "How long must he be a menace to us? Let the men go to worship the LORD, their God. Do you not yet realize that Egypt is being destroyed?" 8 So Moses and Aaron were brought back to Pharaoh, who said to them, "You may go and worship the LORD, your God. But how many of you will go?" 9 "Young and old must go with us," Moses answered, "our sons and daughters as well as our flocks and herds must accompany us. That is what a feast of the LORD means to us." 10 "The LORD help you," Pharaoh replied, "if I ever let your little ones go with you! Clearly, you have some evil in mind. 11 No, no! Just you men can go and worship the LORD. After all, that is what you want." With that they were driven from Pharaoh's presence. 12 The LORD then said to Moses, "Stretch out your hand over the land of Egypt, that locusts may swarm over it and eat up all the vegetation and whatever the hail has left." 13 So Moses stretched out his staff over the land of Egypt, and the LORD sent an east wind blowing over the land all that day and all that night. At dawn the east wind brought the locusts. 14 They swarmed over the whole land of Egypt and settled down on every part of it. Never before had there been such a fierce swarm of locusts, nor will there ever be. 15 They covered the surface of the whole land, till it was black with them. They ate up all the vegetation in the land and the fruit of whatever trees the hail had spared. Nothing green was left on any tree or plant throughout the land of Egypt. 16 Hastily Pharaoh summoned Moses and Aaron and said, "I have sinned against the LORD, your God, and against you. 17 But now, do forgive me my sin once more, and pray the LORD, your God, to take at least this deadly pest from me." 18 When Moses left the presence of Pharaoh, he prayed to the LORD, 19 and the LORD changed the wind to a very strong west wind, which took up the locusts and hurled them into the Red Sea. But though not a single locust remained within the confines of Egypt, 20 the LORD made Pharaoh obstinate, and he would not let the Israelites go. 21 Then the LORD said to Moses, "Stretch out your hand toward the sky, that over the land of Egypt there may be such intense darkness that one can feel it." 22 So Moses stretched out his hand toward the sky, and there was dense darkness throughout the land of Egypt for three days. 23 Men could not see one another, nor could they move from where they were, for three days. But all the Israelites had light where they dwelt. 24 Pharaoh then summoned Moses and Aaron and said, "Go and worship the LORD. Your little ones, too, may go with you. But your flocks and herds must remain." 25 Moses replied, "You must also grant us sacrifices and holocausts to offer up to the LORD, our God. 26 Hence, our livestock also must go with us. Not an animal must be left behind. Some of them we must sacrifice to the LORD, our God, but we ourselves shall not know which ones we must sacrifice to him until we arrive at the place itself." 27 But the LORD made Pharaoh obstinate, and he would not let them go. 28 "Leave my presence," Pharaoh said to him, "and see to it that you do not appear before me again! The day you appear before me you shall die!" 29 Moses replied, "Well said! I will never appear before you again."

Exodus Chapter 11

1 Then the LORD told Moses, "One more plague will I bring upon Pharaoh and upon Egypt. After that he will let you depart. In fact, he will not merely let you go; he will drive you away. 2 Instruct your people that every man is to ask his neighbor, and every woman her neighbor, for silver and gold articles and for clothing." 3 The LORD indeed made the Egyptians well-disposed toward the people; Moses himself was very highly regarded by Pharaoh's servants and the people in the land of Egypt. 4 Moses then said, "Thus says the LORD: At midnight I will go forth through Egypt. 5 Every first-born in this land shall die, from the first-born of Pharaoh on the throne to the first-born of the slave-girl at the handmill, as well as all the first-born of the animals. 6 Then there shall be loud wailing throughout the land of Egypt, such as has never been, nor will ever be again. 7 But among the Israelites and their animals not even a dog shall growl, so that you may know how the LORD distinguishes between the Egyptians and the Israelites. 8 All these servants of yours shall then come down to me, and prostrate

before me, they shall beg me, 'Leave us, you and all your followers!' Only then will I depart." With that he left Pharaoh's presence in hot anger. 9 The LORD said to Moses, "Pharaoh refuses to listen to you that my wonders may be multiplied in the land of Egypt." 10 Thus, although Moses and Aaron performed these various wonders in Pharaoh's presence, the LORD made Pharaoh obstinate, and he would not let the Israelites leave his land.

Exodus Chapter 12

1 The LORD said to Moses and Aaron in the land of Egypt, 2 "This month shall stand at the head of your calendar; you shall reckon it the first month of the year. 3 Tell the whole community of Israel: On the tenth of this month every one of your families must procure for itself a lamb, one apiece for each household. 4 If a family is too small for a whole lamb, it shall join the nearest household in procuring one and shall share in the lamb in proportion to the number of persons who partake of it. 5 The lamb must be a year-old male and without blemish. You may take it from either the sheep or the goats. 6 You shall keep it until the fourteenth day of this month, and then, with the whole assembly of Israel present, it shall be slaughtered during the evening twilight. 7 They shall take some of its blood and apply it to the two doorposts and the lintel of every house in which they partake of the lamb. 8 That same night they shall eat its roasted flesh with unleavened bread and bitter herbs. 9 It shall not be eaten raw or boiled, but roasted whole, with its head and shanks and inner organs. 10 None of it must be kept beyond the next morning; whatever is left over in the morning shall be burned up. 11 "This is how you are to eat it: with your loins girt, sandals on your feet and your staff in hand, you shall eat like those who are in flight. It is the Passover of the LORD. 12 For on this same night I will go through Egypt, striking down every first - born of the land, both man and beast, and executing judgment on all the gods of Egypt-I, the LORD! 13 But the blood will mark the houses where you are. Seeing the blood, I will pass over you; thus, when I strike the land of Egypt, no destructive blow will come upon you. 14 "This day shall be a memorial feast for you, which all your generations shall celebrate with pilgrimage to the LORD, as a perpetual institution. 15 For seven days you must eat unleavened bread. From the very first day you shall have your houses clear of all leaven. Whoever eats leavened bread from the first day to the seventh shall be cut off from Israel. 16 On the first day you shall hold a sacred assembly, and likewise on the seventh. On these days you shall not do any sort of work, except to prepare the food that everyone needs. 17 "Keep, then, this custom of the unleavened bread. Since it was on this very day that I brought your ranks out of the land of Egypt, you must celebrate this day throughout your generations as a perpetual institution. 18 From the evening of the fourteenth day of the first month until the evening of the twenty-first day of this month you shall eat unleavened bread. 19 For seven days no leaven may be found in your houses. Anyone, be he a resident alien or a native, who eats leavened food shall be cut off from the community of Israel. 20 Nothing leavened may you eat; wherever you dwell you may eat only unleavened bread." 21 Moses called all the elders of Israel and said to them, "Go and procure lambs for your families, and slaughter them as Passover victims. 22 Then take a bunch of hyssop, and dipping it in the blood that is in the basin, sprinkle the lintel and the two doorposts with this blood. But none of you shall go outdoors until morning. 23 For the LORD will go by, striking down the Egyptians. Seeing the blood on the lintel and the two doorposts, the LORD will pass over that door and not let the destroyer come into your houses to strike you down. 24 "You shall observe this as a perpetual ordinance for yourselves and your descendants. 25 Thus, you must also observe this rite when you have entered the land which the LORD will give you as he promised. 26 When your children ask you, 'What does this rite of yours mean?' 27 you shall reply, 'This is the Passover sacrifice of the LORD, who passed over the houses of the Israelites in Egypt; when he struck down the Egyptians, he spared our houses.'" Then the people bowed down in worship, 28 and the Israelites went and did as the LORD had commanded Moses and Aaron. 29 At midnight the LORD slew every first-born in the land of Egypt, from the first-born of Pharaoh on the throne to the first-born of the prisoner in the dungeon, as well as the first-born of the animals. 30 Pharaoh arose in the night, he and all his servants and all the Egyptians; and there was loud wailing throughout Egypt, for there was not a house without its dead. 31 During the night Pharaoh summoned Moses and Aaron and said, "Leave my people at once, you and the Israelites with you! Go and worship the LORD as you said. 32 Take your flocks, too, and your herds, as you demanded, and be gone; and you will be doing me a favor." 33 The Egyptians likewise urged the people on, to hasten their departure from the land; they thought that otherwise they would all die. 34 The people, therefore, took their dough before it was leavened, in their kneading bowls wrapped in their cloaks on their shoulders. 35 The Israelites did as Moses had commanded: they asked the Egyptians for articles of silver and gold and for clothing. 36 The LORD indeed had made the Egyptians so well-disposed toward the people that they let them have whatever they asked for. Thus did they despoil the Egyptians. 37 The Israelites set out from Rameses for Succoth, about six hundred thousand men on foot, not counting the children. 38 A crowd of mixed ancestry also went up with them, besides their livestock, very numerous flocks and herds. 39 Since the dough had brought out of Egypt was not leavened, they baked it into unleavened loaves. They had been rushed out of Egypt and had no opportunity even to prepare food for the journey. 40 The time the Israelites had stayed in Egypt was four hundred and thirty years. 41 At the end of four hundred and thirty years, all the hosts of the LORD left the land of Egypt on this very date. 42 This was a night of vigil for the LORD, as he led them out of the land of Egypt; so on this same night all the Israelites must keep a vigil for the LORD throughout their generations. 43 The LORD said to Moses and Aaron, "These are the regulations for the Passover. No foreigner may partake of it. 44 However, any slave who has been bought for money may partake of it, provided you have first circumcised him. 45 But no transient alien or hired servant may partake of it. 46 It must be eaten in one and the same house; you may not take any of its flesh outside the house. You shall not break any of its bones. 47 The whole community of Israel must keep this feast. 48 If any aliens living among you wish to celebrate the Passover of the LORD, all the males among them must first be circumcised, and then they may join in its observance just like the natives. But no man who is uncircumcised may partake of it. 49 The law shall be the same for the resident alien as for the native." 50 All the Israelites did just as the LORD had commanded Moses and Aaron. 51 on that same day the LORD brought the Israelites out of Egypt company by company.

Exodus Chapter 13

1 The LORD spoke to Moses and said, 2 "Consecrate to me every first-born that opens the womb among the Israelites, both of man and beast, for it belongs to me." 3 Moses said to the people, "Remember this day on which you came out of Egypt, that place of slavery. It was with a strong hand that the LORD brought you away. Nothing made with leaven must be eaten. 4 This day of your departure is in the month of Abib. 5 Therefore, it is in this month that you must celebrate this rite, after the LORD, your God, has brought you into the land of the Canaanites, Hittites, Amorites, Hivites and Jebusites, which he swore to your fathers he would give you, a land flowing with milk and honey. 6 For seven days you shall eat unleavened bread, and the seventh day shall also be a festival to the LORD. 7 Only unleavened bread may be eaten during the seven days; no leaven and nothing leavened may be found in all your territory. 8 On this day you shall explain to your son, 'This is because of what the LORD did for me when I came out of Egypt.' 9 It shall be as a sign on your hand and as a reminder on your forehead; thus the law of the LORD will ever be on your lips, because with a strong hand the LORD brought you out of Egypt. 10 Therefore, you shall keep this prescribed rite at its appointed time from year to year. 11 "When the LORD, your God, has brought you into the land of the Canaanites, which he swore to you and your fathers he would give you, 12 you shall dedicate to the LORD every son that opens the womb; and all the male firstlings of your animals shall belong to the LORD. 13 Every first-born of an ass you shall redeem with a sheep. If you do not redeem it, you shall break its neck. Every first-born son you must redeem. 14 If your son should ask you later on, 'What does this mean?' you shall tell him, 'With a strong hand the LORD brought us out of Egypt, that place of slavery. 15 When Pharaoh stubbornly refused to let us go, the LORD killed every first-born in the land of Egypt, every first-born of man and of beast. That is why I sacrifice to the LORD everything of the male sex that opens the womb, and why I redeem every first-born of my sons.' 16 Let this, then, be as a sign on your hand and as a pendant on your forehead: with a strong hand the LORD brought us out of Egypt." 17 Now, when Pharaoh let the people go, God did not lead them by way of the Philistines' land, though this was the nearest; for he thought, should the people see that they would have to fight, they might change their minds and return to Egypt. 18 Instead, he rerouted them toward the Red Sea by way of the desert road. In battle array the Israelites marched out of Egypt. 19 Moses also took Joseph's bones along, for Joseph had made the Israelites swear solemnly that, when God should come to them, they would carry his bones away with them. 20 Setting out from Succoth, they camped at Etham near the edge of the desert. 21 The LORD preceded them, in the daytime by means of a column of cloud to show them the way, and at night by means of a column of fire to give them light. Thus they could travel both day and night. 22 Neither the column of cloud by day nor the column of fire by night ever left its place in front of the people.

Exodus Chapter 14

¹ Then the LORD said to Moses, ² "Tell the Israelites to turn about and camp before Pi-hahiroth, between Migdol and the sea. You shall camp in front of Baal-zephon, just opposite, by the sea. ³ Pharaoh will then say, 'The Israelites are wandering about aimlessly in the land. The desert has closed in on them.' ⁴ Thus will I make Pharaoh so obstinate that he will pursue them. Then I will receive glory through Pharaoh and all his army, and the Egyptians will know that I am the LORD." This the Israelites did. ⁵ When it was reported to the king of Egypt that the people had fled, Pharaoh and his servants changed their minds about them. "What have we done!" they exclaimed. "Why, we have released Israel from our service!" ⁶ So Pharaoh made his chariots ready and mustered his soldiers - ⁷ six hundred first-class chariots and all the other chariots of Egypt, with warriors on them all. ⁸ So obstinate had the LORD made Pharaoh that he pursued the Israelites even while they were marching away in triumph. ⁹ The Egyptians, then, pursued them; Pharaoh's whole army, his horses, chariots and charioteers, caught up with them as they lay encamped by the sea, at Pi-hahiroth, in front of Baal-zephon. ¹⁰ Pharaoh was already near when the Israelites looked up and saw that the Egyptians were on the march in pursuit of them. In great fright they cried out to the LORD. ¹¹ And they complained to Moses, "Were there no burial places in Egypt that you had to bring us out here to die in the desert? Why did you do this to us? Why did you bring us out of Egypt? ¹² Did we not tell you this in Egypt, when we said, 'Leave us alone. Let us serve the Egyptians'? Far better for us to be the slaves of the Egyptians than to die in the desert." ¹³ But Moses answered the people, "Fear not! Stand your ground, and you will see the victory the LORD will win for you today. These Egyptians whom you see today you will never see again. ¹⁴ The LORD himself will fight for you; you have only to keep still." ¹⁵ Then the LORD said to Moses, "Why are you crying out to me? Tell the Israelites to go forward. ¹⁶ And you, lift up your staff and, with hand outstretched over the sea, split the sea in two, that the Israelites may pass through it on dry land. ¹⁷ But I will make the Egyptians so obstinate that they will go in after them. Then I will receive glory through Pharaoh and all his army, his chariots and charioteers. ¹⁸ The Egyptians shall know that I am the LORD, when I receive glory through Pharaoh and his chariots and charioteers." ¹⁹ The angel of God, who had been leading Israel's camp, now moved and went around behind them. The column of cloud also, leaving the front, took up its place behind them, ²⁰ so that it came between the camp of the Egyptians and that of Israel. But the cloud now became dark, and thus the night passed without the rival camps coming any closer together all night long. ²¹ Then Moses stretched out his hand over the sea, and the LORD swept the sea with a strong east wind throughout the night and so turned it into dry land. When the water was thus divided, ²² the Israelites marched into the midst of the sea on dry land, with the water like a wall to their right and to their left. ²³ The Egyptians followed in pursuit; all Pharaoh's horses and chariots and charioteers went after them right into the midst of the sea. ²⁴ In the night watch just before dawn the LORD cast through the column of the fiery cloud upon the Egyptian force a glance that threw it into a panic; ²⁵ and he so clogged their chariot wheels that they could hardly drive. With that the Egyptians sounded the retreat before Israel, because the LORD was fighting for them against the Egyptians. ²⁶ Then the LORD told Moses, "Stretch out your hand over the sea, that the water may flow back upon the Egyptians, upon their chariots and their charioteers." ²⁷ So Moses stretched out his hand over the sea, and at dawn the sea flowed back to its normal depth. The Egyptians were fleeing head on toward the sea, when the LORD hurled them into its midst. ²⁸ As the water flowed back, it covered the chariots and the charioteers of Pharaoh's whole army which had followed the Israelites into the sea. Not a single one of them escaped. ²⁹ But the Israelites had marched on dry land through the midst of the sea, with the water like a wall to their right and to their left. ³⁰ Thus the LORD saved Israel on that day from the power of the Egyptians. When Israel saw the Egyptians lying dead on the seashore ³¹ and beheld the great power that the LORD had shown against the Egyptians, they feared the LORD and believed in him and in his servant Moses.

Exodus Chapter 15

¹ Then Moses and the Israelites sang this song to the LORD: I will sing to the LORD, for he is gloriously triumphant; horse and chariot he has cast into the sea. ² My strength and my courage is the LORD, and he has been my savior. He is my God, I praise him; the God of my father, I extol him. ³ The LORD is a warrior, LORD is his name! ⁴ Pharaoh's chariots and army he hurled into the sea; the elite of his officers were submerged in the Red Sea. ⁵ The flood waters covered them, they sank into the depths like a stone. ⁶ Your right hand, O LORD, magnificent in power, your right hand, O LORD, has shattered the enemy. ⁷ In your great majesty you overthrew your adversaries; you loosed your wrath to consume them like stubble. ⁸ At a breath of your anger the waters piled up, the flowing waters stood like a mound, the flood waters congealed in the midst of the sea. ⁹ The enemy boasted, "I will pursue and overtake them; I will divide the spoils and have my fill of them; I will draw my sword; my hand shall despoil them!" ¹⁰ When your wind blew, the sea covered them; like lead they sank in the mighty waters. ¹¹ Who is like to you among the gods, O LORD? Who is like to you, magnificent in holiness? O terrible in renown, worker of wonders, ¹² when you stretched out your right hand, the earth swallowed them! ¹³ In your mercy you led the people you redeemed; in your strength you guided them to your holy dwelling. ¹⁴ The nations heard and quaked; anguish gripped the dwellers in Philistia. ¹⁵ Then were the princes of Edom dismayed; trembling seized the chieftains of Moab; All the dwellers in Canaan melted away; ¹⁶ terror and dread fell upon them. By the might of your arm they were frozen like stone, while your people, O LORD, passed over, while the people you had made your own passed over. ¹⁷ And you brought them in and planted them on the mountain of your inheritance - the place where you made your seat, O LORD, the sanctuary, O LORD, which your hands established. ¹⁸ The LORD shall reign forever and ever. ¹⁹ They sang thus because Pharaoh's horses and chariots and charioteers had gone into the sea, and the LORD made the waters of the sea flow back upon them, though the Israelites had marched on dry land through the midst of the sea. ²⁰ The prophetess Miriam, Aaron's sister, took a tambourine in her hand, while all the women went out after her with tambourines, dancing; ²¹ and she led them in the refrain: Sing to the LORD, for he is gloriously triumphant; horse and chariot he has cast into the sea. ²² Then Moses led Israel forward from the Red Sea, and they marched out to the desert of Shur. After traveling for three days through the desert without finding water, ²³ they arrived at Marah, where they could not drink the water, because it was too bitter. Hence this place was called Marah. ²⁴ As the people grumbled against Moses, saying, "What are we to drink?" ²⁵ he appealed to the LORD, who pointed out to him a certain piece of wood. When he threw this into the water, the water became fresh.It was here that the LORD, in making rules and regulations for them, put them to the test. ²⁶ "If you really listen to the voice of the LORD, your God," he told them, "and do what is right in his eyes: if you heed his commandments and keep all his precepts, I will not afflict you with any of the diseases with which I afflicted the Egyptians; for I, the LORD, am your healer." ²⁷ Then they came to Elim, where there were twelve springs of water and seventy palm trees, and they camped there near the water.

Exodus Chapter 16

¹ Having set out from Elim, the whole Israelite community came into the desert of Sin, which is between Elim and Sinai, on the fifteenth day of the second month after their departure from the land of Egypt. ² Here in the desert the whole Israelite community grumbled against Moses and Aaron. ³ The Israelites said to them, "Would that we had died at the LORD'S hand in the land of Egypt, as we sat by our fleshpots and ate our fill of bread! But you had to lead us into this desert to make the whole community die of famine!" ⁴ Then the LORD said to Moses, "I will now rain down bread from heaven for you. Each day the people are to go out and gather their daily portion; thus will I test them, to see whether they follow my instructions or not. ⁵ On the sixth day, however, when they prepare what they bring in, let it be twice as much as they gather on the other days." ⁶ So Moses and Aaron told all the Israelites, "At evening you will know that it was the LORD who brought you out of the land of Egypt; ⁷ and in the morning you will see the glory of the LORD, as he heeds your grumbling against him. But what are we that you should grumble against us? ⁸ When the LORD gives you flesh to eat in the evening," continued Moses, "and in the morning your fill of bread, as he heeds the grumbling you utter against him, what then are we? Your grumbling is not against us, but against the LORD." ⁹ Then Moses said to Aaron, "Tell the whole Israelite community: Present yourselves before the LORD, for he has heard your grumbling." ¹⁰ When Aaron announced this to the whole Israelite community, they turned toward the desert, and lo, the glory of the LORD appeared in the cloud! ¹¹ The LORD spoke to Moses and said, ¹² "I have heard the grumbling of the Israelites. Tell them: In the evening twilight you shall eat flesh, and in the morning you shall have your fill of bread, so that you may know that I, the LORD, am your God." ¹³ In the evening quail came up and covered the camp. In the morning a dew lay all about the camp, ¹⁴ and when the dew evaporated, there on the surface of the desert were fine flakes like hoarfrost on the ground. ¹⁵ On seeing it, the Israelites asked one another, "What is this?" for they did not know what it was. But Moses told them, "This is the bread which the LORD has

given you to eat. ¹⁶ "Now, this is what the LORD has commanded. So gather it that everyone has enough to eat, an omer for each person, as many of you as there are, each man providing for those of his own tent." ¹⁷ The Israelites did so. Some gathered a large and some a small amount. ¹⁸ But when they measured it out by the omer, he who had gathered a large amount did not have too much, and he who had gathered a small amount did not have too little. They so gathered that everyone had enough to eat. ¹⁹ Moses also told them, "Let no one keep any of it over until tomorrow morning." ²⁰ But they would not listen to him. When some kept a part of it over until the following morning, it became wormy and rotten. Therefore Moses was displeased with them. ²¹ Morning after morning they gathered it, till each had enough to eat; but when the sun grew hot, the manna melted away. ²² On the sixth day they gathered twice as much food, two omers for each person. When all the leaders of the community came and reported this to Moses, ²³ he told them, "That is what the LORD prescribed. Tomorrow is a day of complete rest, the sabbath, sacred to the LORD. You may either bake or boil the manna, as you please; but whatever is left put away and keep for the morrow." ²⁴ When they put it away for the morrow, as Moses commanded, it did not become rotten or wormy. ²⁵ Moses then said, "Eat it today, for today is the sabbath of the LORD. On this day you will not find any of it on the ground. ²⁶ On the other six days you can gather it, but on the seventh day, the sabbath, none of it will be there." ²⁷ Still, on the seventh day some of the people went out to gather it, although they did not find any. ²⁸ Then the LORD said to Moses, "How long will you refuse to keep my commandments and laws? ²⁹ Take note! The LORD has given you the sabbath. That is why on the sixth day he gives you food for two days. On the seventh day everyone is to stay home and no one is to go out." ³⁰ After that the people rested on the seventh day. ³¹ The Israelites called this food manna. It was like coriander seed, but white, and it tasted like wafers made with honey. ³² Moses said, "This is what the LORD has commanded. Keep an omerful of manna for your descendants, that they may see what food I gave you to eat in the desert when I brought you out of the land of Egypt." ³³ Moses then told Aaron, "Take an urn and put an omer of manna in it. Then place it before the LORD in safekeeping for your descendants." ³⁴ So Aaron placed it in front of the commandments for safekeeping, as the LORD had commanded Moses. ³⁵ The Israelites ate this manna for forty years, until they came to settled land; they ate manna until they reached the borders of Canaan. ³⁶ (An omer is one tenth of an ephah.)

Exodus Chapter 17

¹ From the desert of Sin the whole Israelite community journeyed by stages, as the LORD directed, and encamped at Rephidim. Here there was no water for the people to drink. ² They quarreled, therefore, with Moses and said, "Give us water to drink." Moses replied, "Why do you quarrel with me? Why do you put the LORD to a test?" ³ Here, then, in their thirst for water, the people grumbled against Moses, saying, "Why did you ever make us leave Egypt? Was it just to have us die here of thirst with our children and our livestock?" ⁴ So Moses cried out to the LORD, "What shall I do with this people? A little more and they will stone me!" ⁵ The LORD answered Moses, "Go over there in front of the people, along with some of the elders of Israel, holding in your hand, as you go, the staff with which you struck the river. ⁶ I will be standing there in front of you on the rock in Horeb. Strike the rock, and the water will flow from it for the people to drink." This Moses did, in the presence of the elders of Israel. ⁷ The place was called Massah and Meribah, because the Israelites quarreled there and tested the LORD, saying, "Is the LORD in our midst or not?" ⁸ At Rephidim, Amalek came and waged war against Israel. ⁹ Moses, therefore, said to Joshua, "Pick out certain men, and tomorrow go out and engage Amalek in battle. I will be standing on top of the hill with the staff of God in my hand." ¹⁰ So Joshua did as Moses told him: he engaged Amalek in battle after Moses had climbed to the top of the hill with Aaron and Hur. ¹¹ As long as Moses kept his hands raised up, Israel had the better of the fight, but when he let his hands rest, Amalek had the better of the fight. ¹² Moses' hands, however, grew tired; so they put a rock in place for him to sit on. Meanwhile Aaron and Hur supported his hands, one on one side and one on the other, so that his hands remained steady till sunset. ¹³ And Joshua mowed down Amalek and his people with the edge of the sword. ¹⁴ Then the LORD said to Moses, "Write this down in a document as something to be remembered, and recite it in the ears of Joshua: I will completely blot out the memory of Amalek from under the heavens." ¹⁵ Moses also built an altar there, which he called Yahweh-nissi; ¹⁶ for he said, "The LORD takes in hand his banner; the LORD will war against Amalek through the centuries."

Exodus Chapter 18

¹ Now Moses' father-in-law Jethro, the priest of Midian, heard of all that God had done for Moses and for his people Israel: how the LORD had brought Israel out of Egypt. ² So his father-in-law Jethro took along Zipporah, Moses' wife, whom Moses had sent back to him, ³ and her two sons. One of these was called Gershom; for he said, "I am a stranger in a foreign land." ⁴ The other was called Eliezer; for he said, "My father's God is my helper; he has rescued me from Pharaoh's sword." ⁵ Together with Moses' wife and sons, then, his father-in-law Jethro came to him in the desert where he was encamped near the mountain of God, ⁶ and he sent word to Moses, "I, Jethro, your father-in-law, am coming to you, along with your wife and her two sons." ⁷ Moses went out to meet his father-in-law, bowed down before him, and kissed him. Having greeted each other, they went into the tent. ⁸ Moses then told his father-in-law of all that the LORD had done to Pharaoh and the Egyptians for the sake of Israel, and of all the hardships they had had to endure on their journey, and how the LORD had come to their rescue. ⁹ Jethro rejoiced over all the goodness that the LORD had shown Israel in rescuing them from the hands of the Egyptians. ¹⁰ "Blessed be the LORD," he said, "who has rescued his people from the hands of Pharaoh and the Egyptians. ¹¹ Now I know that the LORD is a deity great beyond any other; for he took occasion of their being dealt with insolently to deliver the people from the power of the Egyptians." ¹² Then Jethro, the father-in-law of Moses, brought a holocaust and other sacrifices to God, and Aaron came with all the elders of Israel to participate with Moses' father-in-law in the meal before God. ¹³ The next day Moses sat in judgment for the people, who waited about him from morning until evening. ¹⁴ When his father-in-law saw all that he was doing for the people, he inquired, "What sort of thing is this that you are doing for the people? Why do you sit alone while all the people have to stand about you from morning till evening?" ¹⁵ Moses answered his father-in-law, "The people come to me to consult God. ¹⁶ Whenever they have a disagreement, they come to me to have me settle the matter between them and make known to them God's decisions and regulations." ¹⁷ "You are not acting wisely," his father-in-law replied. ¹⁸ "You will surely wear yourself out, and not only yourself but also these people with you. The task is too heavy for you; you cannot do it alone. ¹⁹ Now, listen to me, and I will give you some advice, that God may be with you. Act as the people's representative before God, bringing to him whatever they have to say. ²⁰ Enlighten them in regard to the decisions and regulations, showing them how they are to live and what they are to do. ²¹ But you should also look among all the people for able and God-fearing men, trustworthy men who hate dishonest gain, and set them as officers over groups of thousands, of hundreds, of fifties, and of tens. ²² Let these men render decisions for the people in all ordinary cases. More important cases they should refer to you, but all the lesser cases they can settle themselves. Thus, your burden will be lightened, since they will bear it with you. ²³ If you do this, when God gives you orders you will be able to stand the strain, and all these people will go home satisfied." ²⁴ Moses followed the advice of his father-in-law and did all that he had suggested. ²⁵ He picked out able men from all Israel and put them in charge of the people as officers over groups of thousands, of hundreds, of fifties, and of tens. ²⁶ They rendered decisions for the people in all ordinary cases. The more difficult cases they referred to Moses, but all the lesser cases they settled themselves. ²⁷ Then Moses bade farewell to his father-in-law, who went off to his own country.

Exodus Chapter 19

¹ In the third month after their departure from the land of Egypt, on its first day, the Israelites came to the desert of Sinai. ² After the journey from Rephidim to the desert of Sinai, they pitched camp. While Israel was encamped here in front of the mountain, ³ Moses went up the mountain to God. Then the LORD called to him and said, "Thus shall you say to the house of Jacob; ⁴ tell the Israelites: You have seen for yourselves how I treated the Egyptians and how I bore you up on eagle wings and brought you here to myself. ⁵ Therefore, if you hearken to my voice and keep my covenant, you shall be my special possession, dearer to me than all other people, though all the earth is mine. ⁶ You shall be to me a kingdom of priests, a holy nation. That is what you must tell the Israelites." ⁷ So Moses went and summoned the elders of the people. When he set before them all that the LORD had ordered him to tell them, ⁸ the people all answered together, "Everything the LORD has said, we will do." Then Moses brought back to the LORD the response of the people. ⁹ The LORD also told him, "I am coming to you in a dense cloud, so that when the people hear me speaking with you, they may always have faith in you also." When Moses, then, had reported to the LORD the response of the people, ¹⁰ the LORD added, "Go to the people and have them sanctify themselves today and tomorrow. Make them wash their garments ¹¹ and be ready for the third day; for on the third day the LORD will come down on Mount Sinai before the eyes of all the people. ¹² Set limits for the people all around the mountain, and tell

them: Take care not to go up the mountain, or even to touch its base. If anyone touches the mountain, he must be put to death. ¹³ No hand shall touch him; he must be stoned to death or killed with arrows. Such a one, man or beast, must not be allowed to live. Only when the ram's horn resounds may they go up to the mountain." ¹⁴ Then Moses came down from the mountain to the people and had them sanctify themselves and wash their garments. ¹⁵ He warned them, "Be ready for the third day. Have no intercourse with any woman." ¹⁶ On the morning of the third day there were peals of thunder and lightning, and a heavy cloud over the mountain, and a very loud trumpet blast, so that all the people in the camp trembled. ¹⁷ But Moses led the people out of the camp to meet God, and they stationed themselves at the foot of the mountain. ¹⁸ Mount Sinai was all wrapped in smoke, for the LORD came down upon it in fire. The smoke rose from it as though from a furnace, and the whole mountain trembled violently. ¹⁹ The trumpet blast grew louder and louder, while Moses was speaking and God answering him with thunder. ²⁰ When the LORD came down to the top of Mount Sinai, he summoned Moses to the top of the mountain, and Moses went up to him. ²¹ Then the LORD told Moses, "Go down and warn the people not to break through toward the LORD in order to see him; otherwise many of them will be struck down. ²² The priests, too, who approach the LORD must sanctify themselves; else he will vent his anger upon them." ²³ Moses said to the LORD, "The people cannot go up to Mount Sinai, for you yourself warned us to set limits around the mountain to make it sacred." ²⁴ The LORD repeated, "Go down now! Then come up again along with Aaron. But the priests and the people must not break through to come up to the LORD; else he will vent his anger upon them." ²⁵ So Moses went down to the people and told them this.

Exodus Chapter 20

¹ Then God delivered all these commandments: ² "I, the LORD, am your God, who brought you out of the land of Egypt, that place of slavery. ³ You shall not have other gods besides me. ⁴ You shall not carve idols for yourselves in the shape of anything in the sky above or on the earth below or in the waters beneath the earth; ⁵ you shall not bow down before them or worship them. For I, the LORD, your God, am a jealous God, inflicting punishment for their fathers' wickedness on the children of those who hate me, down to the third and fourth generation; ⁶ but bestowing mercy down to the thousandth generation, on the children of those who love me and keep my commandments. ⁷ "You shall not take the name of the LORD, your God, in vain. For the LORD will not leave unpunished him who takes his name in vain. ⁸ "Remember to keep holy the sabbath day. ⁹ Six days you may labor and do all your work, ¹⁰ but the seventh day is the sabbath of the LORD, your God. No work may be done then either by you, or your son or daughter, or your male or female slave, or your beast, or by the alien who lives with you. ¹¹ In six days the LORD made the heavens and the earth, the sea and all that is in them; but on the seventh day he rested. That is why the LORD has blessed the sabbath day and made it holy. ¹² "Honor your father and your mother, that you may have a long life in the land which the LORD, your God, is giving you. ¹³ "You shall not kill. ¹⁴ "You shall not commit adultery. ¹⁵ "You shall not steal. ¹⁶ "You shall not bear false witness against your neighbor. ¹⁷ "You shall not covet your neighbor's house. You shall not covet your neighbor's wife, nor his male or female slave, nor his ox or ass, nor anything else that belongs to him." ¹⁸ When the people witnessed the thunder and lightning, the trumpet blast and the mountain smoking, they all feared and trembled. So they took up a position much farther away ¹⁹ and said to Moses, "You speak to us, and we will listen; but let not God speak to us, or we shall die." ²⁰ Moses answered the people, "Do not be afraid, for God has come to you only to test you and put his fear upon you, lest you should sin." ²¹ Still the people remained at a distance, while Moses approached the cloud where God was. ²² The LORD told Moses, "Thus shall you speak to the Israelites: You have seen for yourselves that I have spoken to you from heaven. ²³ Do not make anything to rank with me; neither gods of silver nor gods of gold shall you make for yourselves. ²⁴ "An altar of earth you shall make for me, and upon it you shall sacrifice your holocausts and peace offerings, your sheep and your oxen. In whatever place I choose for the remembrance of my name I will come to you and bless you. ²⁵ If you make an altar of stone for me, do not build it of cut stone, for by putting a tool to it you desecrate it. ²⁶ You shall not go up by steps to my altar, on which you must not be indecently uncovered.

Exodus Chapter 21

¹ "These are the rules you shall lay before them. ² When you purchase a Hebrew slave, he is to serve you for six years, but in the seventh year he shall be given his freedom without cost. ³ If he comes into service alone, he shall leave alone; if he comes with a wife, his wife shall leave with him. ⁴ But if his master gives him a wife and she bears him sons or daughters, the woman and her children shall remain the master's property and the man shall leave alone. ⁵ If, however, the slave declares, 'I am devoted to my master and my wife and children; I will not go free,' ⁶ his master shall bring him to God and there, at the door or doorpost, he shall pierce his ear with an awl, thus keeping him as his slave forever. ⁷ "When a man sells his daughter as a slave, she shall not go free as male slaves do. ⁸ But if her master, who had destined her for himself, dislikes her, he shall let her be redeemed. He has no right to sell her to a foreigner, since he has broken faith with her. ⁹ If he destines her for his son, he shall treat her like a daughter. ¹⁰ If he takes another wife, he shall not withhold her food, her clothing, or her conjugal rights. ¹¹ If he does not grant her these three things, she shall be given her freedom absolutely, without cost to her. ¹² "Whoever strikes a man a mortal blow must be put to death. ¹³ He, however, who did not hunt a man down, but caused his death by an act of God, may flee to a place which I will set apart for this purpose. ¹⁴ But when a man kills another after maliciously scheming to do so, you must take him even from my altar and put him to death. ¹⁵ Whoever strikes his father or mother shall be put to death. ¹⁶ "A kidnapper, whether he sells his victim or still has him when caught, shall be put to death. ¹⁷ "Whoever curses his father or mother shall be put to death. ¹⁸ "When men quarrel and one strikes the other with a stone or with his fist, not mortally, but enough to put him in bed, ¹⁹ the one who struck the blow shall be acquitted, provided the other can get up and walk around with the help of his staff. Still, he must compensate him for his enforced idleness and provide for his complete cure. ²⁰ "When a man strikes his male or female slave with a rod so hard that the slave dies under his hand, he shall be punished. ²¹ If, however, the slave survives for a day or two, he is not to be punished, since the slave is his own property. ²² "When men have a fight and hurt a pregnant woman, so that she suffers a miscarriage, but no further injury, the guilty one shall be fined as much as the woman's husband demands of him, and he shall pay in the presence of the judges. ²³ But if injury ensues, you shall give life for life, ²⁴ eye for eye, tooth for tooth, hand for hand, foot for foot, ²⁵ burn for burn, wound for wound, stripe for stripe. ²⁶ "When a man strikes his male or female slave in the eye and destroys the use of the eye, he shall let the slave go free in compensation for the eye. ²⁷ If he knocks out a tooth of his male or female slave, he shall let the slave go free in compensation for the tooth. ²⁸ "When an ox gores a man or a woman to death, the ox must be stoned; its flesh may not be eaten. The owner of the ox, however, shall go unpunished. ²⁹ But if an ox was previously in the habit of goring people and its owner, though warned, would not keep it in; should it then kill a man or a woman, not only must the ox be stoned, but its owner also must be put to death. ³⁰ If, however, a fine is imposed on him, he must pay in ransom for his life whatever amount is imposed on him. ³¹ This law applies if it is a boy or a girl that the ox gores. ³² But if it is a male or a female slave that it gores, he must pay the owner of the slave thirty shekels of silver, and the ox must be stoned. ³³ "When a man uncovers or digs a cistern and does not cover it over again, should an ox or an ass fall into it, ³⁴ the owner of the cistern must make good by restoring the value of the animal to its owner; the dead animal, however, he may keep. ³⁵ "When one man's ox hurts another's ox so badly that it dies, they shall sell the live ox and divide this money as well as the dead animal equally between them. ³⁶ But if it was known that the ox was previously in the habit of goring and its owner would not keep it in, he must make full restitution, an ox for an ox; but the dead animal he may keep.

Exodus Chapter 22

¹ "(If a thief is caught in the act of housebreaking and beaten to death, there is no bloodguilt involved. ² But if after sunrise he is thus beaten, there is bloodguilt.) He must make full restitution. If he has nothing, he shall be sold to pay for his theft. ³ If what he stole is found alive in his possession, be it an ox, an ass or a sheep, he shall restore two animals for each one stolen. ⁴ "When a man is burning over a field or a vineyard, if he lets the fire spread so that it burns in another's field, he must make restitution with the best produce of his own field or vineyard. ⁵ If the fire spreads further, and catches on to thorn bushes, so that shocked grain or standing grain or the field itself is burned up, the one who started the fire must make full restitution. ⁶ "When a man gives money or an article to another for safekeeping and it is stolen from the latter's house, the thief, if caught, must make twofold restitution. ⁷ If the thief is not caught, the owner of the house shall be brought to God, to swear that he himself did not lay hands on his neighbor's property. ⁸ In every question of dishonest appropriation, whether it be about an ox, or an ass, or a sheep, or a garment, or anything else that has disappeared, where another claims that the thing is his, both parties shall present their case before God; the one whom God convicts must make twofold restitution to the other. ⁹ "When a man gives an ass, or an ox, or a sheep,

or any other animal to another for safekeeping, if it dies, or is maimed or snatched away, without anyone witnessing the fact, ¹⁰ the custodian shall swear by the LORD that he did not lay hands on his neighbor's property; the owner must accept the oath, and no restitution is to be made. ¹¹ But if the custodian is really guilty of theft, he must make restitution to the owner. ¹² If it has been killed by a wild beast, let him bring it as evidence, and he need not make restitution for the mangled animal. ¹³ "When a man borrows an animal from his neighbor, if it is maimed or dies while the owner is not present, the man must make restitution. ¹⁴ But if the owner is present, he need not make restitution. If it was hired, this was covered by the price of its hire. ¹⁵ "When a man seduces a virgin who is not betrothed, and lies with her, he shall pay her marriage price and marry her. ¹⁶ If her father refuses to give her to him, he must still pay him the customary marriage price for virgins. ¹⁷ "You shall not let a sorceress live. ¹⁸ "Anyone who lies with an animal shall be put to death. ¹⁹ "Whoever sacrifices to any god, except to the LORD alone, shall be doomed. ²⁰ "You shall not molest or oppress an alien, for you were once aliens yourselves in the land of Egypt. ²¹ You shall not wrong any widow or orphan. ²² If ever you wrong them and they cry out to me, I will surely hear their cry. ²³ My wrath will flare up, and I will kill you with the sword; then your own wives will be widows, and your children orphans. ²⁴ "If you lend money to one of your poor neighbors among my people, you shall not act like an extortioner toward him by demanding interest from him. ²⁵ If you take your neighbor's cloak as a pledge, you shall return it to him before sunset; ²⁶ for this cloak of his is the only covering he has for his body. What else has he to sleep in? If he cries out to me, I will hear him; for I am compassionate. ²⁷ "You shall not revile God, nor curse a prince of your people. ²⁸ "You shall not delay the offering of your harvest and your press. You shall give me the first-born of your sons. ²⁹ You must do the same with your oxen and your sheep; for seven days the firstling may stay with its mother, but on the eighth day you must give it to me. ³⁰ "You shall be men sacred to me. Flesh torn to pieces in the field you shall not eat; throw it to the dogs.

Exodus Chapter 23

¹ "You shall not repeat a false report. Do not join the wicked in putting your hand, as an unjust witness, upon anyone. ² Neither shall you allege the example of the many as an excuse for doing wrong, nor shall you, when testifying in a lawsuit, side with the many in perverting justice. ³ You shall not favor a poor man in his lawsuit. ⁴ "When you come upon your enemy's ox or ass going astray, see to it that it is returned to him. ⁵ When you notice the ass of one who hates you lying prostrate under its burden, by no means desert him; help him, rather, to raise it up. ⁶ "You shall not deny one of your needy fellow men his rights in his lawsuit. ⁷ You shall keep away from anything dishonest. The innocent and the just you shall not put to death, nor shall you acquit the guilty. ⁸ Never take a bribe, for a bribe blinds even the most clear-sighted and twists the words even of the just. ⁹ You shall not oppress an alien; you well know how it feels to be an alien, since you were once aliens yourselves in the land of Egypt. ¹⁰ "For six years you may sow your land and gather in its produce. ¹¹ But the seventh year you shall let the land lie untilled and unharvested, that the poor among you may eat of it and the beasts of the field may eat what the poor leave. So also shall you do in regard to your vineyard and your olive grove. ¹² "For six days you may do your work, but on the seventh day you must rest, that your ox and your ass may also have rest, and that the son of your maidservant and the alien may be refreshed. ¹³ Give heed to all that I have told you. "Never mention the name of any other god; it shall not be heard from your lips. ¹⁴ "Three times a year you shall celebrate a pilgrim feast to me. ¹⁵ You shall keep the feast of Unleavened Bread. As I have commanded you, you must eat unleavened bread for seven days at the prescribed time in the month of Abib, for it was then that you came out of Egypt. No one shall appear before me empty-handed. ¹⁶ You shall also keep the feast of the grain harvest with the first of the crop that you have sown in the field; and finally, the feast at the fruit harvest at the end of the year, when you gather in the produce from the fields. ¹⁷ Thrice a year shall all your men appear before the Lord GOD. ¹⁸ "You shall not offer the blood of my sacrifice with leavened bread; nor shall the fat of my feast be kept overnight till the next day. ¹⁹ The choicest first fruits of your soil you shall bring to the house of the LORD, your God. "You shall not boil a kid in its mother's milk. ²⁰ "See, I am sending an angel before you, to guard you on the way and bring you to the place I have prepared. ²¹ Be attentive to him and heed his voice. Do not rebel against him, for he will not forgive your sin. My authority resides in him. ²² If you heed his voice and carry out all I tell you, I will be an enemy to your enemies and a foe to your foes. ²³ "My angel will go before you and bring you to the Amorites, Hittites, Perizzites, Canaanites, Hivites and Jebusites; and I will wipe them out. ²⁴ Therefore, you shall not bow down in worship before their gods, nor

shall you make anything like them; rather, you must demolish them and smash their sacred pillars. ²⁵ The LORD, your God, you shall worship; then I will bless your food and drink, and I will remove all sickness from your midst; ²⁶ no woman in your land will be barren or miscarry; and I will give you a full span of life. ²⁷ "I will have the fear of me precede you, so that I will throw into panic every nation you reach. I will make all your enemies turn from you in flight, ²⁸ and ahead of you I will send hornets to drive the Hivites, Canaanites and Hittites out of your way. ²⁹ But not in one year will I drive them all out before you; else the land will become so desolate that the wild beasts will multiply against you. ³⁰ Instead, I will drive them out little by little before you, until you have grown numerous enough to take possession of the land. ³¹ I will set your boundaries from the Red Sea to the sea of the Philistines, and from the desert to the River; all who dwell in this land I will hand over to you to be driven out of your way. ³² You shall not make a covenant with them or their gods. ³³ They must not abide in your land, lest they make you sin against me by ensnaring you into worshiping their gods."

Exodus Chapter 24

¹ Moses himself was told, "Come up to the LORD, you and Aaron, with Nadab, Abihu, and seventy of the elders of Israel. You shall all worship at some distance, ² but Moses alone is to come close to the LORD; the others shall not come too near, and the people shall not come up at all with Moses." ³ When Moses came to the people and related all the words and ordinances of the LORD, they all answered with one voice, "We will do everything that the LORD has told us." ⁴ Moses then wrote down all the words of the LORD and, rising early the next day, he erected at the foot of the mountain an altar and twelve pillars for the twelve tribes of Israel. ⁵ Then, having sent certain young men of the Israelites to offer holocausts and sacrifice young bulls as peace offerings to the LORD, ⁶ Moses took half of the blood and put it in large bowls; the other half he splashed on the altar. ⁷ Taking the book of the covenant, he read it aloud to the people, who answered, "All that the LORD has said, we will heed and do." ⁸ Then he took the blood and sprinkled it on the people, saying, "This is the blood of the covenant which the LORD has made with you in accordance with all these words of his." ⁹ Moses then went up with Aaron, Nadab, Abihu, and seventy elders of Israel, ¹⁰ and they beheld the God of Israel. Under his feet there appeared to be sapphire tilework, as clear as the sky itself. ¹¹ Yet he did not smite these chosen Israelites. After gazing on God, they could still eat and drink. ¹² The LORD said to Moses, "Come up to me on the mountain and, while you are there, I will give you the stone tablets on which I have written the commandments intended for their instruction." ¹³ So Moses set out with Joshua, his aide, and went up to the mountain of God. ¹⁴ The elders, however, had been told by him, "Wait here for us until we return to you. Aaron and Hur are staying with you. If anyone has a complaint, let him refer the matter to them." ¹⁵ After Moses had gone up, a cloud covered the mountain. ¹⁶ The glory of the LORD settled upon Mount Sinai. The cloud covered it for six days, and on the seventh day he called to Moses from the midst of the cloud. ¹⁷ To the Israelites the glory of the LORD was seen as a consuming fire on the mountaintop. ¹⁸ But Moses passed into the midst of the cloud as he went up on the mountain; and there he stayed for forty days and forty nights.

Exodus Chapter 25

¹ This is what the LORD then said to Moses: ² "Tell the Israelites to take up a collection for me. From every man you shall accept the contribution that his heart prompts him to give me. ³ These are the contributions you shall accept from them: gold, silver and bronze; ⁴ violet, purple and scarlet yarn; fine linen and goat hair; ⁵ rams' skins dyed red, and tahash skins; acacia wood; ⁶ oil for the light; spices for the anointing oil and for the fragrant incense; ⁷ onyx stones and other gems for mounting on the ephod and the breastpiece. ⁸ "They shall make a sanctuary for me, that I may dwell in their midst. ⁹ This Dwelling and all its furnishings you shall make exactly according to the pattern that I will now show you. ¹⁰ "You shall make an ark of acacia wood, two and a half cubits long, one and a half cubits wide, and one and a half cubits high. ¹¹ Plate it inside and outside with pure gold, and put a molding of gold around the top of it. ¹² Cast four gold rings and fasten them on the four supports of the ark, two rings on one side and two on the opposite side. ¹³ Then make poles of acacia wood and plate them with gold. ¹⁴ These poles you are to put through the rings on the sides of the ark, for carrying it; ¹⁵ they must remain in the rings of the ark and never be withdrawn. ¹⁶ In the ark you are to put the commandments which I will give you. ¹⁷ "You shall then make a propitiatory of pure gold, two cubits and a half long, and one and a half cubits wide. ¹⁸ Make two cherubim of beaten gold for the two ends of the propitiatory, ¹⁹ fastening them so that one cherub springs direct

from each end. 20 The cherubim shall have their wings spread out above, covering the propitiatory with them; they shall be turned toward each other, but with their faces looking toward the propitiatory. 21 This propitiatory you shall then place on top of the ark. In the ark itself you are to put the commandments which I will give you. 22 There I will meet you and there, from above the propitiatory, between the two cherubim on the ark of the commandments, I will tell you all the commands that I wish you to give the Israelites. 23 "You shall also make a table of acacia wood, two cubits long, a cubit wide, and a cubit and a half high. 24 Plate it with pure gold and make a molding of gold around it. 25 Surround it with a frame, a handbreadth high, with a molding of gold around the frame. 26 You shall also make four rings of gold for it and fasten them at the four corners, one at each leg, 27 on two opposite sides of the frame as holders for the poles to carry the table. 28 These poles for carrying the table you shall make of acacia wood and plate with gold. 29 Of pure gold you shall make its plates and cups, as well as its pitchers and bowls for pouring libations. 30 On the table you shall always keep showbread set before me. 31 "You shall make a lampstand of pure beaten gold - its shaft and branches - with its cups and knobs and petals springing directly from it. 32 Six branches are to extend from the sides of the lampstand, three branches on one side, and three on the other. 33 On one branch there are to be three cups, shaped like almond blossoms, each with its knob and petals; on the opposite branch there are to be three cups, shaped like almond blossoms, each with its knob and petals; and so for the six branches that extend from the lampstand. 34 On the shaft there are to be four cups, shaped like almond blossoms, with their knobs and petals, 35 including a knob below each of the three pairs of branches that extend from the lampstand. 36 Their knobs and branches shall so spring from it that the whole will form but a single piece of pure beaten gold. 37 You shall then make seven lamps for it and so set up the lamps that they shed their light on the space in front of the lampstand. 38 These, as well as the trimming shears and trays, must be of pure gold. 39 Use a talent of pure gold for the lampstand and all its appurtenances. 40 See that you make them according to the pattern shown you on the mountain.

Exodus Chapter 26

1 "The Dwelling itself you shall make out of sheets woven of fine linen twined and of violet, purple and scarlet yarn, with cherubim embroidered on them. 2 The length of each shall be twenty-eight cubits, and the width four cubits; all the sheets shall be of the same size. 3 Five of the sheets are to be sewed together, edge to edge; and the same for the other five. 4 Make loops of violet yarn along the edge of the end sheet in one set, and the same along the edge of the end sheet in the other set. 5 There are to be fifty loops along the edge of the end sheet in the first set, and fifty loops along the edge of the corresponding sheet in the second set, and so placed that the loops are directly opposite each other. 6 Then make fifty clasps of gold, with which to join the two sets of sheets, so that the Dwelling forms one whole. 7 "Also make sheets woven of goat hair, to be used as a tent covering over the Dwelling. 8 Eleven such sheets are to be made; the length of each shall be thirty cubits, and the width four cubits: all eleven sheets shall be of the same size. 9 Sew five of the sheets, edge to edge, into one set, and the other six sheets into another set. Use the sixth sheet double at the front of the tent. 10 Make fifty loops along the edge of the end sheet in one set, and fifty loops along the edge of the end sheet in the second set. 11 Also make fifty bronze clasps and put them into the loops, to join the tent into one whole. 12 There will be an extra half sheet of tent covering, which shall be allowed to hang down over the rear of the Dwelling. 13 Likewise, the sheets of the tent will have an extra cubit's length to be left hanging down on either side of the Dwelling to protect it. 14 Over the tent itself you shall make a covering of rams' skins dyed red, and above that, a covering of tahash skins. 15 "You shall make boards of acacia wood as walls for the Dwelling. 16 The length of each board is to be ten cubits, and its width one and a half cubits. 17 Each board shall have two arms that shall serve to fasten the boards in line. In this way all the boards of the Dwelling are to be made. 18 Set up the boards of the Dwelling as follows: twenty boards on the south side, 19 with forty silver pedestals under these boards, so that there are two pedestals under each board, at its two arms; 20 twenty boards on the other side of the Dwelling, the north side, 21 with their forty silver pedestals, two under each board; 22 six boards for the rear of the Dwelling, to the west; 23 and two boards for the corners at the rear of the Dwelling. 24 These two shall be double at the bottom, and likewise double at the top, to the first ring. That is how both boards in the corners are to be made. 25 Thus, there shall be in the rear eight boards, with their sixteen silver pedestals, two pedestals under each board. 26 Also make bars of acacia wood: five for the boards on one side of the Dwelling, 27 five for those on the other side, and five for those at the rear, toward the west. 28 The

center bar, at the middle of the boards, shall reach across from end to end. 29 Plate the boards with gold, and make gold rings on them as holders for the bars, which are also to be plated with gold. 30 You shall erect the Dwelling according to the pattern shown you on the mountain. 31 "You shall have a veil woven of violet, purple and scarlet yarn, and of fine linen twined, with cherubim embroidered on it. 32 It is to be hung on four gold-plated columns of acacia wood, which shall have hooks of gold and shall rest on four silver pedestals. 33 Hang the veil from clasps. The ark of the commandments you shall bring inside, behind this veil which divides the holy place from the holy of holies. 34 Set the propitiatory on the ark of the commandments in the holy of holies. 35 "Outside the veil you shall place the table and the lampstand, the latter on the south side of the Dwelling, opposite the table, which is to be put on the north side. 36 For the entrance of the tent make a variegated curtain of violet, purple and scarlet yarn and of fine linen twined. 37 Make five columns of acacia wood for this curtain; have them plated with gold, with their hooks of gold; and cast five bronze pedestals for them.

Exodus Chapter 27

1 "You shall make an altar of acacia wood, on a square, five cubits long and five cubits wide; it shall be three cubits high. 2 At the four corners there are to be horns, so made that they spring directly from the altar. You shall then plate it with bronze. 3 Make pots for removing the ashes, as well as shovels, basins, forks and fire pans, all of which shall be of bronze. 4 Make a grating of bronze network for it; this to have four bronze rings, one at each of its four corners. 5 Put it down around the altar, on the ground. This network is to be half as high as the altar. 6 You shall also make poles of acacia wood for the altar, and plate them with bronze. 7 These poles are to be put through the rings, so that they are on either side of the altar when it is carried. 8 Make the altar itself in the form of a hollow box, just as it was shown you on the mountain. 9 "You shall also make a court for the Dwelling. On the south side the court shall have hangings a hundred cubits long, woven of fine linen twined, 10 with twenty columns and twenty pedestals of bronze; the hooks and bands on the columns shall be of silver. 11 On the north side there shall be similar hangings, a hundred cubits long, with twenty columns and twenty pedestals of bronze; the hooks and bands on the columns shall be of silver. 12 On the west side, across the width of the court, there shall be hangings, fifty cubits long, with ten columns and ten pedestals. 13 The width of the court on the east side shall be fifty cubits. 14 On one side there shall be hangings to the extent of fifteen cubits, with three columns and three pedestals; 15 on the other side there shall be hangings to the extent of fifteen cubits, with three columns and three pedestals. 16 "At the entrance of the court there shall be a variegated curtain, twenty cubits long, woven of violet, purple and scarlet yarn and of fine linen twined. It shall have four columns and four pedestals. 17 "All the columns around the court shall have bands and hooks of silver, and pedestals of bronze. 18 The enclosure of the court is to be one hundred cubits long, fifty cubits wide, and five cubits high. Fine linen twined must be used, and the pedestals must be of bronze. 19 All the fittings of the Dwelling, whatever be their use, as well as all its tent pegs and all the tent pegs of the court, must be of bronze. 20 "You shall order the Israelites to bring you clear oil of crushed olives, to be used for the light, so that you may keep lamps burning regularly. 21 From evening to morning Aaron and his sons shall maintain them before the LORD in the meeting tent, outside the veil which hangs in front of the commandments. This shall be a perpetual ordinance for the Israelites throughout their generations.

Exodus Chapter 28

1 "From among the Israelites have your brother Aaron, together with his sons Nadab, Abihu, Eleazar and Ithamar, brought to you, that they may be my priests. 2 For the glorious adornment of your brother Aaron you shall have sacred vestments made. 3 Therefore, to the various expert workmen whom I have endowed with skill, you shall give instructions to make such vestments for Aaron as will set him apart for his sacred service as my priest. 4 These are the vestments they shall make: a breastpiece, an ephod, a robe, a brocaded tunic, a miter and a sash. In making these sacred vestments which your brother Aaron and his sons are to wear in serving as my priests, 5 they shall use gold, violet, purple and scarlet yarn and fine linen. 6 "The ephod they shall make of gold thread and of violet, purple and scarlet yarn, embroidered on cloth of fine linen twined. 7 It shall have a pair of shoulder straps joined to its two upper ends. 8 The embroidered belt of the ephod shall extend out from it and, like it, be made of gold thread, of violet, purple and scarlet yarn, and of fine linen twined. 9 "Get two onyx stones and engrave on them the names of the sons of Israel: 10 six of their names on one stone, and the other six on the other stone, in the order of their birth. 11 As a

gem-cutter engraves a seal, so shall you have the two stones engraved with the names of the sons of Israel and then mounted in gold filigree work. 12 Set these two stones on the shoulder straps of the ephod as memorial stones of the sons of Israel. Thus Aaron shall bear their names on his shoulders as a reminder before the LORD. 13 Make filigree rosettes of gold, 14 as well as two chains of pure gold, twisted like cords, and fasten the cordlike chains to the filigree rosettes. 15 "The breastpiece of decision you shall also have made, embroidered like the ephod with gold thread and violet, purple and scarlet yarn on cloth of fine linen twined. 16 It is to be square when folded double, a span high and a span wide. 17 On it you shall mount four rows of precious stones: in the first row, a carnelian, a topaz and an emerald; 18 in the second row, a garnet, a sapphire and a beryl; 19 in the third row, a jacinth, an agate and an amethyst; 20 in the fourth row, a chrysolite, an onyx and a jasper. These stones are to be mounted in gold filigree work, 21 twelve of them to match the names of the sons of Israel, each stone engraved like a seal with the name of one of the twelve tribes. 22 "When the chains of pure gold, twisted like cords, have been made for the breastpiece, 23 you shall then make two rings of gold for it and fasten them to the two upper ends of the breastpiece. 24 The gold cords are then to be fastened to the two rings at the upper ends of the breastpiece, 25 the other two ends of the cords being fastened in front to the two filigree rosettes which are attached to the shoulder straps of the ephod. 26 Make two other rings of gold and put them on the two lower ends of the breastpiece, on its edge that faces the ephod. 27 Then make two more rings of gold and fasten them to the bottom of the shoulder straps next to where they join the ephod in front, just above its embroidered belt. 28 Violet ribbons shall bind the rings of the breastpiece to the rings of the ephod, so that the breastpiece will stay right above the embroidered belt of the ephod and not swing loose from it. 29 "Whenever Aaron enters the sanctuary, he will thus bear the names of the sons of Israel on the breastpiece of decision over his heart as a constant reminder before the LORD. 30 In this breastpiece of decision you shall put the Urim and Thummim, that they may be over Aaron's heart whenever he enters the presence of the LORD. Thus he shall always bear the decisions for the Israelites over his heart in the LORD'S presence. 31 "The robe of the ephod you shall make entirely of violet material. 32 It shall have an opening for the head in the center, and around this opening there shall be a selvage, woven as at the opening of a shirt, to keep it from being torn. 33 All around the hem at the bottom you shall make pomegranates, woven of violet, purple and scarlet yarn and fine linen twined, with gold bells between them; 34 first a gold bell, then a pomegranate, and thus alternating all around the hem of the robe. 35 Aaron shall wear it when ministering, that its tinkling may be heard as he enters and leaves the LORD'S presence in the sanctuary; else he will die. 36 "You shall also make a plate of pure gold and engrave on it, as on a seal engraving, 'Sacred to the LORD.' 37 This plate is to be tied over the miter with a violet ribbon in such a way that it rests on the front of the miter, 38 over Aaron's forehead. Since Aaron bears whatever guilt the Israelites may incur in consecrating any of their sacred gifts, this plate must always be over his forehead, so that they may find favor with the LORD. 39 "The tunic of fine linen shall be brocaded. The miter shall be made of fine linen. The sash shall be of variegated work. 40 "Likewise, for the glorious adornment of Aaron's sons you shall have tunics and sashes and turbans made. 41 With these you shall clothe your brother Aaron and his sons. Anoint and ordain them, consecrating them as my priests. 42 You must also make linen drawers for them, to cover their naked flesh from their loins to their thighs. 43 Aaron and his sons shall wear them whenever they go into the meeting tent or approach the altar to minister in the sanctuary, lest they incur guilt and die. This shall be a perpetual ordinance for him and for his descendants.

Exodus Chapter 29

1 "This is the rite you shall perform in consecrating them as my priests. Procure a young bull and two unblemished rams. 2 With fine wheat flour make unleavened cakes mixed with oil, and unleavened wafers spread with oil, 3 and put them in a basket. Take the basket of them along with the bullock and the two rams. 4 Aaron and his sons you shall also bring to the entrance of the meeting tent, and there wash them with water. 5 Take the vestments and clothe Aaron with the tunic, the robe of the ephod, the ephod itself, and the breastpiece, fastening the embroidered belt of the ephod around him. 6 Put the miter on his head, the sacred diadem on the miter. 7 Then take the anointing oil and anoint him with it, pouring it on his head. 8 Bring forward his sons also and clothe them with the tunics, 9 gird them with the sashes, and tie the turbans on them. Thus shall the priesthood be theirs by perpetual law, and thus shall you ordain Aaron and his sons. 10 "Now bring forward the bullock in front of the meeting tent. There Aaron and his sons shall lay their hands on its head. 11 Then slaughter the bullock before the

LORD, at the entrance of the meeting tent. 12 Take some of its blood and with your finger put it on the horns of the altar. All the rest of the blood you shall pour out at the base of the altar. 13 All the fat that covers its inner organs, as well as the lobe of its liver and its two kidneys, together with the fat that is on them, you shall take and burn on the altar. 14 But the flesh and hide and offal of the bullock you must burn up outside the camp, since this is a sin offering. 15 "Then take one of the rams, and after Aaron and his sons have laid their hands on its head, 16 slaughter it. The blood you shall take and splash on all the sides of the altar. 17 Cut the ram into pieces; its inner organs and shanks you shall first wash, and then put them with the pieces and with the head. 18 The entire ram shall then be burned on the altar, since it is a holocaust, a sweet-smelling oblation to the LORD. 19 "After this take the other ram, and when Aaron and his sons have laid their hands on its head, 20 slaughter it. Some of its blood you shall take and put on the tip of Aaron's right ear and on the tips of his sons' right ears and on the thumbs of their right hands and the great toes of their right feet. Splash the rest of the blood on all the sides of the altar. 21 Then take some of the blood that is on the altar, together with some of the anointing oil, and sprinkle this on Aaron and his vestments, as well as on his sons and their vestments, that his sons and their vestments may be sacred. 22 "Now, from this ram you shall take its fat: its fatty tail, the fat that covers its inner organs, the lobe of its liver, its two kidneys with the fat that is on them, and its right thigh, since this is the ordination ram; 23 then, out of the basket of unleavened food that you have set before the LORD, you shall take one of the loaves of bread, one of the cakes made with oil, and one of the wafers. 24 All these things you shall put into the hands of Aaron and his sons, so that they may wave them as a wave offering before the LORD. 25 After you have received them back from their hands, you shall burn them on top of the holocaust on the altar as a sweet-smelling oblation to the LORD. 26 Finally, take the breast of Aaron's ordination ram and wave it as a wave offering before the LORD; this is to be your own portion. 27 "Thus shall you set aside the breast of whatever wave offering is waved, as well as the thigh of whatever raised offering is raised up, whether this be the ordination ram or anything else belonging to Aaron or to his sons. 28 Such things are due to Aaron and his sons from the Israelites by a perpetual ordinance as a contribution. From their peace offerings, too, the Israelites shall make a contribution, their contribution to the LORD. 29 "The sacred vestments of Aaron shall be passed down to his descendants, that in them they may be anointed and ordained. 30 The descendant who succeeds him as priest and who is to enter the meeting tent to minister in the sanctuary shall be clothed with them for seven days. 31 "You shall take the flesh of the ordination ram and boil it in a holy place. 32 At the entrance of the meeting tent Aaron and his sons shall eat the flesh of the ram and the bread that is in the basket. 33 They themselves are to eat of these things by which atonement was made at their ordination and consecration; but no layman may eat of them, since they are sacred. 34 If some of the flesh of the ordination sacrifice or some of the bread remains over on the next day, this remnant must be burned up; it is not to be eaten, since it is sacred. 35 Carry out all these orders in regard to Aaron and his sons just as I have given them to you. "Seven days you shall spend in ordaining them, 36 sacrificing a bullock each day as a sin offering, to make atonement. Thus also shall you purge the altar in making atonement for it; you shall anoint it in order to consecrate it. 37 Seven days you shall spend in making atonement for the altar and in consecrating it. Then the altar will be most sacred, and whatever touches it will become sacred. 38 "Now, this is what you shall offer on the altar: two yearling lambs as the sacrifice established for each day; 39 one lamb in the morning and the other lamb at the evening twilight. 40 With the first lamb there shall be a tenth of an ephah of fine flour mixed with a fourth of a hin of oil of crushed olives and, as its libation, a fourth of a hin of wine. 41 The other lamb you shall offer at the evening twilight, with the same cereal offering and libation as in the morning. You shall offer this as a sweet-smelling oblation to the LORD. 42 Throughout your generations this established holocaust shall be offered before the LORD at the entrance of the meeting tent, where I will meet you and speak to you. 43 "There, at the altar, I will meet the Israelites; hence, it will be made sacred by my glory. 44 Thus I will consecrate the meeting tent and the altar, just as I also consecrate Aaron and his sons to be my priests. 45 I will dwell in the midst of the Israelites and will be their God. 46 They shall know that I, the LORD, am their God who brought them out of the land of Egypt, so that I, the LORD, their God, might dwell among them.

Exodus Chapter 30

1 "For burning incense you shall make an altar of acacia wood, 2 with a square surface, a cubit long, a cubit wide, and two cubits high, with horns that spring directly from it. 3 Its grate on top, its walls on all four

sides, and its horns you shall plate with pure gold. Put a gold molding around it. 4 Underneath the molding you shall put gold rings, two on one side and two on the opposite side, as holders for the poles used in carrying it. 5 Make the poles, too, of acacia wood and plate them with gold. 6 This altar you are to place in front of the veil that hangs before the ark of the commandments where I will meet you. 7 "On it Aaron shall burn fragrant incense. Morning after morning, when he prepares the lamps, 8 and again in the evening twilight, when he lights the lamps, he shall burn incense. Throughout your generations this shall be the established incense offering before the LORD. 9 On this altar you shall not offer up any profane incense, or any holocaust or cereal offering; nor shall you pour out a libation upon it. 10 Once a year Aaron shall perform the atonement rite on its horns. Throughout your generations this atonement is to be made once a year with the blood of the atoning sin offering. This altar is most sacred to the LORD." 11 The LORD also said to Moses, 12 "When you take a census of the Israelites who are to be registered, each one, as he is enrolled, shall give the LORD a forfeit for his life, so that no plague may come upon them for being registered. 13 Everyone who enters the registered group must pay a half-shekel, according to the standard of the sanctuary shekel, twenty gerahs to the shekel. This payment of a half-shekel is a contribution to the LORD. 14 Everyone of twenty years or more who enters the registered group must give this contribution to the LORD. 15 The rich need not give more, nor shall the poor give less, than a half-shekel in this contribution to the LORD to pay the forfeit for their lives. 16 When you receive this forfeit money from the Israelites, you shall donate it to the service of the meeting tent, that there it may be the Israelites' reminder before the LORD, of the forfeit paid for their lives." 17 The LORD said to Moses, 18 "For ablutions you shall make a bronze laver with a bronze base. Place it between the meeting tent and the altar, and put water in it. 19 Aaron and his sons shall use it in washing their hands and feet. 20 When they are about to enter the meeting tent, they must wash with water, lest they die. Likewise when they approach the altar in their ministry, to offer an oblation to the LORD, 21 they must wash their hands and feet, lest they die. This shall be a perpetual ordinance for him and his descendants throughout their generations." 22 The LORD said to Moses, 23 "Take the finest spices: five hundred shekels of free-flowing myrrh; half that amount, that is, two hundred and fifty shekels, of fragrant cinnamon; two hundred and fifty shekels of fragrant cane; 24 five hundred shekels of cassia-all according to the standard of the sanctuary shekel; together with a hin of olive oil; 25 and blend them into sacred anointing oil, perfumed ointment expertly prepared. 26 With this sacred anointing oil you shall anoint the meeting tent and the ark of the commandments, 27 the table and all its appurtenances, the lampstand and its appurtenances, the altar of incense 28 and the altar of holocausts with all its appurtenances, and the laver with its base. 29 When you have consecrated them, they shall be most sacred; whatever touches them shall be sacred. 30 Aaron and his sons you shall also anoint and consecrate as my priests. 31 To the Israelites you shall say: As sacred anointing oil this shall belong to me throughout your generations. 32 It may not be used in any ordinary anointing of the body, nor may you make any other oil of a like mixture. It is sacred, and shall be treated as sacred by you. 33 Whoever prepares a perfume like this, or whoever puts any of this on a layman, shall be cut off from his kinsmen." 34 The LORD told Moses, "Take these aromatic substances: storax and onycha and galbanum, these and pure frankincense in equal parts; 35 and blend them into incense. This fragrant powder, expertly prepared, is to be salted and so kept pure and sacred. 36 Grind some of it into fine dust and put this before the commandments in the meeting tent where I will meet you. This incense shall be treated as most sacred by you. 37 You may not make incense of a like mixture for yourselves; you must treat it as sacred to the LORD. 38 Whoever makes an incense like this for his own enjoyment of its fragrance, shall be cut off from his kinsmen."

Exodus Chapter 31

1 The LORD said to Moses, 2 "See, I have chosen Bezalel, son of Uri, son of Hur, of the tribe of Judah, 3 and I have filled him with a divine spirit of skill and understanding and knowledge in every craft: 4 in the production of embroidery, in making things of gold, silver or bronze, 5 in cutting and mounting precious stones, in carving wood, and in every craft. 6 As his assistant I have appointed Oholiab, son of Ahisamach, of the tribe of Dan. I have also endowed all the experts with the necessary skill to make all the things I have ordered you to make: 7 the meeting tent, the ark of the commandments with the propitiatory on top of it, all the furnishings of the tent, 8 the table with its appurtenances, the pure gold lampstand with all its appurtenances, the altar of incense, 9 the altar of holocausts with all its appurtenances, the laver with its base, 10 the service cloths, the sacred vestments for Aaron the priest, the

vestments for his sons in their ministry, 11 the anointing oil, and the fragrant incense for the sanctuary. All these things they shall make just as I have commanded you." 12 The LORD said to Moses, 13 "You must also tell the Israelites: Take care to keep my sabbaths, for that is to be the token between you and me throughout the generations, to show that it is I, the LORD, who make you holy. 14 Therefore, you must keep the sabbath as something sacred. Whoever desecrates it shall be put to death. If anyone does work on that day, he must be rooted out of his people. 15 Six days there are for doing work, but the seventh day is the sabbath of complete rest, sacred to the LORD. Anyone who does work on the sabbath day shall be put to death. 16 So shall the Israelites observe the sabbath, keeping it throughout their generations as a perpetual covenant. 17 Between me and the Israelites it is to be an everlasting token; for in six days the LORD made the heavens and the earth, but on the seventh day he rested at his ease." 18 When the LORD had finished speaking to Moses on Mount Sinai, he gave him the two tablets of the commandments, the stone tablets inscribed by God's own finger.

Exodus Chapter 32

1 When the people became aware of Moses' delay in coming down from the mountain, they gathered around Aaron and said to him, "Come, make us a god who will be our leader; as for the man Moses who brought us out of the land of Egypt, we do not know what has happened to him." 2 Aaron replied, "Have your wives and sons and daughters take off the golden earrings they are wearing, and bring them to me." 3 So all the people took off their earrings and brought them to Aaron, 4 who accepted their offering, and fashioning this gold with a graving tool, made a molten calf. Then they cried out, "This is your God, O Israel, who brought you out of the land of Egypt." 5 On seeing this, Aaron built an altar before the calf and proclaimed, "Tomorrow is a feast of the LORD." 6 Early the next day the people offered holocausts and brought peace offerings. Then they sat down to eat and drink, and rose up to revel. 7 With that, the LORD said to Moses, "Go down at once to your people, whom you brought out of the land of Egypt, for they have become depraved. 8 They have soon turned aside from the way I pointed out to them, making for themselves a molten calf and worshiping it, sacrificing to it and crying out, 'This is your God, O Israel, who brought you out of the land of Egypt!' 9 I see how stiff-necked this people is," continued the LORD to Moses. 10 "Let me alone, then, that my wrath may blaze up against them to consume them. Then I will make of you a great nation." 11 But Moses implored the LORD, his God, saying, "Why, O LORD, should your wrath blaze up against your own people, whom you brought out of the land of Egypt with such great power and with so strong a hand? 12 Why should the Egyptians say, 'With evil intent he brought them out, that he might kill them in the mountains and exterminate them from the face of the earth'? Let your blazing wrath die down; relent in punishing your people. 13 Remember your servants Abraham, Isaac and Israel, and how you swore to them by your own self, saying, 'I will make your descendants as numerous as the stars in the sky; and all this land that I promised, I will give your descendants as their perpetual heritage.'" 14 So the LORD relented in the punishment he had threatened to inflict on his people. 15 Moses then turned and came down the mountain with the two tablets of the commandments in his hands, tablets that were written on both sides, front and back; 16 tablets that were made by God, having inscriptions on them that were engraved by God himself. 17 Now, when Joshua heard the noise of the people shouting, he said to Moses, "That sounds like a battle in the camp." 18 But Moses answered, "It does not sound like cries of victory, nor does it sound like cries of defeat; the sounds that I hear are cries of revelry." 19 As he drew near the camp, he saw the calf and the dancing. With that, Moses' wrath flared up, so that he threw the tablets down and broke them on the base of the mountain. 20 Taking the calf they had made, he fused it in the fire and then ground it down to powder, which he scattered on the water and made the Israelites drink. 21 Moses asked Aaron, "What did this people ever do to you that you should lead them into so grave a sin?" Aaron replied, "Let not my lord be angry. 22 You know well enough how prone the people are to evil. 23 They said to me, 'Make us a god to be our leader; as for the man Moses who brought us out of the land of Egypt, we do not know what has happened to him.' 24 So I told them, 'Let anyone who has gold jewelry take it off.' They gave it to me, and I threw it into the fire, and this calf came out." 25 When Moses realized that, to the scornful joy of their foes, Aaron had let the people run wild, 26 he stood at the gate of the camp and cried, "Whoever is for the LORD, let him come to me!" All the Levites then rallied to him, 27 and he told them, "Thus says the LORD, the God of Israel: Put your sword on your hip, every one of you! Now go up and down the camp, from gate to gate, and slay your own kinsmen, your friends and neighbors!" 28 The Levites carried out the

command of Moses, and that day there fell about three thousand of the people. 29 Then Moses said, "Today you have been dedicated to the LORD, for you were against your own sons and kinsmen, to bring a blessing upon yourselves this day." 30 On the next day Moses said to the people, "You have committed a grave sin. I will go up to the LORD, then; perhaps I may be able to make atonement for your sin." 31 So Moses went back to the LORD and said, "Ah, this people has indeed committed a grave sin in making a god of gold for themselves! 32 If you would only forgive their sin! If you will not, then strike me out of the book that you have written." 33 The LORD answered, "Him only who has sinned against me will I strike out of my book. 34 Now, go and lead the people whither I have told you. My angel will go before you. When it is time for me to punish, I will punish them for their sin." 35 Thus the LORD smote the people for having had Aaron make the calf for them.

Exodus Chapter 33

1 The LORD told Moses, "You and the people whom you have brought up from the land of Egypt, are to go up from here to the land which I swore to Abraham, Isaac and Jacob I would give to their descendants. 2 Driving out the Canaanites, Amorites, Hittites, Perizzites, Hivites and Jebusites, I will send an angel before you 3 to the land flowing with milk and honey. But I myself will not go up in your company, because you are a stiff-necked people; otherwise I might exterminate you on the way." 4 When the people heard this bad news, they went into mourning, and no one wore his ornaments. 5 The LORD said to Moses, "Tell the Israelites: You are a stiff-necked people. Were I to go up in your company even for a moment, I would exterminate you. Take off your ornaments, therefore; I will then see what I am to do with you." 6 So, from Mount Horeb onward, the Israelites laid aside their ornaments. 7 The tent, which was called the meeting tent, Moses used to pitch at some distance away, outside the camp. Anyone who wished to consult the LORD would go to this meeting tent outside the camp. 8 Whenever Moses went out to the tent, the people would all rise and stand at the entrance of their own tents, watching Moses until he entered the tent. 9 As Moses entered the tent, the column of cloud would come down and stand at its entrance while the LORD spoke with Moses. 10 On seeing the column of cloud stand at the entrance of the tent, all the people would rise and worship at the entrance of their own tents. 11 The LORD used to speak to Moses face to face, as one man speaks to another. Moses would then return to the camp, but his young assistant, Joshua, son of Nun, would not move out of the tent. 12 Moses said to the LORD, "You, indeed, are telling me to lead this people on; but you have not let me know whom you will send with me. Yet you have said, 'You are my intimate friend,' and also, 'You have found favor with me.' 13 Now, if I have found favor with you, do let me know your ways so that, in knowing you, I may continue to find favor with you. Then, too, this nation is, after all, your own people." 14 "I myself," the LORD answered, "will go along, to give you rest." 15 Moses replied, "If you are not going yourself, do not make us go up from here. 16 For how can it be known that we, your people and I, have found favor with you, except by your going with us? Then we, your people and I, will be singled out from every other people on the earth." 17 The LORD said to Moses, "This request, too, which you have just made, I will carry out, because you have found favor with me and you are my intimate friend." 18 Then Moses said, "Do let me see your glory!" 19 He answered, "I will make all my beauty pass before you, and in your presence I will pronounce my name, 'LORD'; I who show favors to whom I will, I who grant mercy to whom I will. 20 But my face you cannot see, for no man sees me and still lives. 21 Here," continued the LORD, "is a place near me where you shall station yourself on the rock. 22 When my glory passes I will set you in the hollow of the rock and will cover you with my hand until I have passed by. 23 Then I will remove my hand, so that you may see my back; but my face is not to be seen."

Exodus Chapter 34

1 The LORD said to Moses, "Cut two stone tablets like the former, that I may write on them the commandments which were on the former tablets that you broke. 2 Get ready for tomorrow morning, when you are to go up Mount Sinai and there present yourself to me on the top of the mountain. 3 No one shall come up with you, and no one is even to be seen on any part of the mountain; even the flocks and the herds are not to go grazing toward this mountain." 4 Moses then cut two stone tablets like the former, and early the next morning he went up Mount Sinai as the LORD had commanded him, taking along the two stone tablets. 5 Having come down in a cloud, the LORD stood with him there and proclaimed his name, "LORD." 6 Thus the LORD passed before him and cried out, "The LORD, the LORD, a merciful and gracious God, slow to anger and rich in kindness and fidelity, 7 continuing his kindness for a thousand generations, and forgiving wickedness and crime and sin; yet not declaring the guilty guiltless, but punishing children and grandchildren to the third and fourth generation for their fathers' wickedness!" 8 Moses at once bowed down to the ground in worship. 9 Then he said, "If I find favor with you, O Lord, do come along in our company. This is indeed a stiff-necked people; yet pardon our wickedness and sins, and receive us as your own." 10 "Here, then," said the LORD, "is the covenant I will make. Before the eyes of all your people I will work such marvels as have never been wrought in any nation anywhere on earth, so that this people among whom you live may see how awe-inspiring are the deeds which I, the LORD, will do at your side. 11 But you, on your part, must keep the commandments I am giving you today. "I will drive out before you the Amorites, Canaanites, Hittites, Perizzites, Hivites and Jebusites. 12 Take care, therefore, not to make a covenant with these inhabitants of the land that you are to enter; else they will become a snare among you. 13 Tear down their altars; smash their sacred pillars, and cut down their sacred poles. 14 You shall not worship any other god, for the LORD is 'the Jealous One'; a jealous God is he. 15 Do not make a covenant with the inhabitants of that land; else, when they render their wanton worship to their gods and sacrifice to them, one of them may invite you and you may partake of his sacrifice. 16 Neither shall you take their daughters as wives for your sons; otherwise, when their daughters render their wanton worship to their gods, they will make your sons do the same. 17 You shall not make for yourselves molten gods. 18 You shall keep the feast of Unleavened Bread. For seven days at the prescribed time in the month of Abib you are to eat unleavened bread, as I commanded you; for in the month of Abib you came out of Egypt. 19 To me belongs every first-born male that opens the womb among all your livestock, whether in the herd or in the flock. 20 The firstling of an ass you shall redeem with one of the flock; if you do not redeem it, you must break its neck. The first-born among your sons you shall redeem. No one shall appear before me empty-handed. 21 For six days you may work, but on the seventh day you shall rest; on that day you must rest even during the seasons of plowing and harvesting. 22 You shall keep the feast of Weeks with the first of the wheat harvest; likewise, the feast at the fruit harvest at the close of the year. 23 Three times a year all your men shall appear before the Lord, the LORD God of Israel. 24 Since I will drive out the nations before you to give you a large territory, there will be no one to covet your land when you go up three times a year to appear before the LORD, your God. 25 You shall not offer me the blood of sacrifice with leavened bread, nor shall the sacrifice of the Passover feast be kept overnight for the next day. 26 The choicest first fruits of your soil you shall bring to the house of the LORD, your God. You shall not boil a kid in its mother's milk." 27 Then the LORD said to Moses, "Write down these words, for in accordance with them I have made a covenant with you and with Israel." 28 So Moses stayed there with the LORD for forty days and forty nights, without eating any food or drinking any water, and he wrote on the tablets the words of the covenant, the ten commandments. 29 As Moses came down from Mount Sinai with the two tablets of the commandments in his hands, he did not know that the skin of his face had become radiant while he conversed with the LORD. 30 When Aaron, then, and the other Israelites saw Moses and noticed how radiant the skin of his face had become, they were afraid to come near him. 31 Only after Moses called to them did Aaron and all the rulers of the community come back to him. Moses then spoke to them. 32 Later on, all the Israelites came up to him, and he enjoined on them all that the LORD had told him on Mount Sinai. 33 When he finished speaking with them, he put a veil over his face. 34 Whenever Moses entered the presence of the LORD to converse with him, he removed the veil until he came out again. On coming out, he would tell the Israelites all that had been commanded. 35 Then the Israelites would see that the skin of Moses' face was radiant; so, he would again put the veil over his face until he went in to converse with the LORD.

Exodus Chapter 35

1 Moses assembled the whole Israelite community and said to them, "This is what the LORD has commanded to be done. 2 On six days work may be done, but the seventh day shall be sacred to you as the sabbath of complete rest to the LORD. Anyone who does work on that day shall be put to death. 3 You shall not even light a fire in any of your dwellings on the sabbath day." 4 Moses told the whole Israelite community, "This is what the LORD has commanded: 5 Take up among you a collection for the LORD. Everyone, as his heart prompts him, shall bring, as a contribution to the LORD, gold, silver and bronze; 6 violet, purple and scarlet yarn; fine linen and goat hair; 7 rams' skins dyed red, and tahash skins; acacia wood; 8 oil for the light; spices for the anointing oil and for the fragrant incense; 9 onyx stones and other gems for mounting on the ephod and on the breastpiece. 10 "Let every expert among you come and make all that the LORD has commanded: the Dwelling, 11 with its

tent, its covering, its clasps, its boards, its bars, its columns and its pedestals; ¹² the ark, with its poles, the propitiatory, and the curtain veil; ¹³ the table, with its poles and all its appurtenances, and the showbread; ¹⁴ the lampstand, with its appurtenances, the lamps, and the oil for the light; ¹⁵ the altar of incense, with its poles; the anointing oil, and the fragrant incense; the entrance curtain for the entrance of the Dwelling; ¹⁶ the altar of holocausts, with its bronze grating, its poles, and all its appurtenances; the laver, with its base; ¹⁷ the hangings of the court, with their columns and pedestals; the curtain for the entrance of the court; ¹⁸ the tent pegs for the Dwelling and for the court, with their ropes; ¹⁹ the service cloths for use in the sanctuary; the sacred vestments for Aaron, the priest, and the vestments worn by his sons in their ministry." ²⁰ When the whole Israelite community left Moses' presence, ²¹ everyone, as his heart suggested and his spirit prompted, brought a contribution to the LORD for the construction of the meeting tent, for all its services, and for the sacred vestments. ²² Both the men and the women, all as their heart prompted them, brought brooches, earrings, rings, necklaces and various other gold articles. Everyone who could presented an offering of gold to the LORD. ²³ Everyone who happened to have violet, purple or scarlet yarn, fine linen or goat hair, rams' skins dyed red or tahash skins, brought them. ²⁴ Whoever could make a contribution of silver or bronze offered it to the LORD; and everyone who happened to have acacia wood for any part of the work, brought it. ²⁵ All the women who were expert spinners brought hand-spun violet, purple and scarlet yarn and fine linen thread. ²⁶ All the women who possessed the skill, spun goat hair. ²⁷ The princes brought onyx stones and other gems for mounting on the ephod and on the breastpiece; ²⁸ as well as spices, and oil for the light, anointing oil, and fragrant incense. ²⁹ Every Israelite man and woman brought to the LORD such voluntary offerings as they thought best, for the various kinds of work which the LORD had commanded Moses to have done. ³⁰ Moses said to the Israelites, "See, the LORD has chosen Bezalel, son of Uri, son of Hur, of the tribe of Judah, ³¹ and has filled him with a divine spirit of skill and understanding and knowledge in every craft: ³² in the production of embroidery, in making things of gold, silver or bronze, ³³ in cutting and mounting precious stones, in carving wood, and in every other craft. ³⁴ He has also given both him and Oholiab, son of Ahisamach, of the tribe of Dan, the ability to teach others. ³⁵ He has endowed them with skill to execute all types of work: engraving, embroidering, the making of variegated cloth of violet, purple and scarlet yarn and fine linen thread, weaving, and all other arts and crafts.

Exodus Chapter 36

¹ "Bezalel, therefore, will set to work with Oholiab and with all the experts whom the LORD has endowed with skill and understanding in knowing how to execute all the work for the service of the sanctuary, just as the LORD has commanded." ² Moses then called Bezalel and Oholiab and all the other experts whom the LORD had endowed with skill, men whose hearts moved them to come and take part in the work. ³ They received from Moses all the contributions which the Israelites had brought for establishing the service of the sanctuary. Still, morning after morning the people continued to bring their voluntary offerings to Moses. ⁴ Thereupon the experts who were executing the various kinds of work for the sanctuary, all left the work they were doing, ⁵ and told Moses, "The people are bringing much more than is needed to carry out the work which the LORD has commanded us to do." ⁶ Moses, therefore, ordered a proclamation to be made throughout the camp: "Let neither man nor woman make any more contributions for the sanctuary." So the people stopped bringing their offerings; ⁷ there was already enough at hand, in fact, more than enough, to complete the work to be done. ⁸ The various experts who were executing the work, made the Dwelling with its ten sheets woven of fine linen twined, having cherubim embroidered on them with violet, purple and scarlet yarn. ⁹ The length of each sheet was twenty-eight cubits, and the width four cubits; all the sheets were of the same size. ¹⁰ Five of the sheets were sewed together, edge to edge; and the same for the other five. ¹¹ Loops of violet yarn were made along the edge of the end sheet in the first set, and the same along the edge of the end sheet in the second set. ¹² Fifty loops were thus put on one inner sheet, and fifty loops on the inner sheet in the other set, with the loops directly opposite each other. ¹³ Then fifty clasps of gold were made, with which the sheets were joined so that the Dwelling formed one whole. ¹⁴ Sheets of goat hair were also woven as a tent over the Dwelling. Eleven such sheets were made. ¹⁵ The length of each sheet was thirty cubits and the width four cubits; all eleven sheets were the same size. ¹⁶ Five of these sheets were sewed edge to edge into one set; and the other six sheets into another set. ¹⁷ Fifty loops were made along the edge of the end sheet in one set, and fifty loops along the edge of the corresponding sheet in the other set. ¹⁸ Fifty bronze clasps were made with which the tent was joined so that it

formed one whole. ¹⁹ A covering for the tent was made of rams' skins dyed red, and above that, a covering of tahash skins. ²⁰ Boards of acacia wood were made as walls for the Dwelling. ²¹ The length of each board was ten cubits, and the width one and a half cubits. ²² Each board had two arms, fastening them in line. In this way all the boards of the Dwelling were made. ²³ They were set up as follows: twenty boards on the south side, ²⁴ with forty silver pedestals under the twenty boards, so that there were two pedestals under each board, at its two arms; ²⁵ twenty boards on the other side of the Dwelling, the north side, ²⁶ with their forty silver pedestals, two under each board; ²⁷ six boards at the rear of the Dwelling, to the west; ²⁸ and two boards at the corners in the rear of the Dwelling. ²⁹ These were double at the bottom, and likewise double at the top, to the first ring. That is how both boards in the corners were made. ³⁰ Thus, there were in the rear eight boards, with their sixteen silver pedestals, two pedestals under each board. ³¹ Bars of acacia wood were also made, five for the boards on one side of the Dwelling, ³² five for those on the other side, and five for those at the rear, to the west. ³³ The center bar, at the middle of the boards, was made to reach across from end to end. ³⁴ The boards were plated with gold, and gold rings were made on them as holders for the bars, which were also plated with gold. ³⁵ The veil was woven of violet, purple and scarlet yarn, and of fine linen twined, with cherubim embroidered on it. ³⁶ Four gold-plated columns of acacia wood, with gold hooks, were made for it, and four silver pedestals were cast for them. ³⁷ The curtain for the entrance of the tent was made of violet, purple and scarlet yarn, and of fine linen twined, woven in a variegated manner. ³⁸ Its five columns, with their hooks as well as their capitals and bands, were plated with gold; their five pedestals were of bronze.

Exodus Chapter 37

¹ Bezalel made the ark of acacia wood, two and a half cubits long, one and a half cubits wide, and one and a half cubits high. ² The inside and outside were plated with gold, and a molding of gold was put around it. ³ Four gold rings were cast and put on its four supports, two rings for one side and two for the opposite side. ⁴ Poles of acacia wood were made and plated with gold; ⁵ these were put through the rings on the sides of the ark, for carrying it. ⁶ The propitiatory was made of pure gold, two and a half cubits long and one and a half cubits wide. ⁷ Two cherubim of beaten gold were made for the two ends of the propitiatory, ⁸ one cherub fastened at one end, the other at the other end, springing directly from the propitiatory at its two ends. ⁹ The cherubim had their wings spread out above, covering the propitiatory with them. They were turned toward each other, but with their faces looking toward the propitiatory. ¹⁰ The table was made of acacia wood, two cubits long, one cubit wide, and one and a half cubits high. ¹¹ It was plated with pure gold, and a molding of gold was put around it. ¹² A frame a handbreadth high was also put around it, with a molding of gold around the frame. ¹³ Four rings of gold were cast for it and fastened, one at each of the four corners. ¹⁴ The rings were alongside the frame as holders for the poles to carry the table. ¹⁵ These poles were made of acacia wood and plated with gold. ¹⁶ The vessels that were set on the table, its plates and cups, as well as its pitchers and bowls for pouring libations, were of pure gold. ¹⁷ The lampstand was made of pure beaten gold - its shaft and branches as well as its cups and knobs and petals springing directly from it. ¹⁸ Six branches extended from its sides, three branches on one side and three on the other. ¹⁹ On one branch there were three cups, shaped like almond blossoms, each with its knob and petals; on the opposite branch there were three cups, shaped like almond blossoms, each with its knob and petals; and so for the six branches that extended from the lampstand. ²⁰ On the shaft there were four cups, shaped like almond blossoms, with their knobs and petals, ²¹ including a knob below each of the three pairs of branches that extended from the lampstand. ²² The knobs and branches sprang so directly from it that the whole formed but a single piece of pure beaten gold. ²³ Its seven lamps, as well as its trimming shears and trays, were made of pure gold. ²⁴ A talent of pure gold was used for the lampstand and its various appurtenances. ²⁵ The altar of incense was made of acacia wood, on a square, a cubit long, a cubit wide, and two cubits high, having horns that sprang directly from it. ²⁶ Its grate on top, its walls on all four sides, and its horns were plated with pure gold; and a molding of gold was put around it. ²⁷ Underneath the molding gold rings were placed, two on one side and two on the opposite side, as holders for the poles to carry it. ²⁸ The poles, too, were made of acacia wood and plated with gold. ²⁹ The sacred anointing oil and the fragrant incense were prepared in their pure form by a perfumer.

Exodus Chapter 38

¹ The altar of holocausts was made of acacia wood, on a square, five cubits long and five cubits wide; its height was three cubits. ² At the four

corners horns were made that sprang directly from the altar. The whole was plated with bronze. 3 All the utensils of the altar, the pots, shovels, basins, forks and fire pans, were likewise made of bronze. 4 A grating of bronze network was made for the altar and placed round it, on the ground, half as high as the altar itself. 5 Four rings were cast for the four corners of the bronze grating, as holders for the poles, 6 which were made of acacia wood and plated with bronze. 7 The poles were put through the rings on the sides of the altar for carrying it. The altar was made in the form of a hollow box. 8 The bronze laver, with its bronze base, was made from the mirrors of the women who served at the entrance of the meeting tent. 9 The court was made as follows. On the south side of the court there were hangings, woven of fine linen twined, a hundred cubits long, 10 with twenty columns and twenty pedestals of bronze, the hooks and bands of the columns being of silver. 11 On the north side there were similar hangings, one hundred cubits long, with twenty columns and twenty pedestals of bronze, the hooks and bands of the columns being of silver. 12 On the west side there were hangings, fifty cubits long, with ten columns and ten pedestals, the hooks and bands of the columns being of silver. 13 On the east side the court was fifty cubits long. 14 Toward one side there were hangings to the extent of fifteen cubits, with three columns and three pedestals; toward the other side, 15 beyond the entrance of the court, there were likewise hangings to the extent of fifteen cubits, with three columns and three pedestals. 16 The hangings on all sides of the court were woven of fine linen twined. 17 The pedestals of the columns were of bronze, while the hooks and bands of the columns were of silver; the capitals were silver-plated, and all the columns of the court were banded with silver. 18 At the entrance of the court there was a variegated curtain, woven of violet, purple and scarlet yarn and of fine linen twined, twenty cubits long and five cubits wide, in keeping with the hangings of the court. 19 There were four columns and four pedestals of bronze for it, while their hooks were of silver. 20 All the tent pegs for the Dwelling and for the court around it were of bronze. 21 The following is an account of the various amounts used on the Dwelling, the Dwelling of the commandments, drawn up at the command of Moses by the Levites under the direction of Ithamar, son of Aaron the priest. 22 However, it was Bezalel, son of Uri, son of Hur, of the tribe of Judah, who made all that the Lord commanded Moses, 23 and he was assisted by Oholiab, son of Ahisamach, of the tribe of Dan, who was an engraver, an embroiderer, and a weaver of variegated cloth of violet, purple and scarlet yarn and of fine linen. 24 All the gold used in the entire construction of the sanctuary, having previously been given as an offering, amounted to twenty-nine talents and seven hundred and thirty shekels, according to the standard of the sanctuary shekel. 25 The amount of the silver received from the community was one hundred talents and one thousand seven hundred and seventy-five shekels, according to the standard of the sanctuary shekel; 26 one bekah apiece, that is, a half-shekel apiece, according to the standard of the sanctuary shekel, was received from every man of twenty years or more who entered the registered group; the number of these was six hundred and three thousand five hundred and fifty men. 27 One hundred talents of silver were used for casting the pedestals of the sanctuary and the pedestals of the veil, one talent for each pedestal, or one hundred talents for the one hundred pedestals. 28 The remaining one thousand seven hundred and seventy-five shekels were used for making the hooks on the columns, for plating the capitals, and for banding them with silver. 29 The bronze, given as an offering, amounted to seventy talents and two thousand four hundred shekels. 30 With this were made the pedestals at the entrance of the meeting tent, the bronze altar with its bronze gratings and all the appurtenances of the altar, 31 the pedestals around the court, the pedestals at the entrance of the court, and all the tent pegs for the Dwelling and for the court around it.

Exodus Chapter 39

1 With violet, purple, and scarlet yarn were woven the service cloths for use in the sanctuary, as well as the sacred vestments for Aaron, as the LORD had commanded Moses. 2 The ephod was woven of gold thread and of violet, purple, and scarlet yarn and of fine linen twined. 3 Gold was first hammered into gold leaf and then cut up into threads, which were woven with the violet, purple, and scarlet yarn into an embroidered pattern on the fine linen. 4 Shoulder straps were made for it and joined to its two upper ends. 5 The embroidered belt on the ephod extended out from it and, like it, was made of gold thread, of violet, purple, and scarlet yarn, and of fine linen twined, as the LORD had commanded Moses. 6 The onyx stones were prepared and mounted in gold filigree work; they were engraved like seal engravings with the names of the sons of Israel. 7 These stones were set on the shoulder straps of the ephod as memorial stones of the sons of Israel, just as the LORD had commanded Moses. 8 The breastpiece was embroidered like the ephod, with gold thread and violet, purple, and scarlet yarn on cloth of fine linen twined. 9 It was square and folded double, a span high and a span wide in its folded form. 10 Four rows of precious stones were mounted on it: in the first row a carnelian, a topaz, and an emerald; 11 in the second row, a garnet, a sapphire, and a beryl; 12 in the third row a jacinth, an agate, and an amethyst; 13 in the fourth row a chrysolite, an onyx, and a jasper. They were mounted in gold filigree work. 14 These stones were twelve, to match the names of the sons of Israel, and each stone was engraved like a seal with the name of one of the twelve tribes. 15 Chains of pure gold, twisted like cords, were made for the breastpiece, 16 together with two gold filigree rosettes and two gold rings. The two rings were fastened to the two upper ends of the breastpiece. 17 The two gold chains were then fastened to the two rings at the ends of the breastpiece. 18 The other two ends of the two chains were fastened in front to the two filigree rosettes, which were attached to the shoulder straps of the ephod. 19 Two other gold rings were made and put on the two lower ends of the breastpiece, on the edge facing the ephod. 20 Two more gold rings were made and fastened to the bottom of the two shoulder straps next to where they joined the ephod in front, just above its embroidered belt. 21 Violet ribbons bound the rings of the breastpiece to the rings of the ephod, so that the breastpiece stayed right above the embroidered belt of the ephod and did not swing loose from it. All this was just as the LORD had commanded Moses. 22 The robe of the ephod was woven entirely of violet yarn, 23 with an opening in its center like the opening of a shirt, with selvage around the opening to keep it from being torn. 24 At the hem of the robe pomegranates were made of violet, purple, and scarlet yarn and of fine linen twined; 25 bells of pure gold were also made and put between the pomegranates all around the hem of the robe: 26 first a bell, then a pomegranate, and thus alternating all around the hem of the robe which was to be worn in performing the ministry—all this, just as the LORD had commanded Moses. 27 For Aaron and his sons there were also woven tunics of fine linen; 28 the miter of fine linen; the ornate turbans of fine linen; drawers of linen (of fine linen twined); 29 and sashes of variegated work made of fine linen twined and of violet, purple, and scarlet yarn, as the LORD had commanded Moses. 30 The plate of the sacred diadem was made of pure gold and inscribed, as on a seal engraving: "Sacred to the LORD." 31 It was tied over the miter with a violet ribbon, as the LORD had commanded Moses. 32 Thus the entire work of the Dwelling of the meeting tent was completed. The Israelites did the work just as the LORD had commanded Moses. 33 They then brought to Moses the Dwelling, the tent with all its appurtenances, the clasps, the boards, the bars, the columns, the pedestals, 34 the covering of rams' skins dyed red, the covering of tahash skins, the curtain veil; 35 the ark of the commandments with its poles, the propitiatory, 36 the table with all its appurtenances and the showbread, 37 the pure gold lampstand with its lamps set up on it and with all its appurtenances, the oil for the light, 38 the golden altar, the anointing oil, the fragrant incense; the curtain for the entrance of the tent, 39 the altar of bronze with its bronze grating, its poles and all its appurtenances, the laver with its base, 40 the hangings of the court with their columns and pedestals, the curtain for the entrance of the court with its ropes and tent pegs, all the equipment for the service of the Dwelling of the meeting tent; 41 the service cloths for use in the sanctuary, the sacred vestments for Aaron the priest, and the vestments to be worn by his sons in their ministry. 42 The Israelites had carried out all the work just as the LORD had commanded Moses. 43 So when Moses saw that all the work was done just as the LORD had commanded, he blessed them.

Exodus Chapter 40

1 Then the LORD said to Moses, 2 "On the first day of the first month you shall erect the Dwelling of the meeting tent. 3 Put the ark of the commandments in it, and screen off the ark with the veil. 4 Bring in the table and set it. Then bring in the lampstand and set up the lamps on it. 5 Put the golden altar of incense in front of the ark of the commandments, and hang the curtain at the entrance of the Dwelling. 6 Put the altar of holocausts in front of the entrance of the Dwelling of the meeting tent. 7 Place the laver between the meeting tent and the altar, and put water in it. 8 Set up the court round about, and put the curtain at the entrance of the court. 9 "Take the anointing oil and anoint the Dwelling and everything in it, consecrating it and all its furnishings, so that it will be sacred. 10 Anoint the altar of holocausts and all its appurtenances, consecrating it, so that it will be most sacred. 11 Likewise, anoint the laver with its base, and thus consecrate it. 12 "Then bring Aaron and his sons to the entrance of the meeting tent, and there wash them with water. 13 Clothe Aaron with the sacred vestments and anoint him, thus consecrating him as my priest. 14 Bring forward his sons also, and clothe them with the tunics. 15 As you have anointed their father, anoint them also as my priests. Thus, by being anointed,

shall they receive a perpetual priesthood throughout all future generations." 16 Moses did exactly as the LORD had commanded him. 17 On the first day of the first month of the second year the Dwelling was erected. 18 It was Moses who erected the Dwelling. He placed its pedestals, set up its boards, put in its bars, and set up its columns. 19 He spread the tent over the Dwelling and put the covering on top of the tent, as the LORD had commanded him. 20 He took the commandments and put them in the ark; he placed poles alongside the ark and set the propitiatory upon it. 21 He brought the ark into the Dwelling and hung the curtain veil, thus screening off the ark of the commandments, as the LORD had commanded him. 22 He put the table in the meeting tent, on the north side of the Dwelling, outside the veil, 23 and arranged the bread on it before the LORD, as the LORD had commanded him. 24 He placed the lampstand in the meeting tent, opposite the table, on the south side of the Dwelling, 25 and he set up the lamps before the LORD, as the LORD had commanded him. 26 He placed the golden altar in the meeting tent, in front of the veil, 27 and on it he burned fragrant incense, as the LORD had commanded him. 28 He hung the curtain at the entrance of the Dwelling. 29 He put the altar of holocausts in front of the entrance of the Dwelling of the meeting tent, and offered holocausts and cereal offerings on it, as the LORD had commanded him. 30 He placed the laver between the meeting tent and the altar, and put water in it for washing. 31 Moses and Aaron and his sons used to wash their hands and feet there, 32 for they washed themselves whenever they went into the meeting tent or approached the altar, as the LORD had commanded Moses. 33 Finally, he set up the court around the Dwelling and the altar and hung the curtain at the entrance of the court. Thus Moses finished all the work. 34 Then the cloud covered the meeting tent, and the glory of the LORD filled the Dwelling. 35 Moses could not enter the meeting tent, because the cloud settled down upon it and the glory of the LORD filled the Dwelling. 36 Whenever the cloud rose from the Dwelling, the Israelites would set out on their journey. 37 But if the cloud did not lift, they would not go forward; only when it lifted did they go forward. 38 In the daytime the cloud of the LORD was seen over the Dwelling; whereas at night, fire was seen in the cloud by the whole house of Israel in all the stages of their journey.

Leviticus

Leviticus chapter 1

1 The LORD called Moses, and from the meeting tent gave him this message: 2 "Speak to the Israelites and tell them: When any one of you wishes to bring an animal offering to the LORD, such an offering must be from the herd or from the flock. 3 "If his holocaust offering is from the herd, it must be a male without blemish. To find favor with the LORD, he shall bring it to the entrance of the meeting tent 4 and there lay his hand on the head of the holocaust, so that it may be acceptable to make atonement for him. 5 He shall then slaughter the bull before the LORD, but Aaron's sons, the priests, shall offer up its blood by splashing it on the sides of the altar which is at the entrance of the meeting tent. 6 Then he shall skin the holocaust and cut it up into pieces. 7 After Aaron's sons, the priests, have put some burning embers on the altar and laid some wood on them, 8 they shall lay the pieces of meat, together with the head and the suet, on top of the wood and embers on the altar. 9 The inner organs and the shanks, however, the offerer shall first wash with water. The priest shall then burn the whole offering on the altar as a holocaust, a sweet-smelling oblation to the LORD. 10 "If his holocaust offering is from the flock, that is, a sheep or a goat, he must bring a male without blemish. 11 This he shall slaughter before the LORD at the north side of the altar. Then Aaron's sons, the priests, shall splash its blood on the sides of the altar. 12 When the offerer has cut it up into pieces, the priest shall lay these, together with the head and suet, on top of the wood and the fire on the altar. 13 The inner organs and the shanks, however, the offerer shall first wash with water. The priest shall offer them up and then burn the whole offering on the altar as a holocaust, a sweet-smelling oblation to the LORD. 14 "If he offers a bird as a holocaust to the LORD, he shall choose a turtledove or a pigeon as his offering. 15 Having brought it to the altar where it is to be burned, the priest shall snap its head loose and squeeze out its blood against the side of the altar. 16 Its crop and feathers shall be removed and thrown on the ash heap at the east side of the altar. 17 Then, having split the bird down the middle without separating the halves, the priest shall burn it on the altar, over the wood on the fire, as a holocaust, a sweet-smelling oblation to the LORD.

Leviticus chapter 2

1 "When anyone wishes to bring a cereal offering to the LORD, his offering must consist of fine flour. He shall pour oil on it and put frankincense over it. 2 When he has brought it to Aaron's sons, the priests, one of them shall take a handful of this fine flour and oil, together with all the frankincense, and this he shall burn on the altar as a token offering, a sweet-smelling oblation to the LORD. 3 The rest of the cereal offering belongs to Aaron and his sons. It is a most sacred oblation to the LORD. 4 "When the cereal offering you present is baked in an oven, it must be in the form of unleavened cakes made of fine flour mixed with oil, or of unleavened wafers spread with oil. 5 If you present a cereal offering that is fried on a griddle, it must be of fine flour mixed with oil and unleavened. 6 Such a cereal offering must be broken into pieces, and oil must be poured over it. 7 If you present a cereal offering that is prepared in a pot, it must be of fine flour, deep-fried in oil. 8 A cereal offering that is made in any of these ways you shall bring to the LORD, offering it to the priest, who shall take it to the altar. 9 Its token offering the priest shall then lift from the cereal offering and burn on the altar as a sweet-smelling oblation to the LORD. 10 The rest of the cereal offering belongs to Aaron and his sons. It is a most sacred oblation to the LORD. 11 "Every cereal offering that you present to the LORD shall be unleavened, for you shall not burn any leaven or honey as an oblation to the LORD. 12 Such you may indeed present to the LORD in the offering of first fruits, but they are not to be placed on the altar for a pleasing odor. 13 However, every cereal offering that you present to the LORD shall be seasoned with salt. Do not let the salt of the covenant of your God be lacking from your cereal offering. On every offering you shall offer salt. 14 "If you present a cereal offering of first fruits to the LORD, you shall offer it in the form of fresh grits of new ears of grain, roasted by fire. 15 On this cereal offering you shall put oil and frankincense. 16 For its token offering the priest shall then burn some of the grits and oil, together with all the frankincense, as an oblation to the LORD.

Leviticus chapter 3

1 "If someone in presenting a peace offering makes his offering from the herd, he may offer before the LORD either a male or a female animal, but it must be without blemish. 2 He shall lay his hand on the head of his offering, and then slaughter it at the entrance of the meeting tent; but Aaron's sons, the priests, shall splash its blood on the sides of the altar. 3 From the peace offering he shall offer as an oblation to the LORD the fatty membrane over the inner organs, and all the fat that adheres to them, 4 as well as the two kidneys, with the fat on them near the loins, and the lobe of the liver, which he shall sever above the kidneys. 5 All this Aaron's sons shall then burn on the altar with the holocaust, on the wood over the fire, as a sweet-smelling oblation to the LORD. 6 "If the peace offering he presents to the LORD is from the flock, he may offer either a male or a female animal, but it must be without blemish. 7 If he presents a lamb as his offering, he shall bring it before the LORD, 8 and after laying his hand on the head of his offering, he shall slaughter it before the meeting tent; but Aaron's sons shall splash its blood on the sides of the altar. 9 As an oblation to the LORD he shall present the fat of the peace offering: the whole fatty tail, which he must sever close to the spine, the fatty membrane over the inner organs, and all the fat that adheres to them, 10 as well as the two kidneys, with the fat on them near the loins, and the lobe of the liver, which he must sever above the kidneys. 11 All this the priest shall burn on the altar as the food of the LORD'S oblation. 12 "If he presents a goat, he shall bring it before the LORD, 13 and after laying his hand on its head, he shall slaughter it before the meeting tent; but Aaron's sons shall splash its blood on the sides of the altar. 14 From it he shall offer as an oblation to the LORD the fatty membrane over the inner organs, and all the fat that adheres to them, 15 as well as the two kidneys, with the fat on them near the loins, and the lobe of the liver, which he must sever above the kidneys. 16 All this the priest shall burn on the altar as the food of the sweet-smelling oblation. All the fat belongs to the LORD. 17 This shall be a perpetual ordinance for your descendants wherever they may dwell. You shall not partake of any fat or any blood."

Leviticus chapter 4

1 "The LORD said to Moses, 2 'Tell the Israelites: When a person inadvertently commits a sin against some command of the LORD by doing one of the forbidden things, 3 if it is the anointed priest who thus sins and thereby makes the people also become guilty, he shall present to the LORD a young, unblemished bull as a sin offering for the sin he committed. 4 Bringing the bullock to the entrance of the meeting tent, before the LORD, he shall lay his hand on its head and slaughter it before the LORD. 5 The anointed priest shall then take some of the bullock's blood and bring it into the meeting tent, 6 where, dipping his finger in the blood, he shall sprinkle it seven times before the LORD, toward the veil of the sanctuary. 7 The priest shall also put some of the blood on the horns of the altar of fragrant incense which is before the

LORD in the meeting tent. The rest of the bullock's blood he shall pour out at the base of the altar of holocausts which is at the entrance of the meeting tent. 8 From the sin-offering bullock he shall remove all the fat: the fatty membrane over the inner organs, and all the fat that adheres to them, 9 as well as the two kidneys, with the fat on them near the loins, and the lobe of the liver, which he must sever above the kidneys. 10 This is the same as is removed from the ox of the peace offering; and the priest shall burn it on the altar of holocausts. 11 The hide of the bullock and all its flesh, with its head, legs, inner organs and offal, 12 in short, the whole bullock, shall be brought outside the camp to a clean place where the ashes are deposited and there be burned up in a wood fire. At the place of the ash heap, there it must be burned. 13 'If the whole community of Israel inadvertently and without even being aware of it does something that the LORD has forbidden and thus makes itself guilty, 14 should it later on become known that the sin was committed, the community shall present a young bull as a sin offering. They shall bring it before the meeting tent, 15 and here, before the LORD, the elders of the community shall lay their hands on the bullock's head. When the bullock has been slaughtered before the LORD, 16 the anointed priest shall bring some of its blood into the meeting tent, 17 and dipping his finger in the blood, he shall sprinkle it seven times before the LORD, toward the veil. 18 He shall also put some of the blood on the horns of the altar of fragrant incense which is before the LORD in the meeting tent. The rest of the blood he shall pour out at the base of the altar of holocausts which is at the entrance of the meeting tent. 19 All of its fat he shall take from it and burn on the altar, 20 doing with this bullock just as he did with the other sin-offering bullock. Thus the priest shall make atonement for them, and they will be forgiven. 21 This bullock must also be brought outside the camp and burned, just as has been prescribed for the other one. This is the sin offering for the community. 22 'Should a prince commit a sin inadvertently by doing one of the things which are forbidden by some commandment of the LORD, his God, and thus become guilty, 23 if later on he learns of the sin he committed, he shall bring as his offering an unblemished male goat. 24 Having laid his hands on its head, he shall slaughter the goat as a sin offering before the LORD, in the place where the holocausts are slaughtered. 25 The priest shall then take some of the blood of the sin offering on his finger and put it on the horns of the altar of holocausts. The rest of the blood he shall pour out at the base of this altar. 26 All of the fat he shall burn on the altar like the fat of the peace offering. Thus the priest shall make atonement for the prince's sin, and it will be forgiven. 27 'If a private person commits a sin inadvertently by doing one of the things which are forbidden by the commandments of the LORD, and thus becomes guilty, 28 should he later on learn of the sin he committed, he shall bring an unblemished she-goat as the offering for his sin. 29 Having laid his hand on the head of the sin offering, he shall slaughter it at the place of the holocausts. 30 The priest shall then take some of its blood on his finger and put it on the horns of the altar of holocausts. The rest of the blood he shall pour out at the base of the altar. 31 All the fat shall be removed, just as the fat is removed from the peace offering, and the priest shall burn it on the altar for an odor pleasing to the LORD. Thus the priest shall make atonement for him, and he will be forgiven. 32 'If, however, for his sin offering he presents a lamb, he shall bring an unblemished female. 33 Having laid his hand on its head, he shall slaughter this sin offering in the place where the holocausts are slaughtered. 34 The priest shall then take some of the blood of the sin offering on his finger and put it on the horns of the altar of holocausts. The rest of the blood he shall pour out at the base of the altar. 35 All the fat shall be removed, just as the fat is removed from the peace-offering lamb, and the priest shall burn it on the altar with the other oblations of the LORD. Thus the priest shall make atonement for the man's sin, and it will be forgiven."

Leviticus chapter 5

1 "If any person refuses to give the information which, as a witness of something he has seen or learned, he has been adjured to give, and thus commits a sin and has guilt to bear; 2 or if someone, without being aware of it, touches any unclean thing, as the carcass of an unclean wild animal, or that of an unclean domestic animal, or that of an unclean swarming creature, and thus becomes unclean and guilty; 3 or if someone, without being aware of it, touches some human uncleanness, whatever kind of uncleanness this may be, and then recognizes his guilt; 4 or if someone, without being aware of it, rashly utters an oath to do good or evil, such as men are accustomed to utter rashly, and then recognizes that he is guilty of such an oath; 5 then whoever is guilty in any of these cases shall confess the sin he has incurred, 6 and as his sin offering for the sin he has committed he shall bring to the LORD a female animal from the flock, a ewe lamb or a she-goat. The priest shall then make atonement for his sin. 7 If, however, he cannot afford an animal of the flock, he shall bring to the LORD as the sin offering for his sin two turtledoves or two pigeons, one for a sin offering and the other for a holocaust. 8 He shall bring them to the priest, who shall offer the one for the sin offering first. Snapping its head loose at the neck, yet without breaking it off completely, 9 he shall sprinkle some of the blood of the sin offering against the side of the altar. The rest of the blood shall be squeezed out against the base of the altar. Such is the offering for sin. 10 The other bird shall be offered as a holocaust in the usual way. Thus the priest shall make atonement for the sin the man committed, and it will be forgiven. 11 If he is unable to afford even two turtledoves or two pigeons, he shall present as a sin offering for his sin one tenth of an ephah of fine flour. He shall not put oil or frankincense on it, because it is a sin offering. 12 When he has brought it to the priest, the latter shall take a handful of this flour as a token offering, and this he shall burn as a sin offering on the altar with the other oblations of the LORD. 13 Thus the priest shall make atonement for the sin that the man committed in any of the above cases, and it will be forgiven. The rest of the flour, like the cereal offerings, shall belong to the priest. 14 The LORD said to Moses, 15 If someone commits a sin by inadvertently cheating in the LORD'S sacred dues, he shall bring to the LORD as his guilt offering an unblemished ram from the flock, valued at two silver shekels according to the standard of the sanctuary shekel. 16 He shall also restore what he has sinfully withheld from the sanctuary, adding to it a fifth of its value. This is to be given to the priest, who shall then make atonement for him with the guilt-offering ram, and he will be forgiven. 17 If someone, without being aware of it, commits such a sin by doing one of the things which are forbidden by some commandment of the LORD, that he incurs guilt for which he must answer, 18 he shall bring as a guilt offering to the priest an unblemished ram of the flock of the established value. The priest shall then make atonement for the fault which was unwittingly committed, and it will be forgiven. 19 Such is the offering for guilt; the penalty of the guilt must be paid to the LORD. 20 The LORD said to Moses, 21 If someone commits a sin of dishonesty against the LORD by denying his neighbor a deposit or a pledge for a stolen article, or by otherwise retaining his neighbor's goods unjustly, 22 or if, having found a lost article, he denies the fact and swears falsely about it with any of the sinful oaths that men make in such cases, 23 he shall therefore, since he has incurred guilt by his sin, restore the thing that was stolen or unjustly retained by him or the deposit left with him or the lost article he found 24 or whatever else he swore falsely about; on the day of his guilt offering he shall make full restitution of the thing itself, and in addition, give the owner one fifth of its value. 25 As his guilt offering he shall bring to the LORD an unblemished ram of the flock of the established value. When he has presented this as his guilt offering to the priest, 26 the latter shall make atonement for him before the LORD, and he will be forgiven whatever guilt he may have incurred.

Leviticus chapter 6

1 The LORD said to Moses, 2 "Give Aaron and his sons the following command: This is the ritual for holocausts. The holocaust is to remain on the hearth of the altar all night until the next morning, and the fire is to be kept burning on the altar. 3 The priest, clothed in his linen robe and wearing linen drawers on his body, shall take away the ashes to which the fire has reduced the holocaust on the altar, and lay them at the side of the altar. 4 Then, having taken off these garments and put on other garments, he shall carry the ashes to a clean place outside the camp. 5 The fire on the altar is to be kept burning; it must not go out. Every morning the priest shall put firewood on it. On this he shall lay out the holocaust and burn the fat of the peace offerings. 6 The fire is to be kept burning continuously on the altar; it must not go out. 7 "This is the ritual of the cereal offering. One of Aaron's sons shall first present it before the LORD, in front of the altar. 8 Then he shall take from it a handful of its fine flour and oil, together with all the frankincense that is on it, and this he shall burn on the altar as its token offering, a sweet-smelling oblation to the LORD. 9 The rest of it Aaron and his sons may eat; but it must be eaten in the form of unleavened cakes and in a sacred place: in the court of the meeting tent they shall eat it. 10 It shall not be baked with leaven. I have given it to them as their portion from the oblations of the LORD; it is most sacred, like the sin offering and the guilt offering. 11 All the male descendants of Aaron may partake of it as their rightful share in the oblations of the LORD perpetually throughout your generations. Whatever touches the oblations becomes sacred." 12 The LORD said to Moses, 13 "This is the offering that Aaron and his sons shall present to the LORD (on the day he is anointed): one tenth of an ephah of fine flour for the established cereal offering, half in the morning and half in the evening. 14 It shall be well kneaded and fried in oil on a griddle when you bring it in. Having broken the offering into pieces, you shall present it as a sweet-smelling oblation to the LORD. 15 Aaron's descendant who succeeds him as the anointed priest shall do

likewise. This is a perpetual ordinance: for the Lord the whole offering shall be burned. [16] Every cereal offering of a priest shall be a whole burnt offering; it may not be eaten." [17] The LORD said to Moses, [18] "Tell Aaron and his sons: This is the ritual for sin offerings. At the place where holocausts are slaughtered, there also, before the LORD, shall the sin offering be slaughtered. It is most sacred. [19] The priest who presents the sin offering may partake of it; but it must be eaten in a sacred place, in the court of the meeting tent. [20] Whatever touches its flesh shall become sacred. If any of its blood is spilled on a garment, the stained part must be washed in a sacred place. [21] A clay vessel in which it has been cooked shall thereafter be broken; if it is cooked in a bronze vessel, this shall be scoured afterward and rinsed with water. [22] All the males of the priestly line may partake of the sin offering, since it is most sacred. [23] But no one may partake of any sin offering of which some blood has been brought into the meeting tent to make atonement in the sanctuary; such an offering must be burned up in the fire.

Leviticus chapter 7

[1] "This is the ritual for guilt offerings, which are most sacred. [2] At the place where the holocausts are slaughtered, there also shall the guilt offering be slaughtered. Its blood shall be splashed on the sides of the altar. [3] All of its fat shall be taken from it and offered up: the fatty tail, the fatty membrane over the inner organs, [4] as well as the two kidneys with the fat on them near the loins, and the lobe of the liver, which must be severed above the kidneys. [5] All this the priest shall burn on the altar as an oblation to the LORD. This is the guilt offering. [6] All the males of the priestly line may partake of it; but it must be eaten in a sacred place, since it is most sacred. [7] Because the sin offering and the guilt offering are alike, both having the same ritual, the guilt offering likewise belongs to the priest who makes atonement with it. [8] Similarly, the priest who offers a holocaust for someone may keep for himself the hide of the holocaust that he has offered. [9] Also, every cereal offering that is baked in an oven or deep-fried in a pot or fried on a griddle shall belong to the priest who offers it, [10] whereas all cereal offerings that are offered up dry or mixed with oil shall belong to all of Aaron's sons without distinction. [11] This is the ritual for the peace offerings that are presented to the LORD. [12] When anyone makes a peace offering in thanksgiving, together with his thanksgiving sacrifice he shall offer unleavened cakes mixed with oil, unleavened wafers spread with oil, and cakes made of fine flour mixed with oil and well kneaded. [13] His offering shall also include loaves of leavened bread along with the victim of his peace offering for thanksgiving. [14] From each of his offerings he shall present one portion as a contribution to the LORD; this shall belong to the priest who splashes the blood of the peace offering. [15] The flesh of the thanksgiving sacrifice shall be eaten on the day it is offered; none of it may be kept till the next day. [16] However, if the sacrifice is a votive or a free-will offering, it should indeed be eaten on the day the sacrifice is offered, but what is left over may be eaten on the next day. [17] Should any flesh from the sacrifice be left over on the third day, it must be burned up in the fire. [18] If, therefore, any of the flesh of the peace offering is eaten on the third day, it shall not win favor for him nor shall it be reckoned to his credit; rather, it shall be considered as refuse, and anyone who eats of it shall have his guilt to bear. [19] Should the flesh touch anything unclean, it may not be eaten, but shall be burned up in the fire. All who are clean may partake of this flesh. [20] If, however, someone while in a state of uncleanness eats any of the flesh of a peace offering belonging to the LORD, that person shall be cut off from his people. [21] Likewise, if someone touches anything unclean, whether the uncleanness be of human or of animal origin or from some loathsome crawling creature, and then eats of a peace offering belonging to the LORD, that person, too, shall be cut off from his people." [22] The LORD said to Moses, [23] "Tell the Israelites: You shall not eat the fat of any ox or sheep or goat. [24] Although the fat of an animal that has died a natural death or has been killed by wild beasts may be put to any other use, you may not eat it. [25] If anyone eats the fat of an animal from which an oblation is made to the LORD, such a one shall be cut off from his people. [26] Wherever you dwell, you shall not partake of any blood, be it of bird or of animal. [27] Every person who partakes of any blood shall be cut off from his people." [28] The LORD said to Moses, [29] "Tell the Israelites: He who presents a peace offering to the LORD shall bring a part of it as his special offering to him, [30] carrying in with his own hands the oblations to the LORD. The fat is to be brought in, together with the breast, which is to be waved as a wave offering before the LORD. [31] The priest shall burn the fat on the altar, but the breast belongs to Aaron and his sons. [32] Moreover, from your peace offering you shall give to the priest the right leg as a raised offering. [33] The descendant of Aaron who offers up the blood and fat of the peace offering shall have the right leg as his portion, [34] for from the peace offerings of the Israelites I have taken the breast that is waved and the leg that is raised up, and I have

given them to Aaron, the priest, and to his sons by a perpetual ordinance as a contribution from the Israelites." [35] This is the priestly share from the oblations of the LORD, allotted to Aaron and his sons on the day he called them to be the priests of the LORD; [36] on the day he anointed them the LORD ordered the Israelites to give them this share by a perpetual ordinance throughout their generations. [37] This is the ritual for holocausts, cereal offerings, sin offerings, guilt offerings, (ordination offerings) and peace offerings, [38] which the LORD enjoined on Moses at Mount Sinai at the time when he commanded the Israelites in the wilderness of Sinai to bring their offerings to the LORD.

Leviticus chapter 8

[1] "The LORD said to Moses, [2] "Take Aaron and his sons, together with the vestments, the anointing oil, the bullock for a sin offering, the two rams, and the basket of unleavened food. [3] Then assemble the whole community at the entrance of the meeting tent.' [4] And Moses did as the LORD had commanded. When the community had assembled at the entrance of the meeting tent, [5] Moses told them what the LORD had ordered to be done. [6] Bringing forward Aaron and his sons, he first washed them with water. [7] Then he put the tunic on Aaron, girded him with the sash, clothed him with the robe, placed the ephod on him, and girded him with the embroidered belt of the ephod, fastening it around him. [8] He then set the breastpiece on him, with the Urim and Thummim in it, [9] and put the miter on his head, attaching the gold plate, the sacred diadem, over the front of the miter, at his forehead, as the LORD had commanded him to do. [10] Taking the anointing oil, Moses anointed and consecrated the Dwelling, with all that was in it. [11] Then he sprinkled some of this oil seven times on the altar, and anointed the altar, with all its appurtenances, and the laver, with its base, thus consecrating them. [12] He also poured some of the anointing oil on Aaron's head, thus consecrating him. [13] Moses likewise brought forward Aaron's sons, clothed them with tunics, girded them with sashes, and put turbans on them, as the LORD had commanded him to do. [14] When he had brought forward the bullock for a sin offering, Aaron and his sons laid their hands on its head. [15] Then Moses slaughtered it, and taking some of its blood, with his finger he put it on the horns around the altar, thus purifying the altar. He also made atonement for the altar by pouring out the blood at its base when he consecrated it. [16] Taking all the fat that was over the inner organs, as well as the lobe of the liver and the two kidneys with their fat, Moses burned them on the altar. [17] The bullock, however, with its hide and flesh and offal he burned in the fire outside the camp, as the LORD had commanded him to do. [18] He next brought forward the holocaust ram, and Aaron and his sons laid their hands on its head. [19] When he had slaughtered it, Moses splashed its blood on all sides of the altar. [20] After cutting up the ram into pieces, he burned the head, the cut-up pieces and the suet; [21] then, having washed the inner organs and the shanks with water, he also burned these remaining parts of the ram on the altar as a holocaust, a sweet-smelling oblation to the LORD, as the LORD had commanded him to do. [22] Then he brought forward the second ram, the ordination ram, and Aaron and his sons laid their hands on its head. [23] When he had slaughtered it, Moses took some of its blood and put it on the tip of Aaron's right ear, on the thumb of his right hand, and on the big toe of his right foot. [24] Moses had the sons of Aaron also come forward, and he put some of the blood on the tips of their right ears, on the thumbs of their right hands, and on the big toes of their right feet. The rest of the blood he splashed on the sides of the altar. [25] He then took the fat: the fatty tail and all the fat over the inner organs, the lobe of the liver and the two kidneys with their fat, and likewise the right leg; [26] from the basket of unleavened food that was set before the LORD he took one unleavened cake, one loaf of bread made with oil, and one wafer; these he placed on top of the portions of fat and the right leg. [27] He then put all these things into the hands of Aaron and his sons, whom he had wave them as a wave offering before the LORD. [28] When he had received them back, Moses burned them with the holocaust on the altar as the ordination offering, a sweet-smelling oblation to the LORD. [29] He then took the breast and waved it as a wave offering before the LORD; this was Moses' own portion of the ordination ram. All this was in keeping with the LORD'S command to Moses. [30] Taking some of the anointing oil and some of the blood that was on the altar, Moses sprinkled with it Aaron and his vestments, as well as his sons and their vestments, thus consecrating both Aaron and his vestments and his sons and their vestments. [31] Finally, Moses said to Aaron and his sons, 'Boil the flesh at the entrance of the meeting tent, and there eat it with the bread that is in the basket of the ordination offering, in keeping with the command I have received: Aaron and his sons shall eat of it.' [32] What is left over of the flesh and the bread you shall burn up in the fire. [33] Moreover, you are not to depart from the entrance of the meeting tent for seven days, until the days of your ordination are completed; for your ordination is to last for seven days.

34The LORD has commanded that what has been done today be done to make atonement for you. 35Hence you must remain at the entrance of the meeting tent day and night for seven days, carrying out the prescriptions of the LORD; otherwise, you shall die; for this is the command I have received.' 36So Aaron and his sons did all that the LORD had commanded through Moses."

Leviticus chapter 9

1"On the eighth day Moses summoned Aaron and his sons, together with the elders of Israel, 2and said to Aaron, 'Take a calf for a sin offering and a ram for a holocaust, both without blemish, and offer them before the LORD. 3Tell the elders of Israel, too: Take a he-goat for a sin offering, a calf and a lamb, both unblemished yearlings, for a holocaust, 4and an ox and a ram for a peace offering, to sacrifice them before the LORD, along with a cereal offering mixed with oil; for today the LORD will reveal himself to you.' 5So they brought what Moses had ordered. When the whole community had come forward and stood before the LORD, 6Moses said, 'This is what the LORD orders you to do, that the glory of the LORD may be revealed to you. 7Come up to the altar,' Moses then told Aaron, 'and offer your sin offering and your holocaust in atonement for yourself and for your family; then present the offering of the people in atonement for them, as the LORD has commanded.' 8Going up to the altar, Aaron first slaughtered the calf that was his own sin offering. 9When his sons presented the blood to him, he dipped his finger in the blood and put it on the horns of the altar. The rest of the blood he poured out at the base of the altar. 10He then burned on the altar the fat, the kidneys and the lobe of the liver that were taken from the sin offering, as the LORD had commanded Moses; 11but the flesh and the hide he burned up in the fire outside the camp. 12Then Aaron slaughtered his holocaust. When his sons brought him the blood, he splashed it on all sides of the altar. 13They then brought him the pieces and the head of the holocaust, and he burned them on the altar. 14Having washed the inner organs and the shanks, he burned these also with the holocaust on the altar. 15Thereupon he had the people's offering brought up. Taking the goat that was for the people's sin offering, he slaughtered it and offered it up for sin as before. 16Then he brought forward the holocaust, other than the morning holocaust, and offered it in the usual manner. 17He then presented the cereal offering; taking a handful of it, he burned it on the altar. 18Finally he slaughtered the ox and the ram, the peace offering of the people. When his sons brought him the blood, Aaron splashed it on all sides of the altar. 19The portions of fat from the ox and from the ram, the fatty tail, the fatty membrane over the inner organs, the two kidneys, with the fat that is on them, and the lobe of the liver, 20he placed on top of the breasts and burned them on the altar, 21having first waved the breasts and the right legs as a wave offering before the LORD, in keeping with the LORD'S command to Moses. 22Aaron then raised his hands over the people and blessed them. When he came down from offering the sin offering and holocaust and peace offering, 23Moses and Aaron went into the meeting tent. On coming out they again blessed the people. Then the glory of the LORD was revealed to all the people. 24Fire came forth from the LORD'S presence and consumed the holocaust and the remnants of the fat on the altar. Seeing this, all the people cried out and fell prostrate."

Leviticus chapter 10

1 "During this time Aaron's sons Nadab and Abihu took their censers and, strewing incense on the fire they had put in them, they offered up before the LORD profane fire, such as he had not authorized. 2 Fire therefore came forth from the LORD'S presence and consumed them, so that they died in his presence. 3 Moses then said to Aaron, 'This is as the LORD said: Through those who approach me I will manifest my sacredness; In the sight of all the people I will reveal my glory.' But Aaron said nothing. 4 Then Moses summoned Mishael and Elzaphan, the sons of Aaron's uncle Uzziel, with the order, 'Come, remove your kinsmen from the sanctuary and carry them to a place outside the camp.' 5 So they went in and took them, in their tunics, outside the camp, as Moses had commanded. 6 Moses said to Aaron and his sons Eleazar and Ithamar, 'Do not bare your heads or tear your garments, lest you bring not only death on yourselves but God's wrath also on the whole community. Your kinsmen, the rest of the house of Israel, shall mourn for those whom the LORD'S fire has smitten; 7 but do not you go beyond the entry of the meeting tent, else you shall die; for the anointing oil of the LORD is upon you.' So they did as Moses told them. 8 The LORD said to Aaron, 9 'When you are to go to the meeting tent, you and your sons are forbidden under pain of death, by a perpetual ordinance throughout your generations, to drink any wine or strong drink. 10 You must be able to distinguish between what is sacred and what is profane, between what is clean and what is unclean; 11 you must teach the Israelites all the laws that the LORD has given them through Moses.' 12 Moses said to Aaron and his surviving sons, Eleazar and Ithamar, 'Take the cereal offering left over from the oblations of the LORD, and eat it beside the altar in the form of unleavened cakes. Since it is most sacred, 13 you must eat it in a sacred place. This is your due from the oblations of the LORD, and that of your sons; such is the command I have received. 14 With your sons and daughters you shall also eat the breast of the wave offering and the leg of the raised offering, in a clean place; for these have been assigned to you and your children as your due from the peace offerings of the Israelites. 15 The leg of the raised offering and the breast of the wave offering shall first be brought in with the oblations, the fatty portions, that are to be waved as a wave offering before the LORD. Then they shall belong to you and your children by a perpetual ordinance, as the LORD has commanded.' 16 When Moses inquired about the goat of the sin offering, he discovered that it had all been burned. So he was angry with the surviving sons of Aaron, Eleazar and Ithamar, and said, 17 'Why did you not eat the sin offering in the sacred place, since it is most sacred? It has been given to you that you might bear the guilt of the community and make atonement for them before the LORD. 18 If its blood was not brought into the inmost part of the sanctuary, you should certainly have eaten the offering in the sanctuary, in keeping with the command I had received.' 19 Aaron answered Moses, 'Even though they presented their sin offering and holocaust before the LORD today, yet this misfortune has befallen me. Had I then eaten of the sin offering today, would it have been pleasing to the LORD?' 20 On hearing this, Moses was satisfied."

Leviticus chapter 11

1 The LORD said to Moses and Aaron, 2 "Speak to the Israelites and tell them: Of all land animals these are the ones you may eat: 3 any animal that has hoofs you may eat, provided it is cloven-footed and chews the cud. 4 But you shall not eat any of the following that only chew the cud or only have hoofs: the camel, which indeed chews the cud, but does not have hoofs and is therefore unclean for you; 5 the rock badger, which indeed chews the cud, but does not have hoofs and is therefore unclean for you; 6 the hare, which indeed chews the cud, but does not have hoofs and is therefore unclean for you; and the pig, 7 which does indeed have hoofs and is cloven-footed, but does not chew the cud and is therefore unclean for you. 8 Their flesh you shall not eat, and their dead bodies you shall not touch; they are unclean for you. 9 "Of the various creatures that live in the water, you may eat the following: whatever in the seas or in river waters has both fins and scales you may eat. 10 But of the various creatures that crawl or swim in the water, whether in the sea or in the rivers, all those that lack either fins or scales are loathsome for you, 11 and you shall treat them as loathsome. Their flesh you shall not eat, and their dead bodies you shall loathe. 12 Every water creature that lacks fins or scales is loathsome for you. 13 "Of the birds, these you shall loathe and, as loathsome, they shall not be eaten: the eagle, the vulture, the osprey, 14 the kite, the various species of falcons, 15 the various species of crows, 16 the ostrich, the nightjar, the gull, the various species of hawks, 17 the owl, the cormorant, the screech owl, 18 the barn owl, the desert owl, the buzzard, 19 the stork, the various species of herons, the hoopoe, and the bat. 20 "The various winged insects that walk on all fours are loathsome for you. 21 But of the various winged insects that walk on all fours you may eat those that have jointed legs for leaping on the ground; 22 hence of these you may eat the following: the various kinds of locusts, the various kinds of grasshoppers, the various kinds of katydids, and the various kinds of crickets. 23 All other winged insects that have four legs are loathsome for you. 24 "Such is the uncleanness that you contract, that everyone who touches their dead bodies shall be unclean until evening, 25 and everyone who picks up any part of their dead bodies shall wash his garments and be unclean until evening. 26 All hoofed animals that are not cloven-footed or do not chew the cud are unclean for you; everyone who touches them becomes unclean. 27 Of the various quadrupeds, all those that walk on paws are unclean for you; everyone who touches their dead bodies shall be unclean until evening, 28 and everyone who picks up their dead bodies shall wash his garments and be unclean until evening. Such is their uncleanness for you. 29 "Of the creatures that swarm on the ground, the following are unclean for you: the rat, the mouse, the various kinds of lizards, 30 the gecko, the chameleon, the agama, the skink, and the mole. 31 Among the various swarming creatures, these are unclean for you. Everyone who touches them when they are dead shall be unclean until evening. 32 Everything on which one of them falls when dead becomes unclean. Any such article that men use, whether it be an article of wood, cloth, leather or goat hair, must be put in water and remain unclean until evening, when it again becomes clean. 33 Should any of these creatures fall into a clay vessel, everything in it becomes unclean, and the vessel itself you must break. 34 Any solid food that was in contact with water,

and any liquid that men drink, in any such vessel become unclean. 35 Any object on which one of their dead bodies falls, becomes unclean; if it is an oven or a jar-stand, this must be broken to pieces; they are unclean and shall be treated as unclean by you. 36 However, a spring or a cistern for collecting water remains clean; but whoever touches the dead body becomes unclean. 37 Any sort of cultivated grain remains clean even though one of their dead bodies falls on it; 38 but if the grain has become moistened, it becomes unclean when one of these falls on it. 39 "When one of the animals that you could otherwise eat, dies of itself, anyone who touches its dead body shall be unclean until evening; 40 and anyone who eats of its dead body shall wash his garments and be unclean until evening; so also, anyone who removes its dead body shall wash his garments and be unclean until evening. 41 "All the creatures that swarm on the ground are loathsome and shall not be eaten. 42 Whether it crawls on its belly, goes on all fours, or has many legs, you shall eat no swarming creature: they are loathsome. 43 Do not make yourselves loathsome or unclean with any swarming creature through being contaminated by them. 44 For I, the LORD, am your God; and you shall make and keep yourselves holy, because I am holy. You shall not make yourselves unclean, then, by any swarming creature that crawls on the ground. 45 Since I, the LORD, brought you up from the land of Egypt that I might be your God, you shall be holy, because I am holy. 46 "This is the law for animals and birds and for all the creatures that move about in the water or swarm on the ground, 47 that you may distinguish between the clean and the unclean, between creatures that may be eaten and those that may not be eaten."

Leviticus chapter 12

1 The LORD said to Moses, 2 "Tell the Israelites: When a woman has conceived and gives birth to a boy, she shall be unclean for seven days, with the same uncleanness as at her menstrual period. 3 On the eighth day, the flesh of the boy's foreskin shall be circumcised, 4 and then she shall spend thirty-three days more in becoming purified of her blood; she shall not touch anything sacred nor enter the sanctuary till the days of her purification are fulfilled. 5 If she gives birth to a girl, for fourteen days she shall be as unclean as at her menstruation, after which she shall spend sixty-six days in becoming purified of her blood. 6 "When the days of her purification for a son or for a daughter are fulfilled, she shall bring to the priest at the entrance of the meeting tent a yearling lamb for a holocaust and a pigeon or a turtledove for a sin offering. 7 The priest shall offer them up before the LORD to make atonement for her, and thus she will be clean again after her flow of blood. Such is the law for the woman who gives birth to a boy or a girl child. 8 If, however, she cannot afford a lamb, she may take two turtledoves or two pigeons, the one for a holocaust and the other for a sin offering. The priest shall make atonement for her, and thus she will again be clean."

Leviticus chapter 13

1 The LORD said to Moses and Aaron, 2 "If someone has on his skin a scab or pustule or blotch which appears to be the sore of leprosy, he shall be brought to Aaron, the priest, or to one of the priests among his descendants, 3 who shall examine the sore on his skin. If the hair on the sore has turned white and the sore itself shows that it has penetrated below the skin, it is indeed the sore of leprosy; the priest, on seeing this, shall declare the man unclean. 4 If, however, the blotch on the skin is white, but does not seem to have penetrated below the skin, nor has the hair turned white, the priest shall quarantine the stricken man for seven days. 5 On the seventh day the priest shall again examine him. If he judges that the sore has remained unchanged and has not spread on the skin, the priest shall quarantine him for another seven days, 6 and once more examine him on the seventh day. If the sore is now dying out and has not spread on the skin, the priest shall declare the man clean; it was merely eczema. The man shall wash his garments and so become clean. 7 But if, after he has shown himself to the priest to be declared clean, the eczema spreads at all on his skin, he shall once more show himself to the priest. 8 Should the priest, on examining it, find that the eczema has indeed spread on the skin, he shall declare the man unclean; it is leprosy. 9 "When someone is stricken with leprosy, he shall be brought to the priest. 10 Should the priest, on examining him, find that there is a white scab on the skin which has turned the hair white and that there is raw flesh in it, 11 it is skin leprosy that has long developed. The priest shall declare the man unclean without first quarantining him, since he is certainly unclean. 12 If leprosy breaks out on the skin and, as far as the priest can see, covers all the skin of the stricken man from head to foot, 13 should the priest then, on examining him, find that the leprosy does cover his whole body, he shall declare the stricken man clean; since it has all turned white, the man is clean. 14 But as soon as raw flesh appears on him, he is unclean; 15 on observing the raw flesh, the priest shall declare him unclean, because raw flesh is unclean; it is leprosy. 16

If, however, the raw flesh again turns white, he shall return to the priest; 17 should the latter, on examining him, find that the sore has indeed turned white, he shall declare the stricken man clean, and thus he will be clean. 18 "If a man who had a boil on his skin which later healed, 19 should now in the place of the boil have a white scab or a pink blotch, he shall show himself to the priest. 20 If the latter, on examination, sees that it is deeper than the skin and that the hair has turned white, he shall declare the man unclean; it is the sore of leprosy that has broken out in the boil. 21 But if the priest, on examining him, finds that there is no white hair in it and that it is not deeper than the skin and is already dying out, the priest shall quarantine him for seven days. 22 If it has then spread on the skin, the priest shall declare him unclean; the man is stricken. 23 But if the blotch remains in its place without spreading, it is merely the scar of the boil; the priest shall therefore declare him clean. 24 "If a man had a burn on his skin, and the proud flesh of the burn now becomes a pink or a white blotch, 25 the priest shall examine it. If the hair has turned white on the blotch and this seems to have penetrated below the skin, it is leprosy that has broken out in the burn; the priest shall therefore declare him unclean and stricken with leprosy. 26 But if the priest, on examining it, finds that there is no white hair on the blotch and that this is not deeper than the skin and is already dying out, the priest shall quarantine him for seven days. 27 Should the priest, when examining it on the seventh day, find that it has spread at all on the skin, he shall declare the man unclean and stricken with leprosy. 28 But if the blotch remains in its place without spreading on the skin and is already dying out, it is merely the scab of the burn; the priest shall therefore declare the man clean, since it is only the scar of the burn. 29 "When a man or a woman has a sore on the head or cheek, 30 should the priest, on examining it, find that the sore has penetrated below the skin and that there is fine yellow hair on it, the priest shall declare the person unclean, for this is scall, a leprous disease of the head or cheek. 31 But if the priest, on examining the scall sore, finds that it has not penetrated below the skin, though the hair on it may not be black, the priest shall quarantine the person with the scall sore for seven days, 32 and on the seventh day again examine the sore. If the scall has not spread and has no yellow hair on it and does not seem to have penetrated below the skin, 33 the man shall shave himself, but not on the diseased spot. Then the priest shall quarantine him for another seven days. 34 If the priest, when examining the scall on the seventh day, finds that it has not spread on the skin and that it has not penetrated below the skin, he shall declare the man clean; the latter shall wash his garments, and thus he will be clean. 35 But if the scall spreads at all on his skin after he has been declared clean, 36 the priest shall again examine it. If the scall has indeed spread on the skin, he need not look for yellow hair; the man is surely unclean. 37 If, however, he judges that the scall has remained in its place and that black hair has grown on it, the disease has been healed; the man is clean, and the priest shall declare him clean. 38 "When the skin of a man or a woman is spotted with white blotches, 39 the priest shall make an examination. If the blotches on the skin are white and already dying out, it is only tetter that has broken out on the skin, and the person therefore is clean. 40 "When a man loses the hair of his head, he is not unclean merely because of his bald crown. 41 So too, if he loses the hair on the front of his head, he is not unclean merely because of his bald forehead. 42 But when there is a pink sore on his bald crown or bald forehead, it is leprosy that is breaking out there. 43 The priest shall examine him; and if the scab on the sore of the bald spot has the same pink appearance as that of skin leprosy of the fleshy part of the body, 44 the man is leprous and unclean, and the priest shall declare him unclean by reason of the sore on his head. 45 "The one who bears the sore of leprosy shall keep his garments rent and his head bare, and shall muffle his beard; he shall cry out, 'Unclean, unclean!' 46 As long as the sore is on him he shall declare himself unclean, since he is in fact unclean. He shall dwell apart, making his abode outside the camp. 47 "When a leprous infection is on a garment of wool or of linen, 48 or on woven or knitted material of linen or wool, or on a hide or anything made of leather, 49 if the infection on the garment or hide, or on the woven or knitted material, or on any leather article is greenish or reddish, the thing is indeed infected with leprosy and must be shown to the priest. 50 Having examined the infection, the priest shall quarantine the infected article for seven days. 51 On the seventh day the priest shall again examine the infection. If it has spread on the garment, or on the woven or knitted material, or on the leather, whatever be its use, the infection is malignant leprosy, and the article is unclean. 52 He shall therefore burn up the garment, or the woven or knitted material of wool or linen, or the leather article, whatever it may be, which is infected; since it has malignant leprosy, it must be destroyed by fire. 53 But if the priest, on examining the infection, finds that it has not spread on the garment, or on the woven or knitted material, or on the leather article, ⁵⁴ he shall give orders to have the infected article washed and then quarantined for another seven days. ⁵⁵ Then the priest shall again examine the infected article after it has been washed. If the infection has not changed its appearance, even though it may not have spread, the article is unclean and shall be destroyed by fire. ⁵⁶ But if the priest, on examining the infection, finds that it is dying out after the washing, he shall tear the infected part out of the garment, or the leather, or the woven or knitted material. ⁵⁷ If, however, the infection again appears on the garment, or on the woven or knitted material, or on the leather article, it is still virulent and the thing infected shall be destroyed by fire. ⁵⁸ But if, after the washing, the infection has left the garment, or the woven or knitted material, or the leather article, the thing shall be washed a second time, and thus it will be clean. ⁵⁹ This is the law for leprous infection on a garment of wool or linen, or on woven or knitted material, or on any leather article, to determine whether it is clean or unclean."

Leviticus chapter 14

¹ The LORD said to Moses, ² "This is the law for the victim of leprosy at the time of his purification. He shall be brought to the priest, ³ who is to go outside the camp to examine him. If the priest finds that the sore of leprosy has healed in the leper, ⁴ he shall order the man who is to be purified, to get two live, clean birds, as well as some cedar wood, scarlet yarn, and hyssop. ⁵ The priest shall then order him to slay one of the birds over an earthen vessel with spring water in it. ⁶ Taking the living bird with the cedar wood, the scarlet yarn and the hyssop, the priest shall dip them all in the blood of the bird that was slain over the spring water, ⁷ and then sprinkle seven times the man to be purified from his leprosy. When he has thus purified him, he shall let the living bird fly away over the countryside. ⁸ The man being purified shall then wash his garments and shave off all his hair and bathe in water; only when he is thus made clean may he come inside the camp; but he shall still remain outside his tent for seven days. ⁹ On the seventh day he shall again shave off all the hair of his head, his beard, his eyebrows, and any other hair he may have, and also wash his garments and bathe his body in water; and so he will be clean. ¹⁰ "On the eighth day he shall take two unblemished male lambs, one unblemished yearling ewe lamb, three tenths of an ephah of fine flour mixed with oil for a cereal offering, and one log of oil. ¹¹ The priest who performs the purification ceremony shall place the man who is being purified, as well as all these offerings, before the LORD at the entrance of the meeting tent. ¹² Taking one of the male lambs, the priest shall present it as a guilt offering, along with the log of oil, waving them as a wave offering before the LORD. ¹³ (This lamb he shall slaughter in the sacred place where the sin offering and the holocaust are slaughtered; because, like the sin offering, the guilt offering belongs to the priest and is most sacred.) ¹⁴ Then the priest shall take some of the blood of the guilt offering and put it on the tip of the man's right ear, the thumb of his right hand, and the big toe of his right foot. ¹⁵ The priest shall also take the log of oil and pour some of it into the palm of his own left hand; ¹⁶ then, dipping his right forefinger in it, he shall sprinkle it seven times before the LORD. ¹⁷ Of the oil left in his hand the priest shall put some on the tip of the man's right ear, the thumb of his right hand, and the big toe of his right foot, over the blood of the guilt offering. ¹⁸ The rest of the oil in his hand the priest shall put on the head of the man being purified. Thus shall the priest make atonement for him before the LORD. ¹⁹ Only after he has offered the sin offering in atonement for the man's uncleanness shall the priest slaughter the holocaust ²⁰ and offer it, together with the cereal offering, on the altar before the LORD. When the priest has thus made atonement for him, the man will be clean. ²¹ "If a man is poor and cannot afford so much, he shall take one male lamb for a guilt offering, to be used as a wave offering in atonement for himself, one tenth of an ephah of fine flour mixed with oil for a cereal offering, a log of oil, ²² and two turtledoves or pigeons, which he can more easily afford, the one as a sin offering and the other as a holocaust. ²³ On the eighth day of his purification he shall bring them to the priest, at the entrance of the meeting tent before the LORD. ²⁴ Taking the guilt-offering lamb, along with the log of oil, the priest shall wave them as a wave offering before the LORD. ²⁵ When he has slaughtered the guilt-offering lamb, he shall take some of its blood, and put it on the tip of the right ear of the man being purified, on the thumb of his right hand, and on the big toe of his right foot. ²⁶ The priest shall then pour some of the oil into the palm of his own left hand ²⁷ and with his right forefinger sprinkle it seven times before the LORD. ²⁸ Some of the oil in his hand the priest shall also put on the tip of the man's right ear, the thumb of his right hand, and the big toe of his right foot, over the blood of the guilt offering. ²⁹ The rest of the oil in his hand the priest shall put on the man's head. Thus shall he make atonement for him before the LORD. ³⁰ Then, of the turtledoves or pigeons, such as the man can afford, ³¹ the priest shall offer up one as a sin offering and the other as a holocaust, along with the cereal offering. Thus shall the priest make atonement before the LORD for the man who is to be purified. ³² This is the law for one afflicted with leprosy who has insufficient means for his purification." ³³ The LORD said to Moses and Aaron, ³⁴ "When you come into the land of Canaan, which I am giving you to possess, if I put a leprous infection on any house of the land you occupy, ³⁵ the owner of the house shall come and report to the priest, 'It looks to me as if my house were infected.' ³⁶ The priest shall then order the house to be cleared out before he goes in to examine the infection, lest everything in the house become unclean. Only after this is he to go in to examine the house. ³⁷ If the priest, on examining it, finds that the infection on the walls of the house consists of greenish or reddish depressions which seem to go deeper than the surface of the wall, ³⁸ he shall close the door of the house behind him and quarantine the house for seven days. ³⁹ On the seventh day the priest shall return to examine the house again. If he finds that the infection has spread on the walls, ⁴⁰ he shall order the infected stones to be pulled out and cast in an unclean place outside the city. ⁴¹ The whole inside of the house shall then be scraped, and the mortar that has been scraped off shall be dumped in an unclean place outside the city. ⁴² Then new stones shall be brought and put in the place of the old stones, and new mortar shall be made and plastered on the house. ⁴³ "If the infection breaks out once more after the stones have been pulled out and the house has been scraped and replastered, ⁴⁴ the priest shall come again; and if he finds that the infection has spread in the house, it is corrosive leprosy, and the house is unclean. ⁴⁵ It shall be pulled down, and all its stones, beams and mortar shall be hauled away to an unclean place outside the city. ⁴⁶ Whoever enters a house while it is quarantined shall be unclean until evening. ⁴⁷ Whoever sleeps or eats in such a house shall also wash his garments. ⁴⁸ If the priest finds, when he comes to examine the house, that the infection has in fact not spread after the plastering, he shall declare the house clean, since the infection has been healed. ⁴⁹ To purify the house, he shall take two birds, as well as cedar wood, scarlet yarn, and hyssop. ⁵⁰ One of the birds he shall slay over an earthen vessel with spring water in it. ⁵¹ Then, taking the cedar wood, the hyssop and the scarlet yarn, together with the living bird, he shall dip them all in the blood of the slain bird and the spring water, and sprinkle the house seven times. ⁵² Thus shall he purify the house with the bird's blood and the spring water, along with the living bird, the cedar wood, the hyssop, and the scarlet yarn. ⁵³ He shall then let the living bird fly away over the countryside outside the city. When he has thus made atonement for it, the house will be clean. ⁵⁴ "This is the law for every kind of human leprosy and scall, ⁵⁵ for leprosy of garments and houses, ⁵⁶ as well as for scabs, pustules and blotches, ⁵⁷ so that it may be manifest when there is a state of uncleanness and when a state of cleanness. This is the law for leprosy."

Leviticus chapter 15

¹ The LORD said to Moses and Aaron, ² "Speak to the Israelites and tell them: Every man who is afflicted with a chronic flow from his private parts is thereby unclean. ³ Such is his uncleanness from this flow that it makes no difference whether the flow drains off or is blocked up; his uncleanness remains. ⁴ Any bed on which the man afflicted with the flow lies, is unclean, and any piece of furniture on which he sits, is unclean. ⁵ Anyone who touches his bed shall wash his garments, bathe in water, and be unclean until evening. ⁶ Whoever sits on a piece of furniture on which the afflicted man was sitting, shall wash his garments, bathe in water, and be unclean until evening. ⁷ Whoever touches the body of the afflicted man shall wash his garments, bathe in water, and be unclean until evening. ⁸ If the afflicted man spits on a clean man, the latter shall wash his garments, bathe in water, and be unclean until evening. ⁹ Any saddle on which the afflicted man rides, is unclean. ¹⁰ Whoever touches anything that was under him shall be unclean until evening; whoever lifts up any such thing shall wash his garments, bathe in water, and be unclean until evening. ¹¹ Anyone whom the afflicted man touches with unrinsed hands shall wash his garments, bathe in water, and be unclean until evening. ¹² Earthenware touched by the afflicted man shall be broken; and every wooden article shall be rinsed with water. ¹³ "When a man who has been afflicted with a flow becomes free of his affliction, he shall wait seven days for his purification. Then he shall wash his garments and bathe his body in fresh water, and so he will be clean. ¹⁴ On the eighth day he shall take two turtledoves or two pigeons, and going before the LORD, to the entrance of the meeting tent, he shall give them to the priest, ¹⁵ who shall offer them up, the one as a sin offering and the other as a holocaust. Thus shall the priest make atonement before the LORD for the man's flow. ¹⁶ "When a man has an emission of seed, he shall bathe his whole body in water and be unclean until evening. ¹⁷ Any piece of

cloth or leather with seed on it shall be washed with water and be unclean until evening. ¹⁸ "If a man lies carnally with a woman, they shall both bathe in water and be unclean until evening. ¹⁹ "When a woman has her menstrual flow, she shall be in a state of impurity for seven days. Anyone who touches her shall be unclean until evening. ²⁰ Anything on which she lies or sits during her impurity shall be unclean. ²¹ Anyone who touches her bed shall wash his garments, bathe in water, and be unclean until evening. ²² Whoever touches any article of furniture on which she was sitting, shall wash his garments, bathe in water, and be unclean until evening. ²³ But if she is on the bed or on the seat when he touches it, he shall be unclean until evening. ²⁴ If a man dares to lie with her, he contracts her impurity and shall be unclean for seven days; every bed on which he then lies also becomes unclean. ²⁵ "When a woman is afflicted with a flow of blood for several days outside her menstrual period, or when her flow continues beyond the ordinary period, as long as she suffers this unclean flow she shall be unclean, just as during her menstrual period. ²⁶ Any bed on which she lies during such a flow becomes unclean, as it would during her menstruation, and any article of furniture on which she sits becomes unclean just as during her menstruation. ²⁷ Anyone who touches them becomes unclean; he shall wash his garments, bathe in water, and be unclean until evening. ²⁸ "If she becomes freed from her affliction, she shall wait seven days, and only then is she to be purified. ²⁹ On the eighth day she shall take two turtledoves or two pigeons and bring them to the priest at the entrance of the meeting tent. ³⁰ The priest shall offer up one of them as a sin offering and the other as a holocaust. Thus shall the priest make atonement before the LORD for her unclean flow. ³¹ "You shall warn the Israelites of their uncleanness, lest by defiling my Dwelling, which is in their midst, their uncleanness be the cause of their death. ³² "This is the law for the man who is afflicted with a chronic flow, or who has an emission of seed, and thereby becomes unclean; ³³ as well as for the woman who has her menstrual period, or who is afflicted with a chronic flow; the law for male and female; and also for the man who lies with an unclean woman."

Leviticus chapter 16

¹ After the death of Aaron's two sons, who died when they approached the LORD'S presence, the LORD spoke to Moses ² and said to him, "Tell your brother Aaron that he is not to come whenever he pleases into the sanctuary, inside the veil, in front of the propitiatory on the ark; otherwise, when I reveal myself in a cloud above the propitiatory, he will die. ³ Only in this way may Aaron enter the sanctuary. He shall bring a young bullock for a sin offering and a ram for a holocaust. ⁴ He shall wear the sacred linen tunic, with the linen drawers next his flesh, gird himself with the linen sash and put on the linen miter. But since these vestments are sacred, he shall not put them on until he has first bathed his body in water. ⁵ From the Israelite community he shall receive two male goats for a sin offering and one ram for a holocaust. ⁶ "Aaron shall bring in the bullock, his sin offering to atone for himself and for his household. ⁷ Taking the two male goats and setting them before the LORD at the entrance of the meeting tent, ⁸ he shall cast lots to determine which one is for the LORD and which for Azazel. ⁹ The goat that is determined by lot for the LORD, Aaron shall bring in and offer up as a sin offering. ¹⁰ But the goat determined by lot for Azazel he shall set alive before the LORD, so that with it he may make atonement by sending it off to Azazel in the desert. ¹¹ "Thus shall Aaron offer up the bullock, his sin offering, to atone for himself and for his family. When he has slaughtered it, ¹² he shall take a censer full of glowing embers from the altar before the LORD, as well as a double handful of finely ground fragrant incense, and bringing them inside the veil, ¹³ there before the LORD he shall put incense on the fire, so that a cloud of incense may cover the propitiatory over the commandments; else he will die. ¹⁴ Taking some of the bullock's blood, he shall sprinkle it with his finger on the fore part of the propitiatory and likewise sprinkle some of the blood with his finger seven times in front of the propitiatory. ¹⁵ "Then he shall slaughter the people's sin-offering goat, and bringing its blood inside the veil, he shall do with it as he did with the bullock's blood, sprinkling it on the propitiatory and before it. ¹⁶ Thus he shall make atonement for the sanctuary because of all the sinful defilements and faults of the Israelites. He shall do the same for the meeting tent, which is set up among them in the midst of their uncleanness. ¹⁷ No one else may be in the meeting tent from the time he enters the sanctuary to make atonement until he departs. When he has made atonement for himself and his household, as well as for the whole Israelite community, ¹⁸ he shall come out to the altar before the LORD and make atonement for it also. Taking some of the bullock's and the goat's blood, he shall put it on the horns around the altar, ¹⁹ and with his finger sprinkle some of the blood on it seven times. Thus he shall render it clean and holy, purged of the defilements of the

Israelites. ²⁰ "When he has completed the atonement rite for the sanctuary, the meeting tent and the altar, Aaron shall bring forward the live goat. ²¹ Laying both hands on its head, he shall confess over it all the sinful faults and transgressions of the Israelites, and so put them on the goat's head. He shall then have it led into the desert by an attendant. ²² Since the goat is to carry off their iniquities to an isolated region, it must be sent away into the desert. ²³ "After Aaron has again gone into the meeting tent, he shall strip off and leave in the sanctuary the linen vestments he had put on when he entered there. ²⁴ After bathing his body with water in a sacred place, he shall put on his vestments, and then come out and offer his own and the people's holocaust, in atonement for himself and for the people, ²⁵ and also burn the fat of the sin offering on the altar. ²⁶ "The man who has led away the goat for Azazel shall wash his garments and bathe his body in water; only then may he enter the camp. ²⁷ The sin-offering bullock and goat whose blood was brought into the sanctuary to make atonement, shall be taken outside the camp, where their hides and flesh and offal shall be burned up in the fire. ²⁸ The one who burns them shall wash his garments and bathe his body in water; only then may he enter the camp. ²⁹ "This shall be an everlasting ordinance for you: on the tenth day of the seventh month every one of you, whether a native or a resident alien, shall mortify himself and shall do no work. ³⁰ Since on this day atonement is made for you to make you clean, so that you may be cleansed of all your sins before the LORD, ³¹ by everlasting ordinance it shall be a most solemn sabbath for you, on which you must mortify yourselves. ³² "This atonement is to be made by the priest who has been anointed and ordained to the priesthood in succession to his father. He shall wear the linen garments, the sacred vestments, ³³ and make atonement for the sacred sanctuary, the meeting tent and the altar, as well as for the priests and all the people of the community. ³⁴ This, then, shall be an everlasting ordinance for you: once a year atonement shall be made for all the sins of the Israelites." Thus was it done, as the LORD had commanded Moses.

Leviticus chapter 17

¹ The LORD said to Moses, ² "Speak to Aaron and his sons, as well as to all the Israelites, and tell them: This is what the LORD has commanded. ³ Any Israelite who slaughters an ox or a sheep or a goat, whether in the camp or outside of it, ⁴ without first bringing it to the entrance of the meeting tent to present it as an offering to the LORD in front of his Dwelling, shall be judged guilty of bloodshed; and for this, such a man shall be cut off from among his people. ⁵ Therefore, such sacrifices as they used to offer up in the open field the Israelites shall henceforth offer to the LORD, bringing them to the priest at the entrance of the meeting tent and sacrificing them there as peace offerings to the LORD. ⁶ The priest shall splash the blood on the altar of the LORD at the entrance of the meeting tent and there burn the fat for an odor pleasing to the LORD. ⁷ No longer shall they offer their sacrifices to the satyrs to whom they used to render their wanton worship. This shall be an everlasting ordinance for them and their descendants. ⁸ "Tell them, therefore: Anyone, whether of the house of Israel or of the aliens residing among them, who offers a holocaust or sacrifice ⁹ without bringing it to the entrance of the meeting tent to offer it to the LORD, shall be cut off from his kinsmen. ¹⁰ And if anyone, whether of the house of Israel or of the aliens residing among them, partakes of any blood, I will set myself against that one who partakes of blood and will cut him off from among his people. ¹¹ Since the life of a living body is in its blood, I have made you put it on the altar, so that atonement may thereby be made for your own lives, because it is the blood, as the seat of life, that makes atonement. ¹² That is why I have told the Israelites: No one among you, not even a resident alien, may partake of blood. ¹³ "Anyone hunting, whether of the Israelites or of the aliens residing among them, who catches an animal or a bird that may be eaten, shall pour out its blood and cover it with earth. ¹⁴ Since the life of every living body is its blood, I have told the Israelites: You shall not partake of the blood of any meat. Since the life of every living body is its blood, anyone who partakes of it shall be cut off. ¹⁵ "Everyone, whether a native or an alien, who eats of an animal that died of itself or was killed by a wild beast, shall wash his garments, bathe in water, and be unclean until evening, and then he will be clean. ¹⁶ If he does not wash or does not bathe his body, he shall have the guilt to bear."

Leviticus chapter 18

¹ The LORD said to Moses, ² "Speak to the Israelites and tell them: I, the LORD, am your God. ³ You shall not do as they do in the land of Egypt, where you once lived, nor shall you do as they do in the land of Canaan, where I am bringing you; do not conform to their customs. ⁴ My decrees you shall carry out, and my statutes you shall take care to follow. I, the LORD, am your God. ⁵ Keep, then, my statutes and

decrees, for the man who carries them out will find life through them. I am the LORD. ⁶ None of you shall approach a close relative to have sexual intercourse with her. I am the LORD. ⁷ You shall not disgrace your father by having intercourse with your mother. Besides, since she is your own mother, you shall not have intercourse with her. ⁸ You shall not have intercourse with your father's wife, for that would be a disgrace to your father. ⁹ You shall not have intercourse with your sister, your father's daughter or your mother's daughter, whether she was born in your own household or born elsewhere. ¹⁰ You shall not have intercourse with your son's daughter or with your daughter's daughter, for that would be a disgrace to your own family. ¹¹ You shall not have intercourse with the daughter whom your father's wife bore to him, since she, too, is your sister. ¹² You shall not have intercourse with your father's sister, since she is your father's relative. ¹³ You shall not have intercourse with your mother's sister, since she is your mother's relative. ¹⁴ You shall not disgrace your father's brother by being intimate with his wife, since she, too, is your aunt. ¹⁵ You shall not have intercourse with your daughter-in-law; she is your son's wife, and therefore you shall not disgrace her. ¹⁶ You shall not have intercourse with your brother's wife, for that would be a disgrace to your brother. ¹⁷ You shall not have intercourse with a woman and also with her daughter, nor shall you marry and have intercourse with her son's daughter or her daughter's daughter; this would be shameful, because they are related to her. ¹⁸ While your wife is still living you shall not marry her sister as her rival; for thus you would disgrace your first wife. ¹⁹ You shall not approach a woman to have intercourse with her while she is unclean from menstruation. ²⁰ You shall not have carnal relations with your neighbor's wife, defiling yourself with her. ²¹ You shall not offer any of your offspring to be immolated to Molech, thus profaning the name of your God. I am the LORD. ²² You shall not lie with a male as with a woman; such a thing is an abomination. ²³ You shall not have carnal relations with an animal, defiling yourself with it; nor shall a woman set herself in front of an animal to mate with it; such things are abhorrent. ²⁴ Do not defile yourselves by any of these things by which the nations whom I am driving out of your way have defiled themselves. ²⁵ Because their land has become defiled, I am punishing it for its wickedness, by making it vomit out its inhabitants. ²⁶ You, however, whether natives or resident aliens, must keep my statutes and decrees forbidding all such abominations ²⁷ by which the previous inhabitants defiled the land; ²⁸ otherwise the land will vomit you out also for having defiled it, just as it vomited out the nations before you. ²⁹ Everyone who does any of these abominations shall be cut off from among his people. ³⁰ Heed my charge, then, not to defile yourselves by observing the abominable customs that have been observed before you. I, the LORD, am your God."

Leviticus chapter 19

¹ The LORD said to Moses, ² "Speak to the whole Israelite community and tell them: Be holy, for I, the LORD your God, am holy. ³ Revere your mother and father, and keep my sabbaths. I, the LORD, am your God. ⁴ Do not turn aside to idols, nor make molten gods for yourselves. I, the LORD, am your God. ⁵ When you sacrifice your peace offering to the LORD, if you wish it to be acceptable, ⁶ it must be eaten on the very day of your sacrifice or on the following day. Whatever is left over until the third day shall be burned up in the fire. ⁷ If any of it is eaten on the third day, the sacrifice will be unacceptable as refuse; ⁸ whoever eats of it then shall pay the penalty for having profaned what is sacred to the LORD. Such a one shall be cut off from his people. ⁹ When you reap the harvest of your land, you shall not be so thorough that you reap the field to its very edge, nor shall you glean the stray ears of grain. ¹⁰ Likewise, you shall not pick your vineyard bare, nor gather up the grapes that have fallen. These things you shall leave for the poor and the alien. I, the LORD, am your God. ¹¹ You shall not steal. You shall not lie or speak falsely to one another. ¹² You shall not swear falsely by my name, thus profaning the name of your God. I am the LORD. ¹³ You shall not defraud or rob your neighbor. You shall not withhold overnight the wages of your day laborer. ¹⁴ You shall not curse the deaf, or put a stumbling block in front of the blind, but you shall fear your God. I am the LORD. ¹⁵ You shall not act dishonestly in rendering judgment. Show neither partiality to the weak nor deference to the mighty, but judge your fellow men justly. ¹⁶ You shall not go about spreading slander among your kinsmen; nor shall you stand by idly when your neighbor's life is at stake. I am the LORD. ¹⁷ You shall not bear hatred for your brother in your heart. Though you may have to reprove your fellow man, do not incur sin because of him. ¹⁸ Take no revenge and cherish no grudge against your fellow countrymen. You shall love your neighbor as yourself. I am the LORD. ¹⁹ Keep my statutes: do not breed any of your domestic animals with others of a different species; do not sow a field of yours with two different kinds of seed; and do not put on

a garment woven with two different kinds of thread. ²⁰ If a man has carnal relations with a female slave who has already been living with another man but has not yet been redeemed or given her freedom, they shall be punished but not put to death, because she is not free. ²¹ The man, moreover, shall bring to the entrance of the meeting tent a ram as his guilt offering to the LORD. ²² With this ram the priest shall make atonement before the LORD for the sin he has committed, and it will be forgiven him. ²³ When you come into the land and plant any fruit tree there, first look upon its fruit as if it were uncircumcised. For three years, while its fruit remains uncircumcised, it may not be eaten. ²⁴ In the fourth year, however, all of its fruit shall be sacred to the LORD as a thanksgiving feast to him. ²⁵ Not until the fifth year may you eat its fruit. Thus it will continue its yield for you. I, the LORD, am your God. ²⁶ Do not eat meat with the blood still in it. Do not practice divination or soothsaying. ²⁷ Do not clip your hair at the temples, nor trim the edges of your beard. ²⁸ Do not lacerate your bodies for the dead, and do not tattoo yourselves. I am the LORD. ²⁹ You shall not degrade your daughter by making a prostitute of her; else the land will become corrupt and full of lewdness. ³⁰ Keep my sabbaths, and reverence my sanctuary. I am the LORD. ³¹ Do not go to mediums or consult fortune-tellers, for you will be defiled by them. I, the LORD, am your God. ³² Stand up in the presence of the aged, and show respect for the old; thus shall you fear your God. I am the LORD. ³³ When an alien resides with you in your land, do not molest him. ³⁴ You shall treat the alien who resides with you no differently than the natives born among you; have the same love for him as for yourself; for you too were once aliens in the land of Egypt. I, the LORD, am your God. ³⁵ Do not act dishonestly in using measures of length or weight or capacity. ³⁶ You shall have a true scale and true weights, an honest ephah and an honest hin. I, the LORD, am your God, who brought you out of the land of Egypt. ³⁷ Be careful, then, to observe all my statutes and decrees. I am the LORD."

Leviticus chapter 20

¹ The LORD said to Moses, ² "Tell the Israelites: Anyone, whether an Israelite or an alien residing in Israel, who gives any of his offspring to Molech shall be put to death. Let his fellow citizens stone him. ³ I myself will turn against such a man and cut him off from the body of his people; for in giving his offspring to Molech, he has defiled my sanctuary and profaned my holy name. ⁴ Even if his fellow citizens connive at such a man's crime of giving his offspring to Molech, and fail to put him to death, ⁵ I myself will set my face against that man and his family and will cut off from their people both him and all who join him in his wanton worship of Molech. ⁶ Should anyone turn to mediums and fortune-tellers and follow their wanton ways, I will turn against such a one and cut him off from his people. ⁷ Sanctify yourselves, then, and be holy; for I, the LORD, your God, am holy. ⁸ Be careful, therefore, to observe what I, the LORD, who make you holy, have prescribed. ⁹ Anyone who curses his father or mother shall be put to death; since he has cursed his father or mother, he has forfeited his life. ¹⁰ If a man commits adultery with his neighbor's wife, both the adulterer and the adulteress shall be put to death. ¹¹ If a man disgraces his father by lying with his father's wife, both the man and his stepmother shall be put to death; they have forfeited their lives. ¹² If a man lies with his daughter-in-law, both of them shall be put to death; since they have committed an abhorrent deed, they have forfeited their lives. ¹³ If a man lies with a male as with a woman, both of them shall be put to death for their abominable deed; they have forfeited their lives. ¹⁴ If a man marries a woman and her mother also, the man and the two women as well shall be burned to death for their shameful conduct, so that such shamefulness may not be found among you. ¹⁵ If a man has carnal relations with an animal, the man shall be put to death, and the animal shall be slain. ¹⁶ If a woman goes up to any animal to mate with it, the woman and the animal shall be slain; let them both be put to death; their lives are forfeit. ¹⁷ If a man consummates marriage with his sister or his half-sister, they shall be publicly cut off from their people for this shameful deed; the man shall pay the penalty of having had intercourse with his own sister. ¹⁸ If a man lies in sexual intercourse with a woman during her menstrual period, both of them shall be cut off from their people, because they have laid bare the flowing fountain of her blood. ¹⁹ You shall not have intercourse with your mother's sister or your father's sister; whoever does so shall pay the penalty of incest. ²⁰ If a man disgraces his uncle by having intercourse with his uncle's wife, the man and his aunt shall pay the penalty by dying childless. ²¹ If a man marries his brother's wife and thus disgraces his brother, they shall be childless because of this incest. ²² Be careful to observe all my statutes and all my decrees; otherwise the land where I am bringing you to dwell will vomit you out. ²³ Do not conform, therefore, to the customs of the nations whom I am driving out of your way, because all these things that they have done have filled me with disgust for them. ²⁴ But to you

I have said: Their land shall be your possession, a land flowing with milk and honey. I am giving it to you as your own, I, the LORD, your God, who have set you apart from the other nations. 25 You, too, must set apart, then, the clean animals from the unclean, and the clean birds from the unclean, so that you may not be contaminated with the uncleanness of any beast or bird or of any swarming creature in the land that I have set apart for you. 26 To me, therefore, you shall be sacred; for I, the LORD, am sacred, I, who have set you apart from the other nations to be my own. 27 A man or a woman who acts as a medium or fortune-teller shall be put to death by stoning; they have no one but themselves to blame for their death."

Leviticus chapter 21

1 The LORD said to Moses, "Speak to Aaron's sons, the priests, and tell them: None of you shall make himself unclean for any dead person among his people, 2 except for his nearest relatives, his mother or father, his son or daughter, his brother 3 or his maiden sister, who is of his own family while she remains unmarried; for these he may make himself unclean. 4 But for a sister who has married out of his family he shall not make himself unclean; this would be a profanation. 5 The priests shall not make bare the crown of the head, nor shave the edges of the beard, nor lacerate the body. 6 To their God they shall be sacred, and not profane his name; since they offer up the oblations of the LORD, the food of their God, they must be holy. 7 A priest shall not marry a woman who has been a prostitute or has lost her honor, nor a woman who has been divorced by her husband; for the priest is sacred to his God. 8 Honor him as sacred who offers up the food of your God; treat him as sacred, because I, the LORD, who have consecrated him, am sacred. 9 A priest's daughter who loses her honor by committing fornication and thereby dishonors her father also, shall be burned to death. 10 The most exalted of the priests, upon whose head the anointing oil has been poured and who has been ordained to wear the special vestments, shall not bare his head or rend his garments, 11 nor shall he go near any dead person. Not even for his father or mother may he thus become unclean 12 or leave the sanctuary; otherwise he will profane the sanctuary of his God, for with the anointing oil upon him, he is dedicated to his God, to me, the LORD. 13 The priest shall marry a virgin. 14 Not a widow or a woman who has been divorced or a woman who has lost her honor as a prostitute, but a virgin, taken from his own people, shall he marry; 15 otherwise he will have base offspring among his people. I, the LORD, have made him sacred." 16 The LORD said to Moses, 17 "Speak to Aaron and tell him: None of your descendants, of whatever generation, who has any defect shall come forward to offer up the food of his God. 18 Therefore, he who has any of the following defects may not come forward: he who is blind, or lame, or who has any disfigurement or malformation, 19 or a crippled foot or hand, 20 or who is hump-backed or weakly or walleyed, or who is afflicted with eczema, ringworm or hernia. 21 No descendant of Aaron the priest who has any such defect may draw near to offer up the oblations of the LORD; on account of his defect he may not draw near to offer up the food of his God. 22 He may, however, partake of the food of his God: of what is most sacred as well as of what is sacred. 23 Only, he may not approach the veil nor go up to the altar on account of his defect; he shall not profane these things that are sacred to me, for it is I, the LORD, who make them sacred." 24 Moses, therefore, told this to Aaron and his sons and to all the Israelites.

Leviticus chapter 22

1 The LORD said to Moses, 2 "Tell Aaron and his sons to respect the sacred offerings which the Israelites consecrate to me; else they will profane my holy name. I am the LORD. 3 Tell them: If any one of you, or of your descendants in any future generation, dares, while he is in a state of uncleanness, to draw near the sacred offerings which the Israelites consecrate to the LORD, such a one shall be cut off from my presence. I am the LORD. 4 No descendant of Aaron who is stricken with leprosy, or who suffers from a flow, may eat of these sacred offerings, unless he again becomes clean. Moreover, if anyone touches a person who has become unclean by contact with a corpse, or if anyone has had an emission of seed, 5 or if anyone touches any swarming creature or any man whose uncleanness, of whatever kind it may be, is contagious, 6 the one who touches such as these shall be unclean until evening and may not eat of the sacred portions until he has first bathed his body in water, 7 then, when the sun sets, he again becomes clean. Only then may he eat of the sacred offerings, which are his food. 8 He shall not make himself unclean by eating of any animal that has died of itself or has been killed by wild beasts. I am the LORD. 9 They shall keep my charge and not do wrong in this matter; else they will die for their profanation. I am the LORD who have consecrated them. 10 Neither a lay person nor a priest's tenant or hired servant may eat of any sacred

offering. 11 But a slave whom a priest acquires by purchase or who is born in his house may eat of his food. 12 A priest's daughter who is married to a layman may not eat of the sacred contributions. 13 But if a priest's daughter is widowed or divorced and, having no children, returns to her father's house, she may then eat of her father's food as in her youth. No layman, however, may eat of it. 14 If such a one eats of a sacred offering through inadvertence, he shall make restitution to the priest for the sacred offering, with an increment of one fifth of the amount. 15 The sacred offerings which the Israelites contribute to the LORD the priests shall not allow to be profaned 16 nor in the eating of the sacred offering shall they bring down guilt that must be punished; it is I, the LORD, who make them sacred. 17 The LORD said to Moses, 18 Speak to Aaron and his sons and to all the Israelites, and tell them: When anyone of the house of Israel, or any alien residing in Israel, who wishes to offer a sacrifice, brings a holocaust as a votive offering or as a free-will offering to the LORD, 19 if it is to be acceptable, the ox or sheep or goat that he offers must be an unblemished male. 20 You shall not offer one that has any defect, for such a one would not be acceptable for you. 21 When anyone presents a peace offering to the LORD from the herd or the flock in fulfillment of a vow, or as a free-will offering, if it is to find acceptance, it must be unblemished; it shall not have any defect. 22 One that is blind or crippled or maimed, or one that has a running sore or mange or ringworm, you shall not offer to the LORD; do not put such an animal on the altar as an oblation to the LORD. 23 An ox or a sheep that is in any way ill-proportioned or stunted you may indeed present as a free-will offering, but it will not be acceptable as a votive offering. 24 One that has its testicles bruised or crushed or torn out or cut off you shall not offer to the LORD. You shall neither do this in your own land 25 nor receive from a foreigner any such animals to offer up as the food of your God; since they are deformed or defective, they will not be acceptable for you. 26 The LORD said to Moses, 27 When an ox or a lamb or a goat is born, it shall remain with its mother for seven days; only from the eighth day onward will it be acceptable, to be offered as an oblation to the LORD. 28 You shall not slaughter an ox or a sheep on one and the same day with its young. 29 Whenever you offer a thanksgiving sacrifice to the LORD, so offer it that it may be acceptable for you; 30 it must, therefore, be eaten on the same day; none of it shall be left over until the next day. I am the LORD. 31 Be careful to observe the commandments which I, the LORD, give you, 32 and do not profane my holy name; in the midst of the Israelites I, the LORD, must be held as sacred. It is I who made you sacred 33 and led you out of the land of Egypt, that I, the LORD, might be your God."

Leviticus chapter 23

1 The LORD said to Moses, 2 "Speak to the Israelites and tell them: The following are the festivals of the LORD, my feast days, which you shall celebrate with a sacred assembly. 3 For six days work may be done; but the seventh day is the sabbath rest, a day for sacred assembly, on which you shall do no work. The sabbath shall belong to the LORD wherever you dwell. 4 These, then, are the festivals of the LORD which you shall celebrate at their proper time with a sacred assembly. 5 The Passover of the LORD falls on the fourteenth day of the first month, at the evening twilight. 6 The fifteenth day of this month is the LORD'S feast of Unleavened Bread. For seven days you shall eat unleavened bread. 7 On the first of these days you shall hold a sacred assembly and do no sort of work. 8 On each of the seven days you shall offer an oblation to the LORD. Then on the seventh day you shall again hold a sacred assembly and do no sort of work. 9 The LORD said to Moses, 10 Speak to the Israelites and tell them: When you come into the land which I am giving you, and reap your harvest, you shall bring a sheaf of the first fruits of your harvest to the priest, 11 who shall wave the sheaf before the LORD that it may be acceptable for you. On the day after the sabbath the priest shall do this. 12 On this day, when your sheaf is waved, you shall offer to the LORD for a holocaust an unblemished yearling lamb. 13 Its cereal offering shall be two tenths of an ephah of fine flour mixed with oil, as a sweet-smelling oblation to the LORD; and its libation shall be a fourth of a hin of wine. 14 Until this day, when you bring your God this offering, you shall not eat any bread or roasted grain or fresh kernels. This shall be a perpetual statute for you and your descendants wherever you dwell. 15 Beginning with the day after the sabbath, the day on which you bring the wave-offering sheaf, you shall count seven full weeks, 16 and then on the day after the seventh week, the fiftieth day, you shall present the new cereal offering to the LORD. 17 For the wave offering of your first fruits to the LORD, you shall bring with you from wherever you live two loaves of bread made of two tenths of an ephah of fine flour and baked with leaven. 18 Besides the bread, you shall offer to the LORD a holocaust of seven unblemished yearling lambs, one young bull, and two rams, along with their cereal offering and libations, as a sweet-smelling oblation to the LORD. 19 One male goat shall be

sacrificed as a sin offering, and two yearling lambs as a peace offering. 20 The priest shall wave the bread of the first fruits and the two lambs as a wave offering before the LORD; these shall be sacred to the LORD and belong to the priest. 21 On this same day you shall by proclamation have a sacred assembly, and no sort of work may be done. This shall be a perpetual statute for you and your descendants wherever you dwell. 22 When you reap the harvest of your land, you shall not be so thorough that you reap the field to its very edge, nor shall you glean the stray ears of your grain. These things you shall leave for the poor and the alien. I, the LORD, am your God. 23 The LORD said to Moses, 24 Tell the Israelites: On the first day of the seventh month you shall keep a sabbath rest, with a sacred assembly and with the trumpet blasts as a reminder; 25 you shall then do no sort of work, and you shall offer an oblation to the LORD. 26 The LORD said to Moses, 27 The tenth of this seventh month is the Day of Atonement, when you shall hold a sacred assembly and mortify yourselves and offer an oblation to the LORD. 28 On this day you shall not do any work, because it is the Day of Atonement, when atonement is made for you before the LORD, your God. 29 Anyone who does not mortify himself on this day shall be cut off from his people, 30 and if anyone does any work on this day, I will remove him from the midst of his people. 31 This is a perpetual statute for you and your descendants wherever you dwell: you shall do no work, 32 but shall keep a sabbath of complete rest and mortify yourselves. Beginning on the evening of the ninth of the month, you shall keep this sabbath of yours from evening to evening. 33 The LORD said to Moses, 34 Tell the Israelites: The fifteenth day of this seventh month is the LORD'S feast of Booths, which shall continue for seven days. 35 On the first day there shall be a sacred assembly, and you shall do no sort of work. 36 For seven days you shall offer an oblation to the LORD, and on the eighth day you shall again hold a sacred assembly and offer an oblation to the LORD. On that solemn closing you shall do no sort of work. 37 These, therefore, are the festivals of the LORD on which you shall proclaim a sacred assembly, and offer as an oblation to the LORD holocausts and cereal offerings, sacrifices and libations, as prescribed for each day, 38 in addition to those of the LORD'S sabbaths, your donations, your various votive offerings and the free-will offerings that you present to the LORD. 39 On the fifteenth day, then, of the seventh month, when you have gathered in the produce of the land, you shall celebrate a pilgrim feast of the LORD for a whole week. The first and the eighth day shall be days of complete rest. 40 On the first day you shall gather foliage from majestic trees, branches of palms and boughs of myrtles and of valley poplars, and then for a week you shall make merry before the LORD, your God. 41 By perpetual statute for you and your descendants you shall keep this pilgrim feast of the LORD for one whole week in the seventh month of the year. 42 During this week every native Israelite among you shall dwell in booths, 43 that your descendants may realize that, when I led the Israelites out of the land of Egypt, I made them dwell in booths. I, the LORD, am your God. 44 Thus did Moses announce to the Israelites the festivals of the LORD.

Leviticus chapter 24

1 The LORD said to Moses, 2 "Order the Israelites to bring you clear oil of crushed olives for the light, so that you may keep lamps burning regularly. 3 In the meeting tent, outside the veil that hangs in front of the commandments, Aaron shall set up the lamps to burn before the LORD regularly, from evening till morning. Thus, by a perpetual statute for you and your descendants, 4 the lamps shall be set up on the pure gold lampstand, to burn regularly before the LORD. 5 You shall take fine flour and bake it into twelve cakes, using two tenths of an ephah of flour for each cake. 6 These you shall place in two piles, six in each pile, on the pure gold table before the LORD. 7 On each pile put some pure frankincense, which shall serve as an oblation to the LORD, a token offering for the bread. 8 Regularly on each sabbath day this bread shall be set out afresh before the LORD, offered on the part of the Israelites by an everlasting agreement. 9 It shall belong to Aaron and his sons, who must eat it in a sacred place, since, as something most sacred among the various oblations to the LORD, it is his by perpetual right. 10 Among the Israelites there was a man born of an Israelite mother (Shelomith, daughter of Dibri, of the tribe of Dan) and an Egyptian father. 11 This man quarreled publicly with another Israelite and cursed and blasphemed the LORD'S name. So the people brought him to Moses, 12 who kept him in custody till a decision from the LORD should settle the case for them. 13 The LORD then said to Moses, 14 Take the blasphemer outside the camp, and when all who heard him have laid their hands on his head, let the whole community stone him. 15 Tell the Israelites: Anyone who curses his God shall bear the penalty of his sin; 16 whoever blasphemes the name of the LORD shall be put to death. The whole community shall stone him; alien and native alike must be put to death for blaspheming the LORD'S name. 17 Whoever takes the

life of any human being shall be put to death; 18 whoever takes the life of an animal shall make restitution of another animal. A life for a life! 19 Anyone who inflicts an injury on his neighbor shall receive the same in return. 20 Limb for limb, eye for eye, tooth for tooth! The same injury that a man gives another shall be inflicted on him in return. 21 Whoever slays an animal shall make restitution, but whoever slays a man shall be put to death. 22 You shall have but one rule, for alien and native alike. I, the LORD, am your God. 23 When Moses told this to the Israelites, they took the blasphemer outside the camp and stoned him; they carried out the command that the LORD had given Moses.

Leviticus chapter 25

1 The LORD said to Moses on Mount Sinai, 2"Speak to the Israelites and tell them: When you enter the land that I am giving you, let the land, too, keep a sabbath for the LORD. 3For six years you may sow your field, and for six years prune your vineyard, gathering in their produce. 4But during the seventh year the land shall have a complete rest, a sabbath for the LORD, when you may neither sow your field nor prune your vineyard. 5The aftergrowth of your harvest you shall not reap, nor shall you pick the grapes of your untrimmed vines in this year of sabbath rest for the land. 6While the land has its sabbath, all its produce will be food equally for you yourself and for your male and female slaves, for your hired help and the tenants who live with you, 7and likewise for your livestock and for the wild animals on your land. 8Seven weeks of years shall you count—seven times seven years—so that the seven cycles amount to forty-nine years. 9Then, on the tenth day of the seventh month let the trumpet resound; on this, the Day of Atonement, the trumpet blast shall re-echo throughout your land. 10This fiftieth year you shall make sacred by proclaiming liberty in the land for all its inhabitants. It shall be a jubilee for you, when every one of you shall return to his own property, every one to his own family estate. 11In this fiftieth year, your year of jubilee, you shall not sow, nor shall you reap the aftergrowth or pick the grapes from the untrimmed vines. 12Since this is the jubilee, which shall be sacred for you, you may not eat of its produce, except as taken directly from the field. 13In this year of jubilee, then, every one of you shall return to his own property. 14Therefore, when you sell any land to your neighbor or buy any from him, do not deal unfairly. 15On the basis of the number of years since the last jubilee shall you purchase the land from him; and so also, on the basis of the number of years for crops, shall he sell it to you. 16When the years are many, the price shall be so much the more; when the years are few, the price shall be so much the less. For it is really the number of crops that he sells you. 17Do not deal unfairly, then; but stand in fear of your God. I, the LORD, am your God. 18Observe my precepts and be careful to keep my regulations, for then you will dwell securely in the land. 19The land will yield its fruit and you will have food in abundance, so that you may live there without worry. 20Therefore, do not say, 'What shall we eat in the seventh year, if we do not then sow or reap our crop?' 21I will bestow such blessings on you in the sixth year that there will then be crop enough for three years. 22When you sow in the eighth year, you will continue to eat from the old crop; and even into the ninth year, when the crop comes in, you will still have the old to eat from. 23The land shall not be sold in perpetuity; for the land is mine, and you are but aliens who have become my tenants. 24Therefore, in every part of the country that you occupy, you must permit the land to be redeemed. 25When one of your countrymen is reduced to poverty and has to sell some of his property, his closest relative, who has the right to redeem it, may go and buy back what his kinsman has sold. 26If, however, the man has no relative to redeem his land, but later on acquires sufficient means to buy it back in his own name, 27he shall make a deduction from the price in proportion to the number of years since the sale, and then pay back the balance to the one to whom he sold it, so that he may thus regain his own property. 28But if he does not acquire sufficient means to buy back his land, what he has sold shall remain in the possession of the purchaser until the jubilee, when it must be released and returned to its original owner. 29When someone sells a dwelling in a walled town, he has the right to buy it back during the time of one full year from its sale. 30But if such a house in a walled town has not been redeemed at the end of a full year, it shall belong in perpetuity to the purchaser and his descendants; nor shall it be released in the jubilee. 31However, houses in villages that are not encircled by walls shall be considered as belonging to the surrounding farm land; they may be redeemed at any time, and in the jubilee they must be released. 32In levitical cities the Levites shall always have the right to redeem the town houses that are their property. 33Any town house of the Levites in their cities that had been sold and not redeemed, shall be released in the jubilee; for the town houses of the Levites are their hereditary property in the midst of the Israelites. 34Moreover, the pasture land belonging to their cities shall not be sold at all; it must always remain their hereditary property.

35When one of your fellow countrymen is reduced to poverty and is unable to hold out beside you, extend to him the privileges of an alien or a tenant, so that he may continue to live with you. 36Do not exact interest from your countryman either in money or in kind, but out of fear of God let him live with you. 37You are to lend him neither money at interest nor food at a profit. 38I, the LORD, am your God, who brought you out of the land of Egypt to give you the land of Canaan and to be your God. 39When, then, your countryman becomes so impoverished beside you that he sells you his services, do not make him work as a slave. 40Rather, let him be like a hired servant or like your tenant, working with you until the jubilee year, 41when he, together with his children, shall be released from your service and return to his kindred and to the property of his ancestors. 42Since those whom I brought out of the land of Egypt are servants of mine, they shall not be sold as slaves to any man. 43Do not lord it over them harshly, but stand in fear of your God. 44Slaves, male and female, you may indeed possess, provided you buy them from among the neighboring nations. 45You may also buy them from among the aliens who reside with you and from their children who are born and reared in your land. Such slaves you may own as chattels, 46and leave to your sons as their hereditary property, making them perpetual slaves. But you shall not lord it harshly over any of the Israelites, your kinsmen. 47When one of your countrymen is reduced to such poverty that he sells himself to a wealthy alien who has a permanent or a temporary residence among you, or to one of the descendants of an immigrant family, 48even after he has thus sold his services he still has the right of redemption; he may be redeemed by one of his own brothers, 49or by his uncle or cousin, or by some other relative or fellow clansman; or, if he acquires the means, he may redeem himself. 50With his purchaser he shall compute the years from the sale to the jubilee, distributing the sale price over these years as though he had been hired as a day laborer. 51The more such years there are, the more of the sale price he shall pay back as ransom; 52the fewer years there are left before the jubilee year, the more he has to his credit; in proportion to his years of service shall he pay his ransom. 53The alien shall treat him as a servant hired on an annual basis, and he shall not lord it over him harshly under your very eyes. 54If he is not thus redeemed, he shall nevertheless be released, together with his children, in the jubilee year. 55For to me the Israelites belong as servants; they are servants of mine, because I brought them out of the land of Egypt, I, the LORD, your God.

Leviticus chapter 26

1 "Do not make false gods for yourselves. You shall not erect an idol or a sacred pillar for yourselves, nor shall you set up a stone figure for worship in your land; for I, the LORD, am your God. 2 Keep my sabbaths and reverence my sanctuary. I am the LORD. 3 If you live in accordance with my precepts and are careful to observe my commandments, 4 I will give you rain in due season, so that the land will bear its crops, and the trees their fruit; 5 your threshing will last till vintage time, and your vintage till the time for sowing, and you will have food to eat in abundance, so that you may dwell securely in your land. 6 I will establish peace in the land, that you may lie down to rest without anxiety. I will rid the country of ravenous beasts, and keep the sword of war from sweeping across your land. 7 You will rout your enemies and lay them low with your sword. 8 Five of you will put a hundred of your foes to flight, and a hundred of you will chase ten thousand of them, till they are cut down by your sword. 9 I will look with favor upon you, and make you fruitful and numerous, as I carry out my covenant with you. 10 So much of the old crops will you have stored up for food that you will have to discard them to make room for the new. 11 I will set my Dwelling among you, and will not disdain you. 12 Ever present in your midst, I will be your God, and you will be my people; 13 for it is I, the LORD, your God, who brought you out of the land of the Egyptians and freed you from their slavery, breaking the yoke they had laid upon you and letting you walk erect. 14 But if you do not heed me and do not keep all these commandments, 15 if you reject my precepts and spurn my decrees, refusing to obey all my commandments and breaking my covenant, 16 then I, in turn, will give you your deserts. I will punish you with terrible woes - with wasting and fever to dim the eyes and sap the life. You will sow your seed in vain, for your enemies will consume the crop. 17 I will turn against you, till you are beaten down before your enemies and lorded over by your foes. You will take to flight though no one pursues you. 18 If even after this you do not obey me, I will increase the chastisement for your sins sevenfold, 19 to break your haughty confidence. I will make the sky above you as hard as iron, and your soil as hard as bronze, 20 so that your strength will be spent in vain; your land will bear no crops, and its trees no fruit. 21 If then you become defiant in your unwillingness to obey me, I will multiply my blows another sevenfold, as your sins deserve. 22 I will unleash the wild beasts against you, to rob you of your children and wipe out your livestock, till your population dwindles away and your roads become deserted. 23 If, with all this, you still refuse to be chastened by me and continue to defy me, 24 I, too, will defy you and will smite you for your sins seven times harder than before. 25 I will make the sword, the avenger of my covenant, sweep over you. Though you then huddle together in your walled cities, I will send in pestilence among you, till you are forced to surrender to the enemy. 26 And as I cut off your supply of bread, ten women will need but one oven for baking all the bread they dole out to you in rations - not enough food to still your hunger. 27 If, despite all this, you still persist in disobeying and defying me, 28 I, also, will meet you with fiery defiance and will chastise you with sevenfold fiercer punishment for your sins, 29 till you begin to eat the flesh of your own sons and daughters. 30 I will demolish your high places, overthrow your incense stands, and cast your corpses on those of your idols. In my abhorrence of you, 31 I will lay waste your cities and devastate your sanctuaries, refusing to accept your sweet-smelling offerings. 32 So devastated will I leave the land that your very enemies who come to live there will stand aghast at the sight of it. 33 You yourselves I will scatter among the nations at the point of my drawn sword, leaving your countryside desolate and your cities deserted. 34 Then shall the land retrieve its lost sabbaths during all the time it lies waste, while you are in the land of your enemies; then shall the land have rest and make up for its sabbaths 35 during all the time that it lies desolate, enjoying the rest that you would not let it have on the sabbaths when you lived there. 36 Those of you who survive in the lands of their enemies I will make so fainthearted that, if leaves rustle behind them, they will flee headlong, as if from the sword, though no one pursues them; 37 stumbling over one another as if to escape a weapon, while no one is after them - so helpless will you be to take a stand against your foes! 38 You will be lost among the Gentiles, swallowed up in your enemies' country. 39 Those of you who survive in the lands of their enemies will waste away for their own and their fathers' guilt. 40 Thus they will have to confess that they and their fathers were guilty of having rebelled against me and of having defied me, 41 so that I, too, had to defy them and bring them into their enemies' land. Then, when their uncircumcised hearts are humbled and they make amends for their guilt, 42 I will remember my covenant with Jacob, my covenant with Isaac, and my covenant with Abraham; and of the land, too, I will be mindful. 43 But the land must first be rid of them, that in its desolation it may make up its lost sabbaths, and that they, too, may make good the debt of their guilt for having spurned my precepts and abhorred my statutes. 44 Yet even so, even while they are in their enemies' land, I will not reject or spurn them, lest, by wiping them out, I make void my covenant with them; for I, the LORD, am their God. 45 I will remember them because of the covenant I made with their forefathers, whom I brought out of the land of Egypt under the very eyes of the Gentiles, that I, the LORD, might be their God. 46 These are the precepts, decrees and laws which the LORD had Moses promulgate on Mount Sinai in the pact between himself and the Israelites.

Leviticus chapter 27

1The LORD said to Moses, 2"Speak to the Israelites and tell them: When anyone fulfills a vow of offering one or more persons to the LORD, who are to be ransomed at a fixed sum of money, 3for persons between the ages of twenty and sixty, the fixed sum, in sanctuary shekels, shall be fifty silver shekels for a man, 4and thirty shekels for a woman; 5for persons between the ages of five and twenty, the fixed sum shall be twenty shekels for a youth, and ten for a maiden; 6for persons between the ages of one month and five years, the fixed sum shall be five silver shekels for a boy, and three for a girl; 7for persons of sixty or more, the fixed sum shall be fifteen shekels for a man, and ten for a woman. 8However, if the one who took the vow is too poor to meet the fixed sum, the person must be set before the priest, who shall determine the sum for his ransom in keeping with the means of the one who made the vow. 9If the offering vowed to the LORD is an animal that may be sacrificed, every such animal, when vowed to the LORD, becomes sacred. 10The offerer shall not present a substitute for it by exchanging either a better for a worse one or a worse for a better one. If he attempts to offer one animal in place of another, both the original and its substitute shall be treated as sacred. 11If the animal vowed to the LORD is unclean and therefore unfit for sacrifice, it must be set before the priest, 12who shall determine its value in keeping with its good or bad qualities, and the value set by the priest shall stand. 13If the offerer wishes to redeem the animal, he shall pay one fifth more than this valuation. 14When someone dedicates his house as sacred to the LORD, the priest shall determine its value in keeping with its good or bad points, and the value set by the priest shall stand. 15If the one who dedicated his house wishes to redeem it, he shall pay one fifth more than the price thus established, and then it will again be his. 16If the object which someone dedicates to the LORD is a piece of his hereditary land, its valuation shall be made according to the amount of seed required to sow it, the acreage sown with a homer of barley seed being valued at fifty silver shekels. 17If the dedication of a field is made at the beginning of a jubilee period, the full valuation shall hold; 18but if it is some time after this, the priest shall estimate its money value according to the number of years left until the next jubilee year, with a corresponding rebate on the valuation. 19If the one who dedicated his field wishes to redeem it, he shall pay one fifth more than the price thus established, and so reclaim it. 20If, instead of redeeming such a field, he sells it to someone else, it may no longer be redeemed; 21but at the jubilee it shall be released as sacred to the LORD; like a field that is doomed, it shall become priestly property. 22If the field that some man dedicates to the LORD is one he had purchased and not a part of his hereditary property, 23the priest shall compute its value in proportion to the number of years until the next jubilee, and on the same day the price thus established shall be given as sacred to the LORD; 24at the jubilee, however, the field shall revert to the hereditary owner of this land from whom it had been purchased. 25Every valuation shall be made according to the standard of the sanctuary shekel. There are twenty gerahs to the shekel. 26Note that a first-born animal, which as such already belongs to the LORD, may not be dedicated by vow to him. If it is an ox or a sheep, it shall be ceded to the LORD; 27but if it is an unclean animal, it may be redeemed by paying one fifth more than its fixed value. If it is not redeemed, it shall be sold at its fixed value. 28Note, also, that any one of his possessions which a man vows as doomed to the LORD, whether it is a human being or an animal or a hereditary field, shall be neither sold nor ransomed; everything that is thus doomed becomes most sacred to the LORD. 29All human beings that are doomed lose the right to be redeemed; they must be put to death. 30All tithes of the land, whether in grain from the fields or in fruit from the trees, belong to the LORD, as sacred to him. 31If someone wishes to buy back any of his tithes, he shall pay one fifth more than their value. 32The tithes of the herd and the flock shall be determined by ceding to the LORD as sacred every tenth animal as they are counted by the herdsman's rod. 33It shall not matter whether good ones or bad ones are thus chosen, and no exchange may be made. If any exchange is attempted, both the original animal and its substitute shall be treated as sacred, without the right of being bought back." 34These are the commandments which the LORD gave Moses on Mount Sinai for the Israelites.

Numbers

Numbers chapter 1

1In the year following that of the Israelites' departure from the land of Egypt, on the first day of the second month, the LORD said to Moses in the meeting tent in the desert of Sinai: 2"Take a census of the whole community of the Israelites, by clans and ancestral houses, registering each male individually. 3You and Aaron shall enroll in companies all the men in Israel of twenty years or more who are fit for military service. 4To assist you there shall be a man from each tribe, the head of his ancestral house. 5These are the names of those who are to assist you: from Reuben: Elizur, son of Shedeur; 6from Simeon: Shelumiel, son of Zurishaddai; 7from Judah: Nahshon, son of Amminadab; 8from Issachar: Nethanel, son of Zuar; 9from Zebulun: Eliab, son of Helon; 10from Ephraim: Elishama, son of Ammihud, and from Manasseh: Gamaliel, son of Pedahzur, for the descendants of Joseph; 11from Benjamin: Abidan, son of Gideoni; 12from Dan: Ahiezer, son of Ammishaddai; 13from Asher: Pagiel, son of Ochran; 14from Gad: Eliasaph, son of Reuel; 15from Naphtali: Ahira, son of Enan." 16These were councilors of the community, princes of their ancestral tribes, chiefs of the troops of Israel. 17So Moses and Aaron took these men who had been designated, 18and assembled the whole community on the first day of the second month. Every man of twenty years or more then declared his name and lineage according to clan and ancestral house, 19as the LORD had commanded Moses. This is their census as taken in the desert of Sinai. 20Of the descendants of Reuben, the first-born of Israel, registered by lineage in clans and ancestral houses: when all the males of twenty years or more who were fit for military service were polled, 21forty-six thousand five hundred were enrolled in the tribe of Reuben. 22Of the descendants of Simeon, registered by lineage in clans and ancestral houses: when all the males of twenty years or more who were fit for military service were polled, 23fifty-nine thousand three hundred were enrolled in the tribe of Simeon. 24Of the descendants of Gad, registered by lineage in clans and ancestral houses: when all the males of twenty years or more who were fit for military service were polled, 25forty-five thousand six hundred and fifty were enrolled in the

tribe of Gad. 26Of the descendants of Judah, registered by lineage in clans and ancestral houses: when all the males of twenty years or more who were fit for military service were polled, 27seventy-four thousand six hundred were enrolled in the tribe of Judah. 28Of the descendants of Issachar, registered by lineage in clans and ancestral houses: when all the males of twenty years or more who were fit for military service were polled, 29fifty-four thousand four hundred were enrolled in the tribe of Issachar. 30Of the descendants of Zebulun, registered by lineage in clans and ancestral houses: when all the males of twenty years or more who were fit for military service were polled, 31fifty-seven thousand four hundred were enrolled in the tribe of Zebulun. 32Of the descendants of Joseph—Of the descendants of Ephraim, registered by lineage in clans and ancestral houses: when all the males of twenty years or more who were fit for military service were polled, 33forty thousand five hundred were enrolled in the tribe of Ephraim. 34Of the descendants of Manasseh, registered by lineage in clans and ancestral houses: when all the males of twenty years or more who were fit for military service were polled, 35thirty-two thousand two hundred were enrolled in the tribe of Manasseh. 36Of the descendants of Benjamin, registered by lineage in clans and ancestral houses: when all the males of twenty years or more who were fit for military service were polled, 37thirty-five thousand four hundred were enrolled in the tribe of Benjamin. 38Of the descendants of Dan, registered by lineage in clans and ancestral houses: when all the males of twenty years or more who were fit for military service were polled, 39sixty-two thousand seven hundred were enrolled in the tribe of Dan. 40Of the descendants of Asher, registered by lineage in clans and ancestral houses: when all the males of twenty years or more who were fit for military service were polled, 41forty-one thousand five hundred were enrolled in the tribe of Asher. 42Of the descendants of Naphtali, registered by lineage in clans and ancestral houses: when all the males of twenty years or more who were fit for military service were polled, 43fifty-three thousand four hundred were enrolled in the tribe of Naphtali. 44It was these who were registered, each according to his ancestral house, in the census taken by Moses and Aaron and the twelve princes of Israel. 45The total number of the Israelites of twenty years or more who were fit for military service, registered by ancestral houses, 46was six hundred and three thousand, five hundred and fifty. 47The Levites, however, were not registered by ancestral tribe with the others. 48For the LORD had told Moses, 49"The tribe of Levi alone you shall not enroll nor include in the census along with the other Israelites. 50You are to give the Levites charge of the Dwelling of the commandments with all its equipment and all that belongs to it. It is they who shall carry the Dwelling with all its equipment and who shall be its ministers. They shall therefore camp around the Dwelling. 51When the Dwelling is to move on, the Levites shall take it down; when the Dwelling is to be pitched, it is the Levites who shall set it up. Any layman who comes near it shall be put to death. 52While the other Israelites shall camp by companies, each in his own division of the camp, 53the Levites shall camp around the Dwelling of the commandments. Otherwise God's wrath will strike the Israelite community. The Levites, then, shall have charge of the Dwelling of the commandments." 54All this the Israelites fulfilled as the LORD had commanded Moses.

Numbers chapter 2

1The LORD said to Moses and Aaron: 2"The Israelites shall camp, each in his own division, under the ensigns of their ancestral houses. They shall camp around the meeting tent, but at some distance from it. 3"Encamped on the east side, toward the sunrise, shall be the divisional camp of Judah, arranged in companies. (The prince of the Judahites was Nahshon, son of Amminadab, 4and his soldiers amounted in the census to seventy-four thousand six hundred.) 5With Judah shall camp the tribe of Issachar (Their prince was Nethanel, son of Zuar, 6and his soldiers amounted in the census to fifty-four thousand four hundred.) 7and the tribe of Zebulun. (Their prince was Eliab, son of Helon, 8and his soldiers amounted in the census to fifty-seven thousand four hundred. 9The total number of those registered by companies in the camp of Judah was one hundred and eighty-six thousand four hundred.) These shall be first on the march. 10"On the south side shall be the divisional camp of Reuben, arranged in companies. (Their prince was Elizur, son of Shedeur, 11and his soldiers amounted in the census to forty-six thousand five hundred.) 12Beside them shall camp the tribe of Simeon (Their prince was Shelumiel, son of Zurishaddai, 13and his soldiers amounted in the census to fifty-nine thousand three hundred.) 14and next the tribe of Gad. (Their prince was Eliasaph, son of Reuel, 15and his soldiers amounted in the census to forty-five thousand six hundred and fifty. 16The total number of those registered by companies in the camp of Reuben was one hundred and fifty-one thousand four hundred and fifty.) These shall be second on the march. 17"Then the meeting tent and the camp of the Levites shall set out in the middle of the line. As in camp, so also on the march, every man shall be in his proper place, with his own division. 18"On the west side shall be the divisional camp of Ephraim, arranged in companies. (Their prince was Elishama, son of Ammihud, 19and his soldiers amounted in the census to forty thousand five hundred.) 20Beside them shall camp the tribe of Manasseh (Their prince was Gamaliel, son of Pedahzur, 21and his soldiers amounted in the census to thirty-two thousand two hundred.) 22and the tribe of Benjamin. (Their prince was Abidan, son of Gideoni, 23and his soldiers amounted in the census to thirty-five thousand four hundred. 24The total number of those registered by companies in the camp of Ephraim was one hundred and eight thousand one hundred.) These shall be third on the march. 25"On the north side shall be the divisional camp of Dan, arranged in companies. (Their prince was Ahiezer, son of Ammishaddai, 26and his soldiers amounted in the census to sixty-two thousand seven hundred.) 27Beside them shall camp the tribe of Asher (Their prince was Pagiel, son of Ochran, 28and his soldiers amounted in the census to forty-one thousand five hundred.) 29and next the tribe of Naphtali. (Their prince was Ahira, son of Enan, 30and his soldiers amounted in the census to fifty-three thousand four hundred. 31The total number of those registered by companies in the camp of Dan was one hundred and fifty-seven thousand six hundred.) These shall be the last of the divisions on the march." 32This was the census of the Israelites taken by ancestral houses. The total number of those registered by companies in the camps was six hundred and three thousand five hundred and fifty. 33The Levites, however, were not registered with the other Israelites, for so the LORD had commanded Moses. 34The Israelites did just as the LORD had commanded Moses; both in camp and on the march, they were in their own divisions, every man according to his clan and his ancestral house.

Numbers chapter 3

1The following were the descendants of Aaron and Moses at the time that the LORD spoke to Moses on Mount Sinai. 2The sons of Aaron were Nadab his first-born, Abihu, Eleazar, and Ithamar. 3These are the names of the sons of Aaron, the anointed priests who were ordained to exercise the priesthood. 4But when Nadab and Abihu offered profane fire before the LORD in the desert of Sinai, they met death in the presence of the LORD, and left no sons. Thereafter only Eleazar and Ithamar performed the priestly functions under the direction of their father Aaron. 5Now the LORD said to Moses: 6"Summon the tribe of Levi and present them to Aaron the priest, as his assistants. 7They shall discharge his obligations and those of the whole community before the meeting tent by serving at the Dwelling. 8They shall have custody of all the furnishings of the meeting tent and discharge the duties of the Israelites in the service of the Dwelling. 9You shall give the Levites to Aaron and his sons; they have been set aside from among the Israelites as dedicated to me. 10But only Aaron and his descendants shall you appoint to have charge of the priestly functions. Any layman who comes near shall be put to death." 11The LORD said to Moses, 12"It is I who have chosen the Levites from the Israelites in place of every first-born that opens the womb among the Israelites. The Levites, therefore, are mine, 13because every first-born is mine. When I slew all the first-born in the land of Egypt, I made all the first-born in Israel sacred to me, both of man and of beast. They belong to me; I am the LORD." 14The LORD said to Moses in the desert of Sinai, 15"Take a census of the Levites by ancestral houses and clans, registering every male of a month or more." 16Moses, therefore, took their census in accordance with the command the LORD had given him. 17The sons of Levi were named Gershon, Kohath and Merari. 18The descendants of Gershon, by clans, were named Libni and Shimei. 19The descendants of Kohath, by clans, were Amram, Izhar, Hebron and Uzziel. 20The descendants of Merari, by clans, were Mahli and Mushi. These were the clans of the Levites by ancestral houses. 21To Gershon belonged the clan of the Libnites and the clan of the Shimeites; these were the clans of the Gershonites. 22When all their males of a month or more were registered, they numbered seven thousand five hundred. 23The clans of the Gershonites camped behind the Dwelling, to the west. 24The prince of their ancestral house was Eliasaph, son of Lael. 25At the meeting tent they had charge of whatever pertained to the Dwelling, the tent and its covering, the curtain at the entrance of the meeting tent, 26the hangings of the court, the curtain at the entrance of the court enclosing both the Dwelling and the altar, and the ropes. 27To Kohath belonged the clans of the Amramites, the Izharites, the Hebronites, and the Uzzielites; these were the clans of the Kohathites. 28When all their males of a month or more were registered, they numbered eight thousand three hundred. They had charge of the sanctuary. 29The clans of the Kohathites camped at the south side of the Dwelling. 30The prince of

their ancestral house was Elizaphan, son of Uzziel. 31They had charge of whatever pertained to the ark, the table, the lampstand, the altars, the utensils with which the ministry of the sanctuary was exercised, and the veil. 32The chief prince of the Levites, however, was Eleazar, son of Aaron the priest; he was supervisor over those who had charge of the sanctuary. 33To Merari belonged the clans of the Mahlites and the Mushites; these were the clans of Merari. 34When all their males of a month or more were registered, they numbered six thousand two hundred. 35The prince of the ancestral house of the clans of Merari was Zuriel, son of Abihail. They camped at the north side of the Dwelling. 36The Merarites were charged with the care of whatever pertained to the boards of the Dwelling, its bars, columns, pedestals, and all its fittings, 37as well as the columns of the surrounding court with their pedestals, pegs and ropes. 38East of the Dwelling, that is, in front of the meeting tent, toward the sunrise, were camped Moses and Aaron and the latter's sons. They discharged the obligations of the sanctuary for the Israelites. Any layman who came near was to be put to death. 39The total number of male Levites a month old or more whom Moses had registered by clans in keeping with the LORD'S command, was twenty-two thousand. 40The LORD then said to Moses, "Take a census of all the first-born males of the Israelites a month old or more, and compute their total number. 41Then assign the Levites to me, the LORD, in place of all the first-born of the Israelites, as well as their cattle in place of all the first-born among the cattle of the Israelites." 42So Moses took a census of all the first-born of the Israelites, as the LORD had commanded him. 43When all the first-born males of a month or more were registered, they numbered twenty-two thousand two hundred and seventy-three. 44The LORD said to Moses: 45"Take the Levites in place of all the first-born of the Israelites, and the Levites' cattle in place of their cattle, that the Levites may belong to me. I am the LORD. 46As ransom for the two hundred and seventy-three first-born of the Israelites who outnumber the Levites, 47you shall take five shekels for each individual, according to the standard of the sanctuary shekel, twenty gerahs to the shekel. 48Give this silver to Aaron and his sons as ransom for the extra number." 49So Moses took the silver as ransom from those who were left when the rest had been redeemed by the Levites. 50From the first-born of the Israelites he received in silver one thousand three hundred and sixty-five shekels according to the sanctuary standard. 51He then gave this ransom silver to Aaron and his sons, as the LORD had commanded him.

Numbers chapter 4

1The LORD said to Moses and Aaron: 2"Among the Levites take a total of the Kohathites, by clans and ancestral houses, all the men of the Kohathites 3between thirty and fifty years of age; these are to undertake obligatory tasks in the meeting tent. 4"The service of the Kohathites in the meeting tent concerns the most sacred objects. 5In breaking camp, Aaron and his sons shall go in and take down the screening curtain and cover the ark of the commandments with it. 6Over these they shall put a cover of tahash skin, and on top of this spread an all-violet cloth. They shall then put the poles in place. 7On the table of the Presence they shall spread a violet cloth and put on it the plates and cups, as well as the bowls and pitchers for libations; the established bread offering shall remain on the table. 8Over these they shall spread a scarlet cloth and cover all this with tahash skin. They shall then put the poles in place. 9They shall use a violet cloth to cover the lampstand with its lamps, trimming shears, and trays, as well as the various containers of oil from which it is supplied. 10The lampstand with all its utensils they shall then enclose in a covering of tahash skin, and place on a litter. 11Over the golden altar they shall spread a violet cloth, and cover this also with a covering of tahash skin. They shall then put the poles in place. 12Taking the utensils of the sanctuary service, they shall wrap them all in violet cloth and cover them with tahash skin. They shall then place them on a litter. 13After cleansing the altar of its ashes, they shall spread a purple cloth over it. 14On this they shall put all the utensils with which it is served: the fire pans, forks, shovels, basins, and all utensils of the altar. They shall then spread a covering of tahash skin over this, and put the poles in place. 15"Only after Aaron and his sons have finished covering the sacred objects and all their utensils on breaking camp, shall the Kohathites enter to carry them. But they shall not touch the sacred objects; if they do they will die. These, then, are the objects in the meeting tent that the Kohathites shall carry. 16"Eleazar, son of Aaron the priest, shall be in charge of the oil for the light, the fragrant incense, the established cereal offering, and the anointing oil. He shall be in charge of the whole Dwelling with all the sacred objects and utensils that are in it." 17The LORD said to Moses and Aaron: 18"Do not let the group of Kohathite clans perish from the body of the Levites. 19That they may live and not die when they approach the most sacred objects, this is what you shall do for them:

Aaron and his sons shall go in and assign to each of them his task and what he must carry; 20but the Kohathites shall not go in to look upon the sacred objects, even for an instant; if they do, they will die." 21The LORD said to Moses, 22"Take a total among the Gershonites also, by ancestral houses and clans, 23of all the men between thirty and fifty years of age; these are to undertake obligatory tasks in the meeting tent. 24This is the task of the clans of the Gershonites, what they must do and what they must carry: 25they shall carry the sheets of the Dwelling, the meeting tent with its covering and the outer wrapping of tahash skin, the curtain at the entrance of the meeting tent, 26the hangings of the court, the curtain at the entrance of the court that encloses both the Dwelling and the altar, together with their ropes and all other objects necessary in their use. Whatever is to be done with these things shall be their task. 27The service of the Gershonites shall be entirely under the direction of Aaron and his sons, with regard to what they must do and what they must carry; you shall make each man of them responsible for what he is to carry. 28This, then, is the task of the Gershonites in the meeting tent; and they shall be under the supervision of Ithamar, son of Aaron the priest. 29"Among the Merarites, too, you shall enroll by clans and ancestral houses 30all their men between thirty and fifty years of age; these are to undertake obligatory tasks in the meeting tent. 31This is what they shall be responsible for carrying, all the years of their service in the meeting tent: the boards of the Dwelling with its bars, columns and pedestals, 32and the columns of the surrounding court with their pedestals, pegs and ropes. You shall designate for each man of them all the objects connected with his service, which he shall be responsible for carrying. 33This, then, is the task of the clans of the Merarites during all their service in the meeting tent under the supervision of Ithamar, son of Aaron the priest." 34So Moses and Aaron and the princes of the community made a registration among the Kohathites, by clans and ancestral houses, 35of all the men between thirty and fifty years of age. These were to undertake obligatory tasks in the meeting tent; 36as registered by clans, they numbered two thousand seven hundred and fifty. 37Such was the census of all the men of the Kohathite clans who were to serve in the meeting tent, which Moses took, together with Aaron, as the LORD bade him. 38The registration was then made among the Gershonites, by clans and ancestral houses, 39of all the men between thirty and fifty years of age. These were to undertake obligatory tasks in the meeting tent; 40as registered by clans and ancestral houses, they numbered two thousand six hundred and thirty. 41Such was the census of all the men of the Gershonite clans who were to serve in the meeting tent, which Moses took, together with Aaron, at the LORD'S bidding. 42Then the registration was made among the Merarites, by clans and ancestral houses, 43of all the men from thirty up to fifty years of age. These were to undertake obligatory tasks in the meeting tent; 44as registered by clans, they numbered three thousand two hundred. 45Such was the census of the men of the Merarite clans which Moses took, together with Aaron, as the LORD bade him. 46Therefore, when Moses and Aaron and the Israelites princes had completed the registration among the Levites, by clans and ancestral houses, 47of all the men between thirty and fifty years of age who were to undertake tasks of service or transport of the meeting tent, 48the total number registered was eight thousand five hundred and eighty. 49According to the LORD'S bidding to Moses, they gave them their individual assignments for service and for transport; so the LORD had commanded Moses.

Numbers chapter 5

1The LORD said to Moses: 2"Order the Israelites to expel from camp every leper, and everyone suffering from a discharge, and everyone who has become unclean by contact with a corpse. 3Male and female alike, you shall compel them to go out of the camp; they are not to defile the camp in which I dwell." 4The Israelites obeyed the command that the LORD had given Moses; they expelled them from the camp. 5The LORD said to Moses, 6"Tell the Israelites: If a man (or a woman) commits a fault against his fellow man and wrongs him, thus breaking faith with the LORD, 7he shall confess the wrong he has done, restore his ill-gotten goods in full, and in addition give one fifth of their value to the one he has wronged. 8However, if the latter has no next of kin to whom restoration of the ill-gotten goods can be made, the goods to be restored shall be the LORD'S and shall fall to the priest; this is apart from the atonement ram with which the priest makes amends for the guilty man. 9Likewise, every sacred contribution that the Israelites are bound to make shall fall to the priest. 10Each Israelite man may dispose of his own sacred contributions; they become the property of the priest to whom he gives them." 11The LORD said to Moses, 12"Speak to the Israelites and tell them: If a man's wife goes astray and becomes unfaithful to him 13by having intercourse with another man, though her husband has not sufficient evidence of the fact, so that her impurity remains unproved for lack of a witness who might have caught her in the act; 14or if a man is overcome by a feeling of jealousy that makes him suspect his wife, whether she was actually impure or not: 15he shall bring his wife to the priest and shall take along as an offering for her a tenth of an ephah of barley meal. However, he shall not pour oil on it nor put frankincense over it, since it is a cereal offering of jealousy, a cereal offering for an appeal in a question of guilt. 16"The priest shall first have the woman come forward and stand before the LORD. 17In an earthen vessel he shall meanwhile put some holy water, as well as some dust that he has taken from the floor of the Dwelling. 18Then, as the woman stands before the LORD, the priest shall uncover her head and place in her hands the cereal offering of her appeal, that is, the cereal offering of jealousy, while he himself shall hold the bitter water that brings a curse. 19Then he shall adjure the woman, saying to her, 'If no other man has had intercourse with you, and you have not gone astray by impurity while under the authority of your husband, be immune to the curse brought by this bitter water. 20But if you have gone astray while under the authority of your husband and have acted impurely by letting a man other than your husband have intercourse with you' - 21so shall the priest adjure the woman with this oath of imprecation - 'may the LORD make you an example of malediction and imprecation among your people by causing your thighs to waste away and your belly to swell! 22May this water, then, that brings a curse, enter your body to make your belly swell and your thighs waste away!' And the woman shall say, 'Amen, amen!' 23The priest shall put these imprecations in writing and shall then wash them off into the bitter water, 24which he is to have the woman drink, so that it may go into her with all its bitter curse. 25But first he shall take the cereal offering of jealousy from the woman's hand, and having waved this offering before the LORD, shall put it near the altar, 26where he shall take a handful of the cereal offering as its token offering and burn it on the altar. Only then shall he have the woman drink the water. 27Once she has done so, if she has been impure and unfaithful to her husband, this bitter water that brings a curse will go into her, and her belly will swell and her thighs will waste away, so that she will become an example of imprecation among her people. 28If, however, the woman has not defiled herself, but is still pure, she will be immune and will still be able to bear children. 29"This, then, is the law for jealousy: When a woman goes astray while under the authority of her husband and acts impurely, 30or when such a feeling of jealousy comes over a man that he becomes suspicious of his wife, he shall have her stand before the LORD, and the priest shall apply this law in full to her. 31The man shall be free from guilt, but the woman shall bear such guilt as she may have."

Numbers chapter 6

1The LORD said to Moses: 2"Speak to the Israelites and tell them: When a man (or a woman) solemnly takes the nazirite vow to dedicate himself to the LORD, 3he shall abstain from wine and strong drink; he may neither drink wine vinegar, other vinegar, of any kind of grape juice, nor eat either fresh or dried grapes. 4As long as he is a nazirite he shall not eat anything of the produce of the vine; not even unripe grapes or grapeskins. 5While he is under the nazirite vow, no razor shall touch his hair. Until the period of his dedication to the LORD is over, he shall be sacred, and shall let the hair of his head grow freely. 6As long as he is dedicated to the LORD, he shall not enter where a dead person is. 7Not even for his father or mother, his sister or brother, should they die, may he become unclean, since his head bears his dedication to God. 8As long as he is a nazirite he is sacred to the LORD. 9"If someone dies very suddenly in his presence, so that his dedicated head becomes unclean, he shall shave his head on the day of his purification, that is, on the seventh day. 10On the eighth day he shall bring two turtledoves or two pigeons to the priest at the entrance of the meeting tent. 11The priest shall offer up the one as a sin offering and the other as a holocaust, thus making atonement for him for the sin he has committed by reason of the dead person. On the same day he shall reconsecrate his head 12and begin anew the period of his dedication to the LORD as a nazirite, bringing a yearling lamb as a guilt offering. The previous period is not valid, because his dedicated head became unclean. 13"This is the ritual for the nazirite: On the day he completes the period of his dedication he shall go to the entrance of the meeting tent, 14bringing as his offering to the LORD one unblemished yearling lamb for a holocaust, one unblemished yearling ewe lamb for a sin offering, one unblemished ram as a peace offering, along with their cereal offerings and libations, 15and a basket of unleavened cakes of fine flour mixed with oil and of unleavened wafers spread with oil. 16The priest shall present them before the LORD, and shall offer up the sin offering and the holocaust for him. 17He shall then offer up the ram as a peace offering to the LORD, with its cereal offering and libation, and the basket of unleavened cakes. 18Then at the entrance of the meeting tent the nazirite shall shave his dedicated head, collect the hair, and put it in the fire that is under the peace offering. ¹⁹After the nazirite has shaved off his dedicated hair, the priest shall take a boiled shoulder of the ram, as well as one unleavened cake and one unleavened wafer from the basket, and shall place them in the hands of the nazirite. ²⁰The priest shall then wave them as a wave offering before the LORD. They become sacred and shall belong to the priest, along with the breast of the wave offering and the leg of the raised offering. Only after this may the nazirite drink wine. ²¹"This, then, is the law for the nazirite; this is the offering to the LORD which is included in his vow of dedication apart from anything else which his means may allow. Thus shall he carry out the law of his dedication in keeping with the vow he has taken." ²²The LORD said to Moses: ²³"Speak to Aaron and his sons and tell them: This is how you shall bless the Israelites. Say to them: ²⁴The LORD bless you and keep you! ²⁵The LORD let his face shine upon you, and be gracious to you! ²⁶The LORD look upon you kindly and give you peace! ²⁷So shall they invoke my name upon the Israelites, and I will bless them."

Numbers chapter 7

¹Now, when Moses had completed the erection of the Dwelling and had anointed and consecrated it with all its equipment (as well as the altar with all its equipment), ²an offering was made by the princes of Israel, who were heads of ancestral houses; the same princes of the tribes who supervised the census. ³The offering they brought before the LORD consisted of six baggage wagons and twelve oxen, that is, a wagon for every two princes, and an ox for every prince. These they presented as their offering before the Dwelling. ⁴The LORD then said to Moses, ⁵"Accept their offering, that these things may be put to use in the service of the meeting tent. Assign them to the Levites, to each group in proportion to its duties." ⁶So Moses accepted the wagons and oxen, and assigned them to the Levites. ⁷He gave two wagons and four oxen to the Gershonites in proportion to their duties, ⁸and four wagons and eight oxen to the Merarites in proportion to their duties, under the supervision of Ithamar, son of Aaron the priest. ⁹He gave none to the Kohathites, because they had to carry on their shoulders the sacred objects which were their charge. ¹⁰For the dedication of the altar also, the princes brought offerings before the altar on the day it was anointed. ¹¹But the LORD said to Moses, "Let one prince a day present his offering for the dedication of the altar." ¹²The one who presented his offering on the first day was Nahshon, son of Amminadab, prince of the tribe of Judah. ¹³His offering consisted of one silver plate weighing a hundred and thirty shekels according to the sanctuary standard and one silver basin weighing seventy shekels, both filled with fine flour mixed with oil for a cereal offering; ¹⁴one gold cup of ten shekels' weight filled with incense; ¹⁵one young bull, one ram, and one yearling lamb for a holocaust; ¹⁶one goat for a sin offering; ¹⁷and two oxen, five rams, five goats, and five yearling lambs for a peace offering. This was the offering of Nahshon, son of Amminadab. ¹⁸On the second day Nethanel, son of Zuar, prince of Issachar, made his offering. ¹⁹He presented as his offering one silver plate weighing a hundred and thirty shekels according to the sanctuary standard and one silver basin weighing seventy shekels, both filled with fine flour mixed with oil for a cereal offering; ²⁰one gold cup of ten shekels' weight filled with incense; ²¹one young bull, one ram, and one yearling lamb for a holocaust; ²²one goat for a sin offering; ²³and two oxen, five rams, five goats, and five yearling lambs for a peace offering. This was the offering of Nethanel, son of Zuar. ²⁴On the third day it was the turn of Eliab, son of Helon, prince of the Zebulunites. ²⁵His offering consisted of one silver plate weighing a hundred and thirty shekels according to the sanctuary standard and one silver basin weighing seventy shekels, both filled with fine flour mixed with oil for a cereal offering; ²⁶one gold cup of ten shekels' weight filled with incense; ²⁷one young bull, one ram, and one yearling lamb for a holocaust; ²⁸one goat for a sin offering; ²⁹and two oxen, five rams, five goats, and five yearling lambs for a peace offering. This was the offering of Eliab, son of Helon. ³⁰On the fourth day it was the turn of Elizur, son of Shedeur, prince of the Reubenites. ³¹His offering consisted of one silver plate weighing a hundred and thirty shekels according to the sanctuary standard and one silver basin weighing seventy shekels, both filled with fine flour mixed with oil for a cereal offering; ³²one gold cup of ten shekels' weight filled with incense; ³³one young bull, one ram, and one yearling lamb for a holocaust; ³⁴one goat for a sin offering; ³⁵and two oxen, five rams, five goats, and five yearling lambs for a peace offering. This was the offering of Elizur, son of Shedeur. ³⁶On the fifth day it was the turn of Shelumiel, son of Zurishaddai, prince of the Simeonites. ³⁷His offering consisted of one silver plate weighing a hundred and thirty shekels according to the sanctuary standard and one silver basin weighing seventy shekels, both filled with fine flour mixed with oil for a cereal offering; ³⁸one gold cup of ten shekels' weight filled with incense; ³⁹one young bull, one ram,

and one yearling lamb for a holocaust; ⁴⁰one goat for a sin offering; ⁴¹and two oxen, five rams, five goats, and five yearling lambs for a peace offering. This was the offering of Shelumiel, son of Zurishaddai. ⁴²On the sixth day it was the turn of Eliasaph, son of Reuel, prince of the Gadites. ⁴³His offering consisted of one silver plate weighing a hundred and thirty shekels according to the sanctuary standard and one silver basin weighing seventy shekels, both filled with fine flour mixed with oil for a cereal offering; ⁴⁴one gold cup of ten shekels' weight filled with incense; ⁴⁵one young bull, one ram, and one yearling lamb for a holocaust; ⁴⁶one goat for a sin offering; ⁴⁷and two oxen, five rams, five goats, and five yearling lambs for a peace offering. This was the offering of Eliasaph, son of Reuel. ⁴⁸On the seventh day it was the turn of Elishama, son of Ammihud, prince of the Ephraimites. ⁴⁹His offering consisted of one silver plate weighing a hundred and thirty shekels according to the sanctuary standard and one silver basin weighing seventy shekels, both filled with fine flour mixed with oil for a cereal offering; ⁵⁰one gold cup of ten shekels' weight filled with incense; ⁵¹one young bull, one ram, and one yearling lamb for a holocaust; ⁵²one goat for a sin offering; ⁵³and two oxen, five rams, five goats, and five yearling lambs for a peace offering. This was the offering of Elishama, son of Ammihud. ⁵⁴On the eighth day it was the turn of Gamaliel, son of Pedahzur, prince of the Manassehites. ⁵⁵His offering consisted of one silver plate weighing a hundred and thirty shekels according to the sanctuary standard and one silver basin weighing seventy shekels, both filled with fine flour mixed with oil for a cereal offering; ⁵⁶one gold cup of ten shekels' weight filled with incense; ⁵⁷one young bull, one ram, and one yearling lamb for a holocaust; ⁵⁸one goat for a sin offering; ⁵⁹and two oxen, five rams, five goats, and five yearling lambs for a peace offering. This was the offering of Gamaliel, son of Pedahzur. ⁶⁰On the ninth day it was the turn of Abidan, son of Gideoni, prince of the Benjaminites. ⁶¹His offering consisted of one silver plate weighing a hundred and thirty shekels according to the sanctuary standard and one silver basin weighing seventy shekels, both filled with fine flour mixed with oil for a cereal offering; ⁶²one gold cup of ten shekels' weight filled with incense; ⁶³one young bull, one ram, and one yearling lamb for a holocaust; ⁶⁴one goat for a sin offering; ⁶⁵and two oxen, five rams, five goats, and five yearling lambs for a peace offering. This was the offering of Abidan, son of Gideoni. ⁶⁶On the tenth day it was the turn of Ahiezer, son of Ammishaddai, prince of the Danites. ⁶⁷His offering consisted of one silver plate weighing a hundred and thirty shekels according to the sanctuary standard and one silver basin weighing seventy shekels, both filled with fine flour mixed with oil for a cereal offering; ⁶⁸one gold cup of ten shekels' weight filled with incense; ⁶⁹one young bull, one ram, and one yearling lamb for a holocaust; ⁷⁰one goat for a sin offering; ⁷¹and two oxen, five rams, five goats, and five yearling lambs for a peace offering. This was the offering of Ahiezer, son of Ammishaddai. ⁷²On the eleventh day it was the turn of Pagiel, son of Ochran, prince of the Asherites. ⁷³His offering consisted of one silver plate weighing one hundred and thirty shekels according to the sanctuary standard and one silver basin weighing seventy shekels, both filled with fine flour mixed with oil for a cereal offering; ⁷⁴one gold cup of ten shekels' weight filled with incense; ⁷⁵one young bull, one ram, and one yearling lamb for a holocaust; ⁷⁶one goat for a sin offering; ⁷⁷and two oxen, five rams, five goats, and five yearling lambs for a peace offering. This was the offering of Pagiel, son of Ochran. ⁷⁸On the twelfth day it was the turn of Ahira, son of Enan, prince of the Naphtalites. ⁷⁹His offering consisted of one silver plate weighing a hundred and thirty shekels according to the sanctuary standard and one silver basin weighing seventy shekels, both filled with fine flour mixed with oil for a cereal offering; ⁸⁰one gold cup of ten shekels' weight filled with incense; ⁸¹one young bull, one ram, and one yearling lamb for a holocaust; ⁸²one goat for a sin offering; ⁸³and two oxen, five rams, five goats, and five yearling lambs for a peace offering. This was the offering of Ahira, son of Enan. ⁸⁴These were the offerings for the dedication of the altar, given by the princes of Israel on the occasion of its anointing: twelve silver plates, twelve silver basins, and twelve gold cups. ⁸⁵Each silver plate weighed a hundred and thirty shekels, and each silver basin seventy, so that all the silver of these vessels amounted to two thousand four hundred shekels, according to the sanctuary standard. ⁸⁶The twelve gold cups that were filled with incense weighed ten shekels apiece, according to the sanctuary standard, so that all the gold of the cups amounted to one hundred and twenty shekels. ⁸⁷The animals for the holocausts were, in all, twelve young bulls, twelve rams, and twelve yearling lambs, with their cereal offerings; those for the sin offerings were twelve goats. ⁸⁸The animals for the peace offerings were, in all, twenty-four oxen, sixty rams, sixty goats, and sixty yearling lambs. These, then, were the offerings for the dedication of the altar after it was anointed. ⁸⁹When Moses entered the meeting tent to speak with him, he heard the voice addressing him from above the propitiatory on the ark of the commandments, from between the two cherubim; and it spoke to him.

Numbers chapter 8

¹The LORD spoke to Moses, and said, ²"Give Aaron this command: When you set up the seven lamps, have them throw their light toward the front of the lampstand." ³Aaron did so, setting up the lamps to face toward the front of the lampstand, just as the LORD had commanded Moses. ⁴The lampstand was made of beaten gold in both its shaft and its branches, according to the pattern which the LORD had shown Moses. ⁵The LORD said to Moses: ⁶"Take the Levites from among the Israelites and purify them. ⁷This is what you shall do to them to purify them. Sprinkle them with the water of remission; then have them shave their whole bodies and wash their clothes, and so purify themselves. ⁸They shall take a young bull, along with its cereal offering of fine flour mixed with oil; you shall take another young bull for a sin offering. ⁹Then have the Levites come forward in front of the meeting tent, where you shall assemble also the whole community of the Israelites. ¹⁰While the Levites are present before the LORD, the Israelites shall lay their hands upon them. ¹¹Let Aaron then offer the Levites before the LORD as a wave offering from the Israelites, thus devoting them to the service of the LORD. ¹²The Levites in turn shall lay their hands on the heads of the bullocks, which shall then be immolated, the one as a sin offering and the other as a holocaust to the LORD, in atonement for the Levites. ¹³Thus, then, shall you have the Levites stand before Aaron and his sons, to be offered as a wave offering to the LORD; ¹⁴and thus shall you set aside the Levites from the rest of the Israelites, that they may be mine. ¹⁵"Only then shall the Levites enter upon their service in the meeting tent. You shall purify them and offer them as a wave offering; ¹⁶because they, among the Israelites, are strictly dedicated to me; I have taken them for myself in place of every first-born that opens the womb among the Israelites. ¹⁷Indeed, all the first-born among the Israelites, both of man and of beast, belong to me; I consecrated them to myself on the day I slew all the first-born in the land of Egypt. ¹⁸But in place of all the first-born Israelites I have taken the Levites; ¹⁹and I have given these dedicated Israelites to Aaron and his sons to discharge the duties of the Israelites in the meeting tent and to make atonement for them, so that no plague may strike among the Israelites should they come near the sanctuary." ²⁰Thus, then, did Moses and Aaron and the whole community of the Israelites deal with the Levites, carrying out exactly the command which the LORD had given Moses concerning them. ²¹When the Levites had cleansed themselves of sin and washed their clothes, Aaron offered them as a wave offering before the LORD, and made atonement for them to purify them. ²²Only then did they enter upon their service in the meeting tent under the supervision of Aaron and his sons. The command which the LORD had given Moses concerning the Levites was carried out. ²³The LORD said to Moses: ²⁴"This is the rule for the Levites. Each from his twenty-fifth year onward shall perform the required service in the meeting tent. ²⁵When he is fifty years old, he shall retire from the required service and work no longer. ²⁶His service with his fellow Levites shall consist in sharing their responsibilities in the meeting tent, but he shall not do the work. This, then, is how you are to regulate the duties of the Levites."

Numbers chapter 9

¹In the first month of the year following their departure from the land of Egypt, the Lord said to Moses in the desert of Sinai, ²"Tell the Israelites to celebrate the Passover at the prescribed time. ³The evening twilight of the fourteenth day of this month is the prescribed time when you shall celebrate it, observing all its rules and regulations." ⁴Moses, therefore, told the Israelites to celebrate the Passover. ⁵And they did so, celebrating the Passover in the desert of Sinai during the evening twilight of the fourteenth day of the first month, just as the LORD had commanded Moses. ⁶There were some, however, who were unclean because of a human corpse and so could not keep the Passover that day. These men came up to Moses and Aaron that same day ⁷and said, "Although we are unclean because of a corpse, why should we be deprived of presenting the LORD'S offering at its proper time along with the other Israelites?" ⁸Moses answered them, "Wait until I learn what the LORD will command in your regard." ⁹The LORD then said to Moses: ¹⁰"Speak to the Israelites and say: If any one of you or of your descendants is unclean because of a corpse, or if he is absent on a journey, he may still keep the LORD'S Passover. ¹¹But he shall keep it in the second month, during the evening twilight of the fourteenth day of that month, eating it with unleavened bread and bitter herbs, ¹²and not leaving any of it over till morning, nor breaking any of its bones, but observing all the rules of the Passover. ¹³However, anyone who is clean and not away on a journey, who yet fails to keep the Passover, shall be cut off from his people, because he did not present the LORD'S offering

at the prescribed time. That man shall bear the consequences of his sin. ¹⁴"If an alien who lives among you wishes to keep the LORD'S Passover, he too shall observe the rules and regulations for the Passover. You shall have the same law for the resident alien as for the native of the land." ¹⁵On the day when the Dwelling was erected, the cloud covered the Dwelling, the tent of the commandments; but from evening until morning it took on the appearance of fire over the Dwelling. ¹⁶It was always so: during the day the Dwelling was covered by the cloud, which at night had the appearance of fire. ¹⁷Whenever the cloud rose from the tent, the Israelites would break camp; wherever the cloud came to rest, they would pitch camp. ¹⁸At the bidding of the LORD the Israelites moved on, and at his bidding they encamped. As long as the cloud stayed over the Dwelling, they remained in camp. ¹⁹Even when the cloud tarried many days over the Dwelling, the Israelites obeyed the LORD and would not move on; ²⁰sometimes the cloud was over the Dwelling only for a few days. It was at the bidding of the LORD that they stayed in camp, and it was at his bidding that they departed. ²¹Sometimes the cloud remained there only from evening until morning; and when it rose in the morning, they would depart. Or if the cloud lifted during the day, or even at night, they would then set out. ²²Whether the cloud tarried over the Dwelling for two days or for a month or longer, the Israelites remained in camp and did not depart; but when it lifted, they moved on. ²³Thus, it was always at the bidding of the LORD that they encamped, and at his bidding that they set out; ever heeding the charge of the LORD, as he had bidden them through Moses.

Numbers chapter 10

¹The LORD said to Moses: ²"Make two trumpets of beaten silver, which you shall use in assembling the community and in breaking camp. ³When both are blown, the whole community shall gather round you at the entrance of the meeting tent; ⁴but when one of them is blown, only the princes, the chiefs of the troops of Israel, shall gather round you. ⁵When you sound the first alarm, those encamped on the east side shall set out; ⁶when you sound the second alarm, those encamped on the south side shall set out; when you sound the third alarm, those encamped on the west side shall set out; when you sound the fourth alarm, those encamped on the north side shall set out. Thus shall the alarm be sounded for them to depart. ⁷But in calling forth an assembly you are to blow an ordinary blast, without sounding the alarm. ⁸"It is the sons of Aaron, the priests, who shall blow the trumpets; and the use of them is prescribed by perpetual statute for you and your descendants. ⁹When in your own land you go to war against an enemy that is attacking you, you shall sound the alarm on the trumpets, and the LORD, your God, will remember you and save you from your foes. ¹⁰On your days of celebration, your festivals, and your new-moon feasts, you shall blow the trumpets over your holocausts and your peace offerings; this will serve as a reminder of you before your God. I, the LORD, am your God." ¹¹In the second year, on the twentieth day of the second month, the cloud rose from the Dwelling of the commandments. ¹²The Israelites moved on from the desert of Sinai by stages, until the cloud came to rest in the desert of Paran. ¹³The first time that they broke camp at the bidding of the LORD through Moses, ¹⁴the camp of the Judahites, under its own standard and arranged in companies, was the first to set out. Nahshon, son of Amminadab, was over their host, ¹⁵and Nethanel, son of Zuar, over the host of the tribe of Issachar, ¹⁶and Eliab, son of Helon, over the host of the tribe of Zebulun. ¹⁷Then, after the Dwelling was dismantled, the clans of Gershon and Merari set out, carrying the Dwelling. ¹⁸The camp of the Reubenites, under its own standard and arranged in companies, was the next to set out, with Elizur, son of Shedeur, over their host, ¹⁹and Shelumiel, son of Zurishaddai, over the host of the tribe of Simeon, ²⁰and Eliasaph, son of Reuel, over the host of the tribe of Gad. ²¹The clan of Kohath then set out, carrying the sacred objects for the Dwelling, which was to be erected before their arrival. ²²The camp of the Ephraimites next set out, under its own standard and arranged in companies, with Elishama, son of Ammihud, over their host, ²³and Gamaliel, son of Pedahzur, over the host of the tribe of Manasseh, ²⁴and Abidan, son of Gideoni, over the host of the tribe of Benjamin. ²⁵Finally, as rear guard for all the camps, the camp of the Danites set out, under its own standard and arranged in companies, with Ahiezer, son of Ammishaddai, over their host, ²⁶and Pagiel, son of Ochran, over the host of the tribe of Asher, ²⁷and Ahira, son of Enan, over the host of the tribe of Naphtali. ²⁸This was the order of departure for the Israelites, company by company. As they were setting out, ²⁹Moses said to his brother-in-law Hobab, son of Reuel the Midianite, "We are setting out for the place which the LORD has promised to give us. Come with us, and we will be generous toward you, for the LORD has promised prosperity to Israel." ³⁰But he answered, "No, I will not come. I am going instead to my own country and to my

own kindred." 31Moses said, "Please, do not leave us; you know where we can camp in the desert, and you will serve as eyes for us. 32If you come with us, we will share with you the prosperity the LORD will bestow on us." 33They moved on from the mountain of the LORD, a three days' journey, and the ark of the covenant of the LORD which was to seek out their resting place went the three days' journey with them. 34And when they set out from camp, the cloud of the LORD was over them by day. 35Whenever the ark set out, Moses would say, "Arise, O LORD, that your enemies may be scattered, and those who hate you may flee before you." 36And when it came to rest, he would say, "Return, O LORD, you who ride upon the clouds, to the troops of Israel."

Numbers chapter 11

1Now the people complained in the hearing of the LORD; and when he heard it his wrath flared up so that the fire of the LORD burned among them and consumed the outskirts of the camp. 2But when the people cried out to Moses, he prayed to the LORD and the fire died out. 3Hence that place was called Taberah, because there the fire of the LORD burned among them." 4The foreign elements among them were so greedy for meat that even the Israelites lamented again, "Would that we had meat for food! 5We remember the fish we used to eat without cost in Egypt, and the cucumbers, the melons, the leeks, the onions, and the garlic. 6But now we are famished; we see nothing before us but this manna." 7Manna was like coriander seed and had the appearance of bdellium. 8When they had gone about and gathered it up, the people would grind it between millstones or pound it in a mortar, then cook it in a pot and make it into loaves, which tasted like cakes made with oil. 9At night, when the dew fell upon the camp, the manna also fell. 10When Moses heard the people, family after family, crying at the entrance of their tents, so that the LORD became very angry, he was grieved. 11"Why do you treat your servant so badly?" Moses asked the LORD. "Why are you so displeased with me that you burden me with all this people? 12Was it I who conceived all this people? or was it I who gave them birth, that you tell me to carry them at my bosom, like a foster father carrying an infant, to the land you have promised under oath to their fathers? 13Where can I get meat to give to all this people? For they are crying to me, 'Give us meat for our food.' 14I cannot carry all this people by myself, for they are too heavy for me. 15If this is the way you will deal with me, then please do me the favor of killing me at once, so that I need no longer face this distress." 16Then the LORD said to Moses, "Assemble for me seventy of the elders of Israel, men you know for true elders and authorities among the people, and bring them to the meeting tent. When they are in place beside you, 17I will come down and speak with you there. I will also take some of the spirit that is on you and will bestow it on them, that they may share the burden of the people with you. You will then not have to bear it by yourself alone. 18"To the people, however, you shall say: Sanctify yourselves for tomorrow, when you shall have meat to eat. For in the hearing of the LORD you have cried, 'Would that we had meat for food! Oh, how well off we were in Egypt!' Therefore the LORD will give you meat for food, 19and you will eat it, not for one day, or two days, or five, or ten, or twenty days, 20but for a whole month—until it comes out of your very nostrils and becomes loathsome to you. For you have spurned the LORD who is in your midst, and in his presence you have wailed, 'Why did we ever leave Egypt?'" 21But Moses said, "The people around me include six hundred thousand soldiers; yet you say, 'I will give them meat to eat for a whole month.' 22Can enough sheep and cattle be slaughtered for them? If all the fish of the sea were caught for them, would they have enough?" 23The LORD answered Moses, "Is this beyond the LORD'S reach? You shall see now whether or not what I have promised you takes place." 24So Moses went out and told the people what the LORD had said. Gathering seventy elders of the people, he had them stand around the tent. 25The LORD then came down in the cloud and spoke to him. Taking some of the spirit that was on Moses, he bestowed it on the seventy elders; and as the spirit came to rest on them, they prophesied. 26Now two men, one named Eldad and the other Medad, were not in the gathering but had been left in the camp. They too had been on the list, but had not gone out to the tent; yet the spirit came to rest on them also, and they prophesied in the camp. 27So, when a young man quickly told Moses, "Eldad and Medad are prophesying in the camp," 28Joshua, son of Nun, who from his youth had been Moses' aide, said, "Moses, my lord, stop them." 29But Moses answered him, "Are you jealous for my sake? Would that all the people of the LORD were prophets! Would that the LORD might bestow his spirit on them all!" 30Then Moses retired to the camp, along with the elders of Israel. 31There arose a wind sent by the LORD, that drove in quail from the sea and brought them down over the campsite at a height of two cubits from the ground for the distance of a day's journey all around the camp. 32All that day, all night,

and all the next day the people gathered in the quail. Even the one who got the least gathered ten homers of them. Then they spread them out all around the camp. 33But while the meat was still between their teeth, before it could be consumed, the LORD'S wrath flared up against the people, and he struck them with a very great plague. 34So that place was named Kibroth-hattaavah, because it was there that the greedy people were buried. 35From Kibroth-hattaavah the people set out for Hazeroth.

Numbers chapter 12

1While they were in Hazeroth, Miriam and Aaron spoke against Moses on the pretext of the marriage he had contracted with a Cushite woman. 2They complained, "Is it through Moses alone that the LORD speaks? Does he not speak through us also?" And the LORD heard this. 3Now, Moses himself was by far the meekest man on the face of the earth. 4So at once the LORD said to Moses and Aaron and Miriam, "Come out, you three, to the meeting tent." And the three of them went. 5Then the LORD came down in the column of cloud, and standing at the entrance of the tent, called Aaron and Miriam. When both came forward, 6he said, "Now listen to the words of the LORD: Should there be a prophet among you, in visions will I reveal myself to him, in dreams will I speak to him; 7Not so with my servant Moses! Throughout my house he bears my trust: 8face to face I speak to him, plainly and not in riddles. The presence of the LORD he beholds. Why, then, did you not fear to speak against my servant Moses?" 9So angry was the LORD against them that when he departed, 10and the cloud withdrew from the tent, there was Miriam, a snow-white leper! When Aaron turned and saw her a leper, 11"Ah, my lord!" he said to Moses, "please do not charge us with the sin that we have foolishly committed! 12Let her not thus be like the stillborn babe that comes forth from its mother's womb with its flesh half consumed." 13Then Moses cried to the LORD, "Please, not this! Pray, heal her!" 14But the LORD answered Moses, "Suppose her father had spit in her face, would she not hide in shame for seven days? Let her be confined outside the camp for seven days; only then may she be brought back." 15So Miriam was confined outside the camp for seven days, and the people did not start out again until she was brought back. 16After that the people set out from Hazeroth and encamped in the desert of Paran.

Numbers chapter 13

1The LORD said to Moses, 2"Send men to reconnoiter the land of Canaan, which I am giving to the Israelites. You shall send one man from each ancestral tribe, all of them princes." 3So Moses dispatched them from the desert of Paran, as the LORD had ordered. All of them were leaders among the Israelites; 4by name they were: Shammua, son of Zaccur, of the tribe of Reuben; 5Shaphat, son of Hori, of the tribe of Simeon; 6Caleb, son of Jephunneh, of the tribe of Judah; 7Igal (son of Joseph), of the tribe of Issachar; 8Hoshea, son of Nun, of the tribe of Ephraim; 9Palti, son of Raphu, of the tribe of Benjamin; 10Gaddiel, son of Sodi, of the tribe of Zebulun; 11Gaddi, son of Susi, of the tribe of Manasseh, for the Josephites, with 12Ammiel, son of Gemalli, of the tribe of Dan; 13Sethur, son of Michael, of the tribe of Asher; 14Nahbi, son of Vophsi, of the tribe of Naphtali; 15Geuel, son of Machi, of the tribe of Gad. 16These are the names of the men whom Moses sent out to reconnoiter the land. But Hoshea, son of Nun, Moses called Joshua. 17In sending them to reconnoiter the land of Canaan, Moses said to them, "Go up here in the Negeb, up into the highlands, 18and see what kind of land it is. Are the people living there strong or weak, few or many? 19Is the country in which they live good or bad? Are the towns in which they dwell open or fortified? 20Is the soil fertile or barren, wooded or clear? And do your best to get some of the fruit of the land." It was then the season for early grapes. 21So they went up and reconnoitered the land from the desert of Zin as far as where Rehob adjoins Labo of Hamath. 22Going up by way of the Negeb, they reached Hebron, where Ahiman, Sheshai and Talmai, descendants of the Anakim, were living. (Hebron had been built seven years before Zoan in Egypt.) 23They also reached the Wadi Eshcol, where they cut down a branch with a single cluster of grapes on it, which two of them carried on a pole, as well as some pomegranates and figs. 24It was because of the cluster the Israelites cut there that they called the place Wadi Eshcol. 25After reconnoitering the land for forty days they returned, 26met Moses and Aaron and the whole community of the Israelites in the desert of Paran at Kadesh, made a report to them all, and showed them the fruit of the country. 27They told Moses: "We went into the land to which you sent us. It does indeed flow with milk and honey, and here is its fruit. 28However, the people who are living in the land are fierce, and the towns are fortified and very strong. Besides, we saw descendants of the Anakim there. 29Amalekites live in the region of the Negeb; Hittites, Jebusites and Amorites dwell in the highlands, and

Canaanites along the seacoast and the banks of the Jordan." ³⁰Caleb, however, to quiet the people toward Moses, said, "We ought to go up and seize the land, for we can certainly do so." ³¹But the men who had gone up with him said, "We cannot attack these people; they are too strong for us." ³²So they spread discouraging reports among the Israelites about the land they had scouted, saying, "The land that we explored is a country that consumes its inhabitants. And all the people we saw there are huge men, ³³veritable giants (the Anakim were a race of giants); we felt like mere grasshoppers, and so we must have seemed to them."

Numbers chapter 14

¹At this, the whole community broke out with loud cries, and even in the night the people wailed. ²All the Israelites grumbled against Moses and Aaron, the whole community saying to them, "Would that we had died in the land of Egypt, or that here in the desert we were dead! ³Why is the LORD bringing us into this land only to have us fall by the sword? Our wives and little ones will be taken as booty. Would it not be better for us to return to Egypt?" ⁴So they said to one another, "Let us appoint a leader and go back to Egypt." ⁵But Moses and Aaron fell prostrate before the whole assembled community of the Israelites; ⁶while Joshua, son of Nun, and Caleb, son of Jephunneh, who had been in the party that scouted the land, tore their garments ⁷and said to the whole community of the Israelites, "The country which we went through and explored is a fine, rich land. ⁸If the LORD is pleased with us, he will bring us in and give us that land, a land flowing with milk and honey. ⁹But do not rebel against the LORD! You need not be afraid of the people of that land; they are but food for us! Their defense has left them, but the LORD is with us. Therefore, do not be afraid of them." ¹⁰In answer, the whole community threatened to stone them. But then the glory of the LORD appeared at the meeting tent to all the Israelites. ¹¹And the LORD said to Moses, "How long will this people spurn me? How long will they refuse to believe in me, despite all the signs I have performed among them? ¹²I will strike them with pestilence and wipe them out. Then I will make of you a nation greater and mightier than they." ¹³But Moses said to the LORD: "Are the Egyptians to hear of this? For by your power you brought out this people from among them. ¹⁴And are they to tell of it to the inhabitants of this land? It has been heard that you, O LORD, are in the midst of this people; you, LORD, who plainly reveal yourself! Your cloud stands over them, and you go before them by day in a column of cloud and by night in a column of fire. ¹⁵If now you slay this whole people, the nations who have heard such reports of you will say, ¹⁶'The LORD was not able to bring this people into the land he swore to give them; that is why he slaughtered them in the desert.' ¹⁷Now then, let the power of my Lord be displayed in its greatness, even as you have said, ¹⁸'The LORD is slow to anger and rich in kindness, forgiving wickedness and crime; yet not declaring the guilty guiltless, but punishing children to the third and fourth generation for their fathers' wickedness.' ¹⁹Pardon, then, the wickedness of this people in keeping with your great kindness, even as you have forgiven them from Egypt until now." ²⁰The LORD answered: "I pardon them as you have asked. ²¹Yet, by my life and the LORD'S glory that fills the whole earth, ²²of all the men who have seen my glory and the signs I worked in Egypt and in the desert, and who nevertheless have put me to the test ten times already and have failed to heed my voice, ²³not one shall see the land which I promised on oath to their fathers. None of these who have spurned me shall see it. ²⁴But because my servant Caleb has a different spirit and follows me unreservedly, I will bring him into the land where he has just been, and his descendants shall possess it. ²⁵But now, since the Amalekites and Canaanites are living in the valleys, turn away tomorrow and set out in the desert on the Red Sea road." ²⁶The LORD also said to Moses and Aaron: ²⁷"How long will this wicked community grumble against me? I have heard the grumblings of the Israelites against me. ²⁸Tell them: By my life, says the LORD, I will do to you just what I have heard you say. ²⁹Here in the desert shall your dead bodies fall. Of all your men of twenty years or more, registered in the census, who grumbled against me, ³⁰not one shall enter the land where I solemnly swore to settle you, except Caleb, son of Jephunneh, and Joshua, son of Nun. ³¹Your little ones, however, who you said would be taken as booty, I will bring in, and they shall appreciate the land you spurned. ³²But as for you, your bodies shall fall here in the desert, ³³here where your children must wander for forty years, suffering for your faithlessness, till the last of you lies dead in the desert. ³⁴Forty days you spent in scouting the land; forty years shall you suffer for your crimes: one year for each day. Thus you will realize what it means to oppose me. ³⁵I, the LORD, have sworn to do this to all this wicked community that conspired against me: here in the desert they shall die to the last man." ³⁶And so it happened to the men whom Moses had sent to reconnoiter the land and who on returning had set the whole

community grumbling against him by spreading discouraging reports about the land; ³⁷these men who had given out the bad report about the land were struck down by the LORD and died. ³⁸Of all the men who had gone to reconnoiter the land, only Joshua, son of Nun, and Caleb, son of Jephunneh, survived. ³⁹When Moses repeated these words to all the Israelites, the people felt great remorse. ⁴⁰Early the next morning they started up into the foothills, saying, "Here we are, ready to go up to the place that the LORD spoke of: for we were indeed doing wrong." ⁴¹But Moses said, "Why are you again disobeying the LORD'S orders? This cannot succeed. ⁴²Do not go up, because the LORD is not in your midst; if you go, you will be beaten down before your enemies. ⁴³For there the Amalekites and Canaanites face you, and you will fall by the sword. You have turned back from following the LORD; therefore the LORD will not be with you." ⁴⁴Yet they dared to go up into the foothills, even though neither the ark of the covenant of the LORD nor Moses left the camp. ⁴⁵And the Amalekites and Canaanites who dwelt in that hill country came down and defeated them, beating them back as far as Hormah.

Numbers chapter 15

¹The LORD said to Moses, ²"Give the Israelites these instructions: When you have entered the land that I will give you for your homesteads, ³if you make to the LORD a sweet-smelling oblation from the herd or from the flock, in holocaust, in fulfillment of a vow, or as a freewill offering, or for one of your festivals, ⁴whoever does so shall also present to the LORD a cereal offering consisting of a tenth of an ephah of fine flour mixed with a fourth of a hin of oil, ⁵as well as a libation of a fourth of a hin of wine, with each lamb sacrificed in holocaust or otherwise. ⁶With each sacrifice of a ram you shall present a cereal offering of two tenths of an ephah of fine flour mixed with a third of a hin of oil, ⁷and a libation of a third of a hin of wine, thus making a sweet-smelling offering to the LORD. ⁸When you sacrifice an ox as a holocaust, or in fulfillment of a vow, or as a peace offering to the LORD, ⁹with it you shall present a cereal offering of three tenths of an ephah of fine flour mixed with half a hin of oil, ¹⁰and a libation of half a hin of wine, as a sweet-smelling oblation to the LORD. ¹¹The same is to be done for each ox, ram, lamb or goat. ¹²Whatever the number you offer, do the same for each of them. ¹³All the native-born shall make these offerings in the same way, whenever they present a sweet-smelling oblation to the LORD. ¹⁴Likewise, in any future generation, any alien residing with you permanently or for a time, who presents a sweet-smelling oblation to the LORD, shall do as you do. ¹⁵There is but one rule for you and for the resident alien, a perpetual rule for all your descendants. Before the LORD you and the alien are alike, ¹⁶with the same law and the same application of it for the alien residing among you as for yourselves." ¹⁷The LORD said to Moses, ¹⁸"Speak to the Israelites and tell them: When you enter the land into which I will bring you ¹⁹and begin to eat of the food of that land, you shall offer the LORD a contribution ²⁰consisting of a cake of your first batch of dough. You shall offer it just as you offer a contribution from the threshing floor. ²¹Throughout your generations you shall give a contribution to the LORD from your first batch of dough. ²²"When through inadvertence you fail to carry out any of these commandments which the LORD gives to Moses, ²³and through Moses to you, from the time the LORD first issues the commandment down through your generations: ²⁴if the community itself unwittingly becomes guilty of the fault of inadvertence, the whole community shall offer the holocaust of one young bull as a sweet-smelling oblation pleasing to the LORD, along with its prescribed cereal offering and libation, as well as one he-goat as a sin offering. ²⁵Then the priest shall make atonement for the whole Israelite community; thus they will be forgiven the inadvertence for which they have brought their holocaust as an oblation to the LORD. ²⁶Not only the whole Israelite community, but also the aliens residing among you, shall be forgiven, since the fault of inadvertence affects all the people. ²⁷"However, if it is an individual who sins inadvertently, he shall bring a yearling she-goat as a sin offering, ²⁸and the priest shall make atonement before the LORD for him who sinned inadvertently; when atonement has been made for him, he will be forgiven. ²⁹You shall have but one law for him who sins inadvertently, whether he be a native Israelite or an alien residing with you. ³⁰"But anyone who sins defiantly, whether he be a native or an alien, insults the LORD, and shall be cut off from among his people. ³¹Since he has despised the word of the LORD and has broken his commandment, he must be cut off. He has only himself to blame." ³²While the Israelites were in the desert, a man was discovered gathering wood on the sabbath day. ³³Those who caught him at it brought him to Moses and Aaron and the whole assembly. ³⁴But they kept him in custody, for there was no clear

decision as to what should be done with him. 35Then the LORD said to Moses, "This man shall be put to death; let the whole community stone him outside the camp." 36So the whole community led him outside the camp and stoned him to death, as the LORD had commanded Moses. 37The LORD said to Moses, 38"Speak to the Israelites and tell them that they and their descendants must put tassels on the corners of their garments, fastening each corner tassel with a violet cord. 39When you use these tassels, let the sight of them remind you to keep all the commandments of the LORD, without going wantonly astray after the desires of your hearts and eyes. 40Thus you will remember to keep all my commandments and be holy to your God. 41I, the LORD, am your God who, as God, brought you out of Egypt that I, the LORD, may be your God."

Numbers chapter 16

1Korah, son of Izhar, son of Kohath, son of Levi, (and Dathan and Abiram, sons of Eliab, son of Pallu, son of Reuben) took 2two hundred and fifty Israelites who were leaders in the community, members of the council and men of note. They stood before Moses, 3and held an assembly against Moses and Aaron, to whom they said, "Enough from you! The whole community, all of them, are holy; the LORD is in their midst. Why then should you set yourselves over the LORD'S congregation?" 4When Moses heard this, he fell prostrate. 5Then he said to Korah and to all his band, "May the LORD make known tomorrow morning who belongs to him and who is the holy one and whom he will have draw near to him! Whom he chooses, he will have draw near him. 6Do this: take your censers (Korah and all his band) 7and put fire in them and place incense in them before the LORD tomorrow. He whom the LORD then chooses is the holy one. Enough from you Levites!" 8Moses also said to Korah, "Listen to me, you Levites! 9Is it too little for you that the God of Israel has singled you out from the community of Israel, to have you draw near him for the service of the LORD'S Dwelling and to stand before the community to minister for them? 10He has allowed you and your kinsmen, the descendants of Levi, to approach him, and yet you now seek the priesthood too. 11It is therefore against the LORD that you and all your band are conspiring. For what has Aaron done that you should grumble against him?" 12Moses summoned Dathan and Abiram, sons of Eliab, but they answered, "We will not go. 13Are you not satisfied with having led us here away from a land flowing with milk and honey, to make us perish in the desert, that you must now lord it over us? 14Far from bringing us to a land flowing with milk and honey, or giving us fields and vineyards for our inheritance, will you also gouge out our eyes? No, we will not go." 15Then Moses became very angry and said to the LORD, "Pay no heed to their offering. I have never taken a single ass from them, nor have I wronged any one of them." 16Moses said to Korah, "You and all your band shall appear before the LORD tomorrow—you and they and Aaron too. 17Then each of your two hundred and fifty followers shall take his own censer, put incense in it, and offer it to the LORD; and you and Aaron, each with his own censer, shall do the same." 18So they all took their censers, and laying incense on the fire they had put in them, they took their stand by the entrance of the meeting tent along with Moses and Aaron. 19Then, when Korah had assembled all his band against them at the entrance of the meeting tent, the glory of the LORD appeared to the entire community, 20and the LORD said to Moses and Aaron, 21"Stand apart from this band, that I may consume them at once." 22But they fell prostrate and cried out, "O God, God of the spirits of all mankind, will one man's sin make you angry with the whole community?" 23The LORD answered Moses, 24"Speak to the community and tell them: Withdraw from the space around the Dwelling" (of Korah, Dathan and Abiram). 25Moses, followed by the elders of Israel, arose and went to Dathan and Abiram. 26Then he warned the community, "Keep away from the tents of these wicked men and do not touch anything that is theirs: otherwise you too will be swept away because of all their sins." 27When Dathan and Abiram had come out and were standing at the entrances of their tents with their wives and sons and little ones, 28Moses said, "This is how you shall know that it was the LORD who sent me to do all I have done, and that it was not I who planned it: 29if these men die an ordinary death, merely suffering the fate common to all mankind, then it was not the LORD who sent me. 30But if the LORD does something entirely new, and the ground opens its mouth and swallows them alive down into the nether world, with all belonging to them, then you will know that these men have defied the LORD." 31No sooner had he finished saying all this than the ground beneath them split open, 32and the earth opened its mouth and swallowed them and their families (and all of Korah's men) and all their possessions. 33They went down alive to the nether world with all belonging to them; the earth closed over them, and they perished from the community. 34But all the Israelites near them fled at their shrieks,

saying, "The earth might swallow us too!" 35So they withdrew from the space around the Dwelling (of Korah, Dathan and Abiram). And fire from the LORD came forth which consumed the two hundred and fifty men who were offering the incense.

Numbers chapter 17

1The LORD said to Moses, 2"Tell Eleazar, son of Aaron the priest, to remove the censers from the embers; and scatter the fire some distance away, 3for these sinners have consecrated the censers at the cost of their lives. Have them hammered into plates to cover the altar, because in being presented before the LORD they have become sacred. In this way they shall serve as a sign to the Israelites." 4So Eleazar the priest had the bronze censers of those burned during the offering hammered into a covering for the altar, 5in keeping with the orders which the LORD had given him through Moses. This cover was to be a reminder to the Israelites that no layman, no one who was not a descendant of Aaron, should approach the altar to offer incense before the LORD, lest he meet the fate of Korah and his band. 6The next day the whole Israelite community grumbled against Moses and Aaron, saying, "It is you who have slain the LORD'S people." 7But while the community was deliberating against them, Moses and Aaron turned toward the meeting tent, and the cloud now covered it and the glory of the LORD appeared. 8Then Moses and Aaron came to the front of the meeting tent, 9and the LORD said to Moses and Aaron, 10"Depart from this community, that I may consume them at once." But they fell prostrate. 11Then Moses said to Aaron, "Take your censer, put fire from the altar in it, lay incense on it, and bring it quickly to the community to make atonement for them; for wrath has come forth from the LORD and the blow is falling." 12Obeying the orders of Moses, Aaron took his censer and ran in among the community, where the blow was already falling on the people. Then, as he offered the incense and made atonement for the people, 13standing there between the living and the dead, the scourge was checked. 14Yet fourteen thousand seven hundred died from the scourge, in addition to those who died because of Korah. 15When the scourge had been checked, Aaron returned to Moses at the entrance of the meeting tent. 16The LORD now said to Moses, 17"Speak to the Israelites and get one staff from them for each ancestral house, twelve staffs in all, one from each of their tribal princes. Mark each man's name on his staff; 18and mark Aaron's name on Levi's staff, for the head of Levi's ancestral house shall also have a staff. 19Then lay them down in the meeting tent, in front of the commandments, where I meet you. 20There the staff of the man of my choice shall sprout. Thus will I suppress from my presence the Israelites' grumbling against you." 21So Moses spoke to the Israelites, and their princes gave him staffs, twelve in all, one from each tribal prince; and Aaron's staff was with them. 22Then Moses laid the staffs down before the LORD in the tent of the commandments. 23The next day, when Moses entered the tent, Aaron's staff, representing the house of Levi, had sprouted and put forth not only shoots, but blossoms as well, and even bore ripe almonds! 24Moses thereupon brought out all the staffs from the LORD'S presence to the Israelites. After each prince identified his own staff and took it, 25the LORD said to Moses, "Put back Aaron's staff in front of the commandments, to be kept there as a warning to the rebellious, so that their grumbling may cease before me; if it does not, they will die." 26And Moses did as the LORD had commanded him. 27Then the Israelites cried out to Moses, "We are perishing; we are lost, we are all lost! 28Every time anyone approaches the Dwelling of the LORD, he dies! Are we to perish to the last man?"

Numbers chapter 18

1The LORD said to Aaron, "You and your sons as well as the other members of your ancestral house shall be responsible for the sanctuary; but the responsibility of the priesthood shall rest on you and your sons alone. 2Bring with you also your other kinsmen of the tribe of Levi, your ancestral tribe, as your associates and assistants, while you and your sons are in front of the tent of the commandments. 3They shall look after your persons and the whole tent; however, they shall not come near the sacred vessels or the altar, lest both they and you die. 4As your associates they shall have charge of all the work connected with the meeting tent. But no layman shall come near you. 5You shall have charge of the sanctuary and of the altar, that wrath may not fall again upon the Israelites. 6"Remember, it is I who have taken your kinsmen, the Levites, from the body of the Israelites; they are a gift to you, dedicated to the LORD for the service of the meeting tent. 7But only you and your sons are to have charge of performing the priestly functions in whatever concerns the altar and the room within the veil. I give you the priesthood as a gift. Any layman who draws near shall be put to death." 8The LORD said to Aaron, "I myself have given you charge of the contributions made to me in the various sacred offerings of the

Israelites; by perpetual ordinance I have assigned them to you and to your sons as your priestly share. ⁹You shall have the right to share in the oblations that are most sacred, in whatever they offer me as cereal offerings or sin offerings or guilt offerings; these shares shall accrue to you and to your sons. ¹⁰In eating them you shall treat them as most sacred; every male among you may partake of them. As sacred, they belong to you. ¹¹You shall also have what is removed from the gift in every wave offering of the Israelites; by perpetual ordinance I have assigned it to you and to your sons and daughters. All in your family who are clean may partake of it. ¹²I have also assigned to you all the best of the new oil and of the new wine and grain that they give to the LORD as their first fruits; ¹³and likewise, of whatever grows on their land, the first products that they bring in to the LORD shall be yours; all of your family who are clean may partake of them. ¹⁴Whatever is doomed in Israel shall be yours. ¹⁵Every living thing that opens the womb, whether of man or of beast, such as are to be offered to the LORD, shall be yours; but you must let the first-born of man, as well as of unclean animals, be redeemed. ¹⁶The ransom for a boy is to be paid when he is a month old; it is fixed at five silver shekels according to the sanctuary standard, twenty gerahs to the shekel. ¹⁷But the first-born of cattle, sheep or goats shall not be redeemed; they are sacred. Their blood you must splash on the altar and their fat you must burn as a sweet-smelling oblation to the LORD. ¹⁸Their meat, however, shall be yours, just as the breast and the right leg of the wave offering belong to you. ¹⁹By perpetual ordinance I have assigned to you and to your sons and daughters all the contributions from the sacred gifts which the Israelites make to the LORD; this is an inviolable covenant to last forever before the LORD, for you and for your descendants." ²⁰Then the LORD said to Aaron, "You shall not have any heritage in the land of the Israelites nor hold any portion among them; I will be your portion and your heritage among them. ²¹To the Levites, however, I hereby assign all tithes in Israel as their heritage in recompense for the service they perform in the meeting tent. ²²The Israelites may no longer approach the meeting tent; else they will incur guilt deserving death. ²³Only the Levites are to perform the service of the meeting tent, and they alone shall be held responsible; this is a perpetual ordinance for all your generations. The Levites, therefore, shall not have any heritage among the Israelites, ²⁴for I have assigned to them as their heritage the tithes which the Israelites give as a contribution to the LORD. That is why I have ordered that they are not to have any heritage among the Israelites." ²⁵The LORD said to Moses, ²⁶"Give the Levites these instructions: When you receive from the Israelites the tithes I have assigned you from them as your heritage, you are to make a contribution from them to the LORD, a tithe of the tithes; ²⁷and your contribution will be credited to you as if it were grain from the threshing floor or new wine from the press. ²⁸Thus you too shall make a contribution from all the tithes you receive from the Israelites, handing over to Aaron the priest the part to be contributed to the LORD. ²⁹From all the gifts that you receive, and from the best parts, you are to consecrate to the LORD your own full contribution. ³⁰Tell them also: Once you have made your contribution from the best part, the rest of the tithes will be credited to you Levites as if it were produce of the threshing floor or of the winepress. ³¹Your families, as well as you, may eat them anywhere, since they are your recompense for service at the meeting tent. ³²You will incur no guilt so long as you make a contribution of the best part. Do not profane the sacred gifts of the Israelites and so bring death on yourselves."

Numbers chapter 19

¹The LORD said to Moses and Aaron: ²"This is the regulation which the law of the LORD prescribes. Tell the Israelites to procure for you a red heifer that is free from every blemish and defect and on which no yoke has ever been laid. ³This is to be given to Eleazar the priest, to be led outside the camp and slaughtered in his presence. ⁴Eleazar the priest shall take some of its blood on his finger and sprinkle it seven times toward the front of the meeting tent. ⁵Then the heifer shall be burned in his sight, with its hide and flesh, its blood and offal; ⁶and the priest shall take some cedar wood, hyssop and scarlet yarn and throw them into the fire in which the heifer is being burned. ⁷The priest shall then wash his garments and bathe his body in water. He remains unclean until the evening, and only afterward may he return to the camp. ⁸Likewise, he who burned the heifer shall wash his garments, bathe his body in water, and be unclean until evening. ⁹Finally, a man who is clean shall gather up the ashes of the heifer and deposit them in a clean place outside the camp. There they are to be kept for preparing lustral water for the Israelite community. The heifer is a sin offering. ¹⁰He who has gathered up the ashes of the heifer shall also wash his garments and be unclean until evening. This is a perpetual ordinance, both for the Israelites and for the aliens residing among them. ¹¹"Whoever touches

the dead body of any human being shall be unclean for seven days; ¹²he shall purify himself with the water on the third and on the seventh day, and then he will be clean again. But if he fails to purify himself on the third and on the seventh day, he will not become clean. ¹³Everyone who fails to purify himself after touching the body of any deceased person, defiles the Dwelling of the LORD and shall be cut off from Israel. Since the lustral water has not been splashed over him, he remains unclean: his uncleanness still clings to him. ¹⁴"This is the law: When a man dies in a tent, everyone who enters the tent, as well as everyone already in it, shall be unclean for seven days; ¹⁵likewise, every vessel that is open, or with its lid unfastened, shall be unclean. ¹⁶Moreover, everyone who in the open country touches a dead person, whether he was slain by the sword or died naturally, or who touches a human bone or a grave, shall be unclean for seven days. ¹⁷For anyone who is thus unclean, ashes from the sin offering shall be put in a vessel, and spring water shall be poured on them. ¹⁸Then a man who is clean shall take some hyssop, dip it in this water, and sprinkle it on the tent and on all the vessels and persons that were in it, or on him who touched a bone, a slain person or other dead body, or a grave. ¹⁹The clean man shall sprinkle the unclean on the third and on the seventh day; thus purified on the seventh day, he shall wash his garments and bathe his body in water, and in the evening he will be clean again. ²⁰Any unclean man who fails to have himself purified shall be cut off from the community, because he defiles the sanctuary of the LORD. As long as the lustral water has not been splashed over him, he remains unclean. ²¹This shall be a perpetual ordinance for you. "One who sprinkles the lustral water shall wash his garments, and anyone who comes in contact with this water shall be unclean until evening. ²²Moreover, whatever the unclean person touches becomes unclean itself, and anyone who touches it becomes unclean until evening."

Numbers chapter 20

¹The whole Israelite community arrived in the desert of Zin in the first month, and the people settled at Kadesh. It was here that Miriam died, and here that she was buried. ²As the community had no water, they held a council against Moses and Aaron. ³The people contended with Moses, exclaiming, "Would that we too had perished with our kinsmen in the LORD'S presence! ⁴Why have you brought the LORD'S community into this desert where we and our livestock are dying? ⁵Why did you lead us out of Egypt, only to bring us to this wretched place which has neither grain nor figs nor vines nor pomegranates? Here there is not even water to drink!" ⁶But Moses and Aaron went away from the assembly to the entrance of the meeting tent, where they fell prostrate. Then the glory of the LORD appeared to them, ⁷and the LORD said to Moses, ⁸"Take the staff and assemble the community, you and your brother Aaron, and in their presence order the rock to yield its waters. From the rock you shall bring forth water for the community and their livestock to drink." ⁹So Moses took the staff from its place before the LORD, as he was ordered. ¹⁰He and Aaron assembled the community in front of the rock, where he said to them, "Listen to me, you rebels! Are we to bring water for you out of this rock?" ¹¹Then, raising his hand, Moses struck the rock twice with his staff, and water gushed out in abundance for the community and their livestock to drink. ¹²But the LORD said to Moses and Aaron, "Because you were not faithful to me in showing forth my sanctity before the Israelites, you shall not lead this community into the land I will give them." ¹³These are the waters of Meribah, where the Israelites contended against the LORD, and where he revealed his sanctity among them. ¹⁴From Kadesh Moses sent men to the king of Edom with the message: "Your brother Israel has this to say: You know of all the hardships that have befallen us, ¹⁵how our fathers went down to Egypt, where we stayed a long time, how the Egyptians maltreated us and our fathers, ¹⁶and how, when we cried to the LORD, he heard our cry and sent an angel who led us out of Egypt. Now here we are at the town of Kadesh at the edge of your territory. ¹⁷Kindly let us pass through your country. We will not cross any fields or vineyards, nor drink any well water, but we will go straight along the royal road without turning to the right or to the left, until we have passed through your territory." ¹⁸But Edom answered him, "You shall not pass through here; if you do, I will advance against you with the sword." ¹⁹The Israelites insisted, "We want only to go up along the highway. If we or our livestock drink any of your water, we will pay for it. Surely there is no harm in merely letting us march through." ²⁰But Edom still said, "No, you shall not pass through," and advanced against them with a large and heavily armed force. ²¹Therefore, since Edom refused to let them pass through their territory, Israel detoured around them. ²²Setting out from Kadesh, the whole Israelite community came to Mount Hor. ²³There at Mount Hor, on the border of the land of Edom, the LORD said to Moses and Aaron, ²⁴"Aaron is about to be taken to his people; he shall not enter the land I am giving to the

Israelites, because you both rebelled against my commandment at the waters of Meribah. ²⁵Take Aaron and his son Eleazar and bring them up on Mount Hor. ²⁶Then strip Aaron of his garments and put them on his son Eleazar; for there Aaron shall be taken in death." ²⁷Moses did as the LORD commanded. When they had climbed Mount Hor in view of the whole community, ²⁸Moses stripped Aaron of his garments and put them on his son Eleazar. Then Aaron died there on top of the mountain. When Moses and Eleazar came down from the mountain, ²⁹all the community understood that Aaron had passed away; and for thirty days the whole house of Israel mourned him.

Numbers chapter 21

¹When the Canaanite king of Arad, who lived in the Negeb, heard that the Israelites were coming along the way of Atharim, he engaged them in battle and took some of them captive. ²Israel then made this vow to the LORD: "If you deliver this people into my hand, I will doom their cities." ³Later, when the LORD heeded Israel's prayer and delivered up the Canaanites, they doomed them and their cities. Hence that place was named Hormah. ⁴From Mount Hor they set out on the Red Sea road, to by-pass the land of Edom. But with their patience worn out by the journey, ⁵the people complained against God and Moses, "Why have you brought us up from Egypt to die in this desert, where there is no food or water? We are disgusted with this wretched food!" ⁶In punishment the LORD sent among the people saraph serpents, which bit the people so that many of them died. ⁷Then the people came to Moses and said, "We have sinned in complaining against the LORD and you. Pray the LORD to take the serpents from us." So Moses prayed for the people, ⁸and the LORD said to Moses, "Make a saraph and mount it on a pole, and if anyone who has been bitten looks at it, he will recover." ⁹Moses accordingly made a bronze serpent and mounted it on a pole, and whenever anyone who had been bitten by a serpent looked at the bronze serpent, he recovered. ¹⁰The Israelites moved on and encamped in Oboth. ¹¹Setting out from Oboth, they encamped in Iye-abarim in the desert fronting Moab on the east. ¹²Setting out from there, they encamped in the Wadi Zered. ¹³Setting out from there, they encamped on the other side of the Arnon, in the desert that extends from the territory of the Amorites; for the Arnon forms Moab's boundary with the Amorites. ¹⁴Hence it is said in the "Book of the Wars of the LORD": "Waheb in Suphah and the wadies, ¹⁵Arnon and the wadi gorges that reach back toward the site of Ar and slant to the border of Moab." ¹⁶From there they went to Beer, where there was the well of which the LORD said to Moses, "Bring the people together, and I will give them water." ¹⁷Then it was that Israel sang this song: "Spring up, O well! - so sing to it - ¹⁸the well that the princes sank, that the nobles of the people dug, with their scepters and their staffs." From Beer they went to Mattanah, ¹⁹from Mattanah to Nahaliel, from Nahaliel to Bamoth, ²⁰from Bamoth to the cleft in the plateau of Moab at the headland of Pisgah that overlooks Jeshimon. ²¹Now Israel sent men to Sihon, king of the Amorites, with the message, ²²"Let us pass through your country. We will not turn aside into any field or vineyard, nor will we drink any well water, but we will go straight along the royal road until we have passed through your territory." ²³Sihon, however, would not let Israel pass through his territory, but mustered all his forces and advanced into the desert against Israel. When he reached Jahaz, he engaged Israel in battle. ²⁴But Israel defeated him at the point of the sword, and took possession of his land from the Arnon to the Jabbok and as far as the country of the Ammonites, whose boundary was at Jazer. ²⁵Israel seized all the towns here and settled in these towns of the Amorites, in Heshbon and all its dependencies. ²⁶Now Heshbon was the capital of Sihon, king of the Amorites, who had fought against the former king of Moab and had seized all his land from Jazer to the Arnon. ²⁷That is why the poets say: "Come to Heshbon, let it be rebuilt, let Sihon's capital be firmly constructed. ²⁸For fire went forth from Heshbon and a blaze from the city of Sihon; it consumed the cities of Moab and swallowed up the high places of the Arnon. ²⁹Woe to you, O Moab! You are ruined, O people of Chemosh! He let his sons become fugitives and his daughters be taken captive by the Amorite king Sihon. ³⁰Their plowland is ruined from Heshbon to Dibon; Ar is laid waste; fires blaze as far as Medeba." ³¹When Israel had settled in the land of the Amorites, ³²Moses sent spies to Jazer; Israel then captured it with its dependencies and dispossessed the Amorites who were there. ³³Then they turned and went up along the road to Bashan. But Og, king of Bashan, advanced against them with all his people to give battle at Edrei. ³⁴The LORD, however, said to Moses, "Do not be afraid of him; for into your hand I will deliver him with all his people and his land. Do to him as you did to Sihon, king of the Amorites, who lived in Heshbon." ³⁵So they struck him down with his sons and all his people, until not a survivor was left to him, and they took possession of his land.

Numbers chapter 22

¹Then the Israelites moved on and encamped in the plains of Moab on the other side of the Jericho stretch of the Jordan. ²Now Balak, son of Zippor, saw all that Israel did to the Amorites. ³Indeed, Moab feared the Israelites greatly because of their numbers, and detested them. ⁴So Moab said to the elders of Midian, "Soon this horde will devour all the country around us as an ox devours the grass of the field." And Balak, Zippor's son, who was king of Moab at that time, ⁵sent messengers to Balaam, son of Beor, at Pethor on the Euphrates, in the land of the Amawites, summoning him with these words, "A people has come here from Egypt who now cover the face of the earth and are settling down opposite us! ⁶Please come and curse this people for us; they are stronger than we are. We may then be able to defeat them and drive them out of the country. For I know that whoever you bless is blessed and whoever you curse is cursed." ⁷Then the elders of Moab and of Midian left with the divination fee in hand and went to Balaam. When they had given him Balak's message, ⁸he said to them in reply, "Stay here overnight, and I will give you whatever answer the LORD gives me." So the princes of Moab lodged with Balaam. ⁹Then God came to Balaam and said, "Who are these men visiting you?" ¹⁰Balaam answered God, "Balak, son of Zippor, king of Moab, sent me the message: ¹¹'This people that came here from Egypt now cover the face of the earth. Please come and lay a curse on them for us; we may then be able to give them battle and drive them out.'" ¹²But God said to Balaam, "Do not go with them and do not curse this people, for they are blessed." ¹³The next morning Balaam arose and told the princes of Balak, "Go back to your own country, for the LORD has refused to let me go with you." ¹⁴So the princes of Moab went back to Balak with the report, "Balaam refused to come with us." ¹⁵Balak again sent princes, who were more numerous and more distinguished than the others. ¹⁶On coming to Balaam they told him, "This is what Balak, son of Zippor, has to say: Please do not refuse to come to me. ¹⁷I will reward you very handsomely and will do anything you ask of me. Please come and lay a curse on this people for me." ¹⁸But Balaam replied to Balak's officials, "Even if Balak gave me his house full of silver and gold, I could not do anything, small or great, contrary to the command of the LORD, my God. ¹⁹But, you too shall stay here overnight, till I learn what else the LORD may tell me." ²⁰That night God came to Balaam and said to him, "If these men have come to summon you, you may go with them; yet only on the condition that you do exactly as I tell you." ²¹So the next morning when Balaam arose, he saddled his ass, and went off with the princes of Moab. ²²But now the anger of God flared up at him for going, and the angel of the LORD stationed himself on the road to hinder him as he was riding along on his ass, accompanied by two of his servants. ²³When the ass saw the angel of the LORD standing on the road with sword drawn, she turned off the road and went into the field, and Balaam had to beat her to bring her back on the road. ²⁴Then the angel of the LORD took his stand in a narrow lane between vineyards with a stone wall on each side. ²⁵When the ass saw the angel of the LORD there, she shrank against the wall; and since she squeezed Balaam's leg against it, he beat her again. ²⁶The angel of the LORD then went ahead, and stopped next in a passage so narrow that there was no room to move either to the right or to the left. ²⁷When the ass saw the angel of the LORD there, she cowered under Balaam. So, in anger, he again beat the ass with his stick. ²⁸But now the LORD opened the mouth of the ass, and she asked Balaam, "What have I done to you that you should beat me these three times?" ²⁹"You have acted so willfully against me," said Balaam to the ass, "that if I but had a sword at hand, I would kill you here and now." ³⁰But the ass said to Balaam, "Am I not your own beast, and have you not always ridden upon me until now? Have I been in the habit of treating you this way before?" "No," replied Balaam. ³¹Then the LORD removed the veil from Balaam's eyes, so that he too saw the angel of the LORD standing on the road with sword drawn; and he fell on his knees and bowed to the ground. ³²But the angel of the LORD said to him, "Why have you beaten your ass these three times? It is I who have come armed to hinder you because this rash journey of yours is directly opposed to me. ³³When the ass saw me, she turned away from me these three times. If she had not turned away from me, I would have killed you; her I would have spared." ³⁴Then Balaam said to the angel of the LORD, "I have sinned. Yet I did not know that you stood against me to oppose my journey. Since it has displeased you, I will go back home." ³⁵But the angel of the LORD said to Balaam, "Go with the men; but you may say only what I tell you." So Balaam went on with the princes of Balak. ³⁶When Balak heard that Balaam was coming, he went out to meet him at the boundary city Ir-Moab on the Arnon at the end of the Moabite territory. ³⁷And he said to Balaam, "I sent an urgent summons to you! Why did you not come to me? Did you think I could not reward you?" ³⁸Balaam answered him, "Well, I have

come to you after all. But what power have I to say anything? I can speak only what God puts in my mouth." ³⁹Then Balaam went with Balak, and they came to Kiriath-huzoth. ⁴⁰Here Balak slaughtered oxen and sheep, and sent portions to Balaam and to the princes who were with him. ⁴¹The next morning Balak took Balaam up on Bamoth-baal, and from there he saw some of the clans.

Numbers chapter 23

1 Then Balaam said to Balak, "Build me seven altars, and prepare seven bullocks and seven rams for me here." ² So he did as Balaam had ordered, offering a bullock and a ram on each altar. And Balak said to him, "I have erected the seven altars, and have offered a bullock and a ram on each." ³ Balaam then said to him, "Stand here by your holocaust while I go over there. Perhaps the LORD will meet me, and then I will tell you whatever he lets me see." He went out on the barren height, ⁴ and God met him. ⁵ When he had put an utterance in Balaam's mouth, the LORD said to him, "Go back to Balak, and speak accordingly." ⁶ So he went back to Balak, who was still standing by his holocaust together with all the princes of Moab. ⁷ Then Balaam gave voice to his oracle: From Aram has Balak brought me here, Moab's king, from the Eastern Mountains: "Come and lay a curse for me on Jacob, come and denounce Israel." ⁸ How can I curse whom God has not cursed? How denounce whom the LORD has not denounced? ⁹ For from the top of the crags I see him, from the heights I behold him. Here is a people that lives apart and does not reckon itself among the nations. ¹⁰ Who has ever counted the dust of Jacob, or numbered Israel's wind-borne particles? May I die the death of the just, may my descendants be as many as theirs! ¹¹ "What have you done to me?" cried Balak to Balaam. "It was to curse my foes that I brought you here; instead, you have even blessed them." ¹² Balaam replied, "Is it not what the LORD puts in my mouth that I must repeat with care?" ¹³ Then Balak said to him, "Please come with me to another place from which you can see only some and not all of them, and from there curse them for me." ¹⁴ So he brought him to the lookout field on the top of Pisgah, where he built seven altars and offered a bullock and a ram on each of them. ¹⁵ Balaam then said to Balak, "Stand here by your holocaust, while I seek a meeting over there." ¹⁶ Then the LORD met Balaam, and having put an utterance in his mouth, he said to him, "Go back to Balak, and speak accordingly." ¹⁷ So he went back to Balak, who was still standing by his holocaust together with the princes of Moab. When Balak asked him, "What did the LORD say?" ¹⁸ Balaam gave voice to his oracle: Be aroused, O Balak, and hearken; give ear to my testimony, O son of Zippor! ¹⁹ God is not man that he should speak falsely, nor human, that he should change his mind. Is he one to speak and not act, to decree and not fulfill? ²⁰ It is a blessing I have been given to pronounce; a blessing which I cannot restrain. ²¹ Misfortune is not observed in Jacob, nor misery seen in Israel. The LORD, his God, is with him; with him is the triumph of his King. ²² It is God who brought him out of Egypt, a wild bull of towering might. ²³ No, there is no sorcery against Jacob, nor omen against Israel. It shall yet be said of Jacob, and of Israel, "Behold what God has wrought!" ²⁴ Here is a people that springs up like a lioness, and stalks forth like a lion; It rests not till it has devoured its prey and has drunk the blood of the slain. ²⁵ "Even though you cannot curse them," said Balak to Balaam, "at least do not bless them." ²⁶ But Balaam answered Balak, "Did I not warn you that I must do all that the LORD tells me?" ²⁷ Then Balak said to Balaam, "Come, let me bring you to another place; perhaps God will approve of your cursing them for me from there." ²⁸ So he took Balaam to the top of Peor, that overlooks Jeshimon. ²⁹ Balaam then said to him, "Here build me seven altars; and here prepare for me seven bullocks and seven rams." ³⁰ And Balak did as Balaam had ordered, offering a bullock and a ram on each altar.

Numbers chapter 24

1 Balaam, however, perceiving that the LORD was pleased to bless Israel, did not go aside as before to seek omens, but turned his gaze toward the desert. ² When he raised his eyes and saw Israel encamped, tribe by tribe, the spirit of God came upon him, ³ and he gave voice to his oracle: The utterance of Balaam, son of Beor, the utterance of the man whose eye is true, ⁴ The utterance of one who hears what God says, and knows what the Most High knows, Of one who sees what the Almighty sees, enraptured, and with eyes unveiled: ⁵ How goodly are your tents, O Jacob; your encampments, O Israel! ⁶ They are like gardens beside a stream, like the cedars planted by the LORD. ⁷ His wells shall yield free-flowing waters, he shall have the sea within reach; His king shall rise higher than... and his royalty shall be exalted. ⁸ It is God who brought him out of Egypt, a wild bull of towering might. He shall devour the nations like grass, their bones he shall strip bare. ⁹ He lies crouching like a lion, or like a lioness; who shall arouse him? Blessed is he who blesses you, and cursed is he who curses you! ¹⁰ Balak

beat his palms together in a blaze of anger at Balaam and said to him, "It was to curse my foes that I summoned you here; yet three times now you have even blessed them instead! ¹¹ Be off at once, then, to your home. I promised to reward you richly, but the LORD has withheld the reward from you!" ¹² Balaam replied to Balak, "Did I not warn the very messengers whom you sent to me, ¹³ 'Even if Balak gave me his house full of silver and gold, I could not of my own accord do anything, good or evil, contrary to the command of the LORD'? Whatever the LORD says I must repeat. ¹⁴ But now that I am about to go to my own people, let me first warn you what this people will do to your people in the days to come." ¹⁵ Then Balaam gave voice to his oracle: The utterance of Balaam, son of Beor, the utterance of the man whose eye is true, ¹⁶ The utterance of one who hears what God says, and knows what the Most High knows, Of one who sees what the Almighty sees, enraptured and with eyes unveiled. ¹⁷ I see him, though not now; I behold him, though not near: A star shall advance from Jacob, and a staff shall rise from Israel, That shall smite the brows of Moab, and the skulls of all the Shuthites, ¹⁸ Till Edom is dispossessed, and no fugitive is left in Seir. Israel shall do valiantly, ¹⁹ and Jacob shall overcome his foes. ²⁰ Upon seeing Amalek, Balaam gave voice to his oracle: First of the peoples was Amalek, but his end is to perish forever. ²¹ Upon seeing the Kenites, he gave voice to his oracle: Your abode is enduring, O smith, and your nest is set on a cliff; ²² Yet destined for burning - even as I watch - are your inhabitants. ²³ Upon seeing... he gave voice to his oracle: Alas, who shall survive of Ishmael, ²⁴ to deliver his people from the hands of the Kittim? When they have conquered Asshur and conquered Eber, He too shall perish forever. ²⁵ Then Balaam set out on his journey home; and Balak also went his way.

Numbers chapter 25

1 While Israel was living at Shittim, the people degraded themselves by having illicit relations with the Moabite women. ² These then invited the people to the sacrifices of their god, and the people ate of the sacrifices and worshiped their god. ³ When Israel thus submitted to the rites of Baal of Peor, the LORD'S anger flared up against Israel, ⁴ and he said to Moses, "Gather all the leaders of the people, and hold a public execution of the guilty ones before the LORD, that his blazing wrath may be turned away from Israel." ⁵ So Moses told the Israelite judges, "Each of you shall kill those of his men who have submitted to the rites of Baal of Peor." ⁶ Yet a certain Israelite came and brought in a Midianite woman to his clansmen in the view of Moses and of the whole Israelite community, while they were weeping at the entrance of the meeting tent. ⁷ When Phinehas, son of Eleazar, son of Aaron the priest, saw this, he left the assembly, and taking a lance in hand, ⁸ followed the Israelite into his retreat where he pierced the pair of them, the Israelite and the woman. Thus the slaughter of Israelites was checked; ⁹ but only after twenty-four thousand had died. ¹⁰ Then the LORD said to Moses, ¹¹ "Phinehas, son of Eleazar, son of Aaron the priest, has turned my anger from the Israelites by his zeal for my honor among them; that is why I did not put an end to the Israelites for the offense to my honor. ¹² Announce, therefore, that I hereby give him my pledge of friendship, ¹³ which shall be for him and for his descendants after him the pledge of an everlasting priesthood, because he was zealous on behalf of his God and thus made amends for the Israelites." ¹⁴ The Israelite slain with the Midianite woman was Zimri, son of Salu, prince of an ancestral house of the Simeonites. ¹⁵ The slain Midianite woman was Cozbi, daughter of Zur, who was head of a clan, an ancestral house, in Midian. ¹⁶ The LORD then said to Moses, ¹⁷ "Treat the Midianites as enemies and crush them, ¹⁸ for they have been your enemies by their wily dealings with you as regards Peor and as regards their kinswoman Cozbi, the daughter of a Midianite prince, who was killed at the time of the slaughter because of Peor." ¹⁹ After the slaughter.

Numbers chapter 26

1 The LORD said to Moses and Eleazar, son of Aaron the priest, ² "Take a census, by ancestral houses, throughout the community of the Israelites of all those of twenty years or more who are fit for military service in Israel." ³ So on the plains of Moab along the Jericho stretch of the Jordan, Moses and the priest Eleazar registered ⁴ those of twenty years or more, as the LORD had commanded Moses. The Israelites who came out of the land of Egypt were as follows: ⁵ Of Reuben, the first-born of Israel, the Reubenites by clans were: through Hanoch the clan of the Hanochites, through Pallu the clan of the Palluites, ⁶ through Hezron the clan of the Hezronites, through Carmi the clan of the Carmites. ⁷ These were the clans of the Reubenites, of whom forty-three thousand seven hundred and thirty men were registered. ⁸ From Pallu descended Eliab, ⁹ and the descendants of Eliab were Dathan and Abiram—the same Dathan and Abiram, councilors of the community, who revolted against Moses and Aaron (like Korah's band when it

rebelled against the LORD). ¹⁰ The earth opened its mouth and swallowed them as a warning (Korah too and the band that died when the fire consumed two hundred and fifty men. ¹¹ The descendants of Korah, however, did not die out). ¹² The Simeonites by clans were: through Nemuel the clan of the Nemuelites, through Jamin the clan of the Jaminites, through Jachin the clan of the Jachinites, ¹³ through Zohar the clan of the Zoharites, through Shaul the clan of the Shaulites. ¹⁴ These were the clans of the Simeonites, of whom twenty-two thousand two hundred men were registered. ¹⁵ The Gadites by clans were: through Zephon the clan of the Zephonites, through Haggi the clan of the Haggites, through Shuni the clan of the Shunites, ¹⁶ through Ozni the clan of the Oznites, through Eri the clan of the Erites, ¹⁷ through Arod the clan of the Arodites, through Areli the clan of the Arelites. ¹⁸ These were the clans of the Gadites, of whom forty thousand five hundred men were registered. ¹⁹ The sons of Judah who died in the land of Canaan were Er and Onan. ²⁰ The Judahites by clans were: through Shelah the clan of the Shelahites, through Perez the clan of the Perezites, through Zerah the clan of the Zerahites. ²¹ The Perezites were: through Hezron the clan of the Hezronites, through Hamul the clan of the Hamulites. ²² These were the clans of Judah, of whom seventy-six thousand five hundred men were registered. ²³ The Issacharites by clans were: through Tola the clan of the Tolaites, through Puvah the clan of the Puvahites, ²⁴ through Jashub the clan of the Jashubites, through Shimron the clan of the Shimronites. ²⁵ These were the clans of Issachar, of whom sixty-four thousand three hundred men were registered. ²⁶ The Zebulunites by clans were: through Sered the clan of the Seredites, through Elon the clan of the Elonites, through Jahleel the clan of the Jahleelites. ²⁷ These were the clans of the Zebulunites, of whom sixty thousand five hundred men were registered. ²⁸ The sons of Joseph were Manasseh and Ephraim. ²⁹ The Manassehites by clans were: through Machir the clan of the Machirites, through Gilead, a descendant of Machir, the clan of the Gileadites. ³⁰ The Gileadites were: through Abiezer the clan of the Abiezrites, through Helek the clan of the Helekites, ³¹ through Asriel the clan of the Asrielites, through Shechem the clan of the Shechemites, ³² through Shemida the clan of the Shemidaites, through Hepher the clan of the Hepherites. ³³ Zelophehad, son of Hepher, had no sons, but only daughters, whose names were Mahlah, Noah, Hoglah, Milcah, and Tirzah. ³⁴ These were the clans of Manasseh, of whom fifty-two thousand seven hundred men were registered. ³⁵ The Ephraimites by clans were: through Shuthelah the clan of the Shuthelahites, through Becher the clan of the Becherites, through Tahan the clan of the Tahanites. ³⁶ The Shuthelahites were: through Eran the clan of the Eranites. ³⁷ These were the clans of the Ephraimites, of whom thirty-two thousand five hundred men were registered. These were the descendants of Joseph by clans. ³⁸ The Benjaminites by clans were: through Bela the clan of the Belaites, through Ashbel the clan of the Ashbelites, through Ahiram the clan of the Ahiramites, ³⁹ through Shupham the clan of the Shuphamites, through Hupham the clan of the Huphamites. ⁴⁰ The descendants of Bela were Ard and Naaman: through Ard the clan of the Ardites, through Naaman the clan of the Naamanites. ⁴¹ These were the Benjaminites by clans, of whom forty-five thousand six hundred men were registered. ⁴² The Danites by clans were: through Shuham the clan of the Shuhamites. These were the clans of Dan, ⁴³ of whom sixty-four thousand four hundred men were registered. ⁴⁴ The Asherites by clans were: through Imnah the clan of the Imnites, through Ishvi the clan of the Ishvites, through Beriah the clan of the Beriites, ⁴⁵ through Heber the clan of the Heberites, through Malchiel the clan of the Malchielites. ⁴⁶ The name of Asher's daughter was Serah. ⁴⁷ These were the clans of Asher, of whom fifty-three thousand four hundred men were registered. ⁴⁸ The Naphtalites by clans were: through Jahzeel the clan of the Jahzeelites, through Guni the clan of the Gunites, ⁴⁹ through Jezer the clan of the Jezerites, through Shillem the clan of the Shillemites. ⁵⁰ These were the clans of Naphtali, of whom forty-five thousand four hundred men were registered. ⁵¹ These six hundred and one thousand seven hundred and thirty were the Israelites who were registered. ⁵² The LORD said to Moses, ⁵³ "Among these groups the land shall be divided as their heritage in keeping with the number of individuals in each group. ⁵⁴ To a large group you shall assign a large heritage, to a small group a small heritage, each group receiving its heritage in proportion to the number of men registered in it. ⁵⁵ But the land shall be divided by lot, as the heritage of the various ancestral tribes. ⁵⁶ As the lot falls shall each group, large or small, be assigned its heritage." ⁵⁷ The Levites registered by clans were: through Gershon the clan of the Gershonites, through Kohath the clan of the Kohathites, through Merari the clan of the Merarites. ⁵⁸ These also were clans of Levi: the clan of the Libnites, the clan of the Hebronites, the clan of the Mahlites, the clan of the

Mushites, the clan of the Korahites. Among the descendants of Kohath was Amram, ⁵⁹ whose wife was named Jochebed. She also was of the tribe of Levi, born to the tribe in Egypt. To Amram she bore Aaron and Moses and their sister Miriam. ⁶⁰ To Aaron were born Nadab and Abihu, Eleazar and Ithamar. ⁶¹ But Nadab and Abihu died when they offered profane fire before the LORD. ⁶² The total number of male Levites one month or more of age, who were registered, was twenty-three thousand. They were not registered with the other Israelites, however, for no heritage was given them among the Israelites. ⁶³ These, then, were the men registered by Moses and the priest Eleazar in the census of the Israelites taken on the plains of Moab along the Jericho stretch of the Jordan. ⁶⁴ Among them there was not a man of those who had been registered by Moses and the priest Aaron in the census of the Israelites taken in the desert of Sinai. ⁶⁵ For the LORD had told them that they would surely die in the desert, and not one of them was left except Caleb, son of Jephunneh, and Joshua, son of Nun.

Numbers chapter 27

¹ Zelophehad, son of Hepher, son of Gilead, son of Machir, son of Manasseh, son of Joseph, had daughters named Mahlah, Noah, Hoglah, Milcah, and Tirzah. They came forward, ² and standing in the presence of Moses, the priest Eleazar, the princes, and the whole community at the entrance of the meeting tent, said: ³ "Our father died in the desert. Although he did not join those who banded together against the LORD (in Korah's band), he died for his own sin without leaving any sons. ⁴ But why should our father's name be withdrawn from his clan merely because he had no son? Let us, therefore, have property among our father's kinsmen." ⁵ When Moses laid their case before the LORD, ⁶ the LORD said to him, ⁷ "The plea of Zelophehad's daughters is just; you shall give them hereditary property among their father's kinsmen, letting their father's heritage pass on to them. ⁸ Therefore, tell the Israelites: If a man dies without leaving a son, you shall let his heritage pass on to his daughter; ⁹ if he has no daughter, you shall give his heritage to his brothers; ¹⁰ if he has no brothers, you shall give his heritage to his father's brothers; ¹¹ if his father had no brothers, you shall give his heritage to his nearest relative in his clan, who shall then take possession of it." This is the legal norm for the Israelites, as the LORD commanded Moses. ¹² The LORD said to Moses, "Go up here into the Abarim Mountains and view the land that I am giving to the Israelites. ¹³ When you have viewed it, you too shall be taken to your people, as was your brother Aaron, ¹⁴ because in the rebellion of the community in the desert of Zin you both rebelled against my order to manifest my sanctity to them by means of the water." (This is the water of Meribah of Kadesh in the desert of Zin.) ¹⁵ Then Moses said to the LORD, ¹⁶ "May the LORD, the God of the spirits of all mankind, set over the community a man ¹⁷ who shall act as their leader in all things, to guide them in all their actions; that the LORD's community may not be like sheep without a shepherd." ¹⁸ And the LORD replied to Moses, "Take Joshua, son of Nun, a man of spirit, and lay your hand upon him. ¹⁹ Have him stand in the presence of the priest Eleazar and of the whole community, and commission him before their eyes. ²⁰ Invest him with some of your own dignity, that the whole Israelite community may obey him. ²¹ He shall present himself to the priest Eleazar, to have him seek out for him the decisions of the Urim in the LORD'S presence; and as he directs, Joshua, all the Israelites with him, and the community as a whole shall perform all their actions." ²² Moses did as the LORD had commanded him. Taking Joshua and having him stand in the presence of the priest Eleazar and of the whole community, ²³ he laid his hands on him and gave him his commission, as the LORD had directed through Moses.

Numbers chapter 28

¹ The LORD said to Moses, ² "Give the Israelites this commandment: At the times I have appointed, you shall be careful to present to me the food offerings that are offered to me as sweet-smelling oblations. ³ "You shall tell them therefore: This is the oblation which you shall offer to the LORD: two unblemished yearling lambs each day as the established holocaust, ⁴ offering one lamb in the morning and the other during the evening twilight, ⁵ each with a cereal offering of one tenth of an ephah of fine flour mixed with a fourth of a hin of oil of crushed olives. ⁶ This is the established holocaust that was offered at Mount Sinai as a sweet-smelling oblation to the LORD. ⁷ And as the libation for the first lamb, you shall pour out to the LORD in the sanctuary a fourth of a hin of wine. ⁸ The other lamb, to be offered during the evening twilight, you shall offer with the same cereal offering and the same libation as in the morning, as a sweet-smelling oblation to the LORD. ⁹ "On the sabbath day you shall offer two unblemished yearling lambs, with their cereal offering, two tenths of an ephah of fine flour mixed with oil, and with their libations. ¹⁰ Each sabbath there shall be the sabbath holocaust in

addition to the established holocaust and its libation. 11 "On the first of each month you shall offer as a holocaust to the LORD two bullocks, one ram, and seven unblemished yearling lambs, 12 with three tenths of an ephah of fine flour mixed with oil as the cereal offering for each bullock, two tenths of an ephah of fine flour mixed with oil as the cereal offering for the ram, 13 and one tenth of an ephah of fine flour mixed with oil as the cereal offering for each lamb, that the holocaust may be a sweet-smelling oblation to the LORD. 14 Their libations shall be half a hin of wine for each bullock, a third of a hin for the ram, and a fourth of a hin for each lamb. This is the new moon holocaust for every new moon of the year. 15 Moreover, one goat shall be sacrificed as a sin offering to the LORD. These are to be offered in addition to the established holocaust and its libation. 16 "On the fourteenth day of the first month falls the Passover of the LORD, 17 and the fifteenth day of this month is the pilgrimage feast. For seven days unleavened bread is to be eaten. 18 On the first of these days you shall hold a sacred assembly, and do no sort of work. 19 As an oblation you shall offer a holocaust to the LORD, which shall consist of two bullocks, one ram, and seven yearling lambs that you are sure are unblemished, 20 with their cereal offerings of fine flour mixed with oil; offering three tenths of an ephah for each bullock, two tenths for the ram, 21 and one tenth for each of the seven lambs; 22 and offer one goat as a sin offering in atonement for yourselves. 23 These offerings you shall make in addition to the established morning holocaust: 24 you shall make exactly the same offerings each day for seven days as food offerings, in addition to the established holocaust with its libation, for a sweet-smelling oblation to the LORD. 25 On the seventh day you shall hold a sacred assembly, and do no sort of work. 26 "On the day of first fruits, on your feast of Weeks, when you present to the LORD the new cereal offering, you shall hold a sacred assembly, and do no sort of work. 27 You shall offer as a sweet-smelling holocaust to the LORD two bullocks, one ram, and seven yearling lambs that you are sure are unblemished, 28 with their cereal offerings of fine flour mixed with oil; offering three tenths of an ephah for each bullock, two tenths for the ram, 29 and one tenth for each of the seven lambs. 30 Moreover, one goat shall be offered as a sin offering in atonement for yourselves. 31 You shall make these offerings, together with their libations, in addition to the established holocaust with its cereal offering.

Numbers chapter 29

1 The LORD said to Moses, 2 "On the first day of the seventh month you shall hold a sacred assembly, and do no sort of work; it shall be a day on which you sound the trumpet. 3 You shall offer as a sweet-smelling holocaust to the LORD one bullock, one ram, and seven unblemished yearling lambs, 4 with their cereal offerings of fine flour mixed with oil; offering three tenths of an ephah for the bullock, two tenths for the ram, 5 and one tenth for each of the seven lambs. 6 Moreover, one goat shall be offered as a sin offering in atonement for yourselves. 7 These are to be offered in addition to the ordinary new-moon holocaust with its cereal offering, and in addition to the established holocaust with its cereal offering, together with the libations prescribed for them, as a sweet-smelling oblation to the LORD. 8 On the tenth day of this seventh month you shall hold a sacred assembly, and mortify yourselves, and do no sort of work. 9 You shall offer as a sweet-smelling holocaust to the LORD one bullock, one ram, and seven yearling lambs that you are sure are unblemished, 10 with their cereal offerings of fine flour mixed with oil; offering three tenths of an ephah for the bullock, two tenths for the ram, 11 and one tenth for each of the seven lambs. 12 Moreover, one goat shall be sacrificed as a sin offering. These are to be offered in addition to the atonement sin offering, the established holocaust with its cereal offering, and their libations. 13 On the fifteenth day of the seventh month you shall hold a sacred assembly, and do no sort of work; then, for seven days following, you shall celebrate a pilgrimage feast to the LORD. 14 You shall offer as a sweet-smelling holocaust to the LORD thirteen bullocks, two rams, and fourteen yearling lambs that are unblemished, 15 with their cereal offerings of fine flour mixed with oil; offering three tenths of an ephah for each of the thirteen bullocks, two tenths for each of the two rams, 16 and one tenth for each of the fourteen lambs. Moreover, one goat shall be sacrificed as a sin offering. These are to be offered in addition to the established holocaust with its cereal offering and libation. 17 On the second day you shall offer twelve bullocks, two rams, and fourteen unblemished yearling lambs, 18 with their cereal offerings and libations as prescribed for the bullocks, rams and lambs in proportion to their number, 19 as well as one goat for a sin offering, besides the established holocaust with its cereal offering and libation. 20 On the third day you shall offer eleven bullocks, two rams, and fourteen unblemished yearling lambs, 21 with their cereal offerings and libations as prescribed for the bullocks, rams and lambs in proportion to their number, 22 as well as one goat for a sin offering,

besides the established holocaust with its cereal offering and libation. 23 On the fourth day you shall offer ten bullocks, two rams, and fourteen unblemished yearling lambs, 24 with their cereal offerings and libations as prescribed for the bullocks, rams and lambs in proportion to their number, 25 as well as one goat for a sin offering, besides the established holocaust with its cereal offering and libation. 26 On the fifth day you shall offer nine bullocks, two rams, and fourteen unblemished yearling lambs, 27 with their cereal offerings and libations as prescribed for the bullocks, rams and lambs in proportion to their number, 28 as well as one goat for a sin offering, besides the established holocaust with its cereal offering and libation. 29 On the sixth day you shall offer eight bullocks, two rams, and fourteen unblemished yearling lambs, 30 with their cereal offerings and libations as prescribed for the bullocks, rams and lambs in proportion to their number, 31 as well as one goat for a sin offering, besides the established holocaust with its cereal offering and libation. 32 On the seventh day you shall offer seven bullocks, two rams, and fourteen unblemished yearling lambs, 33 with their cereal offerings and libations as prescribed for the bullocks, rams and lambs in proportion to their number, 34 as well as one goat for a sin offering, besides the established holocaust with its cereal offering and libation. 35 On the eighth day you shall hold a solemn meeting, and do no sort of work. 36 You shall offer up in holocaust as a sweet-smelling oblation to the LORD one bullock, one ram, and seven unblemished yearling lambs, 37 with their cereal offerings and libations as prescribed for the bullocks, rams and lambs in proportion to their number, 38 as well as one goat for a sin offering, besides the established holocaust with its cereal offering and libation. 39 These are the offerings you shall make to the LORD on your festivals, besides whatever holocausts, cereal offerings, libations, and peace offerings you present as your votive or freewill offerings."

Numbers chapter 30

1 Moses then gave the Israelites these instructions, just as the LORD had ordered him. 2 Moses said to the heads of the Israelite tribes, "This is what the LORD has commanded: 3 When a man makes a vow to the LORD or binds himself under oath to a pledge of abstinence, he shall not violate his word, but must fulfill exactly the promise he has uttered. 4 When a woman, while still a maiden in her father's house, makes a vow to the LORD, or binds herself to a pledge, 5 if her father learns of her vow or the pledge to which she bound herself and says nothing to her about it, then any vow or any pledge she has made remains valid. 6 But if on the day he learns of it her father expresses to her his disapproval, then any vow or any pledge she has made becomes null and void; and the LORD releases her from it, since her father has expressed to her his disapproval. 7 If she marries while under a vow or under a rash pledge to which she bound herself, 8 and her husband learns of it, yet says nothing to her that day about it, then the vow or pledge she had made remains valid. 9 But if on the day he learns of it her husband expresses to her his disapproval, he thereby annuls the vow she had made or the rash pledge to which she had bound herself, and the LORD releases her from it. 10 The vow of a widow or of a divorced woman, or any pledge to which such a woman binds herself, is valid. 11 If it is in her husband's house that she makes a vow or binds herself under oath to a pledge, 12 and her husband learns of it yet says nothing to express to her his disapproval, then any vow or any pledge she has made remains valid. 13 But if on the day he learns of them her husband annuls them, then whatever she has expressly promised in her vow or in her pledge becomes null and void; since her husband has annulled them, the LORD releases her from them. 14 Any vow or any pledge that she makes under oath to mortify herself, her husband can either allow to remain valid or render null and void. 15 But if her husband, day after day, says nothing at all to her about them, he thereby allows as valid any vow or any pledge she has made; he has allowed them to remain valid, because on the day he learned of them he said nothing to her about them. 16 If, however, he countermands them some time after he first learned of them, he is responsible for her guilt. 17 These are the statutes which the LORD prescribed through Moses concerning the relationship between a husband and his wife, as well as between a father and his daughter while she is still a maiden in her father's house.

Numbers chapter 31

1 The LORD said to Moses, 2 "Avenge the Israelites on the Midianites, and then you shall be taken to your people." 3 So Moses told the people, "Select men from your midst and arm them for war, to attack the Midianites and execute the LORD'S vengeance on them. 4 From each of the tribes of Israel you shall send a band of one thousand men to war." 5 From the clans of Israel, therefore, a thousand men of each tribe were levied, so that there were twelve thousand men armed for war. 6 Moses

sent them out on the campaign, a thousand from each tribe, with Phinehas, son of Eleazar, the priest for the campaign, who had with him the sacred vessels and the trumpets for sounding the alarm. 7 They waged war against the Midianites, as the LORD had commanded Moses, and killed every male among them. 8 Besides those slain in battle, they killed the five Midianite kings: Evi, Rekem, Zur, Hur, and Reba; and they also executed Balaam, son of Beor, with the sword. 9 But the Israelites kept the women of the Midianites with their little ones as captives, and all their herds and flocks and wealth as spoil, 10 while they set on fire all the towns where they had settled and all their encampments. 11 Then they took all the booty, with the people and beasts they had captured, and brought the captives, together with the spoils and booty, 12 to Moses and the priest Eleazar and to the Israelite community at their camp on the plains of Moab, along the Jericho stretch of the Jordan. 13 When Moses and the priest Eleazar, with all the princes of the community, went outside the camp to meet them, 14 Moses became angry with the officers of the army, the clan and company commanders, who were returning from combat. 15 "So you have spared all the women!" he exclaimed. 16 "Why, they are the very ones who on Balaam's advice prompted the unfaithfulness of the Israelites toward the LORD in the Peor affair, which began the slaughter of the LORD'S community. 17 Slay, therefore, every male child and every woman who has had intercourse with a man. 18 But you may spare and keep for yourselves all girls who had no intercourse with a man. 19 Moreover, you shall stay outside the camp for seven days, and those of you who have slain anyone or touched anyone slain in battle shall purify yourselves on the third and on the seventh day. This applies both to you and to your captives. 20 You shall also purify every article of cloth, leather, goats' hair, or wood." 21 Eleazar the priest told the soldiers who had returned from combat: "This is what the law, as prescribed by the LORD to Moses, ordains: 22 Whatever can stand fire, such as gold, silver, bronze, iron, tin, and lead, 23 you shall put into the fire, that it may become clean; however, it must also be purified with lustral water. But whatever cannot stand fire you shall put into the water. 24 On the seventh day you shall wash your clothes, and then you will again be clean. After that, you may enter the camp." 25 The LORD said to Moses: 26 "With the help of the priest Eleazar and of the heads of the ancestral houses, count up all the human captives and the beasts that have been taken; 27 then divide them evenly, giving half to those who took an active part in the war by going out to combat, and half to the rest of the community. 28 You shall levy a tax for the LORD on the warriors who went out to combat: one out of every five hundred persons, oxen, asses, and sheep in their half of the spoil you shall turn over to the priest Eleazar as a contribution to the LORD. 30 From the Israelites' half you shall take one out of every fifty persons, and the same from the different beasts, oxen, asses, and sheep, and give them to the Levites, who have charge of the LORD'S Dwelling." 31 So Moses and the priest Eleazar did this, as the LORD had commanded Moses. 32 This booty, what was left of the loot which the soldiers had taken, amounted to six hundred and seventy-five thousand sheep, 33 seventy-two thousand oxen, 34 sixty-one thousand asses, 35 and thirty-two thousand girls who were still virgins. 36 The half that fell to those who had gone out to combat was: three hundred and thirty-seven thousand five hundred sheep, 37 of which six hundred and seventy-five fell as tax to the LORD; 38 thirty-six thousand oxen, of which seventy-two fell as tax to the LORD; 39 thirty thousand five hundred asses, of which sixty-one fell as tax to the LORD; 40 and sixteen thousand persons, of whom thirty-two fell as tax to the LORD. 41 The taxes contributed to the LORD, Moses gave to the priest Eleazar, as the LORD had commanded him. 42 The half for the other Israelites, which fell to the community when Moses had taken it from the soldiers, was: 43 three hundred and thirty-seven thousand five hundred sheep, 44 thirty-six thousand oxen, 45 thirty thousand five hundred asses, 46 and sixteen thousand persons. 47 From this, the Israelites' share, Moses, as the LORD had ordered, took one out of every fifty, both of persons and of beasts, and gave them to the Levites, who had charge of the LORD'S Dwelling. 48 Then the officers who had been clan and company commanders of the army came up to Moses 49 and said to him, "Your servants have counted up the soldiers under our command, and not one is missing. 50 So, to make atonement for ourselves before the LORD, each of us will bring as an offering to the LORD some gold article he has picked up, such as an anklet, a bracelet, a ring, an earring, or a necklace." 51 Moses and the priest Eleazar accepted this gold from them, all of it in well-wrought articles. 52 The gold that they gave as a contribution to the LORD amounted in all to sixteen thousand seven hundred and fifty shekels. This was from the clan and company commanders; 53 what the common soldiers had looted each one kept for himself. 54 Moses, then, and the priest Eleazar accepted the gold from the clan and company

commanders and put it in the meeting tent as a memorial for the Israelites before the LORD.

Numbers chapter 32

1 Now the Reubenites and Gadites had a very large number of livestock. Noticing that the land of Jazer and of Gilead was grazing country, 2 they came to Moses and the priest Eleazar and to the princes of the community and said, 3 "The region of Ataroth, Dibon, Jazer, Nimrah, Heshbon, Elealeh, Sebam, Nebo and Baal-meon, 4 which the LORD has laid low before the community of Israel, is grazing country. Now, since your servants have livestock," 5 they continued, "if we find favor with you, let this land be given to your servants as their property. Do not make us cross the Jordan." 6 But Moses answered the Gadites and Reubenites: "Are your kinsmen, then, to engage in war, while you remain here? 7 Why do you wish to discourage the Israelites from crossing to the land the LORD has given them? 8 That is just what your fathers did when I sent them from Kadesh-barnea to reconnoiter the land. 9 They went up to the Wadi Eshcol and reconnoitered the land, then so discouraged the Israelites that they would not enter the land the LORD had given them. 10 At that time the wrath of the LORD flared up, and he swore, 11 'Because they have not followed me unreservedly, none of these men of twenty years or more who have come up from Egypt shall ever see this country I promised under oath to Abraham and Isaac and Jacob, 12 except the Kenizzite Caleb, son of Jephunneh, and Joshua, son of Nun, who have followed the LORD unreservedly.' 13 So in his anger with the Israelites the LORD made them wander in the desert forty years, until the whole generation that had done evil in the sight of the LORD had died out. 14 And now here you are, a brood of sinners, rising up in your fathers' place to add still more to the LORD'S blazing wrath against the Israelites. 15 If you turn away from following him, he will make them stay still longer in the desert, and so you will bring about the ruin of this whole nation." 16 But they were insistent with him: "We wish only to build sheepfolds here for our flocks, and towns for our families; 17 but we ourselves will march as troops in the van of the Israelites, until we have led them to their destination. Meanwhile, our families can remain here in the fortified towns, safe from attack by the natives. 18 We will not return to our homes until every one of the Israelites has taken possession of his heritage, 19 and will not claim any heritage with them once we cross the Jordan, so long as we receive a heritage for ourselves on this eastern side of the Jordan." 20 Moses said to them in reply: "If you keep your word to march as troops in the LORD'S vanguard 21 and to cross the Jordan in full force before the LORD until he has driven his enemies out of his way 22 and the land is subdued before him, then you may return here, quit of every obligation to the LORD and to Israel, and this region shall be your possession before the LORD. 23 But if you do not do this, you will sin against the LORD, and you can be sure that you will not escape the consequences of your sin. 24 Build the towns, then, for your families, and the folds for your flocks, but also fulfill your express promise." 25 The Gadites and Reubenites answered Moses, "Your servants will do as you command, my lord. 26 While our wives and children, our herds and other livestock remain in the towns of Gilead, 27 all your servants will go across as armed troops to battle before the LORD, just as your lordship says." 28 Moses, therefore, gave this order in their regard to the priest Eleazar, to Joshua, son of Nun, and to the heads of the ancestral tribes of the Israelites: 29 "If all the Gadites and Reubenites cross the Jordan with you as combat troops before the LORD, you shall give them Gilead as their property when the land has been subdued before you. 30 But if they will not go across with you as combat troops before the LORD, you shall bring their wives and children and livestock across before you into Canaan, and they shall have their property with you in the land of Canaan." 31 To this, the Gadites and Reubenites replied, "We will do what the LORD has commanded us, your servants. 32 We ourselves will go across into the land of Canaan as troops before the LORD, but we will retain our hereditary property on this side of the Jordan." 33 So Moses gave them (the Gadites and Reubenites, as well as half the tribe of Manasseh, son of Joseph, the kingdom of Sihon, king of the Amorites, and the kingdom of Og, king of Bashan,) the land with its towns and the districts that surrounded them. 34 The Gadites rebuilt the fortified towns of Dibon, Ataroth, Aroer, 35 Atroth-shophan, Jazer, Jogbehah, 36 Beth-nimrah and Beth-haran, and they built sheepfolds. 37 The Reubenites rebuilt Heshbon, Elealeh, Kiriathaim, 38 Nebo, Baal-meon (names to be changed!), and Sibmah. These towns, which they rebuilt, they called by their old names. 39 The descendants of Machir, son of Manasseh, invaded Gilead and captured it, driving out the Amorites who were there. 40 (Moses gave Gilead to Machir, son of Manasseh, and he settled there.) 41 Jair, a Manassehite clan, campaigned against the tent villages, captured them, and called them Havvoth-jair. 42 Nobah also campaigned against Kenath, captured it

with its dependencies, and called it Nobah after his own name.

Numbers chapter 33

1 The following are the stages by which the Israelites journeyed up by companies from the land of Egypt under the guidance of Moses and Aaron. 2 By the LORD'S command Moses recorded the starting places of the various stages. The starting places of the successive stages were: 3 They set out from Rameses in the first month, on the fifteenth day of the first month. On the Passover morrow the Israelites went forth in triumph, in view of all Egypt, 4 while the Egyptians buried their first-born all of whom the LORD had struck down; on their gods, too, the LORD executed judgments. 5 Setting out from Rameses, the Israelites camped at Succoth. 6 Setting out from Succoth, they camped at Etham near the edge of the desert. 7 Setting out from Etham, they turned back to Pi-hahiroth, which is opposite Baal-zephon, and they camped opposite Migdol. 8 Setting out from Pi-hahiroth, they crossed over through the sea into the desert, and after a three days' journey in the desert of Etham, they camped at Marah. 9 Setting out from Marah, they came to Elim, where there were twelve springs of water and seventy palm trees, and they camped there. 10 Setting out from Elim, they camped beside the Red Sea. 11 Setting out from the Red Sea, they camped in the desert of Sin. 12 Setting out from the desert of Sin, they camped at Dophkah. 13 Setting out from Dophkah, they camped at Alush. 14 Setting out from Alush, they camped at Rephidim, where there was no water for the people to drink. 15 Setting out from Rephidim, they camped in the desert of Sinai. 16 Setting out from the desert of Sinai, they camped at Kibroth-hattaavah. 17 Setting out from Kibroth-hattaavah, they camped at Hazeroth. 18 Setting out from Hazeroth, they camped at Rithmah. 19 Setting out from Rithmah, they camped at Rimmon-perez. 20 Setting out from Rimmon-perez, they camped at Libnah. 21 Setting out from Libnah, they camped at Rissah. 22 Setting out from Rissah, they camped at Kehelathah. 23 Setting out from Kehelathah, they camped at Mount Shepher. 24 Setting out from Mount Shepher, they camped at Haradah. 25 Setting out from Haradah, they camped at Makheloth. 26 Setting out from Makheloth, they camped at Tahath. 27 Setting out from Tahath, they camped at Terah. 28 Setting out from Terah, they camped at Mithkah. 29 Setting out from Mithkah, they camped at Hashmonah. 30 Setting out from Hashmonah, they camped at Moseroth. 31 Setting out from Moseroth, they camped at Bene-jaakan. 32 Setting out from Bene-jaakan, they camped at Mount Gidgad. 33 Setting out from Mount Gidgad, they camped at Jotbathah. 34 Setting out from Jotbathah, they camped at Abronah. 35 Setting out from Abronah, they camped at Ezion-geber. 36 Setting out from Ezion-geber, they camped in the desert of Zin, at Kadesh. 37 Setting out from Kadesh, they camped at Mount Hor on the border of the land of Edom. 38 (Aaron the priest ascended Mount Hor at the LORD'S command, and there he died in the fortieth year from the departure of the Israelites from the land of Egypt, on the first day of the fifth month. 39 Aaron was a hundred and twenty-three years old when he died on Mount Hor. 40 Now, when the Canaanite king of Arad, who lived in the Negeb in the land of Canaan, heard that the Israelites were coming...) 41 Setting out from Mount Hor, they camped at Zalmonah. 42 Setting out from Zalmonah, they camped at Punon. 43 Setting out from Punon, they camped at Oboth. 44 Setting out from Oboth, they camped at Iye-abarim on the border of Moab. 45 Setting out from Iye-abarim, they camped at Dibon-gad. 46 Setting out from Dibon-gad, they camped at Almon-diblathaim. 47 Setting out from Almon-diblathaim, they camped in the Abarim Mountains opposite Nebo. 48 Setting out from the Abarim Mountains, they camped on the plains of Moab along the Jericho stretch of the Jordan. 49 Their camp along the Jordan on the plains of Moab extended from Beth-jeshimoth to Abelshittim. 50 The LORD spoke to Moses on the plains of Moab beside the Jericho stretch of the Jordan and said to him: 51 "Tell the Israelites: When you go across the Jordan into the land of Canaan, 52 drive out all the inhabitants of the land before you; destroy all their stone figures and molten images and demolish all their high places. 53 You shall take possession of the land and settle in it, for I have given you the land as your property. 54 You shall apportion the land among yourselves by lot, clan by clan, assigning a large heritage to a large group and a small heritage to a small group. Wherever anyone's lot falls, there shall his property be within the heritage of his ancestral tribe. 55 But if you do not drive out the inhabitants of the land before you, those whom you allow to remain will become as barbs in your eyes and thorns in your sides, and they will harass you in the country where you live, 56 and I will treat you as I had intended to treat them."

Numbers chapter 34

1 The LORD said to Moses, 2 "Give the Israelites this order: When you enter the land of Canaan, this is the territory that shall fall to you as your heritage - the land of Canaan with its boundaries: 3 Your southern boundary shall be at the desert of Zin along the border of Edom; on the east it shall begin at the end of the Salt Sea, 4 and turning south of the Akrabbim Pass, it shall cross Zin, and extend south of Kadesh-barnea to Hazar-addar; thence it shall cross to Azmon, 5 and turning from Azmon to the Wadi of Egypt, shall terminate at the Sea. 6 For your western boundary you shall have the Great Sea with its coast; this shall be your western boundary. 7 The following shall be your boundary on the north: from the Great Sea you shall draw a line to Mount Hor, 8 and shall continue it from Mount Hor to Labo in the land of Hamath, with the boundary extending through Zedad. 9 Thence the boundary shall reach to Ziphron and terminate at Hazar-enan. This shall be your northern boundary. 10 For your eastern boundary you shall draw a line from Hazar-enan to Shepham. 11 From Shepham the boundary shall go down to Ar-Baal, east of Ain, and descending further, shall strike the ridge on the east side of the Sea of Chinnereth; 12 thence the boundary shall continue along the Jordan and terminate with the Salt Sea. This is the land that shall be yours, with the boundaries that surround it." 13 Moses also gave this order to the Israelites: "This is the land, to be apportioned among you by lot, which the LORD has commanded to be given to the nine and one-half tribes. 14 For all the ancestral houses of the tribe of Reuben, and the ancestral houses of the tribe of Gad, as well as half of the tribe of Manasseh, have already received their heritage; 15 these two and one-half tribes have received their heritage on the eastern side of the Jericho stretch of the Jordan, toward the sunrise." 16 The LORD said to Moses, 17 "These are the names of the men who shall apportion the land among you: Eleazar the priest, and Joshua, son of Nun, 18 and one prince from each of the tribes whom you shall designate for this task. 19 These shall be as follows: from the tribe of Judah: Caleb, son of Jephunneh; 20 from the tribe of Simeon: Samuel, son of Ammihud; 21 from the tribe of Benjamin: Elidad, son of Chislon; 22 from the tribe of Dan: Bukki, son of Jogli; 23 from the tribe of Manasseh: Hanniel, son of Ephod; 24 from the tribe of Ephraim: Kemuel, son of Shiphtan, for the descendants of Joseph; 25 from the tribe of Zebulun: Elizaphan, son of Parnach; 26 from the tribe of Issachar: Paltiel, son of Azzan; 27 from the tribe of Asher: Ahihud, son of Shelomi; 28 from the tribe of Naphtali: Pedahel, son of Ammihud." 29 These are they whom the LORD commanded to assign the Israelites their heritage in the land of Canaan.

Numbers chapter 35

1 The LORD gave these instructions to Moses on the plains of Moab beside the Jericho stretch of the Jordan: 2 "Tell the Israelites that out of their hereditary property they shall give the Levites cities for homes, as well as pasture lands around the cities. 3 The cities shall serve them to dwell in, and the pasture lands shall serve their herds and flocks and other animals. 4 The pasture lands of the cities to be assigned the Levites shall extend a thousand cubits from the city walls in each direction. 5 Thus you shall measure out two thousand cubits outside the city along each side—east, south, west and north—with the city lying in the center. This shall serve them as the pasture lands of their cities. 6 "Now these are the cities you shall give to the Levites: the six cities of asylum which you must establish as places where a homicide can take refuge, and in addition forty-two other cities—a total of forty-eight cities with their pasture lands to be assigned the Levites. 7 In assigning the cities from the property of the Israelites, take more from a larger group and fewer from a smaller one, so that each group will cede cities to the Levites in proportion to its own heritage." 8 The LORD said to Moses, 9 "Tell the Israelites: When you go across the Jordan into the land of Canaan, 10 select for yourselves cities to serve as cities of asylum, where a homicide who has killed someone unintentionally may take refuge. 11 These cities shall serve you as places of asylum from the avenger of blood, so that a homicide shall not be put to death unless he is first tried before the community. 12 Six cities of asylum shall you assign: 13 three beyond the Jordan, and three in the land of Canaan. 14 These six cities of asylum shall serve not only the Israelites but all the resident or transient aliens among them, so that anyone who has killed another unintentionally may take refuge there. 15 "If a man strikes another with an iron instrument and causes his death, he is a murderer and shall be put to death. 16 If a man strikes another with a death-dealing stone in his hand and causes his death, he is a murderer and shall be put to death. 17 If a man strikes another with a death-dealing club in his hand and causes his death, he is a murderer and shall be put to death. 18 The avenger of blood may execute the murderer, putting him to death on sight. 19 "If a man pushes another out of hatred, or after lying in wait for him throws something at him, and causes his death, 20 or if he strikes another out of enmity and causes his death, he shall be put to death as a murderer. The avenger of blood may execute the murderer on sight. 21 "However, if a man pushes another accidentally and not out

of enmity, or if without lying in wait for him he throws some object at him, 22 or without seeing him throws a death-dealing stone which strikes him and causes his death, although he was not his enemy nor seeking to harm him: 23 then the community, deciding the case between the slayer and the avenger of blood in accordance with these norms, 24 shall free the homicide from the avenger of blood and shall remand him to the city of asylum where he took refuge; and he shall stay there until the death of the high priest who has been anointed with sacred oil. 25 If the homicide of his own accord leaves the bounds of the city of asylum where he has taken refuge, 26 and the avenger of blood finds him beyond these bounds and kills him, the avenger incurs no bloodguilt; 27 the homicide was bound to stay in his city of asylum until the death of the high priest. Only after the death of the high priest may the homicide return to his own district. 28 "These shall be norms for you and all your descendants, wherever you live, for rendering judgment. 29 "Whenever someone kills another, the evidence of witnesses is required for the execution of the murderer. The evidence of a single witness is not sufficient for putting a person to death. 30 "You shall not accept indemnity in place of the life of a murderer who deserves the death penalty; he must be put to death. 31 Nor shall you accept indemnity to allow a refugee to leave his city of asylum and again dwell elsewhere in the land before the death of the high priest. 32 You shall not desecrate the land where you live. Since bloodshed desecrates the land, the land can have no atonement for the blood shed on it except through the blood of him who shed it. 33 Do not defile the land in which you live and in the midst of which I dwell; for I am the LORD who dwells in the midst of the Israelites."

Numbers chapter 36

1 The heads of the ancestral houses in the clan of descendants of Gilead, son of Machir, son of Manasseh—one of the Josephite clans—came up and laid this plea before Moses and the priest Eleazar and before the princes who were the heads of the ancestral houses of the other Israelites. 2 They said: "The LORD commanded you, my lord, to apportion the land by lot among the Israelites; and you, my lord, were also commanded by the LORD to give the heritage of our kinsman Zelophehad to his daughters. 3 But if they marry into one of the other Israelite tribes, their heritage will be withdrawn from our ancestral heritage and will be added to that of the tribe into which they marry; thus the heritage that fell to us by lot will be diminished. 4 When the Israelites celebrate the jubilee year, the heritage of these women will be permanently added to that of the tribe into which they marry and will be withdrawn from that of our ancestral tribe." 5 So Moses gave this regulation to the Israelites according to the instructions of the LORD: "The tribe of the Josephites are right in what they say. 6 This is what the LORD commands with regard to the daughters of Zelophehad: They may marry anyone they please, provided they marry into a clan of their ancestral tribe, 7 so that no heritage of the Israelites will pass from one tribe to another, but all the Israelites will retain their own ancestral heritage. 8 Therefore, every daughter who inherits property in any of the Israelite tribes shall marry someone belonging to a clan of her own ancestral tribe, in order that all the Israelites may remain in possession of their own ancestral heritage. 9 Thus, no heritage can pass from one tribe to another, but all the Israelite tribes will retain their own ancestral heritage." 10 The daughters of Zelophehad obeyed the command which the LORD had given to Moses. 11 Mahlah, Tirzah, Hoglah, Milcah and Noah, Zelophehad's daughters, married relatives on their father's side 12 within the clans of the descendants of Manasseh, son of Joseph; hence their heritage remained in the tribe of their father's clan. 13 These are the commandments and decisions which the LORD prescribed for the Israelites through Moses, on the plains of Moab beside the Jericho stretch of the Jordan.

Deuteronomy

Deuteronomy Chapter 1

1These are the words which Moses spoke to all Israel beyond the Jordan, in the desert, in the Arabah, opposite Suph, between Paran and Tophel, Laban, Hazeroth, and Dizahab.2It is a journey of eleven days from Horeb to Kadesh-barnea by way of the highlands of Seir.3In the fortieth year, on the first day of the eleventh month, Moses spoke to the Israelites all the commands that the LORD had given him in their regard.4After he had defeated Sihon, king of the Amorites, who lived in Heshbon, and Og, king of Bashan, who lived in Ashtaroth and in Edrei,5Moses began to explain the law in the land of Moab beyond the Jordan, as follows:6"The LORD, our God, said to us at Horeb, 'You have stayed long enough at this mountain.7Leave here and go to the hill country of the Amorites and to all the surrounding regions, the land of the Canaanites in the Arabah, the mountains, the foothills, the Negeb,

and the seacoast; to Lebanon, and as far as the Great River, the Euphrates.8I have given that land over to you. Go now and occupy the land I swore to your fathers, Abraham, Isaac, and Jacob, I would give to them and to their descendants.'9At that time I said to you, 'Alone, I am unable to carry you.10The LORD, your God, has so multiplied you that you are now as numerous as the stars in the sky.11May the LORD, the God of your fathers, increase you a thousand times over, and bless you as he promised!12But how can I alone bear the crushing burden that you are, along with your bickering?13Choose wise, intelligent, and experienced men from each of your tribes, that I may appoint them as your leaders.'14You answered me, 'We agree to do as you have proposed.'15So I took outstanding men of your tribes, wise and experienced, and made them your leaders as officials over thousands, over hundreds, over fifties, and over tens, and other tribal officers.16I charged your judges at that time, 'Listen to complaints among your kinsmen, and administer true justice to both parties even if one of them is an alien.17In rendering judgment, do not consider who a person is; give ear to the lowly and to the great alike, fearing no man, for judgment is God's. Refer to me any case that is too hard for you and I will hear it.'18Thereupon I gave you all the commands you were to fulfill.19Then, in obedience to the command of the LORD, our God, we set out from Horeb and journeyed through the whole desert, vast and fearful as you have seen, in the direction of the hill country of the Amorites. We had reached Kadesh-barnea20when I said to you, 'You have come to the hill country of the Amorites, which the LORD, our God, is giving us.21The LORD, your God, has given this land over to you. Go up and occupy it, as the LORD, the God of your fathers, commands you. Do not fear or lose heart.'22Then all of you came up to me and said, 'Let us send men ahead to reconnoiter the land for us and report to us on the road we must follow and the cities we must take.'23Agreeing with the proposal, I chose twelve men from your number, one from each tribe.24They set out into the hill country as far as the Wadi Eshcol, and explored it.25Then, taking along some of the fruit of the land, they brought it down to us and reported, 'The land which the LORD, our God, gives us is good.'26But you refused to go up, and after defying the command of the LORD, your God,27you set to murmuring in your tents, 'Out of hatred for us the LORD has brought us up out of the land of Egypt, to deliver us into the hands of the Amorites and destroy us.28What shall we meet with up there? Our kinsmen have made us fainthearted by reporting that the people are stronger and taller than we, and their cities are large and fortified to the sky; besides, they saw the Anakim there.'29But I said to you, 'Have no dread or fear of them.30The LORD, your God, who goes before you, will himself fight for you, just as he took your part before your very eyes in Egypt,31as well as in the desert, where you saw how the LORD, your God, carried you, as a man carries his child, all along your journey until you arrived at this place.'32Despite this, you would not trust the LORD, your God,33who journeys before you to find you a resting place—by day in the cloud, and by night in the fire, to show the way you must go.34When the LORD heard your words, he was angry;35and he swore, 'Not one man of this evil generation shall look upon the good land I swore to give to your fathers,36except Caleb, son of Jephunneh; he shall see it. For to him and to his sons I will give the land he trod upon, because he has followed the LORD unreservedly.'37The LORD was angered against me also on your account, and said, 'Not even you shall enter there, 38 but your aide Joshua, son of Nun, shall enter. Encourage him, for he is to give Israel its heritage.39Your little ones, who you said would become booty, and your children, who as yet do not know good from bad—they shall enter; to them I will give it, and they shall occupy it.40But as for yourselves: turn about and proceed into the desert on the Red Sea road.'41In reply you said to me, 'We have sinned against the LORD. We will go up ourselves and fight, just as the LORD, our God, commanded us.' And each of you girded on his weapons, making light of going up into the hill country. 42 But the LORD said to me, 'Warn them: Do not go up and fight, lest you be beaten down before your enemies, for I will not be in your midst.'43I gave you this warning but you would not listen. In defiance of the LORD'S command you arrogantly marched off into the hill country.44Then the Amorites living there came out against you and, like bees, chased you, cutting you down in Seir as far as Hormah.45On your return you wept before the LORD, but he did not listen to your cry or give ear to you.46That is why you had to stay as long as you did at Kadesh.

Deuteronomy Chapter 2

1"When we did turn and proceed into the desert on the Red Sea road, as the LORD had commanded me, we circled around the highlands of Seir for a long time.2Finally the LORD said to me,3'You have wandered round these highlands long enough; turn and go north.4Give this order to the people: You are now about to pass through the territory of your kinsmen, the descendants of Esau, who live in Seir. Though they are afraid of you, be very careful⁵not to come in conflict with them, for I will not give you so much as a foot of their land, since I have already given Esau possession of the highlands of Seir.⁶You shall purchase from them with silver the food you eat and the well water you drink.⁷The LORD, your God, has blessed you in all your undertakings; he has been concerned about your journey through this vast desert. It is now forty years that he has been with you, and you have never been in want.'⁸Then we left behind us the Arabah route, Elath, Ezion-geber, and Seir, where our kinsmen, the descendants of Esau, live; and we went on toward the desert of Moab.⁹And the LORD said to me, 'Do not show hostility to the Moabites or engage them in battle, for I will not give you possession of any of their land, since I have given Ar to the descendants of Lot as their own.¹⁰(Formerly the Emim lived there, a people strong and numerous and tall like the Anakim;¹¹like them they were considered Rephaim. It was the Moabites who called them Emim.¹²In Seir, however, the former inhabitants were the Horites; the descendants of Esau dispossessed them, clearing them out of the way and taking their place, just as the Israelites have done in the land of their heritage which the LORD has given them.)¹³Get ready, then, to cross the Wadi Zered.' So we crossed it.¹⁴Thirty-eight years had elapsed between our departure from Kadesh-barnea and that crossing; in the meantime the whole generation of soldiers had perished from the camp, as the LORD had sworn they should.¹⁵For it was the LORD'S hand that was against them, till he wiped them out of the camp completely.¹⁶When at length death had put an end to all the soldiers among the people,¹⁷the LORD said to me,¹⁸'You are now about to leave Ar and the territory of Moab behind.¹⁹As you come opposite the Ammonites, do not show hostility or come in conflict with them, for I will not give you possession of any land of the Ammonites, since I have given it to the descendants of Lot as their own.²⁰(This also was considered a country of the Rephaim from its former inhabitants, whom the Ammonites called Zamzummim,²¹a people strong and numerous and tall like the Anakim. But these, too, the LORD cleared out of the way for the Ammonites, who ousted them and took their place.²²He had done the same for the descendants of Esau, who dwell in Seir, by clearing the Horites out of their way, so that the descendants of Esau have taken their place down to the present.²³So also the Caphtorim, migrating from Caphtor, cleared away the Avvim, who once dwelt in villages as far as Gaza, and took their place.)²⁴Advance now across the Wadi Arnon. I now deliver into your hands Sihon, the Amorite king of Heshbon, and his land. Begin the occupation; engage him in battle.²⁵This day I will begin to put a fear and dread of you into every nation under the heavens, so that at the mention of your name they will quake and tremble before you.'²⁶So I sent messengers from the desert of Kedemoth to Sihon, king of Heshbon, with this offer of peace:²⁷'Let me pass through your country by the highway; I will go along it without turning aside to the right or to the left.²⁸For the food I eat which you will supply, and for the water you give me to drink, you shall be paid in silver. Only let me march through,²⁹as the descendants of Esau who dwell in Seir and the Moabites who dwell in Ar have done, until I cross the Jordan into the land which the LORD, our God, is about to give us.'³⁰But Sihon, king of Heshbon, refused to let us pass through his land, because the LORD, your God, made him stubborn in mind and obstinate in heart that he might deliver him up to you, as indeed he has now done.³¹Then the LORD said to me, 'Now that I have already begun to hand over to you Sihon and his land, begin the actual occupation.'³²So Sihon and all his people advanced against us to join battle at Jahaz;³³but since the LORD, our God, had delivered him to us, we defeated him and his sons and all his people.³⁴At that time we seized all his cities and doomed them all, with their men, women, and children; we left no survivor.³⁵Our only booty was the livestock and the loot of the captured cities.³⁶From Aroer on the edge of the Wadi Arnon and from the city in the wadi itself, as far as Gilead, no city was too well fortified for us to whom the LORD had delivered them up.³⁷However, in obedience to the command of the LORD, our God, you did not encroach upon any of the Ammonite land, neither the region bordering on the Wadi Jabbok nor the cities of the highlands.

Deuteronomy Chapter 3

¹"Then we turned and proceeded toward Bashan. But Og, king of Bashan, advanced against us with all his people to give battle at Edrei.²The LORD, however, said to me, 'Do not be afraid of him, for I have delivered him into your hand with all his people and his land. Do to him as you did to Sihon, king of the Amorites, who lived in Heshbon.'³And thus the LORD, our God, delivered into our hands Og, king of Bashan, with all his people. We defeated him so completely that we left him no survivor.⁴At that time we captured all his cities, none of them eluding our grasp, the whole region of Argob, the kingdom of Og

in Bashan: sixty cities in all,⁵to say nothing of the great number of unwalled towns. All the cities were fortified with high walls and gates and bars.⁶As we had done to Sihon, king of Heshbon, so also here we doomed all the cities, with their men, women, and children;⁷but all the livestock and the loot of each city we took as booty for ourselves.⁸And so at that time we took from the two kings of the Amorites beyond the Jordan the territory from the Wadi Arnon to Mount Hermon⁹(which is called Sirion by the Sidonians and Senir by the Amorites),¹⁰comprising all the cities of the plateau and all Gilead and all the cities of the kingdom of Og in Bashan including Salecah and Edrei.¹¹(Og, king of Bashan, was the last remaining survivor of the Rephaim. He had a bed of iron, nine regular cubits long and four wide, which is still preserved in Rabbah of the Ammonites.)¹²When we occupied the land at that time, I gave Reuben and Gad the territory from Aroer, on the edge of the Wadi Arnon, halfway up into the highlands of Gilead, with the cities therein.¹³The rest of Gilead and all of Bashan, the kingdom of Og, the whole Argob region, I gave to the half-tribe of Manasseh. (All this region of Bashan was once called a land of the Rephaim.¹⁴Jair, a Manassehite clan, took all the region of Argob as far as the border of the Geshurites and Maacathites, and called it after his own name Bashan Havvoth-jair, the name it bears today.)¹⁵To Machir I gave Gilead,¹⁶and to Reuben and Gad the territory from Gilead to the Wadi Arnon - including the wadi bed and its banks - and to the Wadi Jabbok, which is the border of the Ammonites,¹⁷as well as the Arabah with the Jordan and its eastern banks from Chinnereth to the Salt Sea of the Arabah, under the slopes of Pisgah.¹⁸At that time I charged them as follows 'The LORD, your God, has given you this land as your own. But all you troops equipped for battle must cross over in the vanguard of your brother Israelites.¹⁹Only your wives and children, as well as your livestock, of which I know you have a large number, shall remain behind in the towns I have given you,²⁰until the LORD has settled your kinsmen as well, and they too possess the land which the LORD, your God, will give them on the other side of the Jordan. Then you may all return to the possessions I have given you.'²¹It was then that I instructed Joshua, 'Your eyes have seen all that the LORD, your God, has done to both these kings; so, too, will the LORD do to all the kingdoms which you will encounter over there.²²Fear them not, for the LORD, your God, will fight for you.'²³And it was then that I besought the LORD,²⁴'O Lord GOD, you have begun to show to your servant your greatness and might. For what god in heaven or on earth can perform deeds as mighty as yours?²⁵Ah, let me cross over and see this good land beyond the Jordan, this fine hill country, and the Lebanon!'²⁶But the LORD was angry with me on your account and would not hear me. 'Enough!' the LORD said to me. 'Speak to me no more of this.²⁷Go up to the top of Pisgah and look out to the west, and to the north, and to the south, and to the east. Look well, for you shall not cross this Jordan.²⁸Commission Joshua, and encourage and strengthen him, for he shall cross at the head of this people and shall put them in possession of the land you are to see.'²⁹This was while we were in the ravine opposite Beth-peor."

Deuteronomy Chapter 4

¹"Now, Israel, hear the statutes and decrees which I am teaching you to observe, that you may live, and may enter in and take possession of the land which the LORD, the God of your fathers, is giving you. ²In your observance of the commandments of the LORD, your God, which I enjoin upon you, you shall not add to what I command you nor subtract from it. ³You have seen with your own eyes what the LORD did at Baal-peor: the LORD, your God, destroyed from your midst everyone that followed the Baal of Peor; ⁴but you, who clung to the LORD, your God, are all alive today. ⁵Therefore, I teach you the statutes and decrees as the LORD, my God, has commanded me, that you may observe them in the land you are entering to occupy. ⁶Observe them carefully, for thus will you give evidence of your wisdom and intelligence to the nations, who will hear of all these statutes and say, 'This great nation is truly a wise and intelligent people.' ⁷For what great nation is there that has gods so close to it as the LORD, our God, is to us whenever we call upon him? ⁸Or what great nation has statutes and decrees that are as just as this whole law which I am setting before you today? ⁹"However, take care and be earnestly on your guard not to forget the things which your own eyes have seen, nor let them slip from your memory as long as you live, but teach them to your children and to your children's children. ¹⁰There was the day on which you stood before the LORD, your God, at Horeb, and he said to me, 'Assemble the people for me; I will have them hear my words, that they may learn to fear me as long as they live in the land and may so teach their children.' ¹¹You came near and stood at the foot of the mountain, which blazed to the very sky with fire and was enveloped in a dense black cloud. ¹²Then the LORD spoke to you from the midst of the fire. You heard the sound of the words, but saw no form; there was only a voice. ¹³He proclaimed to you his covenant, which he

commanded you to keep: the ten commandments, which he wrote on two tablets of stone. ¹⁴The LORD charged me at that time to teach you the statutes and decrees which you are to observe over in the land you will occupy. ¹⁵You saw no form at all on the day the LORD spoke to you at Horeb from the midst of the fire. Be strictly on your guard, therefore, ¹⁶not to degrade yourselves by fashioning an idol to represent any figure, whether it be the form of a man or a woman, ¹⁷of any animal on the earth or of any bird that flies in the sky, ¹⁸of anything that crawls on the ground or of any fish in the waters under the earth. ¹⁹And when you look up to the heavens and behold the sun or the moon or any star among the heavenly hosts, do not be led astray into adoring them and serving them. These the LORD, your God, has let fall to the lot of all other nations under the heavens; ²⁰but you he has taken and led out of that iron foundry, Egypt, that you might be his very own people, as you are today. ²¹Since the LORD was angered against me on your account and swore that I should not cross the Jordan nor enter the good land which he is giving you as a heritage, ²²I myself shall die in this country without crossing the Jordan; but you will cross over and take possession of that good land. ²³Take heed, therefore, lest, forgetting the covenant which the LORD, your God, has made with you, you fashion for yourselves against his command an idol in any form whatsoever. ²⁴For the LORD, your God, is a consuming fire, a jealous God. ²⁵"When you have children and grandchildren, and have grown old in the land, should you then degrade yourselves by fashioning an idol in any form and by this evil done in his sight provoke the LORD, your God, ²⁶I call heaven and earth this day to witness against you, that you shall all quickly perish from the land which you will occupy when you cross the Jordan. You shall not live in it for any length of time but shall be promptly wiped out. ²⁷The LORD will scatter you among the nations, and there shall remain but a handful of you among the nations to which the LORD will lead you. ²⁸There you shall serve gods fashioned by the hands of man out of wood and stone, gods which can neither see nor hear, neither eat nor smell. ²⁹Yet there too you shall seek the LORD, your God; and you shall indeed find him when you search after him with your whole heart and your whole soul. ³⁰In your distress, when all these things shall have come upon you, you shall finally return to the LORD, your God, and heed his voice. ³¹Since the LORD, your God, is a merciful God, he will not abandon and destroy you, nor forget the covenant which under oath he made with your fathers. ³²"Ask now of the days of old, before your time, ever since God created man upon the earth; ask from one end of the sky to the other: Did anything so great ever happen before? Was it ever heard of? ³³Did a people ever hear the voice of God speaking from the midst of fire, as you did, and live? ³⁴Or did any god venture to go and take a nation for himself from the midst of another nation, by testings, by signs and wonders, by war, with his strong hand and outstretched arm, and by great terrors, all of which the LORD, your God, did for you in Egypt before your very eyes? ³⁵All this you were allowed to see that you might know the LORD is God and there is no other. ³⁶Out of the heavens he let you hear his voice to discipline you; on earth he let you see his great fire, and you heard him speaking out of the fire. ³⁷For love of your fathers he chose their descendants and personally led you out of Egypt by his great power, ³⁸driving out of your way nations greater and mightier than you, so as to bring you in and to make their land your heritage, as it is today. ³⁹This is why you must now know, and fix in your heart, that the LORD is God in the heavens above and on earth below, and that there is no other. ⁴⁰You must keep his statutes and commandments which I enjoin on you today, that you and your children after you may prosper, and that you may have long life on the land which the LORD, your God, is giving you forever." ⁴¹Then Moses set apart three cities in the region east of the Jordan, ⁴²that a homicide might take refuge there if he unwittingly killed his neighbor to whom he had previously borne no malice, and that he might save his life by fleeing to one of these cities: ⁴³Bezer in the desert, in the region of the plateau, for the Reubenites; Ramoth in Gilead for the Gadites; and Golan in Bashan for the Manassehites. ⁴⁴This is the law which Moses set before the Israelites. ⁴⁵These are the ordinances, statutes and decrees which he proclaimed to them when they had come out of Egypt ⁴⁶and were beyond the Jordan in the ravine opposite Beth-peor, in the land of Sihon, king of the Amorites, who dwelt in Heshbon and whom Moses and the Israelites defeated after coming out of Egypt. ⁴⁷They occupied his land and the land of Og, king of Bashan, as well - the land of these two kings of the Amorites in the region east of the Jordan: ⁴⁸from Aroer on the edge of the Wadi Arnon to Mount Sion (that is Hermon) ⁴⁹and all the Arabah east of the Jordan, as far as the Arabah Sea under the slopes of Pisgah.

Deuteronomy Chapter 5

¹Moses summoned all Israel and said to them, "Hear, O Israel, the statutes and decrees which I proclaim in your hearing this day, that you

may learn them and take care to observe them. ²The LORD, our God, made a covenant with us at Horeb; ³not with our fathers did he make this covenant, but with us, all of us who are alive here this day. ⁴The LORD spoke with you face to face on the mountain from the midst of the fire. ⁵Since you were afraid of the fire and would not go up the mountain, I stood between the LORD and you at that time, to announce to you these words of the LORD: ⁶'I, the LORD, am your God, who brought you out of the land of Egypt, that place of slavery. ⁷You shall not have other gods besides me. ⁸You shall not carve idols for yourselves in the shape of anything in the sky above or on the earth below or in the waters beneath the earth; ⁹you shall not bow down before them or worship them. For I, the LORD, your God, am a jealous God, inflicting punishments for their fathers' wickedness on the children of those who hate me, down to the third and fourth generation ¹⁰but bestowing mercy, down to the thousandth generation, on the children of those who love me and keep my commandments. ¹¹You shall not take the name of the LORD, your God, in vain. For the LORD will not leave unpunished him who takes his name in vain. ¹²Take care to keep holy the sabbath day as the LORD, your God, commanded you. ¹³Six days you may labor and do all your work; ¹⁴but the seventh day is the sabbath of the LORD, your God. No work may be done then, whether by you, or your son or daughter, or your male or female slave, or your ox or ass or any of your beasts, or the alien who lives with you. Your male and female slave should rest as you do. ¹⁵For remember that you too were once slaves in Egypt, and the LORD, your God, brought you from there with his strong hand and outstretched arm. That is why the LORD, your God, has commanded you to observe the sabbath day. ¹⁶Honor your father and your mother, as the LORD, your God, has commanded you, that you may have a long life and prosperity in the land which the LORD, your God, is giving you. ¹⁷You shall not kill. ¹⁸You shall not commit adultery. ¹⁹You shall not steal. ²⁰You shall not bear dishonest witness against your neighbor. ²¹You shall not covet your neighbor's wife. You shall not desire your neighbor's house or field, nor his male or female slave, nor his ox or ass, nor anything that belongs to him.' ²²These words, and nothing more, the LORD spoke with a loud voice to your entire assembly on the mountain from the midst of the fire and the dense cloud. He wrote them upon two tablets of stone and gave them to me. ²³But when you heard the voice from the midst of the darkness, while the mountain was ablaze with fire, you came to me in the person of all your tribal heads and elders, ²⁴and said, 'The LORD, our God, has indeed let us see his glory and his majesty! We have heard his voice from the midst of the fire and have found out today that a man can still live after God has spoken with him. ²⁵But why should we die now? Surely this great fire will consume us. If we hear the voice of the LORD, our God, any more, we shall die. ²⁶For what mortal has heard, as we have, the voice of the living God speaking from the midst of fire, and survived? ²⁷Go closer, you, and hear all that the LORD, our God, will say, and then tell us what the LORD, our God, tells you; we will listen and obey.' ²⁸The LORD heard your words as you were speaking to me and said to me, 'I have heard the words these people have spoken to you, which are all well said. ²⁹Would that they might always be of such a mind, to fear me and to keep all my commandments! Then they and their descendants would prosper forever. ³⁰Go, tell them to return to their tents. ³¹Then you wait here near me and I will give you all the commandments, the statutes and decrees you must teach them, that they may observe them in the land which I am giving them to possess.' ³²Be careful, therefore, to do as the LORD, your God, has commanded you, not turning aside to the right or to the left, ³³but following exactly the way prescribed for you by the LORD, your God, that you may live and prosper, and may have long life in the land which you are to occupy."

Deuteronomy Chapter 6

¹"These then are the commandments, the statutes and decrees which the LORD, your God, has ordered that you be taught to observe in the land into which you are crossing for conquest, ²so that you and your son and your grandson may fear the LORD, your God, and keep, throughout the days of your lives, all his statutes and commandments which I enjoin on you, and thus have long life. ³Hear then, Israel, and be careful to observe them, that you may grow and prosper the more, in keeping with the promise of the LORD, the God of your fathers, to give you a land flowing with milk and honey. ⁴"Hear, O Israel! The LORD is our God, the LORD alone! ⁵Therefore, you shall love the LORD, your God, with all your heart, and with all your soul, and with all your strength. ⁶Take to heart these words which I enjoin on you today. ⁷Drill them into your children. Speak of them at home and abroad, whether you are busy or at rest. ⁸Bind them at your wrist as a sign and let them be as a pendant on your forehead. ⁹Write them on the doorposts of your houses and on your gates. ¹⁰"When the LORD, your God, brings you

into the land which he swore to your fathers, Abraham, Isaac and Jacob, that he would give you, a land with fine, large cities that you did not build, [11]with houses full of goods of all sorts that you did not garner, with cisterns that you did not dig, with vineyards and olive groves that you did not plant; and when, therefore, you eat your fill, [12]take care not to forget the LORD, who brought you out of the land of Egypt, that place of slavery. [13]The LORD, your God, shall you fear; him shall you serve, and by his name shall you swear. [14]You shall not follow other gods, such as those of the surrounding nations, [15]lest the wrath of the LORD, your God, flare up against you and he destroy you from the face of the land; for the LORD, your God, who is in your midst, is a jealous God. [16]"You shall not put the LORD, your God, to the test, as you did at Massah. [17]But keep the commandments of the LORD, your God, and the ordinances and statutes he has enjoined on you. [18]Do what is right and good in the sight of the LORD, that you may, according to his word, prosper, and may enter in and possess the good land which the LORD promised on oath to your fathers, [19]thrusting all your enemies out of your way. [20]"Later on, when your son asks you what these ordinances, statutes and decrees mean which the LORD, our God, has enjoined on you, [21]you shall say to your son, 'We were once slaves of Pharaoh in Egypt, but the LORD brought us out of Egypt with his strong hand [22]and wrought before our eyes signs and wonders, great and dire, against Egypt and against Pharaoh and his whole house. [23]He brought us from there to lead us into the land he promised on oath to our fathers, and to give it to us. [24]Therefore, the LORD commanded us to observe all these statutes in fear of the LORD, our God, that we may always have as prosperous and happy a life as we have today; [25]and our justice before the LORD, our God, is to consist in carefully observing all these commandments he has enjoined on us.'"

Deuteronomy Chapter 7

[1]"When the LORD, your God, brings you into the land which you are to enter and occupy, and dislodges great nations before you—the Hittites, Girgashites, Amorites, Canaanites, Perizzites, Hivites and Jebusites: seven nations more numerous and powerful than you—[2]and when the LORD, your God, delivers them up to you and you defeat them, you shall doom them. Make no covenant with them and show them no mercy. [3]You shall not intermarry with them, neither giving your daughters to their sons nor taking their daughters for your sons. [4]For they would turn your sons from following me to serving other gods, and then the wrath of the LORD would flare up against you and quickly destroy you. [5]"But this is how you must deal with them: Tear down their altars, smash their sacred pillars, chop down their sacred poles, and destroy their idols by fire. [6]For you are a people sacred to the LORD, your God; he has chosen you from all the nations on the face of the earth to be a people peculiarly his own. [7]It was not because you are the largest of all nations that the LORD set his heart on you and chose you, for you are really the smallest of all nations. [8]It was because the LORD loved you and because of his fidelity to the oath he had sworn to your fathers, that he brought you out with his strong hand from the place of slavery, and ransomed you from the hand of Pharaoh, king of Egypt. [9]Understand, then, that the LORD, your God, is God indeed, the faithful God who keeps his merciful covenant down to the thousandth generation toward those who love him and keep his commandments, [10]but who repays with destruction the person who hates him; he does not dally with such a one, but makes him personally pay for it. [11]You shall therefore carefully observe the commandments, the statutes and the decrees which I enjoin on you today. [12]"As your reward for heeding these decrees and observing them carefully, the LORD, your God, will keep with you the merciful covenant which he promised on oath to your fathers. [13]He will love and bless and multiply you; he will bless the fruit of your womb and the produce of your soil, your grain and wine and oil, the issue of your herds and the young of your flocks, in the land which he swore to your fathers he would give you. [14]You will be blessed above all peoples; no man or woman among you shall be childless nor shall your livestock be barren. [15]The LORD will remove all sickness from you; he will not afflict you with any of the malignant diseases that you know from Egypt, but will leave them with all your enemies. [16]"You shall consume all the nations which the LORD, your God, will deliver up to you. You are not to look on them with pity, lest you be ensnared into serving their gods. [17]Perhaps you will say to yourselves, 'These nations are greater than we. How can we dispossess them?' [18]But do not be afraid of them. Rather, call to mind what the LORD, your God, did to Pharaoh and to all Egypt: [19]the great testings which your own eyes have seen, the signs and wonders, his strong hand and outstretched arm with which the LORD, your God, brought you out. The same also will he do to all the nations of whom you are now afraid. [20]Moreover, the LORD, your God, will send hornets among them, until the survivors who have hidden from you are destroyed. [21]Therefore, do not be terrified by them, for the LORD, your God, who is in your midst, is a great and awesome God. [22]He will dislodge these nations before you little by little. You cannot exterminate them all at once, lest the wild beasts become too numerous for you. [23]The LORD, your God, will deliver them up to you and will rout them utterly until they are annihilated. [24]He will deliver their kings into your hand, that you may make their names perish from under the heavens. No man will be able to stand up against you, till you have put an end to them. [25]The images of their gods you shall destroy by fire. Do not covet the silver or gold on them, nor take it for yourselves, lest you be ensnared by it; for it is an abomination to the LORD, your God. [26]You shall not bring any abominable thing into your house, lest you be doomed with it; loathe and abhor it utterly as a thing that is doomed."

Deuteronomy Chapter 8

[1]"Be careful to observe all the commandments I enjoin on you today, that you may live and increase, and may enter in and possess the land which the LORD promised on oath to your fathers. [2]Remember how for forty years now the LORD, your God, has directed all your journeying in the desert, so as to test you by affliction and find out whether or not it was your intention to keep his commandments. [3]He therefore let you be afflicted with hunger, and then fed you with manna, a food unknown to you and your fathers, in order to show you that not by bread alone does man live, but by every word that comes forth from the mouth of the LORD. [4]The clothing did not fall from you in tatters, nor did your feet swell these forty years. [5]So you must realize that the LORD, your God, disciplines you even as a man disciplines his son. [6]Therefore, keep the commandments of the LORD, your God, by walking in his ways and fearing him. [7]For the LORD, your God, is bringing you into a good country, a land with streams of water, with springs and fountains welling up in the hills and valleys, [8]a land of wheat and barley, of vines and fig trees and pomegranates, of olive trees and of honey, [9]a land where you can eat bread without stint and where you will lack nothing, a land whose stones contain iron and in whose hills you can mine copper. [10]But when you have eaten your fill, you must bless the LORD, your God, for the good country he has given you. [11]Be careful not to forget the LORD, your God, by neglecting his commandments and decrees and statutes which I enjoin on you today: [12]lest, when you have eaten your fill, and have built fine houses and lived in them, [13]and have increased your herds and flocks, your silver and gold, and all your property, [14]you then become haughty of heart and unmindful of the LORD, your God, who brought you out of the land of Egypt, that place of slavery; [15]who guided you through the vast and terrible desert with its saraph serpents and scorpions, its parched and waterless ground; who brought forth water for you from the flinty rock [16]and fed you in the desert with manna, a food unknown to your fathers, that he might afflict you and test you, but also make you prosperous in the end. [17]Otherwise, you might say to yourselves, 'It is my own power and the strength of my own hand that has obtained for me this wealth.' [18]Remember then, it is the LORD, your God, who gives you the power to acquire wealth, by fulfilling, as he has now done, the covenant which he swore to your fathers. [19]But if you forget the LORD, your God, and follow other gods, serving and worshiping them, I forewarn you this day that you will perish utterly. [20]Like the nations which the LORD destroys before you, so shall you too perish for not heeding the voice of the LORD, your God."

Deuteronomy Chapter 9

[1]"Hear, O Israel! You are now about to cross the Jordan to enter in and dispossess nations greater and stronger than yourselves, having large cities fortified to the sky, [2]the Anakim, a people great and tall. You know of them and have heard it said of them, 'Who can stand up against the Anakim?' [3]Understand, then, today that it is the LORD, your God, who will cross over before you as a consuming fire; he it is who will reduce them to nothing and subdue them before you, so that you can drive them out and destroy them quickly, as the LORD promised you. [4]After the LORD, your God, has thrust them out of your way, do not say to yourselves, 'It is because of my merits that the LORD has brought me in to possess this land'; for it is really because of the wickedness of these nations that the LORD is driving them out before you. [5]No, it is not because of your merits or the integrity of your heart that you are going in to take possession of their land; but the LORD, your God, is driving these nations out before you on account of their wickedness and in order to keep the promise which he made on oath to your fathers, Abraham, Isaac and Jacob. [6]Understand this, therefore: it is not because of your merits that the LORD, your God, is giving you this good land to possess, for you are a stiff-necked people. [7]"Bear in mind and do not forget how you angered the LORD, your God, in the desert. From the day you left the land of Egypt until you arrived in this place, you

have been rebellious toward the LORD. 8At Horeb you so provoked the LORD that he was angry enough to destroy you, 9when I had gone up the mountain to receive the stone tablets of the covenant which the LORD made with you. Meanwhile I stayed on the mountain forty days and forty nights without eating or drinking, 10till the LORD gave me the two tablets of stone inscribed, by God's own finger, with a copy of all the words that the LORD spoke to you on the mountain from the midst of the fire on the day of the assembly. 11Then, at the end of the forty days and forty nights, when the LORD had given me the two stone tablets of the covenant, 12he said to me, 'Go down from here now, quickly, for your people whom you have brought out of Egypt have become depraved; they have already turned aside from the way I pointed out to them and have made for themselves a molten idol. 13I have seen now how stiff-necked this people is,' the LORD said to me. 14'Let me be, that I may destroy them and blot out their name from under the heavens. I will then make of you a nation mightier and greater than they.' 15"When I had come down again from the blazing, fiery mountain, with the two tablets of the covenant in both my hands, 16I saw how you had sinned against the LORD, your God: you had already turned aside from the way which the LORD had pointed out to you by making for yourselves a molten calf! 17Raising the two tablets with both hands I threw them from me and broke them before your eyes. 18Then, as before, I lay prostrate before the LORD for forty days and forty nights without eating or drinking, because of all the sin you had committed in the sight of the LORD and the evil you had done to provoke him. 19For I dreaded the fierce anger of the LORD against you: his wrath would destroy you. Yet once again the LORD listened to me. 20With Aaron, too, the LORD was deeply angry, and would have killed him had I not prayed for him also at that time. 21Then, taking the calf, the sinful object you had made, and fusing it with fire, I ground it down to powder as fine as dust, which I threw into the wadi that went down the mountainside. 22"At Taberah, at Massah, and at Kibroth-hattaavah likewise, you provoked the LORD to anger. 23And when he sent you up from Kadesh-barnea to take possession of the land he was giving you, you rebelled against this command of the LORD, your God, and would not trust or obey him. 24Ever since I have known you, you have been rebels against the LORD. 25"Those forty days, then, and forty nights, I lay prostrate before the LORD, because he had threatened to destroy you. 26This was my prayer to him: O Lord GOD, destroy not your people, the heritage which your majesty has ransomed and brought out of Egypt with your strong hand. 27Remember your servants, Abraham, Isaac and Jacob. Look not upon the stubbornness of this people nor upon their wickedness and sin, 28lest the people from whose land you have brought us say, 'The LORD was not able to bring them into the land he promised them'; or 'Out of hatred for them, he brought them out to slay them in the desert.' 29They are, after all, your people and your heritage, whom you have brought out by your great power and with your outstretched arm."

Deuteronomy Chapter 10

1"At that time the LORD said to me, 'Cut two tablets of stone like the former; then come up the mountain to me. Also make an ark of wood. 2I will write upon the tablets the commandments that were on the former tablets that you broke, and you shall place them in the ark.' 3So I made an ark of acacia wood, and cut two tablets of stone like the former, and went up the mountain carrying the two tablets. 4The LORD then wrote on them, as he had written before, the ten commandments which he spoke to you on the mountain from the midst of the fire on the day of the assembly. After the LORD had given them to me, 5I turned and came down the mountain, and placed the tablets in the ark I had made. There they have remained, in keeping with the command the LORD gave me. 6(The Israelites set out from Beeroth Bene-jaakan for Moserah, where Aaron died and was buried, his son Eleazar succeeding him in the priestly office. 7From there they set out for Gudgodah, and from Gudgodah for Jotbathah, a region where there is water in the wadies.) 8"At that time the LORD set apart the tribe of Levi to carry the ark of the covenant of the LORD, to be in attendance before the LORD and minister to him, and to give blessings in his name, as they have done to this day. 9For this reason, Levi has no share in the heritage with his brothers; the LORD himself is his heritage, as the LORD, your God, has told him. 10"After I had spent these other forty days and forty nights on the mountain, and the LORD had once again heard me and decided not to destroy you, 11he said to me, 'Go now and set out at the head of your people, that they may enter in and occupy the land which I swore to their fathers I would give them.' 12"And now, Israel, what does the LORD, your God, ask of you but to fear the LORD, your God, and follow his ways exactly, to love and serve the LORD, your God, with all your heart and all your soul, 13to keep the commandments and statutes of the LORD which I enjoin on you today for your own good? 14Think!

The heavens, even the highest heavens, belong to the LORD, your God, as well as the earth and everything on it. 15Yet in his love for your fathers the LORD was so attached to them as to choose you, their descendants, in preference to all other peoples, as indeed he has now done. 16Circumcise your hearts, therefore, and be no longer stiff-necked. 17For the LORD, your God, is the God of gods, the LORD of lords, the great God, mighty and awesome, who has no favorites, accepts no bribes; 18who executes justice for the orphan and the widow, and befriends the alien, feeding and clothing him. 19So you too must befriend the alien, for you were once aliens yourselves in the land of Egypt. 20The LORD, your God, shall you fear, and him shall you serve; hold fast to him and swear by his name. 21He is your glory, he, your God, who has done for you those great and terrible things which your own eyes have seen. 22Your ancestors went down to Egypt seventy strong, and now the LORD, your God, has made you as numerous as the stars of the sky."

Deuteronomy Chapter 11

1"Love the LORD, your God, therefore, and always heed his charge: his statutes, decrees and commandments. 2It is not your children, who have not known it from experience, but you yourselves who must now understand the discipline of the LORD, your God; his majesty, his strong hand and outstretched arm; 3the signs and deeds he wrought among the Egyptians, on Pharaoh, king of Egypt, and on all his land; 4what he did to the Egyptian army and to their horses and chariots, engulfing them in the water of the Red Sea as they pursued you, and bringing ruin upon them even to this day; 5what he did for you in the desert until you arrived in this place; 6and what he did to the Reubenites Dathan and Abiram, sons of Eliab, when the ground opened its mouth and swallowed them up out of the midst of Israel, with their families and tents and every living thing that belonged to them. 7With your own eyes you have seen all these great deeds that the LORD has done. 8Keep all the commandments, then, which I enjoin on you today, that you may be strong enough to enter in and take possession of the land into which you are crossing, 9and that you may have long life on the land which the LORD swore to your fathers he would give to them and their descendants, a land flowing with milk and honey. 10"For the land which you are to enter and occupy is not like the land of Egypt from which you have come, where you would sow your seed and then water it by hand, as in a vegetable garden. 11No, the land into which you are crossing for conquest is a land of hills and valleys that drinks in rain from the heavens, 12a land which the LORD, your God, looks after; his eyes are upon it continually from the beginning of the year to the end. 13If, then, you truly heed my commandments which I enjoin on you today, loving and serving the LORD, your God, with all your heart and all your soul, 14I will give the seasonal rain to your land, the early rain and the late rain, that you may have your grain, wine and oil to gather in; 15and I will bring forth grass in your fields for your animals. Thus you may eat your fill. 16But be careful lest your heart be so lured away that you serve other gods and worship them. 17For then the wrath of the LORD will flare up against you and he will close up the heavens, so that no rain will fall, and the soil will not yield its crops, and you will soon perish from the good land he is giving you. 18"Therefore, take these words of mine into your heart and soul. Bind them at your wrist as a sign, and let them be a pendant on your forehead. 19Teach them to your children, speaking of them at home and abroad, whether you are busy or at rest. 20And write them on the doorposts of your houses and on your gates, 21so that, as long as the heavens are above the earth, you and your children may live on in the land which the LORD swore to your fathers he would give them. 22"For if you are careful to observe all these commandments I enjoin on you, loving the LORD, your God, and following his ways exactly, and holding fast to him, 23the LORD will drive all these nations out of your way, and you will dispossess nations greater and mightier than yourselves. 24Every place where you set foot shall be yours: from the desert and from Lebanon, from the Euphrates River to the Western Sea, shall be your territory. 25None shall stand up against you; the LORD, your God, will spread the fear and dread of you through any land where you set foot, as he promised you. 26"I set before you here, this day, a blessing and a curse: 27a blessing for obeying the commandments of the LORD, your God, which I enjoin on you today; 28a curse if you do not obey the commandments of the LORD, your God, but turn aside from the way I ordain for you today, to follow other gods, whom you have not known. 29When the LORD, your God, brings you into the land which you are to enter and occupy, then you shall pronounce the blessing on Mount Gerizim, the curse on Mount Ebal. 30(Are they not beyond the Jordan, on the other side of the western road in the country of the Canaanites who live in the Arabah, opposite the Gilgal beside the terebinth of Moreh?) 31For you are about to cross the Jordan to enter and occupy the land which the LORD, your God, is giving you. When, therefore, you take possession of it and settle there, [32]be careful to observe all the statutes and decrees that I set before you today."

Deuteronomy Chapter 12

"[1]These are the statutes and decrees which you must be careful to observe in the land which the LORD, the God of your fathers, has given you to occupy, as long as you live on its soil. [2]Destroy without fail every place on the high mountains, on the hills, and under every leafy tree where the nations you are to dispossess worship their gods. [3]Tear down their altars, smash their sacred pillars, destroy by fire their sacred poles, and shatter the idols of their gods, that you may stamp out the remembrance of them in any such place. [4]That is not how you are to worship the LORD, your God. [5]Instead, you shall resort to the place which the LORD, your God, chooses out of all your tribes and designates as his dwelling [6]and there you shall bring your holocausts and sacrifices, your tithes and personal contributions, your votive and freewill offerings, and the firstlings of your herds and flocks. [7]There, too, before the LORD, your God, you and your families shall eat and make merry over all your undertakings, because the LORD, your God, has blessed you. [8]You shall not do as we are now doing; here, everyone does what seems right to himself, [9]since you have not yet reached your resting place, the heritage which the LORD, your God, will give you. [10]But after you have crossed the Jordan and dwell in the land which the LORD, your God, is giving you as a heritage, when he has given you rest from all your enemies round about and you live there in security, [11]then to the place which the LORD, your God, chooses as the dwelling place for his name you shall bring all the offerings I command you: your holocausts and sacrifices, your tithes and personal contributions, and every special offering you have vowed to the LORD. [12]You shall make merry before the LORD, your God, with your sons and daughters, your male and female slaves, as well as with the Levite who belongs to your community but has no share of his own in your heritage. [13]Take care not to offer up your holocausts in any place you fancy, [14]but offer them up in the place which the LORD chooses from among your tribes; there you shall make whatever offerings I enjoin upon you. [15]However, in any of your communities you may slaughter and eat to your heart's desire as much meat as the LORD, your God, has blessed you with; and the unclean as well as the clean may eat it, as they do the gazelle or the deer. [16]Only, you shall not partake of the blood, but must pour it out on the ground like water. [17]Moreover, you shall not, in your own communities, partake of your tithe of grain or wine or oil, of the first-born of your herd or flock, of any offering you have vowed, of your freewill offerings, or of your personal contributions. [18]These you must eat before the LORD, your God, in the place he chooses, along with your son and daughter, your male and female slave, and the Levite who belongs to your community; and there, before the LORD, you shall make merry over all your undertakings. [19]Take care, also, that you do not neglect the Levite as long as you live in the land. [20]After the LORD, your God, has enlarged your territory, as he promised you, when you wish meat for food, you may eat it at will, to your heart's desire; [21]and if the place which the LORD, your God, chooses for the abode of his name is too far, you may slaughter in the manner I have told you any of your herd or flock that the LORD has given you, and eat it to your heart's desire in your own community. [22]You may eat it as you would the gazelle or the deer: the unclean and the clean eating it alike. [23]But make sure that you do not partake of the blood; for blood is life, and you shall not consume this seat of life with the flesh. [24]Do not partake of the blood, therefore, but pour it out on the ground like water. [25]Abstain from it, that you and your children after you may prosper for doing what is right in the sight of the LORD. [26]However, any sacred gifts or votive offerings that you may have, you shall bring with you to the place which the LORD chooses, [27]and there you must offer both the flesh and the blood of your holocausts on the altar of the LORD, your God; of your other sacrifices the blood indeed must be poured out against the altar of the LORD, your God, but their flesh may be eaten. [28]Be careful to heed all these commandments I enjoin on you, that you and your descendants may always prosper for doing what is good and right in the sight of the LORD, your God. [29]When the LORD, your God, removes the nations from your way as you advance to dispossess them, be on your guard! Otherwise, once they have been wiped out before you and you have replaced them and are settled in their land, [30]you will be lured into following them. Do not inquire regarding their gods, 'How did these nations worship their gods? I, too, would do the same.' [31]You shall not thus worship the LORD, your God, because they offered to their gods every abomination that the LORD detests, even burning their sons and daughters to their gods."

Deuteronomy Chapter 13

"[1]Every command that I enjoin on you, you shall be careful to observe, neither adding to it nor subtracting from it. [2]If there arises among you a prophet or a dreamer who promises you a sign or wonder, [3]urging you to follow other gods, whom you have not known, and to serve them: even though the sign or wonder he has foretold you comes to pass, [4]pay no attention to the words of that prophet or that dreamer; for the LORD, your God, is testing you to learn whether you really love him with all your heart and with all your soul. [5]The LORD, your God, shall you follow, and him shall you fear; his commandment shall you observe, and his voice shall you heed, serving him and holding fast to him alone. [6]But that prophet or that dreamer shall be put to death, because, in order to lead you astray from the way which the LORD, your God, has directed you to take, he has preached apostasy from the LORD, your God, who brought you out of the land of Egypt and ransomed you from that place of slavery. Thus shall you purge the evil from your midst. [7]If your own full brother, or your son or daughter, or your beloved wife, or your intimate friend, entices you secretly to serve other gods, whom you and your fathers have not known, [8]gods of any other nations, near at hand or far away, from one end of the earth to the other: [9]do not yield to him or listen to him, nor look with pity upon him, to spare or shield him, [10]but kill him. Your hand shall be the first raised to slay him; the rest of the people shall join in with you. [11]You shall stone him to death, because he sought to lead you astray from the LORD, your God, who brought you out of the land of Egypt, that place of slavery. [12]And all Israel, hearing of it, shall fear and never again do such evil as this in your midst. [13]If, in any of the cities which the LORD, your God, gives you to dwell in, you hear it said [14]that certain scoundrels have sprung up among you and have led astray the inhabitants of their city to serve other gods whom you have not known, [15]you must inquire carefully into the matter and investigate it thoroughly. If you find that it is true and an established fact that this abomination has been committed in your midst, [16]you shall put the inhabitants of that city to the sword, dooming the city and all life that is in it, even its cattle, to the sword. [17]Having heaped up all its spoils in the middle of its square, you shall burn the city with all its spoils as a whole burnt offering to the LORD, your God. Let it be a heap of ruins forever, never to be rebuilt. [18]You shall not retain anything that is doomed, that the blazing wrath of the LORD may die down and he may show you mercy and in his mercy for you may multiply you as he promised your fathers on oath; [19]because you have heeded the voice of the LORD, your God, keeping all his commandments which I enjoin on you today, doing what is right in his sight."

Deuteronomy Chapter 14

"[1]You are children of the LORD, your God. You shall not gash yourselves nor shave the hair above your foreheads for the dead. [2]For you are a people sacred to the LORD, your God, who has chosen you from all the nations on the face of the earth to be a people peculiarly his own. [3]You shall not eat any abominable thing. [4]These are the animals you may eat: the ox, the sheep, the goat, [5]the red deer, the gazelle, the roe deer, the ibex, the addax, the oryx, and the mountain sheep. [6]Any animal that has hoofs you may eat, provided it is cloven-footed and chews the cud. [7]But you shall not eat any of the following that only chew the cud or only have cloven hoofs: the camel, the hare and the rock badger, which indeed chew the cud, but do not have hoofs and are therefore unclean for you; [8]and the pig, which indeed has hoofs and is cloven-footed, but does not chew the cud and is therefore unclean for you. Their flesh you shall not eat, and their dead bodies you shall not touch. [9]Of the various creatures that live in the water, whatever has both fins and scales you may eat, [10]but all those that lack either fins or scales you shall not eat; they are unclean for you. [11]You may eat all clean birds. [12]But you shall not eat any of the following: the eagle, the vulture, the osprey, [13]the various kites and falcons, [14]all the various species of crows, [15]the ostrich, the nightjar, the gull, the various species of hawks, [16]the owl, the screech owl, the ibis, [17]the desert owl, the buzzard, the cormorant, [18]the stork, the various species of herons, the hoopoe, and the bat. [19]All winged insects, too, are unclean for you and shall not be eaten. [20]But you may eat any clean winged creatures. [21]You must not eat any animal that has died of itself, for you are a people sacred to the LORD, your God. But you may give it to an alien who belongs to your community, and he may eat it, or you may sell it to a foreigner. You shall not boil a kid in its mother's milk. [22]Each year you shall tithe all the produce that grows in the field you have sown; [23]then in the place which the LORD, your God, chooses as the dwelling place of his name you shall eat in his presence your tithe of the grain, wine and oil, as well as the firstlings of your herd and flock, that you may learn always to fear the LORD, your God. [24]If, however, the journey is too much for you and you are not able to bring your tithe, because the place which the LORD, your God, chooses for the abode of his name is too far for you, considering how the LORD has blessed you, 25you may exchange the tithe for money and, with the purse of money in hand, go to the place which the LORD, your God, chooses. 26You may then exchange the money for whatever you desire, oxen or sheep, wine or strong drink, or anything else you would enjoy, and there before the LORD, your God, you shall partake of it and make merry with your family. 27But do not neglect the Levite who belongs to your community, for he has no share in the heritage with you. 28At the end of every third year you shall bring out all the tithes of your produce for that year and deposit them in community stores, 29that the Levite who has no share in the heritage with you, and also the alien, the orphan and the widow who belong to your community, may come and eat their fill; so that the LORD, your God, may bless you in all that you undertake."

Deuteronomy Chapter 15

"1At the end of every seven-year period you shall have a relaxation of debts, 2which shall be observed as follows. Every creditor shall relax his claim on what he has loaned his neighbor; he must not press his neighbor, his kinsman, because a relaxation in honor of the LORD has been proclaimed. 3You may press a foreigner, but you shall relax the claim on your kinsman for what is yours. 4Nay, more! since the LORD, your God, will bless you abundantly in the land he will give you to occupy as your heritage, there should be no one of you in need. 5If you but heed the voice of the LORD, your God, and carefully observe all these commandments which I enjoin on you today, 6you will lend to many nations, and borrow from none; you will rule over many nations, and none will rule over you, since the LORD, your God, will bless you as he promised. 7If one of your kinsmen in any community is in need in the land which the LORD, your God, is giving you, you shall not harden your heart nor close your hand to him in his need. 8Instead, you shall open your hand to him and freely lend him enough to meet his need. 9Be on your guard lest, entertaining the mean thought that the seventh year, the year of relaxation, is near, you grudge help to your needy kinsman and give him nothing; else he will cry to the LORD against you and you will be held guilty. 10When you give to him, give freely and not with ill will; for the LORD, your God, will bless you for this in all your works and undertakings. 112The needy will never be lacking in the land; that is why I command you to open your hand to your poor and needy kinsman in your country. 12If your kinsman, a Hebrew man or woman, sells himself to you, he is to serve you for six years, but in the seventh year you shall dismiss him from your service, a free man. 13When you do so, you shall not send him away empty-handed, 14but shall weight him down with gifts from your flock and threshing floor and wine press, in proportion to the blessing the LORD, your God, has bestowed on you. 15For remember that you too were once slaves in the land of Egypt, and the LORD, your God, ransomed you. That is why I am giving you this command today. 16If, however, he tells you that he does not wish to leave you, because he is devoted to you and your household, since he fares well with you, 173you shall take an awl and thrust it through his ear into the door, and he shall then be your slave forever. Your female slave, also, you shall treat in the same way. 18You must not be reluctant to let your slave go free, since the service he has given you for six years was worth twice a hired man's salary; then also the LORD, your God, will bless you in everything you do. 19You shall consecrate to the LORD, your God, all the male firstlings of your herd and of your flock. You shall not work the firstlings of your cattle, nor shear the firstlings of your flock. 20Year after year you and your family shall eat them before the LORD, your God, in the place he chooses. 21If, however, a firstling is lame or blind or has any other serious defect, you shall not sacrifice it to the LORD, your God, 22but in your own communities you may eat it, the unclean and the clean eating it alike, as you would a gazelle or a deer. 23Only, you shall not partake of its blood, which must be poured out on the ground like water."

Deuteronomy Chapter 16

"1Observe the month of Abib by keeping the Passover of the LORD, your God, since it was in the month of Abib that he brought you by night out of Egypt. 2You shall offer the Passover sacrifice from your flock or your herd to the LORD, your God, in the place which he chooses as the dwelling place of his name. 3You shall not eat leavened bread with it. For seven days you shall eat with it only unleavened bread, the bread of affliction, that you may remember as long as you live the day of your departure from the land of Egypt; for in frightened haste you left the land of Egypt. 4Nothing leavened may be found in all your territory for seven days, and none of the meat which you sacrificed on the evening of the first day shall be kept overnight for the next day. 5You may not sacrifice the Passover in any of the communities which the LORD, your

God, gives you; 6only at the place which he chooses as the dwelling place of his name, and in the evening at sunset, on the anniversary of your departure from Egypt, shall you sacrifice the Passover. 7You shall cook and eat it at the place the LORD, your God, chooses; then in the morning you may return to your tents. 8For six days you shall eat unleavened bread, and on the seventh there shall be a solemn meeting in honor of the LORD, your God; on that day you shall not do any sort of work. 9You shall count off seven weeks, computing them from the day when the sickle is first put to the standing grain. 102You shall then keep the feast of Weeks in honor of the LORD, your God, and the measure of your own freewill offering shall be in proportion to the blessing the LORD, your God, has bestowed on you. 11In the place which the LORD, your God, chooses as the dwelling place of his name, you shall make merry in his presence together with your son and daughter, your male and female slave, and the Levite who belongs to your community, as well as the alien, the orphan and the widow among you. 12Remember that you too were once slaves in Egypt, and carry out these statutes carefully. 133You shall celebrate the feast of Booths for seven days, when you have gathered in the produce from your threshing floor and wine press. 14You shall make merry at your feast, together with your son and daughter, your male and female slave, and also the Levite, the alien, the orphan and the widow who belong to your community. 15For seven days you shall celebrate this pilgrim feast in honor of the LORD, your God, in the place which he chooses; since the LORD, your God, has blessed you in all your crops and in all your undertakings, you shall do nought but make merry. 16Three times a year, then, every male among you shall appear before the LORD, your God, in the place which he chooses: at the feast of Unleavened Bread, at the feast of Weeks, and at the feast of Booths. No one shall appear before the LORD empty-handed, 17but each of you with as much as he can give, in proportion to the blessings which the LORD, your God, has bestowed on you. 18You shall appoint judges and officials throughout your tribes to administer true justice for the people in all the communities which the LORD, your God, is giving you. 19You shall not distort justice; you must be impartial. You shall not take a bribe; for a bribe blinds the eyes even of the wise and twists the words even of the just. 20Justice and justice alone shall be your aim, that you may have life and may possess the land which the LORD, your God, is giving you. 2145You shall not plant a sacred pole of any kind of wood beside the altar of the LORD, your God, which you will build; 22nor shall you erect a sacred pillar, such as the LORD, your God, detests."

Deuteronomy Chapter 17

"1You shall not sacrifice to the LORD, your God, from the herd or from the flock an animal with any serious defect; that would be an abomination to the LORD, your God. 2If there is found among you, in any one of the communities which the LORD, your God, gives you, a man or a woman who does evil in the sight of the LORD, your God, and transgresses his covenant, 3by serving other gods, or by worshiping the sun or the moon or any of the host of the sky, against my command; 4and if, on being informed of it, you find by careful investigation that it is true and an established fact that this abomination has been committed in Israel: 51you shall bring the man (or woman) who has done the evil deed out to your city gates and stone him to death. 6The testimony of two or three witnesses is required for putting a person to death; no one shall be put to death on the testimony of only one witness. 7At the execution, the witnesses are to be the first to raise their hands against him; afterward all the people are to join in. Thus shall you purge the evil from your midst. 8If in your own community there is a case at issue which proves too complicated for you to decide, in a matter of bloodshed or of civil rights or of personal injury, you shall then go up to the place which the LORD, your God, chooses, 9to the levitical priests or to the judge who is in office at that time. They shall study the case and then hand down to you their decision. 10According to this decision that they give you in the place which the LORD chooses, you shall act, being careful to do exactly as they direct. 11You shall carry out the directions they give you and the verdict they pronounce for you, without turning aside to the right or to the left from the decision they hand down to you. 122Any man who has the insolence to refuse to listen to the priest who officiates there in the ministry of the LORD, your God, or to the judge, shall die. Thus shall you purge the evil from your midst. 13And all the people, on hearing of it, shall fear, and never again be so insolent. 14When you have come into the land which the LORD, your God, is giving you, and have occupied it and settled in it, should you then decide to have a king over you like all the surrounding nations, 15you shall set that man over you as your king whom the LORD, your God, chooses. He whom you set over you as king must be your kinsman; a foreigner, who is no kin of yours, you may not set over you. 163But he shall not have a great number of horses; nor shall he make his people go back again to Egypt to acquire them, against the LORD'S warning that you must never go back that way again. [17]Neither shall he have a great number of wives, lest his heart be estranged, nor shall he accumulate a vast amount of silver and gold. [18]When he is enthroned in his kingdom, he shall have a copy of this law made from the scroll that is in the custody of the levitical priests. [19]He shall keep it with him and read it all the days of his life that he may learn to fear the LORD, his God, and to heed and fulfill all the words of this law and these statutes. [20]Let him not become estranged from his countrymen through pride, nor turn aside to the right or to the left from these commandments. Then he and his descendants will enjoy a long reign in Israel."

Deuteronomy Chapter 18

"[1]The whole priestly tribe of Levi shall have no share in the heritage with Israel; they shall live on the oblations of the LORD and the portions due to him. [2]Levi shall have no heritage among his brothers; the LORD himself is his heritage, as he has told him. [3]The priests shall have a right to the following things from the people: from those who are offering a sacrifice, whether the victim is from the herd or from the flock, the priest shall receive the shoulder, the jowls and the stomach. [4]You shall also give him the first fruits of your grain and wine and oil, as well as the first fruits of the shearing of your flock; [5]for the LORD, your God, has chosen him and his sons out of all your tribes to be always in attendance to minister in the name of the LORD. [6]When a Levite goes from one of your communities anywhere in Israel in which he ordinarily resides, to visit, as his heart may desire, the place which the LORD chooses, [7]he may minister there in the name of the LORD, his God, like all his fellow Levites who are in attendance there before the LORD. [8]He shall then receive the same portions to eat as the rest, along with his monetary offerings and heirlooms. [9]When you come into the land which the LORD, your God, is giving you, you shall not learn to imitate the abominations of the peoples there. [10]Let there not be found among you anyone who immolates his son or daughter in the fire, nor a fortune-teller, soothsayer, charmer, diviner, [11]or caster of spells, nor one who consults ghosts and spirits or seeks oracles from the dead. [12]Anyone who does such things is an abomination to the LORD, and because of such abominations the LORD, your God, is driving these nations out of your way. [13]You, however, must be altogether sincere toward the LORD, your God. [14]Though these nations whom you are to dispossess listen to their soothsayers and fortune-tellers, the LORD, your God, will not permit you to do so. [15]A prophet like me will the LORD, your God, raise up for you from among your own kinsmen; to him you shall listen. [16]This is exactly what you requested of the LORD, your God, at Horeb on the day of the assembly, when you said, 'Let us not again hear the voice of the LORD, our God, nor see this great fire any more, lest we die.' [17]And the LORD said to me, 'This was well said. [18]I will raise up for them a prophet like you from among their kinsmen, and will put my words into his mouth; he shall tell them all that I command him. [19]If any man will not listen to my words which he speaks in my name, I myself will make him answer for it. [20]But if a prophet presumes to speak in my name an oracle that I have not commanded him to speak, or speaks in the name of other gods, he shall die.' [21]If you say to yourselves, 'How can we recognize an oracle which the LORD has spoken?', [22]know that, even though a prophet speaks in the name of the LORD, if his oracle is not fulfilled or verified, it is an oracle which the LORD did not speak. The prophet has spoken it presumptuously, and you shall have no fear of him."

Deuteronomy Chapter 19

"[1]When the LORD, your God, removes the nations whose land he is giving you, and you have taken their place and are settled in their cities and houses, [2]you shall set apart three cities in the land which the LORD, your God, is giving you to occupy. [3]You shall thereby divide into three regions the land which the LORD, your God, will give you as a heritage, and so arrange the routes that every homicide will be able to find a refuge. [4]It is in the following case that a homicide may take refuge in such a place to save his life: when someone unwittingly kills his neighbor to whom he had previously borne no malice. [5]For example, if he goes with his neighbor to a forest to cut wood, and as he swings his ax to fell a tree, its head flies off the handle and hits his neighbor a mortal blow, he may take refuge in one of these cities to save his life. [6]Should the distance be too great, the avenger of blood may in the heat of his anger pursue the homicide and overtake him and strike him dead, even though he does not merit death since he had previously borne the slain man no malice. [7]That is why I order you to set apart three cities. [8]But if the LORD, your God, enlarges your territory, as he swore to your fathers, and gives you all the land he promised your fathers he would give [9]in the event that you carefully observe all these commandments which I enjoin on you today, loving the LORD, your God, and ever walking in his ways: then add three cities to these three. [10]Thus, in the land which the LORD, your God, is giving you as a heritage, innocent blood will not be shed and you will not become guilty of bloodshed. [11]However, if someone lies in wait for his neighbor out of hatred for him, and rising up against him, strikes him mortally, and then takes refuge in one of these cities, [12]the elders of his own city shall send for him and have him taken from there, and shall hand him over to be slain by the avenger of blood. [13]Do not look on him with pity, but purge from Israel the stain of shedding innocent blood, that you may prosper. [14]You shall not move your neighbor's landmarks erected by your forefathers in the heritage you receive in the land which the LORD, your God, is giving you to occupy. [15]One witness alone shall not take the stand against a man in regard to any crime or any offense of which he may be guilty; a judicial fact shall be established only on the testimony of two or three witnesses. [16]If an unjust witness takes the stand against a man to accuse him of a defection from the law, [17]the two parties in the dispute shall appear before the LORD in the presence of the priests or judges in office at that time; [18]and if after a thorough investigation the judges find that the witness is a false witness and has accused his kinsman falsely, [19]you shall do to him as he planned to do to his kinsman. Thus shall you purge the evil from your midst. [20]The rest, on hearing of it, shall fear, and never again do a thing so evil among you. [21]Do not look on such a man with pity. Life for life, eye for eye, tooth for tooth, hand for hand, and foot for foot!"

Deuteronomy Chapter 20

"[1]When you go out to war against your enemies and you see horses and chariots and an army greater than your own, do not be afraid of them, for the LORD, your God, who brought you up from the land of Egypt, will be with you. [2]When you are about to go into battle, the priest shall come forward and say to the soldiers: [3]'Hear, O Israel! Today you are going into battle against your enemies. Be not weakhearted or afraid; be neither alarmed nor frightened by them. [4]For it is the LORD, your God, who goes with you to fight for you against your enemies and give you victory.' [5]Then the officials shall say to the soldiers, 'Is there anyone who has built a new house and not yet had the housewarming? Let him return home, lest he die in battle and another dedicate it. [6]Is there anyone who has planted a vineyard and never yet enjoyed its fruits? Let him return home, lest he die in battle and another enjoy its fruits in his stead. [7]Is there anyone who has betrothed a woman and not yet taken her as his wife? Let him return home, lest he die in battle and another take her to wife.' [8]In fine, the officials shall say to the soldiers, 'Is there anyone who is afraid and weakhearted? Let him return home, lest he make his fellows as fainthearted as himself.' [9]When the officials have finished speaking to the soldiers, military officers shall be appointed over the army. [10]When you march up to attack a city, first offer it terms of peace. [11]If it agrees to your terms of peace and opens its gates to you, all the people to be found in it shall serve you in forced labor. [12]But if it refuses to make peace with you and instead offers you battle, lay siege to it, [13]and when the LORD, your God, delivers it into your hand, put every male in it to the sword; [14]but the women and children and livestock and all else in it that is worth plundering you may take as your booty, and you may use this plunder of your enemies which the LORD, your God, has given you. [15]That is how you shall deal with any city at a considerable distance from you, which does not belong to the peoples of this land. [16]But in the cities of those nations which the LORD, your God, is giving you as your heritage, you shall not leave a single soul alive. [17]You must doom them all - the Hittites, Amorites, Canaanites, Perizzites, Hivites and Jebusites - as the LORD, your God, has commanded you, [18]lest they teach you to make any such abominable offerings as they make to their gods, and you thus sin against the LORD, your God. [19]When you are at war with a city and have to lay siege to it for a long time before you capture it, you shall not destroy its trees by putting an ax to them. You may eat their fruit, but you must not cut down the trees. After all, are the trees of the field men, that they should be included in your siege? [20]However, those trees which you know are not fruit trees you may destroy, cutting them down to build siegeworks with which to reduce the city that is resisting you."

Deuteronomy Chapter 21

"[1]If the corpse of a slain man is found lying in the open on the land which the LORD, your God, is giving you to occupy, and it is not known who killed him, [2]your elders and judges shall go out and measure the distances to the cities that are in the neighborhood of the corpse. [3]When it is established which city is nearest the corpse, the elders of that city shall take a heifer that has never been put to work as a draft animal under a yoke, [4]and bringing it down to a wadi with an everflowing stream at a place that has not been plowed or sown, they shall cut the heifer's throat there in the wadi. ⁵The priests, the descendants of Levi, shall also be present, for the LORD, your God, has chosen them to minister to him and to give blessings in his name, and every case of dispute or violence must be settled by their decision. ⁶Then all the elders of that city nearest the corpse shall wash their hands over the heifer whose throat was cut in the wadi, ⁷and shall declare, 'Our hands did not shed this blood, and our eyes did not see the deed. ⁸Absolve, O LORD, your people Israel, whom you have ransomed, and let not the guilt of shedding innocent blood remain in the midst of your people Israel.' Thus they shall be absolved from the guilt of bloodshed, ⁹and you shall purge from your midst the guilt of innocent blood, that you may prosper for doing what is right in the sight of the LORD. ¹⁰When you go out to war against your enemies and the LORD, your God, delivers them into your hand, so that you take captives, ¹¹if you see a comely woman among the captives and become so enamored of her that you wish to have her as wife, ¹²you may take her home to your house. But before she may live there, she must shave her head and pare her nails ¹³and lay aside her captive's garb. After she has mourned her father and mother for a full month, you may have relations with her, and you shall be her husband and she shall be your wife. ¹⁴However, if later on you lose your liking for her, you shall give her her freedom, if she wishes it; but you shall not sell her or enslave her, since she was married to you under compulsion. ¹⁵If a man with two wives loves one and dislikes the other; and if both bear him sons, but the first-born is of her whom he dislikes: ¹⁶when he comes to bequeath his property to his sons he may not consider as his first-born the son of the wife he loves, in preference to his true first-born, the son of the wife whom he dislikes. ¹⁷On the contrary, he shall recognize as his first-born the son of her whom he dislikes, giving him a double share of whatever he happens to own, since he is the first fruits of his manhood, and to him belong the rights of the first-born. ¹⁸If a man has a stubborn and unruly son who will not listen to his father or mother, and will not obey them even though they chastise him, ¹⁹his father and mother shall have him apprehended and brought out to the elders at the gate of his home city, ²⁰where they shall say to those city elders, 'This son of ours is a stubborn and unruly fellow who will not listen to us; he is a glutton and a drunkard.' ²¹Then all his fellow citizens shall stone him to death. Thus shall you purge the evil from your midst, and all Israel, on hearing of it, shall fear. ²²If a man guilty of a capital offense is put to death and his corpse hung on a tree, ²³it shall not remain on the tree overnight. You shall bury him the same day; otherwise, since God's curse rests on him who hangs on a tree, you will defile the land which the LORD, your God, is giving you as an inheritance."

Deuteronomy Chapter 22

"¹You shall not see your kinsman's ox or sheep driven astray without showing concern about it; see to it that it is returned to your kinsman. ²If this kinsman does not live near you, or you do not know who he may be, take it to your own place and keep it with you until he claims it; then give it back to him. ³You shall do the same with his ass, or his garment, or anything else which your kinsman loses and you happen to find; you may not be unconcerned about them. ⁴You shall not see your kinsman's ass or ox foundering on the road without showing concern about it; see to it that you help him lift it up. ⁵A woman shall not wear an article proper to a man, nor shall a man put on a woman's dress; for anyone who does such things is an abomination to the LORD, your God. ⁶If, while walking along, you chance upon a bird's nest with young birds or eggs in it, in any tree or on the ground, and the mother bird is sitting on them, you shall not take away the mother bird along with her brood; ⁷you shall let her go, although you may take her brood away. It is thus that you shall have prosperity and a long life. ⁸When you build a new house, put a parapet around the roof; otherwise, if someone falls off, you will bring bloodguilt upon your house. ⁹You shall not sow your vineyard with two different kinds of seed; if you do, its produce shall become forfeit, both the crop you have sown and the yield of the vineyard. ¹⁰You shall not plow with an ox and an ass harnessed together. ¹¹You shall not wear cloth of two different kinds of thread, wool and linen, woven together. ¹²You shall put twisted cords on the four corners of the cloak that you wrap around you. ¹³If a man, after marrying a woman and having relations with her, comes to dislike her, ¹⁴and makes monstrous charges against her and defames her by saying, 'I married this woman, but when I first had relations with her I did not find her a virgin,' ¹⁵the father and mother of the girl shall take the evidence of her virginity and bring it to the elders at the city gate. ¹⁶There the father of the girl shall say to the elders, 'I gave my daughter to this man in marriage, but he has come to dislike her, ¹⁷and now brings monstrous charges against her, saying: I did not find your daughter a virgin. But here is the evidence of my daughter's virginity!' And they shall spread out the cloth before the elders of the city. ¹⁸Then these city elders shall take the man and chastise him, ¹⁹besides fining him one hundred silver shekels, which they shall give to the girl's father, because the man defamed a virgin in Israel. Moreover, she shall remain his wife, and he may not divorce her as long as he lives. ²⁰But if this charge is true, and evidence of the girl's virginity is not found, ²¹they shall bring the girl to the entrance of her father's house and there her townsmen shall stone her to death, because she committed a crime against Israel by her unchasteness in her father's house. Thus shall you purge the evil from your midst. ²²If a man is discovered having relations with a woman who is married to another, both the man and the woman with whom he has had relations shall die. Thus shall you purge the evil from your midst. ²³If within the city a man comes upon a maiden who is betrothed, and has relations with her, ²⁴you shall bring them both out to the gate of the city and there stone them to death: the girl because she did not cry out for help though she was in the city, and the man because he violated his neighbor's wife. Thus shall you purge the evil from your midst. ²⁵If, however, it is in the open fields that a man comes upon such a betrothed maiden, seizes her and has relations with her, the man alone shall die. ²⁶You shall do nothing to the maiden, since she is not guilty of a capital offense. This case is like that of a man who rises up against his neighbor and murders him: ²⁷it was in the open fields that he came upon her, and though the betrothed maiden may have cried out for help, there was no one to come to her aid. ²⁸If a man comes upon a maiden that is not betrothed, takes her and has relations with her, and their deed is discovered, ²⁹the man who had relations with her shall pay the girl's father fifty silver shekels and take her as his wife, because he has deflowered her. Moreover, he may not divorce her as long as he lives."

Deuteronomy Chapter 23

"¹A man shall not marry his father's wife, nor shall he dishonor his father's bed. ²No one whose testicles have been crushed or whose penis has been cut off may be admitted into the community of the LORD. ³No child of an incestuous union may be admitted into the community of the LORD, nor any descendant of his even to the tenth generation. ⁴No Ammonite or Moabite may ever be admitted into the community of the LORD, nor any descendants of theirs even to the tenth generation, ⁵because they would not succor you with food and water on your journey after you left Egypt, and because Moab hired Balaam, son of Beor, from Pethor in Aram Naharaim, to curse you; ⁶though the LORD, your God, would not listen to Balaam and turned his curse into a blessing for you, because he loves you. ⁷Never promote their peace and prosperity as long as you live. ⁸But do not abhor the Edomite, since he is your brother, nor the Egyptian, since you were an alien in his country. ⁹Children born to them may in the third generation be admitted into the community of the LORD. ¹⁰When you are in camp during an expedition against your enemies, you shall keep yourselves from everything offensive. ¹¹If one of you becomes unclean because of a nocturnal emission, he shall go outside the camp, and not return until, ¹²toward evening, he has bathed in water; then, when the sun has set, he may come back into the camp. ¹³Outside the camp you shall have a place set aside to be used as a latrine. ¹⁴You shall also keep a trowel in your equipment and with it, when you go outside to ease nature, you shall first dig a hole and afterward cover up your excrement. ¹⁵Since the LORD, your God, journeys along within your camp to defend you and to put your enemies at your mercy, your camp must be holy; otherwise, if he sees anything indecent in your midst, he will leave your company. ¹⁶You shall not hand over to his master a slave who has taken refuge from him with you. ¹⁷Let him live with you wherever he chooses, in any one of your communities that pleases him. Do not molest him. ¹⁸There shall be no temple harlot among the Israelite women, nor a temple prostitute among the Israelite men. ¹⁹You shall not offer a harlot's fee or a dog's price as any kind of votive offering in the house of the LORD, your God; both these things are an abomination to the LORD, your God. ²⁰You shall not demand interest from your countrymen on a loan of money or of food or of anything else on which interest is usually demanded. ²¹You may demand interest from a foreigner, but not from your countryman, so that the LORD, your God, may bless you in all your undertakings on the land you are to enter and occupy. ²²When you make a vow to the LORD, your God, you shall not delay in fulfilling it; otherwise you will be held guilty, for the LORD, your God, is strict in requiring it of you. ²³Should you refrain from making a vow, you will not be held guilty. ²⁴But you must keep your solemn word and fulfill the votive offering you have freely promised to the LORD. ²⁵When you go through your neighbor's vineyard, you may eat as many of his grapes as you wish, but do not put them in your basket. ²⁶When you go through your neighbor's grainfield, you may pluck some of the ears with your hand, but do not put a sickle to your neighbor's grain."

Deuteronomy Chapter 24

"¹When a man, after marrying a woman and having relations with her, is later displeased with her because he finds in her something indecent, and therefore he writes out a bill of divorce and hands it to her, thus dismissing her from his house: ²if on leaving his house she goes and becomes the wife of another man, ³and the second husband, too, comes to dislike her and dismisses her from his house by handing her a written bill of divorce; or if this second man who has married her, dies; ⁴then her former husband, who dismissed her, may not again take her as his wife after she has become defiled. That would be an abomination before the LORD, and you shall not bring such guilt upon the land which the LORD, your God, is giving you as a heritage. ⁵When a man is newly wed, he need not go out on a military expedition, nor shall any public duty be imposed on him. He shall be exempt for one year for the sake of his family, to bring joy to the wife he has married. ⁶No one shall take a hand mill or even its upper stone as a pledge for debt, for he would be taking the debtor's sustenance as a pledge. ⁷If any man is caught kidnapping a fellow Israelite in order to enslave him and sell him, the kidnapper shall be put to death. Thus shall you purge the evil from your midst. ⁸In an attack of leprosy you shall be careful to observe exactly and to carry out all the directions of the levitical priests. Take care to act in accordance with the instructions I have given them. ⁹Remember what the LORD, your God, did to Miriam on the journey after you left Egypt. ¹⁰When you make a loan of any kind to your neighbor, you shall not enter his house to receive a pledge from him, ¹¹but shall wait outside until the man to whom you are making the loan brings his pledge outside to you. ¹²If he is a poor man, you shall not sleep in the mantle he gives as a pledge, ¹³but shall return it to him at sunset that he himself may sleep in it. Then he will bless you, and it will be a good deed of yours before the LORD, your God. ¹⁴You shall not defraud a poor and needy hired servant, whether he be one of your own countrymen or one of the aliens who live in your communities. ¹⁵You shall pay him each day's wages before sundown on the day itself, since he is poor and looks forward to them. Otherwise, he will cry to the LORD against you, and you will be held guilty. ¹⁶Fathers shall not be put to death for their children, nor children for their fathers; only for his own guilt shall a man be put to death. ¹⁷You shall not violate the rights of the alien or of the orphan, nor take the clothing of a widow as a pledge. ¹⁸For, remember, you were once slaves in Egypt, and the LORD, your God, ransomed you from there; that is why I command you to observe this rule. ¹⁹When you reap the harvest in your field and overlook a sheaf there, you shall not go back to get it; let it be for the alien, the orphan, or the widow, that the LORD, your God, may bless you in all your undertakings. ²⁰When you knock down the fruit of your olive trees, you shall not go over the branches a second time; let what remains be for the alien, the orphan, and the widow. ²¹When you pick your grapes, you shall not go over the vineyard a second time; let what remains be for the alien, the orphan, and the widow. ²² For remember that you were once slaves in Egypt; that is why I command you to observe this rule."

Deuteronomy Chapter 25

"¹When men have a dispute and bring it to court, and a decision is handed down to them acquitting the innocent party and condemning the guilty party, ²if the latter deserves stripes, the judge shall have him lie down and in his presence receive the number of stripes his guilt deserves. ³Forty stripes may be given him, but no more; lest, if he were beaten with more stripes than these, your kinsman should be looked upon as disgraced because of the severity of the beating. ⁴You shall not muzzle an ox when it is treading out grain. ⁵When brothers live together and one of them dies without a son, the widow of the deceased shall not marry anyone outside the family; but her husband's brother shall go to her and perform the duty of a brother-in-law by marrying her. ⁶The first-born son she bears shall continue the line of the deceased brother, that his name may not be blotted out from Israel. ⁷If, however, a man does not care to marry his brother's wife, she shall go up to the elders at the gate and declare, 'My brother-in-law does not intend to perform his duty toward me and refuses to perpetuate his brother's name in Israel.' ⁸Thereupon the elders of his city shall summon him and admonish him. If he persists in saying, 'I am not willing to marry her,' ⁹his sister-in-law, in the presence of the elders, shall go up to him and strip his sandal from his foot and spit in his face, saying publicly, 'This is how one should be treated who will not build up his brother's family!' ¹⁰And his lineage shall be spoken of in Israel as 'the family of the man stripped of his sandal.' ¹¹When two men are fighting and the wife of one intervenes to save her husband from the blows of his opponent, if she stretches out her hand and seizes the latter by his private parts, ¹²you shall chop off her hand without pity. ¹³You shall not keep two differing weights in your bag, one large and the other small; ¹⁴nor shall you keep two different measures in your house, one large and the other small. ¹⁵But use a true and just weight, and a true and just measure, that you may have a long life on the land which the LORD, your God, is giving you. ¹⁶Everyone who is dishonest in any of these matters is an abomination to the LORD, your God. ¹⁷Bear in mind what Amalek did to you on the journey after you left Egypt, ¹⁸how without fear of any god he harassed you along the way, weak and weary as you were, and cut off at the rear all those who lagged behind. ¹⁹Therefore, when the LORD, your God, gives you rest from all your enemies round about in the land which he is giving you to occupy as your heritage, you shall blot out the memory of Amalek from under the heavens. Do not forget!"

Deuteronomy Chapter 26

"¹When you have come into the land which the LORD, your God, is giving you as a heritage, and have occupied it and settled in it, ²you shall take some first fruits of the various products of the soil which you harvest from the land which the LORD, your God, gives you, and putting them in a basket, you shall go to the place which the LORD, your God, chooses for the dwelling place of his name. ³There you shall go to the priest in office at that time and say to him, 'Today I acknowledge to the LORD, my God, that I have indeed come into the land which he swore to our fathers he would give us.' ⁴The priest shall then receive the basket from you and shall set it in front of the altar of the LORD, your God. ⁵Then you shall declare before the LORD, your God, 'My father was a wandering Aramean who went down to Egypt with a small household and lived there as an alien. But there he became a nation great, strong and numerous. ⁶When the Egyptians maltreated and oppressed us, imposing hard labor upon us, ⁷we cried to the LORD, the God of our fathers, and he heard our cry and saw our affliction, our toil and our oppression. ⁸He brought us out of Egypt with his strong hand and outstretched arm, with terrifying power, with signs and wonders; ⁹and bringing us into this country, he gave us this land flowing with milk and honey. ¹⁰Therefore, I have now brought you the first fruits of the products of the soil which you, O LORD, have given me.' And having set them before the LORD, your God, you shall bow down in his presence. ¹¹Then you and your family, together with the Levite and the aliens who live among you, shall make merry over all these good things which the LORD, your God, has given you. ¹²When you have finished setting aside all the tithes of your produce in the third year, the year of the tithes, and you have given them to the Levite, the alien, the orphan and the widow, that they may eat their fill in your own community, ¹³you shall declare before the LORD, your God, 'I have purged my house of the sacred portion and I have given it to the Levite, the alien, the orphan and the widow, just as you have commanded me. In this I have not broken or forgotten any of your commandments: ¹⁴I have not eaten any of the tithe as a mourner; I have not brought any of it out as one unclean; I have not offered any of it to the dead. I have thus hearkened to the voice of the LORD, my God, doing just as you have commanded me. ¹⁵Look down, then, from heaven, your holy abode, and bless your people Israel and the soil you have given us in the land flowing with milk and honey which you promised on oath to our fathers.' ¹⁶This day the LORD, your God, commands you to observe these statutes and decrees. Be careful, then, to observe them with all your heart and with all your soul. ¹⁷Today you are making this agreement with the LORD: he is to be your God and you are to walk in his ways and observe his statutes, commandments and decrees, and to hearken to his voice. ¹⁸And today the LORD is making this agreement with you: you are to be a people peculiarly his own, as he promised you; and provided you keep all his commandments, ¹⁹he will then raise you high in praise and renown and glory above all other nations he has made, and you will be a people sacred to the LORD, your God, as he promised."

Deuteronomy Chapter 27

"¹Then Moses, with the elders of Israel, gave the people this order: 'Keep all these commandments which I enjoin on you today. ²On the day you cross the Jordan into the land which the LORD, your God, is giving you, set up some large stones and coat them with plaster. ³Also write on them, at the time you cross, all the words of this law, that you may thus enter into the land flowing with milk and honey, which the LORD, your God, and the God of your fathers, is giving you as he promised you. ⁴When, moreover, you have crossed the Jordan, besides setting up on Mount Ebal these stones concerning which I command you today, and coating them with plaster, ⁵you shall also build to LORD, your God, an altar made of stones that no iron tool has touched. ⁶You shall make this altar of the LORD, your God, with undressed stones, and shall offer on it holocausts to the LORD, your God. ⁷You shall also sacrifice peace offerings and eat them there, making merry before the LORD, your God. ⁸On the stones you shall inscribe all the words of this law very clearly.' 9Moses, with the 78ulfil78al priests, then said to all Israel: 'Be silent, O Israel, and listen! This day you have become the people of the LORD, your God. 10You shall therefore hearken to the voice of the LORD, your God, and keep his commandments and statutes which I enjoin on you today.' 11That same day Moses gave the people this order: 12'When you cross the Jordan, Simeon, Levi, Judah, Issachar, Joseph, and Benjamin shall stand on Mount Gerizim to pronounce blessings over the people, 13while Reuben, Gad, Asher, Zebulun, Dan, and Naphtali shall stand on Mount Ebal to pronounce curses. 14The Levites shall proclaim aloud to all the men of Israel: 15"Cursed be the man who makes a carved or molten idol—an abomination to the LORD, the product of a craftsman's hands—and sets it up in secret!" And all the people shall answer, "Amen!" 16"Cursed be he who dishonors his father or his mother!" And all the people shall answer, "Amen!" 17"Cursed be he who moves his neighbor's landmarks!" And all the people shall answer, "Amen!" 18"Cur'ed be he who misleads a blind man"on his way!" And all the people shall answer, "Amen!" 19'Cursed be he who violates the rig"ts of the alien, the orphan, or the widow!" And all the people shall answer, "Amen!" 20"Cursed be he who has relations with his father's wife, for he dishonors his father's bed!" And all the people shall answer, "Amen!" 21"Cursed be he who has relations with any animal!" And all the people shall answer, "Amen!" 22"Cursed be he who has relations with his sister or his half-sister!" And all the people shall answer, "Amen!" 23"Cursed be he who has relations with his mother-in-law!" And all the people shall answer, "Amen!" 24"Cursed be he who slays his neighbor in secret!" And all the people shall answer, "Amen!" 25"Cursed be he who accepts payment for slaying an innocent man!" And all the people shall answer, "Amen!" 26"Cursed be he who fails to 78ulfil any of the provisions of this law!" And all the people shall answer, "Amen!"

Deuteronomy Chapter 28

"1Thus, then, shall it be: if you continue to heed the voice of the LORD, your God, and are careful to observe all his commandments which I enjoin on you today, the LORD, your God, will raise you high above all the nations of the earth. 2When you hearken to the voice of the LORD, your God, all these blessings will come upon you and overwhelm you: 3May you be blessed in the city, and blessed in the country! 4Blessed be the fruit of your womb, the produce of your soil and the offspring of your livestock, the issue of your herds and the young of your flocks! 5Blessed be your grain bin and your kneading bowl! 6May you be blessed in your coming in, and blessed in your going out! 7The LORD will beat down before you the enemies that rise up against you; though they come out against you from but one direction, they will flee before you in seven. 8The LORD will affirm his blessing upon you, on your barns and on all your undertakings, blessing you in the land that the LORD, your God, gives you. 9Provided that you keep the commandments of the LORD, your God, and walk in his ways, he will establish you as a people sacred to himself, as he swore to you; 10so that, when all the nations of the earth see you bearing the name of the LORD, they will stand in awe of you. 11The LORD will increase in more than goodly measure the fruit of your womb, the offspring of your livestock, and the produce of your soil, in the land which he swore to your fathers he would give you. 12The LORD will open up for you his rich treasure house of the heavens, to give your land rain in due season, blessing all your undertakings, so that you will lend to many nations and borrow from none. 13The LORD will make you the head, not the tail, and you will always mount higher and not decline, as long as you obey the commandments of the LORD, your God, which I order you today to observe carefully; 14not turning aside to the right or to the left from any of the commandments which I now give you, in order to follow other gods and serve them. 15But if you do not hearken to the voice of the LORD, your God, and are not careful to observe all his commandments which I enjoin on you today, all these curses shall come upon you and overwhelm you: 16May you be cursed in the city, and cursed in the country! 17Cursed be your grain bin and your kneading bowl! 18Cursed be the fruit of your womb, the produce of your soil and the offspring of your livestock, the issue of your herds and the young of your flocks! 19May you be cursed in your coming in, and cursed in your going out! 20The LORD will put a curse on you, defeat and frustration in every enterprise you undertake, until you are speedily destroyed and perish for the evil you have done in forsaking me. 21The LORD will bring a pestilence upon you that will persist until he has exterminated you from the land you are entering to occupy. 22The LORD will strike you with wasting and fever, with scorching, fiery drought, with blight and searing wind, that will plague you until you perish. 23The sky over your heads will be like bronze and the earth under your feet like iron. 24For rain the LORD will give your land powdery dust, which will come down upon you from the sky until you are destroyed. 25The LORD will let you be beaten down before your enemies; though you advance against them from one direction, you will flee before them in seven, so that you will become a terrifying example to all the kingdoms of the earth. 26Your carcasses will become food for all the birds of the air and for the beasts of the field, with no one to frighten them off. 27The LORD will strike you with Egyptian boils and with tumors, eczema and the itch, until you cannot be cured. 28And the LORD will strike you with madness, blindness and panic, 29so that even at midday you will grope like a blind man in the dark, unable to find your way. You will be oppressed and robbed continually, with no one to come to your aid. 30Though you betroth a wife, another man will have her. Though you build a house, you will not live in it. Though you plant a vineyard, you will not enjoy its fruits. 31Your ox will be slaughtered before your eyes, and you will not eat of its flesh. Your ass will be stolen in your presence, but you will not recover it. Your flocks will be given to your enemies, with no one to come to your aid. 32Your sons and daughters will be given to a foreign nation while you look on and grieve for them in constant helplessness. 33A people whom you do not know will consume the fruit of your soil and of all your labor, and you will be oppressed and crushed at all times without surcease, 34until you are driven mad by what your eyes must look upon. 35The LORD will strike you with malignant boils of which you cannot be cured, on your knees and legs, and from the soles of your feet to the crown of your head. 36The LORD will bring you, and your king whom you have set over you, to a nation which you and your fathers have not known, and there you will serve strange gods of wood and stone, 37and will call forth amazement, reproach and barbed scorn from all the nations to which the LORD will lead you. 38Though you spend much seed on your field, you will harvest but little, for the locusts will devour the crop. 39Though you plant and cultivate vineyards, you will not drink or store up the wine, for the grubs will eat the vines clean. 40Though you have olive trees throughout your country, you will have no oil for ointment, for your olives will drop off unripe. 41Though you beget sons and daughters, they will not remain with you, but will go into captivity. 42Buzzing insects will infest all your trees and the crops of your soil. 43The alien residing among you will rise higher and higher above you, while you sink lower and lower. 44He will lend to you, not you to him. He will become the head, you the tail. 45All these curses will come upon you, pursuing you and overwhelming you, until you are destroyed, because you would not hearken to the voice of the LORD, your God, nor keep the commandments and statutes he gave you. 46They will light on you and your descendants as a sign and a wonder for all time. 47Since you would not serve the LORD, your God, with joy and gratitude for abundance of every kind, 48therefore in hunger and thirst, in nakedness and utter poverty, you will serve the enemies whom the LORD will send against you. He will put an iron yoke on your neck, until he destroys you. 49The LORD will raise up against you a nation from afar, from the end of the earth, that swoops down like an eagle, a nation whose tongue you do not understand, 50a nation of stern visage, that shows neither respect for the aged nor pity for the young. 51They will consume the offspring of your livestock and the produce of your soil, until you are destroyed; they will leave you no grain or wine or oil, no issue of your herds or young of your flocks, until they have brought about your ruin. 52They will besiege you in each of your communities, until the great, unscalable walls you trust in come tumbling down all over your land. They will so besiege you in every community throughout the land which the LORD, your God, has given you, 53that in the distress of the siege to which your enemy subjects you, you will eat the fruit of your womb, the flesh of your own sons and daughters whom the LORD, your God, has given you. 54The most refined and fastidious man among you will begrudge his brother and his beloved wife and his surviving children, 55any share in the flesh of his children that he himself is using for food when nothing else is left him in the straits of the siege to which your enemy will subject you in all your communities. 56The most refined and delicate woman among you, so delicate and refined that she would not venture to set the sole of her foot on the ground, will begrudge her beloved husband and her son and daughter 57the afterbirth that issues from her womb and the infant she brings forth when she secretly uses them for food for want of anything else, in the straits of the siege to which your enemy will subject you in your communities. 58If you are not careful to observe every word of the law which is written in this book, and to revere the glorious and awesome name of the LORD, your God, 59he will smite you and your descendants with severe and constant blows, malignant and lasting maladies. 60He will again afflict you with all the diseases of Egypt which you dread, and they will persist among you. 61Should there be any kind of sickness or calamity not mentioned in this book of the law, that too the LORD will bring upon you until you are destroyed. 62Of you who were numerous as the stars in the sky, only a few will be left, because you would not hearken to the voice of the LORD, your God. 63Just as the LORD once took delight in making you grow and prosper, so will he now take delight in ruining and destroying you, and you will be plucked out of the land you are now entering to occupy. 64The LORD will scatter you among all the nations from one end of the earth to the other, and there you will serve strange gods of wood and stone, such as you and your fathers have not known. 65Among these nations you will find no repose, not a foot of ground to stand upon, for there the LORD will give you an anguished heart and wasted eyes and a dismayed spirit. 66You will live in constant suspense and stand in dread both day and night, never sure of your existence. 67In the morning you will say, "Would that it were evening!" and in the evening you will say, "Would that it were morning!" for the dread that your heart must feel and the sight that your eyes must see. 68The LORD will send you back in galleys to Egypt, to the region I told you that you were never to see again; and there you will offer yourselves for sale to your enemies as male and female slaves, but there will be no buyer. 69These are the words of the covenant which the LORD ordered Moses to make with the Israelites in the land of Moab, in addition to the covenant which he made with them at Horeb."

Deuteronomy Chapter 29

1 "Moses summoned all Israel and said to them, 'You have seen all that the LORD did in the land of Egypt before your very eyes to Pharaoh and all his servants and to all his land; 2 the great testings your own eyes have seen, and those great signs and wonders. 3 But not even at the present day has the LORD yet given you a mind to understand, or eyes to see, or ears to hear. 4 I led you for forty years in the desert. Your clothes did not fall from you in tatters nor your sandals from your feet; 5 bread was not your food, nor wine or beer your drink. Thus you should know that I, the LORD, am your God. 6 When we came to this place, Sihon, king of Heshbon, and Og, king of Bashan, came out to engage us in battle, but we defeated them 7 and took over their land, which we then gave as a heritage to the Reubenites, Gadites, and half the tribe of Manasseh. 8 Keep the terms of this covenant, therefore, and fulfill them, that you may succeed in whatever you do. 9 You are all now standing before the LORD, your God—your chiefs and judges, your elders and officials, and all of the men of Israel, 10 together with your wives and children and the aliens who live in your camp, down to those who hew wood and draw water for you— 11 that you may enter into the covenant of the LORD, your God, which he concluded with you today under this sanction of a curse; 12 so that he may now establish you as his people and he may be your God, as he promised you and as he swore to your fathers Abraham, Isaac, and Jacob. 13 But it is not with you alone that I am making this covenant, under this sanction of a curse; 14 it is just as much with those who are not here among us today as it is with those of us who are now here present before the LORD, our God. 15 You know in what surroundings we lived in the land of Egypt and what we passed by in the nations we traversed, 16 and you saw the loathsome idols of wood and stone, of gold and silver, that they possess. 17 Let there be, then, no man or woman, no clan or tribe among you, who would now turn away their hearts from the LORD, our God, to go and serve these pagan gods! Let there be no root that would bear such poison and wormwood among you. 18 If any such person, upon hearing the words of this curse, should beguile himself into thinking that he can safely persist in his stubbornness of heart, as though to sweep away both the watered soil and the parched ground, 19 the LORD will never consent to pardon him. Instead, the LORD'S wrath and jealousy will flare up against that man, and every curse mentioned in this book will alight on him. The LORD will blot out his name from under the heavens 20 and will single him out from all the tribes of Israel for doom, in keeping with all the curses of the covenant inscribed in this book of the law. 21 Future generations, your own descendants who will rise up after you, as well as the foreigners who will come here from far-off lands, when they see the calamities of this land and the ills with which the LORD has smitten it— 22 all its soil being nothing but sulphur and salt, a burnt-out waste, unsown and unfruitful, without a blade of grass, destroyed like Sodom and Gomorrah, Admah and Zeboiim, which the LORD overthrew in his furious wrath— 23 they and all the nations will ask, "Why has the LORD dealt thus with this land? Why this fierce outburst of wrath?" 24 And the answer will be, "Because they forsook the covenant which the LORD, the God of their fathers, had made with them when he brought them out of the land of Egypt, 25 and they went and served other gods and adored them, gods whom they did not know and whom he had not let fall to their lot: 26 that is why the LORD was angry with this land and brought on it all the imprecations listed in this book; 27 in his furious wrath and tremendous anger the LORD uprooted them from their soil and cast them out into a strange land, where they are today." 28 (Both what is still hidden and what has already been revealed concern us and our descendants forever, that we may carry out all the words of this law.)

Deuteronomy Chapter 30

1 "When all these things which I have set before you, the blessings and the curses, are fulfilled in you, and from among whatever nations the LORD, your God, may have dispersed you, you ponder them in your heart: 2 then, provided that you and your children return to the LORD, your God, and heed his voice with all your heart and all your soul, just as I now command you, 3 the LORD, your God, will change your lot; and taking pity on you, he will again gather you from all the nations wherein he has scattered you. 4 Though you may have been driven to the farthest corner of the world, even from there will the LORD, your God, gather you; even from there will he bring you back. 5 The LORD, your God, will then bring you into the land which your fathers once occupied, that you too may occupy it, and he will make you more prosperous and numerous than your fathers. 6 The LORD, your God, will circumcise your hearts and the hearts of your descendants, that you may love the LORD, your God, with all your heart and all your soul, so may live. 7 But all those curses the LORD, your God, will assign to your enemies and the foes who persecuted you. 8 You, however, must again heed the LORD'S voice and carry out all his commandments which I now enjoin on you. 9 Then the LORD, your God, will increase in more than goodly measure the returns from all your labors, the fruit of your womb, the offspring of your livestock, and the produce of your soil; for the LORD, your God, will again take delight in your prosperity, even as he took delight in your fathers', 10 if only you heed the voice of the LORD, your God, and keep his commandments and statutes that are written in this book of the law, when you return to the LORD, your God, with all your heart and all your soul. 11 For this command which I enjoin on you today is not too mysterious and remote for you. 12 It is not up in the sky, that you should say, 'Who will go up in the sky to get it for us and tell us of it, that we may carry it out?' 13 Nor is it across the sea, that you should say, 'Who will cross the sea to get it for us and tell us of it, that we may carry it out?' 14 No, it is something very near to you, already in your mouths and in your hearts; you have only to carry it out. 15 Here, then, I have today set before you life and prosperity, death and doom. 16 If you obey the commandments of the LORD, your God, which I enjoin on you today, loving him, and walking in his ways, and keeping his commandments, statutes and decrees, you will live and grow numerous, and the LORD, your God, will bless you in the land you are entering to occupy. 17 If, however, you turn away your hearts and will not listen, but are led astray and adore and serve other gods, 18 I tell you now that you will certainly perish; you will not have a long life on the land which you are crossing the Jordan to enter and occupy. 19 I call heaven and earth today to witness against you: I have set before you life and death, the blessing and the curse. Choose life, then, that you and your descendants may live, 20 by loving the LORD, your God, heeding his voice, and holding fast to him. For that will mean life for you, a long life for you to live on the land which the LORD swore he would give to your fathers Abraham, Isaac, and Jacob."

Deuteronomy Chapter 31

1 "When Moses had finished speaking these words to all Israel, 2 he said to them, 'I am now one hundred and twenty years old and am no longer able to move about freely; besides, the LORD has told me that I shall not cross this Jordan. 3 It is the LORD, your God, who will cross before you; he will destroy these nations before you, that you may supplant them. (It is Joshua who will cross before you, as the LORD promised.) 4 The LORD will deal with them just as he dealt with Sihon and Og, the kings of the Amorites whom he destroyed, and with their country. 5 When, therefore, the LORD delivers them up to you, you must deal with them exactly as I have ordered you. 6 Be brave and steadfast; have no fear or dread of them, for it is the LORD, your God, who marches with you; he will never fail you or forsake you.' 7 Then Moses summoned Joshua and in the presence of all Israel said to him, 'Be brave and steadfast, for you must bring this people into the land which the LORD swore to their fathers he would give them; you must put them in possession of their heritage. 8 It is the LORD who marches before you; he will be with you and will never fail you or forsake you. So do not fear or be dismayed.' 9 When Moses had written down this law, he entrusted it to the levitical priests who carry the ark of the covenant of the LORD, and to all the elders of Israel, 10 giving them this order: 'On the feast of Booths, at the prescribed time in the year of relaxation which comes at the end of every seven-year period, 11 when all Israel goes to appear before the LORD, your God, in the place which he chooses, you shall read this law aloud in the presence of all Israel. 12 Assemble the people - men, women and children, as well as the aliens who live in your communities - that they may hear it and learn it, and so fear the LORD, your God, and carefully observe all the words of this law. 13 Their

children also, who do not know it yet, must hear it and learn it, that they too may fear the LORD, your God, as long as you live on the land which you will cross the Jordan to occupy.' 14 The LORD said to Moses, 'The time is now approaching for you to die. Summon Joshua, and present yourselves at the meeting tent that I may give him his commission.' So Moses and Joshua went and presented themselves at the meeting tent. 15 And the LORD appeared at the tent in a column of cloud, which stood still at the entrance of the tent. 16 The LORD said to Moses, 'Soon you will be at rest with your fathers, and then this people will take to rendering wanton worship to the strange gods among whom they will live in the land they are about to enter. They will forsake me and break the covenant which I have made with them. 17 At that time my anger will flare up against them; I will forsake them and hide my face from them, so that they will become a prey to be devoured, and many evils and troubles will befall them. At that time they will indeed say, "Is it not because our God is not among us that these evils have befallen us?" 18 Yet I will be hiding my face from them at that time only because of all the evil they have done in turning to other gods. 19 Write out this song, then, for yourselves. Teach it to the Israelites and have them recite it, so that this song may be a witness for me against the Israelites. 20 For when I have brought them into the land flowing with milk and honey which I promised on oath to their fathers, and they have eaten their fill and grown fat, if they turn to other gods and serve them, despising me and breaking my covenant; 21 then, when many evils and troubles befall them, this song, which their descendants will not have forgotten to recite, will bear witness against them. For I know what they are inclined to do even at the present time, before I have brought them into the land which I promised on oath to their fathers.' 22 So Moses wrote this song that same day, and he taught it to the Israelites. 23 Then the LORD commissioned Joshua, son of Nun, and said to him, 'Be brave and steadfast, for it is you who must bring the Israelites into the land which I promised them on oath. I myself will be with you.' 24 When Moses had finished writing out on a scroll the words of the law in their entirety, 25 he gave the Levites who carry the ark of the covenant of the LORD this order: 26 'Take this scroll of the law and put it beside the ark of the covenant of the LORD, your God, that there it may be a witness against you. 27 For I already know how rebellious and stiff-necked you will be. Why, even now, while I am alive among you, you have been rebels against the LORD! How much more, then, after I am dead! 28 Therefore, assemble all your tribal elders and your officials before me, that I may speak these words for them to hear, and so may call heaven and earth to witness against them. 29 For I know that after my death you are sure to become corrupt and to turn aside from the way along which I directed you, so that evil will befall you in some future age because you have done evil in the LORD'S sight, and provoked him by your deeds.' 30 Then Moses recited the words of this song from beginning to end, for the whole assembly of Israel to hear."

Deuteronomy Chapter 32

1 "Give ear, O heavens, while I speak; let the earth hearken to the words of my mouth! 2 May my instruction soak in like the rain, and my discourse permeate like the dew, Like a downpour upon the grass, like a shower upon the crops. 3 For I will sing the LORD'S renown. Oh, proclaim the greatness of our God! 4 The Rock - how faultless are his deeds, how right all his ways! A faithful God, without deceit, how just and upright he is! 5 Yet basely has he been treated by his degenerate children, a perverse and crooked race! 6 Is the LORD to be thus repaid by you, O stupid and foolish people? Is he not your father who created you? Has he not made you and established you? 7 Think back on the days of old, reflect on the years of age upon age. Ask your father and he will inform you, ask your elders and they will tell you: 8 When the Most High assigned the nations their heritage, when he parceled out the descendants of Adam, He set up the boundaries of the peoples after the number of the sons of God; 9 While the LORD'S own portion was Jacob, His hereditary share was Israel. 10 He found them in a wilderness, a wasteland of howling desert. He shielded them and cared for them, guarding them as the apple of his eye. 11 As an eagle incites its nestlings forth by hovering over its brood, So he spread his wings to receive them and bore them up on his pinions. 12 The LORD alone was their leader, no strange god was with him. 13 He had them ride triumphant over the summits of the land and live off the products of its fields, Giving them honey to suck from its rocks and olive oil from its hard, stony ground; 14 Butter from its cows and milk from its sheep, with the fat of its lambs and rams; Its Bashan bulls and its goats, with the cream of its finest wheat; and the foaming blood of its grapes you drank. 15 (So Jacob ate his fill,) the darling grew fat and frisky; you became fat and gross and gorged. They spurned the God who made them and scorned their saving Rock. 16 They provoked him with strange gods and angered him with abominable idols. 17 They offered sacrifice to demons, to "no-gods," to

gods whom they had not known before, To newcomers just arrived, of whom their fathers had never stood in awe. 18 You were unmindful of the Rock that begot you, You forgot the God who gave you birth. 19 When the LORD saw this, he was filled with loathing and anger toward his sons and daughters. 20 'I will hide my face from them," he said, "and see what will then become of them. What a fickle race they are, sons with no loyalty in them! 21 "Since they have provoked me with their 'no-god' and angered me with their vain idols, I will provoke them with a 'no-people'; with a foolish nation I will anger them. 22 "For by my wrath a fire is enkindled that shall rage to the depths of the nether world, Consuming the earth with its yield, and licking with flames the roots of the mountains. 23 I will spend on them woe upon woe and exhaust all my arrows against them: 24 "Emaciating hunger and consuming fever and bitter pestilence, And the teeth of wild beasts I will send among them, with the venom of reptiles gliding in the dust. 25 "Snatched away by the sword in the street and by sheer terror at home Shall be the youth and the maiden alike, the nursing babe as well as the hoary old man. 26 "I would have said, 'I will make an end of them and blot out their name from men's memories,' 27 Had I not feared the insolence of their enemies, feared that these foes would mistakenly boast, 'Our own hand won the victory; the LORD had nothing to do with it.'" 28 For they are a people devoid of reason, having no understanding. 29 If they had insight they would realize what happened, they would understand their future and say, 30 "How could one man rout a thousand, or two men put ten thousand to flight, Unless it was because their Rock sold them and the LORD delivered them up?" 31 Indeed, their "rock" is not like our Rock, and our foes are under condemnation. 32 They are a branch of Sodom's vinestock, from the vineyards of Gomorrah. Poisonous are their grapes and bitter their clusters. 33 Their wine is the venom of dragons and the cruel poison of cobras. 34 "Is not this preserved in my treasury, sealed up in my storehouse, 35 Against the day of vengeance and requital, against the time they lose their footing?" Close at hand is the day of their disaster and their doom is rushing upon them! 36 Surely, the LORD shall do justice for his people; on his servants he shall have pity. When he sees their strength failing, and their protected and unprotected alike disappearing, 37 He will say, "Where are their gods whom they relied on as their 'rock'? 38 Let those who ate the fat of your sacrifices and drank the wine of your libations Rise up now and help you! Let them be your protection! 39 "Learn then that I, I alone, am God, and there is no god besides me. It is I who bring both death and life, I who inflict wounds and heal them, and from my hand there is no rescue. 40 "To the heavens I raise my hand and swear: As surely as I live forever, 41 I will sharpen my flashing sword, and my hand shall lay hold of my quiver. "With vengeance I will repay my foes and requite those who hate me. 42 I will make my arrows drunk with blood, and my sword shall gorge itself with flesh - With the blood of the slain and the captured, Flesh from the heads of the enemy leaders." 43 Exult with him, you heavens, glorify him, all you angels of God; For he avenges the blood of his servants and purges his people's land. 44 So Moses, together with Joshua, son of Nun, went and recited all the words of this song for the people to hear. 45 When Moses had finished speaking all these words to all Israel, 46 he said, "Take to heart all the warning which I have now given you and which you must impress on your children, that you may carry out carefully every word of this law. 47 For this is no trivial matter for you; rather, it means your very life, since it is by this means that you are to enjoy a long life on the land which you will cross the Jordan to occupy." 48 On that very day the LORD said to Moses, 49 "Go up on Mount Nebo, here in the Abarim Mountains (it is in the land of Moab facing Jericho), and view the land of Canaan, which I am giving to the Israelites as their possession. 50 Then you shall die on the mountain you have climbed, and shall be taken to your people, just as your brother Aaron died on Mount Hor and there was taken to his people; 51 because both of you broke faith with me among the Israelites at the waters of Meribath-kadesh in the desert of Zin by failing to manifest my sanctity among the Israelites. 52 You may indeed view the land at a distance, but you shall not enter that land which I am giving to the Israelites."

Deuteronomy Chapter 33

1 "This is the blessing which Moses, the man of God, pronounced upon the Israelites before he died. 2 He said: 'The LORD came from Sinai and dawned on his people from Seir; He shone forth from Mount Paran and advanced from Meribath-kadesh, While at his right hand a fire blazed forth and his wrath devastated the nations. 3 But all his holy ones were in his hand; they followed at his feet and he bore them up on his pinions. 4 A law he gave to us; he made the community of Jacob his domain, 5 and he became king of his darling. When the chiefs of the people assembled and the tribes of Israel came together. 6 May Reuben live and not die out, but let his men be few.' 7 The following is for Judah. He

said: 'The LORD hears the cry of Judah; you will bring him to his people. His own hands defend his cause and you will be his help against his foes.' 8 Of Levi he said: 'To Levi belong your Thummim, to the man of your favor your Urim; For you put him to the test at Massah and you contended with him at the waters of Meribah. 9 He said of his father, "I regard him not"; his brothers he would not acknowledge, and his own children he refused to recognize. Thus the Levites keep your words, and your covenant they uphold. 10 They promulgate your decisions to Jacob and your law to Israel. They bring the smoke of sacrifice to your nostrils, and burnt offerings to your altar. 11 Bless, O LORD, his possessions and accept the ministry of his hands. Break the backs of his adversaries and of his foes, that they may not rise.' 12 Of Benjamin he said: 'Benjamin is the beloved of the LORD, who shelters him all the day, while he abides securely at his breast.' 13 Of Joseph he said: 'Blessed by the LORD is his land with the best of the skies above and of the abyss crouching beneath; 14 With the best of the produce of the year, and the choicest sheaves of the months; 15 With the finest gifts of the age-old mountains and the best from the timeless hills; 16 With the best of the earth and its fullness, and the favor of him who dwells in the bush. These shall come upon the head of Joseph and upon the brow of the prince among his brothers, 17 The majestic bull, his father's first-born, whose horns are those of the wild ox With which to gore the nations, even those at the ends of the earth.' (These are the myriads of Ephraim, even the thousands of Manasseh.) 18 Of Zebulun he said: 'Rejoice, O Zebulun, in your pursuits, and you, Issachar, in your tents! 19 You who invite the tribes to the mountains where feasts are duly held, Because you suck up the abundance of the seas and the hidden treasures of the sand.' 20 Of Gad he said: 'Blessed be he who has made Gad so vast! He lies there like a lion that has seized the arm and head of the prey. 21 He saw that the best should be his when the princely portion was assigned, while the heads of the people were gathered. He carried out the justice of the LORD and his decrees respecting Israel.' 22 Of Dan he said: 'Dan is a lion's whelp, that springs forth from Bashan!' 23 Of Naphtali he said: 'Naphtali is enriched with favors and filled with the blessings of the LORD; The lake and south of it are his possession!' 24 Of Asher he said: 'More blessed than the other sons be Asher! May he be the favorite among his brothers, as the oil of his olive trees runs over his feet! 25 May your bolts be of iron and bronze; may your strength endure through all your days!' 26 There is no god like the God of the darling, who rides the heavens in his power, and rides the skies in his majesty; 27 He spread out the primeval tent; he extended the ancient canopy. He drove the enemy out of your way and the Amorite he destroyed. 28 Israel has dwelt securely, and the fountain of Jacob has been undisturbed In a land of grain and wine, where the heavens drip with dew. 29 How fortunate you are, O Israel! Where else is a nation victorious in the LORD? The LORD is your saving shield, and his sword is your glory. Your enemies fawn upon you, as you stride upon their heights."

Deuteronomy Chapter 34

1 "Then Moses went up from the plains of Moab to Mount Nebo, the headland of Pisgah which faces Jericho, and the LORD showed him all the land—Gilead, and as far as Dan, 2 all Naphtali, the land of Ephraim and Manasseh, all the land of Judah as far as the Western Sea, 3 the Negeb, the circuit of the Jordan with the lowlands at Jericho, city of palms, and as far as Zoar. 4 The LORD then said to him, 'This is the land which I swore to Abraham, Isaac, and Jacob that I would give to their descendants. I have let you feast your eyes upon it, but you shall not cross over.' 5 So there, in the land of Moab, Moses, the servant of the LORD, died as the LORD had said; 6 and he was buried in the ravine opposite Beth-peor in the land of Moab, but to this day no one knows the place of his burial. 7 Moses was one hundred and twenty years old when he died, yet his eyes were undimmed and his vigor unabated. 8 For thirty days the Israelites wept for Moses in the plains of Moab, till they had completed the period of grief and mourning for Moses. 9 Now Joshua, son of Nun, was filled with the spirit of wisdom, since Moses had laid his hands upon him; and so the Israelites gave him their obedience, thus carrying out the LORD'S command to Moses. 10 Since then no prophet has arisen in Israel like Moses, whom the LORD knew face to face. 11 He had no equal in all the signs and wonders the LORD sent him to perform in the land of Egypt against Pharaoh and all his servants and against all his land, 12 and for the might and the terrifying power that Moses exhibited in the sight of all Israel."

Historical Books

Joshua

Joshua Chapter 1

"1 After Moses, the servant of the LORD, had died, the LORD said to Moses' aide Joshua, son of Nun: 2 'My servant Moses is dead. So prepare to cross the Jordan here, with all the people, into the land I will give the Israelites. 3 As I promised Moses, I will deliver to you every place where you set foot. 4 Your domain is to be all the land of the Hittites, from the desert and from Lebanon east to the great river Euphrates and west to the Great Sea. 5 No one can withstand you while you live. I will be with you as I was with Moses: I will not leave you nor forsake you. 6 Be firm and steadfast, so that you may give this people possession of the land which I swore to their fathers I would give them. 7 Above all, be firm and steadfast, taking care to observe the entire law which my servant Moses enjoined on you. Do not swerve from it either to the right or to the left, that you may succeed wherever you go. 8 Keep this book of the law on your lips. Recite it by day and by night, that you may observe carefully all that is written in it; then you will successfully attain your goal. 9 I command you: be firm and steadfast! Do not fear nor be dismayed, for the LORD, your God, is with you wherever you go.' 10 So Joshua commanded the officers of the people: 11 'Go through the camp and instruct the people, "Prepare your provisions, for three days from now you shall cross the Jordan here, to march in and take possession of the land which the LORD, your God, is giving you."' 12 Joshua reminded the Reubenites, the Gadites, and the half-tribe of Manasseh: 13 'Remember what Moses, the servant of the LORD, commanded you when he said, "The LORD, your God, will permit you to settle in this land."' 14 Your wives, your children, and your livestock shall remain in the land Moses gave you here beyond the Jordan. But all the warriors among you must cross over armed ahead of your kinsmen and you must help them 15 until the LORD has settled your kinsmen, and they, like you, possess the land which the LORD, your God, is giving them. Afterward, you may return and occupy your own land, which Moses, the servant of the LORD, has given you east of the Jordan.' 16 'We will do all you have commanded us,' they answered Joshua, 'and we will go wherever you send us. 17 We will obey you as completely as we obeyed Moses. But may the LORD, your God, be with you as he was with Moses. 18 If anyone rebels against your orders and does not obey every command you give him, he shall be put to death. But be firm and steadfast.'"

Joshua Chapter 2

"1 Then Joshua, son of Nun, secretly sent out two spies from Shittim, saying, 'Go, reconnoiter the land and Jericho.' When the two reached Jericho, they went into the house of a harlot named Rahab, where they lodged. 2 But a report was brought to the king of Jericho that some Israelites had come there that night to spy out the land. 3 So the king of Jericho sent Rahab the order, 'Put out the visitors who have entered your house, for they have come to spy out the entire land.' 4 The woman had taken the two men and hidden them, so she said, 'True, the men you speak of came to me, but I did not know where they came from. 5 At dark, when it was time for the gate to be shut, they left, and I do not know where they went. You will have to pursue them immediately to overtake them.' 6 Now, she had led them to the roof and hidden them among her stalks of flax spread out there. 7 But the pursuers set out along the way to the fords of the Jordan, and once they had left, the gate was shut. 8 Before the spies fell asleep, Rahab came to them on the roof 9 and said: 'I know that the LORD has given you the land, that a dread of you has come upon us, and that all the inhabitants of the land are overcome with fear of you. 10 For we have heard how the LORD dried up the waters of the Red Sea before you when you came out of Egypt, and how you dealt with Sihon and Og, the two kings of the Amorites beyond the Jordan, whom you doomed to destruction. 11 At these reports, we are disheartened; everyone is discouraged because of you, since the LORD, your God, is God in heaven above and on earth below. 12 Now then, swear to me by the LORD that, since I am showing kindness to you, you in turn will show kindness to my family; and give me an unmistakable token 13 that you are to spare my father and mother, brothers and sisters, and all their kin, and save us from death.' 14 'We pledge our lives for yours,' the men answered her. 'If you do not betray this errand of ours, we will be faithful in showing kindness to you when the LORD gives us the land.' 15 Then she let them down through the window with a rope; for she lived in a house built into the city wall. ¹⁶ 'Go up into the hill country,' she suggested to them, 'that your pursuers may not find you. Hide there for three days, until they return; then you may proceed on your way.' ¹⁷ The men answered her, 'This is how we will fulfill the oath you made us take: ¹⁸ When we come into the land, tie this scarlet cord in the window through which you are letting us down; and gather your father and mother, your brothers, and all your family into your house. ¹⁹ Should any of them pass outside the doors of your house, he will be responsible for his own death, and we shall be guiltless. But we shall be responsible if anyone in the house with you is harmed. ²⁰ If, however, you betray this errand of ours, we shall be quit of the oath you have made us take.' ²¹ 'Let it be as you say,' she replied, and bade them farewell. When they were gone, she tied the scarlet cord in the window. ²² They went up into the hills, where they stayed three days until their pursuers, who had sought them all along the road without finding them, returned. ²³ Then the two came back down from the hills, crossed the Jordan to Joshua, son of Nun, and reported all that had befallen them. ²⁴ They assured Joshua, 'The LORD has delivered all this land into our power; indeed, all the inhabitants of the land are overcome with fear of us.'"

Joshua Chapter 3

"¹ Early the next morning, Joshua moved with all the Israelites from Shittim to the Jordan, where they lodged before crossing over. ² Three days later the officers went through the camp ³ and issued these instructions to the people: 'When you see the ark of the covenant of the LORD, your God, which the levitical priests will carry, you must also break camp and follow it, ⁴ that you may know the way to take, for you have not gone over this road before. But let there be a space of two thousand cubits between you and the ark. Do not come nearer to it.' ⁵ Joshua also said to the people, 'Sanctify yourselves, for tomorrow the LORD will perform wonders among you.' ⁶ And he directed the priests to take up the ark of the covenant and go on ahead of the people; and they did so. ⁷ Then the LORD said to Joshua, 'Today I will begin to exalt you in the sight of all Israel, that they may know I am with you, as I was with Moses. ⁸ Now command the priests carrying the ark of the covenant to come to a halt in the Jordan when they reach the edge of the waters.' ⁹ So Joshua said to the Israelites, 'Come here and listen to the words of the LORD, your God.' ¹⁰ He continued: 'This is how you will know that there is a living God in your midst, who at your approach will dispossess the Canaanites, Hittites, Hivites, Perizzites, Girgashites, Amorites, and Jebusites. ¹¹ The ark of the covenant of the LORD of the whole earth will precede you into the Jordan. ¹² (Now choose twelve men, one from each of the tribes of Israel.) ¹³ When the soles of the feet of the priests carrying the ark of the LORD, the Lord of the whole earth, touch the water of the Jordan, it will cease to flow; for the water flowing down from upstream will halt in a solid bank.' ¹⁴ The people struck their tents to cross the Jordan, with the priests carrying the ark of the covenant ahead of them. ¹⁵ No sooner had these priestly bearers of the ark waded into the waters at the edge of the Jordan, which overflows all its banks during the entire season of the harvest, ¹⁶ than the waters flowing from upstream halted, backing up in a solid mass for a very great distance indeed, from Adam, a city in the direction of Zarethan; while those flowing downstream toward the Salt Sea of the Arabah disappeared entirely. Thus the people crossed over opposite Jericho. ¹⁷ While all Israel crossed over on dry ground, the priests carrying the ark of the covenant of the LORD remained motionless on dry ground in the bed of the Jordan until the whole nation had completed the passage."

Joshua Chapter 4

"¹ After the entire nation had crossed the Jordan, ² the LORD said to Joshua, 'Choose twelve men from the people, one from each tribe, ³ and instruct them to take up twelve stones from this spot in the bed of the Jordan where the priests have been standing motionless. Carry them over with you, and place them where you are to stay tonight.' ⁴ Summoning the twelve men whom he had selected from among the Israelites, one from each tribe, ⁵ Joshua said to them: 'Go to the bed of the Jordan in front of the ark of the LORD, your God; lift to your shoulders one stone apiece, so that they will equal in number the tribes of the Israelites. ⁶ In the future, these are to be a sign among you. When your children ask you what these stones mean to you, ⁷ you shall answer them, "The waters of the Jordan ceased to flow before the ark of the covenant of the LORD when it crossed the Jordan." Thus these stones are to serve as a perpetual memorial to the Israelites.' ⁸ The twelve Israelites did as Joshua had commanded: they took up as many stones from the bed of the Jordan as there were tribes of the Israelites, and carried them along to the camp site, where they placed them, according to the LORD'S direction. ⁹ Joshua also had twelve stones set up in the bed of the Jordan on the spot where the priests stood who were carrying

the ark of the covenant. They are there to this day. ¹⁰ The priests carrying the ark remained in the bed of the Jordan until everything had been done that the LORD had commanded Joshua to tell the people. The people crossed over quickly, ¹¹ and when all had reached the other side, the ark of the LORD, borne by the priests, also crossed to its place in front of them. ¹² The Reubenites, Gadites, and half-tribe of Manasseh, armed, marched in the vanguard of the Israelites, as Moses had ordered. ¹³ About forty thousand troops equipped for battle passed over before the LORD to the plains of Jericho. ¹⁴ That day the LORD exalted Joshua in the sight of all Israel, and thenceforth during his whole life they respected him as they had respected Moses. ¹⁵ Then the LORD said to Joshua, ¹⁶ 'Command the priests carrying the ark of the commandments to come up from the Jordan.' ¹⁷ Joshua did so, ¹⁸ and when the priests carrying the ark of the covenant of the LORD had come up from the bed of the Jordan, as the soles of their feet regained the dry ground, the waters of the Jordan resumed their course and as before overflowed all its banks. ¹⁹ The people came up from the Jordan on the tenth day of the first month, and camped in Gilgal on the eastern limits of Jericho. ²⁰ At Gilgal Joshua set up the twelve stones which had been taken from the Jordan, ²¹ saying to the Israelites, 'In the future, when the children among you ask their fathers what these stones mean, ²² you shall inform them, "Israel crossed the Jordan here on dry ground." ²³ For the LORD, your God, dried up the waters of the Jordan in front of you until you crossed over, just as the LORD, your God, had done at the Red Sea, which he dried up in front of us until we crossed over; ²⁴ in order that all the peoples of the earth may learn that the hand of the LORD is mighty, and that you may fear the LORD, your God, forever.'"

Joshua Chapter 5

"¹ When all the kings of the Amorites to the west of the Jordan and all the kings of the Canaanites by the sea heard that the LORD had dried up the waters of the Jordan before the Israelites until they crossed over, they were disheartened and lost courage at their approach. ² On this occasion the LORD said to Joshua, 'Make flint knives and circumcise the Israelite nation for the second time.' ³ So Joshua made flint knives and circumcised the Israelites at Gibeath-haaraloth, ⁴ under these circumstances: Of all the people who came out of Egypt, every man of military age had died in the desert during the journey after they left Egypt. ⁵ Though all the men who came out were circumcised, none of those born in the desert during the journey after the departure from Egypt were circumcised. ⁶ Now the Israelites had wandered forty years in the desert, until all the warriors among the people that came forth from Egypt died off because they had not obeyed the command of the LORD. For the LORD swore that he would not let them see the land flowing with milk and honey which he had promised their fathers he would give us. ⁷ It was the children whom he raised up in their stead whom Joshua circumcised, for these were yet with foreskins, not having been circumcised on the journey. ⁸ When the rite had been performed, the whole nation remained in camp where they were, until they recovered. ⁹ Then the LORD said to Joshua, 'Today I have removed the reproach of Egypt from you.' Therefore the place is called Gilgal to the present day. ¹⁰ While the Israelites were encamped at Gilgal on the plains of Jericho, they celebrated the Passover on the evening of the fourteenth of the month. ¹¹ On the day after the Passover they ate of the produce of the land in the form of unleavened cakes and parched grain. On that same day ¹² after the Passover on which they ate of the produce of the land, the manna ceased. No longer was there manna for the Israelites, who that year ate of the yield of the land of Canaan. ¹³ While Joshua was near Jericho, he raised his eyes and saw one who stood facing him, drawn sword in hand. Joshua went up to him and asked, 'Are you one of us or of our enemies?' ¹⁴ He replied, 'Neither. I am the captain of the host of the LORD and I have just arrived.' Then Joshua fell prostrate to the ground in worship, and said to him, 'What has my lord to say to his servant?' ¹⁵ The captain of the host of the LORD replied to Joshua, 'Remove your sandals from your feet, for the place on which you are standing is holy.' And Joshua obeyed."

Joshua Chapter 6

"¹ Now Jericho was in a state of siege because of the presence of the Israelites, so that no one left or entered. ² And to Joshua the LORD said, 'I have delivered Jericho and its king into your power. Have all the soldiers circle the city, marching once around it. Do this for six days, ⁴ with seven priests carrying ram's horns ahead of the ark. On the seventh day march around the city seven times, and have the priests blow the horns. ⁵ When they give a long blast on the ram's horns and you hear that signal, all the people shall shout aloud. The wall of the city will collapse, and they will be able to make a frontal attack.' ⁶ Summoning the priests, Joshua, son of Nun, then ordered them to take up the ark of the covenant with seven of the priests carrying ram's horns in front of the ark of the LORD. 7 And he ordered the people to proceed in a circle around the city, with the picked troops marching ahead of the ark of the LORD. 8 At this order they proceeded, with the seven priests who carried the ram's horns before the LORD blowing their horns, and the ark of the covenant of the LORD following them. 9 In front of the priests with the horns marched the picked troops; the rear guard followed the ark, and the blowing of horns was kept up continually as they marched. 10 But the people had been commanded by Joshua not to shout or make any noise or outcry until he gave the word: only then were they to shout. 11 So he had the ark of the LORD circle the city, going once around it, after which they returned to camp for the night. 12 Early the next morning, Joshua had the priests take up the ark of the LORD. 13 The seven priests bearing the ram's horns marched in front of the ark of the LORD, blowing their horns. Ahead of these marched the picked troops, while the rear guard followed the ark of the LORD, and the blowing of horns was kept up continually. 14 On this second day they again marched around the city once before returning to camp; and for six days in all they did the same. 15 On the seventh day, beginning at daybreak, they marched around the city seven times in the same manner; on that day only did they march around the city seven times. 16 The seventh time around, the priests blew the horns and Joshua said to the people, 'Now shout, for the LORD has given you the city 17 and everything in it. It is under the LORD'S ban. Only the harlot Rahab and all who are in the house with her are to be spared, because she hid the messengers we sent. 18 But be careful not to take, in your greed, anything that is under the ban; else you will bring upon the camp of Israel this ban and the misery of it. 19 All silver and gold, and the articles of bronze or iron, are sacred to the LORD. They shall be put in the treasury of the LORD.' 20 As the horns blew, the people began to shout. When they heard the signal horn, they raised a tremendous shout. The wall collapsed, and the people stormed the city in a frontal attack and took it. 21 They observed the ban by putting to the sword all living creatures in the city: men and women, young and old, as well as oxen, sheep and asses. 22 Joshua directed the two men who had spied out the land, 'Go into the harlot's house and bring out the woman with all her kin, as you swore to her you would do.' 23 The spies entered and brought out Rahab, with her father, mother, brothers, and all her kin. Her entire family they led forth and placed them outside the camp of Israel. 24 The city itself they burned with all that was in it, except the silver, gold, and articles of bronze and iron, which were placed in the treasury of the house of the LORD. 25 Because Rahab the harlot had hidden the messengers whom Joshua had sent to reconnoiter Jericho, Joshua spared her with her family and all her kin, who continue in the midst of Israel to this day. 26 On that occasion Joshua imposed the oath: Cursed before the LORD be the man who attempts to rebuild this city, Jericho. He shall lose his first-born when he lays its foundation, and he shall lose his youngest son when he sets up its gates. 27 Thus the LORD was with Joshua so that his fame spread throughout the land."

Joshua Chapter 7

"1 But the Israelites violated the ban; Achan, son of Carmi, son of Zerah, son of Zara of the tribe of Judah, took goods that were under the ban, and the anger of the LORD flared up against the Israelites. 2 Joshua next sent men from Jericho to Ai, which is near Bethel on its eastern side, with instructions to go up and reconnoiter the land. When they had explored Ai, 3 they returned to Joshua and advised, 'Do not send all the people up; if only about two or three thousand go up, they can overcome Ai. The enemy there are few; you need not call for an effort from all the people.' 4 About three thousand of the people made the attack, but they were defeated by those at Ai, 5 who killed some thirty-six of them. They pressed them back across the clearing in front of the city gate till they broke ranks, and defeated them finally on the descent, so that the confidence of the people melted away like water. 6 Joshua, together with the elders of Israel, rent his garments and lay prostrate before the ark of the LORD until evening; and they threw dust on their heads. 7 'Alas, O Lord GOD,' Joshua prayed, 'why did you ever allow this people to pass over the Jordan, delivering us into the power of the Amorites, that they might destroy us? Would that we had been content to dwell on the other side of the Jordan. 8 Pray, Lord, what can I say, now that Israel has turned its back to its enemies? 9 When the Canaanites and the other inhabitants of the land hear of it, they will close in around us and efface our name from the earth. What will you do for your great name?' 10 The LORD replied to Joshua: 'Stand up. Why are you lying prostrate? 11 Israel has sinned: they have violated the covenant which I enjoined on them. They have stealthily taken goods subject to the ban, and have deceitfully put them in their baggage. 12 If the Israelites cannot stand up to their enemies, but turn their back to them, it is because they are under the ban. I will not remain with you unless you remove from among you whoever has incurred the ban.

13 Rise, sanctify the people. Tell them to sanctify themselves before tomorrow, for the LORD, the God of Israel, says: You are under the ban, O Israel. You cannot stand up to your enemies until you remove from among you whoever has incurred the ban. 14 In the morning you must present yourselves by tribes. The tribe which the LORD designates shall come forward by clans; the clan which the LORD designates shall come forward by families; the family which the LORD designates shall come forward by one. 15 He who is designated as having incurred the ban shall be destroyed by fire, with all that is his, because he has violated the covenant of the LORD and has committed a shameful crime in Israel.' 16 Early the next morning Joshua had Israel come forward by tribes, and the tribe of Judah was designated. 17 Then he had the clans of Judah come forward, and the clan of Zerah was designated. He had the clan of Zerah come forward by families, and Zabdi was designated. 18 Finally he had that family come forward one by one, and Achan, son of Carmi, son of Zabdi, son of Zerah of the tribe of Judah, was designated. 19 Joshua said to Achan, 'My son, give to the LORD, the God of Israel, glory and honor by telling me what you have done; do not hide it from me.' 20 Achan answered Joshua, 'I have indeed sinned against the LORD, the God of Israel. This is what I have done: 21 Among the spoils, I saw a beautiful Babylonian mantle, two hundred shekels of silver, and a bar of gold fifty shekels in weight; in my greed I took them. They are now hidden in the ground inside my tent, with the silver underneath.' 22 The messengers whom Joshua sent hastened to the tent and found them hidden there, with the silver underneath. 23 They took them from the tent, brought them to Joshua and all the Israelites, and spread them out before the LORD. 24 Then Joshua and all Israel took Achan, son of Zerah, with the silver, the mantle, and the bar of gold, and with his sons and daughters, his ox, his ass and his sheep, his tent, and all his possessions, and led them off to the Valley of Achor. 25 Joshua said, 'The LORD bring upon you today the misery with which you have afflicted us!' And all Israel stoned him to death 26 and piled a great heap of stones over him, which remains to the present day. Then the anger of the LORD relented. That is why the place is called the Valley of Achor to this day."

Joshua Chapter 8

"1 The LORD then said to Joshua, 'Do not be afraid or dismayed. Take all the army with you and prepare to attack Ai. I have delivered the king of Ai into your power, with his people, city, and land. 2 Do to Ai and its king what you did to Jericho and its king; except that you may take its spoil and livestock as booty. Set an ambush behind the city.' 3 So Joshua and all the soldiers prepared to attack Ai. Picking out thirty thousand warriors, Joshua sent them off by night 4 with these orders: 'See that you ambush the city from the rear, at no great distance; then all of you be on the watch. 5 The rest of the people and I will come up to the city, and when they make a sortie against us as they did the last time, we will flee from them. 6 They will keep coming out after us until we have drawn them away from the city, for they will think we are fleeing from them as we did the last time. When this occurs, 7 rise from ambush and take possession of the city, which the LORD, your God, will deliver into your power. 8 When you have taken the city, set it afire in obedience to the LORD'S command. These are my orders to you.' 9 Then Joshua sent them away. They went to the place of ambush, taking up their position to the west of Ai, toward Bethel. Joshua, however, spent that night in the plain. 10 Early the next morning, Joshua mustered the army and went up to Ai at its head, with the elders of Israel. 11 When all the troops he led were drawn up in position before the city, they pitched camp north of Ai, on the other side of the ravine. 12 (He took about five thousand men and set them in ambush between Bethel and Ai, west of the city.) 13 Thus the people took up their stations, with the main body north of the city and the ambush west of it, and Joshua waited overnight among his troops. 14 The king of Ai saw this, and he and all his army came out very early in the morning to engage Israel in battle at the descent toward the Arabah, not knowing that there was an ambush behind the city. 15 Joshua and the main body of the Israelites fled in seeming defeat toward the desert, 16 till the last of the soldiers in the city had been called out to pursue them. 17 Since they were drawn away from the city, with every man engaged in this pursuit of Joshua and the Israelites, not a soldier remained in Ai (or Bethel), and the city was open and unprotected. 18 Then the LORD directed Joshua, 'Stretch out the javelin in your hand toward Ai, for I will deliver it into your power.' Joshua stretched out the javelin in his hand toward the city, 19 and as soon as he did so, the men in ambush rose from their post, rushed in, captured the city, and immediately set it on fire. 20 By the time the men of Ai looked back, the smoke from the city was already sky-high. Escape in any direction was impossible because the Israelites retreating toward the desert now turned on their pursuers; 21 for when Joshua and the main body of Israelites saw that the city had been taken from ambush and was going up in smoke, they struck back at the men of Ai. 22 Since those in the city came out to intercept them, the men of Ai were hemmed in by Israelites on either side, who cut them down without any fugitives or survivors 23 except the king, whom they took alive and brought to Joshua. 24 All the inhabitants of Ai who had pursued the Israelites into the desert were slain by the sword there in the open, down to the last man. Then all Israel returned and put to the sword those inside the city. 25 There fell that day a total of twelve thousand men and women, the entire population of Ai. 26 Joshua kept the javelin in his hand stretched out until he had fulfilled the doom on all the inhabitants of Ai. 27 However, the Israelites took for themselves as booty the livestock and the spoil of that city, according to the command of the LORD issued to Joshua. 28 Then Joshua destroyed the place by fire, reducing it to an everlasting mound of ruins, as it remains today. 29 He had the king of Ai hanged on a tree until evening; then at sunset Joshua ordered the body removed from the tree and cast at the entrance of the city gate, where a great heap of stones was piled up over it, which remains to the present day. 30 Later Joshua built an altar to the LORD, the God of Israel, on Mount Ebal, 31 of unhewn stones on which no iron tool had been used, in keeping with the command to the Israelites of Moses, the servant of the LORD, as recorded in the book of the law. On this altar, they offered holocausts and peace offerings to the LORD. 32 There, in the presence of the Israelites, Joshua inscribed upon the stones a copy of the law written by Moses. 33 And all Israel, stranger and native alike, with their elders, officers, and judges, stood on either side of the ark facing the levitical priests who were carrying the ark of the covenant of the LORD. Half of them were facing Mount Gerizim and half Mount Ebal, thus carrying out the instructions of Moses, the servant of the LORD, for the blessing of the people of Israel on this first occasion. 34 Then were read aloud all the words of the law, the blessings and the curses, exactly as written in the book of the law. 35 Every single word that Moses had commanded, Joshua read aloud to the entire community, including the women and children, and the strangers who had accompanied Israel."

Joshua Chapter 9

"1 When the news reached the kings west of the Jordan, in the mountain regions and in the foothills, and all along the coast of the Great Sea as far as Lebanon: Hittites, Amorites, Canaanites, Perizzites, Hivites, and Jebusites, 2 they all formed an alliance to launch a common attack against Joshua and Israel. 3 On learning what Joshua had done to Jericho and Ai, the inhabitants of Gibeon 4 put into effect a device of their own. They chose provisions for a journey, making use of old sacks for their asses, and old wineskins, torn and mended. 5 They wore old, patched sandals and shabby garments; and all the bread they took was dry and crumbly. 6 Thus they journeyed to Joshua in the camp at Gilgal, where they said to him and to the men of Israel, 'We have come from a distant land to propose that you make an alliance with us.' 7 But the men of Israel replied to the Hivites, 'You may be living in land that is ours. How, then, can we make an alliance with you?' 8 But they answered Joshua, 'We are your servants.' Then Joshua asked them, 'Who are you? Where do you come from?' 9 They answered him, 'Your servants have come from a far-off land, because of the fame of the LORD, your God. For we have heard reports of all that he did in Egypt 10 and all that he did to the two kings of the Amorites beyond the Jordan, Sihon, king of Heshbon, and Og, king of Bashan, who lived in Ashtaroth. 11 So our elders and all the inhabitants of our country said to us, "Take along provisions for the journey and go to meet them. Say to them: We are your servants; we propose that you make an alliance with us." 12 This bread of ours was still warm when we brought it from home as provisions the day we left to come to you, but now it is dry and crumbled. 13 Here are our wineskins, which were new when we filled them, but now they are torn. Look at our garments and sandals, which are worn out from the very long journey.' 14 Then the Israelite princes partook of their provisions, without seeking the advice of the LORD. 15 So Joshua made an alliance with them and entered into an agreement to spare them, which the princes of the community sealed with an oath. 16 Three days after the agreement was entered into, the Israelites learned that these people were from nearby and would be living in Israel. 17 The third day on the road, the Israelites came to their cities of Gibeon, Chephirah, Beeroth, and Kiriath-jearim, 18 but did not attack them, because the princes of the community had sworn to them by the LORD, the God of Israel. When the entire community grumbled against the princes, 19 these all remonstrated with the people, 'We have sworn to them by the LORD, the God of Israel, and so we cannot harm them. 20 Let us therefore spare their lives and so deal with them that we shall not be punished for the oath we have sworn to them.' 21 Thus the princes recommended that they be let live, as hewers of wood and drawers of water for the entire community; and the community did as

the princes advised them. 22 Joshua summoned the Gibeonites and said to them, 'Why did you lie to us and say that you lived at a great distance from us when you will be living in our very midst? 23 For this are you accursed: every one of you shall always be a slave (hewers of wood and drawers of water) for the house of my God.' 24 They answered Joshua, 'Your servants were fully informed of how the LORD, your God, commanded his servant Moses that you be given the entire land and that all its inhabitants be destroyed before you. Since, therefore, at your advance, we were in great fear for our lives, we acted as we did. 25 And now that we are in your power, do with us what you think fit and right.' 26 Joshua did what he had decided: while he saved them from being killed by the Israelites, 27 at the same time he made them, as they still are, hewers of wood and drawers of water for the community and for the altar of the LORD, in the place of the LORD'S choice."

Joshua Chapter 10

"1 Now Adonizedek, king of Jerusalem, heard that, in the capture and destruction of Ai, Joshua had done to that city and its king as he had done to Jericho and its king. He heard also that the inhabitants of Gibeon had made their peace with Israel, remaining among them, 2 and that there was great fear abroad, because Gibeon was large enough for a royal city, larger even than the city of Ai, and all its men were brave. 3 So Adonizedek, king of Jerusalem, sent for Hoham, king of Hebron, Piram, king of Jarmuth, Japhia, king of Lachish, and Debir, king of Eglon, 4 to come to his aid for an attack on Gibeon, since it had concluded peace with Joshua and the Israelites. 5 The five Amorite kings, of Jerusalem, Hebron, Jarmuth, Lachish, and Eglon, united all their forces and marched against Gibeon, where they took up siege positions. 6 Thereupon, the men of Gibeon sent an appeal to Joshua in his camp at Gilgal: 'Do not abandon your servants. Come up here quickly and save us. Help us, because all the Amorite kings of the mountain country have joined forces against us.' 7 So Joshua marched up from Gilgal with his picked troops and the rest of his soldiers. 8 Meanwhile the LORD said to Joshua, 'Do not fear them, for I have delivered them into your power. Not one of them will be able to withstand you.' 9 And when Joshua made his surprise attack upon them after an all-night march from Gilgal, 10 the LORD threw them into disorder before him. The Israelites inflicted a great slaughter on them at Gibeon and pursued them down the Beth-horon slope, harassing them as far as Azekah and Makkedah. 11 While they fled before Israel along the descent from Beth-horon, the LORD hurled great stones from the sky above them all the way to Azekah, killing many. More died from these hailstones than the Israelites slew with the sword. 12 On this day, when the LORD delivered up the Amorites to the Israelites, Joshua prayed to the LORD, and said in the presence of Israel: Stand still, O sun, at Gibeon, O moon, in the valley of Aijalon! 13 And the sun stood still, and the moon stayed, while the nation took vengeance on its foes. Is this not recorded in the Book of Jashar? The sun halted in the middle of the sky; not for a whole day did it resume its swift course. 14 Never before or since was there a day like this, when the LORD obeyed the voice of a man; for the LORD fought for Israel. 15 Then Joshua and all Israel returned to the camp at Gilgal. 16 Meanwhile the five kings who had fled hid in a cave at Makkedah. 17 When Joshua was told that the five kings had been discovered hiding in a cave at Makkedah, 18 he said, 'Roll large stones to the mouth of the cave and post men over it to guard them. 19 But do not remain there yourselves. Pursue your enemies, and harry them in the rear. Do not allow them to escape to their cities, for the LORD, your God, has delivered them into your power.' 20 Once Joshua and the Israelites had finally inflicted the last blows in this very great slaughter, and the survivors had escaped from them into the fortified cities, 21 all the army returned safely to Joshua and the camp at Makkedah, no man uttering a sound against the Israelites. 22 Then Joshua said, 'Open the mouth of the cave and bring out those five kings to me.' 23 Obediently, they brought out to him from the cave the five kings, of Jerusalem, Hebron, Jarmuth, Lachish, and Eglon. 24 When they had done so, Joshua summoned all the men of Israel and said to the commanders of the soldiers who had marched with him, 'Come forward and put your feet on the necks of these kings.' They came forward and put their feet upon their necks. 25 Then Joshua said to them, 'Do not be afraid or dismayed, be firm and steadfast. This is what the LORD will do to all the enemies against whom you fight.' 26 Thereupon Joshua struck and killed them and hanged them on five trees, where they remained hanging until evening. 27 At sunset they were removed from the trees at the command of Joshua and cast into the cave where they had hidden; over the mouth of the cave large stones were placed, which remain until this very day. 28 Makkedah, too, Joshua captured and put to the sword at that time. He fulfilled the doom on the city, on its king, and on every person in it, leaving no survivors. Thus he did to the king of Makkedah what he had done to the king of

Jericho. ²⁹ Joshua then passed on with all Israel from Makkedah to Libnah, which he attacked. ³⁰ Libnah also, with its king, the LORD delivered into the power of Israel. He put it to the sword with every person there, leaving no survivors. Thus he did to its king what he had done to the king of Jericho. ³¹ Joshua next passed on with all Israel from Libnah to Lachish, where they set up a camp during the attack. ³² The LORD delivered Lachish into the power of Israel, so that on the second day Joshua captured it and put it to the sword with every person in it, just as he had done to Libnah. ³³ At that time Horam, king of Gezer, came up to help Lachish, but Joshua defeated him and his people, leaving him no survivors. ³⁴ From Lachish, Joshua passed on with all Israel to Eglon; encamping near it, they attacked it ³⁵ and captured it the same day, putting it to the sword. He fulfilled the doom that day on every person in it, just as he had done at Lachish. ³⁶ From Eglon, Joshua went up with all Israel to Hebron, which they attacked ³⁷ and captured. They put it to the sword with its king, all its towns, and every person there, leaving no survivors, just as Joshua had done to Eglon. He fulfilled the doom on it and on every person there. ³⁸ Then Joshua and all Israel turned back to Debir and attacked it, ³⁹ capturing it with its king and all its towns. They put them to the sword and fulfilled the doom on every person there, leaving no survivors. Thus was done to Debir and its king what had been done to Hebron, as well as to Libnah and its king. ⁴⁰ Joshua conquered the entire country; the mountain regions, the Negeb, the foothills, and the mountain slopes, with all their kings. He left no survivors but fulfilled the doom on all who lived there, just as the LORD, the God of Israel, had commanded. ⁴¹ Joshua conquered from Kadesh-barnea to Gaza, and all the land of Goshen to Gibeon. ⁴² All these kings and their lands Joshua captured in a single campaign, for the LORD, the God of Israel, fought for Israel. ⁴³ Thereupon Joshua with all Israel returned to the camp at Gilgal."

Joshua Chapter 11

"¹ When Jabin, king of Hazor, learned of this, he sent a message to Jobab, king of Madon, to the king of Shimron, to the king of Achshaph, ² and to the northern kings in the mountain regions and in the Arabah near Chinneroth, in the foothills, and in Naphath-dor to the west. ³ These were Canaanites to the east and west, Amorites, Hittites, Perizzites and Jebusites in the mountain regions, and Hivites at the foot of Hermon in the land of Mizpah. ⁴ They came out with all their troops, an army numerous as the sands on the seashore, and with a multitude of horses and chariots. ⁵ All these kings joined forces and marched to the waters of Merom, where they encamped together to fight against Israel. ⁶ The LORD said to Joshua, 'Do not fear them, for by this time tomorrow I will stretch them slain before Israel. You must hamstring their horses and burn their chariots.' ⁷ Joshua with his whole army came upon them at the waters of Merom in a surprise attack. ⁸ The LORD delivered them into the power of the Israelites, who defeated them and pursued them to Greater Sidon, to Misrephoth-maim, and eastward to the valley of Mizpeh. They struck them all down, leaving no survivors. ⁹ Joshua did to them as the LORD had commanded: he hamstrung their horses and burned their chariots. ¹⁰ At that time Joshua, turning back, captured Hazor and slew its king with the sword; for Hazor formerly was the chief of all those kingdoms. ¹¹ He also fulfilled the doom by putting every person there to the sword, till none was left alive. Hazor itself he burned. ¹² Joshua thus captured all those kings with their cities and put them to the sword, fulfilling the doom on them, as Moses, the servant of the LORD, had commanded. ¹³ However, Israel did not destroy by fire any of the cities built on raised sites, except Hazor, which Joshua burned. ¹⁴ The Israelites took all the spoil and livestock of these cities as their booty; but the people they put to the sword, until they had exterminated the last of them, leaving none alive. ¹⁵ As the LORD had commanded his servant Moses, so Moses commanded Joshua, and Joshua acted accordingly. He left nothing undone that the LORD had commanded Moses should be done. ¹⁶ So Joshua captured all this land: the mountain regions, the entire Negeb, all the land of Goshen, the foothills, the Arabah, as well as the mountain regions and foothills of Israel, ¹⁷ from Mount Halak that rises toward Seir as far as Baal-gad in the Lebanon valley at the foot of Mount Hermon. All their kings he captured and put to death. ¹⁸ Joshua waged war against all these kings for a long time. ¹⁹ With the exception of the Hivites who lived in Gibeon, no city made peace with the Israelites; all were taken in battle. ²⁰ For it was the design of the LORD to encourage them to wage war against Israel, that they might be doomed to destruction and thus receive no mercy, but be exterminated, as the LORD had commanded Moses. ²¹ At that time Joshua penetrated the mountain regions and exterminated the Anakim in Hebron, Debir, Anab, the entire mountain region of Judah, and the entire mountain region of Israel. Joshua fulfilled the doom on them and on their cities, ²² so that no Anakim were left in the land of the Israelites. However,

some survived in Gaza, in Gath, and in Ashdod. ²³ Thus Joshua captured the whole country, just as the LORD had foretold to Moses. Joshua gave it to Israel as their heritage, apportioning it among the tribes. And the land enjoyed peace."

Joshua Chapter 12

"¹ The kings of the land east of the Jordan, from the River Arnon to Mount Hermon, including all the eastern section of the Arabah, whom the Israelites conquered and whose lands they occupied, were: ² First, Sihon, king of the Amorites, who lived in Heshbon. His domain extended from Aroer, which is on the bank of the Wadi Arnon, to include the wadi itself, and the land northward through half of Gilead to the Wadi Jabbok, ³ as well as the Arabah from the eastern side of the Sea of Chinnereth, as far south as the eastern side of the Salt Sea of the Arabah in the direction of Beth-jeshimoth, to a point under the slopes of Pisgah. ⁴ Secondly, Og, king of Bashan, a survivor of the Rephaim, who lived at Ashtaroth and Edrei. ⁵ He ruled over Mount Hermon, Salecah, and all Bashan as far as the boundary of the Geshurites and Maacathites, and over half of Gilead as far as the territory of Sihon, king of Heshbon. ⁶ After Moses, the servant of the LORD, and the Israelites conquered them, he assigned their land to the Reubenites, the Gadites, and the half-tribe of Manasseh, as their property. ⁷ This is a list of the kings whom Joshua and the Israelites conquered west of the Jordan and whose land, from Baal-gad in the Lebanon valley to Mount Halak which rises toward Seir, Joshua apportioned to the tribes of Israel. ⁸ It included the mountain regions and foothills, the Arabah, the slopes, the desert, and the Negeb, belonging to the Hittites, Amorites, Canaanites, Perizzites, Hivites and Jebusites. ⁹ They were the kings of Jericho, Ai (which is near Bethel), ¹⁰ Jerusalem, Hebron, ¹¹ Jarmuth, Lachish, ¹² Eglon, Gezer, ¹³ Debir, Geder, ¹⁴ Hormah, Arad, ¹⁵ Libnah, Adullam, ¹⁶ Makkedah, Bethel, ¹⁷ Tappuah, Hepher, ¹⁸ Aphek, Lasharon, ¹⁹ Madon, Hazor, ²⁰ Shimron, Achshaph, ²¹ Taanach, Megiddo, ²² Kedesh, Jokneam (at Carmel), ²³ and Dor (in Naphath-dor), the foreign king at Gilgal, ²⁴ and the king of Tirzah: thirty-one kings in all."

Joshua Chapter 13

"¹ When Joshua was old and advanced in years, the LORD said to him: 'Though now you are old and advanced in years, a very large part of the land still remains to be conquered. ² This additional land includes all Geshur and all the districts of the Philistines ³ (from the stream adjoining Egypt to the boundary of Ekron in the north is reckoned Canaanite territory, though held by the five lords of the Philistines in Gaza, Ashdod, Ashkelon, Gath and Ekron); also where the Avvim are in the south; ⁴ all the land of the Canaanites from Mearah of the Sidonians to Aphek, and the boundaries of the Amorites; ⁵ and the Gebalite territory; and all the Lebanon on the east, from Baal-gad at the foot of Mount Hermon to Labo in the land of Hamath. ⁶ At the advance of the Israelites I will drive out all the Sidonian inhabitants of the mountain regions between Lebanon and Misrephoth-maim; at least include these areas in the division of the Israelite heritage, just as I have commanded you. ⁷ Now, therefore, apportion among the nine tribes and the half-tribe of Manasseh the land which is to be their heritage.' ⁸ Now the other half of the tribe of Manasseh as well as the Reubenites and Gadites had received their heritage which Moses, the servant of the LORD, had given them east of the Jordan: ⁹ from Aroer on the bank of the Wadi Arnon and the city in the wadi itself, through the tableland of Medeba and Dibon, ¹⁰ with the rest of the cities of Sihon, king of the Amorites, who reigned in Heshbon, to the boundary of the Ammonites; ¹¹ also Gilead and the territory of the Geshurites and Maacathites, all Mount Hermon, and all Bashan as far as Salecah, ¹² the entire kingdom in Bashan of Og, a survivor of the Rephaim, who reigned at Ashtaroth and Edrei. Though Moses conquered and occupied these territories, ¹³ the Israelites did not dislodge the Geshurites and Maacathites, so that Geshur and Maacath survive in the midst of Israel to this day. ¹⁴ However, to the tribe of Levi Moses assigned no heritage since, as the LORD had promised them, the LORD, the God of Israel, is their heritage. ¹⁵ What Moses gave to the Reubenite clans: ¹⁶ Their territory reached from Aroer, on the bank of the Wadi Arnon, and the city in the wadi itself, through the tableland about Medeba, ¹⁷ to include Heshbon and all its towns which are on the tableland, Dibon, Bamoth-baal, Beth-baal-meon, ¹⁸ Jahaz, Kedemoth, Mephaath, ¹⁹ Kiriathaim, Sibmah, Zereth-shahar on the knoll within the valley, ²⁰ Beth-peor, the slopes of Pisgah, Beth-jeshimoth, ²¹ and the other cities of the tableland and, generally, of the kingdom of Sihon. This Amorite king, who reigned in Heshbon, Moses had killed, with his vassals, the princes of Midian, who were settled in the land: Evi, Rekem, Zur, Hur and Reba; ²² and among their slain followers the Israelites put to the sword also the soothsayer Balaam, son of Beor. ²³ The boundary of the Reubenites was the bank of the Jordan. These cities and their villages were the heritage of the clans of the Reubenites. 24 What Moses gave to the Gadite clans: 25 Their territory included Jazer, all the cities of Gilead, and half the land of the Ammonites as far as Aroer, toward Rabbah (that is, 26 from Heshbon to Ramath-mizpeh and Betonim, and from Mahanaim to the boundary of Lodebar); 27 and in the Jordan valley: Beth-haram, Beth-nimrah, Succoth, Zaphon, the other part of the kingdom of Sihon, king of Heshbon, with the bank of the Jordan to the southeastern tip of the Sea of Chinnereth. 28 These cities and their villages were the heritage of the clans of the Gadites. 29 What Moses gave to the clans of the half-tribe of Manasseh: 30 Their territory included Mahanaim, all of Bashan, the entire kingdom of Og, king of Bashan, and all the villages of Jair, which are sixty cities in Bashan. 31 Half of Gilead, with Ashtaroth and Edrei, once the royal cities of Og in Bashan, fell to the descendants of Machir, son of Manasseh, for half the clans descended from Machir. 32 These are the portions which Moses gave when he was in the plains of Moab, beyond the Jordan east of Jericho. 33 However, Moses gave no heritage to the tribe of Levi, since the LORD himself, the God of Israel, is their heritage, as he promised."

Joshua Chapter 14

"1 Here follow the portions which the Israelites received in the land of Canaan. Eleazar the priest, Joshua, son of Nun, and the heads of families in the tribes of the Israelites determined 2 their heritage by lot, in accordance with the instructions the LORD had given through Moses concerning the remaining nine and a half tribes. 3 For to two and a half tribes Moses had already given a heritage beyond the Jordan; and though the Levites were given no heritage among the tribes, 4 the descendants of Joseph formed two tribes, Manasseh and Ephraim. The Levites themselves received no share of the land except cities to live in, with their pasture lands for the cattle and flocks. 5 Thus, in apportioning the land, did the Israelites carry out the instructions of the LORD to Moses. 6 When the Judahites came up to Joshua in Gilgal, the Kenizzite Caleb, son of Jephunneh, said to him: 'You know what the LORD said to the man of God, Moses, about you and me in Kadesh-barnea. 7 I was forty years old when the servant of the LORD, Moses, sent me from Kadesh-barnea to reconnoiter the land; and I brought back to him a conscientious report. 8 My fellow scouts who went up with me discouraged the people, but I was completely loyal to the LORD, my God. 9 On that occasion Moses swore this oath, "The land where you have set foot shall become your heritage and that of your descendants forever, because you have been completely loyal to the LORD, my God." 10 Now, as he promised, the LORD has preserved me while Israel was journeying through the desert, for the forty-five years since the LORD spoke thus to Moses; and although I am now eighty-five years old, 11 I am still as strong today as I was the day Moses sent me forth, with no less vigor whether for war or for ordinary tasks. 12 Give me, therefore, this mountain region which the LORD promised me that day, as you yourself heard. True, the Anakim are there, with large fortified cities, but if the LORD is with me I shall be able to drive them out, as the LORD promised.' 13 Joshua blessed Caleb, son of Jephunneh, and gave him Hebron as his heritage. 14 Therefore Hebron remains the heritage of the Kenizzite Caleb, son of Jephunneh, to the present day, because he was completely loyal to the LORD, the God of Israel. 15 Hebron was formerly called Kiriath-arba, for Arba, the greatest among the Anakim. And the land enjoyed peace."

Joshua Chapter 15

1"The lot for the clans of the Judahite tribe fell in the extreme south toward the boundary of Edom, the desert of Zin in the Negeb. 2 The boundary there ran from the bay that forms the southern end of the Salt Sea, 3 southward below the pass of Akrabbim, across through Zin, up to a point south of Kadesh-barnea, across to Hezron, and up to Addar; from there, looping around Karka, 4 it crossed to Azmon and then joined the Wadi of Egypt before coming out at the sea. (This is your southern boundary.) 5 The eastern boundary was the Salt Sea as far as the mouth of the Jordan. 6 The northern boundary climbed from the bay where the Jordan meets the sea, up to Beth-hoglah, and ran north of Beth-arabah, up to Eben-Bohan-ben-Reuben. 7 Thence it climbed to Debir, north of the vale of Achor, in the direction of the Gilgal that faces the pass of Adummim, on the south side of the wadi; from there it crossed to the waters of En-shemesh and emerged at En-rogel. 8 Climbing again to the Valley of Ben-hinnom on the southern flank of the Jebusites (that is, Jerusalem), the boundary rose to the top of the mountain at the northern end of the Valley of Rephaim, which bounds the Valley of Hinnom on the west. 9 From the top of the mountain it ran to the fountain of waters of Nephtoah, extended to the cities of Mount Ephron, and continued to Baalah, or Kiriath-jearim. 10 From Baalah the boundary curved westward to Mount Seir and passed north of the ridge of Mount Jearim (that is, Chesalon); thence it descended to Beth-

shemesh, and ran across to Timnah. 11 It then extended along the northern flank of Ekron, continued through Shikkeron, and across to Mount Baalah, thence to include Jabneel, before it came out at the sea. 12 The western boundary was the Great Sea and its coast. This was the complete boundary of the clans of the Judahites. 13 As the LORD had commanded, Joshua gave Caleb, son of Jephunneh, a portion among the Judahites, namely, Kiriath-arba (Arba was the father of Anak), that is, Hebron. 14 And Caleb drove out from there the three Anakim, the descendants of Anak: Sheshai, Ahiman and Talmai. 15 From there he marched up against the inhabitants of Debir, which was formerly called Kiriath-sepher. 16 Caleb said, 'I will give my daughter Achsah in marriage to the one who attacks Kiriath-sepher and captures it.' 17 Othniel, son of Caleb's brother Kenaz, captured it, and so Caleb gave him his daughter Achsah in marriage. 18 On the day of her marriage to Othniel, she induced him to ask her father for some land. Then, as she alighted from the ass, Caleb asked her, 'What is troubling you?' 19 She answered, 'Give me an additional gift! Since you have assigned to me land in the Negeb, give me also pools of water.' So he gave her the upper and the lower pools. 20 This is the heritage of the clans of the tribe of Judahites: 21 The cities of the tribe of the Judahites in the extreme southern district toward Edom were: Kabzeel, Eder, Jagur, 22 Kinah, Dimonah, Adadah, 23 Kedesh, Hazor and Ithnan; 24 Ziph, Telem, Bealoth, 25 Hazor-hadattah, and Kerioth-hezron (that is, Hazor); 26 Amam, Shema, Moladah, 27 Hazar-gaddah, Heshmon, Beth-pelet, 28 Hazar-shual, Beer-sheba and Biziothiah; 29 Baalah, Iim, Ezem, 30 Eltolad, Chesil, Hormah, 31 Ziklag, Madmannah, Sansannah, 32 Lebaoth, Shilhim and En-rimmon; a total of twenty-nine cities with their villages. 33 In the foothills: Eshtaol, Zorah, Ashnah, 34 Zanoah, Engannim, Tappuah, Enam, 35 Jarmuth, Adullam, Socoh, Azekah, 36 Shaaraim, Adithaim, Gederah, and Gederothaim; fourteen cities and their villages. 37 Zenan, Hadashah, Migdal-gad, 38 Dilean, Mizpeh, Joktheel, 39 Lachish, Bozkath, Eglon, 40 Cabbon, Lahmam, Chitlish, 41 Gederoth, Beth-dagon, Naamah and Makkedah; sixteen cities and their villages. 42 Libnah, Ether, Ashan, 43 Iphtah, Ashnah, Nezib, 44 Keilah, Achzib and Mareshah; nine cities and their villages. 45 Ekron and its towns and villages; 46 from Ekron to the sea, all the towns that lie alongside Ashdod, and their villages; 47 Ashdod and its towns and villages; Gaza and its towns and villages, as far as the Wadi of Egypt and the coast of the Great Sea. 48 In the mountain regions: Shamir, Jattir, Socoh, 49 Dannah, Kiriath-sannah (that is, Debir), 50 Anab, Eshtemoh, Anim, 51 Goshen, Holon and Giloh; eleven cities and their villages. 52 Arab, Dumah, Eshan, 53 Janim, Beth-tappuah, Aphekah, 54 Humtah, Kiriath-arba (that is, Hebron), and Zior; nine cities and their villages. 55 Maon, Carmel, Ziph, Juttah, 56 Jezreel, Jokdeam, Zanoah, 57 Kain, Gibbeah and Timnah; ten cities and their villages. 58 Halhul, Beth-zur, Gedor, 59 Maarath, Beth-anoth and Eltekon; six cities and their villages. Tekoa, Ephrathah (that is, Bethlehem), Peor, Etam, Kulom, Tatam, Zores, Karim, Gallim, Bether and Manoko; eleven cities and their villages. 60 Kiriath-baal (that is, Kiriath-jearim) and Rabbah; two cities and their villages. 61 In the desert: Beth-arabah, Middin, Secacah, 62 Nibshan, Ir-hamelah and En-gedi; six cities and their villages. 63 (But the Jebusites who lived in Jerusalem the Judahites could not drive out; so the Jebusites dwell in Jerusalem beside the Judahites to the present day.)"

Joshua Chapter 16

"1 The lot that fell to the Josephites extended from the Jordan at Jericho to the waters of Jericho east of the desert; then the boundary went up from Jericho to the heights at Bethel. 2 Leaving Bethel for Luz, it crossed the ridge to the border of the Archites at Ataroth, 3 and descended westward to the border of the Japhletites, to that of the Lower Beth-horon, and to Gezer, ending thence at the sea. 4 Within the heritage of Manasseh and Ephraim, sons of Joseph, 5 the dividing line for the heritage of the clans of the Ephraimites ran from east of Ataroth-addar to Upper Beth-horon 6 and thence to the sea. From Michmethath on the north, their boundary curved eastward around Taanath-shiloh, and continued east of it to Janoah; 7 from there it descended to Ataroth and Naarah, and skirting Jericho, it ended at the Jordan. 8 From Tappuah the boundary ran westward to the Wadi Kanah and ended at the sea. This was the heritage of the clans of the Ephraimites, 9 including the villages that belonged to each city set aside for the Ephraimites within the territory of the Manassehites. 10 But they did not drive out the Canaanites living in Gezer, who live on within Ephraim to the present day, though they have been impressed as laborers."

Joshua Chapter 17

"1 Now as for the lot that fell to the tribe of Manasseh as the first-born of Joseph: since his eldest son, Machir, the father of Gilead, was a warrior, who had already obtained Gilead and Bashan, 2 the allotment was now made to the other descendants of Manasseh, the clans of Abiezer, Helek, Asriel, Shechem, Hepher and Shemida, the other male children of Manasseh, son of Joseph. 3Furthermore, Zelophehad, son of Hepher, son of Gilead, son of Machir, son of Manasseh, had had no sons, but only daughters, whose names were Mahlah, Noah, Hoglah, Milcah, and Tirzah. 4These presented themselves to Eleazar the priest, to Joshua, son of Nun, and to the princes, saying, 'The LORD commanded Moses to give us a heritage among our kinsmen.' So in obedience to the command of the LORD a heritage was given to each of them among their father's kinsmen. 5Thus ten shares fell to Manasseh apart from the land of Gilead and Bashan beyond the Jordan, 6since these female descendants of Manasseh received each a portion among his sons. The land of Gilead fell to the rest of the Manassehites. 7Manasseh bordered on Asher. From Michmethath near Shechem, another boundary ran southward to include the natives of En-Tappuah, 8because the district of Tappuah belonged to Manasseh, although Tappuah itself was an Ephraimite city on the border of Manasseh. 9This same boundary continued down to the Wadi Kanah. The cities that belonged to Ephraim from among the cities in Manasseh were those to the south of that wadi; thus the territory of Manasseh ran north of the wadi and ended at the sea. 10The land on the south belonged to Ephraim and that on the north to Manasseh; with the sea as their common boundary, they reached Asher on the north and Issachar on the east. 11Moreover, in Issachar and in Asher Manasseh was awarded Beth-shean and its towns, Ibleam and its towns, Dor and its towns and the natives there, Endor and its towns and natives, Taanach and its towns and natives, and Megiddo and its towns and natives (the third is Naphath-dor). 12Since the Manassehites could not conquer these cities, the Canaanites persisted in this region. 13When the Israelites grew stronger they impressed the Canaanites as laborers, but they did not drive them out. 14The descendants of Joseph said to Joshua, 'Why have you given us only one lot and one share as our heritage? Our people are too many, because of the extent to which the LORD has blessed us.' 15Joshua answered them, 'If you are too many, go up to the forest and clear out a place for yourselves there in the land of the Perizzites and Rephaim, since the mountain regions of Ephraim are so narrow.' 16For the Josephites said, 'Our mountain regions are not enough for us; on the other hand, the Canaanites living in the valley region all have iron chariots, in particular those in Beth-shean and its towns, and those in the valley of Jezreel.' 17Joshua therefore said to Ephraim and Manasseh, the house of Joseph, 'You are a numerous people and very strong. You shall have not merely one share, 18for the mountain region which is now forest shall be yours when you clear it. Its adjacent land shall also be yours if, despite their strength and iron chariots, you drive out the Canaanites.'"

Joshua Chapter 18

"1After they had subdued the land, the whole community of the Israelites assembled at Shiloh, where they set up the meeting tent. 2Seven tribes among the Israelites had not yet received their heritage. 3Joshua therefore said to the Israelites, 'How much longer will you put off taking steps to possess the land which the LORD, the God of your fathers, has given you? 4Choose three men from each of your tribes; I will commission them to begin a survey of the land, which they shall describe for purposes of inheritance. When they return to me 5you shall divide it into seven parts. Judah is to retain its territory in the south, and the house of Joseph its territory in the north. 6You shall bring here to me the description of the land in seven sections. I will then cast lots for you here before the LORD, our God. 7For the Levites have no share among you, because the priesthood of the LORD is their heritage; while Gad, Reuben, and the half-tribe of Manasseh have already received the heritage east of the Jordan which Moses, the servant of the LORD, gave them.' 8When those who were to map out the land were ready for the journey, Joshua instructed them to survey the land, prepare a description of it, and return to him; then he would cast lots for them there before the LORD in Shiloh. 9So they went through the land, listed its cities in writing in seven sections, and returned to Joshua in the camp at Shiloh. 10Joshua then divided up the land for the Israelites into their separate shares, casting lots for them before the LORD in Shiloh. 11One lot fell to the clans of the tribe of Benjaminites. The territory allotted them lay between the descendants of Judah and those of Joseph. 12Their northern boundary began at the Jordan and went over the northern flank of Jericho, up westward into the mountains, till it reached the desert of Beth-aven. 13From there it crossed over to the southern flank of Luz (that is, Bethel). Then it ran down to Ataroth-addar, on the mountaintop south of Lower Beth-horon. 14For the western border, the boundary line swung south from the mountaintop opposite Bethhoron till it reached Kiriath-baal (that is, Kiriath-jearim), which city belonged to the Judahites. This was the western boundary.

15The southern boundary began at the limits of Kiriath-jearim and projected to the spring at Nephtoah. 16It went down to the edge of the mountain on the north of the Valley of Rephaim, where it faces the Valley of Ben-hinnom; and continuing down the Valley of Hinnom along the southern flank of the Jebusites, reached En-rogel. 17Inclining to the north, it extended to En-shemesh, and thence to Geliloth, opposite the pass of Adummim. Then it dropped to Eben-Bohan-ben-Reuben, 18across the northern flank of the Arabah overlook, down into the Aarabah. 19From there the boundary continued across the northern flank of Beth-hoglah and extended to the northern tip of the Salt Sea, at the southern end of the Jordan. This was the southern boundary. 20The Jordan bounded it on the east. This was how the heritage of the clans of the Benjaminites was bounded on all sides. 21Now the cities belonging to the clans of the tribe of the Benjaminites were: Jericho, Beth-hoglah, Emek-keziz, 22Beth-arabah, Zemaraim, Bethel, 23Avvim, Parah, Ophrah, 24Chephar-ammoni, Ophni and Geba; twelve cities and their villages. 25Also Gibeon, Ramah, Beeroth, 26Mizpeh, Chephirah, Mozah, 27Rekem, Irpeel, Taralah, 28Zela, Haeleph, the Jebusite city (that is, Jerusalem), Gibeah and Kiriath; fourteen cities and their villages. This was the heritage of the clans of Benjaminites."

Joshua Chapter 19

"1The second lot fell to Simeon. The heritage of the clans of the tribe of Simeonites lay within that of the Judahites. 2For their heritage they received Beer-sheba, Shema, Moladah, 3Hazar-shual, Balah, Ezem, 4Eltolad, Bethul, Hormah, 5Ziklag, Bethmar-caboth, Hazar-susah, 6Beth-lebaoth and Sharuhen; thirteen cities and their villages. 7Also En-rimmon, Ether and Ashan; four cities and their villages, 8besides all the villages around these cities as far as Baalath-beer (that is, Ramoth-negeb). This was the heritage of the clans of the tribe of the Simeonites. 9This heritage of the Simeonites was within the confines of the Judahites; for since the portion of the latter was too large for them, the Simeonites obtained their heritage within it. 10The third lot fell to the clans of the Zebulunites. The limit of their heritage was at Sarid. 11Their boundary went up west and through Mareal, reaching Dabbesheth and the wadi that is near Jokneam. 12From Sarid eastward it ran to the district of Chisloth-tabor, on to Daberath, and up to Japhia. 13From there it continued eastward to Gath-hepher and to Eth-kazin, extended to Rimmon, and turned to Neah. 14Skirting north of Hannathon, the boundary ended at the valley of Iphtahel. 15Thus, with Kattath, Nahalal, Shimron, Idalah and Bethlehem, there were twelve cities and their villages 16to comprise the heritage of the clans of the Zebulunites. 17The fourth lot fell to Issachar. The territory of the clans of the Issacharites 18included Jezreel, Chesulloth, Shunem, 19Hapharaim, Shion, Anaharath, 20Rabbith, Kishion, Ebez, 21Remeth, En-gannim, En-haddah and Beth-pazzez. 22The boundary reached Tabor, Shahazumah and Beth-shemesh, ending at the Jordan. These sixteen cities and their villages 23were the heritage of the clans of the Issacharites. 24The fifth lot fell to the clans of the tribe of the Asherites. 25Their territory included Helkath, Hali, Beten, Achshaph, 26Allammelech, Amad and Mishal, and reached Carmel on the west, and Shihor-libnath. 27In the other direction, it ran eastward of Beth-dagon, reached Zebulun and the valley of Iphtahel; then north of Beth-emek and Neiel, it extended to Cabul, 28Mishal, Abdon, Rehob, Hammon and Kanah, near Greater Sidon. 29Then the boundary turned back to Ramah and to the fortress city of Tyre; thence it cut back to Hosah and ended at the sea. Thus, with Mahalab, Achzib, 30Ummah, Acco, Aphek and Rehob, there were twenty-two cities and their villages 31to comprise the heritage of the clans of the tribe of the Asherites. 32The sixth lot fell to the Naphtalites. The boundary of the clans of the Naphtalites 33extended from Heleph, from the oak at Zaanannim to Lakkum, including Adami-nekeb and Jabneel, and ended at the Jordan. 34In the opposite direction, westerly, it ran through Aznoth-tabor and from there extended to Hukkok; it touched Zebulun on the south, Asher on the west, and the Jordan on the east. 35The fortified cities were Ziddim, Zer, Hammath, Rakkath, Chinnereth, 36Adamah, Ramah, Hazor, 37Kedesh, Edrei, En-hazor, 38Yiron, Migdal-el, Horem, Beth-anath and Beth-shemesh; nineteen cities and their villages 39to comprise the heritage of the clans of the tribe of the Naphtalites. 40The seventh lot fell to the clans of the tribe of Danites. 41Their heritage was the territory of Zorah, Eshtaol, Ir-shemesh, 42Shaalabbin, Aijalon, Ithlah, 43Elon, Timnah, Ekron, 44Eltekoh, Gibbethon, Baalath, 45Jehud, Bene-berak, Gath-rimmon, 46Me-jarkon and Rakkon, with the coast at Joppa. 47But the territory of the Danites was too small for them; so the Danites marched up and attacked Leshem, which they captured and put to the sword. Once they had taken possession of Leshem, they renamed the settlement after their ancestor Dan. 48These cities and their villages were the heritage of the clans of the tribe of the Danites. 49When the last of them had received the portions of the land they were to inherit, the Israelites assigned a heritage in their midst to Joshua, son of Nun. 50In obedience to the command of the LORD, they gave him the city which he requested, Timnah-serah in the mountain region of Ephraim. He rebuilt the city and made it his home. 51These are the final portions into which Eleazar the priest, Joshua, son of Nun, and the heads of families in the tribes of the Israelites divided the land by lot in the presence of the LORD, at the door of the meeting tent in Shiloh."

Joshua Chapter 20

"1The LORD said to Joshua: 2'Tell the Israelites to designate the cities of which I spoke to them through Moses, 3to which one guilty of accidental and unintended homicide may flee for asylum from the avenger of blood. 4To one of these cities the killer shall flee, and standing at the entrance of the city gate, he shall plead his case before the elders, who must receive him and assign him a place in which to live among them. 5Though the avenger of blood pursues him, they are not to deliver up the homicide who slew his fellow man unintentionally and not out of previous hatred. 6Once he has stood judgment before the community, he shall live on in that city till the death of the high priest who is in office at the time. Then the killer may go back home to his own city from which he fled.' 7So they set apart Kedesh in Galilee in the mountain region of Naphtali, Shechem in the mountain region of Ephraim, and Kiriath-arba (that is, Hebron) in the mountain region of Judah. 8And beyond the Jordan east of Jericho they designated Bezer on the open tableland in the tribe of Reuben, Ramoth in Gilead in the tribe of Gad, and Golan in Bashan in the tribe of Manasseh. 9These were the designated cities to which any Israelite or stranger living among them who had killed a person accidentally might flee to escape death at the hand of the avenger of blood, until he could appear before the community."

Joshua Chapter 21

"1The heads of the Levite families came up to Eleazar the priest, to Joshua, son of Nun, and to the heads of families of the other tribes of the Israelites 2at Shiloh in the land of Canaan, and said to them, 'The LORD commanded, through Moses, that cities be given us to dwell in, with pasture lands for our livestock.' 3Out of their own heritage, in obedience to this command of the LORD, the Israelites gave the Levites the following cities with their pasture lands. 4When the first lot among the Levites fell to the clans of the Kohathites, the descendants of Aaron the priest obtained thirteen cities by lot from the tribes of Judah, Simeon and Benjamin. 5The rest of the Kohathites obtained ten cities by lot from the clans of the tribe of Ephraim, from the tribe of Dan, and from the half-tribe of Manasseh. 6The Gershonites obtained thirteen cities by lot from the clans of the tribe of Issachar, from the tribe of Asher, from the tribe of Naphtali, and from the half-tribe of Manasseh. 7The clans of the Merarites obtained twelve cities from the tribes of Reuben, Gad and Zebulun. 8These cities with their pasture lands the Israelites allotted to the Levites in obedience to the LORD'S command through Moses. 9From the tribes of the Judahites and Simeonites they designated the following cities, 10and assigned them to the descendants of Aaron in the Kohathite clan of the Levites, since the first lot fell to them: 11first, Kiriath-arba (Arba was the father of Anak), that is, Hebron, in the mountain region of Judah, with the adjacent pasture lands, 12although the open country and villages belonging to the city had been given to Caleb, son of Jephunneh, as his property. 13Thus to the descendants of Aaron the priest were given the city of asylum for homicides at Hebron, with its pasture lands; also, Libnah with its pasture lands, 14Jattir with its pasture lands, Eshtemoa with its pasture lands, 15Holon with its pasture lands, Debir with its pasture lands, 16Ashan with its pasture lands, Juttah with its pasture lands, and Beth-shemesh with its pasture lands: nine cities from the two tribes mentioned. 17From the tribe of Benjamin they obtained the four cities of Gibeon with its pasture lands, Geba with its pasture lands, 18Anathoth with its pasture lands, and Almon with its pasture lands. 19These cities which with their pasture lands belonged to the priestly descendants of Aaron, were thirteen in all. 20The rest of the Kohathite clans among the Levites obtained by lot, from the tribe of Ephraim, four cities. 21They were assigned, with its pasture lands, the city of asylum for homicides at Shechem in the mountain region of Ephraim; also Gezer with its pasture lands, 22Kibzaim with its pasture lands, and Beth-horon with its pasture lands. 23From the tribe of Dan they obtained the four cities of Elteke with its pasture lands, Gibbethon with its pasture lands, 24Aijalon with its pasture lands, and Gath-rimmon with its pasture lands; 25and from the half-tribe of Manasseh the two cities of Taanach with its pasture lands and Ibleam with its pasture lands. 26These cities which with their pasture lands belonged to the rest of the Kohathite clans were ten in all. 27The Gershonite clan of the

Levites received from the half-tribe of Manasseh two cities: the city of asylum for homicides at Golan, with its pasture lands; and also Beth-ashtaroth with its pasture lands. 28From the tribe of Issachar they obtained the four cities of Kishion with its pasture lands, Daberath with its pasture lands, 29Jarmuth with its pasture lands, and En-gannim with its pasture lands; from the tribe of Asher, 30the four cities of Mishal with its pasture lands, Abdon with its pasture lands, 31Helkath with its pasture lands, and Rehob with its pasture lands; 32and from the tribe of Naphtali, three cities: the city of asylum for homicides at Kedesh in Galilee, with its pasture lands; also Hammath with its pasture lands, and Rakkath with its pasture lands. 33These cities which with their pasture lands belonged to the Gershonite clans were thirteen in all. 34The Merarite clans, the last of the Levites, received from the tribe of Zebulun the four cities of Jokneam with its pasture lands, Kartah with its pasture lands, 35Rimmon with its pasture lands, and Nahalal with its pasture lands; 36also, across the Jordan, from the tribe of Reuben, four cities: the city of asylum for homicides at Bezer with its pasture lands, Jahaz with its pasture lands, 37Kedemoth with its pasture lands, and Mephaath with its pasture lands; 38and from the tribe of Gad a total of four cities: the city of asylum for homicides at Ramoth in Gilead with its pasture lands, also Mahanaim with its pasture lands, 39Heshbon with its pasture lands, and Jazer with its pasture lands. 40The cities which were allotted to the Merarite clans, the last of the Levites, were therefore twelve in all. 41Thus the total number of cities within the territory of the Israelites which, with their pasture lands, belonged to the Levites, was forty-eight. 42With each and every one of these cities went the pasture lands round about it. 43And so the LORD gave Israel all the land he had sworn to their fathers he would give them. Once they had conquered and occupied it, 44the LORD gave them peace on every side, just as he had promised their fathers. Not one of their enemies could withstand them; the LORD brought all their enemies under their power. 45Not a single promise that the LORD made to the house of Israel was broken; every one was fulfilled."

Joshua Chapter 22

1At that time Joshua summoned the Reubenites, the Gadites, and the half-tribe of Manasseh 2and said to them: "You have done all that Moses, the servant of the LORD, commanded you, and have obeyed every command I gave you. 3For many years now you have not once abandoned your kinsmen, but have faithfully carried out the commands of the LORD, your God. 4Since, therefore, the LORD, your God, has settled your kinsmen as he promised them, you may now return to your tents beyond the Jordan; to your own land, which Moses, the servant of the LORD, gave you. 5But be very careful to observe the precept and law which Moses, the servant of the LORD, enjoined upon you: love the LORD, your God; follow him faithfully; keep his commandments; remain loyal to him; and serve him with your whole heart and soul." 6Joshua then blessed them and sent them away to their own tents. 7(For, to half the tribe of Manasseh Moses had assigned land in Bashan; and to the other half Joshua had given a portion along with their kinsmen west of the Jordan.) What Joshua said to them when he sent them off to their tents with his blessing was, 8"Now that you are returning to your own tents with great wealth, with very numerous livestock, with silver, gold, bronze and iron, and with a very large supply of clothing, divide these spoils of your enemies with your kinsmen there." 9So the Reubenites, the Gadites, and the half-tribe of Manasseh left the other Israelites at Shiloh in the land of Canaan and returned to the land of Gilead, their own property, which they had received according to the LORD'S command through Moses. 10When the Reubenites, the Gadites, and the half-tribe of Manasseh came to the region of the Jordan in the land of Canaan, they built there at Jordan a conspicuously large altar. 11The other Israelites heard the report that the Reubenites, the Gadites, and the half-tribe of Manasseh had built an altar in the region of the Jordan facing the land of Canaan, across from them, 12and therefore they assembled their whole community at Shiloh to declare war on them. 13First, however, they sent to the Reubenites, the Gadites, and the half-tribe of Manasseh in the land of Gilead an embassy consisting of Phinehas, son of Eleazar the priest, 14and ten princes, one from every tribe of Israel, each one being both prince and military leader of his ancestral house. 15When these came to the Reubenites, the Gadites, and the half-tribe of Manasseh in the land of Gilead, they said to them: 16"The whole community of the LORD sends this message: What act of treachery is this you have committed against the God of Israel? You have seceded from the LORD this day, and rebelled against him by building an altar of your own! 17For the sin of Peor, a plague came upon the community of the LORD. 18We are still not free of that; must you now add to it? You are rebelling against the LORD today and by tomorrow he will be angry with the whole community of Israel! 19If you consider the land you now possess unclean, cross over to the land the LORD possesses, where the Dwelling of the LORD stands, and share that with us. But do not rebel against the LORD, nor involve us in rebellion, by building an altar of your own in addition to the altar of the LORD, our God. ²⁰When Achan, son of Zerah, violated the ban, did not wrath fall upon the entire community of Israel? Though he was but a single man, he did not perish alone for his guilt!" ²¹The Reubenites, the Gadites, and the half-tribe of Manasseh replied to the military leaders of the Israelites: "The LORD is the God of gods. ²²The LORD, the God of gods, knows and Israel shall know. If now we have acted out of rebellion or treachery against the LORD, our God, ²³and if we have built an altar of our own to secede from the LORD, or to offer holocausts, grain offerings or peace offerings upon it, the LORD himself will exact the penalty. ²⁴We did it rather out of our anxious concern lest in the future your children should say to our children: 'What have you to do with the LORD, the God of Israel? ²⁵For the LORD has placed the Jordan as a boundary between you and us. You descendants of Reuben and Gad have no share in the LORD.' Thus your children would prevent ours from revering the LORD. ²⁶So we decided to guard our interests by building this altar of our own: not for holocausts or for sacrifices, ²⁷but as evidence for you on behalf of ourselves and our descendants, that we have the right to worship the LORD in his presence with our holocausts, sacrifices, and peace offerings. Now in the future your children cannot say to our children, 'You have no share in the LORD.' ²⁸Our thought was, that if in the future they should speak thus to us or to our descendants, we could answer: 'Look at the model of the altar of the LORD which our fathers made, not for holocausts or for sacrifices, but to witness between you and us.' ²⁹Far be it from us to rebel against the LORD or to secede now from the LORD by building an altar for holocaust, grain offering, or sacrifice in addition to the altar of the LORD, our God, which stands before his Dwelling." ³⁰When Phinehas the priest and the princes of the community, the military leaders of the Israelites, heard what the Reubenites, the Gadites and the Manassehites had to say, they were satisfied. ³¹Phinehas, son of Eleazar the priest, said to the Reubenites, the Gadites and the Manassehites, "Now we know that the LORD is with us. Since you have not committed this act of treachery against the LORD, you have kept the Israelites free from punishment by the LORD." ³²Phinehas, son of Eleazar the priest, and the princes returned from the Reubenites and the Gadites in the land of Gilead to the Israelites in the land of Canaan, and reported the matter to them. ³³The report satisfied the Israelites, who blessed God and decided against declaring war on the Reubenites and Gadites or ravaging the land they occupied. ³⁴The Reubenites and the Gadites gave the altar its name as a witness among them that the LORD is God."

Joshua Chapter 23

¹Many years later, after the LORD had given the Israelites rest from all their enemies round about them, and when Joshua was old and advanced in years, ²he summoned all Israel (including their elders, leaders, judges and officers) and said to them: "I am old and advanced in years. ³You have seen all that the LORD, your God, has done for you against all these nations; for it has been the LORD, your God, himself who fought for you. ⁴Bear in mind that I have apportioned among your tribes as their heritage the nations that survive (as well as those I destroyed) between the Jordan and the Great Sea in the west. ⁵The LORD, your God, will drive them out and dislodge them at your approach, so that you will take possession of their land as the LORD, your God, promised you. ⁶Therefore strive hard to observe and carry out all that is written in the book of the law of Moses, not straying from it in any way, ⁷or mingling with these nations while they survive among you. You must not invoke their gods, or swear by them, or serve them, or worship them, ⁸but you must remain loyal to the LORD, your God, as you have been to this day. ⁹At your approach the LORD has driven out large and strong nations, and to this day no one has withstood you. ¹⁰One of you puts to flight a thousand, because it is the LORD, your God, himself who fights for you, as he promised you. ¹¹Take great care, however, to love the LORD, your God. ¹²For if you ever abandon him and ally yourselves with the remnant of these nations while they survive among you, by intermarrying and intermingling with them, ¹³know for certain that the LORD, your God, will no longer drive these nations out of your way. Instead they will be a snare and a trap for you, a scourge for your sides and thorns for your eyes, until you perish from this good land which the LORD, your God, has given you. ¹⁴"Today, as you see, I am going the way of all men. So now acknowledge with your whole heart and soul that not one of all the promises the LORD, your God, made to you has remained unfulfilled. Every promise has been fulfilled for you, with not one single exception. ¹⁵But just as every promise the LORD, your God, made to you has been fulfilled for you, so will he fulfill every threat, even so far as to exterminate you from this good land which the

LORD, your God, has given you. ¹⁶If you transgress the covenant of the LORD, your God, which he enjoined on you, serve other gods and worship them, the anger of the LORD will flare up against you and you will quickly perish from the good land which he has given you."

Joshua Chapter 24

¹Joshua gathered together all the tribes of Israel at Shechem, summoning their elders, their leaders, their judges, and their officers. When they stood in ranks before God, ²Joshua addressed all the people: "Thus says the LORD, the God of Israel: In times past your fathers, down to Terah, father of Abraham and Nahor, dwelt beyond the River and served other gods. ³But I brought your father Abraham from the region beyond the River and led him through the entire land of Canaan. I made his descendants numerous and gave him Isaac. ⁴To Isaac I gave Jacob and Esau. To Esau, I assigned the mountain region of Seir in which to settle, while Jacob and his children went down to Egypt. ⁵"Then I sent Moses and Aaron and smote Egypt with the prodigies which I wrought in her midst. ⁶Afterward, I led you out of Egypt, and when you reached the sea, the Egyptians pursued your fathers to the Red Sea with chariots and horsemen. ⁷Because they cried out to the LORD, he put darkness between your people and the Egyptians, upon whom he brought the sea so that it engulfed them. After you witnessed what I did to Egypt, and dwelt a long time in the desert, ⁸I brought you into the land of the Amorites who lived east of the Jordan. They fought against you, but I delivered them into your power. You took possession of their land, and I destroyed them (the two kings of the Amorites) before you. ⁹Then Balak, son of Zippor, king of Moab, prepared to war against Israel. He summoned Balaam, son of Beor, to curse you; ¹⁰but I would not listen to Balaam. On the contrary, he had to bless you, and I saved you from him. ¹¹Once you crossed the Jordan and came to Jericho, the men of Jericho fought against you, but I delivered them also into your power. ¹²And I sent the hornets ahead of you which drove them (the Amorites, Perizzites, Canaanites, Hittites, Girgashites, Hivites, and Jebusites) out of your way; it was not your sword or your bow. ¹³"I gave you a land which you had not tilled and cities which you had not built, to dwell in; you have eaten of vineyards and olive groves which you did not plant. ¹⁴"Now, therefore, fear the LORD and serve him completely and sincerely. Cast out the gods your fathers served beyond the River and in Egypt, and serve the LORD. ¹⁵If it does not please you to serve the LORD, decide today whom you will serve, the gods your fathers served beyond the River or the gods of the Amorites in whose country you are dwelling. As for me and my household, we will serve the LORD." ¹⁶But the people answered, "Far be it from us to forsake the LORD for the service of other gods. ¹⁷For it was the LORD, our God, who brought us and our fathers up out of the land of Egypt, out of a state of slavery. He performed those great miracles before our very eyes and protected us along our entire journey and among all the peoples through whom we passed. ¹⁸At our approach, the LORD drove out (all the peoples, including) the Amorites who dwelt in the land. Therefore we also will serve the LORD, for he is our God." ¹⁹Joshua in turn said to the people, "You may not be able to serve the LORD, for he is a holy God; he is a jealous God who will not forgive your transgressions or your sins. ²⁰If, after the good he has done for you, you forsake the LORD and serve strange gods, he will do evil to you and destroy you." ²¹But the people answered Joshua, "We will still serve the LORD." ²²Joshua therefore said to the people, "You are your own witnesses that you have chosen to serve the LORD." They replied, "We are, indeed!" ²³"Now, therefore, put away the strange gods that are among you and turn your hearts to the LORD, the God of Israel." ²⁴Then the people promised Joshua, "We will serve the LORD, our God, and obey his voice." ²⁵So Joshua made a covenant with the people that day and made statutes and ordinances for them at Shechem, ²⁶which he recorded in the book of the law of God. Then he took a large stone and set it up there under the oak that was in the sanctuary of the LORD. ²⁷And Joshua said to all the people, "This stone shall be our witness, for it has heard all the words which the LORD spoke to us. It shall be a witness against you, should you wish to deny your God." ²⁸Then Joshua dismissed the people, each to his own heritage. ²⁹After these events, Joshua, son of Nun, servant of the LORD, died at the age of a hundred and ten. ³⁰He was buried within the limits of his heritage at Timnath-serah in the mountain region of Ephraim north of Mount Gaash. ³¹Israel served the LORD during the entire lifetime of Joshua and that of the elders who outlived Joshua and knew all that the LORD had done for Israel. ³²The bones of Joseph, which the Israelites had brought up from Egypt, were buried in Shechem in the plot of ground Jacob had bought from the sons of Hamor, father of Shechem, for a hundred pieces of money. This was a heritage of the descendants of Joseph. ³³When Eleazar, son of Aaron, also died, he was buried on the hill which had been given to his son Phinehas in the mountain region of

Ephraim.

Judges

Judges Chapter 1

[1]After the death of Joshua, the Israelites consulted the LORD, asking, "Who shall be first among us to attack the Canaanites and to do battle with them?" [2]The LORD answered, "Judah shall attack: I have delivered the land into his power." [3]Judah then said to his brother Simeon, "Come up with me into the territory allotted to me, and let us engage the Canaanites in battle. I will likewise accompany you into the territory allotted to you." So Simeon went with him. [4]When the forces of Judah attacked, the LORD delivered the Canaanites and Perizzites into their power, and they slew ten thousand of them in Bezek. [5]It was in Bezek that they came upon Adonibezek and fought against him. When they defeated the Canaanites and Perizzites, [6]Adonibezek fled. They set out in pursuit, and when they caught him, cut off his thumbs and his big toes. [7]At this, Adonibezek said, "Seventy kings, with their thumbs and big toes cut off, used to pick up scraps under my table. As I have done, so has God repaid me." He was brought to Jerusalem, and there he died. [8](The Judahites fought against Jerusalem and captured it, putting it to the sword; then they destroyed the city by fire.) [9]Afterward, the Judahites went down to fight against the Canaanites who lived in the mountain region, in the Negeb, and in the foothills. [10]Judah also marched against the Canaanites who dwelt in Hebron, which was formerly called Kiriath-arba, and defeated Sheshai, Ahiman, and Talmai. [11]From there, they marched against the inhabitants of Debir, which was formerly called Kiriath-sepher. [12]And Caleb said, "I will give my daughter Achsah in marriage to the one who attacks Kiriath-sepher and captures it." [13]Othniel, son of Caleb's younger brother Kenaz, captured it; so Caleb gave him his daughter Achsah in marriage. [14]On the day of her marriage to Othniel, she induced him to ask her father for some land. Then, as she alighted from the ass, Caleb asked her, "What is troubling you?" [15]"Give me an additional gift," she answered. "Since you have assigned land in the Negeb to me, give me also pools of water." So Caleb gave her the upper and the lower pool. [16]The descendants of the Kenite, Moses' father-in-law, came up with the Judahites from the city of palms to the desert at Arad (which is in the Negeb). But they later left and settled among the Amalekites. [17]Judah then went with his brother Simeon, and they defeated the Canaanites who dwelt in Zephath. After having doomed the city to destruction, they renamed it Hormah. [18]Judah, however, did not occupy Gaza with its territory, Ashkelon with its territory, or Ekron with its territory. [19]Since the LORD was with Judah, he gained possession of the mountain region. Yet he could not dislodge those who lived on the plain, because they had iron chariots. [20]As Moses had commanded, Hebron was given to Caleb, who then drove from it the three sons of Anak. [21]The Benjaminites did not dislodge the Jebusites who dwelt in Jerusalem, with the result that the Jebusites live in Jerusalem beside the Benjaminites to the present day. [22]The house of Joseph, too, marched up against Bethel, and the LORD was with them. [23]The house of Joseph had a reconnaissance made of Bethel, which formerly was called Luz. [24]The scouts saw a man coming out of the city and said to him, "Show us a way into the city, and we will spare you." [25]He showed them a way into the city, which they then put to the sword; but they let the man and his whole clan go free. [26]He then went to the land of the Hittites, where he built a city and called it Luz, as it is still called. [27]Manasseh did not take possession of Beth-shean with its towns or of Taanach with its towns. Neither did he dislodge the inhabitants of Dor and its towns, those of Ibleam and its towns, or those of Megiddo and its towns. The Canaanites kept their hold in this district. [28]When the Israelites grew stronger, they impressed the Canaanites as laborers but did not drive them out. [29]Similarly, the Ephraimites did not drive out the Canaanites living in Gezer, and so the Canaanites live in Gezer in their midst. [30]Zebulun did not dislodge the inhabitants of Kitron or those of Nahalol; the Canaanites live among them but have become forced laborers. [31]Nor did Asher drive out the inhabitants of Acco or those of Sidon, or take possession of Mahaleb, Achzib, Helbah, Aphik, or Rehob. [32]The Asherites live among the Canaanite natives of the land, whom they have not dislodged. [33]Naphtali did not drive out the inhabitants of Beth-shemesh or those of Beth-anath, and so they live among the Canaanite natives of the land. However, the inhabitants of Beth-shemesh and Beth-anath have become forced laborers for them. [34]The Amorites hemmed in the Danites in the mountain region, not permitting them to go down into the plain. [35]The Amorites had a firm hold in Harheres, Aijalon, and Shaalbim, but as the house of Joseph gained the upper hand, they were impressed as laborers. [36]The territory of the Amorites extended from the Akrabbim pass to Sela and beyond.

Judges Chapter 2

[1]An angel of the LORD went up from Gilgal to Bochim and said, "It was I who brought you up from Egypt and led you into the land which I promised on oath to your fathers. I said that I would never break my covenant with you, [2]but that you were not to make a pact with the inhabitants of this land, and you were to pull down their altars. Yet you have not obeyed me. What did you mean by this? [3]For now I tell you, I will not clear them out of your way; they shall oppose you and their gods shall become a snare for you." [4]When the angel of the LORD had made these threats to all the Israelites, the people wept aloud; [5]and so that place came to be called Bochim. They offered sacrifice there to the LORD. [6]When Joshua dismissed the people, each Israelite went to take possession of his own hereditary land. [7]The people served the LORD during the entire lifetime of Joshua, and of those elders who outlived Joshua and who had seen all the great work which the LORD had done for Israel. [8]Joshua, son of Nun, the servant of the LORD, was a hundred and ten years old when he died; [9]and they buried him within the borders of his heritage at Timnath-heres in the mountain region of Ephraim north of Mount Gaash. [10]But once the rest of that generation were gathered to their fathers, and a later generation arose that did not know the LORD, or what he had done for Israel, [11]the Israelites offended the LORD by serving the Baals. [12]Abandoning the LORD, the God of their fathers, who had led them out of the land of Egypt, they followed the other gods of the various nations around them, and by their worship of these gods provoked the LORD. [13]Because they had thus abandoned him and served Baal and the Ashtaroth, [14]the anger of the LORD flared up against Israel, and he delivered them over to plunderers who despoiled them. He allowed them to fall into the power of their enemies round about whom they were no longer able to withstand. [15]Whatever they undertook, the LORD turned into disaster for them, as in his warning he had sworn he would do, till they were in great distress. [16]Even when the LORD raised up judges to deliver them from the power of their despoilers, [17]they did not listen to their judges, but abandoned themselves to the worship of other gods. They were quick to stray from the way their fathers had taken, and did not follow their example of obedience to the commandments of the LORD. [18]Whenever the LORD raised up judges for them, he would be with the judge and save them from the power of their enemies as long as the judge lived; it was thus the LORD took pity on their distressful cries of affliction under their oppressors. [19]But when the judge died, they would relapse and do worse than their fathers, following other gods in service and worship, relinquishing none of their evil practices or stubborn conduct. [20]In his anger toward Israel the LORD said, "Inasmuch as this nation has violated my covenant which I enjoined on their fathers, and has disobeyed me, [21]I for my part will not clear away for them any more of the nations which Joshua left when he died." [22]Through these nations the Israelites were to be made to prove whether or not they would keep to the way of the LORD and continue in it as their fathers had done; [23]therefore the LORD allowed them to remain instead of expelling them immediately, or delivering them into the power of Israel.

Judges Chapter 3

[1]The following are the nations which the LORD allowed to remain, so that through them he might try all those Israelites who had no experience of the battles with Canaan, [2]training them in battle, those generations only of the Israelites who would not have had that previous experience: [3]the five lords of the Philistines; and all the Canaanites, the Sidonians, and the Hivites who dwell in the mountain region of Lebanon between Baal-hermon and the entrance to Hamath. [4]These served to put Israel to the test, to determine whether they would obey the commandments the LORD had enjoined on their fathers through Moses. [5]Besides, the Israelites were living among the Canaanites, Hittites, Amorites, Perizzites, Hivites, and Jebusites. [6]In fact, they took their daughters in marriage, and gave their own daughters to their sons in marriage, and served their gods. [7]Because the Israelites had offended the LORD by forgetting the LORD, their God, and serving the Baals and the Asherahs, [8]the anger of the LORD flared up against them, and he allowed them to fall into the power of Cushan-rishathaim, king of Aram Naharaim, whom they served for eight years. [9]But when the Israelites cried out to the LORD, he raised up for them a savior, Othniel, son of Caleb's younger brother Kenaz, who rescued them. [10]The spirit of the LORD came upon him, and he judged Israel. When he went out to war, the LORD delivered Cushan-rishathaim, king of Aram, into his power, so that he made him subject. [11]The land then was at rest for forty years, until Othniel, son of Kenaz, died. [12]Again the Israelites offended the LORD, who because of this offense strengthened Eglon, king of Moab, against Israel. [13]In alliance with the Ammonites and

Amalekites, he attacked and defeated Israel, taking possession of the city of palms. [14]The Israelites then served Eglon, king of Moab, for eighteen years. [15]But when the Israelites cried out to the LORD, he raised up for them a savior, the Benjaminite Ehud, son of Gera, who was left-handed. It was by him that the Israelites sent their tribute to Eglon, king of Moab. [16]Ehud made himself a two-edged dagger a foot long, and wore it under his clothes over his right thigh. [17]He presented the tribute to Eglon, king of Moab, who was very fat, [18]and after the presentation went off with the tribute bearers. [19]He returned, however, from where the idols are, near Gilgal, and said, "I have a private message for you, O king." And the king said, "Silence!" Then when all his attendants had left his presence, [20]and Ehud went in to him where he sat alone in his cool upper room, Ehud said, "I have a message from God for you." So the king rose from his chair, [21]and then Ehud with his left hand drew the dagger from his right thigh, and thrust it into Eglon's belly. [22]The hilt also went in after the blade, and the fat closed over the blade because he did not withdraw the dagger from his body. [23]Then Ehud went out into the hall, shutting the doors of the upper room on him and locking them. [24]When Ehud had left and the servants came, they saw that the doors of the upper room were locked, and thought, "He must be easing himself in the cool chamber." [25]They waited until they finally grew suspicious. Since he did not open the doors of the upper room, they took the key and opened them. There on the floor, dead, lay their lord! [26]During their delay Ehud made good his escape and, passing the idols, took refuge in Seirah. [27]On his arrival he sounded the horn in the mountain region of Ephraim, and the Israelites went down from the mountains with him as their leader. [28]"Follow me," he said to them, "for the LORD has delivered your enemies the Moabites into your power." So they followed him down and seized the fords of the Jordan leading to Moab, permitting no one to cross. [29]On that occasion they slew about ten thousand Moabites, all of them strong and valiant men. Not a man escaped. [30]Thus was Moab brought under the power of Israel at that time; and the land had rest for eighty years. [31]After him there was Shamgar, son of Anath, who slew six hundred Philistines with an oxgoad. He, too, rescued Israel.

Judges Chapter 4

[1]After Ehud's death, however, the Israelites again offended the LORD. [2]So the LORD allowed them to fall into the power of the Canaanite king, Jabin, who reigned in Hazor. The general of his army was Sisera, who dwelt in Harosheth-ha-goiim. [3]But the Israelites cried out to the LORD; for with his nine hundred iron chariots he sorely oppressed the Israelites for twenty years. [4]At this time the prophetess Deborah, wife of Lappidoth, was judging Israel. [5]She used to sit under Deborah's palm tree, situated between Ramah and Bethel in the mountain region of Ephraim, and there the Israelites came up to her for judgment. [6]She sent and summoned Barak, son of Abinoam, from Kedesh of Naphtali. "This is what the LORD, the God of Israel, commands," she said to him; "go, march on Mount Tabor, and take with you ten thousand Naphtalites and Zebulunites. [7]I will lead Sisera, the general of Jabin's army, out to you at the Wadi Kishon, together with his chariots and troops, and will deliver them into your power." [8]But Barak answered her, "If you come with me, I will go; if you do not come with me, I will not go." [9]"I will certainly go with you," she replied, "but you shall not gain the glory in the expedition on which you are setting out, for the LORD will have Sisera fall into the power of a woman." So Deborah joined Barak and journeyed with him to Kedesh. [10]Barak summoned Zebulun and Naphtali to Kedesh, and ten thousand men followed him. Deborah also went up with him. [11]Now the Kenite Heber had detached himself from his own people, the descendants of Hobab, Moses' brother-in-law, and had pitched his tent by the terebinth of Zaanannim, which was near Kedesh. [12]It was reported to Sisera that Barak, son of Abinoam, had gone up to Mount Tabor. [13]So Sisera assembled from Harosheth-ha-goiim at the Wadi Kishon all nine hundred of his iron chariots and all his forces. [14]Deborah then said to Barak, "Be off, for this is the day on which the LORD has delivered Sisera into your power. The LORD marches before you." So Barak went down Mount Tabor, followed by his ten thousand men. [15]And the LORD put Sisera and all his chariots and all his forces to rout before Barak. Sisera himself dismounted from his chariot and fled on foot. [16]Barak, however, pursued the chariots and the army as far as Harosheth-ha-goiim. The entire army of Sisera fell beneath the sword, not even one man surviving. [17][2]Sisera, in the meantime, had fled on foot to the tent of Jael, wife of the Kenite Heber, since Jabin, king of Hazor, and the family of the Kenite Heber were at peace with one another. [18]Jael went out to meet Sisera and said to him, "Come in, my lord, come in with me; do not be afraid." So he went into her tent, and she covered him with a rug. [19]He said to her, "Please give me a little water to drink. I am thirsty." But she opened a jug of milk for him to drink, and then covered him

over. [20]"Stand at the entrance of the tent," he said to her. "If anyone comes and asks, 'Is there someone here?' say, 'No!'" [21]Instead Jael, wife of Heber, got a tent peg and took a mallet in her hand. While Sisera was sound asleep, she stealthily approached him and drove the peg through his temple down into the ground, so that he perished in death. [22]Then when Barak came in pursuit of Sisera, Jael went out to meet him and said to him, "Come, I will show you the man you seek." So he went in with her, and there lay Sisera dead, with the tent peg through his temple. [23]Thus on that day God humbled the Canaanite king, Jabin, before the Israelites; [24]their power weighed ever heavier upon him, till at length they destroyed the Canaanite king, Jabin.

Judges Chapter 5

[1] On that day Deborah (and Barak, son of Abinoam,) sang this song: [2]Of chiefs who took the lead in Israel, of noble deeds by the people who bless the LORD, [3]Hear, O kings! Give ear, O princes! I to the LORD will sing my song, my hymn to the LORD, the God of Israel. [4]O LORD, when you went out from Seir, when you marched from the land of Edom, the earth quaked and the heavens were shaken, while the clouds sent down showers. [5]Mountains trembled in the presence of the LORD, the One of Sinai, in the presence of the LORD, the God of Israel. [6]In the days of Shamgar, son of Anath, in the days of slavery caravans ceased: those who traveled the roads went by roundabout paths. [7]Gone was freedom beyond the walls, gone indeed from Israel. When I, Deborah, rose, when I rose, a mother in Israel, [8]New gods were their choice; then the war was at their gates. Not a shield could be seen, nor a lance, among forty thousand in Israel! [9]My heart is with the leaders of Israel, nobles of the people who bless the LORD; [10]They who ride on white asses, seated on saddlecloths as they go their way; [11]Sing of them to the strains of the harpers at the wells, where men recount the just deeds of the LORD, his just deeds that brought freedom to Israel. [12]Awake, awake, Deborah! awake, awake, strike up a song. Strength! arise, Barak, make despoilers your spoil, son of Abinoam. [13]Then down came the fugitives with the mighty, the people of the LORD came down for me as warriors. [14]From Ephraim, princes were in the valley; behind you was Benjamin, among your troops. From Machir came down commanders, from Zebulun wielders [15]of the marshal's staff. With Deborah were the princes of Issachar; Barak, too, was in the valley, his course unchecked. Among the clans of Reuben great were the searchings of heart. [16]Why do you stay beside your hearths listening to the lowing of the herds? Among the clans of Reuben great were the searchings of heart! [17]Gilead, beyond the Jordan, rests; why does Dan spend his time in ships? Asher, who dwells along the shore, is resting in his coves. [18]Zebulun is the people defying death; Naphtali, too, on the open heights! [19]The kings came and fought; then they fought, those kings of Canaan, at Taanach by the waters of Megiddo; no silver booty did they take. [20]From the heavens the stars, too, fought; from their courses they fought against Sisera. [21]The Wadi Kishon swept them away; a wadi. . . , the Kishon. [22]Then the hoofs of the horses pounded, with the dashing, dashing of his steeds. [23]"Curse Meroz," says the LORD, "hurl a curse at its inhabitants! For they came not to my help, as warriors to the help of the LORD." [24]Blessed among women be Jael, blessed among tent-dwelling women. [25]He asked for water, she gave him milk; in a princely bowl she offered curds. [26]With her left hand she reached for the peg, with her right, for the workman's mallet. She hammered Sisera, crushed his head; she smashed, stove in his temple. [27]At her feet he sank down, fell, lay still; down at her feet he sank and fell; where he sank down, there he fell, slain. [28]From the window peered down and wailed the mother of Sisera, from the lattice: "Why is his chariot so long in coming? why are the hoofbeats of his chariots delayed?" [29]The wisest of her princesses answers her, and she, too, keeps answering herself: [30]"They must be dividing the spoil they took: there must be a damsel or two for each man, spoils of dyed cloth as Sisera's spoil, an ornate shawl or two for me in the spoil." [31]May all your enemies perish thus, O LORD! but your friends be as the sun rising in its might! And the land was at rest for forty years.

Judges Chapter 6

[1]The Israelites offended the LORD, who therefore delivered them into the power of Midian for seven years, [2]so that Midian held Israel subject. For fear of Midian the Israelites established the fire signals on the mountains, the caves for refuge, and the strongholds. [3]And it used to be that when the Israelites had completed their sowing, Midian, Amalek and the Kedemites would come up, [4]encamp opposite them, and destroy the produce of the land as far as the outskirts of Gaza, leaving no sustenance in Israel, nor sheep, oxen or asses. [5]For they would come up with their livestock, and their tents would become as numerous as locusts; and neither they nor their camels could be numbered, when they came into the land to lay it waste. [6]Thus was Israel reduced to

misery by Midian, and so the Israelites cried out to the LORD. 7When Israel cried out to the LORD because of Midian, 8he sent a prophet to the Israelites who said to them, "The LORD, the God of Israel, says: I led you up from Egypt; I brought you out of the place of slavery. 9I rescued you from the power of Egypt and of all your other oppressors. I drove them out before you and gave you their land. 10And I said to you: I, the LORD, am your God; you shall not venerate the gods of the Amorites in whose land you are dwelling. But you did not obey me." 11Then the angel of the LORD came and sat under the terebinth in Ophrah that belonged to Joash the Abiezrite. While his son Gideon was beating out wheat in the wine press to save it from the Midianites, 12the angel of the LORD appeared to him and said, "The LORD is with you, O champion!" 13"My Lord," Gideon said to him, "if the LORD is with us, why has all this happened to us? Where are his wondrous deeds of which our fathers told us when they said, 'Did not the LORD bring us up from Egypt?' For now the LORD has abandoned us and has delivered us into the power of Midian." 14The LORD turned to him and said, "Go with the strength you have and save Israel from the power of Midian. It is I who send you." 15But he answered him, "Please, my lord, how can I save Israel? My family is the meanest in Manasseh, and I am the most insignificant in my father's house." 16"I shall be with you," the LORD said to him, "and you will cut down Midian to the last man." 17He answered him, "If I find favor with you, give me a sign that you are speaking with me. 18Do not depart from here, I pray you, until I come back to you and bring out my offering and set it before you." He answered, "I will await your return." 19So Gideon went off and prepared a kid and an ephah of flour in the form of unleavened cakes. Putting the meat in a basket and the broth in a pot, he brought them out to him under the terebinth and presented them. 20The angel of God said to him, "Take the meat and unleavened cakes and lay them on this rock; then pour out the broth." When he had done so, 21the angel of the LORD stretched out the tip of the staff he held, and touched the meat and unleavened cakes. Thereupon a fire came up from the rock which consumed the meat and unleavened cakes, and the angel of the LORD disappeared from sight. 22Gideon, now aware that it had been the angel of the LORD, said, "Alas, Lord GOD, that I have seen the angel of the LORD face to face!" 23The LORD answered him, "Be calm, do not fear. You shall not die." 24So Gideon built there an altar to the LORD and called it Yahweh-shalom. To this day it is still in Ophrah of the Abiezrites. 25That same night the LORD said to him, "Take the seven-year-old spare bullock and destroy your father's altar to Baal and cut down the sacred pole that is by it. 26You shall build, instead, the proper kind of altar to the LORD, your God, on top of this stronghold. Then take the spare bullock and offer it as a holocaust on the wood from the sacred pole you have cut down." 27So Gideon took ten of his servants and did as the LORD had commanded him. But through fear of his family and of the townspeople, he would not do it by day, but did it at night. 28Early the next morning the townspeople found that the altar of Baal had been destroyed, the sacred pole near it cut down, and the spare bullock offered on the altar that was built. 29They asked one another, "Who did this?" Their inquiry led them to the conclusion that Gideon, son of Joash, had done it. 30So the townspeople said to Joash, "Bring out your son that he may die, for he has destroyed the altar of Baal and has cut down the sacred pole that was near it." 31But Joash replied to all who were standing around him, "Do you intend to act in Baal's stead, or be his champion? If anyone acts for him, he shall be put to death by morning. If he whose altar has been destroyed is a god, let him act for himself!" 32So on that day Gideon was called Jerubbaal, because of the words, "Let Baal take action against him, since he destroyed his altar." 33Then all Midian and Amalek and the Kedemites mustered and crossed over into the valley of Jezreel, where they encamped. 34The spirit of the LORD enveloped Gideon; he blew the horn that summoned Abiezer to follow him. 35He sent messengers, too, throughout Manasseh, which also obeyed his summons; through Asher, Zebulun and Naphtali, likewise, he sent messengers and these tribes advanced to meet the others. 36Gideon said to God, "If indeed you are going to save Israel through me, as you promised, 37I am putting this woolen fleece on the threshing floor. If dew comes on the fleece alone, while all the ground is dry, I shall know that you will save Israel through me, as you promised." 38That is what took place. Early the next morning he wrung the dew from the fleece, squeezing out of it a bowlful of water. 39Gideon then said to God, "Do not be angry with me if I speak once more. Let me make just one more test with the fleece. Let the fleece alone be dry, but let there be dew on all the ground." 40That night God did so; the fleece alone was dry, but there was dew on all the ground.

Judges Chapter 7

1Early the next morning Jerubbaal (that is, Gideon) encamped by Enharod with all his soldiers. The camp of Midian was in the valley north of Gibeath-hammoreh. 2The LORD said to Gideon, "You have too many soldiers with you for me to deliver Midian into their power, lest Israel vaunt itself against me and say, 'My own power brought me the victory.' 3Now proclaim to all the soldiers, 'If anyone is afraid or fearful, let him leave.'" When Gideon put them to this test on the mountain, twenty-two thousand of the soldiers left, but ten thousand remained. 4The LORD said to Gideon, "There are still too many soldiers. Lead them down to the water and I will test them for you there. If I tell you that a certain man is to go with you, he must go with you. But no one is to go if I tell you he must not." 5When Gideon led the soldiers down to the water, the LORD said to him, "You shall set to one side everyone who laps up the water as a dog does with its tongue; to the other, everyone who kneels down to drink." 6Those who lapped up the water raised to their mouths by hand numbered three hundred, but all the rest of the soldiers knelt down to drink the water. 7The LORD said to Gideon, "By means of the three hundred who lapped up the water I will save you and will deliver Midian into your power. So let all the other soldiers go home." 8Their horns, and such supplies as the soldiers had with them, were taken up, and Gideon ordered the rest of the Israelites to their tents, but kept the three hundred men. Now the camp of Midian was beneath him in the valley. 9That night the LORD said to Gideon, "Go, descend on the camp, for I have delivered it up to you. 10If you are afraid to attack, go down to the camp with your aide Purah. 11When you hear what they are saying, you will have the courage to descend on the camp." So he went down with his aide Purah to the outposts of the camp. 12The Midianites, Amalekites, and all the Kedemites lay in the valley, as numerous as locusts. Nor could their camels be counted, for these were as many as the sands on the seashore. 13When Gideon arrived, one man was telling another about a dream. "I had a dream," he said, "that a round loaf of barley bread was rolling into the camp of Midian. It came to our tent and struck it, and as it fell it turned the tent upside down." 14"This can only be the sword of the Israelite Gideon, son of Joash," the other replied. "God has delivered Midian and all the camp into his power." 15When Gideon heard the description and explanation of the dream, he prostrated himself. Then returning to the camp of Israel, he said, "Arise, for the LORD has delivered the camp of Midian into your power." 16He divided the three hundred men into three companies, and provided them all with horns and with empty jars and torches inside the jars. 17"Watch me and follow my lead," he told them. "I shall go to the edge of the camp, and as I do, you must do also. 18When I and those with me blow horns, you too must blow horns all around the camp and cry out, 'For the LORD and for Gideon!'" 19So Gideon and the hundred men who were with him came to the edge of the camp at the beginning of the middle watch, just after the posting of the guards. They blew the horns and broke the jars they were holding. 20All three companies blew horns and broke their jars. They held the torches in their left hands, and in their right the horns they were blowing, and cried out, "A sword for the LORD and Gideon!" 21They all remained standing in place around the camp, while the whole camp fell to running and shouting and fleeing. 22But the three hundred men kept blowing the horns, and throughout the camp the LORD set the sword of one against another. The army fled as far as Beth-shittah in the direction of Zererath, near the border of Abel-meholah at Tabbath. 23The Israelites were called to arms from Naphtali, from Asher, and from all Manasseh, and they pursued Midian. 24Gideon also sent messengers throughout the mountain region of Ephraim to say, "Go down to confront Midian, and seize the water courses against them as far as Beth-barah, as well as the Jordan." So all the Ephraimites were called to arms, and they seized the water courses as far as Beth-barah, and the Jordan as well. 25They captured the two princes of Midian, Oreb and Zeeb, killing Oreb at the rock of Oreb and Zeeb at the wine press of Zeeb. Then they pursued Midian and carried the heads of Oreb and Zeeb to Gideon beyond the Jordan.

Judges Chapter 8

1But the Ephraimites said to him, "What have you done to us, not calling us when you went to fight against Midian?" And they quarreled bitterly with him. 2"What have I accomplished now in comparison with you?" he answered them. "Is not the gleaning of Ephraim better than the vintage of Abiezer? 3Into your power God delivered the princes of Midian, Oreb and Zeeb. What have I been able to do in comparison with you?" When he said this, their anger against him subsided. 4When Gideon reached the Jordan and crossed it with his three hundred men, they were exhausted and famished. 5So he said to the men of Succoth, "Will you give my followers some loaves of bread? They are exhausted, and I am pursuing Zebah and Zalmunna, kings of Midian." 6But the princes of Succoth replied, "Are the hands of Zebah and Zalmunna already in your possession, that we should give food to your army?" 7Gideon said, "Very well; when the LORD has delivered Zebah and

Zalmunna into my power, I will grind your flesh in with the thorns and briers of the desert." [8]He went up from there to Penuel and made the same request of them, but the men of Penuel answered him as had the men of Succoth. [9]So to the men of Penuel, too, he said, "When I return in triumph, I will demolish this tower." [10]Now Zebah and Zalmunna were in Karkor with their force of about fifteen thousand men; these were all who were left of the whole Kedemite army, a hundred and twenty thousand swordsmen having fallen. Gideon went up by the route of the nomads east of Nobah and Jogbehah, and attacked the camp when it felt secure. [12]Zebah and Zalmunna fled. He pursued them and took the two kings of Midian, Zebah and Zalmunna, captive, throwing the entire army into panic. [13]Then Gideon, son of Joash, returned from battle by the pass of Heres. [14]He captured a young man of Succoth, who upon being questioned listed for him the seventy-seven princes and elders of Succoth. [15]So he went to the men of Succoth and said, "Here are Zebah and Zalmunna, with whom you taunted me, 'Are the hands of Zebah and Zalmunna already in your possession, that we should give food to your weary followers?'" [16]He took the elders of the city, and thorns and briers of the desert, and ground these men of Succoth into them. [17]He also demolished the tower of Penuel and slew the men of the city. [18]Then he said to Zebah and Zalmunna, "Where now are the men you killed at Tabor?" "They all resembled you," they replied. "They appeared to be princes." [19]"They were my brothers, my mother's sons," he said. "As the LORD lives, if you had spared their lives, I should not kill you." [20]Then he said to his first-born, Jether, "Go, kill them." Since Jether was still a boy, he was afraid and did not draw his sword. [21]Zebah and Zalmunna said, "Come, kill us yourself, for a man's strength is like the man." So Gideon stepped forward and killed Zebah and Zalmunna. He also took the crescents that were on the necks of their camels. [22]The Israelites then said to Gideon, "Rule over us— you, your son, and your son's son—for you rescued us from the power of Midian." [23]But Gideon answered them, "I will not rule over you, nor shall my son rule over you. The LORD must rule over you." [24]Gideon went on to say, "I should like to make a request of you. Will each of you give me a ring from his booty?" (For being Ishmaelites, the enemy had gold rings.) [25]"We will gladly give them," they replied, and spread out a cloak into which everyone threw a ring from his booty. [26]The gold rings that he requested weighed seventeen hundred gold shekels, in addition to the crescents and pendants, the purple garments worn by the kings of Midian, and the trappings that were on the necks of their camels. [27]Gideon made an ephod out of the gold and placed it in his city Ophrah. However, all Israel paid idolatrous homage to it there, and caused the ruin of Gideon and his family. [28]Thus was Midian brought into subjection by the Israelites; no longer did they hold their heads high. And the land had rest for forty years, during the lifetime of Gideon. [29]Then Jerubbaal, son of Joash, went back home to stay. [30]Now Gideon had seventy sons, his direct descendants, for he had many wives. [31]His concubine who lived in Shechem also bore him a son, whom he named Abimelech. [32]At a good old age Gideon, son of Joash, died and was buried in the tomb of his father Joash in Ophrah of the Abiezrites. [33]But after Gideon was dead, the Israelites again abandoned themselves to the Baals, making Baal of Berith their god [34]and forgetting the LORD, their God, who had delivered them from the power of their enemies all around them. [35]Nor were they grateful to the family of Jerubbaal (Gideon) for all the good he had done for Israel.

Judges Chapter 9

[1]Abimelech, son of Jerubbaal, went to his mother's kinsmen in Shechem and said to them and to the whole clan to which his mother's family belonged, [2]"Put this question to all the citizens of Shechem: 'Which is better for you: that seventy men, all of Jerubbaal's sons, rule over you, or that one man rule over you?' You must remember that I am your own flesh and bone." [3]When his mother's kin repeated these words to them on his behalf, all the citizens of Shechem sympathized with Abimelech, thinking, "He is our kinsman." [4]They also gave him seventy silver shekels from the temple of Baal of Berith, with which Abimelech hired shiftless men and ruffians as his followers. [5]He then went to his ancestral house in Ophrah and slew his brothers, the seventy sons of Jerubbaal, on one stone. Only the youngest son of Jerubbaal, Jotham, escaped, for he was hidden. [6]Then all the citizens of Shechem and all Beth-millo came together and proceeded to make Abimelech king by the terebinth at the memorial pillar in Shechem. [7]When this was reported to him, Jotham went to the top of Mount Gerizim and, standing there, cried out to them in a loud voice: "Hear me, citizens of Shechem, that God may then hear you! [8]Once the trees went to anoint a king over themselves. So they said to the olive tree, 'Reign over us.' [9]But the olive tree answered them, 'Must I give up my rich oil, whereby men and gods are honored, and go to wave over the trees?' [10]Then the trees said to the fig tree, 'Come; you reign over us!' [11]But the fig tree answered them, 'Must I give up my sweetness and my good fruit, and go to wave over the trees?' [12]Then the trees said to the vine, 'Come you, and reign over us.' [13]But the vine answered them, 'Must I give up my wine that cheers gods and men, and go to wave over the trees?' [14]Then all the trees said to the buckthorn, 'Come; you reign over us!' [15]But the buckthorn replied to the trees, 'If you wish to anoint me king over you in good faith, come and take refuge in my shadow. Otherwise, let fire come from the buckthorn and devour the cedars of Lebanon.' [16]"Now then, if you have acted in good faith and honorably in appointing Abimelech your king, if you have dealt well with Jerubbaal and with his family, and if you have treated him as he deserved— [17]for my father fought for you at the risk of his life when he saved you from the power of Midian; [18]but you have risen against his family this day and have killed his seventy sons upon one stone, and have made Abimelech, the son of his handmaid, king over the citizens of Shechem because he is your kinsman— [19]if, then, you have acted in good faith and with honor toward Jerubbaal and his family this day, rejoice in Abimelech and may he in turn rejoice in you. [20]But if not, let fire come forth from Abimelech to devour the citizens of Shechem and Beth-millo, and let fire come forth from the citizens of Shechem and from Beth-millo to devour Abimelech." [21]Then Jotham went in flight to Beer, where he remained for fear of his brother Abimelech. [22]When Abimelech had ruled Israel for three years, [23]God put bad feelings between Abimelech and the citizens of Shechem, who rebelled against Abimelech. [24]This was to repay the violence done to the seventy sons of Jerubbaal and to avenge their blood upon their brother Abimelech, who killed them, and upon the citizens of Shechem, who encouraged him to kill his brothers. [25]The citizens of Shechem then set men in ambush for him on the mountaintops, and these robbed all who passed them on the road. But it was reported to Abimelech. [26]Now Gaal, son of Ebed, came over to Shechem with his kinsmen. The citizens of Shechem put their trust in him, [27]and went out into the fields, harvested their grapes, and trod them out. Then they held a festival and went to the temple of their god, where they ate and drank and cursed Abimelech. [28]Gaal, son of Ebed, said, "Who is Abimelech? And why should we of Shechem serve him? Were not the son of Jerubbaal and his lieutenant Zebul once subject to the men of Hamor, father of Shechem? Why should we serve him? [29]Would that this people were entrusted to my command! I would depose Abimelech. I would say to Abimelech, 'Get a larger army and come out!'" [30]At the news of what Gaal, son of Ebed, had said, Zebul, the ruler of the city, was angry [31]and sent messengers to Abimelech in Arumah with the information: "Gaal, son of Ebed, and his kinsmen have come to Shechem and are stirring up the city against you. [32]Now rouse yourself; set an ambush tonight in the fields, you and the men who are with you. [33]Promptly at sunrise tomorrow morning, make a raid on the city. When he and his followers come out against you, deal with him as best you can." [34]During the night Abimelech advanced with all his soldiers and set up an ambush for Shechem in four companies. [35]Gaal, son of Ebed, went out and stood at the entrance of the city gate. When Abimelech and his soldiers rose from their place of ambush, [36]Gaal saw them and said to Zebul, "There are men coming down from the hilltops!" But Zebul answered him, "You see the shadow of the hills as men." [37]But Gaal went on to say, "Men are coming down from the region of Tabbur-Haares, and one company is coming by way of Elon-Meonenim." [38]Zebul said to him, "Where now is the boast you uttered, 'Who is Abimelech that we should serve him?' Are these not the men for whom you expressed contempt? Go out now and fight with them." [39]So Gaal went out at the head of the citizens of Shechem and fought against Abimelech. [40]But Abimelech routed him, and he fled before him; and many fell slain right up to the entrance of the gate. [41]Abimelech returned to Arumah, but Zebul drove Gaal and his kinsmen from Shechem, which they had occupied. [42]The next day, when the people were taking the field, it was reported to Abimelech, [43]who divided the men he had into three companies and set up an ambush in the fields. He watched till he saw the people leave the city, and then rose against them for the attack. [44]Abimelech and the company with him dashed in and stood at the entrance of the city gate, while the other two companies rushed upon all who were in the field and attacked them. [45]That entire day Abimelech fought against the city and captured it. He then killed its inhabitants and demolished the city, sowing the site with salt. [46]When they heard of this, all the citizens of Migdal-shechem went into the crypt of the temple of El-berith. [47]It was reported to Abimelech that all the citizens of Migdal-shechem were gathered together. [48]So he went up Mount Zalmon with all his soldiers, took his axe in his hand, and cut down some brushwood. This he lifted to his shoulder, then said to the men with him, "Hurry! Do just as you have seen me do." [49]So all the men likewise cut down brushwood, and following Abimelech,

placed it against the crypt. Then they set the crypt on fire over their heads, so that every one of the citizens of Migdal-shechem, about a thousand men and women, perished. ⁵⁰Abimelech proceeded to Thebez, which he invested and captured. ⁵¹Now there was a strong tower in the middle of the city, and all the men and women, in a word all the citizens of the city, fled there, shutting themselves in and going up to the roof of the tower. ⁵²Abimelech came up to the tower and fought against it, advancing to the very entrance of the tower to set it on fire. ⁵³But a certain woman cast the upper part of a millstone down on Abimelech's head, and it fractured his skull. ⁵⁴He immediately called his armor-bearer and said to him, "Draw your sword and dispatch me, lest they say of me that a woman killed me." So his attendant ran him through and he died. ⁵⁵When the Israelites saw that Abimelech was dead, they all left for their homes. ⁵⁶Thus did God requite the evil Abimelech had done to his father in killing his seventy brothers. ⁵⁷God also brought all their wickedness home to the Shechemites, for the curse of Jotham, son of Jerubbaal, overtook them.

Judges Chapter 10

¹After Abimelech there rose to save Israel the Issacharite Tola, son of Puah, son of Dodo, a resident of Shamir in the mountain region of Ephraim. ²When he had judged Israel twenty-three years, he died and was buried in Shamir. ³Jair the Gileadite came after him and judged Israel twenty-two years. ⁴He had thirty sons who rode on thirty saddle-asses and possessed thirty cities in the land of Gilead; these are called Havvoth-jair to the present day. ⁵Jair died and was buried in Kamon. ⁶The Israelites again offended the LORD, serving the Baals and Ashtaroths, the gods of Aram, the gods of Sidon, the gods of Moab, the gods of the Ammonites, and the gods of the Philistines. Since they had abandoned the LORD and would not serve him, ⁷the LORD became angry with Israel and allowed them to fall into the power of the Philistines and the Ammonites. ⁸For eighteen years they afflicted and oppressed the Israelites in Bashan, and all the Israelites in the Amorite land beyond the Jordan in Gilead. ⁹The Ammonites also crossed the Jordan to fight against Judah, Benjamin, and the house of Ephraim, so that Israel was in great distress. ¹⁰Then the Israelites cried out to the LORD, "We have sinned against you; we have forsaken our God and have served the Baals." ¹¹The LORD answered the Israelites: "Did not the Egyptians, the Amorites, the Ammonites, the Philistines, ¹²the Sidonians, the Amalekites, and the Midianites oppress you? When you cried out to me, and I saved you from their grasp, ¹³you still forsook me and worshiped other gods. Therefore I will save you no more. ¹⁴Go and cry out to the gods you have chosen; let them save you now that you are in distress." ¹⁵But the Israelites said to the LORD, "We have sinned. Do to us whatever you please. Only save us this day." ¹⁶And they cast out the foreign gods from their midst and served the LORD, so that he grieved over the misery of Israel. ¹⁷The Ammonites had gathered for war and encamped in Gilead, while the Israelites assembled and encamped in Mizpah. ¹⁸And among the people, the princes of Gilead said to one another, "The one who begins the war against the Ammonites shall be leader of all the inhabitants of Gilead."

Judges Chapter 11

¹There was a chieftain, the Gileadite Jephthah, born to Gilead of a harlot. ²Gilead's wife had also borne him sons, and on growing up the sons of the wife had driven Jephthah away, saying to him, "You shall inherit nothing in our family, for you are the son of another woman." ³So Jephthah had fled from his brothers and had taken up residence in the land of Tob. A rabble had joined company with him, and went out with him on raids. ⁴Some time later, the Ammonites warred on Israel. ⁵When this occurred, the elders of Gilead went to bring Jephthah from the land of Tob. ⁶"Come," they said to Jephthah, "be our commander that we may be able to fight the Ammonites." ⁷"Are you not the ones who hated me and drove me from my father's house?" Jephthah replied to the elders of Gilead. "Why do you come to me now, when you are in distress?" ⁸The elders of Gilead said to Jephthah, "In any case, we have now come back to you; if you go with us to fight against the Ammonites, you shall be the leader of all of us who dwell in Gilead." ⁹Jephthah answered the elders of Gilead, "If you bring me back to fight against the Ammonites and the LORD delivers them up to me, I shall be your leader." ¹⁰The elders of Gilead said to Jephthah, "The LORD is witness between us that we will do as you say." ¹¹So Jephthah went with the elders of Gilead, and the people made him their leader and commander. In Mizpah, Jephthah settled all his affairs before the LORD. ¹²Then he sent messengers to the king of the Ammonites to say, "What have you against me that you come to fight with me in my land?" ¹³He answered the messengers of Jephthah, "Israel took away my land from the Arnon to the Jabbok and the Jordan when they came up from Egypt. Now restore the same peaceably." ¹⁴Again Jephthah sent messengers to the king of the Ammonites, ¹⁵saying to him, "This is what Jephthah says: Israel did not take the land of Moab or the land of the Ammonites. ¹⁶For when they came up from Egypt, Israel went through the desert to the Red Sea and came to Kadesh. ¹⁷Israel then sent messengers to the king of Edom saying, 'Let me pass through your land.' But the king of Edom did not give consent. They also sent to the king of Moab, but he too was unwilling. So Israel remained in Kadesh. ¹⁸Then they went through the desert, and by-passing the land of Edom and the land of Moab, went east of the land of Moab and encamped across the Arnon. Thus they did not go through the territory of Moab, for the Arnon is the boundary of Moab. ¹⁹Then Israel sent messengers to Sihon, king of the Amorites, king of Heshbon. Israel said to him, 'Let me pass through your land to my own place.' ²⁰But Sihon refused to let Israel pass through his territory. On the contrary, he gathered all his soldiers, who encamped at Jahaz and fought Israel. ²¹But the LORD, the God of Israel, delivered Sihon and all his men into the power of Israel, who defeated them and occupied all the land of the Amorites dwelling in that region, ²²the whole territory from the Arnon to the Jabbok, from the desert to the Jordan. ²³If now the LORD, the God of Israel, has cleared the Amorites out of the way of his people, are you to dislodge Israel? ²⁴Should you not possess that which your god Chemosh gave you to possess, and should we not possess all that the LORD, our God, has cleared out for us? ²⁵Again, are you any better than Balak, son of Zippor, king of Moab? Did he ever quarrel with Israel, or did he war against them ²⁶when Israel occupied Heshbon and its villages, Aroer and its villages, and all the cities on the banks of the Arnon? Three hundred years have passed; why did you not recover them during that time? ²⁷I have not sinned against you, but you wrong me by warring against me. Let the LORD, who is judge, decide this day between the Israelites and the Ammonites!" ²⁸But the king of the Ammonites paid no heed to the message Jephthah sent him. ²⁹The spirit of the LORD came upon Jephthah. He passed through Gilead and Manasseh, and through Mizpah-Gilead as well, and from there he went on to the Ammonites. ³⁰Jephthah made a vow to the LORD. "If you deliver the Ammonites into my power," he said, ³¹"whoever comes out of the doors of my house to meet me when I return in triumph from the Ammonites shall belong to the LORD. I shall offer him up as a holocaust." ³²Jephthah then went on to the Ammonites to fight against them, and the LORD delivered them into his power, ³³so that he inflicted a severe defeat on them, from Aroer to the approach of Minnith (twenty cities in all) and as far as Abel-keramin. Thus were the Ammonites brought into subjection by the Israelites. ³⁴When Jephthah returned to his house in Mizpah, it was his daughter who came forth, playing the tambourines and dancing. She was an only child: he had neither son nor daughter besides her. ³⁵When he saw her, he rent his garments and said, "Alas, daughter, you have struck me down and brought calamity upon me. For I have made a vow to the LORD and I cannot retract." ³⁶"Father," she replied, "you have made a vow to the LORD. Do with me as you have vowed, because the LORD has wrought vengeance for you on your enemies the Ammonites." ³⁷Then she said to her father, "Let me have this favor. Spare me for two months, that I may go off down the mountains to mourn my virginity with my companions." ³⁸"Go," he replied, and sent her away for two months. So she departed with her companions and mourned her virginity on the mountains. ³⁹At the end of the two months she returned to her father, who did to her as he had vowed. She had not been intimate with man. It then became a custom in Israel ⁴⁰for Israelite women to go yearly to mourn the daughter of Jephthah the Gileadite for four days of the year.

Judges Chapter 12

¹The men of Ephraim gathered together and crossed over to Zaphon. They said to Jephthah, "Why do you go on to fight with the Ammonites without calling us to go with you? We will burn your house over you." ²Jephthah answered them, "My soldiers and I were engaged in a critical contest with the Ammonites. I summoned you, but you did not rescue me from their power. ³When I saw that you would not effect a rescue, I took my life in my own hand and went on to the Ammonites, and the LORD delivered them into my power. Why, then, do you come up against me this day to fight with me?" ⁴Then Jephthah called together all the men of Gilead and fought against Ephraim, whom they defeated; for the Ephraimites had said, "You of Gilead are Ephraimite fugitives in territory belonging to Ephraim and Manasseh." ⁵The Gileadites took the fords of the Jordan toward Ephraim. When any of the fleeing Ephraimites said, "Let me pass," the men of Gilead would say to him, "Are you an Ephraimite?" If he answered, "No!" ⁶they would ask him to say "Shibboleth." If he said "Sibboleth," not being able to give the proper pronunciation, they would seize him and kill him at the fords of the Jordan. Thus forty-two thousand Ephraimites fell at that time. ⁷After having judged Israel for six years, Jephthah the Gileadite died

and was buried in his city in Gilead. ⁸After him Ibzan of Bethlehem judged Israel. ⁹He had thirty sons. He also had thirty daughters married outside the family, and he brought in as wives for his sons thirty young women from outside the family. After having judged Israel for seven years, ¹⁰Ibzan died and was buried in Bethlehem. ¹¹After him the Zebulunite Elon judged Israel. When he had judged Israel for ten years, ¹²the Zebulunite Elon died and was buried in Elon in the land of Zebulun. ¹³After him the Pirathonite Abdon, son of Hillel, judged Israel. ¹⁴He had forty sons and thirty grandsons who rode on seventy saddle-asses. After having judged Israel for eight years, ¹⁵the Pirathonite Abdon, son of Hillel, died and was buried in Pirathon in the land of Ephraim on the mountain of the Amalekites.

Judges Chapter 13

¹The Israelites again offended the LORD, who therefore delivered them into the power of the Philistines for forty years. ²There was a certain man from Zorah, of the clan of the Danites, whose name was Manoah. His wife was barren and had borne no children. ³An angel of the LORD appeared to the woman and said to her, "Though you are barren and have had no children, yet you will conceive and bear a son. ⁴Now, then, be careful to take no wine or strong drink and to eat nothing unclean. ⁵As for the son you will conceive and bear, no razor shall touch his head, for this boy is to be consecrated to God from the womb. It is he who will begin the deliverance of Israel from the power of the Philistines." ⁶The woman went and told her husband, "A man of God came to me; he had the appearance of an angel of God, terrible indeed. I did not ask him where he came from, nor did he tell me his name. ⁷But he said to me, 'You will be with child and will bear a son. So take neither wine nor strong drink, and eat nothing unclean. For the boy shall be consecrated to God from the womb, until the day of his death.'" ⁸Manoah then prayed to the LORD. "O LORD, I beseech you," he said, "may the man of God whom you sent, return to us to teach us what to do for the boy who will be born." ⁹God heard the prayer of Manoah, and the angel of God came again to the woman as she was sitting in the field. Since her husband Manoah was not with her, ¹⁰the woman ran in haste and told her husband. "The man who came to me the other day has appeared to me," she said to him; ¹¹so Manoah got up and followed his wife. When he reached the man, he said to him, "Are you the one who spoke to my wife?" "Yes," he answered. ¹²Then Manoah asked, "Now, when that which you say comes true, what are we expected to do for the boy?" ¹³The angel of the LORD answered Manoah, "Your wife is to abstain from all the things of which I spoke to her. ¹⁴She must not eat anything that comes from the vine, nor take wine or strong drink, nor eat anything unclean. Let her observe all that I have commanded her." ¹⁵Then Manoah said to the angel of the LORD, "Can we persuade you to stay, while we prepare a kid for you?" ¹⁶But the angel of the LORD answered Manoah, "Although you press me, I will not partake of your food. But if you will, you may offer a holocaust to the LORD." Not knowing that it was the angel of the LORD, ¹⁷Manoah said to him, "What is your name, that we may honor you when your words come true?" ¹⁸The angel of the LORD answered him, "Why do you ask my name, which is mysterious?" ¹⁹Then Manoah took the kid with a cereal offering and offered it on the rock to the LORD, whose works are mysteries. While Manoah and his wife were looking on, ²⁰as the flame rose to the sky from the altar, the angel of the LORD ascended in the flame of the altar. When Manoah and his wife saw this, they fell prostrate to the ground; ²¹but the angel of the LORD was seen no more by Manoah and his wife. Then Manoah, realizing that it was the angel of the LORD, ²²said to his wife, "We will certainly die, for we have seen God." ²³But his wife pointed out to him, "If the LORD had meant to kill us, he would not have accepted a holocaust and cereal offering from our hands! Nor would he have let us see all this just now, or hear what we have heard." ²⁴The woman bore a son and named him Samson. The boy grew up and the LORD blessed him; ²⁵the spirit of the LORD first stirred him in Mahaneh-dan, which is between Zorah and Eshtaol.

Judges Chapter 14

¹Samson went down to Timnah and saw there one of the Philistine women. ²On his return he told his father and mother, "There is a Philistine woman I saw in Timnah whom I wish you to get as a wife for me." ³His father and mother said to him, "Can you find no wife among your kinsfolk or among all our people, that you must go and take a wife from the uncircumcised Philistines?" But Samson answered his father, "Get her for me, for she pleases me." ⁴Now his father and mother did not know that this had been brought about by the LORD, who was providing an opportunity against the Philistines; for at that time they had dominion over Israel. ⁵So Samson went down to Timnah with his father and mother. When they had come to the vineyards of Timnah, a young lion came roaring to meet him. ⁶But the spirit of the LORD came

upon Samson, and although he had no weapons, he tore the lion in pieces as one tears a kid. ⁷However, on the journey to speak for the woman, he did not mention to his father or mother what he had done. ⁸Later, when he returned to marry the woman who pleased him, he stepped aside to look at the remains of the lion and found a swarm of bees and honey in the lion's carcass. ⁹So he scooped the honey out into his palms and ate it as he went along. When he came to his father and mother, he gave them some to eat, without telling them that he had scooped the honey from the lion's carcass. ¹⁰His father also went down to the woman, and Samson gave a banquet there, since it was customary for the young men to do this. ¹¹When they met him, they brought thirty men to be his companions. ¹²Samson said to them, "Let me propose a riddle to you. If within the seven days of the feast you solve it for me successfully, I will give you thirty linen tunics and thirty sets of garments. ¹³But if you cannot answer it for me, you must give me thirty tunics and thirty sets of garments." "Propose your riddle," they responded; "we will listen to it." ¹⁴So he said to them, "Out of the eater came forth food, and out of the strong came forth sweetness." After three days' failure to answer the riddle, ¹⁵they said on the fourth day to Samson's wife, "Coax your husband to answer the riddle for us, or we will burn you and your family. Did you invite us here to reduce us to poverty?" ¹⁶At Samson's side, his wife wept and said, "You must hate me; you do not love me, for you have proposed a riddle to my countrymen, but have not told me the answer." He said to her, "If I have not told it even to my father or my mother, must I tell it to you?" ¹⁷But she wept beside him during the seven days the feast lasted. On the seventh day, since she importuned him, he told her the answer, and she explained the riddle to her countrymen. ¹⁸On the seventh day, before the sun set, the men of the city said to him, "What is sweeter than honey, and what is stronger than a lion?" He replied to them, "If you had not plowed with my heifer, you would not have solved my riddle." ¹⁹The spirit of the LORD came upon him, and he went down to Ashkelon, where he killed thirty of their men and despoiled them; he gave their garments to those who had answered the riddle. Then he went off to his own family in anger, ²⁰and Samson's wife was married to the one who had been best man at his wedding.

Judges Chapter 15

¹After some time, in the season of the wheat harvest, Samson visited his wife, bringing a kid. But when he said, "Let me be with my wife in private," her father would not let him enter, ²saying, "I thought it certain you wished to repudiate her; so I gave her to your best man. Her younger sister is more beautiful than she; you may have her instead." ³Samson said to them, "This time the Philistines cannot blame me if I harm them." ⁴So Samson left and caught three hundred foxes. Turning them tail to tail, he tied between each pair of tails one of the torches he had at hand. ⁵He then kindled the torches and set the foxes loose in the standing grain of the Philistines, thus burning both the shocks and the standing grain, and the vineyards and olive orchards as well. ⁶When the Philistines asked who had done this, they were told, "Samson, the son-in-law of the Timnite, because his wife was taken and given to his best man." So the Philistines went up and destroyed her and her family by fire. ⁷Samson said to them, "If this is how you act, I will not stop until I have taken revenge on you." ⁸And with repeated blows, he inflicted a great slaughter on them. Then he went down and remained in a cavern of the cliff of Etam. ⁹The Philistines went up and, from a camp in Judah, deployed against Lehi. ¹⁰When the men of Judah asked, "Why have you come up against us?" they answered, "To take Samson prisoner; to do to him as he has done to us." ¹¹Three thousand men of Judah went down to the cavern in the cliff of Etam and said to Samson, "Do you not know that the Philistines are our rulers? Why, then, have you done this to us?" He answered them, "As they have done to me, so have I done to them." ¹²They said to him, "We have come to take you prisoner, to deliver you over to the Philistines." Samson said to them, "Swear to me that you will not kill me yourselves." ¹³"No," they replied, "we will certainly not kill you but will only bind you and deliver you over to them." So they bound him with two new ropes and brought him up from the cliff. ¹⁴When he reached Lehi, and the Philistines came shouting to meet him, the spirit of the LORD came upon him: the ropes around his arms became as flax that is consumed by fire and his bonds melted away from his hands. ¹⁵Near him was the fresh jawbone of an ass; he reached out, grasped it, and with it killed a thousand men. ¹⁶Then Samson said, "With the jawbone of an ass I have piled them in a heap; With the jawbone of an ass I have slain a thousand men." ¹⁷As he finished speaking he threw the jawbone from him; and so that place was named Ramath-lehi. ¹⁸Being very thirsty, he cried to the LORD and said, "You have granted this great victory by the hand of your servant. Must I now die of thirst or fall into the hands of the uncircumcised?" ¹⁹Then God split the cavity in Lehi, and water issued from it, which Samson drank

till his spirit returned and he revived. Hence that spring in Lehi is called En-hakkore to this day. [20]Samson judged Israel for twenty years in the days of the Philistines.

Judges Chapter 16

[1]Once Samson went down to Gaza, where he saw a harlot and visited her. [2]Informed that Samson had come there, the men of Gaza surrounded him with an ambush at the city gate all night long. And all the night they waited, saying, "Tomorrow morning we will kill him." [3]Samson rested there until midnight. Then he rose, seized the doors of the city gate and the two gateposts, and tore them loose, bar and all. He hoisted them on his shoulders and carried them to the top of the ridge opposite Hebron. [4]After that he fell in love with a woman in the Wadi Sorek whose name was Delilah. [5]The lords of the Philistines came to her and said, "Beguile him and find out the secret of his great strength, and how we may overcome and bind him so as to keep him helpless. We will each give you eleven hundred shekels of silver." [6]So Delilah said to Samson, "Tell me the secret of your great strength and how you may be bound so as to be kept helpless." [7]"If they bind me with seven fresh bowstrings which have not dried," Samson answered her, "I shall be as weak as any other man." [8]So the lords of the Philistines brought her seven fresh bowstrings which had not dried, and she bound him with them. [9]She had men lying in wait in the chamber and so she said to him, "The Philistines are upon you, Samson!" But he snapped the strings as a thread of tow is severed by a whiff of flame; and the secret of his strength remained unknown. [10]Delilah said to Samson, "You have mocked me and told me lies. Now tell me how you may be bound." [11]"If they bind me tight with new ropes, with which no work has been done," he answered her, "I shall be as weak as any other man." [12]So Delilah took new ropes and bound him with them. Then she said to him, "The Philistines are upon you, Samson!" For there were men lying in wait in the chamber. But he snapped them off his arms like thread. [13]Delilah said to Samson again, "Up to now you have mocked me and told me lies. Tell me how you may be bound." He said to her, "If you weave my seven locks of hair into the web and fasten them with the pin, I shall be as weak as any other man." [14]So while he slept, Delilah wove his seven locks of hair into the web, and fastened them in with the pin. Then she said, "The Philistines are upon you, Samson!" Awakening from his sleep, he pulled out both the weaver's pin and the web. [15]Then she said to him, "How can you say that you love me when you do not confide in me? Three times already you have mocked me, and not told me the secret of your great strength!" [16]She importuned him continually and vexed him with her complaints till he was deathly weary of them. [17]So he took her completely into his confidence and told her, "No razor has touched my head, for I have been consecrated to God from my mother's womb. If I am shaved, my strength will leave me, and I shall be as weak as any other man." [18]When Delilah saw that he had taken her completely into his confidence, she summoned the lords of the Philistines, saying, "Come up this time, for he has opened his heart to me." So the lords of the Philistines came and brought up the money with them. [19]She had him sleep on her lap, and called for a man who shaved off his seven locks of hair. Then she began to mistreat him, for his strength had left him. [20]When she said, "The Philistines are upon you, Samson!", and he woke from his sleep, he thought he could make good his escape as he had done time and again, for he did not realize that the LORD had left him. [21]But the Philistines seized him and gouged out his eyes. Then they brought him down to Gaza and bound him with bronze fetters, and he was put to grinding in the prison. [22]But the hair of his head began to grow as soon as it was shaved off. [23]The lords of the Philistines assembled to offer a great sacrifice to their god Dagon and to make merry. They said, "Our god has delivered into our power Samson our enemy." [24]When the people saw him, they praised their god. For they said, "Our god has delivered into our power our enemy, the ravager of our land, the one who has multiplied our slain." Then they stationed him between the columns. [25]When their spirits were high, they said, "Call Samson that he may amuse us." So they called Samson from the prison, and he played the buffoon before them. [26]Samson said to the attendant who was holding his hand, "Put me where I may touch the columns that support the temple and may rest against them." [27]The temple was full of men and women: all the lords of the Philistines were there, and from the roof about three thousand men and women looked on as Samson provided amusement. [28]Samson cried out to the LORD and said, "O Lord GOD, remember me! Strengthen me, O God, this last time that for my two eyes I may avenge myself once and for all on the Philistines." [29]Samson grasped the two middle columns on which the temple rested and braced himself against them, one at his right hand, the other at his left. [30]And Samson said, "Let me die with the Philistines!" He pushed hard, and the temple fell upon the lords and all the people who were in it. Those he killed at his

death were more than those he had killed during his lifetime. [31]All his family and kinsmen went down and bore him up for burial in the grave of his father Manoah between Zorah and Eshtaol. He had judged Israel for twenty years.

Judges Chapter 17

[1]There was a man in the mountain region of Ephraim whose name was Micah. [2]He said to his mother, "The eleven hundred shekels of silver over which you pronounced a curse in my hearing when they were taken from you, are in my possession. It is I who took them; so now I will restore them to you." [3]When he restored the eleven hundred shekels of silver to his mother, she took two hundred of them and gave them to the silversmith, who made of them a carved idol overlaid with silver. [4]Then his mother said, "May the LORD bless my son! I have consecrated the silver to the LORD as my gift in favor of my son, by making a carved idol overlaid with silver." It remained in the house of Micah. [5]Thus the layman Micah had a sanctuary. He also made an ephod and household idols, and consecrated one of his sons, who became his priest. [6]In those days there was no king in Israel; everyone did what he thought best. [7]There was a young Levite who had resided within the tribe of Judah at Bethlehem of Judah. [8]From that city he set out to find another place of residence. On his journey he came to the house of Micah in the mountain region of Ephraim. [9]Micah said to him, "Where do you come from?" He answered him, "I am a Levite from Bethlehem in Judah, and am on my way to find some other place of residence." [10]"Stay with me," Micah said to him. "Be father and priest to me, and I will give you ten silver shekels a year, a set of garments, and your food." [11]So the young Levite decided to stay with the man, to whom he became as one of his own sons. [12]Micah consecrated the young Levite, who became his priest, remaining in his house. [13]Therefore Micah said, "Now I know that the LORD will prosper me, since the Levite has become my priest."

Judges Chapter 18

[1]At that time, there was no king in Israel. Moreover, the tribe of Danites were in search of a district to dwell in, for up to that time they had received no heritage among the tribes of Israel. [2]So the Danites sent from their clan a detail of five valiant men of Zorah and Eshtaol to reconnoiter the land and scout it. With their instructions to go and scout the land, they traveled as far as the house of Micah in the mountain region of Ephraim, where they passed the night. [3]Near the house of Micah, they recognized the voice of the young Levite and turned in that direction. "Who brought you here and what are you doing here?" they asked him. "What is your interest here?" [4]"This is how Micah treats me," he replied to them. "He pays me a salary and I am his priest." [5]They said to him, "Consult God, that we may know whether the undertaking we are engaged in will succeed." [6]The priest said to them, "Go and prosper: the LORD is favorable to the undertaking you are engaged in." [7]So the five men went on and came to Laish. They saw that the people dwelling there lived securely after the manner of the Sidonians, quiet and trusting, with no lack of any natural resources. They were distant from the Sidonians and had no contact with other people. [8]When the five returned to their kinsmen in Zorah and Eshtaol and were asked for a report, [9]they replied, "Come, let us attack them, for we have seen the land and it is very good. Are you going to hesitate? Do not be slothful about beginning your expedition to possess the land. [10]Those against whom you go are a trusting people, and the land is ample. God has indeed given it into your power: a place where no natural resource is lacking." [11]So six hundred men of the clan of the Danites, fully armed with weapons of war, set out from where they were in Zorah and Eshtaol, [12]and camped in Judah, up near Kiriath-jearim; hence to this day the place, which lies west of Kiriath-jearim, is called Mahaneh-dan. [13]From there they went on to the mountain region of Ephraim and came to the house of Micah. [14]The five men who had gone to reconnoiter the land of Laish said to their kinsmen, "Do you know that in these houses there are an ephod, household idols, and a carved idol overlaid with silver? Now decide what you must do!" [15]So turning in that direction, they went to the house of the young Levite at the home of Micah and greeted him. [16]The six hundred men girt with weapons of war, who were Danites, stood by the entrance of the gate, and the priest stood there also. [17]Meanwhile, the five men who had gone to reconnoiter the land went up and entered the house of Micah. [18]When they had gone in and taken the ephod, the household idols, and the carved idol overlaid with silver, the priest said to them, "What are you doing?" [19]They said to him, "Be still: put your hand over your mouth. Come with us and be our father and priest. Is it better for you to be a priest for the family of one man or to be a priest for a tribe and a clan in Israel?" [20]The priest, agreeing, took the ephod, household idols, and carved idol and went off in the midst of the band. [21]As they turned to

depart, they placed their little ones, their livestock, and their goods at the head of the column. ²²The Danites had already gone some distance when those in the houses near that of Micah took up arms and overtook them. ²³They called to the Danites, who turned about and said to Micah, "What do you want, that you have taken up arms?" ²⁴"You have taken my god, which I made, and have gone off with my priest as well," he answered. "What is left for me? How, then, can you ask me what I want?" ²⁵The Danites said to him, "Let us hear no further sound from you, lest fierce men fall upon you and you and your family lose your lives." ²⁶The Danites then went on their way, and Micah, seeing that they were stronger than he, returned home. ²⁷Having taken what Micah had made, and the priest he had had, they attacked Laish, a quiet and trusting people; they put them to the sword and destroyed their city by fire. ²⁸No one came to their aid since the city was far from Sidon and they had no contact with other people. The Danites then rebuilt the city, which was in the valley that belongs to Beth-rehob, and lived there. ²⁹They named it Dan after their ancestor Dan, son of Israel. However, the name of the city was formerly Laish. ³⁰The Danites set up the carved idol for themselves, and Jonathan, son of Gershom, son of Moses, and his descendants were priests for the tribe of the Danites until the time of the captivity of the land. ³¹They maintained the carved idol Micah had made as long as the house of God was in Shiloh.

Judges Chapter 19

¹At that time, when there was no king in Israel, there was a Levite residing in remote parts of the mountain region of Ephraim who had taken for himself a concubine from Bethlehem of Judah. ²His concubine was unfaithful to him and left him for her father's house in Bethlehem of Judah, where she stayed for some four months. ³Her husband then set out with his servant and a pair of asses, and went after her to forgive her and take her back. She brought him into her father's house, and on seeing him, the girl's father joyfully made him welcome. ⁴He was detained by the girl's father, and so he spent three days with this father-in-law of his, eating and drinking and passing the night there. ⁵On the fourth day they rose early in the morning and he prepared to go. But the girl's father said to his son-in-law, "Fortify yourself with a little food; you can go later on." ⁶So they stayed and the two men ate and drank together. Then the girl's father said to the husband, "Why not decide to spend the night here and enjoy yourself?" ⁷The man still made a move to go, but when his father-in-law pressed him he went back and spent the night there. ⁸On the fifth morning he rose early to depart, but the girl's father said, "Fortify yourself and tarry until the afternoon." When he and his father-in-law had eaten, ⁹and the husband was ready to go with his concubine and servant, the girl's father said to him, "It is already growing dusk. Stay for the night. See, the day is coming to an end. Spend the night here and enjoy yourself. Early tomorrow you can start your journey home." ¹⁰The man, however, refused to stay another night; he and his concubine set out with a pair of saddled asses and traveled till they came opposite Jebus, which is Jerusalem. ¹¹Since they were near Jebus with the day far gone, the servant said to his master, "Come, let us turn off to this city of the Jebusites and spend the night in it." ¹²But his master said to him, "We will not turn off to a city of foreigners, who are not Israelites, but will go on to Gibeah. ¹³Come," he said to his servant, "let us make for some other place, either Gibeah or Ramah, to spend the night." ¹⁴So they continued on their way till the sun set on them when they were abreast of Gibeah of Benjamin. ¹⁵There they turned off to enter Gibeah for the night. The man waited in the public square of the city he had entered, but no one offered them the shelter of his home for the night. ¹⁶In the evening, however, an old man came from his work in the field; he was from the mountain region of Ephraim, though he lived among the Benjaminite townspeople of Gibeah. ¹⁷When he noticed the traveler in the public square of the city, the old man asked where he was going, and whence he had come. ¹⁸He said to him, "We are traveling from Bethlehem of Judah far up into the mountain region of Ephraim, where I belong. I have been to Bethlehem of Judah and am now going back home; but no one has offered us the shelter of his house. ¹⁹We have straw and fodder for our asses, and bread and wine for the woman and myself and for our servant; there is nothing else we need." ²⁰"You are welcome," the old man said to him, "but let me provide for all your needs, and do not spend the night in the public square." ²¹So he led them to his house and provided fodder for the asses. Then they washed their feet and ate and drank. ²²While they were enjoying themselves, the men of the city, who were corrupt, surrounded the house and beat on the door. They said to the old man whose house it was, "Bring out your guest, that we may abuse him." ²³The owner of the house went out to them and said, "No, my brothers; do not be so wicked. Since this man is my guest, do not commit this crime. ²⁴Rather let me bring out my maiden daughter or his concubine. Ravish them, or do whatever you want with them; but against the man you must not commit this wanton crime." ²⁵When the men would not listen to his host, the husband seized his concubine and thrust her outside to them. They had relations with her and abused her all night until the following dawn, when they let her go. ²⁶Then at daybreak, the woman came and collapsed at the entrance of the house in which her husband was a guest, where she lay until the morning. ²⁷When her husband rose that day and opened the door of the house to start out again on his journey, there lay the woman, his concubine, at the entrance of the house with her hands on the threshold. ²⁸He said to her, "Come, let us go"; but there was no answer. So the man placed her on an ass and started out again for home. ²⁹On reaching home, he took a knife to the body of his concubine, cut her into twelve pieces, and sent them throughout the territory of Israel. ³⁰Everyone who saw this said, "Nothing like this has been done or seen from the day the Israelites came up from the land of Egypt to this day. Take note of it, and state what you propose to do."

Judges Chapter 20

¹So all the Israelites came out as one man: from Dan to Beer-sheba, and from the land of Gilead, the community was gathered to the LORD at Mizpah. ²The leaders of all the people and all the tribesmen of Israel, four hundred thousand foot soldiers who were swordsmen, presented themselves in the assembly of the people of God. ³Meanwhile, the Benjaminites heard that the Israelites had gone up to Mizpah. The Israelites asked to be told how the crime had taken place, ⁴and the Levite, the husband of the murdered woman, testified: "My concubine and I went into Gibeah of Benjamin for the night. ⁵But the citizens of Gibeah rose up against me by night and surrounded the house in which I was. Me they attempted to kill, and my concubine they abused so that she died. ⁶So I took my concubine and cut her up and sent her through every part of the territory of Israel, because of the monstrous crime they had committed in Israel. ⁷Now that you are all here, O Israelites, state what you propose to do." ⁸All the people rose as one man to say, "None of us is to leave for his tent or return to his home. ⁹Now as for Gibeah, this is what we will do: We will proceed against it by lot, ¹⁰taking from all the tribes of Israel ten men for every hundred, a hundred for every thousand, a thousand for every ten thousand, and procuring supplies for the soldiers who will go to deal fully and suitably with Gibeah of Benjamin for the crime it committed in Israel." ¹¹When, therefore, all the men of Israel without exception were leagued together against the city, ¹²the tribes of Israel sent men throughout the tribe of Benjamin to say, "What is this evil which has occurred among you? ¹³Now give up these corrupt men of Gibeah, that we may put them to death and thus purge the evil from Israel." But the Benjaminites refused to accede to the demand of their brothers, the Israelites. ¹⁴Instead, the Benjaminites assembled from their other cities to Gibeah, to do battle with the Israelites. ¹⁵The number of the Benjaminite swordsmen from the other cities on that occasion was twenty-six thousand, in addition to the inhabitants of Gibeah. ¹⁶Included in this total were seven hundred picked men who were left-handed, every one of them able to sling a stone at a hair without missing. ¹⁷Meanwhile, the other Israelites who, without Benjamin, mustered four hundred thousand swordsmen ready for battle, ¹⁸moved on to Bethel and consulted God. When the Israelites asked who should go first in the attack on the Benjaminites, the LORD said, "Judah shall go first." ¹⁹The next day the Israelites advanced on Gibeah with their forces. ²⁰On the day of the combat with Benjamin, the Israelites drew up in battle array at Gibeah for the combat with Benjamin, ²¹the Benjaminites came out of the city and felled twenty-two thousand men of Israel. ²²But though the Israelite soldiers took courage and again drew up for combat in the same place as on the previous day, ²³then the Israelites went up and wept before the LORD until evening. "Shall I again engage my brother Benjamin in battle?" they asked the LORD; and the LORD answered that they should. ²⁴When they met the Benjaminites for the second time, ²⁵once again the Benjaminites who came out of Gibeah against them felled eighteen thousand Israelites, all of them swordsmen. ²⁶So the entire Israelite army went up to Bethel, where they wept and remained fasting before the LORD until evening of that day, besides offering holocausts and peace offerings before the LORD. ²⁷When the Israelites consulted the LORD (for the ark of the covenant of God was there in those days, ²⁸and Phinehas, son of Eleazar, son of Aaron, was ministering to him in those days), and asked, "Shall I go out again to battle with Benjamin, my brother, or shall I desist?" the LORD said, "Attack! for tomorrow I will deliver him into your power." ²⁹So Israel set men in ambush around Gibeah. ³⁰The Israelites went up against the Benjaminites for the third time and formed their line of battle at Gibeah as on other occasions. ³¹The Benjaminites went out to meet them, and in the beginning, they killed off about thirty of the Israelite soldiers in the open field, just as on the other occasions. ³²Therefore the Benjaminites thought, "We are

defeating them as before"; not realizing that disaster was about to overtake them. The Israelites, however, had planned the flight so as to draw them away from the city onto the highways. They were drawn away from the city onto the highways, of which the one led to Bethel, the other to Gibeon. ³³And then all the men of Israel rose from their places. They re-formed their ranks at Baal-tamar, and the Israelites in ambush rushed from their place west of Gibeah, ³⁴ten thousand picked men from all Israel, and advanced against the city itself. In a fierce battle, ³⁵the LORD defeated Benjamin before Israel; and on that day the Israelites killed twenty-five thousand one hundred men of Benjamin, all of them swordsmen. ³⁶To the Benjaminites it had looked as though the enemy were defeated, for the men of Israel gave ground to Benjamin, trusting in the ambush they had set at Gibeah. ³⁷But then the men in ambush made a sudden dash into Gibeah, overran it, and put the whole city to the sword. ³⁸Now, the other Israelites had agreed with the men in ambush on a smoke signal they were to send up from the city. ³⁹And though the men of Benjamin had begun by killing off some thirty of the men of Israel, under the impression that they were defeating them as surely as in the earlier fighting, the Israelites wheeled about to resist ⁴⁰as the smoke of the signal column began to rise up from the city. It was when Benjamin looked back and saw the whole city in flames against the sky ⁴¹that the men of Israel wheeled about. Therefore the men of Benjamin were thrown into confusion, for they realized the disaster that had overtaken them. ⁴²They retreated before the men of Israel in the direction of the desert, with the fight being pressed against them. In their very midst, meanwhile, those who had been in the city were spreading destruction. ⁴³The men of Benjamin had been surrounded and were now pursued to a point east of Gibeah, ⁴⁴while eighteen thousand of them fell, warriors to a man. ⁴⁵The rest turned and fled through the desert to the rock Rimmon. But on the highways, the Israelites picked five thousand men among them, and chasing them up to Gidom, killed another two thousand of them there. ⁴⁶Those of Benjamin who fell on that day were in all twenty-five thousand swordsmen, warriors to a man. ⁴⁷But six hundred others who turned and fled through the desert reached the rock Rimmon, where they remained for four months. ⁴⁸The men of Israel withdrew through the territory of the Benjaminites, putting to the sword the inhabitants of the cities, the livestock, and all they chanced upon. Moreover, they destroyed by fire all the cities they came upon.

Judges Chapter 21

¹Now the men of Israel had sworn at Mizpah that none of them would give his daughter in marriage to anyone from Benjamin. ²So the people went to Bethel and remained there before God until evening, raising their voices in bitter lament. ³They said, "LORD, God of Israel, why has it come to pass in Israel that today one tribe of Israel should be lacking?" ⁴Early the next day the people built an altar there and offered holocausts and peace offerings. ⁵Then the Israelites asked, "Are there any among all the tribes of Israel who did not come up to the LORD for the assembly?" For they had taken a solemn oath that anyone who did not go up to the LORD at Mizpah should be put to death without fail. ⁶The Israelites were disconsolate over their brother Benjamin and said, "Today one of the tribes of Israel has been cut off. ⁷What can we do about wives for the survivors, since we have sworn by the LORD not to give them any of our daughters in marriage?" ⁸And when they asked whether anyone among the tribes of Israel had not come up to the LORD in Mizpah, they found that none of the men of Jabesh-gilead had come to the encampment for the assembly. ⁹A roll call of the army established that none of the inhabitants of that city were present. ¹⁰The community, therefore, sent twelve thousand warriors with orders to go to Jabesh-gilead and put those who lived there to the sword, including the women and children. ¹¹They were told to include under the ban all males and every woman who was not still a virgin. ¹²Finding among the inhabitants of Jabesh-gilead four hundred young virgins, who had had no relations with men, they brought them to the camp at Shiloh in the land of Canaan. ¹³Then the whole community sent a message to the Benjaminites at the rock Rimmon, offering them peace. ¹⁴When Benjamin returned at that time, they gave them as wives the women of Jabesh-gilead whom they had spared; but these proved to be not enough for them. ¹⁵The people were still disconsolate over Benjamin because the LORD had made a breach among the tribes of Israel. ¹⁶And the elders of the community said, "What shall we do for wives for the survivors? For every woman in Benjamin has been put to death." ¹⁷They said, "Those of Benjamin who survive must have heirs, else one of the Israelite tribes will be wiped out. ¹⁸Yet we cannot give them any of our daughters in marriage, because the Israelites have sworn, 'Cursed be he who gives a woman to Benjamin!'" ¹⁹Then they thought of the yearly feast of the LORD at Shiloh, north of Bethel, east of the highway that goes up from Bethel to Shechem, and south of Lebonah. ²⁰And they

instructed the Benjaminites, "Go and lie in wait in the vineyards. ²¹When you see the girls of Shiloh come out to do their dancing, leave the vineyards and each of you seize one of the girls of Shiloh for a wife, and go to the land of Benjamin. ²²When their fathers or their brothers come to complain to us, we shall say to them, 'Release them to us as a kindness, since we did not take a woman apiece in the war. Had you yourselves given them these wives, you would now be guilty.'" ²³The Benjaminites did this; they carried off a wife for each of them from their raid on the dancers, and went back to their own territory, where they rebuilt and occupied the cities. ²⁴Also at that time the Israelites dispersed; each of them left for his own heritage in his own clan and tribe. ²⁵In those days there was no king in Israel; everyone did what he thought best.

Ruth

Ruth Chapter 1

¹Once in the time of the judges there was a famine in the land; so a man from Bethlehem of Judah departed with his wife and two sons to reside on the plateau of Moab. ²The man was named Elimelech, his wife Naomi, and his sons Mahlon and Chilion; they were Ephrathites from Bethlehem of Judah. Some time after their arrival on the Moabite plateau, ³Elimelech, the husband of Naomi, died, and she was left with her two sons, ⁴who married Moabite women, one named Orpah, the other Ruth. When they had lived there about ten years, ⁵both Mahlon and Chilion died also, and the woman was left with neither her two sons nor her husband. ⁶She then made ready to go back from the plateau of Moab because word reached her there that the LORD had visited his people and given them food. ⁷She and her two daughters-in-law left the place where they had been living. Then as they were on the road back to the land of Judah, ⁸Naomi said to her two daughters-in-law, "Go back, each of you, to your mother's house! May the LORD be kind to you as you were to the departed and to me! ⁹May the LORD grant each of you a husband and a home in which you will find rest." She kissed them good-bye, but they wept with loud sobs, ¹⁰and told her they would return with her to her people. ¹¹"Go back, my daughters!" said Naomi. "Why should you come with me? Have I other sons in my womb who may become your husbands? ¹²Go back, my daughters! Go, for I am too old to marry again. And even if I could offer any hopes, or if tonight I had a husband or had borne sons, ¹³would you then wait and deprive yourselves of husbands until those sons grew up? No, my daughters! my lot is too bitter for you, because the LORD has extended his hand against me." ¹⁴Again they sobbed aloud and wept; and Orpah kissed her mother-in-law good-bye, but Ruth stayed with her. ¹⁵"See now!" she said, "your sister-in-law has gone back to her people and her god. Go back after your sister-in-law!" ¹⁶But Ruth said, "Do not ask me to abandon or forsake you! for wherever you go I will go, wherever you lodge I will lodge, your people shall be my people, and your God my God. ¹⁷Wherever you die I will die, and there be buried. May the LORD do so and so to me, and more besides, if aught but death separates me from you!" ¹⁸Naomi then ceased to urge her, for she saw she was determined to go on together until they reached Bethlehem. On their arrival there, the whole city was astir over them, and the women asked, "Can this be Naomi?" ²⁰But she said to them, "Do not call me Naomi. Call me Mara, for the Almighty has made it very bitter for me. ²¹I went away with an abundance, but the LORD has brought me back destitute. Why should you call me Naomi, since the LORD has pronounced against me and the Almighty has brought evil upon me?" ²²Thus it was that Naomi returned with the Moabite daughter-in-law, Ruth, who accompanied her back from the plateau of Moab. They arrived in Bethlehem at the beginning of the barley harvest.

Ruth Chapter 2

¹Naomi had a prominent kinsman named Boaz, of the clan of her husband Elimelech. ²Ruth the Moabite said to Naomi, "Let me go and glean ears of grain in the field of anyone who will allow me that favor." Naomi said to her, "Go, my daughter," ³and she went. The field she entered to glean after the harvesters happened to be the section belonging to Boaz of the clan of Elimelech. ⁴Boaz himself came from Bethlehem and said to the harvesters, "The LORD be with you!" and they replied, "The LORD bless you!" ⁵Boaz asked the overseer of his harvesters, "Whose girl is this?" ⁶The overseer of the harvesters answered, "She is the Moabite girl who returned from the plateau of Moab with Naomi. ⁷She asked leave to gather the gleanings into sheaves after the harvesters; and ever since she came this morning she has remained here until now, with scarcely a moment's rest." ⁸Boaz said to Ruth, "Listen, my daughter! Do not go to glean in anyone else's field; you are not to leave here. Stay here with my women servants. ⁹Watch to see which field is to be harvested, and follow them; I have

commanded the young men to do you no harm. When you are thirsty, you may go and drink from the vessels the young men have filled." ¹⁰Casting herself prostrate upon the ground, she said to him, "Why should I, a foreigner, be favored with your notice?" ¹¹Boaz answered her: "I have had a complete account of what you have done for your mother-in-law after your husband's death; you have left your father and your mother and the land of your birth, and have come to a people whom you did not know previously. ¹²May the LORD reward what you have done! May you receive a full reward from the LORD, the God of Israel, under whose wings you have come for refuge." ¹³She said, "May I prove worthy of your kindness, my lord: you have comforted me, your servant, with your consoling words; would indeed that I were a servant of yours!" ¹⁴At mealtime Boaz said to her, "Come here and have some food; dip your bread in the sauce." Then as she sat near the reapers, he handed her some roasted grain and she ate her fill and had some left over. ¹⁵She rose to glean, and Boaz instructed his servants to let her glean among the sheaves themselves without scolding her, ¹⁶and even to let drop some handfuls and leave them for her to glean without being rebuked. ¹⁷She gleaned in the field until evening, and when she beat out what she had gleaned it came to about an ephah of barley, ¹⁸which she took into the city and showed to her mother-in-law. Next she brought out and gave her what she had left over from lunch. ¹⁹So her mother-in-law said to her, "Where did you glean today? Where did you go to work? May he who took notice of you be blessed!" Then she told her mother-in-law with whom she had worked. "The man at whose place I worked today is named Boaz," she said. ²⁰"May he be blessed by the LORD, who is ever merciful to the living and to the dead," Naomi exclaimed to her daughter-in-law; and she continued, "He is a relative of ours, one of our next of kin." ²¹"He even told me," added Ruth the Moabite, "that I should stay with his servants until they complete his entire harvest." ²²"You would do well, my dear," Naomi rejoined, "to go out with his servants; for in someone else's field you might be insulted." ²³So she stayed gleaning with the servants of Boaz until the end of the barley and wheat harvests.

Ruth Chapter 3

¹When she was back with her mother-in-law, Naomi said to her, "My daughter, I must seek a home for you that will please you. ²Now is not Boaz, with whose servants you were, a relative of ours? This evening he will be winnowing barley at the threshing floor. ³So bathe and anoint yourself; then put on your best attire and go down to the threshing floor. Do not make yourself known to the man before he has finished eating and drinking. ⁴But when he lies down, take note of the place where he does so. Then go, uncover a place at his feet, and lie down. He will tell you what to do." ⁵"I will do whatever you advise," Ruth replied. ⁶So she went down to the threshing floor and did just as her mother-in-law had instructed her. ⁷Boaz ate and drank to his heart's content. Then when he went and lay down at the edge of the sheaves, she stole up, uncovered a place at his feet, and lay down. ⁸In the middle of the night, however, the man gave a start and turned around to find a woman lying at his feet. ⁹He asked, "Who are you?" And she replied, "I am your servant Ruth. Spread the corner of your cloak over me, for you are my next of kin." ¹⁰He said, "May the LORD bless you, my daughter! You have been even more loyal now than before in not going after the young men, whether poor or rich. ¹¹So be assured, daughter, I will do for you whatever you say; all my townspeople know you for a worthy woman. ¹²Now, though indeed I am closely related to you, you have another relative still closer. ¹³Stay as you are for tonight, and tomorrow, if he wishes to claim you, good! let him do so. But if he does not wish to claim you, as the LORD lives, I will claim you myself. Lie there until morning." ¹⁴So she lay at his feet until morning, but rose before men could recognize one another. Boaz said, "Let it not be known that this woman came to the threshing floor." ¹⁵Then he said to her, "Take off your cloak and hold it out." When she did so, he poured out six measures of barley, helped her lift the bundle, and left for the city. ¹⁶Ruth went home to her mother-in-law, who asked, "How have you fared, my daughter?" So she told her all the man had done for her, ¹⁷and concluded, "He gave me these six measures of barley because he did not wish me to come back to my mother-in-law emptyhanded!" ¹⁸Naomi then said, "Wait here, my daughter, until you learn what happens, for the man will not rest, but will settle the matter today."

Ruth Chapter 4

¹Boaz went and took a seat at the gate; and when he saw the closer relative of whom he had spoken come along, he called to him by name, "Come and sit beside me!" And he did so. ²Then Boaz picked out ten of the elders of the city and asked them to sit nearby. When they had done this, ³he said to the near relative: "Naomi, who has come back from the Moabite plateau, is putting up for sale the piece of land that belonged

to our kinsman Elimelech. ⁴So I thought I would inform you, bidding you before those here present, including the elders of my people, to put in your claim for it if you wish to acquire it as next of kin. But if you do not wish to claim it, tell me so, that I may be guided accordingly, for no one has a prior claim to yours, and mine is next." He answered, "I will put in my claim." ⁵Boaz continued, "Once you acquire the field from Naomi, you must take also Ruth the Moabite, the widow of the late heir, and raise up a family for the departed on his estate." ⁶The near relative replied, "I cannot exercise my claim lest I depreciate my own estate. Put in a claim yourself in my stead, for I cannot exercise my claim." ⁷Now it used to be the custom in Israel that, to make binding a contract of redemption or exchange, one party would take off his sandal and give it to the other. This was the form of attestation in Israel. ⁸So the near relative, in saying to Boaz, "Acquire it for yourself," drew off his sandal. ⁹Boaz then said to the elders and to all the people, "You are witnesses today that I have acquired from Naomi all the holdings of Elimelech, Chilion, and Mahlon. ¹⁰I also take Ruth the Moabite, the widow of Mahlon, as my wife, in order to raise up a family for her late husband on his estate, so that the name of the departed may not perish among his kinsmen and fellow citizens. Do you witness this today?" ¹¹All those at the gate, including the elders, said, "We do so. May the LORD make this wife come into your house like Rachel and Leah, who between them built up the house of Israel. May you do well in Ephrathah and win fame in Bethlehem. ¹²With the offspring the LORD will give you from this girl, may your house become like the house of Perez, whom Tamar bore to Judah." ¹³Boaz took Ruth. When they came together as man and wife, the LORD enabled her to conceive and she bore a son. ¹⁴Then the women said to Naomi, "Blessed is the LORD who has not failed to provide you today with an heir! May he become famous in Israel! ¹⁵He will be your comfort and the support of your old age, for his mother is the daughter-in-law who loves you. She is worth more to you than seven sons!" ¹⁶Naomi took the child, placed him on her lap, and became his nurse. ¹⁷And the neighbor women gave him his name, at the news that a grandson had been born to Naomi. They called him Obed. He was the father of Jesse, the father of David. ¹⁸These are the descendants of Perez: Perez was the father of Hezron, ¹⁹Hezron was the father of Ram, Ram was the father of Amminadab, ²⁰Amminadab was the father of Nahshon, Nahshon was the father of Salmon, ²¹Salmon was the father of Boaz, Boaz was the father of Obed, ²²Obed was the father of Jesse, and Jesse became the father of David.

I Samuel

1 Samuel Chapter 1

¹There was a certain man from Ramathaim, Elkanah by name, a Zuphite from the hill country of Ephraim. He was the son of Jeroham, son of Elihu, son of Tohu, son of Zuph, an Ephraimite. ²He had two wives, one named Hannah, the other Peninnah; Peninnah had children, but Hannah was childless. ³This man regularly went on pilgrimage from his city to worship the LORD of hosts and to sacrifice to him at Shiloh, where the two sons of Eli, Hophni and Phinehas, were ministering as priests of the LORD. ⁴When the day came for Elkanah to offer sacrifice, he used to give a portion each to his wife Peninnah and to all her sons and daughters, ⁵but a double portion to Hannah because he loved her, though the LORD had made her barren. ⁶Her rival, to upset her, turned it into a constant reproach to her that the LORD had left her barren. ⁷This went on year after year; each time they made their pilgrimage to the sanctuary of the LORD, Peninnah would approach her, and Hannah would weep and refuse to eat. ⁸Her husband Elkanah used to ask her: "Hannah, why do you weep, and why do you refuse to eat? Why do you grieve? Am I not more to you than ten sons?" ⁹Hannah rose after one such meal at Shiloh, and presented herself before the LORD; at the time, Eli the priest was sitting on a chair near the doorpost of the LORD's temple. ¹⁰In her bitterness she prayed to the LORD, weeping copiously, ¹¹and she made a vow, promising: "O LORD of hosts, if you look with pity on the misery of your handmaid, if you remember me and do not forget me, if you give your handmaid a male child, I will give him to the LORD for as long as he lives; neither wine nor liquor shall he drink, and no razor shall ever touch his head." ¹²As she remained long at prayer before the LORD, Eli watched her mouth, ¹³for Hannah was praying silently; though her lips were moving, her voice could not be heard. Eli, thinking her drunk, ¹⁴said to her, "How long will you make a drunken show of yourself? Sober up from your wine!" ¹⁵"It isn't that, my lord," Hannah answered. "I am an unhappy woman. I have had neither wine nor liquor; I was only pouring out my troubles to the LORD. ¹⁶Do not think your handmaid a ne'er-do-well; my prayer has been prompted by my deep sorrow and misery." ¹⁷Eli said, "Go in peace, and may the God of Israel grant you what you have

asked of him." 18She replied, "Think kindly of your maidservant," and left. She went to her quarters, ate and drank with her husband, and no longer appeared downcast. 19Early the next morning they worshiped before the LORD, and then returned to their home in Ramah. When Elkanah had relations with his wife Hannah, the LORD remembered her. 20She conceived, and at the end of her term bore a son whom she called Samuel, since she had asked the LORD for him. 21The next time her husband Elkanah was going up with the rest of his household to offer the customary sacrifice to the LORD and to fulfill his vows, 22Hannah did not go, explaining to her husband, "Once the child is weaned, I will take him to appear before the LORD and to remain there forever; I will offer him as a perpetual nazirite." 23Her husband Elkanah answered her: "Do what you think best; wait until you have weaned him. Only, may the LORD bring your resolve to fulfillment!" And so she remained at home and nursed her son until she had weaned him. 24Once he was weaned, she brought him up with her, along with a three-year-old bull, an ephah of flour, and a skin of wine, and presented him at the temple of the LORD in Shiloh. 25After the boy's father had sacrificed the young bull, Hannah, his mother, approached Eli 26and said: "Pardon, my lord! As you live, my lord, I am the woman who stood near you here, praying to the LORD. 27I prayed for this child, and the LORD granted my request. 28Now I, in turn, give him to the LORD; as long as he lives, he shall be dedicated to the LORD." She left him there.

1 Samuel Chapter 2

1And as she worshiped the LORD, she said: "My heart exults in the LORD, my horn is exalted in my God. I have swallowed up my enemies; I rejoice in my victory. 2There is no Holy One like the LORD; there is no Rock like our God. 3Speak boastfully no longer, nor let arrogance issue from your mouths. For an all-knowing God is the LORD, a God who judges deeds. 4The bows of the mighty are broken, while the tottering gird on strength. 5The well-fed hire themselves out for bread, while the hungry batten on spoil. The barren wife bears seven sons, while the mother of many languishes. 6The LORD puts to death and gives life; he casts down to the nether world; he raises up again. 7The LORD makes poor and makes rich, he humbles, he also exalts. 8He raises the needy from the dust; from the ash heap he lifts up the poor, to seat them with nobles and make a glorious throne their heritage. He gives to the vower his vow and blesses the sleep of the just. For the pillars of the earth are the LORD's, and he has set the world upon them. 9He will guard the footsteps of his faithful ones, but the wicked shall perish in the darkness. For not by strength does man prevail; 10the LORD's foes shall be shattered. The Most High in heaven thunders; the LORD judges the ends of the earth, now may he give strength to his king, and exalt the horn of his anointed!"11When Elkanah returned home to Ramah, the child remained in the service of the LORD under the priest Eli. 12Now the sons of Eli were wicked; they had respect neither for the LORD 13nor for the priests' duties toward the people. When someone offered a sacrifice, the priest's servant would come with a three-pronged fork, while the meat was still boiling, 14and would thrust it into the basin, kettle, caldron, or pot. Whatever the fork brought up, the priest would keep. That is how all the Israelites were treated who came to the sanctuary at Shiloh. 15In fact, even before the fat was burned, the priest's servant would come and say to the man offering the sacrifice, "Give me some meat to roast for the priest. He will not accept boiled meat from you, only raw meat." 16And if the man protested, "Let the fat be burned first as is the custom, then take whatever you wish," he would reply, "No, give it to me now, or else I will take it by force." 17Thus the young men sinned grievously in the presence of the LORD; they treated the offerings to the LORD with disdain. 18Meanwhile the boy Samuel, girt with a linen apron, was serving in the presence of the LORD. 19His mother used to make a little garment for him, which she would bring him each time she went up with her husband to offer the customary sacrifice. 20And Eli would bless Elkanah and his wife, as they were leaving for home. He would say, "May the LORD repay you with children from this woman for the gift she has made to the LORD!" 21The LORD favored Hannah so that she conceived and gave birth to three more sons and two daughters, while young Samuel grew up in the service of the LORD. 22When Eli was very old, he heard repeatedly how his sons were treating all Israel (and that they were having relations with the women serving at the entry of the meeting tent). 23So he said to them: "Why are you doing such things? 24No, my sons, you must not do these things! It is not a good report that I hear the people of the LORD spreading about you. 25If a man sins against another man, one can intercede for him with the LORD; but if a man sins against the LORD, who can intercede for him?" But they disregarded their father's warning, since the LORD had decided on their death. 26Meanwhile, young Samuel was growing in stature and in worth in the estimation of the LORD and of men. 27A man of God came

to Eli and said to him: "This is what the LORD says: 'I went so far as to reveal myself to your father's family when they were in Egypt as slaves to the house of Pharaoh. 28I chose them out of all the tribes of Israel to be my priests, to go up to my altar, to burn incense, and to wear the ephod before me; and I assigned all the oblations of the Israelites to your father's family. 29Why do you keep a greedy eye on my sacrifices and on the offerings which I have prescribed? And why do you honor your sons in preference to me, fattening yourselves with the choicest part of every offering of my people Israel?' 30This, therefore, is the oracle of the LORD, the God of Israel: 'I said in the past that your family and your father's family should minister in my presence forever. But now,' the LORD declares, 'away with this! for I will honor those who honor me, but those who spurn me shall be accursed. 31Yes, the time is coming when I will break your strength and the strength of your father's family, so that no man in your family shall reach old age. 32You shall witness as a disappointed rival all the benefits enjoyed by Israel, but there shall never be an old man in your family. 33I will permit some of your family to remain at my altar, to wear out their eyes in consuming greed; but the rest of the men of your family shall die by the sword. 34You shall have a sign in what will happen to your two sons, Hophni and Phinehas: both shall die on the same day. 35I will choose a faithful priest who shall do what I have in heart and mind. I will establish a lasting house for him which shall function in the presence of my anointed forever. 36Then whoever is left of your family will come to grovel before him for a piece of silver or a loaf of bread, and will say: "Appoint me, I beg you, to a priestly function, that I may have a morsel of bread to eat."'"

1 Samuel Chapter 3

1During the time young Samuel was minister to the LORD under Eli, a revelation of the LORD was uncommon and vision infrequent. 2One day Eli was asleep in his usual place. His eyes had lately grown so weak that he could not see. 3The lamp of God was not yet extinguished, and Samuel was sleeping in the temple of the LORD where the ark of God was. 4The LORD called to Samuel, who answered, "Here I am." 5He ran to Eli and said, "Here I am. You called me." "I did not call you," Eli said. "Go back to sleep." So he went back to sleep. 6Again the LORD called Samuel, who rose and went to Eli. "Here I am," he said. "You called me." But he answered, "I did not call you, my son. Go back to sleep." 7At that time Samuel was not familiar with the LORD, because the LORD had not revealed anything to him as yet. 8The LORD called Samuel again, for the third time. Getting up and going to Eli, he said, "Here I am. You called me." Then Eli understood that the LORD was calling the youth. 9So he said to Samuel, "Go to sleep, and if you are called, reply, 'Speak, LORD, for your servant is listening.'" When Samuel went to sleep in his place, 10the LORD came and revealed his presence, calling out as before, "Samuel, Samuel!" Samuel answered, "Speak, for your servant is listening." 11The LORD said to Samuel: "I am about to do something in Israel that will cause the ears of everyone who hears it to ring. 12On that day I will carry out in full against Eli everything I threatened against his family. 13I announce to him that I am condemning his family once and for all, because of this crime: though he knew his sons were blaspheming God, he did not reprove them. 14Therefore, I swear to the family of Eli that no sacrifice or offering will ever expiate its crime." 15Samuel then slept until morning, when he got up early and opened the doors of the temple of the LORD. He feared to tell Eli the vision, 16but Eli called to him, "Samuel, my son!" He replied, "Here I am." 17Then Eli asked, "What did he say to you? Hide nothing from me! May God do thus and so to you if you hide a single thing he told you." 18So Samuel told him everything, and held nothing back. Eli answered, "He is the LORD. He will do what he judges best." 19Samuel grew up, and the LORD was with him, not permitting any word of his to be without effect. 20Thus all Israel from Dan to Beer-sheba came to know that Samuel was an accredited prophet of the LORD. 21The LORD continued to appear at Shiloh; he manifested himself to Samuel at Shiloh through his word.

1 Samuel Chapter 4

1And Samuel spoke to all Israel. At that time, the Philistines gathered for an attack on Israel. Israel went out to engage them in battle and camped at Ebenezer, while the Philistines camped at Aphek. 2The Philistines then drew up in battle formation against Israel. After a fierce struggle, Israel was defeated by the Philistines, who slew about four thousand men on the battlefield. 3When the troops retired to the camp, the elders of Israel said, "Why has the LORD permitted us to be defeated today by the Philistines? Let us fetch the ark of the LORD from Shiloh that it may go into battle among us and save us from the grasp of our enemies." 4So the people sent to Shiloh and brought from there the ark of the LORD of hosts, who is enthroned upon the cherubim. The two sons of Eli, Hophni and Phinehas, were with the ark of God. 5When the ark of the LORD arrived in the camp, all Israel shouted so loudly that the earth resounded. 6The Philistines, hearing the noise of shouting, asked, "What can this loud shouting in the camp of the Hebrews mean?" On learning that the ark of the LORD had come into the camp, 7the Philistines were frightened. They said, "Gods have come to their camp." They said also, "Woe to us! This has never happened before. 8Woe to us! Who can deliver us from the power of these mighty gods? These are the gods that struck the Egyptians with various plagues and with pestilence. 9Take courage and be manly, Philistines; otherwise, you will become slaves to the Hebrews, as they were your slaves. So fight manfully!" 10The Philistines fought, and Israel was defeated; every man fled to his own tent. It was a disastrous defeat, in which Israel lost thirty thousand foot soldiers. 11The ark of God was captured, and Eli's two sons, Hophni and Phinehas, were among the dead. 12A Benjaminite fled from the battlefield and reached Shiloh that same day, with his clothes torn and his head covered with dirt. 13When he arrived, Eli was sitting in his chair beside the gate, watching the road, for he was troubled at heart about the ark of God. The man, however, went into the city to divulge his news, which put the whole city in an uproar. 14Hearing the outcry of the men standing near him, Eli inquired, "What does this commotion mean?" 15(Eli was ninety-eight years old, and his eyes would not focus, so that he could not see.) 16The man quickly came up to Eli and said, "It is I who have come from the battlefield; I fled from there today." He asked, "What happened, my son?" 17And the messenger answered: "Israel fled from the Philistines; in fact, the troops suffered heavy losses. Your two sons, Hophni and Phinehas, are among the dead, and the ark of God has been captured." 18At this mention of the ark of God, Eli fell backward from his chair into the gateway; since he was an old man and heavy, he died of a broken neck. He had judged Israel for forty years. 19His daughter-in-law, the wife of Phinehas, was with child and at the point of giving birth. When she heard the news concerning the capture of the ark and the deaths of her father-in-law and her husband, she was seized with the pangs of labor, and gave birth. 20She was about to die when the women standing around her said to her, "Never fear! You have given birth to a son." Yet she neither answered nor paid any attention. 21She named the child Ichabod, saying, "Gone is the glory from Israel," with reference to the capture of the ark of God and to her father-in-law and her husband. 22She said, "Gone is the glory from Israel," because the ark of God had been captured.

1 Samuel Chapter 5

1The Philistines, having captured the ark of God, transferred it from Ebenezer to Ashdod. 2They then took the ark of God and brought it into the temple of Dagon, placing it beside Dagon. 3When the people of Ashdod rose early the next morning, Dagon was lying prone on the ground before the ark of the LORD. So they picked Dagon up and replaced him. 4But the next morning early, when they arose, Dagon lay prone on the ground before the ark of the LORD, his head and hands broken off and lying on the threshold, his trunk alone intact. 5For this reason, neither the priests of Dagon nor any others who enter the temple of Dagon tread on the threshold of Dagon in Ashdod to this very day; they always step over it. 6Now the LORD dealt severely with the people of Ashdod. He ravaged and afflicted the city and its vicinity with hemorrhoids; he brought upon the city a great and deadly plague of mice that swarmed in their ships and overran their fields. 7On seeing how matters stood, the men of Ashdod decided, "The ark of the God of Israel must not remain with us, for he is handling us and our god Dagon severely." 8So they summoned all the Philistine lords and inquired of them, "What shall we do with the ark of the God of Israel?" The men of Gath replied, "Let them move the ark of the God of Israel on to us." 9So they moved the ark of the God of Israel to Gath! But after it had been brought there, the LORD threw the city into utter turmoil: he afflicted its inhabitants, young and old, and hemorrhoids broke out on them. 10The ark of God was next sent to Ekron; but as it entered that city, the people there cried out, "Why have they brought the ark of the God of Israel here to kill us and our kindred?" 11Then they, too, sent a summons to all the Philistine lords and pleaded: "Send away the ark of the God of Israel. Let it return to its own place, that it may not kill us and our kindred." A deadly panic had seized the whole city, since the hand of God had been very heavy upon it. 12Those who escaped death were afflicted with hemorrhoids, and the outcry from the city went up to the heavens.

1 Samuel Chapter 6

1The ark of the LORD had been in the land of the Philistines seven months 2when they summoned priests and fortune-tellers to ask, "What shall we do with the ark of the LORD? Tell us what we should

send back with it." 3They replied: "If you intend to send away the ark of the God of Israel, you must not send it alone, but must, by all means, make amends to him through a guilt offering. Then you will be healed, and will learn why he continues to afflict you." 4When asked further, "What guilt offering should be our amends to him?", they replied: "Five golden hemorrhoids and five golden mice to correspond to the number of Philistine lords, since the same plague has struck all of you and your lords. 5Therefore, make images of the hemorrhoids and of the mice that are infesting your land and give them as a tribute to the God of Israel. Perhaps then he will cease to afflict you, your gods, and your land. 6Why should you become stubborn, as the Egyptians and Pharaoh were stubborn? Was it not after he had dealt ruthlessly with them that the Israelites were released and departed? 7So now set to work and make a new cart. Then take two milch cows that have not borne the yoke; hitch them to the cart, but drive their calves indoors away from them. 8You shall next take the ark of the LORD and place it on the cart, putting in a box beside it the golden articles that you are offering, as amends for your guilt. Start it on its way, and let it go. 9Then watch! If it goes to Beth-shemesh along the route to his own territory, he has brought this great calamity upon us; if not, we will know it was not he who struck us, but that an accident happened to us." 10They acted upon this advice. Taking two milch cows, they hitched them to the cart but shut up their calves indoors. 11Then they placed the ark of the LORD on the cart, along with the box containing the golden mice and the images of the hemorrhoids. 12The cows went straight for the route to Beth-shemesh and continued along this road, mooing as they went, without turning right or left. The Philistine lords followed them as far as the border of Beth-shemesh. 13The people of Beth-shemesh were harvesting the wheat in the valley. When they looked up and spied the ark, they greeted it with rejoicing. 14The cart came to the field of Joshua the Beth-shemite and stopped there. At a large stone in the field, the wood of the cart was split up and the cows were offered as a holocaust to the LORD. 15The Levites, meanwhile, had taken down the ark of God and the box beside it, in which the golden articles were, and had placed them on the great stone. The men of Beth-shemesh also offered other holocausts and sacrifices to the LORD that day. 16After witnessing this, the five Philistine lords returned to Ekron the same day. 17The golden hemorrhoids the Philistines sent back as a guilt offering to the LORD were as follows: one for Ashdod, one for Gaza, one for Ashkelon, one for Gath, and one for Ekron. 18The golden mice, however, corresponded to the number of all the cities of the Philistines belonging to the five lords, including fortified cities and open villages. The large stone on which the ark of the LORD was placed is still in the field of Joshua the Beth-shemite at the present time. 19The descendants of Jeconiah did not join in the celebration with the inhabitants of Beth-shemesh when they greeted the ark of the LORD, and seventy of them were struck down. The people went into mourning at this great calamity with which the LORD had afflicted them. 20The men of Beth-shemesh asked, "Who can stand in the presence of this Holy One? To whom shall he go from us?" 21They then sent messengers to the inhabitants of Kiriath-jearim, saying, "The Philistines have returned the ark of the LORD; come down and get it."

1 Samuel Chapter 7

1So the inhabitants of Kiriath-jearim came for the ark of the LORD and brought it into the house of Abinadab on the hill, appointing his son Eleazar as guardian of the ark of the LORD. 2From the day the ark came to rest in Kiriath-jearim a long time—twenty years—elapsed, and the whole Israelite population turned to the LORD. 3Samuel said to them: "If you wish with your whole heart to return to the LORD, put away your foreign gods and your Ashtaroth, devote yourselves to the LORD, and worship him alone. Then he will deliver you from the power of the Philistines." 4So the Israelites put away their Baals and Ashtaroth, and worshiped the LORD alone. 5Samuel then gave orders, "Gather all Israel to Mizpah, that I may pray to the LORD for you." 6When they were gathered at Mizpah, they drew water and poured it out on the ground before the LORD, and they fasted that day, confessing, "We have sinned against the LORD." It was at Mizpah that Samuel began to judge the Israelites. 7When the Philistines heard that the Israelites had gathered at Mizpah, their lords went up against Israel. Hearing this, the Israelites became afraid of the Philistines 8and said to Samuel, "Implore the LORD our God unceasingly for us, to save us from the clutches of the Philistines." 9Samuel therefore took an unweaned lamb and offered it entire as a holocaust to the LORD. He implored the LORD for Israel, and the LORD heard him. 10While Samuel was offering the holocaust, the Philistines advanced to join battle with Israel. That day, however, the LORD thundered loudly against the Philistines, and threw them into such confusion that they were defeated by Israel. 11Thereupon the Israelites sallied forth from Mizpah and pursued the

Philistines, harrying them down beyond Beth-car. [12]Samuel then took a stone and placed it between Mizpah and Jeshanah; he named it Ebenezer, explaining, "To this point the LORD helped us." [13]Thus were the Philistines subdued, never again to enter the territory of Israel, for the LORD was severe with them as long as Samuel lived. [14]The cities from Ekron to Gath which the Philistines had taken from Israel were restored to them. Israel also freed the territory of these cities from the dominion of the Philistines. Moreover, there was peace between Israel and the Amorites. [15]Samuel judged Israel as long as he lived. [16]He made a yearly journey, passing through Bethel, Gilgal, and Mizpah and judging Israel at each of these sanctuaries. [17]Then he used to return to Ramah, for that was his home. There, too, he judged Israel and built an altar to the LORD.

1 Samuel Chapter 8

[1]In his old age, Samuel appointed his sons judges over Israel. [2]His first-born was named Joel, his second son, Abijah; they judged at Beer-sheba. [3]His sons did not follow his example but sought illicit gain and accepted bribes, perverting justice. [4]Therefore all the elders of Israel came in a body to Samuel at Ramah [5]and said to him, "Now that you are old, and your sons do not follow your example, appoint a king over us, as other nations have, to judge us." [6]Samuel was displeased when they asked for a king to judge them. He prayed to the LORD, however, [7]who said in answer: "Grant the people's every request. It is not you they reject, they are rejecting me as their king. [8]As they have treated me constantly from the day I brought them up from Egypt to this day, deserting me and worshiping strange gods, so do they treat you too. [9]Now grant their request; but at the same time, warn them solemnly and inform them of the rights of the king who will rule them." [10]Samuel delivered the message of the LORD in full to those who were asking him for a king. [11]He told them: "The rights of the king who will rule you will be as follows: He will take your sons and assign them to his chariots and horses, and they will run before his chariot. [12]He will also appoint from among them his commanders of groups of a thousand and of a hundred soldiers. He will set them to do his plowing and his harvesting, and to make his implements of war and the equipment of his chariots. [13]He will use your daughters as ointment-makers, as cooks, and as bakers. [14]He will take the best of your fields, vineyards, and olive groves, and give them to his officials. [15]He will tithe your crops and your vineyards, and give the revenue to his eunuchs and his slaves. [16]He will take your male and female servants, as well as your best oxen and your asses, and use them to do his work. [17]He will tithe your flocks and you yourselves will become his slaves. [18]When this takes place, you will complain against the king whom you have chosen, but on that day the LORD will not answer you." [19]The people, however, refused to listen to Samuel's warning and said, "Not so! There must be a king over us. [20]We too must be like other nations, with a king to rule us and to lead us in warfare and fight our battles." [21]When Samuel had listened to all the people had to say, he repeated it to the LORD, [22]who then said to him, "Grant their request and appoint a king to rule them." Samuel thereupon said to the men of Israel, "Each of you go to his own city."

1 Samuel Chapter 9

[1]There was a stalwart man from Benjamin named Kish, who was the son of Abiel, son of Zeror, son of Becorath, son of Aphiah, a Benjaminite. [2]He had a son named Saul, who was a handsome young man. There was no other Israelite handsomer than Saul; he stood head and shoulders above the people. [3]Now the asses of Saul's father, Kish, had wandered off. Kish said to his son Saul, "Take one of the servants with you and go out and hunt for the asses." [4]Accordingly they went through the hill country of Ephraim, and through the land of Shalishah. Not finding them there, they continued through the land of Shaalim without success. They also went through the land of Benjamin, but they failed to find the animals. [5]When they came to the land of Zuph, Saul said to the servant who was with him, "Come, let us turn back, lest my father forget about the asses and become anxious about us." [6]The servant replied, "Listen! There is a man of God in this city, a man held in high esteem; all that he says is sure to come true. Let us go there now! Perhaps he can tell us how to accomplish our errand." [7]But Saul said to his servant, "If we go, what can we offer the man? There is no bread in our bags, and we have no present to give the man of God. What have we?" [8]Again the servant answered Saul, "I have a quarter of a silver shekel. If I give that to the man of God, he will tell us our way." [9](In former times in Israel, anyone who went to consult God used to say, "Come, let us go to the seer." For he who is now called prophet was formerly called seer.) [10]Saul then said to his servant, "Well said! Come on, let us go!" And they went to the city where the man of God lived. [11]As they were going up the ascent to the city, they met some girls coming out to draw water and inquired of them, "Is the seer in town?"

[12]The girls answered, "Yes, there—straight ahead. Hurry now; just today he came to the city, because the people have a sacrifice today on the high place. [13]When you enter the city, you may reach him before he goes up to the high place to eat. The people will not eat until he arrives; only after he blesses the sacrifice will the invited guests eat. Go up immediately, for you should find him right now." [14]So they went up to the city. As they entered it, Samuel was coming toward them on his way to the high place. [15]The day before Saul's arrival, the LORD had given Samuel the revelation: [16]"At this time tomorrow I will send you a man from the land of Benjamin whom you are to anoint as commander of my people Israel. He shall save my people from the clutches of the Philistines, for I have witnessed their misery and accepted their cry for help." [17]When Samuel caught sight of Saul, the LORD assured him, "This is the man of whom I told you; he is to govern my people." [18]Saul met Samuel in the gateway and said, "Please tell me where the seer lives." [19]Samuel answered Saul: "I am the seer. Go up ahead of me to the high place and eat with me today. In the morning, before dismissing you, I will tell you whatever you wish. [20]As for the asses you lost three days ago, do not worry about them, for they have been found. Whom does Israel desire ardently if not you and your father's family?" [21]Saul replied: "Am I not a Benjaminite, of one of the smallest tribes of Israel, and is not my clan the least among the clans of the tribe of Benjamin? Why say such things to me?" [22]Samuel then took Saul and his servant and brought them to the room, where he placed them at the head of the guests, of whom there were about thirty. [23]He said to the cook, "Bring the portion I gave you and told you to put aside." [24]So the cook took up the leg and what went with it, and placed it before Saul. Samuel said: "This is a reserved portion that has been set before you. Eat, for it was kept for you until your arrival; I explained that I was inviting some guests." Thus Saul dined with Samuel that day. [25]When they came down from the high place into the city, a mattress was spread for Saul on the roof, [26]and he slept there. At daybreak Samuel called to Saul on the roof, "Get up, and I will start you on your journey." Saul rose, and he and Samuel went outside the city together. [27]As they were approaching the edge of the town, Samuel said to Saul, "Tell the servant to go on ahead of us, but stay here yourself for the moment, that I may give you a message from God."

1 Samuel Chapter 10

[1]Then, from a flask he had with him, Samuel poured oil on Saul's head; he also kissed him, saying: "The LORD anoints you commander over his heritage. You are to govern the LORD'S people Israel and to save them from the grasp of their enemies round about. This will be the sign for you that the LORD has anointed you commander over his heritage: [2]When you leave me today, you will meet two men near Rachel's tomb at Zelzah in the territory of Benjamin, who will say to you, 'The asses you went to look for have been found. Your father is no longer worried about the asses but is anxious about you and says, *What shall I do about my son?*' [3]Farther on, when you arrive at the terebinth of Tabor, you will be met by three men going up to God at Bethel; one will be bringing three kids, another three loaves of bread, and the third a skin of wine. [4]They will greet you and offer you two wave offerings of bread, which you will take from them. [5]After that, you will come to Gibeath-elohim, where there is a garrison of the Philistines. As you enter that city, you will meet a band of prophets, in a prophetic state, coming down from the high place preceded by lyres, tambourines, flutes, and harps. [6]The spirit of the LORD will rush upon you, and you will join them in their prophetic state and will be changed into another man. [7]When you see these signs fulfilled, do whatever you judge feasible because God is with you. [8]Now go down ahead of me to Gilgal, for I shall come down to you to offer holocausts and to sacrifice peace offerings. Wait seven days until I come to you; I shall then tell you what you must do." [9]As Saul turned to leave Samuel, God gave him another heart. That very day all these signs came to pass. [10]When they were going from there to Gibeah, a band of prophets met him, and the spirit of God rushed upon him, so that he joined them in their prophetic state. [11]When all who had known him previously saw him in a prophetic state among the prophets, they said to one another, "What has happened to the son of Kish? Is Saul also among the prophets?" [12]And someone from that district added, "And who is their father?" Thus the proverb arose, "Is Saul also among the prophets?" [13]When he came out of the prophetic state, he went home. [14]Saul's uncle inquired of him and his servant, "Where have you been?" Saul replied, "To look for the asses. When we could not find them, we went to Samuel." [15]Then Saul's uncle said, "Tell me, then, what Samuel said to you." [16]Saul said to his uncle, "He assured us that the asses had been found." But he mentioned nothing to him of what Samuel had said about the kingship. [17]Samuel called the people together to the LORD at Mizpah [18]and addressed the Israelites: "Thus says the LORD, the God of Israel, *It was I who brought Israel up

from Egypt and delivered you from the power of the Egyptians and from the power of all the kingdoms that oppressed you.* ¹⁹But today you have rejected your God, who delivers you from all your evils and calamities, by saying to him, *Not so, but you must appoint a king over us.* Now, therefore, take your stand before the LORD according to tribes and families." ²⁰So Samuel had all the tribes of Israel come forward, and the tribe of Benjamin was chosen. ²¹Next, he had the tribe of Benjamin come forward in clans, and the clan of Matri was chosen, and finally Saul, son of Kish, was chosen. But they looked for him in vain. ²²Again they consulted the LORD, "Has he come here?" The LORD answered, "He is hiding among the baggage." ²³They ran to bring him from there; and when he stood among the people, he was head and shoulders above all the crowd. ²⁴Samuel said to all the people, "Do you see the man whom the LORD has chosen? There is none like him among all the people!" Then all the people shouted, "Long live the king!" ²⁵Samuel next explained to the people the law of royalty and wrote it in a book, which he placed in the presence of the LORD. This done, Samuel dismissed the people, each to his own place. ²⁶Saul also went home to Gibeah, accompanied by warriors whose hearts the LORD had touched. ²⁷But certain worthless men said, "How can this fellow save us?" They despised him and brought him no present.

1 Samuel Chapter 11

¹About a month later, Nahash the Ammonite went up and laid siege to Jabesh-gilead. All the men of Jabesh begged Nahash, "Make a treaty with us, and we will be your subjects." ²But Nahash the Ammonite replied, "This is my condition for a treaty with you: I must gouge out every man's right eye, that I may thus bring ignominy on all Israel." ³The elders of Jabesh said to him: "Give us seven days to send messengers throughout the territory of Israel. If no one rescues us, we will surrender to you." ⁴When the messengers arrived at Gibeah of Saul, they related the news to the people, all of whom wept aloud. ⁵Just then Saul came in from the field, behind his oxen. "Why are the people weeping?" he asked. The message of the inhabitants of Jabesh was repeated to him. ⁶As he listened to this report, the spirit of God rushed upon him, and he became very angry. ⁷Taking a yoke of oxen, he cut them into pieces, which he sent throughout the territory of Israel by couriers with the message, "If anyone does not come out to follow Saul (and Samuel), the same as this will be done to his oxen!" In dread of the LORD, the people turned out to a man. ⁸When he reviewed them in Bezek, there were three hundred thousand Israelites and seventy thousand Judahites. ⁹To the messengers who had come, he said, "Tell the inhabitants of Jabesh-gilead that tomorrow, while the sun is hot, they will be rescued." The messengers came and reported this to the inhabitants of Jabesh, who were jubilant, ¹⁰and said to Nahash, "Tomorrow we will surrender to you, and you may do whatever you please with us." ¹¹On the appointed day, Saul arranged his troops in three companies and invaded the camp during the dawn watch. They slaughtered Ammonites until the heat of the day; by then the survivors were so scattered that no two were left together. ¹²The people then said to Samuel, "Who questioned whether Saul should rule over us? Hand over the men, and we will put them to death." ¹³But Saul broke in to say, "No man is to be put to death this day, for today the LORD has saved Israel." ¹⁴Samuel said to the people, "Come, let us go to Gilgal to inaugurate the kingdom there." ¹⁵So all the people went to Gilgal, where, in the presence of the LORD, they made Saul king. They also sacrificed peace offerings there before the LORD, and Saul and all the Israelites celebrated the occasion with great joy.

1 Samuel Chapter 12

¹Samuel addressed all Israel: "I have granted your request in every respect," he said. "I have set a king over you. ²And now the king is your leader. As for me, I am old and gray, and have sons among you. I have lived with you from my youth to the present day. ³Here I stand! Answer me in the presence of the LORD and of his anointed. Whose ox have I taken? Whose ass have I taken? Whom have I cheated? Whom have I oppressed? From whom have I accepted a bribe and overlooked his guilt? I will make restitution to you." ⁴They replied, "You have neither cheated us, nor oppressed us, nor accepted anything from anyone." ⁵So he said to them, "The LORD is witness against you this day, and his anointed as well, that you have found nothing in my possession." "He is witness," they agreed. ⁶Continuing, Samuel said to the people: "The LORD is witness, who appointed Moses and Aaron, and who brought your fathers up from the land of Egypt. ⁷Now, therefore, take your stand, and I shall arraign you before the LORD, and shall recount for you all the acts of mercy the LORD has done for you and your fathers. ⁸When Jacob and his sons went to Egypt and the Egyptians oppressed them, your fathers appealed to the LORD, who sent Moses and Aaron to bring them out of Egypt, and he gave them this place to live in. ⁹But

they forgot the LORD their God; and he allowed them to fall into the clutches of Sisera, the captain of the army of Jabin, king of Hazor, into the grasp of the Philistines, and into the grip of the king of Moab, who made war against them. ¹⁰Each time they appealed to the LORD and said, 'We have sinned in forsaking the LORD and worshiping Baals and Ashtaroth; but deliver us now from the power of our enemies, and we will worship you.' ¹¹Accordingly, the LORD sent Jerubbaal, Barak, Jephthah, and Samuel; he delivered you from the power of your enemies on every side, so that you were able to live in security. ¹²Yet, when you saw Nahash, king of the Ammonites, advancing against you, you said to me, 'Not so, but a king must rule us,' even though the LORD your God is your king. ¹³Now you have the king you want, a king the LORD has given you. ¹⁴If you fear the LORD and worship him, if you are obedient to him and do not rebel against the LORD'S command, if both you and the king who rules you follow the LORD your God—well and good. ¹⁵But if you do not obey the LORD and if you rebel against his command, the LORD will deal severely with you and your king, and destroy you. ¹⁶Now then, stand ready to witness the great marvel the LORD is about to accomplish before your eyes. ¹⁷Are we not in the harvest time for wheat? Yet I shall call to the LORD, and he will send thunder and rain. Thus you will see and understand how greatly the LORD is displeased that you have asked for a king." ¹⁸Samuel then called to the LORD, and the LORD sent thunder and rain that day. As a result, all the people dreaded the LORD and Samuel. ¹⁹They said to Samuel, "Pray to the LORD your God for us, your servants, that we may not die for having added to all our other sins the evil of asking for a king." ²⁰"Do not fear," Samuel answered them. "It is true you have committed all this evil; still, you must not turn from the LORD, but must worship him with your whole heart. ²¹Do not turn to meaningless idols which can neither profit nor save; they are nothing. ²²For the sake of his own great name the LORD will not abandon his people, since the LORD himself chose to make you his people. ²³As for me, far be it from me to sin against the LORD by ceasing to pray for you and to teach you the good and right way. ²⁴But you must fear the LORD and worship him faithfully with your whole heart; keep in mind the great things he has done among you. ²⁵If instead you continue to do evil, both you and your king shall perish.

1 Samuel Chapter 13

¹ Saul was. . . years old when he became king and he reigned. . . (two) years over Israel. ² Saul chose three thousand men of Israel, of whom two thousand remained with him in Michmash and in the hill country of Bethel, and one thousand were with Jonathan in Gibeah of Benjamin. He sent the rest of the people back to their tents. ³ Now Jonathan overcame the Philistine garrison which was in Gibeah, and the Philistines got word of it. Then Saul sounded the horn throughout the land, with a proclamation, "Let the Hebrews hear!" ⁴ Thus all Israel learned that Saul had overcome the garrison of the Philistines and that Israel had brought disgrace upon the Philistines; and the soldiers were called up to Saul in Gilgal. ⁵ The Philistines also assembled for battle, with three thousand chariots, six thousand horsemen, and foot soldiers as numerous as the sands of the seashore. Moving up against Israel, they encamped in Michmash, east of Beth-aven. ⁶ Some Israelites, aware of the danger and of the difficult situation, hid themselves in caves, in thickets, among rocks, in caverns, and in cisterns, ⁷ and other Hebrews passed over the Jordan into the land of Gad and Gilead. Saul, however, held out at Gilgal, although all his followers were seized with fear. ⁸ He waited seven days—the time Samuel had determined. When Samuel did not arrive at Gilgal, the men began to slip away from Saul. ⁹ He then said, "Bring me the holocaust and peace offerings," and he offered up the holocaust. ¹⁰ He had just finished this offering when Samuel arrived. Saul went out to greet him, ¹¹ and Samuel asked him, "What have you done?" Saul replied: "When I saw that the men were slipping away from me, since you had not come by the specified time, and with the Philistines assembled at Michmash, ¹² I said to myself, 'Now the Philistines will come down against me at Gilgal, and I have not yet sought the LORD'S blessing.' So in my anxiety I offered up the holocaust." ¹³ Samuel's response was: "You have been foolish! Had you kept the command the LORD your God gave you, the LORD would now establish your kingship in Israel as lasting; ¹⁴ but as things are, your kingdom shall not endure. The LORD has sought out a man after his own heart and has appointed him commander of his people, because you broke the LORD'S command." ¹⁵ Then Samuel set out from Gilgal and went his own way; but the rest of the people went up after Saul to meet the soldiers, going from Gilgal to Gibeah of Benjamin. Saul then numbered the soldiers he had with him, who were about six hundred. ¹⁶ Saul, his son Jonathan, and the soldiers they had with them were now occupying Geba of Benjamin, and the Philistines were encamped at Michmash. ¹⁷ Meanwhile, raiders left the camp of the Philistines in

three bands. One band took the Ophrah road toward the district of Shual; ¹⁸ another turned in the direction of Beth-horon; and the third took the road for Geba that overlooks the Valley of the Hyenas toward the desert. ¹⁹ Not a single smith was to be found in the whole land of Israel, for the Philistines had said, "Otherwise the Hebrews will make swords or spears." ²⁰ All Israel, therefore, had to go down to the Philistines to sharpen their plowshares, mattocks, axes, and sickles. ²¹ The price for the plowshares and mattocks was two-thirds of a shekel, and a third of a shekel for sharpening the axes and for setting the ox-goads. ²² And so on the day of battle neither sword nor spear could be found in the possession of any of the soldiers with Saul or Jonathan. Only Saul and his son Jonathan had them. ²³ An outpost of the Philistines had pushed forward to the pass of Michmash.

1 Samuel Chapter 14

¹ One day Jonathan, son of Saul, said to his armor-bearer, "Come let us go over to the Philistine outpost on the other side." But he did not inform his father. ² (Saul's command post was under the pomegranate tree near the threshing floor on the outskirts of Geba; those with him numbered about six hundred men. ³ Ahijah, son of Ahitub, brother of Ichabod, who was the son of Phinehas, son of Eli, the priest of the LORD at Shiloh, was wearing the ephod.) Nor did the soldiers know that Jonathan had gone. ⁴ Flanking the ravine through which Jonathan intended to get over to the Philistine outpost there was a rocky crag on each side, one called Bozez, the other Seneh. ⁵ One crag was to the north, toward Michmash, the other to the south, toward Geba. ⁶ Jonathan said to his armor-bearer: "Come let us go over to that outpost of the uncircumcised. Perhaps the LORD will help us, because it is no more difficult for the LORD to grant victory through a few than through many." ⁷ His armor-bearer replied, "Do whatever you are inclined to do; I will match your resolve." ⁸ Jonathan continued: "We shall go over to those men and show ourselves to them. ⁹ If they say to us, 'Stay there until we can come to you,' we shall stop where we are; we shall not go up to them. ¹⁰ But if they say, 'Come up to us,' we shall go up, because the LORD has delivered them into our grasp. That will be our sign." ¹¹ Accordingly, the two of them appeared before the outpost of the Philistines, who said, "Look, some Hebrews are coming out of the holes where they have been hiding." ¹² The men of the outpost called to Jonathan and his armor-bearer. "Come up here," they said, "and we will teach you a lesson." So Jonathan said to his armor-bearer, "Climb up after me, for the LORD has delivered them into the grasp of Israel." ¹³ Jonathan clambered up with his armor-bearer behind him; as the Philistines turned to flee him, he cut them down, and his armor-bearer followed him and finished them off. ¹⁴ In this first exploit Jonathan and his armor-bearer slew about twenty men within half a furlong. ¹⁵ Then panic spread to the army and to the countryside, and all the soldiers, including the outpost and the raiding parties, were terror-stricken. The earth also shook, so that the panic was beyond human endurance. ¹⁶ The lookouts of Saul in Geba of Benjamin saw that the enemy camp had scattered and were running about in all directions. ¹⁷ Saul said to those around him, "Count the troops and find out if any of us are missing." When they had investigated, they found Jonathan and his armor-bearer missing. ¹⁸ Saul then said to Ahijah, "Bring the ephod here." (Ahijah was wearing the ephod in front of the Israelites at that time.) ¹⁹ While Saul was speaking to the priest, the tumult in the Philistine camp kept increasing. So he said to the priest, "Withdraw your hand." ²⁰ And Saul and all his men shouted and rushed into the fight, where the Philistines, wholly confused, were thrusting swords at one another. ²¹ In addition, the Hebrews who had previously sided with the Philistines and had gone up with them to the camp, turned to join the Israelites under Saul and Jonathan. ²² Likewise, all the Israelites who were hiding in the hill country of Ephraim, on hearing that the Philistines were fleeing, pursued them in the rout. ²³ Thus the LORD saved Israel that day. The battle continued past Beth-horon; ²⁴ the whole people, about ten thousand combatants, were with Saul, and there was scattered fighting in every town in the hill country of Ephraim. And Saul swore a very rash oath that day, putting the people under this ban: "Cursed be the man who takes food before evening, before I am able to avenge myself on my enemies." So none of the people tasted food. ²⁵ Indeed, there was a honeycomb lying on the ground, ²⁶ and when the soldiers came to the comb the swarm had left it; yet no one would raise a hand to his mouth from it, because the people feared the oath. ²⁷ Jonathan, who had not heard that his father had put the people under oath, thrust out the end of the staff he was holding and dipped it into the honey. Then he raised it to his mouth and his eyes lit up. ²⁸ At this one of the soldiers spoke up: "Your father put the people under a strict oath, saying, 'Cursed be the man who takes food this day!' As a result the people are weak." ²⁹ Jonathan replied: "My father brings trouble to the land. Look how bright my eyes are from this small taste of honey I have had. ³⁰ What is

more, if the people had eaten freely today of their enemy's booty when they came across it, would not the slaughter of the Philistines by now have been the greater for it?" ³¹ After the Philistines were routed that day from Michmash to Aijalon, the people were completely exhausted. ³² So they pounced upon the spoil and took sheep, oxen and calves, slaughtering them on the ground and eating the flesh with blood. ³³ Informed that the people were sinning against the LORD by eating the flesh with blood, Saul said: "You have broken faith. Roll a large stone here for me." ³⁴ He continued: "Mingle with the people and tell each of them to bring his ox or his sheep to me. Slaughter it here and then eat, but you must not sin against the LORD by eating the flesh with blood." So everyone brought to the LORD whatever ox he had seized, and they slaughtered them there; ³⁵ and Saul built an altar to the LORD—this was the first time he built an altar to the LORD. ³⁶ Then Saul said, "Let us go down in pursuit of the Philistines by night, to plunder among them until daybreak and to kill them all off." They replied, "Do what you think best." But the priest said, "Let us consult God." ³⁷ So Saul inquired of God: "Shall I go down in pursuit of the Philistines? Will you deliver them into the power of Israel?" But he received no answer on this occasion. ³⁸ Saul then said, "Come here, all officers of the army. We must investigate and find out how this sin was committed today. ³⁹ As the LORD lives who has given victory to Israel, even if my son Jonathan has committed it, he shall surely die!" But none of the people answered him. ⁴⁰ So he said to all Israel, "Stand on one side, and I and my son Jonathan will stand on the other." The people responded, "Do what you think best." ⁴¹ And Saul said to the LORD, the God of Israel: "Why did you not answer your servant this time? If the blame for this resides in me or my son Jonathan, LORD, God of Israel, respond with Urim; but if this guilt is in your people Israel, respond with Thummim." Jonathan and Saul were designated, and the people went free. ⁴² Saul then said, "Cast lots between me and my son Jonathan." And Jonathan was designated. ⁴³ Saul said to Jonathan, "Tell me what you have done." Jonathan replied, "I only tasted a little honey from the end of the staff I was holding. Am I to die for this?" ⁴⁴ Saul said, "May God do thus and so to me if you do not indeed die, Jonathan!" ⁴⁵ But the army said to Saul: "Is Jonathan to die, though it was he who brought Israel this great victory? This must not be! As the LORD lives, not a single hair of his head shall fall to the ground, for God was with him in what he did today!" Thus the soldiers were able to rescue Jonathan from death. ⁴⁶ After that Saul gave up the pursuit of the Philistines, who returned to their own territory. ⁴⁷ After taking over the kingship of Israel, Saul waged war on all their surrounding enemies—Moab, the Ammonites, Aram, Beth-rehob, the king of Zobah, and the Philistines. Wherever he turned, he was successful ⁴⁸ and fought bravely. He defeated Amalek and delivered Israel from the hands of those who were plundering them. ⁴⁹ The sons of Saul were Jonathan, Ishvi, and Malchishua; his two daughters were named, the elder, Merob, and the younger, Michal. ⁵⁰ Saul's wife, who was named Ahinoam, was the daughter of Ahimaaz. The name of his general was Abner, son of Saul's uncle, Ner; ⁵¹ Kish, Saul's father, and Ner, Abner's father, were sons of Abiel. ⁵² An unremitting war was waged against the Philistines during Saul's lifetime. When Saul saw any strong or brave man, he took him into his service.

1 Samuel Chapter 15

¹ Samuel said to Saul: "It was I the LORD sent to anoint you king over his people Israel. Now, therefore, listen to the message of the LORD. ² This is what the LORD of hosts has to say: 'I will punish what Amalek did to Israel when he barred his way as he was coming up from Egypt. ³ Go, now, attack Amalek, and deal with him and all that he has under the ban. Do not spare him, but kill men and women, children and infants, oxen and sheep, camels and asses.'" ⁴ Saul alerted the soldiers, and at Telaim reviewed two hundred thousand foot soldiers and ten thousand men of Judah. ⁵ Saul went to the city of Amalek, and after setting an ambush in the wadi, ⁶ warned the Kenites: "Come! Leave Amalek and withdraw, that I may not have to destroy you with them, for you were kind to the Israelites when they came up from Egypt." After the Kenites left, ⁷ Saul routed Amalek from Havilah to the approaches of Shur, on the frontier of Egypt. ⁸ He took Agag, king of Amalek, alive, but on the rest of the people he put into effect the ban of destruction by the sword. ⁹ He and his troops spared Agag and the best of the fat sheep and oxen, and the lambs. They refused to carry out the doom on anything that was worthwhile, dooming only what was worthless and of no account. ¹⁰ Then the LORD spoke to Samuel: ¹¹ "I regret having made Saul king, for he has turned from me and has not kept my command." At this Samuel grew angry and cried out to the LORD all night. ¹² Early in the morning he went to meet Saul, but was informed that Saul had gone to Carmel, where he erected a trophy in his own honor, and that on his return he had passed on and gone down to Gilgal.

13 When Samuel came to him, Saul greeted him: "The LORD bless you! I have kept the command of the LORD." 14 But Samuel asked, "What, then, is the meaning of this bleating of sheep that comes to my ears, and the lowing of oxen that I hear?" 15 Saul replied: "They were brought from Amalek. The men spared the best sheep and oxen to sacrifice to the LORD, your God; but we have carried out the ban on the rest." 16 Samuel said to Saul: "Stop! Let me tell you what the LORD said to me last night." "Speak!" he replied. 17 Samuel then said: "Though little in your own esteem, are you not leader of the tribes of Israel? The LORD anointed you king of Israel 18 and sent you on a mission, saying, 'Go and put the sinful Amalekites under a ban of destruction. Fight against them until you have exterminated them.' 19 Why then have you disobeyed the LORD? You have pounced on the spoil, thus displeasing the LORD." 20 Saul answered Samuel: "I did indeed obey the LORD and fulfill the mission on which the LORD sent me. I have brought back Agag, and I have destroyed Amalek under the ban. 21 But from the spoil the men took sheep and oxen, the best of what had been banned, to sacrifice to the LORD their God in Gilgal." 22 But Samuel said: "Does the LORD so delight in holocausts and sacrifices as in obedience to the command of the LORD? Obedience is better than sacrifice, and submission than the fat of rams. 23 For a sin like divination is rebellion, and presumption is the crime of idolatry. Because you have rejected the command of the LORD, he, too, has rejected you as ruler." 24 Saul replied to Samuel: "I have sinned, for I have disobeyed the command of the LORD and your instructions. In my fear of the people, I did what they said. 25 Now forgive my sin, and return with me, that I may worship the LORD." 26 But Samuel said to Saul, "I will not return with you, because you rejected the command of the LORD and the LORD rejects you as king of Israel." 27 As Samuel turned to go, Saul seized a loose end of his mantle, and it tore off. 28 So Samuel said to him: "The LORD has torn the kingdom of Israel from you this day, and has given it to a neighbor of yours, who is better than you. 29 The Glory of Israel neither retracts nor repents, for he is not man that he should repent." 30 But he answered: "I have sinned, yet honor me now before the elders of my people and before Israel. Return with me that I may worship the LORD your God." 31 And so Samuel returned with him, and Saul worshiped the LORD. 32 Afterward Samuel commanded, "Bring Agag, king of Amalek, to me." Agag came to him struggling and saying, "So it is bitter death!" 33 And Samuel said, "As your sword has made women childless, so shall your mother be childless among women." Then he cut Agag down before the LORD in Gilgal. 34 Samuel departed for Ramah, while Saul went up to his home in Gibeah of Saul. 35 Never again, as long as he lived, did Samuel see Saul. Yet he grieved over Saul, because the LORD regretted having made him king of Israel.

1 Samuel Chapter 16

1 The LORD said to Samuel: "How long will you grieve for Saul, whom I have rejected as king of Israel? Fill your horn with oil, and be on your way. I am sending you to Jesse of Bethlehem, for I have chosen my king from among his sons." 2 But Samuel replied: "How can I go? Saul will hear of it and kill me." To this the LORD answered: "Take a heifer along and say, 'I have come to sacrifice to the LORD.' 3 Invite Jesse to the sacrifice, and I myself will tell you what to do; you are to anoint for me the one I point out to you." 4 Samuel did as the LORD had commanded him. When he entered Bethlehem, the elders of the city came trembling to meet him and inquired, "Is your visit peaceful, O seer?" 5 He replied: "Yes! I have come to sacrifice to the LORD. So cleanse yourselves and join me today for the banquet." He also had Jesse and his sons cleanse themselves and invited them to the sacrifice. 6 As they came, he looked at Eliab and thought, "Surely the LORD'S anointed is here before him." 7 But the LORD said to Samuel: "Do not judge from his appearance or from his lofty stature, because I have rejected him. Not as man sees does God see, because man sees the appearance but the LORD looks into the heart." 8 Then Jesse called Abinadab and presented him before Samuel, who said, "The Lord has not chosen him." 9 Next Jesse presented Shammah, but Samuel said, "The LORD has not chosen this one either." 10 In the same way Jesse presented seven sons before Samuel, but Samuel said to Jesse, "The LORD has not chosen any one of these." 11 Then Samuel asked Jesse, "Are these all the sons you have?" Jesse replied, "There is still the youngest, who is tending the sheep." Samuel said to Jesse, "Send for him; we will not begin the sacrificial banquet until he arrives here." 12 Jesse sent and had the young man brought to them. He was ruddy, a youth handsome to behold and making a splendid appearance. The LORD said, "There—anoint him, for this is he!" 13 Then Samuel, with the horn of oil in hand, anointed him in the midst of his brothers; and from that day on, the spirit of the LORD rushed upon David. When Samuel took his leave, he went to Ramah. 14 The spirit of the LORD had departed from Saul, and he was tormented, by an evil spirit sent by the LORD. 15 So the servants of Saul said to him: "Please! An evil spirit from God is tormenting you. 16 If your lordship will order it, we, your servants here in attendance on you, will look for a man skilled in playing the harp. When the evil spirit from God comes over you, he will play and you will feel better." 17 Saul then told his servants, "Find me a skillful harpist and bring him to me." 18 A servant spoke up to say: "I have observed that one of the sons of Jesse of Bethlehem is a skillful harpist. He is also a stalwart soldier, besides being an able speaker, and handsome. Moreover, the LORD is with him." 19 Accordingly, Saul dispatched messengers to ask Jesse to send him his son David, who was with the flock. 20 Then Jesse took five loaves of bread, a skin of wine, and a kid, and sent them to Saul by his son David. 21 Thus David came to Saul and entered his service. Saul became very fond of him, made him his armor-bearer, 22 and sent Jesse the message, "Allow David to remain in my service, for he meets with my approval." 23 Whenever the spirit from God seized Saul, David would take the harp and play, and Saul would be relieved and feel better, for the evil spirit would leave him.

1 Samuel Chapter 17

1 The Philistines rallied their forces for battle at Socoh in Judah and camped between Socoh and Azekah at Ephes-dammim. 2 Saul and the Israelites also gathered and camped in the Vale of the Terebinth, drawing up their battle line to meet the Philistines. 3 The Philistines were stationed on one hill and the Israelites on an opposite hill, with a valley between them. 4 A champion named Goliath of Gath came out from the Philistine camp; he was six and a half feet tall. 5 He had a bronze helmet on his head and wore a bronze corselet of scale armor weighing five thousand shekels, 6 and bronze greaves, and had a bronze scimitar slung from a baldric. 7 The shaft of his javelin was like a weaver's heddle-bar, and its iron head weighed six hundred shekels. His shield-bearer went before him. 8 He stood and shouted to the ranks of Israel: "Why come out in battle formation? I am a Philistine, and you are Saul's servants. Choose one of your men, and have him come down to me. 9 If he beats me in combat and kills me, we will be your vassals; but if I beat him and kill him, you shall be our vassals and serve us." 10 The Philistine continued: "I defy the ranks of Israel today. Give me a man and let us fight together." 11 Saul and all the men of Israel, when they heard this challenge of the Philistine, were dismayed and terror-stricken. 12 David was the son of an Ephrathite named Jesse, who was from Bethlehem in Judah. He had eight sons, and in the days of Saul was old and well on in years. 13 The three oldest sons of Jesse had followed Saul to war; these three sons who had gone off to war were named, the first-born Eliab, the second son Abinadab, and the third Shammah. 14 David was the youngest. While the three oldest had joined Saul, 15 David would go and come from Saul to tend his father's sheep at Bethlehem. 16 Meanwhile the Philistine came forward and took his stand morning and evening for forty days. 17 Now Jesse said to his son David: "Take this ephah of roasted grain and these ten loaves for your brothers, and bring them quickly to your brothers in the camp. 18 Also take these ten cheeses for the field officer. Greet your brothers and bring home some token from them. 19 Saul, and they, and all Israel are fighting against the Philistines in the Vale of the Terebinth." 20 Early the next morning, having left the flock with a shepherd, David set out on his errand, as Jesse had commanded him. He reached the barricade of the camp just as the army, on their way to the battleground, were shouting their battle cry. 21 The Israelites and the Philistines drew up opposite each other in battle array. 22 David entrusted what he had brought to the keeper of the baggage and hastened to the battle line, where he greeted his brothers. 23 While he was talking with them, the Philistine champion, by name Goliath of Gath, came up from the ranks of the Philistines and spoke as before, and David listened. 24 When the Israelites saw the man, they all retreated before him, very much afraid. 25 The Israelites had been saying: "Do you see this man coming up? He comes up to insult Israel. If anyone should kill him, the king would give him great wealth, and his daughter as well, and would grant exemption to his father's family in Israel." 26 David now said to the men standing by: "What will be done for the man who kills this Philistine and frees Israel of the disgrace? Who is this uncircumcised Philistine in any case, that he should insult the armies of the living God?" 27 They repeated the same words to him and said, "That is how the man who kills him will be rewarded." 28 When Eliab, his oldest brother, heard him speaking with the men, he grew angry with David and said: "Why did you come down? With whom have you left those sheep in the desert meanwhile? I know your arrogance and your evil intent. You came down to enjoy the battle!" 29 David replied, "What have I done now? - I was only talking." 30 Yet he turned from him to another and asked the same question; and everyone gave him the same answer as before. 31 The words that David had spoken were overheard and reported to Saul, who sent for him. 32 Then David spoke to Saul: "Let your majesty not

lose courage. I am at your service to go and fight this Philistine." 33 But Saul answered David, "You cannot go up against this Philistine and fight with him, for you are only a youth, while he has been a warrior from his youth." 34 Then David told Saul: "Your servant used to tend his father's sheep, and whenever a lion or bear came to carry off a sheep from the flock, 35 I would go after it and attack it and rescue the prey from its mouth. If it attacked me, I would seize it by the jaw, strike it, and kill it. 36 Your servant has killed both a lion and a bear, and this uncircumcised Philistine will be as one of them, because he has insulted the armies of the living God." 37 David continued: "The LORD, who delivered me from the claws of the lion and the bear, will also keep me safe from the clutches of this Philistine." Saul answered David, "Go! the LORD will be with you." 38 Then Saul clothed David in his own tunic, putting a bronze helmet on his head and arming him with a coat of mail. 39 David also girded himself with Saul's sword over the tunic. He walked with difficulty, however, since he had never tried armor before. He said to Saul, "I cannot go in these, because I have never tried them before." So he took them off. 40 Then, staff in hand, David selected five smooth stones from the wadi and put them in the pocket of his shepherd's bag. With his sling also ready to hand, he approached the Philistine. 41 With his shield-bearer marching before him, the Philistine also advanced closer and closer to David. 42 When he had sized David up, and seen that he was youthful, and ruddy, and handsome in appearance, he held him in contempt. 43 The Philistine said to David, "Am I a dog that you come against me with a staff?" Then the Philistine cursed David by his gods 44 and said to him, "Come here to me, and I will leave your flesh for the birds of the air and the beasts of the field." 45 David answered him: "You come against me with sword and spear and scimitar, but I come against you in the name of the LORD of hosts, the God of the armies of Israel that you have insulted. 46 Today the LORD shall deliver you into my hand; I will strike you down and cut off your head. This very day I will leave your corpse and the corpses of the Philistine army for the birds of the air and the beasts of the field; thus the whole land shall learn that Israel has a God. 47 All this multitude, too, shall learn that it is not by sword or spear that the LORD saves. For the battle is the LORD'S, and he shall deliver you into our hands." 48 The Philistine then moved to meet David at close quarters, while David ran quickly toward the battle line in the direction of the Philistine. 49 David put his hand into the bag and took out a stone, hurled it with the sling, and struck the Philistine on the forehead. The stone embedded itself in his brow, and he fell prostrate on the ground. 50 Thus David overcame the Philistine with sling and stone; he struck the Philistine mortally, and did it without a sword. 51 Then David ran and stood over him; with the Philistine's own sword (which he drew from its sheath) he dispatched him and cut off his head. When they saw that their hero was dead, the Philistines took to flight. 52 Then the men of Israel and Judah, with loud shouts, went in pursuit of the Philistines to the approaches of Gath and to the gates of Ekron, and Philistines fell wounded along the road from Shaaraim as far as Gath and Ekron. 53 On their return from the pursuit of the Philistines, the Israelites looted their camp. 54 David took the head of the Philistine and brought it to Jerusalem; but he kept Goliath's armor in his own tent. 55 When Saul saw David go out to meet the Philistine, he asked his general Abner, "Abner, whose son is that youth?" Abner replied, "As truly as your majesty is alive, I have no idea." 56 And the king said, "Find out whose son the lad is." 57 So when David returned from slaying the Philistine, Abner took him and presented him to Saul. David was still holding the Philistine's head. 58 Saul then asked him, "Whose son are you, young man?" David replied, "I am the son of your servant Jesse of Bethlehem."

1 Samuel Chapter 18

1 By the time David finished speaking with Saul, Jonathan had become as fond of David as if his life depended on him; he loved him as he loved himself. 2 Saul laid claim to David that day and did not allow him to return to his father's house. 3 And Jonathan entered into a bond with David, because he loved him as himself. 4 Jonathan divested himself of the mantle he was wearing and gave it to David, along with his military dress, and his sword, his bow and his belt. 5 David then carried out successfully every mission on which Saul sent him. So Saul put him in charge of his soldiers, and this was agreeable to the whole army, even to Saul's own officers. 6 At the approach of Saul and David on David's return after slaying the Philistine, women came out from each of the cities of Israel to meet King Saul, singing and dancing, with tambourines, joyful songs, and sistrums. 7 The women played and sang: "Saul has slain his thousands, and David his ten thousands." 8 Saul was very angry and resentful of the song, for he thought: "They give David ten thousands, but only thousands to me. All that remains for him is the kingship." 9 And from that day on, Saul was jealous of David. 10 The next day an evil spirit from God came over Saul, and he raged in his house. David was in attendance, playing the harp as at other times, while Saul was holding his spear. 11 Saul poised the spear, thinking to nail David to the wall, but twice David escaped him. 12 Saul then began to fear David, because the LORD was with him, but had departed from Saul himself. 13 Accordingly, Saul removed him from his presence by appointing him a field officer. So David led the people on their military expeditions, 14 and prospered in all his enterprises, for the LORD was with him. 15 Seeing how successful he was, Saul conceived a fear of David. 16 On the other hand, all Israel and Judah loved him, since he led them on their expeditions. 17 Saul said to David, "There is my older daughter, Merob, whom I will give you in marriage if you become my champion and fight the battles of the LORD." Saul had in mind, "I shall not touch him; let the Philistines strike him." 18 But David answered Saul: "Who am I? And who are my kin or my father's clan in Israel that I should become the king's son-in-law?" 19 However, when it was time for Saul's daughter Merob to be given to David, she was given in marriage to Adriel the Meholathite instead. 20 Now Saul's daughter Michal loved David, and it was reported to Saul, who was pleased at this, 21 for he thought, "I will offer her to him to become a snare for him, so that the Philistines may strike him." Thus for the second time Saul said to David, "You shall become my son-in-law today." 22 Saul then ordered his servants to speak to David privately and to say: "The king is fond of you, and all his officers love you. You should become the king's son-in-law." 23 But when Saul's servants mentioned this to David, he said: "Do you think it easy to become the king's son-in-law? I am poor and insignificant." 24 When his servants reported to him the nature of David's answer, 25 Saul commanded them to say this to David: "The king desires no other price for the bride than the foreskins of one hundred Philistines, that he may thus take vengeance on his enemies." Saul intended in this way to bring about David's death through the Philistines. 26 When the servants reported this offer to David, he was pleased with the prospect of becoming the king's son-in-law. Before the year was up, 27 David made preparations and sallied forth with his men and slew two hundred Philistines. He brought back their foreskins and counted them out before the king, that he might thus become the king's son-in-law. So Saul gave him his daughter Michal in marriage. 28 Saul thus came to recognize that the LORD was with David; besides, his own daughter Michal loved David. 29 Therefore Saul feared David all the more and was his enemy ever after. 30 The Philistine chiefs continued to make forays, but each time they took the field, David was more successful against them than any other of Saul's officers, and as a result acquired great fame.

1 Samuel Chapter 19

1 Saul discussed his intention of killing David with his son Jonathan and with all his servants. But Saul's son Jonathan, who was very fond of David, 2 told him: "My father Saul is trying to kill you. Therefore, please be on your guard tomorrow morning; get out of sight and remain in hiding. 3 I, however, will go out and stand beside my father in the countryside where you are, and will speak to him about you. If I learn anything, I will let you know." 4 Jonathan then spoke well of David to his father Saul, saying to him: "Let not your majesty sin against his servant David, for he has committed no offense against you, but has helped you very much by his deeds. 5 When he took his life in his hands and slew the Philistine, and the LORD brought about a great victory for all Israel through him, you were glad to see it. Why, then, should you become guilty of shedding innocent blood by killing David without cause?" 6 Saul heeded Jonathan's plea and swore, "As the LORD lives, he shall not be killed." 7 So Jonathan summoned David and repeated the whole conversation to him. Jonathan then brought David to Saul, and David served him as before. 8 When war broke out again, David went out to fight against the Philistines and inflicted a great defeat upon them, putting them to flight. 9 Then an evil spirit from the LORD came upon Saul as he was sitting in his house with spear in hand and David was playing the harp nearby. 10 Saul tried to nail David to the wall with the spear, but David eluded Saul, so that the spear struck only the wall, and David got away safe. 11 The same night, Saul sent messengers to David's house to guard it, that he might kill him in the morning. David's wife Michal informed him, "Unless you save yourself tonight, tomorrow you will be killed." 12 Then Michal let David down through a window, and he made his escape in safety. 13 Michal took the household idol and laid it in the bed, putting a net of goat's hair at its head and covering it with a spread. 14 When Saul sent messengers to arrest David, she said, "He is sick." 15 Saul, however, sent the messengers back to see David and commanded them, "Bring him up to me in the bed, that I may kill him." 16 But when the messengers entered, they found the household idol in the bed, with the net of goat's hair at its head. 17 Saul therefore asked Michal: "Why did you play this trick on me? You have helped my enemy to get away!" Michal answered Saul: "He threatened me, 'Let me

go or I will kill you.'" 18 Thus David got safely away; he went to Samuel in Ramah, informing him of all that Saul had done to him. Then he and Samuel went to stay in the sheds. 19 When Saul was told that David was in the sheds near Ramah, 20 he sent messengers to arrest David. But when they saw the band of prophets, presided over by Samuel, in a prophetic frenzy, they too fell into the prophetic state. 21 Informed of this, Saul sent other messengers, who also fell into the prophetic state. For the third time Saul sent messengers, but they too fell into the prophetic state. 22 Saul then went to Ramah himself. Arriving at the cistern of the threshing floor on the bare hilltop, he inquired, "Where are Samuel and David?", and was told, "At the sheds near Ramah." 23 As he set out from the hilltop toward the sheds, the spirit of God came upon him also, and he continued on in a prophetic condition until he reached the spot. At the sheds near Ramah 24 he, too, stripped himself of his garments and he, too, remained in the prophetic state in the presence of Samuel; all that day and night he lay naked. That is why they say, "Is Saul also among the prophets?"

1 Samuel Chapter 20

1 David fled from the sheds near Ramah, and went to Jonathan. "What have I done?" he asked him. "What crime or what offense does your father hold against me that he seeks my life?" 2 Jonathan answered him: "Heaven forbid that you should die! My father does nothing, great or small, without disclosing it to me. Why, then, should my father conceal this from me? This cannot be so!" 3 But David replied: "Your father is well aware that I am favored with your friendship, so he has decided, 'Jonathan must not know of this lest he be grieved.' Nevertheless, as the LORD lives and as you live, there is but a step between me and death." 4 Jonathan then said to David, "I will do whatever you wish." 5 David answered: "Tomorrow is the new moon, when I should in fact dine with the king. Let me go and hide in the open country until evening. 6 If it turns out that your father misses me, say, 'David urged me to let him go on short notice to his city Bethlehem, because his whole clan is holding its seasonal sacrifice there.' 7 If he says, 'Very well,' your servant is safe. But if he becomes quite angry, you can be sure he has planned some harm. 8 Do this kindness for your servant because of the LORD'S bond between us, into which you brought me: if I am guilty, kill me yourself! Why should you give me up to your father?" 9 But Jonathan answered: "Not I! If ever I find out that my father is determined to inflict injury upon you, I will certainly let you know." 10 David then asked Jonathan, "Who will tell me if your father gives you a harsh answer?" 11 Jonathan replied to David, "Come, let us go out into the field." When they were out in the open country together, 12 Jonathan said to David: "As the LORD, the God of Israel, lives, I will sound out my father about this time tomorrow. Whether he is well disposed toward David or not, I will send you the information. 13 Should it please my father to bring any injury upon you, may the LORD do thus and so to Jonathan if I do not apprise you of it and send you on your way in peace. May the LORD be with you even as he was with my father. 14 Only this: if I am still alive, may you show me the kindness of the LORD. But if I die, 15 never withdraw your kindness from my house. And when the LORD exterminates all the enemies of David from the surface of the earth, 16 the name of Jonathan must never be allowed by the family of David to die out from among you, or the LORD will make you answer for it." 17 And in his love for David, Jonathan renewed his oath to him, because he loved him as his very self. 18 Jonathan then said to him: "Tomorrow is the new moon; and you will be missed, since your place will be vacant. 19 On the following day you will be missed all the more. Go to the spot where you hid on the other occasion and wait near the mound there. 20 On the third day of the month I will shoot arrows, as though aiming at a target. 21 I will then send my attendant to go and recover the arrows. If in fact I say to him, 'Look, the arrow is this side of you; pick it up,' come, for you are safe. As the LORD lives, there will be nothing to fear. 22 But if I say to the boy, 'Look, the arrow is beyond you,' go, for the LORD sends you away. 23 However, in the matter which you and I have discussed, the LORD shall be between you and me forever." 24 So David hid in the open country. On the day of the new moon, when the king sat at table to dine, 25 taking his usual place against the wall, Jonathan sat facing him, while Abner sat at the king's side, and David's place was vacant. 26 Saul, however, said nothing that day, for he thought, "He must have become unclean by accident, and not yet have been cleansed." 27 On the next day, the second day of the month, David's place was vacant. Saul inquired of his son Jonathan, "Why has the son of Jesse not come to table yesterday or today?" 28 Jonathan answered Saul: "David urgently asked me to let him go to his city, Bethlehem. 29 'Please let me go,' he begged, 'for we are to have a clan sacrifice in our city, and my brothers insist on my presence. Now, therefore, if you think well of me, give me leave to visit my brothers.' That is why he has not come to the king's

table." 30 But Saul was extremely angry with Jonathan and said to him: "Son of a rebellious woman, do I not know that, to your own shame and to the disclosure of your mother's shame, you are the companion of Jesse's son? 31 Why, as long as the son of Jesse lives upon the earth, you cannot make good your claim to the kingship! So send for him, and bring him to me, for he is doomed." 32 But Jonathan asked his father Saul: "Why should he die? What has he done?" 33 At this Saul brandished his spear to strike him, and thus Jonathan learned that his father was resolved to kill David. 34 Jonathan sprang up from the table in great anger and took no food that second day of the month, for he was grieved on David's account, since his father had railed against him. 35 The next morning Jonathan went out into the field with a little boy for his appointment with David. 36 There he said to the boy, "Run and fetch the arrow." And as the boy ran, he shot an arrow beyond him in the direction of the city. 37 When the boy made for the spot where Jonathan had shot the arrow, Jonathan called after him, "The arrow is farther on!" 38 Again he called to his lad, "Hurry, be quick, don't delay!" Jonathan's boy picked up the arrow and brought it to his master. 39 The boy knew nothing; only Jonathan and David knew what was meant. 40 Then Jonathan gave his weapons to this boy of his and said to him, "Go, take them to the city." 41 When the boy had left, David rose from beside the mound and prostrated himself on the ground three times before Jonathan in homage. They kissed each other and wept aloud together. 42 At length Jonathan said to David, "Go in peace, in keeping with what we two have sworn by the name of the LORD: 'The LORD shall be between you and me, and between your posterity and mine forever.'"

1 Samuel Chapter 21

1 Then David departed on his way, while Jonathan went back into the city. 2 David went to Ahimelech, the priest of Nob, who came trembling to meet him and asked, "Why are you alone? Is there no one with you?" 3 David answered the priest: "The king gave me a commission and told me to let no one know anything about the business on which he sent me or the commission he gave me. For that reason, I have arranged a meeting place with my men. 4 Now what have you on hand? Give me five loaves, or whatever you can find." 5 But the priest replied to David, "I have no ordinary bread on hand, only holy bread; if the men have abstained from women, you may eat some of that." 6 David answered the priest: "We have indeed been segregated from women as on previous occasions. Whenever I go on a journey, all the young men are consecrated—even for a secular journey. All the more so today, when they are consecrated at arms!" 7 So the priest gave him holy bread, for no other bread was on hand except the showbread which had been removed from the LORD's presence and replaced by fresh bread when it was taken away. 8 One of Saul's servants was there that day, detained before the LORD; his name was Doeg the Edomite, and he was Saul's chief henchman. 9 David then asked Ahimelech, "Do you have a spear or a sword on hand? I brought along neither my sword nor my weapons, because the king's business was urgent." 10 The priest replied: "The sword of Goliath the Philistine, whom you killed in the Vale of the Terebinth, is here (wrapped in a mantle) behind an ephod. If you wish to take that, take it; there is no sword here except that one." David said: "There is none to match it. Give it to me!" 11 That same day David took to flight from Saul, going to Achish, king of Gath. 12 But the servants of Achish said, "Is this not David, the king of the land? During their dances do they not sing, 'Saul has slain his thousands, but David his ten thousands'?" 13 David took note of these remarks and became very much afraid of Achish, king of Gath. 14 So, as they watched, he feigned insanity and acted like a madman in their hands, drumming on the doors of the gate and drooling onto his beard. 15 Finally Achish said to his servants: "You see the man is mad. Why did you bring him to me? 16 Do I not have enough madmen, that you bring in this one to carry on in my presence? Should this fellow come into my house?"

1 Samuel Chapter 22

1 David left Gath and escaped to the cave of Adullam. When his brothers and the rest of his family heard about it, they came down to him there. 2 He was joined by all those who were in difficulties or in debt, or who were embittered, and he became their leader. About four hundred men were with him. 3 From there David went to Mizpeh of Moab and said to the king of Moab, "Let my father and mother stay with you, until I learn what God will do for me." 4 He left them with the king of Moab, and they stayed with him as long as David remained in the refuge. 5 But the prophet Gad said to David: "Do not remain in the refuge. Leave, and go to the land of Judah." And so David left and went to the forest of Hereth. 6 Now Saul heard that David and his men had been located. At the time he was sitting in Gibeah under a tamarisk tree on the high place, holding his spear, while all his servants were standing by. 7 So he said to them:

"Listen, men of Benjamin! Will the son of Jesse give all of you fields and vineyards? Will he make each of you an officer over a thousand or a hundred men, 8 that you have all conspired against me and no one tells me that my son has made an agreement with the son of Jesse? None of you shows sympathy for me or discloses to me that my son has stirred up my servant to be an enemy against me, as is the case today." 9 Then Doeg the Edomite, who was standing with the officers of Saul, spoke up: "I saw the son of Jesse come to Ahimelech, son of Ahitub, in Nob. 10 He consulted the LORD for him and gave him supplies, and the sword of Goliath the Philistine as well." 11 At this the king sent a summons to Ahimelech the priest, son of Ahitub, and to all his family who were priests in Nob; and they all came to the king. 12 Then Saul said, "Listen, son of Ahitub!" He replied, "Yes, my lord." 13 Saul asked him, "Why did you conspire against me with the son of Jesse by giving him food and a sword and by consulting God for him, that he might rebel against me and become my enemy, as is the case today?" 14 Ahimelech answered the king: "And who among all your servants is as loyal as David, the king's son-in-law, captain of your bodyguard, and honored in your own house? 15 Is this the first time I have consulted God for him? No indeed! Let not the king accuse his servant or anyone in my family of such a thing. Your servant knows nothing at all, great or small, about the whole matter." 16 But the king said, "You shall die, Ahimelech, with all your family." 17 The king then commanded his henchmen standing by: "Make the rounds and kill the priests of the LORD, for they assisted David. They knew he was a fugitive and yet failed to inform me." But the king's servants refused to lift a hand to strike the priests of the LORD. 18 The king therefore commanded Doeg, "You make the rounds and kill the priests!" So Doeg the Edomite went from one to the next and killed the priests himself, slaying on that day eighty-five who wore the linen ephod. 19 Saul also put the priestly city of Nob to the sword, including men and women, children and infants, and oxen, asses, and sheep. 20 One son of Ahimelech, son of Ahitub, named Abiathar, escaped and fled to David. 21 When Abiathar told David that Saul had slain the priests of the LORD, 22 David said to him: "I knew that day, when Doeg the Edomite was there, that he would surely tell Saul. I am responsible for the death of all your family. 23 Stay with me. Fear nothing; he that seeks your life must seek my life also. You are under my protection."

1 Samuel Chapter 23

1 David received information that the Philistines were attacking Keilah and plundering the threshing floors. 2 So he consulted the LORD, inquiring, "Shall I go and defeat these Philistines?" The LORD answered, "Go, for you will defeat the Philistines and rescue Keilah." 3 But David's men said to him: "We are afraid here in Judah. How much more so if we go to Keilah against the forces of the Philistines!" 4 Again David consulted the LORD, who answered, "Go down to Keilah, for I will deliver the Philistines into your power." 5 David then went with his men to Keilah and fought with the Philistines. He drove off their cattle and inflicted a severe defeat on them, and thus rescued the inhabitants of Keilah. 6 Abiathar, son of Ahimelech, who had fled to David, went down with David to Keilah, taking the ephod with him. 7 When Saul was told that David had entered Keilah, he said: "God has put him in my grip. Now he has shut himself in, for he has entered a city with gates and bars." 8 Saul then called all the people to war, in order to go down to Keilah and besiege David and his men. 9 When David found out that Saul was planning to harm him, he said to the priest Abiathar, "Bring forward the ephod." 10 David then said: "O LORD God of Israel, your servant has heard a report that Saul plans to come to Keilah, to destroy the city on my account. 11 Will they hand me over? And now: will Saul come down as your servant has heard? O LORD God of Israel, tell your servant." The LORD answered, "He will come down." 12 David then asked, "Will the citizens of Keilah deliver me and my men into the grasp of Saul?" And the LORD answered, "Yes." 13 So David and his men, about six hundred in number, left Keilah and wandered from place to place. When Saul was informed that David had escaped from Keilah, he abandoned the expedition. 14 David now lived in the refuges in the desert, or in the barren hill country near Ziph. Though Saul sought him continually, the LORD did not deliver David into his grasp. 15 David was apprehensive because Saul had come out to seek his life; but while he was at Horesh in the barrens near Ziph, 16 Saul's son, Jonathan, came down there to David and strengthened his resolve in the LORD. 17 He said to him: "Have no fear, my father Saul shall not lay a hand to you. You shall be king of Israel and I shall be second to you. Even my father Saul knows this." 18 They made a joint agreement before the LORD in Horesh, where David remained, while Jonathan returned to his home. 19 Some of the Ziphites went up to Saul in Gibeah and said, "David is hiding among us, now in the refuges, and again at Horesh, or on the hill of Hachilah, south of the wasteland. 20 Therefore, whenever

the king wishes to come down, let him do so. It will be our task to deliver him into the king's grasp." 21 Saul replied: "The LORD bless you for your sympathy toward me. 22 Go now and make sure once more! Take note of the place where he sets foot" (for he thought, perhaps they are playing some trick on me). 23 "Look around and learn in which of all the various hiding places he is holding out. Then come back to me with sure information, and I will go with you. If he is in the region, I will search him out among all the families of Judah." 24 So they went off to Ziph ahead of Saul. At this time David and his men were in the desert below Maon, in the Arabah south of the wasteland. 25 When Saul and his men came looking for him, David got word of it and went down to the gorge in the desert below Maon. Saul heard of this and pursued David into the desert below Maon. 26 As Saul moved along one rim of the gorge, David and his men took to the other. David was in anxious flight to escape Saul, and Saul and his men were attempting to outflank David and his men in order to capture them, 27 when a messenger came to Saul, saying, "Come quickly, because the Philistines have invaded the land." 28 Saul interrupted his pursuit of David and went to meet the Philistines. This is how that place came to be called the Gorge of Divisions.

1 Samuel Chapter 24

1 David then went up from there and stayed in the refuges behind Engedi. 2 And when Saul returned from the pursuit of the Philistines, he was told that David was in the desert near Engedi. 3 So Saul took three thousand picked men from all Israel and went in search of David and his men in the direction of the wild goat crags. 4 When he came to the sheepfolds along the way, he found a cave, which he entered to ease nature. David and his men were occupying the inmost recesses of the cave. 5 David's servants said to him, "This is the day of which the LORD said to you, 'I will deliver your enemy into your grasp; do with him as you see fit.'" So David moved up and stealthily cut off an end of Saul's mantle. 6 Afterward, however, David regretted that he had cut off an end of Saul's mantle. 7 He said to his men, "The LORD forbid that I should do such a thing to my master, the LORD'S anointed, as to lay a hand on him, for he is the Lord's anointed." 8 With these words David restrained his men and would not permit them to attack Saul. Saul then left the cave and went on his way. 9 David also stepped out of the cave, calling to Saul, "My lord the king!" When Saul looked back, David bowed to the ground in homage 10 and asked Saul: "Why do you listen to those who say, 'David is trying to harm you'? 11 You see for yourself today that the LORD just now delivered you into my grasp in the cave. I had some thought of killing you, but I took pity on you instead. I decided, 'I will not raise a hand against my lord, for he is the LORD'S anointed and a father to me.' 12 Look here at this end of your mantle which I hold. Since I cut off an end of your mantle and did not kill you, see and be convinced that I plan no harm and no rebellion. I have done you no wrong, though you are hunting me down to take my life. 13 The LORD will judge between me and you, and the LORD will exact justice from you in my case. I shall not touch you. 14 The old proverb says, 'From the wicked comes forth wickedness.' So I will take no action against you. 15 Against whom are you on campaign, O king of Israel? Whom are you pursuing? A dead dog, or a single flea! 16 The LORD will be the judge; he will decide between me and you. May he see this, and take my part, and grant me justice beyond your reach!" 17 When David finished saying these things to Saul, Saul answered, "Is that your voice, my son David?" And he wept aloud. 18 Saul then said to David: "You are in the right rather than I; you have treated me generously, while I have done you harm. 19 Great is the generosity you showed me today, when the LORD delivered me into your grasp and you did not kill me. 20 For if a man meets his enemy, does he send him away unharmed? May the LORD reward you generously for what you have done this day. 21 And now, since I know that you shall surely be king and that sovereignty over Israel shall come into your possession, 22 swear to me by the LORD that you will not destroy my descendants and that you will not blot out my name and family." 23 David gave Saul his oath and Saul returned home, while David and his men went up to the refuge.

1 Samuel Chapter 25

1 Samuel died, and all Israel gathered to mourn him; they buried him at his home in Ramah. Then David went down to the desert of Maon. 2 There was a man of Maon who had property in Carmel; he was very wealthy, owning three thousand sheep and a thousand goats. At this time he was present for the shearing of his flock in Carmel. 3 The man was named Nabal, his wife, Abigail. The woman was intelligent and attractive, but Nabal himself, a Calebite, was harsh and ungenerous in his behavior. 4 When David heard in the desert that Nabal was shearing his flock, 5 he sent ten young men, instructing them: "Go up to Carmel. Pay Nabal a visit and greet him in my name. 6 Say to him, 'Peace be with

you, my brother, and with your family, and with all who belong to you. [7] I have just heard that shearers are with you. Now, when your shepherds were with us, we did them no injury, neither did they miss anything all the while they were in Carmel. [8] Ask your servants and they will tell you so. Look kindly on these young men, since we come at a festival time. Please give your servants and your son David whatever you can manage.'" [9] When David's young men arrived, they delivered this message fully to Nabal in David's name, and then waited. [10] But Nabal answered the servants of David: "Who is David? Who is the son of Jesse? Nowadays there are many servants who run away from their masters. [11] Must I take my bread, my wine, my meat that I have slaughtered for my own shearers, and give them to men who come from I know not where?" [12] So David's young men retraced their steps and on their return reported to him all that had been said. [13] Thereupon David said to his men, "Let everyone gird on his sword." And so everyone, David included, girded on his sword. About four hundred men went up after David, while two hundred remained with the baggage. [14] But Nabal's wife Abigail was informed of this by one of the servants, who said: "David sent messengers from the desert to greet our master, but he flew at them screaming. [15] Yet these men were very good to us. We were done no injury, neither did we miss anything all the while we were living among them during our stay in the open country. [16] For us they were like a rampart night and day the whole time we were pasturing the sheep near them. [17] Now, see what you can do, for you must realize that otherwise evil is in store for our master and for his whole family. He is so mean that no one can talk to him." [18] Abigail quickly got together two hundred loaves, two skins of wine, five dressed sheep, five seahs of roasted grain, a hundred cakes of pressed raisins, and two hundred cakes of pressed figs, and loaded them on asses. [19] She then said to her servants, "Go on ahead; I will follow you." But she did not tell her husband Nabal. [20] As she came down through a mountain defile riding on an ass, David and his men were also coming down from the opposite direction. When she met them, [21] David had just been saying: "Indeed, it was in vain that I guarded all this man's possessions in the desert, so that he missed nothing. He has repaid good with evil. [22] May God do thus and so to David, if by morning I leave a single male alive among all those who belong to him." [23] As soon as Abigail saw David, she dismounted quickly from the ass and, falling prostrate on the ground before David, did him homage. [24] As she fell at his feet she said: "My lord, let the blame be mine. Please let your handmaid speak to you, and listen to the words of your handmaid. [25] Let not my lord pay attention to that worthless man Nabal, for he is just like his name. Fool is his name, and he acts the fool. I, your handmaid, did not see the young men whom my lord sent. [26] Now, therefore, my lord, as the LORD lives, and as you live, it is the LORD who has kept you from shedding blood and from avenging yourself personally. May your enemies and those who seek to harm my lord become as Nabal! [27] Accept this present, then, which your maidservant has brought for my lord, and let it be given to the young men who follow my lord. [28] Please forgive the transgression of your handmaid, for the LORD shall certainly establish a lasting dynasty for my lord, because your lordship is fighting the battles of the LORD, and there is no evil to be found in you your whole life long. [29] If anyone rises to pursue you and to seek your life, may the life of my lord be bound in the bundle of the living in the care of the LORD your God; but may he hurl out the lives of your enemies as from the hollow of a sling. [30] And when the LORD carries out for my lord the promise of success he has made concerning you, and appoints you as commander over Israel, [31] you shall not have this as a qualm or burden on your conscience, my lord, for having shed innocent blood or for having avenged yourself personally. When the LORD confers this benefit on your lordship, remember your handmaid." [32] David said to Abigail: "Blessed be the LORD, the God of Israel, who sent you to meet me today. [33] Blessed be your good judgment and blessed be you yourself, who this day have prevented me from shedding blood and from avenging myself personally. [34] Otherwise, as the LORD, the God of Israel, lives, who has restrained me from harming you, if you had not come so promptly to meet me, by dawn Nabal would not have had a single man or boy left alive." [35] David then took from her what she had brought him and said to her: "Go up to your home in peace! See, I have granted your request as a personal favor." [36] When Abigail came to Nabal, there was a drinking party in his house like that of a king, and Nabal was merry because he was very drunk. So she told him nothing at all before daybreak the next morning. [37] But then, when Nabal had become sober, his wife told him what had happened. At this his courage died within him, and he became like a stone. [38] About ten days later the LORD struck him and he died. [39] On hearing that Nabal was dead, David said: "Blessed be the LORD, who has requited the insult I received at the hand of Nabal, and who restrained his servant from doing evil, but has punished Nabal for his own evil deeds." David then sent a proposal of marriage to Abigail. [40] When David's servants came to Abigail in Carmel, they said to her, "David has sent us to you that he may take you as his wife." [41] Rising and bowing to the ground, she answered, "Your handmaid would become a slave to wash the feet of my lord's servants." [42] She got up immediately, mounted an ass, and followed David's messengers, with her five maids following in attendance upon her. She became his wife, [43] and David also married Ahinoam of Jezreel. Thus both of them were his wives; but Saul gave David's wife Michal, Saul's own daughter, to Palti, son of Laish, who was from Gallim.

1 Samuel Chapter 26

[1] Men from Ziph came to Saul in Gibeah, reporting that David was hiding on the hill of Hachilah at the edge of the wasteland. [2] So Saul went off down to the desert of Ziph with three thousand picked men of Israel, to search for David in the desert of Ziph. [3] Saul camped beside the road on the hill of Hachilah, at the edge of the wasteland. David, who was living in the desert, saw that Saul had come into the desert after him [4] and sent out scouts, who confirmed Saul's arrival. [5] David himself then went to the place where Saul was encamped and examined the spot where Saul and Abner, son of Ner, the general, had their sleeping quarters. Saul's were within the barricade, and all his soldiers were camped around him. [6] David asked Ahimelech the Hittite, and Abishai, son of Zeruiah and brother of Joab, "Who will go down into the camp with me to Saul?" Abishai replied, "I will." [7] So David and Abishai went among Saul's soldiers by night and found Saul lying asleep within the barricade, with his spear thrust into the ground at his head and Abner and his men sleeping around him. [8] Abishai whispered to David: "God has delivered your enemy into your grasp this day. Let me nail him to the ground with one thrust of the spear; I will not need a second thrust!" [9] But David said to Abishai, "Do not harm him, for who can lay hands on the LORD'S anointed and remain unpunished? [10] As the LORD lives," David continued, "it must be the LORD himself who will strike him, whether the time comes for him to die, or he goes out and perishes in battle. [11] But the LORD forbid that I touch his anointed! Now take the spear which is at his head and the water jug, and let us be on our way." [12] So David took the spear and the water jug from their place at Saul's head, and they got away without anyone's seeing or knowing or awakening. All remained asleep, because the LORD had put them into a deep slumber. [13] Going across to an opposite slope, David stood on a remote hilltop at a great distance from Abner, son of Ner, and the troops. [14] He then shouted, "Will you not answer, Abner?" And Abner answered, "Who is it that calls me?" [15] David said to Abner: "Are you not a man whose like does not exist in Israel? Why, then, have you not guarded your lord the king when one of his subjects went to kill the king, your lord? [16] This is no creditable service you have performed. As the LORD lives, you people deserve death because you have not guarded your lord, the LORD'S anointed. Go, look: where are the king's spear and the water jug that was at his head?" [17] Saul recognized David's voice and asked, "Is that your voice, my son David?" David answered, "Yes, my lord the king." [18] He continued: "Why does my lord pursue his servant? What have I done? What evil do I plan? [19] Please, now, let my lord the king listen to the words of his servant. If the LORD has incited you against me, let an offering appease him; but if men, may they be cursed before the LORD, because they have exiled me so that this day I have no share in the LORD'S inheritance, but am told: 'Go serve other gods!' [20] Do not let my blood flow to the ground far from the presence of the LORD. For the king of Israel has come out to seek a single flea as if he were hunting partridge in the mountains." [21] Then Saul said: "I have done wrong. Come back, my son David, I will not harm you again, because you have held my life precious today. Indeed, I have been a fool and have made a serious mistake." [22] But David answered: "Here is the king's spear. Let an attendant come over to get it. [23] The LORD will reward each man for his justice and faithfulness. Today, though the LORD delivered you into my grasp, I would not harm the LORD'S anointed. [24] As I valued your life highly today, so may the LORD value my life highly and deliver me from all difficulties." [25] Then Saul said to David: "Blessed are you, my son David! You shall certainly succeed in whatever you undertake." David went his way, and Saul returned to his home.

1 Samuel Chapter 27

[1] But David said to himself: "I shall perish some day at the hand of Saul. I have no choice but to escape to the land of the Philistines; then Saul will give up his continual search for me throughout the land of Israel, and I shall be out of his reach." [2] Accordingly, David departed with his six hundred men and went over to Achish, son of Maoch, king of Gath. [3] David and his men lived in Gath with Achish; each one had his family,

and David had his two wives, Ahinoam from Jezreel and Abigail, the widow of Nabal from Carmel. 4 When Saul was told that David had fled to Gath, he no longer searched for him. 5 David said to Achish: "If I meet with your approval, let me have a place to live in one of the country towns. Why should your servant live with you in the royal city?" 6 That same day Achish gave him Ziklag, which has, therefore, belonged to the kings of Judah up to the present time. 7 In all, David lived a year and four months in the country of the Philistines. 8 David and his men went up and made raids on the Geshurites, Girzites, and Amalekites—peoples living in the land between Telam, on the approach to Shur, and the land of Egypt. 9 In attacking the land David would not leave a man or woman alive, but would carry off sheep, oxen, asses, camels, and clothes. On his return he brought these to Achish, 10 who asked, "Whom did you raid this time?" And David answered, "The Negeb of Judah," or "The Negeb of Jerahmeel," or "The Negeb of the Kenites." 11 But David would not leave a man or woman alive to be brought to Gath, fearing that they would betray him by saying, "This is what David did." This was his custom as long as he lived in the country of the Philistines. 12 And Achish trusted David, thinking, "He must certainly be detested by his people Israel. I shall have him as my vassal forever."

1 Samuel Chapter 28

1 In those days the Philistines mustered their military forces to fight against Israel. So Achish said to David, "You realize, of course, that you and your men must go out on campaign with me to Jezreel." 2 David answered Achish, "Good! Now you shall learn what your servant can do." Then Achish said to David, "I shall appoint you my permanent bodyguard." 3 Now Samuel had died and, after being mourned by all Israel, was buried in his city, Ramah. Meanwhile Saul had driven mediums and fortune-tellers out of the land. 4 The Philistine levies advanced to Shunem and encamped. Saul, too, mustered all Israel; they camped on Gilboa. 5 When Saul saw the camp of the Philistines, he was dismayed and lost heart completely. 6 He therefore consulted the LORD; but the LORD gave no answer, whether in dreams or by the Urim or through prophets. 7 Then Saul said to his servants, "Find me a woman who is a medium, to whom I can go to seek counsel through her." His servants answered him, "There is a woman in Endor who is a medium." 8 So he disguised himself, putting on other clothes, and set out with two companions. They came to the woman by night, and Saul said to her, "Tell my fortune through a ghost; conjure up for me the one I ask you to." 9 But the woman answered him, "You are surely aware of what Saul has done, in driving the mediums and fortune-tellers out of the land. Why, then, are you laying snares for my life, to have me killed?" 10 But Saul swore to her by the LORD, "As the LORD lives, you shall incur no blame for this." 11 Then the woman asked him, "Whom do you want me to conjure up?" and he answered, "Samuel." 12 When the woman saw Samuel, she shrieked at the top of her voice and said to Saul, "Why have you deceived me? You are Saul!" 13 But the king said to her, "Have no fear. What do you see?" The woman answered Saul, "I see a preternatural being rising from the earth." 14 "What does he look like?" asked Saul. And she replied, "It is an old man who is rising, clothed in a mantle." Saul knew that it was Samuel, and so he bowed face to the ground in homage. 15 Samuel then said to Saul, "Why do you disturb me by conjuring me up?" Saul replied: "I am in great straits, for the Philistines are waging war against me and God has abandoned me. Since he no longer answers me through prophets or in dreams, I have called you to tell me what I should do." 16 To this Samuel said: "But why do you ask me, if the LORD has abandoned you and is with your neighbor? 17 The LORD has done to you what he foretold through me: he has torn the kingdom from your grasp and has given it to your neighbor David. 18 Because you disobeyed the LORD'S directive and would not carry out his fierce anger against Amalek, the LORD has done this to you today. 19 Moreover, the LORD will deliver Israel, and you as well, into the clutches of the Philistines. By tomorrow you and your sons will be with me, and the LORD will have delivered the army of Israel into the hands of the Philistines." 20 Immediately Saul fell full length on the ground, for he was badly shaken by Samuel's message. Moreover, he had no bodily strength left, since he had eaten nothing all that day and night. 21 Then the woman came to Saul, and seeing that he was quite terror-stricken, said to him: "Remember, your maidservant obeyed you: I took my life in my hands and fulfilled the request you made of me. 22 Now you, in turn, please listen to your maidservant. Let me set something before you to eat, so that you may have strength when you go on your way." 23 But he refused, saying, "I will not eat." However, when his servants joined the woman in urging him, he listened to their entreaties, got up from the ground, and sat on a couch. 24 The woman had a stall-fed calf in the house, which she now quickly slaughtered. Then taking flour, she kneaded it and baked unleavened bread. 25 She set the meal before Saul and his servants, and they ate. Then they stood up and left the same night.

1 Samuel Chapter 29

1 Now the Philistines had mustered all their forces in Aphek, and the Israelites were encamped at the spring of Harod near Jezreel. 2 As the Philistine lords were marching their groups of a hundred and a thousand, David and his men were marching in the rear guard with Achish. 3 The Philistine chiefs asked, "What are those Hebrews doing here?" And Achish answered them: "Why, that is David, the officer of Saul, king of Israel. He has been with me now for a year or two, and I have no fault to find with him from the day he came over to me until the present." 4 But the Philistine chiefs were angered at this and said to him: "Send that man back! Let him return to the place you picked out for him. He must not go down into battle with us, lest during the battle he become our enemy. For how else can he win back his master's favor, if not with the heads of these men of ours? 5 Is this not the David of whom they sing during their dances, 'Saul has slain his thousands, but David his ten thousands'?" 6 So Achish summoned David and said to him: "As the LORD lives, you are honest, and I should be pleased to have you active with me in the camp, for I have found nothing wrong with you from the day of your arrival to this day. But you are not welcome to the lords. 7 Withdraw peaceably, now, and do nothing that might displease the Philistine lords." 8 But David said to Achish: "What have I done? Or what have you against your servant from the first day I have been with you to this day, that I cannot go to fight against the enemies of my lord the king?" 9 "You know," Achish answered David, "that you are acceptable to me. But the Philistine chiefs have determined you are not to go up with us to battle. 10 So the first thing tomorrow, you and your lord's servants who came with you, go to the place I picked out for you. Do not decide to take umbrage at this; you are as acceptable to me as an angel of God. But make an early morning start, as soon as it grows light, and be on your way." 11 So David and his men left early in the morning to return to the land of the Philistines. The Philistines, however, went on up to Jezreel.

1 Samuel Chapter 30

1 Before David and his men reached Ziklag on the third day, the Amalekites had raided the Negeb and Ziklag, had stormed the city, and had set it on fire. 2 They had taken captive the women and all who were in the city, young and old, killing no one; they had carried them off when they left. 3 David and his men arrived at the city to find it burned to the ground and their wives, sons, and daughters taken captive. 4 Then David and those who were with him wept aloud until they could weep no more. 5 David's two wives, Ahinoam of Jezreel and Abigail, the widow of Nabal from Carmel, had also been carried off with the rest. 6 Now David found himself in great difficulty, for the men spoke of stoning him, so bitter were they over the fate of their sons and daughters. But with renewed trust in the LORD his God, 7 David said to Abiathar, the priest, son of Ahimelech, "Bring me the ephod!" When Abiathar brought him the ephod, 8 David inquired of the LORD, "Shall I pursue these raiders? Can I overtake them?" The LORD answered him, "Go in pursuit, for you shall surely overtake them and effect a rescue." 9 So David went off with his six hundred men and came as far as the Wadi Besor, where those who were to remain behind halted. 10 David continued the pursuit with four hundred men, but two hundred were too exhausted to cross the Wadi Besor and remained behind. 11 An Egyptian was found in the open country and brought to David. He was provided with food, which he ate, and given water to drink; 12 a cake of pressed figs and two cakes of pressed raisins were also offered to him. When he had eaten, he revived; he had not taken food nor drunk water for three days and three nights. 13 Then David asked him, "To whom do you belong, and where do you come from?" He replied: "I am an Egyptian, the slave of an Amalekite. My master abandoned me because I fell sick three days ago today. 14 We raided the Negeb of the Cherethites, the territory of Judah, and the Negeb of Caleb; and we set Ziklag on fire." 15 David then asked him, "Will you lead me down to this raiding party?" He answered, "Swear to me by God that you will not kill me or deliver me to my master, and I will lead you to the raiding party." 16 He did lead them, and there were the Amalekites scattered all over the ground, eating, drinking, and in a festive mood because of all the rich booty they had taken from the land of the Philistines and from the land of Judah. 17 From dawn to sundown David attacked them, putting them under the ban so that none escaped except four hundred young men, who mounted their camels and fled. 18 David recovered everything the Amalekites had taken and rescued his two wives. 19 Nothing was missing, small or great, booty or sons or daughters, of all that the Amalekites had taken. David brought back everything. 20 Moreover, David took all the sheep and oxen, and as they drove these before him, they shouted, "This is David's spoil!" 21 When David came

to the two hundred men who had been too exhausted to follow him, and whom he had left behind at the Wadi Besor, they came out to meet David and the men with him. On nearing them, David greeted them. 22 But all the stingy and worthless men among those who had accompanied David spoke up to say, "Since they did not accompany us, we will not give them anything from the booty, except to each man his wife and children. Let them take those along and be on their way." 23 But David said: "You must not do this, my brothers, after what the LORD has given us. He has protected us and delivered into our grip the band that came against us. 24 Who could agree with this proposal of yours? Rather, the share of the one who goes down to battle and that of the one who remains with the baggage shall be the same; they shall share alike." 25 And from that day forward he made it a law and a custom in Israel, as it still is today. 26 When David came to Ziklag, he sent part of the spoil to the elders of Judah, city by city, saying, "This is a gift to you from the spoil of the enemies of the LORD": 27 to those in Bethel, to those in Ramoth-negeb, to those in Jattir, 28 to those in Aroer, to those in Siphmoth, to those in Eshtemoa, 29 to those in Racal, to those in the Jerahmeelite cities, to those in the Kenite cities, 30 to those in Hormah, to those in Borashan, to those in Athach, 31 to those in Hebron, and to all the places frequented by David and his men.

1 Samuel Chapter 31

1 As they pressed their attack on Israel, with the Israelites fleeing before them and falling mortally wounded on Mount Gilboa, 2 the Philistines pursued Saul and his sons closely, and slew Jonathan, Abinadab, and Malchishua, sons of Saul. 3 The battle raged around Saul, and the archers hit him; he was pierced through the abdomen. 4 Then Saul said to his armor-bearer, "Draw your sword and run me through, lest these uncircumcised come and make sport of me." But his armor-bearer, badly frightened, refused to do it. So Saul took his own sword and fell upon it. 51 When the armor-bearer saw that Saul was dead, he too fell upon his sword and died with him. 6 Thus Saul, his three sons, and his armor-bearer died together on that same day. 7 When the Israelites on the slope of the valley and those along the Jordan saw that the men of Israel had fled and that Saul and his sons were dead, they too abandoned their cities and fled. Then the Philistines came and lived in those cities. 8 The day after the battle the Philistines came to strip the slain, and found Saul and his three sons lying on Mount Gilboa. 9 They cut off Saul's head and stripped him of his armor, and then sent the good news throughout the land of the Philistines to their idols and to the people. 10 They put his armor in the temple of Astarte, but impaled his body on the wall of Bethshan. 11 When the inhabitants of Jabesh-gilead heard what the Philistines had done to Saul, 122 all their warriors set out, and after marching throughout the night, removed the bodies of Saul and his sons from the wall of Beth-shan, and brought them to Jabesh, where they cremated them. 13 Then they took their bones and buried them under the tamarisk tree in Jabesh, and fasted for seven days.

II Samuel

2 Samuel Chapter 1

1 After the death of Saul, David returned from his defeat of the Amalekites and spent two days in Ziklag. 2 On the third day, a man came from Saul's camp, with his clothes torn and dirt on his head. Going to David, he fell to the ground in homage. 3 David asked him, "Where do you come from?" He replied, "I have escaped from the Israelite camp." 4 "Tell me what happened," David bade him. He answered that the soldiers had fled the battle and that many of them had fallen and were dead, among them Saul and his son Jonathan. 5 Then David said to the youth who was reporting to him, "How do you know that Saul and his son Jonathan are dead?" 6 The youthful informant replied: "It was by chance that I found myself on Mount Gilboa and saw Saul leaning on his spear, with chariots and horsemen closing in on him. 7 He turned around and, seeing me, called me to him. When I said, 'Here I am,' 8 he asked me, 'Who are you?' and I replied, 'An Amalekite.' 9 Then he said to me, 'Stand up to me, please, and finish me off, for I am in great suffering, yet fully alive.' 10 So I stood up to him and dispatched him, for I knew that he could not survive his wound. I removed the crown from his head and the armlet from his arm and brought them here to my lord." 11 David seized his garments and rent them, and all the men who were with him did likewise. 12 They mourned and wept and fasted until evening for Saul and his son Jonathan, and for the soldiers of the LORD of the clans of Israel, because they had fallen by the sword. 13 Then David said to the young man who had brought him the information, "Where are you from?" He replied, "I am the son of an Amalekite immigrant." 14 David said to him, "How is it that you were

not afraid to put forth your hand to desecrate the LORD'S anointed?" 15 David then called one of the attendants and said to him, "Come, strike him down"; and the youth struck him a mortal blow. 16 Meanwhile David said to him, "You are responsible for your own death, for you testified against yourself when you said, 'I dispatched the LORD'S anointed.'" 17 Then David chanted this elegy for Saul and his son Jonathan, 18 which is recorded in the Book of Jashar to be taught to the Judahites. He sang: 19 "Alas! the glory of Israel, Saul, slain upon your heights; how can the warriors have fallen! 20 Tell it not in Gath, herald it not in the streets of Ashkelon, lest the Philistine maidens rejoice, lest the daughters of the strangers exult! 211 Mountains of Gilboa, may there be neither dew nor rain upon you, nor upsurgings of the deeps! Upon you lie begrimed the warriors' shields, the shield of Saul, no longer anointed with oil. 22 From the blood of the slain, from the bodies of the valiant, the bow of Jonathan did not turn back, or the sword of Saul return unstained. 23 Saul and Jonathan, beloved and cherished, separated neither in life nor in death, swifter than eagles, stronger than lions! 24 Women of Israel, weep over Saul, who clothed you in scarlet and in finery, who decked your attire with ornaments of gold. 25 How can the warriors have fallen in the thick of the battle, slain upon your heights! 26 I grieve for you, Jonathan, my brother! most dear have you been to me; more precious have I held love for you than love for women. 27 How can the warriors have fallen, the weapons of war have perished!"

2 Samuel Chapter 2

1 After this David inquired of the LORD, "Shall I go up into one of the cities of Judah?" The LORD replied to him, "Yes." Then David asked, "Where shall I go?" He replied, "To Hebron." 2 So David went up there accompanied by his two wives, Ahinoam of Jezreel and Abigail, the widow of Nabal of Carmel. 3 David also brought up his men with their families, and they dwelt in the cities near Hebron. 4 Then the men of Judah came there and anointed David king of the Judahites. A report reached David that the men of Jabesh-gilead had buried Saul. 5 So David sent messengers to the men of Jabesh-gilead and said to them: "May you be blessed by the LORD for having done this kindness to your lord Saul in burying him. 6 And now may the LORD be kind and faithful to you. I, too, will be generous to you for having done this. 7 Take courage, therefore, and prove yourselves valiant men, for though your lord Saul is dead, the Judahites have anointed me their king." 8 Abner, son of Ner, Saul's general, took Ishbaal, son of Saul, and brought him over to Mahanaim, 9 where he made him king over Gilead, the Ashurites, Jezreel, Ephraim, Benjamin, and the rest of Israel. 10 Ishbaal, son of Saul, was forty years old when he became king over Israel, and he reigned for two years. The Judahites alone followed David. 11 In all, David spent seven years and six months in Hebron as king of the Judahites. 12 Now Abner, son of Ner, and the servants of Ishbaal, Saul's son, left Mahanaim for Gibeon. 13 Joab, son of Zeruiah, and David's servants also set out and met them at the pool of Gibeon. And they sat down, one group on one side of the pool and the other on the opposite side. 14 Then Abner said to Joab, "Let the young men rise and perform for us." Joab replied, "All right!" 15 So they rose and were counted off: twelve of the Benjaminites of Ishbaal, son of Saul, and twelve of David's servants. 16 Then each one grasped his opponent's head and thrust his sword into his opponent's side, and all fell down together. And so that place, which is in Gibeon, was named the Field of the Sides. 17 After a very fierce battle that day, Abner and the men of Israel were defeated by David's servants. 18 The three sons of Zeruiah were there—Joab, Abishai, and Asahel. Asahel, who was as fleet of foot as a gazelle in the open field, 19 set out after Abner, turning neither right nor left in his pursuit. 20 Abner turned around and said, "Is that you, Asahel?" He replied, "Yes." 21 Abner said to him, "Turn right or left; seize one of the young men and take what you can strip from him." But Asahel would not desist from his pursuit. 22 Once more Abner said to Asahel: "Stop pursuing me! Why must I strike you to the ground? How could I face your brother Joab?" 23 Still he refused to stop. So Abner struck him in the abdomen with the heel of his javelin, and the weapon protruded from his back. He fell there and died on the spot. And all who came to the place where Asahel had fallen and died, came to a halt. 24 Joab and Abishai, however, continued the pursuit of Abner. The sun had gone down when they came to the hill of Ammah which lies east of the valley toward the desert near Geba. 25 Here the Benjaminites rallied around Abner, forming a single group, and made a stand on the hilltop. 26 Then Abner called to Joab and said: "Must the sword destroy to the utmost? Do you not know that afterward there will be bitterness? How much longer will you refrain from ordering the people to stop the pursuit of their brothers?" 27 Joab replied, "As God lives, if you had not spoken, the soldiers would not have been withdrawn from the pursuit of their brothers until morning." 28 Joab then sounded the horn, and

all the soldiers came to a halt, pursuing Israel no farther and fighting no more. 29 Abner and his men marched all night long through the Arabah, crossed the Jordan, marched all through the morning, and came to Mahanaim. 30 Joab, after interrupting the pursuit of Abner, assembled all the men. Besides Asahel, nineteen other servants of David were missing. 31 But David's servants had fatally wounded three hundred and sixty men of Benjamin, followers of Abner. 32 They took up Asahel and buried him in his father's tomb in Bethlehem. Joab and his men made an all-night march, and dawn found them in Hebron.

2 Samuel Chapter 3

1 There followed a long war between the house of Saul and that of David, in which David grew stronger, but the house of Saul weaker. 2 Sons were born to David in Hebron: his first-born, Amnon, of Ahinoam from Jezreel; 3 the second, Chileab, of Abigail the widow of Nabal of Carmel; the third, Absalom, son of Maacah the daughter of Talmai, king of Geshur; 4 the fourth, Adonijah, son of Haggith; the fifth, Shephatiah, son of Abital; 5 and the sixth, Ithream, of David's wife Eglah. These were born to David in Hebron. 6 During the war between the house of Saul and that of David, Abner was gaining power in the house of Saul. 7 Now Saul had had a concubine, Rizpah, the daughter of Aiah. And Ishbaal, son of Saul, said to Abner, "Why have you been intimate with my father's concubine?" 8 Enraged at the words of Ishbaal, Abner said, "Am I a dog's head in Judah? At present I am doing a kindness to the house of your father Saul, to his brothers and his friends, by keeping you out of David's clutches; yet this day you charge me with a crime involving a woman! 9 May God do thus and so to Abner if I do not carry out for David what the LORD swore to him - 10 that is, take away the kingdom from the house of Saul and establish the throne of David over Israel and over Judah from Dan to Beersheba." 11 In his fear of Abner, Ishbaal was no longer able to say a word to him. 12 Then Abner sent messengers to David in Telam, where he was at the moment, to say, "Make an agreement with me, and I will aid you by bringing all Israel over to you." 13 He replied, "Very well, I will make an agreement with you. But one thing I require of you. You must not appear before me unless you bring back Michal, Saul's daughter, when you come to present yourself to me." 14 At the same time David sent messengers to Ishbaal, son of Saul, to say, "Give me my wife Michal, whom I espoused by paying a hundred Philistine foreskins." 15 Ishbaal sent for her and took her away from her husband Paltiel, son of Laish, 16 who followed her weeping as far as Bahurim. But Abner said to him, "Go back!" And he turned back. 17 Abner then said in discussion with the elders of Israel: "For a long time you have been seeking David as your king. 18 Now take action, for the LORD has said of David, 'By my servant David I will save my people Israel from the grasp of the Philistines and from the grasp of all their enemies.'" 19 Abner also spoke personally to Benjamin, and then went to make his own report to David in Hebron concerning all that would be agreeable to Israel and to the whole house of Benjamin. 20 When Abner, accompanied by twenty men, came to David in Hebron, David prepared a feast for Abner and for the men who were with him. 21 Then Abner said to David, "I will now go to assemble all Israel for my lord the king, that they may make an agreement with you; you will then be king over all whom you wish to rule." So David bade Abner farewell, and he went away in peace. 22 Just then David's servants and Joab were coming in from an expedition, bringing much plunder with them. Abner, having been dismissed by David, was no longer with him in Hebron but had gone his way in peace. 23 When Joab and the whole force he had with him arrived, he was informed, "Abner, son of Ner, came to David; he has been sent on his way in peace." 24 So Joab went to the king and said: "What have you done? Abner came to you. Why did you let him go peacefully on his way? 25 Are you not aware that Abner came to deceive you and to learn the ins and outs of all that you are doing?" 26 Joab then left David, and without David's knowledge sent messengers after Abner, who brought him back from the cistern of Sirah. 27 When Abner returned to Hebron, Joab took him aside within the city gate as though to speak with him privately. There he stabbed him in the abdomen, and he died in revenge for the killing of Joab's brother Asahel. 28 Later David heard of it and said: "Before the LORD; I and my kingdom are forever innocent. 29 May the full responsibility for the death of Abner, son of Ner, be laid to Joab and to all his family. May the men of Joab's family never be without one suffering from a discharge, or a leper, or one unmanly, or one falling by the sword, or one in need of bread!" 30 (Joab and his brother Abishai had lain in wait for Abner because he killed their brother Asahel in battle at Gibeon.) 31 Then David said to Joab and to all the people who were with him, "Rend your garments, gird yourselves with sackcloth, and mourn over Abner." King David himself followed the bier. 32 When they had buried Abner in Hebron, the king wept aloud at the grave of Abner, and the people also wept. 33 And the king sang this elegy over Abner: "Would Abner

have died like a fool? 34 Your hands were not bound with chains, nor your feet placed in fetters; As men fall before the wicked, you fell." And all the people continued to weep for him. 35 Then they went to console David with food while it was still day. But David swore, "May God do thus and so to me if I eat bread or anything else before sunset." 36 All the people noted this with approval, just as they were pleased with everything that the king did. 37 So on that day all the people and all Israel came to know that the king had no part in the killing of Abner, son of Ner. 38 The king then said to his servants: "You must recognize that a great general has fallen today in Israel. 39 Although I am the anointed king, I am weak this day, and these men, the sons of Zeruiah, are too ruthless for me. May the LORD requite the evildoer in accordance with his evil deed."

2 Samuel Chapter 4

1 When Ishbaal, son of Saul, heard that Abner had died in Hebron, he ceased to resist and all Israel was alarmed. 2 Ishbaal, son of Saul, had two company leaders named Baanah and Rechab, sons of Rimmon the Beerothite, of the tribe of Benjamin. (Beeroth, too, was ascribed to Benjamin: 3 the Beerothites fled to Gittaim, where they have been resident aliens to this day. 4 Jonathan, son of Saul, had a son named Meribbaal with crippled feet. He was five years old when the news about Saul and Jonathan came from Jezreel, and his nurse took him up and fled. But in their hasty flight, he fell and became lame.) 5 The sons of Rimmon the Beerothite, Rechab and Baanah, came into the house of Ishbaal during the heat of the day, while he was taking his siesta. 6 The portress of the house had dozed off while sifting wheat, and was asleep. So Rechab and his brother Baanah slipped past 7 and entered the house while Ishbaal was lying asleep in his bedroom. They struck and killed him, and cut off his head. Then, taking the head, they traveled on the Arabah road all night long. 8 They brought the head of Ishbaal to David in Hebron and said to the king: "This is the head of Ishbaal, son of your enemy Saul, who sought your life. Thus has the LORD this day avenged my lord the king on Saul and his posterity." 9 But David replied to Rechab and his brother Baanah, sons of Rimmon the Beerothite: "As the LORD lives, who rescued me from all difficulty, 10 in Ziklag I seized and put to death the man who informed me of Saul's death, thinking himself the bearer of good news for which I ought to give him a reward. 11 How much more now, when wicked men have slain an innocent man in bed at home, must I hold you responsible for his death and destroy you from the earth!" 12 So at a command from David, the young men killed them and cut off their hands and feet, hanging them up near the pool in Hebron. But he took the head of Ishbaal and buried it in Abner's grave in Hebron.

2 Samuel Chapter 5

1 All the tribes of Israel came to David in Hebron and said: "Here we are, your bone and your flesh. 2 In days past, when Saul was our king, it was you who led the Israelites out and brought them back. And the LORD said to you, 'You shall shepherd my people Israel and shall be commander of Israel.'" 3 When all the elders of Israel came to David in Hebron, King David made an agreement with them there before the LORD, and they anointed him king of Israel. 4 David was thirty years old when he became king, and he reigned for forty years: 5 seven years and six months in Hebron over Judah, and thirty-three years in Jerusalem over all Israel and Judah. 6 Then the king and his men set out for Jerusalem against the Jebusites who inhabited the region. David was told, "You cannot enter here: the blind and the lame will drive you away!" which was their way of saying, "David cannot enter here." 7 But David did take the stronghold of Zion, which is the City of David. 8 On that day David said: "All who wish to attack the Jebusites must strike at them through the water shaft. The lame and the blind shall be the personal enemies of David." That is why it is said, "The blind and the lame shall not enter the palace." 9 David then dwelt in the stronghold, which was called the City of David; he built up the area from Millo to the palace. 10 David grew steadily more powerful, for the LORD of hosts was with him. 11 Hiram, king of Tyre, sent ambassadors to David; he furnished cedar wood, as well as carpenters and masons, who built a palace for David. 12 And David knew that the LORD had established him as king of Israel and had exalted his rule for the sake of his people Israel. 13 David took more concubines and wives in Jerusalem after he had come from Hebron, and more sons and daughters were born to him in Jerusalem. 14 These are the names of those who were born to him in Jerusalem: Shammua, Shobab, Nathan, Solomon, 15 Ibhar, Elishua, Nepheg, Japhia, 16 Elishama, Baaliada, and Eliphelet. 17 When the Philistines heard that David had been anointed king of Israel, they all took the field in search of him. On hearing this, David went down to the refuge. 18 The Philistines came and overran the valley of Rephaim. 19 David inquired of the LORD, "Shall I attack the Philistines - will you

deliver them into my grip?" The LORD replied to David, "Attack, for I will surely deliver the Philistines into your grip." 20 David then went to Baal-perazim, where he defeated them. He said, "The LORD has scattered my enemies before me like waters that have broken free." That is why the place is called Baal-perazim. 21 They abandoned their gods there, and David and his men carried them away. 22 But the Philistines came up again and overran the valley of Rephaim. 23 So David inquired of the LORD, who replied: "You must not attack frontally, but circle their rear and meet them before the mastic trees. 24 When you hear a sound of marching in the tops of the mastic trees, act decisively, for the LORD will have gone forth before you to attack the camp of the Philistines." 25 David obeyed the LORD'S command and routed the Philistines from Gibeon as far as Gezer.

2 Samuel Chapter 6

1 David again assembled all the picked men of Israel, thirty thousand in number. 2 Then David and all the people who were with him set out for Baala of Judah to bring up from there the ark of God, which bears the name of the LORD of hosts enthroned above the cherubim. 3 The ark of God was placed on a new cart and taken away from the house of Abinadab on the hill. Uzzah and Ahio, sons of Abinadab, guided the cart, 4 with Ahio walking before it, 5 while David and all the Israelites made merry before the LORD with all their strength, with singing and with citharas, harps, tambourines, sistrums and cymbals. 6 When they came to the threshing floor of Nodan, Uzzah reached out his hand to the ark of God and steadied it, for the oxen were making it tip. 7 But the LORD was angry with Uzzah; God struck him on that spot, and he died there before God. 8 David was disturbed because the LORD had vented his anger on Uzzah. (The place has been called Perez-uzzah down to the present day.) 9 David feared the LORD that day and said, "How can the ark of the LORD come to me?" 10 So David would not have the ark of the LORD brought to him in the City of David, but diverted it to the house of Obed-edom the Gittite. 11 The ark of the LORD remained in the house of Obed-edom the Gittite for three months, and the LORD blessed Obed-edom and his whole house. 12 When it was reported to King David that the LORD had blessed the family of Obed-edom and all that belonged to him, David went to bring up the ark of God from the house of Obed-edom into the City of David amid festivities. 13 As soon as the bearers of the ark of the LORD had advanced six steps, he sacrificed an ox and a fatling. 14 Then David, girt with a linen apron, came dancing before the LORD with abandon, 15 as he and all the Israelites were bringing up the ark of the LORD with shouts of joy and to the sound of the horn. 16 As the ark of the LORD was entering the City of David, Saul's daughter Michal looked down through the window and saw King David leaping and dancing before the LORD, and she despised him in her heart. 17 The ark of the LORD was brought in and set in its place within the tent David had pitched for it. Then David offered holocausts and peace offerings before the LORD. 18 When he finished making these offerings, he blessed the people in the name of the LORD of hosts. 19 He then distributed among all the people, to each man and each woman in the entire multitude of Israel, a loaf of bread, a cut of roast meat, and a raisin cake. With this, all the people left for their homes. 20 When David returned to bless his own family, Saul's daughter Michal came out to meet him and said, "How the king of Israel has honored himself today, exposing himself to the view of the slave girls of his followers, as a commoner might do!" 21 But David replied to Michal: "I was dancing before the LORD. As the LORD lives, who preferred me to your father and his whole family when he appointed me commander of the LORD'S people, Israel, not only will I make merry before the LORD, 22 but I will demean myself even more. I will be lowly in your esteem, but in the esteem of the slave girls you spoke of I will be honored." 23 And so Saul's daughter Michal was childless to the day of her death.

2 Samuel Chapter 7

1 When King David was settled in his palace, and the LORD had given him rest from his enemies on every side, 2 he said to Nathan the prophet, "Here I am living in a house of cedar, while the ark of God dwells in a tent!" 3 Nathan answered the king, "Go, do whatever you have in mind, for the LORD is with you." 4 But that night the LORD spoke to Nathan and said: 5 "Go, tell my servant David, 'Thus says the LORD: Should you build me a house to dwell in? 6 I have not dwelt in a house from the day on which I led the Israelites out of Egypt to the present, but I have been going about in a tent under cloth. 7 In all my wanderings everywhere among the Israelites, did I ever utter a word to any one of the judges whom I charged to tend my people Israel, to ask: Why have you not built me a house of cedar?' 8 Now then, speak thus to my servant David, 'The LORD of hosts has this to say: It was I who took you from the pasture and from the care of the flock to be commander of

my people Israel. 9 I have been with you wherever you went, and I have destroyed all your enemies before you. And I will make you famous like the great ones of the earth. 10 I will fix a place for my people Israel; I will plant them so that they may dwell in their place without further disturbance. Neither shall the wicked continue to afflict them as they did of old, 11 since the time I first appointed judges over my people Israel. I will give you rest from all your enemies. The LORD also reveals to you that he will establish a house for you. 12 And when your time comes and you rest with your ancestors, I will raise up your heir after you, sprung from your loins, and I will make his kingdom firm. 13 It is he who shall build a house for my name. And I will make his royal throne firm forever. 14 I will be a father to him, and he shall be a son to me. And if he does wrong, I will correct him with the rod of men and with human chastisements; 15 but I will not withdraw my favor from him as I withdrew it from your predecessor Saul, whom I removed from my presence. 16 Your house and your kingdom shall endure forever before me; your throne shall stand firm forever.'" 17 Nathan reported all these words and this entire vision to David. 18 Then King David went in and sat before the LORD and said, "Who am I, Lord GOD, and who are the members of my house, that you have brought me to this point? 19 Yet even this you see as too little, Lord GOD; you have also spoken of the house of your servant for a long time to come: this too you have shown to man, Lord GOD! 20 What more can David say to you? You know your servant, Lord GOD! 21 For your servant's sake and as you have had at heart, you have brought about this entire magnificent disclosure to your servant. 22 And so - 'Great are you, Lord GOD! There is none like you and there is no God but you, just as we have heard it told. 23 What other nation on earth is there like your people Israel, which God has led, redeeming it as his people; so that you have made yourself renowned by doing this magnificent deed, and by doing awe-inspiring things as you cleared nations and their gods out of the way of your people, which you redeemed for yourself from Egypt? 24 You have established for yourself your people Israel as yours forever, and you, LORD, have become their God. 25 And now, LORD God, confirm for all time the prophecy you have made concerning your servant and his house, and do as you have promised. 26 Your name will be forever great, when men say, 'The LORD of hosts is God of Israel,' and the house of your servant David stands firm before you. 27 It is you, LORD of hosts, God of Israel, who said in a revelation to your servant, 'I will build a house for you.' Therefore your servant now finds the courage to make this prayer to you. 28 And now, Lord GOD, you are God and your words are truth; you have made this generous promise to your servant. 29 Do, then, bless the house of your servant that it may be before you forever; for you, Lord GOD, have promised, and by your blessing the house of your servant shall be blessed forever."

2 Samuel Chapter 8

1 After this David attacked the Philistines and conquered them, wresting. . . from the Philistines. 2 He also defeated Moab and then measured them with a line, making them lie down on the ground. He told off two lengths of line for execution, and a full length to be spared. Thus the Moabites became tributary to David. 3 Next David defeated Hadadezer, son of Rehob, king of Zobah, when he went to reestablish his dominion at the Euphrates River. 4 David captured from him one thousand seven hundred horsemen and twenty thousand foot soldiers. And he hamstrung all the chariot horses, preserving only enough for a hundred chariots. 5 When the Arameans of Damascus came to the aid of Hadadezer, king of Zobah, David slew twenty-two thousand of them. 6 David then placed garrisons in Aram of Damascus, and the Arameans became subjects, tributary to David. The LORD brought David victory in all his undertakings. 7 David also took away the golden shields used by Hadadezer's servants and brought them to Jerusalem. (These Shishak, king of Egypt, took away when he came to Jerusalem in the days of Rehoboam, son of Solomon.) 8 From Tebah and Berothai, towns of Hadadezer, King David removed a very large quantity of bronze. 9 When Toi, king of Hamath, heard that David had defeated all the forces of Hadadezer, 10 he sent his son Hadoram to King David to greet him and to congratulate him for his victory over Hadadezer in battle, because Toi had been in many battles with Hadadezer. Hadoram also brought with him articles of silver, gold, and bronze. 11 These, too, King David consecrated to the LORD, together with the silver and gold he had taken from every nation he had conquered: 12 from Edom and Moab, from the Ammonites, from the Philistines, from the Amalekites, and from the plunder of Hadadezer, son of Rehob, king of Zobah. 13 On his return, David became famous for having slain eighteen thousand Edomites in the Salt Valley; 14 after which he placed garrisons in Edom. Thus all the Edomites became David's subjects, and the LORD brought David victory in all his undertakings. 15 David reigned over all Israel,

judging and administering justice to all his people. [16] Joab, son of Zeruiah, was in command of the army. Jehoshaphat, son of Ahilud, was chancellor. [17] Zadok, son of Ahitub, and Ahimelech, son of Abiathar, were priests. Shawsha was scribe. [18] Benaiah, son of Jehoiada, was in command of the Cherethites and Pelethites. And David's sons were priests.

2 Samuel Chapter 9

[1] David asked, "Is there any survivor of Saul's house to whom I may show kindness for the sake of Jonathan?" [2] Now there was a servant of the family of Saul named Ziba. He was summoned to David, and the king asked him, "Are you Ziba?" He replied, "Your servant." [3] Then the king inquired, "Is there any survivor of Saul's house to whom I may show God's kindness?" Ziba answered the king, "There is still Jonathan's son, whose feet are crippled." [4] The king said to him, "Where is he?" and Ziba answered, "He is in the house of Machir, son of Ammiel, in Lodebar." [5] So King David sent for him and had him brought from the house of Machir, son of Ammiel, in Lodebar. [6] When Meribbaal, son of Jonathan, son of Saul, came to David, he fell prostrate in homage. David said, "Meribbaal," and he answered, "Your servant." [7] "Fear not," David said to him, "I will surely be kind to you for the sake of your father Jonathan. I will restore to you all the lands of your grandfather Saul, and you shall always eat at my table." [8] Bowing low, he answered, "What is your servant that you should pay attention to a dead dog like me?" [9] The king then called Ziba, Saul's attendant, and said to him: "I am giving your lord's son all that belonged to Saul and to all his family. [10] You and your sons and servants must till the land for him. You shall bring in the produce, which shall be food for your lord's family to eat. But Meribbaal, your lord's son, shall always eat at my table." Ziba, who had fifteen sons and twenty servants, [11] said to the king, "Your servant shall do just as my lord the king has commanded him." And so Meribbaal ate at David's table like one of the king's sons. [12] Meribbaal had a young son whose name was Mica; and all the tenants of Ziba's family worked for Meribbaal. [13] But Meribbaal lived in Jerusalem, because he always ate at the king's table. He was lame in both feet.

2 Samuel Chapter 10

[1] Some time later the king of the Ammonites died, and his son Hanun succeeded him as king. [2] David thought, "I will be kind to Hanun, son of Nahash, as his father was kind to me." So David sent his servants with condolences to Hanun for the loss of his father. But when David's servants entered the country of the Ammonites, [3] the Ammonite princes said to their lord Hanun: "Do you think that David is honoring your father by sending men with condolences? Is it not rather to explore the city, to spy on it, and to overthrow it, that David has sent his messengers to you?" [4] Hanun, therefore, seized David's servants and, after shaving off half their beards and cutting away the lower halves of their garments at the buttocks, sent them away. [5] When he was told of it, King David sent out word to them, since the men were quite ashamed. "Stay in Jericho until your beards grow," he said, "and then come back." [6] In view of the offense they had given to David, the Ammonites sent for and hired twenty thousand Aramean foot soldiers from Beth-rehob and Zobah, as well as the king of Maacah with one thousand men, and twelve thousand men from Tob. [7] On learning this, David sent out Joab with the entire levy of trained soldiers. [8] The Ammonites came out and drew up in battle formation at the entrance of their city gate, while the Arameans of Zobah and Rehob and the men of Tob and Maacah remained apart in the open country. [9] When Joab saw the battle lines drawn up against him, both front and rear, he made a selection from all the picked troops of Israel and arrayed them against the Arameans. [10] He placed the rest of the soldiers under the command of his brother Abishai, who arrayed them against the Ammonites. [11] Joab said, "If the Arameans are stronger than I, you shall help me. But if the Ammonites are stronger than you, I will come to help you. [12] Be brave; let us prove our valor for the sake of our people and the cities of our God; the LORD will do what he judges best." [13] When Joab and the soldiers who were with him approached the Arameans for battle, they fled before him. [14] The Ammonites, seeing that the Arameans had fled, also fled from Abishai and withdrew into the city. Joab then ceased his attack on the Ammonites and returned to Jerusalem. [15] Then the Arameans responded to their defeat by Israel with a full mustering of troops; [16] Hadadezer sent for and enlisted Arameans from beyond the Euphrates. They came to Helam, with Shobach, general of Hadadezer's army, at their head. [17] On receiving this news, David assembled all Israel, crossed the Jordan, and went to Helam. The Arameans drew up in formation against David and fought with him. [18] But the Arameans gave way before Israel, and David's men killed seven hundred charioteers and forty thousand of the Aramean foot soldiers. Shobach,

general of the army, was struck down and died on the field. [19] All of Hadadezer's vassal kings, in view of their defeat by Israel, then made peace with the Israelites and became their subjects. And the Arameans were afraid to give further aid to the Ammonites.

2 Samuel Chapter 11

[1] At the turn of the year, when kings go out on campaign, David sent out Joab along with his officers and the army of Israel, and they ravaged the Ammonites and besieged Rabbah. David, however, remained in Jerusalem. [2] One evening David rose from his siesta and strolled about on the roof of the palace. From the roof he saw a woman bathing, who was very beautiful. [3] David had inquiries made about the woman and was told, "She is Bathsheba, daughter of Eliam, and wife of (Joab's armor-bearer) Uriah the Hittite." [4] Then David sent messengers and took her. When she came to him, he had relations with her, at a time when she was just purified after her monthly period. She then returned to her house. [5] But the woman had conceived, and sent the information to David, "I am with child." [6] David therefore sent a message to Joab, "Send me Uriah the Hittite." So Joab sent Uriah to David. [7] When he came, David questioned him about Joab, the soldiers, and how the war was going, and Uriah answered that all was well. [8] David then said to Uriah, "Go down to your house and bathe your feet." Uriah left the palace, and a portion was sent out after him from the king's table. [9] But Uriah slept at the entrance of the royal palace with the other officers of his lord, and did not go down to his own house. [10] David was told that Uriah had not gone home. So he said to Uriah, "Have you not come from a journey? Why, then, did you not go down to your house?" [11] Uriah answered David, "The ark and Israel and Judah are lodged in tents, and my lord Joab and your majesty's servants are encamped in the open field. Can I go home to eat and to drink and to sleep with my wife? As the LORD lives and as you live, I will do no such thing." [12] Then David said to Uriah, "Stay here today also, I shall dismiss you tomorrow." So Uriah remained in Jerusalem that day. On the day following, [13] David summoned him, and he ate and drank with David, who made him drunk. But in the evening he went out to sleep on his bed among his lord's servants, and did not go down to his home. [14] The next morning David wrote a letter to Joab which he sent by Uriah. [15] In it he directed: "Place Uriah up front, where the fighting is fierce. Then pull back and leave him to be struck down dead." [16] So while Joab was besieging the city, he assigned Uriah to a place where he knew the defenders were strong. [17] When the men of the city made a sortie against Joab, some officers of David's army fell, and among them Uriah the Hittite died. [18] Then Joab sent David a report of all the details of the battle, [19] instructing the messenger, "When you have finished giving the king all the details of the battle, [20] the king may become angry and say to you: 'Why did you go near the city to fight? Did you not know that they would shoot from the wall above? [21] Who killed Abimelech, son of Jerubbaal? Was it not a woman who threw a millstone down on him from the wall above, so that he died in Thebez? Why did you go near the wall?' Then you in turn shall say, 'Your servant Uriah the Hittite is also dead.'" [22] The messenger set out, and on his arrival he relayed to David all the details as Joab had instructed him. [23] He told David: "The men had us at a disadvantage and came out into the open against us, but we pushed them back to the entrance of the city gate. [24] Then the archers shot at your servants from the wall above, and some of the king's servants died, among them your servant Uriah." [25] David said to the messenger: "This is what you shall convey to Joab: 'Do not be chagrined at this, for the sword devours now here and now there. Strengthen your attack on the city and destroy it.' Encourage him." [26] When the wife of Uriah heard that her husband had died, she mourned her lord. [27] But once the mourning was over, David sent for her and brought her into his house. She became his wife and bore him a son. But the LORD was displeased with what David had done.

2 Samuel Chapter 12

[1] The LORD sent Nathan to David, and when he came to him, he said: "Judge this case for me! In a certain town there were two men, one rich, the other poor. [2] The rich man had flocks and herds in great numbers. [3] But the poor man had nothing at all except one little ewe lamb that he had bought. He nourished her, and she grew up with him and his children. She shared the little food he had and drank from his cup and slept in his bosom. She was like a daughter to him. [4] Now, the rich man received a visitor, but he would not take from his own flocks and herds to prepare a meal for the wayfarer who had come to him. Instead he took the poor man's ewe lamb and made a meal of it for his visitor." [5] David grew very angry with that man and said to Nathan: "As the LORD lives, the man who has done this merits death! [6] He shall restore the ewe lamb fourfold because he has done this and has had no pity." [7] Then Nathan said to David: "You are the man! Thus says the LORD God of

Israel: 'I anointed you king of Israel. I rescued you from the hand of Saul. ⁸ I gave you your lord's house and your lord's wives for your own. I gave you the house of Israel and of Judah. And if this were not enough, I could count up for you still more. ⁹ Why have you spurned the LORD and done evil in his sight? You have cut down Uriah the Hittite with the sword; you took his wife as your own, and him you killed with the sword of the Ammonites. ¹⁰ Now, therefore, the sword shall never depart from your house, because you have despised me and have taken the wife of Uriah to be your wife.' ¹¹ Thus says the LORD: 'I will bring evil upon you out of your own house. I will take your wives while you live to see it, and will give them to your neighbor. He shall lie with your wives in broad daylight. ¹² You have done this deed in secret, but I will bring it about in the presence of all Israel, and with the sun looking down.'" ¹³ Then David said to Nathan, "I have sinned against the LORD." Nathan answered David: "The LORD on his part has forgiven your sin: you shall not die. ¹⁴ But since you have utterly spurned the LORD by this deed, the child born to you must surely die." ¹⁵ Then Nathan returned to his house. The LORD struck the child that the wife of Uriah had borne to David, and it became desperately ill. ¹⁶ David besought God for the child. He kept a fast, retiring for the night to lie on the ground clothed in sackcloth. ¹⁷ The elders of his house stood beside him urging him to rise from the ground; but he would not, nor would he take food with them. ¹⁸ On the seventh day, the child died. David's servants, however, were afraid to tell him that the child was dead, for they said: "When the child was alive, we spoke to him, but he would not listen to what we said. How can we tell him the child is dead? He may do some harm!" ¹⁹ But David noticed his servants whispering among themselves and realized that the child was dead. He asked his servants, "Is the child dead?" They replied, "Yes, he is." ²⁰ Rising from the ground, David washed and anointed himself, and changed his clothes. Then he went to the house of the LORD and worshiped. He returned to his own house, where at his request food was set before him, and he ate. ²¹ His servants said to him: "What is this you are doing? While the child was living, you fasted and wept and kept vigil; now that the child is dead, you rise and take food." ²² He replied: "While the child was living, I fasted and wept, thinking, 'Perhaps the LORD will grant me the child's life.' ²³ But now he is dead. Why should I fast? Can I bring him back again? I shall go to him, but he will not return to me." ²⁴ Then David comforted his wife Bathsheba. He went and slept with her; and she conceived and bore him a son, who was named Solomon. The LORD loved him ²⁵ and sent the prophet Nathan to name him Jedidiah, on behalf of the LORD. ²⁶ Joab fought against Rabbah of the Ammonites and captured this royal city. ²⁷ He sent messengers to David with the word: "I have fought against Rabbah and have taken the water-city. ²⁸ Therefore, assemble the rest of the soldiers, join the siege against the city and capture it, lest it be I that capture the city and it be credited to me." ²⁹ So David assembled the rest of the soldiers and went to Rabbah. When he had fought against it and captured it, ³⁰ he took the crown from Milcom's head. It weighed a talent, of gold and precious stones; it was placed on David's head. He brought out immense booty from the city, ³¹ and also led away the inhabitants, whom he assigned to work with saws, iron picks, and iron axes, or put to work at the brickmold. This is what he did to all the Ammonite cities. David and all the soldiers then returned to Jerusalem.

2 Samuel Chapter 13

¹ Some time later the following incident occurred. David's son Absalom had a beautiful sister named Tamar, and David's son Amnon loved her. ² He was in such straits over his sister Tamar that he became sick; since she was a virgin, Amnon thought it impossible to carry out his designs toward her. ³ Now Amnon had a friend named Jonadab, son of David's brother Shimeah, who was very clever. ⁴ He asked him, "Prince, why are you so dejected morning after morning? Why not tell me?" So Amnon said to him, "I am in love with Tamar, my brother Absalom's sister." ⁵ Then Jonadab replied, "Lie down on your bed and pretend to be sick. When your father comes to visit you, say to him, 'Please let my sister Tamar come and encourage me to take food. If she prepares something appetizing in my presence, for me to see, I will eat it from her hand.'" ⁶ So Amnon lay down and pretended to be sick. When the king came to visit him, Amnon said to the king, "Please let my sister Tamar come and prepare some fried cakes before my eyes, that I may take nourishment from her hand." ⁷ David then sent home a message to Tamar, "Please go to the house of your brother Amnon and prepare some nourishment for him." ⁸ Tamar went to the house of her brother Amnon, who was in bed. Taking dough and kneading it, she twisted it into cakes before his eyes and fried the cakes. ⁹ Then she took the pan and set out the cakes before him. But Amnon would not eat; he said, "Have everyone leave me." When they had all left him, ¹⁰ Amnon said to Tamar, "Bring the nourishment into the bedroom, that I may have it from your hand." So Tamar picked up the cakes she had prepared and brought them to her brother Amnon in the bedroom. ¹¹ But when she brought them to him to eat, he seized her and said to her, "Come! Lie with me, my sister!" ¹² But she answered him, "No my brother! Do not shame me! That is an intolerable crime in Israel. Do not commit this insensate deed. ¹³ Where would I take my shame? And you would be a discredited man in Israel. So please, speak to the king; he will not keep me from you." ¹⁴ Not heeding her plea, he overpowered her; he shamed her and had relations with her. ¹⁵ Then Amnon conceived an intense hatred for her, which far surpassed the love he had had for her. "Get up and leave," he said to her. ¹⁶ She replied, "No, brother, because to drive me out would be far worse than the first injury you have done me." He would not listen to her, ¹⁷ but called the youth who was his attendant and said, "Put her outside, away from me, and bar the door after her." ¹⁸ Now she had on a long tunic, for that is how maiden princesses dressed in olden days. When his attendant put her out and barred the door after her, ¹⁹ Tamar put ashes on her head and tore the long tunic in which she was clothed. Then, putting her hands to her head, she went away crying loudly. ²⁰ Her brother Absalom said to her: "Has your brother Amnon been with you? Be still now, my sister; he is your brother. Do not take this affair to heart." But Tamar remained grief-stricken and forlorn in the house of her brother Absalom. ²¹ King David, who got word of the whole affair, became very angry. He did not, however, spark the resentment of his son Amnon, whom he favored because he was his first-born. ²² Absalom, moreover, said nothing at all to Amnon, although he hated him for having shamed his sister Tamar. ²³ After a period of two years, Absalom had shearers in Baalhazor near Ephraim, and he invited all the princes. ²⁴ Absalom went to the king and said: "Your servant is having shearers. Please, your majesty, come with all your retainers to your servant." ²⁵ But the King said to Absalom, "No, my son, all of us should not go lest we be a burden to you." And though Absalom urged him, he refused to go and began to bid him good-bye. ²⁶ Absalom then said, "If you will not come yourself, please let my brother Amnon come to us." The king asked him, "Why should he go to you?" ²⁷ At Absalom's urging, however, he sent Amnon and all the other princes with him. Absalom prepared a banquet fit for royalty. ²⁸ But he had instructed his servants: "Now watch! When Amnon is merry with wine and I say to you, 'Kill Amnon,' put him to death. Do not be afraid, for it is I who order you to do it. Be resolute and act manfully." ²⁹ When the servants did to Amnon as Absalom had commanded, all the other princes rose, mounted their mules, and fled. ³⁰ While they were still on the road, a report reached David that Absalom had killed all the princes and that not one of them had survived. ³¹ The king stood up, rent his garments, and then lay on the ground. All his servants standing by him also rent their garments. ³² But Jonadab, son of David's brother Shimeah, spoke up: "Let not my lord think that all the young princes have been killed! Amnon alone is dead, for Absalom was determined on this ever since Amnon shamed his sister Tamar. ³³ So let not my lord the king put faith in the report that all the princes are dead. Amnon alone is dead." ³⁴ Meanwhile, Absalom had taken flight. Then the servant on watch looked about and saw a large group coming down the slope from the direction of Bahurim. He came in and reported this, telling the king that he had seen some men coming down the mountainside from the direction of Bahurim. ³⁵ So Jonadab said to the king: "There! The princes have come. It is as your servant said." ³⁶ No sooner had he finished speaking than the princes came in, weeping aloud. The king, too, and all his servants wept very bitterly. ³⁷ But Absalom, who had taken flight, went to Talmai, son of Ammihud, king of Geshur, ³⁸ and stayed in Geshur for three years. ³⁹ The king continued during all that time to mourn over his son; but his longing reached out for Absalom as he became reconciled to the death of Amnon.

2 Samuel Chapter 14

¹ When Joab, son of Zeruiah, observed how the king felt toward Absalom, ² he sent to Tekoa and brought from there a gifted woman, to whom he said: "Pretend to be in mourning. Put on mourning apparel and do not anoint yourself with oil, that you may appear to be a woman who has been long in mourning for a departed one. ³ Then go to the king and speak to him in this manner." And Joab instructed her what to say. ⁴ So the woman of Tekoa went to the king and fell prostrate to the ground in homage, saying, "Help, your majesty!" ⁵ The king said to her, "What do you want?" She replied: "Alas, I am a widow; my husband is dead. ⁶ Your servant had two sons, who quarreled in the field. There being no one to part them, one of them struck his brother and killed him. ⁷ Then the whole clan confronted your servant and demanded: 'Give up the one who killed his brother. We must put him to death for the life of his brother whom he has slain; we must extinguish the heir also.' Thus they will quench my remaining hope and leave my husband neither name nor posterity upon the earth." ⁸ The king then said to the

woman: "Go home. I will issue a command on your behalf." 9 The woman of Tekoa answered him, "Let me and my family be to blame, my lord king; you and your throne are innocent." 10 Then the king said, "If anyone says a word to you, have him brought to me, and he shall not touch you again." 11 But she went on to say, "Please, your majesty, keep in mind the LORD your God, that the avenger of blood may not go too far in destruction and that my son may not be done away with." He replied, "As the LORD lives, not a hair of your son shall fall to the ground." 12 The woman continued, "Please let your servant say still another word to my lord the king." He replied, "Speak." 13 So the woman said: "Why, then, do you think of this same kind of thing against the people of God? In pronouncing as he has, the king shows himself guilty, for not bringing back his own banished son. 14 We must indeed die; we are then like water that is poured out on the ground and cannot be gathered up. Yet, though God does not bring back life, he does take thought how not to banish anyone from him. 15 And now, if I have presumed to speak of this matter to your majesty, it is because the people have given me cause to fear. And so your servant thought: 'Let me speak to the king. Perhaps he will grant the petition of his maidservant. 16 For the king must surely consent to free his servant from the grasp of one who would seek to destroy me and my son as well from God's inheritance.'" 17 And the woman concluded: "Let the word of my lord the king provide a resting place; indeed, my lord the king is like an angel of God, evaluating good and bad. The LORD your God be with you." 18 The king answered the woman, "Now do not conceal from me anything I may ask you!" The woman said, "Let my lord the king speak." 19 So the king asked, "Is Joab involved with you in all this?" And the woman answered: "As you live, my lord the king, it is just as your majesty has said, and not otherwise. It was your servant Joab who instructed me and told your servant all these things she was to say. 20 Your servant Joab did this to come at the issue in a roundabout way. But my lord is as wise as an angel of God, so that he knows all things on earth." 21 Then the king said to Joab: "I hereby grant this request. Go, therefore, and bring back young Absalom." 22 Falling prostrate to the ground in homage and blessing the king, Joab said, "This day I know that I am in good favor with you, my lord the king, since the king has granted the request of his servant." 23 Joab then went off to Geshur and brought Absalom to Jerusalem. 24 But the king said, "Let him go to his own house; he shall not appear before me." So Absalom went off to his house and did not appear before the king. 25 In all Israel there was not a man who could so be praised for his beauty as Absalom, who was without blemish from the sole of his foot to the crown of his head. 26 When he shaved his head - which he used to do at the end of every year, because his hair became too heavy for him - the hair weighed two hundred shekels according to the royal standard. 27 Absalom had three sons born to him, besides a daughter named Tamar, who was a beautiful woman. 28 Absalom lived in Jerusalem for two years without appearing before the king. 29 Then he summoned Joab to send him to the king, but Joab would not come to him. Although he summoned him a second time, Joab refused to come. 30 He therefore instructed his servants: "You see Joab's field that borders mine, on which he has barley. Go, set it on fire." And so Absalom's servants set the field on fire. Joab's farmhands came to him with torn garments and reported to him what had been done. 31 At this, Joab went to Absalom in his house and asked him, "Why have your servants set my field on fire?" 32 Absalom answered Joab: "I was summoning you to come here, that I may send you to the king to say: 'Why did I come back from Geshur? I would be better off if I were still there!' Now, let me appear before the king. If I am guilty, let him put me to death." 33 Joab went to the king and reported this. The king then called Absalom, who came to him and in homage fell on his face to the ground before the king. Then the king kissed him.

2 Samuel Chapter 15

1 After this Absalom provided himself with chariots, horses, and fifty henchmen. 2 Moreover, Absalom used to rise early and stand alongside the road leading to the gate. If someone had a lawsuit to be decided by the king, Absalom would call to him and say, "From what city are you?" And when he replied, "Your servant is of such and such a tribe of Israel," 3 Absalom would say to him, "Your suit is good and just, but there is no one to hear you in the king's name." 4 And he would continue: "If only I could be appointed judge in the land! Then everyone who has a lawsuit to be decided might come to me and I would render him justice." 5 Whenever a man approached him to show homage, he would extend his hand, hold him, and kiss him. 6 By behaving in this way toward all the Israelites who came to the king for judgment, Absalom was stealing away the loyalties of the men of Israel. 7 After a period of four years, Absalom said to the king: "Allow me to go to Hebron and fulfill a vow I made to the LORD. 8 For while living in Geshur in Aram, your servant

made this vow: 'If the LORD ever brings me back to Jerusalem, I will worship him in Hebron.'" 9 The king wished him a safe journey, and he went off to Hebron. 10 Then Absalom sent spies throughout the tribes of Israel to say, "When you hear the sound of the horn, declare Absalom king in Hebron." 11 Two hundred men had accompanied Absalom from Jerusalem. They had been invited and went in good faith, knowing nothing of the plan. 12 Absalom also sent to Ahithophel the Gilonite, David's counselor, an invitation to come from his town, Giloh, for the sacrifices he was about to offer. So the conspiracy gained strength, and the people with Absalom increased in numbers. 13 An informant came to David with the report, "The Israelites have transferred their loyalty to Absalom." 14 At this, David said to all his servants who were with him in Jerusalem: "Up! Let us take flight, or none of us will escape from Absalom. Leave quickly, lest he hurry and overtake us, then visit disaster upon us and put the city to the sword." 15 The king's officers answered him, "Your servants are ready, whatever our lord the king chooses to do." 16 Then the king set out, accompanied by his entire household, except for ten concubines whom he left behind to take care of the palace. 17 As the king left the city, with all his officers accompanying him, they halted opposite the ascent of the Mount of Olives, at a distance, 18 while the whole army marched past him. As all the Cherethites and Pelethites, and the six hundred men of Gath who had accompanied him from that city, were passing in review before the king, 19 he said to Ittai the Gittite: "Why should you also go with us? Go back and stay with the king, for you are a foreigner and you, too, are an exile from your own country. 20 You came only yesterday, and shall I have you wander about with us today, wherever I have to go? Return and take your brothers with you, and may the LORD be kind and faithful to you." 21 But Ittai answered the king, "As the LORD lives, and as my lord the king lives, your servant shall be wherever my lord the king may be, whether for death or for life." 22 So the king said to Ittai, "Go, then, march on." And Ittai the Gittite, with all his men and all the dependents that were with him, marched on. 23 Everyone in the countryside wept aloud as the last of the soldiers went by, and the king crossed the Kidron Valley with all the soldiers moving on ahead of him by way of the Mount of Olives, toward the desert. 24 Zadok, too (with all the Levite bearers of the ark of the covenant of God), and Abiathar brought the ark of God to a halt until the soldiers had marched out of the city. 25 Then the king said to Zadok: "Take the ark of God back to the city. If I find favor with the LORD, he will bring me back and permit me to see it and its lodging. 26 But if he should say, 'I am not pleased with you,' I am ready; let him do to me as he sees fit." 27 The king also said to the priest Zadok: "See to it that you and Abiathar return to the city in peace, and both your sons with you, your own son Ahimaaz, and Abiathar's son Jonathan. 28 Remember, I shall be waiting at the fords near the desert until I receive information from you." 29 So Zadok and Abiathar took the ark of God back to Jerusalem and remained there. 30 As David went up the Mount of Olives, he wept without ceasing. His head was covered, and he was walking barefoot. All those who were with him also had their heads covered and were weeping as they went. 31 When David was informed that Ahithophel was among the conspirators with Absalom, he said, "O LORD, turn the counsel of Ahithophel to folly!" 32 When David reached the top, where men used to worship God, Hushai the Archite was there to meet him, with rent garments and dirt upon his head. 33 David said to him: "If you come with me, you will be a burden to me. 34 But if you return to the city and say to Absalom, 'Let me be your servant, O king; I was formerly your father's servant, but now I will be yours,' you will undo for me the counsel of Ahithophel. 35 You will have the priests Zadok and Abiathar there with you. If you hear anything from the royal palace, you shall report it to the priests Zadok and Abiathar, 36 who have there with them both Zadok's son Ahimaaz and Abiathar's son Jonathan. Through them you shall send on to me whatever you hear." 37 So David's friend Hushai went into the city of Jerusalem as Absalom was about to enter it.

2 Samuel Chapter 16

1 David had gone a little beyond the top when Ziba, the servant of Meribbaal, met him with saddled asses laden with two hundred loaves of bread, an ephah of cakes of pressed raisins, an ephah of summer fruits, and a skin of wine. 2 The king said to Ziba, "What do you plan to do with these?" Ziba replied: "The asses are for the king's household to ride on. The bread and summer fruits are for your servants to eat, and the wine for those to drink who are weary in the desert." 3 Then the king said, "And where is your lord's son?" Ziba answered the king, "He is staying in Jerusalem, for he said, 'Now the Israelites will restore to me my father's kingdom.'" 4 The king therefore said to Ziba, "So! Everything Meribbaal has is yours." Then Ziba said: "I pay you homage, my lord the king. May I find favor with you!" 5 As David was approaching Bahurim, a man named Shimei, the son of Gera of the

same clan as Saul's family, was coming out of the place, cursing as he came. [6] He threw stones at David and at all the king's officers, even though all the soldiers, including the royal guard, were on David's right and on his left. [7] Shimei was saying as he cursed: "Away, away, you murderous and wicked man! [8] The LORD has requited you for all the bloodshed in the family of Saul, in whose stead you became king, and the LORD has given over the kingdom to your son Absalom. And now you suffer ruin because you are a murderer." [9] Abishai, son of Zeruiah, said to the king: "Why should this dead dog curse my lord the king? Let me go over, please, and lop off his head." [10] But the king replied: "What business is it of mine or of yours, sons of Zeruiah, that he curses? Suppose the LORD has told him to curse David; who then will dare to say, 'Why are you doing this?'" [11] Then the king said to Abishai and to all his servants: "If my own son, who came forth from my loins, is seeking my life, how much more might this Benjaminite do so! Let him alone and let him curse, for the LORD has told him to. [12] Perhaps the LORD will look upon my affliction and make it up to me with benefits for the curses he is uttering this day." [13] David and his men continued on the road, while Shimei kept abreast of them on the hillside, all the while cursing and throwing stones and dirt as he went. [14] The king and all the soldiers with him arrived at the Jordan tired out, and stopped there for a rest. [15] In the meantime Absalom, accompanied by Ahithophel, entered Jerusalem with all the Israelites. [16] When David's friend Hushai the Archite came to Absalom, he said to him: "Long live the king! Long live the king!" [17] But Absalom asked Hushai: "Is this your devotion to your friend? Why did you not go with your friend?" [18] Hushai replied to Absalom: "On the contrary, I am his whom the LORD and all this people and all Israel have chosen, and with him I will stay. [19] Furthermore, as I was in attendance upon your father, so will I be before you. Whom should I serve, if not his son?" [20] Then Absalom said to Ahithophel, "Offer your counsel on what we should do." [21] Ahithophel replied to Absalom: "Have relations with your father's concubines, whom he left behind to take care of the palace. When all Israel hears how odious you have made yourself to your father, all your partisans will take courage." [22] So a tent was pitched on the roof for Absalom, and he visited his father's concubines in view of all Israel. [23] Now the counsel given by Ahithophel at that time was as though one had sought divine revelation. Such was all his counsel both to David and to Absalom.

2 Samuel Chapter 17

[1] Ahithophel went on to say to Absalom: "Please let me choose twelve thousand men, and be off in pursuit of David tonight. [2] If I come upon him when he is weary and discouraged, I shall cause him panic. When all the people with him flee, I shall strike down the king alone. [3] Then I can bring back the rest of the people to you, as a bride returns to her husband. It is the death of only one man you are seeking; then all the people will be at peace." [4] This plan was agreeable to Absalom and to all the elders of Israel. [5] Then Absalom said, "Now call Hushai the Archite also; let us hear what he too has to say." [6] When Hushai came to Absalom, Absalom said to him: "This is what Ahithophel proposed. Shall we follow his proposal? If not, speak up." [7] Hushai replied to Absalom, "This time Ahithophel has not given good counsel." [8] And he went on to say: "You know that your father and his men are warriors, and that they are as fierce as a bear in the wild robbed of her cubs. Moreover, since your father is skilled in warfare, he will not spend the night with the people. [9] Even now he lies hidden in one of the caves or in some other place. And if some of our soldiers should fall at the first attack, whoever hears of it will say, 'Absalom's followers have been slaughtered.' [10] Then even the brave man with the heart of a lion will lose courage. For all Israel knows that your father is a warrior and that those who are with him are brave. [11] "This is what I counsel: Let all Israel from Dan to Beer-sheba, who are as numerous as the sands by the sea, be called up for combat; and go with them yourself. [12] We can then attack him wherever we find him, settling down upon him as dew alights on the ground. None shall survive - neither he nor any of his followers. [13] And if he retires into a city, all Israel shall bring ropes to that city and we can drag it into the gorge, so that not even a pebble of it can be found." [14] Then Absalom and all the Israelites pronounced the counsel of Hushai the Archite better than that of Ahithophel. For the LORD had decided to undo Ahithophel's good counsel, in order thus to bring Absalom to ruin. [15] Then Hushai said to the priests Zadok and Abiathar: "This is the counsel Ahithophel gave Absalom and the elders of Israel, and this is what I counseled. [16] So send a warning to David immediately, not to spend the night at the fords near the desert, but to cross over without fail. Otherwise the king and all the people with him will be destroyed." [17] Now Jonathan and Ahimaaz were staying at En-rogel, since they could not risk being seen entering the city. A maidservant was to come with information for them, and they in turn

were to go and report to King David. [18] But an attendant saw them and informed Absalom. They sped on their way and reached the house of a man in Bahurim who had a cistern in his courtyard. They let themselves down into this, [19] and the housewife took the cover and spread it over the cistern, strewing ground grain on the cover so that nothing could be noticed. [20] When Absalom's servants came to the woman at the house, they asked, "Where are Ahimaaz and Jonathan?" The woman replied, "They went by a short while ago toward the water." They searched, found no one, and so returned to Jerusalem. [21] As soon as they left, Ahimaaz and Jonathan came up out of the cistern and went on to inform King David. They said to him: "Leave! Cross the water at once, for Ahithophel has given the following counsel in regard to you." [22] So David and all his people moved on and crossed the Jordan. By daybreak, there was no one left who had not crossed. [23] When Ahithophel saw that his counsel was not acted upon, he saddled his ass and departed, going to his home in his own city. Then, having left orders concerning his family, he hanged himself. And so he died and was buried in his father's tomb. [24] Now David had gone to Mahanaim when Absalom crossed the Jordan accompanied by all the Israelites. [25] Absalom had put Amasa in command of the army in Joab's place. Amasa was the son of an Ishmaelite named Ithra, who had married Abigail, daughter of Jesse and sister of Joab's mother Zeruiah. [26] Israel and Absalom encamped in the territory of Gilead. [27] When David came to Mahanaim, Shobi, son of Nahash from Rabbah of the Ammonites, Machir, son of Ammiel from Lodebar, and Barzillai, the Gileadite from Rogelim, [28] brought couches, coverlets, basins and earthenware, as well as wheat, barley, flour, roasted grain, beans, lentils, [29] honey, butter and cheese from the flocks and herds, for David and those who were with him to eat; for they said, "The people have been hungry and tired and thirsty in the desert."

2 Samuel Chapter 18

[1] After mustering the troops he had with him, David placed officers in command of groups of a thousand and groups of a hundred. [2] David then put a third part of the soldiers under Joab's command, a third under command of Abishai, son of Zeruiah and brother of Joab, and a third under command of Ittai the Gittite. The king then said to the soldiers, "I intend to go out with you myself." [3] But they replied: "You must not come out with us. For if we should flee, we shall not count; even if half of us should die, we shall not count. You are equal to ten thousand of us. Therefore it is better that we have you to help us from the city." [4] So the king said to them, "I will do what you think best"; and he stood by the gate as all the soldiers marched out in units of a hundred and of a thousand. [5] But the king gave this command to Joab, Abishai and Ittai: "Be gentle with young Absalom for my sake." All the soldiers heard the king instruct the various leaders with regard to Absalom. [6] David's army then took the field against Israel, and a battle was fought in the forest near Mahanaim. [7] The forces of Israel were defeated by David's servants, and the casualties there that day were heavy - twenty thousand men. [8] The battle spread out over that entire region, and the thickets consumed more combatants that day than did the sword. [9] Absalom unexpectedly came up against David's servants. He was mounted on a mule, and, as the mule passed under the branches of a large terebinth, his hair caught fast in the tree. He hung between heaven and earth while the mule he had been riding ran off. [10] Someone saw this and reported to Joab that he had seen Absalom hanging from a terebinth. [11] Joab said to his informant: "If you saw him, why did you not strike him to the ground on the spot? Then it would have been my duty to give you fifty pieces of silver and a belt." [12] But the man replied to Joab: "Even if I already held a thousand pieces of silver in my two hands, I would not harm the king's son, for the king charged you and Abishai and Ittai in our hearing to protect the youth Absalom for his sake. [13] Had I been disloyal and killed him, the whole matter would have come to the attention of the king, and you would stand aloof." [14] Joab replied, "I will not waste time with you in this way." And taking three pikes in hand, he thrust for the heart of Absalom, still hanging from the tree alive. [15] Next, ten of Joab's young armor-bearers closed in on Absalom, and killed him with further blows. [16] Joab then sounded the horn, and the soldiers turned back from the pursuit of the Israelites, because Joab called on them to halt. [17] Absalom was taken up and cast into a deep pit in the forest, and a very large mound of stones was erected over him. And all the Israelites fled to their own tents. [18] During his lifetime Absalom had taken a pillar and erected it for himself in the King's Valley, for he said, "I have no son to perpetuate my name." The pillar which he named for himself is called Yadabshalom to the present day. [19] Then Ahimaaz, son of Zadok, said, "Let me run to take the good news to the king that the LORD has set him free from the grasp of his enemies." [20] But Joab said to him: "You are not the man to bring the news today. On some other day you may take the good news, but today

you would not be bringing good news, for in fact the king's son is dead." 21 Then Joab said to a Cushite, "Go, tell the king what you have seen." The Cushite bowed to Joab and sped away. 22 But Ahimaaz, son of Zadok, said to Joab again, "Come what may, permit me also to run after the Cushite." Joab replied: "Why do you want to run, my son? You will receive no reward." 23 But he insisted, "Come what may, I want to run." Joab said to him, "Very well." Ahimaaz sped off by way of the Jordan plain and outran the Cushite. 24 Now David was sitting between the two gates, and a lookout mounted to the roof of the gate above the city wall, where he looked about and saw a man running all alone. 25 The lookout shouted to inform the king, who said, "If he is alone, he has good news to report." As he kept coming nearer, 26 the lookout spied another runner. From his place atop the gate he cried out, "There is another man running by himself." And the king responded, "He, too, is bringing good news." 27 Then the lookout said, "I notice that the first one runs like Ahimaaz, son of Zadok." The king replied, "He is a good man; he comes with good news." 28 Then Ahimaaz called out and greeted the king. With face to the ground he paid homage to the king and said, "Blessed be the LORD your God, who has delivered up the men who rebelled against my lord the king." 29 But the king asked, "Is the youth Absalom safe?" And Ahimaaz replied, "I saw a great disturbance when the king's servant Joab sent your servant on, but I do not know what it was." 30 The king said, "Step aside and remain in attendance here." So he stepped aside and remained there. 31 When the Cushite came in, he said, "Let my lord the king receive the good news that this day the LORD has taken your part, freeing you from the grasp of all who rebelled against you." 32 But the king asked the Cushite, "Is young Absalom safe?" The Cushite replied, "May the enemies of my lord the king and all who rebel against you with evil intent be as that young man!"

2 Samuel Chapter 19

1 The king was shaken, and went up to the room over the city gate to weep. He said as he wept, "My son Absalom! My son, my son Absalom! If only I had died instead of you, Absalom, my son, my son!" 2 Joab was told that the king was weeping and mourning for Absalom; 3 and that day's victory was turned into mourning for the whole army when they heard that the king was grieving for his son. 4 The soldiers stole into the city that day like men shamed by flight in battle. 5 Meanwhile the king covered his face and cried out in a loud voice, "My son Absalom! Absalom! My son, my son!" 6 Then Joab went to his residence and said: "Though they saved your life and your sons' and daughters' lives, also the lives of your wives and those of your concubines, you have put all your servants to shame today 7 by loving those who hate you and hating those who love you. For you have shown today that officers and servants mean nothing to you. Indeed I am now certain that if Absalom were alive today and all of us dead, you would think that more suitable. 8 Now then, get up! Go out and speak kindly to your servants. I swear by the LORD that if you do not go out, not a single man will remain with you overnight, and this will be a far greater disaster for you than any that has afflicted you from your youth until now." 9 So the king stepped out and sat at the gate. When all the people were informed that the king was sitting at the gate, they came into his presence. Now the Israelites had fled to their separate tents, 10 but throughout the tribes of Israel all the people were arguing among themselves, saying to one another: "The king delivered us from the clutches of our enemies, and it was he who rescued us from the grip of the Philistines. But now he has fled from the country before Absalom, 11 and Absalom, whom we anointed over us, died in battle. Why, then, should you remain silent about restoring the king to his palace?" When the talk of all Israel reached the king, 12 David sent word to the priests Zadok and Abiathar: "Say to the elders of Judah: 'Why should you be last to restore the king to his palace? 13 You are my brothers, you are my bone and flesh. Why should you be last to restore the king?' 14 Also say to Amasa: 'Are you not my bone and flesh? May God do thus and so to me, if you do not become my general permanently in place of Joab.'" 15 He won over all the Judahites as one man, and so they summoned the king to return, with all his servants. 16 When the king, on his return, reached the Jordan, Judah had come to Gilgal to meet him and to escort him across the Jordan. 17 Shimei, son of Gera, the Benjaminite from Bahurim, hurried down with the Judahites to meet King David, 18 accompanied by a thousand men from Benjamin. Ziba, too, the servant of the house of Saul, accompanied by his fifteen sons and twenty servants, hastened to the Jordan before the king. 19 They crossed over the ford to bring the king's household over and to do whatever he wished. When Shimei, son of Gera, crossed the Jordan, he fell down before the king 20 and said to him: "May my lord not hold me guilty, and may he not remember and take to heart the wrong that your servant did the day my lord the king left Jerusalem. 21 For your servant knows that he has done wrong. Yet realize that I have been the first of the whole house of Joseph to come down today to meet

my lord the king." 22 But Abishai, son of Zeruiah, countered: "Shimei must be put to death for this. He cursed the LORD'S anointed." 23 David replied: "What has come between you and me, sons of Zeruiah, that you would create enmity for me this day? Should anyone die today in Israel? Am I not aware that today I am king of Israel?" 24 Then the king said to Shimei, "You shall not die." And the king gave him his oath. 25 Meribbaal, son of Saul, also went down to meet the king. He had not washed his feet nor trimmed his mustache nor washed his clothes from the day the king left until he returned safely. 26 When he came from Jerusalem to meet the king, the king asked him, "Why did you not go with me, Meribbaal?" 27 He replied: "My lord the king, my servant betrayed me. For your servant, who is lame, said to him, 'Saddle the ass for me, that I may ride on it and go with the king.' 28 But he slandered your servant before my lord the king. But my lord the king is like an angel of God. Do what you judge best. 29 For though my father's entire house deserved only death from my lord the king, yet you placed your servant among the guests at your table. What right do I still have to make further appeal to the king?" 30 But the king said to him: "Why do you go on talking? I say, 'You and Ziba shall divide the property.'" 31 Meribbaal answered the king, "Indeed let him have it all, now that my lord the king has returned safely to his palace." 32 Barzillai the Gileadite also came down from Rogelim and escorted the king to the Jordan for his crossing, taking leave of him there. 33 It was Barzillai, a very old man of eighty and very wealthy besides, who had provisioned the king during his stay in Mahanaim. 34 The king said to Barzillai, "Cross over with me, and I will provide for your old age as my guest in Jerusalem." 35 But Barzillai answered the king: "How much longer have I to live, that I should go up to Jerusalem with the king? 36 I am now eighty years old. Can I distinguish between good and bad? Can your servant taste what he eats and drinks, or still appreciate the voices of singers and songstresses? Why should your servant be any further burden to my lord the king? 37 In escorting the king across the Jordan, your servant is doing little enough! Why should the king give me this reward? 38 Please let your servant go back to die in his own city by the tomb of his father and mother. Here is your servant Chimham. Let him cross over with my lord the king. Do for him whatever you will." 39 Then the king said to him, "Chimham shall come over with me, and I will do for him as you would wish. And anything else you would like me to do for you, I will do." 40 Then all the people crossed over the Jordan but the king remained; he kissed Barzillai and bade him Godspeed as he returned to his own district. 41 Finally the king crossed over to Gilgal, accompanied by Chimham. All the people of Judah and half of the people of Israel had escorted the king across. 42 But all these Israelites began coming to the king and saying, "Why did our brothers the Judahites steal you away and escort the king and his household across the Jordan, along with all David's men?" 43 All the Judahites replied to the men of Israel: "Because the king is our relative. Why are you angry over this affair? Have we had anything to eat at the king's expense? Or have portions from his table been given to us?" 44 The Israelites answered the Judahites: "We have ten shares in the king. Also, we are the first-born rather than you. Why do you slight us? Were we not first to speak of restoring the king?" Then the Judahites in turn spoke even more fiercely than the Israelites.

2 Samuel Chapter 20

1 Now a rebellious individual from Benjamin named Sheba, the son of Bichri, happened to be there. He sounded the horn and cried out, "We have no portion in David, nor any share in the son of Jesse. Every man to his tent, O Israel!" 2 So all the Israelites left David for Sheba, son of Bichri. But from the Jordan to Jerusalem the Judahites remained loyal to their king. 3 When King David came to his palace in Jerusalem, he took the ten concubines whom he had left behind to take care of the palace and placed them in confinement. He provided for them, but had no further relations with them. And so they remained in confinement to the day of their death, lifelong widows. 4 Then the king said to Amasa: "Summon the Judahites for me within three days. Then present yourself here." 5 Accordingly Amasa set out to summon Judah, but delayed beyond the time set for him by David. 6 Then David said to Abishai: "Sheba, son of Bichri, may now do us more harm than Absalom did. Take your lord's servants and pursue him, lest he find fortified cities and take shelter while we look on." 7 So Joab and the Cherethites and Pelethites and all the warriors marched out behind Abishai from Jerusalem to campaign in pursuit of Sheba, son of Bichri. 8 They were at the great stone in Gibeon when Amasa met them. Now Joab had a belt over his tunic, from which was slung, in its sheath near his thigh, a sword that could be drawn with a downward movement. 9 And Joab asked Amasa, "How are you, my brother?" With his right hand Joab held Amasa's beard as if to kiss him. 10 And since Amasa was not on his guard against the sword in Joab's other hand, Joab stabbed him in the

abdomen with it, so that his entrails burst forth to the ground, and he died without receiving a second thrust. Then Joab and his brother Abishai pursued Sheba, son of Bichri. ¹¹ One of Joab's attendants stood by Amasa and said, "Let him who favors Joab and is for David follow Joab." ¹² Amasa lay covered with blood in the middle of the highroad, and the man noticed that all the soldiers were stopping. So he removed Amasa from the road to the field and placed a garment over him, because all who came up to him were stopping. ¹³ When he had been removed from the road, everyone went on after Joab in pursuit of Sheba, son of Bichri. ¹⁴ Sheba passed through all the tribes of Israel to Abel Beth-maacah. Then all the Bichrites assembled and they too entered the city after him. ¹⁵ So David's servants came and besieged him in Abel Beth-maacah. They threw up a mound against the city, and all the soldiers who were with Joab began battering the wall to throw it down. ¹⁶ Then a wise woman from the city stood on the outworks and called out, "Listen, listen! Tell Joab to come here, that I may speak with him." ¹⁷ When Joab had come near her, the woman said, "Are you Joab?" And he replied, "Yes." She said to him, "Listen to what your maidservant has to say." He replied. "I am listening." ¹⁸ Then she went on to say: "There is an ancient saying, 'Let them ask if they will in Abel ¹⁹ or in Dan whether loyalty is finished or ended in Israel.' You are seeking to beat down a city that is a mother in Israel. Why do you wish to destroy the inheritance of the LORD?" ²⁰ Joab answered, "Not at all, not at all! I do not wish to destroy or to ruin anything. ²¹ That is not the case at all. A man named Sheba, son of Bichri, from the hill country of Ephraim has rebelled against King David. Surrender him alone, and I will withdraw from the city." Then the woman said to Joab, "His head shall be thrown to you across the wall." ²² She went to all the people with her advice, and they cut off the head of Sheba, son of Bichri, and threw it out to Joab. He then sounded the horn, and they scattered from the city to their own tents, while Joab returned to Jerusalem to the king. ²³ Joab was in command of the whole army of Israel. Benaiah, son of Jehoiada, was in command of the Cherethites and Pelethites. ²⁴ Adoram was in charge of the forced labor. Jehoshaphat, son of Ahilud, was the chancellor. ²⁵ Shawsha was the scribe. Zadok and Abiathar were priests. ²⁶ Ira the Jairite was also David's priest.

2 Samuel Chapter 21

¹ During David's reign there was a famine for three successive years. David had recourse to the LORD, who said, "There is bloodguilt on Saul and his family because he put the Gibeonites to death." ² So the king called the Gibeonites and spoke to them. (Now the Gibeonites were not Israelites, but survivors of the Amorites; and although the Israelites had given them their oath, Saul had attempted to kill them off in his zeal for the men of Israel and Judah.) ³ David said to the Gibeonites, "What must I do for you and how must I make atonement, that you may bless the inheritance of the LORD?" ⁴ The Gibeonites answered him, "We have no claim against Saul and his house for silver or gold, nor is it our place to put any man to death in Israel." Then he said, "I will do for you whatever you propose." ⁵ They said to the king, "As for the man who was exterminating us and who intended to destroy us that we might have no place in all the territory of Israel, ⁶ let seven men from among his descendants be given to us, that we may dismember them before the LORD in Gibeon, on the LORD'S mountain." The king replied, "I will give them up." ⁷ The king, however, spared Meribbaal, son of Jonathan, son of Saul, because of the LORD'S oath that formed a bond between David and Saul's son Jonathan. ⁸ But the king took Armoni and Meribbaal, the two sons that Aiah's daughter Rizpah had borne to Saul, and the five sons of Saul's daughter Merob that she had borne to Adriel, son of Barzillai the Meholathite, ⁹ and surrendered them to the Gibeonites. They then dismembered them on the mountain before the LORD. The seven fell at the one time; they were put to death during the first days of the harvest - that is, at the beginning of the barley harvest. ¹⁰ Then Rizpah, Aiah's daughter, took sackcloth and spread it out for herself on the rock from the beginning of the harvest until rain came down on them from the sky, fending off the birds of the sky from settling on them by day, and the wild animals by night. ¹¹ When David was informed of what Rizpah, Aiah's daughter, the concubine of Saul, had done, ¹² he went and obtained the bones of Saul and of his son Jonathan from the citizens of Jabesh-gilead, who had carried them off secretly from the public square of Beth-shan, where the Philistines had hanged them at the time they killed Saul on Gilboa. ¹³ When he had brought up from there the bones of Saul and of his son Jonathan, the bones of those who had been dismembered were also gathered up. ¹⁴ Then the bones of Saul and of his son Jonathan were buried in the tomb of his father Kish at Zela in the territory of Benjamin. After all that the king commanded had been carried out, God granted relief to the land. ¹⁵ There was another battle between the Philistines and Israel. David went down with his servants and fought the Philistines, but David grew

tired. ¹⁶ Dadu, one of the Rephaim, whose bronze spear weighed three hundred shekels, was about to take him captive. Dadu was girt with a new sword and planned to kill David, ¹⁷ but Abishai, son of Zeruiah, came to his assistance and struck and killed the Philistine. Then David's men swore to him, "You must not go out to battle with us again, lest you quench the lamp of Israel." ¹⁸ After this there was another battle with the Philistines in Gob. On that occasion Sibbecai, from Husha, killed Saph, one of the Rephaim. ¹⁹ There was another battle with the Philistines in Gob, in which Elhanan, son of Jair from Bethlehem, killed Goliath of Gath, who had a spear with a shaft like a weaver's heddlebar. ²⁰ There was another battle at Gath in which there was a man of large stature with six fingers on each hand and six toes on each foot - twenty-four in all. He too was one of the Rephaim. ²¹ And when he insulted Israel, Jonathan, son of David's brother Shimei, killed him. ²² These four were Rephaim in Gath, and they fell at the hands of David and his servants.

2 Samuel Chapter 22

¹ David sang the words of this song to the LORD when the LORD had rescued him from the grasp of all his enemies and from the hand of Saul. ² This is what he sang:

I

"O LORD, my rock, my fortress, my deliverer, ³ my God, my rock of refuge! My shield, the horn of my salvation, my stronghold, my refuge, my savior, from violence you keep me safe. ⁴ 'Praised be the LORD,' I exclaim, and I am safe from my enemies.

II

⁵ "The breakers of death surged round about me, the floods of perdition overwhelmed me; ⁶ The cords of the nether world enmeshed me, the snares of death overtook me. ⁷ In my distress I called upon the LORD and cried out to my God; From his temple he heard my voice, and my cry reached his ears.

III

⁸ "The earth swayed and quaked; the foundations of the heavens trembled and shook when his wrath flared up. ⁹ Smoke rose from his nostrils, and a devouring fire from his mouth; he kindled coals into flame. ¹⁰ He inclined the heavens and came down, with dark clouds under his feet. ¹¹ He mounted a cherub and flew, borne on the wings of the wind. ¹² He made darkness the shelter about him, with spattering rain and thickening clouds. ¹³ From the brightness of his presence coals were kindled to flame. ¹⁴ "The LORD thundered from heaven; the Most High gave forth his voice. ¹⁵ He sent forth arrows to put them to flight; he flashed lightning and routed them. ¹⁶ Then the wellsprings of the sea appeared, the foundations of the earth were laid bare, At the rebuke of the LORD, at the blast of the wind of his wrath. ¹⁷ "He reached out from on high and grasped me; he drew me out of the deep waters. ¹⁸ He rescued me from my mighty enemy, from my foes, who were too powerful for me. ¹⁹ They attacked me on my day of calamity, but the LORD came to my support. ²⁰ He set me free in the open, and rescued me, because he loves me.

IV

²¹ "The LORD rewarded me according to my justice; according to the cleanness of my hands he requited me. ²² For I kept the ways of the LORD and was not disloyal to my God. ²³ For his ordinances were all present to me, and his statutes I put not from me; ²⁴ But I was wholehearted toward him, and I was on my guard against guilt. ²⁵ And the LORD requited me according to my justice, according to my innocence in his sight. ²⁶ "Toward the faithful you are faithful; toward the wholehearted you are wholehearted; ²⁷ Toward the sincere you are sincere; but toward the crooked you are astute. ²⁸ You save lowly people, though on the lofty your eyes look down. ²⁹ You are my lamp, O LORD! O my God, you brighten the darkness about me. ³⁰ For with your aid I run against an armed band, and by the help of my God I leap over a wall. ³¹ God's way is unerring; the promise of the LORD is fire-tried; he is a shield to all who take refuge in him."

V

³² "For who is God except the LORD? Who is a rock save our God? ³³ The God who girded me with strength and kept my way unerring; ³⁴ Who made my feet swift as those of hinds and set me on the heights; ³⁵ Who trained my hands for war till my arms could bend a bow of brass.

VI

³⁶ "You have given me your saving shield, and your help has made me great. ³⁷ You made room for my steps; unwavering was my stride. ³⁸ I pursued my enemies and destroyed them, nor did I turn again till I made an end of them. ³⁹ I smote them and they did not rise; they fell beneath my feet.

VII

⁴⁰ "You girded me with strength for war; you subdued my adversaries beneath me. ⁴¹ My enemies you put to flight before me and those who

hated me I destroyed. ⁴² They cried for help-but no one saved them; to the LORD - but he answered them not. ⁴³ I ground them fine as the dust of the earth; like the mud in the streets I trampled them down.

VIII

⁴⁴ "You rescued me from the strife of my people; you made me head over nations. A people I had not known became my slaves; ⁴⁵ as soon as they heard me, they obeyed. ⁴⁶ The foreigners fawned and cringed before me; they staggered forth from their fortresses." ⁴⁷ "The LORD live! And blessed be my Rock! Extolled be my God, rock of my salvation. ⁴⁸ O God, who granted me vengeance, who made peoples subject to me ⁴⁹ and helped me escape from my enemies, Above my adversaries you exalt me and from the violent man you rescue me. ⁵⁰ Therefore will I proclaim you, O LORD, among the nations, and I will sing praise to your name, ⁵¹ You who gave great victories to your king and showed kindness to your anointed, to David and his posterity forever."

2 Samuel Chapter 23

¹ These are the last words of David: "The utterance of David, son of Jesse; the utterance of the man God raised up, Anointed of the God of Jacob, favorite of the Mighty One of Israel. ² The spirit of the LORD spoke through me; his word was on my tongue. ³ The God of Israel spoke; of me the Rock of Israel said, 'He that rules over men in justice, that rules in the fear of God, ⁴ Is like the morning light at sunrise on a cloudless morning, making the greensward sparkle after rain.' ⁵ Is not my house firm before God? He has made an eternal covenant with me, set forth in detail and secured. Will he not bring to fruition all my salvation and my every desire? ⁶ But the wicked are all like thorns to be cast away; they cannot be taken up by hand. ⁷ He who wishes to touch them must arm himself with iron and the shaft of a spear, and they must be consumed by fire." ⁸ These are the names of David's warriors. Ishbaal, son of Hachamoni, was the first of the Three. It was he who brandished his battle-ax over eight hundred slain in a single encounter. ⁹ Next to him, among the Three warriors, was Eleazar, son of Dodo the Ahohite. He was with David at Ephes-dammim when the Philistines assembled there for battle. The Israelites had retreated, ¹⁰ but he stood his ground and fought the Philistines until his hand grew tired and became cramped, holding fast to the sword. The LORD brought about a great victory on that day; the soldiers turned back after Eleazar, but only to strip the slain. ¹¹ Next to him was Shammah, son of Agee the Hararite. The Philistines had assembled at Lehi, where there was a plot of land full of lentils. When the soldiers fled from the Philistines, ¹² he took his stand in the middle of the plot and defended it. He slew the Philistines, and the LORD brought about a great victory. Such were the deeds of the Three warriors. ¹³ During the harvest three of the Thirty went down to David in the cave of Adullam, while a Philistine clan was encamped in the Vale of Rephaim. ¹⁴ At that time David was in the refuge, and there was a garrison of Philistines in Bethlehem. ¹⁵ Now David had a strong craving and said, "Oh, that someone would give me a drink of water from the cistern that is by the gate of Bethlehem!" ¹⁶ So the Three warriors broke through the Philistine camp and drew water from the cistern that is by the gate of Bethlehem. But when they brought it to David he refused to drink it, and instead poured it out to the LORD, ¹⁷ saying: "The LORD forbid that I do this! Can I drink the blood of these men who went at the risk of their lives?" So he refused to drink it. ¹⁸ Abishai, brother of Joab, son of Zeruiah, was at the head of the Thirty. It was he who brandished his spear over three hundred slain. He was listed among the Thirty ¹⁹ and commanded greater respect than the Thirty, becoming their leader. However, he did not attain to the Three. ²⁰ Benaiah, son of Jehoiada, a stalwart from Kabzeel, was a man of great achievements. It was he who slew the two lions in Moab. He also went down and killed the lion in the cistern at the time of the snow. ²¹ It was he, too, who slew an Egyptian of large stature. Although the Egyptian was armed with a spear, he went against him with a club and wrested the spear from the Egyptian's hand, then killed him with his own spear. ²² Such were the deeds performed by Benaiah, son of Jehoiada. He was listed among the Thirty warriors ²³ and commanded greater respect than the Thirty. However, he did not attain to the Three. David put him in command of his bodyguard. ²⁴ Asahel, brother of Joab. . . .Among the Thirty were: Elhanan, son of Dodo, from Bethlehem; ²⁵ Shammah from En-harod; Elika from En-harod; ²⁶ Helez from Beth-pelet; Ira, son of Ikkesh, from Tekoa; ²⁷ Abiezer from Anathoth; Sibbecai from Hushah; ²⁸ Zalmon from Ahoh; Maharai from Netophah; ²⁹ Heled, son of Baanah, from Netophah; Ittai, son of Ribai, from Gibeah of the Benjaminites; ³⁰ Benaiah from Pirathon; Hiddai from Nahale-gaash; ³¹ Abibaal from Beth-arabah; Azmaveth from Bahurim; ³² Eliahba from Shaalbon; Jashen the Gunite; Jonathan, ³³ son of Shammah the Hararite; Ahiam, son of Sharar the Hararite; ³⁴ Eliphelet, son of Ahasbai, from Beth-maacah; Eliam, son of Ahithophel, from Gilo; ³⁵ Hezrai from Carmel; Paarai the Arbite; ³⁶ Igal, son of

Nathan, from Zobah; Bani the Gadite; ³⁷ Zelek the Ammonite; Naharai from Beeroth, armor-bearer of Joab, son of Zeruiah; ³⁸ Ira from Jattir; Gareb from Jattir; ³⁹ Uriah the Hittite-thirty-seven in all.

2 Samuel Chapter 24

¹ The LORD'S anger against Israel flared again, and he incited David against the Israelites by prompting him to number Israel and Judah. ² Accordingly the king said to Joab and the leaders of the army who were with him, "Tour all the tribes in Israel from Dan to Beer-sheba and register the people, that I may know their number." ³ But Joab said to the king: "May the LORD your God increase the number of people a hundredfold for your royal majesty to see it with his own eyes. But why does it please my lord the king to order a thing of this kind?" ⁴ The king, however, overruled Joab and the leaders of the army, so they left the king's presence in order to register the people of Israel. ⁵ Crossing the Jordan, they began near Aroer, south of the city in the wadi, and went in the direction of Gad toward Jazer. ⁶ They continued on to Gilead and to the district below Mount Hermon. Then they proceeded to Dan; from there they turned toward Sidon, ⁷ going to the fortress of Tyre and to all the cities of the Hivites and Canaanites, and ending up at Beer-sheba in the Negeb of Judah. ⁸ Thus they toured the whole country, reaching Jerusalem again after nine months and twenty days. ⁹ Joab then reported to the king the number of people registered: in Israel, eight hundred thousand men fit for military service; in Judah, five hundred thousand. ¹⁰ Afterward, however, David regretted having numbered the people, and said to the LORD: "I have sinned grievously in what I have done. But now, LORD, forgive the guilt of your servant, for I have been very foolish." ¹¹ When David rose in the morning, the LORD had spoken to the prophet Gad, David's seer, saying: ¹² "Go and say to David, 'This is what the LORD says: I offer you three alternatives; choose one of them, and I will inflict it on you.'" ¹³ Gad then went to David to inform him. He asked: "Do you want a three years' famine to come upon your land, or to flee from your enemy three months while he pursues you, or to have a three days' pestilence in your land? Now consider and decide what I must reply to him who sent me." ¹⁴ David answered Gad: "I am in very serious difficulty. Let us fall by the hand of God, for he is most merciful; but let me not fall by the hand of man." ¹⁵ Thus David chose the pestilence. Now it was the time of the wheat harvest when the plague broke out among the people. (The LORD then sent a pestilence over Israel from morning until the time appointed, and seventy thousand of the people from Dan to Beer-sheba died.) ¹⁶ But when the angel stretched forth his hand toward Jerusalem to destroy it, the LORD regretted the calamity and said to the angel causing the destruction among the people, "Enough now! Stay your hand." The angel of the LORD was then standing at the threshing floor of Araunah the Jebusite. ¹⁷ When David saw the angel who was striking the people, he said to the LORD: "It is I who have sinned; it is I, the shepherd, who have done wrong. But these are sheep; what have they done? Punish me and my kindred." ¹⁸ On the same day Gad went to David and said to him, "Go up and build an altar to the LORD on the threshing floor of Araunah the Jebusite." ¹⁹ Following Gad's bidding, David went up as the LORD had commanded. ²⁰ Now Araunah looked down and noticed the king and his servants coming toward him while he was threshing wheat. So he went out and paid homage to the king, with face to the ground. ²¹ Then Araunah asked, "Why does my lord the king come to his servant?" David replied, "To buy the threshing floor from you, to build an altar to the LORD, that the plague may be checked among the people." ²² But Araunah said to David: "Let my lord the king take and offer up whatever he may wish. Here are oxen for holocausts, and threshing sledges and the yokes of the oxen for wood. ²³ All this does Araunah give to the king." Araunah then said to the king, "May the LORD your God accept your offering." ²⁴ The king, however, replied to Araunah, "No, I must pay you for it, for I cannot offer to the LORD my God holocausts that cost nothing." So David bought the threshing floor and the oxen for fifty silver shekels. ²⁵ Then David built an altar there to the LORD, and offered holocausts and peace offerings. The LORD granted relief to the country, and the plague was checked in Israel.

I Kings

1 Kings Chapter 1

¹ When King David was old and advanced in years, though they spread covers over him he could not keep warm. ² His servants therefore said to him, "Let a young virgin be sought to attend you, lord king, and to nurse you. If she sleeps with your royal majesty, you will be kept warm." ³ So they sought for a beautiful girl throughout the territory of Israel, and found Abishag the Shunamite, whom they brought to the king. ⁴ The maiden, who was very beautiful, nursed the king and cared for him, but the king did not have relations with her. ⁵ Adonijah, son of Haggith,

began to display his ambition to be king. He acquired chariots, drivers, and fifty henchmen. 6 Yet his father never rebuked him or asked why he was doing this. Adonijah was also very handsome, and next in age to Absalom by the same mother. 7 He conferred with Joab, son of Zeruiah, and with Abiathar the priest, and they supported him. 8 However, Zadok the priest, Benaiah, son of Jehoiada, Nathan the prophet, and Shimei and his companions, the pick of David's army, did not side with Adonijah. 9 When he slaughtered sheep, oxen, and fatlings at the stone Zoheleth, near En-rogel, Adonijah invited all his brothers, the king's sons, and all the royal officials of Judah. 10 But he did not invite the prophet Nathan, or Benaiah, or the pick of the army, or his brother Solomon. 11 Then Nathan said to Bathsheba, Solomon's mother: "Have you not heard that Adonijah, son of Haggith, has become king without the knowledge of our lord David? 12 Come now, let me advise you so that you may save your life and that of your son Solomon. 13 Go, visit King David, and say to him, 'Did you not, lord king, swear to your handmaid: Your son Solomon shall be king after me and shall sit upon my throne? Why, then, has Adonijah become king?' 14 And while you are still there speaking to the king, I will come in after you and confirm what you have said." 15 So Bathsheba visited the king in his room, while Abishag the Shunamite was attending him because of his advanced age. 16 Bathsheba bowed in homage to the king, who said to her, "What do you wish?" 17 She answered him: "My lord, you swore to me your handmaid by the LORD, your God, that my son Solomon should reign after you and sit upon your throne. 18 But now Adonijah has become king, and you, my lord king, do not know it. 19 He has slaughtered oxen, fatlings, and sheep in great numbers; he has invited all the king's sons, Abiathar the priest, and Joab, the general of the army, but not your servant Solomon. 20 Now, my lord king, all Israel is waiting for you to make known to them who is to sit on the throne after your royal majesty. 21 If this is not done, when my lord the king sleeps with his fathers, I and my son Solomon will be considered criminals." 22 While she was still speaking to the king, the prophet Nathan came in. 23 When he had been announced, the prophet entered the king's presence and, bowing to the floor, did him homage. 24 Then Nathan said: "Have you decided, my lord king, that Adonijah is to reign after you and sit on your throne? 25 He went down today and slaughtered oxen, fatlings, and sheep in great numbers; he invited all the king's sons, the commanders of the army, and Abiathar the priest, and they are eating and drinking in his company and saying, 'Long live King Adonijah!' 26 But me, your servant, he did not invite; nor Zadok the priest, nor Benaiah, son of Jehoiada, nor your servant Solomon. 27 Was this done by my royal master's order without my being told who was to succeed to your majesty's kingly throne?" 28 King David answered, "Call Bathsheba here." When she re-entered the king's presence and stood before him, 29 the king swore, "As the LORD lives, who has delivered me from all distress, 30 this very day I will fulfill the oath I swore to you by the LORD, the God of Israel, that your son Solomon should reign after me and should sit upon my throne in my place." 31 Bowing to the floor in homage to the king, Bathsheba said, "May my lord, King David, live forever!" 32 Then King David summoned Zadok the priest, Nathan the prophet, and Benaiah, son of Jehoiada. When they had entered the king's presence, 33 he said to them: "Take with you the royal attendants. Mount my son Solomon upon my own mule and escort him down to Gihon. 34 There Zadok the priest and Nathan the prophet are to anoint him king of Israel, and you shall blow the horn and cry, 'Long live King Solomon!' 35 When you come back in his train, he is to go in and sit upon my throne and reign in my place. I designate him ruler of Israel and of Judah." 36 In answer to the king, Benaiah, son of Jehoiada, said: "So be it! May the LORD, the God of my lord the king, so decree! 37 As the LORD has been with your royal majesty, so may he be with Solomon, and exalt his throne even more than that of my lord, King David!" 38 So Zadok the priest, Nathan the prophet, Benaiah, son of Jehoiada, and the Cherethites and Pelethites went down, and mounting Solomon on King David's mule, escorted him to Gihon. 39 Then Zadok the priest took the horn of oil from the tent and anointed Solomon. They blew the horn and all the people shouted, "Long live King Solomon!" 40 Then all the people went up after him, playing flutes and rejoicing so much as to split open the earth with their shouting. 41 Adonijah and all the guests who were with him heard it, just as they ended their banquet. When Joab heard the sound of the horn, he asked, "What does this uproar in the city mean?" 42 As he was speaking, Jonathan, son of Abiathar the priest, arrived. "Come," said Adonijah, "you are a man of worth and must bring good news." 43 "On the contrary!" Jonathan answered him. "Our lord, King David, has made Solomon king. 44 The king sent with him Zadok the priest, Nathan the prophet, Benaiah, son of Jehoiada, and the Cherethites and Pelethites, and they mounted him upon the king's own mule. 45 Zadok the priest and Nathan the prophet

anointed him king at Gihon, and they went up from there rejoicing, so that the city is in an uproar. That is the noise you heard. 46 Besides, Solomon took his seat on the royal throne, 47 and the king's servants went in and paid their respects to our lord, King David, saying, 'May God make Solomon more famous than you and exalt his throne more than your own!' And the king in his bed worshiped God, 48 and this is what he said: 'Blessed be the LORD, the God of Israel, who has this day seated one of my sons upon my throne, so that I see it with my own eyes.'" 49 All the guests of Adonijah left in terror, each going his own way. 50 Adonijah, in fear of Solomon, also left; he went and seized the horns of the altar. 51 It was reported to Solomon that Adonijah, in his fear of King Solomon, had seized the horns of the altar and said, "Let King Solomon first swear that he will not kill me, his servant, with the sword." 52 Solomon answered, "If he proves himself worthy, not a hair shall fall from his head. But if he is found guilty of crime, he shall die." 53 King Solomon sent to have him brought down from the altar, and he came and paid homage to the king. Solomon then said to him, "Go to your home."

1 Kings Chapter 2

1 When the time of David's death drew near, he gave these instructions to his son Solomon: 2 "I am going the way of all mankind. Take courage and be a man. 3 Keep the mandate of the LORD, your God, following his ways and observing his statutes, commands, ordinances, and decrees as they are written in the law of Moses, that you may succeed in whatever you do, wherever you turn, 4 and the LORD may fulfill the promise he made on my behalf when he said, 'If your sons so conduct themselves that they remain faithful to me with their whole heart and with their whole soul, you shall always have someone of your line on the throne of Israel.' 5 You yourself know what Joab, son of Zeruiah, did to me when he slew the two generals of Israel's armies, Abner, son of Ner, and Amasa, son of Jether. He took revenge for the blood of war in a time of peace, and put bloodshed without provocation on the belt about my waist and the sandal on my foot. 6 Act with the wisdom you possess; you must not allow him to go down to the grave in peaceful old age. 7 But be kind to the sons of Barzillai the Gileadite, and have them eat at your table. For they received me kindly when I was fleeing your brother Absalom. 8 You also have with you Shimei, son of Gera, the Benjaminite of Bahurim, who cursed me balefully when I was going to Mahanaim. Because he came down to meet me at the Jordan, I swore to him by the LORD that I would not put him to the sword. 9 But you must not let him go unpunished. You are a prudent man and will know how to deal with him to send down his hoary head in blood to the grave." 10 David rested with his ancestors and was buried in the City of David. 11 The length of David's reign over Israel was forty years: he reigned seven years in Hebron and thirty-three years in Jerusalem. 12 When Solomon was seated on the throne of his father David, with his sovereignty firmly established, 13 Adonijah, son of Haggith, went to Bathsheba, the mother of Solomon. "Do you come as a friend?" she asked. "Yes," he answered, 14 and added, "I have something to say to you." She replied, "Say it." 15 So he said: "You know that the kingdom was mine, and all Israel expected me to be king. But the kingdom escaped me and became my brother's, for the LORD gave it to him. 16 But now there is one favor I would ask of you. Do not refuse me." And she said, "Speak on." 17 He said, "Please ask King Solomon, who will not refuse you, to give me Abishag the Shunamite for my wife." 18 "Very well," replied Bathsheba, "I will speak to the king for you." 19 Then Bathsheba went to King Solomon to speak to him for Adonijah, and the king stood up to meet her and paid her homage. Then he sat down upon his throne, and a throne was provided for the king's mother, who sat at his right. 20 "There is one small favor I would ask of you," she said. "Do not refuse me." "Ask it, my mother," the king said to her, "for I will not refuse you." 21 So she said, "Let Abishag the Shunamite be given to your brother Adonijah for his wife." 22 "And why do you ask Abishag the Shunamite for Adonijah?" King Solomon answered his mother. "Ask the kingdom for him as well, for he is my elder brother and has with him Abiathar the priest and Joab, son of Zeruiah." 23 And King Solomon swore by the LORD: "May God do thus and so to me, and more besides, if Adonijah has not proposed this at the cost of his life. 24 And now, as the LORD lives, who has seated me firmly on the throne of my father David and made of me a dynasty as he promised, this day shall Adonijah be put to death." 25 Then King Solomon sent Benaiah, son of Jehoiada, who struck him dead. 26 The king said to Abiathar the priest: "Go to your land in Anathoth. Though you deserve to die, I will not put you to death this time, because you carried the ark of the Lord GOD before my father David and shared in all the hardships my father endured." 27 So Solomon deposed Abiathar from his office of priest of the LORD, thus fulfilling the prophecy which the LORD had made in Shiloh about the house of Eli. 28 When the news came to Joab, who had sided with

Adonijah, though not with Absalom, he fled to the tent of the LORD and seized the horns of the altar. ²⁹ King Solomon was told that Joab had fled to the tent of the LORD and was at the altar. He sent Benaiah, son of Jehoiada, with the order, "Go, strike him down." ³⁰ Benaiah went to the tent of the LORD and said to him, "The king says, 'Come out.'" But he answered, "No! I will die here." Benaiah reported to the king, "This is what Joab said to me in reply." ³¹ The king answered him: "Do as he has said, Strike him down and bury him, and you will remove from me and from my family the blood which Joab shed without provocation. ³² The LORD will hold him responsible for his own blood, because he struck down two men better and more just than himself, and slew them with the sword without my father David's knowledge: Abner, son of Ner, general of Israel's army, and Amasa, son of Jether, general of Judah's army. ³³ Joab and his descendants shall be responsible forever for their blood. But there shall be the peace of the LORD forever for David, and his descendants, and his house, and his throne." ³⁴ Benaiah, son of Jehoiada, went back, struck him down and killed him; he was buried in his house in the desert. ³⁵ The king appointed Benaiah, son of Jehoiada, over the army in his place, and put Zadok the priest in place of Abiathar. ³⁶ Then the king summoned Shimei and said to him: "Build yourself a house in Jerusalem and live there. Do not go anywhere else. ³⁷ For if you leave, and cross the Kidron Valley, be certain you shall die without fail. You shall be responsible for your own blood." ³⁸ Shimei answered the king: "I accept. Your servant will do just as the king's majesty has said." So Shimei stayed in Jerusalem for a long time. ³⁹ But three years later, two of Shimei's servants ran away to Achish, son of Maacah, king of Gath, and Shimei was informed that his servants were in Gath. ⁴⁰ So Shimei rose, saddled his ass, and went to Achish in Gath in search of his servants, whom he brought back. ⁴¹ When Solomon was informed that Shimei had gone from Jerusalem to Gath, and had returned, ⁴² the king summoned Shimei and said to him: "Did I not have you swear by the LORD to your clear understanding of my warning that, if you left and went anywhere else, you should die without fail? And you answered, 'I accept and obey.' ⁴³ Why, then, have you not kept the oath of the LORD and the command that I gave you?" ⁴⁴ And the king said to Shimei: "You know in your heart the evil that you did to my father David. Now the LORD requites you for your own wickedness. ⁴⁵ But King Solomon shall be blessed, and David's throne shall endure before the LORD forever." ⁴⁶ The king then gave the order to Benaiah, son of Jehoiada, who struck him dead as he left.

1 Kings Chapter 3

¹ With the royal power firmly in his grasp, Solomon allied himself by marriage with Pharaoh, king of Egypt. The daughter of Pharaoh, whom he married, he brought to the City of David, until he should finish building his palace, and the temple of the LORD, and the wall around Jerusalem. ² However, the people were sacrificing on the high places, for up to that time no temple had been built to the name of the LORD. ³ Solomon loved the LORD, and obeyed the statutes of his father David; yet he offered sacrifice and burned incense on the high places. ⁴ The king went to Gibeon to sacrifice there, because that was the most renowned high place. Upon its altar Solomon offered a thousand holocausts. ⁵ In Gibeon the LORD appeared to Solomon in a dream at night. God said, "Ask something of me and I will give it to you." ⁶ Solomon answered: "You have shown great favor to your servant, my father David, because he behaved faithfully toward you, with justice and an upright heart; and you have continued this great favor toward him, even today, seating a son of his on his throne. ⁷ O LORD, my God, you have made me, your servant, king to succeed my father David; but I am a mere youth, not knowing at all how to act. ⁸ I serve you in the midst of the people whom you have chosen, a people so vast that it cannot be numbered or counted. ⁹ Give your servant, therefore, an understanding heart to judge your people and to distinguish right from wrong. For who is able to govern this vast people of yours?" ¹⁰ The LORD was pleased that Solomon made this request. ¹¹ So God said to him: "Because you have asked for this - not for a long life for yourself, nor for riches, nor for the life of your enemies, but for understanding so that you may know what is right - ¹² I do as you requested. I give you a heart so wise and understanding that there has never been anyone like you up to now, and after you there will come no one to equal you. ¹³ In addition, I give you what you have not asked for, such riches and glory that among kings there is not your like. ¹⁴ And if you follow me by keeping my statutes and commandments, as your father David did, I will give you a long life." ¹⁵ When Solomon awoke from his dream, he went to Jerusalem, stood before the ark of the covenant of the LORD, offered holocausts and peace offerings, and gave a banquet for all his servants. ¹⁶ Later, two harlots came to the king and stood before him. ¹⁷ One woman said: "By your leave, my lord, this woman and I live in the same house, and I gave birth in the house while she was present. ¹⁸ On the third day after

I gave birth, this woman also gave birth. We were alone in the house; there was no one there but us two. ¹⁹ This woman's son died during the night; she smothered him by lying on him. ²⁰ Later that night she got up and took my son from my side, as I, your handmaid, was sleeping. Then she laid him in her bosom, after she had laid her dead child in my bosom. ²¹ I rose in the morning to nurse my child, and I found him dead. But when I examined him in the morning light, I saw it was not the son whom I had borne." ²² The other woman answered, "It is not so! The living one is my son, the dead one is yours." But the first kept saying, "No, the dead one is your child, the living one is mine!" Thus they argued before the king. ²³ Then the king said: "One woman claims, 'This, the living one, is my child, and the dead one is yours.' The other answers, 'No! The dead one is your child; the living one is mine.'" ²⁴ The king continued, "Get me a sword." When they brought the sword before him, ²⁵ he said, "Cut the living child in two, and give half to one woman and half to the other." ²⁶ The woman whose son it was, in the anguish she felt for it, said to the king, "Please, my lord, give her the living child - please do not kill it!" The other, however, said, "It shall be neither mine nor yours. Divide it!" ²⁷ The king then answered, "Give the first one the living child! By no means kill it, for she is the mother." ²⁸ When all Israel heard the judgment the king had given, they were in awe of him, because they saw that the king had in him the wisdom of God for giving judgment.

1 Kings Chapter 4

¹ Solomon was king over all Israel, ² and these were the officials he had in his service: Azariah, son of Zadok, priest; ³ Elihoreph and Ahijah, sons of Shisha, scribes; Jehoshaphat, son of Ahilud, chancellor; ⁴ (Benaiah, son of Jehoiada, commander of the army; Zadok and Abiathar, priests;) ⁵ Azariah, son of Nathan, chief of the commissaries; Zabud, son of Nathan, companion to the king; ⁶ Ahishar, major-domo of the palace; and Adoniram, son of Abda, superintendent of the forced labor. ⁷ Solomon had twelve commissaries for all Israel who supplied food for the king and his household, each having to provide for one month in the year. ⁸ Their names were: the son of Hur in the hill country of Ephraim; ⁹ the son of Deker in Makaz, Shaalbim, Beth-shemesh, Elon and Beth-hanan; ¹⁰ the son of Hesed in Arubboth, as well as in Socoh and the whole region of Hepher; ¹¹ the son of Abinadab, who was married to Solomon's daughter Taphath, in all the Naphath-dor; ¹² Baana, son of Ahilud, in Taanach and Megiddo, and beyond Jokmeam, and in all Beth-shean, and in the country around Zarethan below Jezreel from Beth-shean to Abel-meholah; ¹³ the son of Geber in Ramoth-gilead, having charge of the villages of Jair, son of Manasseh, in Gilead; and of the district of Argob in Bashan - sixty large walled cities with gates barred with bronze; ¹⁴ Ahinadab, son of Iddo, in Mahanaim; ¹⁵ Ahimaaz, who was married to Basemath, another daughter of Solomon, in Naphtali; ¹⁶ Baana, son of Hushai, in Asher and along the rocky coast; ¹⁷ Jehoshaphat, son of Paruah, in Issachar; ¹⁸ Shimei, son of Ela, in Benjamin; ¹⁹ Geber, son of Uri, in the land of Gilead, the land of Sihon, king of the Amorites, and of Og, king of Bashan. There was one prefect besides, in the king's own land. ²⁰ Judah and Israel were as numerous as the sands by the sea; they ate and drank and made merry.

1 Kings Chapter 5

¹ Solomon ruled over all the kingdoms from the River to the land of the Philistines, down to the border of Egypt; they paid Solomon tribute and were his vassals as long as he lived. ² Solomon's supplies for each day were thirty kors of fine flour, sixty kors of meal, ³ ten fatted oxen, twenty pasture-fed oxen, and a hundred sheep, not counting harts, gazelles, roebucks, and fatted fowl. ⁴ He ruled over all the land west of the Euphrates, from Tiphsah to Gaza, and over all its kings, and he had peace on all his borders round about. ⁵ Thus Judah and Israel lived in security, every man under his vine or under his fig tree from Dan to Beer-sheba, as long as Solomon lived. ⁶ Solomon had four thousand stalls for his twelve thousand chariot horses. ⁷ These commissaries, one for each month, provided food for King Solomon and for all the guests at the royal table. They left nothing unprovided. ⁸ For the chariot horses and draft animals also, each brought his quota of barley and straw to the required place. ⁹ Moreover, God gave Solomon wisdom and exceptional understanding and knowledge, as vast as the sand on the seashore. ¹⁰ Solomon surpassed all the Cedemites and all the Egyptians in wisdom. ¹¹ He was wiser than all other men - than Ethan the Ezrahite, or Heman, Chalcol, and Darda, the musicians - and his fame spread throughout the neighboring nations. ¹² Solomon also uttered three thousand proverbs, and his songs numbered a thousand and five. ¹³ He discussed plants, from the cedar on Lebanon to the hyssop growing out of the wall, and he spoke about beasts, birds, reptiles, and fishes. ¹⁴ Men came to hear Solomon's wisdom from all nations, sent

by all the kings of the earth who had heard of his wisdom. ¹⁵ When Hiram, king of Tyre, heard that Solomon had been anointed king in place of his father, he sent an embassy to him; for Hiram had always been David's friend. ¹⁶ Solomon sent back this message to Hiram: ¹⁷ "You know that my father David, because of the enemies surrounding him on all sides, could not build a temple in honor of the LORD, his God, until such a time as the LORD should put these enemies under the soles of his feet. ¹⁸ But now the LORD, my God, has given me peace on all sides. There is no enemy or threat of danger. ¹⁹ So I purpose to build a temple in honor of the LORD, my God, as the LORD predicted to my father David when he said: 'It is your son whom I will put upon your throne in your place who shall build the temple in my honor.' ²⁰ Give orders, then, to have cedars from the Lebanon cut down for me. My servants shall accompany yours, since you know that there is no one among us who is skilled in cutting timber like the Sidonians, and I will pay you whatever you say for your servants' salary." ²¹ When he had heard the words of Solomon, Hiram was pleased and said, "Blessed be the LORD this day, who has given David a wise son to rule this numerous people." ²² Hiram then sent word to Solomon, "I agree to the proposal you sent me, and I will provide all the cedars and fir trees you wish. ²³ My servants shall bring them down from the Lebanon to the sea, and I will arrange them into rafts in the sea and bring them wherever you say. There I will break up the rafts, and you shall take the lumber. You, for your part, shall furnish the provisions I desire for my household." ²⁴ So Hiram continued to provide Solomon with all the cedars and fir trees he wished; ²⁵ while Solomon every year gave Hiram twenty thousand kors of wheat to provide for his household, and twenty thousand measures of pure oil. ²⁶ The LORD, moreover, gave Solomon wisdom as he promised him, and there was peace between Hiram and Solomon, since they were parties to a treaty. ²⁷ King Solomon conscripted thirty thousand workmen from all Israel. ²⁸ He sent them to the Lebanon each month in relays of ten thousand, so that they spent one month in the Lebanon and two months at home. Adoniram was in charge of the draft. ²⁹ Solomon had seventy thousand carriers and eighty thousand stonecutters in the mountain, ³⁰ in addition to three thousand three hundred overseers, answerable to Solomon's prefects for the work, directing the people engaged in the work. ³¹ By order of the king, fine, large blocks were quarried to give the temple a foundation of hewn stone. ³² Solomon's and Hiram's builders, along with the Gebalites, hewed them out, and prepared the wood and stones for building the temple.

1 Kings Chapter 6

¹ In the four hundred and eightieth year from the departure of the Israelites from the land of Egypt, in the fourth year of Solomon's reign over Israel, in the month of Ziv, which is the second month, the construction of the temple of the LORD was begun. ² The temple which King Solomon built for the LORD was sixty cubits long, twenty wide, and twenty-five high. ³ The porch in front of the temple was twenty cubits from side to side, along the width of the nave, and ten cubits deep in front of the temple. ⁴ Splayed windows with trellises were made for the temple, ⁵ and adjoining the wall of the temple, which enclosed the nave and the sanctuary, an annex of several stories was built. ⁶ Its lowest story was five cubits wide, the middle one six cubits wide, the third seven cubits wide, because there were offsets along the outside of the temple so that the beams would not be fastened into the walls of the temple. ⁷ (The temple was built of stone dressed at the quarry, so that no hammer, axe, or iron tool was to be heard in the temple during its construction.) ⁸ The entrance to the lowest floor of the annex was at the right side of the temple, and stairs with intermediate landings led up to the middle story and from the middle story to the third. ⁹ When the temple was built to its full height, it was roofed in with rafters and boards of cedar. ¹⁰ The annex, with its lowest story five cubits high, was built all along the outside of the temple, to which it was joined by cedar beams. ¹¹ This word of the LORD came to Solomon: ¹² "As to this temple you are building - if you observe my statutes, carry out my ordinances, keep and obey all my commands, I will fulfill toward you the promise I made to your father David. ¹³ I will dwell in the midst of the Israelites and will not forsake my people Israel." ¹⁴ When Solomon finished building the temple, ¹⁵ its walls were lined from floor to ceiling beams with cedar paneling, and its floor was laid with fir planking. ¹⁶ At the rear of the temple a space of twenty cubits was set off by cedar partitions from the floor to the rafters, enclosing the sanctuary, the holy of holies. ¹⁷ The nave, or part of the temple in front of the sanctuary, was forty cubits long. ¹⁸ The cedar in the interior of the temple was carved in the form of gourds and open flowers; all was of cedar, and no stone was to be seen. ¹⁹ In the innermost part of the temple was located the sanctuary to house the ark of the LORD'S covenant, ²⁰ twenty cubits long, twenty wide, and twenty high. ²¹ Solomon overlaid the interior of

the temple with pure gold. He made in front of the sanctuary a cedar altar, overlaid it with gold, and looped it with golden chains. ²² The entire temple was overlaid with gold so that it was completely covered with it; the whole altar before the sanctuary was also overlaid with gold. ²³ In the sanctuary were two cherubim, each ten cubits high, made of olive wood. ²⁴ Each wing of a cherub measured five cubits so that the space from wing tip to wing tip of each was ten cubits. ²⁵ The cherubim were identical in size and shape, ²⁶ and each was exactly ten cubits high. ²⁷ The cherubim were placed in the inmost part of the temple, with their wings spread wide, so that one wing of each cherub touched a side wall while the other wing, pointing toward the middle of the room, touched the corresponding wing of the second cherub. ²⁸ The cherubim, too, were overlaid with gold. ²⁹ The walls on all sides of both the inner and the outer rooms had carved figures of cherubim, palm trees, and open flowers. ³⁰ The floor of both the inner and the outer rooms was overlaid with gold. ³¹ At the entrance of the sanctuary, doors of olive wood were made; the doorframes had beveled posts. ³² The two doors were of olive wood, with carved figures of cherubim, palm trees, and open flowers. The doors were overlaid with gold, which was also molded to the cherubim and the palm trees. ³³ The same was done at the entrance to the nave, where the doorposts of olive wood were rectangular. ³⁴ The two doors were of fir wood; each door was banded by a metal strap, front and back, ³⁵ and had carved cherubim, palm trees, and open flowers, over which gold was evenly applied. ³⁶ The inner court was walled off by means of three courses of hewn stones and one course of cedar beams. ³⁷ The foundations of the LORD'S temple were laid in the month of Ziv ³⁸ in the fourth year, and it was completed in all particulars, exactly according to plan, in the month of Bul, the eighth month, in the eleventh year. Thus it took Solomon seven years to build it.

1 Kings Chapter 7

¹ His own palace Solomon completed after thirteen years of construction. ² He built the hall called the Forest of Lebanon one hundred cubits long, fifty wide, and thirty high; it was supported by four rows of cedar columns, with cedar capitals upon the columns. ³ Moreover, it had a ceiling of cedar above the beams resting on the columns; these beams numbered forty-five, fifteen to a row. ⁴ There were three window frames at either end, with windows in strict alignment. ⁵ The posts of all the doorways were rectangular, and the doorways faced each other, three at either end. ⁶ The porch of the columned hall he made fifty cubits long and thirty wide. The porch extended the width of the columned hall, and there was a canopy in front. ⁷ He also built the vestibule of the throne where he gave judgment - that is, the tribunal; it was paneled with cedar from floor to ceiling beams. ⁸ His living quarters were in another court, set in deeper than the tribunal and of the same construction. A palace like this tribunal was built for Pharaoh's daughter, whom Solomon had married. ⁹ All these buildings were of fine stones, hewn to size and trimmed front and back with a saw, from the foundation to the bonding course. ¹⁰ (The foundation was made of fine, large blocks, some ten cubits and some eight cubits. ¹¹ Above were fine stones hewn to size, and cedar wood.) ¹² The great court was enclosed by three courses of hewn stones and a bonding course of cedar beams. So also were the inner court of the temple of the LORD and the temple porch. ¹³ King Solomon had Hiram brought from Tyre. ¹⁴ He was a bronze worker, the son of a widow from the tribe of Naphtali; his father had been from Tyre. He was endowed with skill, understanding, and knowledge of how to produce any work in bronze. He came to King Solomon and did all his metal work. ¹⁵ Two hollow bronze columns were cast, each eighteen cubits high and twelve cubits in circumference; their metal was of four fingers' thickness. ¹⁶ There were also two capitals cast in bronze, to place on top of the columns, each of them five cubits high. ¹⁷ Two pieces of network with a chainlike mesh were made to cover the (nodes of the) capitals on top of the columns, one for each capital. ¹⁸ Four hundred pomegranates were also cast; two hundred of them in a double row encircled the piece of network on each of the two capitals. ¹⁹ The capitals on top of the columns were finished wholly in a lotus pattern ²⁰ above the level of the nodes and their enveloping network. ²¹ The columns were then erected adjacent to the porch of the temple, one to the right, called Jachin, and the other to the left, called Boaz. ²² Thus the work on the columns was completed. ²³ The sea was then cast; it was made with a circular rim, and measured ten cubits across, five in height, and thirty in circumference. ²⁴ Under the brim, gourds encircled it, ten to the cubit all the way around; the gourds were in two rows and were cast in one mold with the sea. ²⁵ This rested on twelve oxen, three facing north, three facing west, three facing south, and three facing east, with their haunches all toward the center, where the sea was set upon them. ²⁶ It was a handbreadth thick, and its brim resembled that of a cup, being

lily-shaped. Its capacity was two thousand measures. 27 Ten stands were also made of bronze, each four cubits long, four wide, and three high. 28 When these stands were constructed, panels were set within the framework. 29 On the panels between the frames there were lions, oxen, and cherubim; and on the frames likewise, above and below the lions and oxen, there were wreaths in relief. 30 Each stand had four bronze wheels and bronze axles. 31 This was surmounted by a crown one cubit high within which was a rounded opening to provide a receptacle a cubit and a half in depth. There was carved work at the opening, on panels that were angular, not curved. 32 The four wheels were below the paneling, and the axletrees of the wheels and the stand were of one piece. Each wheel was a cubit and a half high. 33 The wheels were constructed like chariot wheels; their axles, fellies, spokes, and hubs were all cast. The four legs of each stand had cast braces, which were under the basin; they had wreaths on each side. 34 These four braces, extending to the corners of each stand, were of one piece with the stand. 35 On top of the stand there was a raised collar half a cubit high, with supports and panels which were of one piece with the top of the stand. 36 On the surfaces of the supports and on the panels, wherever there was a clear space, cherubim, lions, and palm trees were carved, as well as wreaths all around. 37 This was how the ten stands were made, all of the same casting, the same size, the same shape. 38 Ten bronze basins were then made, each four cubits in diameter with a capacity of forty measures, one basin for the top of each of the ten stands. 39 The stands were placed, five on the south side of the temple and five on the north. The sea was placed off to the southeast from the south side of the temple. 40 When Hiram made the pots, shovels, and bowls, he therewith completed all his work for King Solomon in the temple of the LORD: 41 two columns, two nodes for the capitals on top of the columns, two pieces of network covering the nodes for the capitals on top of the columns, 42 four hundred pomegranates in double rows on both pieces of network that covered the two nodes of the capitals where they met the columns, 43 ten stands, ten basins on the stands, 44 one sea, twelve oxen supporting the sea, 45 pots, shovels, and bowls. All these articles which Hiram made for King Solomon in the temple of the LORD were of burnished bronze. 46 The king had them cast in the neighborhood of the Jordan, in the clayey ground between Succoth and Zarethan. 47 Solomon did not weigh all the articles because they were so numerous; the weight of the bronze, therefore, was not determined. 48 Solomon had all the articles made for the interior of the temple of the LORD: the golden altar; the golden table on which the showbread lay; 49 the lampstands of pure gold, five to the right and five to the left before the sanctuary, with their flowers, lamps, and tongs of gold; 50 basins, snuffers, bowls, cups, and fire pans of pure gold; and hinges of gold for the doors of the inner room, or holy of holies, and for the doors of the outer room, the nave. 51 When all the work undertaken by King Solomon in the temple of the LORD was completed, he brought in the dedicated offerings of his father David, putting the silver, gold, and other articles in the treasuries of the temple of the LORD.

1 Kings Chapter 8

1 At the order of Solomon, the elders of Israel and all the leaders of the tribes, the princes in the ancestral houses of the Israelites, came to King Solomon in Jerusalem, to bring up the ark of the LORD'S covenant from the city of David (which is Zion). 2 All the men of Israel assembled before King Solomon during the festival in the month of Ethanim (the seventh month). 3 When all the elders of Israel had arrived, the priests took up the ark; 4 they carried the ark of the LORD and the meeting tent with all the sacred vessels that were in the tent. (The priests and Levites carried them.) 5 King Solomon and the entire community of Israel present for the occasion sacrificed before the ark sheep and oxen too many to number or count. 6 The priests brought the ark of the covenant of the LORD to its place beneath the wings of the cherubim in the sanctuary, the holy of holies of the temple. 7 The cherubim had their wings spread out over the place of the ark, sheltering the ark and its poles from above. 8 The poles were so long that their ends could be seen from that part of the holy place adjoining the sanctuary; however, they could not be seen beyond. (They have remained there to this day.) 9 There was nothing in the ark but the two stone tablets which Moses had put there at Horeb, when the LORD made a covenant with the Israelites at their departure from the land of Egypt. 10 When the priests left the holy place, the cloud filled the temple of the LORD 11 so that the priests could no longer minister because of the cloud, since the LORD'S glory had filled the temple of the LORD. 12 Then Solomon said, "The LORD intends to dwell in the dark cloud; 13 I have truly built you a princely house, a dwelling where you may abide forever." 14 The king turned and greeted the whole community of Israel as they stood. 15 He said to them: "Blessed be the LORD, the God of Israel, who with his own mouth made a promise to my father David and by his hand has brought it to

fulfillment. It was he who said, 16 'Since the day I brought my people Israel out of Egypt, I have not chosen a city out of any tribe of Israel for the building of a temple to my honor; but I choose David to rule my people Israel.' 17 When my father David wished to build a temple to the honor of the LORD, the God of Israel, 18 the LORD said to him, 'In wishing to build a temple to my honor, you do well. 19 It will not be you, however, who will build the temple; but the son who will spring from you, he shall build the temple to my honor.' 20 And now the LORD has fulfilled the promise that he made: I have succeeded my father David and sit on the throne of Israel, as the LORD foretold, and I have built this temple to honor the LORD, the God of Israel. 21 I have provided in it a place for the ark in which is the covenant of the LORD, which he made with our fathers when he brought them out of the land of Egypt." 22 Solomon stood before the altar of the LORD in the presence of the whole community of Israel, and stretching forth his hands toward heaven, 23 he said, "LORD, God of Israel, there is no God like you in heaven above or on earth below; you keep your covenant of kindness with your servants who are faithful to you with their whole heart. 24 You have kept the promise you made to my father David, your servant. You who spoke that promise, have this day, by your own power, brought it to fulfillment. 25 Now, therefore, LORD, God of Israel, keep the further promise you made to my father David, your servant, saying, 'You shall always have someone from your line to sit before me on the throne of Israel, provided only that your descendants look to their conduct so that they live in my presence, as you have lived in my presence.' 26 Now, LORD, God of Israel, may this promise which you made to my father David, your servant, be confirmed. 27 Can it indeed be that God dwells among men on earth? If the heavens and the highest heavens cannot contain you, how much less this temple which I have built! 28 Look kindly on the prayer and petition of your servant, O LORD, my God, and listen to the cry of supplication which I, your servant, utter before you this day. 29 May your eyes watch night and day over this temple, the place where you have decreed you shall be honored; may you heed the prayer which I, your servant, offer in this place. 30 Listen to the petitions of your servant and of your people Israel which they offer in this place. Listen from your heavenly dwelling and grant pardon. 31 If a man sins against his neighbor and is required to take an oath sanctioned by a curse, when he comes and takes the oath before your altar in this temple, 32 listen in heaven; take action and pass judgment on your servants. Condemn the wicked and punish him for his conduct, but acquit the just and establish his innocence. 33 If your people Israel sin against you and are defeated by an enemy, and if then they return to you, praise your name, pray to you, and entreat you in this temple, 34 listen in heaven and forgive the sin of your people Israel, and bring them back to the land you gave their fathers. 35 If the sky is closed, so that there is no rain, because they have sinned against you and you afflict them, and if then they repent of their sin, and pray, and praise your name in this place, 36 listen in heaven and forgive the sin of your servant and of your people Israel, teaching them the right way to live and sending rain upon this land of yours which you have given to your people as their heritage. 37 If there is famine in the land or pestilence; or if blight comes, or mildew, or a locust swarm, or devouring insects; if an enemy of your people besieges them in one of their cities; whatever plague or sickness there may be, 38 if then any one (of your entire people Israel) has remorse of conscience and offers some prayer or petition, stretching out his hands toward this temple, 39 listen from your heavenly dwelling place and forgive. You who alone know the hearts of all men, render to each one of them according to his conduct; knowing their hearts, so treat them 40 that they may fear you as long as they live on the land you gave our fathers. 41 To the foreigner, likewise, who is not of your people Israel, but comes from a distant land to honor you 42 (since men will learn of your great name and your mighty hand and your outstretched arm), when he comes and prays toward this temple, 43 listen from your heavenly dwelling. Do all that the foreigner asks of you, that all the peoples of the earth may know your name, may fear you as do your people Israel, and may acknowledge that this temple which I have built is dedicated to your honor. 44 Whatever the direction in which you may send your people forth to war against their enemies, if they pray to you, O LORD, toward the city you have chosen and the temple I have built in your honor, 45 listen in heaven to their prayer and petition, and defend their cause. 46 When they sin against you (for there is no man who does not sin), and in your anger against them you deliver them to the enemy, so that their captors deport them to a hostile land, far or near, 47 may they repent in the land of their captivity and be converted. If then they entreat you in the land of their captors and say, 'We have sinned and done wrong; we have been wicked'; 48 if with their whole heart and soul they turn back to you in the land of the enemies who took them captive, pray to you toward the land you gave their fathers, the city you have chosen, and the temple I have built in your honor, 49 listen from your heavenly dwelling. 50 Forgive your people their sins and all the offenses they have committed against you, and grant them mercy before their captors, so that these will be merciful to them. 51 For they are your people and your inheritance, whom you brought out of Egypt, from the midst of an iron furnace. 52 Thus may your eyes be open to the petition of your servant and to the petition of your people Israel. Hear them whenever they call upon you, 53 because you have set them apart among all the peoples of the earth for your inheritance, as you declared through your servant Moses when you brought our fathers out of Egypt, O Lord GOD. 54 When Solomon finished offering this entire prayer of petition to the LORD, he rose from before the altar of the LORD, where he had been kneeling with his hands outstretched toward heaven. 55 He stood and blessed the whole community of Israel, saying in a loud voice: 56 Blessed be the LORD who has given rest to his people Israel, just as he promised. Not a single word has gone unfulfilled of the entire generous promise he made through his servant Moses. 57 May the LORD, our God, be with us as he was with our fathers and may he not forsake us nor cast us off. 58 May he draw our hearts to himself, that we may follow him in everything and keep the commands, statutes, and ordinances which he enjoined on our fathers. 59 May this prayer I have offered to the LORD, our God, be present to him day and night, that he may uphold the cause of his servant and of his people Israel as each day requires, 60 that all the peoples of the earth may know the LORD is God and there is no other. 61 You must be wholly devoted to the LORD, our God, observing his statutes and keeping his commandments, as on this day. 62 The king and all Israel with him offered sacrifices before the LORD. 63 Solomon offered as peace offerings to the LORD twenty-two thousand oxen and one hundred twenty thousand sheep. Thus the king and all the Israelites dedicated the temple of the LORD. 64 On that day the king consecrated the middle of the court facing the temple of the LORD; he offered there the holocausts, the cereal offerings, and the fat of the peace offerings, because the bronze altar before the LORD was too small to hold these offerings. 65 On this occasion Solomon and all the Israelites, who had assembled in large numbers from Labo of Hamath to the Wadi of Egypt, celebrated the festival before the LORD, our God, for seven days. 66 On the eighth day he dismissed the people, who bade the king farewell and went to their homes, rejoicing and happy over all the blessings the LORD had given to his servant David and to his people Israel.

1 Kings Chapter 9

1 After Solomon finished building the temple of the LORD, the royal palace, and everything else that he had planned, 2 the LORD appeared to him a second time, as he had appeared to him in Gibeon. 3 The LORD said to him: "I have heard the prayer of petition which you offered in my presence. I have consecrated this temple which you have built; I confer my name upon it forever, and my eyes and my heart shall be there always. 4 As for you, if you live in my presence as your father David lived, sincerely and uprightly, doing just as I have commanded you, keeping my statutes and decrees, 5 I will establish your throne of sovereignty over Israel forever, as I promised your father David when I said, 'You shall always have someone from your line on the throne of Israel.' 6 But if you and your descendants ever withdraw from me, fail to keep the commandments and statutes which I set before you, and proceed to venerate and worship strange gods, 7 I will cut off Israel from the land I gave them and repudiate the temple I have consecrated to my honor. Israel shall become a proverb and a byword among all nations, 8 and this temple shall become a heap of ruins. Every passerby shall catch his breath in amazement, and ask, 'Why has the LORD done this to the land and to this temple?' 9 Men will answer: 'They forsook the LORD, their God, who brought their fathers out of the land of Egypt; they adopted strange gods which they worshiped and served. That is why the LORD has brought down upon them all this evil.'" 10 After the twenty years during which Solomon built the two houses, the temple of the LORD and the palace of the king - 11 Hiram, king of Tyre, supplying Solomon with all the cedar wood, fir wood, and gold he wished - King Solomon gave Hiram twenty cities in the land of Galilee. 12 Hiram left Tyre to see the cities Solomon had given him, but was not satisfied with them. 13 So he said, "What are these cities you have given me, my brother?" And he called them the land of Cabul, as they are called to this day. 14 Hiram, however, had sent king Solomon one hundred and twenty talents of gold. 15 This is an account of the forced labor which King Solomon levied in order to build the temple of the LORD, his palace, Millo, the wall of Jerusalem, Hazor, Megiddo, Gezer 16 (Pharaoh, king of Egypt, had come up and taken Gezer and, after destroying it by fire and slaying all the Canaanites living in the city, had given it as dowry to his daughter, Solomon's wife; 17 Solomon then rebuilt Gezer), Lower Beth-horon, 18 Baalath, Tamar in the desert of

Judah, 19 all his cities for supplies, cities for chariots and for horses, and whatever else Solomon decided should be built in Jerusalem, in Lebanon, and in the entire land under his dominion. 20 All the non-Israelite people who remained in the land, descendants of the Amorites, Hittites, Perizzites, Hivites, and Jebusites 21 whose doom the Israelites had been unable to accomplish, Solomon conscripted as forced laborers, as they are to this day. 22 But Solomon enslaved none of the Israelites, for they were his fighting force, his ministers, commanders, adjutants, chariot officers, and charioteers. 23 The supervisors of Solomon's works who policed the people engaged in the work numbered five hundred and fifty. 24 As soon as Pharaoh's daughter went up from the City of David to her palace, which he had built for her, Solomon built Millo. 25 Three times a year Solomon used to offer holocausts and peace offerings on the altar which he had built to the LORD, and to burn incense before the LORD; and he kept the temple in repair. 26 King Solomon also built a fleet at Ezion-geber, which is near Elath on the shore of the Red Sea in the land of Edom. 27 In this fleet Hiram placed his own expert seamen with the servants of Solomon. 28 They went to Ophir, and brought back four hundred and twenty talents of gold to King Solomon.

1 Kings Chapter 10

1 The queen of Sheba, having heard of Solomon's fame, came to test him with subtle questions. 2 She arrived in Jerusalem with a very numerous retinue, and with camels bearing spices, a large amount of gold, and precious stones. She came to Solomon and questioned him on every subject in which she was interested. 3 King Solomon explained everything she asked about, and there remained nothing hidden from him that he could not explain to her. 4 When the queen of Sheba witnessed Solomon's great wisdom, the palace he had built, 5 the food at his table, the seating of his ministers, the attendance and garb of his waiters, his banquet service, and the holocausts he offered in the temple of the LORD, she was breathless. 6 "The report I heard in my country about your deeds and your wisdom is true," she told the king. 7 "Though I did not believe the report until I came and saw with my own eyes, I have discovered that they were not telling me the half. Your wisdom and prosperity surpass the report I heard. 8 Happy are your men, happy these servants of yours, who stand before you always and listen to your wisdom. 9 Blessed be the LORD, your God, whom it has pleased to place you on the throne of Israel. In his enduring love for Israel, the LORD has made you king to carry out judgment and justice." 10 Then she gave the king one hundred and twenty gold talents, a very large quantity of spices, and precious stones. Never again did anyone bring such an abundance of spices as the queen of Sheba gave to King Solomon. 11 Hiram's fleet, which used to bring gold from Ophir, also brought from there a large quantity of cabinet wood and precious stones. 12 With the wood the king made supports for the temple of the LORD and for the palace of the king, and harps and lyres for the chanters. No more such wood was brought or seen to the present day. 13 King Solomon gave the queen of Sheba everything she desired and asked for, besides such presents as were given her from Solomon's royal bounty. Then she returned with her servants to her own country. 14 The gold that Solomon received every year weighed six hundred and sixty-six gold talents, 15 in addition to what came from the Tarshish fleet, from the traffic of merchants, and from all the kings of Arabia and the governors of the country. 16 Moreover, King Solomon made two hundred shields of beaten gold (six hundred gold shekels went into each shield) 17 and three hundred bucklers of beaten gold (three minas of gold went into each buckler); and he put them in the hall of the Forest of Lebanon. 18 The king also had a large ivory throne made, and overlaid it with refined gold. 19 The throne had six steps, a back with a round top, and an arm on each side of the seat. Next to each arm stood a lion; 20 and twelve other lions stood on the steps, two to a step, one on either side of each step. Nothing like this was produced in any other kingdom. 21 In addition, all King Solomon's drinking vessels were of gold, and all the utensils in the hall of the Forest of Lebanon were of pure gold. There was no silver, for in Solomon's time it was considered worthless. 22 The king had a fleet of Tarshish ships at sea with Hiram's fleet. Once every three years the fleet of Tarshish ships would come with a cargo of gold, silver, ivory, apes, and monkeys. 23 Thus King Solomon surpassed in riches and wisdom all the kings of the earth. 24 And the whole world sought audience with Solomon, to hear from him the wisdom which God had put in his heart. 25 Each one brought his yearly tribute: silver or gold articles, garments, weapons, spices, horses and mules. 26 Solomon collected chariots and drivers; he had one thousand four hundred chariots and twelve thousand drivers; these he allocated among the chariot cities and to the king's service in Jerusalem. 27 The king made silver as common in Jerusalem as stones, and cedars as numerous as the sycamores of the foothills. 28 Solomon's horses were

imported from Cilicia, where the king's agents purchased them. 29 A chariot imported from Egypt cost six hundred shekels, a horse one hundred and fifty shekels; they were exported at these rates to all the Hittite and Aramean kings.

1 Kings Chapter 11

1 King Solomon loved many foreign women besides the daughter of Pharaoh (Moabites, Ammonites, Edomites, Sidonians, and Hittites), 2 from nations with which the LORD had forbidden the Israelites to intermarry, "because," he said, "they will turn your hearts to their gods." But Solomon fell in love with them. 3 He had seven hundred wives of princely rank and three hundred concubines, and his wives turned his heart. 4 When Solomon was old his wives had turned his heart to strange gods, and his heart was not entirely with the LORD, his God, as the heart of his father David had been. 5 By adoring Astarte, the goddess of the Sidonians, and Milcom, the idol of the Ammonites, 6 Solomon did evil in the sight of the LORD; he did not follow him unreservedly as his father David had done. 7 Solomon then built a high place to Chemosh, the idol of Moab, and to Molech, the idol of the Ammonites, on the hill opposite Jerusalem. 8 He did the same for all his foreign wives who burned incense and sacrificed to their gods. 9 The LORD, therefore, became angry with Solomon, because his heart was turned away from the LORD, the God of Israel, who had appeared to him twice 10 (for though the LORD had forbidden him this very act of following strange gods, Solomon had not obeyed him). 11 So the LORD said to Solomon: "Since this is what you want, and you have not kept my covenant and my statutes which I enjoined on you, I will deprive you of the kingdom and give it to your servant. 12 I will not do this during your lifetime, however, for the sake of your father David; it is your son whom I will deprive. 13 Nor will I take away the whole kingdom. I will leave your son one tribe for the sake of my servant David and of Jerusalem, which I have chosen." 14 The LORD then raised up an adversary to Solomon: Hadad the Edomite, who was of the royal line in Edom. 15 Earlier, when David had conquered Edom, Joab, the general of the army, while going to bury the slain, put to death every male in Edom. 16 Joab and all Israel remained there six months until they had killed off every male in Edom. 17 Meanwhile, Hadad, who was only a boy, fled toward Egypt with some Edomite servants of his father. 18 They left Midian and passing through Paran, where they picked up additional men, they went into Egypt to Pharaoh, king of Egypt, who gave Hadad a house, appointed him rations, and assigned him land. 19 Hadad won great favor with Pharaoh, so that he gave him in marriage the sister of Queen Tahpenes, his own wife. 20 Tahpenes' sister bore Hadad a son, Genubath. After his weaning, the queen kept him in Pharaoh's palace, where he then lived with Pharaoh's own sons. 21 When Hadad in Egypt heard that David rested with his ancestors and that Joab, the general of the army, was dead, he said to Pharaoh, "Give me leave to return to my own country." 22 Pharaoh said to him, "What do you lack with me, that you are seeking to return to your own country?" "Nothing," he said, "but please let me go!" 23 God raised up against Solomon another adversary, in Rezon, the son of Eliada, who had fled from his lord, Hadadezer, king of Zobah, 24 when David defeated them with slaughter. Rezon gathered men about him and became leader of a band, went to Damascus, settled there, and became king in Damascus. 25 He was an enemy of Israel as long as Solomon lived; this added to the harm done by Hadad, who made a rift in Israel by becoming king over Edom. 26 Solomon's servant Jeroboam, son of Nebat, an Ephraimite from Zeredah with a widowed mother, Zeruah, also rebelled against the king. 27 This is why he rebelled. King Solomon was building Millo, closing up the breach of his father's City of David. 28 Jeroboam was a man of means, and when Solomon saw that he was also an industrious young man, he put him in charge of the entire labor force of the house of Joseph. 29 At that time Jeroboam left Jerusalem, and the prophet Ahijah the Shilonite met him on the road. The two were alone in the area, and the prophet was wearing a new cloak. 30 Ahijah took off his new cloak, tore it into twelve pieces, 31 and said to Jeroboam: "Take ten pieces for yourself; the LORD, the God of Israel, says: 'I will tear away the kingdom from Solomon's grasp and will give you ten of the tribes. 32 One tribe shall remain to him for the sake of David my servant, and of Jerusalem, the city I have chosen out of all the tribes of Israel. 33 The ten I will give you because he has forsaken me and has worshiped Astarte, goddess of the Sidonians, Chemosh, god of Moab, and Milcom, god of the Ammonites; he has not followed my ways or done what is pleasing to me according to my statutes and my decrees, as his father David did. 34 Yet I will not take any of the kingdom from Solomon himself, but will keep him a prince as long as he lives for the sake of my servant David, whom I chose, who kept my commandments and statutes. 35 But I will take the kingdom from his son and will give it to you - that is, the ten tribes. 36 I will give his son one tribe, that my servant David may always have a lamp before me in Jerusalem, the city in which I choose to be honored. 37 I will take you; you shall reign over all that you desire and shall become king of Israel. 38 If, then, you heed all that I command you, follow my ways, and please me by keeping my statutes and my commandments like my servant David, I will be with you. I will establish for you, as I did for David, a lasting dynasty; I will give Israel to you. 39 I will punish David's line for this, but not forever.'" 40 When Solomon tried to have Jeroboam killed for his rebellion, he escaped to King Shishak, in Egypt, where he remained until Solomon's death. 41 The rest of the acts of Solomon, with all his deeds and his wisdom, are recorded in the book of the chronicles of Solomon. 42 The time that Solomon reigned in Jerusalem over all Israel was forty years. 43 Solomon rested with his ancestors; he was buried in his father's City of David, and his son Rehoboam succeeded him as king.

1 Kings Chapter 12

1 Rehoboam went to Shechem, where all Israel had come to proclaim him king. 2 Jeroboam, son of Nebat, who was still in Egypt, where he had fled from King Solomon, returned from Egypt as soon as he learned this. 3 They said to Rehoboam: 4 "Your father put on us a heavy yoke. If you now lighten the harsh service and the heavy yoke your father imposed on us, we will serve you." 5 "Come back to me in three days," he answered them. When the people had departed, 6 King Rehoboam consulted the elders who had been in his father's service while he was alive, and asked, "What do you advise me to give this people?" 7 They replied, "If today you will be the servant of this people and submit to them, giving them a favorable answer, they will be your servants forever." 8 But he ignored the advice the elders had given him, and consulted the young men who had grown up with him and were in his service. 9 He said to them, "What answer do you advise me to give this people, who have asked me to lighten the yoke my father imposed on them?" 10 The young men who had grown up with him replied, "This is what you must say to this people who have asked you to lighten the yoke your father put on them: 'My little finger is thicker than my father's body. 11 Whereas my father put a heavy yoke on you, I will make it heavier. My father beat you with whips, but I will beat you with scorpions.'" 12 On the third day all Israel came back to King Rehoboam, as he had instructed them to do. 13 Ignoring the advice the elders had given him, the king gave the people a harsh answer. 14 He said to them, as the young men had advised: "My father put on you a heavy yoke, but I will make it heavier. My father beat you with whips, but I will beat you with scorpions." 15 The king did not listen to the people, for the LORD brought this about to fulfill the prophecy he had uttered to Jeroboam, son of Nebat, through Ahijah the Shilonite. 162 When all Israel saw that the king did not listen to them, the people answered the king: "What share have we in David? We have no heritage in the son of Jesse. To your tents, O Israel! Now look to your own house, David." So Israel went off to their tents, 17 but Rehoboam reigned over the Israelites who lived in the cities of Judah. 18 King Rehoboam then sent out Adoram, superintendent of the forced labor, but all Israel stoned him to death. Rehoboam managed to mount his chariot to flee to Jerusalem, 19 and Israel went into rebellion against David's house to this day. 20 When all Israel heard that Jeroboam had returned, they summoned him to an assembly and made him king over all Israel. None remained loyal to David's house except the tribe of Judah alone. 21 On his arrival in Jerusalem, Rehoboam gathered together all the house of Judah and the tribe of Benjamin - one hundred and eighty thousand seasoned warriors - to fight against the house of Israel, to restore the kingdom to Rehoboam, son of Solomon. 22 However, the LORD spoke to Shemaiah, a man of God: 23 "Say to Rehoboam, son of Solomon, king of Judah, and to the house of Judah and to Benjamin, and to the rest of the people: 24 'Thus says the LORD: You must not march out to fight against your brother Israelites. Let every man return home, for I have brought this about.'" They accepted this message of the LORD and gave up the expedition accordingly. 25 Jeroboam built up Shechem in the hill country of Ephraim and lived there. Then he left it and built up Penuel. 263 Jeroboam thought to himself: "The kingdom will return to David's house. 27 If now this people go up to offer sacrifices in the temple of the LORD in Jerusalem, the hearts of this people will return to their master, Rehoboam, king of Judah, and they will kill me." 28 After taking counsel, the king made two calves of gold and said to the people: "You have been going up to Jerusalem long enough. Here is your God, O Israel, who brought you up from the land of Egypt." 294 And he put one in Bethel, the other in Dan. 30 This led to sin, because the people frequented these calves in Bethel and in Dan. 31 He also built temples on the high places and made priests from among the people who were not Levites. 32 Jeroboam established a feast in the eighth month on the fifteenth day of the month to duplicate in Bethel the pilgrimage feast of Judah, with sacrifices to the calves he had made; and he stationed in

Bethel priests of the high places he had built. ³³ Jeroboam ascended the altar he built in Bethel on the fifteenth day of the eighth month, the month in which he arbitrarily chose to establish a feast for the Israelites; he was going to offer sacrifice.

1 Kings Chapter 13

¹ A man of God came from Judah to Bethel by the word of the LORD, while Jeroboam was standing at the altar to offer sacrifice. ² He cried out against the altar the word of the LORD: "O altar, altar, the LORD says, 'A child shall be born to the house of David, Josiah by name, who shall slaughter upon you the priests of the high places who offer sacrifice upon you, and he shall burn human bones upon you.'" ³ He gave a sign that same day and said: "This is the sign that the LORD has spoken: The altar shall break up and the ashes on it shall be strewn about. ⁴ When King Jeroboam heard what the man of God was crying out against the altar, he stretched forth his hand from the altar and said, "Seize him!" But the hand he stretched forth against him withered, so that he could not draw it back. ⁵ Moreover, the altar broke up and the ashes from it were strewn about - the sign the man of God had given as the word of the LORD. ⁶ Then the king appealed to the man of God. "Entreat the LORD, your God," he said, "and intercede for me that I may be able to withdraw my hand." So the man of God entreated the LORD, and the king recovered the normal use of his hand. ⁷ "Come home with me for some refreshment," the king invited the man of God, "and I will give you a present." ⁸ "If you gave me half your kingdom," the man of God said to the king, "I would not go with you, nor eat bread or drink water in this place. ⁹ For I was instructed by the word of the LORD not to eat bread or drink water and not to return by the way I came." ¹⁰ So he departed by another road and did not go back the way he had come to Bethel. ¹¹ There was an old prophet living in the city, whose sons came and told him all that the man of God had done that day in Bethel. When they repeated to their father the words he had spoken to the king, ¹² the father asked them, "Which way did he go?" And his sons pointed out to him the road taken by the man of God who had come from Judah. ¹³ Then he said to his sons, "Saddle the ass for me." When they had saddled it, he mounted ¹⁴ and followed the man of God, whom he found seated under a terebinth. When he asked him, "Are you the man of God who came from Judah?" he answered, "Yes." ¹⁵ Then he said, "Come home with me and have some bread." ¹⁶ "I cannot go back with you, and I cannot eat bread or drink water with you in this place," he answered, ¹⁷ "for I was told by the word of the LORD neither to eat bread nor drink water here, and not to go back the way I came." ¹⁸ But he said to him, "I, too, am a prophet like you, and an angel told me in the word of the LORD to bring you back with me to my house and to have you eat bread and drink water." He was lying to him, however. ¹⁹ So he went back with him, and ate bread and drank water in his house. ²⁰ But while they were sitting at table, the LORD spoke to the prophet who had brought him back, ²¹ and he cried out to the man of God who had come from Judah: "The LORD says, 'Because you rebelled against the command of the LORD and did not keep the command which the LORD, your God, gave you, ²² but returned and ate bread and drank water in the place where he told you to do neither, your corpse shall not be brought to the grave of your ancestors.'" ²³ After he had eaten bread and drunk water, the ass was saddled for him, and he again ²⁴ set out. But a lion met him on the road, and killed him. His corpse lay sprawled on the road, and the ass remained standing by it, and so did the lion. ²⁵ Some passers-by saw the body lying in the road, with the lion standing beside it, and carried the news to the city where the old prophet lived. ²⁶ On hearing it, the prophet who had brought him back from his journey said: "It is the man of God who rebelled against the command of the LORD. He has delivered him to a lion, which mangled and killed him, as the LORD predicted to him." ²⁷ Then he said to his sons, "Saddle the ass for me." When they had saddled it, ²⁸ he went off and found the body lying in the road with the ass and the lion standing beside it. The lion had not eaten the body nor had it harmed the ass. ²⁹ The prophet lifted up the body of the man of God and put it on the ass, and brought it back to the city to mourn over it and to bury it. ³⁰ He laid the man's body in his own grave, and they mourned over it: "Alas, my brother!" ³¹ After he had buried him, he said to his sons, "When I die, bury me in the grave where the man of God is buried. Lay my remains beside his. ³² For the word of the LORD which he proclaimed against the altar in Bethel and against all the shrines on the high places in the cities of Samaria shall certainly come to pass." ³³ Jeroboam did not give up his evil ways after this event, but again made priests for the high places from among the common people. Whoever desired it was consecrated and became a priest of the high places. ³⁴ This was a sin on the part of the house of Jeroboam for which it was to be cut off and destroyed from the earth.

1 Kings Chapter 14

¹ At that time Abijah, son of Jeroboam, took sick. ² So Jeroboam said to his wife, "Get ready and disguise yourself so that none will recognize you as Jeroboam's wife. Then go to Shiloh, where you will find the prophet Ahijah. It was he who predicted my reign over this people. ³ Take along ten loaves, some cakes, and a jar of preserves, and go to him. He will tell you what will happen to the child." ⁴ The wife of Jeroboam obeyed. She made the journey to Shiloh and entered the house of Ahijah who could not see because age had dimmed his sight. ⁵ The LORD had said to Ahijah: "Jeroboam's wife is coming to consult you about her son, for he is sick. This is what you must tell her. When she comes, she will be in disguise." ⁶ So Ahijah, hearing the sound of her footsteps as she entered the door, said, "Come in, wife of Jeroboam. Why are you in disguise? I have been commissioned to give you bitter news. ⁷ Go, tell Jeroboam, 'This is what the LORD, the God of Israel, says: I exalted you from among the people and made you ruler of my people Israel. ⁸ I deprived the house of David of the kingdom and gave it to you. Yet you have not been like my servant David, who kept my commandments and followed me with his whole heart, doing only what pleased me. ⁹ You have done worse than all who preceded you: you have gone and made for yourself strange gods and molten images to provoke me; but me you have cast behind your back. ¹⁰ Therefore, I am bringing evil upon the house of Jeroboam: I will cut off every male in Jeroboam's line, whether slave or freeman in Israel, and will burn up the house of Jeroboam completely, as though dung were being burned. ¹¹ When one of Jeroboam's line dies in the city, dogs will devour him; when one of them dies in the field, he will be devoured by the birds of the sky. For the LORD has spoken!' ¹² So leave; go home! As you step inside the city, the child will die, ¹³ and all Israel will mourn him and bury him, for he alone of Jeroboam's line will be laid in the grave, since in him alone of Jeroboam's house has something pleasing to the LORD, the God of Israel, been found. ¹⁴ Today, at this very moment, the LORD will raise up for himself a king of Israel who will destroy the house of Jeroboam. ¹⁵ The LORD will strike Israel like a reed tossed about in the water and will pluck out Israel from this good land which he gave their fathers, scattering them beyond the River, because they made sacred poles for themselves and thus provoked the LORD. ¹⁶ He will give up Israel because of the sins Jeroboam has committed and caused Israel to commit." ¹⁷ So Jeroboam's wife started back; when she reached Tirzah and crossed the threshold of her house, the child died. ¹⁸ He was buried with all Israel mourning him, as the LORD had prophesied through his servant the prophet Ahijah. ¹⁹ The rest of the acts of Jeroboam, with his warfare and his reign, are recorded in the book of the chronicles of the kings of Israel. ²⁰ The length of Jeroboam's reign was twenty-two years. He rested with his ancestors, and his son Nadab succeeded him as king. ²¹ Rehoboam, son of Solomon, reigned in Judah. He was forty-one years old when he became king, and he reigned seventeen years in Jerusalem, the city in which, out of all the tribes of Israel, the LORD chose to be honored. His mother was the Ammonite named Naamah. ²² Judah did evil in the sight of the LORD, and by their sins angered him even more than their fathers had done. ²³ They, too, built for themselves high places, pillars, and sacred poles, upon every high hill and under every green tree. ²⁴ There were also cult prostitutes in the land. Judah imitated all the abominable practices of the nations whom the LORD had cleared out of the Israelites' way. ²⁵ In the fifth year of King Rehoboam, Shishak, king of Egypt, attacked Jerusalem. ²⁶ He took everything, including the treasures of the temple of the LORD and those of the royal palace, as well as all the gold shields made under Solomon. ²⁷ To replace them, King Rehoboam had bronze shields made, which he entrusted to the officers of the guard on duty at the entrance of the royal palace. ²⁸ Whenever the king visited the temple of the LORD, those on duty would carry the shields, and then return them to the guardroom. ²⁹ The rest of the acts of Rehoboam, with all that he did, are recorded in the book of the chronicles of the kings of Judah. ³⁰ There was constant warfare between Rehoboam and Jeroboam. ³¹ Rehoboam rested with his ancestors; he was buried with them in the City of David. His mother was the Ammonite named Naamah. His son Abijam succeeded him as king.

1 Kings Chapter 15

¹ In the eighteenth year of King Jeroboam, son of Nebat, Abijam became king of Judah; ² he reigned three years in Jerusalem. His mother's name was Maacah, daughter of Abishalom. ³ He imitated all the sins his father had committed before him, and his heart was not entirely with the LORD, his God, like the heart of his grandfather David. ⁴ Yet for David's sake the LORD, his God, gave him a lamp in Jerusalem, raising up his son after him and permitting Jerusalem to endure; ⁵ because David had pleased the LORD and did not disobey any of his

commands as long as he lived, except in the case of Uriah the Hittite. 6 There was war between Abijam and Jeroboam. 7 The rest of Abijam's acts, with all that he did, are written in the book of the chronicles of the kings of Judah. 8 Abijam rested with his ancestors; he was buried in the City of David, and his son Asa succeeded him as king. 9 In the twentieth year of Jeroboam, king of Israel, Asa, king of Judah, began to reign; 10 he reigned forty-one years in Jerusalem. His grandmother's name was Maacah, daughter of Abishalom. 11 Asa pleased the LORD like his forefather David, 12 banishing the temple prostitutes from the land and removing all the idols his father had made. 13 He also deposed his grandmother Maacah from her position as queen mother, because she had made an outrageous object for Asherah. Asa cut down this object and burned it in the Kidron Valley. 14 The high places did not disappear; yet Asa's heart was entirely with the LORD as long as he lived. 15 He brought into the temple of the LORD his father's and his own votive offerings of silver, gold, and various utensils. 16 There was war between Asa and Baasha, king of Israel, as long as they both reigned. 17 Baasha, king of Israel, attacked Judah and fortified Ramah to prevent communication with Asa, king of Judah. 18 Asa then took all the silver and gold remaining in the treasuries of the temple of the LORD and of the royal palace. Entrusting them to his ministers, King Asa sent them to Ben-hadad, son of Tabrimmon, son of Hezion, king of Aram, resident in Damascus. He said: 19 "There is a treaty between you and me, as there was between your father and my father. I am sending you a present of silver and gold. Go, break your treaty with Baasha, king of Israel, that he may withdraw from me." 20 Ben-hadad agreed with King Asa and sent the leaders of his troops against the cities of Israel. They attacked Ijon, Dan, Abel-beth-maacah, and all Chinnereth, besides all the land of Naphtali. 21 When Baasha heard of it, he left off fortifying Ramah, and stayed in Tirzah. 22 Then King Asa summoned all Judah without exception, and they carried away the stones and beams with which Baasha was fortifying Ramah. With them King Asa built Geba of Benjamin and Mizpeh. 23 The rest of the acts of Asa, with all his valor and accomplishments, and the cities he built, are written in the book of the chronicles of the kings of Judah. In his old age, Asa had an infirmity in his feet. 24 He rested with his ancestors; he was buried in his forefather's City of David, and his son Jehoshaphat succeeded him as king. 25 In the second year of Asa, king of Judah, Nadab, son of Jeroboam, became king of Israel; he reigned over Israel two years. 26 He did evil in the LORD'S sight, imitating his father's conduct and the sin which he had caused Israel to commit. 27 Baasha, son of Ahijah, of the house of Issachar, plotted against him and struck him down at Gibbethon of the Philistines, which Nadab and all Israel were besieging. 28 Baasha killed him in the third year of Asa, king of Judah, and reigned in his stead. 29 Once he was king, he killed off the entire house of Jeroboam, not leaving a single soul to Jeroboam but destroying him utterly, according to the warning which the LORD had pronounced through his servant, Ahijah the Shilonite, 30 because of the sins Jeroboam committed and caused Israel to commit, by which he provoked the LORD, the God of Israel, to anger. 31 The rest of the acts of Nadab, with all that he did, are written in the book of the chronicles of the kings of Israel. 32 There was war between Asa and Baasha, king of Israel, as long as they lived. 33 In the third year of Asa, king of Judah, Baasha, son of Ahijah, began his twenty-four-year reign over Israel in Tirzah. 34 He did evil in the LORD'S sight, imitating the conduct of Jeroboam and the sin he had caused Israel to commit.

1 Kings Chapter 16

1 The LORD spoke against Baasha to Jehu, son of Hanani, and said: 2 "Inasmuch as I lifted you up from the dust and made you ruler of my people Israel, but you have imitated the conduct of Jeroboam and have caused my people Israel to sin, provoking me to anger by their sins, 3 I will destroy you, Baasha, and your house; I will make your house like that of Jeroboam, son of Nebat. If anyone of Baasha's line dies in the city, dogs shall devour him; if he dies in the field, he shall be devoured by the birds of the sky." 5 The rest of the acts of Baasha, with all his valor and accomplishments, are written in the book of the chronicles of the kings of Israel. 6 Baasha rested with his ancestors; he was buried in Tirzah, and his son Elah succeeded him as king. 7 (Through the prophet Jehu, son of Hanani, the LORD had threatened Baasha and his house, because of all the evil Baasha did in the sight of the LORD, provoking him to anger by his evil deeds, so that he became like the house of Jeroboam; and because he killed Nadab.) 8 In the twenty-sixth year of Asa, king of Judah, Elah, son of Baasha, began his two-year reign over Israel in Tirzah. 9 His servant Zimri, commander of half his chariots, plotted against him. As he was in Tirzah, drinking to excess in the house of Arza, superintendent of his palace in Tirzah, 10 Zimri entered; he struck and killed him in the twenty-seventh year of Asa, king of Judah, and reigned in his place. 11 Once he was seated on the royal throne, he killed off the whole house of Baasha, not sparing a single male relative or friend of his. 12 Zimri destroyed the entire house of Baasha, as the LORD had prophesied to Baasha through the prophet Jehu, 13 because of all the sins which Baasha and his son Elah committed and caused Israel to commit, provoking the LORD, the God of Israel, to anger by their idols. 14 The rest of the acts of Elah, with all that he did, are written in the book of the chronicles of the kings of Israel. 15 In the twenty-seventh year of Asa, king of Judah, Zimri reigned seven days in Tirzah. The army was besieging Gibbethon of the Philistines 16 when they heard that Zimri had formed a conspiracy and had killed the king. So that day in the camp all Israel proclaimed Omri, general of the army, king of Israel. 17 Omri marched up from Gibbethon, accompanied by all Israel, and laid siege to Tirzah. 18 When Zimri saw the city was captured, he entered the citadel of the royal palace and burned down the palace over him. He died 19 because of the sins he had committed, doing evil in the sight of the LORD by imitating the sinful conduct of Jeroboam, thus causing Israel to sin. 20 The rest of the acts of Zimri, with the conspiracy he carried out, are written in the book of the chronicles of the kings of Israel. 21 At that time the people of Israel were divided, half following Tibni, son of Ginath, to make him king, and half for Omri. 22 The partisans of Omri prevailed over those of Tibni, son of Ginath. Tibni died and Omri became king. 23 In the thirty-first year of Asa, king of Judah, Omri became king; he reigned over Israel twelve years, the first six of them in Tirzah. 24 He then bought the hill of Samaria from Shemer for two silver talents and built upon the hill, naming the city he built Samaria after Shemer, the former owner. 25 But Omri did evil in the LORD'S sight beyond any of his predecessors. 26 He closely imitated the sinful conduct of Jeroboam, son of Nebat, causing Israel to sin and to provoke the LORD, the God of Israel, to anger by their idols. 27 The rest of the acts of Omri, with all his valor and accomplishments, are written in the book of the chronicles of the kings of Israel. 28 Omri rested with his ancestors; he was buried in Samaria, and his son Ahab succeeded him as king. 29 In the thirty-eighth year of Asa, king of Judah, Ahab, son of Omri, became king of Israel; he reigned over Israel in Samaria for twenty-two years. 30 Ahab, son of Omri, did evil in the sight of the LORD more than any of his predecessors. 31 It was not enough for him to imitate the sins of Jeroboam, son of Nebat. He even married Jezebel, daughter of Ethbaal, king of the Sidonians, and went over to the veneration and worship of Baal. 32 Ahab erected an altar to Baal in the temple of Baal which he built in Samaria, 33 and also made a sacred pole. He did more to anger the LORD, the God of Israel, than any of the kings of Israel before him. 34 During his reign, Hiel from Bethel rebuilt Jericho. He lost his first-born son, Abiram, when he laid the foundation, and his youngest son, Segub, when he set up the gates, as the LORD had foretold through Joshua, son of Nun.

1 Kings Chapter 17

1 Elijah the Tishbite, from Tishbe in Gilead, said to Ahab: "As the LORD, the God of Israel, lives, whom I serve, during these years there shall be no dew or rain except at my word." 2 The LORD then said to Elijah: 3 "Leave here, go east and hide in the Wadi Cherith, east of the Jordan. 4 You shall drink of the stream, and I have commanded ravens to feed you there." 5 So he left and did as the LORD had commanded. He went and remained by the Wadi Cherith, east of the Jordan. 6 Ravens brought him bread and meat in the morning, and bread and meat in the evening, and he drank from the stream. 7 After some time, however, the brook ran dry, because no rain had fallen in the land. 8 So the LORD said to him: 9 "Move on to Zarephath of Sidon and stay there. I have designated a widow there to provide for you." 10 He left and went to Zarephath. As he arrived at the entrance of the city, a widow was gathering sticks there; he called out to her, "Please bring me a small cupful of water to drink." 11 She left to get it, and he called out after her, "Please bring along a bit of bread." 12 "As the LORD, your God, lives," she answered, "I have nothing baked; there is only a handful of flour in my jar and a little oil in my jug. Just now I was collecting a couple of sticks, to go in and prepare something for myself and my son; when we have eaten it, we shall die." 13 "Do not be afraid," Elijah said to her. "Go and do as you propose. But first make me a little cake and bring it to me. Then you can prepare something for yourself and your son. 14 For the LORD, the God of Israel, says, 'The jar of flour shall not go empty, nor the jug of oil run dry, until the day when the LORD sends rain upon the earth.'" 15 She left and did as Elijah had said. She was able to eat for a year, and he and her son as well; 16 The jar of flour did not go empty, nor the jug of oil run dry, as the LORD had foretold through Elijah. 17 Some time later the son of the mistress of the house fell sick, and his sickness grew more severe until he stopped breathing. 18 So she said to Elijah, "Why have you done this to me, O man of God? Have you come to me to call attention to my guilt and to kill my son?" 19 "Give me your

son," Elijah said to her. Taking him from her lap, he carried him to the upper room where he was staying, and laid him on his own bed. 20 He called out to the LORD: "O LORD, my God, will you afflict even the widow with whom I am staying by killing her son?" 21 Then he stretched himself out upon the child three times and called out to the LORD: "O LORD, my God, let the life breath return to the body of this child." 22 The LORD heard the prayer of Elijah; the life breath returned to the child's body and he revived. 23 Taking the child, Elijah brought him down into the house from the upper room and gave him to his mother. "See!" Elijah said to her, "your son is alive." 24 "Now indeed I know that you you are a man of God," the woman replied to Elijah. "The word of the LORD comes truly from your mouth."

1 Kings Chapter 18

1 Long afterward, in the third year, the LORD spoke to Elijah, "Go, present yourself to Ahab," he said, "that I may send rain upon the earth." 2 So Elijah went to present himself to Ahab. 3 Now the famine in Samaria was bitter, 4 and Ahab had summoned Obadiah, his vizier, who was a zealous follower of the LORD. When Jezebel was murdering the prophets of the LORD, Obadiah took a hundred prophets, hid them away fifty each in two caves, and supplied them with food and drink. 5 Ahab said to Obadiah, "Come, let us go through the land to all sources of water and to all the streams. We may find grass and save the horses and mules, so that we shall not have to slaughter any of the beasts." 6 Dividing the land to explore between them, Ahab went one way by himself, Obadiah another way by himself. 7 As Obadiah was on his way, Elijah met him. Recognizing him, Obadiah fell prostrate and asked, "Is it you, my lord Elijah?" 8 "Yes," he answered. "Go tell your master, 'Elijah is here!'" 9 But Obadiah said, "What sin have I committed, that you are handing me over to Ahab to have me killed? 10 As the LORD, your God, lives, there is no nation or kingdom where my master has not sent in search of you. When they replied, 'He is not here,' he made each kingdom and nation swear they could not find you. 11 And now you say, 'Go tell your master: Elijah is here!' 12 After I leave you, the spirit of the LORD will carry you to some place I do not know, and when I go to inform Ahab and he does not find you, he will kill me. Your servant has revered the LORD from his youth. 13 Have you not been told, my lord, what I did when Jezebel was murdering the prophets of the LORD - that I hid a hundred of the prophets of the LORD, fifty each in two caves, and supplied them with food and drink? 14 And now you say, 'Go tell your master: Elijah is here!' He will kill me!" 15 Elijah answered, "As the LORD of hosts lives, whom I serve, I will present myself to him today." 16 So Obadiah went to meet Ahab and informed him. Ahab came to meet Elijah, 17 and when he saw Elijah, said to him, "Is it you, you disturber of Israel?" 18 "It is not I who disturb Israel," he answered, "but you and your family, by forsaking the commands of the LORD and following the Baals. 19 Now summon all Israel to me on Mount Carmel, as well as the four hundred and fifty prophets of Baal and the four hundred prophets of Asherah who eat at Jezebel's table." 20 So Ahab sent to all the Israelites and had the prophets assemble on Mount Carmel. 21 Elijah appealed to all the people and said, "How long will you straddle the issue? If the LORD is God, follow him; if Baal, follow him." The people, however, did not answer him. 22 So Elijah said to the people, "I am the only surviving prophet of the LORD, and there are four hundred and fifty prophets of Baal. 23 Give us two young bulls. Let them choose one, cut it into pieces, and place it on the wood, but start no fire. I shall prepare the other and place it on the wood, but shall start no fire. 24 You shall call on the name of your gods, and I will call on the name of the LORD. The God who answers with fire is God." All the people answered, "Agreed!" 25 Elijah then said to the prophets of Baal, "Choose one young bull and prepare it first, for there are more of you. Call upon your gods, but do not start the fire." 26 Taking the young bull that was turned over to them, they prepared it and called on Baal from morning to noon, saying, "Answer us, Baal!" But there was no sound, and no one answering. And they hopped around the altar they had prepared. 27 When it was noon, Elijah taunted them: "Call louder, for he is a god and may be meditating, or may have retired, or may be on a journey. Perhaps he is asleep and must be awakened." 28 They called out louder and slashed themselves with swords and spears, as was their custom, until blood gushed over them. 29 Noon passed and they remained in a prophetic state until the time for offering sacrifice. But there was not a sound; no one answered, and no one was listening. 30 Then Elijah said to all the people, "Come here to me." When they had done so, he repaired the altar of the LORD which had been destroyed. 31 He took twelve stones, for the number of tribes of the sons of Jacob, to whom the LORD had said, "Your name shall be Israel." 32 He built an altar in honor of the LORD with the stones, and made a trench around the altar large enough for two seahs of grain. 33 When he had arranged the wood, he cut up the young bull and laid it on the wood. 34

"Fill four jars with water," he said, "and pour it over the holocaust and over the wood." "Do it again," he said, and they did it again. "Do it a third time," he said, and they did it a third time. 35 The water flowed around the altar, and the trench was filled with the water. 36 At the time for offering sacrifice, the prophet Elijah came forward and said, "LORD, God of Abraham, Isaac, and Israel, let it be known this day that you are God in Israel and that I am your servant and have done all these things by your command. 37 Answer me, LORD! Answer me, that this people may know that you, LORD, are God and that you have brought them back to their senses." 38 The LORD'S fire came down and consumed the holocaust, wood, stones, and dust, and it lapped up the water in the trench. 39 Seeing this, all the people fell prostrate and said, "The LORD is God! The LORD is God!" 40 Then Elijah said to them, "Seize the prophets of Baal. Let none of them escape!" They were seized, and Elijah had them brought down to the brook Kishon and there he slit their throats. 41 Elijah then said to Ahab, "Go up, eat and drink, for there is the sound of a heavy rain." 42 So Ahab went up to eat and drink, while Elijah climbed to the top of Carmel, crouched down to the earth, and put his head between his knees. 43 "Climb up and look out to sea," he directed his servant, who went up and looked, but reported, "There is nothing." Seven times he said, "Go look again!" 44 And the seventh time the youth reported, "There is a cloud as small as a man's hand rising from the sea." Elijah said, "Go and say to Ahab, 'Harness up and leave the mountain before the rain stops you.'" 45 In a trice, the sky grew dark with clouds and wind, and a heavy rain fell. Ahab mounted his chariot and made for Jezreel. 46 But the hand of the LORD was on Elijah, who girded up his clothing and ran before Ahab as far as the approaches to Jezreel.

1 Kings Chapter 19

1 Ahab told Jezebel all that Elijah had done - that he had put all the prophets to the sword. 2 Jezebel then sent a messenger to Elijah and said, "May the gods do thus and so to me if by this time tomorrow I have not done with your life what was done to each of them." 3 Elijah was afraid and fled for his life, going to Beer-sheba of Judah. He left his servant there 4 and went a day's journey into the desert, until he came to a broom tree and sat beneath it. He prayed for death: "This is enough, O LORD! Take my life, for I am no better than my fathers." 5 He lay down and fell asleep under the broom tree, but then an angel touched him and ordered him to get up and eat. 6 He looked and there at his head was a hearth cake and a jug of water. After he ate and drank, he lay down again, 7 but the angel of the LORD came back a second time, touched him, and ordered, "Get up and eat, else the journey will be too long for you!" 8 He got up, ate and drank; then strengthened by that food, he walked forty days and forty nights to the mountain of God, Horeb. 9 There he came to a cave, where he took shelter. But the word of the LORD came to him, "Why are you here, Elijah?" 10 He answered: "I have been most zealous for the LORD, the God of hosts, but the Israelites have forsaken your covenant, torn down your altars, and put your prophets to the sword. I alone am left, and they seek to take my life." 11 Then the LORD said, "Go outside and stand on the mountain before the LORD; the LORD will be passing by." A strong and heavy wind was rending the mountains and crushing rocks before the LORD - but the LORD was not in the wind. After the wind there was an earthquake - but the LORD was not in the earthquake. 12 After the earthquake there was fire - but the LORD was not in the fire. After the fire there was a tiny whispering sound. 13 When he heard this, Elijah hid his face in his cloak and went and stood at the entrance of the cave. A voice said to him, "Elijah, why are you here?" 14 He replied, "I have been most zealous for the LORD, the God of hosts. But the Israelites have forsaken your covenant, torn down your altars, and put your prophets to the sword. I alone am left, and they seek to take my life." 15 "Go, take the road back to the desert near Damascus," the LORD said to him. "When you arrive, you shall anoint Hazael as king of Aram. 16 Then you shall anoint Jehu, son of Nimshi, as king of Israel, and Elisha, son of Shaphat of Abel-meholah, as prophet to succeed you. 17 If anyone escapes the sword of Hazael, Jehu will kill him. If he escapes the sword of Jehu, Elisha will kill him. 18 Yet I will leave seven thousand men in Israel - all those who have not knelt to Baal or kissed him." 19 Elijah set out, and came upon Elisha, son of Shaphat, as he was plowing with twelve yoke of oxen; he was following the twelfth. Elijah went over to him and threw his cloak over him. 20 Elisha left the oxen, ran after Elijah, and said, "Please, let me kiss my father and mother good-bye, and I will follow you." "Go back!" Elijah answered. "Have I done anything to you?" 21 Elisha left him and, taking the yoke of oxen, slaughtered them; he used the plowing equipment for fuel to boil their flesh, and gave it to his people to eat. Then he left and followed Elijah as his attendant.

1 Kings Chapter 20

¹ Ben-hadad, king of Aram, gathered all his forces, and accompanied by thirty-two kings with horses and chariotry, proceeded to invest and attack Samaria. ² He sent couriers to Ahab, king of Israel, within the city, ³ and said to him, "This is Ben-hadad's message: 'Your silver and gold are mine, and your wives and your promising sons are mine.'" ⁴ The king of Israel answered, "As you say, my lord king, I and all I have are yours." ⁵ But the couriers came again and said, "This is Ben-hadad's message: 'I sent you word to give me your silver and gold, your wives and your sons. ⁶ Now, however, at this time tomorrow I will send my servants to you, and they shall ransack your house and the houses of your servants. They shall seize and take away whatever they consider valuable.'" ⁷ The king of Israel then summoned all the elders of the land and said: "Understand clearly that this man wants to ruin us. When he sent to me for my wives and sons, my silver and my gold, I did not refuse him." ⁸ All the elders and all the people said to him, "Do not listen. Do not give in." ⁹ Accordingly he directed the couriers of Ben-hadad, "Say to my lord the king, 'I will do all that you demanded of your servant the first time. But this I cannot do.'" The couriers left and reported this. ¹⁰ Ben-hadad then sent him the message, "May the gods do thus and so to me if there is enough dust in Samaria to make handfuls for all my followers." ¹¹ The king of Israel replied, "Tell him, 'It is not for the man who is buckling his armor to boast as though he were taking it off.'" ¹² Ben-hadad was drinking in the pavilions with the kings when he heard this reply. "Prepare the assault," he commanded his servants; and they made ready to storm the city. ¹³ Then a prophet came up to Ahab, king of Israel and said: "The LORD says, 'Do you see all this huge army? When I deliver it up to you today, you will know that I am the LORD.'" ¹⁴ But Ahab asked, "Through whom will it be delivered up?" He answered, "The LORD says, 'Through the retainers of the governors of the provinces.'" Then Ahab asked, "Who is to attack?" He replied, "You are." ¹⁵ So Ahab called up the retainers of the governors of the provinces, two hundred thirty-two of them. Behind them he mustered all the Israelite soldiery, who numbered seven thousand. ¹⁶ They marched out at noon, while Ben-hadad was drinking heavily in the pavilions with the thirty-two kings who were his allies. ¹⁷ When the retainers of the governors of the provinces marched out first, Ben-hadad received word that some men had marched out of Samaria. ¹⁸ He answered, "Whether they have come out for peace or for war, in any case take them alive." ¹⁹ But when these had come out of the city - the soldiers of the governors of the provinces with the army following them - ²⁰ each of them struck down his man. The Arameans fled with Israel pursuing them, while Ben-hadad, king of Aram, escaped on a chariot steed. ²¹ The king of Israel went out, took the horses and chariots, and inflicted a severe defeat on Aram. ²² Then the prophet went up to the king of Israel and said to him: "Go, regroup your forces. Mark well what you do, for at the beginning of the year the king of Aram will attack you." ²³ On the other hand, the servants of the king of Aram said to him: "Their gods are gods of mountains. That is why they defeated us. But if we fight them on level ground, we shall be sure to defeat them. ²⁴ This is what you must do: Take the kings from their posts and put prefects in their places. ²⁵ Mobilize an army as large as the army that has deserted you, horse for horse, chariot for chariot. Let us fight them on level ground, and we shall surely defeat them." He took their advice and did this. ²⁶ At the beginning of the year, Ben-hadad mobilized Aram and went up to Aphek to fight against Israel. ²⁷ The Israelites, too, were called to arms and supplied with provisions; then they went out to engage the foe. The Israelites, encamped opposite them, seemed like a couple of small flocks of goats, while Aram covered the countryside. ²⁸ A man of God came up and said to the king of Israel: "The LORD says, 'Because Aram has said the LORD is a god of mountains, not a god of plains, I will deliver up to you all this large army, that you may know I am the LORD.'" ²⁹ They were encamped opposite each other for seven days. On the seventh day battle was joined, and the Israelites struck down one hundred thousand foot soldiers of Aram in one day. ³⁰ The survivors, twenty-seven thousand of them, fled into the city of Aphek, and there the wall collapsed. Ben-hadad, too, fled, and took refuge within the city, in an inside room. ³¹ His servants said to him: "We have heard that the kings of the land of Israel are merciful kings. Allow us, therefore, to garb ourselves in sackcloth, with cords around our heads, and go out to the king of Israel. Perhaps he will spare your life." ³² So they dressed in sackcloth girded at the waist, and wearing cords around their heads, they went to the king of Israel. "Your servant Ben-hadad pleads for his life," they said. "Is he still alive?" the king asked. "He is my brother." ³³ Hearing this as a good omen, the men quickly took him at his word and said, "Ben-hadad is your brother." He answered, "Go and get him." When Ben-hadad came out to him, the king had him mount his chariot. ³⁴ Ben-hadad said to him, "I will restore the cities which my father took from your father, and you may make yourself bazaars in Damascus, as my father did in Samaria." "On these terms," Ahab replied, "I will set you free." So he made an agreement with him and then set him free. ³⁵ One of the guild prophets was prompted by the LORD to say to his companion, "Strike me." But he refused to strike him. ³⁶ Then he said to him, "Since you did not obey the voice of the LORD, a lion will kill you when you leave me." When they parted company, a lion came upon him and killed him. ³⁷ The prophet met another man and said, "Strike me." The man struck him a blow and wounded him. ³⁸ The prophet went on and waited for the king on the road, having disguised himself with a bandage over his eyes. ³⁹ As the king was passing, he called out to the king and said: "Your servant went into the thick of the battle, and suddenly someone turned and brought me a man and said, 'Guard this man. If he is missing, you shall have to pay for his life with your life or pay out a talent of silver.' ⁴⁰ But while your servant was looking here and there, the man disappeared." The king of Israel said to him, "That is your sentence. You have decided it yourself." ⁴¹ He immediately removed the bandage from his eyes, and the king of Israel recognized him as one of the prophets. ⁴² He said to him: "The LORD says, 'Because you have set free the man I doomed to destruction, your life shall pay for his life, your people for his people.'" ⁴³ Disturbed and angry, the king of Israel went off homeward and entered Samaria.

1 Kings Chapter 21

¹ Some time after this, as Naboth the Jezreelite had a vineyard in Jezreel next to the palace of Ahab, king of Samaria, ² Ahab said to Naboth, "Give me your vineyard to be my vegetable garden, since it is close by, next to my house. I will give you a better vineyard in exchange, or, if you prefer, I will give you its value in money." ³ "The LORD forbid," Naboth answered him, "that I should give you my ancestral heritage." ⁴ Ahab went home disturbed and angry at the answer Naboth the Jezreelite had made to him: "I will not give you my ancestral heritage." Lying down on his bed, he turned away from food and would not eat. ⁵ His wife Jezebel came to him and said to him, "Why are you so angry that you will not eat?" ⁶ He answered her, "Because I spoke to Naboth the Jezreelite and said to him, 'Sell me your vineyard, or, if you prefer, I will give you a vineyard in exchange.' But he refused to let me have his vineyard." ⁷ "A fine ruler over Israel you are indeed!" his wife Jezebel said to him. "Get up. Eat and be cheerful. I will obtain the vineyard of Naboth the Jezreelite for you." ⁸ So she wrote letters in Ahab's name and, having sealed them with his seal, sent them to the elders and to the nobles who lived in the same city with Naboth. ⁹ This is what she wrote in the letters: "Proclaim a fast and set Naboth at the head of the people. ¹⁰ Next, get two scoundrels to face him and accuse him of having cursed God and king. Then take him out and stone him to death." ¹¹ His fellow citizens - the elders and the nobles who dwelt in his city - did as Jezebel had ordered them in writing, through the letters she had sent them. ¹² They proclaimed a fast and placed Naboth at the head of the people. ¹³ Two scoundrels came in and confronted him with the accusation, "Naboth has cursed God and king." And they led him out of the city and stoned him to death. ¹⁴ Then they sent the information to Jezebel that Naboth had been stoned to death. ¹⁵ When Jezebel learned that Naboth had been stoned to death, she said to Ahab, "Go on, take possession of the vineyard of Naboth the Jezreelite which he refused to sell you, because Naboth is not alive, but dead." ¹⁶ On hearing that Naboth was dead, Ahab started off on his way down to the vineyard of Naboth the Jezreelite, to take possession of it. ¹⁷ But the LORD said to Elijah the Tishbite: ¹⁸ "Start down to meet Ahab, king of Israel, who rules in Samaria. He will be in the vineyard of Naboth, of which he has come to take possession. ¹⁹ This is what you shall tell him, 'The LORD says: After murdering, do you also take possession? For this, the LORD says: In the place where the dogs licked up the blood of Naboth, the dogs shall lick up your blood, too.'" ²⁰ "Have you found me out, my enemy?" Ahab said to Elijah. "Yes," he answered. "Because you have given yourself up to doing evil in the LORD'S sight, ²¹ I am bringing evil upon you: I will destroy you and will cut off every male in Ahab's line, whether slave or freeman, in Israel. ²² I will make your house like that of Jeroboam, son of Nebat, and like that of Baasha, son of Ahijah, because of how you have provoked me by leading Israel into sin." ²³ (Against Jezebel, too, the LORD declared, "The dogs shall devour Jezebel in the district of Jezreel.") ²⁴ "When one of Ahab's line dies in the city, dogs will devour him; when one of them dies in the field, the birds of the sky will devour him." ²⁵ Indeed, no one gave himself up to the doing of evil in the sight of the LORD as did Ahab, urged on by his wife Jezebel. ²⁶ He became completely abominable by following idols, just as the Amorites had done, whom the LORD drove out before the Israelites. ²⁷ When Ahab heard these words, he tore his garments and put on sackcloth over his bare flesh. He fasted, slept in the

sackcloth, and went about subdued. ²⁸ Then the LORD said to Elijah the Tishbite, ²⁹ "Have you seen that Ahab has humbled himself before me? Since he has humbled himself before me, I will not bring the evil in his time. I will bring the evil upon his house during the reign of his son."

1 Kings Chapter 22

¹ Three years passed without war between Aram and Israel. ² In the third year, however, King Jehoshaphat of Judah came down to the king of Israel, ³ who said to his servants, "Do you not know that Ramoth-gilead is ours and we are doing nothing to take it from the king of Aram?" ⁴ He asked Jehoshaphat, "Will you come with me to fight against Ramoth-gilead?" Jehoshaphat answered the king of Israel, "You and I are as one, and your people and my people, your horses and my horses as well." ⁵ Jehoshaphat also said to the king of Israel, "Seek the word of the LORD at once." ⁶ The king of Israel gathered together the prophets, about four hundred of them, and asked, "Shall I go to attack Ramoth-gilead or shall I refrain?" "Go up," they answered. "The LORD will deliver it over to the king." ⁷ But Jehoshaphat said, "Is there no other prophet of the LORD here whom we may consult?" ⁸ The king of Israel answered, "There is one other through whom we might consult the LORD, Micaiah, son of Imlah; but I hate him because he prophesies not good but evil about me." Jehoshaphat said, "Let not your majesty speak of evil against you." ⁹ So the king of Israel called an official and said to him, "Get Micaiah, son of Imlah, at once." ¹⁰ The king of Israel and King Jehoshaphat of Judah were seated, each on his throne, clothed in their robes of state on a threshing floor at the entrance of the gate of Samaria, and all the prophets were prophesying before them. ¹¹ Zedekiah, son of Chenaanah, made himself horns of iron and said, "The LORD says, 'With these you shall gore Aram until you have destroyed them.'" ¹² The other prophets prophesied in a similar vein, saying: "Go up to Ramoth-gilead; you shall succeed. The LORD will deliver it over to the king." ¹³ The messenger who had gone to call Micaiah said to him, "Look now, the prophets are unanimously predicting good for the king. Let your word be the same as any of theirs; predict good." ¹⁴ "As the LORD lives," Micaiah answered, "I shall say whatever the LORD tells me." ¹⁵ When he came to the king, the king said to him, "Micaiah, shall we go to fight against Ramoth-gilead, or shall we refrain?" "Go up," he answered, "you shall succeed! The LORD will deliver it over to the king." ¹⁶ But the king answered him, "How many times must I adjure you to tell me nothing but the truth in the name of the LORD?" ¹⁷ So Micaiah said: "I see all Israel scattered on the mountains, like sheep without a shepherd, and the LORD saying, 'These have no master! Let each of them go back home in peace.'" ¹⁸ The king of Israel said to Jehoshaphat, "Did I not tell you he prophesies not good but evil about me?" ¹⁹ Micaiah continued: "Therefore hear the word of the LORD: I saw the LORD seated on his throne, with the whole host of heaven standing by to his right and to his left. ²⁰ The LORD asked, 'Who will deceive Ahab, so that he will go up and fall at Ramoth-gilead?' And one said this, another that, ²¹ until one of the spirits came forth and presented himself to the LORD, saying, 'I will deceive him.' The LORD asked, 'How?' ²² He answered, 'I will go forth and become a lying spirit in the mouths of all his prophets.' The LORD replied, 'You shall succeed in deceiving him. Go forth and do this.' ²³ So now, the LORD has put a lying spirit in the mouths of all these prophets of yours, but the LORD himself has decreed evil against you." ²⁴ Thereupon Zedekiah, son of Chenaanah, came up and slapped Micaiah on the cheek, saying, "Has the spirit of the LORD, then, left me to speak with you?" ²⁵ "You shall find out," Micaiah replied, "on that day when you retreat into an inside room to hide." ²⁶ The king of Israel then said, "Seize Micaiah and take him back to Amon, prefect of the city, and to Joash, the king's son, ²⁷ and say, 'This is the king's order: Put this man in prison and feed him scanty rations of bread and water until I return in safety.'" ²⁸ But Micaiah said, "If ever you return in safety, the LORD has not spoken through me." ²⁹ The king of Israel and King Jehoshaphat of Judah went up to Ramoth-gilead, ³⁰ and the king of Israel said to Jehoshaphat, "I will disguise myself and go into battle, but you put on your own clothes." So the king of Israel disguised himself and entered the fray. ³¹ In the meantime the king of Aram had given his thirty-two chariot commanders the order, "Do not fight with anyone at all except the king of Israel." ³² When the chariot commanders saw Jehoshaphat, they cried out, "That must be the king of Israel!" and shifted to fight him. But Jehoshaphat shouted his battle cry, ³³ and the chariot commanders, aware that he was not the king of Israel, gave up pursuit of him. ³⁴ Someone, however, drew his bow at random, and hit the king of Israel between the joints of his breastplate. He ordered his charioteer, "Rein about and take me out of the ranks, for I am disabled." ³⁵ The battle grew fierce during the day, and the king, who was propped up in his chariot facing the Arameans, died in the evening. The blood from his wound flowed to the bottom of the chariot. ³⁶ At sunset a cry went through the army, "Every man to his city, every man to his land, ³⁷ for the king is dead!" So they went to Samaria, where they buried the king. ³⁸ When the chariot was washed at the pool of Samaria, the dogs licked up his blood and harlots bathed there, as the LORD had prophesied. ³⁹ The rest of the acts of Ahab, with all that he did, including the ivory palace and all the cities he built, are recorded in the book of the chronicles of the kings of Israel. ⁴⁰ Ahab rested with his ancestors, and his son Ahaziah succeeded him as king. ⁴¹ Jehoshaphat, son of Asa, began to reign over Judah in the fourth year of Ahab, king of Israel. ⁴² Jehoshaphat was thirty-five years old when he began to reign, and he reigned twenty-five years in Jerusalem. His mother's name was Azubah, daughter of Shilhi. ⁴³ He followed all the ways of his father Asa unswervingly, doing what was right in the LORD'S sight. ⁴⁴ Nevertheless, the high places did not disappear, and the people continued to sacrifice and to burn incense on the high places. ⁴⁵ Jehoshaphat also made peace with the king of Israel. ⁴⁶ The rest of the acts of Jehoshaphat, with his prowess, what he did and how he fought, are recorded in the book of the chronicles of the kings of Judah. ⁴⁷ He removed from the land the rest of the cult prostitutes who had remained in the reign of his father Asa. ⁴⁸ There was no king in Edom, but an appointed regent. ⁴⁹ Jehoshaphat made Tarshish ships to go to Ophir for gold; but in fact the ships did not go, because they were wrecked at Ezion-geber. ⁵⁰ Then Ahaziah, son of Ahab, said to Jehoshaphat, "Let my servants accompany your servants in the ships." But Jehoshaphat would not agree. ⁵¹ Jehoshaphat rested with his ancestors; he was buried in his forefathers' City of David. His son Jehoram succeeded him as king. ⁵² Ahaziah, son of Ahab, began to reign over Israel in Samaria in the seventeenth year of Jehoshaphat, king of Judah; he reigned two years over Israel. ⁵³ He did evil in the sight of the LORD, behaving like his father, his mother, and Jeroboam, son of Nebat, who caused Israel to sin. ⁵⁴ He served and worshiped Baal, thus provoking the LORD, the God of Israel, just as his father had done.

II Kings

2 Kings Chapter 1

¹ After Ahab's death, Moab rebelled against Israel. ² Ahaziah had fallen through the lattice of his roof terrace at Samaria and had been injured. So he sent out messengers with the instructions: "Go and inquire of Baalzebub, the god of Ekron, whether I shall recover from this injury." ³ Meanwhile, the angel of the LORD said to Elijah the Tishbite: "Go, intercept the messengers of Samaria's king, and ask them, 'Is it because there is no God in Israel that you are going to inquire of Baalzebub, the god of Ekron?' ⁴ For this, the LORD says: 'You shall not leave the bed upon which you lie; instead, you shall die.'" And with that, Elijah departed. ⁵ The messengers then returned to Ahaziah, who asked them, "Why have you returned?" ⁶ "A man came up to us," they answered, "who said to us, 'Go back to the king who sent you and tell him: The LORD says, Is it because there is no God in Israel that you are sending to inquire of Baalzebub, the god of Ekron? For this you shall not leave the bed upon which you lie; instead, you shall die.'" ⁷ The king asked them, "What was the man like who came up to you and said these things to you?" ⁸ "Wearing a hairy garment," they replied, "with a leather girdle about his loins." "It is Elijah the Tishbite!" he exclaimed. ⁹ Then the king sent a captain with his company of fifty men after Elijah. The prophet was seated on a hilltop when he found him. "Man of God," he ordered, "the king commands you to come down." ¹⁰ "If I am a man of God," Elijah answered the captain, "may fire come down from heaven and consume you and your fifty men." And fire came down from heaven and consumed him and his fifty men. ¹¹ Ahaziah sent another captain with his company of fifty men after Elijah. "Man of God," he called out to Elijah, "the king commands you to come down immediately." ¹² "If I am a man of God," Elijah answered him, "may fire come down from heaven and consume you and your fifty men." And divine fire came down from heaven, consuming him and his fifty men. ¹³ Again, for the third time, Ahaziah sent a captain with his company of fifty men. When the third captain arrived, he fell to his knees before Elijah, pleading with him. "Man of God," he implored him, "let my life and the lives of these fifty men, your servants, count for something in your sight! ¹⁴ Already fire has come down from heaven, consuming two captains with their companies of fifty men. But now, let my life mean something to you!" ¹⁵ Then the angel of the LORD said to Elijah, "Go down with him; you need not be afraid of him." So Elijah left and went down with him and stated to the king: "Thus says the LORD: 'Because you sent messengers to inquire of Baalzebub, the god of Ekron, you shall not leave the bed upon which you lie; instead you shall die.'" ¹⁷ Ahaziah died in fulfillment of the prophecy of the LORD spoken by Elijah. Since he had no son, his brother Joram succeeded him as king, in the second

year of Jehoram, son of Jehoshaphat, king of Judah. ¹⁸ The rest of the acts of Ahaziah are recorded in the book of chronicles of the kings of Israel.

2 Kings Chapter 2

¹ When the LORD was about to take Elijah up to heaven in a whirlwind, he and Elisha were on their way from Gilgal. ² "Stay here, please," Elijah said to Elisha. "The LORD has sent me on to Bethel." "As the LORD lives, and as you yourself live," Elisha replied, "I will not leave you." So they went down to Bethel, ³ where the guild prophets went out to Elisha and asked him, "Do you know that the LORD will take your master from over you today?" "Yes, I know it," he replied. "Keep still." ⁴ Then Elijah said to him, "Stay here, please, Elisha, for the LORD has sent me on to Jericho." "As the LORD lives, and as you yourself live," Elisha replied, "I will not leave you." ⁵ They went on to Jericho, where the guild prophets approached Elisha and asked him, "Do you know that the LORD will take your master from over you today?" "Yes, I know it," he replied. "Keep still." ⁶ Elijah said to Elisha, "Please stay here; the LORD has sent me on to the Jordan." "As the LORD lives, and as you yourself live," Elisha replied, "I will not leave you." And so the two went on together. ⁷ Fifty of the guild prophets followed, and when the two stopped at the Jordan, stood facing them at a distance. ⁸ Elijah took his mantle, rolled it up and struck the water, which divided, and both crossed over on dry ground. ⁹ When they had crossed over, Elijah said to Elisha, "Ask for whatever I may do for you, before I am taken from you." Elisha answered, "May I receive a double portion of your spirit." ¹⁰ "You have asked something that is not easy," he replied. "Still, if you see me taken up from you, your wish will be granted; otherwise not." ¹¹ As they walked on conversing, a flaming chariot and flaming horses came between them, and Elijah went up to heaven in a whirlwind. ¹² When Elisha saw it happen he cried out, "My father! my father! Israel's chariots and drivers!" But when he could no longer see him, Elisha gripped his own garment and tore it in two. ¹³ Then he picked up Elijah's mantle which had fallen from him, and went back and stood at the bank of the Jordan. ¹⁴ Wielding the mantle which had fallen from Elijah, he struck the water in his turn and said, "Where is the LORD, the God of Elijah?" When Elisha struck the water it divided and he crossed over. ¹⁵ The guild prophets in Jericho, who were on the other side, saw him and said, "The spirit of Elijah rests on Elisha." They went to meet him, bowing to the ground before him. ¹⁶ "Among your servants are fifty brave men," they said. "Let them go in search of your master. Perhaps the spirit of the LORD has carried him away to some mountain or some valley." "Do not send them," he answered. ¹⁷ However, they kept urging him, until he was embarrassed and said, "Send them." So they sent the fifty men, who searched for three days without finding him. ¹⁸ When they returned to Elisha in Jericho, where he was staying, he said to them, "Did I not tell you not to go?" ¹⁹ Once the inhabitants of the city complained to Elisha, "The site of the city is fine indeed, as my lord can see, but the water is bad and the land unfruitful." ²⁰ "Bring me a new bowl," Elisha said, "and put salt into it." When they had brought it to him, ²¹ he went out to the spring and threw salt into it, saying, "Thus says the LORD, 'I have purified this water. Never again shall death or miscarriage spring from it.'" ²² And the water has stayed pure even to this day, just as Elisha prophesied. ²³ From there Elisha went up to Bethel. While he was on the way, some small boys came out of the city and jeered at him. "Go up, baldhead," they shouted, "go up, baldhead!" ²⁴ The prophet turned and saw them, and he cursed them in the name of the LORD. Then two she-bears came out of the woods and tore forty-two of the children to pieces. ²⁵ From there he went to Mount Carmel, and thence he returned to Samaria.

2 Kings Chapter 3

¹ Joram, son of Ahab, became king of Israel in Samaria (in the eighteenth year of Jehoshaphat, king of Judah, and he reigned for twelve years). ² He did evil in the LORD'S sight, though not as much as his father and mother. He did away with the pillar of Baal, which his father had made, ³ but he still clung to the sin to which Jeroboam, son of Nebat, had lured Israel; this he did not give up. ⁴ Now Mesha, king of Moab, who raised sheep, used to pay the king of Israel as tribute a hundred thousand lambs and the wool of a hundred thousand rams. ⁵ But when Ahab died, the king of Moab had rebelled against the king of Israel. ⁶ Joram as king mustered all Israel, and when he set out on a campaign from Samaria, ⁷ he sent the king of Judah the message: "The king of Moab is in rebellion against me. Will you join me in battle against Moab?" "I will," he replied. "You and I shall be as one, your people and mine, and your horses and mine as well." ⁸ They discussed the route for their attack, and settled upon the route through the desert of Edom. ⁹ So the king of Israel set out, accompanied by the king of Judah and the king of Edom. After their roundabout journey of seven days the water gave out for the army and for the animals with them. ¹⁰ "Alas!" exclaimed the king of Israel. "The LORD has called together these three kings to put them in the grasp of Moab." ¹¹ But the king of Judah asked, "Is there no prophet of the LORD here through whom we may inquire of the LORD?" One of the officers of the king of Israel replied, "Elisha, son of Shaphat, who poured water on the hands of Elijah, is here." ¹² "He has the word of the LORD," the king of Judah agreed. So the kings of Israel, Judah, and Edom went down to Elisha. ¹³ "What do you want with me?" Elisha asked the king of Israel. "Go to the prophets of your father and to the prophets of your mother." "No," the king of Israel replied. "The LORD has called these three kings together to put them in the grasp of Moab." ¹⁴ Then Elisha said, "As the LORD of hosts lives, whom I serve, were it not that I respect the king of Judah, I should neither look at you nor notice you at all. ¹⁵ Now get me a minstrel." When the minstrel played, the power of the LORD came upon Elisha ¹⁶ and he announced: "Thus says the LORD, 'Provide many catch basins in this wadi.' ¹⁷ For the LORD says, 'Though you will see neither wind nor rain, yet this wadi will be filled with water for you, your livestock, and your pack animals to drink.' ¹⁸ And since the LORD does not consider this enough, he will also deliver Moab into your grasp. ¹⁹ You shall destroy every fortified city, fell every fruit tree, stop up all the springs, and ruin every fertile field with stones." ²⁰ In the morning, at the time of the sacrifice, water came from the direction of Edom and filled the land. ²¹ Meanwhile, all Moab heard that the kings had come to give them battle; every man capable of bearing arms was called up and stationed at the border. ²² Early that morning, when the sun shone on the water, the Moabites saw the water at a distance as red as blood. ²³ "This is blood!" they exclaimed. "The kings have fought among themselves and killed one another. Quick! To the spoils, Moabites!" ²⁴ But when they reached the camp of Israel, the Israelites rose up and attacked the Moabites, who fled from them. They ranged through the countryside striking down the Moabites, ²⁵ destroying the cities; each of them cast stones onto every fertile field till they had loaded it down; all the springs they stopped up and every useful tree they felled. Finally only Kir-hareseth was left behind its stone walls, and the slingers had surrounded it and were attacking it. ²⁶ When he saw that he was losing the battle, the king of Moab took seven hundred swordsmen to break through to the king of Aram, but he failed. ²⁷ So he took his first-born, his heir apparent, and offered him as a holocaust upon the wall. The wrath against Israel was so great that they gave up the siege and returned to their own land.

2 Kings Chapter 4

¹ A certain woman, the widow of one of the guild prophets, complained to Elisha: "My husband, your servant, is dead. You know that he was a God-fearing man, yet now his creditor has come to take my two children as his slaves." ² "How can I help you?" Elisha answered her. "Tell me what you have in the house." "This servant of yours has nothing in the house but a jug of oil," she replied. ³ "Go out," he said, "borrow vessels from all your neighbors - as many empty vessels as you can. ⁴ Then come back and close the door on yourself and your children; pour the oil into all the vessels, and as each is filled, set it aside." ⁵ She went and did so, closing the door on herself and her children. As they handed her the vessels, she would pour in oil. ⁶ When all the vessels were filled, she said to her son, "Bring me another vessel." "There is none left," he answered her. And then the oil stopped. ⁷ She went and told the man of God, who said, "Go and sell the oil to pay off your creditor; with what remains, you and your children can live." ⁸ One day Elisha came to Shunem, where there was a woman of influence, who urged him to dine with her. Afterward, whenever he passed by, he used to stop there to dine. ⁹ So she said to her husband, "I know that he is a holy man of God. Since he visits us often, ¹⁰ let us arrange a little room on the roof and furnish it for him with a bed, table, chair, and lamp, so that when he comes to us he can stay there." ¹¹ Sometime later Elisha arrived and stayed in the room overnight. ¹² Then he said to his servant Gehazi, "Call this Shunammite woman." He did so, and when she stood before Elisha, ¹³ he told Gehazi, "Say to her, 'You have lavished all this care on us; what can we do for you? Can we say a good word for you to the king or to the commander of the army?'" She replied, "I am living among my own people." ¹⁴ Later Elisha asked, "Can something be done for her?" "Yes!" Gehazi answered. "She has no son, and her husband is getting on in years." ¹⁵ "Call her," said Elisha. When she had been called, and stood at the door, ¹⁶ Elisha promised, "This time next year you will be fondling a baby son." "Please, my lord," she protested, "you are a man of God; do not deceive your servant." ¹⁷ Yet the woman conceived, and by the same time the following year she had given birth to a son, as Elisha had promised. ¹⁸ The day came when the child was old enough to go out to his father among the reapers. ¹⁹ "My head hurts!" he complained to his father. "Carry him to his mother," the father said to

a servant. 20 The servant picked him up and carried him to his mother; he stayed with her until noon, when he died in her lap. 21 The mother took him upstairs and laid him on the bed of the man of God. Closing the door on him, she went out 22 and called to her husband, "Let me have a servant and a donkey. I must go quickly to the man of God, and I will be back." 23 "Why are you going to him today?" he asked. "It is neither the new moon nor the sabbath." But she bade him good-bye, 24 and when the donkey was saddled, said to her servant: "Lead on! Do not stop my donkey unless I tell you to." 25 She kept going till she reached the man of God on Mount Carmel. When he spied her at a distance, the man of God said to his servant Gehazi: "There is the Shunammite! 26 Hurry to meet her, and ask if all is well with her, with her husband, and with the boy." "Greetings," she replied. 27 But when she reached the man of God on the mountain, she clasped his feet. Gehazi came near to push her away, but the man of God said: "Let her alone, she is in bitter anguish; the LORD hid it from me and did not let me know." 28 "Did I ask my lord for a son?" she cried out. "Did I not beg you not to deceive me?" 29 "Gird your loins," Elisha said to Gehazi, "take my staff with you and be off; if you meet anyone, do not greet him, and if anyone greets you, do not answer. Lay my staff upon the boy." 30 But the boy's mother cried out: "As the LORD lives and as you yourself live, I will not release you." So he started to go back with her. 31 Meanwhile, Gehazi had gone on ahead and laid the staff upon the boy, but there was no sound or sign of life. He returned to meet Elisha and informed him that the boy had not awakened. 32 When Elisha reached the house, he found the boy lying dead. 33 He went in, closed the door on them both, and prayed to the LORD. 34 Then he lay upon the child on the bed, placing his mouth upon the child's mouth, his eyes upon the eyes, and his hands upon the hands. As Elisha stretched himself over the child, the body became warm. 35 He arose, paced up and down the room, and then once more lay down upon the boy, who now sneezed seven times and opened his eyes. 36 Elisha summoned Gehazi and said, "Call the Shunammite." She came at his call, and Elisha said to her, "Take your son." 37 She came in and fell at his feet in gratitude; then she took her son and left the room. 38 When Elisha returned to Gilgal, there was a famine in the land. Once, when the guild prophets were seated before him, he said to his servant, "Put the large pot on, and make some vegetable stew for the guild prophets." 39 Someone went out into the field to gather herbs and found a wild vine, from which he picked a clothful of wild gourds. On his return he cut them up into the pot of vegetable stew without anybody's knowing it. 40 The stew was poured out for the men to eat, but when they began to eat it, they exclaimed, "Man of God, there is poison in the pot!" And they could not eat it. 41 "Bring some meal," Elisha said. He threw it into the pot and said, "Serve it to the people to eat." And there was no longer anything harmful in the pot. 42 A man came from Baal-shalishah bringing the man of God twenty barley loaves made from the first fruits, and fresh grain in the ear. "Give it to the people to eat," Elisha said. 43 But his servant objected, "How can I set this before a hundred men?" "Give it to the people to eat," Elisha insisted. "For thus says the LORD, 'They shall eat and there shall be some left over.'" 44 And when they had eaten, there was some left over, as the LORD had said.

2 Kings Chapter 5

1 Naaman, the army commander of the king of Aram, was highly esteemed and respected by his master, for through him the LORD had brought victory to Aram. But valiant as he was, the man was a leper. 2 Now the Arameans had captured from the land of Israel in a raid a little girl, who became the servant of Naaman's wife. 3 "If only my master would present himself to the prophet in Samaria," she said to her mistress, "he would cure him of his leprosy." 4 Naaman went and told his lord just what the slave girl from the land of Israel had said. 5 "Go," said the king of Aram. "I will send along a letter to the king of Israel." So Naaman set out, taking along ten silver talents, six thousand gold pieces, and ten festal garments. 6 To the king of Israel he brought the letter, which read: "With this letter I am sending my servant Naaman to you, that you may cure him of his leprosy." 7 When he read the letter, the king of Israel tore his garments and exclaimed: "Am I a god with power over life and death, that this man should send someone to me to be cured of leprosy? Take note! You can see he is only looking for a quarrel with me!" 8 When Elisha, the man of God, heard that the king of Israel had torn his garments, he sent word to the king: "Why have you torn your garments? Let him come to me and find out that there is a prophet in Israel." 9 Naaman came with his horses and chariots and stopped at the door of Elisha's house. 10 The prophet sent him the message: "Go and wash seven times in the Jordan, and your flesh will heal, and you will be clean." 11 But Naaman went away angry, saying, "I thought that he would surely come out and stand there to invoke the LORD his God, and would move his hand over the spot, and thus cure

the leprosy. 12 Are not the rivers of Damascus, the Abana and the Pharpar, better than all the waters of Israel? Could I not wash in them and be cleansed?" With this, he turned about in anger and left. 13 But his servants came up and reasoned with him. "My father," they said, "if the prophet had told you to do something extraordinary, would you not have done it? All the more now, since he said to you, 'Wash and be clean,' should you do as he said." 14 So Naaman went down and plunged into the Jordan seven times at the word of the man of God. His flesh became again like the flesh of a little child, and he was clean. 15 He returned with his whole retinue to the man of God. On his arrival he stood before him and said, "Now I know that there is no God in all the earth, except in Israel. Please accept a gift from your servant." 16 "As the LORD lives whom I serve, I will not take it," Elisha replied; and despite Naaman's urging, he still refused. 17 Naaman said: "If you will not accept, please let me, your servant, have two mule-loads of earth, for I will no longer offer holocaust or sacrifice to any other god except to the LORD. 18 But I trust the LORD will forgive your servant this: when my master enters the temple of Rimmon to worship there, then I, too, as his adjutant, must bow down in the temple of Rimmon. May the LORD forgive your servant this." 19 "Go in peace," Elisha said to him. 20 Naaman had gone some distance when Gehazi, the servant of Elisha, the man of God, thought to himself: "My master was too easy with this Aramean Naaman, not accepting what he brought. As the LORD lives, I will run after him and get something out of him." 21 So Gehazi hurried after Naaman. Aware that someone was running after him, Naaman alighted from his chariot to wait for him. "Is everything all right?" he asked. 22 "Yes," Gehazi replied, "but my master sent me to say, 'Two young men have just come to me, guild prophets from the hill country of Ephraim. Please give them a talent of silver and two festal garments.'" 23 "Please take two talents," Naaman said, and pressed them upon him. He tied up these silver talents in bags and gave them, with the two festal garments, to two of his servants, who carried them before Gehazi. 24 When they reached the hill, Gehazi took what they had, carried it into the house, and sent the men on their way. 25 He went in and stood before Elisha his master, who asked him, "Where have you been, Gehazi?" He answered, "Your servant has not gone anywhere." 26 But Elisha said to him: "Was I not present in spirit when the man alighted from his chariot to wait for you? Is this a time to take money or to take garments, olive orchards or vineyards, sheep or cattle, male or female servants? 27 The leprosy of Naaman shall cling to you and your descendants forever." And Gehazi left Elisha, a leper white as snow.

2 Kings Chapter 6

1 The guild prophets once said to Elisha: "There is not enough room for us to continue to live here with you. 2 Let us go to the Jordan, where by getting one beam apiece we can build ourselves a place to live." "Go," Elisha said. 3 "Please agree to accompany your servants," one of them requested. "Yes, I will come," he replied. 4 So he went with them, and when they arrived at the Jordan they began to fell trees. 5 While one of them was felling a tree trunk, the iron axhead slipped into the water. "O master," he cried out, "it was borrowed!" 6 "Where did it fall?" asked the man of God. When he pointed out the spot, Elisha cut off a stick, threw it into the water, and brought the iron to the surface. 7 "Pick it up," he said. And the man reached down and grasped it. 8 When the king of Aram was waging war on Israel, he would make plans with his servants to attack a particular place. 9 But the man of God would send word to the king of Israel, "Be careful! Do not pass by this place, for Aram will attack there." 10 So the king of Israel would send word to the place which the man of God had indicated, and alert it; then they would be on guard. This happened several times. 11 Greatly disturbed over this, the king of Aram called together his officers. "Will you not tell me," he asked them, "who among us is for the king of Israel?" 12 "No one, my lord king," answered one of the officers. "The Israelite prophet Elisha can tell the king of Israel the very words you speak in your bedroom." 13 "Go, find out where he is," he said, "so that I may take him captive." Informed that Elisha was in Dothan, 14 he sent there a strong force with horses and chariots. They arrived by night and surrounded the city. 15 Early the next morning, when the attendant of the man of God arose and went out, he saw the force with its horses and chariots surrounding the city. "Alas!" he said to Elisha. "What shall we do, my lord?" 16 "Do not be afraid," Elisha answered. "Our side outnumbers theirs." 17 Then he prayed, "O LORD, open his eyes, that he may see." And the LORD opened the eyes of the servant, so that he saw the mountainside filled with horses and fiery chariots around Elisha. 18 When the Arameans came down to get him, Elisha prayed to the LORD, "Strike this people blind, I pray you." And in answer to the prophet's prayer the LORD struck them blind. 19 Then Elisha said to them: "This is the wrong road, and this is the wrong city. Follow me! I will take you to the man you want." And he led them to Samaria. 20 When they entered Samaria,

Elisha prayed, "O LORD, open their eyes that they may see." The LORD opened their eyes, and they saw that they were inside Samaria. 21When the king of Israel saw them, he asked, "Shall I kill them, my father?" 22 "You must not kill them," replied Elisha. "Do you slay those whom you have taken captive with your sword or bow? Serve them bread and water. Let them eat and drink, and then go back to their master." 23The king spread a great feast for them. When they had eaten and drunk he sent them away, and they went back to their master. No more Aramean raiders came into the land of Israel. 24 After this, Ben-hadad, king of Aram, mustered his whole army and laid siege to Samaria. 25 Because of the siege the famine in Samaria was so severe that an ass's head sold for eighty pieces of silver, and a fourth of a kab of wild onion for five pieces of silver. 26 One day, as the king of Israel was walking on the city wall, a woman cried out to him, "Help, my lord king!" 27 "No," he replied, "the LORD help you! Where could I find help for you: from the threshing floor or the winepress?" 28Then the king asked her, "What is your trouble?" She replied: "This woman said to me, 'Give up your son that we may eat him today; then tomorrow we will eat my son.' 29So we boiled my son and ate him. The next day I said to her, 'Now give up your son that we may eat him.' But she hid her son." 30 When the king heard the woman's words, he tore his garments. And as he was walking on the wall, the people saw that he was wearing sackcloth underneath, next to his skin. 31 "May God do thus and so to me," the king exclaimed, "if the head of Elisha, son of Shaphat, stays on him today!" 32 Meanwhile, Elisha was sitting in his house in conference with the elders. The king had sent a man ahead before he himself should come to him. Elisha had said to the elders: "Do you know that this son of a murderer is sending someone to cut off my head? When the messenger comes, see that you close the door and hold it fast against him. His master's footsteps are echoing behind him." 33 While Elisha was still speaking, the king came down to him and said, "This evil is from the LORD. Why should I trust in the LORD any longer?"

2 Kings Chapter 7

1Elisha said: "Hear the word of the LORD! Thus says the LORD, 'At this time tomorrow a seah of fine flour will sell for a shekel, and two seahs of barley for a shekel, in the market of Samaria.'" 2But the adjutant on whose arm the king leaned, answered the man of God, "Even if the LORD were to make windows in heaven, how could this happen?" "You shall see it with your own eyes," Elisha said, "but you shall not eat of it." 3At the city gate were four lepers who were deliberating, "Why should we sit here until we die? 4If we decide to go into the city, we shall die there, for there is famine in the city. If we remain here, we shall die too. Come, let us desert to the camp of the Arameans. If they spare us, we live; if they kill us, we die." 5At twilight they left for the Arameans; but when they reached the edge of the camp, no one was there. 6The LORD had caused the army of the Arameans to hear the sound of chariots and horses, the din of a large army, and they had reasoned among themselves, "The king of Israel has hired the kings of the Hittites and the kings of the borderlands to fight us." 7Then in the twilight they fled, abandoning their tents, their horses, and their asses, the whole camp just as it was, and fleeing for their lives. 8After the lepers reached the edge of the camp, they went first into one tent, ate and drank, and took silver, gold, and clothing from it, and went out and hid them. Back they came into another tent, took things from it, and again went out and hid them. 9Then they said to one another: "We are not doing right. This is a day of good news, and we are keeping silent. If we wait until morning breaks, we shall be blamed. Come, let us go and inform the palace." 10They came and summoned the city gatekeepers. "We went to the camp of the Arameans," they said, "but no one was there - not a human voice, only the horses and asses tethered, and the tents just as they were left." 11The gatekeepers announced this and it was reported within the palace. 12Though it was night, the king got up; he said to his servants: "Let me tell you what the Arameans have done to us. Knowing that we are in famine, they have left their camp to hide in the field, hoping to take us alive and enter our city when we leave it." 13One of his servants, however, suggested: "Since those who are left in the city are no better off than all the throng that has perished, let some of us take five of the abandoned horses and send scouts to investigate." 14They took two chariots, and horses, and the king sent them to reconnoiter the Aramean army. "Go and find out," he ordered. 15They followed the Arameans as far as the Jordan, and the whole route was strewn with garments and other objects that the Arameans had thrown away in their haste. The messengers returned and told the king. 16The people went out and plundered the camp of the Arameans; and then a seah of fine flour sold for a shekel and two seahs of barley for a shekel, as the LORD had said. 17The king put in charge of the gate the officer who was his adjutant; but the people trampled him to death at the gate, just as the man of God had predicted when the king visited him. 18Thus was

fulfilled the prophecy of the man of God to the king, "Two seahs of barley will sell for a shekel, and one seah of fine flour for a shekel at this time tomorrow at the gate of Samaria." 19The adjutant had answered the man of God, "Even if the LORD were to make windows in heaven, how could this happen?" And Elisha had replied, "You shall see it with your own eyes, but you shall not eat of it." 20And that is what happened to him, for the people trampled him to death at the gate.

2 Kings Chapter 8

1Elisha once said to the woman whose son he had restored to life: "Get ready! Leave with your family and settle wherever you can, because the LORD has decreed a seven-year famine which is coming upon the land." 2The woman got ready and did as the man of God said, setting out with her family and settling in the land of the Philistines for seven years. 3At the end of the seven years, the woman returned from the land of the Philistines and went out to the king to claim her house and her field. 4The king was talking with Gehazi, the servant of the man of God. "Tell me," he said, "all the great things that Elisha has done." 5Just as he was relating to the king how his master had restored a dead person to life, the very woman whose son Elisha had restored to life came to the king to claim her house and field. "My lord king," Gehazi said, "this is the woman, and this is that son of hers whom Elisha restored to life." 6The king questioned the woman, and she told him her story. With that the king placed an official at her disposal, saying, "Restore all her property to her, with all that the field produced from the day she left the land until now." 7Elisha came to Damascus at a time when Ben-hadad, king of Aram, lay sick. When he was told that the man of God had come there, 8the king said to Hazael, "Take a gift with you and go call on the man of God. Have him consult the LORD as to whether I shall recover from this sickness." 9Hazael went to visit him, carrying a present, and with forty camel loads of the best goods of Damascus. On his arrival, he stood before the prophet and said, "Your son Ben-hadad, king of Aram, has sent me to ask you whether he will recover from his sickness." 10"Go and tell him," Elisha answered, "that he will surely recover. However, the LORD has showed me that he will in fact die." 11Then he stared him down until Hazael became ill at ease. The man of God wept, 12and Hazael asked, "Why are you weeping, my lord?" Elisha replied, "Because I know the evil that you will inflict upon the Israelites. You will burn their fortresses, you will slay their youth with the sword, you will dash their little children to pieces, you will rip open their pregnant women." 13Hazael exclaimed, "How can a dog like me, your servant, do anything so important?" "The LORD has showed you to me as king over Aram," replied Elisha. 14Hazael left Elisha and returned to his master. "What did Elisha tell you?" asked Ben-hadad. "He told me that you would surely recover," replied Hazael. 15The next day, however, Hazael took a cloth, dipped it in water, and spread it over the king's face, so that he died. And Hazael reigned in his stead. 16In the fifth year of Joram, son of Ahab, king of Israel, Jehoram, son of Jehoshaphat, king of Judah, became king. 17He was thirty-two years old when he began to reign, and he reigned eight years in Jerusalem. 18He conducted himself like the kings of Israel of the line of Ahab, since the sister of Ahab was his wife; and he did evil in the LORD'S sight. 19Even so, the LORD was unwilling to destroy Judah, because of his servant David. For he had promised David that he would leave him a lamp in the LORD'S presence for all time. 20During Jehoram's reign, Edom revolted against the sovereignty of Judah and chose a king of its own. 21Thereupon Jehoram with all his chariots crossed over to Zair. He arose by night and broke through the Edomites when they had surrounded him and the commanders of his chariots. Then his army fled homeward. 22To this day Edom has been in revolt against the rule of Judah. Libnah also revolted at that time. 23The rest of the acts of Jehoram, with all that he did, are recorded in the book of the chronicles of the kings of Judah. 24Jehoram rested with his ancestors and was buried with them in the City of David. His son Ahaziah succeeded him as king. 25Ahaziah, son of Jehoram, king of Judah, became king in the twelfth year of Joram, son of Ahab, king of Israel. 26He was twenty-two years old when he began his reign, and he reigned one year in Jerusalem. His mother's name was Athaliah; she was daughter of Omri, king of Israel. 27He conducted himself like the house of Ahab, doing evil in the LORD'S sight as they did, since he was related to them by marriage. 28He joined Joram, son of Ahab, in battle against Hazael, king of Aram, at Ramoth-gilead, where the Arameans wounded Joram. 29King Joram returned to Jezreel to be healed of the wounds which the Arameans had inflicted on him at Ramah in his battle against Hazael, king of Aram. Then Ahaziah, son of Jehoram, king of Judah, went down to Jezreel to visit him there in his illness.

2 Kings Chapter 9

1The prophet Elisha called one of the guild prophets and said to him:

"Gird your loins, take this flask of oil with you, and go to Ramoth-gilead. ²When you get there, look for Jehu, son of Jehoshaphat, son of Nimshi. Enter and take him away from his companions into an inner chamber. ³From the flask you have, pour oil on his head, and say, 'Thus says the LORD: I anoint you king over Israel.' Then open the door and flee without delay." ⁴The young man (the guild prophet) went to Ramoth-gilead. ⁵When he arrived, the commanders of the army were in session. "I have a message for you, commander," he said. "For which one of us?" asked Jehu. "For you, commander," he answered. ⁶Jehu got up and went into the house. Then the young man poured the oil on his head and said, "Thus says the LORD, the God of Israel: 'I anoint you king over the people of the LORD, over Israel. ⁷You shall destroy the house of Ahab your master; thus will I avenge the blood of my servants the prophets, and the blood of all the other servants of the LORD shed by Jezebel, ⁸and by all the rest of the family of Ahab. I will cut off every male in Ahab's line, whether slave or freeman in Israel. ⁹I will deal with the house of Ahab as I dealt with the house of Jeroboam, son of Nebat, and with the house of Baasha, son of Ahijah. ¹⁰Dogs shall devour Jezebel at the confines of Jezreel, so that no one can bury her.'" Then he opened the door and fled. ¹¹When Jehu rejoined his master's servants, they asked him, "Is all well? Why did that madman come to you?" You know that kind of man and his talk, he replied. ¹²But they said, "Not at all! Come, tell us." So he told them what the young man had said to him, and finally, "Thus says the LORD: 'I anoint you king over Israel.'" ¹³At once each took his garment, spread it under Jehu on the bare steps, blew the trumpet, and cried out, "Jehu is king!" ¹⁴Thus Jehu, son of Jehoshaphat, son of Nimshi, formed a conspiracy against Joram. Joram, with all Israel, had been besieging Ramoth-gilead against Hazael, king of Aram, ¹⁵but had returned to Jezreel to be healed of the wounds the Arameans had inflicted on him in the battle against Hazael, king of Aram. "If you are truly with me," Jehu said, "see that no one escapes from the city to report in Jezreel." ¹⁶Then Jehu mounted his chariot and drove to Jezreel, where Joram lay ill and Ahaziah, king of Judah, had come to visit him. ¹⁷The watchman standing on the tower in Jezreel saw the troop of Jehu coming and reported, "I see chariots." "Get a driver," Joram said, "and send him to meet them and to ask whether all is well." ¹⁸So a driver went out to meet him and said, "The king asks whether all is well." "What does it matter to you how things are?" Jehu said. "Get behind me." The watchman reported to the king, "The messenger has reached them, but is not returning." ¹⁹Joram sent a second driver, who went to them and said, "The king asks whether all is well." "What does it matter to you how things are?" Jehu replied. "Get behind me." ²⁰The watchman reported, "The messenger has reached them, but is not returning. The driving is like that of Jehu, son of Nimshi, in its fury." ²¹"Prepare my chariot," said Joram. When they had done so, Joram, king of Israel, and Ahaziah, king of Judah, set out, each in his own chariot, to meet Jehu. They reached him near the field of Naboth the Jezreelite. ²²When Joram recognized Jehu, he asked, "Is all well, Jehu?" "How can all be well," Jehu replied, "as long as the many fornications and witchcrafts of your mother Jezebel continue?" ²³Joram reined about and fled, crying to Ahaziah, "Treason, Ahaziah!" ²⁴But Jehu drew his bow and shot Joram between the shoulders, so that the arrow went through his heart and he collapsed in his chariot. ²⁵Then Jehu said to his adjutant Bidkar, "Take him and throw him into the field of Naboth the Jezreelite. For I remember that when we were driving teams behind his father Ahab, the LORD delivered this oracle against him: ²⁶'As surely as I saw yesterday the blood of Naboth and the blood of his sons,' says the LORD, 'I will repay you for it in that very plot of ground, says the LORD.' So now take him into this plot of ground, in keeping with the word of the LORD." ²⁷Seeing what was happening, Ahaziah, king of Judah, fled toward Beth-haggan. Jehu pursued him, shouting, "Kill him too!" And they pierced him as he rode through the pass of Gur near Ibleam. He continued his flight as far as Megiddo and died there. ²⁸His servants brought him in a chariot to Jerusalem and buried him in the tomb of his ancestors in the City of David. ²⁹Ahaziah had become king of Judah in the eleventh year of Joram, son of Ahab. ³⁰When Jezebel learned that Jehu had arrived in Jezreel, she shadowed her eyes, adorned her hair, and looked down from her window. ³¹As Jehu came through the gate, she cried out, "Is all well, Zimri, murderer of your master?" ³²Jehu looked up to the window and shouted, "Who is on my side? Anyone?" At this, two or three eunuchs looked down toward him. ³³"Throw her down," he ordered. They threw her down, and some of her blood spurted against the wall and against the horses. Jehu rode in over her body ³⁴and, after eating and drinking, he said: "Attend to that accursed woman and bury her; after all, she was a king's daughter." ³⁵But when they went to bury her, they found nothing of her but the skull, the feet, and the hands. ³⁶They returned to Jehu, and when they told him, he said, "This is the sentence which the LORD pronounced through his servant Elijah the Tishbite: 'In the confines of Jezreel dogs shall eat the flesh of Jezebel. ³⁷The corpse of Jezebel shall be like dung in the field in the confines of Jezreel, so that no one can say: This was Jezebel.'"

2 Kings Chapter 10

¹Ahab had seventy descendants in Samaria. Jehu prepared letters and sent them to the city rulers, to the elders, and to the guardians of Ahab's descendants in Samaria. ²"Since your master's sons are with you," he wrote, "and you have the chariots, the horses, a fortified city, and the weapons, when this letter reaches you ³decide which is the best and the fittest of your master's offspring, place him on his father's throne, and fight for your master's house." ⁴They were overcome with fright and said, "If two kings could not withstand him, how can we?" ⁵So the vizier and the ruler of the city, along with the elders and the guardians, sent this message to Jehu: "We are your servants, and we will do everything you tell us. We will proclaim no one king; do whatever you think best." ⁶So Jehu wrote them a second letter: "If you are on my side and will obey me, count the heads of your master's sons and come to me in Jezreel at this time tomorrow." (The seventy princes were in the care of prominent men of the city, who were rearing them.) ⁷When the letter arrived, they took the princes and slew all seventy of them, put their heads in baskets, and sent them to Jehu in Jezreel. ⁸"They have brought the heads of the princes," a messenger came in and told him. "Pile them in two heaps at the entrance of the city until morning," he ordered. ⁹Going out in the morning, he stopped and said to all the people: "You are not responsible, and although I conspired against my lord and slew him, yet who killed all these? ¹⁰Know that not a single word which the LORD has spoken against the house of Ahab shall go unfulfilled. The LORD has accomplished all that he foretold through his servant Elijah." ¹¹Thereupon Jehu slew all who were left of the family of Ahab in Jezreel, as well as all his powerful supporters, intimates, and priests, leaving him no survivor. ¹²Then he set out for Samaria, and at Beth-eked-haroim on the way, ¹³he came across kinsmen of Ahaziah, king of Judah. "Who are you?" he asked. "We are kinsmen of Ahaziah," they replied. "We are going down to visit the princes and the family of the queen mother." ¹⁴"Take them alive," Jehu ordered. They were taken alive, forty-two in number, then slain at the pit of Beth-eked. Not one of them was spared. ¹⁵When he had left there, Jehu met Jehonadab, son of Rechab, on the road. He greeted him and asked, "Are you sincerely disposed toward me, as I am toward you?" "Yes," replied Jehonadab. "If you are," continued Jehu, "give me your hand." Jehonadab gave him his hand, and Jehu drew him up into his chariot. ¹⁶"Come with me," he said, "and see my zeal for the LORD." And he took him along in his own chariot. ¹⁷When he arrived in Samaria, Jehu slew all who remained there of Ahab's line, doing away with them completely and thus fulfilling the prophecy which the LORD had spoken to Elijah. ¹⁸Jehu gathered all the people together and said to them: "Ahab served Baal to some extent, but Jehu will serve him yet more. ¹⁹Now summon for me all Baal's prophets, all his worshipers, and all his priests. See that no one is absent, for I have a great sacrifice for Baal. Whoever is absent shall not live." This Jehu did as a ruse, so that he might destroy the worshipers of Baal. ²⁰Jehu said further, "Proclaim a solemn assembly in honor of Baal." They did so, ²¹and Jehu sent word of it throughout the land of Israel. All the worshipers of Baal without exception came into the temple of Baal, which was filled to capacity. ²²Then Jehu said to the custodian of the wardrobe, "Bring out the garments for all the worshipers of Baal." When he had brought out the garments for them, ²³Jehu, with Jehonadab, son of Rechab, entered the temple of Baal and said to the worshipers of Baal, "Search and be sure that there is no worshiper of the LORD here with you, but only worshipers of Baal." ²⁴Then they proceeded to offer sacrifices and holocausts. Now Jehu had stationed eighty men outside with this warning, "If one of you lets anyone escape of those whom I shall deliver into your hands, he shall pay life for life." ²⁵As soon as he finished offering the holocaust, Jehu said to the guards and officers, "Go in and slay them. Let no one escape." So the guards and officers put them to the sword and cast them out. Afterward they went into the inner shrine of the temple of Baal, ²⁶took out the stele of Baal, and burned the shrine. ²⁷Then they smashed the stele of Baal, tore down the building, and turned it into a latrine, as it remains today. ²⁸Thus Jehu rooted out the worship of Baal from Israel. ²⁹However, he did not desist from the sins which Jeroboam, son of Nebat, had caused Israel to commit, as regards the golden calves at Bethel and at Dan. ³⁰The LORD said to Jehu, "Because you have done well what I deem right, and have treated the house of Ahab as I desire, your sons to the fourth generation shall sit upon the throne of Israel." ³¹But Jehu was not careful to observe wholeheartedly the law of the LORD, the God of Israel, since he did not desist from the sins which Jeroboam caused Israel to commit. ³²At that

time the LORD began to dismember Israel. Hazael defeated the Israelites throughout their territory 33east of the Jordan (all the land of Gilead, of the Gadites, Reubenites and Manassehites), from Aroer on the river Arnon up through Gilead and Bashan. 34The rest of the acts of Jehu, his valor and all his accomplishments, are written in the book of the chronicles of the kings of Israel. 35Jehu rested with his ancestors and was buried in Samaria. His son Jehoahaz succeeded him as king. 36The length of Jehu's reign over Israel in Samaria was twenty-eight years.

2 Kings Chapter 11

1When Athaliah, the mother of Ahaziah, saw that her son was dead, she began to kill off the whole royal family. 2But Jehosheba, daughter of King Jehoram and sister of Ahaziah, took Joash, his son, and spirited him away, along with his nurse, from the bedroom where the princes were about to be slain. She concealed him from Athaliah, and so he did not die. 3For six years he remained hidden in the temple of the LORD, while Athaliah ruled the land. 4But in the seventh year, Jehoiada summoned the captains of the Carians and of the guards. He had them come to him in the temple of the LORD, exacted from them a sworn commitment, and then showed them the king's son. 5He gave them these orders: "This is what you must do: the third of you who come on duty on the sabbath shall guard the king's palace; 6another third shall be at the gate Sur; and the last third shall be at the gate behind the guards. 7The two of your divisions who are going off duty that week shall keep guard over the temple of the LORD for the king. 8You shall surround the king, each with drawn weapons, and if anyone tries to approach the cordon, kill him; stay with the king, whatever he may do." 9The captains did just as Jehoiada the priest commanded. Each one with his men, both those going on duty for the sabbath and those going off duty that week, came to Jehoiada the priest. 10He gave the captains King David's spears and shields, which were in the temple of the LORD. 11And the guards, with drawn weapons, lined up from the southern to the northern limit of the enclosure, surrounding the altar and the temple on the king's behalf. 12Then Jehoiada led out the king's son and put the crown and the insignia upon him. They proclaimed him king and anointed him, clapping their hands and shouting, "Long live the king!" 13Athaliah heard the noise made by the people, and appeared before them in the temple of the LORD. 14When she saw the king standing by the pillar, as was the custom, and the captains and trumpeters near him, with all the people of the land rejoicing and blowing trumpets, she tore her garments and cried out, "Treason, treason!" 15Then Jehoiada the priest instructed the captains in command of the force: "Bring her outside through the ranks. If anyone follows her," he added, "let him die by the sword." He had given orders that she should not be slain in the temple of the LORD. 16She was led out forcibly to the horse gate of the royal palace, where she was put to death. 17Then Jehoiada made a covenant between the LORD as one party and the king and the people as the other, by which they would be the LORD'S people; and another covenant, between the king and the people. 18Thereupon all the people of the land went to the temple of Baal and demolished it. They shattered its altars and images completely, and slew Mattan, the priest of Baal, before the altars. After appointing a detachment for the temple of the LORD, Jehoiada 19with the captains, the Carians, the guards, and all the people of the land, led the king down from the temple of the LORD through the guards' gate to the palace, where Joash took his seat on the royal throne. 20All the people of the land rejoiced and the city was quiet, now that Athaliah had been slain with the sword at the royal palace.

2 Kings Chapter 12

1Joash was seven years old when he became king. 2Joash began to reign in the seventh year of Jehu, and he reigned forty years in Jerusalem. His mother, who was named Zibiah, was from Beer-sheba. 3Joash did what was pleasing to the LORD as long as he lived, because the priest Jehoiada guided him. 4Still, the high places did not disappear; the people continued to sacrifice and to burn incense there. 5For the priests Joash made this rule: "All the funds for sacred purposes that are brought to the temple of the LORD—the census tax, personal redemption money, and whatever funds are freely brought to the temple of the LORD— 6the priests may take for themselves, each from his own clients. However, they must make whatever repairs on the temple may prove necessary." 7Nevertheless, as late as the twenty-third year of the reign of King Joash, the priests had not made needed repairs on the temple. 8Accordingly, King Joash summoned the priest Jehoiada and the other priests. "Why do you not repair the temple?" he asked them. "You must no longer take funds from your clients, but you shall turn them over for the repairs." 9So the priests agreed that they would neither take funds from the people nor make the repairs on the temple.

10The priest Jehoiada then took a chest, bored a hole in its lid, and set it beside the stele, on the right as one entered the temple of the LORD. The priests who guarded the entry would put into it all the funds that were brought to the temple of the LORD. 11When they noticed that there was a large amount of silver in the chest, the royal scribe (and the priest) would come up, and they would melt down all the funds that were in the temple of the LORD, and weigh them. 12The amount thus realized they turned over to the master workmen in the temple of the LORD. They in turn would give it to the carpenters and builders working in the temple of the LORD, 13and to the lumbermen and stone cutters, and for the purchase of the wood and hewn stone used in repairing the breaches, and for any other expenses that were necessary to repair the temple. 14None of the funds brought to the temple of the LORD were used there to make silver cups, snuffers, basins, trumpets, or any gold or silver article. 15Instead, they were given to the workmen, and with them they repaired the temple of the LORD. 16Moreover, no reckoning was asked of the men who were provided with the funds to give to the workmen, because they held positions of trust. 17The funds from guilt-offerings and from sin-offerings, however, were not brought to the temple of the LORD; they belonged to the priests. 18Then King Hazael of Aram mounted a siege against Gath. When he had taken it, Hazael decided to go on to attack Jerusalem. 19But King Jehoash of Judah took all the dedicated offerings presented by his forebears, Jehoshaphat, Jehoram, and Ahaziah, kings of Judah, as well as his own, and all the gold there was in the treasuries of the temple and the palace, and sent them to King Hazael of Aram, who then led his forces away from Jerusalem. 20The rest of the acts of Joash, with all that he did, are recorded in the book of the chronicles of the kings of Judah. 21Certain of his officials entered into a plot against him and killed him at Beth-millo. 22Jozacar, son of Shimeath, and Jehozabad, son of Shomer, were the officials who killed him. He was buried in his forefathers' City of David, and his son Amaziah succeeded him as king.

2 Kings Chapter 13

1 In the twenty-third year of Joash, son of Ahaziah, king of Judah, Jehoahaz, son of Jehu, began his seventeen-year reign over Israel in Samaria. 2 He did evil in the LORD'S sight, conducting himself like Jeroboam, son of Nebat, and not renouncing the sin he had caused Israel to commit. 3 The LORD was angry with Israel for a long time left them in the power of Hazael, king of Aram, and of Ben-hadad, son of Hazael. 4 Then Jehoahaz entreated the LORD, who heard him, since he saw the oppression to which the king of Aram had subjected Israel. 5 So the LORD gave Israel a savior, and the Israelites, freed from the power of Aram, dwelt in their own homes as formerly. 6 Nevertheless, they did not desist from the sins which the house of Jeroboam had caused Israel to commit, but persisted in them. The sacred pole also remained standing in Samaria. 7 No soldiers were left to Jehoahaz, except fifty horsemen with ten chariots and ten thousand foot soldiers, since the king of Aram had destroyed them and trampled them like dust. 8 The rest of the acts of Jehoahaz, with all his valor and accomplishments, are recorded in the book of the chronicles of the kings of Israel. 9 Jehoahaz rested with his ancestors and was buried in Samaria. His son Joash succeeded him as king. 10 In the thirty-seventh year of Joash, king of Judah, Jehoash, son of Jehoahaz, began his sixteen-year reign over Israel in Samaria. 11 He did evil in the sight of the LORD; he did not desist from any of the sins which Jeroboam, son of Nebat, had caused Israel to commit, but persisted in them. 12 (The rest of the acts of Joash, the valor with which he fought against Amaziah, king of Judah, and all his accomplishments, are recorded in the book of the chronicles of the kings of Israel. 13 Joash rested with his ancestors, and Jeroboam occupied the throne. Joash was buried with the kings of Israel in Samaria.) 14 When Elisha was suffering from the sickness of which he was to die, King Joash of Israel went down to visit him. "My father, my father!" he exclaimed, weeping over him. "Israel's chariots and horsemen!" 15 "Take a bow and some arrows," Elisha said to him. When he had done so, 16 Elisha said to the king of Israel, "Put your hand on the bow." As the king held the bow, Elisha placed his hands over the king's hands 17 and said, "Open the window toward the east." He opened it. Elisha said, "Shoot," and he shot. The prophet exclaimed, "The LORD'S arrow of victory! The arrow of victory over Aram! You will completely conquer Aram at Aphec." 18 Then he said to the king of Israel, "Take the arrows," which he did. Elisha said to him, "Strike the ground!" He struck the ground three times and stopped. 19 Angry with him, the man of God said: "You should have struck five or six times; you would have defeated Aram completely. Now, you will defeat Aram only three times." 20 Elisha died and was buried. At the time, bands of Moabites used to raid the land each year. 21 Once some people were burying a man, when suddenly they spied such a raiding band. So they cast the dead man into the grave of Elisha, and everyone

went off. But when the man came in contact with the bones of Elisha, he came back to life and rose to his feet. 22 King Hazael of Aram oppressed Israel during the entire reign of Jehoahaz. 23 But the LORD was merciful with Israel and looked on them with compassion because of his covenant with Abraham, Isaac, and Jacob. He was unwilling to destroy them or to cast them out from his presence. 24 So when King Hazael of Aram died and his son Ben-hadad succeeded him as king, 25 Joash, son of Jehoahaz, took back from Ben-hadad, son of Hazael, the cities which Hazael had taken in battle from his father Jehoahaz. Joash defeated Ben-hadad three times, and thus recovered the cities of Israel.

2 Kings Chapter 14

1 In the second year of Joash, son of Jehoahaz, king of Israel, Amaziah, son of Joash, king of Judah, began to reign. 2 He was twenty-five years old when he became king, and he reigned twenty-nine years in Jerusalem. His mother, whose name was Jehoaddin, was from Jerusalem. 3 He pleased the LORD, yet not like his forefather David, since he did just as his father Joash had done. 4 Thus the high places did not disappear; the people continued to sacrifice and to burn incense on them. 5 When Amaziah had the kingdom firmly in hand, he slew the officials who had murdered the king, his father. 6 But the children of the murderers he did not put to death, obeying the LORD'S command written in the book of the law of Moses, "Fathers shall not be put to death for their children, nor shall children be put to death for their fathers; each one shall die for his own sin." 7 Amaziah slew ten thousand Edomites in the Salt Valley, and took Sela in battle. He renamed it Joktheel, the name it has to this day. 8 Then Amaziah sent messengers to Jehoash, son of Jehoahaz, son of Jehu, king of Israel, with this challenge, "Come, let us meet face to face." 9 King Jehoash of Israel sent this reply to the king of Judah: "The thistle of Lebanon sent word to the cedar of Lebanon, 'Give your daughter to my son in marriage,' but an animal of Lebanon passed by and trampled the thistle underfoot. 10 You have indeed conquered Edom, and you have become ambitious. Enjoy your glory, but stay at home! Why involve yourself and Judah with you in misfortune and failure?" 11 But Amaziah would not listen. King Jehoash of Israel then advanced, and he and King Amaziah of Judah met in battle at Beth-shemesh of Judah. 12 Judah was defeated by Israel, and all the Judean soldiery fled homeward. 13 King Jehoash of Israel captured Amaziah, son of Jehoash, son of Ahaziah, king of Judah, at Beth-shemesh. He went on to Jerusalem where he tore down four hundred cubits of the city wall, from the Gate of Ephraim to the Corner Gate. 14 He took all the gold and silver and all the utensils there were in the temple of the LORD and the treasuries of the palace, and hostages as well. Then he returned to Samaria. 15 The rest of the acts of Jehoash, his valor, and how he fought Amaziah, king of Judah, are recorded in the book of the chronicles of the kings of Israel. 16 Jehoash rested with his ancestors; he was buried in Samaria with the kings of Israel. His son Jeroboam succeeded him as king. 17 Amaziah, son of Joash, king of Judah, survived Jehoash, son of Jehoahaz, king of Israel, by fifteen years. 18 The rest of the acts of Amaziah are written in the book of the chronicles of the kings of Judah. 19 When a conspiracy was formed against him in Jerusalem, he fled to Lachish. But he was pursued to Lachish and killed there. 20 He was brought back on horses and buried with his ancestors in the City of David in Jerusalem. 21 Thereupon all the people of Judah took the sixteen-year-old Azariah and proclaimed him king to succeed his father Amaziah. 22 It was Azariah who rebuilt Elath and restored it to Judah, after King Amaziah rested with his ancestors. 23 In the fifteenth year of Amaziah, son of Joash, king of Judah, Jeroboam, son of Joash, king of Israel, began his forty-one-year reign in Samaria. 24 He did evil in the sight of the LORD; he did not desist from any of the sins which Jeroboam, son of Nebat, had caused Israel to commit. 25 He restored the boundaries of Israel from Labo-of-Hamath to the sea of the Arabah, just as the LORD, the God of Israel, had prophesied through his servant, the prophet Jonah, son of Amittai, from Gath-hepher. 26 For the LORD saw the very bitter affliction of Israel, where there was neither slave nor freeman, no one at all to help Israel. 27 Since the LORD had not determined to blot out the name of Israel from under the heavens, he saved them through Jeroboam, son of Joash. 28 The rest of the acts of Jeroboam, his valor and all his accomplishments, how he fought with Damascus and turned back Hamath from Israel, are recorded in the book of the chronicles of the kings of Israel. 29 Jeroboam rested with his ancestors, the kings of Israel, and his son Zechariah succeeded him as king.

2 Kings Chapter 15

1 Azariah, son of Amaziah, king of Judah, became king in the twenty-seventh year of Jeroboam, king of Israel. 2 He was sixteen years old when he began to reign, and he reigned fifty-two years in Jerusalem. His mother, whose name was Jecholiah, was from Jerusalem. 3 He

pleased the LORD just as his father Amaziah had done. 4 Yet the high places did not disappear; the people continued to sacrifice and to burn incense on them. 5 The LORD afflicted the king, and he was a leper to the day of his death. He lived in a house apart, while Jotham, the king's son, was vizier and regent for the people of the land. 6 The rest of the acts of Azariah, and all his accomplishments, are recorded in the book of the chronicles of the kings of Judah. 7 Azariah rested with his ancestors, and was buried with them in the City of David. His son Jotham succeeded him as king. 8 In the thirty-eighth year of Azariah, king of Judah, Zechariah, son of Jeroboam, was king of Israel in Samaria for six months. 9 He did evil in the sight of the LORD as his fathers had done, and did not desist from the sins which Jeroboam, son of Nebat, had caused Israel to commit. 10 Shallum, son of Jabesh, conspired against Zechariah, attacked and killed him at Ibleam, and reigned in his place. 11 The rest of the acts of Zechariah are recorded in the book of the chronicles of the kings of Israel. 12 Thus the LORD'S promise to Jehu, "Your descendants to the fourth generation shall sit upon the throne of Israel," was fulfilled. 13 Shallum, son of Jabesh, became king in the thirty-ninth year of Uzziah, king of Judah; he reigned one month in Samaria. 14 Menahem, son of Gadi, came up from Tirzah to Samaria, where he attacked and killed Shallum, son of Jabesh, and reigned in his place. 15 The rest of the acts of Shallum, and the fact of his conspiracy, are recorded in the book of the chronicles of the kings of Israel. 16 At that time, Menahem punished Tappuah, all the inhabitants of the town and of its whole district, because on his way from Tirzah they did not let him in. He punished them even to ripping open all the pregnant women. 17 In the thirty-ninth year of Azariah, king of Judah, Menahem, son of Gadi, began his ten-year reign over Samaria. 18 He did evil in the sight of the LORD, not desisting from the sins which Jeroboam, son of Nebat, had caused Israel to commit. During his reign, 19 Pul, king of Assyria, invaded the land, and Menahem gave him a thousand talents of silver to have his assistance in strengthening his hold on the kingdom. 20 Menahem secured the money to give to the king of Assyria by exacting it from all the men of substance in the country, fifty silver shekels from each. The king of Assyria did not remain in the country but withdrew. 21 The rest of the acts of Menahem, and all his accomplishments, are recorded in the book of the chronicles of the kings of Israel. 22 Menahem rested with his ancestors, and his son Pekahiah succeeded him as king. 23 In the fiftieth year of Azariah, king of Judah, Pekahiah, son of Menahem, began his two-year reign over Israel in Samaria. 24 He did evil in the sight of the LORD, not desisting from the sins which Jeroboam, son of Nebat, had caused Israel to commit. 25 His adjutant Pekah, son of Remaliah, who had with him fifty men from Gilead, conspired against him, killed him within the palace stronghold in Samaria, and reigned in his place. 26 The rest of the acts of Pekahiah, and all his accomplishments, are recorded in the book of the chronicles of the kings of Israel. 27 In the fifty-second year of Azariah, king of Judah, Pekah, son of Remaliah, began his twenty-year reign over Israel in Samaria. 28 He did evil in the sight of the LORD, not desisting from the sins which Jeroboam, son of Nebat, had caused Israel to commit. 29 During the reign of Pekah, king of Israel, Tiglath-pileser, king of Assyria, came and took Ijon, Abel-beth-maacah, Janoah, Kedesh, Hazor, all the territory of Naphtali, Gilead, and Galilee, deporting the inhabitants to Assyria. 30 Hoshea, son of Elah, conspired against Pekah, son of Remaliah; he attacked and killed him, and reigned in his place (in the twentieth year of Jotham, son of Uzziah). 31 The rest of the acts of Pekah, and all his accomplishments, are recorded in the book of the chronicles of the kings of Israel. 32 In the second year of Pekah, son of Remaliah, king of Israel, Jotham, son of Uzziah, king of Judah, began to reign. 33 He was twenty-five years old when he became king, and he reigned sixteen years in Jerusalem. His mother's name was Jerusha, daughter of Zadok. 34 He pleased the LORD, just as his father Uzziah had done. 35 Nevertheless the high places did not disappear and the people continued to sacrifice and to burn incense on them. It was he who built the Upper Gate of the temple of the LORD. 36 The rest of the acts of Jotham, and all his accomplishments, are recorded in the book of the chronicles of the kings of Judah. 37 It was at that time that the LORD first loosed Rezin, king of Aram, and Pekah, son of Remaliah, against Judah. 38 Jotham rested with his ancestors and was buried with them in his forefather's City of David. His son Ahaz succeeded him as king.

2 Kings Chapter 16

1 In the seventeenth year of Pekah, son of Remaliah, Ahaz, son of Jotham, king of Judah, began to reign. 2 Ahaz was twenty years old when he became king, and he reigned sixteen years in Jerusalem. He did not please the LORD, his God, like his forefather David, 3 but conducted himself like the kings of Israel, and even immolated his son

by fire, in accordance with the abominable practice of the nations whom the LORD had cleared out of the way of the Israelites. ⁴ Further, he sacrificed and burned incense on the high places, on hills, and under every leafy tree. ⁵ Then Rezin, king of Aram, and Pekah, son of Remaliah, king of Israel, came up to Jerusalem to attack it. Although they besieged Ahaz, they were unable to conquer him. ⁶ At the same time the king of Edom recovered Elath for Edom, driving the Judeans out of it. The Edomites then entered Elath, which they have occupied until the present. ⁷ Meanwhile, Ahaz sent messengers to Tiglath-pileser, king of Assyria, with the plea: "I am your servant and your son. Come up and rescue me from the clutches of the king of Aram and the king of Israel, who are attacking me." ⁸ Ahaz took the silver and gold that were in the temple of the LORD and in the palace treasuries and sent them as a present to the king of Assyria, ⁹ who listened to him and moved against Damascus, which he captured. He deported its inhabitants to Kir and put Rezin to death. ¹⁰ King Ahaz went to Damascus to meet Tiglath-pileser, king of Assyria. When he saw the altar in Damascus, King Ahaz sent to Uriah the priest a model of the altar and a detailed design of its construction. ¹¹ Uriah the priest built an altar according to the plans which King Ahaz sent him from Damascus, and had it completed by the time the king returned home. ¹² On his arrival from Damascus, the king inspected this altar, then went up to it and offered sacrifice on it, ¹³ burning his holocaust and cereal-offering, pouring out his libation, and sprinkling the blood of his peace-offerings on the altar. ¹⁴ The bronze altar that stood before the LORD he brought from the front of the temple - that is, from the space between the new altar and the temple of the LORD - and set it on the north side of his altar. ¹⁵ "Upon the large altar," King Ahaz commanded Uriah the priest, "burn the morning holocaust and the evening cereal offering, the royal holocaust and cereal offering, as well as the holocausts, cereal offerings, and libations of the people. You must also sprinkle on it all the blood of holocausts and sacrifices. But the old bronze altar shall be mine for consultation." ¹⁶ Uriah the priest did just as King Ahaz had commanded. ¹⁷ King Ahaz detached the frames from the bases and removed the lavers from them; he also took down the bronze sea from the bronze oxen that supported it, and set it on a stone pavement. ¹⁸ In deference to the king of Assyria he removed from the temple of the LORD the emplacement which had been built in the temple for a throne, and the outer entrance for the king. ¹⁹ The rest of the acts of Ahaz are recorded in the book of the chronicles of the kings of Judah. ²⁰ Ahaz rested with his ancestors and was buried with them in the City of David. His son Hezekiah succeeded him as king.

2 Kings Chapter 17

¹ In the twelfth year of Ahaz, king of Judah, Hoshea, son of Elah, began his nine-year reign over Israel in Samaria. ² He did evil in the sight of the LORD, yet not to the extent of the kings of Israel before him. ³ Shalmaneser, king of Assyria, advanced against him, and Hoshea became his vassal and paid him tribute. ⁴ But the king of Assyria found Hoshea guilty of conspiracy for sending envoys to the king of Egypt at Sais, and for failure to pay the annual tribute to his Assyrian overlord. ⁵ For this, the king of Assyria arrested and imprisoned Hoshea; he then occupied the whole land and attacked Samaria, which he besieged for three years. ⁶ In the ninth year of Hoshea, the king of Assyria took Samaria, and deported the Israelites to Assyria, settling them in Halah, at the Habor, a river of Gozan, and in the cities of the Medes. ⁷ This came about because the Israelites sinned against the LORD, their God, who had brought them up from the land of Egypt, from under the domination of Pharaoh, king of Egypt, and because they venerated other gods. ⁸ They followed the rites of the nations whom the LORD had cleared out of the way of the Israelites (and the kings of Israel whom they set up). ⁹ They adopted unlawful practices toward the LORD, their God. They built high places in all their settlements, the watchtowers as well as the walled cities. ¹⁰ They set up pillars and sacred poles for themselves on every high hill and under every leafy tree. ¹¹ There, on all the high places, they burned incense like the nations whom the LORD had sent into exile at their coming. They did evil things that provoked the LORD, ¹² and served idols, although the LORD had told them, "You must not do this." ¹³ And though the LORD warned Israel and Judah by every prophet and seer, "Give up your evil ways and keep my commandments and statutes, in accordance with the entire law which I enjoined on your fathers and which I sent you by my servants the prophets," ¹⁴ they did not listen, but were as stiff-necked as their fathers, who had not believed in the LORD, their God. ¹⁵ They rejected his statutes, the covenant which he had made with their fathers, and the warnings which he had given them. The vanity they pursued, they themselves became: they followed the surrounding nations whom the LORD had commanded them not to imitate. ¹⁶ They disregarded all the commandments of the LORD, their God, and made for themselves two

molten calves; they also made a sacred pole and worshiped all the host of heaven, and served Baal. ¹⁷ They immolated their sons and daughters by fire, practiced fortune-telling and divination, and sold themselves into evil doing in the LORD'S sight, provoking him ¹⁸ till, in his great anger against Israel, the LORD put them away out of his sight. Only the tribe of Judah was left. ¹⁹ Even the people of Judah, however, did not keep the commandments of the LORD, their God, but followed the rites practiced by Israel. ²⁰ So the LORD rejected the whole race of Israel. He afflicted them and delivered them over to plunderers, finally casting them out from before him. ²¹ When he tore Israel away from the house of David, they made Jeroboam, son of Nebat, king; he drove the Israelites away from the LORD, causing them to commit a great sin. ²² The Israelites imitated Jeroboam in all the sins he committed, nor would they desist from them. ²³ Finally, the LORD put Israel away out of his sight as he had foretold through all his servants, the prophets; and Israel went into exile from their native soil to Assyria, an exile lasting to the present. ²⁴ The king of Assyria brought people from Babylon, Cuthah, Avva, Hamath, and Sepharvaim, and settled them in the cities of Samaria in place of the Israelites. They took possession of Samaria and dwelt in its cities. ²⁵ When they first settled there, they did not venerate the LORD, so he sent lions among them that killed some of their number. ²⁶ A report reached the king of Assyria: "The nations whom you deported and settled in the cities of Samaria do not know how to worship the God of the land, and he has sent lions among them that are killing them, since they do not know how to worship the God of the land." ²⁷ The king of Assyria gave the order, "Send back one of the priests whom I deported, to go there and settle, to teach them how to worship the God of the land." ²⁸ So one of the priests who had been deported from Samaria returned and settled in Bethel, and taught them how to venerate the LORD. ²⁹ But these peoples began to make their own gods in the various cities in which they were living; in the shrines on the high places which the Samarians had made, each people set up gods. ³⁰ Thus the Babylonians made Marduk and his consort; the men of Cuth made Nergal; the men of Hamath made Ashima; ³¹ the men of Avva made Nibhaz and Tartak; and the men of Sepharvaim immolated their children by fire to their city gods, King Hadad and his consort Anath. ³² They also venerated the LORD, choosing from their number priests for the high places, who officiated for them in the shrines on the high places. ³³ But, while venerating the LORD, they served their own gods, following the worship of the nations from among whom they had been deported. ³⁴ To this day they worship according to their ancient rites. (They did not venerate the LORD nor observe the statutes and regulations, the law and commandments, which the LORD enjoined on the descendants of Jacob, whom he had named Israel. ³⁵ When he made a covenant with them, he commanded them: "You must not venerate other gods, nor worship them, nor serve them, nor offer sacrifice to them. ³⁶ The LORD, who brought you up from the land of Egypt with great power and outstretched arm: him shall you venerate, him shall you worship, and to him shall you sacrifice. ³⁷ You must be careful to observe forever the statutes and regulations, the law and commandment, which he wrote for you, and you must not venerate other gods. ³⁸ The covenant which I made with you, you must not forget; you must not venerate other gods. ³⁹ But the LORD, your God, you must venerate; it is he who will deliver you from the power of all your enemies." ⁴⁰ They did not listen, however, but continued in their earlier manner.) ⁴¹ Thus these nations venerated the LORD, but also served their idols. And their sons and grandsons, to this day, are doing as their fathers did.

2 Kings Chapter 18

¹ In the third year of Hoshea, son of Elah, king of Israel, Hezekiah, son of Ahaz, king of Judah, began to reign. ² He was twenty-five years old when he became king, and he reigned twenty-nine years in Jerusalem. His mother's name was Abi, daughter of Zechariah. ³ He pleased the LORD, just as his forefather David had done. ⁴ It was he who removed the high places, shattered the pillars, and cut down the sacred poles. He smashed the bronze serpent called Nehushtan which Moses had made, because up to that time the Israelites were burning incense to it. ⁵ He put his trust in the LORD, the God of Israel; and neither before him nor after him was there anyone like him among all the kings of Judah. ⁶ Loyal to the LORD, Hezekiah never turned away from him, but observed the commandments which the LORD had given Moses. ⁷ The LORD was with him, and he prospered in all that he set out to do. He rebelled against the king of Assyria and did not serve him. ⁸ He also subjugated the watchtowers and walled cities of the Philistines, all the way to Gaza and its territory. ⁹ In the fourth year of King Hezekiah, which was the seventh year of Hoshea, son of Elah, king of Israel, Shalmaneser, king of Assyria, attacked Samaria, laid siege to it, ¹⁰ and after three years captured it. In the sixth year of Hezekiah, the ninth

year of Hoshea, king of Israel, Samaria was taken. ¹¹ The king of Assyria then deported the Israelites to Assyria and settled them in Halah, at the Habor, a river of Gozan, and in the cities of the Medes. ¹² This came about because they had not heeded the warning of the LORD, their God, but violated his covenant, not heeding and not fulfilling the commandments of Moses, the servant of the LORD. ¹³ In the fourteenth year of King Hezekiah, Sennacherib, king of Assyria, went on an expedition against all the fortified cities of Judah and captured them. ¹⁴ Hezekiah, king of Judah, sent this message to the king of Assyria at Lachish: "I have done wrong. Leave me, and I will pay whatever tribute you impose on me." The king of Assyria exacted three hundred talents of silver and thirty talents of gold from Hezekiah, king of Judah. ¹⁵ Hezekiah paid him all the funds there were in the temple of the LORD and in the palace treasuries. ¹⁶ He broke up the door panels and the uprights of the temple of the LORD which he himself had ordered to be overlaid with gold, and gave the gold to the king of Assyria. ¹⁷ The king of Assyria sent the general, the lord chamberlain, and the commander from Lachish with a great army to King Hezekiah at Jerusalem. They went up, and on their arrival in Jerusalem, stopped at the conduit of the upper pool on the highway of the fuller's field. ¹⁸ They called for the king, who sent out to them Eliakim, son of Hilkiah, the master of the palace; Shebnah the scribe; and the herald Joah, son of Asaph. ¹⁹ The commander said to them, "Tell Hezekiah, 'Thus says the great king, the king of Assyria: On what do you base this confidence of yours? ²⁰ Do you think mere words substitute for strategy and might in war? On whom, then, do you rely, that you rebel against me? ²¹ This Egypt, the staff on which you rely, is in fact a broken reed which pierces the hand of anyone who leans on it. That is what Pharaoh, king of Egypt, is to all who rely on him. ²² But if you say to me, We rely on the LORD, our God, is not he the one whose high places and altars Hezekiah has removed, commanding Judah and Jerusalem to worship before this altar in Jerusalem?' ²³ "Now, make a wager with my lord, the king of Assyria: I will give you two thousand horses if you can put riders on them. ²⁴ How then can you repulse even one of the least servants of my lord, relying as you do on Egypt for chariots and horsemen? ²⁵ Was it without the LORD'S will that I have come up to destroy this place? The LORD said to me, 'Go up and destroy that land!'" ²⁶ Then Eliakim, son of Hilkiah, and Shebnah and Joah said to the commander: "Please speak to your servants in Aramaic; we understand it. Do not speak to us in Judean within earshot of the people who are on the wall." ²⁷ But the commander replied: "Was it to your master and to you that my lord sent me to speak these words? Was it not rather to the men sitting on the wall, who, with you, will have to eat their own excrement and drink their urine?" ²⁸ Then the commander stepped forward and cried out in a loud voice in Judean, "Listen to the words of the great king, the king of Assyria. ²⁹ Thus says the king: 'Do not let Hezekiah deceive you, since he cannot deliver you out of my hand. ³⁰ Let not Hezekiah induce you to rely on the LORD, saying, The LORD will surely save us; this city will not be handed over to the king of Assyria. ³¹ Do not listen to Hezekiah, for the king of Assyria says: Make peace with me and surrender! Then each of you will eat of his own vine and of his own fig-tree, and drink the water of his own cistern, ³² until I come to take you to a land like your own, a land of grain and wine, of bread and orchards, of olives, oil and fruit syrup. Choose life, not death. Do not listen to Hezekiah when he would seduce you by saying, The LORD will rescue us. ³³ Has any of the gods of the nations ever rescued his land from the hand of the king of Assyria? ³⁴ Where are the gods of Hamath and Arpad? Where are the gods of Sepharvaim, Hena, and Avva? Where are the gods of the land of Samaria? ³⁵ Which of the gods for all these lands ever rescued his land from my hand? Will the LORD then rescue Jerusalem from my hand?'" ³⁶ But the people remained silent and did not answer him one word, for the king had ordered them not to answer him. ³⁷ Then the master of the palace, Eliakim, son of Hilkiah, Shebnah the scribe, and the herald Joah, son of Asaph, came to Hezekiah with their garments torn, and reported to him what the commander had

2 Kings Chapter 19

¹ When King Hezekiah heard this, he tore his garments, wrapped himself in sackcloth, and went into the temple of the LORD. ² He sent Eliakim, the master of the palace, Shebnah the scribe, and the elders of the priests, wrapped in sackcloth, to tell the prophet Isaiah, son of Amoz, ³ "Thus says Hezekiah: 'This is a day of distress, of rebuke, and of disgrace. Children are at the point of birth, but there is no strength to bring them forth. ⁴ Perhaps the LORD, your God, will hear all the words of the commander, whom his master, the king of Assyria, sent to taunt the living God, and will rebuke him for the words which the LORD, your God, has heard. So send up a prayer for the remnant that is here.'" ⁵ When the servants of King Hezekiah had come to Isaiah, ⁶ he said to them, "Tell this to your master: 'Thus says the LORD: Do not

be frightened by the words you have heard, with which the servants of the king of Assyria have blasphemed me. ⁷ I am about to put in him such a spirit that, when he hears a certain report, he will return to his own land, and there I will cause him to fall by the sword.'" ⁸ When the commander, on his return, heard that the king of Assyria had withdrawn from Lachish, he found him besieging Libnah. ⁹ The king of Assyria heard a report that Tirhakah, king of Ethiopia, had come out to fight against him. Again he sent envoys to Hezekiah with this message: ¹⁰ "Thus shall you say to Hezekiah, king of Judah: 'Do not let your God on whom you rely deceive you by saying that Jerusalem will not be handed over to the king of Assyria. ¹¹ You have heard what the kings of Assyria have done to all other countries: they doomed them! Will you, then, be saved? ¹² Did the gods of the nations whom my fathers destroyed save them? Gozan, Haran, Rezeph, or the Edenites in Telassar? ¹³ Where are the king of Hamath, the king of Arpad, or the kings of the cities Sepharvaim, Hena and Avva?'" ¹⁴ Hezekiah took the letter from the hand of the messengers and read it; then he went up to the temple of the LORD, and spreading it out before him, ¹⁵ he prayed in the LORD'S presence: "O LORD, God of Israel, enthroned upon the cherubim! You alone are God over all the kingdoms of the earth. You have made the heavens and the earth. ¹⁶ Incline your ear, O LORD, and listen! Open your eyes, O LORD, and see! Hear the words of Sennacherib which he sent to taunt the living God. ¹⁷ Truly, O LORD, the kings of Assyria have laid waste the nations and their lands, ¹⁸ and cast their gods into the fire; they destroyed them because they were not gods, but the work of human hands, wood and stone. ¹⁹ Therefore, O LORD, our God, save us from the power of this man, that all the kingdoms of the earth may know that you alone, O LORD, are God." ²⁰ Then Isaiah, son of Amoz, sent this message to Hezekiah: "Thus says the LORD, the God of Israel, in answer to your prayer for help against Sennacherib, king of Assyria: I have listened! ²¹ This is the word the LORD has spoken concerning him: 'She despises you, laughs you to scorn, the virgin daughter Zion! Behind you she wags her head, daughter Jerusalem. ²² Whom have you insulted and blasphemed, against whom have you raised your voice and lifted up your eyes on high? Against the Holy One of Israel! ²³ Through your servants you have insulted the LORD. You said: With my many chariots I climbed the mountain heights, the recesses of Lebanon; I cut down its lofty cedars, its choice cypresses; I reached the remotest heights, its forest park. ²⁴ I dug wells and drank water in foreign lands; I dried up with the soles of my feet all the rivers of Egypt. ²⁵ 'Have you not heard? Long ago I prepared it, From days of old I planned it. Now I have brought it to pass: That you should reduce fortified cities into heaps of ruins, ²⁶ While their inhabitants, shorn of power, are dismayed and ashamed, Becoming like the plants of the field, like the green growth, like the scorched grass on the housetops. ²⁷ I am aware whether you stand or sit; I know whether you come or go, ²⁸ and also your rage against me. Because of your rage against me and your fury which has reached my ears, I will put my hook in your nose and my bit in your mouth, and make you return the way you came. ²⁹ 'This shall be a sign for you: this year you shall eat the aftergrowth, next year, what grows of itself; But in the third year, sow and reap, plant vineyards and eat their fruit! ³⁰ The remaining survivors of the house of Judah shall again strike root below and bear fruit above. ³¹ For out of Jerusalem shall come a remnant, and from Mount Zion, survivors. The zeal of the LORD of hosts shall do this.' ³² "Therefore, thus says the LORD concerning the king of Assyria: 'He shall not reach this city, nor shoot an arrow at it, nor come before it with a shield, nor cast up siege-works against it. ³³ He shall return by the same way he came, without entering the city, says the LORD. ³⁴ I will shield and save this city for my own sake, and for the sake of my servant David.'" ³⁵ That night the angel of the LORD went forth and struck down one hundred and eighty-five thousand men in the Assyrian camp. Early the next morning, there they were, all the corpses of the dead. ³⁶ So Sennacherib, the king of Assyria, broke camp, and went back home to Nineveh. ³⁷ When he was worshiping in the temple of his god Nisroch, his sons Adrammelech and Sharezer slew him with the sword and fled into the land of Ararat. His son Esarhaddon reigned in his stead.

2 Kings Chapter 20

¹ In those days, when Hezekiah was mortally ill, the prophet Isaiah, son of Amoz, came and said to him: "Thus says the LORD: 'Put your house in order, for you are about to die; you shall not recover.'" ² He turned his face to the wall and prayed to the LORD: ³ "O LORD, remember how faithfully and wholeheartedly I conducted myself in your presence, doing what was pleasing to you!" And Hezekiah wept bitterly. ⁴ Before Isaiah had left the central courtyard, the word of the LORD came to him: ⁵ "Go back and tell Hezekiah, the leader of my people: 'Thus says the LORD, the God of your forefather David: I have heard your prayer

and seen your tears. I will heal you. In three days you shall go up to the LORD'S temple; 6 I will add fifteen years to your life. I will rescue you and this city from the hand of the king of Assyria; I will be a shield to this city for my own sake, and for the sake of my servant David.'" 7 Isaiah then ordered a poultice of figs to be brought and applied to the boil, that he might recover. 8 Then Hezekiah asked Isaiah, "What is the sign that the LORD will heal me and that I shall go up to the temple of the LORD on the third day?" 9 Isaiah replied, "This will be the sign for you from the LORD that he will do what he has promised: Shall the shadow go forward or back ten steps?" 10 "It is easy for the shadow to advance ten steps," Hezekiah answered. "Rather, let it go back ten steps." 11 So the prophet Isaiah invoked the LORD, who made the shadow retreat the ten steps it had descended on the staircase to the terrace of Ahaz. 12 At that time, when Merodachbaladan, son of Baladan, king of Babylon, heard that Hezekiah had been ill, he sent letters and gifts to him. 13 Hezekiah was pleased at this, and therefore showed the messengers his whole treasury, his silver, gold, spices and fine oil, his armory, and all that was in his storerooms; there was nothing in his house or in all his realm that Hezekiah did not show them. 14 Then Isaiah the prophet came to King Hezekiah and asked him: "What did these men say to you? Where did they come from?" "They came from a distant land, from Babylon," replied Hezekiah. 15 "What did they see in your house?" the prophet asked. "They saw everything in my house," answered Hezekiah. "There is nothing in my storerooms that I did not show them." 16 Then Isaiah said to Hezekiah: "Hear the word of the LORD: 17 The time is coming when all that is in your house, and everything that your fathers have stored up until this day, shall be carried off to Babylon; nothing shall be left, says the LORD. 18 Some of your own bodily descendants shall be taken and made servants in the palace of the king of Babylon." 19 Hezekiah replied to Isaiah, "The word of the LORD which you have spoken is favorable." For he thought, "There will be peace and security in my lifetime." 20 The rest of the acts of Hezekiah, all his valor, and his construction of the pool and conduit by which water was brought into the city, are written in the book of the chronicles of the kings of Judah. 21 Hezekiah rested with his ancestors and his son Manasseh succeeded him as king.

2 Kings Chapter 21

1 Manasseh was twelve years old when he began to reign, and he reigned fifty-five years in Jerusalem. His mother's name was Hephzibah. 2 He did evil in the sight of the LORD, following the abominable practices of the nations whom the LORD had cleared out of the way of the Israelites. 3 He rebuilt the high places which his father Hezekiah had destroyed. He erected altars to Baal, and also set up a sacred pole, as Ahab, king of Israel, had done. He worshiped and served the whole host of heaven. 4 He built altars in the temple of the LORD, about which the LORD had said, "I will establish my name in Jerusalem" - 5 altars for the whole host of heaven, in the two courts of the temple. 6 He immolated his son by fire. He practiced soothsaying and divination, and reintroduced the consulting of ghosts and spirits. He did much evil in the LORD'S sight and provoked him to anger. 7 The Asherah idol he had made, he set up in the temple, of which the LORD had said to David and to his son Solomon: "In this temple and in Jerusalem, which I have chosen out of all the tribes of Israel, I shall place my name forever. 8 I will not in future allow Israel to be driven off the land I gave their fathers, provided that they are careful to observe all I have commanded them, the entire law which my servant Moses enjoined upon them." 9 But they did not listen, and Manasseh misled them into doing even greater evil than the nations whom the LORD had destroyed at the coming of the Israelites. 10 Then the LORD spoke through his servants the prophets: 11 "Because Manasseh, king of Judah, has practiced these abominations and has done greater evil than all that was done by the Amorites before him, and has led Judah into sin by his idols, 12 therefore thus says the LORD, the God of Israel: 'I will bring such evil on Jerusalem and Judah that, whenever anyone hears of it, his ears shall ring. 13 I will measure Jerusalem with the same cord as I did Samaria, and with the plummet I used for the house of Ahab. I will wipe Jerusalem clean as one wipes a dish, wiping it inside and out. 14 I will cast off the survivors of my inheritance and deliver them into enemy hands, to become a prey and a booty for all their enemies, 15 because they have done evil in my sight and provoked me from the day their fathers came forth from Egypt until today.'" 16 In addition to the sin which he caused Judah to commit, Manasseh did evil in the sight of the LORD, shedding so much innocent blood as to fill the length and breadth of Jerusalem. 17 The rest of the acts of Manasseh, the sin he committed, and all that he did, are written in the book of the chronicles of the kings of Judah. 18 Manasseh rested with his ancestors and was buried in his palace garden, the garden of Uzza. His son Amon succeeded him as king. 19 Amon was twenty-two years old when he

began to reign, and he reigned two years in Jerusalem. His mother's name was Meshullemeth, daughter of Haruz of Jotbah. 20 He did evil in the sight of the LORD, as his father Manasseh had done. 21 He followed exactly the path his father had trod, serving and worshiping the idols his father had served. 22 He abandoned the LORD, the God of his fathers, and did not follow the path of the LORD. 23 Subjects of Amon conspired against him and slew the king in his palace, 24 but the people of the land then slew all who had conspired against King Amon, and proclaimed his son Josiah king in his stead. 25 The rest of the acts that Amon did are written in the book of the chronicles of the kings of Judah. 26 He was buried in his own grave in the garden of Uzza, and his son Josiah succeeded him as king.

2 Kings Chapter 22

1 Josiah was eight years old when he began to reign, and he reigned thirty-one years in Jerusalem. His mother's name was Jedidah, daughter of Adaiah of Bozkath. 2 He pleased the LORD and conducted himself unswervingly just as his ancestor David had done. 31 In his eighteenth year, King Josiah sent the scribe Shaphan, son of Azaliah, son of Meshullam, to the temple of the LORD with orders to 4 go to the high priest Hilkiah and have him smelt down the precious metals that had been donated to the temple of the Lord, which the doorkeepers had collected from the people. 5 They were to be consigned to the master workmen in the temple of the LORD, who should then pay them out to the carpenters, builders, and lumbermen making repairs on the temple, 6 and for the purchase of wood and hewn stone for the temple repairs. 7 No reckoning was asked of them regarding the funds consigned to them, because they held positions of trust. 8 The high priest Hilkiah informed the scribe Shaphan, "I have found the book of the law in the temple of the LORD." Hilkiah gave the book to Shaphan, who read it. 9 Then the scribe Shaphan went to the king and reported, "Your servants have smelted down the metals available in the temple and have consigned them to the master workmen in the temple of the LORD." 10 The scribe Shaphan also informed the king that the priest Hilkiah had given him a book, and then read it aloud to the king. 11 When the king had heard the contents of the book of the law, he tore his garments 12 and issued this command to Hilkiah the priest, Ahikam, son of Shaphan, Achbor, son of Micaiah, the scribe Shaphan, and the king's servant Asaiah: 13 "Go, consult the LORD for me, for the people, for all Judah, about the stipulations of this book that has been found, for the anger of the LORD has been set furiously ablaze against us, because our fathers did not obey the stipulations of this book, nor fulfill our written obligations." 14 So Hilkiah the priest, Ahikam, Achbor, Shaphan, and Asaiah betook themselves to the Second Quarter in Jerusalem, where the prophetess Huldah resided. She was the wife of Shallum, son of Tikvah, son of Harhas, keeper of the wardrobe. When they had spoken to her, 15 she said to them, "Thus says the LORD, the God of Israel: 'Say to the man who sent you to me, 16 Thus says the LORD: I will bring upon this place and upon its inhabitants all the evil that is threatened in the book which the king of Judah has read. 17 Because they have forsaken me and have burned incense to other gods, provoking me by everything to which they turn their hands, my anger is ablaze against this place and it cannot be extinguished.' 18 "But to the king of Judah who sent you to consult the LORD, give this response: 'Thus says the LORD, the God of Israel: As for the threats you have heard, 19 because you were heartsick and have humbled yourself before the LORD when you heard my threats that this place and its inhabitants would become a desolation and a curse; because you tore your garments and wept before me; I in turn have listened, says the LORD. 20 I will therefore gather you to your ancestors; you shall go to your grave in peace, and your eyes shall not see all the evil I will bring upon this place.'" This they reported to the king.

2 Kings Chapter 23

1 The king then had all the elders of Judah and of Jerusalem summoned together before him. 2 The king went up to the temple of the LORD with all the men of Judah and all the inhabitants of Jerusalem: priests, prophets, and all the people, small and great. He had the entire contents of the book of the covenant that had been found in the temple of the LORD, read out to them. 3 Standing by the column, the king made a covenant before the LORD that they would follow him and observe his ordinances, statutes and decrees with their whole hearts and souls, thus reviving the terms of the covenant which were written in this book. And all the people stood as participants in the covenant. 4 Then the king commanded the high priest Hilkiah, his vicar, and the doorkeepers to remove from the temple of the LORD all the objects that had been made for Baal, Asherah, and the whole host of heaven. He had these burned outside Jerusalem on the slopes of the Kidron and their ashes carried to Bethel. 5 He also put an end to the pseudo-priests whom the kings of

Judah had appointed to burn incense on the high places in the cities of Judah and in the vicinity of Jerusalem, as well as those who burned incense to Baal, to the sun, moon, and signs of the Zodiac, and to the whole host of heaven. 6 From the temple of the LORD he also removed the sacred pole, to the Kidron Valley, outside Jerusalem; there he had it burned and beaten to dust, which was then scattered over the common graveyard. 7 He tore down the apartments of the cult prostitutes which were in the temple of the LORD, and in which the women wove garments for the Asherah. 8 He brought in all the priests from the cities of Judah, and then defiled, from Geba to Beer-sheba, the high places where they had offered incense. He also tore down the high place of the satyrs, which was at the entrance of the Gate of Joshua, governor of the city, to the left as one enters the city gate. 9 The priests of the high places could not function at the altar of the LORD in Jerusalem; but they, along with their relatives, ate the unleavened bread. 10 The king also defiled Topheth in the Valley of Ben-hinnom, so that there would no longer be an immolation of sons or daughters by fire in honor of Molech. 11 He did away with the horses which the kings of Judah had dedicated to the sun; these were at the entrance of the temple of the LORD, near the chamber of Nathan-melech the eunuch, which was in the large building. The chariots of the sun he destroyed by fire. 12 He also demolished the altars made by the kings of Judah on the roof (the roof terrace of Ahaz), and the altars made by Manasseh in the two courts of the temple of the LORD. He pulverized them and threw the dust into the Kidron Valley. 13 The king defiled the high places east of Jerusalem, south of the Mount of Misconduct, which Solomon, king of Israel, had built in honor of Astarte, the Sidonian horror, of Chemosh, the Moabite horror, and of Milcom, the idol of the Ammonites. 14 He broke to pieces the pillars, cut down the sacred poles, and filled the places where they had been with human bones. 15 Likewise the altar which was at Bethel, the high place built by Jeroboam, son of Nebat, who caused Israel to sin—this same altar and high place he tore down, breaking up the stones and grinding them to powder, and burning the Asherah. 16 When Josiah turned and saw the graves there on the mountainside, he ordered the bones taken from the graves and burned on the altar, and thus defiled it in fulfillment of the word of the LORD which the man of God had proclaimed as Jeroboam was standing by the altar on the feast day. When the king looked up and saw the grave of the man of God who had proclaimed these words, 17 he asked, "What is that tombstone I see?" The men of the city replied, "It is the grave of the man of God who came from Judah and predicted the very things you have done to the altar of Bethel." 18 "Let him be," he said, "let no one move his bones." So they left his bones undisturbed together with the bones of the prophet who had come from Samaria. 19 Josiah also removed all the shrines on the high places near the cities of Samaria which the kings of Israel had erected, thereby provoking the LORD; he did the very same to them as he had done in Bethel. 20 He slaughtered upon the altars all the priests of the high places that were at the shrines, and burned human bones upon them. Then he returned to Jerusalem. 21 The king issued a command to all the people to observe the Passover of the LORD, their God, as it was prescribed in that book of the covenant. 22 No Passover such as this had been observed during the period when the Judges ruled Israel, or during the entire period of the kings of Israel and the kings of Judah, 23 until the eighteenth year of king Josiah, when this Passover of the LORD was kept in Jerusalem. 24 Further, Josiah did away with the consultation of ghosts and spirits, with the household gods, idols, and all the other horrors to be seen in the land of Judah and in Jerusalem, so that he might carry out the stipulations of the law written in the book that the priest Hilkiah had found in the temple of the LORD. 25 Before him there had been no king who turned to the LORD as he did, with his whole heart, his whole soul, and his whole strength, in accord with the entire law of Moses; nor could any after him compare with him. 26 Yet, because of all the provocations that Manasseh had given, the LORD did not desist from his fiercely burning anger against Judah. 27 The LORD said: "Even Judah will I put out of my sight as I did Israel. I will reject this city, Jerusalem, which I chose, and the temple of which I said, 'There shall my name be.'" 28 The rest of the acts of Josiah, with all that he did, are written in the book of the chronicles of the kings of Judah. 29 In his time Pharaoh Neco, king of Egypt, went up toward the river Euphrates to the king of Assyria. King Josiah set out to confront him, but was slain at Megiddo at the first encounter. 30 His servants brought his body on a chariot from Megiddo to Jerusalem, where they buried him in his own grave. Then the people of the land took Jehoahaz, son of Josiah, anointed him, and proclaimed him king to succeed his father. 31 Jehoahaz was twenty-three years old when he began to reign, and he reigned three months in Jerusalem. His mother, whose name was Hamutal, daughter of Jeremiah, was from Libnah. 32 He did evil in the

sight of the LORD, just as his forebears had done. 33 Pharaoh Neco took him prisoner at Riblah in the land of Hamath, thus ending his reign in Jerusalem. He imposed a fine upon the land of a hundred talents of silver and a talent of gold. 34 Pharaoh Neco then appointed Eliakim, son of Josiah, king in place of his father Josiah; he changed his name to Jehoiakim. Jehoahaz he took away with him to Egypt, where he died. 35 Jehoiakim gave the silver and gold to Pharaoh, but taxed the land to raise the amount Pharaoh demanded. He exacted the silver and gold from the people of the land, from each proportionately, to pay Pharaoh Neco. 36 Jehoiakim was twenty-five years old when he began to reign, and he reigned eleven years in Jerusalem. His mother's name was Zebidah, daughter of Pedaiah, from Rumah. 37 He did evil in the sight of the LORD, just as his forebears had done.

2 Kings Chapter 24

1 During his reign Nebuchadnezzar, king of Babylon, moved against him, and Jehoiakim became his vassal for three years. Then Jehoiakim turned and rebelled against him. 2 The LORD loosed against him bands of Chaldeans, Arameans, Moabites, and Ammonites; he loosed them against Judah to destroy it, as the LORD had threatened through his servants the prophets. 3 This befell Judah because the LORD had stated that he would inexorably put them out of his sight for the sins Manasseh had committed in all that he did; 4 and especially because of the innocent blood he shed, with which he filled Jerusalem, the LORD would not forgive. 5 The rest of the acts of Jehoiakim, with all that he did, are written in the book of the chronicles of the kings of Judah. 6 Jehoiakim rested with his ancestors, and his son Jehoiachin succeeded him as king. 7 The king of Egypt did not again leave his own land, for the king of Babylon had taken all that belonged to the king of Egypt from the Wadi of Egypt to the Euphrates River. 8 Jehoiachin was eighteen years old when he began to reign, and he reigned three months in Jerusalem. His mother's name was Nehushta, daughter of Elnathan of Jerusalem. 9 He did evil in the sight of the LORD, just as his forebears had done. 10 At that time the officials of Nebuchadnezzar, king of Babylon, attacked Jerusalem, and the city came under siege. 11 Nebuchadnezzar, king of Babylon, himself arrived at the city while his servants were besieging it. 12 Then Jehoiachin, king of Judah, together with his mother, his ministers, officers, and functionaries, surrendered to the king of Babylon, who, in the eighth year of his reign, took him captive. 13 He carried off all the treasures of the temple of the LORD and those of the palace, and broke up all the gold utensils that Solomon, king of Israel, had provided in the temple of the LORD, as the LORD had foretold. 14 He deported all Jerusalem: all the officers and men of the army, ten thousand in number, and all the craftsmen and smiths. None were left among the people of the land except the poor. 15 He deported Jehoiachin to Babylon, and also led captive from Jerusalem to Babylon the king's mother and wives, his functionaries, and the chief men of the land. 16 The king of Babylon also led captive to Babylon all seven thousand men of the army, and a thousand craftsmen and smiths, all of them trained soldiers. 17 In place of Jehoiachin, the king of Babylon appointed his uncle Mattaniah king, and changed his name to Zedekiah. 18 Zedekiah was twenty-one years old when he became king, and he reigned eleven years in Jerusalem. His mother's name was Hamutal, daughter of Jeremiah of Libnah. 19 He also did evil in the sight of the LORD, just as Jehoiakim had done. 20 The LORD'S anger befell Jerusalem and Judah till he cast them out from his presence. Thus Zedekiah rebelled against the king of Babylon.

2 Kings Chapter 25

1 In the tenth month of the ninth year of Zedekiah's reign, on the tenth day of the month, Nebuchadnezzar, king of Babylon, and his whole army advanced against Jerusalem, encamped around it, and built siege walls on every side. 2 The siege of the city continued until the eleventh year of Zedekiah. 3 On the ninth day of the fourth month, when famine had gripped the city, and the people had no more bread, 4 the city walls were breached. Then the king and all the soldiers left the city by night through the gate between the two walls which was near the king's garden. Since the Chaldeans had the city surrounded, they went in the direction of the Arabah. 5 But the Chaldean army pursued the king and overtook him in the desert near Jericho, abandoned by his whole army. 6 The king was therefore arrested and brought to Riblah to the king of Babylon, who pronounced sentence on him. 7 He had Zedekiah's sons slain before his eyes. Then he blinded Zedekiah, bound him with fetters, and had him brought to Babylon. 8 On the seventh day of the fifth month (this was in the nineteenth year of Nebuchadnezzar, king of Babylon), Nebuzaradan, captain of the bodyguard, came to Jerusalem as the representative of the king of Babylon. 9 He burned the house of the LORD, the palace of the king, and all the houses of Jerusalem; every large building was destroyed by fire. 10 Then the Chaldean troops who

were with the captain of the guard tore down the walls that surrounded Jerusalem. 11 Then Nebuzaradan, captain of the guard, led into exile the last of the people remaining in the city, and those who had deserted to the king of Babylon, and the last of the artisans. 12 But some of the country's poor, Nebuzaradan, captain of the guard, left behind as vinedressers and farmers. 13 The bronze pillars that belonged to the house of the LORD, and the wheeled carts and the bronze sea in the house of the LORD, the Chaldeans broke into pieces; they carried away the bronze to Babylon. 14 They took also the pots, the shovels, the snuffers, the bowls, the pans and all the bronze vessels used for service. 15 The fire-holders and the bowls which were of gold or silver the captain of the guard also carried off. 16 The weight in bronze of the two pillars, the bronze sea, and the wheeled carts, all of them furnishings which Solomon had made for the house of the LORD, was never calculated. 17 Each of the pillars was eighteen cubits high; a bronze capital five cubits high surmounted each pillar, and a network with pomegranates encircled the capital, all of bronze; and so for the other pillar, as regards the network. 18 The captain of the guard also took Seraiah the high priest, Zephaniah the second priest, and the three keepers of the entry. 19 And from the city he took one courtier, a commander of soldiers, five men in the personal service of the king who were still in the city, the scribe of the army commander, who mustered the people of the land, and sixty of the common people still remaining in the city. 20 The captain of the guard, Nebuzaradan, arrested these and brought them to the king of Babylon at Riblah; 21 the king had them struck down and put to death in Riblah, in the land of Hamath. Thus was Judah exiled from her land. 22 As for the people whom he had allowed to remain in the land of Judah, Nebuchadnezzar, king of Babylon, appointed as their governor Gedaliah, son of Ahikam, son of Shaphan. 23 Hearing that the king of Babylon had appointed Gedaliah governor, all the army commanders with their men came to him at Mizpah: Ishmael, son of Nethaniah, Johanan, son of Kareah, Seraiah, son of Tanhumeth the Netophathite, and Jaazaniah, from Beth-maacah. 24 Gedaliah gave the commanders and their men his oath. "Do not be afraid of the Chaldean officials," he said to them. "Remain in the country and serve the king of Babylon, and all will be well with you." 25 But in the seventh month Ishmael, son of Nethaniah, son of Elishama, of royal descent, came with ten men, attacked Gedaliah and killed him, along with the Jews and Chaldeans who were in Mizpah with him. 26 Then all the people, great and small, left with the army commanders and went to Egypt for fear of the Chaldeans. 27 In the thirty-seventh year of the exile of Jehoiachin, king of Judah, on the twenty-seventh day of the twelfth month, Evilmerodach, king of Babylon, in the inaugural year of his own reign, raised up Jehoiachin, king of Judah, from prison. 28 He spoke kindly to him and gave him a throne higher than that of the other kings who were with him in Babylon. 29 Jehoiachin took off his prison garb and ate at the king's table as long as he lived. 30 The allowance granted him by the king was a perpetual allowance, in fixed daily amounts, for as long as he lived.

I Chronicles

1 Chronicles Chapter 1

1 Adam, Seth, Enosh, 2 Kenan, Mahalalel, Jared, 3 Enoch, Methuselah, Lamech, 4 Noah, Shem, Ham, and Japheth. 5 The descendants of Japheth were Gomer, Magog, Madai, Javan, Tubal, Meshech, and Tiras. 6 The descendants of Gomer were Ashkenaz, Riphath, and Togarmah. 7 The descendants of Javan were Elishah, Tarshish, the Kittim, and the Rodanim. 8 The descendants of Ham were Cush, Mesraim, Put, and Canaan. 9 The descendants of Cush were Seba, Havilah, Sabta, Raama, and Sabteca. The descendants of Raama were Sheba and Dedan. 10 Cush became the father of Nimrod, who was the first to be a conqueror on the earth. 11 Mesraim became the father of the Ludim, Anamim, Lehabim, Naphtuhim, 12 Pathrusim, Casluhim, and Caphtorim, from whom the Philistines sprang. 13 Canaan became the father of Sidon, his first-born, and Heth, 14 and the Jebusite, the Amorite, the Girgashite, 15 the Hivite, the Arkite, the Sinite, 16 the Arvadite, the Zemarite, and the Hamathite. 17 The descendants of Shem were Elam, Asshur, Arpachshad, Lud, and Aram. The descendants of Aram were Uz, Hul, Gether, and Mash. 18 Arpachshad became the father of Shelah, and Shelah became the father of Eber. 19 Two sons were born to Eber; the first was named Peleg (for in his time the world was divided), and his brother was Joktan. 20 Joktan became the father of Almodad, Sheleph, Hazarmaveth, Jerah, 21 Hadoram, Uzal, Diklah, 22 Ebal, Abimael, Sheba, 23 Ophir, Havilah, and Jobab; all these were the sons of Joktan. 24 Shem, Arpachshad, Shelah, 25 Eber, Peleg, Reu, 26 Serug, Nahor, Terah, 27 Abram, who was Abraham. 28 The sons of Abraham were Isaac and Ishmael. 29 These were their descendants: Nebaioth, the first-

born of Ishmael, then Kedar, Adbeel, Mibsam, 30 Mishma, Dumah, Massa, Hadad, Tema, 31 Jetur, Naphish, and Kedemah. These were the descendants of Ishmael. 32 The descendants of Keturah, Abraham's concubine: she bore Zimran, Jokshan, Medan, Midian, Ishbak, and Shuah. The sons of Jokshan were Sheba and Dedan. 33 The descendants of Midian were Ephah, Epher, Hanoch, Abida, and Eldaah. All these were the descendants of Keturah. 34 Abraham became the father of Isaac. The sons of Isaac were Esau and Israel. 35 The sons of Esau were Eliphaz, Reuel, Jeush, Jalam, and Korah. 36 The sons of Eliphaz were Teman, Omar, Zephi, Gatam, Kenaz, (Timna,) and Amalek. 37 The sons of Reuel were Nahath, Zerah, Shammah, and Mizzah. 38 The descendants of Seir were Lotan, Shobal, Zibeon, Anah, Dishon, Ezer, and Dishan. 39 The sons of Lotan were Hori and Homam; Timna was the sister of Lotan. 40 The sons of Shobal were Alian, Manahath, Ebal, Shephi, and Onam. The sons of Zibeon were Aiah and Anah. 41 The sons of Anah: Dishon. The sons of Dishon were Hemdan, Eshban, Ithran, and Cheran. 42 The sons of Ezer were Bilhan, Zaavan, and Jaakan. The sons of Dishan were Uz and Aran. 43 The kings who reigned in the land of Edom before they had Israelite kings were the following: Bela, son of Beor, the name of whose city was Dinhabah. 44 When Bela died, Jobab, son of Zerah, from Bozrah, succeeded him. 45 When Jobab died, Husham, from the land of the Temanites, succeeded him. 46 Husham died and Hadad, son of Bedad, succeeded him. He overthrew the Midianites on the Moabite plateau, and the name of his city was Avith. 47 Hadad died and Samlah of Masrekah succeeded him. 48 Samlah died and Shaul from Rehoboth-han-nahar succeeded him. 49 When Shaul died, Baal-hanan, son of Achbor, succeeded him. 50 Baalhanan died and Hadad succeeded him. The name of his city was Pai, and his wife's name was Mehetabel. She was the daughter of Matred, who was the daughter of Mezahab. 51 After Hadad died. . . .These were the chiefs of Edom: the chiefs of Timna, Aliah, Jetheth, 52 Oholibamah, Elah, Pinon, 53 Kenaz, Teman, Mibzar, 54 Magdiel, and Iram were the chiefs of Edom.

1 Chronicles Chapter 2

1 These were the sons of Israel: Reuben, Simeon, Levi, Judah, Issachar, Zebulun, 2 Dan, Joseph, Benjamin, Naphtali, Gad, and Asher. 3 The sons of Judah were: Er, Onan, and Shelah; these three were born to him of Bathshua, a Canaanite woman. But Judah's first-born, Er, was wicked in the sight of the LORD, so he killed him. 4 Judah's daughter-in-law Tamar bore him Perez and Zerah, so that he had five sons in all. 5 The sons of Perez were Hezron and Hamul. 6 The sons of Zerah were Zimri, Ethan, Heman, Calcol, and Darda - five in all. 7 The sons of Zimri: Carmi. The sons of Carmi: Achar, who brought trouble upon Israel by violating the ban. 8 The sons of Ethan: Azariah. 9 The sons born to Hezron were Jerahmeel, Ram, and Chelubai. 10 Ram became the father of Amminadab, and Amminadab became the father of Nahshon, a prince of the Judahites. 11 Nahshon became the father of Salmah. Salmah became the father of Boaz. 12 Boaz became the father of Obed. Obed became the father of Jesse. 13 Jesse became the father of Eliab, his first-born, of Abinadab, the second son, Shimea, the third, 14 Nethanel, the fourth, Raddai, the fifth, 15 Ozem, the sixth, and David, the seventh. 16 Their sisters were Zeruiah and Abigail. Zeruiah had three sons: Abishai, Joab, and Asahel. 17 Abigail bore Amasa, whose father was Jether the Ishmaelite. 18 By his wife Azubah, Caleb, son of Hezron, became the father of a daughter, Jerioth. Her sons were Jesher, Shobab, and Ardon. 19 When Azubah died, Caleb married Ephrath, who bore him Hur. 20 Hur became the father of Uri, and Uri became the father of Bezalel. 21 Then Hezron had relations with the daughter of Machir, the father of Gilead, having married her when he was sixty years old. She bore him Segub. 22 Segub became the father of Jair, who possessed twenty-three cities in the land of Gilead. 23 Geshur and Aram took from them the villages of Jair, that is, Kenath and its towns, sixty cities in all, which had belonged to the sons of Machir, the father of Gilead. 24 After the death of Hezron, Caleb had relations with Ephrathah, the widow of his father Hezron, and she bore him Ashhur, the father of Tekoa. 25 The sons of Jerahmeel, the first-born of Hezron, were Ram, the first-born, then Bunah, Oren, and Ozem, his brothers. 26 Jerahmeel also had another wife, Atarah by name, who was the mother of Onam. 27 The sons of Ram, the first-born of Jerahmeel, were Maaz, Jamin, and Eker. 28 The sons of Onam were Shammai and Jada. The sons of Shammai were Nadab and Abishur. 29 Abishur's wife, who was named Abihail, bore him Ahban and Molid. 30 The sons of Nadab were Seled and Appaim. Seled died without sons. 31 The sons of Appaim: Ishi. The sons of Ishi: Sheshan. The sons of Sheshan: Ahlai. 32 The sons of Jada, the brother of Shammai, were Jether and Jonathan. Jether died without sons. 33 The sons of Jonathan were Peleth and Zaza. These were the descendants of Jerahmeel. 34 Sheshan, who had no sons, only daughters, had an Egyptian slave named Jarha. 35 Sheshan gave his daughter in marriage to his slave Jarha, and she bore

him Attai. ³⁶ Attai became the father of Nathan. Nathan became the father of Zabad. ³⁷ Zabad became the father of Ephlal. Ephlal became the father of Obed. ³⁸ Obed became the father of Jehu. Jehu became the father of Azariah. ³⁹ Azariah became the father of Helez. Helez became the father of Eleasah. ⁴⁰ Eleasah became the father of Sismai. Sismai became the father of Shallum. ⁴¹ Shallum became the father of Jekamiah. Jekamiah became the father of Elishama. ⁴² The descendants of Caleb, the brother of Jerahmeel: (Mesha) his first-born, who was the father of Ziph. Then the sons of Mareshah, who was the father of Hebron. ⁴³ The sons of Hebron were Korah, Tappuah, Rekem, and Shema. ⁴⁴ Shema became the father of Raham, who was the father of Jorkeam. Rekem became the father of Shammai. ⁴⁵ The son of Shammai: Maon, who was the father of Beth-zur. ⁴⁶ Ephah, Caleb's concubine, bore Haran, Moza, and Gazez. Haran became the father of Gazez. ⁴⁷ The sons of Jahdai were Regem, Jotham, Geshan, Pelet, Ephah, and Shaaph. ⁴⁸ Maacah, Caleb's concubine, bore Sheber and Tirhanah. ⁴⁹ She also bore Shaaph, the father of Madmannah, Sheva, the father of Machbenah, and the father of Gibea. Achsah was Caleb's daughter. ⁵⁰ These were descendants of Caleb, sons of Hur, the first-born of Ephrathah: Shobal, the father of Kiriath-jearim, ⁵¹ Salma, the father of Bethlehem, and Hareph, the father of Bethgader. ⁵² The sons of Shobal, the father of Kiriath-jearim, were Reaiah, half the Manahathites, ⁵³ and the clans of Kiriath-jearim: the Ithrites, the Puthites, the Shumathites, and the Mishraites. From these the people of Zorah and the Eshtaolites derived. ⁵⁴ The descendants of Salma were Bethlehem, the Netophathites, Atroth-beth-Joab, half the Manahathites, and the Zorites. ⁵⁵ The clans of the Sopherim dwelling in Jabez were the Tirathites, the Shimeathites, and the Sucathites. They were the Kenites, who came from Hammath of the ancestor of the Rechabites.

1 Chronicles Chapter 3

¹The following were the sons of David who were born to him in Hebron: the first-born, Amnon, by Ahinoam of Jezreel; the second, Daniel, by Abigail of Carmel; ²the third, Absalom, son of Maacah, who was the daughter of Talmai, king of Geshur; the fourth, Adonijah, son of Haggith; ³the fifth, Shephatiah, by Abital; the sixth, Ithream, by his wife Eglah. ⁴Six in all were born to him in Hebron, where he reigned seven years and six months. Then he reigned thirty-three years in Jerusalem, ⁵where the following were born to him: Shimea, Shobab, Nathan, Solomon — four by Bathsheba, the daughter of Ammiel; ⁶Ibhar, Elishua, Eliphelet, ⁷Nogah, Nepheg, Japhia, ⁸Elishama, Eliada, and Eliphelet — nine. ⁹All these were sons of David, in addition to other sons by concubines; and Tamar was their sister. ¹⁰The son of Solomon was Rehoboam, whose son was Abijah, whose son was Asa, whose son was Jehoshaphat, ¹¹whose son was Joram, whose son was Ahaziah, whose son was Joash, whose son was Amaziah, whose son was Azariah, whose son was Jotham, ¹²whose son was Ahaz, whose son was Hezekiah, whose son was Manasseh, ¹⁴whose son was Amon, whose son was Josiah. ¹⁵The sons of Josiah were: the first-born Johanan; the second, Jehoiakim; the third, Zedekiah; the fourth, Shallum. ¹⁶The sons of Jehoiakim were: Jeconiah, his son; Zedekiah, his son. ¹⁷The sons of Jeconiah the captive were: Shealtiel, ¹⁸Malchiram, Pedaiah, Shenazzar, Jekamiah, Shama, and Nedabiah. ¹⁹The sons of Pedaiah were Zerubbabel and Shimei. The sons of Zerubbabel were Meshullam and Hananiah; Shelomith was their sister. ²⁰The sons of Meshullam were Hashubah, Ohel, Berechiah, Hasadiah, Jushabhesed — five. ²¹The sons of Hananiah were Pelatiah, Jeshaiah, Rephaiah, Arnan, Obadiah, and Shecaniah. ²²The sons of Shecaniah were Shemiah, Hattush, Igal, Bariah, Neariah, Shaphat — six. ²³The sons of Neariah were Elioenai, Hizkiah, and Azrikam — three. ²⁴The sons of Elioenai were Hodaviah, Eliashib, Pelaiah, Akkub, Johanan, Delaiah, and Anani — seven.

1 Chronicles Chapter 4

¹The descendants of Judah were: Perez, Hezron, Carmi, Hur, and Shobal. ²Reaiah, the son of Shobal, became the father of Jahath, and Jahath became the father of Ahumai and Lahad. These were the clans of the Zorathites. ³These were the descendants of Hareph, the father of Etam: Jezreel, Ishma, and Idbash; their sister was named Hazzelelponi. ⁴Penuel was the father of Gedor, and Ezer the father of Hushah. These were the descendants of Hur, the first-born of Ephrathah, the father of Bethlehem. ⁵Ashhur, the father of Tekoa, had two wives, Helah and Naarah. ⁶Naarah bore him Ahuzzam, Hepher, the Temenites and the Ahashtarites. These were the descendants of Naarah. ⁷The sons of Helah were Zereth, Izhar, Ethnan, and Koz. ⁸Koz became the father of Anub and Zobebah, as well as of the clans of Aharhel, son of Harum. ⁹Jabez was the most distinguished of the brothers. His mother had named him Jabez, saying, "I bore him with pain." ¹⁰Jabez prayed to the God of Israel: "Oh, that you may truly bless me and extend my boundaries! Help me and make me free of misfortune, without pain!" And God granted his prayer. ¹¹Chelub, the brother of Shuhah, became the father of Mehir, who was the father of Eshton. ¹²Eshton became the father of Bethrapha, Paseah, and Tehinnah, the father of the city of Nahash. These were the men of Recah. ¹³The sons of Kenaz were Othniel and Seraiah. The sons of Othniel were Hathath and Meonothai; ¹⁴Meonothai became the father of Ophrah. Seraiah became the father of Joab, the father of Geharashim, so called because they were craftsmen. ¹⁵The sons of Caleb, son of Jephunneh, were Ir, Elah, and Naam. The sons of Elah were...and Kenaz. ¹⁶The sons of Jehallelel were Ziph, Ziphah, Tiria, and Asarel. ¹⁷The sons of Ezrah were Jether, Mered, Epher, and Jalon. Jether became the father of Miriam, Shammai, and Ishbah, the father of Eshtemoa. ¹⁸His (Mered's) Egyptian wife bore Jered, the father of Gedor, Heber, the father of Soco, and Jekuthiel, the father of Zanoah. These were the sons of Bithiah, the daughter of Pharaoh, whom Mered married. ¹⁹The sons of his Jewish wife, the sister of Naham, the father of Keilah, were Shimon the Garmite and Ishi the Maacathite. ²⁰The sons of Shimon were Amnon, Rinnah, Benhanan, and Tilon. The son of Ishi was Zoheth and the son of Zoheth... ²¹The descendants of Shelah, son of Judah, were: Er, the father of Lecah; Laadah, the father of Mareshah; the clans of the linen weavers' guild in Bethashbea; ²²Jokim; the men of Cozeba; and Joash and Saraph, who held property in Moab, but returned to Bethlehem. (These are events of old.) ²³They were potters and inhabitants of Netaim and Gederah, where they lived in the king's service. ²⁴The sons of Simeon were Nemuel, Jamin, Jachin, Zerah, and Shaul, ²⁵whose son was Shallum, whose son was Mibsam, whose son was Mishma. ²⁶The descendants of Mishma were his son Hammuel, whose son was Zaccur, whose son was Shimei. ²⁷Shimei had sixteen sons and six daughters. His brothers, however, did not have many sons, and as a result all their clans did not equal the number of the Judahites. ²⁸They dwelt in Beer-sheba, Moladah, Hazar-shual, ²⁹Bilhah, Ezem, Tolad, ³⁰Bethuel, Hormah, Ziklag, ³¹Beth-marcaboth, Hazar-susim, Bethbiri, and Shaaraim. Until David came to reign, these were their cities ³²and their villages. Etam, also, and Ain, Rimmon, Tochen, and Ashan — five cities, ³³together with all their outlying villages as far as Baal. Here is where they dwelt, and so it was inscribed of them in their family records. ³⁴Meshobab, Jamlech, Joshah, son of Amaziah, ³⁵Joel, Jehu, son of Joshibiah, son of Seraiah, son of Asiel, ³⁶Elioenai, Jaakobath, Jeshohaiah, Asaiah, Adiel, Jesimiel, Benaiah, ³⁷Ziza, son of Shiphi, son of Allon, son of Jedaiah, son of Shimri, son of Shemaiah — ³⁸these just named were princes in their clans, and their ancestral houses spread out to such an extent ³⁹that they went to the approaches of Gedor, east of the valley, seeking pasture for their flocks. ⁴⁰They found abundant and good pastures, and the land was spacious, quiet, and peaceful. ⁴¹They who have just been listed by name set out during the reign of Hezekiah, king of Judah, and attacked the tents of Ham (for Hamites dwelt there formerly) and also the Meunites who were there. They pronounced against them the ban that is still in force and dwelt in their place because they found pasture there for their flocks. ⁴²Five hundred of them (the Simeonites) went to Mount Seir under the leadership of Pelatiah, Neariah, Rephaiah, and Uzziel, sons of Ishi. ⁴³They attacked the surviving Amalekites who had escaped and have resided there to the present day.

1 Chronicles Chapter 5

¹ The sons of Reuben, the first-born of Israel. (He was indeed the first-born, but because he disgraced the couch of his father his birthright was given to the sons of Joseph, son of Israel, so that he is not listed in the family records according to birthright. ² Judah, in fact, became powerful among his brothers, so that the ruler came from him, though the birthright had been Joseph's.) ³ The sons of Reuben, the first-born of Israel, were Hanoch, Pallu, Hezron, and Carmi. ⁴ His son was Joel, whose son was Shemaiah, whose son was Gog, whose son was Shimei, ⁵ whose son was Micah, whose son was Reaiah, whose son was Baal, ⁶ whose son was Beerah, whom Tiglath-pileser, the king of Assyria, took into exile; he was a prince of the Reubenites. ⁷ His brothers who belonged to his clans, when they were listed in the family records according to their descendants, were: Jeiel, the chief, and Zechariah, ⁸ and Bela, son of Azaz, son of Shema, son of Joel. The Reubenites lived in Aroer and as far as Nebo and Baal-meon; ⁹ toward the east they dwelt as far as the desert which extends from the Euphrates River, for they had much livestock in the land of Gilead. ¹⁰ During the reign of Saul they waged war with the Hagrites, and when they had defeated them they occupied their tents throughout the region east of Gilead. ¹¹ The Gadites lived alongside them in the land of Bashan as far as Salecah. ¹² Joel was chief, Shapham was second in command, and Janai was judge in Bashan. ¹³ Their brothers, corresponding to their ancestral houses, were: Michael, Meshullam, Sheba, Jorai, Jacan, Zia, and Eber—seven.

14 These were the sons of Abihail, son of Huri, son of Jaroah, son of Gilead, son of Michael, son of Jeshishai, son of Jahdo, son of Buz. 15 Ahi, son of Abdiel, son of Guni, was the head of their ancestral houses. 16 They dwelt in Gilead, in Bashan and its towns, and in all the pasture lands of Sirion to the borders. 17 All were listed in the family records in the time of Jotham, king of Judah, and of Jeroboam, king of Israel. 18 The Reubenites, Gadites, and half-tribe of Manasseh were warriors, men who bore shield and sword and who drew the bow, trained in warfare—forty-four thousand seven hundred and sixty men fit for military service. 19 When they waged war against the Hagrites and against Jetur, Naphish, and Nodab, 20 they received help so that they mastered the Hagrites and all who were with them. For during the battle they called on God, and he heard them because they had put their trust in him. 21 Along with one hundred thousand men they also captured their livestock: fifty thousand camels, two hundred fifty thousand sheep, and two thousand asses. 22 Many had fallen in battle, for victory is from God; and they took over their dwelling place until the time of the exile. 23 The numerous members of the half-tribe of Manasseh lived in the land of Bashan as far as Baal-hermon, Senir, and Mount Hermon. 24 The following were the heads of their ancestral houses: Epher, Ishi, Eliel, Azriel, Jeremiah, Hodaviah, and Jahdiel— men who were warriors, famous men, and heads over their ancestral houses. 25 However, they offended the God of their fathers by lusting after the gods of the natives of the land, whom God had cleared out of their way. 26 Therefore the God of Israel incited against them the anger of Pul, king of Assyria, and of Tiglath-pileser, king of Assyria, who deported the Reubenites, the Gadites, and the half-tribe of Manasseh and brought them to Halah, Habor, and Hara, and to the river Gozan, where they have remained to this day. 27 The sons of Levi were Gershon, Kohath, and Merari. 28 The sons of Kohath were Amram, Izhar, Hebron, and Uzziel. 29 The children of Amram were Aaron, Moses, and Miriam. The sons of Aaron were Nadab, Abihu, Eleazar, and Ithamar. 30 Eleazar became the father of Phinehas. Phinehas became the father of Abishua. 31 Abishua became the father of Bukki. Bukki became the father of Uzzi. 32 Uzzi became the father of Zerahiah. Zerahiah became the father of Meraioth. 33 Meraioth became the father of Amariah. Amariah became the father of Ahitub. 34 Ahitub became the father of Zadok. Zadok became the father of Ahimaaz. 35 Ahimaaz became the father of Azariah. Azariah became the father of Johanan. 36 Johanan became the father of Azariah, who served as priest in the temple Solomon built in Jerusalem. 37 Azariah became the father of Amariah. Amariah became the father of Ahitub. 38 Ahitub became the father of Zadok. Zadok became the father of Shallum. 39 Shallum became the father of Hilkiah. Hilkiah became the father of Azariah. 40 Azariah became the father of Seraiah. Seraiah became the father of Jehozadak. 41 Jehozadak was one of those who went into the exile which the LORD inflicted on Judah and Jerusalem through Nebuchadnezzar.

1 Chronicles Chapter 6

1The sons of Levi were Gershon, Kohath, and Merari. 2The sons of Gershon were named Libni and Shimei. 3The sons of Kohath were Amram, Izhar, Hebron, and Uzziel. 4The sons of Merari were Mahli and Mushi.The following were the clans of Levi, distributed according to their ancestors: 5of Gershon: his son Libni, whose son was Jahath, whose son was Zimmah, 6whose son was Joah, whose son was Iddo, whose son was Zerah, whose son was Jetherai. 7The descendants of Kohath were: his son Amminadab, whose son was Korah, whose son was Assir, 8whose son was Elkanah, whose son was Ebiasaph, whose son was Assir, 9whose son was Tahath, whose son was Uriel, whose son was Uzziah, whose son was Shaul. 10The sons of Elkanah were Amasai and Ahimoth, 11whose son was Elkanah, whose son was Zophai, whose son was Nahath, 12whose son was Eliab, whose son was Jeroham, whose son was Elkanah, whose son was Samuel. 13The sons of Samuel were Joel, the first-born, and Abijah, the second. 14The descendants of Merari were Mahli, whose son was Libni, whose son was Shimei, whose son was Uzzah, 15whose son was Shimea, whose son was Haggiah, whose son was Asaiah. 16The following were entrusted by David with the choir services in the LORD'S house from the time when the ark had obtained a permanent resting place. 17They served as singers before the Dwelling of the meeting tent until Solomon built the temple of the LORD in Jerusalem, and they performed their services in an order prescribed for them. 18Those who so performed are the following, together with their descendants. Among the Kohathites: Heman, the chanter, son of Joel, son of Samuel, 19son of Elkanah, son of Jeroham, son of Eliel, son of Toah, 20son of Zuth, son of Elkanah, son of Mahath, son of Amasi, 21son of Elkanah, son of Joel, son of Azariah, son of Zaphaniah, 22son of Tahath, son of Assir, son of Ebiasaph, son of Korah, 23son of Izhar, son of Kohath, son of Levi, son of Israel. 24His

brother Asaph stood at his right hand. Asaph was the son of Berechiah, son of Shimea, 25son of Michael, son of Baaseiah, son of Malchijah, 26son of Ethni, son of Zerah, son of Adaiah, 27son of Ethan, son of Zimmah, son of Shimei, 28son of Jahath, son of Gershon, son of Levi. 29Their brothers, the Merarites, stood at the left: Ethan, son of Kishi, son of Abdi, son of Malluch, 30son of Hashabiah, son of Amaziah, son of Hilkiah, 31son of Amzi, son of Bani, son of Shemer, 32son of Mahli, son of Mushi, son of Merari, son of Levi. 33Their brother Levites were appointed to all the other services of the Dwelling of the house of God. 34However, it was Aaron and his descendants who burnt the offerings on the altar of holocausts and on the altar of incense; they alone had charge of the holy of holies and of making atonement for Israel, as Moses, the servant of God, had ordained. 35These were the descendants of Aaron: his son Eleazar, whose son was Phinehas, whose son was Abishua, 36whose son was Bukki, whose son was Uzzi, whose son was Zerahiah, 37whose son was Meraioth, whose son was Amariah, whose son was Ahitub, 38whose son was Zadok, whose son was Ahimaaz. 39The following were their dwelling places to which their encampment was limited. To the descendants of Aaron who belonged to clan of the Kohathites, since the first lot fell to them, 40was assigned Hebron with its adjacent pasture lands in the land of Judah, 41although the open country and the villages belonging to the city had been given to Caleb, the son of Jephunneh. 42There were assigned to the descendants of Aaron: Hebron a city of asylum, Libnah with its pasture lands, Jattir with its pasture lands, Eshtemoa with its pasture lands, 43Holon with its pasture lands, Debir with its pasture lands, 44Ashan with its pasture lands, Jetta with its pasture lands, and Beth-shemesh with its pasture lands. 45Also from the tribe of Benjamin: Gibeon with its pasture lands, Geba with its pasture lands, Almon with its pasture lands, Anathoth with its pasture lands. In all, they had thirteen cities with their pasture lands. 49The Israelites assigned these cities with their pasture lands to the Levites, 50designating them by name and assigning them by lot from the tribes of the Judahites, Simeonites, and Benjaminites. 46The other Kohathites obtained ten cities by lot for their clans from the tribe of Ephraim, from the tribe of Dan, and from the half-tribe of Manasseh. 47The clans of the Gershonites obtained thirteen cities from the tribes of Issachar, Asher, and Naphtali, and from the half-tribe of Manasseh in Bashan. 48The clans of the Merarites obtained twelve cities by lot from the tribes of Reuben, Gad, and Zebulun. 51The clans of the Kohathites obtained cities by lot from the tribe of Ephraim. 52They were assigned: Shechem in the mountain region of Ephraim, a city of asylum, with its pasture lands, Gezer with its pasture lands, 53Kibzaim with its pasture lands, and Beth-horon with its pasture lands. 54From the tribe of Dan: Elteke with its pasture lands, Gibbethon with its pasture lands, Aijalon with its pasture lands, and Gath-rimmon with its pasture lands. 55From the half-tribe of Manasseh: Taanach with its pasture lands and Ibleam with its pasture lands. These belonged to the rest of the Kohathite clan. 56The clans of the Gershonites received from the half-tribe of Manasseh: Golan in Bashan with its pasture lands and Ashtaroth with its pasture lands. 57From the tribe of Issachar: Kedesh with its pasture lands, Daberath with its pasture lands, 58Ramoth with its pasture lands, and Engannim with its pasture lands. 59From the tribe of Asher: Mashal with its pasture lands, Abdon with its pasture lands, 60Hilkath with its pasture lands, and Rehob with its pasture lands. 61From the tribe of Naphtali: Kedesh in Galilee with its pasture lands, Hammon with its pasture lands, and Kiriathaim with its pasture lands. 62The rest of the Merarites received from the tribe of Zebulun: Jokneam with its pasture lands, Kartah with its pasture lands, Rimmon with its pasture lands, and Tabor with its pasture lands. 63Across the Jordan at Jericho (that is, east of the Jordan) they received from the tribe of Reuben: Bezer in the desert with its pasture lands, Jahzah with its pasture lands, 64Kedemoth with its pasture lands, and Mephaath with its pasture lands. 65From the tribe of Gad: Ramoth in Gilead with its pasture lands, Mahanaim with its pasture lands, 66Heshbon with its pasture lands, and Jazer with its pasture lands.

1 Chronicles Chapter 7

1The sons of Issachar were Tola, Puah, Jashub, and Shimron: four. 2The sons of Tola were Uzzi, Rephaiah, Jeriel, Jahmai, Ibsam, and Shemuel, warrior heads of the ancestral houses of Tola. Their kindred numbered twenty-two thousand six hundred in the time of David. 3The sons of Uzzi: Izarahiah. The sons of Izarahiah were Michael, Obadiah, Joel, and Isshiah. All five of these were chiefs. 4Their kindred, by ancestral houses, numbered thirty-six thousand men in organized military troops, since they had more wives and sons 5than their fellow tribesmen. In all the clans of Issachar there was a total of eighty-seven thousand warriors in their family records. 6The sons of Benjamin were Bela, Becher, and Jediael - three. 7The sons of Bela were Ezbon, Uzzi, Uzziel, Jerimoth, and Iri - five. They were heads of their ancestral houses and warriors. Their family records listed twenty-two thousand and thirty-four. [8]The sons of Becher were Zemirah, Joash, Eliezer, Elioenai, Omri, Jeremoth, Abijah, Anathoth, and Alemeth - all these were sons of Becher. [9]Their family records listed twenty thousand two hundred of their kindred who were heads of their ancestral houses and warriors. [10]The sons of Jediael: Bilhan. The sons of Bilhan were Jeush, Benjamin, Ehud, Chenaanah, Zethan, Tarshish, and Ahishahar. [11]All these were descendants of Jediael, heads of ancestral houses and warriors. They numbered seventeen thousand two hundred men fit for military service... Shupham and Hupham. [12]The sons of Dan: Hushim. [13]The sons of Naphtali were Jahziel, Guni, Jezer, and Shallum. These were descendants of Bilhah. [14]The sons of Manasseh, whom his Aramean concubine bore: she bore Machir, the father of Gilead. [15]Machir took a wife whose name was Maacah; his sister's name was Molecheth. Manasseh's second son was named Zelophehad, but to Zelophehad only daughters were born. [16]Maacah, Machir's wife, bore a son whom she named Peresh. He had a brother named Sheresh, whose sons were Ulam and Rakem. [17]The sons of Ulam: Bedan. These were the descendants of Gilead, the son of Machir, the son of Manasseh. [18]His sister Molecheth bore Ishhod, Abiezer, and Mahlah. [19]The sons of Shemida were Ahian, Shechem, Likhi, and Aniam. [20]The sons of Ephraim: Shuthelah, whose son was Bered, whose son was Tahath, whose son was Eleadah, whose son was Tahath, [21]whose son was Zabad. Ephraim's son Shuthelah, and Ezer and Elead, who were born in the land, were slain by the inhabitants of Gath because they had gone down to take away their livestock. [22]Their father Ephraim mourned a long time, but after his kinsmen had come and comforted him, [23]he visited his wife, who conceived and bore a son whom he named Beriah, since evil had befallen his house. [24]He had a daughter, Sheerah, who built lower and upper Beth-horon and Uzzen-sheerah. [25]Zabad's son was Rephah, whose son was Resheph, whose son was Telah, whose son was Tahan, [26]whose son was Ladan, whose son was Ammihud, whose son was Elishama, [27]whose son was Nun, whose son was Joshua. [28]Their property and their dwellings were in Bethel and its towns, Naaran to the east, Gezer and its towns to the west, and also Shechem and its towns as far as Ayyah and its towns. [29]Manasseh, however, had possession of Beth-shean and its towns, Taanach and its towns, Megiddo and its towns, and Dor and its towns. In these dwelt the descendants of Joseph, the son of Israel. [30]The sons of Asher were Imnah, Iishvah, Ishvi, and Beriah; their sister was Serah. [31]Beriah's sons were Heber and Malchiel, who was the father of Birzaith. [32]Heber became the father of Japhlet, Shomer, Hotham, and their sister Shua. [33]The sons of Japhlet were Pasach, Bimhal, and Ashvath; these were the sons of Japhlet. [34]The sons of Shomer were Ahi, Rohgah, Jehubbah, and Aram. [35]The sons of his brother Hotham were Zophah, Imna, Shelesh, and Amal. [36]The sons of Zophah were Suah, Harnepher, Shual, Beri, Imrah, [37]Bezer, Hod, Shamma, Shilshah, Ithran, and Beera. [38]The sons of Jether were Jephunneh, Pispa, and Ara. [39]The sons of Ulla were Arah, Hanniel, and Rizia. [40]All these were descendants of Asher, heads of ancestral houses, distinguished men, warriors, and chiefs among the princes. Their family records numbered twenty-six thousand men fit for military service.

1 Chronicles Chapter 8

[1]Benjamin became the father of Bela, his first-born, Ashbel, the second son, Aharah, the third, [2]Nohah, the fourth, and Rapha, the fifth. [3]The sons of Bela were Addar and Gera, the father of Ehud. [4]The sons of Ehud were Abishua, Naaman, Ahoah, [5]Gera, Shephuphan, and Huram. [6]These were the sons of Ehud, family heads over those who dwelt in Geba and were deported to Manahath. [7]Also Naaman, Ahijah, and Gera. The last, who led them into exile, became the father of Uzza and Ahihud. [8]Shaharaim became a father on the Moabite plateau after he had put away his wives Hushim and Baara. [9]By his wife Hodesh he became the father of Jobab, Zibia, Mesha, Malcam, [10]Jeuz, Sachia, and Mirmah. These were his sons, family heads. [11]By Hushim he became the father of Abitub and Elpaal. [12]The sons of Elpaal were Eber, Misham, Shemed, who built Ono and Lod with its nearby towns, [13]Beriah and Shema. They were family heads of those who dwelt in Aijalon, and they put the inhabitants of Gath to flight. [14]Their brethren were Elpaal, Shashak, and Jeremoth. [15]Zebadiah, Arad, Eder, [16]Michael, Ishpah, and Joha were the sons of Beriah. [17]Zebadiah, Meshullam, Hizki, Heber, [18]Ishmerai, Izliah, and Jobab were the sons of Elpaal. [19]Jakim, Zichri, Zabdi, [20]Elienai, Zillethai, Eliel, [21]Adaiah, Beraiah, and Shimrath were the sons of Shimei. [22]Ishpan, Eber, Eliel, [23]Abdon, Zichri, Hanan, [24]Hananiah, Elam, Anthothijah, [25]Iphdeiah, and Penuel were the sons of Shashak. [26]Shamsherai, Shehariah, Athaliah, [27]Jaareshiah, Elijah, and Zichri were the sons of Jeroham. [28]These were family heads over their kindred, chiefs who dwelt in Jerusalem. [29]In Gibeon dwelt Jeiel, the founder of Gibeon, whose wife's

name was Maacah; [30]also his first-born son, Abdon, and Zur, Kish, Baal, Ner, Nadab, [31]Gedor, Ahio, Zecher, and Mikloth. [32]Mikloth became the father of Shimeah. These, too, dwelt with their relatives in Jerusalem, opposite their fellow tribesmen. [33]Ner became the father of Kish, and Kish became the father of Saul. Saul became the father of Jonathan, Malchishua, Abinadab, and Eshbaal. [34]The son of Jonathan was Meribbaal, and Meribbaal became the father of Micah. [35]The sons of Micah were Pithon, Melech, Tarea, and Ahaz. [36]Ahaz became the father of Jehoaddah, and Jehoaddah became the father of Alemeth, Azmaveth, and Zimri. Zimri became the father of Moza. [37]Moza became the father of Binea, whose son was Raphah, whose son was Eleasah, whose son was Azel. [38]Azel had six sons, whose names were Azrikam, his first-born, Ishmael, Sheariah, Azariah, Obadiah, and Hanan; all these were the sons of Azel. [39]The sons of Eshek, his brother, were Ulam, his first-born, Jeush, the second son, and Eliphelet, the third. [40]The sons of Ulam were combat archers, and many were their sons and grandsons: one hundred and fifty. All these were the descendants of Benjamin.

1 Chronicles Chapter 9

[1]Thus all Israel was inscribed in its family records which are recorded in the book of the kings of Israel. Now Judah had been carried in captivity to Babylon because of its rebellion. [2]The first to settle again in their cities and dwell there were certain lay Israelites, the priests, the Levites, and the temple slaves. [3]In Jerusalem lived Judahites and Benjaminites; also Ephraimites and Manassehites. [4]Among the Judahites was Uthai, son of Ammihud, son of Omri, son of Imri, son of Bani, one of the descendants of Perez, son of Judah. [5]Among the Shelanites were Asaiah, the first-born, and his sons. [6]Among the Zerahites were Jeuel and six hundred and ninety of their brethren. [7]Among the Benjaminites were Sallu, son of Meshullam, son of Hodaviah, son of Hassenuah; [8]Ibneiah, son of Jeroham; Elah, son of Uzzi, son of Michri; Meshullam, son of Shephatiah, son of Reuel, son of Ibnijah. [9]Their kindred of various families were nine hundred and fifty-six. All those named were heads of their ancestral houses. [10]Among the priests were Jedaiah; Jehoiarib; Jachin; [11]Azariah, son of Hilkiah, son of Meshullam, son of Zadok, son of Meraioth, son of Ahitub, the ruler of the house of God; [12]Adaiah, son of Jeroham, son of Pashhur, son of Malchijah; Maasai, son of Adiel, son of Jahzerah, son of Meshullam, son of Meshillemith, son of Immer. [13]Their brethren, heads of their ancestral houses, were one thousand seven hundred and sixty, valiant for the work of the service of the house of God. [14]Among the Levites were Shemaiah, son of Hasshub, son of Azrikam, son of Hashabiah, one of the descendants of Merari; [15]Bakbakkar; Heresh; Galal; Mattaniah, son of Mica, son of Zichri, a descendant of Asaph; [16]Obadiah, son of Shemaiah, son of Galal, a descendant of Jeduthun; and Berechiah, son of Asa, son of Elkanah, whose family lived in the villages of the Netophathites. [17]The gatekeepers were Shallum, Akkub, Talmon, Ahiman, and their brethren; Shallum was the chief. [18]Previously they had stood guard at the king's gate on the east side; now they became gatekeepers for the encampments of the Levites. [19]Shallum, son of Kore, son of Ebiasaph, a descendant of Korah, and his brethren of the same ancestral house of the Korahites had as their assigned task the guarding of the threshold of the tent, just as their fathers had guarded the entrance to the encampment of the LORD. [20]Phinehas, son of Eleazar, had been their chief in times past - the LORD be with him! [21]Zechariah, son of Meshelemiah, guarded the gate of the meeting tent. [22]In all, those who were chosen for gatekeepers at the threshold were two hundred and twelve. They were inscribed in the family records of their villages. David and Samuel the seer had established them in their position of trust. [23]Thus they and their sons kept guard over the gates of the house of the LORD, the house which was then a tent. [24]The gatekeepers were stationed at the four sides, to the east, the west, the north, and the south. [25]Their kinsmen who lived in their own villages took turns in assisting them for seven-day periods, [26]while the four chief gatekeepers were on constant duty. These were the Levites who also had charge of the chambers and treasures of the house of God. [27]At night they lodged about the house of God, for it was in their charge and they had the duty of opening it each morning. [28]Some of them had charge of the liturgical equipment, tallying it as it was brought in and taken out. [29]Others were appointed to take care of the utensils and all the sacred vessels, as well as the fine flour, the wine, the oil, the frankincense, and the spices. [30]It was the sons of priests, however, who mixed the spiced ointments. [31]Mattithiah, one of the Levites, the first-born of Shallum the Koreite, was entrusted with preparing the cakes. [32]Benaiah the Kohathite, one of their brethren, was in charge of setting out the showbread each sabbath. [33]These were the chanters and the gatekeepers, family heads over the Levites. They stayed in the chambers when free of duty, for day and night they had to be ready for service.

34These were the levitical family heads over their kindred, chiefs who dwelt in Jerusalem. 35In Gibeon dwelt Jeiel, the founder of Gibeon, whose wife's name was Maacah. 36His first-born son was Abdon; then came Zur, Kish, Baal, Ner, Nadab, 37Gedor, Ahio, Zechariah, and Mikloth. 38Mikloth became the father of Shimeam. These, too, with their brethren, dwelt opposite their brethren in Jerusalem. 39Ner became the father of Kish, and Kish became the father of Saul. Saul became the father of Jonathan, Malchishua, Abinadab, and Eshbaal. 40The son of Jonathan was Meribbaal, and Meribbaal became the father of Micah. 41The sons of Micah were Pithon, Melech, Tahrea, and Ahaz. 42Ahaz became the father of Jehoaddah, and Jehoaddah became the father of Alemeth, Azmaveth, and Zimri. Zimri became the father of Moza. 43Moza became the father of Binea, whose son was Rephaiah, whose son was Eleasah, whose son was Azel. 44Azel had six sons, whose names were Azrikam, his first-born, Ishmael, Sheariah, Azariah, Obadiah, and Hanan; these were the sons of Azel.

1 Chronicles Chapter 10

1Now the Philistines were at war with Israel; the Israelites fled before the Philistines, and a number of them fell, slain on Mount Gilboa. 2The Philistines pressed hard after Saul and his sons. When the Philistines had killed Jonathan, Abinadab, and Malchishua, sons of Saul, 3the whole fury of the battle descended upon Saul. Then the archers found him, and wounded him with their arrows. 4Saul said to his armor-bearer, "Draw your sword and thrust me through with it, that these uncircumcised may not come and maltreat me." But the armor-bearer, in great fear, refused. So Saul took his own sword and fell on it; 5and seeing him dead, the armor-bearer also fell on his sword and died. 6Thus, with Saul and his three sons, his whole house died at one time. 7When all the Israelites who were in the valley saw that Saul and his sons had died in the rout, they left their cities and fled; thereupon the Philistines came and occupied them. 8On the following day, when the Philistines came to strip the slain, they found Saul and his sons where they had fallen on Mount Gilboa. 9They stripped him, cut off his head, and took his armor; these they sent throughout the land of the Philistines to convey the good news to their idols and their people. 10His armor they put in the house of their gods, but his skull they impaled on the temple of Dagon. 11When all the inhabitants of Jabesh-gilead had heard what the Philistines had done to Saul, 12its warriors rose to a man, recovered the bodies of Saul and his sons, and brought them to Jabesh. They buried their bones under the oak of Jabesh, and fasted seven days. 13Thus Saul died because of his rebellion against the LORD in disobeying his command, and also because he had sought counsel of a necromancer, 14and had not rather inquired of the LORD. Therefore the LORD slew him, and transferred his kingdom to David, the son of Jesse.

1 Chronicles Chapter 11

1Then all Israel gathered about David in Hebron, and they said: "Surely, we are of the same bone and flesh as you. 2Even formerly, when Saul was still the king, it was you who led Israel in all its battles. And now the LORD, your God, has said to you, 'You shall shepherd my people Israel and be ruler over them.'" 3Then all the elders of Israel came to the king at Hebron, and there David made a covenant with them in the presence of the LORD; and they anointed him king over Israel, in accordance with the word of the LORD as revealed through Samuel. 4Then David and all Israel went to Jerusalem, that is, Jebus, where the natives of the land were called Jebusites. 5The inhabitants of Jebus said to David, "You shall not enter here." David nevertheless captured the fortress of Zion, which is the City of David. 6David said, "Whoever strikes the Jebusites first shall be made the chief commander." Joab, the son of Zeruiah, was the first to go up; and so he became chief. 7David took up his residence in the fortress, which thenceforth was called the City of David. 8He rebuilt the city on all sides, from the Millo all the way around, while Joab restored the rest of the city. 9David became more and more powerful, for the LORD of hosts was with him. 10These were David's chief warriors who, together with all Israel, supported him in his reign in order to make him true king, even as the LORD had commanded concerning Israel. 11Here is the list of David's warriors: Ishbaal, the son of Hachamoni, chief of the Three. He brandished his spear against three hundred, whom he slew in a single encounter. 12Next to him Eleazar, the son of Dodo the Ahohite, one of the Three warriors. 13He was with David at Pas-dammim, where the Philistines had massed for battle. The plow-land was fully planted with barley, but its defenders were retreating before the Philistines. 14He made a stand on the sown ground, kept it safe, and cut down the Philistines. Thus the LORD brought about a great victory. 15Three of the Thirty chiefs went down to the rock, to David, who was in the cave of Adullam while the Philistines were encamped in the valley of Rephaim. 16David was then in the stronghold, and a Philistine garrison was at Bethlehem. 17David expressed a desire: "Oh, that someone would give me a drink from the cistern that is by the gate at Bethlehem!" 18Thereupon the Three broke through the encampment of the Philistines, drew water from the cistern by the gate at Bethlehem, and carried it back to David. But David refused to drink it. Instead, he poured it out as a libation to the LORD, 19saying, "God forbid that I should do such a thing! Could I drink the blood of these men who risked their lives?" For at the risk of their lives they brought it; and so he refused to drink it. Such deeds as these the Three warriors performed. 20Abishai, the brother of Joab. He was the chief of the Thirty; he brandished his spear against three hundred, and slew them. Thus he had a reputation like that of the Three. 21He was twice as famous as any of the Thirty and became their commander, but he did not attain to the Three. 22Benaiah, son of Jehoiada, a valiant man of mighty deeds, from Kabzeel. He killed the two sons of Ariel of Moab, and also, on a snowy day, he went down and killed the lion in the cistern. 23He likewise slew the Egyptian, a huge man five cubits tall. The Egyptian carried a spear that was like a weaver's heddle-bar, but he came against him with a staff, wrested the spear from the Egyptian's hand, and killed him with his own spear. 24Such deeds as these of Benaiah, the son of Jehoiada, gave him a reputation like that of the Three. 25He was more famous than any of the Thirty, but he did not attain to the Three. David put him in charge of his bodyguard. 26Also these warriors: Asahel, the brother of Joab; Elhanan, son of Dodo, from Bethlehem; 27Shammoth, from En-harod; Helez, from Palti; 28Ira, son of Ikkesh, from Tekoa; Abiezer, from Anathoth; 29Sibbecai, from Husha; Ilai, from Ahoh; 30Maharai, from Netophah; Heled, son of Baanah, from Netophah; 31Ithai, son of Ribai, from Gibeah of Benjamin; Benaiah, from Pirathon; 32Hurai, from the valley of Gaash; Abiel, from Beth-arabah; 33Azmaveth, from Bahurim; Eliahba, from Shaalbon; 34Jashen the Gunite; Jonathan, son of Shagee, from En-harod; 35Ahiam, son of Sachar, from En-harod; Eliphelet, son of 36Ahasabi, from Beth-maacah; Ahijah, from Gilo; 37Hezro, from Carmel; Naarai, the son of Ezbai; 38Joel, brother of Nathan, from Rehob, the Gadite; 39Zelek the Ammonite; Naharai, from Beeroth, the armor-bearer of Joab, son of Zeruiah; 40Ira, from Jattir; Gareb, from Jattir; 41Uriah the Hittite; Zabad, son of Ahlai, 42and, in addition to the Thirty, Adina, son of Shiza, the Reubenite, chief of the tribe of Reuben; 43Hanan, from Beth-maacah; Joshaphat the Mithnite; 44Uzzia, from Ashterath; Shama and Jeiel, sons of Hotham, from Aroer; 45Jediael, son of Shimri, and Joha, his brother, the Tizite; 46Eliel the Mahavite; Jeribai and Joshaviah, sons of Elnaam; Ithmah, from Moab; 47Eliel, Obed, and Jaasiel the Mezobian.

1 Chronicles Chapter 12

1The following men came to David in Ziklag while he was still under banishment from Saul, son of Kish; they, too, were among the warriors who helped him in his battles. 2They were archers who could use either the right or the left hand, both in slinging stones and in shooting arrows with the bow. They were some of Saul's kinsmen, from Benjamin. 3Ahiezer was their chief, along with Joash, both sons of Shemaah of Gibeah; also Jeziel and Pelet, sons of Azmaveth; Beracah; Jehu, from Anathoth; 4Ishmaiah the Gibeonite, a warrior on the level of the Thirty, and in addition to their number; 5Jeremiah; Jahaziel; Johanan; Jozabad from Gederah; 6Eluzai; Jerimoth; Bealiah; Shemariah; Shephatiah the Haruphite; 7Elkanah, Isshiah, Azarel, Joezer, and Ishbaal, who were Korahites; 8Joelah, finally, and Zebadiah, sons of Jeroham, from Gedor. 9Some of the Gadites also went over to David when he was at the stronghold in the wilderness. They were valiant warriors, experienced soldiers equipped with shield and spear, who bore themselves like lions, and were as swift as the gazelles on the mountains. 10Ezer was their chief, Obadiah was second, Eliab third, 11Mishmannah fourth, Jeremiah fifth, 12Attai sixth, Eliel seventh, 13Johanan eighth, Elzabad ninth, 14Jeremiah tenth, and Machbannai eleventh. 15These Gadites were army commanders, the lesser placed over hundreds and the greater over thousands. 16It was they who crossed over the Jordan when it was overflowing both its banks in the first month, and dispersed all who were in the valleys to the east and to the west. 17Some Benjaminites and Judahites also came to David at the stronghold. 18David went out to meet them and addressed them in these words: "If you come peacefully, to help me, I am of a mind to have you join me. But if you have come to betray me to my enemies though my hands have done no wrong, may the God of our fathers see and punish you." 19Then spirit enveloped Amasai, the chief of the Thirty, who spoke: "We are yours, O David, we are with you, O son of Jesse. Peace, peace to you, and peace to him who helps you; your God it is who helps you." So David received them and placed them among the leaders of his troops. 20Men from Manasseh also deserted to David when he came with the Philistines to battle against Saul. However, he did not help the Philistines, for their lords took counsel and sent him home, saying, "At the cost of our heads he will desert to his master Saul." ²¹As he was returning to Ziklag, therefore, these deserted to him from Manasseh: Adnah, Jozabad, Jediael, Michael, Jozabad, Elihu, and Zillethai, chiefs of thousands of Manasseh. ²²They helped David by taking charge of his troops, for they were all warriors and became commanders of his army. ²³And from day to day men kept coming to David's help until there was a vast encampment, like an encampment of angels. ²⁴This is the muster of the detachments of armed troops that came to David at Hebron to transfer to him Saul's kingdom, as the LORD had ordained. ²⁵Judahites bearing shields and spears: six thousand eight hundred armed troops. ²⁶Of the Simeonites, warriors fit for battle: seven thousand one hundred. ²⁷Of the Levites: four thousand six hundred, ²⁸along with Jehoiada, leader of the line of Aaron, with another three thousand seven hundred, ²⁹and Zadok, a young warrior, with twenty-two princes of his father's house. ³⁰Of the Benjaminites, the brethren of Saul: three thousand—until this time, most of them had held their allegiance to the house of Saul. ³¹Of the Ephraimites: twenty thousand eight hundred warriors, men renowned in their ancestral houses. ³²Of the half-tribe of Manasseh: eighteen thousand, designated by name to come and make David king. ³³Of the Issacharites, their chiefs who were endowed with an understanding of the times and who knew what Israel had to do: two hundred chiefs, together with all their brethren under their command. ³⁴From Zebulun, men fit for military service, set in battle array with every kind of weapon for war: fifty thousand men rallying with a single purpose. ³⁵From Naphtali: one thousand captains, and with them, armed with shield and lance, thirty-seven thousand men. ³⁶Of the Danites, set in battle array: twenty-eight thousand six hundred. ³⁷From Asher, fit for military service and set in battle array: forty thousand. ³⁸From the other side of the Jordan, of the Reubenites, Gadites, and the half-tribe of Manasseh, men equipped with every kind of weapon of war: one hundred and twenty thousand. ³⁹All these soldiers, drawn up in battle order, came to Hebron with the resolute intention of making David king over all Israel. The rest of Israel was likewise of one mind to make David king. ⁴⁰They remained with David for three days, feasting and drinking, for their brethren had prepared for them. ⁴¹Moreover, their neighbors from as far as Issachar, Zebulun, and Naphtali came bringing food on asses, camels, mules, and oxen—provisions in great quantity of meal, pressed figs, raisins, wine, oil, oxen, and sheep. For there was rejoicing in Israel.

1 Chronicles Chapter 13

¹After David had taken counsel with his commanders of thousands and of hundreds, that is to say, with every one of his leaders, ²he said to the whole assembly of Israel: "If it seems good to you, and is so decreed by the LORD our God, let us summon the rest of our brethren from all the districts of Israel, and also the priests and the Levites from their cities with pasture lands, that they may join us; ³and let us bring the ark of our God here among us, for in the days of Saul we did not visit it." ⁴And the whole assembly agreed to do this, for the idea was pleasing to all the people. ⁵Then David assembled all Israel, from Shihor of Egypt to Labo of Hamath, to bring the ark of God from Kiriath-jearim. ⁶David and all Israel went up to Baalah, that is, to Kiriath-jearim, of Judah, to bring back the ark of God, which was known by the name "LORD enthroned upon the cherubim." ⁷They transported the ark of God on a new cart from the house of Abinadab; Uzzah and Ahio were guiding the cart, ⁸while David and all Israel danced before God with great enthusiasm, amid songs and music on lyres, harps, tambourines, cymbals, and trumpets. ⁹As they reached the threshing floor of Chidon, Uzzah stretched out his hand to steady the ark, for the oxen were upsetting it. ¹⁰Then the LORD became angry with Uzzah and struck him; he died there in God's presence, because he had laid his hand on the ark. ¹¹David was disturbed because the LORD'S anger had broken out against Uzzah. Therefore that place has been called Perez-uzza even to this day. ¹²David was now afraid of God, and he said, "How can I bring the ark of God with me?" ¹³Therefore he did not take the ark back with him to the City of David, but he took it instead to the house of Obed-edom the Gittite. ¹⁴The ark of God remained in the house of Obed-edom with his family for three months, and the LORD blessed Obed-edom's household and all that he possessed.

1 Chronicles Chapter 14

¹Hiram, king of Tyre, sent envoys to David along with masons and carpenters, and cedar wood to build him a house. ²David now understood that the LORD had truly confirmed him as king over Israel, for his kingdom was greatly exalted for the sake of his people Israel. ³David took other wives in Jerusalem and became the father of more

sons and daughters. ⁴These are the names of those who were born to him in Jerusalem: Shammua, Shobab, Nathan, Solomon, ⁵Ibhar, Elishua, Elpelet, ⁶Nogah, Nepheg, Japhia, ⁷Elishama, Beeliada, and Eliphelet. ⁸When the Philistines had heard that David was anointed king over all Israel, they went up in unison to seek him out. But when David heard of this, he marched out against them. ⁹Meanwhile the Philistines had come and raided the valley of Rephaim. ¹⁰David inquired of God, "Shall I advance against the Philistines, and will you deliver them into my power?" The LORD answered him, "Advance, for I will deliver them into your power." ¹¹They advanced, therefore, to Baal-perazim, and David defeated them there. Then David said, "God has used me to break through my enemies just as water breaks through a dam." Therefore that place was called Baal-perazim. ¹²The Philistines had left their gods there, and David ordered them to be burnt. ¹³Once again the Philistines raided the valley, ¹⁴and again David inquired of God. But God answered him: "Do not try to pursue them, but go around them and come upon them from the direction of the mastic trees. ¹⁵When you hear the sound of marching in the tops of the mastic trees, then go forth to battle, for God has already gone before you to strike the army of the Philistines." ¹⁶David did as God commanded him, and they routed the Philistine army from Gibeon to Gezer. ¹⁷Thus David's fame was spread abroad through every land, and the LORD made all the nations fear him.

1 Chronicles Chapter 15

¹David built houses for himself in the City of David and prepared a place for the ark of God, pitching a tent for it there. ²At that time he said, "No one may carry the ark of God except the Levites, for the LORD chose them to carry the ark of the LORD and to minister to him forever." ³Then David assembled all Israel in Jerusalem to bring the ark of the LORD to the place which he had prepared for it. ⁴David also called together the sons of Aaron and the Levites: ⁵of the sons of Kohath, Uriel, their chief, and one hundred and twenty of his brethren; ⁶of the sons of Merari, Asaiah, their chief, and two hundred and twenty of his brethren; ⁷of the sons of Gershon, Joel, their chief, and one hundred and thirty of his brethren; ⁸of the sons of Elizaphan, Shemaiah, their chief, and two hundred of his brethren; ⁹of the sons of Hebron, Eliel, their chief, and eighty of his brethren; ¹⁰of the sons of Uzziel, Amminadab, their chief, and one hundred and twelve of his brethren. ¹¹David summoned the priests Zadok and Abiathar, and the Levites Uriel, Asaiah, Joel, Shemaiah, Eliel, and Amminadab, ¹²and said to them: "You, the heads of the levitical families, must sanctify yourselves along with your brethren and bring the ark of the LORD, the God of Israel, to the place which I have prepared for it. ¹³Because you were not with us the first time, the wrath of the LORD our God burst upon us, for we did not seek him aright." ¹⁴Accordingly, the priests and the Levites sanctified themselves to bring up the ark of the LORD, the God of Israel. ¹⁵The Levites bore the ark of God on their shoulders with poles, as Moses had ordained according to the word of the LORD. ¹⁶David commanded the chiefs of the Levites to appoint their brethren as chanters, to play on musical instruments, harps, lyres, and cymbals, to make a loud sound of rejoicing. ¹⁷Therefore the Levites appointed Heman, son of Joel, and, among his brethren, Asaph, son of Berechiah; and among the sons of Merari, their brethren, Ethan, son of Kushaiah; ¹⁸and, together with these, their brethren of the second rank: the gatekeepers Zechariah, Uzziel, Shemiramoth, Jehiel, Unni, Eliab, Benaiah, Maaseiah, Mattithiah, Eliphelehu, Mikneiah, Obed-edom, and Jeiel. ¹⁹The chanters, Heman, Asaph, and Ethan, sounded brass cymbals. ²⁰Zechariah, Uzziel, Shemiramoth, Jehiel, Unni, Eliab, Maaseiah, and Benaiah played on harps set to "Alamoth." ²¹But Mattithiah, Eliphelehu, Mikneiah, Obed-edom, and Jeiel led the chant on lyres set to "the eighth." ²²Chenaniah was the chief of the Levites in the chanting; he directed the chanting, for he was skillful. ²³Berechiah and Elkanah were gatekeepers before the ark. ²⁴The priests, Shebaniah, Joshaphat, Nethanel, Amasai, Zechariah, Benaiah, and Eliezer, sounded the trumpets before the ark of God. Obed-edom and Jeiel were also gatekeepers before the ark. ²⁵Thus David, the elders of Israel, and the commanders of thousands went to bring up the ark of the covenant of the LORD with joy from the house of Obed-edom. ²⁶While the Levites, with God's help, were bearing the ark of the covenant of the LORD, seven bulls and seven rams were sacrificed. ²⁷David was clothed in a robe of fine linen, as were all the Levites who carried the ark, the singers, and Chenaniah, the leader of the chant; David was also wearing a linen ephod. ²⁸Thus all Israel brought back the ark of the covenant of the LORD with joyful shouting, to the sound of horns, trumpets, and cymbals, and the music of harps and lyres. ²⁹But as the ark of the covenant of the LORD was entering the City of David, Michal, daughter of Saul, looked down from her window, and when she saw King David leaping and dancing, she despised him in her heart.

1 Chronicles Chapter 16

¹They brought in the ark of God and set it within the tent which David had pitched for it. Then they offered up holocausts and peace offerings to God. ²When David had finished offering up the holocausts and peace offerings, he blessed the people in the name of the LORD, ³and distributed to every Israelite, to every man and every woman, a loaf of bread, a piece of meat, and a raisin cake. ⁴He now appointed certain Levites to minister before the ark of the LORD, to celebrate, thank, and praise the LORD, the God of Israel. ⁵Asaph was their chief, and second to him were Zechariah, Uzziel, Shemiramoth, Jehiel, Mattithiah, Eliab, Benaiah, Obed-edom, and Jeiel. These were to play on harps and lyres, while Asaph was to sound the cymbals, ⁶and the priests Benaiah and Jahaziel were to be the regular trumpeters before the ark of the covenant of God. ⁷Then, on that same day, David appointed Asaph and his brethren to sing for the first time these praises of the LORD: ⁸Give thanks to the LORD, invoke his name; make known among the nations his deeds. ⁹Sing to him, sing his praise, proclaim all his wondrous deeds. ¹⁰Glory in his holy name; rejoice, O hearts that seek the LORD! ¹¹Look to the LORD in his strength; seek to serve him constantly. ¹²Recall the wondrous deeds that he has wrought, his portents, and the judgments he has uttered, ¹³You descendants of Israel, his servants, sons of Jacob, his chosen ones! ¹⁴He, the LORD, is our God; throughout the earth his judgments prevail. ¹⁵He remembers forever his covenant which he made binding for a thousand generations - ¹⁶Which he entered into with Abraham and by his oath to Isaac; ¹⁷Which he established for Jacob by statute, for Israel as an everlasting covenant, ¹⁸Saying, "To you will I give the land of Canaan as your allotted inheritance." ¹⁹When they were few in number, a handful, and strangers there, ²⁰Wandering from nation to nation, from one kingdom to another people, ²¹He let no one oppress them, and for their sake he rebuked kings: ²²"Touch not my anointed, and to my prophets do no harm." ²³Sing to the LORD, all the earth, announce his salvation, day after day. ²⁴Tell his glory among the nations; among all peoples, his wondrous deeds. ²⁵For great is the LORD and highly to be praised; and awesome is he, beyond all gods. ²⁶For all the gods of the nations are things of nought, but the LORD made the heavens. ²⁷Splendor and majesty go before him; praise and joy are in his holy place. ²⁸Give to the LORD, you families of nations, give to the LORD glory and praise; ²⁹Give to the LORD the glory due his name! Bring gifts, and enter his presence; worship the LORD in holy attire. ³⁰Tremble before him, all the earth; he has made the world firm, not to be moved. ³¹Let the heavens be glad and the earth rejoice; let them say among the nations: The LORD is king. ³²Let the sea and what fills it resound; let the plains rejoice and all that is in them! ³³Then shall all the trees of the forest exult before the LORD, for he comes: he comes to rule the earth. ³⁴Give thanks to the LORD, for he is good, for his kindness endures forever; ³⁵And say, "Save us, O God, our savior, gather us and deliver us from the nations, That we may give thanks to your holy name and glory in praising you." ³⁶Blessed be the LORD, the God of Israel, through all eternity! Let all the people say, Amen! Alleluia. ³⁷Then David left Asaph and his brethren there before the ark of the covenant of the LORD to minister before the ark regularly according to the daily ritual; ³⁸he also left there Obed-edom and sixty-eight of his brethren, including Obed-edom, son of Jeduthun, and Hosah, to be gatekeepers. ³⁹But the priest Zadok and his priestly brethren he left before the Dwelling of the LORD on the high place at Gibeon, ⁴⁰to offer holocausts to the LORD on the altar of holocausts regularly, morning and evening, and to do all that is written in the law of the LORD which he has decreed for Israel. ⁴¹With them were Heman and Jeduthun and the others who were chosen and designated by name to give thanks to the LORD, "because his kindness endures forever," ⁴²with trumpets and cymbals for accompaniment, and instruments for the sacred chant. The sons of Jeduthun kept the gate. ⁴³Then all the people departed, each to his own home, and David returned to bless his household.

1 Chronicles Chapter 17

¹After David had taken up residence in his house, he said to Nathan the prophet, "See, I am living in a house of cedar, but the ark of the covenant of the LORD dwells under tentcloth." ²Nathan replied to David, "Do, therefore, whatever you desire, for God is with you." ³But that same night the word of God came to Nathan: ⁴"Go and tell my servant David, Thus says the LORD: It is not you who are to build a house for me to dwell in. ⁵For I have never dwelt in a house, from the time when I led Israel onward, even to this day, but I have been lodging in tent or pavilion ⁶as long as I have wandered about with all of Israel. Did I ever say a word to any of the judges of Israel whom I commanded to guide my people, such as, 'Why have you not built me a house of cedar?' ⁷Therefore, tell my servant David, Thus says the LORD of hosts: I took you from the pasture, from following the sheep, that you might become ruler over my people Israel. ⁸I was with you wherever you went, and I cut down all your enemies before you. I will make your name great like that of the greatest on the earth. ⁹I will assign a place for my people Israel and I will plant them in it to dwell there henceforth undisturbed; nor shall wicked men ever again oppress them, as they did at first, ¹⁰and during all that time when I appointed judges over my people Israel. And I will subdue all your enemies. Moreover, I declare to you that I, the LORD, will build you a house; ¹¹so that when your days have been completed and you must join your fathers, I will raise up your offspring after you who will be one of your own sons, and I will establish his kingdom. ¹²He it is who shall build me a house, and I will establish his throne forever. ¹³I will be a father to him, and he shall be a son to me, and I will not withdraw my favor from him as I withdrew it from him who preceded you; ¹⁴but I will maintain him in my house and in my kingdom forever, and his throne shall be firmly established forever." ¹⁵All these words and this whole vision Nathan related exactly to David. ¹⁶Then David came in and sat in the LORD'S presence, saying: "Who am I, O LORD God, and what is my family, that you should have brought me as far as I have come? ¹⁷And yet, even this you now consider too little, O God! For you have made a promise regarding your servant's family reaching into the distant future, and you have looked on me as henceforth the most notable of men, O LORD God. ¹⁸What more can David say to you? You know your servant. ¹⁹O LORD, for your servant's sake and in keeping with your purpose, you have done this great thing. ²⁰O LORD, there is no one like you and there is no God but you, just as we have always understood. ²¹Is there, like your people Israel, whom you redeemed from Egypt, another nation on earth whom a god went to redeem as his people? You won for yourself a name for great and awesome deeds by driving out the nations before your people. ²²You made your people Israel your own forever, and you, O LORD, became their God. ²³Therefore, O LORD, may the promise that you have uttered concerning your servant and his house remain firm forever. Bring about what you have promised, ²⁴that your renown as LORD of hosts, God of Israel, may be great and abide forever, while the house of David, your servant, is established in your presence. ²⁵Because you, O my God, have revealed to your servant that you will build him a house, your servant has made bold to pray before you. ²⁶Since you, O LORD, are truly God and have promised this good thing to your servant, ²⁷and since you have deigned to bless the house of your servant, so that it will remain forever - since it is you, O LORD, who blessed it, it is blessed forever."

1 Chronicles Chapter 18

¹After this, David defeated the Philistines and subdued them; and he took Gath and its towns away from the control of the Philistines. ²He also defeated Moab, and the Moabites became his subjects, paying tribute. ³David then defeated Hadadezer, king of Zobah toward Hamath, when the latter was on his way to set up his victory stele at the river Euphrates. ⁴David took from him twenty thousand foot soldiers, one thousand chariots, and seven thousand horsemen. Of the chariot horses, David hamstrung all but one hundred. ⁵The Arameans of Damascus came to the aid of Hadadezer, king of Zobah, but David also slew twenty-two thousand of their men. ⁶Then David set up garrisons in the Damascus region of Aram, and the Arameans became his subjects, paying tribute. Thus the LORD made David victorious in all his campaigns. ⁷David took the golden shields that were carried by Hadadezer's attendants and brought them to Jerusalem. ⁸He likewise took away from Tibhath and Cun, cities of Hadadezer, large quantities of bronze, which Solomon later used to make the bronze sea and the pillars and the vessels of bronze. ⁹When Tou, the king of Hamath, heard that David had defeated the entire army of Hadadezer, king of Zobah, ¹⁰he sent his son Hadoram to wish King David well and to congratulate him on having waged a victorious war against Hadadezer; for Hadadezer had been at war with Tou. He also sent David gold, silver, and bronze utensils of every sort. ¹¹These also King David consecrated to the LORD along with all the silver and gold that he had taken from the nations: from Edom, Moab, the Ammonites, the Philistines, and Amalek. ¹²Abishai, the son of Zeruiah, also slew eighteen thousand Edomites in the Valley of Salt. ¹³He set up garrisons in Edom, and all the Edomites became David's subjects. Thus the LORD made David victorious in all his campaigns. ¹⁴David reigned over all Israel and dispensed justice and right to all his people. ¹⁵Joab, son of Zeruiah, was in command of the army; Jehoshaphat, son of Ahilud, was herald; ¹⁶Zadok, son of Ahitub, and Ahimelech, son of Abiathar, were priests; Shavsha was scribe; ¹⁷Benaiah, son of Jehoiada, was in command of the Cherethites and the Pelethites; and David's sons were the chief assistants to the king.

1 Chronicles Chapter 19

[1]Afterward Nahash, king of the Ammonites, died and his son succeeded him as king. [2]David said, "I will show kindness to Hanun, the son of Nahash, for his father treated me with kindness." Therefore he sent envoys to him to comfort him over the death of his father. But when David's servants had entered the land of the Ammonites to comfort Hanun, [3]the Ammonite princes said to Hanun, "Do you think David is doing this—sending you these consolers—to honor your father? Have not his servants rather come to you to explore the land, spying it out for its overthrow?" [4]Thereupon Hanun seized David's servants and had them shaved and their garments cut off halfway at the hips. Then he sent them away. [5]When David was informed of what had happened to his men, he sent messengers to meet them, for the men had been greatly disgraced. "Remain at Jericho," the king told them, "until your beards have grown again; and then you may come back here." [6]When the Ammonites realized that they had put themselves in bad odor with David, Hanun and the Ammonites sent a thousand talents of silver to hire chariots and horsemen from Aram Naharaim, from Aram-maacah, and from Zobah. [7]They hired thirty-two thousand chariots along with the king of Maacah and his army, who came and encamped before Medeba. The Ammonites also assembled from their cities and came out for war. [8]When David heard of this, he sent Joab and his whole army of warriors against them. [9]The Ammonites marched out and lined up for a battle at the gate of the city, while the kings who had come to their help remained apart in the open field. [10]When Joab saw that there was a battle line both in front of and behind him, he chose some of the best fighters among the Israelites and set them in array against the Arameans; [11]the rest of the army, which he placed under the command of his brother Abishai, then lined up to oppose the Ammonites. [12]And he said: "If the Arameans prove too strong for me, you must come to my help; and if the Ammonites prove too strong for you, I will save you. [13]Hold steadfast and let us show ourselves courageous for the sake of our people and the cities of our God; then may the LORD do what seems best to him." [14]Joab therefore advanced with his men to engage the Arameans in battle; but they fled before him. [15]And when the Ammonites saw that the Arameans had fled, they also took to flight before his brother Abishai, and reentered the city. Joab then returned to Jerusalem. [16]Seeing themselves vanquished by Israel, the Arameans sent messengers to bring out the Arameans from the other side of the River, with Shophach, the general of Hadadezer's army, at their head. [17]When this was reported to David, he gathered all Israel together, crossed the Jordan, and met them. With the army of David drawn up to fight the Arameans, they gave battle. [18]But the Arameans fled before Israel, and David slew seven thousand of their chariot fighters and forty thousand of their foot soldiers; he also killed Shophach, the general of the army. [19]When the vassals of Hadadezer saw themselves vanquished by Israel, they made peace with David and became his subjects. After this, the Arameans refused to come to the aid of the Ammonites.

1 Chronicles Chapter 20

[1]At the beginning of the following year, the time when kings go to war, Joab led the army out in force, laid waste the land of the Ammonites, and went on to besiege Rabbah, while David himself remained in Jerusalem. When Joab had attacked Rabbah and destroyed it, [2]David took the crown of Milcom from the idol's head. It was found to weigh a talent of gold; and it contained precious stones, which David wore on his own head. He also brought out a great amount of booty from the city. [3]He deported the people of the city and set them to work with saws, iron picks, and axes. Thus David dealt with all the cities of the Ammonites. Then he and his whole army returned to Jerusalem. [4]Afterward there was another battle with the Philistines, at Gezer. At that time, Sibbecai the Hushathite slew Sippai, one of the descendants of the Raphaim, and the Philistines were subdued. [5]Once again there was war with the Philistines, and Elhanan, the son of Jair, slew Lahmi, the brother of Goliath of Gath, whose spear shaft was like a weaver's heddle-bar. [6]In still another battle, at Gath, they encountered a giant, also a descendant of the Raphaim, who had six fingers to each hand and six toes to each foot; twenty-four in all. [7]He defied Israel, and Jonathan, the son of Shimea, David's brother, slew him. [8]These were the descendants of the Raphaim of Gath who died at the hands of David and his servants.

1 Chronicles Chapter 21

[1]A satan rose up against Israel, and he enticed David into taking a census of Israel. [2]David therefore said to Joab and to the other generals of the army, "Go, find out the number of the Israelites from Beer-sheba to Dan, and report back to me that I may know their number." [3]But Joab replied: "May the LORD increase his people a hundredfold! My lord king, are not all of them my lord's subjects? Why does my lord seek to do this thing? Why will he bring guilt upon Israel?" [4]However, the king's command prevailed over Joab, who departed and traversed all of Israel, and then returned to Jerusalem. [5]Joab reported the result of the census to David: of men capable of wielding a sword, there were in all Israel one million one hundred thousand, and in Judah four hundred and seventy thousand. [6]Levi and Benjamin, however, he did not include in the census, for the king's command was repugnant to Joab. [7]This command displeased God, who began to punish Israel. [8]Then David said to God, "I have sinned greatly in doing this thing. Take away your servant's guilt, for I have acted very foolishly." [9]Then the LORD spoke to Gad, David's seer, in these words: [10]"Go, tell David: Thus says the LORD: I offer you three alternatives; choose one of them, and I will inflict it on you." [11]Accordingly, Gad went to David and said to him; "Thus says the LORD: Decide now— [12]will it be three years of famine; or three months of fleeing your enemies, with the sword of your foes ever at your back; or three days of the LORD's own sword, a pestilence in the land, with the LORD's destroying angel in every part of Israel? Therefore choose: What answer am I to give him who sent me?" [13]Then David said to Gad: "I am in dire straits. But I prefer to fall into the hand of the LORD, whose mercy is very great, than into the hands of men." [14]Therefore the LORD sent pestilence upon Israel, and seventy thousand men of Israel died. [15]God also sent an angel to destroy Jerusalem; but as he was on the point of destroying it, the LORD saw and decided against the calamity, and said to the destroying angel, "Enough now! Stay your hand!" The angel of the LORD was then standing by the threshing floor of Ornan the Jebusite. [16]When David raised his eyes, he saw the angel of the LORD standing between earth and heaven, with a naked sword in his hand stretched out against Jerusalem. David and the elders, clothed in sackcloth, prostrated themselves face to the ground, [17]and David prayed to God: "Was it not I who ordered the census of the people? I am the one who sinned, I did this wicked thing. But these sheep, what have they done? O LORD, my God, strike me and my father's family, but do not afflict your people with this plague!" [18]Then the angel of the LORD commanded Gad to tell David to go up and erect an altar to the LORD on the threshing floor of Ornan the Jebusite. [19]David went up at Gad's command, given in the name of the LORD. [20]While Ornan was threshing wheat, he turned around and saw the king, and his four sons who were with him, without recognizing them. [21]But as David came on toward him, he looked up and saw that it was David. Then he left the threshing floor and bowed down before David, his face to the ground. [22]David said to Ornan: "Sell me the ground of this threshing floor, that I may build on it an altar to the LORD. Sell it to me at its full price, that the plague may be stayed from the people." [23]But Ornan said to David: "Take it as your own, and let my lord the king do what seems best to him. See, I also give you the oxen for the holocausts, the threshing sledges for the wood, and the wheat for the cereal offering. I give it all to you." [24]But King David replied to Ornan: "No! I will buy it from you properly, at its full price. I will not take what is yours for the LORD, nor offer up holocausts that cost me nothing." [25]So David paid Ornan six hundred shekels of gold for the place. [26]David then built an altar there to the LORD, and offered up holocausts and peace offerings. When he called upon the LORD, he answered him by sending down fire from heaven upon the altar of holocausts. [27]Then the LORD gave orders to the angel to return his sword to its sheath. [28]Once David saw that the LORD had heard him on the threshing floor of Ornan the Jebusite, he continued to offer sacrifices there. [29]The Dwelling of the LORD, which Moses had built in the desert, and the altar of holocausts were at that time on the high place at Gibeon. [30]But David could not go there to worship God, for he was fearful of the sword of the angel of the LORD.

1 Chronicles Chapter 22

[1]"Therefore David said, 'This is the house of the LORD God, and this is the altar of holocausts for Israel.' [2]David then ordered that all the aliens who lived in the land of Israel be brought together, and he appointed them stonecutters to hew out stone blocks for building the house of God. [3]He also laid up large stores of iron to make nails for the doors of the gates, and clamps, together with so much bronze that it could not be weighed, [4]and cedar trees without number. The Sidonians and Tyrians brought great stores of cedar logs to David, [5]who said: 'My son Solomon is young and immature; but the house that is to be built for the LORD must be made so magnificent that it will be renowned and glorious in all countries. Therefore I will make preparations for it.' Thus before his death David laid up materials in abundance. [6]Then he called for his son Solomon and commanded him to build a house for the LORD, the God of Israel. [7]David said to Solomon: 'My son, it was my purpose to build a house myself for the honor of the LORD, my God. [8]But this word of the LORD came to me: "You have shed much blood, and you have waged great wars. You may not build a house in my honor,

because you have shed too much blood upon the earth in my sight. ⁹However, a son is to be born to you. He will be a peaceful man, and I will give him rest from all his enemies on every side. For Solomon shall be his name, and in his time I will bestow peace and tranquillity on Israel. ¹⁰It is he who shall build a house in my honor; he shall be a son to me, and I will be a father to him, and I will establish the throne of his kingship over Israel forever."' ¹¹Now, my son, the LORD be with you, and may you succeed in building the house of the LORD your God, as he has said you shall. ¹²May the LORD give you prudence and discernment when he brings you to rule over Israel, so that you keep the law of the LORD, your God. ¹³Only then shall you succeed, if you are careful to observe the precepts and decrees which the LORD gave Moses for Israel. Be brave and steadfast; do not fear or lose heart. ¹⁴See, with great effort I have laid up for the house of the LORD a hundred thousand talents of gold, a million talents of silver, and bronze and iron in such great quantities that they cannot be weighed. I have also stored up wood and stones, to which you must add. ¹⁵Moreover, you have available an unlimited supply of workmen, stonecutters, masons, carpenters, and every kind of craftsman skilled in gold, silver, bronze, and iron. Set to work, therefore, and the LORD be with you!' ¹⁷David also commanded all of Israel's leaders to help his son Solomon: ¹⁸'Is not the LORD your God with you? Has he not given you rest on every side? Indeed, he has delivered the occupants of the land into my power, and the land is subdued before the LORD and his people. ¹⁹Therefore, devote your hearts and souls to seeking the LORD your God. Proceed to build the sanctuary of the LORD God, that the ark of the covenant of the LORD and God's sacred vessels may be brought into the house built in honor of the LORD.'"

1 Chronicles Chapter 23

"¹When David had grown old and was near the end of his days, he made his son Solomon king over Israel. ²He then gathered together all the leaders of Israel, together with the priests and the Levites. ³The Levites thirty years old and above were counted, and their total number was found to be thirty-eight thousand men. ⁴Of these, twenty-four thousand were to direct the service of the house of the LORD, six thousand were to be officials and judges, ⁵four thousand were to be gatekeepers, and four thousand were to praise the LORD with the instruments which David had devised for praise. ⁶David divided them into classes according to the sons of Levi: Gershon, Kohath, and Merari. ⁷To the Gershonites belonged Ladan and Shimei. ⁸The sons of Ladan: Jehiel the chief, then Zetham and Joel; three in all. ⁹The sons of Shimei were Shelomoth, Haziel, and Haran; three. These were the heads of the families of Ladan. ¹⁰The sons of Shimei were Jahath, Zizah, Jeush, and Beriah; these were the sons of Shimei, four in all. ¹¹Jahath was the chief and Zizah was second to him; but Jeush and Beriah had not many sons, and therefore they were classed as a single family, fulfilling a single office. ¹²The sons of Kohath: Amram, Izhar, Hebron, and Uzziel; four in all. ¹³The sons of Amram were Aaron and Moses. Aaron was set apart to be consecrated as most holy, he and his sons forever, to offer sacrifice before the LORD, to minister to him, and to bless his name forever. ¹⁴As for Moses, however, the man of God, his sons were counted as part of the tribe of Levi. ¹⁵The sons of Moses were Gershom and Eliezer. ¹⁶The sons of Gershom: Shubael the chief. ¹⁷The sons of Eliezer were Rehabiah the chief - Eliezer had no other sons, but the sons of Rehabiah were very numerous. ¹⁸The sons of Izhar: Shelomith the chief. ¹⁹The sons of Hebron: Jeriah, the chief, Amariah, the second, Jahaziel, the third, and Jekameam, the fourth. ²⁰The sons of Uzziel: Micah, the chief, and Isshiah, the second. ²¹The sons of Merari: Mahli and Mushi. The sons of Mahli: Eleazar and Kish. ²²Eleazar died leaving no sons, only daughters; the sons of Kish, their kinsmen, married them. ²³The sons of Mushi: Mahli, Eder, and Jeremoth; three in all. ²⁴These were the sons of Levi according to their ancestral houses, the family heads as they were enrolled one by one according to their names. They performed the work of the service of the house of the LORD from twenty years of age upward, ²⁵David said: 'The LORD, the God of Israel, has given rest to his people, and has taken up his dwelling in Jerusalem. ²⁶Henceforth the Levites need not carry the Dwelling or any of its furnishings or equipment. ²⁷For David's final orders were to enlist the Levites from the time they were twenty years old. ²⁸Rather, their duty shall be to assist the sons of Aaron in the service of the house of the LORD, having charge of the courts, the chambers, and the preservation of everything holy: they shall take part in the service of the house of God. ²⁹They shall also have charge of the showbread, of the fine flour for the cereal offering, of the wafers of unleavened bread, and of the baking and mixing, and of all measures of quantity and size. ³⁰They must be present every morning to offer thanks and to praise the LORD, and likewise in the evening; ³¹and at every offering of holocausts to the LORD on sabbaths, new moons, and feast days, in such numbers as are

prescribed, they must always be present before the LORD. ³²They shall observe what is prescribed for them concerning the meeting tent, the sanctuary, and the sons of Aaron, their brethren, in the service of the house of the LORD.'"

1 Chronicles Chapter 24

"¹The descendants of Aaron also were divided into classes. The sons of Aaron were Nadab, Abihu, Eleazar, and Ithamar. ²Nadab and Abihu died before their father, leaving no sons; therefore only Eleazar and Ithamar served as priests. ³David, with Zadok, a descendant of Eleazar, and Ahimelech, a descendant of Ithamar, assigned the functions for the priestly service. ⁴But since the descendants of Eleazar were found to be more numerous than those of Ithamar, the former were divided into sixteen groups, and the latter into eight groups, each under its family head. ⁵Their functions were assigned impartially by lot, for there were officers of the holy place, and officers of the divine presence, descended both from Eleazar and from Ithamar. ⁶The scribe Shemaiah, son of Nethanel, a Levite, made a record of it in the presence of the king, and of the leaders, of Zadok the priest, and of Ahimelech, son of Abiathar, and of the heads of the ancestral houses of the priests and of the Levites, listing two successive family groups from Eleazar before each one from Ithamar. ⁷The first lot fell to Jehoiarib, the second to Jedaiah, ⁸the third to Harim, the fourth to Seorim, ⁹the fifth to Malchijah, the sixth to Mijamin, ¹⁰the seventh to Hakkoz, the eighth to Abijah, ¹¹the ninth to Jeshua, the tenth to Shecaniah, ¹²the eleventh to Eliashib, the twelfth to Jakim, ¹³the thirteenth to Huppah, the fourteenth to Ishbaal, ¹⁴the fifteenth to Bilgah, the sixteenth to Immer, ¹⁵the seventeenth to Hezir, the eighteenth to Happizzez, ¹⁶the nineteenth to Pethahiah, the twentieth to Jehezkel, ¹⁷the twenty-first to Jachin, the twenty-second to Gamul, ¹⁸the twenty-third to Delaiah, the twenty-fourth to Maaziah. ¹⁹This was the appointed order of their service when they functioned in the house of the LORD in keeping with the precepts given them by Aaron, their father, as the LORD, the God of Israel, had commanded him. ²⁰Of the remaining Levites, there were Shubael, of the descendants of Amram, and Jehdeiah, of the descendants of Shubael; ²¹Isshiah, the chief, of the descendants of Rehabiah; ²²Shelomith of the Izharites, and Jahath of the descendants of Shelomith. ²³The descendants of Hebron were Jeriah, the chief, Amariah, the second, Jahaziel, the third, Jekameam, the fourth. ²⁴The descendants of Uzziel were Micah; Shamir, of the descendants of Micah; ²⁵Isshiah, the brother of Micah; and Zechariah, a descendant of Isshiah. ²⁶The descendants of Merari were Mahli, Mushi, and the descendants of his son Uzziah. ²⁷The descendants of Merari through his son Uzziah: Shoham, Zaccur, and Ibri. ²⁸Descendants of Mahli were Eleazar, who had no sons, ²⁹and Jerahmeel, of the descendants of Kish. ³⁰The descendants of Mushi were Mahli, Eder, and Jerimoth. These were the descendants of the Levites according to their ancestral houses. ³¹They too, in the same manner as their relatives, the descendants of Aaron, cast lots in the presence of King David, Zadok, Ahimelech, and the heads of the priestly and levitical families; the more important family did so in the same way as the less important one."

1 Chronicles Chapter 25

¹David and the leaders of the liturgical cult set apart for service the descendants of Asaph, Heman, and Jeduthun, as singers of inspired songs to the accompaniment of lyres and harps and cymbals. This is the list of those who performed this service: ²Of the sons of Asaph: Zaccur, Joseph, Nethaniah, and Asharelah, sons of Asaph, under the direction of Asaph, who sang inspired songs under the guidance of the king. ³Of Jeduthun, these sons of Jeduthun: Gedaliah, Zeri, Jeshaiah, Shimei, Hashabiah, and Mattithiah; six, under the direction of their father Jeduthun, who sang inspired songs to the accompaniment of a lyre, to give thanks and praise to the LORD. ⁴Of Heman, these sons of Heman: Bukkiah, Mattaniah, Uzziel, Shubael, and Jerimoth; Hananiah, Hanani, Eliathah, Giddalti, Romamti-ezer, Joshbekashah, Mallothi, Hothir, and Mahazioth. ⁵All these were the sons of Heman, the king's seer in divine matters; to enhance his prestige, God gave Heman fourteen sons and three daughters. ⁶All these, whether of Asaph, Jeduthun, or Heman, were under their fathers' direction in the singing in the house of the LORD to the accompaniment of cymbals, harps, and lyres, serving in the house of God, under the guidance of the king. ⁷Their number, together with that of their brethren who were trained in singing to the LORD, all of them skilled men, was two hundred and eighty-eight. ⁸They cast lots for their functions equally, young and old, master and pupil alike. ⁹The first lot fell to Asaph, the family of Joseph; he and his sons and his brethren were twelve. Gedaliah was the second; he and his brethren and his sons were twelve. ¹⁰The third was Zaccur, his sons, and his brethren: twelve. ¹¹The fourth fell to Izri, his sons, and his brethren: twelve. ¹²The fifth was Nethaniah, his sons, and his brethren:

twelve. [13]The sixth was Bukkiah, his sons, and his brethren: twelve. [14]The seventh was Jesarelah, his sons, and his brethren: twelve. [15]The eighth was Jeshaiah, his sons, and his brethren: twelve. [16]The ninth was Mattaniah, his sons, and his brethren: twelve. [17]The tenth was Shimei, his sons, and his brethren: twelve. [18]The eleventh was Uzziel, his sons, and his brethren: twelve. [19]The twelfth fell to Hashabiah, his sons, and his brethren: twelve. [20]The thirteenth was Shubael, his sons, and his brethren: twelve. [21]The fourteenth was Mattithiah, his sons, and his brethren: twelve. [22]The fifteenth fell to Jeremoth, his sons, and his brethren: twelve. [23]The sixteenth fell to Hananiah, his sons, and his brethren: twelve. [24]The seventeenth fell to Joshbekashah, his sons, and his brethren: twelve. [25]The eighteenth fell to Hanani, his sons, and his brethren: twelve. [26]The nineteenth fell to Mallothi, his sons, and his brethren: twelve. [27]The twentieth fell to Eliathah, his sons, and his brethren: twelve. [28]The twenty-first fell to Hothir, his sons, and his brethren: twelve. [29]The twenty-second fell to Giddalti, his sons, and his brethren: twelve. [30]The twenty-third fell to Mahazioth, his sons, and his brethren: twelve. [31]The twenty-fourth fell to Romamti-ezer, his sons, and his brethren: twelve.

1 Chronicles Chapter 26

[1]As for the classes of gatekeepers. Of the Korahites was Meshelemiah, the son of Kore, one of the sons of Abiasaph. [2]Meshelemiah's sons: Zechariah, the first-born, Jediael, the second son, Zebadiah, the third, Jathniel, the fourth, [3]Elam, the fifth, Jehohanan, the sixth, Eliehoenai, the seventh. [4]Obed-edom's sons: Shemaiah, the first-born, Jehozabad, a second son, Joah, the third, Sachar, the fourth, Nethanel, the fifth, [5]Ammiel, the sixth, Issachar, the seventh, Peullethai, the eighth, for God blessed him. [6]To his son Shemaiah were born sons who ruled over their family, for they were warriors. [7]The sons of Shemaiah were Othni, Rephael, Obed, and Elzabad; also his brethren who were men of might, Elihu and Semachiah. [8]All these were the sons of Obed-edom, who, together with their sons and their brethren, were mighty men, fit for the service. Of Obed-edom, sixty-two. [9]Of Meshelemiah, eighteen sons and brethren, mighty men. [10]Hosah, a descendant of Merari, had these sons: Shimri, the chief (for though he was not the first-born, his father made him chief), [11]Hilkiah, the second son, Tebaliah, the third, Zechariah, the fourth. All the sons and brethren of Hosah were thirteen. [12]To these classes of gatekeepers, under their chief men, were assigned watches in the service of the house of the LORD, for each group in the same way. [13]They cast lots for each gate, the small and the large families alike. [14]When the lot was cast for the east side, it fell to Meshelemiah. Then they cast lots for his son Zechariah, a prudent counselor, and the north side fell to his lot. [15]To Obed-edom fell the south side, and to his sons the storehouse. [16]To Hosah fell the west side with the Shallecheth gate at the ascending highway. For each family, watches were established. [17]On the east, six watched each day, on the north, four each day, on the south, four each day, and at the storehouse they were two and two; [18]as for the large building on the west, there were four at the highway and two at the large building. [19]These were the classes of the gatekeepers, descendants of Kore and Merari. [20]Their brother Levites superintended the stores for the house of God and the stores of votive offerings. [21]Among the descendants of Ladan the Gershonite, the family heads were descendants of Jehiel: the descendants of Jehiel, [22]Zetham and his brother Joel, who superintended the treasures of the house of the LORD. [23]From the Amramites, Izharites, Hebronites, and Uzzielites, [24]Shubael, son of Gershon, son of Moses, was chief superintendent over the treasures. [25]His associate pertained to Eliezer, whose son was Rehabiah, whose son was Jeshaiah, whose son was Joram, whose son was Zichri, whose son was Shelomith. [26]This Shelomith and his brethren superintended all the stores of the votive offerings dedicated by King David, the heads of the families, the commanders of thousands and of hundreds, and the commanders of the army, [27]from the booty they had taken in the wars, for the enhancement of the house of the LORD. [28]Also, whatever Samuel the seer, Saul, son of Kish, Abner, son of Ner, Joab, son of Zeruiah, and all others had consecrated, was under the charge of Shelomith and his brethren. [29]Among the Izharites, Chenaniah and his sons were in charge of Israel's civil affairs as officials and judges. [30]Among the Hebronites, Hashabiah and his brethren, one thousand seven hundred police officers, had the administration of Israel on the western side of the Jordan in all the work of the LORD and in the service of the king. [31]Among the Hebronites, Jerijah was their chief according to their family records. In the fortieth year of David's reign, search was made, and there were found among them outstanding officers at Jazer of Gilead. [32]His brethren were also police officers, two thousand seven hundred heads of families. King David appointed them to the administration of the Reubenites, the Gadites, and the half-tribe of Manasseh in everything pertaining to God and to the king.

1 Chronicles Chapter 27

[1]This is the list of the Israelite family heads, commanders of thousands and of hundreds, and other officers who served the king in all that pertained to the divisions, of twenty-four thousand men each, that came and went month by month throughout the year. [2]Over the first division for the first month was Ishbaal, son of Zabdiel, and in his division were twenty-four thousand men; [3]a descendant of Perez, he was chief over all the commanders of the army for the first month. [4]Over the division of the second month was Eleazar, son of Dodo, from Ahoh, and in his division were twenty-four thousand men. [5]The third army commander, chief for the third month, was Benaiah, son of Jehoiada the priest, and in his division were twenty-four thousand men. [6]This Benaiah was a warrior among the Thirty and over the Thirty. His son Ammizabad was over his division. [7]Fourth, for the fourth month, was Asahel, brother of Joab, and after him his son Zebadiah, and in his division were twenty-four thousand men. [8]Fifth, for the fifth month, was the commander Shamhuth, a descendant of Zerah, and in his division were twenty-four thousand men. [9]Sixth, for the sixth month, was Ira, son of Ikkesh, from Tekoa, and in his division were twenty-four thousand men. [10]Seventh, for the seventh month, was Hellez, from Beth-phelet, of the sons of Ephraim, and in his division were twenty-four thousand men. [11]Eighth, for the eighth month, was Sibbecai the Hushathite, a descendant of Zerah, and in his division were twenty-four thousand men. [12]Ninth, for the ninth month, was Abiezer from Anathoth, of Benjamin, and in his division were twenty-four thousand men. [13]Tenth, for the tenth month, was Maharai from Netophah, a descendant of Zerah, and in his division were twenty-four thousand men. [14]Eleventh, for the eleventh month, was Benaiah the Pirathonite, of Ephraim, and in his division were twenty-four thousand men. [15]Twelfth, for the twelfth month, was Heldai the Netophathite, of the family of Othniel, and in his division were twenty-four thousand men. [16]Over the tribes of Israel, for the Reubenites the leader was Eliezer, son of Zichri; for the Simeonites, Shephatiah, son of Maacah; [17]for Levi, Hashabiah, son of Kemuel; for Aaron, Zadok; [18]for Judah, Eliab, one of David's brothers; for Issachar, Omri, son of Michael; [19]for Zebulun, Ishmaiah, son of Obadiah; for Naphtali, Jeremoth, son of Azriel; [20]for the sons of Ephraim, Hoshea, son of Azaziah; for the half-tribe of Manasseh, Joel, son of Pedaiah; [21]for the half-tribe of Manasseh in Gilead, Iddo, son of Zechariah; for Benjamin, Jaasiel, son of Abner; [22]for Dan, Azarel, son of Jeroham. These were the commanders of the tribes of Israel. [23]David did not count those who were twenty years of age or younger, for the LORD had promised to multiply Israel like the stars of the heavens. [24]Joab, son of Zeruiah, began to take the census, but he did not complete it, for because of it wrath fell upon Israel. Therefore the number did not enter into the book of chronicles of King David. [25]Over the treasures of the king was Azmaveth, the son of Adiel. Over the stores in the country, the cities, the villages, and the towers was Jonathan, son of Uzziah. [26]Over the farm workers who tilled the soil was Ezri, son of Chelub. [27]Over the vineyards was Shimei from Ramah, and over their produce for the wine cellars was Zabdi the Shiphmite. [28]Over the olive trees and sycamores of the foothills was Baalhanan the Gederite, and over the stores of oil was Joash. [29]Over the cattle that grazed in Sharon was Shitrai the Sharonite, and over the cattle in the valleys was Shaphat, son of Adlai; [30]over the camels was Obil the Ishmaelite; over the she-asses was Jehdeiah the Meronothite; [31]and over the flocks was Jaziz the Hagrite. All these were the overseers of King David's possessions. [32]Jonathan, David's uncle and a man of intelligence, was counselor and scribe; he and Jehiel, the son of Hachmoni, were tutors of the king's sons. [33]Ahithophel was also the king's counselor, and Hushai the Archite was the king's confidant. [34]After Ahithophel came Jehoiada, the son of Benaiah, and Abiathar. The commander of the king's army was Joab.

1 Chronicles Chapter 28

[1]David assembled at Jerusalem all the leaders of Israel, the heads of the tribes, the commanders of the divisions who were in the service of the king, the commanders of thousands and of hundreds, the overseers of all the king's estates and possessions, and his sons, together with the courtiers, the warriors, and every important man. [2]King David rose to his feet and said: "Hear me, my brethren and my people. It was my purpose to build a house of repose myself for the ark of the covenant of the LORD, the footstool for the feet of our God; and I was preparing to build it. [3]But God said to me, 'You may not build a house in my honor, for you are a man who fought wars and shed blood.' [4]However, the LORD, the God of Israel, chose me from all my father's family to be king over Israel forever. For he chose Judah as leader, then one family of Judah, that of my father; and finally, among all the sons of my father, it pleased him to make me king over all Israel. [5]And of all my sons - for the LORD has given me many sons - he has chosen my son Solomon to

sit on the LORD'S royal throne over Israel. 6For he said to me: 'It is your son Solomon who shall build my house and my courts, for I have chosen him for my son, and I will be a father to him. 7I will establish his kingdom forever, if he perseveres in keeping my commandments and decrees as he keeps them now.' 8Therefore, in the presence of all Israel, the assembly of the LORD, and in the hearing of our God, I exhort you to keep and to carry out all the commandments of the LORD, your God, that you may continue to possess this good land and afterward leave it as an inheritance to your children forever. 9"As for you, Solomon, my son, know the God of your father and serve him with a perfect heart and a willing soul, for the LORD searches all hearts and understands all the mind's thoughts. If you seek him, he will let himself be found by you; but if you abandon him, he will cast you off forever. 10See, then! The LORD has chosen you to build a house as his sanctuary. Take courage and set to work." 11Then David gave to his son Solomon the pattern of the portico and of the building itself, with its storerooms, its upper rooms and inner chambers, and the room with the propitiatory. 12He provided also the pattern for all else that he had in mind by way of courts for the house of the LORD, with the surrounding compartments for the stores for the house of God and the stores of the votive offerings, 13as well as for the divisions of the priests and Levites, for all the work of the service of the house of the LORD, and for all the liturgical vessels of the house of the LORD. 14He specified the weight of gold to be used in the golden vessels for the various services and the weight of silver to be used in the silver vessels for the various services; 15likewise for the golden lampstands and their lamps he specified the weight of gold for each lampstand and its lamps, and for the silver lampstands he specified the weight of silver for each lampstand and its lamps, depending on the use to which each lampstand was to be put. 16He specified the weight of gold for each table to hold the showbread, and the silver for the silver tables; 17the pure gold to be used for the forks and pitchers; the amount of gold for each golden bowl and the silver for each silver bowl; 18the refined gold, and its weight, to be used for the altar of incense; and, finally, gold for what would suggest a chariot throne: the cherubim that spread their wings and covered the ark of the covenant of the LORD. 19He had successfully committed to writing the exact specifications of the pattern, because the hand of the LORD was upon him. 20Then David said to his son Solomon: "Be firm and steadfast; go to work without fear or discouragement, for the LORD God, my God, is with you. He will not fail you or abandon you before you have completed all the work for the service of the house of the LORD. 21The classes of the priests and Levites are ready for all the service of the house of God; they will help you in all your work with all those who are eager to show their skill in every kind of craftsmanship. Also the leaders and all the people will do everything that you command."

1 Chronicles Chapter 29

1King David then said to the whole assembly: "My son Solomon, whom alone God has chosen, is still young and immature; the work, however, is great, for this castle is not intended for man, but for the LORD God. 2For this reason I have stored up for the house of my God, as far as I was able, gold for what will be made of gold, silver for what will be made of silver, bronze for what will be made of bronze, iron for what will be made of iron, wood for what will be made of wood, onyx stones and settings for them, carnelian and mosaic stones, every other kind of precious stone, and great quantities of marble. 3But now, because of the delight I take in the house of my God, in addition to all that I stored up for the holy house, I give to the house of my God my personal fortune in gold and silver: 4three thousand talents of Ophir gold, and seven thousand talents of refined silver, for overlaying the walls of the rooms, 5for the various utensils to be made of gold and silver, and for every work that is to be done by artisans. Now, who else is willing to contribute generously this day to the LORD?" 6Then the heads of the families, the leaders of the tribes of Israel, the commanders of thousands and of hundreds, and the overseers of the king's affairs came forward willingly 7and contributed for the service of the house of God five thousand talents and ten thousand darics of gold, ten thousand talents of silver, eighteen thousand talents of bronze, and one hundred thousand talents of iron. 8Those who had precious stones gave them into the keeping of Jehiel the Gershonite for the treasury of the house of the LORD. 9The people rejoiced over these free-will offerings, which had been contributed to the LORD wholeheartedly. King David also rejoiced greatly. 10Then David blessed the LORD in the presence of the whole assembly, praying in these words: "Blessed may you be, O LORD, God of Israel our father, from eternity to eternity. 11Yours, O LORD, are grandeur and power, majesty, splendor, and glory. For all in heaven and on earth is yours; yours, O LORD, is the sovereignty; you are exalted as head over all. 12Riches and honor are from you, and you have

dominion over all. In your hand are power and might; it is yours to give grandeur and strength to all. 13Therefore, our God, we give you thanks and we praise the majesty of your name." 14"But who am I, and who are my people, that we should have the means to contribute so freely? For everything is from you, and we only give you what we have received from you. 15For we stand before you as aliens: we are only your guests, like all our fathers. Our life on earth is like a shadow that does not abide. 16O LORD our God, all this wealth that we have brought together to build you a house in honor of your holy name comes from you and is entirely yours. 17I know, O my God, that you put hearts to the test and that you take pleasure in uprightness. With a sincere heart I have willingly given all these things, and now with joy I have seen your people here present also giving to you generously. 18O LORD, God of our fathers Abraham, Isaac, and Israel, keep such thoughts in the hearts and minds of your people forever, and direct their hearts toward you. 19Give to my son Solomon a wholehearted desire to keep your commandments, precepts, and statutes, that he may carry out all these plans and build the castle for which I have made preparation." 20Then David besought the whole assembly, "Now bless the LORD your God!" And the whole assembly blessed the LORD, the God of their fathers, bowing down and prostrating themselves before the LORD and before the king. 21On the following day they offered sacrifices and holocausts to the LORD, a thousand bulls, a thousand rams, and a thousand lambs, together with their libations and many other sacrifices for all Israel; 22and on that day they ate and drank in the LORD'S presence with great rejoicing. Then for a second time they proclaimed David's son Solomon king, and they anointed him as the LORD'S prince, and Zadok as priest. 23Thereafter Solomon sat on the throne of the LORD as king in place of his father David; he prospered, and all Israel obeyed him. 24All the leaders and warriors, and also all the other sons of King David, swore allegiance to King Solomon. 25And the LORD exalted Solomon greatly in the eyes of all Israel, giving him a glorious reign such as had not been enjoyed by any king over Israel before him. 26Thus David, the son of Jesse, had reigned over all Israel. 27The time that he reigned over Israel was forty years: in Hebron he reigned seven years, and in Jerusalem thirty-three. 28He died at a ripe old age, rich in years and wealth and glory, and his son Solomon succeeded him as king. 29Now the deeds of King David, first and last, can be found written in the history of Samuel the seer, the history of Nathan the prophet, and the history of Gad the seer, 30together with the particulars of his reign and valor, and of the events that affected him and all Israel and all the kingdoms of the surrounding lands.

II Chronicles

2 Chronicles Chapter 1

1Solomon, son of David, strengthened his hold on the kingdom, for the LORD, his God, was with him, constantly making him more renowned. 2He sent a summons to all Israel, to the commanders of thousands and of hundreds, the judges, the princes of all Israel, and the family heads; 3and, accompanied by the whole assembly, he went to the high place at Gibeon, because the meeting tent of God, made in the desert by Moses, the LORD'S servant, was there. 4(The ark of God, however, David had brought up from Kiriath-jearim to Jerusalem, where he had provided a place and pitched a tent for it.) 5The bronze altar made by Bezalel, son of Uri, son of Hur, he put in front of the LORD'S Dwelling1 on the high place. There Solomon and the assembly consulted the LORD, 6and Solomon offered sacrifice in the LORD'S presence on the bronze altar at the meeting tent; he offered a thousand holocausts upon it. 7That night God appeared to Solomon and said to him, "Make a request of me, and I will grant it to you." 8Solomon answered God: "You have shown great favor to my father David, and you have allowed me to succeed him as king. 9Now, LORD God, may your promise to my father David be fulfilled, for you have made me king over a people as numerous as the dust of the earth. 10Give me, therefore, wisdom and knowledge to lead this people, for otherwise who could rule this great people of yours?" 11God then replied to Solomon: "Since this has been your wish and you have not asked for riches, treasures and glory, nor for the life of those who hate you, nor even for a long life for yourself, but have asked for wisdom and knowledge in order to rule my people over whom I have made you king, 12wisdom and knowledge are given you; but I will also give you riches, treasures and glory, such as kings before you never had, nor will those have them who come after you." 13Solomon returned to Jerusalem from the high place at Gibeon, from the meeting tent, and became king over Israel. 14He gathered together chariots and drivers, so that he had one thousand four hundred chariots and twelve thousand drivers he could station in the chariot cities and with the king in Jerusalem. 15The king made silver and gold as common in Jerusalem as stones, while cedars became as numerous as the sycamores of the foothills. [16]Solomon also imported horses from Egypt and Cilicia. The king's agents would acquire them by purchase from Cilicia, [17]and would then bring up chariots from Egypt and export them at six hundred silver shekels, with the horses going for a hundred and fifty shekels. At these rates they served as middlemen for all the Hittite and Aramean kings. [18]Solomon gave orders for the building of a house to honor the LORD and also of a house for his own royal estate.

2 Chronicles Chapter 2

[1]He conscripted seventy thousand men to carry stone and eighty thousand to cut the stone in the mountains, and over these he placed three thousand six hundred overseers. [2]Moreover, Solomon sent this message to Huram, king of Tyre: "As you dealt with my father David, sending him cedars to build a house for his dwelling, so deal with me. [3]I intend to build a house for the honor of the LORD, my God, and to consecrate it to him, for the burning of fragrant incense in his presence, for the perpetual display of the showbread, for holocausts morning and evening, and for the sabbaths, new moons, and festivals of the LORD, our God: such is Israel's perpetual obligation. [4]And the house I intend to build must be large, for our God is greater than all other gods. [5]Yet who is really able to build him a house, since the heavens and even the highest heavens cannot contain him? And who am I that I should build him a house, unless it be to offer incense in his presence? [6]Now, send me men skilled at work in gold, silver, bronze and iron, in purple, crimson, and violet fabrics, and who know how to do engraved work, to join the craftsmen who are with me in Judah and Jerusalem, whom my father David appointed. [7]Also send me boards of cedar, cypress and cabinet wood from Lebanon, for I realize that your servants know how to cut the wood of the Lebanon. My servants will labor with yours [8]in order to prepare for me a great quantity of wood, since the house I intend to build must be lofty and wonderful. [9]I will furnish as food for your servants, the hewers who cut the wood, twenty thousand kors of wheat, twenty thousand kors of barley, twenty thousand measures of wine, and twenty thousand measures of oil." [10]Huram, king of Tyre, wrote an answer which he sent to Solomon: "Because the LORD loves his people, he has placed you over them as king." [11]He added: "Blessed be the LORD, the God of Israel, who made heaven and earth, for having given King David a wise son of intelligence and understanding, who will build a house for the LORD and also a house for his royal estate. [12]I am now sending you a craftsman of great skill, Huram-abi, [13]son of a Danite woman and of a father from Tyre; he knows how to work with gold, silver, bronze and iron, with stone and wood, with purple, violet, fine linen and crimson, and also how to do all kinds of engraved work and to devise every type of artistic work that may be given him and your craftsmen and the craftsmen of my lord David your father. [14]And now, let my lord send to his servants the wheat, barley, oil and wine which he has promised. [15]For our part, we will cut trees on Lebanon, as many as you need, and float them down to you at the port of Joppa, whence you may take them up to Jerusalem." [16]Thereupon Solomon took a census of all the alien men who were in the land of Israel (following the census David his father had taken of them), who were found to number one hundred fifty-three thousand six hundred. [17]Of these he made seventy thousand carriers and eighty thousand cutters in the mountains, and three thousand six hundred overseers to keep the people working.

2 Chronicles Chapter 3

[1]Then Solomon began to build the house of the LORD in Jerusalem on Mount Moriah, which had been pointed out to his father David, on the spot which David had selected, the threshing floor of Ornan the Jebusite. [2]He began to build in the second month of the fourth year of his reign. [3]These were the specifications laid down by Solomon for building the house of God: the length was sixty cubits according to the old measure, and the width was twenty cubits; [4]the porch which lay before the nave along the width of the house was also twenty cubits, and it was twenty cubits high. He overlaid its interior with pure gold. [5]The nave he overlaid with cypress wood which he covered with fine gold, embossing on it palms and chains. [6]He also decorated the building with precious stones. [7]The house, its beams and thresholds, as well as its walls and its doors, he overlaid with gold, and he engraved cherubim upon the walls. (The gold was from Parvaim.) [8]He also made the room of the holy of holies. Its length corresponded to the width of the house, twenty cubits, and its width was also twenty cubits. He overlaid it with fine gold to the amount of six hundred talents. [9]The weight of the nails was fifty gold shekels. The upper chambers he likewise covered with gold. [10]For the room of the holy of holies he made two cherubim of carved workmanship, which were then overlaid with gold. [11]The wings of the cherubim spanned twenty cubits: [12]one wing of each cherub, five cubits in length, extended to a wall of the building, while the other wing,

also five cubits in length, touched the corresponding wing of the second cherub. [13]The combined wingspread of the two cherubim was thus twenty cubits. They stood upon their own feet, facing toward the nave. [14]He made the veil of violet, purple, crimson and fine linen, and had cherubim embroidered upon it. [15]In front of the building he set two columns thirty-five cubits high; the capital topping each was of five cubits. [16]He worked out chains in the form of a collar with which he encircled the capitals of the columns, and he made a hundred pomegranates which he set on the chains. [17]He set up the columns to correspond with the nave, one for the right side and the other for the left, and he called the one to the right Jachin and the one to the left Boaz.

2 Chronicles Chapter 4

[1]Then he made a bronze altar twenty cubits long, twenty cubits wide and ten cubits high. [2]He also made the molten sea. It was perfectly round, ten cubits in diameter, five in depth, and thirty in circumference; [3]below the rim a ring of figures of oxen encircled the sea, ten to the cubit, all the way around; there were two rows of these cast in the same mold with the sea. [4]It rested on twelve oxen, three facing north, three west, three south, and three east, with their haunches all toward the center; the sea rested on their backs. [5]It was a handbreadth thick, and its brim was made like that of a cup, being lily-shaped. It had a capacity of three thousand measures. [6]Then he made ten basins for washing, placing five of them to the right and five to the left. Here were cleansed the victims for the holocausts; but the sea was for the priests to wash in. [7]He made the lampstands of gold, ten of them as was prescribed, and placed them in the nave, five to the right and five to the left. [8]He made ten tables and had them set in the nave, five to the right and five to the left; and he made a hundred golden bowls. [9]He made the court of the priests and the great courtyard and the gates of the courtyard; the gates he overlaid with bronze. [10]The sea was placed off to the southeast from the right side of the temple. [11]Huram also made the pots, the shovels and the bowls. Huram thus completed the work he had to do for King Solomon in the house of God: [12]two columns, two nodes for the capitals topping these two columns, and two networks covering the nodes of the capitals topping the columns; [13]also four hundred pomegranates for the two networks, with two rows of pomegranates to each network, to cover the two nodes of the capitals topping the columns. [14]He made the stands, and the basins on the stands; [15]one sea, and the twelve oxen under it; [16]likewise the pots, the shovels and the forks. Huram-abi made all these articles for King Solomon from polished bronze for the house of the LORD. [17]The king had them cast in the Jordan region, in the clayey ground between Succoth and Zeredah. [18]Solomon made all these vessels, so many in number that the weight of the bronze was not ascertained. [19]Solomon had all these articles made for the house of God: the golden altar, the tables on which the showbread lay, [20]the lampstands and their lamps of pure gold which were to burn according to prescription before the sanctuary, [21]flowers, lamps and gold tongs (this was the purest gold), [22]snuffers, bowls, cups and firepans of pure gold. As for the entry to the house, its inner doors to the holy of holies, as well as the doors to the nave, were of gold.

2 Chronicles Chapter 5

[1] When all the work undertaken by Solomon for the temple of the LORD had been completed, he brought in the dedicated offerings of his father David, putting the silver, the gold and all the other articles in the treasuries of the house of God. [2] At Solomon's order the elders of Israel and all the leaders of the tribes, the princes of the Israelite ancestral houses, came to Jerusalem to bring up the ark of the LORD'S covenant from the City of David (which is Zion). [3] All the men of Israel assembled before the king during the festival of the seventh month. [4] When all the elders of Israel had arrived, the Levites took up the ark, [5] and they carried the ark and the meeting tent with all the sacred vessels that were in the tent; it was the levitical priests who carried them. [6] King Solomon and the entire community of Israel gathered about him before the ark were sacrificing sheep and oxen so numerous that they could not be counted or numbered. [7] The priests brought the ark of the covenant of the LORD to its place beneath the wings of the cherubim in the sanctuary, the holy of holies of the temple. [8] The cherubim had their wings spread out over the place of the ark, sheltering the ark and its poles from above. [9] The poles were long enough so that their ends could be seen from that part of the holy place nearest the sanctuary; however, they could not be seen beyond. The ark has remained there to this day. [10] There was nothing in it but the two tablets which Moses put there on Horeb, the tablets of the covenant which the LORD made with the Israelites at their departure from Egypt. [11] When the priests came out of the holy place (all the priests who were present had purified themselves without reference to the rotation of their various classes),

12 the Levites who were singers, all who belonged to Asaph, Heman, Jeduthun, and their sons and brothers, clothed in fine linen, with cymbals, harps and lyres, stood east of the altar, and with them a hundred and twenty priests blowing trumpets. 13 When the trumpeters and singers were heard as a single voice praising and giving thanks to the LORD, and when they raised the sound of the trumpets, cymbals and other musical instruments to "give thanks to the LORD, for he is good, for his mercy endures forever," the building of the LORD'S temple was filled with a cloud. 14 The priests could not continue to minister because of the cloud, since the LORD'S glory filled the house of God.

2 Chronicles Chapter 6

1 Then Solomon said: "The LORD intends to dwell in the dark cloud. 2 I have truly built you a princely house and dwelling, where you may abide forever." 3 Turning about, the king greeted the whole community of Israel as they stood. 4 He said: "Blessed be the LORD, the God of Israel, who with his own mouth made a promise to my father David and by his own hands brought it to fulfillment. He said: 5 'Since the day I brought my people out of the land of Egypt, I have not chosen any city from among all the tribes of Israel for the building of a temple to my honor, nor have I chosen any man to be commander of my people Israel; 6 but now I choose Jerusalem, where I shall be honored, and I choose David to rule my people Israel.' 7 My father David wished to build a temple to the honor of the LORD, the God of Israel, 8 but the LORD said to him: 'In wishing to build a temple to my honor, you do well. 9 However, you shall not build the temple; rather, your son whom you will beget shall build the temple to my honor.' 10 "Now the LORD has fulfilled the promise that he made. I have succeeded my father David and have taken my seat on the throne of Israel, as the LORD foretold, and I have built the temple to the honor of the LORD, the God of Israel. 11 And I have placed there the ark, in which abides the covenant of the LORD which he made with the Israelites." 12 Solomon then took his place before the altar of the LORD in the presence of the whole community of Israel and stretched forth his hands. 13 He had made a bronze platform five cubits long, five cubits wide, and three cubits high, which he had placed in the middle of the courtyard. Having ascended it, Solomon knelt in the presence of the whole of Israel and stretched forth his hands toward heaven. 14 Thus he prayed: "LORD, God of Israel, there is no god like you in heaven or on earth; you keep your covenant and show kindness to your servants who are wholeheartedly faithful to you. 15 You have kept the promise you made to my father David, your servant. With your own mouth you spoke it, and by your own hand you have brought it to fulfillment this day. 16 Now, therefore, LORD, God of Israel, keep the further promise you made to my father David, your servant, when you said, 'You shall always have someone from your line to sit before me on the throne of Israel, provided only that your descendants look to their conduct so as always to live according to my law, even as you have lived in my presence.' 17 Now, LORD, God of Israel, may this promise which you made to your servant David be confirmed. 18 "Can it indeed be that God dwells with mankind on earth? If the heavens and the highest heavens cannot contain you, how much less this temple which I have built! 19 Look kindly on the prayer and petition of your servant, O LORD, my God, and listen to the cry of supplication your servant makes before you. 20 May your eyes watch day and night over this temple, the place where you have decreed you shall be honored; may you heed the prayer which I your servant offer toward this place. 21 Listen to the petitions of your servant and of your people Israel which they direct toward this place. Listen from your heavenly dwelling, and when you have heard, pardon. 22 "When any man sins against his neighbor and is required to take an oath of execration against himself, and when he comes for the oath before your altar in this temple, 23 listen from heaven: take action and pass judgment on your servants, requiting the wicked man and holding him responsible for his conduct, but absolving the innocent and rewarding him according to his virtue. 24 When your people Israel have sinned against you and are defeated by the enemy, but afterward they return and praise your name, and they pray to you and entreat you in this temple, 25 listen from heaven and forgive the sin of your people Israel, and bring them back to the land which you gave them and their fathers. 26 When the sky is closed so that there is no rain, because they have sinned against you, but then they pray toward this place and praise your name, and they withdraw from sin because you afflict them, 27 listen in heaven and forgive the sin of your servants and of your people Israel. But teach them the right way to live, and send rain upon your land which you gave your people as their heritage. 28 When there is famine in the land, when there is pestilence, or blight, or mildew, or locusts, or caterpillars; when their enemies besiege them at any of their gates; whenever there is a plague or sickness of any kind; 29 when any Israelite of all your people offers a prayer or petition of any kind, and in

awareness of his affliction and pain, stretches out his hands toward this temple, 30 listen from your heavenly dwelling place, and forgive. Knowing his heart, render to everyone according to his conduct, for you alone know the hearts of men. 31 So may they fear you and walk in your ways as long as they live on the land you gave our fathers. 32 "For the foreigner, too, who is not of your people Israel, when he comes from a distant land to honor your great name, your mighty power, and your outstretched arm, when they come in prayer to this temple, 33 listen from your heavenly dwelling place, and do whatever the foreigner entreats you, that all the peoples of the earth may know your name, fearing you as do your people Israel, and knowing that this house which I have built is dedicated to your honor. 34 "When your people go forth to war against their enemies, wherever you send them, and pray to you in the direction of this city and of the house I have built to your honor, 35 listen from heaven to their prayer and petition, and defend their cause. 36 When they sin against you (for there is no man who does not sin), and in your anger against them you deliver them to the enemy, so that their captors deport them to another land, far or near, 37 when they repent in the land where they are captive and are converted, when they entreat you in the land of their captivity and say, 'We have sinned and done wrong; we have been wicked,' 38 and with their whole heart and with their whole soul they turn back to you in the land of those who hold them captive, when they pray in the direction of their land which you gave their fathers, and of the city you have chosen, and of the house which I have built to your honor, 39 listen from your heavenly dwelling place, hear their prayer and petitions, and uphold their cause. Forgive your people who have sinned against you. 40 My God, may your eyes be open and your ears attentive to the prayer of this place. 41 And now, "Advance, LORD God, to your resting place, you and the ark of your majesty. May your priests, LORD God, be clothed with salvation, may your faithful ones rejoice in good things. 42 LORD God, reject not the plea of your anointed, remember the devotion of David, your servant."

2 Chronicles Chapter 7

1 When Solomon had ended his prayer, fire came down from heaven and consumed the holocaust and the sacrifices, and the glory of the LORD filled the house. 2 But the priests could not enter the house of the LORD, for the glory of the LORD had filled the house of the LORD. 3 All the Israelites looked on while the fire came down and the glory of the LORD was upon the house, and they fell down upon the pavement with their faces to the earth and adored, praising the LORD, "for he is good, for his mercy endures forever." 4 The king and all the people were offering sacrifices before the LORD. 5 King Solomon offered as sacrifice twenty-two thousand oxen, and one hundred twenty thousand sheep. 6 Thus the king and all the people dedicated the house of God. The priests were standing at their stations, as were the Levites, with the musical instruments of the LORD which King David had made for "praising the LORD, for his mercy endures forever," when David used them to accompany the hymns. Across from them the priests blew the trumpets and all Israel stood. 7 Then Solomon consecrated the middle part of the court which lay before the house of the LORD; there he offered the holocausts and the fat of the peace offerings, since the bronze altar which Solomon had made could not hold the holocausts, the cereal offerings and the fat. 8 On this occasion Solomon and with him all Israel, who had assembled in very large numbers from Labo of Hamath to the Wadi of Egypt, celebrated the festival for seven days. 9 On the eighth day they held a special meeting, for they had celebrated the dedication of the altar for seven days and the feast for seven days. 10 On the twenty-third day of the seventh month he sent the people back to their tents, rejoicing and glad at heart at the good things the LORD had done for David, for Solomon, and for his people Israel. 11 Solomon completed the house of the LORD and the royal palace; he successfully accomplished everything he had planned to do in regard to the house of the LORD and his own house. 12 The LORD appeared to Solomon during the night and said to him: "I have heard your prayer, and I have chosen this place for my house of sacrifice. 13 If I close heaven so that there is no rain, if I command the locust to devour the land, if I send pestilence among my people, 14 and if my people, upon whom my name has been pronounced, humble themselves and pray, and seek my presence and turn from their evil ways, I will hear them from heaven and pardon their sins and revive their land. 15 Now my eyes shall be open and my ears attentive to the prayer of this place. 16 And now I have chosen and consecrated this house that my name may be there forever; my eyes and my heart also shall be there always. 17 "As for you, if you live in my presence as your father David did, doing all that I have commanded you and keeping my statutes and ordinances, 18 I will establish your royal throne as I covenanted with your father David when I said, 'There shall never be lacking someone of yours as ruler in Israel.' 19 But if you turn away and forsake my statutes and commands which

I placed before you, if you proceed to venerate and worship strange gods, 20 then I will uproot the people from the land I gave them; I will cast from my sight this house which I have consecrated to my honor, and I will make it a proverb and a byword among all peoples. 21 This temple which is so exalted - everyone passing by it will be amazed and ask: 'Why has the LORD done this to this land and to this house?' 22 And men will answer: 'They forsook the LORD, the God of their fathers, who brought them out of the land of Egypt, and they adopted strange gods and worshiped them and served them. That is why he has brought down upon them all this evil.'"

2 Chronicles Chapter 8

1 After the twenty years during which Solomon built the house of the LORD and his own house, 2 he built up the cities which Huram had given him, and settled Israelites there. 3 Then Solomon went to Hamath of Zoba and conquered it. 4 He built Tadmor in the desert region and all the supply cities, which he built in Hamath. 5 He built Upper Beth-horon and Lower Beth-horon, fortified cities with walls, gates and bars; 6 also Baalath, all the supply cities belonging to Solomon, and all the cities for the chariots, the cities for the horsemen, and whatever else Solomon decided should be built in Jerusalem, in the Lebanon, and in the entire land under his dominion. 7 All the people that remained of the Hittites, Amorites, Perizzites, Hivites, and Jebusites, who were not of Israel - 8 that is, their descendants remaining in the land, whom the Israelites had not destroyed - Solomon subjected to forced labor, as they continue to this day. 9 But Solomon did not enslave the Israelites for his works. They became soldiers, commanders of his warriors, and commanders of his chariots and his horsemen. 10 They were also King Solomon's two hundred and fifty overseers who had charge of the people. 11 Solomon brought the daughter of Pharaoh up from the City of David to the palace which he had built for her, for he said, "No wife of mine shall dwell in the house of David, king of Israel, for the places where the ark of the LORD has come are holy." 12 In those times Solomon offered holocausts to the LORD upon the altar of the LORD which he had built in front of the porch, 13 as was required day by day according to the command of Moses, and in particular on the sabbaths, at the new moons, and on the fixed festivals three times a year: on the feast of the Unleavened Bread, the feast of Weeks and the feast of Booths. 14 And according to the ordinance of his father David he appointed the various classes of the priests for their service, and the Levites according to their functions of praise and ministry alongside the priests, as the daily duty required. The gatekeepers of the various classes stood guard at each gate, since such was the command of David, the man of God. 15 There was no deviation from the king's command in any respect relating to the priests and Levites or the treasuries. 16 All of Solomon's work was carried out successfully from the day the foundation of the house of the LORD was laid until the house of the LORD had been completed in every detail. 17 In those times Solomon went to Ezion-geber and to Elath on the seashore of the land of Edom. 18 Huram, through his servants, sent him ships and crewmen acquainted with the sea, who accompanied Solomon's servants to Ophir and brought back from there four hundred and fifty talents of gold to King Solomon.

2 Chronicles Chapter 9

1 When the queen of Sheba heard of Solomon's fame, she came to Jerusalem to test him with subtle questions, accompanied by a very numerous retinue and by camels bearing spices, much gold, and precious stones. She came to Solomon and questioned him on every subject in which she was interested. 2 Solomon explained to her everything she asked about, and there remained nothing hidden from Solomon that he could not explain to her. 3 When the queen of Sheba witnessed Solomon's wisdom, the palace he had built, 4 the food at his table, the seating of his ministers, the attendance of his servants and their dress, his cupbearers and their dress, and the holocausts he offered in the house of the LORD, it took her breath away. 5 "The account I heard in my country about your deeds and your wisdom is true," she told the king. 6 "Yet I did not believe the report until I came and saw with my own eyes. I have discovered that they did not tell me the half of your great wisdom; you have surpassed the stories I heard. 7 Happy are your men, happy these servants of yours, who stand before you always and listen to your wisdom. 8 Blessed be the LORD, your God, who has been so pleased with you as to place you on his throne as king for the LORD, your God. Because your God has so loved Israel as to will to make it last forever, he has appointed you over them as king to administer right and justice." 9 Then she gave the king one hundred and twenty gold talents and a very large quantity of spices, as well as precious stones. There was no other spice like that which the queen of Sheba gave to King Solomon. 10 The servants of Huram and of Solomon who brought gold from Ophir also brought cabinet wood and precious stones. 11 With the cabinet wood the king made stairs for the temple of the LORD and the palace of the king; also lyres and harps for the chanters. The like of these had not been seen before in the land of Judah. 12 King Solomon gave the queen of Sheba everything she desired and asked him for, more than she had brought to the king. Then she returned to her own country with her servants. 13 The gold that Solomon received each year weighed six hundred and sixty-six gold talents, 14 in addition to what was collected from travelers and what the merchants brought. All the kings of Arabia also, and the governors of the country, brought gold and silver to Solomon. 15 Moreover, King Solomon made two hundred large shields of beaten gold, six hundred shekels of beaten gold going into each shield, 16 and three hundred bucklers of beaten gold, three hundred shekels of gold going into each buckler; these the king put in the hall of the Forest of Lebanon. 17 King Solomon also made a large ivory throne which he overlaid with fine gold. 18 The throne had six steps; a footstool of gold was fastened to it, and there was an arm on each side of the seat, with two lions standing beside the arms. 19 Twelve other lions also stood there, one on either side of each step. Nothing like this had ever been produced in any other kingdom. 20 Furthermore, all of King Solomon's drinking vessels were of gold, and all the utensils in the hall of the Forest of Lebanon were of pure gold; silver was not considered of value in Solomon's time. 21 For the king had ships that went to Tarshish with the servants of Huram. Once every three years the fleet of Tarshish would return with a cargo of gold and silver, ivory, apes and monkeys. 22 Thus King Solomon surpassed all the other kings of the earth in riches as well as in wisdom. 23 All the kings of the earth sought audience with Solomon, to hear from him the wisdom which God had put in his heart. 24 Year in and year out, each one would bring his tribute-silver and gold articles, garments, weapons, spices, horses and mules. 25 Solomon also had four thousand stalls of horses, chariots, and twelve thousand horsemen, which he assigned to the chariot cities and to the king in Jerusalem. 26 He was ruler over all the kings from the River to the land of the Philistines and down to the border of Egypt. 27 The king made silver as common in Jerusalem as stones, while cedars became as numerous as the sycamores of the foothills. 28 Horses were imported for Solomon from Egypt and from all the lands. 29 The rest of the acts of Solomon, first and last, are written, as is well known, in the acts of Nathan the prophet, in the prophecy of Ahijah the Shilonite, and in the visions of Iddo the seer which concern Jeroboam, son of Nebat. 30 Solomon reigned in Jerusalem over all Israel for forty years. 31 He rested with his ancestors; he was buried in his father's City of David, and his son Rehoboam succeeded him as king.

2 Chronicles Chapter 10

1 Rehoboam went to Shechem, for all Israel had come to Shechem to proclaim him king. 2 When Jeroboam, son of Nebat, heard of this in Egypt where he had fled from King Solomon, he returned from Egypt. 3 Jeroboam was summoned to the assembly, and he and all Israel said to Rehoboam: 4 "Your father laid a heavy yoke upon us. If you now lighten the harsh service and the heavy yoke that your father imposed on us, we will serve you." 5 "In three days," he answered them, "come back to me." When the people had departed, 6 King Rehoboam consulted the elders who had been in the service of his father during Solomon's lifetime, asking, "What answer do you advise me to give this people?" 7 They replied, "If you will deal kindly with this people and give in to them, acceding to their request, they will be your servants forever." 8 But he ignored the advice the elders had given him and consulted the young men who had grown up with him and were in his service. 9 He said to them, "What answer do you advise me to give this people, who have asked me to lighten the yoke my father imposed on them?" 10 The young men who had grown up with him replied: "This is the answer you should give to this people who have said to you, 'Your father laid a heavy yoke upon us, but do you lighten our yoke'; this you should say to them: 'My little finger is thicker than my father's body. 11 Whereas my father put a heavy yoke on you, I will make it heavier! My father beat you with whips, but I will beat you with scorpions!'" 12 On the third day, Jeroboam and all the people came back to King Rehoboam as he had instructed them to do. 13 Ignoring the advice the elders had given him, the king gave them a harsh answer, 14 speaking to them according to the advice of the young men: "My father laid a heavy yoke on you, but I will make it heavier. My father beat you with whips, but I will beat you with scorpions." 15 The king would not listen to the people, for this turn of events was divinely ordained to fulfill the prophecy the LORD had uttered to Jeroboam, the son of Nebat, through Ahijah the Shilonite. 16 When all Israel saw that the king would not listen to them, the people answered the king. "What share have we in David? We have no heritage in the son of Jesse. Everyone to your tents,

O Israel! Now look to your own house, David!" So all Israel went off to their tents. [17] Rehoboam, therefore, reigned over only those Israelites who lived in the cities of Judah. [18] King Rehoboam then sent out Hadoram, who was superintendent of the forced labor, but the Israelites stoned him to death. Rehoboam himself managed to mount his chariot and flee to Jerusalem. [19] Thus Israel has been in rebellion against David's house to this day.

2 Chronicles Chapter 11

[1] On his arrival in Jerusalem Rehoboam gathered together the house of Judah and Benjamin, a hundred and eighty thousand seasoned warriors, to have them fight against Israel and restore the kingdom to him. [2] However, the word of the LORD came to Shemaiah, a man of God: [3] "Say to Rehoboam, son of Solomon, king of Judah, and to all the Israelites in Judah and Benjamin: [4] 'Thus says the LORD: You must not march out to fight against your brothers. Let every man return home, for what has occurred I have brought about.'" They obeyed this message of the LORD and gave up the expedition against Jeroboam. [5] Rehoboam took up residence in Jerusalem and built fortified cities in Judah. [6] He built up Bethlehem, Etam, Tekoa, [7] Beth-zur, Soco, Adullam, [8] Gath, Mareshah, Ziph, [9] Adoraim, Lachish, Azekah, [10] Zorah, Aijalon, and Hebron; these were fortified cities in Judah and Benjamin. [11] Then he strengthened the fortifications and put commanders in them, with supplies of food, oil and wine. [12] In every city were shields and spears, and he made them very strong. Thus Judah and Benjamin remained his. [13] Now the priests and Levites throughout Israel presented themselves to him from all parts of their land, [14] for the Levites left their assigned pasture lands and their holdings and came to Judah and Jerusalem, because Jeroboam and his sons repudiated them as priests of the LORD. [15] In their place, he himself appointed priests for the high places and satyrs and calves he had made. [16] After them, all those of the Israelite tribes who firmly desired to seek the LORD, the God of Israel, came to Jerusalem to sacrifice to the LORD, the God of their fathers. [17] Thus they strengthened the kingdom of Judah and made Rehoboam, son of Solomon, prevail for three years; for they walked in the way of David and Solomon three years. [18] Rehoboam took to himself as wife Mahalath, daughter of Jerimoth, son of David and of Abihail, daughter of Eliab, son of Jesse. [19] She bore him sons: Jehush, Shemariah and Zaham. [20] After her, he married Maacah, daughter of Absalom, who bore him Abijah, Attai, Ziza and Shelomith. [21] Rehoboam loved Maacah, daughter of Absalom, more than all his other wives and concubines; he had taken eighteen wives and sixty concubines, and he fathered twenty-eight sons and sixty daughters. [22] Rehoboam constituted Abijah, son of Maacah, commander among his brothers, for he intended to make him king. [23] He acted prudently, distributing various of his sons throughout all the districts of Judah and Benjamin, in all the fortified cities; and he furnished them with copious provisions and sought an abundance of wives for them.

2 Chronicles Chapter 12

[1] After Rehoboam had consolidated his rule and had become powerful, he abandoned the law of the LORD, he and all Israel with him. [2] Thus it happened that in the fifth year of King Rehoboam, Shishak, king of Egypt, attacked Jerusalem, for they had been unfaithful to the LORD. [3] He came up with twelve hundred chariots and sixty thousand horsemen, and there was no counting the army that came with him from Egypt—Libyans, Sukkites and Ethiopians. [4] They captured the fortified cities of Judah and came as far as Jerusalem. [5] Then Shemaiah the prophet came to Rehoboam and the commanders of Judah who had gathered at Jerusalem because of Shishak, and said to them: "Thus says the LORD: 'You have abandoned me, and therefore I have abandoned you to the power of Shishak.'" [6] However, the commanders of Israel and the king humbled themselves saying, "The LORD is just." [7] When the LORD saw that they had humbled themselves, the word of the LORD came to Shemaiah: "Because they have humbled themselves, I will not destroy them; I will give them some deliverance, and my wrath shall not be poured out upon Jerusalem through Shishak. [8] But they shall be his servants, that they may know what it is to serve me and what it is to serve earthly kingdoms." [9] Therefore Shishak, king of Egypt, attacked Jerusalem and carried off the treasures of the temple of the LORD and of the king's palace. He took everything, including the gold bucklers that Solomon had made. [10] (To replace them, King Rehoboam made bronze bucklers, which he entrusted to the officers of the guard on duty at the entrance of the royal palace. [11] Whenever the king visited the temple of the LORD, the troops would come bearing them, and then they would return them to the guardroom.) [12] Because he had humbled himself, the anger of the LORD turned from him so that it did not destroy him completely; and in Judah, moreover, good deeds were found. [13] King Rehoboam consolidated his power in Jerusalem and continued to rule;

he was forty-one years old when he became king, and he reigned seventeen years in Jerusalem, the city in which, out of all the tribes of Israel, the LORD chose to be honored. Rehoboam's mother was named Naamah, an Ammonite. [14] He did evil, for he had not truly resolved to seek the LORD. [15] The acts of Rehoboam, first and last, are written, as is well known, in the history of Shemaiah the prophet and of Iddo the seer (his family record). There was war continually between Rehoboam and Jeroboam. [16] Rehoboam rested with his ancestors; he was buried in the City of David. His son Abijah succeeded him as king.

2 Chronicles Chapter 13

[1] In the eighteenth year of King Jeroboam, Abijah became king of Judah; [2] he reigned three years in Jerusalem. His mother was named Michaiah, daughter of Uriel of Gibeah. There was war between Abijah and Jeroboam. [3] Abijah joined battle with a force of four hundred thousand picked warriors, while Jeroboam lined up against him in battle with eight hundred thousand picked and valiant warriors. [4] Abijah stood on Mount Zemariam, which is in the highlands of Ephraim, and said: "Listen to me, Jeroboam and all Israel! [5] Do you not know that the LORD, the God of Israel, has given the kingdom of Israel to David forever, to him and to his sons, by a covenant made in salt? [6] Yet Jeroboam, son of Nebat, the servant of Solomon, son of David, has stood up and rebelled against his lord! [7] Worthless men, scoundrels, joined him and overcame Rehoboam, son of Solomon, when Rehoboam was young and unthinking, and no match for them. [8] But now, do you think you are a match for the kingdom of the LORD commanded by the sons of David, simply because you are a huge multitude and have with you the golden calves which Jeroboam made you for gods? [9] "Have you not expelled the priests of the LORD, the sons of Aaron, and the Levites, and made for yourselves priests like the peoples of foreign lands? Everyone who comes to consecrate himself with a young bull and seven rams becomes a priest of no-gods. [10] But as for us, the LORD is our God, and we have not forsaken him. The priests ministering to the LORD are sons of Aaron, and the Levites also have their offices. [11] They burn holocausts to the LORD and fragrant incense morning after morning and evening after evening; they display the showbread on the pure table, and the lamps of the golden lampstand burn evening after evening; for we observe our duties to the LORD, our God, but you have abandoned him. [12] See, God is with us, at our head, and his priests are here with trumpets to sound the attack against you. Do not battle against the LORD, the God of your fathers, O Israelites, for you will not succeed!" [13] But Jeroboam had an ambush go around them to come at them from the rear; so that while his army faced Judah, his ambush lay behind them. [14] When Judah turned and saw that they had to battle on both fronts, they cried out to the LORD and the priests sounded the trumpets. [15] Then the men of Judah shouted; and when they did so, God defeated Jeroboam and all Israel before Abijah and Judah. [16] The Israelites fled before Judah, and God delivered them into their hands. [17] Abijah and his people inflicted a severe defeat upon them; five hundred thousand picked men of Israel fell slain. [18] The Israelites were subdued on that occasion and the Judahites were victorious because they relied on the LORD, the God of their fathers. [19] Abijah pursued Jeroboam and took cities from him: Bethel and its dependencies, Jeshanah and its dependencies, and Ephron and its dependencies. [20] Jeroboam did not regain power during the time of Abijah; the LORD struck him down and he died, [21] while Abijah continued to grow stronger. He took to himself fourteen wives and fathered twenty-two sons and sixteen daughters. [22] The rest of Abijah's acts, his deeds and his words, are written in the midrash of the prophet Iddo. [23] Abijah rested with his ancestors; they buried him in the City of David. His son Asa succeeded him as king. During his time, ten years of peace began in the land.

2 Chronicles Chapter 14

[1] Asa did what was good and pleasing to the LORD, his God, [2] removing the heathen altars and the high places, breaking to pieces the sacred pillars, and cutting down the sacred poles. [3] He commanded Judah to seek the LORD, the God of their fathers, and to observe the law and its commands. [4] He removed the high places and incense stands from all the cities of Judah, and under him the kingdom had peace. [5] He built fortified cities in Judah, for the land had peace and no war was waged against him during these years, because the LORD had given him peace. [6] He said to Judah: "Let us build these cities and surround them with walls, towers, gates and bars. The land is still ours, for we have sought the LORD, our God; we sought him, and he has given us rest on every side." So they built and prospered. [7] Asa had an army of three hundred thousand shield-and lance-bearers from Judah, and two hundred and eighty thousand from Benjamin who carried bucklers and were archers, all of them valiant warriors. [8] Zerah the Ethiopian moved against them

with a force of one million men and three hundred chariots, and he came as far as Mareshah. [9] Asa went out to meet him and set himself in battle array in the valley of Zephathah, near Mareshah. [10] Asa called upon the LORD, his God, praying: "O LORD, there is none like you to help the powerless against the strong. Help us, O LORD, our God, for we rely on you, and in your name we have come against this multitude. You are the LORD, our God; let no man prevail against you." [11] And so the LORD defeated the Ethiopians before Asa and Judah, and they fled. [12] Asa and those with him pursued them as far as Gerar, and the Ethiopians fell until there were no survivors, for they were crushed before the LORD and his army, which carried away enormous spoils. [13] Then the Judahites conquered all the cities around Gerar, for the fear of the LORD was upon them; they despoiled all the cities, for there was much booty in them. [14] They attacked also the tents of the cattle-herders and carried off a great number of sheep and camels. Then they returned to Jerusalem.

2 Chronicles Chapter 15

[1] Upon Azariah, son of Oded, came the spirit of God. [2] He went forth to meet Asa and said to him: "Hear me, Asa and all Judah and Benjamin! The LORD is with you when you are with him, and if you seek him he will be present to you; but if you abandon him, he will abandon you. [3] For a long time Israel had no true God, no priest-teacher and no law, [4] but when in their distress they turned to the LORD, the God of Israel, and sought him, he was present to them. [5] In that former time there was no peace for anyone to go or come, but there were many terrors upon the inhabitants of the lands. [6] Nation crushed nation and city crushed city, for God destroyed them by every kind of adversity. [7] But as for you, be strong and do not relax, for your work shall be rewarded." [8] When Asa heard these words and the prophecy (Oded the prophet), he was encouraged to remove the detestable idols from the whole land of Judah and Benjamin and from the cities he had taken in the highlands of Ephraim, and to restore the altar of the LORD which was before the vestibule of the LORD. [9] Then he convened all Judah and Benjamin, together with those of Ephraim, Manasseh and Simeon who sojourned with them; for many had fled to him from Israel when they saw that the LORD, his God, was with him. [10] They gathered at Jerusalem in the third month of the fifteenth year of Asa's reign, [11] and sacrificed to the LORD at that time seven hundred oxen and seven thousand sheep of the booty they had brought. [12] They entered into a covenant to seek the LORD, the God of their fathers, with all their heart and soul; [13] and everyone who would not seek the LORD, the God of Israel, was to be put to death, whether small or great, whether man or woman. [14] They swore to the LORD with a loud voice, with shouting and with trumpets and horns. [15] All Judah rejoiced over the oath, for they had sworn with their whole heart and sought him with complete desire, so that he was present to them. And the LORD gave them rest on every side. [16] Maacah, the mother of King Asa, he deposed as queen mother because she had made an outrageous object for Asherah; Asa cut this down, smashed it, and burnt it in the Kidron Valley. [17] Although the high places did not disappear from Israel, yet Asa's heart was undivided as long as he lived. [18] He brought into the house of God his father's votive offerings and his own: silver, gold, and various utensils. [19] There was no war until the thirty-fifth year of Asa's reign.

2 Chronicles Chapter 16

[1] In the thirty-sixth year of Asa's reign, Baasha, king of Israel, attacked Judah and fortified Ramah to prevent any communication with Asa, king of Judah. [2] Asa then brought out silver and gold from the treasuries of the temple of the LORD and of the royal palace and sent them to Ben-hadad, king of Aram, who lived in Damascus, with this message: [3] "There is a treaty between you and me, as there was between your father and my father. See, I am sending you silver and gold. Go, break your treaty with Baasha, king of Israel, that he may withdraw from me." [4] Ben-hadad agreed to King Asa's request and sent the leaders of his troops against the cities of Israel. They attacked Ijon, Dan, Abel-maim, and all the store cities of Naphtali. [5] When Baasha heard of it, he left off fortifying Ramah; he stopped his work. [6] Then King Asa commandeered all of Judah to carry away the stone and wood with which Baasha had been fortifying Ramah, and with them he fortified Geba and Mizpah. [7] At that time Hanani the seer came to Asa, king of Judah, and said to him: "Because you relied on the king of Aram and did not rely on the LORD, your God, the army of the king of Aram has escaped your hand. [8] Were not the Ethiopians and Libyans a vast army, with great numbers of chariots and drivers? And yet, because you relied on the LORD, he delivered them into your power. [9] The eyes of the LORD roam over the whole earth, to encourage those who are devoted to him wholeheartedly. You have acted foolishly in this matter, for from now on you will have wars." [10] But Asa became angry with the seer and

imprisoned him in the stocks, so greatly was he enraged at him over this. Asa also oppressed some of his people at this time. [11] Now the acts of Asa, first and last, can be found recorded in the book of the kings of Judah and Israel. [12] In the thirty-ninth year of his reign, Asa contracted a serious disease in his feet. But even in his sickness he did not seek the LORD, but only the physicians. [13] Asa rested with his ancestors; he died in the forty-first year of his reign. [14] They buried him in the tomb he had hewn for himself in the City of David, having laid him upon a couch which was filled with spices and various kinds of aromatics compounded into an ointment. They also burned a very great funeral pyre for him.

2 Chronicles Chapter 17

[1] His son Jehoshaphat succeeded him as king and strengthened his hold against Israel. [2] He placed armed forces in all the fortified cities of Judah, and put garrisons in the land of Judah and in the cities of Ephraim which his father Asa had taken. [3] The LORD was with Jehoshaphat, for he walked in the ways his father had pursued in the beginning, and he did not consult the Baals. [4] Rather, he sought the God of his father and observed his commands, and not the practices of Israel. [5] As a result, the LORD made his kingdom secure, and all Judah gave Jehoshaphat gifts, so that he enjoyed great wealth and glory. [6] Thus he was encouraged to follow the LORD'S ways, and again he removed the high places and the sacred poles from Judah. [7] In the third year of his reign he sent his leading men, Ben-hail, Obadiah, Zechariah, Nethanel and Micaiah, to teach in the cities of Judah. [8] With them he sent the Levites Shemaiah, Nethaniah, Zebadiah, Asahel, Shemiramoth, Jehonathan, Adonijah and Tobijah, together with the priests Elishama and Jehoram. [9] They taught in Judah, having with them the book containing the law of the LORD; they traveled through all the cities of Judah and taught among the people. [10] Now the fear of the LORD was upon all the kingdoms of the countries surrounding Judah, so that they did not war against Jehoshaphat. [11] Some of the Philistines brought Jehoshaphat gifts and a tribute of silver; and the Arabs also brought him a flock of seven thousand seven hundred rams and seven thousand seven hundred he-goats. [12] Jehoshaphat grew steadily greater. He built strongholds and store cities in Judah. [13] He carried out many works in the cities of Judah, and he had soldiers, valiant warriors, in Jerusalem. [14] This was their mustering according to their ancestral houses. Of Judah, the commanders of thousands: Adnah the commander, and with him three hundred thousand valiant warriors. [15] Next to him, Jehohanan the commander, and with him two hundred eighty thousand. [16] Next to him, Amasiah, son of Zichri, who offered himself to the LORD, and with him two hundred thousand valiant warriors. [17] From Benjamin: Eliada, a valiant warrior, and with him two hundred thousand armed with bow and buckler. [18] Next to him, Jozabad, and with him one hundred and eighty thousand equipped for war. [19] These were at the service of the king; in addition were those whom the king had placed in the fortified cities throughout all Judah.

2 Chronicles Chapter 18

[1] Jehoshaphat therefore had wealth and glory in abundance; but he became related to Ahab by marriage. [2] After some years he went down to Ahab at Samaria; Ahab offered numerous sheep and oxen for him and the people with him, and persuaded him to go up against Ramoth-gilead. [3] Ahab, king of Israel, asked Jehoshaphat, king of Judah, "Will you come with me to Ramoth-gilead?" "You and I are as one," was his answer; "your people and my people as well. We will be with you in the battle." [4] But Jehoshaphat also said to the king of Israel, "Seek the word of the LORD at once." [5] The king of Israel gathered his prophets, four hundred in number, and asked them, "Shall we go to attack Ramoth-gilead, or shall I refrain?" "Go up," they answered. "God will deliver it over to the king." [6] But Jehoshaphat said, "Is there no other prophet of the LORD here whom we may consult?" [7] The king of Israel answered Jehoshaphat, "There is still another through whom we may consult the LORD, but I hate him, for he prophesies not good but always evil about me. That is Micaiah, son of Imlah." Jeshoshaphat said, "Let not your Majesty speak of evil against you." [8] So the king of Israel called an official, to whom he said, "Get Micaiah, son of Imlah, at once." [9] The king of Israel and King Jehoshaphat of Judah were seated each on his throne, clothed in their robes of state on a threshing floor at the entrance of the gate of Samaria, and all the prophets were prophesying before them. [10] Zedekiah, son of Chenaanah, made iron horns for himself and said: "The LORD says, 'With these you shall gore Aram until you have destroyed them.'" [11] The other prophets prophesied in the same vein, saying: "Go up to Ramoth-gilead. You shall succeed; the LORD will deliver it over to the king." [12] The messenger who had gone to call Micaiah said to him: "Look now, the prophets unanimously

predict good for the king. Let your word, like each of theirs, predict good." 13 "As the LORD lives," Micaiah answered, "I will say what my God tells me." 14 When he came to the king, the king said to him, "Micaiah, shall we go to fight against Ramoth-gilead, or shall I refrain?" "Go up," he answered, "and succeed; they will be delivered into your power." 15 But the king said to him, "How many times must I adjure you to tell me nothing but the truth in the name of the LORD?" 16 Then Micaiah answered: "I see all Israel scattered on the mountains, like sheep without a shepherd, and the LORD saying, 'These have no master!' Let each of them go back home in peace.'" 17 The king of Israel said to Jehoshaphat, "Did I not tell you that he prophesies no good about me, but only evil?" 18 But Micaiah continued: "Therefore hear the word of the LORD: I saw the LORD seated on his throne, with the whole host of heaven standing by to his right and to his left. 19 The LORD asked, 'Who will deceive Ahab, king of Israel, so that he will go up and fall at Ramoth-gilead?' And one said this, another that, 20 until a spirit came forward and presented himself to the LORD, saying, 'I will deceive him.' The LORD asked, 'How?' 21 He answered, 'I will go forth and become a lying spirit in the mouths of all his prophets.' The LORD agreed: 'You shall succeed in deceiving him. Go forth and do this.' 22 So now the LORD has put a lying spirit in the mouths of these your prophets, but the LORD himself has decreed evil against you." 23 Thereupon Zedekiah, son of Chenaanah, came up and slapped Micaiah on the cheek, saying, "Which way did the spirit of the LORD go when he left me to speak to you?" 24 "You shall find out," Micaiah replied, "on that day when you enter an innermost chamber to hide." 25 The king of Israel then said: "Seize Micaiah and take him back to Amon, prefect of the city, and to Joash the king's son, 26 and say, 'This is the king's order: Put this man in prison and feed him scanty rations of bread and water until I return in safety!'" 27 But Micaiah said, "If ever you return in safety, the LORD has not spoken through me." And he said, "Hear, O peoples, all of you!" 28 The king of Israel and King Jehoshaphat of Judah went up to Ramoth-gilead 29 and the king of Israel said to Jehoshaphat, "I will go into battle disguised, but you put on your own clothes." So the king of Israel disguised himself and they entered the fray. 30 Meanwhile, the king of Aram had given his chariot commanders the order, "Fight with no one, small or great, except the king of Israel." 31 When the commanders saw Jehoshaphat, they exclaimed, "That must be the king of Israel!" and shifted to fight him. But Jehoshaphat cried out and the LORD helped him; God induced them to leave him. 32 The chariot commanders became aware that he was not the king of Israel and gave up their pursuit of him. 33 Someone, however, drew his bow at random and hit the king of Israel between the joints of his breastplate. He ordered his charioteer, "Rein about and take me out of the ranks, for I am disabled." 34 The battle grew fierce during the day, and the king of Israel braced himself up on his chariot facing the Arameans until evening. He died as the sun was setting.

2 Chronicles Chapter 19

1 King Jehoshaphat of Judah returned in safety to his house in Jerusalem. 2 Jehu the seer, son of Hanani, met King Jehoshaphat and said to him: "Should you help the wicked and love those who hate the LORD? For this reason, wrath is upon you from the LORD. 3 Yet some good things are to be found in you, since you have removed the sacred poles from the land and have been determined to seek God." 4 Jehoshaphat dwelt in Jerusalem; but he went out again among the people from Beer-sheba to the highlands of Ephraim and brought them back to the LORD, the God of their fathers. 5 He appointed judges in the land, in all the fortified cities of Judah, city by city, 6 and he said to them: "Take care what you do, for you are judging, not on behalf of man, but on behalf of the LORD; he judges with you. 7 And now, let the fear of the LORD be upon you. Act carefully, for with the LORD, our God there is no injustice, no partiality, no bribe-taking." 8 In Jerusalem also, Jehoshaphat appointed some Levites and priests and some of the family heads of Israel to judge in the name of the LORD and to settle quarrels among the inhabitants of Jerusalem. 9 He gave them this command: "You shall act faithfully and wholeheartedly in the fear of the LORD. 10 And in every dispute that your brethren living in their cities bring to you, whether it concerns bloodguilt or questions of law, command, statutes, or judgments, warn them lest they become guilty before the LORD and his wrath come upon you and your brethren. Do that and you shall be guiltless. 11 See now, Amariah is high priest over you in everything that pertains to the LORD, and Zebadiah, son of Ishmael, is leader of the house of Judah in all that pertains to the king; and the Levites will be your officials. Act firmly, and the LORD will be with the good."

2 Chronicles Chapter 20

1 After this the Moabites, the Ammonites, and with them some

Meunites came to fight against Jehoshaphat. 2 The message was brought to Jehoshaphat: "A great multitude is coming against you from across the sea, from Edom; they are already in Hazazon-tamar" (which is En-gedi). 3 Jehoshaphat was frightened, and he hastened to consult the LORD. He proclaimed a fast for all Judah. 4 Then Judah gathered to seek help from the LORD; from every one of the cities of Judah they came to seek the LORD. 5 Jehoshaphat stood up in the assembly of Judah and Jerusalem in the house of the LORD before the new court, 6 and he said: "LORD, God of our fathers, are you not the God in heaven, and do you not rule over all the kingdoms of the nations? In your hand is power and might, and no one can withstand you. 7 Was it not you, our God, who drove out the inhabitants of this land before your people Israel and gave it forever to the descendants of Abraham, your friend? 8 They have dwelt in it and they built in it a sanctuary to your honor, saying, 9 'When evil comes upon us, the sword of judgment, or pestilence, or famine, we will stand before this house and before you, for your name is in this house, and we will cry out to you in our affliction, and you will hear and save!' 10 And now, see the Ammonites, Moabites, and those of Mount Seir whom you did not allow Israel to invade when they came from the land of Egypt, but instead they passed them by and did not destroy them. 11 See how they are now repaying us by coming to drive us out of the possession you have given us. 12 O our God, will you not pass judgment on them? We are powerless before this vast multitude that comes against us. We are at a loss what to do, hence our eyes are turned toward you." 13 All Judah was standing before the LORD, with their little ones, their wives, and their young sons. 14 And the spirit of the LORD came upon Jahaziel, son of Zechariah, son of Benaiah, son of Jeiel, son of Mattaniah, a Levite of the clan of Asaph, in the midst of the assembly, 15 and he said: "Listen, all of Judah, inhabitants of Jerusalem, and King Jehoshaphat! The LORD says to you: 'Do not fear or lose heart at the sight of this vast multitude, for the battle is not yours but God's. 16 Go down against them tomorrow. You will see them coming up by the ascent of Ziz, and you will come upon them at the end of the wadi which opens on the wilderness of Jeruel. 17 You will not have to fight in this encounter. Take your places, stand firm, and see how the LORD will be with you to deliver you, Judah and Jerusalem. Do not fear or lose heart. Tomorrow go out to meet them, and the LORD will be with you.'" 18 Then Jehoshaphat knelt down with his face to the ground, and all Judah and the inhabitants of Jerusalem fell down before the LORD in worship. 19 Levites from among the Kohathites and Korahites rose to sing the praises of the LORD, the God of Israel, in a resounding chorus. 20 In the early morning they hastened out to the wilderness of Tekoa. As they were going out, Jehoshaphat halted and said: "Listen to me, Judah and inhabitants of Jerusalem! Trust in the LORD, your God, and you will be found firm. Trust in his prophets and you will succeed." 21 After consulting with the people, he appointed some to sing to the LORD and some to praise the holy Appearance as it went forth at the head of the army. They sang: "Give thanks to the LORD, for his mercy endures forever." 22 At the moment they began their jubilant hymn, the LORD laid an ambush against the Ammonites, Moabites, and those of Mount Seir who were coming against Judah, so that they were vanquished. 23 For the Ammonites and Moabites set upon the inhabitants of Mount Seir and completely exterminated them. And when they had finished with the inhabitants of Seir, they began to destroy each other. 24 When Judah came to the watchtower of the desert and looked toward the throng, they saw only corpses fallen on the ground, with no survivors. 25 Jehoshaphat and his people came to take plunder, and they found an abundance of cattle and personal property, garments and precious vessels. They took so much that they were unable to carry it all; they were three days taking the spoil, so great was it. 26 On the fourth day they held an assembly in the Valley of Beracah—for there they blessed the LORD; therefore that place has ever since been called the Valley of Beracah. 27 Then all the men of Judah and Jerusalem, with Jehoshaphat at their head, turned back toward Jerusalem celebrating the joyful victory the LORD had given them over their enemies. 28 They came to Jerusalem, to the house of the LORD, with harps, lyres and trumpets. 29 And the fear of God came upon all the kingdoms of the surrounding lands when they heard how the LORD had fought against the enemies of Israel. 30 Thereafter Jehoshaphat's kingdom enjoyed peace, for his God gave him rest on every side. 31 Thus Jehoshaphat reigned over Judah. He was thirty-five years old when he became king, and he reigned twenty-five years in Jerusalem. His mother was named Azubah, daughter of Shilhi. 32 He followed the path of his father Asa unswervingly, doing what was right in the LORD'S sight. 33 But the high places were not removed, nor as yet had the people fixed their hearts on the God of their fathers. 34 The rest of the acts of Jehoshaphat, first and last, can be found written in the chronicle of Jehu, son of Hanani, which is inserted in the book of the kings of Israel. ³⁵ After this, King Jehoshaphat of Judah allied himself with King Ahaziah of Israel, who did evil. ³⁶ He joined with him in building ships to sail to Tarshish; the fleet was built at Ezion-geber. ³⁷ But Eliezer, son of Dodavahu from Mareshah, prophesied against Jehoshaphat, saying, "Because you have joined with Ahaziah, the LORD will shatter your work." And the ships were wrecked and were unable to sail to Tarshish.

2 Chronicles Chapter 21

¹Jehoshaphat rested with his ancestors; he was buried with them in the City of David. Jehoram, his son, succeeded him as king. ²His brothers, sons of Jehoshaphat, were Azariah, Jehiel, Zechariah, Azariah, Michael and Shephatiah; all these were sons of King Jehoshaphat of Judah. ³Their father gave them numerous gifts of silver, gold and precious objects, together with fortified cities in Judah, but the kingship he gave to Jehoram because he was the first-born. ⁴When Jehoram had come into his father's kingdom and had consolidated his power, he put to the sword all his brothers and also some of the princes of Israel. ⁵Jehoram was thirty-two years old when he became king, and he reigned eight years in Jerusalem. ⁶He conducted himself like the kings of Israel of the line of Ahab, because one of Ahab's daughters was his wife. He did evil in the sight of the LORD, ⁷but the LORD would not destroy the house of David because of the covenant he had made with David and because of his promise to give him and his sons a lamp for all time. ⁸During his time Edom revolted against the sovereignty of Judah; they chose a king of their own. ⁹Thereupon Jehoram crossed over with his officers and all the chariots he had. He arose by night and broke through the Edomites when they had surrounded him and the commanders of his chariots. ¹⁰However, Edom has continued in revolt against the sovereignty of Judah down to the present time. Libnah also revolted at that time against Jehoram's sovereignty because he had forsaken the LORD, the God of his fathers. ¹¹He also set up high places in the mountains of Judah; he led the inhabitants of Jerusalem into idolatry and seduced Judah. ¹²He received a letter from the prophet Elijah with this message: "Thus says the LORD, the God of your ancestor David: 'Because you have not followed the path of your father Jehoshaphat, nor of Asa, king of Judah, ¹³but instead have walked in the way of the kings of Israel and have led Judah and the inhabitants of Jerusalem into idolatry, as did the house of Ahab, and also because you have murdered your brothers of your father's house who were better than you, ¹⁴the LORD will strike your people, your children, your wives, and all that is yours with a great plague; ¹⁵and you shall have severe pains from a disease in your bowels, while your bowels issue forth because of the disease, day after day.'" ¹⁶Then the LORD stirred up against Jehoram the animosity of the Philistines and of the Arabs who bordered on the Ethiopians. ¹⁷They came up against Judah, invaded it, and carried away all the wealth found in the king's palace, along with his sons and his wives; there was left to him only one son, Jehoahaz, his youngest. ¹⁸After these events, the LORD afflicted him with an incurable disease of the bowels. ¹⁹As time went on until a period of two years had elapsed, his bowels issued forth because of the disease and he died in great pain. His people did not make a pyre for him like that of his fathers. ²⁰He was thirty-two years old when he became king, and he reigned eight years in Jerusalem. He departed unloved and was buried in the City of David, but not in the tombs of the kings.

2 Chronicles Chapter 22

¹Then the inhabitants of Jerusalem made Ahaziah, his youngest son, king in his stead, since all the older sons had been slain by the band that had come into the fort with the Arabs. Thus Ahaziah, son of Jehoram, reigned as the king of Judah. ²He was twenty-two years old when he became king, and he reigned one year in Jerusalem. His mother was named Athaliah, daughter of Omri. ³He, too, followed the ways of the house of Ahab, because his mother counseled him to act sinfully. ⁴To his own destruction, he did evil in the sight of the LORD, as did the house of Ahab, since they were his counselors after the death of his father. ⁵He was also following their counsel when he accompanied Jehoram, son of Ahab, king of Israel, to battle against Hazael, king of Aram, at Ramoth-gilead. There Jehoram was wounded by the Arameans. ⁶He returned to Jezreel to be healed of the wounds he had received at Rama in his battle against Hazael, king of Aram. Because of this illness, Ahaziah, son of Jehoram, king of Judah, went down to visit Jehoram, son of Ahab, in Jezreel. ⁷Now it was willed by God for Ahaziah's downfall that he should join Jehoram, for after his arrival he rode out with Jehoram to Jehu, son of Nimshi, whom the LORD had anointed to cut down the house of Ahab. ⁸While Jehu was executing judgment on the house of Ahab, he also encountered the princes of Judah and the nephews of Ahaziah who were his attendants, and he slew them. ⁹Then he looked for Ahaziah himself. They caught him where he was hiding in Samaria and brought him to Jehu, who put him to death. They buried him, for they said, "He was the grandson of Jehoshaphat, who sought the LORD with his whole heart." There remained in Ahaziah's house no one powerful enough to wield the kingship. ¹⁰When Athaliah, mother of Ahaziah, learned that her son was dead, she proceeded to kill off all the royal offspring of the house of Judah. ¹¹But Jehosheba, a royal princess, secretly took Ahaziah's son Joash from among the king's sons who were about to be slain, and put him and his nurse in a bedroom. In this way Jehosheba, who was the daughter of King Jehoram, a sister of Ahaziah, and wife of Jehoiada the priest, hid the child from Athaliah's sight, so that she did not put him to death. ¹²For six years he remained hidden with them in the house of God, while Athaliah ruled over the land.

2 Chronicles Chapter 23

¹In the seventh year, Jehoiada took courage and entered a conspiracy with certain captains: Azariah, son of Jehoram; Ishmael, son of Jehohanan; Azariah, son of Obed; Masseiah, son of Adaiah; and Elishaphat, son of Zichri. ²They journeyed about Judah, gathering the Levites from all the cities of Judah and also the heads of the Israelite families. When they had come to Jerusalem, ³the whole assembly made a covenant with the king in the house of God. Jehoiada said to them: "Here is the king's son who must reign, as the LORD promised concerning the sons of David. ⁴This is what you must do: a third of your number, both priests and Levites, who come in on the sabbath must guard the thresholds, ⁵another third must be at the king's palace, and the final third at the Foundation Gate, when all the people will be in the courts of the LORD'S temple. ⁶Let no one enter the LORD'S house except the priests and those Levites who are ministering. They may enter because they are holy; but all the other people must observe the prescriptions of the LORD. ⁷The Levites shall surround the king on all sides, each with his weapon drawn. Whoever tries to enter the house must be slain. Stay with the king wherever he goes." ⁸The Levites and all Judah did just as Jehoiada the priest commanded. Each brought his men, those who were to come in on the sabbath as well as those who were to depart on the sabbath, since Jehoiada the priest had not dismissed any of the divisions. ⁹Jehoiada the priest gave the captains the spears, shields and bucklers of King David which were in the house of God. ¹⁰He stationed all the people, each with his spear in hand, from the southern to the northern extremity of the enclosure, around the altar and the temple on the king's behalf. ¹¹Then they brought out the king's son, set the crown and the insignia upon him, and made him king. Jehoiada and his sons anointed him, and they cried, "Long live the king!" ¹²When Athaliah heard the din of the people running and acclaiming the king, she went to the people in the temple of the LORD. ¹³She looked, and there was the king standing beside his pillar at the entrance, the officers and the trumpeters around him, and all the people of the land rejoicing and blowing trumpets, while the singers with their musical instruments were leading the acclaim. Athaliah tore her garments and cried out, "Treason! treason!" ¹⁴Then Jehoiada the priest sent out the captains who were in command of the army; he said to them: "Take her outside through the ranks, and if anyone tries to follow her, let him die by the sword. For," the priest continued, "you must not put her to death in the LORD'S temple." ¹⁵So they seized her, and when she arrived at the entrance to the Horse Gate of the palace, they put her to death there. ¹⁶Then Jehoiada made a covenant between himself and all the people and the king, that they should be the LORD'S people. ¹⁷And all the people went to the temple of Baal and tore it down. They smashed its altars and images, and they slew Mattan, the priest of Baal, before the altars. ¹⁸Then Jehoiada gave the charge of the LORD'S temple into the hands of the levitical priests, to whom David had assigned turns in the temple for offering the holocausts of the LORD, as is written in the law of Moses, with rejoicing and song, as David had provided. ¹⁹Moreover, he stationed guards at the gates of the LORD'S temple so that no one unclean in any respect might enter. ²⁰Then he took the captains, the nobles, the rulers among the people, and all the people of the land, and led the king out of the LORD'S house. When they had come within the upper gate of the king's house, they seated the king upon the royal throne. ²¹All the people of the land rejoiced and the city was quiet, now that Athaliah had been put to death by the sword.

2 Chronicles Chapter 24

¹Joash was seven years old when he became king, and he reigned forty years in Jerusalem. His mother, named Zibiah, was from Beer-sheba. ²Joash did what was pleasing to the LORD as long as Jehoiada the priest lived. ³Jehoiada provided him with two wives, and he became the father of sons and daughters. ⁴After some time, Joash decided to restore the LORD'S temple. ⁵He called together the priests and Levites and said to them: "Go out to all the cities of Judah and collect money

from all Israel that you may repair the house of your God over the years. You must hasten this affair." But the Levites did not hasten. 6Then the king summoned Jehoiada, who was in charge, and said to him: "Why have you not required the Levites to bring in from Judah and Jerusalem the tax levied by Moses, the servant of the LORD, and by the assembly of Israel, for the tent of the testimony?" 7For the wicked Athaliah and her sons had damaged the house of God and had even turned over to the Baals the dedicated resources of the LORD'S temple. 8At the king's command, therefore, they made a chest, which they put outside the gate of the LORD'S temple. 9They had it proclaimed throughout Judah and Jerusalem that the tax which Moses, the servant of God, had imposed on Israel in the desert should be brought to the LORD. 10All the princes and the people rejoiced; they brought what was asked and cast it into the chest until it was filled. 11Whenever the chest was brought to the royal officials by the Levites and they saw that it contained much money, the royal scribe and an overseer for the high priest came, emptied the chest, then took it back and returned it to its place. This they did day after day until they had collected a large sum of money. 12Then the king and Jehoiada gave it to the workmen in charge of the labor on the LORD'S temple, who hired masons and carpenters to restore the temple, and also iron- and bronze-smiths to repair it. 13The workmen labored, and the task of restoration progressed under their hands. They restored the house of God according to its original form, and reinforced it. 14After they had finished, they brought the rest of the money to the king and to Jehoiada, who had it made into utensils for the LORD'S temple, utensils for the service and the holocausts, and basins and other gold and silver utensils. They offered holocausts in the LORD'S temple continually throughout the lifetime of Jehoiada. 15Jehoiada lived to a ripe old age; he was a hundred and thirty years old when he died. 16He was buried in the City of David with the kings, because he had done good in Israel, in particular with respect to God and his temple. 17After the death of Jehoiada, the princes of Judah came and paid homage to the king, and the king then listened to them. 18They forsook the temple of the LORD, the God of their fathers, and began to serve the sacred poles and the idols; and because of this crime of theirs, wrath came upon Judah and Jerusalem. 19Although prophets were sent to them to convert them to the LORD, the people would not listen to their warnings. 20Then the spirit of God possessed Zechariah, son of Jehoiada the priest. He took his stand above the people and said to them: "God says, 'Why are you transgressing the LORD'S commands, so that you cannot prosper? Because you have abandoned the LORD, he has abandoned you.'" 21But they conspired against him, and at the king's order they stoned him to death in the court of the LORD'S temple. 22Thus King Joash was unmindful of the devotion shown him by Jehoiada, Zechariah's father, and slew his son. And as he was dying, he said, "May the LORD see and avenge." 23At the turn of the year a force of Arameans came up against Joash. They invaded Judah and Jerusalem, did away with all the princes of the people, and sent all their spoil to the king of Damascus. 24Though the Aramean force came with few men, the LORD surrendered a very large force into their power, because Judah had abandoned the LORD, the God of their fathers. So punishment was meted out to Joash. 25After the Arameans had departed from him, leaving him in grievous suffering, his servants conspired against him because of the murder of the son of Jehoiada the priest. They killed him on his sickbed. He was buried in the City of David, but not in the tombs of the kings. 26These conspired against him: Zabad, son of Shimeath from Ammon, and Jehozabad, son of Shimrith from Moab. 27Of his sons, and the great tribute imposed on him, and of his rebuilding of the house of God, there is a written account in the midrash of the book of the kings. His son Amaziah succeeded him as king.

2 Chronicles Chapter 25

1Amaziah was twenty-five years old when he became king, and he reigned twenty-nine years in Jerusalem. His mother, named Jehoaddan, was from Jerusalem. 2He did what was pleasing in the sight of the LORD, though not wholeheartedly. 3After he had strengthened his hold on the kingdom, he slew those of his servants who had killed the king, his father; 4but he did not put their children to death, for he acted according to what is written in the law, in the Book of Moses, as the LORD commanded: "Fathers shall not be put to death for their children, nor children for their fathers; but only for his own guilt shall a man be put to death." 5Amaziah mustered Judah and placed them, out of all Judah and Benjamin according to their ancestral houses, under leaders of thousands and of hundreds. When he had counted those of twenty years and over, he found them to be three hundred thousand picked men fit for war, capable of handling lance and shield. 6He also hired a hundred thousand valiant warriors from Israel for a hundred talents of silver. 7But a man of God came to him and said: "O

king, let not the army of Israel go with you, for the LORD is not with Israel, with any Ephraimite. 8Instead, go on your own, strongly prepared for the conflict; otherwise the LORD will defeat you in the face of the enemy. It is God who has the power to reinforce or to defeat." 9Amaziah answered the man of God, "But what is to be done about the hundred talents that I paid for the troops of Israel?" The man of God replied, "The LORD can give you much more than that." 10Amaziah then disbanded the troops that had come to him from Ephraim, and sent them home. They, however, became furiously angry with Judah, and returned home blazing with resentment. 11Amaziah now assumed command of his army. They proceeded to the Valley of Salt, and there they killed ten thousand men of Seir. 12The Judahites also brought back another ten thousand alive, whom they led to the summit of the Rock and then cast down, so that they were all crushed. 13Meanwhile, the mercenaries whom Amaziah had dismissed from battle service with him raided the cities of Judah from Samaria to Beth-horon. They killed three thousand of the inhabitants and took away much booty. 14When Amaziah returned from his conquest of the Edomites he brought back with him the gods of the people of Seir, which he set up as his own gods; he bowed down before them and offered sacrifice to them. 15Then the anger of the LORD blazed out against Amaziah, and he sent a prophet to him who said: "Why have you had recourse to this people's gods that could not save their own people from your hand?" 16While he was still speaking, however, the king said to him: "Have you been made the king's counselor? Be silent! Why should it be necessary to kill you?" Therefore the prophet desisted. "I know, however," he said, "that God has let you take counsel to your own destruction, because you have done this thing and have refused to hear my counsel." 17Having taken counsel, King Amaziah of Judah sent messengers to Joash, son of Jehoahaz, son of Jehu, king of Israel, saying, "Come, let us meet each other face to face." 18King Joash of Israel sent this reply to King Amaziah of Judah: "The thistle of the Lebanon sent a message to the cedar of the Lebanon, saying, 'Give your daughter to my son for his wife.' But the wild beasts of the Lebanon passed by and trampled the thistle down. 19You are thinking, 'See, I have beaten Edom!', and thus ambition makes you proud. Remain at home. Why involve yourself, and Judah with you, in misfortune and failure?" 20But Amaziah would not listen, for God had determined to hand them over because they had had recourse to the gods of Edom. 21Therefore King Joash of Israel advanced and he and King Amaziah met in battle at Beth-shemesh of Judah. 22There Judah was defeated by Israel, and all the Judean soldiers fled homeward. 23King Joash of Israel captured Amaziah, king of Judah, son of Joash, son of Jehoahaz, at Beth-shemesh and brought him to Jerusalem. Then he tore down the wall of Jerusalem from the Ephraim Gate to the Corner Gate, a distance of four hundred cubits. 24He took away all the gold and silver and all the vessels he found in the house of God with Obed-edom, together with the treasures of the palace, and hostages as well. Then he returned to Samaria. 25Amaziah, son of Joash, king of Judah, survived Joash, son of Jehoahaz, king of Israel, by fifteen years. 26The rest of the acts of Amaziah, first and last, can be found written, as is well known, in the book of the kings of Judah and Israel. 27Now from the time that Amaziah ceased to follow the LORD, a conspiracy was formed against him in Jerusalem; hence he fled to Lachish. But they pursued him to Lachish and put him to death there. 28They brought him back on horses and buried him with his ancestors in the City of Judah.

2 Chronicles Chapter 26

1All the people of Judah chose Uzziah, though he was but sixteen years of age, and proclaimed him king to succeed his father Amaziah. 2 He rebuilt Elath and restored it to Judah; this was after King Amaziah had gone to rest with his ancestors. 3 Uzziah was sixteen years old when he became king, and he reigned fifty-two years in Jerusalem. His mother, named Jecoliah, was from Jerusalem. 4 He pleased the LORD, just as his father Amaziah had done. 5 He was prepared to seek God as long as Zechariah lived, who taught him to fear God; and as long as he sought the LORD, God made him prosper. 6 He went out and fought the Philistines and razed the walls of Gath, Jabneh, and Ashdod (and built cities in the district of Ashdod and in Philistia). 7 God helped him against the Philistines, against the Arabs who dwelt in Gurbaal, and against the Meunites. 8 The Ammonites paid tribute to Uzziah and his fame spread as far as Egypt, for he grew stronger and stronger. 9 Moreover, Uzziah built towers in Jerusalem at the Corner Gate, at the Valley Gate, and at the Angle, and he fortified them. 10 He built towers in the desert and dug numerous cisterns, for he had many cattle. He had plowmen in the foothills and the plains, and vinedressers in the highlands and the garden land. He was a lover of the soil. 11 Uzziah also had a standing army of fit soldiers divided into bands according to the number in which they were mustered by Jeiel the scribe and Maaseiah the recorder, under the command of Hananiah, one of the king's officials.¹² The entire number of family heads over these valiant warriors was two thousand six hundred,¹³ and at their disposal was a mighty army of three hundred seven thousand five hundred fighting men of great valor to help the king against his enemies.¹⁴ Uzziah provided for them—for the entire army—bucklers, lances, helmets, breastplates, bows, and slingstones.¹⁵ He also built machines in Jerusalem, devices contrived to stand on the towers and at the angles of the walls to shoot arrows and cast large stones. His fame spread far and wide, and his power was ascribed to the marvelous help he had received.¹⁶ But after he had become strong, he became proud to his own destruction and broke faith with the LORD, his God. He entered the temple of the LORD to make an offering on the altar of incense.¹⁷ But Azariah the priest, and with him eighty other priests of the LORD, courageous men, followed him.¹⁸ They opposed King Uzziah, saying to him: "It is not for you, Uzziah, to burn incense to the LORD, but for the priests, the sons of Aaron, who have been consecrated for this purpose. Leave the sanctuary, for you have broken faith and no longer have a part in the glory that comes from the LORD God."¹⁹ Uzziah, who was holding a censer for burning the incense, became angry, but at the moment he showed his anger to the priests, while they were looking at him in the house of the LORD beside the altar of incense, leprosy broke out on his forehead.²⁰ Azariah the chief priest and all the other priests examined him, and when they saw that his forehead was leprous, they expelled him from the temple. He himself fled willingly, for the LORD had afflicted him.²¹ King Uzziah remained a leper to the day of his death. As a leper he dwelt in a segregated house, for he was excluded from the house of the LORD. Therefore his son Jotham was regent of the palace and ruled the people of the land.²² The prophet Isaiah, son of Amos, wrote the rest of the acts of Uzziah, first and last.²³ Uzziah rested with his ancestors; he was buried with them in the field adjoining the royal cemetery, for they said, "He was a leper." His son Jotham succeeded him as king.

2 Chronicles Chapter 27

¹ Jotham was twenty-five years old when he became king, and he reigned sixteen years in Jerusalem. His mother was named Jerusa, daughter of Zadok. ² He pleased the LORD just as his father Uzziah had done, though he did not enter the temple of the LORD; the people, however, continued to act sinfully. ³ He built the upper gate of the LORD'S house and had much construction done on the wall of Ophel. ⁴ Moreover, he built cities in the hill country of Judah, and in the forest land he set up fortresses and towers. ⁵ He fought with the king of the Ammonites and conquered them. That year the Ammonites paid him one hundred talents of silver, together with ten thousand kors of wheat and ten thousand of barley. They brought the same to him also in the second and in the third year. ⁶ Thus Jotham continued to grow strong because he lived resolutely in the presence of the LORD, his God. ⁷ The rest of the acts of Jotham, his wars and his activities, can be found written in the book of the kings of Israel and Judah. ⁸ He was twenty-five years old when he became king, and he reigned sixteen years in Jerusalem. ⁹ Jotham rested with his ancestors and was buried in the City of David, and his son Ahaz succeeded him as king.

2 Chronicles Chapter 28

¹ Ahaz was twenty years old when he became king, and he reigned sixteen years in Jerusalem. He did not please the LORD as his forefather David had done, ² but conducted himself like the kings of Israel and even made molten idols of the Baals. ³ Moreover, he offered sacrifice in the Valley of Ben-hinnom, and immolated his sons by fire according to the abominable practice of the nations which the LORD had cleared out before the Israelites. ⁴ He offered sacrifice and incense on the high places, on hills, and under every leafy tree. ⁵ Therefore the LORD, his God, delivered him into the power of the king of Aram. The Arameans defeated him and carried away captive a large number of his people, whom they brought to Damascus. He was also delivered into the power of the king of Israel, who defeated him with great slaughter. ⁶ For Pekah, son of Remaliah, slew one hundred and twenty thousand of Judah in a single day, all of them valiant men, because they had abandoned the LORD, the God of their fathers. ⁷ Zichri, an Ephraimite warrior, killed Maaseiah, the king's son, and Azrikam, the master of the palace, and also Elkanah, who was second to the king. ⁸ The Israelites took away as captives two hundred thousand of their brethren's wives, sons and daughters; they also took from them much plunder, which they brought to Samaria. ⁹ In Samaria there was a prophet of the LORD by the name of Oded. He went out to meet the army returning to Samaria and said to them: "It was because the LORD, the God of your fathers, was angry with Judah that he delivered them into your hands. You, however, have slaughtered them with a fury that has reached up to

heaven. ¹⁰ And now you are planning to make the children of Judah and Jerusalem your slaves and bondwomen. Are not you yourselves, therefore, guilty of a crime against the LORD, your God? ¹¹ Now listen to me: send back the captives you have carried off from among your brethren, for the burning anger of the LORD is upon you." ¹² At this, some of the Ephraimite leaders, Azariah, son of Johanan, Berechiah, son of Meshillemoth, Jehizkiah, son of Shallum, and Amasa, son of Hadlai, themselves stood up in opposition to those who had returned from the war. ¹³ They said to them: "Do not bring the captives here, for what you propose will make us guilty before the LORD and increase our sins and our guilt. Our guilt is already great, and there is a burning anger upon Israel." ¹⁴ Therefore the soldiers left their captives and the plunder before the princes and the whole assembly. ¹⁵ Then the men just named proceeded to help the captives. All of them who were naked they clothed from the booty; they clothed them, put sandals on their feet, gave them food and drink, anointed them, and all who were weak they set on asses. They brought them to Jericho, the city of palms, to their brethren. Then they returned to Samaria. ¹⁶ At that time King Ahaz sent an appeal for help to the kings of Assyria. ¹⁷ The Edomites had returned, attacked Judah, and carried off captives. ¹⁸ The Philistines too had raided the cities of the foothills and the Negeb of Judah; they captured Beth-shemesh, Aijalon, Gederoth, Soco and its dependencies, Timnah and its dependencies, and Gimzo and its dependencies, and occupied them. ¹⁹ For the LORD had brought Judah low because of Ahaz, king of Israel, who let Judah go its own way and proved utterly faithless to the LORD. ²⁰ Tilgath-pilneser, king of Assyria, did indeed come to him, but to oppress him rather than to help him. ²¹ Though Ahaz plundered the LORD'S house and the houses of the king and the princes to make payment to the king of Assyria, it availed him nothing. ²² While he was already in distress, the same King Ahaz became even more unfaithful to the LORD. ²³ He sacrificed to the gods of Damascus who had defeated him, saying, "Since it was the gods of the kings of Aram who helped them, I will sacrifice to them that they may help me also." However, they only caused further disaster to him and to all Israel. ²⁴ Ahaz gathered up the utensils of God's house and broke them in pieces. He closed the doors of the LORD'S house and had altars made for himself in every corner of Jerusalem. ²⁵ In every city throughout Judah he set up high places to offer sacrifice to other gods. Thus he angered the LORD, the God of his fathers. ²⁶ The rest of his deeds and his activities, first and last, can be found written in the book of the kings of Judah and Israel. ²⁷ Ahaz rested with his ancestors and was buried in Jerusalem - in the city, for they did not bring him to the tombs of the kings of Israel. His son Hezekiah succeeded him as king.

2 Chronicles Chapter 29

¹ Hezekiah was twenty-five years old when he became king, and he reigned twenty-nine years in Jerusalem. His mother was named Abia, daughter of Zechariah. ² He pleased the LORD just as his forefather David had done. ³ It was he who, in the first month of the first year of his reign, opened the doors of the LORD'S house and repaired them. ⁴ He summoned the priests and Levites, gathered them in the open space to the east, ⁵ and said to them: "Listen to me, you Levites! Sanctify yourselves now and sanctify the house of the LORD, the God of your fathers, and clean out the filth from the sanctuary. ⁶ Our fathers acted faithlessly and did evil in the eyes of the LORD, our God. They abandoned him, turned away their faces from the LORD'S dwelling, and turned their backs on him. ⁷ They also closed the doors of the vestibule, extinguished the lamps, and refused to burn incense and offer holocausts in the sanctuary to the honor of the God of Israel. ⁸ Therefore the anger of the LORD has come upon Judah and Jerusalem; he has made them an object of terror, astonishment and mockery, as you see with your own eyes. ⁹ For our fathers, as you know, fell by the sword, and our sons, our daughters and our wives have been taken captive because of this. ¹⁰ Now, I intend to make a covenant with the LORD, the God of Israel, that his burning anger may withdraw from us. ¹¹ My sons, be not negligent any longer, for it is you whom the LORD has chosen to stand before him, to minister to him, to be his ministers and to offer incense." ¹² Then the Levites arose: Mahath, son of Amasai, and Joel, son of Azariah, descendants of the Kohathites; of the sons of Merari: Kish, son of Abdi, and Azariah, son of Jehallel; of the Gershonites: Joah, son of Zimmah, and Eden, son of Joah; ¹³ of the sons of Elizaphan: Shimri and Jeuel; of the sons of Asaph: Zechariah and Mattaniah; ¹⁴ of the sons of Heman: Jehuel and Shimei; of the sons of Jeduthun: Shemiah and Uzziel. ¹⁵ They gathered their brethren together and sanctified themselves; then they came as the king had ordered, to cleanse the LORD'S house in keeping with his words. ¹⁶ The priests entered the interior of the LORD'S house to cleanse it; and whatever they found in the LORD'S temple that was unclean they brought out to the court of the LORD'S house, where the Levites took it

from them and carried it out to the Kidron Valley. 17 They began the work of consecration on the first day of the first month, and on the eighth day of the month they arrived at the vestibule of the LORD; they consecrated the LORD'S house during eight days, and on the sixteenth day of the first month, they had finished. 18 Then they went inside to King Hezekiah and said: "We have cleansed the entire house of the LORD, the altar of holocausts with all its utensils, and the table for the showbread with all its utensils. 19 All the articles which King Ahaz during his reign had thrown away because of his apostasy, we have restored and consecrated, and they are now before the LORD'S altar." 20 Then King Hezekiah hastened to convoke the princes of the city and went up to the LORD'S house. 21 Seven bulls, seven rams, seven lambs and seven he-goats were brought for a sin offering for the kingdom, for the sanctuary, and for Judah, and he ordered the sons of Aaron, the priests, to offer them on the altar of the LORD. 22 They slaughtered the bulls, and the priests collected the blood and cast it on the altar. Then they slaughtered the rams and cast the blood on the altar; then they slaughtered the lambs and cast the blood on the altar. 23 Then the he-goats for the sin offering were led before the king and the assembly, who laid their hands upon them. 24 The priests then slaughtered them and offered their blood on the altar to atone for the sin of all Israel; for "The holocaust and the sin offering," the king had said, "is for all Israel." 25 He stationed the Levites in the LORD'S house with cymbals, harps and lyres according to the prescriptions of David, of Gad the king's seer, and of Nathan the prophet; for the prescriptions were from the LORD through his prophets. 26 The Levites were stationed with the instruments of David, and the priests with the trumpets. 27 Then Hezekiah ordered the holocaust to be sacrificed on the altar, and in the same instant that the holocaust began, they also began the song of the LORD, to the accompaniment of the trumpets and the instruments of David, king of Israel. 28 The entire assembly prostrated itself, and they continued to sing the song and to sound the trumpets until the holocaust had been completed. 29 As the holocaust was completed, the king and all who were with him knelt and prostrated themselves. 30 King Hezekiah and the princes then commanded the Levites to sing the praises of the LORD in the words of David and of Asaph the seer. They sang praises till their joy was full, then fell down and prostrated themselves. 31 Hezekiah now spoke out this command: "You have undertaken a work for the LORD. Approach, and bring forward the sacrifices and thank offerings for the house of the LORD." Then the assembly brought forward the sacrifices and thank offerings and all the holocausts which were free-will offerings. 32 The number of holocausts that the assembly brought forward was seventy oxen, one hundred rams, and two hundred lambs: all of these as a holocaust to the LORD. 33 As consecrated gifts there were six hundred oxen and three thousand sheep. 34 Since the priests were too few in number to be able to skin all the victims for the holocausts, their brethren the Levites assisted them until the task was completed and the priests had sanctified themselves; the Levites, in fact, were more willing than the priests to sanctify themselves. 35 Also, the holocausts were many, along with the fat of the peace offerings and the libations for the holocausts. Thus the service of the house of the LORD was reestablished. 36 Hezekiah and all the people rejoiced over what God had reestablished for the people, and at how suddenly this had been done.

2 Chronicles Chapter 30

1 Hezekiah sent a message to all Israel and Judah, and even wrote letters to Ephraim and Manasseh saying that they should come to the house of the LORD in Jerusalem to celebrate the Passover in honor of the LORD, the God of Israel. 2 The king, his princes, and the entire assembly in Jerusalem had agreed to celebrate the Passover during the second month, 3 for they could not celebrate it at the time of the restoration: the priests had not sanctified themselves in sufficient numbers, and the people were not gathered at Jerusalem. 4 When this proposal had been approved by the king and the entire assembly, 5 they issued a decree to be proclaimed throughout all Israel from Beer-sheba to Dan, that everyone should come to Jerusalem to celebrate the Passover in honor of the LORD, the God of Israel; for not many had kept it in the manner prescribed. 6 Accordingly the couriers, with the letters written by the king and his princes, traversed all Israel and Judah, and at the king's command they said: "Israelites, return to the LORD, the God of Abraham, Isaac and Israel, that he may return to you, the remnant left from the hands of the Assyrian kings. 7 Be not like your fathers and your brethren who proved faithless to the LORD, the God of their fathers, so that he delivered them over to desolation, as you yourselves now see. 8 Be not obstinate, as your fathers were; extend your hands to the LORD and come to his sanctuary that he has consecrated forever, and serve the LORD, your God, that he may turn away his burning anger from you. 9 For when you return to the LORD,

your brethren and your children will find mercy with their captors and return to this land; for merciful and compassionate is the LORD, your God, and he will not turn away his face from you if you return to him." 10 So the couriers passed from city to city in the land of Ephraim and Manasseh and as far as Zebulun, but they were derided and scoffed at. 11 Nevertheless, some from Asher, Manasseh and Zebulun humbled themselves and came to Jerusalem. 12 In Judah, however, the power of God brought it about that the people were of one mind to carry out the command of the king and the princes in accordance with the word of the LORD. 13 Thus many people gathered in Jerusalem to celebrate the feast of Unleavened Bread in the second month; it was a very great assembly. 14 They proceeded to take down the altars that were in Jerusalem; also they removed all the altars of incense and cast them into the Kidron Valley. 15 They slaughtered the Passover on the fourteenth day of the second month. The priests and Levites, touched with shame, sanctified themselves and brought holocausts into the house of the LORD. 16 They stood in the places prescribed for them according to the law of Moses, the man of God. The priests sprinkled the blood given them by the Levites; 17 for many in the assembly had not sanctified themselves, and the Levites were in charge of slaughtering the Passover victims for all who were unclean and therefore could not consecrate them to the LORD. 18 The greater part of the people, in fact, chiefly from Ephraim, Manasseh, Issachar and Zebulun, had not cleansed themselves. Nevertheless they ate the Passover, contrary to the prescription; for Hezekiah prayed for them, saying, "May the LORD, who is good, grant pardon to 19 everyone who has resolved to seek God, the LORD, the God of his fathers, though he be not clean as holiness requires." 20 The LORD heard Hezekiah and spared the people. 21 Thus the Israelites who were in Jerusalem celebrated the feast of Unleavened Bread with great rejoicing for seven days, and the Levites and the priests sang the praises of the LORD day after day with all their strength. 22 Hezekiah spoke encouragingly to all the Levites who had shown themselves well skilled in the service of the LORD. And when they had completed the seven days of festival, slaying peace offerings and singing praises to the LORD, the God of their fathers, 23 the whole assembly agreed to celebrate another seven days. With joy, therefore, they continued the festivity seven days longer. 24 King Hezekiah of Judah had contributed a thousand bulls and seven thousand sheep to the assembly, and the princes had contributed to the assembly a thousand bulls and ten thousand sheep. The priests sanctified themselves in great numbers, 25 and the whole assembly of Judah rejoiced, together with the priests and Levites and the rest of the assembly that had come from Israel, as well as the sojourners from the land of Israel and those that lived in Judah. 26 There was great rejoicing in Jerusalem, for since the days of Solomon, son of David, king of Israel, there had not been the like in the city. 27 Then the levitical priests rose and blessed the people; their voice was heard and their prayer reached heaven, God's holy dwelling.

2 Chronicles Chapter 31

1 After all this was over, those Israelites who had been present went forth to the cities of Judah and smashed the sacred pillars, cut down the sacred poles, and tore down the high places and altars throughout Judah, Benjamin, Ephraim and Manasseh, until all were destroyed. Then the Israelites returned to their various cities, each to his own possession. 2 Hezekiah reestablished the classes of the priests and the Levites according to their former classification, assigning to each priest and Levite his proper service, whether in regard to holocausts or peace offerings, thanksgiving or praise, or ministering in the gates of the encampment of the LORD. 3 From his own wealth the king allotted a portion for holocausts, those of morning and evening and those on sabbaths, new moons and festivals, as prescribed in the law of the LORD. 4 He also commanded the people living in Jerusalem to provide the support of the priests and Levites, that they might devote themselves entirely to the law of the LORD. 5 As soon as the order was promulgated, the Israelites brought, in great quantities, the best of their grain, wine, oil and honey, and all the produce of the fields; they gave a generous tithe of everything. 6 Israelites and Judahites living in other cities of Judah also brought in tithes of oxen, sheep, and things that had been consecrated to the LORD, their God; these they brought in and set out in heaps. 7 It was in the third month that they began to establish these heaps, and they completed them in the seventh month. 8 When Hezekiah and the princes had come and seen the heaps, they blessed the LORD and his people Israel. 9 Then Hezekiah questioned the priests and the Levites concerning the heaps, 10 and the priest Azariah, head of the house of Zadoc, answered him, "Since they began to bring the offerings to the house of the LORD, we have eaten to the full and have had much left over, for the LORD has blessed his people. This great supply is what was left over." 11 Hezekiah then gave orders that

chambers be constructed in the house of the LORD. When this had been done, 12 the offerings, tithes and consecrated things were deposited there in safekeeping. The overseer of these things was Conaniah the Levite, and his brother Shimei was second in charge. 13 Jehiel, Azaziah, Nahath, Asahel, Jerimoth, Jozabad, Eliel, Ismachiah, Mahath and Benaiah were supervisors subject to Conaniah and his brother Shimei by appointment of King Hezekiah and of Azariah, the prefect of the house of God. 14 Kore, the son of Imnah, a Levite and the keeper of the eastern gate, was in charge of the free-will gifts made to God; he distributed the offerings made to the LORD and the most holy of the consecrated things. 15 Under him in the priestly cities were Eden, Miniamin, Jeshua, Shemaiah, Amariah and Shecaniah, who faithfully made the distribution to their brethren, great and small alike, according to their classes. 16 There was also a register by ancestral houses of males thirty years of age and over, for all priests who were eligible to enter the house of the LORD according to the daily rule to fulfill their service in the order of their classes. 17 The priests were inscribed in their family records according to their ancestral houses, and the Levites of twenty years and over according to their various offices and classes. 18 A distribution was also made to all who were inscribed in the family records, for their little ones, wives, sons and daughters - thus for the entire assembly, since they were to sanctify themselves by sharing faithfully in the consecrated things. 19 The sons of Aaron, the priests who lived on the lands attached to their cities, had in every city men designated by name to distribute portions to every male among the priests and to every Levite listed in the family records. 20 This Hezekiah did in all Judah. He did what was good, upright and faithful before the LORD, his God. 21 Everything that he undertook, for the service of the house of God or for the law and the commandments, was to do the will of his God. He did this wholeheartedly, and he prospered.

2 Chronicles Chapter 32

1 But after he had proved his fidelity by such deeds, Sennacherib, king of Assyria, came. He invaded Judah, besieged the fortified cities, and proposed to take them by storm. 2 When Hezekiah saw that Sennacherib was coming with the intention of attacking Jerusalem, 3 he decided in counsel with his princes and warriors to stop the waters of the springs outside the city. When they had pledged him their support, 4 a large crowd was gathered which stopped all the springs and also the running stream in the valley nearby. For they said, "Why should the kings of Assyria come and find an abundance of water?" 5 He then looked to his defenses: he rebuilt the wall where it was broken down, raised towers upon it, and built another wall outside. He strengthened the Millo of the City of David and had a great number of spears and shields prepared. 6 Then he appointed army commanders over the people. He gathered them together in his presence in the open space at the gate of the city and encouraged them with these words: 7 "Be brave and steadfast; do not be afraid or dismayed because of the king of Assyria and all the throng that is coming with him, for there is more with us than with him. 8 For he has only an arm of flesh, but we have the LORD, our God, to help us and to fight our battles." And the people took confidence from the words of King Hezekiah of Judah. 9 After this, while Sennacherib, king of Assyria, himself remained at Lachish with all his forces, he sent his officials to Jerusalem with this message for King Hezekiah of Judah, and all the Judahites who were in Jerusalem: 10 "King Sennacherib of Assyria has this to say: On what are you relying, while you remain under siege in Jerusalem? 11 Has not Hezekiah deceived you, delivering you over to a death of famine and thirst, by his claim that 'the LORD, our God, will save us from the grasp of the king of Assyria'? 12 Has not this same Hezekiah removed his high places and altars and commanded Judah and Jerusalem, 'You shall prostrate yourselves before one altar only, and on it alone you shall offer incense'? 13 Do you not know what my fathers and I have done to all the peoples of other lands? Were the gods of the nations in those lands able to save their lands from my hand? 14 Who among all the gods of those nations which my fathers put under the ban was able to save his people from my hand? Will your god, then, be able to save you from my hand? 15 Let not Hezekiah mislead you further and deceive you in any such way. Do not believe him! Since no other god of any other nation or kingdom has been able to save his people from my hand or the hands of my fathers, how much the less shall your god save you from my hand!" 16 His officials said still more against the LORD God and against his servant Hezekiah, 17 for he had written letters to deride the LORD, the God of Israel, speaking of him in these terms: "As the gods of the nations in other lands have not saved their people from my hand, neither shall Hezekiah's god save his people from my hand." 18 In a loud voice they shouted in the Judean language to the people of Jerusalem who were on the wall, to frighten and terrify them so that they might capture their city. 19 They spoke of the God of Israel as though he were one of the gods of the other peoples of the earth, a work of human hands. 20 But because of this, King Hezekiah and the prophet Isaiah, son of Amos, prayed and called out to heaven. 21 Then the LORD sent an angel, who destroyed every valiant warrior, leader and commander in the camp of the Assyrian king, so that he had to return shamefaced to his own country. And when he entered the temple of his god, some of his own offspring struck him down there with the sword. 22 Thus the LORD saved Hezekiah and the inhabitants of Jerusalem from the hand of Sennacherib, king of Assyria, as from every other power; he gave them rest on every side. 23 Many brought gifts for the LORD to Jerusalem and costly objects for King Hezekiah of Judah, who thereafter was exalted in the eyes of all the nations. 24 In those days Hezekiah became mortally ill. He prayed to the LORD, who answered him by giving him a sign. 25 Hezekiah, however, did not then discharge his debt of gratitude, for he had become proud. Therefore anger descended upon him and upon Judah and Jerusalem. 26 But then Hezekiah humbled himself for his pride - both he and the inhabitants of Jerusalem; and therefore the LORD did not vent his anger on them during the time of Hezekiah. 27 Hezekiah possessed very great wealth and glory. He had treasuries made for his silver, gold, precious stones, spices, jewels, and other precious things of all kinds; 28 also storehouses for the harvest of grain, for wine and oil, and barns for the various kinds of cattle and for the flocks. 29 He built cities for himself, and he acquired sheep and oxen in great numbers, for God gave him very great riches. 30 This same Hezekiah stopped the upper outflow of water from Gihon and led it underground westward to the City of David. Hezekiah prospered in all his undertakings. 31 Nevertheless, in respect to the ambassadors (princes) sent to him from Babylon to investigate the sign that had occurred in the land, God forsook him to test him, that he might know all that was in his heart. 32 The rest of Hezekiah's acts, including his pious works, can be found written in the Vision of the Prophet Isaiah, son of Amos, and in the book of the kings of Judah and Israel. 33 Hezekiah rested with his ancestors; he was buried at the approach to the tombs of the descendants of David. All Judah and the inhabitants of Jerusalem paid him honor at his death. His son Manasseh succeeded him as king.

2 Chronicles Chapter 33

1 Manasseh was twelve years old when he became king, and he reigned fifty-five years in Jerusalem. 2 He did evil in the sight of the LORD, following the abominable practices of the nations whom the LORD had cleared out of the way of the Israelites. 3 He rebuilt the high places which his father Hezekiah had torn down, erected altars for the Baals, made sacred poles, and prostrated himself before the whole host of heaven and worshiped them. 4 He even built altars in the temple of the LORD, of which the LORD had said, "In Jerusalem shall my name be forever": 5 he built altars to the whole host of heaven in the two courts of the LORD'S house. 6 It was he, too, who immolated his sons by fire in the Valley of Ben-hinnom. He practiced augury, divination and magic, and appointed necromancers and diviners of spirits, so that he provoked the LORD with the great evil that he did in his sight. 7 He placed an idol that he had carved in the house of God, of which God had said to David and his son Solomon: "In this house and in Jerusalem which I have chosen from all the tribes of Israel I shall place my name forever. 8 I will not again allow Israel's feet to leave the land which I assigned to your fathers, provided they are careful to observe all that I commanded them, keeping the whole law and the statutes and the ordinances given by Moses." 9 Manasseh misled Judah and the inhabitants of Jerusalem into doing even greater evil than the nations which the LORD had destroyed at the coming of the Israelites. 10 The LORD spoke to Manasseh and his people, but they paid no attention. 11 Therefore the LORD brought against them the army commanders of the Assyrian king; they took Manasseh with hooks, shackled him with chains, and transported him to Babylon. 12 In this distress, he began to appease the LORD, his God. He humbled himself abjectly before the God of his fathers 13 and prayed to him. The LORD let himself be won over: he heard his prayer and restored him to his kingdom in Jerusalem. Then Manasseh understood that the LORD is indeed God. 14 Afterward he built an outer wall for the City of David to the west of Gihon in the valley, extending to the Fish Gate and encircling Ophel; he built it very high. He stationed army officers in all the fortified cities of Judah. 15 He removed the foreign gods and the idol from the LORD'S house and all the altars he had built on the mount of the LORD'S house and in Jerusalem, and he cast them outside the city. 16 He restored the altar of the LORD, and sacrificed on it peace offerings and thank offerings, and commanded Judah to serve the LORD, the God of Israel. 17 Though the people continued to sacrifice on the high places, they now did so to the LORD, their God. 18 The rest of the acts of Manasseh, his prayer to his God, and the words of the seers who spoke to him in

the name of the LORD, the God of Israel, can be found written in the chronicles of the kings of Israel. [19] His prayer and how his supplication was heard, all his sins and his infidelity, the sites where he built high places and erected sacred poles and carved images before he humbled himself, all can be found written down in the history of his seers. [20] Manasseh rested with his ancestors and was buried in his own palace. His son Amon succeeded him as king. [21] Amon was twenty-two years old when he became king, and he reigned two years in Jerusalem. [22] He did evil in the sight of the LORD, just as his father Manasseh had done. Amon offered sacrifice to all the idols which his father Manasseh had made, and worshiped them. [23] Moreover, he did not humble himself before the LORD as his father Manasseh had done; on the contrary, Amon only increased his guilt. [24] His servants conspired against him and put him to death in his own house. [25] But the people of the land slew all those who had conspired against King Amon, and then they, the people of the land, made his son Josiah king in his stead.

2 Chronicles Chapter 34

[1] Josiah was eight years old when he became king, and he reigned thirty-one years in Jerusalem. [2] He pleased the LORD, following the path of his ancestor David. [3] In the eighth year of his reign, while he was still a youth, he began to seek after the God of his forefather David, and in his twelfth year he began to purge Judah and Jerusalem of the high places, the sacred poles and the carved and molten images. [4] In his presence, the altars of the Baals were destroyed; the incense stands erected above them were torn down; the sacred poles and the carved and molten images were shattered and beaten into dust, which was strewn over the tombs of those who had sacrificed to them; [5] and the bones of the priests he burned upon their altars. Thus he purged Judah and Jerusalem. [6] He did likewise in the cities of Manasseh, Ephraim, Simeon, and in the ruined villages of the surrounding country as far as Naphtali; [7] he destroyed the altars, broke up the sacred poles and carved images and beat them into dust, and tore down the incense stands throughout the land of Israel. Then he returned to Jerusalem. [8] In the eighteenth year of his reign, in order to cleanse the temple as well as the land, he sent Shaphan, son of Azaliah, Maaseiah, the ruler of the city, and Joah, son of Joahaz, the chamberlain, to restore the house of the LORD, his God. [9] They came to Hilkiah the high priest and turned over the money brought to the house of God which the Levites, the guardians of the threshold, had collected from Manasseh, Ephraim, and all the remnant of Israel, as well as from all of Judah, Benjamin, and the inhabitants of Jerusalem. [10] They turned it over to the master workmen in the house of the LORD, and these in turn used it to pay the workmen in the LORD'S house who were restoring and repairing the temple. [11] They also gave it to the carpenters and the masons to buy hewn stone and timber for the tie beams and rafters of the buildings which the kings of Judah had allowed to fall into ruin. [12] The men worked faithfully at their task; their overseers were Jahath and Obadiah, Levites of the line of Merari, and Zechariah and Meshullam, of the Kohathites, who directed them. All those Levites who were skillful with musical instruments [13] were in charge of the men who carried the burdens, and they directed all the workers in every kind of labor. Some of the other Levites were scribes, officials and gatekeepers. [14] When they brought out the money that had been deposited in the house of the LORD, Hilkiah the priest found the book of the law of the LORD given through Moses. [15] He reported this to Shaphan the scribe, saying, "I have found the book of the law in the house of the LORD." Hilkiah gave the book to Shaphan, [16] who brought it to the king at the same time that he was making his report to him. He said, "Your servants are doing everything that has been entrusted to them; [17] they have turned into bullion the metals deposited in the LORD'S house and have handed it over to the overseers and the workmen." [18] Then Shaphan the scribe announced to the king, "Hilkiah the priest has given me a book." And Shaphan read from it before the king. [19] When the king heard the words of the law, he tore his garments [20] and issued this command to Hilkiah, to Ahikam, son of Shaphan, to Abdon, son of Michah, to Shaphan the scribe, and to Asaiah, the king's servant: [21] "On behalf of myself and those who are left in Israel and Judah, go, consult the LORD concerning the words of the book that has been found. For the anger of the LORD has been set furiously ablaze against us, since our fathers have not kept the word of the LORD and have not done all that is written in this book." [22] Then Hilkiah and the other men from the king went to the prophetess Huldah, the wife of Shallum, son of Tokhath, son of Hasrah, the guardian of the wardrobe; she dwelt in Jerusalem, in the new quarter. They spoke to her as they had been instructed, [23] and she said to them: "Thus says the LORD, the God of Israel: 'Tell the one who sent you to me, [24] The LORD says: I am prepared to bring evil upon this place and upon its inhabitants, all the curses written in the book that has been read before the king of Judah. [25] Because they have abandoned me and

have offered incense to other gods, provoking me by every deed that they have performed, my anger is ablaze against this place and cannot be extinguished.' [26] But to the king of Judah who sent you to consult the LORD, give this response: 'Thus says the LORD, the God of Israel, concerning the threats you have heard: [27] Because you were heartsick and have humbled yourself before God on hearing his words spoken against this place and its inhabitants; because you have humbled yourself before me, have torn your garments, and have wept before me, I in turn have listened - so declares the LORD. [28] I will gather you to your ancestors and you shall be taken to your grave in peace. Your eyes shall not see all the evil I will bring upon this place and upon its inhabitants.'" They brought back this message to the king. [29] The king now convened all the elders of Judah and Jerusalem. [30] He went up to the house of the LORD with all the men of Judah and the inhabitants of Jerusalem, the priests, the Levites, and all the people, great and small; and he had read aloud to them the entire text of the book of the covenant that had been found in the house of the LORD. [31] Standing at his post, the king made a covenant before the LORD to follow the LORD and to keep his commandments, decrees, and statutes with his whole heart and soul, thus observing the terms of the covenant written in this book. [32] He thereby committed all who were of Jerusalem and Benjamin, and the inhabitants of Jerusalem conformed themselves to the covenant of God, the God of their fathers. [33] Josiah removed every abominable thing from all the territory belonging to the Israelites, and he obliged all who were in Israel to serve the LORD, their God. During his lifetime they did not desert the LORD, the God of their fathers.

2 Chronicles Chapter 35

[1] Josiah celebrated in Jerusalem a Passover to honor the LORD; the Passover sacrifice was slaughtered on the fourteenth day of the first month. [2] He reappointed the priests to their duties and encouraged them in the service of the LORD'S house. [3] He said to the Levites who were to instruct all Israel, and who were consecrated to the LORD: "Put the holy ark in the house built by Solomon, son of David, king of Israel. It shall no longer be a burden on your shoulders. Serve now the LORD, your God, and his people Israel. [4] Prepare yourselves in your ancestral houses and your classes according to the prescriptions of King David of Israel and his son Solomon. [5] Stand in the sanctuary according to the divisions of the ancestral houses of your brethren, the common people, so that the distribution of the Levites and the families may be the same. [6] Slay the Passover sacrifice, sanctify yourselves, and be at the disposition of your brethren, that all may be carried out according to the word of the LORD given through Moses." [7] Josiah contributed to the common people a flock of lambs and kids, thirty thousand in number, each to serve as a Passover victim for any who were present, and also three thousand oxen; these were from the king's property. [8] His princes also gave a free-will gift to the people, the priests and the Levites. Hilkiah, Zechariah and Jehiel, prefects of the house of God, gave to the priests two thousand six hundred Passover victims together with three hundred oxen. [9] Conaniah and his brothers Shemaiah, Nethanel, Hashabiah, Jehiel and Jozabad, the rulers of the Levites, contributed to the Levites five thousand Passover victims, together with five hundred oxen. [10] When the service had been arranged, the priests took their places, as did the Levites in their classes according to the king's command. [11] The Passover sacrifice was slaughtered, whereupon the priests sprinkled some of the blood and the Levites proceeded to the skinning. [12] They separated what was destined for the holocaust and gave it to various groups of the ancestral houses of the common people to offer to the LORD, as is prescribed in the book of Moses. They did the same with the oxen. [13] They cooked the Passover on the fire as prescribed, and also cooked the sacred meals in pots, caldrons and pans, then brought them quickly to all the common people. [14] Afterward they prepared the Passover for themselves and for the priests. Indeed the priests, the sons of Aaron, were busy offering holocausts and the fatty portions until night; therefore the Levites prepared for themselves and for the priests, the sons of Aaron. [15] The singers, the sons of Asaph, were at their posts as prescribed by David: Asaph, Heman and Jeduthun, the king's seer. The gatekeepers were at every gate; there was no need for them to leave their stations, for their brethren, the Levites, prepared for them. [16] Thus the entire service of the LORD was arranged that day so that the Passover could be celebrated and the holocausts offered on the altar of the LORD, as King Josiah had commanded. [17] The Israelites who were present on that occasion kept the Passover and the feast of the Unleavened Bread for seven days. [18] No such Passover had been observed in Israel since the time of the prophet Samuel, nor had any king of Israel kept a Passover like that of Josiah, the priests and Levites, all of Judah and Israel that were present, and the inhabitants of Jerusalem. [19] It was in the eighteenth year of Josiah's reign that this Passover was observed. [20]

After Josiah had done all this to restore the temple, Neco, king of Egypt, came up to fight at Carchemish on the Euphrates, and Josiah went out to intercept him. 21 Neco sent messengers to him, saying: "What quarrel is between us, king of Judah? I have not come against you this day, for my war is with another kingdom, and God has told me to hasten. Do not interfere with God who is with me, as otherwise he will destroy you." 22 But Josiah would not withdraw from him, for he had sought a pretext for fighting with him. Therefore he would not listen to the words of Neco that came from the mouth of God, but went out to fight in the plain of Megiddo. 23 Then the archers shot King Josiah, who said to his servants, "Take me away, for I am seriously wounded." 24 His servants removed him from his own chariot, placed him in another he had in reserve, and brought him to Jerusalem, where he died. He was buried in the tombs of his ancestors, and all Judah and Jerusalem mourned him. 25 Jeremiah also composed a lamentation over Josiah, which is recited to this day by all the male and female singers in their lamentations over Josiah. These have been made obligatory for Israel, and can be found written in the Lamentations. 26 The rest of the chronicle of Josiah, his pious deeds in regard to what is written in the law of the LORD, and his acts, first and last, can be found written in the book of the kings of Israel and Judah.

2 Chronicles Chapter 36

1 The people of the land took Jehoahaz, son of Josiah, and made him king in Jerusalem in his father's stead. 2 Jehoahaz was twenty-three years old when he became king, and he reigned three months in Jerusalem. 3 The king of Egypt deposed him in Jerusalem and fined the land one hundred talents of silver and a talent of gold. 4 Then the king of Egypt made his brother Eliakim king over Judah and Jerusalem, and changed his name to Jehoiakim. Neco took his brother Jehoahaz away and brought him to Egypt. 5 Jehoiakim was twenty-five years old when he became king, and he reigned eleven years in Jerusalem. He did evil in the sight of the LORD, his God. 6 Nebuchadnezzar, king of Babylon, came up against him and bound him with chains to take him to Babylon. 7 Nebuchadnezzar also carried away to Babylon some of the vessels of the house of the LORD and put them in his palace in Babylon. 8 The rest of the acts of Jehoiakim, the abominable things that he did, and what therefore happened to him, can be found written in the book of the kings of Israel and Judah. His son Jehoiachin succeeded him as king. 9 Jehoiachin was eighteen years old when he became king, and he reigned three months (and ten days) in Jerusalem. He did evil in the sight of the LORD. 10 At the turn of the year, King Nebuchadnezzar sent for him and had him brought to Babylon, along with precious vessels from the temple of the LORD. He made his brother Zedekiah king over Judah and Jerusalem. 11 Zedekiah was twenty-one years old when he became king, and he reigned eleven years in Jerusalem. 12 He did evil in the sight of the LORD, his God, and he did not humble himself before the prophet Jeremiah, who spoke the word of the LORD. 13 He also rebelled against King Nebuchadnezzar, who had made him swear by God. He became stiff-necked and hardened his heart rather than return to the LORD, the God of Israel. 14 Likewise all the princes of Judah, the priests and the people added infidelity to infidelity, practicing all the abominations of the nations and polluting the LORD'S temple which he had consecrated in Jerusalem. 15 Early and often did the LORD, the God of their fathers, send his messengers to them, for he had compassion on his people and his dwelling place. 16 But they mocked the messengers of God, despised his warnings, and scoffed at his prophets, until the anger of the LORD against his people was so inflamed that there was no remedy. 17 Then he brought up against them the king of the Chaldeans, who slew their young men in their own sanctuary building, sparing neither young man nor maiden, neither the aged nor the decrepit; he delivered all of them over into his grip. 18 All the utensils of the house of God, the large and the small, and the treasures of the LORD'S house and of the king and his princes, all these he brought to Babylon. 19 They burnt the house of God, tore down the walls of Jerusalem, set all its palaces afire, and destroyed all its precious objects. 20 Those who escaped the sword he carried captive to Babylon, where they became his and his sons' servants until the kingdom of the Persians came to power. 21 All this was to fulfill the word of the LORD spoken by Jeremiah: "Until the land has retrieved its lost sabbaths, during all the time it lies waste it shall have rest while seventy years are fulfilled." 22 In the first year of Cyrus, king of Persia, in order to fulfill the word of the LORD spoken by Jeremiah, the LORD inspired King Cyrus of Persia to issue this proclamation throughout his kingdom, both by word of mouth and in writing: 23 "Thus says Cyrus, king of Persia: 'All the kingdoms of the earth the LORD, the God of heaven, has given to me, and he has also charged me to build him a house in Jerusalem, which is in Judah. Whoever, therefore, among you belongs to any part of his people, let him go up, and may his God be with him!'"

Ezra

Ezra Chapter 1

1 In the first year of Cyrus, king of Persia, in order to fulfill the word of the LORD spoken by Jeremiah, the LORD inspired King Cyrus of Persia to issue this proclamation throughout his kingdom, both by word of mouth and in writing: 2 "Thus says Cyrus, king of Persia: 'All the kingdoms of the earth the LORD, the God of heaven, has given to me, and he has also charged me to build him a house in Jerusalem, which is in Judah. 3 Whoever, therefore, among you belongs to any part of his people, let him go up, and may his God be with him! 4 Let everyone who has survived, in whatever place he may have dwelt, be assisted by the people of that place with silver, gold, goods, and cattle, together with free-will offerings for the house of God in Jerusalem.'" 5 Then the family heads of Judah and Benjamin and the priests and Levites—everyone, that is, whom God had inspired to do so—prepared to go up to build the house of the LORD in Jerusalem. 6 All their neighbors gave them help in every way, with silver, gold, goods, and cattle, and with many precious gifts besides all their free-will offerings. 7 King Cyrus, too, had the utensils of the house of the LORD brought forth which Nebuchadnezzar had taken away from Jerusalem and placed in the house of his god. 8 Cyrus, king of Persia, had them brought forth by the treasurer Mithredath, and counted out to Sheshbazzar, the prince of Judah. 9 This was the inventory: sacks of goldware, thirty; sacks of silverware, one thousand and twenty-nine; 10 golden bowls, thirty; silver bowls, four hundred and ten; other ware, one thousand pieces. 11 Total of the gold and silver ware: five thousand four hundred pieces. All these Sheshbazzar took with him when the exiles were brought back from Babylon to Jerusalem.

Ezra Chapter 2

1 These are the inhabitants of the province who returned from the captivity of the exiles, whom Nebuchadnezzar, king of Babylon, had carried away to Babylon, and who came back to Jerusalem and Judah, each man in his own city 2 (those who returned with Zerubbabel, Jeshua, Nehemiah, Seraiah, Reelaiah, Mordecai, Bilshan, Mispereth, Bigvai, Rehum, and Baanah): The census of the men of Israel: 3 sons of Parosh, two thousand one hundred and seventy-two; 4 sons of Shephatiah, three hundred and seventy-two; 5 sons of Arah, seven hundred and seventy-five; 6 sons of Pahath-moab, who were sons of Jeshua and Joab, two thousand eight hundred and twelve; 7 sons of Elam, one thousand two hundred and fifty-four; 8 sons of Zattu, nine hundred and forty-five; 9 sons of Zaccai, seven hundred and sixty; 10 sons of Bani, six hundred and forty-two; 11 sons of Bebai, six hundred and twenty-three; 12 sons of Azgad, one thousand two hundred and twenty-two; 13 sons of Adonikam, six hundred and sixty-six; 14 sons of Bigvai, two thousand and fifty-six; 15 sons of Adin, four hundred and fifty-four; 16 sons of Ater, who were sons of Hezekiah, ninety-eight; 17 sons of Bezai, three hundred and twenty-three; 18 sons of Jorah, one hundred and twelve; 19 sons of Hashum, two hundred and twenty-three; 20 sons of Gibeon, ninety-five; 21 sons of Bethlehem, one hundred and twenty-three; 22 men of Netophah, fifty-six; 23 men of Anathoth, one hundred and twenty-eight; 24 men of Beth-azmaveth, forty-two; 25 men of Kiriath-jearim, Chephirah, and Beeroth, seven hundred and forty-three; 26 men of Ramah and Geba, six hundred and twenty-one; 27 men of Michmas, one hundred and twenty-two; 28 men of Bethel and Ai, two hundred and twenty-three; 29 sons of Nebo, fifty-two; 30 sons of Magbish, one hundred and fifty-six; 31 sons of the other Elam, one thousand two hundred and fifty-four; 32 sons of Harim, three hundred and twenty; 33 sons of Lod, Hadid, and Ono, seven hundred and twenty-five; 34 sons of Jericho, three hundred and forty-five; 35 sons of Senaah, three thousand six hundred and thirty. 36 The priests: sons of Jedaiah, who were of the house of Jeshua, nine hundred and seventy-three; 37 sons of Immer, one thousand and fifty-two; 38 sons of Pashhur, one thousand two hundred and forty-seven; 39 sons of Harim, one thousand and seventeen. 40 The Levites: sons of Jeshua, Kadmiel, Binnui, and Hodaviah, seventy-four. 41 The singers: sons of Asaph, one hundred and twenty-eight. 42 The gatekeepers: sons of Shallum, sons of Ater, sons of Talmon, sons of Akkub, sons of Hatita, sons of Shobai, one hundred and thirty-nine in all. 43 The temple slaves: sons of Ziha, sons of Hasupha, sons of Tabbaoth, 44 sons of Keros, sons of Siaha, sons of Padon, 45 sons of Lebanah, sons of Hagabah, sons of Akkub, 46 sons of Hagab, sons of Shamlai, sons of Hanan, 47 sons of Giddel, sons of Gahar, sons of Reaiah, 48 sons of Rezin, sons of Nekoda, sons of Gazzam, 49 sons of Uzza, sons of Paseah, sons of Besai, 50 sons of Asnah, sons of the Meunites, sons of the Nephusites, 51 sons of Bakbuk, sons of Hakupha, sons of Harhur, 52 sons of Bazluth, sons of Mehida, sons of Harsha, 53 sons of Barkos, sons of Sisera, sons of Temah, 54

sons of Neziah, sons of Hatipha. 55 Descendants of the slaves of Solomon: sons of Sotai, sons of Hassophereth, sons of Peruda, 56 sons of Jaalah, sons of Darkon, sons of Giddel, 57 sons of Shephatiah, sons of Hattil, sons of Pochereth-hazzebaim, sons of Ami. 58 The total of the temple slaves and the descendants of the slaves of Solomon was three hundred and ninety-two. 59 The following who returned from Tel-melah, Tel-harsha, Cherub, Addan, and Immer were unable to prove that their ancestral houses and their descent were Israelite: 60 sons of Delaiah, sons of Tobiah, sons of Nekoda, six hundred and fifty-two. 61 Also, of the priests: sons of Habaiah, sons of Hakkoz, sons of Barzillai (he had married one of the daughters of Barzillai the Gileadite and became known by his name). 62 These men searched their family records, but their names could not be found written there; hence they were degraded from the priesthood, 63 and His Excellency ordered them not to partake of the most holy foods until there should be a priest bearing the Urim and Thummim. 64 The entire assembly taken together came to forty-two thousand three hundred and sixty, 65 not counting their male and female slaves, who were seven thousand three hundred and thirty-seven. They also had two hundred male and female singers. 66 Their horses were seven hundred and thirty-six, their mules two hundred and forty-five, 67 their camels four hundred and thirty-five, their asses six thousand seven hundred and twenty. 68 When they arrived at the house of the LORD in Jerusalem, some of the family heads made free-will offerings for the house of God, to rebuild it in its place. 69 According to their means they contributed to the treasury for the temple service: sixty-one thousand drachmas of gold, five thousand minas of silver, and one hundred garments for the priests. 70 The priests, the Levites, and some of the common people took up residence in Jerusalem; but the singers, the gatekeepers, and the temple slaves dwelt in their cities. Thus all the Israelites dwelt in their cities.

Ezra Chapter 3

1 Now when the seventh month came, after the Israelites had settled in their cities, the people gathered at Jerusalem as one man. 2 Then Jeshua, son of Jozadak, together with his brethren the priests, and Zerubbabel, son of Shealtiel, together with his brethren, set about rebuilding the altar of the God of Israel in order to offer on it the holocausts prescribed in the law of Moses, the man of God. 3 Despite their fear of the peoples of the land, they replaced the altar on its foundations and offered holocausts to the LORD on it, both morning and evening. 4 They also kept the feast of Booths in the manner prescribed, and they offered the daily holocausts in the proper number required for each day. 5 Thereafter they offered the established holocaust, the sacrifices prescribed for the new moons and all the festivals sacred to the LORD, and those which anyone might offer as a free-will gift to the LORD. 6 From the first day of the seventh month they began to offer holocausts to the LORD, though the foundation of the temple of the LORD had not yet been laid. 7 Then they hired stonecutters and carpenters, and sent food and drink and oil to the Sidonians and Tyrians that they might ship cedar trees from the Lebanon to the port of Joppa, as Cyrus, king of Persia, had authorized. 8 In the year after their coming to the house of God in Jerusalem, in the second month, Zerubbabel, son of Shealtiel, and Jeshua, son of Jozadak, together with the rest of their brethren, the priests and Levites and all who had come from the captivity to Jerusalem, began by appointing the Levites twenty years of age and over to supervise the work on the house of the LORD. 9 Jeshua and his sons and brethren, with Kadmiel and Binnui, son of Henadad, and their sons and their brethren, the Levites, stood as one man to supervise those who were engaged in the work on the house of God. 10 When the builders had laid the foundation of the LORD'S temple, the vested priests with the trumpets and the Levites, sons of Asaph, were stationed there with the cymbals to praise the LORD in the manner laid down by David, king of Israel. 11 They alternated in songs of praise and thanksgiving to the LORD, "for he is good, for his kindness to Israel endures forever"; and all the people raised a great shout of joy, praising the LORD because the foundation of the LORD'S house had been laid. 12 Many of the priests, Levites, and family heads, the old men who had seen the former house, cried out in sorrow as they watched the foundation of the present house being laid. Many others, however, lifted up their voices in shouts of joy, 13 and no one could distinguish the sound of the joyful shouting from the sound of those who were weeping; for the people raised a mighty clamor which was heard afar off.

Ezra Chapter 4

1 When the enemies of Judah and Benjamin heard that the exiles were building a temple for the LORD, the God of Israel, 2 they approached Zerubbabel and the family heads and said to them, "Let us build with you, for we seek your God just as you do, and we have sacrificed to him

since the days of Esarhaddon, king of Assyria, who had us brought here." 3 But Zerubbabel, Jeshua, and the rest of the family heads of Israel answered them, "It is not your responsibility to build with us a house for our God, but we alone must build it for the LORD, the God of Israel, as King Cyrus of Persia has commanded us." 4 Thereupon the people of the land set out to intimidate and dishearten the people of Judah so as to keep them from building. 5 They also suborned counselors to work against them and thwart their plans during the remaining years of Cyrus, king of Persia, and until the reign of Darius, king of Persia. 6 Also at the beginning of the reign of Ahashuerus they prepared a written accusation against the inhabitants of Judah and Jerusalem. 7 Again, in the time of Artaxerxes, Mithredath wrote in concert with Tabeel and the rest of his fellow officials to Artaxerxes, king of Persia. The document was written in Aramaic and was accompanied by a translation. (Aramaic:) 8 Then Rehum, the governor, and Shimshai, the scribe, wrote the following letter against Jerusalem to King Artaxerxes: 9 "Rehum, the governor, Shimshai, the scribe, and their fellow judges, officials, and agents from among the Persian, Urukian, Babylonian, Susian (that is Elamite), 10 and the other peoples whom the great and illustrious Assurbanipal transported and settled in the city of Samaria and elsewhere in the province West-of-Euphrates, as follows. . . ." 11 This is a copy of the letter that they sent to him: "To King Artaxerxes, your servants, the men of West-of-Euphrates, as follows: 12 Let it be known to the king that the Jews who came up from you to us have arrived at Jerusalem and are now rebuilding this rebellious and evil city. They are raising up its walls, and the foundations have already been laid. 13 Now let it be known to the king that if this city is rebuilt and its walls are raised up again, they will no longer pay taxes, tributes, or tolls; thus it can only result in harm to the throne. 14 Now, since we partake of the salt of the palace, we ought not simply to look on while the king is being dishonored. Therefore we have sent this message to inform you, O king, 15 so that inquiry may be made in the historical records of your fathers. In the historical records you can discover and verify that this city is a rebellious city which has proved fatal to kings and provinces, and that sedition has been fostered there since ancient times. For that reason this city was destroyed. 16 We inform you, O king, that if this city is rebuilt and its walls are raised up again, by that very fact you will no longer own any part of West-of-Euphrates." 17 The king sent this answer: "To Rehum, the governor, Shimshai, the scribe, and their fellow officials living in Samaria and elsewhere in the province West-of-Euphrates, greetings and the following: 18 The communication which you sent us has been read plainly in my presence. 19 When at my command inquiry was made, it was verified that from ancient times this city has risen up against kings and that rebellion and sedition have been fostered there. 20 Powerful kings were once in Jerusalem who ruled over all West-of-Euphrates, and taxes, tributes, and tolls were paid to them. 21 Give orders, therefore, that will stop the work of these men. This city may not be rebuilt until a further decree has been issued by me. 22 Take care that you do not neglect this matter, lest the evil grow to the detriment of the throne." 23 As soon as a copy of King Artaxerxes' letter had been read before Rehum, the governor, Shimshai, the scribe, and their fellow officials, they went in all haste to the Jews in Jerusalem and stopped their work by force of arms. 24 Thus it was that the work on the house of God in Jerusalem was halted. This inaction lasted until the second year of the reign of Darius, king of Persia.

Ezra Chapter 5

1 Then the prophets Haggai and Zechariah, son of Iddo, began to prophesy to the Jews in Judah and Jerusalem in the name of the God of Israel. 2 Thereupon Zerubbabel, son of Shealtiel, and Jeshua, son of Jozadak, began again to build the house of God in Jerusalem, with the prophets of God giving them support. 3 At that time there came to them Tattenai, governor of West-of-Euphrates, and Shethar-bozenai, and their fellow officials, who asked of them: "Who issued the decree for you to build this house and raise this edifice? 4 What are the names of the men who are building this structure?" 5 But their God watched over the elders of the Jews so that they were not hindered, until a report could go to Darius and then a written order be sent back concerning this matter. 6 A copy of the letter sent to King Darius by Tattenai, governor of West-of-Euphrates, and Shethar-bozenai, and their fellow officials from West-of-Euphrates; 7 they sent him a report in which was written the following: "To King Darius, all good wishes! 8 Let it be known to the king that we have visited the province of Judah and the house of the great God: it is being rebuilt of cut stone and the walls are being reinforced with timber; the work is being carried on diligently and is making good progress under their hands. 9 We then questioned the elders, addressing to them the following words: 'Who issued the decree for you to build this house and raise this edifice?' 10 We also asked them

their names, to report them to you in a list of the men who are their leaders. ¹¹ This was their answer to us: 'We are the servants of the God of heaven and earth, and we are rebuilding the house built here long years ago, which a great king of Israel built and finished. ¹² But because our fathers provoked the wrath of the God of heaven, he delivered them into the power of the Chaldean, Nebuchadnezzar, king of Babylon, who destroyed this house and led the people captive to Babylon. ¹³ However, in the first year of Cyrus, king of Babylon, King Cyrus issued a decree for the rebuilding of this house of God. ¹⁴ Moreover, the gold and silver utensils of the house of God which Nebuchadnezzar had taken from the temple in Jerusalem and carried off to the temple in Babylon, King Cyrus ordered to be removed from the temple in Babylon and consigned to a certain Sheshbazzar, whom he named governor. ¹⁵ And he commanded him: Take these utensils and deposit them in the temple of Jerusalem, and let the house of God be rebuilt on its former site. ¹⁶ Then this same Sheshbazzar came and laid the foundations of the house of God in Jerusalem. Since that time the building has been going on, and it is not yet completed.' ¹⁷ Now, if it please the king, let a search be made in the royal archives of Babylon to discover whether a decree really was issued by King Cyrus for the rebuilding of this house of God in Jerusalem. And may the king's pleasure in this matter be communicated to us."

Ezra Chapter 6

¹ Thereupon King Darius issued an order to search the archives in which the Babylonian records were stored away; ² and in Ecbatana, the stronghold in the province of Media, a scroll was found containing the following text: "Memorandum. ³ In the first year of King Cyrus, King Cyrus issued a decree: The house of God in Jerusalem. The house is to be rebuilt as a place for offering sacrifices and bringing burnt offerings. Its height is to be sixty cubits and its width sixty cubits. ⁴ It shall have three courses of cut stone for each one of timber. The costs are to be borne by the royal palace. ⁵ Also, the gold and silver utensils of the house of God which Nebuchadnezzar took from the temple of Jerusalem and brought to Babylon are to be sent back: to be returned to their place in the temple of Jerusalem and deposited in the house of God. ⁶ "Now, therefore, Tattenai, governor of West-of-Euphrates, and Shethar-bozenai, and you, their fellow officials in West-of-Euphrates, do not interfere in that place. ⁷ Let the governor and the elders of the Jews continue the work on that house of God; they are to rebuild it on its former site. ⁸ I also issue this decree concerning your dealing with these elders of the Jews in the rebuilding of that house of God: From the royal revenue, the taxes of West-of-Euphrates, let these men be repaid for their expenses, in full and without delay. ⁹ Whatever else is required - young bulls, rams, and lambs for holocausts to the God of heaven, wheat, salt, wine, and oil, according to the requirements of the priests who are in Jerusalem - is to be delivered to them day by day without fail, ¹⁰ that they may continue to offer sacrifices of pleasing odor to the God of heaven and pray for the life of the king and his sons. ¹¹ I also issue this decree: If any man violates this edict, a beam is to be taken from his house, and he is to be lifted up and impaled on it; and his house is to be reduced to rubble for this offense. ¹² And may the God who causes his name to dwell there overthrow every king or people who may undertake to alter this or to destroy this house of God in Jerusalem. I, Darius, have issued this decree; let it be carefully executed." ¹³ Then Tattenai, the governor of West-of-Euphrates, and Shethar-bozenai, and their fellow officials carried out fully the instructions King Darius had sent them. ¹⁴ The elders of the Jews continued to make progress in the building, supported by the message of the prophets, Haggai and Zechariah, son of Iddo. They finished the building according to the command of the God of Israel and the decrees of Cyrus and Darius (and of Artaxerxes, king of Persia). ¹⁵ They completed this house on the third day of the month Adar, in the sixth year of the reign of King Darius. ¹⁶ The Israelites - priests, Levites, and the other returned exiles - celebrated the dedication of this house of God with joy. ¹⁷ For the dedication of this house of God, they offered one hundred bulls, two hundred rams, and four hundred lambs, together with twelve he-goats as a sin-offering for all Israel, in keeping with the number of the tribes of Israel. ¹⁸ Finally, they set up the priests in their classes and the Levites in their divisions for the service of God in Jerusalem, as is prescribed in the book of Moses. ¹⁹ The exiles kept the Passover on the fourteenth day of the first month. ²⁰ The Levites, every one of whom had purified himself for the occasion, sacrificed the Passover for the rest of the exiles, for their brethren the priests, and for themselves. ²¹ The Israelites who had returned from the exile partook of it together with all those who had separated themselves from the uncleanness of the peoples of the land to join them in seeking the LORD, the God of Israel. ²² They joyfully kept the feast of Unleavened Bread for seven days, for the LORD had filled them with joy by making the king of Assyria

favorable to them, so that he gave them help in their work on the house of God, the God of Israel.

Ezra Chapter 7

¹ After these events, during the reign of Artaxerxes, king of Persia, Ezra, son of Seraiah, son of Azariah, son of Hilkiah, ² son of Shallum, son of Zadok, son of Ahitub, ³ son of Amariah, son of Azariah, son of Meraioth, ⁴ son of Zerahiah, son of Uzzi, son of Bukki, ⁵ son of Abishua, son of Phinehas, son of Eleazar, son of the high priest Aaron - ⁶ this Ezra came up from Babylon. He was a scribe, well-versed in the law of Moses which was given by the LORD, the God of Israel. Because the hand of the LORD, his God, was upon him, the king granted him all that he requested. ⁷ Some of the Israelites and some priests, Levites, singers, gatekeepers, and temple slaves also came up to Jerusalem in the seventh year of King Artaxerxes. ⁸ Ezra came to Jerusalem in the fifth month of that seventh year of the king. ⁹ On the first day of the first month he resolved on the journey up from Babylon, and on the first day of the fifth month he arrived at Jerusalem, for the favoring hand of his God was upon him. ¹⁰ Ezra had set his heart on the study and practice of the law of the LORD and on teaching statutes and ordinances in Israel. ¹¹ This is a copy of the rescript which King Artaxerxes gave to Ezra the priest-scribe, the scribe of the text of the LORD'S commandments and statutes for Israel: ¹² "Artaxerxes, king of kings, to Ezra the priest, scribe of the law of the God of heaven (then, after greetings): ¹³ I have issued this decree, that anyone in my kingdom belonging to the people of Israel, its priests or Levites, who is minded to go up to Jerusalem with you, may do so. ¹⁴ You are the envoy from the king and his seven counselors to supervise Judah and Jerusalem in respect of the law of your God which is in your possession, ¹⁵ and to bring with you the silver and gold which the king and his counselors have freely contributed to the God of Israel, whose dwelling is in Jerusalem, ¹⁶ as well as all the silver and gold which you may receive throughout the province of Babylon, together with the free-will offerings which the people and priests freely contribute for the house of their God in Jerusalem. ¹⁷ You must take care, therefore, to use this money to buy bulls, rams, lambs, and the cereal offerings and libations proper to these, and to offer them on the altar of the house of your God in Jerusalem. ¹⁸ You and your brethren may do whatever seems best to you with the remainder of the silver and gold, conformably to the will of your God. ¹⁹ The utensils consigned to you for the service of the house of your God you are to deposit before the God of Jerusalem. ²⁰ Whatever else you may be required to supply for the needs of the house of your God, you may draw from the royal treasury. ²¹ I, Artaxerxes the king, issue this decree to all the treasurers of West-of-Euphrates: Whatever Ezra the priest, scribe of the law of the God of heaven, requests of you, dispense to him accurately, ²² within these limits: silver, one hundred talents; wheat, one hundred kors; wine, one hundred baths; oil, one hundred baths; salt, without limit. ²³ Let everything that is ordered by the God of heaven be carried out exactly for the house of the God of heaven, that wrath may not come upon the realm of the king and his sons. ²⁴ We also inform you that it is not permitted to impose taxes, tributes, or tolls on any priest, Levite, singer, gatekeeper, temple slave, or any other servant of that house of God. ²⁵ "As for you, Ezra, in accordance with the wisdom of your God which is in your possession, appoint magistrates and judges to administer justice to all the people in West-of-Euphrates, to all, that is, who know the laws of your God. Instruct those who do not know these laws. ²⁶ Whoever does not obey the law of your God and the law of the king, let strict judgment be executed upon him, whether death, or corporal punishment, or a fine on his goods, or imprisonment." ²⁷ Blessed be the LORD, the God of our fathers, who thus disposed the mind of the king to glorify the house of the LORD in Jerusalem, ²⁸ and who let me find favor with the king, with his counselors, and with all the most influential royal officials. I therefore took courage and, with the hand of the LORD, my God, upon me, I gathered together Israelite family heads to make the return journey with me.

Ezra Chapter 8

¹ This is the list of the family heads who returned with me from Babylon during the reign of King Artaxerxes: ² Of the sons of Phinehas, Gershon; of the sons of Ithamar, Daniel; of the sons of David, Hattush, ³ son of Shecaniah; of the sons of Parosh, Zechariah, and with him one hundred and fifty males were enrolled; ⁴ of the sons of Pahath-moab, Eliehoenai, son of Zerahiah, and with him two hundred males; ⁵ of the sons of Zattu, Shecaniah, son of Jahaziel, and with him three hundred males; ⁶ of the sons of Adin, Ebed, son of Jonathan, and with him fifty males; ⁷ of the sons of Elam, Jeshaiah, son of Athaliah, and with him seventy males; ⁸ of the sons of Shephatiah, Zebadiah, son of Michael, and with him eighty males; ⁹ of the sons of Joab, Obadiah, son of Jehiel, and with

him two hundred and eighteen males; ¹⁰ of the sons of Bani, Shelomith, son of Josiphiah, and with him one hundred and sixty males; ¹¹ of the sons of Bebai, Zechariah, son of Bebai, and with him twenty-eight males; ¹² of the sons of Azgad, Johanan, son of Hakkatan, and with him one hundred and ten males; ¹³ of the sons of Adonikam, younger sons, whose names were Eliphelet, Jeiel, and Shemaiah, and with them sixty males; ¹⁴ of the sons of Bigvai, Uthai, son of Zakkur, and with him seventy males. ¹⁵ I had them assemble by the river that flows toward Ahava, where we made camp for three days. There I perceived that both laymen and priests were present, but I could not discover a single Levite. ¹⁶ Therefore I sent Eliezer, Ariel, Shemaiah, Jarib, Elnathan, Nathan, Zechariah, and Meshullam, wise leaders, ¹⁷ with a command for Iddo, the leader in the place Casiphia, instructing them what to say to Iddo and his brethren, and to the temple slaves in Casiphia, in order to procure for us ministers for the house of our God. ¹⁸ They sent to us—for the favoring hand of our God was upon us—a well-instructed man, one of the sons of Mahli, son of Levi, son of Israel, namely Sherebiah, with his sons and brethren, eighteen men. ¹⁹ They also sent us Hashabiah, and with him Jeshaiah, sons of Merari, and their brethren and their sons, twenty men. ²⁰ Of the temple slaves (those whom David and the princes appointed to serve the Levites) there were two hundred and twenty. All these men were enrolled by name. ²¹ Then I proclaimed a fast, there by the river of Ahava, that we might humble ourselves before our God to petition from him a safe journey for ourselves, our children, and all our possessions. ²² For I would have been ashamed to ask the king for troops and horsemen to protect us against enemies along the way, since we had said to the king, "The favoring hand of our God is upon all who seek him, but his mighty wrath is against all who forsake him." ²³ So we fasted, and prayed to our God for this, and our petition was granted. ²⁴ Next I selected twelve of the priestly leaders along with Sherebiah, Hashabiah, and ten of their brethren, ²⁵ and I weighed out before them the silver and the gold and the utensils offered for the house of our God by the king, his counselors, his officials, and all the Israelites of that region. ²⁶ I consigned it to them in these amounts: silver, six hundred and fifty talents; silver utensils, one hundred; gold, one hundred talents; ²⁷ twenty golden bowls valued at a thousand darics; two vases of excellent polished bronze, as precious as gold. ²⁸ I addressed them in these words: "You are consecrated to the LORD, and the utensils are also consecrated; the silver and the gold are a free-will offering to the LORD, the God of your fathers. ²⁹ Keep good watch over them till you weigh them out in Jerusalem in the presence of the chief priests and Levites and the family leaders of Israel, in the chambers of the house of the LORD." ³⁰ The priests and the Levites then took over the silver, the gold, and the utensils that had been weighed out, to bring them to Jerusalem, to the house of our God. ³¹ We set out for Jerusalem from the river of Ahava on the twelfth day of the first month. The hand of our God remained upon us, and he protected us from enemies and bandits along the way. ³² Thus we arrived in Jerusalem, where we first rested for three days. ³³ On the fourth day, the silver, the gold, and the utensils were weighed out in the house of our God and consigned to the priest Meremoth, son of Uriah, who was assisted by Eleazar, son of Phinehas; they were assisted by the Levites Jozabad, son of Jeshua, and Noadiah, son of Binnui. ³⁴ Everything was in order as to number and weight, and the total weight was registered. At that same time, ³⁵ those who had returned from the captivity, the exiles, offered as holocausts to the God of Israel twelve bulls for all Israel, ninety-six rams, seventy-seven lambs, and twelve goats as sin-offerings: all these as a holocaust to the LORD. ³⁶ Finally, the orders of the king were presented to the king's satraps and to the governors in West-of-Euphrates, who gave their support to the people and to the house of God.

Ezra Chapter 9

¹ When these matters had been concluded, the leaders approached me with this report: "Neither the Israelite laymen nor the priests nor the Levites have kept themselves aloof from the peoples of the land and their abominations (Canaanites, Hittites, Perizzites, Jebusites, Ammonites, Moabites, Egyptians, and Amorites); ² for they have taken some of their daughters as wives for themselves and their sons, and thus they have desecrated the holy race with the peoples of the land. Furthermore, the leaders and rulers have taken a leading part in this apostasy!" ³ When I had heard this thing, I tore my cloak and my mantle, plucked hair from my head and beard, and sat there stupefied. ⁴ Around me gathered all who were in dread of the sentence of the God of Israel on this apostasy of the exiles, while I remained motionless until the evening sacrifice. ⁵ Then, at the time of the evening sacrifice, I rose in my wretchedness, and with cloak and mantle torn I fell on my knees, stretching out my hands to the LORD, my God. ⁶ I said: "My God, I am too ashamed and confounded to raise my face to you, O my God, for our

wicked deeds are heaped up above our heads and our guilt reaches up to heaven. ⁷ From the time of our fathers even to this day great has been our guilt, and for our wicked deeds we have been delivered over, we and our kings and our priests, to the will of the kings of foreign lands, to the sword, to captivity, to pillage, and to disgrace, as is the case today. ⁸ "And now, but a short time ago, mercy came to us from the LORD, our God, who left us a remnant and gave us a stake in his holy place; thus our God has brightened our eyes and given us relief in our servitude. ⁹ For slaves we are, but in our servitude our God has not abandoned us; rather, he has turned the good will of the kings of Persia toward us. Thus he has given us new life to raise again the house of our God and restore its ruins, and has granted us a fence in Judah and Jerusalem. ¹⁰ But now, O our God, what can we say after all this? For we have abandoned your commandments, ¹¹ which you gave through your servants the prophets: the land which you are entering to take as your possession is a land unclean with the filth of the peoples of the land, with the abominations with which they have filled it from one end to the other in their uncleanness. ¹² Do not, then, give your daughters to their sons in marriage, and do not take their daughters for your sons. Never promote their peace and prosperity; thus you will grow strong, enjoy the produce of the land, and leave it as an inheritance to your children forever. ¹³ "After all that has come upon us for our evil deeds and our great guilt—though you, our God, have made less of our sinfulness than it deserved and have allowed us to survive as we do— ¹⁴ shall we again violate your commandments by intermarrying with these abominable peoples? Would you not become so angered with us as to destroy us without remnant or survivor? ¹⁵ O LORD, God of Israel, you are just; yet we have been spared, the remnant we are today. Here we are before you in our sins. Because of all this, we can no longer stand in your presence."

Ezra Chapter 10

¹ While Ezra prayed and acknowledged their guilt, weeping and prostrate before the house of God, a very large assembly of Israelites gathered about him, men, women, and children; and the people wept profusely. ² Then Shecaniah, the son of Jehiel, one of the sons of Elam, made this appeal to Ezra: "We have indeed betrayed our God by taking as wives foreign women of the peoples of the land. Yet even now there remains a hope for Israel. ³ Let us therefore enter into a covenant before our God to dismiss all our foreign wives and the children born of them, in keeping with what you, my lord, advise, and those who fear the commandments of our God. Let the law be observed! ⁴ Rise, then, for this is your duty! We will stand by you, so have courage and take action!" ⁵ Ezra rose to his feet and demanded an oath from the chiefs of the priests, from the Levites and from all Israel that they would do as had been proposed; and they swore it. ⁶ Then Ezra retired from his place before the house of God and entered the chamber of Johanan, son of Eliashib, where he spent the night neither eating food nor drinking water, for he was in mourning over the betrayal by the exiles. ⁷ A proclamation was made throughout Judah and Jerusalem that all the exiles should gather together in Jerusalem, ⁸ and that whoever failed to appear within three days would, according to the judgment of the leaders and elders, suffer the confiscation of all his possessions, and himself be excluded from the assembly of the exiles. ⁹ All the men of Judah and Benjamin gathered together in Jerusalem within the three-day period: it was in the ninth month, on the twentieth day of the month. All the people, standing in the open place before the house of God, were trembling both over the matter at hand and because it was raining. ¹⁰ Then Ezra, the priest, stood up and said to them: "Your unfaithfulness in taking foreign women as wives has added to Israel's guilt. ¹¹ But now, give praise to the LORD, the God of your fathers, and do his will: separate yourselves from the peoples of the land and from these foreign women." ¹² In answer, the whole assembly cried out with a loud voice: "Yes, it is our duty to do as you say! ¹³ But the people are numerous and it is the rainy season, so that we cannot remain out-of-doors; besides, this is not a task that can be performed in a single day or even two, for those of us who have sinned in this regard are many. ¹⁴ Let our leaders represent the whole assembly; then let all those in our cities who have taken foreign women for wives appear at appointed times, accompanied by the elders and magistrates of each city in question, till we have turned away from us our God's burning anger over this affair." ¹⁵ Only Jonathan, son of Asahel, and Jahzeiah, son of Tikvah, were against this proposal, with Meshullam and Shabbethai the Levite supporting them. ¹⁶ The exiles did as agreed. Ezra appointed as his assistants men who were family heads, one for each family, all of them designated by name. They held sessions to examine the matter, beginning with the first day of the tenth month. ¹⁷ By the first day of the first month they had passed judgment on all the men who had taken foreign women for wives. ¹⁸ Among the priests, the following were

found to have taken foreign women for wives: Of the sons of Jeshua, son of Jozadak, and his brethren: Maaseiah, Eliezer, Jarib, and Gedaliah. ¹⁹ They pledged themselves to dismiss their wives, and as a guilt-offering for their guilt they gave a ram from the flock. ²⁰ Of the sons of Immer: Hanani and Zebadiah; ²¹ of the sons of Harim: Maaseiah, Elijah, Shemaiah, Jehiel, and Uzziah; ²² of the sons of Pashhur: Elioenai, Maaseiah, Ishmael, Nethanel, Jozabad, and Elasah. ²³ Of the Levites: Jozabad, Shimei, Kelaiah (also called Kelita), Pethahiah, Judah and Eliezer. ²⁴ Of the singers: Eliashib and Zakkur; of the gatekeepers: Shallum, Telem, and Uri. ²⁵ Among the other Israelites: Of the sons of Parosh: Ramiah, Izziah, Malchijah, Mijamin, Eleazar, Malchijah, and Benaiah; ²⁶ of the sons of Elam: Mattaniah, Zechariah, Jehiel, Abdi, Jeremoth, and Elijah; ²⁷ of the sons of Zattu: Elioenai, Eliashib, Mattaniah, Jeremoth, Zabad, and Aziza; ²⁸ of the sons of Bebai: Jehohanan, Hananiah, Zabbai, and Athlai; ²⁹ of the sons of Bani: Meshullam, Malluch, Adaiah, Jashub, Sheal, and Jeremoth; ³⁰ of the sons of Pahath-moab: Adna, Chelal, Benaiah, Maaseiah, Mattaniah, Bezalel, Binnui, and Manasseh; ³¹ of the sons of Harim: Eliezer, Isshijah, Malchijah, Shemaiah, Shimeon, ³² Benjamin, Malluch, Shemariah, ³³ of the sons of Hashum: Mattenai, Mattattah, Zabad, Eliphelet, Jeremai, Manasseh, Shimei, ³⁴ of the sons of Begui: Maadai, Amram, Uel, ³⁵ Benaiah, Bedeiah, Cheluhi, ³⁶ Vaniah, Meremoth, Eliashib, ³⁷ Mattaniah, Mattenai, and Jaasu; ³⁸ of the sons of Binnui: Shimei, ³⁹ Shelemiah, Nathan, and Adaiah; ⁴⁰ of the sons of Zachai: Shashai, Sharai, ⁴¹ Azarel, Shelemiah, Shemariah, ⁴² Shallum, Amariah, Joseph; ⁴³ of the sons of Nebo: Jeiel, Mattithiah, Zabad, Zebina, Jaddai, Joel, Benaiah. ⁴⁴ All these had taken foreign wives; but they sent them away, both the women and their children.

Nehemiah

Nehemiah Chapter 1

¹ The words of Nehemiah, the son of Hacaliah. In the month Chislev of the twentieth year, I was in the citadel of Susa ² when Hanani, one of my brothers, came with other men from Judah. I asked them about the Jews, the remnant preserved after the captivity, and about Jerusalem, ³ and they answered me: "The survivors of the captivity there in the province are in great distress and under reproach. Also, the wall of Jerusalem lies breached, and its gates have been gutted with fire." ⁴ When I heard this report, I began to weep and continued mourning for several days; I fasted and prayed before the God of heaven. ⁵ I prayed: "O LORD, God of heaven, great and awesome God, you who preserve your covenant of mercy toward those who love you and keep your commandments, ⁶ may your ear be attentive, and your eyes open, to heed the prayer which I, your servant, now offer in your presence day and night for your servants the Israelites, confessing the sins which we of Israel have committed against you, I and my father's house included. ⁷ Grievously have we offended you, not keeping the commandments, the statutes, and the ordinances which you committed to your servant Moses. ⁸ But remember, I pray, the promise which you gave through Moses, your servant, when you said: 'Should you prove faithless, I will scatter you among the nations; ⁹ but should you return to me and carefully keep my commandments, even though your outcasts have been driven to the farthest corner of the world, I will gather them from there, and bring them back to the place which I have chosen as the dwelling place for my name.' ¹⁰ They are your servants, your people, whom you freed by your great might and your strong hand. ¹¹ O Lord, may your ear be attentive to my prayer and that of all your willing servants who revere your name. Grant success to your servant this day, and let him find favor with this man"—for I was cupbearer to the king.

Nehemiah Chapter 2

¹ In the month Nisan of the twentieth year of King Artaxerxes, when the wine was in my charge, I took some and offered it to the king. As I had never before been sad in his presence, ² the king asked me, "Why do you look sad? If you are not sick, you must be sad at heart." Though I was seized with great fear, ³ I answered the king: "May the king live forever! How could I not look sad when the city where my ancestors are buried lies in ruins, and its gates have been eaten out by fire?" ⁴ The king asked, "What is it, then, that you wish?" I prayed to the God of heaven ⁵ and then answered the king: "If it please the king, and if your servant is deserving of your favor, send me to Judah, to the city of my ancestors' graves, to rebuild it." ⁶ Then the king, and the queen seated beside him, asked me how long my journey would take and when I would return. I set a date that was acceptable to him, and the king agreed that I might go. ⁷ I asked the king further: "If it please the king, let letters be given to me for the governors of West-of-Euphrates, that they may afford me safe-conduct till I arrive in Judah; ⁸ also a letter for Asaph, the keeper of the royal park, that he may give me wood for timbering the gates of the temple-citadel and for the city wall and the house that I shall occupy." The king granted my requests, for the favoring hand of my God was upon me. ⁹ Thus I proceeded to the governors of West-of-Euphrates and presented the king's letters to them. The king also sent with me army officers and cavalry. ¹⁰ When Sanballat the Horonite and Tobiah the Ammonite slave had heard of this, they were very much displeased that someone had come to seek the welfare of the Israelites. ¹¹ When I had arrived in Jerusalem, I first rested there for three days. ¹² Then I set out by night with only a few other men (for I had not told anyone what my God had inspired me to do for Jerusalem) and with no other animals but my own mount. ¹³ I rode out at night by the Valley Gate, passed by the Dragon Spring, and came to the Dung Gate, observing how the walls of Jerusalem lay in ruins and its gates had been eaten out by fire. ¹⁴ Then I passed over to the Spring Gate and to the King's Pool. Since there was no room here for my mount to pass with me astride, ¹⁵ I continued on foot up the wadi by night, inspecting the wall all the while till I once more reached the Valley Gate, by which I went back in. ¹⁶ The magistrates knew nothing of where I had gone or what I was doing, for as yet I had disclosed nothing to the Jews, neither to the priests, nor to the nobles, nor to the magistrates, nor to the others who would be concerned about the matter. ¹⁷ Afterward I said to them: "You see the evil plight in which we stand: how Jerusalem lies in ruins and its gates have been gutted by fire. Come, let us rebuild the wall of Jerusalem, so that we may no longer be an object of derision!" ¹⁸ Then I explained to them how the favoring hand of my God had rested upon me, and what the king had said to me. They replied, "Let us be up and building!" And they undertook the good work with vigor. ¹⁹ On hearing of this, Sanballat the Horonite, Tobiah the Ammonite slave, and Geshem the Arab mocked us and ridiculed us. "What is this that you are about?" they asked. "Are you rebelling against the king?" ²⁰ My answer to them was this: "It is the God of heaven who will grant us success. We, his servants, shall set about the rebuilding; but for you there is to be neither share nor claim nor memorial in Jerusalem."

Nehemiah Chapter 3

¹ Eliashib the high priest and his priestly brethren took up the task of rebuilding the Sheep Gate. They timbered it and set up its doors, its bolts, and its bars, then continued the rebuilding to the Tower of Hananel. ² At their side the men of Jericho were rebuilding, and next to them was Zaccur, son of Imri. ³ The Fish Gate was rebuilt by the sons of Hassenaah; they timbered it and set up its doors, its bolts, and its bars. ⁴ At their side Meremoth, son of Uriah, son of Hakkoz, carried out the work of repair; next to him was Meshullam, son of Berechiah, son of Meshezabel; and next to him was Zadok, son of Baana. ⁵ Next to him the Tekoites carried out the work of repair; however, some of their outstanding men would not submit to the labor asked by their lords. ⁶ The New City Gate was repaired by Joiada, son of Paseah; and Meshullam, son of Besodeiah; they timbered it and set up its doors, its bolts, and its bars. ⁷ At their side were Melatiah the Gibeonite, Jadon the Meronothite, and the men of Gibeon and of Mizpah, who were under the jurisdiction of the governor of West-of-Euphrates. ⁸ Next to them the work of repair was carried out by Uzziel, son of Harhaiah, a member of the goldsmiths' guild, and at his side was Hananiah, one of the perfumers' guild. They restored Jerusalem as far as the wall of the public square. ⁹ Next to them the work of repair was carried out by Rephaiah, son of Hur, leader of half the district of Jerusalem, ¹⁰ and at his side was Jedaiah, son of Harumaph, who repaired opposite his own house. Next to him Hattush, son of Hashabneiah, carried out the work of repair. ¹¹ The adjoining sector, as far as the Oven Tower, was repaired by Malchijah, son of Harim, and Hasshub, of Pahath-moab. ¹² At their side the work of repair was carried out by Shallum, son of Hallohesh, leader of half the district of Jerusalem, by himself and his daughters. ¹³ The Valley Gate was repaired by Hanun and the inhabitants of Zanoah; they rebuilt it and set up its doors, its bolts, and its bars. They also repaired a thousand cubits of the wall up to the Dung Gate. ¹⁴ The Dung Gate was repaired by Malchijah, son of Rechab, leader of the district of Beth-haccherem; he rebuilt it and set up its doors, its bolts, and its bars. ¹⁵ The Spring Gate was repaired by Shallum, son of Colhozeh, leader of the district of Mizpah; he rebuilt it, roofed it over, and set up its doors, its bolts, and its bars. He also repaired the wall of the Aqueduct Pool near the king's garden as far as the steps that lead down from the City of David. ¹⁶ After him, the work of repair was carried out by Nehemiah, son of Azbuk, leader of half the district of Beth-zur, to a place opposite the tombs of David, as far as the artificial pool and the barracks. ¹⁷ After him, the Levites carried out the work of repair: Rehum, son of Bani. Next to him, for his own district, was Hashabiah, leader of half the district of Keilah. ¹⁸ After him, their brethren carried out the work of repair: Binnui, son of Henadad, leader

of half the district of Keilah; ¹⁹ next to him Ezer, son of Jeshua, leader of Mizpah, who repaired the adjoining sector, the Corner, opposite the ascent to the arsenal. ²⁰ After him, Baruch, son of Zabbai, repaired the adjoining sector from the Corner to the entrance of the house of Eliashib, the high priest. ²¹ After him, Meremoth, son of Uriah, son of Hakkoz, repaired the adjoining sector from the entrance of Eliashib's house to the end of the house. ²² After him, the work of repair was carried out by the priests, men of the surrounding country. ²³ After them, Benjamin and Hasshub carried out the repair in front of their houses; after them, Azariah, son of Maaseiah, son of Ananiah, made the repairs alongside his house. ²⁴ After him, Binnui, son of Henadad, repaired the adjoining sector from the house of Azariah to the Corner (that is, to the Angle). ²⁵ After him, Palal, son of Uzai, carried out the work of repair opposite the Corner and the tower projecting from the Upper Palace at the quarters of the guard. After him, Pedaiah, son of Parosh, carried out the work of repair ²⁶ to a point opposite the Water Gate on the east, and the projecting tower. ²⁷ After him, the Tekoites repaired the adjoining sector opposite the great projecting tower, to the wall of Ophel (the temple slaves were dwelling on Ophel). ²⁸ Above the Horse Gate the priests carried out the work of repair, each before his own house. ²⁹ After them Zadok, son of Immer, carried out the repair before his house, and after him the repair was carried out by Shemaiah, son of Shecaniah, keeper of the East Gate. ³⁰ After him, Hananiah, son of Shelemiah, and Hanun, the sixth son of Zalaph, repaired the adjoining sector; after them, Meshullam, son of Berechiah, repaired the place opposite his own lodging. ³¹ After him, Malchijah, a member of the goldsmiths' guild, carried out the work of repair as far as the quarters of the temple slaves and the merchants, before the Gate of Inspection and as far as the upper chamber of the Angle. ³² Between the upper chamber of the Angle and the Sheep Gate, the goldsmiths and the merchants carried out the work of repair. ³³ When Sanballat heard that we were rebuilding the wall, it roused his anger and he became very much incensed. He ridiculed the Jews, ³⁴ saying in the presence of his brethren and the troops of Samaria: "What are these miserable Jews trying to do? Will they complete their restoration in a single day? Will they recover these stones, burnt as they are, from the heaps of dust?" ³⁵ Tobiah the Ammonite was beside him, and he said: "It is a rubble heap they are building. Any fox that attacked it would breach their wall of stones!" ³⁶ Take note, O our God, how we were mocked! Turn back their derision upon their own heads and let them be carried away to a land of captivity! ³⁷ Hide not their crime and let not their sin be blotted out in your sight, for they insulted the builders to their face! ³⁸ We, however, continued to build the wall, which was soon filled in and completed up to half its height. The people worked with a will.

Nehemiah Chapter 4

¹ When Sanballat, Tobiah, the Arabs, the Ammonites, and the Ashdodites heard that the restoration of the walls of Jerusalem was progressing - for the gaps were beginning to be closed up - they became extremely angry. ² Thereupon they all plotted together to come and fight against Jerusalem and thus to throw us into confusion. ³ We prayed to our God and posted a watch against them day and night for fear of what they might do. ⁴ Meanwhile the Judahites were saying: "Slackened is the bearers' strength, there is no end to the rubbish; Never shall we be able the wall to rebuild." ⁵ Our enemies thought, "Before they are aware of it or see us, we shall come into their midst, kill them, and put an end to the work." ⁶ When the Jews who lived near them had come to us from one place after another, and had told us ten times over that they were about to attack us, ⁷ I stationed guards down below, behind the wall, near the exposed points, assigning them by family groups with their swords, their spears, and their bows. ⁸ I made an inspection, then addressed these words to the nobles, the magistrates, and the rest of the people: "Have no fear of them! Keep in mind the LORD, who is great and to be feared, and fight for your brethren, your sons and daughters, your wives and your homes." ⁹ When our enemies became aware that we had been warned and that God had upset their plan, we all went back, each to his own task at the wall. ¹⁰ From that time on, however, only half my able men took a hand in the work, while the other half, armed with spears, bucklers, bows, and breastplates, stood guard behind the whole house of Judah ¹¹ as they rebuilt the wall. The load carriers, too, were armed; each did his work with one hand and held a weapon with the other. ¹² Every builder, while he worked, had his sword girt at his side. Also, a trumpeter stood beside me, ¹³ for I had said to the nobles, the magistrates, and the rest of the people: "Our work is scattered and extensive, and we are widely separated from one another along the wall; ¹⁴ wherever you hear the trumpet sound, join us there; our God will fight with us." ¹⁵ Thus we went on with the work, half of the men with spears at the ready, from daybreak till the stars came out. ¹⁶ At the same time I told the people to spend the nights inside Jerusalem, each man with his own attendant, so that they might serve as a guard by night and a working force by day. ¹⁷ Neither I, nor my kinsmen, nor any of my attendants, nor any of the bodyguard that accompanied me took off his clothes; everyone kept his weapon at his right hand.

Nehemiah Chapter 5

¹ Then there rose a great outcry of the common people and their wives against certain of their fellow Jews. ² Some said: "We are forced to pawn our sons and daughters in order to get grain to eat that we may live." ³ Others said: "We are forced to pawn our fields, our vineyards, and our houses, that we may have grain during the famine." ⁴ Still others said: "To pay the king's tax we have borrowed money on our fields and our vineyards. ⁵ And though these are our own kinsmen and our children are as good as theirs, we have had to reduce our sons and daughters to slavery, and violence has been done to some of our daughters! Yet we can do nothing about it, for our fields and our vineyards belong to others." ⁶ I was extremely angry when I heard the reasons they had for complaint. ⁷ After some deliberation, I called the nobles and magistrates to account, saying to them, "You are exacting interest from your own kinsmen!" I then rebuked them severely, ⁸ saying to them: "As far as we were able, we bought back our fellow Jews who had been sold to Gentiles; you, however, are selling your own brothers, to have them bought back by us." They remained silent, for they could find no answer. ⁹ I continued: "What you are doing is not good. Should you not walk in the fear of our God, and put an end to the derision of our Gentile enemies? ¹⁰ I myself, my kinsmen, and my attendants have lent the people money and grain without charge. Let us put an end to this usury! ¹¹ I ask that you return to them this very day their fields, their vineyards, their olive groves, and their houses, together with the interest on the money, the grain, the wine, and the oil that you have lent them." ¹² They answered: "We will return everything and exact nothing further from them. We will do just what you ask." Then I called for the priests and had them administer an oath to these men that they would do as they had promised. ¹³ I also shook out the folds of my garment, saying, "Thus may God shake from his home and his fortune every man who fails to keep this promise, and may he thus be shaken out and emptied!" And the whole assembly answered, "Amen," and praised the LORD. Then the people did as they had promised. ¹⁴ Moreover, from the time that King Artaxerxes appointed me governor in the land of Judah, from his twentieth to his thirty-second year - during these twelve years neither I nor my brethren lived from the governor's allowance. ¹⁵ The earlier governors, my predecessors, had laid a heavy burden on the people, taking from them each day forty silver shekels for their food; then too, their men oppressed the people. But I, because I feared God, did not act thus. ¹⁶ Moreover, though I had acquired no land of my own, I did my part in this work on the wall, and all my men were gathered there for the work. ¹⁷ Though I set my table for a hundred and fifty persons, Jews and magistrates, as well as those who came to us from the nations round about, ¹⁸ and though the daily preparations were made at my expense - one beef, six choice muttons, poultry - besides all kinds of wine in abundance every ten days, despite this I did not claim the governor's allowance, for the labor lay heavy upon this people. ¹⁹ Keep in mind, O my God, in my favor all that I did for this people.

Nehemiah Chapter 6

¹ When it had been reported to Sanballat, Tobiah, Geshem the Arab, and our other enemies that I had rebuilt the wall and that there was no breach left in it (though up to that time I had not yet set up the doors in the gates), ² Sanballat and Geshem sent me this message: "Come, let us hold council together at Caphirim in the plain of Ono." They were planning to do me harm. ³ However, I sent messengers to them with this reply: "I am engaged in a great enterprise and am unable to come down; why should the work stop, while I leave it to come down to you?" ⁴ Four times they sent me this same proposal, and each time I gave the same reply. ⁵ Then, the fifth time, Sanballat sent me the same message by one of his servants, who bore an unsealed letter ⁶ containing this text: "Among the nations it has been reported - Geshem is witness to this - that you and the Jews are planning a rebellion; that for this reason you are rebuilding the wall; and that you are to be their king" - and so on. ⁷ "Also, that you have set up prophets in Jerusalem to proclaim you king of Judah. Now, since matters like these must reach the ear of the king, come, let us hold council together." ⁸ I sent him this answer: "Nothing of what you report has taken place; rather, it is the invention of your own mind." ⁹ They were all trying to frighten us, thinking, "Their hands will slacken in the work, and it will never be completed." But instead, I now redoubled my efforts. ¹⁰ I went to the house of Shemaiah, son of Delaiah, son of Mehetabel, who was unable to go about, and he

said: "Let us meet in the house of God, inside the temple building; let us lock the doors of the temple. For men are coming to kill you; by night they are coming to kill you." 11 My answer was: "A man like me take flight? Can a man like me enter the temple to save his life? I will not go!" 12 For on consideration it was plain to me that God had not sent him; rather, because Tobiah and Sanballat had bribed him, he voiced this prophecy concerning me 13 that I might act on it out of fear and commit this sin. Then they would have had a shameful story with which to discredit me. 14 Keep in mind Tobiah and Sanballat, O my God, because of these things they did; keep in mind as well Noadiah the prophetess and the other prophets who were trying to frighten me. 15 The wall was finished on the twenty-fifth day of Elul; it had taken fifty-two days. 16 When all our enemies had heard of this, and all the nations round about had taken note of it, our enemies lost face in the eyes of the nations, for they knew that it was with our God's help that this work had been completed. 17 At that same time, however, many letters were going to Tobiah from the nobles of Judah, and Tobiah's letters were reaching them, 18 for many in Judah were in league with him, since he was the son-in-law of Shecaniah, son of Arah, and his son Jehohanan had married the daughter of Meshullam, son of Berechiah. 19 Thus they would praise his good deeds in my presence and relate to him whatever I said; and Tobiah sent letters trying to frighten me.

Nehemiah Chapter 7

1 When the wall had been rebuilt, I had the doors set up, and the gatekeepers (and the singers and the Levites) were put in charge of them. 2 Over Jerusalem I placed Hanani, my brother, and Hananiah, the commander of the citadel, who was a more trustworthy and God-fearing man than most. 3 I said to them: "The gates of Jerusalem are not to be opened until the sun is hot, and while the sun is still shining they shall shut and bar the doors. Appoint as watchmen the inhabitants of Jerusalem, some at their watch posts, and others before their own houses." 4 Now the city was quite wide and spacious, but its population was small, and none of the houses had been rebuilt. 5 When my God had put it into my mind to gather together the nobles, the magistrates, and the common people, and to examine their family records, I came upon the family list of those who had returned in the earliest period. There I found the following written: 6 These are the inhabitants of the province who returned from the captivity of the exiles whom Nebuchadnezzar, king of Babylon, had carried away, and who came back to Jerusalem and Judah, each man to his own city 7 (those who returned with Zerubbabel, Jeshua, Nehemiah, Azariah, Raamiah, Nahamani, Mordecai, Bilshan, Mispereth, Bigvai, Nehum, and Baanah). The census of the men of Israel: 8 sons of Parosh, two thousand one hundred and seventy-two; 9 sons of Shephatiah, three hundred and seventy-two; 10 sons of Arah, six hundred and fifty-two; 11 sons of Pahath-moab who were sons of Jeshua and Joab, two thousand eight hundred and eighteen; 12 sons of Elam, one thousand two hundred and fifty-four; 13 sons of Zattu, eight hundred and forty-five; 14 sons of Zaccai, seven hundred and sixty; 15 sons of Binnui, six hundred and forty-eight; 16 sons of Bebai, six hundred and twenty-eight; 17 sons of Azgad, two thousand three hundred and twenty-two; 18 sons of Adonikam, six hundred and sixty-seven; 19 sons of Bigvai, two thousand and sixty-seven; 20 sons of Adin, six hundred and fifty-five; 21 sons of Ater who were sons of Hezekiah, ninety-eight; 22 sons of Hashum, three hundred and twenty-eight; 23 sons of Bezai, three hundred and twenty-four; 24 sons of Hariph, one hundred and twelve; 25 sons of Gibeon, ninety-five; 26 men of Bethlehem and Netophah, one hundred and eighty-eight; 27 men of Anathoth, one hundred and twenty-eight; 28 men of Beth-azmaveth, forty-two; 29 men of Kiriath-jearim, Chephirah, and Beeroth, seven hundred and forty-three; 30 men of Ramah and Geba, six hundred and twenty-one; 31 men of Michmas, one hundred and twenty-two; 32 men of Bethel and Ai, one hundred and twenty-three; 33 men of Nebo, fifty-two; 34 sons of another Elam, one thousand two hundred and fifty-four; 35 sons of Harim, three hundred and twenty; 36 sons of Jericho, three hundred and forty-five; 37 sons of Lod, Hadid, and Ono, seven hundred and twenty-one; 38 sons of Senaah, three thousand nine hundred and thirty. 39 The priests: sons of Jedaiah who were of the house of Jeshua, nine hundred and seventy-three; 40 sons of Immer, one thousand and fifty-two; 41 sons of Pashhur, one thousand two hundred and forty-seven; 42 sons of Harim, one thousand and seventeen. 43 The Levites: sons of Jeshua, Kadmiel, Binnui, Hodeviah, seventy-four. 44 The singers: sons of Asaph, one hundred and forty-eight. 45 The gatekeepers: sons of Shallum, sons of Ater, sons of Talmon, sons of Akkub, sons of Hatita, sons of Shobai, one hundred and thirty-eight. 46 The temple slaves: sons of Ziha, sons of Hasupha, sons of Tabbaoth, 47 sons of Keros, sons of Sia, sons of Padon, 48 sons of Lebana, sons of Hagaba, sons of Shalmai, 49 sons of Hanan, sons of Giddel, sons of Gahar, 50 sons of Reaiah, sons of Rezin, sons of

Nekoda, 51 sons of Gazzam, sons of Uzza, sons of Paseah, 52 sons of Besai, sons of the Meunites, sons of the Nephusites, 53 sons of Bakbuk, sons of Hakupha, sons of Harhur, 54 sons of Bazlith, sons of Mehida, sons of Harsha, 55 sons of Barkos, sons of Sisera, sons of Temah, 56 sons of Neziah, sons of Hatipha. 57 Descendants of the slaves of Solomon: sons of Sotai, sons of Sophereth, sons of Perida, 58 sons of Jaala, sons of Darkon, sons of Giddel, 59 sons of Shephatiah, sons of Hattil, sons of Pochereth-hazzebaim, sons of Amon. 60 The total of the temple slaves and the descendants of the slaves of Solomon was three hundred and ninety-two. 61 The following who returned from Tel-melah, Tel-harsha, Cherub, Addon, and Immer were unable to prove that their ancestral houses and their descent were Israelite: 62 sons of Delaiah, sons of Tobiah, sons of Nekoda, six hundred and forty-two. 63 Also, of the priests: sons of Hobaiah, sons of Hakkoz, sons of Barzillai (he had married one of the daughters of Barzillai the Gileadite and became known by his name). 64 These men searched their family records, but their names could not be found written there; hence they were degraded from the priesthood, 65 and His Excellency ordered them not to partake of the most holy foods until there should be a priest bearing the Urim and Thummim. 66 The entire assembly taken together came to forty-two thousand three hundred and sixty, 67 not counting their male and female slaves, who were seven thousand three hundred and thirty-seven. They also had two hundred male and female singers. Their horses were seven hundred and thirty-six, their mules two hundred and forty-five, 68 their camels four hundred and thirty-five, their asses six thousand seven hundred and twenty. 69 Certain of the family heads contributed to the service. His Excellency put into the treasury one thousand drachmas of gold, fifty basins, thirty garments for priests, and five hundred minas of silver. 70 Some of the family heads contributed to the treasury for the temple service: twenty thousand drachmas of gold and two thousand two hundred minas of silver. 71 The contributions of the rest of the people amounted to twenty thousand drachmas of gold, two thousand minas of silver, and sixty-seven garments for priests. 72 The priests, the Levites, the gatekeepers, the singers, the temple slaves, and all Israel took up residence in their cities.

Nehemiah Chapter 8

1 Now when the seventh month came, the whole people gathered as one man in the open space before the Water Gate, and they called upon Ezra the scribe to bring forth the book of the law of Moses which the LORD prescribed for Israel. 2 On the first day of the seventh month, therefore, Ezra the priest brought the law before the assembly, which consisted of men, women, and those children old enough to understand. 3 Standing at one end of the open place that was before the Water Gate, he read out of the book from daybreak till midday, in the presence of the men, the women, and those children old enough to understand; and all the people listened attentively to the book of the law. 4 Ezra the scribe stood on a wooden platform that had been made for the occasion; at his right side stood Mattithiah, Shema, Anaiah, Uriah, Hilkiah, and Maaseiah, and on his left Pedaiah, Mishael, Malchijah, Hashum, Hashbaddanah, Zechariah, Meshullam. 5 Ezra opened the scroll so that all the people might see it (for he was standing higher up than any of the people); and, as he opened it, all the people rose. 6 Ezra blessed the LORD, the great God, and all the people, their hands raised high, answered, "Amen, amen!" Then they bowed down and prostrated themselves before the LORD, their faces to the ground. 7 (The Levites Jeshua, Bani, Sherebiah, Jamin, Akkub, Shabbethai, Hodiah, Maaseiah, Kelita, Azariah, Jozabad, Hanan, and Pelaiah explained the law to the people, who remained in their places.) 8 Ezra read plainly from the book of the law of God, interpreting it so that all could understand what was read. 9 Then (Nehemiah, that is, His Excellency, and) Ezra the priest-scribe (and the Levites who were instructing the people) said to all the people: "Today is holy to the LORD your God. Do not be sad, and do not weep"— for all the people were weeping as they heard the words of the law. 10 He said further: "Go, eat rich foods and drink sweet drinks, and allot portions to those who had nothing prepared; for today is holy to our LORD. Do not be saddened this day, for rejoicing in the LORD must be your strength!" 11 (And the Levites quieted all the people, saying, "Hush, for today is holy, and you must not be saddened.") 12 Then all the people went to eat and drink, to distribute portions, and to celebrate with great joy, for they understood the words that had been expounded to them. 13 On the second day, the family heads of the whole people and also the priests and the Levites gathered around Ezra the scribe and examined the words of the law more closely. 14 They found it written in the law prescribed by the LORD through Moses that the Israelites must dwell in booths during the feast of the seventh month; 15 and that they should have this proclamation made throughout their cities and in Jerusalem: "Go out into the hill country and bring in branches of olive

trees, oleasters, myrtle, palm, and other leafy trees, to make booths, as the law prescribes." 16The people went out and brought in branches with which they made booths for themselves, on the roof of their houses, in their courtyards, in the courts of the house of God, and in the open spaces of the Water Gate and the Gate of Ephraim. 17Thus the entire assembly of the returned exiles made booths and dwelt in them. Now the Israelites had done nothing of this sort from the days of Jeshua, son of Nun, until this occasion; therefore there was very great joy. 18Ezra read from the book of the law of God day after day, from the first day to the last. They kept the feast for seven days, and the solemn assembly on the eighth day, as was required.

Nehemiah Chapter 9

1On the twenty-fourth day of this month, the Israelites gathered together fasting and in sackcloth, their heads covered with dust. 2Those of Israelite descent separated themselves from all who were of foreign extraction, then stood forward and confessed their sins and the guilty deeds of their fathers. 3When they had taken their places, they read from the book of the law of the LORD their God, for a fourth part of the day, and during another fourth part they made their confession and prostrated themselves before the LORD their God. 4Standing on the platform of the Levites were Jeshua, Binnui, Kadmiel, Shebaniah, Bunni, Sherebiah, Bani, and Chenani, who cried out to the LORD their God with a loud voice. 5The Levites Jeshua, Kadmiel, Bani, Hashabneiah, Sherebiah, Hodiah, Shebaniah, and Pethahiah said, "Arise, bless the LORD, your God, from eternity to eternity!" The Israelites answered with the blessing, "Blessed is your glorious name, and exalted above all blessing and praise." 6Then Ezra said: "It is you, O LORD, you are the only one; you made the heavens, the highest heavens and all their host, the earth and all that is upon it, the seas and all that is in them. To all of them you give life, and the heavenly hosts bow down before you. 7You, O LORD, are the God who chose Abram, who brought him out from Ur of the Chaldees, and named him Abraham. 8When you had found his heart faithful in your sight, you made the covenant with him to give to him and his posterity the land of the Canaanites, Hittites, Amorites, Perizzites, Jebusites, and Girgashites. These promises of yours you fulfilled, for you are just. 9You saw the affliction of our fathers in Egypt, you heard their cry by the Red Sea; 10You worked signs and wonders against Pharaoh, against all his servants and the people of his land, because you knew of their insolence toward them; thus you made for yourself a name even to this day. 11The sea you divided before them, on dry ground they passed through the midst of the sea; their pursuers you hurled into the depths, like a stone into the mighty waters. 12With a column of cloud you led them by day, and by night with a column of fire, to light the way of their journey, the way in which they must travel. 13On Mount Sinai you came down, you spoke with them just ordinances, firm laws, good statutes, and commandments; 14Your holy sabbath you made known to them, commandments, statutes, and law you prescribed for them, by the hand of Moses your servant. 15Food from heaven you gave them in their hunger, water from a rock you sent them in their thirst. You bade them enter and occupy the land which you had sworn with upraised hand to give them. 16But they, our fathers, proved to be insolent; they held their necks stiff and would not obey your commandments. 17They refused to obey and no longer remembered the miracles you had worked for them. They stiffened their necks and turned their heads to return to their slavery in Egypt. But you are a God of pardons, gracious and compassionate, slow to anger and rich in mercy; you did not forsake them. 18Though they made for themselves a molten calf, and proclaimed, 'Here is your God who brought you up out of Egypt,' and were guilty of great effronteries, 19yet in your great mercy you did not forsake them in the desert. The column of cloud did not cease to lead them by day on their journey, nor did the column of fire by night cease to light for them the way by which they were to travel. 20Your good spirit you bestowed on them, to give them understanding; your manna you did not withhold from their mouths, and you gave them water in their thirst. 21Forty years in the desert you sustained them: they did not want; their garments did not become worn, and their feet did not become swollen. 22You gave them kingdoms and peoples, which you divided up among them as border lands. They possessed the land of Sihon, king of Heshbon, and the land of Og, king of Bashan. 23You made their children as numerous as the stars of the heavens, and you brought them into the land which you had commanded their fathers to enter and possess. 24The sons went in to take possession of the land, and you humbled before them the Canaanite inhabitants of the land and delivered them over into their power, their kings as well as the peoples of the land, to do with them as they would. 25They captured fortified cities and fertile land; they took possession of houses filled with all good things, cisterns already dug, vineyards, olive groves, and fruit trees in abundance. They could eat and have their fill, fatten and feast themselves on your immense good gifts. 26But they were contemptuous and rebellious: they cast your law behind their backs, they slew your prophets who bore witness against them in order to bring them back to you, and they were guilty of great effronteries. 27Therefore you delivered them into the power of their enemies, who oppressed them. But in the time of their oppression they would cry out to you, and you would hear them from heaven, and according to your great mercy give them saviors to deliver them from the power of their enemies. 28As soon as they had relief, they would go back to doing evil in your sight. Then again you abandoned them to the power of their enemies, who crushed them. Then they cried out to you, and you heard them from heaven and delivered them according to your mercy, many times over. 29You bore witness against them, in order to bring them back to your law. But they were insolent and would not obey your commandments; they sinned against your ordinances, from which men draw life when they practice them. They turned stubborn backs, stiffened their necks, and would not obey. 30You were patient with them for many years, bearing witness against them through your spirit, by means of your prophets; still they would not listen. Thus you delivered them over into the power of the peoples of the lands. 31Yet in your great mercy you did not completely destroy them and you did not forsake them, for you are a kind and merciful God. 32Now, therefore, O our God, great, mighty, and awesome God, you who in your mercy preserve the covenant, take into account all the disasters that have befallen us, our kings, our princes, our priests, our prophets, our fathers, and your entire people, from the time of the kings of Assyria until this day! 33In all that has come upon us you have been just, for you kept faith while we have done evil. 34Yes, our kings, our princes, our priests, and our fathers have not kept your law; they paid no attention to your commandments and the obligations of which you reminded them. 35While they were yet in their kingdom, in the midst of the many good things that you had given them and in the wide and fertile land that you had spread out before them, they did not serve you nor did they turn away from their evil deeds. 36But, see, we today are slaves; and as for the land which you gave our fathers that they might eat its fruits and good things—see, we have become slaves upon it! 37Its rich produce goes to the kings whom you set over us because of our sins, who rule over our bodies and our cattle as they please. We are in great distress!"

Nehemiah Chapter 10

1 In view of all this, we are entering into a firm pact, which we are putting into writing. On the sealed document appear the names of our princes, our Levites, and our priests. 2 On the sealed document: His Excellency Nehemiah, son of Hacaliah, and Zedekiah. 3 Seraiah, Azariah, Jeremiah, 4 Pashhur, Amariah, Malchijah, 5 Hattush, Shebaniah, Malluch, 6 Harim, Meremoth, Obadiah, 7 Daniel, Ginnethon, Baruch, 8 Meshullam, Abijah, Mijamin, 9 Maaziah, Bilgai, Shemaiah: these are the priests. 10 The Levites: Jeshua, son of Azaniah; Binnui, of the sons of Henadad; Kadmiel; 11 and their brethren Shebaniah, Hodiah, Kelita, Pelaiah, Hanan, 12 Mica, Rehob, Hashabiah, 13 Zaccur, Sherebiah, Shebaniah, 14 Hodiah, Bani, Beninu. 15 The leaders of the people: Parosh, Pahath-moab, Elam, Zattu, Bani, 16 Bunni, Azgad, Bebai, 17 Adonijah, Bigvai, Adin, 18 Ater, Hezekiah, Azzur, 19 Hodiah, Hashum, Bezai, 20 Hariph, Anathoth, Nebai, 21 Magpiash, Meshullam, Hezir, 22 Meshezabel, Zadok, Jaddua, 23 Pelatiah, Hanan, Anaiah, 24 Hoshea, Hananiah, Hasshub, 25 Halhohesh, Pilha, Shobek, 26 Rehum, Hashabnah, Maaseiah, 27 Ahiah, Hanan, Anan, 28 Malluch, Harim, Baanah. 29 The rest of the people, priests, Levites, gatekeepers, singers, temple slaves, and all others who have separated themselves from the peoples of the lands in favor of the law of God, with their wives, their sons, their daughters, all who are of the age of discretion, 30 join with their brethren who are their princes, and with the sanction of a curse take this oath to follow the law of God which was given through Moses, the servant of God, and to observe carefully all the commandments of the LORD, our LORD, his ordinances and his statutes. 31 Agreed, that we will not marry our daughters to the peoples of the land, and that we will not take their daughters for our sons. 32 When the peoples of the land bring in merchandise or any kind of grain for sale on the sabbath day, we will not buy from them on the sabbath or on any other holy day. We will forgo the seventh year, as well as every kind of debt. 33 We impose these commandments on ourselves: to give a third of a shekel each year for the service of the house of our God, 34 for the showbread, for the daily cereal offering, for the daily holocaust, for the sabbaths, new moons, and festivals, for the holy offerings, for sin offerings to make atonement for Israel, and for every service of the house of our God. 35 We, priests, Levites, and people, have determined by lot concerning the procurement of wood: it is to be brought to the house of our God by

each of our family houses at stated times each year, to be burnt on the altar of the LORD, our God, as the law prescribes. 36 We have agreed to bring each year to the house of the LORD the first fruits of our fields and of our fruit trees, of whatever kind; 37 also, as is prescribed in the law, to bring to the house of our God, to the priests who serve in the house of our God, the first-born of our children and our animals, including the first-born of our flocks and herds. 38 The first batch of our dough, and our offerings of the fruit of every tree, of wine and of oil, we will bring to the priests, to the chambers of the house of our God. The tithe of our fields we will bring to the Levites; they, the Levites, shall take the tithe in all the cities of our service. 39 An Aaronite priest shall be with the Levites when they take the tithe, and the Levites shall bring the tithe of the tithes to the house of our God, to the chambers of the treasury. 40 For to these chambers the Israelites and Levites bring the offerings of grain, wine, and oil; there also are housed the utensils of the sanctuary, and the ministering priests, the gatekeepers, and the singers. We will not neglect the house of our God.

Nehemiah Chapter 11

1 The leaders of the people took up residence in Jerusalem, and the rest of the people cast lots to bring one man in ten to reside in Jerusalem, the holy city, while the other nine would remain in the other cities. 2 The people applauded all those men who willingly agreed to take up residence in Jerusalem. 3 These are the heads of the province who took up residence in Jerusalem. (In the cities of Judah dwelt lay Israelites, priests, Levites, temple slaves, and the descendants of the slaves of Solomon, each man on the property he owned in his own city.) 4 In Jerusalem dwelt both Judahites and Benjaminites. Of the Judahites: Athaiah, son of Uzziah, son of Zechariah, son of Amariah, son of Shephatiah, son of Mehallalel, of the sons of Perez; 5 Maaseiah, son of Baruch, son of Colhozeh, son of Hazaiah, son of Adaiah, son of Joiarib, son of Zechariah, a son of the Shelanites. 6 The total of the sons of Perez who dwelt in Jerusalem was four hundred and sixty-eight valiant men. 7 These were the Benjaminites: Sallu, son of Meshullam, son of Joed, son of Pedaiah, son of Kolaiah, son of Maaseiah, son of Ithiel, son of Jeshaiah, 8 and his brethren, warriors, nine hundred and twenty-eight in number. 9 Joel, son of Zichri, was their commander, and Judah, son of Hassenuah, was second in charge of the city. 10 Among the priests were: Jedaiah; Joiarib; Jachin; 11 Seraiah, son of Hilkiah, son of Meshullam, son of Zadok, son of Meraioth, son of Ahitub, the ruler of the house of God, 12 and their brethren who carried out the temple service, eight hundred and twenty-two; Adaiah, son of Jeroham, son of Pelaliah, son of Amzi, son of Zechariah, son of Pashhur, son of Malchijah, 13 and his brethren, family heads, two hundred and forty-two; and Amasai, son of Azarel, son of Ahzai, son of Meshillemoth, son of Immer, 14 and his brethren, warriors, one hundred and twenty-eight. Their commander was Zabdiel, son of Haggadol. 15 Among the Levites were Shemaiah, son of Hasshub, son of Azrikam, son of Hashabiah, son of Bunni; 16 Shabbethai and Jozabad, levitical chiefs who were placed over the external affairs of the house of God; 17 Mattaniah, son of Micah, son of Zabdi, son of Asaph, director of the psalms, who led the thanksgiving at prayer; Bakbukiah, second in rank among his brethren; and Abda, son of Shammua, son of Galal, son of Jeduthun. 18 The total of the Levites in the holy city was two hundred and eighty-four. 19 The gatekeepers were Akkub, Talmon, and their brethren, who kept watch over the gates; one hundred and seventy-two in number. 20 The rest of Israel, including priests and Levites, were in all the other cities of Judah, each man in his inheritance. 21 The temple slaves lived on Ophel. Ziha and Gishpa were in charge of the temple slaves. 22 The prefect of the Levites in Jerusalem was Uzzi, son of Bani, son of Hashabiah, son of Mattaniah, son of Micah; he was one of the sons of Asaph, the singers appointed to the service of the house of God - 23 for they had been appointed by royal decree, and there was a fixed schedule for the singers assigning them their daily duties. 24 Pethahiah, son of Meshezabel, a descendant of Zerah, son of Judah, was royal deputy in all affairs that concerned the people. 25 As concerns their villages in the country: Judahites lived in Kiriath-arba and its dependencies, in Dibon and its dependencies, in Jekabzeel and its villages, 26 in Jeshua, Moladah, Beth-pelet, 27 in Hazarshual, in Beer-sheba and its dependencies, 28 in Ziklag, in Meconah and its dependencies, 29 in En-rimmon, Zorah, Jarmuth, 30 Zanoah, Adullam, and their villages, Lachish and its countryside, Azekah and its dependencies. They were settled from Beer-sheba to Ge-hinnom. 31 Benjaminites were in Geba, Michmash, Aija, Bethel and its dependencies, 32 Anathoth, Nob, Ananiah, 33 Hazor, Ramah, Gittaim, 34 Hadid, Zeboim, Neballat, 35 Lod, Ono, and the Valley of the Artisans. 36 Some sections of the Levites from Judah settled in Benjamin.

Nehemiah Chapter 12

1 The following are the priests and Levites who returned with Zerubbabel, son of Shealtiel, and Jeshua: Seraiah, Jeremiah, Ezra, 2 Amariah, Malluch, Hattush, 3 Shecaniah, Rehum, Meremoth, 4 Iddo, Ginnethon, Abijah, 5 Mijamin, Maadiah, Bilgah, 6 Shemaiah, and Joiarib, Jedaiah, 7 Sallu, Amok, Hilkiah, Jedaiah. These were the priestly heads and their brethren in the days of Jeshua. 8 The Levites were Jeshua, Binnui, Kadmiel, Sherebiah, Judah, Mattaniah; the last-mentioned, together with his brethren, was in charge of the hymns, 9 while Bakbukiah and Unno and their brethren ministered opposite them by turns. 10 Jeshua became the father of Joiakim, Joiakim became the father of Eliashib, and Eliashib became the father of Joiada. 11 Joiada became the father of Johanan, and Johanan became the father of Jaddua. 12 In the days of Joiakim these were the priestly family heads: for Seraiah, Meraiah; for Jeremiah, Hananiah; 13 for Ezra, Meshullam; for Amariah, Jehohanan; 14 for Malluchi, Jonathan; for Shebaniah, Joseph; 15 for Harim, Adna; for Meremoth, Helkai; 16 for Iddo, Zechariah; for Ginnethon, Meshullam; 17 for Abijah, Zichri; for Miamin, . . . ; for Maadiah, Piltai; 18 for Bilgah, Shammua; for Shemaiah, Jehonathan; 19 and for Joiarib, Mattenai; for Jedaiah, Uzzi; 20 for Sallu, Kallai; for Amok, Eber; 21 for Hilkiah, Hashabiah; for Jedaiah, Nethanel. 22 In the time of Eliashib, Joiada, Johanan, and Jaddua, the family heads of the priests were written down in the Book of Chronicles, up until the reign of Darius the Persian. 23 The sons of Levi: the family heads were written down in the Book of Chronicles, up until the time of Johanan, the son of Eliashib. 24 The heads of the Levites were Hashabiah, Sherebiah, Jeshua, Binnui, Kadmiel. Their brethren who stood opposite them to sing praises and thanksgiving in fulfillment of the command of David, the man of God, one section opposite the other, 25 were Mattaniah, Bakbukiah, Obadiah. Meshullam, Talmon, and Akkub were gatekeepers. They kept watch over the storerooms at the gates. 26 All these lived in the time of Joiakim, son of Jeshua, son of Jozadak (and in the time of Nehemiah the governor and of Ezra the priest-scribe). 27 At the dedication of the wall of Jerusalem, the Levites were sought out wherever they lived and were brought to Jerusalem to celebrate a joyful dedication with thanksgiving hymns and the music of cymbals, harps, and lyres. 28 The levitical singers gathered together from the region about Jerusalem, from the villages of the Netophathites, 29 from Beth-gilgal, and from the plains of Geba and Azmaveth (for the singers had built themselves settlements about Jerusalem). 30 The priests and Levites first purified themselves, then they purified the people, the gates, and the wall. 31 I had the princes of Judah mount the wall, and I arranged two great choirs. The first of these proceeded to the right, along the top of the wall, in the direction of the Dung Gate, 32 followed by Hoshaiah and half the princes of Judah, 33 along with Azariah, Ezra, Meshullam, 34 Judah, Benjamin, Shemaiah, and Jeremiah, 35 priests with the trumpets, and also Zechariah, son of Jonathan, son of Shemaiah, son of Mattaniah, son of Micaiah, son of Zaccur, son of Asaph, 36 and his brethren Shemaiah, Azarel, Milalai, Gilalai, Maai, Nethanel, Judah, and Hanani, with the musical instruments of David, the man of God. (Ezra the scribe was at their head.) 37 At the Spring Gate they went straight up by the steps of the City of David and continued along the top of the wall above the house of David until they came to the Water Gate on the east. 38 The second choir proceeded to the left, followed by myself and the other half of the princes of the people, along the top of the wall past the Oven Tower as far as the Broad Wall, 39 then past the Ephraim Gate (the New City Gate), the Fish Gate, the Tower of Hananel, and the Hundred Tower, as far as the Sheep Gate (and they came to a halt at the Prison Gate). 40 The two choirs took up a position in the house of God; I, too, who had with me half the magistrates, 41 the priests Eliakim, Maaseiah, Minjamin, Micaiah, Elioenai, Zechariah, Hananiah, with the trumpets, 42 and Maaseiah, Shemaiah, Eleazar, Uzzi, Jehohanan, Malchijah, Elam, and Ezer. The singers were heard under the leadership of Jezrahiah. 43 Great sacrifices were offered on that day, and there was rejoicing over the great feast of the LORD in which they shared. The women and the children joined in, and the rejoicing at Jerusalem could be heard from afar off. 44 At that time men were appointed over the chambers set aside for stores, offerings, first fruits, and tithes; in them they were to collect from the fields of the various cities the portions legally assigned to the priests and Levites. For Judah rejoiced in its appointed priests and Levites 45 who carried out the ministry of their God and the ministry of purification (as did the singers and the gatekeepers) in accordance with the prescriptions of David and of Solomon, his son. 46 For the heads of the families of the singers and the hymns of praise and thanksgiving to God came down from the days of David and Asaph in times of old. 47 Thus all Israel, in the days of Zerubbabel (and in the days of Nehemiah), gave the singers and the

gatekeepers their portions, according to their daily needs. They made their consecrated offering to the Levites, and the Levites made theirs to the sons of Aaron.

Nehemiah Chapter 13

1 At that time, when there was reading from the book of Moses in the hearing of the people, it was found written there that "no Ammonite or Moabite may ever be admitted into the assembly of God; 2 for they would not succor the Israelites with food and water, but they hired Balaam to curse them, though our God turned the curse into a blessing." 3 When they had heard the law, they separated from Israel every foreign element. 4 Before this, the priest Eliashib, who had been placed in charge of the chambers of the house of our God and who was an associate of Tobiah, 5 had set aside for the latter's use a large chamber in which had previously been stored the cereal offerings, incense and utensils, the tithes in grain, wine, and oil allotted to the Levites, singers, and gatekeepers, and the offerings due the priests. 6 During all this time I had not been in Jerusalem, for in the thirty-second year of Artaxerxes, king of Babylon, I had gone back to the king. After due time, however, I asked leave of the king 7 and returned to Jerusalem, where I discovered the evil thing that Eliashib had done for Tobiah, in setting aside for him a chamber in the courts of the house of God. 8 This displeased me very much, and I had all of Tobiah's household goods thrown outside the chamber. 9 Then I gave orders to purify the chambers, and I had them replace there the utensils of the house of God, the cereal offerings, and the incense. 10 I learned, too, that the portions due the Levites were no longer being given, so that the Levites and the singers who should have been carrying out the services had deserted, each man to his own field. 11 I took the magistrates to task, demanding, "Why is the house of God abandoned?" Then I brought the Levites together and had them resume their stations. 12 All Judah once more brought in the tithes of grain, wine, and oil to the storerooms; 13 and in charge of the storerooms I appointed the priest Shelemiah, Zadok the scribe, and Pedaiah, one of the Levites, together with Hanan, son of Zaccur, son of Mattaniah, as their assistant; for these men were held to be trustworthy. It was their duty to make the distribution to their brethren. 14 Remember this to my credit, O my God! Let not the devotion which I showed for the house of my God and its services be forgotten! 15 In those days I perceived that men in Judah were treading the winepresses on the sabbath; that they were bringing in sheaves of grain, loading them on their asses, together with wine, grapes, figs, and every other kind of burden, and bringing them to Jerusalem on the sabbath day. I warned them to sell none of these victuals. 16 In Jerusalem itself the Tyrians who were resident there were importing fish and every other kind of merchandise and selling it to the Judahites on the sabbath. 17 I took the nobles of Judah to task, demanding of them: "What is this evil thing that you are doing, profaning the sabbath day? 18 Did not your fathers act in this same way, with the result that our God has brought all this evil upon us and upon this city? Would you add to the wrath against Israel by once more profaning the sabbath?" 19 When the shadows were falling on the gates of Jerusalem before the sabbath, I ordered the doors to be closed and forbade them to be reopened till after the sabbath. I posted some of my own men at the gates so that no burden might enter on the sabbath day. 20 The merchants and sellers of various kinds of merchandise spent the night once or twice outside Jerusalem, 21 but then I warned them, saying to them: "Why do you spend the night alongside the wall? If you keep this up, I will lay hands on you!" From that time on, they did not return on the sabbath. 22 Then I ordered the Levites to purify themselves and to go and watch the gates, so that the sabbath day might be kept holy. This, too, remember in my favor, O my God, and have mercy on me in accordance with your great mercy! 23 Also in those days I saw Jews who had married Ashdodite, Ammonite, or Moabite wives. 24 Of their children, half spoke Ashdodite, and none of them knew how to speak Jewish; and so it was in regard to the languages of the various other peoples. 25 I took them to task and cursed them; I had some of them beaten and their hair pulled out; and I adjured them by God: "You shall not marry your daughters to their sons nor take any of their daughters for your sons or for yourselves! 26 Did not Solomon, the king of Israel, sin because of them? Though among the many nations there was no king like him, and though he was beloved of his God and God had made him king over all Israel, yet even he was made to sin by foreign women. 27 Must it also be heard of you that you have done this same very great evil, betraying our God by marrying foreign women?" 28 One of the sons of Joiada, son of Eliashib the high priest, was the son-in-law of Sanballat the Horonite! I drove him from my presence. 29 Remember against them, O my God, how they defiled the priesthood and the covenant of the priesthood and the Levites! 30 Thus I cleansed them of all foreign contamination. I established the various functions for the priests and Levites, so that each had his appointed task. 31 I also provided for the procurement of wood at stated times and for the first fruits. Remember this in my favor, O my God!

Esther

Esther Chapter 1

1 During the reign of Ahasuerus—this was the Ahasuerus who ruled over a hundred and twenty-seven provinces from India to Ethiopia—2 while he was occupying the royal throne in the stronghold of Susa, 3 in the third year of his reign, he presided over a feast for all his officers and ministers: the Persian and Median aristocracy, the nobles, and the governors of the provinces. 4 For as many as a hundred and eighty days, he displayed the glorious riches of his kingdom and the resplendent wealth of his royal estate. 5 At the end of this time the king gave a feast of seven days in the garden court of the royal palace for all the people, great and small, who were in the stronghold of Susa. 6 There were white cotton draperies and violet hangings, held by cords of crimson byssus from silver rings on marble pillars. Gold and silver couches were on the pavement, which was of porphyry, marble, mother-of-pearl, and colored stones. 7 Liquor was served in a variety of golden cups, and the royal wine flowed freely, as befitted the king's munificence. 8 By ordinance of the king the drinking was unstinted, for he had instructed all the stewards of his household to comply with the good pleasure of everyone. 9 Queen Vashti also gave a feast for the women inside the royal palace of King Ahasuerus. 10 On the seventh day, when the king was merry with wine, he instructed Mehuman, Biztha, Harbona, Bigtha, Abagtha, Zethar, and Carkas, the seven eunuchs who attended King Ahasuerus, 11 to bring Queen Vashti into his presence wearing the royal crown, that he might display her beauty to the populace and the officials, for she was lovely to behold. 12 But Queen Vashti refused to come at the royal order issued through the eunuchs. At this the king's wrath flared up, and he burned with fury. 13 He conferred with the wise men versed in the law, because the king's business was conducted in general consultation with lawyers and jurists. 14 He summoned Carshena, Shethar, Admatha, Tarshish, Meres, Marsena and Memucan, the seven Persian and Median officials who were in the king's personal service and held first rank in the realm, 15 and asked them, "What is to be done by law with Queen Vashti for disobeying the order of King Ahasuerus issued through the eunuchs?" 16 In the presence of the king and of the officials, Memucan answered: "Queen Vashti has not wronged the king alone, but all the officials and the populace throughout the provinces of King Ahasuerus. 17 For the queen's conduct will become known to all the women, and they will look with disdain upon their husbands when it is reported, 'King Ahasuerus commanded that Queen Vashti be ushered into his presence, but she would not come.' 18 This very day the Persian and Median ladies who hear of the queen's conduct will rebel against all the royal officials, with corresponding disdain and rancor. 19 If it please the king, let an irrevocable royal decree be issued by him and inscribed among the laws of the Persians and Medes, forbidding Vashti to come into the presence of King Ahasuerus and authorizing the king to give her royal dignity to one more worthy than she. 20 Thus, when the decree which the king will issue is published throughout his realm, vast as it is, all wives will honor their husbands, from the greatest to the least." 21 This proposal found acceptance with the king and the officials, and the king acted on the advice of Memucan. 22 He sent letters to all the royal provinces, to each province in its own script and to each people in its own language, to the effect that every man should be lord in his own home.

Esther Chapter 2

1 After this, when King Ahasuerus' wrath had cooled, he thought over what Vashti had done and what had been decreed against her. 2 Then the king's personal attendants suggested: "Let beautiful young virgins be sought for the king. 3 Let the king appoint commissaries in all the provinces of his realm to bring together all beautiful young virgins to the harem in the stronghold of Susa. Under the care of the royal eunuch Hegai, custodian of the women, let cosmetics be given them. 4 Then the girl who pleases the king shall reign in place of Vashti." This suggestion pleased the king, and he acted accordingly. 5 There was in the stronghold of Susa a certain Jew named Mordecai, son of Jair, son of Shimei, son of Kish, a Benjaminite, 6 who had been exiled from Jerusalem with the captives taken with Jeconiah, king of Judah, whom Nebuchadnezzar, king of Babylon, had deported. 7 He was foster father to Hadassah, that is, Esther, his cousin; for she had lost both father and mother. The girl was beautifully formed and lovely to behold. On the death of her father and mother, Mordecai had taken her as his own daughter. 8 When the king's order and decree had been obeyed and many maidens brought together to the stronghold of Susa under the

care of Hegai, Esther also was brought in to the royal palace under the care of Hegai, custodian of the women. 9The girl pleased him and won his favor. So he promptly furnished her with cosmetics and provisions. Then picking out seven maids for her from the royal palace, he transferred both her and her maids to the best place in the harem. 10Esther did not reveal her nationality or family, for Mordecai had commanded her not to do so. 11Day by day Mordecai would walk about in front of the court of the harem, to learn how Esther was faring and what was to become of her. 12Each girl went in turn to visit King Ahasuerus after the twelve months' preparation decreed for the women. Of this period of beautifying treatment, six months were spent with oil of myrrh, and the other six months with perfumes and cosmetics. 13Then, when the girl was to visit the king, she was allowed to take with her from the harem to the royal palace whatever she chose. 14She would go in the evening and return in the morning to a second harem under the care of the royal eunuch Shaashgaz, custodian of the concubines. She could not return to the king unless he was pleased with her and had her summoned by name. 15As for Esther, daughter of Abihail and adopted daughter of his nephew Mordecai, when her turn came to visit the king, she did not ask for anything but what the royal eunuch Hegai, custodian of the women, suggested. Yet she won the admiration of all who saw her. 16Esther was led to King Ahasuerus in his palace in the tenth month, Tebeth, in the seventh year of his reign. 17The king loved Esther more than all other women, and of all the virgins she won his favor and benevolence. So he placed the royal diadem on her head and made her queen in place of Vashti. 18Then the king gave a great feast in honor of Esther to all his officials and ministers, granting a holiday to the provinces and bestowing gifts with royal bounty. 19[To resume: From the time the virgins had been brought together, and while Mordecai was passing his time at the king's gate, 20Esther had not revealed her family or nationality, because Mordecai had told her not to; and Esther continued to follow Mordecai's instructions, just as she had when she was being brought up by him. 21And during the time that Mordecai spent at the king's gate, Bagathan and Thares, two of the royal eunuchs who guarded the entrance, had plotted in anger to lay hands on King Ahasuerus. 22When the plot became known to Mordecai, he told Queen Esther, who in turn informed the king for Mordecai. 23The matter was investigated and verified, and both of them were hanged on a gibbet. This was written in the annals for the king's use.]

Esther Chapter 3

1After these events King Ahasuerus raised Haman, son of Hammedatha the Agagite, to high rank, seating him above all his fellow officials. 2All the king's servants who were at the royal gate would kneel and bow down to Haman, for that is what the king had ordered in his regard. Mordecai, however, would not kneel and bow down. 3The king's servants who were at the royal gate said to Mordecai, "Why do you disobey the king's order?" 4When they had reminded him day after day and he would not listen to them, they informed Haman, to see whether Mordecai's explanation was acceptable, since he had told them that he was a Jew. 5When Haman observed that Mordecai would not kneel and bow down to him, he was filled with anger. 6Moreover, he thought it was not enough to lay hands on Mordecai alone. Since they had told Haman of Mordecai's nationality, he sought to destroy all the Jews, Mordecai's people, throughout the realm of King Ahasuerus. 7In the first month, Nisan, in the twelfth year of King Ahasuerus, the pur, or lot, was cast in Haman's presence to determine the day and the month for the destruction of Mordecai's people on a single day, and the lot fell on the thirteenth day of the twelfth month, Adar. 8Then Haman said to King Ahasuerus: "Dispersed among the nations throughout the provinces of your kingdom, there is a certain people living apart, with laws differing from those of every other people. They do not obey the laws of the king, and so it is not proper for the king to tolerate them. 9If it please the king, let a decree be issued to destroy them; and I will deliver to the procurators ten thousand silver talents for deposit in the royal treasury." 10The king took the signet ring from his hand and gave it to Haman, son of Hammedatha the Agagite, the enemy of the Jews. 11"The silver you may keep," the king said to Haman, "but as for this people, do with them whatever you please." 12So the royal scribes were summoned; and on the thirteenth day of the first month they wrote, at the dictation of Haman, an order to the royal satraps, the governors of every province, and the officials of every people, to each province in its own script and to each people in its own language. It was written in the name of King Ahasuerus and sealed with the royal signet ring. 13Letters were sent by couriers to all the royal provinces, that all the Jews, young and old, including women and children, should be killed, destroyed, wiped out in one day, the thirteenth day of the twelfth month, Adar, and that their goods should be seized as spoil.

Esther Chapter 4

1When Mordecai learned all that was happening, he tore his garments, put on sackcloth and ashes, and walked through the city crying out loudly and bitterly, 2till he came before the royal gate, which no one clothed in sackcloth might enter. 3(Likewise in each of the provinces, wherever the king's legal enactment reached, the Jews went into deep mourning, with fasting, weeping, and lament; they all slept on sackcloth and ashes.) 4Queen Esther's maids and eunuchs came and told her. Overwhelmed with anguish, she sent garments for Mordecai to put on, so that he might take off his sackcloth; but he refused. 5Esther then summoned Hathach, one of the king's eunuchs whom he had placed at her service, and commanded him to find out what this action of Mordecai meant and the reason for it. 6So Hathach went out to Mordecai in the public square in front of the royal gate, 7and Mordecai told him all that had happened, as well as the exact amount of silver Haman had promised to pay to the royal treasury for the slaughter of the Jews. 8He also gave him a copy of the written decree for their destruction which had been promulgated in Susa, to show and explain to Esther. He was to instruct her to go to the king; she was to plead and intercede with him on behalf of her people. 9"Remember the days of your lowly estate," Mordecai had him say, "when you were brought up in my charge; for Haman, who is second to the king, has asked for our death. 10Invoke the Lord and speak to the king for us: save us from death." Hathach returned to Esther and told her what Mordecai had said. 11Then Esther replied to Hathach and gave him this message for Mordecai: "All the servants of the king and the people of his provinces know that any man or woman who goes to the king in the inner court without being summoned, suffers the automatic penalty of death, unless the king extends to him the golden scepter, thus sparing his life. Now as for me, I have not been summoned to the king for thirty days." 12When Esther's words were reported to Mordecai, 13he had this reply brought to her: "Do not imagine that because you are in the king's palace, you alone of all the Jews will escape. 14Even if you now remain silent, relief and deliverance will come to the Jews from another source; but you and your father's house will perish. Who knows but that it was for a time like this that you obtained the royal dignity?" 15Esther sent back to Mordecai the response: 16"Go and assemble all the Jews who are in Susa; fast on my behalf, all of you, not eating or drinking, night or day, for three days. I and my maids will also fast in the same way. Thus prepared, I will go to the king, contrary to the law. If I perish, I perish!"

Esther Chapter 5

1[Now on the third day, Esther put on her royal garments and stood in the inner courtyard, looking toward the royal palace, while the king was seated on his royal throne in the audience chamber, facing the palace doorway. 2He saw Queen Esther standing in the courtyard, and made her welcome by extending toward her the golden staff which he held. She came up to him, and touched the top of the staff.] 3Then the king said to her, "What is it, Queen Esther? What is your request? Even if it is half of my kingdom, it shall be granted you." 4"If it please your majesty," Esther replied, "come today with Haman to a banquet I have prepared." 5And the king ordered, "Have Haman make haste to fulfill the wish of Esther." So the king went with Haman to the banquet Esther had prepared. 6During the drinking of the wine, the king said to Esther, "Whatever you ask for shall be granted, and whatever request you make shall be honored, even if it is for half my kingdom." 7Esther replied: "This is my petition and request: 8if I have found favor with the king and if it pleases your majesty to grant my petition and honor my request, come with Haman tomorrow to a banquet which I shall prepare for you; and then I will do as you ask." 9That day Haman left happy and in good spirits. But when he saw that Mordecai at the royal gate did not rise, and showed no fear of him, he was filled with anger toward him. 10Haman restrained himself, however, and went home, where he summoned his friends and his wife Zeresh. 11He recounted the greatness of his riches, the large number of his sons, and just how the king had promoted him and placed him above the officials and royal servants. 12"Moreover," Haman added, "Queen Esther invited no one but me to the banquet with the king; again tomorrow I am to be her guest, with the king. 13Yet none of this satisfies me as long as I continue to see the Jew Mordecai sitting at the royal gate." 14His wife Zeresh and all his friends said to him, "Have a gibbet set up, fifty cubits in height, and in the morning ask the king to have Mordecai hanged on it. Then go to the banquet with the king in good cheer." This suggestion pleased Haman, and he had the gibbet erected.

Esther Chapter 6

1That night the king, unable to sleep, asked that the chronicle of notable events be brought in. While this was being read to him, 2the passage occurred in which Mordecai reported Bagathan and Teresh, two of the royal eunuchs who guarded the entrance, for seeking to lay hands on King Ahasuerus. 3The king asked, "What was done to reward and honor Mordecai for this?" The king's attendants replied, "Nothing was done for him." 4"Who is in the court?" the king asked. Now Haman had entered the outer court of the king's palace to suggest to the king that Mordecai should be hanged on the gibbet he had raised for him. 5The king's servants answered him, "Haman is waiting in the court." "Let him come in," the king said. 6When Haman entered, the king said to him, "What should be done for the man whom the king wishes to reward?" Now Haman thought to himself, "Whom would the king more probably wish to reward than me?" 7So he replied to the king: "For the man whom the king wishes to reward 8there should be brought the royal robe which the king wore and the horse on which the king rode when the royal crown was placed on his head. 9The robe and the horse should be consigned to one of the noblest of the king's officials, who must clothe the man the king wishes to reward, have him ride on the horse in the public square of the city, and cry out before him, 'This is what is done for the man whom the king wishes to reward!'" 10Then the king said to Haman: "Hurry! Take the robe and horse as you have proposed, and do this for the Jew Mordecai, who is sitting at the royal gate. Do not omit anything you proposed." 11So Haman took the robe and horse, clothed Mordecai, had him ride in the public square of the city, and cried out before him, "This is what is done for the man whom the king wishes to reward!" 12Mordecai then returned to the royal gate, while Haman hurried home, his head covered in grief. 13When he told his wife Zeresh and all his friends everything that had happened to him, his advisers and his wife Zeresh said to him, "If Mordecai, before whom you are beginning to decline, is of the Jewish race, you will not prevail against him, but will surely be defeated by him." 14While they were speaking with him, the king's eunuchs arrived and hurried Haman off to the banquet Esther had prepared.

Esther Chapter 7

1So the king and Haman went to the banquet with Queen Esther. 2Again, on this second day, during the drinking of the wine, the king said to Esther, "Whatever you ask, Queen Esther, shall be granted you. Whatever request you make shall be honored, even for half the kingdom." 3Queen Esther replied: "If I have found favor with you, O king, and if it pleases your majesty, I ask that my life be spared, and I beg that you spare the lives of my people. 4For my people and I have been delivered to destruction, slaughter, and extinction. If we were to be sold into slavery I would remain silent, but as it is, the enemy will be unable to compensate for the harm done to the king." 5"Who and where," said King Ahasuerus to Queen Esther, "is the man who has dared to do this?" 6Esther replied, "The enemy oppressing us is this wicked Haman." At this, Haman was seized with dread of the king and queen. 7The king left the banquet in anger and went into the garden of the palace, but Haman stayed to beg Queen Esther for his life, since he saw that the king had decided on his doom. 8When the king returned from the garden of the palace to the banquet hall, Haman had thrown himself on the couch on which Esther was reclining; and the king exclaimed, "Will he also violate the queen while she is with me in my own house!" Scarcely had the king spoken when the face of Haman was covered over. 9Harbona, one of the eunuchs who attended the king, said, "At the house of Haman stands a gibbet fifty cubits high. Haman prepared it for Mordecai, who gave the report that benefited the king." The king answered, "Hang him on it." 10So they hanged Haman on the gibbet which he had made ready for Mordecai, and the anger of the king abated.

Esther Chapter 8

1That day King Ahasuerus gave the house of Haman, enemy of the Jews, to Queen Esther; and Mordecai was admitted to the king's presence, for Esther had revealed his relationship to her. 2The king removed his signet ring from Haman, and transferred it into the keeping of Mordecai; and Esther put Mordecai in charge of the house of Haman. 3In another audience with the king, Esther fell at his feet and tearfully implored him to revoke the harm done by Haman the Agagite, and the plan he had devised against the Jews. 4The king stretched forth the golden scepter to Esther. So she rose and, standing in his presence, 5said: "If it pleases your majesty and seems proper to you, and if I have found favor with you and you love me, let a document be issued to revoke the letters which that schemer Haman, son of Hammedatha the Agagite, wrote for the destruction of the Jews in all the royal provinces. 6For how can I witness the evil that is to befall my people, and how can I behold the destruction of my race?" 7King Ahasuerus then said to Queen Esther and to the Jew Mordecai: "Now that I have given Esther the house of Haman, and they have hanged him on the gibbet because

he attacked the Jews, 8you in turn may write in the king's name what you see fit concerning the Jews and seal the letter with the royal signet ring." For whatever is written in the name of the king and sealed with the royal signet ring cannot be revoked. 9At that time, on the twenty-third day of the third month, Sivan, the royal scribes were summoned. Exactly as Mordecai dictated, they wrote to the Jews and to the satraps, governors, and officials of the hundred and twenty-seven provinces from India to Ethiopia: to each province in its own script and to each people in its own language, and to the Jews in their own script and language. 10These letters, which he wrote in the name of King Ahasuerus and sealed with the royal signet ring, he sent by mounted couriers riding thoroughbred royal steeds. 11In these letters the king authorized the Jews in each and every city to group together and defend their lives, and to kill, destroy, wipe out, along with their wives and children, every armed group of any nation or province which should attack them, and to seize their goods as spoil 12throughout the provinces of King Ahasuerus, on a single day, the thirteenth of the twelfth month, Adar. 13A copy of the letter to be promulgated as law in each and every province was published among all the peoples, so that the Jews might be prepared on that day to avenge themselves on their enemies. 14Couriers mounted on royal steeds sped forth in haste at the king's order, and the decree was promulgated in the stronghold of Susa. 15Mordecai left the king's presence clothed in a royal robe of violet and of white cotton, with a large crown of gold and a cloak of crimson byssus. The city of Susa shouted with joy, 16and there was splendor and merriment for the Jews, exultation and triumph. 17In each and every province and in each and every city, wherever the king's order arrived, there was merriment and exultation, banqueting and feasting for the Jews. And many of the peoples of the land embraced Judaism, for they were seized with a fear of the Jews.

Esther Chapter 9

1When the day arrived on which the order decreed by the king was to be carried out, the thirteenth day of the twelfth month, Adar, on which the enemies of the Jews had expected to become masters of them, the situation was reversed: the Jews became masters of their enemies. 2The Jews mustered in their cities throughout the provinces of King Ahasuerus to attack those who sought to do them harm, and no one could withstand them, but all peoples were seized with a fear of them. 3Moreover, all the officials of the provinces, the satraps, governors, and royal procurators supported the Jews from fear of Mordecai; 4for Mordecai was powerful in the royal palace, and the report was spreading through all the provinces that he was continually growing in power. 5The Jews struck down all their enemies with the sword, killing and destroying them; they did to their enemies as they pleased. 6In the stronghold of Susa, the Jews killed and destroyed five hundred men. 7They also killed Parshandatha, Dalphon, Aspatha, 8Porathai, Adalia, Aridatha, 9Parmashta, Arisai, Aridai, and Vaizatha, 10the ten sons of Haman, son of Hammedatha, the foe of the Jews. However, they did not engage in plundering. 11On the same day, when the number of those killed in the stronghold of Susa was reported to the king, 12he said to Queen Esther: "In the stronghold of Susa the Jews have killed and destroyed five hundred men, as well as the ten sons of Haman. What must they have done in the other royal provinces! You shall again be granted whatever you ask, and whatever you request shall be honored." 13So Esther said, "If it pleases your majesty, let the Jews in Susa be permitted again tomorrow to act according to today's decree, and let the ten sons of Haman be hanged on gibbets." 14The king then gave an order to this effect, and the decree was published in Susa. So the ten sons of Haman were hanged, 15and the Jews in Susa mustered again on the fourteenth of the month of Adar and killed three hundred men in Susa. However, they did not engage in plundering. 16The other Jews, who dwelt in the royal provinces, also mustered and defended themselves, and obtained rest from their enemies. They killed seventy-five thousand of their foes, without engaging in plunder, 17on the thirteenth day of the month of Adar. On the fourteenth of the month they rested, and made it a day of feasting and rejoicing. 18(The Jews in Susa, however, mustered on the thirteenth and fourteenth of the month. But on the fifteenth they rested, and made it a day of feasting and rejoicing.) 19That is why the rural Jews, who dwell in villages, celebrate the fourteenth of the month of Adar as a day of rejoicing and feasting, a holiday on which they send gifts of food to one another. 20Mordecai recorded these events and sent letters to all the Jews, both near and far, in all the provinces of King Ahasuerus. 21He ordered them to celebrate every year both the fourteenth and the fifteenth of the month of Adar 22as the days on which the Jews obtained rest from their enemies and as the month which was turned for them from sorrow into joy, from mourning into festivity. They were to observe these days with feasting and gladness, sending food to one another and gifts to the poor.

23The Jews took upon themselves for the future this observance which they instituted at the written direction of Mordecai. 24Haman, son of Hammedatha the Agagite, the foe of all the Jews, had planned to destroy them and had cast the pur, or lot, for the time of their defeat and destruction. 25Yet, when Esther entered the royal presence, the king ordered in writing that the wicked plan Haman had devised against the Jews should instead be turned against Haman and that he and his sons should be hanged on gibbets. 26And so these days have been named Purim after the word pur. Thus, because of all that was contained in this letter, and because of what they had witnessed and experienced in this affair, 27the Jews established and took upon themselves, their descendants, and all who should join them, the inviolable obligation of celebrating these two days every year in the manner prescribed by this letter, and at the time appointed. 28These days were to be commemorated and kept in every generation, by every clan, in every province, and in every city. These days of Purim were never to fall into disuse among the Jews, nor into oblivion among their descendants. 29Queen Esther, daughter of Abihail and of Mordecai the Jew, wrote to confirm with full authority this second letter about Purim, 30when Mordecai sent documents concerning peace and security to all the Jews in the hundred and twenty-seven provinces of Ahasuerus' kingdom. 31Thus were established, for their appointed time, these days of Purim which Mordecai the Jew and Queen Esther had designated for the Jews, just as they had previously enjoined upon themselves and upon their race the duty of fasting and supplication. 32The command of Esther confirmed these prescriptions for Purim and was recorded in the book.

Esther Chapter 10

1King Ahasuerus laid tribute on the land and on the islands of the sea. 2All the acts of his power and valor, as well as a detailed account of the greatness of Mordecai, whom the king promoted, are recorded in the chronicles of the kings of Media and Persia. 3The Jew Mordecai was next in rank to King Ahasuerus, in high standing among the Jews, and was regarded with favor by his many brethren, as the promoter of his people's welfare and the herald of peace for his whole race.

Additions to Esther

Additions to Esther chapter 1

1 [In the second year of the reign of Ahasuerus the great king, on the first day of Nisan, Mordecai the son of Jair, the son of Shimei, the son of Kish, of the tribe of Benjamin, a Jew dwelling in the city Susa, a great man, serving in the king's palace, saw a vision. Now he was one of the captives whom Nebuchadnezzar king of Babylon had carried captive from Jerusalem with Jeconiah the king of Judea. This was his dream: Behold, voices and a noise, thunders and earthquake, tumult upon the earth. And, behold, two great serpents came out, both ready for conflict. A great voice came from them. Every nation was prepared for battle by their voice, even to fight against the nation of the just. Behold, a day of darkness and blackness, suffering and anguish, affection and tumult upon the earth. And all the righteous nation was troubled, fearing their own afflictions. They prepared to die, and cried to God. Something like a great river from a little spring with much water, came from their cry. Light and the sun arose, and the lowly were exalted, and devoured the honorable. Mordecai, who had seen this vision and what God desired to do, having arisen, kept it in his heart, and desired by all means to interpret it, even until night. Mordecai rested quietly in the palace with Gabatha and Tharrha the king's two chamberlains, eunuchs who guarded the palace. He heard their conversation and searched out their plans. He learned that they were preparing to lay hands on King Ahasuerus; and he informed the king concerning them. The king examined the two chamberlains. They confessed, and were led away and executed. The king wrote these things for a record. Mordecai also wrote concerning these matters. The king commanded Mordecai to serve in the palace, and gave gifts for this service. But Haman the son of Hammedatha the Bougean was honored in the sight of the king, and he endeavored to harm Mordecai and his people, because of the king's two chamberlains.]2 And it came to pass after these things in the days of Ahasuerus, —(this Ahasuerus ruled over one hundred twenty-seven provinces from India)—3 in those days, when King Ahasuerus was on the throne in the city of Susa, 4 in the third year of his reign, he made a feast for his friends, for people from the rest of the nations, for the nobles of the Persians and Medes, and for the chief of the local governors. 5 After this—after he had shown them the wealth of his kingdom and the abundant glory of his wealth during one hundred eighty days—6 when the days of the wedding feast were completed, the king made a banquet lasting six days for the people of the nations who were present in the city, in the court of the king's house, 7 which was

adorned with fine linen and flax on cords of fine linen and purple, fastened to golden and silver studs on pillars of white marble and stone. There were golden and silver couches on a pavement of emerald stone, and of mother-of-pearl, and of white marble, with transparent coverings variously flowered, having roses arranged around it. 8 There were gold and silver cups, and a small cup of carbuncle set out, of the value of thirty thousand talents, with abundant and sweet wine, which the king himself drank. 9 This banquet was not according to the appointed law, but as the king desired to have it. He charged the stewards to perform his will and that of the company. 10 Also Vashti the queen made a banquet for the women in the palace where King Ahasuerus lived.11 Now on the seventh day, the king, being merry, told Haman, Bazan, Tharrha, Baraze, Zatholtha, Abataza, and Tharaba, the seven chamberlains, servants of King Ahasuerus, 12 to bring in the queen to him, to enthrone her, and crown her with the diadem, and to show her to the princes, and her beauty to the nations, for she was beautiful.13 But queen Vashti refused to come with the chamberlains; so the king was grieved and angered.14 And he said to his friends, "This is what Vashti said. Therefore pronounce your legal judgment on this case."15 So Arkesaeus, Sarsathaeus, and Malisear, the princes of the Persians and Medes, who were near the king, who sat chief in rank by the king, drew near to him,16 and reported to him according to the laws what it was proper to do to queen Vashti, because she had not done the things commanded by the king through the chamberlains.17 And Memucan said to the king and to the princes, "Queen Vashti has not wronged the king only, but also all the king's rulers and princes;18 for he has told them the words of the queen, and how she disobeyed the king. As she then refused to obey King Ahasuerus,19 so this day the other wives of the chiefs of the Persians and Medes, having heard what she said to the king, will dare in the same way to dishonor their husbands.20 If then it seems good to the king, let him make a royal decree, and let it be written according to the laws of the Medes and Persians, and let him not alter it: 'Don't allow the queen to come in to him any more. Let the king give her royalty to a woman better than she.'21 Let the law of the king which he will have made be widely proclaimed in his kingdom. Then all the women will give honor to their husbands, from the poor even to the rich."22 This advice pleased the king and the princes; and the king did as Memucan had said, and sent into all his kingdom through the several provinces, according to their language, so that men might be feared in their own houses.

Additions to Esther chapter 2

1 After this, the king's anger was pacified, and he no more mentioned Vashti, bearing in mind what she had said, and how he had condemned her.2 Then the servants of the king said, "Let chaste, beautiful young virgins be sought for the king.3 Let the king appoint local governors in all the provinces of his kingdom, and let them select beautiful, chaste young ladies and bring them to the city Susa, into the women's apartment. Let them be consigned to the king's chamberlain, the keeper of the women. Then let things for purification and other needs be given to them. 4 Let the woman who pleases the king be queen instead of Vashti." This thing pleased the king; and he did so..5 Now there was a Jew in the city Susa, and his name was Mordecai, the son of Jairus, the son of Shimei, the son of Kish, of the tribe of Benjamin. 6 He had been brought as a prisoner from Jerusalem, whom Nebuchadnezzar king of Babylon had carried into captivity. 7 He had a foster child, daughter of Aminadab his father's brother. Her name was Esther. When her parents died, he brought her up to womanhood as his own. This lady was beautiful. 8 And because the king's ordinance was published, many ladies were gathered to the city of Susa under the hand of Hegai; and Esther was brought to Hegai, the keeper of the women. 9 The lady pleased him, and she found favor in his sight. He hurried to give her the things for purification, her portion, and the seven maidens appointed her out of the palace. He treated her and her maidens well in the women's apartment. 10 But Esther didn't reveal her family or her kindred, for Mordecai had charged her not to tell. 11 But Mordecai used to walk every day by the women's court, to see what would become of Esther. 12 Now this was the time for a virgin to go into the king, when she had completed twelve months; for so are the days of purification fulfilled, six months while they are anointing themselves with oil of myrrh, and six months with spices and women's purifications. 13 And then the lady goes in to the king. The officer that he commands to do so will bring her to come in with him from the women's apartment to the king's chamber. 14 She enters in the evening, and in the morning she departs to the second women's apartment, where Hegai the king's chamberlain is keeper of the women. She doesn't go in to the king again, unless she is called by name. 15 And when the time was fulfilled for Esther the daughter of Aminadab the brother of Mordecai's father to go

in to the king, she neglected nothing which the chamberlain, the women's keeper, commanded; for Esther found grace in the sight of all who looked at her. 16 So Esther went in to King Ahasuerus in the twelfth month, which is Adar, in the seventh year of his reign. 17 The king loved Esther, and she found favor beyond all the other virgins. He put the queen's crown on her. 18 The king made a banquet for all his friends and great men for seven days, and he highly celebrated the marriage of Esther; and he granted a remission of taxes to those who were under his dominion. 19 Meanwhile, Mordecai served in the courtyard. 20 Now Esther had not revealed her country, for so Mordecai commanded her, to fear God, and perform his commandments, as when she was with him. Esther didn't change her manner of life. 21 Two chamberlains of the king, the chiefs of the body-guard, were grieved, because Mordecai was promoted; and they sought to kill King Ahasuerus. 22 And the matter was discovered by Mordecai, and he made it known to Esther, and she declared to the king the matter of the conspiracy. 23 And the king examined the two chamberlains and hanged them. Then the king gave orders to make a note for a memorial in the royal library of the goodwill shown by Mordecai, as a commendation.

Additions to Esther chapter 3

1 After this, King Ahasuerus highly honored Haman the son of Hammedatha, the Bugaean. He exalted him and set his seat above all his friends. 2 All in the palace bowed down to him, for so the king had given orders to do; but Mordecai didn't bow down to him. 3 And they in the king's palace said to Mordecai, "Mordecai, why do you transgress the commands of the king?" 4 They questioned him daily, but he didn't listen to them; so they reported to Haman that Mordecai resisted the commands of the king; and Mordecai had shown to them that he was a Jew. 5 When Haman understood that Mordecai didn't bow down to him, he was greatly enraged, 6 and plotted to utterly destroy all the Jews who were under the rule of Ahasuerus. 7 In the twelfth year of the reign of Ahasuerus, Haman made a decision by casting lots by day and month, to kill the race of Mordecai in one day. The lot fell on the fourteenth day of the month of Adar. 8 So he spoke to King Ahasuerus, saying, "There is a nation scattered among the nations in all your kingdom, and their laws differ from all the other nations. They disobey the king's laws. It is not expedient for the king to tolerate them. 9 If it seem good to the king, let him make a decree to destroy them, and I will remit into the king's treasury ten thousand talents of silver." 10 So the king took off his ring, and gave it into the hands of Haman to seal the decrees against the Jews. 11 The king said to Haman, "Keep the silver, and treat the nation as you will." 12 So the king's recorders were called in the first month, on the thirteenth day, and they wrote as Haman commanded to the captains and governors in every province, from India even to Ethiopia, to one hundred twenty-seven provinces; and to the rulers of the nations according to their languages, in the name of King Ahasuerus. 13 The message was sent by couriers throughout the kingdom of Ahasuerus, to utterly destroy the race of the Jews on the first day of the twelfth month, which is Adar, and to plunder their goods. 14 Copies of the letters were published in every province; and an order was given to all the nations to be ready for that day. 15 This business was hastened also in Susa. The king and Haman began to drink, but the city was confused.

Additions to Esther chapter 4

1 But Mordecai, having perceived what was done, tore his garments, put on sackcloth, and sprinkled dust upon himself. Having rushed forth through the open street of the city, he cried with a loud voice, "A nation that has done no wrong is going to be destroyed!" 2 He came to the king's gate, and stood; for it was not lawful for him to enter into the palace wearing sackcloth and ashes. 3 And in every province where the letters were published, there was crying, lamentation, and great mourning on the part of the Jews. They wore sackcloth and ashes. 4 The queen's maids and chamberlains went in and told her; and when she had heard what was done, she was deeply troubled. She sent clothes to Mordecai to replace his sackcloth, but he refused. 5 So Esther called for her chamberlain Hathach, who waited upon her; and she sent to learn the truth from Mordecai. 7 Mordecai showed him what was done, and the promise which Haman had made the king of ten thousand talents to be paid into the treasury, that he might destroy the Jews. 8 And he gave him the copy of what was published in Susa concerning their destruction to show to Esther; and told him to charge her to go in and entreat the king, and to beg him for the people. "Remember," he said, "the days of your humble condition, how you were nursed by my hand; because Haman, who holds the next place to the king, has spoken against us to cause our death. Call upon the Lord, and speak to the king concerning us, to deliver us from death." 9 So Hathach went in and told her all these words. 10 Esther said to Hathach, "Go to Mordecai, and

say, 11'All the nations of the empire know than any man or woman who goes in to the king into the inner court without being called, that person must die, unless the king stretches out his golden sceptre; then he shall live. I haven't been called to go into the king for thirty days.'" 12 So Hathach reported to Mordecai all the words of Esther. 13 Then Mordecai said to Hathach, "Go, and say to her, 'Esther, don't say to yourself that you alone will escape in the kingdom, more than all the other Jews. 14 For if you keep quiet on this occasion, help and protection will come to the Jews from another place; but you and your father's house will perish. Who knows if you have been made queen for this occasion?'" 15 And Esther sent the messenger who came to her to Mordecai, saying, 16"Go and assemble the Jews that are in Susa, and all of you fast for me. Don't eat or drink for three days, night and day. My maidens and I will also fast. Then I will go in to the king contrary to the law, even if I must die." 17 So Mordecai went and did all that Esther commanded him. 18[He prayed to the Lord, making mention of all the works of the Lord. 19 He said, "Lord God, you are king ruling over all, for all things are in your power, and there is no one who can oppose you in your purpose to save Israel; 20 for you have made the heaven and the earth and every wonderful thing under heaven. 21 You are Lord of all, and there is no one who can resist you, Lord. 22 You know all things. You know, Lord, that it is not in insolence, nor arrogance, nor love of glory, that I have done this, to refuse to bow down to the arrogant Haman. 23 For I would gladly have kissed the soles of his feet for the safety of Israel. 24 But I have done this that I might not set the glory of man above the glory of God. I will not worship anyone except you, my Lord, and I will not do these things in arrogance. 25 And now, O Lord God, the King, the God of Abraham, spare your people, for our enemies are planning our destruction, and they have desired to destroy your ancient inheritance. 26 Do not overlook your people, whom you have redeemed for yourself out of the land of Egypt. 27 Listen to my prayer. Have mercy on your inheritance and turn our mourning into gladness, that we may live and sing praise to your name, O Lord. Don't utterly destroy the mouth of those who praise you, O Lord." 28 All Israel cried with all their might, for death was before their eyes.]

Additions to Esther chapter 5

1 It came to pass on the third day, when she had ceased praying, that she took off her servant's dress and put on her glorious apparel. Being splendidly dressed and having called upon God the Overseer and Preserver of all things, she took her two maids, and she leaned upon one, as a delicate female, and the other followed bearing her train. She was blooming in the perfection of her beauty. Her face was cheerful and looked lovely, but her heart was filled with fear. 2 Having passed through all the doors, she stood before the king. He was sitting on his royal throne. He had put on all his glorious apparel, covered all over with gold and precious stones, and was very terrifying. 3 And having raised his face resplendent with glory, he looked with intense anger. The queen fell, and changed her color as she fainted. She bowed herself upon the head of the maid who went before her. 4 But God changed the spirit of the king to gentleness, and in intense feeling, he sprang from off his throne, and took her into his arms, until she recovered. He comforted her with peaceful words, and said to her, "What is the matter, Esther? I am your relative. Cheer up! You shall not die, for our command is openly declared to you: 'Draw near.'" 5 And having raised the golden sceptre, he laid it upon her neck, and embraced her. He said, "Speak to me." So she said to him, "I saw you, my lord, as an angel of God, and my heart was troubled for fear of your glory; for you, my lord, are to be wondered at, and your face is full of grace." 6 While she was speaking, she fainted and fell. Then the king was troubled, and all his servants comforted her. 7 The king said, "What do you desire, Esther? What is your request? Ask even to the half of my kingdom, and it shall be yours." 8 Esther said, "Today is a special day. So if it seems good to the king, let both him and Haman come to the feast which I will prepare this day." 9 The king said, "Hurry and bring Haman here, that we may do as Esther said." So they both came to the feast about which Esther had spoken. 10 At the banquet, the king said to Esther, "What is your request, queen Esther? You shall have all that you require." 11 She said, "My request and my petition is: 12 if I have found favor in the king's sight, let the king and Haman come again tomorrow to the feast which I shall prepare for them, and tomorrow I will do as I have done today." 13 So Haman went out from the king very glad and merry; but when Haman saw Mordecai the Jew in the court, he was greatly enraged. 14 Having gone into his own house, he called his friends, and his wife Zeresh. 15 He showed them his wealth and the glory with which the king had invested him, and how he had promoted him to be chief ruler in the kingdom. 16 Haman said, "The queen has called no one to the feast with the king but me, and I am invited tomorrow. 17 But these things don't please me while I see Mordecai the Jew in the court." 18 Then Zeresh

his wife and his friends said to him, "Let a fifty cubit tall gallows be made for you. In the morning you speak to the king, and let Mordecai be hanged on the gallows; but you go in to the feast with the king, and be merry." The saying pleased Haman, and the gallows was prepared.

Additions to Esther chapter 6

1 The Lord removed sleep from the king that night; so he told his servant to bring in the books, the registers of daily events, to read to him. 2 And he found the records written concerning Mordecai, how he had told the king about the king's two chamberlains, when they were keeping guard, and sought to lay hands on Ahasuerus. 3 The king said, "What honor or favor have we done for Mordecai?" The king's servants said, "You haven't done anything for him." 4 And while the king was enquiring about the kindness of Mordecai, behold, Haman was in the court. The king said, "Who is in the court? Now Haman had come in to speak to the king about hanging Mordecai on the gallows which he had prepared. 5 The king's servants said, "Behold, Haman stands in the court." And the king said, "Call him!" 6 The king said to Haman, "What should I do for the man whom I wish to honor?" Haman said within himself, "Whom would the king honor but myself?" 7 He said to the king, "As for the man whom the king wishes to honor, 8 let the king's servants bring the robe of fine linen which the king puts on, and the horse on which the king rides, 9 and let him give it to one of the king's noble friends, and let him dress the man whom the king loves. Let him mount him on the horse, and proclaim through the streets of the city, saying, 'This is what will be done for every man whom the king honors!'" 10 Then the king said to Haman, "You have spoken well. Do so for Mordecai the Jew, who waits in the palace, and let not a word of what you have spoken be neglected!" 11 So Haman took the robe and the horse, dressed Mordecai, mounted him on the horse, and went through the streets of the city, proclaiming, "This is what will be done for every man whom the king wishes to honor." 12 Then Mordecai returned to the palace; but Haman went home mourning, with his head covered. 13 Haman related the events that had happened to him to Zeresh his wife and to his friends. His friends and his wife said to him, "If Mordecai is of the race of the Jews, and you have begun to be humbled before him, you will assuredly fall; and you will not be able to withstand him, for the living God is with him." 14 While they were still speaking, the chamberlains arrived to rush Haman to the banquet which Esther had prepared.

Additions to Esther chapter 7

1 So the king and Haman went in to drink with the queen. 2 The king said to Esther at the banquet on the second day, "What is it, queen Esther? What is your request? What is your petition? It shall be done for you, up to half of my kingdom." 3 She answered and said, "If I have found favor in the sight of the king, let my life be granted as my petition, and my people as my request. 4 For both I and my people are sold for destruction, pillage, and genocide. If both we and our children were sold for male and female slaves, I would not have bothered you, for this isn't worthy of the king's palace." 5 The king said, "Who has dared to do this thing?" 6 Esther said, "The enemy is Haman, this wicked man!" Then Haman was terrified in the presence of the king and the queen. 7 The king rose up from the banquet to go into the garden. Haman began to beg the queen for mercy, for he saw that he was in serious trouble. 8 The king returned from the garden; and Haman had fallen upon the couch, begging the queen for mercy. The king said, "Will you even assault my wife in my house?" And when Haman heard it, he changed countenance. 9 And Bugathan, one of the chamberlains, said to the king, "Behold, Haman has also prepared a gallows for Mordecai, who spoke concerning the king, and a fifty cubit high gallows has been set up on Haman's property." The king said, "Let him be hanged on it!" 10 So Haman was hanged on the gallows that had been prepared for Mordecai. Then the king's wrath was abated.

Additions to Esther chapter 8

1 On that day, King Ahasuerus gave to Esther all that belonged to Haman the slanderer. The king called Mordecai, for Esther had told that he was related to her. 2 The king took the ring which he had taken away from Haman and gave it to Mordecai. Esther appointed Mordecai over all that had been Haman's. 3 She spoke yet again to the king, and fell at his feet, and implored him to undo Haman's mischief and all that he had done against the Jews. 4 Then the king extended the golden sceptre to Esther; and Esther arose to stand near the king. 5 Esther said, "If it seems good to you, and I have found favor in your sight, let an order be sent that the letters sent by Haman may be reversed—letters that were written for the destruction of the Jews who are in your kingdom. 6 For how could I see the affliction of my people, and how could I survive the destruction of my kindred?" 7 Then the king said to Esther, "If I have given and freely granted you all that was Haman's,

and hanged him on a gallows because he laid his hands upon the Jews, what more do you seek? 8 Write in my name whatever seems good to you, and seal it with my ring; for whatever is written at the command of the king, and sealed with my ring, cannot be countermanded." 9 So the scribes were called in the first month, which is Nisan, on the twenty-third day of the same year; and orders were written to the Jews, whatever the king had commanded to the local governors and chiefs of the local governors, from India even to Ethiopia—one hundred twenty-seven local governors, according to the several provinces, in their own languages. 10 They were written by order of the king, sealed with his ring, and the letters were sent by the couriers. 11 In them, he charged them to use their own laws in every city, to help each other, and to treat their adversaries and those who attacked them as they pleased, 12 on one day in all the kingdom of Ahasuerus, on the thirteenth day of the twelfth month, which is Adar. 13 Let the copies be posted in conspicuous places throughout the kingdom. Let all the Jews be ready against this day, to fight against their enemies. 14 So the horsemen went forth with haste to perform the king's commands. The ordinance was also published in Susa. 15 Mordecai went out robed in royal apparel, wearing a golden crown and a diadem of fine purple linen. The people in Susa saw it and rejoiced. 16 The Jews had light and gladness 17 in every city and province where the ordinance was published. Wherever the proclamation took place, the Jews had joy and gladness, feasting and mirth. Many of the Gentiles were circumcised and became Jews for fear of the Jews.

Additions to Esther chapter 9

1 Now in the twelfth month, on the thirteenth day of the month, which is Adar, the letters written by the king arrived. 2 In that day, the adversaries of the Jews perished; for no one resisted, through fear of them. 3 For the chiefs of the local governors, and the princes and the royal scribes, honored the Jews; for the fear of Mordecai was upon them. 4 For the order of the king was in force, that he should be celebrated in all the kingdom. 6 In the city Susa the Jews killed five hundred men, 7 including Pharsannes, Delphon, Phasga, 8 Pharadatha, Barea, Sarbaca, 9 Marmasima, Ruphaeus, Arsaeus, and Zabuthaeus, 10 the ten sons of Haman the son of Hammedatha the Bugaean, the enemy of the Jews; and they plundered their property on the same day. 11 The number of those who perished in Susa was reported to the king. 12 Then the king said to Esther, "The Jews have slain five hundred men in the city Susa. What do you think they have done in the rest of the country? What more do you ask, that it may be done for you?" 13 Esther said to the king, "Let it be granted to the Jews to do the same to them tomorrow. Also, hang the bodies of the ten sons of Haman." 14 He permitted it to be done; and he gave up to the Jews of the city the bodies of the sons of Haman to hang. 15 The Jews assembled in Susa on the fourteenth day of Adar and killed three hundred men, but plundered no property. 16 The rest of the Jews who were in the kingdom assembled, and helped one another, and obtained rest from their enemies; for they destroyed fifteen thousand of them on the thirteenth day of Adar, but took no spoil. 17 They rested on the fourteenth of the same month, and kept it as a day of rest with joy and gladness. 18 The Jews in the city of Susa assembled also on the fourteenth day and rested; and they also observed the fifteenth with joy and gladness. 19 On this account then, the Jews dispersed in every foreign land keep the fourteenth of Adar as a holy day with joy, each sending gifts of food to his neighbor. 20 Mordecai wrote these things in a book and sent them to the Jews, as many as were in the kingdom of Ahasuerus, both those who were near and those who were far away, 21 to establish these as joyful days and to keep the fourteenth and fifteenth of Adar; 22 for on these days the Jews obtained rest from their enemies; and in that month, which was Adar, in which a change was made for them from mourning to joy, and from sorrow to a holiday, to spend the whole of it in good days of feasting and gladness, sending portions to their friends and to the poor. 23 And the Jews consented to this as Mordecai wrote to them, 24 showing how Haman the son of Hammedatha the Macedonian fought against them, how he made a decree and cast lots to destroy them utterly; 25 also how he went in to the king, telling him to hang Mordecai; but all the calamities he tried to bring upon the Jews came upon himself, and he was hanged, along with his children. 26 Therefore these days were called Purim, because of the lots (for in their language they are called Purim) because of the words of this letter, and because of all they suffered on this account, and all that happened to them. 27 Mordecai established it, and the Jews took upon themselves, upon their offspring, and upon those who were joined to them to observe it, neither would they on any account behave differently; but these days were to be a memorial kept in every generation, city, family, and province. 28 These days of Purim shall be kept forever, and their memorial shall not fail in any generation. 29 Queen Esther the daughter of Aminadab and

Mordecai the Jew wrote all that they had done, and gave the confirmation of the letter about Purim. 31 Mordecai and Esther the queen established this decision on their own, pledging their own well-being to their plan. 32 And Esther established it by a command forever, and it was written for a memorial.

Additions to Esther chapter 10

1 The king levied a tax upon his kingdom both by land and sea. 2 As for his strength and valour, and the wealth and glory of his kingdom, behold, they are written in the book of the Persians and Medes for a memorial. 3 Mordecai was viceroy to King Ahasuerus, and was a great man in the kingdom, honored by the Jews, and lived his life loved by all his nation.4[Mordecai said, "These things have come from God. 5 For I remember the dream which I had concerning these matters; for not one detail of them has failed. 6 There was the little spring which became a river, and there was light, and the sun and much water. The river is Esther, whom the king married and made queen. 7 The two serpents are Haman and me. 8 The nations are those which combined to destroy the name of the Jews. 9 But as for my nation, this is Israel, even those who cried to God and were delivered; for the Lord delivered his people. The Lord rescued us out of all these calamities; and God worked such signs and great wonders as have not been done among the nations. 10 Therefore he ordained two lots. One for the people of God, and one for all the other nations. 11 And these two lots came for an appointed season, and for a day of judgment, before God, and for all the nations. 12 God remembered his people and vindicated his inheritance. 13 They shall observe these days in the month Adar, on the fourteenth and on the fifteenth day of the month, with an assembly, joy, and gladness before God, throughout the generations forever among his people Israel. 14 In the fourth year of the reign of Ptolemeus and Cleopatra, Dositheus, who said he was a priest and Levite, and Ptolemeus his son brought this letter of Purim, which they said was authentic, and that Lysimachus the son of Ptolemeus, who was in Jerusalem, had interpreted.]

Tobit

Tobit Chapter 1

1 This book tells the story of Tobit, son of Tobiel, son of Hananiel, son of Aduel, son of Gabael of the family of Asiel, of the tribe of Naphtali, 2 who during the reign of Shalmaneser, king of Assyria, was taken captive from Thisbe, which is south of Kedesh Naphtali in upper Galilee, above and to the west of Asser, north of Phogor. 3 I, Tobit, have walked all the days of my life on the paths of truth and righteousness. I performed many charitable works for my kinsmen and my people who had been deported with me to Nineveh, in Assyria. 4 When I lived as a young man in my own country, Israel, the entire tribe of my forefather Naphtali had broken away from the house of David and from Jerusalem. This city had been singled out of all Israel's tribes, so that they all might offer sacrifice in the place where the temple, God's dwelling, had been built and consecrated for all generations to come. 5 All my kinsmen, like the rest of the tribe of my forefather Naphtali, used to offer sacrifice on all the mountains of Galilee as well as to the young bull which Jeroboam, king of Israel, had made in Dan. 6 I, for my part, would often make the pilgrimage alone to Jerusalem for the festivals, as is prescribed for all Israel by perpetual decree. Bringing with me the first fruits of the field and the firstlings of the flock, together with a tenth of my income and the first shearings of the sheep, I would hasten to Jerusalem 7 and present them to the priests, Aaron's sons, at the altar. To the Levites who were doing service in Jerusalem I would give the tithe of grain, wine, olive oil, pomegranates, figs, and other fruits. And except for sabbatical years, I used to give a second tithe in money, which each year I would go and disburse in Jerusalem. 8 The third tithe I gave to orphans and widows, and to converts who were living with the Israelites. Every third year I would bring them this offering, and we ate it in keeping with the decree of the Mosaic law and the commands of Deborah, the mother of my father Tobiel; for when my father died, he left me an orphan. 9 When I reached manhood, I married Anna, a woman of our own lineage. By her I had a son whom I named Tobiah. 10 Now, after I had been deported to Nineveh, all my brothers and relatives ate the food of heathens, 11 but I refrained from eating that kind of food. 12 Because of this wholehearted service of God, 13 the Most High granted me favor and status with Shalmaneser, so that I became purchasing agent for all his needs. 14 Every now and then until his death I would go to Media to buy goods for him. I also deposited several pouches containing a great sum of money with my kinsman Gabael, son of Gabri, who lived at Rages, in Media. 15 But when Shalmaneser died and his son Sennacherib succeeded him as king, the roads to Media became unsafe, so I could no longer go there. 16 During

Shalmaneser's reign I performed many charitable works for my kinsmen and my people. 17 I would give my bread to the hungry and my clothing to the naked. If I saw one of my people who had died and been thrown outside the walls of Nineveh, I would bury him. 18 I also buried anyone whom Sennacherib slew when he returned as a fugitive from Judea during the days of judgment decreed against him by the heavenly King because of the blasphemies he had uttered. In his rage he killed many Israelites, but I used to take their bodies by stealth and bury them; so when Sennacherib looked for them, he could not find them. 19 But a certain citizen of Nineveh informed the king that it was I who buried the dead. When I found out that the king knew all about me and wanted to put me to death, I went into hiding; then in my fear I took to flight. 20 Afterward, all my property was confiscated; I was left with nothing. All that I had was taken to the king's palace, except for my wife Anna and my son Tobiah. 21 But less than forty days later the king was assassinated by two of his sons, who then escaped into the mountains of Ararat. His son Esarhaddon, who succeeded him as king, placed Ahiqar, my brother Anael's son, in charge of all the accounts of his kingdom, so that he took control over the entire administration. 22 Then Ahiqar interceded on my behalf, and I was able to return to Nineveh. For under Sennacherib, king of Assyria, Ahiqar had been chief cupbearer, keeper of the seal, administrator, and treasurer; and Esarhaddon reappointed him. He was a close relative—in fact, my nephew.

Tobit Chapter 2

1 Thus under King Esarhaddon I returned to my home, and my wife Anna and my son Tobiah were restored to me. Then on our festival of Pentecost, the feast of Weeks, a fine dinner was prepared for me, and I reclined to eat. 2 The table was set for me, and when many different dishes were placed before me, I said to my son Tobiah: "My son, go out and try to find a poor man from among our kinsmen exiled here in Nineveh. If he is a sincere worshiper of God, bring him back with you, so that he can share this meal with me. Indeed, son, I shall wait for you to come back." 3 Tobiah went out to look for some poor kinsman of ours. When he returned he exclaimed, "Father!" I said to him, "What is it, son?" He answered, "Father, one of our people has been murdered! His body lies in the market place where he was just strangled!" 4 I sprang to my feet, leaving the dinner untouched; and I carried the dead man from the street and put him in one of the rooms, so that I might bury him after sunset. 5 Returning to my own quarters, I washed myself and ate my food in sorrow. 6 I was reminded of the oracle pronounced by the prophet Amos against Bethel: "Your festivals shall be turned into mourning, And all your songs into lamentation." 7 And I wept. Then at sunset I went out, dug a grave, and buried him. 8 The neighbors mocked me, saying to one another: "Will this man never learn! Once before he was hunted down for execution because of this very thing; yet now that he has escaped, here he is again burying the dead!" 9 That same night I bathed, and went to sleep next to the wall of my courtyard. Because of the heat I left my face uncovered. 10 I did not know there were birds perched on the wall above me, till their warm droppings settled in my eyes, causing cataracts. I went to see some doctors for a cure, but the more they anointed my eyes with various salves, the worse the cataracts became, until I could see no more. For four years I was deprived of eyesight, and all my kinsmen were grieved at my condition. Ahiqar, however, took care of me for two years, until he left for Elymais. 11 At that time my wife Anna worked for hire at weaving cloth, the kind of work women do. 12 When she sent back the goods to their owners, they would pay her. Late in winter she finished the cloth and sent it back to the owners. They paid her the full salary, and also gave her a young goat for the table. 13 On entering my house the goat began to bleat. I called to my wife and said: "Where did this goat come from? Perhaps it was stolen! Give it back to its owners; we have no right to eat stolen food!" 14 But she said to me, "It was given to me as a bonus over and above my wages." Yet I would not believe her, and told her to give it back to its owners. I became very angry with her over this. So she retorted: "Where are your charitable deeds now? Where are your virtuous acts? See! Your true character is finally showing itself!"

Tobit Chapter 3

1 Grief-stricken in spirit, I groaned and wept aloud. Then with sobs I began to pray: 2 "You are righteous, O Lord, and all your deeds are just; All your ways are mercy and truth; you are the judge of the world. 3 And now, O Lord, may you be mindful of me, and look with favor upon me. Punish me not for my sins, nor for my inadvertent offenses, nor for those of my fathers. They sinned against you, 4 and disobeyed your commandments. So you handed us over to plundering, exile, and death, till we were an object lesson, a byword, a reproach in all the nations among whom you scattered us. 5 Yes, your judgments are many and

true in dealing with me as my sins and those of my fathers deserve. For we have not kept your commandments, nor have we trodden the paths of truth before you. 6 So now, deal with me as you please, and command my life breath to be taken from me, that I may go from the face of the earth into dust. It is better for me to die than to live, because I have heard insulting calumnies, and I am overwhelmed with grief. Lord, command me to be delivered from such anguish; let me go to the everlasting abode; Lord, refuse me not. For it is better for me to die than to endure so much misery in life, and to hear these insults!" 7 On the same day, at Ecbatana in Media, it so happened that Raguel's daughter Sarah also had to listen to abuse, from one of her father's maids. 8 For she had been married to seven husbands, but the wicked demon Asmodeus killed them off before they could have intercourse with her, as it is prescribed for wives. So the maid said to her: "You are the one who strangles your husbands! Look at you! You have already been married seven times, but you have had no joy with any one of your husbands. 9 Why do you beat us? Because your husbands are dead? Then why not join them! May we never see a son or daughter of yours!" 10 That day she was deeply grieved in spirit. She went in tears to an upstairs room in her father's house with the intention of hanging herself. But she reconsidered, saying to herself: "No! People would level this insult against my father: 'You had only one beloved daughter, but she hanged herself because of ill fortune!' And thus would I cause my father in his old age to go down to the nether world laden with sorrow. It is far better for me not to hang myself, but to beg the Lord to have me die, so that I need no longer live to hear such insults." 11 At that time, then, she spread out her hands, and facing the window, poured out this prayer: "Blessed are you, O Lord, merciful God! Forever blessed and honored is your holy name; may all your works forever bless you. 12 And now, O Lord, to you I turn my face and raise my eyes. 13 Bid me to depart from the earth, never again to hear such insults. 14 You know, O Master, that I am innocent of any impure act with a man, 15 And that I have never defiled my own name or my father's name in the land of my exile. I am my father's only daughter, and he has no other child to make his heir, Nor does he have a close kinsman or other relative whom I might bide my time to marry. I have already lost seven husbands; why then should I live any longer? But if it please you, Lord, not to slay me, look favorably upon me and have pity on me; never again let me hear these insults!" 16 At that very time, the prayer of these two suppliants was heard in the glorious presence of Almighty God. 17 So Raphael was sent to heal them both: to remove the cataracts from Tobit's eyes, so that he might again see God's sunlight; and to marry Raguel's daughter Sarah to Tobit's son Tobiah, and then drive the wicked demon Asmodeus from her. For Tobiah had the right to claim her before any other who might wish to marry her. In the very moment that Tobit returned from the courtyard to his house, Raguel's daughter Sarah came downstairs from her room.

Tobit Chapter 4

1 That same day Tobit remembered the money he had deposited with Gabael at Rages in Media, and he thought, 2 "Now that I have asked for death, why should I not call my son Tobiah and let him know about this money before I die?" 3 So he called his son Tobiah; and when he came, he said to him: "My son, when I die, give me a decent burial. Honor your mother, and do not abandon her as long as she lives. Do whatever pleases her, and do not grieve her spirit in any way. 4 Remember, my son, that she went through many trials for your sake while you were in her womb. And when she dies, bury her in the same grave with me. 5 Through all your days, my son, keep the Lord in mind, and suppress every desire to sin or to break his commandments. Perform good works all the days of your life, and do not tread the paths of wrongdoing. 6 For if you are steadfast in your service, your good works will bring success, not only to you, but also to all those who live uprightly. 7 Give alms from your possessions. Do not turn your face away from any of the poor, and God's face will not be turned away from you. 8 Son, give alms in proportion to what you own. If you have great wealth, give alms out of your abundance; if you have but little, distribute even some of that. But do not hesitate to give alms; 9 you will be storing up a goodly treasure for yourself against the day of adversity. 10 Almsgiving frees one from death, and keeps one from going into the dark abode. 11 Alms are a worthy offering in the sight of the Most High for all who give them. 12 Be on your guard, son, against every form of immorality, and above all, marry a woman of the lineage of your forefathers. Do not marry a stranger who is not of your father's tribe, because we are sons of the prophets. My boy, keep in mind Noah, Abraham, Isaac, and Jacob, our fathers from of old: all of them took wives from among their own kinsmen and were blessed in their children. Remember that their posterity shall inherit the land. 13 Therefore, my son, love your kinsmen. Do not be so proudhearted toward your kinsmen, the sons

and daughters of your people, as to refuse to take a wife for yourself from among them. For in such arrogance there is ruin and great disorder. Likewise, in worthlessness there is decay and dire poverty, for worthlessness is the mother of famine. 14 Do not keep with you overnight the wages of any man who works for you, but pay him immediately. If you thus behave as God's servant, you will receive your reward. Keep a close watch on yourself, my son, in everything you do, and discipline yourself in all your conduct. 15 Do to no one what you yourself dislike. Do not drink wine till you become drunk, nor let drunkenness accompany you on your way. 16 Give to the hungry some of your bread, and to the naked some of your clothing. Whatever you have left over, give away as alms; and do not begrudge the alms you give. 17 Be lavish with your bread and wine at the burial of the virtuous, but do not share them with sinners. 18 Seek counsel from every wise man, and do not think lightly of any advice that can be useful. 19 At all times bless the Lord God, and ask him to make all your paths straight and to grant success to all your endeavors and plans. For no pagan nation possesses good counsel, but the Lord himself gives all good things. If the Lord chooses, he raises a man up; but if he should decide otherwise, he casts him down to the deepest recesses of the nether world. So now, my son, keep in mind my commandments, and never let them be erased from your heart. 20 And now, son, I wish to inform you that I have deposited a great sum of money with Gabri's son Gabael at Rages in Media. 21 Do not be discouraged, my child, because of our poverty. You will be a rich man if you fear God, avoid all sin, and do what is right before the Lord your God."

Tobit Chapter 5

1 Then Tobiah replied to his father Tobit: "Everything that you have commanded me, father, I will do. 2 But how shall I be able to obtain the money from him, since he does not know me nor do I know him? What can I show him to make him recognize me and trust me, so that he will give me the money? I do not even know which roads to take for the journey into Media!" 3 Tobit answered his son Tobiah: "We exchanged signatures on a document written in duplicate; I divided it into two parts, and each of us kept one; his copy I put with the money. Think of it, twenty years have already passed since I deposited that money! So now, my son, find yourself a trustworthy man who will make the journey with you. We will, of course, give him a salary when you return; but get back that money from Gabael." 4 Tobiah went to look for someone acquainted with the roads who would travel with him to Media. As soon as he went out, he found the angel Raphael standing before him, though he did not know that this was an angel of God. 5 Tobiah said to him, "Who are you, young man?" He replied "I am an Israelite, one of your kinsmen. I have come here to work." Tobiah said, "Do you know the way to Media?" 6 The other replied: "Yes, I have been there many times. I know the place well and I know all the routes. I have often traveled to Media; I used to stay with our kinsman Gabael, who lives at Rages in Media. It is a good two days' travel from Ecbatana to Rages, for Rages is situated at the mountains, Ecbatana out on the plateau." 7 Tobiah said to him, "Wait for me, young man, till I go back and tell my father; for I need you to make the journey with me. I will, of course, pay you." 8 Raphael replied, "Very well, I will wait for you; but do not be long." 9 Tobiah went back to tell his father Tobit what had happened. He said to him, "I have just found a man who is one of our own Israelite kinsmen!" Tobit said, "Call the man, so that I may find out what family and tribe he comes from, and whether he is trustworthy enough to travel with you, son." Tobiah went out to summon the man, saying, "Young man, my father would like to see you." 10 When Raphael entered the house, Tobit greeted him first. Raphael said, "Hearty greetings to you!" Tobit replied: "What joy is left for me any more? Here I am, a blind man who cannot see God's sunlight, but must remain in darkness, like the dead who no longer see the light! Though alive, I am among the dead. I can hear a man's voice, but I cannot see him." Raphael said, "Take courage! God has healing in store for you; so take courage!" Tobit then said: "My son Tobiah wants to go to Media. Can you go with him to show him the way? I will of course pay you, brother." Raphael answered: "Yes, I can go with him, for I know all the routes. I have often traveled to Media and crossed all its plains and mountains; so I know every road well." 11 Tobit asked, "Brother, tell me, please, what family and tribe are you from?" 12 Raphael said: "Why? Do you need a tribe and a family? Or are you looking for a hired man to travel with your son?" Tobit replied, "I wish to know truthfully whose son you are, brother, and what your name is." 13 Raphael answered, "I am Azariah, son of Hananiah the elder, one of your own kinsmen." 14 Tobit exclaimed: "Welcome! God save you, brother! Do not be provoked with me, brother, for wanting to learn the truth about your family. So it turns out that you are a kinsman, and from a noble and good line! I knew Hananiah and Nathaniah, the two sons of Shemaiah the elder; with me

they used to make the pilgrimage to Jerusalem, where we would worship together. No, they did not stray from the right path; your kinsmen are good men. You are certainly of good lineage, and welcome!" 15 Then he added: "For each day you are away I will give you the normal wages, plus expenses for you and for my son. If you go with my son, 16 I will even add a bonus to your wages!" Raphael replied: "I will go with him; have no fear. In good health we shall leave you, and in good health we shall return to you, for the way is safe." 17 Tobit said, "God bless you, brother." Then he called his son and said to him: "My son, prepare whatever you need for the journey, and set out with your kinsman. May God in heaven protect you on the way and bring you back to me safe and sound; and may his angel accompany you for safety, my son." Before setting out on his journey, Tobiah kissed his father and mother. Tobit said to him, "Have a safe journey." 18 But his mother began to weep. She said to Tobit: "Why have you decided to send my child away? Is he not the staff to which we cling, ever there with us in all that we do? 19 I hope more money is not your chief concern! Rather let it be a ransom for our son! 20 What the Lord has given us to live on is certainly enough for us." 21 Tobit reassured her: "Have no such thought. Our son will leave in good health and come back to us in good health. Your own eyes will see the day when he returns to you safe and sound. 22 So, no such thought; do not worry about them, my love. For a good angel will go with him, his journey will be successful, and he will return unharmed."

Tobit Chapter 6

1 Then she stopped weeping. 2 When the boy left home, accompanied by the angel, the dog followed Tobiah out of the house and went with them. The travelers walked till nightfall, and made camp beside the Tigris River. 3 Now when the boy went down to wash his feet in the river, a large fish suddenly leaped out of the water and tried to swallow his foot. He shouted in alarm. 4 But the angel said to him, "Take hold of the fish and don't let it get away!" The boy seized the fish and hauled it up on the shore. 5 The angel then told him: "Cut the fish open and take out its gall, heart, and liver, and keep them with you; but throw away the entrails. Its gall, heart, and liver make useful medicines." 6 After the lad had cut the fish open, he put aside the gall, heart, and liver. Then he broiled and ate part of the fish; the rest he salted and kept for the journey. 7 Afterward they traveled on together till they were near Media. The boy asked the angel this question: "Brother Azariah, what medicinal value is there in the fish's heart, liver, and gall?" 8 He answered: "As regards the fish's heart and liver, if you burn them so that the smoke surrounds a man or a woman who is afflicted by a demon or evil spirit, the affliction will leave him completely, and no demons will ever return to him again. 9 And as for the gall, if you rub it on the eyes of a man who has cataracts, blowing into his eyes right on the cataracts, his sight will be restored." 10 When they had entered Media and were getting close to Ecbatana, 11 Raphael said to the boy, "Brother Tobiah!" He answered, "Yes, what is it?" Raphael continued: "Tonight we must stay with Raguel, who is a relative of yours. He has a daughter named Sarah, 12 but no other child. Since you are Sarah's closest relative, you before all other men have the right to marry her. Also, her father's estate is rightfully yours to inherit. Now the girl is sensible, courageous, and very beautiful; and her father loves her dearly." 13 He continued: "Since you have the right to marry her, listen to me, brother. Tonight I will ask the girl's father to let us have her as your bride. When we return from Rages, we will hold the wedding feast for her. I know that Raguel cannot keep her from you or let her become engaged to another man; that would be a capital crime according to the decree in the Book of Moses, and he knows that it is your right, before all other men, to marry his daughter. So heed my words, brother; tonight we must speak for the girl, so that we may have her engaged to you. And when we return from Rages, we will take her and bring her back with us to your house." 14 Tobiah objected, however: "Brother Azariah, I have heard that this woman has already been married seven times, and that her husbands died in their bridal chambers. On the very night they approached her, they dropped dead. And I have heard it said that it was a demon who killed them. 15 So now I too am afraid of this demon. Because he loves her, he does not harm her; but he does slay any man who wishes to come close to her. I am my father's only child. If I should die, ever bring my father and mother down to their grave in sorrow over me. And they have no other son to bury them!" 16 Raphael said to him: "Do you not remember your father's orders? He commanded you to marry a woman from your own family. So now listen to me, brother; do not give another thought to this demon, but marry Sarah. I know that tonight you shall have her for your wife! 17 When you go into the bridal chamber, take the fish's liver and heart, and place them on the embers for the incense. 18 As soon as the demon smells the odor they give off, he will flee and never again show himself near her. Then when you are about to have

intercourse with her, both of you first rise up to pray. Beg the Lord of heaven to show you mercy and grant you deliverance. But do not be afraid, for she was set apart for you before the world existed. You will save her, and she will go with you. And I suppose that you will have children by her, who will take the place of brothers for you. So do not worry." When Tobiah heard Raphael say that she was his kinswoman, of his own family's lineage, he fell deeply in love with her, and his heart became set on her.

Tobit Chapter 7

1 When they entered Ecbatana, Tobiah said, "Brother Azariah, lead me straight to our kinsman Raguel." So he brought him to the house of Raguel, whom they found seated by his courtyard gate. They greeted him first. He said to them, "Greetings to you too, brothers! Good health to you, and welcome!" When he brought them into his home, 2 he said to his wife Edna, "This young man looks just like my kinsman Tobit!" 3 So Edna asked them, "Who are you, brothers?" They answered, "We are of the exiles from Naphtali at Nineveh." 4 She said, "Do you know our kinsman Tobit?" They answered, "Indeed we do!" She asked, "Is he well?" 5 They answered, "Yes, he is alive and well." Then Tobiah exclaimed, "He is my father!" 6 Raguel sprang up and kissed him, shedding tears of joy. 7 But when he heard that Tobit had lost his eyesight, he was grieved and wept aloud. He said to Tobiah: "My child, God bless you! You are the son of a noble and good father. But what a terrible misfortune that such a righteous and charitable man should be afflicted with blindness!" He continued to weep in the arms of his kinsman Tobiah. 8 His wife Edna also wept for Tobit; and even their daughter Sarah began to weep. 9 Afterward, Raguel slaughtered a ram from the flock and gave them a cordial reception. When they had bathed and reclined to eat, Tobiah said to Raphael, "Brother Azariah, ask Raguel to let me marry my kinswoman Sarah." 10 Raguel overheard the words; so he said to the boy: "Eat and drink and be merry tonight, for no man is more entitled to marry my daughter Sarah than you, brother. Besides, not even I have the right to give her to anyone but you, because you are my closest relative. But I will explain the situation to you very frankly. 11 I have given her in marriage to seven men, all of whom were kinsmen of ours, and all died on the very night they approached her. But now, son, eat and drink. I am sure the Lord will look after you both." Tobiah answered, "I will eat or drink nothing until you set aside what belongs to me." Raguel said to him: "I will do it. She is yours according to the decree of the Book of Moses. Your marriage to her has been decided in heaven! Take your kinswoman; from now on you are her love, and she is your beloved. She is yours today and ever after. And tonight, son, may the Lord of heaven prosper you both. May he grant you mercy and peace." 12 Then Raguel called his daughter Sarah, and she came to him. He took her by the hand and gave her to Tobiah with the words: "Take her according to the law. According to the decree written in the Book of Moses she is your wife. Take her and bring her back safely to your father. And may the God of heaven grant both of you peace and prosperity." 13 He then called her mother and told her to bring a scroll, so that he might draw up a marriage contract stating that he gave Sarah to Tobiah as his wife according to the decree of the Mosaic law. Her mother brought the scroll, and he drew up the contract, to which they affixed their seals. 14 Afterward they began to eat and drink. 15 Later Raguel called his wife Edna and said, "My love, prepare the other bedroom and bring the girl there." 16 She went and made the bed in the room, as she was told, and brought the girl there. After she had cried over her, she wiped away the tears and said: 17 "Be brave, my daughter. May the Lord of heaven grant you joy in place of your grief. Courage, my daughter." Then she left.

Tobit Chapter 8

1 When they had finished eating and drinking, the girl's parents wanted to retire. They brought the young man out of the dining room and led him into the bedroom. 2 At this point Tobiah, mindful of Raphael's instructions, took the fish's liver and heart from the bag which he had with him, and placed them on the embers for the incense. 3 The demon, repelled by the odor of the fish, fled into Upper Egypt; Raphael pursued him there and bound him hand and foot. Then Raphael returned immediately. 4 When the girl's parents left the bedroom and closed the door behind them, Tobiah arose from bed and said to his wife, "My love, get up. Let us pray and beg our Lord to have mercy on us and to grant us deliverance." 5 She got up, and they started to pray and beg that deliverance might be theirs. He began with these words: "Blessed are you, O God of our fathers; praised be your name forever and ever. Let the heavens and all your creation praise you forever. 6 You made Adam and you gave him his wife Eve to be his help and support; and from these two the human race descended. You said, 'It is not good for the man to be alone; let us make him a partner like himself.' 7 Now, Lord,

you know that I take this wife of mine not because of lust, but for a noble purpose. Call down your mercy on me and on her, and allow us to live together to a happy old age." 8 They said together, "Amen, amen," 9 and went to bed for the night. But Raguel got up and summoned his servants. With him they went out to dig a grave, 10 for he said, "I must do this, because if Tobiah should die, we would be subjected to ridicule and insult." 11 When they had finished digging the grave, Raguel went back into the house and called his wife, 12 saying, "Send one of the maids in to see whether Tobiah is alive or dead, so that if necessary we may bury him without anyone's knowing about it." 13 She sent the maid, who lit a lamp, opened the bedroom door, went in, and found them sound asleep together. 14 The maid went out and told the girl's parents that Tobiah was alive, and that there was nothing wrong. 15 Then Raguel praised the God of heaven in these words: "Blessed are you, O God, with every holy and pure blessing! Let all your chosen ones praise you; let them bless you forever! 16 Blessed are you, who have made me glad; what I feared did not happen. Rather you have dealt with us according to your great mercy. 17 Blessed are you, for you were merciful toward two only children. Grant them, Master, mercy and deliverance, and bring their lives to fulfillment with happiness and mercy." 18 Then he told his servants to fill in the grave before dawn. 19 He asked his wife to bake many loaves of bread; he himself went out to the herd and picked out two steers and four rams which he ordered to be slaughtered. So the servants began to prepare the feast. 20 He summoned Tobiah and made an oath in his presence, saying: "For fourteen days you shall not stir from here, but shall remain here eating and drinking with me; and you shall bring joy to my daughter's sorrowing spirit. 21 Take, to begin with, half of whatever I own when you go back in good health to your father; the other half will be yours when I and my wife die. Be of good cheer, my son! I am your father, and Edna is your mother; and we belong to you and to your beloved now and forever. So be happy, son!"

Tobit Chapter 9

1 Then Tobiah called Raphael and said to him: 2 "Brother Azariah, take along with you four servants and two camels and travel to Rages. Go to Gabael's house and give him this bond. Get the money and then bring him along with you to the wedding celebration. 3 You witnessed the oath that Raguel has sworn; I cannot violate his oath." 4 "For you know that my father is counting the days. If I should delay my return by a single day, I would cause him intense grief." 5 So Raphael, together with the four servants and two camels, traveled to Rages in Media, where they stayed at Gabael's house. Raphael gave Gabael his bond and told him about Tobit's son Tobiah, and that he had married and was inviting him to the wedding celebration. Gabael promptly checked over the sealed moneybags, and they placed them on the camels. 6 The following morning they got an early start and traveled to the wedding celebration. When they entered Raguel's house, they found Tobiah reclining at table. He sprang up and greeted Gabael, who wept and blessed him, exclaiming: "O noble and good child, son of a noble and good, upright and charitable man, may the Lord grant heavenly blessing to you and to your wife, and to your wife's father and mother. Blessed be God, because I have seen the very image of my cousin Tobit!"

Tobit Chapter 10

1 Meanwhile, day by day, Tobit was keeping track of the time Tobiah would need to go and to return. When the number of days was reached and his son did not appear, 2 he said, "I wonder what has happened. Perhaps he has been detained there; or perhaps Gabael is dead, and there is no one to give him the money." 3 And he began to worry. 4 His wife Anna said, "My son has perished and is no longer among the living!" And she began to weep aloud and to wail over her son: 5 "Alas, my child, light of my eyes, that I let you make this journey!" 6 But Tobit kept telling her: "Hush, do not think about it, my love; he is safe! Probably they have to take care of some unexpected business there. The man who is traveling with him is trustworthy, and is one of our own kinsmen. So do not worry over him, my love. He will be here soon." 7 But she retorted, "Stop it, and do not lie to me! My child has perished!" She would go out and keep watch all day at the road her son had taken, and she ate nothing. At sunset she would go back home to wail and cry the whole night through, getting no sleep at all. Now at the end of the fourteen-day wedding celebration which Raguel had sworn to hold for his daughter, Tobiah went to him and said: "Please let me go, for I know that my father and mother do not believe they will ever see me again. So I beg you, father, let me go back to my father. I have already told you how I left him." 8 Raguel said to Tobiah: "Stay, my child, stay with me. I am sending messengers to your father Tobit, and they will give him news of you." 9 But Tobiah insisted, "No, I beg you to let me go back to my father." 10 Raguel then promptly handed over to Tobiah Sarah his

wife, together with half of all his property: male and female slaves, oxen and sheep, asses and camels, clothing, money, and household goods. 11 Bidding them farewell, he let them go. He embraced Tobiah and said to him: "Good-bye, my son. Have a safe journey. May the Lord of heaven grant prosperity to you and to your wife Sarah. And may I see children of yours before I die!" 12 Then he kissed his daughter Sarah and said to her: "My daughter, honor your father-in-law and your mother-in-law, because from now on they are as much your parents as the ones who brought you into the world. Go in peace, my daughter; let me hear good reports about you as long as I live." Finally he said good-bye to them and sent them away. 13 Then Edna said to Tobiah: "My child and beloved kinsman, may the Lord bring you back safely, and may I live long enough to see children of you and of my daughter Sarah before I die. Before the Lord, I entrust my daughter to your care. Never cause her grief at any time in your life. Go in peace, my child. From now on I am your mother, and Sarah is your beloved. May all of us be prosperous all the days of our lives." She kissed them both and sent them away in peace. 14 When Tobiah left Raguel, he was full of happiness and joy, and he blessed the Lord of heaven and earth, the King of all, for making his journey so successful. Finally he said good-bye to Raguel and his wife Edna, and added, "May I honor you all the days of my life!"

Tobit Chapter 11

1 Then they left and began their return journey. When they were near Kaserin, just before Nineveh, 2 Raphael said: "You know how we left your father. 3 Let us hurry on ahead of your wife to prepare the house while the rest of the party are still on the way." 4 So they both went on ahead and Raphael said to Tobiah, "Have the gall in your hand!" And the dog ran along behind them. 5 Meanwhile, Anna sat watching the road by which her son was to come. 6 When she saw him coming, she exclaimed to her father, "Tobit, your son is coming, and the man who traveled with him!" 7 Raphael said to Tobiah before he reached his father: "I am certain that his eyes will be opened. 8 Smear the fish gall on them. This medicine will make the cataracts shrink and peel off from his eyes; then your father will again be able to see the light of day." 9 Then Anna ran up to her son, threw her arms around him, and said to him, "Now that I have seen you again, son, I am ready to die!" And she sobbed aloud. 10 Tobit got up and stumbled out through the courtyard gate. Tobiah went up to him 11 with the fish gall in his hand, and holding him firmly, blew into his eyes. "Courage, father," he said. 12 Next he smeared the medicine on his eyes, 13 and it made them smart. Then, beginning at the corners of Tobit's eyes, Tobiah used both hands to peel off the cataracts. When Tobit saw his son, he threw his arms around him 14 and wept. He exclaimed, "I can see you, son, the light of my eyes!" Then he said: "Blessed be God, and praised be his great name, and blessed be all his holy angels. May his holy name be praised throughout all the ages, 15 Because it was he who scourged me, and it is he who has had mercy on me. Behold, I now see my son Tobiah!" Then Tobit went back in, rejoicing and praising God with full voice. Tobiah told his father that his journey had been a success; that he had brought back the money; and that he had married Raguel's daughter Sarah, who would arrive shortly, for she was approaching the gate of Nineveh. 16 Rejoicing and praising God, Tobit went out to the gate of Nineveh to meet his daughter-in-law. When the people of Nineveh saw him walking along briskly, with no one leading him by the hand, they were amazed. 17 Before them all Tobit proclaimed how God had mercifully restored sight to his eyes. When Tobit reached Sarah, the wife of his son Tobiah, he greeted her: "Welcome, my daughter! Blessed be your God for bringing you to us, daughter! Blessed are your father and your mother. Blessed is my son Tobiah, and blessed are you, daughter! Welcome to your home with blessing and joy. Come in, daughter!" That day there was joy for all the Jews who lived in Nineveh. 18 Ahiqar and his nephew Nadab also came to rejoice with Tobit. They celebrated Tobiah's wedding feast for seven happy days, and he received many gifts.

Tobit Chapter 12

1 When the wedding celebration came to an end, Tobit called his son Tobiah and said to him, "Son, see to it that you give what is due to the man who made the journey; give him a bonus too." 2 Tobiah said: "Father, how much shall I pay him? It would not hurt me at all to give him half of all the wealth he brought back with me. 3 He led me back safe and sound; he cured my wife; he brought the money back with me; and he cured you. How much of a bonus should I give him?" 4 Tobit answered, "It is only fair, son, that he should receive half of all that he brought back." 5 So Tobiah called Raphael and said, "Take as your wages half of all that you have brought back, and go in peace." 6 Raphael called the two men aside privately and said to them: "Thank God! Give him the praise and the glory. Before all the living, acknowledge the

many good things he has done for you, by blessing and extolling his name in song. Before all men, honor and proclaim God's deeds, and do not be slack in praising him. 7 A king's secret it is prudent to keep, but the works of God are to be declared and made known. Praise them with due honor. Do good, and evil will not find its way to you. 8 Prayer and fasting are good, but better than either is almsgiving accompanied by righteousness. A little with righteousness is better than abundance with wickedness. It is better to give alms than to store up gold; 9 for almsgiving saves one from death and expiates every sin. Those who regularly give alms shall enjoy a full life; 10 but those habitually guilty of sin are their own worst enemies. 11 "I will now tell you the whole truth; I will conceal nothing at all from you. I have already said to you, 'A king's secret it is prudent to keep, but the works of God are to be made known with due honor.' 12 I can now tell you that when you, Tobit, and Sarah prayed, it was I who presented and read the record of your prayer before the Glory of the Lord; and I did the same thing when you used to bury the dead. 13 When you did not hesitate to get up and leave your dinner in order to go and bury the dead, 14 I was sent to put you to the test. At the same time, however, God commissioned me to heal you and your daughter-in-law Sarah. 15 I am Raphael, one of the seven angels who enter and serve before the Glory of the Lord." 16 Stricken with fear, the two men fell to the ground. 17 But Raphael said to them: "No need to fear; you are safe. Thank God now and forever. 18 As for me, when I came to you it was not out of any favor on my part, but because it was God's will. So continue to thank him every day; praise him with song. 19 Even though you watched me eat and drink. I did not really do so; what you were seeing was a vision. 20 So now get up from the ground and praise God. Behold, I am about to ascend to him who sent me; write down all these things that have happened to you." 21 When Raphael ascended they rose to their feet and could no longer see him. 22 They kept thanking God and singing his praises; and they continued to acknowledge these marvelous deeds which he had done when the angel of God appeared to them.

Tobit Chapter 13

1 Then Tobit composed this joyful prayer: Blessed be God who lives forever, because his kingdom lasts for all ages. 2 For he scourges and then has mercy; he casts down to the depths of the nether world, and he brings up from the great abyss. No one can escape his hand. 3 Praise him, you Israelites, before the Gentiles, for though he has scattered you among them, 4 he has shown you his greatness even there. Exalt him before every living being, because he is the Lord our God, our Father and God forever. 5 He scourged you for your iniquities, but will again have mercy on you all. He will gather you from all the Gentiles among whom you have been scattered. 6 When you turn back to him with all your heart, to do what is right before him, Then he will turn back to you, and no longer hide his face from you. So now consider what he has done for you, and praise him with full voice. Bless the Lord of righteousness, and exalt the King of the ages. In the land of my exile I praise him, and show his power and majesty to a sinful nation. "Turn back, you sinners! do the right before him: perhaps he may look with favor upon you and show you mercy. 7 As for me, I exalt my God, and my spirit rejoices in the King of heaven. 8 Let all men speak of his majesty, and sing his praises in Jerusalem." 9 O Jerusalem, holy city, he scourged you for the works of your hands, but will again pity the children of the righteous. 10 Praise the Lord for his goodness, and bless the King of the ages, so that his tent may be rebuilt in you with joy. May he gladden within you all who were captives; all who were ravaged may he cherish within you for all generations to come. 11 A bright light will shine to all parts of the earth; many nations shall come to you from afar, And the inhabitants of all the limits of the earth, drawn to you by the name of the Lord God, Bearing in their hands their gifts for the King of heaven. Every generation shall give joyful praise in you, and shall call you the chosen one, through all ages forever. 12 Accursed are all who speak a harsh word against you; accursed are all who destroy you and pull down your walls, And all who overthrow your towers and set fire to your homes; but forever blessed are all those who build you up. 13 Go, then, rejoice over the children of the righteous, who shall all be gathered together and shall bless the Lord of the ages. 14 Happy are those who love you, and happy those who rejoice in your prosperity. Happy are all the men who shall grieve over you, over all your chastisements, For they shall rejoice in you as they behold all your joy forever. 15 My spirit blesses the Lord, the great King; 16 Jerusalem shall be rebuilt as his home forever. Happy for me if a remnant of my offspring survive to see your glory and to praise the King of heaven! The gates of Jerusalem shall be built with sapphire and emerald, and all your walls with precious stones. The towers of Jerusalem shall be built with gold, and their battlements with pure gold. 17 The streets of Jerusalem shall be paved with rubies and stones of Ophir; 18 The gates of Jerusalem shall sing

hymns of gladness, and all her houses shall cry out, "Alleluia! Blessed be God who has raised you up! may he be blessed for all ages!" For in you they shall praise his holy name forever. The end of Tobit's hymn of praise.

Tobit Chapter 14

1 Tobit died peacefully at the age of a hundred and twelve, and received an honorable burial in Nineveh. 2 He was sixty-two years old when he lost his eyesight, and after he recovered it he lived in prosperity, giving alms and continually blessing God and praising the divine Majesty. 3 Just before he died, he called his son Tobiah and Tobiah's seven sons, and gave him this command: "Son, take your children 4 and flee into Media, for I believe God's word which was spoken by Nahum against Nineveh. It shall all happen, and shall overtake Assyria and Nineveh; indeed, whatever was said by Israel's prophets, whom God commissioned, shall occur. Not one of all the oracles shall remain unfulfilled, but everything shall take place in the time appointed for it. So it will be safer in Media than in Assyria or Babylon. For I know and believe that whatever God has spoken will be accomplished. It shall happen, and not a single word of the prophecies shall prove false. As for our kinsmen who dwell in Israel, they shall all be scattered and led away into exile from the Good Land. The entire country of Israel shall become desolate; even Samaria and Jerusalem shall become desolate! God's temple there shall be burnt to the ground and shall be desolate for a while. 5 But God will again have mercy on them and bring them back to the land of Israel. They shall rebuild the temple, but it will not be like the first one, until the era when the appointed times shall be completed. Afterward all of them shall return from their exile, and they shall rebuild Jerusalem with splendor. In her temple of God shall also be rebuilt; yes, it will be rebuilt for all generations to come, just as the prophets of Israel said of her. 6 All the nations of the world shall be converted and shall offer God true worship; all shall abandon their idols which have deceitfully led them into error, 7 and shall bless the God of the ages in righteousness. Because all the Israelites who are to be saved in those days will truly be mindful of God, they shall be gathered together and go to Jerusalem; in security shall they dwell forever in the land of Abraham, which will be given over to them. Those who sincerely love God shall rejoice, but those who become guilty of sin shall completely disappear from the land. 8 "Now, as for you, my son, depart from Nineveh; do not remain here. 9 Now, children, I give you this command: serve God faithfully and do what is right before him; you must tell your children to do what is upright and to give alms, to be mindful of God and at all times to bless his name sincerely and with all their strength. 10 The day you bury your mother next to me, do not even stay overnight within the confines of the city. For I see that people here shamelessly commit all sorts of wickedness and treachery. Think, my son, of all that Nadab did to Ahiqar, the very one who brought him up: Ahiqar went down alive into the earth! Yet God made Nadab's disgraceful crime rebound against him. Ahiqar came out again into the light, but Nadab went into the everlasting darkness, for he had tried to kill Ahiqar. Because Ahiqar had given alms to me, he escaped from the deadly trap Nadab had set for him. But Nadab himself fell into the deadly trap, and it destroyed him. 11 So, my children, note well what almsgiving does, and also what wickedness does - it kills! But now my spirit is about to leave me." 12 They placed him on his bed and he died; and he received an honorable burial. When Tobiah's mother died, he buried her next to his father. He then departed with his wife and children for Media, where he settled in Ecbatana with his father-in-law Raguel. 13 He took respectful care of his aging father-in-law and mother-in-law; and he buried them at Ecbatana in Media. Then he inherited Raguel's estate as well as that of his father Tobit. 14 He died at the venerable age of a hundred and seventeen. 15 But before he died, he heard of the destruction of Nineveh and saw its effects. He witnessed the exile of the city's inhabitants when Cyaxares, king of Media, led them captive into Media. Tobiah praised God for all that he had done against the citizens of Nineveh and Assyria. Before dying he rejoiced over Nineveh's destruction, and he blessed the Lord God forever and ever. Amen.

Judith

Judith Chapter 1

1 It was the twelfth year of the reign of Nebuchadnezzar, king of the Assyrians in the great city of Nineveh. At that time Arphaxad ruled over the Medes in Ecbatana. 2 Around this city he built a wall of blocks of stone, each three cubits in height and six in length. He made the wall seventy cubits high and fifty thick. 3 At the gates he raised towers of a hundred cubits, with a thickness of sixty cubits at the base. 4 The gateway he built to a height of seventy cubits, with an opening forty

cubits wide for the passage of his chariot forces and the marshaling of his infantry. 5 Then King Nebuchadnezzar waged war against King Arphaxad in the vast plain, in the district of Ragae. 6 To him there rallied all the inhabitants of the mountain region, all who dwelt along the Euphrates, the Tigris, and the Hydaspes, and King Arioch of the Elamites, in the plain. Thus many nations came together to resist the people of Cheleoud. 7 Now Nebuchadnezzar, king of the Assyrians, sent messengers to all the inhabitants of Persia, and to all those who dwelt in the West: to the inhabitants of Cilicia and Damascus, Lebanon and Anti-Lebanon, to all who dwelt along the seacoast, 8 to the peoples of Carmel, Gilead, Upper Galilee, and the vast plain of Esdraelon, 9 to all those in Samaria and its cities, and west of the Jordan as far as Jerusalem, Bethany, Chelous, Kadesh, and the River of Egypt; to Tahpanhes, Raamses, all the land of Goshen, 10 Tanis, Memphis and beyond, and to all the inhabitants of Egypt as far as the borders of Ethiopia. 11 But the inhabitants of all that land disregarded the summons of Nebuchadnezzar, king of the Assyrians, and would not go with him to the war. They were not afraid of him but regarded him as a lone individual opposed to them, and turned away his envoys empty-handed, in disgrace. 12 Then Nebuchadnezzar fell into a violent rage against all that land, and swore by his throne and his kingdom that he would avenge himself on all the territories of Cilicia and Damascus and Syria, and also destroy with his sword all the inhabitants of Moab, Ammon, the whole of Judea, and those living anywhere in Egypt as far as the borders of the two seas. 13 In the seventeenth year he proceeded with his army against King Arphaxad, and was victorious in his campaign. He routed the whole force of Arphaxad, his entire cavalry and all his chariots, 14 and took possession of his cities. He pressed on to Ecbatana and took its towers, sacked its marketplaces, and turned its glory into shame. 15 Arphaxad himself he overtook in the mountains of Ragae, ran him through with spears, and utterly destroyed him. 16 Then he returned home with all his numerous, motley horde of warriors; and there he and his army relaxed and feasted for a hundred and twenty days.

Judith Chapter 2

1 In the eighteenth year, on the twenty-second day of the first month, there was a discussion in the palace of Nebuchadnezzar, king of the Assyrians, about taking revenge on the whole world, as he had threatened. 2 He summoned all his ministers and nobles, laid before them his secret plan, and urged the total destruction of those countries. 3 They decided to do away with all those who had refused to comply with the order he had issued. 4 When he had completed his plan, Nebuchadnezzar, king of the Assyrians, summoned Holofernes, general in chief of his forces, second to himself in command, and said to him: 5 "Thus says the great king, the lord of all the earth: Go forth from my presence, take with you men of proven valor, a hundred and twenty thousand infantry and twelve thousand cavalry, 6 and proceed against all the land of the West, because they did not comply with the order I issued. 7 Tell them to have earth and water ready, for I will come against them in my wrath; I will cover all the land with the feet of my soldiers, to whom I will deliver them as spoils. 8 Their slain shall fill their ravines and wadies, the swelling torrent shall be choked with their dead; 9 and I will deport them as exiles to the very ends of the earth. 10 You go before me and take possession of all their territories for me. If they surrender to you, guard them for me till the day of their punishment. 11 As for those who resist, show them no quarter, but deliver them up to slaughter and plunder in each country you occupy. 12 For as I live, and by the strength of my kingdom, what I have spoken I will accomplish by my power. 13 Do not disobey a single one of the orders of your lord; fulfill them exactly as I have commanded you, and do it without delay." 14 So Holofernes left the presence of his lord, and summoned all the princes, and the generals and officers of the Assyrian army. 15 He mustered a hundred and twenty thousand picked troops, as his lord had commanded, and twelve thousand mounted archers, 16 and grouped them into a complete combat force. 17 He took along a very large number of camels, asses, and mules for their baggage; innumerable sheep, cattle, and goats for their food supply; 18 abundant provisions for each man, and much gold and silver from the royal palace. 19 Then he and his whole army proceeded on their expedition in advance of King Nebuchadnezzar, to cover all the western region with their chariots and cavalry and regular infantry. 20 A huge, irregular force, too many to count, like locusts or the dust of the earth, went along with them. 21 After a three-day march from Nineveh, they reached the plain of Bectileth, and from Bectileth they next encamped near the mountains to the north of Upper Cilicia. 22 From there Holofernes took his whole force, the infantry, cavalry, and chariots, and marched into the mountain region. 23 He devastated Put and Lud, and plundered all the Rassisites and the Ishmaelites on the border of the desert toward the south of Chaldea. 24 Then, following the Euphrates, he went through Mesopotamia, and battered down every fortified city along the Wadi Abron, until he reached the sea. 25 He seized the territory of Cilicia, and cut down everyone who resisted him. Then he proceeded to the southern borders of Japheth, toward Arabia. 26 He surrounded all the Midianites, burned their tents, and plundered their sheepfolds. 27 Descending to the plain of Damascus at the time of the wheat harvest, he set fire to all their fields, destroyed their flocks and herds, despoiled their cities, devastated their plains, and put all their youths to the sword. 28 The fear and dread of him fell upon all the inhabitants of the coastland, upon those in Sidon and Tyre, and those who dwelt in Sur and Ocina, and the inhabitants of Jamnia. Those in Azotus and Ascalon also feared him greatly.

Judith Chapter 3

1 They therefore sent messengers to him to sue for peace in these words: 2 "We, the servants of Nebuchadnezzar the great king, lie prostrate before you; do with us as you will. 3 Our dwellings and all our wheat fields, our flocks and herds, and all our encampments are at your disposal; make use of them as you please. 4 Our cities and their inhabitants are also at your service; come and deal with them as you see fit." 5 After the spokesmen had reached Holofernes and given him this message, 6 he went down with his army to the seacoast, and stationed garrisons in the fortified cities; from them he impressed picked troops as auxiliaries. 7 The people of these cities and all the inhabitants of the countryside received him with garlands and dancing to the sound of timbrels. 8 Nevertheless, he devastated their whole territory and cut down their sacred groves, for he had been commissioned to destroy all the gods of the earth, so that every nation might worship Nebuchadnezzar alone, and every people and tribe invoke him as a god. 9 At length Holofernes reached Esdraelon in the neighborhood of Dothan, the approach to the main ridge of the Judean mountains; 10 he set up his camp between Geba and Scythopolis, and stayed there a whole month to refurbish all the equipment of his army.

Judith Chapter 4

1 When the Israelites who dwelt in Judea heard of all that Holofernes, commander-in-chief of Nebuchadnezzar, king of the Assyrians, had done to the nations, and how he had despoiled all their temples and destroyed them, 2 they were in extreme dread of him, and greatly alarmed for Jerusalem and the temple of the Lord, their God. 3 Now, they had lately returned from exile, and only recently had all the people of Judea been gathered together, and the vessels, the altar, and the temple been purified from profanation. 4 So they sent word to the whole region of Samaria, to Kona, Beth-horon, Belmain, and Jericho, to Choba and Aesora, and to the valley of Salem. 5 The people there posted guards on all the summits of the high mountains, fortified their villages, and since their fields had recently been harvested, stored up provisions in preparation for war. 6 Joakim, who was high priest in Jerusalem in those days, wrote to the inhabitants of Bethulia (and Betomesthaim), which is on the way to Esdraelon, facing the plain near Dothan, 7 and instructed them to keep firm hold of the mountain passes, since these offered access to Judea. It would be easy to ward off the attacking forces, as the defile was only wide enough for two abreast. 8 The Israelites carried out the orders given them by Joakim, the high priest, and the senate of the whole people of Israel, which met in Jerusalem. 9 All the men of Israel cried to God with great fervor and did penance— 10 they, along with their wives, and children, and domestic animals. All their resident aliens, hired laborers, and slaves also girded themselves with sackcloth. 11 And all the Israelite men, women and children who lived in Jerusalem prostrated themselves in front of the temple building, with ashes strewn on their heads, displaying their sackcloth covering before the Lord. 12 The altar, too, they draped in sackcloth; and with one accord they cried out fervently to the God of Israel not to allow their children to be seized, their wives to be taken captive, the cities of their inheritance to be ruined, or the sanctuary to be profaned and mocked for the nations to gloat over. 13 The Lord heard their cry and had regard for their distress. For the people observed a fast of many days' duration throughout Judea, and before the sanctuary of the Lord Almighty in Jerusalem. 14 The high priest Joakim, and all the priests in attendance on the Lord who served his altar, were also girded with sackcloth as they offered the daily holocaust, the votive offerings, and the freewill offerings of the people. 15 With ashes upon their turbans, they cried to the Lord with all their strength to look with favor on the whole house of Israel.

Judith Chapter 5

1 It was reported to Holofernes, commander-in-chief of the Assyrian army, that the Israelites were ready for battle, and had blocked the mountain passes, fortified the summits of all the higher peaks, and

placed roadblocks in the plains. ² In great anger he summoned all the rulers of the Moabites, the generals of the Ammonites, and all the satraps of the seacoast ³ and said to them: "Now tell me, you Canaanites, what sort of people is this that dwells in the mountains? Which cities do they inhabit? How large is their army? In what does their power and strength consist? Who has set himself up as their king and the leader of their army? ⁴ Why have they refused to come out to meet me along with all the other inhabitants of the West?" ⁵ Then Achior, the leader of all the Ammonites, said to him: "My lord, hear this account from your servant; I will tell you the truth about this people that lives near you (that inhabits this mountain region); no lie shall escape your servant's lips. ⁶ These people are descendants of the Chaldeans. ⁷ They formerly dwelt in Mesopotamia, for they did not wish to follow the gods of their forefathers who were born in the land of the Chaldeans. ⁸ Since they abandoned the way of their ancestors, and acknowledged with divine worship the God of heaven, their forefathers expelled them from the presence of their gods. So they fled to Mesopotamia and dwelt there a long time. ⁹ Their God bade them leave their abode and proceed to the land of Canaan. Here they settled, and grew very rich in gold, silver, and a great abundance of livestock. ¹⁰ Later, when famine had gripped the whole land of Canaan, they went down into Egypt. They stayed there as long as they found sustenance, and grew into such a great multitude that the number of their race could not be counted. ¹¹ The king of Egypt, however, rose up against them, shrewdly forced them to labor at brickmaking, oppressed and enslaved them. ¹² But they cried to their God, and he struck the land of Egypt with plagues for which there was no remedy. When the Egyptians expelled them, ¹³ God dried up the Red Sea before them, ¹⁴ and led them along the route to Sinai and Kadesh-barnea. First they drove out all the inhabitants of the desert; ¹⁵ then they settled in the land of the Amorites, destroyed all the Heshbonites by main force, crossed the Jordan, and took possession of the whole mountain region. ¹⁶ They expelled the Canaanites, the Perizzites, the Jebusites, the Shechemites, and all the Gergesites; and they lived in these mountains a long time. ¹⁷ "As long as the Israelites did not sin in the sight of their God, they prospered, for their God, who hates wickedness, was with them. ¹⁸ But when they deviated from the way he prescribed for them, they were ground down steadily, more and more, by frequent wars, and finally taken as captives into foreign lands. The temple of their God was razed to the ground, and their cities were occupied by their enemies. ¹⁹ But now that they have returned to their God, they have come back from the Dispersion wherein they were scattered, and have repossessed Jerusalem, where their sanctuary is, and have settled again in the mountain region which was unoccupied. ²⁰ "So now, my lord and master, if these people are at fault, and are sinning against their God, and if we verify this offense of theirs, then we shall be able to go up and conquer them. ²¹ But if they are not a guilty nation, then your lordship should keep his distance; otherwise their Lord and God will shield them, and we shall become the laughing stock of the whole world." ²² Now when Achior had concluded his recommendation, all the people standing round about the tent murmured; and the officers of Holofernes and all the inhabitants of the seacoast and of Moab alike said he should be cut to pieces. ²³ "We are not afraid of the Israelites," they said, "for they are a powerless people, incapable of a strong defense. ²⁴ Let us therefore attack them; your great army, Lord Holofernes, will swallow them up."

Judith Chapter 6

¹ When the noise of the crowd surrounding the council had subsided, Holofernes, commander-in-chief of the Assyrian army, said to Achior, in the presence of the whole throng of coastland peoples, of the Moabites, and of the Ammonite mercenaries: ² "Who are you, Achior, to prophesy among us as you have done today, and to tell us not to fight against the Israelites because their God protects them? What god is there beside Nebuchadnezzar? He will send his force and destroy them from the face of the earth. Their God will not save them; ³ but we, the servants of Nebuchadnezzar, will strike them down as one man, for they will be unable to withstand the force of our cavalry. ⁴ We will overwhelm them with it, and the mountains shall be drunk with their blood, and their plains filled with their corpses. Not a trace of them shall survive our attack: they shall utterly perish, says King Nebuchadnezzar, lord of all the earth; for he has spoken, and his words shall not remain unfulfilled. ⁵ As for you, Achior, you Ammonite mercenary, for saying these things in a moment of perversity you shall not see my face after today, until I have taken revenge on this race of people from Egypt. ⁶ Then at my return, the sword of my army or the spear of my servants will pierce your sides, and you shall fall among their slain. ⁷ My servants will now conduct you to the mountain region, and leave you at one of the towns along the ascent. ⁸ You shall not die till you are destroyed

together with them. ⁹ If you still cherish the hope that they will not be taken, then there is no need for you to be downcast. I have spoken, and my words shall not prove false in any respect." ¹⁰ Then Holofernes ordered the servants who were standing by in his tent to seize Achior, conduct him to Bethulia, and hand him over to the Israelites. ¹¹ So the servants took him in custody and brought him out of the camp into the plain. From there they led him into the mountain region till they reached the springs below Bethulia. ¹² When the men of the city saw them, they seized their weapons and ran out of the city to the crest of the ridge; and all the slingers blocked the ascent of Holofernes' servants by hurling stones upon them. ¹³ So they took cover below the mountain, where they bound Achior and left him lying at the foot of the mountain; then they returned to their lord. ¹⁴ The Israelites came down to him from their city, loosed him, and brought him into Bethulia. They haled him before the rulers of the city, ¹⁵ who in those days were Uzziah, son of Micah of the tribe of Simeon, Chabris, son of Gothoniel, and Charmis, son of Melchiel. ¹⁶ They then convened all the elders of the city; and all their young men, as well as the women, gathered in haste at the place of assembly. They placed Achior in the center of the throng, and Uzziah questioned him about what had happened. ¹⁷ He replied by giving them an account of what was said in the council of Holofernes, and of all his own words among the Assyrian officers, and of all the boasting threats of Holofernes against the house of Israel. ¹⁸ At this the people fell prostrate and worshiped God; and they cried out: ¹⁹ "Lord, God of heaven, behold their arrogance! Have pity on the lowliness of our people, and look with favor this day on those who are consecrated to you." ²⁰ Then they reassured Achior and praised him highly. ²¹ Uzziah brought him from the assembly to his home, where he gave a banquet for the elders. That whole night they called upon the God of Israel for help.

Judith Chapter 7

¹ The following day Holofernes ordered his whole army, and all the allied troops that had come to his support, to move against Bethulia, seize the mountain passes, and engage the Israelites in battle. ² That same day all their fighting men went into action. Their forces numbered a hundred and seventy thousand infantry and twelve thousand horsemen, not counting the baggage train or the men who accompanied it on foot—a very great army. ³ They encamped at the spring in the valley near Bethulia, and spread out in breadth toward Dothan as far as Balbaim, and in length from Bethulia to Cyamon, which faces Esdraelon. ⁴ When the Israelites saw how many there were, they said to one another in great dismay: "Soon they will devour the whole country. Neither the high mountains nor the valleys and hills can support the mass of them." ⁵ Yet they all seized their weapons, lighted fires on their bastions, and kept watch throughout the night. ⁶ On the second day Holofernes led out all his cavalry in the sight of the Israelites who were in Bethulia. ⁷ He reconnoitered the approaches to their city and located their sources of water; these he seized, stationing armed detachments around them, while he himself returned to his troops. ⁸ All the commanders of the Edomites and all the leaders of the Ammonites, together with the generals of the seacoast, came to Holofernes and said: ⁹ "Sir, listen to what we have to say, that there may be no losses among your troops. ¹⁰ These Israelites do not rely on their spears, but on the height of the mountains where they dwell; it is not easy to reach the summit of their mountains. ¹¹ Therefore, sir, do not attack them in regular formation; thus not a single one of your troops will fall. ¹² Stay in your camp, and spare all your soldiers. Have some of your servants keep control of the source of water that flows out at the base of the mountain, ¹³ for that is where the inhabitants of Bethulia get their water. Then thirst will begin to carry them off, and they will surrender their city. Meanwhile, we and our men will go up to the summits of the nearby mountains, and encamp there to guard against anyone's leaving the city. ¹⁴ They and their wives and children will languish with hunger, and even before the sword strikes them they will be laid low in the streets of their city. ¹⁵ Thus you will render them dire punishment for their rebellion and their refusal to meet you peacefully." ¹⁶ Their words pleased Holofernes and all his ministers, and he ordered their proposal to be carried out. ¹⁷ Thereupon the Moabites moved camp, together with five thousand Assyrians. They encamped in the valley, and held the water supply and the springs of the Israelites. ¹⁸ The Edomites and the Ammonites went up and encamped in the mountain region opposite Dothan; and they sent some of their men to the south and to the east opposite Egrebel, near Chusi, which is on Wadi Mochmur. The rest of the Assyrian army was encamped in the plain, covering the whole countryside. Their enormous store of tents and equipment was spread out in profusion everywhere. ¹⁹ The Israelites cried to the Lord, their God, for they were disheartened, since all their enemies had them surrounded, and there was no way of slipping through their lines. ²⁰

The whole Assyrian camp, infantry, chariots, and cavalry, kept them thus surrounded for thirty-four days. All the reservoirs of water failed the inhabitants of Bethulia, ²¹ and the cisterns ran dry, so that on no day did they have enough to drink, but their drinking water was rationed. ²² Their children fainted away, and the women and youths were consumed with thirst and were collapsing in the streets and gateways of the city, with no strength left in them. ²³ All the people, therefore, including youths, women, and children, went in a crowd to Uzziah and the rulers of the city. They set up a great clamor and said before the elders: ²⁴ "God judge between you and us! You have done us grave injustice in not making peace with the Assyrians. ²⁵ There is no help for us now! Instead, God has sold us into their power by laying us prostrate before them in thirst and utter exhaustion. ²⁶ Therefore, summon them and deliver the whole city as booty to the troops of Holofernes and to all his forces; ²⁷ we would be better off to become their prey. We should indeed be made slaves, but at least we should live, and not have to behold our little ones dying before our eyes and our wives and children breathing out their souls. ²⁸ We adjure you by heaven and earth, and by our God, the Lord of our forefathers, who is punishing us for our sins and those of our forefathers, to do as we have proposed, this very day." ²⁹ All in the assembly with one accord broke into shrill wailing and loud cries to the Lord their God. ³⁰ But Uzziah said to them, "Courage, my brothers! Let us wait five days more for the Lord our God, to show his mercy toward us; he will not utterly forsake us. ³¹ But if those days pass without help coming to us, I will do as you say." ³² Then he dispersed the men to their posts, and they returned to the walls and towers of the city; the women and children he sent to their homes. Throughout the city they were in great misery.

Judith Chapter 8

¹ Now in those days Judith, daughter of Merari, son of Joseph, son of Oziel, son of Elkiah, son of Ananias, son of Gideon, son of Raphain, son of Ahitob, son of Elijah, son of Hilkiah, son of Eliab, son of Nathanael, son of Salamiel, son of Sarasadai, son of Simeon, son of Israel, heard of this. ² Her husband, Manasseh, of her own tribe and clan, had died at the time of the barley harvest. ³ While he was in the field supervising those who bound the sheaves, he suffered sunstroke; and he died of this illness in Bethulia, his native city. He was buried with his forefathers in the field between Dothan and Balamon. ⁴ The widowed Judith remained three years and four months at home, ⁵ where she set up a tent for herself on the roof of her house. She put sackcloth about her loins and wore widow's weeds. ⁶ She fasted all the days of her widowhood, except sabbath eves and sabbaths, new moon eves and new moons, feastdays and holidays of the house of Israel. ⁷ She was beautifully formed and lovely to behold. Her husband, Manasseh, had left her gold and silver, servants and maids, livestock and fields, which she was maintaining. ⁸ No one had a bad word to say about her, for she was a very God-fearing woman. ⁹ When Judith, therefore, heard of the harsh words which the people, discouraged by their lack of water, had spoken against their ruler, and of all that Uzziah had said to them in reply, swearing that he would hand over the city to the Assyrians at the end of five days, ¹⁰ she sent the maid who was in charge of all her things to ask Uzziah, Chabris, and Charmis, the elders of the city, to visit her. ¹¹ When they came, she said to them: "Listen to me, you rulers of the people of Bethulia. What you said to the people today is not proper. When you promised to hand over the city to our enemies at the end of five days unless within that time the Lord comes to our aid, you interposed between God and yourselves this oath which you took. ¹² Who are you, then, that you should have put God to the test this day, setting yourselves in the place of God in human affairs? ¹³ It is the Lord Almighty for whom you are laying down conditions; will you never understand anything? ¹⁴ You cannot plumb the depths of the human heart or grasp the workings of the human mind; how then can you fathom God, who has made all these things, discern his mind, and understand his plan? "No, my brothers, do not anger the Lord our God. ¹⁵ For if he does not wish to come to our aid within the five days, he has it equally within his power to protect us at such time as he pleases, or to destroy us in the face of our enemies. ¹⁶ It is not for you to make the Lord our God give surety for his plans. "God is not man that he should be moved by threats, nor human, that he may be given an ultimatum. ¹⁷ "So while we wait for the salvation that comes from him, let us call upon him to help us, and he will hear our cry if it is his good pleasure. ¹⁸ For there has not risen among us in recent generations, nor does there exist today, any tribe, or clan, or town, or city of ours that worships gods made by hands, as happened in former days. ¹⁹ It was for such conduct that our forefathers were handed over to the sword and to pillage, and fell with great destruction before our enemies. ²⁰ But since we acknowledge no other god but the Lord, we hope that he will not disdain us or any of our people. ²¹ If we are taken, all Judea will fall,

our sanctuary will be plundered, and God will make us pay for its profanation with our life's blood. ²² For the slaughter of our kinsmen, for the taking of exiles from the land, and for the devastation of our inheritance, he will lay the guilt on our heads. Wherever we shall be enslaved among the nations, we shall be a mockery and a reproach in the eyes of our masters. ²³ Our enslavement will not be turned to our benefit, but the Lord our God, will maintain it to our disgrace. ²⁴ "Therefore, my brothers, let us set an example for our kinsmen. Their lives depend on us, and the defense of the sanctuary, the temple, and the altar rests with us. ²⁵ Besides all this, we should be grateful to the Lord our God, for putting us to the test, as he did our forefathers. ²⁶ Recall how he dealt with Abraham, and how he tried Isaac, and all that happened to Jacob in Syrian Mesopotamia while he was tending the flocks of Laban, his mother's brother. ²⁷ Not for vengeance did the Lord put them in the crucible to try their hearts, nor has he done so with us. It is by way of admonition that he chastises those who are close to him." ²⁸ Then Uzziah said to her: "All that you have said was spoken with good sense, and no one can gainsay your words. ²⁹ Not today only is your wisdom made evident, but from your earliest years all the people have recognized your prudence, which corresponds to the worthy dispositions of your heart. ³⁰ The people, however, were so tortured with thirst that they forced us to speak to them as we did, and to bind ourselves by an oath that we cannot break. ³¹ But now, God-fearing woman that you are, pray for us that the Lord may send rain to fill up our cisterns, lest we be weakened still further." ³² Then Judith said to them: "Listen to me! I will do something that will go down from generation to generation among the descendants of our race. ³³ Stand at the gate tonight to let me pass through with my maid; and within the days you have specified before you will surrender the city to our enemies, the Lord will rescue Israel by my hand. ³⁴ You must not inquire into what I am doing, for I will not tell you until my plan has been accomplished." ³⁵ Uzziah and the rulers said to her, "Go in peace, and may the Lord God go before you to take vengeance upon our enemies!" ³⁶ Then they withdrew from the tent and returned to their posts.

Judith Chapter 9

¹ Judith threw herself down prostrate, with ashes strewn upon her head, and wearing nothing over her sackcloth. While the incense was being offered in the temple of God in Jerusalem that evening, Judith prayed to the Lord with a loud voice: ² "Lord, God of my forefather Simeon! You put a sword into his hand to take revenge upon the foreigners who had immodestly loosened the maiden's girdle, shamefully exposed her thighs, and disgracefully violated her body. This they did, though you forbade it. ³ Therefore you had their rulers slaughtered; and you covered with their blood the bed in which they lay deceived, the same bed that had felt the shame of their own deceiving. You smote the slaves together with their princes, and the princes together with their servants. ⁴ Their wives you handed over to plunder, and their daughters to captivity; and all the spoils you divided among your favored sons, who burned with zeal for you, and in their abhorrence of the defilement of their kinswoman, called on you for help. ⁵ "O God, my God, hear me also, a widow. It is you who were the author of those events and of what preceded and followed them. The present, also, and the future you have planned. Whatever you devise comes into being; ⁶ the things you decide on come forward and say, 'Here we are!' All your ways are in readiness, and your judgment is made with foreknowledge. ⁷ "Here are the Assyrians, a vast force, priding themselves on horse and rider, boasting of the power of their infantry, trusting in shield and spear, bow and sling. They do not know that ⁸ 'You, the Lord, crush warfare; Lord is your name. Shatter their strength in your might, and crush their force in your wrath; for they have resolved to profane your sanctuary, to defile the tent where your glorious name resides, and to overthrow with iron the horns of your altar. ⁹ See their pride, and send forth your wrath upon their heads. Give me, a widow, the strong hand to execute my plan. ¹⁰ With the guile of my lips, smite the slave together with the ruler, the ruler together with his servant; crush their pride by the hand of a woman. ¹¹ "Your strength is not in numbers, nor does your power depend upon stalwart men; but you are the God of the lowly, the helper of the oppressed, the supporter of the weak, the protector of the forsaken, the savior of those without hope. ¹² "Please, please, God of my forefather, God of the heritage of Israel, Lord of heaven and earth, Creator of the waters, King of all you have created, hear my prayer! ¹³ Let my guileful speech bring wound and wale on those who have planned dire things against your covenant, your holy temple, Mount Zion, and the homes your children have inherited. ¹⁴ Let your whole nation and all the tribes know clearly that you are the god of all power and might, and that there is no other who protects the people of Israel but you alone."

Judith Chapter 10

1 As soon as Judith had thus concluded, and ceased her invocation to the God of Israel, 2 she rose from the ground. She called her maid and they went down into the house, which she used only on sabbaths and feast days. 3 She took off the sackcloth she had on, laid aside the garments of her widowhood, washed her body with water, and anointed it with rich ointment. She arranged her hair and bound it with a fillet, and put on the festive attire she had worn while her husband, Manasseh, was living. 4 She chose sandals for her feet, and put on her anklets, bracelets, rings, earrings, and all her other jewelry. Thus she made herself very beautiful, to captivate the eyes of all the men who should see her. 5 She gave her maid a leather flask of wine and a cruse of oil. She filled a bag with roasted grain, fig cakes, bread and cheese; all these provisions she wrapped up and gave to the maid to carry. 6 Then they went out to the gate of the city of Bethulia and found Uzziah and the elders of the city, Chabri and Charmis, standing there. 7 When these men saw Judith transformed in looks and differently dressed, they were very much astounded at her beauty and said to her, 8 "May the God of our fathers bring you to favor, and make your undertaking a success, for the glory of the Israelites and the exaltation of Jerusalem." Judith bowed down to God. Then she said to them, 9 "Order the gate of the city opened for me, that I may go to carry out the business we discussed." So they ordered the youths to open the gate for her as she requested. 10 When they did so, Judith and her maid went out. The men of the city kept her in view as she went down the mountain and crossed the valley; then they lost sight of her. 11 As Judith and her maid walked directly across the valley, they encountered the Assyrian outpost. 12 The men took her in custody and asked her, "To what people do you belong? Where do you come from, and where are you going?" She replied: "I am a daughter of the Hebrews, and I am fleeing from them, because they are about to be delivered up to you as prey. 13 I have come to see Holofernes, the general in chief of your forces, to give him a trustworthy report; I will show him the route by which he can ascend and take possession of the whole mountain district without a single one of his men suffering injury or loss of life." 14 When the men heard her words and gazed upon her face, which appeared wondrously beautiful to them, they said to her, 15 "By coming down thus promptly to see our master, you have saved your life. Now go to his tent; some of our men will accompany you to present you to him. 16 When you stand before him, have no fear in your heart; give him the report you speak of, and he will treat you well." 17 So they detailed a hundred of their men as an escort for her and her maid, and these conducted them to the tent of Holofernes. 18 When the news of her arrival spread among the tents, a crowd gathered in the camp. They came and stood around her as she waited outside the tent of Holofernes, while he was being informed about her. 19 They marveled at her beauty, regarding the Israelites with wonder because of her, and they said to one another, "Who can despise this people that has such women among them? It is not wise to leave one man of them alive, for if any were to be spared they could beguile the whole world." 20 The guard of Holofernes and all his servants came out and ushered her into the tent. 21 Now Holofernes was reclining on his bed under a canopy with a netting of crimson and gold, emeralds and other precious stones. 22 When they announced her to him, he came out to the antechamber, preceded by silver lamps; 23 and when Holofernes and his servants beheld Judith, they all marveled at the beauty of her face. She threw herself down prostrate before him, but his servants raised her up.

Judith Chapter 11

1 Then Holofernes said to her: "Take courage, lady; have no fear in your heart! Never have I harmed anyone who chose to serve Nebuchadnezzar, king of all the earth. 2 Nor would I have raised my spear against your people who dwell in the mountain region, had they not despised me and brought this upon themselves. 3 But now tell me why you fled from them and came to us. In any case, you have come to safety. Take courage! Your life is spared tonight and for the future. 4 No one at all will harm you. Rather, you will be well treated, as are all the servants of my lord, King Nebuchadnezzar." 5 Judith answered him: "Listen to the words of your servant, and let your handmaid speak in your presence! I will tell no lie to my lord this night, 6 and if you follow out the words of your handmaid, God will give you complete success, and my lord will not fail in any of his undertakings. 7 By the life of Nebuchadnezzar, king of all the earth, and by the power of him who has sent you to set all creatures aright! Not only do men serve him through you; but even the wild beasts and the cattle and the birds of the air, because of your strength, will live for Nebuchadnezzar and his whole house. 8 Indeed, we have heard of your wisdom and sagacity, and all the world is aware that throughout the kingdom you alone are competent,

rich in experience, and distinguished in military strategy. 9 "As for Achior's speech in your council, we have heard of it. When the men of Bethulia spared him, he told them all he had said to you. 10 So then, my lord and master, do not disregard his word, but bear it in mind, for it is true. For our people are not punished, nor does the sword prevail against them, except when they sin against their God. 11 But now their guilt has caught up with them, by which they bring the wrath of their God upon them whenever they do wrong; so that my lord will not be repulsed and fail, but death will overtake them. 12 Since their food gave out and all their water ran low, they decided to kill their animals, and determined to consume all the things which God in his laws forbade them to eat. 13 They decreed that they would use up the first fruits of grain and the tithes of wine and oil which they had sanctified and reserved for the priests who minister in the presence of our God in Jerusalem: things which no layman should even touch with his hands. 14 They have sent messengers to Jerusalem to bring back to them authorization from the council of the elders; for the inhabitants there have also done these things. 15 On the very day when the response reaches them and they act upon it, they will be handed over to you for destruction. 16 "As soon as I, your handmaid, learned all this, I fled from them. God has sent me to perform with you such deeds that people throughout the world will be astonished on hearing of them. 17 Your handmaid is, indeed, a God-fearing woman, serving the God of heaven night and day. Now I will remain with you, my lord; but each night your handmaid will go out to the ravine and pray to God. He will tell me when the Israelites have committed their crimes. 18 Then I will come and let you know, so that you may go out with your whole force, and not one of them will be able to withstand you. 19 I will lead you through Judea, till you come to Jerusalem, and there I will set up your judgment seat. You will drive them like sheep that have no shepherd, and not even a dog will growl at you. This was told me, and announced to me in advance, and I in turn have been sent to tell you." 20 Her words pleased Holofernes and all his servants; they marveled at her wisdom and exclaimed, 21 "No other woman from one end of the world to the other looks so beautiful and speaks so wisely!" 22 Then Holofernes said to her: "God has done well in sending you ahead of your people, to bring victory to our arms, and destruction to those who have despised my lord. 23 You are fair to behold, and your words are well spoken. If you do as you have said, your God will be my God; you shall dwell in the palace of King Nebuchadnezzar, and shall be renowned throughout the earth."

Judith Chapter 12

1 Then he ordered them to lead her into the room where his silverware was kept, and bade them set a table for her with his own delicacies to eat and his own wine to drink. 2 But Judith said, "I will not partake of them, lest it be an occasion of sin; but I shall be amply supplied from the things I brought with me." 3 Holofernes asked her: "But if your provisions give out, where shall we get more of the same to provide for you? None of your people are with us." 4 Judith answered him, "As surely as you, my lord, live, your handmaid will not use up her supplies till the Lord accomplishes by my hand what he has determined." 5 Then the servants of Holofernes led her into the tent, where she slept till midnight. 6 In the night watch just before dawn, she rose and sent this message to Holofernes, "Give orders, my lord, to let your handmaid go out for prayer." 7 So Holofernes ordered his bodyguard not to hinder her. Thus she stayed in the camp three days. Each night she went out to the ravine of Bethulia, where she washed herself at the spring of the camp. 8 After bathing, she besought the Lord, the God of Israel, to direct her way for the triumph of his people. 9 Then she returned purified to the tent, and remained there until her food was brought to her toward evening. 10 On the fourth day Holofernes gave a banquet for his servants alone, to which he did not invite any of the officers. 11 And he said to Bagoas, the eunuch in charge of his household: "Go and persuade this Hebrew woman in your care to come to and to eat and drink with us. 12 It would be a disgrace for us to have such a woman with us without enjoying her company. If we do not entice her, she will laugh us to scorn." 13 So Bagoas left the presence of Holofernes, and came to Judith and said, "So fair a maiden should not be reluctant to come to my lord to be honored by him, to enjoy drinking wine with us, and to be like one of the Assyrian women who live in the palace of Nebuchadnezzar." 14 She replied, "Who am I to refuse my lord? Whatever is pleasing to him I will promptly do. This will be a joy for me till the day of my death." 15 Thereupon she proceeded to put on her festive garments and all her feminine adornments. Meanwhile, her maid went ahead and spread out on the ground for her in front of Holofernes the fleece Bagoas had furnished for her daily use in reclining at her dinner. 16 Then Judith came in and reclined on it. The heart of Holofernes was in rapture over her, and his spirit was shaken. He was burning with the desire to

possess her, for he had been biding his time to seduce her from the day he saw her. [17] Holofernes said to her, "Drink and be merry with us!" [18] Judith replied, "I will gladly drink, my lord, for at no time since I was born have I ever enjoyed life as much as I do today." [19] She then took the things her maid had prepared, and ate and drank in his presence. [20] Holofernes, charmed by her, drank a great quantity of wine, more than he had ever drunk on one single day in his life.

Judith Chapter 13

[1] When it grew late, his servants quickly withdrew. Bagoas closed the tent from the outside and excluded the attendants from their master's presence. They went off to their beds, for they were all tired from the prolonged banquet. [2] Judith was left alone in the tent with Holofernes, who lay prostrate on his bed, for he was sodden with wine. [3] She had ordered her maid to stand outside the bedroom and wait, as on the other days, for her to come out; she said she would be going out for her prayer. To Bagoas she had said this also. [4] When all had departed, and no one, small or great, was left in the bedroom, Judith stood by Holofernes' bed and said within herself: "O Lord, God of all might, in this hour look graciously on my undertaking for the exaltation of Jerusalem; [5] now is the time for aiding your heritage and for carrying out my design to shatter the enemies who have risen against us." [6] She went to the bedpost near the head of Holofernes, and taking his sword from it, [7] drew close to the bed, grasped the hair of his head, and said, "Strengthen me this day, O God of Israel!" [8] Then with all her might she struck him twice in the neck and cut off his head. [9] She rolled his body off the bed and took the canopy from its supports. Soon afterward, she came out and handed over the head of Holofernes to her maid, [10] who put it into her food pouch; and the two went off together as they were accustomed to do for prayer. They passed through the camp, and skirting the ravine, reached Bethulia on the mountain. As they approached its gates, [11] Judith shouted to the guards from a distance: "Open! Open the gate! God, our God, is with us. Once more he has made manifest his strength in Israel and his power against our enemies; he has done it this very day." [12] When the citizens heard her voice, they quickly descended to their city gate and summoned the city elders. [13] All the people, from the least to the greatest, hurriedly assembled, for her return seemed unbelievable. They opened the gate and welcomed the two women. They made a fire for light; and when they gathered around the two, [14] Judith urged them with a loud voice: "Praise God, praise him! Praise God, who has not withdrawn his mercy from the house of Israel, but has shattered our enemies by my hand this very night." [15] Then she took the head out of the pouch, showed it to them, and said: "Here is the head of Holofernes, general in charge of the Assyrian army, and here is the canopy under which he lay in his drunkenness. The Lord struck him down by the hand of a woman. [16] As the Lord lives, who has protected me in the path I have followed, I swear that it was my face that seduced Holofernes to his ruin, and that he did not sin with me to my defilement or disgrace." [17] All the people were greatly astonished. They bowed down and worshiped God, saying with one accord, "Blessed are you, our God, who today have brought to nought the enemies of your people." [18] Then Uzziah said to her: "Blessed are you, daughter, by the Most High God, above all the women on earth; and blessed be the Lord God, the creator of heaven and earth, who guided your blow at the head of the chief of our enemies. [19] Your deed of hope will never be forgotten by those who tell of the might of God. [20] May God make this redound to your everlasting honor, rewarding you with blessings, because you risked your life when your people were being oppressed, and you averted our disaster, walking uprightly before our God." And all the people answered, "Amen! Amen!"

Judith Chapter 14

[1] Then Judith said to them: "Listen to me, my brothers. Take this head and hang it on the parapet of your wall. [2] At daybreak, when the sun rises on the earth, let each of you seize his weapons, and let all the able-bodied men rush out of the city under command of a captain, as if about to go down into the plain against the advance guard of the Assyrians, but without going down. [3] They will seize their armor and hurry to their camp to awaken the generals of the Assyrian army. When they run to the tent of Holofernes and do not find him, panic will seize them, and they will flee before you. [4] Then you and all the other inhabitants of the whole territory of Israel will pursue them and strike them down in their tracks. [5] But before doing this, summon for me Achior the Ammonite, that he may see and recognize the one who despised the house of Israel and sent him here to meet his death." [6] So they called Achior from the house of Uzziah. When he came and saw the head of Holofernes in the hand of one of the men in the assembly of the people, he fell forward in a faint. [7] Then, after they lifted him up, he threw himself at the feet of Judith in homage, saying: "Blessed are you in every tent of Judah; and in every foreign nation, all who hear of you will be struck with terror. [8] But now, tell me all that you did during these days." So Judith told him, in the presence of the people, all that she had been doing from the day she left till the time she began speaking to them. [9] When she finished her account, the people cheered loudly, and their city resounded with shouts of joy. [10] Now Achior, seeing all that the God of Israel had done, believed firmly in him. He had the flesh of his foreskin circumcised, and he has been united with the house of Israel to the present day. [11] At daybreak they hung the head of Holofernes on the wall. Then all the Israelite men took up their arms and went to the slopes of the mountain. [12] When the Assyrians saw them, they notified their captains; these, in turn, went to the generals and division leaders and all their other commanders. [13] They came to the tent of Holofernes and said to the one in charge of all his things, "Waken our master, for the slaves have dared come down to give us battle, to their utter destruction." [14] Bagoas went in, and knocked at the entry of the tent, presuming that he was sleeping with Judith. [15] As no one answered, he parted the curtains, entered the bedroom, and found him lying on the floor, a headless corpse. [16] He broke into a loud clamor of weeping, groaning, and howling, and rent his garments. [17] Then he entered the tent where Judith had her quarters; and, not finding her, he rushed out to the troops and cried: [18] "The slaves have duped us! A single Hebrew woman has brought disgrace on the house of King Nebuchadnezzar. Here is Holofernes headless on the ground!" [19] When the commanders of the Assyrian army heard these words, they rent their tunics and were seized with consternation. Loud screaming and howling arose in the camp.

Judith Chapter 15

[1] On hearing what had happened, those still in their tents were amazed, [2] and overcome with fear and trembling. No one kept ranks any longer; they scattered in all directions, and fled along every road, both through the valley and in the mountains. [3] Those also who were stationed in the mountain district around Bethulia took to flight. Then all the Israelite warriors overwhelmed them. [4] Uzziah sent messengers to Betomasthaim, to Choba and Kona, and to the whole country of Israel to report what had happened, that all might fall upon the enemy and destroy them. [5] On hearing this, all the Israelites, with one accord, attacked them and cut them down as far as Choba. Even those from Jerusalem and the rest of the mountain region took part in this, for they too had been notified of the happenings in the camp of their enemies. The Gileadites and the Galileans struck the enemy's flanks with great slaughter, even beyond Damascus and its territory. [6] The remaining inhabitants of Bethulia swept down on the camp of the Assyrians, plundered it, and acquired great riches. [7] The Israelites who returned from the slaughter took possession of what was left, till the towns and villages in the mountains and on the plain were crammed with the enormous quantity of booty they had seized. [8] The high priest Joakim and the elders of the Israelites, who dwelt in Jerusalem, came to see for themselves the good things that the Lord had done for Israel, and to meet and congratulate Judith. [9] When they had visited her, all with one accord blessed her, saying: "You are the glory of Jerusalem, the surpassing joy of Israel; You are the splendid boast of our people. [10] With your own hand you have done all this; You have done good to Israel, and God is pleased with what you have wrought. May you be blessed by the Lord Almighty forever and ever!" And all the people answered, "Amen!" [11] For thirty days the whole populace plundered the camp, giving Judith the tent of Holofernes, with all his silver, his couches, his dishes, and all his furniture, which she accepted. She harnessed her mules, hitched her wagons to them, and loaded these things on them. [12] All the women of Israel gathered to see her; and they blessed her and performed a dance in her honor. She took branches in her hands and distributed them to the women around her, [13] and she and the other women crowned themselves with garlands of olive leaves. At the head of all the people, she led the women in the dance, while men of Israel followed in their armor, wearing garlands and singing hymns. [14] Judith led all Israel in this song of thanksgiving, and the people swelled this hymn of praise:

Judith Chapter 16

[1] "Strike up the instruments, a song to my God with timbrels, chant to the Lord with cymbals; Sing to him a new song, exalt and acclaim his name. [2] For the Lord is God; he crushes warfare, and sets his encampment among his people; he snatched me from the hands of my persecutors. [3] The Assyrian came from the mountains of the north, with the myriads of his forces he came; Their numbers blocked the torrents, their horses covered the hills. [4] He threatened to burn my land, put my youths to the sword, Dash my babes to the ground, make my children a

prey, and seize my virgins as spoil. 5But the Lord Almighty thwarted them, by a woman's hand he confounded them. 6Not by youths was their mighty one struck down, nor did titans bring him low, nor huge giants attack him; But Judith, the daughter of Merari, by the beauty of her countenance disabled him. 7She took off her widow's garb to raise up the afflicted in Israel. She anointed her face with fragrant oil; 8with a fillet she fastened her tresses, and put on a linen robe to beguile him. 9Her sandals caught his eyes, and her beauty captivated his mind. The sword cut through his neck. 10The Persians were dismayed at her daring, the Medes appalled at her boldness. 11When my lowly ones shouted, they were terrified; when my weaklings cried out, they trembled; at the sound of their war cry, they took to flight. 12Sons of slave girls pierced them through; the supposed sons of rebel mothers cut them down; they perished before the ranks of my Lord. 13A new hymn I will sing to my God. O Lord, great are you and glorious, wonderful in power and unsurpassable. 14Let your every creature serve you; for you spoke, and they were made, You sent forth your spirit, and they were created; no one can resist your word. 15The mountains to their bases, and the seas, are shaken; the rocks, like wax, melt before your glance. But to those who fear you, you are very merciful. 16Though the sweet odor of every sacrifice is a trifle, and the fat of all holocausts but little in your sight, one who fears the Lord is forever great. 17Woe to the nations that rise against my people! The Lord Almighty will requite them; in the day of judgment he will punish them: He will send fire and worms into their flesh, and they shall burn and suffer forever." 18The people then went to Jerusalem to worship God; when they were purified, they offered their holocausts, freewill offerings, and gifts. 19Judith dedicated, as a votive offering to God, all the things of Holofernes that the people had given her, as well as the canopy that she herself had taken from his bedroom. 20For three months the people continued their celebration in Jerusalem before the sanctuary, and Judith remained with them. 21When those days were over, each one returned to his inheritance. Judith went back to Bethulia and remained on her estate. For the rest of her life she was renowned throughout the land. 22Many wished to marry her, but she gave herself to no man all the days of her life from the time of the death and burial of her husband, Manasseh. 23She lived to be very old in the house of her husband, reaching the advanced age of a hundred and five. She died in Bethulia, where they buried her in the tomb of her husband, Manasseh; 24and the house of Israel mourned her for seven days. Before she died, she distributed her goods to the relatives of her husband, Manasseh, and to her own relatives; and to the maid she gave her freedom. 25During the life of Judith and for a long time after her death, no one again disturbed the Israelites.

Esdras I

Esdras 1 Chapter 1

1 Josias held the Passover in Jerusalem to his Lord, and offered the Passover the fourteenth day of the first month, 2 having set the priests according to their daily courses, being arrayed in their vestments, in the Lord's temple. 3 He spoke to the Levites, the temple servants of Israel, that they should make themselves holy to the Lord, to set the holy ark of the Lord in the house that King Solomon the son of David had built. 4 He said, "You no longer need to carry it on your shoulders. Now therefore serve the Lord your God, and minister to his people Israel, and prepare yourselves by your fathers' houses and kindred, 5 according to the writing of King David of Israel, and according to the magnificence of Solomon his son. Stand in the holy place according to the divisions of your Levite families who minister in the presence of your kindred the descendants of Israel. 6 Offer the Passover in order, prepare the sacrifices for your kindred, and keep the Passover according to the Lord's commandment, which was given to Moses. 7 To the people which were present, Josias gave thirty thousand lambs and kids, and three thousand calves. These things were given from the king's possessions, as he promised, to the people and to the priests and Levites. 8 Helkias, Zacharias, and Esyelus, the rulers of the temple, gave to the priests for the Passover two thousand six hundred sheep, and three hundred calves. 9 Jeconias, Samaias, Nathanael his brother, Sabias, Ochielus, and Joram, captains over thousands, gave to the Levites for the Passover five thousand sheep and seven hundred calves. 10 When these things were done, the priests and Levites, having the unleavened bread, stood in proper order according to the kindred, 11 and according to the several divisions by fathers' houses, before the people, to offer to the Lord as it is written in the book of Moses. They did this in the morning. 12 They roasted the Passover lamb with fire, as required. They boiled the sacrifices in the brazen vessels and caldrons with a pleasing smell, 13 and set them before all the people. Afterward

they prepared for themselves and for their kindred the priests, the sons of Aaron. 14 For the priests offered the fat until night. The Levites prepared for themselves and for their kindred the priests, the sons of Aaron. 15 The holy singers also, the sons of Asaph, were in their order, according to the appointment of David: Asaph, Zacharias, and Eddinus, who represented the king. 16 Moreover the gatekeepers were at every gate. No one needed to depart from his daily duties, for their kindred the Levites prepared for them. 17 So the things that belonged to the Lord's sacrifices were accomplished in that day, in holding the Passover, 18 and offering sacrifices on the altar of the Lord, according to the commandment of King Josias. 19 So the children of Israel which were present at that time held the Passover and the feast of unleavened bread seven days. 20 Such a Passover had not been held in Israel since the time of the prophet Samuel. 21 Indeed, none of the kings of Israel held such a Passover as Josias with the priests, the Levites, and the Jews, held with all Israel that were present in their dwelling place at Jerusalem. 22 This Passover was held in the eighteenth year of the reign of Josias. 23 The works of Josias were upright before his Lord with a heart full of godliness. 24 Moreover the things that came to pass in his days have been written in times past, concerning those who sinned and did wickedly against the Lord more than any other people or kingdom, and how they grieved him exceedingly, so that the Lord's words were confirmed against Israel. 25 Now after all these acts of Josias, it came to pass that Pharaoh the king of Egypt came to make war at Carchemish on the Euphrates; and Josias went out against him. 26 But the king of Egypt sent to him, saying, "What do I have to do with you, O king of Judea? 27 I wasn't sent out from the Lord God against you, for my war is against the Euphrates. Now the Lord is with me, yes, the Lord is with me hastening me forward. Depart from me, and don't be against the Lord." 28 However, Josias didn't turn back to his chariot, but tried to fight with him, not regarding the words of the prophet Jeremy from the Lord's mouth, 29 but joined battle with him in the plain of Megiddo, and the commanders came down against King Josias. 30 Then the king said to his servants, "Carry me away out of the battle, for I am very weak!" Immediately his servants carried him away out of the army. 31 Then he got into his second chariot. After he was brought back to Jerusalem he died, and was buried in the tomb of his ancestors. 32 All Judea mourned for Josias. Jeremy the prophet lamented for Josias, and the chief men with the women made lamentation for him to this day. This was given out for an ordinance to be done continually in all the nation of Israel. 33 These things are written in the book of the histories of the kings of Judea, and every one of the acts that Josias did, and his glory, and his understanding in the law of the Lord, and the things that he had done before, and the things now told, are reported in the book of the kings of Israel and Judah. 34 The people took Joachaz the son of Josias, and made him king instead of Josias his father, when he was twenty-three years old. 35 He reigned in Judah and Jerusalem for three months. Then the king of Egypt deposed him from reigning in Jerusalem. 36 He set a tax upon the people of one hundred talents of silver and one talent of gold. 37 The king of Egypt also made King Joakim his brother king of Judea and Jerusalem. 38 And Joakim imprisoned the nobles and apprehended his brother Zarakes, and brought him up out of Egypt. 39 Joakim was twenty-five years old when he began to reign in Judea and Jerusalem. He did that which was evil in the sight of the Lord. 40 King Nabuchodonosor of Babylon came up against him, bound him with a chain of brass, and carried him to Babylon. 41 Nabuchodonosor also took some of the Lord's holy vessels, carried them away, and stored them in his own temple at Babylon. 42 But those things that are reported of him, and of his uncleanness and impiety, are written in the chronicles of the kings. 43 Then Joakim his son reigned in his place. When he was made king, he was eighteen years old. 44 He reigned three months and ten days in Jerusalem. He did that which was evil before the Lord. 45 So after a year Nabuchodonosor sent and caused him to be brought to Babylon with the holy vessels of the Lord, 46 and made Sedekias king of Judea and Jerusalem when he was twenty-one years old. He reigned eleven years. 47 He also did that which was evil in the sight of the Lord, and didn't heed the words that were spoken by Jeremy the prophet from the Lord's mouth. 48 After King Nabuchodonosor had made him to swear by the name of the Lord, he broke his oath and rebelled. Hardening his neck and his heart, he transgressed the laws of the Lord, the God of Israel. 49 Moreover the governors of the people and of the priests did many things wickedly, exceeding all the defilements of all nations, and defiled the temple of the Lord, which was sanctified in Jerusalem. 50 The God of their ancestors sent by his messenger to call them back, because he had compassion on them and on his dwelling place. 51 But they mocked his messengers. In the day when the Lord spoke, they scoffed at his prophets 52 until he, being angry with his people for their great ungodliness, commanded to bring up the kings of the Chaldeans against them. ⁵³ They killed their young men with the sword around their holy temple, and spared neither young man or young woman, old man or child; but he delivered all of them into their hands. ⁵⁴ They took all the holy vessels of the Lord, both great and small, with the treasure chests of the Lord's ark and the king's treasures, and carried them away to Babylon. ⁵⁵ They burned the Lord's house, broke down Jerusalem's walls, and burned its towers with fire. ⁵⁶ As for her glorious things, they didn't stop until they had brought them all to nothing. He carried the people who weren't slain with the sword to Babylon. ⁵⁷ They were servants to him and to his children until the Persians reigned, to fulfill the word of the Lord by the mouth of Jeremy: ⁵⁸ "Until the land has enjoyed its Sabbaths, the whole time of her desolation shall she keep Sabbath, to fulfill seventy years."

Esdras 1 Chapter 2

¹ In the first year of King Cyrus of the Persians, that the word of the Lord by the mouth of Jeremy might be accomplished, ² the Lord stirred up the spirit of King Cyrus of the Persians, and he made a proclamation throughout all his kingdom, and also by writing, ³ saying, "Cyrus king of the Persians says: The Lord of Israel, the Most High Lord, has made me king of the whole world, ⁴ and commanded me to build him a house at Jerusalem that is in Judea. ⁵ If therefore there are any of you that are of his people, let the Lord, even his Lord, be with him, and let him go up to Jerusalem that is in Judea, and build the house of the Lord of Israel. He is the Lord who dwells in Jerusalem. ⁶ Therefore, of those who dwell in various places, let those who are in his own place help each one with gold, with silver, ⁷ with gifts, with horses, and cattle, beside the other things which have been added by vow for the temple of the Lord which is in Jerusalem. ⁸ Then the chief of the families of Judah and of the tribe of Benjamin stood up, with the priests, the Levites, and all whose spirit the Lord had stirred to go up, to build the house for the Lord which is in Jerusalem. ⁹ Those who lived around them helped them in all things with silver and gold, with horses and cattle, and with very many gifts that were vowed by a great number whose minds were so moved. ¹⁰ King Cyrus also brought out the holy vessels of the Lord, which Nabuchodonosor had carried away from Jerusalem and had stored in his temple of idols. ¹¹ Now when King Cyrus of the Persians had brought them out, he delivered them to Mithradates his treasurer, ¹² and by him they were delivered to Sanabassar the governor of Judea. ¹³ This was the number of them: one thousand gold cups, one thousand silver cups, twenty-nine silver censers, thirty gold bowls, two thousand four hundred ten silver bowls, and one thousand other vessels. ¹⁴ So all the vessels of gold and of silver were brought up, even five thousand four hundred seventy-nine, ¹⁵ and were carried back by Sanabassar, together with the returning exiles, from Babylon to Jerusalem. ¹⁶ In the time of King Artaxerxes of the Persians, Belemus, Mithradates, Tabellius, Rathumus, Beeltethmus, and Samellius the scribe, with their other associates, dwelling in Samaria and other places, wrote to him against those who lived in Judea and Jerusalem the following letter: ¹⁷"To King Artaxerxes our Lord, from your servants, Rathumus the recorder, Samellius the scribe, and the rest of their council, and the judges who are in Coelesyria and Phoenicia: ¹⁸ Let it now be known to our lord the king, that the Jews that have come up from you to us, having come to Jerusalem, are building that rebellious and wicked city, and are repairing its marketplaces and walls, and are laying the foundation of a temple. ¹⁹ Now if this city is built and its walls are finished, they will not only refuse to give tribute, but will even stand up against kings. ²⁰ Since the things pertaining to the temple are now in hand, we think it appropriate not to neglect such a matter, ²¹ but to speak to our lord the king, to the intent that, if it is your pleasure, search may be made in the books of your ancestors. ²² You will find in the chronicles what is written concerning these things, and will understand that that city was rebellious, troubling both kings and cities, ²³ and that the Jews were rebellious, and kept starting wars there in the past. For this cause, this city was laid waste. ²⁴ Therefore now we do declare to you, O lord the king, that if this city is built again, and its walls set up again, you will from then on have no passage into Coelesyria and Phoenicia." ²⁵ Then the king wrote back again to Rathumus the recorder, Beeltethmus, Samellius the scribe, and to the rest that of their associates who lived in Samaria, Syria, and Phoenicia, as follows: ²⁶"I have read the letter which you have sent to me. Therefore I commanded to make search, and it has been found that that city of old time has fought against kings, ²⁷ and the men were given to rebellion and war in it, and that mighty and fierce kings were in Jerusalem, who reigned and exacted tribute in Coelesyria and Phoenicia. ²⁸ Now therefore I have commanded to prevent those men from building the city, and heed to be taken that there be nothing done contrary to this order, ²⁹ and that those wicked doings proceed no further to the annoyance of kings." ³⁰

Then King Artaxerxes, his letters being read, Rathumus, and Samellius the scribe, and the rest of their associates, went in haste to Jerusalem with cavalry and a multitude of people in battle array, and began to hinder the builders. So the building of the temple in Jerusalem ceased until the second year of the reign of King Darius of the Persians.

Esdras 1 Chapter 3

¹ Now King Darius made a great feast for all his subjects, for all who were born in his house, for all the princes of Media and of Persia, ² and for all the local governors and captains and governors who were under him, from India to Ethiopia, in the one hundred twenty seven provinces. ³ They ate and drank, and when they were satisfied went home. Then King Darius went into his bedchamber slept, but awakened out of his sleep. ⁴ Then the three young men of the bodyguard, who guarded the king, spoke one to another: ⁵"Let every one of us state what one thing is strongest. King Darius will give he whose statement seems wiser than the others great gifts and great honors in token of victory. ⁶ He shall be clothed in purple, drink from gold cups, sleep on a gold bed, and have a chariot with bridles of gold, a fine linen turban, and a chain around his neck. ⁷ He shall sit next to Darius because of his wisdom, and shall be called cousin of Darius." ⁸ Then they each wrote his sentence, sealed them, and laid them under King Darius' pillow, ⁹ and said, "When the king wakes up, someone will give him the writing. Whoever the king and the three princes of Persia judge that his sentence is the wisest, to him shall the victory be given, as it is written." ¹⁰ The first wrote, "Wine is the strongest." ¹¹ The second wrote, "The king is strongest." ¹² The third wrote, "Women are strongest, but above all things Truth is the victor." ¹³ Now when the king woke up, they took the writing and gave it to him, so he read it. ¹⁴ Sending out, he called all the princes of Persia and of Media, the local governors, the captains, the governors, and the chief officers ¹⁵ and sat himself down in the royal seat of judgment; and the writing was read before them. ¹⁶ He said, "Call the young men, and they shall explain their own sentences. So they were called and came in. ¹⁷ They said to them, "Explain what you have written." Then the first, who had spoken of the strength of wine, began ¹⁸ and said this: "O sirs, how exceedingly strong wine is! It causes all men who drink it to go astray. ¹⁹ It makes the mind of the king and of the fatherless child to be the same, likewise of the bondman and of the freeman, of the poor man and of the rich. ²⁰ It also turns every thought into cheer and mirth, so that a man remembers neither sorrow nor debt. ²¹ It makes every heart rich, so that a man remembers neither king nor local governor. It makes people say things in large amounts. ²² When they are in their cups, they forget their love both to friends and kindred, and before long draw their swords. ²³ But when they awake from their wine, they don't remember what they have done. ²⁴ O sirs, isn't wine the strongest, seeing that it forces people to do this?" And when he had said this, he stopped speaking.

Esdras 1 Chapter 4

¹ Then the second, who had spoken of the strength of the king, began to say, ²"O sirs, don't men excel in strength who rule over the sea and land, and all things in them? ³ But yet the king is stronger. He is their lord and has dominion over them. In whatever he commands them, they obey him. ⁴ If he tells them to make war the one against the other, they do it. If he sends them out against the enemies, they go, and conquer mountains, walls, and towers. ⁵ They kill and are killed, and don't disobey the king's commandment. If they win the victory, they bring everything to the king—all the plunder and everything else. ⁶ Likewise for those who are not soldiers, and don't have anything to do with wars, but farm, when they have reaped again that which they had sown, they bring some to the king and compel one another to pay tribute to the king. ⁷ He is just one man! If he commands people to kill, they kill. If he commands them to spare, they spare. ⁸ If he commands them to strike, they strike. If he commands them to make desolate, they make desolate. If he commands to build, they build. ⁹ If he commands them to cut down, they cut down. If he commands them to plant, they plant. ¹⁰ So all his people and his armies obey him. Furthermore, he lies down, he eats and drinks, and takes his rest; ¹¹ and these keep watch around him. None of them may depart and do his own business. They don't disobey him in anything. ¹² O sirs, how could the king not be the strongest, seeing that he is obeyed like this?" Then he stopped talking. ¹³ Then the third, who had spoken of women, and of truth, (this was Zorobabel) began to speak: ¹⁴"O sirs, isn't the king great, and men are many, and isn't wine strong? Who is it then who rules them, or has the lordship over them? Aren't they women? ¹⁵ Women have given birth to the king and all the people who rule over sea and land. ¹⁶ They came from women. Women nourished up those who planted the vineyards, from where the wine comes..." ¹⁶ ...They came from women. Women nourished up those who planted the vineyards, from where the wine

comes. 17 Women also make garments for men. These bring glory to men. Without women, men can't exist. 18 Yes, and if men have gathered together gold and silver and any other beautiful thing, and see a woman who is lovely in appearance and beauty, 19 they let all those things go and gape at her, and with open mouth stare at her. They all have more desire for her than for gold, or silver, or any other beautiful thing. 20 A man leaves his own father who brought him up, leaves his own country, and joins with his wife. 21 With his wife he ends his days, with no thought for his father, mother, or country. 22 By this also you must know that women have dominion over you. Don't you labor and toil, and bring it all to give to women? 23 Yes, a man takes his sword and goes out to travel, to rob, to steal, and to sail on the sea and on rivers. 24 He sees a lion and walks in the darkness. When he has stolen, plundered, and robbed, he brings it to the woman he loves. 25 Therefore a man loves his wife better than father or mother. 26 Yes, there are many who have lost their minds for women, and become slaves for their sakes. 27 Many also have perished, have stumbled, and sinned, for women. 28 Now don't you believe me? Isn't the king great in his power? Don't all regions fear to touch him? 29 Yet I saw him and Apame the king's concubine, the daughter of the illustrious Barticus, sitting at the right hand of the king, 30 and taking the crown from the king's head, and setting it upon her own head. Yes, she struck the king with her left hand. 31 At this, the king gaped and gazed at her with open mouth. If she smiles at him, he laughs. But if she takes any displeasure at him, he flatters her, that she might be reconciled to him again. 32 O sirs, how can it not be that women are strong, seeing they do this?" 33 Then the king and the nobles looked at one another. So he began to speak concerning truth. 34 "O sirs, aren't women strong? The earth is great. The sky is high. The sun is swift in its course, for it circles around the sky, and returns on its course again in one day. 35 Isn't he who makes these things great? Therefore the truth is great, and stronger than all things. 36 All the earth calls upon truth, and the sky blesses truth. All works shake and tremble, but with truth there is no unrighteous thing. 37 Wine is unrighteous. The king is unrighteous. Women are unrighteous. All the children of men are unrighteous, and all their works are unrighteous. There is no truth in them. They shall also perish in their unrighteousness. 38 But truth remains, and is strong forever. Truth lives and conquers forevermore. 39 With truth there is no partiality toward persons or rewards, but truth does the things that are just, instead of any unrighteous or wicked things. All men approve truth's works. 40 In truth's judgment is not any unrighteousness. Truth is the strength, the kingdom, the power, and the majesty of all ages. Blessed be the God of truth!" 41 With that, he stopped speaking. Then all the people shouted and said, "Great is truth, and strong above all things!" 42 Then the king said to him, "Ask what you wish, even more than is appointed in writing, and we will give it to you, because you are found wisest. You shall sit next to me, and shall be called my cousin." 43 Then he said to the king, "Remember your vow, which you vowed to build Jerusalem, in the day when you came to your kingdom, 44 and to send back all the vessels that were taken out of Jerusalem, which Cyrus set apart when he vowed to destroy Babylon, and vowed to send them back there. 45 You also vowed to build the temple which the Edomites burned when Judea was made desolate by the Chaldeans. 46 Now, O lord the king, this is what I request, and what I desire of you, and this is the princely generosity that may proceed from you: I ask therefore that you make good the vow, the performance of which you have vowed to the King of Heaven with your own mouth." 47 Then King Darius stood up, kissed him, and wrote letters for him to all the treasurers and governors and captains and local governors, that they should safely bring on their way both him, and all those who would go up with him to build Jerusalem. 48 He wrote letters also to all the governors who were in Coelesyria and Phoenicia, and to them in Libanus, that they should bring cedar wood from Libanus to Jerusalem, and that they should help him build the city. 49 Moreover he wrote for all the Jews who would go out of his realm up into Judea concerning their freedom, that no officer, no governor, no local governor, nor treasurer, should forcibly enter into their doors, 50 and that all the country which they occupied should be free to them without tribute, and that the Edomites should give up the villages of the Jews which they held at that time, 51 and that there should be given twenty talents yearly toward the building of the temple, until the time that it was built, 52 and another ten talents yearly for burnt offerings to be presented upon the altar every day, as they had a commandment to make seventeen offerings, 53 and that all those who would come from Babylonia to build the city should have their freedom—they and their descendants, and all the priests that came. 54 He wrote also to give them their support and the priests' vestments in which they minister. 55 For the Levites he wrote that their support should be given them until the day that the house was finished and

Jerusalem built up. 56 He commanded that land and wages should be given to all who guarded the city. 57 He also sent away all the vessels from Babylon that Cyrus had set apart, and all that Cyrus had given in commandment, he commanded also to be done and to be sent to Jerusalem. 58 Now when this young man had gone out, he lifted up his face to heaven toward Jerusalem, and praised the King of heaven, 59 and said, "From you comes victory. From you comes wisdom. Yours is the glory, and I am your servant. 60 Blessed are you, who have given me wisdom. I give thanks to you, O Lord of our fathers. 61 So he took the letters, went out, came to Babylon, and told it all his kindred. 62 They praised the God of their ancestors, because he had given them freedom and liberty 63 to go up and to build Jerusalem and the temple which is called by his name. They feasted with instruments of music and gladness seven days.

Esdras 1 Chapter 5

1 After this, the chiefs of fathers' houses were chosen to go up according to their tribes, with their wives, sons, and daughters, with their menservants and maidservants, and their livestock. 2 Darius sent with them one thousand cavalry to bring them back to Jerusalem with peace, with musical instruments, drums, and flutes. 3 All their kindred were making merry, and he made them go up together with them. 4 These are the names of the men who went up, according to their families among their tribes, after their several divisions. 5 The priests, the sons of Phinees, the sons of Aaron: Jesus the son of Josedek, the son of Saraias, and Joakim the son of Zorobabel, the son of Salathiel, of the house of David, of the lineage of Phares, of the tribe of Judah, 6 who spoke wise words before Darius the king of Persia in the second year of his reign, in the month Nisan, which is the first month. 7 These are the of Judeans who came up from the captivity, where they lived as foreigners, whom Nabuchodonosor the king of Babylon had carried away to Babylon. 8 They returned to Jerusalem and to the other parts of Judea, every man to his own city, who came with Zorobabel, with Jesus, Nehemias, Zaraias, Resaias, Eneneus, Mardocheus, Beelsarus, Aspharsus, Reelias, Roimus, and Baana, their leaders. 9 The number of them of the nation and their leaders: the sons of Phoros, two thousand one hundred seventy two; the sons of Saphat, four hundred seventy two; 10 the sons of Ares, seven hundred fifty six; 11 the sons of Phaath Moab, of the sons of Jesus and Joab, two thousand eight hundred twelve; 12 the sons of Elam, one thousand two hundred fifty four; the sons of Zathui, nine hundred forty five; the sons of Chorbe, seven hundred five; the sons of Bani, six hundred forty eight; 13 the sons of Bebai, six hundred twenty three; the sons of Astad, one thousand three hundred twenty two; 14 the sons of Adonikam, six hundred sixty seven; the sons of Bagoi, two thousand sixty six; the sons of Adinu, four hundred fifty four; 15 the sons of Ater, of Ezekias, ninety two; the sons of Kilan and Azetas, sixty seven; the sons of Azaru, four hundred thirty two; 16 the sons of Annis, one hundred one; the sons of Arom; the sons of Bassai, three hundred twenty three; the sons of Arsiphurith, one hundred twelve; 17 the sons of Baiterus, three thousand five; the sons of Bethlomon, one hundred twenty three; 18 those from Netophas, fifty five; those from Anathoth, one hundred fifty eight; those from Bethasmoth, forty two; 19 those from Kariathiarius, twenty five: those from Caphira and Beroth, seven hundred forty three; 20 the Chadiasai and Ammidioi, four hundred twenty two; those from Kirama and Gabbe, six hundred twenty one; 21 those from Macalon, one hundred twenty two; those from Betolion, fifty two; the sons of Niphis, one hundred fifty six; 22 the sons of Calamolalus and Onus, seven hundred twenty five; the sons of Jerechu, three hundred forty five; 23 and the sons of Sanaas, three thousand three hundred thirty... 24 The priests: the sons of Jeddu, the son of Jesus, among the sons of Sanasib, nine hundred seventy two; the sons of Emmeruth, one thousand fifty two; 25 the sons of Phassurus, one thousand two hundred forty seven; and the sons of Charme, one thousand seventeen. 26 The Levites: the sons of Jesus, Kadmiel, Bannas, and Sudias, seventy four. 27 The holy singers: the sons of Asaph, one hundred twenty eight. 28 The gatekeepers: the sons of Salum, the sons of Atar, the sons of Tolman, the sons of Dacubi, the sons of Ateta, the sons of Sabi, in all one hundred thirty nine. 29 The temple servants: the sons of Esau, the sons of Asipha, the sons of Tabaoth, the sons of Keras, the sons of Sua, the sons of Phaleas, the sons of Labana, the sons of Aggaba. 30 The sons of Acud, the sons of Uta, the sons of Ketab, the sons of Accaba, the sons of Subai, the sons of Anan, the sons of Cathua, the sons of Geddur, 31 the sons of Jairus, the sons of Daisan, the sons of Noeba, the sons of Chaseba, the sons of Gazera, the sons of Ozias, the sons of Phinoe, the sons of Asara, the sons of Basthai, the sons of Asana, the sons of Maani, the sons of Naphisi, the sons of Acub, the sons of Achipha, the sons of Asur, the sons of Pharakim, the sons of Basaloth, 32 the sons of Meedda, the sons of Cutha, the sons of Charea, the sons of Barchus, the sons of Serar, the

sons of Thomei, the sons of Nasi, the sons of Atipha. 33 The sons of the servants of Solomon: the sons of Assaphioth, the sons of Pharida, the sons of Jeeli, the sons of Lozon, the sons of Isdael, the sons of Saphuthi, 34 the sons of Agia, the sons of Phacareth, the sons of Sabie, the sons of Sarothie, the sons of Masias, the sons of Gas, the sons of Addus, the sons of Subas, the sons of Apherra, the sons of Barodis, the sons of Saphat, the sons of Allon. 35 All the temple-servants and the sons of the servants of Solomon were three hundred seventy two. 36 These came up from Thermeleth, and Thelersas, Charaathalan leading them, and Allar; 37 and they could not show their families, nor their stock, how they were of Israel: the sons of Dalan the son of Ban, the sons of Nekodan, six hundred fifty two. 38 Of the priests, those who usurped the office of the priesthood and were not found: the sons of Obdia, the sons of Akkos, the sons of Jaddus, who married Augia one of the daughters of Zorzelleus, and was called after his name. 39 When the description of the kindred of these men was sought in the register and was not found, they were removed from executing the office of the priesthood; 40 for Nehemias and Attharias told them that they should not be partakers of the holy things until a high priest wearing Urim and Thummim should arise. 41 So all those of Israel, from twelve years old and upward, beside menservants and women servants, were in number forty two thousand three hundred sixty. 42 Their menservants and handmaids were seven thousand three hundred thirty and seven; the minstrels and singers, two hundred forty five; 43 four hundred thirty and five camels, seven thousand thirty six horses, two hundred forty five mules, and five thousand five hundred twenty five beasts of burden. 44 And some of the chief men of their families, when they came to the temple of God that is in Jerusalem, vowed to set up the house again in its own place according to their ability, 45 and to give into the holy treasury of the works one thousand minas of gold, five thousand minas of silver, and one hundred priestly vestments. 46 The priests and the Levites and some of the people lived in Jerusalem and the country. The holy singers also and the gatekeepers and all Israel lived in their villages. 47 But when the seventh month was at hand, and when the children of Israel were each in their own place, they all came together with one purpose into the broad place before the first porch which is toward the east. 48 Then Jesus the son of Josedek, his kindred the priests, Zorobabel the son of Salathiel, and his kindred stood up and made the altar of the God of Israel ready 49 to offer burned sacrifices upon it, in accordance with the express commands in the book of Moses the man of God. 50 Some people joined them out of the other nations of the land, and they erected the altar upon its own place, because all the nations of the land were hostile to them and oppressed them; and they offered sacrifices at the proper times and burnt offerings to the Lord both morning and evening. 51 They also held the feast of tabernacles, as it is commanded in the law, and offered sacrifices daily, as appropriate. 52 After that, they offered the continual oblations and the sacrifices of the Sabbaths, of the new moons, and of all the consecrated feasts. 53 All those who had made any vow to God began to offer sacrifices to God from the new moon of the seventh month, although the temple of God was not yet built. 54 They gave money, food, and drink to the masons and carpenters. 55 They also gave carts to the people of Sidon and Tyre, that they should bring cedar trees from Libanus, and convey them in rafts to the harbor of Joppa, according to the commandment which was written for them by Cyrus king of the Persians. 56 In the second year after his coming to the temple of God at Jerusalem, in the second month, Zorobabel the son of Salathiel, Jesus the son of Josedek, their kindred, the Levitical priests, and all those who had come to Jerusalem out of the captivity began work. 57 They laid the foundation of God's temple on the new moon of the second month, in the second year after they had come to Judea and Jerusalem. 58 They appointed the Levites who were at least twenty years old over the Lord's works. Then Jesus, with his sons and kindred, Kadmiel his brother, the sons of Jesus, Emadabun, and the sons of Joda the son of Iliadun, and their sons and kindred, all the Levites, with one accord stood up and started the business, laboring to advance the works in the house of God. So the builders built the Lord's temple. 59 The priests stood arrayed in their vestments with musical instruments and trumpets, and the Levites the sons of Asaph with their cymbals, 60 singing songs of thanksgiving and praising the Lord, according to the directions of King David of Israel. 61 They sang aloud, praising the Lord in songs of thanksgiving, because his goodness and his glory are forever in all Israel. 62 All the people sounded trumpets and shouted with a loud voice, singing songs of thanksgiving to the Lord for the raising up of the Lord's house. 63 Some of the Levitical priests and of the heads of their families, the elderly who had seen the former house came to the building of this one with lamentation and great weeping. 64 But many with trumpets and joy shouted with a loud voice, 65 so that the people

couldn't hear the trumpets for the weeping of the people, for the multitude sounded loudly, so that it was heard far away. 66 Therefore when the enemies of the tribe of Judah and Benjamin heard it, they came to know what that noise of trumpets meant. 67 They learned that those who returned from captivity built the temple for the Lord, the God of Israel. 68 So they went to Zorobabel and Jesus, and to the chief men of the families, and said to them, "We will build together with you. 69 For we, just like you, obey your Lord, and sacrifice to him from the days of King Asbasareth of the Assyrians, who brought us here." 70 Then Zorobabel, Jesus and the chief men of the families of Israel said to them, "It is not for you to build the house for the Lord our God. 71 We ourselves alone will build for the Lord of Israel, as King Cyrus of the Persians has commanded us." 72 But the heathen of the land pressed hard upon the inhabitants of Judea, cut off their supplies, and hindered their building. 73 By their secret plots, and popular persuasions and commotions, they hindered the finishing of the building all the time that King Cyrus lived. So they were hindered from building for two years, until the reign of Darius.

Esdras 1 Chapter 6

1 Now in the second year of the reign of Darius, Aggaeus and Zacharius the son of Addo, the prophets, prophesied to the Jews in Judea and Jerusalem in the name of the Lord, the God of Israel. 2 Then Zorobabel the son of Salathiel and Jesus the son of Josedek stood up and began to build the house of the Lord at Jerusalem, the prophets of the Lord being with them and helping them. 3 At the same time Sisinnes the governor of Syria and Phoenicia came to them, with Sathrabuzanes and his companions, and said to them, 4"By whose authority do you build this house and this roof, and perform all the other things? Who are the builders who do these things?" 5 Nevertheless, the elders of the Jews obtained favor, because the Lord had visited the captives; 6 and they were not hindered from building until such time as communication was made to Darius concerning them, and his answer received. 7 A copy of the letter which Sisinnes, governor of Syria and Phoenicia, and Sathrabuzanes, with their companions, the rulers in Syria and Phoenicia, wrote and sent to Darius: 8"To King Darius, greetings. Let it be fully known to our lord the king, that having come into the country of Judea, and entered into the city of Jerusalem, we found in the city of Jerusalem the elders of the Jews that were of the captivity 9 building a great new house for the Lord of hewn and costly stones, with timber laid in the walls. 10 Those works are being done with great speed. The work goes on prosperously in their hands, and it is being accomplished with all glory and diligence. 11 Then asked we these elders, saying, 'By whose authority are you building this house and laying the foundations of these works?' 12 Therefore, to the intent that we might give knowledge to you by writing who were the leaders, we questioned them, and we required of them the names in writing of their principal men. 13 So they gave us this answer, 'We are the servants of the Lord who made heaven and earth. 14 As for this house, it was built many years ago by a great and strong king of Israel, and was finished. 15 But when our fathers sinned against the Lord of Israel who is in heaven, and provoked him to wrath, he gave them over into the hands of King Nabuchodonosor of Babylon, king of the Chaldeans. 16 They pulled down the house, burned it, and carried away the people captive to Babylon. 17 But in the first year that Cyrus reigned over the country of Babylon, King Cyrus wrote that this house should be rebuilt. 18 The holy vessels of gold and of silver that Nabuchodonosor had carried away out of the house at Jerusalem and had set up in his own temple, those King Cyrus brought out of the temple in Babylonia, and they were delivered to Zorobabel and to Sanabassarus the governor, 19 with commandment that he should carry away all these vessels, and put them in the temple at Jerusalem, and that the Lord's temple should be built on its site. 20 Then Sanabassarus, having come here, laid the foundations of the Lord's house which is in Jerusalem. From that time to this we are still building. It is not yet fully completed.' 21 Now therefore, if it seems good, O king, let a search be made among the royal archives of our lord the king that are in Babylon. 22 If it is found that the building of the house of the Lord which is in Jerusalem has been done with the consent of King Cyrus, and it seems good to our lord the king, let him send us directions concerning these things." 23 Then King Darius commanded that a search be made among the archives that were laid up at Babylon. So at Ekbatana the palace, which is in the country of Media, a scroll was found where these things were recorded: 24"In the first year of the reign of Cyrus, King Cyrus commanded to build up the house of the Lord which is in Jerusalem, where they sacrifice with continual fire. 25 Its height shall be sixty cubits, and the breadth sixty cubits, with three rows of hewn stones, and one row of new wood out of that country. 26 The holy vessels of the house of the Lord, both gold and silver, that

Nabuchodonosor took out of the house at Jerusalem and carried away to Babylon, should be restored to the house at Jerusalem, and be set in the place where they were before." 27 Also he commanded that Sisinnes the governor of Syria and Phoenicia, and Sathrabuzanes, and their companions, and those who were appointed rulers in Syria and Phoenicia, should be careful not to meddle with the place, but allow Zorobabel, the servant of the Lord, and governor of Judea, and the elders of the Jews, to build that house of the Lord in its place. 28 "I also command to have it built up whole again; and that they look diligently to help those who are of the captivity of Judea, until the house of the Lord is finished, 29 and that out of the tribute of Coelesyria and Phoenicia a portion shall be carefully given to these men for the sacrifices of the Lord, that is, to Zorobabel the governor for bulls, rams, and lambs, 30 and also corn, salt, wine and oil, and that continually every year without further question, according as the priests who are in Jerusalem may direct to be daily spent, 31 that drink offerings may be made to the Most High God for the king and for his children, and that they may pray for their lives." 32 He commanded that whoever should transgress, yes, or neglect anything written here, a beam shall be taken out of his own house, and he shall be hanged on it, and all his goods seized for the king. 33 "Therefore may the Lord, whose name is called upon there, utterly destroy every king and nation that stretches out his hand to hinder or damage that house of the Lord in Jerusalem. 34 I, King Darius have ordained that these things be done with diligence."

Esdras 1 Chapter 7

1 Then Sisinnes the governor of Coelesyria and Phoenicia, and Sathrabuzanes, with their companions, following the commandments of King Darius, 2 very carefully supervised the holy work, assisting the elders of the Jews and rulers of the temple. 3 So the holy work prospered, while Aggaeus and Zacharias the prophets prophesied. 4 They finished these things by the commandment of the Lord, the God of Israel, and with the consent of Cyrus, Darius, and Artaxerxes, kings of the Persians. 5 So the holy house was finished by the twenty-third day of the month Adar, in the sixth year of King Darius. 6 The children of Israel, the priests, the Levites, and the others who returned from captivity who joined them did what was written in the book of Moses. 7 For the dedication of the Lord's temple, they offered one hundred bulls, two hundred rams, four hundred lambs, 8 and twelve male goats for the sin of all Israel, according to the number of the twelve princes of the tribes of Israel. 9 The priests and the Levites stood arrayed in their vestments, according to their kindred, for the services of the Lord, the God of Israel, according to the book of Moses. The gatekeepers were at every gate. 10 The children of Israel who came out of captivity held the Passover the fourteenth day of the first month, when the priests and the Levites were sanctified together, 11 with all those who returned from captivity; for they were sanctified. For the Levites were all sanctified together, 12 and they offered the Passover for all who returned from captivity, for their kindred the priests, and for themselves. 13 The children of Israel who came out of the captivity ate, even all those who had separated themselves from the abominations of the heathen of the land, and sought the Lord. 14 They kept the feast of unleavened bread seven days, rejoicing before the Lord, 15 because he had turned the counsel of the king of Assyria toward them, to strengthen their hands in the works of the Lord, the God of Israel.

Esdras 1 Chapter 8

1 After these things, when Artaxerxes the king of the Persians reigned, Esdras came, who was the son of Azaraias, the son of Zechrias, the son of Helkias, 2 the son of Salem, the son of Sadduk, the son of Ahitob, the son of Amarias, the son of Ozias, the son of Memeroth, the son of Zaraias, the son of Savias, the son of Boccas, the son of Abisne, the son of Phinees, the son of Eleazar, the son of Aaron, the chief priest. 3 This Esdras went up from Babylon as a skilled scribe in the law of Moses, which was given by the God of Israel. 4 The king honored him, for he found favor in his sight in all his requests. 5 There went up with him also some of the children of Israel, and of the priests, Levites, holy singers, gatekeepers, and temple servants to Jerusalem 6 in the seventh year of the reign of Artaxerxes, in the fifth month (this was the king's seventh year); for they left Babylon on the new moon of the first month and came to Jerusalem, by the prosperous journey which the Lord gave them for his sake. 7 For Esdras had very great skill, so that he omitted nothing of the law and commandments of the Lord, but taught all Israel the ordinances and judgments. 8 Now the commission, which was written from King Artaxerxes, came to Esdras the priest and reader of the law of the Lord, was as follows: 9 "King Artaxerxes to Esdras the priest and reader of the law of the Lord, greetings. 10 Having determined to deal graciously, I have given orders that those of the nation of the Jews, and of the priests and Levites, and of those within

our realm who are willing and freely choose to, should go with you to Jerusalem. 11 As many therefore as are so disposed, let them depart with you, as it has seemed good both to me and my seven friends the counselors, 12 that they may look to the affairs of Judea and Jerusalem, in accordance with what is in the Lord's law, 13 and carry the gifts to the Lord of Israel to Jerusalem, which I and my friends have vowed, and that all the gold and silver that can be found in the country of Babylonia for the Lord in Jerusalem, 14 with that also which is given of the people for the temple of the Lord their God that is at Jerusalem, be collected: even the gold and silver for bulls, rams, and lambs, and what goes with them, 15 to the end that they may offer sacrifices to the Lord upon the altar of the Lord their God, which is in Jerusalem. 16 Whatever you and your kindred decide to do with gold and silver, do that according to the will of your God. 17 The holy vessels of the Lord, which are given you for the use of the temple of your God, which is in Jerusalem, 18 and whatever else you shall remember for the use of the temple of your God, you shall give it out of the king's treasury. 19 I, King Artaxerxes, have also commanded the keepers of the treasures in Syria and Phoenicia, that whatever Esdras the priest and reader of the law of the Most High God shall send for, they should give it to him with all diligence, 20 to the sum of one hundred talents of silver, likewise also of wheat even to one hundred cors, and one hundred firkins of wine, and salt in abundance. 21 Let all things be performed after God's law diligently to the most high God, that wrath come not upon the kingdom of the king and his sons. 22 I command you also that no tax, nor any other imposition, be laid upon any of the priests, or Levites, or holy singers, or gatekeepers, or temple servants, or any that have employment in this temple, and that no man has authority to impose any tax on them. 23 You, Esdras, according to the wisdom of God, ordain judges and justices that they may judge in all Syria and Phoenicia all those who know the law of your God; and those who don't know it, you shall teach. 24 Whoever transgresses the law of your God and of the king shall be punished diligently, whether it be by death, or other punishment, by penalty of money, or by imprisonment." 25 Then Esdras the scribe said, "Blessed be the only Lord, the God of my fathers, who has put these things into the heart of the king, to glorify his house that is in Jerusalem, 26 and has honored me in the sight of the king, his counselors, and all his friends and nobles. 27 Therefore I was encouraged by the help of the Lord my God, and gathered together out of Israel men to go up with me. 28 These are the chief according to their families and their several divisions, who went up with me from Babylon in the reign of King Artaxerxes: 29 of the sons of Phinees, Gerson; of the sons of Ithamar, Gamael; of the sons of David, Attus the son of Sechenias; 30 of the sons of Phoros, Zacharais; and with him were counted one hundred fifty men; 31 of the sons of Phaath Moab, Eliaonias the son of Zaraias, and with him two hundred men; 32 of the sons of Zathoes, Sechenias the son of Jezelus, and with him three hundred men; of the sons of Adin, Obeth the son of Jonathan, and with him two hundred fifty men; 33 of the sons of Elam, Jesias son of Gotholias, and with him seventy men; 34 of the sons of Saphatias, Zaraias son of Michael, and with him seventy men; 35 of the sons of Joab, Abadias son of Jehiel. Jezelus, and with him two hundred twelve men; 36 of the sons of Banias, Salimoth son of Josaphias, and with him one hundred sixty men; 37 of the sons of Babi, Zacharias son of Bebai, and with him twenty-eight men; 38 of the sons of Azgad: Astath, Joannes son of Hakkatan Akatan, and with him one hundred ten men; 39 of the sons of Adonikam, the last, and these are the names of them, Eliphalat, Jeuel, and Samaias, and with them seventy men; 40 of the sons of Bago, Uthi the son of Istalcurus, and with him seventy men. 41 I gathered them together to the river called Theras. There we pitched our tents three days, and I inspected them. 42 When I had found there none of the priests and Levites, 43 then sent I to Eleazar, Iduel, Maasmas, 44 Elnathan, Samaias, Joribus, Nathan, Ennatan, Zacharias, and Mosollamus, principal men and men of understanding. 45 I asked them to go to Loddeus the captain, who was in the place of the treasury, 46 and commanded them that they should speak to Loddeus, to his kindred, and to the treasurers in that place, to send us such men as might execute the priests' office in our Lord's house. 47 By the mighty hand of our Lord, they brought to us men of understanding of the sons of Mooli the son of Levi, the son of Israel, Asebebias, and his sons, and his kindred, who were eighteen, 48 and Asebias, Annuus, and Osaias his brother, of the sons of Chanuneus, and their sons were twenty men; 49 and of the temple servants whom David and the principal men had appointed for the servants of the Levites, two hundred twenty temple servants. The list of all their names was reported. 50 There I vowed a fast for the young men before our Lord, to seek from him a prosperous journey both for us and for our children and livestock that were with us; 51 for I was ashamed to ask of the king infantry, cavalry, and an escort for protection against our adversaries.

52 For we had said to the king that the power of our Lord would be with those who seek him, to support them in all ways. 53 Again we prayed to our Lord about these things, and found him to be merciful. 54 Then I set apart twelve men of the chiefs of the priests, Eserebias, Assamias, and ten men of their kindred with them. 55 I weighed out to them the silver, the gold, and the holy vessels of the house of our Lord, which the king, his counselors, the nobles, and all Israel had given. 56 When I had weighed it, I delivered to them six hundred fifty talents of silver, silver vessels weighing one hundred talents, one hundred talents of gold, 57 twenty golden vessels, and twelve vessels of brass, even of fine brass, glittering like gold. 58 I said to them, "You are holy to the Lord, the vessels are holy, and the gold and the silver are a vow to the Lord, the Lord of our fathers. 59 Watch and keep them until you deliver them to the chiefs of the priests and Levites, and to the principal men of the families of Israel in Jerusalem, in the chambers of our Lord's house." 60 So the priests and the Levites who received the silver, the gold, and the vessels which were in Jerusalem, brought them into the temple of the Lord. 61 We left the river Theras on the twelfth day of the first month. We came to Jerusalem by the mighty hand of our Lord which was upon us. The Lord delivered us from every enemy on the way, and so we came to Jerusalem. 62 When we had been there three days, the silver and gold was weighed and delivered in our Lord's house on the fourth day to Marmoth the priest the son of Urias. 63 With him was Eleazar the son of Phinees, and with them were Josabdus the son of Jesus and Moeth the son of Sabannus, the Levites. All was delivered to them by number and weight. 64 All the weight of them was recorded at the same hour. 65 Moreover those who had come out of captivity offered sacrifices to the Lord, the God of Israel, even twelve bulls for all Israel, ninety-six rams, 66 seventy-two lambs, and twelve goats for a peace offering—all of them a sacrifice to the Lord. 67 They delivered the king's commandments to the king's stewards and to the governors of Coelesyria and Phoenicia; and they honored the people and the temple of the Lord. 68 Now when these things were done, the principal men came to me and said, 69 "The nation of Israel, the princes, the priests, and the Levites haven't put away from themselves the foreign people of the land nor the uncleannesses of the Gentiles—the Canaanites, Hittites, Pherezites, Jebusites, Moabites, Egyptians, and Edomites. 70 For both they and their sons have married with their daughters, and the holy seed is mixed with the foreign people of the land. From the beginning of this matter the rulers and the nobles have been partakers of this iniquity." 71 And as soon as I had heard these things, I tore my clothes and my holy garment, and plucked the hair from off my head and beard, and sat down sad and full of heaviness. 72 So all those who were moved at the word of the Lord, the God of Israel, assembled to me while I mourned for the iniquity, but I sat still full of heaviness until the evening sacrifice. 73 Then rising up from the fast with my clothes and my holy garment torn, and bowing my knees and stretching out my hands to the Lord, 74 I said, "O Lord, I am ashamed and confounded before your face, 75 for our sins are multiplied above our heads, and our errors have reached up to heaven 76 ever since the time of our fathers. We are in great sin, even to this day. 77 For our sins and our fathers' we with our kindred, our kings, and our priests were given up to the kings of the earth, to the sword, and to captivity, and for a prey with shame, to this day. 78 Now in some measure mercy has been shown to us from you, O Lord, that there should be left us a root and a name in the place of your sanctuary, 79 and to uncover a light in the house of the Lord our God, and to give us food in the time of our servitude. 80 Yes, when we were in bondage, we were not forsaken by our Lord, but he gave us favor before the kings of Persia, so that they gave us food, 81 glorified the temple of our Lord, and raised up the desolate Zion, to give us a sure dwelling in Judea and Jerusalem. 82 "Now, O Lord, what shall we say, having these things? For we have transgressed your commandments which you gave by the hand of your servants the prophets, saying, 83 'The land, which you enter into to possess as an inheritance, is a land polluted with the pollutions of the foreigners of the land, and they have filled it with their uncleanness. 84 Therefore now you shall not join your daughters to their sons, neither shall you take their daughters for your sons. 85 You shall never seek to have peace with them, that you may be strong, and eat the good things of the land, and that you may leave it for an inheritance to your children for evermore.' 86 All that has happened is done to us for our wicked works and great sins, for you, O Lord, made our sins light, 87 and gave to us such a root; but we have turned back again to transgress your law in mingling ourselves with the uncleanness of the heathen of the land. 88 You weren't angry with us to destroy us until you had left us neither root, seed, nor name. 89 O Lord of Israel, you are true, for we are left a root this day. 90 Behold, now we are before you in our iniquities, for we can't stand any longer before you because of these things." 91 As Esdras in his prayer made his confession, weeping, and lying flat on the ground before the temple, a very great throng of men, women, and children gathered to him from Jerusalem; for there was great weeping among the multitude. 92 Then Jechonias the son of Jeelus, one of the sons of Israel, called out, and said, "O Esdras, we have sinned against the Lord God, we have married foreign women of the heathen of the land, but there is still hope for Israel. 93 Let's make an oath to the Lord about this, that we will put away all our foreign wives with their children, 94 as seems good to you, and to as many as obey the Lord's Law. 95 Arise, and take action, for this is your task, and we will be with you to do valiantly." 96 So Esdras arose, and took an oath from the chief of the priests and Levites of all Israel to do these things; and they swore to it.

Esdras 1 Chapter 9

1 Then Esdras rose up from the court of the temple and went to the chamber of Jonas the son of Eliasib, 2 and lodged there, and ate no bread and drank no water, mourning for the great iniquities of the multitude. 3 A proclamation was made in all Judea and Jerusalem to all those who returned from captivity, that they should be gathered together at Jerusalem, 4 and that whoever didn't meet there within two or three days, in accordance with the ruling of the elders, that their livestock would be seized for the use of the temple, and they would be expelled from the multitude of those who returned from captivity. 5 Within three days, all those of the tribe of Judah and Benjamin gathered together at Jerusalem. This was the ninth month, on the twentieth day of the month. 6 All the multitude sat together shivering in the broad place before the temple because of the present foul weather. 7 So Esdras arose up and said to them, "You have transgressed the law and married foreign wives, increasing the sins of Israel. 8 Now make confession and give glory to the Lord, the God of our fathers, 9 and do his will, and separate yourselves from the heathen of the land, and from the foreign women." 10 Then the whole multitude cried out, and said with a loud voice, "Just as you have spoken, so we will do. 11 But because the multitude is great, and it is foul weather, so that we can't stand outside, and this is not a work of one day or two, seeing our sin in these things has spread far, 12 therefore let the rulers of the multitude stay, and let all those of our settlements that have foreign wives come at the time appointed, 13 and with them the rulers and judges of every place, until we turn away the wrath of the Lord from us for this matter." 14 So Jonathan the son of Azael and Ezekias the son of Thocanus took the matter on themselves. Mosollamus and Levis and Sabbateus were judges with them. 15 Those who returned from captivity did according to all these things. 16 Esdras the priest chose for himself principal men of their families, all by name. On the new moon of the tenth month they met together to examine the matter. 17 So their cases of men who had foreign wives was brought to an end by the new moon of the first month. 18 Of the priests who had come together and had foreign wives, there were found 19 of the sons of Jesus the son of Josedek, and his kindred, Mathelas, Eleazar, and Joribus, and Joadanus. 20 They gave their hands to put away their wives, and to offer rams to make reconciliation for their error. 21 Of the sons of Emmer: Ananias, Zabdeus, Manes, Sameus, Hiereel, and Azarias. 22 Of the sons of Phaisur: Elionas, Massias, Ishmael, Nathanael, Ocidelus, and Saloas. 23 Of the Levites: Jozabdus, Semeis, Colius who was called Calitas, Patheus, Judas, and Jonas. 24 Of the holy singers: Eliasibus and Bacchurus. 25 Of the gatekeepers: Sallumus and Tolbanes. 26 Of Israel, of the sons of Phoros: Hiermas, Ieddias, Melchias, Maelus, Eleazar, Asibas, and Banneas. 27 Of the sons of Ela: Matthanias, Zacharias, Jezrielus, Oabdius, Hieremoth, and Aedias. 28 Of the sons of Zamoth: Eliadas, Eliasimus, Othonias, Jarimoth, Sabathus, and Zardeus. 29 Of the sons of Bebai: Joannes, Ananias, Jozabdus, and Ematheis. 30 Of the sons of Mani: Olamus, Mamuchus, Jedeus, Jasubas, Jasaelus, and Hieremoth. 31 Of the sons of Addi: Naathus, Moossias, Laccunus, Naidus, Matthanias, Sesthel, Balnuus, and Manasseas. 32 Of the sons of Annas: Elionas, Aseas, Melchias, Sabbeus, and Simon Chosameus. 33 Of the sons of Asom: Maltanneus, Mattathias, Sabanneus, Eliphalat, Manasses, and Semei. 34 Of the sons of Baani: Jeremias, Momdis, Ismaerus, Juel, Mamdai, Pedias, Anos, Carabasion, Enasibus, Mamnitamenus, Eliasis, Bannus, Eliali, Someis, Selemias, and Nathanias. Of the sons of Ezora: Sesis, Ezril, Azaelus, Samatus, Zambri, and Josephus. 35 Of the sons of Nooma: Mazitias, Zabadeas, Edos, Juel, and Banaias. 36 All these had taken foreign wives, and they put them away with their children. 37 The priests and Levites, and those who were of Israel, lived in Jerusalem and in the country, on the new moon of the seventh month, and the children of Israel in their settlements. 38 The whole multitude gathered together with one accord into the broad place before the porch of the temple toward the east. 39 They said to Esdras the priest and reader, "Bring the law of Moses that was given by the Lord, the God of Israel." 40 So Esdras the chief priest brought the law to the whole multitude

both of men and women, and to all the priests, to hear the law on the new moon of the seventh month. 41 He read in the broad place before the porch of the temple from morning until midday, before both men and women; and all the multitude gave attention to the law. 42 Esdras the priest and reader of the law stood up upon the pulpit of wood which had been prepared. 43 Beside him stood Mattathias, Sammus, Ananias, Azarias, Urias, Ezekias, and Baalsamus on the right hand, 44 and on his left hand, Phaldeus, Misael, Melchias, Lothasubus, Nabarias, and Zacharias. 45 Then Esdras took the book of the law before the multitude, and sat honorably in the first place before all. 46 When he opened the law, they all stood straight up. So Esdras blessed the Lord God Most High, the God of armies, the Almighty. 47 All the people answered, "Amen." Lifting up their hands, they fell to the ground and worshiped the Lord. 48 Also Jesus, Annus, Sarabias, Iadinus, Jacubus, Sabateus, Auteas, Maiannas, Calitas, Azarias, Jozabdus, Ananias, and Phalias, the Levites, taught the law of the Lord, and read to the multitude the law of the Lord, explaining what was read. 49 Then Attharates said to Esdras the chief priest and reader, and to the Levites who taught the multitude, even to all, 50 "This day is holy to the Lord— now they all wept when they heard the law— 51 go then, eat the fat, drink the sweet, and send portions to those who have nothing; 52 for the day is holy to the Lord. Don't be sorrowful, for the Lord will bring you to honor." 53 So the Levites commanded all things to the people, saying, "This day is holy. Don't be sorrowful." 54 Then they went their way, every one to eat, drink, enjoy themselves, to give portions to those who had nothing, and to rejoice greatly, 55 because they understood the words they were instructed with, and for which they had been assembled.

Esdras II

Esdras 2 Chapter 1

1 The second book of the prophet Esdras, the son of Saraias, the son of Azaraias, the son of Helkias, the son of Salemas, the son of Sadoc, the son of Ahitob, 2 the son of Achias, the son of Phinees, the son of Heli, the son of Amarias, the son of Aziei, the son of Marimoth, the son of Arna, the son of Ozias, the son of Borith, the son of Abissei, the son of Phinees, the son of Eleazar, 3 the son of Aaron, of the tribe of Levi, who was captive in the land of the Medes, in the reign of Artaxerxes king of the Persians. 4 The Lord's word came to me, saying, 5 "Go your way and show my people their sinful deeds, and their children their wickedness which they have done against me, that they may tell their children's children, 6 because the sins of their fathers have increased in them, for they have forgotten me, and have offered sacrifices to foreign gods. 7 Didn't I bring them out of the land of Egypt, out of the house of bondage? But they have provoked me to wrath and have despised my counsels. 8 So pull out the hair of your head and cast all evils upon them, for they have not been obedient to my law, but they are a rebellious people. 9 How long shall I endure them, to whom I have done so much good? 10 I have overthrown many kings for their sakes. I have struck down Pharaoh with his servants and all his army. 11 I have destroyed all the nations before them. In the east, I have scattered the people of two provinces, even of Tyre and Sidon, and have slain all their adversaries. 12 Speak therefore to them, saying: 13 "The Lord says, truly I brought you through the sea, and where there was no path I made highways for you. I gave you Moses for a leader and Aaron for a priest. 14 I gave you light in a pillar of fire. I have done great wonders among you, yet you have forgotten me, says the Lord. 15 "The Lord Almighty says: The quails were for a token to you. I gave you a camp for your protection, but you complained there. 16 You didn't celebrate in my name for the destruction of your enemies, but even to this day you still complain. 17 Where are the benefits that I have given you? When you were hungry and thirsty in the wilderness, didn't you cry to me, 18 saying, 'Why have you brought us into this wilderness to kill us? It would have been better for us to have served the Egyptians than to die in this wilderness.' 19 I had pity on your mourning and gave you manna for food. You ate angels' bread. 20 When you were thirsty, didn't I split the rock, and water flowed out in abundance? Because of the heat, I covered you with the leaves of the trees. 21 I divided fruitful lands among you. I drove out the Canaanites, the Perizzites, and the Philistines before you. What more shall I do for you?" says the Lord. 22 The Lord Almighty says, "When you were in the wilderness, at the bitter stream, being thirsty and blaspheming my name, 23 I gave you not fire for your blasphemies, but threw a tree in the water, and made the river sweet. 24 What shall I do to you, O Jacob? You, Judah, would not obey me. I will turn myself to other nations, and I will give my name to them, that they may keep my statutes. 25 Since you have forsaken me, I also will forsake you. When you ask me to be merciful to you, I will have no mercy upon you.

26 Whenever you call upon me, I will not hear you, for you have defiled your hands with blood, and your feet are swift to commit murder. 27 It is not as though you have forsaken me, but your own selves," says the Lord. 28 The Lord Almighty says, "Haven't I asked you as a father his sons, as a mother her daughters, and a nurse her young babies, 29 that you would be my people, and I would be your God, that you would be my children, and I would be your father? 30 I gathered you together, as a hen gathers her chicks under her wings. But now, what should I do to you? I will cast you out from my presence. 31 When you offer burnt sacrifices to me, I will turn my face from you, for I have rejected your solemn feast days, your new moons, and your circumcisions of the flesh. 32 I sent to you my servants the prophets, whom you have taken and slain, and torn their bodies in pieces, whose blood I will require from you," says the Lord. 33 The Lord Almighty says, "Your house is desolate. I will cast you out as the wind blows stubble. 34 Your children won't be fruitful, for they have neglected my commandment to you, and done that which is evil before me. 35 I will give your houses to a people that will come, which not having heard of me yet believe me. Those to whom I have shown no signs will do what I have commanded. 36 They have seen no prophets, yet they will remember their former condition. 37 I call to witness the gratitude of the people who will come, whose little ones rejoice with gladness. Although they see me not with bodily eyes, yet in spirit they will believe what I say." 38 And now, father, behold with glory, and see the people that come from the east: 39 to whom I will give for leaders, Abraham, Isaac, and Jacob, Oseas, Amos, and Micheas, Joel, Abdias, and Jonas, 40 Nahum, and Abacuc, Sophonias, Aggaeus, Zachary, and Malachy, who is also called the Lord's messenger.

Esdras 2 Chapter 2

1 Thus saith the Lord, I brought this people out of bondage, and I gave them my commandments by menservants the prophets; whom they would not hear, but despised my counsels. 2 The mother that bare them saith unto them, Go your way, ye children; for I am a widow and forsaken. 3 I brought you up with gladness; but with sorrow and heaviness have I lost you: for ye have sinned before the Lord your God, and done that thing that is evil before him. 4 But what shall I now do unto you? I am a widow and forsaken: go your way, O my children, and ask mercy of the Lord. 5 As for me, O father, I call upon thee for a witness over the mother of these children, which would not keep my covenant, 6 That thou bring them to confusion, and their mother to a spoil, that there may be no offspring of them. 7 Let them be scattered abroad among the heathen, let their names be put out of the earth: for they have despised my covenant. 8 Woe be unto thee, Assur, thou that hidest the unrighteous in thee! O thou wicked people, remember what I did unto Sodom and Gomorrha; 9 Whose land lieth in clods of pitch and heaps of ashes: even so also will I do unto them that hear me not, saith the Almighty Lord. 10 Thus saith the Lord unto Esdras, Tell my people that I will give them the kingdom of Jerusalem, which I would have given unto Israel. 11 Their glory also will I take unto me, and give these the everlasting tabernacles, which I had prepared for them. 12 They shall have the tree of life for an ointment of sweet savour; they shall neither labour, nor be weary. 13 Go, and ye shall receive: pray for few days unto you, that they may be shortened: the kingdom is already prepared for you: watch. 14 Take heaven and earth to witness: for I have broken the evil in pieces, and created the good: for I live, saith the Lord. 15 Mother, embrace thy children, and bring them up with gladness, make their feet as fast as a pillar: for I have chosen thee, saith the Lord. 16 And those that be dead will I raise up again from their places, and bring them out of the graves: for I have known my name in Israel. 17 Fear not, thou mother of the children: for I have chosen thee, saith the Lord. 18 For thy help will I send my servants Esau and Jeremy, after whose counsel I have sanctified and prepared for thee twelve trees laden with divers fruits, 19 And as many fountains flowing with milk and honey, and seven mighty mountains, whereupon there grow roses and lilies, whereby I will fill thy children with joy. 20 Do right to the widow, judge for the fatherless, give to the poor, defend the orphan, clothe the naked, 21 Heal the broken and the weak, laugh not a lame man to scorn, defend the maimed, and let the blind man come into the sight of my clearness. 22 Keep the old and young within thy walls. 23 Wheresoever thou findest the dead, take them, and bury them, and I will give thee the first place in my resurrection. 24 Abide still, O my people, and take thy rest, for thy quietness still come. 25 Nourish thy children, O thou good nurse; stablish their feet. 26 As for the servants whom I have given thee, there shall not one of them perish; for I will require them from among thy number. 27 Be not weary: for when the day of trouble and heaviness cometh, others shall weep and be sorrowful, but thou shalt be merry and have abundance. 28 The heathen shall envy thee, but they shall be able to do nothing against thee, saith the Lord. 29 My hands shall cover thee, so that thy children shall not see hell. 30 Be joyful, O thou mother,

with thy children; for I will deliver thee, saith the Lord. ³¹Remember thy children that sleep, for I shall bring them out of the sides of the earth, and shew mercy unto them: for I am merciful, saith the Lord Almighty. ³²Embrace thy children until I come and shew mercy unto them: for my wells run over, and my grace shall not fail. ³³I Esdras received a charge of the Lord upon the mount Oreb, that I should go unto Israel; but when I came unto them, they set me at nought, and despised the commandment of the Lord. ³⁴And therefore I say unto you, O ye heathen, that hear and understand, Look for your Shepherd, he shall give you everlasting rest; for he is nigh at hand, that shall come in the end of the world. ³⁵Be ready to the reward of the kingdom, for the everlasting light shall shine upon you for evermore. ³⁶Flee the shadow of this world, receive the joyfulness of your glory: I testify my Saviour openly. ³⁷O receive the gift that is given you, and be glad, giving thanks unto him that hath led you to the heavenly kingdom. ³⁸Arise up and stand, behold the number of those that be sealed in the feast of the Lord; ³⁹Which are departed from the shadow of the world, and have received glorious garments of the Lord. ⁴⁰Take thy number, O Sion, and shut up those of thine that are clothed in white, which have fulfilled the law of the Lord. ⁴¹The number of thy children, whom thou longedst for, is fulfilled: beseech the power of the Lord, that thy people, which have been called from the beginning, may be hallowed. ⁴²I Esdras saw upon the mount Sion a great people, whom I could not number, and they all praised the Lord with songs. ⁴³And in the midst of them there was a young man of a high stature, taller than all the rest, and upon every one of their heads he set crowns, and was more exalted; which I marvelled at greatly. ⁴⁴So I asked the angel, and said, Sir, what are these? ⁴⁵He answered and said unto me, These be they that have put off the mortal clothing, and put on the immortal, and have confessed the name of God: now are they crowned, and receive palms. ⁴⁶Then said I unto the angel, What young person is it that crowneth them, and giveth them palms in their hands? ⁴⁷So he answered and said unto me, It is the Son of God, whom they have confessed in the world. Then began I greatly to commend them that stood so stiffly for the name of the Lord. ⁴⁸Then the angel said unto me, Go thy way, and tell my people what manner of things, and how great wonders of the Lord thy God, thou hast seen.

Esdras 2 Chapter 3

¹ In the thirtieth year after the ruin of the city, I Salathiel, also called Esdras, was in Babylon, and lay troubled upon my bed, and my thoughts came up over my heart, ² for I saw the desolation of Zion and the wealth of those who lived at Babylon. ³ My spirit was very agitated, so that I began to speak words full of fear to the Most High, and said, ⁴ "O sovereign Lord, didn't you speak at the beginning when you formed the earth—and that yourself alone—and commanded the dust ⁵ and it gave you Adam, a body without a soul? Yet it was the workmanship of your hands, and you breathed into him the breath of life, and he was made alive in your presence. ⁶ You led him into the garden which your right hand planted before the earth appeared. ⁷ You gave him your one commandment, which he transgressed, and immediately you appointed death for him and his descendants. From him were born nations, tribes, peoples, and kindred without number. ⁸ Every nation walked after their own will, did ungodly things in your sight, and despised your commandments, and you didn't hinder them. ⁹ Nevertheless, again in process of time, you brought the flood on those who lived in the world and destroyed them. ¹⁰ It came to pass that the same thing happened to them. Just as death came to Adam, so was the flood to these. ¹¹ Nevertheless, you left one of them, Noah with his household, and all the righteous men who descended from him. ¹² "It came to pass that when those who lived upon the earth began to multiply, they also multiplied children, peoples, and many nations, and began again to be more ungodly than their ancestors. ¹³ It came to pass, when they did wickedly before you, you chose one from among them, whose name was Abraham. ¹⁴ You loved, and to him only you showed the end of the times secretly by night, ¹⁵ and made an everlasting covenant with him, promising him that you would never forsake his descendants. To him, you gave Isaac, and to Isaac you gave Jacob and Esau. ¹⁶ You set apart Jacob for yourself, but rejected Esau. Jacob became a great multitude. ¹⁷ It came to pass that when you led his descendants out of Egypt, you brought them up to Mount Sinai. ¹⁸ You bowed the heavens also, shook the earth, moved the whole world, made the depths tremble, and troubled the age. ¹⁹ Your glory went through four gates, of fire, of earthquake, of wind, and of ice, that you might give the law to the descendants of Jacob, and the commandment to the descendants of Israel. ²⁰ "Yet you didn't take away from them their wicked heart, that your law might produce fruit in them. ²¹ For the first Adam, burdened with a wicked heart transgressed and was overcome, as were all who are descended from him. ²² Thus disease was made permanent. The law was in the heart of the people along with the wickedness of the root. So

the good departed away and that which was wicked remained. ²³ So the times passed away, and the years were brought to an end. Then you raised up a servant, called David, ²⁴ whom you commanded to build a city to your name, and to offer burnt offerings to you in it from what is yours. ²⁵ When this was done many years, then those who inhabited the city did evil, ²⁶ in all things doing as Adam and all his generations had done, for they also had a wicked heart. ²⁷ So you gave your city over into the hands of your enemies. ²⁸ "Then I said in my heart, 'Are their deeds of those who inhabit Babylon any better? Is that why it gained dominion over Zion?' ²⁹ For it came to pass when I came here, that I also saw impieties without number, and my soul saw many sinners in this thirtieth year, so that my heart failed me. ³⁰ For I have seen how you endure them sinning, and have spared those who act ungodly, and have destroyed your people, and have preserved your enemies; ³¹ and you have not shown how your way may be comprehended. Are the deeds of Babylon better than those of Zion? ³² Or is there any other nation that knows you beside Israel? Or what tribes have so believed your covenants as these tribes of Jacob? ³³ Yet their reward doesn't appear, and their labor has no fruit, for I have gone here and there through the nations, and I see that they abound in wealth, and don't think about your commandments. ³⁴ Weigh therefore our iniquities now in the balance, and theirs also who dwell in the world, and so will it be found which way the scale inclines. ³⁵ Or when was it that they who dwell on the earth have not sinned in your sight? Or what nation has kept your commandments so well? ³⁶ You will find some men by name who have kept your precepts, but you won't find nations."

Esdras 2 Chapter 4

¹ The angel who was sent to me, whose name was Uriel, gave me an answer, ² and said to me, "Your understanding has utterly failed you regarding this world. Do you think you can comprehend the way of the Most High?" ³ Then I said, "Yes, my Lord." He answered me, "I have been sent to show you three ways, and to set before you three problems. ⁴ If you can solve one for me, I also will show you the way that you desire to see, and I will teach you why the heart is wicked." ⁵ I said, "Say on, my Lord." Then said he to me, "Go, weigh for me the weight of fire, or measure for me blast of wind, or call back for me the day that is past." ⁶ Then answered I and said, "Who of the sons of men is able to do this, that you should ask me about such things?" ⁷ He said to me, "If I had asked you, 'How many dwellings are there in the heart of the sea? Or how many springs are there at the fountain head of the deep? Or how many streams are above the firmament? Or which are the exits of hell? Or which are the entrances of paradise?' ⁸ perhaps you would say to me, 'I never went down into the deep, or as yet into hell, neither did I ever climb up into heaven.' ⁹ Nevertheless now I have only asked you about the fire, wind, and the day, things which you have experienced, and from which you can't be separated, and yet have you given me no answer about them." ¹⁰ He said moreover to me, "You can't understand your own things that you grew up with. ¹¹ How then can your mind comprehend the way of the Most High? How can he who is already worn out with the corrupted world understand incorruption?" When I heard these things, I fell on my face ¹² and said to him, "It would have been better if we weren't here at all, than that we should come here and live in the midst of ungodliness, and suffer, and not know why." ¹³ He answered me, and said, "A forest of the trees of the field went out, and took counsel together, ¹⁴ and said, 'Come! Let's go and make war against the sea, that it may depart away before us, and that we may make ourselves more forests.' ¹⁵ The waves of the sea also in like manner took counsel together, and said, 'Come! Let's go up and subdue the forest of the plain, that there also we may gain more territory.' ¹⁶ The counsel of the wood was in vain, for the fire came and consumed it. ¹⁷ Likewise also the counsel of the waves of the sea, for the sand stood up and stopped them. ¹⁸ If you were judge now between these two, which would you justify, or which would you condemn?" ¹⁹ I answered and said, "It is a foolish counsel that they both have taken, for the ground is given to the wood, and the place of the sea is given to bear its waves." ²⁰ Then answered he me, and said, "You have given a right judgment. Why don't you judge your own case? ²¹ For just as the ground is given to the wood, and the sea to its waves, even so those who dwell upon the earth may understand nothing but what is upon the earth. Only he who dwells above the heavens understands the things that are above the height of the heavens." ²² Then answered I and said, "I beg you, O Lord, why has the power of understanding been given to me? ²³ For it was not in my mind to be curious of the ways above, but of such things as pass by us daily, because Israel is given up as a reproach to the heathen. The people whom you have loved have been given over to ungodly nations. The law of our forefathers is made of no effect, and the written covenants are nowhere regarded. ²⁴ We pass away out of the world like locusts. Our life is like a vapor, and we aren't

worthy to obtain mercy. 25 What will he then do for his name by which we are called? I have asked about these things." 26 Then he answered me, and said, "If you are alive you will see, and if you live long, you will marvel, for the world hastens quickly to pass away. 27 For it is not able to bear the things that are promised to the righteous in the times to come; for this world is full of sadness and infirmities. 28 For the evil about which you asked me has been sown, but its harvest hasn't yet come. 29 If therefore that which is sown isn't reaped, and if the place where the evil is sown doesn't pass away, the field where the good is sown won't come. 30 For a grain of evil seed was sown in the heart of Adam from the beginning, and how much wickedness it has produced to this time! How much more it will yet produce until the time of threshing comes! 31 Ponder now by yourself, how much fruit of wickedness a grain of evil seed has produced. 32 When the grains which are without number are sown, how great a threshing floor they will fill!" 33 Then I answered and said, "How long? When will these things come to pass? Why are our years few and evil?" 34 He answered me, and said, "Don't hurry faster than the Most High; for your haste is for your own self, but he who is above hurries on behalf of many. 35 Didn't the souls of the righteous ask question of these things in their chambers, saying, 'How long will we be here? When does the fruit of the threshing floor come?' 36 To them, Jeremiel the archangel answered, 'When the number is fulfilled of those who are like you. For he has weighed the world in the balance. 37 By measure, he has measured the times. By number, he has counted the seasons. He won't move or stir them until that measure is fulfilled.'" 38 Then I answered, "O sovereign Lord, all of us are full of ungodliness. 39 Perhaps it is for our sakes that the threshing time of the righteous is kept back—because of the sins of those who dwell on the earth." 40 So he answered me, "Go your way to a woman with child, and ask of her when she has fulfilled her nine months, if her womb may keep the baby any longer within her." 41 Then I said, "No, Lord, that can it not." He said to me, "In Hades, the chambers of souls are like the womb. 42 For just like a woman in labor hurries to escape the anguish of the labor pains, even so these places hurry to deliver those things that are committed to them from the beginning. 43 Then you will be shown those things which you desire to see." 44 Then I answered, "If I have found favor in your sight, and if it is possible, and if I am worthy, 45 show me this also, whether there is more to come than is past, or whether the greater part has gone over us. 46 For what is gone I know, but I don't know what is to come." 47 He said to me, "Stand up on my right side, and I will explain the parable to you." 48 So I stood, looked, and saw a hot burning oven passed by before me. It happened that when the flame had gone by I looked, and saw that the smoke remained. 49 After this, a watery cloud passed in front of me, and sent down much rain with a storm. When the stormy rain was past, the drops still remained in it." 50 Then said he to me, "Consider with yourself; as the rain is more than the drops, and the fire is greater than the smoke, so the quantity which is past was far greater; but the drops and the smoke still remained." 51 Then I prayed, and said, "Do you think that I will live until that time? Or who will be alive in those days?" 52 He answered me, "As for the signs you asked me about, I may tell you of them in part; but I wasn't sent to tell you about your life, for I don't know.

Esdras 2 Chapter 5

1 "Nevertheless, concerning the signs, behold, the days will come when those who dwell on earth will be taken with great amazement, and the way of truth will be hidden, and the land will be barren of faith. 2 Iniquity will be increased above what now you see, and beyond what you have heard long ago. 3 The land that you now see ruling will be a trackless waste, and men will see it desolate. 4 But if the Most High grants you to live, you will see what is after the third period will be troubled. The sun will suddenly shine in the night, and the moon in the day. 5 Blood will drop out of wood, and the stone will utter its voice. The peoples will be troubled, and the stars will fall. 6 He will rule whom those who dwell on the earth don't expect, and the birds will fly away together. 7 The Sodomite sea will cast out fish, and make a noise in the night, which many have not known; but all will hear its voice. 8 There will also be chaos in many places. Fires will break out often, and the wild animals will change their places, and women will bring forth monsters. 9 Salt waters will be found in the sweet, and all friends will destroy one another. Then reason will hide itself, and understanding withdraw itself into its chamber. 10 It will be sought by many, and won't be found. Unrighteousness and lack of restraint will be multiplied on earth. 11 One country will ask another, 'Has righteousness, or a man that does righteousness, gone through you?' And it will say, 'No.' 12 It will come to pass at that time that men will hope, but won't obtain. They will labor, but their ways won't prosper. 13 I am permitted to show you such signs. If you will pray again, and weep as now, and fast seven days,

you will hear yet greater things than these." 14 Then I woke up, and an extreme trembling went through my body, and my mind was so troubled that it fainted. 15 So the angel who had come to talk with me held me, comforted me, and set me on my feet. 16 In the second night, it came to pass that Phaltiel the captain of the people came to me, saying, "Where have you been? Why is your face sad? 17 Or don't you know that Israel is committed to you in the land of their captivity? 18 Get up then, and eat some bread, and don't forsake us, like a shepherd who leaves the flock in the power of cruel wolves." 19 Then said I to him, "Go away from me and don't come near me for seven days, and then you shall come to me." He heard what I said and left me. 20 So I fasted seven days, mourning and weeping, like Uriel the angel had commanded me. 21 After seven days, the thoughts of my heart were very grievous to me again, 22 and my soul recovered the spirit of understanding, and I began to speak words before the Most High again. 23 I said, "O sovereign Lord of all the woods of the earth, and of all the trees thereof, you have chosen one vine for yourself. 24 Of all the lands of the world you have chosen one country for yourself. Of all the flowers of the world, you have chosen one lily for yourself. 25 Of all the depths of the sea, you have filled one river for yourself. Of all built cities, you have consecrated Zion for yourself. 26 Of all the birds that are created you have named for yourself one dove. Of all the livestock that have been made, you have provided for yourself one sheep. 27 Among all the multitudes of peoples you have gotten yourself one people. To this people, whom you loved, you gave a law that is approved by all. 28 Now, O Lord, why have you given this one people over to many, and have dishonored the one root above others, and have scattered your only one among many? 29 Those who opposed your promises have trampled down those who believed your covenants. 30 If you really do hate your people so much, they should be punished with your own hands." 31 Now when I had spoken these words, the angel that came to me the night before was sent to me, 32 and said to me, "Hear me, and I will instruct you. Listen to me, and I will tell you more." 33 I said, "Speak on, my Lord." Then said he to me, "You are very troubled in mind for Israel's sake. Do you love that people more than he who made them?" 34 I said, "No, Lord; but I have spoken out of grief; for my heart is in agony every hour while I labor to comprehend the way of the Most High, and to seek out part of his judgment." 35 He said to me, "You can't." And I said, "Why, Lord? Why was I born? Why wasn't my mother's womb my grave, that I might not have seen the travail of Jacob, and the wearisome toil of the people of Israel?" 36 He said to me, "Count for me those who haven't yet come. Gather together for me the drops that are scattered abroad, and make the withered flowers green again for me. 37 Open for me the chambers that are closed, and bring out the winds for me that are shut up in them. Or show me the image of a voice. Then I will declare to you the travail that you asked to see." 38 And I said, "O sovereign Lord, who may know these things except he who doesn't have his dwelling with men? 39 As for me, I lack wisdom. How can I then speak of these things you asked me about?" 40 Then said he to me, "Just as you can do none of these things that I have spoken of, even so you can't find out my judgment, or the end of the love that I have promised to my people." 41 I said, "But, behold, O Lord, you have made the promise to those who are alive at the end. What should they do who have been before us, or we ourselves, or those who will come after us?" 42 He said to me, "I will compare my judgment to a ring. Just as there is no slowness of those who are last, even so there is no swiftness of those who be first." 43 So I answered, "Couldn't you make them all at once that have been made, and that are now, and that are yet to come, that you might show your judgment sooner?" 44 Then he answered me, "The creature may not move faster than the creator, nor can the world hold them at once who are to be created in it." 45 And I said, "How have you said to your servant, that you will surely make alive at once the creature that you have created? If therefore they will be alive at once, and the creation will sustain them, even so it might now also support them to be present at once." 46 And he said to me, "Ask the womb of a woman, and say to her, 'If you bear ten children, why do you it at different times? Ask her therefore to give birth to ten children at once." 47 I said, "She can't, but must do it each in their own time." 48 Then said he to me, "Even so, I have given the womb of the earth to those who are sown in it in their own times. 49 For just as a young child may not give birth, neither she who has grown old any more, even so have I organized the world which I created." 50 I asked, "Seeing that you have now shown me the way, I will speak before you. Is our mother, of whom you have told me, still young? Or does she now draw near to old age?" 51 He answered me, "Ask a woman who bears children, and she will tell you. 52 Say to her, 'Why aren't they whom you have now brought forth like those who were before, but smaller in stature?' 53 She also will answer you, 'Those who are born in the strength of youth are different from those who are born in the time of old age, when the womb fails.' ⁵⁴ Consider therefore you also, how you are shorter than those who were before you. ⁵⁵ So are those who come after you smaller than you, as born of the creature which now begins to be old, and is past the strength of youth." ⁵⁶ Then I said, "Lord, I implore you, if I have found favor in your sight, show your servant by whom you visit your creation."

Esdras 2 Chapter 6

¹ He said to me, "In the beginning, when the earth was made, before the portals of the world were fixed and before the gatherings of the winds blew, ² before the voices of the thunder sounded and before the flashes of the lightning shone, before the foundations of paradise were laid, ³ before the fair flowers were seen, before the powers of the earthquake were established, before the innumerable army of angels were gathered together, ⁴ before the heights of the air were lifted up, before the measures of the firmament were named, before the footstool of Zion was established, ⁵ before the present years were reckoned, before the imaginations of those who now sin were estranged, and before they were sealed who have gathered faith for a treasure— ⁶ then I considered these things, and they all were made through me alone, and not through another; just as by me also they will be ended, and not by another." ⁷ Then I answered, "What will be the dividing of the times? Or when will be the end of the first and the beginning of the age that follows?" ⁸ He said to me, "From Abraham to Isaac, because Jacob and Esau were born to him, for Jacob's hand held Esau's heel from the beginning. ⁹ For Esau is the end of this age, and Jacob is the beginning of the one that follows. ¹⁰ The beginning of a man is his hand, and the end of a man is his heel. Seek nothing else between the heel and the hand, Esdras!" ¹¹ Then I answered, "O sovereign Lord, if I have found favor in your sight, ¹² I beg you, show your servant the end of your signs which you showed me part on a previous night." ¹³ So he answered, "Stand up upon your feet, and you will hear a mighty sounding voice. ¹⁴ If the place you stand on is greatly moved ¹⁵ when it speaks don't be afraid, for the word is of the end, and the foundations of the earth will understand ¹⁶ that the speech is about them. They will tremble and be moved, for they know that their end must be changed." ¹⁷ It happened that when I had heard it, I stood up on my feet, and listened, and, behold, there was a voice that spoke, and its sound was like the sound of many waters. ¹⁸ It said, "Behold, the days come when I draw near to visit those who dwell upon the earth, ¹⁹ and when I investigate those who have caused harm unjustly with their unrighteousness, and when the affliction of Zion is complete, ²⁰ and when the seal will be set on the age that is to pass away, then I will show these signs: the books will be opened before the firmament, and all will see together. ²¹ The children a year old will speak with their voices. The women with child will deliver premature children at three or four months, and they will live and dance. ²² Suddenly the sown places will appear unsown. The full storehouses will suddenly be found empty. ²³ The trumpet will give a sound which when every man hears, they will suddenly be afraid. ²⁴ At that time friends will make war against one another like enemies. The earth will stand in fear with those who dwell in it. The springs of the fountains will stand still, so that for three hours they won't flow. ²⁵ "It will be that whoever remains after all these things that I have told you of, he will be saved and will see my salvation, and the end of my world. ²⁶ They will see the men who have been taken up, who have not tasted death from their birth. The heart of the inhabitants will be changed and turned into a different spirit. ²⁷ For evil will be blotted out and deceit will be quenched. ²⁸ Faith will flourish. Corruption will be overcome, and the truth, which has been so long without fruit, will be declared." ²⁹ When he talked with me, behold, little by little, the place I stood on rocked back and forth. ³⁰ He said to me, "I came to show you these things tonight. ³¹ If therefore you will pray yet again, and fast seven more days, I will again tell you greater things than these. ³² For your voice has surely been heard before the Most High. For the Mighty has seen your righteousness. He has also seen your purity, which you have maintained ever since your youth. ³³ Therefore he has sent me to show you all these things, and to say to you, 'Believe, and don't be afraid! ³⁴ Don't be hasty to think vain things about the former times, that you may not hasten in the latter times.'" ³⁵ It came to pass after this, that I wept again, and fasted seven days in like manner, that I might fulfill the three weeks which he told me. ³⁶ On the eighth night, my heart was troubled within me again, and I began to speak in the presence of the Most High. ³⁷ For my spirit was greatly aroused, and my soul was in distress. ³⁸ I said, "O Lord, truly you spoke at the beginning of the creation, on the first day, and said this: 'Let heaven and earth be made,' and your word perfected the work. ³⁹ Then the spirit was hovering, and darkness and silence were on every side. The sound of man's voice was not yet there. ⁴⁰ Then you commanded a ray of light to be brought out of your treasuries, that your works might then appear. ⁴¹ "On the second day, again you made the spirit of the firmament and commanded it to divide and to separate the waters, that

the one part might go up, and the other remain beneath. ⁴² "On the third day, you commanded that the waters should be gathered together in the seventh part of the earth. You dried up six parts and kept them, to the intent that of these some being both planted and tilled might serve before you. ⁴³ For as soon as your word went out, the work was done. ⁴⁴ Immediately, great and innumerable fruit grew, with many pleasant tastes, and flowers of inimitable color, and fragrances of most exquisite smell. This was done the third day. ⁴⁵ "On the fourth day, you commanded that the sun should shine, the moon give its light, and the stars should be in their order; ⁴⁶ and gave them a command to serve mankind, who was to be made. ⁴⁷ "On the fifth day, you said to the seventh part, where the water was gathered together, that it should produce living creatures, fowls and fishes; and so it came to pass ⁴⁸ that the mute and lifeless water produced living things as it was told, that the nations might therefore praise your wondrous works. ⁴⁹ "Then you preserved two living creatures. The one you called Behemoth, and the other you called Leviathan. ⁵⁰ You separated the one from the other; for the seventh part, namely, where the water was gathered together, might not hold them both. ⁵¹ To Behemoth, you gave one part, which was dried up on the third day, that he should dwell in it, in which are a thousand hills; ⁵² but to Leviathan you gave the seventh part, namely, the watery part. You have kept them to be devoured by whom you wish, when you wish. ⁵³ "But on the sixth day, you commanded the earth to produce before you cattle, animals, and creeping things. ⁵⁴ Over these, you ordained Adam as ruler over all the works that you have made. Of him came all of us, the people whom you have chosen. ⁵⁵ "All this have I spoken before you, O Lord, because you have said that for our sakes you made this world. ⁵⁶ As for the other nations, which also come from Adam, you have said that they are nothing, and are like spittle. You have likened the abundance of them to a drop that falls from a bucket. ⁵⁷ Now, O Lord, behold these nations, which are reputed as nothing, being rulers over us and devouring us. ⁵⁸ But we your people, whom you have called your firstborn, your only children, and your fervent lover, are given into their hands. ⁵⁹ Now if the world is made for our sakes, why don't we possess our world for an inheritance? How long will this endure?

Esdras 2 Chapter 7

¹ When I had finished speaking these words, the angel which had been sent to me the nights before was sent to me. ² He said to me, "Rise, Esdras, and hear the words that I have come to tell you." ³ I said, "Speak on, my Lord." Then he said to me, "There is a sea set in a wide place, that it might be broad and vast, ⁴ but its entrance is set in a narrow place so as to be like a river. ⁵ Whoever desires to go into the sea to look at it, or to rule it, if he didn't go through the narrow entrance, how could he come into the broad part? ⁶ Another thing also: There is a city built and set in a plain country, and full of all good things, ⁷ but its entrance is narrow, and is set in a dangerous place to fall, having fire on the right hand, and deep water on the left. ⁸ There is one only path between them both, even between the fire and the water, so that only one person can go there at once. ⁹ If this city is now given to a man for an inheritance, if the heir doesn't pass the danger before him, how will he receive his inheritance?" ¹⁰ I said, "That is so, Lord." Then said he to me, "Even so also is Israel's portion. ¹¹ I made the world for their sakes. What is now done was decreed when Adam transgressed my statutes. ¹² Then the entrances of this world were made narrow, sorrowful, and toilsome. They are but few and evil, full of perils, and involved in great toils. ¹³ For the entrances of the greater world are wide and safe, and produce fruit of immortality. ¹⁴ So if those who live don't enter these difficult and vain things, they can never receive those that are reserved for them. ¹⁵ Now therefore why are you disturbed, seeing you are but a corruptible man? Why are you moved, since you are mortal? ¹⁶ Why haven't you considered in your mind that which is to come, rather than that which is present?" ¹⁷ Then I answered and said, "O sovereign Lord, behold, you have ordained in your law that the righteous will inherit these things, but that the ungodly will perish. ¹⁸ The righteous therefore will suffer difficult things, and hope for easier things, but those who have done wickedly have suffered the difficult things, and yet will not see the easier things." ¹⁹ He said to me, "You are not a judge above God, neither do you have more understanding than the Most High. ²⁰ Yes, let many perish who now live, rather than that the law of God which is set before them be despised. ²¹ For God strictly commanded those who came, even as they came, what they should do to live, and what they should observe to avoid punishment. ²² Nevertheless, they weren't obedient to him, but spoke against him and imagined for themselves vain things. ²³ They made cunning plans of wickedness, and said moreover of the Most High that he doesn't exist, and they didn't know his ways. ²⁴ They despised his law and denied his covenants. They haven't been faithful to his statutes, and haven't performed his works.

25 Therefore, Esdras, for the empty are empty things, and for the full are the full things. 26 For behold, the time will come, and it will be, when these signs of which I told you before will come to pass, that the bride will appear, even the city coming forth, and she will be seen who now is withdrawn from the earth. 27 Whoever is delivered from the foretold evils will see my wonders. 28 For my son Jesus will be revealed with those who are with him, and those who remain will rejoice four hundred years. 29 After these years my son Christ will die, along with all of those who have the breath of life. 30 Then the world will be turned into the old silence seven days, like as in the first beginning, so that no human will remain. 31 After seven days the world that is not yet awake will be raised up, and what is corruptible will die. 32 The earth will restore those who are asleep in it, and the dust those who dwell in it in silence, and the secret places will deliver those souls that were committed to them. 33 The Most High will be revealed on the judgment seat, and compassion will pass away, and patience will be withdrawn. 34 Only judgment will remain. Truth will stand. Faith will grow strong. 35 Recompense will follow. The reward will be shown. Good deeds will awake, and wicked deeds won't sleep. 36 The pit of torment will appear, and near it will be the place of rest. The furnace of hell will be shown, and near it the paradise of delight. 37 Then the Most High will say to the nations that are raised from the dead, 'Look and understand whom you have denied, whom you haven't served, whose commandments you have despised. 38 Look on this side and on that. Here is delight and rest, and there fire and torments.' Thus he will speak to them in the day of judgment. 39 This is a day that has neither sun, nor moon, nor stars, 40 neither cloud, nor thunder, nor lightning, neither wind, nor water, nor air, neither darkness, nor evening, nor morning, 41 neither summer, nor spring, nor heat, nor winter, neither frost, nor cold, nor hail, nor rain, nor dew, 42 neither noon, nor night, nor dawn, neither shining, nor brightness, nor light, except only the splendor of the glory of the Most High, by which all will see the things that are set before them. 43 It will endure as though it were a week of years. 44 This is my judgment and its prescribed order; but I have only shown these things to you." 45 I answered, "I said then, O Lord, and I say now: Blessed are those who are now alive and keep your commandments! 46 But what about those for whom I prayed? For who is there of those who are alive who has not sinned, and who of the children of men hasn't transgressed your covenant? 47 Now I see that the world to come will bring delight to few, but torments to many. 48 For an evil heart has grown up in us, which has led us astray from these commandments and has brought us into corruption and into the ways of death. It has shown us the paths of perdition and removed us far from life—and that, not a few only, but nearly all who have been created." 49 He answered me, "Listen to me, and I will instruct you. I will admonish you yet again. 50 For this reason, the Most High has not made one world, but two. 51 For because you have said that the just are not many, but few, and the ungodly abound, hear the explanation. 52 If you have just a few precious stones, will you add them to lead and clay?" 53 I said, "Lord, how could that be?" 54 He said to me, "Not only that, but ask the earth, and she will tell you. Defer to her, and she will declare it to you. 55 Say to her, 'You produce gold, silver, and brass, and also iron, lead, and clay; 56 but silver is more abundant than gold, and brass than silver, and iron than brass, and lead than iron, and clay than lead.' 57 Judge therefore which things are precious and to be desired, what is abundant or what is rare?" 58 I said, "O sovereign Lord, that which is plentiful is of less worth, for that which is more rare is more precious." 59 He answered me, "Weigh within yourself the things that you have thought, for he who has what is hard to get rejoices over him who has what is plentiful. 60 So also is the judgment which I have promised; for I will rejoice over the few that will be saved, because these are those who have made my glory to prevail now, and through them, my name is now honored. 61 I won't grieve over the multitude of those who perish; for these are those who are now like mist, and have become like flame and smoke; they are set on fire and burn hotly, and are extinguished." 62 I answered, "O earth, why have you produced, if the mind is made out of dust, like all other created things? 63 For it would have been better that the dust itself had been unborn, so that the mind might not have been made from it. 64 But now the mind grows with us, and because of this we are tormented, because we perish and we know it. 65 Let the race of men lament and the animals of the field be glad. Let all who are born lament, but let the four-footed animals and the livestock rejoice. 66 For it is far better with them than with us; for they don't look forward to judgment, neither do they know of torments or of salvation promised to them after death. 67 For what does it profit us, that we will be preserved alive, but yet be afflicted with torment? 68 For all who are born are defiled with iniquities, and are full of sins and laden with transgressions. 69 If after death we were not to come into judgment, perhaps it would have been better for us." 70 He answered me, "When the Most High made the world and Adam and all those who came from him, he first prepared the judgment and the things that pertain to the judgment. 71 Now understand from your own words, for you have said that the mind grows with us. 72 They therefore who dwell on the earth will be tormented for this reason, that having understanding they have committed iniquity, and receiving commandments have not kept them, and having obtained a law they dealt unfaithfully with that which they received. 73 What then will they have to say in the judgment, or how will they answer in the last times? 74 For how long a time has the Most High been patient with those who inhabit the world, and not for their sakes, but because of the times which he has foreordained!" 75 I answered, "If I have found grace in your sight, O Lord, show this also to your servant, whether after death, even now when every one of us gives up his soul, we will be kept in rest until those times come, in which you renew the creation, or whether we will be tormented immediately." 76 He answered me, "I will show you this also; but don't join yourself with those who are scorners, nor count yourself with those who are tormented. 77 For you have a treasure of works laid up with the Most High, but it won't be shown you until the last times. 78 For concerning death the teaching is: When the decisive sentence has gone out from the Most High that a man shall die, as the spirit leaves the body to return again to him who gave it, it adores the glory of the Most High first of all. 79 And if it is one of those who have been scorners and have not kept the way of the Most High, and that have despised his law, and who hate those who fear God, 80 these spirits won't enter into habitations, but will wander and be in torments immediately, ever grieving and sad, in seven ways. 81 The first way, because they have despised the law of the Most High. 82 The second way, because they can't now make a good repentance that they may live. 83 The third way, they will see the reward laid up for those who have believed the covenants of the Most High. 84 The fourth way, they will consider the torment laid up for themselves in the last days. 85 The fifth way, they will see the dwelling places of the others guarded by angels, with great quietness. 86 The sixth way, they will see how immediately some of them will pass into torment. 87 The seventh way, which is more grievous than all the aforesaid ways, because they will pine away in confusion and be consumed with shame, and will be withered up by fears, seeing the glory of the Most High before whom they have sinned while living, and before whom they will be judged in the last times. 88 "Now this is the order of those who have kept the ways of the Most High, when they will be separated from their mortal body. 89 In the time that they lived in it, they painfully served the Most High, and were in jeopardy every hour, that they might keep the law of the lawgiver perfectly. 90 Therefore this is the teaching concerning them: 91 First of all they will see with great joy the glory of him who takes them up, for they will have rest in seven orders. 92 The first order, because they have labored with great effort to overcome the evil thought which was fashioned together with them, that it might not lead them astray from life into death. 93 The second order, because they see the perplexity in which the souls of the ungodly wander, and the punishment that awaits them. 94 The third order, they see the testimony which he who fashioned them gives concerning them, that while they lived they kept the law which was given them in trust. 95 The fourth order, they understand the rest which, being gathered in their chambers, they now enjoy with great quietness, guarded by angels, and the glory that awaits them in the last days. 96 The fifth order, they rejoice that they have now escaped from that which is corruptible, and that they will inherit that which is to come, while they see in addition the difficulty and the pain from which they have been delivered, and the spacious liberty which they will receive with joy and immortality. 97 The sixth order, when it is shown to them how their face will shine like the sun, and how they will be made like the light of the stars, being incorruptible from then on. 98 The seventh order, which is greater than all the previously mentioned orders, because they will rejoice with confidence, and because they will be bold without confusion, and will be glad without fear, for they hurry to see the face of him whom in their lifetime they served, and from whom they will receive their reward in glory. 99 This is the order of the souls of the just, as from henceforth is announced to them. Previously mentioned are the ways of torture which those who would not give heed will suffer from after this." 100 I answered, "Will time therefore be given to the souls after they are separated from the bodies, that they may see what you have described to me?" 101 He said, "Their freedom will be for seven days, that for seven days they may see the things you have been told, and afterwards they will be gathered together in their habitations." 102 I answered, "If I have found favor in your sight, show further to me your servant whether in the day of judgment the just will be able to intercede for the ungodly or to entreat the Most High for them, 103 whether fathers for children, or children

for parents, or kindred for kindred, or kinsfolk for their next of kin, or friends for those who are most dear." 104 He answered me, "Since you have found favor in my sight, I will show you this also. The day of judgment is a day of decision, and displays to all the seal of truth. Even as now a father doesn't send his son, or a son his father, or a master his slave, or a friend him that is most dear, that in his place he may understand, or sleep, or eat, or be healed, 105 so no one will ever pray for another in that day, neither will one lay a burden on another, for then everyone will each bear his own righteousness or unrighteousness." 106 I answered, "How do we now find that first Abraham prayed for the people of Sodom, and Moses for the ancestors who sinned in the wilderness, 107 and Joshua after him for Israel in the days of Achan, 108 and Samuel in the days of Saul, and David for the plague, and Solomon for those who would worship in the sanctuary, 109 and Elijah for those that received rain, and for the dead, that he might live, 110 and Hezekiah for the people in the days of Sennacherib, and many others prayed for many? 111 If therefore now, when corruption has grown and unrighteousness increased, the righteous have prayed for the ungodly, why will it not be so then also?" 112 He answered me, "This present world is not the end. The full glory doesn't remain in it. Therefore those who were able prayed for the weak. 113 But the day of judgment will be the end of this age, and the beginning of the immortality to come, in which corruption has passed away, 114 intemperance is at an end, infidelity is cut off, but righteousness has grown, and truth has sprung up. 115 Then no one will be able to have mercy on him who is condemned in judgment, nor to harm someone who is victorious." 116 I answered then, "This is my first and last saying, that it would have been better if the earth had not produced Adam, or else, when it had produced him, to have restrained him from sinning. 117 For what profit is it for all who are in this present time to live in heaviness, and after death to look for punishment? 118 O Adam, what have you done? For though it was you who sinned, the evil hasn't fallen on you alone, but on all of us who come from you. 119 For what profit is it to us, if an immortal time is promised to us, but we have done deeds that bring death? 120 And that there is promised us an everlasting hope, but we have most miserably failed? 121 And that there are reserved habitations of health and safety, but we have lived wickedly? 122 And that the glory of the Most High will defend those who have led a pure life, but we have walked in the most wicked ways of all? 123 And that a paradise will be revealed, whose fruit endures without decay, in which is abundance and healing, but we won't enter into it, 124 for we have lived in perverse ways? 125 And that the faces of those who have practiced self-control will shine more than the stars, but our faces will be blacker than darkness? 126 For while we lived and committed iniquity, we didn't consider what we would have to suffer after death." 127 Then he answered, "This is the significance of the battle which humans born on the earth will fight: 128 if they are overcome, they will suffer as you have said, but if they get the victory, they will receive the thing that I say. 129 For this is the way that Moses spoke to the people while he lived, saying, 'Choose life, that you may live!' 130 Nevertheless they didn't believe him or the prophets after him, not even me, who have spoken to them. 131 Therefore there won't be such heaviness in their destruction, as there will be joy over those who are assured of salvation." 132 Then I answered, "I know, Lord, that the Most High is now called merciful, in that he has mercy upon those who have not yet come into the world; 133 and compassionate, in that he has compassion upon those who turn to his law; 134 and patient, in that he is patient with those who have sinned, since they are his creatures; 135 and bountiful, in that he is ready to give rather than to take away; 136 and very merciful, in that he multiplies more and more mercies to those who are present, and who are past, and also to those who are to come— 137 for if he wasn't merciful, the world wouldn't continue with those who dwell in it— 138 and one who forgives, for if he didn't forgive out of his goodness, that those who have committed iniquities might be relieved of them, not even one ten thousandth part of mankind would remain living; 139 and a judge, for if he didn't pardon those who were created by his word, and blot out the multitude of sins, 140 there would perhaps be very few left of an innumerable multitude."

Esdras 2 Chapter 8

1 He answered me, "The Most High has made this world for many, but the world to come for few. 2 Now I will tell you a parable, Esdras. Just as when you ask the earth, it will say to you that it gives very much clay from which earthen vessels are made, but little dust that gold comes from. Even so is the course of the present world. 3 Many have been created, but few will be saved." 4 I answered, "Drink your fill of understanding then, O my soul, and let my heart devour wisdom. 5 For you have come apart from your will, and depart against your will, for you have only been given a short time to live. 6 O Lord over us, grant to your servant that we may pray before you, and give us seed for our heart and cultivation for our understanding, that fruit may grow from it, by which everyone who is corrupt, who bears the likeness of a man, may live. 7 For you alone exist, and we all are one workmanship of your hands, just as you have said. 8 Because you give life to the body that is now fashioned in the womb, and give it members, your creature is preserved in fire and water, and your workmanship endures nine months as your creation which is created in it. 9 But that which keeps and that which is kept will both be kept by your keeping. When the womb gives up again what has grown in it, 10 you have commanded that out of the parts of the body, that is to say, out of the breasts, be given milk, which is the fruit of the breasts, 11 that the body that is fashioned may be nourished for a time, and afterwards you guide it in your mercy. 12 Yes, you have brought it up in your righteousness, nurtured it in your law, and corrected it with your judgment. 13 You put it to death as your creation, and make it live as your work. 14 If therefore you lightly and suddenly destroy him which with so great labor was fashioned by your commandment, to what purpose was he made? 15 Now therefore I will speak. About man in general, you know best, but about your people for whose sake I am sorry, 16 and for your inheritance, for whose cause I mourn, for Israel, for whom I am heavy, and for the seed of Jacob, for whose sake I am troubled, 17 therefore I will begin to pray before you for myself and for them; for I see the failings of us who dwell in the land, 18 but I have heard the swiftness of the judgment which is to come. 19 Therefore hear my voice, and understand my saying, and I will speak before you." The beginning of the words of Esdras, before he was taken up. He said, 20 "O Lord, you who remain forever, whose eyes are exalted, and whose chambers are in the air, 21 whose throne is beyond measure, whose glory is beyond comprehension, before whom the army of angels stand with trembling, 22 at whose bidding they are changed to wind and fire, whose word is sure, and sayings constant, whose ordinance is strong, and commandment fearful, 23 whose look dries up the depths, and whose indignation makes the mountains to melt away, and whose truth bears witness— 24 hear, O Lord, the prayer of your servant, and give ear to the petition of your handiwork. 25 Attend to my words, for as long as I live, I will speak, and as long as I have understanding, I will answer. 26 Don't look at the sins of your people, but on those who have served you in truth. 27 Don't regard the doings of those who act wickedly, but of those who have kept your covenants in affliction. 28 Don't think about those who have lived wickedly before you, but remember those who have willingly known your fear. 29 Let it not be your will to destroy those who have lived like cattle, but look at those who have clearly taught your law. 30 Don't be indignant at those who are deemed worse than animals, but love those who have always put their trust in your glory. 31 For we and our fathers have passed our lives in ways that bring death, but you are called merciful because of us sinners. 32 For if you have a desire to have mercy upon us who have no works of righteousness, then you will be called merciful. 33 For the just, which have many good works laid up with you, will be rewarded for their own deeds. 34 For what is man, that you should take displeasure at him? Or what is a corruptible race, that you should be so bitter toward it? 35 For in truth, there is no man among those who are born who has not done wickedly, and among them who have lived, there is none which have not done wrong. 36 For in this, O Lord, your righteousness and your goodness will be declared, if you are merciful to those who have no store of good works." 37 Then he answered me, "Some things you have spoken rightly, and it will happen according to your words. 38 For indeed I will not think about the fashioning of those who have sinned, or about their death, their judgment, or their destruction; 39 but I will rejoice over the creation of the righteous and their pilgrimage, their salvation, and the reward that they will have. 40 Therefore as I have spoken, so it will be. 41 For as the farmer sows many seeds in the ground, and plants many trees, and yet not all that is sown will come up in due season, neither will all that is planted take root, even so those who are sown in the world will not all be saved." 42 Then I answered, "If I have found favor, let me speak before you. 43 If the farmer's seed doesn't come up because it hasn't received your rain in due season, or if it is ruined by too much rain and perishes, 44 likewise man, who is formed with your hands and is called your own image, because he is made like you, for whose sake you have formed all things, even him have you made like the farmer's seed. 45 Don't be angry with us, but spare your people and have mercy upon your inheritance, for you have mercy upon your own creation." 46 Then he answered me, "Things present are for those who live now, and things to come for those who will live hereafter. 47 For you come far short of being able to love my creature more than I. But you have compared yourself to the unrighteous. Don't do that! 48 Yet in this will you be admirable to the Most High, 49 in that you have humbled yourself, as it becomes you,

and have not judged yourself among the righteous, so as to be much glorified. ⁵⁰ For many grievous miseries will fall on those who dwell in the world in the last times, because they have walked in great pride. ⁵¹ But understand for yourself, and for those who inquire concerning the glory of those like you, ⁵² because paradise is opened to you. The tree of life is planted. The time to come is prepared. Plenteousness is made ready. A city is built. Rest is allowed. Goodness is perfected, and wisdom is perfected beforehand. ⁵³ The root of evil is sealed up from you. Weakness is done away from you, and death is hidden. Hell and corruption have fled into forgetfulness. ⁵⁴ Sorrows have passed away, and in the end, the treasure of immortality is shown. ⁵⁵ Therefore ask no more questions concerning the multitude of those who perish. ⁵⁶ For when they had received liberty, they despised the Most High, scorned his law, and forsook his ways. ⁵⁷ Moreover they have trodden down his righteous, ⁵⁸ and said in their heart that there is no God—even knowing that they must die. ⁵⁹ For as the things I have said will welcome you, so thirst and pain which are prepared for them. For the Most High didn't intend that men should be destroyed, ⁶⁰ but those who are created have themselves defiled the name of him who made them, and were unthankful to him who prepared life for them. ⁶¹ Therefore my judgment is now at hand, ⁶² which I have not shown to all men, but to you, and a few like you." Then I answered, ⁶³"Behold, O Lord, now you have shown me the multitude of the wonders which you will do in the last times, but you haven't shown me when."

Esdras 2 Chapter 9

¹He answered me, "Measure diligently within yourself. When you see that a certain part of the signs are past, which have been told you beforehand, ² then will you understand that it is the very time in which the Most High will visit the world which was made by him. ³ When earthquakes, tumult of peoples, plans of nations, wavering of leaders, and confusion of princes are seen in the world, ⁴ then will you understand that the Most High spoke of these things from the days that were of old, from the beginning. ⁵ For just as with everything that is made in the world, the beginning is evident and the end manifest, ⁶ so also are the times of the Most High: the beginnings are manifest in wonders and mighty works, and the end in effects and signs. ⁷ Everyone who will be saved, and will be able to escape by his works, or by faith by which they have believed, ⁸ will be preserved from the said perils, and will see my salvation in my land and within my borders, which I have sanctified for myself from the beginning. ⁹ Then those who now have abused my ways will be amazed. Those who have cast them away despitefully will live in torments. ¹⁰ For as many as in their life have received benefits, and yet have not known me, ¹¹ and as many as have scorned my law, while they still had liberty and when an opportunity to repent was open to them, didn't understand, but despised it, ¹² must know it in torment after death. ¹³ Therefore don't be curious any longer how the ungodly will be punished, but inquire how the righteous will be saved, those who the world belongs to, and for whom the world was created." ¹⁴ I answered, ¹⁵ "I have said before, and now speak, and will say it again hereafter, that there are more of those who perish than of those who will be saved, ¹⁶ like a wave is greater than a drop." ¹⁷ He answered me, "Just as the field is, so also the seed. As the flowers are, so are the colors. As the work is, so also is the judgment on it. As is the farmer, so also is his threshing floor. For there was a time in the world ¹⁸ when I was preparing for those who now live, before the world was made for them to dwell in. Then no one spoke against me, ¹⁹ for no one existed. But now those who are created in this world that is prepared, both with a table that doesn't fail and a law which is unsearchable, are corrupted in their ways. ²⁰ So I considered my world, and behold, it was destroyed, and my earth, and behold, it was in peril, because of the plans that had come into it. ²¹ I saw and spared them, but not greatly, and saved myself a grape out of a cluster, and a plant out of a great forest. ²² Let the multitude perish then, which were born in vain. Let my grape be saved, and my plant, for I have made them perfect with great labor. ²³ Nevertheless, if you will wait seven more days—however don't fast in them, ²⁴ but go into a field of flowers, where no house is built, and eat only of the flowers of the field, and you shall taste no flesh, and shall drink no wine, but shall eat flowers only— ²⁵ and pray to the Most High continually, then I will come and talk with you." ²⁶ So I went my way, just as he commanded me, into the field which is called Ardat. There I sat among the flowers, and ate of the herbs of the field, and this food satisfied me. ²⁷ It came to pass after seven days that I lay on the grass, and my heart was troubled again, like before. ²⁸ My mouth was opened, and I began to speak before the Lord Most High, and said, ²⁹ "O Lord, you showed yourself among us, to our fathers in the wilderness, when they went out of Egypt, and when they came into the wilderness, where no man treads and that bears no fruit. ³⁰ You said, 'Hear me, O Israel. Heed my words, O seed of Jacob. ³¹ For behold, I

sow my law in you, and it will bring forth fruit in you, and you will be glorified in it forever.' ³² But our fathers, who received the law, didn't keep it, and didn't observe the statutes. The fruit of the law didn't perish, for it couldn't, because it was yours. ³³ Yet those who received it perished, because they didn't keep the thing that was sown in them. ³⁴ Behold, it is a custom that when the ground has received seed, or the sea a ship, or any vessel food or drink, and when it comes to pass that that which is sown, or that which is launched, ³⁵ or the things which have been received, should come to an end, these come to an end, but the receptacles remain. Yet with us, it doesn't happen that way. ³⁶ For we who have received the law will perish by sin, along with our heart which received it. ³⁷ Notwithstanding the law doesn't perish, but remains in its honor." ³⁸ When I spoke these things in my heart, I looked around me with my eyes, and on my right side I saw a woman, and behold, she mourned and wept with a loud voice, and was much grieved in mind. Her clothes were torn, and she had ashes on her head. ³⁹ Then let I my thoughts go in which I was occupied, and turned myself to her, ⁴⁰ and said to her, "Why are you weeping? Why are you grieved in your mind?" ⁴¹ She said to me, "Leave me alone, my Lord, that I may weep for myself and add to my sorrow, for I am very troubled in my mind, and brought very low." ⁴² I said to her, "What ails you? Tell me." ⁴³ She said to me, "I, your servant, was barren and had no child, though I had a husband thirty years. ⁴⁴ Every hour and every day these thirty years I made my prayer to the Most High day and night. ⁴⁵ It came to pass after thirty years that God heard me, your handmaid, and saw my low estate, and considered my trouble, and gave me a son. I rejoiced in him greatly, I and my husband, and all my neighbors. We gave great honor to the Mighty One. ⁴⁶ I nourished him with great care. ⁴⁷ So when he grew up, and I came to take him a wife, I made him a feast day.

Esdras 2 Chapter 10

¹"So it came to pass that when my son was entered into his wedding chamber, he fell down and died. ² Then we all put out the lamps, and all my neighbors rose up to comfort me. I remained quiet until the second day at night. ³ It came to pass, when they had all stopped consoling me, encouraging me to be quiet, then rose I up by night, and fled, and came here into this field, as you see. ⁴ Now I don't intend to return into the city, but to stay here, and not eat or drink, but to continually mourn and fast until I die." ⁵ Then I left the reflections I was engaged in, and answered her in anger, ⁶ "You most foolish woman, don't you see our mourning, and what has happened to us? ⁷ For Zion the mother of us all is full of sorrow, and much humbled. ⁸ It is right now to mourn deeply, since we all mourn, and to be sorrowful, since we are all in sorrow, but you are mourning for one son. ⁹ Ask the earth, and she will tell you that it is she which ought to mourn for so many that grow upon her. ¹⁰ For out of her, all had their beginnings, and others will come; and, behold, almost all of them walk into destruction, and the multitude of them is utterly doomed. ¹¹ Who then should mourn more, she who has lost so great a multitude, or you, who are grieved but for one? ¹² But if you say to me, 'My lamentation is not like the earth's, for I have lost the fruit of my womb, which I brought forth with pains, and bare with sorrows;' ¹³ but it is with the earth after the manner of the earth. The multitude present in it has gone as it came. ¹⁴ Then say I to you, 'Just as you have brought forth with sorrow, even so the earth also has given her fruit, namely, people, ever since the beginning to him who made her.' ¹⁵ Now therefore keep your sorrow to yourself, and bear with a good courage the adversities which have happened to you. ¹⁶ For if you will acknowledge the decree of God to be just, you will both receive your son in time, and will be praised among women. ¹⁷ Go your way then into the city to your husband." ¹⁸ She said to me, "I won't do that. I will not go into the city, but I will die here." ¹⁹ So I proceeded to speak further to her, and said, ²⁰ "Don't do so, but allow yourself to be persuaded by reason of the adversities of Zion; and be comforted by reason of the sorrow of Jerusalem. ²¹ For you see that our sanctuary has been laid waste, our altar broken down, our temple destroyed, ²² our lute has been brought low, our song is put to silence, our rejoicing is at an end, the light of our candlestick is put out, the ark of our covenant is plundered, our holy things are defiled, and the name that we are called is profaned. Our free men are despitefully treated, our priests are burned, our Levites have gone into captivity, our virgins are defiled and our wives ravished, our righteous men carried away, our little ones betrayed, our young men are brought into bondage, and our strong men have become weak. ²³ What is more than all, the seal of Zion has now lost the seal of her honor, and is delivered into the hands of those who hate us. ²⁴ Therefore shake off your great heaviness, and put away from yourself the multitude of sorrows, that the Mighty One may be merciful to you again, and the Most High may give you rest, even ease from your troubles." ²⁵ It came to pass while I was talking with her, behold, her face suddenly began to shine exceedingly, and her

countenance glistered like lightning, so that I was very afraid of her, and wondered what this meant. 26 Behold, suddenly she made a great and very fearful cry, so that the earth shook at the noise. 27 I looked, and behold, the woman appeared to me no more, but there was a city built, and a place shown itself from large foundations. Then I was afraid, and cried with a loud voice, 28 "Where is Uriel the angel, who came to me at the first? For he has caused me to fall into this great trance, and my end has turned into corruption, and my prayer a reproach!" 29 As I was speaking these words, behold, the angel who had come to me at first came to me, and he looked at me. 30 Behold, I lay as one who had been dead, and my understanding was taken from me. He took me by the right hand, and comforted me, and set me on my feet, and said to me, 31 "What ails you? Why are you so troubled? Why is your understanding and the thoughts of your heart troubled?" 32 I said, "Because you have forsaken me; yet I did according to your words, and went into the field, and, behold, I have seen, and still see, that which I am not able to explain." 33 He said to me, "Stand up like a man, and I will instruct you." 34 Then I said, "Speak on, my Lord; only don't forsake me, lest I die before my time. 35 For I have seen what I didn't know, and hear what I don't know. 36 Or is my sense deceived, or my soul in a dream? 37 Now therefore I beg you to explain to your servant what this vision means." 38 He answered me, "Listen to me, and I will inform you, and tell you about the things you are afraid of, for the Most High has revealed many secret things to you. 39 He has seen that your way is righteous, because you are continually sorry for your people, and make great lamentation for Zion. 40 This therefore is the meaning of the vision. 41 The woman who appeared to you a little while ago, whom you saw mourning, and began to comfort her, 42 but now you no longer see the likeness of the woman, but a city under construction appeared to you, 43 and she told you of the death of her son, this is the interpretation: 44 This woman, whom you saw, is Zion, whom you now see as a city being built. 45 She told you that she had been barren for thirty years because there were three thousand years in the world in which there was no offering as yet offered in her. 46 And it came to pass after three thousand years that Solomon built the city and offered offerings. It was then that the barren bore a son. 47 She told you that she nourished him with great care. That was the dwelling in Jerusalem. 48 When she said to you, 'My son died when he entered into his marriage chamber, and that misfortune befell her,' this was the destruction that came to Jerusalem. 49 Behold, you saw her likeness, how she mourned for her son, and you began to comfort her for what has happened to her. These were the things to be opened to you. 50 For now the Most High, seeing that you are sincerely grieved and suffer from your whole heart for her, has shown you the brightness of her glory and the attractiveness of her beauty. 51 Therefore I asked you to remain in the field where no house was built, 52 for I knew that the Most High would show you this to you. 53 Therefore I commanded you to come into the field, where no foundation of any building was. 54 For no human construction could stand in the place in which the city of the Most High was to be shown. 55 Therefore don't be afraid nor let your heart be terrified, but go your way in and see the beauty and greatness of the building, as much as your eyes are able to see. 56 Then will you hear as much as your ears may comprehend. 57 For you are more blessed than many, and are called by name to be with the Most High, like only a few. 58 But tomorrow at night you shall remain here, 59 and so the Most High will show you those visions in dreams of what the Most High will do to those who live on the earth in the last days." So I slept that night and another, as he commanded me.

Esdras 2 Chapter 11

1 "It came to pass the second night that I saw a dream, and behold, an eagle which had twelve feathered wings and three heads came up from the sea. 2 I saw, and behold, she spread her wings over all the earth, and all the winds of heaven blew on her, and the clouds were gathered together against her. 3 I saw, and out of her wings there grew other wings near them; and they became little, tiny wings. 4 But her heads were at rest. The head in the middle was larger than the other heads, yet rested it with them. 5 Moreover I saw, and behold, the eagle flew with her wings to reign over the earth and over those who dwell therein. 6 I saw how all things under heaven were subject to her, and no one spoke against her—no, not one creature on earth. 7 I saw, and behold, the eagle rose on her talons, and uttered her voice to her wings, saying, 8 'Don't all watch at the same time. Let each one sleep in his own place and watch in turn; 9 but let the heads be preserved for the last.' 10 I saw, and behold, the voice didn't come out of her heads, but from the midst of her body. 11 I counted her wings that were near the others, and behold, there were eight of them. 12 I saw, and behold, on the right side one wing arose and reigned over all the earth. 13 When it reigned, the end of it came, and it disappeared, so that its place appeared no more. The next wing rose up and reigned, and it ruled a long time. 14 It

happened that when it reigned, its end came also, so that it disappeared, like the first. 15 Behold, a voice came to it, and said, 16 'Listen, you who have ruled over the earth all this time! I proclaim this to you, before you disappear, 17 none after you will rule as long as you, not even half as long.' 18 Then the third arose, and ruled as the others before, and it also disappeared. 19 So it went with all the wings one after another, as every one ruled, and then disappeared. 20 I saw, and behold, in process of time the wings that followed were set up on the right side, that they might rule also. Some of them ruled, but in a while they disappeared. 21 Some of them also were set up, but didn't rule. 22 After this I saw, and behold, the twelve wings disappeared, along with two of the little wings. 23 There was no more left on the eagle's body, except the three heads that rested, and six little wings. 24 I saw, and behold, two little wings divided themselves from the six and remained under the head that was on the right side; but four remained in their place. 25 I saw, and behold, these under wings planned to set themselves up and to rule. 26 I saw, and behold, there was one set up, but in a while it disappeared. 27 A second also did so, and it disappeared faster than the first. 28 I saw, and behold, the two that remained also planned between themselves to reign. 29 While they thought about it, behold, one of the heads that were at rest awakened, the one that was in the middle, for that was greater than the two other heads. 30 I saw how it joined the two other heads with it. 31 Behold, the head turned with those who were with it, and ate the two under wings that planned to reign. 32 But this head held the whole earth in possession, and ruled over those who dwell in it with much oppression. It had stronger governance over the world than all the wings that had gone before. 33 After this I saw, and behold, the head also that was in the middle suddenly disappeared, like the wings. 34 But the two heads remained, which also reigned the same way over the earth and over those who dwell in it. 35 I saw, and behold, the head on the right side devoured the one that was on the left side. 36 Then I heard a voice, which said to me, 'Look in front of you, and consider the thing that you see.' 37 I saw, and behold, something like a lion roused out of the woods roaring. I heard how he sent out a man's voice to the eagle, and spoke, saying, 38 'Listen and I will talk with you. The Most High will say to you, 39 "Aren't you the one that remains of the four animals whom I made to reign in my world, that the end of my times might come through them? 40 The fourth came and overcame all the animals that were past, and ruled the world with great trembling, and the whole extent of the earth with grievous oppression. He lived on the earth such a long time with deceit. 41 You have judged the earth, but not with truth. 42 For you have afflicted the meek, you have hurt the peaceful, you have hated those who speak truth, you have loved liars, destroyed the dwellings of those who produced fruit, and threw down the walls of those who did you no harm. 43 Your insolence has come up to the Most High, and your pride to the Mighty. 44 The Most High also has looked at his times, and behold, they are ended, and his ages are fulfilled. 45 Therefore appear no more, you eagle, nor your horrible wings, nor your evil little wings, nor your cruel heads, nor your hurtful talons, nor all your worthless body, 46 that all the earth may be refreshed and relieved, being delivered from your violence, and that she may hope for the judgment and mercy of him who made her."'"

Esdras 2 Chapter 12

1 "It came to pass, while the lion spoke these words to the eagle, I saw, 2 and behold, the head that remained disappeared, and the two wings which went over to it arose and set themselves up to reign; and their kingdom was brief and full of uproar. 3 I saw, and behold, they disappeared, and the whole body of the eagle was burned, so that the earth was in great fear. Then I woke up because of great perplexity of mind and great fear, and said to my spirit, 4 'Behold, you have done this to me, because you search out the ways of the Most High. 5 Behold, I am still weary in my mind, and very weak in my spirit. There isn't even a little strength in me, because of the great fear with which I was frightened tonight. 6 Therefore I will now ask the Most High that he would strengthen me to the end.' 7 Then I said, 'O sovereign Lord, if I have found favor in your sight, and if I am justified with you more than many others, and if my prayer has indeed come up before your face, 8 strengthen me then, and show me, your servant, the interpretation and plain meaning of this fearful vision, that you may fully comfort my soul. 9 For you have judged me worthy to show me the end of time and the last events of the times.' 10 He said to me, 'This is the interpretation of this vision which you saw: 11 The eagle, whom you saw come up from the sea, is the fourth kingdom which appeared in a vision to your brother Daniel. 12 But it was not explained to him, as I now explain it to you or have explained it. 13 Behold, the days come that a kingdom will rise up on earth, and it will be feared more than all the kingdoms that were before it. 14 Twelve kings will reign in it, one after another. 15 Of those, the second will begin to reign, and will reign a longer time

than others of the twelve. 16 This is the interpretation of the twelve wings which you saw. 17 As for when you heard a voice which spoke, not going out from the heads, but from the midst of its body, this is the interpretation: 18 That after the time of that kingdom, there will arise no small contentions, and it will stand in peril of falling. Nevertheless, it won't fall then, but will be restored again to its former power. 19 You saw the eight under wings sticking to her wings. This is the interpretation: 20 That in it eight kings will arise, whose times will be short and their years swift. 21 Two of them will perish when the middle time approaches. Four will be kept for a while until the time of the ending of it will approach; but two will be kept to the end. 22 You saw three heads resting. This is the interpretation: 23 In its last days, the Most High will raise up three kingdoms and renew many things in them. They will rule over the earth, 24 and over those who dwell in it, with much oppression, more than all those who were before them. Therefore they are called the heads of the eagle. 25 For these are those who will accomplish her wickedness, and who will finish her last actions. 26 You saw that the great head disappeared. It signifies that one of them will die on his bed, and yet with pain. 27 But for the two that remained, the sword will devour them. 28 For the sword of the one will devour him that was with him, but he will also fall by the sword in the last days. 29 You saw two under wings passing over to the head that is on the right side. 30 This is the interpretation: These are they whom the Most High has kept to his end. This is the brief reign that was full of trouble, as you saw. 31 'The lion, whom you saw rising up out of the forest, roaring, speaking to the eagle, and rebuking her for her unrighteousness, and all her words which you have heard, 32 this is the anointed one, whom the Most High has kept to the end [of days, who will spring up out of the seed of David, and he will come and speak] to them and reprove them for their wickedness and unrighteousness, and will heap up before them their contemptuous dealings. 33 For at first he will set them alive in his judgment, and when he has reproved them, he will destroy them. 34 For he will deliver the rest of my people with mercy, those who have been preserved throughout my borders, and he will make them joyful until the coming of the end, even the day of judgment, about which I have spoken to you from the beginning. 35 This is the dream that you saw, and this is its interpretation. 36 Only you have been worthy to know the secret of the Most High. 37 Therefore write all these things that you have seen in a book, and put it in a secret place. 38 You shall teach them to the wise of your people, whose hearts you know are able to comprehend and keep these secrets. 39 But wait here yourself seven more days, that you may be shown whatever it pleases the Most High to show you.' Then he departed from me. 40 It came to pass, when all the people saw that the seven days were past, and I had not come again into the city, they all gathered together, from the least to the greatest, and came to me, and spoke to me, saying, 41 'How have we offended you? What evil have we done against you, that you have utterly forsaken us, and sit in this place? 42 For of all the prophets, only you are left to us, like a cluster of the vintage, and like a lamp in a dark place, and like a harbor for a ship saved from the tempest. 43 Aren't the evils which have come to us sufficient? 44 If you will forsake us, how much better had it been for us if we also had been consumed in the burning of Zion! 45 For we are not better than those who died there.' Then they wept with a loud voice. I answered them, 46 'Take courage, O Israel! Don't be sorrowful, you house of Jacob; 47 for the Most High remembers you. The Mighty has not forgotten you forever. 48 As for me, I have not forsaken you. I haven't departed from you; but I have come into this place to pray for the desolation of Zion, and that I might seek mercy for the humiliation of your sanctuary. 49 Now go your way, every man to his own house, and after these days I will come to you.' 50 So the people went their way into the city, as I told them to do. 51 But I sat in the field seven days, as the angel commanded me. In those days, I ate only of the flowers of the field, and my food was from plants."

Esdras 2 Chapter 13

1 "It came to pass after seven days, I dreamed a dream by night. 2 Behold, a wind arose from the sea that moved all its waves. 3 I saw, and behold, [this wind caused to come up from the midst of the sea something like the appearance of a man. I saw, and behold,] that man flew with the clouds of heaven. When he turned his face to look, everything that he saw trembled. 4 Whenever the voice went out of his mouth, all who heard his voice melted, like the wax melts when it feels the fire. 5 After this I saw, and behold, an innumerable multitude of people was gathered together from the four winds of heaven to make war against the man who came out of the sea. 6 I saw, and behold, he carved himself a great mountain, and flew up onto it. 7 I tried to see the region or place from which the mountain was carved, and I couldn't. 8 After this I saw, and behold, all those who were gathered together to fight against him were very afraid, and yet they dared to fight. 9 Behold, as he saw the assault of the multitude that came, he didn't lift up his hand, or hold a spear or any weapon of war; 10 but I saw only how he sent out of his mouth something like a flood of fire, and out of his lips a flaming breath, and out of his tongue he shot out a storm of sparks. 11 These were all mixed together: the flood of fire, the flaming breath, and the great storm, and fell upon the assault of the multitude which was prepared to fight, and burned up every one of them, so that all of a sudden an innumerable multitude was seen to be nothing but dust of ashes and smell of smoke. When I saw this, I was amazed. 12 Afterward, I saw the same man come down from the mountain, and call to himself another multitude which was peaceful. 13 Many people came to him. Some of them were glad. Some were sorry. Some of them were bound, and some others brought some of those as offerings. Then through great fear I woke up and prayed to the Most High, and said, 14 'You have shown your servant these wonders from the beginning, and have counted me worthy that you should receive my prayer. 15 Now show me also the interpretation of this dream. 16 For as I conceive in my understanding, woe to those who will be left in those days! Much more woe to those who are not left! 17 For those who were not left will be in heaviness, 18 understanding the things that are laid up in the latter days, but not attaining to them. 19 But woe to them also who are left, because they will see great perils and much distress, like these dreams declare. 20 Yet is it better for one to be in peril and to come into these things, than to pass away as a cloud out of the world, and not to see the things that will happen in the last days.' He answered me, 21 'I will tell you the interpretation of the vision, and I will also open to you the things about which you mentioned. 22 You have spoken of those who are left behind. This is the interpretation: 23 He that will endure the peril in that time will protect those who fall into danger, even those who have works and faith toward the Almighty. 24 Know therefore that those who are left behind are more blessed than those who are dead. 25 These are the interpretations of the vision: Whereas you saw a man coming up from the midst of the sea, 26 this is he whom the Most High has been keeping for many ages, who by his own self will deliver his creation. He will direct those who are left behind. 27 Whereas you saw that out of his mouth came wind, fire, and storm, 28 and whereas he held neither spear, nor any weapon of war, but destroyed the assault of that multitude which came to fight against him, this is the interpretation: 29 Behold, the days come when the Most High will begin to deliver those who are on the earth. 30 Astonishment of mind will come upon those who dwell on the earth. 31 One will plan to make war against another, city against city, place against place, people against people, and kingdom against kingdom. 32 It will be, when these things come to pass, and the signs happen which I showed you before, then my Son will be revealed, whom you saw as a man ascending. 33 It will be, when all the nations hear his voice, every man will leave his own land and the battle they have against one another. 34 An innumerable multitude will be gathered together, as you saw, desiring to come and to fight against him. 35 But he will stand on the top of Mount Zion. 36 Zion will come, and will be shown to all men, being prepared and built, like you saw the mountain carved without hands. 37 My Son will rebuke the nations which have come for their wickedness, with plagues that are like a storm, 38 and will rebuke them to their face with their evil thoughts, and the torments with which they will be tormented, which are like a flame. He will destroy them without labor by the law, which is like fire. 39 Whereas you saw that he gathered to himself another multitude that was peaceful, 40 these are the ten tribes which were led away out of their own land in the time of Osea the king, whom Salmanasar the king of the Assyrians led away captive, and he carried them beyond the River, and they were taken into another land. 41 But they made this plan among themselves, that they would leave the multitude of the heathen, and go out into a more distant region, where mankind had never lived, 42 that there they might keep their statutes which they had not kept in their own land. 43 They entered by the narrow passages of the river Euphrates. 44 For the Most High then did signs for them, and stopped the springs of the River until they had passed over. 45 For through that country there was a long way to go, namely, of a year and a half. The same region is called Arzareth. 46 Then they lived there until the latter time. Now when they begin to come again, 47 the Most High stops the springs of the River again, that they may go through. Therefore you saw the multitude gathered together with peace. 48 But those who are left behind of your people are those who are found within my holy border. 49 It will be therefore when he will destroy the multitude of the nations that are gathered together, he will defend the people who remain. 50 Then will he show them very many wonders.' 51 Then I said, 'O sovereign Lord, explain this to me: Why have I seen the man coming up from the midst of the sea?' 52 He said to me, as no one can explore or

know what is in the depths of the sea, even so no man on earth can see my Son, or those who are with him, except in the time of his day. ⁵³ This is the interpretation of the dream which you saw, and for this only you are enlightened about this, ⁵⁴ for you have forsaken your own ways, and applied your diligence to mine, and have searched out my law. ⁵⁵ You have ordered your life in wisdom, and have called understanding your mother. ⁵⁶ Therefore I have shown you this, for there is a reward laid up with the Most High. It will be, after another three days I will speak other things to you, and declare to you mighty and wondrous things.' ⁵⁷ Then I went out and passed into the field, giving praise and thanks greatly to the Most High because of his wonders, which he did from time to time, ⁵⁸ and because he governs the time, and such things as happen in their seasons. So I sat there three days."

Esdras 2 Chapter 14

¹ It came to pass upon the third day, I sat under an oak, and, behold, a voice came out of a bush near me, and said, "Esdras, Esdras!" ² I said, "Here I am, Lord," and I stood up on my feet. ³ Then he said to me, "I revealed myself in a bush and talked with Moses when my people were in bondage in Egypt. ⁴ I sent him, and he led my people out of Egypt. I brought him up to Mount Sinai, where I kept him with me for many days. ⁵ I told him many wondrous things, and showed him the secrets of the times and the end of the seasons. I commanded him, saying, ⁶ 'You shall publish these openly, and these you shall hide.' ⁷ Now I say to you: ⁸ Lay up in your heart the signs that I have shown, the dreams that you have seen, and the interpretations which you have heard; ⁹ for you will be taken away from men, and from now on you will live with my Son and with those who are like you, until the times have ended. ¹⁰ For the world has lost its youth, and the times begin to grow old. ¹¹ For the age is divided into twelve parts, and ten parts of it are already gone, even the half of the tenth part. ¹² There remain of it two parts after the middle of the tenth part. ¹³ Now therefore set your house in order, reprove your people, comfort the lowly among them, and instruct those of them who are wise, and now renounce the life that is corruptible, ¹⁴ and let go of the mortal thoughts, cast away from you the burdens of man, put off now your weak nature, ¹⁵ lay aside the thoughts that are most grievous to you, and hurry to escape from these times. ¹⁶ For worse evils than those which you have seen happen will be done after this. ¹⁷ For look how much the world will be weaker through age, so much that more evils will increase on those who dwell in it. ¹⁸ For the truth will withdraw itself further off, and falsehood will be near. For now the eagle which you saw in vision hurries to come." ¹⁹ Then I answered and said, "Let me speak in your presence, O Lord. ²⁰ Behold, I will go, as you have commanded me, and reprove the people who now live, but who will warn those who will be born afterward? For the world is set in darkness, and those who dwell in it are without light. ²¹ For your law has been burned, therefore no one knows the things that are done by you, or the works that will be done. ²² But if I have found favor before you, send the Holy Spirit to me, and I will write all that has been done in the world since the beginning, even the things that were written in your law, that men may be able to find the path, and that those who would live in the latter days may live." ²³ He answered me and said, "Go your way, gather the people together, and tell them not to seek you for forty days. ²⁴ But prepare for yourself many tablets, and take with you Sarea, Dabria, Selemia, Ethanus, and Asiel, these five, which are ready to write swiftly; ²⁵ and come here, and I will light a lamp of understanding in your heart which will not be put out until the things have ended about which you will write. ²⁶ When you are done, some things you shall publish openly, and some things you shall deliver in secret to the wise. Tomorrow at this hour you will begin to write." ²⁷ Then went I out, as he commanded me, and gathered all the people together, and said, ²⁸ "Hear these words, O Israel! ²⁹ Our fathers at the beginning were foreigners in Egypt, and they were delivered from there, ³⁰ and received the law of life, which they didn't keep, which you also have transgressed after them. ³¹ Then the land of Zion was given to you for a possession; but you yourselves and your ancestors have done unrighteousness, and have not kept the ways which the Most High commanded you. ³² Because he is a righteous judge, in due time, he took from you what he had given you. ³³ Now you are here, and your kindred are among you. ³⁴ Therefore if you will rule over your own understanding and instruct your hearts, you will be kept alive, and after death you will obtain mercy. ³⁵ For after death the judgment will come, when we will live again. Then the names of the righteous will become manifest, and the works of the ungodly will be declared. ³⁶ Let no one therefore come to me now, nor seek me for forty days." ³⁷ So I took the five men, as he commanded me, and we went out into the field, and remained there. ³⁸ It came to pass on the next day that, behold, a voice called me, saying, "Esdras, open your mouth, and drink what I give you to drink." ³⁹ Then opened I my mouth, and behold, a full cup was handed to me. It was full of something like water, but its color was like fire. ⁴⁰ I took it, and drank. When I had drunk it, my heart uttered understanding, and wisdom grew in my chest, for my spirit retained its memory. ⁴¹ My mouth was opened, and shut no more. ⁴² The Most High gave understanding to the five men, and they wrote by course the things that were told them, in characters which they didn't know, and they sat forty days. Now they wrote in the day-time, and at night they ate bread. ⁴³ As for me, I spoke in the day, and by night I didn't hold my tongue. ⁴⁴ So in forty days, ninety-four books were written. ⁴⁵ It came to pass, when the forty days were fulfilled, that the Most High spoke to me, saying, "The first books that you have written, publish openly, and let the worthy and unworthy read them; ⁴⁶ but keep the last seventy, that you may deliver them to those who are wise among your people; ⁴⁷ for in them is the spring of understanding, the fountain of wisdom, and the stream of knowledge." ⁴⁸ I did so.

Esdras 2 Chapter 15

¹ "Behold, speak in the ears of my people the words of prophecy which I will put in your mouth," says the Lord. ² "Cause them to be written on paper, for they are faithful and true. ³ Don't be afraid of their plots against you. Don't let the unbelief of those who speak against you trouble you. ⁴ For all the unbelievers will die in their unbelief. ⁵ "Behold," says the Lord, "I bring evils on the whole earth: sword, famine, death, and destruction. ⁶ For wickedness has prevailed over every land, and their hurtful works have reached their limit. ⁷ Therefore," says the Lord, ⁸ "I will hold my peace no more concerning their wickedness which they profanely commit, neither will I tolerate them in these things, which they wickedly practice. Behold, the innocent and righteous blood cries to me, and the souls of the righteous cry out continually. ⁹ I will surely avenge them," says the Lord, "and will receive to me all the innocent blood from among them. ¹⁰ Behold, my people is led like a flock to the slaughter. I will not allow them now to dwell in the land of Egypt, ¹¹ but I will bring them out with a mighty hand and with a high arm, and will strike Egypt with plagues, as before, and will destroy all its land." ¹² Let Egypt and its foundations mourn, for the plague of the chastisement and the punishment that God will bring upon it. ¹³ Let the farmers that till the ground mourn, for their seeds will fail and their trees will be ruined through the blight and hail, and a terrible tempest. ¹⁴ Woe to the world and those who dwell in it! ¹⁵ For the sword and their destruction draws near, and nation will rise up against nation to battle with weapons in their hands. ¹⁶ For there will be sedition among men, and growing strong against one another. In their might, they won't respect their king or the chief of their great ones. ¹⁷ For a man will desire to go into a city, and will not be able. ¹⁸ For because of their pride the cities will be troubled, the houses will be destroyed, and men will be afraid. ¹⁹ A man will have no pity on his neighbors, but will assault their houses with the sword and plunder their goods, because of the lack of bread, and for great suffering. ²⁰ "Behold," says God, "I call together all the kings of the earth to stir up those who are from the rising of the sun, from the south, from the east, and Libanus, to turn themselves one against another, and repay the things that they have done to them. ²¹ Just as they do yet this day to my chosen, so I will do also, and repay into their bosom." The Lord God says: ²² "My right hand won't spare the sinners, and my sword won't cease over those who shed innocent blood on the earth. ²³ A fire has gone out from his wrath and has consumed the foundations of the earth and the sinners, like burnt straw. ²⁴ Woe to those who sin and don't keep my commandments!" says the Lord. ²⁵ "I will not spare them. Go your way, you rebellious children! Don't defile my sanctuary!" ²⁶ For the Lord knows all those who trespass against him, therefore he will deliver them to death and destruction. ²⁷ For now evils have come upon the whole earth, and you will remain in them; for God will not deliver you, because you have sinned against him. ²⁸ Behold, a horrible sight appearing from the east! ²⁹ The nations of the dragons of Arabia will come out with many chariots. From the day that they set out, their hissing is carried over the earth, so that all those who will hear them may also fear and tremble. ³⁰ Also the Carmonians, raging in wrath, will go out like the wild boars of the forest. They will come with great power and join battle with them, and will devastate a portion of the land of the Assyrians with their teeth. ³¹ Then the dragons will have the upper hand, remembering their nature. If they will turn themselves, conspiring together in great power to persecute them, ³² then these will be troubled, and keep silence through their power, and will turn and flee. ³³ From the land of the Assyrians, an enemy in ambush will attack them and destroy one of them. Upon their army will be fear and trembling, and indecision upon their kings. ³⁴ Behold, clouds from the east, and from the north to the south! They are very horrible to look at, full of wrath and storm. ³⁵ They will clash against one another. They will pour out a heavy storm on the earth, even their own storm. There

will be blood from the sword to the horse's belly, 36 and to the thigh of man, and to the camel's hock. 37 There will be fearfulness and great trembling upon earth. They who see that wrath will be afraid, and trembling will seize them. 38 After this, great storms will be stirred up from the south, from the north, and another part from the west. 39 Strong winds will arise from the east, and will shut it up, even the cloud which he raised up in wrath; and the storm that was to cause destruction by the east wind will be violently driven toward the south and west. 40 Great and mighty clouds, full of wrath, will be lifted up with the storm, that they may destroy all the earth and those who dwell in it. They will pour out over every high and lofty one a terrible storm, 41 fire, hail, flying swords, and many waters, that all plains may be full, and all rivers, with the abundance of those waters. 42 They will break down the cities and walls, mountains and hills, trees of the forest, and grass of the meadows, and their grain. 43 They will go on steadily to Babylon and destroy her. 44 They will come to it and surround it. They will pour out the storm and all wrath on her. Then the dust and smoke will go up to the sky, and all those who are around it will mourn for it. 45 Those who remain will serve those who have destroyed it. 46 You, Asia, who are partaker in the beauty of Babylon, and in the glory of her person— 47 woe to you, you wretch, because you have made yourself like her. You have decked out your daughters for prostitution, that they might please and glory in your lovers, which have always lusted after you! 48 You have followed her who is hateful in all her works and inventions. Therefore God says, 49"I will send evils on you: widowhood, poverty, famine, sword, and pestilence, to lay waste your houses and bring you to destruction and death. 50 The glory of your power will be dried up like a flower when the heat rises that is sent over you. 51 You will be weakened like a poor woman who is beaten and wounded, so that you won't be able to receive your mighty ones and your lovers. 52 Would I have dealt with you with such jealousy," says the Lord, 53"if you had not always slain my chosen, exalting and clapping of your hands, and saying over their dead, when you were drunk? 54"Beautify your face! 55 The reward of a prostitute will be in your bosom, therefore you will be repaid. 56 Just as you will do to my chosen," says the Lord, "even so God will do to you, and will deliver you to your adversaries. 57 Your children will die of hunger. You will fall by the sword. Your cities will be broken down, and all your people in the field will perish by the sword. 58 Those who are in the mountains will die of hunger, eat their own flesh, and drink their own blood, because of hunger for bread and thirst for water. 59 You, unhappy above all others, will come and will again receive evils. 60 In the passage, they will rush on the hateful city and will destroy some portion of your land, and mar part of your glory, and will return again to Babylon that was destroyed. 61 You will be cast down by them as stubble, and they will be to you as fire. 62 They will devour you, your cities, your land, and your mountains. They will burn all your forests and your fruitful trees with fire. 63 They will carry your children away captive, and will plunder your wealth, and mar the glory of your face."

Esdras 2 Chapter 16

1"Woe to you, Babylon, and Asia! Woe to you, Egypt and Syria! 2 Put on sackcloth and garments of goats' hair, wail for your children and lament; for your destruction is at hand. 3 A sword has been sent upon you, and who is there to turn it back? 4 A fire has been sent upon you, and who is there to quench it? 5 Calamities are sent upon you, and who is there to drive them away? 6 Can one drive away a hungry lion in the forest? Can one quench a fire in stubble, once it has begun to burn? 7 Can one turn back an arrow that is shot by a strong archer? 8 The Lord God sends the calamities, and who will drive them away? 9 A fire will go out from his wrath, and who may quench it? 10 He will flash lightning, and who will not fear? He will thunder, and who wouldn't tremble? 11 The Lord will threaten, and who will not be utterly broken in pieces at his presence? 12 The earth and its foundations quake. The sea rises up with waves from the deep, and its waves will be troubled, along with the fish in them, at the presence of the Lord, and before the glory of his power. 13 For his right hand that bends the bow is strong, his arrows that he shoots are sharp, and will not miss when they begin to be shot into the ends of the world. 14 Behold, the calamities are sent out, and will not return again until they come upon the earth. 15 The fire is kindled and will not be put out until it consumes the foundations of the earth. 16 Just as an arrow which is shot by a mighty archer doesn't return backward, even so the calamities that are sent out upon earth won't return again. 17 Woe is me! Woe is me! Who will deliver me in those days? 18 The beginning of sorrows, when there will be great mourning; the beginning of famine, and many will perish; the beginning of wars, and the powers will stand in fear; the beginning of calamities, and all will tremble! What will they do when the calamities come? 19 Behold, famine and plague, suffering and anguish! They are

sent as scourges for correction. 20 But for all these things they will not turn them from their wickedness, nor be always mindful of the scourges. 21 Behold, food will be so cheap on earth that they will think themselves to be in good condition, and even then calamities will grow on earth: sword, famine, and great confusion. 22 For many of those who dwell on earth will perish of famine; and others who escape the famine, the sword will destroy. 23 The dead will be cast out like dung, and there will be no one to comfort them; for the earth will be left desolate, and its cities will be cast down. 24 There will be no farmer left to cultivate the earth or to sow it. 25 The trees will give fruit, but who will gather it? 26 The grapes will ripen, but who will tread them? For in all places there will be a great solitude; 27 for one man will desire to see another, or to hear his voice. 28 For of a city there will be ten left, and two of the field, who have hidden themselves in the thick groves, and in the clefts of the rocks. 29 As in an orchard of olives upon every tree there may be left three or four olives, 30 or as when a vineyard is gathered, there are some clusters left by those who diligently search through the vineyard, 31 even so in those days, there will be three or four left by those who search their houses with the sword. 32 The earth will be left desolate, and its fields will be for briers, and its roads and all her paths will grow thorns, because no sheep will pass along them. 33 The virgins will mourn, having no bridegrooms. The women will mourn, having no husbands. Their daughters will mourn, having no helpers. 34 Their bridegrooms will be destroyed in the wars, and their husbands will perish of famine. 35 Hear now these things, and understand them, you servants of the Lord. 36 Behold, the Lord's word: receive it. Don't doubt the things about which the Lord speaks. 37 Behold, the calamities draw near, and are not delayed. 38 Just as a woman with child in the ninth month, when the hour of her delivery draws near, within two or three hours great pains surround her womb, and when the child comes out from the womb, there will be no waiting for a moment, 39 even so the calamities won't delay coming upon the earth. The world will groan, and sorrows will seize it on every side. 40"O my people, hear my word: prepare for battle, and in those calamities be like strangers on the earth. 41 He who sells, let him be as he who flees away, and he who buys, as one who will lose. 42 Let he who does business be as he who has no profit by it, and he who builds, as he who won't dwell in it, 43 and he who sows, as if he wouldn't reap, so also he who prunes the vines, as he who won't gather the grapes, 44 those who marry, as those who will have no children, and those who don't marry, as the widowed. 45 Because of this, those who labor, labor in vain; 46 for foreigners will reap their fruits, plunder their goods, overthrow their houses, and take their children captive, for in captivity and famine they will conceive their children. 47 Those who conduct business, do so only to be plundered. The more they adorn their cities, their houses, their possessions, and their own persons, 48 the more I will hate them for their sins," says the Lord. 49 Just as a respectable and virtuous woman hates a prostitute, 50 so will righteousness hate iniquity, when she adorns herself, and will accuse her to her face, when he comes who will defend him who diligently searches out every sin on earth. 51 Therefore don't be like her or her works. 52 For yet a little while, and iniquity will be taken away out of the earth, and righteousness will reign over us. 53 Don't let the sinner say that he has not sinned; for God will burn coals of fire on the head of one who says "I haven't sinned before God and his glory." 54 Behold, the Lord knows all the works of men, their imaginations, their thoughts, and their hearts. 55 He said, "Let the earth be made," and it was made, "Let the sky be made," and it was made. 56 At his word, the stars were established, and he knows the number of the stars. 57 He searches the deep and its treasures. He has measured the sea and what it contains. 58 He has shut the sea in the midst of the waters, and with his word, he hung the earth over the waters. 59 He has spread out the sky like a vault. He has founded it over the waters. 60 He has made springs of water in the desert and pools on the tops of the mountains to send out rivers from the heights to water the earth. 61 He formed man, and put a heart in the midst of the body, and gave him breath, life, and understanding, 62 yes, the spirit of God Almighty. He who made all things and searches out hidden things in hidden places, 63 surely he knows your imagination, and what you think in your hearts. Woe to those who sin, and try to hide their sin! 64 Because the Lord will exactly investigate all your works, and he will put you all to shame. 65 When your sins are brought out before men, you will be ashamed, and your own iniquities will stand as your accusers in that day. 66 What will you do? Or how will you hide your sins before God and his angels? 67 Behold, God is the judge. Fear him! Stop sinning, and forget your iniquities, to never again commit them. So will God lead you out, and deliver you from all suffering. 68 For, behold, the burning wrath of a great multitude is kindled over you, and they will take away some of you, and feed you with that which is sacrificed to idols. 69 Those who consent to them will be held in derision and in contempt, and be trodden under foot. [70] For there will be in various places, and in the next cities, a great insurrection against those who fear the Lord. [71] They will be like mad men, sparing none, but spoiling and destroying those who still fear the Lord. [72] For they will destroy and plunder their goods, and throw them out of their houses. [73] Then the trial of my elect will be made known, even as the gold that is tried in the fire. [74] Hear, my elect ones, says the Lord: "Behold, the days of suffering are at hand, and I will deliver you from them. [75] Don't be afraid, and don't doubt, for God is your guide. [76] You who keep my commandments and precepts," says the Lord God, "don't let your sins weigh you down, and don't let your iniquities lift themselves up." [77] Woe to those who are choked with their sins and covered with their iniquities, like a field is choked with bushes, and its path covered with thorns, that no one may travel through! [78] It is shut off and given up to be consumed by fire."

Baruch I

Baruch I Chapter 1

[1] Now these are the words of the scroll which Baruch, son of Neriah, son of Mahseiah, son of Zedekiah, son of Hasadiah, son of Hilkiah, wrote in Babylon, [2] in the fifth year (on the seventh day of the month, at the time when the Chaldeans took Jerusalem and burnt it with fire). [3] And Baruch read the words of this scroll for Jeconiah, son of Jehoiakim, king of Judah, to hear it, as well as all the people who came to the reading: [4] the nobles, the kings' sons, the elders, and the whole people, small and great alike - all who lived in Babylon by the river Sud. [5] They wept and fasted and prayed before the LORD, [6] and collected such funds as each could furnish. [7] These they sent to Jerusalem, to Jehoiakim, son of Hilkiah, son of Shallum, the priest, and to the priests and the whole people who were with him in Jerusalem. [8] (This was when he received the vessels of the house of the Lord that had been removed from the temple, to restore them to the land of Judah, on the tenth of Sivan. These silver vessels Zedekiah, son of Josiah, king of Judah, had had made [9] after Nebuchadnezzar, king of Babylon, carried off Jeconiah, and the princes, and the skilled workers, and the nobles, and the people of the land from Jerusalem, as captives, and brought them to Babylon.) [10] Their message was: "We send you funds, with which you are to procure holocausts, sin offerings, and frankincense, and to prepare cereal offerings; offer these on the altar of the LORD our God, [11] and pray for the life of Nebuchadnezzar, king of Babylon, and that of Belshazzar, his son, that their lifetimes may equal the duration of the heavens above the earth; [12] and that the LORD may give us strength, and light to our eyes, that we may live under the protective shadow of Nebuchadnezzar, king of Babylon, and that of Belshazzar, his son, and serve them long, finding favor in their sight. [13] "Pray for us also to the LORD, our God; for we have sinned against the LORD, our God, and the wrath and anger of the LORD have not yet been withdrawn from us at the present day. [14] And read out publicly this scroll which we send you, in the house of the LORD, on the feast day and during the days of assembly: [15] "Justice is with the LORD, our God; and we today are flushed with shame, we men of Judah and citizens of Jerusalem, [16] that we, with our kings and rulers and priests and prophets, and with our fathers, [17] have sinned in the LORD'S sight [18] and disobeyed him. We have neither heeded the voice of the LORD, our God, nor followed the precepts which the LORD set before us. [19] From the time the LORD led our fathers out of the land of Egypt until the present day, we have been disobedient to the LORD, our God, and only too ready to disregard his voice. [20] And the evils and the curse which the LORD enjoined upon Moses, his servant, at the time he led our fathers forth from the land of Egypt to give us the land flowing with milk and honey, cling to us even today. [21] For we did not heed the voice of the LORD, our God, in all the words of the prophets whom he sent us, [22] but each one of us went off after the devices of our own wicked hearts, served other gods, and did evil in the sight of the LORD, our God.

Baruch I Chapter 2

[1] "And the LORD fulfilled the warning he had uttered against us: against our judges, who governed Israel, against our kings and princes, and against the men of Israel and Judah. [2] He brought down upon us evils so great that there has not been done anywhere under heaven what has been done in Jerusalem, as was written in the law of Moses: [3] that one after another of us should eat the flesh of his son or of his daughter. [4] He has made us subject to all the kingdoms round about us, a reproach and a horror among all the nations round about to which the LORD has scattered us. [5] We are brought low, not raised up, because we sinned against the LORD, our God, not heeding his voice. [6] "Justice is with the LORD, our God; and we, like our fathers, are flushed with shame even today. [7] All the evils of which the LORD had warned us have come upon us: [8] and we did not plead before the LORD, or turn, each from the figments of his evil heart. [9] And the LORD kept watch over the evils, and brought them home to us; for the LORD is just in all the works he commanded us to do, [10] but we did not heed his voice, or follow the precepts of the LORD which he set before us. [11] "And now, LORD, God of Israel, you who led your people out of the land of Egypt with your mighty hand, with signs and wonders and great might, and with your upraised arm, so that you have made for yourself a name till the present day: [12] we have sinned, been impious, and violated, O LORD, our God, all your statutes. [13] Let your anger be withdrawn from us, for we are left few in number among the nations to which you scattered us. [14] Hear, O LORD, our prayer of supplication, and deliver us for your own sake: grant us favor in the presence of our captors, [15] that the whole earth may know that you are the LORD, our God, and that Israel and his descendants bear your name. [16] O LORD, look down from your holy dwelling and take thought of us; turn, O LORD, your ear to hear us. [17] Look directly at us, and behold: it is not the dead in the nether world, whose spirits have been taken from within them, who will give glory and vindication to the LORD. [18] He whose soul is deeply grieved, who walks bowed and feeble, with failing eyes and famished soul, will declare your glory and justice, LORD! [19] "Not on the just deeds of our fathers and our kings do we base our plea for mercy in your sight, O LORD, our God. [20] You have brought your wrath and anger down upon us, as you had warned us through your servants the prophets: [21] 'Thus says the LORD: Bend your shoulders to the service of the king of Babylon, that you may continue in the land I gave your fathers: [22] for if you do not hear the LORD'S voice so as to serve the king of Babylon, [23] I will make to cease from the cities of Judah and from the streets of Jerusalem The sounds of joy and the sounds of gladness, the voice of the bridegroom and the voice of the bride; And all the land shall be deserted, without inhabitants.' [24] But we did not heed your voice, or serve the king of Babylon, and you fulfilled the threats you had made through your servants the prophets, to have the bones of our kings and the bones of our fathers brought out from their burial places. [25] And indeed, they lie exposed to the heat of day and the frost of night. They died in dire anguish, by hunger and the sword and plague. [26] And you reduced the house which bears your name to what it is today, for the wickedness of the kingdom of Israel and the kingdom of Judah. [27] "But with us, O Lord, our God, you have dealt in all your clemency and in all your great mercy. [28] This was your warning through your servant Moses, the day you ordered him to write down your law in the presence of the Israelites: [29] If you do not heed my voice, surely this great and numerous throng will dwindle away among the nations to which I will scatter them. [30] For I know they will not heed me, because they are a stiff-necked people. But in the land of their captivity they shall have a change of heart; [31] they shall know that I, the LORD, am their God. I will give them hearts, and heedful ears; [32] and they shall praise me in the land of their captivity, and shall invoke my name. [33] Then they shall turn back from their stiff-necked stubbornness, and from their evil deeds, because they shall remember the fate of their fathers who sinned against the LORD. [34] And I will bring them back to the land which with my oath I promised to their fathers, to Abraham, Isaac and Jacob; and they shall rule it. I will make them increase; they shall not then diminish. [35] And I will establish for them, as an eternal covenant, that I will be their God, and they shall be my people; and I will not again remove my people Israel from the land I gave them."

Baruch I Chapter 3

[1] "LORD Almighty, God of Israel, afflicted souls and dismayed spirits call to you. [2] Hear, O LORD, for you are a God of mercy; and have mercy on us, who have sinned against you: [3] for you are enthroned forever, while we are perishing forever. [4] LORD Almighty, God of Israel, hear the prayer of Israel's few, the sons of those who sinned against you; they did not heed the voice of the LORD, their God, and the evils cling to us. [5] Remember at this time not the misdeeds of our fathers, but your own hand and name: [6] for you are the LORD our God; and you, O LORD, we will praise! [7] For this, you put into our hearts the fear of you: that we may call upon your name, and praise you in our captivity, when we have removed from our hearts all the wickedness of our fathers who sinned against you. [8] Behold us today in our captivity, where you scattered us, a reproach, a curse, and a requital for all the misdeeds of our fathers, who withdrew from the LORD, our God." [9] Hear, O Israel, the commandments of life: listen, and know prudence! [10] How is it, Israel, that you are in the land of your foes, grown old in a foreign land, defiled with the dead, [11] accounted with those destined for the nether world? [12] You have forsaken the fountain of wisdom! [13] Had you walked in the way of God, you would have dwelt in enduring peace. [14] Learn where prudence is, where strength, where understanding; that you may know also where are length of days, and life, where light of the eyes, and

peace. 15 Who has found the place of wisdom, who has entered into her treasuries? 16 Where are the rulers of the nations, they who lorded it over the wild beasts of the earth, 17 and made sport of the birds of the heavens: they who heaped up the silver and the gold in which men trust; of whose possessions there was no end? 18 They schemed anxiously for money, but there is no trace of their work: 19 They have vanished down into the nether world, and others have risen up in their stead. 20 Later generations have seen the light, have dwelt in the land, but the way to understanding they have not known, 21 they have not perceived her paths, or reached her; their offspring were far from the way to her. 22 She has not been heard of in Canaan, nor seen in Teman. 23 The sons of Hagar who seek knowledge on earth, the merchants of Midian and Teman, the phrasemakers seeking knowledge, these have not known the way to wisdom, nor have they her paths in mind. 24 O Israel, how vast is the house of God, how broad the scope of his dominion: 25 Vast and endless, high and immeasurable! 26 In it were born the giants, renowned at the first, stalwarts, skilled in war. 27 Not these did God choose, nor did he give them the way of understanding; 28 They perished for lack of prudence, perished through their folly. 29 Who has gone up to the heavens and taken her, or brought her down from the clouds? 30 Who has crossed the sea and found her, bearing her away rather than choice gold? 31 None knows the way to her, nor has any understood her paths. 32 Yet he who knows all things knows her; he has probed her by his knowledge—he who established the earth for all time, and filled it with four-footed beasts; 33 He who dismisses the light, and it departs, calls it, and it obeys him trembling; 34 Before whom the stars at their posts shine and rejoice; 35 When he calls them, they answer, "Here we are!" shining with joy for their Maker. 36 Such is our God; no other is to be compared to him: 37 He has traced out all the way of understanding, and has given her to Jacob, his servant, to Israel, his beloved son. 38 Since then she has appeared on earth, and moved among men."

Baruch I Chapter 4

1 "She is the book of the precepts of God, the law that endures forever; All who cling to her will live, but those will die who forsake her. 2 Turn, O Jacob, and receive her: walk by her light toward splendor. 3 Give not your glory to another, your privileges to an alien race. 4 Blessed are we, O Israel; for what pleases God is known to us! 5 Fear not, my people! Remember, Israel, 6 You were sold to the nations not for your destruction; it was because you angered God that you were handed over to your foes. 7 For you provoked your Maker with sacrifices to demons, to no-gods; 8 You forsook the Eternal God who nourished you, and you grieved Jerusalem who fostered you. 9 She indeed saw coming upon you the anger of God; and she said: 'Hear, you neighbors of Zion! God has brought great mourning upon me, 10 For I have seen the captivity that the Eternal God has brought upon my sons and daughters. 11 With joy I fostered them; but with mourning and lament I let them go. 12 Let no one gloat over me, a widow, bereft of many: for the sins of my children I am left desolate, because they turned from the law of God, 13 and did not acknowledge his statutes; in the ways of God's commandments they did not walk, nor did they tread the disciplined paths of his justice. 14 'Let Zion's neighbors come, to take note of the captivity of my sons and daughters, brought upon them by the Eternal God. 15 He has brought against them a nation from afar, a nation ruthless and of alien speech, that has neither reverence for age nor tenderness for childhood; 16 They have led away this widow's cherished sons, have left me solitary, without daughters. 17 What can I do to help you? 18 He who has brought this evil upon you must himself deliver you from your enemies' hands. 19 Farewell, my children, farewell: I am left desolate. 20 I have taken off the garment of peace, have put on sackcloth for my prayer of supplication, and while I live I will cry out to the Eternal God. 21 'Fear not, my children; call upon God, who will deliver you from oppression at enemy hands. 22 I have trusted in the Eternal God for your welfare, and joy has come to me from the Holy One because of the mercy that will swiftly reach you from your eternal savior. 23 With mourning and lament I sent you forth, but God will give you back to me with enduring gladness and joy. 24 As Zion's neighbors lately saw you taken captive, so shall they soon see God's salvation come to you, with great glory and the splendor of the Eternal God. 25 'My children, bear patiently the anger that has come from God upon you; your enemies have persecuted you, and you will soon see their destruction and trample upon their necks. 26 My pampered children have trodden rough roads, carried off by their enemies like sheep in a raid. 27 Fear not, my children; call out to God! He who brought this upon you will remember you. 28 As your hearts have been disposed to stray from God, turn now ten times the more to seek him; 29 For he who has brought disaster upon you will, in saving you, bring you back enduring joy.' 30 Fear not, Jerusalem! He who gave you your name is your encouragement. 31 Fearful are those

who harmed you, who rejoiced at your downfall; 32 Fearful are the cities where your children were enslaved, fearful the city that took your sons. 33 As that city rejoiced at your collapse, and made merry at your downfall, so shall she grieve over her own desolation. 34 I will take from her the joyous throngs, and her exultation shall be turned to mourning: 35 For fire shall come upon her from the Eternal God, for a long time, and demons shall dwell in her from that time on. 36 Look to the east, Jerusalem! behold the joy that comes to you from God. 37 Here come your sons whom you once let go, gathered in from the east and from the west by the word of the Holy One, rejoicing in the glory of God."

Baruch I Chapter 5

1 "Jerusalem, take off your robe of mourning and misery; put on the splendor of glory from God forever: 2 Wrapped in the cloak of justice from God, bear on your head the mitre that displays the glory of the eternal name. 3 For God will show all the earth your splendor: 4 you will be named by God forever the peace of justice, the glory of God's worship. 5 Up, Jerusalem! stand upon the heights; look to the east and see your children gathered from the east and the west at the word of the Holy One, rejoicing that they are remembered by God. 6 Led away on foot by their enemies they left you: but God will bring them back to you borne aloft in glory as on royal thrones. 7 For God has commanded that every lofty mountain be made low, and that the age-old depths and gorges be filled to level ground, that Israel may advance secure in the glory of God. 8 The forests and every fragrant kind of tree have overshadowed Israel at God's command; 9 For God is leading Israel in joy by the light of his glory, with his mercy and justice for company."

Baruch I Chapter 6

1 "A copy of the letter which Jeremiah sent to those who were being led captive to Babylon by the king of the Babylonians, to convey to them what God had commanded him: For the sins you committed before God, you are being led captive to Babylon by Nebuchadnezzar, king of the Babylonians. 2 When you reach Babylon you will be there many years, a period seven generations long; after which I will bring you back from there in peace. 3 And now in Babylon you will see borne upon men's shoulders gods of silver and gold and wood, which cast fear upon the pagans. 4 Take care that you yourselves do not imitate their alien example and stand in fear of them, 5 when you see the crowd before them and behind worshiping them. Rather, say in your hearts, 'You, O LORD, are to be worshiped!'; 6 for my angel is with you, and he is the custodian of your lives. 7 Their tongues are smoothed by woodworkers; they are covered with gold and silver—but they are a fraud, and cannot speak. 8 People bring gold, as to a maiden in love with ornament, 9 and furnish crowns for the heads of their gods. Then sometimes the priests take the silver and gold from their gods and spend it on themselves, 10 or give part of it to the harlots on the terrace. They trick them out in garments like men, these gods of silver and gold and wood; 11 but though they are wrapped in purple clothing, they are not safe from corrosion or insects. 12 They wipe their faces clean of the house dust which is thick upon them. 13 Each has a scepter, like the human ruler of a district; but none does away with those that offend against it. 14 Each has in its right hand an axe or dagger, but it cannot save itself from war or pillage. Thus it is known they are not gods; do not fear them. 15 As useless as one's broken tools 16 are their gods, set up in their houses; their eyes are full of dust from the feet of those who enter. 17 Their courtyards are walled in like those of a man brought to execution for a crime against the king; the priests reinforce their houses with gates and bars and bolts, lest they be carried off by robbers. 18 They light more lamps for them than for themselves, yet not one of these can they see. 19 They are like any beam in the house; it is said their hearts are eaten away. Though the insects out of the ground consume them and their garments, they do not feel it. 20 Their faces are blackened by the smoke of the house. 21 Bats and swallows alight on their bodies and on their heads; and cats as well as birds. 22 Know, therefore, that they are not gods, and do not fear them. 23 Despite the gold that covers them for adornment, unless someone wipes away the corrosion, they do not shine; nor did they feel anything when they were molded. 24 They are bought at any price, and there is no spirit in them. 25 Having no feet, they are carried on men's shoulders, displaying their shame to all; and those who worship them are put to confusion 26 because, if they fall to the ground, the worshipers must raise them up. They neither move of themselves if one sets them upright, nor come upright if they fall; but one puts gifts beside them as beside the dead. 27 Their priests resell their sacrifices for their own advantage. Even their wives cure parts of the meat, but do not share it with the poor and the weak; 28 the menstruous and women in childbed handle their sacrifices. Knowing from this that they are not gods, do not fear them. 29 How can they be called gods? For women bring the offerings to these gods of silver and

gold and wood; 30 and in their temples the priests squat with torn tunic and with shaven hair and beard, and with their heads uncovered. 31 They shout and wail before their gods as others do at a funeral banquet. 32 The priests take some of their clothing and put it on their wives and children. 33 Whether they are treated well or ill by anyone, they cannot requite it; they can neither set up a king nor remove him. 34 Similarly, they cannot give anyone riches or coppers; if one fails to fulfill a vow to them, they cannot exact it of him. 35 They neither save a man from death, nor deliver the weak from the strong. 36 To no blind man do they restore his sight, nor do they save any man in an emergency. 37 They neither pity the widow nor benefit the orphan. 38 These gilded and silvered wooden statues are like stones from the mountains; and their worshipers will be put to shame. 39 How then can it be thought or claimed that they are gods? 40 Even the Chaldeans themselves have no respect for them; for when they see a deaf mute, incapable of speech, they bring forward Bel and ask the god to make noise, as though the man could understand; 41 and they are themselves unable to reflect and abandon these gods, for they have no sense. 42 And their women, girt with cords, sit by the roads, burning chaff for incense; 43 and whenever one of them is drawn aside by some passer-by who lies with her, she mocks her neighbor who has not been dignified as she has, and has not had her cord broken. 44 All that takes place around these gods is a fraud: how then can it be thought or claimed that they are gods? 45 They are produced by woodworkers and goldsmiths, and they are nothing else than what these craftsmen wish them to be. 46 Even those who produce them are not long-lived; 47 how then can what they have produced be gods? They have left frauds and opprobrium to their successors. 48 For when war or disaster comes upon them, the priests deliberate among themselves where they can hide with them. 49 How then can one not know that these are no-gods, which do not save themselves either from war or from disaster? 50 They are wooden, gilded and silvered; they will later be known for frauds. To all peoples and kings it will be clear that they are not gods, but human handiwork; and that God's work is not in them. 51 Who does not know that they are not gods? 52 They set no king over the land, nor do they give men rain. 53 They neither vindicate their own rights, nor do they recover what is unjustly taken, for they are unable; 54 they are like crows between heaven and earth. For when fire breaks out in the temple of these wooden or gilded or silvered gods, though the priests flee and are safe, they themselves are burnt up in the fire like beams. 55 They cannot resist a king, or enemy forces. 56 How then can it be admitted or thought that they are gods? They are safe from neither thieves nor bandits, these wooden and silvered and gilded gods; 57 those who seize them strip off the gold and the silver, and go away with the clothing that was on them, and they cannot help themselves. 58 How much better to be a king displaying his valor, or a handy tool in a house, the joy of its owner, than these false gods; or the door of a house, that keeps safe those who are within, rather than these false gods; or a wooden post in a palace, rather than these false gods! 59 The sun and moon and stars are bright, and obedient in the service for which they are sent. 60 Likewise the lightning, when it flashes, is a goodly sight; and the same wind blows over all the land. 61 The clouds, too, when commanded by God to proceed across the whole world, fulfill the order; 62 and fire, sent from on high to burn up the mountains and the forests, does what has been commanded. But these false gods are not their equal, whether in beauty or in power; 63 so that it is unthinkable, and cannot be claimed, that they are gods. They can neither execute judgment, nor benefit man. 64 Know, therefore, that they are not gods, and do not fear them. 65 Kings they neither curse nor bless. 66 They show the nations no signs in the heavens, nor are they brilliant like the sun, nor shining like the moon. 67 The beasts which can help themselves by fleeing to shelter are better than they are. 68 Thus in no way is it clear to us that they are gods; so do not fear them. 69 For like a scarecrow in a cucumber patch, that is no protection, are their wooden, gilded, silvered gods. 70 Just like a thornbush in a garden on which perches every kind of bird, or like a corpse hurled into darkness, are their silvered and gilded wooden gods. 71 From the rotting of the purple and the linen upon them, it can be known that they are not gods; they themselves will in the end be consumed, and be a disgrace in the land. 72 The better for the just man who has no idols: he shall be far from disgrace!"

Baruch II

Baruch II Chapter 1

1 It came to pass, when the children of Israel were taken captive by the king of the Chaldeans, that God spoke to Jeremiah saying: Jeremiah, my chosen [one] [servant], arise and depart from this city, you and Baruch, since I am going to destroy it because of the multitude of the sins of those who dwell in it. 2 For your prayers are like a solid pillar in its midst, and like an indestructible wall surrounding it. 3 Now, then, arise and depart before the host of the Chaldeans surrounds it. 4 And Jeremiah answered, saying: I beseech you, Lord, permit me, your servant, to speak in your presence. 5 And the Lord said to him: Speak, my chosen [one] [servant] Jeremiah. 6 And Jeremiah spoke, saying: Lord Almighty, would you deliver the chosen city into the hands of the Chaldeans, so that the king with the multitude of his people might boast and say: "I have prevailed over the holy city of God"? 7 No, my Lord, but if it is your will, let it be destroyed by your hands. 8 And the Lord said to Jeremiah: Since you are my chosen one, arise and depart from this city, you and Baruch, for I am going to destroy it because of the multitude of the sins of those who dwell in it. 9 For neither the king nor his host will be able to enter it unless I first open its gates. 10 Arise, then, and go to Baruch, and tell him these words. 11 And when you have arisen at the sixth hour of the night, go out on the city walls and I will show you that unless I first destroy the city, they cannot enter it. 12 When the Lord had said this, he departed from Jeremiah.

Baruch II - Chapter 2

1 And Jeremiah ran and told these things to Baruch; and as they went into the temple of God, Jeremiah tore his garments and put dust on his head and entered the holy place of God. 2 And when Baruch saw him with dust sprinkled on his head and his garments torn, he cried out in a loud voice, saying: Father Jeremiah, what are you doing? What sin has the people committed? 3 (For whenever the people sinned, Jeremiah would sprinkle dust on his head and would pray for the people until their sin was forgiven.) 4 So Baruch asked him, saying: Father, what is this? 5 And Jeremiah said to him: Refrain from rending your garments — rather, let us rend our hearts! And let us not draw water for the trough, but let us weep and fill them with tears! For the Lord will not have mercy on this people. 6 And Baruch said: Father Jeremiah, what has happened? 7 And Jeremiah said: God is delivering the city into the hands of the king of the Chaldeans, to take the people captive into Babylon. 8 And when Baruch heard these things, he also tore his garments and said: Father Jeremiah, who has made this known to you? 9 And Jeremiah said to him: Stay with me awhile, until the sixth hour of the night, so that you may know that this word is true. 10 Therefore they both remained in the altar-area weeping, and their garments were torn.

Baruch II - Chapter 3

1 And when the hour of the night arrived, as the Lord had told Jeremiah they came up together on the walls of the city, Jeremiah and Baruch. 2 And behold, there came a sound of trumpets; and angels emerged from heaven holding torches in their hands, and they set them on the walls of the city. 3 And when Jeremiah and Baruch saw them, they wept, saying: Now we know that the word is true! 4 And Jeremiah besought the angels, saying: I beseech you, do not destroy the city yet, until I say something to the Lord. 5 And the Lord spoke to the angels, saying: Do not destroy the city until I speak to my chosen one, Jeremiah. 6 Then Jeremiah spoke, saying: I beg you, Lord, bid me to speak in your presence. 7 And the Lord said: Speak, my chosen [one] [servant] Jeremiah. 8 And Jeremiah said: Behold, Lord, now we know that you are delivering the city into the hands of its enemies, and they will take the people away to Babylon. What do you want me to do with the holy vessels of the temple service? 10 And the Lord said to him: Take them and consign them to the earth, saying: Hear, Earth, the voice of your creator who formed you in the abundance of waters, who sealed you with seven seals for seven epochs, and after this you will receive your ornaments (?) — 11 Guard the vessels of the temple service until the gathering of the beloved. 12 And Jeremiah spoke, saying: I beseech you, Lord, show me what I should do for Abimelech the Ethiopian, for he has done many kindnesses to your servant Jeremiah. 13 For he pulled me out of the miry pit; and I do not wish that he should see the destruction and desolation of this city, but that you should be merciful to him and that he should not be grieved. 14 And the Lord said to Jeremiah: Send him to the vineyard of Agrippa, and I will hide him in the shadow of the mountain until I cause the people to return to the city. 15 And you, Jeremiah, go with your people into Babylon and stay with them, preaching to them, until I cause them to return to the city. 16 But leave Baruch here until I speak with him. 17 When he had said these things, the Lord ascended from Jeremiah into heaven. 18 But Jeremiah and Baruch entered the holy place, and taking the vessels of the temple service, they consigned them to the earth as the Lord had told them. 19 And immediately the earth swallowed them. 20 And they both sat down and wept. 21 And when morning came, Jeremiah sent Abimelech, saying: Take a basket and go to the estate of Agrippa by the mountain road, and bring back some figs to give to the sick among the people; for

the favor of the Lord is on you and his glory is on your head. ²²And when he had said this, Jeremiah sent him away; and Abimelech went as he told him.

Baruch II - Chapter 4

¹ And when morning came, behold the host of the Chaldeans surrounded the city. ²And the great angel trumpeted, saying: Enter the city, host of the Chaldeans; for behold, the gate is opened for you. ³Therefore let the king enter, with his multitudes, and let him take all the people captive. ⁴But taking the keys of the temple, Jeremiah went outside the city and threw them away in the presence of the sun, saying: I say to you, Sun, take the keys of the temple of God and guard them until the day in which the Lord asks you for them. ⁵For we have not been found worthy to keep them, for we have become unfaithful guardians. ⁶While Jeremiah was still weeping for the people, they brought him out with the people and dragged him into Babylon. ⁷But Baruch put dust on his head and sat and wailed this lamentation, saying: Why has Jerusalem been devastated? Because of the sins of the beloved people she was delivered into the hands of enemies—because of our sins and those of the people. ⁸But let not the lawless ones boast and say: "We were strong enough to take the city of God by our might;" but it was delivered to you because of our sins. ⁹And God will pity us and cause us to return to our city, but you will not survive! ¹⁰Blessed are our fathers, Abraham, Isaac and Jacob, for they departed from this world and did not see the destruction of this city. ¹¹When he had said this, Baruch departed from the city, weeping and saying: Grieving because of you, Jerusalem, I went out from you. ¹²And he remained sitting in a tomb, while the angels came to him and explained to him everything that the Lord revealed to him through them.

Baruch II - Chapter 5

¹ But Abimelech took the figs in the burning heat; and coming upon a tree, he sat under its shade to rest a bit. ²And leaning his head on the basket of figs, he fell asleep and slept for 66 years; and he was not awakened from his slumber. ³And afterward, when he awoke from his sleep, he said: I slept sweetly for a little while, but my head is heavy because I did not get enough sleep. ⁴Then he uncovered the basket of figs and found them dripping milk. ⁵And he said: I would like to sleep a little longer, because my head is heavy. But I am afraid that I might fall asleep and be late in awakening and my father Jeremiah would think badly of me; for if he were not in a hurry, he would not have sent me today at daybreak. ⁶So I will get up, and proceed in the burning heat; for isn't there heat, isn't there toil every day? ⁷So he got up and took the basket of figs and placed it on his shoulders, and he entered into Jerusalem and did not recognize it — neither his own house, nor the place — nor did he find his own family or any of his acquaintances. ⁸And he said: The Lord be blessed, for a great trance has come over me today! ⁹This is not the city Jerusalem — and I have lost my way because I came by the mountain road when I arose from my sleep; and since my head was heavy because I did not get enough sleep, I lost my way. ¹⁰It will seem incredible to Jeremiah that I lost my way! ¹¹And he departed from the city; and as he searched he saw the landmarks of the city, and he said: Indeed, this is the city; I lost my way. ¹²And again he returned to the city and searched, and found no one of his own people; and he said: The Lord be blessed, for a great trance has come over me! ¹³And again he departed from the city, and he stayed there grieving, not knowing where he should go. ¹⁴And he put down the basket, saying: I will sit here until the Lord takes this trance from me. ¹⁵And as he sat, he saw an old man coming from the field; and Abimelech said to him: I say to you, old man, what city is this? ¹⁶And he said to him: It is Jerusalem. ¹⁷And Abimelech said to him: Where is Jeremiah the priest, and Baruch the secretary, and all the people of this city, for I could not find them? ¹⁸And the old man said to him: Are you not from this city, seeing that you remember Jeremiah, because you are asking about him after such a long time? ¹⁹For Jeremiah is in Babylon with the people; for they were taken captive by king Nebuchadnezzar, and Jeremiah is with them to preach the good news to them and to teach them the word. ²⁰As soon as Abimelech heard this from the old man, he said: If you were not an old man, and if it were not for the fact that it is not lawful for a man to upbraid one older than himself, I would laugh at you and say that you are out of your mind — since you say that the people have been taken captive into Babylon. ²¹Even if the heavenly torrents had descended on them, there has not yet been time for them to go into Babylon! ²²For how much time has passed since my father Jeremiah sent me to the estate of Agrippa to bring a few figs, so that I might give them to the sick among the people? ²³And I went and got them, and when I came to a certain tree in the burning heat, I sat to rest a little; and I leaned my head on the basket and fell asleep. ²⁴And when I awoke I uncovered the basket of figs, supposing that I was late; and I found the

figs dripping milk, just as I had collected them. ²⁵But you claim that the people have been taken captive into Babylon. ²⁶But that you might know, take the figs and see! ²⁷And he uncovered the basket of figs for the old man, and he saw them dripping milk. ²⁸And when the old man saw them, he said: O my son, you are a righteous man, and God did not want you to see the desolation of the city, so he brought this trance upon you. ²⁹For behold it is 66 years today since the people were taken captive into Babylon. ³⁰But that you might learn, my son, that what I tell you is true — look into the field and see that the ripening of the crops has not appeared. ³¹And notice that the figs are not in season, and be enlightened. ³²Then Abimelech cried out in a loud voice, saying: I bless you, God of heaven and earth, the Rest of the souls of the righteous in every place! ³³Then he said to the old man: What month is this? ³⁴And he said: Nisan (which is Abib). ³⁵And taking some of figs, he gave them to the old man and said to him: May God illumine your way to the city above, Jerusalem.

Baruch II - Chapter 6

¹After this, Abimelech went out of the city and prayed to the Lord. ²And behold, an angel of the Lord came and took him by the right hand and brought him back to where Baruch was sitting, and he found him in a tomb. ³And when they saw each other, they both wept and kissed each other. ⁴But when Baruch looked up he saw with his own eyes the figs that were covered in Abimelech's basket. ⁵And lifting his eyes to heaven, he prayed, saying: ⁶You are the God who gives a reward to those who love you. Prepare yourself, my heart, and rejoice and be glad while you are in your tabernacle, saying to your fleshly house, "your grief has been changed to joy;" for the Sufficient One is coming and will deliver you in your tabernacle — for there is no sin in you. ⁷Revive in your tabernacle, in your virginal faith, and believe that you will live! ⁸Look at this basket of figs — for behold, they are 66 years old and have not become shrivelled or rotten, but they are dripping milk. ⁹So it will be with you, my flesh, if you do what is commanded you by the angel of righteousness. ¹⁰He who preserved the basket of figs, the same will again preserve you by his power. ¹¹When Baruch had said this, he said to Abimelech: Stand up and let us pray that the Lord may make known to us how we shall be able to send to Jeremiah in Babylon the report about the shelter provided for you on the way. ¹²And Baruch prayed, saying: Lord God, our strength is the elect light which comes forth from your mouth. ¹³We beseech and beg of your goodness — you whose great name no one is able to know — hear the voice of your servants and let knowledge come into our hearts. ¹⁴What shall we do, and how shall we send this report to Jeremiah in Babylon? ¹⁵And while Baruch was still praying, behold an angel of the Lord came and said all these words to Baruch: Agent of the light, do not be anxious about how you will send to Jeremiah; for an eagle is coming to you at the hour of light tomorrow, and you will direct him to Jeremiah. ¹⁶Therefore, write in a letter: Say to the children of Israel: Let the stranger who comes among you be set apart and let 15 days go by; and after this I will lead you into your city, says the Lord. ¹⁷He who is not separated from Babylon will not enter into the city; and I will punish them by keeping them from being received back by the Babylonians, says the Lord. ¹⁸And when the angel had said this, he departed from Baruch. ¹⁹And Baruch sent to the market of the gentiles and got papyrus and ink and wrote a letter as follows: Baruch, the servant of God, writes to Jeremiah in the captivity of Babylon: ²⁰Greetings! Rejoice, for God has not allowed us to depart from this body grieving for the city which was laid waste and outraged. ²¹Wherefore the Lord has had compassion on our tears, and has remembered the covenant which he established with our fathers Abraham, Isaac and Jacob. ²²And he sent his angel to me, and he told me these words which I send to you. ²³These, then, are the words which the Lord, the God of Israel, spoke, who led us out of Egypt, out of the great furnace: Because you did not keep my ordinances, but your heart was lifted up, and you were haughty before me, in anger and wrath I delivered you to the furnace in Babylon. ²⁴If, therefore, says the Lord, you listen to my voice, from the mouth of Jeremiah my servant, I will bring the one who listens up from Babylon; but the one who does not listen will become a stranger to Jerusalem and to Babylon. ²⁵And you will test them by means of the water of the Jordan; whoever does not listen will be exposed — this is the sign of the great seal.

Baruch II - Chapter 7

¹ And Baruch got up and departed from the tomb and found the eagle sitting outside the tomb. ²And the eagle said to him in a human voice: Hail, Baruch, steward of the faith. ³And Baruch said to him: You who speak are chosen from among all the birds of heaven, for this is clear from the gleam of your eyes; tell me, then, what are you doing here? ⁴And the eagle said to him: I was sent here so that you might through me send whatever message you want. ⁵And Baruch said to him: Can you

carry this message to Jeremiah in Babylon? [6]And the eagle said to him: Indeed, it was for this reason I was sent. [7]And Baruch took the letter, and 15 figs from Abimelech's basket, and tied them to the eagle's neck and said to him: I say to you, king of the birds, go in peace with good health and carry the message for me. [8]Do not be like the raven which Noah sent out and which never came back to him in the ark; but be like the dove which, the third time, brought a report to the righteous one. [9]So you also, take this good message to Jeremiah and to those in bondage with him, that it may be well with you — take this papyrus to the people and to the chosen one of God. [10]Even if all the birds of heaven surround you and want to fight with you, struggle — the Lord will give you strength. [11]And do not turn aside to the right or to the left, but straight as a speeding arrow, go in the power of God, and the glory of the Lord will be with you the entire way. [12]Then the eagle took flight and went away to Babylon, having the letter tied to his neck; and when he arrived he rested on a post outside the city in a desert place. [13]And he kept silent until Jeremiah came along, for he and some of the people were coming out to bury a corpse outside the city. [14](For Jeremiah had petitioned king Nebuchadnezzar, saying: "Give me a place where I may bury those of my people who have died;" and the king gave it to him.) [15]And as they were coming out with the body, and weeping, they came to where the eagle was. [16]And the eagle cried out in a loud voice, saying: I say to you, Jeremiah the chosen [one] [servant] of God, go and gather together the people and come here so that they may hear a letter which I have brought to you from Baruch and Abimelech. [17]And when Jeremiah heard this, he glorified God; and he went and gathered together the people along with their wives and children, and he came to where the eagle was. [18]And the eagle came down on the corpse, and it revived. [19](Now this took place so that they might believe.) [20]And all the people were astounded at what had happened, and said: This is the God who appeared to our fathers in the wilderness through Moses, and now he has appeared to us through the eagle. [21]And the eagle said: I say to you, Jeremiah, come, untie this letter and read it to the people — So he untied the letter and read it to the people. [22]And when the people heard it, they wept and put dust on their heads, and they said to Jeremiah: Deliver us and tell us what to do that we may once again enter our city. [23]And Jeremiah answered and said to them: Do whatever you heard from the letter, and the Lord will lead us into our city. [24]And Jeremiah wrote a letter to Baruch, saying thus: My beloved son, do not be negligent in your prayers, beseeching God on our behalf, that he might direct our way until we come out of the jurisdiction of this lawless king. [25]For you have been found righteous before God, and he did not let you come here, lest you see the affliction which has come upon the people at the hands of the Babylonians. [26]For it is like a father with an only son, who is given over for punishment; and those who see his father and console them cover his face, lest he see how his son is being punished, and are even more ravaged by grief. [27]For thus God took pity on you and did not let you enter Babylon lest you see the affliction of the people. [28]For since we came here, grief has not left us, for 66 years today. [29]For many times when I went out I found some of the people hung up by king Nebuchadnezzar, crying and saying: "Have mercy on us, God-ZAR!" [30]When I heard this, I grieved and cried with two-fold mourning, not only because they were hung up, but because they were calling on a foreign God, saying "Have mercy on us." [31]But I remembered days of festivity which we celebrated in Jerusalem before our captivity; and when I remembered, I groaned, and returned to my house wailing and weeping. [32]Now, then, pray in the place where you are — you and Abimelech — for this people, that they may listen to my voice and to the decrees of my mouth, so that we may depart from here. [33]For I tell you that the entire time that we have spent here they have kept us in subjection, saying: Recite for us a song from the songs of Zion — the song of your God. Psalm 3-4 [34]And we reply to them: How shall we sing for you since we are in a foreign land? [35]And after this, Jeremiah tied the letter to the eagle's neck, saying: Go in peace, and may the Lord watch over both of us. [36]And the eagle took flight and came to Jerusalem and gave the letter to Baruch; and when he had untied it he read it and kissed it and wept when he heard about the distresses and afflictions of the people. [37]But Jeremiah took the figs and distributed them to the sick among the people, and he kept teaching them to abstain from the pollutions of the gentiles of Babylon.

Baruch II - Chapter 8

[1]And the day came in which the Lord brought the people out of Babylon. [2]And the Lord said to Jeremiah: Rise up — you and the people — and come to the Jordan and say to the people: Let anyone who desires the Lord forsake the works of Babylon. [3]As for the men who took wives from them and the women who took husbands from them — those who listen to you shall cross over, and you take them into Jerusalem; but those who do not listen to you, do not lead them there. [4]And Jeremiah

spoke these words to the people, and they arose and came to the Jordan to cross over. [5]As he told them the words that the Lord had spoken to him, half of those who had taken spouses from them did not wish to listen to Jeremiah, but said to him: We will never forsake our wives, but we will bring them back with us into our city. [6]So they crossed the Jordan and came to Jerusalem. [7]And Jeremiah and Baruch and Abimelech stood up and said: No man joined with Babylonians shall enter this city! [8]And they said to one another: Let us arise and return to Babylon to our place — And they departed. [9]But while they were coming to Babylon, the Babylonians came out to meet them, saying: You shall not enter our city, for you hated us and you left us secretly; therefore you cannot come in with us. [10]For we have taken a solemn oath together in the name of our god to receive neither you nor your children, since you left us secretly. [11]And when they heard this, they returned and came to a desert place some distance from Jerusalem and built a city for themselves and named it 'SAMARIA.' [12]And Jeremiah sent to them, saying: Repent, for the angel of righteousness is coming and will lead you to your exalted place.

Baruch II - Chapter 9

[1] Now those who were with Jeremiah were rejoicing and offering sacrifices on behalf of the people for nine days. [2]But on the tenth, Jeremiah alone offered sacrifice. [3]And he prayed a prayer, saying: Holy, holy, holy, fragrant aroma of the living trees, true light that enlightens me until I ascend to you; [4]For your mercy, I beg you — for the sweet voice of the two seraphim, I beg — for another fragrant aroma. [5]And may Michael, archangel of righteousness, who opens the gates to the righteous, be my guardian until he causes the righteous to enter. [6]I beg you, almighty Lord of all creation, unbegotten and incomprehensible, in whom all judgment was hidden before these things came into existence. [7]When Jeremiah had said this, and while he was standing in the altar-area with Baruch and Abimelech, he became as one whose soul had departed. [8]And Baruch and Abimelech were weeping and crying out in a loud voice: Woe to us! For our father Jeremiah has left us — the priest of God has departed! [9]And all the people heard their weeping and they all ran to them and saw Jeremiah lying on the ground as if dead. [10]And they tore their garments and put dust on their heads and wept bitterly. [11]And after this they prepared to bury him. [12]And behold, there came a voice saying: Do not bury the one who yet lives, for his soul is returning to his body! [13]And when they heard the voice they did not bury him, but stayed around his tabernacle for three days saying, "when will he arise?" [14]And after three days his soul came back into his body and he raised his voice in the midst of them all and said: Glorify God with one voice! All of you glorify God and the son of God who awakens us — messiah Jesus — the light of all the ages, the inextinguishable lamp, the life of faith. [15]But after these times there shall be 477 years more and he comes to earth. [16]And the tree of life planted in the midst of paradise will cause all the unfruitful trees to bear fruit, and will grow and sprout forth. [17]And the trees that had sprouted and became haughty and said: "We have supplied our power to the air," he will cause them to wither, with the grandeur of their branches, and he will cause them to be judged — that firmly rooted tree! [18]And what is crimson will become white as wool — the snow will be blackened — the sweet waters will become salty, and the salty sweet, in the intense light of the joy of God. [19]And he will bless the isles so that they become fruitful by the word of the mouth of his messiah. [20]For he shall come, and he will go out and choose for himself twelve apostles to proclaim the news among the nations– he whom I have seen adorned by his father and coming into the world on the Mount of Olives — and he shall fill the hungry souls. [21]When Jeremiah was saying this concerning the son of God — that he is coming into the world — the people became very angry and said: This is a repetition of the words spoken by Isaiah son of Amos, when he said: I saw God and the son of God. [22]Come, then, and let us not kill him by the same sort of death with which we killed Isaiah, but let us stone him with stones. [23]And Baruch and Abimelech were greatly grieved because they wanted to hear in full the mysteries that he had seen. [24]But Jeremiah said to them: Be silent and weep not, for they cannot kill me until I describe for you everything I saw. [25]And he said to them: Bring a stone here to me. [26]And he set it up and said: Light of the ages, make this stone to become like me in appearance, until I have described to Baruch and Abimelech everything I saw. [27]Then the stone, by God's command, took on the appearance of Jeremiah. [28]And they were stoning the stone, supposing that it was Jeremiah! [29]But Jeremiah delivered to Baruch and to Abimelech all the mysteries he had seen, and forthwith he stood in the midst of the people desiring to complete his ministry. [30]Then the stone cried out, saying: O foolish children of Israel, why do you stone me, supposing that I am Jeremiah? Behold, Jeremiah is standing in your midst! [31]And when they saw him, immediately they rushed upon him with many stones, and his ministry

was fulfilled. 32And when Baruch and Abimelech came, they buried him, and taking the stone they placed it on his tomb and inscribed it thus: This is the stone that was the ally of Jeremiah.

Wisdom Books (Poetic Books)

Job

Job Chapter 1

1In the land of Uz, there was a blameless and upright man named Job, who feared God and avoided evil. 2Seven sons and three daughters were born to him; 3and he had seven thousand sheep, three thousand camels, five hundred yoke of oxen, five hundred she-asses, and a great number of work animals, so that he was greater than any of the men of the East. His sons used to take turns giving feasts, sending invitations to their three sisters to eat and drink with them. And when each feast had run its course, Job would send for them and sanctify them, rising early and offering holocausts for every one of them. For Job said, "It may be that my sons have sinned and blasphemed God in their hearts." This Job did habitually. 4One day, when the sons of God came to present themselves before the LORD, Satan also came among them. 7And the LORD said to Satan, "Whence do you come?" Then Satan answered the LORD and said, "From roaming the earth and patrolling it." And the LORD said to Satan, "Have you noticed my servant Job, and that there is no one on earth like him, blameless and upright, fearing God and avoiding evil?" 9But Satan answered the LORD and said, "Is it for nothing that Job is God-fearing? 10Have you not surrounded him and his family and all that he has with your protection? You have blessed the work of his hands, and his livestock are spread over the land. 11But now put forth your hand and touch anything that he has, and surely he will blaspheme you to your face." 12And the LORD said to Satan, "Behold, all that he has is in your power; only do not lay a hand upon his person." So Satan went forth from the presence of the LORD. 13And so one day, while his sons and his daughters were eating and drinking wine in the house of their eldest brother, 14a messenger came to Job and said, "The oxen were plowing and the asses grazing beside them, 15and the Sabeans carried them off in a raid. They put the herdsmen to the sword, and I alone have escaped to tell you." 16While he was yet speaking, another came and said, "Lightning has fallen from heaven and struck the sheep and their shepherds and consumed them; and I alone have escaped to tell you." 17While he was yet speaking, another came and said, "The Chaldeans formed three columns, seized the camels, carried them off, and put those tending them to the sword, and I alone have escaped to tell you." 18While he was yet speaking, another came and said, "Your sons and daughters were eating and drinking wine in the house of their eldest brother, 19when suddenly a great wind came across the desert and smote the four corners of the house. It fell upon the young people and they are dead; and I alone have escaped to tell you." 20Then Job began to tear his cloak and cut off his hair. He cast himself prostrate upon the ground, 21and said, "Naked I came forth from my mother's womb, and naked shall I go back again. The LORD gave and the LORD has taken away; blessed be the name of the LORD!" 22In all this Job did not sin, nor did he say anything disrespectful of God.

Job Chapter 2

1Once again the sons of God came to present themselves before the LORD, and Satan also came with them. 2And the LORD said to Satan, "Whence do you come?" And Satan answered the LORD and said, "From roaming the earth and patrolling it." 3And the LORD said to Satan, "Have you noticed my servant Job, and that there is no one on earth like him, faultless and upright, fearing God and avoiding evil? He still holds fast to his innocence although you incited me against him to ruin him without cause." 4And Satan answered the LORD and said, "Skin for skin! All that a man has will he give for his life. 5But now put forth your hand and touch his bone and his flesh, and surely he will blaspheme you to your face." 6And the LORD said to Satan, "He is in your power; only spare his life." 7So Satan went forth from the presence of the LORD and smote Job with severe boils from the soles of his feet to the crown of his head. 8And he took a potsherd to scrape himself, as he sat among the ashes. 9Then his wife said to him, "Are you still holding to your innocence? Curse God and die." 10But he said to her, "Are even you going to speak as senseless women do? We accept good things from God; and should we not accept evil?" Through all this, Job said nothing sinful. 11Now when three of Job's friends heard of all the misfortune that had come upon him, they set out each one from his own

place: Eliphaz from Teman, Bildad from Shuh, and Zophar from Naamath. They met and journeyed together to give him sympathy and comfort. 12But when, at a distance, they lifted up their eyes and did not recognize him, they began to weep aloud; they tore their cloaks and threw dust upon their heads. 13Then they sat down upon the ground with him seven days and seven nights, but none of them spoke a word to him; for they saw how great was his suffering.

Job Chapter 3

1After this, Job opened his mouth and cursed his day. 2Job spoke out and said: 3Perish the day on which I was born, the night when they said, "The child is a boy!" 4May that day be darkness: let not God above call for it, nor light shine upon it! 5May darkness and gloom claim it, clouds settle upon it, the blackness of night affright it! 6May obscurity seize that day; let it not occur among the days of the year, nor enter into the count of the months! 7May that night be barren; let no joyful outcry greet it! 8Let them curse it who curse the sea, the appointed disturbers of Leviathan! 9May the stars of its twilight be darkened; may it look for daylight, but have none, nor gaze on the eyes of the dawn, 10Because it kept not shut the doors of the womb to shield my eyes from trouble! 11Why did I not perish at birth, come forth from the womb and expire? 12Wherefore did the knees receive me? or why did I suck at the breasts? 13For then I should have lain down and been tranquil; had I slept, I should then have been at rest 14With kings and counselors of the earth who built where now there are ruins 15Or with princes who had gold and filled their houses with silver. 16Or why was I not buried away like an untimely birth, like babes that have never seen the light? 17There the wicked cease from troubling, there the weary are at rest. 18There the captives are at ease together, and hear not the voice of the slave driver. 19Small and great are there the same, and the servant is free from his master. 20Why is light given to the toilers, and life to the bitter in spirit? 21They wait for death and it comes not; they search for it rather than for hidden treasures, 22Rejoice in it exultingly, and are glad when they reach the grave: 23Men whose path is hidden from them, and whom God has hemmed in! 24For sighing comes more readily to me than food, and my groans well forth like water. 25For what I fear overtakes me, and what I shrink from comes upon me. 26I have no peace nor ease; I have no rest, for trouble comes!

Job Chapter 4

1Then spoke Eliphaz the Temanite, who said: 2If someone attempts a word with you, will you mind? For how can anyone refrain from speaking? 3Behold, you have instructed many, and have made firm their feeble hands. 4Your words have upheld the stumbler; you have strengthened his faltering knees. 5But now that it comes to you, you are impatient; when it touches yourself, you are dismayed. 6Is not your piety a source of confidence, and your integrity of life your hope? 7Reflect now, what innocent person perishes? Since when are the upright destroyed? 8As I see it, those who plow for mischief and sow trouble, reap the same. 9By the breath of God they perish, and by the blast of his wrath they are consumed. 10Though the lion roars, though the king of beasts cries out, yet the teeth of the young lions are broken; 11The old lion perishes for lack of prey, and the cubs of the lioness are scattered. 12For a word was stealthily brought to me, and my ear caught a whisper of it. 13In my thoughts during visions of the night, when deep sleep falls on men, 14Fear came upon me, and shuddering, that terrified me to the bones. 15Then a spirit passed before me, and the hair of my flesh stood up. 16It paused, but its likeness I could not discern; a figure was before my eyes, and I heard a still voice: 17"Can a man be righteous as against God? Can a mortal be blameless against his Maker? 18Lo, he puts no trust in his servants, and with his angels he can find fault. 19How much more with those that dwell in houses of clay, whose foundation is in the dust, who are crushed more easily than the moth! 20Morning or evening they may be shattered; with no heed paid to it, they perish forever. 21The pegs of their tent are plucked up; they die without knowing wisdom."

Job Chapter 5

1Call now! Will anyone respond to you? To which of the holy ones will you appeal? 2Nay, impatience kills the fool and indignation slays the simpleton. 3I have seen a fool spreading his roots, but his household suddenly decayed. 4His children shall be far from safety; they shall be crushed at the gate without a rescuer. 5What they have reaped the hungry shall eat up; and the thirsty shall swallow their substance. 6For mischief comes not out of the earth, nor does trouble spring out of the ground; 7but man himself begets mischief, as sparks fly upward. 8In your place, I would appeal to God, and to God I would state my plea. 9He does great things beyond searching out, and marvelous things beyond number. 10He gives rain upon the earth and sends water upon the fields; 11He sets up on high the lowly, and those who mourn he exalts to safety. [12]He frustrates the plans of the cunning, so that their hands achieve no success; [13]He catches the wise in their own ruses, and the designs of the crafty are routed. [14]They meet with darkness in the daytime, and at noonday they grope as though it were night. [15]But the poor from the edge of the sword and from the hand of the mighty, he saves. [16]Thus the unfortunate have hope, and iniquity closes her mouth. [17]Happy is the man whom God reproves! The Almighty's chastening do not reject. [18]For he wounds, but he binds up; he smites, but his hands give healing. [19]Out of six troubles he will deliver you, and at the seventh no evil shall touch you. [20]In famine he will deliver you from death, and in war from the threat of the sword; [21]From the scourge of the tongue you shall be hidden, and shall not fear approaching ruin. [22]At destruction and want you shall laugh; the beasts of the earth you need not dread. [23]You shall be in league with the stones of the field, and the wild beasts shall be at peace with you. [24]And you shall know that your tent is secure; taking stock of your household, you shall miss nothing. [25]You shall know that your descendants are many, and your offspring as the grass of the earth. [26]You shall approach the grave in full vigor, as a shock of grain comes in at its season. [27]Lo, this we have searched out; so it is! This we have heard, and you should know.

Job Chapter 6

[1]Then Job answered and said: [2]"Ah, could my anguish but be measured and my calamity laid with it in the scales, [3]they would now outweigh the sands of the sea! Because of this I speak without restraint. [4]For the arrows of the Almighty pierce me, and my spirit drinks in their poison; the terrors of God are arrayed against me. [5]Does the wild ass bray when he has grass? Does the ox low over his fodder? [6]Can a thing insipid be eaten without salt? Is there flavor in the white of an egg? [7]I refuse to touch them; they are loathsome food to me. [8]Oh, that I might have my request, and that God would grant what I long for: [9]Even that God would decide to crush me, that he would put forth his hand and cut me off! [10]Then I should still have consolation and could exult through unremitting pain, because I have not transgressed the commands of the Holy One. [11]What strength have I that I should endure, and what is my limit that I should be patient? [12]Have I the strength of stones, or is my flesh of bronze? [13]Have I no helper, and has advice deserted me? [14]A friend owes kindness to one in despair, though he have forsaken the fear of the Almighty. [15]My brethren are undependable as a brook, as watercourses that run dry in the wadies; [16]though they may be black with ice, and with snow heaped upon them, [17]yet once they flow, they cease to be; in the heat, they disappear from their place. [18]Caravans turn aside from their routes; they go into the desert and perish. [19]The caravans of Tema search, the companies of Sheba have hopes; [20]they are disappointed, though they were confident; they come there and are frustrated. [21]It is thus that you have now become for me; you see a terrifying thing and are afraid. [22]Have I asked you to give me anything, to offer a gift for me from your possessions, [23]or to deliver me from the enemy, or to redeem me from oppressors? [24]Teach me, and I will be silent; prove to me wherein I have erred. [25]How agreeable are honest words; yet how unconvincing is your argument! [26]Do you consider your words as proof, but the sayings of a desperate man as wind? [27]You would even cast lots for the orphan, and would barter away your friend! [28]Come, now, give me your attention; surely I will not lie to your face. [29]Think it over; let there be no injustice. Think it over; I still am right. [30]Is there insincerity on my tongue, or cannot my taste discern falsehood?"

Job Chapter 7

[1]"Is not man's life on earth a drudgery? Are not his days those of a hireling? [2]He is a slave who longs for the shade, a hireling who waits for his wages. [3]So I have been assigned months of misery, and troubled nights have been told off for me. [4]If in bed I say, 'When shall I arise?' then the night drags on; I am filled with restlessness until the dawn. [5]My flesh is clothed with worms and scabs; my skin cracks and festers; [6]my days are swifter than a weaver's shuttle; they come to an end without hope. [7]Remember that my life is like the wind; I shall not see happiness again. [8]The eye that now sees me shall no more behold me; as you look at me, I shall be gone. [9]As a cloud dissolves and vanishes, so he who goes down to the nether world shall come up no more. [10]He shall not again return to his house; his place shall know him no more. [11]My own utterance I will not restrain; I will speak in the anguish of my spirit; I will complain in the bitterness of my soul. [12]Am I the sea, or a monster of the deep, that you place a watch over me? [13]When I say, 'My bed shall comfort me, my couch shall ease my complaint,' [14]then you affright me with dreams and with visions terrify me, [15]so that I should prefer choking and death rather than my pains. [16]I waste away: I cannot live forever; let me alone, for my days are but a breath. [17]What

is man, that you make much of him, or pay him any heed? [18]You observe him with each new day and try him at every moment! [19]How long will it be before you look away from me, and let me alone long enough to swallow my spittle? [20]Though I have sinned, what can I do to you, O watcher of men? [21]Why do you not pardon my offense, or take away my guilt? For soon I shall lie down in the dust; and should you seek me I shall then be gone."

Job Chapter 8

[1]"Bildad the Shuhite spoke out and said: [2]How long will you utter such things? The words from your mouth are like a mighty wind! [3]Does God pervert judgment, and does the Almighty distort justice? [4]If your children have sinned against him and he has left them in the grip of their guilt, [5]still, if you yourself have recourse to God and make supplication to the Almighty, [6]should you be blameless and upright, surely now he will awake for you and restore your rightful domain; [7]your former state will be of little moment, for in time to come you will flourish indeed. [8]If you inquire of the former generations, and give heed to the experience of the fathers [9](as we are but of yesterday and have no knowledge, because our days on earth are but a shadow), [10]will they not teach you and tell you and utter their words of understanding? [11]Can the papyrus grow up without mire? Can the reed grass flourish without water? [12]While it is yet green and uncut, it withers quicker than any grass. [13]So is the end of everyone who forgets God, and so shall the hope of the godless man perish. [14]His confidence is but a gossamer thread and his trust is a spider's web. [15]He shall rely upon his family, but it shall not last; he shall cling to it, but it shall not endure. [16]He is full of sap before sunrise, and beyond his garden his shoots go forth; [17]about a heap of stones are his roots entwined; among the rocks he takes hold. [18]Yet if one tears him from his place, it will disown him: 'I have never seen you!' [19]There he lies rotting beside the road, and out of the soil another sprouts. [20]Behold, God will not cast away the upright; neither will he take the hand of the wicked. [21]Once more will he fill your mouth with laughter, and your lips with rejoicing. [22]They that hate you shall be clothed with shame, and the tent of the wicked shall be no more."

Job Chapter 9

"[1]Then Job answered and said: [2]I know well that it is so; but how can a man be justified before God? [3]Should one wish to contend with him, he could not answer him once in a thousand times. [4]God is wise in heart and mighty in strength; who has withstood him and remained unscathed? [5]He removes the mountains before they know it; he overturns them in his anger. [6]He shakes the earth out of its place, and the pillars beneath it tremble. [7]He commands the sun, and it rises not; he seals up the stars. [8]He alone stretches out the heavens and treads upon the crests of the sea. [9]He made the Bear and Orion, the Pleiades and the constellations of the south; [10]He does great things past finding out, marvelous things beyond reckoning. [11]Should he come near me, I see him not; should he pass by, I am not aware of him; [12]Should he seize me forcibly, who can say him nay? Who can say to him, 'What are you doing?' [13]He is God and he does not relent; the helpers of Rahab bow beneath him. [14]How much less shall I give him any answer, or choose out arguments against him! [15]Even though I were right, I could not answer him, but should rather beg for what was due me. [16]If I appealed to him and he answered my call, I could not believe that he would hearken to my words; [17]With a tempest he might overwhelm me, and multiply my wounds without cause; [18]He need not suffer me to draw breath, but might fill me with bitter griefs. [19]If it be a question of strength, he is mighty; and if of judgment, who will call him to account? [20]Though I were right, my own mouth might condemn me; were I innocent, he might put me in the wrong. [21]Though I am innocent, I myself cannot know it; I despise my life. [22]It is all one! therefore I say: Both the innocent and the wicked he destroys. [23]When the scourge slays suddenly, he laughs at the despair of the innocent. [24]The earth is given into the hands of the wicked; he covers the faces of its judges. If it is not he, who then is it? [25]My days are swifter than a runner, they flee away; they see no happiness; [26]They shoot by like skiffs of reed, like an eagle swooping upon its prey. [27]If I say: I will forget my complaining, I will lay aside my sadness and be of good cheer, [28]Then I am in dread of all my pains; I know that you will not hold me innocent. [29]If I must be accounted guilty, why then should I strive in vain? [30]If I should wash myself with snow and cleanse my hands with lye, [31]Yet you would plunge me in the ditch, so that my garments would abhor me. [32]For he is not a man like myself, that I should answer him, that we should come together in judgment. [33]Would that there were an arbiter between us, who could lay his hand upon us both [34]and withdraw his rod from me. Would that his terrors did not frighten me; [35]that I might speak without being afraid of him. Since this is not the case with me."

Job Chapter 10

"¹I loathe my life. I will give myself up to complaint; I will speak from the bitterness of my soul. ²I will say to God: Do not put me in the wrong! Let me know why you oppose me. ³Is it a pleasure for you to oppress, to spurn the work of your hands, and smile on the plan of the wicked? ⁴Have you eyes of flesh? Do you see as man sees? ⁵Are your days as the days of a mortal, and are your years as a man's lifetime, ⁶That you seek for guilt in me and search after my sins, ⁷Even though you know that I am not wicked, and that none can deliver me out of your hand? ⁸Your hands have formed me and fashioned me; will you then turn and destroy me? ⁹Oh, remember that you fashioned me from clay! Will you then bring me down to dust again? ¹⁰Did you not pour me out as milk, and thicken me like cheese? ¹¹With skin and flesh you clothed me, with bones and sinews knit me together. ¹²Grace and favor you granted me, and your providence has preserved my spirit. ¹³Yet these things you have hidden in your heart; I know that they are your purpose: ¹⁴If I should sin, you would keep a watch against me, and from my guilt you would not absolve me. ¹⁵If I should be wicked, alas for me! if righteous, I dare not hold up my head, filled with ignominy and sodden with affliction! ¹⁶Should it lift up, you hunt me like a lion: repeatedly you show your wondrous power against me, ¹⁷You renew your attack upon me and multiply your harassment of me; in waves your troops come against me. ¹⁸Why then did you bring me forth from the womb? I should have died and no eye have seen me. ¹⁹I should be as though I had never lived; I should have been taken from the womb to the grave. ²⁰Are not the days of my life few? Let me alone, that I may recover a little ²¹Before I go whence I shall not return, to the land of darkness and of gloom, ²²The black, disordered land where darkness is the only light."

Job Chapter 11

"¹And Zophar the Naamathite spoke out and said: ²Should not the man of many words be answered, or must the garrulous man necessarily be right? ³Shall your babblings keep men silent, and shall you deride and no one give rebuke? ⁴Shall you say: 'My teaching is pure, and I am clean in your sight'? ⁵But oh, that God would speak, and open his lips against you, ⁶And tell you that the secrets of wisdom are twice as effective: So you might learn that God will make you answer for your guilt. ⁷Can you penetrate the designs of God? Dare you vie with the perfection of the Almighty? ⁸It is higher than the heavens; what can you do? It is deeper than the netherworld; what can you know? ⁹It is longer than the earth in measure, and broader than the sea. ¹⁰If he seize and imprison or call to judgment, who then can say him nay? ¹¹For he knows the worthlessness of men and sees iniquity; will he then ignore it? ¹²Will empty man then gain understanding, and the wild jackass be made docile? ¹³If you set your heart aright and stretch out your hands toward him, ¹⁴If you remove all iniquity from your conduct, and let not injustice dwell in your tent, ¹⁵Surely then you may lift up your face in innocence; you may stand firm and unafraid. ¹⁶For then you shall forget your misery, or recall it like waters that have ebbed away. ¹⁷Then your life shall be brighter than the noonday; its gloom shall become as the morning, ¹⁸And you shall be secure, because there is hope; you shall look round you and lie down in safety, ¹⁹and you shall take your rest with none to disturb. Many shall entreat your favor, ²⁰but the wicked, looking on, shall be consumed with envy. Escape shall be cut off from them, they shall wait to expire."

Job Chapter 12

"¹Then Job replied and said: ²No doubt you are the intelligent folk, and with you wisdom shall die! ³But I have intelligence as well as you; for who does not know such things as these? ⁴I have become the sport of my neighbors: 'The one whom God answers when he calls upon him, The just, the perfect man,' is a laughing-stock; ⁵The undisturbed esteem my downfall a disgrace such as awaits unsteady feet; ⁶Yet the tents of robbers are prosperous, and those who provoke God are secure. ⁷But now ask the beasts to teach you, and the birds of the air to tell you; ⁸Or the reptiles on earth to instruct you, and the fish of the sea to inform you. ⁹Which of all these does not know that the hand of God has done this? ¹⁰In his hand is the soul of every living thing, and the life breath of all mankind. ¹¹Does not the ear judge words as the mouth tastes food? ¹²So with old age is wisdom, and with length of days understanding. ¹³With him are wisdom and might; his are counsel and understanding. ¹⁴If he breaks a thing down, there is no rebuilding; if he imprisons a man, there is no release. ¹⁵He holds back the waters and there is drought; he sends them forth and they overwhelm the land. ¹⁶With him are strength and prudence; the misled and the misleaders are his. ¹⁷He sends counselors away barefoot, and of judges he makes fools. ¹⁸He loosens the bonds imposed by kings and leaves but a waistcloth to bind the king's own loins. ¹⁹He silences the trusted adviser, and takes discretion from the aged. ²⁰He breaks down the barriers of the streams and lets their never-failing waters flow away. ²¹The recesses of the darkness he discloses, and brings the gloom forth to the light. ²²He makes nations great and he destroys them; he spreads peoples abroad and he abandons them. ²³He takes understanding from the leaders of the land, ²⁴till they grope in the darkness without light; he makes them stagger like drunken men."

Job Chapter 13

"¹Lo, all this my eye has seen; my ear has heard and perceived it. ²What you know, I also know; I fall not short of you. ³But I would speak with the Almighty; I wish to reason with God. ⁴You are glossing over falsehoods and offering vain remedies, every one of you! ⁵Oh, that you would be altogether silent! This for you would be wisdom. ⁶Hear now the rebuke I shall utter and listen to the reproof from my lips. ⁷Is it for God that you speak falsehood? Is it for him that you utter deceit? ⁸Is it for him that you show partiality? Do you play advocate on behalf of God? ⁹Will it be well when he shall search you out? Would you impose on him as one does on men? ¹⁰He will openly rebuke you if even in secret you show partiality. ¹¹Surely will his majesty affright you and the dread of him fall upon you. ¹²Your reminders are ashy maxims, your fabrications are mounds of clay. ¹³Be silent, let me alone! that I may speak and give vent to my feelings. ¹⁴I will carry my flesh between my teeth, and take my life in my hand. ¹⁵Slay me though he might, I will wait for him; I will defend my conduct before him. ¹⁶And this shall be my salvation, that no impious man can come into his presence. ¹⁷Pay careful heed to my speech, and give my statement a hearing. ¹⁸Behold, I have prepared my case, I know that I am in the right. ¹⁹If anyone can make a case against me, then I shall be silent and die. ²⁰These things only do not use against me, then from your presence I need not hide: ²¹Withdraw your hand far from me, and let not the terror of you frighten me. ²²Then call me, and I will respond; or let me speak first, and answer me. ²³What are my faults and my sins? My misdeeds and my sins make known to me! ²⁴Why do you hide your face and consider me your enemy? ²⁵Will you harass a wind-driven leaf, or pursue a withered straw? ²⁶For you draw up bitter indictments against me, and punish in me the faults of my youth. ²⁷You put my feet in the stocks; you watch all my paths and trace out all my footsteps. ²⁸Though he wears out like a leather bottle, like a garment that the moth has consumed?"

Job Chapter 14

"¹Man born of woman is short-lived and full of trouble, ²Like a flower that springs up and fades, swift as a shadow that does not abide. ³Upon such a one will you cast your eyes so as to bring him into judgment before you, ⁴Can a man be found who is clean of defilement? There is none, ⁵however short his days. You know the number of his months; you have fixed the limit which he cannot pass. ⁶Look away from him and let him be, while, like a hireling, he completes his day. ⁷For a tree there is hope, if it be cut down, that it will sprout again and that its tender shoots will not cease. ⁸Even though its root grow old in the earth, and its stump die in the dust, ⁹Yet at the first whiff of water it may flourish again and put forth branches like a young plant. ¹⁰But when a man dies, all vigor leaves him; when man expires, where then is he? ¹¹As when the waters of a lake fail, or a stream grows dry and parches, ¹²So men lie down and rise not again. Till the heavens are no more, they shall not awake, nor be roused out of their sleep. ¹³Oh, that you would hide me in the nether world and keep me sheltered till your wrath is past; would fix a time for me, and then remember me! ¹⁴When a man has died, were he to live again, all the days of my drudgery I would wait, until my relief should come. ¹⁵You would call, and I would answer you; you would esteem the work of your hands. ¹⁶Surely then you would count my steps, and not keep watch for sin in me. ¹⁷My misdeeds would be sealed up in a pouch, and you would cover over my guilt. ¹⁸But as a mountain falls at last and its rock is moved from its place, ¹⁹As waters wear away the stones and floods wash away the soil of the land, so you destroy the hope of man. ²⁰You prevail once for all against him and he passes on; with changed appearance you send him away. ²¹If his sons are honored, he is not aware of it; if they are in disgrace, he does not know about them. ²²Only his own flesh pains him, and his soul grieves for him."

Job Chapter 15

"¹Then Eliphaz the Temanite spoke and said: ²Should a wise man answer with airy opinions, or puff himself up with wind? ³Should he argue in speech which does not avail, and in words which are to no profit? ⁴You in fact do away with piety, and you lessen devotion toward God, ⁵Because your wickedness instructs your mouth, and you choose to speak like the crafty. ⁶Your own mouth condemns you, not I; your own lips refute you. ⁷Are you indeed the first-born of mankind, or were you brought forth before the hills? 8Are you privy to the counsels of God, and do you restrict wisdom to yourself? 9What do you know that we do not know? What intelligence have you which we have not? 10There are gray-haired old men among us more advanced in years than your father. 11Are the consolations of God not enough for you, and speech that deals gently with you? 12Why do your notions carry you away, and why do your eyes blink, 13So that you turn your anger against God and let such words escape your mouth! 14What is a man that he should be blameless, one born of woman that he should be righteous? 15If in his holy ones God places no confidence, and if the heavens are not clean in his sight, 16How much less so is the abominable, the corrupt: man, who drinks in iniquity like water! 17I will show you, if you listen to me; what I have seen I will tell—18What wise men relate and have not contradicted since the days of their fathers, 19To whom alone the land was given, when no foreigner moved among them. 20The wicked man is in torment all his days, and limited years are in store for the tyrant; 21The sound of terrors is in his ears; when all is prosperous, the spoiler comes upon him. 22He despairs of escaping the darkness, and looks ever for the sword; 23A wanderer, food for the vultures, he knows that his destruction is imminent. 24By day the darkness fills him with dread; distress and anguish overpower him. 25Because he has stretched out his hand against God and bade defiance to the Almighty, 26One shall rush sternly upon him with the stout bosses of his shield, like a king prepared for the charge. 27Because he has blinded himself with his crassness, padding his loins with fat, 28He shall dwell in ruinous cities, in houses that are deserted, that are crumbling into clay 29with no shadow to lengthen over the ground. He shall not be rich, and his possessions shall not endure; 30A flame shall wither him up in his early growth, and with the wind his blossoms shall disappear. 31His stalk shall wither before its time, and his branches shall be green no more. 32He shall be like a vine that sheds its grapes unripened, and like an olive tree casting off its bloom. 33For the breed of the impious shall be sterile, and fire shall consume the tents of extortioners. 34They conceive malice and bring forth emptiness; they give birth to failure."

Job Chapter 16

1Then Job answered and said: 2I have heard this sort of thing many times. Wearisome comforters are you all! 3Is there no end to windy words? Or what sickness have you that you speak on? 4I also could talk as you do, were you in my place. I could declaim over you, or wag my head at you; 5I could strengthen you with talk, or shake my head with silent lips. 6If I speak, this pain I have will not be checked; if I leave off, it will not depart from me. 7But now that I am exhausted and stunned, all my company has closed in on me. 8As a witness there rises up my traducer, speaking openly against me; 9I am the prey his wrath assails, he gnashes his teeth against me. My enemies lord it over me; 10their mouths are agape to bite me. They smite me on the cheek insultingly; they are all enlisted against me. 11God has given me over to the impious; into the clutches of the wicked he has cast me. 12I was in peace, but he dislodged me; he seized me by the neck and dashed me to pieces. He has set me up for a target; 13his arrows strike me from all directions, He pierces my sides without mercy, he pours out my gall upon the ground. 14He pierces me with thrust upon thrust; he attacks me like a warrior. 15I have fastened sackcloth over my skin, and have laid my brow in the dust. 16My face is inflamed with weeping and there is darkness over my eyes, 17Although my hands are free from violence, and my prayer is sincere. 18O earth, cover not my blood, nor let my outcry come to rest! 19Even now, behold, my witness is in heaven, and my spokesman is on high. 20My friends it is who wrong me; before God my eyes drop tears, 21That he may do justice for a mortal in his presence and decide between a man and his neighbor. 22For my years are numbered now, and I am on a journey from which I shall not return.

Job Chapter 17

1My spirit is broken, my lamp of life extinguished; my burial is at hand. 2I am indeed mocked, and, as their provocation mounts, my eyes grow dim. 3Grant me one to offer you a pledge on my behalf: who is there that will give surety for me? 4You darken their minds to knowledge; therefore they do not understand. 5My lot is described as evil, 6and I am made a byword of the people; their object lesson I have become. 7My eye has grown blind with anguish, and all my frame is shrunken to a shadow. 8Upright men are astonished at this, and the innocent aroused against the wicked. 9Yet the righteous shall hold to his way, and he who has clean hands increase in strength. 10But turn now, and come on again; for I shall not find a wise man among you! 11My days are passed away, my plans are at an end, the cherished purposes of my heart. 12Such men change the night into day; where there is darkness they talk of approaching light. 13If I look for the nether world as my dwelling, if I spread my couch in the darkness, 14If I must call corruption "my

father," and the maggot "my mother" and "my sister," 15Where then is my hope, and my prosperity, who shall see? 16Will they descend with me into the nether world? Shall we go down together into the dust?

Job Chapter 18

1Then Bildad the Shuhite replied and said: 2When will you put an end to words? Reflect, and then we can have discussion. 3Why are we accounted like the beasts, their equals in your sight? 4You who tear yourself in your anger, shall the earth be neglected on your account, or the rock be moved out of its place? 5Truly, the light of the wicked is extinguished; no flame brightens his hearth. 6The light is darkened in his tent; in spite of him, his lamp goes out. 7His vigorous steps are hemmed in, and his own counsel casts him down. 8For he rushes headlong into a net, and he wanders into a pitfall. 9A trap seizes him by the heel, and a snare lays hold of him. 10A noose for him is hid on the ground, and the toils for him on the way. 11On every side terrors affright him; they harry him at each step. 12Disaster is ready at his side, 13the first-born of death consumes his limbs. 14Fiery destruction lodges in his tent, and marches him off to the king of terrors. He is plucked from the security of his tent; 15over his abode brimstone is scattered. 16Below, his roots dry up, and above, his branches wither. 17His memory perishes from the land, and he has no name on the earth. 18He is driven from light into darkness, and banished out of the world. 19He has neither son nor grandson among his people, nor any survivor where once he dwelt. 20They who come after shall be appalled at his fate; they who went before are struck with horror. 21So is it then with the dwelling of the impious man, and such is the place of him who knows not God!

Job Chapter 19

1Then Job answered and said: 2How long will you vex my soul, grind me down with words? 3These ten times you have reviled me, have assailed me without shame! 4Be it indeed that I am at fault and that my fault remains with me, 5Even so, if you would vaunt yourselves against me and cast up to me any reproach, 6Know then that God has dealt unfairly with me, and compassed me round with his net. 7If I cry out "Injustice!" I am not heard. I cry for help, but there is no redress. 8He has barred my way and I cannot pass; he has veiled my path in darkness; 9He has stripped me of my glory, and taken the diadem from my brow. 10He breaks me down on every side, and I am gone; my hope he has uprooted like a tree. 11His wrath he has kindled against me; he counts me among his enemies. 12His troops advance as one man; they build up their road to attack me, and they encamp around my tent. 13My brethren have withdrawn from me, and my friends are wholly estranged. 14My kinsfolk and companions neglect me, and my guests have forgotten me. 15Even my handmaids treat me as a stranger; I am an alien in their sight. 16I call my servant, but he gives no answer, though in my speech I plead with him. 17My breath is abhorred by my wife; I am loathsome to the men of my family. 18The young children, too, despise me; when I appear, they speak against me. 19All my intimate friends hold me in horror; those whom I loved have turned against me! 20My bones cleave to my skin, and I have escaped with my flesh between my teeth. 21Pity me, pity me, O you my friends, for the hand of God has struck me! 22Why do you hound me as though you were divine, and insatiably prey upon me? 23Oh, would that my words were written down! Would that they were inscribed in a record: 24That with an iron chisel and with lead they were cut in the rock forever! 25But as for me, I know that my Vindicator lives, and that he will at last stand forth upon the dust; 26And from my flesh I shall see God; my inmost being is consumed with longing. 27Whom I myself shall see: my own eyes, not another's, shall behold him. 28But you who say, "How shall we persecute him, seeing that the root of the matter is found in him?" 29Be afraid of the sword for yourselves, for these crimes deserve the sword; that you may know that there is a judgment.

Job Chapter 20

1Then Zophar the Naamathite spoke and said: 2"Therefore my thoughts answer me, and because of this I am disturbed. 3I hear a rebuke that dishonors me, and my understanding inspires me to reply. 4Do you not know this from olden time, since man was placed upon the earth, 5that the triumph of the wicked is short, and the joy of the godless but for a moment? 6Though his pride mounts up to the heavens and his head reaches to the clouds, 7he will perish forever like his own dung; those who have seen him will say, 'Where is he?' 8He will fly away like a dream and not be found; he will be chased away like a vision of the night. 9The eye that saw him will see him no more, nor will his place behold him any longer. 10His children will seek the favor of the poor, and his hands will give back his wealth. 11Though his bones are full of youthful vigor, they will lie down with him in the dust. 12Though evil is sweet in his mouth, though he hides it under his tongue, 13though he is loath to let it go and holds it in his mouth, [14]yet his food will turn sour in his stomach; it will become the venom of serpents within him. [15]He will spit out the riches he swallowed; God will make his stomach vomit them up. [16]He will suck the poison of serpents; the fangs of an adder will kill him. [17]He will not enjoy the streams, the rivers flowing with honey and cream. [18]What he toiled for he must give back uneaten; he will not enjoy the profit from his trading. [19]For he has oppressed and forsaken the poor; he has seized houses he did not build. [20]"Because his greed knew no bounds, he will not escape with his treasure. [21]Nothing is left for him to devour; his prosperity will not endure. [22]In the midst of his plenty, distress will overtake him; the full force of misery will come upon him. [23]When he has filled his belly, God will vent his burning anger against him and rain down his blows on him. [24]Though he flees from an iron weapon, a bronze-tipped arrow will pierce him. [25]He pulls it out of his back, the gleaming point out of his liver. Terrors will come over him; [26]total darkness lies in wait for his treasure. A fire unfanned will consume him and devour what is left in his tent. [27]The heavens will expose his guilt; the earth will rise up against him. [28]A flood will carry off his house, rushing waters on the day of God's wrath. [29]Such is the fate God allots the wicked, the heritage appointed for them by God."

Job Chapter 21

[1]Then Job said in reply: [2]"At least listen to my words, and let that be the consolation you offer. [3]Bear with me while I speak; and after I have spoken, you can mock! [4]Is my complaint toward man? And why should I not be impatient? [5]Look at me and be astonished, put your hands over your mouths. [6]When I think of it, I am dismayed, and horror takes hold on my flesh. [7]Why do the wicked survive, grow old, become mighty in power? [8]Their progeny is secure in their sight; they see before them their kinsfolk and their offspring. [9]Their homes are safe and without fear, nor is the scourge of God upon them. [10]Their bulls gender without fail; their cows calve and do not miscarry. [11]These folk have infants numerous as lambs, and their children dance. [12]They sing to the timbrel and harp, and make merry to the sound of the flute. [13]They live out their days in prosperity, and tranquilly go down to the nether world. [14]Yet they say to God, 'Depart from us, for we have no wish to learn your ways! [15]What is the Almighty that we should serve him? And what gain shall we have if we pray to him?' [16]If their happiness is not in their own hands and if the counsel of the wicked is repulsive to God, [17]How often is the lamp of the wicked put out? How often does destruction come upon them, the portion he allots in his anger? [18]Let them be like straw before the wind, and like chaff which the storm snatches away! [19]May God not store up the man's misery for his children; let him requite the man himself so that he feels it, [20]Let his own eyes see the calamity, and the wrath of the Almighty let him drink! [21]For what interest has he in his family after him, when the number of his months is finished? [22]Can anyone teach God knowledge, seeing that he judges those on high? [23]One dies in his full vigor, wholly at ease and content; [24]His figure is full and nourished, and his bones are rich in marrow. [25]Another dies in bitterness of soul, having never tasted happiness. [26]Alike they lie down in the dust, and worms cover them both. [27]Behold, I know your thoughts, and the arguments you rehearse against me. [28]For you say, 'Where is the house of the magnate, and where the dwelling place of the wicked?' [29]Have you not asked the wayfarers and do you not recognize their monuments? [30]Nay, the evil man is spared calamity when it comes; [31]Who will charge him with his conduct to his face, and for what he has done who will repay him? [32]He is carried to the grave, and the clods of the valley are sweet to him. [33]Over him the funeral mound keeps watch, while all the line of mankind follows him, and the countless others who have gone before. [34]How then can you offer me vain comfort, while in your answers perfidy remains?"

Job Chapter 22

[1]Then Eliphaz the Temanite answered and said: [2]Can a man be profitable to God? Though to himself a wise man be profitable! [3]Is it of advantage to the Almighty if you are just? Or is it a gain to him if you make your ways perfect? [4]Is it because of your piety that he reproves you— that he enters with you into judgment? [5]Is not your wickedness manifold? Are not your iniquities endless? [6]You have unjustly kept your kinsmen's goods in pawn, left them stripped naked of their clothing, [7]To the thirsty you have given no water to drink, and from the hungry you have withheld bread; [8]As if the land belonged to the man of might, and only the privileged were to dwell in it. [9]You have sent widows away empty-handed, and the resources of orphans you have destroyed. [10]Therefore snares are round about you, and a sudden terror causes you dismay, [11]Or darkness, in which you cannot see; a deluge of waters covers you. [12]Does not God, in the heights of the heavens, behold the stars, high though they are? [13]Yet you say, "What does God know? Can

he judge through the thick darkness? [14]Clouds hide him so that he cannot see; he walks upon the vault of the heavens!" [15]Do you indeed keep to the ancient way trodden by worthless men, [16]Who were snatched away before their time; whose foundations a flood swept away? [17]These men said to God, "Depart from us!" and, "What can the Almighty do to us?" [18](Yet he had filled their houses with good things! But far be from me the mind of the impious!) [19]The just look on and are gladdened, and the innocent deride them: [20]"Truly these have been destroyed where they stood, and such as were left, fire has consumed!" [21]Come to terms with him to be at peace. In this shall good come to you: [22]Receive instruction from his mouth, and lay up his words in your heart. [23]If you return to the Almighty, you will be restored; if you put iniquity far from your tent, [24]And treat raw gold like dust, and the fine gold of Ophir as pebbles from the brook, [25]Then the Almighty himself shall be your gold and your sparkling silver. [26]For then you shall delight in the Almighty and you shall lift up your face toward God. [27]You shall entreat him and he will hear you, and your vows you shall fulfill. [28]When you make a decision, it shall succeed for you, and upon your ways the light shall shine. [29]For he brings down the pride of the haughty, but the man of humble mien he saves. [30]God delivers him who is innocent; you shall be delivered through cleanness of hands.

Job Chapter 23

[1]Again Job answered and said: [2]Though I know my complaint is bitter, his hand is heavy upon me in my groanings. [3]Oh, that today I might find him, that I might come to his judgment seat! [4]I would set out my cause before him, and fill my mouth with arguments; [5]I would learn the words with which he would answer, and understand what he would reply to me. [6]Even should he contend against me with his great power, yet, would that he himself might heed me! [7]There the upright man might reason with him, and I should once and for all preserve my rights. [8]But if I go to the east, he is not there; or to the west, I cannot perceive him; [9]Where the north enfolds him, I behold him not; by the south he is veiled, and I see him not. [10]Yet he knows my way; if he proved me, I should come forth as gold. [11]My foot has always walked in his steps; his way I have kept and have not turned aside. [12]From the commands of his lips I have not departed; the words of his mouth I have treasured in my heart. [13]But he had decided, and who can say him nay? What he desires, that he does. [14]For he will carry out what is appointed for me; and many such things may yet be in his mind. [15]Therefore am I dismayed before him; when I take thought, I fear him. [16]Indeed God has made my courage fail; the Almighty has put me in dismay. [17]Yes, would that I had vanished in darkness, and that thick gloom were before me to conceal me.

Job Chapter 24

[1]Why are not times set by the Almighty, and why do his friends not see his days? [2]The wicked remove landmarks; they steal away herds and pasture them. [3]The asses of orphans they drive away; they take the widow's ox for a pledge. [4]They force the needy off the road; all the poor of the land are driven into hiding. [5]Like wild asses in the desert, these go forth to their task of seeking food; the steppe provides food for the young among them; [6]they harvest at night in the untilled land. [7]They pass the night naked, without clothing, for they have no covering against the cold; [8]They are drenched with the rain of the mountains, and for want of shelter they cling to the rock. [11]Between the rows they press out the oil; they glean in the vineyard of the wicked. They tread the wine presses, yet suffer thirst, [10]and famished are those who carry the sheaves. [12]From the dust the dying groan, and the souls of the wounded cry out (yet God does not treat it as unseemly). [13]There are those who are rebels against the light; they know not its ways; they abide not in its paths. [14]When there is no light the murderer rises, to kill the poor and needy. [15]The eye of the adulterer watches for the twilight; he says, "No eye will see me." In the night the thief roams about, and he puts a mask over his face; [16]in the dark he breaks into houses. By day they shut themselves in; none of them know the light, [17]for daylight they regard as darkness. [18]Their portion in the land is accursed, [20]and wickedness is splintered like wood. [22]To him who rises without assurance of his life [23]he gives safety and support. He sustains the mighty by his strength, and his eyes are on their ways. [24]They are exalted for a while, and then they are gone; they are laid low and, like all others, are gathered up; like ears of grain they shrivel. [25]If this be not so, who will confute me, and reduce my argument to nought?

Job Chapter 25

[1]Then Bildad the Shuhite answered and said: [2]Dominion and awesomeness are his who brings about harmony in his heavens. [3]Is there any numbering of his troops? Yet to which of them does not his light extend? [4]How can a man be just in God's sight, or how can any woman's child be innocent? [5]Behold, even the moon is not bright and

the stars are not clear in his sight. 6How much less man, who is but a maggot, the son of man, who is only a worm?

Job Chapter 26

1Then Job spoke again and said: 2What help you give to the powerless, what strength to the feeble arm! 3How you counsel, as though he had no wisdom; how profuse is the advice you offer! 4With whose help have you uttered those words, and whose is the breath that comes forth from you? 5The shades beneath writhe in terror, the waters, and their inhabitants. 6Naked before him is the nether world, and Abaddon has no covering. 7He stretches out the North over empty space, and suspends the earth over nothing at all; 8He binds up the waters in his clouds, yet the cloud is not rent by their weight; 9He holds back the appearance of the full moon by spreading his clouds before it. 10He has marked out a circle on the surface of the deep as the boundary of light and darkness. 11The pillars of the heavens tremble and are stunned at his thunderous rebuke; 12By his power he stirs up the sea, and by his might he crushes Rahab; 13With his angry breath he scatters the waters, and he hurls the lightning against them relentlessly; 14Lo, these are but the outlines of his ways, and how faint is the word we hear!

Job Chapter 27

1I will teach you the manner of God's dealings, and the way of the Almighty I will not conceal. 2As God lives, who withholds my deserts, the Almighty, who has made bitter my soul, 3So long as I still have life in me and the breath of God is in my nostrils, 4My lips shall not speak falsehood, nor my tongue utter deceit! 5Far be it from me to account you right; till I die I will not renounce my innocence. 6My justice I maintain and I will not relinquish it; my heart does not reproach me for any of my days. 7Let my enemy be as the wicked and my adversary as the unjust! 8For what can the impious man expect when he is cut off, when God requires his life? 9Will God then attend to his cry when calamity comes upon him? 10Will he then delight in the Almighty and call upon him constantly? 12Behold, you yourselves have all seen it; why then do you spend yourselves in idle words! 13This is the portion of a wicked man from God, the inheritance an oppressor receives from the Almighty: 14Though his children be many, the sword is their destiny. His offspring shall not be filled with bread. 15His survivors, when they die, shall have no burial, and their widows shall not be mourned. 16Though he heap up silver like dust and store away mounds of clothing, 17What he has stored the just man shall wear, and the innocent shall divide the silver. 18He builds his house as of cobwebs, or like a booth put up by the vine-keeper. 19He lies down a rich man, one last time; he opens his eyes and nothing remains to him. 20Terrors rush upon him by day; at night the tempest carries him off. 21The storm wind seizes him and he disappears; it sweeps him out of his place.

Job Chapter 28

1There is indeed a mine for silver, and a place for gold which men refine. 2Iron is taken from the earth, and copper is melted out of stone. 3He sets an end to darkness, and searches out all perfection: the stones of darkness, and the shadow of death. 4He breaks open a shaft away from where people live; they are forgotten by travelers, they hang far from mankind, they swing to and fro. 5The earth, from it comes bread, but underneath it is turned up as by fire. 6Its stones are the place of sapphires, and it has dust of gold. 7That path no bird of prey knows, nor has the falcon's eye seen it. 8The proud beasts have not trodden it, nor has the fierce lion passed over it. 9He puts forth his hand on the flinty rock; he overturns the mountains by the roots. 10He cuts out channels in the rocks, and his eye sees every precious thing. 11He dams up the streams from trickling; what is hidden he brings forth to light. 12But where shall wisdom be found? And where is the place of understanding? 13Man does not know its worth, and it is not found in the land of the living. 14The deep says, 'It is not in me,' and the sea says, 'It is not with me.' 15It cannot be bought for gold, and silver cannot be weighed as its price. 16It cannot be valued in the gold of Ophir, in precious onyx or sapphire. 17Gold and glass cannot equal it, nor can it be exchanged for jewels of fine gold. 18No mention shall be made of coral or of crystal; the price of wisdom is above pearls. 19The topaz of Ethiopia cannot equal it, nor can it be valued in pure gold. 20From where, then, does wisdom come? And where is the place of understanding? 21It is hidden from the eyes of all living and concealed from the birds of the air. 22Abaddon and Death say, 'We have heard a rumor of it with our ears.' 23God understands the way to it, and he knows its place. 24For he looks to the ends of the earth and sees everything under the heavens. 25When he gave to the wind its weight and apportioned the waters by measure, 26when he made a decree for the rain and a way for the lightning of the thunder, 27then he saw it and declared it; he established it, and searched it out. 28And he said to man, 'Behold, the fear of the Lord, that is wisdom, and to depart from evil is understanding.'

Job Chapter 29

1Job took up his theme anew and said: 2Oh, that I were as in the months past! as in the days when God watched over me, 3While he kept his lamp shining above my head, and by his light I walked through darkness; 4As I was in my flourishing days, when God sheltered my tent; 5When the Almighty was yet with me, and my children were round about me; 6When my footsteps were bathed in milk, and the rock flowed with streams of oil; 7When I went forth to the gate of the city and set up my seat in the square – 8Then the young men saw me and withdrew, while the elders rose up and stood; 9The chief men refrained from speaking and covered their mouths with their hands; 10The voice of the princes was silenced, and their tongues stuck to the roofs of their mouths. 11Whoever heard of me blessed me; those who saw me commended me. 12For I rescued the poor who cried out for help, the orphans, and the unassisted; 13The blessing of those in extremity came upon me, and the heart of the widow I made joyful. 14I wore my honesty like a garment; justice was my robe and my turban. 15I was eyes to the blind, and feet to the lame was I; 16I was a father to the needy; the rights of the stranger I studied, 17And I broke the jaws of the wicked man; from his teeth I forced the prey. 18Then I said: "In my own nest I shall grow old; I shall multiply years like the phoenix. 19My root is spread out to the waters; the dew rests by night on my branches. 20My glory is fresh within me, and my bow is renewed in my hand!"

Job Chapter 30

1But now they hold me in derision who are younger in years than I; whose fathers I should have disdained to rank with the dogs of my flock. 2Such strength as they had, to me meant nought; they were utterly destitute. 3In want and hunger was their lot, they who fled to the parched wastelands: 4They plucked saltwort and shrubs; the roots of the broom plant were their food. 5They were banished from among men, with an outcry like that against a thief– 6to dwell on the slopes of the wadies, in caves of sand and stone; 7among the bushes they raised their raucous cry; under the nettles they huddled together. 8Irresponsible, nameless men, they were driven out of the land. 9Yet now they sing of me in mockery; I am become a byword among them. 10They abhor me, they stand aloof from me, they do not hesitate to spit in my face! 11Indeed, they have loosed their bonds; they lord it over me, and have thrown off restraint in my presence. 12To subvert my paths they rise up; they build their approaches for my ruin. 13To destroy me, they attack with none to stay them; 14as through a wide breach they advance. Amid the uproar they come on in waves; 15over me rolls the terror. My dignity is borne off on the wind, and my welfare vanishes like a cloud. 18One with great power lays hold of my clothing; by the collar of my tunic he seizes me: 19He has cast me into the mire; I am leveled with the dust and ashes. 20I cry to you, but you do not answer me; you stand off and look at me, 21Then you turn upon me without mercy and with your strong hand you buffet me. 22You raise me up and drive me before the wind; I am tossed about by the tempest. 23Indeed I know you will turn me back in death to the destined place of everyone alive. 24Yet should not a hand be held out to help a wretched man in his calamity? 25Or have I not wept for the hardships of others; was not my soul grieved for the destitute? 26Yet when I looked for good, then evil came; when I expected light, then came darkness. 27My soul ebbs away from me; days of affliction have overtaken me. 28My frame takes no rest by night; my inward parts seethe and will not be stilled. 29I go about in gloom, without the sun; I rise up in public to voice my grief. 30I have become the brother of jackals, companion to the ostrich. 31My blackened skin falls away from me; the heat scorches my very frame. 32My harp is turned to mourning, and my reed pipe to sounds of weeping.

Job Chapter 31

1But what is man's lot from God above, his inheritance from the Almighty on high? 2Is it not calamity for the unrighteous, and woe for evildoers? 3Does he not see my ways, and number all my steps? 4Let God weigh me in the scales of justice; thus will he know my innocence! 5If I have walked in falsehood and my foot has hastened to deceit; 6If my steps have turned out of the way, and my heart has followed my eyes, or any stain clings to my hands, 7Then may I sow, but another eat of it, or may my planting be rooted up! 8If my land has cried out against me till its very furrows complained; 9If I have eaten its produce without payment and grieved the hearts of its tenants; 10Then let the thistles grow instead of wheat and noxious weeds instead of barley! 11If I have made an agreement with my eyes and entertained any thoughts against a maiden; 12If my heart has been enticed toward a woman, and I have lain in wait at my neighbor's door; 13Then may my wife grind for another, and may others cohabit with her! 14For that would be heinous, a crime to be condemned; 15A fire that should burn down to the abyss till it consumed all my possessions to the roots. 16Had I refused justice to my manservant or to my maid, when they had a claim against me, 17What then should I do when God rose up; what could I answer when he demanded an account? 18Did not he who made me in the womb make him? Did not the same One fashion us before our birth? 19If I have denied anything to the poor, or allowed the eyes of the widow to languish 20While I ate my portion alone, with no share in it for the fatherless, 21Though like a father God has reared me from my youth, guiding me even from my mother's womb - 22If I have seen a wanderer without clothing, or a poor man without covering, 23Whose limbs have not blessed me when warmed with the fleece of my sheep; 24If I have raised my hand against the innocent because I saw that I had supporters at the gate - 25Then may my arm fall from the shoulder, my forearm be broken at the elbow! 26For the dread of God will be upon me, and his majesty will overpower me. 27Had I put my trust in gold or called fine gold my security; 28Or had I rejoiced that my wealth was great, or that my hand had acquired abundance - 29Had I looked upon the sun as it shone, or the moon in the splendor of its progress, 30And had my heart been secretly enticed to waft them a kiss with my hand; 31This too would be a crime for condemnation, for I should have denied God above. 32Had I rejoiced at the destruction of my enemy or exulted when evil fell upon him, 33Even though I had not suffered my mouth to sin by uttering a curse against his life - 34Had not the men of my tent exclaimed, "Who has not been fed with his meat!" 35Because no stranger lodged in the street, but I opened my door to wayfarers - 36Had I, out of human weakness, hidden my sins and buried my guilt in my bosom 37Because I feared the noisy multitude and the scorn of the tribes terrified me - then I should have remained silent, and not come out of doors! 38Oh, that I had one to hear my case, and that my accuser would write out his indictment! 39Surely, I should wear it on my shoulder or put it on me like a diadem; 40Of all my steps I should give him an account; like a prince, I should present myself before him. 41This is my final plea; let the Almighty answer me! The words of Job are ended.

Job Chapter 32

1Then the three men ceased to answer Job, because he was righteous in his own eyes. 2But the anger of Elihu, son of Barachel the Buzite, of the family of Ram, was kindled. He was angry with Job for considering himself rather than God to be in the right. 3He was angry also with the three friends because they had not found a good answer and had not condemned Job. 4But since these men were older than he, Elihu bided his time before addressing Job. 5When, however, Elihu saw that there was no reply in the mouths of the three men, his wrath was inflamed. 6So Elihu, son of Barachel the Buzite, spoke out and said: I am young and you are very old; therefore I held back and was afraid to declare to you my knowledge. 7Days should speak, I thought, and many years teach wisdom! 8But it is a spirit in man, the breath of the Almighty, that gives him understanding. 9It is not those of many days who are wise, nor the aged who understand the right. 10Therefore I say, hearken to me; let me too set forth my knowledge! 11Behold, I have waited for your discourses, and have given ear to your arguments. 12Yes, I followed you attentively as you searched out what to say; And behold, there is none who has convicted Job, not one of you who could refute his statements. 13Yet do not say, "We have met wisdom. God may vanquish him but not man!" 14For had he addressed his words to me, I should not then have answered him as you have done. 15They are dismayed, they make no more reply; words fail them. 16Must I wait? Now that they speak no more, and have ceased to make reply, 17I too will speak my part; I also will show my knowledge! 18For I am full of matters to utter; the spirit within me compels me. 19Like a new wineskin with wine under pressure, my bosom is ready to burst. 20Let me speak and obtain relief; let me open my lips, and make reply. 21I would not be partial to anyone, nor give flattering titles to any. 22For I know nought of flattery; if I did, my Maker would soon take me away.

Job Chapter 33

1Therefore, O Job, hear my discourse, and hearken to all my words. 2Behold, now I open my mouth; my tongue and my voice form words. 3I will state directly what is in my mind, my lips shall utter knowledge sincerely; 4For the spirit of God has made me, the breath of the Almighty keeps me alive. 5If you are able, refute me; draw up your arguments and stand forth. 6Behold I, like yourself, have been taken from the same clay by God. 7Therefore no fear of me should dismay you, nor should my presence weigh heavily upon you. 8But you have said in my hearing, as I listened to the sound of your words: 9"I am clean and without transgression; I am innocent, there is no guilt in me. 10Yet he invents pretexts against me and reckons me as his enemy. 11He puts my feet in the stocks; he watches all my ways!" 12In this you are not just, let me tell you; for God is greater than man. 13Why, then, do you make complaint against him that he gives no account of his doings? 14For God does speak, perhaps once, or even twice, though one perceive it not. 15In a dream, in a vision of the night, (when deep sleep falls upon men) as they slumber in their beds, 16It is then he opens the ears of men and as a warning to them, terrifies them; 17By turning man from evil and keeping pride away from him, 18He withholds his soul from the pit and his life from passing to the grave. 19Or a man is chastened on his bed by pain and unceasing suffering within his frame, 20So that to his appetite food becomes repulsive, and his senses reject the choicest nourishment. 21His flesh is wasted so that it cannot be seen, and his bones, once invisible, appear; 22His soul draws near to the pit, his life to the place of the dead. 23If then there be for him an angel, one out of a thousand, a mediator, to show him what is right for him and bring the man back to justice, 24He will take pity on him and say, "Deliver him from going down to the pit; I have found him a ransom." 25Then his flesh shall become soft as a boy's; he shall be again as in the days of his youth. 26He shall pray and God will favor him; he shall see God's face with rejoicing. 27He shall sing before men and say, "I sinned and did wrong, yet he has not punished me accordingly. 28He delivered my soul from passing to the pit, and I behold the light of life." 29Lo, all these things God does, twice, or thrice, for a man, 30Bringing back his soul from the pit to the light, in the land of the living. 31Be attentive, O Job; listen to me! Be silent and I will speak. 32If you have aught to say, then answer me. Speak out! I should like to see you justified. 33If not, then do you listen to me; be silent while I teach you wisdom.

Job Chapter 34

1Then Elihu continued and said: 2Hear, O wise men, my discourse, and you that have knowledge, hear me! 3For the ear tests words, as the taste does food. 4Let us discern for ourselves what is right; let us learn between us what is good. 5For Job has said, "I am innocent, but God has taken what is my due. 6Notwithstanding my right I am set at nought; in my wound the arrow rankles, sinless though I am." 7What man is like Job? He drinks in blasphemies like water, 8Keeps company with evildoers and goes along with wicked men, 9When he says, "It profits a man nought that he is pleasing to God." 10Therefore, men of understanding, hearken to me: far be it from God to do wickedness; far from the Almighty to do wrong! 11Rather, he requites men for their conduct, and brings home to a man his way of life. 12Surely, God cannot act wickedly, the Almighty cannot violate justice. 13Who gave him government over the earth, or who else set all the land in its place? 14If he were to take back his spirit to himself, withdraw to himself his breath, 15All flesh would perish together, and man would return to the dust. 16Now, do you, O Job, hear this! Hearken to the words I speak! 17Can an enemy of justice indeed be in control, or will you condemn the supreme Just One, 18Who says to a king, "You are worthless!" and to nobles, "You are wicked!" 19Who neither favors the person of princes, nor respects the rich more than the poor? For they are all the work of his hands; 20in a moment they die, even at midnight. He brings on nobles, and takes them away, removing the powerful without lifting a hand; 21For his eyes are upon the ways of man, and he beholds all his steps. 22There is no darkness so dense that evildoers can hide in it. 25Therefore he discerns their works; he turns at night and crushes them. 23For he forewarns no man of his time to come before God in judgment. 24Without a trial he breaks the mighty, and sets others in their stead, 27Because they turned away from him and heeded none of his ways, 28But caused the cries of the poor to reach him, so that he heard the plea of the afflicted. 29If he remains tranquil, who then can condemn? If he hides his face, who then can behold him? 31When anyone says to God, "I was misguided; I will offend no more. 32Teach me wherein I have sinned; if I have done wrong, I will do so no more," 33Would you then say that God must punish, since you reject what he is doing? It is you who must choose, not I; speak, therefore, what you know. 34Men of understanding will say to me, every wise man who hears my views: 35"Job speaks without intelligence, and his words are without sense." 36Let Job be tried to the limit, since his answers are those of the impious; 37For he is adding rebellion to his sin by brushing off our arguments and addressing many words to God.

Job Chapter 35

1Then Elihu proceeded and said: 2Do you think it right to say, "I am just rather than God?" 3To say, "What does it profit me; what advantage have I more than if I had sinned?" 4I have words for a reply to you and your three companions as well. 5Look up to the skies and behold; regard the heavens high above you. 6If you sin, what injury do you do to God? Even if your offenses are many, how do you hurt him? 7If you are righteous, what do you give him, or what does he receive from your

218

hand? [8]Your wickedness can affect only a man like yourself; and your justice only a fellow human being. [9]In great oppression men cry out; they call for help because of the power of the mighty, [10]Saying, "Where is God, my Maker, who has given visions in the night, [11]Taught us rather than the beasts of the earth, and made us wise rather than the birds of the heavens?" [12]Though thus they cry out, he answers not against the pride of the wicked. [13]But it is idle to say God does not hear or that the Almighty does not take notice. [14]Even though you say that you see him not, the case is before him; with trembling should you wait upon him. [15]But now that you have done otherwise, God's anger punishes, nor does he show concern that a man will die. [16]Yet Job to no purpose opens his mouth, and without knowledge multiplies words.

Job Chapter 36

[1]Elihu proceeded further and said: [2]Wait yet a little and I will instruct you, for there are still words to be said on God's behalf. [3]I will bring my knowledge from afar, and to my Maker I will accord the right. [4]For indeed, my theme cannot fail me: the one perfect in knowledge I set before you. [5]Behold, God rejects the obstinate in heart; he preserves not the life of the wicked. [6]He withholds not the just man's rights, but grants vindication to the oppressed, [7]And with kings upon thrones he sets them, exalted forever. [8]Or if they are bound with fetters and held fast by bonds of affliction, [9]Then he makes known to them what they have done and their sins of boastful pride. [10]He opens their ears to correction and exhorts them to turn back from evil. [11]If they obey and serve him, they spend their days in prosperity, their years in happiness. [12]But if they obey not, they perish; they die for lack of knowledge. [13]The impious in heart lay up anger for themselves; they cry not for help when he enchains them; [14]Therefore they expire in youth, and perish among the reprobate. [15]But he saves the unfortunate through their affliction, and instructs them through distress. [16]Take heed, turn not to evil; for you have preferred carousal to affliction. [17]Behold, God is sublime in his power. What teacher is there like him? [18]Who prescribes for him his conduct, or who can say, "You have done wrong"? [19]Remember, you should extol his work, which men have praised in song. [20]All men contemplate it; man beholds it from afar. [21]Lo, God is great beyond our knowledge; the number of his years is past searching out. [22]He holds in check the waterdrops that filter in rain through his mists, [23]Till the skies run with them and the showers rain down on mankind. [24]For by these he nourishes the nations, and gives them food in abundance. [25]Lo! he spreads the clouds in layers as the carpeting of his tent. [26]In his hands he holds the lightning, and he commands it to strike the mark. [27]His thunder speaks for him and incites the fury of the storm.

Job Chapter 37

[1]At this my heart trembles and leaps out of its place, [2]To hear his angry voice as it rumbles forth from his mouth! [3]Everywhere under the heavens he sends it, with his lightning, to the ends of the earth. [4]Again his voice roars—the majestic sound of his thunder. [5]He does great things beyond our knowing; wonders past our searching out. [6]For he says to the snow, "Fall to the earth"; likewise to his heavy, drenching rain. [7]He shuts up all mankind indoors; [8]the wild beasts take to cover and remain quietly in their dens. [9]Out of its chamber comes forth the tempest; from the north winds, the cold. [10]With his breath God brings the frost, and the broad waters become congealed. [11]With hail, also, the clouds are laden, as they scatter their flashes of light. [12]He it is who changes their rounds, according to his plans, in their task upon the surface of the earth, [13]whether for punishment or mercy, as he commands. [14]Hearken to this, O Job! Stand and consider the wondrous works of God! [15]Do you know how God lays his commands upon them, and makes the light shine forth from his clouds? [16]Do you know how the clouds are banked, the wondrous work of him who is perfect in knowledge? [17]You, whom the streams of water fail when a calm from the south comes over the land, [18]Do you spread out with him the firmament of the skies, hard as a brazen mirror? [19]Teach us then what we shall say to him; we cannot, for the darkness, make our plea. [20]Will he be told about it when I speak, or when a man says he is being destroyed? [21]Nay, rather, it is as the light which men see not while it is obscured among the clouds, till the wind comes by and sweeps the clouds away. [22]From the North the splendor comes, surrounding God's awesome majesty! [23]The Almighty! we cannot discover him, pre-eminent in power and judgment; his great justice owes no one an accounting. [24]Therefore men revere him, though none can see him, however wise their hearts.

Job Chapter 38

[1]Then the LORD addressed Job out of the storm and said: [2]Who is this that obscures divine plans with words of ignorance? [3]Gird up your loins now, like a man; I will question you, and you tell me the answers! [4]Where were you when I founded the earth? Tell me, if you have understanding. [5]Who determined its size; do you know? Who stretched out the measuring line for it? [6]Into what were its pedestals sunk, and who laid the cornerstone, [7]While the morning stars sang in chorus and all the sons of God shouted for joy? [8]And who shut within doors the sea, when it burst forth from the womb; [9]When I made the clouds its garment and thick darkness its swaddling bands? [10]When I set limits for it and fastened the bar of its door, [11]And said: Thus far shall you come but no farther, and here shall your proud waves be stilled! [12]Have you ever in your lifetime commanded the morning and shown the dawn its place [13]For taking hold of the ends of the earth, till the wicked are shaken from its surface? [14]The earth is changed as is clay by the seal, and dyed as though it were a garment; [15]But from the wicked the light is withheld, and the arm of pride is shattered. [16]Have you entered into the sources of the sea, or walked about in the depths of the abyss? [17]Have the gates of death been shown to you, or have you seen the gates of darkness? [18]Have you comprehended the breadth of the earth? Tell me, if you know all: [19]Which is the way to the dwelling place of light, and where is the abode of darkness, [20]That you may take them to their boundaries and set them on their homeward paths? [21]You know, because you were born before them, and the number of your years is great! [22]Have you entered the storehouse of the snow, and seen the treasury of the hail [23]Which I have reserved for times of stress, for the days of war and of battle? [24]Which way to the parting of the winds, whence the east wind spreads over the earth? [25]Who has laid out a channel for the downpour and for the thunderstorm a path [26]To bring rain to no man's land, the unpeopled wilderness; [27]To enrich the waste and desolate ground till the desert blooms with verdure? [28]Has the rain a father; or who has begotten the drops of dew? [29]Out of whose womb comes the ice, and who gives the hoarfrost its birth in the skies, [30]When the waters lie covered as though with stone that holds captive the surface of the deep? [31]Have you fitted a curb to the Pleiades, or loosened the bonds of Orion? [32]Can you bring forth the Mazzaroth in their season, or guide the Bear with its train? [33]Do you know the ordinances of the heavens; can you put into effect their plan on the earth? [34]Can you raise your voice among the clouds, or veil yourself in the waters of the storm? [35]Can you send forth the lightnings on their way, or will they say to you, "Here we are"? [36]Who puts wisdom in the heart, and gives the cock its understanding? [37]Who counts the clouds in his wisdom? Or who tilts the water jars of heaven [38]So that the dust of earth is fused into a mass and its clods made solid? [39]Do you hunt the prey for the lioness or appease the hunger of her cubs, [40]While they crouch in their dens, or lie in wait in the thicket? [41]Who provides nourishment for the ravens when their young ones cry out to God, and they rove abroad without food?

Job Chapter 39

[1]Do you know about the birth of the mountain goats, watch for the birth pangs of the hinds, [2]Number the months that they must fulfill, and fix the time of their bringing forth? [3]They crouch down and bear their young; they deliver their progeny in the desert. [4]When their offspring thrive and grow, they leave and do not return. [5]Who has given the wild ass his freedom, and who has loosed him from bonds? [6]I have made the wilderness his home and the salt flats his dwelling. [7]He scoffs at the uproar of the city, and hears no shouts of a driver. [8]He ranges the mountains for pasture, and seeks out every patch of green. [9]Will the wild ox consent to serve you, and to pass the nights by your manger? [10]Will a rope bind him in the furrow, and will he harrow the valleys after you? [11]Will you trust him for his great strength and leave to him the fruits of your toil? [12]Can you rely on him to thresh out your grain and gather in the yield of your threshing floor? [13]The wings of the ostrich beat idly; her plumage is lacking in pinions. [14]When she leaves her eggs on the ground and deposits them in the sand, [15]Unmindful that a foot may crush them, that the wild beasts may trample them, [16]She cruelly disowns her young and ruthlessly makes nought of her brood; [17]For God has withheld wisdom from her and has given her no share in understanding. [18]Yet in her swiftness of foot she makes sport of the horse and his rider. [19]Do you give the horse his strength, and endow his neck with splendor? [20]Do you make the steed to quiver while his thunderous snorting spreads terror? [21]He jubilantly paws the plain and rushes in his might against the weapons. [22]He laughs at fear and cannot be deterred; he turns not back from the sword. [23]Around him rattles the quiver, flashes the spear and the javelin. [24]Frenzied and trembling he devours the ground; he holds not back at the sound of the trumpet, [25]but at each blast he cries, "Aha!" Even from afar he scents the battle, the roar of the chiefs and the shouting. [26]Is it by your discernment that the hawk soars, that he spreads his wings toward the south? [27]Does the eagle fly up at your command to build his nest aloft? [28]On the cliff he dwells and spends the night, on the spur of the cliff or the fortress. [29]From thence he watches for his prey; his eyes behold it

afar off. ³⁰His young ones greedily drink blood; where the slain are, there is he.

Job Chapter 40

¹The LORD then said to Job: ²Will we have arguing with the Almighty by the critic? Let him who would correct God give answer! ³Then Job answered the LORD and said: ⁴Behold, I am of little account; what can I answer you? I put my hand over my mouth. ⁵Though I have spoken once, I will not do so again; though twice, I will do so no more. ⁶Then the LORD addressed Job out of the storm and said: ⁷Gird up your loins now, like a man. I will question you, and you tell me the answers! ⁸Would you refuse to acknowledge my right? Would you condemn me that you may be justified? ⁹Have you an arm like that of God, or can you thunder with a voice like his? ¹⁰Adorn yourself with grandeur and majesty, and array yourself with glory and splendor. ¹¹Let loose the fury of your wrath; ¹²tear down the wicked and shatter them. Bring down the haughty with a glance; ¹³bury them in the dust together; in the hidden world imprison them. ¹⁴Then will I too acknowledge that your own right hand can save you. ¹⁵See, besides you I made Behemoth, that feeds on grass like an ox. ¹⁶Behold the strength in his loins, and his vigor in the sinews of his belly. ¹⁷He carries his tail like a cedar; the sinews of his thighs are like cables. ¹⁸His bones are like tubes of bronze; his frame is like iron rods. ¹⁹He came at the beginning of God's ways, and was made the taskmaster of his fellows; ²⁰For the produce of the mountains is brought to him, and of all wild animals he makes sport. ²¹Under the lotus trees he lies, in coverts of the reedy swamp. ²²The lotus trees cover him with their shade; all about him are the poplars on the bank. ²³If the river grows violent, he is not disturbed; he is tranquil though the torrent surges about his mouth. ²⁴Who can capture him by his eyes, or pierce his nose with a trap? ²⁵Can you lead about Leviathan with a hook, or curb his tongue with a bit? ²⁶Can you put a rope into his nose, or pierce through his cheek with a gaff? ²⁷Will he then plead with you, time after time, or address you with tender words? ²⁸Will he make an agreement with you that you may have him as a slave forever? ²⁹Can you play with him, as with a bird? Can you put him in leash for your maidens? ³⁰Will the traders bargain for him? Will the merchants divide him up? ³¹Can you fill his hide with barbs, or his head with fish spears? ³²Once you but lay a hand upon him, no need to recall any other conflict!

Job Chapter 41

¹Is he not relentless when aroused; who then dares stand before him? ²Whoever might vainly hope to do so need only see him to be overthrown. ³Who has assailed him and come off safe—Who under all the heavens? ⁴I need hardly mention his limbs, his strength, and the fitness of his armor. ⁵Who can strip off his outer garment, or penetrate his double corselet? ⁶Who can force open the doors of his mouth, close to his terrible teeth? ⁷Rows of scales are on his back, tightly sealed together; ⁸They are fitted each so close to the next that no space intervenes; ⁹So joined one to another that they hold fast and cannot be parted. ¹⁰When he sneezes, light flashes forth; his eyes are like those of the dawn. ¹¹Out of his mouth go forth firebrands; sparks of fire leap forth. ¹²From his nostrils issues steam, as from a seething pot or bowl. ¹³His breath sets coals afire; a flame pours from his mouth. ¹⁴Strength abides in his neck, and terror leaps before him. ¹⁵His heart is hard as stone; his flesh, as the lower millstone. ¹⁶When he rises up, the mighty are afraid; the waves of the sea fall back. ¹⁷Should the sword reach him, it will not avail; nor will the spear, nor the dart, nor the javelin. ¹⁸He regards iron as straw, and bronze as rotten wood. ¹⁹The arrow will not put him to flight; slingstones used against him are but straws. ²⁰Clubs he esteems as splinters; he laughs at the crash of the spear. ²¹His belly is sharp as pottery fragments; he spreads like a threshing sledge upon the mire. ²²He makes the depths boil like a pot; the sea he churns like perfume in a kettle. ²³Behind him he leaves a shining path; you would think the deep had the hoary head of age. ²⁴Upon the earth there is not his like, intrepid he was made. ²⁵All, however lofty, fear him; he is king over all proud beasts.

Job Chapter 42

¹Then Job answered the LORD and said: ²I know that you can do all things, and that no purpose of yours can be hindered. ³I have dealt with great things that I do not understand; things too wonderful for me, which I cannot know. ⁴I had heard of you by word of mouth, but now my eye has seen you. ⁵Therefore I disown what I have said, and repent in dust and ashes. ⁶And it came to pass after the LORD had spoken these words to Job, that the LORD said to Eliphaz the Temanite, "I am angry with you and with your two friends; for you have not spoken rightly concerning me, as has my servant Job. ⁷Now, therefore, take seven bullocks and seven rams, and go to my servant Job, and offer up a holocaust for yourselves; and let my servant Job pray for you; for his

prayer I will accept, not to punish you severely. For you have not spoken rightly concerning me, as has my servant Job." ⁸Then Eliphaz the Temanite, and Bildad the Shuhite, and Zophar the Naamathite, went and did as the LORD had commanded them. And the LORD accepted the intercession of Job. ⁹Also, the LORD restored the prosperity of Job, after he had prayed for his friends; the LORD even gave to Job twice as much as he had before. ¹⁰Then all his brethren and his sisters came to him, and all his former acquaintances, and they dined with him in his house. They condoled with him and comforted him for all the evil which the LORD had brought upon him; and each one gave him a piece of money and a gold ring. ¹¹Thus the LORD blessed the latter days of Job more than his earlier ones. For he had fourteen thousand sheep, six thousand camels, a thousand yoke of oxen, and a thousand she-asses. ¹²And he had seven sons and three daughters, ¹³of whom he called the first Jemimah, the second Keziah, and the third Keren-happuch. ¹⁴In all the land no other women were as beautiful as the daughters of Job; and their father gave them an inheritance among their brethren. ¹⁵After this, Job lived a hundred and forty years; and he saw his children, his grandchildren, and even his great-grandchildren. ¹⁶Then Job died, old and full of years.

Psalms

Psalms Book 1

Psalm Book 1 Chapter 1

¹Blessed is the man who doesn't walk in the counsel of the wicked, nor stand on the path of sinners, nor sit in the seat of scoffers; ²but his delight is in Yahweh's law. On his law he meditates day and night. ³He will be like a tree planted by the streams of water, that produces its fruit in its season, whose leaf also does not wither. Whatever he does shall prosper. ⁴The wicked are not so, but are like the chaff which the wind drives away. ⁵Therefore the wicked shall not stand in the judgment, nor sinners in the congregation of the righteous. ⁶For Yahweh knows the way of the righteous, but the way of the wicked shall perish.

Psalm Book 1 Chapter 2

¹Why do the nations rage, and the peoples plot a vain thing? ²The kings of the earth take a stand, and the rulers take counsel together, against Yahweh, and against his Anointed, saying, ³"Let's break their bonds apart, and cast their cords from us." ⁴He who sits in the heavens will laugh. The Lord will have them in derision. ⁵Then he will speak to them in his anger, and terrify them in his wrath: ⁶"Yet I have set my King on my holy hill of Zion." ⁷I will tell of the decree: Yahweh said to me, "You are my son. Today I have become your father. ⁸Ask of me, and I will give the nations for your inheritance, the uttermost parts of the earth for your possession. ⁹You shall break them with a rod of iron. You shall dash them in pieces like a potter's vessel." ¹⁰Now therefore be wise, you kings. Be instructed, you judges of the earth. ¹¹Serve Yahweh with fear, and rejoice with trembling. ¹²Give sincere homage to the Son, lest he be angry, and you perish on the way, for his wrath will soon be kindled. Blessed are all those who take refuge in him.

Psalm Book 1 Chapter 3

¹Yahweh, how my adversaries have increased! Many are those who rise up against me. ²Many there are who say of my soul, "There is no help for him in God." Selah. ³But you, Yahweh, are a shield around me, my glory, and the one who lifts up my head. ⁴I cry to Yahweh with my voice, and he answers me out of his holy hill. Selah. ⁵I laid myself down and slept. I awakened, for Yahweh sustains me. ⁶I will not be afraid of tens of thousands of people who have set themselves against me on every side. ⁷Arise, Yahweh! Save me, my God! For you have struck all of my enemies on the cheek bone. You have broken the teeth of the wicked. ⁸Salvation belongs to Yahweh. May your blessing be on your people. Selah.

Psalm Book 1 Chapter 4

¹Answer me when I call, God of my righteousness. Give me relief from my distress. Have mercy on me, and hear my prayer. ²You sons of men, how long shall my glory be turned into dishonor? Will you love vanity and seek after falsehood? Selah. ³But know that Yahweh has set apart for himself him who is godly; Yahweh will hear when I call to him. ⁴Stand in awe, and don't sin. Search your own heart on your bed, and be still. Selah. ⁵Offer the sacrifices of righteousness. Put your trust in Yahweh. ⁶Many say, "Who will show us any good?" Yahweh, let the light of your face shine on us. ⁷You have put gladness in my heart, more than when their grain and their new wine are increased. ⁸In peace I will both lay myself down and sleep, for you alone, Yahweh, make me live in safety.

Psalm Book 1 Chapter 5

¹Give ear to my words, Yahweh. Consider my meditation. ²Listen to the

voice of my cry, my King and my God, for I pray to you. ³Yahweh, in the morning you will hear my voice. In the morning I will lay my requests before you, and will watch expectantly. ⁴For you are not a God who has pleasure in wickedness. Evil can't live with you. ⁵The arrogant will not stand in your sight. You hate all workers of iniquity. ⁶You will destroy those who speak lies. Yahweh abhors the bloodthirsty and deceitful man. ⁷But as for me, in the abundance of your loving kindness I will come into your house. I will bow toward your holy temple in reverence of you. ⁸Lead me, Yahweh, in your righteousness because of my enemies. Make your way straight before my face. ⁹For there is no faithfulness in their mouth. Their heart is destruction. Their throat is an open tomb. They flatter with their tongue. ¹⁰Hold them guilty, God. Let them fall by their own counsels. Thrust them out in the multitude of their transgressions, for they have rebelled against you. ¹¹But let all those who take refuge in you rejoice. Let them always shout for joy, because you defend them. Let them also who love your name be joyful in you. ¹²For you will bless the righteous. Yahweh, you will surround him with favor as with a shield.

Psalm Book 1 Chapter 6

¹Yahweh, don't rebuke me in your anger, neither discipline me in your wrath. ²Have mercy on me, Yahweh, for I am faint. Yahweh, heal me, for my bones are troubled. ³My soul is also in great anguish. But you, Yahweh—how long? ⁴Return, Yahweh. Deliver my soul, and save me for your loving kindness' sake. ⁵For in death there is no memory of you. In Sheol, who shall give you thanks? ⁶I am weary with my groaning. Every night I flood my bed. I drench my couch with my tears. ⁷My eye wastes away because of grief. It grows old because of all my adversaries. ⁸Depart from me, all you workers of iniquity, for Yahweh has heard the voice of my weeping. ⁹Yahweh has heard my supplication. Yahweh accepts my prayer. ¹⁰May all my enemies be ashamed and dismayed. They shall turn back, they shall be disgraced suddenly.

Psalm Book 1 Chapter 7

¹Yahweh, my God, I take refuge in you. Save me from all those who pursue me, and deliver me, ²lest they tear apart my soul like a lion, ripping it in pieces, while there is no one to deliver. ³Yahweh, my God, if I have done this, if there is iniquity in my hands, ⁴if I have rewarded evil to him who was at peace with me (yes, I have plundered him who without cause was my adversary), ⁵let the enemy pursue my soul, and overtake it; yes, let him tread my life down to the earth, and lay my glory in the dust. Selah. ⁶Arise, Yahweh, in your anger. Lift up yourself against the rage of my adversaries. Awake for me. You have commanded judgment. ⁷Let the congregation of the peoples surround you. Rule over them on high. ⁸Yahweh administers judgment to the peoples. Judge me, Yahweh, according to my righteousness, and to my integrity that is in me. ⁹Oh let the wickedness of the wicked come to an end, but establish the righteous; their minds and hearts are searched by the righteous God. ¹⁰My shield is with God, who saves the upright in heart. ¹¹God is a righteous judge, yes, a God who has indignation every day. ¹²If a man doesn't repent, he will sharpen his sword; he has bent and strung his bow. ¹³He has also prepared for himself the instruments of death. He makes ready his flaming arrows. ¹⁴Behold, he travails with iniquity. Yes, he has conceived mischief, and brought out falsehood. ¹⁵He has dug a hole, and has fallen into the pit which he made. ¹⁶The trouble he causes shall return to his own head. His violence shall come down on the crown of his own head. ¹⁷I will give thanks to Yahweh according to his righteousness, and will sing praise to the name of Yahweh Most High.

Psalm Book 1 Chapter 8

¹Yahweh, our Lord, how majestic is your name in all the earth! You have set your glory above the heavens! ²From the lips of babes and infants you have established strength, because of your adversaries, that you might silence the enemy and the avenger. ³When I consider your heavens, the work of your fingers, the moon and the stars, which you have ordained, ⁴what is man, that you think of him? What is the son of man, that you care for him? ⁵For you have made him a little lower than the angels, and crowned him with glory and honor. ⁶You make him ruler over the works of your hands. You have put all things under his feet: ⁷All sheep and cattle, yes, and the animals of the field, ⁸the birds of the sky, the fish of the sea, and whatever passes through the paths of the seas. ⁹Yahweh, our Lord, how majestic is your name in all the earth!

Psalm Book 1 Chapter 9

¹I will give thanks to Yahweh with my whole heart. I will tell of all your marvelous works. ²I will be glad and rejoice in you. I will sing praise to your name, O Most High. ³When my enemies turn back, they stumble and perish in your presence. ⁴For you have maintained my just cause. You sit on the throne judging righteously. ⁵You have rebuked the nations. You have destroyed the wicked. You have blotted out their name forever and ever. ⁶The enemy is overtaken by endless ruin. The very memory of the cities which you have overthrown has perished. ⁷But Yahweh reigns forever. He has prepared his throne for judgment. ⁸He will judge the world in righteousness. He will administer judgment to the peoples in uprightness. ⁹Yahweh will also be a high tower for the oppressed; a high tower in times of trouble. ¹⁰Those who know your name will put their trust in you, for you, Yahweh, have not forsaken those who seek you. ¹¹Sing praises to Yahweh, who dwells in Zion, and declare among the people what he has done. ¹²For he who avenges blood remembers them. He doesn't forget the cry of the afflicted. ¹³Have mercy on me, Yahweh. See my affliction by those who hate me, and lift me up from the gates of death, ¹⁴that I may show all of your praise. I will rejoice in your salvation in the gates of the daughter of Zion. ¹⁵The nations have sunk down in the pit that they made. In the net which they hid, their own foot is taken. ¹⁶Yahweh has made himself known. He has executed judgment. The wicked is snared by the work of his own hands. Meditation. Selah. ¹⁷The wicked shall be turned back to Sheol, even all the nations that forget God. ¹⁸For the needy shall not always be forgotten, nor the hope of the poor perish forever. ¹⁹Arise, Yahweh! Don't let man prevail. Let the nations be judged in your sight. ²⁰Put them in fear, Yahweh. Let the nations know that they are only men. Selah.

Psalm Book 1 Chapter 10

¹Why do you stand far off, Yahweh? Why do you hide yourself in times of trouble? ²In arrogance, the wicked hunt down the weak. They are caught in the schemes that they devise. ³For the wicked boasts of his heart's cravings. He blesses the greedy and condemns Yahweh. ⁴The wicked, in the pride of his face, has no room in his thoughts for God. ⁵His ways are prosperous at all times. He is arrogant, and your laws are far from his sight. As for all his adversaries, he sneers at them. ⁶He says in his heart, "I shall not be shaken. For generations I shall have no trouble." ⁷His mouth is full of cursing, deceit, and oppression. Under his tongue is mischief and iniquity. ⁸He lies in wait near the villages. From ambushes, he murders the innocent. His eyes are secretly set against the helpless. ⁹He lurks in secret as a lion in his ambush. He lies in wait to catch the helpless. He catches the helpless when he draws him in his net. ¹⁰The helpless are crushed. They collapse. They fall under his strength. ¹¹He says in his heart, "God has forgotten. He hides his face. He will never see it." ¹²Arise, Yahweh! God, lift up your hand! Don't forget the helpless. ¹³Why does the wicked person condemn God, and say in his heart, "God won't call me into account"? ¹⁴But you do see trouble and grief. You consider it to take it into your hand. You help the victim and the fatherless. ¹⁵Break the arm of the wicked. As for the evil man, seek out his wickedness until you find none. ¹⁶Yahweh is King forever and ever! The nations will perish out of his land. ¹⁷Yahweh, you have heard the desire of the humble. You will prepare their heart. You will cause your ear to hear, ¹⁸to judge the fatherless and the oppressed, that man who is of the earth may terrify no more.

Psalm Book 1 Chapter 11

¹In Yahweh, I take refuge. How can you say to my soul, "Flee as a bird to your mountain"? ²For, behold, the wicked bend their bows. They set their arrows on the strings, that they may shoot in darkness at the upright in heart. ³If the foundations are destroyed, what can the righteous do? ⁴Yahweh is in his holy temple. Yahweh is on his throne in heaven. His eyes observe. His eyes examine the children of men. ⁵Yahweh examines the righteous, but his soul hates the wicked and him who loves violence. ⁶On the wicked he will rain blazing coals; fire, sulfur, and scorching wind shall be the portion of their cup. ⁷For Yahweh is righteous. He loves righteousness. The upright shall see his face.

Psalm Book 1 Chapter 12

¹Help, Yahweh; for the godly man ceases. For the faithful fail from among the children of men. ²Everyone lies to his neighbor. They speak with flattering lips, and with a double heart. ³May Yahweh cut off all flattering lips, and the tongue that boasts, ⁴who have said, "With our tongue we will prevail. Our lips are our own. Who is lord over us?" ⁵"Because of the oppression of the weak and because of the groaning of the needy, I will now arise," says Yahweh; "I will set him in safety from those who malign him." ⁶Yahweh's words are flawless words, as silver refined in a clay furnace, purified seven times. ⁷You will keep them, Yahweh. You will preserve them from this generation forever. ⁸The wicked walk on every side, when what is vile is exalted among the sons of men.

Psalm Book 1 Chapter 13

¹How long, Yahweh? Will you forget me forever? How long will you hide your face from me? ²How long shall I take counsel in my soul, having sorrow in my heart every day? How long shall my enemy

triumph over me? ³Behold, and answer me, Yahweh, my God. Give light to my eyes, lest I sleep in death; ⁴lest my enemy say, "I have prevailed against him;" lest my adversaries rejoice when I fall. ⁵But I trust in your loving kindness. My heart rejoices in your salvation. ⁶I will sing to Yahweh, because he has been good to me.

Psalm Book 1 Chapter 14

¹The fool has said in his heart, "There is no God." They are corrupt. They have done abominable deeds. There is no one who does good. ²Yahweh looked down from heaven on the children of men, to see if there were any who understood, who sought after God. ³They have all gone aside. They have together become corrupt. There is no one who does good, no, not one. ⁴Have all the workers of iniquity no knowledge, who eat up my people as they eat bread, and don't call on Yahweh? ⁵There they were in great fear, for God is in the generation of the righteous. ⁶You frustrate the plan of the poor, because Yahweh is his refuge. ⁷Oh that the salvation of Israel would come out of Zion! When Yahweh restores the fortunes of his people, then Jacob shall rejoice, and Israel shall be glad.

Psalm Book 1 Chapter 15

¹Yahweh, who shall dwell in your sanctuary? Who shall live on your holy hill? ²He who walks blamelessly and does what is right, and speaks truth in his heart; ³he who doesn't slander with his tongue, nor does evil to his friend, nor casts slurs against his fellow man; ⁴in whose eyes a vile man is despised, but who honors those who fear Yahweh; he who keeps an oath even when it hurts, and doesn't change; ⁵he who doesn't lend out his money for usury, nor take a bribe against the innocent. He who does these things shall never be shaken.

Psalm Book 1 Chapter 16

¹Preserve me, God, for I take refuge in you. ²My soul, you have said to Yahweh, "You are my Lord. Apart from you I have no good thing." ³As for the saints who are in the earth, they are the excellent ones in whom is all my delight. ⁴Their sorrows shall be multiplied who give gifts to another god. Their drink offerings of blood I will not offer, nor take their names on my lips. ⁵Yah weh assigned my portion and my cup. You made my lot secure. ⁶The lines have fallen to me in pleasant places. Yes, I have a good inheritance. ⁷I will bless Yahweh, who has given me counsel. Yes, my heart instructs me in the night seasons. ⁸I have set Yahweh always before me. Because he is at my right hand, I shall not be moved. ⁹Therefore my heart is glad, and my tongue rejoices. My body shall also dwell in safety. ¹⁰For you will not leave my soul in Sheol, neither will you allow your holy one to see corruption. ¹¹You will show me the path of life. In your presence is fullness of joy. In your right hand there are pleasures forever more.

Psalm Book 1 Chapter 17

¹Hear, Yahweh, my righteous plea. Give ear to my prayer that doesn't go out of deceitful lips. ²Let my sentence come out of your presence. Let your eyes look on equity. ³You have proved my heart. You have visited me in the night. You have tried me, and found nothing. I have resolved that my mouth shall not disobey. ⁴As for the deeds of men, by the word of your lips, I have kept myself from the ways of the violent. ⁵My steps have held fast to your paths. My feet have not slipped. ⁶I have called on you, for you will answer me, God. Turn your ear to me. Hear my speech. ⁷Show your marvelous loving kindness, you who save those who take refuge by your right hand from their enemies. ⁸Keep me as the apple of your eye. Hide me under the shadow of your wings, ⁹from the wicked who oppress me, my deadly enemies, who surround me. ¹⁰They close up their callous hearts. With their mouth they speak proudly. ¹¹They have now surrounded us in our steps. They set their eyes to cast us down to the earth. ¹²He is like a lion that is greedy of his prey, as it were a young lion lurking in secret places. ¹³Arise, Yahweh, confront him. Cast him down. Deliver my soul from the wicked by your sword, ¹⁴from men by your hand, Yahweh, from men of the world, whose portion is in this life. You fill the belly of your cherished ones. Your sons have plenty, and they store up wealth for their children. ¹⁵As for me, I shall see your face in righteousness. I shall be satisfied, when I awake, with seeing your form.

Psalm Book 1 Chapter 18

¹I love you, Yahweh, my strength. ²Yahweh is my rock, my fortress, and my deliverer; my God, my rock, in whom I take refuge; my shield, and the horn of my salvation, my high tower. ³I call on Yahweh, who is worthy to be praised; and I am saved from my enemies. ⁴The cords of death surrounded me. The floods of ungodliness made me afraid. ⁵The cords of Sheol were around me. The snares of death came on me. ⁶In my distress I called on Yahweh, and cried to my God. He heard my voice out of his temple. My cry before him came into his ears. ⁷Then the earth shook and trembled. The foundations also of the mountains quaked and were shaken, because he was angry. ⁸Smoke went out of his nostrils.

Consuming fire came out of his mouth. Coals were kindled by it. ⁹He bowed the heavens also, and came down. Thick darkness was under his feet. ¹⁰He rode on a cherub, and flew. Yes, he soared on the wings of the wind. ¹¹He made darkness his hiding place, his pavilion around him, darkness of waters, thick clouds of the skies. ¹²At the brightness before him his thick clouds passed, hailstones and coals of fire. ¹³Yahweh also thundered in the sky. The Most High uttered his voice: hailstones and coals of fire. ¹⁴He sent out his arrows, and scattered them. He routed them with great lightning bolts. ¹⁵Then the channels of waters appeared. The foundations of the world were laid bare at your rebuke, Yahweh, at the blast of the breath of your nostrils. ¹⁶He sent from on high. He took me. He drew me out of many waters. ¹⁷He delivered me from my strong enemy, from those who hated me; for they were too mighty for me. ¹⁸They came on me in the day of my calamity, but Yahweh was my support. ¹⁹He brought me out also into a large place. He delivered me, because he delighted in me. ²⁰Yahweh has rewarded me according to my righteousness. According to the cleanness of my hands, he has recompensed me. ²¹For I have kept the ways of Yahweh, and have not wickedly departed from my God. ²²For all his ordinances were before me. I didn't put away his statutes from me. ²³I was also blameless with him. I kept myself from my iniquity. ²⁴Therefore Yahweh has rewarded me according to my righteousness, according to the cleanness of my hands in his eyesight. ²⁵With the merciful you will show yourself merciful. With the perfect man, you will show yourself perfect. ²⁶With the pure, you will show yourself pure. With the crooked you will show yourself shrewd. ²⁷For you will save the afflicted people, but the arrogant eyes you will bring down. ²⁸For you will light my lamp, Yahweh. My God will light up my darkness. ²⁹For by you, I advance through a troop. By my God, I leap over a wall. ³⁰As for God, his way is perfect. Yahweh's word is tried. He is a shield to all those who take refuge in him. ³¹For who is God, except Yahweh? Who is a rock, besides our God, ³²the God who arms me with strength, and makes my way perfect? ³³He makes my feet like deer's feet, and sets me on my high places. ³⁴He teaches my hands to war, so that my arms bend a bow of bronze. ³⁵You have also given me the shield of your salvation. Your right hand sustains me. Your gentleness has made me great. ³⁶You have enlarged my steps under me, My feet have not slipped. ³⁷I will pursue my enemies, and overtake them. I won't turn away until they are consumed. ³⁸I will strike them through, so that they will not be able to rise. They shall fall under my feet. ³⁹For you have armed me with strength to the battle. You have subdued under me those who rose up against me. ⁴⁰You have also made my enemies turn their backs to me, that I might cut off those who hate me. ⁴¹They cried, but there was no one to save; even to Yahweh, but he didn't answer them. ⁴²Then I beat them small as the dust before the wind. I cast them out as the mire of the streets. ⁴³You have delivered me from the strivings of the people. You have made me the head of the nations. A people whom I have not known shall serve me. ⁴⁴As soon as they hear of me they shall obey me. The foreigners shall submit themselves to me. ⁴⁵The foreigners shall fade away, and shall come trembling out of their strongholds. ⁴⁶Yahweh lives! Blessed be my rock. Exalted be the God of my salvation, ⁴⁷even the God who executes vengeance for me, and subdues peoples under me. ⁴⁸He rescues me from my enemies. Yes, you lift me up above those who rise up against me. You deliver me from the violent man. ⁴⁹Therefore I will give thanks to you, Yahweh, among the nations, and will sing praises to your name. ⁵⁰He gives great deliverance to his king, and shows loving kindness to his anointed, to David and to his offspring, forever more.

Psalm Book 1 Chapter 19

¹The heavens declare the glory of God. The expanse shows his handiwork. ²Day after day they pour out speech, and night after night they display knowledge. ³There is no speech nor language where their voice is not heard. ⁴Their voice has gone out through all the earth, their words to the end of the world. In them he has set a tent for the sun, ⁵which is as a bridegroom coming out of his room, like a strong man rejoicing to run his course. ⁶His going out is from the end of the heavens, his circuit to its ends. There is nothing hidden from its heat. ⁷Yahweh's law is perfect, restoring the soul. Yahweh's covenant is sure, making wise the simple. ⁸Yahweh's precepts are right, rejoicing the heart. Yahweh's commandment is pure, enlightening the eyes. ⁹The fear of Yahweh is clean, enduring forever. Yahweh's ordinances are true, and righteous altogether. ¹⁰They are more to be desired than gold, yes, than much fine gold, sweeter also than honey and the extract of the honeycomb. ¹¹Moreover your servant is warned by them. In keeping them there is great reward. ¹²Who can discern his errors? Forgive me from hidden errors. ¹³Keep back your servant also from presumptuous sins. Let them not have dominion over me. Then I will be upright. I will be blameless and innocent of great transgression. ¹⁴Let the words of

my mouth and the meditation of my heart be acceptable in your sight, Yahweh, my rock, and my redeemer.

Psalm Book 1 Chapter 20

[1]May Yahweh answer you in the day of trouble. May the name of the God of Jacob set you up on high, [2]send you help from the sanctuary, grant you support from Zion, [3]remember all your offerings, and accept your burned sacrifice. Selah. [4]May he grant you your heart's desire, and fulfill all your counsel. [5]We will triumph in your salvation. In the name of our God, we will set up our banners. May Yahweh grant all your requests. [6]Now I know that Yahweh saves his anointed. He will answer him from his holy heaven, with the saving strength of his right hand. [7]Some trust in chariots, and some in horses, but we trust in the name of Yahweh our God. [8]They are bowed down and fallen, but we rise up, and stand upright. [9]Save, Yahweh! Let the King answer us when we call!

Psalm Book 1 Chapter 21

[1]The king rejoices in your strength, Yahweh! How greatly he rejoices in your salvation! [2]You have given him his heart's desire, and have not withheld the request of his lips. Selah. [3]For you meet him with the blessings of goodness. You set a crown of fine gold on his head. [4]He asked life of you and you gave it to him, even length of days forever and ever. [5]His glory is great in your salvation. You lay honor and majesty on him. [6]For you make him most blessed forever. You make him glad with joy in your presence. [7]For the king trusts in Yahweh. Through the loving kindness of the Most High, he shall not be moved. [8]Your hand will find out all of your enemies. Your right hand will find out those who hate you. [9]You will make them as a fiery furnace in the time of your anger. Yahweh will swallow them up in his wrath. The fire shall devour them. [10]You will destroy their descendants from the earth, their posterity from among the children of men. [11]For they intended evil against you. They plotted evil against you which cannot succeed. [12]For you will make them turn their back, when you aim drawn bows at their face. [13]Be exalted, Yahweh, in your strength, so we will sing and praise your power.

Psalm Book 1 Chapter 22

[1]My God, my God, why have you forsaken me? Why are you so far from helping me, and from the words of my groaning? [2]My God, I cry in the daytime, but you don't answer; in the night season, and am not silent. [3]But you are holy, you who inhabit the praises of Israel. [4]Our fathers trusted in you. They trusted, and you delivered them. [5]They cried to you, and were delivered. They trusted in you, and were not disappointed. [6]But I am a worm, and no man; a reproach of men, and despised by the people. [7]All those who see me mock me. They insult me with their lips. They shake their heads, saying, [8]"He trusts in Yahweh. Let him deliver him. Let him rescue him, since he delights in him." [9]But you brought me out of the womb. You made me trust while at my mother's breasts. [10]I was thrown on you from my mother's womb. You are my God since my mother bore me. [11]Don't be far from me, for trouble is near. For there is no one to help. [12]Many bulls have surrounded me. Strong bulls of Bashan have encircled me. [13]They open their mouths wide against me, lions tearing prey and roaring. [14]I am poured out like water. All my bones are out of joint. My heart is like wax. It is melted within me. [15]My strength is dried up like a potsherd. My tongue sticks to the roof of my mouth. You have brought me into the dust of death. [16]For dogs have surrounded me. A company of evildoers have enclosed me. They have pierced my hands and feet. [17]I can count all of my bones. They look and stare at me. [18]They divide my garments among them. They cast lots for my clothing. [19]But don't be far off, Yahweh. You are my help. Hurry to help me! [20]Deliver my soul from the sword, my precious life from the power of the dog. [21]Save me from the lion's mouth! Yes, you have rescued me from the horns of the wild oxen. [22]I will declare your name to my brothers. Among the assembly, I will praise you. [23]You who fear Yahweh, praise him! All you descendants of Jacob, glorify him! Stand in awe of him, all you descendants of Israel! [24]For he has not despised nor abhorred the affliction of the afflicted, neither has he hidden his face from him; but when he cried to him, he heard. [25]My praise of you comes in the great assembly. I will pay my vows before those who fear him. [26]The humble shall eat and be satisfied. They shall praise Yahweh who seek after him. Let your hearts live forever. [27]All the ends of the earth shall remember and turn to Yahweh. All the relatives of the nations shall worship before you. [28]For the kingdom is Yahweh's. He is the ruler over the nations. [29]All the rich ones of the earth shall eat and worship. All those who go down to the dust shall bow before him, even he who can't keep his soul alive. [30]Posterity shall serve him. Future generations shall be told about the Lord. [31]They shall come and shall declare his righteousness to a people that shall be born, for he has done it.

Psalm Book 1 Chapter 23

[1]Yahweh is my shepherd; I shall lack nothing. [2]He makes me lie down in green pastures. He leads me beside still waters. [3]He restores my soul. He guides me in the paths of righteousness for his name's sake. [4]Even though I walk through the valley of the shadow of death, I will fear no evil, for you are with me. Your rod and your staff, they comfort me. [5]You prepare a table before me in the presence of my enemies. You anoint my head with oil. My cup runs over. [6]Surely goodness and loving kindness shall follow me all the days of my life, and I will dwell in Yahweh's house forever.

Psalm Book 1 Chapter 24

[1]The earth is Yahweh's, with its fullness; the world, and those who dwell in it. [2]For he has founded it on the seas, and established it on the floods. [3]Who may ascend to Yahweh's hill? Who may stand in his holy place? [4]He who has clean hands and a pure heart; who has not lifted up his soul to falsehood, and has not sworn deceitfully. [5]He shall receive a blessing from Yahweh, righteousness from the God of his salvation. [6]This is the generation of those who seek Him, who seek your face— even Jacob. Selah. [7]Lift up your heads, you gates! Be lifted up, you everlasting doors, and the King of glory will come in. [8]Who is the King of glory? Yahweh strong and mighty, Yahweh mighty in battle. [9]Lift up your heads, you gates; yes, lift them up, you everlasting doors, and the King of glory will come in. [10]Who is this King of glory? Yahweh of Armies is the King of glory! Selah.

Psalm Book 1 Chapter 25

[1]To you, Yahweh, I lift up my soul. [2]My God, I have trusted in you. Don't let me be shamed. Don't let my enemies triumph over me. [3]Yes, no one who waits for you will be shamed. They will be shamed who deal treacherously without cause. [4]Show me your ways, Yahweh. Teach me your paths. [5]Guide me in your truth, and teach me, for you are the God of my salvation. I wait for you all day long. [6]Yahweh, remember your tender mercies and your loving kindness, for they are from old times. [7]Don't remember the sins of my youth, nor my transgressions. Remember me according to your loving kindness, for your goodness' sake, Yahweh. [8]Good and upright is Yahweh, therefore he will instruct sinners in the way. [9]He will guide the humble in justice. He will teach the humble his way. [10]All the paths of Yahweh are loving kindness and truth to such as keep his covenant and his testimonies. [11]For your name's sake, Yahweh, pardon my iniquity, for it is great. [12]What man is he who fears Yahweh? He shall instruct him in the way that he shall choose. [13]His soul will dwell at ease. His offspring will inherit the land. [14]The friendship of Yahweh is with those who fear him. He will show them his covenant. [15]My eyes are ever on Yahweh, for he will pluck my feet out of the net. [16]Turn to me, and have mercy on me, for I am desolate and afflicted. [17]The troubles of my heart are enlarged. Oh bring me out of my distresses. [18]Consider my affliction and my travail. Forgive all my sins. [19]Consider my enemies, for they are many. They hate me with cruel hatred. [20]Oh keep my soul, and deliver me. Let me not be disappointed, for I take refuge in you. [21]Let integrity and uprightness preserve me, for I wait for you. [22]God, redeem Israel out of all his troubles.

Psalm Book 1 Chapter 26

[1]Judge me, Yahweh, for I have walked in my integrity. I have trusted also in Yahweh without wavering. [2]Examine me, Yahweh, and prove me. Try my heart and my mind. [3]For your loving kindness is before my eyes. I have walked in your truth. [4]I have not sat with deceitful men, neither will I go in with hypocrites. [5]I hate the assembly of evildoers, and will not sit with the wicked. [6]I will wash my hands in innocence, so I will go about your altar, Yahweh, [7]that I may make the voice of thanksgiving to be heard and tell of all your wondrous deeds. [8]Yahweh, I love the habitation of your house, the place where your glory dwells. [9]Don't gather my soul with sinners, nor my life with bloodthirsty men [10]in whose hands is wickedness; their right hand is full of bribes. [11]But as for me, I will walk in my integrity. Redeem me, and be merciful to me. [12]My foot stands in an even place. In the congregations I will bless Yahweh.

Psalm Book 1 Chapter 27

[1]Yahweh is my light and my salvation. Whom shall I fear? Yahweh is the strength of my life. Of whom shall I be afraid? [2]When evildoers came at me to eat up my flesh, even my adversaries and my foes, they stumbled and fell. [3]Though an army should encamp against me, my heart shall not fear. Though war should rise against me, even then I will be confident. [4]One thing I have asked of Yahweh, that I will seek after: that I may dwell in Yahweh's house all the days of my life, to see Yahweh's beauty, and to inquire in his temple. [5]For in the day of trouble, he will keep me secretly in his pavilion. In the secret place of his tabernacle, he will hide me. He will lift me up on a rock. [6]Now my

head will be lifted up above my enemies around me. I will offer sacrifices of joy in his tent. I will sing, yes, I will sing praises to Yahweh. [7]Hear, Yahweh, when I cry with my voice. Have mercy also on me, and answer me. [8]When you said, "Seek my face," my heart said to you, "I will seek your face, Yahweh." [9]Don't hide your face from me. Don't put your servant away in anger. You have been my help. Don't abandon me, neither forsake me, God of my salvation. [10]When my father and my mother forsake me, then Yahweh will take me up. [11]Teach me your way, Yahweh. Lead me in a straight path, because of my enemies. [12]Don't deliver me over to the desire of my adversaries, for false witnesses have risen up against me, such as breathe out cruelty. [13]I am still confident of this: I will see the goodness of Yahweh in the land of the living. [14]Wait for Yahweh. Be strong, and let your heart take courage. Yes, wait for Yahweh.

Psalm Book 1 Chapter 28

[1]To you, Yahweh, I call. My rock, don't be deaf to me, lest, if you are silent to me, I would become like those who go down into the pit. [2]Hear the voice of my petitions, when I cry to you, when I lift up my hands toward your Most Holy Place. [3]Don't draw me away with the wicked, with the workers of iniquity who speak peace with their neighbors, but mischief is in their hearts. [4]Give them according to their work, and according to the wickedness of their doings. Give them according to the operation of their hands. Bring back on them what they deserve. [5]Because they don't respect the works of Yahweh, nor the operation of his hands, he will break them down and not build them up. [6]Blessed be Yahweh, because he has heard the voice of my petitions. [7]Yahweh is my strength and my shield. My heart has trusted in him, and I am helped. Therefore my heart greatly rejoices. With my song I will thank him. [8]Yahweh is their strength. He is a stronghold of salvation to his anointed. [9]Save your people, and bless your inheritance. Be their shepherd also, and bear them up forever.

Psalm Book 1 Chapter 29

[1]Ascribe to Yahweh, you sons of the mighty, ascribe to Yahweh glory and strength. [2]Ascribe to Yahweh the glory due to his name. Worship Yahweh in holy array. [3]Yahweh's voice is on the waters. The God of glory thunders, even Yahweh on many waters. [4]Yahweh's voice is powerful. Yahweh's voice is full of majesty. [5]Yahweh's voice breaks the cedars. Yes, Yahweh breaks in pieces the cedars of Lebanon. [6]He makes them also to skip like a calf; Lebanon and Sirion like a young, wild ox. [7]Yahweh's voice strikes with flashes of lightning. [8]Yahweh's voice shakes the wilderness. Yahweh shakes the wilderness of Kadesh. [9]Yahweh's voice makes the deer calve, and strips the forests bare. In his temple everything says, "Glory!" [10]Yahweh sat enthroned at the Flood. Yes, Yahweh sits as King forever. [11]Yahweh will give strength to his people. Yahweh will bless his people with peace.

Psalm Book 1 Chapter 30

[1]I will extol you, Yahweh, for you have raised me up, and have not made my foes to rejoice over me. [2]Yahweh my God, I cried to you, and you have healed me. [3]Yahweh, you have brought up my soul from Sheol. You have kept me alive, that I should not go down to the pit. [4]Sing praise to Yahweh, you saints of his. Give thanks to his holy name. [5]For his anger is but for a moment. His favor is for a lifetime. Weeping may stay for the night, but joy comes in the morning. [6]As for me, I said in my prosperity, "I shall never be moved." [7]You, Yahweh, when you favored me, made my mountain stand strong; but when you hid your face, I was troubled. [8]I cried to you, Yahweh. I made supplication to the Lord: [9]"What profit is there in my destruction, if I go down to the pit? Shall the dust praise you? Shall it declare your truth? [10]Hear, Yahweh, and have mercy on me. Yahweh, be my helper." [11]You have turned my mourning into dancing for me. You have removed my sackcloth, and clothed me with gladness, [12]to the end that my heart may sing praise to you, and not be silent. Yahweh my God, I will give thanks to you forever!

Psalm Book 1 Chapter 31

[1]In you, Yahweh, I take refuge. Let me never be disappointed. Deliver me in your righteousness. [2]Bow down your ear to me. Deliver me speedily. Be to me a strong rock, a house of defense to save me. [3]For you are my rock and my fortress, therefore for your name's sake lead me and guide me. [4]Pluck me out of the net that they have laid secretly for me, for you are my stronghold. [5]Into your hand I commend my spirit. You redeem me, Yahweh, God of truth. [6]I hate those who regard lying vanities, but I trust in Yahweh. [7]I will be glad and rejoice in your loving kindness, for you have seen my affliction. You have known my soul in adversities. [8]You have not shut me up into the hand of the enemy. You have set my feet in a large place. [9]Have mercy on me, Yahweh, for I am in distress. My eye, my soul, and my body waste away with grief. [10]For my life is spent with sorrow, my years with sighing. My strength fails because of my iniquity. My bones are wasted away.

[11]Because of all my adversaries I have become utterly contemptible to my neighbors, a horror to my acquaintances. Those who saw me on the street fled from me. [12]I am forgotten from their hearts like a dead man. I am like broken pottery. [13]For I have heard the slander of many, terror on every side, while they conspire together against me, they plot to take away my life. [14]But I trust in you, Yahweh. I said, "You are my God." [15]My times are in your hand. Deliver me from the hand of my enemies, and from those who persecute me. [16]Make your face to shine on your servant. Save me in your loving kindness. [17]Let me not be disappointed, Yahweh, for I have called on you. Let the wicked be disappointed. Let them be silent in Sheol. [18]Let the lying lips be mute, which speak against the righteous insolently, with pride and contempt. [19]Oh how great is your goodness, which you have laid up for those who fear you, which you have worked for those who take refuge in you, before the sons of men! [20]In the shelter of your presence you will hide them from the plotting of man. You will keep them secretly in a dwelling away from the strife of tongues. [21]Praise be to Yahweh, for he has shown me his marvelous loving kindness in a strong city. [22]As for me, I said in my haste, "I am cut off from before your eyes." Nevertheless you heard the voice of my petitions when I cried to you. [23]Oh love Yahweh, all you his saints! Yahweh preserves the faithful, and fully recompenses him who behaves arrogantly. [24]Be strong, and let your heart take courage, all you who hope in Yahweh.

Psalm Book 1 Chapter 32

[1]Blessed is he whose disobedience is forgiven, whose sin is covered. [2]Blessed is the man to whom Yahweh doesn't impute iniquity, in whose spirit there is no deceit. [3]When I kept silence, my bones wasted away through my groaning all day long. [4]For day and night your hand was heavy on me. My strength was sapped in the heat of summer. Selah. [5]I acknowledged my sin to you. I didn't hide my iniquity. I said, I will confess my transgressions to Yahweh, and you forgave the iniquity of my sin. Selah. [6]For this, let everyone who is godly pray to you in a time when you may be found. Surely when the great waters overflow, they shall not reach to him. [7]You are my hiding place. You will preserve me from trouble. You will surround me with songs of deliverance. Selah. [8]I will instruct you and teach you in the way which you shall go. I will counsel you with my eye on you. [9]Don't be like the horse, or like the mule, which have no understanding, who are controlled by bit and bridle, or else they will not come near to you. [10]Many sorrows come to the wicked, but loving kindness shall surround him who trusts in Yahweh. [11]Be glad in Yahweh, and rejoice, you righteous! Shout for joy, all you who are upright in heart!

Psalm Book 1 Chapter 33

[1]Rejoice in Yahweh, you righteous! Praise is fitting for the upright. [2]Give thanks to Yahweh with the lyre. Sing praises to him with the harp of ten strings. [3]Sing to him a new song. Play skillfully with a shout of joy! [4]For Yahweh's word is right. All his work is done in faithfulness. [5]He loves righteousness and justice. The earth is full of the loving kindness of Yahweh. [6]By Yahweh's word, the heavens were made: all their army by the breath of his mouth. [7]He gathers the waters of the sea together as a heap. He lays up the deeps in storehouses. [8]Let all the earth fear Yahweh. Let all the inhabitants of the world stand in awe of him. [9]For he spoke, and it was done. He commanded, and it stood firm. [10]Yahweh brings the counsel of the nations to nothing. He makes the thoughts of the peoples to be of no effect. [11]The counsel of Yahweh stands fast forever, the thoughts of his heart to all generations. [12]Blessed is the nation whose God is Yahweh, the people whom he has chosen for his own inheritance. [13]Yahweh looks from heaven. He sees all the sons of men. [14]From the place of his habitation he looks out on all the inhabitants of the earth, [15]he who fashions all of their hearts; and he considers all of their works. [16]There is no king saved by the multitude of army. A mighty man is not delivered by great strength. [17]A horse is a vain thing for safety, neither does he deliver any by his great power. [18]Behold, Yahweh's eye is on those who fear him, on those who hope in his loving kindness, [19]to deliver their soul from death, to keep them alive in famine. [20]Our soul has waited for Yahweh. He is our help and our shield. [21]For our heart rejoices in him, because we have trusted in his holy name. [22]Let your loving kindness be on us, Yahweh, since we have hoped in you.

Psalm Book 1 Chapter 34

[1]I will bless Yahweh at all times. His praise will always be in my mouth. [2]My soul shall boast in Yahweh. The humble shall hear of it and be glad. [3]Oh magnify Yahweh with me. Let's exalt his name together. [4]I sought Yahweh, and he answered me, and delivered me from all my fears. [5]They looked to him, and were radiant. Their faces shall never be covered with shame. [6]This poor man cried, and Yahweh heard him, and saved him out of all his troubles. [7]Yahweh's angel encamps around

those who fear him, and delivers them. [8]Oh taste and see that Yahweh is good. Blessed is the man who takes refuge in him. [9]Oh fear Yahweh, you his saints, for there is no lack with those who fear him. [10]The young lions do lack, and suffer hunger, but those who seek Yahweh shall not lack any good thing. [11]Come, you children, listen to me. I will teach you the fear of Yahweh. [12]Who is someone who desires life, and loves many days, that he may see good? [13]Keep your tongue from evil, and your lips from speaking lies. [14]Depart from evil, and do good. Seek peace, and pursue it. [15]Yahweh's eyes are toward the righteous. His ears listen to their cry. [16]Yahweh's face is against those who do evil, to cut off their memory from the earth. [17]The righteous cry, and Yahweh hears, and delivers them out of all their troubles. [18]Yahweh is near to those who have a broken heart, and saves those who have a crushed spirit. [19]Many are the afflictions of the righteous, but Yahweh delivers him out of them all. [20]He protects all of his bones. Not one of them is broken. [21]Evil shall kill the wicked. Those who hate the righteous shall be condemned. [22]Yahweh redeems the soul of his servants. None of those who take refuge in him shall be condemned.

Psalm Book 1 Chapter 35

[1]Contend, Yahweh, with those who contend with me. Fight against those who fight against me. [2]Take hold of shield and buckler, and stand up for my help. [3]Brandish the spear and block those who pursue me. Tell my soul, "I am your salvation." [4]Let those who seek after my soul be disappointed and brought to dishonor. Let those who plot my ruin be turned back and confounded. [5]Let them be as chaff before the wind, Yahweh's angel driving them on. [6]Let their way be dark and slippery, Yahweh's angel pursuing them. [7]For without cause they have hidden their net in a pit for me. Without cause they have dug a pit for my soul. [8]Let destruction come on him unawares. Let his net that he has hidden catch himself. Let him fall into that destruction. [9]My soul shall be joyful in Yahweh. It shall rejoice in his salvation. [10]All my bones shall say, "Yahweh, who is like you, who delivers the poor from him who is too strong for him; yes, the poor and the needy from him who robs him?" [11]Unrighteous witnesses rise up. They ask me about things that I don't know about. [12]They reward me evil for good, to the bereaving of my soul. [13]But as for me, when they were sick, my clothing was sackcloth. I afflicted my soul with fasting. My prayer returned into my own bosom. [14]I behaved myself as though it had been my friend or my brother. I bowed down mourning, as one who mourns his mother. [15]But in my adversity, they rejoiced, and gathered themselves together. The attackers gathered themselves together against me, and I didn't know it. They tore at me, and didn't cease. [16]Like the profane mockers in feasts, they gnashed their teeth at me. [17]Lord, how long will you look on? Rescue my soul from their destruction, my precious life from the lions. [18]I will give you thanks in the great assembly. I will praise you among many people. [19]Don't let those who are my enemies wrongfully rejoice over me; neither let those who hate me without a cause wink their eyes. [20]For they don't speak peace, but they devise deceitful words against those who are quiet in the land. [21]Yes, they opened their mouth wide against me. They said, "Aha! Aha! Our eye has seen it!" [22]You have seen it, Yahweh. Don't keep silent. Lord, don't be far from me. [23]Wake up! Rise up to defend me, my God! My Lord, contend for me! [24]Vindicate me, Yahweh my God, according to your righteousness. Don't let them gloat over me. [25]Don't let them say in their heart, "Aha! That's the way we want it!" Don't let them say, "We have swallowed him up!" [26]Let them be disappointed and confounded together who rejoice at my calamity. Let them be clothed with shame and dishonor who magnify themselves against me. [27]Let those who favor my righteous cause shout for joy and be glad. Yes, let them say continually, "May Yahweh be magnified, who has pleasure in the prosperity of his servant!" [28]My tongue shall talk about your righteousness and about your praise all day long.

Psalm Book 1 Chapter 36

[1]A revelation is within my heart about the disobedience of the wicked: There is no fear of God before his eyes. [2]For he flatters himself in his own eyes, too much to detect and hate his sin. [3]The words of his mouth are iniquity and deceit. He has ceased to be wise and to do good. [4]He plots iniquity on his bed. He sets himself in a way that is not good. He doesn't abhor evil. [5]Your loving kindness, Yahweh, is in the heavens. Your faithfulness reaches to the skies. [6]Your righteousness is like the mountains of God. Your judgments are like a great deep. Yahweh, you preserve man and animal. [7]How precious is your loving kindness, God! The children of men take refuge under the shadow of your wings. [8]They shall be abundantly satisfied with the abundance of your house. You will make them drink of the river of your pleasures. [9]For with you is the spring of life. In your light we will see light. [10]Oh continue your loving kindness to those who know you, your righteousness to the upright in heart. [11]Don't let the foot of pride come against me. Don't let the hand of the wicked drive me away. [12]There the workers of iniquity are fallen. They are thrust down, and shall not be able to rise.

Psalm Book 1 Chapter 37

[1]Don't fret because of evildoers, neither be envious against those who work unrighteousness. [2]For they shall soon be cut down like the grass, and wither like the green herb. [3]Trust in Yahweh, and do good. Dwell in the land, and enjoy safe pasture. [4]Also delight yourself in Yahweh, and he will give you the desires of your heart. [5]Commit your way to Yahweh. Trust also in him, and he will do this: [6]he will make your righteousness shine out like light, and your justice as the noon day sun. [7]Rest in Yahweh, and wait patiently for him. Don't fret because of him who prospers in his way, because of the man who makes wicked plots happen. [8]Cease from anger, and forsake wrath. Don't fret; it leads only to evildoing. [9]For evildoers shall be cut off, but those who wait for Yahweh shall inherit the land. [10]For yet a little while, and the wicked will be no more. Yes, though you look for his place, he isn't there. [11]But the humble shall inherit the land, and shall delight themselves in the abundance of peace. [12]The wicked plots against the just, and gnashes at him with his teeth. [13]The Lord will laugh at him, for he sees that his day is coming. [14]The wicked have drawn out the sword, and have bent their bow, to cast down the poor and needy, to kill those who are upright on the path. [15]Their sword shall enter into their own heart. Their bows shall be broken. [16]Better is a little that the righteous has, than the abundance of many wicked. [17]For the arms of the wicked shall be broken, but Yahweh upholds the righteous. [18]Yahweh knows the days of the perfect. Their inheritance shall be forever. [19]They shall not be disappointed in the time of evil. In the days of famine they shall be satisfied. [20]But the wicked shall perish. The enemies of Yahweh shall be like the beauty of the fields. They will vanish— vanish like smoke. [21]The wicked borrow, and don't pay back, but the righteous give generously. [22]For such as are blessed by him shall inherit the land. Those who are cursed by him shall be cut off. [23]A man's steps are established by Yahweh. He delights in his way. [24]Though he stumble, he shall not fall, for Yahweh holds him up with his hand. [25]I have been young, and now am old, yet I have not seen the righteous forsaken, nor his children begging for bread. [26]All day long he deals graciously, and lends. His offspring is blessed. [27]Depart from evil, and do good. Live securely forever. [28]For Yahweh loves justice, and doesn't forsake his saints. They are preserved forever, but the children of the wicked shall be cut off. [29]The righteous shall inherit the land, and live in it forever. [30]The mouth of the righteous talks of wisdom. His tongue speaks justice. [31]The law of his God is in his heart. None of his steps shall slide. [32]The wicked watch the righteous, and seek to kill him. [33]Yahweh will not leave him in his hand, nor condemn him when he is judged. [34]Wait for Yahweh, and keep his way, and he will exalt you to inherit the land. When the wicked are cut off, you shall see it. [35]I have seen the wicked in great power, spreading himself like a green tree in its native soil. [36]But he passed away, and behold, he was not. Yes, I sought him, but he could not be found. [37]Mark the perfect man, and see the upright, for there is a future for the man of peace. [38]As for transgressors, they shall be destroyed together. The future of the wicked shall be cut off. [39]But the salvation of the righteous is from Yahweh. He is their stronghold in the time of trouble. [40]Yahweh helps them and rescues them. He rescues them from the wicked and saves them, because they have taken refuge in him.

Psalm Book 1 Chapter 38

[1]Yahweh, don't rebuke me in your wrath, neither chasten me in your hot displeasure. [2]For your arrows have pierced me, your hand presses hard on me. [3]There is no soundness in my flesh because of your indignation, neither is there any health in my bones because of my sin. [4]For my iniquities have gone over my head. As a heavy burden, they are too heavy for me. [5]My wounds are loathsome and corrupt because of my foolishness. [6]I am in pain and bowed down greatly. I go mourning all day long. [7]For my waist is filled with burning. There is no soundness in my flesh. [8]I am faint and severely bruised. I have groaned by reason of the anguish of my heart. [9]Lord, all my desire is before you. My groaning is not hidden from you. [10]My heart throbs. My strength fails me. As for the light of my eyes, it has also left me. [11]My lovers and my friends stand aloof from my plague. My kinsmen stand far away. [12]They also who seek after my life lay snares. Those who seek my hurt speak mischievous things, and meditate deceits all day long. [13]But I, as a deaf man, don't hear. I am as a mute man who doesn't open his mouth. [14]Yes, I am as a man who doesn't hear, in whose mouth are no reproofs. [15]For I hope in you, Yahweh. You will answer, Lord my God. [16]For I said, "Don't let them gloat over me, or exalt themselves over me when my foot slips." [17]For I am ready to fall. My pain is continually before

me. [18]For I will declare my iniquity. I will be sorry for my sin. [19]But my enemies are vigorous and many. Those who hate me without reason are numerous. [20]They who render evil for good are also adversaries to me, because I follow what is good. [21]Don't forsake me, Yahweh. My God, don't be far from me. [22]Hurry to help me, Lord, my salvation.

Psalm Book 1 Chapter 39

[1]I said, "I will watch my ways, so that I don't sin with my tongue. I will keep my mouth with a bridle while the wicked is before me." [2]I was mute with silence. I held my peace, even from good. My sorrow was stirred. [3]My heart was hot within me. While I meditated, the fire burned. I spoke with my tongue: [4]"Yahweh, show me my end, what is the measure of my days. Let me know how frail I am. [5]Behold, you have made my days hand widths. My lifetime is as nothing before you. Surely every man stands as a breath." Selah. [6]"Surely every man walks like a shadow. Surely they busy themselves in vain. He heaps up, and doesn't know who shall gather. [7]Now, Lord, what do I wait for? My hope is in you. [8]Deliver me from all my transgressions. Don't make me the reproach of the foolish. [9]I was mute. I didn't open my mouth, because you did it. [10]Remove your scourge away from me. I am overcome by the blow of your hand. [11]When you rebuke and correct man for iniquity, you consume his wealth like a moth. Surely every man is but a breath." Selah. [12]"Hear my prayer, Yahweh, and give ear to my cry. Don't be silent at my tears. For I am a stranger with you, a foreigner, as all my fathers were. [13]Oh spare me, that I may recover strength, before I go away and exist no more."

Psalm Book 1 Chapter 40

[1]I waited patiently for Yahweh. He turned to me, and heard my cry. [2]He brought me up also out of a horrible pit, out of the miry clay. He set my feet on a rock, and gave me a firm place to stand. [3]He has put a new song in my mouth, even praise to our God. Many shall see it, and fear, and shall trust in Yahweh. [4]Blessed is the man who makes Yahweh his trust, and doesn't respect the proud, nor such as turn away to lies. [5]Many, Yahweh, my God, are the wonderful works which you have done, and your thoughts which are toward us. They can't be declared back to you. If I would declare and speak of them, they are more than can be counted. [6]Sacrifice and offering you didn't desire. You have opened my ears. You have not required burnt offering and sin offering. [7]Then I said, "Behold, I have come. It is written about me in the book in the scroll. [8]I delight to do your will, my God. Yes, your law is within my heart." [9]I have proclaimed glad news of righteousness in the great assembly. Behold, I will not seal my lips, Yahweh, you know. [10]I have not hidden your righteousness within my heart. I have declared your faithfulness and your salvation. I have not concealed your loving kindness and your truth from the great assembly. [11]Don't withhold your tender mercies from me, Yahweh. Let your loving kindness and your truth continually preserve me. [12]For innumerable evils have surrounded me. My iniquities have overtaken me, so that I am not able to look up. They are more than the hairs of my head. My heart has failed me. [13]Be pleased, Yahweh, to deliver me. Hurry to help me, Yahweh. [14]Let them be disappointed and confounded together who seek after my soul to destroy it. Let them be turned backward and brought to dishonor who delight in my hurt. [15]Let them be desolate by reason of their shame that tell me, "Aha! Aha!" [16]Let all those who seek you rejoice and be glad in you. Let such as love your salvation say continually, "Let Yahweh be exalted!" [17]But I am poor and needy. May the Lord think about me. You are my help and my deliverer. Don't delay, my God.

Psalm Book 1 Chapter 41

[1]Blessed is he who considers the poor. Yahweh will deliver him in the day of evil. [2]Yahweh will preserve him, and keep him alive. He shall be blessed on the earth, and he will not surrender him to the will of his enemies. [3]Yahweh will sustain him on his sickbed, and restore him from his bed of illness. [4]I said, "Yahweh, have mercy on me! Heal me, for I have sinned against you." [5]My enemies speak evil against me: "When will he die, and his name perish?" [6]If he comes to see me, he speaks falsehood. His heart gathers iniquity to itself. When he goes abroad, he tells it. [7]All who hate me whisper together against me. They imagine the worst for me. [8]"An evil disease", they say, "has afflicted him. Now that he lies he shall rise up no more." [9]Yes, my own familiar friend, in whom I trusted, who ate bread with me, has lifted up his heel against me. [10]But you, Yahweh, have mercy on me, and raise me up, that I may repay them. [11]By this I know that you delight in me, because my enemy doesn't triumph over me. [12]As for me, you uphold me in my integrity, and set me in your presence forever. [13]Blessed be Yahweh, the God of Israel, from everlasting and to everlasting! Amen and amen.

Psalms Book 2

Psalms Book 2 Chapter 42

[1] As the deer pants for the water brooks, so my soul pants after you, God. [2] My soul thirsts for God, for the living God. When shall I come and appear before God? [3] My tears have been my food day and night, while they continually ask me, "Where is your God?" [4] These things I remember, and pour out my soul within me, how I used to go with the crowd, and led them to God's house, with the voice of joy and praise, a multitude keeping a holy day. [5] Why are you in despair, my soul? Why are you disturbed within me? Hope in God! For I shall still praise him for the saving help of his presence. [6] My God, my soul is in despair within me. Therefore I remember you from the land of the Jordan, the heights of Hermon, from the hill Mizar. [7] Deep calls to deep at the noise of your waterfalls. All your waves and your billows have swept over me. [8] Yahweh will command his loving kindness in the daytime. In the night his song shall be with me: a prayer to the God of my life. [9] I will ask God, my rock, "Why have you forgotten me? Why do I go mourning because of the oppression of the enemy?" [10] As with a sword in my bones, my adversaries reproach me, while they continually ask me, "Where is your God?" [11] Why are you in despair, my soul? Why are you disturbed within me? Hope in God! For I shall still praise him, the saving help of my countenance, and my God.

Psalms Book 2 Chapter 43

[1] Vindicate me, God, and plead my cause against an ungodly nation. Oh, deliver me from deceitful and wicked men. [2] For you are the God of my strength. Why have you rejected me? Why do I go mourning because of the oppression of the enemy? [3] Oh, send out your light and your truth. Let them lead me. Let them bring me to your holy hill, to your tents. [4] Then I will go to the altar of God, to God, my exceeding joy. I will praise you on the harp, God, my God. [5] Why are you in despair, my soul? Why are you disturbed within me? Hope in God! For I shall still praise him: my Savior, my helper, and my God.

Psalms Book 2 Chapter 44

[1] We have heard with our ears, God; our fathers have told us what work you did in their days, in the days of old. [2] You drove out the nations with your hand, but you planted them. You afflicted the peoples, but you spread them abroad. [3] For they didn't get the land in possession by their own sword, neither did their own arm save them; but your right hand, your arm, and the light of your face, because you were favorable to them. [4] God, you are my King. Command victories for Jacob! [5] Through you, we will push down our adversaries. Through your name, we will tread down those who rise up against us. [6] For I will not trust in my bow, neither will my sword save me. [7] But you have saved us from our adversaries, and have shamed those who hate us. [8] In God we have made our boast all day long. We will give thanks to your name forever. Selah. [9] But now you rejected us, and brought us to dishonor, and don't go out with our armies. [10] You make us turn back from the adversary. Those who hate us take plunder for themselves. [11] You have made us like sheep for food, and have scattered us among the nations. [12] You sell your people for nothing, and have gained nothing from their sale. [13] You make us a reproach to our neighbors, a scoffing and a derision to those who are around us. [14] You make us a byword among the nations, a shaking of the head among the peoples. [15] All day long my dishonor is before me, and shame covers my face, [16] at the taunt of one who reproaches and verbally abuses, because of the enemy and the avenger. [17] All this has come on us, yet we haven't forgotten you. We haven't been false to your covenant. [18] Our heart has not turned back, neither have our steps strayed from your path, [19] though you have crushed us in the haunt of jackals, and covered us with the shadow of death. [20] If we have forgotten the name of our God, or spread out our hands to a strange god, [21] won't God search this out? For he knows the secrets of the heart. [22] Yes, for your sake we are killed all day long. We are regarded as sheep for the slaughter. [23] Wake up! Why do you sleep, Lord? Arise! Don't reject us forever. [24] Why do you hide your face, and forget our affliction and our oppression? [25] For our soul is bowed down to the dust. Our body clings to the earth. [26] Rise up to help us. Redeem us for your loving kindness' sake.

Psalms Book 2 Chapter 45

[1] My heart overflows with a noble theme. I recite my verses for the king. My tongue is like the pen of a skillful writer. [2] You are the most excellent of the sons of men. Grace has anointed your lips, therefore God has blessed you forever. [3] Strap your sword on your thigh, O mighty one, in your splendor and your majesty. [4] In your majesty ride on victoriously on behalf of truth, humility, and righteousness. Let your right hand display awesome deeds. [5] Your arrows are sharp. The nations fall under you, with arrows in the heart of the king's enemies. [6] Your throne, God, is forever and ever. A scepter of equity is the scepter of your kingdom.

7 You have loved righteousness, and hated wickedness. Therefore God, your God, has anointed you with the oil of gladness above your fellows. 8 All your garments smell like myrrh, aloes, and cassia. Out of ivory palaces stringed instruments have made you glad. 9 Kings' daughters are among your honorable women. At your right hand the queen stands in gold of Ophir. 10 Listen, daughter, consider, and turn your ear. Forget your own people, and also your father's house. 11 So the king will desire your beauty, honor him, for he is your lord. 12 The daughter of Tyre comes with a gift. The rich among the people entreat your favor. 13 The princess inside is all glorious. Her clothing is interwoven with gold. 14 She shall be led to the king in embroidered work. The virgins, her companions who follow her, shall be brought to you. 15 With gladness and rejoicing they shall be led. They shall enter into the king's palace. 16 Your sons will take the place of your fathers. You shall make them princes in all the earth. 17 I will make your name to be remembered in all generations. Therefore the peoples shall give you thanks forever and ever.

Psalms Book 2 Chapter 46

1 God is our refuge and strength, a very present help in trouble. 2 Therefore we won't be afraid, though the earth changes, though the mountains are shaken into the heart of the seas; 3 though its waters roar and are troubled, though the mountains tremble with their swelling. Selah. 4 There is a river, the streams of which make the city of God glad, the holy place of the tents of the Most High. 5 God is within her. She shall not be moved. God will help her at dawn. 6 The nations raged. The kingdoms were moved. He lifted his voice and the earth melted. 7 Yahweh of Armies is with us. The God of Jacob is our refuge. Selah. 8 Come, see Yahweh's works, what desolations he has made in the earth. 9 He makes wars cease to the end of the earth. He breaks the bow, and shatters the spear. He burns the chariots in the fire. 10 "Be still, and know that I am God. I will be exalted among the nations. I will be exalted in the earth." 11 Yahweh of Armies is with us. The God of Jacob is our refuge. Selah.

Psalms Book 2 Chapter 47

1 Oh clap your hands, all you nations. Shout to God with the voice of triumph! 2 For Yahweh Most High is awesome. He is a great King over all the earth. 3 He subdues nations under us, and peoples under our feet. 4 He chooses our inheritance for us, the glory of Jacob whom he loved. Selah. 5 God has gone up with a shout, Yahweh with the sound of a trumpet. 6 Sing praises to God! Sing praises! Sing praises to our King! Sing praises! 7 For God is the King of all the earth. Sing praises with understanding. 8 God reigns over the nations. God sits on his holy throne. 9 The princes of the peoples are gathered together, the people of the God of Abraham. For the shields of the earth belong to God. He is greatly exalted!

Psalms Book 2 Chapter 48

1 Great is Yahweh, and greatly to be praised, in the city of our God, in his holy mountain. 2 Beautiful in elevation, the joy of the whole earth, is Mount Zion, on the north sides, the city of the great King. 3 God has shown himself in her citadels as a refuge. 4 For, behold, the kings assembled themselves, they passed by together. 5 They saw it, then they were amazed. They were dismayed. They hurried away. 6 Trembling took hold of them there, pain, as of a woman in travail. 7 With the east wind, you break the ships of Tarshish. 8 As we have heard, so we have seen, in the city of Yahweh of Armies, in the city of our God. God will establish it forever. Selah. 9 We have thought about your loving kindness, God, in the middle of your temple. 10 As is your name, God, so is your praise to the ends of the earth. Your right hand is full of righteousness. 11 Let Mount Zion be glad! Let the daughters of Judah rejoice because of your judgments. 12 Walk about Zion, and go around her. Number its towers. 13 Notice her bulwarks. Consider her palaces, that you may tell it to the next generation. 14 For this God is our God forever and ever. He will be our guide even to death.

Psalms Book 2 Chapter 49

1 Hear this, all you peoples. Listen, all you inhabitants of the world, 2 both low and high, rich and poor together. 3 My mouth will speak words of wisdom. My heart will utter understanding. 4 I will incline my ear to a proverb. I will solve my riddle on the harp. 5 Why should I fear in the days of evil, when iniquity at my heels surrounds me? 6 Those who trust in their wealth, and boast in the multitude of their riches— 7 none of them can by any means redeem his brother, nor give God a ransom for him. 8 For the redemption of their life is costly, no payment is ever enough, 9 that he should live on forever, that he should not see corruption. 10 For he sees that wise men die; likewise the fool and the senseless perish, and leave their wealth to others. 11 Their inward thought is that their houses will endure forever, and their dwelling places to all generations. They name their lands after themselves. 12 But

man, despite his riches, doesn't endure. He is like the animals that perish. 13 This is the destiny of those who are foolish, and of those who approve their sayings. Selah. 14 They are appointed as a flock for Sheol. Death shall be their shepherd. The upright shall have dominion over them in the morning. Their beauty shall decay in Sheol, far from their mansion. 15 But God will redeem my soul from the power of Sheol, for he will receive me. Selah. 16 Don't be afraid when a man is made rich, when the glory of his house is increased; 17 for when he dies he will carry nothing away. His glory won't descend after him. 18 Though while he lived he blessed his soul— and men praise you when you do well for yourself— 19 he shall go to the generation of his fathers. They shall never see the light. 20 A man who has riches without understanding, is like the animals that perish.

Psalms Book 2 Chapter 50

1 The Mighty One, God, Yahweh, speaks, and calls the earth from sunrise to sunset. 2 Out of Zion, the perfection of beauty, God shines out. 3 Our God comes, and does not keep silent. A fire devours before him. It is very stormy around him. 4 He calls to the heavens above, to the earth, that he may judge his people: 5 "Gather my saints together to me, those who have made a covenant with me by sacrifice." 6 The heavens shall declare his righteousness, for God himself is judge. Selah. 7 "Hear, my people, and I will speak. Israel, I will testify against you. I am God, your God. 8 I don't rebuke you for your sacrifices. Your burnt offerings are continually before me. 9 I have no need for a bull from your stall, nor male goats from your pens. 10 For every animal of the forest is mine, and the livestock on a thousand hills. 11 I know all the birds of the mountains. The wild animals of the field are mine. 12 If I were hungry, I would not tell you, for the world is mine, and all that is in it. 13 Will I eat the meat of bulls, or drink the blood of goats? 14 Offer to God the sacrifice of thanksgiving. Pay your vows to the Most High. 15 Call on me in the day of trouble. I will deliver you, and you will honor me." 16 But to the wicked God says, "What right do you have to declare my statutes, that you have taken my covenant on your lips, 17 since you hate instruction, and throw my words behind you? 18 When you saw a thief, you consented with him, and have participated with adulterers. 19 You give your mouth to evil. Your tongue frames deceit. 20 You sit and speak against your brother. You slander your own mother's son. 21 You have done these things, and I kept silent. You thought that I was just like you. I will rebuke you, and accuse you in front of your eyes. 22 "Now consider this, you who forget God, lest I tear you into pieces, and there be no one to deliver. 23 Whoever offers the sacrifice of thanksgiving glorifies me, and prepares his way so that I will show God's salvation to him."

Psalms Book 2 Chapter 51

1 Have mercy on me, God, according to your loving kindness. According to the multitude of your tender mercies, blot out my transgressions. 2 Wash me thoroughly from my iniquity. Cleanse me from my sin. 3 For I know my transgressions. My sin is constantly before me. 4 Against you, and you only, I have sinned, and done that which is evil in your sight, so you may be proved right when you speak, and justified when you judge. 5 Behold, I was born in iniquity. My mother conceived me in sin. 6 Behold, you desire truth in the inward parts. You teach me wisdom in the inmost place. 7 Purify me with hyssop, and I will be clean. Wash me, and I will be whiter than snow. 8 Let me hear joy and gladness, that the bones which you have broken may rejoice. 9 Hide your face from my sins, and blot out all of my iniquities. 10 Create in me a clean heart, O God. Renew a right spirit within me. 11 Don't throw me from your presence, and don't take your Holy Spirit from me. 12 Restore to me the joy of your salvation. Uphold me with a willing spirit. 13 Then I will teach transgressors your ways. Sinners will be converted to you. 14 Deliver me from the guilt of bloodshed, O God, the God of my salvation. My tongue will sing aloud of your righteousness. 15 Lord, open my lips. My mouth shall declare your praise. 16 For you don't delight in sacrifice, or else I would give it. You have no pleasure in burnt offering. 17 The sacrifices of God are a broken spirit. O God, you will not despise a broken and contrite heart. 18 Do well in your good pleasure to Zion. Build the walls of Jerusalem. 19 Then you will delight in the sacrifices of righteousness, in burnt offerings and in whole burnt offerings. Then they will offer bulls on your altar.

Psalms Book 2 Chapter 52

1 Why do you boast of mischief, mighty man? God's loving kindness endures continually. 2 Your tongue plots destruction, like a sharp razor, working deceitfully. 3 You love evil more than good, lying rather than speaking the truth. Selah. 4 You love all devouring words, you deceitful tongue. 5 God will likewise destroy you forever. He will take you up, and pluck you out of your tent, and root you out of the land of the living. Selah. 6 The righteous also will see it, and fear, and laugh at him, saying,

7 "Behold, this is the man who didn't make God his strength, but trusted in the abundance of his riches, and strengthened himself in his wickedness." 8 But as for me, I am like a green olive tree in God's house. I trust in God's loving kindness forever and ever. 9 I will give you thanks forever, because you have done it. I will hope in your name, for it is good, in the presence of your saints.

Psalms Book 2 Chapter 53

1 The fool has said in his heart, "There is no God." They are corrupt, and have done abominable iniquity. There is no one who does good. 2 God looks down from heaven on the children of men, to see if there are any who understood, who seek after God. 3 Every one of them has gone back. They have become filthy together. There is no one who does good, no, not one. 4 Have the workers of iniquity no knowledge, who eat up my people as they eat bread, and don't call on God? 5 There they were in great fear, where no fear was, for God has scattered the bones of him who encamps against you. You have put them to shame, because God has rejected them. 6 Oh that the salvation of Israel would come out of Zion! When God brings back his people from captivity, then Jacob shall rejoice, and Israel shall be glad.

Psalms Book 2 Chapter 54

1 Save me, God, by your name. Vindicate me in your might. 2 Hear my prayer, God. Listen to the words of my mouth. 3 For strangers have risen up against me. Violent men have sought after my soul. They haven't set God before them. Selah. 4 Behold, God is my helper. The Lord is the one who sustains my soul. 5 He will repay the evil to my enemies. Destroy them in your truth. 6 With a free will offering, I will sacrifice to you. I will give thanks to your name, Yahweh, for it is good. 7 For he has delivered me out of all trouble. My eye has seen triumph over my enemies.

Psalms Book 2 Chapter 55

1 Listen to my prayer, God. Don't hide yourself from my supplication. 2 Attend to me, and answer me. I am restless in my complaint, and moan 3 because of the voice of the enemy, because of the oppression of the wicked. For they bring suffering on me. In anger they hold a grudge against me. 4 My heart is severely pained within me. The terrors of death have fallen on me. 5 Fearfulness and trembling have come on me. Horror has overwhelmed me. 6 I said, "Oh that I had wings like a dove! Then I would fly away, and be at rest. 7 Behold, then I would wander far off. I would lodge in the wilderness." Selah. 8 "I would hurry to a shelter from the stormy wind and storm." 9 Confuse them, Lord, and confound their language, for I have seen violence and strife in the city. 10 Day and night they prowl around on its walls. Malice and abuse are also within her. 11 Destructive forces are within her. Threats and lies don't depart from her streets. 12 For it was not an enemy who insulted me, then I could have endured it. Neither was it he who hated me who raised himself up against me, then I would have hidden myself from him. 13 But it was you, a man like me, my companion, and my familiar friend. 14 We took sweet fellowship together. We walked in God's house with company. 15 Let death come suddenly on them. Let them go down alive into Sheol. For wickedness is among them, in their dwelling. 16 As for me, I will call on God. Yahweh will save me. 17 Evening, morning, and at noon, I will cry out in distress. He will hear my voice. 18 He has redeemed my soul in peace from the battle that was against me, although there are many who oppose me. 19 God, who is enthroned forever, will hear and answer them. Selah. They never change and don't fear God. 20 He raises his hands against his friends. He has violated his covenant. 21 His mouth was smooth as butter, but his heart was war. His words were softer than oil, yet they were drawn swords. 22 Cast your burden on Yahweh and he will sustain you. He will never allow the righteous to be moved. 23 But you, God, will bring them down into the pit of destruction. Bloodthirsty and deceitful men shall not live out half their days, but I will trust in you.

Psalms Book 2 Chapter 56

1 Be merciful to me, God, for man wants to swallow me up. All day long, he attacks and oppresses me. 2 My enemies want to swallow me up all day long, for they are many who fight proudly against me. 3 When I am afraid, I will put my trust in you. 4 In God, I praise his word. In God, I put my trust. I will not be afraid. What can flesh do to me? 5 All day long they twist my words. All their thoughts are against me for evil. 6 They conspire and lurk, watching my steps. They are eager to take my life. 7 Shall they escape by iniquity? In anger cast down the peoples, God. 8 You count my wanderings. You put my tears into your container. Aren't they in your book? 9 Then my enemies shall turn back in the day that I call. I know this: that God is for me. 10 In God, I will praise his word. In Yahweh, I will praise his word. 11 I have put my trust in God. I will not be afraid. What can man do to me? 12 Your vows are on me, God. I will give thank offerings to you. 13 For you have delivered my soul from

death, and prevented my feet from falling, that I may walk before God in the light of the living.

Psalms Book 2 Chapter 57

1 Be merciful to me, God, be merciful to me, for my soul takes refuge in you. Yes, in the shadow of your wings, I will take refuge, until disaster has passed. 2 I cry out to God Most High, to God who accomplishes my requests for me. 3 He will send from heaven, and save me, he rebukes the one who is pursuing me. Selah. God will send out his loving kindness and his truth. 4 My soul is among lions. I lie among those who are set on fire, even the sons of men, whose teeth are spears and arrows, and their tongue a sharp sword. 5 Be exalted, God, above the heavens! Let your glory be above all the earth! 6 They have prepared a net for my steps. My soul is bowed down. They dig a pit before me. They fall into the middle of it themselves. Selah. 7 My heart is steadfast, God. My heart is steadfast. I will sing, yes, I will sing praises. 8 Wake up, my glory! Wake up, lute and harp! I will wake up the dawn. 9 I will give thanks to you, Lord, among the peoples. I will sing praises to you among the nations. 10 For your great loving kindness reaches to the heavens, and your truth to the skies. 11 Be exalted, God, above the heavens. Let your glory be over all the earth.

Psalms Book 2 Chapter 58

1 Do you indeed speak righteousness, silent ones? Do you judge blamelessly, you sons of men? 2 No, in your heart you plot injustice. You measure out the violence of your hands in the earth. 3 The wicked go astray from the womb. They are wayward as soon as they are born, speaking lies. 4 Their poison is like the poison of a snake, like a deaf cobra that stops its ear, 5 which doesn't listen to the voice of charmers, no matter how skillful the charmer may be. 6 Break their teeth, God, in their mouth. Break out the great teeth of the young lions, Yahweh. 7 Let them vanish like water that flows away. When they draw the bow, let their arrows be made blunt. 8 Let them be like a snail which melts and passes away, like the stillborn child, who has not seen the sun. 9 Before your pots can feel the heat of the thorns, he will sweep away the green and the burning alike. 10 The righteous shall rejoice when he sees the vengeance. He shall wash his feet in the blood of the wicked, 11 so that men shall say, "Most certainly there is a reward for the righteous. Most certainly there is a God who judges the earth."

Psalms Book 2 Chapter 59

1 Deliver me from my enemies, my God. Set me on high from those who rise up against me. 2 Deliver me from the workers of iniquity. Save me from the bloodthirsty men. 3 For, behold, they lie in wait for my soul. The mighty gather themselves together against me, not for my disobedience, nor for my sin, Yahweh. 4 I have done no wrong, yet they are ready to attack me. Rise up, behold, and help me! 5 You, Yahweh God of Armies, the God of Israel, rouse yourself to punish the nations. Show no mercy to the wicked traitors. Selah. 6 They return at evening, howling like dogs, and prowl around the city. 7 Behold, they spew with their mouth. Swords are in their lips, "For," they say, "who hears us?" 8 But you, Yahweh, laugh at them. You scoff at all the nations. 9 Oh, my Strength, I watch for you, for God is my high tower. 10 My God will go before me with his loving kindness. God will let me look at my enemies in triumph. 11 Don't kill them, or my people may forget. Scatter them by your power, and bring them down, Lord our shield. 12 For the sin of their mouth, and the words of their lips, let them be caught in their pride, for the curses and lies which they utter. 13 Consume them in wrath. Consume them, and they will be no more. Let them know that God rules in Jacob, to the ends of the earth. Selah. 14 At evening let them return. Let them howl like a dog, and go around the city. 15 They shall wander up and down for food, and wait all night if they aren't satisfied. 16 But I will sing of your strength. Yes, I will sing aloud of your loving kindness in the morning. For you have been my high tower, a refuge in the day of my distress. 17 To you, my strength, I will sing praises. For God is my high tower, the God of my mercy.

Psalms Book 2 Chapter 60

1 God, you have rejected us. You have broken us down. You have been angry. Restore us, again. 2 You have made the land tremble. You have torn it. Mend its fractures, for it quakes. 3 You have shown your people hard things. You have made us drink the wine that makes us stagger. 4 You have given a banner to those who fear you, that it may be displayed because of the truth. Selah. 5 So that your beloved may be delivered, save with your right hand, and answer us. 6 God has spoken from his sanctuary: "I will triumph. I will divide Shechem, and measure out the valley of Succoth. 7 Gilead is mine, and Manasseh is mine. Ephraim also is the defense of my head. Judah is my scepter. 8 Moab is my wash basin. I will throw my sandal on Edom. I shout in triumph over Philistia." 9 Who will bring me into the strong city? Who has led me to Edom? 10 Haven't you, God, rejected us? You don't go out with our

armies, God. ¹¹ Give us help against the adversary, for the help of man is vain. ¹² Through God we will do valiantly, for it is he who will tread down our adversaries.

Psalms Book 2 Chapter 61

¹ Hear my cry, God. Listen to my prayer. ² From the end of the earth, I will call to you when my heart is overwhelmed. Lead me to the rock that is higher than I. ³ For you have been a refuge for me, a strong tower from the enemy. ⁴ I will dwell in your tent forever. I will take refuge in the shelter of your wings. Selah. ⁵ For you, God, have heard my vows. You have given me the heritage of those who fear your name. ⁶ You will prolong the king's life. His years will be for generations. ⁷ He shall be enthroned in God's presence forever. Appoint your loving kindness and truth, that they may preserve him. ⁸ So I will sing praise to your name forever, that I may fulfill my vows daily.

Psalms Book 2 Chapter 62

¹ My soul rests in God alone. My salvation is from him. ² He alone is my rock, my salvation, and my fortress. I will never be greatly shaken. ³ How long will you assault a man? Would all of you throw him down, like a leaning wall, like a tottering fence? ⁴ They fully intend to throw him down from his lofty place. They delight in lies. They bless with their mouth, but they curse inwardly. Selah. ⁵ My soul, wait in silence for God alone, for my expectation is from him. ⁶ He alone is my rock and my salvation, my fortress. I will not be shaken. ⁷ My salvation and my honor is with God. The rock of my strength, and my refuge, is in God. ⁸ Trust in him at all times, you people. Pour out your heart before him. God is a refuge for us. Selah. ⁹ Surely men of low degree are just a breath, and men of high degree are a lie. In the balances they will go up. They are together lighter than a breath. ¹⁰ Don't trust in oppression. Don't become vain in robbery. If riches increase, don't set your heart on them. ¹¹ God has spoken once; twice I have heard this, that power belongs to God. ¹² Also to you, Lord, belongs loving kindness, for you reward every man according to his work.

Psalms Book 2 Chapter 63

¹ God, you are my God. I will earnestly seek you. My soul thirsts for you. My flesh longs for you, in a dry and weary land, where there is no water. ² So I have seen you in the sanctuary, watching your power and your glory. ³ Because your loving kindness is better than life, my lips shall praise you. ⁴ So I will bless you while I live. I will lift up my hands in your name. ⁵ My soul shall be satisfied as with the richest food. My mouth shall praise you with joyful lips, ⁶ when I remember you on my bed, and think about you in the night watches. ⁷ For you have been my help. I will rejoice in the shadow of your wings. ⁸ My soul stays close to you. Your right hand holds me up. ⁹ But those who seek my soul to destroy it shall go into the lower parts of the earth. ¹⁰ They shall be given over to the power of the sword. They shall be jackal food. ¹¹ But the king shall rejoice in God. Everyone who swears by him will praise him, for the mouth of those who speak lies shall be silenced.

Psalms Book 2 Chapter 64

¹ Hear my voice, God, in my complaint. Preserve my life from fear of the enemy. ² Hide me from the conspiracy of the wicked, from the noisy crowd of the ones doing evil; ³ who sharpen their tongue like a sword, and aim their arrows, deadly words, ⁴ to shoot innocent men from ambushes. They shoot at him suddenly and fearlessly. ⁵ They encourage themselves in evil plans. They talk about laying snares secretly. They say, "Who will see them?" ⁶ They plot injustice, saying, "We have made a perfect plan!" Surely man's mind and heart are cunning. ⁷ But God will shoot at them. They will be suddenly struck down with an arrow. ⁸ Their own tongues shall ruin them. All who see them will shake their heads. ⁹ All mankind shall be afraid. They shall declare the work of God, and shall wisely ponder what he has done. ¹⁰ The righteous shall be glad in Yahweh, and shall take refuge in him. All the upright in heart shall praise him!

Psalms Book 2 Chapter 65

¹ Praise waits for you, God, in Zion. Vows shall be performed to you. ² You who hear prayer, all men will come to you. ³ Sins overwhelmed me, but you atoned for our transgressions. ⁴ Blessed is the one whom you choose and cause to come near, that he may live in your courts. We will be filled with the goodness of your house, your holy temple. ⁵ By awesome deeds of righteousness, you answer us, God of our salvation. You who are the hope of all the ends of the earth, of those who are far away on the sea. ⁶ By your power, you form the mountains, having armed yourself with strength. ⁷ You still the roaring of the seas, the roaring of their waves, and the turmoil of the nations. ⁸ They also who dwell in faraway places are afraid at your wonders. You call the morning's dawn and the evening with songs of joy. ⁹ You visit the earth, and water it. You greatly enrich it. The river of God is full of water. You provide them grain, for so you have ordained it. ¹⁰ You drench its

furrows. You level its ridges. You soften it with showers. You bless it with a crop. ¹¹ You crown the year with your bounty. Your carts overflow with abundance. ¹² The wilderness grasslands overflow. The hills are clothed with gladness. ¹³ The pastures are covered with flocks. The valleys also are clothed with grain. They shout for joy! They also sing.

Psalms Book 2 Chapter 66

¹ Make a joyful shout to God, all the earth! ² Sing to the glory of his name! Offer glory and praise! ³ Tell God, "How awesome are your deeds! Through the greatness of your power, your enemies submit themselves to you. ⁴ All the earth will worship you, and will sing to you; they will sing to your name." Selah. ⁵ Come, and see God's deeds— awesome work on behalf of the children of men. ⁶ He turned the sea into dry land. They went through the river on foot. There, we rejoiced in him. ⁷ He rules by his might forever. His eyes watch the nations. Don't let the rebellious rise up against him. Selah. ⁸ Praise our God, you peoples! Make the sound of his praise heard, ⁹ who preserves our life among the living, and doesn't allow our feet to be moved. ¹⁰ For you, God, have tested us. You have refined us, as silver is refined. ¹¹ You brought us into prison. You laid a burden on our backs. ¹² You allowed men to ride over our heads. We went through fire and through water, but you brought us to the place of abundance. ¹³ I will come into your temple with burnt offerings. I will pay my vows to you, ¹⁴ which my lips promised, and my mouth spoke, when I was in distress. ¹⁵ I will offer to you burnt offerings of fat animals, with the offering of rams, I will offer bulls with goats. Selah. ¹⁶ Come and hear, all you who fear God. I will declare what he has done for my soul. ¹⁷ I cried to him with my mouth. He was extolled with my tongue. ¹⁸ If I cherished sin in my heart, the Lord wouldn't have listened. ¹⁹ But most certainly, God has listened. He has heard the voice of my prayer. ²⁰ Blessed be God, who has not turned away my prayer, nor his loving kindness from me.

Psalms Book 2 Chapter 67

¹ May God be merciful to us, bless us, and cause his face to shine on us. Selah. ² That your way may be known on earth, and your salvation among all nations, ³ let the peoples praise you, God. Let all the peoples praise you. ⁴ Oh let the nations be glad and sing for joy, for you will judge the peoples with equity, and govern the nations on earth. Selah. ⁵ Let the peoples praise you, God. Let all the peoples praise you. ⁶ The earth has yielded its increase. God, even our own God, will bless us. ⁷ God will bless us. All the ends of the earth shall fear him.

Psalms Book 2 Chapter 68

¹ Let God arise! Let his enemies be scattered! Let them who hate him also flee before him. ² As smoke is driven away, so drive them away. As wax melts before the fire, so let the wicked perish at the presence of God. ³ But let the righteous be glad. Let them rejoice before God. Yes, let them rejoice with gladness. ⁴ Sing to God! Sing praises to his name! Extol him who rides on the clouds: to Yah, his name! Rejoice before him! ⁵ A father of the fatherless, and a defender of the widows, is God in his holy habitation. ⁶ God sets the lonely in families. He brings out the prisoners with singing, but the rebellious dwell in a sun-scorched land. ⁷ God, when you went out before your people, when you marched through the wilderness... Selah. ⁸ The earth trembled. The sky also poured down rain at the presence of the God of Sinai— at the presence of God, the God of Israel. ⁹ You, God, sent a plentiful rain. You confirmed your inheritance when it was weary. ¹⁰ Your congregation lived therein. You, God, prepared your goodness for the poor. ¹¹ The Lord announced the word. The ones who proclaim it are a great company. ¹² "Kings of armies flee! They flee!" She who waits at home divides the plunder, ¹³ while you sleep among the camp fires, the wings of a dove sheathed with silver, her feathers with shining gold. ¹⁴ When the Almighty scattered kings in her, it snowed on Zalmon. ¹⁵ The mountains of Bashan are majestic mountains. The mountains of Bashan are rugged. ¹⁶ Why do you look in envy, you rugged mountains, at the mountain where God chooses to reign? Yes, Yahweh will dwell there forever. ¹⁷ The chariots of God are tens of thousands and thousands of thousands. The Lord is among them, from Sinai, into the sanctuary. ¹⁸ You have ascended on high. You have led away captives. You have received gifts among people, yes, among the rebellious also, that Yah God might dwell there. ¹⁹ Blessed be the Lord, who daily bears our burdens, even the God who is our salvation. Selah. ²⁰ God is to us a God of deliverance. To Yahweh, the Lord, belongs escape from death. ²¹ But God will strike through the head of his enemies, the hairy scalp of such a one as still continues in his guiltiness. ²² The Lord said, "I will bring you again from Bashan, I will bring you again from the depths of the sea, ²³ that you may crush them, dipping your foot in blood, that the tongues of your dogs may have their portion from your enemies." ²⁴ They have seen your processions, God, even the processions of my God,

my King, into the sanctuary. 25 The singers went before, the minstrels followed after, among the ladies playing with tambourines, 26 "Bless God in the congregations, even the Lord in the assembly of Israel!" 27 There is little Benjamin, their ruler, the princes of Judah, their council, the princes of Zebulun, and the princes of Naphtali. 28 Your God has commanded your strength. Strengthen, God, that which you have done for us. 29 Because of your temple at Jerusalem, kings shall bring presents to you. 30 Rebuke the wild animal of the reeds, the multitude of the bulls with the calves of the peoples. Trample under foot the bars of silver. Scatter the nations who delight in war. 31 Princes shall come out of Egypt. Ethiopia shall hurry to stretch out her hands to God. 32 Sing to God, you kingdoms of the earth! Sing praises to the Lord— Selah— 33 to him who rides on the heaven of heavens, which are of old; behold, he utters his voice, a mighty voice. 34 Ascribe strength to God! His excellency is over Israel, his strength is in the skies. 35 You are awesome, God, in your sanctuaries. The God of Israel gives strength and power to his people. Praise be to God!

Psalms Book 2 Chapter 69

1 Save me, God, for the waters have come up to my neck! 2 I sink in deep mire, where there is no foothold. I have come into deep waters, where the floods overflow me. 3 I am weary with my crying. My throat is dry. My eyes fail looking for my God. 4 Those who hate me without a cause are more than the hairs of my head. Those who want to cut me off, being my enemies wrongfully, are mighty. I have to restore what I didn't take away. 5 God, you know my foolishness. My sins aren't hidden from you. 6 Don't let those who wait for you be shamed through me, Lord Yahweh of Armies. Don't let those who seek you be brought to dishonor through me, God of Israel. 7 Because for your sake, I have borne reproach. Shame has covered my face. 8 I have become a stranger to my brothers, an alien to my mother's children. 9 For the zeal of your house consumes me. The reproaches of those who reproach you have fallen on me. 10 When I wept and I fasted, that was to my reproach. 11 When I made sackcloth my clothing, I became a byword to them. 12 Those who sit in the gate talk about me. I am the song of the drunkards. 13 But as for me, my prayer is to you, Yahweh, in an acceptable time. God, in the abundance of your loving kindness, answer me in the truth of your salvation. 14 Deliver me out of the mire, and don't let me sink. Let me be delivered from those who hate me, and out of the deep waters. 15 Don't let the flood waters overwhelm me, neither let the deep swallow me up. Don't let the pit shut its mouth on me. 16 Answer me, Yahweh, for your loving kindness is good. According to the multitude of your tender mercies, turn to me. 17 Don't hide your face from your servant, for I am in distress. Answer me speedily! 18 Draw near to my soul and redeem it. Ransom me because of my enemies. 19 You know my reproach, my shame, and my dishonor. My adversaries are all before you. 20 Reproach has broken my heart, and I am full of heaviness. I looked for some to take pity, but there was none; for comforters, but I found none. 21 They also gave me poison for my food. In my thirst, they gave me vinegar to drink. 22 Let their table before them become a snare. May it become a retribution and a trap. 23 Let their eyes be darkened, so that they can't see. Let their backs be continually bent. 24 Pour out your indignation on them. Let the fierceness of your anger overtake them. 25 Let their habitation be desolate. Let no one dwell in their tents. 26 For they persecute him whom you have wounded. They tell of the sorrow of those whom you have hurt. 27 Charge them with crime upon crime. Don't let them come into your righteousness. 28 Let them be blotted out of the book of life, and not be written with the righteous. 29 But I am in pain and distress. Let your salvation, God, protect me. 30 I will praise the name of God with a song, and will magnify him with thanksgiving. 31 It will please Yahweh better than an ox, or a bull that has horns and hoofs. 32 The humble have seen it, and are glad. You who seek after God, let your heart live. 33 For Yahweh hears the needy, and doesn't despise his captive people. 34 Let heaven and earth praise him; the seas, and everything that moves therein! 35 For God will save Zion, and build the cities of Judah. They shall settle there, and own it. 36 The children also of his servants shall inherit it. Those who love his name shall dwell therein.

Psalms Book 2 Chapter 70

1 Hurry, God, to deliver me. Come quickly to help me, Yahweh. 2 Let them be disappointed and confounded who seek my soul. Let those who desire my ruin be turned back in disgrace. 3 Let them be turned because of their shame who say, "Aha! Aha!" 4 Let all those who seek you rejoice and be glad in you. Let those who love your salvation continually say, "Let God be exalted!" 5 But I am poor and needy. Come to me quickly, God. You are my help and my deliverer. Yahweh, don't delay.

Psalms Book 2 Chapter 71

1In you, Yahweh, I take refuge. Never let me be disappointed. 2 Deliver me in your righteousness, and rescue me. Turn your ear to me, and save me. 3 Be to me a rock of refuge to which I may always go. Give the command to save me, for you are my rock and my fortress. 4 Rescue me, my God, from the hand of the wicked, from the hand of the unrighteous and cruel man. 5 For you are my hope, Lord Yahweh, my confidence from my youth. 6 I have relied on you from the womb. You are he who took me out of my mother's womb. I will always praise you. 7 I am a marvel to many, but you are my strong refuge. 8 My mouth shall be filled with your praise, with your honor all day long. 9 Don't reject me in my old age. Don't forsake me when my strength fails. 10 For my enemies talk about me. Those who watch for my soul conspire together, 11 saying, "God has forsaken him. Pursue and take him, for no one will rescue him." 12 God, don't be far from me. My God, hurry to help me. 13 Let my accusers be disappointed and consumed. Let them be covered with disgrace and scorn who want to harm me. 14 But I will always hope, and will add to all of your praise. 15 My mouth will tell about your righteousness, and of your salvation all day, though I don't know its full measure. 16 I will come with the mighty acts of the Lord Yahweh. I will make mention of your righteousness, even of yours alone. 17 God, you have taught me from my youth. Until now, I have declared your wondrous works. 18 Yes, even when I am old and gray-haired, God, don't forsake me, until I have declared your strength to the next generation, your might to everyone who is to come. 19 God, your righteousness also reaches to the heavens. You have done great things. God, who is like you? 20 You, who have shown us many and bitter troubles, you will let me live. You will bring us up again from the depths of the earth. 21 Increase my honor and comfort me again. 22 I will also praise you with the harp for your faithfulness, my God. I sing praises to you with the lyre, Holy One of Israel. 23 My lips shall shout for joy! My soul, which you have redeemed, sings praises to you! 24 My tongue will also talk about your righteousness all day long, for they are disappointed, and they are confounded, who want to harm me.

Psalms Book 2 Chapter 72

1 God, give the king your justice; your righteousness to the royal son. 2 He will judge your people with righteousness, and your poor with justice. 3 The mountains shall bring prosperity to the people. The hills bring the fruit of righteousness. 4 He will judge the poor of the people. He will save the children of the needy, and will break the oppressor in pieces. 5 They shall fear you while the sun endures; and as long as the moon, throughout all generations. 6 He will come down like rain on the mown grass, as showers that water the earth. 7 In his days, the righteous shall flourish, and abundance of peace, until the moon is no more. 8 He shall have dominion also from sea to sea, from the River to the ends of the earth. 9 Those who dwell in the wilderness shall bow before him. His enemies shall lick the dust. 10 The kings of Tarshish and of the islands will bring tribute. The kings of Sheba and Seba shall offer gifts. 11 Yes, all kings shall fall down before him. All nations shall serve him. 12 For he will deliver the needy when he cries; the poor, who has no helper. 13 He will have pity on the poor and needy. He will save the souls of the needy. 14 He will redeem their soul from oppression and violence. Their blood will be precious in his sight. 15 He will live; and Sheba's gold will be given to him. Men will pray for him continually. They will bless him all day long. 16 Abundance of grain shall be throughout the land. Its fruit sways like Lebanon. Let it flourish, thriving like the grass of the field. 17 His name endures forever. His name continues as long as the sun. Men shall be blessed by him. All nations will call him blessed. 18 Praise be to Yahweh God, the God of Israel, who alone does marvelous deeds. 19 Blessed be his glorious name forever! Let the whole earth be filled with his glory! Amen and amen. 20 This ends the prayers by David, the son of Jesse.

Psalms Book 3

Psalms Book 3 Chapter 73

1 Surely God is good to Israel, to those who are pure in heart. 2 But as for me, my feet were almost gone. My steps had nearly slipped. 3 For I was envious of the arrogant, when I saw the prosperity of the wicked. 4 For there are no struggles in their death, but their strength is firm. 5 They are free from burdens of men, neither are they plagued like other men. 6 Therefore pride is like a chain around their neck. Violence covers them like a garment. 7 Their eyes bulge with fat. Their minds pass the limits of conceit. 8 They scoff and speak with malice. In arrogance, they threaten oppression. 9 They have set their mouth in the heavens. Their tongue walks through the earth. 10 Therefore their people return to them, and they drink up waters of abundance. 11 They say, "How does God know? Is there knowledge in the Most High?" 12 Behold, these are the wicked. Being always at ease, they increase in riches. 13 Surely I have cleansed my heart in vain, and washed my hands in innocence, 14 For all day long I have been plagued, and punished every morning. 15

If I had said, "I will speak thus", behold, I would have betrayed the generation of your children. ¹⁶ When I tried to understand this, it was too painful for me— ¹⁷ until I entered God's sanctuary, and considered their latter end. ¹⁸ Surely you set them in slippery places. You throw them down to destruction. ¹⁹ How they are suddenly destroyed! They are completely swept away with terrors. ²⁰ As a dream when one wakes up, so, Lord, when you awake, you will despise their fantasies. ²¹ For my soul was grieved. I was embittered in my heart. ²² I was so senseless and ignorant. I was a brute beast before you. ²³ Nevertheless, I am continually with you. You have held my right hand. ²⁴ You will guide me with your counsel, and afterward receive me to glory. ²⁵ Whom do I have in heaven? There is no one on earth whom I desire besides you. ²⁶ My flesh and my heart fails, but God is the strength of my heart and my portion forever. ²⁷ For, behold, those who are far from you shall perish. You have destroyed all those who are unfaithful to you. ²⁸ But it is good for me to come close to God. I have made the Lord Yahweh my refuge, that I may tell of all your works.

Psalms Book 3 Chapter 74

¹ God, why have you rejected us forever? Why does your anger smolder against the sheep of your pasture? ² Remember your congregation, which you purchased of old, which you have redeemed to be the tribe of your inheritance: Mount Zion, in which you have lived. ³ Lift up your feet to the perpetual ruins, all the evil that the enemy has done in the sanctuary. ⁴ Your adversaries have roared in the middle of your assembly. They have set up their standards as signs. ⁵ They behaved like men wielding axes, cutting through a thicket of trees. ⁶ Now they break all its carved work down with hatchet and hammers. ⁷ They have burned your sanctuary to the ground. They have profaned the dwelling place of your Name. ⁸ They said in their heart, "We will crush them completely." They have burned up all the places in the land where God was worshiped. ⁹ We see no miraculous signs. There is no longer any prophet, neither is there among us anyone who knows how long. ¹⁰ How long, God, shall the adversary reproach? Shall the enemy blaspheme your name forever? ¹¹ Why do you draw back your hand, even your right hand? Take it from your chest and consume them! ¹² Yet God is my King of old, working salvation throughout the earth. ¹³ You divided the sea by your strength. You broke the heads of the sea monsters in the waters. ¹⁴ You broke the heads of Leviathan in pieces. You gave him as food to people and desert creatures. ¹⁵ You opened up spring and stream. You dried up mighty rivers. ¹⁶ The day is yours, the night is also yours. You have prepared the light and the sun. ¹⁷ You have set all the boundaries of the earth. You have made summer and winter. ¹⁸ Remember this, that the enemy has mocked you, Yahweh. Foolish people have blasphemed your name. ¹⁹ Don't deliver the soul of your dove to wild beasts. Don't forget the life of your poor forever. ²⁰ Honor your covenant, for haunts of violence fill the dark places of the earth. ²¹ Don't let the oppressed return ashamed. Let the poor and needy praise your name. ²² Arise, God! Plead your own cause. Remember how the foolish man mocks you all day. ²³ Don't forget the voice of your adversaries. The tumult of those who rise up against you ascends continually.

Psalms Book 3 Chapter 75

¹ We give thanks to you, God. We give thanks, for your Name is near. Men tell about your wondrous works. ² When I choose the appointed time, I will judge blamelessly. ³ The earth and all its inhabitants quake. I firmly hold its pillars. Selah. ⁴ I said to the arrogant, "Don't boast!" I said to the wicked, "Don't lift up the horn. ⁵ Don't lift up your horn on high. Don't speak with a stiff neck." ⁶ For neither from the east, nor from the west, nor yet from the south, comes exaltation. ⁷ But God is the judge. He puts down one, and lifts up another. ⁸ For in Yahweh's hand there is a cup, full of foaming wine mixed with spices. He pours it out. Indeed the wicked of the earth drink and drink it to its very dregs. ⁹ But I will declare this forever: I will sing praises to the God of Jacob. ¹⁰ I will cut off all the horns of the wicked, but the horns of the righteous shall be lifted up.

Psalms Book 3 Chapter 76

¹ In Judah, God is known. His name is great in Israel. ² His tabernacle is also in Salem. His dwelling place in Zion. ³ There he broke the flaming arrows of the bow, the shield, and the sword, and the weapons of war. Selah. ⁴ Glorious are you, and excellent, more than mountains of game. ⁵ Valiant men lie plundered, they have slept their last sleep. None of the men of war can lift their hands. ⁶ At your rebuke, God of Jacob, both chariot and horse are cast into a dead sleep. ⁷ You, even you, are to be feared. Who can stand in your sight when you are angry? ⁸ You pronounced judgment from heaven. The earth feared, and was silent, ⁹ when God arose to judgment, to save all the afflicted ones of the earth. Selah. ¹⁰ Surely the wrath of man praises you. The survivors of your wrath are restrained. ¹¹ Make vows to Yahweh your God, and fulfill them! Let all of his neighbors bring presents to him who is to be feared. ¹² He will cut off the spirit of princes. He is feared by the kings of the earth.

Psalms Book 3 Chapter 77

¹ My cry goes to God! Indeed, I cry to God for help, and for him to listen to me. ² In the day of my trouble I sought the Lord. My hand was stretched out in the night, and didn't get tired. My soul refused to be comforted. ³ I remember God, and I groan. I complain, and my spirit is overwhelmed. Selah. ⁴ You hold my eyelids open. I am so troubled that I can't speak. ⁵ I have considered the days of old, the years of ancient times. ⁶ I remember my song in the night. I consider in my own heart; my spirit diligently inquires: ⁷"Will the Lord reject us forever? Will he be favorable no more? ⁸ Has his loving kindness vanished forever? Does his promise fail for generations? ⁹ Has God forgotten to be gracious? Has he, in anger, withheld his compassion?" Selah. ¹⁰ Then I thought, "I will appeal to this: the years of the right hand of the Most High." ¹¹ I will remember Yah's deeds; for I will remember your wonders of old. ¹² I will also meditate on all your work, and consider your doings. ¹³ Your way, God, is in the sanctuary. What god is great like God? ¹⁴ You are the God who does wonders. You have made your strength known among the peoples. ¹⁵ You have redeemed your people with your arm, the sons of Jacob and Joseph. Selah. ¹⁶ The waters saw you, God. The waters saw you, and they writhed. The depths also convulsed. ¹⁷ The clouds poured out water. The skies resounded with thunder. Your arrows also flashed around. ¹⁸ The voice of your thunder was in the whirlwind. The lightnings lit up the world. The earth trembled and shook. ¹⁹ Your way was through the sea, your paths through the great waters. Your footsteps were not known. ²⁰ You led your people like a flock, by the hand of Moses and Aaron.

Psalms Book 3 Chapter 78

¹ Hear my teaching, my people. Turn your ears to the words of my mouth. ² I will open my mouth in a parable. I will utter dark sayings of old, ³ which we have heard and known, and our fathers have told us. ⁴ We will not hide them from their children, telling to the generation to come the praises of Yahweh, his strength, and his wondrous deeds that he has done. ⁵ For he established a covenant in Jacob, and appointed a teaching in Israel, which he commanded our fathers, that they should make them known to their children; ⁶ that the generation to come might know, even the children who should be born; who should arise and tell their children, ⁷ that they might set their hope in God, and not forget God's deeds, but keep his commandments, ⁸ and might not be as their fathers— a stubborn and rebellious generation, a generation that didn't make their hearts loyal, whose spirit was not steadfast with God. ⁹ The children of Ephraim, being armed and carrying bows, turned back in the day of battle. ¹⁰ They didn't keep God's covenant, and refused to walk in his law. ¹¹ They forgot his doings, his wondrous deeds that he had shown them. ¹² He did marvelous things in the sight of their fathers, in the land of Egypt, in the field of Zoan. ¹³ He split the sea, and caused them to pass through. He made the waters stand as a heap. ¹⁴ In the daytime he also led them with a cloud, and all night with a light of fire. ¹⁵ He split rocks in the wilderness, and gave them drink abundantly as out of the depths. ¹⁶ He brought streams also out of the rock, and caused waters to run down like rivers. ¹⁷ Yet they still went on to sin against him, to rebel against the Most High in the desert. ¹⁸ They tempted God in their heart by asking food according to their desire. ¹⁹ Yes, they spoke against God. They said, "Can God prepare a table in the wilderness? ²⁰ Behold, he struck the rock, so that waters gushed out, and streams overflowed. Can he give bread also? Will he provide meat for his people?" ²¹ Therefore Yahweh heard, and was angry. A fire was kindled against Jacob, anger also went up against Israel, ²² because they didn't believe in God, and didn't trust in his salvation. ²³ Yet he commanded the skies above, and opened the doors of heaven. ²⁴ He rained down manna on them to eat, and gave them food from the sky. ²⁵ Man ate the bread of angels. He sent them food to the full. ²⁶ He caused the east wind to blow in the sky. By his power he guided the south wind. ²⁷ He also rained meat on them as the dust, winged birds as the sand of the seas. ²⁸ He let them fall in the middle of their camp, around their habitations. ²⁹ So they ate, and were well filled. He gave them their own desire. ³⁰ They didn't turn from their cravings. Their food was yet in their mouths, ³¹ when the anger of God went up against them, killed some of their strongest, and struck down the young men of Israel. ³² For all this they still sinned, and didn't believe in his wondrous works. ³³ Therefore he consumed their days in vanity, and their years in terror. ³⁴ When he killed them, then they inquired after him. They returned and sought God earnestly. ³⁵ They remembered that God was their rock, the Most High God, their

redeemer. 36 But they flattered him with their mouth, and lied to him with their tongue. 37 For their heart was not right with him, neither were they faithful in his covenant. 38 But he, being merciful, forgave iniquity, and didn't destroy them. Yes, many times he turned his anger away, and didn't stir up all his wrath. 39 He remembered that they were but flesh, a wind that passes away, and doesn't come again. 40 How often they rebelled against him in the wilderness, and grieved him in the desert! 41 They turned again and tempted God, and provoked the Holy One of Israel. 42 They didn't remember his hand, nor the day when he redeemed them from the adversary; 43 how he set his signs in Egypt, his wonders in the field of Zoan, 44 he turned their rivers into blood, and their streams, so that they could not drink. 45 He sent among them swarms of flies, which devoured them; and frogs, which destroyed them. 46 He also gave their increase to the caterpillar, and their labor to the locust. 47 He destroyed their vines with hail, their sycamore fig trees with frost. 48 He also gave over their livestock to the hail, and their flocks to hot thunderbolts. 49 He threw on them the fierceness of his anger, wrath, indignation, and trouble, and a band of angels of evil. 50 He made a path for his anger. He didn't spare their soul from death, but gave their life over to the pestilence, 51 and struck all the firstborn in Egypt, the chief of their strength in the tents of Ham. 52 But he led out his own people like sheep, and guided them in the wilderness like a flock. 53 He led them safely, so that they weren't afraid, but the sea overwhelmed their enemies. 54 He brought them to the border of his sanctuary, to this mountain, which his right hand had taken. 55 He also drove out the nations before them, allotted them for an inheritance by line, and made the tribes of Israel to dwell in their tents. 56 Yet they tempted and rebelled against the Most High God, and didn't keep his testimonies, 57 but turned back, and dealt treacherously like their fathers. They were twisted like a deceitful bow. 58 For they provoked him to anger with their high places, and moved him to jealousy with their engraved images. 59 When God heard this, he was angry, and greatly abhorred Israel, 60 so that he abandoned the tent of Shiloh, the tent which he placed among men, 61 and delivered his strength into captivity, his glory into the adversary's hand. 62 He also gave his people over to the sword, and was angry with his inheritance. 63 Fire devoured their young men. Their virgins had no wedding song. 64 Their priests fell by the sword, and their widows couldn't weep. 65 Then the Lord awakened as one out of sleep, like a mighty man who shouts by reason of wine. 66 He struck his adversaries backward. He put them to a perpetual reproach. 67 Moreover he rejected the tent of Joseph, and didn't choose the tribe of Ephraim, 68 But chose the tribe of Judah, Mount Zion which he loved. 69 He built his sanctuary like the heights, like the earth which he has established forever. 70 He also chose David his servant, and took him from the sheepfolds; 71 from following the ewes that have their young, he brought him to be the shepherd of Jacob, his people, and Israel, his inheritance. 72 So he was their shepherd according to the integrity of his heart, and guided them by the skillfulness of his hands.

Psalms Book 3 Chapter 79

1 God, the nations have come into your inheritance. They have defiled your holy temple. They have laid Jerusalem in heaps. 2 They have given the dead bodies of your servants to be food for the birds of the sky, the flesh of your saints to the animals of the earth. 3 They have shed their blood like water around Jerusalem. There was no one to bury them. 4 We have become a reproach to our neighbors, a scoffing and derision to those who are around us. 5 How long, Yahweh? Will you be angry forever? Will your jealousy burn like fire? 6 Pour out your wrath on the nations that don't know you, on the kingdoms that don't call on your name, 7 for they have devoured Jacob, and destroyed his homeland. 8 Don't hold the iniquities of our forefathers against us. Let your tender mercies speedily meet us, for we are in desperate need. 9 Help us, God of our salvation, for the glory of your name. Deliver us, and forgive our sins, for your name's sake. 10 Why should the nations say, "Where is their God?" Let it be known among the nations, before our eyes, that vengeance for your servants' blood is being poured out. 11 Let the sighing of the prisoner come before you. According to the greatness of your power, preserve those who are sentenced to death. 12 Pay back to our neighbors seven times into their bosom their reproach with which they have reproached you, Lord. 13 So we, your people and sheep of your pasture, will give you thanks forever. We will praise you forever, to all generations.

Psalms Book 3 Chapter 80

1 Hear us, Shepherd of Israel, you who lead Joseph like a flock, you who sit above the cherubim, shine out. 2 Before Ephraim, Benjamin, and Manasseh, stir up your might! Come to save us! 3 Turn us again, God. Cause your face to shine, and we will be saved. 4 Yahweh God of Armies,

how long will you be angry against the prayer of your people? 5 You have fed them with the bread of tears, and given them tears to drink in large measure. 6 You make us a source of contention to our neighbors. Our enemies laugh among themselves. 7 Turn us again, God of Armies. Cause your face to shine, and we will be saved. 8 You brought a vine out of Egypt. You drove out the nations, and planted it. 9 You cleared the ground for it. It took deep root, and filled the land. 10 The mountains were covered with its shadow. Its boughs were like God's cedars. 11 It sent out its branches to the sea, its shoots to the River. 12 Why have you broken down its walls, so that all those who pass by the way pluck it? 13 The boar out of the wood ravages it. The wild animals of the field feed on it. 14 Turn again, we beg you, God of Armies. Look down from heaven, and see, and visit this vine, 15 the stock which your right hand planted, the branch that you made strong for yourself. 16 It's burned with fire. It's cut down. They perish at your rebuke. 17 Let your hand be on the man of your right hand, on the son of man whom you made strong for yourself. 18 So we will not turn away from you. Revive us, and we will call on your name. 19 Turn us again, Yahweh God of Armies. Cause your face to shine, and we will be saved.

Psalms Book 3 Chapter 81

1 Sing aloud to God, our strength! Make a joyful shout to the God of Jacob! 2 Raise a song, and bring here the tambourine, the pleasant lyre with the harp. 3 Blow the trumpet at the New Moon, at the full moon, on our feast day. 4 For it is a statute for Israel, an ordinance of the God of Jacob. 5 He appointed it in Joseph for a covenant, when he went out over the land of Egypt, I heard a language that I didn't know. 6 "I removed his shoulder from the burden. His hands were freed from the basket. 7 You called in trouble, and I delivered you. I answered you in the secret place of thunder. I tested you at the waters of Meribah." Selah. 8 "Hear, my people, and I will testify to you, Israel, if you would listen to me! 9 There shall be no strange god in you, neither shall you worship any foreign god. 10 I am Yahweh, your God, who brought you up out of the land of Egypt. Open your mouth wide, and I will fill it. 11 But my people didn't listen to my voice. Israel desired none of me. 12 So I let them go after the stubbornness of their hearts, that they might walk in their own counsels. 13 Oh that my people would listen to me, that Israel would walk in my ways! 14 I would soon subdue their enemies, and turn my hand against their adversaries. 15 The haters of Yahweh would cringe before him, and their punishment would last forever. 16 But he would have also fed them with the finest of the wheat. I will satisfy you with honey out of the rock."

Psalms Book 3 Chapter 82

1 God presides in the great assembly. He judges among the gods. 2 "How long will you judge unjustly, and show partiality to the wicked?" Selah. 3 "Defend the weak, the poor, and the fatherless. Maintain the rights of the poor and oppressed. 4 Rescue the weak and needy. Deliver them out of the hand of the wicked." 5 They don't know, neither do they understand. They walk back and forth in darkness. All the foundations of the earth are shaken. 6 I said, "You are gods, all of you are sons of the Most High. 7 Nevertheless you shall die like men, and fall like one of the rulers." 8 Arise, God, judge the earth, for you inherit all of the nations.

Psalms Book 3 Chapter 83

1 God, don't keep silent. Don't keep silent, and don't be still, God. 2 For, behold, your enemies are stirred up. Those who hate you have lifted up their heads. 3 They conspire with cunning against your people. They plot against your cherished ones. 4 "Come," they say, "let's destroy them as a nation, that the name of Israel may be remembered no more." 5 For they have conspired together with one mind. They form an alliance against you. 6 The tents of Edom and the Ishmaelites; Moab, and the Hagrites; 7 Gebal, Ammon, and Amalek; Philistia with the inhabitants of Tyre; 8 Assyria also is joined with them. They have helped the children of Lot. Selah. 9 Do to them as you did to Midian, as to Sisera, as to Jabin, at the river Kishon; 10 who perished at Endor, who became as dung for the earth. 11 Make their nobles like Oreb and Zeeb, yes, all their princes like Zebah and Zalmunna, 12 who said, "Let's take possession of God's pasture lands." 13 My God, make them like tumbleweed, like chaff before the wind. 14 As the fire that burns the forest, as the flame that sets the mountains on fire, 15 so pursue them with your tempest, and terrify them with your storm. 16 Fill their faces with confusion, that they may seek your name, Yahweh. 17 Let them be disappointed and dismayed forever. Yes, let them be confounded and perish; 18 that they may know that you alone, whose name is Yahweh, are the Most High over all the earth.

Psalms Book 3 Chapter 84

1 How lovely are your dwellings, Yahweh of Armies! 2 My soul longs, and even faints for the courts of Yahweh. My heart and my flesh cry out for the living God. 3 Yes, the sparrow has found a home, and the swallow

a nest for herself, where she may have her young, near your altars, Yahweh of Armies, my King, and my God. 4 Blessed are those who dwell in your house. They are always praising you. Selah. 5 Blessed are those whose strength is in you, who have set their hearts on a pilgrimage. 6 Passing through the valley of Weeping, they make it a place of springs. Yes, the autumn rain covers it with blessings. 7 They go from strength to strength. Every one of them appears before God in Zion. 8 Yahweh, God of Armies, hear my prayer. Listen, God of Jacob. Selah. 9 Behold, God our shield, look at the face of your anointed. 10 For a day in your courts is better than a thousand. I would rather be a doorkeeper in the house of my God, than to dwell in the tents of wickedness. 11 For Yahweh God is a sun and a shield. Yahweh will give grace and glory. He withholds no good thing from those who walk blamelessly. 12 Yahweh of Armies, blessed is the man who trusts in you.

Psalms Book 3 Chapter 85

1 Yahweh, you have been favorable to your land. You have restored the fortunes of Jacob. 2 You have forgiven the iniquity of your people. You have covered all their sin. Selah. 3 You have taken away all your wrath. You have turned from the fierceness of your anger. 4 Turn us, God of our salvation, and cause your indignation toward us to cease. 5 Will you be angry with us forever? Will you draw out your anger to all generations? 6 Won't you revive us again, that your people may rejoice in you? 7 Show us your loving kindness, Yahweh. Grant us your salvation. 8 I will hear what God, Yahweh, will speak, for he will speak peace to his people, his saints; but let them not turn again to folly. 9 Surely his salvation is near those who fear him, that glory may dwell in our land. 10 Mercy and truth meet together. Righteousness and peace have kissed each other. 11 Truth springs out of the earth. Righteousness has looked down from heaven. 12 Yes, Yahweh will give that which is good. Our land will yield its increase. 13 Righteousness goes before him, and prepares the way for his steps.

Psalms Book 3 Chapter 86

1 Hear, Yahweh, and answer me, for I am poor and needy. 2 Preserve my soul, for I am godly. You, my God, save your servant who trusts in you. 3 Be merciful to me, Lord, for I call to you all day long. 4 Bring joy to the soul of your servant, for to you, Lord, do I lift up my soul. 5 For you, Lord, are good, and ready to forgive, abundant in loving kindness to all those who call on you. 6 Hear, Yahweh, my prayer. Listen to the voice of my petitions. 7 In the day of my trouble I will call on you, for you will answer me. 8 There is no one like you among the gods, Lord, nor any deeds like your deeds. 9 All nations you have made will come and worship before you, Lord. They shall glorify your name. 10 For you are great, and do wondrous things. You are God alone. 11 Teach me your way, Yahweh. I will walk in your truth. Make my heart undivided to fear your name. 12 I will praise you, Lord my God, with my whole heart. I will glorify your name forever more. 13 For your loving kindness is great toward me. You have delivered my soul from the lowest Sheol. 14 God, the proud have risen up against me. A company of violent men have sought after my soul, and they don't hold regard for you before them. 15 But you, Lord, are a merciful and gracious God, slow to anger, and abundant in loving kindness and truth. 16 Turn to me, and have mercy on me! Give your strength to your servant. Save the son of your servant. 17 Show me a sign of your goodness, that those who hate me may see it, and be shamed, because you, Yahweh, have helped me, and comforted me.

Psalms Book 3 Chapter 87

1 His foundation is in the holy mountains. 2 Yahweh loves the gates of Zion more than all the dwellings of Jacob. 3 Glorious things are spoken about you, city of God. Selah. 4 I will record Rahab and Babylon among those who acknowledge me. Behold, Philistia, Tyre, and also Ethiopia: "This one was born there." 5 Yes, of Zion it will be said, "This one and that one was born in her;" the Most High himself will establish her. 6 Yahweh will count, when he writes up the peoples, "This one was born there." Selah. 7 Those who sing as well as those who dance say, "All my springs are in you."

Psalms Book 3 Chapter 88

1 Yahweh, the God of my salvation, I have cried day and night before you. 2 Let my prayer enter into your presence. Turn your ear to my cry. 3 For my soul is full of troubles. My life draws near to Sheol. 4 I am counted among those who go down into the pit. I am like a man who has no help, 5 set apart among the dead, like the slain who lie in the grave, whom you remember no more. They are cut off from your hand. 6 You have laid me in the lowest pit, in the darkest depths. 7 Your wrath lies heavily on me. You have afflicted me with all your waves. Selah. 8 You have taken my friends from me. You have made me an abomination to them. I am confined, and I can't escape. 9 My eyes are dim from grief. I have called on you daily, Yahweh. I have spread out my hands to you.

10 Do you show wonders to the dead? Do the departed spirits rise up and praise you? Selah. 11 Is your loving kindness declared in the grave? Or your faithfulness in Destruction? 12 Are your wonders made known in the dark? Or your righteousness in the land of forgetfulness? 13 But to you, Yahweh, I have cried. In the morning, my prayer comes before you. 14 Yahweh, why do you reject my soul? Why do you hide your face from me? 15 I am afflicted and ready to die from my youth up. While I suffer your terrors, I am distracted. 16 Your fierce wrath has gone over me. Your terrors have cut me off. 17 They came around me like water all day long. They completely engulfed me. 18 You have put lover and friend far from me, and my friends into darkness.

Psalms Book 3 Chapter 89

1 I will sing of the loving kindness of Yahweh forever. With my mouth, I will make known your faithfulness to all generations. 2 I indeed declare, "Love stands firm forever. You established the heavens. Your faithfulness is in them." 3 "I have made a covenant with my chosen one, I have sworn to David, my servant, 4 'I will establish your offspring forever, and build up your throne to all generations.'" Selah. 5 The heavens will praise your wonders, Yahweh, your faithfulness also in the assembly of the holy ones. 6 For who in the skies can be compared to Yahweh? Who among the sons of the heavenly beings is like Yahweh, 7 a very awesome God in the council of the holy ones, to be feared above all those who are around him? 8 Yahweh, God of Armies, who is a mighty one, like you? Yah, your faithfulness is around you. 9 You rule the pride of the sea. When its waves rise up, you calm them. 10 You have broken Rahab in pieces, like one of the slain. You have scattered your enemies with your mighty arm. 11 The heavens are yours. The earth also is yours, the world and its fullness. You have founded them. 12 You have created the north and the south. Tabor and Hermon rejoice in your name. 13 You have a mighty arm. Your hand is strong, and your right hand is exalted. 14 Righteousness and justice are the foundation of your throne. Loving kindness and truth go before your face. 15 Blessed are the people who learn to acclaim you. They walk in the light of your presence, Yahweh. 16 In your name they rejoice all day. In your righteousness, they are exalted. 17 For you are the glory of their strength. In your favor, our horn will be exalted. 18 For our shield belongs to Yahweh, our king to the Holy One of Israel. 19 Then you spoke in vision to your saints, and said, "I have given strength to the warrior. I have exalted a young man from the people. 20 I have found David, my servant. I have anointed him with my holy oil, 21 with whom my hand shall be established. My arm will also strengthen him. 22 No enemy will tax him. No wicked man will oppress him. 23 I will beat down his adversaries before him, and strike those who hate him. 24 But my faithfulness and my loving kindness will be with him. In my name, his horn will be exalted. 25 I will set his hand also on the sea, and his right hand on the rivers. 26 He will call to me, 'You are my Father, my God, and the rock of my salvation!' 27 I will also appoint him my firstborn, the highest of the kings of the earth. 28 I will keep my loving kindness for him forever more. My covenant will stand firm with him. 29 I will also make his offspring endure forever, and his throne as the days of heaven. 30 If his children forsake my law, and don't walk in my ordinances; 31 if they break my statutes, and don't keep my commandments; 32 then I will punish their sin with the rod, and their iniquity with stripes. 33 But I will not completely take my loving kindness from him, nor allow my faithfulness to fail. 34 I will not break my covenant, nor alter what my lips have uttered. 35 Once I have sworn by my holiness, I will not lie to David. 36 His offspring will endure forever, his throne like the sun before me. 37 It will be established forever like the moon, the faithful witness in the sky." Selah. 38 But you have rejected and spurned. You have been angry with your anointed. 39 You have renounced the covenant of your servant. You have defiled his crown in the dust. 40 You have broken down all his hedges. You have brought his strongholds to ruin. 41 All who pass by the way rob him. He has become a reproach to his neighbors. 42 You have exalted the right hand of his adversaries. You have made all of his enemies rejoice. 43 Yes, you turn back the edge of his sword, and haven't supported him in battle. 44 You have ended his splendor, and thrown his throne down to the ground. 45 You have shortened the days of his youth. You have covered him with shame. Selah. 46 How long, Yahweh? Will you hide yourself forever? Will your wrath burn like fire? 47 Remember how short my time is, for what vanity you have created all the children of men! 48 What man is he who shall live and not see death, who shall deliver his soul from the power of Sheol? Selah. 49 Lord, where are your former loving kindnesses, which you swore to David in your faithfulness? 50 Remember, Lord, the reproach of your servants, how I bear in my heart the taunts of all the mighty peoples, 51 With which your enemies have mocked, Yahweh, with which they have mocked the footsteps of your anointed one. 52 Blessed be Yahweh forever more.

Amen, and Amen.

Psalms Book 4

Psalms Book 4 Chapter 90

1 Lord, you have been our dwelling place for all generations. 2 Before the mountains were born, before you had formed the earth and the world, even from everlasting to everlasting, you are God. 3 You turn man to destruction, saying, "Return, you children of men." 4 For a thousand years in your sight are just like yesterday when it is past, like a watch in the night. 5 You sweep them away as they sleep. In the morning they sprout like new grass. 6 In the morning it sprouts and springs up. By evening, it is withered and dry. 7 For we are consumed in your anger. We are troubled in your wrath. 8 You have set our iniquities before you, our secret sins in the light of your presence. 9 For all our days have passed away in your wrath. We bring our years to an end as a sigh. 10 The days of our years are seventy, or even by reason of strength eighty years; yet their pride is but labor and sorrow, for it passes quickly, and we fly away. 11 Who knows the power of your anger, your wrath according to the fear that is due to you? 12 So teach us to count our days, that we may gain a heart of wisdom. 13 Relent, Yahweh! How long? Have compassion on your servants! 14 Satisfy us in the morning with your loving kindness, that we may rejoice and be glad all our days. 15 Make us glad for as many days as you have afflicted us, for as many years as we have seen evil. 16 Let your work appear to your servants, your glory to their children. 17 Let the favor of the Lord our God be on us. Establish the work of our hands for us. Yes, establish the work of our hands.

Psalms Book 4 Chapter 91

1 He who dwells in the secret place of the Most High will rest in the shadow of the Almighty. 2 I will say of Yahweh, "He is my refuge and my fortress; my God, in whom I trust." 3 For he will deliver you from the snare of the fowler, and from the deadly pestilence. 4 He will cover you with his feathers. Under his wings you will take refuge. His faithfulness is your shield and rampart. 5 You shall not be afraid of the terror by night, nor of the arrow that flies by day, 6 nor of the pestilence that walks in darkness, nor of the destruction that wastes at noonday. 7 A thousand may fall at your side, and ten thousand at your right hand; but it will not come near you. 8 You will only look with your eyes, and see the recompense of the wicked. 9 Because you have made Yahweh your refuge, and the Most High your dwelling place, 10 no evil shall happen to you, neither shall any plague come near your dwelling. 11 For he will put his angels in charge of you, to guard you in all your ways. 12 They will bear you up in their hands, so that you won't dash your foot against a stone. 13 You will tread on the lion and cobra. You will trample the young lion and the serpent underfoot. 14 "Because he has set his love on me, therefore I will deliver him. I will set him on high, because he has known my name. 15 He will call on me, and I will answer him. I will be with him in trouble. I will deliver him, and honor him. 16 I will satisfy him with long life, and show him my salvation."

Psalms Book 4 Chapter 92

1 It is a good thing to give thanks to Yahweh, to sing praises to your name, Most High, 2 to proclaim your loving kindness in the morning, and your faithfulness every night, 3 with the ten-stringed lute, with the harp, and with the melody of the lyre. 4 For you, Yahweh, have made me glad through your work. I will triumph in the works of your hands. 5 How great are your works, Yahweh! Your thoughts are very deep. 6 A senseless man doesn't know, neither does a fool understand this: 7 though the wicked spring up as the grass, and all the evildoers flourish, they will be destroyed forever. 8 But you, Yahweh, are on high forever more. 9 For behold, your enemies, Yahweh, for behold, your enemies shall perish. All the evildoers will be scattered. 10 But you have exalted my horn like that of the wild ox. I am anointed with fresh oil.

Psalms Book 4 Chapter 93

1 Yahweh reigns! He is clothed with majesty! Yahweh is armed with strength. The world also is established. It can't be moved. 2 Your throne is established from long ago. You are from everlasting. 3 The floods have lifted up, Yahweh, the floods have lifted up their voice. The floods lift up their waves. 4 Above the voices of many waters, the mighty breakers of the sea, Yahweh on high is mighty. 5 Your statutes stand firm. Holiness adorns your house, Yahweh, forever more.

Psalms Book 4 Chapter 94

1 Yahweh, you God to whom vengeance belongs, you God to whom vengeance belongs, shine out. 2 Rise up, you judge of the earth. Pay back the proud what they deserve. 3 Yahweh, how long will the wicked, how long will the wicked triumph? 4 They pour out arrogant words. All the evildoers boast. 5 They break your people in pieces, Yahweh, and afflict your heritage. 6 They kill the widow and the alien, and murder the fatherless. 7 They say, "Yah will not see, neither will Jacob's God consider." 8 Consider, you senseless among the people; you fools, when will you be wise? 9 He who implanted the ear, won't he hear? He who formed the eye, won't he see? 10 He who disciplines the nations, won't he punish? He who teaches man knows. 11 Yahweh knows the thoughts of man, that they are futile. 12 Blessed is the man whom you discipline, Yah, and teach out of your law, 13 that you may give him rest from the days of adversity, until the pit is dug for the wicked. 14 For Yahweh won't reject his people, neither will he forsake his inheritance. 15 For judgment will return to righteousness. All the upright in heart shall follow it. 16 Who will rise up for me against the wicked? Who will stand up for me against the evildoers? 17 Unless Yahweh had been my help, my soul would have soon lived in silence. 18 When I said, "My foot is slipping!" Your loving kindness, Yahweh, held me up. 19 In the multitude of my thoughts within me, your comforts delight my soul. 20 Shall the throne of wickedness have fellowship with you, which brings about mischief by statute? 21 They gather themselves together against the soul of the righteous, and condemn the innocent blood. 22 But Yahweh has been my high tower, my God, the rock of my refuge. 23 He has brought on them their own iniquity, and will cut them off in their own wickedness. Yahweh, our God, will cut them off.

Psalms Book 4 Chapter 95

1 Oh come, let's sing to Yahweh. Let's shout aloud to the rock of our salvation! 2 Let's come before his presence with thanksgiving. Let's extol him with songs! 3 For Yahweh is a great God, a great King above all gods. 4 In his hand are the deep places of the earth. The heights of the mountains are also his. 5 The sea is his, and he made it. His hands formed the dry land. 6 Oh come, let's worship and bow down. Let's kneel before Yahweh, our Maker, 7 for he is our God. We are the people of his pasture, and the sheep in his care. Today, oh that you would hear his voice! 8 Don't harden your heart, as at Meribah, as in the day of Massah in the wilderness, 9 when your fathers tempted me, tested me, and saw my work. 10 Forty long years I was grieved with that generation, and said, "They are a people who err in their heart. They have not known my ways." 11 Therefore I swore in my wrath, "They won't enter into my rest."

Psalms Book 4 Chapter 96

1 Sing to Yahweh a new song! Sing to Yahweh, all the earth. 2 Sing to Yahweh! Bless his name! Proclaim his salvation from day to day! 3 Declare his glory among the nations, his marvelous works among all the peoples. 4 For Yahweh is great, and greatly to be praised! He is to be feared above all gods. 5 For all the gods of the peoples are idols, but Yahweh made the heavens. 6 Honor and majesty are before him. Strength and beauty are in his sanctuary. 7 Ascribe to Yahweh, you families of nations, ascribe to Yahweh glory and strength. 8 Ascribe to Yahweh the glory due to his name. Bring an offering, and come into his courts. 9 Worship Yahweh in holy array. Tremble before him, all the earth. 10 Say among the nations, "Yahweh reigns." The world is also established. It can't be moved. He will judge the peoples with equity. 11 Let the heavens be glad, and let the earth rejoice. Let the sea roar, and its fullness! 12 Let the field and all that is in it exult! Then all the trees of the woods shall sing for joy 13 before Yahweh; for he comes, for he comes to judge the earth. He will judge the world with righteousness, the peoples with his truth.

Psalms Book 4 Chapter 97

1 Yahweh reigns! Let the earth rejoice! Let the multitude of islands be glad! 2 Clouds and darkness are around him. Righteousness and justice are the foundation of his throne. 3 A fire goes before him, and burns up his adversaries on every side. 4 His lightning lights up the world. The earth sees, and trembles. 5 The mountains melt like wax at the presence of Yahweh, at the presence of the Lord of the whole earth. 6 The heavens declare his righteousness. All the peoples have seen his glory. 7 Let them be shamed who serve engraved images, who boast in their idols. Worship him, all you gods! 8 Zion heard and was glad. The daughters of Judah rejoiced because of your judgments, Yahweh. 9 For you, Yahweh, are most high above all the earth. You are exalted far above all gods. 10 You who love Yahweh, hate evil! He preserves the souls of his saints. He delivers them out of the hand of the wicked. 11 Light is sown for the righteous, and gladness for the upright in heart. 12 Be glad in Yahweh, you righteous people! Give thanks to his holy Name.

Psalms Book 4 Chapter 98

1 Sing to Yahweh a new song, for he has done marvelous things! His right hand and his holy arm have worked salvation for him. 2 Yahweh has made known his salvation. He has openly shown his righteousness in the sight of the nations. 3 He has remembered his loving kindness and his faithfulness toward the house of Israel. All the ends of the earth have seen the salvation of our God. 4 Make a joyful noise to Yahweh, all the earth! Burst out and sing for joy, yes, sing praises! 5 Sing praises to

Yahweh with the harp, with the harp and the voice of melody. ⁶ With trumpets and sound of the ram's horn, make a joyful noise before the King, Yahweh. ⁷ Let the sea roar with its fullness; the world, and those who dwell therein. ⁸ Let the rivers clap their hands. Let the mountains sing for joy together ⁹ Let them sing before Yahweh, for he comes to judge the earth. He will judge the world with righteousness, and the peoples with equity.

Psalms Book 4 Chapter 99

¹ Yahweh reigns! Let the peoples tremble. He sits enthroned among the cherubim. Let the earth be moved. ² Yahweh is great in Zion. He is high above all the peoples. ³ Let them praise your great and awesome name. He is Holy! ⁴ The King's strength also loves justice. You establish equity. You execute justice and righteousness in Jacob. ⁵ Exalt Yahweh our God. Worship at his footstool. He is Holy! ⁶ Moses and Aaron were among his priests, Samuel was among those who call on his name. They called on Yahweh, and he answered them. ⁷ He spoke to them in the pillar of cloud. They kept his testimonies, the statute that he gave them. ⁸ You answered them, Yahweh our God. You are a God who forgave them, although you took vengeance for their doings. ⁹ Exalt Yahweh, our God. Worship at his holy hill, for Yahweh, our God, is holy!

Psalms Book 4 Chapter 100

¹ Shout for joy to Yahweh, all you lands! ² Serve Yahweh with gladness. Come before his presence with singing. ³ Know that Yahweh, he is God. It is he who has made us, and we are his. We are his people, and the sheep of his pasture. ⁴ Enter into his gates with thanksgiving, and into his courts with praise. Give thanks to him, and bless his name. ⁵ For Yahweh is good. His loving kindness endures forever, his faithfulness to all generations.

Psalms Book 4 Chapter 101

¹ I will sing of loving kindness and justice. To you, Yahweh, I will sing praises. ² I will be careful to live a blameless life. When will you come to me? I will walk within my house with a blameless heart. ³ I will set no vile thing before my eyes. I hate the deeds of faithless men. They will not cling to me. ⁴ A perverse heart will be far from me. I will have nothing to do with evil. ⁵ I will silence whoever secretly slanders his neighbor. I won't tolerate one who is arrogant and conceited. ⁶ My eyes will be on the faithful of the land, that they may dwell with me. He who walks in a perfect way, he will serve me. ⁷ He who practices deceit won't dwell within my house. He who speaks falsehood won't be established before my eyes. ⁸ Morning by morning, I will destroy all the wicked of the land, to cut off all the workers of iniquity from Yahweh's city.

Psalms Book 4 Chapter 102

¹ Hear my prayer, Yahweh! Let my cry come to you. ² Don't hide your face from me in the day of my distress. Turn your ear to me. Answer me quickly in the day when I call. ³ For my days consume away like smoke. My bones are burned as a torch. ⁴ My heart is blighted like grass, and withered, for I forget to eat my bread. ⁵ By reason of the voice of my groaning, my bones stick to my skin. ⁶ I am like a pelican of the wilderness. I have become as an owl of the waste places. ⁷ I watch, and have become like a sparrow that is alone on the housetop. ⁸ My enemies reproach me all day. Those who are mad at me use my name as a curse. ⁹ For I have eaten ashes like bread, and mixed my drink with tears, ¹⁰ because of your indignation and your wrath; for you have taken me up and thrown me away. ¹¹ My days are like a long shadow. I have withered like grass. ¹² But you, Yahweh, will remain forever; your renown endures to all generations. ¹³ You will arise and have mercy on Zion, for it is time to have pity on her. Yes, the set time has come. ¹⁴ For your servants take pleasure in her stones, and have pity on her dust. ¹⁵ So the nations will fear Yahweh's name, all the kings of the earth your glory. ¹⁶ For Yahweh has built up Zion. He has appeared in his glory. ¹⁷ He has responded to the prayer of the destitute, and has not despised their prayer. ¹⁸ This will be written for the generation to come. A people which will be created will praise Yah, ¹⁹ for he has looked down from the height of his sanctuary. From heaven, Yahweh saw the earth, ²⁰ to hear the groans of the prisoner, to free those who are condemned to death, ²¹ that men may declare Yahweh's name in Zion, and his praise in Jerusalem, ²² when the peoples are gathered together, the kingdoms, to serve Yahweh. ²³ He weakened my strength along the course. He shortened my days. ²⁴ I said, "My God, don't take me away in the middle of my days. Your years are throughout all generations. ²⁵ Of old, you laid the foundation of the earth. The heavens are the work of your hands. ²⁶ They will perish, but you will endure. Yes, all of them will wear out like a garment. You will change them like a cloak, and they will be changed. ²⁷ But you are the same. Your years will have no end. ²⁸ The children of your servants will continue. Their offspring will be established before you."

Psalms Book 4 Chapter 103

¹ Praise Yahweh, my soul! All that is within me, praise his holy name! ² Praise Yahweh, my soul, and don't forget all his benefits, ³ who forgives all your sins, who heals all your diseases, ⁴ who redeems your life from destruction, who crowns you with loving kindness and tender mercies, ⁵ who satisfies your desire with good things, so that your youth is renewed like the eagle's. ⁶ Yahweh executes righteous acts, and justice for all who are oppressed. ⁷ He made known his ways to Moses, his deeds to the children of Israel. ⁸ Yahweh is merciful and gracious, slow to anger, and abundant in loving kindness. ⁹ He will not always accuse; neither will he stay angry forever. ¹⁰ He has not dealt with us according to our sins, nor repaid us for our iniquities. ¹¹ For as the heavens are high above the earth, so great is his loving kindness toward those who fear him. ¹² As far as the east is from the west, so far has he removed our transgressions from us. ¹³ Like a father has compassion on his children, so Yahweh has compassion on those who fear him. ¹⁴ For he knows how we are made. He remembers that we are dust. ¹⁵ As for man, his days are like grass. As a flower of the field, so he flourishes. ¹⁶ For the wind passes over it, and it is gone. Its place remembers it no more. ¹⁷ But Yahweh's loving kindness is from everlasting to everlasting with those who fear him, his righteousness to children's children, ¹⁸ to those who keep his covenant, to those who remember to obey his precepts. ¹⁹ Yahweh has established his throne in the heavens. His kingdom rules over all. ²⁰ Praise Yahweh, you angels of his, who are mighty in strength, who fulfill his word, obeying the voice of his word. ²¹ Praise Yahweh, all you armies of his, you servants of his, who do his pleasure. ²² Praise Yahweh, all you works of his, in all places of his dominion. Praise Yahweh, my soul!

Psalms Book 4 Chapter 104

¹ Bless Yahweh, my soul. Yahweh, my God, you are very great. You are clothed with honor and majesty. ² He covers himself with light as with a garment. He stretches out the heavens like a curtain. ³ He lays the beams of his rooms in the waters. He makes the clouds his chariot. He walks on the wings of the wind. ⁴ He makes his messengers winds, and his servants flames of fire. ⁵ He laid the foundations of the earth, that it should not be moved forever. ⁶ You covered it with the deep as with a cloak. The waters stood above the mountains. ⁷ At your rebuke they fled. At the voice of your thunder they hurried away. ⁸ The mountains rose, the valleys sank down, to the place which you had assigned to them. ⁹ You have set a boundary that they may not pass over, that they don't turn again to cover the earth. ¹⁰ He sends springs into the valleys. They run among the mountains. ¹¹ They give drink to every animal of the field. The wild donkeys quench their thirst. ¹² The birds of the sky nest by them. They sing among the branches. ¹³ He waters the mountains from his rooms. The earth is filled with the fruit of your works. ¹⁴ He causes the grass to grow for the livestock, and plants for man to cultivate, that he may produce food out of the earth: ¹⁵ wine that makes the heart of man glad, oil to make his face to shine, and bread that strengthens man's heart. ¹⁶ Yahweh's trees are well watered, the cedars of Lebanon, which he has planted, ¹⁷ where the birds make their nests. The stork makes its home in the cypress trees. ¹⁸ The high mountains are for the wild goats. The rocks are a refuge for the rock badgers. ¹⁹ He appointed the moon for seasons. The sun knows when to set. ²⁰ You make darkness, and it is night, in which all the animals of the forest prowl. ²¹ The young lions roar after their prey, and seek their food from God. ²² The sun rises, and they steal away, and lie down in their dens. ²³ Man goes out to his work, to his labor until the evening. ²⁴ Yahweh, how many are your works! In wisdom, you have made them all. The earth is full of your riches. ²⁵ There is the sea, great and wide, in which are innumerable living things, both small and large animals. ²⁶ There the ships go, and leviathan, whom you formed to play there. ²⁷ These all wait for you, that you may give them their food in due season. ²⁸ You give to them; they gather. You open your hand; they are satisfied with good. ²⁹ You hide your face; they are troubled. You take away their breath; they die and return to the dust. ³⁰ You send out your Spirit and they are created. You renew the face of the ground. ³¹ Let Yahweh's glory endure forever. Let Yahweh rejoice in his works. ³² He looks at the earth, and it trembles. He touches the mountains, and they smoke. ³³ I will sing to Yahweh as long as I live. I will sing praise to my God while I have any being. ³⁴ Let my meditation be sweet to him. I will rejoice in Yahweh. ³⁵ Let sinners be consumed out of the earth. Let the wicked be no more. Bless Yahweh, my soul. Praise Yah!

Psalms Book 4 Chapter 105

¹ Give thanks to Yahweh! Call on his name! Make his doings known among the peoples. ² Sing to him, sing praises to him! Tell of all his marvelous works. ³ Glory in his holy name. Let the heart of those who seek Yahweh rejoice. ⁴ Seek Yahweh and his strength. Seek his face

forever more. 5 Remember his marvelous works that he has done: his wonders, and the judgments of his mouth, 6 you offspring of Abraham, his servant, you children of Jacob, his chosen ones. 7 He is Yahweh, our God. His judgments are in all the earth. 8 He has remembered his covenant forever, the word which he commanded to a thousand generations, 9 the covenant which he made with Abraham, his oath to Isaac, 10 and confirmed it to Jacob for a statute; to Israel for an everlasting covenant, 11 saying, "To you I will give the land of Canaan, the lot of your inheritance," 12 when they were but a few men in number, yes, very few, and foreigners in it. 13 They went about from nation to nation, from one kingdom to another people. 14 He allowed no one to do them wrong. Yes, he reproved kings for their sakes, 15 "Don't touch my anointed ones! Do my prophets no harm!" 16 He called for a famine on the land. He destroyed the food supplies. 17 He sent a man before them. Joseph was sold for a slave. 18 They bruised his feet with shackles. His neck was locked in irons, 19 until the time that his word happened, and Yahweh's word proved him true. 20 The king sent and freed him, even the ruler of peoples, and let him go free. 21 He made him lord of his house, and ruler of all of his possessions, 22 to discipline his princes at his pleasure, and to teach his elders wisdom. 23 Israel also came into Egypt. Jacob lived in the land of Ham. 24 He increased his people greatly, and made them stronger than their adversaries. 25 He turned their heart to hate his people, to conspire against his servants. 26 He sent Moses, his servant, and Aaron, whom he had chosen. 27 They performed miracles among them, and wonders in the land of Ham. 28 He sent darkness, and made it dark. They didn't rebel against his words. 29 He turned their waters into blood, and killed their fish. 30 Their land swarmed with frogs, even in the rooms of their kings. 31 He spoke, and swarms of flies came, and lice in all their borders. 32 He gave them hail for rain, with lightning in their land. 33 He struck their vines and also their fig trees, and shattered the trees of their country. 34 He spoke, and the locusts came with the grasshoppers, without number. 35 They ate up every plant in their land, and ate up the fruit of their ground. 36 He struck also all the firstborn in their land, the first fruits of all their manhood. 37 He brought them out with silver and gold. There was not one feeble person among his tribes. 38 Egypt was glad when they departed, for the fear of them had fallen on them. 39 He spread a cloud for a covering, fire to give light in the night. 40 They asked, and he brought quails, and satisfied them with the bread of the sky. 41 He opened the rock, and waters gushed out. They ran as a river in the dry places. 42 For he remembered his holy word, and Abraham, his servant. 43 He brought his people out with joy, his chosen with singing. 44 He gave them the lands of the nations. They took the labor of the peoples in possession, 45 that they might keep his statutes, and observe his laws. Praise Yah!

Psalms Book 4 Chapter 106

1 Praise Yahweh! Give thanks to Yahweh, for he is good, for his loving kindness endures forever. 2 Who can utter the mighty acts of Yahweh, or fully declare all his praise? 3 Blessed are those who keep justice. Blessed is one who does what is right at all times. 4 Remember me, Yahweh, with the favor that you show to your people. Visit me with your salvation, 5 that I may see the prosperity of your chosen, that I may rejoice in the gladness of your nation, that I may glory with your inheritance. 6 We have sinned with our fathers. We have committed iniquity. We have done wickedly. 7 Our fathers didn't understand your wonders in Egypt. They didn't remember the multitude of your loving kindnesses, but were rebellious at the sea, even at the Red Sea. 8 Nevertheless he saved them for his name's sake, that he might make his mighty power known. 9 He rebuked the Red Sea also, and it was dried up; so he led them through the depths, as through a desert. 10 He saved them from the hand of him who hated them, and redeemed them from the hand of the enemy. 11 The waters covered their adversaries. There was not one of them left. 12 Then they believed his words. They sang his praise. 13 They soon forgot his works. They didn't wait for his counsel, 14 but gave in to craving in the desert, and tested God in the wasteland. 15 He gave them their request, but sent leanness into their soul. 16 They envied Moses also in the camp, and Aaron, Yahweh's saint. 17 The earth opened and swallowed up Dathan, and covered the company of Abiram. 18 A fire was kindled in their company. The flame burned up the wicked. 19 They made a calf in Horeb, and worshiped a molten image. 20 Thus they exchanged their glory for an image of a bull that eats grass. 21 They forgot God, their Savior, who had done great things in Egypt, 22 wondrous works in the land of Ham, and awesome things by the Red Sea. 23 Therefore he said that he would destroy them, had Moses, his chosen, not stood before him in the breach, to turn away his wrath, so that he wouldn't destroy them. 24 Yes, they despised the pleasant land. They didn't believe his word, 25 but murmured in their tents, and didn't listen to Yahweh's voice. 26 Therefore he swore to them that he would

overthrow them in the wilderness, 27 that he would overthrow their offspring among the nations, and scatter them in the lands. 28 They joined themselves also to Baal Peor, and ate the sacrifices of the dead. 29 Thus they provoked him to anger with their deeds. The plague broke in on them. 30 Then Phinehas stood up and executed judgment, so the plague was stopped. 31 That was credited to him for righteousness, for all generations to come. 32 They angered him also at the waters of Meribah, so that Moses was troubled for their sakes; 33 because they were rebellious against his spirit, he spoke rashly with his lips. 34 They didn't destroy the peoples, as Yahweh commanded them, 35 but mixed themselves with the nations, and learned their works. 36 They served their idols, which became a snare to them. 37 Yes, they sacrificed their sons and their daughters to demons. 38 They shed innocent blood, even the blood of their sons and of their daughters, whom they sacrificed to the idols of Canaan. The land was polluted with blood. 39 Thus they were defiled with their works, and prostituted themselves in their deeds. 40 Therefore Yahweh burned with anger against his people. He abhorred his inheritance. 41 He gave them into the hand of the nations. Those who hated them ruled over them. 42 Their enemies also oppressed them. They were brought into subjection under their hand. 43 He rescued them many times, but they were rebellious in their counsel, and were brought low in their iniquity. 44 Nevertheless he regarded their distress, when he heard their cry. 45 He remembered for them his covenant, and repented according to the multitude of his loving kindnesses. 46 He made them also to be pitied by all those who carried them captive. 47 Save us, Yahweh, our God, gather us from among the nations, to give thanks to your holy name, to triumph in your praise! 48 Blessed be Yahweh, the God of Israel, from everlasting even to everlasting! Let all the people say, "Amen." Praise Yah!

Psalms Book 5

Psalms Book 5 Chapter 107

1 Give thanks to Yahweh, for he is good, for his loving kindness endures forever. 2 Let the redeemed by Yahweh say so, whom he has redeemed from the hand of the adversary, 3 and gathered out of the lands, from the east and from the west, from the north and from the south. 4 They wandered in the wilderness in a desert way. They found no city to live in. 5 Hungry and thirsty, their soul fainted in them. 6 Then they cried to Yahweh in their trouble, and he delivered them out of their distresses. 7 He led them also by a straight way, that they might go to a city to live in. 8 Let them praise Yahweh for his loving kindness, for his wonderful deeds to the children of men! 9 For he satisfies the longing soul. He fills the hungry soul with good. 10 Some sat in darkness and in the shadow of death, being bound in affliction and iron, 11 because they rebelled against the words of God, and condemned the counsel of the Most High. 12 Therefore he brought down their heart with labor. They fell down, and there was no one to help. 13 Then they cried to Yahweh in their trouble, and he saved them out of their distresses. 14 He brought them out of darkness and the shadow of death, and broke away their chains. 15 Let them praise Yahweh for his loving kindness, for his wonderful deeds to the children of men! 16 For he has broken the gates of bronze, and cut through bars of iron. 17 Fools are afflicted because of their disobedience, and because of their iniquities. 18 Their soul abhors all kinds of food. They draw near to the gates of death. 19 Then they cry to Yahweh in their trouble, and he saves them out of their distresses. 20 He sends his word, and heals them, and delivers them from their graves. 21 Let them praise Yahweh for his loving kindness, for his wonderful deeds to the children of men! 22 Let them offer the sacrifices of thanksgiving, and declare his deeds with singing. 23 Those who go down to the sea in ships, who do business in great waters, 24 these see Yahweh's deeds, and his wonders in the deep. 25 For he commands, and raises the stormy wind, which lifts up its waves. 26 They mount up to the sky; they go down again to the depths. Their soul melts away because of trouble. 27 They reel back and forth, and stagger like a drunken man, and are at their wits' end. 28 Then they cry to Yahweh in their trouble, and he brings them out of their distress. 29 He makes the storm a calm, so that its waves are still. 30 Then they are glad because it is calm, so he brings them to their desired haven. 31 Let them praise Yahweh for his loving kindness, for his wonderful deeds for the children of men! 32 Let them exalt him also in the assembly of the people, and praise him in the seat of the elders. 33 He turns rivers into a desert, water springs into a thirsty ground, 34 and a fruitful land into a salt waste, for the wickedness of those who dwell in it. 35 He turns a desert into a pool of water, and a dry land into water springs. 36 There he makes the hungry live, that they may prepare a city to live in, 37 sow fields, plant vineyards, and reap the fruits of increase. 38 He blesses them also, so that they are multiplied greatly. He doesn't allow their

livestock to decrease. ³⁹ Again, they are diminished and bowed down through oppression, trouble, and sorrow. ⁴⁰ He pours contempt on princes, and causes them to wander in a trackless waste. ⁴¹ Yet he lifts the needy out of their affliction, and increases their families like a flock. ⁴² The upright will see it, and be glad. All the wicked will shut their mouths. ⁴³ Whoever is wise will pay attention to these things. They will consider the loving kindnesses of Yahweh.

Psalms Book 5 Chapter 108

¹ My heart is steadfast, God. I will sing and I will make music with my soul. ² Wake up, harp and lyre! I will wake up the dawn. ³ I will give thanks to you, Yahweh, among the nations. I will sing praises to you among the peoples. ⁴ For your loving kindness is great above the heavens. Your faithfulness reaches to the skies. ⁵ Be exalted, God, above the heavens! Let your glory be over all the earth. ⁶ That your beloved may be delivered, save with your right hand, and answer us. ⁷ God has spoken from his sanctuary: "In triumph, I will divide Shechem, and measure out the valley of Succoth. ⁸ Gilead is mine. Manasseh is mine. Ephraim also is my helmet. Judah is my scepter. ⁹ Moab is my wash pot. I will toss my sandal on Edom. I will shout over Philistia." ¹⁰ Who will bring me into the fortified city? Who will lead me to Edom? ¹¹ Haven't you rejected us, God? You don't go out, God, with our armies. ¹² Give us help against the enemy, for the help of man is vain. ¹³ Through God, we will do valiantly, for it is he who will tread down our enemies.

Psalms Book 5 Chapter 109

¹ God of my praise, don't remain silent, ² for they have opened the mouth of the wicked and the mouth of deceit against me. They have spoken to me with a lying tongue. ³ They have also surrounded me with words of hatred, and fought against me without a cause. ⁴ In return for my love, they are my adversaries; but I am in prayer. ⁵ They have rewarded me evil for good, and hatred for my love. ⁶ Set a wicked man over him. Let an adversary stand at his right hand. ⁷ When he is judged, let him come out guilty. Let his prayer be turned into sin. ⁸ Let his days be few. Let another take his office. ⁹ Let his children be fatherless, and his wife a widow. ¹⁰ Let his children be wandering beggars. Let them be sought from their ruins. ¹¹ Let the creditor seize all that he has. Let strangers plunder the fruit of his labor. ¹² Let there be no one to extend kindness to him, neither let there be anyone to have pity on his fatherless children. ¹³ Let his posterity be cut off. In the generation following let their name be blotted out. ¹⁴ Let the iniquity of his fathers be remembered by Yahweh. Don't let the sin of his mother be blotted out. ¹⁵ Let them be before Yahweh continually, that he may cut off their memory from the earth; ¹⁶ because he didn't remember to show kindness, but persecuted the poor and needy man, the broken in heart, to kill them. ¹⁷ Yes, he loved cursing, and it came to him. He didn't delight in blessing, and it was far from him. ¹⁸ He clothed himself also with cursing as with his garment. It came into his inward parts like water, like oil into his bones. ¹⁹ Let it be to him as the clothing with which he covers himself, for the belt that is always around him. ²⁰ This is the reward of my adversaries from Yahweh, of those who speak evil against my soul. ²¹ But deal with me, Yahweh the Lord, for your name's sake, because your loving kindness is good, deliver me; ²² for I am poor and needy. My heart is wounded within me. ²³ I fade away like an evening shadow. I am shaken off like a locust. ²⁴ My knees are weak through fasting. My body is thin and lacks fat. ²⁵ I have also become a reproach to them. When they see me, they shake their head. ²⁶ Help me, Yahweh, my God. Save me according to your loving kindness; ²⁷ that they may know that this is your hand; that you, Yahweh, have done it. ²⁸ They may curse, but you bless. When they arise, they will be shamed, but your servant shall rejoice. ²⁹ Let my adversaries be clothed with dishonor. Let them cover themselves with their own shame as with a robe. ³⁰ I will give great thanks to Yahweh with my mouth. Yes, I will praise him among the multitude. ³¹ For he will stand at the right hand of the needy, to save him from those who judge his soul.

Psalms Book 5 Chapter 110

¹ Yahweh says to my Lord, "Sit at my right hand, until I make your enemies your footstool for your feet." ² Yahweh will send out the rod of your strength out of Zion. Rule among your enemies. ³ Your people offer themselves willingly in the day of your power, in holy array. Out of the womb of the morning, you have the dew of your youth. ⁴ Yahweh has sworn, and will not change his mind: "You are a priest forever in the order of Melchizedek." ⁵ The Lord is at your right hand. He will crush kings in the day of his wrath. ⁶ He will judge among the nations. He will heap up dead bodies. He will crush the ruler of the whole earth. ⁷ He will drink of the brook on the way; therefore he will lift up his head.

Psalms Book 5 Chapter 111

¹ Praise Yah! I will give thanks to Yahweh with my whole heart, in the council of the upright, and in the congregation. ² Yahweh's works are great, pondered by all those who delight in them. ³ His work is honor and majesty. His righteousness endures forever. ⁴ He has caused his wonderful works to be remembered. Yahweh is gracious and merciful. ⁵ He has given food to those who fear him. He always remembers his covenant. ⁶ He has shown his people the power of his works, in giving them the heritage of the nations. ⁷ The works of his hands are truth and justice. All his precepts are sure. ⁸ They are established forever and ever. They are done in truth and uprightness. ⁹ He has sent redemption to his people. He has ordained his covenant forever. His name is holy and awesome! ¹⁰ The fear of Yahweh is the beginning of wisdom. All those who do his work have a good understanding. His praise endures forever!

Psalms Book 5 Chapter 112

¹ Praise Yah! Blessed is the man who fears Yahweh, who delights greatly in his commandments. ² His offspring will be mighty in the land. The generation of the upright will be blessed. ³ Wealth and riches are in his house. His righteousness endures forever. ⁴ Light dawns in the darkness for the upright, gracious, merciful, and righteous. ⁵ It is well with the man who deals graciously and lends. He will maintain his cause in judgment. ⁶ For he will never be shaken. The righteous will be remembered forever. ⁷ He will not be afraid of evil news. His heart is steadfast, trusting in Yahweh. ⁸ His heart is established. He will not be afraid in the end when he sees his adversaries. ⁹ He has dispersed, he has given to the poor. His righteousness endures forever. His horn will be exalted with honor. ¹⁰ The wicked will see it, and be grieved. He shall gnash with his teeth, and melt away. The desire of the wicked will perish.

Psalms Book 5 Chapter 113

¹ Praise Yah! Praise, you servants of Yahweh, praise Yahweh's name. ² Blessed be Yahweh's name, from this time forward and forever more. ³ From the rising of the sun to its going down, Yahweh's name is to be praised. ⁴ Yahweh is high above all nations, his glory above the heavens. ⁵ Who is like Yahweh, our God, who has his seat on high, ⁶ who stoops down to see in heaven and in the earth? ⁷ He raises up the poor out of the dust, and lifts up the needy from the ash heap, ⁸ that he may set him with princes, even with the princes of his people. ⁹ He settles the barren woman in her home as a joyful mother of children. Praise Yah!

Psalms Book 5 Chapter 114

¹ When Israel went out of Egypt, the house of Jacob from a people of foreign language, ² Judah became his sanctuary, Israel his dominion. ³ The sea saw it, and fled. The Jordan was driven back. ⁴ The mountains skipped like rams, the little hills like lambs. ⁵ What was it, you sea, that you fled? You Jordan, that you turned back? ⁶ You mountains, that you skipped like rams? You little hills, like lambs? ⁷ Tremble, you earth, at the presence of the Lord, at the presence of the God of Jacob, ⁸ who turned the rock into a pool of water, the flint into a spring of waters.

Psalms Book 5 Chapter 115

¹ Not to us, Yahweh, not to us, but to your name give glory, for your loving kindness, and for your truth's sake. ² Why should the nations say, "Where is their God, now?" ³ But our God is in the heavens. He does whatever he pleases. ⁴ Their idols are silver and gold, the work of men's hands. ⁵ They have mouths, but they don't speak. They have eyes, but they don't see. ⁶ They have ears, but they don't hear. They have noses, but they don't smell. ⁷ They have hands, but they don't feel. They have feet, but they don't walk, neither do they speak through their throat. ⁸ Those who make them will be like them; yes, everyone who trusts in them. ⁹ Israel, trust in Yahweh! He is their help and their shield. ¹⁰ House of Aaron, trust in Yahweh! He is their help and their shield. ¹¹ You who fear Yahweh, trust in Yahweh! He is their help and their shield. ¹² Yahweh remembers us. He will bless us. He will bless the house of Israel. He will bless the house of Aaron. ¹³ He will bless those who fear Yahweh, both small and great. ¹⁴ May Yahweh increase you more and more, you and your children. ¹⁵ Blessed are you by Yahweh, who made heaven and earth. ¹⁶ The heavens are Yahweh's heavens, but he has given the earth to the children of men. ¹⁷ The dead don't praise Yah, nor any who go down into silence, ¹⁸ but we will bless Yah, from this time forward and forever more. Praise Yah!

Psalms Book 5 Chapter 116

¹ I love Yahweh, because he listens to my voice, and my cries for mercy. ² Because he has turned his ear to me, therefore I will call on him as long as I live. ³ The cords of death surrounded me, the pains of Sheol got a hold of me. I found trouble and sorrow. ⁴ Then I called on Yahweh's name: "Yahweh, I beg you, deliver my soul." ⁵ Yahweh is gracious and righteous. Yes, our God is merciful. ⁶ Yahweh preserves the simple. I was brought low, and he saved me. ⁷ Return to your rest, my soul, for Yahweh has dealt bountifully with you. ⁸ For you have

delivered my soul from death, my eyes from tears, and my feet from falling. 9 I will walk before Yahweh in the land of the living. 10 I believed, therefore I said, "I was greatly afflicted." 11 I said in my haste, "All people are liars." 12 What will I give to Yahweh for all his benefits toward me? 13 I will take the cup of salvation, and call on Yahweh's name. 14 I will pay my vows to Yahweh, yes, in the presence of all his people. 15 Precious in Yahweh's sight is the death of his saints. 16 Yahweh, truly I am your servant. I am your servant, the son of your servant girl. You have freed me from my chains. 17 I will offer to you the sacrifice of thanksgiving, and will call on Yahweh's name. 18 I will pay my vows to Yahweh, yes, in the presence of all his people, 19 in the courts of Yahweh's house, in the middle of you, Jerusalem. Praise Yah!

Psalms Book 5 Chapter 117

1 Praise Yahweh, all you nations! Extol him, all you peoples! 2 For his loving kindness is great toward us. Yahweh's faithfulness endures forever. Praise Yah!

Psalms Book 5 Chapter 118

1 Give thanks to Yahweh, for he is good, for his loving kindness endures forever. 2 Let Israel now say that his loving kindness endures forever. 3 Let the house of Aaron now say that his loving kindness endures forever. 4 Now let those who fear Yahweh say that his loving kindness endures forever. 5 Out of my distress, I called on Yah. Yah answered me with freedom. 6 Yahweh is on my side. I will not be afraid. What can man do to me? 7 Yahweh is on my side among those who help me. Therefore I will look in triumph at those who hate me. 8 It is better to take refuge in Yahweh, than to put confidence in man. 9 It is better to take refuge in Yahweh, than to put confidence in princes. 10 All the nations surrounded me, but in Yahweh's name I cut them off. 11 They surrounded me, yes, they surrounded me. In Yahweh's name I indeed cut them off. 12 They surrounded me like bees. They are quenched like the burning thorns. In Yahweh's name I cut them off. 13 You pushed me back hard, to make me fall, but Yahweh helped me. 14 Yah is my strength and song. He has become my salvation. 15 The voice of rejoicing and salvation is in the tents of the righteous. "The right hand of Yahweh does valiantly. 16 The right hand of Yahweh is exalted! The right hand of Yahweh does valiantly!" 17 I will not die, but live, and declare Yah's works. 18 Yah has punished me severely, but he has not given me over to death. 19 Open to me the gates of righteousness. I will enter into them. I will give thanks to Yah. 20 This is the gate of Yahweh; the righteous will enter into it. 21 I will give thanks to you, for you have answered me, and have become my salvation. 22 The stone which the builders rejected has become the cornerstone. 23 This is Yahweh's doing. It is marvelous in our eyes. 24 This is the day that Yahweh has made. We will rejoice and be glad in it! 25 Save us now, we beg you, Yahweh! Yahweh, we beg you, send prosperity now. 26 Blessed is he who comes in Yahweh's name! We have blessed you out of Yahweh's house. 27 Yahweh is God, and he has given us light. Bind the sacrifice with cords, even to the horns of the altar. 28 You are my God, and I will give thanks to you. You are my God, I will exalt you. 29 Oh give thanks to Yahweh, for he is good, for his loving kindness endures forever.

Psalms Book 5 Chapter 119

1 Blessed are those whose ways are blameless, who walk according to Yahweh's law. 2 Blessed are those who keep his statutes, who seek him with their whole heart. 3 Yes, they do nothing wrong. They walk in his ways. 4 You have commanded your precepts, that we should fully obey them. 5 Oh that my ways were steadfast to obey your statutes! 6 Then I wouldn't be disappointed, when I consider all of your commandments. 7 I will give thanks to you with uprightness of heart, when I learn your righteous judgments. 8 I will observe your statutes. Don't utterly forsake me. **BETH** 9 How can a young man keep his way pure? By living according to your word. 10 With my whole heart I have sought you. Don't let me wander from your commandments. 11 I have hidden your word in my heart, that I might not sin against you. 12 Blessed are you, Yahweh. Teach me your statutes. 13 With my lips, I have declared all the ordinances of your mouth. 14 I have rejoiced in the way of your testimonies, as much as in all riches. 15 I will meditate on your precepts, and consider your ways. 16 I will delight myself in your statutes. I will not forget your word. **GIMEL** 17 Do good to your servant. I will live and I will obey your word. 18 Open my eyes, that I may see wondrous things out of your law. 19 I am a stranger on the earth. Don't hide your commandments from me. 20 My soul is consumed with longing for your ordinances at all times. 21 You have rebuked the proud who are cursed, who wander from your commandments. 22 Take reproach and contempt away from me, for I have kept your statutes. 23 Though princes sit and slander me, your servant will meditate on your statutes. 24 Indeed your statutes are my delight, and my counselors. **DALETH** 25 My soul is laid low in the dust. Revive me according to your word! 26

I declared my ways, and you answered me. Teach me your statutes. 27 Let me understand the teaching of your precepts! Then I will meditate on your wondrous works. 28 My soul is weary with sorrow; strengthen me according to your word. 29 Keep me from the way of deceit. Grant me your law graciously! 30 I have chosen the way of truth. I have set your ordinances before me. 31 I cling to your statutes, Yahweh. Don't let me be disappointed. 32 I run in the path of your commandments, for you have set my heart free. **HE** 33 Teach me, Yahweh, the way of your statutes. I will keep them to the end. 34 Give me understanding, and I will keep your law. Yes, I will obey it with my whole heart. 35 Direct me in the path of your commandments, for I delight in them. 36 Turn my heart toward your statutes, not toward selfish gain. 37 Turn my eyes away from looking at worthless things. Revive me in your ways. 38 Fulfill your promise to your servant, that you may be feared. 39 Take away my disgrace that I dread, for your ordinances are good. 40 Behold, I long for your precepts! Revive me in your righteousness. **VAV** 41 Let your loving kindness also come to me, Yahweh, your salvation, according to your word. 42 So I will have an answer for him who reproaches me, for I trust in your word. 43 Don't snatch the word of truth out of my mouth, for I put my hope in your ordinances. 44 So I will obey your law continually, forever and ever. 45 I will walk in liberty, for I have sought your precepts. 46 I will also speak of your statutes before kings, and will not be disappointed. 47 I will delight myself in your commandments, because I love them. 48 I reach out my hands for your commandments, which I love. I will meditate on your statutes. **ZAYIN** 49 Remember your word to your servant, because you gave me hope. 50 This is my comfort in my affliction, for your word has revived me. 51 The arrogant mock me excessively, but I don't swerve from your law. 52 I remember your ordinances of old, Yahweh, and have comforted myself. 53 Indignation has taken hold on me, because of the wicked who forsake your law. 54 Your statutes have been my songs in the house where I live. 55 I have remembered your name, Yahweh, in the night, and I obey your law. 56 This is my way, that I keep your precepts. **HETH** 57 Yahweh is my portion. I promised to obey your words. 58 I sought your favor with my whole heart. Be merciful to me according to your word. 59 I considered my ways, and turned my steps to your statutes. 60 I will hurry, and not delay, to obey your commandments. 61 The ropes of the wicked bind me, but I won't forget your law. 62 At midnight I will rise to give thanks to you, because of your righteous ordinances. 63 I am a friend of all those who fear you, of those who observe your precepts. 64 The earth is full of your loving kindness, Yahweh. Teach me your statutes. **TETH** 65 You have treated your servant well, according to your word, Yahweh. 66 Teach me good judgment and knowledge, for I believe in your commandments. 67 Before I was afflicted, I went astray; but now I observe your word. 68 You are good, and do good. Teach me your statutes. 69 The proud have smeared a lie upon me. With my whole heart, I will keep your precepts. 70 Their heart is as callous as the fat, but I delight in your law. 71 It is good for me that I have been afflicted, that I may learn your statutes. 72 The law of your mouth is better to me than thousands of pieces of gold and silver. **YODH** 73 Your hands have made me and formed me. Give me understanding, that I may learn your commandments. 74 Those who fear you will see me and be glad, because I have put my hope in your word. 75 Yahweh, I know that your judgments are righteous, that in faithfulness you have afflicted me. 76 Please let your loving kindness be for my comfort, according to your word to your servant. 77 Let your tender mercies come to me, that I may live; for your law is my delight. 78 Let the proud be disappointed, for they have overthrown me wrongfully. I will meditate on your precepts. 79 Let those who fear you turn to me. They will know your statutes. 80 Let my heart be blameless toward your decrees, that I may not be disappointed. **KAPF** 81 My soul faints for your salvation. I hope in your word. 82 My eyes fail for your word. I say, "When will you comfort me?" 83 For I have become like a wineskin in the smoke. I don't forget your statutes. 84 How many are the days of your servant? When will you execute judgment on those who persecute me? 85 The proud have dug pits for me, contrary to your law. 86 All of your commandments are faithful. They persecute me wrongfully. Help me! 87 They had almost wiped me from the earth, but I didn't forsake your precepts. 88 Preserve my life according to your loving kindness, so I will obey the statutes of your mouth. **LAMEDH** 89 Yahweh, your word is settled in heaven forever. 90 Your faithfulness is to all generations. You have established the earth, and it remains. 91 Your laws remain to this day, for all things serve you. 92 Unless your law had been my delight, I would have perished in my affliction. 93 I will never forget your precepts, for with them, you have revived me. 94 I am yours. Save me, for I have sought your precepts. 95 The wicked have waited for me, to destroy me. I will consider your statutes. 96 I have seen a limit to all perfection, but your commands are boundless.

MEM 97 How I love your law! It is my meditation all day. 98 Your commandments make me wiser than my enemies, for your commandments are always with me. 99 I have more understanding than all my teachers, for your testimonies are my meditation. 100 I understand more than the aged, because I have kept your precepts. 101 I have kept my feet from every evil way, that I might observe your word. 102 I have not turned away from your ordinances, for you have taught me. 103 How sweet are your promises to my taste, more than honey to my mouth! 104 Through your precepts, I get understanding; therefore I hate every false way. **NUN** 105 Your word is a lamp to my feet, and a light for my path. 106 I have sworn, and have confirmed it, that I will obey your righteous ordinances. 107 I am afflicted very much. Revive me, Yahweh, according to your word. 108 Accept, I beg you, the willing offerings of my mouth. Yahweh, teach me your ordinances. 109 My soul is continually in my hand, yet I won't forget your law. 110 The wicked have laid a snare for me, yet I haven't gone astray from your precepts. 111 I have taken your testimonies as a heritage forever, for they are the joy of my heart. 112 I have set my heart to perform your statutes forever, even to the end. **SAMEKH** 113 I hate double-minded men, but I love your law. 114 You are my hiding place and my shield. I hope in your word. 115 Depart from me, you evildoers, that I may keep the commandments of my God. 116 Uphold me according to your word, that I may live. Let me not be ashamed of my hope. 117 Hold me up, and I will be safe, and will have respect for your statutes continually. 118 You reject all those who stray from your statutes, for their deceit is in vain. 119 You put away all the wicked of the earth like dross. Therefore I love your testimonies. 120 My flesh trembles for fear of you. I am afraid of your judgments. **AYIN** 121 I have done what is just and righteous. Don't leave me to my oppressors. 122 Ensure your servant's well-being. Don't let the proud oppress me. 123 My eyes fail looking for your salvation, for your righteous word. 124 Deal with your servant according to your loving kindness. Teach me your statutes. 125 I am your servant. Give me understanding, that I may know your testimonies. 126 It is time to act, Yahweh, for they break your law. 127 Therefore I love your commandments more than gold, yes, more than pure gold. 128 Therefore I consider all of your precepts to be right. I hate every false way. **PE** 129 Your testimonies are wonderful, therefore my soul keeps them. 130 The entrance of your words gives light. It gives understanding to the simple. 131 I opened my mouth wide and panted, for I longed for your commandments. 132 Turn to me, and have mercy on me, as you always do to those who love your name. 133 Establish my footsteps in your word. Don't let any iniquity have dominion over me. 134 Redeem me from the oppression of man, so I will observe your precepts. 135 Make your face shine on your servant. Teach me your statutes. 136 Streams of tears run down my eyes, because they don't observe your law. **TZADHE** 137 You are righteous, Yahweh. Your judgments are upright. 138 You have commanded your statutes in righteousness. They are fully trustworthy. 139 My zeal wears me out, because my enemies ignore your words. 140 Your promises have been thoroughly tested, and your servant loves them. 141 I am small and despised. I don't forget your precepts. 142 Your righteousness is an everlasting righteousness. Your law is truth. 143 Trouble and anguish have taken hold of me. Your commandments are my delight. 144 Your testimonies are righteous forever. Give me understanding, that I may live. **QOPH** 145 I have called with my whole heart. Answer me, Yahweh! I will keep your statutes. 146 I have called to you. Save me! I will obey your statutes. 147 I rise before dawn and cry for help. I put my hope in your words. 148 My eyes stay open through the night watches, that I might meditate on your word. 149 Hear my voice according to your loving kindness. Revive me, Yahweh, according to your ordinances. 150 They draw near who follow after wickedness. They are far from your law. 151 You are near, Yahweh. All your commandments are truth. 152 Of old I have known from your testimonies, that you have founded them forever. **RESH** 153 Consider my affliction, and deliver me, for I don't forget your law. 154 Plead my cause, and redeem me! Revive me according to your promise. 155 Salvation is far from the wicked, for they don't seek your statutes. 156 Great are your tender mercies, Yahweh. Revive me according to your ordinances. 157 Many are my persecutors and my adversaries. I haven't swerved from your testimonies. 158 I look at the faithless with loathing, because they don't observe your word. 159 Consider how I love your precepts. Revive me, Yahweh, according to your loving kindness. 160 All of your words are truth. Every one of your righteous ordinances endures forever. **SIN AND SHIN** 161 Princes have persecuted me without a cause, but my heart stands in awe of your words. 162 I rejoice at your word, as one who finds great plunder. 163 I hate and abhor falsehood. I love your law. 164 Seven times a day, I praise you, because of your righteous ordinances. 165 Those who love your law have great peace. Nothing causes them to stumble. 166 I have hoped for your salvation, Yahweh. I have done your commandments. 167 My soul has observed your testimonies. I love them exceedingly. 168 I have obeyed your precepts and your testimonies, for all my ways are before you. **TAV** 169 Let my cry come before you, Yahweh. Give me understanding according to your word. 170 Let my supplication come before you. Deliver me according to your word. 171 Let my lips utter praise, for you teach me your statutes. 172 Let my tongue sing of your word, for all your commandments are righteousness. 173 Let your hand be ready to help me, for I have chosen your precepts. 174 I have longed for your salvation, Yahweh. Your law is my delight. 175 Let my soul live, that I may praise you. Let your ordinances help me. 176 I have gone astray like a lost sheep. Seek your servant, for I don't forget your commandments.

Psalms Book 5 Chapter 120

1 In my distress, I cried to Yahweh. He answered me. 2 Deliver my soul, Yahweh, from lying lips, from a deceitful tongue. 3 What will be given to you, and what will be done more to you, you deceitful tongue? 4 Sharp arrows of the mighty, with coals of juniper. 5 Woe is me, that I live in Meshech, that I dwell among the tents of Kedar! 6 My soul has had her dwelling too long with him who hates peace. 7 I am for peace, but when I speak, they are for war.

Psalms Book 5 Chapter 121

1 I will lift up my eyes to the hills. Where does my help come from? 2 My help comes from Yahweh, who made heaven and earth. 3 He will not allow your foot to be moved. He who keeps you will not slumber. 4 Behold, he who keeps Israel will neither slumber nor sleep. 5 Yahweh is your keeper. Yahweh is your shade on your right hand. 6 The sun will not harm you by day, nor the moon by night. 7 Yahweh will keep you from all evil. He will keep your soul. 8 Yahweh will keep your going out and your coming in, from this time forward, and forever more.

Psalms Book 5 Chapter 122

1 I was glad when they said to me, "Let's go to Yahweh's house!" 2 Our feet are standing within your gates, Jerusalem! 3 Jerusalem is built as a city that is compact together, 4 where the tribes go up, even Yah's tribes, according to an ordinance for Israel, to give thanks to Yahweh's name. 5 For there are set thrones for judgment, the thrones of David's house. 6 Pray for the peace of Jerusalem. Those who love you will prosper. 7 Peace be within your walls, and prosperity within your palaces. 8 For my brothers' and companions' sakes, I will now say, "Peace be within you." 9 For the sake of the house of Yahweh our God, I will seek your good.

Psalms Book 5 Chapter 123

1 I lift up my eyes to you, you who sit in the heavens. 2 Behold, as the eyes of servants look to the hand of their master, as the eyes of a maid to the hand of her mistress, so our eyes look to Yahweh, our God, until he has mercy on us. 3 Have mercy on us, Yahweh, have mercy on us, for we have endured much contempt. 4 Our soul is exceedingly filled with the scoffing of those who are at ease, with the contempt of the proud.

Psalms Book 5 Chapter 124

1 If it had not been Yahweh who was on our side, let Israel now say, 2 if it had not been Yahweh who was on our side, when men rose up against us, 3 then they would have swallowed us up alive, when their wrath was kindled against us, 4 then the waters would have overwhelmed us, the stream would have gone over our soul. 5 Then the proud waters would have gone over our soul. 6 Blessed be Yahweh, who has not given us as a prey to their teeth. 7 Our soul has escaped like a bird out of the fowler's snare. The snare is broken, and we have escaped. 8 Our help is in Yahweh's name, who made heaven and earth.

Psalms Book 5 Chapter 125

1 Those who trust in Yahweh are as Mount Zion, which can't be moved, but remains forever. 2 As the mountains surround Jerusalem, so Yahweh surrounds his people from this time forward and forever more. 3 For the scepter of wickedness won't remain over the allotment of the righteous, so that the righteous won't use their hands to do evil. 4 Do good, Yahweh, to those who are good, to those who are upright in their hearts. 5 But as for those who turn away to their crooked ways, Yahweh will lead them away with the workers of iniquity. Peace be on Israel.

Psalms Book 5 Chapter 126

1 When Yahweh brought back those who returned to Zion, we were like those who dream. 2 Then our mouth was filled with laughter, and our tongue with singing. Then they said among the nations, "Yahweh has done great things for them." 3 Yahweh has done great things for us, and we are glad. 4 Restore our fortunes again, Yahweh, like the streams in the Negev. 5 Those who sow in tears will reap in joy. 6 He who goes out weeping, carrying seed for sowing, will certainly come again with joy, carrying his sheaves.

Psalms Book 5 Chapter 127

¹ Unless Yahweh builds the house, they who build it labor in vain. Unless Yahweh watches over the city, the watchman guards it in vain. ² It is vain for you to rise up early, to stay up late, eating the bread of toil, for he gives sleep to his loved ones. ³ Behold, children are a heritage of Yahweh. The fruit of the womb is his reward. ⁴ As arrows in the hand of a mighty man, so are the children of youth. ⁵ Happy is the man who has his quiver full of them. They won't be disappointed when they speak with their enemies in the gate.

Psalms Book 5 Chapter 128

¹ Blessed is everyone who fears Yahweh, who walks in his ways. ² For you will eat the labor of your hands. You will be happy, and it will be well with you. ³ Your wife will be as a fruitful vine in the innermost parts of your house, your children like olive shoots around your table. ⁴ Behold, this is how the man who fears Yahweh is blessed. ⁵ May Yahweh bless you out of Zion, and may you see the good of Jerusalem all the days of your life. ⁶ Yes, may you see your children's children. Peace be upon Israel.

Psalms Book 5 Chapter 129

¹ Many times they have afflicted me from my youth up. Let Israel now say: ² many times they have afflicted me from my youth up, yet they have not prevailed against me. ³ The plowers plowed on my back. They made their furrows long. ⁴ Yahweh is righteous. He has cut apart the cords of the wicked. ⁵ Let them be disappointed and turned backward, all those who hate Zion. ⁶ Let them be as the grass on the housetops, which withers before it grows up, ⁷ with which the reaper doesn't fill his hand, nor he who binds sheaves, his bosom. ⁸ Neither do those who go by say, "The blessing of Yahweh be on you. We bless you in Yahweh's name."

Psalms Book 5 Chapter 130

¹ Out of the depths I have cried to you, Yahweh. ² Lord, hear my voice. Let your ears be attentive to the voice of my petitions. ³ If you, Yah, kept a record of sins, Lord, who could stand? ⁴ But there is forgiveness with you, therefore you are feared. ⁵ I wait for Yahweh. My soul waits. I hope in his word. ⁶ My soul longs for the Lord more than watchmen long for the morning, more than watchmen for the morning. ⁷ Israel, hope in Yahweh, for there is loving kindness with Yahweh. Abundant redemption is with him. ⁸ He will redeem Israel from all their sins.

Psalms Book 5 Chapter 131

¹ Yahweh, my heart isn't arrogant, nor my eyes lofty; nor do I concern myself with great matters, or things too wonderful for me. ² Surely I have stilled and quieted my soul, like a weaned child with his mother, like a weaned child is my soul within me. ³ Israel, hope in Yahweh, from this time forward and forever more.

Psalms Book 5 Chapter 132

¹ Yahweh, remember David and all his affliction, ² how he swore to Yahweh, and vowed to the Mighty One of Jacob: ³ "Surely I will not come into the structure of my house, nor go up into my bed; ⁴ I will not give sleep to my eyes, or slumber to my eyelids, ⁵ until I find out a place for Yahweh, a dwelling for the Mighty One of Jacob." ⁶ Behold, we heard of it in Ephrathah. We found it in the field of Jaar. ⁷ "We will go into his dwelling place. We will worship at his footstool." ⁸ Arise, Yahweh, into your resting place, you, and the ark of your strength. ⁹ Let your priests be clothed with righteousness. Let your saints shout for joy! ¹⁰ For your servant David's sake, don't turn away the face of your anointed one. ¹¹ Yahweh has sworn to David in truth. He will not turn from it: "I will set the fruit of your body on your throne. ¹² If your children will keep my covenant, my testimony that I will teach them, their children also will sit on your throne forever more." ¹³ For Yahweh has chosen Zion. He has desired it for his habitation. ¹⁴ "This is my resting place forever. I will live here, for I have desired it. ¹⁵ I will abundantly bless her provision. I will satisfy her poor with bread. ¹⁶ I will also clothe her priests with salvation. Her saints will shout aloud for joy. ¹⁷ I will make the horn of David to bud there. I have ordained a lamp for my anointed. ¹⁸ I will clothe his enemies with shame, but on himself, his crown will shine."

Psalms Book 5 Chapter 133

¹ See how good and how pleasant it is for brothers to live together in unity! ² It is like the precious oil on the head, that ran down on the beard, even Aaron's beard, that came down on the edge of his robes, ³ like the dew of Hermon, that comes down on the hills of Zion; for there Yahweh gives the blessing, even life forever more.

Psalms Book 5 Chapter 134

¹ Look! Praise Yahweh, all you servants of Yahweh, who stand by night in Yahweh's house! ² Lift up your hands in the sanctuary. Praise Yahweh! ³ May Yahweh bless you from Zion, even he who made heaven and earth.

Psalms Book 5 Chapter 135

¹ Praise Yah! Praise Yahweh's name! Praise him, you servants of Yahweh, ² you who stand in Yahweh's house, in the courts of our God's house. ³ Praise Yah, for Yahweh is good. Sing praises to his name, for that is pleasant. ⁴ For Yah has chosen Jacob for himself, Israel for his own possession. ⁵ For I know that Yahweh is great, that our Lord is above all gods. ⁶ Whatever Yahweh pleased, that he has done, in heaven and in earth, in the seas and in all deeps. ⁷ He causes the clouds to rise from the ends of the earth. He makes lightnings with the rain. He brings the wind out of his treasuries. ⁸ He struck the firstborn of Egypt, both of man and animal. ⁹ He sent signs and wonders into the middle of you, Egypt, on Pharaoh, and on all his servants. ¹⁰ He struck many nations, and killed mighty kings— ¹¹ Sihon king of the Amorites, Og king of Bashan, and all the kingdoms of Canaan— ¹² and gave their land for a heritage, a heritage to Israel, his people. ¹³ Your name, Yahweh, endures forever; your renown, Yahweh, throughout all generations. ¹⁴ For Yahweh will judge his people and have compassion on his servants. ¹⁵ The idols of the nations are silver and gold, the work of men's hands. ¹⁶ They have mouths, but they can't speak. They have eyes, but they can't see. ¹⁷ They have ears, but they can't hear, neither is there any breath in their mouths. ¹⁸ Those who make them will be like them, yes, everyone who trusts in them. ¹⁹ House of Israel, praise Yahweh! House of Aaron, praise Yahweh! ²⁰ House of Levi, praise Yahweh! You who fear Yahweh, praise Yahweh! ²¹ Blessed be Yahweh from Zion, who dwells in Jerusalem. Praise Yah!

Psalms Book 5 Chapter 136

¹ Give thanks to Yahweh, for he is good, for his loving kindness endures forever. ² Give thanks to the God of gods, for his loving kindness endures forever. ³ Give thanks to the Lord of lords, for his loving kindness endures forever; ⁴ to him who alone does great wonders, for his loving kindness endures forever; ⁵ to him who by understanding made the heavens, for his loving kindness endures forever; ⁶ to him who spread out the earth above the waters, for his loving kindness endures forever; ⁷ to him who made the great lights, for his loving kindness endures forever; ⁸ the sun to rule by day, for his loving kindness endures forever; ⁹ the moon and stars to rule by night, for his loving kindness endures forever; ¹⁰ to him who struck down the Egyptian firstborn, for his loving kindness endures forever; ¹¹ and brought out Israel from among them, for his loving kindness end ures forever; ¹² with a strong hand, and with an outstretched arm, for his loving kindness endures forever; ¹³ to him who divided the Red Sea apart, for his loving kindness endures forever; ¹⁴ and made Israel to pass through the middle of it, for his loving kindness endures forever; ¹⁵ but overthrew Pharaoh and his army in the Red Sea, for his loving kindness endures forever; ¹⁶ to him who led his people through the wilderness, for his loving kindness endures forever; ¹⁷ to him who struck great kings, for his loving kindness endures forever; ¹⁸ and killed mighty kings, for his loving kindness endures forever; ¹⁹ Sihon king of the Amorites, for his loving kindness endures forever; ²⁰ Og king of Bashan, for his loving kindness endures forever; ²¹ and gave their land as an inheritance, for his loving kindness endures forever; ²² even a heritage to Israel his servant, for his loving kindness endures forever; ²³ who remembered us in our low estate, for his loving kindness endures forever; ²⁴ and has delivered us from our adversaries, for his loving kindness endures forever; ²⁵ who gives food to every creature, for his loving kindness endures forever. ²⁶ Oh give thanks to the God of heaven, for his loving kindness endures forever.

Psalms Book 5 Chapter 137

¹ By the rivers of Babylon, there we sat down. Yes, we wept, when we remembered Zion. ² On the willows in that land, we hung up our harps. ³ For there, those who led us captive asked us for songs. Those who tormented us demanded songs of joy: "Sing us one of the songs of Zion!" ⁴ How can we sing Yahweh's song in a foreign land? ⁵ If I forget you, Jerusalem, let my right hand forget its skill. ⁶ Let my tongue stick to the roof of my mouth if I don't remember you, if I don't prefer Jerusalem above my chief joy. ⁷ Remember, Yahweh, against the children of Edom in the day of Jerusalem, who said, "Raze it! Raze it even to its foundation!" ⁸ Daughter of Babylon, doomed to destruction, he will be happy who repays you, as you have done to us. ⁹ Happy shall he be, who takes and dashes your little ones against the rock.

Psalms Book 5 Chapter 138

¹ I will give you thanks with my whole heart. Before the gods, I will sing praises to you. ² I will bow down toward your holy temple, and give thanks to your name for your loving kindness and for your truth; for you have exalted your name and your word above all. ³ In the day that I called, you answered me. You encouraged me with strength in my soul. ⁴ All the kings of the earth will give you thanks, Yahweh, for they have

heard the words of your mouth. ⁵ Yes, they will sing of the ways of Yahweh, for Yahweh's glory is great! ⁶ For though Yahweh is high, yet he looks after the lowly; but he knows the proud from afar. ⁷ Though I walk in the middle of trouble, you will revive me. You will stretch out your hand against the wrath of my enemies. Your right hand will save me. ⁸ Yahweh will fulfill that which concerns me. Your loving kindness, Yahweh, endures forever. Don't forsake the works of your own hands.

Psalms Book 5 Chapter 139

¹ Yahweh, you have searched me, and you know me. ² You know my sitting down and my rising up. You perceive my thoughts from afar. ³ You search out my path and my lying down, and are acquainted with all my ways. ⁴ For there is not a word on my tongue, but behold, Yahweh, you know it altogether. ⁵ You hem me in behind and before. You laid your hand on me. ⁶ This knowledge is beyond me. It's lofty. I can't attain it. ⁷ Where could I go from your Spirit? Or where could I flee from your presence? ⁸ If I ascend up into heaven, you are there. If I make my bed in Sheol, behold, you are there! ⁹ If I take the wings of the dawn, and settle in the uttermost parts of the sea, ¹⁰ even there your hand will lead me, and your right hand will hold me. ¹¹ If I say, "Surely the darkness will overwhelm me. The light around me will be night," ¹² even the darkness doesn't hide from you, but the night shines as the day. The darkness is like light to you. ¹³ For you formed my inmost being. You knit me together in my mother's womb. ¹⁴ I will give thanks to you, for I am fearfully and wonderfully made. Your works are wonderful. My soul knows that very well. ¹⁵ My frame wasn't hidden from you, when I was made in secret, woven together in the depths of the earth. ¹⁶ Your eyes saw my body. In your book they were all written, the days that were ordained for me, when as yet there were none of them. ¹⁷ How precious to me are your thoughts, God! How vast is their sum! ¹⁸ If I would count them, they are more in number than the sand. When I wake up, I am still with you. ¹⁹ If only you, God, would kill the wicked. Get away from me, you bloodthirsty men! ²⁰ For they speak against you wickedly. Your enemies take your name in vain. ²¹ Yahweh, don't I hate those who hate you? Am I not grieved with those who rise up against you? ²² I hate them with perfect hatred. They have become my enemies. ²³ Search me, God, and know my heart. Try me, and know my thoughts. ²⁴ See if there is any wicked way in me, and lead me in the everlasting way.

Psalms Book 5 Chapter 140

¹ Deliver me, Yahweh, from evil men. Preserve me from violent men: ² those who devise mischief in their hearts. They continually gather themselves together for war. ³ They have sharpened their tongues like a serpent. Viper's poison is under their lips. Selah. ⁴ Yahweh, keep me from the hands of the wicked. Preserve me from the violent men who have determined to trip my feet. ⁵ The proud have hidden a snare for me, they have spread the cords of a net by the path. They have set traps for me. Selah. ⁶ I said to Yahweh, "You are my God." Listen to the cry of my petitions, Yahweh. ⁷ Yahweh, the Lord, the strength of my salvation, you have covered my head in the day of battle. ⁸ Yahweh, don't grant the desires of the wicked. Don't let their evil plans succeed, or they will become proud. Selah. ⁹ As for the head of those who surround me, let the mischief of their own lips cover them. ¹⁰ Let burning coals fall on them. Let them be thrown into the fire, into miry pits, from where they never rise. ¹¹ An evil speaker won't be established in the earth. Evil will hunt the violent man to overthrow him. ¹² I know that Yahweh will maintain the cause of the afflicted, and justice for the needy. ¹³ Surely the righteous will give thanks to your name. The upright will dwell in your presence.

Psalms Book 5 Chapter 141

¹ Yahweh, I have called on you. Come to me quickly! Listen to my voice when I call to you. ² Let my prayer be set before you like incense; the lifting up of my hands like the evening sacrifice. ³ Set a watch, Yahweh, before my mouth. Keep the door of my lips. ⁴ Don't incline my heart to any evil thing, to practice deeds of wickedness with men who work iniquity. Don't let me eat of their delicacies. ⁵ Let the righteous strike me, it is kindness; let him reprove me, it is like oil on the head; don't let my head refuse it; Yet my prayer is always against evil deeds. ⁶ Their judges are thrown down by the sides of the rock. They will hear my words, for they are well spoken. ⁷ "As when one plows and breaks up the earth, our bones are scattered at the mouth of Sheol." ⁸ For my eyes are on you, Yahweh, the Lord. I take refuge in you. Don't leave my soul destitute. ⁹ Keep me from the snare which they have laid for me, from the traps of the workers of iniquity. ¹⁰ Let the wicked fall together into their own nets while I pass by.

Psalms Book 5 Chapter 142

¹ I cry with my voice to Yahweh. With my voice, I ask Yahweh for mercy. ² I pour out my complaint before him. I tell him my troubles. ³ When my spirit was overwhelmed within me, you knew my route. On the path in which I walk, they have hidden a snare for me. ⁴ Look on my right, and see; for there is no one who is concerned for me. Refuge has fled from me. No one cares for my soul. ⁵ I cried to you, Yahweh. I said, "You are my refuge, my portion in the land of the living." ⁶ Listen to my cry, for I am in desperate need. Deliver me from my persecutors, for they are too strong for me. ⁷ Bring my soul out of prison, that I may give thanks to your name. The righteous will surround me, for you will be good to me.

Psalms Book 5 Chapter 143

¹ Hear my prayer, Yahweh. Listen to my petitions. In your faithfulness and righteousness, relieve me. ² Don't enter into judgment with your servant, for in your sight no man living is righteous. ³ For the enemy pursues my soul. He has struck my life down to the ground. He has made me live in dark places, as those who have been long dead. ⁴ Therefore my spirit is overwhelmed within me. My heart within me is desolate. ⁵ I remember the days of old. I meditate on all your doings. I contemplate the work of your hands. ⁶ I spread out my hands to you. My soul thirsts for you, like a parched land. Selah. ⁷ Hurry to answer me, Yahweh. My spirit fails. Don't hide your face from me, so that I don't become like those who go down into the pit. ⁸ Cause me to hear your loving kindness in the morning, for I trust in you. Cause me to know the way in which I should walk, for I lift up my soul to you. ⁹ Deliver me, Yahweh, from my enemies. I flee to you to hide me. ¹⁰ Teach me to do your will, for you are my God. Your Spirit is good. Lead me in the land of uprightness. ¹¹ Revive me, Yahweh, for your name's sake. In your righteousness, bring my soul out of trouble. ¹² In your loving kindness, cut off my enemies, and destroy all those who afflict my soul, for I am your servant.

Psalms Book 5 Chapter 144

¹ Blessed be Yahweh, my rock, who trains my hands to war, and my fingers to battle— ² my loving kindness, my fortress, my high tower, my deliverer, my shield, and he in whom I take refuge, who subdues my people under me. ³ Yahweh, what is man, that you care for him? Or the son of man, that you think of him? ⁴ Man is like a breath. His days are like a shadow that passes away. ⁵ Part your heavens, Yahweh, and come down. Touch the mountains, and they will smoke. ⁶ Throw out lightning, and scatter them. Send out your arrows, and rout them. ⁷ Stretch out your hand from above, rescue me, and deliver me out of great waters, out of the hands of foreigners, ⁸ whose mouths speak deceit, whose right hand is a right hand of falsehood. ⁹ I will sing a new song to you, God. On a ten-stringed lyre, I will sing praises to you. ¹⁰ You are he who gives salvation to kings, who rescues David, his servant, from the deadly sword. ¹¹ Rescue me, and deliver me out of the hands of foreigners, whose mouths speak deceit, whose right hand is a right hand of falsehood. ¹² Then our sons will be like well-nurtured plants, our daughters like pillars carved to adorn a palace. ¹³ Our barns are full, filled with all kinds of provision. Our sheep produce thousands and tens thousands in our fields. ¹⁴ Our oxen will pull heavy loads. There is no breaking in, and no going away, and no outcry in our streets. ¹⁵ Happy are the people who are in such a situation. Happy are the people whose God is Yahweh.

Psalms Book 5 Chapter 145

¹ I will exalt you, my God, the King. I will praise your name forever and ever. ² Every day I will praise you. I will extol your name forever and ever. ³ Great is Yahweh, and greatly to be praised! His greatness is unsearchable. ⁴ One generation will commend your works to another, and will declare your mighty acts. ⁵ I will meditate on the glorious majesty of your honor, on your wondrous works. ⁶ Men will speak of the might of your awesome acts. I will declare your greatness. ⁷ They will utter the memory of your great goodness, and will sing of your righteousness. ⁸ Yahweh is gracious, merciful, slow to anger, and of great loving kindness. ⁹ Yahweh is good to all. His tender mercies are over all his works. ¹⁰ All your works will give thanks to you, Yahweh. Your saints will extol you. ¹¹ They will speak of the glory of your kingdom, and talk about your power, ¹² to make known to the sons of men his mighty acts, the glory of the majesty of his kingdom. ¹³ Your kingdom is an everlasting kingdom. Your dominion endures throughout all generations. Yahweh is faithful in all his words, and loving in all his deeds. ¹⁴ Yahweh upholds all who fall, and raises up all those who are bowed down. ¹⁵ The eyes of all wait for you. You give them their food in due season. ¹⁶ You open your hand, and satisfy the desire of every living thing. ¹⁷ Yahweh is righteous in all his ways, and gracious in all his works. ¹⁸ Yahweh is near to all those who call on him, to all who call on him in truth. ¹⁹ He will fulfill the desire of those who fear him. He also will hear their cry, and will save them. ²⁰ Yahweh preserves all those who love him, but he will destroy all the wicked. ²¹ My mouth will speak the praise of Yahweh. Let all flesh bless his holy

name forever and ever.

Psalms Book 5 Chapter 146

¹ Praise Yah! Praise Yahweh, my soul. ² While I live, I will praise Yahweh. I will sing praises to my God as long as I exist. ³ Don't put your trust in princes, in a son of man in whom there is no help. ⁴ His spirit departs, and he returns to the earth. In that very day, his thoughts perish. ⁵ Happy is he who has the God of Jacob for his help, whose hope is in Yahweh, his God, ⁶ who made heaven and earth, the sea, and all that is in them; who keeps truth forever; ⁷ who executes justice for the oppressed; who gives food to the hungry. Yahweh frees the prisoners. ⁸ Yahweh opens the eyes of the blind. Yahweh raises up those who are bowed down. Yahweh loves the righteous. ⁹ Yahweh preserves the foreigners. He upholds the fatherless and widow, but he turns the way of the wicked upside down. ¹⁰ Yahweh will reign forever; your God, O Zion, to all generations. Praise Yah!

Psalms Book 5 Chapter 147

¹ Praise Yah, for it is good to sing praises to our God; for it is pleasant and fitting to praise him. ² Yahweh builds up Jerusalem. He gathers together the outcasts of Israel. ³ He heals the broken in heart, and binds up their wounds. ⁴ He counts the number of the stars. He calls them all by their names. ⁵ Great is our Lord, and mighty in power. His understanding is infinite. ⁶ Yahweh upholds the humble. He brings the wicked down to the ground. ⁷ Sing to Yahweh with thanksgiving. Sing praises on the harp to our God, ⁸ who covers the sky with clouds, who prepares rain for the earth, who makes grass grow on the mountains. ⁹ He provides food for the livestock, and for the young ravens when they call. ¹⁰ He doesn't delight in the strength of the horse. He takes no pleasure in the legs of a man. ¹¹ Yahweh takes pleasure in those who fear him, in those who hope in his loving kindness. ¹² Praise Yahweh, Jerusalem! Praise your God, Zion! ¹³ For he has strengthened the bars of your gates. He has blessed your children within you. ¹⁴ He makes peace in your borders. He fills you with the finest of the wheat. ¹⁵ He sends out his commandment to the earth. His word runs very swiftly. ¹⁶ He gives snow like wool, and scatters frost like ashes. ¹⁷ He hurls down his hail like pebbles. Who can stand before his cold? ¹⁸ He sends out his word, and melts them. He causes his wind to blow, and the waters flow. ¹⁹ He shows his word to Jacob, his statutes and his ordinances to Israel. ²⁰ He has not done this for just any nation. They don't know his ordinances. Praise Yah!

Psalms Book 5 Chapter 148

¹ Praise Yah! Praise Yahweh from the heavens! Praise him in the heights! ² Praise him, all his angels! Praise him, all his army! ³ Praise him, sun and moon! Praise him, all you shining stars! ⁴ Praise him, you heavens of heavens, you waters that are above the heavens. ⁵ Let them praise Yahweh's name, for he commanded, and they were created. ⁶ He has also established them forever and ever. He has made a decree which will not pass away. ⁷ Praise Yahweh from the earth, you great sea creatures, and all depths, ⁸ lightning and hail, snow and clouds, stormy wind, fulfilling his word, ⁹ mountains and all hills, fruit trees and all cedars, ¹⁰ wild animals and all livestock, small creatures and flying birds, ¹¹ kings of the earth and all peoples, princes and all judges of the earth, ¹² both young men and maidens, old men and children. ¹³ Let them praise Yahweh's name, for his name alone is exalted. His glory is above the earth and the heavens. ¹⁴ He has lifted up the horn of his people, the praise of all his saints, even of the children of Israel, a people near to him. Praise Yah!

Psalms Book 5 Chapter 149

¹ Praise Yahweh! Sing to Yahweh a new song, his praise in the assembly of the saints. ² Let Israel rejoice in him who made them. Let the children of Zion be joyful in their King. ³ Let them praise his name in the dance! Let them sing praises to him with tambourine and harp! ⁴ For Yahweh takes pleasure in his people. He crowns the humble with salvation. ⁵ Let the saints rejoice in honor. Let them sing for joy on their beds. ⁶ May the high praises of God be in their mouths, and a two-edged sword in their hand, ⁷ to execute vengeance on the nations, and punishments on the peoples; ⁸ to bind their kings with chains, and their nobles with fetters of iron; ⁹ to execute on them the written judgment. All his saints have this honor. Praise Yah!

Psalms Book 5 Chapter 150

¹ Praise Yah! Praise God in his sanctuary! Praise him in his heavens for his acts of power! ² Praise him for his mighty acts! Praise him according to his excellent greatness! ³ Praise him with the sounding of the trumpet! Praise him with harp and lyre! ⁴ Praise him with tambourine and dancing! Praise him with stringed instruments and flute! ⁵ Praise him with loud cymbals! Praise him with resounding cymbals! ⁶ Let everything that has breath praise Yah! Praise Yah!

Psalm 151

Psalm 151

This Psalm is a genuine one of David, though extra, composed when he fought in single combat with Goliath. ¹ I was small among my brothers, and youngest in my father's house. I tended my father's sheep. ² My hands formed a musical instrument, and my fingers tuned a lyre. ³ Who shall tell my Lord? The Lord himself, he himself hears. ⁴ He sent forth his angel and took me from my father's sheep, and he anointed me with his anointing oil. ⁵ My brothers were handsome and tall; but the Lord didn't take pleasure in them. ⁶ I went out to meet the Philistine, and he cursed me by his idols. ⁷ But I drew his own sword and beheaded him, and removed reproach from the children of Israel.

Proverbs

Proverbs Chapter 1

¹ The Proverbs of Solomon, the son of David, king of Israel: ² That men may appreciate wisdom and discipline, may understand words of intelligence; ³ May receive training in wise conduct, in what is right, just and honest; ⁴ That resourcefulness may be imparted to the simple, to the young man knowledge and discretion. ⁵ A wise man by hearing them will advance in learning, an intelligent man will gain sound guidance, ⁶ That he may comprehend proverb and parable, the words of the wise and their riddles. ⁷ The fear of the LORD is the beginning of knowledge; wisdom and instruction fools despise. ⁸ Hear, my son, your father's instruction, and reject not your mother's teaching; ⁹ A graceful diadem will they be for your head; a torque for your neck. ¹⁰ My son, should sinners entice you, ¹¹ and say, "Come along with us! Let us lie in wait for the honest man, let us, unprovoked, set a trap for the innocent; ¹² Let us swallow them up, as the nether world does, alive, in the prime of life, like those who go down to the pit! ¹³ All kinds of precious wealth shall we gain, we shall fill our houses with booty; ¹⁴ Cast in your lot with us, we shall all have one purse!" ¹⁵ My son, walk not in the way with them, hold back your foot from their path! ¹⁶ (For their feet run to evil, they hasten to shed blood.) ¹⁷ It is in vain that a net is spread before the eyes of any bird - ¹⁸ These men lie in wait for their own blood, they set a trap for their own lives. ¹⁹ This is the fate of everyone greedy of loot: unlawful gain takes away the life of him who acquires it. ²⁰ Wisdom cries aloud in the street, in the open squares she raises her voice; ²¹ Down the crowded ways she calls out, at the city gates she utters her words: ²² "How long, you simple ones, will you love inanity, ²³ how long will you turn away at my reproof? Lo! I will pour out to you my spirit, I will acquaint you with my words. ²⁴ "Because I called and you refused, I extended my hand and no one took notice; ²⁵ Because you disdained all my counsel, and my reproof you ignored - ²⁶ I, in my turn, will laugh at your doom; I will mock when terror overtakes you; ²⁷ When terror comes upon you like a storm, and your doom approaches like a whirlwind; when distress and anguish befall you. ²⁸ "Then they call me, but I answer not; they seek me, but find me not; ²⁹ Because they hated knowledge, and chose not the fear of the LORD; ³⁰ They ignored my counsel, they spurned all my reproof; And in their arrogance they preferred arrogance, and like fools they hated knowledge: ³¹ "Now they must eat the fruit of their own way, and with their own devices be glutted. ³² For the self-will of the simple kills them, the smugness of fools destroys them. ³³ But he who obeys me dwells in security, in peace, without fear of harm."

Proverbs Chapter 2

¹ My son, if you receive my words and treasure my commands, ² Turning your ear to wisdom, inclining your heart to understanding; ³ Yes, if you call to intelligence, and to understanding raise your voice; ⁴ If you seek her like silver, and like hidden treasures search her out; ⁵ Then will you understand the fear of the LORD; the knowledge of God you will find; ⁶ For the LORD gives wisdom, from his mouth come knowledge and understanding; ⁷ He has counsel in store for the upright, he is the shield of those who walk honestly, ⁸ Guarding the paths of justice, protecting the way of his pious ones. ⁹ Then you will understand rectitude and justice, honesty, every good path; ¹⁰ For wisdom will enter your heart, knowledge will please your soul, ¹¹ Discretion will watch over you, understanding will guard you; ¹² Saving you from the way of evil men, from men of perverse speech, ¹³ Who leave the straight paths to walk in the way of darkness, ¹⁴ Who delight in doing evil, rejoice in perversity; ¹⁵ Whose ways are crooked, and devious their paths; ¹⁶ Saving you from the wife of another, from the adulteress with her smooth words, ¹⁷ Who forsakes the companion of her youth and forgets the pact with her God; ¹⁸ For her path sinks down to death, and her footsteps lead to the shades; ¹⁹ None who enter thereon come back again, or gain the paths of life. ²⁰ Thus you may walk

in the way of good men, and keep to the paths of the just. ²¹ For the upright will dwell in the land, the honest will remain in it; ²² But the wicked will be cut off from the land, the faithless will be rooted out of it.

Proverbs Chapter 3

¹ My son, forget not my teaching, keep in mind my commands; ² For many days, and years of life, and peace, will they bring you. ³ Let not kindness and fidelity leave you; bind them around your neck; ⁴ Then will you win favor and good esteem before God and man. ⁵ Trust in the LORD with all your heart, on your own intelligence rely not; ⁶ In all your ways be mindful of him, and he will make straight your paths. ⁷ Be not wise in your own eyes, fear the LORD and turn away from evil; ⁸ This will mean health for your flesh and vigor for your bones. ⁹ Honor the LORD with your wealth, with first fruits of all your produce; ¹⁰ Then will your barns be filled with grain, with new wine your vats will overflow. ¹¹ The discipline of the LORD, my son, disdain not; spurn not his reproof; ¹² For whom the LORD loves he reproves, and he chastises the son he favors. ¹³ Happy the man who finds wisdom, the man who gains understanding! ¹⁴ For her profit is better than profit in silver, and better than gold is her revenue; ¹⁵ She is more precious than corals, and none of your choice possessions can compare with her. ¹⁶ Long life is in her right hand, in her left are riches and honor; ¹⁷ Her ways are pleasant ways, and all her paths are peace; ¹⁸ She is a tree of life to those who grasp her, and he is happy who holds her fast. ¹⁹ The LORD by wisdom founded the earth, established the heavens by understanding; ²⁰ By his knowledge the depths break open, and the clouds drop down dew. ²¹ My son, let not these slip out of your sight: keep advice and counsel in view; ²² So will they be life to your soul, and an adornment for your neck. ²³ Then you may securely go your way; your foot will never stumble; ²⁴ When you lie down, you need not be afraid, when you rest, your sleep will be sweet. ²⁵ Be not afraid of sudden terror, of the ruin of the wicked when it comes; ²⁶ For the LORD will be your confidence, and will keep your foot from the snare. ²⁷ Refuse no one the good on which he has a claim when it is in your power to do it for him. ²⁸ Say not to your neighbor, "Go, and come again, tomorrow I will give," when you can give at once. ²⁹ Plot no evil against your neighbor, against him who lives at peace with you. ³⁰ Quarrel not with a man without cause, with one who has done you no harm. ³¹ Envy not the lawless man and choose none of his ways; ³² To the LORD the perverse man is an abomination, but with the upright is his friendship. ³³ The curse of the LORD is on the house of the wicked, but the dwelling of the just he blesses; ³⁴ When he is dealing with the arrogant, he is stern, but to the humble he shows kindness. ³⁵ Honor is the possession of wise men, but fools inherit shame.

Proverbs Chapter 4

¹ Hear, O children, a father's instruction, be attentive, that you may gain understanding! ² Yes, excellent advice I give you; my teaching do not forsake. ³ When I was my father's child, frail, yet the darling of my mother, ⁴ He taught me, and said to me: "Let your heart hold fast my words: keep my commands, that you may live! ⁵ Get wisdom, get understanding! Do not forget or turn aside from the words I utter. ⁶ Forsake her not, and she will preserve you; love her, and she will safeguard you; ⁷ The beginning of wisdom is: get wisdom; at the cost of all you have, get understanding. ⁸ Extol her, and she will exalt you; she will bring you honors if you embrace her; ⁹ She will put on your head a graceful diadem; a glorious crown will she bestow on you." ¹⁰ Hear, my son, and receive my words, and the years of your life shall be many. ¹¹ On the way of wisdom I direct you, I lead you on straightforward paths. ¹² When you walk, your step will not be impeded, and should you run, you will not stumble. ¹³ Hold fast to instruction, never let her go; keep her, for she is your life. ¹⁴ The path of the wicked enter not, walk not on the way of evil men; ¹⁵ Shun it, cross it not, turn aside from it, and pass on. ¹⁶ For they cannot rest unless they have done evil; to have made no one stumble steals away their sleep. ¹⁷ For they eat the bread of wickedness and drink the wine of violence. ¹⁸ But the path of the just is like shining light, that grows in brilliance till perfect day. ¹⁹ The way of the wicked is like darkness; they know not on what they stumble. ²⁰ My son, to my words be attentive, to my sayings incline your ear; ²¹ Let them not slip out of your sight, keep them within your heart; ²² For they are life to those who find them, to man's whole being they are health. ²³ With closest custody, guard your heart, for in it are the sources of life. ²⁴ Put away from you dishonest talk, deceitful speech put far from you. ²⁵ Let your eyes look straight ahead and your glance be directly forward. ²⁶ Survey the path for your feet, and let all your ways be sure. ²⁷ Turn neither to right nor to left, keep your foot far from evil.

Proverbs Chapter 5

¹ My son, to my wisdom be attentive, to my knowledge incline your ear,

² That discretion may watch over you, and understanding may guard you. ³ The lips of an adulteress drip with honey, and her mouth is smoother than oil; ⁴ But in the end she is as bitter as wormwood, as sharp as a two-edged sword. ⁵ Her feet go down to death, to the nether world her steps attain; ⁶ Lest you see before you the road to life, her paths will ramble, you know not where. ⁷ So now, O children, listen to me, go not astray from the words of my mouth. ⁸ Keep your way far from her, approach not the door of her house, ⁹ Lest you give your honor to others, and your years to a merciless one; ¹⁰ Lest strangers have their fill of your wealth, your hard-won earnings go to an alien's house; ¹¹ And you groan in the end, when your flesh and your body are consumed; ¹² And you say, "Oh, why did I hate instruction, and my heart spurn reproof! ¹³ Why did I not listen to the voice of my teachers, nor to my instructors incline my ear! ¹⁴ I have all but come to utter ruin, condemned by the public assembly!" ¹⁵ Drink water from your own cistern, running water from your own well. ¹⁶ How may your water sources be dispersed abroad, streams of water in the streets? ¹⁷ Let your fountain be yours alone, not one shared with strangers; ¹⁸ And have joy of the wife of your youth, ¹⁹ your lovely hind, your graceful doe. Her love will invigorate you always, through her love you will flourish continually, ²⁰ Why then, my son, should you go astray for another's wife and accept the embraces of an adulteress? ²¹ For each man's ways are plain to the LORD'S sight; all their paths he surveys; ²² By his own iniquities the wicked man will be caught, in the meshes of his own sin he will be held fast; ²³ He will die from lack of discipline, through the greatness of his folly he will be lost.

Proverbs Chapter 6

¹ My son, if you have become surety to your neighbor, given your hand in pledge to another, ² You have been snared by the utterance of your lips, caught by the words of your mouth; ³ So do this, my son, to free yourself, since you have fallen into your neighbor's power: Go, hurry, stir up your neighbor! ⁴ Give no sleep to your eyes, nor slumber to your eyelids; ⁵ Free yourself as a gazelle from the snare, or as a bird from the hand of the fowler. ⁶ Go to the ant, O sluggard, study her ways and learn wisdom; ⁷ For though she has no chief, no commander or ruler, ⁸ She procures her food in the summer, stores up her provisions in the harvest. ⁹ How long, O sluggard, will you rest? when will you rise from your sleep? ¹⁰ A little sleep, a little slumber, a little folding of the arms to rest— ¹¹ Then will poverty come upon you like a highwayman, and want like an armed man. ¹² A scoundrel, a villain, is he who deals in crooked talk. ¹³ He winks his eyes, shuffles his feet, makes signs with his fingers; ¹⁴ He has perversity in his heart, is always plotting evil, sows discord. ¹⁵ Therefore suddenly ruin comes upon him; in an instant he is crushed beyond cure. ¹⁶ There are six things the LORD hates, yes, seven are an abomination to him; ¹⁷ Haughty eyes, a lying tongue, and hands that shed innocent blood; ¹⁸ A heart that plots wicked schemes, feet that run swiftly to evil, ¹⁹ The false witness who utters lies, and he who sows discord among brothers. ²⁰ Observe, my son, your father's bidding, and reject not your mother's teaching; ²¹ Keep them fastened over your heart always, put them around your neck; ²² When you walk, they will guide you; when you lie down, they will watch over you; when you wake, they will converse with you. ²³ For the bidding is a lamp, and the teaching a light, and a way to life are the reproofs of discipline; ²⁴ To keep you from your neighbor's wife, from the smooth tongue of the adulteress. ²⁵ Lust not in your heart after her beauty, let her not captivate you with her glance! ²⁶ For the price of a loose woman may be scarcely a loaf of bread, But if she is married, she is a trap for your precious life. ²⁷ Can a man take fire to his bosom, and his garments not be burned? ²⁸ Or can a man walk on live coals, and his feet not be scorched? ²⁹ So with him who goes in to his neighbor's wife—none who touches her shall go unpunished. ³⁰ Men despise not the thief if he steals to satisfy his appetite when he is hungry; ³¹ Yet if he be caught he must pay back sevenfold; all the wealth of his house he may yield up. ³² But he who commits adultery is a fool; he who would destroy himself does it. ³³ A degrading beating will he get, and his disgrace will not be wiped away; ³⁴ For vindictive is the husband's wrath, he will have no pity on the day of vengeance; ³⁵ He will not consider any restitution, nor be satisfied with the greatest gifts.

Proverbs Chapter 7

¹ My son, keep my words, and treasure my commands. ² Keep my commands and live, my teaching as the apple of your eye; ³ Bind them on your fingers, write them on the tablet of your heart. ⁴ Say to Wisdom, "You are my sister!" call Understanding, "Friend!" ⁵ That they may keep you from another's wife, from the adulteress with her smooth words. ⁶ For at the window of my house, through my lattice I looked out— ⁷ And I saw among the simple ones, I observed among the young men, a youth with no sense, ⁸ Going along the street near the corner, then walking in

the direction of her house— 9 In the twilight, at dusk of day, at the time of the dark of night. 10 And lo! the woman comes to meet him, robed like a harlot, with secret designs— 11 She is fickle and unruly, in her home her feet cannot rest; 12 Now she is in the streets, now in the open squares, and at every corner she lurks in ambush 13 When she seizes him, she kisses him, and with an impudent look says to him: 14 "I owed peace offerings, and today I have fulfilled my vows; 15 So I came out to meet you, to look for you, and I have found you! 16 With coverlets I have spread my couch, with brocaded cloths of Egyptian linen; 17 I have sprinkled my bed with myrrh, with aloes, and with cinnamon. 18 "Come, let us drink our fill of love, until morning, let us feast on love! 19 For my husband is not at home, he has gone on a long journey; 20 A bag of money he took with him, not till the full moon will he return home." 21 She wins him over by her repeated urging, with her smooth lips she leads him astray; 22 He follows her stupidly, like an ox that is led to slaughter; Like a stag that minces toward the net, 23 till an arrow pierces its liver; Like a bird that rushes into a snare, unaware that its life is at stake. 24 So now, O children, listen to me, be attentive to the words of my mouth! 25 Let not your heart turn to her ways, go not astray in her paths; 26 For many are those she has struck down dead, numerous, those she has slain. 27 Her house is made up of ways to the nether world, leading down into the chambers of death.

Proverbs Chapter 8

1 Does not Wisdom call, and Understanding raise her voice? 2 On the top of the heights along the road, at the crossroads she takes her stand; 3 By the gates at the approaches of the city, in the entryways she cries aloud: 4 "To you, O men, I call; my appeal is to the children of men. 5 You simple ones, gain resource, you fools, gain sense. 6 Give heed! for noble things I speak; honesty opens my lips. 7 Yes, the truth my mouth recounts, but wickedness my lips abhor. 8 Sincere are all the words of my mouth, no one of them is wily or crooked; 9 All of them are plain to the man of intelligence, and right to those who attain knowledge. 10 Receive my instruction in preference to silver, and knowledge rather than choice gold. 11 (For Wisdom is better than corals, and no choice possessions can compare with her.) 12 I, Wisdom, dwell with experience, and judicious knowledge I attain. 13 (The fear of the LORD is to hate evil;) Pride, arrogance, the evil way, and the perverse mouth I hate. 14 Mine are counsel and advice; Mine is strength; I am understanding. 15 By me kings reign, and lawgivers establish justice; 16 By me princes govern, and nobles; all the rulers of earth. 17 Those who love me I also love, and those who seek me find me. 18 With me are riches and honor, enduring wealth and prosperity. 19 My fruit is better than gold, yes, than pure gold, and my revenue than choice silver. 20 On the way of duty I walk, along the paths of justice, 21 Granting wealth to those who love me, and filling their treasuries. 22 The LORD begot me, the first-born of his ways, the forerunner of his prodigies of long ago; 23 From of old I was poured forth, at the first, before the earth. 24 When there were no depths I was brought forth, when there were no fountains or springs of water; 25 Before the mountains were settled into place, before the hills, I was brought forth; 26 While as yet the earth and the fields were not made, nor the first clods of the world. 27 When he established the heavens I was there, when he marked out the vault over the face of the deep; 28 When he made firm the skies above, when he fixed fast the foundations of the earth; 29 When he set for the sea its limit, so that the waters should not transgress his command; 30 Then was I beside him as his craftsman, and I was his delight day by day, Playing before him all the while, 31 playing on the surface of his earth; and I found delight in the sons of men. 32 So now, O children, listen to me; 33 instruction and wisdom do not reject! Happy the man who obeys me, and happy those who keep my ways, 34 Happy the man watching daily at my gates, waiting at my doorposts; 35 For he who finds me finds life, and wins favor from the LORD; 36 But he who misses me harms himself; all who hate me love death."

Proverbs Chapter 9

1 Wisdom has built her house, she has set up her seven columns; 2 She has dressed her meat, mixed her wine, yes, she has spread her table. 3 She has sent out her maidens; she calls from the heights out over the city: 4 "Let whoever is simple turn in here; to him who lacks understanding, I say, 5 Come, eat of my food, and drink of the wine I have mixed! 6 Forsake foolishness that you may live; advance in the way of understanding. 11 For by me your days will be multiplied and the years of your life increased." 7 He who corrects an arrogant man earns insult; and he who reproves a wicked man incurs opprobrium. 8 Reprove not an arrogant man, lest he hate you; reprove a wise man, and he will love you. 9 Instruct a wise man, and he becomes still wiser; teach a just man, and he advances in learning. 10 The beginning of wisdom is

the fear of the LORD, and knowledge of the Holy One is understanding. 12 If you are wise, it is to your own advantage; and if you are arrogant, you alone shall bear it. 13 The woman Folly is fickle, she is inane, and knows nothing. 14 She sits at the door of her house upon a seat on the city heights, 15 Calling to passers-by as they go on their straight way: 16 "Let whoever is simple turn in here, or who lacks understanding; for to him I say, 17 Stolen water is sweet, and bread gotten secretly is pleasing!" 18 Little he knows that the shades are there, that in the depths of the nether world are her guests!

Proverbs Chapter 10

1 The Proverbs of Solomon: A wise son makes his father glad, but a foolish son is a grief to his mother. 2 Ill-gotten treasures profit nothing, but virtue saves from death. 3 The LORD permits not the just to hunger, but the craving of the wicked he thwarts. 4 The slack hand impoverishes, but the hand of the diligent enriches. 5 A son who fills the granaries in summer is a credit; a son who slumbers during harvest, a disgrace. 6 Blessings are for the head of the just, but a rod for the back of the fool. 7 The memory of the just will be blessed, but the name of the wicked will rot. 8 A wise man heeds commands, but a prating fool will be overthrown. 9 He who walks honestly walks securely, but he whose ways are crooked will fare badly. 10 He who winks at a fault causes trouble, but he who frankly reproves promotes peace. 11 A fountain of life is the mouth of the just, but the mouth of the wicked conceals violence. 12 Hatred stirs up disputes, but love covers all offenses. 13 On the lips of the intelligent is found wisdom, but the mouth of the wicked conceals violence. 14 Wise men store up knowledge, but the mouth of a fool is imminent ruin. 15 The rich man's wealth is his strong city; the ruination of the lowly is their poverty. 16 The just man's recompense leads to life, the gains of the wicked, to sin. 17 A path to life is his who heeds admonition, but he who disregards reproof goes astray. 18 It is the lips of the liar that conceal hostility; but he who spreads accusations is a fool. 19 Where words are many, sin is not wanting; but he who restrains his lips does well. 20 Like choice silver is the just man's tongue; the heart of the wicked is of little worth. 21 The just man's lips nourish many, but fools die for want of sense. 22 It is the LORD'S blessing that brings wealth, and no effort can substitute for it. 23 Crime is the entertainment of the fool; so is wisdom for the man of sense. 24 What the wicked man fears will befall him, but the desire of the just will be granted. 25 When the tempest passes, the wicked man is no more; but the just man is established forever. 26 As vinegar to the teeth, and smoke to the eyes, is the sluggard to those who use him as a messenger. 27 The fear of the LORD prolongs life, but the years of the wicked are brief. 28 The hope of the just brings them joy, but the expectation of the wicked comes to nought. 29 The LORD is a stronghold to him who walks honestly, but to evildoers, their downfall. 30 The just man will never be disturbed, but the wicked will not abide in the land. 31 The mouth of the just yields wisdom, but the perverse tongue will be cut off. 32 The lips of the just know how to please, but the mouth of the wicked, how to pervert.

Proverbs Chapter 11

1 False scales are an abomination to the LORD, but a full weight is his delight. 2 When pride comes, disgrace comes; but with the humble is wisdom. 3 The honesty of the upright guides them; the faithless are ruined by their duplicity. 4 Wealth is useless on the day of wrath, but virtue saves from death. 5 The honest man's virtue makes his way straight, but by his wickedness the wicked man falls. 6 The virtue of the upright saves them, but the faithless are caught in their own intrigue. 7 When a wicked man dies his hope perishes, and what is expected from strength comes to nought. 8 The just man escapes trouble, and the wicked man falls into it in his stead. 9 With his mouth the impious man would ruin his neighbor, but through their knowledge the just make their escape. 10 When the just prosper, the city rejoices; and when the wicked perish, there is jubilation. 11 Through the blessing of the righteous the city is exalted, but through the mouth of the wicked it is overthrown. 12 He who reviles his neighbor has no sense, but the intelligent man keeps silent. 13 A newsmonger reveals secrets, but a trustworthy man keeps a confidence. 14 For lack of guidance a people falls; security lies in many counselors. 15 He is in a bad way who becomes surety for another, but he who hates giving pledges is safe. 16 A gracious woman wins esteem, but she who hates virtue is covered with shame. The slothful become impoverished, but the diligent gain wealth. 17 A kindly man benefits himself, but a merciless man harms himself. 18 The wicked man makes empty profits, but he who sows virtue has a sure reward. 19 Virtue directs toward life, but he who pursues evil does so to his death. 20 The depraved in heart are an abomination to the LORD, but those who walk blamelessly are his delight. 21 Truly the evil man shall not go unpunished, but those who

are just shall escape. 22 Like a golden ring in a swine's snout is a beautiful woman with a rebellious disposition. 23 The desire of the just ends only in good; the expectation of the wicked is wrath. 24 One man is lavish yet grows still richer; another is too sparing, yet is the poorer. 25 He who confers benefits will be amply enriched, and he who refreshes others will himself be refreshed. 26 Him who monopolizes grain, the people curse, but blessings upon the head of him who distributes it! 27 He who seeks the good commands favor, but he who pursues evil will have evil befall him. 28 He who trusts in his riches will fall, but like green leaves the just flourish. 29 He who upsets his household has empty air for a heritage; and the fool will become slave to the wise man. 30 The fruit of virtue is a tree of life, but violence takes lives away. 31 If the just man is punished on earth, how much more the wicked and the sinner!

Proverbs Chapter 12

1 He who loves correction loves knowledge, but he who hates reproof is stupid. 2 The good man wins favor from the LORD, but the schemer is condemned by him. 3 No man is built up by wickedness, but the root of the just will never be disturbed. 4 A worthy wife is the crown of her husband, but a disgraceful one is like rot in his bones. 5 The plans of the just are legitimate; the designs of the wicked are deceitful. 6 The words of the wicked are a deadly ambush, but the speech of the upright saves them. 7 The wicked are overthrown and are no more, but the house of the just stands firm. 8 According to his good sense a man is praised, but one with a warped mind is despised. 9 Better a lowly man who supports himself than one of assumed importance who lacks bread. 10 The just man takes care of his beast, but the heart of the wicked is merciless. 11 He who tills his own land has food in plenty, but he who follows idle pursuits is a fool. 12 The stronghold of evil men will be demolished, but the root of the just is enduring. 13 In the sin of his lips the evil man is ensnared, but the just comes free of trouble. 14 From the fruit of his words a man has his fill of good things, and the work of his hands comes back to reward him. 15 The way of the fool seems right in his own eyes, but he who listens to advice is wise. 16 The fool immediately shows his anger, but the shrewd man passes over an insult. 17 He tells the truth who states what he is sure of, but a lying witness speaks deceitfully. 18 The prating of some men is like sword thrusts, but the tongue of the wise is healing. 19 Truthful lips endure forever, the lying tongue, for only a moment. 20 Deceit is in the hands of those who plot evil, but those who counsel peace have joy. 21 No harm befalls the just, but the wicked are overwhelmed with misfortune. 22 Lying lips are an abomination to the LORD, but those who are truthful are his delight. 23 A shrewd man conceals his knowledge, but the hearts of fools gush forth folly. 24 The diligent hand will govern, but the slothful will be enslaved. 25 Anxiety in a man's heart depresses it, but a kindly word makes it glad. 26 The just man surpasses his neighbor, but the way of the wicked leads them astray. 27 The slothful man catches not his prey, but the wealth of the diligent man is great. 28 In the path of justice there is life, but the abominable way leads to death.

Proverbs Chapter 13

1 A wise son loves correction, but the senseless one heeds no rebuke. 2 From the fruit of his words a man eats good things, but the treacherous one craves violence. 3 He who guards his mouth protects his life; to open wide one's lips brings downfall. 4 The soul of the sluggard craves in vain, but the diligent soul is amply satisfied. 5 Anything deceitful the just man hates, but the wicked brings shame and disgrace. 6 Virtue guards one who walks honestly, but the downfall of the wicked is sin. 7 One man pretends to be rich, yet has nothing; another pretends to be poor, yet has great wealth. 8 A man's riches serve as ransom for his life, but the poor man heeds no rebuke. 9 The light of the just shines gaily, but the lamp of the wicked goes out. 10 The stupid man sows discord by his insolence, but with those who take counsel is wisdom. 11 Wealth quickly gotten dwindles away, but amassed little by little, it grows. 12 Hope deferred makes the heart sick, but a wish fulfilled is a tree of life. 13 He who despises the word must pay for it, but he who reveres the commandment will be rewarded. 14 The teaching of the wise is a fountain of life, that a man may avoid the snares of death. 15 Good sense brings favor, but the way of the faithless is their ruin. 16 The shrewd man does everything with prudence, but the fool peddles folly. 17 A wicked messenger brings on disaster, but a trustworthy envoy is a healing remedy. 18 Poverty and shame befall the man who disregards correction, but he who heeds reproof is honored. 19 Lust indulged starves the soul, but fools hate to turn from evil. 20 Walk with wise men and you will become wise, but the companion of fools will fare badly. 21 Misfortune pursues sinners, but the just shall be recompensed with good. 22 The good man leaves an inheritance to his children's children, but the wealth of the sinner is stored up for the just. 23 A lawsuit devours the tillage of the poor, but some men perish for lack of a law court. 24 He who spares his rod hates his son, but he who loves him takes care to chastise him. 25 When the just man eats, his hunger is appeased; but the belly of the wicked suffers want.

Proverbs Chapter 14

1 Wisdom builds her house, but Folly tears hers down with her own hands. 2 He who walks uprightly fears the LORD, but he who is devious in his ways spurns him. 3 In the mouth of the fool is a rod for his back, but the lips of the wise preserve them. 4 Where there are no oxen, the crib remains empty; but large crops come through the strength of the bull. 5 A truthful witness does not lie, but a false witness utters lies. 6 The senseless man seeks in vain for wisdom, but knowledge is easy to the man of intelligence. 7 To avoid the foolish man, take steps! But knowing lips one meets with by surprise. 8 The shrewd man's wisdom gives him knowledge of his way, but the folly of fools is their deception. 9 Guilt lodges in the tents of the arrogant, but favor in the house of the just. 10 The heart knows its own bitterness, and in its joy no one else shares. 11 The house of the wicked will be destroyed, but the tent of the upright will flourish. 12 Sometimes a way seems right to a man, but the end of it leads to death! 13 Even in laughter the heart may be sad, and the end of joy may be sorrow. 14 The scoundrel suffers the consequences of his ways, and the good man reaps the fruit of his paths. 15 The simpleton believes everything, but the shrewd man measures his steps. 16 The wise man is cautious and shuns evil; the fool is reckless and sure of himself. 17 The quick-tempered man makes a fool of himself, but the prudent man is at peace. 18 The adornment of simpletons is folly, but shrewd men gain the crown of knowledge. 19 Evil men must bow down before the good, and the wicked, at the gates of the just. 20 Even by his neighbor the poor man is hated, but the friends of the rich are many. 21 He sins who despises the hungry; but happy is he who is kind to the poor! 22 Do not those who plot evil go astray? But those intent on good gain kindness and constancy. 23 In all labor there is profit, but mere talk tends only to penury. 24 The crown of the wise is resourcefulness; the diadem of fools is folly. 25 The truthful witness saves lives, but he who utters lies is a betrayer. 26 In the fear of the LORD is a strong defense; even for one's children he will be a refuge. 27 The fear of the LORD is a fountain of life, that a man may avoid the snares of death. 28 In many subjects lies the glory of the king; but if his people are few, it is the prince's ruin. 29 The patient man shows much good sense, but the quick-tempered man displays folly at its height. 30 A tranquil mind gives life to the body, but jealousy rots the bones. 31 He who oppresses the poor blasphemes his Maker, but he who is kind to the needy glorifies him. 32 The wicked man is overthrown by his wickedness, but the just man finds a refuge in his honesty. 33 In the heart of the intelligent wisdom abides, but in the bosom of fools it is unknown. 34 Virtue exalts a nation, but sin is a people's disgrace. 35 The king favors the intelligent servant, but the worthless one incurs his wrath.

Proverbs Chapter 15

1 A mild answer calms wrath, but a harsh word stirs up anger. 2 The tongue of the wise pours out knowledge, but the mouth of fools spurts forth folly. 3 The eyes of the LORD are in every place, keeping watch on the evil and the good. 4 A soothing tongue is a tree of life, but a perverse one crushes the spirit. 5 The fool spurns his father's admonition, but prudent is he who heeds reproof. 6 In the house of the just there are ample resources, but the earnings of the wicked are in turmoil. 7 The lips of the wise disseminate knowledge, but the heart of fools is perverted. 8 The sacrifice of the wicked is an abomination to the LORD, but the prayer of the upright is his delight. 9 The way of the wicked is an abomination to the LORD, but he loves the man who pursues virtue. 10 Severe punishment is in store for the man who goes astray; he who hates reproof will die. 11 The nether world and the abyss lie open before the LORD; how much more the hearts of men! 12 The senseless man loves not to be reproved; to wise men he will not go. 13 A glad heart lights up the face, but by mental anguish the spirit is broken. 14 The mind of the intelligent man seeks knowledge, but the mouth of fools feeds on folly. 15 Every day is miserable for the depressed, but a lighthearted man has a continual feast. 16 Better a little with fear of the LORD than a great fortune with anxiety. 17 Better a dish of herbs where love is than a fatted ox and hatred with it. 18 An ill-tempered man stirs up strife, but a patient man allays discord. 19 The way of the sluggard is hemmed in as with thorns, but the path of the diligent is a highway. 20 A wise son makes his father glad, but a fool of a man despises his mother. 21 Folly is joy to the senseless man, but the man of understanding goes the straight way. 22 Plans fail when there is no counsel, but they succeed when counselors are many. 23 There is joy for a man in his utterance; a word in season, how good it is! 24 The path of

life leads the prudent man upward, that he may avoid the nether world below. 25 The LORD overturns the house of the proud, but he preserves intact the widow's landmark. 26 The wicked man's schemes are an abomination to the LORD, but the pure speak what is pleasing to him. 27 He who is greedy of gain brings ruin on his own house, but he who hates bribes will live. 28 The just man weighs well his utterance, but the mouth of the wicked pours out evil. 29 The LORD is far from the wicked, but the prayer of the just he hears. 30 A cheerful glance brings joy to the heart; good news invigorates the bones. 31 He who listens to salutary reproof will abide among the wise. 32 He who rejects admonition despises his own soul, but he who heeds reproof gains understanding. 33 The fear of the LORD is training for wisdom, and humility goes before honors.

Proverbs Chapter 16

1 Man may make plans in his heart, but what the tongue utters is from the LORD. 2 All the ways of a man may be pure in his own eyes, but it is the LORD who proves the spirit. 3 Entrust your works to the LORD, and your plans will succeed. 4 The LORD has made everything for his own ends, even the wicked for the evil day. 5 Every proud man is an abomination to the LORD; I assure you that he will not go unpunished. 6 By kindness and piety guilt is expiated, and by the fear of the LORD man avoids evil. 7 When the LORD is pleased with a man's ways, he makes even his enemies be at peace with him. 8 Better a little with virtue, than a large income with injustice. 9 In his mind a man plans his course, but the LORD directs his steps. 10 The king's lips are an oracle; no judgment he pronounces is false. 11 Balance and scales belong to the LORD; all the weights used with them are his concern. 12 Kings have a horror of wrongdoing, for by righteousness the throne endures. 13 The king takes delight in honest lips, and the man who speaks what is right he loves. 14 The king's wrath is like messengers of death, but a wise man can pacify it. 15 In the light of the king's countenance is life, and his favor is like a rain cloud in spring. 16 How much better to acquire wisdom than gold! To acquire understanding is more desirable than silver. 17 The path of the upright avoids misfortune; he who pays attention to his way safeguards his life. 18 Pride goes before disaster, and a haughty spirit before a fall. 19 It is better to be humble with the meek than to share plunder with the proud. 20 He who plans a thing will be successful; happy is he who trusts in the LORD! 21 The wise man is esteemed for his discernment, yet pleasing speech increases his persuasiveness. 22 Good sense is a fountain of life to its possessor, but folly brings chastisement on fools. 23 The mind of the wise man makes him eloquent, and augments the persuasiveness of his lips. 24 Pleasing words are a honeycomb, sweet to the taste and healthful to the body. 25 Sometimes a way seems right to a man, but the end of it leads to death! 26 The laborer's appetite labors for him, for his mouth urges him on. 27 A scoundrel is a furnace of evil, and on his lips there is a scorching fire. 28 An intriguer sows discord, and a talebearer separates bosom friends. 29 A lawless man allures his neighbor, and leads him into a way that is not good. 30 He who winks his eye is plotting trickery; he who compresses his lips has mischief ready. 31 Gray hair is a crown of glory; it is gained by virtuous living. 32 A patient man is better than a warrior, and he who rules his temper, than he who takes a city. 33 When the lot is cast into the lap, its decision depends entirely on the LORD.

Proverbs Chapter 17

1 Better a dry crust with peace than a house full of feasting with strife. 2 An intelligent servant will rule over a worthless son, and will share the inheritance with the brothers. 3 The crucible for silver, and the furnace for gold, but the tester of hearts is the LORD. 4 The evil man gives heed to wicked lips, and listens to falsehood from a mischievous tongue. 5 He who mocks the poor blasphemes his Maker; he who is glad at calamity will not go unpunished. 6 Grandchildren are the crown of old men, and the glory of children is their parentage. 7 Fine words are out of place in a fool; how much more, lying words in a noble! 8 A man who has a bribe to offer rates it a magic stone; at every turn it brings him success. 9 He who covers up a misdeed fosters friendship, but he who gossips about it separates friends. 10 A single reprimand does more for a man of intelligence than a hundred lashes for a fool. 11 On rebellion alone is the wicked man bent, but a merciless messenger will be sent against him. 12 Face a bear robbed of her cubs, but never a fool in his folly! 13 If a man returns evil for good, from his house evil will not depart. 14 The start of strife is like the opening of a dam; therefore, check a quarrel before it begins! 15 He who condones the wicked, he who condemns the just, are both an abomination to the LORD. 16 Of what use in the fool's hand are the means to buy wisdom, since he has no mind for it? 17 He who is a friend is always a friend, and a brother is born for the time of stress. 18 Senseless is the man who gives his hand in pledge, who becomes surety for his neighbor. 19 He who loves strife loves guilt; he

who builds his gate high courts disaster. 20 He who is perverse in heart finds no good, and a double-tongued man falls into trouble. 21 To be a fool's parent is grief for a man; the father of a numskull has no joy. 22 A joyful heart is the health of the body, but a depressed spirit dries up the bones. 23 The wicked man accepts a concealed bribe to pervert the course of justice. 24 The man of intelligence fixes his gaze on wisdom, but the eyes of a fool are on the ends of the earth. 25 A foolish son is vexation to his father, and bitter sorrow to her who bore him. 26 It is wrong to fine an innocent man, but beyond reason to scourge princes. 27 He who spares his words is truly wise, and he who is chary of speech is a man of intelligence. 28 Even a fool, if he keeps silent, is considered wise; if he closes his lips, intelligent.

Proverbs Chapter 18

1 In estrangement one seeks pretexts: with all persistence he picks a quarrel. 2 The fool takes no delight in understanding, but rather in displaying what he thinks. 3 With wickedness comes contempt, and with disgrace comes scorn. 4 The words from a man's mouth are deep waters, but the source of wisdom is a flowing brook. 5 It is not good to be partial to the guilty, and so to reject a rightful claim. 6 The fool's lips lead him into strife, and his mouth provokes a beating. 7 The fool's mouth is his ruin; his lips are a snare to his life. 8 The words of a talebearer are like dainty morsels that sink into one's inmost being. 9 The man who is slack in his work is own brother to the man who is destructive. 10 The name of the LORD is a strong tower; the just man runs to it and is safe. 11 The rich man's wealth is his strong city; he fancies it a high wall. 12 Before his downfall a man's heart is haughty, but humility goes before honors. 13 He who answers before he hears—his is the folly and the shame. 14 A man's spirit sustains him in infirmity—but a broken spirit who can bear? 15 The mind of the intelligent gains knowledge, and the ear of the wise seeks knowledge. 16 A man's gift clears the way for him, and gains him access to great men. 17 The man who pleads his case first seems to be in the right; then his opponent comes and puts him to the test. 18 The lot puts an end to disputes, and is decisive in a controversy between the mighty. 19 A brother is a better defense than a strong city, and a friend is like the bars of a castle. 20 From the fruit of his mouth a man has his fill; with the yield of his lips he sates himself. 21 Death and life are in the power of the tongue; those who make it a friend shall eat its fruit. 22 He who finds a wife finds happiness; it is a favor he receives from the LORD. 23 The poor man implores, but the rich man answers harshly. 24 Some friends bring ruin on us, but a true friend is more loyal than a brother.

Proverbs Chapter 19

1 Better a poor man who walks in his integrity than he who is crooked in his ways and rich. 2 Without knowledge even zeal is not good; and he who acts hastily, blunders. 3 A man's own folly upsets his way, but his heart is resentful against the LORD. 4 Wealth adds many friends, but the friend of the poor man deserts him. 5 The false witness will not go unpunished, and he who utters lies will not escape. 6 Many curry favor with a noble; all are friends of the man who has something to give. 7 All the poor man's brothers hate him; how much more do his friends shun him! 8 He who gains intelligence is his own best friend; he who keeps understanding will be successful. 9 The false witness will not go unpunished, and he who utters lies will perish. 10 Luxury is not befitting a fool; much less should a slave rule over princes. 11 It is good sense in a man to be slow to anger, and it is his glory to overlook an offense. 12 The king's wrath is like the roaring of a lion, but his favor, like dew on the grass. 13 The foolish son is ruin to his father, and the nagging of a wife is a persistent leak. 14 Home and possessions are an inheritance from parents, but a prudent wife is from the LORD. 15 Laziness plunges a man into deep sleep, and the sluggard must go hungry. 16 He who keeps the precept keeps his life, but the despiser of the word will die. 17 He who has compassion on the poor lends to the LORD, and he will repay him for his good deed. 18 Chastise your son, for in this there is hope; but do not desire his death. 19 The man of violent temper pays the penalty; even if you rescue him, you will have it to do again. 20 Listen to counsel and receive instruction, that you may eventually become wise. 21 Many are the plans in a man's heart, but it is the decision of the LORD that endures. 22 From a man's greed comes his shame; rather be a poor man than a liar. 23 The fear of the LORD is an aid to life; one eats and sleeps without being visited by misfortune. 24 The sluggard loses his hand in the dish; he will not even lift it to his mouth. 25 If you beat an arrogant man, the simple learn a lesson; if you rebuke an intelligent man, he gains knowledge. 26 He who mistreats his father, or drives away his mother, is a worthless and disgraceful son. 27 If a son ceases to hear instruction, he wanders from words of knowledge. 28 An unprincipled witness perverts justice, and the mouth of the wicked pours out iniquity. 29 Rods are prepared for the arrogant,

and blows for the backs of fools.

Proverbs Chapter 20

¹ Wine is arrogant, strong drink is riotous; none who goes astray for it is wise. ² The dread of the king is as when a lion roars; he who incurs his anger forfeits his life. ³ It is honorable for a man to shun strife, while every fool starts a quarrel. ⁴ In seedtime the sluggard plows not; when he looks for the harvest, it is not there. ⁵ The intention in the human heart is like water far below the surface, but the man of intelligence draws it forth. ⁶ Many are declared to be men of virtue: but who can find one worthy of trust? ⁷ When a man walks in integrity and justice, happy are his children after him! ⁸ A king seated on the throne of judgment dispels all evil with his glance. ⁹ Who can say, "I have made my heart clean, I am cleansed of my sin"? ¹⁰ Varying weights, varying measures, are both an abomination to the LORD. ¹¹ Even by his manners the child betrays whether his conduct is innocent and right. ¹² The ear that hears, and the eye that sees—the LORD has made them both. ¹³ Love not sleep, lest you be reduced to poverty; eyes wide open mean abundant food. ¹⁴ "Bad, bad!" says the buyer; but once he has gone his way, he boasts. ¹⁵ Like gold or a wealth of corals, wise lips are a precious ornament. ¹⁶ Take his garment who becomes surety for another, and for strangers yield it up! ¹⁷ The bread of deceit is sweet to a man, but afterward his mouth will be filled with gravel. ¹⁸ Plans made after advice succeed; so with wise guidance wage your war. ¹⁹ A newsmonger reveals secrets; so have nothing to do with a babbler! ²⁰ If one curses his father or mother, his lamp will go out at the coming of darkness. ²¹ Possessions gained hastily at the outset will in the end not be blessed. ²² Say not, "I will repay evil!" Trust in the LORD and he will help you. ²³ Varying weights are an abomination to the LORD, and false scales are not good. ²⁴ Man's steps are from the LORD; how, then, can a man understand his way? ²⁵ Rashly to pledge a sacred gift is a trap for a man, or to regret a vow once made. ²⁶ A wise king winnows the wicked, and threshes them under the cartwheel. ²⁷ A lamp from the LORD is the breath of man; it searches through all his inmost being. ²⁸ Kindness and piety safeguard the king, and he upholds his throne by justice. ²⁹ The glory of young men is their strength, and the dignity of old men is gray hair. ³⁰ Evil is cleansed away by bloody lashes, and a scourging to the inmost being.

Proverbs Chapter 21

¹ Like a stream is the king's heart in the hand of the LORD; wherever it pleases him, he directs it. ² All the ways of a man may be right in his own eyes, but it is the LORD who proves hearts. ³ To do what is right and just is more acceptable to the LORD than sacrifice. ⁴ Haughty eyes and a proud heart—the tillage of the wicked is sin. ⁵ The plans of the diligent are sure of profit, but all rash haste leads certainly to poverty. ⁶ He who makes a fortune by a lying tongue is chasing a bubble over deadly snares. ⁷ The oppression of the wicked will sweep them away, because they refuse to do what is right. ⁸ The way of the culprit is crooked, but the conduct of the innocent is right. ⁹ It is better to dwell in a corner of the housetop than in a roomy house with a quarrelsome woman. ¹⁰ The soul of the wicked man desires evil; his neighbor finds no pity in his eyes. ¹¹ When the arrogant man is punished, the simple are the wiser; when the wise man is instructed, he gains knowledge. ¹² The just man appraises the house of the wicked: there is one who brings down the wicked to ruin. ¹³ He who shuts his ear to the cry of the poor will himself also call and not be heard. ¹⁴ A secret gift allays anger, and a concealed present, violent wrath. ¹⁵ To practice justice is a joy for the just, but terror for evildoers. ¹⁶ The man who strays from the way of good sense will abide in the assembly of the shades. ¹⁷ He who loves pleasure will suffer want; he who loves wine and perfume will not be rich. ¹⁸ The wicked man serves as ransom for the just, and the faithless man for the righteous. ¹⁹ It is better to dwell in a wilderness than with a quarrelsome and vexatious wife. ²⁰ Precious treasure remains in the house of the wise, but the fool consumes it. ²¹ He who pursues justice and kindness will find life and honor. ²² The wise man storms a city of the mighty, and overthrows the stronghold in which it trusts. ²³ He who guards his mouth and his tongue keeps himself from trouble. ²⁴ Arrogant is the name for the man of overbearing pride who acts with scornful effrontery. ²⁵ The sluggard's propensity slays him, for his hands refuse to work. ²⁶ Some are consumed with avarice all the day, but the just man gives unsparingly. ²⁷ The sacrifice of the wicked is an abomination, the more so when they offer it with a bad intention. ²⁸ The false witness will perish, but he who listens will finally have his say. ²⁹ The wicked man is brazenfaced, but the upright man pays heed to his ways. ³⁰ There is no wisdom, no understanding, no counsel, against the LORD. ³¹ The horse is equipped for the day of battle, but victory is the LORD'S.

Proverbs Chapter 22

¹ A good name is more desirable than great riches, and high esteem than gold and silver. ² Rich and poor have a common bond: the LORD is the maker of them all. ³ The shrewd man perceives evil and hides, while simpletons continue on and suffer the penalty. ⁴ The reward of humility and fear of the LORD is riches, honor, and life. ⁵ Thorns and snares are on the path of the crooked; he who would safeguard his life will shun them. ⁶ Train a boy in the way he should go; even when he is old, he will not swerve from it. ⁷ The rich rule over the poor, and the borrower is the slave of the lender. ⁸ He who sows iniquity reaps calamity, and the rod destroys his labors. ⁹ The kindly man will be blessed, for he gives of his sustenance to the poor. ¹⁰ Expel the arrogant man and discord goes out; strife and insult cease. ¹¹ The LORD loves the pure of heart; the man of winning speech has the king for his friend. ¹² The eyes of the LORD safeguard knowledge, but he defeats the projects of the faithless. ¹³ The sluggard says, "A lion is outside; in the streets, I might be slain." ¹⁴ The mouth of the adulteress is a deep pit; he with whom the LORD is angry will fall into it. ¹⁵ Folly is close to the heart of a child, but the rod of discipline will drive it far from him. ¹⁶ He who oppresses the poor to enrich himself will yield up his gains to the rich as sheer loss. ¹⁷ Incline your ear, and hear my words, and apply your heart to my doctrine; ¹⁸ For it will be well if you keep them in your bosom, if they all are ready on your lips. ¹⁹ That your trust may be in the LORD, I make known to you the words of Amen-em-Ope. ²⁰ Have I not written for you the "Thirty," with counsels and knowledge, ²¹ To teach you truly how to give a dependable report to one who sends you? ²² Injure not the poor because they are poor, nor crush the needy at the gate; ²³ For the LORD will defend their cause, and will plunder the lives of those who plunder them. ²⁴ Be not friendly with a hotheaded man, nor the companion of a wrathful man, ²⁵ Lest you learn his ways, and get yourself into a snare. ²⁶ Be not one of those who give their hand in pledge, of those who become surety for debts; ²⁷ For if you have not the means to pay, your bed will be taken from under you. ²⁸ Remove not the ancient landmark which your fathers set up. ²⁹ You see a man skilled at his work? He will stand in the presence of kings; he will not stand in the presence of obscure men.

Proverbs Chapter 23

¹ When you sit down to dine with a ruler, keep in mind who is before you; ² And put a knife to your throat if you have a ravenous appetite. ³ Do not desire his delicacies; they are deceitful food. ⁴ Toil not to gain wealth, cease to be concerned about it; ⁵ While your glance flits to it, it is gone! For assuredly it grows wings, like the eagle that flies toward heaven. ⁶ Do not take food with a grudging man, and do not desire his dainties; ⁷ For in his greed he is like a storm. "Eat and drink," he says to you, though his heart is not with you; ⁸ The little you have eaten you will vomit up, and you will have wasted your agreeable words. ⁹ Speak not for the fool's hearing; he will despise the wisdom of your words. ¹⁰ Remove not the ancient landmark, nor invade the fields of orphans; ¹¹ For their redeemer is strong; he will defend their cause against you. ¹² Apply your heart to instruction, and your ears to words of knowledge. ¹³ Withhold not chastisement from a boy; if you beat him with the rod, he will not die. ¹⁴ Beat him with the rod, and you will save him from the nether world. ¹⁵ My son, if your heart be wise, my own heart also will rejoice; ¹⁶ And my inmost being will exult, when your lips speak what is right. ¹⁷ Let not your heart emulate sinners, but be zealous for the fear of the LORD always; ¹⁸ For you will surely have a future, and your hope will not be cut off. ¹⁹ Hear, my son, and be wise, and guide your heart in the right way. ²⁰ Consort not with winebibbers, nor with those who eat meat to excess; ²¹ For the drunkard and the glutton come to poverty, and torpor clothes a man in rags. ²² Listen to your father who begot you, and despise not your mother when she is old. ²³ Get the truth, and sell it not - wisdom, instruction and understanding. ²⁴ The father of a just man will exult with glee; he who begets a wise son will have joy in him. ²⁵ Let your father and mother have joy; let her who bore you exult. ²⁶ My son, give me your heart, and let your eyes keep to my ways. ²⁷ For the harlot is a deep ditch, and the adulteress a narrow pit; ²⁸ Yes, she lies in wait like a robber, and increases the faithless among men. ²⁹ Who scream? Who shriek? Who have strife? Who have anxiety? Who have wounds for nothing? Who have black eyes? ³⁰ Those who linger long over wine, those who engage in trials of blended wine. ³¹ Look not on the wine when it is red, when it sparkles in the glass. It goes down smoothly; ³² But in the end it bites like a serpent, or like a poisonous adder. ³³ Your eyes behold strange sights, and your heart utters disordered thoughts; ³⁴ You are like one now lying in the depths of the sea, now sprawled at the top of the mast. ³⁵ "They struck me, but it pained me not; They beat me, but I felt it not; When shall I awake to seek wine once again?"

Proverbs Chapter 24

1 Be not emulous of evil men, and desire not to be with them; 2 For their hearts plot violence, and their lips speak of foul play. 3 By wisdom is a house built, by understanding is it made firm; 4 And by knowledge are its rooms filled with every precious and pleasing possession. 5 A wise man is more powerful than a strong man, and a man of knowledge than a man of might; 6 For it is by wise guidance that you wage your war, and the victory is due to a wealth of counselors. 7 For a fool, to be silent is wisdom; not to open his mouth at the gate. 8 He who plots evil doing—men call him an intriguer. 9 Beyond intrigue and folly and sin, it is arrogance that men find abominable. 10 If you remain indifferent in time of adversity, your strength will depart from you. 11 Rescue those who are being dragged to death, and from those tottering to execution withdraw not. 12 If you say, "I know not this man!" does not he who tests hearts perceive it? He who guards your life knows it, and he will repay each one according to his deeds. 13 If you eat honey, my son, because it is good, if virgin honey is sweet to your taste; 14 Such, you must know, is wisdom to your soul. If you find it, you will have a future, and your hope will not be cut off. 15 Lie not in wait against the home of the just man, ravage not his dwelling place; 16 For the just man falls seven times and rises again, but the wicked stumble to ruin. 17 Rejoice not when your enemy falls, and when he stumbles, let not your heart exult, 18 Lest the LORD see it, be displeased with you, and withdraw his wrath from your enemy. 19 Be not provoked with evildoers, nor envious of the wicked; 20 For the evil man has no future, the lamp of the wicked will be put out. 21 My son, fear the LORD and the king; have nothing to do with those who rebel against them; 22 For suddenly arises the destruction they send, and the ruin from either one, who can measure? 23 These also are sayings of the wise: To show partiality in judgment is not good. 24 He who says to the wicked man, "You are just"—men will curse him, people will denounce him; 25 But those who convict the evildoer will fare well, and on them will come the blessing of prosperity. 26 He gives a kiss on the lips who makes an honest reply. 27 Complete your outdoor tasks, and arrange your work in the field; afterward you can establish your house. 28 Be not a witness against your neighbor without just cause, thus committing folly with your lips. 29 Say not, "As he did to me, so will I do to him; I will repay the man according to his deeds." 30 I passed by the field of the sluggard, by the vineyard of the man without sense; 31 And behold! it was all overgrown with thistles; its surface was covered with nettles, and its stone wall broken down. 32 And as I gazed at it, I reflected; I saw and learned the lesson: 33 A little sleep, a little slumber, a little folding of the arms to rest— 34 Then will poverty come upon you like a highwayman, and want like an armed man.

Proverbs Chapter 25

1 These also are proverbs of Solomon. The men of Hezekiah, king of Judah, transmitted them. 2 God has glory in what he conceals, kings have glory in what they fathom. 3 As the heavens in height, and the earth in depth, the heart of kings is unfathomable. 4 Remove the dross from silver, and it comes forth perfectly purified; 5 Remove the wicked from the presence of the king, and his throne is made firm through righteousness. 6 Claim no honor in the king's presence, nor occupy the place of great men; 7 For it is better that you be told, "Come up closer!" than that you be humbled before the prince. 8 What your eyes have seen bring not forth hastily against an opponent; what will you do later on when your neighbor puts you to shame? 9 Discuss your case with your neighbor, but another man's secret do not disclose; 10 Lest, hearing it, he reproach you, and your ill repute cease not. 11 Like golden apples in silver settings are words spoken at the proper time. 12 Like a golden earring, or a necklace of fine gold, is a wise reprover to an obedient ear. 13 Like the coolness of snow in the heat of the harvest is a faithful messenger for the one who sends him. (He refreshes the soul of his master.) 14 Like clouds and wind when no rain follows is the man who boastfully promises what he never gives. 15 By patience is a ruler persuaded, and a soft tongue will break a bone. 16 If you find honey, eat only what you need, lest you become glutted with it and vomit it up. 17 Let your foot be seldom in your neighbor's house, lest he have more than enough of you, and hate you. 18 Like a club, or a sword, or a sharp arrow, is the man who bears false witness against his neighbor. 19 Like an infected tooth or an unsteady foot is (dependence on) a faithless man in time of trouble. 20 Like a moth in clothing, or a maggot in wood, sorrow gnaws at the human heart. 21 If your enemy be hungry, give him food to eat, if he be thirsty, give him to drink; 22 For live coals you will heap on his head, and the LORD will vindicate you. 23 The north wind brings rain, and a backbiting tongue an angry countenance. 24 It is better to dwell in a corner of the housetop than in a roomy house with a quarrelsome woman. 25 Like cool water to one faint from thirst is good news from a far country. 26 Like a troubled fountain or a polluted spring is a just man who gives way before the wicked. 27 To eat too much honey is not good; nor to seek honor after honor. 28 Like an open city with no defenses is the man with no check on his feelings.

Proverbs Chapter 26

1 Like snow in summer, or rain in harvest, honor for a fool is out of place. 2 Like the sparrow in its flitting, like the swallow in its flight, a curse uncalled-for arrives nowhere. 3 The whip for the horse, the bridle for the ass, and the rod for the back of fools. 4 Answer not the fool according to his folly, lest you too become like him. 5 Answer the fool according to his folly, lest he become wise in his own eyes. 6 He cuts off his feet, he drinks down violence, who sends messages by a fool. 7 A proverb in the mouth of a fool hangs limp, like crippled legs. 8 Like one who entangles the stone in the sling is he who gives honor to a fool. 9 Like a thorn stick brandished by the hand of a drunkard is a proverb in the mouth of fools. 10 Like an archer wounding all who pass by is he who hires a drunken fool. 11 As the dog returns to his vomit, so the fool repeats his folly. 12 You see a man wise in his own eyes? There is more hope for a fool than for him. 13 The sluggard says, "There is a lion in the street, a lion in the middle of the square!" 14 The door turns on its hinges, the sluggard, on his bed! 15 The sluggard loses his hand in the dish; he is too weary to lift it to his mouth. 16 The sluggard imagines himself wiser than seven men who answer with good sense. 17 Like the man who seizes a passing dog by the ears is he who meddles in a quarrel not his own. 18 Like a crazed archer scattering firebrands and deadly arrows 19 Is the man who deceives his neighbor, and then says, "I was only joking." 20 For lack of wood, the fire dies out; and when there is no talebearer, strife subsides. 21 What a bellows is to live coals, what wood is to fire, such is a contentious man in enkindling strife. 22 The words of a talebearer are like dainty morsels that sink into one's inmost being. 23 Like a glazed finish on earthenware are smooth lips with a wicked heart. 24 With his lips an enemy pretends, but in his inmost being he maintains deceit; 25 When he speaks graciously, trust him not, for seven abominations are in his heart. 26 A man may conceal hatred under dissimulation, but his malice will be revealed in the assembly. 27 He who digs a pit falls into it; and a stone comes back upon him who rolls it. 28 The lying tongue is its owner's enemy, and the flattering mouth works ruin.

Proverbs Chapter 27

1 Boast not of tomorrow, for you know not what any day may bring forth. 2 Let another praise you—not your own mouth; someone else—not your own lips. 3 Stone is heavy, and sand a burden, but a fool's provocation is heavier than both. 4 Anger is relentless, and wrath overwhelming—but before jealousy who can stand? 5 Better is an open rebuke than a love that remains hidden. 6 Wounds from a friend may be accepted as well meant, but the greetings of an enemy one prays against. 7 One who is full tramples on virgin honey, but to the man who is hungry, any bitter thing is sweet. 8 Like a bird that is far from its nest is a man who is far from his home. 9 Perfume and incense gladden the heart, but by grief the soul is torn asunder. 10 Your own friend and your father's friend forsake not; but if ruin befalls you, enter not a kinsman's house. Better is a neighbor near at hand than a brother far away. 11 If you are wise, my son, you will gladden my heart, and I will be able to rebut him who taunts me. 12 The shrewd man perceives evil and hides; simpletons continue on and suffer the penalty. 13 Take his garment who becomes surety for another, and for the sake of a stranger, yield it up! 14 When one greets his neighbor with a loud voice in the early morning, a curse can be laid to his charge. 15 For a persistent leak on a rainy day, the match is a quarrelsome woman. 16 He who keeps her stores up a stormwind; he cannot tell north from south. 17 As iron sharpens iron, so man sharpens his fellow man. 18 He who tends a fig tree eats its fruit, and he who is attentive to his master will be enriched. 19 As one face differs from another, so does one human heart from another. 20 The nether world and the abyss are never satisfied; so too the eyes of men. 21 As the crucible tests silver and the furnace gold, so a man is tested by the praise he receives. 22 Though you should pound the fool to bits with the pestle, amid the grits in a mortar, his folly would not go out of him. 23 Take good care of your flocks, give careful attention to your herds; 24 For wealth lasts not forever, nor even a crown from age to age. 25 When the grass is taken away and the aftergrowth appears, and the mountain greens are gathered in, 26 The lambs will provide you with clothing, and the goats will bring the price of a field, 27 And there will be ample goat's milk to supply you, to supply your household, and maintenance for your maidens.

Proverbs Chapter 28

1 The wicked man flees although no one pursues him; but the just man, like a lion, feels sure of himself. 2 If a land is rebellious, its princes will

be many; but with a prudent man, it knows security. ³ A rich man who oppresses the poor is like a devastating rain that leaves no food. ⁴ Those who abandon the law praise the wicked man, but those who keep the law war against him. ⁵ Evil men understand nothing of justice, but those who seek the LORD understand all. ⁶ Better a poor man who walks in his integrity than he who is crooked in his ways and rich. ⁷ He who keeps the law is a wise son, but the gluttons' companion disgraces his father. ⁸ He who increases his wealth by interest and overcharge gathers it for him who is kind to the poor. ⁹ When one turns away his ear from hearing the law, even his prayer is an abomination. ¹⁰ He who seduces the upright into an evil way will himself fall into his own pit. (And blameless men will gain prosperity.) ¹¹ The rich man is wise in his own eyes, but a poor man who is intelligent sees through him. ¹² When the just are triumphant, there is great jubilation; but when the wicked gain preeminence, people hide. ¹³ He who conceals his sins prospers not, but he who confesses and forsakes them obtains mercy. ¹⁴ Happy the man who is always on his guard; but he who hardens his heart will fall into evil. ¹⁵ Like a roaring lion or a ravenous bear is a wicked ruler over a poor people. ¹⁶ The less prudent the prince, the more his deeds oppress. He who hates ill-gotten gain prolongs his days. ¹⁷ Though a man burdened with human blood were to flee to the grave, none should support him. ¹⁸ He who walks uprightly is safe, but he whose ways are crooked falls into the pit. ¹⁹ He who cultivates his land will have plenty of food, but from idle pursuits a man has his fill of poverty. ²⁰ The trustworthy man will be richly blessed; he who is in haste to grow rich will not go unpunished. ²¹ To show partiality is never good: for even a morsel of bread a man may do wrong. ²² The avaricious man is perturbed about his wealth, and he knows not when want will come upon him. ²³ He who rebukes a man gets more thanks in the end than one with a flattering tongue. ²⁴ He who defrauds father or mother and calls it no sin is a partner of the brigand. ²⁵ The greedy man stirs up disputes, but he who trusts in the LORD will prosper. ²⁶ He who trusts in himself is a fool, but he who walks in wisdom is safe. ²⁷ He who gives to the poor suffers no want, but he who ignores them gets many a curse. ²⁸ When the wicked gain pre-eminence, other men hide; but at their fall, the just flourish.

Proverbs Chapter 29

¹ The man who remains stiff-necked and hates rebuke will be crushed suddenly beyond cure. ² When the just prevail, the people rejoice; but when the wicked rule, the people groan. ³ He who loves wisdom makes his father glad, but he who consorts with harlots squanders his wealth. ⁴ By justice a king gives stability to the land; but he who imposes heavy taxes ruins it. ⁵ The man who flatters his neighbor is spreading a net under his feet. ⁶ The wicked man steps into a snare, but the just man runs on joyfully. ⁷ The just man has a care for the rights of the poor; the wicked man has no such concern. ⁸ Arrogant men set the city ablaze, but wise men calm the fury. ⁹ If a wise man disputes with a fool, he may rage or laugh but can have no peace. ¹⁰ Bloodthirsty men hate the honest man, but the upright show concern for his life. ¹¹ The fool gives vent to all his anger; but by biding his time, the wise man calms it. ¹² If a ruler listens to lying words, his servants all become wicked. ¹³ The poor and the oppressor have a common bond: the LORD gives light to the eyes of both. ¹⁴ If a king is zealous for the rights of the poor, his throne stands firm forever. ¹⁵ The rod of correction gives wisdom, but a boy left to his whims disgraces his mother. ¹⁶ When the wicked prevail, crime increases; but their downfall the just will behold. ¹⁷ Correct your son, and he will bring you comfort, and give delight to your soul. ¹⁸ Without prophecy the people become demoralized; but happy is he who keeps the law. ¹⁹ By words no servant can be trained; for he understands what is said, but obeys not. ²⁰ Do you see a man hasty in his words? More can be hoped for from a fool! ²¹ If a man pampers his servant from childhood, he will turn out to be stubborn. ²² An ill-tempered man stirs up disputes, and a hotheaded man is the cause of many sins. ²³ Man's pride causes his humiliation, but he who is humble of spirit obtains honor. ²⁴ The accomplice of a thief is his own enemy: he hears himself put under a curse, yet discloses nothing. ²⁵ The fear of man brings a snare, but he who trusts in the LORD is safe. ²⁶ Many curry favor with the ruler, but the rights of each are from the LORD. ²⁷ The evildoer is an abomination to the just, and he who walks uprightly is an abomination to the wicked.

Proverbs Chapter 30

¹ The words of Agur, son of Jakeh the Massaite: The pronouncement of mortal man: "I am not God; I am not God, that I should prevail. ² Why, I am the most stupid of men, and have not even human intelligence; ³ Neither have I learned wisdom, nor have I the knowledge of the Holy One. ⁴ Who has gone up to heaven and come down again - who has cupped the wind in his hands? Who has bound up the waters in a cloak - who has marked out all the ends of the earth? What is his name, what is his son's name, if you know it?" ⁵ Every word of God is tested; he is a shield to those who take refuge in him. ⁶ Add nothing to his words, lest he reprove you, and you be exposed as a deceiver. ⁷ Two things I ask of you, deny them not to me before I die: ⁸ Put falsehood and lying far from me, give me neither poverty nor riches; (provide me only with the food I need;) ⁹ Lest, being full, I deny you, saying, "Who is the LORD?" Or, being in want, I steal, and profane the name of my God. ¹⁰ Slander not a servant to his master, lest he curse you, and you have to pay the penalty. ¹¹ There is a group of people that curses its father, and blesses not its mother. ¹² There is a group that is pure in its own eyes, yet is not purged of its filth. ¹³ There is a group - how haughty their eyes! how overbearing their glance! ¹⁴ There is a group whose incisors are swords, whose teeth are knives, Devouring the needy from the earth, and the poor from among men. ¹⁵ The two daughters of the leech are, "Give, Give." Three things are never satisfied, four never say, "Enough!" ¹⁶ The nether world, and the barren womb; the earth, that is never saturated with water, and fire, that never says, "Enough!" ¹⁷ The eye that mocks a father, or scorns an aged mother, Will be plucked out by the ravens in the valley; the young eagles will devour it. ¹⁸ Three things are too wonderful for me, yes, four I cannot understand: ¹⁹ The way of an eagle in the air, the way of a serpent upon a rock, The way of a ship on the high seas, and the way of a man with a maiden. ²⁰ Such is the way of an adulterous woman: she eats, wipes her mouth, and says, "I have done no wrong." ²¹ Under three things the earth trembles, yes, under four it cannot bear up: ²² Under a slave when he becomes king, and a fool when he is glutted with food; ²³ Under an odious woman when she is wed, and a maidservant when she displaces her mistress. ²⁴ Four things are among the smallest on the earth, and yet are exceedingly wise: ²⁵ Ants - a species not strong, yet they store up their food in the summer; ²⁶ Rock-badgers - a species not mighty, yet they make their home in the crags; ²⁷ Locusts - they have no king, yet they migrate all in array; ²⁸ Lizards - you can catch them with your hands, yet they find their way into king's palaces. ²⁹ Three things are stately in their stride, yes, four are stately in their carriage: ³⁰ The lion, mightiest of beasts, who retreats before nothing; ³¹ The strutting cock, and the he-goat, and the king at the head of his people. ³² If you have foolishly been proud or presumptuous - put your hand on your mouth; ³³ For the stirring of milk brings forth curds, and the stirring of anger brings forth blood.

Proverbs Chapter 31

¹ The words of Lemuel, king of Massa. The advice which his mother gave him: ² What, my son, my first-born! what, O son of my womb; what, O son of my vows! ³ Give not your vigor to women, nor your strength to those who ruin kings. ⁴ It is not for kings, O Lemuel, not for kings to drink wine; strong drink is not for princes! ⁵ Lest in drinking they forget what the law decrees, and violate the rights of all who are in need. ⁶ Give strong drink to one who is perishing, and wine to the sorely depressed; ⁷ When they drink, they will forget their misery, and think no more of their burdens. ⁸ Open your mouth in behalf of the dumb, and for the rights of the destitute; ⁹ Open your mouth, decree what is just, defend the needy and the poor! ¹⁰ When one finds a worthy wife, her value is far beyond pearls. ¹¹ Her husband, entrusting his heart to her, has an unfailing prize. ¹² She brings him good, and not evil, all the days of her life. ¹³ She obtains wool and flax and makes cloth with skillful hands. ¹⁴ Like merchant ships, she secures her provisions from afar. ¹⁵ She rises while it is still night, and distributes food to her household. ¹⁶ She picks out a field to purchase; out of her earnings she plants a vineyard. ¹⁷ She is girt about with strength, and sturdy are her arms. ¹⁸ She enjoys the success of her dealings; at night her lamp is undimmed. ¹⁹ She puts her hands to the distaff, and her fingers ply the spindle. ²⁰ She reaches out her hands to the poor, and extends her arms to the needy. ²¹ She fears not the snow for her household; all her charges are doubly clothed. ²² She makes her own coverlets; fine linen and purple are her clothing. ²³ Her husband is prominent at the city gates as he sits with the elders of the land. ²⁴ She makes garments and sells them, and stocks the merchants with belts. ²⁵ She is clothed with strength and dignity, and she laughs at the days to come. ²⁶ She opens her mouth in wisdom, and on her tongue is kindly counsel. ²⁷ She watches the conduct of her household, and eats not her food in idleness. ²⁸ Her children rise up and praise her; her husband, too, extols her: ²⁹ "Many are the women of proven worth, but you have excelled them all." ³⁰ Charm is deceptive and beauty fleeting; the woman who fears the LORD is to be praised. ³¹ Give her a reward of her labors, and let her works praise her at the city gates.

Ecclesiastes

Ecclesiastes Chapter 1

1 The words of David's son, Qoheleth, king in Jerusalem: 2 Vanity of vanities, says Qoheleth, vanity of vanities! All things are vanity! 3 What profit has man from all the labor which he toils at under the sun? 4 One generation passes and another comes, but the world forever stays. 5 The sun rises and the sun goes down; then it presses on to the place where it rises. 6 Blowing now toward the south, then toward the north, the wind turns again and again, resuming its rounds. 7 All rivers go to the sea, yet never does the sea become full. To the place where they go, the rivers keep on going. 8 All speech is labored; there is nothing man can say. The eye is not satisfied with seeing nor is the ear filled with hearing. 9 What has been, that will be; what has been done, that will be done. Nothing is new under the sun. 10 Even the thing of which we say, "See, this is new!" has already existed in the ages that preceded us. 11 There is no remembrance of the men of old; nor of those to come will there be any remembrance among those who come after them. 12 I, Qoheleth, was king over Israel in Jerusalem, 13 and I applied my mind to search and investigate in wisdom all things that are done under the sun. A thankless task God has appointed for men to be busied about. 14 I have seen all things that are done under the sun, and behold, all is vanity and a chase after wind. 15 What is crooked cannot be made straight, and what is missing cannot be supplied. 16 Though I said to myself, "Behold, I have become great and stored up wisdom beyond all who were before me in Jerusalem, and my mind has broad experience of wisdom and knowledge"; 17 yet when I applied my mind to know wisdom and knowledge, madness and folly, I learned that this also is a chase after wind. 18 For in much wisdom there is much sorrow, and he who stores up knowledge stores up grief.

Ecclesiastes Chapter 2

1 I said to myself, "Come, now, let me try you with pleasure and the enjoyment of good things." But behold, this too was vanity. 2 Of laughter I said: "Mad!" and of mirth: "What good does this do?" 3 I thought of beguiling my senses with wine, though my mind was concerned with wisdom, and of taking up folly, until I should understand what is best for men to do under the heavens during the limited days of their life. 4 I undertook great works; I built myself houses and planted vineyards; 5 I made gardens and parks, and set out in them fruit trees of all sorts. 6 And I constructed for myself reservoirs to water a flourishing woodland. 7 I acquired male and female slaves, and slaves were born in my house. I also had growing herds of cattle and flocks of sheep, more than all who had been before me in Jerusalem. 8 I amassed for myself silver and gold, and the wealth of kings and provinces. I got for myself male and female singers and all human luxuries. 9 I became great, and I stored up more than all others before me in Jerusalem; my wisdom, too, stayed with me. 10 Nothing that my eyes desired did I deny them, nor did I deprive myself of any joy, but my heart rejoiced in the fruit of all my toil. This was my share for all my toil. 11 But when I turned to all the works that my hands had wrought, and to the toil at which I had taken such pains, behold! all was vanity and a chase after wind, with nothing gained under the sun. 12 For what will the man do who is to come after the king? What men have already done! I went on to the consideration of wisdom, madness and folly. 13 And I saw that wisdom has the advantage over folly as much as light has the advantage over darkness. 14 The wise man has eyes in his head, but the fool walks in darkness. Yet I knew that one lot befalls both of them. 15 So I said to myself, if the fool's lot is to befall me also, why then should I be wise? Where is the profit for me? And I concluded in my heart that this too is vanity. 16 Neither of the wise man nor of the fool will there be an abiding remembrance, for in days to come both will have been forgotten. How is it that the wise man dies as well as the fool! 17 Therefore I loathed life, since for me the work that is done under the sun is evil; for all is vanity and a chase after wind. 18 And I detested all the fruits of my labor under the sun, because I must leave them to a man who is to come after me. 19 And who knows whether he will be a wise man or a fool? Yet he will have control over all the fruits of my wise labor under the sun. This also is vanity. 20 So my feelings turned to despair of all the fruits of my labor under the sun. 21 For here is a man who has labored with wisdom and knowledge and skill, and to another, who has not labored over it, he must leave his property. This also is vanity and a great misfortune. 22 For what profit comes to a man from all the toil and anxiety of heart with which he has labored under the sun? 23 All his days sorrow and grief are his occupation; even at night his mind is not at rest. This also is vanity. 24 There is nothing better for man than to eat and drink and provide himself with good things by his labors. Even this, I realized, is from the hand of God. 25 For who can eat or drink apart from him? 26 For to whatever man he sees fit he gives wisdom and knowledge and joy; but to the sinner he gives the task of gathering possessions to be given to whatever man God sees fit. This also is vanity and a chase after wind.

Ecclesiastes Chapter 3

1 There is an appointed time for everything, and a time for every affair under the heavens. 2 A time to be born, and a time to die; a time to plant, and a time to uproot the plant. 3 A time to kill, and a time to heal; a time to tear down, and a time to build. 4 A time to weep, and a time to laugh; a time to mourn, and a time to dance. 5 A time to scatter stones, and a time to gather them; a time to embrace, and a time to be far from embraces. 6 A time to seek, and a time to lose; a time to keep, and a time to cast away. 7 A time to rend, and a time to sew; a time to be silent, and a time to speak. 8 A time to love, and a time to hate; a time of war, and a time of peace. 9 What advantage has the worker from his toil? 10 I have considered the task which God has appointed for men to be busied about. 11 He has made everything appropriate to its time, and has put the timeless into their hearts, without men's ever discovering, from beginning to end, the work which God has done. 12 I recognized that there is nothing better than to be glad and to do well during life. 13 For every man, moreover, to eat and drink and enjoy the fruit of all his labor is a gift of God. 14 I recognized that whatever God does will endure forever; there is no adding to it, or taking from it. Thus has God done that he may be revered. 15 What now is has already been; what is to be, already is; and God restores what would otherwise be displaced. 16 And still under the sun in the judgment place I saw wickedness, and in the seat of justice, iniquity. 17 And I said to myself, both the just and the wicked God will judge, since there is a time for every affair and on every work a judgment. 18 I said to myself: As for the children of men, it is God's way of testing them and of showing that they are in themselves like beasts. 19 For the lot of man and of beast is one lot; the one dies as well as the other. Both have the same life-breath, and man has no advantage over the beast; but all is vanity. 20 Both go to the same place; both were made from the dust, and to the dust they both return. 21 Who knows if the life-breath of the children of men goes upward and the life-breath of beasts goes earthward? 22 And I saw that there is nothing better for a man than to rejoice in his work; for this is his lot. Who will let him see what is to come after him?

Ecclesiastes Chapter 4

1 Again I considered all the oppressions that take place under the sun: the tears of the victims with none to comfort them! From the hand of their oppressors comes violence, and there is none to comfort them! 2 And those now dead, I declared more fortunate in death than are the living to be still alive. 3 And better off than both is the yet unborn, who has not seen the wicked work that is done under the sun. 4 Then I saw that all toil and skillful work is the rivalry of one man for another. This also is vanity and a chase after wind. 5 "The fool folds his arms and consumes his own flesh" - 6 Better is one handful with tranquility than two with toil and a chase after wind! 7 Again I found this vanity under the sun: 8 a solitary man with no companion; with neither son nor brother. Yet there is no end to all his toil, and riches do not satisfy his greed. "For whom do I toil and deprive myself of good things?" This also is vanity and a worthless task. 9 Two are better than one: they get a good wage for their labor. 10 If the one falls, the other will lift up his companion. Woe to the solitary man! For if he should fall, he has no one to lift him up. 11 So also, if two sleep together, they keep each other warm. How can one alone keep warm? 12 Where a lone man may be overcome, two together can resist. A three-ply cord is not easily broken. 13 Better is a poor but wise youth than an old but foolish king who no longer knows caution; 14 for from a prison house one comes forth to rule, since even in his royalty he was poor at birth. 15 Then I saw all those who are to live and move about under the sun with the heir apparent who will succeed to his place. 16 There is no end to all these people, to all over whom he takes precedence; yet the later generations will not applaud him. This also is vanity and a chase after wind. 17 Guard your step when you go to the house of God. Let your approach be obedience, rather than the fools' offering of sacrifice; for they know not how to keep from doing evil.

Ecclesiastes Chapter 5

1 Be not hasty in your utterance and let not your heart be quick to make a promise in God's presence. God is in heaven and you are on earth; therefore let your words be few. 2 For nightmares come with many cares, and a fool's utterance with many words. 3 When you make a vow to God, delay not its fulfillment. For God has no pleasure in fools; fulfill what you have vowed. 4 You had better not make a vow than make it and not fulfill it. 5 Let not your utterances make you guilty, and say not before his representative, "It was a mistake," lest God be angered by

such words and destroy the works of your hands. 6 Rather, fear God! 7 If you see oppression of the poor, and violation of rights and justice in the realm, do not be shocked by the fact, for the high official has another higher than he watching him and above these are others higher still. 8 Yet an advantage for a country in every respect is a king for the arable land. 9 The covetous man is never satisfied with money, and the lover of wealth reaps no fruit from it; so this too is vanity. 10 Where there are great riches, there are also many to devour them. Of what use are they to the owner except to feast his eyes upon? 11 Sleep is sweet to the laboring man, whether he eats little or much, but the rich man's abundance allows him no sleep. 12 This is a grievous evil which I have seen under the sun: riches kept by their owner to his hurt. 13 Should the riches be lost through some misfortune, he may have a son when he is without means. 14 As he came forth from his mother's womb, so again shall he depart, naked as he came, having nothing from his labor that he can carry in his hand. 15 This too is a grievous evil, that he goes just as he came. What then does it profit him to toil for wind? 16 All the days of his life are passed in gloom and sorrow, under great vexation, sickness, and wrath. 17 Here is what I recognize as good: it is well for a man to eat and drink and enjoy all the fruits of his labor under the sun during the limited days of the life which God gives him; for this is his lot. 18 Any man to whom God gives riches and property, and grants power to partake of them, so that he receives his lot and finds joy in the fruits of his toil, has a gift from God. 19 For he will hardly dwell on the shortness of his life, because God lets him busy himself with the joy of his heart.

Ecclesiastes Chapter 6

1 There is another evil which I have seen under the sun, and it weighs heavily upon man: 2 there is the man to whom God gives riches and property and honor, so that he lacks none of all the things he craves; yet God does not grant him power to partake of them, but a stranger devours them. This is vanity and a dire plague. 3 Should a man have a hundred children and live many years, no matter to what great age, still if he has not the full benefit of his goods, or if he is deprived of burial, of this man I proclaim that the child born dead is more fortunate than he. 4 Though it came in vain and goes into darkness and its name is enveloped in darkness; 5 though it has not seen or known the sun, yet the dead child is at rest rather than such a man. 6 Should he live twice a thousand years and not enjoy his goods, do not both go to the same place? 7 All man's toil is for his mouth, yet his desire is not fulfilled. 8 For what advantage has the wise man over the fool, or what advantage has the poor man in knowing how to conduct himself in life? 9 "What the eyes see is better than what the desires wander after." This also is vanity and a chase after wind. 10 Whatever is, was long ago given its name, and the nature of man is known, and that he cannot contend in judgment with one who is stronger than he. 11 For though there are many sayings that multiply vanity, what profit is there for a man? 12 For who knows what is good for a man in life, the limited days of his vain life (which God has made like a shadow)? Because—who is there to tell a man what will come after him under the sun?

Ecclesiastes Chapter 7

1 A good name is better than good ointment, and the day of death than the day of birth. 2 It is better to go to the house of mourning than to the house of feasting, for that is the end of every man, and the living should take it to heart. 3 Sorrow is better than laughter, because when the face is sad the heart grows wiser. 4 The heart of the wise is in the house of mourning, but the heart of fools is in the house of mirth. 5 It is better to hearken to the wise man's rebuke than to hearken to the song of fools; 6 for as the crackling of thorns under a pot, so is the fool's laughter. 7 For oppression can make a fool of a wise man, and a bribe corrupts the heart. 8 Better is the end of speech than its beginning; better is the patient spirit than the lofty spirit. 9 Do not in spirit become quickly discontented, for discontent lodges in the bosom of a fool. 10 Do not say: How is it that former times were better than these? For it is not in wisdom that you ask about this. 11 Wisdom and an inheritance are good, and an advantage to those that see the sun. 12 For the protection of wisdom is as the protection of money; and the advantage of knowledge is that wisdom preserves the life of its owner. 13 Consider the work of God. Who can make straight what he has made crooked? 14 On a good day enjoy good things, and on an evil day consider: Both the one and the other God has made, so that man cannot find fault with him in anything. 15 I have seen all manner of things in my vain days: a just man perishing in his justice, and a wicked one surviving in his wickedness. 16 "Be not just to excess, and be not overwise, lest you be ruined. 17 Be not wicked to excess, and be not foolish. Why should you die before your time?" 18 It is good to hold to this rule, and not to let that one go; but he who fears God will win through at all events. 19

Wisdom is a better defense for the wise man than would be ten princes in the city, 20 yet there is no man on earth so just as to do good and never sin. 21 Do not give heed to every word that is spoken lest you hear your servant speaking ill of you, 22 for you know in your heart that you have many times spoken ill of others. 23 All these things I probed in wisdom. I said, "I will acquire wisdom"; but it was beyond me. 24 What exists is far-reaching; it is deep, very deep: who can find it out? 25 I turned my thoughts toward knowledge; I sought and pursued wisdom and reason, and I recognized that wickedness is foolish and folly is madness. 26 More bitter than death I find the woman who is a hunter's trap, whose heart is a snare and whose hands are prison bonds. He who is pleasing to God will escape her, but the sinner will be entrapped by her. 27 Behold, this have I found, says Qoheleth, adding one thing to another that I might discover the answer 28 which my soul still seeks and has not found: One man out of a thousand have I come upon, but a woman among them all I have not found. 29 Behold, only this have I found out: God made mankind straight, but men have had recourse to many calculations.

Ecclesiastes Chapter 8

1 Who is like the wise man, and who knows the explanation of things? A man's wisdom illumines his face, but an impudent look is resented. 2 Observe the precept of the king, and in view of your oath to God, 3 be not hasty to withdraw from the king; do not join in with a base plot, for he does whatever he pleases, 4 because his word is sovereign, and who can say to him, "What are you doing?" 5 He who keeps the commandment experiences no evil, and the wise man's heart knows times and judgments; 6 for there is a time and a judgment for everything. Yet it is a great affliction for man 7 that he is ignorant of what is to come; for who will make known to him how it will be? 8 There is no man who is master of the breath of life so as to retain it, and none has mastery of the day of death. There is no exemption from the struggle, nor are the wicked saved by their wickedness. 9 All these things I considered and I applied my mind to every work that is done under the sun, while one man tyrannizes over another to his hurt. 10 Meanwhile I saw wicked men approach and enter; and as they left the sacred place, they were praised in the city for what they had done. This also is vanity. 11 Because the sentence against evildoers is not promptly executed, therefore the hearts of men are filled with the desire to commit evil, 12 because the sinner does evil a hundred times and survives. Though indeed I know that it shall be well with those who fear God, for their reverence toward him; 13 and that it shall not be well with the wicked man, and he shall not prolong his shadowy days, for his lack of reverence toward God. 14 This is a vanity which occurs on earth: there are just men treated as though they had done evil and wicked men treated as though they had done justly. This, too, I say is vanity. 15 Therefore I commend mirth, because there is nothing good for man under the sun except eating and drinking and mirth: for this is the accompaniment of his toil during the limited days of the life which God gives him under the sun. 16 When I applied my heart to know wisdom and to observe what is done on earth, 17 I recognized that man is unable to find out all God's work that is done under the sun, even though neither by day nor by night do his eyes find rest in sleep. However much man toils in searching, he does not find it out; and even if the wise man says that he knows, he is unable to find it out.

Ecclesiastes Chapter 9

1 All this I have kept in mind and recognized: the just, the wise, and their deeds are in the hand of God. Love from hatred man cannot tell; both appear equally vain, 2 in that there is the same lot for all, for the just and the wicked, for the good and the bad, for the clean and the unclean, for him who offers sacrifice and him who does not. As it is for the good man, so it is for the sinner; as it is for him who swears rashly, so it is for him who fears an oath. 3 Among all the things that happen under the sun, this is the worst, that things turn out the same for all. Hence the minds of men are filled with evil, and madness is in their hearts during life; and afterward they go to the dead. 4 Indeed, for any among the living there is hope; a live dog is better off than a dead lion. 5 For the living know that they are to die, but the dead no longer know anything. There is no further recompense for them, because all memory of them is lost. 6 For them, love and hatred and rivalry have long since perished. They will never again have part in anything that is done under the sun. 7 Go, eat your bread with joy and drink your wine with a merry heart, because it is now that God favors your works. 8 At all times let your garments be white, and spare not the perfume for your head. 9 Enjoy life with the wife whom you love, all the days of the fleeting life that is granted you under the sun. This is your lot in life, for the toil of your labors under the sun. 10 Anything you can turn your hand to, do with what power you have; for there will be no work, nor reason, nor

knowledge, nor wisdom in the nether world where you are going. ¹¹ Again I saw under the sun that the race is not won by the swift, nor the battle by the valiant, nor a livelihood by the wise, nor riches by the shrewd, nor favor by the experts; for a time of calamity comes to all alike. ¹² Man no more knows his own time than fish taken in the fatal net, or birds trapped in the snare; like these the children of men are caught when the evil time falls suddenly upon them. ¹³ On the other hand I saw this wise deed under the sun, which I thought sublime. ¹⁴ Against a small city with few men in it advanced a mighty king, who surrounded it and threw up great siegeworks about it. ¹⁵ But in the city lived a man who, though poor, was wise, and he delivered it through his wisdom. Yet no one remembered this poor man. ¹⁶ Though I had said, "Wisdom is better than force," yet the wisdom of the poor man is despised and his words go unheeded. ¹⁷ The quiet words of the wise are better heeded than the shout of a ruler of fools. ¹⁸ A fly that dies can spoil the perfumer's ointment, and a single slip can ruin much that is good.

Ecclesiastes Chapter 10

¹ More weighty than wisdom or wealth is a little folly! ² The wise man's understanding turns him to his right; the fool's understanding turns him to his left. ³ When the fool walks through the street, in his lack of understanding he calls everything foolish. ⁴ Should the anger of the ruler burst upon you, forsake not your place; for mildness abates great offenses. ⁵ I have seen under the sun another evil, like a mistake that proceeds from the ruler: ⁶ a fool put in a lofty position while the rich sit in lowly places. ⁷ I have seen slaves on horseback, while princes walked on the ground like slaves. ⁸ He who digs a pit may fall into it, and he who breaks through a wall may be bitten by a serpent. ⁹ He who moves stones may be hurt by them, and he who chops wood is in danger from it. ¹⁰ If the iron becomes dull, though at first he made easy progress, he must increase his efforts; but the craftsman has the advantage of his skill. ¹¹ If the serpent bites because it has not been charmed, then there is no advantage for the charmer. ¹² Words from the wise man's mouth win favor, but the fool's lips consume him. ¹³ The beginning of his words is folly, and the end of his talk is utter madness; ¹⁴ yet the fool multiplies words. Man knows not what is to come, for who can tell him what is to come after him? ¹⁵ When will the fool be weary of his labor, he who knows not the way to the city? ¹⁶ Woe to you, O land, whose king was a servant, and whose princes dine in the morning! ¹⁷ Blessed are you, O land, whose king is of noble birth, and whose princes dine at the right time (for vigor and not in drinking bouts). ¹⁸ When hands are lazy, the rafters sag; when hands are slack, the house leaks. ¹⁹ Bread and oil call forth merriment and wine makes the living glad, but money answers for everything. ²⁰ Even in your thoughts do not make light of the king, nor in the privacy of your bedroom revile the rich. Because the birds of the air may carry your voice, a winged creature may tell what you say.

Ecclesiastes Chapter 11

¹ Cast your bread upon the waters; after a long time you may find it again. ² Make seven or eight portions; you know not what misfortune may come upon the earth. ³ When the clouds are full, they pour out rain upon the earth. Whether a tree falls to the south or to the north, wherever it falls, there shall it lie. ⁴ One who pays heed to the wind will not sow, and one who watches the clouds will never reap. ⁵ Just as you know not how the breath of life fashions the human frame in the mother's womb, so you know not the work of God which he is accomplishing in the universe. ⁶ In the morning sow your seed, and at evening let not your hand be idle: for you know not which of the two will be successful, or whether both alike will turn out well. ⁷ Light is sweet! and it is pleasant for the eyes to see the sun. ⁸ However many years a man may live, let him, as he enjoys them all, remember that the days of darkness will be many. All that is to come is vanity. ⁹ Rejoice, O young man, while you are young and let your heart be glad in the days of your youth. Follow the ways of your heart, the vision of your eyes; yet understand that as regards all this God will bring you to judgment. ¹⁰ Ward off grief from your heart and put away trouble from your presence, though the dawn of youth is fleeting.

Ecclesiastes Chapter 12

¹ Remember your Creator in the days of your youth, before the evil days come and the years approach of which you will say, "I have no pleasure in them"; ² before the sun is darkened, and the light, and the moon, and the stars, while the clouds return after the rain; ³ when the guardians of the house tremble, and the strong men are bent, and the grinders are idle because they are few, and they who look through the windows grow blind; ⁴ when the doors to the street are shut, and the sound of the mill is low; when one waits for the chirp of a bird, but all the daughters of song are suppressed; ⁵ and one fears heights, and perils in the street;

when the almond tree blooms, and the locust grows sluggish and the caper berry is without effect, because man goes to his lasting home, and mourners go about the streets; ⁶ before the silver cord is snapped and the golden bowl is broken, and the pitcher is shattered at the spring, and the broken pulley falls into the well, ⁷ and the dust returns to the earth as it once was, and the life breath returns to God who gave it. ⁸ Vanity of vanities, says Qoheleth, all things are vanity! ⁹ Besides being wise, Qoheleth taught the people knowledge, and weighed, scrutinized and arranged many proverbs. ¹⁰ Qoheleth sought to find pleasing sayings, and to write down true sayings with precision. ¹¹ The sayings of the wise are like goads; like fixed spikes are the topics given by one collector. ¹² As to more than these, my son, beware. Of the making of many books there is no end, and in much study there is weariness for the flesh. ¹³ The last word, when all is heard: Fear God and keep his commandments, for this is man's all; ¹⁴ because God will bring to judgment every work, with all its hidden qualities, whether good or bad.

The Song of Songs

The Song of Songs Chapter 1

¹ The Song of songs, which is Solomon's. **B** ² Let him kiss me with kisses of his mouth! More delightful is your love than wine! ³ Your name spoken is a spreading perfume—that is why the maidens love you. ⁴ Draw me!— **D** We will follow you eagerly! **B** Bring me, O king, to your chambers. **D** With you we rejoice and exult, we extol your love; it is beyond wine: how rightly you are loved! ⁵ **B** I am as dark—but lovely, O daughters of Jerusalem—As the tents of Kedar, as the curtains of Salma. ⁶ Do not stare at me because I am swarthy, because the sun has burned me. My brothers have been angry with me; they charged me with the care of the vineyards: my own vineyard I have not cared for. ⁷ Tell me, you whom my heart loves, where you pasture your flock, where you give them rest at midday, Lest I be found wandering after the flocks of your companions. ⁸ **G** If you do not know, O most beautiful among women, Follow the tracks of the flock and pasture the young ones near the shepherds' camps. ⁹ To the steeds of Pharaoh's chariots would I liken you, my beloved: ¹⁰ Your cheeks lovely in pendants, your neck in jewels. ¹¹ We will make pendants of gold for you, and silver ornaments. ¹² **B** For the king's banquet my nard gives forth its fragrance. ¹³ My lover is for me a sachet of myrrh to rest in my bosom. ¹⁴ My lover is for me a cluster of henna from the vineyards of Engedi. ¹⁵ **G** Ah, you are beautiful, my beloved, ah, you are beautiful; your eyes are doves! ¹⁶ **B** Ah, you are beautiful, my lover—yes, you are lovely. Our couch, too, is verdant; ¹⁷ the beams of our house are cedars, our rafters, cypresses.

Caption: The marginal letters indicate the speakers of the verses:

- **B**: Bride - The beloved woman expressing her love for the bridegroom.
- **D**: Daughters of Jerusalem - A chorus commenting on and supporting the bride's feelings.
- **G**: Bridegroom - The beloved man responding to the bride's affection.

The Song of Songs Chapter 2

¹ I am a flower of Sharon, a lily of the valley. ² **G** As a lily among thorns, so is my beloved among women. ³ **B** As an apple tree among the trees of the woods, so is my lover among men. I delight to rest in his shadow, and his fruit is sweet to my mouth. ⁴ **B** He brings me into the banquet hall and his emblem over me is love. ⁵ Strengthen me with raisin cakes, refresh me with apples, for I am faint with love. ⁶ His left hand is under my head and his right arm embraces me. ⁷ **B** I adjure you, daughters of Jerusalem, by the gazelles and hinds of the field, Do not arouse, do not stir up love before its own time. ⁸ **B** Hark! my lover—here he comes springing across the mountains, leaping across the hills. ⁹ My lover is like a gazelle or a young stag. Here he stands behind our wall, gazing through the windows, peering through the lattices. ¹⁰ My lover speaks; he says to me, "Arise, my beloved, my beautiful one, and come! ¹¹ For see, the winter is past, the rains are over and gone. ¹² The flowers appear on the earth, the time of pruning the vines has come, and the song of the dove is heard in our land. ¹³ The fig tree puts forth its figs, and the vines, in bloom, give forth fragrance. Arise, my beloved, my beautiful one, and come! ¹⁴ **G** O my dove in the clefts of the rock, in the secret recesses of the cliff, Let me see you, let me hear your voice, For your voice is sweet, and you are lovely." ¹⁵ **B** Catch us the foxes, the little foxes that damage the vineyards; for our vineyards are in bloom! ¹⁶ My lover belongs to me and I to him; he browses among the lilies. ¹⁷ **B** Until the day breathes cool and the shadows lengthen, roam, my lover, Like a gazelle or a young stag upon the mountains of Bether.

Caption: The marginal letters indicate the speakers of the verses:

- **B**: Bride - The beloved woman expressing her love for the bridegroom.
- **G**: Bridegroom - The beloved man responding to the bride's affection.

The Song of Songs Chapter 3

¹ **B** On my bed at night I sought him whom my heart loves—I sought him but I did not find him. ² I will rise then and go about the city; in the streets and crossings I will seek him whom my heart loves. I sought him but I did not find him. ³ The watchmen came upon me as they made their rounds of the city: Have you seen him whom my heart loves? ⁴ I had hardly left them when I found him whom my heart loves. I took hold of him and would not let him go till I should bring him to the home of my mother, to the room of my parent. ⁵ I adjure you, daughters of Jerusalem, by the gazelles and hinds of the field, do not arouse, do not stir up love before its own time. ⁶ **D** What is this coming up from the desert, like a column of smoke laden with myrrh, with frankincense, and with the perfume of every exotic dust? ⁷ Ah, it is the litter of Solomon; sixty valiant men surround it, of the valiant men of Israel: ⁸ All of them expert with the sword, skilled in battle, each with his sword at his side against danger in the watches of the night. ⁹ King Solomon made himself a carriage of wood from Lebanon. ¹⁰ He made its columns of silver, its roof of gold, its seat of purple cloth, its framework inlaid with ivory. ¹¹ Daughters of Jerusalem, come forth and look upon King Solomon in the crown with which his mother has crowned him on the day of his marriage, on the day of the joy of his heart.

Caption: The marginal letters indicate the speakers of the verses:

- **B**: Bride - The beloved woman expressing her love for the bridegroom.
- **D**: Daughters of Jerusalem - The chorus of women observing and commenting on the love between the bride and bridegroom.

The Song of Songs Chapter 4

¹ **G** Ah, you are beautiful, my beloved, ah, you are beautiful! Your eyes are doves behind your veil. Your hair is like a flock of goats streaming down the mountains of Gilead. ² Your teeth are like a flock of ewes to be shorn, which come up from the washing, all of them big with twins, none of them thin and barren. ³ Your lips are like a scarlet strand; your mouth is lovely. Your cheek is like a half-pomegranate behind your veil. ⁴ Your neck is like David's tower girt with battlements; a thousand bucklers hang upon it, all the shields of valiant men. ⁵ Your breasts are like twin fawns, the young of a gazelle that browse among the lilies. ⁶ Until the day breathes cool and the shadows lengthen, I will go to the mountain of myrrh, to the hill of incense. ⁷ You are all-beautiful, my beloved, and there is no blemish in you. ⁸ Come from Lebanon, my bride, come from Lebanon, come! Descend from the top of Amana, from the top of Senir and Hermon, from the haunts of lions, from the leopards' mountains. ⁹ You have ravished my heart, my sister, my bride; you have ravished my heart with one glance of your eyes, with one bead of your necklace. ¹⁰ How beautiful is your love, my sister, my bride, how much more delightful is your love than wine, and the fragrance of your ointments than all spices! ¹¹ Your lips drip honey, my bride, sweetmeats and milk are under your tongue; and the fragrance of your garments is the fragrance of Lebanon. ¹² **G** You are an enclosed garden, my sister, my bride, an enclosed garden, a fountain sealed. ¹³ You are a park that puts forth pomegranates, with all choice fruits; ¹⁴ nard and saffron, calamus and cinnamon, with all kinds of incense; myrrh and aloes, with all the finest spices. ¹⁵ You are a garden fountain, a well of water flowing fresh from Lebanon. ¹⁶ Arise, north wind! Come, south wind! blow upon my garden that its perfumes may spread abroad. **B** Let my lover come to his garden and eat its choice fruits.

Caption: The marginal letters indicate the speakers of the verses:

- **B**: Bride - The beloved woman expressing her love for the bridegroom.
- **G**: Bridegroom - The beloved man expressing his admiration and love for the bride.

The Song of Songs Chapter 5

¹ **G** I have come to my garden, my sister, my bride; I gather my myrrh and my spices, I eat my honey and my sweetmeats, I drink my wine and my milk. **D** Eat, friends; drink! Drink freely of love! ² **B** I was sleeping, but my heart kept vigil; I heard my lover knocking: "Open to me, my sister, my beloved, my dove, my perfect one! For my head is wet with dew, my locks with the moisture of the night." ³ I have taken off my robe, am I then to put it on? I have bathed my feet, am I then to soil them? ⁴ My lover put his hand through the opening; my heart trembled within me, and I grew faint when he spoke. ⁵ I rose to open to my lover,

with my hands dripping myrrh: With my fingers dripping choice myrrh upon the fittings of the lock. ⁶ I opened to my lover—but my lover had departed, gone. I sought him but I did not find him; I called to him but he did not answer me. ⁷ **B** The watchmen came upon me as they made their rounds of the city; they struck me, and wounded me, and took my mantle from me, the guardians of the walls. ⁸ I adjure you, daughters of Jerusalem, if you find my lover—what shall you tell him?—that I am faint with love. ⁹ **D** How does your lover differ from any other, O most beautiful among women? How does your lover differ from any other, that you adjure us so? ¹⁰ **B** My lover is radiant and ruddy; he stands out among thousands. ¹¹ His head is pure gold; his locks are palm fronds, black as the raven. ¹² His eyes are like doves beside running waters, his teeth would seem bathed in milk, and are set like jewels. ¹³ His cheeks are like beds of spice with ripening aromatic herbs. His lips are red blossoms; they drip choice myrrh. ¹⁴ His arms are rods of gold adorned with chrysolites. His body is a work of ivory covered with sapphires. ¹⁵ His legs are columns of marble resting on golden bases. His stature is like the trees on Lebanon, imposing as the cedars. ¹⁶ His mouth is sweetness itself; he is all delight. Such is my lover, and such my friend, O daughters of Jerusalem.

Caption: The marginal letters indicate the speakers of the verses:

- **B**: Bride - The beloved woman expressing her love for the bridegroom.
- **D**: Daughters of Jerusalem - The chorus of women addressing the bride.
- **G**: Bridegroom - The beloved man expressing his admiration and love for the bride.

The Song of Songs Chapter 6

¹ **D** Where has your lover gone, O most beautiful among women? Where has your lover gone that we may seek him with you? ² **B** My lover has come down to his garden, to the beds of spice, to browse in the garden and to gather lilies. ³ My lover belongs to me and I to him; he browses among the lilies. ⁴ **G** You are as beautiful as Tirzah, my beloved, as lovely as Jerusalem, as awe-inspiring as bannered troops. ⁵ Turn your eyes from me, for they torment me. Your hair is like a flock of goats streaming down from Gilead. ⁶ Your teeth are like a flock of ewes which come up from the washing, all of them big with twins, none of them thin and barren. ⁷ Your cheek is like a half-pomegranate behind your veil. ⁸ There are sixty queens, eighty concubines, and maidens without number— ⁹ one alone is my dove, my perfect one, her mother's chosen, the dear one of her parent. The daughters saw her and declared her fortunate, the queens and concubines, and they sang her praises; ¹⁰ **D** Who is this that comes forth like the dawn, as beautiful as the moon, as resplendent as the sun, as awe-inspiring as bannered troops? ¹¹ **B** I came down to the nut garden to look at the fresh growth of the valley, to see if the vines were in bloom, if the pomegranates had blossomed. ¹² Before I knew it, my heart had made me the blessed one of my kinswomen.

Caption: The marginal letters indicate the speakers of the verses:

- **B**: Bride - The beloved woman expressing her love for the bridegroom.
- **D**: Daughters of Jerusalem - The chorus of women addressing the bride.
- **G**: Bridegroom - The beloved man expressing his admiration and love for the bride.

The Song of Songs Chapter 7

¹ **D** Turn, turn, O Shulammite, turn, turn, that we may look at you! **B** Why would you look at the Shulammite as at the dance of the two companies? ² **D** How beautiful are your feet in sandals, O prince's daughter! Your rounded thighs are like jewels, the handiwork of an artist. ³ Your navel is a round bowl that should never lack for mixed wine. Your body is a heap of wheat encircled with lilies. ⁴ Your breasts are like twin fawns, the young of a gazelle. ⁵ Your neck is like a tower of ivory. Your eyes are like the pools in Heshbon by the gate of Bathrabbim. Your nose is like the tower on Lebanon that looks toward Damascus. ⁶ You head rises like Carmel; your hair is like draperies of purple; a king is held captive in its tresses. ⁷ **G** How beautiful you are, how pleasing, my love, my delight! ⁸ Your very figure is like a palm tree, your breasts are like clusters. ⁹ I said: I will climb the palm tree, I will take hold of its branches. Now let your breasts be like clusters of the vine and the fragrance of your breath like apples, ¹⁰ And your mouth like an excellent wine - **B** that flows smoothly for my lover, spreading over the lips and the teeth. ¹¹ I belong to my lover and for me he yearns. ¹² Come, my lover, let us go forth to the fields and spend the night among the villages. ¹³ Let us go early to the vineyards, and see if the vines are in bloom, if the buds have opened, if the pomegranates have

blossomed; there will I give you my love. ¹⁴ The mandrakes give forth fragrance, and at our doors are all choice fruits; both fresh and mellowed fruits, my lover, I have kept in store for you.

Caption: The marginal letters indicate the speakers of the verses:

- **B**: Bride - The beloved woman expressing her love for the bridegroom.
- **D**: Daughters of Jerusalem - The chorus of women addressing the bride.
- **G**: Bridegroom - The beloved man expressing his admiration and love for the bride.

The Song of Songs Chapter 8

¹ Oh, that you were my brother, nursed at my mother's breasts! If I met you out of doors, I would kiss you and none would taunt me. ² I would lead you, bring you in to the home of my mother. There you would teach me to give you spiced wine to drink and pomegranate juice. ³ His left hand is under my head and his right arm embraces me. ⁴ I adjure you, daughters of Jerusalem, by the gazelles and hinds of the field, do not arouse, do not stir up love, before its own time. ⁵ **D** Who is this coming up from the desert, leaning upon her lover? **G** Under the apple tree I awakened you; it was there that your mother conceived you, it was there that your parent conceived. ⁶ **B** Set me as a seal on your heart, as a seal on your arm; for stern as death is love, relentless as the nether world is devotion; its flames are a blazing fire. ⁷ Deep waters cannot quench love, nor floods sweep it away. Were one to offer all he owns to purchase love, he would be roundly mocked. ⁸ "Our sister is little and she has no breasts as yet. What shall we do for our sister when her courtship begins? ⁹ If she is a wall, we will build upon it a silver parapet; if she is a door, we will reinforce it with a cedar plank." ¹⁰ I am a wall, and my breasts are like towers. So now in his eyes I have become one to be welcomed. ¹¹ **B** Solomon had a vineyard at Baal-hamon; he gave over the vineyard to caretakers. For its fruit, one would have to pay a thousand silver pieces. ¹² My vineyard is at my own disposal; the thousand pieces are for you, O Solomon, and two hundred for the caretakers of its fruit. ¹³ **G** O garden-dweller, my friends are listening for your voice, let me hear it! ¹⁴ **B** Be swift, my lover, like a gazelle or a young stag on the mountains of spices!

Caption: The marginal letters indicate the speakers of the verses:

- **B**: Bride - The beloved woman expressing her love for the bridegroom.
- **D**: Daughters of Jerusalem - The chorus of women addressing the bride.
- **G**: Bridegroom - The beloved man expressing his admiration and love for the bride.

The Wisdom of Solomon

The Wisdom of Solomon Chapter 1

¹ Love justice, you who judge the earth; think of the LORD in goodness, and seek him in integrity of heart; ² Because he is found by those who test him not, and he manifests himself to those who do not disbelieve him. ³ For perverse counsels separate a man from God, and his power, put to the proof, rebukes the foolhardy; ⁴ Because into a soul that plots evil wisdom enters not, nor dwells she in a body under debt of sin. ⁵ For the holy spirit of discipline flees deceit and withdraws from senseless counsels; and when injustice occurs it is rebuked. ⁶ For wisdom is a kindly spirit, yet she acquits not the blasphemer of his guilty lips; because God is the witness of his inmost self and the sure observer of his heart and the listener to his tongue. ⁷ For the spirit of the LORD fills the world, is all-embracing, and knows what man says. ⁸ Therefore no one who utters wicked things can go unnoticed, nor will chastising condemnation pass him by. ⁹ For the devices of the wicked man shall be scrutinized, and the sound of his words shall reach the LORD, for the chastisement of his transgressions; ¹⁰ Because a jealous ear hearkens to everything, and discordant grumblings are no secret. ¹¹ Therefore guard against profitless grumbling, and from calumny withhold your tongues; for a stealthy utterance does not go unpunished, and a lying mouth slays the soul. ¹² Court not death by your erring way of life, nor draw to yourselves destruction by the works of your hands. ¹³ Because God did not make death, nor does he rejoice in the destruction of the living. ¹⁴ For he fashioned all things that they might have being; and the creatures of the world are wholesome, and there is not a destructive drug among them nor any domain of the nether world on earth, ¹⁵ For justice is undying. ¹⁶ It was the wicked who with hands and words invited death, considered it a friend, and pined for it, and made a covenant with it, because they deserve to be in its possession.

The Wisdom of Solomon Chapter 2

¹ They who said among themselves, thinking not aright: "Brief and troublous is our lifetime; neither is there any remedy for man's dying, nor is anyone known to have come back from the nether world. ² For haphazard were we born, and hereafter we shall be as though we had not been; because the breath in our nostrils is a smoke and reason is a spark at the beating of our hearts, ³ and when this is quenched, our body will be ashes and our spirit will be poured abroad like unresisting air. ⁴ Even our name will be forgotten in time, and no one will recall our deeds. So our life will pass away like the traces of a cloud, and will be dispersed like a mist pursued by the sun's rays and overpowered by its heat. ⁵ For our lifetime is the passing of a shadow; and our dying cannot be deferred because it is fixed with a seal; and no one returns. ⁶ Come, therefore, let us enjoy the good things that are real, and use the freshness of creation avidly. ⁷ Let us have our fill of costly wine and perfumes, and let no springtime blossom pass us by; ⁸ let us crown ourselves with rosebuds ere they wither. ⁹ Let no meadow be free from our wantonness; everywhere let us leave tokens of our rejoicing, for this our portion is, and this our lot. ¹⁰ Let us oppress the needy just man; let us neither spare the widow nor revere the old man for his hair grown white with time. ¹¹ But let our strength be our norm of justice; for weakness proves itself useless. ¹² Let us beset the just one, because he is obnoxious to us; he sets himself against our doings, reproaches us for transgressions of the law and charges us with violations of our training. ¹³ He professes to have knowledge of God and styles himself a child of the LORD. ¹⁴ To us he is the censure of our thoughts; merely to see him is a hardship for us, ¹⁵ because his life is not like other men's, and different are his ways. ¹⁶ He judges us debased; he holds aloof from our paths as from things impure. He calls blest the destiny of the just and boasts that God is his Father. ¹⁷ Let us see whether his words be true; let us find out what will happen to him. ¹⁸ For if the just one be the son of God, he will defend him and deliver him from the hand of his foes. ¹⁹ With revilement and torture let us put him to the test that we may have proof of his gentleness and try his patience. ²⁰ Let us condemn him to a shameful death; for according to his own words, God will take care of him." ²¹ These were their thoughts, but they erred; for their wickedness blinded them, ²² and they knew not the hidden counsels of God; neither did they count on a recompense of holiness nor discern the innocent souls' reward. ²³ For God formed man to be imperishable; the image of his own nature he made him. ²⁴ But by the envy of the devil, death entered the world, and they who are in his possession experience it.

The Wisdom of Solomon Chapter 3

¹ But the souls of the just are in the hand of God, and no torment shall touch them. ² They seemed, in the view of the foolish, to be dead; and their passing away was thought an affliction ³ and their going forth from us, utter destruction. But they are in peace. ⁴ For if before men, indeed, they be punished, yet is their hope full of immortality; ⁵ chastised a little, they shall be greatly blessed, because God tried them and found them worthy of himself. ⁶ As gold in the furnace, he proved them, and as sacrificial offerings he took them to himself. ⁷ In the time of their visitation they shall shine, and shall dart about as sparks through stubble; ⁸ they shall judge nations and rule over peoples, and the LORD shall be their King forever. ⁹ Those who trust in him shall understand truth, and the faithful shall abide with him in love: because grace and mercy are with his holy ones, and his care is with the elect. ¹⁰ But the wicked shall receive a punishment to match their thoughts, since they neglected justice and forsook the LORD. ¹¹ For he who despises wisdom and instruction is doomed. Vain is their hope, fruitless are their labors, and worthless are their works. ¹² Their wives are foolish and their children wicked; accursed is their brood. ¹³ Yes, blessed is she who, childless and undefiled, knew not transgression of the marriage bed; she shall bear fruit at the visitation of souls. ¹⁴ So also the eunuch whose hand wrought no misdeed, who held no wicked thoughts against the LORD—for he shall be given fidelity's choice reward and a more gratifying heritage in the LORD'S temple. ¹⁵ For the fruit of noble struggles is a glorious one; and unfailing is the root of understanding. ¹⁶ But the children of adulterers will remain without issue, and the progeny of an unlawful bed will disappear. ¹⁷ For should they attain long life, they will be held in no esteem, and dishonored will their old age be at last; ¹⁸ while should they die abruptly, they have no hope nor comfort in the day of scrutiny; ¹⁹ for dire is the end of the wicked generation.

The Wisdom of Solomon Chapter 4

¹ Better is childlessness with virtue; for immortal is its memory: because both by God is it acknowledged, and by men. ² When it is present men imitate it, and they long for it when it is gone; and forever it marches crowned in triumph, victorious in unsullied deeds of valor.

3 But the numerous progeny of the wicked shall be of no avail; their spurious offshoots shall not strike deep root nor take firm hold. 4 For even though their branches flourish for a time, they are unsteady and shall be rocked by the wind and, by the violence of the winds, uprooted; 5 their twigs shall be broken off untimely, and their fruit be useless, unripe for eating, and fit for nothing. 6 For children born of lawless unions give evidence of the wickedness of their parents, when they are examined. 7 But the just man, though he die early, shall be at rest. 8 For the age that is honorable comes not with the passing of time, nor can it be measured in terms of years. 9 Rather, understanding is the hoary crown for men, and an unsullied life, the attainment of old age. 10 He who pleased God was loved; he who lived among sinners was transported. 11 Snatched away, lest wickedness pervert his mind or deceit beguile his soul; 12 for the witchery of paltry things obscures what is right and the whirl of desire transforms the innocent mind. 13 Having become perfect in a short while, he reached the fullness of a long career; 14 for his soul was pleasing to the LORD, therefore he sped him out of the midst of wickedness. But the people saw and did not understand, nor did they take this into account. 15 Yes, the just man dead condemns the sinful who live, and youth swiftly completed condemns the many years of the wicked man grown old. 16 For they see the death of the wise man and do not understand what the LORD intended for him, or why he made him secure. 17 They see, and hold him in contempt; but the LORD laughs them to scorn. 18 And they shall afterward become dishonored corpses and an unceasing mockery among the dead. For he shall strike them down speechless and prostrate and rock them to their foundations; they shall be utterly laid waste and shall be in grief and their memory shall perish. 19 Fearful shall they come, at the counting up of their sins, and their lawless deeds shall convict them to their face.

The Wisdom of Solomon Chapter 5

1 Then shall the just one with great assurance confront his oppressors who set at nought his labors. 2 Seeing this, they shall be shaken with dreadful fear, and amazed at the unlooked-for salvation. 3 They shall say among themselves, rueful and groaning through anguish of spirit: "This is he whom once we held as a laughingstock and as a type for mockery, 4 fools that we were! His life we accounted madness, and his death dishonored. 5 See how he is accounted among the sons of God; how his lot is with the saints! 6 We, then, have strayed from the way of truth, and the light of justice did not shine for us, and the sun did not rise for us. 7 We had our fill of the ways of mischief and of ruin; we journeyed through impassable deserts, but the way of the LORD we knew not. 8 What did our pride avail us? What have wealth and its boastfulness afforded us? 9 All of them passed like a shadow and like a fleeting rumor; 10 Like a ship traversing the heaving water, of which, when it has passed, no trace can be found, no path of its keel in the waves. 11 Or like a bird flying through the air; no evidence of its course is to be found - But the fluid air, lashed by the beat of pinions, and cleft by the rushing force of speeding wings, is traversed: and afterward no mark of passage can be found in it. 12 Or as, when an arrow has been shot at a mark, the parted air straightway flows together again so that none discerns the way it went through - 13 Even so we, once born, abruptly came to nought and held no sign of virtue to display; but were consumed in our wickedness." 14 Yes, the hope of the wicked is like thistledown borne on the wind, and like fine, tempest-driven foam; like smoke scattered by the wind, and like the passing memory of the nomad camping for a single day. 15 But the just live forever, and in the LORD is their recompense, and the thought of them is with the Most High. 16 Therefore shall they receive the splendid crown, the beauteous diadem, from the hand of the LORD - for he shall shelter them with his right hand, and protect them with his arm. 17 He shall take his zeal for armor and he shall arm creation to requite the enemy; 18 He shall don justice for a breastplate and shall wear sure judgment for a helmet; 19 He shall take invincible rectitude as a shield 20 and whet his sudden anger for a sword, and the universe shall war with him against the foolhardy. 21 Well-aimed shafts of lightnings shall go forth and from the clouds as from a well-drawn bow shall leap to the mark; 22 and as from his sling, wrathful hailstones shall be hurled. The water of the sea shall be enraged against them and the streams shall abruptly overflow; 23 A mighty wind shall confront them and a tempest winnow them out; thus lawlessness shall lay the whole earth waste and evildoing overturn the thrones of potentates.

The Wisdom of Solomon Chapter 6

1 Hear, therefore, kings, and understand; learn, you magistrates of the earth's expanse! 2 Hearken, you who are in power over the multitude and lord it over throngs of peoples! 3 Because authority was given you by the LORD and sovereignty by the Most High, who shall probe your works and scrutinize your counsels! 41 Because, though you were ministers of his kingdom, you judged not rightly, and did not keep the law, nor walk according to the will of God, 5 Terribly and swiftly shall he come against you, because judgment is stern for the exalted - 6 For the lowly may be pardoned out of mercy but the mighty shall be mightily put to the test. 7 For the Lord of all shows no partiality, nor does he fear greatness, because he himself made the great as well as the small, and he provides for all alike; 8 but for those in power a rigorous scrutiny impends. 9 To you, therefore, O princes, are my words addressed that you may learn wisdom and that you may not sin. 10 2 For those who keep the holy precepts hallowed shall be found holy, and those learned in them will have ready a response. 11 Desire therefore my words; long for them and you shall be instructed. 12 Resplendent and unfading is Wisdom, and she is readily perceived by those who love her, and found by those who seek her. 13 She hastens to make herself known in anticipation of men's desire; 14 he who watches for her at dawn shall not be disappointed, for he shall find her sitting by his gate. 15 For taking thought of her is the perfection of prudence, and he who for her sake keeps vigil shall quickly be free from care; 16 Because she makes her own rounds, seeking those worthy of her, and graciously appears to them in the ways, and meets them with all solicitude. 17 For the first step toward discipline is a very earnest desire for her; then, care for discipline is love of her; 18 love means the keeping of her laws; to observe her laws is the basis for incorruptibility; 19 and incorruptibility makes one close to God; 20 thus the desire for Wisdom leads up to a kingdom. 21 If, then, you find pleasure in throne and scepter, you princes of the peoples, honor Wisdom, that you may reign as kings forever. 22 Now what wisdom is, and how she came to be I shall relate; and I shall hide no secrets from you, but from the very beginning I shall search out and bring to light knowledge of her, nor shall I diverge from the truth. 23 Neither shall I admit consuming jealousy to my company, because that can have no fellowship with Wisdom. 24 A great number of wise men is the safety of the world, and a prudent king, the stability of his people; 25 so take instruction from my words, to your profit.

The Wisdom of Solomon Chapter 7

1 I too am a mortal man, the same as all the rest, and a descendant of the first man formed on earth. And in my mother's womb I was molded into flesh, 2 in a ten-months' period-body and blood, from the seed of man, and the pleasure that accompanies marriage. 3 And I too, when born, inhaled the common air, and fell upon the kindred earth; wailing, I uttered that first sound common to all. 4 In swaddling clothes and with constant care I was nurtured. 5 For no king has any different origin or birth, 6 but one is the entry into life for all; and in one same way they leave it. 7 Therefore I prayed, and prudence was given me; I pleaded and the spirit of Wisdom came to me. 8 I preferred her to scepter and throne, and deemed riches nothing in comparison with her, 9 nor did I liken any priceless gem to her; because all gold, in view of her, is a little sand, and before her, silver is to be accounted mire. 10 Beyond health and comeliness I loved her, and I chose to have her rather than the light, because the splendor of her never yields to sleep. 11 Yet all good things together came to me in her company, and countless riches at her hands; 12 and I rejoiced in them all, because Wisdom is their leader, though I had not known that she is the mother of these. 13 Simply I learned about her, and ungrudgingly do I share—her riches I do not hide away; 14 for to men she is an unfailing treasure; those who gain this treasure win the friendship of God, to whom the gifts they have from discipline commend them. 15 Now God grant I speak suitably and value these endowments at their worth: for he is the guide of Wisdom and the director of the wise. 16 For both we and our words are in his hand, as well as all prudence and knowledge of crafts. 17 For he gave me sound knowledge of existing things, that I might know the organization of the universe and the force of its elements, 18 the beginning and the end and the midpoint of times, the changes in the sun's course and the variations of the seasons. 19 Cycles of years, positions of the stars, 20 natures of animals, tempers of beasts, powers of the winds and thoughts of men, uses of plants and virtues of roots— 21 such things as are hidden I learned and such as are plain; 22 for Wisdom, the artificer of all, taught me. For in her is a spirit intelligent, holy, unique, manifold, subtle, agile, clear, unstained, certain, not baneful, loving the good, keen, unhampered, beneficent, 23 kindly, firm, secure, tranquil, all-powerful, all-seeing, and pervading all spirits, though they be intelligent, pure and very subtle. 24 For Wisdom is mobile beyond all motion, and she penetrates and pervades all things by reason of her purity. 25 For she is an aura of the might of God and a pure effusion of the glory of the Almighty; therefore nought that is sullied enters into her. 26 For she is the refulgence of eternal light, the spotless mirror of the power of God, the image of his goodness. 27 And she, who is one, can do all things, and renews everything while herself perduring; and passing into holy souls

from age to age, she produces friends of God and prophets. 28 For there is nought God loves, be it not one who dwells with Wisdom. 29 For she is fairer than the sun and surpasses every constellation of the stars. Compared to light, she takes precedence; 30 for that, indeed, night supplants, but wickedness prevails not over Wisdom.

The Wisdom of Solomon Chapter 8

1 Indeed, she reaches from end to end mightily and governs all things well. 2 Her I loved and sought after from my youth; I sought to take her for my bride and was enamored of her beauty. 3 She adds to nobility the splendor of companionship with God; even the LORD of all loved her. 4 For she is instructress in the understanding of God, the selector of his works. 5 And if riches be a desirable possession in life, what is more rich than Wisdom, who produces all things? 6 And if prudence renders service, who in the world is a better craftsman than she? 7 Or if one loves justice, the fruits of her works are virtues; for she teaches moderation and prudence, justice and fortitude, and nothing in life is more useful for men than these. 8 Or again, if one yearns for copious learning, she knows the things of old, and infers those yet to come. She understands the turns of phrases and the solutions of riddles; signs and wonders she knows in advance and the outcome of times and ages. 9 So I determined to take her to live with me, knowing that she would be my counselor while all was well, and my comfort in care and grief. 10 For her sake I should have glory among the masses, and esteem from the elders, though I be but a youth. 11 I should become keen in judgment, and should be a marvel before rulers. 12 They would abide my silence and attend my utterance; and as I spoke on further, they would place their hands upon their mouths. 13 For her sake I should have immortality and leave to those after me an everlasting memory. 14 I should govern peoples, and nations would be my subjects— 15 terrible princes, hearing of me, would be afraid; in the assembly I should appear noble, and in war courageous. 16 Within my dwelling, I should take my repose beside her; for association with her involves no bitterness and living with her no grief, but rather joy and gladness. 17 Thinking thus within myself, and reflecting in my heart that there is immortality in kinship with Wisdom, 18 and good pleasure in her friendship, and unfailing riches in the works of her hands, and that in frequenting her society there is prudence, and fair renown in sharing her discourses, I went about seeking to take her for my own. 19 Now, I was a well-favored child, and I came by a noble nature; 20 or rather, being noble, I attained an unsullied body. 21 And knowing that I could not otherwise possess her except God gave it—and this, too, was prudence, to know whose is the gift—I went to the LORD and besought him, and said with all my heart:

The Wisdom of Solomon Chapter 9

1 God of my fathers, LORD of mercy. you who have made all things by your word 2 And in your wisdom have established man to rule the creatures produced by you, 3 To govern the world in holiness and justice, and to render judgment in integrity of heart: 4 Give me Wisdom, the attendant at your throne, and reject me not from among your children; 5 For I am your servant, the son of your handmaid, a man weak and short-lived and lacking in comprehension of judgment and of laws. 6 Indeed, though one be perfect among the sons of men, if Wisdom, who comes from you, be not with him, he shall be held in no esteem. 7 You have chosen me king over your people and magistrate for your sons and daughters. 8 You have bid me build a temple on your holy mountain and an altar in the city that is your dwelling place, a copy of the holy tabernacle which you had established from of old. 9 Now with you is Wisdom, who knows your works and was present when you made the world; Who understands what is pleasing in your eyes and what is conformable with your commands. 10 Send her forth from your holy heavens and from your glorious throne dispatch her that she may be with me and work with me, that I may know what is your pleasure. 11 For she knows and understands all things, and will guide me discreetly in my affairs and safeguard me by her glory; 12 Thus my deeds will be acceptable, and I shall judge your people justly and be worthy of my father's throne. 13 For what man knows God's counsel, or who can conceive what our LORD intends? 14 For the deliberations of mortals are timid, and unsure are our plans. 15 For the corruptible body burdens the soul and the earthen shelter weighs down the mind that has many concerns. 16 And scarce do we guess the things on earth, and what is within our grasp we find with difficulty; but when things are in heaven, who can search them out? 17 Or who ever knew your counsel, except you had given Wisdom and sent your holy spirit from on high? 18 And thus were the paths of those on earth made straight, and men learned what was your pleasure, and were saved by Wisdom.

The Wisdom of Solomon Chapter 10

1 She preserved the first-formed father of the world when he alone had been created; And she raised him up from his fall, 2 and gave him power to rule all things. 3 But when the unjust man withdrew from her in his anger, he perished through his fratricidal wrath. 4 When on his account the earth was flooded, Wisdom again saved it, piloting the just man on frailest wood. 5 She, when the nations were sunk in universal wickedness, knew the just man, kept him blameless before God, and preserved him resolute against pity for his child. 6 She delivered the just man from among the wicked who were being destroyed, when he fled as fire descended upon Pentapolis— 7 Where as a testimony to its wickedness, there yet remain a smoking desert, Plants bearing fruit that never ripens, and the tomb of a disbelieving soul, a standing pillar of salt. 8 For those who forsook Wisdom first were bereft of knowledge of the right, And then they left mankind a memorial of their folly—so that they could not even be hidden in their fall. 9 But Wisdom delivered from tribulations those who served her. 10 She, when the just man fled from his brother's anger, guided him in direct ways, Showed him the kingdom of God and gave him knowledge of holy things; She prospered him in his labors and made abundant the fruit of his works, 11 Stood by him against the greed of his defrauders, and enriched him; 12 She preserved him from foes, and secured him against ambush, And she gave him the prize for his stern struggle that he might know that devotion to God is mightier than all else. 13 She did not abandon the just man when he was sold, but delivered him from sin. 14 She went down with him into the dungeon, and did not desert him in his bonds, Until she brought him the scepter of royalty and authority over his oppressors, Showed those who had defamed him false, and gave him eternal glory. 15 The holy people and blameless race—it was she who delivered them from the nation that oppressed them. 16 She entered the soul of the LORD'S servant, and withstood fearsome kings with signs and portents; 17 she gave the holy ones the recompense of their labors, Conducted them by a wondrous road, and became a shelter for them by day and a starry flame by night. 18 She took them across the Red Sea and brought them through the deep waters— 19 But their enemies she overwhelmed, and cast them up from the bottom of the depths. 20 Therefore the just despoiled the wicked; and they sang, O LORD, your holy name 21 Because Wisdom opened the mouths of the dumb, and gave ready speech to infants.

The Wisdom of Solomon Chapter 11

1 She made their affairs prosper through the holy prophet. 2 They journeyed through the uninhabited desert, and in solitudes they pitched their tents; 3 they withstood enemies and took vengeance on their foes. 4 When they thirsted, they called upon you, and water was given them from the sheer rock, assuagement for their thirst from the hard stone. 5 For by the things through which their foes were punished they in their need were benefited. 6 Instead of a spring, when the perennial river was troubled with impure blood 7 as a rebuke to the decree for the slaying of infants, You gave them abundant water in an unhoped-for way, 8 once you had shown by the thirst they then had how you punished their adversaries. 9 For when they had been tried, though only mildly chastised, they recognized how the wicked, condemned in anger, were being tormented. 10 Both those afar off and those close by were afflicted: the latter you tested, admonishing them as a father; the former as a stern king you probed and condemned. 11 For a twofold grief took hold of them and a groaning at the remembrance of the ones who had departed. 12 For when they heard that the cause of their own torments was a benefit to these others, they recognized the Lord. 13 Him who of old had been cast out in exposure they indeed mockingly rejected; but in the end of events, they marveled at him, since their thirst proved unlike that of the just. 14 And in return for their senseless, wicked thoughts, which misled them into worshiping dumb serpents and worthless insects, You sent upon them swarms of dumb creatures for vengeance; 15 that they might recognize that a man is punished by the very things through which he sins. 16 For not without means was your almighty hand, that had fashioned the universe from formless matter, to send upon them a drove of bears or fierce lions, 17 Or new-created, wrathful, unknown beasts to breathe forth fiery breath, Or pour out roaring smoke, or flash terrible sparks from their eyes. 18 Not only could these attack and completely destroy them; even their frightful appearance itself could slay. 19 Even without these, they could have been killed at a single blast, pursued by retribution and winnowed out by your mighty spirit; But you have disposed all things by measure and number and weight. 20 For with you great strength abides always; who can resist the might of your arm? 21 Indeed, before you the whole universe is as a grain from a balance, or a drop of morning dew come down upon the earth. 22 But you have mercy on all, because you can do all things; and you overlook the sins of men that they may repent. 23 For you love all things that are and loathe nothing that you have made; for what you hated, you would not have fashioned. 24 And how could a

thing remain, unless you willed it; or be preserved, had it not been called forth by you? 25 But you spare all things, because they are yours, O LORD and lover of souls.

The Wisdom of Solomon Chapter 12

1 For your imperishable spirit is in all things! 2 Therefore you rebuke offenders little by little, warn them, and remind them of the sins they are committing, that they may abandon their wickedness and believe in you, O LORD! 3 For truly, the ancient inhabitants of your holy land, 4 whom you hated for deeds most odious—works of witchcraft and impious sacrifices; 5 a cannibal feast of human flesh and blood from the midst of...—these merciless murderers of children, 6 and parents who took with their own hands defenseless lives, you willed to destroy by the hands of our fathers, 7 that the land that is dearest of all to you might receive a worthy colony of God's children. 8 But even these, as they were men, you spared, and sent wasps as forerunners of your army that they might exterminate them by degrees. 9 Not that you were without power to have the wicked vanquished in battle by the just, or wiped out at once by terrible beasts or by one decisive word; 10 but condemning them bit by bit, you gave them space for repentance. You were not unaware that their race was wicked and their malice ingrained, and that their dispositions would never change; 11 for they were a race accursed from the beginning. Neither out of fear for anyone did you grant amnesty for their sins. 12 For who can say to you, "What have you done?" or who can oppose your decree? Or when peoples perish, who can challenge you, their maker; or who can come into your presence as vindicator of unjust men? 13 For neither is there any god besides you who have the care of all, that you need show you have not unjustly condemned; 14 nor can any king or prince confront you on behalf of those you have punished. 15 But as you are just, you govern all things justly; you regard it as unworthy of your power to punish one who has incurred no blame. 16 For your might is the source of justice; your mastery over all things makes you lenient to all. 17 For you show your might when the perfection of your power is disbelieved; and in those who know you, you rebuke temerity. 18 But though you are master of might, you judge with clemency, and with much lenience you govern us; for power, whenever you will, attends you. 19 And you taught your people, by these deeds, that those who are just must be kind; and you gave your sons good ground for hope that you would permit repentance for their sins. 20 For these were enemies of your servants, doomed to death; yet, while you punished them with such solicitude and pleading, granting time and opportunity to abandon wickedness, 21 with what exactitude you judged your sons, to whose fathers you gave the sworn covenants of goodly promises! 22 Us, therefore, you chastise, and our enemies with a thousand blows you punish, that we may think earnestly of your goodness when we judge, and, when being judged, may look for mercy. 23 Hence those unjust also, who lived a life of folly, you tormented through their own abominations. 24 For they went far astray in the paths of error, taking for gods the worthless and disgusting among beasts, deceived like senseless infants. 25 Therefore, as though upon unreasoning children, you sent your judgment on them as a mockery; 26 but they who took no heed of punishment, which was but child's play, were to experience a condemnation worthy of God. 27 For in the things through which they suffered distress, since they were tortured by the very things they deemed gods, they saw and recognized the true God whom before they had refused to know; with this, their final condemnation came upon them.

The Wisdom of Solomon Chapter 13

1 For all men were by natur foolish who were in ignorance of God, and who from the good things seen did not succeed in knowing Him who is, and from studying the works did not discern the artisan; 2 but either fire, or wind, or the swift air, or the circuit of the stars, or the mighty water, or the luminaries of heaven, the governors of the world, they considered gods. 3 Now if out of joy in their beauty they thought them gods, let them know how far more excellent is the Lord than these; for the original source of beauty fashioned them. 4 Or if they were struck by their might and energy, let them from these things realize how much more powerful is He who made them. 5 For from the greatness and the beauty of created things their original author, by analogy, is seen. 6 But yet, for these the blame is less; for they indeed have gone astray perhaps, though they seek God and wish to find Him. 7 For they search busily among His works, but are distracted by what they see, because the things seen are fair. 8 But again, not even these are pardonable. 9 For if they so far succeeded in knowledge that they could speculate about the world, how did they not more quickly find its Lord? 10 But doomed are they, and in dead things are their hopes, who termed gods things made by human hands: gold and silver, the product of art, and likenesses of beasts, or useless stone, the work of an ancient hand. 11 A carpenter may saw out a suitable tree and skillfully scrape off all its bark, and deftly plying his art, produce something fit for daily use, 12 and use up the refuse from his handiwork in preparing his food, and have his fill; 13 then the good-for-nothing refuse from these remnants, crooked wood grown full of knots, he takes and carves to occupy his spare time. This wood he models with listless skill, and patterns it on the image of a man 14 or makes it resemble some worthless beast. When he has daubed it with red and crimsoned its surface with red stain, and daubed over every blemish in it, 15 he makes a fitting shrine for it and puts it on the wall, fastening it with a nail. 16 Thus lest it fall down he provides for it, knowing that it cannot help itself; for, truly, it is an image and needs help. 17 But when he prays about his goods or marriage or children, he is not ashamed to address the thing without a soul. And for vigor he invokes the powerless; 18 and for life he entreats the dead; and for aid he beseeches the wholly incompetent, and about travel, something that cannot even walk. 19 And for profit in business and success with his hands, he asks facility of a thing with hands completely inert.

The Wisdom of Solomon Chapter 14

1 Again, one preparing for a voyage and about to traverse the wild waves cries out to wood more unsound than the boat that bears him. 2 For the urge for profits devised this latter, and Wisdom the artificer produced it. 3 But your providence, O Father! guides it, for you have furnished even in the sea a road, and through the waves a steady path, 4 showing that you can save from any danger, so that even one without skill may embark. 5 But you will that the products of your Wisdom be not idle; therefore men trust their lives even to frailest wood, and have been safe crossing the surge on a raft. 6 For of old, when the proud giants were being destroyed, the hope of the universe, who took refuge on a raft, left to the world a future for his race, under the guidance of your hand. 7 For blest is the wood through which justice comes about; 8 but the handmade idol is accursed, and its maker as well: he for having produced it, and it, because though corruptible, it was termed a god. 9 Equally odious to God are the evildoer and his evil deed; 10 and the thing made shall be punished with its contriver. 11 Therefore upon even the idols of the nations shall a visitation come, since they have become abominable amid God's works, snares for the souls of men and a trap for the feet of the senseless. 12 For the source of wantonness is the devising of idols; and their invention was a corruption of life. 13 For in the beginning they were not, nor shall they continue forever; 14 for by the vanity of men they came into the world, and therefore a sudden end is devised for them. 15 For a father, afflicted with untimely mourning, made an image of the child so quickly taken from him, and now honored as a god what was formerly a dead man and handed down to his subjects mysteries and sacrifices. 16 Then, in time, the impious practice gained strength and was observed as law, and graven things were worshiped by princely decrees. 17 Men who lived so far away that they could not honor him in his presence copied the appearance of the distant king and made a public image of him they wished to honor, out of zeal to flatter him when absent, as though present. 18 And to promote this observance among those to whom it was strange, the artisan's ambition provided a stimulus. 19 For he, mayhap in his determination to please the ruler, labored over the likeness to the best of his skill; 20 and the masses, drawn by the charm of the workmanship, soon thought he should be worshiped who shortly before was honored as a man. 21 And this became a snare for mankind, that men enslaved to either grief or tyranny conferred the incommunicable Name on stocks and stones. 22 Then it was not enough for them to err in their knowledge of God; but even though they live in a great war of ignorance, they call such evils peace. 23 For while they celebrate either child-slaying sacrifices or clandestine mysteries, or frenzied carousals in unheard-of rites, 24 they no longer safeguard either lives or pure wedlock; but each either waylays and kills his neighbor, or aggrieves him by adultery. 25 And all is confusion—blood and murder, theft and guile, corruption, faithlessness, turmoil, perjury, 26 disturbance of good men, neglect of gratitude, besmirching of souls, unnatural lust, disorder in marriage, adultery, and shamelessness. 27 For the worship of infamous idols is the reason and source and extremity of all evil. 28 For they either go mad with enjoyment, or prophesy lies, or live lawlessly, or lightly forswear themselves. 29 For as their trust is in soulless idols, they expect no harm when they have sworn falsely. 30 But on both counts shall justice overtake them: because they thought ill of God and devoted themselves to idols, and because they deliberately swore false oaths, despising piety. 31 For not the might of those that are sworn by but the retribution of sinners ever follows upon the transgression of the wicked.

The Wisdom of Solomon Chapter 15

1 But you, our God, are good and true, slow to anger, and governing all

with mercy. 2 For even if we sin, we are yours, and know your might; but we will not sin, knowing that we belong to you. 3 For to know you well is complete justice, and to know your might is the root of immortality. 4 For neither did the evil creation of men's fancy deceive us, nor the fruitless labor of painters, a form smeared with varied colors, 5 the sight of which arouses yearning in the senseless man, till he longs for the inanimate form of a dead image. 6 Lovers of evil things, and worthy of such hopes are they who make them and long for them and worship them. 7 For truly the potter, laboriously working the soft earth, molds for our service each several article: Both the vessels that serve for clean purposes and their opposites, all alike; as to what shall be the use of each vessel of either class the worker in clay is the judge. 8 And with misspent toil he molds a meaningless god from the selfsame clay; though he himself shortly before was made from the earth and after a little, is to go whence he was taken, when the life that was lent him is demanded back. 9 But his concern is not that he is to die nor that his span of life is brief; rather, he vies with goldsmiths and silversmiths and emulates molders of bronze, and takes pride in modeling counterfeits. 10 Ashes his heart is! More worthless than earth is his hope, and more ignoble than clay his life; 11 because he knew not the one who fashioned him, and breathed into him a quickening soul, and infused a vital spirit. 12 Instead, he esteemed our life a plaything, and our span of life a holiday for gain; "For one must," says he, "make profit every way, be it even out of evil." 13 For this man more than any knows that he is sinning, when out of earthen stuff he creates fragile vessels and idols alike. 14 But all quite senseless, and worse than childish in mind, are the enemies of your people who enslaved them. 15 For they esteemed all the idols of the nations gods, which have no use of the eyes for vision, nor nostrils to snuff the air, nor ears to hear, nor fingers on their hands for feeling; even their feet are useless to walk with. 16 For a man made them; one whose own spirit has been lent him fashioned them. For no man succeeds in fashioning a god like himself; 17 being mortal, he makes a dead thing with his lawless hands. For he is better than the things he worships; he at least lives, but never they. 18 And besides, they worship the most loathsome beasts — for compared as to folly, these are worse than the rest, 19 nor for their looks are they good or desirable beasts, but they have escaped both the approval of God and his blessing.

The Wisdom of Solomon Chapter 16

1 Therefore they were fittingly punished by similar creatures, and were tormented by a swarm of insects. 2 Instead of this punishment, you benefited your people with a novel dish, the delight they craved, by providing quail for their food; 3 that those others, when they desired food, since the creatures sent to plague them were so loathsome, should be turned from even the craving of necessities, while these, after a brief period of privation, partook of a novel dish. 4 For upon those oppressors, inexorable want had to come; but these needed only be shown how their enemies were being tormented. 5 For when the dire venom of beasts came upon them and they were dying from the bite of crooked serpents, your anger endured not to the end. 6 But as a warning, for a short time they were terrorized, though they had a sign of salvation, to remind them of the precept of your law. 7 For he who turned toward it was saved, not by what he saw, but by you, the savior of all. 8 And by this also you convinced our foes that you are he who delivers from all evil. 9 For the bites of locusts and of flies slew them, and no remedy was found to save their lives because they deserved to be punished by such means; 10 but not even the fangs of poisonous reptiles overcame your sons, for your mercy brought the antidote to heal them. 11 For as a reminder of your injunctions, they were stung, and swiftly they were saved, lest they should fall into deep forgetfulness and become unresponsive to your beneficence. 12 For indeed, neither herb nor application cured them, but your all-healing word, O LORD! 13 For you have dominion over life and death; you lead down to the gates of the nether world, and lead back. 14 Man, however, slays in his malice, but when the spirit has come away, it does not return, nor can he bring back the soul once it is confined. 15 But your hand none can escape. 16 For the wicked who refused to know you were punished by the might of your arm, pursued by unwonted rains and hailstorms and unremitting downpours, and consumed by fire. 17 For against all expectation, in water which quenches anything, the fire grew more active; for the universe fights on behalf of the just. 18 For now the flame was tempered so that the beasts might not be burnt up that were sent upon the wicked, but that these might see and know they were struck by the judgment of God; 19 and again, even in the water, fire blazed beyond its strength so as to consume the produce of the wicked land. 20 Instead of this, you nourished your people with food of angels and furnished them bread from heaven, ready to hand, untoiled-for, endowed with all delights and conforming to every taste. 21 For this substance of yours revealed your sweetness toward your children, and

serving the desire of him who received it, was blended to whatever flavor each one wished. 22 Yet snow and ice withstood fire and were not melted, that they might know that their enemies' fruits were consumed by a fire that blazed in the hail and flashed lightning in the rain. 23 But this fire, again, that the just might be nourished, forgot even its proper strength; 24 for your creation, serving you, its maker, grows tense for punishment against the wicked, but is relaxed in benefit for those who trust in you. 25 Therefore at that very time, transformed in all sorts of ways, it was serving your all-nourishing bounty according to what they needed and desired; 26 that your sons whom you loved might learn, O LORD, that it is not the various kinds of fruits that nourish man, but it is your word that preserves those who believe you! 27 For what was not destroyed by fire, when merely warmed by a momentary sunbeam, melted; 28 so that men might know that one must give you thanks before the sunrise, and turn to you at daybreak. 29 For the hope of the ingrate melts like a wintry frost and runs off like useless water.

The Wisdom of Solomon Chapter 17

1 For great are your judgments, and hardly to be described; therefore the unruly souls were wrong. 2 For when the lawless thought to enslave the holy nation, shackled with darkness, fettered by the long night, they lay confined beneath their own roofs as exiles from the eternal providence. 3 For they who supposed their secret sins were hid under the dark veil of oblivion were scattered in fearful trembling, terrified by apparitions. 4 For not even their inner chambers kept them fearless, for crashing sounds on all sides terrified them, and mute phantoms with somber looks appeared. 5 No force, even of fire, was able to give light, nor did the flaming brilliance of the stars succeed in lighting up that gloomy night. 6 But only intermittent, fearful fires flashed through upon them; and in their terror, they thought beholding these was worse than the times when that sight was no longer to be seen. 7 And mockeries of the magic art were in readiness, and a jeering reproof of their vaunted shrewdness. 8 For they who undertook to banish fears and terrors from the sick soul themselves sickened with a ridiculous fear. 9 For even though no monstrous thing frightened them, they shook at the passing of insects and the hissing of reptiles, 10 and perished trembling, reluctant to face even the air that they could nowhere escape. 11 For wickedness, of its nature cowardly, testifies in its own condemnation, and because of a distressed conscience, always magnifies misfortunes. 12 For fear is nought but the surrender of the helps that come from reason; 13 and the more one's expectation is of itself uncertain, the more one makes of not knowing the cause that brings on torment. 14 So they, during that night, powerless though it was, that had come upon them from the recesses of a powerless nether world, while all sleeping the same sleep, 15 were partly smitten by fearsome apparitions and partly stricken by their souls' surrender; for fear came upon them, sudden and unexpected. 16 Thus, then, whoever was there fell into that unbarred prison and was kept confined. 17 For whether one was a farmer, or a shepherd, or a worker at tasks in the wasteland, taken unawares, he served out the inescapable sentence; 18 for all were bound by the one bond of darkness. And were it only the whistling wind, or the melodious song of birds in the spreading branches, or the steady sound of rushing water, 19 or the rude crash of overthrown rocks, or the unseen gallop of bounding animals, or the roaring cry of the fiercest beasts, or an echo resounding from the hollow of the hills, these sounds, inspiring terror, paralyzed them. 20 For the whole world shone with brilliant light and continued its works without interruption; 21 over them alone was spread oppressive night, an image of the darkness that next should come upon them; yet they were to themselves more burdensome than the darkness.

The Wisdom of Solomon Chapter 18

1 But your holy ones had very great light; and those others, who heard their voices but did not see their forms, since now they themselves had suffered, called them blessed. 2 And because they who formerly had been wronged did not harm them, they thanked them and pleaded with them, for the sake of the difference between them. 3 Instead of this, you furnished the flaming pillar which was a guide on the unknown way, and the mild sun for an honorable migration. 4 For those deserved to be deprived of light and imprisoned by darkness, who had kept your sons confined through whom the imperishable light of the law was to be given to the world. 5 When they determined to put to death the infants of the holy ones, and when a single boy had been cast forth but saved, as a reproof you carried off their multitude of sons and made them perish all at once in the mighty water. 6 That night was known beforehand to our fathers, that, with sure knowledge of the oaths in which they put their faith, they might have courage. 7 Your people awaited the salvation of the just and the destruction of their foes. 8 For when you punished our adversaries, in this you glorified us whom you

had summoned. 9 For in secret the holy children of the good were offering sacrifice and putting into effect with one accord the divine institution, that your holy ones should share alike the same good things and dangers, having previously sung the praises of the fathers. 10 But the discordant cry of their enemies responded, and the piteous wail of mourning for children was borne to them. 11 And the slave was smitten with the same retribution as his master; even the plebeian suffered the same as the king. 12 And all alike by a single death had countless dead; for the living were not even sufficient for the burial, since at a single instant their nobler offspring were destroyed. 13 For though they disbelieved at every turn on account of sorceries, at the destruction of the first-born they acknowledged that the people was God's son. 14 For when peaceful stillness compassed everything and the night in its swift course was half spent, 15 your all-powerful word from heaven's royal throne bounded, a fierce warrior, into the doomed land, 16 bearing the sharp sword of your inexorable decree. And as he alighted, he filled every place with death; he still reached to heaven while he stood upon the earth. 17 Then, forthwith, visions in horrible dreams perturbed them and unexpected fears assailed them; 18 and cast half-dead, one here, another there, each was revealing the reason for his dying. 19 For the dreams that disturbed them had proclaimed this beforehand, lest they perish unaware of why they suffered ill. 20 But the trial of death touched at one time even the just, and in the desert a plague struck the multitude; yet not for long did the anger last. 21 For the blameless man hastened to be their champion, bearing the weapon of his special office, prayer and the propitiation of incense; he withstood the wrath and put a stop to the calamity, showing that he was your servant. 22 And he overcame the bitterness not by bodily strength, not by force of arms; but by word he overcame the smiter, recalling the sworn covenants with their fathers. 23 For when corpses had already fallen one on another in heaps, he stood in the midst and checked the anger and cut off the way to the living. 24 For on his full-length robe was the whole world, and the glories of the fathers were carved in four rows upon the stones, and your grandeur was on the crown upon his head. 25 To these names the destroyer yielded, and these he feared; for the mere trial of anger was enough.

The Wisdom of Solomon Chapter 19

1 But the wicked, merciless wrath assailed until the end. For he knew beforehand what they were yet to do: 2 that though they themselves had agreed to the departure and had anxiously sent them on their way, they would regret it and pursue them. 3 For while they were still engaged in funeral rites and were mourning at the burials of the dead, they adopted another senseless plan; and those whom they had sent away with entreaty, they pursued as fugitives. 4 For a compulsion suited to this ending drew them on, and made them forgetful of what had befallen them, that they might fill out the torments of their punishment, 5 and your people might experience a glorious journey while those others met an extraordinary death. 6 For all creation, in its several kinds, was being made over anew, serving its natural laws, that your children might be preserved unharmed. 7 The cloud overshadowed their camp; and out of what had before been water, dry land was seen emerging: out of the Red Sea an unimpeded road, and a grassy plain out of the mighty flood. 8 Over this crossed the whole nation sheltered by your hand, after they beheld stupendous wonders. 9 For they ranged about like horses, and bounded about like lambs, praising you, O LORD! their deliverer. 10 For they were still mindful of what had happened in their sojourn: how instead of the young of animals the land brought forth gnats, and instead of fishes the river swarmed with countless frogs. 11 And later they saw also a new kind of bird when, prompted by desire, they asked for pleasant foods; 12 for to appease them quail came to them from the sea. 13 And the punishments came upon the sinners only after forewarnings from the violence of the thunderbolts. For they justly suffered for their own misdeeds, since indeed they treated their guests with the more grievous hatred. 14 For those others did not receive unfamiliar visitors, but these were enslaving beneficent guests. 15 And not that only; but what punishment was to be theirs since they received strangers unwillingly! 16 Yet these, after welcoming them with festivities, oppressed with awful toils those who now shared with them the same rights. 17 And they were struck with blindness, as those others had been at the portals of the just—when, surrounded by yawning darkness, each sought the entrance of his own gate. 18 For the elements, in variable harmony among themselves, like strings of the harp, produce new melody, while the flow of music steadily persists. And this can be perceived exactly from a review of what took place. 19 For land creatures were changed into water creatures, and those that swam went over onto the land. 20 Fire in water maintained its own strength, and water forgot its quenching nature; 21 flames, by contrast, neither consumed the flesh of the perishable animals that went about in them,

nor melted the icelike, quick-melting kind of ambrosial food. 22 For every way, O LORD! you magnified and glorified your people; unfailing, you stood by them in every time and circumstance.

Sirach

Sirach Chapter 1

1 All wisdom comes from the LORD and with him it remains forever. 2 The sand of the seashore, the drops of rain, the days of eternity: who can number these? 3 Heaven's height, earth's breadth, the depths of the abyss: who can explore these? 4 Before all things else wisdom was created; and prudent understanding, from eternity. 5 To whom has wisdom's root been revealed? Who knows her subtleties? 6 There is but one, wise and truly awe-inspiring, seated upon his throne: 7 It is the LORD; he created her, has seen and taken note of her. 8 He has poured her forth upon all his works, upon every living thing according to his bounty; he has lavished her upon his friends. 9 Fear of the LORD is glory and splendor, gladness and a festive crown. 10 Fear of the LORD warms the heart, giving gladness and joy and length of days. 11 He who fears the LORD will have a happy end; even on the day of his death he will be blessed. 12 The beginning of wisdom is fear of the LORD, which is formed with the faithful in the womb. 13 With devoted men was she created from of old, and with their children her beneficence abides. 14 Fullness of wisdom is fear of the LORD; she inebriates men with her fruits. 15 Her entire house she fills with choice foods, her granaries with her harvest. 16 Wisdom's garland is fear of the LORD, with blossoms of peace and perfect health. 17 Knowledge and full understanding she showers down; she heightens the glory of those who possess her. 18 The root of wisdom is fear of the LORD; her branches are length of days. 19 One cannot justify unjust anger; anger plunges a man to his downfall. 20 A patient man need stand firm but for a time, and then contentment comes back to him. 21 For a while he holds back his words, then the lips of many herald his wisdom. 22 Among wisdom's treasures is the paragon of prudence; but fear of the LORD is an abomination to the sinner. 23 If you desire wisdom, keep the commandments, and the LORD will bestow her upon you; 24 For fear of the LORD is wisdom and culture; loyal humility is his delight. 25 Be not faithless to the fear of the LORD, nor approach it with duplicity of heart. 26 Play not the hypocrite before men; over your lips keep watch. 27 Exalt not yourself lest you fall and bring upon you dishonor; 28 For then the LORD will reveal your secrets and publicly cast you down, 29 Because you approached the fear of the LORD with your heart full of guile.

Sirach Chapter 2

1 My son, when you come to serve the LORD, prepare yourself for trials. 2 Be sincere of heart and steadfast, undisturbed in time of adversity. 3 Cling to him, forsake him not; thus will your future be great. 4 Accept whatever befalls you, in crushing misfortune be patient; 5 For in fire gold is tested, and worthy men in the crucible of humiliation. 6 Trust God and he will help you; make straight your ways and hope in him. 7 You who fear the LORD, wait for his mercy, turn not away lest you fall. 8 You who fear the LORD, trust him, and your reward will not be lost. 9 You who fear the LORD, hope for good things, for lasting joy and mercy. 10 Study the generations long past and understand; has anyone hoped in the LORD and been disappointed? Has anyone persevered in his fear and been forsaken? has anyone called upon him and been rebuffed? 11 Compassionate and merciful is the LORD; he forgives sins, he saves in time of trouble. 12 Woe to craven hearts and drooping hands, to the sinner who treads a double path! 13 Woe to the faint of heart who trust not, who therefore will have no shelter! 14 Woe to you who have lost hope! what will you do at the visitation of the LORD? 15 Those who fear the LORD disobey not his words; those who love him keep his ways. 16 Those who fear the LORD seek to please him, those who love him are filled with his law. 17 Those who fear the LORD prepare their hearts and humble themselves before him. 18 Let us fall into the hands of the LORD and not into the hands of men, for equal to his majesty is the mercy that he shows.

Sirach Chapter 3

1 Children, pay heed to a father's right; do so that you may live. 2 For the LORD sets a father in honor over his children; a mother's authority he confirms over her sons. 3 He who honors his father atones for sins; 4 he stores up riches who reveres his mother. 5 He who honors his father is gladdened by children, and when he prays he is heard. 6 He who reveres his father will live a long life; he obeys the LORD who brings comfort to his mother. 7 He who fears the LORD honors his father, and serves his parents as rulers. 8 In word and deed honor your father that his blessing may come upon you; 9 For a father's blessing gives a family firm roots, but a mother's curse uproots the growing plant. 10 Glory not in your father's shame, for his shame is no glory to you! 11 His father's

honor is a man's glory; disgrace for her children, a mother's shame. 12 My son, take care of your father when he is old; grieve him not as long as he lives. 13 Even if his mind fail, be considerate with him; revile him not in the fullness of your strength. 14 For kindness to a father will not be forgotten, it will serve as a sin offering—it will take lasting root. 15 In time of tribulation it will be recalled to your advantage, like warmth upon frost it will melt away your sins. 16 A blasphemer is he who despises his father; accursed of his Creator, he who angers his mother. 17 My son, conduct your affairs with humility, and you will be loved more than a giver of gifts. 18 Humble yourself the more, the greater you are, and you will find favor with God. 19 For great is the power of God; by the humble he is glorified. 20 What is too sublime for you, seek not, into things beyond your strength search not. 21 What is committed to you, attend to; for what is hidden is not your concern. 22 With what is too much for you meddle not, when shown things beyond human understanding. 23 Their own opinion has misled many, and false reasoning unbalanced their judgment. 24 Where the pupil of the eye is missing, there is no light, and where there is no knowledge, there is no wisdom. 25 A stubborn man will fare badly in the end, and he who loves danger will perish in it. 26 A stubborn man will be burdened with sorrow; a sinner will heap sin upon sin. 27 For the affliction of the proud man there is no cure; he is the offshoot of an evil plant. 28 The mind of a sage appreciates proverbs, and an attentive ear is the wise man's joy. 29 Water quenches a flaming fire, and alms atone for sins. 30 He who does a kindness is remembered afterward; when he falls, he finds a support.

Sirach Chapter 4

1 My son, rob not the poor man of his livelihood; force not the eyes of the needy to turn away. 2 A hungry man grieve not, a needy man anger not; 3 Do not exasperate the downtrodden; delay not to give to the needy. 4 A beggar in distress do not reject; avert not your face from the poor. 5 From the needy turn not your eyes, give no man reason to curse you; 6 For if in the bitterness of his soul he curse you, his Creator will hear his prayer. 7 Endear yourself to the assembly; before a ruler bow your head. 8 Give a hearing to the poor man, and return his greeting with courtesy; 9 Deliver the oppressed from the hand of the oppressor; let not justice be repugnant to you. 10 To the fatherless be as a father, and help their mother as a husband would; Thus will you be like a son to the Most High, and he will be more tender to you than a mother. 11 Wisdom instructs her children and admonishes those who seek her. 12 He who loves her loves life; those who seek her out win her favor. 13 He who holds her fast inherits glory; wherever he dwells, the LORD bestows blessings. 14 Those who serve her serve the Holy One; those who love her the LORD loves. 15 He who obeys her judges nations; he who hearkens to her dwells in her inmost chambers. 16 If one trusts her, he will possess her; his descendants too will inherit her. 17 She walks with him as a stranger, and at first she puts him to the test; Fear and dread she brings upon him and tries him with her discipline; With her precepts she puts him to the proof, until his heart is fully with her. 18 Then she comes back to bring him happiness and reveal her secrets to him. 19 But if he fails her, she will abandon him and deliver him into the hands of despoilers. 20 Use your time well; guard yourself from evil, and bring upon yourself no shame. 21 There is a sense of shame laden with guilt, and a shame that merits honor and respect. 22 Show no favoritism to your own discredit; let no one intimidate you to your own downfall. 23 Refrain not from speaking at the proper time, and hide not away your wisdom; 24 For it is through speech that wisdom becomes known, and knowledge through the tongue's rejoinder. 25 Never gainsay the truth, and struggle not against the rushing stream. 26 Be not ashamed to acknowledge your guilt, but of your ignorance rather be ashamed. 27 Do not abase yourself before an impious man, nor refuse to do so before rulers. 28 Even to the death fight for truth, and the LORD your God will battle for you. 29 Be not surly in your speech, nor lazy and slack in your deeds. 30 Be not a lion at home, nor sly and suspicious at work. 31 Let not your hand be open to receive and clenched when it is time to give.

Sirach Chapter 5

1 Rely not on your wealth; say not: "I have the power." 2 Rely not on your strength in following the desires of your heart. 3 Say not: "Who can prevail against me?" for the LORD will exact the punishment. 4 Say not: "I have sinned, yet what has befallen me?" for the LORD bides his time. 5 Of forgiveness be not overconfident, adding sin upon sin. 6 Say not: "Great is his mercy; my many sins he will forgive." 7 For mercy and anger alike are with him; upon the wicked alights his wrath. 8 Delay not your conversion to the LORD, put it not off from day to day; 9 For suddenly his wrath flames forth; at the time of vengeance, you will be destroyed. 10 Rely not upon deceitful wealth, for it will be no help on the day of wrath. 11 Winnow not in every wind, and start not off in every direction. 12 Be consistent in your thoughts; steadfast be your words. 13 Be swift to hear, but slow to answer. 14 If you have the knowledge, answer your neighbor; if not, put your hand over your mouth. 15 Honor and dishonor through talking! A man's tongue can be his downfall. 16 Be not called a detractor; use not your tongue for calumny; 17 For shame has been created for the thief, and the reproach of his neighbor for the double-tongued.

Sirach Chapter 6

1 Say nothing harmful, small or great; be not a foe instead of a friend; A bad name and disgrace will you acquire: "That for the evil man with double tongue!" 2 Fall not into the grip of desire, lest, like fire, it consume your strength; 3 Your leaves it will eat, your fruits destroy, and you will be left a dry tree, 4 For contumacious desire destroys its owner and makes him the sport of his enemies. 5 A kind mouth multiplies friends, and gracious lips prompt friendly greetings. 6 Let your acquaintances be many, but one in a thousand your confidant. 7 When you gain a friend, first test him, and be not too ready to trust him. 8 For one sort of friend is a friend when it suits him, but he will not be with you in time of distress. 9 Another is a friend who becomes an enemy, and tells of the quarrel to your shame. 10 Another is a friend, a boon companion, who will not be with you when sorrow comes. 11 When things go well, he is your other self, and lords it over your servants; 12 But if you are brought low, he turns against you and avoids meeting you. 13 Keep away from your enemies; be on your guard with your friends. 14 A faithful friend is a sturdy shelter; he who finds one finds a treasure. 15 A faithful friend is beyond price, no sum can balance his worth. 16 A faithful friend is a life-saving remedy, such as he who fears God finds; 17 For he who fears God behaves accordingly, and his friend will be like himself. 18 My son, from your youth embrace discipline; thus will you find wisdom with graying hair. 19 As though plowing and sowing, draw close to her; then await her bountiful crops. 20 For in cultivating her you will labor but little, and soon you will eat of her fruits. 21 How irksome she is to the unruly! The fool cannot abide her. 22 She will be like a burdensome stone to test him, and he will not delay in casting her aside. 23 For discipline is like her name, she is not accessible to many. 24 Listen, my son, and heed my advice; refuse not my counsel. 25 Put your feet into her fetters, and your neck under her yoke. 26 Stoop your shoulders and carry her and be not irked at her bonds. 27 With all your soul draw close to her; with all your strength keep her ways. 28 Search her out, discover her; seek her and you will find her. Then when you have her, do not let her go; 29 Thus will you afterward find rest in her, and she will become your joy. 30 Her fetters will be your throne of majesty; her bonds, your purple cord. 31 You will wear her as your robe of glory, bear her as your splendid crown. 32 My son, if you wish, you can be taught; if you apply yourself, you will be shrewd. 33 If you are willing to listen, you will learn; if you give heed, you will be wise. 34 Frequent the company of the elders; whoever is wise, stay close to him. 35 Be eager to hear every godly discourse; let no wise saying escape you. 36 If you see a man of prudence, seek him out; let your feet wear away his doorstep! 37 Reflect on the precepts of the LORD, let his commandments be your constant meditation; Then he will enlighten your mind, and the wisdom you desire he will grant.

Sirach Chapter 7

1 Do no evil, and evil will not overtake you; 2 avoid wickedness, and it will turn aside from you. 3 Sow not in the furrows of injustice, lest you harvest it sevenfold. 4 Seek not from the LORD authority, nor from the king a place of honor. 5 Parade not your justice before the Lord, and before the king flaunt not your wisdom. 6 Seek not to become a judge if you have not strength to root out crime, Or you will show favor to the ruler and mar your integrity. 7 Be guilty of no evil before the city's populace, nor disgrace yourself before the assembly. 8 Do not plot to repeat a sin; not even for one will you go unpunished. 9 Say not: "He will appreciate my many gifts; the Most High will accept my offerings." 10 Be not impatient in prayers, and neglect not the giving of alms. 11 Laugh not at an embittered man; be mindful of him who exalts and humbles. 12 Plot no mischief against your brother, nor against your friend and companion. 13 Delight not in telling lie after lie, for it never results in good. 14 Thrust not yourself into the deliberations of princes, and repeat not the words of your prayer. 15 Hate not laborious tasks, nor farming, which was ordained by the Most High. 16 Do not esteem yourself better than your fellows; remember, his wrath will not delay. 17 More and more, humble your pride; what awaits man is worms. 18 Barter not a friend for money, nor a dear brother for the gold of Ophir. 19 Dismiss not a sensible wife; a gracious wife is more precious than corals. 20 Mistreat not a servant who faithfully serves, nor a laborer who devotes himself to his task. 21 Let a wise servant be dear to you as your

own self; refuse him not his freedom. 22 If you have livestock, look after them; if they are dependable, keep them. 23 If you have sons, chastise them; bend their necks from childhood. 24 If you have daughters, keep them chaste, and be not indulgent to them. 25 Giving your daughter in marriage ends a great task; but give her to a worthy man. 26 If you have a wife, let her not seem odious to you; but where there is ill-feeling, trust her not. 27 With your whole heart honor your father; your mother's birthpangs forget not. 28 Remember, of these parents you were born; what can you give them for all they gave you? 29 With all your soul, fear God, revere his priests. 30 With all your strength, love your Creator, forsake not his ministers. 31 Honor God and respect the priest; give him his portion as you have been commanded: First fruits and contributions, due sacrifices and holy offerings. 32 To the poor man also extend your hand, that your blessing may be complete; 33 Be generous to all the living, and withhold not your kindness from the dead. 34 Avoid not those who weep, but mourn with those who mourn; 35 Neglect not to visit the sick - for these things you will be loved. 36 In whatever you do, remember your last days, and you will never sin.

Sirach Chapter 8

1 Contend not with an influential man, lest you fall into his power. 2 Quarrel not with a rich man, lest he pay out the price of your downfall; for gold has dazzled many, and perverts the character of princes. 3 Dispute not with a man of railing speech, heap no wood upon his fire. 4 Be not too familiar with an unruly man, lest he speak ill of your forebears. 5 Shame not a repentant sinner; remember, we all are guilty. 6 Insult no man when he is old, for some of us, too, will grow old. 7 Rejoice not when a man dies; remember, we are all to die. 8 Spurn not the discourse of the wise, but acquaint yourself with their proverbs; from them you will acquire the training to serve in the presence of princes. 9 Reject not the tradition of old men which they have learned from their fathers; from it you will obtain the knowledge how to answer in time of need. 10 Kindle not the coals of a sinner, lest you be consumed in his flaming fire. 11 Let not the impious man intimidate you; it will set him in ambush against you. 12 Lend not to one more powerful than yourself; and whatever you lend, count it as lost. 13 Go not surety beyond your means; think any pledge a debt you must pay. 14 Contend not at law with a judge, for he will settle it according to his whim. 15 Travel not with a ruthless man, lest he weigh you down with calamity; for he will go his own way straight, and through his folly you will perish with him. 16 Provoke no quarrel with a quick-tempered man, nor ride with him through the desert, for bloodshed is nothing to him; when there is no one to help you, he will destroy you. 17 Take no counsel with a fool, for he can keep nothing to himself. 18 Before a stranger do nothing that should be kept secret, for you know not what it will engender. 19 Open your heart to no man, and banish not your happiness.

Sirach Chapter 9

1 Be not jealous of the wife of your bosom, lest you teach her to do evil against you. 2 Give no woman power over you to trample upon your dignity. 3 Be not intimate with a strange woman, lest you fall into her snares. 4 With a singing girl be not familiar, lest you be caught in her wiles. 5 Entertain no thoughts against a virgin, lest you be enmeshed in damages for her. 6 Give not yourself to harlots, lest you surrender your inheritance. 7 Gaze not about the lanes of the city and wander not through its squares; 8 Avert your eyes from a comely woman; gaze not upon the beauty of another's wife—through woman's beauty many perish, for lust for it burns like fire. 9 With a married woman dine not, recline not at table to drink by her side, lest your heart be drawn to her and you go down in blood to the grave. 10 Discard not an old friend, for the new one cannot equal him. A new friend is like new wine which you drink with pleasure only when it has aged. 11 Envy not a sinner's fame, for you know not what disaster awaits him. 12 Rejoice not at a proud man's success; remember he will not reach death unpunished. 13 Keep far from the man who has power to kill, and you will not be filled with the dread of death. But if you approach him, offend him not, lest he take away your life; know that you are stepping among snares and walking over a net. 14 As best you can, take your neighbors' measure, and associate with the wise. 15 With the learned be intimate; let all your conversation be about the law of the LORD. 16 Have just men for your table companions; in the fear of God be your glory. 17 Skilled artisans are esteemed for their deftness; but the ruler of his people is the skilled sage. 18 Feared in the city is the man of railing speech, and he who talks rashly is hated.

Sirach Chapter 10

1 A wise magistrate lends stability to his people, and the government of a prudent man is well ordered. 2 As the people's judge, so are his ministers; as the head of a city, its inhabitants. 3 A wanton king destroys his people, but a city grows through the wisdom of its princes. 4 Sovereignty over the earth is in the hand of God, who raises up on it the man of the hour; 5 Sovereignty over every man is in the hand of God, who imparts his majesty to the ruler. 6 No matter the wrong, do no violence to your neighbor, and do not walk the path of arrogance. 7 Odious to the LORD and to men is arrogance, and the sin of oppression they both hate. 8 Dominion is transferred from one people to another because of the violence of the arrogant. 9 Why are dust and ashes proud? Even during life man's body decays; 10 A slight illness—the doctor jests, a king today—tomorrow he is dead. 11 When a man dies, he inherits corruption; worms and gnats and maggots. 12 The beginning of pride is man's stubbornness in withdrawing his heart from his Maker; 13 For pride is the reservoir of sin, a source which runs over with vice; because of it God sends unheard-of afflictions and brings men to utter ruin. 14 The thrones of the arrogant God overturns and establishes the lowly in their stead. 15 The roots of the proud God plucks up, to plant the humble in their place: 16 He breaks down their stem to the level of the ground, then digs their roots from the earth. 17 The traces of the proud God sweeps away and effaces the memory of them from the earth. 18 Insolence is not allotted to a man, nor stubborn anger to one born of woman. 19 Whose offspring can be in honor? Those of men. Which offspring are in honor? Those who fear God. Whose offspring can be in disgrace? Those of men. Which offspring are in disgrace? Those who transgress the commandments. 20 Among brethren their leader is in honor; he who fears God is in honor among his people. 21 Be it tenant or wayfarer, alien or pauper, his glory is the fear of the LORD. 22 It is not just to despise a man who is wise but poor, nor proper to honor any sinner. 23 The prince, the ruler, the judge are in honor; but none is greater than he who fears God. 24 When free men serve a prudent slave, the wise man does not complain. 25 Flaunt not your wisdom in managing your affairs, and boast not in your time of need. 26 Better the worker who has plenty of everything than the boaster who is without bread. 27 My son, with humility have self-esteem; prize yourself as you deserve. 28 Who will acquit him who condemns himself? Who will honor him who discredits himself? 29 The poor man is honored for his wisdom as the rich man is honored for his wealth; 30 Honored in poverty, how much more so in wealth! Dishonored in wealth, in poverty how much the more!

Sirach Chapter 11

1 The poor man's wisdom lifts his head high and sets him among princes. 2 Praise not a man for his looks; despise not a man for his appearance. 3 Least is the bee among winged things, but she reaps the choicest of all harvests. 4 Mock not the worn cloak and jibe at no man's bitter day: For strange are the works of the LORD, hidden from men his deeds. 5 The oppressed often rise to a throne, and some that none would consider wear a crown. 6 The exalted often fall into utter disgrace; the honored are given into enemy hands. 7 Before investigating, find no fault; examine first, then criticize. 8 Before hearing, answer not, and interrupt no one in the middle of his speech. 9 Dispute not about what is not your concern; in the strife of the arrogant take no part. 10 My son, why increase your cares, since he who is avid for wealth will not be blameless? Even if you run after it, you will never overtake it; however you seek it, you will not find it. 11 One may toil and struggle and drive, and fall short all the more. 12 Another goes his way a weakling and a failure, with little strength and great misery—yet the eyes of the LORD look favorably upon him; he raises him free of the vile dust, 13 lifts up his head and exalts him to the amazement of the many. 14 Good and evil, life and death, poverty and riches, are from the LORD. 15 Wisdom and understanding and knowledge of affairs, love and virtuous paths are from the LORD. 16 Error and darkness were formed with sinners from their birth, and evil grows old with evildoers. 17 The LORD'S gift remains with the just; his favor brings continued success. 18 A man may become rich through a miser's life, and this is his allotted reward: 19 When he says: "I have found rest, now I will feast on my possessions," he does not know how long it will be till he dies and leaves them to others. 20 My son, hold fast to your duty, busy yourself with it, grow old while doing your task. 21 Admire not how sinners live, but trust in the LORD and wait for his light; for it is easy with the LORD suddenly, in an instant, to make a poor man rich. 22 God's blessing is the lot of the just man, and in due time his hopes bear fruit. 23 Say not: "What do I need? What further pleasure can be mine?" 24 Say not: "I am independent. What harm can come to me now?" 25 The day of prosperity makes one forget adversity; the day of adversity makes one forget prosperity. 26 For it is easy with the LORD on the day of death to repay man according to his deeds. 27 A moment's affliction brings forgetfulness of past delights; when a man dies, his life is revealed. 28 Call no man happy before his death, for by how he ends, a man is known. 29 Bring not every man into your house, for many are the snares

of the crafty one; 30 though he seem like a bird confined in a cage, yet like a spy he will pick out the weak spots. 31 The talebearer turns good into evil; with a spark he sets many coals afire. 32 The evil man lies in wait for blood, and plots against your choicest possessions. 33 Avoid a wicked man, for he breeds only evil, lest you incur a lasting stain. 34 Lodge a stranger with you, and he will subvert your course, and make a stranger of you to your own household.

Sirach Chapter 12

1 If you do good, know for whom you are doing it, and your kindness will have its effect. 2 Do good to the just man and reward will be yours, if not from him, from the LORD. 3 No good comes to him who gives comfort to the wicked, nor is it an act of mercy that he does. 4 Give to the good man, refuse the sinner; refresh the downtrodden, give nothing to the proud man. 5 No arms for combat should you give him, lest he use them against yourself; 6 with twofold evil you will meet for every good deed you do for him. 7 The Most High himself hates sinners, and upon the wicked he takes vengeance. 8 In our prosperity we cannot know our friends; in adversity an enemy will not remain concealed. 9 When a man is successful even his enemy is friendly; in adversity even his friend disappears. 10 Never trust your enemy, for his wickedness is like corrosion in bronze. 11 Even though he acts humbly and peaceably toward you, take care to be on your guard against him. Rub him as one polishes a brazen mirror, and you will find that there is still corrosion. 12 Let him not stand near you, lest he oust you and take your place. Let him not sit at your right hand, lest he then demand your seat, and in the end you appreciate my advice, when you groan with regret, as I warned you. 13 Who pities a snake charmer when he is bitten, or anyone who goes near a wild beast? 14 So is it with the companion of the proud man, who is involved in his sins: 15 While you stand firm, he makes no bold move; but if you slip, he cannot hold back. 16 With his lips an enemy speaks sweetly, but in his heart he schemes to plunge you into the abyss. Though your enemy has tears in his eyes, if given the chance, he will never have enough of your blood. 17 If evil comes upon you, you will find him at hand; feigning to help, he will trip you up, 18 then he will nod his head and clap his hands and hiss repeatedly, and show his true face.

Sirach Chapter 13

1 He who touches pitch blackens his hand; he who associates with an impious man learns his ways. 2 Bear no burden too heavy for you; go with no one greater or wealthier than yourself. How can the earthen pot go with the metal cauldron? When they knock together, the pot will be smashed: 3 The rich man does wrong and boasts of it, the poor man is wronged and begs forgiveness. 4 As long as the rich man can use you he will enslave you, but when you are exhausted, he will abandon you. 5 As long as you have anything he will speak fair words to you, and with smiles he will win your confidence; 6 When he needs something from you he will cajole you, then without regret he will impoverish you. 7 While it serves his purpose he will beguile you, then twice or three times he will terrify you; when later he sees you he will pass you by, and shake his head over you. 8 Guard against being presumptuous; be not as those who lack sense. 9 When invited by a man of influence, keep your distance; then he will urge you all the more. 10 Be not bold with him lest you be rebuffed, but keep not too far away lest you be forgotten. 11 Engage not freely in discussion with him, trust not his many words; for by prolonged talk he will test you, and though smiling he will probe you. 12 Mercilessly he will make of you a laughingstock, and will not refrain from injury or chains. 13 Be on your guard and take care never to accompany men of violence. 14 Every living thing loves its own kind, every man a man like himself. 15 Every being is drawn to its own kind; with his own kind every man associates. 16 Is a wolf ever allied with a lamb? So it is with the sinner and the just. 17 Can there be peace between the hyena and the dog? Or between the rich and the poor can there be peace? 18 Lion's prey are the wild asses of the desert; so too the poor are feeding grounds for the rich. 19 A proud man abhors lowliness; so does the rich man abhor the poor. 20 When a rich man stumbles he is supported by a friend; when a poor man trips he is pushed down by a friend. 21 Many are the supporters for a rich man when he speaks; though what he says is odious, it wins approval. When a poor man speaks they make sport of him; he speaks wisely and no attention is paid him. 22 A rich man speaks and all are silent, his wisdom they extol to the clouds. A poor man speaks and they say: "Who is that?" If he slips they cast him down. 23 Wealth is good when there is no sin; but poverty is evil by the standards of the proud. 24 The heart of a man changes his countenance, either for good or for evil. 25 The sign of a good heart is a cheerful countenance; withdrawn and perplexed is the laborious schemer.

Sirach Chapter 14

1 Happy the man whose mouth brings him no grief, who is not stung by remorse for sin. 2 Happy the man whose conscience does not reproach him, who has not lost hope. 3 Wealth ill becomes the mean man; and to the miser, of what use is gold? 4 What he denies himself he collects for others, and in his possessions a stranger will revel. 5 To whom will he be generous who is stingy with himself and does not enjoy what is his own? 6 None is more stingy than he who is stingy with himself; he punishes his own miserliness. 7 If ever he is generous, it is by mistake; and in the end he displays his greed. 8 In the miser's opinion his share is too small; 9 he refuses his neighbor and brings ruin on himself. 10 The miser's eye is rapacious for bread, but on his own table he sets it stale. 11 My son, use freely whatever you have and enjoy it as best you can; 12 Remember that death does not tarry, nor have you been told the grave's appointed time. 13 Before you die, be good to your friend, and give him a share in what you possess. 14 Deprive not yourself of present good things, let no choice portion escape you. 15 Will you not leave your riches to others, and your earnings to be divided by lot? 16 Give, take, and treat yourself well, for in the nether world there are no joys to seek. 17 All flesh grows old, like a garment; the age-old law is: All must die. 18 As with the leaves that grow on a vigorous tree: one falls off and another sprouts - So with the generations of flesh and blood: one dies and another is born. 19 All man's works will perish in decay, and his handiwork will follow after him. 20 Happy the man who meditates on wisdom, and reflects on knowledge; 21 Who ponders her ways in his heart, and understands her paths; 22 Who pursues her like a scout, and lies in wait at her entry way; 23 Who peeps through her windows, and listens at her doors; 24 Who encamps near her house, and fastens his tent pegs next to her walls; 25 Who pitches his tent beside her, and lives as her welcome neighbor; 26 Who builds his nest in her leafage, and lodges in her branches; 27 Who takes shelter with her from the heat, and dwells in her home.

Sirach Chapter 15

1 He who fears the LORD will do this; he who is practiced in the law will come to wisdom. 2 Motherlike she will meet him, like a young bride she will embrace him, 3 Nourish him with the bread of understanding, and give him the water of learning to drink. 4 He will lean upon her and not fall, he will trust in her and not be put to shame. 5 She will exalt him above his fellows; in the assembly she will make him eloquent. 6 Joy and gladness he will find, an everlasting name inherit. 7 Worthless men will not attain to her, haughty men will not behold her. 8 Far from the impious is she, not to be spoken of by liars. 9 Unseemly is praise on a sinner's lips, for it is not accorded to him by God. 10 But praise is offered by the wise man's tongue; its rightful steward will proclaim it. 11 Say not: "It was God's doing that I fell away"; for what he hates he does not do. 12 Say not: "It was he who set me astray"; for he has no need of wicked man. 13 Abominable wickedness the LORD hates, he does not let it befall those who fear him. 14 When God, in the beginning, created man, he made him subject to his own free choice. 15 If you choose you can keep the commandments; it is loyalty to do his will. 16 There are set before you fire and water; to whichever you choose, stretch forth your hand. 17 Before man are life and death, whichever he chooses shall be given him. 18 Immense is the wisdom of the LORD; he is mighty in power, and all-seeing. 19 The eyes of God see all he has made; he understands man's every deed. 20 No man does he command to sin, to none does he give strength for lies.

Sirach Chapter 16

1 Desire not a brood of worthless children, nor rejoice in wicked offspring. 2 Many though they be, exult not in them if they have not the fear of the LORD. 3 Count not on their length of life, have no hope in their future. For one can be better than a thousand; rather die childless than have godless children! 4 Through one wise man can a city be peopled; through a clan of rebels it becomes desolate. 5 Many such things has my eye seen, even more than these has my ear heard. 6 Against a sinful band fire is enkindled, upon a godless people wrath flames out. 7 He forgave not the leaders of old who rebelled long ago in their might; 8 He spared not the neighbors of Lot whom he detested for their pride; 9 Nor did he spare the doomed people who were uprooted because of their sin; 10 Nor the six hundred thousand foot soldiers who perished for the impiety of their hearts. 11 And had there been but one stiffnecked man, it were a wonder had he gone unpunished. For mercy and anger alike are with him who remits and forgives, though on the wicked alights his wrath. 12 Great as his mercy is his punishment; he judges men, each according to his deeds. 13 A criminal does not escape with his plunder; a just man's hope God does not leave unfulfilled. 14 Whoever does good has his reward, which each receives according to his deeds. 15 Say not: "I am hidden from God; in heaven who

remembers me? Among so many people I cannot be known; what am I in the world of spirits? ¹⁶ Behold, the heavens, the heaven of heavens, the earth and the abyss tremble at his visitation; ¹⁷ The roots of the mountains, the earth's foundations, at his mere glance, quiver and quake. ¹⁸ Of me, therefore, he will take no thought; with my ways who will concern himself? ¹⁹ If I sin, no eye will see me; if all in secret I am disloyal, who is to know? ²⁰ Who tells him of just deeds and what could I expect for doing my duty?" ²¹ Such are the thoughts of senseless men, which only the foolish knave will think. ²² Hearken to me, my son, take my advice, apply your mind to my words, ²³ While I propose measured wisdom, and impart accurate knowledge. ²⁴ When at the first God created his works and, as he made them, assigned their tasks, ²⁵ He ordered for all time what they were to do and their domains from generation to generation. They were not to hunger, nor grow weary, nor ever cease from their tasks. ²⁶ Not one should ever crowd its neighbor, nor should they ever disobey his word. ²⁷ Then the LORD looked upon the earth, and filled it with his blessings. ²⁸ Its surface he covered with all manner of life which must return into it again.

Sirach Chapter 17

¹ The LORD from the earth created man, and in his own image he made him. ² Limited days of life he gives him and makes him return to earth again. ³ He endows man with a strength of his own, and with power over all things else on earth. ⁴ He puts the fear of him in all flesh, and gives him rule over beasts and birds. ⁵ He forms men's tongues and eyes and ears, and imparts to them an understanding heart. ⁶ With wisdom and knowledge he fills them; good and evil he shows them. ⁷ He looks with favor upon their hearts, and shows them his glorious works, ⁸ That they may describe the wonders of his deeds and praise his holy name. ⁹ He has set before them knowledge, a law of life as their inheritance; ¹⁰ An everlasting covenant he has made with them, his commandments he has revealed to them. ¹¹ His majestic glory their eyes beheld, his glorious voice their ears heard. ¹² He says to them, "Avoid all evil"; each of them he gives precepts about his fellow men. ¹³ Their ways are ever known to him, they cannot be hidden from his eyes. ¹⁴ Over every nation he places a ruler, but the LORD'S own portion is Israel. ¹⁵ All their actions are clear as the sun to him, his eyes are ever upon their ways. ¹⁶ Their wickedness cannot be hidden from him; all of their sins are before the LORD. ¹⁷ A man's goodness God cherishes like a signet ring, a man's virtue, like the apple of his eye. ¹⁸ Later he will rise up and repay them, and require each one of them as they deserve. ¹⁹ But to the penitent he provides a way back, he encourages those who are losing hope! ²⁰ Return to the LORD and give up sin, pray to him and make your offenses few. ²¹ Turn again to the Most High and away from sin, hate intensely what he loathes; ²² Who in the nether world can glorify the Most High in place of the living who offer their praise? ²³ No more can the dead give praise than those who have never lived; they glorify the LORD who are alive and well. ²⁴ How great the mercy of the LORD, his forgiveness of those who return to him! ²⁵ The like cannot be found in men, for not immortal is any son of man. ²⁶ Is anything brighter than the sun? Yet it can be eclipsed. How obscure then the thoughts of flesh and blood! ²⁷ God watches over the hosts of highest heaven, while all men are dust and ashes.

Sirach Chapter 18

¹ The Eternal is the judge of all things without exception; the LORD alone is just. ² Whom has he made equal to describing his works, and who can probe his mighty deeds? ³ Who can measure his majestic power, or exhaust the tale of his mercies? ⁴ One cannot lessen, nor increase, nor penetrate the wonders of the LORD. ⁵ When a man ends he is only beginning, and when he stops he is still bewildered. ⁶ What is man, of what worth is he? the good, the evil in him, what are these? ⁷ The sum of a man's days is great if it reaches a hundred years: ⁸ Like a drop of sea water, like a grain of sand, so are these few years among the days of eternity. ⁹ That is why the LORD is patient with men and showers upon them his mercy. ¹⁰ He sees and understands that their death is grievous, and so he forgives them all the more. ¹¹ Man may be merciful to his fellow man, but the LORD'S mercy reaches all flesh, ¹² Reproving, admonishing, teaching, as a shepherd guides his flock; ¹³ Merciful to those who accept his guidance, who are diligent in his precepts. ¹⁴ My son, to your charity add no reproach, nor spoil any gift by harsh words. ¹⁵ Like dew that abates a burning wind, so does a word improve a gift. ¹⁶ Sometimes the word means more than the gift; both are offered by a kindly man. ¹⁷ Only a fool upbraids before giving; a grudging gift wears out the expectant eyes. ¹⁸ Be informed before speaking; before sickness prepare the cure. ¹⁹ Before you are judged, seek merit for yourself, and at the time of visitation you will have a ransom. ²⁰ Before you have fallen, humble yourself; when you have sinned, show repentance. ²¹ Delay not to forsake sins, neglect it not till

you are in distress. ²² Let nothing prevent the prompt payment of your vows; wait not to fulfill them when you are dying. ²³ Before making a vow have the means to fulfill it; be not one who tries the LORD. ²⁴ Think of wrath and the day of death, the time of vengeance when he will hide his face. ²⁵ Remember the time of hunger in the time of plenty, poverty and want in the day of wealth. ²⁶ Between morning and evening the weather changes; before the LORD all things are fleeting. ²⁷ A wise man is circumspect in all things; when sin is rife he keeps himself from wrongdoing. ²⁸ Any learned man should make wisdom known, and he who attains to her should declare her praise; ²⁹ Those trained in her words must show their wisdom, dispensing sound proverbs like life-giving waters. ³⁰ Go not after your lusts, but keep your desires in check. ³¹ If you satisfy your lustful appetites they will make you the sport of your enemies. ³² Have no joy in the pleasures of a moment which bring on poverty redoubled; ³³ Become not a glutton and a winebibber with nothing in your purse.

Sirach Chapter 19

¹ He who does so grows no richer; he who wastes the little he has will be stripped bare. ² Wine and women make the mind giddy, and the companion of harlots becomes reckless. ³ He who lightly trusts in them has no sense, and he who strays after them sins against his own life. ⁴ Rottenness and worms will possess him, for contumacious desire destroys its owner. ⁵ He who gloats over evil will meet with evil, and he who repeats an evil report has no sense. ⁶ Never repeat gossip, and you will not be reviled. ⁷ Tell nothing to friend or foe; if you have a fault, reveal it not, ⁸ For he who hears it will hold it against you, and in time become your enemy. ⁹ Let anything you hear die within you; be assured it will not make you burst. ¹⁰ When a fool hears something, he is in labor, like a woman giving birth to a child. ¹¹ Like an arrow lodged in a man's thigh is gossip in the breast of a fool. ¹² Admonish your friend - he may not have done it; and if he did, that he may not do it again. ¹³ Admonish your neighbor - he may not have said it; and if he did, that he may not say it again. ¹⁴ Admonish your friend - often it may be slander; every story you must not believe. ¹⁵ Then, too, a man can slip and not mean it; who has not sinned with his tongue? ¹⁶ Admonish your neighbor before you break with him; thus will you fulfill the law of the Most High. ¹⁷ All wisdom is fear of the LORD; perfect wisdom is the fulfillment of the law. ¹⁸ The knowledge of wickedness is not wisdom, nor is there prudence in the counsel of sinners. ¹⁹ There is a shrewdness that is detestable, while the simple man may be free from sin. ²⁰ There are those with little understanding who fear God, and those of great intelligence who violate the law. ²¹ There is a shrewdness keen but dishonest, which by duplicity wins a judgment. ²² There is the wicked man who is bowed in grief, but is full of guile within; ²³ He bows his head and feigns not to hear, but when not observed, he will take advantage of you: ²⁴ Even though his lack of strength keeps him from sinning, when he finds the opportunity, he will do harm. ²⁵ One can tell a man by his appearance; a wise man is known as such when first met. ²⁶ A man's attire, his hearty laughter and his gait, proclaim him for what he is.

Sirach Chapter 20

¹ An admonition can be inopportune, and a man may be wise to hold his peace. ² It is much better to admonish than to lose one's temper, for one who admits his fault will be kept from disgrace. ³ Like a eunuch lusting for intimacy with a maiden is he who does right under compulsion. ⁴ One man is silent and is thought wise, another is talkative and is disliked. ⁵ One man is silent because he has nothing to say; another is silent, biding his time. ⁶ A wise man is silent till the right time comes, but a boasting fool ignores the proper time. ⁷ He who talks too much is detested; he who pretends to authority is hated. ⁸ Some misfortunes bring success; some things gained are a man's loss. ⁹ Some gifts do one no good, and some must be paid back double. ¹⁰ Humiliation can follow fame, while from obscurity a man can lift up his head. ¹¹ A man may buy much for little, but pay for it seven times over. ¹² A wise man makes himself popular by a few words, but fools pour forth their blandishments in vain. ¹³ A gift from a rogue will do you no good, for in his eyes his one gift is equal to seven. ¹⁴ He gives little and criticizes often, and like a crier he shouts aloud. He lends today, he asks it back tomorrow; hateful indeed is such a man. ¹⁵ A fool has no friends, nor thanks for his generosity. ¹⁶ Those who eat his bread have an evil tongue. How many times they laugh him to scorn! ¹⁷ A fall to the ground is less sudden than a slip of the tongue; that is why the downfall of the wicked comes so quickly. ¹⁸ Insipid food is the untimely tale; the unruly are always ready to offer it. ¹⁹ A proverb when spoken by a fool is unwelcome, for he does not utter it at the proper time. ²⁰ A man through want may be unable to sin, yet in this tranquility he cannot rest. ²¹ One may lose his life through shame, and perish through a fool's

intimation. 22 A man makes a promise to a friend out of shame, and has him for his enemy needlessly. 23 A lie is a foul blot in a man, yet it is constantly on the lips of the unruly. 24 Better a thief than an inveterate liar, yet both will suffer disgrace. 25 A liar's way leads to dishonor, his shame remains ever with him. 26 A wise man advances himself by his words, a prudent man pleases the great. 27 He who works his land has abundant crops, he who pleases the great is pardoned his faults. 28 Favors and gifts blind the eyes; like a muzzle over the mouth they silence reproof. 29 Hidden wisdom and unseen treasure—of what value is either? 30 Better the man who hides his folly than the one who hides his wisdom.

Sirach Chapter 21

1 My son, if you have sinned, do so no more, and for your past sins pray to be forgiven. 2 Flee from sin as from a serpent, that will bite you if you go near it; its teeth are lion's teeth, destroying the souls of men. 3 Every offense is a two-edged sword; when it cuts, there can be no healing. 4 Violence and arrogance wipe out wealth; so too a proud man's home is destroyed. 5 Prayer from a poor man's lips is heard at once, and justice is quickly granted him. 6 He who hates correction walks the sinner's path, but he who fears the LORD repents in his heart. 7 Widely known is the boastful speaker, but the wise man knows his own faults. 8 He who builds his house with another's money is collecting stones for his funeral mound. 9 A band of criminals is like a bundle of tow; they will end in a flaming fire. 10 The path of sinners is smooth stones that end in the depths of the nether world. 11 He who keeps the law controls his impulses; he who is perfect in fear of the LORD has wisdom. 12 He can never be taught who is not shrewd, but one form of shrewdness is thoroughly bitter. 13 A wise man's knowledge wells up in a flood, and his counsel, like a living spring. 14 A fool's mind is like a broken jar—no knowledge at all can it hold. 15 When an intelligent man hears words of wisdom, he approves them and adds to them; the wanton hears them with scorn and casts them behind his back. 16 A fool's chatter is like a load on a journey, but there is charm to be found upon the lips of the wise. 17 The views of a prudent man are sought in an assembly, and his words are considered with care. 18 Like a house in ruins is wisdom to a fool; the stupid man knows it only as inscrutable words. 19 Like fetters on the legs is learning to a fool, like a manacle on his right hand. 20 A fool raises his voice in laughter, but the prudent man at the most smiles gently. 21 Like a chain of gold is learning to a wise man, like a bracelet on his right arm. 22 The fool steps boldly into a house, while the well-bred man remains outside. 23 A boor peeps through the doorway of a house, but a cultured man keeps his glance cast down. 24 It is rude for one to listen at a door; a cultured man would be overwhelmed by the disgrace of it. 25 The lips of the impious talk of what is not their concern, but the words of the prudent are carefully weighed. 26 Fools' thoughts are in their mouths, wise men's words are in their hearts. 27 When a godless man curses his adversary, he really curses himself. 28 A slanderer besmirches himself and is hated by his neighbors.

Sirach Chapter 22

1 The sluggard is like a stone in the mud; everyone hisses at his disgrace. 2 The sluggard is like a lump of dung; whoever touches him wipes his hands. 3 An unruly child is a disgrace to its father; if it be a daughter she brings him to poverty. 4 A thoughtful daughter becomes a treasure to her husband, a shameless one is her father's grief. 5 A hussy shames her father and her husband; by both she is despised. 6 Like a song in time of mourning is inopportune talk, but lashes and discipline are at all times wisdom. 7 Teaching a fool is like gluing a broken pot, or like disturbing a man in the depths of sleep; 8 He talks with a slumberer who talks with a fool, for when it is over, he will say, "What was that?" 9 Weep over the dead man, for his light has gone out; weep over the fool, for sense has left him. 10 Weep but a little over the dead man, for he is at rest; but worse than death is the life of a fool. 11 Seven days of mourning for the dead, but for the wicked fool a whole lifetime. 12 Speak but seldom with the stupid man, be not the companion of a brute; 13 Beware of him lest you have trouble and be spattered when he shakes himself; Turn away from him and you will find rest and not be wearied by his lack of sense. 14 What is heavier than lead, and what is its name but "Fool"? 15 Sand and salt and an iron mass are easier to bear than a stupid man. 16 Masonry bonded with wooden beams is not loosened by an earthquake; Neither is a resolve constructed with careful deliberation shaken in a moment of fear. 17 A resolve that is backed by prudent understanding is like the polished surface of a smooth wall. 18 Small stones lying on an open height will not remain when the wind blows; Neither can a timid resolve based on foolish plans withstand fear of any kind. 19 One who jabs the eye brings tears: he who pierces the heart bares its feelings. 20 He who throws stones at birds drives them away, and he who insults a friend breaks up the friendship. 21 Should you draw a sword against a friend, despair not, it can be undone. 22 Should you speak sharply to a friend, fear not, you can be reconciled. But a contemptuous insult, a confidence broken, or a treacherous attack will drive away any friend. 23 Make fast friends with a man while he is poor; thus will you enjoy his prosperity with him. In time of trouble remain true to him, so as to share in his inheritance when it comes. 24 Before flames burst forth an oven smokes; so does abuse come before bloodshed. 25 From a friend in need of support no one need hide in shame; 26 But from him who brings harm to his friend all will stand aloof who hear of it. 27 Who will set a guard over my mouth, and upon my lips an effective seal, That I may not fail through them, that my tongue may not destroy me?

Sirach Chapter 23

1 LORD, Father and Master of my life, permit me not to fall by them! 2 Who will apply the lash to my thoughts, to my mind the rod of discipline, That my failings may not be spared, nor the sins of my heart overlooked; 3 Lest my failings increase, and my sins be multiplied; Lest I succumb to my foes, and my enemy rejoice over me? 4 LORD, Father and God of my life, abandon me not into their control! 5 A brazen look allow me not; ward off passion from my heart, 6 Let not the lustful cravings of the flesh master me, surrender me not to shameless desires. 7 Give heed, my children, to the instruction that I pronounce, for he who keeps it will not be enslaved. 8 Through his lips is the sinner ensnared; the railer and the arrogant man fall thereby. 9 Let not your mouth form the habit of swearing, or becoming too familiar with the Holy Name. 10 Just as a slave that is constantly under scrutiny will not be without welts, So one who swears continually by the Holy Name will not remain free from sin. 11 A man who often swears heaps up obligations; the scourge will never be far from his house. If he swears in error, he incurs guilt; if he neglects his obligation, his sin is doubly great. If he swears without reason he cannot be found just, and all his house will suffer affliction. 12 There are words which merit death; may they never be heard among Jacob's heirs. For all such words are foreign to the devout, who do not wallow in sin. 13 Let not your mouth become used to coarse talk, for in it lies sinful matter. 14 Keep your father and mother in mind when you sit among the mighty, Lest in their presence you commit a blunder and disgrace your upbringing, By wishing you had never been born or cursing the day of your birth. 15 A man who has the habit of abusive language will never mature in character as long as he lives. 16 Two types of men multiply sins, a third draws down wrath; For burning passion is a blazing fire, not to be quenched till it burns itself out: A man given to sins of the flesh, who never stops until the fire breaks forth; 17 The rake to whom all bread is sweet and who is never through till he dies; 18 And the man who dishonors his marriage bed and says to himself "Who can see me? Darkness surrounds me, walls hide me; no one sees me; why should I fear to sin?" Of the Most High he is not mindful, 19 fearing only the eyes of men; He does not understand that the eyes of the LORD, ten thousand times brighter than the sun, Observe every step a man takes and peer into hidden corners. 20 He who knows all things before they exist still knows them all after they are made. 21 Such a man will be punished in the streets of the city; when he least expects it, he will be apprehended. 22 So also with the woman who is unfaithful to her husband and offers as heir her son by a stranger. 23 First, she has disobeyed the law of the Most High; secondly, she has wronged her husband; Thirdly, in her wanton adultery she has borne children by another man. 24 Such a woman will be dragged before the assembly, and her punishment will extend to her children; 25 Her children will not take root; her branches will not bring forth fruit. 26 She will leave an accursed memory; her disgrace will never be blotted out. 27 Thus all who dwell on the earth shall know, and all who inhabit the world shall understand, That nothing is better than the fear of the LORD, nothing more salutary than to obey his commandments.

Sirach Chapter 24

1 Wisdom sings her own praises, before her own people she proclaims her glory; 2 In the assembly of the Most High she opens her mouth, in the presence of his hosts she declares her worth: 3 "From the mouth of the Most High I came forth, and mistlike covered the earth. 4 In the highest heavens did I dwell, my throne on a pillar of cloud. 5 The vault of heaven I compassed alone, through the deep abyss I wandered. 6 Over waves of the sea, over all the land, over every people and nation I held sway. 7 Among all these I sought a resting place; in whose inheritance should I abide? 8 "Then the Creator of all gave me his command, and he who formed me chose the spot for my tent, Saying, 'In Jacob make your dwelling, in Israel your inheritance.' 9 Before all ages, in the beginning, he created me, and through all ages I shall not cease to be. 10 In the holy tent I ministered before him, and in Zion I fixed my abode. 11 Thus in the chosen city he has given me rest, in

Jerusalem is my domain. 12 I have struck root among the glorious people, in the portion of the LORD, his heritage. 13 "Like a cedar on Lebanon I am raised aloft, like a cypress on Mount Hermon, 14 Like a palm tree in En-gedi, like a rosebush in Jericho, Like a fair olive tree in the field, like a plane tree growing beside the water. 15 Like cinnamon, or fragrant balm, or precious myrrh, I give forth perfume; Like galbanum and onycha and sweet spices, like the odor of incense in the holy place. 16 I spread out my branches like a terebinth, my branches so bright and so graceful. 17 I bud forth delights like the vine, my blossoms become fruit fair and rich. 18 Come to me, all you that yearn for me, and be filled with my fruits; 19 You will remember me as sweeter than honey, better to have than the honeycomb. 20 He who eats of me will hunger still, he who drinks of me will thirst for more; 21 He who obeys me will not be put to shame, he who serves me will never fail." 22 All this is true of the book of the Most High's covenant, the law which Moses commanded us as an inheritance for the community of Jacob. 23 It overflows, like the Pishon, with wisdom - like the Tigris in the days of the new fruits. 24 It runs over, like the Euphrates, with understanding, like the Jordan at harvest time. 25 It sparkles like the Nile with knowledge, like the Gihon at vintage time. 26 The first man never finished comprehending wisdom, nor will the last succeed in fathoming her. 27 For deeper than the sea are her thoughts; her counsels, than the great abyss. 28 Now I, like a rivulet from her stream, channeling the waters into a garden, 29 Said to myself, "I will water my plants, my flower bed I will drench"; And suddenly this rivulet of mine became a river, then this stream of mine, a sea. 30 Thus do I send my teachings forth shining like the dawn, to become known afar off. 31 Thus do I pour out instruction like prophecy and bestow it on generations to come.

Sirach Chapter 25

1 With three things I am delighted, for they are pleasing to the LORD and to men: Harmony among brethren, friendship among neighbors, and the mutual love of husband and wife. 2 Three kinds of men I hate; their manner of life I loathe indeed: A proud pauper, a rich dissembler, and an old man lecherous in his dotage. 3 What you have not saved in your youth, how will you acquire in your old age? 4 How becoming to the gray-haired is judgment, and a knowledge of counsel to those on in years! 5 How becoming to the aged is wisdom, understanding and prudence to the venerable! 6 The crown of old men is wide experience; their glory, the fear of the LORD. 7 There are nine who come to my mind as blessed, a tenth whom my tongue proclaims: The man who finds joy in his children, and he who lives to see his enemies' downfall. 8 Happy is he who dwells with a sensible wife, and he who plows not like a donkey yoked with an ox. Happy is he who sins not with his tongue, and he who serves not his inferior. 9 Happy is he who finds a friend and he who speaks to attentive ears. 10 He who finds wisdom is great indeed, but not greater than he who fears the LORD. 11 Fear of the LORD surpasses all else. Its possessor is beyond compare. 12 Worst of all wounds is that of the heart, worst of all evils is that of a woman. 13 Worst of all sufferings is that from one's foes, worst of all vengeance is that of one's enemies: 14 No poison worse than that of a serpent, no venom greater than that of a woman. 15 With a dragon or a lion I would rather dwell than live with an evil woman. 16 Wickedness changes a woman's looks, and makes her sullen as a female bear. 17 When her husband sits among his neighbors, a bitter sigh escapes him unawares. 18 There is scarce any evil like that in a woman; may she fall to the lot of the sinner! 19 Like a sandy hill to aged feet is a railing wife to a quiet man. 20 Stumble not through woman's beauty, nor be greedy for her wealth; 21 The man is a slave, in disgrace and shame, when a wife supports her husband. 22 Depressed mind, saddened face, broken heart - this from an evil wife. Feeble hands and quaking knees - from a wife who brings no happiness to her husband. 23 In woman was sin's beginning, and because of her we all die. 24 Allow water no outlet, and be not indulgent to an erring wife. 25 If she walks not by your side, cut her away from you.

Sirach Chapter 26

1 Happy the husband of a good wife, twice-lengthened are his days; 2 A worthy wife brings joy to her husband, peaceful and full is his life. 3 A good wife is a generous gift bestowed upon him who fears the LORD; 4 Be he rich or poor, his heart is content, and a smile is ever on his face. 5 There are three things at which my heart quakes, a fourth before which I quail: Though false charges in public, trial before all the people, and lying testimony are harder to bear than death, 6 A jealous wife is heartache and mourning and a scourging tongue like the other three. 7 A bad wife is a chafing yoke; he who marries her seizes a scorpion. 8 A drunken wife arouses great anger, for she does not hide her shame. 9 By her eyelids and her haughty stare an unchaste wife can be recognized. 10 Keep a strict watch over an unruly wife, lest, finding an opportunity, she make use of it; 11 Follow close if her eyes are bold, and be not surprised if she betrays you: 12 As a thirsty traveler with eager mouth drinks from any water that he finds, So she settles down before every tent peg and opens her quiver for every arrow. 13 A gracious wife delights her husband, her thoughtfulness puts flesh on his bones; 14 A gift from the LORD is her governed speech, and her firm virtue is of surpassing worth. 15 Choicest of blessings is a modest wife, priceless her chaste person. 16 Like the sun rising in the LORD'S heavens, the beauty of a virtuous wife is the radiance of her home. 17 Like the light which shines above the holy lampstand, are her beauty of face and graceful figure. 18 Golden columns on silver bases are her shapely limbs and steady feet. 19 These two bring grief to my heart, and the third arouses my horror: A wealthy man reduced to want; illustrious men held in contempt; And the man who passes from justice to sin, for whom the LORD makes ready the sword. 20 A merchant can hardly remain upright, nor a shopkeeper free from sin.

Sirach Chapter 27

1 For the sake of profit many sin, and the struggle for wealth blinds the eyes. 2 Like a peg driven between fitted stones, between buying and selling sin is wedged in. 3 Unless you earnestly hold fast to the fear of the LORD, suddenly your house will be thrown down. 4 When a sieve is shaken, the husks appear; so do a man's faults when he speaks. 5 As the test of what the potter molds is in the furnace, so in his conversation is the test of a man. 6 The fruit of a tree shows the care it has had; so too does a man's speech disclose the bent of his mind. 7 Praise no man before he speaks, for it is then that men are tested. 8 If you strive after justice you will attain it, and put it on like a splendid robe. 9 Birds nest with their own kind, and fidelity comes to those who live by it. 10 As a lion crouches in wait for prey, so do sins for evildoers. 11 Ever wise are the discourses of the devout, but the godless man, like the moon, is inconstant. 12 Limit the time you spend among fools, but frequent the company of thoughtful men. 13 The conversation of the wicked is offensive, their laughter is wanton guilt. 14 Their oath-filled talk makes the hair stand on end, their brawls make one stop one's ears. 15 Wrangling among the haughty ends in bloodshed, their cursing is painful to hear. 16 He who betrays a secret cannot be trusted, he will never find an intimate friend. 17 Cherish your friend, keep faith with him; but if you betray his confidence, follow him not; 18 For as an enemy might kill a man, you have killed your neighbor's friendship. 19 Like a bird released from the hand, you have let your friend go and cannot recapture him; 20 Follow him not, for he is far away, he has fled like a gazelle from the trap. 21 A wound can be bound up, and an insult forgiven, but he who betrays secrets does hopeless damage. 22 He who has shifty eyes plots mischief and no one can ward him off; 23 In your presence he uses honeyed talk, and admires your every word, But later he changes his tone and twists your words to your ruin. 24 There is nothing that I hate so much, and the LORD hates him as well. 25 As a stone falls back on him who throws it up, so a blow struck in treachery injures more than one. 26 As he who digs a pit falls into it, and he who lays a snare is caught in it, 27 Whoever does harm will be involved in it without knowing how it came upon him. 28 Mockery and abuse will be the lot of the proud, and vengeance lies in wait for them like a lion. 29 The trap seizes those who rejoice in pitfalls, and pain will consume them before they die; 30 Wrath and anger are hateful things, yet the sinner hugs them tight.

Sirach Chapter 28

1 The vengeful will suffer the LORD'S vengeance, for he remembers their sins in detail. 2 Forgive your neighbor's injustice; then when you pray, your own sins will be forgiven. 3 Should a man nourish anger against his fellows and expect healing from the LORD? 4 Should a man refuse mercy to his fellows, yet seek pardon for his own sins? 5 If he who is but flesh cherishes wrath, who will forgive his sins? 6 Remember your last days, set enmity aside; remember death and decay, and cease from sin! 7 Think of the commandments, hate not your neighbor; of the Most High's covenant, and overlook faults. 8 Avoid strife and your sins will be fewer, for a quarrelsome man kindles disputes, 9 Commits the sin of disrupting friendship and sows discord among those at peace. 10 The more wood, the greater the fire, the more underlying it, the fiercer the fight; The greater a man's strength, the sterner his anger, the greater his power, the greater his wrath. 11 Pitch and resin make fires flare up, and insistent quarrels provoke bloodshed. 12 If you blow upon a spark, it quickens into flame, if you spit on it, it dies out; yet both you do with your mouth! 13 Cursed be gossips and the double-tongued, for they destroy the peace of many. 14 A meddlesome tongue subverts many, and makes them refugees among the peoples; It destroys walled cities, and overthrows powerful dynasties. 15 A meddlesome tongue can drive virtuous women from their homes and rob them of the fruit of their toil;

16 Whoever heeds it has no rest, nor can he dwell in peace. 17 A blow from a whip raises a welt, but a blow from the tongue smashes bones; 18 Many have fallen by the edge of the sword, but not as many as by the tongue. 19 Happy he who is sheltered from it, and has not endured its wrath; Who has not borne its yoke nor been fettered with its chain; 20 For its yoke is a yoke of iron and its chains are chains of bronze! 21 Dire is the death it inflicts, besides which even the nether world is a gain; 22 It will not take hold among the just nor scorch them in its flame, 23 But those who forsake the LORD will fall victims to it, as it burns among them unquenchably! It will hurl itself against them like a lion; like a panther, it will tear them to pieces. 24 As you hedge round your vineyard with thorns, set barred doors over your mouth; 25 As you seal up your silver and gold, so balance and weigh your words. 26 Take care not to slip by your tongue and fall victim to your foe waiting in ambush.

Sirach Chapter 29

1 He does a kindness who lends to his neighbor, and he fulfills the precepts who holds out a helping hand. 2 Lend to your neighbor in his hour of need, and pay back your neighbor when a loan falls due; 3 Keep your promise, be honest with him, and you will always come by what you need. 4 Many a man who asks for a loan adds to the burdens of those who help him; 5 When he borrows, he kisses the lender's hand and speaks with respect of his creditor's wealth; But when payment is due he disappoints him and says he is helpless to meet the claim. 6 If the lender is able to recover barely half, he considers this an achievement; If not, he is cheated of his wealth and acquires an enemy at no extra charge; With curses and insults the borrower pays him back, with abuse instead of honor. 7 Many refuse to lend, not out of meanness, but from fear of being cheated. 8 To a poor man, however, be generous; keep him not waiting for your alms; 9 Because of the precept, help the needy, and in their want, do not send them away empty-handed. 10 Spend your money for your brother and friend, and hide it not under a stone to perish; 11 Dispose of your treasure as the Most High commands, for that will profit you more than the gold. 12 Store up almsgiving in your treasure house, and it will save you from every evil; 13 Better than a stout shield and a sturdy spear it will fight for you against the foe. 14 A good man goes surety for his neighbor, and only the shameless would play him false; 15 Forget not the kindness of your backer, for he offers his very life for you. 16 The wicked turn a pledge on their behalf into misfortune, and the ingrate abandons his protector; 17 Going surety has ruined many prosperous men and tossed them about like waves of the sea, 18 Has exiled men of prominence and sent them wandering through foreign lands. 19 The sinner through surety comes to grief, and he who undertakes too much falls into lawsuits. 20 Go surety for your neighbor according to your means, but take care lest you fall thereby. 21 Life's prime needs are water, bread, and clothing, a house, too, for decent privacy. 22 Better a poor man's fare under the shadow of one's own roof than sumptuous banquets among strangers. 23 Be it little or much, be content with what you have, and pay no heed to him who would disparage your home; 24 A miserable life it is to go from house to house, for as a guest you dare not open your mouth. 25 The visitor has no thanks for filling the cups; besides, you will hear these bitter words: 26 "Come here, stranger, set the table, give me to eat the food you have! 27 Away, stranger, for one more worthy; for my brother's visit I need the room!" 28 Painful things to a sensitive man are abuse at home and insults from his creditors.

Sirach Chapter 30

1 He who loves his son chastises him often, that he may be his joy when he grows up. 2 He who disciplines his son will benefit from him, and boast of him among his intimates. 3 He who educates his son makes his enemy jealous, and shows his delight in him among his friends. 4 At the father's death, he will seem not dead, since he leaves after him one like himself, 5 Whom he looks upon through life with joy, and even in death, without regret: 6 The avenger he leaves against his foes, and the one to repay his friends with kindness. 7 He who spoils his son will have wounds to bandage, and will quake inwardly at every outcry. 8 A colt untamed turns out stubborn; a son left to himself grows up unruly. 9 Pamper your child and he will be a terror for you, indulge him and he will bring you grief. 10 Share not in his frivolity lest you share in his sorrow, when finally your teeth are clenched in remorse. 11 Give him not his own way in his youth, and close not your eyes to his follies. 12 Bend him to the yoke when he is young, thrash his sides while he is still small, lest he become stubborn, disobey you, and leave you disconsolate. 13 Discipline your son, make heavy his yoke, lest his folly humiliate you. 14 Better a poor man strong and robust, than a rich man with wasted frame. 15 More precious than gold is health and well-being, contentment of spirit than coral. 16 No treasure greater than a healthy body; no happiness, than a joyful heart! 17 Preferable is death to a bitter life, unending sleep to constant illness. 18 Dainties set before one who cannot eat are like the offerings placed before a tomb. 19 What good is an offering to an idol that can neither taste nor smell? 20 So it is with the afflicted man who groans at the good things his eyes behold! 21 Do not give in to sadness, torment not yourself with brooding; 22 Gladness of heart is the very life of man, cheerfulness prolongs his days. 23 Distract yourself, renew your courage, drive resentment far away from you; for worry has brought death to many, nor is there aught to be gained from resentment. 24 Envy and anger shorten one's life, worry brings on premature old age. 25 One who is cheerful and gay while at table benefits from his food.

Sirach Chapter 31

1 Keeping watch over riches wastes the flesh, and the care of wealth drives away rest. 2 Concern for one's livelihood banishes slumber; more than a serious illness it disturbs repose. 3 The rich man labors to pile up wealth, and his only rest is wanton pleasure; 4 The poor man toils for a meager subsistence, and if ever he rests, he finds himself in want. 5 The lover of gold will not be free from sin, for he who pursues wealth is led astray by it. 6 Many have been ensnared by gold, though destruction lay before their eyes; 7 It is a stumbling block to those who are avid for it, a snare for every fool. 8 Happy the rich man found without fault, who turns not aside after gain! 9 Who is he, that we may praise him? he, of all his kindred, has done wonders, 10 For he has been tested by gold and come off safe, and this remains his glory; He could have sinned but did not, could have done evil but would not, 11 So that his possessions are secure, and the assembly recounts his praises. 12 If you are dining with a great man, bring not a greedy gullet to his table, Nor cry out, "How much food there is here!" 13 Remember that gluttony is evil. No creature is greedier than the eye: therefore it weeps for any cause. 14 Recognize that your neighbor feels as you do, and keep in mind your own dislikes: 15 Toward what he eyes, do not put out a hand; nor reach when he does for the same dish. 16 Behave at table like a favored guest, and be not greedy, lest you be despised. 17 Be the first to stop, as befits good manners; gorge not yourself, lest you give offense. 18 If there are many with you at table, be not the first to reach out your hand. 19 Does not a little suffice for a well-bred man? When he lies down, it is without discomfort. 20 Distress and anguish and loss of sleep, and restless tossing for the glutton! Moderate eating ensures sound slumber and a clear mind next day on rising. 21 If perforce you have eaten too much, once you have emptied your stomach, you will have relief. 22 Listen to me, my son, and scorn me not; later you will find my advice good. In whatever you do, be moderate, and no sickness will befall you. 23 On a man generous with food, blessings are invoked, and this testimony to his goodness is lasting; 24 He who is miserly with food is denounced in public, and this testimony to his stinginess is lasting. 25 Let not wine-drinking be the proof of your strength, for wine has been the ruin of many. 26 As the furnace probes the work of the smith, so does wine the hearts of the insolent. 27 Wine is very life to man if taken in moderation. Does he really live who lacks the wine which was created for his joy? 28 Joy of heart, good cheer and merriment are wine drunk freely at the proper time. 29 Headache, bitterness and disgrace is wine drunk amid anger and strife. 30 More and more wine is a snare for the fool; it lessens his strength and multiplies his wounds. 31 Rebuke not your neighbor when wine is served, nor put him to shame while he is merry; Use no harsh words with him and distress him not in the presence of others.

Sirach Chapter 32

1 If you are chosen to preside at dinner, be not puffed up, but with the guests be as one of themselves; Take care of them first before you sit down; 2 when you have fulfilled your duty, then take your place, to share in their joy and win praise for your hospitality. 3 Being older, you may talk; that is only your right, but temper your wisdom, not to disturb the singing. 4 When wine is present, do not pour out discourse, and flaunt not your wisdom at the wrong time. 5 Like a seal of carnelian in a setting of gold is a concert when wine is served. 6 Like a gold mounting with an emerald seal is string music with delicious wine. 7 Young man, speak only when necessary, when they have asked you more than once; 8 Be brief, but say much in those few words, be like the wise man, taciturn. 9 When among your elders be not forward, and with officials be not too insistent. 10 Like the lightning that flashes before a storm is the esteem that shines on modesty. 11 When it is time to leave, tarry not; be off for home! There take your ease, 12 And there enjoy doing as you wish, but without sin or words of pride. 13 Above all, give praise to your Creator, who showers his favors upon you. 14 He who would find God must accept discipline; he who seeks him obtains his request. 15 He who studies the law masters it, but the hypocrite finds it a trap. 16 His judgment is sound who fears the LORD; out of obscurity he draws forth a clear plan. 17 The sinner turns aside reproof and distorts the law to

suit his purpose. 18 The thoughtful man will not neglect direction; the proud and insolent man is deterred by nothing. 19 Do nothing without counsel, and then you need have no regrets. 20 Go not on a way that is set with snares, and let not the same thing trip you twice. 21 Be not too sure even of smooth roads, 22 be careful on all your paths. 23 Whatever you do, be on your guard, for in this way you will keep the commandments. 24 He who keeps the law preserves himself; and he who trusts in the LORD shall not be put to shame.

Sirach Chapter 33

1 No evil can harm the man who fears the LORD; through trials, again and again he is safe. 2 He who hates the law is without wisdom, and is tossed about like a boat in a storm. 3 The prudent man trusts in the word of the LORD, and the law is dependable for him as a divine oracle. 4 Prepare your words and you will be listened to; draw upon your training, and then give your answer. 5 Like the wheel of a cart is the mind of a fool; his thoughts revolve in circles. 6 A fickle friend is like the stallion that neighs, no matter who the rider. 7 Why is one day more important than another, when it is the sun that lights up every day? 8 It is due to the LORD'S wisdom that they differ; it is through him the seasons and feasts come and go. 9 Some he dignifies and sanctifies, and others he lists as ordinary days. 10 So too, all men are of clay, for from earth man was formed; 11 Yet with his great knowledge the LORD makes men unlike; in different paths he has them walk. 12 Some he blesses and makes great, some he sanctifies and draws to himself. Others he curses and brings low, and expels them from their place. 13 Like clay in the hands of a potter, to be molded according to his pleasure, so are men in the hands of their Creator, to be assigned by him their function. 14 As evil contrasts with good, and death with life, so are sinners in contrast with the just; 15 See now all the works of the Most High: they come in pairs, the one the opposite of the other. 16 Now I am the last to keep vigil, like a gleaner after the vintage; 17 Since by the LORD'S blessing I have made progress till like a vintager I have filled my wine press, 18 I would inform you that not for myself only have I toiled, but for every seeker after wisdom. 19 Listen to me, O leaders of the multitude; O rulers of the assembly, give ear! 20 Let neither son nor wife, neither brother nor friend, have power over you as long as you live. 21 While breath of life is still in you, let no man have dominion over you. Give not to another your wealth, lest then you have to plead with him; 22 Far better that your children plead with you than that you should look to their generosity. 23 Keep control over all your affairs; let no one tarnish your glory. 24 When your few days reach their limit, at the time of death distribute your inheritance. 25 Fodder and whip and loads for an ass; the yoke and harness and the rod of his master. 26 Food, correction and work for a slave; and for a wicked slave, punishment in the stocks. 27 Make a slave work and he will look for his rest; let his hands be idle and he will seek to be free. 28 Force him to work that he be not idle, for idleness is an apt teacher of mischief. 29 Put him to work, for that is what befits him; if he becomes unruly, load him with chains. 30 But never lord it over any human being, and do nothing unjust. 31 If you have but one slave, treat him like yourself, for you have acquired him with your life's blood; 32 If you have but one slave, deal with him as a brother, for you need him as you need your life: 33 If you mistreat him and he runs away, in what direction will you look for him?

Sirach Chapter 34

1 Empty and false are the hopes of the senseless, and fools are borne aloft by dreams. 2 Like a man who catches at shadows or chases the wind, is the one who believes in dreams. 3 What is seen in dreams is to reality what the reflection of a face is to the face itself. 4 Can the unclean produce the clean? can the liar ever speak the truth? 5 Divination, omens and dreams all are unreal; what you already expect, the mind depicts. 6 Unless it be a vision specially sent by the Most High, fix not your heart on it; 7 For dreams have led many astray, and those who believed in them have perished. 8 The law is fulfilled without fail, and perfect wisdom is found in the mouth of the faithful man. 9 A man with training gains wide knowledge; a man of experience speaks sense. 10 One never put to the proof knows little, whereas with travel a man adds to his resourcefulness. 11 I have seen much in my travels, learned more than ever I could say. 12 Often I was in danger of death, but by these attainments I was saved. 13 Lively is the courage of those who fear the LORD, for they put their hope in their savior; 14 He who fears the LORD is never alarmed, never afraid; for the LORD is his hope. 15 Happy the soul that fears the LORD! In whom does he trust, and who is his support? 16 The eyes of the LORD are upon those who love him; he is their mighty shield and strong support, a shelter from the heat, a shade from the noonday sun, a guard against stumbling, a help against falling. 17 He buoys up the spirits, brings a sparkle to the eyes, gives health and life and blessing. 18 Tainted his gifts who offers in sacrifice ill-gotten goods! Mock presents from the lawless win not God's favor. 19 The Most High approves not the gifts of the godless, nor for their many sacrifices does he forgive their sins. 20 Like the man who slays a son in his father's presence is he who offers sacrifice from the possessions of the poor. 21 The bread of charity is life itself for the needy; he who withholds it is a man of blood. 22 He slays his neighbor who deprives him of his living: he sheds blood who denies the laborer his wages. 23 If one man builds up and another tears down, what do they gain but trouble? 24 If one man prays and another curses, whose voice will the LORD hear? 25 If a man again touches a corpse after he has bathed, what did he gain by the purification? 26 So with a man who fasts for his sins, but then goes and commits them again: who will hear his prayer, and what has he gained by his mortification?

Sirach Chapter 35

1 To keep the law is a great oblation, and he who observes the commandments sacrifices a peace offering. 2 In works of charity one offers fine flour, and when he gives alms he presents his sacrifice of praise. 3 To refrain from evil pleases the LORD, and to avoid injustice is an atonement. 4 Appear not before the LORD empty-handed, for all that you offer is in fulfillment of the precepts. 5 The just man's offering enriches the altar and rises as a sweet odor before the Most High. 6 The just man's sacrifice is most pleasing, nor will it ever be forgotten. 7 In generous spirit pay homage to the LORD, be not sparing of freewill gifts. 8 With each contribution show a cheerful countenance, and pay your tithes in a spirit of joy. 9 Give to the Most High as he has given to you, generously, according to your means. 10 For the LORD is one who always repays, and he will give back to you sevenfold. 11 But offer no bribes, these he does not accept! Trust not in sacrifice of the fruits of extortion, 12 For he is a God of justice, who knows no favorites. 13 Though not unduly partial toward the weak, yet he hears the cry of the oppressed. 14 He is not deaf to the wail of the orphan, nor to the widow when she pours out her complaint; 15 Do not the tears that stream down her cheek cry out against him that causes them to fall? 16 He who serves God willingly is heard; his petition reaches the heavens. 17 The prayer of the lowly pierces the clouds; it does not rest till it reaches its goal, 18 Nor will it withdraw till the Most High responds, judges justly and affirms the right. 19 God indeed will not delay, and like a warrior, will not be still 20 Till he breaks the backs of the merciless and wreaks vengeance upon the proud; 21 Till he destroys the haughty root and branch, and smashes the scepter of the wicked; 22 Till he requites mankind according to its deeds, and repays men according to their thoughts; 23 Till he defends the cause of his people, and gladdens them by his mercy. 24 Welcome is his mercy in time of distress as rain clouds in time of drought.

Sirach Chapter 36

1 Come to our aid, O God of the universe, and put all the nations in dread of you! 2 Raise your hand against the heathen, that they may realize your power. 3 As you have used us to show them your holiness, so now use them to show us your glory. 4 Thus they will know, as we know, that there is no God but you. 5 Give new signs and work new wonders; show forth the splendor of your right hand and arm; 6 Rouse your anger, pour out wrath, humble the enemy, scatter the foe. 7 Hasten the day, bring on the time; 9 crush the heads of the hostile rulers. 8 Let raging fire consume the fugitive, and your people's oppressors meet destruction. 10 Gather all the tribes of Jacob, that they may inherit the land as of old, 11 Show mercy to the people called by your name; Israel, whom you named your first-born. 12 Take pity on your holy city, Jerusalem, your dwelling place. 13 Fill Zion with your majesty, your temple with your glory. 14 Give evidence of your deeds of old; fulfill the prophecies spoken in your name, 15 Reward those who have hoped in you, and let your prophets be proved true. 16 Hear the prayer of your servants, for you are ever gracious to your people; 17 Thus it will be known to the very ends of the earth that you are the eternal God. 18 The throat can swallow any food, yet some foods are more agreeable than others; 19 As the palate tests meat by its savor, so does a keen mind insincere words. 20 A deceitful character causes grief, but an experienced man can turn the tables on him. 21 Though any man may be accepted as a husband, yet one girl will be more suitable than another: 22 A woman's beauty makes her husband's face light up, for it surpasses all else that charms the eye; 23 And if, besides, her speech is kindly, his lot is beyond that of mortal men. 24 A wife is her husband's richest treasure, a helpmate, a steadying column. 25 A vineyard with no hedge will be overrun; a man with no wife becomes a homeless wanderer. 26 Who will trust an armed band that shifts from city to city? 27 Or a man who has no nest, but lodges where night overtakes him?

Sirach Chapter 37

1 Every friend declares his friendship, but there are friends who are friends in name only. 2 Is it not a sorrow unto death when your bosom companion becomes your enemy? 3 "Alas, my companion! Why were you created to blanket the earth with deceit?" 4 A false friend will share your joys, but in time of trouble he stands afar off. 5 A true friend will fight with you against the foe, against your enemies he will be your shield-bearer. 6 Forget not your comrade during the battle, and neglect him not when you distribute your spoils. 7 Every counselor points out a way, but some counsel ways of their own; 8 Be on the alert when one proffers advice, find out first of all what he wants. For he may be thinking of himself alone; why should the profit fall to him? 9 He may tell you how good your way will be, and then stand by to watch your misfortune. 10 Seek no advice from one who regards you with hostility; from those who envy you, keep your intentions hidden. 11 Speak not to a woman about her rival, nor to a coward about war, to a merchant about business, to a buyer about value, to a miser about generosity, to a cruel man about mercy, to a lazy man about work, to a seasonal laborer about the harvest, to an idle slave about a great task: pay no attention to any advice they give. 12 Instead, associate with a religious man, who you are sure keeps the commandments; Who is like-minded with yourself and will feel for you if you fall. 13 Then, too, heed your own heart's counsel; for what have you that you can depend on more? 14 A man's conscience can tell him his situation better than seven watchmen in a lofty tower. 15 Most important of all, pray to God to set your feet in the path of truth. 16 A word is the source of every deed; a thought, of every act. 17 The root of all conduct is the mind; four branches it shoots forth: 18 Good and evil, death and life, their absolute mistress is the tongue. 19 A man may be wise and benefit many, yet be of no use to himself. 20 Though a man may be wise, if his words are rejected he will be deprived of all enjoyment. 21 When a man is wise to his own advantage, the fruits of his knowledge are seen in his own person; 22 When a man is wise to his people's advantage, the fruits of his knowledge are enduring: 23 Limited are the days of one man's life, but the life of Israel is days without number. 24 One wise for himself has full enjoyment, and all who see him praise him; 25 One wise for his people wins a heritage of glory, and his name endures forever. 26 My son, while you are well, govern your appetite so that you allow it not what is bad for you; 27 For not every food is good for everyone, nor is everything suited to every taste. 28 Be not drawn after every enjoyment, neither become a glutton for choice foods, 29 For sickness comes with overeating, and gluttony brings on biliousness. 30 Through lack of self-control many have died, but the abstemious man prolongs his life.

Sirach Chapter 38

1 Hold the physician in honor, for he is essential to you, and God it was who established his profession. 2 From God the doctor has his wisdom, and the king provides for his sustenance. 3 His knowledge makes the doctor distinguished, and gives him access to those in authority. 4 God makes the earth yield healing herbs which the prudent man should not neglect; 5 Was not the water sweetened by a twig that men might learn his power? 6 He endows men with the knowledge to glory in his mighty works, 7 Through which the doctor eases pain and the druggist prepares his medicines; 8 Thus God's creative work continues without cease in its efficacy on the surface of the earth. 9 My son, when you are ill, delay not, but pray to God, who will heal you: 10 Flee wickedness; let your hands be just, cleanse your heart of every sin; 11 Offer your sweet-smelling oblation and petition, a rich offering according to your means. 12 Then give the doctor his place lest he leave; for you need him too. 13 There are times that give him an advantage, 14 and he too beseeches God that his diagnosis may be correct and his treatment bring about a cure. 15 He who is a sinner toward his Maker will be defiant toward the doctor. 16 My son, shed tears for one who is dead with wailing and bitter lament; as is only proper, prepare the body, absent not yourself from his burial: 17 Weeping bitterly, mourning fully, pay your tribute of sorrow, as he deserves, 18 One or two days, to prevent gossip; then compose yourself after your grief, 19 For grief can bring on an extremity and heartache destroy one's health. 20 Turn not your thoughts to him again; cease to recall him; think rather of the end. 21 Recall him not, for there is no hope of his return; it will not help him, but will do you harm. 22 Remember that his fate will also be yours; for him it was yesterday, for you today. 23 With the departed dead, let memory fade; rally your courage, once the soul has left. 24 The scribe's profession increases his wisdom; whoever is free from toil can become a wise man. 25 How can he become learned who guides the plow, who thrills in wielding the goad like a lance, who guides the ox and urges on the bullock, and whose every concern is for cattle? 26 His care is for plowing furrows, and he keeps a watch on the beasts in the stalls. 27 So with every engraver and designer who, laboring night and day, fashions carved seals, and whose concern is to vary the pattern. His care is to produce a vivid impression, and he keeps watch till he finishes his design. 28 So with the smith standing near his anvil, forging crude iron. The heat from the fire sears his flesh, yet he toils away in the furnace heat. The clang of the hammer deafens his ears, his eyes are fixed on the tool he is shaping. His care is to finish his work, and he keeps watch till he perfects it in detail. 29 So with the potter sitting at his labor, revolving the wheel with his feet. He is always concerned for his products, and turns them out in quantity. 30 With his hands he molds the clay, and with his feet softens it. His care is for proper coloring, and he keeps watch on the fire of his kiln. 31 All these men are skilled with their hands, each one an expert at his own task; 32 Without them no city could be lived in, and wherever they stay, they need not hunger. 33 They do not occupy the judge's bench, nor are they prominent in the assembly; they set forth no decisions or judgments, nor are they found among the rulers; 34 Yet they maintain God's ancient handiwork, and their concern is for exercise of their skill.

Sirach Chapter 39

1 How different the man who devotes himself to the study of the law of the Most High! He explores the wisdom of the men of old and occupies himself with the prophecies; 2 He treasures the discourses of famous men, and goes to the heart of involved sayings; 3 He studies obscure parables, and is busied with the hidden meanings of the sages. 4 He is in attendance on the great, and has entrance to the ruler. 5 He travels among the peoples of foreign lands to learn what is good and evil among men. 6 His care is to seek the LORD, his Maker, to petition the Most High, to open his lips in prayer, to ask pardon for his sins. Then, if it pleases the LORD Almighty, he will be filled with the spirit of understanding; He will pour forth his words of wisdom and in prayer give thanks to the LORD, 7 Who will direct his knowledge and his counsel, as he meditates upon his mysteries. 8 He will show the wisdom of what he has learned and glory in the law of the LORD'S covenant. 9 Many will praise his understanding; his fame can never be effaced; Unfading will be his memory, through all generations his name will live; 10 Peoples will speak of his wisdom, and in assembly sing his praises. 11 While he lives he is one out of a thousand, and when he dies his renown will not cease. 12 Once more I will set forth my theme to shine like the moon in its fullness! 13 Listen, my faithful children: open up your petals, like roses planted near running waters; 14 Send up the sweet odor of incense, break forth in blossoms like the lily. Send up the sweet odor of your hymn of praise; bless the LORD for all he has done! 15 Proclaim the greatness of his name, loudly sing his praises, with music on the harp and all stringed instruments; sing out with joy as you proclaim: 16 The works of God are all of them good; in its own time every need is supplied. 17 At his word the waters become still as in a flask; he had but to speak and the reservoirs were made. 18 He has but to command and his will is done; nothing can limit his achievement. 19 The works of all mankind are present to him; not a thing escapes his eye. 20 His gaze spans all the ages; to him there is nothing unexpected. 21 No cause then to say: "What is the purpose of this?" Everything is chosen to satisfy a need. 22 His blessing overflows like the Nile; like the Euphrates it enriches the surface of the earth. 23 Again, his wrath expels the nations and turns fertile land into a salt marsh. 24 For the virtuous his paths are level, to the haughty they are steep; 25 Good things for the good he provided from the beginning, but for the wicked good things and bad. 26 Chief of all needs for human life are water and fire, iron and salt, the heart of the wheat, milk and honey, the blood of the grape, and oil, and cloth; 27 For the good all these are good, but for the wicked they turn out evil. 28 There are storm winds created to punish, which in their fury can dislodge mountains; when destruction must be, they hurl all their force and appease the anger of their Maker. 29 In his treasury also, kept for the proper time, are fire and hail, famine, disease, 30 ravenous beasts, scorpions, vipers, and the avenging sword to exterminate the wicked; 31 In doing his bidding they rejoice, in their assignments they disobey not his command. 32 So from the first I took my stand, and wrote down as my theme: 33 The works of God are all of them good; every need when it comes he fills. 34 No cause then to say: "This is not as good as that"; for each shows its worth at the proper time. 35 So now with full joy of heart proclaim and bless the name of the Holy One.

Sirach Chapter 40

1 A great anxiety has God allotted, and a heavy yoke, to the sons of men; from the day one leaves his mother's womb to the day he returns to the mother of all the living, 2 his thoughts, the fear in his heart, and his troubled forebodings till the day he dies— 3 whether he sits on a lofty throne or grovels in dust and ashes, 4 whether he bears a splendid crown or is wrapped in the coarsest of cloaks— 5 are of wrath and envy, trouble and dread, terror of death, fury and strife. Even when he lies on

his bed to rest, his cares at night disturb his sleep. 6 So short is his rest it seems like none, till in his dreams he struggles as he did by day, terrified by what his mind's eye sees, like a fugitive being pursued; 7 as he reaches safety, he wakes up astonished that there was nothing to fear. 8 So it is with all flesh, with man and with beast, but for sinners seven times more. 9 Plague and bloodshed, wrath and the sword, plunder and ruin, famine and death: 10 for the wicked, these were created evil, and it is they who bring on destruction. 11 All that is of earth returns to earth, and what is from above returns above. 12 All that comes from bribes or injustice will be wiped out, but loyalty remains for ages. 13 Wealth out of wickedness is like a wadi in spate: like a mighty stream with lightning and thunder, 14 which, in its rising, rolls along the stones, but suddenly, once and for all, comes to an end. 15 The offshoot of violence will not flourish, for the root of the godless is on sheer rock; 16 or they are like reeds on the riverbank, withered before all other plants; 17 but goodness will never be cut off, and justice endures forever. Wealth or wages can make life sweet, but better than either is finding a treasure. 18 A child or a city will preserve one's name, but better than either, attaining wisdom. 19 Sheepfolds and orchards bring flourishing health; but better than either, a devoted wife; 20 wine and music delight the soul, but better than either, conjugal love. 21 The flute and the harp offer sweet melody, but better than either, a voice that is true. 22 Charm and beauty delight the eye, but better than either, the flowers of the field. 23 A friend, a neighbor, are timely guides, but better than either, a prudent wife. 24 A brother, a helper, for times of stress; but better than either, charity that rescues. 25 Gold and silver make one's way secure, but better than either, sound judgment. 26 Wealth and vigor build up confidence, but better than either, fear of God. Fear of the LORD leaves nothing wanting; he who has it need seek no other support: 27 the fear of God is a paradise of blessings; its canopy, all that is glorious. 28 My son, live not the life of a beggar, better to die than to beg; 29 when one has to look to another's table, his life is not really a life. His neighbor's delicacies bring revulsion of spirit to one who understands inward feelings: 30 in the mouth of the shameless man begging is sweet, but within him it burns like fire.

Sirach Chapter 41

1 O death! how bitter the thought of you for the man at peace amid his possessions, for the man unruffled and always successful, who still can enjoy life's pleasures. 2 O death! how welcome your sentence to the weak man of failing strength, tottering and always rebuffed, with no more sight, with vanished hope. 3 Fear not death's decree for you; remember, it embraces those before you, and those after. 4 Thus God has ordained for all flesh; why then should you reject the will of the Most High? Whether one has lived a thousand years, a hundred, or ten, in the nether world he has no claim on life. 5 A reprobate line are the children of sinners, and witless offspring are in the homes of the wicked. 6 Their dominion is lost to sinners' children, and reproach abides with their descendants. 7 Children curse their wicked father, for they suffer disgrace through him. 8 Woe to you, O sinful men, who forsake the law of the Most High. 9 If you have children, calamity will seize them; you will beget them only for groaning. When you stumble, there is lasting joy; at death, you become a curse. 10 Whatever is of nought returns to nought, so too the godless from void to void. 11 Man's body is a fleeting thing, but a virtuous name will never be annihilated. 12 Have a care for your name, for it will stand by you better than precious treasures in the thousands; 13 The boon of life is for limited days, but a good name, for days without number. 14 My children, heed my instruction about shame; judge of disgrace only according to my rules, for it is not always well to be ashamed, nor is it always the proper thing to blush: 15 Before father and mother be ashamed of immorality, before master and mistress, of falsehood; 16 Before prince and ruler, of flattery; before the public assembly, of crime; 17 Before friend and companion, of disloyalty, and of breaking an oath or agreement. 18 Be ashamed of theft from the people where you settle, and of stretching out your elbow when you dine; 19 Of refusing to give when asked, of defrauding another of his appointed share, 20 Of failing to return a greeting, and of rebuffing a friend; 21 Of gazing at a married woman, and of entertaining thoughts about another's wife; of trifling with a servant girl you have, and of violating her couch; 22 Of using harsh words with friends, and of following up your gifts with insults; 23 Of repeating what you hear, and of betraying secrets— 24 these are the things you should rightly avoid as shameful if you would be looked upon by everyone with favor.

Sirach Chapter 42

1 But of these things be not ashamed, lest you sin through human respect: 2 Of the law of the Most High and his precepts, or of the sentence to be passed upon the sinful; 3 Of sharing the expenses of a business or a journey, or of dividing an inheritance or property; 4 Of accuracy of scales and balances, or of tested measures and weights; 5 Of acquiring much or little, or of bargaining in dealing with a merchant; of constant training of children, or of beating the sides of a disloyal servant; 6 Of a seal to keep an erring wife at home, or of a lock placed where there are many hands; 7 Of numbering every deposit, or of recording all that is given or received; 8 Of chastisement of the silly and the foolish, or of the aged and infirm answering for wanton conduct. Thus you will be truly cautious and recognized by all men as discreet. 9 A daughter is a treasure that keeps her father wakeful, and worry over her drives away rest: lest she pass her prime unmarried, or when she is married, lest she be disliked; 10 While unmarried, lest she be seduced, or, as a wife, lest she prove unfaithful; lest she conceive in her father's home, or be sterile in that of her husband. 11 Keep a close watch on your daughter, lest she make you the sport of your enemies, a byword in the city, a reproach among the people, an object of derision in public gatherings. See that there is no lattice in her room, no place that overlooks the approaches to the house. 12 Let her not parade her charms before men, or spend her time with married women; 13 For just as moths come from garments, so harm to women comes from women: 14 Better a man's harshness than a woman's indulgence, and a frightened daughter than any disgrace. 15 Now will I recall God's works; what I have seen, I will describe. At God's word were his works brought into being; they do his will as he has ordained for them. 16 As the rising sun is clear to all, so the glory of the LORD fills all his works; 17 Yet even God's holy ones must fail in recounting the wonders of the LORD, though God has given these, his hosts, the strength to stand firm before his glory. 18 He plumbs the depths and penetrates the heart; their innermost being he understands. The Most High possesses all knowledge, and sees from of old the things that are to come: 19 He makes known the past and the future, and reveals the deepest secrets. 20 No understanding does he lack; no single thing escapes him. 21 Perennial is his almighty wisdom; he is from all eternity one and the same, 22 With nothing added, nothing taken away; no need of a counselor for him! 23 How beautiful are all his works! even to the spark and the fleeting vision! 24 The universe lives and abides forever; to meet each need, each creature is preserved. 25 All of them differ, one from another, yet none of them has he made in vain, for each in turn, as it comes, is good; can one ever see enough of their splendor?

Sirach Chapter 43

1 The clear vault of the sky shines forth like heaven itself, a vision of glory. 2 The orb of the sun, resplendent at its rising: what a wonderful work of the Most High! 3 At noon it seethes the surface of the earth, and who can bear its fiery heat? 4 Like a blazing furnace of solid metal, it sets the mountains aflame with its rays; by its fiery darts the land is consumed; the eyes are dazzled by its light. 5 Great indeed is the LORD who made it, at whose orders it urges on its steeds. 6 The moon, too, that marks the changing times, governing the seasons, their lasting sign, 7 by which we know the feast days and fixed dates, this light-giver which wanes in its course: 8 as its name says, each month it renews itself; how wondrous in this change! 9 The beauty, the glory, of the heavens are the stars that adorn with their sparkling the heights of God, 10 at whose command they keep their place and never relax in their vigils. A weapon against the flood waters stored on high, lighting up the firmament by its brilliance, 11 Behold the rainbow! Then bless its Maker, for majestic indeed is its splendor; 12 it spans the heavens with its glory, this bow bent by the mighty hand of God. 13 His rebuke marks out the path for the lightning, and speeds the arrows of his judgment to their goal. 14 At it the storehouse is opened, and like vultures the clouds hurry forth. 15 In his majesty he gives the storm its power and breaks off the hailstones. 16 The thunder of his voice makes the earth writhe; before his might the mountains quake. 17 A word from him drives on the south wind, the angry north wind, the hurricane, and the storm. 18 He sprinkles the snow like fluttering birds; it comes to settle like swarms of locusts. 19 Its shining whiteness blinds the eyes, the mind is baffled by its steady fall. 20 He scatters frost like so much salt; it shines like blossoms on the thornbush. 21 Cold northern blasts he sends that turn the ponds to lumps of ice. He freezes over every body of water, and clothes each pool with a coat of mail. 22 When the mountain growth is scorched with heat, and the flowering plains as though by flames, 23 the dripping clouds restore them all, and the scattered dew enriches the parched land. 24 His is the plan that calms the deep, and plants the islands in the sea. 25 Those who go down to the sea tell part of its story, and when we hear them we are thunderstruck; 26 in it are his creatures, stupendous, amazing, all kinds of life, and the monsters of the deep. 27 For him each messenger succeeds, and at his bidding accomplishes his will. 28 More than this we need not add; let the last word be, he is all in all! 29 Let us praise him the more, since we cannot fathom him, for greater is he than all his works; 30 awful indeed is the LORD'S majesty,

and wonderful is his power. 31 Lift up your voices to glorify the LORD, though he is still beyond your power to praise; 32 extol him with renewed strength, and weary not, though you cannot reach the end: 33 for who can see him and describe him? or who can praise him as he is? 34 Beyond these, many things lie hid; only a few of his works have we seen. 35 It is the LORD who has made all things, and to those who fear him he gives wisdom.

Sirach Chapter 44

1 Now will I praise those godly men, our ancestors, each in his own time: 2 The abounding glory of the Most High's portion, his own part, since the days of old. Subduers of the land in kingly fashion, men of renown for their might, 3 or counselors in their prudence, or seers of all things in prophecy; 4 resolute princes of the folk, and governors with their staves; authors skilled in composition, and forgers of epigrams with their spikes; 5 composers of melodious psalms, or discoursers on lyric themes; 6 stalwart men, solidly established and at peace in their own estates— 7 all these were glorious in their time, each illustrious in his day. 8 Some of them have left behind a name and men recount their praiseworthy deeds; 9 but of others there is no memory, for when they ceased, they ceased. And they are as though they had not lived, they and their children after them. 10 Yet these also were godly men whose virtues have not been forgotten; 11 their wealth remains in their families, their heritage with their descendants; 12 through God's covenant with them their family endures, their posterity, for their sake. 13 And for all time their progeny will endure, their glory will never be blotted out; 14 their bodies are peacefully laid away, but their name lives on and on. 15 At gatherings their wisdom is retold, and the assembly proclaims their praise. 16 ENOCH walked with the LORD and was taken up, that succeeding generations might learn by his example. 17 NOAH, found just and perfect, renewed the race in the time of devastation. Because of his worth there were survivors, and with a sign to him the deluge ended; 18 a lasting agreement was made with him, that never should all flesh be destroyed. 19 ABRAHAM, father of many peoples, kept his glory without stain: 20 He observed the precepts of the Most High, and entered into an agreement with him; in his own flesh he incised the ordinance, and when tested he was found loyal. 21 For this reason, God promised him with an oath that in his descendants the nations would be blessed, that he would make him numerous as the grains of dust, and exalt his posterity like the stars; 22 that he would give them an inheritance from sea to sea, and from the River to the ends of the earth. And for ISAAC he renewed the same promise because of Abraham, his father. 23 The covenant with all his forebears was confirmed, and the blessing rested upon the head of JACOB. God acknowledged him as the first-born, and gave him his inheritance. He fixed the boundaries for his tribes, and their division into twelve.

Sirach Chapter 45

1 From him was to spring the man who won the favor of all: Dear to God and men, Moses, whose memory is held in benediction. 2 God's honor devolved upon him, and the Lord strengthened him with fearful powers; 3 God wrought swift miracles at his words and sustained him in the king's presence. He gave him the commandments for his people, and revealed to him his glory. 4 For his trustworthiness and meekness God selected him from all mankind; 5 He permitted him to hear his voice, and led him into the cloud, where, face to face, he gave him the commandments, the law of life and understanding, that he might teach his precepts to Jacob, his judgments and decrees to Israel. 6 He raised up also, like Moses in holiness, his brother Aaron, of the tribe of Levi. 7 He made him perpetual in his office when he bestowed on him the priesthood of his people; he established him in honor and crowned him with lofty majesty; 8 he clothed him with splendid apparel, and adorned him with the glorious vestments: breeches and tunic and robe with pomegranates around the hem, 9 and a rustle of bells round about, through whose pleasing sound at each step he would be heard within the sanctuary, and the children of his race would be remembered; 10 the sacred vestments of gold, of violet, and of crimson, wrought with embroidery; the breastpiece for decision, the ephod and cincture 11 with scarlet yarn, the work of the weaver; precious stones with seal engravings in golden settings, the work of the jeweler, to commemorate in incised letters each of the tribes of Israel; 12 on his turban the diadem of gold, its plate wrought with the insignia of holiness, majestic, glorious, renowned for splendor, a delight to the eyes, beauty supreme. 13 Before him, no one was adorned with these, nor may they ever be worn by any except his sons and them alone, generation after generation, for all time. 14 His cereal offering is wholly burnt with the established sacrifice twice each day; 15 for Moses ordained him and anointed him with the holy oil, in a lasting covenant with him and with his family, as permanent as the heavens, that he should serve God in his priesthood and bless his people in his name. 16 He chose him from all mankind to offer holocausts and choice offerings, to burn sacrifices of sweet odor for a memorial, and to atone for the people of Israel. 17 He gave to him his laws, and authority to prescribe and to judge: to teach the precepts to his people, and the ritual to the descendants of Israel. 18 Men of other families were inflamed against him, were jealous of him in the desert, the followers of Dathan and Abiram, and the band of Korah in their defiance. 19 But the Lord saw this and became angry, he destroyed them in his burning wrath. He brought down upon them a miracle, and consumed them with his flaming fire. 20 Then he increased the glory of Aaron and bestowed upon him his inheritance: the sacred offerings he allotted to him, with the showbread as his portion; 21 the oblations of the Lord are his food, a gift to him and his descendants. 22 But he holds no land among the people nor shares with them their heritage; for the Lord himself is his portion, his inheritance in the midst of Israel. 23 Phinehas too, the son of Eleazar, was the courageous third of his line when, zealous for the God of all, he met the crisis of his people and, at the prompting of his noble heart, atoned for the children of Israel. 24 Therefore on him again God conferred the right, in a covenant of friendship, to provide for the sanctuary, so that he and his descendants should possess the high priesthood forever. 25 For even his covenant with David, the son of Jesse of the tribe of Judah, was an individual heritage through one son alone; but the heritage of Aaron is for all his descendants. 26 And now bless the Lord who has crowned you with glory! May he grant you wisdom of heart to govern his people in justice, lest their welfare should ever be forgotten, or your authority, throughout all time.

Sirach Chapter 46

1 Valiant leader was JOSHUA, son of Nun, assistant to Moses in the prophetic office, formed to be, as his name implies, the great savior of God's chosen ones, to punish the enemy and to win the inheritance for Israel. 2 What glory was his when he raised his arm, to brandish his javelin against the city! 3 And who could withstand him when he fought the battles of the LORD? 4 Did he not by his power stop the sun, so that one day became two? 5 He called upon the Most High God when his enemies beset him on all sides, and God Most High gave answer to him in hailstones of tremendous power, 6 which he rained down upon the hostile army till on the slope he destroyed the foe; that all the doomed nations might know that the LORD was watching over his people's battles. 7 And because he was a devoted follower of God and in Moses' lifetime showed himself loyal, he and CALEB, son of Jephunneh, when they opposed the rebel assembly, averted God's anger from the people and suppressed the wicked complaint. 8 Because of this, they were the only two spared from the six hundred thousand infantry, to lead the people into their inheritance, the land flowing with milk and honey. 9 And the strength he gave to Caleb remained with him even in his old age till he won his way onto the summits of the land; his family too received an inheritance, 10 that all the people of Jacob might know how good it is to be a devoted follower of the LORD. 11 The JUDGES, too, each one of them, whose hearts were not deceived, who did not abandon God: may their memory be ever blessed, 12 their bones return to life from their resting place, and their names receive fresh luster in their children! 13 Beloved of his people, dear to his Maker, dedicated from his mother's womb, consecrated to the LORD as a prophet, was SAMUEL, the judge and priest. At God's word he established the kingdom and anointed princes to rule the people. 14 By the law of the LORD he judged the nation, when he visited the encampments of Jacob. 15 As a trustworthy prophet he was sought out and his words proved him true as a seer. 16 He, too, called upon God, and offered him a suckling lamb; 17 then the LORD thundered forth from heaven, and the tremendous roar of his voice was heard. 18 He brought low the rulers of the enemy and destroyed all the lords of the Philistines. 19 When Samuel approached the end of his life, he testified before the LORD and his anointed prince, "No bribe or secret gift have I taken from any man!" and no one dared gainsay him. 20 Even when he lay buried, his guidance was sought; he made known to the king his fate, and from the grave he raised his voice as a prophet, to put an end to wickedness.

Sirach Chapter 47

1 After him came **NATHAN** who served in the presence of David. 2 Like the choice fat of the sacred offerings, so was **DAVID** in Israel. 3 He made sport of lions as though they were kids, and of bears, like lambs of the flock. 4 As a youth he slew the giant and wiped out the people's disgrace, when his hand let fly the slingstone that crushed the pride of Goliath. 5 Since he called upon the Most High God, who gave strength to his right arm to defeat the skilled warrior and raise up the might of his people, 6 therefore the women sang his praises and ascribed to him tens of thousands. When he assumed the royal crown, he battled 7 and

subdued the enemy on every side. He destroyed the hostile Philistines and shattered their power till our own day. 8 With his every deed he offered thanks to God Most High, in words of praise. With his whole being he loved his Maker and daily had his praises sung; 9 He added beauty to the feasts and solemnized the seasons of each year with string music before the altar, providing sweet melody for the psalms, 10 so that when the Holy Name was praised, before daybreak the sanctuary would resound. 11 The LORD forgave him his sins and exalted his strength forever; He conferred on him the rights of royalty and established his throne in Israel. 12 Because of his merits he had as his successor a wise son, who lived in security: 13 **SOLOMON** reigned during an era of peace, for God made tranquil all his borders. He built a house to the name of God, and established a lasting sanctuary. 14 How wise you were when you were young, overflowing with instruction, like the Nile in flood! 15 Your understanding covered the whole earth, and, like a sea, filled it with knowledge. 16 Your fame reached distant coasts, and their peoples came to hear you; 17 With song and story and riddle, and with your answers, you astounded the nations. 18 You were called by that glorious name which was conferred upon Israel. 19 Gold you gathered like so much iron, you heaped up silver as though it were lead; 20 But you abandoned yourself to women and gave them dominion over your body. 21 You brought dishonor upon your reputation, shame upon your marriage, wrath upon your descendants, and groaning upon your domain; 22 Thus two governments came into being, when in Ephraim kingship was usurped. 23 But God does not withdraw his mercy, nor permit even one of his promises to fail. He does not uproot the posterity of his chosen one, nor destroy the offspring of his friend. So he gave to Jacob a remnant, to David a root from his own family. 24 **Solomon** finally slept with his fathers, and left behind him one of his sons, expansive in folly, limited in sense, **REHOBOAM**, who by his policy made the people rebel; until one arose who should not be remembered, the sinner who led Israel into sin, who brought ruin to Ephraim 25 and caused them to be exiled from their land. Their sinfulness grew more and more, and they lent themselves to every evil.

Sirach Chapter 48

1 Till like a fire there appeared the prophet whose words were as a flaming furnace. 2 Their staff of bread he shattered, in his zeal he reduced them to straits; 3 By God's word he shut up the heavens and three times brought down fire. 4 How awesome are you, **ELIJAH!** Whose glory is equal to yours? 5 You brought a dead man back to life from the nether world, by the will of the LORD. 6 You sent kings down to destruction, and nobles, from their beds of sickness. 7 You heard threats at Sinai, at Horeb avenging judgments. 8 You anointed kings who should inflict vengeance, and a prophet as your successor. 9 You were taken aloft in a whirlwind, in a chariot with fiery horses. 10 You are destined, it is written, in time to come to put an end to wrath before the day of the LORD, to turn back the hearts of fathers toward their sons, and to reestablish the tribes of Jacob. 11 Blessed is he who shall have seen you before he dies, 12 O **ELIJAH**, enveloped in the whirlwind! Then **ELISHA**, filled with a twofold portion of his spirit, wrought many marvels by his mere word. During his lifetime he feared no one, nor was any man able to intimidate his will. 13 Nothing was beyond his power; beneath him flesh was brought back into life. 14 In life he performed wonders, and after death, marvelous deeds. 15 Despite all this the people did not repent, nor did they give up their sins, until they were rooted out of their land and scattered all over the earth. But **Judah** remained, a tiny people, with its rulers from the house of David. 16 Some of these did what was right, but others were extremely sinful. 17 **HEZEKIAH** fortified his city and had water brought into it; with iron tools he cut through the rock and he built reservoirs for water. 18 During his reign **Sennacherib** led an invasion and sent his adjutant; he shook his fist at Zion and blasphemed God in his pride. 19 The people's hearts melted within them, and they were in anguish like that of childbirth. 20 But they called upon the Most High God and lifted up their hands to him; he heard the prayer they uttered, and saved them through **ISAIAH**. 21 God struck the camp of the **Assyrians** and routed them with a plague. 22 For **Hezekiah** did what was right and held fast to the paths of **David**, as ordered by the illustrious prophet **Isaiah**, who saw the truth in visions. 23 In his lifetime he turned back the sun and prolonged the life of the king. 24 By his powerful spirit he looked into the future and consoled the mourners of Zion; 25 He foretold what should be till the end of time, hidden things yet to be fulfilled.

Sirach Chapter 49

1 The name **JOSIAH** is like blended incense, made lasting by a skilled perfumer. Precious is his memory, like honey to the taste, like music at a banquet. 2 For he grieved over our betrayals, and destroyed the abominable idols. 3 He turned to God with his whole heart, and, though

times were evil, he practiced virtue. 4 Except for **David**, **Hezekiah**, and **Josiah**, they all were wicked; they abandoned the Law of the Most High, these kings of Judah, right to the very end. 5 So he gave over their power to others, their glory to a foolish foreign nation 6 who burned the holy city and left its streets desolate, as **JEREMIAH** had foretold; 7 for they had treated him badly who even in the womb had been made a prophet, to root out, pull down, and destroy, and then to build and to plant. 8 **EZEKIEL** beheld the vision and described the different creatures of the chariot; 9 he also referred to **JOB**, who always persevered in the right path. 10 Then, too, the **TWELVE PROPHETS**—may their bones return to life from their resting place!— gave new strength to Jacob and saved him by their faith and hope. 11 How can we fittingly praise **ZERUBBABEL**, who was like a signet ring on God's right hand, 12 and **Jeshua**, **Jozadak's** son? In their time they built the house of God; they erected the holy temple, destined for everlasting glory. 13 Extolled be the memory of **NEHEMIAH!** He rebuilt our ruined walls, restored our shattered defenses, and set up gates and bars. 14 Few on earth have been made the equal of **ENOCH**, for he was taken up bodily. 15 Was ever a man born like **JOSEPH**? Even his dead body was provided for. 16 Glorious, too, were **SHEM**, **SETH**, and **ENOS**; but beyond that of any living being was the splendor of **ADAM**.

Sirach Chapter 50

1 The greatest among his brethren, the glory of his people, was SIMON the priest**, son of Jochanan, in whose time the house of God was renovated, in whose days the temple was reinforced. 2 In his time also the wall was built with powerful turrets for the temple precincts; 3 in his time the reservoir was dug, the pool with a vastness like the sea's. 4 He protected his people against brigands and strengthened his city against the enemy. 5 How splendid he was as he appeared from the tent, as he came from within the veil! 6 Like a star shining among the clouds, like the full moon at the holyday season; 7 like the sun shining upon the temple, like the rainbow appearing in the cloudy sky; 8 like the blossoms on the branches in springtime, like a lily on the banks of a stream; like the trees of Lebanon in summer, 9 like the fire of incense at the sacrifice; like a vessel of beaten gold, studded with precious stones; 10 like a luxuriant olive tree thick with fruit, like a cypress standing against the clouds; 11 vested in his magnificent robes, and wearing his garments of splendor, as he ascended the glorious altar and lent majesty to the court of the sanctuary. 12 When he received the sundered victims from the priests while he stood before the sacrificial wood, his brethren ringed him about like a garland, like a stand of cedars on Lebanon; 13 all the sons of Aaron in their dignity clustered around him like poplars, with the offerings to the LORD in their hands, in the presence of the whole assembly of Israel. 14 Once he had completed the services at the altar with the arranging of the sacrifices for the Most High, 15 and had stretched forth his hand for the cup, to offer blood of the grape, and poured it out at the foot of the altar, a sweet-smelling odor to the Most High God, 16 the sons of Aaron would sound a blast, the priests, on their trumpets of beaten metal; a blast to resound mightily as a reminder before the Most High. 17 Then all the people with one accord would quickly fall prostrate to the ground in adoration before the Most High, before the Holy One of Israel. 18 Then hymns would re-echo, and over the throng sweet strains of praise resound. 19 All the people of the land would shout for joy, praying to the Merciful One, as the high priest completed the services at the altar by presenting to God the sacrifice due; 20 then coming down he would raise his hands over all the congregation of Israel. The blessing of the LORD would be upon his lips, the name of the LORD would be his glory. 21 Then again the people would lie prostrate to receive from him the blessing of the Most High. 22 And now, bless the God of all, who has done wondrous things on earth; who fosters men's growth from their mother's womb, and fashions them according to his will! 23 May he grant you joy of heart and may peace abide among you; 24 may his goodness toward us endure in Israel as long as the heavens are above. 25 My whole being loathes two nations, the third is not even a people: 26 those who live in Seir and Philistia, and the degenerate folk who dwell in Shechem. 27 Wise instruction, appropriate proverbs, I have written in this book, I, **Jesus, son of Eleazar, son of Sirach**, as they gushed forth from my heart's understanding. 28 Happy the man who meditates upon these things, wise the man who takes them to heart! 29 If he puts them into practice, he can cope with anything, for the fear of the LORD is his lamp.

Sirach Chapter 51

1 I give you thanks, O God of my father; I praise you, O God my savior! I will make known your name, refuge of my life; 2 you have been my helper against my adversaries. You have saved me from death, and kept back my body from the pit, from the clutches of the nether world you

have snatched my feet; 3 you have delivered me, in your great mercy, from the scourge of a slanderous tongue, and from lips that went over to falsehood; from the snare of those who watched for my downfall, and from the power of those who sought my life; from many a danger you have saved me, 4 from flames that hemmed me in on every side; from the midst of unremitting fire, 5 from the deep belly of the nether world; from deceiving lips and painters of lies, 6 from the arrows of dishonest tongues. I was at the point of death, my soul was nearing the depths of the nether world; 7 I turned every way, but there was no one to help me, I looked for one to sustain me, but could find no one. 8 But then I remembered the mercies of the LORD, his kindness through ages past; for he saves those who take refuge in him, and rescues them from every evil. 9 So I raised my voice from the very earth, from the gates of the nether world, my cry. 10 I called out: O Lord, you are my father, you are my champion and my savior; do not abandon me in time of trouble, in the midst of storms and dangers. 11 I will ever praise your name and be constant in my prayers to you. Thereupon the LORD heard my voice, he listened to my appeal; 12 He saved me from evil of every kind and preserved me in time of trouble. For this reason I thank him and I praise him; I bless the name of the LORD. 13 When I was young and innocent, I sought wisdom. 14 She came to me in her beauty, and until the end I will cultivate her. 15 As the blossoms yielded to ripening grapes, the heart's joy, my feet kept to the level path because from earliest youth I was familiar with her. 16 In the short time I paid heed, I met with great instruction. 17 Since in this way I have profited, I will give my teacher grateful praise. 18 I became resolutely devoted to her—the good I persistently strove for. 19 I burned with desire for her, never turning back. I became preoccupied with her, never weary of extolling her. My hand opened her gate and I came to know her secrets. 20 For her I purified my hands; in cleanness I attained to her. At first acquaintance with her, I gained understanding such that I will never forsake her. 21 My whole being was stirred as I learned about her; therefore I have made her my prize possession. 22 The LORD has granted me my lips as a reward, and my tongue will declare his praises. 23 Come aside to me, you untutored, and take up lodging in the house of instruction; 24 How long will you be deprived of wisdom's food, how long will you endure such bitter thirst? 25 I open my mouth and speak of her: gain, at no cost, wisdom for yourselves. 26 Submit your neck to her yoke, that your mind may accept her teaching. For she is close to those who seek her, and the one who is in earnest finds her. 27 See for yourselves! I have labored only a little, but have found much. 28 Acquire but a little instruction; you will win silver and gold through her. 29 Let your spirits rejoice in the mercy of God, and be not ashamed to give him praise. 30 Work at your tasks in due season, and in his own time God will give you your reward.

Prophetic Books
Major Prophets

Isaiah

Isaiah Chapter 1

1 The vision which Isaiah, son of Amoz, had concerning Judah and Jerusalem in the days of Uzziah, Jotham, Ahaz, and Hezekiah, kings of Judah. 2 Hear, O heavens, and listen, O earth, for the LORD speaks: Sons have I raised and reared, but they have disowned me! 3 An ox knows its owner, and an ass, its master's manger; but Israel does not know, my people has not understood. 4 Ah! sinful nation, people laden with wickedness, evil race, corrupt children! They have forsaken the LORD, spurned the Holy One of Israel, apostatized. 5 Where would you yet be struck, you that rebel again and again? The whole head is sick, the whole heart faint. 6 From the sole of the foot to the head there is no sound spot: Wound and welt and gaping gash, not drained, or bandaged, or eased with salve. 7 Your country is waste, your cities burnt with fire; your land before your eyes strangers devour—a waste, like Sodom overthrown. 8 And daughter Zion is left like a hut in a vineyard, like a shed in a melon patch, like a city blockaded. 9 Unless the LORD of hosts had left us a scanty remnant, we had become as Sodom, we should be like Gomorrah. 10 Hear the word of the LORD, princes of Sodom! Listen to the instruction of our God, people of Gomorrah! 11 What care I for the number of your sacrifices? says the LORD. I have had enough of whole-burnt rams and fat of fatlings; in the blood of calves, lambs, and goats I find no pleasure. 12 When you come in to visit me, who asks these things of you? 13 Trample my courts no more! Bring no more worthless offerings; your incense is loathsome to me. New moon and sabbath, calling of assemblies, octaves with wickedness:

these I cannot bear. 14 Your new moons and festivals I detest; they weigh me down, I tire of the load. 15 When you spread out your hands, I close my eyes to you; though you pray the more, I will not listen. Your hands are full of blood! 16 Wash yourselves clean! Put away your misdeeds from before my eyes; cease doing evil; 17 learn to do good. Make justice your aim: redress the wronged, hear the orphan's plea, defend the widow. 18 Come now, let us set things right, says the LORD: Though your sins be like scarlet, they may become white as snow; though they be crimson red, they may become white as wool. 19 If you are willing, and obey, you shall eat the good things of the land; 20 but if you refuse and resist, the sword shall consume you: for the mouth of the LORD has spoken! 21 How has she turned adulteress, the faithful city, so upright! Justice used to lodge within her, but now, murderers. 22 Your silver is turned to dross, your wine is mixed with water. 23 Your princes are rebels and comrades of thieves; each one of them loves a bribe and looks for gifts. The fatherless they defend not, and the widow's plea does not reach them. 24 Now, therefore, says the Lord, the LORD of hosts, the Mighty One of Israel: Ah! I will take vengeance on my foes and fully repay my enemies! 25 I will turn my hand against you, and refine your dross in the furnace, removing all your alloy. 26 I will restore your judges as at first, and your counselors as in the beginning; after that you shall be called city of justice, faithful city. 27 Zion shall be redeemed by judgment, and her repentant ones by justice. 28 Rebels and sinners alike shall be crushed, those who desert the LORD shall be consumed. 29 You shall be ashamed of the terebinths which you prized, and blush for the groves which you chose. 30 You shall become like a tree with falling leaves, like a garden that has no water. 31 The strong man shall turn to tow, and his work shall become a spark; both shall burn together, and there shall be none to quench the flames.

Isaiah Chapter 2

1 This is what Isaiah, son of Amoz, saw concerning Judah and Jerusalem. 2 In days to come, the mountain of the LORD's house shall be established as the highest mountain and raised above the hills. All nations shall stream toward it; 3 many peoples shall come and say: "Come, let us climb the LORD's mountain, to the house of the God of Jacob, that he may instruct us in his ways, and we may walk in his paths." For from Zion shall go forth instruction, and the word of the LORD from Jerusalem. 4 He shall judge between the nations, and impose terms on many peoples. They shall beat their swords into plowshares and their spears into pruning hooks; one nation shall not raise the sword against another, nor shall they train for war again. 5 O house of Jacob, come, let us walk in the light of the LORD! 6 You have abandoned your people, the house of Jacob, because they are filled with fortunetellers and soothsayers, like the Philistines; they covenant with strangers. 7 Their land is full of silver and gold, and there is no end to their treasures; their land is full of horses, and there is no end to their chariots. 8 Their land is full of idols; they worship the works of their hands, that which their fingers have made. 9 But man is abased, each one brought low. (Do not pardon them!) 10 Get behind the rocks, hide in the dust, from the terror of the LORD and the splendor of his majesty! 11 The haughty eyes of man will be lowered, the arrogance of men will be abased, and the LORD alone will be exalted, on that day. 12 For the LORD of hosts will have his day against all that is proud and arrogant, all that is high, and it will be brought low; 13 Yes, against all the cedars of Lebanon and all the oaks of Bashan, 14 against all the lofty mountains and all the high hills, 15 against every lofty tower and every fortified wall, 16 against all the ships of Tarshish and all stately vessels. 17 Human pride will be abased, the arrogance of men brought low, and the LORD alone will be exalted, on that day. 18 The idols will perish forever. 19 Men will go into caves in the rocks and into holes in the earth, from the terror of the LORD and the splendor of his majesty, when he arises to overawe the earth. 20 On that day men will throw to the moles and the bats the idols of silver and gold which they made for worship. 21 They go into caverns in the rocks and into crevices in the cliffs, from the terror of the LORD and the splendor of his majesty, when he arises to overawe the earth. 22 As for you, let man alone, in whose nostrils is but a breath; for what is he worth?

Isaiah Chapter 3

1 The Lord, the LORD of hosts, shall take away from Jerusalem and from Judah support and prop (all supplies of bread and water): 2 Hero and warrior, judge and prophet, fortune-teller and elder, 3 The captain of fifty and the nobleman, counselor, skilled magician, and expert charmer. 4 I will make striplings their princes; the fickle shall govern them, 5 And the people shall oppress one another, yes, every man his neighbor. The child shall be bold toward the elder, and the base toward the honorable. 6 When a man seizes his brother in his father's house, saying, "You have clothes! Be our ruler, and take in hand this ruin!" —

7 Then shall he answer in that day: "I will not undertake to cure this, when in my own house there is no bread or clothing! You shall not make me ruler of the people." 8 Jerusalem is crumbling, Judah is falling; for their speech and their deeds are before the LORD, a provocation in the sight of his majesty. 9 Their very look bears witness against them; their sin like Sodom they vaunt, they hide it not. Woe to them! they deal out evil to themselves. 10 Happy the just, for it will be well with them, the fruit of their works they will eat. 11 Woe to the wicked man! All goes ill, with the work of his hands he will be repaid. 12 My people — a babe in arms will be their tyrant, and women will rule them! O my people, your leaders mislead, they destroy the paths you should follow. 13 The LORD rises to accuse, standing to try his people. 14 The Lord enters into judgment with his people's elders and princes: It is you who have devoured the vineyard; the loot wrested from the poor is in your houses. 15 What do you mean by crushing my people, and grinding down the poor when they look to you? says the Lord, the GOD of hosts. 16 The LORD said: Because the daughters of Zion are haughty, and walk with necks outstretched, ogling and mincing as they go, their anklets tinkling with every step, 17 The Lord shall cover the scalps of Zion's daughters with scabs, and the LORD shall bare their heads. 18 On that day the LORD will do away with the finery of the anklets, sunbursts, and crescents; 19 the pendants, bracelets, and veils; 20 the headdresses, bangles, cinctures, perfume boxes, and amulets; 21 the signet rings, and the nose rings; 22 the court dresses, wraps, cloaks, and purses; 23 the mirrors, linen tunics, turbans, and shawls. 24 Instead of perfume there will be stench, instead of the girdle, a rope, and for the coiffure, baldness; for the rich gown, a sackcloth skirt. Then, instead of beauty: 25 Your men will fall by the sword, and your champions, in war; 26 Her gates will lament and mourn, as the city sits desolate on the ground.

Isaiah Chapter 4

1 Seven women will take hold of one man on that day, saying: "We will eat our own food and wear our own clothing; only let your name be given us, put an end to our disgrace!" 2 On that day, the branch of the LORD will be luster and glory, and the fruit of the earth will be honor and splendor for the survivors of Israel. 3 He who remains in Zion and he that is left in Jerusalem will be called holy: every one marked down for life in Jerusalem. 4 When the Lord washes away the filth of the daughters of Zion, and purges Jerusalem's blood from her midst with a blast of searing judgment, 5 then will the LORD create, over the whole site of Mount Zion and over her place of assembly, a smoking cloud by day and a light of flaming fire by night. 6 For over all, his glory will be shelter and protection: shade from the parching heat of day, refuge and cover from storm and rain.

Isaiah Chapter 5

1 Let me now sing of my friend, my friend's song concerning his vineyard. My friend had a vineyard on a fertile hillside; 2 He spaded it, cleared it of stones, and planted the choicest vines; within it, he built a watchtower, and hewed out a wine press. Then he looked for the crop of grapes, but what it yielded was wild grapes. 3 Now, inhabitants of Jerusalem and men of Judah, judge between me and my vineyard: 4 What more was there to do for my vineyard that I had not done? Why, when I looked for the crop of grapes, did it bring forth wild grapes? 5 Now, I will let you know what I mean to do to my vineyard: Take away its hedge, give it to grazing, break through its wall, let it be trampled! 6 Yes, I will make it a ruin: it shall not be pruned or hoed, but overgrown with thorns and briers; I will command the clouds not to send rain upon it. 7 The vineyard of the LORD of hosts is the house of Israel, and the men of Judah are his cherished plant; He looked for judgment, but see, bloodshed! for justice, but hark, the outcry! 8 Woe to you who join house to house, who connect field with field, till no room remains, and you are left to dwell alone in the midst of the land! 9 In my hearing the LORD of hosts has sworn: Many houses shall be in ruins, large ones and fine, with no one to live in them. 10 Ten acres of vineyard shall yield but one liquid measure, and a homer of seed shall yield but an ephah. 11 Woe to those who demand strong drink as soon as they rise in the morning, and linger into the night while wine inflames them! 12 With harp and lyre, timbrel and flute, they feast on wine; but what the LORD does, they regard not, the work of his hands they see not. 13 Therefore my people go into exile because they do not understand; their nobles die of hunger, and their masses are parched with thirst. 14 Therefore the nether world enlarges its throat and opens its maw without limit; down go their nobility and their masses, their throngs and their revelry. 15 Men shall be abased, each one brought low, and the eyes of the haughty lowered, 16 But the LORD of hosts shall be exalted by his judgment, and God the Holy shall be shown holy by his justice. 17 Lambs shall graze there at pasture, and kids shall eat in the ruins of the rich. 18 Woe to those who tug at guilt with cords of perversity, and at

sin as if with cart ropes! 19 To those who say, "Let him make haste and speed his work, that we may see it; on with the plan of the Holy One of Israel! let it come to pass, that we may know it!" 20 Woe to those who call evil good, and good evil, who change darkness into light, and light into darkness, who change bitter into sweet, and sweet into bitter! 21 Woe to those who are wise in their own sight, and prudent in their own esteem! 22 Woe to the champions at drinking wine, the valiant at mixing strong drink! 23 To those who acquit the guilty for bribes, and deprive the just man of his rights! 24 Therefore, as the tongue of fire licks up stubble, as dry grass shrivels in the flame, even so their root shall become rotten and their blossom scatter like dust; for they have spurned the law of the LORD of hosts and scorned the word of the Holy One of Israel. 25 Therefore the wrath of the LORD blazes against his people, he raises his hand to strike them; when the mountains quake, their corpses shall be like refuse in the streets. For all this, his wrath is not turned back, and his hand is still outstretched. 26 He will give a signal to a far-off nation, and whistle to them from the ends of the earth; speedily and promptly will they come. 27 None of them will stumble with weariness, none will slumber, and none will sleep. None will have his waist belt loose, nor the thong of his sandal broken. 28 Their arrows are sharp, and all their bows are bent. The hoofs of their horses seem like flint, and their chariot wheels like the hurricane. 29 Their roar is that of the lion, like the lion's whelps they roar; they growl and seize the prey, they carry it off and none will rescue it. 30 They will roar over it, on that day, with a roaring like that of the sea.

Isaiah Chapter 6

1 In the year King Uzziah died, I saw the Lord seated on a high and lofty throne, with the train of his garment filling the temple. 2 Seraphim were stationed above; each of them had six wings: with two they veiled their faces, with two they veiled their feet, and with two they hovered aloft. 3 "Holy, holy, holy is the LORD of hosts!" they cried one to the other. "All the earth is filled with his glory!" 4 At the sound of that cry, the frame of the door shook and the house was filled with smoke. 5 Then I said, "Woe is me, I am doomed! For I am a man of unclean lips, living among a people of unclean lips; yet my eyes have seen the King, the LORD of hosts!" 6 Then one of the seraphim flew to me, holding an ember which he had taken with tongs from the altar. 7 He touched my mouth with it. "See," he said, "now that this has touched your lips, your wickedness is removed, your sin purged." 8 Then I heard the voice of the Lord saying, "Whom shall I send? Who will go for us?" "Here I am," I said; "send me!" 9 And he replied: Go and say to this people: Listen carefully, but you shall not understand! Look intently, but you shall know nothing! 10 You are to make the heart of this people sluggish, to dull their ears and close their eyes; Else their eyes will see, their ears hear, their heart understand, and they will turn and be healed. 11 "How long, O Lord?" I asked. And he replied: Until the cities are desolate, without inhabitants, houses, without a man, and the earth is a desolate waste. 12 Until the LORD removes men far away, and the land is abandoned more and more. 13 If there be still a tenth part in it, then this in turn shall be laid waste; as with a terebinth or an oak whose trunk remains when its leaves have fallen. (Holy offspring is the trunk.)

Isaiah Chapter 7

1 In the days of Ahaz, king of Judah, son of Jotham, son of Uzziah, Rezin, king of Aram, and Pekah, king of Israel, son of Remaliah, went up to attack Jerusalem, but they were not able to conquer it. 2 When word came to the house of David that Aram was encamped in Ephraim, the heart of the king and heart of the people trembled, as the trees of the forest tremble in the wind. 3 Then the LORD said to Isaiah: Go out to meet Ahaz, you and your son Shear-jashub, at the end of the conduit of the upper pool, on the highway of the fuller's field, 4 and say to him: Take care you remain tranquil and do not fear; let not your courage fail before these two stumps of smoldering brands (the blazing anger of Rezin and the Arameans, and of the son of Remaliah), 5 because of the mischief that Aram (Ephraim and the son of Remaliah) plots against you, saying, 6 "Let us go up and tear Judah asunder, make it our own by force, and appoint the son of Tabeel king there." 7 Thus says the LORD: This shall not stand, it shall not be! 8 Damascus is the capital of Aram, and Rezin the head of Damascus; Samaria is the capital of Ephraim, and Remaliah's son the head of Samaria. 9 But within sixty years and five, Ephraim shall be crushed, no longer a nation. Unless your faith is firm you shall not be firm! 10 Again the LORD spoke to Ahaz: 11 Ask for a sign from the LORD, your God; let it be deep as the nether world, or high as the sky! 12 But Ahaz answered, "I will not ask! I will not tempt the LORD!" 13 Then he said: Listen, O house of David! Is it not enough for you to weary men, must you also weary my God? 14 Therefore the Lord himself will give you this sign: the virgin shall be with child, and bear a son, and shall name him Immanuel. 15 He shall

be living on curds and honey by the time he learns to reject the bad and choose the good. 16 For before the child learns to reject the bad and choose the good, the land of those two kings whom you dread shall be deserted. 17 The LORD shall bring upon you and your people and your father's house days worse than any since Ephraim seceded from Judah. (This means the king of Assyria.) 18 On that day the LORD shall whistle for the fly that is in the farthest streams of Egypt, and for the bee in the land of Assyria. 19 All of them shall come and settle in the steep ravines and in the rocky clefts, on all thornbushes and in all pastures. 20 On that day the LORD shall shave with the razor hired from across the River (with the king of Assyria) the head, and the hair between the legs. It shall also shave off the beard. 21 On that day a man shall keep a heifer or a couple of sheep, 22 and from their abundant yield of milk he shall live on curds; curds and honey shall be the food of all who remain in the land. 23 On that day every place where there used to be a thousand vines, worth a thousand pieces of silver, shall be turned to briers and thorns. 24 Men shall go there with bow and arrows; for all the country shall be briers and thorns. 25 For fear of briers and thorns you shall not go upon any mountainside which used to be hoed with the mattock; they shall be grazing land for cattle and shall be trampled upon by sheep.

Isaiah Chapter 8

1 The LORD said to me: Take a large cylinder-seal, and inscribe on it in ordinary letters: "Belonging to Maher-shalal-hash-baz." 2 And I took reliable witnesses, Uriah the priest, and Zechariah, son of Jeberechiah. 3 Then I went to the prophetess and she conceived and bore a son. The LORD said to me: Name him Maher-shalal-hash-baz, 4 for before the child knows how to call his father or mother by name, the wealth of Damascus and the spoil of Samaria shall be carried off by the king of Assyria. 5 Again the LORD spoke to me: 6 Because this people has rejected the waters of Shiloah that flow gently, and melts with fear before the loftiness of Rezin and Remaliah's son, 7 Therefore the LORD raises against them the waters of the River, great and mighty (the king of Assyria and all his power). It shall rise above all its channels, and overflow all its banks; 8 It shall pass into Judah, and flood it all throughout: up to the neck it shall reach; It shall spread its wings the full width of your land, Immanuel! 9 Know, O peoples, and be appalled! Give ear, all you distant lands! Arm, but be crushed! Arm, but be crushed! 10 Form a plan, and it shall be thwarted; make a resolve, and it shall not be carried out, for "With us is God!" 11 For thus said the LORD to me, taking hold of me and warning me not to walk in the way of this people: 12 Call not alliance what this people calls alliance, and fear not, nor stand in awe of what they fear. 13 But with the LORD of hosts make your alliance—for him be your fear and your awe. 14 Yet he shall be a snare, an obstacle and a stumbling stone to both the houses of Israel, a trap and a snare to those who dwell in Jerusalem; 15 And many among them shall stumble and fall, broken, snared, and captured. 16 The record is to be folded and the sealed instruction kept among my disciples. 17 For I will trust in the LORD, who is hiding his face from the house of Jacob; yes, I will wait for him. 18 Look at me and the children whom the Lord has given me: we are signs and portents in Israel from the LORD of hosts who dwells on Mount Zion. 19 And when they say to you, "Inquire of mediums and fortune-tellers (who chirp and mutter!); should not a people inquire of their gods, apply to the dead on behalf of the living?"—20 then this document will furnish its instruction. That kind of thing they will surely say. 21 First he degraded the land of Zebulun and the land of Naphtali; but in the end he has glorified the seaward road, the land West of the Jordan, the District of the Gentiles. Anguish has taken wing, dispelled is darkness; for there is no gloom where but now there was distress.

Isaiah Chapter 9

1The people who walked in darkness have seen a great light; Upon those who dwelt in the land of gloom a light has shone. 2You have brought them abundant joy and great rejoicing, As they rejoice before you as at the harvest, as men make merry when dividing spoils. 3For the yoke that burdened them, the pole on their shoulder, And the rod of their taskmaster you have smashed, as on the day of Midian. 4For every boot that tramped in battle, every cloak rolled in blood, will be burned as fuel for flames. 5For a child is born to us, a son is given us; upon his shoulder dominion rests. They name him Wonder-Counselor, God-Hero, Father-Forever, Prince of Peace. 6His dominion is vast and forever peaceful, From David's throne, and over his kingdom, which he confirms and sustains By judgment and justice, both now and forever. The zeal of the LORD of hosts will do this! 7The Lord has sent word against Jacob, it falls upon Israel; 8And all the people know it, Ephraim and those who dwell in Samaria, those who say in arrogance and pride of heart, 9"Bricks have fallen, but we will build with cut stone; Sycamores are

felled, but we will replace them with cedars." 10But the LORD raises up their foes against them and stirs up their enemies to action: 11Aram on the east and the Philistines on the west devour Israel with open mouth. For all this, his wrath is not turned back, and his hand is still outstretched! 12The people do not turn to him who struck them, nor seek the LORD of hosts. 13So the LORD severs from Israel head and tail, palm branch and reed in one day. 14(The elder and the noble are the head, the prophet who teaches falsehood is the tail.) 15The leaders of this people mislead them and those to be led are engulfed. 16For this reason, the Lord does not spare their young men, and their orphans and widows he does not pity; They are wholly profaned and sinful, and every mouth gives vent to folly. For all this, his wrath is not turned back, his hand is still outstretched! 17For wickedness burns like fire, devouring brier and thorn; It kindles the forest thickets, which go up in columns of smoke. 18At the wrath of the LORD of hosts the land quakes, and the people are like fuel for fire; No man spares his brother, each devours the flesh of his neighbor. 19Though they hack on the right, they are hungry; though they eat on the left, they are not filled. 20Manasseh devours Ephraim, and Ephraim Manasseh; together they turn on Judah. For all this, his wrath is not turned back, his hand is still outstretched!

Isaiah Chapter 10

1Woe to those who enact unjust statutes and who write oppressive decrees, 2Depriving the needy of judgment and robbing my people's poor of their rights, Making widows their plunder, and orphans their prey! 3What will you do on the day of punishment, when ruin comes from afar? To whom will you flee for help? Where will you leave your wealth, 4Lest it sink beneath the captive or fall beneath the slain? For all this, his wrath is not turned back, his hand is still outstretched! 5Woe to Assyria! My rod in anger, my staff in wrath. 6Against an impious nation I send him, and against a people under my wrath I order him to seize plunder, carry off loot, and tread them down like the mud of the streets. 7But this is not what he intends, nor does he have this in mind; Rather, it is in his heart to destroy, to make an end of nations not a few. 8"Are not my commanders all kings?" he says, 9"Is not Calno like Carchemish, Or Hamath like Arpad, or Samaria like Damascus? 10Just as my hand reached out to idolatrous kingdoms that had more images than Jerusalem and Samaria, 11Just as I treated Samaria and her idols, shall I not do to Jerusalem and her graven images?" 12But when the LORD has brought to an end all his work on Mount Zion and in Jerusalem, I will punish the utterance of the king of Assyria's proud heart, and the boastfulness of his haughty eyes. For he says: 13"By my own power I have done it, and by my wisdom, for I am shrewd. I have moved the boundaries of peoples, their treasures I have pillaged, and, like a giant, I have put down the enthroned. 14My hand has seized like a nest the riches of nations; As one takes eggs left alone, so I took in all the earth; No one fluttered a wing, or opened a mouth, or chirped!" 15Will the axe boast against him who hews with it? Will the saw exalt itself above him who wields it? As if a rod could sway him who lifts it, or a staff him who is not wood! 16Therefore the Lord, the LORD of hosts, will send among his fat ones leanness, And instead of his glory there will be kindling like the kindling of fire. 17The Light of Israel will become a fire, Israel's Holy One a flame, That burns and consumes his briers and his thorns in a single day. 18His splendid forests and orchards will be consumed, soul and body; 19And the remnant of the trees in his forest will be so few, Like poles set up for signals, that any boy can record them. 20On that day, The remnant of Israel, the survivors of the house of Jacob, will no more lean upon him who struck them; But they lean upon the LORD, the Holy One of Israel, in truth. 21A remnant will return, the remnant of Jacob, to the mighty God. 22For though your people, O Israel, were like the sand of the sea, Only a remnant of them will return; their destruction is decreed as overwhelming justice demands. 23Yes, the destruction he has decreed, the Lord, the GOD of hosts, will carry out within the whole land. 24Therefore thus says the Lord, the GOD of hosts: O my people, who dwell in Zion, do not fear the Assyrian, though he strikes you with a rod, and raises his staff against you. 25For only a brief moment more, and my anger shall be over; but them I will destroy in wrath. 26Then the LORD of hosts will raise against them a scourge such as struck Midian at the rock of Oreb; and he will raise his staff over the sea as he did against Egypt. 27On that day, His burden shall be taken from your shoulder, and his yoke shattered from your neck. He has come up from the direction of Rimmon, 28he has reached Aiath, passed through Migron, at Michmash his supplies are stored. 29They cross the ravine: "We will spend the night at Geba." Ramah is in terror, Gibeah of Saul has fled. 30Cry and shriek, O daughter of Gallim! Hearken, Laishah! Answer her, Anathoth! 31Madmenah is in flight, the inhabitants of Gebim seek refuge. 32Even today he will halt at Nob, he will shake his fist at the mount of daughter Zion, the hill of Jerusalem! 33Behold, the Lord, the LORD of hosts, lops off the boughs with terrible violence; The tall of stature are felled, and the lofty ones brought low; 34The forest thickets are felled with the axe, and Lebanon in its splendor falls.

Isaiah Chapter 11

1But a shoot shall sprout from the stump of Jesse, and from his roots a bud shall blossom. 2The spirit of the LORD shall rest upon him: a spirit of wisdom and of understanding, a spirit of counsel and of strength, a spirit of knowledge and of fear of the LORD, 3and his delight shall be the fear of the LORD. Not by appearance shall he judge, nor by hearsay shall he decide, 4But he shall judge the poor with justice, and decide aright for the land's afflicted. He shall strike the ruthless with the rod of his mouth, and with the breath of his lips he shall slay the wicked. 5Justice shall be the band around his waist, and faithfulness a belt upon his hips. 6Then the wolf shall be a guest of the lamb, and the leopard shall lie down with the kid; the calf and the young lion shall browse together, with a little child to guide them. 7The cow and the bear shall be neighbors, together their young shall rest; the lion shall eat hay like the ox. 8The baby shall play by the cobra's den, and the child lay his hand on the adder's lair. 9There shall be no harm or ruin on all my holy mountain; for the earth shall be filled with knowledge of the LORD, as water covers the sea. 10On that day, The root of Jesse, set up as a signal for the nations, The Gentiles shall seek out, for his dwelling shall be glorious. 11On that day, The Lord shall again take it in hand to reclaim the remnant of his people that is left from Assyria and Egypt, Pathros, Ethiopia, and Elam, Shinar, Hamath, and the isles of the sea. 12He shall raise a signal to the nations and gather the outcasts of Israel; the dispersed of Judah he shall assemble from the four corners of the earth. 13The envy of Ephraim shall pass away, and the rivalry of Judah be removed; Ephraim shall not be jealous of Judah, and Judah shall not be hostile to Ephraim; 14But they shall swoop down on the foothills of the Philistines to the west, together they shall plunder the Kedemites; Edom and Moab shall be their possessions, and the Ammonites their subjects. 15The LORD shall dry up the tongue of the Sea of Egypt, and wave his hand over the Euphrates in his fierce anger and shatter it into seven streamlets, so that it can be crossed in sandals. 16There shall be a highway for the remnant of his people that is left from Assyria, as there was for Israel when he came up from the land of Egypt.

Isaiah Chapter 12

1On that day, you will say: I give you thanks, O LORD; though you have been angry with me, your anger has abated, and you have consoled me. 2God indeed is my savior; I am confident and unafraid. My strength and my courage is the LORD, and he has been my savior. 3With joy you will draw water at the fountain of salvation, 4and say on that day: Give thanks to the LORD, acclaim his name; among the nations make known his deeds, proclaim how exalted is his name. 5Sing praise to the LORD for his glorious achievement; let this be known throughout all the earth. 6Shout with exultation, O city of Zion, for great in your midst is the Holy One of Israel!

Isaiah Chapter 13

1An oracle concerning Babylon; a vision of Isaiah, son of Amoz. 2Upon the bare mountains set up a signal; cry out to them, wave for them to enter the gates of the volunteers. 3I have commanded my dedicated soldiers, I have summoned my warriors, eager and bold to carry out my anger. 4Listen! the rumble on the mountains: that of an immense throng! Listen! the noise of kingdoms, nations assembled! The LORD of hosts is mustering an army for battle. 5They come from a far-off country, and from the end of the heavens, the LORD and the instruments of his wrath, to destroy all the land. 6Howl, for the day of the LORD is near; as destruction from the Almighty it comes. 7Therefore all hands fall helpless, the bows of the young men fall from their hands. Every man's heart melts 8in terror. Pangs and sorrows take hold of them, like a woman in labor they writhe; they look aghast at each other, their faces aflame. 9Lo, the day of the LORD comes, cruel, with wrath and burning anger; to lay waste the land and destroy the sinners within it! 10The stars and constellations of the heavens send forth no light; the sun is dark when it rises, and the light of the moon does not shine. 11Thus I will punish the world for its evil and the wicked for their guilt. I will put an end to the pride of the arrogant, the insolence of tyrants I will humble. 12I will make mortals more rare than pure gold, men, than gold of Ophir. 13For this I will make the heavens tremble and the earth shall be shaken from its place, at the wrath of the LORD of hosts on the day of his burning anger. 14Like a hunted gazelle, or a flock that no one gathers, every man shall turn to his kindred and flee to his own land. 15Everyone who is caught shall be run through; to a man, they shall fall by the sword. 16Their infants shall be dashed to pieces in their sight; their houses shall be plundered and their wives

ravished. 17I am stirring up against them the Medes, who think nothing of silver and take no delight in gold. 18The fruit of the womb they shall not spare, nor shall they have eyes of pity for children. 19And Babylon, the jewel of kingdoms, the glory and pride of the Chaldeans, shall be overthrown by God like Sodom and like Gomorrah. 20She shall never be inhabited, nor dwelt in, from age to age; the Arab shall not pitch his tent there, nor shepherds couch their flocks. 21But wildcats shall rest there and owls shall fill the houses; there ostriches shall dwell, and satyrs shall dance. 22Desert beasts shall howl in her castles, and jackals in her luxurious palaces. Her time is near at hand and her days shall not be prolonged.

Isaiah Chapter 14

1When the LORD has pity on Jacob and again chooses Israel and settles them on their own soil, the aliens will join them and be counted with the house of Jacob. 2The house of Israel will take them and bring them along to its place, and possess them as male and female slaves on the Lord's soil, making captives of its captors and ruling over its oppressors. 3On the day the LORD relieves you of sorrow and unrest and the hard service in which you have been enslaved, 4you will take up this taunt-song against the king of Babylon: How the oppressor has reached his end! How the turmoil is stilled! 5The LORD has broken the rod of the wicked, the staff of the tyrants 6that struck the peoples in wrath, relentless blows; that beat down the nations in anger, with oppression unchecked. 7The whole earth rests peacefully, song breaks forth; 8the very cypresses rejoice over you, and the cedars of Lebanon: "Now that you are laid to rest, there will be none to cut us down." 9The nether world below is all astir preparing for your coming; it awakens the shades to greet you, all the leaders of the earth; it has the kings of all nations rise from their thrones. 10All of them speak out and say to you, "You too have become weak like us, you are the same as we." 11Down to the nether world your pomp is brought, the music of your harps. The couch beneath you is the maggot, your covering, the worm. 12How have you fallen from the heavens, O morning star, son of the dawn! How are you cut down to the ground, you who mowed down the nations! 13You said in your heart: "I will scale the heavens; above the stars of God I will set up my throne; I will take my seat on the Mount of Assembly, in the recesses of the North. 14I will ascend above the tops of the clouds; I will be like the Most High!" 15Yet down to the nether world you go to the recesses of the pit! 16When they see you, they will stare, pondering over you: "Is this the man who made the earth tremble, and kingdoms quake? 17Who made the world a desert, razed its cities, and gave his captives no release?" 18All the kings of the nations lie in glory, each in his own tomb; 19but you are cast forth without burial, loathsome and corrupt, clothed as those slain at sword-point, a trampled corpse. Going down to the pavement of the pit, 20you will never be one with them in the grave. For you have ruined your land, you have slain your people! Let him not be named forever, that scion of an evil race! 21Make ready to slaughter his sons for the guilt of their fathers; lest they rise and possess the earth, and fill the breadth of the world with tyrants. 22I will rise up against them, says the LORD of hosts, and cut off from Babylon name and remnant, progeny and offspring, says the LORD. 23I will make it a haunt of hoot owls and a marshland; I will sweep it with the broom of destruction, says the LORD of hosts. 24The LORD of hosts has sworn: As I have resolved, so shall it be; as I have proposed, so shall it stand: 25I will break the Assyrian in my land and trample him on my mountains. 21He shall pass through it hard-pressed and hungry, and in his hunger he shall become enraged, and curse his king and his gods. He shall look upward, but there shall be strict darkness without any dawn; 22he shall gaze at the earth, but there shall be distress and darkness, with the light blacked out by its clouds. 25Then his yoke shall be removed from them, and his burden from their shoulder. 26This is the plan proposed for the whole earth, and this the hand outstretched over all nations. 27The LORD of hosts has planned; who can thwart him? His hand is stretched out; who can turn it back? 28In the year that King Ahaz died, there came this oracle: 29Rejoice not, O Philistia, not a man of you, that the rod which smote you is broken; for out of the serpent's root shall come an adder, its fruit shall be a flying saraph. 30In my pastures the poor shall eat, and the needy lie down in safety; but I will kill your root with famine that shall slay even your remnant. 31Howl, O gate; cry out, O city! Philistia, all of you melts away! For there comes a smoke from the north, without a straggler in the ranks. 32What will one answer the messengers of the nation? "The LORD has established Zion, and in her the afflicted of his people find refuge."

Isaiah Chapter 15

1Oracle on Moab: Laid waste in a night, Ar of Moab is destroyed; laid waste in a night, Kir of Moab is destroyed. 2Up goes daughter Dibon to the high places to weep; over Nebo and over Medeba, Moab wails. Every head is shaved, every beard sheared off. ³In the streets they wear sackcloth, lamenting and weeping; on the rooftops and in the squares, everyone wails. ⁴Heshbon and Elealeh cry out, they are heard as far as Jahaz. At this the loins of Moab tremble, his soul quivers within him. ⁵The heart of Moab cries out, his fugitives reach Zoar (Eglath-shelishiyah). The ascent of Luhith they climb weeping; on the way to Horonaim they utter rending cries. ⁶The waters of Nimrim have become a waste; the grass is withered, new growth is gone, nothing is green. ⁷So now whatever they have acquired or stored away they carry across the Gorge of the Poplars, ⁸for the cry has gone round the land of Moab; as far as Eglaim the wailing, and to Beer-elim, the wail. ⁹The waters of Dimon are filled with blood, but I will bring still more upon Dimon: lions for those who are fleeing from Moab and for those who remain in the land!

Isaiah Chapter 16

¹Send them forth, hugging the earth like reptiles, from Sela across the desert, to the mount of daughter Zion. ²Like flushed birds, like startled nestlings, are the daughters of Moab at the fords of the Arnon. ³Offer counsel, take their part: at high noon let your shadow be like the night, to hide the outcasts, to conceal the fugitives. ⁴Let the outcasts of Moab live with you, be their shelter from the destroyer. When the struggle is ended, the ruin complete, and they have done with trampling the land, ⁵a throne shall be set up in mercy, and on it shall sit in fidelity (in David's tent) a judge upholding right and prompt to do justice. ⁶We have heard of the pride of Moab, how very proud he is, with his haughty, arrogant insolence that his empty words do not match. ⁷Therefore Moab wails for Moab, everywhere they wail; for the raisin cakes of Kir-hareseth they sigh, stricken with grief. ⁸The terraced slopes of Heshbon languish, the vines of Sibmah, whose clusters overpowered the lords of nations, while they reached as far as Jazer and scattered over the desert, and whose branches spread forth and extended over the sea. ⁹Therefore I weep with Jazer for the vines of Sibmah; I water you with tears, Heshbon and Elealeh; for on your summer fruits and harvests the battle cry has fallen. ¹⁰From the orchards are taken away joy and gladness, in the vineyards there is no singing, no shout of joy; in the wine presses no one treads grapes, the vintage shout is stilled. ¹¹Therefore for Moab my breast moans like a lyre, and my heart for Kir-hareseth. ¹²When Moab grows weary on the high places, he shall enter his sanctuary to pray, but it shall avail him nothing. ¹³This is the word the LORD spoke against Moab in times past. ¹⁴But now the LORD has spoken: In three years, like those of a hireling, the glory of Moab shall be degraded despite all its great multitude; there shall be a remnant, very small and weak.

Isaiah Chapter 17

¹ Oracle on Damascus: Lo, Damascus shall cease to be a city and become a ruin; ² her cities shall be forever abandoned, given over to flocks to lie in undisturbed. ³ The fortress shall be lost to Ephraim and the kingdom to Damascus; the remnant of Aram shall have the same glory as the Israelites, says the LORD of hosts. ⁴ On that day, the glory of Jacob shall fade, and his full body grow thin, ⁵ like the reaper's mere armful of stalks when he gathers the standing grain; or as when one gleans the ears in the Valley of Rephaim. ⁶ Only a scattering of grapes shall be left! As when an olive tree has been beaten, two or three olives remain at the very top, four or five on its fruitful branches, says the LORD, the God of Israel. ⁷ On that day man shall look to his maker, his eyes turned toward the Holy One of Israel. ⁸ He shall not look to the altars, his handiwork, nor shall he regard what his fingers have made: the sacred poles or the incense stands. ⁹ On that day his strong cities shall be like those abandoned by the Hivites and Amorites when faced with the children of Israel: they shall be laid waste. ¹⁰ For you have forgotten God, your savior, and remembered not the Rock, your strength. Therefore, though you plant your pagan plants and set out your foreign vine slips, ¹¹ though you make them grow the day you plant them and make your sprouts blossom on the next morning, the harvest shall disappear on the day of the grievous blow, the incurable blight. ¹² Ah! the roaring of many peoples that roar like the roar of the seas! The surging of nations that surge like the surging of mighty waves! ¹³ But God shall rebuke them, and they shall flee far away; windswept, like chaff on the mountains, like tumbleweed in a storm. ¹⁴ In the evening, they spread terror, before morning, they are gone! Such is the portion of those who despoil us, the lot of those who plunder us.

Isaiah Chapter 18

¹ Ah, land of buzzing insects, beyond the rivers of Ethiopia,² sending ambassadors by sea, in papyrus boats on the waters! Go, swift messengers, to a nation tall and bronzed, to a people dreaded near and far, a nation strong and conquering, whose land is washed by rivers. ³ All you who inhabit the world, who dwell on earth, when the signal is raised on the mountain, look! When the trumpet blows, listen! ⁴ For thus says the LORD to me: I will quietly look on from where I dwell, like the glowing heat of sunshine, like a cloud of dew at harvest time. ⁵ Before the vintage, when the flowering is ended, and the blooms are succeeded by ripening grapes, then comes the cutting of branches with pruning hooks and the discarding of the lopped-off shoots. ⁶ They shall all be left to the mountain birds of prey, and to the beasts in the land; the birds of prey shall summer on them, and on them all the beasts of the earth shall winter. ⁷ Then will gifts be brought to the LORD of hosts from a people tall and bronzed, from a people dreaded near and far, a nation strong and conquering, whose land is washed by rivers—to Mount Zion where dwells the name of the LORD of hosts.

Isaiah Chapter 19

¹ Oracle on Egypt: See, the LORD is riding on a swift cloud on his way to Egypt; the idols of Egypt tremble before him, the hearts of the Egyptians melt within them. ² I will rouse Egypt against Egypt: brother will war against brother, neighbor against neighbor, city against city, kingdom against kingdom. ³ The courage of the Egyptians ebbs away within them, and I will bring to nought their counsel; they shall consult idols and charmers, ghosts and spirits. ⁴ I will deliver Egypt into the power of a cruel master, a harsh king who shall rule over them, says the Lord, the LORD of hosts. ⁵ The waters shall be drained from the sea, the river shall shrivel and dry up; ⁶ its streams shall become foul, and the canals of Egypt shall dwindle and dry up. Reeds and rushes shall wither away, ⁷ and bulrushes on the bank of the Nile; all the sown land along the Nile shall dry up and blow away, and be no more. ⁸ The fishermen shall mourn and lament, all who cast hook in the Nile; those who spread their nets in the water shall pine away. ⁹ The linen-workers shall be disappointed, the combers and weavers shall turn pale; ¹⁰ the spinners shall be crushed, all the hired laborers shall be despondent. ¹¹ Utter fools are the princes of Zoan! The wisest of Pharaoh's advisers give stupid counsel. How can you say to Pharaoh, "I am a disciple of wise men, of ancient kings"? ¹² Where then are your wise men? Let them tell you and make known what the LORD of hosts has planned against Egypt. ¹³ The princes of Zoan have become fools, the princes of Memphis have been deceived. The chiefs of her tribes have led Egypt astray. ¹⁴ The LORD has prepared among them a spirit of dizziness, and they have made Egypt stagger in whatever she does, as a drunkard staggers in his vomit. ¹⁵ Egypt shall have no work to do for head or tail, palm branch or reed. ¹⁶ On that day the Egyptians shall be like women, trembling with fear, because of the LORD of hosts shaking his fist at them. ¹⁷ And the land of Judah shall be a terror to the Egyptians. Every time they remember Judah, they shall stand in dread because of the plan which the LORD of hosts has in mind for them. ¹⁸ On that day there shall be five cities in the land of Egypt speaking the language of Canaan and swearing by the LORD of hosts; one shall be called "City of the Sun." ¹⁹ On that day there shall be an altar to the LORD in the land of Egypt, and a sacred pillar to the LORD near the boundary. ²⁰ It shall be a sign and a witness to the LORD of hosts in the land of Egypt, when they cry out to the LORD against their oppressors, and he sends them a savior to defend and deliver them. ²¹ The LORD shall make himself known to Egypt, and the Egyptians shall know the LORD in that day; they shall offer sacrifices and oblations, and fulfill the vows they make to the LORD. ²² Although the LORD shall smite Egypt severely, he shall heal them; they shall turn to the LORD and he shall be won over and heal them. ²³ On that day there shall be a highway from Egypt to Assyria; the Assyrians shall enter Egypt, and the Egyptians enter Assyria, and Egypt shall serve Assyria. ²⁴ On that day Israel shall be a third party with Egypt and Assyria, a blessing in the midst of the land, ²⁵ when the LORD of hosts blesses it: "Blessed be my people Egypt, and the work of my hands Assyria, and my inheritance, Israel."

Isaiah Chapter 20

¹ In the year the general sent by Sargon, king of Assyria, fought against Ashdod and captured it, ² the LORD gave a warning through Isaiah, the son of Amoz: "Go and take off the sackcloth from your waist, and remove the sandals from your feet." This he did, walking naked and barefoot. ³ Then the LORD said: "Just as my servant Isaiah has gone naked and barefoot for three years as a sign and portent against Egypt and Ethiopia, ⁴ so shall the king of Assyria lead away captives from Egypt, and exiles from Ethiopia, young and old, naked and barefoot, with buttocks uncovered (the shame of Egypt)." ⁵ They shall be dismayed and ashamed because of Ethiopia, their hope, and because of Egypt, their boast. ⁶ The inhabitants of this coastland shall say on that day, "Look at our hope! We have fled here for help and deliverance from the king of Assyria; where can we flee now?"

Isaiah Chapter 21

¹ **Oracle on the wastelands by the sea:** Like whirlwinds sweeping in waves through the Negeb, there comes from the desert, from the

fearful land, ² A cruel sight, revealed to me: the traitor betrays, the despoiler spoils. "Go up, Elam; besiege, O Media; I will put an end to all groaning!" ³ Therefore my loins are filled with anguish, pangs have seized me like those of a woman in labor; I am too bewildered to hear, too dismayed to look. ⁴ My mind reels, shuddering assails me; My yearning for twilight has turned into dread. ⁵ They set the table, spread out the rugs; they eat, they drink. Rise up, O princes, oil the shield! ⁶ For thus says my Lord to me: Go, station a watchman, let him tell what he sees. ⁷ If he sees a chariot, a pair of horses, someone riding an ass, someone riding a camel, then let him pay heed, very close heed. ⁸ Then the watchman cried, "On the watchtower, O my Lord, I stand constantly by day; And I stay at my post through all the watches of the night. ⁹ Here he comes now: a single chariot, a pair of horses; He calls out and says, 'Fallen, fallen is Babylon, and all the images of her gods are smashed to the ground.'" ¹⁰ O my people who have been threshed, beaten on my threshing floor! What I have heard from the LORD of hosts, the God of Israel, I have announced to you. ¹¹ **Oracle on Edom:** They call to me from Seir, "Watchman, how much longer the night? Watchman, how much longer the night?" ¹² The watchman replies, "Morning has come, and again night. If you will ask, ask; come back again." ¹³ **Oracle on Arabia:** In the thicket in the nomad country spend the night, O caravans of Dedanites. ¹⁴ Meet the thirsty, bring them water; you who dwell in the land of Tema, greet the fugitives with bread. ¹⁵ They flee from the sword, from the whetted sword, from the taut bow, from the fury of battle. ¹⁶ For thus says the Lord to me: In another year, like those of a hireling, all the glory of Kedar shall come to an end. ¹⁷ Few of Kedar's stalwart archers shall remain, for the LORD, the God of Israel, has spoken.

Isaiah Chapter 22

¹ **Oracle of the Valley of Vision:** What is the matter with you now, that you have gone up, all of you, to the housetops, ² O city full of noise and chaos, O wanton town! Your slain are not slain with the sword, nor killed in battle. ³ All your leaders fled away together, fled afar off; All who were in you were captured together, captured without the use of a bow. ⁴ At this I say: Turn away from me, let me weep bitterly; Do not try to comfort me for the ruin of the daughter of my people. ⁵ It is a day of panic, rout, and confusion, from the Lord, the GOD of hosts, in the Valley of Vision. Walls crash; they cry for help to the mountains. ⁶ Elam takes up the quivers, Aram mounts the horses, and Kir uncovers the shields. ⁷ Your choice valleys are filled with chariots, and horses are posted at the gates, ⁸ and shelter over Judah is removed. On that day you looked to the weapons in the House of the Forest; ⁹ you saw that the breaches in the City of David were many; you collected the water of the lower pool. ¹⁰ You numbered the houses of Jerusalem, tearing some down to strengthen the wall; ¹¹ you made a reservoir between the two walls for the water of the old pool. But you did not look to the city's Maker, nor did you consider him who built it long ago. ¹² On that day the Lord, the GOD of hosts, called on you to weep and mourn, to shave your head and put on sackcloth. ¹³ But look! you feast and celebrate, you slaughter oxen and butcher sheep, You eat meat and drink wine: "Eat and drink, for tomorrow we die!" ¹⁴ This reaches the ears of the LORD of hosts: You shall not be pardoned this wickedness till you die, says the Lord, the GOD of hosts. ¹⁵ **Thus says the Lord, the GOD of hosts:** Up, go to that official, Shebna, master of the palace, ¹⁶ who has hewn for himself a sepulcher on a height and carved his tomb in the rock: "What are you doing here, and what people have you here, that here you have hewn for yourself a tomb?" ¹⁷ The LORD shall hurl you down headlong, mortal man! He shall grip you firmly ¹⁸ and roll you up and toss you like a ball into an open land to perish there, you and the chariots you glory in, you disgrace to your master's house! ¹⁹ I will thrust you from your office and pull you down from your station. ²⁰ On that day I will summon my servant Eliakim, son of Hilkiah; ²¹ I will clothe him with your robe, and gird him with your sash, and give over to him your authority. He shall be a father to the inhabitants of Jerusalem, and to the house of Judah. ²² I will place the key of the House of David on his shoulder; when he opens, no one shall shut, when he shuts, no one shall open. ²³ I will fix him like a peg in a sure spot, to be a place of honor for his family; ²⁴ On him shall hang all the glory of his family: descendants and offspring, all the little dishes, from bowls to jugs. ²⁵ On that day, says the LORD of hosts, the peg fixed in a sure spot shall give way, break off and fall, and the weight that hung on it shall be done away with; for the LORD has spoken.

Isaiah Chapter 23

¹ Oracle on Tyre: Wail, O ships of Tarshish, for your port is destroyed; from the land of the Kittim, the news reaches them. ² Silence! you who dwell on the coast, you merchants of Sidon, whose messengers crossed the sea ³ over the deep waters. The grain of Shihor, the harvest of the Nile, was her revenue, and she the merchant among nations. ⁴ Shame, O Sidon, fortress on the sea, for the sea has spoken: "I have not been in labor, nor given birth, nor raised young men, nor reared virgins." ⁵ When it is heard in Egypt they shall be in anguish at the news of Tyre. ⁶ Pass over to Tarshish, wailing, you who dwell on the coast! ⁷ Is this your wanton city, whose origin is from old, whose feet have taken her to dwell in distant lands? ⁸ Who has planned such a thing against Tyre, the bestower of crowns, whose merchants are princes, whose traders are the earth's honored men? ⁹ The LORD of hosts has planned it, to disgrace all pride of majesty, to degrade all the earth's honored men. ¹⁰ Cross to your own land, O ship of Tarshish; the harbor is no more. ¹¹ His hand he stretches out over the sea, he shakes kingdoms; the LORD has ordered the destruction of Canaan's strongholds. ¹² You shall exult no more, he says, you who are now oppressed, virgin daughter Sidon. Arise, pass over to the Kittim, even there you shall find no rest. ¹³ (This people is the land of the Chaldeans, not Assyria.) She whom the impious founded, setting up towers for her, has had her castles destroyed, and has been turned into a ruin. ¹⁴ Lament, O ships of Tarshish, for your haven is destroyed. ¹⁵ On that day, Tyre shall be forgotten for seventy years. With the days of another king, at the end of seventy years, it shall be for Tyre as in the song about the harlot: ¹⁶ Take a harp, go about the city, O forgotten harlot; pluck the strings skillfully, sing many songs, that they may remember you. ¹⁷ At the end of the seventy years the LORD shall visit Tyre. She shall return to her hire and deal with all the world's kingdoms on the face of the earth. ¹⁸ But her merchandise and her hire shall be sacred to the LORD. It shall not be stored up or laid away, but from her merchandise those who dwell before the LORD shall eat their fill and clothe themselves in choice attire.

Isaiah Chapter 24

¹ Lo, the LORD empties the land and lays it waste; he turns it upside down, scattering its inhabitants; ² Layman and priest alike, servant and master, the maid as her mistress, the buyer as the seller, the lender as the borrower, the creditor as the debtor. ³ The earth is utterly laid waste, utterly stripped, for the LORD has decreed this thing. ⁴ The earth mourns and fades, the world languishes and fades; both heaven and earth languish. ⁵ The earth is polluted because of its inhabitants, who have transgressed laws, violated statutes, broken the ancient covenant. ⁶ Therefore a curse devours the earth, and its inhabitants pay for their guilt; therefore they who dwell on earth turn pale, and few men are left. ⁷ The wine mourns, the vine languishes, all the merry-hearted groan. ⁸ Stilled are the cheerful timbrels, ended the shouts of the jubilant, stilled is the cheerful harp. ⁹ They cannot sing and drink wine; strong drink is bitter to those who partake of it. ¹⁰ Broken down is the city of chaos, shut against entry, every house. ¹¹ In the streets they cry out for lack of wine; all joy has disappeared and cheer has left the land. ¹² In the city nothing remains but ruin; its gates are battered and desolate. ¹³ Thus it is within the land, and among the peoples, as with an olive tree after it is beaten, as with a gleaning when the vintage is done. ¹⁴ These lift up their voice in acclaim; from the sea they proclaim the majesty of the LORD: ¹⁵ "For this, in the coastlands, give glory to the LORD! In the coastlands of the sea, to the name of the LORD, the God of Israel!" ¹⁶ From the end of the earth we hear songs: "Splendor to the Just One!" But I said, "I am wasted, wasted away. Woe is me! The traitors betray: with treachery have the traitors betrayed! ¹⁷ Terror, pit, and trap are upon you, inhabitant of the earth; ¹⁸ He who flees at the sound of terror will fall into the pit; he who climbs out of the pit will be caught in the trap. For the windows on high will be opened and the foundations of the earth will shake. ¹⁹ The earth will burst asunder, the earth will be shaken apart, the earth will be convulsed. ²⁰ The earth will reel like a drunkard, and it will sway like a hut; its rebellion will weigh it down, until it falls, never to rise again." ²¹ On that day the LORD will punish the host of the heavens in the heavens, and the kings of the earth on the earth. ²² They will be gathered together like prisoners into a pit; they will be shut up in a dungeon, and after many days they will be punished. ²³ Then the moon will blush and the sun grow pale, for the LORD of hosts will reign on Mount Zion and in Jerusalem, glorious in the sight of his elders.

Isaiah Chapter 25

¹ O LORD, you are my God, I will extol you and praise your name; for you have fulfilled your wonderful plans of old, faithful and true. ² For you have made the city a heap, the fortified city a ruin; the castle of the insolent is a city no more, nor ever to be rebuilt. ³ Therefore a strong people will honor you, fierce nations will fear you. ⁴ For you are a refuge to the poor, a refuge to the needy in distress; shelter from the rain, shade from the heat. As with the cold rain, ⁵ as with the desert heat, even so you quell the uproar of the wanton. ⁶ On this mountain the LORD of hosts will provide for all peoples a feast of rich food and choice

wines, juicy, rich food and pure, choice wines. 7 On this mountain he will destroy the veil that veils all peoples, the web that is woven over all nations; 8 he will destroy death forever. The Lord GOD will wipe away the tears from all faces; the reproach of his people he will remove from the whole earth; for the LORD has spoken. 9 On that day it will be said: "Behold our God, to whom we looked to save us! This is the LORD for whom we looked; let us rejoice and be glad that he has saved us!" 10 For the hand of the LORD will rest on this mountain, but Moab will be trodden down as a straw is trodden down in the mire. 11 He will stretch forth his hands in Moab as a swimmer extends his hands to swim; he will bring low their pride as his hands sweep over them. 12 The high-walled fortress he will raze, and strike it down level with the earth, with the very dust.

Isaiah Chapter 26

1 On that day they will sing this song in the land of Judah: "A strong city have we; he sets up walls and ramparts to protect us. 2 Open up the gates to let in a nation that is just, one that keeps faith. 3 A nation of firm purpose you keep in peace; in peace, for its trust in you." 4 Trust in the LORD forever! For the LORD is an eternal Rock. 5 He humbles those in high places, and the lofty city he brings down; he tumbles it to the ground, levels it with the dust. 6 It is trampled underfoot by the needy, by the footsteps of the poor. 7 The way of the just is smooth; the path of the just you make level. 8 Yes, for your way and your judgments, O LORD, we look to you; your name and your title are the desire of our souls. 9 My soul yearns for you in the night, yes, my spirit within me keeps vigil for you; when your judgment dawns upon the earth, the world's inhabitants learn justice. 10 The wicked man, spared, does not learn justice; in an upright land he acts perversely, and sees not the majesty of the LORD. 11 O LORD, your hand is uplifted, but they behold it not; let them be shamed when they see your zeal for your people: let the fire prepared for your enemies consume them. 12 O LORD, you mete out peace to us, for it is you who have accomplished all we have done. 13 O LORD, our God, other lords than you have ruled us; it is from you only that we can call upon your name. 14 Dead they are, they have no life, shades that cannot rise; for you have punished and destroyed them, and wiped out all memory of them. 15 You have increased the nation, O LORD, increased the nation to your own glory, and extended far all the borders of the land. 16 O LORD, oppressed by your punishment, we cried out in anguish under your chastising. 17 As a woman about to give birth writhes and cries out in her pains, so were we in your presence, O LORD. 18 We conceived and writhed in pain, giving birth to wind; salvation we have not achieved for the earth, the inhabitants of the world cannot bring it forth. 19 But your dead shall live, their corpses shall rise; awake and sing, you who lie in the dust. For your dew is a dew of light, and the land of shades gives birth. 20 Go, my people, enter your chambers, and close your doors behind you; hide yourselves for a brief moment, until the wrath is past. 21 See, the LORD goes forth from his place, to punish the wickedness of the earth's inhabitants; the earth will reveal the blood upon her, and no longer conceal her slain.

Isaiah Chapter 27

1 On that day, the LORD will punish with his cruel, great, and strong sword, Leviathan the fleeing serpent, Leviathan the coiled serpent; and he will slay the dragon that is in the sea. 2 On that day—sing about the pleasant vineyard! 3 I, the LORD, am its keeper; I water it every moment. Lest anyone harm it, night and day I guard it. 4 I am not angry, but if I were to find briers and thorns, I would march against them in battle and burn them all. 8 Expunging and expelling, I would strive against them, carrying them off with my cruel wind in a time of storm. 6 In days to come, Jacob shall take root, Israel shall sprout and blossom, covering all the world with fruit. 7 Is he to be smitten as his smiter was smitten? Or slain as his slayer was slain? 5 Or shall he cling to me for refuge? He must make peace with me; peace shall he make with me! 9 This, then, shall be the expiation of Jacob's guilt, this the whole fruit of the removal of his sin: He shall pulverize all the stones of the altars like pieces of chalk; no sacred poles or incense altars shall stand. 10 For the fortified city shall be desolate, an abandoned pasture, a forsaken wilderness where calves shall browse and lie. Its boughs shall be destroyed, 11 its branches shall wither and be broken off, and women shall come to build a fire with them. This is not an understanding people; therefore, their maker shall not spare them, nor shall he who formed them have mercy on them. 12 On that day, the LORD shall beat out the grain between the Euphrates and the Wadi of Egypt, and you shall be gleaned one by one, O sons of Israel. 13 On that day, a great trumpet shall blow, and the lost in the land of Assyria and the outcasts in the land of Egypt shall come and worship the LORD on the holy mountain in Jerusalem.

Isaiah Chapter 28

1 Woe to the majestic garland of the drunkard Ephraim, to the fading blooms of his glorious beauty, on the head of him who is stupefied with wine. 2 Behold, the LORD has a strong one and a mighty, who, like a downpour of hail, a destructive storm, like a flood of water, great and overflowing, levels to the ground with violence; 3 with feet that will trample the majestic garland of the drunkard Ephraim. 4 The fading blooms of his glorious beauty on the head of the fertile valley will be like an early fig before summer: when a man sees it, he picks and swallows it at once. 5 On that day the LORD of hosts will be a glorious crown and a brilliant diadem to the remnant of his people, 6 a spirit of justice to him who sits in judgment, and strength to those who turn back the battle at the gate. 7 But these also stagger from wine and stumble from strong drink: priest and prophet stagger from strong drink, overpowered by wine; led astray by strong drink, staggering in their visions, tottering when giving judgment. 8 Yes, all the tables are covered with filthy vomit, with no place left clean. 9 "To whom would he impart knowledge? To whom would he convey the message? To those just weaned from milk, those taken from the breast? 10 For he says, 'Command on command, command on command, rule on rule, rule on rule, here a little, there a little!'" 11 Yes, with stammering lips and in a strange language he will speak to this people 12 to whom he said: This is the resting place, give rest to the weary; here is repose—but they would not listen. 13 So for them, the word of the LORD shall be: "Command on command, command on command, rule on rule, rule on rule, here a little, there a little!" So that when they walk, they stumble backward, broken, ensnared, and captured. 14 Therefore, hear the word of the LORD, you arrogant, who rule this people in Jerusalem: 15 because you say, "We have made a covenant with death, and with the nether world we have made a pact; when the overwhelming scourge passes, it will not reach us; for we have made lies our refuge, and in falsehood we have found a hiding place,"— 16 therefore, thus says the Lord GOD: See, I am laying a stone in Zion, a stone that has been tested, a precious cornerstone as a sure foundation; he who puts his faith in it shall not be shaken. 17 I will make of right a measuring line, of justice a level—hail shall sweep away the refuge of lies, and waters shall flood the hiding place. 18 Your covenant with death shall be canceled, and your pact with the nether world shall not stand. When the overwhelming scourge passes, you shall be trampled down by it. 19 Whenever it passes, it shall take you; morning after morning it shall pass, by day and by night; terror alone shall convey the message. 20 For the bed shall be too short to stretch out in, and the cover too narrow to wrap in. 21 For the LORD shall rise up as on Mount Perazim, bestir himself as in the Valley of Gibeon, to carry out his work, his singular work, to perform his deed, his strange deed. 22 Now, be arrogant no more lest your bonds be tightened, for I have heard from the Lord, the GOD of hosts, the destruction decreed for the whole earth. 23 Give ear and hear my voice, pay attention and listen to what I say: 24 Is the plowman forever plowing, always loosening and harrowing his land for planting? 25 When he has leveled the surface, does he not scatter gith and sow cumin, put in wheat and barley, with spelt as its border? 26 He has learned this rule, instructed by his God. 27 Gith is not threshed with a sledge, nor does a cartwheel roll over cumin. But gith is beaten out with a staff, and cumin crushed for food with a rod. 28 No, he does not thresh it unendingly, nor does he crush it with his noisy cartwheels and horses. 29 This too comes from the LORD of hosts; wonderful is his counsel and great his wisdom.

Isaiah Chapter 29

1 Woe to Ariel, Ariel, the city where David encamped! Add year to year, let the feasts come round. 2 But I will bring distress upon Ariel, with mourning and grief. You shall be to me like Ariel, 3 I will encamp like David against you; I will encircle you with outposts and set up siege works against you. 4 Prostrate you shall speak from the earth, and from the base dust your words shall come. Your voice shall be like a ghost's from the earth, and your words like chirping from the dust. 5 The horde of your arrogant shall be like fine dust, the horde of the tyrants like flying chaff. Then suddenly, in an instant, 6 you shall be visited by the LORD of hosts, with thunder, earthquake, and great noise, whirlwind, storm, and the flame of consuming fire. 7 Then like a dream, a vision in the night, shall be the horde of all the nations who war against Ariel with all the earthworks of her besiegers. 8 As when a hungry man dreams he is eating and awakens with an empty stomach, or when a thirsty man dreams he is drinking and awakens faint and dry, so shall the horde of all the nations be, who make war against Zion. 9 Be irresolute, stupefied; blind yourselves and stay blind! Be drunk, but not from wine, stagger, but not from strong drink! 10 For the LORD has poured out on you a spirit of deep sleep. He has shut your eyes (the

prophets) and covered your heads (the seers). 11 For you the revelation of all this has become like the words of a sealed scroll. When it is handed to one who can read, with the request, "Read this," he replies, "I cannot; it is sealed." 12 When it is handed to one who cannot read, with the request, "Read this," he replies, "I cannot read." 13 The Lord said: Since this people draws near with words only and honors me with their lips alone, though their hearts are far from me, and their reverence for me has become routine observance of the precepts of men, 14 therefore I will again deal with this people in surprising and wondrous fashion: The wisdom of its wise men shall perish and the understanding of its prudent men be hid. 15 Woe to those who would hide their plans too deep for the LORD! Who work in the dark, saying, "Who sees us, or who knows us?" 16 Your perversity is as though the potter were taken to be the clay: As though what is made should say of its maker, "He made me not!" Or the vessel should say of the potter, "He does not understand." 17 But a very little while, and Lebanon shall be changed into an orchard, and the orchard be regarded as a forest! 18 On that day the deaf shall hear the words of a book; and out of gloom and darkness, the eyes of the blind shall see. 19 The lowly will ever find joy in the LORD, and the poor rejoice in the Holy One of Israel. 20 For the tyrant will be no more and the arrogant will have gone; all who are alert to do evil will be cut off, 21 those whose mere word condemns a man, who ensnare his defender at the gate, and leave the just man with an empty claim. 22 Therefore thus says the LORD, the God of the house of Jacob, who redeemed Abraham: Now Jacob shall have nothing to be ashamed of, nor shall his face grow pale. 23 When his children see the work of my hands in his midst, they shall keep my name holy; they shall reverence the Holy One of Jacob, and be in awe of the God of Israel. 24 Those who err in spirit shall acquire understanding, and those who find fault shall receive instruction.

Isaiah Chapter 30

1 Woe to the rebellious children, says the LORD, who carry out plans that are not mine, who weave webs that are not inspired by me, adding sin upon sin. 2 They go down to Egypt, but my counsel they do not seek. They find their strength in Pharaoh's protection and take refuge in Egypt's shadow; 3 Pharaoh's protection shall be your shame, and refuge in Egypt's shadow your disgrace. 4 When their princes are at Zoan and their messengers reach Hanes, 5 all shall be ashamed of a people that gain them nothing, neither help nor benefit, but only shame and reproach. 6 (Oracle on the Beasts of the Negeb) Through the distressed and troubled land of the lioness and roaring lion, of the viper and flying saraph, they carry their riches on the backs of asses and their treasures on the humps of camels to a people good for nothing, 7 to Egypt whose help is futile and vain. Therefore I call her "Rahab quelled." 8 Now come, write it on a tablet they can keep, inscribe it in a record; that it may be in future days an eternal witness: 9 This is a rebellious people, deceitful children, children who refuse to obey the law of the LORD. 10 They say to the seers, "Have no visions"; to the prophets, "Do not descry for us what is right; speak flatteries to us, conjure up illusions. 11 Out of the way! Out of our path! Let us hear no more of the Holy One of Israel." 12 Therefore, thus says the Holy One of Israel: Because you reject this word, and put your trust in what is crooked and devious, and depend on it, 13 this guilt of yours shall be like a descending rift bulging out in a high wall whose crash comes suddenly, in an instant. 14 It crashes like a potter's jar smashed beyond rescue, and among its fragments cannot be found a sherd to scoop fire from the hearth or dip water from the cistern. 15 For thus said the Lord GOD, the Holy One of Israel: By waiting and by calm you shall be saved, in quiet and in trust your strength lies. But this you did not wish. 16 "No," you said, "Upon horses we will flee." —Very well, flee! "Upon swift steeds we will ride." —Not so swift as your pursuers. 17 A thousand shall tremble at the threat of one; if five threaten you, you shall flee, until you are left like a flagstaff on the mountaintop, like a flag on the hill. 18 Yet the LORD is waiting to show you favor, and he rises to pity you; for the LORD is a God of justice: blessed are all who wait for him! 19 O people of Zion, who dwell in Jerusalem, no more will you weep; he will be gracious to you when you cry out, as soon as he hears he will answer you. 20 The Lord will give you the bread you need and the water for which you thirst. No longer will your Teacher hide himself, but with your own eyes you shall see your Teacher, 21 while from behind, a voice shall sound in your ears: "This is the way; walk in it," when you would turn to the right or to the left. 22 And you shall consider unclean your silver-plated idols and your gold-covered images; you shall throw them away like filthy rags to which you say, "Begone!" 23 He will give rain for the seed that you sow in the ground, and the wheat that the soil produces will be rich and abundant. On that day your cattle will graze in spacious meadows; 24 the oxen and the asses that till the ground will eat silage tossed to them with shovel and pitchfork. 25 Upon every high mountain and lofty

hill there will be streams of running water. On the day of the great slaughter, when the towers fall, 26 the light of the moon will be like that of the sun and the light of the sun will be seven times greater (like the light of seven days). On the day the LORD binds up the wounds of his people, he will heal the bruises left by his blows. 27 See the name of the LORD coming from afar in burning wrath, with lowering clouds! His lips are filled with fury, his tongue is like a consuming fire; 28 his breath, like a flood in a ravine that reaches suddenly to the neck, will winnow the nations with a destructive winnowing, and with repeated winnowings will he battle against them (and a bridle on the jaws of the peoples to send them astray). 29 You will sing as on a night when a feast is observed, and be merry of heart, as one marching along with a flute toward the mountain of the LORD, toward the Rock of Israel, accompanied by the timbrels and lyres. 30 The LORD will make his glorious voice heard, and let it be seen how his arm descends in raging fury and flame of consuming fire, in driving storm and hail. 31 When the LORD speaks, Assyria will be shattered, as he strikes with the rod; 32 while at every sweep of the rod which the LORD will bring down on him in punishment, 33 for the pyre has long been ready, prepared for the king; broad and deep it is piled with dry grass and wood in abundance, and the breath of the LORD, like a stream of sulfur, will set it afire.

Isaiah Chapter 31

1 Woe to those who go down to Egypt for help, who depend upon horses: who put their trust in chariots because of their number, and in horsemen because of their combined power, but look not to the Holy One of Israel nor seek the LORD! 2 Yet he too is wise and will bring disaster; he will not turn from what he has threatened to do. He will rise up against the house of the wicked and against those who help evildoers. 3 The Egyptians are men, not God, their horses are flesh, not spirit; when the LORD stretches forth his hand, the helper shall stumble, the one helped shall fall, and both of them shall perish together. 4 Thus says the LORD to me: As a lion or a lion cub growling over its prey, with a band of shepherds assembled against it, is neither frightened by their shouts nor disturbed by their noise, so shall the LORD of hosts come down to wage war upon the mountain and hill of Zion. 5 Like hovering birds, so the LORD of hosts shall shield Jerusalem, to protect and deliver, to spare and rescue it. 6 Return, O children of Israel, to him whom you have utterly deserted. 7 On that day each one of you shall spurn his sinful idols of silver and gold, which you made with his hands. 8 Assyria shall fall by a sword not wielded by man, no mortal sword shall devour him; he shall flee before the sword, and his young men shall be impressed as laborers. 1 He shall rush past his crag in panic, and his princes shall flee in terror from his standard, says the LORD who has a fire in Zion and a furnace in Jerusalem.

Isaiah Chapter 32

1 See, a king will reign justly and princes will rule rightly. 2 Each of them will be a shelter from the wind, a retreat from the rain. They will be like streams of water in a dry country, like the shade of a great rock in a parched land. 3 The eyes of those who see will not be closed; the ears of those who hear will be attentive. 4 The flighty will become wise and capable, and the stutterers will speak fluently and clearly. 5 No more will the fool be called noble, nor the trickster be considered honorable. 6 For the fool speaks foolishly, planning evil in his heart: how to do wickedness, to speak perversely against the LORD, to let the hungry go empty and the thirsty be without drink. 7 And the trickster uses wicked trickery, planning crimes: how to ruin the poor with lies, and the needy when they plead their case. 8 But the noble man plans noble things, and by noble things he stands. 9 O complacent ladies, rise up and hear my voice, overconfident women, give heed to my words. 10 In a little more than a year, you overconfident ones will be shaken; the vintage will fail, there will be no harvest. 11 Tremble, you who are complacent! Shudder, you who are overconfident! Strip yourselves bare, with only a loincloth to cover you. 12 Beat your breasts for the pleasant fields, the fruitful vine, 13 and the soil of my people, overgrown with thorns and briers; for all the joyful houses, the wanton city. 14 Yes, the castle will be forsaken, the noisy city deserted. 15 Down it comes, as trees come down in the forest! The city will be utterly laid low. Hill and tower will become wasteland forever for wild asses to frolic in, and flocks to pasture, 16 until the spirit from on high is poured out on us. Then will the desert become an orchard and the orchard be regarded as a forest. 17 Right will dwell in the desert and justice abide in the orchard. 18 Justice will bring about peace; right will produce calm and security. 19 My people will live in peaceful country, in secure dwellings and quiet resting places. 20 Happy are you who sow beside every stream, and let the ox and the ass go freely!

Isaiah Chapter 33

1 Woe, O destroyer never destroyed, O traitor never betrayed! When you finish destroying, you will be destroyed; when wearied with betraying, you will be betrayed. 2 O LORD, have pity on us, for you we wait. Be our strength every morning, our salvation in time of trouble! 3 At the roaring sound, peoples flee; when you rise in your majesty, nations are scattered. 4 Men gather spoil as caterpillars are gathered up; they rush upon it like the onrush of locusts. 5 The LORD is exalted, enthroned on high; he fills Zion with right and justice. 6 That which makes her seasons lasting, the riches that save her, are wisdom and knowledge; the fear of the LORD is her treasure. 7 See, the men of Ariel cry out in the streets, the messengers of Shalem weep bitterly. 8 The highways are desolate, travelers have quit the paths, covenants are broken, their terms are spurned; yet no man gives it a thought. 9 The country languishes in mourning, Lebanon withers with shame; Sharon is like the steppe, Bashan and Carmel are stripped bare. 10 Now will I rise up, says the LORD, now will I be exalted, now be lifted up. 11 You conceive dry grass, bring forth stubble; my spirit shall consume you like fire. 12 The peoples shall be as in a limekiln, like brushwood cut down for burning in the fire. 13 Hear, you who are far off, what I have done; you who are near, acknowledge my might. 14 On Zion sinners are in dread, trembling grips the impious: "Who of us can live with the consuming fire? Who of us can live with the everlasting flames?" 15 He who practices virtue and speaks honestly, who spurns what is gained by oppression, brushing his hands free of contact with a bribe, stopping his ears lest he hear of bloodshed, closing his eyes lest he look on evil – 16 He shall dwell on the heights, his stronghold shall be the rocky fastness, his food and drink in steady supply. 17 Your eyes will see a king in his splendor, they will look upon a vast land. 18 Your mind will dwell on the terror: "Where is he who counted, where is he who weighed? Where is he who counted the towers?" 19 To the people of alien tongue you will look no more, the people of obscure speech, stammering in a language not understood. 20 Look to Zion, the city of our festivals; let your eyes see Jerusalem as a quiet abode, a tent not to be struck, whose pegs will never be pulled up, nor any of its ropes severed. 21 Indeed the LORD will be there with us, majestic; yes, the LORD our judge, the LORD our lawgiver, the LORD our king, he it is who will save us. 22 In a place of rivers and wide streams on which no boat is rowed, where no majestic ship passes, 23 the rigging hangs slack; it cannot hold the mast in place, nor keep the sail spread out. Then the blind will divide great spoils and the lame will carry off the loot. 24 No one who dwells there will say, "I am sick"; the people who live there will be forgiven their guilt.

Isaiah Chapter 34

1 Come near, O nations, and hear; be attentive, O peoples! Let the earth and what fills it listen, the world and all it produces. 2 The LORD is angry with all the nations and is wrathful against all their host; he has doomed them and given them over to slaughter. 3 Their slain shall be cast out, their corpses shall send up a stench; the mountains shall run with their blood, 4 and all the hills shall rot; the heavens shall be rolled up like a scroll, and all their host shall wither away, as the leaf wilts on the vine, or as the fig withers on the tree. 5 When my sword has drunk its fill in the heavens, lo, it shall come down in judgment upon Edom, a people I have doomed. 6 The LORD has a sword filled with blood, greasy with fat, with the blood of lambs and goats, with the fat of rams' kidneys; for the LORD has a sacrifice in Bozrah, a great slaughter in the land of Edom. 7 Wild oxen shall be struck down with fatlings, and bullocks with bulls; their land shall be soaked with blood, and their earth greasy with fat. 8 For the LORD has a day of vengeance, a year of requital by Zion's defender. 9 Edom's streams shall be changed into pitch and her earth into sulphur, and her land shall become burning pitch; 10 night and day it shall not be quenched, its smoke shall rise forever. From generation to generation she shall lie waste, never again shall anyone pass through her. 11 But the desert owl and hoot owl shall possess her, the screech owl and raven shall dwell in her. The LORD will measure her with line and plummet to be an empty waste for satyrs to dwell in. 12 Her nobles shall be no more, nor shall kings be proclaimed there; all her princes are gone. 13 Her castles shall be overgrown with thorns, her fortresses with thistles and briers. She shall become an abode for jackals and a haunt for ostriches. 14 Wildcats shall meet with desert beasts, satyrs shall call to one another; there shall the lilith repose, and find for herself a place to rest. 15 There the hoot owl shall nest and lay eggs, hatch them out and gather them in her shadow; there shall the kites assemble, none shall be missing its mate. 16 Look in the book of the LORD and read: No one of these shall be lacking, for the mouth of the LORD has ordered it, and his spirit shall gather them there. 17 It is he who casts the lot for them, and with his hands he marks off their shares of her; they shall possess her forever, and dwell there from generation to generation.

Isaiah Chapter 35

1 The desert and the parched land will exult; the steppe will rejoice and bloom. 2 They will bloom with abundant flowers, and rejoice with joyful song. The glory of Lebanon will be given to them, the splendor of Carmel and Sharon; they will see the glory of the LORD, the splendor of our God. 3 Strengthen the hands that are feeble, make firm the knees that are weak, 4 say to those whose hearts are frightened: Be strong, fear not! Here is your God, he comes with vindication; with divine recompense he comes to save you. 5 Then will the eyes of the blind be opened, the ears of the deaf be cleared; 6 then will the lame leap like a stag, then the tongue of the dumb will sing. Streams will burst forth in the desert, and rivers in the steppe. 7 The burning sands will become pools, and the thirsty ground, springs of water; the abode where jackals lurk will be a marsh for the reed and papyrus. 8 A highway will be there, called the holy way; no one unclean may pass over it, nor fools go astray on it. 9 No lion will be there, nor beast of prey go up to be met upon it. It is for those with a journey to make, and on it the redeemed will walk. 10 Those whom the LORD has ransomed will return and enter Zion singing, crowned with everlasting joy; they will meet with joy and gladness, sorrow and mourning will flee.

Isaiah Chapter 36

1 In the fourteenth year of King Hezekiah, Sennacherib, king of Assyria, went on an expedition against all the fortified cities of Judah and captured them. 2 From Lachish, the king of Assyria sent his commander with a great army to King Hezekiah in Jerusalem. When he stopped at the conduit of the upper pool, on the highway of the fuller's field, 3 there came out to him the master of the palace, Eliakim, son of Hilkiah, and Shebna the scribe, and the herald Joah, son of Asaph. 4 The commander said to them, "Tell King Hezekiah: Thus says the great king, the king of Assyria, 'On what do you base this confidence of yours? 5 Do you think mere words substitute for strategy and might in war? On whom, then, do you rely, that you rebel against me? 6 This Egypt, the staff on which you rely, is in fact a broken reed which pierces the hand of anyone who leans on it. That is what Pharaoh, king of Egypt, is to all who rely on him. 7 But if you say to me: "We rely on the LORD, our God," is not he the one whose high places and altars Hezekiah removed, commanding Judah and Jerusalem to worship before this altar?' 8 'Now, make a wager with my lord the king of Assyria: "I will give you two thousand horses, if you can put riders on them."' 9 How then can you repulse even one of the least servants of my lord? And yet you rely on Egypt for chariots and horsemen! 10 'Was it without the LORD'S will that I have come up to destroy this land? The LORD said to me, "Go up and destroy that land!"' 11 Then Eliakim and Shebna and Joah said to the commander, "Please speak to your servants in Aramaic; we understand it. Do not speak to us in Judean within earshot of the people who are on the wall." 12 But the commander replied, "Was it to you and your master that my lord sent me to speak these words? Was it not rather to the men sitting on the wall, who, with you, will have to eat their own excrement and drink their own urine?" 13 Then the commander stepped forward and cried out in a loud voice in Judean, "Listen to the words of the great king, the king of Assyria. 14 Thus says the king: 'Do not let Hezekiah deceive you, since he cannot deliver you. 15 Let not Hezekiah induce you to rely on the LORD, saying, "The LORD will surely save us; this city will not be handed over to the king of Assyria."' 16 Do not listen to Hezekiah, for the king of Assyria says: 'Make peace with me and surrender! Then each of you will eat of his own vine and of his own fig tree, and drink the water of his own cistern, 17 until I come to take you to a land like your own, a land of grain and wine, of bread and vineyards. 18 Do not let Hezekiah seduce you by saying, "The LORD will save us." Has any of the gods of the nations ever rescued his land from the hand of the king of Assyria? 19 Where are the gods of Hamath and Arpad? Where are the gods of Sepharvaim? Where are the gods of Samaria? Have they saved Samaria from my hand? 20 Which of all the gods of these lands ever rescued his land from my hand? Will the LORD then save Jerusalem from my hand?'" 21 But they remained silent and did not answer him one word, for the king had ordered them not to answer him. 22 Then the master of the palace, Eliakim, son of Hilkiah, Shebna the scribe, and the herald Joah, son of Asaph, came to Hezekiah with their garments torn, and reported to him what the commander had said.

Isaiah Chapter 37

1 When King Hezekiah heard this, he tore his garments, wrapped himself in sackcloth, and went into the temple of the LORD. 2 He sent Eliakim, the master of the palace, and Shebna the scribe, and the elders of the priests, wrapped in sackcloth, to tell the prophet Isaiah, son of

Amoz: 3 "Thus says Hezekiah: 'This is a day of distress, of rebuke, and of disgrace. Children are at the point of birth, but there is no strength to bring them forth. 4 Perhaps the LORD, your God, will hear the words of the commander, whom his master, the king of Assyria, sent to taunt the living God, and will rebuke him for the words which the LORD, your God, has heard. Send up a prayer for the remnant that is here.'" 5 When the servants of King Hezekiah had come to Isaiah, 6 he said to them: "Tell this to your master: 'Thus says the LORD: Do not be frightened by the words you have heard, with which the servants of the king of Assyria have blasphemed me. 7 I am about to put in him such a spirit that, when he hears a certain report, he will return to his own land, and there I will cause him to fall by the sword.'" 8 When the commander returned to Lachish and heard that the king of Assyria had left there, he found him besieging Libnah. 9 The king of Assyria heard a report that Tirhakah, king of Ethiopia, had come out to fight against him. Again he sent envoys to Hezekiah with this message: "Thus shall you say to Hezekiah, king of Judah: 10 'Do not let your God on whom you rely deceive you by saying that Jerusalem will not be handed over to the king of Assyria. 11 You yourself have heard what the kings of Assyria have done to all the countries: They doomed them! Will you, then, be saved? 12 Did the gods of the nations whom my fathers destroyed save them? Gozen, Haran, Rezeph, and the Edenites in Telassar? 13 Where is the king of Hamath, the king of Arpad, or a king of the cities of Sepharvaim, Hena or Ivvah?'" 14 Hezekiah took the letter from the hand of the messengers and read it; then he went up to the temple of the LORD, and spreading it out before him, 15 he prayed to the LORD: 16 "O LORD of hosts, God of Israel, enthroned upon the cherubim! You alone are God over all the kingdoms of the earth. You have made the heavens and the earth. 17 Incline your ear, O LORD, and listen! Open your eyes, O LORD, and see! Hear all the words of the letter that Sennacherib sent to taunt the living God. 18 Truly, O LORD, the kings of Assyria have laid waste all the nations and their lands, 19 and cast their gods into the fire; they destroyed them because they were not gods but the work of human hands, wood and stone. 20 Therefore, O LORD, our God, save us from his hand, that all the kingdoms of the earth may know that you, O LORD, alone are God." 21 Then Isaiah, son of Amoz, sent this message to Hezekiah: Thus says the LORD, the God of Israel: In answer to your prayer for help against Sennacherib, king of Assyria, 22 this is the word the LORD has spoken concerning him: She despises you, laughs you to scorn, the virgin daughter Zion; Behind you she wags her head, daughter Jerusalem. 23 Whom have you insulted and blasphemed, against whom have you raised your voice and lifted up your eyes on high? Against the Holy One of Israel! 24 Through your servants you have insulted the Lord: You said, "With my many chariots I climbed the mountain heights, the recesses of Lebanon; I cut down its lofty cedars, its choice cypresses; I reached the remotest heights, its forest park. 25 I dug wells and drank water in foreign lands; I dried up with the soles of my feet all the rivers of Egypt. 26 Have you not heard? Long ago I prepared it, from days of old I planned it, now I have brought it to pass: that you should reduce fortified cities into heaps of ruins, 27 while their inhabitants, shorn of power, are dismayed and ashamed, becoming like the plants of the field, like the green growth, like the scorched grass on the housetops. 28 I am aware whether you stand or sit; I know whether you come or go, and also your rage against me. 29 Because of your rage against me and your fury which has reached my ears, I will put my hook in your nose and my bit in your mouth, and make you return the way you came. 30 This shall be a sign for you: this year you shall eat the aftergrowth, next year, what grows of itself; but in the third year, sow and reap, plant vineyards and eat their fruit! 31 The remaining survivors of the house of Judah shall again strike root below and bear fruit above. 32 For out of Jerusalem shall come a remnant, and from Mount Zion, survivors. The zeal of the LORD of hosts shall do this. 33 Therefore, thus says the LORD concerning the king of Assyria: He shall not reach this city, nor shoot an arrow at it, nor come before it with a shield, nor cast up siegeworks against it. 34 He shall return by the same way he came, without entering the city, says the LORD. 35 I will shield and save this city for my own sake, and for the sake of my servant David. 36 The angel of the LORD went forth and struck down one hundred and eighty-five thousand in the Assyrian camp. Early the next morning, there they were, all the corpses of the dead. 37 So Sennacherib, the king of Assyria, broke camp and went back home to Nineveh. 38 When he was worshiping in the temple of his god Nisroch, his sons Adrammelech and Sharezer slew him with the sword and fled into the land of Ararat. His son Esarhaddon reigned in his stead.

Isaiah Chapter 38

1 In those days, when Hezekiah was mortally ill, the prophet Isaiah, son of Amoz, came and said to him: "Thus says the LORD: Put your house in order, for you are about to die; you shall not recover." 2 Then

Hezekiah turned his face to the wall and prayed to the LORD: 3 "O LORD, remember how faithfully and wholeheartedly I conducted myself in your presence, doing what was pleasing to you!" And Hezekiah wept bitterly. 4 Then the word of the LORD came to Isaiah: 5 "Go, tell Hezekiah: Thus says the LORD, the God of your father David: I have heard your prayer and seen your tears. I will heal you: in three days you shall go up to the LORD'S temple; I will add fifteen years to your life. 6 I will rescue you and this city from the hand of the king of Assyria; I will be a shield to this city." 21 Isaiah then ordered a poultice of figs to be taken and applied to the boil, that he might recover. 22 Then Hezekiah asked, "What is the sign that I shall go up to the temple of the LORD?" 7 Isaiah answered: "This will be the sign for you from the LORD that he will do what he has promised: 8 See, I will make the shadow cast by the sun on the stairway to the terrace of Ahaz go back the ten steps it has advanced." So the sun came back the ten steps it had advanced. 9 The song of Hezekiah, king of Judah, after he had been sick and had recovered from his illness: 10 "Once I said, 'In the noontime of life I must depart! To the gates of the nether world I shall be consigned for the rest of my years.' 11 I said, 'I shall see the LORD no more in the land of the living. No longer shall I behold my fellow men among those who dwell in the world.' 12 My dwelling, like a shepherd's tent, is struck down and borne away from me; You have folded up my life, like a weaver who severs the last thread. Day and night you give me over to torment; 13 I cry out until the dawn. Like a lion, he breaks all my bones; day and night you give me over to torment. 14 Like a swallow, I utter shrill cries; I moan like a dove. My eyes grow weak, gazing heavenward: O Lord, I am in straits; be my surety! 15 What am I to say or tell him? He has done it! I shall go on through all my years despite the bitterness of my soul. 16 Those live whom the LORD protects; yours is the life of my spirit. You have given me health and life; 17 thus is my bitterness transformed into peace. You have preserved my life from the pit of destruction when you cast behind your back all my sins. 18 For it is not the nether world that gives you thanks, nor death that praises you; neither do those who go down into the pit await your kindness. 19 The living, the living give you thanks, as I do today. Fathers declare to their sons, O God, your faithfulness. 20 The LORD is our savior; we shall sing to stringed instruments in the house of the LORD all the days of our life."

Isaiah Chapter 39

1 At that time, when Merodach-baladan, son of Baladan, king of Babylon, heard that Hezekiah had recovered from his sickness, he sent letters and gifts to him. 2 Hezekiah was pleased with this, and therefore showed the messengers his treasury—the silver and gold, the spices and fine oil, his whole armory, and everything in his storerooms. There was nothing in his house or in his whole realm that he did not show them. 3 Then Isaiah the prophet came to King Hezekiah and asked him, "What did these men say to you? Where did they come from?" Hezekiah answered, "They came to me from a distant land, from Babylon." 4 "What did they see in your house?" he asked. Hezekiah replied, "They saw everything in my house; there is nothing in my storerooms that I did not show them." 5 Then Isaiah said to Hezekiah, "Hear the word of the LORD of hosts: 6 Behold, the days shall come when all that is in your house, and everything that your fathers have stored up until this day, shall be carried off to Babylon; nothing shall be left, says the LORD. 7 Some of your own bodily descendants shall be taken and made servants in the palace of the king of Babylon." 8 Hezekiah replied to Isaiah, "The word of the LORD which you have spoken is favorable." For he thought, "There will be peace and security in my lifetime."

Isaiah Chapter 40

1 Comfort, give comfort to my people, says your God. 2 Speak tenderly to Jerusalem, and proclaim to her that her service is at an end, her guilt is expiated; indeed, she has received from the hand of the LORD double for all her sins. 3 A voice cries out: In the desert prepare the way of the LORD! Make straight in the wasteland a highway for our God! 4 Every valley shall be filled in, every mountain and hill shall be made low; the rugged land shall be made a plain, the rough country, a broad valley. 5 Then the glory of the LORD shall be revealed, and all mankind shall see it together; for the mouth of the LORD has spoken. 6 A voice says, "Cry out!" I answer, "What shall I cry out?" "All mankind is grass, and all their glory like the flower of the field. 7 The grass withers, the flower wilts, when the breath of the LORD blows upon it. (So then, the people is the grass.) 8 Though the grass withers and the flower wilts, the word of our God stands forever." 9 Go up onto a high mountain, Zion, herald of glad tidings; cry out at the top of your voice, Jerusalem, herald of good news! Fear not to cry out and say to the cities of Judah: Here is your God! 10 Here comes with power the Lord GOD, who rules by his strong arm; here is his reward with him, his recompense before him. 11

Like a shepherd he feeds his flock; in his arms he gathers the lambs, carrying them in his bosom, and leading the ewes with care. 12 Who has cupped in his hand the waters of the sea, and marked off the heavens with a span? Who has held in a measure the dust of the earth, weighed the mountains in scales and the hills in a balance? 13 Who has directed the spirit of the LORD, or has instructed him as his counselor? 14 Whom did he consult to gain knowledge? Who taught him the path of judgment, or showed him the way of understanding? 15 Behold, the nations count as a drop in the bucket, as dust on the scales; the coastlands weigh no more than powder. 16 Lebanon would not suffice for fuel, nor its animals be enough for holocausts. 17 Before him all the nations are as nought, as nothing and void he accounts them. 18 To whom can you liken God? With what equal can you confront him? 19 An idol, cast by a craftsman, which the smith plates with gold and fits with silver chains? 20 Mulberry wood, the choice portion which a skilled craftsman picks out for himself, choosing timber that will not rot, to set up an idol that will not be unsteady? 21 Do you not know? Have you not heard? Was it not foretold you from the beginning? Have you not understood since the earth was founded? 22 He sits enthroned above the vault of the earth, and its inhabitants are like grasshoppers; he stretches out the heavens like a veil, spreads them out like a tent to dwell in. 23 He brings princes to nought and makes the rulers of the earth as nothing. 24 Scarcely are they planted or sown, scarcely is their stem rooted in the earth, when he breathes upon them and they wither, and the stormwind carries them away like straw. 25 To whom can you liken me as an equal? says the Holy One. 26 Lift up your eyes on high and see who has created these: he leads out their army and numbers them, calling them all by name. By his great might and the strength of his power not one of them is missing! 27 Why, O Jacob, do you say, and declare, O Israel, "My way is hidden from the LORD, and my right is disregarded by my God"? 28 Do you not know or have you not heard? The LORD is the eternal God, creator of the ends of the earth. He does not faint nor grow weary, and his knowledge is beyond scrutiny. 29 He gives strength to the fainting; for the weak he makes vigor abound. 30 Though young men faint and grow weary, and youths stagger and fall, 31 they that hope in the LORD will renew their strength, they will soar as with eagles' wings; they will run and not grow weary, walk and not grow faint.

Isaiah Chapter 41

1 Keep silence before me, O coastlands; you peoples, wait for my words! Let them draw near and speak; let us come together for judgment. 2 Who has stirred up from the East the champion of justice, and summoned him to be his attendant? To him he delivers the nations and subdues the kings; with his sword he reduces them to dust, with his bow, to driven straw. 3 He pursues them, passing on without loss, by a path his feet do not even tread. 4 Who has performed these deeds? He who has called forth the generations since the beginning. I, the LORD, am the first, and with the last I will also be. 5 The coastlands see, and fear; the ends of the earth tremble: these things are near, they come to pass. 6 They help one another; one says to the other, "Courage!" 7 The craftsman encourages the goldsmith, the one who beats with the hammer, him who strikes on the anvil; He says the soldering is good, and he fastens it with nails to steady it. 8 But you, Israel, my servant, Jacob, whom I have chosen, offspring of Abraham my friend—9 you whom I have taken from the ends of the earth and summoned from its far-off places, you whom I have called my servant, whom I have chosen and will not cast off—10 fear not, I am with you; be not dismayed; I am your God. I will strengthen you, and help you, and uphold you with my right hand of justice. 11 Yes, all shall be put to shame and disgrace who vent their anger against you; those shall perish and come to nought who offer resistance. 12 You shall seek out, but shall not find, those who strive against you; they shall be as nothing at all who do battle with you. 13 For I am the LORD, your God, who grasp your right hand; it is I who say to you, "Fear not, I will help you." 14 Fear not, O worm Jacob, O maggot Israel; I will help you, says the LORD; your redeemer is the Holy One of Israel. 15 I will make of you a threshing sledge, sharp, new, and double-edged, to thresh the mountains and crush them, to make the hills like chaff. 16 When you winnow them, the wind shall carry them off and the storm shall scatter them. But you shall rejoice in the LORD, and glory in the Holy One of Israel. 17 The afflicted and the needy seek water in vain, their tongues are parched with thirst. I, the LORD, will answer them; I, the God of Israel, will not forsake them. 18 I will open up rivers on the bare heights, and fountains in the broad valleys; I will turn the desert into a marshland, and the dry ground into springs of water. 19 I will plant in the desert the cedar, acacia, myrtle, and olive; I will set in the wasteland the cypress, together with the plane tree and the pine, 20 that all may see and know, observe and understand, that the hand of the LORD has done this, the Holy One of Israel has created

it. 21 Present your case, says the LORD; bring forward your reasons, says the King of Jacob. 22 Let them come near and foretell to us what it is that shall happen! What are the things of long ago? Tell us, that we may reflect on them and know their outcome; or declare to us the things to come! 23 Foretell the things that shall come afterward, that we may know that you are gods! Do something, good or evil, that will put us in awe and in fear. 24 Why, you are nothing and your work is nought! To choose you is an abomination. 25 I have stirred up one from the north, and he comes; from the east I summon him by name; he shall trample the rulers down like red earth, as the potter treads the clay. 26 Who announced this from the beginning, that we might know; beforehand, that we might say it is true? Not one of you foretold it, not one spoke; no one heard you say, 27 "The first news for Zion: they are coming now," or, "For Jerusalem I will pick out a bearer of the glad tidings." 28 When I look, there is not one, no one of them to give counsel, to make an answer when I question them. 29 Ah, all of them are nothing, their works are nought, their idols are empty wind!

Isaiah Chapter 42

1 Here is my servant whom I uphold, my chosen one with whom I am pleased, upon whom I have put my spirit; he shall bring forth justice to the nations, 2 not crying out, not shouting, not making his voice heard in the street. 3 A bruised reed he shall not break, and a smoldering wick he shall not quench, 4 until he establishes justice on the earth; the coastlands will wait for his teaching. 5 Thus says God, the LORD, who created the heavens and stretched them out, who spreads out the earth with its crops, who gives breath to its people and spirit to those who walk on it: 6 I, the LORD, have called you for the victory of justice, I have grasped you by the hand; I formed you, and set you as a covenant of the people, a light for the nations, 7 to open the eyes of the blind, to bring out prisoners from confinement, and from the dungeon, those who live in darkness. 8 I am the LORD, this is my name; my glory I give to no other, nor my praise to idols. 9 See, the earlier things have come to pass, new ones I now foretell; before they spring into being, I announce them to you. 10 Sing to the LORD a new song, his praise from the end of the earth: let the sea and what fills it resound, the coastlands, and those who dwell in them. 11 Let the steppe and its cities cry out, the villages where Kedar dwells; let the inhabitants of Sela exult, and shout from the top of the mountains. 12 Let them give glory to the LORD, and utter his praise in the coastlands. 13 The LORD goes forth like a hero, like a warrior he stirs up his ardor; he shouts out his battle cry, against his enemies he shows his might: 14 I have looked away, and kept silence, I have said nothing, holding myself in; but now, I cry out as a woman in labor, gasping and panting. 15 I will lay waste mountains and hills, all their herbage I will dry up; I will turn the rivers into marshes, and the marshes I will dry up. 16 I will lead the blind on their journey; by paths unknown I will guide them. I will turn darkness into light before them, and make crooked ways straight. These things I do for them, and I will not forsake them. 17 They shall be turned back in utter shame who trust in idols, who say to molten images, "You are our gods." 18 You who are deaf, listen, you who are blind, look and see! 19 Who is blind but my servant, or deaf like the messenger I send? 20 You see many things without taking note; your ears are open, but without hearing. 21 Though it pleased the LORD in his justice to make his law great and glorious, 22 this is a people despoiled and plundered, all of them trapped in holes, hidden away in prisons. They are taken as booty, with no one to rescue them, as spoil, with no one to demand their return. 23 Who of you gives ear to this? Who listens and pays heed for the time to come? 24 Who was it that gave Jacob to be plundered, Israel to the despoilers? Was it not the LORD, against whom we have sinned? In his ways they refused to walk, his law they disobeyed. 25 So he poured out wrath upon them, his anger, and the fury of battle; it blazed round about them, yet they did not realize, it burned them, but they took it not to heart.

Isaiah Chapter 43

1 But now, thus says the LORD, who created you, O Jacob, and formed you, O Israel: Fear not, for I have redeemed you; I have called you by name: you are mine. 2 When you pass through the water, I will be with you; in the rivers, you shall not drown. When you walk through fire, you shall not be burned; the flames shall not consume you. 3 For I am the LORD, your God, the Holy One of Israel, your savior. I give Egypt as your ransom, Ethiopia and Seba in return for you. 4 Because you are precious in my eyes and glorious, and because I love you, I give men in return for you and peoples in exchange for your life. 5 Fear not, for I am with you; from the east I will bring back your descendants, from the west I will gather you. 6 I will say to the north: Give them up! and to the south: Hold not back! Bring back my sons from afar, and my daughters from the ends of the earth: 7 Everyone who is named as mine, whom I created for my glory, whom I formed and made. 8 Lead out the people

who are blind though they have eyes, who are deaf though they have ears. 9 Let all the nations gather together, let the peoples assemble! Who among them could have revealed this, or foretold to us the earlier things? Let them produce witnesses to prove themselves right, that one may hear and say, "It is true!" 10 You are my witnesses, says the LORD, my servants whom I have chosen to know and believe in me and understand that it is I. Before me no god was formed, and after me there shall be none. 11 It is I, the LORD; there is no savior but me. 12 It is I who foretold, I who saved; I made it known, not any strange god among you; you are my witnesses, says the LORD. I am God, 13 yes, from eternity I am He; there is none who can deliver from my hand: who can countermand what I do? 14 Thus says the LORD, your redeemer, the Holy One of Israel: For your sakes I send to Babylon; I will lower all the bars, and the Chaldeans shall cry out in lamentation. 15 I am the LORD, your Holy One, the creator of Israel, your King. 16 Thus says the LORD, who opens a way in the sea and a path in the mighty waters, 17 who leads out chariots and horsemen, a powerful army, till they lie prostrate together, never to rise, snuffed out and quenched like a wick. 18 Remember not the events of the past, the things of long ago consider not; 19 See, I am doing something new! Now it springs forth, do you not perceive it? In the desert, I make a way, in the wasteland, rivers. 20 Wild beasts honor me, jackals and ostriches, for I put water in the desert and rivers in the wasteland for my chosen people to drink, 21 the people whom I formed for myself, that they might announce my praise. 22 Yet you did not call upon me, O Jacob, for you grew weary of me, O Israel. 23 You did not bring me sheep for your holocausts, nor honor me with your sacrifices. I did not exact from you the service of offerings, nor weary you for frankincense. 24 You did not buy me sweet cane for money, nor fill me with the fat of your sacrifices; instead, you burdened me with your sins, and wearied me with your crimes. 25 It is I, I, who wipe out, for my own sake, your offenses; your sins I remember no more. 26 Would you have me remember, have us come to trial? Speak up, prove your innocence! 27 Your first father sinned; your spokesmen rebelled against me 28 till I repudiated the holy gates, put Jacob under the ban, and exposed Israel to scorn.

Isaiah Chapter 44

1 Hear then, O Jacob, my servant, Israel, whom I have chosen. 2 Thus says the LORD who made you, your help, who formed you from the womb: Fear not, O Jacob, my servant, the darling whom I have chosen. 3 I will pour out water upon the thirsty ground, and streams upon the dry land; I will pour out my spirit upon your offspring, and my blessing upon your descendants. 4 They shall spring up amid the verdure like poplars beside the flowing waters. 5 One shall say, "I am the LORD'S," another shall be named after Jacob, and this one shall write on his hand, "The LORD'S," and Israel shall be his surname. 6 Thus says the LORD, Israel's King and redeemer, the LORD of hosts: I am the first and I am the last; there is no God but me. 7 Who is like me? Let him stand up and speak, make it evident, and confront me with it. Who of old announced future events? Let them foretell to us the things to come. 8 Fear not, be not troubled: did I not announce and foretell it long ago? You are my witnesses! Is there a God or any Rock besides me? 9 Idol makers all amount to nothing, and their precious works are of no avail, as they themselves give witness. To their shame, they neither see nor know anything; and they are more deaf than men are. 10 Indeed, all the associates of anyone who forms a god, or casts an idol to no purpose, will be put to shame; 11 they will all assemble and stand forth, to be reduced to fear and shame. 12 The smith fashions an iron image, works it over the coals, shapes it with hammers, and forges it with his strong arm. He is hungry and weak, drinks no water and becomes exhausted. 13 The carpenter stretches a line and marks with a stylus the outline of an idol. He shapes it with a plane and measures it off with a compass, making it like a man in appearance and dignity, to occupy a shrine. 14 He cuts down cedars, takes a holm or an oak, and lays hold of other trees of the forest, which the Lord had planted and the rain made grow 15 to serve man for fuel. With a part of their wood he warms himself, or makes a fire for baking bread; but with another part he makes a god which he adores, an idol which he worships. 16 Half of it he burns in the fire, and on its embers he roasts his meat; he eats what he has roasted until he is full, and then warms himself and says, "Ah! I am warm, I feel the fire." 17 Of what remains he makes a god, his idol, and prostrate before it in worship, he implores it, "Rescue me, for you are my god." 18 The idols have neither knowledge nor reason; their eyes are coated so that they cannot see, and their hearts so that they cannot understand. 19 Yet he does not reflect, nor have the intelligence and sense to say, "Half of the wood I burned in the fire, and on its embers I baked bread and roasted meat which I ate. Shall I then make an abomination out of the rest, or worship a block of wood?" 20 He is chasing ashes—a thing that cannot save itself when the flame consumes it; yet he does not say,

"Is not this thing in my right hand a fraud?" 21 Remember this, O Jacob, you, O Israel, who are my servant! I formed you to be a servant to me; O Israel, by me you shall never be forgotten: 22 I have brushed away your offenses like a cloud, your sins like a mist; return to me, for I have redeemed you. 23 Raise a glad cry, you heavens: the LORD has done this; shout, you depths of the earth. Break forth, you mountains, into song, you forest, with all your trees. For the LORD has redeemed Jacob, and shows his glory through Israel. 24 Thus says the LORD, your redeemer, who formed you from the womb: I am the LORD, who made all things, who alone stretched out the heavens; when I spread out the earth, who was with me? 25 It is I who bring to nought the omens of liars, who make fools of diviners; I turn wise men back and make their knowledge foolish. 26 It is I who confirm the words of my servants, I carry out the plan announced by my messengers; I say to Jerusalem: Be inhabited; to the cities of Judah: Be rebuilt; I will raise up their ruins. 27 It is I who said to the deep: Be dry; I will dry up your wellsprings. 28 I say of Cyrus: My shepherd, who fulfills my every wish; He shall say of Jerusalem, "Let her be rebuilt," and of the temple, "Let its foundations be laid."

Isaiah Chapter 45

1 Thus says the LORD to his anointed, Cyrus, whose right hand I grasp, subduing nations before him and making kings run in his service, opening doors before him and leaving the gates unbarred: 2 I will go before you and level the mountains; bronze doors I will shatter, and iron bars I will snap. 3 I will give you treasures out of the darkness, and riches that have been hidden away, that you may know that I am the LORD, the God of Israel, who calls you by your name. 4 For the sake of Jacob, my servant, of Israel my chosen one, I have called you by your name, giving you a title, though you knew me not. 5 I am the LORD and there is no other, there is no God besides me. It is I who arm you, though you know me not, 6 so that toward the rising and the setting of the sun men may know that there is none besides me. I am the LORD, there is no other; 7 I form the light and create the darkness, I make well-being and create woe; I, the LORD, do all these things. 8 Let justice descend, O heavens, like dew from above, like gentle rain let the skies drop it down. Let the earth open and salvation bud forth; let justice also spring up! I, the LORD, have created this. 9 Woe to him who contends with his Maker; a potsherd among potsherds of the earth! Dare the clay say to its modeler, "What are you doing?" or, "What you are making has no hands"? 10 Woe to him who asks a father, "What are you begetting?" or a woman, "What are you giving birth to?" 11 Thus says the LORD, the Holy One of Israel, his maker: You question me about my children, or prescribe the work of my hands for me! 12 It was I who made the earth and created mankind upon it; it was my hands that stretched out the heavens; I gave the order to all their host. 13 It was I who stirred up one for the triumph of justice; all his ways I make level. He shall rebuild my city and let my exiles go free without price or ransom, says the LORD of hosts. 14 Thus says the LORD: The earnings of Egypt, the gain of Ethiopia, and the Sabeans, tall of stature, shall come over to you and belong to you; they shall follow you, coming in chains. Before you they shall fall prostrate, saying in prayer: "With you only is God, and nowhere else; the gods are nought." 15 Truly with you God is hidden, the God of Israel, the savior! 16 Those are put to shame and disgrace who vent their anger against him; those go in disgrace who carve images. 17 Israel, you are saved by the LORD, saved forever! You shall never be put to shame or disgrace in future ages. 18 For thus says the LORD, the creator of the heavens, who is God, the designer and maker of the earth who established it, not creating it to be a waste, but designing it to be lived in: I am the LORD, and there is no other. 19 I have not spoken from hiding nor from some dark place of the earth, and I have not said to the descendants of Jacob, "Look for me in an empty waste." I, the LORD, promise justice, I foretell what is right. 20 Come and assemble, gather together, you fugitives from among the gentiles! They are without knowledge who bear wooden idols and pray to gods that cannot save. 21 Come here and declare in counsel together: Who announced this from the beginning and foretold it from of old? Was it not I, the LORD, besides whom there is no other God? There is no just and saving God but me. 22 Turn to me and be safe, all you ends of the earth, for I am God; there is no other! 23 By myself I swear, uttering my just decree and my unalterable word: To me every knee shall bend; by me every tongue shall swear, 24 saying, "Only in the LORD are just deeds and power. Before him in shame shall come all who vent their anger against him. 25 In the LORD shall be the vindication and the glory of all the descendants of Israel."

Isaiah Chapter 46

1 Bel bows down, Nebo stoops, their idols are upon beasts and cattle; they must be borne up on shoulders, carried as burdens by the weary. 2

They stoop and bow down together; unable to save those who bear them, they too go into captivity. 3 Hear me, O house of Jacob, all who remain of the house of Israel, my burden since your birth, whom I have carried from your infancy. 4 Even to your old age I am the same, even when your hair is gray I will bear you; it is I who have done this, I who will continue, and I who will carry you to safety. 5 Whom would you compare me with, as an equal, or match me against, as though we were alike? 6 There are those who pour out gold from a purse and weigh out silver on the scales; then they hire a goldsmith to make it into a god before which they fall down in worship. 7 They lift it to their shoulders to carry; when they set it in place again, it stays, and does not move from the spot. Although they cry out to it, it cannot answer; it delivers no one from distress. 8 Remember this and be firm, bear it well in mind, you rebels; remember the former things, those long ago: 9 I am God, there is no other; I am God, there is none like me. 10 At the beginning I foretell the outcome; in advance, things not yet done. I say that my plan shall stand, I accomplish my every purpose. 11 I call from the east a bird of prey, from a distant land, one to carry out my plan. Yes, I have spoken, I will accomplish it; I have planned it, and I will do it. 12 Listen to me, you fainthearted, you who seem far from the victory of justice: 13 I am bringing on my justice, it is not far off, my salvation shall not tarry; I will put salvation within Zion, and give to Israel my glory.

Isaiah Chapter 47

1 Come down, sit in the dust, O virgin daughter Babylon; sit on the ground, dethroned, O daughter of the Chaldeans. No longer shall you be called dainty and delicate. 2 Take the millstone and grind flour, remove your veil; strip off your train, bare your legs, pass through the streams. 3 Your nakedness shall be uncovered and your shame be seen; I will take vengeance, I will yield to no entreaty, says our redeemer, 4 whose name is the LORD of hosts, the Holy One of Israel. 5 Go into darkness and sit in silence, O daughter of the Chaldeans, no longer shall you be called sovereign mistress of kingdoms. 6 Angry at my people, I profaned my inheritance, and I gave them into your hand; but you showed them no mercy, and upon old men you laid a very heavy yoke. 7 You said, "I shall remain always, a sovereign mistress forever!" But you did not lay these things to heart, you disregarded their outcome. 8 Now hear this, voluptuous one, enthroned securely, saying to yourself, "I, and no one else! I shall never be a widow, or suffer the loss of my children" - 9 Both these things shall come to you suddenly, in a single day: complete bereavement and widowhood shall come upon you for your many sorceries and the great number of your spells; 10 because you felt secure in your wickedness, and said, "No one sees me." Your wisdom and your knowledge led you astray, and you said to yourself, "I, and no one else!" 11 But upon you shall come evil you will not know how to predict; disaster shall befall you which you cannot allay. Suddenly there shall come upon you ruin which you will not expect. 12 Keep up, now, your spells and your many sorceries. Perhaps you can make them avail, perhaps you can strike terror! 13 You wearied yourself with many consultations, at which you toiled from your youth; let the astrologers stand forth to save you, the stargazers who forecast at each new moon what would happen to you. 14 Lo, they are like stubble, fire consumes them; they cannot save themselves from the spreading flames. This is no warming ember, no fire to sit before. 15 Thus do your wizards serve you with whom you have toiled from your youth; each wanders his own way, with none to save you.

Isaiah Chapter 48

1 Hear this, O house of Jacob, called by the name Israel, sprung from the stock of Judah, you who swear by the name of the LORD and invoke the God of Israel without sincerity or justice, 2 though you are named after the holy city and rely on the God of Israel, whose name is the LORD of hosts. 3 Things of the past I foretold long ago, they went forth from my mouth, I let you hear of them; then suddenly I took action and they came to be. 4 Because I know that you are stubborn and that your neck is an iron sinew and your forehead bronze, 5 I foretold them to you of old; before they took place I let you hear of them, that you might not say, "My idol did them, my statue, my molten image commanded them." 6 Now that you have heard, look at all this; must you not admit it? From now on I announce new things to you, hidden events of which you knew not. 7 Now, not long ago, they are brought into being, and beforetime you did not hear of them, so that you cannot claim to have known them; 8 You neither heard nor knew, they did not reach your ears beforehand. Yes, I know you are utterly treacherous, a rebel you were called from birth. 9 For the sake of my name I restrain my anger, for the sake of my renown I hold it back from you, lest I should destroy you. 10 See, I have refined you like silver, tested you in the furnace of affliction. 11 For my sake, for my own sake, I do this; why should I suffer profanation? My glory I will not give to another. 12 Listen to me, Jacob,

Israel, whom I named! I, it is I who am the first, and also the last am I. 13 Yes, my hand laid the foundations of the earth; my right hand spread out the heavens. When I call them, they stand forth at once. 14 All of you assemble and listen: Who among you foretold these things? The LORD'S friend shall do his will against Babylon and the progeny of Chaldea. 15 I myself have spoken, I have called him, I have brought him, and his way succeeds! 16 Come near to me and hear this! Not from the beginning did I speak it in secret; At the time it comes to pass, I am present: "Now the Lord GOD has sent me, and his spirit." 17 Thus says the LORD, your redeemer, the Holy One of Israel: I, the LORD, your God, teach you what is for your good, and lead you on the way you should go. 18 If you would hearken to my commandments, your prosperity would be like a river, and your vindication like the waves of the sea; 19 Your descendants would be like the sand, and those born of your stock like its grains, their name never cut off or blotted out from my presence. 20 Go forth from Babylon, flee from Chaldea! With shouts of joy proclaim this, make it known; publish it to the ends of the earth, and say, "The LORD has redeemed his servant Jacob. 21 They did not thirst when he led them through dry lands; Water from the rock he set flowing for them; he cleft the rock, and waters welled forth." 22 (There is no peace for the wicked, says the LORD.)

Isaiah Chapter 49

1 Hear me, O coastlands, listen, O distant peoples. The LORD called me from birth, from my mother's womb he gave me my name. 2 He made of me a sharp-edged sword and concealed me in the shadow of his arm. He made me a polished arrow, in his quiver he hid me. 3 You are my servant, he said to me, Israel, through whom I show my glory. 4 Though I thought I had toiled in vain, and for nothing, uselessly, spent my strength, yet my reward is with the LORD, my recompense is with my God. 5 For now the LORD has spoken who formed me as his servant from the womb, that Jacob may be brought back to him and Israel gathered to him; and I am made glorious in the sight of the LORD, and my God is now my strength! 6 It is too little, he says, for you to be my servant, to raise up the tribes of Jacob, and restore the survivors of Israel; I will make you a light to the nations, that my salvation may reach to the ends of the earth. 7 Thus says the LORD, the redeemer and the Holy One of Israel, to the one despised, whom the nations abhor, the slave of rulers: When kings see you, they shall stand up, and princes shall prostrate themselves because of the LORD who is faithful, the Holy One of Israel who has chosen you. 8 Thus says the LORD: In a time of favor I answer you, on the day of salvation I help you, to restore the land and allot the desolate heritages, 9 saying to the prisoners: Come out! To those in darkness: Show yourselves! Along the ways they shall find pasture, on every bare height shall their pastures be. 10 They shall not hunger or thirst, nor shall the scorching wind or the sun strike them; for he who pities them leads them and guides them beside springs of water. 11 I will cut a road through all my mountains, and make my highways level. 12 See, some shall come from afar, others from the north and the west, and some from the land of Syene. 13 Sing out, O heavens, and rejoice, O earth, break forth into song, you mountains. For the LORD comforts his people and shows mercy to his afflicted. 14 But Zion said, "The LORD has forsaken me; my Lord has forgotten me." 15 Can a mother forget her infant, be without tenderness for the child of her womb? Even should she forget, I will never forget you. 16 See, upon the palms of my hands I have written your name; your walls are ever before me. 17 Your rebuilders make haste, as those who tore you down and laid you waste go forth from you; 18 Look about and see, they are all gathering and coming to you. As I live, says the LORD, you shall be arrayed with them all as with adornments, like a bride you shall fasten them on you. 19 Though you were waste and desolate, a land of ruins, now you shall be too small for your inhabitants, while those who swallowed you up will be far away. 20 The children whom you had lost shall yet say to you, "This place is too small for me, make room for me to live in." 21 You shall ask yourself: "Who has borne me these? I was bereft and barren (exiled and repudiated); who has reared them? I was left all alone; where then do these come from?" 22 Thus says the Lord GOD: See, I will lift up my hand to the nations, and raise my signal to the peoples; they shall bring your sons in their arms, and your daughters shall be carried on their shoulders. 23 Kings shall be your foster fathers, their princesses your nurses; bowing to the ground, they shall worship you and lick the dust at your feet. Then you shall know that I am the LORD, and those who hope in me shall never be disappointed. 24 Thus says the LORD: Can booty be taken from a warrior? or captives be rescued from a tyrant? 25 Yes, captives can be taken from a warrior, and booty be rescued from a tyrant; those who oppose you I will oppose, and your sons I will save. 26 I will make your oppressors eat their own flesh, and they shall be drunk with their own

blood as with the juice of the grape. All mankind shall know that I, the LORD, am your savior, your redeemer, the Mighty One of Jacob.

Isaiah Chapter 50

1 Thus says the LORD: Where is the bill of divorce with which I dismissed your mother? Or to which of my creditors have I sold you? It was for your sins that you were sold, for your crimes that your mother was dismissed. 2 Why was no one there when I came? Why did no one answer when I called? Is my hand too short to ransom? Have I not the strength to deliver? Lo, with my rebuke I dry up the sea, I turn rivers into a desert; their fish rot for lack of water, and die of thirst. 3 I clothe the heavens in mourning, and make sackcloth their vesture. 4 The Lord GOD has given me a well-trained tongue, that I might know how to speak to the weary a word that will rouse them. Morning after morning he opens my ear that I may hear; 5 And I have not rebelled, have not turned back. 6 I gave my back to those who beat me, my cheeks to those who plucked my beard; my face I did not shield from buffets and spitting. 7 The Lord GOD is my help, therefore I am not disgraced; I have set my face like flint, knowing that I shall not be put to shame. 8 He is near who upholds my right; if anyone wishes to oppose me, let us appear together. Who disputes my right? Let him confront me. 9 See, the Lord GOD is my help; who will prove me wrong? Lo, they will all wear out like cloth, the moth will eat them up. 10 Who among you fears the LORD, heeds his servant's voice, and walks in darkness without any light, trusting in the name of the LORD and relying on his God? 11 All of you kindle flames and carry about you fiery darts; walk by the light of your own fire and by the flares you have burnt! This is your fate from my hand: you shall lie down in a place of pain.

Isaiah Chapter 51

1 Listen to me, you who pursue justice, who seek the LORD; look to the rock from which you were hewn, to the pit from which you were quarried. 2 Look to Abraham, your father, and to Sarah, who gave you birth; when he was but one I called him, I blessed him and made him many. 3 Yes, the LORD shall comfort Zion and have pity on all her ruins; her deserts he shall make like Eden, her wasteland like the garden of the LORD; joy and gladness shall be found in her, thanksgiving and the sound of song. 4 Be attentive to me, my people; my folk, give ear to me. For law shall go forth from my presence, and my judgment, as the light of the peoples. 5 I will make my justice come speedily; my salvation shall go forth and my arm shall judge the nations. In me shall the coastlands hope, and my arm they shall await. 6 Raise your eyes to the heavens, and look at the earth below; though the heavens grow thin like smoke, the earth wears out like a garment and its inhabitants die like flies, my salvation shall remain forever, and my justice shall never be dismayed. 7 Hear me, you who know justice, you people who have my teaching at heart: fear not the reproach of men, be not dismayed at their revilings. 8 They shall be like a garment eaten by moths, like wool consumed by grubs; but my justice shall remain forever and my salvation for all generations. 9 Awake, awake, put on strength, O arm of the LORD! Awake as in the days of old, in ages long ago! Was it not you who crushed Rahab, you who pierced the dragon? 10 Was it not you who dried up the sea, the waters of the great deep, who made the depths of the sea into a way for the redeemed to pass over? 11 Those whom the LORD has ransomed will return and enter Zion singing, crowned with everlasting joy; they will meet with joy and gladness, sorrow and mourning will flee. 12 I, it is I who comfort you. Can you then fear mortal man, who is human only, to be looked upon as grass, 13 and forget the LORD, your maker, who stretched out the heavens and laid the foundations of the earth? All the day you are in constant dread of the fury of the oppressor; but when he sets himself to destroy, what is there of the oppressor's fury? 14 The oppressed shall soon be released; they shall not die and go down into the pit, nor shall they want for bread. 15 For I am the LORD, your God, who stirs up the sea so that its waves roar; the LORD of hosts by name. 16 I have put my words into your mouth and shielded you in the shadow of my hand, I, who stretched out the heavens, who laid the foundations of the earth, who say to Zion: You are my people. 17 Awake, awake! Arise, O Jerusalem, you who drank at the LORD'S hand the cup of his wrath; who drained to the dregs the bowl of staggering! 18 She has no one to guide her of all the sons she bore; she has no one to grasp her by the hand, of all the sons she reared! 19 Your misfortunes are double; who is there to condole with you? Desolation and destruction, famine and sword! Who is there to comfort you? 20 Your sons lie helpless at every street corner like antelopes in a net. They are filled with the wrath of the LORD, the rebuke of your God. 21 But now, hear this, O afflicted one, drunk, but not with wine, 22 thus says the LORD, your Master, your God, who defends his people: See, I am taking from your hand the cup of staggering; the bowl of my wrath you shall no longer drink. 23 I will put it into the hands of your

tormentors, those who ordered you to bow down, that they might walk over you, while you offered your back like the ground, like the street for them to walk on.

Isaiah Chapter 52

1 Awake, awake! Put on your strength, O Zion; put on your glorious garments, O Jerusalem, holy city. No longer shall the uncircumcised or the unclean enter you. 2 Shake off the dust, ascend to the throne, Jerusalem; loose the bonds from your neck, O captive daughter Zion! 3 For thus says the LORD: You were sold for nothing, and without money you shall be redeemed. 4 Thus says the Lord GOD: To Egypt in the beginning my people went down, to sojourn there; Assyria, too, oppressed them for nought. 5 But now, what am I to do here? says the LORD. My people have been taken away without redress; their rulers make a boast of it, says the LORD; all the day my name is constantly reviled. 6 Therefore on that day my people shall know my renown, that it is I who have foretold it. Here I am! 7 How beautiful upon the mountains are the feet of him who brings glad tidings, announcing peace, bearing good news, announcing salvation, and saying to Zion, "Your God is King!" 8 Hark! Your watchmen raise a cry, together they shout for joy, for they see directly, before their eyes, the LORD restoring Zion. 9 Break out together in song, O ruins of Jerusalem! For the LORD comforts his people, he redeems Jerusalem. 10 The LORD has bared his holy arm in the sight of all the nations; all the ends of the earth will behold the salvation of our God. 11 Depart, depart, come forth from there, touch nothing unclean! Out from there! Purify yourselves, you who carry the vessels of the LORD. 12 Yet not in fearful haste will you come out, nor leave in headlong flight, for the LORD comes before you, and your rear guard is the God of Israel. 13 See, my servant shall prosper, he shall be raised high and greatly exalted. 14 Even as many were amazed at him—so marred was his look beyond that of man, and his appearance beyond that of mortals— 15 so shall he startle many nations, because of him kings shall stand speechless; for those who have not been told shall see, those who have not heard shall ponder it.

Isaiah Chapter 53

1 Who will believe what we have heard? To whom has the arm of the LORD been revealed? 2 He grew up like a sapling before him, like a shoot from the parched earth; there was in him no stately bearing to make us look at him, nor appearance that would attract us to him. 3 He was spurned and avoided by men, a man of suffering, accustomed to infirmity, one of those from whom men hide their faces, spurned, and we held him in no esteem. 4 Yet it was our infirmities that he bore, our sufferings that he endured, while we thought of him as stricken, as one smitten by God and afflicted. 5 But he was pierced for our offenses, crushed for our sins; upon him was the chastisement that makes us whole, by his stripes we were healed. 6 We had all gone astray like sheep, each following his own way; but the LORD laid upon him the guilt of us all. 7 Though he was harshly treated, he submitted and opened not his mouth; like a lamb led to the slaughter or a sheep before the shearers, he was silent and opened not his mouth. 8 Oppressed and condemned, he was taken away, and who would have thought any more of his destiny? When he was cut off from the land of the living, and smitten for the sin of his people, 9 a grave was assigned him among the wicked and a burial place with evildoers, though he had done no wrong nor spoken any falsehood. 10 But the LORD was pleased to crush him in infirmity. If he gives his life as an offering for sin, he shall see his descendants in a long life, and the will of the LORD shall be accomplished through him. 11 Because of his affliction he shall see the light in fullness of days; through his suffering, my servant shall justify many, and their guilt he shall bear. 12 Therefore I will give him his portion among the great, and he shall divide the spoils with the mighty, because he surrendered himself to death and was counted among the wicked; and he shall take away the sins of many, and win pardon for their offenses.

Isaiah Chapter 54

1 Raise a glad cry, you barren one who did not bear, break forth in jubilant song, you who were not in labor, for more numerous are the children of the deserted wife than the children of her who has a husband, says the LORD. 2 Enlarge the space for your tent, spread out your tent cloths unsparingly; lengthen your ropes and make firm your stakes. 3 For you shall spread abroad to the right and to the left; your descendants shall dispossess the nations and shall people the desolate cities. 4 Fear not, you shall not be put to shame; you need not blush, for you shall not be disgraced. The shame of your youth you shall forget, the reproach of your widowhood no longer remember. 5 For he who has become your husband is your Maker; his name is the LORD of hosts; your redeemer is the Holy One of Israel, called God of all the earth. 6 The LORD calls you back, like a wife forsaken and grieved in spirit, a

wife married in youth and then cast off, says your God. 7 For a brief moment I abandoned you, but with great tenderness I will take you back. 8 In an outburst of wrath, for a moment I hid my face from you; but with enduring love I take pity on you, says the LORD, your redeemer. 9 This is for me like the days of Noah, when I swore that the waters of Noah should never again deluge the earth; so I have sworn not to be angry with you, or to rebuke you. 10 Though the mountains leave their place and the hills be shaken, my love shall never leave you nor my covenant of peace be shaken, says the LORD, who has mercy on you. 11 O afflicted one, storm-battered and unconsoled, I lay your pavements in carnelians, and your foundations in sapphires; 12 I will make your battlements of rubies, your gates of carbuncles, and all your walls of precious stones. 13 All your sons shall be taught by the LORD, and great shall be the peace of your children. 14 In justice shall you be established, far from the fear of oppression, where destruction cannot come near you. 15 Should there be any attack, it shall not be of my making; whoever attacks you shall fall before you. 16 Lo, I have created the craftsman who blows on the burning coals and forges weapons as his work; it is I also who have created the destroyer to work havoc. 17 No weapon fashioned against you shall prevail; every tongue you shall prove false that launches an accusation against you. This is the lot of the servants of the LORD, their vindication from me, says the LORD.

Isaiah Chapter 55

1 All you who are thirsty, come to the water! You who have no money, come, receive grain and eat; come, without paying and without cost, drink wine and milk! 2 Why spend your money for what is not bread; your wages for what fails to satisfy? Heed me, and you shall eat well, you shall delight in rich fare. 3 Come to me heedfully, listen, that you may have life. I will renew with you the everlasting covenant, the benefits assured to David. 4 As I made him a witness to the peoples, a leader and commander of nations, 5 so shall you summon a nation you knew not, and nations that knew you not shall run to you, because of the LORD, your God, the Holy One of Israel, who has glorified you. 6 Seek the LORD while he may be found, call him while he is near. 7 Let the scoundrel forsake his way, and the wicked man his thoughts; let him turn to the LORD for mercy; to our God, who is generous in forgiving. 8 For my thoughts are not your thoughts, nor are your ways my ways, says the LORD. 9 As high as the heavens are above the earth, so high are my ways above your ways and my thoughts above your thoughts. 10 For just as from the heavens the rain and snow come down and do not return there till they have watered the earth, making it fertile and fruitful, giving seed to him who sows and bread to him who eats, 11 so shall my word be that goes forth from my mouth; it shall not return to me void, but shall do my will, achieving the end for which I sent it. 12 Yes, in joy you shall depart, in peace you shall be brought back; mountains and hills shall break out in song before you, and all the trees of the countryside shall clap their hands. 13 In place of the thornbush, the cypress shall grow, instead of nettles, the myrtle. This shall be to the LORD'S renown, an everlasting imperishable sign.

Isaiah Chapter 56

1 Thus says the LORD: Observe what is right, do what is just; for my salvation is about to come, my justice, about to be revealed. 2 Happy is the man who does this, the son of man who holds to it; who keeps the sabbath free from profanation, and his hand from any evildoing. 3 Let not the foreigner say, when he would join himself to the LORD, "The LORD will surely exclude me from his people"; nor let the eunuch say, "See, I am a dry tree." 4 For thus says the LORD: To the eunuchs who observe my sabbaths and choose what pleases me and hold fast to my covenant, 5 I will give, in my house and within my walls, a monument and a name better than sons and daughters; an eternal, imperishable name will I give them. 6 And the foreigners who join themselves to the LORD, ministering to him, loving the name of the LORD, and becoming his servants—all who keep the sabbath free from profanation and hold to my covenant, 7 them I will bring to my holy mountain and make joyful in my house of prayer; their holocausts and sacrifices will be acceptable on my altar, for my house shall be called a house of prayer for all peoples. 8 Thus says the Lord GOD, who gathers the dispersed of Israel: Others will I gather to him besides those already gathered. 9 All you wild beasts of the field, come and eat, all you beasts in the forest! 10 My watchmen are blind, all of them unaware; they are all dumb dogs, they cannot bark; dreaming as they lie there, loving their sleep. 11 They are relentless dogs, they know not when they have enough. These are the shepherds who know no discretion; each of them goes his own way, every one of them to his own gain: 12 "Come, I will fetch some wine; let us carouse with strong drink, and tomorrow will be like today, or even greater."

Isaiah Chapter 57

1 The just man perishes, but no one takes it to heart; devout men are swept away, with no one giving it a thought. Though he is taken away from the presence of evil, the just man 2 enters into peace; there is rest on his couch for the sincere, straightforward man. 3 But you, draw near, you sons of a sorceress, adulterous, wanton race! 4 Of whom do you make sport, at whom do you open wide your mouth, and put out your tongue? Are you not rebellious children, a worthless race; 5 you who are in heat among the terebinths, under every green tree; you who immolate children in the wadies, behind the crevices in the cliffs? 6 Among the smooth stones of the wadi is your portion, these are your lot; to these you poured out libations, and brought offerings. Should I decide not to punish these things? 7 Upon a high and lofty mountain you made your bed, and there you went up to offer sacrifice. 8 Behind the door and the doorpost you placed your indecent symbol. Deserting me, you spread out your high, wide bed; and of those whose embraces you love you carved the symbol and gazed upon it 9 while you approached the king with scented oil, and multiplied your perfumes; while you sent your ambassadors far away, down even to the nether world. 10 Though worn out by your many misdeeds, you never said, "It is hopeless"; new strength you found, and so you did not weaken. 11 Of whom were you afraid? Whom did you fear, that you became false and did not remember me or give me any thought? Was I to remain silent and unseeing, so that you would not have me to fear? 12 I will expose your justice and your works; 13 they shall not help you when you cry out, nor save you in your distress. All these the wind shall carry off, the breeze shall bear away; but he who takes refuge in me shall inherit the land, and possess my holy mountain. 14 Build up, build up, prepare the way, remove the stumbling blocks from my people's path. 15 For thus says he who is high and exalted, living eternally, whose name is the Holy One: On high I dwell, and in holiness, and with the crushed and dejected in spirit, to revive the spirits of the dejected, to revive the hearts of the crushed. 16 I will not accuse forever, nor always be angry; for their spirits would faint before me, the souls that I have made. 17 Because of their wicked avarice I was angry, and struck them, hiding myself in wrath, as they went their own rebellious way. 18 I saw their ways, but I will heal them and lead them; I will give full comfort to them and to those who mourn for them, 19 I, the Creator, who gave them life. Peace, peace to the far and the near, says the LORD; and I will heal them. 20 But the wicked are like the tossing sea which cannot be calmed, and its waters cast up mud and filth. 21 No peace for the wicked! says my God.

Isaiah Chapter 58

1 Cry out full-throated and unsparingly, lift up your voice like a trumpet blast; tell my people their wickedness, and the house of Jacob their sins. 2 They seek me day after day, and desire to know my ways, like a nation that has done what is just and not abandoned the law of their God; they ask me to declare what is due them, pleased to gain access to God. 3 "Why do we fast, and you do not see it? Afflict ourselves, and you take no note of it?" Lo, on your fast day you carry out your own pursuits, and drive all your laborers. 4 Yes, your fast ends in quarreling and fighting, striking with wicked claw. Would that today you might fast so as to make your voice heard on high! 5 Is this the manner of fasting I wish, of keeping a day of penance: that a man bow his head like a reed, and lie in sackcloth and ashes? Do you call this a fast, a day acceptable to the LORD? 6 This, rather, is the fasting that I wish: releasing those bound unjustly, untying the thongs of the yoke; setting free the oppressed, breaking every yoke; 7 sharing your bread with the hungry, sheltering the oppressed and the homeless; clothing the naked when you see them, and not turning your back on your own. 8 Then your light shall break forth like the dawn, and your wound shall quickly be healed; your vindication shall go before you, and the glory of the LORD shall be your rear guard. 9 Then you shall call, and the LORD will answer; you shall cry for help, and he will say: Here I am! If you remove from your midst oppression, false accusation, and malicious speech; 10 if you bestow your bread on the hungry and satisfy the afflicted; then light shall rise for you in the darkness, and the gloom shall become for you like midday. 11 Then the LORD will guide you always and give you plenty even on the parched land. He will renew your strength, and you shall be like a watered garden, like a spring whose water never fails. 12 The ancient ruins shall be rebuilt for your sake, and the foundations from ages past you shall raise up; "Repairer of the breach," they shall call you, "Restorer of ruined homesteads." 13 If you hold back your foot on the sabbath from following your own pursuits on my holy day; if you call the sabbath a delight, and the LORD'S holy day honorable; if you honor it by not following your ways, seeking your own interests, or speaking with malice – 14 then you shall delight in the LORD, and I will

make you ride on the heights of the earth; I will nourish you with the heritage of Jacob, your father, for the mouth of the LORD has spoken.

Isaiah Chapter 59

1 Lo, the hand of the LORD is not too short to save, nor his ear too dull to hear. 2 Rather, it is your crimes that separate you from your God, it is your sins that make him hide his face so that he will not hear you. 3 For your hands are stained with blood, your fingers with guilt; your lips speak falsehood, and your tongue utters deceit. 4 No one brings suit justly, no one pleads truthfully; they trust in emptiness and tell lies; they conceive mischief and bring forth malice. 5 They hatch adders' eggs, and weave spiders' webs: whoever eats their eggs will die, if one of them is pressed, it will hatch as a viper. 6 Their webs cannot serve as clothing, nor can they cover themselves with their works. Their works are evil works, and deeds of violence come from their hands. 7 Their feet run to evil, and they are quick to shed innocent blood; their thoughts are destructive thoughts, plunder and ruin are on their highways. 8 The way of peace they know not, and there is nothing that is right in their paths; their ways they have made crooked, whoever treads them knows no peace. 9 That is why right is far from us and justice does not reach us. We look for light, and lo, darkness; for brightness, but we walk in gloom! 10 Like blind men we grope along the wall, like people without eyes we feel our way. We stumble at midday as at dusk, in Stygian darkness, like the dead. 11 We all growl like bears, like doves we moan without ceasing. We look for right, but it is not there; for salvation, and it is far from us. 12 For our offenses before you are many, our sins bear witness against us. Yes, our offenses are present to us, and our crimes we know: 13 transgressing, and denying the LORD, turning back from following our God, threatening outrage, and apostasy, uttering words of falsehood the heart has conceived. 14 Right is repelled, and justice stands far off; for truth stumbles in the public square, uprightness cannot enter. 15 Honesty is lacking, and the man who turns from evil is despoiled. The LORD saw this, and was aggrieved that right did not exist. 16 He saw that there was no one, and was appalled that there was none to intervene; so his own arm brought about the victory, and his justice lent him its support. 17 He put on justice as his breastplate, salvation as the helmet on his head; he clothed himself with garments of vengeance, wrapped himself in a mantle of zeal. 18 He repays his enemies their deserts, and requites his foes with wrath. 19 Those in the west shall fear the name of the LORD, and those in the east, his glory; for it shall come like a pent-up river which the breath of the LORD drives on. 20 He shall come to Zion a redeemer to those of Jacob who turn from sin, says the LORD. 21 This is the covenant with them which I myself have made, says the LORD: My spirit which is upon you and my words that I have put into your mouth shall never leave your mouth, nor the mouths of your children nor the mouths of your children's children from now on and forever, says the LORD.

Isaiah Chapter 60

1 Rise up in splendor! Your light has come, the glory of the Lord shines upon you. 2 See, darkness covers the earth, and thick clouds cover the peoples; but upon you the LORD shines, and over you appears his glory. 3 Nations shall walk by your light, and kings by your shining radiance. 4 Raise your eyes and look about; they all gather and come to you: your sons come from afar, and your daughters in the arms of their nurses. 5 Then you shall be radiant at what you see, your heart shall throb and overflow, for the riches of the sea shall be emptied out before you, the wealth of nations shall be brought to you. 6 Caravans of camels shall fill you, dromedaries from Midian and Ephah; all from Sheba shall come bearing gold and frankincense, and proclaiming the praises of the LORD. 7 All the flocks of Kedar shall be gathered for you, the rams of Nebaioth shall be your sacrifices; they will be acceptable offerings on my altar, and I will enhance the splendor of my house. 8 What are these that fly along like clouds, like doves to their cotes? 9 All the vessels of the sea are assembled, with the ships of Tarshish in the lead, to bring your children from afar with their silver and gold, in the name of the LORD, your God, the Holy One of Israel, who has glorified you. 10 Foreigners shall rebuild your walls, and their kings shall be your attendants; though I struck you in my wrath, yet in my good will I have shown you mercy. 11 Your gates shall stand open constantly; day and night they shall not be closed but shall admit to you the wealth of nations, and their kings, in the vanguard. 12 For the people or kingdom shall perish that does not serve you; those nations shall be utterly destroyed. 13 The glory of Lebanon shall come to you: the cypress, the plane, and the pine, to bring beauty to my sanctuary, and glory to the place where I set my feet. 14 The children of your oppressors shall come, bowing low before you; all those who despised you shall fall prostrate at your feet. They shall call you "City of the LORD," "Zion of the Holy

One of Israel." 15 Once you were forsaken, hated, and unvisited, now I will make you the pride of the ages, a joy to generation after generation. 16 You shall suck the milk of nations and be nursed at royal breasts; you shall know that I, the LORD, am your savior, your redeemer, the Mighty One of Jacob. 17 In place of bronze I will bring gold, instead of iron, silver; in place of wood, bronze, instead of stones, iron; I will appoint peace your governor, and justice your ruler. 18 No longer shall violence be heard of in your land, or plunder and ruin within your boundaries. You shall call your walls "Salvation" and your gates "Praise." 19 No longer shall the sun be your light by day, nor the brightness of the moon shine upon you at night; the LORD shall be your light forever, your God shall be your glory. 20 No longer shall your sun go down, or your moon withdraw, for the LORD will be your light forever, and the days of your mourning shall be at an end. 21 Your people shall all be just; they shall always possess the land. They, the bud of my planting, my handiwork to show my glory. 22 The smallest shall become a thousand, the youngest, a mighty nation; I, the LORD, will swiftly accomplish these things when their time comes.

Isaiah Chapter 61

1 The spirit of the Lord GOD is upon me, because the LORD has anointed me; He has sent me to bring glad tidings to the lowly, to heal the brokenhearted, to proclaim liberty to the captives and release to the prisoners, 2 to announce a year of favor from the LORD and a day of vindication by our God, to comfort all who mourn; 3 to place on those who mourn in Zion a diadem instead of ashes, to give them oil of gladness in place of mourning, a glorious mantle instead of a listless spirit. They will be called oaks of justice, planted by the LORD to show his glory. 4 They shall rebuild the ancient ruins, the former wastes they shall raise up, and restore the ruined cities, desolate now for generations. 5 Strangers shall stand ready to pasture your flocks, foreigners shall be your farmers and vinedressers. 6 You yourselves shall be named priests of the LORD, ministers of our God you shall be called. You shall eat the wealth of the nations and boast of riches from them. 7 Since their shame was double and disgrace and spittle were their portion, they shall have a double inheritance in their land, everlasting joy shall be theirs. 8 For I, the LORD, love what is right, I hate robbery and injustice; I will give them their recompense faithfully, a lasting covenant I will make with them. 9 Their descendants shall be renowned among the nations, and their offspring among the peoples; all who see them shall acknowledge them as a race the LORD has blessed. 10 I rejoice heartily in the LORD, in my God is the joy of my soul; for he has clothed me with a robe of salvation, and wrapped me in a mantle of justice, like a bridegroom adorned with a diadem, like a bride bedecked with her jewels. 11 As the earth brings forth its plants, and a garden makes its growth spring up, so will the Lord GOD make justice and praise spring up before all the nations.

Isaiah Chapter 62

1 For Zion's sake I will not be silent, for Jerusalem's sake I will not be quiet, until her vindication shines forth like the dawn and her victory like a burning torch. 2 Nations shall behold your vindication, and all kings your glory; you shall be called by a new name pronounced by the mouth of the LORD. 3 You shall be a glorious crown in the hand of the LORD, a royal diadem held by your God. 4 No more shall men call you "Forsaken," or your land "Desolate," but you shall be called "My Delight," and your land "Espoused." For the LORD delights in you, and makes your land his spouse. 5 As a young man marries a virgin, your Builder shall marry you; and as a bridegroom rejoices in his bride, so shall your God rejoice in you. 6 Upon your walls, O Jerusalem, I have stationed watchmen; never, by day or by night, shall they be silent. O you who are to remind the LORD, take no rest 7 and give no rest to him, until he re-establishes Jerusalem and makes of it the pride of the earth. 8 The LORD has sworn by his right hand and by his mighty arm: No more will I give your grain as food to your enemies; nor shall foreigners drink your wine, for which you toiled. 9 But you who harvest the grain shall eat it, and you shall praise the LORD; you who gather the grapes shall drink the wine in the courts of my sanctuary. 10 Pass through, pass through the gates, prepare the way for the people; build up, build up the highway, clear it of stones, raise up a standard over the nations. 11 See, the LORD proclaims to the ends of the earth: Say to daughter Zion, your savior comes! Here is his reward with him, his recompense before him. 12 They shall be called the holy people, the redeemed of the LORD, and you shall be called "Frequented," a city that is not forsaken.

Isaiah Chapter 63

1 Who is this that comes from Edom, in crimsoned garments, from Bozrah—this one arrayed in majesty, marching in the greatness of his strength? "It is I, I who announce vindication, I who am mighty to save." 2 Why is your apparel red, and your garments like those of the wine

presser? 3 "The wine press I have trodden alone, and of my people there was no one with me. I trod them in my anger, and trampled them down in my wrath; their blood spurted on my garments; all my apparel I stained. 4 For the day of vengeance was in my heart, my year for redeeming was at hand. 5 I looked about, but there was no one to help, I was appalled that there was no one to lend support; so my own arm brought about the victory and my own wrath lent me its support. 6 I trampled down the peoples in my anger, I crushed them in my wrath, and I let their blood run out upon the ground." 7 The favors of the LORD I will recall, the glorious deeds of the LORD, because of all he has done for us; for he is good to the house of Israel, he has favored us according to his mercy and his great kindness. 8 He said: They are indeed my people, children who are not disloyal; so he became their savior 9 in their every affliction. It was not a messenger or an angel, but he himself who saved them. Because of his love and pity he redeemed them himself, lifting them and carrying them all the days of old. 10 But they rebelled, and grieved his holy spirit; so he turned on them like an enemy, and fought against them. 11 Then they remembered the days of old and Moses, his servant; where is he who brought up out of the sea the shepherd of his flock? Where is he who put his holy spirit in their midst; 12 whose glorious arm was the guide at Moses' right; who divided the waters before them, winning for himself eternal renown; 13 who led them without stumbling through the depths like horses in the open country, 14 like cattle going down into the plain, the spirit of the LORD guiding them? Thus you led your people, bringing glory to your name. 15 Look down from heaven and regard us from your holy and glorious palace! Where is your zealous care and your might, your surge of pity and your mercy? O Lord, hold not back, 16 for you are our father. Were Abraham not to know us, nor Israel to acknowledge us, you, LORD, are our father, our redeemer you are named forever. 17 Why do you let us wander, O LORD, from your ways, and harden our hearts so that we fear you not? Return for the sake of your servants, the tribes of your heritage. 18 Why have the wicked invaded your holy place, why have our enemies trampled your sanctuary? 19 Too long have we been like those you do not rule, who do not bear your name. Oh, that you would rend the heavens and come down, with the mountains quaking before you.

Isaiah Chapter 64

1 As when brushwood is set ablaze, or fire makes the water boil! Thus your name would be made known to your enemies and the nations would tremble before you, 2 While you wrought awesome deeds we could not hope for, 3 such as they had not heard of from of old. No ear has ever heard, no eye ever seen, any God but you doing such deeds for those who wait for him. 4 Would that you might meet us doing right, that we were mindful of you in our ways! Behold, you are angry, and we are sinful; 5 all of us have become like unclean men, all our good deeds are like polluted rags; we have all withered like leaves, and our guilt carries us away like the wind. 6 There is none who calls upon your name, who rouses himself to cling to you; for you have hidden your face from us and have delivered us up to our guilt. 7 Yet, O LORD, you are our father; we are the clay and you the potter: we are all the work of your hands. 8 Be not so very angry, LORD, keep not our guilt forever in mind; look upon us, who are all your people. 9 Your holy cities have become a desert, Zion is a desert, Jerusalem a waste. 10 Our holy and glorious temple in which our fathers praised you has been burned with fire; all that was dear to us is laid waste. 11 Can you hold back, O LORD, after all this? Can you remain silent, and afflict us so severely?

Isaiah Chapter 65

1 I was ready to respond to those who asked me not, to be found by those who sought me not. I said: Here I am! Here I am! To a nation that did not call upon my name. 2 I have stretched out my hands all the day to a rebellious people, who walk in evil paths and follow their own thoughts, 3 People who provoke me continually, to my face, offering sacrifices in the groves and burning incense on bricks, 4 Living among the graves and spending the night in caverns, eating swine's flesh, with carrion broth in their dishes, 5 Crying out, "Hold back, do not touch me; I am too sacred for you!" These things enkindle my wrath, a fire that burns all the day. 6 Lo, before me it stands written; I will not be quiet until I have paid in full 7 your crimes and the crimes of your fathers as well, says the LORD. Since they burned incense on the mountains, and disgraced me on the hills, I will at once pour out in full measure their recompense into their laps. 8 Thus says the LORD: When the juice is pressed from grapes, men say, "Do not discard them, for there is still good in them"; thus will I do with my servants: I will not discard them all; 9 From Jacob I will save offspring, from Judah, those who are to inherit my mountains; my chosen ones shall inherit the land, my servants shall dwell there. 10 Sharon shall be a pasture for the flocks and the valley of Achor a resting place for the cattle of my people who have sought me. 11 But you who forsake the LORD, forgetting my holy mountain, you who spread a table for Fortune and fill cups of blended wine for Destiny, 12 You I will destine for the sword; you shall all go down in slaughter. Since I called and you did not answer, I spoke and you did not listen, but did what was evil in my sight and preferred things which displease me, 13 therefore thus says the Lord GOD: Lo, my servants shall eat, but you shall go hungry; my servants shall drink, but you shall be thirsty; my servants shall rejoice, but you shall be put to shame; 14 My servants shall shout for joy of heart, but you shall cry out for grief of heart and howl for anguish of spirit. 15 The Lord GOD shall slay you, and the name you leave shall be used by my chosen ones for cursing; but my servants shall be called by another name. 16 By which he will be blessed on whom a blessing is invoked in the land; he who takes an oath in the land shall swear by the God of truth; for the hardships of the past shall be forgotten, and hidden from my eyes. 17 Lo, I am about to create new heavens and a new earth; the things of the past shall not be remembered or come to mind. 18 Instead, there shall always be rejoicing and happiness in what I create; for I create Jerusalem to be a joy and its people to be a delight; 19 I will rejoice in Jerusalem and exult in my people. No longer shall the sound of weeping be heard there, or the sound of crying; 20 No longer shall there be in it an infant who lives but a few days, or an old man who does not round out his full lifetime; he dies a mere youth who reaches but a hundred years, and he who fails of a hundred shall be thought accursed. 21 They shall live in the houses they build, and eat the fruit of the vineyards they plant; 22 They shall not build houses for others to live in, or plant for others to eat. As the years of a tree, so the years of my people; and my chosen ones shall long enjoy the produce of their hands. 23 They shall not toil in vain, nor beget children for sudden destruction; for a race blessed by the LORD are they and their offspring. 24 Before they call, I will answer; while they are yet speaking, I will hearken to them. 25 The wolf and the lamb shall graze alike, and the lion shall eat hay like the ox (but the serpent's food shall be dust). None shall hurt or destroy on all my holy mountain, says the LORD.

Isaiah Chapter 66

1 Thus says the LORD: The heavens are my throne, the earth is my footstool. What kind of house can you build for me; what is to be my resting place? 2 My hand made all these things when all of them came to be, says the LORD. This is the one whom I approve: the lowly and afflicted man who trembles at my word. 3 Merely slaughtering an ox is like slaying a man; sacrificing a lamb, like breaking a dog's neck; bringing a cereal offering, like offering swine's blood; burning incense, like paying homage to an idol. Since these have chosen their own ways and taken pleasure in their own abominations, 4 I in turn will choose ruthless treatment for them and bring upon them what they fear. Because, when I called, no one answered, when I spoke, no one listened; because they did what was evil in my sight, and chose what gave me displeasure. 5 Hear the word of the LORD, you who tremble at his word: Your brethren who, because of my name, hate and reject you, say, "Let the LORD show his glory that we may see your joy"; but they shall be put to shame. 6 A sound of roaring from the city, a sound from the temple, the sound of the LORD repaying his enemies their deserts! 7 Before she comes to labor, she gives birth; before the pains come upon her, she safely delivers a male child. 8 Who ever heard of such a thing, or saw the like? Can a country be brought forth in one day, or a nation be born in a single moment? Yet Zion is scarcely in labor when she gives birth to her children. 9 Shall I bring a mother to the point of birth, and yet not let her child be born? says the LORD; or shall I who allow her to conceive, yet close her womb? says your God. 10 Rejoice with Jerusalem and be glad because of her, all you who love her; exult, exult with her, all you who were mourning over her! 11 Oh, that you may suck fully of the milk of her comfort, that you may nurse with delight at her abundant breasts! 12 For thus says the LORD: Lo, I will spread prosperity over her like a river, and the wealth of the nations like an overflowing torrent. As nurslings, you shall be carried in her arms, and fondled in her lap; 13 as a mother comforts her son, so will I comfort you; in Jerusalem you shall find your comfort. 14 When you see this, your heart shall rejoice, and your bodies flourish like the grass; the LORD'S power shall be known to his servants, but to his enemies, his wrath. 15 Lo, the LORD shall come in fire, his chariots like the whirlwind, to wreak his wrath with burning heat and his punishment with fiery flames. 16 For the LORD shall judge all mankind by fire and sword, and many shall be slain by the LORD. 17 They who sanctify and purify themselves to go to the groves, as followers of one who stands within, they who eat swine's flesh, loathsome things and mice, shall all perish with their deeds and their thoughts, says the LORD. 18 I come to gather nations of every language; they shall come and see my glory. 19

I will set a sign among them; from them I will send fugitives to the nations: to Tarshish, Put and Lud, Mosoch, Tubal and Javan, to the distant coastlands that have never heard of my fame, or seen my glory; and they shall proclaim my glory among the nations. 20 They shall bring all your brethren from all the nations as an offering to the LORD, on horses and in chariots, in carts, upon mules and dromedaries, to Jerusalem, my holy mountain, says the LORD, just as the Israelites bring their offering to the house of the LORD in clean vessels. 21 Some of these I will take as priests and Levites, says the LORD. 22 As the new heavens and the new earth which I will make shall endure before me, says the LORD, so shall your race and your name endure. 23 From one new moon to another, and from one sabbath to another, all mankind shall come to worship before me, says the LORD. 24 They shall go out and see the corpses of the men who rebelled against me; their worm shall not die, nor their fire be extinguished; and they shall be abhorrent to all mankind.

Jeremiah

Jeremiah Chapter 1

1 The words of Jeremiah, son of Hilkiah, of a priestly family in Anathoth, in the land of Benjamin. 2 The word of the LORD first came to him in the days of Josiah, son of Amon, king of Judah, in the thirteenth year of his reign, 3 and continued through the reign of Jehoiakim, son of Josiah, king of Judah, and until the downfall and exile of Jerusalem in the fifth month of the eleventh year of Zedekiah, son of Josiah, king of Judah. 4 The word of the LORD came to me thus: 5 Before I formed you in the womb I knew you, before you were born I dedicated you, a prophet to the nations I appointed you. 6 "Ah, Lord GOD!" I said, "I know not how to speak; I am too young." 7 But the LORD answered me, Say not, "I am too young." To whomever I send you, you shall go; whatever I command you, you shall speak. 8 Have no fear before them, because I am with you to deliver you, says the LORD. 9 Then the LORD extended his hand and touched my mouth, saying, See, I place my words in your mouth! 10 This day I set you over nations and over kingdoms, To root up and to tear down, to destroy and to demolish, to build and to plant. 11 The word of the LORD came to me with the question: What do you see, Jeremiah? "I see a branch of the watching-tree," I replied. 12 Then the LORD said to me: Well have you seen, for I am watching to fulfill my word. 13 A second time the word of the LORD came to me with the question: What do you see? "I see a boiling cauldron," I replied, "that appears from the north." 14 And from the north, said the LORD to me, evil will boil over upon all who dwell in the land. 15 Lo, I am summoning all the kingdoms of the north, says the LORD; Each king shall come and set up his throne at the gateways of Jerusalem, Opposite her walls all around and opposite all the cities of Judah. 16 I will pronounce my sentence against them for all their wickedness in forsaking me, And in burning incense to strange gods and adoring their own handiwork. 17 But do you gird your loins; stand up and tell them all that I command you. Be not crushed on their account, as though I would leave you crushed before them; 18 For it is I this day who have made you a fortified city, A pillar of iron, a wall of brass, against the whole land: Against Judah's kings and princes, against its priests and people. 19 They will fight against you, but not prevail over you, for I am with you to deliver you, says the LORD.

Jeremiah Chapter 2

1 This word of the LORD came to me: 2 Go, cry out this message for Jerusalem to hear! I remember the devotion of your youth, how you loved me as a bride, Following me in the desert, in a land unsown. 3 Sacred to the LORD was Israel, the first fruits of his harvest; Should anyone presume to partake of them, evil would befall him, says the LORD. 4 Listen to the word of the LORD, O house of Jacob! All you clans of the house of Israel, 5 thus says the LORD: What fault did your fathers find in me that they withdrew from me, Went after empty idols, and became empty themselves? 6 They did not ask, "Where is the LORD who brought us up from the land of Egypt, Who led us through the desert, through a land of wastes and gullies, Through a land of drought and darkness, through a land which no one crosses, where no man dwells?" 7 When I brought you into the garden land to eat its goodly fruits, You entered and defiled my land, you made my heritage loathsome. 8 The priests asked not, "Where is the LORD?" Those who dealt with the law knew me not: the shepherds rebelled against me. The prophets prophesied by Baal, and went after useless idols. 9 Therefore will I yet accuse you, says the LORD, and even your children's children I will accuse. 10 Pass over to the coast of the Kittim and see, send to Kedar and carefully inquire: Where has the like of this been done? 11 Does any other nation change its gods? — yet they are not gods at all! But my people have changed their glory for useless things. 12 Be amazed at this, O heavens, and shudder with sheer horror, says the LORD. 13 Two evils have my people done: they have forsaken me, the source of living waters; They have dug themselves cisterns, broken cisterns, that hold no water. 14 Is Israel a slave, a bondman by birth? Why then has he become booty? 15 Against him lions roar full-throated cries. They have made his land a waste; his cities are charred ruins, without inhabitant. 16 Yes, the people of Memphis and Tahpanhes shave the crown of your head. 17 Has not the forsaking of the LORD, your God, done this to you? 18 And now, why go to Egypt, to drink the waters of the Nile? Why go to Assyria, to drink the waters of the Euphrates? 19 Your own wickedness chastises you, your own infidelities punish you. Know then, and see, how evil and bitter is your forsaking the LORD, your God, And showing no fear of me, says the Lord, the GOD of hosts. 20 Long ago you broke your yoke, you tore off your bonds. "I will not serve," you said. On every high hill, under every green tree, you gave yourself to harlotry. 21 I had planted you, a choice vine of fully tested stock; How could you turn out obnoxious to me, a spurious vine? 22 Though you scour it with soap, and use much lye, The stain of your guilt is still before me, says the Lord GOD. 23 How can you say, "I am not defiled, I have not gone after the Baals"? Consider your conduct in the Valley, recall what you have done: A frenzied she-camel, coursing near and far, 24 breaking away toward the desert, Snuffing the wind in her ardor — who can restrain her lust? No beasts need tire themselves seeking her; in her month they will meet her. 25 Stop wearing out your shoes and parching your throat! But you say, "No use! no! I love these strangers, and after them I must go." 26 As the thief is shamed when caught, so shall the house of Israel be shamed: They, their kings and their princes, their priests and their prophets; 27 They who say to a piece of wood, "You are my father," and to a stone, "You gave me birth." They turn to me their backs, not their faces; yet, in their time of trouble they cry out, "Rise up and save us!" 28 Where are the gods you made for yourselves? Let them rise up! Will they save you in your time of trouble? For as numerous as your cities are your gods, O Judah! And as many as the streets of Jerusalem are the altars you have set up for Baal. 29 How dare you still plead with me? You have all rebelled against me, says the LORD. 30 In vain I struck your children; the correction they did not take. Your sword devoured your prophets like a ravening lion. 31 You, of this generation, take note of the word of the Lord: Have I been a desert to Israel, a land of darkness? Why do my people say, "We have moved on, we will come to you no more"? 32 Does a virgin forget her jewelry, a bride her sash? Yet my people have forgotten me days without number. 33 How well you pick your way when seeking love! You who, in your wickedness, have gone by ways unclean! 34 You, on whose clothing there is the life-blood of the innocent, whom you found committing no burglary; 35 Yet withal you say, "I am innocent; at least, his anger is turned away from me." Behold, I will judge you on that word of yours, "I have not sinned." 36 How very base you have become in changing your course! By Egypt will you be shamed, as you were shamed by Assyria. 37 From there also shall you go away with hands upon your head; For the LORD has rejected those in whom you trust, with them you will have no success.

Jeremiah Chapter 3

1 If a man sends away his wife and, after leaving her, she marries another man, Does the first husband come back to her? Would not the land be wholly defiled? But you have sinned with many lovers, and yet you would return to me! says the LORD. 2 Lift your eyes to the heights, and see, where have men not lain with you? By the waysides you waited for them like an Arab in the desert. You defiled the land by your wicked harlotry. 3 Therefore the showers were withheld, the spring rain failed. But because you have a harlot's brow, you refused to blush. 4 Even now do you not call me, "My father, you who are the bridegroom of my youth"? 5 "Will he keep his wrath forever, will he hold his grudge to the end?" This is what you say; yet you do all the evil you can. 6 The LORD said to me in the days of King Josiah: See now what rebellious Israel has done! She has gone up every high mountain, and under every green tree she has played the harlot. 7 And I thought, after she has done all this she will return to me. But she did not return. Then, even though her traitor sister Judah saw 8 that for all the adulteries rebellious Israel had committed, I put her away and gave her a bill of divorce, nevertheless her traitor sister Judah was not frightened; she too went off and played the harlot. 9 Eager to sin, she polluted the land, committing adultery with stone and wood. 10 With all this, the traitor sister Judah did not return to me wholeheartedly, but insincerely, says the LORD. 11 Then the LORD said to me: Rebel Israel is inwardly more just than traitorous Judah. 12 Go, proclaim these words toward the north, and say: Return, rebel Israel, says the LORD, I will not remain angry with you; For I am merciful, says the LORD, I will not continue my wrath forever. 13 Only know your guilt: how you rebelled against the LORD, your God, How

you ran hither and yon to strangers (under every green tree) and would not listen to my voice, says the LORD. 14 Return, rebellious children, says the LORD, for I am your Master; I will take you, one from a city, two from a clan, and bring you to Zion. 15 I will appoint over you shepherds after my own heart, who will shepherd you wisely and prudently. 16 When you multiply and become fruitful in the land, says the LORD, They will in those days no longer say, "The ark of the covenant of the LORD!" They will no longer think of it, or remember it, or miss it, or make another. 17 At that time they will call Jerusalem the LORD'S throne; there all nations will be gathered together to honor the name of the LORD at Jerusalem, and they will walk no longer in their hardhearted wickedness. 18 In those days the house of Judah will join the house of Israel; together they will come from the land of the north to the land which I gave to your fathers as a heritage. 19 I had thought: How I should like to treat you as sons, And give you a pleasant land, a heritage most beautiful among the nations! You would call me, "My Father," I thought, and never cease following me. 20 But like a woman faithless to her lover, even so have you been faithless to me, O house of Israel, says the LORD. 21 A cry is heard on the heights! the plaintive weeping of Israel's children, Because they have perverted their ways and forgotten the LORD, their God. 22 Return, rebellious children, and I will cure you of your rebelling. "Here we are, we now come to you because you are the LORD, our God. 23 Deceptive indeed are the hills, the thronging mountains; In the LORD, our God, alone is the salvation of Israel. 24 The shame-god has devoured our fathers' toil from our youth, Their sheep and their cattle, their sons and their daughters. 25 Let us lie down in our shame, let our disgrace cover us, for we have sinned against the LORD, our God, From our youth to this day, we and our fathers also; we listened not to the voice of the LORD, our God."

Jeremiah Chapter 4

1 If you wish to return, O Israel, says the LORD, return to me. If you put your detestable things out of my sight, and do not stray, 2 Then you can swear, "As the LORD lives," in truth, in judgment, and in justice; Then shall the nations use his name in blessing, and glory in him. 3 For to the men of Judah and to Jerusalem, thus says the LORD: Till your untilled ground, sow not among thorns. 4 For the sake of the LORD, be circumcised, remove the foreskins of your hearts, O men of Judah and citizens of Jerusalem; Lest my anger break out like fire, and burn till none can quench it, because of your evil deeds. 5 Proclaim it in Judah, make it heard in Jerusalem; Blow the trumpet through the land, summon the recruits! Say, "Fall in, let us march to the fortified cities." 6 Bear the standard to Zion, seek refuge without delay! Evil I bring from the north, and great destruction. 7 Up comes the lion from his lair, the destroyer of nations has set out, has left his place, To turn your land into desolation, till your cities lie waste and empty. 8 So gird yourselves with sackcloth, mourn and wail: "The blazing wrath of the LORD is not turned away from us." 9 In that day, says the LORD, The king will lose heart, and the princes; the priests will be amazed, and the prophets stunned. 10 "Alas! Lord GOD," they will say, "You only deceived us When you said: Peace shall be yours; for the sword touches our very soul." 11 At that time it will be said of this people and of Jerusalem, "From the glaring heights through the desert a wind comes toward the daughter of my people." Not to winnow, not to cleanse; 12 does this wind from the heights come at my bidding; And I myself now pronounce sentence upon them. 13 See! like storm clouds he advances, like a hurricane his chariots; Swifter than eagles are his steeds: "Woe to us! we are ruined." 14 Cleanse your heart of evil, O Jerusalem, that you may be saved. How long must your pernicious thoughts lodge within you? 15 Listen! They proclaim it from Dan, from Mount Ephraim they announce destruction. 16 "Make this known to the nations, announce it to Jerusalem: The besiegers are coming from the distant land, shouting their war cry against the cities of Judah." 17 Like watchmen of the fields they surround her, for she has rebelled against me, says the LORD. 18 Your conduct, your misdeeds, have done this to you; how bitter is this disaster of yours, how it reaches to your very heart! 19 My breast! my breast! how I suffer! The walls of my heart! My heart beats wildly, I cannot be still; For I have heard the sound of the trumpet, the alarm of war. 20 Ruin after ruin is reported; the whole earth is laid waste. In an instant my tents are ravaged; in a flash, my shelters. 21 How long must I see that signal, hear that trumpet sound? 22 Fools my people are, they know me not; Senseless children they are, having no understanding; They are wise in evil, but know not how to do good. 23 I looked at the earth, and it was waste and void; at the heavens, and their light had gone out! 24 I looked at the mountains, and they were trembling, and all the hills were crumbling! 25 I looked and behold, there was no man; even the birds of the air had flown away! 26 I looked and behold, the garden land was a desert, with all its cities destroyed before the LORD, before his blazing wrath. 27 For thus says the LORD: Waste shall the

whole land be; I will (not) wholly destroy it. 28 Because of this the earth shall mourn, the heavens above shall darken; I have spoken, I will not repent, I have resolved, I will not turn back. 29 At the shout of horseman and bowman each city takes to flight; They shrink into the thickets, they scale the rocks: All the cities are abandoned, and no one dwells in them. 30 You now who are doomed, what do you mean by putting on purple, bedecking yourself with gold, Shading your eyes with cosmetics, beautifying yourself in vain? Your lovers spurn you, they seek your life. 31 Yes, I hear the moaning, as of a woman in travail, like the anguish of a mother with her first child — The cry of daughter Zion gasping, as she stretches forth her hands: "Ah, woe is me! I sink exhausted before the slayers!"

Jeremiah Chapter 5

1 Roam the streets of Jerusalem, look about and observe, Search through her public places, to find even one Who lives uprightly and seeks to be faithful, and I will pardon her! 2 Though they say, "As the LORD lives," they swear falsely. 3 O LORD, do your eyes not look for honesty? You struck them, but they did not cringe; you laid them low, but they refused correction; They set their faces harder than stone, and refused to return to you. 4 It is only the lowly, I thought, who are foolish; For they know not the way of the LORD, their duty to their God. 5 I will go to the great ones and speak with them; For they know the way of the LORD, their duty to their God. But, one and all, they had broken the yoke, torn off the harness. 6 Therefore lions from the forest slay them, wolves of the desert ravage them, Leopards keep watch round their cities: all who come out are torn to pieces For their many crimes and their numerous rebellions. 7 Why should I pardon you these things? Your sons have forsaken me, they swear by gods that are not. I fed them, but they committed adultery; to the harlot's house they throng. 8 Lustful stallions they are, each neighs after another's wife. 9 Shall I not punish them for these things? says the LORD; On a nation such as this shall I not take vengeance? 10 Climb to her terraces, and ravage them, destroy them (not) wholly. Tear away her tendrils, they do not belong to the LORD. 11 For they have openly rebelled against me, both the house of Israel and the house of Judah, says the LORD. 12 They denied the LORD, saying, "Not he — No evil shall befall us, neither sword nor famine shall we see. 13 The prophets have become wind, and the word is not in them. May their threats be carried out against themselves!" 14 Now, for this that you have said, says the LORD, the God of hosts — Behold, I make my words in your mouth, a fire, And this people is the wood that it shall devour! 15 Beware, I will bring against you a nation from afar, O house of Israel, says the LORD; A long-lived nation, an ancient nation, a people whose language you know not, whose speech you cannot understand. 16 Their quivers are like open graves; all of them are warriors. 17 They will devour your harvest and your bread, devour your sons and your daughters, Devour your sheep and cattle, devour your vines and fig trees; They will beat flat with the sword the fortified city in which you trust. 18 Yet even in those days, says the LORD, I will not wholly destroy you. 19 And when they ask, "Why has the LORD done all these things to us?" say to them, "As you have forsaken me to serve strange gods in your own land, so shall you serve strangers in a land not your own." 20 Announce this to the house of Jacob, proclaim it in Judah: 21 Pay attention to this, foolish and senseless people Who have eyes and see not, who have ears and hear not. 22 Should you not fear me, says the LORD, should you not tremble before me? I made the sandy shore the sea's limit, which by eternal decree it may not overstep. Toss though it may, it is to no avail; though its billows roar, they cannot pass. 23 But this people's heart is stubborn and rebellious; they turn and go away, 24 And say not in their hearts, "Let us fear the LORD, our God, Who gives us rain early and late, in its time; Who watches for us over the appointed weeks of harvest." 25 Your crimes have prevented these things, your sins have turned back these blessings from you. 26 For there are among my people criminals; like fowlers they set traps, but it is men they catch. 27 Their houses are as full of treachery as a bird-cage is of birds; Therefore they grow powerful and rich, 28 fat and sleek. They go their wicked way; justice they do not defend By advancing the claim of the fatherless or judging the cause of the poor. 29 Shall I not punish these things? says the LORD; on a nation such as this shall I not take vengeance? 30 A shocking, horrible thing has happened in the land: 31 The prophets prophesy falsely, and the priests teach as they wish; Yet my people will have it so; what will you do when the end comes?

Jeremiah Chapter 6

1 Flee, sons of Benjamin, out of Jerusalem! Blow the trumpet in Tekoa, raise a signal over Beth-haccherem; For evil threatens from the north, and mighty destruction. 2 O lovely and delicate daughter Zion, you are ruined! 3 Against her, shepherds come with their flocks; all around, they

pitch their tents, each one grazes his portion. 4 "Prepare for war against her, Up! let us rush upon her at midday! Alas! the day is waning, evening shadows lengthen; 5 Up! let us rush upon her by night, destroy her palaces!" 6 For thus says the LORD of hosts: Hew down her trees, throw up a siege mound against Jerusalem. Woe to the city marked for punishment; nought but oppression within her! 7 As the well gushes out its waters, so she gushes out her wickedness. Violence and destruction resound in her; ever before me are wounds and blows. 8 Be warned, O Jerusalem, lest I be estranged from you; Lest I turn you into a desert, a land where no man dwells. 9 Thus says the LORD of hosts: Glean, glean like a vine the remnant of Israel; Pass your hand, like a vintager, repeatedly over the tendrils. 10 To whom shall I speak? whom shall I warn, and be heard? See! their ears are uncircumcised, they cannot give heed; See, the word of the LORD has become for them an object of scorn, which they will not have. 11 Therefore my wrath brims up within me, I am weary of holding it in; I will pour it out upon the child in the street, upon the young men gathered together. Yes, all will be taken, husband and wife, graybeard with ancient. 12 Their houses will fall to strangers, their fields and their wives as well; For I will stretch forth my hand against those who dwell in this land, says the LORD. 13 Small and great alike, all are greedy for gain; prophet and priest, all practice fraud. 14 They would repair, as though it were nought, the injury to my people: "Peace, peace!" they say, though there is no peace. 15 They are odious; they have done abominable things, yet they are not at all ashamed, they know not how to blush. Hence they shall be among those who fall; in their time of punishment they shall go down, says the LORD. 16 Thus says the LORD: Stand beside the earliest roads, ask the pathways of old Which is the way to good, and walk it; thus you will find rest for your souls. But they said, "We will not walk it." 17 When I raised up watchmen for them: "Hearken to the sound of the trumpet!" they said, "We will not hearken." 18 Therefore hear, O nations, and know, O earth, what I will do with them: 19 See, I bring evil upon this people, the fruit of their own schemes; Because they heeded not my words, because they despised my law. 20 Of what use to me incense that comes from Sheba, or sweet cane from far-off lands? Your holocausts find no favor with me, your sacrifices please me not. 21 Therefore, thus says the LORD: See, I will place before this people obstacles to bring them down; Fathers and sons alike, neighbors and friends shall perish. 22 Thus says the LORD: See, a people comes from the land of the north, a great nation, roused from the ends of the earth. 23 Bow and javelin they wield; cruel and pitiless are they. They sound like the roaring sea as they ride forth on steeds, Each in his place, for battle against you, daughter Zion. 24 We hear the report of them; helpless fall our hands, Anguish takes hold of us, throes like a mother's in childbirth. 25 Go not forth into the field, step not into the street, Beware of the enemy's sword; terror on every side! 26 O daughter of my people, gird on sackcloth, roll in the ashes. Mourn as for an only child with bitter wailing, For sudden upon us comes the destroyer. 27 A tester among my people I have appointed you, to search and test their way. 28 Arch-rebels are they all, dealers in slander, all of them corrupt. 29 The bellows roars, the lead is consumed by the fire; In vain has the smelter refined, the wicked are not drawn off. 30 "Silver rejected" they shall be called, for the LORD has rejected them.

Jeremiah Chapter 7

1 The following message came to Jeremiah from the LORD: 2 Stand at the gate of the house of the LORD, and there proclaim this message: Hear the word of the LORD, all you of Judah who enter these gates to worship the LORD! 3 Thus says the LORD of hosts, the God of Israel: Reform your ways and your deeds, so that I may remain with you in this place. 4 Put not your trust in the deceitful words: "This is the temple of the LORD! The temple of the LORD! The temple of the LORD!" 5 Only if you thoroughly reform your ways and your deeds; if each of you deals justly with his neighbor; 6 if you no longer oppress the resident alien, the orphan, and the widow; if you no longer shed innocent blood in this place, or follow strange gods to your own harm, 7 will I remain with you in this place, in the land which I gave your fathers long ago and forever. 8 But here you are, putting your trust in deceitful words to your own loss! 9 Are you to steal and murder, commit adultery and perjury, burn incense to Baal, go after strange gods that you know not, 10 and yet come to stand before me in this house which bears my name, and say: "We are safe; we can commit all these abominations again"? 11 Has this house which bears my name become in your eyes a den of thieves? I too see what is being done, says the LORD. 12 You may go to Shiloh, which I made the dwelling place of my name in the beginning. See what I did to it because of the wickedness of my people Israel. 13 And now, because you have committed all these misdeeds, says the LORD, because you did not listen, though I spoke to you untiringly; because you did not answer, though I called you, 14 I will do to this house named after me,

in which you trust, and to this place which I gave to you and your fathers, just as I did to Shiloh. 15 I will cast you away from me, as I cast away all your brethren, all the offspring of Ephraim. 16 You, now, do not intercede for this people; raise not in their behalf a pleading prayer! Do not urge me, for I will not listen to you. 17 Do you not see what they are doing in the cities of Judah, in the streets of Jerusalem? 18 The children gather wood, their fathers light the fire, and the women knead dough to make cakes for the queen of heaven, while libations are poured out to strange gods in order to hurt me. 19 Is it whom they hurt, says the LORD; is it not rather themselves, to their own confusion? 20 See now, says the Lord GOD, my anger and my wrath will pour out upon this place, upon man and beast, upon the trees of the field and the fruits of the earth; it will burn without being quenched. 21 Thus says the LORD of hosts, the God of Israel: Heap your holocausts upon your sacrifices; eat up the flesh! 22 In speaking to your fathers on the day I brought them out of the land of Egypt, I gave them no command concerning holocaust or sacrifice. 23 This rather is what I commanded them: Listen to my voice; then I will be your God and you shall be my people. Walk in all the ways that I command you, so that you may prosper. 24 But they obeyed not, nor did they pay heed. They walked in the hardness of their evil hearts and turned their backs, not their faces, to me. 25 From the day that your fathers left the land of Egypt even to this day, I have sent you untiringly all my servants the prophets. 26 Yet they have not obeyed me nor paid heed; they have stiffened their necks and done worse than their fathers. 27 When you speak all these words to them, they will not listen to you either; when you call to them, they will not answer you. 28 Say to them: This is the nation which does not listen to the voice of the LORD, its God, or take correction. Faithfulness has disappeared; the word itself is banished from their speech. 29 Cut off your dedicated hair and throw it away! on the heights intone an elegy; For the LORD has rejected and cast off the generation that draws down his wrath. 30 The people of Judah have done what is evil in my eyes, says the LORD. They have defiled the house which bears my name by setting up in it their abominable idols. 31 In the Valley of Ben-hinnom they have built the high place of Topheth to immolate in fire their sons and their daughters, such a thing as I never commanded or had in mind. 32 Therefore, beware! days will come, says the LORD, when Topheth and the Valley of Ben-hinnom will no longer be called such, but rather the Valley of Slaughter. For lack of space, Topheth will be a burial place. 33 The corpses of this people will be food for the birds of the sky and for the beasts of the field, which no one will drive away. 34 In the cities of Judah and in the streets of Jerusalem I will silence the cry of joy, the cry of gladness, the voice of the bridegroom and the voice of the bride; for the land will be turned to rubble.

Jeremiah Chapter 8

1 At that time, says the LORD, the bones of the kings and princes of Judah, the bones of the priests and the prophets, and the bones of the citizens of Jerusalem will be emptied out of their graves 2 and spread out before the sun and the moon and the whole army of heaven, which they loved and served, which they followed, consulted, and worshiped. They will not be gathered up for burial, but will lie like dung upon the ground. 3 Death will be preferred to life by all the survivors of this wicked race who remain in any of the places to which I banish them, says the LORD of hosts. 4 Tell them: Thus says the LORD: When someone falls, does he not rise again? if he goes astray, does he not turn back? 5 Why do these people rebel with obstinate resistance? Why do they cling to deceptive idols, refuse to turn back? 6 I listen closely: they speak what is not true; No one repents of his wickedness, saying, "What have I done!" Everyone keeps on running his course, like a steed dashing into battle. 7 Even the stork in the air knows its seasons; Turtledove, swallow and thrush observe their time of return, But my people do not know the ordinance of the LORD. 8 How can you say, "We are wise, we have the law of the LORD"? Why, that has been changed into falsehood by the lying pen of the scribes! 9 The wise are confounded, dismayed and ensnared; Since they have rejected the word of the LORD, of what avail is their wisdom? 10 Therefore, I will give their wives to strangers, their fields to spoilers. Small and great alike, all are greedy for gain, prophet and priest, all practice fraud. 11 They would repair, as though it were nought, the injury to the daughter of my people: "Peace, peace!" they say, though there is no peace. 12 They are odious; they have done abominable things, yet they are not at all ashamed, they know not how to blush. Hence they shall be among those who fall; in their time of punishment they shall go down, says the LORD. 13 I will gather them all in, says the LORD: no grapes on the vine, No figs on the fig trees, foliage withered! 14 Why do we remain here? Let us form ranks and enter the walled cities, to perish there; For the LORD has wrought our destruction, he has given us poison to drink, because we have sinned against the LORD. 15 We wait for peace to no

avail; for a time of healing, but terror comes instead. ¹⁶ From Dan is heard the snorting of his steeds; The neighing of his stallions shakes the whole land. They come devouring the land and all it contains, the city and those who dwell in it. ¹⁷ Yes, I will send against you poisonous snakes, Against which no charm will work when they bite you, says the LORD. ¹⁸ My grief is incurable, my heart within me is faint. ¹⁹ Listen! the cry of the daughter of my people, far and wide in the land! Is the LORD no longer in Zion, is her King no longer in her midst? (Why do they provoke me with their idols, with their foreign nonentities?) ²⁰ "The harvest has passed, the summer is at an end, and yet we are not safe!" ²¹ I am broken by the ruin of the daughter of my people. I am disconsolate; horror has seized me. ²² Is there no balm in Gilead, no physician there? Why grows not new flesh over the wound of the daughter of my people? ²³ Oh, that my head were a spring of water, my eyes a fountain of tears, That I might weep day and night over the slain of the daughter of my people!

Jeremiah Chapter 9

¹ Would that I had in the desert a travelers' lodge! That I might leave my people and depart from them. They are all adulterers, a faithless band. ² They ready their tongues like a drawn bow; with lying, and not with truth, they hold forth in the land. They go from evil to evil, but me they know not, says the LORD. ³ Be on your guard, everyone against his neighbor; put no trust in any brother. Every brother apes Jacob, the supplanter, every friend is guilty of slander. ⁴ Each one deceives the other, no one speaks the truth. They have accustomed their tongues to lying, and are perverse, and cannot repent. ⁵ Violence upon violence, deceit upon deceit: They refuse to recognize me, says the LORD. ⁶ Therefore, thus says the LORD of hosts: I will smelt them and test them; how else should I deal with their wickedness? ⁷ A murderous arrow is his tongue, his mouth utters deceit; He speaks cordially with his friends, but in his heart he lays an ambush! ⁸ For these things, says the LORD, shall I not punish them? On a nation such as this shall I not take vengeance? ⁹ Over the mountains, break out in cries of lamentation, over the pasture lands, intone a dirge: They are scorched, and no man crosses them, unheard is the bleat of the flock; Birds of the air as well as beasts, all have fled, and are gone. ¹⁰ I will turn Jerusalem into a heap of ruins, a haunt of jackals; The cities of Judah I will make into a waste, where no one dwells. ¹¹ Who is so wise that he can understand this? Let him to whom the mouth of the LORD has spoken make it known: Why is the land ravaged, scorched like a wasteland untraversed? ¹² The LORD answered: Because they have abandoned my law, which I set before them, and have not followed it or listened to my voice, ¹³ but followed rather the hardness of their hearts and the Baals, as their fathers had taught them; ¹⁴ therefore, thus says the LORD of hosts, the God of Israel: See now, I will give them wormwood to eat and poison to drink. ¹⁵ I will scatter them among nations whom neither they nor their fathers have known; I will send the sword to pursue them until I have completely destroyed them. ¹⁶ Thus says the LORD of hosts: Attention! tell the wailing women to come, summon the best of them; ¹⁷ Let them come quickly and intone a dirge for us, That our eyes may be wet with weeping, our cheeks run with tears. ¹⁸ The dirge is heard from Zion: Ruined we are, and greatly ashamed; We must leave the land, give up our homes! ¹⁹ Hear, you women, the word of the LORD, let your ears receive his message. Teach your daughters this dirge, and each other this lament. ²⁰ Death has come up through our windows, has entered our palaces; It cuts down the children in the street, young people in the squares. ²¹ The corpses of the slain lie like dung on a field, Like sheaves behind the harvester, with no one to gather them. ²² Thus says the LORD: Let not the wise man glory in his wisdom, nor the strong man glory in his strength, nor the rich man glory in his riches; ²³ But rather, let him who glories, glory in this, that in his prudence he knows me, Knows that I, the LORD, bring about kindness, justice and uprightness on the earth; For with such am I pleased, says the LORD. ²⁴ See, days are coming, says the LORD, when I will demand an account of all those circumcised in their flesh: ²⁵ Egypt and Judah, Edom and the Ammonites, Moab and the desert dwellers who shave their temples. For all these nations, like the whole house of Israel, are uncircumcised in heart.

Jeremiah Chapter 10

¹ Hear the word which the LORD speaks to you, O house of Israel. ² Thus says the LORD: Learn not the customs of the nations, and have no fear of the signs of the heavens, though the nations fear them. ³ For the cult idols of the nations are nothing, wood cut from the forest, Wrought by craftsmen with the adze, ⁴ adorned with silver and gold. With nails and hammers they are fastened, that they may not totter. ⁵ Like a scarecrow in a cucumber field are they, they cannot speak; They must be carried about, for they cannot walk. Fear them not, they can do no

harm, neither is it in their power to do good. ⁶ No one is like you, O LORD, great are you, great and mighty is your name. ⁷ Who would not fear you, King of the nations, for it is your due! Among all the wisest of the nations, and in all their domain, there is none like you. ⁸ One and all they are dumb and senseless, these idols they teach about are wooden: ⁹ Silver strips brought from Tarshish, and gold from Ophir, The work of the craftsman and the handiwork of the smelter, Clothed with violet and purple — all of them the work of artisans. ¹¹ Thus shall you say of them: Let the gods that did not make heaven and earth perish from the earth, and from beneath these heavens! ¹⁰ The LORD is true God, he is the living God, the eternal King, Before whose anger the earth quakes, whose wrath the nations cannot endure: ¹² He who made the earth by his power, established the world by his wisdom, and stretched out the heavens by his skill. ¹³ When he thunders, the waters in the heavens roar, and he brings up clouds from the end of the earth; He makes the lightning flash in the rain, and releases stormwinds from their chambers. ¹⁴ Every man is stupid, ignorant; every artisan is put to shame by his idol: He has molded a fraud, without breath of life. ¹⁵ Nothingness are they, a ridiculous work; they will perish in their time of punishment. ¹⁶ Not like these is the portion of Jacob: he is the creator of all things; Israel is his very own tribe, LORD of hosts is his name. ¹⁷ Lift up your bundle and leave the land, O city living in a state of siege! ¹⁸ For thus says the LORD: Behold, this time I will sling away the inhabitants of the land; I will hem them in, that they may be taken. ¹⁹ Woe is me! I am undone, my wound is incurable; Yet I had thought: if I make light of my wound, I can bear it. ²⁰ My tent is ruined, all its cords are severed. My sons have left me, they are no more: no one to pitch my tent, no one to raise its curtains. ²¹ Yes, the shepherds were stupid as cattle, the LORD they sought not; Therefore they had no success, and all their flocks were scattered. ²² Listen! a noise! it comes closer, a great uproar from the northern land: To turn the cities of Judah into a desert haunt of jackals. ²³ You know, O LORD, that man is not master of his way; Man's course is not within his choice, nor is it for him to direct his step. ²⁴ Punish us, O LORD, but with equity, not in anger, lest you have us dwindle away. ²⁵ Pour out your wrath on the nations that know you not, on the tribes that call not upon your name; For they have devoured Jacob utterly, and laid waste his dwelling.

Jeremiah Chapter 11

¹ The following message came to Jeremiah from the LORD: ² Speak to the men of Judah and to the citizens of Jerusalem, ³ saying to them: Thus says the LORD, the God of Israel: Cursed be the man who does not observe the terms of this covenant, ⁴ which I enjoined upon your fathers the day I brought them up out of the land of Egypt, that iron foundry, saying: Listen to my voice and do all that I command you. Then you shall be my people, and I will be your God. ⁵ Thus I will fulfill the oath which I swore to your fathers, to give them a land flowing with milk and honey: the one you have today. "Amen, LORD," I answered. ⁶ Then the LORD said to me: Proclaim all these words in the cities of Judah and in the streets of Jerusalem: Hear the words of this covenant and obey them. ⁷ Urgently and constantly I warned your fathers to obey my voice, from the day I brought them up out of the land of Egypt even to this day. ⁸ But they did not listen or give ear. Each one followed the hardness of his evil heart, till I brought upon them all the threats of this covenant which they had failed to observe as I commanded them. ⁹ A conspiracy has been found, the LORD said to me, among the men of Judah and the citizens of Jerusalem. ¹⁰ They have returned to the crimes of their forefathers who refused to obey my words. They also have followed and served strange gods; the covenant which I had made with their fathers, the house of Israel and the house of Judah have broken. ¹¹ Therefore, thus says the LORD: See, I bring upon them misfortune which they cannot escape. Though they cry out to me, I will not listen to them. ¹² Then the cities of Judah and the citizens of Jerusalem will go and cry out to the gods to which they have been offering incense. But these gods will give them no help whatever when misfortune strikes. ¹³ For as numerous as your cities are your gods, O Judah! And as many as the streets of Jerusalem are the altars for offering sacrifice to Baal. ¹⁴ Do not intercede on behalf of this people, nor utter a plea for them. I will not listen when they call to me at the time of their misfortune. ¹⁵ What right has my beloved in my house, while she prepares her plots? Can vows and sacred meat turn away your misfortune from you? Will you still be jubilant ¹⁶ when you hear the great invasion? A spreading olive tree, goodly to behold, the LORD has named you; Now he sets fire to it, its branches burn. ¹⁷ The LORD of hosts who planted you has decreed misfortune for you because of the evil done by the house of Israel and by the house of Judah, who provoked me by sacrificing to Baal. ¹⁸ I knew it because the LORD informed me; at that time you, O LORD, showed me their doings.

Jeremiah Chapter 12

1 You would be in the right, O LORD, if I should dispute with you; even so, I must discuss the case with you. Why does the way of the godless prosper, why live all the treacherous in contentment? 2 You planted them; they have taken root, they keep on growing and bearing fruit. You are upon their lips, but far from their inmost thoughts. 3 You, O Lord, know me, you see me, you have found that at heart I am with you. Pick them out like sheep for the slaughter, set them apart for the day of carnage. 4 How long must the earth mourn, the green of the whole countryside wither? For the wickedness of those who dwell in it beasts and birds disappear, because they say, "God does not see our ways." 5 If running against men has wearied you, how will you race against horses? And if in a land of peace you fall headlong, what will you do in the thickets of the Jordan? 6 For even your own brothers, the members of your father's house, betray you; they have recruited a force against you. Do not believe them, even if they are friendly to you in their words. 19 Yet I, like a trusting lamb led to slaughter, had not realized that they were hatching plots against me: "Let us destroy the tree in its vigor; let us cut him off from the land of the living, so that his name will be spoken no more." 20 But, you, O LORD of hosts, O just Judge, searcher of mind and heart, Let me witness the vengeance you take on them, for to you I have entrusted my cause! 21 Therefore, thus says the LORD concerning the men of Anathoth who seek your life, saying, "Do not prophesy in the name of the LORD; else you shall die by our hand." 22 Therefore, thus says the LORD of hosts: I am going to punish them. The young men shall die by the sword; their sons and daughters shall die by famine. 23 None shall be spared among them, for I will bring misfortune upon the men of Anathoth, the year of their punishment. 7 I abandon my house, cast off my heritage; The beloved of my soul I deliver into the hand of her foes. 8 My heritage has turned on me like a lion in the jungle; Because she has roared against me, I treat her as an enemy. 9 My heritage is a prey for hyenas, is surrounded by vultures; Come, gather together, all you beasts of the field, come and eat! 10 Many shepherds have ravaged my vineyard, have trodden my heritage underfoot; The portion that delighted me they have turned into a desert waste. 11 They have made it a mournful waste, desolate it lies before me, Desolate, all the land, because no one takes it to heart. 12 Upon every desert height brigands have come up. The LORD has a sword which consumes the land, from end to end: no peace for all mankind. 13 They have sown wheat and reaped thorns, they have tired themselves out to no purpose; They recoil before their harvest, the flaming anger of the LORD. 14 Thus says the LORD against all my evil neighbors who plunder the heritage which I gave my people Israel as their own: See, I will pluck them up from their land; the house of Judah I will pluck up in their midst. 15 But after plucking them up, I will pity them again and bring them back, each to his heritage, each to his land. 16 And if they carefully learn my people's custom of swearing by my name, "As the LORD lives," they who formerly taught my people to swear by Baal shall be built up in the midst of my people. 17 But if they do not obey, I will uproot and destroy that nation entirely, says the LORD.

Jeremiah Chapter 13

1 The LORD said to me: Go buy yourself a linen loincloth; wear it on your loins, but do not put it in water. 2 I bought the loincloth, as the LORD commanded, and put it on. 3 A second time the word of the LORD came to me thus: 4 Take the loincloth which you bought and are wearing, and go now to the Parath; there hide it in a cleft of the rock. 5 Obedient to the LORD'S command, I went to the Parath and buried the loincloth. 6 After a long interval, he said to me: Go now to the Parath and fetch the loincloth which I told you to hide there. 7 Again I went to the Parath, sought out and took the loincloth from the place where I had hid it. But it was rotted, good for nothing! 8 Then the message came to me from the LORD: 9 Thus says the LORD: So also I will allow the pride of Judah to rot, the great pride of Jerusalem. 10 This wicked people who refuse to obey my words, who walk in the stubbornness of their hearts, and follow strange gods to serve and adore them, shall be like this loincloth which is good for nothing. 11 For, as close as the loincloth clings to a man's loins, so had I made the whole house of Israel and the whole house of Judah cling to me, says the LORD; to be my people, my renown, my praise, my beauty. But they did not listen. 12 Now speak to them this word: Thus says the LORD, the God of Israel: Every wineflask is meant to be filled with wine. If they reply, "Do we not know that every wineflask is meant to be filled with wine?" 13 say to them: Thus says the LORD: Beware! I am filling with drunkenness all the inhabitants of this land, the kings who succeed to David's throne, the priests and prophets, and all the citizens of Jerusalem. 14 I will dash them against each other, fathers and sons together, says the LORD; I will show no compassion, I will not spare or pity, but will destroy them. 15 Give ear, listen humbly,

for the LORD speaks. 16 Give glory to the LORD, your God, before it grows dark; Before your feet stumble on darkening mountains; Before the light you look for turns to darkness, changes into black clouds. 17 If you do not listen to this in your pride, I will weep in secret many tears; My eyes will run with tears for the LORD'S flock, led away to exile. 18 Say to the king and to the queen mother: come down from your throne; From your heads fall your magnificent crowns. 19 The cities of the Negeb are besieged, with no one to relieve them; All Judah is banished in universal exile. 20 Lift up your eyes and see men coming from the north. Where is the flock entrusted to you, the sheep that were your glory? 21 What will you say when they place as rulers over you those whom you taught to be your lovers? Will not pangs seize you like those of a woman giving birth? 22 If you ask in your heart why these things befall you: For your great guilt your skirts are stripped away and you are violated. 23 Can the Ethiopian change his skin? the leopard his spots? As easily would you be able to do good, accustomed to evil as you are. 24 I will scatter them like chaff that flies when the desert wind blows. 25 This is your lot, the portion measured out to you from me, says the LORD. Because you have forgotten me, and trusted in the lying idol, 26 I now will strip off your skirts from you, so that your shame will appear. 27 Your adulteries, your neighings, your shameless prostitutions: On the hills in the highlands I see these horrible crimes of yours. Woe to you, Jerusalem, how long will it yet be before you become clean!

Jeremiah Chapter 14

1 The word of the LORD that came to Jeremiah concerning the drought: 2 Judah mourns, her gates are lifeless; Her people sink down in mourning: from Jerusalem ascends a cry of anguish. 3 The nobles send their servants for water, but when they come to the cisterns They find no water and return with empty jars. Ashamed, despairing, they cover their heads 4 because of the stricken soil; Because there is no rain in the land the farmers are ashamed, they cover their heads. 5 Even the hind in the field deserts her offspring because there is no grass. 6 The wild asses stand on the bare heights, gasping for breath like jackals; Their eyes grow dim, because there is no vegetation to be seen. 7 Even though our crimes bear witness against us, take action, O LORD, for the honor of your name — Even though our rebellions are many, though we have sinned against you. 8 O Hope of Israel, O LORD, our savior in time of need! Why should you be a stranger in this land, like a traveler who has stopped but for a night? 9 Why are you like a man dumbfounded, a champion who cannot save? You are in our midst, O LORD, your name we bear: do not forsake us! 10 Thus says the LORD of this people: They so love to wander that they do not spare their feet. The LORD has no pleasure in them; now he remembers their guilt, and will punish their sins. 11 Then the LORD said to me: Do not intercede for this people. 12 If they fast, I will not listen to their supplication. If they offer holocausts or cereal offerings, I will not accept them. Rather, I will destroy them with the sword, famine, and pestilence. 13 Ah! Lord GOD, I replied, it is the prophets who say to them, "You shall not see the sword; famine shall not befall you. Indeed, I will give you lasting peace in this place." 14 Lies these prophets utter in my name, the LORD said to me. I did not send them; I gave them no command nor did I speak to them. Lying visions, foolish divination, dreams of their own imagination, they prophesy to you. 15 Therefore, thus says the LORD: Concerning the prophets who prophesy in my name, though I did not send them; who say, "Sword and famine shall not befall this land": by the sword and famine shall these prophets meet their end. 16 The people to whom they prophesy shall be cast out into the streets of Jerusalem by famine and the sword. No one shall bury them, their wives, their sons, or their daughters, for I will pour out upon them their own wickedness. 17 Speak to them this word: Let my eyes stream with tears day and night, without rest, Over the great destruction which overwhelms the virgin daughter of my people, over her incurable wound. 18 If I walk out into the field, look! those slain by the sword; If I enter the city, look! those consumed by hunger. Even the prophet and the priest forage in a land they know not. 19 Have you cast Judah off completely? Is Zion loathsome to you? Why have you struck us a blow that cannot be healed? We wait for peace, to no avail; for a time of healing, but terror comes instead. 20 We recognize, O LORD, our wickedness, the guilt of our fathers; that we have sinned against you. 21 For your name's sake spurn us not, disgrace not the throne of your glory; remember your covenant with us, and break it not. 22 Among the nations' idols is there any that gives rain? Or can the mere heavens send showers? Is it not you alone, O LORD, our God, to whom we look? You alone have done all these things.

Jeremiah Chapter 15

1 The LORD said to me: Even if Moses and Samuel stood before me, my

heart would not turn toward this people. Send them away from me. 2 If they ask you where they should go, tell them, Thus says the LORD: Whoever is marked for death, to death; whoever is marked for the sword, to the sword; whoever is marked for famine, to famine; whoever is marked for captivity, to captivity. 3 Four kinds of scourge I have decreed against them, says the LORD: the sword to slay them; dogs to drag them about; the birds of the sky and the beasts of the earth to devour and destroy them. 4 And I will make them an object of horror to all the kingdoms of the earth because of what Manasseh, son of Hezekiah, king of Judah, did in Jerusalem. 5 Who will pity you, Jerusalem, who will console you? Who will stop to ask about your welfare? 6 You have disowned me, says the LORD, turned your back upon me; And so I stretched out my hand to destroy you, I was weary of sparing you. 7 I winnowed them with the fan in every city gate. I destroyed my people through bereavement; they returned not from their evil ways. 8 Their widows were more numerous before me than the sands of the sea. I brought against the mother of youths the spoiler at midday; Suddenly I struck her with anguish and terror. 9 The mother of seven swoons away, gasping out her life; Her sun sets in full day, she is disgraced, despairing. Their survivors I will give to the sword before their enemies, says the LORD. 10 Woe to me, mother, that you gave me birth! a man of strife and contention to all the land! I neither borrow nor lend, yet all curse me. 11 Tell me, LORD, have I not served you for their good? Have I not interceded with you in the time of misfortune and anguish? 12 You know I have. Remember me, LORD, visit me, and avenge me on my persecutors. Because of your long-suffering banish me not; know that for you I have borne insult. 13 When I found your words, I devoured them; they became my joy and the happiness of my heart, Because I bore your name, O LORD, God of hosts. 14 I did not sit celebrating in the circle of merrymakers; Under the weight of your hand I sat alone because you filled me with indignation. 15 Why is my pain continuous, my wound incurable, refusing to be healed? You have indeed become for me a treacherous brook, whose waters do not abide! 16 Thus the LORD answered me: If you repent, so that I restore you, in my presence you shall stand; If you bring forth the precious without the vile, you shall be my mouthpiece. Then it shall be they who turn to you, and you shall not turn to them; 17 And I will make you toward this people a solid wall of brass. Though they fight against you, they shall not prevail, For I am with you, to deliver and rescue you, says the LORD. 18 I will free you from the hand of the wicked, and rescue you from the grasp of the violent.

Jeremiah Chapter 16

1 This message came to me from the LORD: 2 Do not marry any woman; you shall not have sons or daughters in this place, 3 for thus says the LORD concerning the sons and daughters who will be born in this place, the mothers who will give them birth, the fathers who will beget them in this land: 4 Of deadly disease they shall die. Unlamented and unburied they will lie like dung on the ground. Sword and famine will make an end of them, and their corpses will become food for the birds of the sky and the beasts of the field. 5 Go not into a house of mourning, the LORD continued: go not there to lament or offer sympathy. For I have withdrawn my friendship from this people, says the LORD, my kindness and my pity. 6 They shall die, the great and the lowly, in this land, and shall go unburied and unlamented. No one will gash himself or shave his head for them. 7 They will not break bread with the bereaved to console them in their bereavement; they will not give them the cup of consolation to drink over the death of father or mother. 8 Enter not a house where people are celebrating, to sit with them eating and drinking. 9 For thus says the LORD of hosts, the God of Israel: Before your very eyes and during your lifetime I will silence from this place the cry of joy and the cry of gladness, the voice of the bridegroom and the voice of the bride. 10 When you proclaim all these words to this people and they ask you: "Why has the LORD pronounced all these great evils against us? What is our crime? What sin have we committed against the LORD, our God?" — 11 you shall answer them: It is because your fathers have forsaken me, says the LORD, and followed strange gods, which they served and worshiped; but me they have forsaken, and my law they have not observed. 12 And you have done worse than your fathers. Here you are, every one of you, walking in the hardness of his evil heart instead of listening to me. 13 I will cast you out of this land into a land that neither you nor your fathers have known; there you can serve strange gods day and night, because I will not grant you my mercy. 14 However, days will surely come, says the LORD, when it will no longer be said, "As the LORD lives, who brought the Israelites out of Egypt"; 15 but rather, "As the LORD lives, who brought the Israelites out of the land of the north and out of all the countries to which he had banished them." I will bring them back to the land which I gave their fathers. 16 Look! I will send many fishermen, says the LORD, to catch them. After that, I will send many hunters to hunt them out from every mountain and hill and from the clefts of the rocks. 17 For my eyes are upon all their ways; they are not hidden from me, nor does their guilt escape my view. 18 I will at once repay them double for their crime and their sin of profaning my land with their detestable corpses of idols, and filling my heritage with their abominations. 19 O LORD, my strength, my fortress, my refuge in the day of distress! To you will the nations come from the ends of the earth, and say, "Mere frauds are the heritage of our fathers, empty idols of no use." 20 Can man make for himself gods? These are not gods. 21 Look, then: I will give them knowledge; this time I will leave them in no doubt Of my strength and my power: they shall know that my name is LORD.

Jeremiah Chapter 17

1 The sin of Judah is written with an iron stylus, Engraved with a diamond point upon the tablets of their hearts. (And the horns of their altars, 2 when their sons remember their altars and their sacred poles, beside the green trees, on the high hills, 3 the peaks in the highland.) Your wealth and all your treasures I will give as spoil. In recompense for all your sins throughout your borders, 4 You will relinquish your hold on your heritage which I have given you. I will enslave you to your enemies in a land that you know not: For a fire has been kindled by my wrath that will burn forever. 5 Thus says the LORD: Cursed is the man who trusts in human beings, who seeks his strength in flesh, whose heart turns away from the LORD. 6 He is like a barren bush in the desert that enjoys no change of season, But stands in a lava waste, a salt and empty earth. 7 Blessed is the man who trusts in the LORD, whose hope is the LORD. 8 He is like a tree planted beside the waters that stretches out its roots to the stream: It fears not the heat when it comes, its leaves stay green; In the year of drought it shows no distress, but still bears fruit. 9 More tortuous than all else is the human heart, beyond remedy; who can understand it? 10 I, the LORD, alone probe the mind and test the heart, To reward everyone according to his ways, according to the merit of his deeds. 11 A partridge that mothers a brood not her own is the man who acquires wealth unjustly: In midlife it will desert him; in the end he is only a fool. 12 A throne of glory, exalted from the beginning, such is our holy place. 13 O hope of Israel, O LORD! all who forsake you shall be in disgrace; The rebels in the land shall be put to shame; they have forsaken the source of living waters (the LORD). 14 Heal me, LORD, that I may be healed; save me, that I may be saved, for it is you whom I praise. 15 See how they say to me, "Where is the word of the LORD? Let it come to pass!" 16 Yet I did not press you to send calamity; the day without remedy I have not desired. You know what passed my lips; it is present before you. 17 Do not be my ruin, you, my refuge in the day of misfortune. 18 Let my persecutors, not me, be confounded; let them, not me, be broken. Bring upon them the day of misfortune, crush them with repeated destruction. 19 Thus said the LORD to me: Go, stand at the Gate of Benjamin, where the kings of Judah enter and leave, and at the other gates of Jerusalem. 20 There say to them: Hear the word of the LORD, you kings of Judah, and all Judah, and all you citizens of Jerusalem who enter these gates! 21 Thus says the LORD: As you love your lives, take care not to carry burdens on the sabbath day, to bring them in through the gates of Jerusalem. 22 Bring no burden from your homes on the sabbath. Do no work whatever, but keep holy the sabbath, as I commanded your fathers, 23 though they did not listen or give ear, but stiffened their necks so as not to hear or take correction. 24 If you obey me wholeheartedly, says the LORD, and carry no burden through the gates of this city on the sabbath, keeping the sabbath holy and abstaining from all work on it, 25 then, through the gates of this city, kings who sit upon the throne of David will continue to enter, riding in their chariots or upon their horses, along with their princes, and the men of Judah, and the citizens of Jerusalem. This city will remain inhabited forever. 26 To it people will come from the cities of Judah and the neighborhood of Jerusalem, from the land of Benjamin and from the foothills, from the hill country and the Negeb, to bring holocausts and sacrifices, cereal offerings and incense and thank offerings to the house of the LORD. 27 But if you do not obey me and keep holy the sabbath, if you carry burdens and come through the gates of Jerusalem on the sabbath, I will set unquenchable fire to its gates, which will consume the palaces of Jerusalem.

Jeremiah Chapter 18

1 This word came to Jeremiah from the LORD: 2 Rise up, be off to the potter's house; there I will give you my message. 3 I went down to the potter's house and there he was, working at the wheel. 4 Whenever the object of clay which he was making turned out badly in his hand, he tried again, making of the clay another object of whatever sort he pleased. 5 Then the word of the Lord came to me: 6 Can I not do to you, house of Israel, as this potter has done? says the LORD. Indeed, like

clay in the hand of the potter, so are you in my hand, house of Israel. 7 Sometimes I threaten to uproot and tear down and destroy a nation or a kingdom. 8 But if that nation which I have threatened turns from its evil, I also repent of the evil which I threatened to do. 9 Sometimes, again, I promise to build up and plant a nation or a kingdom. 10 But if that nation does what is evil in my eyes, refusing to obey my voice, I repent of the good with which I promised to bless it. 11 And now, tell this to the men of Judah and the citizens of Jerusalem: Thus says the LORD: Take care! I am fashioning evil against you and making a plan. Return, each of you, from his evil way; reform your ways and your deeds. 12 But they will say, "No use! We will follow our own devices; each one of us will behave according to the stubbornness of his evil heart!" 13 Therefore thus says the LORD: Ask among the nations — who has ever heard the like? Truly horrible things has virgin Israel done! 14 Does the snow of Lebanon desert the rocky heights? Do the gushing waters dry up that flow fresh down the mountains? 15 Yet my people have forgotten me: they burn incense to a thing that does not exist. They stumble out of their ways, the paths of old, To travel on bypaths, not the beaten track. 16 Their land shall be turned into a desert, an object of lasting ridicule: All passers-by will be amazed, will shake their heads. 17 Like the east wind, I will scatter them before their enemies; I will show them my back, not my face, in their day of disaster. 18 "Come," they said, "let us contrive a plot against Jeremiah. It will not mean the loss of instruction from the priests, nor of counsel from the wise, nor of messages from the prophets. And so, let us destroy him by his own tongue; let us carefully note his every word." 19 Heed me, O LORD, and listen to what my adversaries say. 20 Must good be repaid with evil that they should dig a pit to take my life? Remember that I stood before you to speak in their behalf, to turn away your wrath from them. 21 So now, deliver their children to famine, do away with them by the sword. Let their wives be made childless and widows; let their men die of pestilence, their young men be slain by the sword in battle. 22 May cries be heard from their homes, when suddenly you send plunderers against them. For they have dug a pit to capture me, they have hid snares for my feet; 23 But you, O LORD, know all their plans to slay me. Forgive not their crime, blot not out their sin in your sight! Let them go down before you, proceed against them in the time of your anger.

Jeremiah Chapter 19

1 Thus said the LORD: Go, buy a potter's earthen flask. Take along some of the elders of the people and of the priests, 2 and go out toward the Valley of Ben-hinnom, at the entrance of the Potsherd Gate; there proclaim the words which I will speak to you: 3 Listen to the word of the LORD, kings of Judah and citizens of Jerusalem: Thus says the LORD of hosts, the God of Israel: I am going to bring such evil upon this place that all who hear of it will feel their ears tingle. 4 This is because they have forsaken me and alienated this place by burning in it incense to strange gods which neither they nor their fathers knew; and the kings of Judah have filled this place with the blood of the innocent. 5 They have built high places for Baal to immolate their sons in fire as holocausts to Baal: such a thing as I neither commanded nor spoke of, nor did it ever enter my mind. 6 Therefore, days will come, says the LORD, when this place will no longer be called Topheth, or the Valley of Ben-hinnom, but rather, the Valley of Slaughter. 7 In this place I will foil the plan of Judah and Jerusalem; I will make them fall by the sword before their enemies, by the hand of those that seek their lives. Their corpses I will give as food to the birds of the sky and the beasts of the field. 8 I will make this city an object of amazement and derision. Because of all its wounds, every passer-by will be amazed and will catch his breath. 9 I will have them eat the flesh of their sons and daughters; they shall eat one another's flesh during the strict siege by which their enemies and those who seek their lives will confine them. 10 And you shall break the flask in the sight of the men who went with you, 11 and say to them: Thus says the LORD of hosts: Thus will I smash this people and this city, as one smashes a clay pot so that it cannot be repaired. And Topheth shall be a burial place, for lack of place to bury elsewhere. 12 Thus I will do to this place and to its inhabitants, says the LORD; I will make this city like Topheth. 13 And the houses of Jerusalem and the palaces of the kings of Judah shall be defiled like the place of Topheth, all the houses upon whose roofs they burnt incense to the whole host of heaven and poured out libations to strange gods. 14 When Jeremiah returned from Topheth, where the LORD had sent him to prophesy, he stood in the court of the house of God and said to all the people: 15 Thus says the LORD of hosts, the God of Israel: I will surely bring upon this city all the evil with which I threatened it, because they have stiffened their necks and have not obeyed my words.

Jeremiah Chapter 20

1 Jeremiah was heard prophesying these things by the priest Pashhur, son of Immer, chief officer in the house of the Lord. 2 So he had the prophet scourged and placed in the stocks at the upper Gate of Benjamin in the house of the Lord. 3 The next morning, after Pashhur had released Jeremiah from the stocks, the prophet said to him: Instead of Pashhur, the Lord will name you "Terror on every side." 4 For thus says the Lord: Indeed, I will deliver you to terror, you and all your friends. Your own eyes shall see them fall by the sword of their enemies. All Judah I will deliver to the king of Babylon, who shall take them captive to Babylon or slay them with the sword. 5 All the wealth of this city, all it has toiled for and holds dear, all the treasures of the kings of Judah, I will give as plunder into the hands of their foes, who shall seize it and carry it away to Babylon. 6 You, Pashhur, and all the members of your household shall go into exile. To Babylon you shall go, you and all your friends; there you shall die and be buried, because you have prophesied lies to them. 7 You duped me, O Lord, and I let myself be duped; you were too strong for me, and you triumphed. All the day I am an object of laughter; everyone mocks me. 8 Whenever I speak, I must cry out, violence and outrage is my message; the word of the Lord has brought me derision and reproach all the day. 9 I say to myself, I will not mention him, I will speak in his name no more. But then it becomes like fire burning in my heart, imprisoned in my bones; I grow weary holding it in, I cannot endure it. 10 Yes, I hear the whisperings of many: "Terror on every side! Denounce! Let us denounce him!" All those who were my friends are on the watch for any misstep of mine. "Perhaps he will be trapped; then we can prevail, and take our vengeance on him." 11 But the Lord is with me, like a mighty champion: my persecutors will stumble, they will not triumph. In their failure they will be put to utter shame, to lasting, unforgettable confusion. 12 O Lord of hosts, you who test the just, who probe mind and heart, let me witness the vengeance you take on them, for to you I have entrusted my cause. 13 Sing to the Lord, praise the Lord, for he has rescued the life of the poor from the power of the wicked! 14 Cursed be the day on which I was born! May the day my mother gave me birth never be blessed! 15 Cursed be the man who brought the news to my father, saying, "A child, a son, has been born to you!" filling him with great joy. 16 Let that man be like the cities which the Lord relentlessly overthrew; let him hear war cries in the morning, battle alarms at noonday, 17 because he did not dispatch me in the womb! Then my mother would have been my grave, her womb confining me forever. 18 Why did I come forth from the womb, to see sorrow and pain, to end my days in shame?

Jeremiah Chapter 21

1 The message which came to Jeremiah from the LORD when King Zedekiah sent him Pashhur, son of Malchiah, and the priest Zephaniah, son of Maaseiah, with this request: 2 Inquire for us of the LORD, because Nebuchadnezzar, king of Babylon, is attacking us. Perhaps the LORD will deal with us according to all his wonderful works, so that he will withdraw from us. 3 But Jeremiah answered them: This is what you shall report to Zedekiah: 4 Thus says the LORD, the God of Israel: I will turn back in your hands the weapons with which you intend to fight the king of Babylon and the Chaldeans who besiege you outside the walls. These weapons I will pile up in the midst of this city, 5 and I myself will fight against you with outstretched hand and mighty arm, in anger, and wrath, and great rage! 6 I will strike the inhabitants of this city, both man and beast; they shall die in a great pestilence. 7 After that, says the LORD, I will hand over Zedekiah, king of Judah, and his ministers and the people in this city who survive pestilence, sword, and famine, into the hand of Nebuchadnezzar, king of Babylon, into the hands of their enemies and those who seek their lives. He shall strike them with the edge of the sword, without quarter, without pity or mercy. 8 And to this people you shall say: Thus says the LORD: See, I am giving you a choice between life and death. 9 Whoever remains in this city shall die by the sword or famine or pestilence. But whoever leaves and surrenders to the besieging Chaldeans shall live and have his life as booty. 10 For I have turned against this city, for its woe and not for its good, says the LORD. It shall be given into the power of the king of Babylon who shall burn it with fire. 11 To the royal house of Judah: Hear the word of the LORD, 12 O house of David! Thus says the LORD: Each morning dispense justice, rescue the oppressed from the hand of the oppressor, Lest my fury break out like fire which burns without being quenched, because of the evil of your deeds. 13 Beware! I am against you, Valley-site, Rock of the Plain, says the LORD. You who say, "Who will attack us, who can penetrate our retreats?" 14 I will punish you, says the LORD, as your deeds deserve! I will kindle a fire in its forest that shall devour all its surroundings.

Jeremiah Chapter 22

1 The LORD told me this: Go down to the palace of the king of Judah and there deliver this message: 2 You shall say: Listen to the word of the

LORD, king of Judah, who sit on the throne of David, you, your ministers, and your people that enter by these gates! 3 Thus says the LORD: Do what is right and just. Rescue the victim from the hand of his oppressor. Do not wrong or oppress the resident alien, the orphan, or the widow, and do not shed innocent blood in this place. 4 If you carry out these commands, kings who succeed to the throne of David will continue to enter the gates of this palace, riding in chariots or mounted on horses, with their ministers, and their people. 5 But if you do not obey these commands, I swear by myself, says the LORD: this palace shall become rubble. 6 For thus says the LORD concerning the palace of the king of Judah: Though you be to me like Gilead, like the peak of Lebanon, I will turn you into a waste, a city uninhabited. 7 Against you I will send destroyers, each with his axe: They shall cut down your choice cedars, and cast them into the fire. 8 Many people will pass by this city and ask one another: "Why has the LORD done this to so great a city?" 9 And the answer will be given: "Because they have deserted their covenant with the LORD, their God, by worshiping and serving strange gods." 10 Weep not for him who is dead, mourn not for him! Weep rather for him who is going away; never again will he see the land of his birth. 11 Thus says the LORD concerning Shallum, son of Josiah, king of Judah, who succeeded his father as king. He has left this place never to return. 12 Rather, he shall die in the place where they exiled him; this land he shall not see again. 13 Woe to him who builds his house on wrong, his terraces on injustice; Who works his neighbor without pay, and gives him no wages. 14 Who says, "I will build myself a spacious house, with airy rooms," Who cuts out windows for it, panels it with cedar, and paints it with vermilion. 15 Must you prove your rank among kings by competing with them in cedar? Did not your father eat and drink? He did what was right and just, and it went well with him. 16 Because he dispensed justice to the weak and the poor, it went well with him. Is this not true knowledge of me? says the LORD. 17 But your eyes and heart are set on nothing except on your own gain, On shedding innocent blood, on practicing oppression and extortion. 18 Therefore, thus says the LORD concerning Jehoiakim, son of Josiah, king of Judah: They shall not lament him, "Alas! my brother"; "Alas! sister." They shall not lament him, "Alas, Lord! alas, Majesty!" 19 The burial of an ass shall he be given, dragged forth and cast out beyond the gates of Jerusalem. 20 Scale Lebanon and cry out, in Bashan lift up your voice; Cry out from Abarim, for all your lovers are crushed. 21 I spoke to you when you were secure, but you answered, "I will not listen." This has been your way from your youth, not to listen to my voice. 22 The wind shall shepherd all your shepherds, your lovers shall go into exile. Surely then you shall be ashamed and confounded because of all your wickedness. 23 You who dwell on Lebanon, who nest in the cedars, How you shall groan when pains come upon you, like the pangs of a woman in travail! 24 As I live, says the LORD, if you, Coniah, son of Jehoiakim, king of Judah, are a signet ring on my right hand, I will snatch you from it. 25 I will deliver you into the hands of those who seek your life; the hands of those whom you fear; the hands of Nebuchadnezzar, king of Babylon, and the Chaldeans. 26 I will cast you out, you and the mother who bore you, into a different land from the one you were born in; and there you shall die. 27 Neither of them shall come back to the land for which they yearn. 28 Is this man Coniah a vessel despised, to be broken up, an instrument that no one wants? Why are he and his descendants cast out? why thrown into a land they know not? 29 O land, land, land, hear the word of the LORD — 30 Thus says the LORD: Write this man down as one childless, who will never thrive in his lifetime! No descendant of his shall achieve a seat on the throne of David as ruler again over Judah.

Jeremiah Chapter 23

1 Woe to the shepherds who mislead and scatter the flock of my pasture, says the LORD. 2 Therefore, thus says the LORD, the God of Israel, against the shepherds who shepherd my people: You have scattered my sheep and driven them away. You have not cared for them, but I will take care to punish your evil deeds. 3 I myself will gather the remnant of my flock from all the lands to which I have driven them and bring them back to their meadow; there they shall increase and multiply. 4 I will appoint shepherds for them who will shepherd them so that they need no longer fear and tremble; and none shall be missing, says the LORD. 5 Behold, the days are coming, says the LORD, when I will raise up a righteous shoot to David; As king he shall reign and govern wisely, he shall do what is just and right in the land. 6 In his days Judah shall be saved, Israel shall dwell in security. This is the name they give him: "The LORD our justice." 7 Therefore, the days will come, says the LORD, when they shall no longer say, "As the LORD lives, who brought the Israelites out of the land of Egypt"; 8 but rather, "As the LORD lives, who brought the descendants of the house of Israel up from the land of the north"—and from all the lands to which I banished them; they shall

again live on their own land. 9 Concerning the prophets: My heart within me is broken, my bones all tremble; I am like a man who is drunk, overcome by wine, Because of the LORD, because of his holy words. 10 With adulterers the land is filled; on their account the land mourns, the pasture ranges are seared. Theirs is an evil course, theirs is unjust power. 11 Both prophet and priest are godless! In my very house I find their wickedness, says the LORD. 12 Hence their way shall become for them slippery ground. In the darkness they shall lose their footing, and fall headlong; Evil I will bring upon them: the year of their punishment, says the LORD. 13 Among Samaria's prophets I saw unseemly deeds: They prophesied by Baal and led my people Israel astray. 14 But among Jerusalem's prophets I saw deeds still more shocking: Adultery, living in lies, siding with the wicked, so that no one turns from evil; To me they are all like Sodom, its citizens like Gomorrah. 15 Therefore, thus says the LORD of hosts against the prophets: Behold, I will give them wormwood to eat, and poison to drink; For from Jerusalem's prophets ungodliness has gone forth into the whole land. 16 Thus says the LORD of hosts: Listen not to the words of your prophets, who fill you with emptiness; Visions of their own fancy they speak, not from the mouth of the LORD. 17 They say to those who despise the word of the LORD, "Peace shall be yours"; And to everyone who walks in hardness of heart, "No evil shall overtake you." 18 Now, who has stood in the council of the LORD, to see him and to hear his word? Who has heeded his word, so as to announce it? 19 See, the storm of the LORD! His wrath breaks forth In a whirling storm that bursts upon the heads of the wicked. 20 The anger of the LORD shall not abate until he has done and fulfilled what he has determined in his heart. When the time comes, you shall fully understand. 21 I did not send these prophets, yet they ran; I did not speak to them, yet they prophesied. 22 Had they stood in my council, and did they but proclaim to my people my words, They would have brought them back from evil ways and from their wicked deeds. 23 Am I a God near at hand only, says the LORD, and not a God far off? 24 Can a man hide in secret without my seeing him? says the LORD. Do I not fill both heaven and earth? says the LORD. 25 I have heard the prophets who prophesy lies in my name say, "I had a dream! I had a dream!" 26 How long will this continue? Is my name in the hearts of the prophets who prophesy lies and their own deceitful fancies? 27 By their dreams which they recount to each other, they think to make my people forget my name, just as their fathers forgot my name for Baal. 28 Let the prophet who has a dream recount his dream; let him who has my word speak my word truthfully! What has straw to do with the wheat? says the LORD. 29 Is not my word like fire, says the LORD, like a hammer shattering rocks? 30 Therefore I am against the prophets, says the LORD, who steal my words from each other. 31 Yes, I am against the prophets, says the LORD, who borrow speeches to pronounce oracles. 32 Yes, I am against the prophets who prophesy lying dreams, says the LORD, and who lead my people astray by recounting their lies and by their empty boasting. From me they have no mission or command, and they do this people no good at all, says the LORD. 33 And when this people, or a prophet or a priest asks you, "What is the burden of the LORD?" you shall answer, "You are the burden, and I cast you off, says the LORD." 34 If a prophet or a priest or anyone else mentions "the burden of the LORD," I will punish that man and his house. 35 Thus you shall ask, when speaking to one another, "What answer did the LORD give?" or, "What did the LORD say?" 36 But the burden of the LORD you shall mention no more. For each man his own word becomes the burden so that you pervert the words of the living God, the LORD of hosts, our God. 37 Thus shall you ask the prophet, "What answer did the LORD give?" or, "What did the LORD say?" 38 But if you ask about "the burden of the LORD," then thus says the LORD: Because you use this phrase, "the burden of the LORD," though I forbade you to use it, 39 therefore I will lift you on high and cast you from my presence, you and the city which I gave to you and your fathers. 40 And I will bring upon you eternal reproach, eternal, unforgettable shame.

Jeremiah Chapter 24

1 The LORD showed me two baskets of figs placed before the temple of the LORD. This was after Nebuchadnezzar, king of Babylon, had exiled from Jerusalem Jeconiah, son of Jehoiakim, king of Judah, and the princes of Judah, the artisans and the skilled workers, and brought them to Babylon. 2 One basket contained excellent figs, the early-ripening kind. But the other basket contained very bad figs, so bad they could not be eaten. 3 Then the LORD said to me: What do you see, Jeremiah? "Figs," I replied; "the good ones are very good, but the bad ones very bad, so bad they cannot be eaten." 4 Thereupon this word of the LORD came to me: 5 Thus says the LORD, the God of Israel: Like these good figs, even so will I regard with favor Judah's exiles whom I sent away from this place into the land of the Chaldeans. 6 I will look

after them for their good, and bring them back to this land, to build them up, not to tear them down; to plant them, not to pluck them out. [7] I will give them a heart with which to understand that I am the LORD. They shall be my people and I will be their God, for they shall return to me with their whole heart. [8] And like the figs that are bad, so bad they cannot be eaten—yes, thus says the LORD—even so will I treat Zedekiah, king of Judah, and his princes, the remnant of Jerusalem remaining in this land and those who have settled in the land of Egypt. [9] I will make them an object of horror to all the kingdoms of the earth, a reproach and a byword, a taunt and a curse, in all the places to which I will drive them. [10] I will send upon them the sword, famine, and pestilence, until they have disappeared from the land which I gave them and their fathers.

Jeremiah Chapter 25

[1] The word that came to Jeremiah concerning all the people of Judah, in the fourth year of Jehoiakim, son of Josiah, king of Judah (the first year of Nebuchadnezzar, king of Babylon). [2] This word the prophet Jeremiah spoke to all the people of Judah and all the citizens of Jerusalem: [3] Since the thirteenth year of Josiah, son of Amon, king of Judah, to this day—these three and twenty years—the word of the LORD has come to me and I spoke to you untiringly, but you would not listen. [4] Though you refused to listen or pay heed, the LORD has sent you without fail all his servants the prophets [5] with this message: Turn back, each of you, from your evil way and from your evil deeds; then you shall remain in the land which the LORD gave you and your fathers, from of old and forever. [6] Do not follow strange gods to serve and adore them, lest you provoke me with your handiwork, and I bring evil upon you. [7] But you would not listen to me, says the LORD, and so you provoked me with your handiwork to your own harm. [8] Hence, thus says the LORD of hosts: Since you would not listen to my words, [9] lo! I will send for and fetch all the tribes of the north, says the LORD (and I will send to Nebuchadnezzar, king of Babylon, my servant); I will bring them against this land, against its inhabitants, and against all these neighboring nations. I will doom them, making them an object of horror, of ridicule, of everlasting reproach. [10] Among them I will bring to an end the song of joy and the song of gladness, the voice of the bridegroom and the voice of the bride, the sound of the millstone and the light of the lamp. [11] This whole land shall be a ruin and a desert. Seventy years these nations shall be enslaved to the king of Babylon; [12] but when the seventy years have elapsed, I will punish the king of Babylon and the nation and the land of the Chaldeans for their guilt, says the LORD. Their land I will turn into everlasting desert. [13] Against that land I will fulfill all the words I have spoken against it (all that is written in this book, which Jeremiah prophesied against all the nations). [14] They also shall be enslaved to great nations and mighty kings, and thus I will repay them according to their own deeds and according to their own handiwork. [15] For thus said the LORD, the God of Israel, to me: Take this cup of foaming wine from my hand, and have all the nations to whom I will send you drink it. [16] They shall drink, and be convulsed, and go mad, because of the sword I will send among them. [17] I took the cup from the hand of the LORD and gave drink to all the nations to which the LORD sent me: [18] (Jerusalem, the cities of Judah, her kings and her princes, to make them a ruin and a desert, an object of ridicule and cursing, as they are today;) [19] Pharaoh, king of Egypt, and his servants, his princes, all the people under him, native [20] and foreign; all the kings of the land of Uz; all the kings of the land of the Philistines: Ashkelon, Gaza, Ekron, and the remnant of Ashdod; [21] Edom, Moab, and the Ammonites; [22] all the kings of Tyre, of Sidon, and of the shores beyond the sea; [23] Dedan and Tema and Buz, all the desert dwellers who shave their temples; [24] all the kings of Arabia; [25] all the kings of Zimri, of Elam, of the Medes; [26] all the kings of the north, near and far, one after the other; all the kingdoms upon the face of the earth (and after them the king of Sheshach shall drink). [27] Tell them: Thus says the LORD of hosts, the God of Israel: Drink! become drunk and vomit; fall, never to rise, before the sword that I will send among you! [28] If they refuse to take the cup from your hand and drink, say to them: Thus says the LORD of hosts: You must drink! [29] For since with this city, which is called by my name, I begin to inflict evil, how can you possibly be spared? You shall not be spared! I will call down the sword upon all who inhabit the earth, says the LORD of hosts. [30] Prophesy against them all these things and say to them: The LORD roars from on high, from his holy dwelling he raises his voice; Mightily he roars over the range, a shout like that of vintagers over the grapes. [31] To all who inhabit the earth to its very ends the uproar spreads; For the LORD has an indictment against the nations, he is to pass judgment upon all mankind: The godless shall be given to the sword, says the LORD. [32] Thus says the LORD of hosts: Lo! calamity stalks from nation to nation; A great storm is unleashed from the ends of the earth. [33] On that day,

those whom the LORD has slain will be strewn from one end of the earth to the other. None will mourn them, none will gather them for burial; they shall lie like dung on the field. [34] Howl, you shepherds, and wail! roll in the dust, leaders of the flock! The time for your slaughter has come; like choice rams you shall fall. [35] There is no flight for the shepherds, no escape for the leaders of the flock. [36] Listen! Wailing from the shepherds, howling by the leaders of the flock! For the LORD lays waste their grazing place, [37] desolate lie the peaceful pastures; [38] The lion leaves his lair, and their land is made desolate By the sweeping sword, by the burning wrath of the LORD.

Jeremiah Chapter 26

[1] In the beginning of the reign of Jehoiakim, son of Josiah, king of Judah, this message came from the LORD: [2] Thus says the LORD: Stand in the court of the house of the LORD and speak to the people of all the cities of Judah who come to worship in the house of the LORD; whatever I command you, tell them, and omit nothing. [3] Perhaps they will listen and turn back, each from his evil way, so that I may repent of the evil I have planned to inflict upon them for their evil deeds. [4] Say to them: Thus says the LORD: If you disobey me, not living according to the law I placed before you [5] and not listening to the words of my servants the prophets, whom I send you constantly though you do not obey them, [6] I will treat this house like Shiloh, and make this the city which all the nations of the earth shall refer to when cursing another. [7] Now the priests, the prophets, and all the people heard Jeremiah speak these words in the house of the LORD. [8] When Jeremiah finished speaking all that the LORD bade him speak to all the people, the priests and prophets laid hold of him, crying, "You must be put to death! [9] Why do you prophesy in the name of the LORD: 'This house shall be like Shiloh,' and 'This city shall be desolate and deserted'?" And all the people gathered about Jeremiah in the house of the LORD. [10] When the princes of Judah were informed of these things, they came up from the king's palace to the house of the LORD and held court at the New Gate of the house of the LORD. [11] The priests and prophets said to the princes and to all the people, "This man deserves death; he has prophesied against this city, as you have heard with your own ears." [12] Jeremiah gave this answer to the princes and all the people: "It was the LORD who sent me to prophesy against this house and city all that you have heard. [13] Now, therefore, reform your ways and your deeds; listen to the voice of the LORD your God, so that the LORD will repent of the evil with which he threatens you. [14] As for me, I am in your hands; do with me what you think good and right. [15] But mark well: if you put me to death, it is innocent blood you bring on yourselves, on this city and its citizens. For in truth it was the LORD who sent me to you, to speak all these things for you to hear." [16] Thereupon the princes and all the people said to the priests and the prophets, "This man does not deserve death; it is in the name of the LORD, our God, that he speaks to us." [17] At this, some of the elders of the land came forward and said to all the people assembled, [18] "Micah of Moresheth used to prophesy in the days of Hezekiah, king of Judah, and he told all the people of Judah: Thus says the LORD of hosts: Zion shall become a plowed field, Jerusalem a heap of ruins, and the temple mount a forest ridge. [19] Did Hezekiah, king of Judah, and all Judah condemn him to death? Did they not rather fear the LORD and entreat the favor of the LORD, so that he repented of the evil with which he had threatened them? But we are on the point of committing this great evil to our own undoing." [20] There was another man who prophesied in the name of the LORD, Uriah, son of Shemaiah, from Kiriath-jearim; he prophesied the same things against this city and land as Jeremiah did. [21] When King Jehoiakim and all his officers and princes were informed of his words, the king sought to kill him. But Uriah heard of it and fled in fear to Egypt. [22] Thereupon King Jehoiakim sent Elnathan, son of Achbor, and others with him into Egypt [23] to bring Uriah back to the king, who had him slain by the sword and his corpse cast into the common grave. [24] But Ahikam, son of Shaphan, protected Jeremiah, so that he was not handed over to the people to be put to death.

Jeremiah Chapter 27

[1] In the beginning of the reign of Jehoiakim, son of Josiah, king of Judah, this message came to Jeremiah from the LORD: [2] Thus said the LORD to me: Make for yourself bands and yoke bars and put them over your shoulders. [3] Send to the kings of Edom, of Moab, of the Ammonites, of Tyre, and of Sidon, through the ambassadors who have come to Jerusalem to Zedekiah, king of Judah, [4] and charge them thus: Tell your masters: Thus says the LORD of hosts, the God of Israel: It was I who made the earth, and man and beast on the face of the earth, by my great power, with my outstretched arm; and I can give them to whomever I think fit. [6] Now I have given all these lands into the hand of Nebuchadnezzar, king of Babylon, my servant; even the beasts of the

field I have given him for his use. 7 All nations shall serve him and his son and his grandson, until the time of his land, too, shall come. Then it in turn shall serve great nations and mighty kings. 8 Meanwhile, if any nation or kingdom will not serve Nebuchadnezzar, king of Babylon, or will not bend its neck under the yoke of the king of Babylon, I will punish that nation with sword, famine, and pestilence, says the LORD, until I give them into his hand. 9 You, however, must not listen to your prophets, to your diviners and dreamers, to your soothsayers and sorcerers, who say to you, "You need not serve the king of Babylon." 10 For they prophesy lies to you, in order to drive you far from your land, to make me banish you so that you will perish. 11 The people that submits its neck to the yoke of the king of Babylon to serve him I will leave in peace on its own land, says the LORD, to till it and dwell in it. 12 To Zedekiah, king of Judah, I spoke the same words: Submit your necks to the yoke of the king of Babylon; serve him and his people, so that you may live. 13 Why should you and your people die by sword, famine, and pestilence, with which the LORD has threatened the nation that will not serve the king of Babylon? 14 Do not listen to the words of those prophets who say, "You need not serve the king of Babylon," for they prophesy lies to you. 15 I did not send them, says the LORD, but they prophesy falsely in my name, with the result that I must banish you, and you will perish, you and the prophets who are prophesying to you. 16 To the priests and to all the people I spoke as follows: Thus says the LORD: Do not listen to the words of your prophets who prophesy to you: "The vessels of the house of the LORD will be brought back from Babylon soon now," for they prophesy lies to you. 17 Do not listen to them! Serve the king of Babylon that you may live; else this city will become a heap of ruins. 18 If they were prophets, if the word of the LORD were with them, they would intercede with the LORD of hosts, that the vessels which remain in the house of the LORD and in the palace of the king of Judah and in Jerusalem might not be taken to Babylon. 19 For thus says the LORD of hosts concerning the pillars, the bronze sea, the stands, and the rest of the vessels that remain in this city, 20 which Nebuchadnezzar, king of Babylon, did not take when he exiled Jeconiah, son of Jehoiakim, king of Judah, from Jerusalem to Babylon, along with all the nobles of Judah and Jerusalem— 21 yes, thus says the LORD of hosts, the God of Israel, concerning the vessels that remain in the house of the LORD, in the palace of the king of Judah, and in Jerusalem: 22 To Babylon they shall be brought, and there they shall remain, until the day I look for them, says the LORD; then I will bring them back and restore them to this place.

Jeremiah Chapter 28

1 That same year, in the beginning of the reign of Zedekiah, king of Judah, in the fifth month of the fourth year, the prophet Hananiah, son of Azzur, from Gibeon, said to me in the house of the LORD in the presence of the priests and all the people: 2 "Thus says the LORD of hosts, the God of Israel: 'I will break the yoke of the king of Babylon. 3 Within two years I will restore to this place all the vessels of the temple of the LORD which Nebuchadnezzar, king of Babylon, took away from this place to Babylon. 4 And I will bring back to this place Jeconiah, son of Jehoiakim, king of Judah, and all the exiles of Judah who went to Babylon,' says the LORD. 'For I will break the yoke of the king of Babylon.'" 5 The prophet Jeremiah answered the prophet Hananiah in the presence of the priests and all the people assembled in the house of the LORD, 6 and said: Amen! thus may the LORD do! May he fulfill the things you have prophesied by bringing the vessels of the house of the LORD and all the exiles back from Babylon to this place! 7 But now, listen to what I am about to state in your hearing and the hearing of all the people. 8 From of old, the prophets who were before you and me prophesied war, woe, and pestilence against many lands and mighty kingdoms. 9 But the prophet who prophesies peace is recognized as truly sent by the LORD only when his prophetic prediction is fulfilled. 10 Thereupon the prophet Hananiah took the yoke from the neck of the prophet Jeremiah, broke it, 11 and said in the presence of all the people: "Thus says the LORD: 'Even so, within two years I will break the yoke of Nebuchadnezzar, king of Babylon, from off the neck of all the nations.'" At that, the prophet Jeremiah went away. 12 Some time after the prophet Hananiah had broken the yoke from off the neck of the prophet Jeremiah, the word of the LORD came to Jeremiah: 13 Go tell Hananiah this: Thus says the LORD: By breaking a wooden yoke, you forge an iron yoke! 14 For thus says the LORD of hosts, the God of Israel: A yoke of iron I will place on the necks of all these nations serving Nebuchadnezzar, king of Babylon, and they shall serve him; even the beasts of the field I give him. 15 To the prophet Hananiah the prophet Jeremiah said: Hear this, Hananiah! The LORD has not sent you, and you have raised false confidence in this people. 16 For this, says the LORD, I will dispatch you from the face of the earth; this very year you shall die, because you have preached rebellion against the LORD. 17

That same year, in the seventh month, Hananiah the prophet died.

Jeremiah Chapter 29

1 This is the contents of the letter which the prophet Jeremiah sent from Jerusalem to the remaining elders among the exiles, to the priests, the prophets, and all the people who were exiled by Nebuchadnezzar from Jerusalem to Babylon. 2 This was after King Jeconiah and the queen mother, the courtiers, the princes of Judah and Jerusalem, the artisans, and the skilled workmen had left Jerusalem. 3 Delivered in Babylon by Elasah, son of Shaphan, and by Gemariah, son of Hilkiah, whom Zedekiah, king of Judah, sent to the king of Babylon, the letter read: 4 Thus says the LORD of hosts, the God of Israel, to all the exiles whom I exiled from Jerusalem to Babylon: 5 Build houses to dwell in; plant gardens, and eat their fruits. 6 Take wives and beget sons and daughters; find wives for your sons and give your daughters husbands, so that they may bear sons and daughters. There you must increase in number, not decrease. 7 Promote the welfare of the city to which I have exiled you; pray for it to the LORD, for upon its welfare depends your own. 10 Thus says the LORD: Only after seventy years have elapsed for Babylon will I visit you and fulfill for you my promise to bring you back to this place. 11 For I know well the plans I have in mind for you, says the LORD, plans for your welfare, not for woe! plans to give you a future full of hope. 12 When you call me, when you go to pray to me, I will listen to you. 13 When you look for me, you will find me. Yes, when you seek me with all your heart, 14 you will find me with you, says the LORD, and I will change your lot; I will gather you together from all the nations and all the places to which I have banished you, says the LORD, and bring you back to the place from which I have exiled you. 16 Thus says the LORD concerning the king who sits on David's throne, and all the people who remain in this city, your brethren who did not go with you into exile; 17 thus says the LORD of hosts: I am sending against them sword, famine, and pestilence. I will make them like rotten figs, too bad to be eaten. 18 I will pursue them with sword, famine, and pestilence, and make them an object of horror to all the kingdoms of the earth, of malediction, astonishment, ridicule, and reproach to all the nations among which I will banish them. 19 For they did not listen to my words, says the LORD, though I kept sending them my servants the prophets, only to have them go unheeded, says the LORD. 20 You, now, listen to the word of the LORD, all you exiles whom I sent away from Jerusalem to Babylon. 15 As for your saying, "The LORD has raised up for us prophets here in Babylon"— 8 thus says the LORD of hosts, the God of Israel: Do not let yourselves be deceived by the prophets and diviners who are among you; do not listen to those among you who dream dreams. 9 For they prophesy lies to you in my name; I did not send them, says the LORD. 21 This is what the LORD of hosts, the God of Israel, has to say about those who prophesy lies to you in my name, Ahab, son of Kolaiah, and Zedekiah, son of Maaseiah: I am handing them over to Nebuchadnezzar, king of Babylon, who will slay them before your eyes. 22 All the exiles of Judah in Babylon will pattern a curse after them: "May the LORD make you like Zedekiah and Ahab, whom the king of Babylon roasted in the flames." 23 For they are criminals in Israel, committing adultery with their neighbors' wives, and alleging in my name things I did not command. I know, I am witness, says the LORD. 24 Say this to Shemaiah, the Nehelamite: 25 Thus says the LORD of hosts, the God of Israel: Because you sent letters on your own authority to all the people of Jerusalem, to all the priests and to Zephaniah, the priest, son of Maaseiah, with this message: 26 "The LORD has appointed you priest in place of the priest Jehoiada, so that there may be police officers in the house of the LORD, to take action against all madmen and those who pose as prophets, by putting them into the stocks or the pillory. 27 Why, then, do you not rebuke Jeremiah of Anathoth who poses as a prophet among you? 28 For he sent us in Babylon this message: It will be a long time; build houses to live in; plant gardens and eat their fruits." 29 When the priest Zephaniah read this letter to the prophet, 30 the word of the LORD came to Jeremiah: 31 Send the message to all the exiles: Thus says the LORD concerning Shemaiah, the Nehelamite: Because Shemaiah prophesies to you without a mission from me, and raises false confidence, 32 says the LORD, I will therefore punish Shemaiah, the Nehelamite, and his offspring. None of them shall survive among this people to see the good I will do to this people, says the LORD, because he preached rebellion against the LORD.

Jeremiah Chapter 30

1 The following message came to Jeremiah from the LORD: 2 Thus says the LORD, the God of Israel: Write all the words I have spoken to you in a book. 3 For behold, the days will come, says the LORD, when I will change the lot of my people (of Israel and Judah, says the LORD), and bring them back to the land which I gave to their fathers; they shall have

it as their possession. 4 These are the words which the LORD spoke to Israel and to Judah: 5 thus says the LORD: A cry of dismay we hear; fear reigns, not peace. 6 Inquire, and see: since when do men bear children? Why, then, do I see all these men, with their hands on their loins like women in childbirth? Why have all their faces turned deathly pale? 7 How mighty is that day—none like it! A time of distress for Jacob, though he shall be saved from it. 8 On that day, says the LORD of hosts, "I will break his yoke from off your necks and snap your bonds." Strangers shall no longer enslave them; 9 instead, they shall serve the LORD, their God, and David, their king, whom I will raise up for them. 10 But you, my servant Jacob, fear not, says the LORD, be not dismayed, O Israel! Behold, I will deliver you from the far-off land, your descendants, from their land of exile; Jacob shall again find rest, shall be tranquil and undisturbed, 11 for I am with you, says the LORD, to deliver you. I will make an end of all the nations among which I have scattered you; but of you I will not make an end. I will chastise you as you deserve, I will not let you go unpunished. 12 For thus says the LORD: Incurable is your wound, grievous your bruise; 13 There is none to plead your cause, no remedy for your running sore, no healing for you. 14 All your lovers have forgotten you, they do not seek you. I struck you as an enemy would strike, punished you cruelly; 15 Why cry out over your wound? your pain is without relief. Because of your great guilt, your numerous sins, I have done this to you. 16 Yet all who devour you shall be devoured, all your enemies shall go into exile. All who plunder you shall be plundered, all who pillage you I will hand over to pillage. 17 For I will restore you to health; of your wounds I will heal you, says the LORD. "The outcast" they have called you, "with no avenger." 18 Thus says the LORD: See! I will restore the tents of Jacob, his dwellings I will pity; City shall be rebuilt upon hill, and palace restored as it was. 19 From them will resound songs of praise, the laughter of happy men. I will make them not few, but many; they will not be tiny, for I will glorify them. 20 His sons shall be as of old, his assembly before me shall stand firm; I will punish all his oppressors. 21 His leader shall be one of his own, and his rulers shall come from his kin. When I summon him, he shall approach me; how else should one take the deadly risk of approaching me? says the LORD. 22 You shall be my people, and I will be your God. 23 See, the storm of the LORD! His wrath breaks forth In a whirling storm that bursts upon the heads of the wicked. 24 The anger of the LORD will not abate until he has done and fulfilled what he has determined in his heart. When the time comes, you will fully understand.

Jeremiah Chapter 31

1 At that time, says the LORD, I will be the God of all the tribes of Israel, and they shall be my people. 2 Thus says the LORD: The people that escaped the sword have found favor in the desert. As Israel comes forward to be given his rest, 3 the LORD appears to him from afar: With age-old love I have loved you; so I have kept my mercy toward you. 4 Again I will restore you, and you shall be rebuilt, O virgin Israel; Carrying your festive tambourines, you shall go forth dancing with the merrymakers. 5 Again you shall plant vineyards on the mountains of Samaria; those who plant them shall enjoy the fruits. 6 Yes, a day will come when the watchmen will call out on Mount Ephraim: "Rise up, let us go to Zion, to the LORD, our God." 7 For thus says the LORD: Shout with joy for Jacob, exult at the head of the nations; proclaim your praise and say: The LORD has delivered his people, the remnant of Israel. 8 Behold, I will bring them back from the land of the north; I will gather them from the ends of the world, with the blind and the lame in their midst, The mothers and those with child; they shall return as an immense throng. 9 They departed in tears, but I will console them and guide them; I will lead them to brooks of water, on a level road, so that none shall stumble. For I am a father to Israel, Ephraim is my first-born. 10 Hear the word of the LORD, O nations, proclaim it on distant coasts, and say: He who scattered Israel, now gathers them together, he guards them as a shepherd his flock. 11 The LORD shall ransom Jacob, he shall redeem him from the hand of his conqueror. 12 Shouting, they shall mount the heights of Zion, they shall come streaming to the LORD'S blessings: The grain, the wine, and the oil, the sheep and the oxen; They themselves shall be like watered gardens, never again shall they languish. 13 Then the virgins shall make merry and dance, and young men and old as well. I will turn their mourning into joy, I will console and gladden them after their sorrows. 14 I will lavish choice portions upon the priests, and my people shall be filled with my blessings, says the LORD. 15 Thus says the LORD: In Ramah is heard the sound of moaning, of bitter weeping! Rachel mourns her children, she refuses to be consoled because her children are no more. 16 Thus says the LORD: Cease your cries of mourning, wipe the tears from your eyes. The sorrow you have shown shall have its reward, says the LORD, they shall return from the enemy's land. 17 There is hope for your

future, says the LORD; your sons shall return to their own borders. 18 I hear, I hear Ephraim pleading: You chastised me, and I am chastened; I was an untamed calf. If you allow me, I will return, for you are the LORD, my God. 19 I turn in repentance; I have come to myself, I strike my breast; I blush with shame, I bear the disgrace of my youth. 20 Is Ephraim not my favored son, the child in whom I delight? Often as I threaten him, I still remember him with favor; My heart stirs for him, I must show him mercy, says the LORD. 21 Set up road markers, put up guideposts; Turn your attention to the highway, the road by which you went. Turn back, O virgin Israel, turn back to these your cities. 22 How long will you continue to stray, rebellious daughter? The LORD has created a new thing upon the earth: the woman must encompass the man with devotion. 23 Thus says the LORD of hosts, the God of Israel: When I change their lot in the land of Judah and her cities, they shall again repeat this greeting: "May the LORD bless you, holy mountain, abode of justice!" 24 Judah and all her cities, the farmers and those who lead the flock, shall dwell there together. 25 For I will refresh the weary soul; every soul that languishes I will replenish. 26 Upon this I awoke and opened my eyes; but my sleep was sweet to me. 27 The days are coming, says the LORD, when I will seed the house of Israel and the house of Judah with the seed of man and the seed of beast. 28 As I once watched over them to uproot and pull down, to destroy, to ruin, and to harm, so I will watch over them to build and to plant, says the LORD. 29 In those days they shall no longer say, "The fathers ate unripe grapes, and the children's teeth are set on edge," 30 but through his own fault only shall anyone die: the teeth of him who eats the unripe grapes shall be set on edge. 31 The days are coming, says the LORD, when I will make a new covenant with the house of Israel and the house of Judah. 32 It will not be like the covenant I made with their fathers the day I took them by the hand to lead them forth from the land of Egypt; for they broke my covenant and I had to show myself their master, says the LORD. 33 But this is the covenant which I will make with the house of Israel after those days, says the LORD. I will place my law within them, and write it upon their hearts; I will be their God, and they shall be my people. 34 No longer will they have need to teach their friends and kinsmen how to know the LORD. All, from least to greatest, shall know me, says the LORD, for I will forgive their evildoing and remember their sin no more. 35 Thus says the LORD, He who gives the sun to light the day, moon and stars to light the night; Who stirs up the sea till its waves roar, whose name is LORD of hosts: 36 If ever these natural laws give way in spite of me, says the LORD, Then shall the race of Israel cease as a nation before me forever. 37 Thus says the LORD: If the heavens on high can be measured, or the foundations below the earth be sounded, Then will I cast off the whole race of Israel because of all they have done, says the LORD. 38 The days are coming, says the LORD, when the city shall be rebuilt as the LORD'S, from the Tower of Hananel to the Corner Gate. 39 The measuring line shall be stretched from there straight to the hill Gareb and then turn to Goah. 40 The whole valley of corpses and ashes, all the slopes toward the Kidron Valley, as far as the corner of the Horse Gate at the east, shall be holy to the LORD. Never again shall the city be rooted up or thrown down.

Jeremiah Chapter 32

1 The message came to Jeremiah from the LORD in the tenth year of Zedekiah, king of Judah, and the eighteenth year of Nebuchadnezzar. 2 At that time, the army of the king of Babylon was besieging Jerusalem, and the prophet Jeremiah was imprisoned in the quarters of the guard at the king's palace. 3 Zedekiah, king of Judah, had imprisoned him, saying: "How dare you prophesy: Thus says the LORD: I am handing over this city to the king of Babylon, who will capture it. 4 Neither shall Zedekiah, king of Judah, escape from the hands of the Chaldeans; rather, he will be handed over to the king of Babylon. They will meet and speak face to face. 5 Zedekiah will be taken to Babylon and will remain there until I attend to him, says the LORD. You will not succeed in fighting the Chaldeans!" 6 This message came to me from the LORD, said Jeremiah: 7 "Hanamel, son of your uncle Shallum, will come to you with the offer: 'Buy for yourself my field in Anathoth, since you, as nearest relative, have the first right of purchase.'" 8 Then, as the LORD foretold, Hanamel, my uncle's son, came to me at the quarters of the guard and said, "Please buy my field in Anathoth, in the district of Benjamin, for you have the first claim to possess it." I knew this was what the LORD meant. 9 So, I bought the field in Anathoth from my cousin Hanamel, paying him seventeen silver shekels. 10 When I had written and sealed the deed, called witnesses, and weighed out the silver on the scales, 11 I accepted the deed of purchase, both the sealed copy and the open one. 12 I gave the deed to Baruch, son of Neriah, in the presence of my cousin Hanamel and the witnesses who signed the deed, before all the men of Judah in the quarters of the guard. 13 In their presence, I gave Baruch this charge: 14 "Thus says the LORD of hosts:

Take these deeds, both the sealed and open ones, and put them in an earthen jar to be kept for a long time." 15 For the LORD says: Houses, fields, and vineyards shall again be bought in this land. 16 After I gave the deed to Baruch, I prayed to the LORD: 17 "Ah, Lord GOD, you have made the heavens and the earth by your great might; nothing is impossible for you. 18 You continue your kindness for a thousand generations and repay the guilt of fathers to their children after them. O great and mighty God, whose name is the LORD of hosts, 19 great in counsel, mighty in deed, whose eyes are open to all the ways of men, you reward everyone according to their ways and the fruits of their deeds. 20 You performed signs and wonders in Egypt and to this day, in Israel and among all mankind, you have gained renown. 21 With strong hand and outstretched arm, you brought your people Israel out of Egypt with signs, wonders, and great terror. 22 You gave them this land, as you promised their fathers, a land flowing with milk and honey. 23 But they did not obey your voice, nor live according to your law. Therefore, you brought all this disaster upon them. 24 The siege ramps have reached the city to capture it; the city is handed over to the Chaldeans, amid sword, famine, and pestilence. Yet you tell me, 'Buy the field with money and call in witnesses,' even though the city is being captured!" 25 Then this word came to Jeremiah from the LORD: 26 "I am the LORD, the God of all mankind! Is anything impossible for me? 27 Therefore, I will hand over this city to Nebuchadnezzar, king of Babylon, to capture. 28 The Chaldeans will enter and burn the city and its houses, where incense was burned to Baal and offerings were made to strange gods, provoking me. 29 From their youth, the Israelites and Judeans have done only evil in my sight, constantly provoking me. 30 This city has excited my wrath from the day it was built until now, and I must remove it from my sight 31 because of the wickedness of Israel and Judah, their kings, princes, priests, prophets, and the people of Judah and Jerusalem. 32 They have turned their backs to me, not their faces, and although I taught them repeatedly, they would not listen. 33 They defiled my house with their idols, 34 and they built high places to Baal and offered their sons and daughters as sacrifices to Molech. This I never commanded, nor did it ever enter my mind to do such abominable things."35 "Nevertheless, I will gather them from the lands where I banished them in my wrath and fury. I will bring them back to this place and settle them in safety. 36 They shall be my people, and I will be their God. 37 I will give them one heart and one way so that they will always fear me for their own good and the good of their children. 38 I will make with them an everlasting covenant. I will never cease to do good for them, and I will put the fear of me into their hearts so they will never turn away from me. 39 I will rejoice in doing good for them and will plant them firmly in this land." 40 "Just as I brought upon this people all the disaster, so I will bring upon them all the good that I promise them. 41 Fields will again be bought in this land, which you now call a desolate place, handed over to the Chaldeans. 42 Fields will be bought, deeds will be signed, sealed, and witnessed, in the land of Benjamin, in the cities of Judah, and in the cities of the hill country and the Negeb, for I will restore their fortunes, says the LORD."

Jeremiah Chapter 33

1 The word of the LORD came to Jeremiah a second time while he was still imprisoned in the quarters of the guard: 2 Thus says the LORD who made the earth and gave it form and firmness, whose name is LORD: 3 Call to me, and I will answer you; I will tell to you things great beyond reach of your knowledge. 4 Thus says the LORD, the God of Israel, concerning the houses of this city and the palaces of Judah's kings, which are being destroyed in the face of siegeworks and the sword: 5 men come to battle the Chaldeans, and these houses will be filled with the corpses of those whom I slay in my anger and wrath, when I hide my face from this city for all their wickedness. 6 Behold, I will treat and assuage the city's wounds; I will heal them, and reveal to them an abundance of lasting peace. 7 I will change the lot of Judah and the lot of Israel, and rebuild them as of old. 8 I will cleanse them of all the guilt they incurred by sinning against me; all their offenses by which they sinned and rebelled against me, I will forgive. 9 Then Jerusalem shall be my joy, my praise, my glory, before all the nations of the earth, as they hear of all the good I will do among them. They shall be in fear and trembling over all the peaceful benefits I will give her. 10 Thus says the LORD: In this place of which you say, "How desolate it is, without man, without beast!" and in the cities of Judah, in the streets of Jerusalem that are now deserted, without man, without citizen, without beast, there shall yet be heard 11 the cry of joy, the cry of gladness, the voice of the bridegroom, the voice of the bride, the sound of those who bring thank offerings to the house of the LORD, singing, "Give thanks to the LORD of hosts, for the LORD is good; his mercy endures forever." For I will restore this country as of old, says the LORD. 12 Thus says the LORD of hosts: In this place, now desolate, without man or beast, and

in all its cities there shall again be sheepfolds for the shepherds to couch their flocks. 13 In the cities of the hill country, of the foothills, and of the Negeb, in the land of Benjamin and the suburbs of Jerusalem, and in the cities of Judah, flocks will again pass under the hands of the one who counts them, says the LORD. 14 The days are coming, says the LORD, when I will fulfill the promise I made to the house of Israel and Judah. 15 In those days, in that time, I will raise up for David a just shoot; he shall do what is right and just in the land. 16 In those days Judah shall be safe and Jerusalem shall dwell secure; this is what they shall call her: "The LORD our justice." 17 For thus says the LORD: Never shall David lack a successor on the throne of the house of Israel, 18 nor shall priests of Levi ever be lacking, to offer holocausts before me, to burn cereal offerings, and to sacrifice victims. 19 This word of the LORD also came to Jeremiah: 20 Thus says the LORD: If you can break my covenant with day, and my covenant with night, so that day and night no longer alternate in sequence, 21 then can my covenant with my servant David also be broken, so that he will not have a son to be king upon his throne, and my covenant with the priests of Levi who minister to me. 22 Like the host of heaven which cannot be numbered, and the sands of the sea which cannot be counted, I will multiply the descendants of my servant David and the Levites who minister to me. 23 This word of the LORD came to Jeremiah: 24 Have you not noticed what these people are saying: "The LORD has rejected the two tribes which he had chosen"? They spurn my people as if it were no longer a nation in their eyes. 25 Thus says the LORD: When I have no covenant with day and night, and have given no laws to heaven and earth, 26 then too will I reject the descendants of Jacob and of my servant David, so as not to take from his descendants rulers for the race of Abraham, Isaac, and Jacob. For I will change their lot and show them mercy.

Jeremiah Chapter 34

1 This word came to Jeremiah from the LORD while Nebuchadnezzar, king of Babylon, and his armies and the earth's kingdoms subject to him, as well as the other peoples, were all attacking Jerusalem and all her cities: 2 Thus says the LORD, the God of Israel: Go to Zedekiah, king of Judah, and tell him: Thus says the LORD: I am handing this city over to the king of Babylon; he will destroy it with fire. 3 Neither shall you escape his hand; rather you will be captured and fall into his hands. You shall see the king of Babylon and speak to him face to face. Then you shall be taken to Babylon. 4 But if you obey the word of the LORD, Zedekiah, king of Judah, then, says the LORD to you, you shall not die by the sword. 5 You shall die in peace, and they will lament you as their lord, and burn spices for your burial as they did for your fathers, the kings who preceded you from the first; it is I who make this promise, says the LORD. 6 The prophet Jeremiah told all these things to Zedekiah, king of Judah, in Jerusalem, 7 while the armies of the king of Babylon were attacking Jerusalem and the remaining cities of Judah, Lachish, and Azekah, since these alone were left of the fortified cities of Judah. 8 This is the word that came to Jeremiah from the LORD after King Zedekiah had made an agreement with all the people in Jerusalem to issue an edict of emancipation. 9 Everyone was to free his Hebrew slaves, male and female, so that no one should hold a man of Judah, his brother, in slavery. 10 All the princes and the others who entered the agreement consented to set free their male and female servants, so that they should be slaves no longer. But though they agreed and freed them, 11 afterward they took back their male and female slaves whom they had set free and again forced them into service. 12 Then this word of the LORD came to Jeremiah: 13 Thus says the LORD, the God of Israel: The day I brought your fathers out of the land of Egypt, out of the place where they were slaves, I made this covenant with them: 14 Every seventh year each of you shall set free his Hebrew brother who has sold himself to you; six years he shall serve you, but then you shall let him go free. Your fathers, however, did not heed me or obey me. 15 Today you indeed repented and did what is right in my eyes by proclaiming the emancipation of your brethren and making an agreement before me in the house that is named after me. 16 But then you changed your mind and profaned my name by taking back your male and female slaves to whom you had given their freedom; you forced them once more into slavery. 17 Therefore, thus says the LORD: You did not obey me by proclaiming your neighbors and kinsmen free. I now proclaim you free, says the LORD, for the sword, famine, and pestilence. I will make you an object of horror to all the kingdoms of the earth. 18 The men who violated my covenant and did not observe the terms of the agreement which they made before me, I will make like the calf which they cut in two, between whose two parts they passed. 19 The princes of Judah and of Jerusalem, the courtiers, the priests, and the common people, who passed between the parts of the calf, 20 I will hand over, all of them, to their enemies, to those who seek their lives: their corpses shall be food for the birds of the air and the beasts of the field. 21 Zedekiah, too, king

of Judah, and his princes, I will hand over to their enemies, to those who seek their lives, to the soldiers of the king of Babylon who have at present withdrawn from you. ²² I will give the command, says the LORD, and bring them back to this city. They shall attack and capture it, and destroy it with fire; the cities of Judah I will turn into a desert where no man dwells.

Jeremiah Chapter 35

¹ This word came to Jeremiah from the LORD in the days of Jehoiakim, son of Josiah, king of Judah: ² Approach the Rechabites and speak to them; bring them into the house of the LORD, to one of the rooms, and give them wine to drink. ³ So I went and brought Jaazaniah, son of Jeremiah, son of Habazziniah, his brothers and all his sons, the whole company of the Rechabites, ⁴ into the house of the LORD, to the room of the sons of Hanan, son of Igdaliah, the man of God, next to the princes' room, above the room of Maaseiah, son of Shallum, keeper of the doorway. ⁵ I set before these Rechabite men bowls full of wine and offered them cups to drink the wine. ⁶ "We do not drink wine," they said to me: "Jonadab, Rechab's son, our father, forbade us in these words: 'Neither you nor your children shall ever drink wine. ⁷ Build no house and sow no seed; neither plant nor own a vineyard. You shall dwell in tents all your life, so that you may live long on the earth where you are wayfarers.' ⁸ Now we have heeded Jonadab, Rechab's son, our father, in all his prohibitions. All our lives we have not drunk wine, neither we, nor our wives, nor our sons, nor our daughters. ⁹ We build no houses to live in; we own no vineyards or fields or crops, ¹⁰ and we live in tents; we obediently do everything our father Jonadab commanded us. ¹¹ But when Nebuchadnezzar, king of Babylon, invaded this land, we decided to come into Jerusalem to escape the army of the Chaldeans and the army of Aram; that is why we are now living in Jerusalem." ¹² Then this word of the LORD came to Jeremiah: ¹³ Thus says the LORD of hosts, the God of Israel: Go, say to the men of Judah and to the citizens of Jerusalem: Will you not take correction and obey my words? says the LORD. ¹⁴ The advice of Jonadab, Rechab's son, by which he forbade his children to drink wine, has been followed: to this day they have not drunk it; they obeyed their father's command. Me, however, you have not obeyed, although I spoke to you untiringly and insistently. ¹⁵ I kept sending you all my servants the prophets, telling you to turn back, all of you, from your evil way; to reform your conduct, and not follow strange gods or serve them, if you would remain on the land which I gave you and your fathers; but you did not heed me or obey me. ¹⁶ Yes, the children of Jonadab, Rechab's son, observed the command which their father laid on them; but this people does not obey me! ¹⁷ Now, therefore, says the LORD God of hosts, the God of Israel: I will bring upon Judah and all the citizens of Jerusalem every evil that I threatened; because when I spoke they did not obey, when I called they did not answer. ¹⁸ But to the company of the Rechabites Jeremiah said: Thus says the LORD of hosts, the God of Israel: Since you have obeyed the command of Jonadab, your father, kept all his commands and done everything he commanded you, ¹⁹ thus therefore says the LORD of hosts, the God of Israel: Never shall there fail to be a descendant of Jonadab, Rechab's son, standing in my service.

Jeremiah Chapter 36

¹ In the fourth year of Jehoiakim, son of Josiah, king of Judah, this word came to Jeremiah from the LORD: ² "Take a scroll and write on it all the words I have spoken to you against Israel, Judah, and all the nations, from the day I first spoke to you, in the days of Josiah, until today. ³ Perhaps, when the house of Judah hears all the evil I have in mind to do to them, they will turn back each from his evil way, so that I may forgive their wickedness and their sin." ⁴ So Jeremiah called Baruch, son of Neriah, who wrote down on a scroll, as Jeremiah dictated, all the words which the LORD had spoken to him. ⁹ In the ninth month, in the fifth year of Jehoiakim, son of Josiah, king of Judah, a fast to placate the LORD was proclaimed for all the people of Jerusalem and all who came from Judah's cities to Jerusalem. ⁵ Then Jeremiah charged Baruch: "I cannot go to the house of the LORD; I am prevented from doing so. ⁶ Do you go on the fast day and read publicly in the LORD'S house the LORD'S words from the scroll you wrote at my dictation; read them also to all the men of Judah who come up from their cities. ⁷ Perhaps they will lay their supplication before the LORD and will all turn back from their evil way; for great is the fury of anger with which the LORD has threatened this people." ⁸ Baruch, son of Neriah, did everything the prophet Jeremiah commanded; from the book-scroll he read the LORD'S words in the LORD'S house. ¹⁰ It was in the room of Gemariah, son of the scribe Shaphan, in the upper court of the LORD'S house, at the entrance of the New Temple-Gate, that Baruch publicly read the words of Jeremiah from his book. ¹¹ Now Micaiah, son of Gemariah, son of Shaphan, heard all the words of the LORD read from the book. ¹² So he went down to the king's palace, into the scribe's chamber, where the princes were just then in session: Elishama, the scribe, Delaiah, son of Shemaiah, Elnathan, son of Achbor, Gemariah, son of Shaphan, Zedekiah, son of Hananiah, and the other princes. ¹³ To them Micaiah reported all that he had heard Baruch read publicly from his book. ¹⁴ Thereupon the princes sent Jehudi, son of Nethaniah, son of Shelemiah, son of Cushi, to Baruch with the order: "Come, and bring with you the scroll you read publicly to the people." Scroll in hand, Baruch, son of Neriah, went to them. ¹⁵ "Sit down," they said to him, "and read it to us." Baruch read it to them, ¹⁶ and when they heard all its words, they were frightened and said to one another, "We must certainly tell the king all these things." ¹⁷ Then they asked Baruch: "Tell us, please, how you came to write down all these words." ¹⁸ "Jeremiah dictated all these words to me," Baruch answered them, "and I wrote them down with ink in the book." ¹⁹ At this the princes said to Baruch, "Go into hiding, you and Jeremiah; let no one know where you are." ²⁰ Leaving the scroll in safekeeping in the room of Elishama the scribe, they entered the room where the king was. When they told him everything that had happened, ²¹ he sent Jehudi to fetch the scroll. Jehudi brought it from the room of Elishama the scribe, and read it to the king and to all the princes who were in attendance on the king. ²² Now the king was sitting in his winter house, since it was the ninth month, and fire was burning in a brazier before him. ²³ Each time Jehudi finished reading three or four columns, the king would cut off the piece with a scribe's knife and cast it into the brazier, until the entire roll was consumed in the fire. ²⁴ Hearing all these words did not frighten the king and his ministers or cause them to rend their garments. ²⁵ And though Elnathan, Delaiah, and Gemariah urged the king not to burn the scroll, he would not listen to them, ²⁶ but commanded Jerahmeel, a royal prince, and Seraiah, son of Azriel, and Shelemiah, son of Abdeel, to arrest Baruch, the secretary, and the prophet Jeremiah. But the LORD kept them concealed. ²⁷ This word of the LORD came to Jeremiah, after the king burned the scroll with the text Jeremiah had dictated to Baruch: ²⁸ "Take another scroll, and write on it everything that the first scroll contained, which Jehoiakim, king of Judah, burned up. ²⁹ And against Jehoiakim, king of Judah, say this: Thus says the LORD: You burned that scroll, saying, 'Why did you write on it: Babylon's king shall surely come and lay waste this land and empty it of man and beast?' ³⁰ The LORD now says of Jehoiakim, king of Judah: No descendant of his shall succeed to David's throne; his corpse shall be cast out, exposed to the heat of day, to the cold of night. ³¹ I will punish him and his descendants and his ministers for their wickedness; against them and the citizens of Jerusalem and the men of Judah I will fulfill all the threats of evil which went unheeded." ³² Jeremiah took another scroll, and gave it to his secretary, Baruch, son of Neriah; he wrote on it at Jeremiah's dictation all the words contained in the book which Jehoiakim, king of Judah, had burned in the fire, and many others of the same kind in addition.

Jeremiah Chapter 37

¹ Coniah, son of Jehoiakim, was succeeded by King Zedekiah, son of Josiah; he was made king over the land of Judah by Nebuchadnezzar, king of Babylon. ² Neither he, nor his ministers, nor the people of the land would listen to the words of the LORD spoken by Jeremiah the prophet. ³ Yet King Zedekiah sent Jehucal, son of Shelemiah, and Zephaniah, son of Maaseiah the priest, to the prophet Jeremiah with this request: "Pray to the LORD, our God, for us." ⁴ At this time Jeremiah had not yet been put into prison; he still came and went freely among the people. ⁵ Also, Pharaoh's army had set out from Egypt, and when the Chaldeans who were besieging Jerusalem heard this report they marched away from the city. ⁶ This word of the LORD then came to the prophet Jeremiah: ⁷ "Thus says the LORD, the God of Israel: Give this answer to the king of Judah who sent you to me to consult me: Pharaoh's army which has set out to help you will return to its own land, Egypt. ⁸ The Chaldeans shall return to the fight against this city; they shall capture it and destroy it with fire. ⁹ Thus says the LORD: Do not deceive yourselves with the thought that the Chaldeans will leave you for good, because they shall not leave! ¹⁰ Even if you were to defeat the whole Chaldean army now attacking you, and only the wounded remained, each in his tent, these would rise up and destroy the city with fire." ¹¹ When the Chaldean army lifted the siege of Jerusalem at the threat of the army of Pharaoh, ¹² Jeremiah set out from Jerusalem for the district of Benjamin, to take part with his family in the division of an inheritance. ¹³ But when he reached the Gate of Benjamin, he met the captain of the guard, a man named Irijah, son of Shelemiah, son of Hananiah; he seized the prophet Jeremiah, saying, "You are deserting to the Chaldeans!" ¹⁴ "That is a lie!" Jeremiah answered, "I am not deserting to the Chaldeans." Without listening, Irijah kept Jeremiah in custody and brought him to the princes. ¹⁵ The princes were enraged,

and had Jeremiah beaten and thrown into prison in the house of Jonathan the scribe, which they were using as a jail. 16 And so Jeremiah entered the vaulted dungeon, where he remained a long time. 17 Once King Zedekiah had him brought to his palace and he asked him secretly whether there was any message from the LORD. Yes! Jeremiah answered: you shall be handed over to the king of Babylon. 18 Jeremiah then asked King Zedekiah: In what have I wronged you, or your ministers, or this people, that you should put me in prison? 19 And where are your own prophets now, 20 who prophesied to you that the king of Babylon would not attack you or this land? Hear now, my lord king, and grant my petition: do not send me back into the house of Jonathan the scribe, or I shall die there. 21 King Zedekiah ordered that Jeremiah be confined in the quarters of the guard, and given a loaf of bread each day from the bakers' shop until all the bread in the city was eaten up. Thus Jeremiah remained in the quarters of the guard.

Jeremiah Chapter 38

1 Shephatiah, son of Mattan, Gedaliah, son of Pashhur, Jucal, son of Shelemiah, and Pashhur, son of Malchiah, heard Jeremiah speaking these words to all the people: 2 Thus says the LORD: He who remains in this city shall die by sword, or famine, or pestilence; but he who goes out to the Chaldeans shall live; his life shall be spared him as booty, and he shall live. 3 Thus says the LORD: This city shall certainly be handed over to the army of the king of Babylon; he shall capture it. 4 "This man ought to be put to death," the princes said to the king; "he demoralizes the soldiers who are left in this city, and all the people, by speaking such things to them; he is not interested in the welfare of our people, but in their ruin." 5 King Zedekiah answered: "He is in your power"; for the king could do nothing with them. 6 And so they took Jeremiah and threw him into the cistern of Prince Malchiah, which was in the quarters of the guard, letting him down with ropes. There was no water in the cistern, only mud, and Jeremiah sank into the mud. 7 Now Ebed-melech, a Cushite, a courtier in the king's palace, heard that they had put Jeremiah into the cistern. The king happened just then to be at the Gate of Benjamin, 8 and Ebed-melech went there from the palace and said to him, 9 "My lord king, these men have been at fault in all they have done to the prophet Jeremiah, casting him into the cistern. He will die of famine on the spot, for there is no more food in the city." 10 Then the king ordered Ebed-melech the Cushite to take three men along with him, and draw the prophet Jeremiah out of the cistern before he should die. 11 Ebed-melech took the men along with him, and went first to the linen closet in the palace, from which he took some old, tattered rags; these he sent down to Jeremiah in the cistern, with ropes. 12 Then he said to Jeremiah, "Put the old, tattered rags between your armpits and the ropes." Jeremiah did so, 13 and they drew him up with the ropes out of the cistern. But Jeremiah remained in the quarters of the guard. 14 Once King Zedekiah summoned the prophet Jeremiah to come to him at the third entrance to the house of the LORD. "I have a question to ask you," the king said to Jeremiah; "hide nothing from me." Jeremiah answered Zedekiah: 15 If I tell you anything, you will have me killed, will you not? If I counsel you, you will not listen to me! 16 But King Zedekiah swore to Jeremiah secretly: "As the LORD lives who gave us the breath of life, I will not kill you; nor will I hand you over to these men who seek your life." 17 Thereupon Jeremiah said to Zedekiah: Thus says the LORD God of hosts, the God of Israel: If you surrender to the princes of Babylon's king, you shall save your life; this city shall not be destroyed with fire, and you and your family shall live. 18 But if you do not surrender to the princes of Babylon's king, this city shall fall into the hands of the Chaldeans, who shall destroy it with fire, and you shall not escape their hands. 19 King Zedekiah, however, said to Jeremiah, "I am afraid of the men of Judah who have deserted to the Chaldeans; I may be handed over to them, and they will mistreat me." 20 "You will not be handed over," Jeremiah answered. "Please obey the voice of the LORD and do as I tell you; then it shall go well with you, and your life will be spared. 21 But if you refuse to surrender, this is what the LORD shows me: 22 All the women left in the house of Judah's king shall be brought out to the princes of Babylon's king, and they shall taunt you thus: 'They betrayed you, outdid you, your good friends! Now that your feet are stuck in the mud, they slink away.' 23 All your wives and sons shall be led forth to the Chaldeans, and you shall not escape their hands; you shall be handed over to the king of Babylon, and this city shall be destroyed with fire." 24 Then Zedekiah said to Jeremiah, "Let no one know about this conversation, or you shall die. 25 If the princes hear I spoke to you, if they come and ask you, 'Tell us what you said to the king; do not hide it from us, or we will kill you,' or, 'What did the king say to you?' 26 give them this answer: 'I petitioned the king not to send me back to Jonathan's house to die there.'" 27 When all the princes came to Jeremiah, they questioned him, and he answered them in the very words the king had commanded. They said no more to him, for

nothing had been heard of the earlier conversation. 28 Thus Jeremiah stayed in the quarters of the guard till the day Jerusalem was taken. When Jerusalem was taken...

Jeremiah Chapter 39

1 In the tenth month of the ninth year of Zedekiah, king of Judah, Nebuchadnezzar, king of Babylon, and all his army marched against Jerusalem and besieged it. 2 On the ninth day of the fourth month, in the eleventh year of Zedekiah, a breach was made in the city's defenses. 3 All the princes of the king of Babylon came and occupied the middle gate: Nergal-sharezer, of Simmagir, the chief officer, Nebushazban, the high dignitary, and all the other princes of the king of Babylon. 4 When Zedekiah, king of Judah, saw them, he and all his warriors fled by night, leaving the city on the Royal Garden Road through the gate between the two walls. He went in the direction of the Arabah, 5 but the Chaldean army pursued them, and overtook and captured Zedekiah in the desert near Jericho. He was brought to Riblah, in the land of Hamath, where Nebuchadnezzar, king of Babylon, pronounced sentence upon him. 6 As Zedekiah looked on, his sons were slain at Riblah by order of the king of Babylon, who slew also all the nobles of Judah. 7 He then blinded Zedekiah and bound him in chains to bring him to Babylon. 8 The Chaldeans set fire to the king's palace and the houses of the people, and demolished the walls of Jerusalem. 9 Nebuzaradan, chief of the bodyguard, deported to Babylon the rest of the people left in the city, those who had deserted to him, and the rest of the workmen. 10 But some of the poor who had no property were left in the land of Judah by Nebuzaradan, chief of the bodyguard, and were given at the same time vineyards and farms. 11 Concerning Jeremiah, Nebuchadnezzar, king of Babylon, gave the following orders through Nebuzaradan, chief of the bodyguard: 12 "Take him and look after him; let no harm befall him, but treat him as he himself requests." 13 Thereupon Nebuzaradan, chief of the bodyguard, and Nebushazban, the high dignitary, and Nergal-sharezer, the chief officer, and all the nobles of the king of Babylon, 14 had Jeremiah taken out of the quarters of the guard, and entrusted to Gedaliah, son of Ahikam, son of Shaphan, to be brought home. And so he remained among the people. 15 While Jeremiah was still imprisoned in the quarters of the guard, the word of the LORD came to him: 16 Go, tell this to Ebed-melech the Cushite: Thus says the LORD of hosts, the God of Israel: Behold, I am now fulfilling the words I spoke against this city, for evil and not for good; and this before your very eyes. 17 But on that day I will rescue you, says the LORD; you shall not be handed over to the men of whom you are afraid. 18 I will make certain that you escape and do not fall by the sword. Your life shall be spared as booty, because you trusted in me, says the LORD.

Jeremiah Chapter 40

1 This word came to Jeremiah from the LORD, after Nebuzaradan, captain of the bodyguard, had released him in Ramah, where he had found him a prisoner in chains, among the captives of Jerusalem and Judah who were being exiled to Babylon. 2 When the captain of the bodyguard took charge of Jeremiah, he said to him, "The LORD, your God, foretold the ruin of this place. 3 Now he has brought about in deed what he threatened; because you sinned against the LORD and did not obey his voice, this fate has befallen you. 4 And now, I am freeing you today from the fetters that bind your hands; if it seems good to you to come with me to Babylon, you may come: I will look after you well. But if it does not please you to come to Babylon, you need not come. See, the whole land is before you; go wherever you think good and proper"; 5 and then, before he left - "or go to Gedaliah, son of Ahikam, son of Shaphan, whom the king of Babylon has appointed ruler over the cities of Judah; stay with him among the people, or go wherever you please." The captain of the bodyguard gave him food and gifts and let him go. 6 Jeremiah went to Gedaliah, son of Ahikam, in Mizpah, and stayed with him among the people left in the land. 7 When the army leaders who were still in the field with all their men heard that the king of Babylon had given Gedaliah, son of Ahikam, charge of the land, of men, women, and children, and of those poor who had not been led captive to Babylon, 8 they came with their men to Gedaliah in Mizpah: Ishmael, son of Nethaniah; Johanan, son of Kareah; Seraiah, son of Tanhumeth; the sons of Ephai of Netophah; and Jezaniah of Beth-maacah. 9 Gedaliah, son of Ahikam, son of Shaphan, adjured them and their men not to be afraid to serve the Chaldeans: to stay in the land and submit to the king of Babylon, for their own welfare; 10 saying that he himself would remain in Mizpah, as their intermediary with the Chaldeans who should come to them. They were to collect the wine, the fruit, and the oil, to store them in jars, and to settle in the cities they occupied. 11 When the people of Judah in Moab, those among the Ammonites, those in Edom, and those in all other lands heard that the king of Babylon had left a remnant in Judah, and had appointed over them Gedaliah, son of

Ahikam, son of Shaphan, 12 they all returned to the land of Judah from the places to which they had scattered. They went to Gedaliah at Mizpah and had a rich harvest of wine and fruit. 13 Now Johanan, son of Kareah, and all the leaders of the armies in the field came to Gedaliah in Mizpah 14 and asked him whether he did not know that Baalis, the king of the Ammonites, had sent Ishmael, son of Nethaniah, to assassinate him. 15 But Gedaliah, son of Ahikam, would not believe them. Then Johanan, son of Kareah, said secretly to Gedaliah in Mizpah: "Let me go and kill Ishmael, son of Nethaniah; no one will know it. Why should he be allowed to kill you? All the Jews who have now rallied to you will be dispersed and the remnant of Judah will perish." 16 Nevertheless, Gedaliah, son of Ahikam, answered Johanan, son of Kareah, "You shall do nothing of the kind; you have lied about Ishmael."

Jeremiah Chapter 41

1 In the seventh month, Ishmael, son of Nethaniah, son of Elishama, of royal descent, one of the king's nobles, came with ten men to Gedaliah, son of Ahikam, at Mizpah. And while they were together at table in Mizpah, 2 Ishmael, son of Nethaniah, and the ten who were with him, rose up and attacked with swords Gedaliah, son of Ahikam, son of Shaphan, whom the king of Babylon had made ruler over the land; and they killed him. 3 Ishmael also slew all the men of Judah of military age who were with Gedaliah and the Chaldean soldiers who were there. 4 The second day after the murder of Gedaliah, before anyone knew of it, 5 eighty men with beards shaved off, clothes in rags, and with gashes on their bodies came from Shechem, Shiloh, and Samaria, bringing food offerings and incense for the house of the LORD. 6 Ishmael, son of Nethaniah, went out from Mizpah to meet them, weeping as he went. 7 "Come to Gedaliah, son of Ahikam," he said as he met them. When they were once inside the city, Ishmael, son of Nethaniah, and his men slew them and threw them into the cistern. 8 But there were ten among them who pleaded with Ishmael: "Do not kill us; we have stores buried in the field: wheat and barley, oil and honey." And so he spared them and did not kill them, as he had killed their companions. 9 The cistern into which Ishmael threw all the corpses of the men he had killed was the large one made by King Asa to defend himself against Baasha, king of Israel; this cistern Ishmael, son of Nethaniah, filled with the slain. 10 Ishmael, son of Nethaniah, led away the remnant of the people left in Mizpah and the princesses, whom Nebuzaradan, captain of the bodyguard, had confided to Gedaliah, son of Ahikam. With these captives, Ishmael, son of Nethaniah, set out to make his way to the Ammonites. 11 But when Johanan, son of Kareah, and the other army leaders with him heard of the crimes Ishmael, son of Nethaniah, had committed, 12 they took all their men and set out to attack Ishmael, son of Nethaniah. They overtook him at the Great Waters in Gibeon. 13 At the sight of Johanan, son of Kareah, and the other army leaders, the people who were Ishmael's captives rejoiced. 14 All of those whom Ishmael had brought away from Mizpah went over to Johanan, son of Kareah. 15 But Ishmael, son of Nethaniah, escaped from Johanan and fled to the Ammonites with eight men. 16 Then Johanan, son of Kareah, and all his army leaders took charge of the remnant of the people, both the soldiers and the women and children with their guardians, whom Ishmael, son of Nethaniah, had brought away from Mizpah after he killed Gedaliah, son of Ahikam. From Gibeon, 17 they retreated to the lodging place of Chimham near Bethlehem, where they stopped, intending to flee into Egypt. 18 They were afraid of the Chaldeans, because Ishmael, son of Nethaniah, had slain Gedaliah, son of Ahikam, whom the king of Babylon had made ruler in the land of Judah.

Jeremiah Chapter 42

1 Then all the army leaders, Johanan, son of Kareah, Azariah, son of Hoshaiah, and all the people, high and low, approached the prophet Jeremiah 2 and said, "Grant our petition; pray for us to the LORD, your God, for all this remnant. We are now few who once were many, as you well see. 3 Let the LORD, your God, show us what way we should take and what we should do." 4 Very well! the prophet Jeremiah answered them: I will pray to the LORD, your God, as you desire; whatever the LORD answers you, I will tell you; I will withhold nothing from you. 5 And they said to Jeremiah, "May the LORD be our witness: we will truly and faithfully follow all the instructions the LORD, your God, will send us. 6 Whether it is pleasant or difficult, we will obey the command of the LORD, our God, to whom we are sending you, so that it will go well with us for obeying the command of the LORD, our God." 7 Ten days passed before the word of the LORD came to Jeremiah. 8 Then he called Johanan, son of Kareah, his army leaders, and all the people, high and low, 9 and said to them: Thus says the LORD, the God of Israel, to whom you sent me to offer your prayer: 10 If you remain quietly in this land I will build you up, and not tear you down; I will plant you, not uproot

you; for I regret the evil I have done you. 11 Do not fear the king of Babylon, before whom you are now afraid; do not fear him, says the LORD, for I am with you to save you, to rescue you from his power. 12 I will grant you mercy, so that he will be sorry for you and let you return to your land. 13 But if you disobey the voice of the LORD, your God, and decide not to remain in this land, 14 saying, "No, we will go to Egypt, where we will see no more of war, hear the trumpet alarm no longer, nor hunger for bread; there we will live"; 15 then listen to the word of the LORD, remnant of Judah: Thus says the LORD of hosts, the God of Israel: If you are determined to go to Egypt, when you arrive there to stay, 16 the sword you fear shall reach you in the land of Egypt; the hunger you dread shall cling to you no less in Egypt, and there you shall die. 17 All those men who determine to go to Egypt to stay, shall die by the sword, famine, and pestilence; not one shall survive or escape the evil that I will bring upon them. 18 For thus says the LORD of hosts, the God of Israel: Just as my furious anger was poured out upon the citizens of Jerusalem, so shall my anger be poured out on you when you reach Egypt. You shall become an example of malediction and horror, a curse and a reproach, and you shall never see this place again. 19 It is the LORD who has spoken to you, remnant of Judah; do not go to Egypt! You can never say that I did not warn you this day. 20 At the cost of your lives you have deceived me, sending me to the LORD, your God, saying, "Pray for us to the LORD, our God; make known to us all that the LORD, our God, shall say, and we will do it." 21 Today I proclaim his message, but you obey the voice of the LORD, your God, in nothing that he has commissioned me to make known to you. 22 Have no doubt of this, you shall die by the sword, famine, and pestilence in the place where you wish to go and settle.

Jeremiah Chapter 43

1 When Jeremiah finished speaking to the people all these words of the LORD, their God, with which the LORD had sent him to them, 2 Azariah, son of Hoshaiah, Johanan, son of Kareah, and all the insolent men shouted to Jeremiah: "You lie; it was not the LORD, our God, who sent you to tell us not to go to Egypt to settle. 3 It is Baruch, son of Neriah, who stirs you up against us, to hand us over to the Chaldeans to be killed or exiled to Babylon." 4 Johanan, son of Kareah, and the rest of the leaders and the people did not obey the LORD'S command to stay in the land of Judah. 5 Instead, Johanan, son of Kareah, and all the army leaders took along the whole remnant of Judah that had been dispersed among the nations and had returned thence to dwell again in the land of Judah: 6 men, women, and children, the princesses and everyone whom Nebuzaradan, captain of the bodyguard, had entrusted to Gedaliah, son of Ahikam, son of Shaphan; also Jeremiah, the prophet, and Baruch, son of Neriah. 7 Against the LORD'S command they went to Egypt, and arrived at Tahpanhes. 8 This word of the LORD came to Jeremiah in Tahpanhes: 9 "Take with you large stones and sink them in mortar in the brickyard at the entrance to the royal building in Tahpanhes, while the men of Judah look on, 10 and then say to them: Thus says the LORD of hosts, the God of Israel: I will send for my servant Nebuchadnezzar, king of Babylon, and bring him here. He will set his throne upon these stones which I, Jeremiah, have sunk, and stretch his canopy over them. 11 He shall come and strike the land of Egypt: with death, whoever is marked for death; with exile, everyone destined for exile; with the sword, all who are intended for the sword. 12 He shall set fire to the temples of Egypt's gods, and burn the gods or carry them off. As a shepherd delouses his cloak, he shall delouse the land of Egypt and depart victorious. 13 He shall smash the obelisks of the temple of the sun in the land of Egypt and destroy with fire the temples of the Egyptian gods."

Jeremiah Chapter 44

1 This word came to Jeremiah for all the people of Judah who were living in Egypt, at Migdol, Tahpanhes, and Memphis, and in Upper Egypt: 2 Thus says the LORD of hosts, the God of Israel: You have seen all the evil I brought on Jerusalem and the other cities of Judah. Today they are ruins and uninhabited, 3 because of the evil they did to provoke me, going after strange gods, serving them and sacrificing to them, gods which neither they, nor you, nor your fathers knew. 4 Though I kept sending to you all my servants the prophets, with the plea not to commit this horrible deed which I hate, 5 they would not listen or accept the warning to turn away from the evil of sacrificing to strange gods. 6 Therefore the fury of my anger poured forth in flame over the cities of Judah and the streets of Jerusalem, so that they became the ruinous waste they are today. 7 Now thus says the LORD God of hosts, the God of Israel: Why do you inflict so great an evil upon yourselves? Will you root out from Judah man and wife, child and nursling, and not leave yourselves even a remnant? 8 Will you go on provoking me by the works of your hands, by sacrificing to strange gods here in the land of Egypt

where you have come to live? Will you be rooted out and become a curse and a disgrace among all the nations of the earth? 9 Have you forgotten the evil deeds which your fathers, and the kings of Judah and their wives, and you yourselves and your wives have done in the land of Judah and the streets of Jerusalem? 10 To this day they have not been crushed; they do not fear or follow the law and the statutes which I set before you and your fathers. 11 Hence, thus says the LORD of hosts, the God of Israel: I have determined evil against you; and I will uproot all Judah. 12 I will take away the remnant of Judah who insisted on coming to dwell in Egypt, so that they shall be wholly destroyed. In the land of Egypt they shall fall by the sword or be consumed by hunger. High and low, they shall die by the sword, or by hunger, and become an example of malediction, a horror, a curse and a reproach. 13 Thus will I punish those who live in Egypt, just as I punished Jerusalem with sword, hunger, and pestilence. None of the remnant of Judah that have come to settle in the land of Egypt shall escape or survive. 14 None shall return to the land of Judah, though they yearn to return and live there. Only scattered refugees shall return. 15 From all the men who knew that their wives were burning incense to strange gods, from all the women who were present in the immense crowd, and from all the people who lived in Lower and Upper Egypt, Jeremiah received this answer: 16 "We will not listen to what you say in the name of the LORD. 17 Rather will we continue doing what we had proposed; we will burn incense to the queen of heaven and pour out libations to her, as we and our fathers, our kings and princes have done in the cities of Judah and the streets of Jerusalem. Then we had enough food to eat and we were well off; we suffered no misfortune. 18 But since we stopped burning incense to the queen of heaven and pouring out libations to her, we are in need of everything and are being destroyed by the sword and by hunger. 19 And when we burned incense to the queen of heaven and poured out libations to her, was it without our husbands' consent that we baked for her cakes in her image and poured out libations to her?" 20 To all the people, men and women, who gave him this answer, Jeremiah said: 21 Was it not this that the LORD remembered and brought to mind, that you burned incense in the cities of Judah and the streets of Jerusalem: you, your fathers, your kings and princes, and the people generally? 22 The LORD could no longer bear your evil deeds, the horrible things which you were doing; and so your land became a waste, a desert, a thing accursed and without inhabitants, as it is today. 23 Because you burned incense and sinned against the LORD, not obeying the voice of the LORD, not living by his law, his statutes, and his decrees, this evil has befallen you at the present day. 24 Jeremiah said further to all the people, including the women: Hear the word of the LORD, all you Judeans in the land of Egypt: 25 Thus says the LORD of hosts, the God of Israel: You and your wives have stated your intentions, and kept them in fact: "We will continue to fulfill the vows we have made to burn incense to the queen of heaven and to pour out libations to her." Very well! keep your vows, carry out your resolutions! 26 But listen then to the word of the LORD, all you people of Judah who live in Egypt; I swear by my own great name, says the LORD, in the whole land of Egypt no man of Judah shall henceforth pronounce my name, saying, "As the Lord GOD lives." 27 I am watching over them to do evil, not good. All the men of Judah in Egypt shall perish by the sword or famine until they are utterly destroyed. 28 Those who escape the sword to return from the land of Egypt to the land of Judah shall be few in number. The whole remnant of Judah who came to settle in Egypt shall know whose word stands, mine or theirs. 29 That you may know how surely my threats of punishment for you shall be fulfilled, this shall be a sign to you, says the LORD, that I will punish you in this place. 30 Thus says the LORD: See! I will hand over Pharaoh Hophra, king of Egypt, to his enemies, to those who seek his life, just as I handed over Zedekiah, king of Judah, to his enemy and mortal foe, Nebuchadnezzar, king of Babylon.

Jeremiah Chapter 45

1 This is the message that the prophet Jeremiah gave to Baruch, son of Neriah, when he wrote in a book the prophecies that Jeremiah dictated in the fourth year of Jehoiakim, son of Josiah, king of Judah: 2 Thus says the LORD, God of Israel, to you, Baruch, 3 because you said, "Alas! the LORD adds grief to my pain; I am weary from groaning, and can find no rest": 4 say this to him, says the LORD: What I have built, I am tearing down; what I have planted, I am uprooting: even the whole land. 5 And do you seek great things for yourself? Seek them not! I am bringing evil on all mankind, says the LORD, but your life I will leave you as booty, wherever you may go.

Jeremiah Chapter 46

1 This is the word of the LORD that came to the prophet Jeremiah against the nations. 2 Concerning Egypt. Against the army of Pharaoh Neco, king of Egypt, which was defeated at Carchemish on the Euphrates by Nebuchadnezzar, king of Babylon, in the fourth year of Jehoiakim, son of Josiah, king of Judah: 3 Prepare shield and buckler! march to battle! 4 Harness the horses, mount, charioteers! Fall in with your helmets; polish your spears, put on your breastplates. 5 What do I see? With broken ranks they fall back; their heroes are routed, they flee headlong without making a stand. Terror on every side, says the LORD! 6 The swift cannot flee, nor the hero escape: there in the north, on the Euphrates' bank, they stumble and fall. 7 Who is this that surges forward like the Nile, like rivers of billowing waters? 8 Egypt surges like the Nile, like rivers of billowing waters. "I will surge forward," he says, "and cover the earth, destroying the city and its people. 9 Forward, horses! drive madly, chariots! Set out, warriors, Cush and Put, bearing your shields, men of Lud, stretching your bows!" 10 But this is the day of the Lord GOD of hosts, a day of vengeance, vengeance on his foes! The sword devours, is sated, drunk with their blood: for the Lord GOD of hosts holds a slaughter feast in the northland, on the Euphrates. 11 Go up to Gilead, and take balm, O virgin daughter Egypt! No use to multiply remedies; for you there is no cure. 12 The nations hear of your shame, your cries fill the earth. Warrior trips over warrior, both fall together. 13 The message which the LORD gave to the prophet Jeremiah concerning the advance of Nebuchadnezzar, king of Babylon, to attack the land of Egypt: 14 Announce it in Egypt, publish it in Migdol, proclaim it in Memphis and Tahpanhes! Say: Take your stand, prepare yourselves, the sword has already devoured your neighbors. 15 Why has Apis fled, your mighty one failed to stand? The LORD thrust him down; 16 he stumbled repeatedly, and fell. They said one to another, "Up! let us return to our own people, to the land of our birth, away from the destroying sword." 17 Call Pharaoh, king of Egypt, by the name "The noise that let its time go by." 18 As I live, says the King whose name is LORD of hosts, like Tabor among the mountains he shall come, like Carmel above the sea. 19 Pack your baggage for exile, capital city of daughter Egypt; Memphis shall become a desert, an empty ruin. 20 Egypt is a pretty heifer, from the north a horsefly lights upon her. 21 The mercenaries in her ranks are like fatted calves; they too turn and flee together, stand not their ground, when the day of their ruin comes upon them, the time of their punishment. 22 She sounds like a retreating reptile! Yes, they come in force; like woodchoppers, they attack her with axes. 23 They cut down her forest, says the LORD, impenetrable though it be; more numerous than locusts, they cannot be counted. 24 Disgraced is daughter Egypt, handed over to the people of the north. 25 The LORD of hosts, the God of Israel, has said: See! I will punish Amon of Thebes, and Egypt, her gods and her kings, Pharaoh, and those who trust in him. 26 I will hand them over to those who seek their lives, to Nebuchadnezzar, king of Babylon, and his ministers. But later on Egypt shall be inhabited again, as in times past, says the LORD. 27 But you, my servant Jacob, fear not; be not dismayed, O Israel. Behold, I will deliver you from the far-off land, your descendants, from their land of exile. Jacob shall again find rest, shall be tranquil and undisturbed. 28 You, my servant Jacob, never fear, says the LORD, for I am with you; I will make an end of all the nations to which I have driven you, but of you I will not make an end: I will chastise you as you deserve, I will not let you go unpunished.

Jeremiah Chapter 47

1 This is the word that came from the LORD to the prophet Jeremiah concerning the Philistines, before Pharaoh attacked Gaza: 2 Thus says the LORD: Behold: waters are rising from the north, a torrent in flood; it shall flood the land and all that is in it, the cities and their people. All the people of the land set up a wailing cry. 3 They hear the stamping hooves of his steeds, the rattling chariots, the rumbling wheels. Fathers turn not to save their children; their hands fall helpless 4 because of the day which has come to ruin all the Philistines, and cut off from Tyre and Sidon the last of their allies. Yes, the LORD is destroying the Philistines, the remnant from the coasts of Caphtor. 5 Gaza is shaved bald, Ashkelon is reduced to silence; Ashdod, the remnant of their strength, how long will you gash yourself? 6 Alas, sword of the LORD! how long till you find rest? Return into your scabbard; stop, be still! 7 How can it find rest when the LORD has commanded it? Against Ashkelon and the seashore he has appointed it.

Jeremiah Chapter 48

1 Concerning Moab, thus says the LORD of hosts, the God of Israel: Woe to Nebo, it is laid waste; Kiriathaim is disgraced and captured, disgraced and overthrown is the stronghold: 2 Moab's glory is no more. Evil they plan against Heshbon: "Come, let us put an end to her as a people." You, too, Madmen, shall be reduced to silence; behind you stalks the sword. 3 Listen! a cry from Horonaim of ruin and great destruction! 4 Moab is crushed, their outcry is heard in Zoar. 5 The ascent of Luhith they climb weeping; on the descent to Horonaim the

cry of destruction is heard. 6 "Flee, save your lives, to survive like the wild ass in the desert!" 7 Because you trusted in your works and your treasures, you also shall be captured. Chemosh shall go into exile, his priests and princes with him. 8 The destroyer comes upon every city, not a city escapes; ruined is the valley, wasted the plain, as the LORD has said. 9 Set up a memorial for Moab, for it is an utter wasteland; its cities are turned into ruins where no one dwells. 10 (Cursed be he who does the LORD'S work remissly, cursed he who holds back his sword from blood.) 11 Moab has been tranquil from his youth, has rested upon his lees; he was not poured from one flask to another, he went not into exile. Thus he kept his taste, and his scent was not lost. 12 Hence, the days shall come, says the LORD, when I will send him coopers to turn him over; they shall empty his flasks and break his jars. 13 Chemosh shall disappoint Moab, as Israel was disappointed by Bethel in which they trusted. 14 How can you say, "We are heroes, men valiant in war"? 15 The ravager of Moab and his cities advances, the flower of his youth goes down to be slaughtered, says the King, the LORD of hosts by name. 16 Near at hand is Moab's ruin, his disaster hastens apace. 17 Mourn for him, all you his neighbors, all you who knew him well! Say: How the strong staff is broken, the glorious rod! 18 Come down from glory, sit on the ground, you that dwell in Dibon; Moab's ravager has come up against you, he has ruined your strongholds. 19 Stand by the wayside, watch closely, you that dwell in Aroer; ask the man who flees, the woman who tries to escape: say to them, "What has happened?" 20 Moab is disgraced, yes, destroyed, howl and cry out; publish it at the Arnon, Moab is ruined! 21 For judgment has come on the land of the plateau: on Holon, Jahzah, and Mephaath, 22 on Dibon, Nebo, and Beth-diblathaim, 23 on Kiriathaim, Beth-gamul, and Beth-meon, 24 on Kerioth and on Bozrah: on all the cities of Moab, far and near. 25 Moab's strength is broken, his might is shattered, says the LORD. 26 Because he boasted against the LORD, make Moab drunk so that he retches and vomits, and he too becomes a laughingstock. 27 Is Israel a laughingstock to you? Was she caught among thieves, that you shake your head whenever you speak of her? 28 Leave the cities, dwell in the crags, you that dwell in Moab. Be like a dove that nests out of reach on the edge of a chasm. 29 We have heard of the pride of Moab, pride beyond bounds: his loftiness, his pride, his scorn, his insolence of heart. 30 I know, says the LORD, his arrogance; liar in boast, liar in deed. 31 And so I wail over Moab, over all Moab I cry, over the men of Kir-heres I moan. 32 More than for Jazer I weep over you, vineyard of Sibmah. Your tendrils trailed down to the sea, as far as Jazer they stretched. Upon your harvest, upon your vintage, the ravager has fallen. 33 Joy and jubilation are at an end in the fruit gardens of the land of Moab. I drain the wine from the wine vats, the treader treads no more, the vintage shout is stilled. 34 The cry of Heshbon and Elealeh is heard as far as Jahaz; they call from Zoar to Horonaim, and to Eglath-shelishiyah, for even the waters of Nimrim turn into a desert. 35 I will leave no one in Moab, says the LORD, to offer a holocaust on the high place, or to burn incense to his gods. 36 Hence the wail of flutes for Moab is in my heart; for the men of Kir-heres the wail of flutes is in my heart: the wealth they acquired has perished. 37 Every head has been made bald, every beard shaved; every hand is gashed, and the loins of all are clothed in sackcloth. 38 On every roof of Moab and in all his squares there is mourning; I have shattered Moab like a pot that no one wants, says the LORD. 39 How terror seizes Moab, and wailing! How he turns his back in shame! Moab has become a laughingstock and a horror to all his neighbors! 40 For thus says the LORD: Behold, like an eagle he soars, spreads his wings over Moab. 41 Cities are taken, strongholds seized: on that day the hearts of Moab's heroes are like the heart of a woman in travail. 42 Moab shall be destroyed, no more a people, because he boasted against the LORD. 43 Terror, pit, and trap be upon you, people of Moab, says the LORD. 44 He who flees from the terror falls into the pit; he who climbs from the pit is caught in the trap; for I will bring these things upon Moab in the year of their punishment, says the LORD. 45 In Heshbon's shadow stop short the exhausted refugees; for fire breaks forth from Heshbon, and a blaze from the house of Sihon: it consumes the brow of Moab, the skull of the noisemakers. 46 Woe to you, O Moab, you are ruined, O people of Chemosh! Your sons are taken into exile, your daughters into captivity. 47 But I will change the lot of Moab in the days to come, says the LORD. Thus far the judgment on Moab.

Jeremiah Chapter 49

1 Concerning the Ammonites, thus says the LORD: Has Israel no sons? has he no heir? Why then has Milcom disinherited Gad, why have his people settled in Gad's cities? 2 But the days are coming, says the LORD, when against Rabbah of the Ammonites I will sound the battle alarm; she shall become a mound of ruins, and her daughter cities shall be destroyed by fire. Israel shall inherit those who disinherited her, says the LORD. 3 Howl, Heshbon, for the ravager approaches, shriek, daughters of Rabbah! Put on sackcloth and mourn, run to and fro, gashing yourselves; for Milcom goes into exile along with his priests and captains. 4 Why do you glory in your strength, your ebbing strength, rebellious daughter? You who trust in your treasures, saying, "Who can come against me?" 5 I am bringing terror upon you, says the Lord GOD of hosts, from all around you; you shall be scattered, each man in headlong flight, with no one to rally the fugitives. 6 But afterward I will change the lot of the Ammonites, says the LORD. 7 Concerning Edom, thus says the LORD of hosts: Is there no more wisdom in Teman, has counsel perished from the prudent, has their wisdom become corrupt? 8 Flee, retreat, hide in deep holes, you who live in Dedan: for I will bring destruction upon Esau when I come to punish him. 9 If vintagers came upon you, they would leave no gleanings; if thieves by night, they would destroy as they pleased. 10 So I myself will strip Esau; I will uncover his retreats so that he cannot hide. He is ruined: sons, and brothers, and neighbors, so that he is no more. 11 Leave your orphans behind, I will keep them alive; your widows, let them trust in me. 12 For thus says the LORD: Even those not sentenced to drink the cup must drink it! Shall you then go unpunished? You shall not go unpunished; you shall surely drink it. 13 By my own self I have sworn, says the LORD: Bozrah shall become an object of horror and a disgrace, a desolation and a curse; she and all her cities shall become ruins forever. 14 I have heard a report from the LORD, a herald has been sent among the nations: Gather together, move against her, rise up for battle. 15 Small will I make you among the nations, despised among men! 16 The terror you spread beguiled you, and your presumption of heart; you that live in rocky crags, that hold the heights of the hill: though you build your nest high as the eagle, from there I will drag you down, says the LORD. 17 Edom shall become an object of horror. Every passerby shall be appalled and catch his breath at all her wounds. 18 As when Sodom, Gomorrah, and their neighbors were overthrown, says the LORD, not a man shall dwell there: no one shall visit there. 19 As when a lion comes up from the thicket of Jordan to the permanent feeding grounds, so I, in an instant, will drive men off; and whom I choose I will establish there! For who is like me? Who can call me to account? What shepherd can stand against me? 20 Therefore, hear the counsel of the LORD, which he has taken against Edom; hear the plans he has made against those that live in Teman: they shall be dragged away, even the smallest sheep, their own pasture shall be aghast because of them. 21 At the noise of their fall the earth quakes, to the Red Sea the outcry is heard! 22 See! like an eagle he soars aloft, and spreads his wings over Bozrah; on that day the hearts of Edom's heroes shall be like the heart of a woman in travail. 23 Concerning Damascus: Hamath and Arpad are covered with shame, they have heard bad news; worried, they toss like the sea which cannot rest. 24 Damascus is weakened, she turns to flee, panic has seized her. Distress and pangs take hold of her, like those of a woman in travail. 25 How can the city of glory be forsaken, the town of delight! 26 But now her young men shall fall in her streets, and all her warriors shall be stilled. On that day, says the LORD of hosts, 27 I will set fire to the wall of Damascus, and it shall devour the palaces of Ben-hadad. 28 Of Kedar and the kingdoms of Hazor, defeated by Nebuchadnezzar, king of Babylon, thus says the LORD: Rise up, attack Kedar, ravage the Easterners. 29 Their tents and herds shall be taken away, their tent curtains and all their goods; their camels they shall carry off for themselves, and shout from upon them, "Terror on every side!" 30 Flee! Leave your homes, hide in deep holes, you that live in Hazor, says the LORD; for counsel has been taken against you, a plan has been formed against you (Nebuchadnezzar, king of Babylon). 31 Rise up! Set out against a nation that is at peace, that lives secure, says the LORD, that has no gates or bars, and dwells alone. 32 Their camels shall be your booty, their many herds your spoil; I will scatter to the winds those who shave their temples, from all sides I will bring ruin upon them, says the LORD. 33 Hazor shall become a haunt of jackals, a desert forever, where no man lives, no human being stays. 34 The following word of the LORD against Elam came to the prophet Jeremiah at the beginning of the reign of Zedekiah, king of Judah: 35 Thus says the LORD of hosts: Behold, I will break the bow of Elam, the mainstay of their might. 36 I will bring upon Elam the four winds from the four ends of the heavens: I will scatter them to all these winds, till there is no nation to which the outcasts of Elam shall not come. 37 I will break Elam before their foes, before those who seek their life; I will bring evil upon them, my burning wrath, says the LORD. I will send the sword to pursue them until I have completely made an end of them; 38 my throne I will set up in Elam and destroy from there king and princes, says the LORD. 39 But in the days to come I will change the lot of Elam, says the LORD.

Jeremiah Chapter 50

1 The word which the LORD spoke against Babylon, against the land of

the Chaldeans, through the prophet Jeremiah: ² Announce and publish it among the nations; publish it, hide it not, but say: Babylon is taken, Bel confounded, Merodach shattered; her images are put to shame, her idols shattered. ³ A people from the north advances against her to turn her land into a desert, so that no one shall live there, because man and beast have fled away. ⁴ In those days, at that time, says the LORD, the men of Israel and of Judah shall come, weeping as they come, to seek the LORD, their God; ⁵ to their goal in Zion they shall ask the way. "Come, let us join ourselves to the LORD with covenant everlasting, never to be forgotten." ⁶ Lost sheep were my people, their shepherds misled them, straggling on the mountains; from mountain to hill they wandered, losing the way to their fold. ⁷ Whoever came upon them devoured them, and their enemies said, "We incur no guilt, because they sinned against the LORD, the hope of their fathers, their abode of justice." ⁸ Flee from Babylon, leave the land of the Chaldeans, be like the rams at the head of the flock. ⁹ See, I am stirring up against Babylon a band of great nations from the north; from there they advance, and she shall be taken. Their arrows are arrows of the skilled warrior; none shall return without effect. ¹⁰ Chaldea shall be their plunder, and all her plunderers shall be enriched, says the LORD. ¹¹ Yes, rejoice and exult, you that plunder my portion; frisk like calves on the green, snort like stallions! ¹² Your mother shall be sorely put to shame, she that bore you shall be abashed; see, the last of the nations, a desert, dry and waste. ¹³ Because of the LORD'S wrath she shall be empty, and become a total desert; everyone who passes by Babylon will be appalled and catch his breath, at all her wounds. ¹⁴ Take your posts encircling Babylon, you who bend the bow; shoot at her, spare not your arrows, ¹⁵ raise the war cry against her on all sides. She surrenders, her bastions fall, her walls are torn down: vengeance of the LORD is this! Take revenge on her, as she has done, do to her; for she sinned against the LORD. ¹⁶ Cut off from Babylon the sower and him who wields the sickle in harvest time! Before the destroying sword, each of them turns to his own people, everyone flees to his own land. ¹⁷ A stray sheep was Israel that lions pursued; formerly the king of Assyria devoured her, now Nebuchadnezzar of Babylon gnaws her bones. ¹⁸ Therefore, thus says the LORD of hosts, the God of Israel: I will punish the king of Babylon and his land, as once I punished the king of Assyria; ¹⁹ but I will bring back Israel to her fold, to feed on Carmel and Bashan, and on Mount Ephraim and Gilead, till she has her fill. ²⁰ In those days, at that time, says the LORD: They shall seek Israel's guilt, but it shall be no more, and Judah's sins, but these shall no longer be found; for I will forgive the remnant I preserve. ²¹ Attack the land of Merathaim, and those who live in Pekod; slaughter and doom them, says the LORD, do all I have commanded you. ²² Battle alarm in the land, dire destruction! ²³ How has the hammer of the whole earth been broken and shattered! What an object of horror Babylon has become among the nations! ²⁴ You ensnared yourself, and were caught, O Babylon, before you knew it! You were discovered and seized, because you challenged the LORD. ²⁵ The LORD opens his armory and brings forth the weapons of his wrath; for the Lord GOD of hosts has work to do in the land of the Chaldeans. ²⁶ Come upon her from every side, open her granaries, pile up her goods in heaps and doom it, leave not a remnant. ²⁷ Slay all her oxen, let them go down to the slaughter; woe to them! Their day has come, the time of their punishment. ²⁸ Listen! the fugitives, the escaped from the land of Babylon: they announce in Zion the vengeance of the LORD, our God. ²⁹ Call up against Babylon archers, all who bend the bow; encamp around her, let no one escape. Repay her for her deeds; as she has done, do to her, for she insulted the LORD, the Holy One of Israel. ³⁰ Therefore her young men shall fall in her streets, all her warriors shall perish on that day, says the LORD. ³¹ I am against you, man of insolence, says the Lord GOD of hosts; for your day has come, the time for me to punish you. ³² Insolence stumbles and falls; there is no one to raise him up. I will kindle in his cities a fire that shall devour everything around him. ³³ Thus says the LORD of hosts: Oppressed are the men of Israel, and with them the men of Judah; all their captors hold them fast and refuse to let them go. ³⁴ Strong is their avenger, whose name is LORD of hosts; he will defend their cause with success, and give rest to the earth, but unrest to those who live in Babylon. ³⁵ A sword upon the Chaldeans, says the LORD, upon Babylon's people, her princes and wise men! ³⁶ A sword upon the soothsayers, that they may become fools! A sword upon her warriors, that they may tremble; ³⁷ a sword upon her motley throng, that they may become women! A sword upon her treasures, that they may be plundered; ³⁸ a sword upon her waters, that they may dry up! For it is a land of idols, and they shall be made frantic by fearful things. ³⁹ Hence, wildcats and desert beasts shall dwell there, and ostriches shall occupy it; never again shall it be peopled, or lived in, from age to age. ⁴⁰ As when God overturned Sodom and Gomorrah, with their neighbors, says the LORD, not a man shall dwell there, no

human being shall tarry there. ⁴¹ See! a people comes from the north, a great nation, and mighty kings roused from the ends of the earth. ⁴² Bow and javelin they wield, cruel and pitiless are they; they sound like the roaring sea, as they ride forth on steeds, each in his place for battle against you, daughter Babylon. ⁴³ The king of Babylon hears news of them, and helpless fall his hands; anguish seizes him, throes like a mother's in childbirth. ⁴⁴ As when a lion comes up from the Jordan's thicket to the permanent feeding grounds, so I, in one instant, will drive them off, and whom I choose I will establish there; for who is like me? Who calls me to account? What shepherd can stand against me? ⁴⁵ Therefore hear the counsel of the LORD which he has taken against Babylon; hear the plans he has made against the land of the Chaldeans: they shall be dragged away, even the smallest sheep; their own pasture shall be aghast because of them. ⁴⁶ At the cry "Babylon is captured!" the earth quakes; the outcry is heard among the nations.

Jeremiah Chapter 51

¹ Thus says the LORD: See! I rouse against Babylon, and against those who live in Chaldea, a destroying wind. ² Against Babylon I will send winnowers to winnow her and lay waste her land; They shall besiege her from all sides on the day of affliction. ³ Let the bowman draw his bow, and flaunt his coat of mail; Spare not her young men, doom her entire army. ⁴ The slain shall fall in the land of Chaldea, the transfixed, in her streets; ⁵ For Israel and Judah are not widowed of their God, the LORD of hosts, And the Chaldean land is full of guilt to be punished by the Holy One of Israel. ⁶ Flee out of Babylon; let each one save his life, perish not for her guilt; This is a time of vengeance for the LORD, he pays her her due. ⁷ Babylon was a golden cup in the hand of the LORD which made the whole earth drunk; The nations drank its wine, with this they have become mad. ⁸ Babylon suddenly falls and is crushed: howl over her! Bring balm for her wounds, in case she can be healed. ⁹ "We have tried to heal Babylon, but she cannot be healed. Leave her, let us go, each to his own land." Her judgment reaches heaven, it touches the clouds. ¹⁰ The LORD has brought to light our just cause; come, let us tell in Zion what the LORD, our God, has done. ¹¹ Sharpen the arrows, fill the quivers; The LORD has stirred up the spirit of Media's kings; Babylon he is resolved to destroy. Yes, it is the vengeance of the LORD, vengeance for his temple. ¹² Against the walls of Babylon raise a signal, make strong the watch; Post sentries, arrange ambushes! For the LORD has planned and he will carry out his threat against the inhabitants of Babylon. ¹³ You who dwell by mighty waters, rich in treasure, Your end has come, the term at which you shall be cut off! ¹⁴ The LORD of hosts has sworn by himself: I will fill you with men as numerous as locusts, who shall raise over you the vintage shout! ¹⁵ He has sworn who made the earth by his power, and established the world by his wisdom, and stretched out the heavens by his skill. ¹⁶ When he thunders, the waters in the heavens roar, and he brings up clouds from the end of the earth; He makes the lightning flash in the rain, and releases stormwinds from their chambers. ¹⁷ Every man is stupid, ignorant; every artisan is put to shame by his idol: He molded a fraud, without breath of life. ¹⁸ Nothingness are they, a ridiculous work, that will perish in their time of punishment. ¹⁹ Not like these is the portion of Jacob, he is the creator of all things; Israel is his very own tribe, LORD of hosts is his name. ²⁰ You are my hammer, my weapon for war; With you I shatter nations, with you I destroy kingdoms. ²¹ With you I shatter horse and rider, with you I shatter chariot and driver. ²² With you I shatter man and wife, with you I shatter old and young, with you I shatter the youth and maiden. ²³ With you I shatter the shepherd and his flock, with you I shatter the farmer and his team, with you I shatter satraps and prefects. ²⁴ Thus will I repay Babylon, and all who live in Chaldea All the evil they did to Zion, as you shall see with your own eyes, says the LORD. ²⁵ Beware! I am against you, destroying mountain, destroyer of the entire earth, says the LORD; I will stretch forth my hand against you, roll you down over the cliffs, and make you a burnt mountain: ²⁶ They will not take from you a cornerstone, or a foundation stone; Ruins forever shall you be, says the LORD. ²⁷ Raise a signal on the earth, blow the trumpet among the nations; Dedicate peoples to war against her, summon against her the kingdoms, Ararat, Minni, and Ashkenaz; Appoint recruiting officers against her, send up horses like bristling locusts. ²⁸ Dedicate peoples to war against her: the king of Media, Its governors and all its prefects, every land in his domain. ²⁹ The earth quakes and writhes, the LORD'S plan against Babylon is carried out, Turning the land of Babylon into a desert where no one lives. ³⁰ Babylon's warriors have ceased to fight, they remain in their strongholds; Dried up is their strength, they have become women. Burned are their homes, and broken their bars. ³¹ One runner meets another, herald meets herald, Telling the king of Babylon that all his city is taken. ³² The fords have been seized, and the fortresses set on fire, while warriors are in panic. ³³ For thus says the LORD of hosts, the

God of Israel: Daughter Babylon is like a threshing floor at the time it is trodden; Yet a little while, and the harvest time will come for her. ³⁴ He has consumed me, routed me, (Nebuchadnezzar, king of Babylon,) he has left me as an empty vessel; He has swallowed me like a dragon: filled his belly with my delights, and cast me out. ³⁵ My torn flesh be upon Babylon, says the city on Zion; My blood upon the people of Chaldea, says Jerusalem. ³⁶ But now, thus says the LORD: Surely I will defend your cause, I will avenge you; I will dry up her sea, and drain her fountain. ³⁷ Babylon shall become a heap of ruins, a haunt of jackals; A place of horror and ridicule, where no one lives. ³⁸ They all roar like lions, growl like lion cubs. ³⁹ When they are parched, I will set a drink before them to make them drunk, that they may be overcome with perpetual sleep, never to awaken, says the LORD. ⁴⁰ I will bring them down like lambs to the slaughter, like rams and goats. ⁴¹ How has she been seized, made captive, the glory of the whole world! What a horror has Babylon become among nations: ⁴² against Babylon the sea rises, she is overwhelmed by the roaring waves! ⁴³ Her cities have become a desert, parched and arid land Where no man lives, and no one passes through. ⁴⁴ I will punish Bel in Babylon, and make him disgorge what he swallowed; peoples shall stream to him no more. The wall of Babylon falls! ⁴⁵ Leave her, my people, let each one save himself from the burning wrath of the LORD. ⁴⁶ Be not discouraged for fear of rumors spread in the land; this year the rumor comes, then violence in the land, tyrant against tyrant. ⁴⁷ But behold, the days are coming when I will punish the idols of Babylon; her whole land shall be put to shame, and all her slain shall lie fallen within her. ⁴⁸ Then heaven, and earth, and everything in them shall shout over Babylon with joy, when the destroyers come against her from the north, says the LORD. ⁴⁹ Babylon, too, must fall, O slain of Israel, as at the hands of Babylon have fallen the slain of all the earth. ⁵⁰ You who have escaped the sword, go on, stand not still; Remember the LORD from afar, let Jerusalem come to your minds. ⁵¹ We are ashamed because we have heard taunts, confusion covers our faces; strangers have entered the holy places of the house of the LORD. ⁵² But behold, the days are coming, says the LORD, when I will punish her idols, and in her whole land the wounded will groan. ⁵³ Though Babylon scale the heavens, and make her strong heights inaccessible, destroyers from me shall reach her, says the LORD. ⁵⁴ Hear! loud cries from Babylon, dire destruction from the land of the Chaldeans; ⁵⁵ For the LORD lays Babylon waste, stills her loud cry, Though her waves were roaring like mighty waters, and their clamor was heard afar. ⁵⁶ For the destroyer comes upon her, (Babylon,) her heroes are captured, their bows broken; The LORD is a God who requites, he will surely repay. ⁵⁷ I will make her princes and her wise men drunk, her governors, her prefects, and her warriors, so that they sleep an eternal sleep, never to awaken, says the King, whose name is the LORD of hosts. ⁵⁸ Thus says the LORD of hosts: The walls of spacious Babylon shall be leveled utterly; her lofty gates shall be destroyed by fire. The toil of the nations is for nothing; for the flames the peoples weary themselves. ⁵⁹ This was the errand given by the prophet Jeremiah to Seraiah, son of Neriah, son of Mahseiah, when he went to Babylon for the king in the fourth year of the reign of Zedekiah; Seraiah was chief quartermaster. ⁶⁰ Jeremiah had written all the misfortune that was to befall Babylon in a single book: all these words that were written against Babylon. ⁶¹ And Jeremiah said to Seraiah: When you reach Babylon, see that you read aloud all these words, ⁶² and then say: O LORD, you yourself threatened to destroy this place, so that neither man nor beast should dwell in it, since it would remain an everlasting desert. ⁶³ When you have finished reading this book, tie a stone to it and throw it in the Euphrates, ⁶⁴ and say: Thus shall Babylon sink. Never shall she rise, because of the evil I am bringing upon her. (To "weary themselves" are the words of Jeremiah.)

Jeremiah Chapter 52

¹ Zedekiah was twenty-one years old when he became king, and he reigned eleven years in Jerusalem. His mother's name was Hamutal, daughter of Jeremiah of Libnah. ² He did what was evil in the eyes of the LORD, just as Jehoiakim had done. ³ Indeed, what was done in Jerusalem and in Judah so angered the LORD that he cast them out from his presence. Zedekiah rebelled against the king of Babylon. ⁴ In the tenth month of the ninth year of his reign, on the tenth day of the month, Nebuchadnezzar, king of Babylon, and his whole army advanced against Jerusalem, encamped around it, and built siege walls on every side. ⁵ The siege of the city continued until the eleventh year of King Zedekiah. ⁶ On the ninth day of the fourth month, when famine had gripped the city and the people had no more bread, ⁷ the city walls were breached. Then all the soldiers took to flight and left the city by night through the gate between the two walls which was near the king's garden. With the Chaldeans surrounding the city, they went in the direction of the Arabah. ⁸ But the Chaldean army pursued the king and

overtook Zedekiah in the desert near Jericho, while his whole army fled from him. ⁹ The king, therefore, was arrested and brought to Riblah, in the land of Hamath, to the king of Babylon, who pronounced sentence on him. ¹⁰ As Zedekiah looked on, the king of Babylon slew his sons as well as all the princes of Judah at Riblah. ¹¹ Then he blinded Zedekiah, bound him with fetters, and had him brought to Babylon and kept in prison until the day of his death. ¹² On the tenth day of the fifth month (this was in the nineteenth year of Nebuchadnezzar, king of Babylon), Nebuzaradan, captain of the bodyguard, came to Jerusalem as the representative of the king of Babylon. ¹³ He burned the house of the LORD, the palace of the king, and all the houses of Jerusalem; every large building he destroyed with fire. ¹⁴ And the Chaldean troops who were with the captain of the guard tore down all the walls that surrounded Jerusalem. ¹⁵ Then Nebuzaradan, captain of the guard, led into exile the rest of the people left in the city, and those who had deserted to the king of Babylon, and the rest of the artisans. ¹⁶ But some of the country's poor, Nebuzaradan, captain of the guard, left behind as vinedressers and farmers. ¹⁷ The bronze pillars that belonged to the house of the LORD, and the wheeled carts and the bronze sea in the house of the LORD, the Chaldeans broke into pieces; they carried away all the bronze to Babylon. ¹⁸ They took also the pots, the shovels, the snuffers, the bowls, the pans, and all the bronze vessels used for service. ¹⁹ The basins also, the fire holders, the bowls, the pots, the lampstands, the pans, the sacrificial bowls which were of gold or silver, these too the captain of the guard carried off, ²⁰ as well as the two pillars, the one sea, and the twelve oxen of bronze under the sea, and the wheeled carts which King Solomon had made for the house of the LORD. The bronze of all these furnishings could not be weighed. ²¹ Each of the pillars was eighteen cubits high and twelve cubits in diameter; each was four fingers thick, and hollow inside. ²² A bronze capital five cubits high surmounted the one pillar, and a network with pomegranates encircled the capital, all of brass; and so for the other pillar. The pomegranates. . . ²³ there were ninety-six pomegranates. There were a hundred pomegranates, all around the network. ²⁴ The captain of the guard also took Seraiah, the high priest, Zephaniah, the second priest, and the three keepers of the entry. ²⁵ And from the city he took one courtier, a commander of soldiers, and seven men in the personal service of the king who were present in the city, and the scribe of the army commander who mustered the people of the land, and sixty of the common people who were in the city. ²⁶ The captain of the guard, Nebuzaradan, arrested these and brought them to the king of Babylon at Riblah, ²⁷ who had them struck down and put to death in Riblah, in the land of Hamath. Thus was Judah exiled from her land. ²⁸ This is the number of the people whom Nebuchadnezzar led away captive: in his seventh year, three thousand and twenty-three people of Judah; ²⁹ in the eighteenth year of Nebuchadnezzar, eight hundred and thirty-two persons from Jerusalem; ³⁰ in the twenty-third year of Nebuchadnezzar, Nebuzaradan, captain of the guard, exiled seven hundred and forty-five people of Judah: four thousand six hundred persons in all. ³¹ In the thirty-seventh year of the exile of Jehoiachin, king of Judah, on the twenty-fifth day of the twelfth month, Evil-merodach, king of Babylon, in the inaugural year of his reign, took up the case of Jehoiachin, king of Judah, and released him from prison. ³² He spoke kindly to him and gave him a throne higher than that of the other kings who were with him in Babylon. ³³ Jehoiachin took off his prison garb and ate at the king's table as long as he lived. ³⁴ The allowance given him by the king of Babylon was a perpetual allowance, in fixed daily amounts, all the days of his life until the day of his death.

The Letter of Jeremiah

¹A copy of a letter that Jeremy sent to those who were to be led captives into Babylon by the king of the Babylonians, to give them the message that God commanded him. ²Because of the sins which you have committed before God, you will be led away captives to Babylon by Nabuchodonosor king of the Babylonians. ³So when you come to Babylon, you will remain there many years, and for a long season, even for seven generations. After that, I will bring you out peacefully from there. ⁴But now you will see in Babylon gods of silver, gold, wood carried on shoulders, which cause the nations to fear. ⁵Beware therefore that you in no way become like these foreigners. Don't let fear take hold of you because of them when you see the multitude before them and behind them, worshiping them. ⁶But say in your hearts, "O Lord, we must worship you." ⁷For my angel is with you, and I myself care for your souls. ⁸For their tongue is polished by the workman, and they themselves are overlaid with gold and with silver; yet they are only fake, and can't speak. ⁹And taking gold, as if it were for a virgin who loves to be happy, they make crowns for the heads of their gods.

10Sometimes also the priests take gold and silver from their gods, and spend it on themselves. 11They will even give some of it to the common prostitutes. They dress them like men with garments, even the gods of silver, gods of gold, and gods of wood. 12Yet these gods can't save themselves from rust and moths, even though they are covered with purple garments. 13They wipe their faces because of the dust of the temple, which is thick upon them. 14And he who can't put to death one who offends against him holds a sceptre, as though he were judge of a country. 15He has also a dagger in his right hand, and an axe, but can't deliver himself from war and robbers. 16By this they are known not to be gods. Therefore don't fear them. 17For like a vessel that a man uses is worth nothing when it is broken, even so it is with their gods. When they are set up in the temples, their eyes are full of dust through the feet of those who come in. 18As the courts are secured on every side upon him who offends the king, as being committed to suffer death, even so the priests secure their temples with doors, with locks, and bars, lest they be carried off by robbers. 19They light candles for them, yes, more than for themselves, even though they can't see one. 20They are like one of the beams of the temple. Men say their hearts are eaten out when things creeping out of the earth devour both them and their clothing. They don't feel it 21when their faces are blackened through the smoke that comes out of the temple. 22Bats, swallows, and birds land on their bodies and heads. So do the cats. 23By this you may know that they are no gods. Therefore don't fear them. 24Notwithstanding the gold with which they are covered to make them beautiful, unless someone wipes off the tarnish, they won't shine; for they didn't even feel it when they were molten. 25Things in which there is no breath are bought at any cost. 26Having no feet, they are carried upon shoulders. By this, they declare to men that they are worth nothing. 27Those who serve them are also ashamed, for if they fall to the ground at any time, they can't rise up again by themselves. If they are bowed down, they can't make themselves straight; but the offerings are set before them, as if they were dead men. 28And the things that are sacrificed to them, their priests sell and spend. In like manner, their wives also lay up part of it in salt; but to the poor and to the impotent they give none of it. 29The menstruous woman and the woman in childbed touch their sacrifices, knowing therefore by these things that they are no gods. Don't fear them. 30For how can they be called gods? Because women set food before the gods of silver, gold, and wood. 31And in their temples the priests sit on seats, having their clothes torn and their heads and beards shaven, and nothing on their heads. 32They roar and cry before their gods, as men do at the feast when one is dead. 33The priests also take off garments from them and clothe their wives and children with them. 34Whether it is evil or good what one does to them, they are not able to repay it. They can't set up a king or put him down. 35In like manner, they can neither give riches nor money. Though a man make a vow to them and doesn't keep it, they will never exact it. 36They can save no man from death. They can't deliver the weak from the mighty. 37They can't restore a blind man to his sight, or deliver anyone who is in distress. 38They can show no mercy to the widow, or do good to the fatherless. 39They are like the stones that are cut out of the mountain, these gods of wood that are overlaid with gold and with silver. Those who minister to them will be confounded. 40How could a man then think or say that they are gods, when even the Chaldeans themselves dishonor them? 41If they shall see one mute who can't speak, they bring him and ask him to call upon Bel, as though he were able to understand. 42Yet they can't perceive this themselves, and forsake them; for they have no understanding. 43The women also with cords around them sit in the ways, burning bran for incense; but if any of them, drawn by someone who passes by, lies with him, she reproaches her fellow, that she was not thought as worthy as herself and her cord wasn't broken. 44Whatever is done among them is false. How could a man then think or say that they are gods? 45They are fashioned by carpenters and goldsmiths. They can be nothing else than what the workmen make them to be. 46And they themselves who fashioned them can never continue long. How then should the things that are fashioned by them? 47For they have left lies and reproaches to those who come after. 48For when there comes any war or plague upon them, the priests consult with themselves, where they may be hidden with them. 49How then can't men understand that they are no gods, which can't save themselves from war or from plague? 50For seeing they are only wood and overlaid with gold and silver, it will be known hereafter that they are false. 51It will be manifest to all nations and kings that they are no gods, but the works of men's hands, and that there is no work of God in them. 52Who then may not know that they are not gods? 53For they can't set up a king in a land or give rain to men. 54They can't judge their own cause, or redress a wrong, being unable; for they are like crows between heaven and earth. 55For even when fire falls upon the house of

gods of wood overlaid with gold or with silver, their priests will flee away, and escape, but they themselves will be burned apart like beams. 56Moreover they can't withstand any king or enemies. How could a man then admit or think that they are gods? 57Those gods of wood overlaid with silver or with gold aren't able to escape from thieves or robbers. 58The gold, silver, and garments with which they are clothed—those who are strong will take from them, and go away with them. They won't be able to help themselves. 59Therefore it is better to be a king who shows his manhood, or else a vessel in a house profitable for whatever the owner needs, than such false gods—or even a door in a house, to keep the things safe that are in it, than such false gods; or better to be a pillar of wood in a palace than such false gods. 60For sun, moon, and stars, being bright and sent to do their jobs, are obedient. 61Likewise also the lightning when it flashes is beautiful to see. In the same way, the wind also blows in every country. 62And when God commands the clouds to go over the whole world, they do as they are told. 63And the fire sent from above to consume mountains and woods does as it is commanded; but these are to be compared to them neither in show nor power. 64Therefore a man shouldn't think or say that they are gods, seeing they aren't able to judge causes or to do good to men. 65Knowing therefore that they are no gods, don't fear them. 66For they can neither curse nor bless kings. 67They can't show signs in the heavens among the nations, or shine as the sun, or give light as the moon. 68The beasts are better than they; for they can get under a covert, and help themselves. 69In no way then is it manifest to us that they are gods. Therefore don't fear them. 70For as a scarecrow in a garden of cucumbers that keeps nothing, so are their gods of wood overlaid with gold and silver. 71Likewise also their gods of wood overlaid with gold and with silver, are like a white thorn in an orchard that every bird sits upon. They are also like a dead body that is thrown out into the dark. 72You will know them to be no gods by the bright purple that rots upon them. They themselves will be consumed afterwards, and will be a reproach in the country. 73Better therefore is the just man who has no idols; for he will be far from reproach.

Lamentations

Lamentations Chapter 1

1 How lonely she is now, the once crowded city! Widowed is she who was mistress over nations; The princess among the provinces has been made a toiling slave. 2 Bitterly she weeps at night, tears upon her cheeks, With not one to console her of all her dear ones; Her friends have all betrayed her and become her enemies. 3 Judah has fled into exile from oppression and cruel slavery; Yet where she lives among the nations she finds no place to rest: All her persecutors come upon her where she is narrowly confined. 4 The roads to Zion mourn for lack of pilgrims going to her feasts; All her gateways are deserted, her priests groan, Her virgins sigh; she is in bitter grief. 5 Her foes are uppermost, her enemies are at ease; The LORD has punished her for her many sins. Her little ones have gone away, captive before the foe. 6 Gone from daughter Zion is all her glory: Her princes, like rams that find no pasture, Have gone off without strength before their captors. 7 Jerusalem is mindful of the days of her wretched homelessness, When her people fell into enemy hands, and she had no one to help her; When her foes gloated over her, laughed at her ruin. 8 Through the sin of which she is guilty, Jerusalem is defiled; All who esteemed her think her vile now that they see her nakedness; She herself groans and turns away. 9 Her filth is on her skirt; she gave no thought how she would end. Astounding is her downfall, with no one to console her. Look, O LORD, upon her misery, for the enemy has triumphed! 10 The foe stretched out his hand to all her treasures; She has seen those nations enter her sanctuary Whom you forbade to come into your assembly. 11 All her people groan, searching for bread; They give their treasures for food, to retain the breath of life. "Look O LORD, and see how worthless I have become! 12 "Come, all you who pass by the way, look and see Whether there is any suffering like my suffering, which has been dealt me When the LORD afflicted me on the day of his blazing wrath. 13 "From on high he sent fire down into my very frame; He spread a net for my feet, and overthrew me. He left me desolate, in pain all the day. 14 "He has kept watch over my sins; by his hand they have been plaited: They have settled about my neck, he has brought my strength to its knees; The Lord has delivered me into their grip, I am unable to rise. 15 "All the mighty ones in my midst the Lord has cast away; He summoned an army against me to crush my young men; The LORD has trodden in the wine press virgin daughter Judah. 16 "At this I weep, my eyes run with tears: Far from me are all who could console me, any who might revive me; My sons were reduced to silence when the enemy prevailed." 17 Zion stretched out her hands, but there was no one to console her;

The LORD gave orders against Jacob for his neighbors to be his foes; Jerusalem has become in their midst a thing unclean. 18 "The LORD is just; I had defied his command. Listen, all you peoples, and behold my suffering: My maidens and my youths have gone into captivity. 19 "I cried out to my lovers, but they failed me. My priests and my elders perished in the city; Where they sought food for themselves, they found it not. 20 "Look, O LORD, upon my distress: all within me is in ferment, My heart recoils within me from my monstrous rebellion. In the streets the sword bereaves, at home death stalks. 21 "Give heed to my groaning; there is no one to console me. All my enemies rejoice at my misfortune: it is you who have wrought it. Bring on the day you have proclaimed, that they may be even as I. 22 "Let all their evil come before you; deal with them As you have dealt with me for all my sins; My groans are many, and I am sick at heart."

Lamentations Chapter 2

1 How the Lord in his wrath has detested daughter Zion! He has cast down from heaven to earth the glory of Israel, Unmindful of his footstool on the day of his wrath. 2 The Lord has consumed without pity all the dwellings of Jacob; He has torn down in his anger the fortresses of daughter Judah; He has brought to the ground in dishonor her king and her princes. 3 He broke off, in fiery wrath, the horn that was Israel's whole strength; He withheld the support of his right hand when the enemy approached; He blazed up in Jacob like a flaming fire devouring all about it. 4 Like an enemy he made taut his bow; with his arrows in his right hand He took his stand as a foe, and slew all on whom the eye doted; Over the tent of daughter Zion he poured out his wrath like fire. 5 The Lord has become an enemy, he has consumed Israel: Consumed all her castles and destroyed her fortresses; For daughter Judah he has multiplied moaning and groaning. 6 He has demolished his shelter like a garden booth, he has destroyed his dwelling; In Zion the LORD has made feast and sabbath to be forgotten; He has scorned in fierce wrath both king and priest. 7 The Lord has disowned his altar, rejected his sanctuary; The walls of her towers he has handed over to the enemy, Who shout in the house of the LORD as on a feast day. 8 The LORD marked for destruction the wall of daughter Zion: He stretched out the measuring line; his hand brought ruin, yet he did not relent - He brought grief on wall and rampart till both succumbed. 9 Sunk into the ground are her gates; he has removed and broken her bars. Her king and her princes are among the pagans; priestly instruction is wanting, And her prophets have not received any vision from the LORD. 10 On the ground in silence sit the old men of daughter Zion; They strew dust on their heads and gird themselves with sackcloth; The maidens of Jerusalem bow their heads to the ground. 11 Worn out from weeping are my eyes, within me all is in ferment; My gall is poured out on the ground because of the downfall of the daughter of my people, As child and infant faint away in the open spaces of the town. 12 They ask their mothers, "Where is the cereal?" - in vain, As they faint away like the wounded in the streets of the city, And breathe their last in their mothers' arms. 13 To what can I liken or compare you, O daughter Jerusalem? What example can I show you for your comfort, virgin daughter Zion? For great as the sea is your downfall; who can heal you? 14 Your prophets had for you false and specious visions; They did not lay bare your guilt, to avert your fate; They beheld for you in vision false and misleading portents. 15 All who pass by clap their hands at you; They hiss and wag their heads over daughter Jerusalem: "Is this the all-beautiful city, the joy of the whole earth?" 16 All your enemies open their mouths against you; They hiss and gnash their teeth. They say, "We have devoured her. This at last is the day we hoped for; we have lived to see it!" 17 The LORD has done as he decreed: he has fulfilled the threat He set forth from days of old; he has destroyed and had no pity, Letting the enemy gloat over you and exalting the horn of your foes. 18 Cry out to the Lord; moan, O daughter Zion! Let your tears flow like a torrent day and night; Let there be no respite for you, no repose for your eyes. 19 Rise up, shrill in the night, at the beginning of every watch; Pour out your heart like water in the presence of the Lord; Lift up your hands to him for the lives of your little ones (Who faint from hunger at the corner of every street). 20 "Look, O LORD, and consider: whom have you ever treated thus? Must women eat their offspring, their well-formed children? Are priest and prophet to be slain in the sanctuary of the LORD? 21 "Dead in the dust of the streets lie young and old; My maidens and young men have fallen by the sword; You have slain on the day of your wrath, slaughtered without pity. 22 "You summoned as for a feast day terrors against me from all sides; There was not, on the day of your wrath, either fugitive or survivor; Those whom I bore and reared my enemy has utterly destroyed."

Lamentations Chapter 3

1 I am a man who knows affliction from the rod of his anger, 2 One

whom he has led and forced to walk in darkness, not in the light; 3 Against me alone he brings back his hand again and again all the day. 4 He has worn away my flesh and my skin, he has broken my bones; 5 He has beset me round about with poverty and weariness; 6 He has left me to dwell in the dark like those long dead. 7 He has hemmed me in with no escape and weighed me down with chains; 8 Even when I cry out for help, he stops my prayer; 9 He has blocked my ways with fitted stones, and turned my paths aside. 10 A lurking bear he has been to me, a lion in ambush! 11 He deranged my ways, set me astray, left me desolate. 12 He bent his bow, and set me up as the target for his arrow. 13 He pierces my sides with shafts from his quiver. 14 I have become a laughingstock for all nations, their taunt all the day long; 15 He has sated me with bitter food, made me drink my fill of wormwood. 16 He has broken my teeth with gravel, pressed my face in the dust; 17 My soul is deprived of peace, I have forgotten what happiness is; 18 I tell myself my future is lost, all that I hoped for from the LORD. 19 The thought of my homeless poverty is wormwood and gall; 20 Remembering it over and over leaves my soul downcast within me. 21 But I will call this to mind, as my reason to have hope: 22 The favors of the LORD are not exhausted, his mercies are not spent; 23 They are renewed each morning, so great is his faithfulness. 24 My portion is the LORD, says my soul; therefore will I hope in him. 25 Good is the LORD to one who waits for him, to the soul that seeks him; 26 It is good to hope in silence for the saving help of the LORD. 27 It is good for a man to bear the yoke from his youth. 28 Let him sit alone and in silence, when it is laid upon him. 29 Let him put his mouth to the dust; there may yet be hope. 30 Let him offer his cheek to be struck, let him be filled with disgrace. 31 For the Lord's rejection does not last forever; 32 Though he punishes, he takes pity, in the abundance of his mercies; 33 He has no joy in afflicting or grieving the sons of men. 34 When anyone tramples underfoot all the prisoners in the land, 35 When he distorts men's rights in the very sight of the Most High, 36 When he presses a crooked claim, the Lord does not look on unconcerned. 37 Who commands so that it comes to pass, except the Lord ordains it; 38 Except it proceeds from the mouth of the Most High, whether the thing be good or bad! 39 Why should any living man complain, any mortal, in the face of his sins? 40 Let us search and examine our ways that we may return to the LORD! 41 Let us reach out our hearts toward God in heaven! 42 We have sinned and rebelled; you have not forgiven us. 43 You veiled yourself in wrath and pursued us, you slew us and took no pity; 44 You wrapped yourself in a cloud which prayer could not pierce. 45 You have made us offscourings and refuse among the nations. 46 All our enemies have opened their mouths against us; 47 Terror and the pit have been our lot, desolation and destruction; 48 My eyes run with streams of water over the downfall of the daughter of my people. 49 My eyes flow without ceasing, there is no respite, 50 Till the LORD from heaven looks down and sees. 51 My eyes torment my soul at the sight of all the daughters of my city. 52 Those who were my enemies without cause hunted me down like a bird; 53 They struck me down alive in the pit, and sealed me in with a stone. 54 The waters flowed over my head, and I said, "I am lost!" 55 I called upon your name, O LORD, from the bottom of the pit; 56 You heard my call, "Let not your ear be deaf to my cry for help!" 57 You came to my aid when I called to you; you said, "Have no fear!" 58 You defended me in mortal danger, you redeemed my life. 59 You see, O LORD, how I am wronged; do me justice! 60 You see all their vindictiveness, all their plots against me. 61 You hear their insults, O LORD, (all their plots against me), 62 The whispered murmurings of my foes, against me all the day; 63 Whether they sit or stand, see, I am their taunt song. 64 Requite them as they deserve, O LORD, according to their deeds; 65 Give them hardness of heart, as your curse upon them; 66 Pursue them in wrath and destroy them from under your heavens!

Lamentations Chapter 4

1 How tarnished is the gold, how changed the noble metal; How the sacred stones lie strewn at every street corner! 2 Zion's precious sons, fine gold their counterpart, now worth no more than earthen jars made by the hands of a potter! 3 Even the jackals bare their breasts and suckle their young; the daughter of my people has become as cruel as the ostrich in the desert. 4 The tongue of the suckling cleaves to the roof of its mouth in thirst; the babes cry for food, but there is no one to give it to them. 5 Those accustomed to dainty food perish in the streets; those brought up in purple now cling to the ash heaps. 6 The punishment of the daughter of my people is greater than the penalty of Sodom, which was overthrown in an instant without the turning of a hand. 7 Brighter than snow were her princes, whiter than milk, more ruddy than coral, more precious than sapphire. 8 Now their appearance is blacker than soot, they are unrecognized on the streets; their skin shrinks on their bones, as dry as wood. 9 Better for those who perish by the sword than for those who die of hunger, who waste away, as though pierced

through, lacking the fruits of the field! ¹⁰ The hands of compassionate women boiled their own children, to serve them as mourners' food in the downfall of the daughter of my people. ¹¹ The LORD has spent his anger, poured out his blazing wrath; he has kindled a fire in Zion that has consumed her foundations. ¹² The kings of the earth did not believe, nor any of the world's inhabitants, that enemy or foe could enter the gates of Jerusalem. ¹³ Because of the sins of her prophets and the crimes of her priests, who shed in her midst the blood of the just! ¹⁴ They staggered blindly in the streets, soiled with blood, so that people could not touch even their garments: ¹⁵ "Away you unclean!" they cried to them, "Away, away, do not draw near!" If they left and wandered among the nations, nowhere could they remain. ¹⁶ The LORD himself has dispersed them, he regards them no more; he does not receive the priests with favor, nor show kindness to the elders. ¹⁷ Our eyes ever wasted away, looking in vain for aid; from our watchtower we watched for a nation that could not save us. ¹⁸ Men dogged our steps so that we could not walk in our streets; our end drew near, and came; our time had expired. ¹⁹ Our pursuers were swifter than eagles in the air, they harassed us on the mountains and waylaid us in the desert. ²⁰ The anointed one of the LORD, our breath of life, was caught in their snares, he in whose shadow we thought we could live on among the nations. ²¹ Though you rejoice and are glad, O daughter Edom, you who dwell in the land of Uz, to you also shall the cup be passed; you shall become drunk and naked. ²² Your chastisement is completed, O daughter Zion, he will not prolong your exile; but your wickedness, O daughter Edom, he will punish, he will lay bare your sins.

Lamentations Chapter 5

¹ Remember, O LORD, what has befallen us, look, and see our disgrace: ² Our inherited lands have been turned over to strangers, our homes to foreigners. ³ We have become orphans, fatherless; widowed are our mothers. ⁴ The water we drink we must buy, for our own wood we must pay. ⁵ On our necks is the yoke of those who drive us; we are worn out, but allowed no rest. ⁶ To Egypt we submitted, and to Assyria, to fill our need of bread. ⁷ Our fathers, who sinned, are no more; but we bear their guilt. ⁸ Slaves rule over us; there is no one to rescue us from their hands. ⁹ At the peril of our lives we bring in our sustenance, in the face of the desert heat; ¹⁰ Our skin is shriveled up, as though in a furnace, with the searing blasts of famine. ¹¹ The wives in Zion were ravished by the enemy, the maidens in the cities of Judah; ¹² Princes were gibbeted by them, elders shown no respect. ¹³ The youths carry the millstones, boys stagger under their loads of wood; ¹⁴ The old men have abandoned the gate, the young men their music. ¹⁵ The joy of our hearts has ceased, our dance has turned into mourning; ¹⁶ The garlands have fallen from our heads: woe to us, for we have sinned! ¹⁷ Over this our hearts are sick, at this our eyes grow dim: ¹⁸ That Mount Zion should be desolate, with jackals roaming there! ¹⁹ You, O LORD, are enthroned forever; your throne stands from age to age. ²⁰ Why, then, should you forget us, abandon us so long a time? ²¹ Lead us back to you, O LORD, that we may be restored: give us anew such days as we had of old. ²² For now you have indeed rejected us, and in full measure turned your wrath against us.

Ezekiel

Ezekiel Chapter 1

¹ "In the thirtieth year, on the fifth day of the fourth month, while I was among the exiles by the river Chebar, the heavens opened, and I saw divine visions. ² On the fifth day of the month, the fifth year, that is, of King Jehoiachin's exile, ³ the word of the LORD came to the priest Ezekiel, the son of Buzi, in the land of the Chaldeans by the river Chebar. There the hand of the LORD came upon me. ⁴ As I looked, a stormwind came from the North, a huge cloud with flashing fire (enveloped in brightness), from the midst of which (the midst of the fire) something gleamed like electrum. ⁵ Within it were figures resembling four living creatures that looked like this: their form was human, ⁶ but each had four faces and four wings, ⁷ and their legs went straight down; the soles of their feet were round. They sparkled with a gleam like burnished bronze. ⁸ Human hands were under their wings, and the wings of one touched those of another. ⁹ Their faces (and their wings) looked out on all their four sides; they did not turn when they moved, but each went straight forward. ¹⁰ Their faces were like this: each of the four had the face of a man, but on the right side was the face of a lion, and on the left side the face of an ox, and finally each had the face of an eagle. ¹¹ Each had two wings spread out above so that they touched one another's, while the other two wings of each covered his body. ¹² Each went straight forward; wherever the spirit wished to go, there they went; they did not turn when they moved. ¹³ In among the living creatures something like burning coals of fire could be seen; they

seemed like torches, moving to and fro among the living creatures. The fire gleamed, and from it came forth flashes of lightning. ¹⁴ The living creatures darted back and forth like flashes of lightning. ¹⁵ As I looked at the living creatures, I saw wheels on the ground, one beside each of the four living creatures. ¹⁶ The wheels had the sparkling appearance of chrysolite, and all four of them looked the same: they were constructed as though one wheel were within another. ¹⁷ They could move in any of the four directions they faced, without veering as they moved. ¹⁸ The four of them had rims, and I saw that their rims were full of eyes all around. ¹⁹ When the living creatures moved, the wheels moved with them; and when the living creatures were raised from the ground, the wheels also were raised. ²⁰ Wherever the spirit wished to go, there the wheels went, and they were raised together with the living creatures; for the spirit of the living creatures was in the wheels. ²¹ When the living creatures moved, the wheels moved; when the living creatures stood still, the wheels stood still; and when the living creatures were raised from the ground, the wheels were raised with them, for the spirit of the living creatures was in the wheels. ²² Over the heads of the living creatures, something like a firmament could be seen, seeming like glittering crystal, stretched straight out above their heads. ²³ Beneath the firmament their wings were stretched out, one toward the other. Each of them had two wings covering his body. ²⁴ Then I heard the sound of their wings, like the roaring of mighty waters, like the voice of the Almighty. When they moved, the sound of the tumult was like the din of an army. And when they stood still, they lowered their wings. ²⁵ A voice came from above the firmament over their heads; when they stood still, they lowered their wings. ²⁶ Above the firmament over their heads something like a throne could be seen, looking like sapphire. Upon it was seated, up above, one who had the appearance of a man. ²⁷ Upward from what resembled his waist I saw what gleamed like electrum; downward from what resembled his waist I saw what looked like fire; he was surrounded with splendor. ²⁸ Like the bow which appears in the clouds on a rainy day was the splendor that surrounded him. Such was the vision of the likeness of the glory of the LORD. When I had seen it, I fell upon my face and heard a voice that said to me:"

Ezekiel Chapter 2

¹ "Son of man, stand up! I wish to speak with you. ² As he spoke to me, spirit entered into me and set me on my feet, and I heard the one who was speaking ³ say to me: Son of man, I am sending you to the Israelites, rebels who have rebelled against me; they and their fathers have revolted against me to this very day. ⁴ Hard of face and obstinate of heart are they to whom I am sending you. But you shall say to them: Thus says the Lord GOD! ⁵ And whether they heed or resist—for they are a rebellious house—they shall know that a prophet has been among them. ⁶ But as for you, son of man, fear neither them nor their words when they contradict you and reject you, and when you sit on scorpions. Neither fear their words nor be dismayed at their looks, for they are a rebellious house. ⁷ But speak my words to them, whether they heed or resist, for they are rebellious. ⁸ As for you, son of man, obey me when I speak to you: be not rebellious like this house of rebellion, but open your mouth and eat what I shall give you. ⁹ It was then I saw a hand stretched out to me, in which was a written scroll ¹⁰ which he unrolled before me. It was covered with writing front and back, and written on it was: Lamentation and wailing and woe!"

Ezekiel Chapter 3

¹ "He said to me: Son of man, eat what is before you; eat this scroll, then go, speak to the house of Israel. ² So I opened my mouth and he gave me the scroll to eat. ³ Son of man, he then said to me, feed your belly and fill your stomach with this scroll I am giving you. I ate it, and it was as sweet as honey in my mouth. He said: ⁴ Son of man, go now to the house of Israel, and speak my words to them. ⁵ Not to a people with difficult speech and barbarous language am I sending you, ⁶ nor to the many peoples with difficult speech and barbarous language whose words you cannot understand. If I were to send you to these, they would listen to you; ⁷ but the house of Israel will refuse to listen to you, since they will not listen to me. For the whole house of Israel is stubborn of brow and obstinate in heart. ⁸ But I will make your face as hard as theirs, and your brow as stubborn as theirs; ⁹ like diamond, harder than flint. Fear them not, nor be dismayed at their looks, for they are a rebellious house. ¹⁰ Son of man, he said to me, take into your heart all my words that I speak to you; hear them well. ¹¹ Now go to the exiles, to your countrymen, and say to them: Thus says the Lord GOD! - whether they heed or resist! ¹² Then spirit lifted me up, and I heard behind me the noise of a loud rumbling as the glory of the LORD rose from its place: ¹³ the noise made by the wings of the living creatures striking one another, and by the wheels alongside them, a loud

rumbling. [14] The spirit which had lifted me up seized me, and I went off spiritually stirred, while the hand of the LORD rested heavily upon me. [15] Thus I came to the exiles who lived at Tel-abib by the river Chebar, and for seven days I sat among them distraught. [17] Thus the word of the LORD came to me: Son of man, I have appointed you a watchman for the house of Israel. When you hear a word from my mouth, you shall warn them for me. [18] If I say to the wicked man, 'You shall surely die,' and you do not warn him or speak out to dissuade him from his wicked conduct so that he may live, that wicked man shall die for his sin, but I will hold you responsible for his death. [19] If, on the other hand, you have warned the wicked man, yet he has not turned away from his evil nor from his wicked conduct, then he shall die for his sin, but you shall save your life. [20] If a virtuous man turns away from virtue and does wrong when I place a stumbling block before him, he shall die. He shall die for his sin, and his virtuous deeds shall not be remembered; but I will hold you responsible for his death if you did not warn him. [21] When, on the other hand, you have warned a virtuous man not to sin, and he has in fact not sinned, he shall surely live because of the warning, and you shall save your own life. [22] The hand of the LORD came upon me, and he said to me: Get up and go out into the plain, where I will speak with you. [23] So I got up and went out into the plain, and I saw that the glory of the LORD was in that place, like the glory I had seen by the river Chebar. I fell prone, [24] but then spirit entered into me and set me on my feet, and he spoke with me. He said to me: Go shut yourself up in your house. [25] As for you, son of man, they will put cords upon you and bind you with them, so that you cannot go out among them. [26] I will make your tongue stick to your palate so that you will be dumb and unable to rebuke them for being a rebellious house. [27] Only when I speak with you and open your mouth, shall you say to them: Thus says the Lord GOD! Let him heed who will, and let him resist who will, for they are a rebellious house. [16] At the end of seven days..."

Ezekiel Chapter 4

[1] "As for you, son of man, take a clay tablet; lay it in front of you, and draw on it a city (Jerusalem). [2] Raise a siege against it: build a tower, lay out a ramp, pitch camps, and set up battering rams all around. [3] Then take an iron griddle and set it up as an iron wall between you and the city. Fix your gaze on it: it shall be in the state of siege, and you shall besiege it. This shall be a sign for the house of Israel. [4] Then you shall lie on your left side, while I place the sins of the house of Israel upon you. As many days as you lie thus, you shall bear their sins. [5] For the years of their sins I allot you the same number of days, three hundred and ninety, during which you will bear the sins of the house of Israel. [6] When you finish this, you are to lie down again, but on your right side, and bear the sins of the house of Judah forty days; one day for each year I have allotted you. [7] Fixing your gaze on the siege of Jerusalem, with bared arm you shall prophesy against it. [8] See, I will bind you with cords so that you cannot turn from one side to the other until you have completed the days of your siege. [9] Again, take wheat and barley, and beans and lentils, and millet and spelt; put them in a single vessel and make bread out of them. Eat it for as many days as you lie upon your side, three hundred and ninety. [10] The food you eat shall be twenty shekels a day by weight; each day the same. [11] And the water you drink shall be the sixth of a hin by measure; each day the same. [12] For your food you must bake barley loaves over human excrement in their sight, said the LORD. [13] Thus the Israelites shall eat their food unclean among the nations where I scatter them. [14] 'Oh no, Lord GOD!' I protested. 'Never have I been made unclean, and from my youth till now, never have I eaten carrion flesh or that torn by wild beasts; never has any unclean meat entered my mouth.' [15] Very well, he replied, I allow you cow's dung in place of human excrement; bake your bread on that. [16] Then he said to me: Son of man, I am breaking the staff of bread in Jerusalem. They shall eat bread which they have weighed out anxiously, and they shall drink water which they have measured out fearfully, [17] so that, owing to the scarcity of bread and water, everyone shall be filled with terror and waste away because of his sins."

Ezekiel Chapter 5

[1] As for you, son of man, take a sharp sword and use it like a barber's razor, passing it over your head and beard. Then take a set of scales and divide the hair you have cut. [2] Burn a third in the fire, within the city, when the days of your siege are completed; place another third around the city and strike it with the sword; the final third strew in the wind, and pursue it with the sword. [3] (But of the last take a small number and tie them in the hem of your garment. [4] Then take some of these and throw them in the midst of the fire and burn them.) Say to the whole house of Israel: [5] Thus says the Lord GOD: This is Jerusalem! In the midst of the nations I placed her, surrounded by foreign countries. [6]

But she rebelled against my ordinances more wickedly than the nations, and against my statutes more than the foreign countries surrounding her; she has spurned my ordinances and has not lived by my statutes. [7] Therefore thus says the Lord GOD: Because you have been more rebellious than the nations surrounding you, not living by my statutes nor fulfilling my ordinances, but acting according to the ordinances of the surrounding nations; [8] therefore thus says the Lord GOD: See, I am coming at you! I will inflict punishments in your midst while the nations look on. [9] Because of all your abominations I will do with you what I have never done before, the like of which I will never do again. [10] This means that fathers within you shall eat sons, and sons shall eat fathers. I will inflict punishments upon you and scatter all that remain of your people in every direction. [11] Therefore, as I live, says the Lord GOD, because you have defiled my sanctuary with all your detestable abominations, I swear to cut you down. I will not look upon you with pity nor have mercy. [12] A third of your people shall die of pestilence and perish of hunger within you; another third shall fall by the sword all around you; and a third I will scatter in every direction, and I will pursue them with the sword. [13] Thus shall my anger spend itself, and I will wreak my fury upon them till I am appeased; they shall know that I, the LORD, have spoken in my jealousy when I spend my fury upon them. [14] I will make you a waste and a reproach among the nations that surround you, which every passer-by may see. [15] When I execute judgment upon you in anger and fury and with furious chastisements, you shall be a reproach and an object of scorn, a terrible warning to the nations that surround you. I, the LORD, have spoken! [16] When I loose against you the cruel, destructive arrows of hunger, I will break your staff of bread; [17] I will send famine against you, and wild beasts that shall rob you of your children. Pestilence and bloodshed shall stalk through you, and I will bring the sword upon you. I, the LORD, have spoken!

Ezekiel Chapter 6

"[1] Thus the word of the LORD came to me: [2] Son of man, turn toward the mountains of Israel, and prophesy against them: [3] Mountains of Israel, hear the word of the Lord GOD. Thus says the Lord GOD to the mountains and hills, the ravines and valleys: See, I am bringing a sword against you, and I will destroy your high places. [4] Your altars shall be laid waste, your incense stands shall be broken, and I will cast down your slain ones before your idols; [5] I will scatter their bones all around your altars. [6] In all your dwelling places cities shall be made desolate and high places laid waste, so that your altars will be made desolate and laid waste, your idols broken and removed, and your incense stands smashed to bits. [7] The slain shall fall in your midst, and you shall know that I am the LORD. [8] I have warned you. When some of your people have escaped to other nations from the sword, and have been scattered over the foreign lands, [9] then those who have escaped will remember me among the nations to which they have been exiled, after I have broken their adulterous hearts that turned away from me and their eyes which lusted after idols. They shall loathe themselves because of their evil deeds, all their abominations. [10] Then they shall know that it was not in vain that I, the LORD, threatened to inflict this calamity upon them. [11] Thus says the Lord GOD: Clap your hands, stamp your feet, and cry 'Alas!' because of all the abominations of the house of Israel, for which they shall fall by the sword, by famine, and by pestilence. [12] He that is far off shall die of pestilence, he that is near shall fall by the sword, and he that is besieged shall perish by famine; so will I spend my fury upon them. [13] Then shall they know that I am the LORD, when their slain shall lie amid their idols, all about their altars, on every high hill and mountaintop, beneath every green tree and leafy oak, wherever they offered appeasing odors to any of their gods. [14] I will stretch out my hand against them, and wherever they live I will make the land a desolate waste, from the desert to Riblah; thus shall they know that I am the LORD."

Ezekiel Chapter 7

[1] Thus the word of the LORD came to me: [2] Son of man, now say: Thus says the Lord GOD to the land of Israel: An end! The end has come upon the four corners of the land! [3] Now the end is upon you; I will unleash my anger against you and judge you according to your conduct and lay upon you the consequences of all your abominations. [4] I will not look upon you with pity nor have mercy; I will bring your conduct down upon you, and the consequences of your abominations shall be in your midst; then shall you know that I am the LORD. [5] Thus says the Lord GOD: Disaster upon disaster! See it coming! [6] An end is coming, the end is coming upon you! See it coming! [7] The climax has come for you who dwell in the land! The time has come, near is the day: a time of consternation, not of rejoicing. [8] Soon now I will pour out my fury upon you and spend my anger upon you; I will judge you according to your

conduct and lay upon you the consequences of all your abominations. 9 I will not look upon you with pity nor have mercy; I will deal with you according to your conduct, and the consequences of your abominations shall be in your midst; then shall you know that it is I, the LORD, who strike. 10 See, the day of the LORD! See, the end is coming! Lawlessness is in full bloom, insolence flourishes, 11 violence has risen to support wickedness. It shall not be long in coming, nor shall it delay. 12 The time has come, the day dawns. Let not the buyer rejoice nor the seller mourn, for wrath shall be upon all the throng. 13 The seller shall not regain what he sold as long as he lives, for wrath shall be upon all the throng. Because of his sins, no one shall preserve his life. 14 They shall sound the trumpet and make everything ready, yet no one shall go to war, for my wrath is upon all the throng. 15 The sword is outside; pestilence and hunger are within. He that is in the country shall die by the sword; pestilence and famine shall devour those in the city. 16 Even those who escape and flee to the mountains like the doves of the valleys—I will put them all to death, each one for his own sins. 17 All their hands shall be limp, and all their knees shall run with water. 18 They shall put on sackcloth, and horror shall cover them; shame shall be on all their faces and baldness on all their heads. 19 They shall fling their silver into the streets, and their gold shall be considered refuse. Their silver and gold cannot save them on the day of the LORD'S wrath. They shall not be allowed to satisfy their craving or fill their bellies, for this has been the occasion of their sin. 20 In the beauty of their ornaments they put their pride: they made of them their abominable images (their idols). For this reason I make them refuse. 21 I will hand them over as booty to foreigners, to be spoiled and defiled by the wicked of the earth. 22 I will turn away my face from them, and my treasure shall be profaned: robbers shall enter and profane it. 23 They shall wreak slaughter, for the land is filled with bloodshed and the city full of violence. 24 I will bring in the worst of the nations, who shall take possession of their houses. I will put an end to their proud strength, and their sanctuaries shall be profaned. 25 When anguish comes they shall seek peace, but there will be none. 26 There shall be disaster after disaster, rumor after rumor. Prophetic vision shall fade; instruction shall be lacking to the priest, and counsel to the elders, 27 while the prince shall be enveloped in terror, and the hands of the common people shall tremble. I will deal with them according to their conduct, and according to their judgments I will judge them; thus they shall know that I am the LORD.

Ezekiel Chapter 8

1 Spirit lifted me up in the air and brought me in divine visions to Jerusalem, to the entrance of the north gate, where stood the statue of jealousy which stirs up jealousy. 2 He said to me: Son of man, look toward the north! I looked toward the north and saw northward of the gate the altar of the statue of jealousy. 3 Son of man, he asked me, do you see what they are doing? Do you see the great abominations that the house of Israel is practicing here, so that I must depart from my sanctuary? But you shall see still greater abominations! 4 Then he brought me to the entrance of the court, where I saw there was a hole in the wall. 5 Son of man, he ordered, dig through the wall. I dug through the wall and saw a door. 6 Enter, he said to me, and see the abominable evils which they are doing here. 7 I entered and saw that all around upon the wall were pictured the figures of all kinds of creeping things and loathsome beasts (all the idols of the house of Israel). 8 Before these stood seventy of the elders of the house of Israel, among whom stood Jaazaniah, son of Shaphan, each of them with his censer in his hand, and the fragrance of the incense was rising upward. 9 Then he said to me: Do you see, son of man, what each of these elders of the house of Israel is doing in his idol room? They think: "The LORD cannot see us; the LORD has forsaken the land." 10 He continued: You shall see still greater abominations that they are practicing. 11 Then he brought me to the entrance of the north gate of the temple, and I saw sitting there the women who were weeping for Tammuz. 12 Then he said to me: Do you see this, son of man? You shall see other abominations, greater than these! 13 Then he brought me into the inner court of the LORD'S house, and there at the door of the LORD'S temple, between the vestibule and the altar, were about twenty-five men with their backs to the LORD'S temple and their faces toward the east; they were bowing down to the sun. 14 Do you see, son of man? he asked me. Is it such a trivial matter for the house of Judah to do the abominable things they have done here—for they have filled the land with violence, and again and again they have provoked me—that now they must also put the branch to my nose? 15 Therefore I in turn will act furiously: I will not look upon them with pity nor will I show mercy.

Ezekiel Chapter 9

1 Then he cried loud for me to hear: Come, you scourges of the city! 2 With that I saw six men coming from the direction of the upper gate which faces the north, each with a destroying weapon in his hand. In their midst was a man dressed in linen, with a writer's case at his waist. They entered and stood beside the bronze altar. 3 Then he called to the man dressed in linen with the writer's case at his waist, 4 saying to him: Pass through the city (through Jerusalem) and mark an X on the foreheads of those who moan and groan over all the abominations that are practiced within it. 5 To the others I heard him say: Pass through the city after him and strike! Do not look on them with pity nor show any mercy! 6 Old men, youths and maidens, women and children—wipe them out! But do not touch any marked with the X; begin at my sanctuary. So they began with the men (the elders) who were in front of the temple. 7 Defile the temple, he said to them, and fill the courts with the slain; then go out and strike in the city. 8 As they began to strike, I was left alone. I fell prone, crying out, Alas, Lord GOD! Will you destroy all that is left of Israel when you pour out your fury on Jerusalem? 9 He answered me: The sins of the house of Israel are great beyond measure; the land is filled with bloodshed, the city with lawlessness. They think that the LORD has forsaken the land, that he does not see them. 10 I, however, will not look upon them with pity, nor show any mercy. I will bring down their conduct upon their heads. 11 Then I saw the man dressed in linen with the writing case at his waist make his report: "I have done as you ordered." 24 Spirit lifted me up and brought me back to the exiles in Chaldea (in a vision, by God's spirit). Then the vision I had seen left me, 25 and I told the exiles everything the LORD had shown me.

Ezekiel Chapter 10

1 On the fifth day of the sixth month, in the sixth year, as I was sitting in my house, and the elders of Judah sat before me, the hand of the Lord GOD fell upon me there. 2 I looked up and saw a form that looked like a man. Downward from what seemed to be his waist, there was fire; from his waist upward there seemed to be a brightness like the sheen of electrum. He stretched out what appeared to be a hand and seized me by the hair of my head. . . . 4 I saw there the glory of the God of Israel, like the vision I had seen in the plain. The cherubim were stationed to the right of the temple; 20 these were the living creatures I had seen beneath the God of Israel by the river Chebar, whom I now recognized to be cherubim. 21 Each had four faces and four wings; something like human hands were under their wings. 22 Their faces looked just like those I had seen by the river Chebar; each one went straight forward. 14 Each had four faces: the first face was that of an ox, the second that of a man, the third that of a lion, and the fourth that of an eagle. 15 Such were the living creatures I had seen by the river Chebar. 9 I also saw four wheels beside them, one wheel beside each cherub; the wheels appeared to have the luster of chrysolite stone. 10 All four of them seemed to be made the same, as though they were a wheel within a wheel. 11 When they moved, they went in any one of their four directions without veering as they moved; for in whichever direction they were faced, they went straight toward it without veering as they moved. 12 The rims of the four wheels were full of eyes all around. 13 I heard the wheels given the name "wheelwork." 16 When the cherubim moved, the wheels went beside them; when the cherubim lifted their wings to rise from the earth, even then the wheels did not leave their sides. 17 When they stood still, the wheels stood still; when they rose, the wheels rose with them; for the living creatures' spirit was in them. 1 I looked and saw in the firmament above the cherubim what appeared to be sapphire stone; something like a throne could be seen upon it. 2 He said to the man dressed in linen: Go within the wheelwork under the cherubim; fill both your hands with burning coals from among the cherubim, then scatter them over the city. As I looked on, he entered. The glory of the God of Israel had gone up from the cherubim, upon which it had been, to the threshold of the temple. 3 As the man entered, the cloud filled the inner court, 4 and the glory of the LORD rose from over the cherubim to the threshold of the temple; the temple was filled with the cloud, and all the court was bright with the glory of the LORD. 5 The noise of the wings of the cherubim could be heard as far as the outer court; it was like the voice of God the Almighty when he speaks. 6 When he had commanded the man dressed in linen to take fire from within the wheelwork, among the cherubim, the man entered and stood by one of the wheels. 7 Thereupon its cherub stretched out his hand toward the fire that was among the cherubim. He took up some of it and put it in the hands of the one dressed in linen, who took it and came out. 8 (Something like human hands could be seen under the wings of the cherubim.) 18 Then the glory of the LORD left the threshold of the temple and rested upon the cherubim. 19 These lifted their wings, and I saw them rise from the earth, the wheels rising along with them. They stood at the entrance of the eastern gate of the LORD'S house, and the glory of the God of Israel was up above them.

Ezekiel Chapter 11

1 Then the cherubim lifted their wings, and the wheels went along with them, while up above them was the glory of the God of Israel. 2 And the glory of the LORD rose from the city and took a stand on the mountain which is to the east of the city. 3 Spirit lifted me up and brought me to the east gate of the temple. At the entrance of the gate I saw twenty-five men, among whom were Jaazaniah, son of Azzur, and Pelatiah, son of Benaiah, princes of the people. 4 The LORD said to me: Son of man, these are the men who are planning evil and giving wicked counsel in this city. 5 "Shall we not," they say, "be building houses soon? The city is the kettle, and we are the meat." 6 Therefore prophesy against them, son of man, prophesy! 7 Then the spirit of the LORD fell upon me, and he told me to say: Thus says the LORD: This is the way you talk, house of Israel, and what you are plotting I well know. 8 You have slain many in this city and have filled its streets with your slain. 9 Therefore thus says the Lord GOD: Your slain whom you have placed within it, they are the meat, and the city is the kettle; but you I will take out of it. 10 You fear the sword, but the sword I will bring upon you, says the Lord GOD. 11 I will bring you out of the city, and hand you over to foreigners, and inflict punishments upon you. 12 By the sword you shall fall; at the boundaries of Israel I will judge you; thus you shall know that I am the LORD. 13 The city shall not be a kettle for you, nor shall you be the meat within it. At the boundaries of Israel I will judge you, 14 and you shall know that I am the LORD, by whose statutes you have not lived, and whose ordinances you have not kept; rather, you have acted according to the ordinances of the nations around you. 15 While I was prophesying, Pelatiah, the son of Benaiah, died. I fell prone and cried out in a loud voice: "Alas, Lord GOD! will you utterly wipe out what remains of Israel?" 16 Thus the word of the LORD came to me: 17 Son of man, it is about your kinsmen, your fellow exiles, and the whole house of Israel that the inhabitants of Jerusalem say, "They are far away from the LORD; to us the land of Israel has been given as our possession." 18 Therefore say: Thus says the Lord GOD: Though I have removed them far among the nations and scattered them over foreign countries—and was for a while their only sanctuary in the countries to which they had gone— 19 I will gather you from the nations and assemble you from the countries over which you have been scattered, and I will restore to you the land of Israel. 20 They shall return to it and remove from it all its detestable abominations. 21 I will give them a new heart and put a new spirit within them; I will remove the stony heart from their bodies, and replace it with a natural heart, 22 so that they will live according to my statutes, and observe and carry out my ordinances; thus they shall be my people and I will be their God. 23 But as for those whose hearts are devoted to their detestable abominations, I will bring down their conduct upon their heads, says the Lord GOD.

Ezekiel Chapter 12

1 Thus the word of the LORD came to me: 2 Son of man, you live in the midst of a rebellious house; they have eyes to see but do not see, and ears to hear but do not hear, for they are a rebellious house. 3 Now, son of man, during the day while they are looking on, prepare your baggage as though for exile, and again while they are looking on, migrate from where you live to another place; perhaps they will see that they are a rebellious house. 4 You shall bring out your baggage like an exile in the daytime while they are looking on; in the evening, again while they are looking on, you shall go out like one of those driven into exile; 5 while they look on, dig a hole in the wall and pass through it; 6 while they look on, shoulder the burden and set out in the darkness; cover your face that you may not see the land, for I have made you a sign for the house of Israel. 7 I did as I was told. During the day I brought out my baggage as though it were that of an exile, and at evening I dug a hole through the wall with my hand and, while they looked on, set out in the darkness, shouldering my burden. 8 Then, in the morning, the word of the LORD came to me: 9 Son of man, did not the house of Israel, that rebellious house, ask you what you were doing? 10 Tell them: Thus says the Lord GOD: This oracle concerns Jerusalem and the whole house of Israel within it. 11 I am a sign for you: as I have done, so shall it be done to them; as captives they shall go into exile. 12 The prince who is among them shall shoulder his burden and set out in darkness, going through a hole that he has dug in the wall, and covering his face lest he be seen by anyone. 13 But I will spread my net over him, and he shall be taken in my snare. I will bring him to Babylon, into the land of the Chaldeans—but he shall not see it—and there he shall die. 14 All his retinue, his aides, and his troops I will scatter in every direction, and pursue them with the sword. 15 Then shall they know that I am the LORD, when I disperse them among the nations and scatter them over foreign lands. 16 Yet I will leave a few of them to escape the sword, famine and pestilence, so that they may tell of all their abominations

among the nations to which they will come; thus they shall know that I am the LORD. 17 Thus the word of the LORD came to me: 18 Son of man, eat your bread trembling, and drink your water shaking with anxiety. 19 Then say to the people of the land: Thus says the Lord GOD of the inhabitants of Jerusalem (to the land of Israel): They shall eat their bread in anxiety and drink their water in horror, that their land may be emptied of the violence of all its inhabitants that now fills it. 20 Inhabited cities shall be in ruins, and the land shall be a waste; thus you shall know that I am the LORD. 21 Thus the word of the LORD came to me: 22 Son of man, what is this proverb that you have in the land of Israel: "The days drag on, and no vision ever comes to anything"? 23 Say to them therefore: Thus says the Lord GOD: I will put an end to this proverb; they shall never quote it again in Israel. Rather, say to them: The days are at hand, and also the fulfillment of every vision. 24 Whatever I speak is final, and it shall be done without further delay. In your days, rebellious house, whatever I speak I will bring about, says the Lord GOD. 25 There shall no longer be any false visions or deceitful divinations within the house of Israel, because it is I, the LORD, who will speak. 26 Thus the word of the LORD came to me: 27 Son of man, listen to the house of Israel saying, "The vision he sees is a long way off; he prophesies of the distant future!" 28 Say to them therefore: Thus says the Lord GOD: None of my words shall be delayed any longer; whatever I speak is final, and it shall be done, says the Lord GOD.

Ezekiel Chapter 13

1 Thus the word of the LORD came to me: 2 Son of man, prophesy against the prophets of Israel, prophesy! Say to those who prophesy their own thought: Hear the word of the LORD: 3 Thus says the Lord GOD: Woe to those prophets who are fools, who follow their own spirit and have seen no vision. 4 Like foxes among ruins are your prophets, O Israel! 5 You did not step into the breach, nor did you build a wall about the house of Israel that would stand firm against attack on the day of the LORD. 6 Their visions are false and their divination lying. They say, "Thus says the LORD!" though the LORD did not send them; then they wait for him to fulfill their word! 7 Was not the vision you saw false, and your divination lying? 8 Therefore thus says the Lord GOD: Because you have spoken falsehood and have seen lying visions, therefore see! I am coming at you, says the Lord GOD. 9 But I will stretch out my hand against the prophets who have false visions and who foretell lies. They shall not belong to the community of my people, nor be recorded in the register of the house of Israel, nor enter the land of Israel; thus you shall know that I am the LORD. 10 For the very reason that they led my people astray, saying, "Peace!" when there was no peace, and that, as one built a wall, they would cover it with whitewash, 11 say then to the whitewashers: I will bring down a flooding rain; hailstones shall fall, and a stormwind shall break out. 12 And when the wall has fallen, will you not be asked: Where is the whitewash you spread on? 13 Therefore thus says the Lord GOD: In my fury I will let loose stormwinds; because of my anger there shall be a flooding rain, and hailstones shall fall with destructive wrath. 14 I will tear down the wall that you have whitewashed and level it to the ground, laying bare its foundations. When it falls, you shall be crushed beneath it; thus you shall know that I am the LORD. 15 When I have spent my fury on the wall and its whitewashers, I tell you there shall be no wall, nor shall there be whitewashers— 16 those prophets of Israel who prophesied to Jerusalem and saw for it visions of peace when there was no peace, says the Lord GOD. 17 Now, son of man, turn toward the daughters of your people who prophesy their own thoughts; against these, prophesy: Thus says the Lord GOD: 18 Woe to those who sew bands for everyone's wrists and make veils for every size of head so as to entrap their owners. Do you think to entrap the lives of my people, yet keep yourselves alive? 19 You dishonor me before my people with handfuls of barley and crumbs of bread, killing those who should not die and keeping alive those who should not live, lying to my people who willingly hear lies. 20 Therefore thus says the Lord GOD: See! I am coming at those bands of yours in which you entrap men's lives: I will tear them from their arms and set free those you have caught. 21 I will tear off your veils and rescue my people from your power, so that they shall no longer be prey to your hands. Thus you shall know that I am the LORD. 22 Because you have disheartened the upright man with lies when I did not wish him grieved, and have encouraged the wicked man not to turn from his evil conduct and save his life; 23 therefore you shall no longer see false visions and practice divination, but I will rescue my people from your power. Thus you shall know that I am the LORD.

Ezekiel Chapter 14

1 When certain elders of Israel came and sat down before me, 2 the word of the LORD came to me: 3 Son of man, these men have the memory of their idols fresh in their hearts, and they keep the occasion of their sin

before them. Why should I allow myself to be consulted by them? 4 Therefore speak with them, and say to them: Thus says the Lord GOD: If anyone of the house of Israel, holding the memory of his idols in his heart and keeping the occasion of his sin before him, has recourse to a prophet, I, the LORD, will be his answer in person because of his many idols. 5 Thus would I bring back to their senses the house of Israel, who have become estranged from me through all their idols. 6 Therefore say to the house of Israel: Thus says the Lord GOD: Return and be converted from your idols; turn yourselves away from all your abominations. 7 For if anyone of the house of Israel or any alien resident in Israel is estranged from me, and holds the memory of his idols in his heart and keeps the occasion of his sin before him, yet asks a prophet to consult me for him, I, the LORD, will be his answer in person. 8 I will turn against that man, and make of him an example and a byword. I will cut him off from the midst of my people. Thus you shall know that I am the LORD. 9 As for the prophet, if he is beguiled into speaking a word, I, the LORD, shall have beguiled that prophet; I will stretch out my hand against him and root him out of my people Israel. 10 Each shall receive punishment for his sin, the inquirer and the prophet shall be punished alike, 11 so that the house of Israel may no longer stray from me and may no longer be defiled by all their sins. Thus they shall be my people, and I will be their God, says the Lord GOD. 12 Thus the word of the LORD came to me: 13 Son of man, when a land sins against me by breaking faith, I stretch out my hand against it and break its staff of bread, I let famine loose upon it and cut off from it both man and beast; 14 and even if these three men were in it, Noah, Daniel, and Job, they could save only themselves by their virtue, says the Lord GOD. 15 If I were to cause wild beasts to prowl the land, depopulating it so that it became a waste, traversed by none because of the wild beasts, 16 and these three men were in it, as I live, says the Lord GOD, I swear they could save neither sons nor daughters; they alone would be saved, and the land would be a waste. 17 Or if I brought the sword upon this country, commanding the sword to pass through the land cutting off from it man and beast, 18 and these three men were in it, as I live, says the Lord GOD, they would be unable to save either sons or daughters; they alone would be saved. 19 Or if I were to send pestilence into this land, pouring out upon it my bloodthirsty fury, cutting off from it man and beast, 20 even if Noah, Daniel, and Job were in it, as I live, says the Lord GOD, I swear that they could save neither son nor daughter; they would save only themselves by their virtue. 21 Thus says the Lord GOD: Even though I send Jerusalem my four cruel punishments, the sword, famine, wild beasts, and pestilence, to cut off from it man and beast, 22 still some survivors shall be left in it who will bring out sons and daughters; when they come out to you, you shall see their conduct and their actions and be consoled regarding the evil I have brought on Jerusalem (all that I have brought upon it). 23 They shall console you when you see their conduct and actions, for you shall then know that it was not without reason that I did to it what I did, says the Lord GOD.

Ezekiel Chapter 15

1 Thus the word of the LORD came to me: 2 Son of man, what makes the wood of the vine better than any other wood? That branch among the trees of the forest! 3 Can you use its wood to make anything worthwhile? Can you make even a peg from it, to hang on it any kind of vessel? 4 If you throw it on the fire as fuel and the fire devours both ends and even the middle is scorched, is it still good for anything? 5 Why, even when it was whole it was good for nothing; how much less, when the fire has devoured and scorched it, can it be used for anything! 6 Therefore, thus says the Lord GOD: Like the wood of the vine among the trees of the forest, which I have destined as fuel for the fire, do I make the inhabitants of Jerusalem. 7 I will set my face against them; they have escaped from the fire, but the fire shall devour them. Thus you shall know that I am the LORD, when I turn my face against them. 8 I will make the land a waste, because they have broken faith, says the Lord GOD.

Ezekiel Chapter 16

1 Thus the word of the LORD came to me: 2 Son of man, make known to Jerusalem her abominations. 3 Thus says the Lord GOD to Jerusalem: By origin and birth you are of the land of Canaan; your father was an Amorite and your mother a Hittite. 4 As for your birth, the day you were born your navel cord was not cut; you were neither washed with water nor anointed, nor were you rubbed with salt, nor swathed in swaddling clothes. 5 No one looked on you with pity or compassion to do any of these things for you. Rather, you were thrown out on the ground as something loathsome, the day you were born. 6 Then I passed by and saw you weltering in your blood. I said to you: Live in your blood 7 and grow like a plant in the field. You grew and developed, you came to the age of puberty; your breasts were formed,

your hair had grown, but you were still stark naked. 8 Again I passed by you and saw that you were now old enough for love. So I spread the corner of my cloak over you to cover your nakedness; I swore an oath to you and entered into a covenant with you; you became mine, says the Lord GOD. 9 Then I bathed you with water, washed away your blood, and anointed you with oil. 10 I clothed you with an embroidered gown, put sandals of fine leather on your feet; I gave you a fine linen sash and silk robes to wear. 11 I adorned you with jewelry: I put bracelets on your arms, a necklace about your neck, 12 a ring in your nose, pendants in your ears, and a glorious diadem upon your head. 13 Thus you were adorned with gold and silver; your garments were of fine linen, silk, and embroidered cloth. Fine flour, honey, and oil were your food. You were exceedingly beautiful, with the dignity of a queen. 14 You were renowned among the nations for your beauty, perfect as it was, because of my splendor which I had bestowed on you, says the Lord GOD. 15 But you were captivated by your own beauty, you used your renown to make yourself a harlot, and you lavished your harlotry on every passer-by, whose own you became. 16 You took some of your gowns and made for yourself gaudy high places, where you played the harlot. 17 You took the splendid gold and silver ornaments that I had given you and made for yourself male images, with which also you played the harlot. 18 You took your embroidered gowns to cover them; my oil and my incense you set before them; 19 the food that I had given you, the fine flour, the oil, and the honey with which I fed you, you set before them as an appeasing odor, says the Lord GOD. 20 The sons and daughters you had borne me you took and offered as sacrifices to be devoured by them! Was it not enough that you had become a harlot? 21 You slaughtered and immolated my children to them, making them pass through fire. 22 And through all your abominations and harlotries you remembered nothing of when you were a girl, stark naked and weltering in your blood. 23 Then after all your evildoing—woe, woe to you! says the Lord GOD— 24 you raised for yourself a platform and a dais in every public place. 25 At every street corner you built a dais for yourself to use your beauty obscenely, spreading your legs for every passer-by, playing the harlot countless times. 26 You played the harlot with the Egyptians, your lustful neighbors, so many times that I was provoked to anger. 27 Therefore I stretched out my hand against you, I diminished your allowance and delivered you over to the will of your enemies, the Philistines, who revolted at your lewd conduct. 28 You also played the harlot with the Assyrians, because you were not satisfied; and after playing the harlot with them, you were still not satisfied. 29 Again and again you played the harlot, now going to Chaldea, the land of the traders; but despite this, you were still not satisfied. 30 How wild your lust! says the Lord GOD, that you did all these things, acting like a shameless prostitute, 31 building your platform at every street corner and erecting your dais in every public place! Yet you were unlike a prostitute, since you disdained payment. 32 The adulterous wife receives, instead of her husband, payment. 33 All harlots receive gifts. But you rather bestowed your gifts on all your lovers, bribing them to come to you from all sides for your harlotry. 34 Thus in your harlotry you were different from all other women. No one sought you out for prostitution. Since you gave payment instead of receiving it, how different you were! 35 Therefore, harlot, hear the word of the LORD! 36 Thus says the Lord GOD: Because you poured out your lust and revealed your nakedness in your harlotry with your lovers and abominable idols, and because you sacrificed the life-blood of your children to them, 37 I will now gather together all your lovers whom you tried to please, whether you loved them or loved them not; I will gather them against you from all sides and expose you naked for them to see. 38 I will inflict on you the sentence of adulteresses and murderesses; I will wreak fury and jealousy upon you. 39 I will hand you over to them to tear down your platform and demolish your dais; they shall strip you of your garments and take away your splendid ornaments, leaving you stark naked. 40 They shall lead an assembly against you to stone you and hack you with their swords. 41 They shall burn your apartments with fire and inflict punishments on you while many women look on. Thus I will put an end to your harlotry, and you shall never again give payment. 42 When I have wreaked my fury upon you I will cease to be jealous of you, I will be quiet and no longer vexed. 43 Because you did not remember what happened when you were a girl, but enraged me with all these things, therefore in return I am bringing down your conduct upon your head, says the Lord GOD. For did you not add lewdness to the rest of your abominable deeds? 44 See, everyone who is fond of proverbs will say of you, 'Like mother, like daughter.' 45 Yes, you are the true daughter of the mother who spurned her husband and children, and you are a true sister to those who spurned their husbands and children—your mother was a Hittite and your father an Amorite. 46 Your elder sister was Samaria with her daughters, living to the north of you; and your younger sister, living to the south of you, was Sodom with her daughters. 47 Yet not only in their ways did you walk, and act as abominably as they did; in a very short time you became more corrupt in all your ways than they. 48 As I live, says the Lord GOD, I swear that your sister Sodom, with her daughters, has not done as you and your daughters have done! 49 And look at the guilt of your sister Sodom: she and her daughters were proud, sated with food, complacent in their prosperity, and they gave no help to the poor and needy. 50 Rather, they became haughty and committed abominable crimes in my presence; then, as you have seen, I removed them. 51 Samaria did not commit half your sins! You have done more abominable things than they, and have even made your sisters appear just, with all the abominable deeds you have done. 52 You, then, bear your shame; you are an argument in favor of your sisters! In view of your sinful deeds, more abominable than theirs, they appear just in comparison with you. Blush for shame, and bear the shame of having made your sisters appear just. 53 I will restore their fortunes, the fortune of Sodom and her daughters and of Samaria and her daughters (and I will restore your fortune along with them), 54 that you may bear your shame and be disgraced for all the comfort you brought them. 55 Yes, your sisters, Sodom and her daughters, Samaria and her daughters, shall return to their former state (you and your daughters shall return to your former state). 56 Was not your sister Sodom kept in bad repute by you while you felt proud of yourself, 57 before your wickedness became evident? Now you are like her, reproached by the Edomites and all your neighbors, despised on all sides by the Philistines. 58 The penalty of your lewdness and your abominations—you must bear it all, says the LORD. 59 For thus speaks the Lord GOD: I will deal with you according to what you have done, you who despised your oath, breaking a covenant. 60 Yet I will remember the covenant I made with you when you were a girl, and I will set up an everlasting covenant with you. 61 Then you shall remember your conduct and be ashamed when I take your sisters, those older and younger than you, and give them to you as daughters, even though I am not bound by my covenant with you. 62 For I will re-establish my covenant with you, that you may know that I am the LORD, 63 that you may remember and be covered with confusion, and that you may be utterly silenced for shame when I pardon you for all you have done, says the Lord GOD.

Ezekiel Chapter 17

1 Thus the word of the LORD came to me: 2 Son of man, propose a riddle, and speak this proverb to the house of Israel: 3 Thus speaks the Lord GOD: The great eagle, with great wings, with long pinions, with thick plumage, many-hued, came to Lebanon. He took the crest of the cedar, 4 tearing off its topmost branch, and brought it to a land of tradesmen, set it in a city of merchants. 5 Then he took some seed of the land, and planted it in a seedbed; a shoot by plentiful waters, like a willow he placed it, 6 to sprout and grow up a vine, dense and low-lying, its branches turned toward him, its roots lying under him. Thus it became a vine, produced branches and put forth shoots. 7 But there was another great eagle, great of wing, rich in plumage; to him this vine bent its roots, sent out its branches, that he might water it more freely than the bed where it was planted. 8 In a fertile field by plentiful waters it was planted, to grow branches, bear fruit, and become a majestic vine. 9 Say: Thus says the Lord GOD: Can it prosper? Will he not rather tear it out by the roots and strip off its fruit, so that all its green growth will wither when he pulls it up by the roots? (No need of a mighty arm or many people to do this.) 10 True, it is planted, but will it prosper? Will it not rather wither, when touched by the east wind, in the bed where it grew? 11 Thus the word of the LORD came to me: 12 Son of man, say now to the rebellious house: Do you not understand what this means? It is this: The king of Babylon came to Jerusalem and took away its king and princes with him to Babylon. 13 Then he selected a man of the royal line with whom he made a covenant, binding him under oath, while removing the nobles of the land, 14 so that the kingdom would remain a modest one, without aspirations, and would keep his covenant and obey him. 15 But this man rebelled against him, sending envoys to Egypt to obtain horses and a great army. Can he prosper? Can he who does such things escape? Can he break a covenant and still go free? 16 As I live, says the Lord GOD, in the home of the king who set him up to rule, whose oath he spurned, whose covenant with him he broke, there in Babylon I swear he shall die! 17 When ramps are cast up and siege towers are built for the destruction of many lives, he shall not be saved in the conflict by Pharaoh with a great army and numerous troops. 18 He spurned his oath, breaking his covenant. Though he gave his hand in pledge, he did all these things. He shall not escape! 19 Therefore say: Thus says the Lord GOD: As I live, my oath which he spurned, my covenant which he broke, I swear to bring down upon his head. 20 I will spread my net over him, and he shall be taken in my snare. I will bring him to Babylon and enter into judgment with him there over his breaking faith with me. 21 All the crack troops among his forces shall fall by the sword, and the survivors shall be scattered in every direction. Thus you shall know that I, the LORD, have spoken. 22 Therefore say: Thus says the Lord GOD: I, too, will take from the crest of the cedar, from its topmost branches tear off a tender shoot, and plant it on a high and lofty mountain; 23 on the mountain heights of Israel I will plant it. It shall put forth branches and bear fruit, and become a majestic cedar. Birds of every kind shall dwell beneath it, every winged thing in the shade of its boughs. 24 And all the trees of the field shall know that I, the LORD, bring low the high tree, lift high the lowly tree, wither up the green tree, and make the withered tree bloom. As I, the LORD, have spoken, so will I do.

Ezekiel Chapter 18

1 Thus the word of the LORD came to me: Son of man, 2 what is the meaning of this proverb that you recite in the land of Israel: "Fathers have eaten green grapes, thus their children's teeth are on edge"? 3 As I live, says the Lord GOD: I swear that there shall no longer be anyone among you who will repeat this proverb in Israel. 4 For all lives are mine; the life of the father is like the life of the son, both are mine; only the one who sins shall die. 5 If a man is virtuous—if he does what is right and just, 6 if he does not eat on the mountains, nor raise his eyes to the idols of the house of Israel; if he does not defile his neighbor's wife, nor have relations with a woman in her menstrual period; 7 if he oppresses no one, gives back the pledge received for a debt, commits no robbery; if he gives food to the hungry and clothes the naked; 8 if he does not lend at interest nor exact usury; if he holds off from evildoing, judges fairly between a man and his opponent; 9 if he lives by my statutes and is careful to observe my ordinances, that man is virtuous—he shall surely live, says the Lord GOD. 10 But if he begets a son who is a thief, a murderer, or who does any of these things 11 (though the father does none of them), a son who eats on the mountains, defiles the wife of his neighbor, 12 oppresses the poor and needy, commits robbery, does not give back a pledge, raises his eyes to idols, does abominable things, 13 lends at interest and exacts usury—this son certainly shall not live. Because he practiced all these abominations, he shall surely die; his death shall be his own fault. 14 On the other hand, if a man begets a son who, seeing all the sins his father commits, yet fears and does not imitate him; 15 a son who does not eat on the mountains, or raise his eyes to the idols of the house of Israel, or defile his neighbor's wife; 16 who does not oppress anyone, or exact a pledge, or commit robbery; who gives his food to the hungry and clothes the naked; 17 who holds off from evildoing, accepts no interest or usury, but keeps my ordinances and lives by my statutes—this one shall not die for the sins of his father, but shall surely live. 18 Only the father, since he violated rights, and robbed, and did what was not good among his people, shall in truth die for his sins. 19 You ask: "Why is not the son charged with the guilt of his father?" Because the son has done what is right and just, and has been careful to observe all my statutes, he shall surely live. 20 Only the one who sins shall die. The son shall not be charged with the guilt of his father, nor shall the father be charged with the guilt of his son. The virtuous man's virtue shall be his own, as the wicked man's wickedness shall be his own. 21 But if the wicked man turns away from all the sins he committed, if he keeps all my statutes and does what is right and just, he shall surely live, he shall not die. 22 None of the crimes he committed shall be remembered against him; he shall live because of the virtue he has practiced. 23 Do I indeed derive any pleasure from the death of the wicked? says the Lord GOD. Do I not rather rejoice when he turns from his evil way that he may live? 24 And if the virtuous man turns from the path of virtue to do evil, the same kind of abominable things that the wicked man does, can he do this and still live? None of his virtuous deeds shall be remembered, because he has broken faith and committed sin; because of this, he shall die. 25 You say, "The LORD'S way is not fair!" Hear now, house of Israel: Is it my way that is unfair, or rather, are not your ways unfair? 26 When a virtuous man turns away from virtue to commit iniquity, and dies, it is because of the iniquity he committed that he must die. 27 But if a wicked man, turning from the wickedness he has committed, does what is right and just, he shall preserve his life; 28 since he has turned away from all the sins which he committed, he shall surely live, he shall not die. 29 And yet the house of Israel says, "The LORD'S way is not fair!" Is it my way that is not fair, house of Israel, or rather, is it not that your ways are not fair? 30 Therefore I will judge you, house of Israel, each one according to his ways, says the Lord GOD. Turn and be converted from all your crimes, that they may be no cause of guilt for you. 31 Cast away from you all the crimes you have committed, and make for yourselves a new heart and a new spirit. Why should you die, O house of Israel? 32 For I have no pleasure in the death of anyone who dies, says the Lord

GOD. Return and live!

Ezekiel Chapter 19

1 As for you, son of man, raise a lamentation over the prince of Israel: 2 What a lioness was your mother, a lion of lions! Among young lions she couched to rear her whelps. 3 One whelp she raised up, a young lion he became; He learned to seize prey, men he devoured. 4 Then nations raised cries against him, in their pit he was caught; They took him away with hooks to the land of Egypt. 5 Then she saw that in vain she had waited, her hope was destroyed. She took another of her whelps, him she made a young lion. 6 He prowled among the lions, a young lion he became; He learned to seize prey, men he devoured; 7 He ravaged their strongholds, their cities he wasted. The land and all in it were appalled at the noise of his roar. 8 Nations laid out against him snares all about him; They spread their net to take him, in their pit he was caught. 9 They put him in a cage and took him away to the king of Babylon, so that his voice would not be heard on the mountains of Israel. 10 Your mother was like a vine planted by the water; fruitful and branchy was she because of the abundant water. 11 One strong branch she put out as a royal scepter. Stately was her height amid the dense foliage; notably tall was she with her many clusters. 12 But she was torn up in fury and flung to the ground; the east wind withered her up, her fruit was torn off; then her strong branch withered up, fire devoured it. 13 So now she is planted in the desert, in a land dry and parched, 14 for fire came out of the branch and devoured her shoots; she is now without a strong branch, a ruler's scepter. This is a lamentation and serves as a lamentation.

Ezekiel Chapter 20

1 In the seventh year, on the tenth day of the fifth month, some of the elders of Israel came to consult the LORD and sat down before me. 2 Then the word of the LORD came to me: 3 Son of man, speak with the elders of Israel and say to them: Thus says the Lord GOD: Have you come to consult me? As I live! I swear I will not allow myself to be consulted by you, says the Lord GOD. 4 Will you judge them? Will you judge, son of man? Make known to them the abominations of their ancestors 5 in these words: Thus speaks the Lord GOD: The day I chose Israel, I swore to the descendants of the house of Jacob; in the land of Egypt I revealed myself to them and swore: I am the LORD, your God. 6 That day I swore to bring them out of the land of Egypt to the land I had scouted for them, a land flowing with milk and honey, a jewel among all lands. 7 Then I said to them: Throw away, each of you, the detestable things that have held your eyes; do not defile yourselves with the idols of Egypt: I am the LORD, your God. 8 But they rebelled against me and refused to listen to me; none of them threw away the detestable things that had held their eyes, they did not abandon the idols of Egypt. Then I thought of pouring out my fury on them and spending my anger on them there in the land of Egypt; 9 but I acted for my name's sake, that it should not be profaned in the sight of the nations among whom they were, in whose presence I had made myself known to them, revealing that I would bring them out of the land of Egypt. 10 Therefore I led them out of the land of Egypt and brought them into the desert. 11 Then I gave them my statutes and made known to them my ordinances, which everyone must keep, to have life through them. 12 I also gave them my sabbaths to be a sign between me and them, to show that it was I, the LORD, who made them holy. 13 But the house of Israel rebelled against me in the desert. They did not observe my statutes, and they despised my ordinances that bring life to those who keep them. My sabbaths, too, they desecrated grievously. Then I thought of pouring out my fury on them in the desert to put an end to them, 14 but I acted for my name's sake, that it should not be profaned in the sight of the nations in whose presence I had brought them out. 15 Nevertheless I swore to them in the desert not to bring them to the land I had given them, a land flowing with milk and honey, a jewel among all lands. 16 So much were their hearts devoted to their idols, they had not lived by my statutes, but despised my ordinances and desecrated my sabbaths. 17 But I looked on them with pity, not wanting to destroy them, so I did not put an end to them in the desert. 18 Then I said to their children in the desert: Do not observe the statutes of your parents or keep their ordinances; do not defile yourselves with their idols. 19 I am the LORD, your God: observe my statutes and be careful to keep my ordinances; 20 keep holy my sabbaths, as a sign between me and you to show that I am the LORD, your God. 21 But their children rebelled against me: they did not observe my statutes or keep my ordinances that bring life to those who observe them, and my sabbaths they desecrated. Then I thought of pouring out my fury on them, of spending my anger on them in the desert; 22 but I stayed my hand, acting for my name's sake, lest it be profaned in the sight of the nations in whose presence I brought them out. 23 Nevertheless I swore to them in the desert that I would disperse them among the nations and scatter them over foreign lands; 24 for they did not keep my ordinances, but despised my statutes and desecrated my sabbaths, with eyes only for the idols of their fathers. 25 Therefore I gave them statutes that were not good, and ordinances through which they could not live. 26 I let them become defiled by their gifts, by their immolation of every first-born, so as to make them an object of horror. 27 Therefore speak to the house of Israel, son of man, and tell them: Thus says the Lord GOD: In this way also your fathers blasphemed me, breaking faith with me: 28 when I had brought them to the land I had sworn to give them, and they saw all its high hills and leafy trees, there they offered their sacrifices (there they brought their offensive offerings), there they sent up appeasing odors, and there they poured out their libations. 29 I asked them: To what sort of high place do you betake yourselves? - and so they call it a high place even to the present day. 30 Therefore say to the house of Israel: Thus says the Lord GOD: Will you defile yourselves like your fathers? Will you lust after their detestable idols? 31 By offering your gifts, by making your children pass through the fire, you defile yourselves with all your idols even to this day. Shall I let myself be consulted by you, house of Israel? As I live! says the Lord GOD: I swear I will not let myself be consulted by you. 32 What you are thinking of shall never happen: "We shall be like the nations, like the peoples of foreign lands, serving wood and stone." 33 As I live, says the Lord GOD, with a mighty hand and outstretched arm, with poured-out wrath, I swear I will be king over you! 34 With a mighty hand and outstretched arm, with poured-out wrath, I will bring you out from the nations and gather you from the countries over which you are scattered; 35 then I will lead you to the desert of the peoples, where I will enter into judgment with you face to face. 36 Just as I entered into judgment with your fathers in the desert of the land of Egypt, so will I enter into judgment with you, says the Lord GOD. 37 I will count you with the staff and bring back but a small number. 38 I will separate from you those who have rebelled and transgressed against me; from the land where they sojourned as aliens I will bring them out, but they shall not return to the land of Israel. Thus you shall know that I am the LORD. 39 As for you, house of Israel, thus says the Lord GOD: Come, each one of you, destroy your idols! Then listen to me, and never again profane my holy name with your gifts and your idols. 40 For on my holy mountain, on the mountain height of Israel, says the Lord GOD, there the whole house of Israel without exception shall worship me; there I will accept them, and there I will claim your tributes and the first fruits of your offerings, and all that you dedicate. 41 As a pleasing odor I will accept you, when I have brought you from among the nations and gathered you out of the countries over which you were scattered; and by means of you I will manifest my holiness in the sight of the nations. 42 Thus you shall know that I am the LORD, when I bring you back to the land of Israel, the land which I swore to give to your fathers. 43 There you shall recall your conduct and all the deeds by which you defiled yourselves; and you shall loathe yourselves because of all the evil things you did. 44 And you shall know that I am the LORD when I deal with you thus, for my name's sake, and not according to your evil conduct and corrupt actions, O house of Israel, says the Lord GOD.

Ezekiel Chapter 21

1 Thus the word of the LORD came to me: 2 Son of man, look southward, preach toward the south, and prophesy against the forest of the southern land. 3 Hear the word of the LORD! You shall say to the southern forest: Thus says the Lord GOD: See! I am kindling a fire in you that shall devour all trees, the green as well as the dry. The blazing flame shall not be quenched, but from south to north every face shall be scorched by it. 4 Everyone shall see that I, the LORD, have kindled it, and it shall not be quenched. 5 But I said, "Alas! Lord GOD, they say to me, 'Is not this the one who is forever spinning parables?'" 6 Then the word of the LORD came to me: 7 Son of man, look toward Jerusalem, preach against their sanctuary, and prophesy against the land of Israel, 8 saying to the land of Israel: Thus says the LORD: See! I am coming at you; I will draw my sword from its sheath and cut off from you the virtuous and the wicked. 9 Thus my sword shall leave its sheath against everyone from south to north, 10 and everyone shall know that I, the LORD, have drawn my sword from its sheath, and it shall not be sheathed again. 11 As for you, son of man, groan! With shattered strength, groan bitterly while they look on. 12 And when they ask you, "Why are you groaning?" you shall say: Because of a report; when it comes, every heart shall fail, every hand shall fall helpless, every spirit shall be daunted, and every knee shall run with water. See, it is coming, it is here! says the Lord GOD. 13 Thus the word of the LORD came to me: 14 Son of man, prophesy! Say: Thus says the LORD: A sword, a sword has been sharpened, a sword, a sword has been burnished. 15 To work slaughter has it been sharpened, to flash lightning has it been burnished. Why should I now withdraw it? You have spurned the rod

and every judgment! 16 I have given it over to the burnisher, that he might hold it in his hand, a sword sharpened and burnished to be put in the hand of a slayer. 17 Cry out and wail, son of man, for it is destined for my people; it is for all the princes of Israel, victims of the sword with my people. Therefore, slap your thigh, 18 for the sword has been tested; and why should it not be so? says the Lord GOD, since you have spurned the rod. 19 As for you, son of man, prophesy, brushing one hand against the other: While the sword is doubled and tripled, this sword of slaughter, this great sword of slaughter which threatens all around, 20 that every heart may tremble; for many will be the fallen. At all their gates, I have appointed for slaughter, fashioned to flash lightning, burnished for slaughter. 21 Cleave to the right! Destroy! To the left! Wherever your edge is turned. 22 Then I, too, shall brush one hand against the other and wreak my fury. I, the LORD, have spoken. 23 Thus the word of the LORD came to me: 24 Son of man, make for yourself two roads over which the sword of the king of Babylon can come. Both roads shall lead out from the same land. Then put a signpost at the head of each road, 25 so that the sword can come to Rabbah of the Ammonites or to Judah's capital, Jerusalem. 26 For at the fork where the two roads divide stands the king of Babylon, divining; he has shaken the arrows, inquired of the teraphim, inspected the liver. 27 In his right hand is the divining arrow marked "Jerusalem," bidding him to give the order for slaying, to raise his voice in the battle cry, to post battering rams at the gates, to cast up a ramp, to build a siege tower. 28 In their eyes, this is but a lying oracle; yet they are bound by the oaths they have sworn, and the arrow taken in hand marks their guilt. 29 Therefore, thus says the Lord GOD: Because you have drawn attention to your guilt, with your crimes laid bare and your sinfulness in all your wicked deeds revealed (because attention has been drawn to you), you shall be taken in hand. 30 And as for you, depraved and wicked prince of Israel, whose day is coming when your life of crime will be ended, 31 thus says the Lord GOD: Off with the turban and away with the crown! Nothing shall be as it was! Up with the low and down with the high! 32 Twisted, twisted, twisted will I leave it; it shall not be the same until he comes who has the claim against the city; and to him, I will hand it over. 33 As for you, son of man, prophesy: Thus says the Lord GOD against the Ammonites and their insults: A sword, a sword is drawn for slaughter, burnished to consume and to flash lightning, 34 because you planned with false visions and lying divinations to lay it on the necks of depraved and wicked men whose day has come when their crimes are at an end. 35 Return it to its sheath! In the place where you were created, in the land of your origin, I will judge you. 36 I will pour out my indignation upon you, breathing my fiery wrath upon you, I will hand you over to ravaging men, artisans of destruction. 37 You shall be fuel for the fire, your blood shall flow throughout the land. You shall not be remembered, for I, the LORD, have spoken.

Ezekiel Chapter 22

1 Thus the word of the LORD came to me: 2 You, son of man, would you judge, would you judge the bloody city? Then make known all her abominations, 3 and say: Thus says the Lord GOD: Woe to the city which sheds blood within herself so that her time has come, and which has made idols for her own defilement. 4 By the blood which you shed you have been made guilty, and with the idols you made you have become defiled; you have brought on your day, so that the end of your years has come. Therefore I make you an object of scorn to the nations and a laughingstock to all foreign lands. 5 Those near you and those far off shall deride you because of your foul reputation and your great perversity. 6 See! the princes of Israel, family by family, are in you only for bloodshed. 7 Within you, father and mother are despised; in your midst, they extort from the resident alien; within you, they oppress orphans and widows. 8 What is holy to me you have spurned, and my sabbaths you have desecrated. 9 There are those in you who slander to cause bloodshed; within you are those who feast on the mountains; in your midst are those who do lewd things. 10 In you are those who uncover the nakedness of their fathers, and in you those who coerce women in their menstrual period. 11 There are those in you who do abominable things with the wives of their neighbors, men who defile their daughters-in-law by incest, men who coerce their sisters, the daughters of their own fathers. 12 There are those in you who take bribes to shed blood. You exact interest and usury; you despoil your neighbors violently; and me you have forgotten, says the Lord GOD. 13 See, I am brushing one hand against the other because of the unjust profits you have made and because of the blood shed in your midst. 14 Can your heart remain firm, will your hands be strong, in the days when I deal with you? I, the LORD, have spoken, and I will act. 15 I will disperse you among the nations and scatter you over foreign lands, so that I may purge your uncleanness. 16 In you I will allow myself to be profaned in the eyes of the nations; thus you shall know that I am the LORD. 17 Thus the word of the LORD came to me: 18 Son of man, the house of Israel has become dross for me. All of them are bronze and tin, iron and lead (in the midst of a furnace): dross from silver have they become. 19 Therefore thus says the Lord GOD: Because all of you have become dross, therefore I must gather you together within Jerusalem. 20 Just as silver, bronze, iron, lead, and tin are gathered into a furnace and smelted in the roaring flames, so I will gather you together in my furious wrath, put you in, and smelt you. 21 When I have assembled you, I will blast you with the fire of my anger and smelt you with it. 22 You shall be smelted by it just as silver is smelted in a furnace. Thus you shall know that I, the LORD, have poured out my fury on you. 23 Thus the word of the LORD came to me: 24 Son of man, say to her: You are a land unrained on (that is, not rained on) at the time of my fury. 25 Her princes are like roaring lions that tear prey; they devour people, seizing their wealth and precious things, and make widows of many within her. 26 Her priests violate my law and profane what is holy to me; they do not distinguish between the sacred and the profane, nor teach the difference between the unclean and the clean; they pay no attention to my sabbaths, so that I have been profaned in their midst. 27 Her nobles within her are like wolves that tear prey, shedding blood and destroying lives to get unjust gain. 28 Her prophets cover them with whitewash, pretending to visions that are false and performing lying divinations, saying, "Thus says the Lord GOD," although the LORD has not spoken. 29 The people of the land practice extortion and commit robbery; they afflict the poor and the needy, and oppress the resident alien without justice. 30 Thus I have searched among them for someone who could build a wall or stand in the breach before me to keep me from destroying the land; but I found no one. 31 Therefore I have poured out my fury upon them; with my fiery wrath I have consumed them; I have brought down their conduct upon their heads, says the Lord GOD.

Ezekiel Chapter 23

1 Thus the word of the LORD came to me: 2 Son of man, there were two women, daughters of the same mother, 3 who even as young girls played the harlot in Egypt. There the Egyptians caressed their bosoms and fondled their virginal breasts. 4 Oholah was the name of the elder, and the name of her sister was Oholibah. They became mine and bore sons and daughters. (As for their names: Samaria is Oholah, and Jerusalem is Oholibah.) 5 Oholah became a harlot faithless to me; she lusted after her lovers, the Assyrians, warriors 6 dressed in purple, governors and officers, all of them attractive young men, knights mounted on horses. 7 Thus she gave herself as a harlot to them, to all the elite of the Assyrians, and she defiled herself with all those for whom she lusted (with all their idols). 8 She did not give up the harlotry which she had begun in Egypt, when they had lain with her as a young girl, fondling her virginal breasts and pouring out their impurities on her. 9 Therefore I handed her over to her lovers, the Assyrians for whom she had lusted. 10 They exposed her nakedness, her sons and daughters they took away, and herself they slew with the sword. Thus she became a byword for women, for they punished her grievously. 11 Though her sister Oholibah saw all this, her lust was more depraved than her sister's, and she outdid her in harlotry. 12 She too lusted after the Assyrians, governors and officers, warriors impeccably clothed, knights mounted on horses, all of them attractive young men. 13 I saw that she had defiled herself. Both had gone down the same path, 14 yet she went further in her harlotry. When she saw men drawn on the wall, the images of Chaldeans drawn with vermillion, 15 with sashes girded about their waists, flowing turbans on their heads, all looking like chariot warriors, the portraits of Babylonians, natives of Chaldea, 16 she lusted for them; no sooner had she set eyes on them than she sent messengers to them in Chaldea. 17 Then the Babylonians came to her, to the love couch, and defiled her with their intercourse. As soon as she was defiled by them, she became disgusted with them. 18 Her harlotry was discovered and her shame was revealed, and I became disgusted with her as I had become disgusted with her sister. 19 But she played the harlot all the more, recalling the days of her girlhood, when she had been a harlot in the land of Egypt. 20 She lusted for the lechers of Egypt, whose members are like that of an ass, and whose heat is like that of stallions. 21 You yearned for the lewdness of your girlhood, when the Egyptians fondled your breasts, caressing your bosom. 22 Therefore, Oholibah, thus says the Lord GOD: I will now stir up your lovers against you, those with whom you are disgusted, and I will bring them against you from every side: 23 the men of Babylon and all of Chaldea, Pekod, Shoa, and Koa, along with all those of Assyria, attractive young men, all of them governors and officers, charioteers and warriors, all of them horsemen. 24 They shall come against you from the north with chariots and wagons and many peoples. Shields, bucklers, and helmets they shall array against you everywhere. 25 I will leave it to them to judge, and they will judge you by their own ordinances. I will let loose my

jealousy against you, so that they shall deal with you in fury, cutting off your nose and ears; and what is left of you shall fall by the sword. They shall take away your sons and daughters, and what is left of you shall be devoured by fire. 26 They shall strip off your clothes and seize your splendid ornaments. 27 I will put an end to your lewdness and to the harlotry you began in Egypt; you shall no longer look toward it, nor shall you remember Egypt again. 28 For thus says the Lord GOD: I am now handing you over to those whom you hate, to those who fill you with disgust. 29 They shall deal with you in hatred, seizing all that you have worked for and leaving you stark naked, so that your indecent nakedness is exposed. Your lewdness and harlotry 30 have brought these things upon you, because you played the harlot with the nations by defiling yourself with their idols. 31 Because you followed in the path of your sister, I will hand you her cup. 32 Thus says the Lord GOD: The cup of your sister you shall drink, so wide and deep, which holds so much, 33 filled with destruction and grief, a cup of dismay, the cup of your sister. 34 You shall drain it dry, and gnaw at the very sherds of the cup, and you shall tear out your breasts; for I have spoken, says the Lord GOD. 35 Therefore thus says the Lord GOD: Because you have forgotten me and cast me behind your back, it is for you to bear the penalty of your lewdness and harlotry. 36 Then the LORD said to me: Son of man, would you judge Oholah and Oholibah? Then make known to them their abominations. 37 For they committed adultery, and blood is on their hands. They committed adultery with their idols; to feed them they immolated the children they had borne me. 38 This, too, they did to me: they defiled my sanctuary and desecrated my sabbaths. 39 On the very day they slew their children for their idols, they entered my sanctuary to desecrate it. Thus they acted within my house. 40 Moreover, they sent for men who had to come from afar, to whom messengers were sent. And so they came — and for them you bathed yourself, painted your eyes, and put on ornaments. 41 You sat on a couch prepared for them, with a table spread before it, on which you had set my incense and oil. 42 Then was heard the shout of a carefree mob in the city, and these were men brought in from the desert, who put bracelets on the women's arms and splendid diadems on their heads. 43 So I said: "Oh, this woman jaded with adulteries! Now they will commit whoredom with her, and as for her. . . ." 44 And indeed they did come to her as men come to a harlot. Thus they came to Oholah and Oholibah, the lewd women. 45 But just men shall punish them with the sentence meted out to adulteresses and murderesses, for they have committed adultery, and blood is on their hands. 46 Thus says the Lord GOD: Summon an assembly against them, and deliver them over to terror and plunder. 47 The assembly shall stone them and hack them to pieces with their swords. They shall slay their sons and daughters, and burn their houses with fire. 48 Thus I will put an end to lewdness in the land, and all the women will be warned not to imitate your lewdness. 49 They shall inflict on you the penalty of your lewdness, and you shall pay for your sins of idolatry. Thus you shall know that I am the LORD.

Ezekiel Chapter 24

1 On the tenth day of the tenth month, in the ninth year, the word of the LORD came to me: 2 Son of man, write down this date today, for this very day the king of Babylon has invested Jerusalem. 3 Propose this parable to the rebellious house: Thus says the Lord GOD: Set up the pot, set it up, then pour in some water. 4 Put in it pieces of meat, all good pieces: thigh and shoulder; fill it with the choicest joints 5 taken from the pick of the flock. Then pile the wood beneath it; bring to a boil these pieces and the joints that are in it. 6 Take out its pieces, one by one, without casting lots for it. Therefore, thus says the Lord GOD: Woe to the bloody city, a pot containing rust, whose rust has not been removed. 7 For the blood she shed is in her midst; she poured it on the bare rock; she did not pour it out on the earth, to be covered with dust. 8 To work up my wrath, to excite my vengeance, she put her blood on the bare rock, not to be covered. 9 Therefore, thus says the Lord GOD: I, too, will heap up a great bonfire, 10 piling on wood and kindling the fire, till the meat has been cooked, till the broth has boiled. 11 Then I will set the pot empty on the coals till its metal glows red hot, till the impurities in it melt, and its rust disappears. 12 Yet not even with fire will its great rust be removed. 13 Because you have sullied yourself with lewdness when I would have purified you, and you refused to be purified of your uncleanness, therefore you shall not be purified until I wreak my fury on you. 14 I, the LORD, have spoken; it is coming, for I will bring it about without fail. I will not have pity nor repent. By your conduct and your deeds you shall be judged, says the Lord GOD. 15 Thus the word of the LORD came to me: 16 Son of man, by a sudden blow I am taking away from you the delight of your eyes, but do not mourn or weep or shed any tears. 17 Groan in silence, make no lament for the dead, bind on your turban, put your sandals on your feet, do not cover your beard, and do not eat the customary bread. 18 That evening my wife died, and

the next morning I did as I had been commanded. 19 Then the people asked me, "Will you not tell us what all these things that you are doing mean for us?" I therefore spoke to the people that morning, 20 saying to them: Thus the word of the LORD came to me: 21 Say to the house of Israel: Thus says the Lord GOD: I will now desecrate my sanctuary, the stronghold of your pride, the delight of your eyes, the desire of your soul. The sons and daughters you left behind shall fall by the sword. 22 You shall do as I have done, not covering your beards nor eating the customary bread. 23 Your turbans shall remain on your heads, your sandals on your feet. You shall not mourn or weep, but you shall rot away because of your sins and groan one to another. 24 Ezekiel shall be a sign for you: all that he did you shall do when it happens. Thus you shall know that I am the LORD. 25 As for you, son of man, truly, on the day I take away from them their bulwark, their glorious joy, the delight of their eyes, the desire of their soul, and the pride of their hearts, their sons and daughters, 26 that day the fugitive will come to you, that you may hear it for yourself; 27 that day your mouth shall be opened and you shall be dumb no longer. Thus you shall be a sign to them, and they shall know that I am the LORD.

Ezekiel Chapter 25

1 Thus the word of the LORD came to me: 2 Son of man, turn toward the Ammonites and prophesy against them. 3 Say to the Ammonites: Hear the word of the LORD! Thus says the Lord GOD: Because you cried out your joy over the desecration of my sanctuary, the devastation of the land of Israel, and the exile of the house of Judah, 4 therefore I will deliver you into the possession of the Easterners. They shall set up their encampments among you and pitch their tents; they shall eat your fruits and drink your milk. 5 I will make Rabbah a pasture for camels, and the villages of the Ammonites a resting place for flocks. Thus you shall know that I am the LORD. 6 For thus says the Lord GOD: Because you clapped your hands and stamped your feet, rejoicing most maliciously in your heart over the land of Israel, 7 therefore I will stretch out my hand against you. I will make you plunder for the nations, I will cut you off from the peoples, and remove you from the lands. I will destroy you, and thus you shall know that I am the LORD. 8 Thus says the Lord GOD: Because Moab said, "See! the house of Judah is like all other nations," 9 therefore I will clear the shoulder of Moab totally of its cities, the jewels of the land: Beth-jesimoth, Baalmeon, and Kiriathaim. 10 I will hand her over, along with the Ammonites, into the possession of the Easterners, that she may not be remembered among the peoples. 11 Thus I will execute judgment upon Moab, that they may know that I am the LORD. 12 Thus says the Lord GOD: Because Edom has taken vengeance on the house of Judah and has made itself grievously guilty by taking vengeance on them, 13 therefore thus says the Lord GOD: I will stretch out my hand against Edom and cut off from it man and beast. I will make it a waste from Teman to Dedan; they shall fall by the sword. 14 My vengeance upon Edom I will entrust to my people Israel, who will deal with Edom in accordance with my anger and my fury; thus they shall know my vengeance, says the Lord GOD. 15 Thus says the Lord GOD: Because the Philistines have acted revengefully, and have taken vengeance with destructive malice in their hearts, with an undying enmity, 16 therefore thus says the Lord GOD: See! I am stretching out my hand against the Philistines; I will cut off the Cherethites and wipe out the remnant on the seacoast. 17 I will execute great acts of vengeance on them, punishing them furiously. Thus they shall know that I am the LORD, when I wreak my vengeance on them.

Ezekiel Chapter 26

1 On the first day of the. . . month in the eleventh year, the word of the LORD came to me: 2 Son of man, because of what Tyre said of Jerusalem: "Aha! it is broken, the gateway to the peoples; now that it is ruined, its wealth reverts to me!" 3 therefore thus says the Lord GOD: See! I am coming at you, Tyre; I will churn up against you many nations, even as the sea churns up its waves; 4 They shall destroy the walls of Tyre and raze her towers. I will scrape the ground from her and leave her a bare rock; 5 She shall be a drying place for nets in the midst of the sea. I have spoken, says the Lord GOD: and she shall be booty for the nations. 6 And her daughters on the mainland shall be slaughtered by the sword; thus they shall know that I am the LORD. 7 For thus says the Lord GOD: I am now bringing up against Tyre from the north Nebuchadnezzar the king of Babylon, the king of kings, with horses and chariots, with cavalry and a great and mighty army. 8 Your daughters on the mainland he shall slay with the sword; He shall place a siege tower against you, cast up a ramp about you, and raise his shields against you. 9 He shall pound your walls with battering-rams and break down your towers with his weapons. 10 The surge of his horses shall cover you with dust, amid the noise of steeds, of wheels and of chariots.

Your walls shall shake as he enters your gates, even as one enters a city that is breached. [11] With the hoofs of his horses he shall trample all your streets; Your people he shall slay by the sword; your mighty pillars he shall pull to the ground. [12] Your wealth shall be plundered, your merchandise pillaged; Your walls shall be torn down, your precious houses demolished; Your stones, your timber, and your clay shall be cast into the sea. [13] I will put an end to the noise of your songs, and the sound of your lyres shall be heard no more. [14] I will make you a bare rock; a drying place for nets shall you be. Never shall you be rebuilt, for I have spoken, says the Lord GOD. [15] Thus says the Lord GOD to Tyre: At the noise of your fall, at the groaning of the wounded, when the sword slays in your midst, shall not the isles quake? [16] All the princes of the sea shall step down from their thrones, lay aside their robes, and strip off their embroidered garments. They shall be clothed in mourning and, sitting on the ground, they shall tremble at every moment and be horrified at you. [17] Then they shall utter a lament over you: How have you perished, gone from the seas, city most prized! Once she was mighty on the sea, she and her dwellers, Who spread terror into all that dwelt by the sea. [18] On this, the day of your fall, the islands quake! The isles in the sea are terrified at your passing. [19] For thus says the Lord GOD: When I make you a city desolate like cities that are no longer inhabited, when I churn up the abyss against you, and its mighty waters cover you, [20] then I will thrust you down with those who descend into the pit, those of the bygone age; and I will make you dwell in the nether lands, in the everlasting ruins, with those who go down to the pit, so that you may never return to take your place in the land of the living. [21] I will make you a devastation, and you shall be no more; you shall be sought, but never again found, says the Lord GOD.

Ezekiel Chapter 27

[1] Thus the word of the LORD came to me: [2] Son of man, utter a lament over Tyre, [3] and say to Tyre that is situated at the approaches of the sea, that brought the trade of the peoples to many a coastland: Thus says the Lord GOD: Tyre, you said, "I am a ship, perfect in beauty." [4] In the midst of the sea your builders placed you, perfected your beauty. [5] With cypress from Senir they built for you all of your decks; Cedar from Lebanon they took to make you a mast; [6] From the highest oaks of Bashan they made your oars; Your bridge they made of cypress wood from the coasts of Kittim. [7] Fine embroidered linen from Egypt became your sail (to serve you as a banner). Purple and scarlet from the coasts of Elishah covered your cabin. [8] Citizens of Sidon and Arvad served as your oarsmen; Skilled men of Zemer were in you to be your mariners; [9] The elders and experts of Gebal were in you to caulk your seams. Every ship and sailor on the sea came to you to carry trade. [10] Persia and Lud and Put were in your army as warriors; shield and helmet they hung upon you, increasing your splendor. [11] The men of Arvad were all about your walls, and the Gamadites were in your towers; they hung their bucklers all around on your walls, and made perfect your beauty. [12] Tarshish traded with you, so great was your wealth, exchanging silver, iron, tin, and lead for your wares. [13] Javan, Tubal, and Meshech were also traders with you, exchanging slaves and articles of bronze for your goods. [14] From Beth-togarmah horses, steeds, and mules were exchanged for your wares. [15] The Rhodanites trafficked with you; many coastlands traded with you; ivory tusks and ebony wood they gave you for payment. [16] Edom traded with you, so many were your products, exchanging garnets, purple, embroidered cloth, fine linen, coral, and rubies for your wares. [17] Judah and the land of Israel trafficked with you, exchanging Minnith wheat, figs, honey, oil, and balm for your goods. [18] Damascus traded with you, so great was your wealth, exchanging Helbon wine and Zahar wool. [19] Javan exchanged wrought iron, cassia, and aromatic cane from Uzal for your wares. [20] Dedan traded with you for riding gear. [21] The trade of Arabia and of all the sheikhs of Kedar belonged to you; they dealt in lambs, rams, and goats. [22] The merchants of Sheba and Raamah also traded with you, exchanging for your wares the very choicest spices, all kinds of precious stones, and gold. [23] Haran, Canneh, and Eden, the merchants of Sheba, Asshur, and Chilmad [24] traded with you, marketing with you rich garments, violet mantles, embroidered cloth, varicolored carpets, and firmly woven cords. [25] Ships of Tarshish journeyed for you in your merchandising. You were full and heavily laden in the heart of the sea. [26] Through the deep waters your oarsmen brought you home, But the east wind smashed you in the heart of the sea. [27] Your wealth, your goods, your wares, your sailors, and your crew, (the caulkers of your seams, those who traded for your goods, all your warriors who were in you, and all the great crowd within you) Sank into the heart of the sea on the day of your shipwreck. [28] Hearing the shouts of your mariners, the shores begin to quake. [29] Down from their ships come all who ply the oar; The sailors, all the mariners of the sea, stand on the shore, [30] Making their voice heard on your behalf, shouting bitter cries, Strewing

dust on their heads, rolling in the ashes. [31] For you they shave their heads and put on sackcloth, For you they weep in anguish, with bitter lament. [32] In their mourning they utter a lament over you; thus they wail over you: Who was ever destroyed like Tyre in the midst of the sea? [33] With your goods which you drew from the seas you filled many peoples; With your great wealth and merchandise you enriched the kings of the earth. [34] Now you are wrecked in the sea, in the watery depths; Your wares and all your crew have gone down with you. [35] All who dwell on the coastlands are aghast over you, Their kings are terrified, their faces convulsed. [36] The traders among the peoples now hiss at you; You have become a horror, and you shall be no more.

Ezekiel Chapter 28

[1] Thus the word of the LORD came to me: [2] Son of man, say to the prince of Tyre: Thus says the Lord GOD: Because you are haughty of heart, you say, "A god am I! I occupy a godly throne in the heart of the sea!" - And yet you are a man, and not a god, however you may think yourself like a god. [3] Oh yes, you are wiser than Daniel, there is no secret that is beyond you. [4] By your wisdom and your intelligence you have made riches for yourself; You have put gold and silver into your treasuries. [5] By your great wisdom applied to your trading you have heaped up your riches; your heart has grown haughty from your riches - [6] therefore thus says the Lord GOD: Because you have thought yourself to have the mind of a god, [7] Therefore I will bring against you foreigners, the most barbarous of nations. They shall draw their swords against your beauteous wisdom, they shall run them through your splendid apparel. [8] They shall thrust you down to the pit, there to die a bloodied corpse, in the heart of the sea. [9] Will you then say, "I am a god!" when you face your murderers? No, you are a man, not a god, handed over to those who will slay you. [10] You shall die the death of the uncircumcised at the hands of foreigners, for I have spoken, says the Lord GOD. [11] Thus the word of the LORD came to me: [12] Son of man, utter a lament over the king of Tyre, saying to him: Thus says the Lord GOD: You were stamped with the seal of perfection, of complete wisdom and perfect beauty. [13] In Eden, the garden of God, you were, and every precious stone was your covering (carnelian, topaz, and beryl; chrysolite, onyx, and jasper, sapphire, garnet, and emerald); Of gold your pendants and jewels were made, on the day you were created. [14] With the Cherub I placed you; you were on the holy mountain of God, walking among the fiery stones. [15] Blameless you were in your conduct from the day you were created, Until evil was found in you, [16] the result of your far-flung trade; violence was your business, and you sinned. Then I banned you from the mountain of God; the Cherub drove you from among the fiery stones. [17] You became haughty of heart because of your beauty; for the sake of splendor you debased your wisdom. I cast you to the earth, so great was your guilt; I made you a spectacle in the sight of kings. [18] Because of your guilt, your sinful trade, I have profaned your sanctuaries, And I have brought out fire from your midst which will devour you. I have reduced you to dust on the earth in the sight of all who should see you. [19] Among the peoples, all who knew you stand aghast at you; You have become a horror, you shall be no more. [20] Thus the word of the LORD came to me: [21] Son of man, look toward Sidon, and prophesy against it: [22] Thus says the Lord GOD: See! I am coming at you, Sidon; I will be glorified in your midst. Then they shall know that I am the LORD, when I inflict punishments upon it and use it to manifest my holiness. [23] Into it I will send pestilence, and blood shall flow in its streets. Within it shall fall those slain by the sword that comes against it from every side. Thus they shall know that I am the LORD. [24] Sidon shall no longer be a tearing thorn for the house of Israel, a brier that scratches them more than all the others about them who despise them; thus they shall know that I am the LORD. [25] Thus says the Lord GOD: When I gather the house of Israel from the peoples among whom they are scattered, then I will manifest my holiness through them in the sight of the nations. Then they shall live on their land which I gave to my servant Jacob; [26] they shall live on it in security, building houses and planting vineyards. They shall dwell secure while I inflict punishments on all their neighbors who despised them; thus they shall know that I, the LORD, am their God.

Ezekiel Chapter 29

[1] On the twelfth day of the tenth month in the tenth year, the word of the LORD came to me: [2] Son of man, set your face against Pharaoh, king of Egypt, and prophesy against him and against all Egypt. [3] Say this to him: Thus says the Lord GOD: See! I am coming at you, Pharaoh, king of Egypt, Great crouching monster amidst your Niles: Who say, "The Niles are mine; it is I who made them!" [4] I will put hooks in your jaws and make the fish of your Niles stick to your scales, then draw you up from the midst of your Niles along with all the fish of your Niles sticking to your scales. [5] I will cast you into the desert, you and all the

fish of your Niles; You shall fall upon the open field, you shall not be taken up or buried; To the beasts of the earth and the birds of the air I give you as food, 6 That all who dwell in Egypt may know that I am the LORD. Because you have been a reed staff for the house of Israel: 7 When they held you in hand, you splintered, throwing every shoulder out of joint; When they leaned on you, you broke, bringing each one of them down headlong; 8 therefore thus says the Lord GOD: See! I will bring the sword against you, and cut off from you both man and beast. 9 The land of Egypt shall become a desolate waste; thus they shall know that I am the LORD. Because you said, "The Niles are mine; it is I who made them," 10 therefore see! I am coming at you and against your Niles; I will make the land of Egypt a waste and a desolation from Migdol to Syene, and even to the frontier of Ethiopia. 11 No foot of man or beast shall pass through it; they shall not pass through it, and it will be uninhabited for forty years. 12 I will make the land of Egypt the most desolate of lands, and its cities shall be the most deserted of cities for forty years; and I will scatter the Egyptians among the nations and strew them over foreign lands. 13 Yet thus says the Lord GOD: At the end of forty years I will gather the Egyptians from the peoples among whom they are scattered, 14 and I will restore Egypt's fortune, bringing them back to the land of Pathros, the land of their origin, where it will be the lowliest 15 of kingdoms, never more to set itself above the nations. I will make them few, that they may not dominate the nations. 16 No longer shall they be for the house of Israel to trust in, but the living reminder of its guilt for having turned to follow after them. Thus they shall know that I am the LORD. 17 On the first day of the first month in the twenty-seventh year, the word of the LORD came to me: 18 Son of man, Nebuchadnezzar, the king of Babylon, has led his army in an exhausting campaign against Tyre. Their heads became bald and their shoulders were galled; but neither he nor his army received any wages from Tyre for the campaign he led against it. 19 Therefore thus says the Lord GOD: I am now giving the land of Egypt to Nebuchadnezzar, king of Babylon. He shall carry off its riches, plundering and pillaging it for the wages of his soldiers, who did it for me; 20 as payment for his toil I have given him the land of Egypt, says the Lord GOD. 21 On that day I will make a horn sprout for the house of Israel, and I will cause you to speak out in their midst; thus they shall know that I am the LORD.

Ezekiel Chapter 30

1 Thus the word of the LORD came to me: 2 Son of man, speak this prophecy: Thus says the Lord GOD: Cry, Oh, the day! 3 for near is the day, near is the day of the LORD; a day of clouds, doomsday for the nations shall it be. 4 Then a sword shall come upon Egypt, and anguish shall be in Ethiopia, when the slain fall in Egypt, when her riches are seized and her foundations are overthrown. 5 Ethiopia, Put, Lud, all Arabia, Libya, and people of the allied territory shall fall by the sword with them. 6 Those who support Egypt shall fall, and down shall come her proud strength; from Migdol to Syene they shall fall there by the sword, says the Lord GOD. 7 She shall be the most devastated of lands, and her cities shall be the most desolate of all. 8 Then they shall know that I am the LORD, when I set fire to Egypt and when all who help her are broken. 9 On that day messengers shall hasten forth at my command to terrify unsuspecting Ethiopia; they shall be in anguish on the day of Egypt, which is surely coming. 10 Thus says the Lord GOD: I will put an end to the throngs of Egypt by the hand of Nebuchadnezzar, king of Babylon. 11 He and his people with him, the most ruthless of nations, shall be brought in to devastate the land. They shall draw their swords against Egypt, and fill the land with the slain. 12 I will turn the Niles into dry land and sell the land over to the power of the wicked. The land and everything in it I will hand over to foreigners to devastate. I, the LORD, have spoken. 13 Thus says the Lord GOD: I will put an end to the great ones of Memphis and the princes of the land of Egypt, that they may be no more. I will cast fear into the land of Egypt, and devastate Pathros. 14 I will set fire to Zoan, and inflict punishments on Thebes. 15 I will pour out my wrath on Pelusium, Egypt's stronghold, and cut down the crowds in Memphis. 16 I will set fire to Egypt; Syene shall writhe in anguish; Thebes shall be breached and its walls shall be demolished. 17 The young men of On and of Pibeseth shall fall by the sword, and the cities themselves shall go into captivity. 18 In Tehaphnehes the day shall be darkened when I break the scepter of Egypt. Her haughty pride shall cease from her, clouds shall cover her, and her daughters shall go into captivity. 19 Thus will I inflict punishments on Egypt, that they may know that I am the LORD. 20 On the seventh day of the first month in the eleventh year, the word of the LORD came to me: 21 Son of man, I have broken the arm of Pharaoh, the king of Egypt, and see, it has not been bound up with bandages and healing remedies that it may be strong enough to hold the sword. 22 Therefore thus says the Lord GOD: See! I am coming at Pharaoh, the

king of Egypt. I will break his strong arm, so that the sword drops from his hand. 23 I will scatter the Egyptians among the nations and strew them over foreign lands. 24 But I will strengthen the arms of the king of Babylon, and put my sword in his hand, which he will bring against Egypt so as to plunder and pillage it. 25 I will make the arms of the king of Babylon strong, but the arms of Pharaoh shall drop. Then they shall know that I am the LORD, when I put my sword in the hand of the king of Babylon for him to wield against the land of Egypt. 26 I will scatter the Egyptians among the nations and strew them over foreign lands. Thus they shall know that I am the LORD.

Ezekiel Chapter 31

1 On the first day of the third month in the eleventh year, the word of the LORD came to me: 2 Son of man, say to Pharaoh, the king of Egypt, and to his hordes: What are you like in your greatness? 3 Behold, a cypress (cedar) in Lebanon, beautiful of branch, lofty of stature, amid the very clouds lifted its crest. 4 Waters made it grow, the abyss made it flourish, sending its rivers round where it was planted, turning its streams to all the trees of the field. 5 Thus it grew taller than every other tree of the field, and longer of branch because of the abundant water. 6 In its boughs nested all the birds of the air, under its branches all beasts of the field gave birth, in its shade dwelt numerous peoples of every race. 7 It became beautiful and stately in its spread of foliage, for its roots were turned toward abundant water. 8 The cedars in the garden of God were not its equal, nor could the fir trees match its boughs, neither were the plane trees like it for branches; no tree in the garden of God matched its beauty. 9 I made it beautiful, with much foliage, the envy of all Eden's trees in the garden of God. 10 Therefore thus says the Lord GOD: Because it became lofty in stature, raising its crest among the clouds, and because it became proud in heart at its height, 11 I have handed it over to the mightiest of the nations, which has dealt with it in keeping with its wickedness. I humiliated it. 12 Foreigners, the most ruthless of the nations, cut it down and left it on the mountains. Its foliage was brought low in all the valleys, its branches lay broken in all the ravines of the land, and all the peoples of the land withdrew from its shade, abandoning it. 13 On its fallen trunk rested all the birds of the air, and by its branches were all the beasts of the field. 14 Thus no tree may grow lofty in stature or raise its crest among the clouds; no tree fed by water may stand by itself in its loftiness. For all of them are destined for death, for the land below, for the company of mortals, those who go down into the pit. 15 Thus says the Lord GOD: On the day he went down to the nether world I made the abyss close up over him; I stopped its streams so that the deep waters were held back. I cast gloom over Lebanon because of him, so that all the trees in the land drooped on his account. 16 At the crash of his fall I made the nations rock, when I cast him down to the nether world with those who go down into the pit. In the land below, all Eden's trees were consoled, Lebanon's choice and best, all that were fed by water. 17 They too have come down with him to the nether world, to those slain by the sword; those who dwelt in his shade are dispersed among the nations. 18 Which was your equal in glory or size among the trees of Eden? Yet you have been brought down with the trees of Eden to the land below. You shall lie with the uncircumcised, with those slain by the sword. Such are Pharaoh and all his hordes, says the Lord GOD.

Ezekiel Chapter 32

1 On the first day of the twelfth month in the twelfth year, the word of the LORD came to me: 2 Son of man, utter a lament over Pharaoh, the king of Egypt, saying to him: Lion of the nations, you are destroyed. You were like a monster in the sea, spouting in your streams, stirring the water with your feet and churning its streams. 3 Thus says the Lord GOD: I will spread my net over you (with a host of many nations), and draw you up in my seine. 4 I will leave you on the land; on the open field I will cast you. I will have all the birds of the air alight on you, and all the beasts of the earth eat their fill of you. 5 I will leave your flesh on the mountains, and fill the valleys with your carcass. 6 I will water the land with what flows from you, and the riverbeds shall be filled with your blood. 7 When I snuff you out I will cover the heavens, and all their stars I will darken; the sun I will cover with clouds, and the moon shall not give its light. 8 All the shining lights in the heavens I will darken on your account, and I will spread darkness over your land, says the Lord GOD. 9 I will grieve the hearts of many peoples when I lead you captive among the nations, to lands which you do not know. 10 Many peoples shall be appalled at you, and their kings shall shudder over you in horror when they see me brandish my sword, and on the day of your downfall every one of them shall continuously tremble for his own life. 11 For thus says the Lord GOD: The sword of the king of Babylon shall come upon you. 12 I will cut down your horde with the blades of warriors, all of them the most ruthless of nations; they shall lay waste the glory of Egypt, and

all her hordes shall be destroyed. 13 I will have all of her animals perish beside her abundant waters; the foot of man shall stir them no longer, nor shall the hoof of beast disturb them. 14 Then will I make their waters clear, and their streams flow like oil, says the Lord GOD. 15 When I turn Egypt into a waste, the land shall be devastated of all that is in it; when I strike all who live there, they shall know that I am the LORD. 16 This is a dirge, and it shall be sung: the daughters of the nations shall chant it; over Egypt and all its hordes shall they chant it, says the Lord GOD. 17 On the fifteenth day of the first month in the twelfth year, the word of the LORD came to me: 18 Son of man, lament over the throngs of Egypt, for the mighty nations have thrust them down to the bottom of the earth, with those who go down into the pit. 19 "Whom do you excel in beauty? 20 In the midst of those slain by the sword shall they fall, and place shall be made with them for all their hordes." Then from the midst of the nether world, the mighty warriors shall speak to Egypt: 21 "Come down, you and your allies, lie with the uncircumcised, with those slain by the sword." 22 There is Assyria with all her company, all of them slain, 23 whose graves have been made in the recesses of the pit; her company is around Egypt's grave, all of them slain, fallen by the sword, who spread terror in the land of the living. 24 There is Elam with all her throng about Egypt's grave, all of them slain, fallen by the sword: they have gone down uncircumcised to the bottom of the earth, who spread their terror in the land of the living, and they bear their disgrace with those who go down into the pit; 25 in the midst of the slain they are placed. 26 There are Meshech and Tubal and all their throng about her grave, all of them uncircumcised, slain by the sword, for they spread their terror in the land of the living. 27 They do not lie with the mighty men fallen of old, who went down to the nether world with their weapons of war, whose swords were placed under their heads and whose shields were laid over their bones, though the mighty men caused terror in the land of the living. 28 But in the midst of the uncircumcised shall you lie, with those slain by the sword. 29 There are Edom, her kings, and all her princes, who despite their might have been placed with those slain by the sword; with the uncircumcised they lie, and with those who go down into the pit. 30 There are all the princes of the north and all the Sidonians, who have gone down with the slain, because of the terror their might inspired; they lie uncircumcised with those slain by the sword and bear their disgrace with those who go down to the pit. 31 When Pharaoh sees these, he shall be comforted for all his hordes slain by the sword - Pharaoh and all his army, says the Lord GOD. 32 Since he spread his terror in the land of the living, therefore is he laid to rest among the uncircumcised, with those slain by the sword - Pharaoh and all his hordes, says the Lord GOD.

Ezekiel Chapter 33

1 Thus the word of the LORD came to me: 2 Son of man, speak thus to your countrymen: When I bring the sword against a country, and the people of this country select one of their number to be their watchman, 3 and the watchman, seeing the sword coming against the country, blows the trumpet to warn the people, 4 anyone hearing but not heeding the warning of the trumpet and therefore slain by the sword that comes against him, shall be responsible for his own death. 5 He heard the trumpet blast yet refused to take warning; he is responsible for his own death, for had he taken warning he would have escaped with his life. 6 But if the watchman sees the sword coming and fails to blow the warning trumpet, so that the sword comes and takes anyone, I will hold the watchman responsible for that person's death, even though that person is taken because of his own sin. 7 You, son of man, I have appointed watchman for the house of Israel; when you hear me say anything, you shall warn them for me. 8 If I tell the wicked man that he shall surely die, and you do not speak out to dissuade the wicked man from his way, he (the wicked man) shall die for his guilt, but I will hold you responsible for his death. 9 But if you warn the wicked man, trying to turn him from his way, and he refuses to turn from his way, he shall die for his guilt, but you shall save yourself. 10 As for you, son of man, speak to the house of Israel: You people say, "Our crimes and our sins weigh us down; we are rotting away because of them. How can we survive?" 11 Answer them: As I live, says the Lord GOD, I swear I take no pleasure in the death of the wicked man, but rather in the wicked man's conversion, that he may live. Turn, turn from your evil ways! Why should you die, O house of Israel? 12 As for you, son of man, tell your countrymen: The virtue which a man has practiced will not save him on the day that he sins; neither will the wickedness that a man has done bring about his downfall on the day that he turns from his wickedness (nor can the virtuous man, when he sins, remain alive). 13 Though I say to the virtuous man that he shall surely live, if he then presumes on his virtue and does wrong, none of his virtuous deeds shall be remembered; because of the wrong he has done, he shall die. 14 And though I say to the wicked man that he shall surely die, if he turns away from his sin and does what is right and just, 15 giving back pledges, restoring stolen goods, living by the statutes that bring life, and doing no wrong, he shall surely live, he shall not die. 16 None of the sins he committed shall be held against him; he has done what is right and just, he shall surely live. 17 Yet your countrymen say, "The way of the LORD is not fair!"; but it is their way that is not fair. 18 When a virtuous man turns away from what is right and does wrong, he shall die for it. 19 But when a wicked man turns away from wickedness and does what is right and just, because of this he shall live. 20 And still you say, "The way of the LORD is not fair!"? I will judge every one of you according to his ways, O house of Israel. 21 On the fifth day of the tenth month, in the twelfth year of our exile, the fugitive came to me from Jerusalem and said, "The city is taken!" 22 The hand of the LORD had come upon me the evening before the fugitive arrived, and he opened my mouth when the fugitive reached me in the morning. My mouth was opened, and I was dumb no longer. 23 Thus the word of the LORD came to me: 24 Son of man, they who live in the ruins on the land of Israel reason thus: "Abraham, though but a single individual, received possession of the land; we, therefore, being many, have as permanent possession the land that has been given to us." 25 Give them this answer: Thus says the Lord GOD: You eat on the mountains, you raise your eyes to your idols, you shed blood - yet you would keep possession of the land? 26 You rely on your sword, you do abominable things, each one of you defiles his neighbor's wife - yet you would keep possession of the land? 27 Tell them this: Thus says the Lord GOD: As I live, those who are in the ruins I swear shall fall by the sword; those who are in the open field I have given to the wild beasts for food; and those who are in fastnesses and in caves shall die by the plague. 28 I will make the land a desolate waste, so that its proud strength will come to an end, and the mountains of Israel shall be so desolate that no one will cross them. 29 Thus they shall know that I am the LORD, when I make the land a desolate waste because of all the abominable things they have done. 30 As for you, son of man, your countrymen are talking about you along the walls and in the doorways of houses. They say to one another, "Come and hear the latest word that comes from the LORD." 31 My people come to you as people always do; they sit down before you and hear your words, but they will not obey them, for lies are on their lips and their desires are fixed on dishonest gain. 32 For them you are only a ballad singer, with a pleasant voice and a clever touch. They listen to your words, but they will not obey them. 33 But when it comes - and it is surely coming! - they shall know that there was a prophet among them.

Ezekiel Chapter 34

1 Thus the word of the LORD came to me: 2 Son of man, prophesy against the shepherds of Israel, in these words prophesy to them (to the shepherds): Thus says the Lord GOD: Woe to the shepherds of Israel who have been pasturing themselves! Should not shepherds, rather, pasture sheep? 3 You have fed off their milk, worn their wool, and slaughtered the fatlings, but the sheep you have not pastured. 4 You did not strengthen the weak nor heal the sick nor bind up the injured. You did not bring back the strayed nor seek the lost, but you lorded it over them harshly and brutally. 5 So they were scattered for lack of a shepherd, and became food for all the wild beasts. My sheep were scattered 6 and wandered over all the mountains and high hills; my sheep were scattered over the whole earth, with no one to look after them or to search for them. 7 Therefore, shepherds, hear the word of the LORD: 8 As I live, says the Lord GOD, because my sheep have been given over to pillage, and because my sheep have become food for every wild beast, for lack of a shepherd; because my shepherds did not look after my sheep, but pastured themselves and did not pasture my sheep; 9 because of this, shepherds, hear the word of the LORD: 10 Thus says the Lord GOD: I swear I am coming against these shepherds. I will claim my sheep from them and put a stop to their shepherding my sheep so that they may no longer pasture themselves. I will save my sheep, that they may no longer be food for their mouths. 11 For thus says the Lord GOD: I myself will look after and tend my sheep. 12 As a shepherd tends his flock when he finds himself among his scattered sheep, so will I tend my sheep. I will rescue them from every place where they were scattered when it was cloudy and dark. 13 I will lead them out from among the peoples and gather them from the foreign lands; I will bring them back to their own country and pasture them upon the mountains of Israel (in the land's ravines and all its inhabited places). 14 In good pastures will I pasture them, and on the mountain heights of Israel shall be their grazing ground. There they shall lie down on good grazing ground, and in rich pastures shall they be pastured on the mountains of Israel. 15 I myself will pasture my sheep; I myself will give them rest, says the Lord GOD. 16 The lost I will seek out, the strayed I will bring back, the injured I will bind up, the sick I will heal (but the sleek and the strong I will destroy), shepherding them rightly. 17 As for you, my

sheep, says the Lord GOD, I will judge between one sheep and another, between rams and goats. 18 Was it not enough for you to graze on the best pasture, that you had to trample the rest of your pastures with your feet? Was it not enough for you to drink the clearest water, that you had to foul the remainder with your feet? 19 Thus my sheep had to graze on what your feet had trampled and drink what your feet had fouled. 20 Therefore thus says the Lord GOD: Now will I judge between the fat and the lean sheep. 21 Because you push with side and shoulder, and butt all the weak sheep with your horns until you have driven them out, 22 I will save my sheep so that they may no longer be despoiled, and I will judge between one sheep and another. 23 I will appoint one shepherd over them to pasture them, my servant David; he shall pasture them and be their shepherd. 24 I, the LORD, will be their God, and my servant David shall be prince among them. I, the LORD, have spoken. 25 I will make a covenant of peace with them, and rid the country of ravenous beasts, that they may dwell securely in the desert and sleep in the forests. 26 I will place them about my hill, sending rain in due season, rains that shall be a blessing to them. 27 The trees of the field shall bear their fruits, and the land its crops, and they shall dwell securely on their own soil. Thus they shall know that I am the LORD when I break the bonds of their yoke and free them from the power of those who enslaved them. 28 They shall no longer be despoiled by the nations or devoured by beasts of the earth, but shall dwell secure, with no one to frighten them. 29 I will prepare for them peaceful fields for planting; they shall no longer be carried off by famine in the land, or bear the reproaches of the nations. 30 Thus they shall know that I, the LORD, am their God, and they are my people, the house of Israel, says the Lord GOD. 31 (You, my sheep, you are the sheep of my pasture, and I am your God, says the Lord GOD.)

Ezekiel Chapter 35

1 Thus the word of the LORD came to me: 2 Son of man, set your face against Mount Seir, and prophesy against it. 3 Say to it: Thus says the Lord GOD: See! I am coming at you, Mount Seir. I will stretch out my hand against you and make you a desolate waste. 4 Your cities I will turn into ruins, and you shall be a waste; thus you shall know that I am the LORD. 5 Because you never let die your hatred for the Israelites, whom you delivered over to the power of the sword at the time of their trouble, when their crimes came to an end, 6 therefore, as I live, says the Lord GOD, you have been guilty of blood, and blood, I swear, shall pursue you. 7 I will make Mount Seir a desolate waste, and cut off from it any traveler. 8 With the slain I will fill your hills, your valleys, and all your ravines (in them the slain shall fall by the sword): 9 desolate will I make you forever, and leave your cities without inhabitants; thus you shall know that I am the LORD. 10 Because you said: The two nations and the two lands have become mine; we shall possess them - although the LORD was there - 11 therefore, as I live, says the Lord GOD, I will deal with you according to your anger and your envy which you have exercised (in your hatred) against them. I will make myself known among you when I judge you, 12 and you shall know that I am the LORD. I have heard all the contemptuous things you have uttered against the mountains of Israel: "They are desolate, they have been given us to devour." 13 I have heard the insolent and wild words you have spoken against me. 14 Thus says the Lord GOD: Just as you rejoiced over my land because it was desolate, so will I do to you. 15 In keeping with your glee over the devastation of the inheritance of the house of Israel, so will I treat you. A waste shall you be, Mount Seir, you and the whole of Edom. Thus they shall know that I am the LORD.

Ezekiel Chapter 36

1 Thus the word of the LORD came to me: 2 Son of man, prophesy to the mountains of Israel: Mountains of Israel, hear the word of the LORD! 3 Thus says the Lord GOD: Because the enemy has said of you, "Ha! the everlasting heights have become our possession" 4 (therefore prophesy in these words: Thus says the Lord GOD:); because you have been ridiculed and despised on all sides for having become a possession for the rest of the nations, and have become a byword and a popular jeer; 5 therefore, mountains of Israel, hear the word of the LORD: (Thus says the Lord GOD to the mountains and hills, the ravines and valleys, the desolate ruins and abandoned cities, which have been given over to the pillage and mockery of the remaining nations round about; 6 therefore thus says the Lord GOD:) Truly, with burning jealousy I speak against the rest of the nations (and against all of Edom) who with wholehearted joy and utter contempt have considered my land their possession to be delivered over to plunder. 7 (Therefore, prophesy concerning the land of Israel, and say to the mountains and hills, the ravines and valleys: Thus says the Lord GOD:) With jealous fury I speak, because you have borne the reproach of the nations. 8 Therefore do I solemnly swear that your neighboring nations shall bear their own

reproach. 9 As for you, mountains of Israel, you shall grow branches and bear fruit for my people Israel, for they shall soon return. 10 See, I come to you, it is to you that I turn; you will be tilled and sown, 11 and I will settle crowds of men upon you, the whole house of Israel; cities shall be repeopled, and ruins rebuilt. 12 I will settle crowds of men and beasts upon you, to multiply and be fruitful. I will repeople you as in the past, and be more generous to you than in the beginning; thus you shall know that I am the LORD. 13 (My people Israel are the ones whom I will have walk upon you; they shall take possession of you, and you shall be their heritage. Never again shall you rob them of their children.) 14 Thus says the Lord GOD: Because they have said of you, "You are a land that devours men, and you rob your people of their children"; 15 therefore, never again shall you devour men or rob your people of their children, says the Lord GOD. 16 No more will I permit you to hear the reproach of nations, or bear insults from peoples, or rob your people of their children, says the Lord GOD. 17 Thus the word of the LORD came to me: 18 Son of man, when the house of Israel lived in their land, they defiled it by their conduct and deeds. In my sight their conduct was like the defilement of a menstruous woman. 19 Therefore I poured out my fury upon them (because of the blood which they poured out on the ground, and because they defiled it with idols). 20 I scattered them among the nations, dispersing them over foreign lands; according to their conduct and deeds I judged them. 21 But when they came among the nations (wherever they came), they served to profane my holy name, because it was said of them: "These are the people of the LORD, yet they had to leave their land." 22 So I have relented because of my holy name which the house of Israel profaned among the nations where they came. 23 Therefore say to the house of Israel: Thus says the Lord GOD: Not for your sakes do I act, house of Israel, but for the sake of my holy name, which you profaned among the nations to which you came. 24 I will prove the holiness of my great name, profaned among the nations, in whose midst you have profaned it. Thus the nations shall know that I am the LORD, says the Lord GOD, when in their sight I prove my holiness through you. 25 For I will take you away from among the nations, gather you from all the foreign lands, and bring you back to your own land. 26 I will sprinkle clean water upon you to cleanse you from all your impurities, and from all your idols I will cleanse you. 27 I will give you a new heart and place a new spirit within you, taking from your bodies your stony hearts and giving you natural hearts. 28 I will put my spirit within you and make you live by my statutes, careful to observe my decrees. 29 You shall live in the land I gave your fathers; you shall be my people, and I will be your God. 30 I will save you from all your impurities; I will order the grain to be abundant, and I will not send famine against you. 31 I will increase the fruit on your trees and the crops in your fields; thus you shall no longer bear among the nations the reproach of famine. 32 Then you shall remember your evil conduct, and that your deeds were not good; you shall loathe yourselves for your sins and your abominations. 33 Not for your sakes do I act, says the Lord GOD - let this be known to you! Be ashamed and abashed because of your conduct, O house of Israel. 34 Thus says the Lord GOD: When I purify you from all your crimes, I will repeople the cities, and the ruins shall be rebuilt; 35 the desolate land shall be tilled, which was formerly a wasteland exposed to the gaze of every passer-by. 36 "This desolate land has been made into a garden of Eden," they shall say. "The cities that were in ruins, laid waste, and destroyed are now repeopled and fortified." 37 Thus the neighboring nations that remain shall know that I, the LORD, have rebuilt what was destroyed and replanted what was desolate. I, the LORD, have promised, and I will do it. 38 Thus says the Lord GOD: This also I will be persuaded to do for the house of Israel: to multiply them like sheep. 39 As with sacrificial sheep, the sheep of Jerusalem on its feast days, the cities which were in ruins shall be filled with flocks of men; thus they shall know that I am the LORD.

Ezekiel Chapter 37

1 The hand of the LORD came upon me, and he led me out in the spirit of the LORD and set me in the center of the plain, which was now filled with bones. 2 He made me walk among them in every direction so that I saw how many they were on the surface of the plain. How dry they were! 3 He asked me: Son of man, can these bones come to life? "Lord GOD," I answered, "you alone know that." 4 Then he said to me: Prophesy over these bones, and say to them: Dry bones, hear the word of the LORD! 5 Thus says the Lord GOD to these bones: See! I will bring spirit into you, that you may come to life. 6 I will put sinews upon you, make flesh grow over you, cover you with skin, and put spirit in you so that you may come to life and know that I am the LORD. 7 I prophesied as I had been told, and even as I was prophesying I heard a noise; it was a rattling as the bones came together, bone joining bone. 8 I saw the sinews and the flesh come upon them, and the skin cover them, but there was no spirit in them. 9 Then he said to me: Prophesy to the spirit,

prophesy, son of man, and say to the spirit: Thus says the Lord GOD: From the four winds come, O spirit, and breathe into these slain that they may come to life. ¹⁰ I prophesied as he told me, and the spirit came into them; they came alive and stood upright, a vast army. ¹¹ Then he said to me: Son of man, these bones are the whole house of Israel. They have been saying, "Our bones are dried up, our hope is lost, and we are cut off." ¹² Therefore, prophesy and say to them: Thus says the Lord GOD: O my people, I will open your graves and have you rise from them, and bring you back to the land of Israel. ¹³ Then you shall know that I am the LORD, when I open your graves and have you rise from them, O my people! ¹⁴ I will put my spirit in you that you may live, and I will settle you upon your land; thus you shall know that I am the LORD. I have promised, and I will do it, says the LORD. ¹⁵ Thus the word of the LORD came to me: ¹⁶ Now, son of man, take a single stick, and write on it: Judah and those Israelites who are associated with him. Then take another stick and write on it: Joseph (the stick of Ephraim) and all the house of Israel associated with him. ¹⁷ Then join the two sticks together, so that they form one stick in your hand. ¹⁸ When your countrymen ask you, "Will you not tell us what you mean by all this?", ¹⁹ answer them: Thus says the Lord GOD: (I will take the stick of Joseph, which is in the hand of Ephraim, and of the tribes of Israel associated with him, and I will join to it the stick of Judah, making them a single stick; they shall be one in my hand. ²⁰ The sticks on which you write you shall hold up before them to see. ²¹ Tell them: Thus speaks the Lord GOD:) I will take the Israelites from among the nations to which they have come, and gather them from all sides to bring them back to their land. ²² I will make them one nation upon the land, in the mountains of Israel, and there shall be one prince for them all. Never again shall they be two nations, and never again shall they be divided into two kingdoms. ²³ No longer shall they defile themselves with their idols, their abominations, and all their transgressions. I will deliver them from all their sins of apostasy, and cleanse them so that they may be my people and I may be their God. ²⁴ My servant David shall be prince over them, and there shall be one shepherd for them all; they shall live by my statutes and carefully observe my decrees. ²⁵ They shall live on the land which I gave to my servant Jacob, the land where their fathers lived; they shall live on it forever, they, and their children, and their children's children, with my servant David their prince forever. ²⁶ I will make with them a covenant of peace; it shall be an everlasting covenant with them, and I will multiply them, and put my sanctuary among them forever. ²⁷ My dwelling shall be with them; I will be their God, and they shall be my people. ²⁸ Thus the nations shall know that it is I, the LORD, who make Israel holy, when my sanctuary shall be set up among them forever.

Ezekiel Chapter 38

¹ Thus the word of the LORD came to me: ² Son of man, turn toward Gog (the land of Magog), the chief prince of Meshech and Tubal, and prophesy against him: ³ Thus says the Lord GOD: See! I am coming at you, Gog, chief prince of Meshech and Tubal. ⁴ I will lead you forth with all your army, horses and riders all handsomely outfitted, a great horde with bucklers and shields, all of them carrying swords: ⁵ Persia, Cush, and Put with them (all with shields and helmets), ⁶ Gomer with all its troops, Beth-togarmah from the recesses of the north with all its troops, many peoples with you. ⁷ Prepare yourself, be ready, you and all your horde assembled about you, and be at my disposal. ⁸ After many days you will be mustered (in the last years you will come) against a nation which has survived the sword, which has been assembled from many peoples (on the mountains of Israel which were long a ruin), which has been brought forth from among the peoples and all of whom now dwell in security. ⁹ You shall come up like a sudden storm, advancing like a cloud to cover the earth, you and all your troops and the many peoples with you. ¹⁰ Thus says the Lord GOD: At that time thoughts shall arise in your mind, and you shall devise an evil scheme: ¹¹ "I will go up against a land of open villages and attack the peaceful people who are living in security, all of them living without walls, having neither bars nor gates, ¹² to plunder and pillage, turning my hand against the ruins that were repeopled and against a people gathered from the nations, a people concerned with cattle and goods, who dwell at the navel of the earth." ¹³ Sheba and Dedan, the merchants of Tarshish and all her young lions shall ask you: "Is it for plunder that you have come? Is it for pillage that you have summoned your horde, to carry off silver and gold, to take away cattle and goods, to seize much plunder?" ¹⁴ Therefore prophesy, son of man, and say to Gog: Thus says the Lord GOD: When my people Israel are dwelling in security, will you not bestir yourself ¹⁵ and come from your home in the recesses of the north, you and many peoples with you, all mounted on horses, a great horde and a mighty army? ¹⁶ You shall come up against my people Israel like a cloud covering the land. In the last days I will bring you against my land, that the nations may know of me, when in their sight I prove my holiness through you, O Gog. ¹⁷ Thus says the Lord GOD: It is of you that I spoke in ancient times through my servants, the prophets of Israel, who prophesied in those days that I would bring you against them. ¹⁸ But on that day, the day when Gog invades the land of Israel, says the Lord GOD, my fury shall be aroused. ¹⁹ In my anger and in my jealousy, in my fiery wrath, I swear: On that day there shall be a great shaking upon the land of Israel. ²⁰ Before me shall tremble the fish of the sea and the birds of the air, the beasts of the field and all the reptiles that crawl upon the ground, and all men who are on the land. Mountains shall be overturned, and cliffs shall tumble, and every wall shall fall to the ground. ²¹ Against him I will summon every terror, says the Lord GOD, every man's sword against his brother. ²² I will hold judgment with him in pestilence and bloodshed; flooding rain and hailstones, fire and brimstone, I will rain upon him, upon his troops, and upon the many peoples with him. ²³ I will prove my greatness and holiness and make myself known in the sight of many nations; thus they shall know that I am the LORD.

Ezekiel Chapter 39

¹ Now, son of man, prophesy against Gog in these words: Thus says the Lord GOD: See! I am coming at you, Gog, chief prince of Meshech and Tubal. ² I will turn you about, I will urge you on, and I will make you come up from the recesses of the north; I will lead you against the mountains of Israel. ³ Then I will strike the bow from your left hand, and make the arrows drop from your right. ⁴ Upon the mountains of Israel you shall fall, you and all your troops and the peoples who are with you. To birds of prey of every kind and to the wild beasts I am giving you to be eaten. ⁵ On the open field you shall fall, for I have decreed it, says the Lord GOD. ⁶ I will send fire upon Magog and upon those who live securely in the coastlands; thus they shall know that I am the LORD. ⁷ I will make my holy name known among my people Israel; I will no longer allow my holy name to be profaned. Thus the nations shall know that I am the LORD, the Holy One in Israel. ⁸ Yes, it is coming and shall be fulfilled, says the Lord GOD. This is the day I have decreed. ⁹ Then shall those who live in the cities of Israel go out and burn weapons: (shields and bucklers,) bows and arrows, clubs and lances; for seven years they shall make fires with them. ¹⁰ They shall not have to bring in wood from the fields or cut it down in the forests, for they shall make fires with the weapons. Thus they shall plunder those who plundered them and pillage those who pillaged them, says the Lord GOD. ¹¹ On that day I will give Gog for his tomb a well-known place in Israel, the Valley of Abarim east of the sea (it is blocked to travelers). Gog shall be buried there with all his horde, and it shall be named "Valley of Hamon-gog." ¹² To purify the land, the house of Israel shall need seven months to bury them. ¹³ All the people of the land shall bury them and gain renown for it, when I reveal my glory, says the Lord GOD. ¹⁴ Men shall be permanently employed to pass through the land burying those who lie unburied, so as to purify the land. For seven months they shall keep searching. ¹⁵ When they pass through, should they see a human bone, let them put up a marker beside it, until others have buried it in the Valley of Hamon-gog. ¹⁶ (Also the name of the city shall be Hamonah.) Thus the land shall be purified. ¹⁷ As for you, son of man, says the Lord GOD, say to birds of every kind and to all the wild beasts: Come together, from all sides gather for the slaughter I am about to provide for you, a great slaughter on the mountains of Israel: you shall have flesh to eat and blood to drink. ¹⁸ You shall eat the flesh of warriors and drink the blood of the princes of the land (rams, lambs, and goats, bullocks, fatlings of Bashan, all of them). ¹⁹ From the slaughter which I will provide for you, you shall eat fat until you are filled and drink blood until you are drunk. ²⁰ You shall be filled at my table with horses and riders, with warriors and soldiers of every kind, says the Lord GOD. ²¹ Thus I will display my glory among the nations, and all the nations shall see the judgment I have executed and the hand I have laid upon them. ²² From that day forward the house of Israel shall know that I am the LORD, their God. ²³ The nations shall know that because of its sins the house of Israel went into exile; for they transgressed against me, and I hid my face from them and handed them over to their foes, so that all of them fell by the sword. ²⁴ According to their uncleanness and their transgressions I dealt with them, hiding my face from them. ²⁵ Therefore, thus says the Lord GOD: Now I will restore the fortunes of Jacob and have pity on the whole house of Israel, and I will be jealous for my holy name. ²⁶ They shall forget their disgrace and all the times they broke faith with me, when they live in security on their land with no one to frighten them. ²⁷ When I bring them back from among the peoples, I will gather them from the lands of their enemies, and will prove my holiness through them in the sight of many nations. ²⁸ Thus they shall know that I, the LORD, am their God, since I who exiled them among the nations, will gather them back

on their land, not leaving any of them behind. 29 No longer will I hide my face from them, for I have poured out my spirit upon the house of Israel, says the Lord GOD.

Ezekiel Chapter 40

1 On the tenth day of the month beginning the twenty-fifth year of our exile, fourteen years after the city was taken, that very day the hand of the LORD came upon me and brought me 2 in divine visions to the land of Israel, where he set me down on a very high mountain. On it there seemed to be a city being built before me. 3 When he had brought me there, all at once I saw a man whose appearance was that of bronze; he was standing in the gate, holding a linen cord and a measuring rod. 4 The man said to me, "Son of man, look carefully and listen intently, and pay strict attention to all that I will show you, for you have been brought here so that I might show it to you. Tell the house of Israel all that you see." 5 (Then I saw an outer wall that completely surrounded the temple. The man was holding a measuring rod six cubits long, each cubit being a cubit and a handbreadth; he measured the width and the height of the structure, each of which were found to be one rod.) 6 Then he went to the gate which faced the east, climbed its steps, and measured the gate's threshold, which was found to be a rod wide. 7 The cells were a rod long and a rod wide, and the pilasters between the cells measured five cubits. The threshold of the gate adjoining the vestibule of the gate toward the inside measured one rod. 8 He measured the vestibule of the gate, 9 which was eight cubits, and its pilasters, which were two cubits. The vestibule of the gate was toward the inside. 10 The cells of the east gate were three on either side, of equal size, and the pilasters on either side were also of equal size. 11 He measured the gate's entrance, which was ten cubits wide, while the width of the gate's passage itself was thirteen cubits. 12 The border before each of the cells on both sides was one cubit; the cells themselves were six cubits on either side, from opening to opening. 13 He measured the gate from the back wall of one cell to the back wall of the cell on the opposite side: the width was twenty-five cubits. 14 He measured the vestibule, which was twenty-five cubits. The pilasters adjoining the court on either side were six cubits. 15 The length of the gate from the front entrance to the front of the vestibule on the inside was fifty cubits. 16 Within the gateway on both sides there were splayed windows let into the cells (and into their pilasters); likewise, within the vestibule on both sides there were windows. The pilasters were decorated with palms. 17 Then he brought me to the outer court, where there were chambers and a pavement. The pavement was laid all around the court, and the chambers, which were on the pavement, were thirty in number. 18 The pavement lay alongside the gates, as wide as the gates were long; this was the lower pavement. 19 He measured the width of the court from the front of the lower gate to the front of the inner gate; it was one hundred cubits between them. Then he proceeded north, 20 where, on the outer court, there was a gate facing north, whose length and width he measured. 21 Its cells, three on either side, its pilasters, and its vestibule had the same measurements as those of the first gate; it was fifty cubits long and twenty-five cubits wide. 22 Its windows, the windows of its vestibule, and its palm decorations were of the same proportions as those of the gate facing the east. Seven steps led up to it, and its vestibule was toward the inside. 23 The inner court had a gate opposite the north gate, just as at the east gate; he measured one hundred cubits from one gate to the other. 24 Then he led me south, to where there was a southern gate, whose cells, pilasters, and vestibule he measured; they were the same size as the others. 25 The gate and its vestibule had windows on both sides, like the other windows. It was fifty cubits long and twenty-five cubits wide. 26 It was ascended by seven steps; its vestibule was toward the inside; and it was decorated with palms here and there on its pilasters. 27 The inner court also had a southern gate; from gate to gate he measured one hundred cubits. 28 Then he brought me to the inner court by the south gate, where he measured the south gate. Its dimensions were the same as the others; 29 its cells, its pilasters, and its vestibule were the same size as the others. The gate and its vestibule had windows on both sides; and it was fifty cubits long and twenty-five cubits wide. 31 But its vestibule was toward the outer court; palms were on its pilasters, and it had a stairway of eight steps. 32 Then he brought me to the gate facing the east, where he measured the gate, whose dimensions were found to be the same. 33 Its cells, its pilasters, and its vestibule were the same size as the others; the gate and its vestibule had windows on both sides; it was fifty cubits long and twenty-five cubits wide. 34 But its vestibule was toward the outer court; palms were on its pilasters here and there, and it had a stairway of eight steps. 35 Then he brought me to the north gate, where he measured the dimensions 36 of its cells, its pilasters, and its vestibule, and found them the same. The gate and its vestibule had windows on both sides; it was fifty cubits long and twenty-five cubits wide. 37 Its vestibule was toward the outer court; palms were on its

pilasters here and there, and it had a stairway of eight steps. 38 There was a chamber opening off the vestibule of the gate, where the holocausts were rinsed. 39 In the vestibule of the gate there were two tables on either side, on which were slaughtered the sin offerings and guilt offerings. 40 Along the wall of the vestibule, but outside, near the entrance of the north gate, were two tables, and on the other side of the vestibule of the gate there were two tables. 41 There were four tables on either side of the gate (eight tables), on which the sacrifices were slaughtered. 42 There were four tables for holocausts, made of cut stone, one and a half cubits long, one and a half cubits wide, and one cubit high. 43 The ledges, a handbreadth wide, were set on the inside all around, and on them were laid the instruments with which the holocausts were slaughtered. On the tables themselves the flesh was laid. 44 He then led me to the inner court where there were two chambers, one beside the north gate, facing south, and the other beside the south gate, facing north. 45 He said to me, "This chamber which faces south is for the priests who have charge of the temple, 46 and the chamber which faces north is for the priests who have charge of the altar. These are the Zadokites, the only Levites who may come near to minister to the LORD." 47 Then he measured the court, which was a hundred cubits long and a hundred cubits wide, a perfect square. The altar stood in front of the temple. 48 Then he brought me into the vestibule of the temple and measured the pilasters on each side, which were five cubits. The width of the doorway was fourteen cubits, and the side walls on either side of the door measured three cubits. 49 The vestibule was twenty cubits wide and twelve cubits deep; ten steps led up to it, and there were columns by the pilasters, one on either side.

Ezekiel Chapter 41

1 Then he brought me to the nave and measured the pilasters, which were six cubits thick on either side. 2 The width of the entrance was ten cubits, and the walls at either side of it measured five cubits each. He measured the length of the nave, which was found to be forty cubits, while its width was twenty. 3 Then he went in beyond and measured the pilasters flanking that entrance, which were two cubits; the width of the entrance was six cubits, and the walls at either side of it extended seven cubits each. 4 He measured the space beyond the nave, twenty cubits long and twenty cubits wide, and said to me, "This is the holy of holies." 5 Then he measured the wall of the temple, which was six cubits thick; the side chambers, which extended all the way around the temple, had a width of four cubits. 6 There were thirty side chambers built one above the other in three stories, and there were offsets in the outside wall of the temple that enclosed the side chambers; these served as supports, so that there were no supports in the temple wall proper. 7 There was a broad circular passageway that led upward to the side chambers, for the temple was enclosed all the way around and all the way upward; therefore the temple had a broad way running upward so that one could pass from the lowest to the middle and the highest story. 8 About the temple was a raised pavement completely enclosing it - the foundations of the side chambers - a full rod of six cubits in extent. 9 The width of the outside wall which enclosed the side chambers was five cubits. Between the side chambers of the temple 10 and the chambers of the court was an open space twenty cubits wide going all around the temple. 11 The side chambers had entrances to the open space, one entrance on the north and another on the south. The width of the wall surrounding the open space was five cubits. 12 The building fronting the free area on the west side was seventy cubits front to back; the wall of the building was five cubits thick all around, and it measured ninety cubits from side to side. 13 He measured the temple, which was one hundred cubits long. The free area, together with the building and its walls, was a hundred cubits in length. 14 The facade of the temple, along with the free area, on the east side, was one hundred cubits wide. 15 He measured the building which lay the length of the free area and behind it, and together with its walls on both sides it was one hundred cubits. The inner nave and the outer vestibule 16 were paneled with precious wood all around, covered from the ground to the windows. There were splayed windows with trellises about them (facing the threshold). 17 As high as the lintel of the door, even into the interior part of the temple as well as outside, on every wall on every side in both the inner and outer rooms were carved 18 the figures of cherubim and palmtrees: a palmtree between every two cherubim. Each cherub had two faces: 19 a man's face looking at a palmtree on one side, and a lion's face looking at a palmtree on the other; thus they were figured on every side throughout the whole temple. 20 From the ground to the lintel of the door the cherubim and palmtrees were carved on the walls. 21 The way into the nave was a square doorframe. In front of the holy place was something that looked like 22 a wooden altar, three cubits in height, two cubits long, and two cubits wide. It had corners, and its base and sides were of wood. He said to me, "This is the table which is before the LORD." 23 The nave had a

double door, and also the holy place had ²⁴ a double door. Each door had two movable leaves; two leaves were on one doorjamb and two on the other. ²⁵ Carved upon them (on the doors of the nave) were cherubim and palmtrees, like those carved on the walls. Before the vestibule outside was a wooden lattice. ²⁶ There were splayed windows (and palmtrees) on both side walls of the vestibule, and the side chambers of the temple.

Ezekiel Chapter 42

¹ Then he led me north to the outer court, bringing me to some chambers on the north that lay across the free area and which were also across from the building. ² Their length was a hundred cubits on the north side, and they were fifty cubits wide. ³ Across the twenty cubits of the inner court and the pavement of the outer court, there were three parallel rows of them on different levels. ⁴ In front of the chambers, to the inside, was a walk ten cubits broad and a wall of one cubit; but the entrances of the chambers were on the north. ⁵ The outermost chambers were the lowest, for the system of levels set them at a level lower than the closest chambers and those in between; ⁶ for they were in three rows and had no foundations to conform with the foundations of the courts, therefore they were on a lower terrace of the ground than the closest and the middle chambers. ⁷ On the far side there was a wall running parallel to the chambers along the outer court; its length before these chambers was fifty cubits, ⁸ for the length of the chambers belonging to the outer court was fifty cubits, but along its entire length the wall measured one hundred cubits. ⁹ Below these chambers there was the way in from the east, so that one could enter from the outer court ¹⁰ where the wall of the court began. To the south along the side of the free area and the building there were also chambers, ¹¹ before which was a passage. These looked like the chambers to the north, just as long and just as wide, with the same exits and plan and entrances. ¹² Below the chambers to the south there was an entrance at the beginning of the way which led to the back wall, by which one could enter from the east. ¹³ He said to me, "The north and south chambers which border on the free area are the sanctuary chambers; here the priests who draw near to the LORD shall eat the most sacred meals, and here they shall keep the most sacred offerings: cereal offerings, sin offerings, and guilt offerings; for it is a holy place. ¹⁴ When the priests have once entered, they shall not leave the holy place for the outer court until they have left here the clothing in which they ministered, for it is holy. They shall put on other garments, and then approach the place destined for the people." ¹⁵ When he had finished measuring the inner temple area, he brought me out by way of the gate which faces east and measured all the limits of the court. ¹⁶ He measured the east side: five hundred cubits by his measuring rod. Then he turned ¹⁷ and measured the north side: five hundred cubits by the measuring rod. He turned ¹⁸ to the south and measured five hundred cubits by the measuring rod. ¹⁹ Then he turned to the west and measured five hundred cubits by the measuring rod. ²⁰ Thus he measured it in the four directions, five hundred cubits long and five hundred cubits wide. It was surrounded by a wall, to separate the sacred from the profane.

Ezekiel Chapter 43

¹ Then he led me to the gate which faces the east, ² and there I saw the glory of the God of Israel coming from the east. I heard a sound like the roaring of many waters, and the earth shone with his glory. ³ The vision was like that which I had seen when he came to destroy the city, and like that which I had seen by the river Chebar. I fell prone ⁴ as the glory of the LORD entered the temple by way of the gate which faces the east, ⁵ but spirit lifted me up and brought me to the inner court. And I saw that the temple was filled with the glory of the LORD. ⁶ Then I heard someone speaking to me from the temple, while the man stood beside me. ⁷ The voice said to me: Son of man, this is where my throne shall be, this is where I will set the soles of my feet; here I will dwell among the Israelites forever. Never again shall they and their kings profane my holy name with their harlotries and with the corpses of their kings (their high places). ⁸ When they placed their threshold against my threshold and their doorpost next to mine, so that only a wall was between us, they profaned my holy name by their abominable deeds; therefore I consumed them in my wrath. ⁹ From now on they shall put far from me their harlotry and the corpses of their kings, and I will dwell in their midst forever. ¹⁰ As for you, son of man, describe the temple to the house of Israel (that they may be ashamed of their sins), both its measurements and its design; ¹¹ (and if they are ashamed of all that they have done,) make known to them the form and design of the temple, its exits and entrances, all its statutes and laws; write these down for them to see, that they may carefully observe all its laws and statutes. ¹² This is the law of the temple: its whole surrounding area on the mountain top shall be most sacred. ¹³ These were the

measurements of the altar in cubits of one cubit plus a handbreadth. Its base was one cubit high and one cubit deep, with a rim around its edges of one span. The height of the altar itself was as follows: ¹⁴ from its base at the bottom up to the lower edge it was two cubits high, and this ledge was one cubit deep; from the lower to the upper ledge it was four cubits high, and this ledge also was one cubit deep; ¹⁵ the hearth of the altar was four cubits high, and extending from the top of the hearth were the four horns of the altar. ¹⁶ The hearth was a square: twelve cubits long and twelve cubits wide. ¹⁷ The upper ledge was also a square: fourteen cubits long and fourteen cubits wide. The lower ledge, likewise a square, was sixteen cubits long and sixteen cubits wide, with a half-cubit rim surrounding it. And there was a base of one cubit all around. The steps of the altar face the east. ¹⁸ Then he said to me: Son of man, thus says the Lord GOD: These are the statutes for the altar when it is set up for the offering of holocausts upon it and for the sprinkling of blood against it. ¹⁹ Give a young bull as a sin offering to the priests, the Levites who are of the line of Zadok, who draw near me to minister to me, says the Lord GOD. ²⁰ Take some of its blood and put it on the four horns of the altar, and on the four corners of the ledge, and on the rim all around. Thus you shall purify it and make atonement for it. ²¹ Then take the bull of the sin offering, which is to be burnt in a designated part of the temple, outside the sanctuary. ²² On the second day present an unblemished he-goat as a sin offering, to purify the altar as was done with the bull. ²³ When you have finished the purification, bring an unblemished young bull and an unblemished ram from the flock, ²⁴ and present them before the LORD; the priests shall strew salt on them and offer them to the LORD as holocausts. ²⁵ Daily for seven days you shall offer a he-goat as a sin offering, and a young bull and a ram from the flock, all unblemished, shall be offered ²⁶ for seven days. Thus atonement shall be made for the altar, and it shall be purified and dedicated. ²⁷ And when these days are over, from the eighth day on, the priests shall offer your holocausts and peace offerings on the altar. Then I will accept you, says the Lord GOD.

Ezekiel Chapter 44

¹ Then he brought me back to the outer gate of the sanctuary, facing the east; but it was closed. ² He said to me: This gate is to remain closed; it is not to be opened for anyone to enter by it; since the LORD, the God of Israel, has entered by it, it shall remain closed. ³ Only the prince may sit down in it to eat his meal in the presence of the LORD. He must enter by way of the vestibule of the gate, and leave by the same way. ⁴ Then he brought me by way of the north gate to the facade of the temple, and when I looked I saw the glory of the LORD filling the LORD'S temple, and I fell prone. ⁵ Then he said to me: Son of man, pay strict attention, look carefully, and listen intently to all that I will tell you about the statutes and laws of the LORD'S temple; be attentive in regard to those who are to be admitted to the temple and all those who are to be excluded from the sanctuary. ⁶ Say to that rebellious house, the house of Israel: Thus says the Lord GOD: Enough of all these abominations of yours, O house of Israel! ⁷ You have admitted foreigners, uncircumcised both in heart and flesh, to my sanctuary to profane it when you offered me food, fat, and blood; thus you have broken my covenant by all your abominations. ⁸ Instead of caring for the service of my temple, you have appointed such as these to serve me in my sanctuary in your stead. ⁹ Thus says the Lord GOD: No foreigners, uncircumcised in heart and in flesh, shall ever enter my sanctuary; none of the foreigners who live among the Israelites. ¹⁰ But as for the Levites who departed from me when Israel strayed from me to pursue their idols, they shall bear the consequences of their sin. ¹¹ They shall serve in my sanctuary as gatekeepers and temple servants; they shall slaughter the holocausts and the sacrifices for the people, and they shall stand before the people to minister for them. ¹² Because they used to minister for them before their idols, and became an occasion of sin to the house of Israel, therefore I have sworn an oath against them, says the Lord GOD: they shall bear the consequences of their sin. ¹³ They shall no longer draw near me to serve as my priests, nor shall they touch any of my sacred things, or the most sacred things. Thus they shall bear their disgrace because of all their abominable deeds. ¹⁴ But I will set them to the service of the temple, for all its work and for everything that is to be done in it. ¹⁵ As for the levitical priests, however, the Zadokites who cared for my sanctuary when the Israelites strayed from me, they shall draw near me to minister to me, and they shall stand before me to offer me fat and blood, says the Lord GOD. ¹⁶ It is they who shall enter my sanctuary, they who shall approach my table to minister to me, and they who shall carry out my service. ¹⁷ Whenever they enter the gates of the inner court, they shall wear linen garments; they shall not put on anything woolen when they minister at the gates of the inner court or within the temple. ¹⁸ They shall have linen turbans on their heads and linen drawers on their loins; they shall not gird themselves with

anything that causes sweat. 19 When they are to go out to the people in the outer court, they shall take off the garments in which they ministered and leave them in the chambers of the sanctuary, putting on other garments; thus they will not transmit holiness to the people with their garments. 20 They shall not shave their heads nor let their hair hang loose, but they shall keep their hair carefully trimmed. 21 No priest shall drink wine when he is to enter the inner court. 22 They shall not take for their wives either widows or divorced women, but only virgins of the race of Israel; however, they may marry women who are the widows of priests. 23 They shall teach my people to distinguish between the sacred and the profane, and make known to them the difference between the clean and the unclean. 24 In capital cases they shall stand as judges, judging them according to my decrees. They shall observe my laws and statutes on all my festivals, and keep my sabbaths holy. 25 They shall not make themselves unclean by coming near any dead person, unless it be their father, mother, son, daughter, brother, or maiden sister; for these they may make themselves unclean. 26 After a priest has been cleansed, he must wait an additional seven days, 27 and on the day he enters the inner court to minister in the sanctuary, he shall present his sin offering, says the Lord GOD. 28 They shall have no inheritance, for I am their inheritance; you shall give them no property in Israel, for I am their property. 29 They shall eat the cereal offering, the sin offering, and the guilt offering; whatever is under the ban in Israel shall be theirs. 30 All the choicest first fruits of every kind, and all the best of your offerings of every kind, shall belong to the priests; likewise the best of your dough you shall give to the priests to bring a blessing down upon your house. 31 The priests shall not eat anything, whether flesh or fowl, that has died of itself or has been killed by wild beasts.

Ezekiel Chapter 45

1 When you apportion the land into inheritances, you shall set apart a sacred tract of land for the LORD, twenty-five thousand cubits long and twenty thousand wide; its whole area shall be sacred. 2 Of this land a square plot, five hundred by five hundred cubits, surrounded by a free space of fifty cubits, shall be assigned to the sanctuary. 3 Also from this sector measure off a strip, twenty-five thousand cubits long and ten thousand wide, within which shall be the sanctuary, the holy of holies. 4 This shall be the sacred part of the land belonging to the priests, the ministers of the sanctuary, who draw near to minister to the LORD; it shall be a place for their homes and pasture land for their cattle. 5 Also there shall be a strip twenty-five thousand cubits long and ten thousand wide as property for the Levites, the ministers of the temple, that they may have cities to live in. 6 As property of the City you shall designate a strip five thousand cubits wide and twenty-five thousand long, parallel to the sacred tract; this shall belong to the whole house of Israel. 7 The prince shall have a section bordering on both sides of the combined sacred tract and City property, extending westward on the western side and eastward on the eastern side, corresponding in length to one of the tribal portions from the western boundary to the eastern boundary 8 of the land. This shall be his property in Israel, so that the princes of Israel will no longer oppress my people, but will leave the land to the house of Israel according to their tribes. 9 Thus says the Lord GOD: Enough, you princes of Israel! Put away violence and oppression, and do what is right and just! Stop evicting my people! says the Lord GOD. 10 You shall have honest scales, an honest ephah, and an honest liquid measure. 11 The ephah and the liquid measure shall be of the same size: the liquid measure equal to a tenth of a homer, and the ephah equal to a tenth of a homer; by the homer they shall be determined. 12 The shekel shall be twenty gerahs. Twenty shekels, twenty-five shekels, plus fifteen shekels shall be your mina. 13 These are the offerings you shall make: one sixth of an ephah from each homer of wheat, and one sixth of an ephah from each homer of barley. 14 The regulation for oil: for every measure of oil, a tenth of a measure, computed by the kor of ten liquid measures (or a homer, for ten liquid measures make a homer). 15 One sheep from the flock for every two hundred from the pasturage of Israel, for sacrifice - holocausts and peace offerings and atonement sacrifices, says the Lord GOD. 16 All the people of the land shall be bound to this offering (for the prince in Israel). 17 It shall be the duty of the prince to provide the holocausts, cereal offerings, and libations on the feasts, new moons, and sabbaths, on all the festivals of the house of Israel. He shall offer the sin offerings, cereal offerings, holocausts, and peace offerings, to make atonement on behalf of the house of Israel. 18 Thus says the Lord GOD: On the first day of the first month you shall use an unblemished young bull as a sacrifice to purify the sanctuary. 19 Then the priest shall take some of the blood from the sin offering and put it on the doorposts of the temple, on the four corners of the ledge of the altar, and on the doorposts of the gates of the inner court. 20 You shall repeat this on the first day of the seventh month for those who have sinned through

inadvertence or ignorance; thus you shall make atonement for the temple. 21 On the fourteenth day of the first month you shall observe the feast of the Passover; for seven days unleavened bread is to be eaten. 22 On that day the prince shall offer on his own behalf, and on behalf of all the people of the land, a bull as a sin offering. 23 On each of the seven days of the feast he shall offer as a holocaust to the LORD seven bulls and seven rams without blemish, and as a sin offering he shall offer one male goat each day. 24 As a cereal offering he shall offer one ephah for each bull and one ephah for each ram; and he shall offer one hin of oil for each ephah. 25 On the fifteenth day of the seventh month, the feast day, and for seven days, he shall perform the same rites, making the same sin offerings, the same holocausts, the same cereal offerings and offerings of oil.

Ezekiel Chapter 46

1 Thus says the Lord GOD: The gate toward the east of the inner court shall remain closed throughout the six working days, but on the sabbath and on the day of the new moon it shall be open. 2 The prince shall enter from outside by way of the vestibule of the gate and remain standing at the doorpost of the gate; then while the priests offer his holocausts and peace offerings, he shall worship at the threshold of the gate and then leave; the gate shall not be closed until evening. 3 The people of the land shall worship before the LORD at the door of this gate on the sabbaths and new moons. 4 The holocausts which the prince presents to the LORD on the sabbath shall consist of six unblemished lambs and an unblemished ram, 5 together with a cereal offering of one ephah for the ram, whatever he pleases for the lambs, and a hin of oil for each ephah. 6 On the day of the new moon he shall provide an unblemished young bull, also six lambs and a ram without blemish, 7 with a cereal offering of one ephah for the bull and one for the ram, for the lambs as much as he has at hand, and for each ephah a hin of oil. 8 The prince shall always enter and depart by the vestibule of the gate. 9 When the people of the land enter the presence of the LORD to worship on the festivals, if they enter by the north gate they shall leave by the south gate, and if they enter by the south gate they shall leave by the north gate; no one shall return by the gate through which he has entered, but he shall leave by the opposite gate. 10 The prince shall be in their midst when they enter, and he shall also leave with them. 11 On the feasts and festivals the cereal offering shall be an ephah for a bull, an ephah for a ram, but for the lambs as much as one pleases, and a hin of oil with each ephah. 12 When the prince makes a freewill offering to the LORD, whether holocausts or peace offerings, the eastern gate shall be opened for him, and he shall offer his holocausts or his peace offerings as on the sabbath; then he shall leave, and the gate shall be closed after his departure. 13 He shall offer as a daily holocaust to the LORD an unblemished yearling lamb; this he shall offer every morning. 14 With it every morning he shall provide as a cereal offering one sixth of an ephah, with a third of a hin of oil to moisten the fine flour. This cereal offering to the LORD is mandatory with the established holocaust. 15 The lamb, the cereal offering, and the oil are to be offered every morning as an established holocaust. 16 Thus says the Lord GOD: If the prince makes a gift of part of his inheritance to any of his sons, it shall belong to his sons; that property is theirs by inheritance. 17 But if he makes a gift of part of his inheritance to one of his servants, it shall belong to the latter only until the year of release, when it shall revert to the prince. Only the inheritance given to his sons is permanent. 18 The prince shall not seize any part of the inheritance of the people by evicting them from their property. He shall provide an inheritance for his sons from his own property, so that none of my people will be driven from their property. 19 Then he brought me by the entrance which is on the side of the gate to the chambers (of the sanctuary, reserved to the priests) which face the north. There, at their west end, I saw a place, 20 concerning which he said to me, "Here the priests cook the guilt offerings and the sin offerings, and bake the cereal offerings, so that they do not have to take them into the outer court at the risk of transmitting holiness to the people." 21 Then he led me into the outer court and had me pass around the four corners of the court, and I saw that in each corner there was another court: 22 in the four corners of the court, minor courts, forty cubits long and thirty wide, all four of them the same size. 23 A wall of stones surrounded each of the four, and hearths were built beneath the stones all the way around. 24 He said to me, "These are the kitchens where the temple ministers cook the sacrifices of the people."

Ezekiel Chapter 47

1 Then he brought me back to the entrance of the temple, and I saw water flowing out from beneath the threshold of the temple toward the east, for the facade of the temple was toward the east; the water flowed down from the southern side of the temple, south of the altar. 2 He led

me outside by the north gate, and around to the outer gate facing the east, where I saw water trickling from the southern side. ³ Then when he had walked off to the east with a measuring cord in his hand, he measured off a thousand cubits and had me wade through the water, which was ankle-deep. ⁴ He measured off another thousand and once more had me wade through the water, which was now knee-deep. Again he measured off a thousand and had me wade; the water was up to my waist. ⁵ Once more he measured off a thousand, but there was now a river through which I could not wade; for the water had risen so high it had become a river that could not be crossed except by swimming. ⁶ He asked me, "Have you seen this, son of man?" Then he brought me to the bank of the river, where he had me sit. ⁷ Along the bank of the river I saw very many trees on both sides. ⁸ He said to me, "This water flows into the eastern district down upon the Arabah, and empties into the sea, the salt waters, which it makes fresh. ⁹ Wherever the river flows, every sort of living creature that can multiply shall live, and there shall be abundant fish, for wherever this water comes the sea shall be made fresh. ¹⁰ Fishermen shall be standing along it from En-gedi to En-eglaim, spreading their nets there. Its kinds of fish shall be like those of the Great Sea, very numerous. ¹¹ Only its marshes and swamps shall not be made fresh; they shall be left for salt. ¹² Along both banks of the river, fruit trees of every kind shall grow; their leaves shall not fade, nor their fruit fail. Every month they shall bear fresh fruit, for they shall be watered by the flow from the sanctuary. Their fruit shall serve for food, and their leaves for medicine." ¹³ Thus says the Lord GOD: These are the boundaries within which you shall apportion the land among the twelve tribes of Israel (Joseph having two portions). ¹⁴ All of you shall have a like portion in this land which I swore to give to your fathers, that it might fall to you as your inheritance. ¹⁵ This is the boundary of the land on the north side: from the Great Sea in the direction of Hethlon, past Labo of Hamath, to Zedad, ¹⁶ Berothah and Sibraim, along the frontiers of Hamath and Damascus, to Hazar-enon which is on the border of the Hauran. ¹⁷ Thus the border shall extend from the sea to Hazar-enon, with the frontier of Hamath and Damascus to the north. This is the northern boundary. ¹⁸ The eastern boundary: between the Hauran - toward Damascus - and Gilead on the one side, and the land of Israel on the other side, the Jordan shall form the boundary down to the eastern sea as far as Tamar. This is the eastern boundary. ¹⁹ The southern boundary: from Tamar to the waters of Meribath-kadesh, thence to the Wadi of Egypt, and on to the Great Sea. This is the southern boundary. ²⁰ The western boundary: the Great Sea forms the boundary up to a point parallel to Labo of Hamath. This is the western boundary. ²¹ You shall distribute this land among yourselves according to the tribes of Israel. ²² You shall allot it as inheritances for yourselves and for the aliens resident in your midst who have bred children among you. The latter shall be to you like native Israelites; along with you they shall receive inheritances among the tribes of Israel. ²³ In whatever tribe the alien may be resident, there you shall assign him his inheritance, says the Lord GOD.

Ezekiel Chapter 48

¹ This is the list of the tribes. Dan: at the northern extremity, adjoining Hamath, all along from the approaches to Hethlon through Labo of Hamath to Hazar-enon, on the northerly border with Damascus, with his possession reaching from the eastern to the western boundary. ² Asher: on the frontier of Dan, from the eastern to the western boundary. ³ Naphtali: on the frontier of Asher, from the eastern to the western boundary. ⁴ Manasseh: on the frontier of Naphtali, from the eastern to the western boundary. ⁵ Ephraim: on the frontier of Manasseh, from the eastern to the western boundary. ⁶ Reuben: on the frontier of Ephraim, from the eastern to the western boundary. ⁷ Judah: on the frontier of Reuben, from the eastern to the western boundary. ⁸ On the frontier of Judah, from the eastern to the western boundary there shall be the tract which you shall set apart, twenty-five thousand cubits from north to south, and as wide as one of the tribal portions from the eastern to the western boundary. In the center of the tract shall be the sanctuary. ⁹ The tract that you set aside for the LORD shall be twenty-five thousand cubits across by twenty thousand north and south. ¹⁰ In this sacred tract the priests shall have twenty-five thousand cubits on the north, ten thousand on the west, ten thousand on the east, and twenty-five thousand on the south; and the sanctuary of the LORD shall be in its center. ¹¹ The consecrated priests, the Zadokites, who fulfilled my service and did not stray along with the Israelites as the Levites did, ¹² shall have within this tract of land their own most sacred domain, next to the territory of the Levites. ¹³ The Levites shall have a territory corresponding to that of the priests, twenty-five thousand cubits by ten thousand. The whole tract shall be twenty-five thousand cubits across and twenty thousand north and south. ¹⁴ They may not sell or exchange or alienate this, the best part of the land, for it is sacred to the LORD.

¹⁵ The remaining five thousand cubits along the twenty-five-thousand-cubit line are profane land, assigned to the City for dwellings and pasture; the City shall be at their center. ¹⁶ These are the dimensions of the City: the north side, forty-five hundred cubits; the south side, forty-five hundred cubits; the east side, forty-five hundred cubits; and the west side, forty-five hundred cubits. ¹⁷ The pasture lands of the City shall extend north two hundred and fifty cubits, south two hundred and fifty cubits, east two hundred and fifty cubits, and west two hundred and fifty cubits. ¹⁸ There shall remain an area along the sacred tract, ten thousand cubits to the east and ten thousand to the west, whose produce shall provide food for the workers of the City. ¹⁹ The workers in the City shall be taken from all the tribes of Israel. ²⁰ The entire tract shall be twenty-five thousand by twenty-five thousand cubits; as a perfect square you shall set apart the sacred tract together with the City property. ²¹ The remainder shall belong to the prince: the land on both sides of the sacred tract and the City property, extending along the twenty-five-thousand-cubit line eastward to the eastern boundary, and westward along the twenty-five-thousand-cubit line to the western boundary, a territory parallel with the tribal portions for the prince. The sacred tract and the sanctuary of the temple shall be in the middle. ²² Thus, except for the property of the Levites and the City property, which lie in the midst of the prince's property, the territory between the portions of Judah and of Benjamin shall belong to the prince. ²³ These are the remaining tribes. Benjamin: from the eastern to the western boundary. ²⁴ Simeon: on the frontier of Benjamin, from the eastern to the western boundary. ²⁵ Issachar: on the frontier of Simeon, from the eastern to the western boundary. ²⁶ Zebulun: on the frontier of Issachar, from the eastern to the western boundary. ²⁷ Gad: on the frontier of Zebulun, from the eastern to the western boundary. ²⁸ Along the frontier of Gad shall be the southern boundary, which shall extend from Tamar to the waters of Meribath-kadesh, and from there to the Wadi of Egypt, and on to the Great Sea. ²⁹ Such is the land which you shall apportion as inheritances among the tribes of Israel, and these are their portions, says the Lord GOD. ³⁰ These are the exits of the City, the gates of which are named after the tribes of Israel. On the north side, measuring forty-five hundred cubits, ³¹ there shall be three gates: the gate of Reuben, the gate of Judah, and the gate of Levi. ³² On the east side, measuring forty-five hundred cubits, there shall be three gates: the gate of Joseph, the gate of Benjamin, and the gate of Dan. ³³ On the south side, measuring forty-five hundred cubits, there shall be three gates: the gate of Simeon, the gate of Issachar, and the gate of Zebulun. ³⁴ On the west side, measuring forty-five hundred cubits, there shall be three gates: the gate of Gad, the gate of Asher, and the gate of Naphtali. ³⁵ The perimeter of the City is eighteen thousand cubits. The name of the City shall henceforth be "The LORD is here."

Daniel

Daniel Chapter 1

¹ In the third year of the reign of Jehoiakim, king of Judah, King Nebuchadnezzar of Babylon came and laid siege to Jerusalem. ² The Lord handed over to him Jehoiakim, king of Judah, and some of the vessels of the temple of God, which he carried off to the land of Shinar, and placed in the temple treasury of his god. ³ The king told Ashpenaz, his chief chamberlain, to bring in some of the Israelites of royal blood and of the nobility, ⁴ young men without any defect, handsome, intelligent and wise, quick to learn, and prudent in judgment, such as could take their place in the king's palace; they were to be taught the language and literature of the Chaldeans; ⁵ after three years' training they were to enter the king's service. The king allotted them a daily portion of food and wine from the royal table. ⁶ Among these were men of Judah: Daniel, Hananiah, Mishael, and Azariah. ⁷ The chief chamberlain changed their names: Daniel to Belteshazzar, Hananiah to Shadrach, Mishael to Meshach, and Azariah to Abednego. ⁸ But Daniel was resolved not to defile himself with the king's food or wine; so he begged the chief chamberlain to spare him this defilement. ⁹ Though God had given Daniel the favor and sympathy of the chief chamberlain, ¹⁰ he nevertheless said to Daniel, "I am afraid of my lord the king; it is he who allotted your food and drink. If he sees that you look wretched by comparison with the other young men of your age, you will endanger my life with the king." ¹¹ Then Daniel said to the steward whom the chief chamberlain had put in charge of Daniel, Hananiah, Mishael, and Azariah, ¹² "Please test your servants for ten days. Give us vegetables to eat and water to drink. ¹³ Then see how we look in comparison with the other young men who eat from the royal table, and treat your servants according to what you see." ¹⁴ He acceded to this request, and tested them for ten days; ¹⁵ after ten days they looked healthier and better fed than any of the young men who ate from the royal table. ¹⁶ So the

steward continued to take away the food and wine they were to receive, and gave them vegetables. 17 To these four young men God gave knowledge and proficiency in all literature and science, and to Daniel the understanding of all visions and dreams. 18 At the end of the time the king had specified for their preparation, the chief chamberlain brought them before Nebuchadnezzar. 19 When the king had spoken with all of them, none was found equal to Daniel, Hananiah, Mishael, and Azariah; and so they entered the king's service. 20 In any question of wisdom or prudence which the king put to them, he found them ten times better than all the magicians and enchanters in his kingdom. 21 Daniel remained there until the first year of King Cyrus.

Daniel Chapter 2

1 In the second year of his reign, King Nebuchadnezzar had a dream which left his spirit no rest and robbed him of his sleep. 2 So he ordered that the magicians, enchanters, sorcerers, and Chaldeans be summoned to interpret the dream for him. When they came and presented themselves to the king, 3 he said to them, "I had a dream which will allow my spirit no rest until I know what it means." 4 The Chaldeans answered the king (Aramaic): "O king, live forever! Tell your servants the dream and we will give its meaning." 5 The king answered the Chaldeans, "This is what I have decided: unless you tell me the dream and its meaning, you shall be cut to pieces and your houses destroyed. 6 But if you tell me the dream and its meaning, you shall receive from me gifts and presents and great honors. Now tell me the dream and its meaning." 7 Again they answered, "Let the king tell his servants the dream and we will give its meaning." 8 But the king replied: "I know for certain that you are bargaining for time, since you know what I have decided. 9 If you do not tell me the dream, there can be but one decree for you. You have framed a false and deceitful interpretation to present me with till the crisis is past. Tell me the dream, therefore, that I may be sure that you can also give its correct interpretation." 10 The Chaldeans answered the king: "There is not a man on earth who can do what you ask, O king; never has any king, however great and mighty, asked such a thing of any magician, enchanter, or Chaldean. 11 What you demand, O king, is too difficult; there is no one who can tell it to the king except the gods who do not dwell among men." 12 At this the king became violently angry and ordered all the wise men of Babylon to be put to death. 13 When the decree was issued that the wise men should be slain, Daniel and his companions were also sought out. 14 Then Daniel prudently took counsel with Arioch, the captain of the king's guard, who had set out to kill the wise men of Babylon: 15 "O officer of the king," he asked, "what is the reason for this harsh order from the king?" When Arioch told him, 16 Daniel went and asked for time from the king, that he might give him the interpretation. 17 Daniel went home and informed his companions Hananiah, Mishael, and Azariah, 18 that they might implore the mercy of the God of heaven in regard to this mystery, so that Daniel and his companions might not perish with the rest of the wise men of Babylon. 19 During the night the mystery was revealed to Daniel in a vision, and he blessed the God of heaven: 20 "Blessed be the name of God forever and ever, for wisdom and power are his. 21 He causes the changes of the times and seasons, makes kings and unmakes them. He gives wisdom to the wise and knowledge to those who understand. 22 He reveals deep and hidden things and knows what is in the darkness, for the light dwells with him. 23 To you, O God of my fathers, I give thanks and praise, because you have given me wisdom and power. Now you have shown me what we asked of you, you have made known to us the king's dream." 24 So Daniel went to Arioch, whom the king had appointed to destroy the wise men of Babylon, and said to him, "Do not put the wise men of Babylon to death. Bring me before the king, and I will tell him the interpretation of the dream." Arioch quickly brought Daniel to the king and said, 25 "I have found a man among the Judean captives who can give the interpretation to the king." 26 The king asked Daniel, whose name was Belteshazzar, "Can you tell me the dream that I had, and its meaning?" 27 In the king's presence Daniel made this reply: "The mystery about which the king has inquired, the wise men, enchanters, magicians, and astrologers could not explain to the king. 28 But there is a God in heaven who reveals mysteries, and he has shown King Nebuchadnezzar what is to happen in days to come; this was the dream you saw as you lay in bed. 29 To you in your bed there came thoughts about what should happen in the future, and he who reveals mysteries showed you what is to be. 30 To me also this mystery has been revealed; not that I am wiser than any other living person, but in order that its meaning may be made known to the king, that you may understand the thoughts in your own mind. 31 "In your vision, O king, you saw a statue, very large and exceedingly bright, terrifying in appearance as it stood before you. 32 The head of the statue was pure gold, its chest and arms were silver, its belly and thighs bronze, 33 the legs iron, its feet partly iron and partly

tile. 34 While you looked at the statue, a stone which was hewn from a mountain without a hand being put to it, struck its iron and tile feet, breaking them in pieces. 35 The iron, tile, bronze, silver, and gold all crumbled at once, fine as the chaff on the threshing floor in summer, and the wind blew them away without leaving a trace. But the stone that struck the statue became a great mountain and filled the whole earth. 36 "This was the dream; the interpretation we shall give in the king's presence. 37 You, O king, are the king of kings; to you the God of heaven has given dominion and strength, power and glory; 38 men, wild beasts, and birds of the air, wherever they may dwell, he has handed over to you, making you ruler over them all; you are the head of gold. 39 Another kingdom shall take your place, inferior to yours, then a third kingdom, of bronze, which shall rule over the whole earth. 40 There shall be a fourth kingdom, strong as iron; it shall break in pieces and subdue all these others, just as iron breaks in pieces and crushes everything else. 41 The feet and toes you saw, partly of potter's tile and partly of iron, mean that it shall be a divided kingdom, but yet have some of the hardness of iron. As you saw the iron mixed with clay tile, 42 and the toes partly iron and partly tile, the kingdom shall be partly strong and partly fragile. 43 The iron mixed with clay tile means that they shall seal their alliances by intermarriage, but they shall not stay united, any more than iron mixes with clay. 44 In the lifetime of those kings the God of heaven will set up a kingdom that shall never be destroyed or delivered up to another people; rather, it shall break in pieces all these kingdoms and put an end to them, and it shall stand forever. 45 That is the meaning of the stone you saw hewn from the mountain without a hand being put to it, which broke in pieces the tile, iron, bronze, silver, and gold. The great God has revealed to the king what shall be in the future; this is exactly what you dreamed, and its meaning is sure." 46 Then King Nebuchadnezzar fell down and worshiped Daniel and ordered sacrifice and incense offered to him. 47 To Daniel the king said, "Truly your God is the God of gods and Lord of kings and a revealer of mysteries; that is why you were able to reveal this mystery." 48 He advanced Daniel to a high post, gave him many generous presents, made him ruler of the whole province of Babylon and chief prefect over all the wise men of Babylon. 49 At Daniel's request the king made Shadrach, Meshach, and Abednego administrators of the province of Babylon, while Daniel himself remained at the king's court.

Daniel Chapter 3

1 King Nebuchadnezzar had a golden statue made, sixty cubits high and six cubits wide, which he set up in the plain of Dura in the province of Babylon. 2 He then ordered the satraps, prefects, and governors, the counselors, treasurers, judges, magistrates and all the officials of the provinces to be summoned to the dedication of the statue which he had set up. 3 The satraps, prefects, and governors, the counselors, treasurers, judges, and magistrates and all the officials of the provinces, all these came together for the dedication and stood before the statue which King Nebuchadnezzar had set up. 4 A herald cried out: "Nations and peoples of every language, when you hear the sound of the trumpet, flute, lyre, harp, psaltery, bagpipe, and all the other musical instruments, 5 you are ordered to fall down and worship the golden statue which King Nebuchadnezzar has set up. 6 Whoever does not fall down and worship shall be instantly cast into a white-hot furnace." 7 Therefore, as soon as they heard the sound of the trumpet, flute, lyre, harp, psaltery, bagpipe, and all the other musical instruments, the nations and peoples of every language all fell down and worshiped the golden statue which King Nebuchadnezzar had set up. 8 At that point, some of the Chaldeans came and accused the Jews 9 to King Nebuchadnezzar: "O king, live forever! 10 O king, you issued a decree that everyone who heard the sound of the trumpet, flute, lyre, harp, psaltery, bagpipe, and all the other musical instruments should fall down and worship the golden statue; 11 whoever did not was to be cast into a white-hot furnace. 12 There are certain Jews whom you have made administrators of the province of Babylon: Shadrach, Meshach, Abednego; these men, O king, have paid no attention to you; they will not serve your god or worship the golden statue which you set up." 13 Nebuchadnezzar flew into a rage and sent for Shadrach, Meshach, and Abednego, who were promptly brought before the king. 14 King Nebuchadnezzar questioned them: "Is it true, Shadrach, Meshach, and Abednego, that you will not serve my god, or worship the golden statue that I set up? 15 Be ready now to fall down and worship the statue I had made, whenever you hear the sound of the trumpet, flute, lyre, harp, psaltery, bagpipe, and all the other musical instruments; otherwise, you shall be instantly cast into the white-hot furnace; and who is the God that can deliver you out of my hands?" 16 Shadrach, Meshach, and Abednego answered King Nebuchadnezzar, "There is no need for us to defend ourselves before you in this matter. 17 If our God, whom we

serve, can save us from the white-hot furnace and from your hands, O king, may he save us! 18 But even if he will not, know, O king, that we will not serve your god or worship the golden statue which you set up." 19 Nebuchadnezzar's face became livid with utter rage against Shadrach, Meshach, and Abednego. He ordered the furnace to be heated seven times more than usual 20 and had some of the strongest men in his army bind Shadrach, Meshach, and Abednego and cast them into the white-hot furnace. 21 They were bound and cast into the white-hot furnace with their coats, hats, shoes and other garments, 22 for the king's order was urgent. So huge a fire was kindled in the furnace that the flames devoured the men who threw Shadrach, Meshach, and Abednego into it. 23 But these three fell, bound, into the midst of the white-hot furnace

Prayer of Azariah and the Songs of the Three Holy Children

(Continuation of Daniel Chapter 3)
The Three Holy Children Chapter 3

24 They walked about in the flames, singing to God and blessing the Lord. 25 In the fire Azariah stood up and prayed aloud: 26 "Blessed are you, and praiseworthy, O Lord, the God of our fathers, and glorious forever is your name. 27 For you are just in all you have done; all your deeds are faultless, all your ways right, and all your judgments proper. 28 You have executed proper judgments in all that you have brought upon us and upon Jerusalem, the holy city of our fathers. By a proper judgment you have done all this because of our sins; 29 For we have sinned and transgressed by departing from you, and we have done every kind of evil. 30 Your commandments we have not heeded or observed, nor have we done as you ordered us for our good. 31 Therefore all you have brought upon us, all you have done to us, you have done by a proper judgment. 32 You have handed us over to our enemies, lawless and hateful rebels; to an unjust king, the worst in all the world. 33 Now we cannot open our mouths; we, your servants, who revere you, have become a shame and a reproach. 34 For your name's sake, do not deliver us up forever, or make void your covenant. 35 Do not take away your mercy from us, for the sake of Abraham, your beloved, Isaac your servant, and Israel your holy one, 36 To whom you promised to multiply their offspring like the stars of heaven, or the sand on the shore of the sea. 37 For we are reduced, O Lord, beyond any other nation, brought low everywhere in the world this day because of our sins. 38 We have in our day no prince, prophet, or leader, no holocaust, sacrifice, oblation, or incense, no place to offer first fruits, to find favor with you. 39 But with contrite heart and humble spirit let us be received; 40 As though it were holocausts of rams and bullocks, or thousands of fat lambs, So let our sacrifice be in your presence today as we follow you unreservedly; for those who trust in you cannot be put to shame. 41 And now we follow you with our whole heart, we fear you and we pray to you. 42 Do not let us be put to shame, but deal with us in your kindness and great mercy. 43 Deliver us by your wonders, and bring glory to your name, O Lord: 44 Let all those be routed who inflict evils on your servants; Let them be shamed and powerless, and their strength broken; 45 Let them know that you alone are the Lord God, glorious over the whole world." 46 Now the king's men who had thrown them in continued to stoke the furnace with brimstone, pitch, tow, and faggots. 47 The flames rose forty-nine cubits above the furnace, 48 and spread out, burning the Chaldeans nearby. 49 But the angel of the Lord went down into the furnace with Azariah and his companions, drove the fiery flames out of the furnace, 50 and made the inside of the furnace as though a dew-laden breeze were blowing through it. The fire in no way touched them or caused them pain or harm. 51 Then these three in the furnace with one voice sang, glorifying and blessing God: 52 "Blessed are you, O Lord, the God of our fathers, praiseworthy and exalted above all forever; And blessed is your holy and glorious name, praiseworthy and exalted above all for all ages. 53 Blessed are you in the temple of your holy glory, praiseworthy and glorious above all forever. 54 Blessed are you on the throne of your kingdom, praiseworthy and exalted above all forever. 55 Blessed are you who look into the depths from your throne upon the cherubim, praiseworthy and exalted above all forever. 56 Blessed are you in the firmament of heaven, praiseworthy and glorious forever. 57 Bless the Lord, all you works of the Lord, praise and exalt him above all forever. 58 Angels of the Lord, bless the Lord, praise and exalt him above all forever. 59 You heavens, bless the Lord, praise and exalt him above all forever. 60 All you waters above the heavens, bless the Lord, praise and exalt him above all forever. 61 All you hosts of the Lord, bless the Lord; praise and exalt him above all forever. 62 Sun and moon, bless the Lord; praise and exalt him above all forever. 63 Stars of heaven,

bless the Lord; praise and exalt him above all forever. 64 Every shower and dew, bless the Lord; praise and exalt him above all forever. 65 All you winds, bless the Lord; praise and exalt him above all forever. 66 Fire and heat, bless the Lord; praise and exalt him above all forever. 67 Cold and chill, bless the Lord; praise and exalt him above all forever. 68 Dew and rain, bless the Lord; praise and exalt him above all forever. 69 Frost and chill, bless the Lord; praise and exalt him above all forever. 70 Ice and snow, bless the Lord; praise and exalt him above all forever. 71 Nights and days, bless the Lord; praise and exalt him above all forever. 72 Light and darkness, bless the Lord; praise and exalt him above all forever. 73 Lightnings and clouds, bless the Lord; praise and exalt him above all forever. 74 Let the earth bless the Lord, praise and exalt him above all forever. 75 Mountains and hills, bless the Lord; praise and exalt him above all forever. 76 Everything growing from the earth, bless the Lord; praise and exalt him above all forever. 77 You springs, bless the Lord; praise and exalt him above all forever. 78 Seas and rivers, bless the Lord; praise and exalt him above all forever. 79 You dolphins and all water creatures, bless the Lord; praise and exalt him above all forever. 80 All you birds of the air, bless the Lord; praise and exalt him above all forever. 81 All you beasts, wild and tame, bless the Lord; praise and exalt him above all forever. 82 You sons of men, bless the Lord; praise and exalt him above all forever. 83 O Israel, bless the Lord; praise and exalt him above all forever. 84 Priests of the Lord, bless the Lord; praise and exalt him above all forever. 85 Servants of the Lord, bless the Lord; praise and exalt him above all forever. 86 Spirits and souls of the just, bless the Lord; praise and exalt him above all forever. 87 Holy men of humble heart, bless the Lord; praise and exalt him above all forever. 88 Hananiah, Azariah, Mishael, bless the Lord; praise and exalt him above all forever. For he has delivered us from the nether world, and saved us from the power of death; He has freed us from the raging flame and delivered us from the fire. 89 Give thanks to the Lord, for he is good, for his mercy endures forever. 90 Bless the God of gods, all you who fear the Lord; praise him and give him thanks, because his mercy endures forever." Hearing them sing, and astonished at seeing them alive, 91 King Nebuchadnezzar rose in haste and asked his nobles, "Did we not cast three men bound into the fire?" "Assuredly, O king," they answered. 92 "But," he replied, "I see four men unfettered and unhurt, walking in the fire, and the fourth looks like a son of God." 93 Then Nebuchadnezzar came to the opening of the white-hot furnace and called to Shadrach, Meshach, and Abednego: "Servants of the most high God, come out." Thereupon Shadrach, Meshach, and Abednego came out of the fire. 94 When the satraps, prefects, governors, and nobles of the king came together, they saw that the fire had had no power over the bodies of these men; not a hair of their heads had been singed, nor were their garments altered; there was not even a smell of fire about them. 95 Nebuchadnezzar exclaimed, "Blessed be the God of Shadrach, Meshach, and Abednego, who sent his angel to deliver the servants that trusted in him; they disobeyed the royal command and yielded their bodies rather than serve or worship any god except their own God. 96 Therefore I decree for nations and peoples of every language that whoever blasphemes the God of Shadrach, Meshach, and Abednego shall be cut to pieces and his house destroyed. For there is no other God who can rescue like this." 97 Then the king promoted Shadrach, Meshach, and Abednego in the province of Babylon. 98 King Nebuchadnezzar to the nations and peoples of every language, wherever they dwell on earth: abundant peace! 99 It has seemed good to me to publish the signs and wonders which the most high God has accomplished in my regard. 100 How great are his signs, how mighty his wonders; his kingdom is an everlasting kingdom, and his dominion endures through all generations.

The Three Holy Children Chapter 4

1 I, Nebuchadnezzar, was at home in my palace, content and prosperous. 2 I had a terrifying dream as I lay in bed, and the images and the visions of my mind frightened me. 3 So I issued a decree that all the wise men of Babylon should be brought before me to give the interpretation of the dream. 4 When the magicians, enchanters, Chaldeans, and astrologers had come in, I related the dream before them; but none of them could tell me its meaning. 5 Finally there came before me Daniel, whose name is Belteshazzar after the name of my god, and in whom is the spirit of the holy God. I repeated the dream to him: 6 "Belteshazzar, chief of the magicians, I know that the spirit of the holy God is in you and no mystery is too difficult for you; tell me the meaning of the visions that I saw in my dream. 7 "These were the visions I saw while in bed: I saw a tree of great height at the center of the world. 8 It was large and strong, with its top touching the heavens, and it could be seen to the ends of the earth. 9 Its leaves were beautiful and its fruit abundant, providing food for all. Under it the wild beasts found shade, in its branches the birds of the air nested; all men ate of it. 10 In the

vision I saw while in bed, a holy sentinel came down from heaven, 11 and cried out: 'Cut down the tree and lop off its branches, strip off its leaves and scatter its fruit; let the beasts flee its shade, and the birds its branches. 12 But leave in the earth its stump and roots, fettered with iron and bronze, in the grass of the field. Let him be bathed with the dew of heaven; his lot be to eat, among beasts, the grass of the earth. 13 Let his mind be changed from the human; let him be given the sense of a beast, till seven years pass over him. 14 By decree of the sentinels is this decided, by order of the holy ones, this sentence; that all who live may know that the Most High rules over the kingdom of men: He can give it to whom he will, or set over it the lowliest of men.' 15 "This is the dream that I, King Nebuchadnezzar, had. Now, Belteshazzar, tell me its meaning. Although none of the wise men in my kingdom can tell me the meaning, you can, because the spirit of the holy God is in you." 16 Then Daniel, whose name was Belteshazzar, was appalled for a while, terrified by his thoughts. "Belteshazzar," the king said to him, "let not the dream or its meaning terrify you." 17 "My lord," Belteshazzar replied, "this dream should be for your enemies, and its meaning for your foes. The large, strong tree that you saw, with its top touching the heavens, that could be seen by the whole earth, 18 which had beautiful foliage and abundant fruit, providing food for all, under which the wild beasts lived, and in whose branches the birds of the air dwelt— 19 you are that tree, O king, large and strong! Your majesty has become so great as to touch the heavens, and your rule extends over the whole earth. 20 As for the king's vision of a holy sentinel that came down from heaven and proclaimed: 'Cut down the tree and destroy it, but leave in the earth its stump and roots, fettered with iron and bronze in the grass of the field; let him be bathed with the dew of heaven, and let his lot be among wild beasts till seven years pass over him'—this is its meaning, O king; this is the sentence which the Most High has passed upon my lord king: 21 You shall be cast out from among men and dwell with wild beasts; you shall be given grass to eat like an ox and be bathed with the dew of heaven; seven years shall pass over you, until you know that the Most High rules over the kingdom of men and gives it to whom he will. 22 The command that the stump and roots of the tree are to be left means that your kingdom shall be preserved for you, once you have learned it is heaven that rules. 23 Therefore, O king, take my advice; atone for your sins by good deeds, and for your misdeeds by kindness to the poor; then your prosperity will be long." 24 All this happened to King Nebuchadnezzar. 25 Twelve months later, as he was walking on the roof of the royal palace in Babylon, 26 the king said, "Babylon the great! Was it not I, with my great strength, who built it as a royal residence for my splendor and majesty?" 27 While these words were still on the king's lips, a voice spoke from heaven, "It has been decreed for you, King Nebuchadnezzar, that your kingdom is taken from you! 28 You shall be cast out from among men, and shall dwell with wild beasts; you shall be given grass to eat like an ox, and seven years shall pass over you, until you learn that the Most High rules over the kingdom of men and gives it to whom he will." 29 At once this was fulfilled. Nebuchadnezzar was cast out from among men, he ate grass like an ox, and his body was bathed with the dew of heaven, until his hair grew like the feathers of an eagle, and his nails like the claws of a bird. 30 When this period was over, I, Nebuchadnezzar, raised my eyes to heaven; my reason was restored to me, and I blessed the Most High, I praised and glorified him who lives forever: His dominion is an everlasting dominion, and his kingdom endures through all generations. 31 All who live on the earth are counted as nothing; he does as he pleases with the powers of heaven as well as with those who live on the earth. There is no one who can stay his hand or say to him, "What have you done?" 32 At the same time my reason returned to me, and for the glory of my kingdom, my majesty and my splendor returned to me. My nobles and lords sought me out; I was restored to my kingdom, and became much greater than before. 33 Therefore, I, Nebuchadnezzar, now praise and exalt and glorify the King of heaven, because all his works are right and his ways just; and those who walk in pride he is able to humble.

The Three Holy Children Chapter 5

1 King Belshazzar gave a great banquet for a thousand of his lords, with whom he drank. 2 Under the influence of the wine, he ordered the gold and silver vessels which Nebuchadnezzar, his father, had taken from the temple in Jerusalem, to be brought in so that the king, his lords, his wives and his entertainers might drink from them. 3 When the gold and silver vessels taken from the house of God in Jerusalem had been brought in, and while the king, his lords, his wives and his entertainers were drinking 4 wine from them, they praised their gods of gold and silver, bronze and iron, wood and stone. 5 Suddenly, opposite the lampstand, the fingers of a human hand appeared, writing on the plaster of the wall in the king's palace. When the king saw the wrist and hand that wrote, 6 his face blanched; his thoughts terrified him, his hip

joints shook, and his knees knocked. 7 The king shouted for the enchanters, Chaldeans, and astrologers to be brought in. "Whoever reads this writing and tells me what it means," he said to the wise men of Babylon, "shall be clothed in purple, wear a golden collar about his neck, and be third in the government of the kingdom." 8 But though all the king's wise men came in, none of them could either read the writing or tell the king what it meant. 9 Then King Belshazzar was greatly terrified; his face went ashen, and his lords were thrown into confusion. 10 When the queen heard of the discussion between the king and his lords, she entered the banquet hall and said, "O king, live forever! Be not troubled in mind, nor look so pale! 11 There is a man in your kingdom in whom is the spirit of the holy God; during the lifetime of your father he was seen to have brilliant knowledge and god-like wisdom. In fact, King Nebuchadnezzar, your father, made him chief of the magicians, enchanters, Chaldeans, and astrologers, 12 because of the extraordinary mind possessed by this Daniel, whom the king named Belteshazzar. He knew and understood how to interpret dreams, explain enigmas, and solve difficulties. Now therefore, summon Daniel to tell you what this means." 13 Then Daniel was brought into the presence of the king. The king asked him, "Are you the Daniel, the Jewish exile, whom my father, the king, brought from Judah? 14 I have heard that the spirit of God is in you, that you possess brilliant knowledge and extraordinary wisdom. 15 Now, the wise men and enchanters were brought in to me to read this writing and tell me its meaning, but they could not say what the words meant. 16 But I have heard that you can interpret dreams and solve difficulties; if you are able to read the writing and tell me what it means, you shall be clothed in purple, wear a gold collar about your neck, and be third in the government of the kingdom." 17 Daniel answered the king: "You may keep your gifts, or give your presents to someone else; but the writing I will read for you, O king, and tell you what it means. 18 The Most High God gave your father Nebuchadnezzar a great kingdom and glorious majesty. 19 Because he made him so great, the nations and peoples of every language dreaded and feared him. Whomever he wished, he killed or let live; whomever he wished, he exalted or humbled. 20 But when his heart became proud and his spirit hardened by insolence, he was put down from his royal throne and deprived of his glory; 21 he was cast out from among men and was made insensate as a beast; he lived with wild asses, and ate grass like an ox; his body was bathed with the dew of heaven, until he learned that the Most High God rules over the kingdom of men and appoints over it whom he will. 22 You, his son, Belshazzar, have not humbled your heart, though you knew all this; 23 you have rebelled against the Lord of heaven. You had the vessels of his temple brought before you, so that you and your nobles, your wives and your entertainers, might drink wine from them; and you praised the gods of silver and gold, bronze and iron, wood and stone, that neither see nor hear nor have intelligence. But the God in whose hand is your life breath and the whole course of your life, you did not glorify. 24By him were the wrist and hand sent, and the writing set down. 25 "This is the writing that was inscribed: MENE, TEKEL, and PERES. These words mean: 26 MENE, God has numbered your kingdom and put an end to it; 27 TEKEL, you have been weighed on the scales and found wanting; 28 PERES, your kingdom has been divided and given to the Medes and Persians." 29 Then by order of Belshazzar they clothed Daniel in purple, with a gold collar about his neck, and proclaimed him third in the government of the kingdom. 30 The same night Belshazzar, the Chaldean king, was slain:

The Three Holy Children Chapter 6

1 And Darius the Mede succeeded to the kingdom at the age of sixty-two. 2 Darius decided to appoint over his entire kingdom one hundred and twenty satraps, to safeguard his interests; 3 these were accountable to three supervisors, one of whom was Daniel. 4 Daniel outshone all the supervisors and satraps because an extraordinary spirit was in him, and the king thought of giving him authority over the entire kingdom. 5 Therefore the supervisors and satraps tried to find grounds for accusation against Daniel as regards the administration. But they could accuse him of no wrongdoing; because he was trustworthy, no fault of neglect or misconduct was to be found in him. 6 Then these men said to themselves, "We shall find no grounds for accusation against this Daniel unless by way of the law of his God." 7 So these supervisors and satraps went thronging to the king and said to him, "King Darius, live forever! 8 All the supervisors of the kingdom, the prefects, satraps, nobles, and governors are agreed that the following prohibition ought to be put in force by royal decree: no one is to address any petition to god or man for thirty days, except to you, O king; otherwise he shall be cast into a den of lions. 9 Now, O king, issue the prohibition over your signature, immutable and irrevocable under Mede and Persian law." 10 So King Darius signed the prohibition and made it law. 11 Even after

Daniel heard that this law had been signed, he continued his custom of going home to kneel in prayer and give thanks to his God in the upper chamber three times a day, with the windows open toward Jerusalem. [12] So these men rushed in and found Daniel praying and pleading before his God. [13] Then they went to remind the king about the prohibition: "Did you not decree, O king, that no one is to address a petition to god or man for thirty days, except to you, O king; otherwise he shall be cast into a den of lions?" The king answered them, "The decree is absolute, irrevocable under the Mede and Persian law." [14] To this they replied, "Daniel, the Jewish exile, has paid no attention to you, O king, or to the decree you issued; three times a day he offers his prayer." [15] The king was deeply grieved at this news and he made up his mind to save Daniel; he worked till sunset to rescue him. [16] But these men insisted. "Keep in mind, O king," they said, "that under the Mede and Persian law every royal prohibition or decree is irrevocable." [17] So the king ordered Daniel to be brought and cast into the lions' den. To Daniel he said, "May your God, whom you serve so constantly, save you." [18] To forestall any tampering, the king sealed with his own ring and the rings of the lords the stone that had been brought to block the opening of the den. [19] Then the king returned to his palace for the night; he refused to eat and he dismissed the entertainers. Since sleep was impossible for him, [20] the king rose very early the next morning and hastened to the lions' den. [21] As he drew near, he cried out to Daniel sorrowfully, "O Daniel, servant of the living God, has the God whom you serve so constantly been able to save you from the lions?" [22] Daniel answered the king: "O king, live forever! [23] My God has sent his angel and closed the lions' mouths so that they have not hurt me. For I have been found innocent before him; neither to you have I done any harm, O king!" [24] This gave the king great joy. At his order Daniel was removed from the den, unhurt because he trusted in his God. [25] The king then ordered the men who had accused Daniel, along with their children and their wives, to be cast into the lions' den. Before they reached the bottom of the den, the lions overpowered them and crushed all their bones. [26] Then King Darius wrote to the nations and peoples of every language, wherever they dwell on the earth: "All peace to you! [27] I decree that throughout my royal domain the God of Daniel is to be reverenced and feared: 'For he is the living God, enduring forever; his kingdom shall not be destroyed, and his dominion shall be without end. [28] He is a deliverer and savior, working signs and wonders in heaven and on earth, and he delivered Daniel from the lions' power.'" [29] So Daniel fared well during the reign of Darius and the reign of Cyrus the Persian.

The Three Holy Children Chapter 7

[1] In the first year of King Belshazzar of Babylon, Daniel had a dream as he lay in bed, and was terrified by the visions of his mind. Then he wrote down the dream; the account began: [2] In the vision I saw during the night, suddenly the four winds of heaven stirred up the great sea, [3] from which emerged four immense beasts, each different from the others. [4] The first was like a lion, but with eagle's wings. While I watched, the wings were plucked; it was raised from the ground to stand on two feet like a man, and given a human mind. [5] The second was like a bear; it was raised up on one side, and among the teeth in its mouth were three tusks. It was given the order, "Up, devour much flesh." [6] After this I looked and saw another beast, like a leopard; on its back were four wings like those of a bird, and it had four heads. To this beast dominion was given. [7] After this, in the visions of the night I saw the fourth beast, different from all the others, terrifying, horrible, and of extraordinary strength; it had great iron teeth with which it devoured and crushed, and what was left it trampled with its feet. [8] I was considering the ten horns it had, when suddenly another, a little horn, sprang out of their midst, and three of the previous horns were torn away to make room for it. This horn had eyes like a man, and a mouth that spoke arrogantly. [9] As I watched, Thrones were set up and the Ancient One took his throne. His clothing was snow bright, and the hair on his head as white as wool; His throne was flames of fire, with wheels of burning fire. [10] A surging stream of fire flowed out from where he sat; Thousands upon thousands were ministering to him, and myriads upon myriads attended him. The court was convened, and the books were opened. [11] I watched, then, from the first of the arrogant words which the horn spoke, until the beast was slain and its body thrown into the fire to be burnt up. [12] The other beasts, which also lost their dominion, were granted a prolongation of life for a time and a season. [13] As the visions during the night continued, I saw One like a son of man coming, on the clouds of heaven; When he reached the Ancient One and was presented before him, [14] He received dominion, glory, and kingship; nations and peoples of every language serve him. His dominion is an everlasting dominion that shall not be taken away, his kingship shall not be destroyed. [15] I, Daniel, found my spirit anguished within its sheath of

flesh, and I was terrified by the visions of my mind. [16] I approached one of those present and asked him what all this meant in truth; in answer, he made known to me the meaning of the things: [17] "These four great beasts stand for four kingdoms which shall arise on the earth. [18] But the holy ones of the Most High shall receive the kingship, to possess it forever and ever." [19] But I wished to make certain about the fourth beast, so very terrible and different from the others, devouring and crushing with its iron teeth and bronze claws, and trampling with its feet what was left; [20] about the ten horns on its head, and the other one that sprang up, before which three horns fell; about the horn with the eyes and the mouth that spoke arrogantly, which appeared greater than its fellows. [21] For, as I watched, that horn made war against the holy ones and was victorious [22] until the Ancient One arrived; judgment was pronounced in favor of the holy ones of the Most High, and the time came when the holy ones possessed the kingdom. [23] He answered me thus: "The fourth beast shall be a fourth kingdom on earth, different from all the others; It shall devour the whole earth, beat it down, and crush it. [24] The ten horns shall be ten kings rising out of that kingdom; another shall rise up after them, Different from those before him, who shall lay low three kings. [25] He shall speak against the Most High and oppress the holy ones of the Most High, thinking to change the feast days and the law. They shall be handed over to him for a year, two years, and a half-year. [26] But when the court is convened, and his power is taken away by final and absolute destruction, [27] Then the kingship and dominion and majesty of all the kingdoms under the heavens shall be given to the holy people of the Most High, Whose kingdom shall be everlasting: all dominions shall serve and obey him." [28] The report concluded: I, Daniel, was greatly terrified by my thoughts, and my face blanched, but I kept the matter to myself.

The Three Holy Children Chapter 8

[1] After this first vision, I, Daniel, had another, in the third year of the reign of King Belshazzar. [2] In my vision I saw myself in the fortress of Susa in the province of Elam; I was beside the river Ulai. [3] I looked up and saw standing by the river a ram with two great horns, the one larger and newer than the other. [4] I saw the ram butting toward the west, north, and south. No beast could withstand it or be rescued from its power; it did what it pleased and became very powerful. [5] As I was reflecting, a he-goat with a prominent horn on its forehead suddenly came from the west across the whole earth without touching the ground. [6] It approached the two-horned ram I had seen standing by the river, and rushed toward it with savage force. [7] I saw it attack the ram with furious blows when they met, and break both its horns. It threw the ram, which had not the force to withstand it, to the ground, and trampled upon it; and no one could rescue it from its power. [8] The he-goat became very powerful, but at the height of its power the great horn was shattered, and in its place came up four others, facing the four winds of heaven. [9] Out of one of them came a little horn which kept growing toward the south, the east, and the glorious country. [10] Its power extended to the host of heaven, so that it cast down to earth some of the host and some of the stars and trampled on them. [11] It boasted even against the prince of the host, from whom it removed the daily sacrifice, and whose sanctuary it cast down, [12] as well as the host, while sin replaced the daily sacrifice. It cast truth to the ground, and was succeeding in its undertaking. [13] I heard a holy one speaking, and another said to whichever one it was that spoke, "How long shall the events of this vision last concerning the daily sacrifice, the desolating sin which is placed there, the sanctuary, and the trampled host?" [14] He answered him, "For two thousand three hundred evenings and mornings; then the sanctuary shall be purified." [15] While I, Daniel, sought the meaning of the vision I had seen, a manlike figure stood before me, [16] and on the Ulai I heard a human voice that cried out, "Gabriel, explain the vision to this man." [17] When he came near where I was standing, I fell prostrate in terror. But he said to me, "Understand, son of man, that the vision refers to the end time." [18] As he spoke to me, I fell forward in a faint; he touched me and made me stand up. [19] "I will show you," he said, "what is to happen later in the period of wrath; for at the appointed time, there will be an end. [20] The two-horned ram you saw represents the kings of the Medes and Persians. [21] The he-goat is the king of the Greeks, and the great horn on its forehead is the first king. [22] The four that rose in its place when it was broken are four kingdoms that will issue from his nation, but without his strength. [23] After their reign, when sinners have reached their measure, there shall arise a king, impudent and skilled in intrigue. [24] He shall be strong and powerful, bring about fearful ruin, and succeed in his undertaking. He shall destroy powerful peoples; [25] his cunning shall be against the holy ones, his treacherous conduct shall succeed. He shall be proud of heart and destroy many by stealth. But when he rises against the prince of princes, he shall be broken without a hand being raised. [26] The vision

of the evenings and the mornings is true, as spoken; do you, however, keep this vision undisclosed, because the days are to be many." 27 I, Daniel, was weak and ill for some days; then I arose and took care of the king's affairs. But I was appalled at the vision, which I could not understand.

The Three Holy Children Chapter 9

1 It was the first year that Darius, son of Ahasuerus, of the race of the Medes, reigned over the kingdom of the Chaldeans; 2 in the first year of his reign I, Daniel, tried to understand in the Scriptures the counting of the years of which the LORD spoke to the prophet Jeremiah: that for the ruins of Jerusalem seventy years must be fulfilled. 3 I turned to the Lord God, pleading in earnest prayer, with fasting, sackcloth, and ashes. 4 I prayed to the LORD, my God, and confessed, "Ah, Lord, great and awesome God, you who keep your merciful covenant toward those who love you and observe your commandments! 5 We have sinned, been wicked and done evil; we have rebelled and departed from your commandments and your laws. 6 We have not obeyed your servants the prophets, who spoke in your name to our kings, our princes, our fathers, and all the people of the land. 7 Justice, O Lord, is on your side; we are shamefaced even to this day: the men of Judah, the residents of Jerusalem, and all Israel, near and far, in all the countries to which you have scattered them because of their treachery toward you. 8 O LORD, we are shamefaced, like our kings, our princes, and our fathers, for having sinned against you. 9 But yours, O Lord, our God, are compassion and forgiveness! Yet we rebelled against you 10 and paid no heed to your command, O LORD, our God, to live by the law you gave us through your servants the prophets. 11 Because all Israel transgressed your law and went astray, not heeding your voice, the sworn malediction, recorded in the law of Moses, the servant of God, was poured out over us for our sins. 12 You carried out the threats you spoke against us and against those who governed us, by bringing upon us in Jerusalem the greatest calamity that has ever occurred under heaven. 13 As it is written in the law of Moses, this calamity came full upon us. As we did not appease the LORD, our God, by turning back from our wickedness and recognizing his constancy, 14 so the LORD kept watch over the calamity and brought it upon us. You, O LORD, our God, are just in all that you have done, for we did not listen to your voice. 15 "Now, O Lord, our God, who led your people out of the land of Egypt with a strong hand, and made a name for yourself even to this day, we have sinned, we are guilty. 16 O Lord, in keeping with all your just deeds, let your anger and your wrath be turned away from your city Jerusalem, your holy mountain. On account of our sins and the crimes of our fathers, Jerusalem and your people have become the reproach of all our neighbors. 17 Hear, therefore, O God, the prayer and petition of your servant; and for your own sake, O Lord, let your face shine upon your desolate sanctuary. 18 Give ear, O my God, and listen; open your eyes and see our ruins and the city which bears your name. When we present our petition before you, we rely not on our just deeds, but on your great mercy. 19 O Lord, hear! O Lord, pardon! O Lord, be attentive and act without delay, for your own sake, O my God, because this city and your people bear your name!" 20 I was still occupied with my prayer, confessing my sin and the sin of my people Israel, presenting my petition to the LORD, my God, on behalf of his holy mountain I 21 was still occupied with this prayer, when Gabriel, the one whom I had seen before in vision, came to me in rapid flight at the time of the evening sacrifice. 22 He instructed me in these words: "Daniel, I have now come to give you understanding. 23 When you began your petition, an answer was given which I have come to announce, because you are beloved. Therefore, mark the answer and understand the vision. 24 Seventy weeks are decreed for your people and for your holy city: Then transgression will stop and sin will end, guilt will be expiated, Everlasting justice will be introduced, vision and prophecy ratified, and a most holy will be anointed. 25 Know and understand this: From the utterance of the word that Jerusalem was to be rebuilt until one who is anointed and a leader, there shall be seven weeks. During sixty-two weeks it shall be rebuilt, with streets and trenches, in time of affliction. 26 After the sixty-two weeks an anointed shall be cut down when he does not possess the city; and the people of a leader who will come shall destroy the sanctuary. Then the end shall come like a torrent; until the end there shall be war, the desolation that is decreed. 27 For one week he shall make a firm compact with the many; half the week he shall abolish sacrifice and oblation; on the temple wing shall be the horrible abomination until the ruin that is decreed is poured out upon the horror."

The Three Holy Children Chapter 10

1 In the third year of Cyrus, king of Persia, a revelation was given to Daniel, who had been named Belteshazzar. The revelation was certain:

a great war; he understood it from the vision. 2 In those days, I, Daniel, mourned three full weeks. 3 I ate no savory food, I took no meat or wine, and I did not anoint myself at all until the end of the three weeks. 4 On the twenty-fourth day of the first month I was on the bank of the great river, the Tigris. 5 As I looked up, I saw a man dressed in linen with a belt of fine gold around his waist. 6 His body was like chrysolite, his face shown like lightning, his eyes were like fiery torches, his arms and feet looked like burnished bronze, and his voice sounded like the roar of a multitude. 7 I alone, Daniel, saw the vision; but great fear seized the men who were with me; they fled and hid themselves, although they did not see the vision. 8 So I was left alone, seeing this great vision. No strength remained in me; I turned the color of death and was powerless. 9 When I heard the sound of his voice, I fell face forward in a faint. 10 But then a hand touched me, raising me to my hands and knees. 11 "Daniel, beloved," he said to me, "understand the words which I am speaking to you; stand up, for my mission now is to you." When he said this to me, I stood up trembling. 12 "Fear not, Daniel," he continued; "from the first day you made up your mind to acquire understanding and humble yourself before God, your prayer was heard. Because of it I started out, 13 but the prince of the kingdom of Persia stood in my way for twenty-one days, until finally Michael, one of the chief princes, came to help me. I left him there with the prince of the kings of Persia, 14 and came to make you understand what shall happen to your people in the days to come; for there is yet a vision concerning those days." 15 While he was speaking thus to me, I fell forward and kept silent. 16 Then something like a man's hand touched my lips; I opened my mouth and said to the one facing me, "My lord, I was seized with pangs at the vision and I was powerless. 17 How can my lord's servant speak with you, my lord? For now no strength or even breath is left in me." 18 The one who looked like a man touched me again and strengthened me, saying, 19 "Fear not, beloved, you are safe; take courage and be strong." 20 When he spoke to me, I grew strong and said, "Speak, my lord, for you have strengthened me." "Do you know," he asked, "why I have come to you? Soon I must fight the prince of Persia again. When I leave, the prince of Greece will come; 21 but I shall tell you what is written in the truthful book. No one supports me against all these except Michael, your prince.

The Three Holy Children Chapter 11

1 Standing as a reinforcement and a bulwark for me. 2 Now I shall tell you the truth. "Three kings of Persia are yet to come; and a fourth shall acquire the greatest riches of all. Strengthened by his riches, he shall rouse all the kingdom of Greece. 3 But a powerful king shall appear and rule with great might, doing as he pleases. 4 No sooner shall he appear than his kingdom shall be broken and divided in four directions under heaven; but not among his descendants or in keeping with his mighty rule, for his kingdom shall be torn to pieces and belong to others than they. 5 "The king of the south shall grow strong, but one of his princes shall grow stronger still and govern a domain greater than his. 6 After some years they shall become allies: the daughter of the king of the south shall come to the king of the north in the interest of peace. But her bid for power shall fail: and her line shall not be recognized, and she shall be given up, together with those who brought her, her son and her husband. But later 7 a descendant of her line shall succeed to his rank, and shall come against the rampart and enter the stronghold of the king of the north, and conquer them. 8 Even their gods, with their molten images and their precious vessels of silver and gold, he shall carry away as booty into Egypt. For years he shall have nothing to do with the king of the north. 9 Then the latter shall invade the land of the king of the south, and return to his own country. 10 But his sons shall prepare and assemble a great armed host, which shall advance like a flood, then withdraw. When it returns and surges around the stronghold, 11 the king of the south, provoked, shall go out to fight against the king of the north, whose great host shall make a stand but shall be given into his hand 12 and be carried off. In the pride of his heart, he shall lay low tens of thousands, but he shall not triumph. 13 For the king of the north shall raise another army, greater than before; after some years he shall attack with this large army and great resources. 14 In those times many shall resist the king of the south, and outlaws of your people shall rise up in fulfillment of vision, but they shall fail. 15 When the king of the north comes, he shall set up siegeworks and take the fortified city by storm. The power of the south shall not withstand him, and not even his picked troops shall have the strength to resist. 16 He shall attack him and do as he pleases, with no one to withstand him. He shall stop in the glorious land, dealing destruction. 17 He shall set himself to penetrate the entire strength of his kingdom. He shall conclude an agreement with him and give him a daughter in marriage in order to destroy the kingdom, but this shall not succeed in his favor. 18 He shall turn to the coastland and take many, but a leader shall put an end to his shameful conduct, so that he cannot renew it against him. 19 He shall turn to the

strongholds of his own land, but shall stumble and fall, to be found no more. ²⁰ In his stead one shall arise who will send a tax collector through the glorious kingdom, but he shall soon be destroyed, though not in conflict or in battle. ²¹ "There shall rise in his place a despicable person, to whom the royal insignia shall not be given. By stealth and fraud he shall seize the kingdom. ²² Armed might shall be completely overwhelmed by him and crushed, and even the prince of the covenant. ²³ After allying with him, he shall treacherously rise to power with a small party. ²⁴ By stealth he shall enter prosperous provinces and do that which his fathers or grandfathers never did; he shall distribute spoil, booty, and riches among them and devise plots against their strongholds; but only for a time. ²⁵ He shall call on his strength and cleverness to meet the king of the south with a great army; the king of the south shall prepare for battle with a very large and strong army, but he shall not succeed because of the plots devised against him. ²⁶ Even his table companions shall seek to destroy him, his army shall be overwhelmed, and many shall fall slain. ²⁷ The two kings, resolved on evil, shall sit at table together and exchange lies, but they shall have no success, because the appointed end is not yet. ²⁸ "He shall turn back toward his land with great riches, his mind set against the holy covenant; he shall arrange matters and return to his land. ²⁹ At the time appointed he shall come again to the south, but this time it shall not be as before. ³⁰ When ships of the Kittim confront him, he shall lose heart and retreat. Then he shall direct his rage and energy against the holy covenant; those who forsake it he shall once more single out. ³¹ Armed forces shall move at his command and defile the sanctuary stronghold, abolishing the daily sacrifice and setting up the horrible abomination. ³² By his deceit he shall make some who were disloyal to the covenant apostatize; but those who remain loyal to their God shall take strong action. ³³ The nation's wise men shall instruct the many; though for a time they will become victims of the sword, of flames, exile, and plunder. ³⁴ When they fall, few people shall help them, but many shall join them out of treachery. ³⁵ Of the wise men, some shall fall, so that the rest may be tested, refined, and purified, until the end time which is still appointed to come. ³⁶ "The king shall do as he pleases, exalting himself and making himself greater than any god; he shall utter dreadful blasphemies against the God of gods. He shall prosper only till divine wrath is ready, for what is determined must take place. ³⁷ He shall have no regard for the gods of his ancestors or for the one in whom women delight; for no god shall he have regard, because he shall make himself greater than all. ³⁸ Instead, he shall give glory to the god of strongholds; a god unknown to his fathers he shall glorify with gold, silver, precious stones, and other treasures. ³⁹ To defend the strongholds he shall station a people of a foreign god. Whoever acknowledges him he shall provide with abundant honor; he shall make them rule over the many and distribute the land as a reward. ⁴⁰ "At the appointed time the king of the south shall come to grips with him, but the king of the north shall overwhelm him with chariots and horsemen and a great fleet, passing through the countries like a flood. ⁴¹ He shall enter the glorious land and many shall fall, except Edom, Moab, and the chief part of Ammon, which shall escape from his power. ⁴² He shall extend his power over the countries, and not even the land of Egypt shall escape. ⁴³ He shall control the riches of gold and silver and all the treasures of Egypt; Libya and Ethiopia shall be in his train. ⁴⁴ When news from the east and the north terrifies him, he shall set out with great fury to slay and to doom many. ⁴⁵ He shall pitch the tents of his royal pavilion between the sea and the glorious holy mountain, but he shall come to his end with none to help him.

The Three Holy Children Chapter 12

¹ "At that time there shall arise Michael, the great prince, guardian of your people; It shall be a time unsurpassed in distress since nations began until that time. At that time your people shall escape, everyone who is found written in the book. ² Many of those who sleep in the dust of the earth shall awake; some shall live forever, others shall be an everlasting horror and disgrace. ³ But the wise shall shine brightly like the splendor of the firmament, And those who lead the many to justice shall be like the stars forever. ⁴ "As for you, Daniel, keep secret the message and seal the book until the end time; many shall fall away and evil shall increase." ⁵ I, Daniel, looked and saw two others, one standing on either bank of the river. ⁶ One of them said to the man clothed in linen, who was upstream, "How long shall it be to the end of these appalling things?" ⁷ The man clothed in linen, who was upstream, lifted his right and left hands to heaven; and I heard him swear by him who lives forever that it should be for a year, two years, a half-year; and that, when the power of the destroyer of the holy people was brought to an end, all these things should end. ⁸ I heard, but I did not understand; so I asked, "My lord, what follows this?" ⁹ "Go, Daniel," he said, "because the words are to be kept secret and sealed until the end time. ¹⁰ Many

shall be refined, purified, and tested, but the wicked shall prove wicked; none of them shall have understanding, but the wise shall have it. ¹¹ From the time that the daily sacrifice is abolished and the horrible abomination is set up, there shall be one thousand two hundred and ninety days. ¹² Blessed is the man who has patience and perseveres until the one thousand three hundred and thirty-five days. ¹³ Go, take your rest, you shall rise for your reward at the end of days."

Susanna

(Continuation the Three Holy Children Chapter 12)
Susanna Chapter 13

¹ In Babylon there lived a man named Joakim, ² who married a very beautiful and God-fearing woman, Susanna, the daughter of Hilkiah; ³ her pious parents had trained their daughter according to the law of Moses. ⁴ Joakim was very rich; he had a garden near his house, and the Jews had recourse to him often because he was the most respected of them all. ⁵ That year, two elders of the people were appointed judges, of whom the Lord said, "Wickedness has come out of Babylon: from the elders who were to govern the people as judges." ⁶ These men, to whom all brought their cases, frequented the house of Joakim. ⁷ When the people left at noon, Susanna used to enter her husband's garden for a walk. ⁸ When the old men saw her enter every day for her walk, they began to lust for her. ⁹ They suppressed their consciences; they would not allow their eyes to look to heaven, and did not keep in mind just judgments. ¹⁰ Though both were enamored of her, they did not tell each other their trouble, ¹¹ for they were ashamed to reveal their lustful desire to have her. ¹² Day by day they watched eagerly for her. ¹³ One day they said to each other, "Let us be off for home, it is time for lunch." So they went out and parted; ¹⁴ but both turned back, and when they met again, they asked each other the reason. They admitted their lust, and then they agreed to look for an occasion when they could meet her alone. ¹⁵ One day, while they were waiting for the right moment, she entered the garden as usual, with two maids only. She decided to bathe, for the weather was warm. ¹⁶ Nobody else was there except the two elders, who had hidden themselves and were watching her. ¹⁷ "Bring me oil and soap," she said to the maids, "and shut the garden doors while I bathe." ¹⁸ They did as she said; they shut the garden doors and left by the side gate to fetch what she had ordered, unaware that the elders were hidden inside. ¹⁹ As soon as the maids had left, the two old men got up and hurried to her. ²⁰ "Look," they said, "the garden doors are shut, and no one can see us; give in to our desire, and lie with us. ²¹ If you refuse, we will testify against you that you dismissed your maids because a young man was here with you." ²² "I am completely trapped," Susanna groaned. "If I yield, it will be my death; if I refuse, I cannot escape your power. ²³ Yet it is better for me to fall into your power without guilt than to sin before the Lord." ²⁴ Then Susanna shrieked, and the old men also shouted at her, ²⁵ as one of them ran to open the garden doors. ²⁶ When the people in the house heard the cries from the garden, they rushed in by the side gate to see what had happened to her. ²⁷ At the accusations by the old men, the servants felt very much ashamed, for never had any such thing been said about Susanna. ²⁸ When the people came to her husband Joakim the next day, the two wicked elders also came, fully determined to put Susanna to death. Before all the people they ordered: ²⁹ "Send for Susanna, the daughter of Hilkiah, the wife of Joakim." When she was sent for, ³⁰ she came with her parents, children, and all her relatives. ³¹ Susanna, very delicate and beautiful, ³² was veiled; but those wicked men ordered her to uncover her face so as to sate themselves with her beauty. ³³ All her relatives and the onlookers were weeping. ³⁴ In the midst of the people the two elders rose up and laid their hands on her head. ³⁵ Through her tears she looked up to heaven, for she trusted in the Lord wholeheartedly. ³⁶ The elders made this accusation: "As we were walking in the garden alone, this woman entered with two girls and shut the doors of the garden, dismissing the girls. ³⁷ A young man, who was hidden there, came and lay with her. ³⁸ When we, in a corner of the garden, saw this crime, we ran toward them. ³⁹ We saw them lying together, but the man we could not hold, because he was stronger than we; he opened the doors and ran off. ⁴⁰ Then we seized this one and asked who the young man was, ⁴¹ but she refused to tell us. We testify to this." The assembly believed them, since they were elders and judges of the people, and they condemned her to death. ⁴² But Susanna cried aloud: "O eternal God, you know what is hidden and are aware of all things before they come to be: ⁴³ you know that they have testified falsely against me. Here I am about to die, though I have done none of the things with which these wicked men have charged me." ⁴⁴ The Lord heard her prayer. ⁴⁵ As she was being led to execution, God stirred up the holy spirit of a young boy named Daniel, ⁴⁶ and he cried aloud: "I

will have no part in the death of this woman." ⁴⁷ All the people turned and asked him, "What is this you are saying?" ⁴⁸ He stood in their midst and continued, "Are you such fools, O Israelites! To condemn a woman of Israel without examination and without clear evidence? ⁴⁹ Return to court, for they have testified falsely against her." ⁵⁰ Then all the people returned in haste. To Daniel the elders said, "Come, sit with us and inform us, since God has given you the prestige of old age." ⁵¹ But he replied, "Separate these two far from one another that I may examine them." ⁵² After they were separated one from the other, he called one of them and said: "How you have grown evil with age! Now have your past sins come to term: ⁵³ passing unjust sentences, condemning the innocent, and freeing the guilty, although the Lord says, 'The innocent and the just you shall not put to death.' ⁵⁴ Now, then, if you were a witness, tell me under what tree you saw them together." ⁵⁵ "Under a mastic tree," he answered. "Your fine lie has cost you your head," said Daniel; "for the angel of God shall receive the sentence from him and split you in two." ⁵⁶ Putting him to one side, he ordered the other one to be brought. "Offspring of Canaan, not of Judah," Daniel said to him, "beauty has seduced you, lust has subverted your conscience. ⁵⁷ This is how you acted with the daughters of Israel, and in their fear they yielded to you; but a daughter of Judah did not tolerate your wickedness. ⁵⁸ Now, then, tell me under what tree you surprised them together." ⁵⁹ "Under an oak," he said. "Your fine lie has cost you also your head," said Daniel; "for the angel of God waits with a sword to cut you in two so as to make an end of you both." ⁶⁰ The whole assembly cried aloud, blessing God who saves those that hope in him. ⁶¹ They rose up against the two elders, for by their own words Daniel had convicted them of perjury. According to the law of Moses, they inflicted on them the penalty they had plotted to impose on their neighbor: ⁶² they put them to death. Thus was innocent blood spared that day. ⁶³ Hilkiah and his wife praised God for their daughter Susanna, as did Joakim her husband and all her relatives, because she was found innocent of any shameful deed. ⁶⁴ And from that day onward Daniel was greatly esteemed by the people.

Bel and the Dragon

(Continuation Susanna Chapter 13)
Bel and the Dragon Chapter 14

¹ After King Astyages was laid with his fathers, Cyrus the Persian succeeded to his kingdom. ² Daniel was the king's favorite and was held in higher esteem than any of the friends of the king. ³ The Babylonians had an idol called Bel, and every day they provided for it six barrels of fine flour, forty sheep, and six measures of wine. ⁴ The king worshiped it and went every day to adore it; but Daniel adored only his God. ⁵ When the king asked him, "Why do you not adore Bel?" Daniel replied, "Because I worship not idols made with hands, but only the living God who made heaven and earth and has dominion over all mankind." ⁶ Then the king continued, "You do not think Bel is a living god? Do you not see how much he eats and drinks every day?" ⁷ Daniel began to laugh. "Do not be deceived, O king," he said; "it is only clay inside and bronze outside; it has never taken any food or drink." ⁸ Enraged, the king called his priests and said to them, "Unless you tell me who it is that consumes these provisions, you shall die. ⁹ But if you can show that Bel consumes them, Daniel shall die for blaspheming Bel." Daniel said to the king, "Let it be as you say!" ¹⁰ There were seventy priests of Bel, besides their wives and children. When the king went with Daniel into the temple of Bel, ¹¹ the priests of Bel said, "See, we are going to leave. Do you, O king, set out the food and prepare the wine; then shut the door and seal it with your ring. ¹² If you do not find that Bel has eaten it all when you return in the morning, we are to die; otherwise Daniel shall die for his lies against us." ¹³ They were not perturbed, because under the table they had made a secret entrance through which they always came in to consume the food. ¹⁴ After they departed the king set the food before Bel, while Daniel ordered his servants to bring some ashes, which they scattered through the whole temple; the king alone was present. Then they went outside, sealed the closed door with the king's ring, and departed. ¹⁵ The priests entered that night as usual, with their wives and children, and they ate and drank everything. ¹⁶ Early the next morning, the king came with Daniel. ¹⁷ "Are the seals unbroken, Daniel?" he asked. And Daniel answered, "They are unbroken, O king." ¹⁸ As soon as he had opened the door, the king looked at the table and cried aloud, "Great you are, O Bel; there is no trickery in you." ¹⁹ But Daniel laughed and kept the king from entering. "Look at the floor," he said; "whose footprints are these?" ²⁰ "I see the footprints of men, women, and children!" said the king. ²¹ The angry king arrested the priests, their wives, and their children. They showed him the secret door by which they used to enter to consume what was

on the table. ²² He put them to death, and handed Bel over to Daniel, who destroyed it and its temple. ²³ There was a great dragon which the Babylonians worshiped. ²⁴ "Look!" said the king to Daniel, "you cannot deny that this is a living god, so adore it." ²⁵ But Daniel answered, "I adore the Lord, my God, for he is the living God. ²⁶ Give me permission, O king, and I will kill this dragon without sword or club." "I give you permission," the king said. ²⁷ Then Daniel took some pitch, fat, and hair; these he boiled together and made into cakes. He put them into the mouth of the dragon, and when the dragon ate them, he burst asunder. "This," he said, "is what you worshiped." ²⁸ When the Babylonians heard this, they were angry and turned against the king. "The king has become a Jew," they said; "he has destroyed Bel, killed the dragon, and put the priests to death." ²⁹ They went to the king and demanded: "Hand Daniel over to us, or we will kill you and your family." ³⁰ When he saw himself threatened with violence, the king was forced to hand Daniel over to them. ³¹ They threw Daniel into a lions' den, where he remained six days. ³² In the den were seven lions, and two carcasses and two sheep had been given to them daily. But now they were given nothing, so that they would devour Daniel. ³³ In Judea there was a prophet, Habakkuk; he mixed some bread in a bowl with the stew he had boiled, and was going to bring it to the reapers in the field, ³⁴ when an angel of the Lord told him, "Take the lunch you have to Daniel in the lions' den at Babylon." ³⁵ But Habakkuk answered, "Babylon, sir, I have never seen, and I do not know the den!" ³⁶ The angel of the Lord seized him by the crown of his head and carried him by the hair; with the speed of the wind, he set him down in Babylon above the den. ³⁷ "Daniel, Daniel," cried Habakkuk, "take the lunch God has sent you." ³⁸ "You have remembered me, O God," said Daniel; "you have not forsaken those who love you." ³⁹ While Daniel began to eat, the angel of the Lord at once brought Habakkuk back to his own place. ⁴⁰ On the seventh day the king came to mourn for Daniel. As he came to the den and looked in, there was Daniel, sitting there! ⁴¹ The king cried aloud, "You are great, O Lord, the God of Daniel, and there is no other besides you!" ⁴² Daniel he took out, but those who had tried to destroy him he threw into the den, and they were devoured in a moment before his eyes.

Minor Prophets

Hosea

Hosea Chapter 1

¹ The word of the LORD that came to Hosea, the son of Beeri, in the days of Uzziah, Jotham, Ahaz, Hezekiah, kings of Judah, and in the days of Jeroboam, son of Joash, king of Israel. ² In the beginning of the LORD'S speaking to Hosea, the LORD said to Hosea: Go, take a harlot wife and harlot's children, for the land gives itself to harlotry, turning away from the LORD. ³ So he went and took Gomer, the daughter of Diblaim; and she conceived and bore him a son. ⁴ Then the LORD said to him: Give him the name Jezreel, for in a little while I will punish the house of Jehu for the bloodshed at Jezreel and bring to an end the kingdom of the house of Israel; ⁵ On that day I will break the bow of Israel in the valley of Jezreel. ⁶ When she conceived again and bore a daughter, the LORD said to him: Give her the name Lo-ruhama; I no longer feel pity for the house of Israel: rather, I abhor them utterly. ⁷ Yet for the house of Judah I feel pity; I will save them by the LORD, their God; but I will not save them by war, by sword or bow, by horses or horsemen. ⁸ After she weaned Lo-ruhama, she conceived and bore a son. ⁹ Then the LORD said: Give him the name Lo-ammi, for you are not my people, and I will not be your God.

Hosea Chapter 2

¹ Protest against your mother, protest! for she is not my wife, and I am not her husband. Let her remove her harlotry from before her, her adultery from between her breasts, ² Or I will strip her naked, leaving her as on the day of her birth; I will make her like the desert, reduce her to an arid land, and slay her with thirst. ³ I will have no pity on her children, for they are the children of harlotry. ⁴ Yes, their mother played the harlot; she that conceived them has acted shamefully. "I will go after my lovers," she said, "who give me my bread and my water, my wool and my flax, my oil and my drink." ⁵ Since she has not known that it was I who gave her the grain, the wine, and the oil, and her abundance of silver, and of gold, which they used for Baal, ⁶ Therefore I will take back my grain in its time, and my wine in its season; I will snatch away my wool and my flax, with which she covers her nakedness. ⁷ So now I will lay bare her shame before the eyes of her lovers, and no one can deliver her out of my hand. ⁸ I will bring an end to all her joy, her feasts, her new moons, her sabbaths, and all her solemnities. ⁹ I will lay waste her vines and fig trees, of which she said, "These are the hire my lovers

have given me"; I will turn them into rank growth and wild beasts shall devour them. [10] I will punish her for the days of the Baals, for whom she burnt incense while she decked herself out with her rings and her jewels, and, in going after her lovers, forgot me, says the LORD. [11] Therefore, I will hedge in her way with thorns and erect a wall against her, so that she cannot find her paths. [12] If she runs after her lovers, she shall not overtake them; if she looks for them she shall not find them. Then she shall say, "I will go back to my first husband, for it was better with me then than now." [13] So I will allure her; I will lead her into the desert and speak to her heart. [14] From there I will give her the vineyards she had, and the valley of Achor as a door of hope. She shall respond there as in the days of her youth, when she came up from the land of Egypt. [15] On that day, says the LORD, she shall call me "My husband," and never again "My baal." [16] Then will I remove from her mouth the names of the Baals, so that they shall no longer be invoked. [17] I will make a covenant for them on that day, with the beasts of the field, with the birds of the air, and with the things that crawl on the ground. Bow and sword and war I will destroy from the land, and I will let them take their rest in security. [18] I will espouse you to me forever: I will espouse you in right and in justice, in love and in mercy; [19] I will espouse you in fidelity, and you shall know the LORD. [20] On that day I will respond, says the LORD; I will respond to the heavens, and they shall respond to the earth; [21] The earth shall respond to the grain, and wine, and oil, and these shall respond to Jezreel. [22] I will sow him for myself in the land, and I will have pity on Lo-ruhama. I will say to Lo-ammi, "You are my people," and he shall say, "My God!"

Hosea Chapter 3

[1] Again the LORD said to me: Give your love to a woman beloved of a paramour, an adulteress; even as the LORD loves the people of Israel, though they turn to other gods and are fond of raisin cakes. [2] So I bought her for fifteen pieces of silver and a homer and a lethech of barley. [3] Then I said to her: "Many days you shall wait for me; you shall not play the harlot or belong to any man; I in turn will wait for you." [4] For the people of Israel shall remain many days without king or prince, without sacrifice or sacred pillar, without ephod or household idols. [5] Then the people of Israel shall turn back and seek the LORD, their God, and David, their king; they shall come trembling to the LORD and to his bounty, in the last days. [6] The number of the Israelites shall be like the sand of the sea, which can be neither measured nor counted. Whereas they were called, "Lo-ammi," they shall be called, "Children of the living God." Then the people of Judah and of Israel shall be gathered together; they shall appoint for themselves one head and come up from other lands, for great shall be the day of Jezreel. Say to your brothers, "Ammi," and to your sisters, "Ruhama."

Hosea Chapter 4

[1] Hear the word of the LORD, O people of Israel, for the LORD has a grievance against the inhabitants of the land: There is no fidelity, no mercy, no knowledge of God in the land. [2] False swearing, lying, murder, stealing and adultery! In their lawlessness, bloodshed follows bloodshed. [3] Therefore the land mourns, and everything that dwells in it languishes: The beasts of the field, the birds of the air, and even the fish of the sea perish. [4] But let no one protest, let no one complain; with you is my grievance, O priests! [5] You shall stumble in the day, and the prophets shall stumble with you at night; I will destroy your mother. [6] My people perish for want of knowledge! Since you have rejected knowledge, I will reject you from my priesthood; since you have ignored the law of your God, I will also ignore your sons. [7] One and all they sin against me, exchanging their glory for shame. [8] They feed on the sin of my people, and are greedy for their guilt. [9] The priests shall fare no better than the people: I will punish them for their ways, and repay them for their deeds. [10] They shall eat but not be satisfied, they shall play the harlot but not increase, because they have abandoned the LORD [11] to practice harlotry. Old wine and new deprive my people of understanding. [12] They consult their piece of wood, and their wand makes pronouncements for them, for the spirit of harlotry has led them astray; they commit harlotry, forsaking their God. [13] On the mountaintops they offer sacrifice and on the hills they burn incense, beneath oak and poplar and terebinth, because of their pleasant shade. That is why your daughters play the harlot, and your daughters-in-law are adulteresses. [14] Am I then to punish your daughters for their harlotry, your daughters-in-law for their adultery? You yourselves consort with harlots, and with prostitutes you offer sacrifice! So must a people without understanding come to ruin. [15] Though you play the harlot, O Israel, let not Judah become guilty! Come not to Gilgal, nor up to Beth-aven, to swear, "As the LORD lives!" [16] For Israel is as stubborn as a heifer; will the LORD now give them broad pastures as though they were lambs? [17] Ephraim is an associate of idols, let him alone! [18] When

their carousing is over, they give themselves to harlotry; in their arrogance they love shame. [19] The wind has bound them up in its pinions; they shall have only shame from their altars.

Hosea Chapter 5

[1] Hear this, O priests, Pay attention, O house of Israel, O household of the king, give ear! It is you who are called to judgment. For you have become a snare at Mizpah, and a net spread upon Tabor. [2] In their perversity they have sunk into wickedness, and I am rejected by them all. [3] I know Ephraim, and Israel is not hidden from me; now Ephraim has played the harlot, Israel is defiled. [4] Their deeds do not allow them to return to their God; for the spirit of harlotry is in them, and they do not recognize the LORD. [5] The arrogance of Israel bears witness against him; Ephraim stumbles in his guilt, and Judah stumbles with them. [6] With their flocks and their herds they shall go to seek the LORD, but they shall not find him; he has withdrawn himself from them. [7] They have been untrue to the LORD, for they have begotten illegitimate children; now shall the new moon devour them together with their fields. [8] Blow the horn in Gibeah, the trumpet in Ramah! Sound the alarm in Beth-aven: "Look behind you, O Benjamin!" [9] Ephraim shall become a waste on the day of chastisement: against the tribes of Israel I announce what is sure to be. [10] The princes of Judah have become like those that move a boundary line; upon them I will pour out my wrath like water. [11] Is Ephraim maltreated, his rights violated? No, he has willingly gone after filth! [12] I am like a moth for Ephraim, like maggots for the house of Judah. [13] When Ephraim saw his infirmity, and Judah his sore, Ephraim went to Assyria, and Judah sent to the great king. But he cannot heal you nor take away your sore. [14] For I am like a lion to Ephraim, like a young lion to the house of Judah; it is I who rend the prey and depart, I carry it away and no one can save it from me. [15] I will go back to my place until they pay for their guilt and seek my presence.

Hosea Chapter 6

[1] In their affliction, they shall look for me: "Come, let us return to the LORD, for it is he who has rent, but he will heal us; he has struck us, but he will bind our wounds. [2] He will revive us after two days; on the third day he will raise us up, to live in his presence. [3] Let us know, let us strive to know the LORD; as certain as the dawn is his coming, and his judgment shines forth like the light of day! He will come to us like the rain, like spring rain that waters the earth." [4] What can I do with you, Ephraim? What can I do with you, Judah? Your piety is like a morning cloud, like the dew that early passes away. [5] For this reason I smote them through the prophets, I slew them by the words of my mouth; [6] for it is love that I desire, not sacrifice, and knowledge of God rather than holocausts. [7] But they, in their land, violated the covenant; there they were untrue to me. [8] Gilead is a city of evildoers, tracked with blood. [9] As brigands ambush a man, a band of priests slay on the way to Shechem, committing monstrous crime. [10] In the house of Israel I have seen a horrible thing: there harlotry is found in Ephraim, Israel is defiled. [11] For you also, O Judah, a harvest has been appointed.

Hosea Chapter 7

[1] When I would bring about the restoration of my people, when I would heal Israel, the guilt of Ephraim stands out, the wickedness of Samaria; they practice falsehood, thieves break in, bandits plunder abroad. [2] Yet they do not remind themselves that I remember all their wickedness. Even now their crimes surround them, present to my sight. [3] In their wickedness they regale the king, the princes too, with their deceits. [4] They are all kindled to wrath like a blazing oven, whose fire the baker desists from stirring once the dough is kneaded until it has risen. [5] On the day of our king, the princes are overcome with the heat of wine. He extends his hand among dissemblers; [6] the plotters approach with hearts like ovens. All the night their anger sleeps; in the morning it flares like a blazing fire. [7] They are all heated like ovens, and consume their rulers. All their kings have fallen; none of them calls upon me. [8] Ephraim mingles with the nations, Ephraim is a hearth cake unturned. [9] Strangers have sapped his strength, but he takes no notice of it; of gray hairs, too, there is a sprinkling, but he takes no notice of it. [10] The arrogance of Israel bears witness against him; yet they do not return to the LORD, their God, nor seek him, for all that. [11] Ephraim is like a dove, silly and senseless; they call upon Egypt, they go to Assyria. [12] Even as they go I will spread my net around them, like birds in the air I will bring them down. In an instant I will send them captive from their land. [13] Woe to them, they have strayed from me! Ruin to them, they have sinned against me! Though I wished to redeem them, they spoke lies against me. [14] They have not cried to me from their hearts when they wailed upon their beds; for wheat and wine they lacerated themselves, while they rebelled against me. [15] Though I trained and strengthened their arms, yet they devised evil against me. [16] They have again become useless, like a treacherous bow. Their princes shall fall by

the sword because of the insolence of their tongues; thus they shall be mocked in the land of Egypt.

Hosea Chapter 8

1 A trumpet to your lips, you who watch over the house of the LORD! Since they have violated my covenant, and sinned against my law, 2 while to me they cry out, "O, God of Israel, we know you!" 3 The men of Israel have thrown away what is good; the enemy shall pursue them. 4 They made kings, but not by my authority; they established princes, but without my approval. With their silver and gold they made idols for themselves, to their own destruction. 5 Cast away your calf, O Samaria! my wrath is kindled against them; how long will they be unable to attain innocence in Israel? 6 The work of an artisan, no god at all, destined for the flames—such is the calf of Samaria! 7 When they sow the wind, they shall reap the whirlwind; the stalk of grain that forms no ear can yield no flour; even if it could, strangers would swallow it. 8 Israel is swallowed up; he is now among the nations a thing of no value. 9 They went up to Assyria—a wild ass off on its own—Ephraim bargained for lovers. 10 Even though they bargain with the nations, I will now gather an army; king and princes shall shortly succumb under the burden. 11 When Ephraim made many altars to expiate sin, his altars became occasions of sin. 12 Though I write for him my many ordinances, they are considered as a stranger's. 13 Though they offer sacrifice, immolate flesh and eat it, the LORD is not pleased with them. He shall still remember their guilt and punish their sins; they shall return to Egypt. 14 Israel has forgotten his maker and built palaces. Judah, too, has fortified many cities, but I will send fire upon his cities, to devour their castles.

Hosea Chapter 9

1 Rejoice not, O Israel, exult not like the nations! For you have been unfaithful to your God, loving a harlot's hire upon every threshing floor. 2 Threshing floor and wine press shall not nourish them, the new wine shall fail them. 3 They shall not dwell in the LORD'S land; Ephraim shall return to Egypt, and in Assyria they shall eat unclean food. 4 They shall not pour libations of wine to the LORD, or proffer their sacrifices before him. Theirs will be like mourners' bread, that makes unclean all who eat of it; such food as they have shall be for themselves; it cannot enter the house of the LORD. 5 What will you do on the festival day, the day of the LORD'S feast? 6 When they go from the ruins, Egypt shall gather them in, Memphis shall bury them. Weeds shall overgrow their silver treasures, and thorns invade their tents. 7 They have come, the days of punishment! they have come, the days of recompense! Let Israel know it! "The prophet is a fool, the man of the spirit is mad!" Because your iniquity is great, great, too, is your hostility. 8 A prophet is Ephraim's watchman with God, yet a fowler's snare is on all his ways, hostility in the house of his God. 9 They have sunk to the depths of corruption, as in the days of Gibeah; he shall remember their iniquity and punish their sins. 10 Like grapes in the desert, I found Israel; like the first fruits of the fig tree in its prime, I considered your fathers. When they came to Baal-peor and consecrated themselves to the Shame, they became as abhorrent as the thing they loved. 11 The glory of Ephraim flies away like a bird: no birth, no carrying in the womb, no conception. Were they to bear children, I would slay the darlings of their womb. 12 Even though they bring up their children, I will make them childless, till not one is left. Woe to them when I turn away from them! 13 Ephraim, as I saw, was like Tyre, planted in a beauteous spot; but Ephraim shall bring out his children to the slayer. 14 Give them, O LORD! give them what? Give them an unfruitful womb, and dry breasts! 15 All their wickedness is in Gilgal; yes, there they incurred my hatred. Because of their wicked deeds I will drive them out of my house. I will love them no longer; all their princes are rebels. 16 Ephraim is stricken, their root is dried up; they shall bear no fruit. 17 My God will disown them because they have not listened to him; they shall be wanderers among the nations.

Hosea Chapter 10

1 Israel is a luxuriant vine whose fruit matches its growth. The more abundant his fruit, the more altars he built; the more productive his land, the more sacred pillars he set up. 2 Their heart is false, now they pay for their guilt; God shall break down their altars and destroy their sacred pillars. 3 If they would say, "We have no king"—since they do not fear the LORD, what can the king do for them? 4 Nothing but make promises, swear false oaths, and make alliances, while justice grows wild like wormwood in a plowed field! 5 The inhabitants of Samaria fear for the calf of Beth-aven; the people mourn for it and its priests wail over it, because the glory has departed from it. 6 It too shall be carried to Assyria, as an offering to the great king. Ephraim shall be taken into captivity, Israel be shamed by his schemes. 7 The king of Samaria shall disappear, like foam upon the waters. 8 The high places of Aven shall be destroyed, the sin of Israel; thorns and thistles shall overgrow their altars. Then they shall cry out to the mountains, "Cover us!" and to the hills, "Fall upon us!" 9 Since the days of Gibeah you have sinned, O Israel. There they took their stand; war was not to reach them in Gibeah. 10 Against the wanton people I came and I chastised them; I gathered troops against them when I chastised them for their two crimes. 11 Ephraim was a trained heifer, willing to thresh; I myself laid a yoke upon her fair neck; Ephraim was to be harnessed, Judah was to plow, Jacob was to break his furrows: 12 "Sow for yourselves justice, reap the fruit of piety; break up for yourselves a new field, for it is time to seek the LORD, till he come and rain down justice upon you." 13 But you have cultivated wickedness, reaped perversity, and eaten the fruit of falsehood. Because you have trusted in your chariots, and in your many warriors, 14 Turmoil shall break out among your tribes and all your fortresses shall be ravaged as Salman ravaged Beth-arbel in time of war, smashing mothers and their children. 15 So shall it be done to you, Bethel, because of your utter wickedness: at dawn the king of Israel shall perish utterly.

Hosea Chapter 11

1 When Israel was a child I loved him, out of Egypt I called my son. 2 The more I called them, the farther they went from me, sacrificing to the Baals and burning incense to idols. 3 Yet it was I who taught Ephraim to walk, who took them in my arms; 4 I drew them with human cords, with bands of love; I fostered them like one who raises an infant to his cheeks; yet, though I stooped to feed my child, they did not know that I was their healer. 5 He shall return to the land of Egypt, and Assyria shall be his king; 6 the sword shall begin with his cities and end by consuming his solitudes. Because they refused to repent, their own counsels shall devour them. 7 His people are in suspense about returning to him; and God, though in unison they cry out to him, shall not raise them up. 8 How could I give you up, O Ephraim, or deliver you up, O Israel? How could I treat you as Admah, or make you like Zeboiim? My heart is overwhelmed, my pity is stirred. 9 I will not give vent to my blazing anger, I will not destroy Ephraim again; for I am God and not man, the Holy One present among you; I will not let the flames consume you. 10 They shall follow the LORD, who roars like a lion; when he roars, his sons shall come frightened from the west, 11 out of Egypt they shall come trembling, like sparrows, from the land of Assyria, like doves; and I will resettle them in their homes, says the LORD.

Hosea Chapter 12

1 Ephraim has surrounded me with lies, the house of Israel, with deceit; Judah is still rebellious against God, against the Holy One, who is faithful. 2 Ephraim chases the wind, ever pursuing the gale. His lies and falsehoods are many: he comes to terms with Assyria, and carries oil to Egypt. 3 The LORD has a grievance against Israel: he shall punish Jacob for his conduct, for his deeds he shall repay him. 4 In the womb he supplanted his brother, and as a man he contended with God; 5 he contended with the angel and triumphed, entreating him with tears. At Bethel he met God and there he spoke with him: 6 The LORD, the God of hosts, the LORD is his name! 7 You shall return by the help of your God, if you remain loyal and do right and always hope in your God. 8 A merchant who holds a false balance, who loves to defraud! 9 Though Ephraim says, "How rich I have become; I have made a fortune!" All his gain shall not suffice him for the guilt of his sin. 10 I am the LORD, your God, since the land of Egypt; I will again have you live in tents, as in that appointed time. 11 I granted many visions and spoke to the prophets, through whom I set forth examples. 12 In Gilead is falsehood, they have come to nought, in Gilgal they sacrifice to bullocks; their altars are like heaps of stones in the furrows of the field. 13 When Jacob fled to the land of Aram, he served for a wife; for a wife Israel tended sheep. 14 By a prophet the LORD brought Israel out of Egypt, and by a prophet they were protected. 15 Ephraim has exasperated his lord; therefore he shall cast his blood-guilt upon him and repay him for his outrage.

Hosea Chapter 13

1 Ephraim's word caused fear, for he was exalted in Israel; but he sinned through Baal and died. 2 Now they continue to sin, making for themselves molten images, silver idols according to their fancy, all of them the work of artisans. "To these," they say, "offer sacrifice." Men kiss calves! 3 Therefore, they shall be like a morning cloud or like the dew that early passes away, like chaff storm-driven from the threshing floor or like smoke out of the window. 4 I am the LORD, your God, since the land of Egypt; you know no God besides me, and there is no savior but me. 5 I fed you in the desert, in the torrid land. 6 They ate their fill; when filled, they became proud of heart and forgot me. 7 Therefore, I will be like a lion to them, like a panther by the road I will keep watch. 8 I will attack them like a bear robbed of its young, and tear their hearts

from their breasts; I will devour them on the spot like a lion, as though a wild beast were to rend them. 9 Your destruction, O Israel! who is there to help you? 10 Where now is your king, that he may rescue you in all your cities? And your rulers, of whom you said, "Give me a king and princes"? 11 I give you a king in my anger, and I take him away in my wrath. 12 The guilt of Israel is wrapped up, his sin is stored away. 13 The birth pangs shall come for him, but he shall be an unwise child; for when it is time he shall not present himself where children break forth. 14 Shall I deliver them from the power of the nether world? Shall I redeem them from death? Where are your plagues, O death! Where is your sting, O nether world! My eyes are closed to compassion. 15 Though he be fruitful among his fellows, an east wind shall come, a wind from the LORD, rising from the desert, that shall dry up his spring, and leave his fountain dry. It shall loot his land of every precious thing.

Hosea Chapter 14

1 Samaria shall expiate her guilt, for she has rebelled against her God. They shall fall by the sword, their little ones shall be dashed to pieces, their expectant mothers shall be ripped open. 2 Return, O Israel, to the LORD, your God; you have collapsed through your guilt. 3 Take with you words, and return to the LORD; say to him, "Forgive all iniquity, and receive what is good, that we may render as offerings the bullocks from our stalls. 4 Assyria will not save us, nor shall we have horses to mount; we shall say no more, 'Our god,' to the work of our hands; for in you the orphan finds compassion." 5 I will heal their defection, I will love them freely; for my wrath is turned away from them. 6 I will be like the dew for Israel: he shall blossom like the lily; he shall strike root like the Lebanon cedar, 7 and put forth his shoots. His splendor shall be like the olive tree and his fragrance like the Lebanon cedar. 8 Again they shall dwell in his shade and raise grain; they shall blossom like the vine, and his fame shall be like the wine of Lebanon. 9 Ephraim! What more has he to do with idols? I have humbled him, but I will prosper him. "I am like a verdant cypress tree" - because of me you bear fruit! 10 Let him who is wise understand these things; let him who is prudent know them. Straight are the paths of the LORD, in them the just walk, but sinners stumble in them.

Joel

Joel Chapter 1

1 The word of the LORD which came to Joel, the son of Pethuel. 2 Hear this, you elders! Pay attention, all you who dwell in the land! Has the like of this happened in your days, or in the days of your fathers? 3 Tell it to your children, and your children to their children, and their children to the next generation. 4 What the cutter left, the locust swarm has eaten; what the locust swarm left, the grasshopper has eaten; and what the grasshopper left, the devourer has eaten. 5 Wake up, you drunkards, and weep; wail, all you drinkers of wine, because the juice of the grape will be withheld from your mouths. 6 For a people has invaded my land, mighty and without number; his teeth are the teeth of a lion, and his molars those of a lioness. 7 He has laid waste my vine, and blighted my fig tree; he has stripped it, sheared off its bark; its branches are made white. 8 Lament like a virgin girt with sackcloth for the spouse of her youth. 9 Abolished are offering and libation from the house of the LORD; in mourning are the priests, the ministers of the LORD. 10 The field is ravaged, the earth mourns, because the grain is ravaged, the must has failed, the oil languishes. 11 Be appalled, you husbandmen! wail, you vinedressers! Over the wheat and the barley, because the harvest of the field has perished. 12 The vine has dried up, the fig tree is withered; the pomegranate, the date palm also, and the apple, all the trees of the field are dried up; yes, joy has withered away from among mankind. 13 Gird yourselves and weep, O priests! wail, O ministers of the altar! Come, spend the night in sackcloth, O ministers of my God! The house of your God is deprived of offering and libation. 14 Proclaim a fast, call an assembly; gather the elders, all who dwell in the land, into the house of the LORD, your God, and cry to the LORD! 15 Alas, the day! for near is the day of the LORD, and it comes as ruin from the Almighty. 16 From before our very eyes has not the food been cut off; and from the house of our God, joy and gladness? 17 The seed lies shriveled under its clods; the stores are destroyed, the barns are broken down, for the grain has failed. 18 How the beasts groan! The herds of cattle are bewildered! Because they have no pasturage, even the flocks of sheep have perished. 19 To you, O LORD, I cry! for fire has devoured the pastures of the plain, and flame has enkindled all the trees of the field. 20 Even the beasts of the field cry out to you; for the streams of water are dried up, and fire has devoured the pastures of the plain.

Joel Chapter 2

1 Blow the trumpet in Zion, sound the alarm on my holy mountain! Let all who dwell in the land tremble, for the day of the LORD is coming; 2

Yes, it is near, a day of darkness and of gloom, a day of clouds and somberness! Like dawn spreading over the mountains, a people numerous and mighty! Their like has not been from of old, nor will it be after them, even to the years of distant generations. 3 Before them a fire devours, and after them a flame enkindles; like the garden of Eden is the land before them, and after them a desert waste; from them there is no escape. 4 Their appearance is that of horses; like steeds they run. 5 As with the rumble of chariots they leap on the mountaintops; as with the crackling of a fiery flame devouring stubble; like a mighty people arrayed for battle. 6 Before them peoples are in torment, every face blanches. 7 Like warriors they run, like soldiers they scale the wall; they advance, each in his own lane, without swerving from their paths. 8 No one crowds another, each advances in his own track; though they fall into the ditches, they are not checked. 9 They assault the city, they run upon the wall, they climb into the houses; in at the windows they come like thieves. 10 Before them the earth trembles, the heavens shake; the sun and the moon are darkened, and the stars withhold their brightness. 11 The LORD raises his voice at the head of his army; for immense indeed is his camp, yes, mighty, and it does his bidding. For great is the day of the LORD, and exceedingly terrible; who can bear it? 12 Yet even now, says the LORD, return to me with your whole heart, with fasting, and weeping, and mourning; 13 Rend your hearts, not your garments, and return to the LORD, your God. For gracious and merciful is he, slow to anger, rich in kindness, and relenting in punishment. 14 Perhaps he will again relent and leave behind him a blessing, offerings and libations for the LORD, your God. 15 Blow the trumpet in Zion! proclaim a fast, call an assembly; 16 gather the people, notify the congregation; assemble the elders, gather the children and the infants at the breast; let the bridegroom quit his room, and the bride her chamber. 17 Between the porch and the altar let the priests, the ministers of the LORD, weep, and say, "Spare, O LORD, your people, and make not your heritage a reproach, with the nations ruling over them! Why should they say among the peoples, 'Where is their God?'" 18 Then the LORD was stirred to concern for his land and took pity on his people. 19 The LORD answered and said to his people: See, I will send you grain, and wine, and oil, and you shall be filled with them; no more will I make you a reproach among the nations. 20 No, the northerner I will remove far from you, and drive him out into a land arid and waste, with his van toward the eastern sea, and his rear toward the western sea; and his foulness shall go up, and his stench shall go up. 21 Fear not, O land! exult and rejoice! for the LORD has done great things. 22 Fear not, beasts of the field! for the pastures of the plain are green; the tree bears its fruit, the fig tree and the vine give their yield. 23 And do you, O children of Zion, exult and rejoice in the LORD, your God! He has given you the teacher of justice: he has made the rain come down for you, the early and the late rain as before. 24 The threshing floors shall be full of grain and the vats shall overflow with wine and oil. 25 And I will repay you for the years which the locust has eaten, the grasshopper, the devourer, and the cutter, my great army which I sent among you. 26 You shall eat and be filled, and shall praise the name of the LORD, your God, because he has dealt wondrously with you; my people shall nevermore be put to shame. 27 And you shall know that I am in the midst of Israel; I am the LORD, your God, and there is no other; my people shall nevermore be put to shame.

Joel Chapter 3

1 Then afterward I will pour out my spirit upon all mankind. Your sons and daughters shall prophesy, your old men shall dream dreams, your young men shall see visions; 2 even upon the servants and the handmaids, in those days, I will pour out my spirit. 3 And I will work wonders in the heavens and on the earth, blood, fire, and columns of smoke; 4 the sun will be turned to darkness, and the moon to blood, at the coming of the Day of the LORD, the great and terrible day. 5 Then everyone shall be rescued who calls on the name of the LORD; for on Mount Zion there shall be a remnant, as the LORD has said, and in Jerusalem survivors whom the LORD shall call.

Joel Chapter 4

1 Yes, in those days, and at that time, when I would restore the fortunes of Judah and Jerusalem, 2 I will assemble all the nations and bring them down to the Valley of Jehoshaphat, and I will enter into judgment with them there on behalf of my people and my inheritance, Israel; because they have scattered them among the nations, and divided my land. 3 Over my people they have cast lots; they gave a boy for a harlot, and sold a girl for the wine they drank. 4 Moreover, what are you to me, Tyre and Sidon, and all the regions of Philistia? Would you take vengeance upon me by some action? But if you do take action against me, swiftly, speedily, I will return your deed upon your own head. 5 You took my silver and my gold, and brought my precious treasures into your

temples! 6 You sold the people of Judah and Jerusalem to the Greeks, removing them far from their own country! 7 See, I will rouse them from the place into which you have sold them, and I will return your deed upon your own head. 8 I will sell your sons and your daughters to the people of Judah, who shall sell them to the Sabeans, a nation far off. Indeed, the LORD has spoken. 9 Declare this among the nations: proclaim a war, rouse the warriors to arms! Let all the soldiers report and march! 10 Beat your plowshares into swords, and your pruning hooks into spears; let the weak man say, "I am a warrior!" 11 Hasten and come, all you neighboring peoples, assemble there! (Bring down, O Lord, your warriors!) 12 Let the nations bestir themselves and come up to the Valley of Jehoshaphat; for there I will sit in judgment upon all the neighboring nations. 13 Apply the sickle, for the harvest is ripe; come and tread, for the wine press is full; the vats overflow, for great is their malice. 14 Crowd upon crowd in the valley of decision; for near is the day of the LORD in the valley of decision. 15 Sun and moon are darkened, and the stars withhold their brightness. 16 The LORD roars from Zion, and from Jerusalem raises his voice; the heavens and the earth quake, but the LORD is a refuge to his people, a stronghold to the men of Israel. 17 Then shall you know that I, the LORD, am your God, dwelling on Zion, my holy mountain; Jerusalem shall be holy, and strangers shall pass through her no more. 18 And then, on that day, the mountains shall drip new wine, and the hills shall flow with milk; and the channels of Judah shall flow with water: a fountain shall issue from the house of the LORD, to water the Valley of Shittim. 19 Egypt shall be a waste, and Edom a desert waste, because of violence done to the people of Judah, because they shed innocent blood in their land. 20 But Judah shall abide forever, and Jerusalem for all generations. 21 I will avenge their blood, and not leave it unpunished. The LORD dwells in Zion.

Amos

Amos Chapter 1

1 The words of Amos, a shepherd from Tekoa, which he received in vision concerning Israel, in the days of Uzziah, king of Judah, and in the days of Jeroboam, son of Joash, king of Israel, two years before the earthquake: 2 The LORD will roar from Zion, and from Jerusalem raise his voice: The pastures of the shepherds will languish, and the summit of Carmel wither. 3 Thus says the LORD: For three crimes of Damascus, and for four, I will not revoke my word; because they threshed Gilead with sledges of iron, 4 I will send fire upon the house of Hazael, to devour the castles of Ben-hadad. 5 I will break the bar of Damascus; I will root out those who live in the Valley of Aven, and the sceptered ruler of Beth-eden; the people of Aram shall be exiled to Kir, says the LORD. 6 Thus says the LORD: For three crimes of Gaza, and for four, I will not revoke my word; because they took captive whole groups to hand over to Edom, 7 I will send fire upon the wall of Gaza, to devour her castles; 8 I will root out those who live in Ashdod, and the sceptered ruler of Ashkelon; I will turn my hand against Ekron, and the last of the Philistines shall perish, says the Lord God. 9 Thus says the LORD: For three crimes of Tyre, and for four, I will not revoke my word; because they delivered whole groups captive to Edom, and did not remember the pact of brotherhood, 10 I will send fire upon the wall of Tyre, to devour her castles. 11 Thus says the LORD: For three crimes of Edom, and for four, I will not revoke my word; because he pursued his brother with the sword, choking up all pity; because he persisted in his anger and kept his wrath to the end, 12 I will send fire upon Teman, and it will devour the castles of Bozrah. 13 Thus says the LORD: For three crimes of the Ammonites, and for four, I will not revoke my word; because they ripped open expectant mothers in Gilead, while extending their territory, 14 I will kindle a fire upon the wall of Rabbah, and it will devour her castles amid clamor on the day of battle and stormwind in a time of tempest. 15 Their king shall go into captivity, he and his princes with him, says the LORD.

Amos Chapter 2

1 Thus says the LORD: For three crimes of Moab, and for four, I will not revoke my word; because he burned to ashes the bones of Edom's king, 2 I will send fire upon Moab, to devour the castles of Kerioth; Moab shall meet death amid uproar and shouts and trumpet blasts. 3 I will root out the judge from her midst, and her princes I will slay with him, says the LORD. 4 Thus says the LORD: For three crimes of Judah, and for four, I will not revoke my word; because they spurned the law of the LORD, and did not keep his statutes; because the lies which their fathers followed have led them astray, 5 I will send fire upon Judah, to devour the castles of Jerusalem. 6 Thus says the LORD: For three crimes of Israel, and for four, I will not revoke my word; because they sell the just man for silver, and the poor man for a pair of sandals. 7

They trample the heads of the weak into the dust of the earth, and force the lowly out of the way. Son and father go to the same prostitute, profaning my holy name. 8 Upon garments taken in pledge they recline beside any altar; and the wine of those who have been fined they drink in the house of their god. 9 Yet it was I who destroyed the Amorites before them, who were as tall as the cedars, and as strong as the oak trees. I destroyed their fruit above, and their roots beneath. 10 It was I who brought you up from the land of Egypt, and who led you through the desert for forty years, to occupy the land of the Amorites. 11 I who raised up prophets among your sons, and nazirites among your young men. Is this not so, O men of Israel? says the LORD. 12 But you gave the nazirites wine to drink, and commanded the prophets not to prophesy. 13 Beware, I will crush you into the ground as a wagon crushes when laden with sheaves. 14 Flight shall perish from the swift, and the strong man shall not retain his strength; the warrior shall not save his life, 15 nor the bowman stand his ground; the swift of foot shall not escape, nor the horseman save his life. 16 And the most stouthearted of warriors shall flee naked on that day, says the LORD.

Amos Chapter 3

1 Hear this word, O men of Israel, that the LORD pronounces over you, over the whole family that I brought up from the land of Egypt: 2 You alone have I favored, more than all the families of the earth; therefore I will punish you for all your crimes. 3 Do two walk together unless they have agreed? 4 Does a lion roar in the forest when it has no prey? Does a young lion cry out from its den unless it has seized something? 5 Is a bird brought to earth by a snare when there is no lure for it? Does a snare spring up from the ground without catching anything? 6 If the trumpet sounds in a city, will the people not be frightened? If evil befalls a city, has not the LORD caused it? 7 Indeed, the Lord GOD does nothing without revealing his plan to his servants, the prophets. 8 The lion roars - who will not be afraid! The Lord GOD speaks - who will not prophesy! 9 Proclaim this in the castles of Ashdod, in the castles of the land of Egypt: "Gather about the mountain of Samaria, and see the great disorders within her, the oppression in her midst." 10 For they know not how to do what is right, says the LORD, storing up in their castles what they have extorted and robbed. 11 Therefore, thus says the Lord GOD: An enemy shall surround the land, and strip you of your strength, and pillage your castles. 12 Thus says the LORD: As the shepherd snatches from the mouth of the lion a pair of legs or the tip of an ear of his sheep, so the Israelites who dwell in Samaria shall escape with the corner of a couch or a piece of a cot. 13 Hear and bear witness against the house of Jacob, says the Lord GOD, the God of hosts: 14 On the day when I punish Israel for his crimes, I will visit also the altars of Bethel: the horns of the altar shall be broken off and fall to the ground. 15 Then will I strike the winter house and the summer house; the ivory apartments shall be ruined, and their many rooms shall be no more, says the LORD.

Amos Chapter 4

1 Hear this word, women of the mountain of Samaria, you cows of Bashan, you who oppress the weak and abuse the needy; who say to your lords, "Bring drink for us!" 2 The Lord GOD has sworn by his holiness: Truly the days are coming upon you when they shall drag you away with hooks, the last of you with fishhooks; 3 you shall go out through the breached walls each by the most direct way, and you shall be cast into the mire, says the LORD. 4 Come to Bethel and sin, to Gilgal, and sin the more; each morning bring your sacrifices, every third day, your tithes; 5 burn leavened food as a thanksgiving sacrifice, proclaim publicly your freewill offerings, for so you love to do, O men of Israel, says the Lord GOD. 6 Though I have made your teeth clean of food in all your cities, and have made bread scarce in all your dwellings, yet you returned not to me, says the LORD. 7 Though I also withheld the rain from you when the harvest was still three months away; I sent rain upon one city but not upon another; one field was watered by rain, but another without rain dried up; 8 though two or three cities staggered to one city for water that did not quench their thirst; yet you returned not to me, says the LORD. 9 I struck you with blight and searing wind; your many gardens and vineyards, your fig trees and olive trees the locust devoured; yet you returned not to me, says the LORD. 10 I sent upon you a pestilence like that of Egypt, and with the sword I slew your young men; your horses I let be captured, to your nostrils I brought the stench of your camps; yet you returned not to me, says the LORD. 11 I brought upon you such upheaval as when God overthrew Sodom and Gomorrah: you were like a brand plucked from the fire; yet you returned not to me, says the LORD. 12 So now I will deal with you in my own way, O Israel! and since I will deal thus with you, prepare to meet your God, O Israel: 13 him who formed the mountains, and created the wind, and declares to man his thoughts; who made the dawn and the darkness, and strides

upon the heights of the earth: the LORD, the God of hosts by name.

Amos Chapter 5

¹Hear this word which I utter over you, a lament, O house of Israel: ²She is fallen, to rise no more, the virgin Israel; she lies abandoned upon her land, with no one to raise her up. ³For thus says the Lord GOD: The city that marched out with a thousand shall be left without a hundred, another that marched out with a hundred shall be left with ten, of the house of Israel. ⁴For thus says the LORD to the house of Israel: Seek me, that you may live, ⁵but do not seek Bethel; do not come to Gilgal, and do not cross to Beer-sheba. For Gilgal shall be led into exile, and Bethel shall become nought. ⁶Seek the LORD, that you may live, lest he come upon the house of Joseph like a fire that shall consume, with none to quench it for the house of Israel: ⁷Woe to those who turn judgment to wormwood and cast justice to the ground! ⁸He who made the Pleiades and Orion, who turns darkness into dawn, and darkens day into night; who summons the waters of the sea, and pours them out upon the surface of the earth; ⁹who flashes destruction upon the strong, and brings ruin upon the fortress; whose name is LORD. ¹⁰They hate him who reproves at the gate and abhor him who speaks the truth. ¹¹Therefore, because you have trampled upon the weak and exacted of them levies of grain, though you have built houses of hewn stone, you shall not live in them! Though you have planted choice vineyards, you shall not drink their wine! ¹²Yes, I know how many are your crimes, how grievous your sins: Oppressing the just, accepting bribes, repelling the needy at the gate! ¹³Therefore the prudent man is silent at this time, for it is an evil time. ¹⁴Seek good and not evil, that you may live; then truly will the LORD, the God of hosts, be with you as you claim! ¹⁵Hate evil and love good, and let justice prevail at the gate; then it may be that the LORD, the God of hosts, will have pity on the remnant of Joseph. ¹⁶Therefore, thus says the LORD, the God of hosts, the Lord: In every square there shall be lamentation, and in every street they shall cry, Alas! Alas! They shall summon the farmers to wail and professional mourners to lament, ¹⁷and in every vineyard there shall be lamentation when I pass through your midst, says the LORD. ¹⁸Woe to those who yearn for the day of the LORD! What will this day of the LORD mean for you? Darkness and not light! ¹⁹As if a man went to flee from a lion, and a bear should meet him; or as if on entering his house he were to rest his hand against the wall, and a snake should bite him. ²⁰Will not the day of the LORD be darkness and not light, gloom without any brightness? ²¹I hate, I spurn your feasts, I take no pleasure in your solemnities; ²²your cereal offerings I will not accept, nor consider your stall-fed peace offerings. ²³Away with your noisy songs! I will not listen to the melodies of your harps. But if you would offer me holocausts, ²⁴then let justice surge like water, and goodness like an unfailing stream. ²⁵Did you bring me sacrifices and offerings for forty years in the desert, O house of Israel? ²⁶You will carry away Sakkuth, your king, and Kaiwan, your star god, the images that you have made for yourselves; ²⁷for I will exile you beyond Damascus, say I, the LORD, the God of hosts by name.

Amos Chapter 6

¹Woe to the complacent in Zion, to the overconfident on the mount of Samaria, leaders of a nation favored from the first, to whom the people of Israel have recourse! ²Pass over to Calneh and see, go from there to Hamath the great, and down to Gath of the Philistines! Are you better than these kingdoms, or is your territory wider than theirs? ³You would put off the evil day, yet you hasten the reign of violence! ⁴Lying upon beds of ivory, stretched comfortably on their couches, they eat lambs taken from the flock, and calves from the stall! ⁵Improvising to the music of the harp, like David, they devise their own accompaniment. ⁶They drink wine from bowls and anoint themselves with the best oils; yet they are not made ill by the collapse of Joseph! ⁷Therefore, now they shall be the first to go into exile, and their wanton revelry shall be done away with. ⁸The Lord GOD has sworn by his very self, say I, the LORD, the God of hosts: I abhor the pride of Jacob, I hate his castles, and I give over the city with everything in it; ⁹Should there remain ten men in a single house, these shall die. ¹⁰Only a few shall be left to carry the dead out of the houses; if one says to a man inside a house, "Is anyone with you?" and he answers, "No one," then he shall say, "Silence!" for no one must mention the name of the LORD. ¹¹Indeed, the LORD has given the command to shatter the great house to bits, and reduce the small house to rubble. ¹²Can horses run across a cliff? or can one plow the sea with oxen? Yet you have turned judgment into gall, and the fruit of justice into wormwood. ¹³You rejoice in Lodebar, and say, "Have we not, by our own strength, seized for ourselves Karnaim?" ¹⁴Beware, I am raising up against you, O house of Israel, say I, the LORD, the God of hosts, a nation that shall oppress you from Labo of Hamath even to the Wadi Arabah.

Amos Chapter 7

¹This is what the Lord GOD showed me: He was forming a locust swarm when the late growth began to come up (the late growth after the king's mowing). ²While they were eating all the grass in the land, I said: Forgive, O Lord GOD! How can Jacob stand? He is so small! ³And the LORD repented of this. "It shall not be," said the Lord GOD. ⁴Then the Lord GOD showed me this: he called for a judgment by fire. It had devoured the great abyss, and was consuming the land, ⁵when I said: Cease, O Lord GOD! How can Jacob stand? He is so small! ⁶The LORD repented of this. "This also shall not be," said the Lord GOD. ⁷Then the Lord GOD showed me this: he was standing by a wall, plummet in hand. ⁸The LORD asked me, "What do you see, Amos?" And when I answered, "A plummet," the Lord said: See, I will lay the plummet in the midst of my people Israel; I will forgive them no longer. ⁹The high places of Isaac shall be laid waste, and the sanctuaries of Israel made desolate; I will attack the house of Jeroboam with the sword. ¹⁰Amaziah, the priest of Bethel, sent word to Jeroboam, king of Israel: "Amos has conspired against you here within Israel; the country cannot endure all his words. ¹¹For this is what Amos says: Jeroboam shall die by the sword, and Israel shall surely be exiled from its land." ¹²To Amos, Amaziah said: "Off with you, visionary, flee to the land of Judah! There earn your bread by prophesying, ¹³but never again prophesy in Bethel; for it is the king's sanctuary and a royal temple." ¹⁴Amos answered Amaziah, "I was no prophet, nor have I belonged to a company of prophets; I was a shepherd and a dresser of sycamores. ¹⁵The LORD took me from following the flock, and said to me, Go, prophesy to my people Israel. ¹⁶Now hear the word of the LORD!" You say: prophesy not against Israel, preach not against the house of Isaac. ¹⁷Now thus says the LORD: Your wife shall be made a harlot in the city, and your sons and daughters shall fall by the sword; your land shall be divided by measuring line, and you yourself shall die in an unclean land; Israel shall be exiled far from its land.

Amos Chapter 8

¹This is what the Lord GOD showed me: a basket of ripe fruit. ²"What do you see, Amos?" he asked. I answered, "A basket of ripe fruit." Then the LORD said to me: The time is ripe to have done with my people Israel; I will forgive them no longer. ³The temple songs shall become wailings on that day, says the Lord GOD. Many shall be the corpses, strewn everywhere. - Silence! ⁴Hear this, you who trample upon the needy and destroy the poor of the land! ⁵"When will the new moon be over," you ask, "that we may sell our grain, and the sabbath, that we may display the wheat? We will diminish the ephah, add to the shekel, and fix our scales for cheating! ⁶We will buy the lowly man for silver, and the poor man for a pair of sandals; even the refuse of the wheat we will sell!" ⁷The LORD has sworn by the pride of Jacob: Never will I forget a thing they have done! ⁸Shall not the land tremble because of this, and all who dwell in it mourn, while it rises up and tosses like the Nile, and settles back like the river of Egypt? ⁹On that day, says the Lord GOD, I will make the sun set at midday and cover the earth with darkness in broad daylight. ¹⁰I will turn your feasts into mourning and all your songs into lamentations. I will cover the loins of all with sackcloth and make every head bald. I will make them mourn as for an only son, and bring their day to a bitter end. ¹¹Yes, days are coming, says the Lord GOD, when I will send famine upon the land: Not a famine of bread, or thirst for water, but for hearing the word of the LORD. ¹²Then shall they wander from sea to sea and rove from the north to the east in search of the word of the LORD, but they shall not find it. ¹³On that day, fair virgins and young men shall faint from thirst; ¹⁴Those who swear by the shameful idol of Samaria, "By the life of your god, O Dan!" "By the life of your love, O Beersheba!" those shall fall, never to rise again.

Amos Chapter 9

¹I saw the Lord standing beside the altar, and he said: Strike the bases, so that the doorjambs totter till you break them off on the heads of them all! Those who are left I will slay with the sword; not one shall flee, no survivor shall escape. ²Though they break through to the nether world, even from there my hand shall bring them out; Though they climb to the heavens, I will bring them down; ³Though they hide on the summit of Carmel, there too I will hunt them out and take them away; Though they hide from my gaze in the bottom of the sea, I will command the serpent there to bite them; ⁴Though they are led into captivity by their enemies, there will I command the sword to slay them. I will fix my gaze upon them for evil, and not for good, ⁵I, the Lord GOD of hosts. I melt the earth with my touch, so that all who dwell on it mourn, while it all rises up like the Nile, and settles back like the river of Egypt; ⁶I have built heaven, my upper chamber, and established my vault over the earth; I summon the waters of the sea and pour them upon the surface

of the earth, I, the LORD by name. 7Are you not like the Ethiopians to
me, O men of Israel, says the LORD? Did I not bring the Israelites from
the land of Egypt as I brought the Philistines from Caphtor and the
Arameans from Kir? 8The eyes of the Lord GOD are on this sinful
kingdom; I will destroy it from off the face of the earth. But I will not
destroy the house of Jacob completely, says the LORD. 9For see, I have
given the command to sift the house of Israel among all the nations, as
one sifts with a sieve, letting no pebble fall to the ground. 10By the
sword shall all sinners among my people die, those who say, "Evil will
not reach or overtake us." 11On that day I will raise up the fallen hut of
David; I will wall up its breaches, raise up its ruins, and rebuild it as in
the days of old, 12that they may conquer what is left of Edom and all
the nations that shall bear my name, say I, the LORD, who will do this.
13Yes, days are coming, says the LORD, when the plowman shall
overtake the reaper, and the vintager, him who sows the seed; The juice
of grapes shall drip down the mountains, and all the hills shall run with
it. 14I will bring about the restoration of my people Israel; they shall
rebuild and inhabit their ruined cities, plant vineyards and drink the
wine, set out gardens and eat the fruits. 15I will plant them upon their
own ground; never again shall they be plucked from the land I have
given them, say I, the LORD, your God.

Obadiah

Obadiah Chapter 1

1The vision of Obadiah. (Thus says the Lord GOD:) Of Edom we have
heard a message from the LORD, and a herald has been sent among the
nations: "Up! let us go to war against him!" 2See, I make you small
among the nations; you are held in dire contempt. 3The pride of your
heart has deceived you: you who dwell in the clefts of the rock, whose
abode is in the heights, Who say in your heart, "Who will bring me down
to earth?" 4Though you go as high as the eagle, and your nest be set
among the stars, From there will I bring you down, says the LORD. 5If
thieves came to you, if robbers by night, how could you be thus
destroyed: would they not steal merely till they had enough? If vintagers
came to you, would they not leave some gleanings? 6How they search
Esau, seek out his hiding places! 7To the border they drive you - all your
allies; They deceive you, they overpower you - those at peace with you;
Those who eat your bread lay snares beneath you: There is no
understanding in him! 8Shall I not, says the LORD, on that day make
the wise men disappear from Edom, and understanding from the
mount of Esau? 9Your warriors, O Teman, shall be crushed, till all on
Mount Esau are destroyed. 10Because of violence to your brother Jacob,
disgrace shall cover you and you shall be destroyed forever. 11On the
day when you stood by, on the day when aliens carried off his
possessions, And strangers entered his gates and cast lots over
Jerusalem, you too were one of them. 12Gaze not upon the day of your
brother, the day of his disaster; Exult not over the children of Judah on
the day of their ruin; Speak not haughtily on the day of distress! 13Enter
not the gate of my people on the day of their calamity; Gaze not, you at
least, upon his misfortune on the day of his calamity; Lay not hands
upon his possessions on the day of his calamity! 14Stand not at the
crossroads to slay his refugees; Betray not his fugitives on the day of
distress! 15For near is the day of the LORD for all the nations! As you
have done, so shall it be done to you, your deed shall come back upon
your own head; 16As you have drunk upon my holy mountain, so shall
all the nations drink continually. Yes, they shall drink and swallow, and
shall become as though they had not been. 17But on Mount Zion there
shall be a portion saved; the mountain shall be holy, And the house of
Jacob shall take possession of those that dispossessed them. 18The
house of Jacob shall be a fire, and the house of Joseph a flame; The
house of Esau shall be stubble, and they shall set them ablaze and
devour them; Then none shall survive of the house of Esau, for the
LORD has spoken. 19They shall occupy the Negeb, the mount of Esau,
and the foothills of the Philistines; And they shall occupy the lands of
Ephraim and the lands of Samaria, and Benjamin shall occupy Gilead.
20The captives of the host of the children of Israel shall occupy the
Canaanite land as far as Zarephath, And the captives of Jerusalem who
are in Sepharad shall occupy the cities of the Negeb. 21And saviors shall
ascend Mount Zion to rule the mount of Esau, and the kingship shall be
the LORD'S.

Jonah

Jonah Chapter 1

1This is the word of the LORD that came to Jonah, son of Amittai: 2"Set
out for the great city of Nineveh, and preach against it; their wickedness
has come up before me." 3But Jonah made ready to flee to Tarshish
away from the LORD. He went down to Joppa, found a ship going to
Tarshish, paid the fare, and went aboard to journey with them to
Tarshish, away from the LORD. 4The LORD, however, hurled a violent
wind upon the sea, and in the furious tempest that arose the ship was
on the point of breaking up. 5Then the mariners became frightened and
each one cried to his god. To lighten the ship for themselves, they threw
its cargo into the sea. Meanwhile, Jonah had gone down into the hold
of the ship, and lay there fast asleep. 6The captain came to him and said,
"What are you doing asleep? Rise up, call upon your God! Perhaps God
will be mindful of us so that we may not perish." 7Then they said to one
another, "Come, let us cast lots to find out on whose account we have
met with this misfortune." So they cast lots, and thus singled out Jonah.
8"Tell us," they said, "what is your business? Where do you come from?
What is your country, and to what people do you belong?" 9"I am a
Hebrew," Jonah answered them; "I worship the LORD, the God of
heaven, who made the sea and the dry land." 10Now the men were
seized with great fear and said to him, "How could you do such a thing!"
- They knew that he was fleeing from the LORD, because he had told
them. - 11"What shall we do with you," they asked, "that the sea may
quiet down for us?" For the sea was growing more and more turbulent.
12Jonah said to them, "Pick me up and throw me into the sea, that it
may quiet down for you; since I know it is because of me that this violent
storm has come upon you." 13Still the men rowed hard to regain the
land, but they could not, for the sea grew ever more turbulent. 14Then
they cried to the LORD: "We beseech you, O LORD, let us not perish for
taking this man's life; do not charge us with shedding innocent blood,
for you, LORD, have done as you saw fit." 15Then they took Jonah and
threw him into the sea, and the sea's raging abated. 16Struck with great
fear of the LORD, the men offered sacrifice and made vows to him.

Jonah Chapter 2

1 But the LORD sent a large fish, that swallowed Jonah; and he
remained in the belly of the fish three days and three nights. 2 From the
belly of the fish Jonah said this prayer to the LORD, his God: 3 Out of
my distress I called to the LORD, and he answered me; From the midst
of the nether world I cried for help, and you heard my voice. 4 For you
cast me into the deep, into the heart of the sea, and the flood enveloped
me; All your breakers and your billows passed over me. 5 Then I said,
"I am banished from your sight! yet would I again look upon your holy
temple." 6 The waters swirled about me, threatening my life; the abyss
enveloped me; seaweed clung about my head. 7 Down I went to the
roots of the mountains; the bars of the nether world were closing behind
me forever, But you brought my life up from the pit, O LORD, my God.
8 When my soul fainted within me, I remembered the LORD; My prayer
reached you in your holy temple. 9 Those who worship vain idols
forsake their source of mercy. 10 But I, with resounding praise, will
sacrifice to you; What I have vowed I will pay: deliverance is from the
LORD. 11 Then the LORD commanded the fish to spew Jonah upon the
shore. The word of the LORD came to Jonah a second time: 12 "Set out
for the great city of Nineveh, and announce to it the message that I will
tell you." 13 So Jonah made ready and went to Nineveh, according to
the LORD'S bidding. Now Nineveh was an enormously large city; it took
three days to go through it. 14 Jonah began his journey through the city,
and had gone but a single day's walk announcing, "Forty days more and
Nineveh shall be destroyed," 15 when the people of Nineveh believed
God; they proclaimed a fast and all of them, great and small, put on
sackcloth. 16 When the news reached the king of Nineveh, he rose from
his throne, laid aside his robe, covered himself with sackcloth, and sat
in the ashes. 17 Then he had this proclaimed throughout Nineveh, by
decree of the king and his nobles: "Neither man nor beast, neither cattle
nor sheep, shall taste anything; they shall not eat, nor shall they drink
water. 18 Man and beast shall be covered with sackcloth and call loudly
to God; every man shall turn from his evil way and from the violence he
has in hand. 19 Who knows, God may relent and forgive, and withhold
his blazing wrath, so that we shall not perish." 20 When God saw by
their actions how they turned from their evil way, he repented of the
evil that he had threatened to do to them; he did not carry it out.

Jonah Chapter 3

1 The word of the LORD came to Jonah a second time: 2 "Set out for the
great city of Nineveh, and announce to it the message that I will tell
you." 3 So Jonah made ready and went to Nineveh, according to the
LORD'S bidding. Now Nineveh was an enormously large city; it took
three days to go through it. 4 Jonah began his journey through the city,
and had gone but a single day's walk announcing, "Forty days more and
Nineveh shall be destroyed," 5 when the people of Nineveh believed
God; they proclaimed a fast and all of them, great and small, put on
sackcloth. 6 When the news reached the king of Nineveh, he rose from
his throne, laid aside his robe, covered himself with sackcloth, and sat

in the ashes. 7 Then he had this proclaimed throughout Nineveh, by decree of the king and his nobles: "Neither man nor beast, neither cattle nor sheep, shall taste anything; they shall not eat, nor shall they drink water. 8 Man and beast shall be covered with sackcloth and call loudly to God; every man shall turn from his evil way and from the violence he has in hand. 9 Who knows, God may relent and forgive, and withhold his blazing wrath, so that we shall not perish." 10 When God saw by their actions how they turned from their evil way, he repented of the evil that he had threatened to do to them; he did not carry it out.

Jonah Chapter 4

1 But this was greatly displeasing to Jonah, and he became angry. 2 "I beseech you, LORD," he prayed, "is not this what I said while I was still in my own country? This is why I fled at first to Tarshish. I knew that you are a gracious and merciful God, slow to anger, rich in clemency, loathe to punish. 3 And now, LORD, please take my life from me; for it is better for me to die than to live." 4 But the LORD asked, "Have you reason to be angry?" 5 Jonah then left the city for a place to the east of it, where he built himself a hut and waited under it in the shade, to see what would happen to the city. 6 And when the LORD God provided a gourd plant, that grew up over Jonah's head, giving shade that relieved him of any discomfort, Jonah was very happy over the plant. 7 But the next morning at dawn God sent a worm which attacked the plant, so that it withered. 8 And when the sun arose, God sent a burning east wind; and the sun beat upon Jonah's head till he became faint. Then he asked for death, saying, "I would be better off dead than alive." 9 But God said to Jonah, "Have you reason to be angry over the plant?" "I have reason to be angry," Jonah answered, "angry enough to die." 10 Then the LORD said, "You are concerned over the plant which cost you no labor and which you did not raise; it came up in one night and in one night it perished. 11 And should I not be concerned over Nineveh, the great city, in which there are more than a hundred and twenty thousand persons who cannot distinguish their right hand from their left, not to mention the many cattle?"

Micah

Micah Chapter 1

1 The word of the LORD which came to Micah of Moresheth in the days of Jotham, Ahaz, and Hezekiah, kings of Judah: that is, the vision he received concerning Samaria and Jerusalem. 2 Hear, O peoples, all of you, give heed, O earth, and all that fills you! Let the Lord GOD be witness against you, the Lord from his holy temple! 3 For see, the LORD comes forth from his place, he descends and treads upon the heights of the earth. 4 The mountains melt under him and the valleys split open, like wax before the fire, like water poured down a slope. 5 For the crime of Jacob all this comes to pass, and for the sins of the house of Israel. What is the crime of Jacob? Is it not Samaria? And what is the sin of the house of Judah? Is it not Jerusalem? 6 I will make Samaria a stone heap in the field, a place to plant for vineyards; I will throw down into the valley her stones, and lay bare her foundations. 7 All her idols shall be broken to pieces, all her wages shall be burned in the fire, and all her statues I will destroy. As the wages of a harlot they were gathered, and to the wages of a harlot shall they return. 8 For this reason I lament and wail, I go barefoot and naked; I utter lamentation like the jackals, and mourning like the ostriches. 9 There is no remedy for the blow she has been struck; rather, it has come even to Judah, it reaches to the gate of my people, even to Jerusalem. 10 Publish it not in Gath, weep not at all; in Beth-leaphrah roll in the dust. 11 Pass by, you who dwell in Shaphir! The inhabitants of Zaanan come not forth from their city. The lamentation of Beth-ezel finds in you its grounds. 12 How can the inhabitants of Maroth hope for good? For evil has come down from the LORD to the gate of Jerusalem. 13 Harness steeds to the chariots, O inhabitants of Lachish; Lachish, the beginning of sin for daughter Zion, because there were in you the crimes of Israel. 14 Therefore you shall give parting gifts to Moresheth-gath; Beth-achzib is a deception to the kings of Israel. 15 Yet must I bring to you the conqueror, O inhabitants of Mareshah; even to Adullam shall go the glory of Israel. 16 Make yourself bald, pluck out your hair, for the children whom you cherish; let your baldness be as the eagle's, because they are exiled from you.

Micah Chapter 2

1 Woe to those who plan iniquity, and work out evil on their couches; in the morning light they accomplish it when it lies within their power. 2 They covet fields, and seize them; houses, and they take them; they cheat an owner of his house, a man of his inheritance. 3 Therefore thus says the LORD: Behold, I am planning against this race an evil from which you shall not withdraw your necks; nor shall you walk with head high, for it will be a time of evil. 4 On that day a satire shall be sung over you, and there shall be a plaintive chant: "Our ruin is complete, our

fields are portioned out among our captors, the fields of my people are measured out, and no one can get them back!" 5 Thus you shall have no one to mark out boundaries by lot in the assembly of the LORD. 6 "Preach not," they preach, "let them not preach of these things!" The shame will not withdraw. 7 How can it be said, O house of Jacob, "Is the LORD short of patience, or are such his deeds?" Do not my words promise good to him who walks uprightly? 8 But of late my people has risen up as an enemy: you have stripped off the mantle covering the tunic of those who go their way in confidence, as though it were spoils of war. 9 The women of my people you drive out from their pleasant houses; from their children you take away forever the honor I gave them. 10 "Up! Be off, this is no place to rest"; for any trifle you exact a crippling pledge. 11 If one, acting on impulse, should make the futile claim: "I pour you wine and strong drink as my prophecy," then he would be the prophet of this people. 12 I will gather you, O Jacob, each and every one, I will assemble all the remnant of Israel; I will group them like a flock in the fold, like a herd in the midst of its corral; they shall not be thrown into panic by men. 13 With a leader to break the path they shall burst open the gate and go out through it; their king shall go through before them, and the LORD at their head.

Micah Chapter 3

1 And I said: Hear, you leaders of Jacob, rulers of the house of Israel! Is it not your duty to know what is right, 2 you who hate what is good, and love evil? You who tear their skin from them, and their flesh from their bones! 3 They eat the flesh of my people, and flay their skin from them, and break their bones. They chop them in pieces like flesh in a kettle, and like meat in a caldron. 4 When they cry to the LORD, he shall not answer them; rather shall he hide his face from them at that time, because of the evil they have done. 5 Thus says the LORD regarding the prophets who lead my people astray; who, when their teeth have something to bite, announce peace, but when one fails to put something in their mouth, proclaim war against him. 6 Therefore you shall have night, not vision, darkness, not divination; the sun shall go down upon the prophets, and the day shall be dark for them. 7 Then shall the seers be put to shame, and the diviners confounded; they shall cover their lips, all of them, because there is no answer from God. 8 But as for me, I am filled with power, with the spirit of the LORD, with authority and with might; to declare to Jacob his crimes and to Israel his sins. 9 Hear this, you leaders of the house of Jacob, you rulers of the house of Israel! You who abhor what is just, and pervert all that is right; 10 who build up Zion with bloodshed, and Jerusalem with wickedness! 11 Her leaders render judgment for a bribe, her priests give decisions for a salary, her prophets divine for money, while they rely on the LORD, saying, "Is not the LORD in the midst of us? No evil can come upon us!" 12 Therefore, because of you, Zion shall be plowed like a field, and Jerusalem reduced to rubble, and the mount of the temple to a forest ridge.

Micah Chapter 4

1 In days to come the mount of the LORD'S house shall be established higher than the mountains; it shall rise high above the hills, and peoples shall stream to it. 2 Many nations shall come, and say, "Come, let us climb the mount of the LORD, to the house of the God of Jacob, that he may instruct us in his ways, that we may walk in his paths." For from Zion shall go forth instruction, and the word of the LORD from Jerusalem. 3 He shall judge between many peoples and impose terms on strong and distant nations; they shall beat their swords into plowshares, and their spears into pruning hooks; one nation shall not raise the sword against another, nor shall they train for war again. 4 Every man shall sit under his own vine or under his own fig tree, undisturbed; for the mouth of the LORD of hosts has spoken. 5 For all the peoples walk each in the name of its god, but we will walk in the name of the LORD, our God, forever and ever. 6 On that day, says the LORD, I will gather the lame, and I will assemble the outcasts, and those whom I have afflicted. 7 I will make of the lame a remnant, and of those driven far off a strong nation; and the LORD shall be king over them on Mount Zion, from now on forever. 8 And you, O Magdal-eder, hillock of daughter Zion! Unto you shall it come: the former dominion shall be restored, the kingdom of daughter Jerusalem. 9 Now why do you cry out so? Are you without a king? Or has your counselor perished, that you are seized with pains like a woman in travail? 10 Writhe in pain, grow faint, O daughter Zion, like a woman in travail; for now shall you go forth from the city and dwell in the fields; to Babylon shall you go, there shall you be rescued. There shall the LORD redeem you from the hand of your enemies. 11 How many nations are gathered against you! They say, "Let her be profaned, let our eyes see Zion's downfall!" 12 But they know not the thoughts of the LORD, nor understand his counsel, when he has gathered them like sheaves on the threshing floor. 13 Arise

and thresh, O daughter Zion; your horn I will make iron and your hoofs bronze, that you may crush many peoples; you shall devote their spoils to the LORD, and their riches to the Lord of the whole earth. 14 Now fence yourself in, Bat-gader! "They have laid siege against us!" With the rod they strike on the cheek the ruler of Israel.

Micah Chapter 5

1 But you, Bethlehem-Ephrathah, too small to be among the clans of Judah, from you shall come forth for me one who is to be ruler in Israel; whose origin is from of old, from ancient times. 2 Therefore the Lord will give them up, until the time when she who is to give birth has borne, and the rest of his brethren shall return to the children of Israel. 3 He shall stand firm and shepherd his flock by the strength of the LORD, in the majestic name of the LORD, his God; and they shall remain, for now his greatness shall reach to the ends of the earth; 4 he shall be peace. If Assyria invades our country and treads upon our land, we shall raise against it seven shepherds, eight men of royal rank. 5 And they shall tend the land of Assyria with the sword, and the land of Nimrod with the drawn sword; and we shall be delivered from Assyria, if it invades our land and treads upon our borders. 6 The remnant of Jacob shall be in the midst of many peoples, like dew coming from the LORD, like raindrops on the grass, which wait for no man, nor tarry for the sons of men. 7 And the remnant of Jacob shall be among the nations, in the midst of many peoples, like a lion among beasts of the forest, like a young lion among flocks of sheep; when it passes through, it tramples and tears, and there is none to deliver. 8 Your hand shall be lifted above your foes, and all your enemies shall be destroyed. 9 On that day, says the LORD, I will destroy the horses from your midst and ruin your chariots. 10 I will demolish the cities of your land and tear down all your fortresses. 11 I will abolish the means of divination from your use, and there shall no longer be soothsayers among you. 12 I will abolish your carved images and the sacred pillars from your midst, and you shall no longer adore the works of your hands. 13 I will tear out the sacred poles from your midst, and destroy your cities. 14 I will wreak vengeance in anger and wrath upon the nations that have not hearkened.

Micah Chapter 6

1 Hear, then, what the LORD says: Arise, present your plea before the mountains, and let the hills hear your voice! 2 Hear, O mountains, the plea of the LORD, pay attention, O foundations of the earth! For the LORD has a plea against his people, and he enters into trial with Israel. 3 O my people, what have I done to you, or how have I wearied you? Answer me! 4 For I brought you up from the land of Egypt, from the place of slavery I released you; and I sent before you Moses, Aaron, and Miriam. 5 My people, remember what Moab's King Balak planned, and how Balaam, the son of Beor, answered him... from Shittim to Gilgal, that you may know the just deeds of the LORD. 6 With what shall I come before the LORD, and bow before God most high? Shall I come before him with holocausts, with calves a year old? 7 Will the LORD be pleased with thousands of rams, with myriad streams of oil? Shall I give my first-born for my crime, the fruit of my body for the sin of my soul? 8 You have been told, O man, what is good, and what the LORD requires of you: Only to do right and to love goodness, and to walk humbly with your God. 9 Hark! the LORD cries to the city. (It is wisdom to fear your name!) Hear, O tribe and city council, 10 Am I to bear any longer criminal hoarding and the meager ephah that is accursed? 11 Shall I acquit criminal balances, bags of false weights? 12 You whose rich men are full of violence, whose inhabitants speak falsehood with deceitful tongues in their heads! 13 Rather I will begin to strike you with devastation because of your sins. 14 You shall eat, without being satisfied, food that will leave you empty; what you acquire, you cannot save; what you do save, I will deliver up to the sword. 15 You shall sow, yet not reap, tread out the olive, yet pour no oil, and the grapes, yet drink no wine. 16 You have kept the decrees of Omri, and all the works of the house of Ahab, and you have walked in their counsels; therefore I will deliver you up to ruin, and your citizens to derision; and you shall bear the reproach of the nations.

Micah Chapter 7

1 Alas! I am as when the fruit is gathered, as when the vines have been gleaned; there is no cluster to eat, no early fig that I crave. 2 The faithful are gone from the earth, among men the upright are no more! They all lie in wait to shed blood, each one ensnares the other. 3 Their hands succeed at evil; the prince makes demands, the judge is had for a price, the great man speaks as he pleases. 4 The best of them is like a brier, the most upright like a thorn hedge. The day announced by your watchmen! Your punishment has come; now is the time of your confusion. 5 Put no trust in a friend, have no confidence in a companion; against her who lies in your bosom guard the portals of your mouth. 6 For the son dishonors his father, the daughter rises up

against her mother, the daughter-in-law against her mother-in-law, and a man's enemies are those of his household. 7 But as for me, I will look to the LORD, I will put my trust in God my savior; my God will hear me! 8 Rejoice not over me, O my enemy! Though I have fallen, I will arise; though I sit in darkness, the LORD is my light. 9 The wrath of the LORD I will endure because I have sinned against him, until he takes up my cause, and establishes my right. He will bring me forth to the light; I will see his justice. 10 When my enemy sees this, shame shall cover her: she who said to me, "Where is the LORD, thy God?" My eyes shall see her downfall; now shall she be trampled underfoot, like the mire in the streets. 11 It is the day for building your walls; on that day the boundary shall be taken away. 12 It is the day; and they shall come to you from Assyria and from Egypt, from Tyre even to the River, from sea to sea, and from mountain to mountain. 13 And the land shall be a waste because of its citizens, as a result of their deeds. 14 Shepherd your people with your staff, the flock of your inheritance, that dwells apart in a woodland, in the midst of Carmel. Let them feed in Bashan and Gilead, as in the days of old; 15 as in the days when you came from the land of Egypt, show us wonderful signs. 16 The nations shall behold and be put to shame, in spite of all their strength; they shall put their hands over their mouths; their ears shall become deaf. 17 They shall lick the dust like the serpent, like reptiles on the ground; they shall come quaking from their fastnesses, trembling in fear of you (the LORD, our God). 18 Who is there like you, the God who removes guilt and pardons sin for the remnant of his inheritance; who does not persist in anger forever, but delights rather in clemency, 19 and will again have compassion on us, treading underfoot our guilt? You will cast into the depths of the sea all our sins; 20 you will show faithfulness to Jacob, and grace to Abraham, as you have sworn to our fathers from days of old.

Nahum

Nahum Chapter 1

1 Oracle about Nineveh. The book of the vision of Nahum of Elkosh. 2 A jealous and avenging God is the LORD, an avenger is the LORD, and angry; the LORD brings vengeance on his adversaries, and lays up wrath for his enemies; 3 The LORD is slow to anger, yet great in power, and the LORD never leaves the guilty unpunished. In hurricane and tempest is his path, and clouds are the dust at his feet; 4 He rebukes the sea and leaves it dry, and all the rivers he dries up. Withered are Bashan and Carmel, and the bloom of Lebanon fades; 5 The mountains quake before him, and the hills dissolve; the earth is laid waste before him, the world and all who dwell in it. 6 Before his wrath, who can stand firm, and who can face his blazing anger? His fury is poured out like fire, and the rocks are rent asunder before him. 7 The LORD is good, a refuge on the day of distress; he takes care of those who have recourse to him, 8 when the flood rages; he makes an end of his opponents, and his enemies he pursues with darkness. 9 What are you imputing to the LORD? It is he who will make an end! The enemy shall not rise a second time; 10 As when a tangle of thornbushes is set aflame, like dry stubble, they shall be utterly consumed. 11 From you he came who devised evil against the LORD, the scoundrel planner. 12 For, says the LORD, be they ever so many and so vigorous, still they shall be mown down and disappear. Though I have humbled you, I will humble you no more. 13 Now will I break his yoke from off you, and burst asunder your bonds. 14 The LORD has commanded regarding you: no descendant shall come to bear your name; from your temple I will abolish the carved and the molten image; I will make your grave a mockery.

Nahum Chapter 2

1 See, upon the mountains there advances the bearer of good news, announcing peace! Celebrate your feasts, O Judah, fulfill your vows! For nevermore shall you be invaded by the scoundrel; he is completely destroyed. 2 The LORD will restore the vine of Jacob, the pride of Israel, though ravagers have ravaged them and ruined the tendrils. 3 The hammer comes up against you; guard the rampart, keep watch on the road, gird your loins, marshall all your strength! 4 The shields of his warriors are crimsoned, the soldiers colored in scarlet; fiery steel are the chariots on the day of his mustering. The horses are frenzied; 5 The chariots dash madly through the streets and wheel in the squares, looking like firebrands, flashing like lightning bolts. 6 His picked troops are called, ranks break at their charge; to the wall they rush, the mantelet is set up. 7 The river gates are opened, the palace shudders, 8 Its mistress is led forth captive, and her handmaids, under guard, moaning like doves, beating their breasts. 9 Nineveh is like a pool whose waters escape; "Stop! Stop!" but none turns back. 10 "Plunder the silver, plunder the gold!" There is no end to the treasure, to their wealth in precious things of every kind! 11 Emptiness, desolation, waste; melting hearts and trembling knees, writhing in every frame, every face

blanched! 12 Where is the lions' cave, the young lions' den, where the lion went in and out, and the cub, with no one to disturb them? 13 The lion snatched enough for his cubs, and strangled for his lionesses; he filled his dens with prey, and his caves with plunder. 14 I come against you, says the LORD of hosts; I will consume in smoke your chariots, and the sword shall devour your young lions; your preying on the land I will bring to an end, the cry of your lionesses shall be heard no more.

Nahum Chapter 3

1 Woe to the bloody city, all lies, full of plunder, whose looting never stops! 2 The crack of the whip, the rumbling sounds of wheels; horses a-gallop, chariots bounding, 3 Cavalry charging, the flame of the sword, the flash of the spear, the many slain, the heaping corpses, the endless bodies to stumble upon! 4 For the many debaucheries of the harlot, fair and charming, a mistress of witchcraft, who enslaved nations with her harlotries, and peoples by her witchcraft: 5 I am come against you, and I will strip your skirt from you; I will show your nakedness to the nations, to the kingdoms your shame! 6 I will cast filth upon you, disgrace you and put you to shame; 7 Till everyone who sees you runs from you, saying, "Nineveh is destroyed; who can pity her? Where can one find any to console her?" 8 Are you better than No-amon that was set among the streams, surrounded by waters, with the flood for her rampart and water her wall? 9 Ethiopia was her strength, and Egypt, and others without end; Put and the Libyans were her auxiliaries. 10 Yet even she went captive into exile, even her little ones were dashed to pieces at the corner of every street; for her nobles they cast lots, and all her great men were put into chains. 11 You too, shall drink of this till you faint away; you, too, shall seek a refuge from the foe. 12 All your fortresses are but fig trees, bearing early figs that fall, when shaken, into the hungry mouth. 13 See, the troops are women in your midst; to your foes the gates of your land are open wide, fire has consumed their bars. 14 Draw water for the siege, strengthen your fortresses; go down into the mud and tread the clay, take hold of the brick mold! 15 There the fire shall consume you, the sword shall cut you down. Multiply like the grasshoppers, multiply like the locusts! 16 Make your couriers more numerous than the stars, your garrisons as many as grasshoppers, and your scribes as locust swarms gathered on the rubble fences on a cold day! 17 Yet when the sun warms them, the grasshoppers will spread their wings and fly, and vanish, no one knows where. 18 Alas! how your shepherds slumber, O king of Assyria, your nobles have gone to rest; your people are scattered upon the mountains, with none to gather them. 19 There is no healing for your hurt, your wound is mortal. All who hear this news of you clap their hands over you; for who has not been overwhelmed, steadily, by your malice?

Habakkuk

Habakkuk Chapter 1

1 The oracle which Habakkuk the prophet received in vision. 2 How long, O LORD? I cry for help but you do not listen! I cry out to you, "Violence!" but you do not intervene. 3 Why do you let me see ruin; why must I look at misery? Destruction and violence are before me; there is strife, and clamorous discord. 4 This is why the law is benumbed, and judgment is never rendered: Because the wicked circumvent the just; this is why judgment comes forth perverted. 5 Look over the nations and see, and be utterly amazed! For a work is being done in your days that you would not have believed, were it told. 6 For see, I am raising up Chaldea, that bitter and unruly people, That marches the breadth of the land to take dwellings not his own. 7 Terrible and dreadful is he, from himself derive his law and his majesty. 8 Swifter than leopards are his horses, and keener than wolves at evening. His horses prance, his horsemen come from afar: They fly like the eagle hastening to devour; 9 each comes for the rapine, Their combined onset is that of a stormwind that heaps up captives like sand. 10 He scoffs at kings, and princes are his laughingstock; He laughs at any fortress, heaps up a ramp, and conquers it. 11 Then he veers like the wind and is gone—this culprit who makes his own strength his god! 12 Are you not from eternity, O LORD, my holy God, immortal? O LORD you have marked him for judgment, O Rock, you have readied him for punishment! 13 Too pure are your eyes to look upon evil, and the sight of misery you cannot endure. Why, then, do you gaze on the faithless in silence while the wicked man devours one more just than himself? 14 You have made man like the fish of the sea, like creeping things without a ruler. 15 He brings them all up with his hook, he hauls them away with his net, He gathers them in his seine; and so he rejoices and exults. 16 Therefore he sacrifices to his net, and burns incense to his seine; For thanks to them his portion is generous, and his repast sumptuous. 17 Shall he, then, keep on brandishing his sword to slay peoples without mercy?

Habakkuk Chapter 2

1 I will stand at my guard post, and station myself upon the rampart, And keep watch to see what he will say to me, and what answer he will give to my complaint. 2 Then the LORD answered me and said: Write down the vision Clearly upon the tablets, so that one can read it readily. 3 For the vision still has its time, presses on to fulfillment, and will not disappoint; If it delays, wait for it, it will surely come, it will not be late. 4 The rash man has no integrity; but the just man, because of his faith, shall live. Wealth, too, is treacherous: the proud, unstable man— 5 He who opens wide his throat like the nether world, and is insatiable as death, Who gathers to himself all the nations, and rallies to himself all the peoples— 6 Shall not all these take up a taunt against him, satire and epigrams about him, to say: Woe to him who stores up what is not his: how long can it last! he loads himself down with debts. 7 Shall not your creditors rise suddenly? Shall not they who make you tremble awake? You shall become their spoil! 8 Because you despoiled many peoples all the rest of the nations shall despoil you; Because of men's blood shed, and violence done to the land, to the city and to all who dwell in it. 9 Woe to him who pursues evil gain for his household, setting his nest on high to escape the reach of misfortune! 10 You have devised shame for your household, cutting off many peoples, forfeiting your own life: 11 For the stone in the wall shall cry out, and the beam in the woodwork shall answer it! 12 Woe to him who builds a city by bloodshed, and establishes a town by wickedness! 13 Is not this from the LORD of hosts: peoples toil for the flames, and nations grow weary for nought! 14 But the earth shall be filled with the knowledge of the LORD'S glory as water covers the sea. 15 Woe to you who give your neighbors a flood of your wrath to drink, and make them drunk, till their nakedness is seen! 16 You are filled with shame instead of glory; drink, you too, and stagger! On you shall revert the cup from the LORD'S right hand, and utter shame on your glory. 17 For the violence done to Lebanon shall cover you, and the destruction of the beasts shall terrify you; Because of men's blood shed, and violence done to the land, to the city and to all who dwell in it. 18 Woe to him who says to wood, "Awake!" to dumb stone, "Arise!" Can such a thing give oracles? See, it is overlaid with gold and silver, but there is no life breath in it. 19 Of what avail is the carved image, that its maker should carve it? Or the molten image and lying oracle, that its very maker should trust in it, and make dumb idols? 20 But the LORD is in his holy temple; silence before him, all the earth!

Habakkuk Chapter 3

1 Prayer of Habakkuk, the prophet. To a plaintive tune. 2 O LORD, I have heard your renown, and feared, O LORD, your work. In the course of the years revive it, in the course of the years make it known; in your wrath remember compassion! 3 God comes from Teman, the Holy One from Mount Paran. Covered are the heavens with his glory, and with his praise the earth is filled. 4 His splendor spreads like the light; rays shine forth from beside him, where his power is concealed. 5 Before him goes pestilence, and the plague follows in his steps. 6 He pauses to survey the earth; his look makes the nations tremble. The eternal mountains are shattered, the age-old hills bow low along his ancient ways. 7 I see the tents of Cushan collapse; trembling are the pavilions of the land of Midian. 8 Is your anger against the streams, O LORD? Is your wrath against the streams, your rage against the sea, that you drive the steeds of your victorious chariot? 9 Bared and ready is your bow, filled with arrows is your quiver. Into streams you split the earth; 10 at sight of you the mountains tremble. A torrent of rain descends; the ocean gives forth its roar. The sun forgets to rise, 11 the moon remains in its shelter, at the light of your flying arrows, at the gleam of your flashing spear. 12 In wrath you bestride the earth, in fury you trample the nations. 13 You come forth to save your people, to save your anointed one. You crush the heads of the wicked, you lay bare their bases at the neck. 14 You pierce with your shafts the heads of their princes whose boast would be of devouring the wretched in their lair. 15 You tread the sea with your steeds amid the churning of the deep waters. 16 I hear, and my body trembles; at the sound, my lips quiver. Decay invades my bones, my legs tremble beneath me. I await the day of distress that will come upon the people who attack us. 17 For though the fig tree blossom not nor fruit be on the vines, though the yield of the olive fail and the terraces produce no nourishment, though the flocks disappear from the fold and there be no herd in the stalls, 18 yet will I rejoice in the LORD and exult in my saving God. 19 GOD, my Lord, is my strength; he makes my feet swift as those of hinds and enables me to go upon the heights. For the leader; with stringed instruments.

Zephaniah

Zephaniah Chapter 1

1 The word of the LORD which came to Zephaniah, the son of Cushi, the

son of Gedaliah, the son of Amariah, the son of Hezekiah, in the days of Josiah, the son of Amon, king of Judah. ²I will completely sweep away all things from the face of the earth, says the LORD. ³I will sweep away man and beast, I will sweep away the birds of the sky, and the fishes of the sea. I will overthrow the wicked; I will destroy mankind from the face of the earth, says the LORD. ⁴I will stretch out my hand against Judah, and against all the inhabitants of Jerusalem; I will destroy from this place the last vestige of Baal, the very names of his priests. ⁵And those who adore the host of heaven on the roofs, with those who adore the LORD but swear by Milcom; ⁶and those who have fallen away from the LORD, and those who do not seek the LORD. ⁷Silence in the presence of the Lord GOD! for near is the day of the LORD, yes, the LORD has prepared a slaughter feast, he has consecrated his guests. ⁸On the day of the LORD'S slaughter feast I will punish the princes, and the king's sons, and all that dress in foreign apparel. ⁹I will punish, on that day, all who leap over the threshold, who fill the house of their master with violence and deceit. ¹⁰On that day, says the LORD, a cry will be heard from the Fish Gate, a wail from the New Quarter, loud crashing from the hills. ¹¹Wail, O inhabitants of the Mortar! for all the merchants will be destroyed, all who weigh out silver, done away with. ¹²At that time I will explore Jerusalem with lamps; I will punish the men who thicken on their lees, who say in their hearts, "Neither good nor evil can the LORD do." ¹³Their wealth shall be given to pillage and their houses to devastation; they will build houses, but shall not dwell in them, plant vineyards, but not drink their wine. ¹⁴Near is the great day of the LORD, near and very swiftly coming, Hark, the day of the LORD! bitter, then, the warrior's cry. ¹⁵A day of wrath is that day, a day of anguish and distress, a day of destruction and desolation, a day of darkness and gloom, a day of thick black clouds, ¹⁶a day of trumpet blasts and battle alarm against fortified cities, against battlements on high. ¹⁷I will hem men in till they walk like the blind, because they have sinned against the LORD; and their blood shall be poured out like dust, and their brains like dung. ¹⁸Neither their silver nor their gold shall be able to save them on the day of the LORD'S wrath, when in the fire of his jealousy all the earth shall be consumed. For he shall make an end, yes, a sudden end, of all who live on the earth.

Zephaniah Chapter 2

¹Gather, gather yourselves together, O nation without shame! ²Before you are driven away, like chaff that passes on; before there comes upon you the blazing anger of the LORD: before there comes upon you the day of the LORD'S anger. ³Seek the LORD, all you humble of the earth, who have observed his law; seek justice, seek humility; perhaps you may be sheltered on the day of the LORD'S anger. ⁴For Gaza shall be forsaken, and Ashkelon shall be a waste, Ashdod they shall drive out at midday, and Ekron shall be uprooted. ⁵Woe to you who dwell by the seacoast, to the Cretan folk! The word of the LORD is against you, I will humble you, land of the Philistines, and leave you to perish without an inhabitant! ⁶The coastland of the Cretans shall become fields for shepherds, and folds for flocks. ⁷The coast shall belong to the remnant of the house of Judah; by the sea they shall pasture. In the houses of Ashkelon at evening they shall couch their flocks, for the LORD their God shall visit them, and bring about their restoration. ⁸I have heard the revilings uttered by Moab, and the insults of the Ammonites, when they reviled my people and made boasts against their territory. ⁹Therefore, as I live, says the LORD of hosts, the God of Israel, Moab shall become like Sodom, the land of Ammon like Gomorrah: a field of nettles and a salt pit and a waste forever. The remnant of my people shall plunder them, the survivors of my nation dispossess them. ¹⁰Such shall be the requital of their pride, because they reviled and boasted against the people of the LORD of hosts. ¹¹The LORD shall inspire them with fear when he makes all the gods of earth to waste away; then, each from its own place, all the coastlands of the nations shall adore him. ¹²You too, O Cushites, shall be slain by the sword of the LORD. ¹³He will stretch out his hand against the north, to destroy Assyria; he will make Nineveh a waste, dry as the desert. ¹⁴In her midst shall settle in droves all the wild life of the hollows; the screech owl and the desert owl shall roost in her columns; their call shall resound from the window, the raven's croak from the doorway. ¹⁵Is this the exultant city that dwelt secure; that told herself, "There is no other than I!" How has she become a waste, a lair for wild beasts? Whoever passes by her hisses, and shakes his fist!

Zephaniah Chapter 3

¹Woe to the city, rebellious and polluted, to the tyrannical city! ²She hears no voice, accepts no correction; in the LORD she has not trusted, to her God she has not drawn near. ³Her princes in her midst are roaring lions; her judges are wolves of the night that have had no bones to gnaw by morning. ⁴Her prophets are insolent, treacherous men; her

priests profane what is holy, and do violence to the law. ⁵The LORD within her is just, who does no wrong; morning after morning he renders judgment unfailingly, at dawn. ⁶I have destroyed nations, their battlements are laid waste; I have made their streets deserted, with no one passing through; their cities are devastated, with no man dwelling in them. ⁷I said, "Surely now you will fear me, you will accept correction"; she should not fail to see all I have visited upon her. Yet all the more eagerly have they done all their corrupt deeds. ⁸Therefore, wait for me, says the LORD, against the day when I arise as accuser; for it is my decision to gather together the nations, to assemble the kingdoms, in order to pour out upon them my wrath, all my blazing anger; for in the fire of my jealousy shall all the earth be consumed. ⁹For then I will change and purify the lips of the peoples, that they all may call upon the name of the LORD, to serve him with one accord; ¹⁰from beyond the rivers of Ethiopia and as far as the recesses of the North, they shall bring me offerings. ¹¹On that day you need not be ashamed of all your deeds, your rebellious actions against me; for then will I remove from your midst the proud braggarts, and you shall no longer exalt yourself on my holy mountain. ¹²But I will leave as a remnant in your midst a people humble and lowly, who shall take refuge in the name of the LORD; ¹³the remnant of Israel. They shall do no wrong and speak no lies; nor shall there be found in their mouths a deceitful tongue; they shall pasture and couch their flocks with none to disturb them. ¹⁴Shout for joy, O daughter Zion! Sing joyfully, O Israel! Be glad and exult with all your heart, O daughter Jerusalem! ¹⁵The LORD has removed the judgment against you, he has turned away your enemies; the King of Israel, the LORD, is in your midst, you have no further misfortune to fear. ¹⁶On that day, it shall be said to Jerusalem: Fear not, O Zion, be not discouraged! ¹⁷The LORD, your God, is in your midst, a mighty savior; he will rejoice over you with gladness, and renew you in his love, he will sing joyfully because of you, ¹⁸as one sings at festivals. I will remove disaster from among you, so that none may recount your disgrace. ¹⁹Yes, at that time I will deal with all who oppress you; I will save the lame, and assemble the outcasts; I will give them praise and renown in all the earth, when I bring about their restoration. ²⁰At that time I will bring you home, and at that time I will gather you; for I will give you renown and praise, among all the peoples of the earth, when I bring about your restoration before your very eyes, says the LORD.

Haggai

Haggai Chapter 1

¹On the first day of the sixth month in the second year of King Darius, the word of the LORD came through the prophet Haggai to the governor of Judah, Zerubbabel, son of Shealtiel, and to the high priest Joshua, son of Jehozadak: ²Thus says the LORD of hosts: This people says: "Not now has the time come to rebuild the house of the LORD." ³(Then this word of the LORD came through Haggai, the prophet:) ⁴Is it time for you to dwell in your own paneled houses, while this house lies in ruins? ⁵Now thus says the LORD of hosts: Consider your ways! ⁶You have sown much, but have brought in little; you have eaten, but have not been satisfied; you have drunk, but have not been exhilarated; have clothed yourselves, but not been warmed; and he who earned wages earned them for a bag with holes in it. ⁷Thus says the LORD of hosts: Consider your ways! ⁸Go up into the hill country; bring timber, and build the house that I may take pleasure in it and receive my glory, says the LORD. ⁹You expected much, but it came to little; and what you brought home, I blew away. For what cause? says the LORD of hosts. Because my house lies in ruins, while each of you hurries to his own house. ¹⁰Therefore the heavens withheld from you their dew, and the earth her crops. ¹¹And I called for a drought upon the land and upon the mountains; upon the grain, and upon the wine, and upon the oil, and upon all that the ground brings forth; upon men and upon beasts, and upon all that is produced by hand. ¹²Then Zerubbabel, son of Shealtiel, and the high priest Joshua, son of Jehozadak, and the remnant of the people listened to the voice of the LORD, their God, and to the words of the prophet Haggai, because the LORD, their God, had sent him, and the people feared because of the LORD. ¹³And the LORD'S messenger, Haggai, proclaimed to the people as the message of the LORD: I am with you, says the LORD. ¹⁴Then the LORD stirred up the spirit of the governor of Judah, Zerubbabel, son of Shealtiel, and the spirit of the high priest Joshua, son of Jehozadak, and the spirit of all the remnant of the people, so that they came and set to work on the house of the LORD of hosts, their God, ¹⁵on the twenty-fourth day of the sixth month. In the second year of King Darius.

Haggai Chapter 2

¹On the twenty-first day of the seventh month, the word of the LORD

came through the prophet Haggai: ²Tell this to the governor of Judah, Zerubbabel, son of Shealtiel, and to the high priest Joshua, son of Jehozadak, and to the remnant of the people: ³Who is left among you that saw this house in its former glory? And how do you see it now? Does it not seem like nothing in your eyes? ⁴But now take courage, Zerubbabel, says the LORD, and take courage, Joshua, high priest, son of Jehozadak, and take courage, all you people of the land, says the LORD, and work! For I am with you, says the LORD of hosts. ⁵This is the pact that I made with you when you came out of Egypt, and my spirit continues in your midst; do not fear! ⁶For thus says the LORD of hosts: One moment yet, a little while, and I will shake the heavens and the earth, the sea and the dry land. ⁷I will shake all the nations, and the treasures of all the nations will come in, and I will fill this house with glory, says the LORD of hosts. ⁸Mine is the silver and mine the gold, says the LORD of hosts. ⁹Greater will be the future glory of this house than the former, says the LORD of hosts; and in this place, I will give you peace, says the LORD of hosts. ¹⁰On the twenty-fourth day of the ninth month, in the second year of King Darius, the word of the LORD came to the prophet Haggai: ¹¹Thus says the LORD of hosts: Ask the priests for a decision: ¹²If a man carries sanctified flesh in the fold of his garment and the fold touches bread, or pottage, or wine, or oil, or any other food, do they become sanctified? "No," the priests answered. ¹³Then Haggai said: If a person unclean from contact with a corpse touches any of these, do they become unclean? The priests answered, "They become unclean." ¹⁴Then Haggai continued: So is this people, and so is this nation in my sight, says the LORD: And so are all the works of their hands; and what they offer there is unclean. ¹⁵But now, consider from this day forward. Before there was a stone laid upon a stone in the temple of the LORD, ¹⁶how did you fare? When one went to a heap of grain for twenty measures, it would yield but ten; when another went to the vat to draw fifty measures, there would be but twenty. ¹⁷I struck you in all the works of your hands with blight, searing wind, and hail, yet you did not return to me, says the LORD. ¹⁸(Consider from this day forward: from the twenty-fourth day of the ninth month. From the day on which the temple of the LORD was founded, consider!) ¹⁹Indeed, the seed has not sprouted, nor have the vine, the fig, the pomegranate, and the olive tree yet borne. From this day, I will bless! ²⁰The message of the LORD came a second time to Haggai on the twenty-fourth day of the month: ²¹Tell this to Zerubbabel, the governor of Judah: I will shake the heavens and the earth; ²²I will overthrow the thrones of kingdoms, destroy the power of the kingdoms of the nations. I will overthrow the chariots and their riders, and the riders with their horses shall go down by one another's sword. ²³On that day, says the LORD of hosts, I will take you, Zerubbabel, son of Shealtiel, my servant, says the LORD, and I will set you as a signet ring; for I have chosen you, says the LORD of hosts.

Zechariah

Zechariah Chapter 1

¹In the second year of Darius, in the eighth month, the word of the LORD came to the prophet Zechariah, son of Berechiah, son of Iddo: ²The LORD was indeed angry with your fathers. ³And say to them: Thus says the LORD of hosts: Return to me, says the LORD of hosts, and I will return to you, says the LORD of hosts. ⁴Be not like your fathers whom the former prophets warned: Thus says the LORD of hosts: Turn from your evil ways and from your wicked deeds. But they would not listen or pay attention to me, says the LORD. ⁵Your fathers, where are they? And the prophets, can they live forever? ⁶But my words and my decrees, which I entrusted to my servants the prophets, did not these overtake your fathers? Then they repented and admitted: "The LORD of hosts has treated us according to our ways and deeds, just as he had determined he would." ⁷In the second year of Darius, on the twenty-fourth day of Shebat, the eleventh month, the word of the LORD came to the prophet Zechariah, son of Berechiah, son of Iddo, in the following way: ⁸I had a vision during the night. There appeared the driver of a red horse, standing among myrtle trees in a shady place, and behind him were red, sorrel, and white horses. ⁹Then I asked, "What are these, my lord?"; and the angel who spoke with me answered me, "I will show you what these are." ¹⁰The man who was standing among the myrtle trees spoke up and said, "These are they whom the LORD has sent to patrol the earth." ¹¹And they answered the angel of the LORD who was standing among the myrtle trees and said, "We have patrolled the earth; see, the whole earth is tranquil and at rest!" ¹²Then the angel of the Lord spoke out and said, "O LORD of hosts, how long will you be without mercy for Jerusalem and the cities of Judah that have felt your anger these seventy years?" ¹³To the angel who spoke with me, the LORD replied with comforting words. ¹⁴And the angel who spoke with

me said to me, Proclaim: Thus says the LORD of hosts: I am deeply moved for the sake of Jerusalem and Zion, ¹⁵and I am exceedingly angry with the complacent nations; whereas I was but a little angry, they added to the harm. ¹⁶Therefore, says the LORD: I will turn to Jerusalem in mercy; my house shall be built in it, says the LORD of hosts, and a measuring line shall be stretched over Jerusalem. ¹⁷Proclaim further: Thus says the LORD of hosts: My cities shall again overflow with prosperity; the LORD will again comfort Zion, and again choose Jerusalem.

Zechariah Chapter 2

¹I raised my eyes and looked; there were four horns. ²Then I asked the angel who spoke with me what these were. He answered me, "These are the horns that scattered Judah and Israel and Jerusalem." ³Then the LORD showed me four blacksmiths. And I asked, "What are these coming to do?" ⁴And he said, "Here are the horns that scattered Judah, so that no man raised his head any more; but these have come to terrify them: to cast down the horns of the nations that raised their horns to scatter the land of Judah." ⁵Again I raised my eyes and looked: there was a man with a measuring line in his hand. ⁶"Where are you going?" I asked. "To measure Jerusalem," he answered; "to see how great is its width and how great its length." ⁷Then the angel who spoke with me advanced, and another angel came out to meet him, ⁸and said to him, "Run, tell this to that young man: People will live in Jerusalem as though in open country, because of the multitude of men and beasts in her midst. ⁹But I will be for her an encircling wall of fire, says the LORD, and I will be the glory in her midst." ¹⁰Up, up! Flee from the land of the north, says the LORD; for I scatter you to the four winds of heaven, says the LORD. ¹¹Up, escape to Zion! you who dwell in daughter Babylon. ¹²For thus said the LORD of hosts (after he had already sent me) concerning the nations that have plundered you: Whoever touches you touches the apple of my eye. ¹³See, I wave my hand over them; they become plunder for their slaves. Thus you shall know that the LORD of hosts has sent me. ¹⁴Sing and rejoice, O daughter Zion! See, I am coming to dwell among you, says the LORD. ¹⁵Many nations shall join themselves to the LORD on that day, and they shall be his people, and he will dwell among you, and you shall know that the LORD of hosts has sent me to you. ¹⁶The LORD will possess Judah as his portion of the holy land, and he will again choose Jerusalem. ¹⁷Silence, all mankind, in the presence of the LORD! for he stirs forth from his holy dwelling.

Zechariah Chapter 3

¹Then he showed me Joshua the high priest standing before the angel of the LORD, while Satan stood at his right hand to accuse him. ²And the angel of the LORD said to Satan, "May the LORD rebuke you, Satan; may the LORD who has chosen Jerusalem rebuke you! Is not this man a brand snatched from the fire?" ³Now Joshua was standing before the angel, clad in filthy garments. ⁴He spoke and said to those who were standing before him, "Take off his filthy garments, and clothe him in festal garments." ⁵He also said, "Put a clean miter on his head." And they put a clean miter on his head and clothed him with the garments. Then the angel of the LORD, standing, said, "See, I have taken away your guilt." ⁶The angel of the LORD then gave Joshua this assurance: ⁷"Thus says the LORD of hosts: If you walk in my ways and heed my charge, you shall judge my house and keep my courts, and I will give you access among these standing here. ⁸Listen, O Joshua, high priest! You and your associates who sit before you are men of good omen. Yes, I will bring my servant the Shoot. ⁹Look at the stone that I have placed before Joshua, one stone with seven facets. I will engrave its inscription, says the LORD of hosts, and I will take away the guilt of the land in one day. ¹⁰On that day, says the LORD of hosts, you will invite one another under your vines and fig trees."

Zechariah Chapter 4

¹Then I said to the angel who spoke with me, "What are these things, my lord?" ²And the angel who spoke with me replied, "Do you not know what these things are?" "No, my lord," I answered. ³Then he said to me, "This is the LORD'S message to Zerubbabel: Not by an army, nor by might, but by my spirit, says the LORD of hosts. ⁴What are you, O great mountain? Before Zerubbabel you are but a plain. He shall bring out the capstone amid exclamations of 'Hail, Hail' to it." ⁵This word of the LORD then came to me: ⁶The hands of Zerubbabel have laid the foundations of this house, and his hands shall finish it; then you shall know that the LORD of hosts has sent me to you. ⁷For even they who were scornful on that day of small beginnings shall rejoice to see the select stone in the hands of Zerubbabel. These seven facets are the eyes of the LORD that range over the whole earth. ⁸Then the angel who spoke with me returned and awakened me, like a man awakened from his sleep. ⁹"What do you see?" he asked me. "I see a lampstand all of

gold, with a bowl at the top," I replied; "on it are seven lamps with their tubes, 10and beside it are two olive trees, one on the right and the other on the left." 11I then asked him, "What are these two olive trees at each side of the lampstand?" 12And again I asked, "What are the two olive tufts which freely pour out fresh oil through the two golden channels?" 13"Do you not know what these are?" he said to me. "No, my lord," I answered him. 14He said, "These are the two anointed who stand by the LORD of the whole earth."

Zechariah Chapter 5

1Then I raised my eyes again and saw a scroll flying. 2"What do you see?" he asked me. I answered, "I see a scroll flying; it is twenty cubits long and ten cubits wide." 3Then he said to me: "This is the curse which is to go forth over the whole earth; in accordance with it shall every thief be swept away, and in accordance with it shall every perjurer be expelled from here. 4I will send it forth, says the LORD of hosts, and it shall come into the house of the thief, or into the house of him who perjures himself with my name; it shall lodge within his house, consuming it, timber and stones." 5Then the angel who spoke with me came forward and said to me, "Raise your eyes and see what this is that comes forth." 6"What is it?" I asked. And he answered, "This is a bushel container coming. This is their guilt in all the land." 7Then a leaden cover was lifted, and there was a woman sitting inside the bushel. 8"This is Wickedness," he said; and he thrust her inside the bushel, pushing the leaden cover into the opening. 9Then I raised my eyes and saw two women coming forth with a wind ruffling their wings, for they had wings like the wings of a stork. As they lifted up the bushel into the air, 10I said to the angel who spoke with me, "Where are they taking the bushel?" 11He replied, "To build a temple for it in the land of Shinar; when the temple is ready, they will deposit it there in its place."

Zechariah Chapter 6

1Again I raised my eyes and saw four chariots coming out from between two mountains; and the mountains were of bronze. 2The first chariot had red horses, the second chariot black horses, 3the third chariot white horses, and the fourth chariot spotted horses—all of them strong horses. 4I asked the angel who spoke with me, "What are these, my lord?" 5The angel said to me in reply, "These are the four winds of the heavens, which are coming forth after being reviewed by the LORD of all the earth." 6The chariot with the black horses was turning toward the land of the north, the red and the white horses went after them, and the spotted ones went toward the land of the south. 7As these strong horses emerged, eager to set about patrolling the earth, he said, "Go, patrol the earth!" Then, as they patrolled the earth, 8he called out to me and said, "See, they that go forth to the land of the north will make my spirit rest in the land of the north." 9This word of the LORD then came to me: 10Take from the returned captives Heldai, Tobijah, Jedaiah; and go the same day to the house of Josiah, son of Zephaniah (these had come from Babylon). 11Silver and gold you shall take, and make a crown; place it on the head of (Joshua, son of Jehozadak, the high priest) Zerubbabel. 12And say to him: Thus says the LORD of hosts: Here is a man whose name is Shoot, and where he is he shall sprout, and he shall build the temple of the LORD. 13Yes, he shall build the temple of the LORD, and taking up the royal insignia, he shall sit as ruler upon his throne. The priest shall be put at his right hand, and between the two of them there shall be friendly understanding. 14The crown itself shall be a memorial offering in the temple of the LORD in favor of Heldai, Tobijah, Jedaiah, and the son of Zephaniah. 15And they who are from afar shall come and build the temple of the LORD, and you shall know that the LORD of hosts has sent me to you. And if you heed carefully the voice of the LORD your God...

Zechariah Chapter 7

1In the fourth year of Darius the king (the word of the LORD came to Zechariah), on the fourth day of Chislev, the ninth month, 2Bethelsarezer sent Regemmelech and his men to implore favor of the LORD 3and to ask the priests of the house of the LORD of hosts, and the prophets, "Must I mourn and abstain in the fifth month as I have been doing these many years?" 4Thereupon this word of the LORD of hosts came to me: 5Say to all the people of the land and to the priests: When you fasted and mourned in the fifth and in the seventh month these seventy years, was it really for me that you fasted? 6And when you were eating and drinking, was it not for yourselves that you ate, and for yourselves that you drank? 7Were not these the words which the LORD spoke through the former prophets, when Jerusalem and the surrounding cities were inhabited and at peace, when the Negeb and the foothills were inhabited? 8(This word of the LORD came to Zechariah: 9Thus says the LORD of hosts:) Render true judgment, and show kindness and compassion toward each other. 10Do not oppress the widow or the orphan, the alien or the poor; do not plot evil against one another in your hearts. 11But they refused to listen; they stubbornly turned their backs and stopped their ears so as not to hear. 12And they made their hearts diamond-hard so as not to hear the teaching and the message that the LORD of hosts had sent by his spirit through the former prophets. 13Then the LORD of hosts in his great anger said that, as they had not listened when he called, so he would not listen when they called, 14but would scatter them with a whirlwind among all the nations that they did not know. Thus the land was left desolate after them with no one traveling to and fro; they made the pleasant land into a desert.

Zechariah Chapter 8

1This word of the LORD of hosts came: Thus says the LORD of hosts: 2I am intensely jealous for Zion, stirred to jealous wrath for her. 3Thus says the LORD: I will return to Zion, and I will dwell within Jerusalem; Jerusalem shall be called the faithful city, and the mountain of the LORD of hosts, the holy mountain. 4Thus says the LORD of hosts: Old men and old women, each with staff in hand because of old age, shall again sit in the streets of Jerusalem. 5The city shall be filled with boys and girls playing in her streets. 6Thus says the LORD of hosts: Even if this should seem impossible in the eyes of the remnant of this people, shall it in those days be impossible in my eyes also, says the LORD of hosts? 7Thus says the LORD of hosts: Lo, I will rescue my people from the land of the rising sun, and from the land of the setting sun. 8I will bring them back to dwell within Jerusalem. They shall be my people, and I will be their God, with faithfulness and justice. 9Thus says the LORD of hosts: Let your hands be strong, you who in these days hear these words spoken by the prophets on the day when the foundation of the house of the LORD of hosts was laid for the building of the temple. 10For before those days there were no wages for men, or hire for beasts; those who came and went had no security from the enemy, for I set every man against his neighbor. 11But now I will not deal with the remnant of this people as in former days, says the LORD of hosts, 12for it is the seedtime of peace: the vine shall yield its fruit, the land shall bear its crops, and the heavens shall give their dew; all these things I will have the remnant of the people possess. 13Just as you were a curse among the nations, O house of Judah and house of Israel, so will I save you that you may be a blessing; do not fear, but let your hands be strong. 14Thus says the LORD of hosts: As I determined to harm you when your fathers provoked me to wrath, says the LORD of hosts, and I did not relent, 15so again in these days I have determined to favor Jerusalem and the house of Judah; do not fear! 16These then are the things you should do: Speak the truth to one another; let there be honesty and peace in the judgments at your gates, 17and let none of you plot evil against another in his heart, nor love a false oath. For all these things I hate, says the LORD. 18This word of the LORD of hosts came to me: 191Thus says the LORD of hosts: The fast days of the fourth, the fifth, the seventh, and the tenth months shall become occasions of joy and gladness, cheerful festivals for the house of Judah; only love faithfulness and peace. 20Thus says the LORD of hosts: There shall yet come peoples, the inhabitants of many cities; 21and the inhabitants of one city shall approach those of another, and say, "Come! let us go to implore the favor of the LORD"; and, "I too will go to seek the LORD." 22Many peoples and strong nations shall come to seek the LORD of hosts in Jerusalem and to implore the favor of the LORD. 23Thus says the LORD of hosts: In those days ten men of every nationality, speaking different tongues, shall take hold, yes, take hold of every Jew by the edge of his garment and say, "Let us go with you, for we have heard that God is with you."

Zechariah Chapter 9

1An oracle: The word of the LORD is upon the land of Hadrach, and Damascus is its resting place, For the cities of Aram are the LORD'S, as are all the tribes of Israel, 2Hamath also, on its border, Tyre too, and Sidon, however wise they be. 3Tyre built herself a stronghold, and heaped up silver like dust, and gold like the mire of the streets. 4Lo, the LORD will strip her of her possessions, and smite her power on the sea, and she shall be devoured by fire. 5Ashkelon shall see it and be afraid; Gaza also: she shall be in great anguish; Ekron, too, for her hope shall come to nought. The king shall disappear from Gaza, and Ashkelon shall not be inhabited, 2and the baseborn shall occupy Ashdod. I will destroy the pride of the Philistine 3and take from his mouth his bloody meat, and his abominations from between his teeth: He also shall become a remnant for our God, and shall be like a family in Judah, and Ekron shall be like the Jebusites. 4I will encamp by my house as a guard that none may pass to and fro; No oppressor shall pass over them again, for now I have regard for their affliction. 5Rejoice heartily, O daughter Zion, shout for joy, O daughter Jerusalem! See, your king shall come to you; a just savior is he, Meek, and riding on an ass, on a colt, the foal of an ass. ⁶He shall banish the chariot from Ephraim, and the horse from Jerusalem; The warrior's bow shall be banished, and he shall proclaim peace to the nations. His dominion shall be from sea to sea, and from the River to the ends of the earth. ⁷As for you, for the blood of your covenant with me, I will bring forth your prisoners from the dungeon. ⁸In the return to the fortress of the waiting prisoners, This very day, I will return you double for your exile. ¹³For I will bend Judah as my bow, I will arm myself with Ephraim; I will arouse your sons, O Zion, (against your sons, O Yavan,) and I will use you as a warrior's sword. ¹⁴The LORD shall appear over them, and his arrow shall shoot forth as lightning; The LORD God shall sound the trumpet, and come in a storm from the south. ¹⁵The LORD of hosts shall be a shield over them, they shall overcome sling stones and trample them underfoot; They shall drink blood like wine, till they are filled with it like libation bowls, like the corners of the altar. ¹⁶And the LORD, their God, shall save them on that day, his people, like a flock. For they are the jewels in a crown raised aloft over his land. ¹⁷For what wealth is theirs, and what beauty! grain that makes the youths flourish, and new wine, the maidens!

Zechariah Chapter 10

¹Ask of the LORD rain in the spring season! It is the LORD who makes storm clouds. And sends men the pouring rain; for everyone, grassy fields. ²For the teraphim speak nonsense, the diviners have false visions: Deceitful dreams they tell, empty comfort they offer. This is why they wander like sheep, wretched: they have no shepherd. ³My wrath is kindled against the shepherds, and I will punish the leaders; For the LORD of hosts will visit his flock, the house of Judah, and make them his stately war horse. ⁴From him shall come leader and chief, from him warrior's bow and every officer. ⁵They shall all be warriors, trampling the mire of the streets in battle; They shall wage war because the LORD is with them, and shall put the horsemen to rout. ⁶I will strengthen the house of Judah, the house of Joseph I will save; I will bring them back, because I have mercy on them, they shall be as though I had never cast them off, for I am the LORD, their God, and I will hear them. ⁷Then Ephraim shall be valiant men, and their hearts shall be cheered as by wine. Their children shall see it and be glad, their hearts shall rejoice in the LORD. ⁸I will whistle for them to come together, and when I redeem them they will be as numerous as before. ⁹I sowed them among the nations, yet in distant lands they remember me; they shall rear their children and return. ¹⁰I will bring them back from the land of Egypt, and gather them from Assyria. I will bring them into Gilead and into Lebanon, but these shall not suffice them; ¹¹I will cross over to Egypt and smite the waves of the sea and all the depths of the Nile shall be dried up. The pride of Assyria shall be cast down, and the scepter of Egypt taken away. ¹²I will strengthen them in the LORD, and they shall walk in his name, says the LORD.

Zechariah Chapter 11

¹Open your doors, O Lebanon, that the fire may devour your cedars! ²Wail, you cypress trees, for the cedars are fallen, the mighty have been despoiled. Wail, you oaks of Bashan, for the impenetrable forest is cut down! ³Hark! the wailing of the shepherds, their glory has been ruined. Hark! the roaring of the young lions, the jungle of the Jordan is laid waste. ⁴Thus said the LORD, my God: Shepherd the flock to be slaughtered. ⁵For they who buy them slay them with impunity; while those who sell them say, "Blessed be the LORD, I have become rich!" Even their own shepherds do not feel for them. ⁶(Nor shall I spare the inhabitants of the earth any more, says the LORD. Yes, I will deliver each of them into the power of his neighbor, or into the power of his king; they shall crush the earth, and I will not deliver it out of their power.) ⁷So I became the shepherd of the flock to be slaughtered for the sheep merchants. I took two staffs, one of which I called "Favor," and the other, "Bonds," and I fed the flock. ⁸In a single month I did away with the three shepherds. I wearied of them, and they behaved badly toward me. ⁹"I will not feed you," I said. "What is to die, let it die; what is to perish, let it perish, and let those that are left devour one another's flesh." ¹⁰Then I took my staff "Favor" and snapped it asunder, breaking off the covenant which I had made with all peoples; ¹¹that day it was broken off. The sheep merchants who were watching me understood that this was the word of the LORD. ¹²I said to them, "If it seems good to you, give me my wages; but if not, let it go." And they counted out my wages, thirty pieces of silver. ¹³But the LORD said to me, "Throw it in the treasury, the handsome price at which they valued me." So I took the thirty pieces of silver and threw them into the treasury in the house of the LORD. ¹⁴Then I snapped asunder my other staff, "Bonds," breaking off the brotherhood between Judah and Israel. ¹⁵The LORD said to me: This time take the gear of a foolish shepherd. ¹⁶For I will raise up a shepherd in the land who will take no note of those that perish, nor seek the strays, nor heal the injured, nor feed what

survives—he will eat the flesh of the fat ones and tear off their hoofs! ¹⁷Woe to my foolish shepherd who forsakes the flock! May the sword fall upon his arm and upon his right eye; let his arm wither away entirely, and his right eye be blind forever!

Zechariah Chapter 12

¹An oracle: the word of the LORD concerning Israel. Thus says the LORD, who spreads out the heavens, lays the foundations of the earth, and forms the spirit of man within him: ²See, I will make Jerusalem a bowl to stupefy all peoples round about. (Judah will be besieged, even Jerusalem.) ³On that day I will make Jerusalem a weighty stone for all peoples. All who attempt to lift it shall injure themselves badly, and all the nations of the earth shall be gathered against her. ⁴On that day, says the LORD, I will strike every horse with fright, and its rider with madness. I will strike blind all the horses of the peoples, but upon the house of Judah I will open my eyes, ⁵and the princes of Judah shall say to themselves, "The inhabitants of Jerusalem have their strength in the LORD of hosts, their God." ⁶On that day I will make the princes of Judah like a brazier of fire in the woodland, and like a burning torch among sheaves, and they shall devour right and left all the surrounding peoples; but Jerusalem shall still abide on its own site. ⁷The LORD shall save the tents of Judah first, that the glory of the house of David and the glory of the inhabitants of Jerusalem may not be exalted over Judah. ⁸On that day, the LORD will shield the inhabitants of Jerusalem, and the weakling among them shall be like David on that day, and the house of David godlike, like an angel of the LORD before them. ⁹On that day I will seek the destruction of all nations that come against Jerusalem. ¹⁰I will pour out on the house of David and on the inhabitants of Jerusalem a spirit of grace and petition; and they shall look on him whom they have thrust through, and they shall mourn for him as one mourns for an only son, and they shall grieve over him as one grieves over a first-born. ¹¹On that day the mourning in Jerusalem shall be as great as the mourning of Hadadrimmon in the plain of Megiddo. ¹²And the land shall mourn, each family apart: the family of the house of David, and their wives; the family of the house of Nathan, and their wives; ¹³the family of the house of Levi, and their wives; the family of Shemei, and their wives; ¹⁴and all the rest of the families, each family apart, and the wives apart.

Zechariah Chapter 13

¹On that day there shall be open to the house of David and to the inhabitants of Jerusalem, a fountain to purify from sin and uncleanness. ²On that day, says the LORD of hosts, I will destroy the names of the idols from the land, so that they shall be mentioned no more; I will also take away the prophets and the spirit of uncleanness from the land. ³If a man still prophesies, his parents, father and mother, shall say to him, "You shall not live, because you have spoken a lie in the name of the LORD." When he prophesies, his parents, father and mother, shall thrust him through. ⁴On that day, every prophet shall be ashamed to prophesy his vision, neither shall he assume the hairy mantle to mislead, ⁵but he shall say, "I am no prophet, I am a tiller of the soil, for I have owned land since my youth." ⁶And if anyone asks him, "What are these wounds on your chest?" he shall answer, "With these I was wounded in the house of my dear ones." ⁷Awake, O sword, against my shepherd, against the man who is my associate, says the LORD of hosts. Strike the shepherd that the sheep may be dispersed, and I will turn my hand against the little ones. ⁸In all the land, says the LORD, two thirds of them shall be cut off and perish, and one third shall be left. ⁹I will bring the one third through fire, and I will refine them as silver is refined, and I will test them as gold is tested. They shall call upon my name, and I will hear them. I will say, "They are my people," and they shall say, "The LORD is my God.

Zechariah Chapter 14

¹Lo, a day shall come for the LORD when the spoils shall be divided in your midst. ²And I will gather all the nations against Jerusalem for battle: the city shall be taken, houses plundered, women ravished; half of the city shall go into exile, but the rest of the people shall not be removed from the city. ³Then the LORD shall go forth and fight against those nations, fighting as on a day of battle. ⁴That day his feet shall rest upon the Mount of Olives, which is opposite Jerusalem to the east. The Mount of Olives shall be cleft in two from east to west by a very deep valley, and half of the mountain shall move to the north and half of it to the south. ⁵And the valley of the LORD'S mountain shall be filled up when the valley of those two mountains reaches its edge; it shall be filled up as it was filled up by the earthquake in the days of King Uzziah of Judah. Then the LORD, my God, shall come, and all his holy ones with him. ⁶On that day there shall no longer be cold or frost. ⁷There shall be one continuous day, known to the LORD, not day and night, for in the evening time there shall be light. ⁸On that day, living waters shall flow

from Jerusalem, half to the eastern sea, and half to the western sea, and it shall be so in summer and in winter. 9The LORD shall become king over the whole earth; on that day the LORD shall be the only one, and his name the only one. 10And from Geba to Rimmon in the Negeb, all the land shall turn into a plain; but Jerusalem shall remain exalted in its place. From the Gate of Benjamin to the place of the First Gate, to the Corner Gate; and from the Tower of Hananel to the king's wine presses, 11they shall occupy her. Never again shall she be doomed; Jerusalem shall abide in security. 12And this shall be the plague with which the LORD shall strike all the nations that have fought against Jerusalem: their flesh shall rot while they stand upon their feet, and their eyes shall rot in their sockets, and their tongues shall rot in their mouths. 13On that day there shall be among them a great tumult from the LORD: every man shall seize the hand of his neighbor, and the hand of each shall be raised against that of his neighbor. 14Judah also shall fight against Jerusalem. The riches of all the surrounding nations shall be gathered together, gold, silver, and garments, in great abundance. 15Similar to this plague shall be the plague upon the horses, mules, camels, asses, and upon all the beasts that are in those camps. 16All who are left of all the nations that came against Jerusalem shall come up year after year to worship the King, the LORD of hosts, and to celebrate the feast of Booths. 17If any of the families of the earth does not come up to Jerusalem to worship the King, the LORD of hosts, no rain shall fall upon them. 18And if the family of Egypt does not come up, or enter, upon them shall fall the plague which the LORD will inflict upon all the nations that do not come up to celebrate the feast of Booths. 19This shall be the punishment of Egypt, and the punishment of all the nations that do not come up to celebrate the feast of Booths. 20On that day there shall be upon the bells of the horses, "Holy to the LORD." The pots in the house of the LORD shall be as the libation bowls before the altar. 21And every pot in Jerusalem and in Judah shall be holy to the LORD of hosts; and all who come to sacrifice shall take them and cook in them. On that day there shall no longer be any merchant in the house of the LORD of hosts.

Malachi

Malachi Chapter 1

1An oracle. The word of the LORD to Israel through Malachi. 2I have loved you, says the LORD; but you say, "How have you loved us?" 31Was not Esau Jacob's brother? says the LORD: yet I loved Jacob, but hated Esau; I made his mountains a waste, his heritage a desert for jackals. 4If Edom says, "We have been crushed but we will rebuild the ruins," Thus says the LORD of hosts: They indeed may build, but I will tear down, And they shall be called the land of guilt, the people with whom the LORD is angry forever. 5Your own eyes shall see it, and you will say, "Great is the LORD, even beyond the land of Israel." 6A son honors his father, and a servant fears his master; If then I am a father, where is the honor due to me? And if I am a master, where is the reverence due to me? - So says the LORD of hosts to you, O priests, who despise his name. But you ask, "How have we despised your name?" 7By offering polluted food on my altar! Then you ask, "How have we polluted it?" By saying the table of the LORD may be slighted! 82When you offer a blind animal for sacrifice, is this not evil? When you offer the lame or the sick, is it not evil? Present it to your governor; see if he will accept it, or welcome you, says the LORD of hosts. 9So now if you implore God for mercy on us, when you have done the like Will he welcome any of you? says the LORD of hosts. 103Oh, that one among you would shut the temple gates to keep you from kindling fire on my altar in vain! I have no pleasure in you, says the LORD of hosts; neither will I accept any sacrifice from your hands, 11For from the rising of the sun, even to its setting, my name is great among the nations; And everywhere they bring sacrifice to my name, and a pure offering; For great is my name among the nations, says the LORD of hosts. 12But you behave profanely toward me by thinking the LORD'S table and its offering may be polluted, and its food slighted. 13You also say, "What a burden!" and you scorn it, says the LORD of hosts; You bring in what you seize, or the lame, or the sick; yes, you bring it as a sacrifice. Shall I accept it from your hands? says the LORD. 14Cursed is the deceiver, who has in his flock a male, but under his vow sacrifices to the LORD a gelding; For a great King am I, says the LORD of hosts, and my name will be feared among the nations.

Malachi Chapter 2

1And now, O priests, this commandment is for you: If you do not listen, 2And if you do not lay it to heart, to give glory to my name, says the LORD of hosts, I will send a curse upon you and of your blessing I will make a curse. Yes, I have already cursed it, because you do not lay it to heart. 31Lo, I will deprive you of the shoulder and I will strew dung in your faces, The dung of your feasts, and you will be carried off with it. 4Then you will know that I sent you this commandment because I have a covenant with Levi, says the LORD of hosts. 5My covenant with him was one of life and peace; fear I put in him, and he feared me, and stood in awe of my name. 6True doctrine was in his mouth, and no dishonesty was found upon his lips; He walked with me in integrity and in uprightness, and turned many away from evil. 7For the lips of the priest are to keep knowledge, and instruction is to be sought from his mouth, because he is the messenger of the LORD of hosts. 8But you have turned aside from the way, and have caused many to falter by your instruction; You have made void the covenant of Levi, says the LORD of hosts. 9I, therefore, have made you contemptible and base before all the people, Since you do not keep my ways, but show partiality in your decisions. 102Have we not all the one Father? Has not the one God created us? Why then do we break faith with each other, violating the covenant of our fathers? 11Judah has broken faith; an abominable thing has been done in Israel and in Jerusalem. Judah has profaned the temple which the LORD loves, and has married an idolatrous woman. 12May the LORD cut off from the man who does this both witness and advocate out of the tents of Jacob, and anyone to offer sacrifice to the LORD of hosts! 13This also you do: the altar of the LORD you cover with tears, weeping and groaning, Because he no longer regards your sacrifice nor accepts it favorably from your hand; 14And you say, "Why is it?" - Because the LORD is witness between you and the wife of your youth, With whom you have broken faith though she is your companion, your betrothed wife. 15Did he not make one being, with flesh and spirit: and what does that one require but godly offspring? You must then safeguard life that is your own, and not break faith with the wife of your youth. 16For I hate divorce, says the LORD, the God of Israel, And covering one's garment with injustice, says the LORD of hosts; You must then safeguard life that is your own, and not break faith. 17You have wearied the LORD with your words, yet you say, "How have we wearied him?" By your saying, "Every evildoer is good in the sight of the LORD, And he is pleased with him"; or else, "Where is the just God?"

Malachi Chapter 3

1Lo, I am sending my messenger to prepare the way before me; And suddenly there will come to the temple the LORD whom you seek, And the messenger of the covenant whom you desire. Yes, he is coming, says the LORD of hosts. 2But who will endure the day of his coming? And who can stand when he appears? For he is like the refiner's fire, or like the fuller's lye. 3He will sit refining and purifying (silver), and he will purify the sons of Levi, Refining them like gold or like silver that they may offer due sacrifice to the LORD. 4Then the sacrifice of Judah and Jerusalem will please the LORD, as in days of old, as in years gone by. 5I will draw near to you for judgment, and I will be swift to bear witness Against the sorcerers, adulterers, and perjurers, those who defraud the hired man of his wages, Against those who defraud widows and orphans; those who turn aside the stranger, and those who do not fear me, says the LORD of hosts. 62Surely I, the LORD, do not change, nor do you cease to be sons of Jacob. 7Since the days of your fathers you have turned aside from my statutes, and have not kept them. Return to me, and I will return to you, says the LORD of hosts. Yet you say, "How must we return?" 8Dare a man rob God? Yet you are robbing me! And you say, "How do we rob you?" In tithes and in offerings. 9You are indeed accursed, for you, the whole nation, rob me. 103Bring the whole tithe into the storehouse, That there may be food in my house, and try me in this, says the LORD of hosts: Shall I not open for you the floodgates of heaven, to pour down blessing upon you without measure? 11For your sake I will forbid the locust to destroy your crops; And the vine in the field will not be barren, says the LORD of hosts. 12Then all nations will call you blessed, for you will be a delightful land, says the LORD of hosts. 13You have defied me in word, says the LORD, yet you ask, "What have we spoken against you?" 14You have said, "It is vain to serve God, and what do we profit by keeping his command, And going about in penitential dress in awe of the LORD of hosts? 15Rather must we call the proud blessed; for indeed evildoers prosper, and even tempt God with impunity." 164Then they who fear the LORD spoke with one another, and the LORD listened attentively; And a record book was written before him of those who fear the LORD and trust in his name. 17And they shall be mine, says the LORD of hosts, my own special possession, on the day I take action. And I will have compassion on them, as a man has compassion on his son who serves him. 18Then you will again see the distinction between the just and the wicked; Between him who serves God, and him who does not serve him. 19For lo, the day is coming, blazing like an oven, when all the proud and all evildoers will be stubble, And the day that is coming will set them on fire, leaving them neither root nor branch, says the LORD of hosts. 20But for you who fear my name, there will arise the sun of justice with its healing

rays; And you will gambol like calves out of the stall 211) and tread
down the wicked; They will become ashes under the soles of your feet,
on the day I take action, says the LORD of hosts. 22Remember the law
of Moses my servant, which I enjoined him on Horeb, The statutes and
ordinances for all Israel. 235Lo, I will send you Elijah, the prophet,
Before the day of the LORD comes, the great and terrible day, 246To
turn the hearts of the fathers to their children, and the hearts of the
children to their fathers, Lest I come and strike the land with doom. Lo,
I will send you Elijah, the prophet, Before the day of the LORD comes,
the great and terrible day.

New Testament

The Gospels

Matthew

Matthew Chapter 1

1The book of the genealogy of Jesus Christ, the
son of David, the son of Abraham. 2Abraham
became the father of Isaac, Isaac the father of
Jacob, Jacob the father of Judah and his
brothers.3Judah became the father of Perez
and Zerah, whose mother was Tamar. Perez
became the father of Hezron, Hezron the
father of Ram,4Ram the father of Amminadab.
Amminadab became the father of Nahshon,
Nahshon the father of Salmon,5Salmon the
father of Boaz, whose mother was Rahab. Boaz became the father of
Obed, whose mother was Ruth. Obed became the father of Jesse,6Jesse
the father of David the king. David became the father of Solomon,
whose mother had been the wife of Uriah.7Solomon became the father
of Rehoboam, Rehoboam the father of Abijah, Abijah the father of
Asaph.8Asaph became the father of Jehoshaphat, Jehoshaphat the
father of Joram, Joram the father of Uzziah.9Uzziah became the father
of Jotham, Jotham the father of Ahaz, Ahaz the father of
Hezekiah.10Hezekiah became the father of Manasseh, Manasseh the
father of Amos, Amos the father of Josiah.11Josiah became the father of
Jechoniah and his brothers at the time of the Babylonian exile.12After
the Babylonian exile, Jechoniah became the father of Shealtiel, Shealtiel
the father of Zerubbabel,13Zerubbabel the father of Abiud. Abiud
became the father of Eliakim, Eliakim the father of Azor,14Azor the
father of Zadok. Zadok became the father of Achim, Achim the father of
Eliud,15Eliud the father of Eleazar. Eleazar became the father of
Matthan, Matthan the father of Jacob,16Jacob the father of Joseph, the
husband of Mary. Of her was born Jesus who is called the
Messiah.17Thus the total number of generations from Abraham to David
is fourteen generations; from David to the Babylonian exile, fourteen
generations; from the Babylonian exile to the Messiah, fourteen
generations. 18Now this is how the birth of Jesus Christ came about.
When his mother Mary was betrothed to Joseph, but before they lived
together, she was found with child through the holy Spirit.19Joseph her
husband, since he was a righteous man, yet unwilling to expose her to
shame, decided to divorce her quietly.20Such was his intention when,
behold, the angel of the Lord appeared to him in a dream and said,
"Joseph, son of David, do not be afraid to take Mary your wife into your
home. For it is through the holy Spirit that this child has been conceived
in her.21She will bear a son and you are to name him Jesus, because he
will save his people from their sins."22All this took place to fulfill what
the Lord had said through the prophet:23"Behold, the virgin shall be
with child and bear a son, and they shall name him Emmanuel," which
means "God is with us."24When Joseph awoke, he did as the angel of the
Lord had commanded him and took his wife into his home.25He had no
relations with her until she bore a son, and he named him Jesus.

Matthew Chapter 2

1When Jesus was born in Bethlehem of Judea, in the days of King
Herod, behold, magi from the east arrived in Jerusalem,2saying,
"Where is the newborn king of the Jews? We saw his star at its rising
and have come to do him homage."3When King Herod heard this, he
was greatly troubled, and all Jerusalem with him.4Assembling all the
chief priests and the scribes of the people, he inquired of them where
the Messiah was to be born. 5They said to him, "In Bethlehem of Judea,
for thus it has been written through the prophet:6'And you, Bethlehem,
land of Judah, are by no means least among the rulers of Judah; since
from you shall come a ruler, who is to shepherd my people
Israel.'"7Then Herod called the magi secretly and ascertained from
them the time of the star's appearance.8He sent them to Bethlehem and
said, "Go and search diligently for the child. When you have found him,
bring me word, that I too may go and do him homage."9After their
audience with the king they set out. And behold, the star that they had
seen at its rising preceded them, until it came and stopped over the
place where the child was.10They were overjoyed at seeing the star,11and
on entering the house they saw the child with Mary his mother. They
prostrated themselves and did him homage. Then they opened their
treasures and offered him gifts of gold, frankincense, and myrrh.12And
having been warned in a dream not to return to Herod, they departed
for their country by another way.13When they had departed, behold, the
angel of the Lord appeared to Joseph in a dream and said, "Rise, take
the child and his mother, flee to Egypt, and stay there until I tell you.
Herod is going to search for the child to destroy him."14Joseph rose and
took the child and his mother by night and departed for Egypt.15He
stayed there until the death of Herod, that what the Lord had said
through the prophet might be fulfilled, "Out of Egypt I called my
son."16When Herod realized that he had been deceived by the magi, he
became furious. He ordered the massacre of all the boys in Bethlehem
and its vicinity two years old and under, in accordance with the time he
had ascertained from the magi.17Then was fulfilled what had been said
through Jeremiah the prophet:18"A voice was heard in Ramah, sobbing
and loud lamentation; Rachel weeping for her children, and she would
not be consoled, since they were no more."19When Herod had died,
behold, the angel of the Lord appeared in a dream to Joseph in
Egypt20and said, "Rise, take the child and his mother and go to the land
of Israel, for those who sought the child's life are dead." 21He rose, took
the child and his mother, and went to the land of Israel.22But when he
heard that Archelaus was ruling over Judea in place of his father
Herod, he was afraid to go back there. And because he had been warned
in a dream, he departed for the region of Galilee.23He went and dwelt in
a town called Nazareth, so that what had been spoken through the
prophets might be fulfilled, "He shall be called a Nazorean."

Matthew Chapter 3

1In those days John the Baptist appeared, preaching in the desert of
Judea2(and) saying, "Repent, for the kingdom of heaven is at hand!"3It
was of him that the prophet Isaiah had spoken when he said: "A voice
of one crying out in the desert, 'Prepare the way of the Lord, make
straight his paths.'"4John wore clothing made of camel's hair and had a
leather belt around his waist. His food was locusts and wild honey.5At
that time Jerusalem, all Judea, and the whole region around the Jordan

were going out to him[6]and were being baptized by him in the Jordan River as they acknowledged their sins. [7]When he saw many of the Pharisees and Sadducees coming to his baptism, he said to them, "You brood of vipers! Who warned you to flee from the coming wrath?[8]Produce good fruit as evidence of your repentance.[9]And do not presume to say to yourselves, 'We have Abraham as our father.' For I tell you, God can raise up children to Abraham from these stones.[10]Even now the ax lies at the root of the trees. Therefore every tree that does not bear good fruit will be cut down and thrown into the fire.[11]I am baptizing you with water, for repentance, but the one who is coming after me is mightier than I. I am not worthy to carry his sandals. He will baptize you with the holy Spirit and fire. [12]His winnowing fan is in his hand. He will clear his threshing floor and gather his wheat into his barn, but the chaff he will burn with unquenchable fire."[13]Then Jesus came from Galilee to John at the Jordan to be baptized by him.[14]John tried to prevent him, saying, "I need to be baptized by you, and yet you are coming to me?"[15]Jesus said to him in reply, "Allow it now; for thus it is fitting for us to fulfill all righteousness." Then he allowed him.[16]After Jesus was baptized, he came up from the water and behold, the heavens were opened (for him), and he saw the Spirit of God descending like a dove (and) coming upon him.[17]And a voice came from the heavens, saying, "This is my beloved Son, with whom I am well pleased."

Matthew Chapter 4

[1]Then Jesus was led by the Spirit into the desert to be tempted by the devil.[2]He fasted for forty days and forty nights, and afterwards he was hungry.[3]The tempter approached and said to him, "If you are the Son of God, command that these stones become loaves of bread."[4]He said in reply, "It is written: 'One does not live by bread alone, but by every word that comes forth from the mouth of God.'"[5]Then the devil took him to the holy city, and made him stand on the parapet of the temple,[6]and said to him, "If you are the Son of God, throw yourself down. For it is written: 'He will command his angels concerning you and 'with their hands they will support you, lest you dash your foot against a stone.'"[7]Jesus answered him, "Again it is written, 'You shall not put the Lord, your God, to the test.'"[8]Then the devil took him up to a very high mountain, and showed him all the kingdoms of the world in their magnificence,[9]and he said to him, "All these I shall give to you, if you will prostrate yourself and worship me."[10]At this, Jesus said to him, "Get away, Satan! It is written: 'The Lord, your God, shall you worship and him alone shall you serve.'"[11]Then the devil left him and, behold, angels came and ministered to him.[12]When he heard that John had been arrested, he withdrew to Galilee.[13]He left Nazareth and went to live in Capernaum by the sea, in the region of Zebulun and Naphtali,[14]that what had been said through Isaiah the prophet might be fulfilled:[15]"Land of Zebulun and land of Naphtali, the way to the sea, beyond the Jordan, Galilee of the Gentiles,[16]the people who sit in darkness have seen a great light, on those dwelling in a land overshadowed by death light has arisen."[17]From that time on, Jesus began to preach and say, "Repent, for the kingdom of heaven is at hand."[18]As he was walking by the Sea of Galilee, he saw two brothers, Simon who is called Peter, and his brother Andrew, casting a net into the sea; they were fishermen.[19]He said to them, "Come after me, and I will make you fishers of men."[20]At once they left their nets and followed him.[21]He walked along from there and saw two other brothers, James, the son of Zebedee, and his brother John. They were in a boat, with their father Zebedee, mending their nets. He called them,[22]and immediately they left their boat and their father and followed him.[23]He went around all of Galilee, teaching in their synagogues, proclaiming the gospel of the kingdom, and curing every disease and illness among the people.[24]His fame spread to all of Syria, and they brought to him all who were sick with various diseases and racked with pain, those who were possessed, lunatics, and paralytics, and he cured them.[25]And great crowds from Galilee, the Decapolis, Jerusalem, and Judea, and from beyond the Jordan followed him.

Matthew Chapter 5

[1]When he saw the crowds, he went up the mountain, and after he had sat down, his disciples came to him.[2]He began to teach them, saying:[3]"Blessed are the poor in spirit, for theirs is the kingdom of heaven.[4]Blessed are they who mourn, for they will be comforted.[5]Blessed are the meek, for they will inherit the land.[6]Blessed are they who hunger and thirst for righteousness, for they will be satisfied.[7]Blessed are the merciful, for they will be shown mercy.[8]Blessed are the clean of heart, for they will see God.[9]Blessed are the peacemakers, for they will be called children of God.[10]Blessed are they who are persecuted for the sake of righteousness, for theirs is the kingdom of heaven.[11]Blessed are you when they insult you and

persecute you and utter every kind of evil against you (falsely) because of me.[12]Rejoice and be glad, for your reward will be great in heaven. Thus they persecuted the prophets who were before you.[13]"You are the salt of the earth. But if salt loses its taste, with what can it be seasoned? It is no longer good for anything but to be thrown out and trampled underfoot.[14]You are the light of the world. A city set on a mountain cannot be hidden.[15]Nor do they light a lamp and then put it under a bushel basket; it is set on a lampstand, where it gives light to all in the house.[16]Just so, your light must shine before others, that they may see your good deeds and glorify your heavenly Father.[17]"Do not think that I have come to abolish the law or the prophets. I have come not to abolish but to fulfill.[18]Amen, I say to you, until heaven and earth pass away, not the smallest letter or the smallest part of a letter will pass from the law, until all things have taken place.[19]Therefore, whoever breaks one of the least of these commandments and teaches others to do so will be called least in the kingdom of heaven. But whoever obeys and teaches these commandments will be called greatest in the kingdom of heaven.[20]I tell you, unless your righteousness surpasses that of the scribes and Pharisees, you will not enter into the kingdom of heaven.[21]"You have heard that it was said to your ancestors, 'You shall not kill; and whoever kills will be liable to judgment.'[22]But I say to you, whoever is angry with his brother will be liable to judgment, and whoever says to his brother, 'Raqa,' will be answerable to the Sanhedrin, and whoever says, 'You fool,' will be liable to fiery Gehenna.[23]Therefore, if you bring your gift to the altar, and there recall that your brother has anything against you,[24]leave your gift there at the altar, go first and be reconciled with your brother, and then come and offer your gift.[25]Settle with your opponent quickly while on the way to court with him. Otherwise your opponent will hand you over to the judge, and the judge will hand you over to the guard, and you will be thrown into prison.[26]Amen, I say to you, you will not be released until you have paid the last penny.[27]"You have heard that it was said, 'You shall not commit adultery.'[28]But I say to you, everyone who looks at a woman with lust has already committed adultery with her in his heart.[29]If your right eye causes you to sin, tear it out and throw it away. It is better for you to lose one of your members than to have your whole body thrown into Gehenna.[30]And if your right hand causes you to sin, cut it off and throw it away. It is better for you to lose one of your members than to have your whole body go into Gehenna.[31]"It was also said, 'Whoever divorces his wife must give her a bill of divorce.'[32]But I say to you, whoever divorces his wife (unless the marriage is unlawful) causes her to commit adultery, and whoever marries a divorced woman commits adultery.[33]"Again you have heard that it was said to your ancestors, 'Do not take a false oath, but make good to the Lord all that you vow.'[34]But I say to you, do not swear at all; not by heaven, for it is God's throne;[35]nor by the earth, for it is his footstool; nor by Jerusalem, for it is the city of the great King.[36]Do not swear by your head, for you cannot make a single hair white or black.[37]Let your 'Yes' mean 'Yes,' and your 'No' mean 'No.' Anything more is from the evil one.[38]"You have heard that it was said, 'An eye for an eye and a tooth for a tooth.'[39]But I say to you, offer no resistance to one who is evil. When someone strikes you on (your) right cheek, turn the other one to him as well.[40]If anyone wants to go to law with you over your tunic, hand him your cloak as well.[41]Should anyone press you into service for one mile, go with him for two miles.[42]Give to the one who asks of you, and do not turn your back on one who wants to borrow.[43]"You have heard that it was said, 'You shall love your neighbor and hate your enemy.'[44]But I say to you, love your enemies, and pray for those who persecute you,[45]that you may be children of your heavenly Father, for he makes his sun rise on the bad and the good, and causes rain to fall on the just and the unjust.[46]For if you love those who love you, what recompense will you have? Do not the tax collectors do the same?[47]And if you greet your brothers only, what is unusual about that? Do not the pagans do the same? [48]So be perfect, just as your heavenly Father is perfect.

Matthew Chapter 6

[1]"(But) take care not to perform righteous deeds in order that people may see them; otherwise, you will have no recompense from your heavenly Father.[2]When you give alms, do not blow a trumpet before you, as the hypocrites do in the synagogues and in the streets to win the praise of others. Amen, I say to you, they have received their reward.[3]But when you give alms, do not let your left hand know what your right is doing,[4]so that your almsgiving may be secret. And your Father who sees in secret will repay you.[5]"When you pray, do not be like the hypocrites, who love to stand and pray in the synagogues and on street corners so that others may see them. Amen, I say to you, they have received their reward.[6]But when you pray, go to your inner room, close the door, and pray to your Father in secret. And your Father who sees in secret will repay you.[7]In praying, do not babble like the pagans,

who think that they will be heard because of their many words.⁸Do not be like them. Your Father knows what you need before you ask him.⁹"This is how you are to pray: Our Father in heaven, hallowed be your name,¹⁰your kingdom come, your will be done, on earth as in heaven.¹¹Give us today our daily bread;¹²and forgive us our debts, as we forgive our debtors;¹³and do not subject us to the final test, but deliver us from the evil one.¹⁴If you forgive others their transgressions, your heavenly Father will forgive you.¹⁵But if you do not forgive others, neither will your Father forgive your transgressions.¹⁶"When you fast, do not look gloomy like the hypocrites. They neglect their appearance, so that they may appear to others to be fasting. Amen, I say to you, they have received their reward.¹⁷But when you fast, anoint your head and wash your face,¹⁸so that you may not appear to be fasting, except to your Father who is hidden. And your Father who sees what is hidden will repay you.¹⁹"Do not store up for yourselves treasures on earth, where moth and decay destroy, and thieves break in and steal.²⁰But store up treasures in heaven, where neither moth nor decay destroys, nor thieves break in and steal.²¹For where your treasure is, there also will your heart be.²²"The lamp of the body is the eye. If your eye is sound, your whole body will be filled with light;²³but if your eye is bad, your whole body will be in darkness. And if the light in you is darkness, how great will the darkness be.²⁴"No one can serve two masters. He will either hate one and love the other, or be devoted to one and despise the other. You cannot serve God and mammon.²⁵"Therefore I tell you, do not worry about your life, what you will eat (or drink), or about your body, what you will wear. Is not life more than food and the body more than clothing?²⁶Look at the birds in the sky; they do not sow or reap, they gather nothing into barns, yet your heavenly Father feeds them. Are not you more important than they?²⁷Can any of you by worrying add a single moment to your life-span? ²⁸Why are you anxious about clothes? Learn from the way the wild flowers grow. They do not work or spin.²⁹But I tell you that not even Solomon in all his splendor was clothed like one of them.³⁰If God so clothes the grass of the field, which grows today and is thrown into the oven tomorrow, will he not much more provide for you, O you of little faith?³¹So do not worry and say, 'What are we to eat?' or 'What are we to drink?' or 'What are we to wear?'³²All these things the pagans seek. Your heavenly Father knows that you need them all.³³But seek first the kingdom (of God) and his righteousness, and all these things will be given you besides.³⁴Do not worry about tomorrow; tomorrow will take care of itself. Sufficient for a day is its own evil.

Matthew Chapter 7

¹ "Stop judging, that you may not be judged.²For as you judge, so will you be judged, and the measure with which you measure will be measured out to you.³Why do you notice the splinter in your brother's eye, but do not perceive the wooden beam in your own eye?⁴How can you say to your brother, 'Let me remove that splinter from your eye,' while the wooden beam is in your eye?⁵You hypocrite, remove the wooden beam from your eye first; then you will see clearly to remove the splinter from your brother's eye.⁶"Do not give what is holy to dogs, or throw your pearls before swine, lest they trample them underfoot, and turn and tear you to pieces.⁷"Ask and it will be given to you; seek and you will find; knock and the door will be opened to you.⁸For everyone who asks, receives; and the one who seeks, finds; and to the one who knocks, the door will be opened.⁹Which one of you would hand his son a stone when he asks for a loaf of bread,¹⁰or a snake when he asks for a fish?¹¹If you then, who are wicked, know how to give good gifts to your children, how much more will your heavenly Father give good things to those who ask him.¹²"Do to others whatever you would have them do to you. This is the law and the prophets.¹³"Enter through the narrow gate; for the gate is wide and the road broad that leads to destruction, and those who enter through it are many.¹⁴How narrow the gate and constricted the road that leads to life. And those who find it are few.¹⁵"Beware of false prophets, who come to you in sheep's clothing, but underneath are ravenous wolves.¹⁶By their fruits you will know them. Do people pick grapes from thornbushes, or figs from thistles?¹⁷Just so, every good tree bears good fruit, and a rotten tree bears bad fruit.¹⁸A good tree cannot bear bad fruit, nor can a rotten tree bear good fruit.¹⁹Every tree that does not bear good fruit will be cut down and thrown into the fire.²⁰So by their fruits you will know them.²¹"Not everyone who says to me, 'Lord, Lord,' will enter the kingdom of heaven, but only the one who does the will of my Father in heaven.²²Many will say to me on that day, 'Lord, Lord, did we not prophesy in your name? Did we not drive out demons in your name? Did we not do mighty deeds in your name?'²³Then I will declare to them solemnly, 'I never knew you. Depart from me, you evildoers.'²⁴ "Everyone who listens to these words of mine and acts on them will be like a wise man who built his house on rock.²⁵The rain fell,

the floods came, and the winds blew and buffeted the house. But it did not collapse; it had been set solidly on rock.²⁶And everyone who listens to these words of mine but does not act on them will be like a fool who built his house on sand.²⁷The rain fell, the floods came, and the winds blew and buffeted the house. And it collapsed and was completely ruined."²⁸When Jesus finished these words, the crowds were astonished at his teaching,²⁹for he taught them as one having authority, and not as their scribes.

Matthew Chapter 8

¹When Jesus came down from the mountain, great crowds followed him.²And then a leper approached, did him homage, and said, "Lord, if you wish, you can make me clean."³He stretched out his hand, touched him, and said, "I will do it. Be made clean." His leprosy was cleansed immediately.⁴Then Jesus said to him, "See that you tell no one, but go show yourself to the priest, and offer the gift that Moses prescribed; that will be proof for them."⁵When he entered Capernaum, a centurion approached him and appealed to him,⁶saying, "Lord, my servant is lying at home paralyzed, suffering dreadfully."⁷He said to him, "I will come and cure him."⁸The centurion said in reply, "Lord, I am not worthy to have you enter under my roof; only say the word and my servant will be healed.⁹For I too am a person subject to authority, with soldiers subject to me. And I say to one, 'Go,' and he goes; and to another, 'Come here,' and he comes; and to my slave, 'Do this,' and he does it."¹⁰When Jesus heard this, he was amazed and said to those following him, "Amen, I say to you, in no one in Israel have I found such faith.¹¹I say to you, many will come from the east and the west, and will recline with Abraham, Isaac, and Jacob at the banquet in the kingdom of heaven,¹²but the children of the kingdom will be driven out into the outer darkness, where there will be wailing and grinding of teeth."¹³And Jesus said to the centurion, "You may go; as you have believed, let it be done for you." And at that very hour (his) servant was healed.¹⁴Jesus entered the house of Peter, and saw his mother-in-law lying in bed with a fever.¹⁵He touched her hand, the fever left her, and she rose and waited on him.¹⁶When it was evening, they brought him many who were possessed by demons, and he drove out the spirits by a word and cured all the sick,¹⁷to fulfill what had been said by Isaiah the prophet: "He took away our infirmities and bore our diseases."¹⁸When Jesus saw a crowd around him, he gave orders to cross to the other side.¹⁹A scribe approached and said to him, "Teacher, I will follow you wherever you go."²⁰Jesus answered him, "Foxes have dens and birds of the sky have nests, but the Son of Man has nowhere to rest his head."²¹Another of (his) disciples said to him, "Lord, let me go first and bury my father."²²But Jesus answered him, "Follow me, and let the dead bury their dead."²³He got into a boat and his disciples followed him.²⁴Suddenly a violent storm came up on the sea, so that the boat was being swamped by waves; but he was asleep.²⁵They came and woke him, saying, "Lord, save us! We are perishing!"²⁶He said to them, "Why are you terrified, O you of little faith?"Then he got up, rebuked the winds and the sea, and there was great calm.²⁷The men were amazed and said, "What sort of man is this, whom even the winds and the sea obey?"²⁸When he came to the other side, to the territory of the Gadarenes, two demoniacs who were coming from the tombs met him. They were so savage that no one could travel by that road.²⁹They cried out, "What have you to do with us, Son of God? Have you come here to torment us before the appointed time?"³⁰Some distance away a herd of many swine was feeding. ³¹The demons pleaded with him, "If you drive us out, send us into the herd of swine."³²And he said to them, "Go then!" They came out and entered the swine, and the whole herd rushed down the steep bank into the sea where they drowned.³³The swineherds ran away, and when they came to the town they reported everything, including what had happened to the demoniacs.³⁴Thereupon the whole town came out to meet Jesus, and when they saw him they begged him to leave their district.

Matthew Chapter 9

¹He entered a boat, made the crossing, and came into his own town.²And there people brought to him a paralytic lying on a stretcher. When Jesus saw their faith, he said to the paralytic, "Courage, child, your sins are forgiven."³At that, some of the scribes said to themselves, "This man is blaspheming."⁴Jesus knew what they were thinking, and said, "Why do you harbor evil thoughts?⁵Which is easier, to say, 'Your sins are forgiven,' or to say, 'Rise and walk'?⁶But that you may know that the Son of Man has authority on earth to forgive sins" - he then said to the paralytic, "Rise, pick up your stretcher, and go home."⁷He rose and went home.⁸When the crowds saw this they were struck with awe and glorified God who had given such authority to human beings.⁹As Jesus passed on from there, he saw a man named Matthew sitting at the customs post. He said to him, "Follow me." And he got up

and followed him.¹⁰While he was at table in his house, many tax collectors and sinners came and sat with Jesus and his disciples.¹¹The Pharisees saw this and said to his disciples, "Why does your teacher eat with tax collectors and sinners?"¹²He heard this and said, "Those who are well do not need a physician, but the sick do. ¹³Go and learn the meaning of the words, 'I desire mercy, not sacrifice.' I did not come to call the righteous but sinners."¹⁴Then the disciples of John approached him and said, "Why do we and the Pharisees fast (much), but your disciples do not fast?"¹⁵Jesus answered them, "Can the wedding guests mourn as long as the bridegroom is with them? The days will come when the bridegroom is taken away from them, and then they will fast. ¹⁶No one patches an old cloak with a piece of unshrunken cloth, for its fullness pulls away from the cloak and the tear gets worse.¹⁷People do not put new wine into old wineskins. Otherwise the skins burst, the wine spills out, and the skins are ruined. Rather, they pour new wine into fresh wineskins, and both are preserved."¹⁸While he was saying these things to them, an official came forward, knelt down before him, and said, "My daughter has just died. But come, lay your hand on her, and she will live."¹⁹Jesus rose and followed him, and so did his disciples.²⁰A woman suffering hemorrhages for twelve years came up behind him and touched the tassel on his cloak.²¹She said to herself, "If only I can touch his cloak, I shall be cured."²²Jesus turned around and saw her, and said, "Courage, daughter! Your faith has saved you." And from that hour the woman was cured.²³When Jesus arrived at the official's house and saw the flute players and the crowd who were making a commotion,²⁴he said, "Go away! The girl is not dead but sleeping." And they ridiculed him.²⁵When the crowd was put out, he came and took her by the hand, and the little girl arose.²⁶And news of this spread throughout all that land.²⁷And as Jesus passed on from there, two blind men followed (him), crying out, "Son of David, have pity on us!"²⁸When he entered the house, the blind men approached him and Jesus said to them, "Do you believe that I can do this?" "Yes, Lord," they said to him.²⁹Then he touched their eyes and said, "Let it be done for you according to your faith."³⁰And their eyes were opened. Jesus warned them sternly, "See that no one knows about this."³¹But they went out and spread word of him through all that land.³²As they were going out, a demoniac who could not speak was brought to him,³³and when the demon was driven out the mute person spoke. The crowds were amazed and said, "Nothing like this has ever been seen in Israel."³⁴But the Pharisees said, "He drives out demons by the prince of demons."³⁵Jesus went around to all the towns and villages, teaching in their synagogues, proclaiming the gospel of the kingdom, and curing every disease and illness.³⁶At the sight of the crowds, his heart was moved with pity for them because they were troubled and abandoned, like sheep without a shepherd.³⁷Then he said to his disciples, "The harvest is abundant but the laborers are few;³⁸so ask the master of the harvest to send out laborers for his harvest."

Matthew Chapter 10

¹Then he summoned his twelve disciples and gave them authority over unclean spirits to drive them out and to cure every disease and every illness.²The names of the twelve apostles are these: first, Simon called Peter, and his brother Andrew; James, the son of Zebedee, and his brother John;³Philip and Bartholomew, Thomas and Matthew the tax collector; James, the son of Alphaeus, and Thaddeus;⁴Simon the Cananean, and Judas Iscariot who betrayed him.⁵Jesus sent out these twelve after instructing them thus, "Do not go into pagan territory or enter a Samaritan town.⁶Go rather to the lost sheep of the house of Israel.⁷As you go, make this proclamation: 'The kingdom of heaven is at hand.'⁸Cure the sick, raise the dead, cleanse lepers, drive out demons. Without cost you have received; without cost you are to give.⁹Do not take gold or silver or copper for your belts;¹⁰no sack for the journey, or a second tunic, or sandals, or walking stick. The laborer deserves his keep.¹¹Whatever town or village you enter, look for a worthy person in it, and stay there until you leave.¹²As you enter a house, wish it peace.¹³If the house is worthy, let your peace come upon it; if not, let your peace return to you. ¹⁴Whoever will not receive you or listen to your words - go outside that house or town and shake the dust from your feet.¹⁵Amen, I say to you, it will be more tolerable for the land of Sodom and Gomorrah on the day of judgment than for that town.¹⁶"Behold, I am sending you like sheep in the midst of wolves; so be shrewd as serpents and simple as doves.¹⁷But beware of people, for they will hand you over to courts and scourge you in their synagogues,¹⁸and you will be led before governors and kings for my sake as a witness before them and the pagans.¹⁹When they hand you over, do not worry about how you are to speak or what you are to say. You will be given at that moment what you are to say.²⁰For it will not be you who speak but the Spirit of your Father speaking through you.²¹Brother will hand over brother to death, and the father his child; children will rise up against parents and have

them put to death.²²You will be hated by all because of my name, but whoever endures to the end will be saved.²³When they persecute you in one town, flee to another. Amen, I say to you, you will not finish the towns of Israel before the Son of Man comes.²⁴No disciple is above his teacher, no slave above his master.²⁵It is enough for the disciple that he become like his teacher, for the slave that he become like his master. If they have called the master of the house Beelzebul, how much more those of his household!²⁶"Therefore do not be afraid of them. Nothing is concealed that will not be revealed, nor secret that will not be known.²⁷What I say to you in the darkness, speak in the light; what you hear whispered, proclaim on the housetops.²⁸And do not be afraid of those who kill the body but cannot kill the soul; rather, be afraid of the one who can destroy both soul and body in Gehenna.²⁹Are not two sparrows sold for a small coin? Yet not one of them falls to the ground without your Father's knowledge.³⁰Even all the hairs of your head are counted.³¹So do not be afraid; you are worth more than many sparrows.³²Everyone who acknowledges me before others I will acknowledge before my heavenly Father.³³But whoever denies me before others, I will deny before my heavenly Father.³⁴"Do not think that I have come to bring peace upon the earth. I have come to bring not peace but the sword.³⁵For I have come to set a man 'against his father, a daughter against her mother, and a daughter-in-law against her mother-in-law;³⁶and one's enemies will be those of his household.'³⁷"Whoever loves father or mother more than me is not worthy of me, and whoever loves son or daughter more than me is not worthy of me;³⁸and whoever does not take up his cross and follow after me is not worthy of me.³⁹Whoever finds his life will lose it, and whoever loses his life for my sake will find it.⁴⁰"Whoever receives you receives me, and whoever receives me receives the one who sent me.⁴¹Whoever receives a prophet because he is a prophet will receive a prophet's reward, and whoever receives a righteous man because he is righteous will receive a righteous man's reward.⁴²And whoever gives only a cup of cold water to one of these little ones to drink because he is a disciple - amen, I say to you, he will surely not lose his reward."

Matthew Chapter 11

¹When Jesus finished giving these commands to his twelve disciples, he went away from that place to teach and to preach in their towns.²When John heard in prison of the works of the Messiah, he sent his disciples to him³with this question, "Are you the one who is to come, or should we look for another?"⁴Jesus said to them in reply, "Go and tell John what you hear and see:⁵the blind regain their sight, the lame walk, lepers are cleansed, the deaf hear, the dead are raised, and the poor have the good news proclaimed to them.⁶And blessed is the one who takes no offense at me.⁷As they were going off, Jesus began to speak to the crowds about John, "What did you go out to the desert to see? A reed swayed by the wind?⁸Then what did you go out to see? Someone dressed in fine clothing? Those who wear fine clothing are in royal palaces.⁹Then why did you go out? To see a prophet? Yes, I tell you, and more than a prophet.¹⁰This is the one about whom it is written: 'Behold, I am sending my messenger ahead of you; he will prepare your way before you.'¹¹Amen, I say to you, among those born of women there has been none greater than John the Baptist; yet the least in the kingdom of heaven is greater than he. ¹²From the days of John the Baptist until now, the kingdom of heaven suffers violence, and the violent are taking it by force.¹³All the prophets and the law prophesied up to the time of John.¹⁴And if you are willing to accept it, he is Elijah, the one who is to come.¹⁵Whoever has ears ought to hear.¹⁶"To what shall I compare this generation? It is like children who sit in marketplaces and call to one another,¹⁷'We played the flute for you, but you did not dance, we sang a dirge but you did not mourn.'¹⁸For John came neither eating nor drinking, and they said, 'He is possessed by a demon.'¹⁹The Son of Man came eating and drinking and they said, 'Look, he is a glutton and a drunkard, a friend of tax collectors and sinners.' But wisdom is vindicated by her works."²⁰Then he began to reproach the towns where most of his mighty deeds had been done, since they had not repented.²¹"Woe to you, Chorazin! Woe to you, Bethsaida! For if the mighty deeds done in your midst had been done in Tyre and Sidon, they would long ago have repented in sackcloth and ashes.²²But I tell you, it will be more tolerable for Tyre and Sidon on the day of judgment than for you.²³And as for you, Capernaum: 'Will you be exalted to heaven? You will go down to the netherworld.' For if the mighty deeds done in your midst had been done in Sodom, it would have remained until this day.²⁴But I tell you, it will be more tolerable for the land of Sodom on the day of judgment than for you."²⁵At that time Jesus said in reply, "I give praise to you, Father, Lord of heaven and earth, for although you have hidden these things from the wise and the learned you have revealed them to the childlike.²⁶Yes, Father, such has been your gracious will.²⁷All things have been handed over to me by my Father.

No one knows the Son except the Father, and no one knows the Father except the Son and anyone to whom the Son wishes to reveal him.²⁸"Come to me, all you who labor and are burdened, and I will give you rest.²⁹Take my yoke upon you and learn from me, for I am meek and humble of heart; and you will find rest for your selves.³⁰For my yoke is easy, and my burden light."

Matthew Chapter 12

¹At that time Jesus was going through a field of grain on the sabbath. His disciples were hungry and began to pick the heads of grain and eat them.²When the Pharisees saw this, they said to him, "See, your disciples are doing what is unlawful to do on the sabbath."³He said to them, "Have you not read what David did when he and his companions were hungry,⁴how he went into the house of God and ate the bread of offering, which neither he nor his companions but only the priests could lawfully eat?⁵Or have you not read in the law that on the sabbath the priests serving in the temple violate the sabbath and are innocent?⁶I say to you, something greater than the temple is here.⁷If you knew what this meant, 'I desire mercy, not sacrifice,' you would not have condemned these innocent men.⁸For the Son of Man is Lord of the sabbath."⁹Moving on from there, he went into their synagogue.¹⁰And behold, there was a man there who had a withered hand. They questioned him, "Is it lawful to cure on the sabbath?" ⁷ so that they might accuse him.¹¹He said to them, "Which one of you who has a sheep that falls into a pit on the sabbath will not take hold of it and lift it out?¹²How much more valuable a person is than a sheep. So it is lawful to do good on the sabbath."¹³Then he said to the man, "Stretch out your hand." He stretched it out, and it was restored as sound as the other.¹⁴But the Pharisees went out and took counsel against him to put him to death.¹⁵When Jesus realized this, he withdrew from that place. Many (people) followed him, and he cured them all,¹⁶but he warned them not to make him known.¹⁷This was to fulfill what had been spoken through Isaiah the prophet:¹⁸"Behold, my servant whom I have chosen, my beloved in whom I delight; I shall place my spirit upon him, and he will proclaim justice to the Gentiles.¹⁹He will not contend or cry out, nor will anyone hear his voice in the streets.²⁰A bruised reed he will not break, a smoldering wick he will not quench, until he brings justice to victory.²¹And in his name the Gentiles will hope." ²²Then they brought to him a demoniac who was blind and mute. He cured the mute person so that he could speak and see.²³All the crowd was astounded, and said, "Could this perhaps be the Son of David?"²⁴But when the Pharisees heard this, they said, "This man drives out demons only by the power of Beelzebul, the prince of demons."²⁵But he knew what they were thinking and said to them, "Every kingdom divided against itself will be laid waste, and no town or house divided against itself will stand.²⁶And if Satan drives out Satan, he is divided against himself; how, then, will his kingdom stand?²⁷And if I drive out demons by Beelzebul, by whom do your own people drive them out? Therefore they will be your judges.²⁸But if it is by the Spirit of God that I drive out demons, then the kingdom of God has come upon you.²⁹How can anyone enter a strong man's house and steal his property, unless he first ties up the strong man? Then he can plunder his house.³⁰Whoever is not with me is against me, and whoever does not gather with me scatters.³¹Therefore, I say to you, every sin and blasphemy will be forgiven people, but blasphemy against the Spirit will not be forgiven.³²And whoever speaks a word against the Son of Man will be forgiven; but whoever speaks against the holy Spirit will not be forgiven, either in this age or in the age to come.³³"Either declare the tree good and its fruit is good, or declare the tree rotten and its fruit is rotten, for a tree is known by its fruit.³⁴You brood of vipers, how can you say good things when you are evil? For from the fullness of the heart the mouth speaks.³⁵A good person brings forth good out of a store of goodness, but an evil person brings forth evil out of a store of evil.³⁶I tell you, on the day of judgment people will render an account for every careless word they speak.³⁷By your words you will be acquitted, and by your words you will be condemned."³⁸Then some of the scribes and Pharisees said to him, "Teacher, we wish to see a sign from you."³⁹He said to them in reply, "An evil and unfaithful generation seeks a sign, but no sign will be given it except the sign of Jonah the prophet.⁴⁰Just as Jonah was in the belly of the whale three days and three nights, so will the Son of Man be in the heart of the earth three days and three nights.⁴¹At the judgment, the men of Nineveh will arise with this generation and condemn it, because they repented at the preaching of Jonah; and there is something greater than Jonah here.⁴²At the judgment the queen of the south will arise with this generation and condemn it, because she came from the ends of the earth to hear the wisdom of Solomon; and there is something greater than Solomon here.⁴³"When an unclean spirit goes out of a person it roams through arid regions searching for rest but finds none.⁴⁴Then it says, 'I will return to my home from which

I came.' But upon returning, it finds it empty, swept clean, and put in order.⁴⁵Then it goes and brings back with itself seven other spirits more evil than itself, and they move in and dwell there; and the last condition of that person is worse than the first. Thus it will be with this evil generation."⁴⁶While he was still speaking to the crowds, his mother and his brothers appeared outside, wishing to speak with him.⁴⁷(Someone told him, "Your mother and your brothers are standing outside, asking to speak with you.") ⁴⁸But he said in reply to the one who told him, "Who is my mother? Who are my brothers?"⁴⁹And stretching out his hand toward his disciples, he said, "Here are my mother and my brothers.⁵⁰For whoever does the will of my heavenly Father is my brother, and sister, and mother."

Matthew Chapter 13

¹On that day, Jesus went out of the house and sat down by the sea.²Such large crowds gathered around him that he got into a boat and sat down, and the whole crowd stood along the shore.³And he spoke to them at length in parables, saying: "A sower went out to sow. ⁴And as he sowed, some seed fell on the path, and birds came and ate it up.⁵Some fell on rocky ground, where it had little soil. It sprang up at once because the soil was not deep,⁶and when the sun rose it was scorched, and it withered for lack of roots.⁷Some seed fell among thorns, and the thorns grew up and choked it.⁸But some seed fell on rich soil, and produced fruit, a hundred or sixty or thirtyfold.⁹Whoever has ears ought to hear."¹⁰The disciples approached him and said, "Why do you speak to them in parables?"¹¹He said to them in reply, "Because knowledge of the mysteries of the kingdom of heaven has been granted to you, but to them it has not been granted.¹²To anyone who has, more will be given and he will grow rich; from anyone who has not, even what he has will be taken away.¹³This is why I speak to them in parables, because 'they look but do not see and hear but do not listen or understand.'¹⁴Isaiah's prophecy is fulfilled in them, which says: 'You shall indeed hear but not understand you shall indeed look but never see.¹⁵Gross is the heart of this people, they will hardly hear with their ears, they have closed their eyes, lest they see with their eyes and hear with their ears and understand with their heart and be converted, and I heal them.'¹⁶"But blessed are your eyes, because they see, and your ears, because they hear.¹⁷Amen, I say to you, many prophets and righteous people longed to see what you see but did not see it, and to hear what you hear but did not hear it.¹⁸"Hear then the parable of the sower.¹⁹The seed sown on the path is the one who hears the word of the kingdom without understanding it, and the evil one comes and steals away what was sown in his heart.²⁰The seed sown on rocky ground is the one who hears the word and receives it at once with joy.²¹But he has no root and lasts only for a time. When some tribulation or persecution comes because of the word, he immediately falls away.²²The seed sown among thorns is the one who hears the word, but then worldly anxiety and the lure of riches choke the word and it bears no fruit.²³But the seed sown on rich soil is the one who hears the word and understands it, who indeed bears fruit and yields a hundred or sixty or thirtyfold."²⁴He proposed another parable to them. "The kingdom of heaven may be likened to a man who sowed good seed in his field.²⁵While everyone was asleep his enemy came and sowed weeds all through the wheat, and then went off.²⁶When the crop grew and bore fruit, the weeds appeared as well.²⁷The slaves of the householder came to him and said, 'Master, did you not sow good seed in your field? Where have the weeds come from?'²⁸He answered, 'An enemy has done this.' His slaves said to him, 'Do you want us to go and pull them up?'²⁹He replied, 'No, if you pull up the weeds you might uproot the wheat along with them.³⁰Let them grow together until harvest; then at harvest time I will say to the harvesters, "First collect the weeds and tie them in bundles for burning; but gather the wheat into my barn."'"³¹He proposed another parable to them. "The kingdom of heaven is like a mustard seed that a person took and sowed in a field.³²It is the smallest of all the seeds, yet when full-grown it is the largest of plants. It becomes a large bush, and the 'birds of the sky come and dwell in its branches.'"³³He spoke to them another parable. "The kingdom of heaven is like yeast that a woman took and mixed with three measures of wheat flour until the whole batch was leavened."³⁴All these things Jesus spoke to the crowds in parables. He spoke to them only in parables,³⁵to fulfill what had been said through the prophet: "I will open my mouth in parables, I will announce what has lain hidden from the foundation (of the world)."³⁶Then, dismissing the crowds, he went into the house. His disciples approached him and said, "Explain to us the parable of the weeds in the field."³⁷He said in reply, "He who sows good seed is the Son of Man,³⁸the field is the world, the good seed the children of the kingdom. The weeds are the children of the evil one,³⁹and the enemy who sows them is the devil. The harvest is the end of the age, and the harvesters are angels.⁴⁰Just as weeds are collected and burned (up) with fire, so will it be at the end of the age.⁴¹The Son of

Man will send his angels, and they will collect out of his kingdom all who cause others to sin and all evildoers.⁴²They will throw them into the fiery furnace, where there will be wailing and grinding of teeth.⁴³Then the righteous will shine like the sun in the kingdom of their Father. Whoever has ears ought to hear.⁴⁴"The kingdom of heaven is like a treasure buried in a field, which a person finds and hides again, and out of joy goes and sells all that he has and buys that field.⁴⁵Again, the kingdom of heaven is like a merchant searching for fine pearls.⁴⁶When he finds a pearl of great price, he goes and sells all that he has and buys it.⁴⁷Again, the kingdom of heaven is like a net thrown into the sea, which collects fish of every kind.⁴⁸When it is full they haul it ashore and sit down to put what is good into buckets. What is bad they throw away.⁴⁹Thus it will be at the end of the age. The angels will go out and separate the wicked from the righteous⁵⁰and throw them into the fiery furnace, where there will be wailing and grinding of teeth.⁵¹"Do you understand all these things?" They answered, "Yes."⁵²And he replied, "Then every scribe who has been instructed in the kingdom of heaven is like the head of a household who brings from his storeroom both the new and the old."⁵³When Jesus finished these parables, he went away from there.⁵⁴He came to his native place and taught the people in their synagogue. They were astonished and said, "Where did this man get such wisdom and mighty deeds?⁵⁵Is he not the carpenter's son? Is not his mother named Mary and his brothers James, Joseph, Simon, and Judas?⁵⁶Are not his sisters all with us? Where did this man get all this?"⁵⁷And they took offense at him. But Jesus said to them, "A prophet is not without honor except in his native place and in his own house."⁵⁸And he did not work many mighty deeds there because of their lack of faith.

Matthew Chapter 14

¹At that time Herod the tetrarch heard of the reputation of Jesus²and said to his servants, "This man is John the Baptist. He has been raised from the dead; that is why mighty powers are at work in him."³Now Herod had arrested John, bound (him), and put him in prison on account of Herodias, the wife of his brother Philip,⁴for John had said to him, "It is not lawful for you to have her."⁵Although he wanted to kill him, he feared the people, for they regarded him as a prophet.⁶But at a birthday celebration for Herod, the daughter of Herodias performed a dance before the guests and delighted Herod⁷so much that he swore to give her whatever she might ask for.⁸Prompted by her mother, she said, "Give me here on a platter the head of John the Baptist."⁹The king was distressed, but because of his oaths and the guests who were present, he ordered that it be given,¹⁰and he had John beheaded in the prison.¹¹His head was brought in on a platter and given to the girl, who took it to her mother.¹²His disciples came and took away the corpse and buried him; and they went and told Jesus.¹³When Jesus heard of it, he withdrew in a boat to a deserted place by himself. The crowds heard of this and followed him on foot from their towns.¹⁴When he disembarked and saw the vast crowd, his heart was moved with pity for them, and he cured their sick.¹⁵When it was evening, the disciples approached him and said, "This is a deserted place and it is already late; dismiss the crowds so that they can go to the villages and buy food for themselves."¹⁶(Jesus) said to them, "There is no need for them to go away; give them some food yourselves."¹⁷But they said to him, "Five loaves and two fish are all we have here."¹⁸Then he said, "Bring them here to me,"¹⁹and he ordered the crowds to sit down on the grass. Taking the five loaves and the two fish, and looking up to heaven, he said the blessing, broke the loaves, and gave them to the disciples, who in turn gave them to the crowds.²⁰They all ate and were satisfied, and they picked up the fragments left over - twelve wicker baskets full.²¹Those who ate were about five thousand men, not counting women and children.²²Then he made the disciples get into the boat and precede him to the other side, while he dismissed the crowds.²³After doing so, he went up on the mountain by himself to pray. When it was evening he was there alone.²⁴Meanwhile the boat, already a few miles offshore, was being tossed about by the waves, for the wind was against it.²⁵During the fourth watch of the night, he came toward them, walking on the sea.²⁶When the disciples saw him walking on the sea they were terrified. "It is a ghost," they said, and they cried out in fear.²⁷At once (Jesus) spoke to them, "Take courage, it is I; do not be afraid."²⁸Peter said to him in reply, "Lord, if it is you, command me to come to you on the water."²⁹He said, "Come." Peter got out of the boat and began to walk on the water toward Jesus.³⁰But when he saw how (strong) the wind was he became frightened; and, beginning to sink, he cried out, "Lord, save me!"³¹Immediately Jesus stretched out his hand and caught him, and said to him, "O you of little faith, why did you doubt?"³²After they got into the boat, the wind died down.³³Those who were in the boat did him homage, saying, "Truly, you are the Son of God."³⁴After making the crossing, they came to land at Gennesaret.³⁵When the men of that place recognized him, they sent word to all the surrounding country. People brought to him all those who were sick³⁶and begged him that they might touch only the tassel on his cloak, and as many as touched it were healed.

Matthew Chapter 15

¹Then Pharisees and scribes came to Jesus from Jerusalem and said,²"Why do your disciples break the tradition of the elders? They do not wash (their) hands when they eat a meal."³He said to them in reply, "And why do you break the commandment of God for the sake of your tradition?⁴For God said, 'Honor your father and your mother,' and 'Whoever curses father or mother shall die.'⁵But you say, 'Whoever says to father or mother, "Any support you might have had from me is dedicated to God,"⁶need not honor his father.' You have nullified the word of God for the sake of your tradition.⁷Hypocrites, well did Isaiah prophesy about you when he said:⁸'This people honors me with their lips, but their hearts are far from me;⁹in vain do they worship me, teaching as doctrines human precepts.'"¹⁰He summoned the crowd and said to them, "Hear and understand.¹¹It is not what enters one's mouth that defiles that person; but what comes out of the mouth is what defiles one."¹²Then his disciples approached and said to him, "Do you know that the Pharisees took offense when they heard what you said?"¹³He said in reply, "Every plant that my heavenly Father has not planted will be uprooted.¹⁴Let them alone; they are blind guides (of the blind). If a blind person leads a blind person, both will fall into a pit."¹⁵Then Peter said to him in reply, "Explain (this) parable to us."¹⁶He said to them, "Are even you still without understanding?¹⁷Do you not realize that everything that enters the mouth passes into the stomach and is expelled into the latrine?¹⁸But the things that come out of the mouth come from the heart, and they defile.¹⁹For from the heart come evil thoughts, murder, adultery, unchastity, theft, false witness, blasphemy.²⁰These are what defile a person, but to eat with unwashed hands does not defile."²¹Then Jesus went from that place and withdrew to the region of Tyre and Sidon.²²And behold, a Canaanite woman of that district came and called out, "Have pity on me, Lord, Son of David! My daughter is tormented by a demon."²³But he did not say a word in answer to her. His disciples came and asked him, "Send her away, for she keeps calling out after us."²⁴He said in reply, "I was sent only to the lost sheep of the house of Israel."²⁵But the woman came and did him homage, saying, "Lord, help me."²⁶He said in reply, "It is not right to take the food of the children and throw it to the dogs."²⁷She said, "Please, Lord, for even the dogs eat the scraps that fall from the table of their masters."²⁸Then Jesus said to her in reply, "O woman, great is your faith! Let it be done for you as you wish." And her daughter was healed from that hour.²⁹Moving on from there Jesus walked by the Sea of Galilee, went up on the mountain, and sat down there.³⁰Great crowds came to him, having with them the lame, the blind, the deformed, the mute, and many others. They placed them at his feet, and he cured them.³¹The crowds were amazed when they saw the mute speaking, the deformed made whole, the lame walking, and the blind able to see, and they glorified the God of Israel.³²Jesus summoned his disciples and said, "My heart is moved with pity for the crowd, for they have been with me now for three days and have nothing to eat. I do not want to send them away hungry, for fear they may collapse on the way."³³The disciples said to him, "Where could we ever get enough bread in this deserted place to satisfy such a crowd?"³⁴Jesus said to them, "How many loaves do you have?" "Seven," they replied, "and a few fish."³⁵He ordered the crowd to sit down on the ground.³⁶Then he took the seven loaves and the fish, gave thanks, broke the loaves, and gave them to the disciples, who in turn gave them to the crowds.³⁷They all ate and were satisfied. They picked up the fragments left over - seven baskets full.³⁸Those who ate were four thousand men, not counting women and children.³⁹And when he had dismissed the crowds, he got into the boat and came to the district of Magadan.

Matthew Chapter 16

¹The Pharisees and Sadducees came and, to test him, asked him to show them a sign from heaven.²He said to them in reply, "(In the evening you say, 'Tomorrow will be fair, for the sky is red';³and, in the morning, 'Today will be stormy, for the sky is red and threatening.' You know how to judge the appearance of the sky, but you cannot judge the signs of the times.)⁴An evil and unfaithful generation seeks a sign, but no sign will be given it except the sign of Jonah." Then he left them and went away.⁵In coming to the other side of the sea, the disciples had forgotten to bring bread.⁶Jesus said to them, "Look out, and beware of the leaven of the Pharisees and Sadducees."⁷They concluded among themselves, saying, "It is because we have brought no bread."⁸When Jesus became aware of this he said, "You of little faith, why do you conclude among yourselves that it is because you have no bread?⁹Do

you not yet understand, and do you not remember the five loaves for the five thousand, and how many wicker baskets you took up?¹⁰Or the seven loaves for the four thousand, and how many baskets you took up?¹¹How do you not comprehend that I was not speaking to you about bread? Beware of the leaven of the Pharisees and Sadducees."¹²Then they understood that he was not telling them to beware of the leaven of bread, but of the teaching of the Pharisees and Sadducees.¹³When Jesus went into the region of Caesarea Philippi he asked his disciples, "Who do people say that the Son of Man is?"¹⁴They replied, "Some say John the Baptist, others Elijah, still others Jeremiah or one of the prophets."¹⁵He said to them, "But who do you say that I am?"¹⁶Simon Peter said in reply, "You are the Messiah, the Son of the living God."¹⁷Jesus said to him in reply, "Blessed are you, Simon son of Jonah. For flesh and blood has not revealed this to you, but my heavenly Father.¹⁸And so I say to you, you are Peter, and upon this rock I will build my church, and the gates of the netherworld shall not prevail against it.¹⁹I will give you the keys to the kingdom of heaven. Whatever you bind on earth shall be bound in heaven; and whatever you loose on earth shall be loosed in heaven."²⁰Then he strictly ordered his disciples to tell no one that he was the Messiah.²¹From that time on, Jesus began to show his disciples that he must go to Jerusalem and suffer greatly from the elders, the chief priests, and the scribes, and be killed and on the third day be raised.²²Then Peter took him aside and began to rebuke him, "God forbid, Lord! No such thing shall ever happen to you."²³He turned and said to Peter, "Get behind me, Satan! You are an obstacle to me. You are thinking not as God does, but as human beings do."²⁴Then Jesus said to his disciples, "Whoever wishes to come after me must deny himself, take up his cross, and follow me.²⁵For whoever wishes to save his life will lose it, but whoever loses his life for my sake will find it.²⁶What profit would there be for one to gain the whole world and forfeit his life? Or what can one give in exchange for his life?²⁷For the Son of Man will come with his angels in his Father's glory, and then he will repay everyone according to his conduct.²⁸Amen, I say to you, there are some standing here who will not taste death until they see the Son of Man coming in his kingdom."

Matthew Chapter 17

¹After six days Jesus took Peter, James, and John his brother, and led them up a high mountain by themselves.²And he was transfigured before them; his face shone like the sun and his clothes became white as light.³And behold, Moses and Elijah appeared to them, conversing with him.⁴Then Peter said to Jesus in reply, "Lord, it is good that we are here. If you wish, I will make three tents here, one for you, one for Moses, and one for Elijah.⁵While he was still speaking, behold, a bright cloud cast a shadow over them, then from the cloud came a voice that said, "This is my beloved Son, with whom I am well pleased; listen to him."⁶When the disciples heard this, they fell prostrate and were very much afraid.⁷But Jesus came and touched them, saying, "Rise, and do not be afraid."⁸And when the disciples raised their eyes, they saw no one else but Jesus alone.⁹As they were coming down from the mountain, Jesus charged them, "Do not tell the vision to anyone until the Son of Man has been raised from the dead."¹⁰Then the disciples asked him, "Why do the scribes say that Elijah must come first?"¹¹He said in reply, "Elijah will indeed come and restore all things;¹²but I tell you that Elijah has already come, and they did not recognize him but did to him whatever they pleased. So also will the Son of Man suffer at their hands."¹³Then the disciples understood that he was speaking to them of John the Baptist.¹⁴When they came to the crowd a man approached, knelt down before him,¹⁵and said, "Lord, have pity on my son, for he is a lunatic and suffers severely; often he falls into fire, and often into water.¹⁶I brought him to your disciples, but they could not cure him."¹⁷Jesus said in reply, "O faithless and perverse generation, how long will I be with you? How long will I endure you? Bring him here to me."¹⁸Jesus rebuked him and the demon came out of him, and from that hour the boy was cured.¹⁹Then the disciples approached Jesus in private and said, "Why could we not drive it out?"²⁰He said to them, "Because of your little faith. Amen, I say to you, if you have faith the size of a mustard seed, you will say to this mountain, 'Move from here to there,' and it will move. Nothing will be impossible for you."²¹ But this kind doesn't go out except by prayer and fasting."²²As they were gathering in Galilee, Jesus said to them, "The Son of Man is to be handed over to men,²³and they will kill him, and he will be raised on the third day." And they were overwhelmed with grief.²⁴When they came to Capernaum, the collectors of the temple tax approached Peter and said, "Doesn't your teacher pay the temple tax?"²⁵"Yes," he said. When he came into the house, before he had time to speak, Jesus asked him, "What is your opinion, Simon? From whom do the kings of the earth take tolls or census tax? From their subjects or from foreigners?"²⁶When he said, "From foreigners," Jesus said to him,

"Then the subjects are exempt.²⁷But that we may not offend them, go to the sea, drop in a hook, and take the first fish that comes up. Open its mouth and you will find a coin worth twice the temple tax. Give that to them for me and for you."

Matthew Chapter 18

¹At that time the disciples approached Jesus and said, "Who is the greatest in the kingdom of heaven?"²He called a child over, placed it in their midst,³and said, "Amen, I say to you, unless you turn and become like children, you will not enter the kingdom of heaven.⁴Whoever humbles himself like this child is the greatest in the kingdom of heaven.⁵And whoever receives one child such as this in my name receives me.⁶"Whoever causes one of these little ones who believe in me to sin, it would be better for him to have a great millstone hung around his neck and to be drowned in the depths of the sea.⁷Woe to the world because of things that cause sin! Such things must come, but woe to the one through whom they come!⁸If your hand or foot causes you to sin, cut it off and throw it away. It is better for you to enter into life maimed or crippled than with two hands or two feet to be thrown into eternal fire.⁹And if your eye causes you to sin, tear it out and throw it away. It is better for you to enter into life with one eye than with two eyes to be thrown into fiery Gehenna.¹⁰"See that you do not despise one of these little ones, for I say to you that their angels in heaven always look upon the face of my heavenly Father.¹¹For the Son of Man came to save that which was lost.¹²What is your opinion? If a man has a hundred sheep and one of them goes astray, will he not leave the ninety-nine in the hills and go in search of the stray?¹³And if he finds it, amen, I say to you, he rejoices more over it than over the ninety-nine that did not stray.¹⁴In just the same way, it is not the will of your heavenly Father that one of these little ones be lost.¹⁵"If your brother sins (against you), go and tell him his fault between you and him alone. If he listens to you, you have won over your brother.¹⁶If he does not listen, take one or two others along with you, so that 'every fact may be established on the testimony of two or three witnesses.'¹⁷If he refuses to listen to them, tell the church. If he refuses to listen even to the church, then treat him as you would a Gentile or a tax collector.¹⁸Amen, I say to you, whatever you bind on earth shall be bound in heaven, and whatever you loose on earth shall be loosed in heaven.¹⁹Again, (amen,) I say to you, if two of you agree on earth about anything for which they are to pray, it shall be granted to them by my heavenly Father.²⁰For where two or three are gathered together in my name, there am I in the midst of them."²¹Then Peter approaching asked him, "Lord, if my brother sins against me, how often must I forgive him? As many as seven times?"²²Jesus answered, "I say to you, not seven times but seventy-seven times.²³That is why the kingdom of heaven may be likened to a king who decided to settle accounts with his servants.²⁴When he began the accounting, a debtor was brought before him who owed him a huge amount.²⁵Since he had no way of paying it back, his master ordered him to be sold, along with his wife, his children, and all his property, in payment of the debt.²⁶At that, the servant fell down, did him homage, and said, 'Be patient with me, and I will pay you back in full.'²⁷Moved with compassion the master of that servant let him go and forgave him the loan.²⁸When that servant had left, he found one of his fellow servants who owed him a much smaller amount. He seized him and started to choke him, demanding, 'Pay back what you owe.'²⁹Falling to his knees, his fellow servant begged him, 'Be patient with me, and I will pay you back.'³⁰But he refused. Instead, he had him put in prison until he paid back the debt.³¹Now when his fellow servants saw what had happened, they were deeply disturbed, and went to their master and reported the whole affair.³²His master summoned him and said to him, 'You wicked servant! I forgave you your entire debt because you begged me to.³³Should you not have had pity on your fellow servant, as I had pity on you?'³⁴Then in anger his master handed him over to the torturers until he should pay back the whole debt.³⁵So will my heavenly Father do to you, unless each of you forgives his brother from his heart."

Matthew Chapter 19

¹When Jesus finished these words, he left Galilee and went to the district of Judea across the Jordan.²Great crowds followed him, and he cured them there.³Some Pharisees approached him, and tested him, saying, "Is it lawful for a man to divorce his wife for any cause whatever?"⁴He said in reply, "Have you not read that from the beginning the Creator 'made them male and female'⁵and said, 'For this reason a man shall leave his father and mother and be joined to his wife, and the two shall become one flesh'?⁶So they are no longer two, but one flesh. Therefore, what God has joined together, no human being must separate."⁷They said to him, "Then why did Moses command that the man give the woman a bill of divorce and dismiss (her)?"⁸He said to them, "Because of the hardness of your hearts Moses allowed you to

divorce your wives, but from the beginning it was not so.9I say to you, whoever divorces his wife (unless the marriage is unlawful) and marries another commits adultery."10[His] disciples said to him, "If that is the case of a man with his wife, it is better not to marry."11He answered, "Not all can accept [this] word, but only those to whom that is granted.12Some are incapable of marriage because they were born so; some, because they were made so by others; some, because they have renounced marriage for the sake of the kingdom of heaven. Whoever can accept this ought to accept it."13Then children were brought to him that he might lay his hands on them and pray. The disciples rebuked them,14but Jesus said, "Let the children come to me, and do not prevent them; for the kingdom of heaven belongs to such as these."15After he placed his hands on them, he went away.16Now someone approached him and said, "Teacher, what good must I do to gain eternal life?"17He answered him, "Why do you ask me about the good? There is only One who is good. If you wish to enter into life, keep the commandments."18He asked him, "Which ones?" And Jesus replied, " 'You shall not kill; you shall not commit adultery; you shall not steal; you shall not bear false witness;19honor your father and your mother'; and 'you shall love your neighbor as yourself.'"20The young man said to him, "All of these I have observed. What do I still lack?"21Jesus said to him, "If you wish to be perfect, go, sell what you have and give to (the) poor, and you will have treasure in heaven. Then come, follow me."22When the young man heard this statement, he went away sad, for he had many possessions.23Then Jesus said to his disciples, "Amen, I say to you, it will be hard for one who is rich to enter the kingdom of heaven.24Again I say to you, it is easier for a camel to pass through the eye of a needle than for one who is rich to enter the kingdom of God."25When the disciples heard this, they were greatly astonished and said, "Who then can be saved?"26Jesus looked at them and said, "For human beings this is impossible, but for God all things are possible."27Then Peter said to him in reply, "We have given up everything and followed you. What will there be for us?"28Jesus said to them, "Amen, I say to you that you who have followed me, in the new age, when the Son of Man is seated on his throne of glory, will yourselves sit on twelve thrones, judging the twelve tribes of Israel.29And everyone who has given up houses or brothers or sisters or father or mother or children or lands for the sake of my name will receive a hundred times more, and will inherit eternal life.30But many who are first will be last, and the last will be first.

Matthew Chapter 20

1"The kingdom of heaven is like a landowner who went out at dawn to hire laborers for his vineyard.2After agreeing with them for the usual daily wage, he sent them into his vineyard.3Going out about nine o'clock, he saw others standing idle in the marketplace,4and he said to them, 'You too go into my vineyard, and I will give you what is just.'5So they went off. (And) he went out again around noon, and around three o'clock, and did likewise.6Going out about five o'clock, he found others standing around, and said to them, 'Why do you stand here idle all day?'7They answered, 'Because no one has hired us.' He said to them, 'You too go into my vineyard.'8When it was evening the owner of the vineyard said to his foreman, 'Summon the laborers and give them their pay, beginning with the last and ending with the first.'9When those who had started about five o'clock came, each received the usual daily wage.10So when the first came, they thought that they would receive more, but each of them also got the usual wage.11And on receiving it they grumbled against the landowner,12saying, 'These last ones worked only one hour, and you have made them equal to us, who bore the day's burden and the heat.'13He said to one of them in reply, 'My friend, I am not cheating you. Did you not agree with me for the usual daily wage?14Take what is yours and go. What if I wish to give this last one the same as you?15(Or) am I not free to do as I wish with my own money? Are you envious because I am generous?'16Thus, the last will be first, and the first will be last."17As Jesus was going up to Jerusalem, he took the twelve (disciples) aside by themselves, and said to them on the way,18"Behold, we are going up to Jerusalem, and the Son of Man will be handed over to the chief priests and the scribes, and they will condemn him to death,19and hand him over to the Gentiles to be mocked and scourged and crucified, and he will be raised on the third day."20Then the mother of the sons of Zebedee approached him with her sons and did him homage, wishing to ask him for something.21He said to her, "What do you wish?" She answered him, "Command that these two sons of mine sit, one at your right and the other at your left, in your kingdom."22Jesus said in reply, "You do not know what you are asking. Can you drink the cup that I am going to drink?" They said to him, "We can."23He replied, "My cup you will indeed drink, but to sit at my right and at my left (, this) is not mine to give but is for those for whom it has been prepared by my Father."24When the ten heard this,

they became indignant at the two brothers.25But Jesus summoned them and said, "You know that the rulers of the Gentiles lord it over them, and the great ones make their authority over them felt.26But it shall not be so among you. Rather, whoever wishes to be great among you shall be your servant;27whoever wishes to be first among you shall be your slave.28Just so, the Son of Man did not come to be served but to serve and to give his life as a ransom for many."29As they left Jericho, a great crowd followed him.30Two blind men were sitting by the roadside, and when they heard that Jesus was passing by, they cried out, "[Lord,] Son of David, have pity on us!"31The crowd warned them to be silent, but they called out all the more, "Lord, Son of David, have pity on us!"32Jesus stopped and called them and said, "What do you want me to do for you?"33They answered him, "Lord, let our eyes be opened."34Moved with pity, Jesus touched their eyes. Immediately they received their sight, and followed him.

Matthew Chapter 21

1When they drew near Jerusalem and came to Bethphage on the Mount of Olives, Jesus sent two disciples,2saying to them, "Go into the village opposite you, and immediately you will find an ass tethered, and a colt with her. Untie them and bring them here to me.3And if anyone should say anything to you, reply, 'The master has need of them.' Then he will send them at once."4This happened so that what had been spoken through the prophet might be fulfilled:5"Say to daughter Zion, 'Behold, your king comes to you, meek and riding on an ass, and on a colt, the foal of a beast of burden.'"6The disciples went and did as Jesus had ordered them.7They brought the ass and the colt and laid their cloaks over them, and he sat upon them.8The very large crowd spread their cloaks on the road, while others cut branches from the trees and strewed them on the road.9The crowds preceding him and those following kept crying out and saying: "Hosanna to the Son of David; blessed is he who comes in the name of the Lord; hosanna in the highest."10And when he entered Jerusalem the whole city was shaken and asked, "Who is this?"11And the crowds replied, "This is Jesus the prophet, from Nazareth in Galilee."12Jesus entered the temple area and drove out all those engaged in selling and buying there. He overturned the tables of the money changers and the seats of those who were selling doves.13And he said to them, "It is written: 'My house shall be a house of prayer,' but you are making it a den of thieves."14The blind and the lame approached him in the temple area, and he cured them.15When the chief priests and the scribes saw the wondrous things he was doing, and the children crying out in the temple area, "Hosanna to the Son of David," they were indignant16and said to him, "Do you hear what they are saying?" Jesus said to them, "Yes; and have you never read the text, 'Out of the mouths of infants and nurslings you have brought forth praise'?"17And leaving them, he went out of the city to Bethany, and there he spent the night.18When he was going back to the city in the morning, he was hungry.19Seeing a fig tree by the road, he went over to it, but found nothing on it except leaves. And he said to it, "May no fruit ever come from you again." And immediately the fig tree withered.20When the disciples saw this, they were amazed and said, "How was it that the fig tree withered immediately?"21Jesus said to them in reply, "Amen, I say to you, if you have faith and do not waver, not only will you do what has been done to the fig tree, but even if you say to this mountain, 'Be lifted up and thrown into the sea,' it will be done.22Whatever you ask for in prayer with faith, you will receive."23When he had come into the temple area, the chief priests and the elders of the people approached him as he was teaching and said, "By what authority are you doing these things? And who gave you this authority?"24Jesus said to them in reply, "I shall ask you one question, and if you answer it for me, then I shall tell you by what authority I do these things.25Where was John's baptism from? Was it of heavenly or of human origin?" They discussed this among themselves and said, "If we say 'Of heavenly origin,' he will say to us, 'Then why did you not believe him?'26But if we say, 'Of human origin,' we fear the crowd, for they all regard John as a prophet."27So they said to Jesus in reply, "We do not know." He himself said to them, "Neither shall I tell you by what authority I do these things. 28What is your opinion? A man had two sons. He came to the first and said, 'Son, go out and work in the vineyard today.'29He said in reply, 'I will not,' but afterwards he changed his mind and went.30The man came to the other son and gave the same order. He said in reply, 'Yes, sir,' but did not go.31Which of the two did his father's will?" They answered, "The first." Jesus said to them, "Amen, I say to you, tax collectors and prostitutes are entering the kingdom of God before you.32When John came to you in the way of righteousness, you did not believe him; but tax collectors and prostitutes did. Yet even when you saw that, you did not later change your minds and believe him.33"Hear another parable. There was a landowner who planted a vineyard, put a hedge around it, dug a wine press in it, and built a tower. Then he leased it to tenants and went on a journey.³⁴When vintage time drew near, he sent his servants to the tenants to obtain his produce.³⁵But the tenants seized the servants and one they beat, another they killed, and a third they stoned.³⁶Again he sent other servants, more numerous than the first ones, but they treated them in the same way.³⁷Finally, he sent his son to them, thinking, 'They will respect my son.'³⁸But when the tenants saw the son, they said to one another, 'This is the heir. Come, let us kill him and acquire his inheritance.'³⁹They seized him, threw him out of the vineyard, and killed him.⁴⁰What will the owner of the vineyard do to those tenants when he comes?"⁴¹They answered him, "He will put those wretched men to a wretched death and lease his vineyard to other tenants who will give him the produce at the proper times."⁴²Jesus said to them, "Did you never read in the scriptures: 'The stone that the builders rejected has become the cornerstone; by the Lord has this been done, and it is wonderful in our eyes'?⁴³Therefore, I say to you, the kingdom of God will be taken away from you and given to a people that will produce its fruit.⁴⁴(The one who falls on this stone will be dashed to pieces; and it will crush anyone on whom it falls.)"⁴⁵When the chief priests and the Pharisees heard his parables, they knew that he was speaking about them.⁴⁶And although they were attempting to arrest him, they feared the crowds, for they regarded him as a prophet.

Matthew Chapter 22

¹Jesus again in reply spoke to them in parables, saying,²"The kingdom of heaven may be likened to a king who gave a wedding feast for his son.³He dispatched his servants to summon the invited guests to the feast, but they refused to come.⁴A second time he sent other servants, saying, 'Tell those invited: "Behold, I have prepared my banquet, my calves and fattened cattle are killed, and everything is ready; come to the feast."'⁵Some ignored the invitation and went away, one to his farm, another to his business.⁶The rest laid hold of his servants, mistreated them, and killed them.⁷The king was enraged and sent his troops, destroyed those murderers, and burned their city.⁸Then he said to his servants, 'The feast is ready, but those who were invited were not worthy to come.⁹Go out, therefore, into the main roads and invite to the feast whomever you find.'¹⁰The servants went out into the streets and gathered all they found, bad and good alike, and the hall was filled with guests.¹¹But when the king came in to meet the guests he saw a man there not dressed in a wedding garment.¹²He said to him, 'My friend, how is it that you came in here without a wedding garment?' But he was reduced to silence.¹³Then the king said to his attendants, 'Bind his hands and feet, and cast him into the darkness outside, where there will be wailing and grinding of teeth.'¹⁴Many are invited, but few are chosen."¹⁵Then the Pharisees went off and plotted how they might entrap him in speech.¹⁶They sent their disciples to him, with the Herodians, saying, "Teacher, we know that you are a truthful man and that you teach the way of God in accordance with the truth. And you are not concerned with anyone's opinion, for you do not regard a person's status.¹⁷Tell us, then, what is your opinion: Is it lawful to pay the census tax to Caesar or not?"¹⁸Knowing their malice, Jesus said, "Why are you testing me, you hypocrites?¹⁹Show me the coin that pays the census tax." Then they handed him the Roman coin.²⁰He said to them, "Whose image is this and whose inscription?"²¹They replied, "Caesar's." At that he said to them, "Then repay to Caesar what belongs to Caesar and to God what belongs to God."²²When they heard this they were amazed, and leaving him they went away.²³On that day Sadducees approached him, saying that there is no resurrection. They put this question to him,²⁴saying, "Teacher, Moses said, 'If a man dies without children, his brother shall marry his wife and raise up descendants for his brother.'²⁵Now there were seven brothers among us. The first married and died and, having no descendants, left his wife to his brother.²⁶The same happened with the second and the third, through all seven.²⁷Finally the woman died.²⁸Now at the resurrection, of the seven, whose wife will she be? For they all had been married to her."²⁹Jesus said to them in reply, "You are misled because you do not know the scriptures or the power of God.³⁰At the resurrection they neither marry nor are given in marriage but are like the angels in heaven.³¹And concerning the resurrection of the dead, have you not read what was said to you by God,³²'I am the God of Abraham, the God of Isaac, and the God of Jacob'? He is not the God of the dead but of the living."³³When the crowds heard this, they were astonished at his teaching.³⁴When the Pharisees heard that he had silenced the Sadducees, they gathered together,³⁵and one of them [a scholar of the law] tested him by asking,³⁶"Teacher, which commandment in the law is the greatest?"³⁷He said to him, "You shall love the Lord, your God, with all your heart, with all your soul, and with all your mind.³⁸This is the greatest and the first commandment.³⁹The second is like it: You shall love your neighbor as yourself.⁴⁰The whole law and the prophets

depend on these two commandments."⁴¹While the Pharisees were gathered together, Jesus questioned them,⁴²saying, "What is your opinion about the Messiah? Whose son is he?" They replied, "David's."⁴³He said to them, "How, then, does David, inspired by the Spirit, call him 'lord,' saying:⁴⁴'The Lord said to my lord, "Sit at my right hand until I place your enemies under your feet"'?⁴⁵If David calls him 'lord,' how can he be his son?"⁴⁶No one was able to answer him a word, nor from that day on did anyone dare to ask him any more questions.

Matthew Chapter 23

¹Then Jesus spoke to the crowds and to his disciples,²saying, "The scribes and the Pharisees have taken their seat on the chair of Moses.³Therefore, do and observe all things whatsoever they tell you, but do not follow their example. For they preach but they do not practice.⁴They tie up heavy burdens (hard to carry) and lay them on people's shoulders, but they will not lift a finger to move them.⁵All their works are performed to be seen. They widen their phylacteries and lengthen their tassels.⁶They love places of honor at banquets, seats of honor in synagogues,⁷greetings in marketplaces, and the salutation 'Rabbi.'⁸As for you, do not be called 'Rabbi.' You have but one teacher, and you are all brothers.⁹Call no one on earth your father; you have but one Father in heaven.¹⁰Do not be called 'Master'; you have but one master, the Messiah.¹¹The greatest among you must be your servant.¹²Whoever exalts himself will be humbled; but whoever humbles himself will be exalted.¹³ "Woe to you, scribes and Pharisees, hypocrites! For you devour widows' houses, and as a pretense you make long prayers. Therefore you will receive greater condemnation.¹⁴ "But woe to you, scribes and Pharisees, hypocrites! Because you shut up the Kingdom of Heaven against men; for you don't enter in yourselves, neither do you allow those who are entering in to enter. ¹⁵"Woe to you, scribes and Pharisees, you hypocrites. You traverse sea and land to make one convert, and when that happens you make him a child of Gehenna twice as much as yourselves.¹⁶"Woe to you, blind guides, who say, 'If one swears by the temple, it means nothing, but if one swears by the gold of the temple, one is obligated.'¹⁷Blind fools, which is greater, the gold, or the temple that made the gold sacred?¹⁸And you say, 'If one swears by the altar, it means nothing, but if one swears by the gift on the altar, one is obligated.'¹⁹You blind ones, which is greater, the gift, or the altar that makes the gift sacred?²⁰One who swears by the altar swears by it and all that is upon it;²¹one who swears by the temple swears by it and by him who dwells in it;²²one who swears by heaven swears by the throne of God and by him who is seated on it.²³"Woe to you, scribes and Pharisees, you hypocrites. You pay tithes of mint and dill and cummin, and have neglected the weightier things of the law: judgment and mercy and fidelity. (But) these you should have done, without neglecting the others.²⁴Blind guides, who strain out the gnat and swallow the camel!²⁵"Woe to you, scribes and Pharisees, you hypocrites. You cleanse the outside of cup and dish, but inside they are full of plunder and self-indulgence.²⁶Blind Pharisee, cleanse first the inside of the cup, so that the outside also may be clean.²⁷"Woe to you, scribes and Pharisees, you hypocrites. You are like whitewashed tombs, which appear beautiful on the outside, but inside are full of dead men's bones and every kind of filth.²⁸Even so, on the outside you appear righteous, but inside you are filled with hypocrisy and evildoing.²⁹"Woe to you, scribes and Pharisees, you hypocrites. You build the tombs of the prophets and adorn the memorials of the righteous,³⁰and you say, 'If we had lived in the days of our ancestors, we would not have joined them in shedding the prophets' blood.'³¹Thus you bear witness against yourselves that you are the children of those who murdered the prophets;³²now fill up what your ancestors measured out!³³You serpents, you brood of vipers, how can you flee from the judgment of Gehenna?³⁴Therefore, behold, I send to you prophets and wise men and scribes; some of them you will kill and crucify, some of them you will scourge in your synagogues and pursue from town to town,³⁵so that there may come upon you all the righteous blood shed upon earth, from the righteous blood of Abel to the blood of Zechariah, the son of Barachiah, whom you murdered between the sanctuary and the altar.³⁶Amen, I say to you, all these things will come upon this generation.³⁷"Jerusalem, Jerusalem, you who kill the prophets and stone those sent to you, how many times I yearned to gather your children together, as a hen gathers her young under her wings, but you were unwilling!³⁸Behold, your house will be abandoned, desolate.³⁹I tell you, you will not see me again until you say, 'Blessed is he who comes in the name of the Lord.'"

Matthew Chapter 24

¹Jesus left the temple area and was going away, when his disciples approached him to point out the temple buildings.²He said to them in reply, "You see all these things, do you not? Amen, I say to you, there

will not be left here a stone upon another stone that will not be thrown down."3As he was sitting on the Mount of Olives, the disciples approached him privately and said, "Tell us, when will this happen, and what sign will there be of your coming, and of the end of the age?"4Jesus said to them in reply, "See that no one deceives you.5For many will come in my name, saying, 'I am the Messiah,' and they will deceive many.6You will hear of wars and reports of wars; see that you are not alarmed, for these things must happen, but it will not yet be the end.7Nation will rise against nation, and kingdom against kingdom; there will be famines and earthquakes from place to place.8All these are the beginning of the labor pains.9Then they will hand you over to persecution, and they will kill you. You will be hated by all nations because of my name.10And then many will be led into sin; they will betray and hate one another.11Many false prophets will arise and deceive many;12and because of the increase of evildoing, the love of many will grow cold.13But the one who perseveres to the end will be saved.14And this gospel of the kingdom will be preached throughout the world as a witness to all nations, and then the end will come.15"When you see the desolating abomination spoken of through Daniel the prophet standing in the holy place (let the reader understand),16then those in Judea must flee to the mountains,17a person on the housetop must not go down to get things out of his house,18a person in the field must not return to get his cloak.19Woe to pregnant women and nursing mothers in those days.20Pray that your flight not be in winter or on the sabbath,21for at that time there will be great tribulation, such as has not been since the beginning of the world until now, nor ever will be.22And if those days had not been shortened, no one would be saved; but for the sake of the elect they will be shortened.23If anyone says to you then, 'Look, here is the Messiah!' or, 'There he is!' do not believe it.24False messiahs and false prophets will arise, and they will perform signs and wonders so great as to deceive, if that were possible, even the elect.25Behold, I have told it to you beforehand.26So if they say to you, 'He is in the desert,' do not go out there; if they say, 'He is in the inner rooms,' do not believe it. 27For just as lightning comes from the east and is seen as far as the west, so will the coming of the Son of Man be.28Wherever the corpse is, there the vultures will gather.29"Immediately after the tribulation of those days, the sun will be darkened, and the moon will not give its light, and the stars will fall from the sky, and the powers of the heavens will be shaken.30And then the sign of the Son of Man will appear in heaven, and all the tribes of the earth will mourn, and they will see the Son of Man coming upon the clouds of heaven with power and great glory.31And he will send out his angels with a trumpet blast, and they will gather his elect from the four winds, from one end of the heavens to the other.32"Learn a lesson from the fig tree. When its branch becomes tender and sprouts leaves, you know that summer is near.33In the same way, when you see all these things, know that he is near, at the gates.34Amen, I say to you, this generation will not pass away until all these things have taken place.35Heaven and earth will pass away, but my words will not pass away.36"But of that day and hour no one knows, neither the angels of heaven, nor the Son, but the Father alone.37For as it was in the days of Noah, so it will be at the coming of the Son of Man.38In (those) days before the flood, they were eating and drinking, marrying and giving in marriage, up to the day that Noah entered the ark.39They did not know until the flood came and carried them all away. So will it be (also) at the coming of the Son of Man.40Two men will be out in the field; one will be taken, and one will be left.41Two women will be grinding at the mill; one will be taken, and one will be left.42Therefore, stay awake! For you do not know on which day your Lord will come.43Be sure of this: if the master of the house had known the hour of night when the thief was coming, he would have stayed awake and not let his house be broken into.44So too, you also must be prepared, for at an hour you do not expect, the Son of Man will come.45"Who, then, is the faithful and prudent servant, whom the master has put in charge of his household to distribute to them their food at the proper time?46Blessed is that servant whom his master on his arrival finds doing so.47Amen, I say to you, he will put him in charge of all his property.48But if that wicked servant says to himself, 'My master is long delayed,'49and begins to beat his fellow servants, and eat and drink with drunkards,50the servant's master will come on an unexpected day and at an unknown hour51and will punish him severely and assign him a place with the hypocrites, where there will be wailing and grinding of teeth.

Matthew Chapter 25

1"Then the kingdom of heaven will be like ten virgins who took their lamps and went out to meet the bridegroom.2Five of them were foolish and five were wise.3The foolish ones, when taking their lamps, brought no oil with them,4but the wise brought flasks of oil with their lamps.5Since the bridegroom was long delayed, they all became drowsy and fell asleep.6At midnight, there was a cry, 'Behold, the bridegroom! Come out to meet him!'7Then all those virgins got up and trimmed their lamps.8The foolish ones said to the wise, 'Give us some of your oil, for our lamps are going out.'9But the wise ones replied, 'No, for there may not be enough for us and you. Go instead to the merchants and buy some for yourselves.'10While they went off to buy it, the bridegroom came and those who were ready went into the wedding feast with him. Then the door was locked.11Afterwards the other virgins came and said, 'Lord, Lord, open the door for us!'12But he said in reply, 'Amen, I say to you, I do not know you.'13Therefore, stay awake, for you know neither the day nor the hour.14"It will be as when a man who was going on a journey called in his servants and entrusted his possessions to them.15To one he gave five talents; to another, two; to a third, one - to each according to his ability. Then he went away. Immediately16the one who received five talents went and traded with them, and made another five.17Likewise, the one who received two made another two.18But the man who received one went off and dug a hole in the ground and buried his master's money.19After a long time the master of those servants came back and settled accounts with them.20The one who had received five talents came forward bringing the additional five. He said, 'Master, you gave me five talents. See, I have made five more.'21His master said to him, 'Well done, my good and faithful servant. Since you were faithful in small matters, I will give you great responsibilities. Come, share your master's joy.'22(Then) the one who had received two talents also came forward and said, 'Master, you gave me two talents. See, I have made two more.'23His master said to him, 'Well done, my good and faithful servant. Since you were faithful in small matters, I will give you great responsibilities. Come, share your master's joy.'24Then the one who had received the one talent came forward and said, 'Master, I knew you were a demanding person, harvesting where you did not plant and gathering where you did not scatter;25so out of fear I went off and buried your talent in the ground. Here it is back.'26His master said to him in reply, 'You wicked, lazy servant! So you knew that I harvest where I did not plant and gather where I did not scatter?27Should you not then have put my money in the bank so that I could have got it back with interest on my return?28Now then! Take the talent from him and give it to the one with ten.29For to everyone who has, more will be given and he will grow rich; but from the one who has not, even what he has will be taken away.30And throw this useless servant into the darkness outside, where there will be wailing and grinding of teeth.'31"When the Son of Man comes in his glory, and all the angels with him, he will sit upon his glorious throne,32and all the nations will be assembled before him. And he will separate them one from another, as a shepherd separates the sheep from the goats.33He will place the sheep on his right and the goats on his left.34Then the king will say to those on his right, 'Come, you who are blessed by my Father. Inherit the kingdom prepared for you from the foundation of the world.35For I was hungry and you gave me food, I was thirsty and you gave me drink, a stranger and you welcomed me,36naked and you clothed me, ill and you cared for me, in prison and you visited me.'37Then the righteous will answer him and say, 'Lord, when did we see you hungry and feed you, or thirsty and give you drink?38When did we see you a stranger and welcome you, or naked and clothe you?39When did we see you ill or in prison, and visit you?'40And the king will say to them in reply, 'Amen, I say to you, whatever you did for one of these least brothers of mine, you did for me.'41Then he will say to those on his left, 'Depart from me, you accursed, into the eternal fire prepared for the devil and his angels.42For I was hungry and you gave me no food, I was thirsty and you gave me no drink,43a stranger and you gave me no welcome, naked and you gave me no clothing, ill and in prison, and you did not care for me.'44Then they will answer and say, 'Lord, when did we see you hungry or thirsty or a stranger or naked or ill or in prison, and not minister to your needs?'45He will answer them, 'Amen, I say to you, what you did not do for one of these least ones, you did not do for me.'46And these will go off to eternal punishment, but the righteous to eternal life."

Matthew Chapter 26

1When Jesus finished all these words, he said to his disciples,2"You know that in two days' time it will be Passover, and the Son of Man will be handed over to be crucified."3Then the chief priests and the elders of the people assembled in the palace of the high priest, who was called Caiaphas,4and they consulted together to arrest Jesus by treachery and put him to death.5But they said, "Not during the festival, that there may not be a riot among the people."6Now when Jesus was in Bethany in the house of Simon the leper,7a woman came up to him with an alabaster jar of costly perfumed oil, and poured it on his head while he was reclining at table.8When the disciples saw this, they were indignant and said, "Why this waste?9It could have been sold for much, and the money given to the poor."10Since Jesus knew this, he said to them, "Why do you make trouble for the woman? She has done a good thing for me.[11]The poor you will always have with you; but you will not always have me.[12]In pouring this perfumed oil upon my body, she did it to prepare me for burial.[13]Amen, I say to you, wherever this gospel is proclaimed in the whole world, what she has done will be spoken of, in memory of her."[14]Then one of the Twelve, who was called Judas Iscar iot, went to the chief priests[15]and said, "What are you willing to give me if I hand him over to you?" They paid him thirty pieces of silver,[16]and from that time on he looked for an opportunity to hand him over.[17]On the first day of the Feast of Unleavened Bread, the disciples approached Jesus and said, "Where do you want us to prepare for you to eat the Passover?"[18]He said, "Go into the city to a certain man and tell him, 'The teacher says, "My appointed time draws near; in your house I shall celebrate the Passover with my disciples."'"[19]The disciples then did as Jesus had ordered, and prepared the Passover.[20]When it was evening, he reclined at table with the Twelve.[21]And while they were eating, he said, "Amen, I say to you, one of you will betray me."[22]Deeply distressed at this, they began to say to him one after another, "Surely it is not I, Lord?"[23]He said in reply, "He who has dipped his hand into the dish with me is the one who will betray me.[24]The Son of Man indeed goes, as it is written of him, but woe to that man by whom the Son of Man is betrayed. It would be better for that man if he had never been born."[25]Then Judas, his betrayer, said in reply, "Surely it is not I, Rabbi?" He answered, "You have said so."[26]While they were eating, Jesus took bread, said the blessing, broke it, and giving it to his disciples said, "Take and eat; this is my body."[27]Then he took a cup, gave thanks, and gave it to them, saying, "Drink from it, all of you,[28]for this is my blood of the covenant, which will be shed on behalf of many for the forgiveness of sins.[29]I tell you, from now on I shall not drink this fruit of the vine until the day when I drink it with you new in the kingdom of my Father."[30]Then, after singing a hymn, they went out to the Mount of Olives.[31]Then Jesus said to them, "This night all of you will have your faith in me shaken, for it is written: 'I will strike the shepherd, and the sheep of the flock will be dispersed';[32]but after I have been raised up, I shall go before you to Galilee."[33]Peter said to him in reply, "Though all may have their faith in you shaken, mine will never be."[34]Jesus said to him, "Amen, I say to you, this very night before the cock crows, you will deny me three times."[35]Peter said to him, "Even though I should have to die with you, I will not deny you." And all the disciples spoke likewise.[36]Then Jesus came with them to a place called Gethsemane, and he said to his disciples, "Sit here while I go over there and pray."[37]He took along Peter and the two sons of Zebedee, and began to feel sorrow and distress.[38]Then he said to them, "My soul is sorrowful even to death. Remain here and keep watch with me."[39]He advanced a little and fell prostrate in prayer, saying, "My Father, if it is possible, let this cup pass from me; yet, not as I will, but as you will."[40]When he returned to his disciples he found them asleep. He said to Peter, "So you could not keep watch with me for one hour?[41]Watch and pray that you may not undergo the test. The spirit is willing, but the flesh is weak."[42]Withdrawing a second time, he prayed again, "My Father, if it is not possible that this cup pass without my drinking it, your will be done!"[43]Then he returned once more and found them asleep, for their eyes could not keep their eyes open.[44]He left them and withdrew again and prayed a third time, saying the same thing again.[45]Then he returned to his disciples and said to them, "Are you still sleeping and taking your rest? Behold, the hour is at hand when the Son of Man is to be handed over to sinners.[46]Get up, let us go. Look, my betrayer is at hand."[47]While he was still speaking, Judas, one of the Twelve, arrived, accompanied by a large crowd, with swords and clubs, who had come from the chief priests and the elders of the people.[48]His betrayer had arranged a sign with them, saying, "The man I shall kiss is the one; arrest him."[49]Immediately he went over to Jesus and said, "Hail, Rabbi!" and he kissed him.[50]Jesus answered him, "Friend, do what you have come for." Then stepping forward they laid hands on Jesus and arrested him.[51]And behold, one of those who accompanied Jesus put his hand to his sword, drew it, and struck the high priest's servant, cutting off his ear.[52]Then Jesus said to him, "Put your sword back into its sheath, for all who take the sword will perish by the sword.[53]Do you think that I cannot call upon my Father and he will not provide me at this moment with more than twelve legions of angels?[54]But then how would the scriptures be fulfilled which say that it must come to pass in this way?"[55]At that hour Jesus said to the crowds, "Have you come out as against a robber, with swords and clubs to seize me? Day after day I sat teaching in the temple area, yet you did not arrest me.[56]But all this has come to pass that the writings of the prophets may be fulfilled." Then all the disciples left him and fled.[57]Those who had arrested Jesus led him away to Caiaphas the high priest, where the scribes and the elders were assembled.[58]Peter was following him at a distance as far as the high priest's courtyard, and going inside he sat down with the servants to see the outcome.[59]The chief priests and the entire Sanhedrin kept trying to obtain false testimony against Jesus in order to put him to death,[60]but they found none, though many false witnesses came forward. Finally two came forward[61]who stated, "This man said, 'I can destroy the temple of God and within three days rebuild it.'"[62]The high priest rose and addressed him, "Have you no answer? What are these men testifying against you?"[63]But Jesus was silent. Then the high priest said to him, "I order you to tell us under oath before the living God whether you are the Messiah, the Son of God."[64]Jesus said to him in reply, "You have said so. But I tell you: From now on you will see 'the Son of Man seated at the right hand of the Power' and 'coming on the clouds of heaven.'"[65]Then the high priest tore his robes and said, "He has blasphemed! What further need have we of witnesses? You have now heard the blasphemy;[66]what is your opinion?" They said in reply, "He deserves to die!"[67]Then they spat in his face and struck him, while some slapped him,[68]saying, "Prophesy for us, Messiah: who is it that struck you?"[69]Now Peter was sitting outside in the courtyard. One of the maids came over to him and said, "You too were with Jesus the Galilean."[70]But he denied it in front of everyone, saying, "I do not know what you are talking about!"[71]As he went out to the gate, another girl saw him and said to those who were there, "This man was with Jesus the Nazorean."[72]Again he denied it with an oath, "I do not know the man!"[73]A little later the bystanders came over and said to Peter, "Surely you too are one of them; even your speech gives you away."[74]At that he began to curse and to swear, "I do not know the man." And immediately a cock crowed.[75]Then Peter remembered the word that Jesus had spoken: "Before the cock crows you will deny me three times." He went out and began to weep bitterly.

Matthew Chapter 27

[1]When it was morning, all the chief priests and the elders of the people took counsel against Jesus to put him to death.[2]They bound him, led him away, and handed him over to Pilate, the governor.[3]Then Judas, his betrayer, seeing that Jesus had been condemned, deeply regretted what he had done. He returned the thirty pieces of silver to the chief priests and elders,[4]saying, "I have sinned in betraying innocent blood." They said, "What is that to us? Look to it yourself."[5]Flinging the money into the temple, he departed and went off and hanged himself.[6]The chief priests gathered up the money, but said, "It is not lawful to deposit this in the temple treasury, for it is the price of blood."[7]After consultation, they used it to buy the potter's field as a burial place for foreigners.[8]That is why that field even today is called the Field of Blood.[9]Then was fulfilled what had been said through Jeremiah the prophet, "And they took the thirty pieces of silver, the value of a man with a price on his head, a price set by some of the Israelites,[10]and they paid it out for the potter's field just as the Lord had commanded me."[11]Now Jesus stood before the governor, and he questioned him, "Are you the king of the Jews?" Jesus said, "You say so."[12]And when he was accused by the chief priests and elders, he made no answer.[13]Then Pilate said to him, "Do you not hear how many things they are testifying against you?"[14]But he did not answer him one word, so that the governor was greatly amazed.[15]Now on the occasion of the feast the governor was accustomed to release to the crowd one prisoner whom they wished.[16]And at that time they had a notorious prisoner called (Jesus) Barabbas.[17]So when they had assembled, Pilate said to them, "Which one do you want me to release to you, (Jesus) Barabbas, or Jesus called Messiah?"[18]For he knew that it was out of envy that they had handed him over.[19]While he was still seated on the bench, his wife sent him a message, "Have nothing to do with that righteous man. I suffered much in a dream today because of him."[20]The chief priests and the elders persuaded the crowds to ask for Barabbas but to destroy Jesus.[21]The governor said to them in reply, "Which of the two do you want me to release to you?" They answered, "Barabbas!"[22]Pilate said to them, "Then what shall I do with Jesus called Messiah?" They all said, "Let him be crucified!"[23]But he said, "Why? What evil has he done?" They only shouted the louder, "Let him be crucified!"[24]When Pilate saw that he was not succeeding at all, but that a riot was breaking out instead, he took water and washed his hands in the sight of the crowd, saying, "I am innocent of this man's blood. Look to it yourselves."[25]And the whole people said in reply, "His blood be upon us and upon our children."[26]Then he released Barabbas to them, but after he had Jesus scourged, he handed him over to be crucified.[27]Then the soldiers of the governor took Jesus inside the praetorium and gathered the whole cohort around him.[28]They stripped off his clothes and threw a scarlet military cloak about him.[29]Weaving a crown out of thorns, they placed it on his head, and a reed in his right hand. And kneeling before him, they mocked him, saying, "Hail, King of the Jews!"[30]They spat upon him and took the reed and kept striking him on the head.[31]And when

they had mocked him, they stripped him of the cloak, dressed him in his own clothes, and led him off to crucify him.³²As they were going out, they met a Cyrenian named Simon; this man they pressed into service to carry his cross.³³And when they came to a place called Golgotha (which means Place of the Skull),³⁴they gave Jesus wine to drink mixed with gall. But when he had tasted it, he refused to drink.³⁵After they had crucified him, they divided his garments by casting lots;³⁶then they sat down and kept watch over him there.³⁷And they placed over his head the written charge against him: This is Jesus, the King of the Jews.³⁸Two revolutionaries were crucified with him, one on his right and the other on his left.³⁹Those passing by reviled him, shaking their heads⁴⁰and saying, "You who would destroy the temple and rebuild it in three days, save yourself, if you are the Son of God, (and) come down from the cross!"⁴¹Likewise the chief priests with the scribes and elders mocked him and said,⁴²"He saved others; he cannot save himself. So he is the king of Israel! Let him come down from the cross now, and we will believe in him.⁴³He trusted in God; let him deliver him now if he wants him. For he said, 'I am the Son of God.'"⁴⁴The revolutionaries who were crucified with him also kept abusing him in the same way.⁴⁵From noon onward, darkness came over the whole land until three in the afternoon.⁴⁶And about three o'clock Jesus cried out in a loud voice, "Eli, Eli, lema sabachthani?" which means, "My God, my God, why have you forsaken me?"⁴⁷Some of the bystanders who heard it said, "This one is calling for Elijah."⁴⁸Immediately one of them ran to get a sponge; he soaked it in wine, and putting it on a reed, gave it to him to drink.⁴⁹But the rest said, "Wait, let us see if Elijah comes to save him."⁵⁰But Jesus cried out again in a loud voice, and gave up his spirit.⁵¹And behold, the veil of the sanctuary was torn in two from top to bottom. The earth quaked, rocks were split,⁵²tombs were opened, and the bodies of many saints who had fallen asleep were raised.⁵³And coming forth from their tombs after his resurrection, they entered the holy city and appeared to many.⁵⁴The centurion and the men with him who were keeping watch over Jesus feared greatly when they saw the earthquake and all that was happening, and they said, "Truly, this was the Son of God!"⁵⁵There were many women there, looking on from a distance, who had followed Jesus from Galilee, ministering to him.⁵⁶Among them were Mary Magdalene and Mary the mother of James and Joseph, and the mother of the sons of Zebedee.⁵⁷When it was evening, there came a rich man from Arimathea named Joseph, who was himself a disciple of Jesus.⁵⁸He went to Pilate and asked for the body of Jesus; then Pilate ordered it to be handed over.⁵⁹Taking the body, Joseph wrapped it (in) clean linen⁶⁰and laid it in his new tomb that he had hewn in the rock. Then he rolled a huge stone across the entrance to the tomb and departed.⁶¹But Mary Magdalene and the other Mary remained sitting there, facing the tomb.⁶²The next day, the one following the day of preparation, the chief priests and the Pharisees gathered before Pilate⁶³and said, "Sir, we remember that this impostor while still alive said, 'After three days I will be raised up.'⁶⁴Give orders, then, that the grave be secured until the third day, lest his disciples come and steal him and say to the people, 'He has been raised from the dead.' This last imposture would be worse than the first." ⁶⁵Pilate said to them, "The guard is yours; go secure it as best you can."⁶⁶So they went and secured the tomb by fixing a seal to the stone and setting the guard.

Matthew Chapter 28

¹After the sabbath, as the first day of the week was dawning, Mary Magdalene and the other Mary came to see the tomb.²And behold, there was a great earthquake; for an angel of the Lord descended from heaven, approached, rolled back the stone, and sat upon it.³His appearance was like lightning and his clothing was white as snow.⁴The guards were shaken with fear of him and became like dead men.⁵Then the angel said to the women in reply, "Do not be afraid! I know that you are seeking Jesus the crucified.⁶He is not here, for he has been raised just as he said. Come and see the place where he lay.⁷Then go quickly and tell his disciples, 'He has been raised from the dead, and he is going before you to Galilee; there you will see him.' Behold, I have told you."⁸Then they went away quickly from the tomb, fearful yet overjoyed, and ran to announce this to his disciples.⁹And behold, Jesus met them on their way and greeted them. They approached, embraced his feet, and did him homage.¹⁰Then Jesus said to them, "Do not be afraid. Go tell my brothers to go to Galilee, and there they will see me."¹¹While they were going, some of the guard went into the city and told the chief priests all that had happened.¹²They assembled with the elders and took counsel; then they gave a large sum of money to the soldiers,¹³telling them, "You are to say, 'His disciples came by night and stole him while we were asleep.'¹⁴And if this gets to the ears of the governor, we will satisfy (him) and keep you out of trouble."¹⁵The soldiers took the money and did as they were instructed. And this story has circulated among the Jews to the present (day).¹⁶The

eleven disciples went to Galilee, to the mountain to which Jesus had ordered them.¹⁷When they saw him, they worshiped, but they doubted.¹⁸Then Jesus approached and said to them, "All power in heaven and on earth has been given to me.¹⁹Go, therefore, and make disciples of all nations, baptizing them in the name of the Father, and of the Son, and of the holy Spirit,²⁰teaching them to observe all that I have commanded you. And behold, I am with you always, until the end of the age."

Mark

Mark Chapter 1

¹The beginning of the gospel of Jesus Christ (the Son of God).²As it is written in Isaiah the prophet: "Behold, I am sending my messenger ahead of you; he will prepare your way.³A voice of one crying out in the desert: 'Prepare the way of the Lord, make straight his paths.'"⁴John (the) Baptist appeared in the desert proclaiming a baptism of repentance for the forgiveness of sins.⁵People of the whole Judean countryside and all the inhabitants of Jerusalem were going out to him and were being baptized by him in the Jordan River as they acknowledged their sins.⁶John was clothed in camel's hair, with a leather belt around his waist. He fed on locusts and wild honey.⁷And this is what he proclaimed: "One mightier than I is coming after me. I am not worthy to stoop and loosen the thongs of his sandals.⁸I have baptized you with water; he will baptize you with the holy Spirit.⁹It happened in those days that Jesus came from Nazareth of Galilee and was baptized in the Jordan by John.¹⁰On coming up out of the water he saw the heavens being torn open and the Spirit, like a dove, descending upon him. ¹¹And a voice came from the heavens, "You are my beloved Son; with you I am well pleased."¹²At once the Spirit drove him out into the desert,¹³and he remained in the desert for forty days, tempted by Satan. He was among wild beasts, and the angels ministered to him.¹⁴After John had been arrested, Jesus came to Galilee proclaiming the gospel of God:¹⁵"This is the time of fulfillment. The kingdom of God is at hand. Repent, and believe in the gospel."¹⁶As he passed by the Sea of Galilee, he saw Simon and his brother Andrew casting their nets into the sea; they were fishermen.¹⁷Jesus said to them, "Come after me, and I will make you fishers of men."¹⁸Then they abandoned their nets and followed him.¹⁹He walked along a little farther and saw James, the son of Zebedee, and his brother John. They too were in a boat mending their nets.²⁰Then he called them. So they left their father Zebedee in the boat along with the hired men and followed him.²¹Then they came to Capernaum, and on the sabbath he entered the synagogue and taught.²²The people were astonished at his teaching, for he taught them as one having authority and not as the scribes.²³In their synagogue was a man with an unclean spirit;²⁴he cried out, "What have you to do with us, Jesus of Nazareth? Have you come to destroy us? I know who you are - the Holy One of God!"²⁵Jesus rebuked him and said, "Quiet! Come out of him!"²⁶The unclean spirit convulsed him and with a loud cry came out of him.²⁷All were amazed and asked one another, "What is this? A new teaching with authority. He commands even the unclean spirits and they obey him."²⁸His fame spread everywhere throughout the whole region of Galilee.²⁹On leaving the synagogue he entered the house of Simon and Andrew with James and John.³⁰Simon's mother-in-law lay sick with a fever. They immediately told him about her.³¹He approached, grasped her hand, and helped her up. Then the fever left her and she waited on them.³²When it was evening, after sunset, they brought to him all who were ill or possessed by demons.³³The whole town was gathered at the door.³⁴He cured many who were sick with various diseases, and he drove out many demons, not permitting them to speak because they knew him.³⁵Rising very early before dawn, he left and went off to a deserted place, where he prayed.³⁶Simon and those who were with him pursued him³⁷and on finding him said, "Everyone is looking for you."³⁸He told them, "Let us go on to the nearby villages that I may preach there also. For this purpose have I come."³⁹So he went into their synagogues, preaching and driving out demons throughout the whole of Galilee.⁴⁰A leper came to him (and kneeling down) begged him and said, "If you wish, you can make me clean."⁴¹Moved with pity, he stretched out his hand, touched him, and said to him, "I do will it. Be made clean."⁴²The leprosy left him immediately, and he was made clean.⁴³Then, warning him sternly, he dismissed him at once.⁴⁴Then he said to him, "See that you tell no one anything, but go, show yourself to the priest and offer for your cleansing what Moses prescribed; that will be proof for them."⁴⁵The man went away and began to publicize the whole matter. He spread the report abroad so that it was impossible for Jesus to enter a town openly. He remained outside in deserted places, and people kept coming to him from everywhere.

Mark Chapter 2

[1]When Jesus returned to Capernaum after some days, it became known that he was at home.[2]Many gathered together so that there was no longer room for them, not even around the door, and he preached the word to them.[3]They came bringing to him a paralytic carried by four men.[4]Unable to get near Jesus because of the crowd, they opened up the roof above him. After they had broken through, they let down the mat on which the paralytic was lying.[5]When Jesus saw their faith, he said to the paralytic, "Child, your sins are forgiven."[6]Now some of the scribes were sitting there asking themselves,[7]"Why does this man speak that way? He is blaspheming. Who but God alone can forgive sins?"[8]Jesus immediately knew in his mind what they were thinking to themselves, so he said, "Why are you thinking such things in your hearts?[9]Which is easier, to say to the paralytic, 'Your sins are forgiven,' or to say, 'Rise, pick up your mat and walk'?[10]But that you may know that the Son of Man has authority to forgive sins on earth" - [11]he said to the paralytic, "I say to you, rise, pick up your mat, and go home."[12]He rose, picked up his mat at once, and went away in the sight of everyone. They were all astounded and glorified God, saying, "We have never seen anything like this."[13]Once again he went out along the sea. All the crowd came to him and he taught them.[14]As he passed by, he saw Levi, son of Alphaeus, sitting at the customs post. He said to him, "Follow me." And he got up and followed him.[15]While he was at table in his house, many tax collectors and sinners sat with Jesus and his disciples; for there were many who followed him.[16]Some scribes who were Pharisees saw that he was eating with sinners and tax collectors and said to his disciples, "Why does he eat with tax collectors and sinners?"[17]Jesus heard this and said to them (that), "Those who are well do not need a physician, but the sick do. I did not come to call the righteous but sinners."[18]The disciples of John and of the Pharisees were accustomed to fast. People came to him and objected, "Why do the disciples of John and the disciples of the Pharisees fast, but your disciples do not fast?"[19]Jesus answered them, "Can the wedding guests fast while the bridegroom is with them? As long as they have the bridegroom with them they cannot fast.[20]But the days will come when the bridegroom is taken away from them, and then they will fast on that day.[21]No one sews a piece of unshrunken cloth on an old cloak. If he does, its fullness pulls away, the new from the old, and the tear gets worse.[22]Likewise, no one pours new wine into old wineskins. Otherwise, the wine will burst the skins, and both the wine and the skins are ruined. Rather, new wine is poured into fresh wineskins."[23]As he was passing through a field of grain on the sabbath, his disciples began to make a path while picking the heads of grain.[24]At this the Pharisees said to him, "Look, why are they doing what is unlawful on the sabbath?"[25]He said to them, "Have you never read what David did when he was in need and he and his companions were hungry?[26]How he went into the house of God when Abiathar was high priest and ate the bread of offering that only the priests could lawfully eat, and shared it with his companions?"[27]Then he said to them, "The sabbath was made for man, not man for the sabbath.[28]That is why the Son of Man is lord even of the sabbath."

Mark Chapter 3

[1]Again he entered the synagogue. There was a man there who had a withered hand.[2]They watched him closely to see if he would cure him on the sabbath so that they might accuse him.[3]He said to the man with the withered hand, "Come up here before us."[4]Then he said to them, "Is it lawful to do good on the sabbath rather than to do evil, to save life rather than to destroy it?" But they remained silent.[5]Looking around at them with anger and grieved at their hardness of heart, he said to the man, "Stretch out your hand." He stretched it out and his hand was restored.[6]The Pharisees went out and immediately took counsel with the Herodians against him to put him to death.[7]Jesus withdrew toward the sea with his disciples. A large number of people (followed) from Galilee and from Judea.[8]Hearing what he was doing, a large number of people came to him also from Jerusalem, from Idumea, from beyond the Jordan, and from the neighborhood of Tyre and Sidon.[9]He told his disciples to have a boat ready for him because of the crowd, so that they would not crush him.[10]He had cured many and, as a result, those who had diseases were pressing upon him to touch him.[11]And whenever unclean spirits saw him they would fall down before him and shout, "You are the Son of God."[12]He warned them sternly not to make him known.[13]He went up the mountain and summoned those whom he wanted and they came to him.[14]He appointed twelve (whom he also named apostles) that they might be with him and he might send them forth to preach[15]and to have authority to drive out demons:[16](he appointed the twelve:) Simon, whom he named Peter;[17]James, son of Zebedee, and John the brother of James, whom he named Boanerges, that is, sons of thunder;[18]Andrew, Philip, Bartholomew, Matthew, Thomas, James the son of Alphaeus; Thaddeus, Simon the Cananean,[19]and Judas Iscariot who betrayed him.[20]He came home. Again (the) crowd gathered, making it impossible for them even to eat.[21]When his relatives heard of this they set out to seize him, for they said, "He is out of his mind."[22]The scribes who had come from Jerusalem said, "He is possessed by Beelzebul," and "By the prince of demons he drives out demons."[23]Summoning them, he began to speak to them in parables, "How can Satan drive out Satan?[24]If a kingdom is divided against itself, that kingdom cannot stand.[25]And if a house is divided against itself, that house will not be able to stand.[26]And if Satan has risen up against himself and is divided, he cannot stand; that is the end of him.[27]But no one can enter a strong man's house to plunder his property unless he first ties up the strong man. Then he can plunder his house.[28]Amen, I say to you, all sins and all blasphemies that people utter will be forgiven them.[29]But whoever blasphemes against the holy Spirit will never have forgiveness, but is guilty of an everlasting sin."[30]For they had said, "He has an unclean spirit."[31]His mother and his brothers arrived. Standing outside they sent word to him and called him.[32]A crowd seated around him told him, "Your mother and your brothers (and your sisters) are outside asking for you."[33]But he said to them in reply, "Who are my mother and (my) brothers?"[34]And looking around at those seated in the circle he said, "Here are my mother and my brothers.[35](For) whoever does the will of God is my brother and sister and mother."

Mark Chapter 4

[1]On another occasion he began to teach by the sea. A very large crowd gathered around him so that he got into a boat on the sea and sat down. And the whole crowd was beside the sea on land.[2]And he taught them at length in parables, and in the course of his instruction he said to them,[3]"Hear this! A sower went out to sow.[4]And as he sowed, some seed fell on the path, and the birds came and ate it up.[5]Other seed fell on rocky ground where it had little soil. It sprang up at once because the soil was not deep.[6]And when the sun rose, it was scorched and it withered for lack of roots.[7]Some seed fell among thorns, and the thorns grew up and choked it and it produced no grain.[8]And some seed fell on rich soil and produced fruit. It came up and grew and yielded thirty, sixty, and a hundredfold."[9]He added, "Whoever has ears to hear ought to hear."[10]And when he was alone, those present along with the Twelve questioned him about the parables.[11]He answered them, "The mystery of the kingdom of God has been granted to you. But to those outside everything comes in parables,[12]so that 'they may look and see but not perceive, and hear and listen but not understand, in order that they may not be converted and be forgiven.'"[13]Jesus said to them, "Do you not understand this parable? Then how will you understand any of the parables?[14]The sower sows the word.[15]These are the ones on the path where the word is sown. As soon as they hear, Satan comes at once and takes away the word sown in them.[16]And these are the ones sown on rocky ground who, when they hear the word, receive it at once with joy.[17]But they have no root; they last only for a time. Then when tribulation or persecution comes because of the word, they quickly fall away.[18]Those sown among thorns are another sort. They are the people who hear the word,[19]but worldly anxiety, the lure of riches, and the craving for other things intrude and choke the word, and it bears no fruit.[20]But those sown on rich soil are the ones who hear the word and accept it and bear fruit thirty and sixty and a hundredfold."[21]He said to them, "Is a lamp brought in to be placed under a bushel basket or under a bed, and not to be placed on a lampstand?[22]For there is nothing hidden except to be made visible; nothing is secret except to come to light.[23]Anyone who has ears to hear ought to hear."[24]He also told them, "Take care what you hear. The measure with which you measure will be measured out to you, and still more will be given to you.[25]To the one who has, more will be given; from the one who has not, even what he has will be taken away."[26]He said, "This is how it is with the kingdom of God; it is as if a man were to scatter seed on the land[27]and would sleep and rise night and day and the seed would sprout and grow, he knows not how.[28]Of its own accord the land yields fruit, first the blade, then the ear, then the full grain in the ear.[29]And when the grain is ripe, he wields the sickle at once, for the harvest has come."[30]He said, "To what shall we compare the kingdom of God, or what parable can we use for it?[31]It is like a mustard seed that, when it is sown in the ground, is the smallest of all the seeds on the earth.[32]But once it is sown, it springs up and becomes the largest of plants and puts forth large branches, so that the birds of the sky can dwell in its shade."[33]With many such parables he spoke the word to them as they were able to understand it.[34]Without parables he did not speak to them, but to his own disciples he explained everything in private.[35]On that day, as evening drew on, he said to them, "Let us cross to the other side."[36]Leaving the crowd, they took him with them in the boat just as he was. And other boats were with him.[37]A

violent squall came up and waves were breaking over the boat, so that it was already filling up.³⁸Jesus was in the stern, asleep on a cushion. They woke him and said to him, "Teacher, do you not care that we are perishing?"³⁹He woke up, rebuked the wind, and said to the sea, "Quiet! Be still!" The wind ceased and there was great calm.⁴⁰Then he asked them, "Why are you terrified? Do you not yet have faith?"⁴¹They were filled with great awe and said to one another, "Who then is this whom even wind and sea obey?"

Mark Chapter 5

¹They came to the other side of the sea, to the territory of the Gerasenes.²When he got out of the boat, at once a man from the tombs who had an unclean spirit met him.³The man had been dwelling among the tombs, and no one could restrain him any longer, even with a chain.⁴In fact, he had frequently been bound with shackles and chains, but the chains had been pulled apart by him and the shackles smashed, and no one was strong enough to subdue him.⁵Night and day among the tombs and on the hillsides he was always crying out and bruising himself with stones.⁶Catching sight of Jesus from a distance, he ran up and prostrated himself before him,⁷crying out in a loud voice, "What have you to do with me, Jesus, Son of the Most High God? I adjure you by God, do not torment me!"⁸(He had been saying to him, "Unclean spirit, come out of the man!")⁹He asked him, "What is your name?" He replied, "Legion is my name. There are many of us."¹⁰And he pleaded earnestly with him not to drive them away from that territory.¹¹Now a large herd of swine was feeding there on the hillside.¹²And they pleaded with him, "Send us into the swine. Let us enter them."¹³And he let them, and the unclean spirits came out and entered the swine. The herd of about two thousand rushed down a steep bank into the sea, where they were drowned.¹⁴The swineherds ran away and reported the incident in the town and throughout the countryside. And people came out to see what had happened.¹⁵As they approached Jesus, they caught sight of the man who had been possessed by Legion, sitting there clothed and in his right mind. And they were seized with fear.¹⁶Those who witnessed the incident explained to them what had happened to the possessed man and to the swine.¹⁷Then they began to beg him to leave their district.¹⁸As he was getting into the boat, the man who had been possessed pleaded to remain with him.¹⁹But he would not permit him but told him instead, "Go home to your family and announce to them all that the Lord in his pity has done for you."²⁰Then the man went off and began to proclaim in the Decapolis what Jesus had done for him; and all were amazed.²¹When Jesus had crossed again (in the boat) to the other side, a large crowd gathered around him, and he stayed close to the sea.²²One of the synagogue officials, named Jairus, came forward. Seeing him he fell at his feet²³and pleaded earnestly with him, saying, "My daughter is at the point of death. Please, come lay your hands on her that she may get well and live."²⁴He went off with him, and a large crowd followed him and pressed upon him.²⁵There was a woman afflicted with hemorrhages for twelve years.²⁶She had suffered greatly at the hands of many doctors and had spent all that she had. Yet she was not helped but only grew worse.²⁷She had heard about Jesus and came up behind him in the crowd and touched his cloak.²⁸She said, "If I but touch his clothes, I shall be cured."²⁹Immediately her flow of blood dried up. She felt in her body that she was healed of her affliction.³⁰Jesus, aware at once that power had gone out from him, turned around in the crowd and asked, "Who has touched my clothes?"³¹But his disciples said to him, "You see how the crowd is pressing upon you, and yet you ask, 'Who touched me?'"³²And he looked around to see who had done it.³³The woman, realizing what had happened to her, approached in fear and trembling. She fell down before Jesus and told him the whole truth.³⁴He said to her, "Daughter, your faith has saved you. Go in peace and be cured of your affliction."³⁵While he was still speaking, people from the synagogue official's house arrived and said, "Your daughter has died; why trouble the teacher any longer?"³⁶Disregarding the message that was reported, Jesus said to the synagogue official, "Do not be afraid; just have faith."³⁷He did not allow anyone to accompany him inside except Peter, James, and John, the brother of James.³⁸When they arrived at the house of the synagogue official, he caught sight of a commotion, people weeping and wailing loudly.³⁹So he went in and said to them, "Why this commotion and weeping? The child is not dead but asleep."⁴⁰And they ridiculed him. Then he put them all out. He took along the child's father and mother and those who were with him and entered the room where the child was.⁴¹He took the child by the hand and said to her, "Talitha koum," which means, "Little girl, I say to you, arise!"⁴²The girl, a child of twelve, arose immediately and walked around. (At that) they were utterly astounded.⁴³He gave strict orders that no one should know this and said that she should be given something to eat.

Mark Chapter 6

¹He departed from there and came to his native place, accompanied by his disciples.²When the sabbath came he began to teach in the synagogue, and many who heard him were astonished. They said, "Where did this man get all this? What kind of wisdom has been given him? What mighty deeds are wrought by his hands!³Is he not the carpenter, the son of Mary, and the brother of James and Joses and Judas and Simon? And are not his sisters here with us?" And they took offense at him.⁴Jesus said to them, "A prophet is not without honor except in his native place and among his own kin and in his own house."⁵So he was not able to perform any mighty deed there, ⁵ apart from curing a few sick people by laying his hands on them.⁶He was amazed at their lack of faith. He went around to the villages in the vicinity teaching.⁷He summoned the Twelve and began to send them out two by two and gave them authority over unclean spirits.⁸He instructed them to take nothing for the journey but a walking stick - no food, no sack, no money in their belts.⁹They were, however, to wear sandals but not a second tunic.¹⁰He said to them, "Wherever you enter a house, stay there until you leave from there.¹¹Whatever place does not welcome you or listen to you, leave there and shake the dust off your feet in testimony against them."¹²So they went off and preached repentance.¹³They drove out many demons, and they anointed with oil many who were sick and cured them.¹⁴King Herod heard about it, for his fame had become widespread, and people were saying, "John the Baptist has been raised from the dead; that is why mighty powers are at work in him."¹⁵Others were saying, "He is Elijah"; still others, "He is a prophet like any of the prophets."¹⁶But when Herod learned of it, he said, "It is John whom I beheaded. He has been raised up."¹⁷Herod was the one who had John arrested and bound in prison on account of Herodias, the wife of his brother Philip, whom he had married.¹⁸John had said to Herod, "It is not lawful for you to have your brother's wife."¹⁹Herodias harbored a grudge against him and wanted to kill him but was unable to do so.²⁰Herod feared John, knowing him to be a righteous and holy man, and kept him in custody. When he heard him speak he was very much perplexed, yet he liked to listen to him.²¹She had an opportunity one day when Herod, on his birthday, gave a banquet for his courtiers, his military officers, and the leading men of Galilee.²²Herodias's own daughter came in and performed a dance that delighted Herod and his guests. The king said to the girl, "Ask of me whatever you wish and I will grant it to you."²³He even swore (many things) to her, "I will grant you whatever you ask of me, even to half of my kingdom."²⁴She went out and said to her mother, "What shall I ask for?" She replied, "The head of John the Baptist."²⁵The girl hurried back to the king's presence and made her request, "I want you to give me at once on a platter the head of John the Baptist."²⁶The king was deeply distressed, but because of his oaths and the guests he did not wish to break his word to her.²⁷So he promptly dispatched an executioner with orders to bring back his head. He went off and beheaded him in the prison.²⁸He brought in the head on a platter and gave it to the girl. The girl in turn gave it to her mother.²⁹When his disciples heard about it, they came and took his body and laid it in a tomb.³⁰The apostles gathered together with Jesus and reported all they had done and taught.³¹He said to them, "Come away by yourselves to a deserted place and rest a while." People were coming and going in great numbers, and they had no opportunity even to eat.³²So they went off in the boat by themselves to a deserted place.³³People saw them leaving and many came to know about it. They hastened there on foot from all the towns and arrived at the place before them.³⁴When he disembarked and saw the vast crowd, his heart was moved with pity for them, for they were like sheep without a shepherd; and he began to teach them many things.³⁵By now it was already late and his disciples approached him and said, "This is a deserted place and it is already very late.³⁶Dismiss them so that they can go to the surrounding farms and villages and buy themselves something to eat."³⁷He said to them in reply, "Give them some food yourselves." But they said to him, "Are we to buy two hundred days' wages worth of food and give it to them to eat?"³⁸He asked them, "How many loaves do you have? Go and see." And when they had found out they said, "Five loaves and two fish."³⁹So he gave orders to have them all sit down in groups on the green grass.⁴⁰The people took their places in rows by hundreds and by fifties.⁴¹Then, taking the five loaves and the two fish and looking up to heaven, he said the blessing, broke the loaves, and gave them to (his) disciples to set before the people; he also divided the two fish among them all. ⁴²They all ate and were satisfied.⁴³And they picked up twelve wicker baskets full of fragments and what was left of the fish.⁴⁴Those who ate (of the loaves) were five thousand men.⁴⁵Then he made his disciples get into the boat and precede him to the other side toward Bethsaida, while he dismissed the crowd.⁴⁶And when he had taken leave of them, he went off to the

mountain to pray.₄₇When it was evening, the boat was far out on the sea and he was alone on shore.₄₈Then he saw that they were tossed about while rowing, for the wind was against them. About the fourth watch of the night, he came toward them walking on the sea. He meant to pass by them.₄₉But when they saw him walking on the sea, they thought it was a ghost and cried out.₅₀They had all seen him and were terrified. But at once he spoke with them, "Take courage, it is I, do not be afraid!"₅₁He got into the boat with them and the wind died down. They were (completely) astounded.₅₂They had not understood the incident of the loaves. On the contrary, their hearts were hardened.₅₃After making the crossing, they came to land at Gennesaret and tied up there.₅₄As they were leaving the boat, people immediately recognized him.₅₅They scurried about the surrounding country and began to bring in the sick on mats to wherever they heard he was.₅₆Whatever villages or towns or countryside he entered, they laid the sick in the marketplaces and begged him that they might touch only the tassel on his cloak; and as many as touched it were healed.

Mark Chapter 7

¹Now when the Pharisees with some scribes who had come from Jerusalem gathered around him,²they observed that some of his disciples ate their meals with unclean, that is, unwashed, hands.³(For the Pharisees and, in fact, all Jews, do not eat without carefully washing their hands, keeping the tradition of the elders.⁴And on coming from the marketplace they do not eat without purifying themselves. And there are many other things that they have traditionally observed, the purification of cups and jugs and kettles (and beds).)⁵So the Pharisees and scribes questioned him, "Why do your disciples not follow the tradition of the elders but instead eat a meal with unclean hands?"⁶He responded, "Well did Isaiah prophesy about you hypocrites, as it is written: 'This people honors me with their lips, but their hearts are far from me;⁷In vain do they worship me, teaching as doctrines human precepts.'⁸You disregard God's commandment but cling to human tradition."⁹He went on to say, "How well you have set aside the commandment of God in order to uphold your tradition!¹⁰For Moses said, 'Honor your father and your mother,' and 'Whoever curses father or mother shall die.'¹¹Yet you say, 'If a person says to father or mother, "Any support you might have had from me is qorban"' (meaning, dedicated to God),¹²you allow him to do nothing more for his father or mother.¹³You nullify the word of God in favor of your tradition that you have handed on. And you do many such things."¹⁴He summoned the crowd again and said to them, "Hear me, all of you, and understand.¹⁵Nothing that enters one from outside can defile that person; but the things that come out from within are what defile."¹⁶If anyone has ears to hear, let him hear!¹⁷When he got home away from the crowd his disciples questioned him about the parable.¹⁸He said to them, "Are even you likewise without understanding? Do you not realize that everything that goes into a person from outside cannot defile,¹⁹since it enters not the heart but the stomach and passes out into the latrine?" (Thus he declared all foods clean.)²⁰"But what comes out of a person, that is what defiles.²¹From within people, from their hearts, come evil thoughts, unchastity, theft, murder,²²adultery, greed, malice, deceit, licentiousness, envy, blasphemy, arrogance, folly.²³All these evils come from within and they defile."²⁴From that place he went off to the district of Tyre. He entered a house and wanted no one to know about it, but he could not escape notice.²⁵Soon a woman whose daughter had an unclean spirit heard about him. She came and fell at his feet.²⁶The woman was a Greek, a Syrophoenician by birth, and she begged him to drive the demon out of her daughter.²⁷He said to her, "Let the children be fed first. For it is not right to take the food of the children and throw it to the dogs."²⁸She replied and said to him, "Lord, even the dogs under the table eat the children's scraps."²⁹Then he said to her, "For saying this, you may go. The demon has gone out of your daughter."³⁰When the woman went home, she found the child lying in bed and the demon gone.³¹Again he left the district of Tyre and went by way of Sidon to the Sea of Galilee, into the district of the Decapolis.³²And people brought to him a deaf man who had a speech impediment and begged him to lay his hand on him.³³He took him off by himself away from the crowd. He put his finger into the man's ears and, spitting, touched his tongue;³⁴then he looked up to heaven and groaned, and said to him, "Ephphatha!"(that is, "Be opened!")³⁵And (immediately) the man's ears were opened, his speech impediment was removed, and he spoke plainly.³⁶He ordered them not to tell anyone. But the more he ordered them not to, the more they proclaimed it.³⁷They were exceedingly astonished and they said, "He has done all things well. He makes the deaf hear and (the) mute speak."

Mark Chapter 8

¹ In those days when there again was a great crowd without anything to

eat, he summoned the disciples and said, 2 "My heart is moved with pity for the crowd, because they have been with me now for three days and have nothing to eat. 3 If I send them away hungry to their homes, they will collapse on the way, and some of them have come a great distance." 4 His disciples answered him, "Where can anyone get enough bread to satisfy them here in this deserted place?" 5 Still he asked them, "How many loaves do you have?" "Seven," they replied. 6 He ordered the crowd to sit down on the ground. Then, taking the seven loaves he gave thanks, broke them, and gave them to his disciples to distribute, and they distributed them to the crowd. 7 They also had a few fish. He said the blessing over them and ordered them distributed also. 8 They ate and were satisfied. They picked up the fragments left over - seven baskets. 9 There were about four thousand people. He dismissed them 10 and got into the boat with his disciples and came to the region of Dalmanutha. 11 The Pharisees came forward and began to argue with him, seeking from him a sign from heaven to test him. 12 He sighed from the depth of his spirit and said, "Why does this generation seek a sign? Amen, I say to you, no sign will be given to this generation." 13 Then he left them, got into the boat again, and went off to the other shore. 14 They had forgotten to bring bread, and they had only one loaf with them in the boat. 15 He enjoined them, "Watch out, guard against the leaven of the Pharisees and the leaven of Herod." 16 They concluded among themselves that it was because they had no bread. 17 When he became aware of this he said to them, "Why do you conclude that it is because you have no bread? Do you not yet understand or comprehend? Are your hearts hardened? 18 Do you have eyes and not see, ears and not hear? And do you not remember, 19 when I broke the five loaves for the five thousand, how many wicker baskets full of fragments you picked up?" They answered him, "Twelve." 20 "When I broke the seven loaves for the four thousand, how many full baskets of fragments did you pick up?" They answered (him), "Seven." 21 He said to them, "Do you still not understand?" 22 When they arrived at Bethsaida, they brought to him a blind man and begged him to touch him. 23 He took the blind man by the hand and led him outside the village. Putting spittle on his eyes he laid his hands on him and asked, "Do you see anything?" 24 Looking up he replied, "I see people looking like trees and walking." 25 Then he laid hands on his eyes a second time and he saw clearly; his sight was restored and he could see everything distinctly. 26 Then he sent him home and said, "Do not even go into the village." 27 Now Jesus and his disciples set out for the villages of Caesarea Philippi. Along the way he asked his disciples, "Who do people say that I am?" 28 They said in reply, "John the Baptist, others Elijah, still others one of the prophets." 29 And he asked them, "But who do you say that I am?" Peter said to him in reply, "You are the Messiah." 30 Then he warned them not to tell anyone about him. 31 He began to teach them that the Son of Man must suffer greatly and be rejected by the elders, the chief priests, and the scribes, and be killed, and rise after three days. 32 He spoke this openly. Then Peter took him aside and began to rebuke him. 33 At this he turned around and, looking at his disciples, rebuked Peter and said, "Get behind me, Satan. You are thinking not as God does, but as human beings do." 34 He summoned the crowd with his disciples and said to them, "Whoever wishes to come after me must deny himself, take up his cross, and follow me. 35 For whoever wishes to save his life will lose it, but whoever loses his life for my sake and that of the gospel will save it. 36 What profit is there for one to gain the whole world and forfeit his life? 37 What could one give in exchange for his life? 38 Whoever is ashamed of me and of my words in this faithless and sinful generation, the Son of Man will be ashamed of when he comes in his Father's glory with the holy angels."

Mark Chapter 9

1 He also said to them, "Amen, I say to you, there are some standing here who will not taste death until they see that the kingdom of God has come in power." 2 After six days Jesus took Peter, James, and John and led them up a high mountain apart by themselves. And he was transfigured before them, 3 and his clothes became dazzling white, such as no fuller on earth could bleach them. 4 Then Elijah appeared to them along with Moses, and they were conversing with Jesus. 5 Then Peter said to Jesus in reply, "Rabbi, it is good that we are here! Let us make three tents: one for you, one for Moses, and one for Elijah." 6 He hardly knew what to say, they were so terrified. 7 Then a cloud came, casting a shadow over them; then from the cloud came a voice, "This is my beloved Son. Listen to him." 8 Suddenly, looking around, they no longer saw anyone but Jesus alone with them. 9 As they were coming down from the mountain, he charged them not to relate what they had seen to anyone, except when the Son of Man had risen from the dead. 10 So they kept the matter to themselves, questioning what rising from the dead meant. 11 Then they asked him, "Why do the scribes say that Elijah must come first?" 12 He told them, "Elijah will indeed come first

and restore all things, yet how is it written regarding the Son of Man that he must suffer greatly and be treated with contempt? 13 But I tell you that Elijah has come and they did to him whatever they pleased, as it is written of him." 14 When they came to the disciples, they saw a large crowd around them and scribes arguing with them. 15 Immediately on seeing him, the whole crowd was utterly amazed. They ran up to him and greeted him. 16 He asked them, "What are you arguing about with them?" 17 Someone from the crowd answered him, "Teacher, I have brought to you my son possessed by a mute spirit. 18 Wherever it seizes him, it throws him down; he foams at the mouth, grinds his teeth, and becomes rigid. I asked your disciples to drive it out, but they were unable to do so." 19 He said to them in reply, "O faithless generation, how long will I be with you? How long will I endure you? Bring him to me." 20 They brought the boy to him. And when he saw him, the spirit immediately threw the boy into convulsions. As he fell to the ground, he began to roll around and foam at the mouth. 21 Then he questioned his father, "How long has this been happening to him?" He replied, "Since childhood. 22 It has often thrown him into fire and into water to kill him. But if you can do anything, have compassion on us and help us." 23 Jesus said to him, " 'If you can!' Everything is possible to one who has faith." 24 Then the boy's father cried out, "I do believe, help my unbelief!" 25 Jesus, on seeing a crowd rapidly gathering, rebuked the unclean spirit and said to it, "Mute and deaf spirit, I command you: come out of him and never enter him again!" 26 Shouting and throwing the boy into convulsions, it came out. He became like a corpse, which caused many to say, "He is dead!" 27 But Jesus took him by the hand, raised him, and he stood up. 28 When he entered the house, his disciples asked him in private, "Why could we not drive it out?" 29 He said to them, "This kind can only come out through prayer." 30 They left from there and began a journey through Galilee, but he did not wish anyone to know about it. 31 He was teaching his disciples and telling them, "The Son of Man is to be handed over to men and they will kill him, and three days after his death he will rise." 32 But they did not understand the saying, and they were afraid to question him. 33 They came to Capernaum and, once inside the house, he began to ask them, "What were you arguing about on the way?" 34 But they remained silent. They had been discussing among themselves on the way who was the greatest. 35 Then he sat down, called the Twelve, and said to them, "If anyone wishes to be first, he shall be the last of all and the servant of all." 36 Taking a child he placed it in their midst, and putting his arms around it he said to them, 37 "Whoever receives one child such as this in my name, receives me; and whoever receives me, receives not me but the one who sent me." 38 John said to him, "Teacher, we saw someone driving out demons in your name, and we tried to prevent him because he does not follow us." 39 Jesus replied, "Do not prevent him. There is no one who performs a mighty deed in my name who can at the same time speak ill of me. 40 For whoever is not against us is for us. 41 Anyone who gives you a cup of water to drink because you belong to Christ, amen, I say to you, will surely not lose his reward. 42 "Whoever causes one of these little ones who believe (in me) to sin, it would be better for him if a great millstone were put around his neck and he were thrown into the sea. 43 If your hand causes you to sin, cut it off. It is better for you to enter into life maimed than with two hands to go into Gehenna, into the unquenchable fire. 44 'where their worm doesn't die, and the fire is not quenched.' 45 And if your foot causes you to sin, cut it off. It is better for you to enter into life crippled than with two feet to be thrown into Gehenna. 47 And if your eye causes you to sin, pluck it out. Better for you to enter into the kingdom of God with one eye than with two eyes to be thrown into Gehenna, 48 where 'their worm does not die, and the fire is not quenched.' 49 "Everyone will be salted with fire. 50 Salt is good, but if salt becomes insipid, with what will you restore its flavor? Keep salt in yourselves and you will have peace with one another."

Mark Chapter 10

1 He set out from there and went into the district of Judea (and) across the Jordan. Again crowds gathered around him and, as was his custom, he again taught them. 2 The Pharisees approached and asked, "Is it lawful for a husband to divorce his wife?" They were testing him. 3 He said to them in reply, "What did Moses command you?" 4 They replied, "Moses permitted him to write a bill of divorce and dismiss her." 5 But Jesus told them, "Because of the hardness of your hearts he wrote you this commandment. 6 But from the beginning of creation, 'God made them male and female. 7 For this reason a man shall leave his father and mother (and be joined to his wife), 8 and the two shall become one flesh.' So they are no longer two but one flesh. 9 Therefore what God has joined together, no human being must separate." 10 In the house the disciples again questioned him about this. 11 He said to them, "Whoever divorces his wife and marries another commits adultery

against her; 12 and if she divorces her husband and marries another, she commits adultery." 13 And people were bringing children to him that he might touch them, but the disciples rebuked them. 14 When Jesus saw this he became indignant and said to them, "Let the children come to me; do not prevent them, for the kingdom of God belongs to such as these. 15 Amen, I say to you, whoever does not accept the kingdom of God like a child will not enter it." 16 Then he embraced them and blessed them, placing his hands on them. 17 As he was setting out on a journey, a man ran up, knelt down before him, and asked him, "Good teacher, what must I do to inherit eternal life?" 18 Jesus answered him, "Why do you call me good? No one is good but God alone. 19 You know the commandments: 'You shall not kill; you shall not commit adultery; you shall not steal; you shall not bear false witness; you shall not defraud; honor your father and your mother.'" 20 He replied and said to him, "Teacher, all of these I have observed from my youth." 21 Jesus, looking at him, loved him and said to him, "You are lacking in one thing. Go, sell what you have, and give to (the) poor and you will have treasure in heaven; then come, follow me." 22 At that statement his face fell, and he went away sad, for he had many possessions. 23 Jesus looked around and said to his disciples, "How hard it is for those who have wealth to enter the kingdom of God!" 24 The disciples were amazed at his words. So Jesus again said to them in reply, "Children, how hard it is to enter the kingdom of God! 25 It is easier for a camel to pass through (the) eye of (a) needle than for one who is rich to enter the kingdom of God." 26 They were exceedingly astonished and said among themselves, "Then who can be saved?" 27 Jesus looked at them and said, "For human beings it is impossible, but not for God. All things are possible for God." 28 Peter began to say to him, "We have given up everything and followed you." 29 Jesus said, "Amen, I say to you, there is no one who has given up house or brothers or sisters or mother or father or children or lands for my sake and for the sake of the gospel 30 who will not receive a hundred times more now in this present age: houses and brothers and sisters and mothers and children and lands, with persecutions, and eternal life in the age to come. 31 But many that are first will be last, and (the) last will be first." 32 They were on the way, going up to Jerusalem, and Jesus went ahead of them. They were amazed, and those who followed were afraid. Taking the Twelve aside again, he began to tell them what was going to happen to him. 33 "Behold, we are going up to Jerusalem, and the Son of Man will be handed over to the chief priests and the scribes, and they will condemn him to death and hand him over to the Gentiles 34 who will mock him, spit upon him, scourge him, and put him to death, but after three days he will rise." 35 Then James and John, the sons of Zebedee, came to him and said to him, "Teacher, we want you to do for us whatever we ask of you." 36 He replied, "What do you wish (me) to do for you?" 37 They answered him, "Grant that in your glory we may sit one at your right and the other at your left." 38 Jesus said to them, "You do not know what you are asking. Can you drink the cup that I drink or be baptized with the baptism with which I am baptized?" 39 They said to him, "We can." Jesus said to them, "The cup that I drink, you will drink, and with the baptism with which I am baptized, you will be baptized; 40 but to sit at my right or at my left is not mine to give but is for those for whom it has been prepared." 41 When the ten heard this, they became indignant at James and John. 42 Jesus summoned them and said to them, "You know that those who are recognized as rulers over the Gentiles lord it over them, and their great ones make their authority over them felt. 43 But it shall not be so among you. Rather, whoever wishes to be great among you will be your servant; 44 whoever wishes to be first among you will be the slave of all. 45 For the Son of Man did not come to be served but to serve and to give his life as a ransom for many." 46 They came to Jericho. And as he was leaving Jericho with his disciples and a sizable crowd, Bartimaeus, a blind man, the son of Timaeus, sat by the roadside begging. 47 On hearing that it was Jesus of Nazareth, he began to cry out and say, "Jesus, son of David, have pity on me." 48 And many rebuked him, telling him to be silent. But he kept calling out all the more, "Son of David, have pity on me." 49 Jesus stopped and said, "Call him." So they called the blind man, saying to him, "Take courage; get up, he is calling you." 50 He threw aside his cloak, sprang up, and came to Jesus. 51 Jesus said to him in reply, "What do you want me to do for you?" The blind man replied to him, "Master, I want to see." 52 Jesus told him, "Go your way; your faith has saved you." Immediately he received his sight and followed him on the way.

Mark Chapter 11

1 When they drew near to Jerusalem, to Bethphage and Bethany at the Mount of Olives, he sent two of his disciples 2 and said to them, "Go into the village opposite you, and immediately on entering it, you will find a colt tethered on which no one has ever sat. Untie it and bring it

here. ³ If anyone should say to you, 'Why are you doing this?' reply, 'The Master has need of it and will send it back here at once.'" ⁴ So they went off and found a colt tethered at a gate outside on the street, and they untied it. ⁵ Some of the bystanders said to them, "What are you doing, untying the colt?" ⁶ They answered them just as Jesus had told them to, and they permitted them to do it. ⁷ So they brought the colt to Jesus and put their cloaks over it. And he sat on it. ⁸ Many people spread their cloaks on the road, and others spread leafy branches that they had cut from the fields. ⁹ Those preceding him as well as those following kept crying out: "Hosanna! Blessed is he who comes in the name of the Lord! ¹⁰ Blessed is the kingdom of our father David that is to come! Hosanna in the highest!" ¹¹ He entered Jerusalem and went into the temple area. He looked around at everything and, since it was already late, went out to Bethany with the Twelve. ¹² The next day as they were leaving Bethany he was hungry. ¹³ Seeing from a distance a fig tree in leaf, he went over to see if he could find anything on it. When he reached it he found nothing but leaves; it was not the time for figs. ¹⁴ And he said to it in reply, "May no one ever eat of your fruit again!" And his disciples heard it. ¹⁵ They came to Jerusalem, and on entering the temple area he began to drive out those selling and buying there. He overturned the tables of the money changers and the seats of those who were selling doves. ¹⁶ He did not permit anyone to carry anything through the temple area. ¹⁷ Then he taught them saying, "Is it not written: 'My house shall be called a house of prayer for all peoples'? But you have made it a den of thieves." ¹⁸ The chief priests and the scribes came to hear of it and were seeking a way to put him to death, yet they feared him because the whole crowd was astonished at his teaching. ¹⁹ When evening came, they went out of the city. ²⁰ Early in the morning, as they were walking along, they saw the fig tree withered to its roots. ²¹ Peter remembered and said to him, "Rabbi, look! The fig tree that you cursed has withered." ²² Jesus said to them in reply, "Have faith in God. ²³ Amen, I say to you, whoever says to this mountain, 'Be lifted up and thrown into the sea,' and does not doubt in his heart but believes that what he says will happen, it shall be done for him. ²⁴ Therefore I tell you, all that you ask for in prayer, believe that you will receive it and it shall be yours. ²⁵ When you stand to pray, forgive anyone against whom you have a grievance, so that your heavenly Father may in turn forgive you your transgressions." ²⁶ But if you do not forgive, neither will your Father in heaven forgive your transgressions. ²⁷ They returned once more to Jerusalem. As he was walking in the temple area, the chief priests, the scribes, and the elders approached him ²⁸ and said to him, "By what authority are you doing these things? Or who gave you this authority to do them?" ²⁹ Jesus said to them, "I shall ask you one question. Answer me, and I will tell you by what authority I do these things. ³⁰ Was John's baptism of heavenly or of human origin? Answer me." ³¹ They discussed this among themselves and said, "If we say, 'Of heavenly origin,' he will say, '(Then) why did you not believe him?' ³² But shall we say, 'Of human origin'?" - they feared the crowd, for they all thought John really was a prophet. ³³ So they said to Jesus in reply, "We do not know." Then Jesus said to them, "Neither shall I tell you by what authority I do these things."

Mark Chapter 12

¹ He began to speak to them in parables. "A man planted a vineyard, put a hedge around it, dug a wine press, and built a tower. Then he leased it to tenant farmers and left on a journey. ² At the proper time he sent a servant to the tenants to obtain from them some of the produce of the vineyard. ³ But they seized him, beat him, and sent him away empty-handed. ⁴ Again he sent them another servant. And that one they beat over the head and treated shamefully. ⁵ He sent yet another whom they killed. So, too, many others; some they beat, others they killed. ⁶ He had one other to send, a beloved son. He sent him to them last of all, thinking, 'They will respect my son.' ⁷ But those tenants said to one another, 'This is the heir. Come, let us kill him, and the inheritance will be ours.' ⁸ So they seized him and killed him, and threw him out of the vineyard. ⁹ What (then) will the owner of the vineyard do? He will come, put the tenants to death, and give the vineyard to others. ¹⁰ Have you not read this scripture passage: 'The stone that the builders rejected has become the cornerstone; ¹¹ by the Lord has this been done, and it is wonderful in our eyes'?" ¹² They were seeking to arrest him, but they feared the crowd, for they realized that he had addressed the parable to them. So they left him and went away. ¹³ They sent some Pharisees and Herodians to him to ensnare him in his speech. ¹⁴ They came and said to him, "Teacher, we know that you are a truthful man and that you are not concerned with anyone's opinion. You do not regard a person's status but teach the way of God in accordance with the truth. Is it lawful to pay the census tax to Caesar or not? Should we pay or should we not pay?" ¹⁵ Knowing their hypocrisy he said to them, "Why are you testing me? Bring me a denarius to look at." ¹⁶ They brought one to him and

he said to them, "Whose image and inscription is this?" They replied to him, "Caesar's." ¹⁷ So Jesus said to them, "Repay to Caesar what belongs to Caesar and to God what belongs to God.' They were utterly amazed at him. ¹⁸ Some Sadducees, who say there is no resurrection, came to him and put this question to him, ¹⁹ saying, "Teacher, Moses wrote for us, 'If someone's brother dies, leaving a wife but no child, his brother must take the wife and raise up descendants for his brother.' ²⁰ Now there were seven brothers. The first married a woman and died, leaving no descendants. ²¹ So the second married her and died, leaving no descendants, and the third likewise. ²² And the seven left no descendants. Last of all the woman also died. ²³ At the resurrection (when they arise) whose wife will she be? For all seven had been married to her." ²⁴ Jesus said to them, "Are you not misled because you do not know the scriptures or the power of God? ²⁵ When they rise from the dead, they neither marry nor are given in marriage, but they are like the angels in heaven. ²⁶ As for the dead being raised, have you not read in the Book of Moses, in the passage about the bush, how God told him, 'I am the God of Abraham, (the) God of Isaac, and (the) God of Jacob'? ²⁷ He is not God of the dead but of the living. You are greatly misled." ²⁸ One of the scribes, when he came forward and heard them disputing and saw how well he had answered them, asked him, "Which is the first of all the commandments?" ²⁹ Jesus replied, "The first is this: 'Hear, O Israel! The Lord our God is Lord alone! ³⁰ You shall love the Lord your God with all your heart, with all your soul, with all your mind, and with all your strength.' ³¹ The second is this: 'You shall love your neighbor as yourself.' There is no other commandment greater than these." ³² The scribe said to him, "Well said, teacher. You are right in saying, 'He is One and there is no other than he.' ³³ And 'to love him with all your heart, with all your understanding, with all your strength, and to love your neighbor as yourself' is worth more than all burnt offerings and sacrifices." ³⁴ And when Jesus saw that (he) answered with understanding, he said to him, "You are not far from the kingdom of God." And no one dared to ask him any more questions. ³⁵ As Jesus was teaching in the temple area he said, "How do the scribes claim that the Messiah is the son of David? ³⁶ David himself, inspired by the holy Spirit, said: 'The Lord said to my lord, "Sit at my right hand until I place your enemies under your feet."' ³⁷ David himself calls him 'lord'; so how is he his son?" (The) great crowd heard this with delight. ³⁸ In the course of his teaching he said, "Beware of the scribes, who like to go around in long robes and accept greetings in the marketplaces, ³⁹ seats of honor in synagogues, and places of honor at banquets. ⁴⁰ They devour the houses of widows and, as a pretext, recite lengthy prayers. They will receive a very severe condemnation." ⁴¹ He sat down opposite the treasury and observed how the crowd put money into the treasury. Many rich people put in large sums. ⁴² A poor widow also came and put in two small coins worth a few cents. ⁴³ Calling his disciples to himself, he said to them, "Amen, I say to you, this poor widow put in more than all the other contributors to the treasury. ⁴⁴ For they have all contributed from their surplus wealth, but she, from her poverty, has contributed all she had, her whole livelihood."

Mark Chapter 13

¹ As he was making his way out of the temple area one of his disciples said to him, "Look, teacher, what stones and what buildings!" ² Jesus said to him, "Do you see these great buildings? There will not be one stone left upon another that will not be thrown down." ³ As he was sitting on the Mount of Olives opposite the temple area, Peter, James, John, and Andrew asked him privately, ⁴ "Tell us, when will this happen, and what sign will there be when all these things are about to come to an end?" ⁵ Jesus began to say to them, "See that no one deceives you. ⁶ Many will come in my name saying, 'I am he,' and they will deceive many. ⁷ When you hear of wars and reports of wars do not be alarmed; such things must happen, but it will not yet be the end. ⁸ Nation will rise against nation and kingdom against kingdom. There will be earthquakes from place to place and there will be famines. These are the beginnings of the labor pains. ⁹ Watch out for yourselves. They will hand you over to the courts. You will be beaten in synagogues. You will be arraigned before governors and kings because of me, as a witness before them. ¹⁰ But the gospel must first be preached to all nations. ¹¹ When they lead you away and hand you over, do not worry beforehand about what you are to say. But say whatever will be given to you at that hour. For it will not be you who are speaking but the holy Spirit. ¹² Brother will hand over brother to death, and the father his child; children will rise up against parents and have them put to death. ¹³ You will be hated by all because of my name. But the one who perseveres to the end will be saved. ¹⁴ When you see the desolating abomination standing where he should not (let the reader understand), then those in Judea must flee to the mountains, ¹⁵ (and) a person on a housetop must not go down or enter to get anything out of his house, ¹⁶ and a person

in a field must not return to get his cloak. ¹⁷ Woe to pregnant women and nursing mothers in those days. ¹⁸ Pray that this does not happen in winter. ¹⁹ For those times will have tribulation such as has not been since the beginning of God's creation until now, nor ever will be. ²⁰ If the Lord had not shortened those days, no one would be saved; but for the sake of the elect whom he chose, he did shorten the days. ²¹ If anyone says to you then, 'Look, here is the Messiah! Look, there he is!' do not believe it. ²² False messiahs and false prophets will arise and will perform signs and wonders in order to mislead, if that were possible, the elect. ²³ Be watchful! I have told it all to you beforehand. ²⁴ But in those days after that tribulation the sun will be darkened, and the moon will not give its light, ²⁵ and the stars will be falling from the sky, and the powers in the heavens will be shaken. ²⁶ And then they will see 'the Son of Man coming in the clouds' with great power and glory, ²⁷ and then he will send out the angels and gather (his) elect from the four winds, from the end of the earth to the end of the sky. ²⁸ Learn a lesson from the fig tree. When its branch becomes tender and sprouts leaves, you know that summer is near. ²⁹ In the same way, when you see these things happening, know that he is near, at the gates. ³⁰ Amen, I say to you, this generation will not pass away until all these things have taken place. ³¹ Heaven and earth will pass away, but my words will not pass away. ³² But of that day or hour, no one knows, neither the angels in heaven, nor the Son, but only the Father. ³³ Be watchful! Be alert! You do not know when the time will come. ³⁴ It is like a man traveling abroad. He leaves home and places his servants in charge, each with his work, and orders the gatekeeper to be on the watch. ³⁵ Watch, therefore; you do not know when the lord of the house is coming, whether in the evening, or at midnight, or at cockcrow, or in the morning. ³⁶ May he not come suddenly and find you sleeping. ³⁷ What I say to you, I say to all: 'Watch!'"

Mark Chapter 14

¹ The Passover and the Feast of Unleavened Bread were to take place in two days' time. So the chief priests and the scribes were seeking a way to arrest him by treachery and put him to death. ² They said, "Not during the festival, for fear that there may be a riot among the people." ³ When he was in Bethany reclining at table in the house of Simon the leper, a woman came with an alabaster jar of perfumed oil, costly genuine spikenard. She broke the alabaster jar and poured it on his head. ⁴ There were some who were indignant. "Why has there been this waste of perfumed oil? ⁵ It could have been sold for more than three hundred days' wages and the money given to the poor." They were infuriated with her. ⁶ Jesus said, "Let her alone. Why do you make trouble for her? She has done a good thing for me. ⁷ The poor you will always have with you, and whenever you wish you can do good to them, but you will not always have me. ⁸ She has done what she could. She has anticipated anointing my body for burial. ⁹ Amen, I say to you, wherever the gospel is proclaimed to the whole world, what she has done will be told in memory of her." ¹⁰ Then Judas Iscariot, one of the Twelve, went off to the chief priests to hand him over to them. ¹¹ When they heard him they were pleased and promised to pay him money. Then he looked for an opportunity to hand him over. ¹² On the first day of the Feast of Unleavened Bread, when they sacrificed the Passover lamb, his disciples said to him, "Where do you want us to go and prepare for you to eat the Passover?" ¹³ He sent two of his disciples and said to them, "Go into the city and a man will meet you, carrying a jar of water. Follow him. ¹⁴ Wherever he enters, say to the master of the house, 'The Teacher says, "Where is my guest room where I may eat the Passover with my disciples?"' ¹⁵ Then he will show you a large upper room furnished and ready. Make the preparations for us there." ¹⁶ The disciples then went off, entered the city, and found it just as he had told them; and they prepared the Passover. ¹⁷ When it was evening, he came with the Twelve. ¹⁸ And as they reclined at table and were eating, Jesus said, "Amen, I say to you, one of you will betray me, one who is eating with me." ¹⁹ They began to be distressed and to say to him, one by one, "Surely it is not I?" ²⁰ He said to them, "One of the Twelve, the one who dips with me into the dish. ²¹ For the Son of Man indeed goes, as it is written of him, but woe to that man by whom the Son of Man is betrayed. It would be better for that man if he had never been born." ²² While they were eating, he took bread, said the blessing, broke it, and gave it to them, and said, "Take it; this is my body." ²³ Then he took a cup, gave thanks, and gave it to them, and they all drank from it. ²⁴ He said to them, "This is my blood of the covenant, which will be shed for many. ²⁵ Amen, I say to you, I shall not drink again the fruit of the vine until the day when I drink it new in the kingdom of God." ²⁶ Then, after singing a hymn, they went out to the Mount of Olives. ²⁷ Then Jesus said to them, "All of you will have your faith shaken, for it is written: 'I will strike the shepherd, and the sheep will be dispersed.' ²⁸ But after I have been raised up, I shall go before you to Galilee." ²⁹ Peter said to

him, "Even though all should have their faith shaken, mine will not be." ³⁰ Then Jesus said to him, "Amen, I say to you, this very night before the cock crows twice you will deny me three times." ³¹ But he vehemently replied, "Even though I should have to die with you, I will not deny you." And they all spoke similarly. ³² Then they came to a place named Gethsemane, and he said to his disciples, "Sit here while I pray." ³³ He took with him Peter, James, and John, and began to be troubled and distressed. ³⁴ Then he said to them, "My soul is sorrowful even to death. Remain here and keep watch." ³⁵ He advanced a little and fell to the ground and prayed that if it were possible the hour might pass by him; ³⁶ he said, "Abba, Father, all things are possible to you. Take this cup away from me, but not what I will but what you will." ³⁷ When he returned he found them asleep. He said to Peter, "Simon, are you asleep? Could you not keep watch for one hour? ³⁸ Watch and pray that you may not undergo the test. The spirit is willing but the flesh is weak." ³⁹ Withdrawing again, he prayed, saying the same thing. ⁴⁰ Then he returned once more and found them asleep, for they could not keep their eyes open and did not know what to answer him. ⁴¹ He returned a third time and said to them, "Are you still sleeping and taking your rest? It is enough. The hour has come. Behold, the Son of Man is to be handed over to sinners. ⁴² Get up, let us go. See, my betrayer is at hand." ⁴³ Then, while he was still speaking, Judas, one of the Twelve, arrived, accompanied by a crowd with swords and clubs who had come from the chief priests, the scribes, and the elders. ⁴⁴ His betrayer had arranged a signal with them, saying, "The man I shall kiss is the one; arrest him and lead him away securely." ⁴⁵ He came and immediately went over to him and said, "Rabbi." And he kissed him. ⁴⁶ At this they laid hands on him and arrested him. ⁴⁷ One of the bystanders drew his sword, struck the high priest's servant, and cut off his ear. ⁴⁸ Jesus said to them in reply, "Have you come out as against a robber, with swords and clubs, to seize me? ⁴⁹ Day after day I was with you teaching in the temple area, yet you did not arrest me; but that the scriptures may be fulfilled." ⁵⁰ And they all left him and fled. ⁵¹ Now a young man followed him wearing nothing but a linen cloth about his body. They seized him, ⁵² but he left the cloth behind and ran off naked. ⁵³ They led Jesus away to the high priest, and all the chief priests and the elders and the scribes came together. ⁵⁴ Peter followed him at a distance into the high priest's courtyard and was seated with the guards, warming himself at the fire. ⁵⁵ The chief priests and the entire Sanhedrin kept trying to obtain testimony against Jesus in order to put him to death, but they found none. ⁵⁶ Many gave false witness against him, but their testimony did not agree. ⁵⁷ Some took the stand and testified falsely against him, alleging, ⁵⁸ "We heard him say, 'I will destroy this temple made with hands and within three days I will build another not made with hands.'" ⁵⁹ Even so their testimony did not agree. ⁶⁰ The high priest rose before the assembly and questioned Jesus, saying, "Have you no answer? What are these men testifying against you?" ⁶¹ But he was silent and answered nothing. Again the high priest asked him and said to him, "Are you the Messiah, the son of the Blessed One?" ⁶² Then Jesus answered, "I am; and 'you will see the Son of Man seated at the right hand of the Power and coming with the clouds of heaven.'" ⁶³ At that the high priest tore his garments and said, "What further need have we of witnesses? ⁶⁴ You have heard the blasphemy. What do you think?" They all condemned him as deserving to die. ⁶⁵ Some began to spit on him. They blindfolded him and struck him and said to him, "Prophesy!" And the guards greeted him with blows. ⁶⁶ While Peter was below in the courtyard, one of the high priest's maids came along. ⁶⁷ Seeing Peter warming himself, she looked intently at him and said, "You too were with the Nazarene, Jesus." ⁶⁸ But he denied it saying, "I neither know nor understand what you are talking about." So he went out into the outer court. [Then the cock crowed.] ⁶⁹ The maid saw him and began again to say to the bystanders, "This man is one of them." ⁷⁰ Once again he denied it. A little later the bystanders said to Peter once more, "Surely you are one of them; for you too are a Galilean." ⁷¹ He began to curse and to swear, "I do not know this man about whom you are talking." ⁷² And immediately a cock crowed a second time. Then Peter remembered the word that Jesus had said to him, "Before the cock crows twice you will deny me three times." He broke down and wept.

Mark Chapter 15

¹ As soon as morning came, the chief priests with the elders and the scribes, that is, the whole Sanhedrin, held a council. They bound Jesus, led him away, and handed him over to Pilate. ² Pilate questioned him, "Are you the king of the Jews?" He said to him in reply, "You say so." ³ The chief priests accused him of many things. ⁴ Again Pilate questioned him, "Have you no answer? See how many things they accuse you of." ⁵ Jesus gave him no further answer, so that Pilate was amazed. ⁶ Now on the occasion of the feast he used to release to them one prisoner whom

they requested. 7 A man called Barabbas was then in prison along with the rebels who had committed murder in a rebellion. 8 The crowd came forward and began to ask him to do for them as he was accustomed. 9 Pilate answered, "Do you want me to release to you the king of the Jews?" 10 For he knew that it was out of envy that the chief priests had handed him over. 11 But the chief priests stirred up the crowd to have him release Barabbas for them instead. 12 Pilate again said to them in reply, "Then what (do you want) me to do with (the man you call) the king of the Jews?" 13 They shouted again, "Crucify him." 14 Pilate said to them, "Why? What evil has he done?" They only shouted the louder, "Crucify him." 15 So Pilate, wishing to satisfy the crowd, released Barabbas to them and, after he had Jesus scourged, handed him over to be crucified. 16 The soldiers led him away inside the palace, that is, the praetorium, and assembled the whole cohort. 17 They clothed him in purple and, weaving a crown of thorns, placed it on him. 18 They began to salute him with, "Hail, King of the Jews!" 19 and kept striking his head with a reed and spitting upon him. They knelt before him in homage. 20 And when they had mocked him, they stripped him of the purple cloak, dressed him in his own clothes, and led him out to crucify him. 21 They pressed into service a passer-by, Simon, a Cyrenian, who was coming in from the country, the father of Alexander and Rufus, to carry his cross. 22 They brought him to the place of Golgotha (which is translated Place of the Skull). 23 They gave him wine drugged with myrrh, but he did not take it. 24 Then they crucified him and divided his garments by casting lots for them to see what each should take. 25 It was nine o'clock in the morning when they crucified him. 26 The inscription of the charge against him read, "The King of the Jews." 27 With him they crucified two revolutionaries, one on his right and one on his left. 28 The Scripture was fulfilled which says, "He was counted with transgressors." 29 Those passing by reviled him, shaking their heads and saying, "Aha! You who would destroy the temple and rebuild it in three days, 30 save yourself by coming down from the cross." 31 Likewise the chief priests, with the scribes, mocked him among themselves and said, "He saved others; he cannot save himself. 32 Let the Messiah, the King of Israel, come down now from the cross that we may see and believe." Those who were crucified with him also kept abusing him. 33 At noon darkness came over the whole land until three in the afternoon. 34 And at three o'clock Jesus cried out in a loud voice, "Eloi, Eloi, lema sabachthani?" which is translated, "My God, my God, why have you forsaken me?" 35 Some of the bystanders who heard it said, "Look, he is calling Elijah." 36 One of them ran, soaked a sponge with wine, put it on a reed, and gave it to him to drink, saying, "Wait, let us see if Elijah comes to take him down." 37 Jesus gave a loud cry and breathed his last. 38 The veil of the sanctuary was torn in two from top to bottom. 39 When the centurion who stood facing him saw how he breathed his last he said, "Truly this man was the Son of God!" 40 There were also women looking on from a distance. Among them were Mary Magdalene, Mary the mother of the younger James and of Joses, and Salome. 41 These women had followed him when he was in Galilee and ministered to him. There were also many other women who had come up with him to Jerusalem. 42 When it was already evening, since it was the day of preparation, the day before the sabbath, 43 Joseph of Arimathea, a distinguished member of the council, who was himself awaiting the kingdom of God, came and courageously went to Pilate and asked for the body of Jesus. 44 Pilate was amazed that he was already dead. He summoned the centurion and asked him if Jesus had already died. 45 And when he learned of it from the centurion, he gave the body to Joseph. 46 Having bought a linen cloth, he took him down, wrapped him in the linen cloth and laid him in a tomb that had been hewn out of the rock. Then he rolled a stone against the entrance to the tomb. 47 Mary Magdalene and Mary the mother of Joses watched where he was laid.

Mark Chapter 16

1 When the sabbath was over, Mary Magdalene, Mary, the mother of James, and Salome bought spices so that they might go and anoint him. 2 Very early when the sun had risen, on the first day of the week, they came to the tomb. 3 They were saying to one another, "Who will roll back the stone for us from the entrance to the tomb?" 4 When they looked up, they saw that the stone had been rolled back; it was very large. 5 On entering the tomb they saw a young man sitting on the right side, clothed in a white robe, and they were utterly amazed. 6 He said to them, "Do not be amazed! You seek Jesus of Nazareth, the crucified. He has been raised; he is not here. Behold the place where they laid him. 7 But go and tell his disciples and Peter, 'He is going before you to Galilee; there you will see him, as he told you.'" 8 Then they went out and fled from the tomb, seized with trembling and bewilderment. They said nothing to anyone, for they were afraid. 9 When he had risen, early on the first day of the week, he appeared first to Mary Magdalene, out

of whom he had driven seven demons. 10 She went and told his companions who were mourning and weeping. 11 When they heard that he was alive and had been seen by her, they did not believe. 12 After this he appeared in another form to two of them walking along on their way to the country. 13 They returned and told the others; but they did not believe them either. 14 (But) later, as the eleven were at table, he appeared to them and rebuked them for their unbelief and hardness of heart because they had not believed those who saw him after he had been raised. 15 He said to them, "Go into the whole world and proclaim the gospel to every creature. 16 Whoever believes and is baptized will be saved; whoever does not believe will be condemned. 17 These signs will accompany those who believe: in my name they will drive out demons, they will speak new languages. 18 They will pick up serpents (with their hands), and if they drink any deadly thing, it will not harm them. They will lay hands on the sick, and they will recover." 19 So then the Lord Jesus, after he spoke to them, was taken up into heaven and took his seat at the right hand of God. 20 But they went forth and preached everywhere, while the Lord worked with them and confirmed the word through accompanying signs.

Luke

Luke Chapter 1

1 Since many have undertaken to compile a narrative of the events that have been fulfilled among us, 2 just as those who were eyewitnesses from the beginning and ministers of the word have handed them down to us, 3 I too have decided, after investigating everything accurately anew, to write it down in an orderly sequence for you, most excellent Theophilus, 4 so that you may realize the certainty of the teachings you have received. 5 In the days of Herod, King of Judea, there was a priest named Zechariah of the priestly division of Abijah; his wife was from the daughters of Aaron, and her name was Elizabeth. 6 Both were righteous in the eyes of God, observing all the commandments and ordinances of the Lord blamelessly. 7 But they had no child, because Elizabeth was barren and both were advanced in years. 8 Once when he was serving as priest in his division's turn before God, 9 according to the practice of the priestly service, he was chosen by lot to enter the sanctuary of the Lord to burn incense. 10 Then, when the whole assembly of the people was praying outside at the hour of the incense offering, 11 the angel of the Lord appeared to him, standing at the right of the altar of incense. 12 Zechariah was troubled by what he saw, and fear came upon him. 13 But the angel said to him, "Do not be afraid, Zechariah, because your prayer has been heard. Your wife Elizabeth will bear you a son, and you shall name him John. 14 And you will have joy and gladness, and many will rejoice at his birth, 15 for he will be great in the sight of (the) Lord. He will drink neither wine nor strong drink. He will be filled with the holy Spirit even from his mother's womb, 16 and he will turn many of the children of Israel to the Lord their God. 17 He will go before him in the spirit and power of Elijah to turn the hearts of fathers toward children and the disobedient to the understanding of the righteous, to prepare a people fit for the Lord." 18 Then Zechariah said to the angel, "How shall I know this? For I am an old man, and my wife is advanced in years." 19 And the angel said to him in reply, "I am Gabriel, who stand before God. I was sent to speak to you and to announce to you this good news. 20 But now you will be speechless and unable to talk until the day these things take place, because you did not believe my words, which will be fulfilled at their proper time." 21 Meanwhile the people were waiting for Zechariah and were amazed that he stayed so long in the sanctuary. 22 But when he came out, he was unable to speak to them, and they realized that he had seen a vision in the sanctuary. He was gesturing to them but remained mute. 23 Then, when his days of ministry were completed, he went home. 24 After this time his wife Elizabeth conceived, and she went into seclusion for five months, saying, 25 "So has the Lord done for me at a time when he has seen fit to take away my disgrace before others." 26 In the sixth month, the angel Gabriel was sent from God to a town of Galilee called Nazareth, 27 to a virgin betrothed to a man named Joseph, of the house of David, and the virgin's name was Mary. 28 And coming to her, he said, "Hail, favored one! The Lord is with you." 29 But she was greatly troubled at what was said and pondered what sort of greeting this might be. 30 Then the angel said to her, "Do not be afraid, Mary, for you have found favor with God. 31 Behold, you will conceive in your womb and bear a son, and you shall name him Jesus. 32 He will be great and will be called Son of the Most High, and the Lord God will give him the throne of David his father, 33 and he will rule over the house of Jacob forever, and of his kingdom there will be no end." 34 But Mary said to the angel, "How can this be, since I have no relations with a man?" 35 And the angel said to her in reply, "The holy Spirit will come upon you,

and the power of the Most High will overshadow you. Therefore the child to be born will be called holy, the Son of God. 36 And behold, Elizabeth, your relative, has also conceived a son in her old age, and this is the sixth month for her who was called barren; 37 for nothing will be impossible for God." 38 Mary said, "Behold, I am the handmaid of the Lord. May it be done to me according to your word." Then the angel departed from her. 39 During those days Mary set out and traveled to the hill country in haste to a town of Judah, 40 where she entered the house of Zechariah and greeted Elizabeth. 41 When Elizabeth heard Mary's greeting, the infant leaped in her womb, and Elizabeth, filled with the holy Spirit, 42 cried out in a loud voice and said, "Most blessed are you among women, and blessed is the fruit of your womb. 43 And how does this happen to me, that the mother of my Lord should come to me? 44 For at the moment the sound of your greeting reached my ears, the infant in my womb leaped for joy. 45 Blessed are you who believed that what was spoken to you by the Lord would be fulfilled." 46 And Mary said: "My soul proclaims the greatness of the Lord; 47 my spirit rejoices in God my savior. 48 For he has looked upon his handmaid's lowliness; behold, from now on will all ages call me blessed. 49 The Mighty One has done great things for me, and holy is his name. 50 His mercy is from age to age to those who fear him. 51 He has shown might with his arm, dispersed the arrogant of mind and heart. 52 He has thrown down the rulers from their thrones but lifted up the lowly. 53 The hungry he has filled with good things; the rich he has sent away empty. 54 He has helped Israel his servant, remembering his mercy, 55 according to his promise to our fathers, to Abraham and to his descendants forever." 56 Mary remained with her about three months and then returned to her home. 57 When the time arrived for Elizabeth to have her child she gave birth to a son. 58 Her neighbors and relatives heard that the Lord had shown his great mercy toward her, and they rejoiced with her. 59 When they came on the eighth day to circumcise the child, they were going to call him Zechariah after his father, 60 but his mother said in reply, "No. He will be called John." 61 But they answered her, "There is no one among your relatives who has this name." 62 So they made signs, asking his father what he wished him to be called. 63 He asked for a tablet and wrote, "John is his name," and all were amazed. 64 Immediately his mouth was opened, his tongue freed, and he spoke blessing God. 65 Then fear came upon all their neighbors, and all these matters were discussed throughout the hill country of Judea. 66 All who heard these things took them to heart, saying, "What, then, will this child be?" For surely the hand of the Lord was with him. 67 Then Zechariah his father, filled with the holy Spirit, prophesied, saying: 68 "Blessed be the Lord, the God of Israel, for he has visited and brought redemption to his people. 69 He has raised up a horn for our salvation within the house of David his servant, 70 even as he promised through the mouth of his holy prophets from of old: 71 salvation from our enemies and from the hand of all who hate us, 72 to show mercy to our fathers and to be mindful of his holy covenant 73 and of the oath he swore to Abraham our father, and to grant us that, 74 rescued from the hand of enemies, without fear we might worship him 75 in holiness and righteousness before him all our days. 76 And you, child, will be called prophet of the Most High, for you will go before the Lord to prepare his ways, 77 to give his people knowledge of salvation through the forgiveness of their sins, 78 because of the tender mercy of our God by which the daybreak from on high will visit us 79 to shine on those who sit in darkness and death's shadow, to guide our feet into the path of peace." 80 The child grew and became strong in spirit, and he was in the desert until the day of his manifestation to Israel.

Luke Chapter 2

1 In those days a decree went out from Caesar Augustus that the whole world should be enrolled. 2 This was the first enrollment, when Quirinius was governor of Syria. 3 So all went to be enrolled, each to his own town. 4 And Joseph too went up from Galilee from the town of Nazareth to Judea, to the city of David that is called Bethlehem, because he was of the house and family of David, 5 to be enrolled with Mary, his betrothed, who was with child. 6 While they were there, the time came for her to have her child, 7 and she gave birth to her firstborn son. She wrapped him in swaddling clothes and laid him in a manger, because there was no room for them in the inn. 8 Now there were shepherds in that region living in the fields and keeping the night watch over their flock. 9 The angel of the Lord appeared to them and the glory of the Lord shone around them, and they were struck with great fear. 10 The angel said to them, "Do not be afraid; for behold, I proclaim to you good news of great joy that will be for all the people. 11 For today in the city of David a savior has been born for you who is Messiah and Lord. 12 And this will be a sign for you: you will find an infant wrapped in swaddling clothes and lying in a manger." 13 And suddenly there was a multitude of the heavenly host with the angel, praising God and saying: 14 "Glory to God in the highest and on earth peace to those on whom his favor rests." 15 When the angels went away from them to heaven, the shepherds said to one another, "Let us go, then, to Bethlehem to see this thing that has taken place, which the Lord has made known to us." 16 So they went in haste and found Mary and Joseph, and the infant lying in the manger. 17 When they saw this, they made known the message that had been told them about this child. 18 All who heard it were amazed by what had been told them by the shepherds. 19 And Mary kept all these things, reflecting on them in her heart. 20 Then the shepherds returned, glorifying and praising God for all they had heard and seen, just as it had been told to them. 21 When eight days were completed for his circumcision, he was named Jesus, the name given him by the angel before he was conceived in the womb. 22 When the days were completed for their purification according to the law of Moses, they took him up to Jerusalem to present him to the Lord, 23 just as it is written in the law of the Lord, "Every male that opens the womb shall be consecrated to the Lord," 24 and to offer the sacrifice of "a pair of turtledoves or two young pigeons," in accordance with the dictate in the law of the Lord. 25 Now there was a man in Jerusalem whose name was Simeon. This man was righteous and devout, awaiting the consolation of Israel, and the holy Spirit was upon him. 26 It had been revealed to him by the holy Spirit that he should not see death before he had seen the Messiah of the Lord. 27 He came in the Spirit into the temple; and when the parents brought in the child Jesus to perform the custom of the law in regard to him, 28 he took him into his arms and blessed God, saying: 29 "Now, Master, you may let your servant go in peace, according to your word, 30 for my eyes have seen your salvation, 31 which you prepared in sight of all the peoples, 32 a light for revelation to the Gentiles, and glory for your people Israel." 33 The child's father and mother were amazed at what was said about him; 34 and Simeon blessed them and said to Mary his mother, "Behold, this child is destined for the fall and rise of many in Israel, and to be a sign that will be contradicted 35 (and you yourself a sword will pierce) so that the thoughts of many hearts may be revealed." 36 There was also a prophetess, Anna, the daughter of Phanuel, of the tribe of Asher. She was advanced in years, having lived seven years with her husband after her marriage, 37 and then as a widow until she was eighty-four. She never left the temple, but worshiped night and day with fasting and prayer. 38 And coming forward at that very time, she gave thanks to God and spoke about the child to all who were awaiting the redemption of Jerusalem. 39 When they had fulfilled all the prescriptions of the law of the Lord, they returned to Galilee, to their own town of Nazareth. 40 The child grew and became strong, filled with wisdom; and the favor of God was upon him. 41 Each year his parents went to Jerusalem for the feast of Passover, 42 and when he was twelve years old, they went up according to festival custom. 43 After they had completed its days, as they were returning, the boy Jesus remained behind in Jerusalem, but his parents did not know it. 44 Thinking that he was in the caravan, they journeyed for a day and looked for him among their relatives and acquaintances, 45 but not finding him, they returned to Jerusalem to look for him. 46 After three days they found him in the temple, sitting in the midst of the teachers, listening to them and asking them questions, 47 and all who heard him were astounded at his understanding and his answers. 48 When his parents saw him, they were astonished, and his mother said to him, "Son, why have you done this to us? Your father and I have been looking for you with great anxiety." 49 And he said to them, "Why were you looking for me? Did you not know that I must be in my Father's house?" 50 But they did not understand what he said to them. 51 He went down with them and came to Nazareth, and was obedient to them; and his mother kept all these things in her heart. 52 And Jesus advanced (in) wisdom and age and favor before God and man.

Luke Chapter 3

1 In the fifteenth year of the reign of Tiberius Caesar, when Pontius Pilate was governor of Judea, and Herod was tetrarch of Galilee, and his brother Philip tetrarch of the region of Ituraea and Trachonitis, and Lysanias was tetrarch of Abilene, 2 during the high priesthood of Annas and Caiaphas, the word of God came to John the son of Zechariah in the desert. 3 He went throughout (the) whole region of the Jordan, proclaiming a baptism of repentance for the forgiveness of sins, 4 as it is written in the book of the words of the prophet Isaiah: "A voice of one crying out in the desert: 'Prepare the way of the Lord, make straight his paths. 5 Every valley shall be filled and every mountain and hill shall be made low. The winding roads shall be made straight, and the rough ways made smooth, 6 and all flesh shall see the salvation of God.'" 7 He said to the crowds who came out to be baptized by him, "You brood of

vipers! Who warned you to flee from the coming wrath? 8 Produce good fruits as evidence of your repentance; and do not begin to say to yourselves, 'We have Abraham as our father,' for I tell you, God can raise up children to Abraham from these stones. 9 Even now the ax lies at the root of the trees. Therefore every tree that does not produce good fruit will be cut down and thrown into the fire." 10 And the crowds asked him, "What then should we do?" 11 He said to them in reply, "Whoever has two cloaks should share with the person who has none. And whoever has food should do likewise." 12 Even tax collectors came to be baptized and they said to him, "Teacher, what should we do?" 13 He answered them, "Stop collecting more than what is prescribed." 14 Soldiers also asked him, "And what is it that we should do?" He told them, "Do not practice extortion, do not falsely accuse anyone, and be satisfied with your wages." 15 Now the people were filled with expectation, and all were asking in their hearts whether John might be the Messiah. 16 John answered them all, saying, "I am baptizing you with water, but one mightier than I is coming. I am not worthy to loosen the thongs of his sandals. He will baptize you with the holy Spirit and fire. 17 His winnowing fan is in his hand to clear his threshing floor and to gather the wheat into his barn, but the chaff he will burn with unquenchable fire." 18 Exhorting them in many other ways, he preached good news to the people. 19 Now Herod the tetrarch, who had been censured by him because of Herodias, his brother's wife, and because of all the evil deeds Herod had committed, 20 added still another to these by (also) putting John in prison. 21 After all the people had been baptized and Jesus also had been baptized and was praying, heaven was opened 22 and the holy Spirit descended upon him in bodily form like a dove. And a voice came from heaven, "You are my beloved Son; with you I am well pleased." 23 When Jesus began his ministry he was about thirty years of age. He was the son, as was thought, of Joseph, the son of Heli, 24 the son of Matthat, the son of Levi, the son of Melchi, the son of Jannai, the son of Joseph, 25 the son of Mattathias, the son of Amos, the son of Nahum, the son of Esli, the son of Naggai, 26 the son of Maath, the son of Mattathias, the son of Semein, the son of Josech, the son of Joda, 27 the son of Joanan, the son of Rhesa, the son of Zerubbabel, the son of Shealtiel, the son of Neri, 28 the son of Melchi, the son of Addi, the son of Cosam, the son of Elmadam, the son of Er, 29 the son of Joshua, the son of Eliezer, the son of Jorim, the son of Matthat, the son of Levi, 30 the son of Simeon, the son of Judah, the son of Joseph, the son of Jonam, the son of Eliakim, 31 the son of Melea, the son of Menna, the son of Mattatha, the son of Nathan, the son of David, 32 the son of Jesse, the son of Obed, the son of Boaz, the son of Sala, the son of Nahshon, 33 the son of Amminadab, the son of Admin, the son of Arni, the son of Hezron, the son of Perez, the son of Judah, 34 the son of Jacob, the son of Isaac, the son of Abraham, the son of Terah, the son of Nahor, 35 the son of Serug, the son of Reu, the son of Peleg, the son of Eber, the son of Shelah, 36 the son of Cainan, the son of Arphaxad, the son of Shem, the son of Noah, the son of Lamech, 37 the son of Methuselah, the son of Enoch, the son of Jared, the son of Mahalaleel, the son of Cainan, 38 the son of Enos, the son of Seth, the son of Adam, the son of God.

Luke Chapter 4

1 Filled with the holy Spirit, Jesus returned from the Jordan and was led by the Spirit into the desert 2 for forty days, to be tempted by the devil. He ate nothing during those days, and when they were over he was hungry. 3 The devil said to him, "If you are the Son of God, command this stone to become bread." 4 Jesus answered him, "It is written, 'One does not live by bread alone.'" 5 Then he took him up and showed him all the kingdoms of the world in a single instant. 6 The devil said to him, "I shall give to you all this power and their glory; for it has been handed over to me, and I may give it to whomever I wish. 7 All this will be yours, if you worship me." 8 Jesus said to him in reply, "It is written: 'You shall worship the Lord, your God, and him alone shall you serve.'" 9 Then he led him to Jerusalem, made him stand on the parapet of the temple, and said to him, "If you are the Son of God, throw yourself down from here, 10 for it is written: 'He will command his angels concerning you, to guard you,' 11 and: 'With their hands they will support you, lest you dash your foot against a stone.'" 12 Jesus said to him in reply, "It also says, 'You shall not put the Lord, your God, to the test.'" 13 When the devil had finished every temptation, he departed from him for a time. 14 Jesus returned to Galilee in the power of the Spirit, and news of him spread throughout the whole region. 15 He taught in their synagogues and was praised by all. 16 He came to Nazareth, where he had grown up, and went according to his custom into the synagogue on the sabbath day. He stood up to read 17 and was handed a scroll of the prophet Isaiah. He unrolled the scroll and found the passage where it was written: 18 "The Spirit of the Lord is upon me,

because he has anointed me to bring glad tidings to the poor. He has sent me to proclaim liberty to captives and recovery of sight to the blind, to let the oppressed go free, 19 and to proclaim a year acceptable to the Lord." 20 Rolling up the scroll, he handed it back to the attendant and sat down, and the eyes of all in the synagogue looked intently at him. 21 He said to them, "Today this scripture passage is fulfilled in your hearing." 22 And all spoke highly of him and were amazed at the gracious words that came from his mouth. They also asked, "Isn't this the son of Joseph?" 23 He said to them, "Surely you will quote me this proverb, 'Physician, cure yourself,' and say, 'Do here in your native place the things that we heard were done in Capernaum.'" 24 And he said, "Amen, I say to you, no prophet is accepted in his own native place. 25 Indeed, I tell you, there were many widows in Israel in the days of Elijah when the sky was closed for three and a half years and a severe famine spread over the entire land. 26 It was to none of these that Elijah was sent, but only to a widow in Zarephath in the land of Sidon. 27 Again, there were many lepers in Israel during the time of Elisha the prophet; yet not one of them was cleansed, but only Naaman the Syrian." 28 When the people in the synagogue heard this, they were all filled with fury. 29 They rose up, drove him out of the town, and led him to the brow of the hill on which their town had been built, to hurl him down headlong. 30 But he passed through the midst of them and went away. 31 Jesus then went down to Capernaum, a town of Galilee. He taught them on the sabbath, 32 and they were astonished at his teaching because he spoke with authority. 33 In the synagogue there was a man with the spirit of an unclean demon, and he cried out in a loud voice, 34 "Ha! What have you to do with us, Jesus of Nazareth? Have you come to destroy us? I know who you are - the Holy One of God!" 35 Jesus rebuked him and said, "Be quiet! Come out of him!" Then the demon threw the man down in front of them and came out of him without doing him any harm. 36 They were all amazed and said to one another, "What is there about his word? For with authority and power he commands the unclean spirits, and they come out." 37 And news of him spread everywhere in the surrounding region. 38 After he left the synagogue, he entered the house of Simon. Simon's mother-in-law was afflicted with a severe fever, and they interceded with him about her. 39 He stood over her, rebuked the fever, and it left her. She got up immediately and waited on them. 40 At sunset, all who had people sick with various diseases brought them to him. He laid his hands on each of them and cured them. 41 And demons also came out from many, shouting, "You are the Son of God." But he rebuked them and did not allow them to speak because they knew that he was the Messiah. 42 At daybreak, Jesus left and went to a deserted place. The crowds went looking for him, and when they came to him, they tried to prevent him from leaving them. 43 But he said to them, "To the other towns also I must proclaim the good news of the kingdom of God, because for this purpose I have been sent." 44 And he was preaching in the synagogues of Judea.

Luke Chapter 5

1 While the crowd was pressing in on Jesus and listening to the word of God, he was standing by the Lake of Gennesaret. 2 He saw two boats there alongside the lake; the fishermen had disembarked and were washing their nets. 3 Getting into one of the boats, the one belonging to Simon, he asked him to put out a short distance from the shore. Then he sat down and taught the crowds from the boat. 4 After he had finished speaking, he said to Simon, "Put out into deep water and lower your nets for a catch." 5 Simon said in reply, "Master, we have worked hard all night and have caught nothing, but at your command I will lower the nets." 6 When they had done this, they caught a great number of fish and their nets were tearing. 7 They signaled to their partners in the other boat to come to help them. They came and filled both boats so that they were in danger of sinking. 8 When Simon Peter saw this, he fell at the knees of Jesus and said, "Depart from me, Lord, for I am a sinful man." 9 For astonishment at the catch of fish they had made seized him and all those with him, 10 and likewise James and John, the sons of Zebedee, who were partners of Simon. Jesus said to Simon, "Do not be afraid; from now on you will be catching men." 11 When they brought their boats to the shore, they left everything and followed him. 12 Now there was a man full of leprosy in one of the towns where he was; and when he saw Jesus, he fell prostrate, pleaded with him, and said, "Lord, if you wish, you can make me clean." 13 Jesus stretched out his hand, touched him, and said, "I do will it. Be made clean." And the leprosy left him immediately. 14 Then he ordered him not to tell anyone, but "Go, show yourself to the priest and offer for your cleansing what Moses prescribed; that will be proof for them." 15 The report about him spread all the more, and great crowds assembled to listen to him and to be cured of their ailments, 16 but he would withdraw to

deserted places to pray. ¹⁷ One day as Jesus was teaching, Pharisees and teachers of the law were sitting there who had come from every village of Galilee and Judea and Jerusalem, and the power of the Lord was with him for healing. ¹⁸ And some men brought on a stretcher a man who was paralyzed; they were trying to bring him in and set (him) in his presence. ¹⁹ But not finding a way to bring him in because of the crowd, they went up on the roof and lowered him on the stretcher through the tiles into the middle in front of Jesus. ²⁰ When he saw their faith, he said, "As for you, your sins are forgiven." ²¹ Then the scribes and Pharisees began to ask themselves, "Who is this who speaks blasphemies? Who but God alone can forgive sins?" ²² Jesus knew their thoughts and said to them in reply, "What are you thinking in your hearts? ²³ Which is easier, to say, 'Your sins are forgiven,' or to say, 'Rise and walk'? ²⁴ But that you may know that the Son of Man has authority on earth to forgive sins" - he said to the man who was paralyzed, "I say to you, rise, pick up your stretcher, and go home." ²⁵ He stood up immediately before them, picked up what he had been lying on, and went home, glorifying God. ²⁶ Then astonishment seized them all and they glorified God, and, struck with awe, they said, "We have seen incredible things today." ²⁷ After this he went out and saw a tax collector named Levi sitting at the customs post. He said to him, "Follow me." ²⁸ And leaving everything behind, he got up and followed him. ²⁹ Then Levi gave a great banquet for him in his house, and a large crowd of tax collectors and others were at table with them. ³⁰ The Pharisees and their scribes complained to his disciples, saying, "Why do you eat and drink with tax collectors and sinners?" ³¹ Jesus said to them in reply, "Those who are healthy do not need a physician, but the sick do. ³² I have not come to call the righteous to repentance but sinners." ³³ And they said to him, "The disciples of John fast often and offer prayers, and the disciples of the Pharisees do the same; but yours eat and drink." ³⁴ Jesus answered them, "Can you make the wedding guests fast while the bridegroom is with them? ³⁵ But the days will come, and when the bridegroom is taken away from them, then they will fast in those days." ³⁶ And he also told them a parable. "No one tears a piece from a new cloak to patch an old one. Otherwise, he will tear the new and the piece from it will not match the old cloak. ³⁷ Likewise, no one pours new wine into old wineskins. Otherwise, the new wine will burst the skins, and it will be spilled, and the skins will be ruined. ³⁸ Rather, new wine must be poured into fresh wineskins. ³⁹ (And) no one who has been drinking old wine desires new, for he says, 'The old is good.'"

Luke Chapter 6

¹ While he was going through a field of grain on a sabbath, his disciples were picking the heads of grain, rubbing them in their hands, and eating them. ² Some Pharisees said, "Why are you doing what is unlawful on the sabbath?" ³ Jesus said to them in reply, "Have you not read what David did when he and those (who were) with him were hungry? ⁴ (How) he went into the house of God, took the bread of offering, which only the priests could lawfully eat, ate of it, and shared it with his companions." ⁵ Then he said to them, "The Son of Man is lord of the sabbath." ⁶ On another sabbath he went into the synagogue and taught, and there was a man there whose right hand was withered. ⁷ The scribes and the Pharisees watched him closely to see if he would cure on the sabbath so that they might discover a reason to accuse him. ⁸ But he realized their intentions and said to the man with the withered hand, "Come up and stand before us." And he rose and stood there. ⁹ Then Jesus said to them, "I ask you, is it lawful to do good on the sabbath rather than to do evil, to save life rather than to destroy it?" ¹⁰ Looking around at them all, he then said to him, "Stretch out your hand." He did so and his hand was restored. ¹¹ But they became enraged and discussed together what they might do to Jesus. ¹² In those days he departed to the mountain to pray, and he spent the night in prayer to God. ¹³ When day came, he called his disciples to himself, and from them he chose Twelve, whom he also named apostles: ¹⁴ Simon, whom he named Peter, and his brother Andrew, James, John, Philip, Bartholomew, ¹⁵ Matthew, Thomas, James the son of Alphaeus, Simon who was called a Zealot, ¹⁶ and Judas the son of James, and Judas Iscariot, who became a traitor. ¹⁷ And he came down with them and stood on a stretch of level ground. A great crowd of his disciples and a large number of the people from all Judea and Jerusalem and the coastal region of Tyre and Sidon ¹⁸ came to hear him and to be healed of their diseases; and even those who were tormented by unclean spirits were cured. ¹⁹ Everyone in the crowd sought to touch him because power came forth from him and healed them all. ²⁰ And raising his eyes toward his disciples he said: "Blessed are you who are poor, for the kingdom of God is yours. ²¹ Blessed are you who are now hungry, for you will be satisfied. Blessed are you who are now weeping, for you will laugh. ²² Blessed are you when people hate you, and when they exclude and insult you, and

denounce your name as evil on account of the Son of Man. ²³ Rejoice and leap for joy on that day! Behold, your reward will be great in heaven. For their ancestors treated the prophets in the same way. ²⁴ But woe to you who are rich, for you have received your consolation. ²⁵ But woe to you who are filled now, for you will be hungry. Woe to you who laugh now, for you will grieve and weep. ²⁶ Woe to you when all speak well of you, for their ancestors treated the false prophets in this way. ²⁷ "But to you who hear I say, love your enemies, do good to those who hate you, ²⁸ bless those who curse you, pray for those who mistreat you. ²⁹ To the person who strikes you on one cheek, offer the other one as well, and from the person who takes your cloak, do not withhold even your tunic. ³⁰ Give to everyone who asks of you, and from the one who takes what is yours do not demand it back. ³¹ Do to others as you would have them do to you. ³² For if you love those who love you, what credit is that to you? Even sinners love those who love them. ³³ And if you do good to those who do good to you, what credit is that to you? Even sinners do the same. ³⁴ If you lend money to those from whom you expect repayment, what credit (is) that to you? Even sinners lend to sinners, and get back the same amount. ³⁵ But rather, love your enemies and do good to them, and lend expecting nothing back; then your reward will be great and you will be children of the Most High, for he himself is kind to the ungrateful and the wicked. ³⁶ Be merciful, just as (also) your Father is merciful. ³⁷ "Stop judging and you will not be judged. Stop condemning and you will not be condemned. Forgive and you will be forgiven. ³⁸ Give and gifts will be given to you; a good measure, packed together, shaken down, and overflowing, will be poured into your lap. For the measure with which you measure will in return be measured out to you." ³⁹ And he told them a parable, "Can a blind person guide a blind person? Will not both fall into a pit? ⁴⁰ No disciple is superior to the teacher; but when fully trained, every disciple will be like his teacher. ⁴¹ Why do you notice the splinter in your brother's eye, but do not perceive the wooden beam in your own? ⁴² How can you say to your brother, 'Brother, let me remove that splinter in your eye,' when you do not even notice the wooden beam in your own eye? You hypocrite! Remove the wooden beam from your eye first; then you will see clearly to remove the splinter in your brother's eye. ⁴³ "A good tree does not bear rotten fruit, nor does a rotten tree bear good fruit. ⁴⁴ For every tree is known by its own fruit. For people do not pick figs from thornbushes, nor do they gather grapes from brambles. ⁴⁵ A good person out of the store of goodness in his heart produces good, but an evil person out of a store of evil produces evil; for from the fullness of the heart the mouth speaks. ⁴⁶ "Why do you call me, 'Lord, Lord,' but not do what I command? ⁴⁷ I will show you what someone is like who comes to me, listens to my words, and acts on them. ⁴⁸ That one is like a person building a house, who dug deeply and laid the foundation on rock; when the flood came, the river burst against that house but could not shake it because it had been well built. ⁴⁹ But the one who listens and does not act is like a person who built a house on the ground without a foundation. When the river burst against it, it collapsed at once and was completely destroyed."

Luke Chapter 7

¹ When he had finished all his words to the people, he entered Capernaum. ² A centurion there had a slave who was ill and about to die, and he was valuable to him. ³ When he heard about Jesus, he sent elders of the Jews to him, asking him to come and save the life of his slave. ⁴ They approached Jesus and strongly urged him to come, saying, "He deserves to have you do this for him, ⁵ for he loves our nation and he built the synagogue for us." ⁶ And Jesus went with them, but when he was only a short distance from the house, the centurion sent friends to tell him, "Lord, do not trouble yourself, for I am not worthy to have you enter under my roof. ⁷ Therefore, I did not consider myself worthy to come to you; but say the word and let my servant be healed. ⁸ For I too am a person subject to authority, with soldiers subject to me. And I say to one, 'Go,' and he goes; and to another, 'Come here,' and he comes; and to my slave, 'Do this,' and he does it." ⁹ When Jesus heard this he was amazed at him and, turning, said to the crowd following him, "I tell you, not even in Israel have I found such faith." ¹⁰ When the messengers returned to the house, they found the slave in good health. ¹¹ Soon afterward he journeyed to a city called Nain, and his disciples and a large crowd accompanied him. ¹² As he drew near to the gate of the city, a man who had died was being carried out, the only son of his mother, and she was a widow. A large crowd from the city was with her. ¹³ When the Lord saw her, he was moved with pity for her and said to her, "Do not weep." ¹⁴ He stepped forward and touched the coffin; at this the bearers halted, and he said, "Young man, I tell you, arise!" ¹⁵ The dead man sat up and began to speak, and Jesus gave him to his mother. ¹⁶ Fear seized them all, and they glorified God, exclaiming, "A

great prophet has arisen in our midst," and "God has visited his people."[17]This report about him spread through the whole of Judea and in all the surrounding region.[18]The disciples of John told him about all these things. John summoned two of his disciples[19]and sent them to the Lord to ask, "Are you the one who is to come, or should we look for another?"[20]When the men came to him, they said, "John the Baptist has sent us to you to ask, 'Are you the one who is to come, or should we look for another?'"[21]At that time he cured many of their diseases, sufferings, and evil spirits; he also granted sight to many who were blind.[22]And he said to them in reply, "Go and tell John what you have seen and heard: the blind regain their sight, the lame walk, lepers are cleansed, the deaf hear, the dead are raised, the poor have the good news proclaimed to them.[23]And blessed is the one who takes no offense at me."[24]When the messengers of John had left, Jesus began to speak to the crowds about John. "What did you go out to the desert to see - a reed swayed by the wind?[25]Then what did you go out to see? Someone dressed in fine garments? Those who dress luxuriously and live sumptuously are found in royal palaces.[26]Then what did you go out to see? A prophet? Yes, I tell you, and more than a prophet.[27]This is the one about whom scripture says: 'Behold, I am sending my messenger ahead of you, he will prepare your way before you.'[28]I tell you, among those born of women, no one is greater than John; yet the least in the kingdom of God is greater than he."[29](All the people who listened, including the tax collectors, and who were baptized with the baptism of John, acknowledged the righteousness of God;[30]but the Pharisees and scholars of the law, who were not baptized by him, rejected the plan of God for themselves.)[31]"Then to what shall I compare the people of this generation? What are they like?[32]They are like children who sit in the marketplace and call to one another, 'We played the flute for you, but you did not dance. We sang a dirge, but you did not weep.'[33]For John the Baptist came neither eating food nor drinking wine, and you said, 'He is possessed by a demon.'[34]The Son of Man came eating and drinking and you said, 'Look, he is a glutton and a drunkard, a friend of tax collectors and sinners.'[35]But wisdom is vindicated by all her children."[36]A Pharisee invited him to dine with him, and he entered the Pharisee's house and reclined at table.[37]Now there was a sinful woman in the city who learned that he was at table in the house of the Pharisee. Bringing an alabaster flask of ointment,[38]she stood behind him at his feet weeping and began to bathe his feet with her tears. Then she wiped them with her hair, kissed them, and anointed them with the ointment.[39]When the Pharisee who had invited him saw this he said to himself, "If this man were a prophet, he would know who and what sort of woman this is who is touching him, that she is a sinner."[40]Jesus said to him in reply, "Simon, I have something to say to you." "Tell me, teacher," he said.[41]"Two people were in debt to a certain creditor; one owed five hundred days' wages and the other owed fifty.[42]Since they were unable to repay the debt, he forgave it for both. Which of them will love him more?"[43]Simon said in reply, "The one, I suppose, whose larger debt was forgiven." He said to him, "You have judged rightly."[44]Then he turned to the woman and said to Simon, "Do you see this woman? When I entered your house, you did not give me water for my feet, but she has bathed them with her tears and wiped them with her hair.[45]You did not give me a kiss, but she has not ceased kissing my feet since the time I entered.[46]You did not anoint my head with oil, but she anointed my feet with ointment.[47]So I tell you, her many sins have been forgiven; hence, she has shown great love. But the one to whom little is forgiven, loves little."[48]He said to her, "Your sins are forgiven."[49]The others at table said to themselves, "Who is this who even forgives sins?"[50]But he said to the woman, "Your faith has saved you; go in peace."

Luke Chapter 8

[1]Afterward he journeyed from one town and village to another, preaching and proclaiming the good news of the kingdom of God. Accompanying him were the Twelve[2]and some women who had been cured of evil spirits and infirmities, Mary, called Magdalene, from whom seven demons had gone out,[3]Joanna, the wife of Herod's steward Chuza, Susanna, and many others who provided for them out of their resources.[4]When a large crowd gathered, with people from one town after another journeying to him, he spoke in a parable.[5]"A sower went out to sow his seed. And as he sowed, some seed fell on the path and was trampled, and the birds of the sky ate it up.[6]Some seed fell on rocky ground, and when it grew, it withered for lack of moisture.[7]Some seed fell among thorns, and the thorns grew with it and choked it.[8]And some seed fell on good soil, and when it grew, it produced fruit a hundredfold." After saying this, he called out, "Whoever has ears to hear ought to hear."[9]Then his disciples asked him what the meaning of this parable might be.[10]He answered, "Knowledge of the mysteries of the kingdom of God has been granted to you; but to the rest, they are made known through parables so that 'they may look but not see, and hear but not understand.'[11]"This is the meaning of the parable. The seed is the word of God.[12]Those on the path are the ones who have heard, but the devil comes and takes away the word from their hearts that they may not believe and be saved.[13]Those on rocky ground are the ones who, when they hear, receive the word with joy, but they have no root; they believe only for a time and fall away in time of trial.[14]As for the seed that fell among thorns, they are the ones who have heard, but as they go along, they are choked by the anxieties and riches and pleasures of life, and they fail to produce mature fruit.[15]But as for the seed that fell on rich soil, they are the ones who, when they have heard the word, embrace it with a generous and good heart, and bear fruit through perseverance.[16]"No one who lights a lamp conceals it with a vessel or sets it under a bed; rather, he places it on a lampstand so that those who enter may see the light.[17]For there is nothing hidden that will not become visible, and nothing secret that will not be known and come to light.[18]Take care, then, how you hear. To anyone who has, more will be given, and from the one who has not, even what he seems to have will be taken away."[19]Then his mother and his brothers came to him but were unable to join him because of the crowd.[20]He was told, "Your mother and your brothers are standing outside and they wish to see you."[21]He said to them in reply, "My mother and my brothers are those who hear the word of God and act on it."[22]One day he got into a boat with his disciples and said to them, "Let us cross to the other side of the lake." So they set sail,[23]and while they were sailing he fell asleep. A squall blew over the lake, and they were taking in water and were in danger.[24]They came and woke him saying, "Master, master, we are perishing!" He awakened, rebuked the wind and the waves, and they subsided and there was a calm.[25]Then he asked them, "Where is your faith?" But they were filled with awe and amazed and said to one another, "Who then is this, who commands even the winds and the sea, and they obey him?"[26]Then they sailed to the territory of the Gerasenes, which is opposite Galilee.[27]When he came ashore a man from the town who was possessed by demons met him. For a long time he had not worn clothes; he did not live in a house, but lived among the tombs.[28]When he saw Jesus, he cried out and fell down before him; in a loud voice he shouted, "What have you to do with me, Jesus, son of the Most High God? I beg you, do not torment me!"[29]For he had ordered the unclean spirit to come out of the man. (It had taken hold of him many times, and he used to be bound with chains and shackles as a restraint, but he would break his bonds and be driven by the demon into deserted places.)[30]Then Jesus asked him, "What is your name?" He replied, "Legion," because many demons had entered him.[31]And they pleaded with him not to order them to depart to the abyss.[32]A herd of many swine was feeding there on the hillside, and they pleaded with him to allow them to enter those swine; and he let them.[33]The demons came out of the man and entered the swine, and the herd rushed down the steep bank into the lake and was drowned.[34]When the swineherds saw what had happened, they ran away and reported the incident in the town and throughout the countryside.[35]People came out to see what had happened and, when they approached Jesus, they discovered the man from whom the demons had come out sitting at his feet. He was clothed and in his right mind, and they were seized with fear.[36]Those who witnessed it told them how the possessed man had been saved.[37]The entire population of the region of the Gerasenes asked Jesus to leave them because they were seized with great fear. So he got into a boat and returned.[38]The man from whom the demons had come out begged to remain with him, but he sent him away, saying,[39]"Return home and recount what God has done for you." The man went off and proclaimed throughout the whole town what Jesus had done for him.[40]When Jesus returned, the crowd welcomed him, for they were all waiting for him.[41]And a man named Jairus, an official of the synagogue, came forward. He fell at the feet of Jesus and begged him to come to his house,[42]because he had an only daughter, about twelve years old, and she was dying. As he went, the crowds almost crushed him.[43]And a woman afflicted with hemorrhages for twelve years, who (had spent her whole livelihood on doctors and) was unable to be cured by anyone,[44]came up behind him and touched the tassel on his cloak. Immediately her bleeding stopped.[45]Jesus then asked, "Who touched me?" While all were denying it, Peter said, "Master, the crowds are pushing and pressing in upon you."[46]But Jesus said, "Someone has touched me; for I know that power has gone out from me."[47]When the woman realized that she had not escaped notice, she came forward trembling. Falling down before him, she explained in the presence of all the people why she had touched him and how she had been healed immediately.[48]He said to her, "Daughter, your faith has saved you; go in peace."[49]While he was still speaking, someone from the synagogue

official's house arrived and said, "Your daughter is dead; do not trouble the teacher any longer."⁵⁰On hearing this, Jesus answered him, "Do not be afraid; just have faith and she will be saved."⁵¹When he arrived at the house he allowed no one to enter with him except Peter and John and James, and the child's father and mother.⁵²All were weeping and mourning for her, when he said, "Do not weep any longer, for she is not dead, but sleeping."⁵³And they ridiculed him, because they knew that she was dead.⁵⁴But he took her by the hand and called to her, "Child, arise!"⁵⁵Her breath returned and she immediately arose. He then directed that she should be given something to eat.⁵⁶Her parents were astounded, and he instructed them to tell no one what had happened.

Luke Chapter 9

¹He summoned the Twelve and gave them power and authority over all demons and to cure diseases,²and he sent them to proclaim the kingdom of God and to heal (the sick).³He said to them, "Take nothing for the journey, neither walking stick, nor sack, nor food, nor money, and let no one take a second tunic.⁴Whatever house you enter, stay there and leave from there.⁵And as for those who do not welcome you, when you leave that town, shake the dust from your feet in testimony against them."⁶Then they set out and went from village to village proclaiming the good news and curing diseases everywhere.⁷Herod the tetrarch heard about all that was happening, and he was greatly perplexed because some were saying, "John has been raised from the dead";⁸others were saying, "Elijah has appeared"; still others, "One of the ancient prophets has arisen."⁹But Herod said, "John I beheaded. Who then is this about whom I hear such things?" And he kept trying to see him.¹⁰When the apostles returned, they explained to him what they had done. He took them and withdrew in private to a town called Bethsaida.¹¹The crowds, meanwhile, learned of this and followed him. He received them and spoke to them about the kingdom of God, and he healed those who needed to be cured.¹²As the day was drawing to a close, the Twelve approached him and said, "Dismiss the crowd so that they can go to the surrounding villages and farms and find lodging and provisions; for we are in a deserted place here."¹³He said to them, "Give them some food yourselves." They replied, "Five loaves and two fish are all we have, unless we ourselves go and buy food for all these people."¹⁴Now the men there numbered about five thousand. Then he said to his disciples, "Have them sit down in groups of (about) fifty."¹⁵They did so and made them all sit down.¹⁶Then taking the five loaves and the two fish, and looking up to heaven, he said the blessing over them, broke them, and gave them to the disciples to set before the crowd.¹⁷They all ate and were satisfied. And when the leftover fragments were picked up, they filled twelve wicker baskets.¹⁸Once when Jesus was praying in solitude, and the disciples were with him, he asked them, "Who do the crowds say that I am?"¹⁹They said in reply, "John the Baptist; others, Elijah; still others, 'One of the ancient prophets has arisen.'"²⁰Then he said to them, "But who do you say that I am?" Peter said in reply, "The Messiah of God."²¹He rebuked them and directed them not to tell this to anyone.²²He said, "The Son of Man must suffer greatly and be rejected by the elders, the chief priests, and the scribes, and be killed and on the third day be raised."²³Then he said to all, "If anyone wishes to come after me, he must deny himself and take up his cross daily and follow me.²⁴For whoever wishes to save his life will lose it, but whoever loses his life for my sake will save it.²⁵What profit is there for one to gain the whole world yet lose or forfeit himself?²⁶Whoever is ashamed of me and of my words, the Son of Man will be ashamed of when he comes in his glory and in the glory of the Father and of the holy angels.²⁷Truly I say to you, there are some standing here who will not taste death until they see the kingdom of God."²⁸About eight days after he said this, he took Peter, John, and James and went up the mountain to pray.²⁹While he was praying his face changed in appearance and his clothing became dazzling white.³⁰And behold, two men were conversing with him, Moses and Elijah, ³¹who appeared in glory and spoke of his exodus that he was going to accomplish in Jerusalem.³²Peter and his companions had been overcome by sleep, but becoming fully awake, they saw his glory and the two men standing with him.³³As they were about to part from him, Peter said to Jesus, "Master, it is good that we are here; let us make three tents, one for you, one for Moses, and one for Elijah." But he did not know what he was saying.³⁴While he was still speaking, a cloud came and cast a shadow over them, and they became frightened when they entered the cloud.³⁵Then from the cloud came a voice that said, "This is my chosen Son; listen to him."³⁶After the voice had spoken, Jesus was found alone. They fell silent and did not at that time tell anyone what they had seen.³⁷On the next day, when they came down from the mountain, a large crowd met him.³⁸There was a man in the crowd who cried out, "Teacher, I beg you, look at my son; he is my only

child.³⁹For a spirit seizes him and he suddenly screams and it convulses him until he foams at the mouth; it releases him only with difficulty, wearing him out.⁴⁰I begged your disciples to cast it out but they could not.⁴¹Jesus said in reply, "O faithless and perverse generation, how long will I be with you and endure you? Bring your son here."⁴²As he was coming forward, the demon threw him to the ground in a convulsion; but Jesus rebuked the unclean spirit, healed the boy, and returned him to his father.⁴³And all were astonished by the majesty of God. While they were all amazed at his every deed, he said to his disciples,⁴⁴"Pay attention to what I am telling you. The Son of Man is to be handed over to men."⁴⁵But they did not understand this saying; its meaning was hidden from them so that they should not understand it, and they were afraid to ask him about this saying.⁴⁶An argument arose among the disciples about which of them was the greatest.⁴⁷Jesus realized the intention of their hearts and took a child and placed it by his side⁴⁸and said to them, "Whoever receives this child in my name receives me, and whoever receives me receives the one who sent me. For the one who is least among all of you is the one who is the greatest."⁴⁹Then John said in reply,"Master, we saw someone casting out demons in your name and we tried to prevent him because he does not follow in our company."⁵⁰Jesus said to him, "Do not prevent him, for whoever is not against you is for you."⁵¹When the days for his being taken up were fulfilled, he resolutely determined to journey to Jerusalem,⁵²and he sent messengers ahead of him. On the way they entered a Samaritan village to prepare for his reception there,⁵³but they would not welcome him because the destination of his journey was Jerusalem.⁵⁴When the disciples James and John saw this they asked, "Lord, do you want us to call down fire from heaven to consume them?"⁵⁵Jesus turned and rebuked them,⁵⁶and they journeyed to another village.⁵⁷As they were proceeding on their journey someone said to him, "I will follow you wherever you go."⁵⁸Jesus answered him, "Foxes have dens and birds of the sky have nests, but the Son of Man has nowhere to rest his head."⁵⁹And to another he said, "Follow me." But he replied, "(Lord,) let me go first and bury my father."⁶⁰But he answered him, "Let the dead bury their dead. But you, go and proclaim the kingdom of God."⁶¹And another said, "I will follow you, Lord, but first let me say farewell to my family at home."⁶²(To him) Jesus said, "No one who sets a hand to the plow and looks to what was left behind is fit for the kingdom of God."

Luke Chapter 10

¹After this the Lord appointed seventy (-two) others whom he sent ahead of him in pairs to every town and place he intended to visit.²He said to them, "The harvest is abundant but the laborers are few; so ask the master of the harvest to send out laborers for his harvest.³Go on your way; behold, I am sending you like lambs among wolves.⁴Carry no money bag, no sack, no sandals; and greet no one along the way.⁵Into whatever house you enter, first say, 'Peace to this household.'⁶If a peaceful person lives there, your peace will rest on him; but if not, it will return to you.⁷Stay in the same house and eat and drink what is offered to you, for the laborer deserves his payment. Do not move about from one house to another.⁸Whatever town you enter and they welcome you, eat what is set before you,⁹cure the sick in it and say to them, 'The kingdom of God is at hand for you.'¹⁰Whatever town you enter and they do not receive you, go out into the streets and say,¹¹'The dust of your town that clings to our feet, even that we shake off against you.' Yet know this: the kingdom of God is at hand.¹²I tell you, it will be more tolerable for Sodom on that day than for that town.¹³"Woe to you, Chorazin! Woe to you, Bethsaida! For if the mighty deeds done in your midst had been done in Tyre and Sidon, they would long ago have repented, sitting in sackcloth and ashes.¹⁴But it will be more tolerable for Tyre and Sidon at the judgment than for you.¹⁵And as for you, Capernaum, 'Will you be exalted to heaven? You will go down to the netherworld.'¹⁶Whoever listens to you listens to me. Whoever rejects you rejects me. And whoever rejects me rejects the one who sent me."¹⁷The seventy (-two) returned rejoicing, and said, "Lord, even the demons are subject to us because of your name."¹⁸Jesus said, "I have observed Satan fall like lightning from the sky.¹⁹Behold, I have given you the power 'to tread upon serpents' and scorpions and upon the full force of the enemy and nothing will harm you.²⁰Nevertheless, do not rejoice because the spirits are subject to you, but rejoice because your names are written in heaven."²¹At that very moment he rejoiced (in) the holy Spirit and said, "I give you praise, Father, Lord of heaven and earth, for although you have hidden these things from the wise and the learned you have revealed them to the childlike. Yes, Father, such has been your gracious will.²²All things have been handed over to me by my Father. No one knows who the Son is except the Father, and who the Father is except the Son and anyone to whom the Son wishes to reveal

him."[23]Turning to the disciples in private he said, "Blessed are the eyes that see what you see.[24]For I say to you, many prophets and kings desired to see what you see, but did not see it, and to hear what you hear, but did not hear it."[25]There was a scholar of the law who stood up to test him and said, "Teacher, what must I do to inherit eternal life?"[26]Jesus said to him, "What is written in the law? How do you read it?"[27]He said in reply, "You shall love the Lord, your God, with all your heart, with all your being, with all your strength, and with all your mind, and your neighbor as yourself."[28]He replied to him, "You have answered correctly; do this and you will live."[29]But because he wished to justify himself, he said to Jesus, "And who is my neighbor?"[30]Jesus replied, "A man fell victim to robbers as he went down from Jerusalem to Jericho. They stripped and beat him and went off leaving him half-dead.[31]A priest happened to be going down that road, but when he saw him, he passed by on the opposite side.[32]Likewise a Levite came to the place, and when he saw him, he passed by on the opposite side.[33]But a Samaritan traveler who came upon him was moved with compassion at the sight.[34]He approached the victim, poured oil and wine over his wounds and bandaged them. Then he lifted him up on his own animal, took him to an inn and cared for him.[35]The next day he took out two silver coins and gave them to the innkeeper with the instruction, 'Take care of him. If you spend more than what I have given you, I shall repay you on my way back.'[36]Which of these three, in your opinion, was neighbor to the robbers' victim?"[37]He answered, "The one who treated him with mercy." Jesus said to him, "Go and do likewise."[38]As they continued their journey he entered a village where a woman whose name was Martha welcomed him.[39]She had a sister named Mary (who) sat beside the Lord at his feet listening to him speak.[40]Martha, burdened with much serving, came to him and said, "Lord, do you not care that my sister has left me by myself to do the serving? Tell her to help me."[41]The Lord said to her in reply, "Martha, Martha, you are anxious and worried about many things.[42]There is need of only one thing. Mary has chosen the better part and it will not be taken from her."

Luke Chapter 11

[1]He was praying in a certain place, and when he had finished, one of his disciples said to him, "Lord, teach us to pray just as John taught his disciples."[2]He said to them, "When you pray, say: Father, hallowed be your name, your kingdom come.[3]Give us each day our daily bread[4]and forgive us our sins for we ourselves forgive everyone in debt to us, and do not subject us to the final test."[5]And he said to them, "Suppose one of you has a friend to whom he goes at midnight and says, 'Friend, lend me three loaves of bread,[6]for a friend of mine has arrived at my house from a journey and I have nothing to offer him,'[7]and he says in reply from within, 'Do not bother me; the door has already been locked and my children and I are already in bed. I cannot get up to give you anything.'[8]I tell you, if he does not get up to give him the loaves because of their friendship, he will get up to give him whatever he needs because of his persistence.[9]"And I tell you, ask and you will receive; seek and you will find; knock and the door will be opened to you.[10]For everyone who asks, receives; and the one who seeks, finds; and to the one who knocks, the door will be opened.[11]What father among you would hand his son a snake when he asks for a fish?[12]Or hand him a scorpion when he asks for an egg?[13]If you then, who are wicked, know how to give good gifts to your children, how much more will the Father in heaven give the holy Spirit to those who ask him?"[14]He was driving out a demon (that was) mute, and when the demon had gone out, the mute person spoke and the crowds were amazed.[15]Some of them said, "By the power of Beelzebul, the prince of demons, he drives out demons."[16]Others, to test him, asked him for a sign from heaven.[17]But he knew their thoughts and said to them, "Every kingdom divided against itself will be laid waste and house will fall against house.[18]And if Satan is divided against himself, how will his kingdom stand? For you say that it is by Beelzebul that I drive out demons.[19]If I, then, drive out demons by Beelzebul, by whom do your own people drive them out? Therefore they will be your judges.[20]But if it is by the finger of God that (I) drive out demons, then the kingdom of God has come upon you.[21]When a strong man fully armed guards his palace, his possessions are safe.[22]But when one stronger than he attacks and overcomes him, he takes away the armor on which he relied and distributes the spoils.[23]Whoever is not with me is against me, and whoever does not gather with me scatters.[24]"When an unclean spirit goes out of someone, it roams through arid regions searching for rest but, finding none, it says, 'I shall return to my home from which I came.'[25]But upon returning, it finds it swept clean and put in order.[26]Then it goes and brings back seven other spirits more wicked than itself who move in and dwell there, and the last condition of that person is worse than the first."[27]While he was speaking, a woman from the crowd called out and said to him, "Blessed

is the womb that carried you and the breasts at which you nursed."[28]He replied, "Rather, blessed are those who hear the word of God and observe it."[29]While still more people gathered in the crowd, he said to them, "This generation is an evil generation; it seeks a sign, but no sign will be given it, except the sign of Jonah.[30]Just as Jonah became a sign to the Ninevites, so will the Son of Man be to this generation.[31]At the judgment the queen of the south will rise with the men of this generation and she will condemn them, because she came from the ends of the earth to hear the wisdom of Solomon, and there is something greater than Solomon here.[32]At the judgment the men of Nineveh will arise with this generation and condemn it, because at the preaching of Jonah they repented, and there is something greater than Jonah here.[33]"No one who lights a lamp hides it away or places it (under a bushel basket), but on a lampstand so that those who enter might see the light.[34]The lamp of the body is your eye. When your eye is sound, then your whole body is filled with light, but when it is bad, then your body is in darkness.[35]Take care, then, that the light in you not become darkness.[36]If your whole body is full of light, and no part of it is in darkness, then it will be as full of light as a lamp illuminating you with its brightness."[37]After he had spoken, a Pharisee invited him to dine at his home. He entered and reclined at table to eat.[38]The Pharisee was amazed to see that he did not observe the prescribed washing before the meal.[39]The Lord said to him, "Oh you Pharisees! Although you cleanse the outside of the cup and the dish, inside you are filled with plunder and evil.[40]You fools! Did not the maker of the outside also make the inside?[41]But as to what is within, give alms, and behold, everything will be clean for you.[42]Woe to you Pharisees! You pay tithes of mint and of rue and of every garden herb, but you pay no attention to judgment and to love for God. These you should have done, without overlooking the others.[43]Woe to you Pharisees! You love the seat of honor in synagogues and greetings in marketplaces.[44]Woe to you! You are like unseen graves over which people unknowingly walk."[45]Then one of the scholars of the law said to him in reply, "Teacher, by saying this you are insulting us too."[46]And he said, "Woe also to you scholars of the law! You impose on people burdens hard to carry, but you yourselves do not lift one finger to touch them.[47]Woe to you! You build the memorials of the prophets whom your ancestors killed.[48]Consequently, you bear witness and give consent to the deeds of your ancestors, for they killed them and you do the building.[49]Therefore, the wisdom of God said, 'I will send to them prophets and apostles; some of them they will kill and persecute'[50]in order that this generation might be charged with the blood of all the prophets shed since the foundation of the world,[51]from the blood of Abel to the blood of Zechariah who died between the altar and the temple building. Yes, I tell you, this generation will be charged with their blood![52]Woe to you, scholars of the law! You have taken away the key of knowledge. You yourselves did not enter and you stopped those trying to enter."[53]When he left, the scribes and Pharisees began to act with hostility toward him and to interrogate him about many things,[54]for they were plotting to catch him at something he might say.

Luke Chapter 12

[1]Meanwhile, so many people were crowding together that they were trampling one another underfoot. He began to speak, first to his disciples, "Beware of the leaven - that is, the hypocrisy - of the Pharisees. [2]"There is nothing concealed that will not be revealed, nor secret that will not be known.[3]Therefore whatever you have said in the darkness will be heard in the light, and what you have whispered behind closed doors will be proclaimed on the housetops. [4]I tell you, my friends, do not be afraid of those who kill the body but after that can do no more. [5]I shall show you whom to fear. Be afraid of the one who after killing has the power to cast into Gehenna; yes, I tell you, be afraid of that one. [6]Are not five sparrows sold for two small coins? Yet not one of them has escaped the notice of God. [7]Even the hairs of your head have all been counted. Do not be afraid. You are worth more than many sparrows. [8]I tell you, everyone who acknowledges me before others the Son of Man will acknowledge before the angels of God. [9]But whoever denies me before others will be denied before the angels of God. [10]"Everyone who speaks a word against the Son of Man will be forgiven, but the one who blasphemes against the holy Spirit will not be forgiven. [11]When they take you before synagogues and before rulers and authorities, do not worry about how or what your defense will be or about what you are to say. [12]For the holy Spirit will teach you at that moment what you should say." [13]Someone in the crowd said to him, "Teacher, tell my brother to share the inheritance with me." [14]He replied to him, "Friend, who appointed me as your judge and arbitrator?" [15]Then he said to the crowd, "Take care to guard against all greed, for though one may be rich, one's life does not consist of possessions." [16]Then he told them a parable. "There was a rich man

whose land produced a bountiful harvest. ¹⁷He asked himself, 'What shall I do, for I do not have space to store my harvest?' ¹⁸And he said, 'This is what I shall do: I shall tear down my barns and build larger ones. There I shall store all my grain and other goods ¹⁹and I shall say to myself, "Now as for you, you have so many good things stored up for many years, rest, eat, drink, be merry!" ²⁰But God said to him, 'You fool, this night your life will be demanded of you; and the things you have prepared, to whom will they belong?' ²¹Thus will it be for the one who stores up treasure for himself but is not rich in what matters to God." ²²He said to (his) disciples, "Therefore I tell you, do not worry about your life and what you will eat, or about your body and what you will wear. ²³For life is more than food and the body more than clothing. ²⁴Notice the ravens: they do not sow or reap; they have neither storehouse nor barn, yet God feeds them. How much more important are you than birds? ²⁵Can any of you by worrying add a moment to your lifespan? ²⁶If even the smallest things are beyond your control, why are you anxious about the rest? ²⁷Notice how the flowers grow. They do not toil or spin. But I tell you, not even Solomon in all his splendor was dressed like one of them. ²⁸If God so clothes the grass in the field that grows today and is thrown into the oven tomorrow, will he not much more provide for you, O you of little faith? ²⁹As for you, do not seek what you are to eat and what you are to drink, and do not worry anymore. ³⁰All the nations of the world seek for these things, and your Father knows that you need them. ³¹Instead, seek his kingdom, and these other things will be given you besides. ³²Do not be afraid any longer, little flock, for your Father is pleased to give you the kingdom. ³³Sell your belongings and give alms. Provide money bags for yourselves that do not wear out, an inexhaustible treasure in heaven that no thief can reach nor moth destroy. ³⁴For where your treasure is, there also will your heart be. ³⁵"Gird your loins and light your lamps ³⁶and be like servants who await their master's return from a wedding, ready to open immediately when he comes and knocks. ³⁷Blessed are those servants whom the master finds vigilant on his arrival. Amen, I say to you, he will gird himself, have them recline at table, and proceed to wait on them. ³⁸And should he come in the second or third watch and find them prepared in this way, blessed are those servants. ³⁹Be sure of this: if the master of the house had known the hour when the thief was coming, he would not have let his house be broken into. ⁴⁰You also must be prepared, for at an hour you do not expect, the Son of Man will come." ⁴¹Then Peter said, "Lord, is this parable meant for us or for everyone?" ⁴²And the Lord replied, "Who, then, is the faithful and prudent steward whom the master will put in charge of his servants to distribute (the) food allowance at the proper time? ⁴³Blessed is that servant whom his master on arrival finds doing so. ⁴⁴Truly, I say to you, he will put him in charge of all his property. ⁴⁵But if that servant says to himself, 'My master is delayed in coming,'and begins to beat the menservants and the maidservants, to eat and drink and get drunk, ⁴⁶then that servant's master will come on an unexpected day and at an unknown hour and will punish him severely and assign him a place with the unfaithful. ⁴⁷That servant who knew his master's will but did not make preparations nor act in accord with his will shall be beaten severely; ⁴⁸and the servant who was ignorant of his master's will but acted in a way deserving of a severe beating shall be beaten only lightly. Much will be required of the person entrusted with much, and still more will be demanded of the person entrusted with more. ⁴⁹I have come to set the earth on fire, and how I wish it were already blazing! ⁵⁰There is a baptism with which I must be baptized, and how great is my anguish until it is accomplished! ⁵¹Do you think that I have come to establish peace on the earth? No, I tell you, but rather division. ⁵²From now on a household of five will be divided, three against two and two against three; ⁵³a father will be divided against his son and a son against his father, a mother against her daughter and a daughter against her mother, a mother-in-law against her daughter-in-law and a daughter-in-law against her mother-in-law." ⁵⁴He also said to the crowds, "When you see (a) cloud rising in the west you say immediately that it is going to rain - and so it does; ⁵⁵and when you notice that the wind is blowing from the south you say that it is going to be hot - and so it is. ⁵⁶You hypocrites! You know how to interpret the appearance of the earth and the sky; why do you not know how to interpret the present time? ⁵⁷"Why do you not judge for yourselves what is right? ⁵⁸If you are to go with your opponent before a magistrate, make an effort to settle the matter on the way; otherwise your opponent will turn you over to the judge, and the judge hand you over to the constable, and the constable throw you into prison. ⁵⁹I say to you, you will not be released until you have paid the last penny."

Luke Chapter 13

¹At that time some people who were present there told him about the

Galileans whose blood Pilate had mingled with the blood of their sacrifices. ²He said to them in reply, "Do you think that because these Galileans suffered in this way they were greater sinners than all other Galileans? ³By no means! But I tell you, if you do not repent, you will all perish as they did! ⁴Or those eighteen people who were killed when the tower at Siloam fell on them - do you think they were more guilty than everyone else who lived in Jerusalem? ⁵By no means! But I tell you, if you do not repent, you will all perish as they did!" ⁶And he told them this parable: "There once was a person who had a fig tree planted in his orchard, and when he came in search of fruit on it but found none, ⁷he said to the gardener, 'For three years now I have come in search of fruit on this fig tree but have found none. (So) cut it down. Why should it exhaust the soil?' ⁸He said to him in reply, 'Sir, leave it for this year also, and I shall cultivate the ground around it and fertilize it; ⁹it may bear fruit in the future. If not you can cut it down.'" ¹⁰He was teaching in a synagogue on the sabbath. ¹¹And a woman was there who for eighteen years had been crippled by a spirit; she was bent over, completely incapable of standing erect. ¹²When Jesus saw her, he called to her and said, "Woman, you are set free of your infirmity." ¹³He laid his hands on her, and she at once stood up straight and glorified God. ¹⁴But the leader of the synagogue, indignant that Jesus had cured on the sabbath, said to the crowd in reply, "There are six days when work should be done. Come on those days to be cured, not on the sabbath day." ¹⁵The Lord said to him in reply, "Hypocrites! Does not each one of you on the sabbath untie his ox or his ass from the manger and lead it out for watering? ¹⁶This daughter of Abraham, whom Satan has bound for eighteen years now, ought she not to have been set free on the sabbath day from this bondage?" ¹⁷When he said this, all his adversaries were humiliated; and the whole crowd rejoiced at all the splendid deeds done by him. ¹⁸Then he said, "What is the kingdom of God like? To what can I compare it? ¹⁹It is like a mustard seed that a person took and planted in the garden. When it was fully grown, it became a large bush and 'the birds of the sky dwelt in its branches.'" ²⁰Again he said, "To what shall I compare the kingdom of God? ²¹It is like yeast that a woman took and mixed (in) with three measures of wheat flour until the whole batch of dough was leavened." ²²He passed through towns and villages, teaching as he went and making his way to Jerusalem. ²³Someone asked him, "Lord, will only a few people be saved?" He answered them, ²⁴"Strive to enter through the narrow gate, for many, I tell you, will attempt to enter but will not be strong enough. ²⁵After the master of the house has arisen and locked the door, then will you stand outside knocking and saying, 'Lord, open the door for us.' He will say to you in reply, 'I do not know where you are from.' ²⁶And you will say, 'We ate and drank in your company and you taught in our streets.' ²⁷Then he will say to you, 'I do not know where (you) are from. Depart from me, all you evildoers!' ²⁸And there will be wailing and grinding of teeth when you see Abraham, Isaac, and Jacob and all the prophets in the kingdom of God and you yourselves cast out. ²⁹And people will come from the east and the west and from the north and the south and will recline at table in the kingdom of God. ³⁰For behold, some are last who will be first, and some are first who will be last." ³¹At that time some Pharisees came to him and said, "Go away, leave this area because Herod wants to kill you." ³²He replied, "Go and tell that fox, 'Behold, I cast out demons and I perform healings today and tomorrow, and on the third day I accomplish my purpose. ³³Yet I must continue on my way today, tomorrow, and the following day, for it is impossible that a prophet should die outside of Jerusalem.' ³⁴"Jerusalem, Jerusalem, you who kill the prophets and stone those sent to you, how many times I yearned to gather your children together as a hen gathers her brood under her wings, but you were unwilling! ³⁵Behold, your house will be abandoned. (But) I tell you, you will not see me until (the time comes when) you say, 'Blessed is he who comes in the name of the Lord.'"

Luke Chapter 14

¹On a sabbath he went to dine at the home of one of the leading Pharisees, and the people there were observing him carefully. ²In front of him there was a man suffering from dropsy. ³Jesus spoke to the scholars of the law and Pharisees in reply, asking, "Is it lawful to cure on the sabbath or not?" ⁴But they kept silent; so he took the man and, after he had healed him, dismissed him. ⁵Then he said to them, "Who among you, if your son or ox falls into a cistern, would not immediately pull him out on the sabbath day?" ⁶But they were unable to answer his question. ⁷He told a parable to those who had been invited, noticing how they were choosing the places of honor at the table. ⁸"When you are invited by someone to a wedding banquet, do not recline at table in the place of honor. A more distinguished guest than you may have been invited by him, ⁹and the host who invited both of you may approach

you and say, 'Give your place to this man,' and then you would proceed with embarrassment to take the lowest place. [10]Rather, when you are invited, go and take the lowest place so that when the host comes to you he may say, 'My friend, move up to a higher position.' Then you will enjoy the esteem of your companions at the table. [11]For everyone who exalts himself will be humbled, but the one who humbles himself will be exalted." [12]Then he said to the host who invited him, "When you hold a lunch or a dinner, do not invite your friends or your brothers or your relatives or your wealthy neighbors, in case they may invite you back and you have repayment. [13]Rather, when you hold a banquet, invite the poor, the crippled, the lame, the blind; [14]blessed indeed will you be because of their inability to repay you. For you will be repaid at the resurrection of the righteous." [15]One of his fellow guests on hearing this said to him, "Blessed is the one who will dine in the kingdom of God." [16]He replied to him, "A man gave a great dinner to which he invited many. [17]When the time for the dinner came, he dispatched his servant to say to those invited, 'Come, everything is now ready.' [18]But one by one, they all began to excuse themselves. The first said to him, 'I have purchased a field and must go to examine it; I ask you, consider me excused.' [19]And another said, 'I have purchased five yoke of oxen and am on my way to evaluate them; I ask you, consider me excused.' [20]And another said, 'I have just married a woman, and therefore I cannot come.' [21]The servant went and reported this to his master. Then the master of the house in a rage commanded his servant, 'Go out quickly into the streets and alleys of the town and bring in here the poor and the crippled, the blind and the lame.' [22]The servant reported, 'Sir, your orders have been carried out and still there is room.' [23]The master then ordered the servant, 'Go out to the highways and hedgerows and make people come in that my home may be filled. [24]For, I tell you, none of those men who were invited will taste my dinner.'" [25]Great crowds were traveling with him, and he turned and addressed them, [26]"If any one comes to me without hating his father and mother, wife and children, brothers and sisters, and even his own life, he cannot be my disciple. [27]Whoever does not carry his own cross and come after me cannot be my disciple. [28]Which of you wishing to construct a tower does not first sit down and calculate the cost to see if there is enough for its completion? [29]Otherwise, after laying the foundation and finding himself unable to finish the work the onlookers should laugh at him [30]and say, 'This one began to build but did not have the resources to finish.' [31]Or what king marching into battle would not first sit down and decide whether with ten thousand troops he can successfully oppose another king advancing upon him with twenty thousand troops? [32]But if not, while he is still far away, he will send a delegation to ask for peace terms. [33]In the same way, everyone of you who does not renounce all his possessions cannot be my disciple. [34]"Salt is good, but if salt itself loses its taste, with what can its flavor be restored? [35]It is fit neither for the soil nor for the manure pile; it is thrown out. Whoever has ears to hear ought to hear."

Luke Chapter 15

[1]The tax collectors and sinners were all drawing near to listen to him, [2]but the Pharisees and scribes began to complain, saying, "This man welcomes sinners and eats with them." [3]So to them he addressed this parable. [4]"What man among you having a hundred sheep and losing one of them would not leave the ninety-nine in the desert and go after the lost one until he finds it? [5]And when he does find it, he sets it on his shoulders with great joy [6]and, upon his arrival home, he calls together his friends and neighbors and says to them, 'Rejoice with me because I have found my lost sheep.' [7]I tell you, in just the same way there will be more joy in heaven over one sinner who repents than over ninety-nine righteous people who have no need of repentance. [8]"Or what woman having ten coins and losing one would not light a lamp and sweep the house, searching carefully until she finds it? [9]And when she does find it, she calls together her friends and neighbors and says to them, 'Rejoice with me because I have found the coin that I lost.' [10]In just the same way, I tell you, there will be rejoicing among the angels of God over one sinner who repents." [11]Then he said, "A man had two sons, [12]and the younger son said to his father, 'Father, give me the share of your estate that should come to me.' So the father divided the property between them. [13]After a few days, the younger son collected all his belongings and set off to a distant country where he squandered his inheritance on a life of dissipation. [14]When he had freely spent everything, a severe famine struck that country, and he found himself in dire need. [15]So he hired himself out to one of the local citizens who sent him to his farm to tend the swine. [16]And he longed to eat his fill of the pods on which the swine fed, but nobody gave him any. [17]Coming to his senses he thought, 'How many of my father's hired workers have more than enough food to eat, but here am I, dying from hunger. [18]I

shall get up and go to my father and I shall say to him, "Father, I have sinned against heaven and against you. [19]I no longer deserve to be called your son; treat me as you would treat one of your hired workers."' [20]So he got up and went back to his father. While he was still a long way off, his father caught sight of him, and was filled with compassion. He ran to his son, embraced him and kissed him. [21]His son said to him, 'Father, I have sinned against heaven and against you; I no longer deserve to be called your son.' [22]But his father ordered his servants, 'Quickly bring the finest robe and put it on him; put a ring on his finger and sandals on his feet. [23]Take the fattened calf and slaughter it. Then let us celebrate with a feast, [24]because this son of mine was dead, and has come to life again; he was lost, and has been found.' Then the celebration began. [25]Now the older son had been out in the field and, on his way back, as he neared the house, he heard the sound of music and dancing. [26]He called one of the servants and asked what this might mean. [27]The servant said to him, 'Your brother has returned and your father has slaughtered the fattened calf because he has him back safe and sound.' [28]He became angry, and when he refused to enter the house, his father came out and pleaded with him. [29]He said to his father in reply, 'Look, all these years I served you and not once did I disobey your orders; yet you never gave me even a young goat to feast on with my friends. [30]But when your son returns who swallowed up your property with prostitutes, for him you slaughter the fattened calf.' [31]He said to him, 'My son, you are here with me always; everything I have is yours. [32]But now we must celebrate and rejoice, because your brother was dead and has come to life again; he was lost and has been found.'"

Luke Chapter 16

[1]Then he also said to his disciples, "A rich man had a steward who was reported to him for squandering his property. [2]He summoned him and said, 'What is this I hear about you? Prepare a full account of your stewardship, because you can no longer be my steward.' [3]The steward said to himself, 'What shall I do, now that my master is taking the position of steward away from me? I am not strong enough to dig and I am ashamed to beg. [4]I know what I shall do so that, when I am removed from the stewardship, they may welcome me into their homes.' [5]He called in his master's debtors one by one. To the first he said, 'How much do you owe my master?' [6]He replied, 'One hundred measures of olive oil.' He said to him, 'Here is your promissory note. Sit down and quickly write one for fifty.' [7]Then to another he said, 'And you, how much do you owe?' He replied, 'One hundred kors of wheat.' He said to him, 'Here is your promissory note; write one for eighty.' [8]And the master commended that dishonest steward for acting prudently. "For the children of this world are more prudent in dealing with their own generation than are the children of light. [9]I tell you, make friends for yourselves with dishonest wealth, so that when it fails, you will be welcomed into eternal dwellings. [10]The person who is trustworthy in very small matters is also trustworthy in great ones; and the person who is dishonest in very small matters is also dishonest in great ones. [11]If, therefore, you are not trustworthy with dishonest wealth, who will trust you with true wealth? [12]If you are not trustworthy with what belongs to another, who will give you what is yours? [13]No servant can serve two masters. He will either hate one and love the other, or be devoted to one and despise the other. You cannot serve God and mammon." [14]The Pharisees, who loved money, heard all these things and sneered at him. [15]And he said to them, "You justify yourselves in the sight of others, but God knows your hearts; for what is of human esteem is an abomination in the sight of God. [16]"The law and the prophets lasted until John; but from then on the kingdom of God is proclaimed, and everyone who enters does so with violence. [17]It is easier for heaven and earth to pass away than for the smallest part of a letter of the law to become invalid. [18]"Everyone who divorces his wife and marries another commits adultery, and the one who marries a woman divorced from her husband commits adultery. [19]"There was a rich man who dressed in purple garments and fine linen and dined sumptuously each day. [20]And lying at his door was a poor man named Lazarus, covered with sores, [21]who would gladly have eaten his fill of the scraps that fell from the rich man's table. Dogs even used to come and lick his sores. [22]When the poor man died, he was carried away by angels to the bosom of Abraham. The rich man also died and was buried, [23]and from the netherworld, where he was in torment, he raised his eyes and saw Abraham far off and Lazarus at his side. [24]And he cried out, 'Father Abraham, have pity on me. Send Lazarus to dip the tip of his finger in water and cool my tongue, for I am suffering torment in these flames.' [25]Abraham replied, 'My child, remember that you received what was good during your lifetime while Lazarus likewise received what was bad; but now he is comforted here, whereas you are tormented. [26]Moreover, between us and you a great chasm is established to prevent anyone from crossing who might wish

to go from our side to yours or from your side to ours.' 27He said, 'Then I beg you, father, send him to my father's house, 28for I have five brothers, so that he may warn them, lest they too come to this place of torment.' 29But Abraham replied, 'They have Moses and the prophets. Let them listen to them.' 30He said, 'Oh no, father Abraham, but if someone from the dead goes to them, they will repent.' 31Then Abraham said, 'If they will not listen to Moses and the prophets, neither will they be persuaded if someone should rise from the dead.'"

Luke Chapter 17

1He said to his disciples, "Things that cause sin will inevitably occur, but woe to the person through whom they occur.2It would be better for him if a millstone were put around his neck and he be thrown into the sea than for him to cause one of these little ones to sin.3Be on your guard! If your brother sins, rebuke him; and if he repents, forgive him.4And if he wrongs you seven times in one day and returns to you seven times saying, 'I am sorry,' you should forgive him."5And the apostles said to the Lord, "Increase our faith."6The Lord replied, "If you have faith the size of a mustard seed, you would say to (this) mulberry tree, 'Be uprooted and planted in the sea,' and it would obey you.7"Who among you would say to your servant who has just come in from plowing or tending sheep in the field, 'Come here immediately and take your place at table'?8Would he not rather say to him, 'Prepare something for me to eat. Put on your apron and wait on me while I eat and drink. You may eat and drink when I am finished'?9Is he grateful to that servant because he did what was commanded?10So should it be with you. When you have done all you have been commanded, say, 'We are unprofitable servants; we have done what we were obliged to do.'"11As he continued his journey to Jerusalem, he traveled through Samaria and Galilee.12As he was entering a village, ten lepers met (him). They stood at a distance from him13and raised their voice, saying, "Jesus, Master! Have pity on us!"14And when he saw them, he said, "Go show yourselves to the priests." As they were going they were cleansed.15And one of them, realizing he had been healed, returned, glorifying God in a loud voice;16and he fell at the feet of Jesus and thanked him. He was a Samaritan.17Jesus said in reply, "Ten were cleansed, were they not? Where are the other nine?18Has none but this foreigner returned to give thanks to God?"19Then he said to him, "Stand up and go; your faith has saved you."20Asked by the Pharisees when the kingdom of God would come, he said in reply, "The coming of the kingdom of God cannot be observed,21and no one will announce, 'Look, here it is,' or, 'There it is.' For behold, the kingdom of God is among you."22Then he said to his disciples, "The days will come when you will long to see one of the days of the Son of Man, but you will not see it.23There will be those who will say to you, 'Look, there he is,' (or) 'Look, here he is.' Do not go off, do not run in pursuit.24For just as lightning flashes and lights up the sky from one side to the other, so will the Son of Man be (in his day).25But first he must suffer greatly and be rejected by this generation.26As it was in the days of Noah, so it will be in the days of the Son of Man;27they were eating and drinking, marrying and giving in marriage up to the day that Noah entered the ark, and the flood came and destroyed them all.28Similarly, as it was in the days of Lot: they were eating, drinking, buying, selling, planting, building;29on the day when Lot left Sodom, fire and brimstone rained from the sky to destroy them all.30So it will be on the day the Son of Man is revealed.31On that day, a person who is on the housetop and whose belongings are in the house must not go down to get them, and likewise a person in the field must not return to what was left behind.32Remember the wife of Lot.33Whoever seeks to preserve his life will lose it, but whoever loses it will save it.34I tell you, on that night there will be two people in one bed; one will be taken, the other left.35And there will be two women grinding meal together; one will be taken, the other left."36 37They said to him in reply, "Where, Lord?" He said to them, "Where the body is, there also the vultures will gather."

Luke Chapter 18

1Then he told them a parable about the necessity for them to pray always without becoming weary. He said,2"There was a judge in a certain town who neither feared God nor respected any human being.3And a widow in that town used to come to him and say, 'Render a just decision for me against my adversary.'4For a long time the judge was unwilling, but eventually he thought, 'While it is true that I neither fear God nor respect any human being,5because this widow keeps bothering me I shall deliver a just decision for her lest she finally come and strike me.'"6The Lord said, "Pay attention to what the dishonest judge says.7Will not God then secure the rights of his chosen ones who call out to him day and night? Will he be slow to answer them?8I tell you, he will see to it that justice is done for them speedily. But when the Son of Man comes, will he find faith on earth?"9He then addressed this parable to those who were convinced of their own righteousness and despised everyone else.10"Two people went up to the temple area to pray; one was a Pharisee and the other was a tax collector.11The Pharisee took up his position and spoke this prayer to himself, 'O God, I thank you that I am not like the rest of humanity - greedy, dishonest, adulterous - or even like this tax collector.12I fast twice a week, and I pay tithes on my whole income.'13But the tax collector stood off at a distance and would not even raise his eyes to heaven but beat his breast and prayed, 'O God, be merciful to me a sinner.'14I tell you, the latter went home justified, not the former; for everyone who exalts himself will be humbled, and the one who humbles himself will be exalted."15People were bringing even infants to him that he might touch them, and when the disciples saw this, they rebuked them.16Jesus, however, called the children to himself and said, "Let the children come to me and do not prevent them; for the kingdom of God belongs to such as these.17Amen, I say to you, whoever does not accept the kingdom of God like a child will not enter it."18An official asked him this question, "Good teacher, what must I do to inherit eternal life?"19Jesus answered him, "Why do you call me good? No one is good but God alone.20You know the commandments, 'You shall not commit adultery; you shall not kill; you shall not steal; you shall not bear false witness; honor your father and your mother.'"21And he replied, "All of these I have observed from my youth."22When Jesus heard this he said to him, "There is still one thing left for you: sell all that you have and distribute it to the poor, and you will have a treasure in heaven. Then come, follow me."23But when he heard this he became quite sad, for he was very rich.24Jesus looked at him (now sad) and said, "How hard it is for those who have wealth to enter the kingdom of God!25For it is easier for a camel to pass through the eye of a needle than for a rich person to enter the kingdom of God."26Those who heard this said, "Then who can be saved?"27And he said, "What is impossible for human beings is possible for God."28Then Peter said, "We have given up our possessions and followed you."29He said to them, "Amen, I say to you, there is no one who has given up house or wife or brothers or parents or children for the sake of the kingdom of God30who will not receive (back) an overabundant return in this present age and eternal life in the age to come."31Then he took the Twelve aside and said to them, "Behold, we are going up to Jerusalem and everything written by the prophets about the Son of Man will be fulfilled.32He will be handed over to the Gentiles and he will be mocked and insulted and spat upon;33and after they have scourged him they will kill him, but on the third day he will rise."34But they understood nothing of this; the word remained hidden from them and they failed to comprehend what he said.35Now as he approached Jericho a blind man was sitting by the roadside begging,36and hearing a crowd going by, he inquired what was happening.37They told him, "Jesus of Nazareth is passing by."38He shouted, "Jesus, Son of David, have pity on me!"39The people walking in front rebuked him, telling him to be silent, but he kept calling out all the more, "Son of David, have pity on me!"40Then Jesus stopped and ordered that he be brought to him; and when he came near, Jesus asked him,41"What do you want me to do for you?" He replied, "Lord, please let me see."42Jesus told him, "Have sight; your faith has saved you."43He immediately received his sight and followed him, giving glory to God. When they saw this, all the people gave praise to God.

Luke Chapter 19

1He came to Jericho and intended to pass through the town.2Now a man there named Zacchaeus, who was a chief tax collector and also a wealthy man,3was seeking to see who Jesus was; but he could not see him because of the crowd, for he was short in stature.4So he ran ahead and climbed a sycamore tree in order to see Jesus, who was about to pass that way.5When he reached the place, Jesus looked up and said to him, "Zacchaeus, come down quickly, for today I must stay at your house."6And he came down quickly and received him with joy.7When they all saw this, they began to grumble, saying, "He has gone to stay at the house of a sinner."8But Zacchaeus stood there and said to the Lord, "Behold, half of my possessions, Lord, I shall give to the poor, and if I have extorted anything from anyone I shall repay it four times over."9And Jesus said to him, "Today salvation has come to this house because this man too is a descendant of Abraham.10For the Son of Man has come to seek and to save what was lost."11While they were listening to him speak, he proceeded to tell a parable because he was near Jerusalem and they thought that the kingdom of God would appear there immediately.12So he said, "A nobleman went off to a distant country to obtain the kingship for himself and then to return.13He called ten of his servants and gave them ten gold coins and told them, 'Engage in trade with these until I return.'14His fellow citizens, however, despised him and sent a delegation after him to announce,

'We do not want this man to be our king.'¹⁵But when he returned after obtaining the kingship, he had the servants called, to whom he had given the money, to learn what they had gained by trading.¹⁶The first came forward and said, 'Sir, your gold coin has earned ten additional ones.'¹⁷He replied, 'Well done, good servant! You have been faithful in this very small matter; take charge of ten cities.'¹⁸Then the second came and reported, 'Your gold coin, sir, has earned five more.'¹⁹And to this servant too he said, 'You, take charge of five cities.'²⁰Then the other servant came and said, 'Sir, here is your gold coin; I kept it stored away in a handkerchief,²¹for I was afraid of you, because you are a demanding person; you take up what you did not lay down and you harvest what you did not plant.'²²He said to him, 'With your own words I shall condemn you, you wicked servant. You knew I was a demanding person, taking up what I did not lay down and harvesting what I did not plant;²³why did you not put my money in a bank? Then on my return I would have collected it with interest.'²⁴And to those standing by he said, 'Take the gold coin from him and give it to the servant who has ten.'²⁵But they said to him, 'Sir, he has ten gold coins.'²⁶'I tell you, to everyone who has, more will be given, but from the one who has not, even what he has will be taken away.²⁷Now as for those enemies of mine who did not want me as their king, bring them here and slay them before me.'"²⁸After he had said this, he proceeded on his journey up to Jerusalem.²⁹As he drew near to Bethphage and Bethany at the place called the Mount of Olives, he sent two of his disciples.³⁰He said, "Go into the village opposite you, and as you enter it you will find a colt tethered on which no one has ever sat. Untie it and bring it here.³¹And if anyone should ask you, 'Why are you untying it?' you will answer, 'The Master has need of it.'"³²So those who had been sent went off and found everything just as he had told them.³³And as they were untying the colt, its owners said to them, "Why are you untying this colt?"³⁴They answered, "The Master has need of it."³⁵So they brought it to Jesus, threw their cloaks over the colt, and helped Jesus to mount.³⁶As he rode along, the people were spreading their cloaks on the road;³⁷and now as he was approaching the slope of the Mount of Olives, the whole multitude of his disciples began to praise God aloud with joy for all the mighty deeds they had seen.³⁸They proclaimed: "Blessed is the king who comes in the name of the Lord. Peace in heaven and glory in the highest."³⁹Some of the Pharisees in the crowd said to him, "Teacher, rebuke your disciples."⁴⁰He said in reply, "I tell you, if they keep silent, the stones will cry out!"⁴¹As he drew near, he saw the city and wept over it,⁴²saying, "If this day you only knew what makes for peace - but now it is hidden from your eyes.⁴³For the days are coming upon you when your enemies will raise a palisade against you; they will encircle you and hem you in on all sides.⁴⁴They will smash you to the ground and your children within you, and they will not leave one stone upon another within you because you did not recognize the time of your visitation."⁴⁵Then Jesus entered the temple area and proceeded to drive out those who were selling things,⁴⁶saying to them, "It is written, 'My house shall be a house of prayer, but you have made it a den of thieves.'"⁴⁷And every day he was teaching in the temple area. The chief priests, the scribes, and the leaders of the people, meanwhile, were seeking to put him to death,⁴⁸but they could find no way to accomplish their purpose because all the people were hanging on his words.

Luke Chapter 20

¹One day as he was teaching the people in the temple area and proclaiming the good news, the chief priests and scribes, together with the elders, approached him²and said to him, "Tell us, by what authority are you doing these things? Or who is the one who gave you this authority?"³He said to them in reply, "I shall ask you a question. Tell me,⁴was John's baptism of heavenly or of human origin?"⁵They discussed this among themselves, and said, "If we say, 'Of heavenly origin,' he will say, 'Why did you not believe him?'⁶But if we say, 'Of human origin,' then all the people will stone us, for they are convinced that John was a prophet.'⁷So they answered that they did not know from where it came.⁸Then Jesus said to them, "Neither shall I tell you by what authority I do these things."⁹Then he proceeded to tell the people this parable. "(A) man planted a vineyard, leased it to tenant farmers, and then went on a journey for a long time.¹⁰At harvest time he sent a servant to the tenant farmers to receive some of the produce of the vineyard. But they beat the servant and sent him away empty-handed.¹¹So he proceeded to send another servant, but him also they beat and insulted and sent away empty-handed.¹²Then he proceeded to send a third, but this one too they wounded and threw out.¹³The owner of the vineyard said, 'What shall I do? I shall send my beloved son; maybe they will respect him.'¹⁴But when the tenant farmers saw him they said to one another, 'This is the heir. Let us kill him that the inheritance may become ours.'¹⁵So they threw him out of the vineyard

and killed him. What will the owner of the vineyard do to them?¹⁶He will come and put those tenant farmers to death and turn over the vineyard to others." When the people heard this, they exclaimed, "Let it not be so!"¹⁷But he looked at them and asked, "What then does this scripture passage mean: 'The stone which the builders rejected has become the cornerstone'?¹⁸Everyone who falls on that stone will be dashed to pieces; and it will crush anyone on whom it falls."¹⁹The scribes and chief priests sought to lay their hands on him at that very hour, but they feared the people, for they knew that he had addressed this parable to them.²⁰They watched him closely and sent agents pretending to be righteous who were to trap him in speech, in order to hand him over to the authority and power of the governor.²¹They posed this question to him, "Teacher, we know that what you say and teach is correct, and you show no partiality, but teach the way of God in accordance with the truth.²²Is it lawful for us to pay tribute to Caesar or not?" ²³Recognizing their craftiness he said to them,²⁴"Show me a denarius; whose image and name does it bear?" They replied, "Caesar's."²⁵So he said to them, "Then repay to Caesar what belongs to Caesar and to God what belongs to God."²⁶They were unable to trap him by something he might say before the people, and so amazed were they at his reply that they fell silent.²⁷Some Sadducees, those who deny that there is a resurrection, came forward and put this question to him,²⁸saying, "Teacher, Moses wrote for us, 'If someone's brother dies leaving a wife but no child, his brother must take the wife and raise up descendants for his brother.'²⁹Now there were seven brothers; the first married a woman but died childless.³⁰Then the second³¹and the third married her, and likewise all the seven died childless.³²Finally the woman also died.³³Now at the resurrection whose wife will that woman be? For all seven had been married to her."³⁴Jesus said to them, "The children of this age marry and remarry;³⁵but those who are deemed worthy to attain to the coming age and to the resurrection of the dead neither marry nor are given in marriage.³⁶They can no longer die, for they are like angels; and they are the children of God because they are the ones who will rise. ³⁷That the dead will rise even Moses made known in the passage about the bush, when he called 'Lord' the God of Abraham, the God of Isaac, and the God of Jacob;³⁸and he is not God of the dead, but of the living, for to him all are alive."³⁹Some of the scribes said in reply, "Teacher, you have answered well."⁴⁰And they no longer dared to ask him anything.⁴¹Then he said to them, "How do they claim that the Messiah is the Son of David?⁴²For David himself in the Book of Psalms says: 'The Lord said to my lord, "Sit at my right hand⁴³till I make your enemies your footstool."'⁴⁴Now if David calls him 'lord,' how can he be his son?"⁴⁵Then, within the hearing of all the people, he said to (his) disciples,⁴⁶"Be on guard against the scribes, who like to go around in long robes and love greetings in marketplaces, seats of honor in synagogues, and places of honor at banquets.⁴⁷They devour the houses of widows and, as a pretext, recite lengthy prayers. They will receive a very severe condemnation."

Luke Chapter 21

¹When he looked up he saw some wealthy people putting their offerings into the treasury²and he noticed a poor widow putting in two small coins.³He said, "I tell you truly, this poor widow put in more than all the rest;⁴for those others have all made offerings from their surplus wealth, but she, from her poverty, has offered her whole livelihood."⁵While some people were speaking about how the temple was adorned with costly stones and votive offerings, he said,⁶"All that you see here - the days will come when there will not be left a stone upon another stone that will not be thrown down."⁷Then they asked him, "Teacher, when will this happen? And what sign will there be when all these things are about to happen?"⁸He answered, "See that you not be deceived, for many will come in my name, saying, 'I am he,' and 'The time has come.' Do not follow them!⁹When you hear of wars and insurrections, do not be terrified; for such things must happen first, but it will not immediately be the end."¹⁰Then he said to them, "Nation will rise against nation, and kingdom against kingdom.¹¹There will be powerful earthquakes, famines, and plagues from place to place; and awesome sights and mighty signs will come from the sky.¹²"Before all this happens, however, they will seize and persecute you, they will hand you over to the synagogues and to prisons, and they will have you led before kings and governors because of my name.¹³It will lead to your giving testimony.¹⁴Remember, you are not to prepare your defense beforehand,¹⁵for I myself shall give you a wisdom in speaking that all your adversaries will be powerless to resist or refute.¹⁶You will even be handed over by parents, brothers, relatives, and friends, and they will put some of you to death.¹⁷You will be hated by all because of my name,¹⁸but not a hair on your head will be destroyed.¹⁹By your perseverance you will secure your lives.²⁰"When you see Jerusalem

surrounded by armies, know that its desolation is at hand. [21]Then those in Judea must flee to the mountains. Let those within the city escape from it, and let those in the countryside not enter the city, [22]for these days are the time of punishment when all the scriptures are fulfilled. [23]Woe to pregnant women and nursing mothers in those days, for a terrible calamity will come upon the earth and a wrathful judgment upon this people. [24]They will fall by the edge of the sword and be taken as captives to all the Gentiles; and Jerusalem will be trampled underfoot by the Gentiles until the times of the Gentiles are fulfilled. [25]"There will be signs in the sun, the moon, and the stars, and on earth nations will be in dismay, perplexed by the roaring of the sea and the waves. [26]People will die of fright in anticipation of what is coming upon the world, for the powers of the heavens will be shaken. [27]And then they will see the Son of Man coming in a cloud with power and great glory. [28]But when these signs begin to happen, stand erect and raise your heads because your redemption is at hand." [29]He taught them a lesson. "Consider the fig tree and all the other trees. [30]When their buds burst open, you see for yourselves and know that summer is now near; [31]in the same way, when you see these things happening, know that the kingdom of God is near. [32]Amen, I say to you, this generation will not pass away until all these things have taken place. [33]Heaven and earth will pass away, but my words will not pass away. [34]"Beware that your hearts do not become drowsy from carousing and drunkenness and the anxieties of daily life, and that day catch you by surprise [35]like a trap. For that day will assault everyone who lives on the face of the earth. [36]Be vigilant at all times and pray that you have the strength to escape the tribulations that are imminent and to stand before the Son of Man." [37]During the day, Jesus was teaching in the temple area, but at night he would leave and stay at the place called the Mount of Olives. [38]And all the people would get up early each morning to listen to him in the temple area.

Luke Chapter 22

[1]Now the feast of Unleavened Bread, called the Passover, was drawing near, [2]and the chief priests and the scribes were seeking a way to put him to death, for they were afraid of the people. [3]Then Satan entered into Judas, the one surnamed Iscariot, who was counted among the Twelve, [4]and he went to the chief priests and temple guards to discuss a plan for handing him over to them. [5]They were pleased and agreed to pay him money. [6]He accepted their offer and sought a favorable opportunity to hand him over to them in the absence of a crowd. [7]When the day of the Feast of Unleavened Bread arrived, the day for sacrificing the Passover lamb, [8]he sent out Peter and John, instructing them, "Go and make preparations for us to eat the Passover." [9]They asked him, "Where do you want us to make the preparations?" [10]And he answered them, "When you go into the city, a man will meet you carrying a jar of water. Follow him into the house that he enters [11]and say to the master of the house, 'The teacher says to you, "Where is the guest room where I may eat the Passover with my disciples?"' [12]He will show you a large upper room that is furnished. Make the preparations there." [13]Then they went off and found everything exactly as he had told them, and there they prepared the Passover. [14]When the hour came, he took his place at table with the apostles. [15]He said to them, "I have eagerly desired to eat this Passover with you before I suffer, [16]for, I tell you, I shall not eat it (again) until there is fulfillment in the kingdom of God." [17]Then he took a cup, gave thanks, and said, "Take this and share it among yourselves; [18]for I tell you (that) from this time on I shall not drink of the fruit of the vine until the kingdom of God comes." [19]Then he took the bread, said the blessing, broke it, and gave it to them, saying, "This is my body, which will be given for you; do this in memory of me." [20]And likewise the cup after they had eaten, saying, "This cup is the new covenant in my blood, which will be shed for you. [21]"And yet behold, the hand of the one who is to betray me is with me on the table; [22]for the Son of Man indeed goes as it has been determined; but woe to that man by whom he is betrayed." [23]And they began to debate among themselves who among them would do such a deed. [24]Then an argument broke out among them about which of them should be regarded as the greatest. [25]He said to them, "The kings of the Gentiles lord it over them and those in authority over them are addressed as 'Benefactors'; [26]but among you it shall not be so. Rather, let the greatest among you be as the youngest, and the leader as the servant. [27]For who is greater: the one seated at table or the one who serves? Is it not the one seated at table? I am among you as the one who serves. [28]It is you who have stood by me in my trials; [29]and I confer a kingdom on you, just as my Father has conferred one on me, [30]that you may eat and drink at my table in my kingdom; and you will sit on thrones judging the twelve tribes of Israel. [31]"Simon, Simon, behold Satan has demanded to sift all of you like wheat, [32]but I have prayed that your own faith may not fail; and once you have turned back, you must strengthen your brothers." [33]He said to him, "Lord, I am prepared to go to prison and to die with you." [34]But he replied, "I tell you, Peter, before the cock crows this day, you will deny three times that you know me." [35]He said to them, "When I sent you forth without a money bag or a sack or sandals, were you in need of anything?" "No, nothing," they replied. [36]He said to them, "But now one who has a money bag should take it, and likewise a sack, and one who does not have a sword should sell his cloak and buy one. [37]For I tell you that this scripture must be fulfilled in me, namely, 'He was counted among the wicked'; and indeed what is written about me is coming to fulfillment." [38]Then they said, "Lord, look, there are two swords here." But he replied, "It is enough!" [39]Then going out he went, as was his custom, to the Mount of Olives, and the disciples followed him. [40]When he arrived at the place he said to them, "Pray that you may not undergo the test." [41]After withdrawing about a stone's throw from them and kneeling, he prayed, [42]saying, "Father, if you are willing, take this cup away from me; still, not my will but yours be done." [43](And to strengthen him an angel from heaven appeared to him. [44]He was in such agony and he prayed so fervently that his sweat became like drops of blood falling on the ground.) [45]When he rose from prayer and returned to his disciples, he found them sleeping from grief. [46]He said to them, "Why are you sleeping? Get up and pray that you may not undergo the test." [47]While he was still speaking, a crowd approached and in front was one of the Twelve, a man named Judas. He went up to Jesus to kiss him. [48]Jesus said to him, "Judas, are you betraying the Son of Man with a kiss?" [49]His disciples realized what was about to happen, and they asked, "Lord, shall we strike with a sword?" [50]And one of them struck the high priest's servant and cut off his right ear. [51]But Jesus said in reply, "Stop, no more of this!" Then he touched the servant's ear and healed him. [52]And Jesus said to the chief priests and temple guards and elders who had come for him, "Have you come out as against a robber, with swords and clubs? [53]Day after day I was with you in the temple area, and you did not seize me; but this is your hour, the time for the power of darkness." [54]After arresting him they led him away and took him into the house of the high priest; Peter was following at a distance. [55]They lit a fire in the middle of the courtyard and sat around it, and Peter sat down with them. [56]When a maid saw him seated in the light, she looked intently at him and said, "This man too was with him." [57]But he denied it saying, "Woman, I do not know him." [58]A short while later someone else saw him and said, "You too are one of them"; but Peter answered, "My friend, I am not." [59]About an hour later, still another insisted, "Assuredly, this man too was with him, for he also is a Galilean." [60]But Peter said, "My friend, I do not know what you are talking about." Just as he was saying this, the cock crowed, [61]and the Lord turned and looked at Peter; and Peter remembered the word of the Lord, how he had said to him, "Before the cock crows today, you will deny me three times." [62]He went out and began to weep bitterly. [63]The men who held Jesus in custody were ridiculing and beating him. [64]They blindfolded him and questioned him, saying, "Prophesy! Who is it that struck you?" [65]And they reviled him in saying many other things against him. [66]When day came the council of elders of the people met, both chief priests and scribes, and they brought him before their Sanhedrin. [67]They said, "If you are the Messiah, tell us," but he replied to them, "If I tell you, you will not believe, [68]and if I question, you will not respond. [69]But from this time on the Son of Man will be seated at the right hand of the power of God." [70]They all asked, "Are you then the Son of God?" He replied to them, "You say that I am." [71]Then they said, "What further need have we for testimony? We have heard it from his own mouth."

Luke Chapter 23

[1]Then the whole assembly of them arose and brought him before Pilate. [2]They brought charges against him, saying, "We found this man misleading our people; he opposes the payment of taxes to Caesar and maintains that he is the Messiah, a king." [3]Pilate asked him, "Are you the king of the Jews?" He said to him in reply, "You say so." [4]Pilate then addressed the chief priests and the crowds, "I find this man not guilty." [5]But they were adamant and said, "He is inciting the people with his teaching throughout all Judea, from Galilee where he began even to here." [6]On hearing this Pilate asked if the man was a Galilean; [7]and upon learning that he was under Herod's jurisdiction, he sent him to Herod who was in Jerusalem at that time. [8]Herod was very glad to see Jesus; he had been wanting to see him for a long time, for he had heard about him and had been hoping to see him perform some sign. [9]He questioned him at length, but he gave him no answer. [10]The chief priests and scribes, meanwhile, stood by accusing him harshly. [11](Even) Herod and his soldiers treated him contemptuously and mocked him, and after clothing him in resplendent garb, he sent him back to

Pilate.¹²Herod and Pilate became friends that very day, even though they had been enemies formerly.¹³Pilate then summoned the chief priests, the rulers, and the people¹⁴and said to them, "You brought this man to me and accused him of inciting the people to revolt. I have conducted my investigation in your presence and have not found this man guilty of the charges you have brought against him,¹⁵nor did Herod, for he sent him back to us. So no capital crime has been committed by him.¹⁶Therefore I shall have him flogged and then release him."¹⁷Now he had to release one prisoner to them at the feast.¹⁸But all together they shouted out, "Away with this man! Release Barabbas to us."¹⁹(Now Barabbas had been imprisoned for a rebellion that had taken place in the city and for murder.)²⁰Again Pilate addressed them, still wishing to release Jesus,²¹but they continued their shouting, "Crucify him! Crucify him!"²²Pilate addressed them a third time, "What evil has this man done? I found him guilty of no capital crime. Therefore I shall have him flogged and then release him."²³With loud shouts, however, they persisted in calling for his crucifixion, and their voices prevailed.²⁴The verdict of Pilate was that their demand should be granted.²⁵So he released the man who had been imprisoned for rebellion and murder, for whom they asked, and he handed Jesus over to them to deal with as they wished.²⁶As they led him away they took hold of a certain Simon, a Cyrenian, who was coming in from the country; and after laying the cross on him, they made him carry it behind Jesus.²⁷A large crowd of people followed Jesus, including many women who mourned and lamented him.²⁸Jesus turned to them and said, "Daughters of Jerusalem, do not weep for me; weep instead for yourselves and for your children,²⁹for indeed, the days are coming when people will say, 'Blessed are the barren, the wombs that never bore and the breasts that never nursed.'³⁰At that time people will say to the mountains, 'Fall upon us!' and to the hills, 'Cover us!'³¹for if these things are done when the wood is green what will happen when it is dry?"³²Now two others, both criminals, were led away with him to be executed.³³When they came to the place called the Skull, they crucified him and the criminals there, one on his right, the other on his left.³⁴[Then Jesus said, "Father, forgive them, they know not what they do."] They divided his garments by casting lots.³⁵The people stood by and watched; the rulers, meanwhile, sneered at him and said, "He saved others, let him save himself if he is the chosen one, the Messiah of God."³⁶Even the soldiers jeered at him. As they approached to offer him wine³⁷they called out, "If you are King of the Jews, save yourself."³⁸Above him there was an inscription that read, "This is the King of the Jews."³⁹Now one of the criminals hanging there reviled Jesus, saying, "Are you not the Messiah? Save yourself and us."⁴⁰The other, however, rebuking him, said in reply, "Have you no fear of God, for you are subject to the same condemnation?⁴¹And indeed, we have been condemned justly, for the sentence we received corresponds to our crimes, but this man has done nothing criminal."⁴²Then he said, "Jesus, remember me when you come into your kingdom."⁴³He replied to him, "Amen, I say to you, today you will be with me in Paradise."⁴⁴It was now about noon and darkness came over the whole land until three in the afternoon⁴⁵because of an eclipse of the sun. Then the veil of the temple was torn down the middle.⁴⁶Jesus cried out in a loud voice, "Father, into your hands I commend my spirit"; and when he had said this he breathed his last.⁴⁷The centurion who witnessed what had happened glorified God and said, "This man was innocent beyond doubt."⁴⁸When all the people who had gathered for this spectacle saw what had happened, they returned home beating their breasts;⁴⁹but all his acquaintances stood at a distance, including the women who had followed him from Galilee and saw these events.⁵⁰Now there was a virtuous and righteous man named Joseph who, though he was a member of the council,⁵¹had not consented to their plan of action. He came from the Jewish town of Arimathea and was awaiting the kingdom of God.⁵²He went to Pilate and asked for the body of Jesus.⁵³After he had taken the body down, he wrapped it in a linen cloth and laid him in a rock-hewn tomb in which no one had yet been buried.⁵⁴It was the day of preparation, and the sabbath was about to begin.⁵⁵The women who had come from Galilee with him followed behind, and when they had seen the tomb and the way in which his body was laid in it,⁵⁶they returned and prepared spices and perfumed oils. Then they rested on the sabbath according to the commandment.

Luke Chapter 24

¹But at daybreak on the first day of the week they took the spices they had prepared and went to the tomb.²They found the stone rolled away from the tomb;³but when they entered, they did not find the body of the Lord Jesus.⁴While they were puzzling over this, behold, two men in dazzling garments appeared to them.⁵They were terrified and bowed their faces to the ground. They said to them, "Why do you seek the living one among the dead?⁶He is not here, but he has been raised. Remember what he said to you while he was still in Galilee,⁷that the Son of Man must be handed over to sinners and be crucified, and rise on the third day."⁸And they remembered his words.⁹Then they returned from the tomb and announced all these things to the eleven and to all the others.¹⁰The women were Mary Magdalene, Joanna, and Mary the mother of James; the others who accompanied them also told this to the apostles,¹¹but their story seemed like nonsense and they did not believe them.¹²But Peter got up and ran to the tomb, bent down, and saw the burial cloths alone; then he went home amazed at what had happened.¹³Now that very day two of them were going to a village seven miles from Jerusalem called Emmaus,¹⁴and they were conversing about all the things that had occurred.¹⁵And it happened that while they were conversing and debating, Jesus himself drew near and walked with them,¹⁶but their eyes were prevented from recognizing him.¹⁷He asked them, "What are you discussing as you walk along?" They stopped, looking downcast.¹⁸One of them, named Cleopas, said to him in reply, "Are you the only visitor to Jerusalem who does not know of the things that have taken place there in these days?"¹⁹And he replied to them, "What sort of things?" They said to him, "The things that happened to Jesus the Nazarene, who was a prophet mighty in deed and word before God and all the people,²⁰how our chief priests and rulers both handed him over to a sentence of death and crucified him.²¹But we were hoping that he would be the one to redeem Israel; and besides all this, it is now the third day since this took place.²²Some women from our group, however, have astounded us: they were at the tomb early in the morning²³and did not find his body; they came back and reported that they had indeed seen a vision of angels who announced that he was alive.²⁴Then some of those with us went to the tomb and found things just as the women had described, but him they did not see."²⁵And he said to them, "Oh, how foolish you are! How slow of heart to believe all that the prophets spoke!²⁶Was it not necessary that the Messiah should suffer these things and enter into his glory?"²⁷Then beginning with Moses and all the prophets, he interpreted to them what referred to him in all the scriptures.²⁸As they approached the village to which they were going, he gave the impression that he was going on farther.²⁹But they urged him, "Stay with us, for it is nearly evening and the day is almost over." So he went in to stay with them.³⁰And it happened that, while he was with them at table, he took bread, said the blessing, broke it, and gave it to them.³¹With that their eyes were opened and they recognized him, but he vanished from their sight.³²Then they said to each other, "Were not our hearts burning (within us) while he spoke to us on the way and opened the scriptures to us?"³³So they set out at once and returned to Jerusalem where they found gathered together the eleven and those with them³⁴who were saying, "The Lord has truly been raised and has appeared to Simon!"³⁵Then the two recounted what had taken place on the way and how he was made known to them in the breaking of the bread.³⁶While they were still speaking about this, he stood in their midst and said to them, "Peace be with you."³⁷But they were startled and terrified and thought that they were seeing a ghost.³⁸Then he said to them, "Why are you troubled? And why do questions arise in your hearts?³⁹Look at my hands and my feet, that it is I myself. Touch me and see, because a ghost does not have flesh and bones as you can see I have."⁴⁰And as he said this, he showed them his hands and his feet.⁴¹While they were still incredulous for joy and were amazed, he asked them, "Have you anything here to eat?"⁴²They gave him a piece of baked fish;⁴³he took it and ate it in front of them.⁴⁴He said to them, "These are my words that I spoke to you while I was still with you, that everything written about me in the law of Moses and in the prophets and psalms must be fulfilled."⁴⁵Then he opened their minds to understand the scriptures.⁴⁶And he said to them, "Thus it is written that the Messiah would suffer and rise from the dead on the third day⁴⁷and that repentance, for the forgiveness of sins, would be preached in his name to all the nations, beginning from Jerusalem.⁴⁸You are witnesses of these things.⁴⁹And (behold) I am sending the promise of my Father upon you; but stay in the city until you are clothed with power from on high."⁵⁰Then he led them (out) as far as Bethany, raised his hands, and blessed them.⁵¹As he blessed them he parted from them and was taken up to heaven.⁵²They did him homage and then returned to Jerusalem with great joy,⁵³and they were continually in the temple praising God.

John

John Chapter 1

¹In the beginning was the Word, and the Word was with God, and the Word was God.²He was in the beginning with God.³All things came to

be through him, and without him nothing came to be. What came to be⁴through him was life, and this life was the light of the human race;⁵the light shines in the darkness, and the darkness has not overcome it.⁶A man named John was sent from God.⁷He came for testimony, to testify to the light, so that all might believe through him.⁸He was not the light, but came to testify to the light.⁹The true light, which enlightens everyone, was coming into the world.¹⁰He was in the world, and the world came to be through him, but the world did not know him.¹¹He came to what was his own, but his own people did not accept him.¹²But to those who did accept him he gave power to become children of God, to those who believe in his name,¹³who were born not by natural generation nor by human choice nor by a man's decision but of God.¹⁴And the Word became flesh and made his dwelling among us, and we saw his glory, the glory as of the Father's only Son, full of grace and truth.¹⁵John testified to him and cried out, saying, "This is he of whom I said, 'The one who is coming after me ranks ahead of me because he existed before me.'"¹⁶From his fullness we have all received, grace in place of grace,¹⁷because while the law was given through Moses, grace and truth came through Jesus Christ.¹⁸No one has ever seen God. The only Son, God, who is at the Father's side, has revealed him.¹⁹And this is the testimony of John. When the Jews from Jerusalem sent priests and Levites (to him) to ask him, "Who are you?"²⁰he admitted and did not deny it, but admitted, "I am not the Messiah."²¹So they asked him, "What are you then? Are you Elijah?" And he said, "I am not." "Are you the Prophet?" He answered, "No."²²So they said to him, "Who are you, so we can give an answer to those who sent us? What do you have to say for yourself?"²³He said: "I am 'the voice of one crying out in the desert, "Make straight the way of the Lord,"' as Isaiah the prophet said."²⁴Some Pharisees were also sent.²⁵They asked him, "Why then do you baptize if you are not the Messiah or Elijah or the Prophet?"²⁶John answered them, "I baptize with water; but there is one among you whom you do not recognize,²⁷the one who is coming after me, whose sandal strap I am not worthy to untie."²⁸This happened in Bethany across the Jordan, where John was baptizing.²⁹The next day he saw Jesus coming toward him and said, "Behold, the Lamb of God, who takes away the sin of the world.³⁰He is the one of whom I said, 'A man is coming after me who ranks ahead of me because he existed before me.'³¹I did not know him, but the reason why I came baptizing with water was that he might be made known to Israel."³²John testified further, saying, "I saw the Spirit come down like a dove from the sky and remain upon him.³³I did not know him, but the one who sent me to baptize with water told me, 'On whomever you see the Spirit come down and remain, he is the one who will baptize with the holy Spirit.'³⁴Now I have seen and testified that he is the Son of God."³⁵The next day John was there again with two of his disciples,³⁶and as he watched Jesus walk by, he said, "Behold, the Lamb of God."³⁷The two disciples heard what he said and followed Jesus.³⁸Jesus turned and saw them following him and said to them, "What are you looking for?" They said to him, "Rabbi" (which translated means Teacher), "where are you staying?"³⁹He said to them,"Come, and you will see." So they went and saw where he was staying, and they stayed with him that day. It was about four in the afternoon.⁴⁰Andrew, the brother of Simon Peter, was one of the two who heard John and followed Jesus.⁴¹He first found his own brother Simon and told him, "We have found the Messiah" (which is translated Anointed).⁴²Then he brought him to Jesus. Jesus looked at him and said, "You are Simon the son of John; you will be called Kephas" (which is translated Peter).⁴³The next day he decided to go to Galilee, and he found Philip. And Jesus said to him, "Follow me."⁴⁴Now Philip was from Bethsaida, the town of Andrew and Peter.⁴⁵Philip found Nathanael and told him, "We have found the one about whom Moses wrote in the law, and also the prophets, Jesus, son of Joseph, from Nazareth."⁴⁶But Nathanael said to him, "Can anything good come from Nazareth?" Philip said to him, "Come and see."⁴⁷Jesus saw Nathanael coming toward him and said of him, "Here is a true Israelite. There is no duplicity in him."⁴⁸Nathanael said to him, "How do you know me?" Jesus answered and said to him, "Before Philip called you, I saw you under the fig tree."⁴⁹Nathanael answered him, "Rabbi, you are the Son of God; you are the King of Israel."⁵⁰Jesus answered and said to him, "Do you believe because I told you that I saw you under the fig tree? You will see greater things than this."⁵¹And he said to him, "Amen, amen, I say to you, you will see the sky opened and the angels of God ascending and descending on the Son of Man."

John Chapter 2

¹On the third day there was a wedding in Cana in Galilee, and the mother of Jesus was there.²Jesus and his disciples were also invited to the wedding.³When the wine ran short, the mother of Jesus said to him, "They have no wine."⁴(And) Jesus said to her, "Woman, how does your concern affect me? My hour has not yet come."⁵His mother said to the servers, "Do whatever he tells you."⁶Now there were six stone water jars there for Jewish ceremonial washings, each holding twenty to thirty gallons.⁷Jesus told them, "Fill the jars with water." So they filled them to the brim.⁸Then he told them, "Draw some out now and take it to the headwaiter." So they took it.⁹And when the headwaiter tasted the water that had become wine, without knowing where it came from (although the servers who had drawn the water knew), the headwaiter called the bridegroom¹⁰and said to him, "Everyone serves good wine first, and then when people have drunk freely, an inferior one; but you have kept the good wine until now."¹¹Jesus did this as the beginning of his signs in Cana in Galilee and so revealed his glory, and his disciples began to believe in him.¹²After this, he and his mother, (his) brothers, and his disciples went down to Capernaum and stayed there only a few days.¹³Since the Passover of the Jews was near, Jesus went up to Jerusalem.¹⁴He found in the temple area those who sold oxen, sheep, and doves, as well as the money-changers seated there.¹⁵He made a whip out of cords and drove them all out of the temple area, with the sheep and oxen, and spilled the coins of the money-changers and overturned their tables,¹⁶and to those who sold doves he said, "Take these out of here, and stop making my Father's house a marketplace."¹⁷His disciples recalled the words of scripture, "Zeal for your house will consume me."¹⁸At this the Jews answered and said to him, "What sign can you show us for doing this?"¹⁹Jesus answered and said to them, "Destroy this temple and in three days I will raise it up."²⁰The Jews said, "This temple has been under construction for forty-six years, and you will raise it up in three days?"²¹But he was speaking about the temple of his body.²²Therefore, when he was raised from the dead, his disciples remembered that he had said this, and they came to believe the scripture and the word Jesus had spoken.²³While he was in Jerusalem for the feast of Passover, many began to believe in his name when they saw the signs he was doing.²⁴But Jesus would not trust himself to them because he knew them all,²⁵and did not need anyone to testify about human nature. He himself understood it well.

John Chapter 3

¹Now there was a Pharisee named Nicodemus, a ruler of the Jews.²He came to Jesus at night and said to him, "Rabbi, we know that you are a teacher who has come from God, for no one can do these signs that you are doing unless God is with him."³Jesus answered and said to him, "Amen, amen, I say to you, no one can see the kingdom of God without being born from above."⁴Nicodemus said to him, "How can a person once grown old be born again? Surely he cannot reenter his mother's womb and be born again, can he?"⁵Jesus answered, "Amen, amen, I say to you, no one can enter the kingdom of God without being born of water and Spirit.⁶What is born of flesh is flesh and what is born of spirit is spirit.⁷Do not be amazed that I told you, 'You must be born from above.'⁸The wind blows where it wills, and you can hear the sound it makes, but you do not know where it comes from or where it goes; so it is with everyone who is born of the Spirit.⁹Nicodemus answered and said to him, "How can this happen?"¹⁰Jesus answered and said to him, "You are the teacher of Israel and you do not understand this?¹¹Amen, amen, I say to you, we speak of what we know and we testify to what we have seen, but you people do not accept our testimony.¹²If I tell you about earthly things and you do not believe, how will you believe if I tell you about heavenly things?¹³No one has gone up to heaven except the one who has come down from heaven, the Son of Man.¹⁴And just as Moses lifted up the serpent in the desert, so must the Son of Man be lifted up,¹⁵so that everyone who believes in him may have eternal life."¹⁶For God so loved the world that he gave his only Son, so that everyone who believes in him might not perish but might have eternal life.¹⁷For God did not send his Son into the world to condemn the world, but that the world might be saved through him.¹⁸Whoever believes in him will not be condemned, but whoever does not believe has already been condemned, because he has not believed in the name of the only Son of God.¹⁹And this is the verdict, that the light came into the world, but people preferred darkness to light, because their works were evil.²⁰For everyone who does wicked things hates the light and does not come toward the light, so that his works might not be exposed.²¹But whoever lives the truth comes to the light, so that his works may be clearly seen as done in God.²²After this, Jesus and his disciples went into the region of Judea, where he spent some time with them baptizing.²³John was also baptizing in Aenon near Salim, because there was an abundance of water there, and people came to be baptized,²⁴for John had not yet been imprisoned.²⁵Now a dispute arose between the disciples of John and a Jew about ceremonial washings.²⁶So they came to John and said to him, "Rabbi, the one who was with you across the Jordan, to whom you testified, here he is baptizing and everyone is coming to him."²⁷John answered and said,

"No one can receive anything except what has been given him from heaven.[28]You yourselves can testify that I said (that) I am not the Messiah, but that I was sent before him.[29]The one who has the bride is the bridegroom; the best man, who stands and listens for him, rejoices greatly at the bridegroom's voice. So this joy of mine has been made complete.[30]He must increase; I must decrease."[31]The one who comes from above is above all. The one who is of the earth is earthly and speaks of earthly things. But the one who comes from heaven (is above all).[32]He testifies to what he has seen and heard, but no one accepts his testimony.[33]Whoever does accept his testimony certifies that God is trustworthy.[34]For the one whom God sent speaks the words of God. He does not ration his gift of the Spirit.[35]The Father loves the Son and has given everything over to him.[36]Whoever believes in the Son has eternal life, but whoever disobeys the Son will not see life, but the wrath of God remains upon him.

John Chapter 4

[1]Now when Jesus learned that the Pharisees had heard that Jesus was making and baptizing more disciples than John[2](although Jesus himself was not baptizing, just his disciples),[3]he left Judea and returned to Galilee.[4]He had to pass through Samaria.[5]So he came to a town of Samaria called Sychar, near the plot of land that Jacob had given to his son Joseph.[6]Jacob's well was there. Jesus, tired from his journey, sat down there at the well. It was about noon.[7]A woman of Samaria came to draw water. Jesus said to her, "Give me a drink."[8]His disciples had gone into the town to buy food.[9]The Samaritan woman said to him, "How can you, a Jew, ask me, a Samaritan woman, for a drink?" (For Jews use nothing in common with Samaritans.)[10]Jesus answered and said to her, "If you knew the gift of God and who is saying to you, 'Give me a drink,' you would have asked him and he would have given you living water."[11](The woman) said to him, "Sir, you do not even have a bucket and the cistern is deep; where then can you get this living water?[12]Are you greater than our father Jacob, who gave us this cistern and drank from it himself with his children and his flocks?[13]Jesus answered and said to her, "Everyone who drinks this water will be thirsty again;[14]but whoever drinks the water I shall give will never thirst; the water I shall give will become in him a spring of water welling up to eternal life."[15]The woman said to him, "Sir, give me this water, so that I may not be thirsty or have to keep coming here to draw water."[16]Jesus said to her, "Go call your husband and come back."[17]The woman answered and said to him, "I do not have a husband." Jesus answered her, "You are right in saying, 'I do not have a husband.'[18]For you have had five husbands, and the one you have now is not your husband. What you have said is true."[19]The woman said to him, "Sir, I can see that you are a prophet.[20]Our ancestors worshiped on this mountain; but you people say that the place to worship is in Jerusalem."[21]Jesus said to her, "Believe me, woman, the hour is coming when you will worship the Father neither on this mountain nor in Jerusalem.[22]You people worship what you do not understand; we worship what we understand, because salvation is from the Jews.[23]But the hour is coming, and is now here, when true worshipers will worship the Father in Spirit and truth; and indeed the Father seeks such people to worship him.[24]God is Spirit, and those who worship him must worship in Spirit and truth."[25]The woman said to him, "I know that the Messiah is coming, the one called the Anointed; when he comes, he will tell us everything."[26]Jesus said to her, "I am he, the one who is speaking with you."[27]At that moment his disciples returned, and were amazed that he was talking with a woman, but still no one said, "What are you looking for?" or "Why are you talking with her?"[28]The woman left her water jar and went into the town and said to the people,[29]"Come see a man who told me everything I have done. Could he possibly be the Messiah?"[30]They went out of the town and came to him.[31]Meanwhile, the disciples urged him, "Rabbi, eat."[32]But he said to them, "I have food to eat of which you do not know."[33]So the disciples said to one another, "Could someone have brought him something to eat?"[34]Jesus said to them, "My food is to do the will of the one who sent me and to finish his work.[35]Do you not say, 'In four months the harvest will be here'? I tell you, look up and see the fields ripe for the harvest.[36]The reaper is already receiving his payment and gathering crops for eternal life, so that the sower and reaper can rejoice together.[37]For here the saying is verified that 'One sows and another reaps.'[38]I sent you to reap what you have not worked for; others have done the work, and you are sharing the fruits of their work."[39]Many of the Samaritans of that town began to believe in him because of the word of the woman who testified, "He told me everything I have done."[40]When the Samaritans came to him, they invited him to stay with them; and he stayed there two days.[41]Many more began to believe in him because of his word,[42]and they said to the woman, "We no longer believe because of your word; for we have heard for ourselves,

and we know that this is truly the savior of the world."[43]After the two days, he left there for Galilee.[44]For Jesus himself testified that a prophet has no honor in his native place.[45]When he came into Galilee, the Galileans welcomed him, since they had seen all he had done in Jerusalem at the feast; for they themselves had gone to the feast.[46]Then he returned to Cana in Galilee, where he had made the water wine. Now there was a royal official whose son was ill in Capernaum.[47]When he heard that Jesus had arrived in Galilee from Judea, he went to him and asked him to come down and heal his son, who was near death.[48]Jesus said to him, "Unless you people see signs and wonders, you will not believe."[49]The royal official said to him, "Sir, come down before my child dies."[50]Jesus said to him, "You may go; your son will live." The man believed what Jesus said to him and left.[51]While he was on his way back, his slaves met him and told him that his boy would live.[52]He asked them when he began to recover. They told him, "The fever left him yesterday, about one in the afternoon."[53]The father realized that just at that time Jesus had said to him, "Your son will live," and he and his whole household came to believe.[54](Now) this was the second sign Jesus did when he came to Galilee from Judea.

John Chapter 5

[1]After this, there was a feast of the Jews, and Jesus went up to Jerusalem.[2]Now there is in Jerusalem at the Sheep (Gate) a pool called in Hebrew Bethesda, with five porticoes.[3]In these lay a large number of ill, blind, lame, and crippled.[4]For an angel went down at certain times into the pool and stirred up the water. Whoever stepped in first after the stirring of the water was healed of whatever disease he had.[5]One man was there who had been ill for thirty-eight years.[6]When Jesus saw him lying there and knew that he had been ill for a long time, he said to him, "Do you want to be well?"[7]The sick man answered him, "Sir, I have no one to put me into the pool when the water is stirred up; while I am on my way, someone else gets down there before me."[8]Jesus said to him, "Rise, take up your mat, and walk."[9]Immediately the man became well, took up his mat, and walked. Now that day was a sabbath.[10]So the Jews said to the man who was cured, "It is the sabbath, and it is not lawful for you to carry your mat."[11]He answered them, "The man who made me well told me, 'Take up your mat and walk.'"[12]They asked him, "Who is the man who told you, 'Take it up and walk'?"[13]The man who was healed did not know who it was, for Jesus had slipped away, since there was a crowd there.[14]After this Jesus found him in the temple area and said to him, "Look, you are well; do not sin any more, so that nothing worse may happen to you."[15]The man went and told the Jews that Jesus was the one who had made him well.[16]Therefore, the Jews began to persecute Jesus because he did this on a sabbath.[17]But Jesus answered them, "My Father is at work until now, so I am at work."[18]For this reason the Jews tried all the more to kill him, because he not only broke the sabbath but he also called God his own father, making himself equal to God.[19]Jesus answered and said to them, "Amen, amen, I say to you, a son cannot do anything on his own, but only what he sees his father doing; for what he does, his son will do also.[20]For the Father loves his Son and shows him everything that he himself does, and he will show him greater works than these, so that you may be amazed.[21]For just as the Father raises the dead and gives life, so also does the Son give life to whomever he wishes.[22]Nor does the Father judge anyone, but he has given all judgment to his Son,[23]so that all may honor the Son just as they honor the Father. Whoever does not honor the Son does not honor the Father who sent him.[24]Amen, amen, I say to you, whoever hears my word and believes in the one who sent me has eternal life and will not come to condemnation, but has passed from death to life.[25]Amen, amen, I say to you, the hour is coming and is now here when the dead will hear the voice of the Son of God, and those who hear will live.[26]For just as the Father has life in himself, so also he gave to his Son the possession of life in himself.[27]And he gave him power to exercise judgment, because he is the Son of Man.[28]Do not be amazed at this, because the hour is coming in which all who are in the tombs will hear his voice[29]and will come out, those who have done good deeds to the resurrection of life, but those who have done wicked deeds to the resurrection of condemnation.[30]"I cannot do anything on my own; I judge as I hear, and my judgment is just, because I do not seek my own will but the will of the one who sent me.[31]If I testify on my own behalf, my testimony cannot be verified.[32]But there is another who testifies on my behalf, and I know that the testimony he gives on my behalf is true.[33]You sent emissaries to John, and he testified to the truth.[34]I do not accept testimony from a human being, but I say this so that you may be saved.[35]He was a burning and shining lamp, and for a while you were content to rejoice in his light.[36]But I have testimony greater than John's. The works that the Father gave me to accomplish, these works that I perform testify on my behalf that the Father has sent me.[37]Moreover, the Father who sent me has testified on my behalf. But

you have never heard his voice nor seen his form,[38]and you do not have his word remaining in you, because you do not believe in the one whom he has sent.[39]You search the scriptures, because you think you have eternal life through them; even they testify on my behalf.[40]But you do not want to come to me to have life.[41]"I do not accept human praise;[42]moreover, I know that you do not have the love of God in you.[43]I came in the name of my Father, but you do not accept me; yet if another comes in his own name, you will accept him.[44]How can you believe, when you accept praise from one another and do not seek the praise that comes from the only God?[45]Do not think that I will accuse you before the Father: the one who will accuse you is Moses, in whom you have placed your hope.[46]For if you had believed Moses, you would have believed me, because he wrote about me.[47]But if you do not believe his writings, how will you believe my words?"

John Chapter 6

[1]After this, Jesus went across the Sea of Galilee (of Tiberias).[2]A large crowd followed him, because they saw the signs he was performing on the sick.[3]Jesus went up on the mountain, and there he sat down with his disciples.[4]The Jewish feast of Passover was near.[5]When Jesus raised his eyes and saw that a large crowd was coming to him, he said to Philip, "Where can we buy enough food for them to eat?"[6]He said this to test him, because he himself knew what he was going to do.[7]Philip answered him, "Two hundred days' wages worth of food would not be enough for each of them to have a little (bit)."[8]One of his disciples, Andrew, the brother of Simon Peter, said to him,[9]"There is a boy here who has five barley loaves and two fish; but what good are these for so many?"[10]Jesus said, "Have the people recline." Now there was a great deal of grass in that place. So the men reclined, about five thousand in number.[11]Then Jesus took the loaves, gave thanks, and distributed them to those who were reclining, and also as much of the fish as they wanted.[12]When they had had their fill, he said to his disciples, "Gather the fragments left over, so that nothing will be wasted."[13]So they collected them, and filled twelve wicker baskets with fragments from the five barley loaves that had been more than they could eat.[14]When the people saw the sign he had done, they said, "This is truly the Prophet, the one who is to come into the world."[15]Since Jesus knew that they were going to come and carry him off to make him king, he withdrew again to the mountain alone.[16]When it was evening, his disciples went down to the sea,[17]embarked in a boat, and went across the sea to Capernaum. It had already grown dark, and Jesus had not yet come to them.[18]The sea was stirred up because a strong wind was blowing.[19]When they had rowed about three or four miles, they saw Jesus walking on the sea and coming near the boat, and they began to be afraid.[20]But he said to them, "It is I. Do not be afraid."[21]They wanted to take him into the boat, but the boat immediately arrived at the shore to which they were heading.[22]The next day, the crowd that remained across the sea saw that there had been only one boat there, and that Jesus had not gone along with his disciples in the boat, but only his disciples had left.[23]Other boats came from Tiberias near the place where they had eaten the bread when the Lord gave thanks.[24]When the crowd saw that neither Jesus nor his disciples were there, they themselves got into boats and came to Capernaum looking for Jesus.[25]And when they found him across the sea they said to him, "Rabbi, when did you get here?"[26]Jesus answered them and said, "Amen, amen, I say to you, you are looking for me not because you saw signs but because you ate the loaves and were filled.[27]Do not work for food that perishes but for the food that endures for eternal life, which the Son of Man will give you. For on him the Father, God, has set his seal."[28]So they said to him, "What can we do to accomplish the works of God?"[29]Jesus answered and said to them, "This is the work of God, that you believe in the one he sent."[30]So they said to him, "What sign can you do, that we may see and believe in you? What can you do?[31]Our ancestors ate manna in the desert, as it is written: 'He gave them bread from heaven to eat.'"[32]So Jesus said to them, "Amen, amen, I say to you, it was not Moses who gave the bread from heaven; my Father gives you the true bread from heaven.[33]For the bread of God is that which comes down from heaven and gives life to the world."[34]So they said to him, "Sir, give us this bread always."[35]Jesus said to them, "I am the bread of life; whoever comes to me will never hunger, and whoever believes in me will never thirst.[36]But I told you that although you have seen (me), you do not believe.[37]Everything that the Father gives me will come to me, and I will not reject anyone who comes to me,[38]because I came down from heaven not to do my own will but the will of the one who sent me.[39]And this is the will of the one who sent me, that I should not lose anything of what he gave me, but that I should raise it (on) the last day.[40]For this is the will of my Father, that everyone who sees the Son and believes in him may have eternal life, and I shall raise him (on) the last day."[41]The Jews murmured about him because he said, "I am

the bread that came down from heaven,"[42]and they said, "Is this not Jesus, the son of Joseph? Do we not know his father and mother? Then how can he say, 'I have come down from heaven'?[43]Jesus answered and said to them, "Stop murmuring among yourselves.[44]No one can come to me unless the Father who sent me draw him, and I will raise him on the last day.[45]It is written in the prophets: 'They shall all be taught by God.' Everyone who listens to my Father and learns from him comes to me.[46]Not that anyone has seen the Father except the one who is from God; he has seen the Father.[47]Amen, amen, I say to you, whoever believes has eternal life.[48]I am the bread of life.[49]Your ancestors ate the manna in the desert, but they died;[50]this is the bread that comes down from heaven so that one may eat it and not die.[51]I am the living bread that came down from heaven; whoever eats this bread will live forever; and the bread that I will give is my flesh for the life of the world."[52]The Jews quarreled among themselves, saying, "How can this man give us (his) flesh to eat?"[53]Jesus said to them, "Amen, amen, I say to you, unless you eat the flesh of the Son of Man and drink his blood, you do not have life within you.[54]Whoever eats my flesh and drinks my blood has eternal life, and I will raise him on the last day.[55]For my flesh is true food, and my blood is true drink.[56]Whoever eats my flesh and drinks my blood remains in me and I in him.[57]Just as the living Father sent me and I have life because of the Father, so also the one who feeds on me will have life because of me.[58]This is the bread that came down from heaven. Unlike your ancestors who ate and still died, whoever eats this bread will live forever."[59]These things he said while teaching in the synagogue in Capernaum.[60]Then many of his disciples who were listening said, "This saying is hard; who can accept it?"[61]Since Jesus knew that his disciples were murmuring about this, he said to them, "Does this shock you?[62]What if you were to see the Son of Man ascending to where he was before?[63]It is the spirit that gives life, while the flesh is of no avail. The words I have spoken to you are spirit and life.[64]But there are some of you who do not believe." Jesus knew from the beginning the ones who would not believe and the one who would betray him.[65]And he said, "For this reason I have told you that no one can come to me unless it is granted him by my Father."[66]As a result of this, many (of) his disciples returned to their former way of life and no longer accompanied him.[67]Jesus then said to the Twelve, "Do you also want to leave?"[68]Simon Peter answered him, "Master, to whom shall we go? You have the words of eternal life.[69]We have come to believe and are convinced that you are the Holy One of God."[70]Jesus answered them, "Did I not choose you twelve? Yet is not one of you a devil?"[71]He was referring to Judas, son of Simon the Iscariot; it was he who would betray him, one of the Twelve.

John Chapter 7

[1]After this, Jesus moved about within Galilee; but he did not wish to travel in Judea, because the Jews were trying to kill him.[2]But the Jewish feast of Tabernacles was near.[3]So his brothers said to him, "Leave here and go to Judea, so that your disciples also may see the works you are doing.[4]No one works in secret if he wants to be known publicly. If you do these things, manifest yourself to the world."[5]For his brothers did not believe in him.[6]So Jesus said to them, "My time is not yet here, but the time is always right for you.[7]The world cannot hate you, but it hates me, because I testify to it that its works are evil.[8]You go up to the feast. I am not going up to this feast, because my time has not yet been fulfilled."[9]After he had said this, he stayed on in Galilee.[10]But when his brothers had gone up to the feast, he himself also went up, not openly but (as it were) in secret.[11]The Jews were looking for him at the feast and saying, "Where is he?"[12]And there was considerable murmuring about him in the crowds. Some said, "He is a good man," (while) others said, "No; on the contrary, he misleads the crowd."[13]Still, no one spoke openly about him because they were afraid of the Jews.[14]When the feast was already half over, Jesus went up into the temple area and began to teach.[15]The Jews were amazed and said, "How does he know scripture without having studied?"[16]Jesus answered them and said, "My teaching is not my own but is from the one who sent me.[17]Whoever chooses to do his will shall know whether my teaching is from God or whether I speak on my own.[18]Whoever speaks on his own seeks his own glory, but whoever seeks the glory of the one who sent him is truthful, and there is no wrong in him.[19]Did not Moses give you the law? Yet none of you keeps the law. Why are you trying to kill me?"[20]The crowd answered, "You are possessed! Who is trying to kill you?"[21]Jesus answered and said to them, "I performed one work and all of you are amazed[22]because of it. Moses gave you circumcision - not that it came from Moses but rather from the patriarchs - and you circumcise a man on the sabbath.[23]If a man can receive circumcision on a sabbath so that the law of Moses may not be broken, are you angry with me because I made a whole person well on a sabbath?[24]Stop judging by appearances, but judge justly."[25]So some

of the inhabitants of Jerusalem said, "Is he not the one they are trying to kill?²⁶And look, he is speaking openly and they say nothing to him. Could the authorities have realized that he is the Messiah?²⁷But we know where he is from. When the Messiah comes, no one will know where he is from."²⁸So Jesus cried out in the temple area as he was teaching and said, "You know me and also know where I am from. Yet I did not come on my own, but the one who sent me, whom you do not know, is true.²⁹I know him, because I am from him, and he sent me."³⁰So they tried to arrest him, but no one laid a hand upon him, because his hour had not yet come.³¹But many of the crowd began to believe in him, and said, "When the Messiah comes, will he perform more signs than this man has done?"³²The Pharisees heard the crowd murmuring about him to this effect, and the chief priests and the Pharisees sent guards to arrest him.³³So Jesus said, "I will be with you only a little while longer, and then I will go to the one who sent me.³⁴You will look for me but not find (me), and where I am you cannot come."³⁵So the Jews said to one another, "Where is he going that we will not find him? Surely he is not going to the dispersion among the Greeks to teach the Greeks, is he?³⁶What is the meaning of his saying, 'You will look for me and not find (me), and where I am you cannot come'?"³⁷On the last and greatest day of the feast, Jesus stood up and exclaimed, "Let anyone who thirsts come to me and drink.³⁸Whoever believes in me, as scripture says: 'Rivers of living water will flow from within him.'"³⁹He said this in reference to the Spirit whom those who came to believe in him were to receive. There was, of course, no Spirit yet, because Jesus had not yet been glorified.⁴⁰Some in the crowd who heard these words said, "This is truly the Prophet."⁴¹Others said, "This is the Messiah." But others said, "The Messiah will not come from Galilee, will he?⁴²Does not scripture say that the Messiah will be of David's family and come from Bethlehem, the village where David lived?"⁴³So a division occurred in the crowd because of him.⁴⁴Some of them even wanted to arrest him, but no one laid hands on him.⁴⁵So the guards went to the chief priests and Pharisees, who asked them, "Why did you not bring him?"⁴⁶The guards answered, "Never before has anyone spoken like this one."⁴⁷So the Pharisees answered them, "Have you also been deceived?⁴⁸Have any of the authorities or the Pharisees believed in him?⁴⁹But this crowd, which does not know the law, is accursed."⁵⁰Nicodemus, one of their members who had come to him earlier, said to them,⁵¹"Does our law condemn a person before it first hears him and finds out what he is doing?"⁵²They answered and said to him, "You are not from Galilee also, are you? Look and see that no prophet arises from Galilee."⁵³Then each went to his own house.

John Chapter 8

¹While Jesus went to the Mount of Olives.²But early in the morning he arrived again in the temple area, and all the people started coming to him, and he sat down and taught them.³Then the scribes and the Pharisees brought a woman who had been caught in adultery and made her stand in the middle.⁴They said to him, "Teacher, this woman was caught in the very act of committing adultery.⁵Now in the law, Moses commanded us to stone such women. So what do you say?"⁶They said this to test him, so that they could have some charge to bring against him. Jesus bent down and began to write on the ground with his finger.⁷But when they continued asking him, he straightened up and said to them, "Let the one among you who is without sin be the first to throw a stone at her."⁸Again he bent down and wrote on the ground.⁹And in response, they went away one by one, beginning with the elders. So he was left alone with the woman before him.¹⁰Then Jesus straightened up and said to her, "Woman, where are they? Has no one condemned you?"¹¹She replied, "No one, sir." Then Jesus said, "Neither do I condemn you. Go, (and) from now on do not sin any more."¹²Jesus spoke to them again, saying, "I am the light of the world. Whoever follows me will not walk in darkness, but will have the light of life."¹³So the Pharisees said to him, "You testify on your own behalf, so your testimony cannot be verified."¹⁴Jesus answered and said to them, "Even if I do testify on my own behalf, my testimony can be verified, because I know where I came from and where I am going. But you do not know where I come from or where I am going.¹⁵You judge by appearances, but I do not judge anyone.¹⁶And even if I should judge, my judgment is valid, because I am not alone, but it is I and the Father who sent me.¹⁷Even in your law it is written that the testimony of two men can be verified.¹⁸I testify on my behalf and so does the Father who sent me."¹⁹So they said to him, "Where is your father?" Jesus answered, "You know neither me nor my Father. If you knew me, you would know my Father also."²⁰He spoke these words while teaching in the treasury in the temple area. But no one arrested him, because his hour had not yet come.²¹He said to them again, "I am going away and you will look for me, but you will die in your sin. Where I am going you cannot come."²²So the Jews said, "He is not going to kill himself, is he,

because he said, 'Where I am going you cannot come'?"²³He said to them, "You belong to what is below, I belong to what is above. You belong to this world, but I do not belong to this world.²⁴That is why I told you that you will die in your sins. For if you do not believe that I AM, you will die in your sins."²⁵So they said to him, "Who are you?" Jesus said to them, "What I told you from the beginning.²⁶I have much to say about you in condemnation. But the one who sent me is true, and what I heard from him I tell the world."²⁷They did not realize that he was speaking to them of the Father.²⁸So Jesus said (to them), "When you lift up the Son of Man, then you will realize that I AM, and that I do nothing on my own, but I say only what the Father taught me.²⁹The one who sent me is with me. He has not left me alone, because I always do what is pleasing to him."³⁰Because he spoke this way, many came to believe in him.³¹Jesus then said to those Jews who believed in him, "If you remain in my word, you will truly be my disciples,³²and you will know the truth, and the truth will set you free."³³They answered him, "We are descendants of Abraham and have never been enslaved to anyone. How can you say, 'You will become free'?"³⁴Jesus answered them, "Amen, amen, I say to you, everyone who commits sin is a slave of sin.³⁵A slave does not remain in a household forever, but a son always remains.³⁶So if a son frees you, then you will truly be free.³⁷I know that you are descendants of Abraham. But you are trying to kill me, because my word has no room among you.³⁸I tell you what I have seen in the Father's presence; then do what you have heard from the Father."³⁹They answered and said to him, "Our father is Abraham." Jesus said to them, "If you were Abraham's children, you would be doing the works of Abraham.⁴⁰But now you are trying to kill me, a man who has told you the truth that I heard from God; Abraham did not do this.⁴¹You are doing the works of your father!" (So) they said to him, "We are not illegitimate. We have one Father, God."⁴²Jesus said to them, "If God were your Father, you would love me, for I came from God and am here; I did not come on my own, but he sent me.⁴³Why do you not understand what I am saying? Because you cannot bear to hear my word.⁴⁴You belong to your father the devil and you willingly carry out your father's desires. He was a murderer from the beginning and does not stand in truth, because there is no truth in him. When he tells a lie, he speaks in character, because he is a liar and the father of lies.⁴⁵But because I speak the truth, you do not believe me.⁴⁶Can any of you charge me with sin? If I am telling the truth, why do you not believe me?⁴⁷Whoever belongs to God hears the words of God; for this reason you do not listen, because you do not belong to God."⁴⁸The Jews answered and said to him, "Are we not right in saying that you are a Samaritan and are possessed?"⁴⁹Jesus answered, "I am not possessed; I honor my Father, but you dishonor me.⁵⁰I do not seek my own glory; there is one who seeks it and he is the one who judges.⁵¹Amen, amen, I say to you, whoever keeps my word will never see death."⁵²(So) the Jews said to him, "Now we are sure that you are possessed. Abraham died, as did the prophets, yet you say, 'Whoever keeps my word will never taste death.'⁵³Are you greater than our father Abraham, who died? Or the prophets, who died? Who do you make yourself out to be?"⁵⁴Jesus answered, "If I glorify myself, my glory is worth nothing; but it is my Father who glorifies me, of whom you say, 'He is our God.'⁵⁵You do not know him, but I know him. And if I should say that I do not know him, I would be like you a liar. But I do know him and I keep his word.⁵⁶Abraham your father rejoiced to see my day; he saw it and was glad.⁵⁷So the Jews said to him, "You are not yet fifty years old and you have seen Abraham?"⁵⁸Jesus said to them, "Amen, amen, I say to you, before Abraham came to be, I AM."⁵⁹So they picked up stones to throw at him; but Jesus hid and went out of the temple area.

John Chapter 9

¹As he passed by he saw a man blind from birth.²His disciples asked him, "Rabbi, who sinned, this man or his parents, that he was born blind?"³Jesus answered, "Neither he nor his parents sinned; it is so that the works of God might be made visible through him.⁴We have to do the works of the one who sent me while it is day. Night is coming when no one can work.⁵While I am in the world, I am the light of the world."⁶When he had said this, he spat on the ground and made clay with the saliva, and smeared the clay on his eyes,⁷and said to him, "Go wash in the Pool of Siloam" (which means Sent). So he went and washed, and came back able to see.⁸His neighbors and those who had seen him earlier as a beggar said, "Isn't this the one who used to sit and beg?"⁹Some said, "It is," but others said, "No, he just looks like him." He said, "I am."¹⁰So they said to him, "(So) how were your eyes opened?"¹¹He replied, "The man called Jesus made clay and anointed my eyes and told me, 'Go to Siloam and wash.' So I went there and washed and was able to see."¹²And they said to him, "Where is he?" He said, "I don't know."¹³They brought the one who was once blind to the Pharisees.¹⁴Now Jesus had made clay and opened his eyes on a

sabbath.¹⁵So then the Pharisees also asked him how he was able to see. He said to them, "He put clay on my eyes, and I washed, and now I can see."¹⁶So some of the Pharisees said, "This man is not from God, because he does not keep the sabbath." (But) others said, "How can a sinful man do such signs?" And there was a division among them.¹⁷So they said to the blind man again, "What do you have to say about him, since he opened your eyes?" He said, "He is a prophet."¹⁸Now the Jews did not believe that he had been blind and gained his sight until they summoned the parents of the one who had gained his sight.¹⁹They asked them, "Is this your son, who you say was born blind? How does he now see?"²⁰His parents answered and said, "We know that this is our son and that he was born blind.²¹We do not know how he sees now, nor do we know who opened his eyes. Ask him, he is of age; he can speak for himself."²²His parents said this because they were afraid of the Jews, for the Jews had already agreed that if anyone acknowledged him as the Messiah, he would be expelled from the synagogue.²³For this reason his parents said, "He is of age; question him."²⁴So a second time they called the man who had been blind and said to him, "Give God the praise! We know that this man is a sinner."²⁵He replied, "If he is a sinner, I do not know. One thing I do know is that I was blind and now I see."²⁶So they said to him, "What did he do to you? How did he open your eyes?"²⁷He answered them, "I told you already and you did not listen. Why do you want to hear it again? Do you want to become his disciples, too?"²⁸They ridiculed him and said, "You are that man's disciple; we are disciples of Moses!²⁹We know that God spoke to Moses, but we do not know where this one is from."³⁰The man answered and said to them, "This is what is so amazing, that you do not know where he is from, yet he opened my eyes.³¹We know that God does not listen to sinners, but if one is devout and does his will, he listens to him.³²It is unheard of that anyone ever opened the eyes of a person born blind.³³If this man were not from God, he would not be able to do anything."³⁴They answered and said to him, "You were born totally in sin, and are you trying to teach us?" Then they threw him out.³⁵When Jesus heard that they had thrown him out, he found him and said, "Do you believe in the Son of Man?"³⁶He answered and said, "Who is he, sir, that I may believe in him?"³⁷Jesus said to him, "You have seen him and the one speaking with you is he."³⁸He said, "I do believe, Lord," and he worshiped him.³⁹Then Jesus said, "I came into this world for judgment, so that those who do not see might see, and those who do see might become blind."⁴⁰Some of the Pharisees who were with him heard this and said to him, "Surely we are not also blind, are we?"⁴¹Jesus said to them, "If you were blind, you would have no sin; but now you are saying, 'We see,' so your sin remains."

John Chapter 10

¹"Amen, amen, I say to you, whoever does not enter a sheepfold through the gate but climbs over elsewhere is a thief and a robber.²But whoever enters through the gate is the shepherd of the sheep.³The gatekeeper opens it for him, and the sheep hear his voice, as he calls his own sheep by name and leads them out.⁴When he has driven out all his own, he walks ahead of them, and the sheep follow him, because they recognize his voice.⁵But they will not follow a stranger; they will run away from him, because they do not recognize the voice of strangers."⁶Although Jesus used this figure of speech, they did not realize what he was trying to tell them.⁷So Jesus said again, "Amen, amen, I say to you, I am the gate for the sheep.⁸All who came [before me] are thieves and robbers, but the sheep did not listen to them.⁹I am the gate. Whoever enters through me will be saved, and will come in and go out and find pasture.¹⁰A thief comes only to steal and slaughter and destroy; I came so that they might have life and have it more abundantly.¹¹I am the good shepherd. A good shepherd lays down his life for the sheep.¹²A hired man, who is not a shepherd and whose sheep are not his own, sees a wolf coming and leaves the sheep and runs away, and the wolf catches and scatters them.¹³This is because he works for pay and has no concern for the sheep.¹⁴I am the good shepherd, and I know mine and mine know me,¹⁵just as the Father knows me and I know the Father; and I will lay down my life for the sheep.¹⁶I have other sheep that do not belong to this fold. These also I must lead, and they will hear my voice, and there will be one flock, one shepherd.¹⁷This is why the Father loves me, because I lay down my life in order to take it up again.¹⁸No one takes it from me, but I lay it down on my own. I have power to lay it down, and power to take it up again. This command I have received from my Father."¹⁹Again there was a division among the Jews because of these words.²⁰Many of them said, "He is possessed and out of his mind; why listen to him?"²¹Others said, "These are not the words of one possessed; surely a demon cannot open the eyes of the blind, can he?"²²The feast of the Dedication was then taking place in Jerusalem. It was winter.²³And Jesus walked about in the temple area on the Portico of Solomon.²⁴So the Jews gathered

around him and said to him, "How long are you going to keep us in suspense? If you are the Messiah, tell us plainly."²⁵Jesus answered them, "I told you and you do not believe. The works I do in my Father's name testify to me.²⁶But you do not believe, because you are not among my sheep.²⁷My sheep hear my voice; I know them, and they follow me.²⁸I give them eternal life, and they shall never perish. No one can take them out of my hand.²⁹My Father, who has given them to me, is greater than all, and no one can take them out of the Father's hand.³⁰The Father and I are one."³¹The Jews again picked up rocks to stone him.³²Jesus answered them, "I have shown you many good works from my Father. For which of these are you trying to stone me?"³³The Jews answered him, "We are not stoning you for a good work but for blasphemy. You, a man, are making yourself God."³⁴Jesus answered them, "Is it not written in your law, 'I said, "You are gods"'?³⁵If it calls them gods to whom the word of God came, and scripture cannot be set aside,³⁶can you say that the one whom the Father has consecrated and sent into the world blasphemes because I said, 'I am the Son of God'?³⁷If I do not perform my Father's works, do not believe me;³⁸but if I perform them, even if you do not believe me, believe the works, so that you may realize (and understand) that the Father is in me and I am in the Father."³⁹(Then) they tried again to arrest him; but he escaped from their power.⁴⁰He went back across the Jordan to the place where John first baptized, and there he remained.⁴¹Many came to him and said, "John performed no sign, but everything John said about this man was true."⁴²And many there began to believe in him.

John Chapter 11

¹Now a man was ill, Lazarus from Bethany, the village of Mary and her sister Martha. ²Mary was the one who had anointed the Lord with perfumed oil and dried his feet with her hair; it was her brother Lazarus who was ill. ³So the sisters sent word to him, saying, "Master, the one you love is ill." ⁴When Jesus heard this he said, "This illness is not to end in death, but is for the glory of God, that the Son of God may be glorified through it." ⁵Now Jesus loved Martha and her sister and Lazarus. ⁶So when he heard that he was ill, he remained for two days in the place where he was. ⁷Then after this he said to his disciples, "Let us go back to Judea." ⁸The disciples said to him, "Rabbi, the Jews were just trying to stone you, and you want to go back there?" ⁹Jesus answered, "Are there not twelve hours in a day? If one walks during the day, he does not stumble, because he sees the light of this world. ¹⁰But if one walks at night, he stumbles, because the light is not in him." ¹¹He said this, and then told them, "Our friend Lazarus is asleep, but I am going to awaken him." ¹²So the disciples said to him, "Master, if he is asleep, he will be saved." ¹³But Jesus was talking about his death, while they thought that he meant ordinary sleep. ¹⁴So then Jesus said to them clearly, "Lazarus has died. ¹⁵And I am glad for you that I was not there, that you may believe. Let us go to him." ¹⁶So Thomas, called Didymus, said to his fellow disciples, "Let us also go to die with him." ¹⁷When Jesus arrived, he found that Lazarus had already been in the tomb for four days. ¹⁸Now Bethany was near Jerusalem, only about two miles away. ¹⁹And many of the Jews had come to Martha and Mary to comfort them about their brother. ²⁰When Martha heard that Jesus was coming, she went to meet him; but Mary sat at home. ²¹Martha said to Jesus, "Lord, if you had been here, my brother would not have died. ²²(But) even now I know that whatever you ask of God, God will give you." ²³Jesus said to her, "Your brother will rise." ²⁴Martha said to him, "I know he will rise, in the resurrection on the last day." ²⁵Jesus told her, "I am the resurrection and the life; whoever believes in me, even if he dies, will live, ²⁶and everyone who lives and believes in me will never die. Do you believe this?" ²⁷She said to him, "Yes, Lord. I have come to believe that you are the Messiah, the Son of God, the one who is coming into the world." ²⁸When she had said this, she went and called her sister Mary secretly, saying, "The teacher is here and is asking for you." ²⁹As soon as she heard this, she rose quickly and went to him. ³⁰For Jesus had not yet come into the village, but was still where Martha had met him. ³¹So when the Jews who were with her in the house comforting her saw Mary get up quickly and go out, they followed her, presuming that she was going to the tomb to weep there. ³²When Mary came to where Jesus was and saw him, she fell at his feet and said to him, "Lord, if you had been here, my brother would not have died." ³³When Jesus saw her weeping and the Jews who had come with her weeping, he became perturbed and deeply troubled, ³⁴and said, "Where have you laid him?" They said to him, "Sir, come and see." ³⁵And Jesus wept. ³⁶So the Jews said, "See how he loved him." ³⁷But some of them said, "Could not the one who opened the eyes of the blind man have done something so that this man would not have died?" ³⁸So Jesus, perturbed again, came to the tomb. It was a cave, and a stone lay across it. ³⁹Jesus said, "Take away the stone." Martha, the dead man's sister, said to him, "Lord, by now there will be a stench; he has been dead for

four days." 40Jesus said to her, "Did I not tell you that if you believe you will see the glory of God?" 41So they took away the stone. And Jesus raised his eyes and said, "Father, I thank you for hearing me. 42I know that you always hear me; but because of the crowd here I have said this, that they may believe that you sent me." 43And when he had said this, he cried out in a loud voice, "Lazarus, come out!" 44The dead man came out, tied hand and foot with burial bands, and his face was wrapped in a cloth. So Jesus said to them, "Untie him and let him go." 45Now many of the Jews who had come to Mary and seen what he had done began to believe in him. 46But some of them went to the Pharisees and told them what Jesus had done. 47So the chief priests and the Pharisees convened the Sanhedrin and said, "What are we going to do? This man is performing many signs. 48If we leave him alone, all will believe in him, and the Romans will come and take away both our land and our nation." 49But one of them, Caiaphas, who was high priest that year, said to them, "You know nothing, 50nor do you consider that it is better for you that one man should die instead of the people, so that the whole nation may not perish." 51He did not say this on his own, but since he was high priest for that year, he prophesied that Jesus was going to die for the nation, 52and not only for the nation, but also to gather into one the dispersed children of God. 53So from that day on they planned to kill him. 54So Jesus no longer walked about in public among the Jews, but he left for the region near the desert, to a town called Ephraim, and there he remained with his disciples. 55Now the Passover of the Jews was near, and many went up from the country to Jerusalem before Passover to purify themselves. 56They looked for Jesus and said to one another as they were in the temple area, "What do you think? That he will not come to the feast?" 57For the chief priests and the Pharisees had given orders that if anyone knew where he was, he should inform them, so that they might arrest him.

John Chapter 12

1Six days before Passover Jesus came to Bethany, where Lazarus was, whom Jesus had raised from the dead. 2They gave a dinner for him there, and Martha served, while Lazarus was one of those reclining at table with him. 3Mary took a liter of costly perfumed oil made from genuine aromatic nard and anointed the feet of Jesus and dried them with her hair; the house was filled with the fragrance of the oil. 4Then Judas the Iscariot, one (of) his disciples, and the one who would betray him, said, 5"Why was this oil not sold for three hundred days' wages and given to the poor?" 6He said this not because he cared about the poor but because he was a thief and held the money bag and used to steal the contributions. 7So Jesus said, "Leave her alone. Let her keep this for the day of my burial. 8You always have the poor with you, but you do not always have me." 9(The) large crowd of the Jews found out that he was there and came, not only because of Jesus, but also to see Lazarus, whom he had raised from the dead. 10And the chief priests plotted to kill Lazarus too, 11because many of the Jews were turning away and believing in Jesus because of him. 12On the next day, when the great crowd that had come to the feast heard that Jesus was coming to Jerusalem, 13they took palm branches and went out to meet him, and cried out: "Hosanna! Blessed is he who comes in the name of the Lord, (even) the king of Israel." 14Jesus found an ass and sat upon it, as is written: 15"Fear no more, O daughter Zion; see, your king comes, seated upon an ass's colt." 16His disciples did not understand this at first, but when Jesus had been glorified they remembered that these things were written about him and that they had done this for him. 17So the crowd that was with him when he called Lazarus from the tomb and raised him from death continued to testify. 18This was (also) why the crowd went to meet him, because they heard that he had done this sign. 19So the Pharisees said to one another, "You see that you are gaining nothing. Look, the whole world has gone after him." 20Now there were some Greeks among those who had come up to worship at the feast. 21They came to Philip, who was from Bethsaida in Galilee, and asked him, "Sir, we would like to see Jesus." 22Philip went and told Andrew; then Andrew and Philip went and told Jesus. 23Jesus answered them, "The hour has come for the Son of Man to be glorified. 24Amen, amen, I say to you, unless a grain of wheat falls to the ground and dies, it remains just a grain of wheat; but if it dies, it produces much fruit. 25Whoever loves his life loses it, and whoever hates his life in this world will preserve it for eternal life. 26Whoever serves me must follow me, and where I am, there also will my servant be. The Father will honor whoever serves me. 27"I am troubled now. Yet what should I say? 'Father, save me from this hour'? But it was for this purpose that I came to this hour. 28Father, glorify your name." Then a voice came from heaven, "I have glorified it and will glorify it again." 29The crowd there heard it and said it was thunder; but others said, "An angel has spoken to him." 30Jesus answered and said, "This voice did not come for my sake but for yours. 31Now is the time of judgment on this world; now

the ruler of this world will be driven out. 32And when I am lifted up from the earth, I will draw everyone to myself." 33He said this indicating the kind of death he would die. 34So the crowd answered him, "We have heard from the law that the Messiah remains forever. Then how can you say that the Son of Man must be lifted up? Who is this Son of Man?" 35Jesus said to them, "The light will be among you only a little while. Walk while you have the light, so that darkness may not overcome you. Whoever walks in the dark does not know where he is going. 36While you have the light, believe in the light, so that you may become children of the light." After he had said this, Jesus left and hid from them. 37Although he had performed so many signs in their presence they did not believe in him, 38in order that the word which Isaiah the prophet spoke might be fulfilled: "Lord, who has believed our preaching, to whom has the might of the Lord been revealed?" 39For this reason they could not believe, because again Isaiah said: 40"He blinded their eyes and hardened their heart, so that they might not see with their eyes and understand with their heart and be converted, and I would heal them." 41Isaiah said this because he saw his glory and spoke about him. 42Nevertheless, many, even among the authorities, believed in him, but because of the Pharisees they did not acknowledge it openly in order not to be expelled from the synagogue. 43For they preferred human praise to the glory of God. 44Jesus cried out and said, "Whoever believes in me believes not only in me but also in the one who sent me, 45and whoever sees me sees the one who sent me. 46I came into the world as light, so that everyone who believes in me might not remain in darkness. 47And if anyone hears my words and does not observe them, I do not condemn him, for I did not come to condemn the world but to save the world. 48Whoever rejects me and does not accept my words has something to judge him: the word that I spoke, it will condemn him on the last day, 49because I did not speak on my own, but the Father who sent me commanded me what to say and speak. 50And I know that his commandment is eternal life. So what I say, I say as the Father told me."

John Chapter 13

1Before the feast of Passover, Jesus knew that his hour had come to pass from this world to the Father. He loved his own in the world and he loved them to the end. 2The devil had already induced Judas, son of Simon the Iscariot, to hand him over. So, during supper, 3fully aware that the Father had put everything into his power and that he had come from God and was returning to God, 4he rose from supper and took off his outer garments. He took a towel and tied it around his waist. 5Then he poured water into a basin and began to wash the disciples' feet and dry them with the towel around his waist. 6He came to Simon Peter, who said to him, "Master, are you going to wash my feet?" 7Jesus answered and said to him, "What I am doing, you do not understand now, but you will understand later." 8Peter said to him, "You will never wash my feet." Jesus answered him, "Unless I wash you, you will have no inheritance with me." 9Simon Peter said to him, "Master, then not only my feet, but my hands and head as well." 10Jesus said to him, "Whoever has bathed has no need except to have his feet washed, for he is clean all over; so you are clean, but not all." 11For he knew who would betray him; for this reason, he said, "Not all of you are clean." 12So when he had washed their feet (and) put his garments back on and reclined at table again, he said to them, "Do you realize what I have done for you? 13You call me 'teacher' and 'master,' and rightly so, for indeed I am. 14If I, therefore, the master and teacher, have washed your feet, you ought to wash one another's feet. 15I have given you a model to follow, so that as I have done for you, you should also do. 16Amen, amen, I say to you, no slave is greater than his master nor any messenger greater than the one who sent him. 17If you understand this, blessed are you if you do it. 18I am not speaking of all of you. I know those whom I have chosen. But so that the scripture might be fulfilled, 'The one who ate my food has raised his heel against me.' 19From now on I am telling you before it happens, so that when it happens you may believe that I AM. 20Amen, amen, I say to you, whoever receives the one I send receives me, and whoever receives me receives the one who sent me." 21When he had said this, Jesus was deeply troubled and testified, "Amen, amen, I say to you, one of you will betray me." 22The disciples looked at one another, at a loss as to whom he meant. 23One of his disciples, the one whom Jesus loved, was reclining at Jesus' side. 24So Simon Peter nodded to him to find out whom he meant. 25He leaned back against Jesus' chest and said to him, "Master, who is it?" 26Jesus answered, "It is the one to whom I hand the morsel after I have dipped it." So he dipped the morsel and (took it and) handed it to Judas, son of Simon the Iscariot. 27After he took the morsel, Satan entered him. So Jesus said to him, "What you are going to do, do quickly." 28(Now) none of those reclining at table realized why he said this to him. 29Some thought that since Judas kept the money bag, Jesus had told him, "Buy what we need for the feast," or to give something to the poor. ³⁰So he took the morsel and left at once. And it was night. ³¹When he had left, Jesus said, "Now is the Son of Man glorified, and God is glorified in him. ³²(If God is glorified in him,) God will also glorify him in himself, and he will glorify him at once. ³³My children, I will be with you only a little while longer. You will look for me, and as I told the Jews, 'Where I go you cannot come,' so now I say it to you. ³⁴I give you a new commandment: love one another. As I have loved you, so you also should love one another. ³⁵This is how all will know that you are my disciples, if you have love for one another." ³⁶Simon Peter said to him, "Master, where are you going?" Jesus answered (him), "Where I am going, you cannot follow me now, though you will follow later." ³⁷Peter said to him, "Master, why can't I follow you now? I will lay down my life for you." ³⁸Jesus answered, "Will you lay down your life for me? Amen, amen, I say to you, the cock will not crow before you deny me three times."

John Chapter 14

¹"Do not let your hearts be troubled. You have faith in God; have faith also in me. ²In my Father's house there are many dwelling places. If there were not, would I have told you that I am going to prepare a place for you? ³And if I go and prepare a place for you, I will come back again and take you to myself, so that where I am you also may be. ⁴Where (I) am going you know the way." ⁵Thomas said to him, "Master, we do not know where you are going; how can we know the way?" ⁶Jesus said to him, "I am the way and the truth and the life. No one comes to the Father except through me. ⁷If you know me, then you will also know my Father. From now on you do know him and have seen him." ⁸Philip said to him, "Master, show us the Father, and that will be enough for us." ⁹Jesus said to him, "Have I been with you for so long a time and you still do not know me, Philip? Whoever has seen me has seen the Father. How can you say, 'Show us the Father'? ¹⁰Do you not believe that I am in the Father and the Father is in me? The words that I speak to you I do not speak on my own. The Father who dwells in me is doing his works. ¹¹Believe me that I am in the Father and the Father is in me, or else, believe because of the works themselves. ¹²Amen, amen, I say to you, whoever believes in me will do the works that I do, and will do greater ones than these, because I am going to the Father. ¹³And whatever you ask in my name, I will do, so that the Father may be glorified in the Son. ¹⁴If you ask anything of me in my name, I will do it. ¹⁵"If you love me, you will keep my commandments. ¹⁶And I will ask the Father, and he will give you another Advocate to be with you always, ¹⁷the Spirit of truth, which the world cannot accept, because it neither sees nor knows it. But you know it, because it remains with you, and will be in you. ¹⁸I will not leave you orphans; I will come to you. ¹⁹In a little while the world will no longer see me, but you will see me, because I live and you will live. ²⁰On that day you will realize that I am in my Father and you are in me and I in you. ²¹Whoever has my commandments and observes them is the one who loves me. And whoever loves me will be loved by my Father, and I will love him and reveal myself to him." ²²Judas, not the Iscariot, said to him, "Master, (then) what happened that you will reveal yourself to us and not to the world?" ²³Jesus answered and said to him, "Whoever loves me will keep my word, and my Father will love him, and we will come to him and make our dwelling with him. ²⁴Whoever does not love me does not keep my words; yet the word you hear is not mine but that of the Father who sent me. ²⁵I have told you this while I am with you. ²⁶The Advocate, the holy Spirit that the Father will send in my name - he will teach you everything and remind you of all that (I) told you. ²⁷Peace I leave with you; my peace I give to you. Not as the world gives do I give it to you. Do not let your hearts be troubled or afraid. ²⁸You heard me tell you, 'I am going away and I will come back to you.' If you loved me, you would rejoice that I am going to the Father; for the Father is greater than I. ²⁹And now I have told you this before it happens, so that when it happens you may believe. ³⁰I will no longer speak much with you, for the ruler of the world is coming. He has no power over me, ³¹but the world must know that I love the Father and that I do just as the Father has commanded me. Get up, let us go."

John Chapter 15

¹"I am the true vine, and my Father is the vine grower. ²He takes away every branch in me that does not bear fruit, and everyone that does he prunes so that it bears more fruit. ³You are already pruned because of the word that I spoke to you. ⁴Remain in me, as I remain in you. Just as a branch cannot bear fruit on its own unless it remains on the vine, so neither can you unless you remain in me. ⁵I am the vine, you are the branches. Whoever remains in me and I in him will bear much fruit, because without me you can do nothing. ⁶Anyone who does not remain in me will be thrown out like a branch and wither; people will gather

them and throw them into a fire and they will be burned. ⁷If you remain in me and my words remain in you, ask for whatever you want and it will be done for you. ⁸By this is my Father glorified, that you bear much fruit and become my disciples. ⁹As the Father loves me, so I also love you. Remain in my love. ¹⁰If you keep my commandments, you will remain in my love, just as I have kept my Father's commandments and remain in his love. ¹¹"I have told you this so that my joy may be in you and your joy may be complete. ¹²This is my commandment: love one another as I love you. ¹³No one has greater love than this, to lay down one's life for one's friends. ¹⁴You are my friends if you do what I command you. ¹⁵I no longer call you slaves, because a slave does not know what his master is doing. I have called you friends, because I have told you everything I have heard from my Father. ¹⁶It was not you who chose me, but I who chose you and appointed you to go and bear fruit that will remain, so that whatever you ask the Father in my name he may give you. ¹⁷This I command you: love one another. ¹⁸"If the world hates you, realize that it hated me first. ¹⁹If you belonged to the world, the world would love its own; but because you do not belong to the world, and I have chosen you out of the world, the world hates you. ²⁰Remember the word I spoke to you, 'No slave is greater than his master.' If they persecuted me, they will also persecute you. If they kept my word, they will also keep yours. ²¹And they will do all these things to you on account of my name, because they do not know the one who sent me. ²²If I had not come and spoken to them, they would have no sin; but as it is they have no excuse for their sin. ²³Whoever hates me also hates my Father. ²⁴If I had not done works among them that no one else ever did, they would not have sin; but as it is, they have seen and hated both me and my Father. ²⁵But in order that the word written in their law might be fulfilled, 'They hated me without cause.' ²⁶"When the Advocate comes whom I will send you from the Father, the Spirit of truth that proceeds from the Father, he will testify to me. ²⁷And you also testify, because you have been with me from the beginning."

John Chapter 16

¹"I have told you this so that you may not fall away. ²They will expel you from the synagogues; in fact, the hour is coming when everyone who kills you will think he is offering worship to God. ³They will do this because they have not known either the Father or me. ⁴I have told you this so that when their hour comes you may remember that I told you. I did not tell you this from the beginning, because I was with you. ⁵But now I am going to the one who sent me, and not one of you asks me, 'Where are you going?' ⁶But because I told you this, grief has filled your hearts. ⁷But I tell you the truth, it is better for you that I go. For if I do not go, the Advocate will not come to you. But if I go, I will send him to you. ⁸And when he comes he will convict the world in regard to sin and righteousness and condemnation: ⁹sin, because they do not believe in me; ¹⁰righteousness, because I am going to the Father and you will no longer see me; ¹¹condemnation, because the ruler of this world has been condemned. ¹²"I have much more to tell you, but you cannot bear it now. ¹³But when he comes, the Spirit of truth, he will guide you to all truth. He will not speak on his own, but he will speak what he hears, and will declare to you the things that are coming. ¹⁴He will glorify me, because he will take from what is mine and declare it to you. ¹⁵Everything that the Father has is mine; for this reason I told you that he will take from what is mine and declare it to you. ¹⁶"A little while and you will no longer see me, and again a little while later and you will see me." ¹⁷So some of his disciples said to one another, "What does this mean that he is saying to us, 'A little while and you will not see me, and again a little while and you will see me,' and 'Because I am going to the Father'?" ¹⁸So they said, "What is this 'little while' (of which he speaks)? We do not know what he means." ¹⁹Jesus knew that they wanted to ask him, so he said to them, "Are you discussing with one another what I said, 'A little while and you will not see me, and again a little while and you will see me'? ²⁰Amen, amen, I say to you, you will weep and mourn, while the world rejoices; you will grieve, but your grief will become joy. ²¹When a woman is in labor, she is in anguish because her hour has arrived; but when she has given birth to a child, she no longer remembers the pain because of her joy that a child has been born into the world. ²²So you also are now in anguish. But I will see you again, and your hearts will rejoice, and no one will take your joy away from you. ²³On that day you will not question me about anything. Amen, amen, I say to you, whatever you ask the Father in my name he will give you. ²⁴Until now you have not asked anything in my name; ask and you will receive, so that your joy may be complete. ²⁵"I have told you this in figures of speech. The hour is coming when I will no longer speak to you in figures but I will tell you clearly about the Father. ²⁶On that day you will ask in my name, and I do not tell you that I will ask the Father for you. ²⁷For the Father himself loves you, because you have loved me and have come to believe that I came from God. ²⁸I came from the Father

and have come into the world. Now I am leaving the world and going back to the Father." ²⁹His disciples said, "Now you are talking plainly, and not in any figure of speech. ³⁰Now we realize that you know everything and that you do not need to have anyone question you. Because of this we believe that you came from God." ³¹Jesus answered them, "Do you believe now? ³²Behold, the hour is coming and has arrived when each of you will be scattered to his own home and you will leave me alone. But I am not alone, because the Father is with me. ³³I have told you this so that you might have peace in me. In the world you will have trouble, but take courage, I have conquered the world."

John Chapter 17

¹When Jesus had said this, he raised his eyes to heaven and said, "Father, the hour has come. Give glory to your son, so that your son may glorify you, ²just as you gave him authority over all people, so that he may give eternal life to all you gave him. ³Now this is eternal life, that they should know you, the only true God, and the one whom you sent, Jesus Christ. ⁴I glorified you on earth by accomplishing the work that you gave me to do. ⁵Now glorify me, Father, with you, with the glory that I had with you before the world began. ⁶"I revealed your name to those whom you gave me out of the world. They belonged to you, and you gave them to me, and they have kept your word. ⁷Now they know that everything you gave me is from you, ⁸because the words you gave to me I have given to them, and they accepted them and truly understood that I came from you, and they have believed that you sent me. ⁹I pray for them. I do not pray for the world but for the ones you have given me, because they are yours, ¹⁰and everything of mine is yours and everything of yours is mine, and I have been glorified in them. ¹¹And now I will no longer be in the world, but they are in the world, while I am coming to you. Holy Father, keep them in your name that you have given me, so that they may be one just as we are. ¹²When I was with them I protected them in your name that you gave me, and I guarded them, and none of them was lost except the son of destruction, in order that the scripture might be fulfilled. ¹³But now I am coming to you. I speak this in the world so that they may share my joy completely. ¹⁴I gave them your word, and the world hated them, because they do not belong to the world any more than I belong to the world. ¹⁵I do not ask that you take them out of the world but that you keep them from the evil one. ¹⁶They do not belong to the world any more than I belong to the world. ¹⁷Consecrate them in the truth. Your word is truth. ¹⁸As you sent me into the world, so I sent them into the world. ¹⁹And I consecrate myself for them, so that they also may be consecrated in truth. ²⁰"I pray not only for them, but also for those who will believe in me through their word, ²¹so that they may all be one, as you, Father, are in me and I in you, that they also may be in us, that the world may believe that you sent me. ²²And I have given them the glory you gave me, so that they may be one, as we are one, ²³I in them and you in me, that they may be brought to perfection as one, that the world may know that you sent me, and that you loved them even as you loved me. ²⁴Father, they are your gift to me. I wish that where I am they also may be with me, that they may see my glory that you gave me, because you loved me before the foundation of the world. ²⁵Righteous Father, the world also does not know you, but I know you, and they know that you sent me. ²⁶I made known to them your name and I will make it known, that the love with which you loved me may be in them and I in them."

John Chapter 18

¹When he had said this, Jesus went out with his disciples across the Kidron valley to where there was a garden, into which he and his disciples entered. ²Judas his betrayer also knew the place, because Jesus had often met there with his disciples. ³So Judas got a band of soldiers and guards from the chief priests and the Pharisees and went there with lanterns, torches, and weapons. ⁴Jesus, knowing everything that was going to happen to him, went out and said to them, "Whom are you looking for?" ⁵They answered him, "Jesus the Nazorean." He said to them, "I AM." Judas his betrayer was also with them. ⁶When he said to them, "I AM," they turned away and fell to the ground. ⁷So he again asked them, "Whom are you looking for?" They said, "Jesus the Nazorean." ⁸Jesus answered, "I told you that I AM. So if you are looking for me, let these men go." ⁹This was to fulfill what he had said, "I have not lost any of those you gave me." ¹⁰Then Simon Peter, who had a sword, drew it, struck the high priest's slave, and cut off his right ear. The slave's name was Malchus. ¹¹Jesus said to Peter, "Put your sword into its scabbard. Shall I not drink the cup that the Father gave me?" ¹²So the band of soldiers, the tribune, and the Jewish guards seized Jesus, bound him, ¹³and brought him to Annas first. He was the father-in-law of Caiaphas, who was high priest that year. ¹⁴It was Caiaphas who had counseled the Jews that it was better that one man should die rather than the people. ¹⁵Simon Peter and another disciple followed Jesus. Now the other disciple was known to the high priest, and he entered the courtyard of the high priest with Jesus. ¹⁶But Peter stood at the gate outside. So the other disciple, the acquaintance of the high priest, went out and spoke to the gatekeeper and brought Peter in. ¹⁷Then the maid who was the gatekeeper said to Peter, "You are not one of this man's disciples, are you?" He said, "I am not." ¹⁸Now the slaves and the guards were standing around a charcoal fire that they had made, because it was cold, and were warming themselves. Peter was also standing there keeping warm. ¹⁹The high priest questioned Jesus about his disciples and about his doctrine. ²⁰Jesus answered him, "I have spoken publicly to the world. I have always taught in a synagogue or in the temple area where all the Jews gather, and in secret I have said nothing. ²¹Why ask me? Ask those who heard me what I said to them. They know what I said." ²²When he had said this, one of the temple guards standing there struck Jesus and said, "Is this the way you answer the high priest?" ²³Jesus answered him, "If I have spoken wrongly, testify to the wrong; but if I have spoken rightly, why do you strike me?" ²⁴Then Annas sent him bound to Caiaphas the high priest. ²⁵Now Simon Peter was standing there keeping warm. And they said to him, "You are not one of his disciples, are you?" He denied it and said, "I am not." ²⁶One of the slaves of the high priest, a relative of the one whose ear Peter had cut off, said, "Didn't I see you in the garden with him?" ²⁷Again Peter denied it. And immediately the cock crowed. ²⁸Then they brought Jesus from Caiaphas to the praetorium. It was morning. And they themselves did not enter the praetorium, in order not to be defiled so that they could eat the Passover. ²⁹So Pilate came out to them and said, "What charge do you bring (against) this man?" ³⁰They answered and said to him, "If he were not a criminal, we would not have handed him over to you." ³¹At this, Pilate said to them, "Take him yourselves, and judge him according to your law." The Jews answered him, "We do not have the right to execute anyone," ³²in order that the word of Jesus might be fulfilled that he said indicating the kind of death he would die. ³³So Pilate went back into the praetorium and summoned Jesus and said to him, "Are you the King of the Jews?" ³⁴Jesus answered, "Do you say this on your own or have others told you about me?" ³⁵Pilate answered, "I am not a Jew, am I? Your own nation and the chief priests handed you over to me. What have you done?" ³⁶Jesus answered, "My kingdom does not belong to this world. If my kingdom did belong to this world, my attendants (would) be fighting to keep me from being handed over to the Jews. But as it is, my kingdom is not here." ³⁷So Pilate said to him, "Then you are a king?" Jesus answered, "You say I am a king. For this I was born and for this I came into the world, to testify to the truth. Everyone who belongs to the truth listens to my voice." ³⁸Pilate said to him, "What is truth?" When he had said this, he again went out to the Jews and said to them, "I find no guilt in him. ³⁹But you have a custom that I release one prisoner to you at Passover. Do you want me to release to you the King of the Jews?" ⁴⁰They cried out again, "Not this one but Barabbas!" Now Barabbas was a revolutionary.

John Chapter 19

¹Then Pilate took Jesus and had him scourged. ²And the soldiers wove a crown out of thorns and placed it on his head, and clothed him in a purple cloak, ³and they came to him and said, "Hail, King of the Jews!" And they struck him repeatedly. ⁴Once more Pilate went out and said to them, "Look, I am bringing him out to you, so that you may know that I find no guilt in him." ⁵So Jesus came out, wearing the crown of thorns and the purple cloak. ⁶When the chief priests and the guards saw him they cried out, "Crucify him, crucify him!" Pilate said to them, "Take him yourselves and crucify him. I find no guilt in him." ⁷The Jews answered, "We have a law, and according to that law he ought to die, because he made himself the Son of God." ⁸Now when Pilate heard this statement, he became even more afraid, ⁹and went back into the praetorium and said to Jesus, "Where are you from?" Jesus did not answer him. ¹⁰So Pilate said to him, "Do you not speak to me? Do you not know that I have power to release you and I have power to crucify you?" ¹¹Jesus answered (him), "You would have no power over me if it had not been given to you from above. For this reason the one who handed me over to you has the greater sin." ¹²Consequently, Pilate tried to release him; but the Jews cried out, "If you release him, you are not a Friend of Caesar. Everyone who makes himself a king opposes Caesar." ¹³When Pilate heard these words he brought Jesus out and seated him on the judge's bench in the place called Stone Pavement, in Hebrew, Gabbatha. ¹⁴It was preparation day for Passover, and it was about noon. And he said to the Jews, "Behold, your king!" ¹⁵They cried out, "Take him away, take him away! Crucify him!" Pilate said to them, "Shall I crucify your king?" The chief priests answered, "We have no king but Caesar." ¹⁶Then he handed him over to them to be crucified. So they took Jesus, ¹⁷and carrying the cross himself he went out to what

is called the Place of the Skull, in Hebrew, Golgotha. [18]There they crucified him, and with him two others, one on either side, with Jesus in the middle. [19]Pilate also had an inscription written and put on the cross. It read, "Jesus the Nazorean, the King of the Jews." [20]Now many of the Jews read this inscription, because the place where Jesus was crucified was near the city; and it was written in Hebrew, Latin, and Greek. [21]So the chief priests of the Jews said to Pilate, "Do not write 'The King of the Jews,' but that he said, 'I am the King of the Jews.'" [22]Pilate answered, "What I have written, I have written." [23]When the soldiers had crucified Jesus, they took his clothes and divided them into four shares, a share for each soldier. They also took his tunic, but the tunic was seamless, woven in one piece from the top down. [24]So they said to one another, "Let's not tear it, but cast lots for it to see whose it will be," in order that the passage of scripture might be fulfilled (that says): "They divided my garments among them, and for my vesture they cast lots." This is what the soldiers did. [25]Standing by the cross of Jesus were his mother and his mother's sister, Mary the wife of Clopas, and Mary of Magdala. [26]When Jesus saw his mother and the disciple there whom he loved, he said to his mother, "Woman, behold, your son." [27]Then he said to the disciple, "Behold, your mother." And from that hour the disciple took her into his home. [28]After this, aware that everything was now finished, in order that the scripture might be fulfilled, Jesus said, "I thirst." [29]There was a vessel filled with common wine. So they put a sponge soaked in wine on a sprig of hyssop and put it up to his mouth. [30]When Jesus had taken the wine, he said, "It is finished." And bowing his head, he handed over the spirit. [31]Now since it was preparation day, in order that the bodies might not remain on the cross on the sabbath, for the sabbath day of that week was a solemn one, the Jews asked Pilate that their legs be broken and they be taken down. [32]So the soldiers came and broke the legs of the first and then of the other one who was crucified with Jesus. [33]But when they came to Jesus and saw that he was already dead, they did not break his legs, [34]but one soldier thrust his lance into his side, and immediately blood and water flowed out. [35]An eyewitness has testified, and his testimony is true; he knows that he is speaking the truth, so that you also may (come to) believe. [36]For this happened so that the scripture passage might be fulfilled: "Not a bone of it will be broken." [37]And again another passage says: "They will look upon him whom they have pierced." [38]After this, Joseph of Arimathea, secretly a disciple of Jesus for fear of the Jews, asked Pilate if he could remove the body of Jesus. And Pilate permitted it. So he came and took his body. [39]Nicodemus, the one who had first come to him at night, also came bringing a mixture of myrrh and aloes weighing about one hundred pounds. [40]They took the body of Jesus and bound it with burial cloths along with the spices, according to the Jewish burial custom. [41]Now in the place where he had been crucified there was a garden, and in the garden a new tomb, in which no one had yet been buried. [42]So they laid Jesus there because of the Jewish preparation day; for the tomb was close by.

John Chapter 20

[1]On the first day of the week, Mary of Magdala came to the tomb early in the morning, while it was still dark, and saw the stone removed from the tomb. [2]So she ran and went to Simon Peter and to the other disciple whom Jesus loved, and told them, "They have taken the Lord from the tomb, and we don't know where they put him." [3]So Peter and the other disciple went out and came to the tomb. [4]They both ran, but the other disciple ran faster than Peter and arrived at the tomb first; [5]he bent down and saw the burial cloths there, but did not go in. [6]When Simon Peter arrived after him, he went into the tomb and saw the burial cloths there, [7]and the cloth that had covered his head, not with the burial cloths but rolled up in a separate place. [8]Then the other disciple also went in, the one who had arrived at the tomb first, and he saw and believed. [9]For they did not yet understand the scripture that he had to rise from the dead. [10]Then the disciples returned home. [11]But Mary stayed outside the tomb weeping. And as she wept, she bent over into the tomb [12]and saw two angels in white sitting there, one at the head and one at the feet where the body of Jesus had been. [13]And they said to her, "Woman, why are you weeping?" She said to them, "They have taken my Lord, and I don't know where they laid him." [14]When she had said this, she turned around and saw Jesus there, but did not know it was Jesus. [15]Jesus said to her, "Woman, why are you weeping? Whom are you looking for?" She thought it was the gardener and said to him, "Sir, if you carried him away, tell me where you laid him, and I will take him." [16]Jesus said to her, "Mary!" She turned and said to him in Hebrew, "Rabbouni," which means Teacher. [17]Jesus said to her, "Stop holding on to me, for I have not yet ascended to the Father. But go to my brothers and tell them, 'I am going to my Father and your Father, to my God and your God.'" [18]Mary of Magdala went and announced to the disciples, "I have seen the Lord," and what he told her. [19]On the evening of that first day of the week, when the doors were locked, where the disciples were, for fear of the Jews, Jesus came and stood in their midst and said to them, "Peace be with you." [20]When he had said this, he showed them his hands and his side. The disciples rejoiced when they saw the Lord. [21](Jesus) said to them again, "Peace be with you. As the Father has sent me, so I send you." [22]And when he had said this, he breathed on them and said to them, "Receive the holy Spirit. [23]Whose sins you forgive are forgiven them, and whose sins you retain are retained." [24]Thomas, called Didymus, one of the Twelve, was not with them when Jesus came. [25]So the other disciples said to him, "We have seen the Lord." But he said to them, "Unless I see the mark of the nails in his hands and put my finger into the nailmarks and put my hand into his side, I will not believe." [26]Now a week later his disciples were again inside and Thomas was with them. Jesus came, although the doors were locked, and stood in their midst and said, "Peace be with you." [27]Then he said to Thomas, "Put your finger here and see my hands, and bring your hand and put it into my side, and do not be unbelieving, but believe." [28]Thomas answered and said to him, "My Lord and my God!" [29]Jesus said to him, "Have you come to believe because you have seen me? Blessed are those who have not seen and have believed." [30]Now Jesus did many other signs in the presence of (his) disciples that are not written in this book. [31]But these are written that you may (come to) believe that Jesus is the Messiah, the Son of God, and that through this belief you may have life in his name.

John Chapter 21

[1]After this, Jesus revealed himself again to his disciples at the Sea of Tiberias. He revealed himself in this way. [2]Together were Simon Peter, Thomas called Didymus, Nathanael from Cana in Galilee, Zebedee's sons, and two others of his disciples. [3]Simon Peter said to them, "I am going fishing." They said to him, "We also will come with you." So they went out and got into the boat, but that night they caught nothing. [4]When it was already dawn, Jesus was standing on the shore; but the disciples did not realize that it was Jesus. [5]Jesus said to them, "Children, have you caught anything to eat?" They answered him, "No." [6]So he said to them, "Cast the net over the right side of the boat and you will find something." So they cast it, and were not able to pull it in because of the number of fish. [7]So the disciple whom Jesus loved said to Peter, "It is the Lord." When Simon Peter heard that it was the Lord, he tucked in his garment, for he was lightly clad, and jumped into the sea. [8]The other disciples came in the boat, for they were not far from shore, only about a hundred yards, dragging the net with the fish. [9]When they climbed out on shore, they saw a charcoal fire with fish on it and bread. [10]Jesus said to them, "Bring some of the fish you just caught." [11]So Simon Peter went over and dragged the net ashore full of one hundred fifty-three large fish. Even though there were so many, the net was not torn. [12]Jesus said to them, "Come, have breakfast." And none of the disciples dared to ask him, "Who are you?" because they realized it was the Lord. [13]Jesus came over and took the bread and gave it to them, and in like manner the fish. [14]This was now the third time Jesus was revealed to his disciples after being raised from the dead. [15]When they had finished breakfast, Jesus said to Simon Peter, "Simon, son of John, do you love me more than these?" He said to him, "Yes, Lord, you know that I love you." He said to him, "Feed my lambs." [16]He then said to him a second time, "Simon, son of John, do you love me?" He said to him, "Yes, Lord, you know that I love you." He said to him, "Tend my sheep." [17]He said to him the third time, "Simon, son of John, do you love me?" Peter was distressed that he had said to him a third time, "Do you love me?" and he said to him, "Lord, you know everything; you know that I love you." (Jesus) said to him, "Feed my sheep. [18]Amen, amen, I say to you, when you were younger, you used to dress yourself and go where you wanted; but when you grow old, you will stretch out your hands, and someone else will dress you and lead you where you do not want to go." [19]He said this signifying by what kind of death he would glorify God. And when he had said this, he said to him, "Follow me." [20]Peter turned and saw the disciple following whom Jesus loved, the one who had also reclined upon his chest during the supper and had said, "Master, who is the one who will betray you?" [21]When Peter saw him, he said to Jesus, "Lord, what about him?" [22]Jesus said to him, "What if I want him to remain until I come? What concern is it of yours? You follow me." [23]So the word spread among the brothers that that disciple would not die. But Jesus had not told him that he would not die, just "What if I want him to remain until I come? (What concern is it of yours?)" [24]It is this disciple who testifies to these things and has written them, and we know that his testimony is true. [25]There are also many other things that Jesus did, but if these were to be described individually, I do not think the whole world would contain the books that would be written.

Historical Book

Acts

Acts Chapter 1

¹In the first book, Theophilus, I dealt with all that Jesus did and taught ²until the day he was taken up, after giving instructions through the holy Spirit to the apostles whom he had chosen. ³He presented himself alive to them by many proofs after he had suffered, appearing to them during forty days and speaking about the kingdom of God. ⁴While meeting with them, he enjoined them not to depart from Jerusalem, but to wait for "the promise of the Father about which you have heard me speak; ⁵for John baptized with water, but in a few days you will be baptized with the holy Spirit." ⁶When they had gathered together they asked him, "Lord, are you at this time going to restore the kingdom to Israel?" ⁷He answered them, "It is not for you to know the times or seasons that the Father has established by his own authority. ⁸But you will receive power when the holy Spirit comes upon you, and you will be my witnesses in Jerusalem, throughout Judea and Samaria, and to the ends of the earth." ⁹When he had said this, as they were looking on, he was lifted up, and a cloud took him from their sight. ¹⁰While they were looking intently at the sky as he was going, suddenly two men dressed in white garments stood beside them. ¹¹They said, "Men of Galilee, why are you standing there looking at the sky? This Jesus who has been taken up from you into heaven will return in the same way as you have seen him going into heaven." ¹²Then they returned to Jerusalem from the mount called Olivet, which is near Jerusalem, a sabbath day's journey away. ¹³When they entered the city they went to the upper room where they were staying, Peter and John and James and Andrew, Philip and Thomas, Bartholomew and Matthew, James son of Alphaeus, Simon the Zealot, and Judas son of James. ¹⁴All these devoted themselves with one accord to prayer, together with some women, and Mary the mother of Jesus, and his brothers. ¹⁵During those days Peter stood up in the midst of the brothers (there was a group of about one hundred and twenty persons in the one place). He said, ¹⁶"My brothers, the scripture had to be fulfilled which the holy Spirit spoke beforehand through the mouth of David, concerning Judas, who was the guide for those who arrested Jesus. ¹⁷He was numbered among us and was allotted a share in this ministry. ¹⁸He bought a parcel of land with the wages of his iniquity, and falling headlong, he burst open in the middle, and all his insides spilled out. ¹⁹This became known to everyone who lived in Jerusalem, so that the parcel of land was called in their language 'Akeldama,' that is, Field of Blood. ²⁰For it is written in the Book of Psalms: 'Let his encampment become desolate, and may no one dwell in it.' And: 'May another take his office.' ²¹Therefore, it is necessary that one of the men who accompanied us the whole time the Lord Jesus came and went among us, ²²beginning from the baptism of John until the day on which he was taken up from us, become with us a witness to his resurrection." ²³So they proposed two, Joseph called Barsabbas, who was also known as Justus, and Matthias. ²⁴Then they prayed, "You, Lord, who know the hearts of all, show which one of these two you have chosen ²⁵to take the place in this apostolic ministry from which Judas turned away to go to his own place." ²⁶Then they gave lots to them, and the lot fell upon Matthias, and he was counted with the eleven apostles.

Acts Chapter 2

¹When the time for Pentecost was fulfilled, they were all in one place together. ²And suddenly there came from the sky a noise like a strong driving wind, and it filled the entire house in which they were. ³Then there appeared to them tongues as of fire, which parted and came to rest on each one of them. ⁴And they were all filled with the holy Spirit and began to speak in different tongues, as the Spirit enabled them to proclaim. ⁵Now there were devout Jews from every nation under heaven staying in Jerusalem. ⁶At this sound, they gathered in a large crowd, but they were confused because each one heard them speaking in his own language. ⁷They were astounded, and in amazement they asked, "Are not all these people who are speaking Galileans? ⁸Then how does each of us hear them in his own native language? ⁹We are Parthians, Medes, and Elamites, inhabitants of Mesopotamia, Judea and Cappadocia, Pontus and Asia, ¹⁰Phrygia and Pamphylia, Egypt and the districts of Libya near Cyrene, as well as travelers from Rome, ¹¹both Jews and converts to Judaism, Cretans and Arabs, yet we hear them speaking in our own tongues of the mighty acts of God." ¹²They were all astounded and bewildered, and said to one another, "What does this mean?" ¹³But others said, scoffing, "They have had too much new wine." ¹⁴Then Peter stood up with the Eleven, raised his voice, and proclaimed to them, "You who are Jews, indeed all of you staying in Jerusalem. Let this be known to you, and listen to my words. ¹⁵These people are not drunk, as you suppose, for it is only nine o'clock in the morning. ¹⁶No, this is what was spoken through the prophet Joel: ¹⁷'It will come to pass in the last days,' God says, 'that I will pour out a portion of my spirit upon all flesh. Your sons and your daughters shall prophesy, your young men shall see visions, your old men shall dream dreams. ¹⁸Indeed, upon my servants and my handmaids I will pour out a portion of my spirit in those days, and they shall prophesy. ¹⁹And I will work wonders in the heavens above and signs on the earth below: blood, fire, and a cloud of smoke. ²⁰The sun shall be turned to darkness, and the moon to blood, before the coming of the great and splendid day of the Lord, ²¹and it shall be that everyone shall be saved who calls on the name of the Lord.' ²²You who are Israelites, hear these words. Jesus the Nazorean was a man commended to you by God with mighty deeds, wonders, and signs, which God worked through him in your midst, as you yourselves know. ²³This man, delivered up by the set plan and foreknowledge of God, you killed, using lawless men to crucify him. ²⁴But God raised him up, releasing him from the throes of death, because it was impossible for him to be held by it. ²⁵For David says of him: 'I saw the Lord ever before me, with him at my right hand I shall not be disturbed. ²⁶Therefore my heart has been glad and my tongue has exulted; my flesh, too, will dwell in hope, ²⁷because you will not abandon my soul to the netherworld, nor will you suffer your holy one to see corruption. ²⁸You have made known to me the paths of life; you will fill me with joy in your presence.' ²⁹My brothers, one can confidently say to you about the patriarch David that he died and was buried, and his tomb is in our midst to this day. ³⁰But since he was a prophet and knew that God had sworn an oath to him that he would set one of his descendants upon his throne, ³¹he foresaw and spoke of the resurrection of the Messiah, that neither was he abandoned to the netherworld nor did his flesh see corruption. ³²God raised this Jesus; of this we are all witnesses. ³³Exalted at the right hand of God, he received the promise of the holy Spirit from the Father and poured it forth, as you (both) see and hear. ³⁴For David did not go up into heaven, but himself said: 'The Lord said to my Lord, "Sit at my right hand ³⁵until I make your enemies your footstool."' ³⁶Therefore let the whole house of Israel know for certain that God has made him both Lord and Messiah, this Jesus whom you crucified." ³⁷Now when they heard this, they were cut to the heart, and they asked Peter and the other apostles, "What are we to do, my brothers?" ³⁸Peter (said) to them, "Repent and be baptized, every one of you, in the name of Jesus Christ for the forgiveness of your sins; and you will receive the gift of the holy Spirit. ³⁹For the promise is made to you and to your children and to all those far off, whomever the Lord our God will call." ⁴⁰He testified with many other arguments, and was exhorting them, "Save yourselves from this corrupt generation." ⁴¹Those who accepted his message were baptized, and about three thousand persons were added that day. ⁴²They devoted themselves to the teaching of the apostles and to the communal life, to the breaking of the bread and to the prayers. ⁴³Awe came upon everyone, and many wonders and signs were done through the apostles. ⁴⁴All who believed were together and had all things in common; ⁴⁵they would sell their property and possessions and divide them among all according to each one's need. ⁴⁶Every day they devoted themselves to meeting together in the temple area and to breaking bread in their homes. They ate their meals with exultation and sincerity of heart, ⁴⁷praising God and enjoying favor with all the people. And every day the Lord added to their number those who were being saved.

Acts Chapter 3

¹Now Peter and John were going up to the temple area for the three o'clock hour of prayer. ²And a man crippled from birth was carried and placed at the gate of the temple called "the Beautiful Gate" every day to beg for alms from the people who entered the temple. ³When he saw Peter and John about to go into the temple, he asked for alms. ⁴But Peter looked intently at him, as did John, and said, "Look at us." ⁵He paid attention to them, expecting to receive something from them. ⁶Peter said, "I have neither silver nor gold, but what I do have I give you: in the name of Jesus Christ the Nazorean, (rise and) walk." ⁷Then Peter took him by the right hand and raised him up, and immediately his feet and ankles grew strong. ⁸He leaped up, stood, and walked around, and went into the temple with them, walking and jumping and praising God. ⁹When all the people saw him walking and praising God, ¹⁰they recognized him as the one who used to sit begging at the Beautiful Gate of the temple, and they were filled with amazement and astonishment at what had happened to him. ¹¹As he clung to Peter and John, all the people hurried in amazement toward them in the portico called "Solomon's Portico." ¹²When Peter saw this, he addressed the people, "You Israelites, why are you amazed at this, and why do you look

so intently at us as if we had made him walk by our own power or piety? 13The God of Abraham, (the God) of Isaac, and (the God) of Jacob, the God of our ancestors, has glorified his servant Jesus whom you handed over and denied in Pilate's presence, when he had decided to release him. 14You denied the Holy and Righteous One and asked that a murderer be released to you. 15The author of life you put to death, but God raised him from the dead; of this we are witnesses. 16And by faith in his name, this man, whom you see and know, his name has been made strong, and the faith that comes through it has given him this perfect health, in the presence of all of you. 17Now I know, brothers, that you acted out of ignorance, just as your leaders did; 18but God has thus brought to fulfillment what he had announced beforehand through the mouth of all the prophets, that his Messiah would suffer. 19Repent, therefore, and be converted, that your sins may be wiped away, 20and that the Lord may grant you times of refreshment and send you the Messiah already appointed for you, Jesus, 21whom heaven must receive until the times of universal restoration of which God spoke through the mouth of his holy prophets from of old. 22For Moses said: 'A prophet like me will the Lord, your God, raise up for you from among your own kinsmen; to him you shall listen in all that he may say to you. 23Everyone who does not listen to that prophet will be cut off from the people.' 24Moreover, all the prophets who spoke, from Samuel and those afterwards, also announced these days. 25You are the children of the prophets and of the covenant that God made with your ancestors when he said to Abraham, 'In your offspring all the families of the earth shall be blessed.' 26For you first, God raised up his servant and sent him to bless you by turning each of you from your evil ways."

Acts Chapter 4

1While they were still speaking to the people, the priests, the captain of the temple guard, and the Sadducees confronted them, 2disturbed that they were teaching the people and proclaiming in Jesus the resurrection of the dead. 3They laid hands on them and put them in custody until the next day, since it was already evening. 4But many of those who heard the word came to believe and (the) number of men grew to (about) five thousand. 5On the next day, their leaders, elders, and scribes were assembled in Jerusalem, 6with Annas the high priest, Caiaphas, John, Alexander, and all who were of the high-priestly class. 7They brought them into their presence and questioned them, "By what power or by what name have you done this?" 8Then Peter, filled with the holy Spirit, answered them, "Leaders of the people and elders: 9If we are being examined today about a good deed done to a cripple, namely, by what means he was saved, 10then all of you and all the people of Israel should know that it was in the name of Jesus Christ the Nazarean whom you crucified, whom God raised from the dead; in his name this man stands before you healed. 11He is 'the stone rejected by you, the builders, which has become the cornerstone.' 12There is no salvation through anyone else, nor is there any other name under heaven given to the human race by which we are to be saved." 13Observing the boldness of Peter and John and perceiving them to be uneducated, ordinary men, they were amazed, and they recognized them as the companions of Jesus. 14Then when they saw the man who had been cured standing there with them, they could say nothing in reply. 15So they ordered them to leave the Sanhedrin, and conferred with one another, saying, 16"What are we to do with these men? Everyone living in Jerusalem knows that a remarkable sign was done through them, and we cannot deny it. 17But so that it may not be spread any further among the people, let us give them a stern warning never again to speak to anyone in this name." 18So they called them back and ordered them not to speak or teach at all in the name of Jesus. 19Peter and John, however, said to them in reply, "Whether it is right in the sight of God for us to obey you rather than God, you be the judges. 20It is impossible for us not to speak about what we have seen and heard." 21After threatening them further, they released them, finding no way to punish them, on account of the people who were all praising God for what had happened. 22For the man on whom this sign of healing had been done was over forty years old. 23After their release they went back to their own people and reported what the chief priests and elders had told them. 24And when they heard it, they raised their voices to God with one accord and said, "Sovereign Lord, maker of heaven and earth and the sea and all that is in them, 25you said by the holy Spirit through the mouth of our father David, your servant: 'Why did the Gentiles rage and the peoples entertain folly? 26The kings of the earth took their stand and the princes gathered together against the Lord and against his anointed.' 27Indeed they gathered in this city against your holy servant Jesus whom you anointed, Herod and Pontius Pilate, together with the Gentiles and the peoples of Israel, 28to do what your hand and (your) will had long ago planned to take place. 29And now, Lord, take note of their threats, and enable your servants to speak your word with

all boldness, 30as you stretch forth (your) hand to heal, and signs and wonders are done through the name of your holy servant Jesus." 31As they prayed, the place where they were gathered shook, and they were all filled with the holy Spirit and continued to speak the word of God with boldness. 32The community of believers was of one heart and mind, and no one claimed that any of his possessions was his own, but they had everything in common. 33With great power the apostles bore witness to the resurrection of the Lord Jesus, and great favor was accorded them all. 34There was no needy person among them, for those who owned property or houses would sell them, bring the proceeds of the sale, 35and put them at the feet of the apostles, and they were distributed to each according to need. 36Thus Joseph, also named by the apostles Barnabas (which is translated "son of encouragement"), a Levite, a Cypriot by birth, 37sold a piece of property that he owned, then brought the money and put it at the feet of the apostles.

Acts Chapter 5

1A man named Ananias, however, with his wife Sapphira, sold a piece of property. 2He retained for himself, with his wife's knowledge, some of the purchase price, took the remainder, and put it at the feet of the apostles. 3But Peter said, "Ananias, why has Satan filled your heart so that you lied to the holy Spirit and retained part of the price of the land? 4While it remained unsold, did it not remain yours? And when it was sold, was it not still under your control? Why did you contrive this deed? You have lied not to human beings, but to God." 5When Ananias heard these words, he fell down and breathed his last, and great fear came upon all who heard of it. 6The young men came and wrapped him up, then carried him out and buried him. 7After an interval of about three hours, his wife came in, unaware of what had happened. 8Peter said to her, "Tell me, did you sell the land for this amount?" She answered, "Yes, for that amount." 9Then Peter said to her, "Why did you agree to test the Spirit of the Lord? Listen, the footsteps of those who have buried your husband are at the door, and they will carry you out." 10At once, she fell down at his feet and breathed her last. When the young men entered they found her dead, so they carried her out and buried her beside her husband. 11And great fear came upon the whole church and upon all who heard of these things. 12Many signs and wonders were done among the people at the hands of the apostles. They were all together in Solomon's portico. 13None of the others dared to join them, but the people esteemed them. 14Yet more than ever, believers in the Lord, great numbers of men and women, were added to them. 15Thus they even carried the sick out into the streets and laid them on cots and mats so that when Peter came by, at least his shadow might fall on one or another of them. 16A large number of people from the towns in the vicinity of Jerusalem also gathered, bringing the sick and those disturbed by unclean spirits, and they were all cured. 17Then the high priest rose up and all his companions, that is, the party of the Sadducees, and, filled with jealousy, 18laid hands upon the apostles and put them in the public jail. 19But during the night, the angel of the Lord opened the doors of the prison, led them out, and said, 20"Go and take your place in the temple area, and tell the people everything about this life." 21When they heard this, they went to the temple early in the morning and taught. When the high priest and his companions arrived, they convened the Sanhedrin, the full senate of the Israelites, and sent to the jail to have them brought in. 22But the court officers who went did not find them in the prison, so they came back and reported, 23"We found the jail securely locked and the guards stationed outside the doors, but when we opened them, we found no one inside." 24When they heard this report, the captain of the temple guard and the chief priests were at a loss about them, as to what this would come to. 25Then someone came in and reported to them, "The men whom you put in prison are in the temple area and are teaching the people." 26Then the captain and the court officers went and brought them in, but without force, because they were afraid of being stoned by the people. 27When they had brought them in and made them stand before the Sanhedrin, the high priest questioned them, 28"We gave you strict orders (did we not?) to stop teaching in that name. Yet you have filled Jerusalem with your teaching and want to bring this man's blood upon us." 29But Peter and the apostles said in reply, "We must obey God rather than men. 30The God of our ancestors raised Jesus, though you had him killed by hanging him on a tree. 31God exalted him at his right hand as leader and savior to grant Israel repentance and forgiveness of sins. 32We are witnesses of these things, as is the holy Spirit that God has given to those who obey him." 33When they heard this, they became infuriated and wanted to put them to death. 34But a Pharisee in the Sanhedrin named Gamaliel, a teacher of the law, respected by all the people, stood up, ordered the men to be put outside for a short time, 35and said to them, "Fellow Israelites, be careful what you are about to do to these men. 36Some time ago, Theudas appeared, claiming to be someone important, and about four hundred men joined him, but he was killed, and all those who were loyal to him were disbanded and came to nothing. [37]After him came Judas the Galilean at the time of the census. He also drew people after him, but he too perished and all who were loyal to him were scattered. [38]So now I tell you, have nothing to do with these men, and let them go. For if this endeavor or this activity is of human origin, it will destroy itself. [39]But if it comes from God, you will not be able to destroy them; you may even find yourselves fighting against God." They were persuaded by him. [40]After recalling the apostles, they had them flogged, ordered them to stop speaking in the name of Jesus, and dismissed them. [41]So they left the presence of the Sanhedrin, rejoicing that they had been found worthy to suffer dishonor for the sake of the name. [42]And all day long, both at the temple and in their homes, they did not stop teaching and proclaiming the Messiah, Jesus.

Acts Chapter 6

[1]At that time, as the number of disciples continued to grow, the Hellenists complained against the Hebrews because their widows were being neglected in the daily distribution. [2]So the Twelve called together the community of the disciples and said, "It is not right for us to neglect the word of God to serve at table. [3]Brothers, select from among you seven reputable men, filled with the Spirit and wisdom, whom we shall appoint to this task, [4]whereas we shall devote ourselves to prayer and to the ministry of the word." [5]The proposal was acceptable to the whole community, so they chose Stephen, a man filled with faith and the holy Spirit, also Philip, Prochorus, Nicanor, Timon, Parmenas, and Nicholas of Antioch, a convert to Judaism. [6]They presented these men to the apostles who prayed and laid hands on them. [7]The word of God continued to spread, and the number of the disciples in Jerusalem increased greatly; even a large group of priests were becoming obedient to the faith. [8]Now Stephen, filled with grace and power, was working great wonders and signs among the people. [9]Certain members of the so-called Synagogue of Freedmen, Cyrenians, and Alexandrians, and people from Cilicia and Asia, came forward and debated with Stephen, [10]but they could not withstand the wisdom and the spirit with which he spoke. [11]Then they instigated some men to say, "We have heard him speaking blasphemous words against Moses and God." [12]They stirred up the people, the elders, and the scribes, accosted him, seized him, and brought him before the Sanhedrin. [13]They presented false witnesses who testified, "This man never stops saying things against (this) holy place and the law. [14]For we have heard him claim that this Jesus the Nazorean will destroy this place and change the customs that Moses handed down to us." [15]All those who sat in the Sanhedrin looked intently at him and saw that his face was like the face of an angel.

Acts Chapter 7

[1]Then the high priest asked, "Is this so?" [2]And he replied, "My brothers and fathers, listen. The God of glory appeared to our father Abraham while he was in Mesopotamia, before he had settled in Haran, [3]and said to him, 'Go forth from your land and (from) your kinsfolk to the land that I will show you.' [4]So he went forth from the land of the Chaldeans and settled in Haran. And from there, after his father died, he made him migrate to this land where you now dwell. [5]Yet he gave him no inheritance in it, not even a foot's length, but he did promise to give it to him and his descendants as a possession, even though he was childless. [6]And God spoke thus, 'His descendants shall be aliens in a land not their own, where they shall be enslaved and oppressed for four hundred years; [7]but I will bring judgment on the nation they serve,' God said, 'and after that they will come out and worship me in this place.' [8]Then he gave him the covenant of circumcision, and so he became the father of Isaac, and circumcised him on the eighth day, as Isaac did Jacob, and Jacob the twelve patriarchs. [9]"And the patriarchs, jealous of Joseph, sold him into slavery in Egypt; but God was with him [10]and rescued him from all his afflictions. He granted him favor and wisdom before Pharaoh, the king of Egypt, who put him in charge of Egypt and (of) his entire household. [11]Then a famine and great affliction struck all Egypt and Canaan, and our ancestors could find no food; [12]but when Jacob heard that there was grain in Egypt, he sent our ancestors there a first time. [13]The second time, Joseph made himself known to his brothers, and Joseph's family became known to Pharaoh. [14]Then Joseph sent for his father Jacob, inviting him and his whole clan, seventy-five persons; [15]and Jacob went down to Egypt. And he and our ancestors died [16]and were brought back to Shechem and placed in the tomb that Abraham had purchased for a sum of money from the sons of Hamor at Shechem. [17]"When the time drew near for the fulfillment of the promise that God pledged to Abraham, the people had increased and become very numerous in Egypt, [18]until another king who knew nothing of Joseph came to power (in Egypt). [19]He dealt shrewdly with our people and oppressed (our) ancestors by forcing them to expose their infants, that they might not survive. [20]At this time Moses was born, and he was extremely beautiful. For three months he was nursed in his father's house; [21]but when he was exposed, Pharaoh's daughter adopted him and brought him up as her own son. [22]Moses was educated (in) all the wisdom of the Egyptians and was powerful in his words and deeds. [23]"When he was forty years old, he decided to visit his kinsfolk, the Israelites. [24]When he saw one of them treated unjustly, he defended and avenged the oppressed man by striking down the Egyptian. [25]He assumed (his) kinsfolk would understand that God was offering them deliverance through him, but they did not understand. [26]The next day he appeared to them as they were fighting and tried to reconcile them peacefully, saying, 'Men, you are brothers. Why are you harming one another?' [27]Then the one who was harming his neighbor pushed him aside, saying, 'Who appointed you ruler and judge over us? [28]Are you thinking of killing me as you killed the Egyptian yesterday?' [29]Moses fled when he heard this and settled as an alien in the land of Midian, where he became the father of two sons. [30]"Forty years later, an angel appeared to him in the desert near Mount Sinai in the flame of a burning bush. [31]When Moses saw it, he was amazed at the sight, and as he drew near to look at it, the voice of the Lord came, [32]'I am the God of your fathers, the God of Abraham, of Isaac, and of Jacob.' Then Moses, trembling, did not dare to look at it. [33]But the Lord said to him, 'Remove the sandals from your feet, for the place where you stand is holy ground. [34]I have witnessed the affliction of my people in Egypt and have heard their groaning, and I have come down to rescue them. Come now, I will send you to Egypt.' [35]This Moses, whom they had rejected with the words, 'Who appointed you ruler and judge?' God sent as (both) ruler and deliverer, through the angel who appeared to him in the bush. [36]This man led them out, performing wonders and signs in the land of Egypt, at the Red Sea, and in the desert for forty years. [37]It was this Moses who said to the Israelites, 'God will raise up for you, from among your own kinsfolk, a prophet like me.' [38]It was he who, in the assembly in the desert, was with the angel who spoke to him on Mount Sinai and with our ancestors, and he received living utterances to hand on to us. [39]"Our ancestors were unwilling to obey him; instead, they pushed him aside and in their hearts turned back to Egypt, [40]saying to Aaron, 'Make us gods who will be our leaders. As for that Moses who led us out of the land of Egypt, we do not know what has happened to him.' [41]So they made a calf in those days, offered sacrifice to the idol, and reveled in the works of their hands. [42]Then God turned and handed them over to worship the host of heaven, as it is written in the book of the prophets: 'Did you bring me sacrifices and offerings for forty years in the desert, O house of Israel? [43]No, you took up the tent of Moloch and the star of (your) god Rephan, the images that you made to worship. So I shall take you into exile beyond Babylon.' [44]"Our ancestors had the tent of testimony in the desert just as the One who spoke to Moses directed him to make it according to the pattern he had seen. [45]Our ancestors who inherited it brought it with Joshua when they dispossessed the nations that God drove out from before our ancestors, up to the time of David, [46]who found favor in the sight of God and asked that he might find a dwelling place for the house of Jacob. [47]But Solomon built a house for him. [48]Yet the Most High does not dwell in houses made by human hands. As the prophet says: [49]'The heavens are my throne, the earth is my footstool. What kind of house can you build for me? says the Lord, or what is to be my resting place? [50]Did not my hand make all these things?' [51]"You stiff-necked people, uncircumcised in heart and ears, you always oppose the holy Spirit; you are just like your ancestors. [52]Which of the prophets did your ancestors not persecute? They put to death those who foretold the coming of the righteous one, whose betrayers and murderers you have now become. [53]You received the law as transmitted by angels, but you did not observe it." [54]When they heard this, they were infuriated, and they ground their teeth at him. [55]But he, filled with the holy Spirit, looked up intently to heaven and saw the glory of God and Jesus standing at the right hand of God, [56]and he said, "Behold, I see the heavens opened and the Son of Man standing at the right hand of God." [57]But they cried out in a loud voice, covered their ears, and rushed upon him together. [58]They threw him out of the city, and began to stone him. The witnesses laid down their cloaks at the feet of a young man named Saul. [59]As they were stoning Stephen, he called out, "Lord Jesus, receive my spirit." [60]Then he fell to his knees and cried out in a loud voice, "Lord, do not hold this sin against them"; and when he said this, he fell asleep.

Acts Chapter 8

[1]Now Saul was consenting to his execution. On that day, there broke out a severe persecution of the church in Jerusalem, and all were scattered throughout the countryside of Judea and Samaria, except the apostles. [2]Devout men buried Stephen and made a loud lament over

him. ³Saul, meanwhile, was trying to destroy the church; entering house after house and dragging out men and women, he handed them over for imprisonment. ⁴Now those who had been scattered went about preaching the word. ⁵Thus Philip went down to (the) city of Samaria and proclaimed the Messiah to them. ⁶With one accord, the crowds paid attention to what was said by Philip when they heard it and saw the signs he was doing. ⁷For unclean spirits, crying out in a loud voice, came out of many possessed people, and many paralyzed and crippled people were cured. ⁸There was great joy in that city. ⁹A man named Simon used to practice magic in the city and astounded the people of Samaria, claiming to be someone great. ¹⁰All of them, from the least to the greatest, paid attention to him, saying, "This man is the 'Power of God' that is called 'Great.'" ¹¹They paid attention to him because he had astounded them by his magic for a long time, ¹²but once they began to believe Philip as he preached the good news about the kingdom of God and the name of Jesus Christ, men and women alike were baptized. ¹³Even Simon himself believed and, after being baptized, became devoted to Philip; and when he saw the signs and mighty deeds that were occurring, he was astounded. ¹⁴Now when the apostles in Jerusalem heard that Samaria had accepted the word of God, they sent them Peter and John, ¹⁵who went down and prayed for them, that they might receive the holy Spirit, ¹⁶for it had not yet fallen upon any of them; they had only been baptized in the name of the Lord Jesus. ¹⁷Then they laid hands on them and they received the holy Spirit. ¹⁸When Simon saw that the Spirit was conferred by the laying on of the apostles' hands, he offered them money ¹⁹and said, "Give me this power too, so that anyone upon whom I lay my hands may receive the holy Spirit." ²⁰But Peter said to him, "May your money perish with you, because you thought that you could buy the gift of God with money. ²¹You have no share or lot in this matter, for your heart is not upright before God. ²²Repent of this wickedness of yours and pray to the Lord that, if possible, your intention may be forgiven. ²³For I see that you are filled with bitter gall and are in the bonds of iniquity." ²⁴Simon said in reply, "Pray for me to the Lord, that nothing of what you have said may come upon me." ²⁵So when they had testified and proclaimed the word of the Lord, they returned to Jerusalem and preached the good news to many Samaritan villages. ²⁶Then the angel of the Lord spoke to Philip, "Get up and head south on the road that goes down from Jerusalem to Gaza, the desert route." ²⁷So he got up and set out. Now there was an Ethiopian eunuch, a court official of the Candace, that is, the queen of the Ethiopians, in charge of her entire treasury, who had come to Jerusalem to worship, ²⁸and was returning home. Seated in his chariot, he was reading the prophet Isaiah. ²⁹The Spirit said to Philip, "Go and join up with that chariot." ³⁰Philip ran up and heard him reading Isaiah the prophet and said, "Do you understand what you are reading?" ³¹He replied, "How can I, unless someone instructs me?" So he invited Philip to get in and sit with him. ³²This was the scripture passage he was reading: "Like a sheep he was led to the slaughter, and as a lamb before its shearer is silent, so he opened not his mouth. ³³In (his) humiliation justice was denied him. Who will tell of his posterity? For his life is taken from the earth." ³⁴Then the eunuch said to Philip in reply, "I beg you, about whom is the prophet saying this? About himself, or about someone else?" ³⁵Then Philip opened his mouth and, beginning with this scripture passage, he proclaimed Jesus to him. ³⁶As they traveled along the road they came to some water, and the eunuch said, "Look, there is water. What is to prevent my being baptized?" ³⁷ ³⁸Then he ordered the chariot to stop, and Philip and the eunuch both went down into the water, and he baptized him. ³⁹When they came out of the water, the Spirit of the Lord snatched Philip away, and the eunuch saw him no more, but continued on his way rejoicing. ⁴⁰Philip came to Azotus, and went about proclaiming the good news to all the towns until he reached Caesarea.

Acts Chapter 9

¹Now Saul, still breathing murderous threats against the disciples of the Lord, went to the high priest ²and asked him for letters to the synagogues in Damascus, that, if he should find any men or women who belonged to the Way, he might bring them back to Jerusalem in chains. ³On his journey, as he was nearing Damascus, a light from the sky suddenly flashed around him. ⁴He fell to the ground and heard a voice saying to him, "Saul, Saul, why are you persecuting me?" ⁵He said, "Who are you, sir?" The reply came, "I am Jesus, whom you are persecuting. ⁶Now get up and go into the city and you will be told what you must do." ⁷The men who were traveling with him stood speechless, for they heard the voice but could see no one. ⁸Saul got up from the ground, but when he opened his eyes he could see nothing; so they led him by the hand and brought him to Damascus. ⁹For three days he was unable to see, and he neither ate nor drank. ¹⁰There was a disciple in Damascus named Ananias, and the Lord said to him in a vision,

"Ananias." He answered, "Here I am, Lord." ¹¹The Lord said to him, "Get up and go to the street called Straight and ask at the house of Judas for a man from Tarsus named Saul. He is there praying, ¹²and (in a vision) he has seen a man named Ananias come in and lay (his) hands on him, that he may regain his sight." ¹³But Ananias replied, "Lord, I have heard from many sources about this man, what evil things he has done to your holy ones in Jerusalem. ¹⁴And here he has authority from the chief priests to imprison all who call upon your name." ¹⁵But the Lord said to him, "Go, for this man is a chosen instrument of mine to carry my name before Gentiles, kings, and Israelites, ¹⁶and I will show him what he will have to suffer for my name." ¹⁷So Ananias went and entered the house; laying his hands on him, he said, "Saul, my brother, the Lord has sent me, Jesus who appeared to you on the way by which you came, that you may regain your sight and be filled with the holy Spirit." ¹⁸Immediately things like scales fell from his eyes and he regained his sight. He got up and was baptized, ¹⁹and when he had eaten, he recovered his strength. He stayed some days with the disciples in Damascus, ²⁰and he began at once to proclaim Jesus in the synagogues, that he is the Son of God. ²¹All who heard him were astounded and said, "Is not this the man who in Jerusalem ravaged those who call upon this name, and came here expressly to take them back in chains to the chief priests?" ²²But Saul grew all the stronger and confounded (the) Jews who lived in Damascus, proving that this is the Messiah. ²³After a long time had passed, the Jews conspired to kill him, ²⁴but their plot became known to Saul. Now they were keeping watch on the gates day and night so as to kill him, ²⁵but his disciples took him one night and let him down through an opening in the wall, lowering him in a basket. ²⁶When he arrived in Jerusalem he tried to join the disciples, but they were all afraid of him, not believing that he was a disciple. ²⁷Then Barnabas took charge of him and brought him to the apostles, and he reported to them how on the way he had seen the Lord and that he had spoken to him, and how in Damascus he had spoken out boldly in the name of Jesus. ²⁸He moved about freely with them in Jerusalem, and spoke out boldly in the name of the Lord. ²⁹He also spoke and debated with the Hellenists, but they tried to kill him. ³⁰And when the brothers learned of this, they took him down to Caesarea and sent him on his way to Tarsus. ³¹The church throughout all Judea, Galilee, and Samaria was at peace. It was being built up and walked in the fear of the Lord, and with the consolation of the holy Spirit it grew in numbers. ³²As Peter was passing through every region, he went down to the holy ones living in Lydda. ³³There he found a man named Aeneas, who had been confined to bed for eight years, for he was paralyzed. ³⁴Peter said to him, "Aeneas, Jesus Christ heals you. Get up and make your bed." He got up at once. ³⁵And all the inhabitants of Lydda and Sharon saw him, and they turned to the Lord. ³⁶Now in Joppa there was a disciple named Tabitha (which translated means Dorcas). She was completely occupied with good deeds and almsgiving. ³⁷Now during those days she fell sick and died, so after washing her, they laid (her) out in a room upstairs. ³⁸Since Lydda was near Joppa, the disciples, hearing that Peter was there, sent two men to him with the request, "Please come to us without delay." ³⁹So Peter got up and went with them. When he arrived, they took him to the room upstairs where all the widows came to him weeping and showing him the tunics and cloaks that Dorcas had made while she was with them. ⁴⁰Peter sent them all out and knelt down and prayed. Then he turned to her body and said, "Tabitha, rise up." She opened her eyes, saw Peter, and sat up. ⁴¹He gave her his hand and raised her up, and when he had called the holy ones and the widows, he presented her alive. ⁴²This became known all over Joppa, and many came to believe in the Lord. ⁴³And he stayed a long time in Joppa with Simon, a tanner.

Acts Chapter 10

¹Now in Caesarea there was a man named Cornelius, a centurion of the Cohort called the Italica, ²devout and God-fearing along with his whole household, who used to give alms generously to the Jewish people and pray to God constantly. ³One afternoon about three o'clock, he saw plainly in a vision an angel of God come in to him and say to him, "Cornelius." ⁴He looked intently at him and, seized with fear, said, "What is it, sir?" He said to him, "Your prayers and almsgiving have ascended as a memorial offering before God. ⁵Now send some men to Joppa and summon one Simon who is called Peter. ⁶He is staying with another Simon, a tanner, who has a house by the sea." ⁷When the angel who spoke to him had left, he called two of his servants and a devout soldier from his staff, ⁸explained everything to them, and sent them to Joppa. ⁹The next day, while they were on their way and nearing the city, Peter went up to the roof terrace to pray at about noontime. ¹⁰He was hungry and wished to eat, and while they were making preparations he fell into a trance. ¹¹He saw heaven opened and something resembling a large sheet coming down, lowered to the ground by its four corners.

¹²In it were all the earth's four-legged animals and reptiles and the birds of the sky. ¹³A voice said to him, "Get up, Peter. Slaughter and eat." ¹⁴But Peter said, "Certainly not, sir. For never have I eaten anything profane and unclean." ¹⁵The voice spoke to him again, a second time, "What God has made clean, you are not to call profane." ¹⁶This happened three times, and then the object was taken up into the sky. ¹⁷While Peter was in doubt about the meaning of the vision he had seen, the men sent by Cornelius asked for Simon's house and arrived at the entrance. ¹⁸They called out inquiring whether Simon, who is called Peter, was staying there. ¹⁹As Peter was pondering the vision, the Spirit said (to him), "There are three men here looking for you. ²⁰So get up, go downstairs, and accompany them without hesitation, because I have sent them." ²¹Then Peter went down to the men and said, "I am the one you are looking for. What is the reason for your being here?" ²²They answered, "Cornelius, a centurion, an upright and God-fearing man, respected by the whole Jewish nation, was directed by a holy angel to summon you to his house and to hear what you have to say." ²³So he invited them in and showed them hospitality. The next day he got up and went with them, and some of the brothers from Joppa went with him. ²⁴On the following day he entered Caesarea. Cornelius was expecting them and had called together his relatives and close friends. ²⁵When Peter entered, Cornelius met him and, falling at his feet, paid him homage. ²⁶Peter, however, raised him up, saying, "Get up. I myself am also a human being." ²⁷While he conversed with him, he went in and found many people gathered together ²⁸and said to them, "You know that it is unlawful for a Jewish man to associate with, or visit, a Gentile, but God has shown me that I should not call any person profane or unclean. ²⁹And that is why I came without objection when sent for. May I ask, then, why you summoned me?" ³⁰Cornelius replied, "Four days ago at this hour, three o'clock in the afternoon, I was at prayer in my house when suddenly a man in dazzling robes stood before me and said, ³¹'Cornelius, your prayer has been heard and your almsgiving remembered before God. ³²Send therefore to Joppa and summon Simon, who is called Peter. He is a guest in the house of Simon, a tanner, by the sea.' ³³So I sent for you immediately, and you were kind enough to come. Now therefore we are all here in the presence of God to listen to all that you have been commanded by the Lord." ³⁴Then Peter proceeded to speak and said, "In truth, I see that God shows no partiality. ³⁵Rather, in every nation whoever fears him and acts uprightly is acceptable to him. ³⁶You know the word (that) he sent to the Israelites as he proclaimed peace through Jesus Christ, who is Lord of all, ³⁷what has happened all over Judea, beginning in Galilee after the baptism that John preached, ³⁸how God anointed Jesus of Nazareth with the holy Spirit and power. He went about doing good and healing all those oppressed by the devil, for God was with him. ³⁹We are witnesses of all that he did both in the country of the Jews and (in) Jerusalem. They put him to death by hanging him on a tree. ⁴⁰This man God raised (on) the third day and granted that he be visible, ⁴¹not to all the people, but to us, the witnesses chosen by God in advance, who ate and drank with him after he rose from the dead. ⁴²He commissioned us to preach to the people and testify that he is the one appointed by God as judge of the living and the dead. ⁴³To him all the prophets bear witness, that everyone who believes in him will receive forgiveness of sins through his name." ⁴⁴While Peter was still speaking these things, the holy Spirit fell upon all who were listening to the word. ⁴⁵The circumcised believers who had accompanied Peter were astounded that the gift of the holy Spirit should have been poured out on the Gentiles also, ⁴⁶for they could hear them speaking in tongues and glorifying God. Then Peter responded, ⁴⁷"Can anyone withhold the water for baptizing these people, who have received the holy Spirit even as we have?" ⁴⁸He ordered them to be baptized in the name of Jesus Christ. ⁴⁹Then they invited him to stay for a few days.

Acts Chapter 11

¹Now the apostles and the brothers who were in Judea heard that the Gentiles too had accepted the word of God. ²So when Peter went up to Jerusalem the circumcised believers confronted him, ³saying, "You entered the house of uncircumcised people and ate with them." ⁴Peter began and explained it to them step by step, saying, ⁵"I was at prayer in the city of Joppa when in a trance I had a vision, something resembling a large sheet coming down, lowered from the sky by its four corners, and it came to me. ⁶Looking intently into it, I observed and saw the four-legged animals of the earth, the wild beasts, the reptiles, and the birds of the sky. ⁷I also heard a voice say to me, 'Get up, Peter. Slaughter and eat.' ⁸But I said, 'Certainly not, sir, because nothing profane or unclean has ever entered my mouth.' ⁹But a second time a voice from heaven answered, 'What God has made clean, you are not to call profane.' ¹⁰This happened three times, and then everything was drawn up again into the sky. ¹¹Just then three men appeared at the house

where we were, who had been sent to me from Caesarea. ¹²The Spirit told me to accompany them without discriminating. These six brothers also went with me, and we entered the man's house. ¹³He related to us how he had seen (the) angel standing in his house, saying, 'Send someone to Joppa and summon Simon, who is called Peter, ¹⁴who will speak words to you by which you and all your household will be saved.' ¹⁵As I began to speak, the holy Spirit fell upon them as it had upon us at the beginning, ¹⁶and I remembered the word of the Lord, how he had said, 'John baptized with water but you will be baptized with the holy Spirit.' ¹⁷If then God gave them the same gift he gave to us when we came to believe in the Lord Jesus Christ, who was I to be able to hinder God?" ¹⁸When they heard this, they stopped objecting and glorified God, saying, "God has then granted life-giving repentance to the Gentiles too." ¹⁹Now those who had been scattered by the persecution that arose because of Stephen went as far as Phoenicia, Cyprus, and Antioch, preaching the word to no one but Jews. ²⁰There were some Cypriots and Cyrenians among them, however, who came to Antioch and began to speak to the Greeks as well, proclaiming the Lord Jesus. ²¹The hand of the Lord was with them and a great number who believed turned to the Lord. ²²The news about them reached the ears of the church in Jerusalem, and they sent Barnabas (to go) to Antioch. ²³When he arrived and saw the grace of God, he rejoiced and encouraged them all to remain faithful to the Lord in firmness of heart, ²⁴for he was a good man, filled with the holy Spirit and faith. And a large number of people was added to the Lord. ²⁵Then he went to Tarsus to look for Saul, ²⁶and when he had found him he brought him to Antioch. For a whole year they met with the church and taught a large number of people, and it was in Antioch that the disciples were first called Christians. ²⁷At that time some prophets came down from Jerusalem to Antioch, ²⁸and one of them named Agabus stood up and predicted by the Spirit that there would be a severe famine all over the world, and it happened under Claudius. ²⁹So the disciples determined that, according to ability, each should send relief to the brothers who lived in Judea. ³⁰This they did, sending it to the presbyters in care of Barnabas and Saul.

Acts Chapter 12

¹About that time King Herod laid hands upon some members of the church to harm them. ²He had James, the brother of John, killed by the sword, ³and when he saw that this was pleasing to the Jews he proceeded to arrest Peter also. (It was (the) feast of Unleavened Bread.) ⁴He had him taken into custody and put in prison under the guard of four squads of four soldiers each. He intended to bring him before the people after Passover. ⁵Peter thus was being kept in prison, but prayer by the church was fervently being made to God on his behalf. ⁶On the very night before Herod was to bring him to trial, Peter, secured by double chains, was sleeping between two soldiers, while outside the door guards kept watch on the prison. ⁷Suddenly the angel of the Lord stood by him and a light shone in the cell. He tapped Peter on the side and awakened him, saying, "Get up quickly." The chains fell from his wrists. ⁸The angel said to him, "Put on your belt and your sandals." He did so. Then he said to him, "Put on your cloak and follow me." ⁹So he followed him out, not realizing that what was happening through the angel was real; he thought he was seeing a vision. ¹⁰They passed the first guard, then the second, and came to the iron gate leading out to the city, which opened for them by itself. They emerged and made their way down an alley, and suddenly the angel left him. ¹¹Then Peter recovered his senses and said, "Now I know for certain that (the) Lord sent his angel and rescued me from the hand of Herod and from all that the Jewish people had been expecting." ¹²When he realized this, he went to the house of Mary, the mother of John who is called Mark, where there were many people gathered in prayer. ¹³When he knocked on the gateway door, a maid named Rhoda came to answer it. ¹⁴She was so overjoyed when she recognized Peter's voice that, instead of opening the gate, she ran in and announced that Peter was standing at the gate. ¹⁵They told her, "You are out of your mind," but she insisted that it was so. But they kept saying, "It is his angel." ¹⁶But Peter continued to knock, and when they opened it, they saw him and were astounded. ¹⁷He motioned to them with his hand to be quiet and explained (to them) how the Lord had led him out of the prison, and said, "Report this to James and the brothers." Then he left and went to another place. ¹⁸At daybreak there was no small commotion among the soldiers over what had become of Peter. ¹⁹Herod, after instituting a search but not finding him, ordered the guards tried and executed. Then he left Judea to spend some time in Caesarea. ²⁰He had long been very angry with the people of Tyre and Sidon, who now came to him in a body. After winning over Blastus, the king's chamberlain, they sued for peace because their country was supplied with food from the king's territory. ²¹On an appointed day, Herod, attired in royal robes, (and)

seated on the rostrum, addressed them publicly. 22The assembled crowd cried out, "This is the voice of a god, not of a man." 23At once the angel of the Lord struck him down because he did not ascribe the honor to God, and he was eaten by worms and breathed his last. 24But the word of God continued to spread and grow. 25After Barnabas and Saul completed their relief mission, they returned to Jerusalem, taking with them John, who is called Mark.

Acts Chapter 13

1Now there were in the church at Antioch prophets and teachers: Barnabas, Symeon who was called Niger, Lucius of Cyrene, Manaen who was a close friend of Herod the tetrarch, and Saul. 2While they were worshiping the Lord and fasting, the holy Spirit said, "Set apart for me Barnabas and Saul for the work to which I have called them." 3Then, completing their fasting and prayer, they laid hands on them and sent them off. 4So they, sent forth by the holy Spirit, went down to Seleucia and from there sailed to Cyprus. 5When they arrived in Salamis, they proclaimed the word of God in the Jewish synagogues. They had John also as their assistant. 6When they had traveled through the whole island as far as Paphos, they met a magician named Bar-Jesus who was a Jewish false prophet. 7He was with the proconsul Sergius Paulus, a man of intelligence, who had summoned Barnabas and Saul and wanted to hear the word of God. 8But Elymas the magician (for that is what his name means) opposed them in an attempt to turn the proconsul away from the faith. 9But Saul, also known as Paul, filled with the holy Spirit, looked intently at him 10and said, "You son of the devil, you enemy of all that is right, full of every sort of deceit and fraud. Will you not stop twisting the straight paths of (the) Lord? 11Even now the hand of the Lord is upon you. You will be blind, and unable to see the sun for a time." Immediately a dark mist fell upon him, and he went about seeking people to lead him by the hand. 12When the proconsul saw what had happened, he came to believe, for he was astonished by the teaching about the Lord. 13From Paphos, Paul and his companions set sail and arrived at Perga in Pamphylia. But John left them and returned to Jerusalem. 14They continued on from Perga and reached Antioch in Pisidia. On the sabbath they entered (into) the synagogue and took their seats. 15After the reading of the law and the prophets, the synagogue officials sent word to them, "My brothers, if one of you has a word of exhortation for the people, please speak." 16So Paul got up, motioned with his hand, and said, "Fellow Israelites and you others who are God-fearing, listen. 17The God of this people Israel chose our ancestors and exalted the people during their sojourn in the land of Egypt. With uplifted arm he led them out of it 18and for about forty years he put up with them in the desert. 19When he had destroyed seven nations in the land of Canaan, he gave them their land as an inheritance 20at the end of about four hundred and fifty years. After these things he provided judges up to Samuel (the) prophet. 21Then they asked for a king. God gave them Saul, son of Kish, a man from the tribe of Benjamin, for forty years. 22Then he removed him and raised up David as their king; of him he testified, 'I have found David, son of Jesse, a man after my own heart; he will carry out my every wish.' 23From this man's descendants God, according to his promise, has brought to Israel a savior, Jesus. 24John heralded his coming by proclaiming a baptism of repentance to all the people of Israel; 25and as John was completing his course, he would say, 'What do you suppose that I am? I am not he. Behold, one is coming after me; I am not worthy to unfasten the sandals of his feet.' 26"My brothers, children of the family of Abraham, and those others among you who are God-fearing, to us this word of salvation has been sent. 27The inhabitants of Jerusalem and their leaders failed to recognize him, and by condemning him they fulfilled the oracles of the prophets that are read sabbath after sabbath. 28For even though they found no grounds for a death sentence, they asked Pilate to have him put to death, 29and when they had accomplished all that was written about him, they took him down from the tree and placed him in a tomb. 30But God raised him from the dead, 31and for many days he appeared to those who had come up with him from Galilee to Jerusalem. These are (now) his witnesses before the people. 32We ourselves are proclaiming this good news to you that what God promised our ancestors 33he has brought to fulfillment for us, (their) children, by raising up Jesus, as it is written in the second psalm, 'You are my son; this day I have begotten you.' 34And that he raised him from the dead never to return to corruption he declared in this way, 'I shall give you the benefits assured to David.' 35That is why he also says in another psalm, 'You will not suffer your holy one to see corruption.' 36Now David, after he had served the will of God in his lifetime, fell asleep, was gathered to his ancestors, and did see corruption. 37But the one whom God raised up did not see corruption. 38You must know, my brothers, that through him forgiveness of sins is being proclaimed to you, (and) in regard to everything from which you could not be justified

under the law of Moses, 39in him every believer is justified. 40Be careful, then, that what was said in the prophets not come about: 41'Look on, you scoffers, be amazed and disappear. For I am doing a work in your days, a work that you will never believe even if someone tells you.'" 42As they were leaving, they invited them to speak on these subjects the following sabbath. 43After the congregation had dispersed, many Jews and worshipers who were converts to Judaism followed Paul and Barnabas, who spoke to them and urged them to remain faithful to the grace of God. 44On the following sabbath almost the whole city gathered to hear the word of the Lord. 45When the Jews saw the crowds, they were filled with jealousy and with violent abuse contradicted what Paul said. 46Both Paul and Barnabas spoke out boldly and said, "It was necessary that the word of God be spoken to you first, but since you reject it and condemn yourselves as unworthy of eternal life, we now turn to the Gentiles. 47For so the Lord has commanded us, 'I have made you a light to the Gentiles, that you may be an instrument of salvation to the ends of the earth.'" 48The Gentiles were delighted when they heard this and glorified the word of the Lord. All who were destined for eternal life came to believe, 49and the word of the Lord continued to spread through the whole region. 50The Jews, however, incited the women of prominence who were worshipers and the leading men of the city, stirred up a persecution against Paul and Barnabas, and expelled them from their territory. 51So they shook the dust from their feet in protest against them and went to Iconium. 52The disciples were filled with joy and the holy Spirit.

Acts Chapter 14

1In Iconium they entered the Jewish synagogue together and spoke in such a way that a great number of both Jews and Greeks came to believe, 2although the disbelieving Jews stirred up and poisoned the minds of the Gentiles against the brothers. 3So they stayed for a considerable period, speaking out boldly for the Lord, who confirmed the word about his grace by granting signs and wonders to occur through their hands. 4The people of the city were divided: some were with the Jews; others, with the apostles. 5When there was an attempt by both the Gentiles and the Jews, together with their leaders, to attack and stone them, 6they realized it and fled to the Lycaonian cities of Lystra and Derbe and to the surrounding countryside, 7where they continued to proclaim the good news. 8At Lystra there was a crippled man, lame from birth, who had never walked. 9He listened to Paul speaking, who looked intently at him, saw that he had the faith to be healed, 10and called out in a loud voice, "Stand up straight on your feet." He jumped up and began to walk about. 11When the crowds saw what Paul had done, they cried out in Lycaonian, "The gods have come down to us in human form." 12They called Barnabas "Zeus" and Paul "Hermes," because he was the chief speaker. 13And the priest of Zeus, whose temple was at the entrance to the city, brought oxen and garlands to the gates, for he together with the people intended to offer sacrifice. 14The apostles Barnabas and Paul tore their garments when they heard this and rushed out into the crowd, shouting, 15"Men, why are you doing this? We are of the same nature as you, human beings. We proclaim to you good news that you should turn from these idols to the living God, 'who made heaven and earth and sea and all that is in them.' 16In past generations he allowed all Gentiles to go their own ways; 17yet, in bestowing his goodness, he did not leave himself without witness, for he gave you rains from heaven and fruitful seasons, and filled you with nourishment and gladness for your hearts." 18Even with these words, they scarcely restrained the crowds from offering sacrifice to them. 19However, some Jews from Antioch and Iconium arrived and won over the crowds. They stoned Paul and dragged him out of the city, supposing that he was dead. 20But when the disciples gathered around him, he got up and entered the city. On the following day he left with Barnabas for Derbe. 21After they had proclaimed the good news to that city and made a considerable number of disciples, they returned to Lystra and to Iconium and to Antioch. 22They strengthened the spirits of the disciples and exhorted them to persevere in the faith, saying, "It is necessary for us to undergo many hardships to enter the kingdom of God." 23They appointed presbyters for them in each church and, with prayer and fasting, commended them to the Lord in whom they had put their faith. 24Then they traveled through Pisidia and reached Pamphylia. 25After proclaiming the word at Perga they went down to Attalia. 26From there they sailed to Antioch, where they had been commended to the grace of God for the work they had now accomplished. 27And when they arrived, they called the church together and reported what God had done with them and how he had opened the door of faith to the Gentiles. 28Then they spent no little time with the disciples.

Acts Chapter 15

[1]Some who had come down from Judea were instructing the brothers, "Unless you are circumcised according to the Mosaic practice, you cannot be saved." [2]Because there arose no little dissension and debate by Paul and Barnabas with them, it was decided that Paul, Barnabas, and some of the others should go up to Jerusalem to the apostles and presbyters about this question. [3]They were sent on their journey by the church, and passed through Phoenicia and Samaria telling of the conversion of the Gentiles, and brought great joy to all the brothers. [4]When they arrived in Jerusalem, they were welcomed by the church, as well as by the apostles and the presbyters, and they reported what God had done with them. [5]But some from the party of the Pharisees who had become believers stood up and said, "It is necessary to circumcise them and direct them to observe the Mosaic law." [6]The apostles and the presbyters met together to see about this matter. [7]After much debate had taken place, Peter got up and said to them, "My brothers, you are well aware that from early days God made his choice among you that through my mouth the Gentiles would hear the word of the gospel and believe. [8]And God, who knows the heart, bore witness by granting them the holy Spirit just as he did us. [9]He made no distinction between us and them, for by faith he purified their hearts. [10]Why, then, are you now putting God to the test by placing on the shoulders of the disciples a yoke that neither our ancestors nor we have been able to bear? [11]On the contrary, we believe that we are saved through the grace of the Lord Jesus, in the same way as they." [12]The whole assembly fell silent, and they listened while Paul and Barnabas described the signs and wonders God had worked among the Gentiles through them. [13]After they had fallen silent, James responded, "My brothers, listen to me. [14]Symeon has described how God first concerned himself with acquiring from among the Gentiles a people for his name. [15]The words of the prophets agree with this, as is written: [16]'After this I shall return and rebuild the fallen hut of David; from its ruins I shall rebuild it and raise it up again, [17]so that the rest of humanity may seek out the Lord, even all the Gentiles on whom my name is invoked. Thus says the Lord who accomplishes these things, [18]known from of old.' [19]It is my judgment, therefore, that we ought to stop troubling the Gentiles who turn to God, [20]but tell them by letter to avoid pollution from idols, unlawful marriage, the meat of strangled animals, and blood. [21]For Moses, for generations now, has had those who proclaim him in every town, as he has been read in the synagogues every sabbath." [22]Then the apostles and presbyters, in agreement with the whole church, decided to choose representatives and to send them to Antioch with Paul and Barnabas. The ones chosen were Judas, who was called Barsabbas, and Silas, leaders among the brothers. [23]This is the letter delivered by them: "The apostles and the presbyters, your brothers, to the brothers in Antioch, Syria, and Cilicia of Gentile origin: greetings. [24]Since we have heard that some of our number (who went out) without any mandate from us have upset you with their teachings and disturbed your peace of mind, [25]we have with one accord decided to choose representatives and to send them to you along with our beloved Barnabas and Paul, [26]who have dedicated their lives to the name of our Lord Jesus Christ. [27]So we are sending Judas and Silas who will also convey this same message by word of mouth: [28]'It is the decision of the holy Spirit and of us not to place on you any burden beyond these necessities, [29]namely, to abstain from meat sacrificed to idols, from blood, from meats of strangled animals, and from unlawful marriage. If you keep free of these, you will be doing what is right. Farewell.'" [30]And so they were sent on their journey. Upon their arrival in Antioch they called the assembly together and delivered the letter. [31]When the people read it, they were delighted with the exhortation. [32]Judas and Silas, who were themselves prophets, exhorted and strengthened the brothers with many words. [33]After they had spent some time there, they were sent off with greetings of peace from the brothers to those who had commissioned them. [34] [35]But Paul and Barnabas remained in Antioch, teaching and proclaiming with many others the word of the Lord. [36]After some time, Paul said to Barnabas, "Come, let us make a return visit to see how the brothers are getting on in all the cities where we proclaimed the word of the Lord." [37]Barnabas wanted to take with them also John, who was called Mark, [38]but Paul insisted that they should not take with them someone who had deserted them at Pamphylia and who had not continued with them in their work. [39]So sharp was their disagreement that they separated. Barnabas took Mark and sailed to Cyprus. [40]But Paul chose Silas and departed after being commended by the brothers to the grace of the Lord. [41]He traveled through Syria and Cilicia bringing strength to the churches.

Acts Chapter 16

[1]He reached (also) Derbe and Lystra where there was a disciple named Timothy, the son of a Jewish woman who was a believer, but his father was a Greek. [2]The brothers in Lystra and Iconium spoke highly of him, [3]and Paul wanted him to come along with him. On account of the Jews of that region, Paul had him circumcised, for they all knew that his father was a Greek. [4]As they traveled from city to city, they handed on to the people for observance the decisions reached by the apostles and presbyters in Jerusalem. [5]Day after day the churches grew stronger in faith and increased in number. [6]They traveled through the Phrygian and Galatian territory because they had been prevented by the holy Spirit from preaching the message in the province of Asia. [7]When they came to Mysia, they tried to go on into Bithynia, but the Spirit of Jesus did not allow them, [8]so they crossed through Mysia and came down to Troas. [9]During (the) night Paul had a vision. A Macedonian stood before him and implored him with these words, "Come over to Macedonia and help us." [10]When he had seen the vision, we sought passage to Macedonia at once, concluding that God had called us to proclaim the good news to them. [11]We set sail from Troas, making a straight run for Samothrace, and on the next day to Neapolis, [12]and from there to Philippi, a leading city in that district of Macedonia and a Roman colony. We spent some time in that city. [13]On the sabbath we went outside the city gate along the river where we thought there would be a place of prayer. We sat and spoke with the women who had gathered there. [14]One of them, a woman named Lydia, a dealer in purple cloth, from the city of Thyatira, a worshiper of God, listened, and the Lord opened her heart to pay attention to what Paul was saying. [15]After she and her household had been baptized, she offered us an invitation, "If you consider me a believer in the Lord, come and stay at my home," and she prevailed on us. [16]As we were going to the place of prayer, we met a slave girl with an oracular spirit, who used to bring a large profit to her owners through her fortune-telling. [17]She began to follow Paul and us, shouting, "These people are slaves of the Most High God, who proclaim to you a way of salvation." [18]She did this for many days. Paul became annoyed, turned, and said to the spirit, "I command you in the name of Jesus Christ to come out of her." Then it came out at that moment. [19]When her owners saw that their hope of profit was gone, they seized Paul and Silas and dragged them to the public square before the local authorities. [20]They brought them before the magistrates and said, "These people are Jews and are disturbing our city [21]and are advocating customs that are not lawful for us Romans to adopt or practice." [22]The crowd joined in the attack on them, and the magistrates had them stripped and ordered them to be beaten with rods. [23]After inflicting many blows on them, they threw them into prison and instructed the jailer to guard them securely. [24]When he received these instructions, he put them in the innermost cell and secured their feet to a stake. [25]About midnight, while Paul and Silas were praying and singing hymns to God as the prisoners listened, [26]there was suddenly such a severe earthquake that the foundations of the jail shook; all the doors flew open, and the chains of all were pulled loose. [27]When the jailer woke up and saw the prison doors wide open, he drew (his) sword and was about to kill himself, thinking that the prisoners had escaped. [28]But Paul shouted out in a loud voice, "Do no harm to yourself; we are all here." [29]He asked for a light and rushed in and, trembling with fear, he fell down before Paul and Silas. [30]Then he brought them out and said, "Sirs, what must I do to be saved?" [31]And they said, "Believe in the Lord Jesus and you and your household will be saved." [32]So they spoke the word of the Lord to him and to everyone in his house. [33]He took them in at that hour of the night and bathed their wounds; then he and all his family were baptized at once. [34]He brought them up into his house and provided a meal and with his household rejoiced at having come to faith in God. [35]But when it was day, the magistrates sent the lictors with the order, "Release those men." [36]The jailer reported the (se) words to Paul, "The magistrates have sent orders that you be released. Now, then, come out and go in peace." [37]But Paul said to them, "They have beaten us publicly, even though we are Roman citizens and have not been tried, and have thrown us into prison. And now, are they going to release us secretly? By no means. Let them come themselves and lead us out." [38]The lictors reported these words to the magistrates, and they became alarmed when they heard that they were Roman citizens. [39]So they came and placated them, and led them out and asked that they leave the city. [40]When they had come out of the prison, they went to Lydia's house where they saw and encouraged the brothers, and then they left.

Acts Chapter 17

[1]When they took the road through Amphipolis and Apollonia, they reached Thessalonica, where there was a synagogue of the Jews. [2]Following his usual custom, Paul joined them, and for three sabbaths he entered into discussions with them from the scriptures, [3]expounding and demonstrating that the Messiah had to suffer and rise from the

dead, and that "This is the Messiah, Jesus, whom I proclaim to you." [4]Some of them were convinced and joined Paul and Silas; so, too, a great number of Greeks who were worshipers, and not a few of the prominent women. [5]But the Jews became jealous and recruited some worthless men loitering in the public square, formed a mob, and set the city in turmoil. They marched on the house of Jason, intending to bring them before the people's assembly. [6]When they could not find them, they dragged Jason and some of the brothers before the city magistrates, shouting, "These people who have been creating a disturbance all over the world have now come here, [7]and Jason has welcomed them. They all act in opposition to the decrees of Caesar and claim instead that there is another king, Jesus." [8]They stirred up the crowd and the city magistrates who, upon hearing these charges, [9]took a surety payment from Jason and the others before releasing them. [10]The brothers immediately sent Paul and Silas to Beroea during the night. Upon arrival they went to the synagogue of the Jews. [11]These Jews were more fair-minded than those in Thessalonica, for they received the word with all willingness and examined the scriptures daily to determine whether these things were so. [12]Many of them became believers, as did not a few of the influential Greek women and men. [13]But when the Jews of Thessalonica learned that the word of God had now been proclaimed by Paul in Beroea also, they came there too to cause a commotion and stir up the crowds. [14]So the brothers at once sent Paul on his way to the seacoast, while Silas and Timothy remained behind. [15]After Paul's escorts had taken him to Athens, they came away with instructions for Silas and Timothy to join him as soon as possible. [16]While Paul was waiting for them in Athens, he grew exasperated at the sight of the city full of idols. [17]So he debated in the synagogue with the Jews and with the worshipers, and daily in the public square with whoever happened to be there. [18]Even some of the Epicurean and Stoic philosophers engaged him in discussion. Some asked, "What is this scavenger trying to say?" Others said, "He sounds like a promoter of foreign deities," because he was preaching about 'Jesus' and 'Resurrection.' [19]They took him and led him to the Areopagus and said, "May we learn what this new teaching is that you speak of? [20]For you bring some strange notions to our ears; we should like to know what these things mean." [21]Now all the Athenians as well as the foreigners residing there used their time for nothing else but telling or hearing something new. [22]Then Paul stood up at the Areopagus and said: "You Athenians, I see that in every respect you are very religious. [23]For as I walked around looking carefully at your shrines, I even discovered an altar inscribed, 'To an Unknown God.' What therefore you unknowingly worship, I proclaim to you. [24]The God who made the world and all that is in it, the Lord of heaven and earth, does not dwell in sanctuaries made by human hands, [25]nor is he served by human hands because he needs anything. Rather it is he who gives to everyone life and breath and everything. [26]He made from one the whole human race to dwell on the entire surface of the earth, and he fixed the ordered seasons and the boundaries of their regions, [27]so that people might seek God, even perhaps grope for him and find him, though indeed he is not far from any one of us. [28]For 'In him we live and move and have our being,' as even some of your poets have said, 'For we too are his offspring.' [29]Since therefore we are the offspring of God, we ought not to think that the divinity is like an image fashioned from gold, silver, or stone by human art and imagination. [30]God has overlooked the times of ignorance, but now he demands that all people everywhere repent [31]because he has established a day on which he will 'judge the world with justice' through a man he has appointed, and he has provided confirmation for all by raising him from the dead." [32]When they heard about resurrection of the dead, some began to scoff, but others said, "We should like to hear you on this some other time." [33]And so Paul left them. [34]But some did join him, and became believers. Among them were Dionysius, a member of the Court of the Areopagus, a woman named Damaris, and others with them.

Acts Chapter 18

[1]After this he left Athens and went to Corinth. [2]There he met a Jew named Aquila, a native of Pontus, who had recently come from Italy with his wife Priscilla because Claudius had ordered all the Jews to leave Rome. He went to visit them [3]and, because he practiced the same trade, stayed with them and worked, for they were tentmakers by trade. [4]Every sabbath, he entered into discussions in the synagogue, attempting to convince both Jews and Greeks. [5]When Silas and Timothy came down from Macedonia, Paul began to occupy himself totally with preaching the word, testifying to the Jews that the Messiah was Jesus. [6]When they opposed him and reviled him, he shook out his garments and said to them, "Your blood be on your heads! I am clear of responsibility. From now on I will go to the Gentiles." [7]So he left there and went to a house belonging to a man named Titus Justus, a

worshiper of God; his house was next to a synagogue. [8]Crispus, the synagogue official, came to believe in the Lord along with his entire household, and many of the Corinthians who heard believed and were baptized. [9]One night in a vision the Lord said to Paul, "Do not be afraid. Go on speaking, and do not be silent, [10]for I am with you. No one will attack and harm you, for I have many people in this city." [11]He settled there for a year and a half and taught the word of God among them. [12]But when Gallio was proconsul of Achaia, the Jews rose up together against Paul and brought him to the tribunal, [13]saying, "This man is inducing people to worship God contrary to the law." [14]When Paul was about to reply, Gallio spoke to the Jews, "If it were a matter of some crime or malicious fraud, I should with reason hear the complaint of you Jews; [15]but since it is a question of arguments over doctrine and titles and your own law, see to it yourselves. I do not wish to be a judge of such matters." [16]And he drove them away from the tribunal. [17]They all seized Sosthenes, the synagogue official, and beat him in full view of the tribunal. But none of this was of concern to Gallio. [18]Paul remained for quite some time, and after saying farewell to the brothers he sailed for Syria, together with Priscilla and Aquila. At Cenchreae he had his hair cut because he had taken a vow. [19]When they reached Ephesus, he left them there, while he entered the synagogue and held discussions with the Jews. [20]Although they asked him to stay for a longer time, he did not consent, [21]but as he said farewell he promised, "I shall come back to you again, God willing." Then he set sail from Ephesus. [22]Upon landing at Caesarea, he went up and greeted the church and then went down to Antioch. [23]After staying there some time, he left and traveled in orderly sequence through the Galatian country and Phrygia, bringing strength to all the disciples. [24]A Jew named Apollos, a native of Alexandria, an eloquent speaker, arrived in Ephesus. He was an authority on the scriptures. [25]He had been instructed in the Way of the Lord and, with ardent spirit, spoke and taught accurately about Jesus, although he knew only the baptism of John. [26]He began to speak boldly in the synagogue; but when Priscilla and Aquila heard him, they took him aside and explained to him the Way (of God) more accurately. [27]And when he wanted to cross to Achaia, the brothers encouraged him and wrote to the disciples there to welcome him. After his arrival he gave great assistance to those who had come to believe through grace. [28]He vigorously refuted the Jews in public, establishing from the scriptures that the Messiah is Jesus.

Acts Chapter 19

[1]While Apollos was in Corinth, Paul traveled through the interior of the country and came (down) to Ephesus where he found some disciples. [2]He said to them, "Did you receive the holy Spirit when you became believers?" They answered him, "We have never even heard that there is a holy Spirit." [3]He said, "How were you baptized?" They replied, "With the baptism of John." [4]Paul then said, "John baptized with a baptism of repentance, telling the people to believe in the one who was to come after him, that is, in Jesus." [5]When they heard this, they were baptized in the name of the Lord Jesus. [6]And when Paul laid (his) hands on them, the holy Spirit came upon them, and they spoke in tongues and prophesied. [7]Altogether there were about twelve men. [8]He entered the synagogue, and for three months debated boldly with persuasive arguments about the kingdom of God. [9]But when some in their obstinacy and disbelief disparaged the Way before the assembly, he withdrew and took his disciples with him and began to hold daily discussions in the lecture hall of Tyrannus. [10]This continued for two years with the result that all the inhabitants of the province of Asia heard the word of the Lord, Jews and Greeks alike. [11]So extraordinary were the mighty deeds God accomplished at the hands of Paul [12]that when face cloths or aprons that touched his skin were applied to the sick, their diseases left them and the evil spirits came out of them. [13]Then some itinerant Jewish exorcists tried to invoke the name of the Lord Jesus over those with evil spirits, saying, "I adjure you by the Jesus whom Paul preaches." [14]When the seven sons of Sceva, a Jewish high priest, tried to do this, [15]the evil spirit said to them in reply, "Jesus I recognize, Paul I know, but who are you?" [16]The person with the evil spirit then sprang at them and subdued them all. He so overpowered them that they fled naked and wounded from that house. [17]When this became known to all the Jews and Greeks who lived in Ephesus, fear fell upon them all, and the name of the Lord Jesus was held in great esteem. [18]Many of those who had become believers came forward and openly acknowledged their former practices. [19]Moreover, a large number of those who had practiced magic collected their books and burned them in public. They calculated their value and found it to be fifty thousand silver pieces. [20]Thus did the word of the Lord continue to spread with influence and power. [21]When this was concluded, Paul made up his mind to travel through Macedonia and Achaia, and then to go on to Jerusalem, saying, "After I have been there, I must visit Rome

also." ²²Then he sent to Macedonia two of his assistants, Timothy and Erastus, while he himself stayed for a while in the province of Asia. ²³About that time a serious disturbance broke out concerning the Way. ²⁴There was a silversmith named Demetrius who made miniature silver shrines of Artemis and provided no little work for the craftsmen. ²⁵He called a meeting of these and other workers in related crafts and said, "Men, you know well that our prosperity derives from this work. ²⁶As you can now see and hear, not only in Ephesus but throughout most of the province of Asia this Paul has persuaded and misled a great number of people by saying that gods made by hands are not gods at all. ²⁷The danger grows, not only that our business will be discredited, but also that the temple of the great goddess Artemis will be of no account, and that she whom the whole province of Asia and all the world worship will be stripped of her magnificence." ²⁸When they heard this, they were filled with fury and began to shout, "Great is Artemis of the Ephesians!" ²⁹The city was filled with confusion, and the people rushed with one accord into the theater, seizing Gaius and Aristarchus, the Macedonians, Paul's traveling companions. ³⁰Paul wanted to go before the crowd, but the disciples would not let him, ³¹and even some of the Asiarchs who were friends of his sent word to him advising him not to venture into the theater. ³²Meanwhile, some were shouting one thing, others something else; the assembly was in chaos, and most of the people had no idea why they had come together. ³³Some of the crowd prompted Alexander, as the Jews pushed him forward, and Alexander signaled with his hand that he wished to explain something to the gathering. ³⁴But when they recognized that he was a Jew, they all shouted in unison, for about two hours, "Great is Artemis of the Ephesians!" ³⁵Finally the town clerk restrained the crowd and said, "You Ephesians, what person is there who does not know that the city of the Ephesians is the guardian of the temple of the great Artemis and of her image that fell from the sky? ³⁶Since these things are undeniable, you must calm yourselves and not do anything rash. ³⁷The men you brought here are not temple robbers, nor have they insulted our goddess. ³⁸If Demetrius and his fellow craftsmen have a complaint against anyone, courts are in session, and there are proconsuls. Let them bring charges against one another. ³⁹If you have anything further to investigate, let the matter be settled in the lawful assembly, ⁴⁰for, as it is, we are in danger of being charged with rioting because of today's conduct. There is no cause for it. We shall (not) be able to give a reason for this demonstration." With these words he dismissed the assembly.

Acts Chapter 20

¹When the disturbance was over, Paul had the disciples summoned and, after encouraging them, he bade them farewell and set out on his journey to Macedonia. ²As he traveled throughout those regions, he provided many words of encouragement for them. Then he arrived in Greece, ³where he stayed for three months. But when a plot was made against him by the Jews as he was about to set sail for Syria, he decided to return by way of Macedonia. ⁴Sopater, the son of Pyrrhus, from Beroea, accompanied him, as did Aristarchus and Secundus from Thessalonica, Gaius from Derbe, Timothy, and Tychicus and Trophimus from Asia ⁵who went on ahead and waited for us at Troas. ⁶We sailed from Philippi after the feast of Unleavened Bread, and rejoined them five days later in Troas, where we spent a week. ⁷On the first day of the week when we gathered to break bread, Paul spoke to them because he was going to leave on the next day, and he kept on speaking until midnight. ⁸There were many lamps in the upstairs room where we were gathered, ⁹and a young man named Eutychus who was sitting on the window sill was sinking into a deep sleep as Paul talked on and on. Once overcome by sleep, he fell down from the third story and when he was picked up, he was dead. ¹⁰Paul went down, threw himself upon him, and said as he embraced him, "Don't be alarmed; there is life in him." ¹¹Then he returned upstairs, broke the bread, and ate; after a long conversation that lasted until daybreak, he departed. ¹²And they took the boy away alive and were immeasurably comforted. ¹³We went ahead to the ship and set sail for Assos where we were to take Paul on board, as he had arranged, since he was going overland. ¹⁴When he met us in Assos, we took him aboard and went on to Mitylene. ¹⁵We sailed away from there on the next day and reached a point off Chios, and a day later we reached Samos, and on the following day we arrived at Miletus. ¹⁶Paul had decided to sail past Ephesus in order not to lose time in the province of Asia, for he was hurrying to be in Jerusalem, if at all possible, for the day of Pentecost. ¹⁷From Miletus he had the presbyters of the church at Ephesus summoned. ¹⁸When they came to him, he addressed them, "You know how I lived among you the whole time from the day I first came to the province of Asia. ¹⁹I served the Lord with all humility and with the tears and trials that came to me because of the plots of the Jews, ²⁰and I did not at all shrink from telling you what was for your benefit, or from teaching you in public or

in your homes. ²¹I earnestly bore witness for both Jews and Greeks to repentance before God and to faith in our Lord Jesus. ²²But now, compelled by the Spirit, I am going to Jerusalem. What will happen to me there I do not know, ²³except that in one city after another the holy Spirit has been warning me that imprisonment and hardships await me. ²⁴Yet I consider life of no importance to me, if only I may finish my course and the ministry that I received from the Lord Jesus, to bear witness to the gospel of God's grace. ²⁵"But now I know that none of you to whom I preached the kingdom during my travels will ever see my face again. ²⁶And so I solemnly declare to you this day that I am not responsible for the blood of any of you, ²⁷for I did not shrink from proclaiming to you the entire plan of God. ²⁸Keep watch over yourselves and over the whole flock of which the holy Spirit has appointed you overseers, in which you tend the church of God that he acquired with his own blood. ²⁹I know that after my departure savage wolves will come among you, and they will not spare the flock. ³⁰And from your own group, men will come forward perverting the truth to draw the disciples away after them. ³¹So be vigilant and remember that for three years, night and day, I unceasingly admonished each of you with tears. ³²And now I commend you to God and to that gracious word of his that can build you up and give you the inheritance among all who are consecrated. ³³I have never wanted anyone's silver or gold or clothing. ³⁴You know well that these very hands have served my needs and my companions. ³⁵In every way I have shown you that by hard work of that sort we must help the weak, and keep in mind the words of the Lord Jesus who himself said, 'It is more blessed to give than to receive.'" ³⁶When he had finished speaking he knelt down and prayed with them all. ³⁷They were all weeping loudly as they threw their arms around Paul and kissed him, ³⁸for they were deeply distressed that he had said that they would never see his face again. Then they escorted him to the ship.

Acts Chapter 21

¹When we had taken leave of them we set sail, made a straight run for Cos, and on the next day for Rhodes, and from there to Patara. ²Finding a ship crossing to Phoenicia, we went on board and put out to sea. ³We caught sight of Cyprus but passed by it on our left and sailed on toward Syria and put in at Tyre where the ship was to unload cargo. ⁴There we sought out the disciples and stayed for a week. They kept telling Paul through the Spirit not to embark for Jerusalem. ⁵At the end of our stay we left and resumed our journey. All of them, women and children included, escorted us out of the city, and after kneeling on the beach to pray, ⁶we bade farewell to one another. Then we boarded the ship, and they returned home. ⁷We continued the voyage and came from Tyre to Ptolemais, where we greeted the brothers and stayed a day with them. ⁸On the next day we resumed the trip and came to Caesarea, where we went to the house of Philip the evangelist, who was one of the Seven, and stayed with him. ⁹He had four virgin daughters gifted with prophecy. ¹⁰We had been there several days when a prophet named Agabus came down from Judea. ¹¹He came up to us, took Paul's belt, bound his own feet and hands with it, and said, "Thus says the holy Spirit: This is the way the Jews will bind the owner of this belt in Jerusalem, and they will hand him over to the Gentiles." ¹²When we heard this, we and the local residents begged him not to go up to Jerusalem. ¹³Then Paul replied, "What are you doing, weeping and breaking my heart? I am prepared not only to be bound but even to die in Jerusalem for the name of the Lord Jesus." ¹⁴Since he would not be dissuaded we let the matter rest, saying, "The Lord's will be done." ¹⁵After these days we made preparations for our journey, then went up to Jerusalem. ¹⁶Some of the disciples from Caesarea came along to lead us to the house of Mnason, a Cypriot, a disciple of long standing, with whom we were to stay. ¹⁷When we reached Jerusalem the brothers welcomed us warmly. ¹⁸The next day, Paul accompanied us on a visit to James, and all the presbyters were present. ¹⁹He greeted them, then proceeded to tell them in detail what God had accomplished among the Gentiles through his ministry. ²⁰They praised God when they heard it but said to him, "Brother, you see how many thousands of believers there are from among the Jews, and they are all zealous observers of the law. ²¹They have been informed that you are teaching all the Jews who live among the Gentiles to abandon Moses and that you are telling them not to circumcise their children or to observe their customary practices. ²²What is to be done? They will surely hear that you have arrived. ²³So do what we tell you. We have four men who have taken a vow. ²⁴Take these men and purify yourself with them, and pay their expenses that they may have their heads shaved. In this way everyone will know that there is nothing to the reports they have been given about you but that you yourself live in observance of the law. ²⁵As for the Gentiles who have come to believe, we sent them our decision that they abstain from meat sacrificed to idols, from blood, from the meat of strangled

animals, and from unlawful marriage." 26So Paul took the men, and on the next day after purifying himself together with them entered the temple to give notice of the day when the purification would be completed and the offering made for each of them. 27When the seven days were nearly completed, the Jews from the province of Asia noticed him in the temple, stirred up the whole crowd, and laid hands on him, 28shouting, "Fellow Israelites, help us. This is the man who is teaching everyone everywhere against the people and the law and this place, and what is more, he has even brought Greeks into the temple and defiled this sacred place." 29For they had previously seen Trophimus the Ephesian in the city with him and supposed that Paul had brought him into the temple. 30The whole city was in turmoil with people rushing together. They seized Paul and dragged him out of the temple, and immediately the gates were closed. 31While they were trying to kill him, a report reached the cohort commander that all Jerusalem was rioting. 32He immediately took soldiers and centurions and charged down on them. When they saw the commander and the soldiers they stopped beating Paul. 33The cohort commander came forward, arrested him, and ordered him to be secured with two chains; he tried to find out who he might be and what he had done. 34Some in the mob shouted one thing, others something else; so, since he was unable to ascertain the truth because of the uproar, he ordered Paul to be brought into the compound. 35When he reached the steps, he was carried by the soldiers because of the violence of the mob, 36for a crowd of people followed and shouted, "Away with him!" 37Just as Paul was about to be taken into the compound, he said to the cohort commander, "May I say something to you?" He replied, "Do you speak Greek? 38So then you are not the Egyptian who started a revolt some time ago and led the four thousand assassins into the desert?" 39Paul answered, "I am a Jew, of Tarsus in Cilicia, a citizen of no mean city; I request you to permit me to speak to the people." 40When he had given his permission, Paul stood on the steps and motioned with his hand to the people; and when all was quiet he addressed them in Hebrew.

Acts Chapter 22

1"My brothers and fathers, listen to what I am about to say to you in my defense." 2When they heard him addressing them in Hebrew they became all the more quiet. And he continued, 3"I am a Jew, born in Tarsus in Cilicia, but brought up in this city. At the feet of Gamaliel I was educated strictly in our ancestral law and was zealous for God, just as all of you are today. 4I persecuted this Way to death, binding both men and women and delivering them to prison. 5Even the high priest and the whole council of elders can testify on my behalf. For from them I even received letters to the brothers and set out for Damascus to bring back to Jerusalem in chains for punishment those there as well. 6"On that journey as I drew near to Damascus, about noon a great light from the sky suddenly shone around me. 7I fell to the ground and heard a voice saying to me, 'Saul, Saul, why are you persecuting me?' 8I replied, 'Who are you, sir?' And he said to me, 'I am Jesus the Nazorean whom you are persecuting.' 9My companions saw the light but did not hear the voice of the one who spoke to me. 10I asked, 'What shall I do, sir?' The Lord answered me, 'Get up and go into Damascus, and there you will be told about everything appointed for you to do.' 11Since I could see nothing because of the brightness of that light, I was led by hand by my companions and entered Damascus. 12"A certain Ananias, a devout observer of the law, and highly spoken of by all the Jews who lived there, 13came to me and stood there and said, 'Saul, my brother, regain your sight.' And at that very moment I regained my sight and saw him. 14Then he said, 'The God of our ancestors designated you to know his will, to see the Righteous One, and to hear the sound of his voice; 15for you will be his witness before all to what you have seen and heard. 16Now, why delay? Get up and have yourself baptized and your sins washed away, calling upon his name.' 17"After I had returned to Jerusalem and while I was praying in the temple, I fell into a trance 18and saw the Lord saying to me, 'Hurry, leave Jerusalem at once, because they will not accept your testimony about me.' 19But I replied, 'Lord, they themselves know that from synagogue to synagogue I used to imprison and beat those who believed in you. 20And when the blood of your witness Stephen was being shed, I myself stood by giving my approval and keeping guard over the cloaks of his murderers.' 21Then he said to me, 'Go, I shall send you far away to the Gentiles.'" 22They listened to him until he said this, but then they raised their voices and shouted, "Take such a one as this away from the earth. It is not right that he should live." 23And as they were yelling and throwing off their cloaks and flinging dust into the air, 24the cohort commander ordered him to be brought into the compound and gave instruction that he be interrogated under the lash to determine the reason why they were making such an outcry against him. 25But when they had stretched him out for the whips, Paul said to the centurion on duty, "Is it lawful for

you to scourge a man who is a Roman citizen and has not been tried?" 26When the centurion heard this, he went to the cohort commander and reported it, saying, "What are you going to do? This man is a Roman citizen." 27Then the commander came and said to him, "Tell me, are you a Roman citizen?" "Yes," he answered. 28The commander replied, "I acquired this citizenship for a large sum of money." Paul said, "But I was born one." 29At once those who were going to interrogate him backed away from him, and the commander became alarmed when he realized that he was a Roman citizen and that he had had him bound. 30The next day, wishing to determine the truth about why he was being accused by the Jews, he freed him and ordered the chief priests and the whole Sanhedrin to convene. Then he brought Paul down and made him stand before them.

Acts Chapter 23

1Paul looked intently at the Sanhedrin and said, "My brothers, I have conducted myself with a perfectly clear conscience before God to this day." 2The high priest Ananias ordered his attendants to strike his mouth. 3Then Paul said to him, "God will strike you, you whitewashed wall. Do you indeed sit in judgment upon me according to the law and yet in violation of the law order me to be struck?" 4The attendants said, "Would you revile God's high priest?" 5Paul answered, "Brothers, I did not realize he was the high priest. For it is written, 'You shall not curse a ruler of your people.'" 6Paul was aware that some were Sadducees and some Pharisees, so he called out before the Sanhedrin, "My brothers, I am a Pharisee, the son of Pharisees; (I) am on trial for hope in the resurrection of the dead." 7When he said this, a dispute broke out between the Pharisees and Sadducees, and the group became divided. 8For the Sadducees say that there is no resurrection or angels or spirits, while the Pharisees acknowledge all three. 9A great uproar occurred, and some scribes belonging to the Pharisee party stood up and sharply argued, "We find nothing wrong with this man. Suppose a spirit or an angel has spoken to him?" 10The dispute was so serious that the commander, afraid that Paul would be torn to pieces by them, ordered his troops to go down and rescue him from their midst and take him into the compound. 11The following night the Lord stood by him and said, "Take courage. For just as you have borne witness to my cause in Jerusalem, so you must also bear witness in Rome." 12When day came, the Jews made a plot and bound themselves by oath not to eat or drink until they had killed Paul. 13There were more than forty who formed this conspiracy. 14They went to the chief priests and elders and said, "We have bound ourselves by a solemn oath to taste nothing until we have killed Paul. 15You, together with the Sanhedrin, must now make an official request to the commander to have him bring him down to you, as though you meant to investigate his case more thoroughly. We on our part are prepared to kill him before he arrives." 16The son of Paul's sister, however, heard about the ambush; so he went and entered the compound and reported it to Paul. 17Paul then called one of the centurions and requested, "Take this young man to the commander; he has something to report to him." 18So he took him and brought him to the commander and explained, "The prisoner Paul called me and asked that I bring this young man to you; he has something to say to you." 19The commander took him by the hand, drew him aside, and asked him privately, "What is it you have to report to me?" 20He replied, "The Jews have conspired to ask you to bring Paul down to the Sanhedrin tomorrow, as though they meant to inquire about him more thoroughly, 21but do not believe them. More than forty of them are lying in wait for him; they have bound themselves by oath not to eat or drink until they have killed him. They are now ready and only wait for your consent." 22As the commander dismissed the young man he directed him, "Tell no one that you gave me this information." 23Then he summoned two of the centurions and said, "Get two hundred soldiers ready to go to Caesarea by nine o'clock tonight, along with seventy horsemen and two hundred auxiliaries. 24Provide mounts for Paul to ride and give him safe conduct to Felix the governor." 25Then he wrote a letter with this content: 26"Claudius Lysias to his excellency the governor Felix, greetings. 27This man, seized by the Jews and about to be murdered by them, I rescued after intervening with my troops when I learned that he was a Roman citizen. 28I wanted to learn the reason for their accusations against him so I brought him down to their Sanhedrin. 29I discovered that he was accused in matters of controversial questions of their law and not of any charge deserving death or imprisonment. 30Since it was brought to my attention that there will be a plot against the man, I am sending him to you at once, and have also notified his accusers to state (their case) against him before you." 31So the soldiers, according to their orders, took Paul and escorted him by night to Antipatris. 32The next day they returned to the compound, leaving the horsemen to complete the journey with him. 33When they arrived in Caesarea they delivered the letter to the governor and presented Paul to him. ³⁴When he had read it and asked to what province he belonged, and learned that he was from Cilicia, ³⁵he said, "I shall hear your case when your accusers arrive." Then he ordered that he be held in custody in Herod's praetorium.

Acts Chapter 24

¹Five days later the high priest Ananias came down with some elders and an advocate, a certain Tertullus, and they presented formal charges against Paul to the governor. ²When he was called, Tertullus began to accuse him, saying, "Since we have attained much peace through you, and reforms have been accomplished in this nation through your provident care, ³we acknowledge this in every way and everywhere, most excellent Felix, with all gratitude. ⁴But in order not to detain you further, I ask you to give us a brief hearing with your customary graciousness. ⁵We found this man to be a pest; he creates dissension among Jews all over the world and is a ringleader of the sect of the Nazoreans. ⁶He even tried to desecrate our temple, but we arrested him. ⁷ ⁸If you examine him you will be able to learn from him for yourself about everything of which we are accusing him." ⁹The Jews also joined in the attack and asserted that these things were so. ¹⁰Then the governor motioned to him to speak and Paul replied, "I know that you have been a judge over this nation for many years and so I am pleased to make my defense before you. ¹¹As you can verify, not more than twelve days have passed since I went up to Jerusalem to worship. ¹²Neither in the temple, nor in the synagogues, nor anywhere in the city did they find me arguing with anyone or instigating a riot among the people. ¹³Nor can they prove to you the accusations they are now making against me. ¹⁴But this I do admit to you, that according to the Way, which they call a sect, I worship the God of our ancestors and I believe everything that is in accordance with the law and written in the prophets. ¹⁵I have the same hope in God as they themselves have that there will be a resurrection of the righteous and the unrighteous. ¹⁶Because of this, I always strive to keep my conscience clear before God and man. ¹⁷After many years, I came to bring alms for my nation and offerings. ¹⁸While I was so engaged, they found me, after my purification, in the temple without a crowd or disturbance. ¹⁹But some Jews from the province of Asia, who should be here before you to make whatever accusation they might have against me - ²⁰or let these men themselves state what crime they discovered when I stood before the Sanhedrin, ²¹unless it was my one outcry as I stood among them, that 'I am on trial before you today for the resurrection of the dead.'" ²²Then Felix, who was accurately informed about the Way, postponed the trial, saying, "When Lysias the commander comes down, I shall decide your case." ²³He gave orders to the centurion that he should be kept in custody but have some liberty, and that he should not prevent any of his friends from caring for his needs. ²⁴Several days later Felix came with his wife Drusilla, who was Jewish. He had Paul summoned and listened to him speak about faith in Christ Jesus. ²⁵But as he spoke about righteousness and self-restraint and the coming judgment, Felix became frightened and said, "You may go for now; when I find an opportunity I shall summon you again." ²⁶At the same time he hoped that a bribe would be offered him by Paul, and so he sent for him very often and conversed with him. ²⁷Two years passed and Felix was succeeded by Porcius Festus. Wishing to ingratiate himself with the Jews, Felix left Paul in prison.

Acts Chapter 25

¹Three days after his arrival in the province, Festus went up from Caesarea to Jerusalem ²where the chief priests and Jewish leaders presented him their formal charges against Paul. They asked him ³as a favor to have him sent to Jerusalem, for they were plotting to kill him along the way. ⁴Festus replied that Paul was being held in custody in Caesarea and that he himself would be returning there shortly. ⁵He said, "Let your authorities come down with me, and if this man has done something improper, let them accuse him." ⁶After spending no more than eight or ten days with them, he went down to Caesarea, and on the following day took his seat on the tribunal and ordered that Paul be brought in. ⁷When he appeared, the Jews who had come down from Jerusalem surrounded him and brought many serious charges against him, which they were unable to prove. ⁸In defending himself Paul said, "I have committed no crime either against the Jewish law or against the temple or against Caesar." ⁹Then Festus, wishing to ingratiate himself with the Jews, said to Paul in reply, "Are you willing to go up to Jerusalem and there stand trial before me on these charges?" ¹⁰Paul answered, "I am standing before the tribunal of Caesar; this is where I should be tried. I have committed no crime against the Jews, as you very well know. ¹¹If I have committed a crime or done anything deserving death, I do not seek to escape the death penalty; but if there is no substance to the charges they are bringing against me, then no one

has the right to hand me over to them. I appeal to Caesar." ¹²Then Festus, after conferring with his council, replied, "You have appealed to Caesar. To Caesar you will go." ¹³When a few days had passed, King Agrippa and Bernice arrived in Caesarea on a visit to Festus. ¹⁴Since they spent several days there, Festus referred Paul's case to the king, saying, "There is a man here left in custody by Felix. ¹⁵When I was in Jerusalem the chief priests and the elders of the Jews brought charges against him and demanded his condemnation. ¹⁶I answered them that it was not Roman practice to hand over an accused person before he has faced his accusers and had the opportunity to defend himself against their charge. ¹⁷So when (they) came together here, I made no delay; the next day I took my seat on the tribunal and ordered the man to be brought in. ¹⁸His accusers stood around him, but did not charge him with any of the crimes I suspected. ¹⁹Instead they had some issues with him about their own religion and about a certain Jesus who had died but who Paul claimed was alive. ²⁰Since I was at a loss how to investigate this controversy, I asked if he were willing to go to Jerusalem and there stand trial on these charges. ²¹And when Paul appealed that he be held in custody for the Emperor's decision, I ordered him held until I could send him to Caesar." ²²Agrippa said to Festus, "I too should like to hear this man." He replied, "Tomorrow you will hear him." ²³The next day Agrippa and Bernice came with great ceremony and entered the audience hall in the company of cohort commanders and the prominent men of the city and, by command of Festus, Paul was brought in. ²⁴And Festus said, "King Agrippa and all you here present with us, look at this man about whom the whole Jewish populace petitioned me here and in Jerusalem, clamoring that he should live no longer. ²⁵I found, however, that he had done nothing deserving death, and so when he appealed to the Emperor, I decided to send him. ²⁶But I have nothing definite to write about him to our sovereign; therefore I have brought him before all of you, and particularly before you, King Agrippa, so that I may have something to write as a result of this investigation. ²⁷For it seems senseless to me to send up a prisoner without indicating the charges against him."

Acts Chapter 26

¹Then Agrippa said to Paul, "You may now speak on your own behalf." So Paul stretched out his hand and began his defense. ²"I count myself fortunate, King Agrippa, that I am to defend myself before you today against all the charges made against me by the Jews, ³especially since you are an expert in all the Jewish customs and controversies. And therefore I beg you to listen patiently. ⁴My manner of living from my youth, a life spent from the beginning among my people and in Jerusalem, all (the) Jews know. ⁵They have known about me from the start, if they are willing to testify, that I have lived my life as a Pharisee, the strictest party of our religion. ⁶But now I am standing trial because of my hope in the promise made by God to our ancestors. ⁷Our twelve tribes hope to attain to that promise as they fervently worship God day and night; and on account of this hope I am accused by Jews, O king. ⁸Why is it thought unbelievable among you that God raises the dead? ⁹I myself once thought that I had to do many things against the name of Jesus the Nazorean, ¹⁰and I did so in Jerusalem. I imprisoned many of the holy ones with the authorization I received from the chief priests, and when they were to be put to death I cast my vote against them. ¹¹Many times, in synagogue after synagogue, I punished them in an attempt to force them to blaspheme; I was so enraged against them that I pursued them even to foreign cities. ¹²"On one such occasion I was traveling to Damascus with the authorization and commission of the chief priests. ¹³At midday, along the way, O king, I saw a light from the sky, brighter than the sun, shining around me and my traveling companions. ¹⁴We all fell to the ground and I heard a voice saying to me in Hebrew, 'Saul, Saul, why are you persecuting me? It is hard for you to kick against the goad.' ¹⁵And I said, 'Who are you, sir?' And the Lord replied, 'I am Jesus whom you are persecuting. ¹⁶Get up now, and stand on your feet. I have appeared to you for this purpose, to appoint you as a servant and witness of what you have seen (of me) and what you will be shown. ¹⁷I shall deliver you from this people and from the Gentiles to whom I send you, ¹⁸to open their eyes that they may turn from darkness to light and from the power of Satan to God, so that they may obtain forgiveness of sins and an inheritance among those who have been consecrated by faith in me.' ¹⁹"And so, King Agrippa, I was not disobedient to the heavenly vision. ²⁰On the contrary, first to those in Damascus and in Jerusalem and throughout the whole country of Judea, and then to the Gentiles, I preached the need to repent and turn to God, and to do works giving evidence of repentance. ²¹That is why the Jews seized me (when I was) in the temple and tried to kill me. ²²But I have enjoyed God's help to this very day, and so I stand here testifying to small and great alike, saying nothing different from what the prophets and Moses foretold, ²³that the Messiah must suffer and

that, as the first to rise from the dead, he would proclaim light both to our people and to the Gentiles." 24While Paul was so speaking in his defense, Festus said in a loud voice, "You are mad, Paul; much learning is driving you mad." 25But Paul replied, "I am not mad, most excellent Festus; I am speaking words of truth and reason. 26The king knows about these matters and to him I speak boldly, for I cannot believe that (any) of this has escaped his notice; this was not done in a corner. 27King Agrippa, do you believe the prophets? I know you believe." 28Then Agrippa said to Paul, "You will soon persuade me to play the Christian." 29Paul replied, "I would pray to God that sooner or later not only you but all who listen to me today might become as I am except for these chains." 30Then the king rose, and with him the governor and Bernice and the others who sat with them. 31And after they had withdrawn they said to one another, "This man is doing nothing (at all) that deserves death or imprisonment." 32And Agrippa said to Festus, "This man could have been set free if he had not appealed to Caesar."

Acts Chapter 27

1When it was decided that we should sail to Italy, they handed Paul and some other prisoners over to a centurion named Julius of the Cohort Augusta. 2We went on board a ship from Adramyttium bound for ports in the province of Asia and set sail. Aristarchus, a Macedonian from Thessalonica, was with us. 3On the following day we put in at Sidon where Julius was kind enough to allow Paul to visit his friends who took care of him. 4From there we put out to sea and sailed around the sheltered side of Cyprus because of the headwinds, 5and crossing the open sea off the coast of Cilicia and Pamphylia we came to Myra in Lycia. 6There the centurion found an Alexandrian ship that was sailing to Italy and put us on board. 7For many days we made little headway, arriving at Cnidus only with difficulty, and because the wind would not permit us to continue our course we sailed for the sheltered side of Crete off Salmone. 8We sailed past it with difficulty and reached a place called Fair Havens, near which was the city of Lasea. 9Much time had now passed and sailing had become hazardous because the time of the fast had already gone by, so Paul warned them, 10"Men, I can see that this voyage will result in severe damage and heavy loss not only to the cargo and the ship, but also to our lives." 11The centurion, however, paid more attention to the pilot and to the owner of the ship than to what Paul said. 12Since the harbor was unfavorably situated for spending the winter, the majority planned to put out to sea from there in the hope of reaching Phoenix, a port in Crete facing west-northwest, to spend the winter. 13A south wind blew gently, and thinking they had attained their objective, they weighed anchor and sailed along close to the coast of Crete. 14Before long an offshore wind of hurricane force called a "Northeaster" struck. 15Since the ship was caught up in it and could not head into the wind we gave way and let ourselves be driven. 16We passed along the sheltered side of an island named Cauda and managed only with difficulty to get the dinghy under control. 17They hoisted it aboard, then used cables to undergird the ship. Because of their fear that they would run aground on the shoal of Syrtis, they lowered the drift anchor and were carried along in this way. 18We were being pounded by the storm so violently that the next day they jettisoned some cargo, 19and on the third day with their own hands they threw even the ship's tackle overboard. 20Neither the sun nor the stars were visible for many days, and no small storm raged. Finally, all hope of our surviving was taken away. 21When many would no longer eat, Paul stood among them and said, "Men, you should have taken my advice and not have set sail from Crete and you would have avoided this disastrous loss. 22I urge you now to keep up your courage; not one of you will be lost, only the ship. 23For last night an angel of the God to whom (I) belong and whom I serve stood by me 24and said, 'Do not be afraid, Paul. You are destined to stand before Caesar; and behold, for your sake, God has granted safety to all who are sailing with you.' 25Therefore, keep up your courage, men; I trust in God that it will turn out as I have been told. 26We are destined to run aground on some island." 27On the fourteenth night, as we were still being driven about on the Adriatic Sea, toward midnight the sailors began to suspect that they were nearing land. 28They took soundings and found twenty fathoms; a little farther on, they again took soundings and found fifteen fathoms. 29Fearing that we would run aground on a rocky coast, they dropped four anchors from the stern and prayed for day to come. 30The sailors then tried to abandon ship; they lowered the dinghy to the sea on the pretext of going to lay out anchors from the bow. 31But Paul said to the centurion and the soldiers, "Unless these men stay with the ship, you cannot be saved." 32So the soldiers cut the ropes of the dinghy and set it adrift. 33Until the day began to dawn, Paul kept urging all to take some food. He said, "Today is the fourteenth day that you have been waiting, going hungry and eating nothing. 34I urge you, therefore, to take some food; it will help you survive. Not a hair of the head of anyone

of you will be lost." 35When he said this, he took bread, gave thanks to God in front of them all, broke it, and began to eat. 36They were all encouraged, and took some food themselves. 37In all, there were two hundred seventy-six of us on the ship. 38After they had eaten enough, they lightened the ship by throwing the wheat into the sea. 39When day came they did not recognize the land, but made out a bay with a beach. They planned to run the ship ashore on it, if they could. 40So they cast off the anchors and abandoned them to the sea, and at the same time they unfastened the lines of the rudders, and hoisting the foresail into the wind, they made for the beach. 41But they struck a sandbar and ran the ship aground. The bow was wedged in and could not be moved, but the stern began to break up under the pounding (of the waves). 42The soldiers planned to kill the prisoners so that none might swim away and escape, 43but the centurion wanted to save Paul and so kept them from carrying out their plan. He ordered those who could swim to jump overboard first and get to the shore, 44and then the rest, some on planks, others on debris from the ship. In this way, all reached shore safely.

Acts Chapter 28

1Once we had reached safety we learned that the island was called Malta.2The natives showed us extraordinary hospitality; they lit a fire and welcomed all of us because it had begun to rain and was cold.3Paul had gathered a bundle of brushwood and was putting it on the fire when a viper, escaping from the heat, fastened on his hand.4When the natives saw the snake hanging from his hand, they said to one another, "This man must certainly be a murderer; though he escaped the sea, Justice has not let him remain alive."5But he shook the snake off into the fire and suffered no harm.6They were expecting him to swell up or suddenly to fall down dead but, after waiting a long time and seeing nothing unusual happen to him, they changed their minds and began to say that he was a god.7In the vicinity of that place were lands belonging to a man named Publius, the chief of the island. He welcomed us and received us cordially as his guests for three days.8It so happened that the father of Publius was sick with a fever and dysentery. Paul visited him and, after praying, laid his hands on him and healed him.9After this had taken place, the rest of the sick on the island came to Paul and were cured.10They paid us great honor and when we eventually set sail they brought us the provisions we needed.11Three months later we set sail on a ship that had wintered at the island. It was an Alexandrian ship with the Dioscuri as its figurehead.12We put in at Syracuse and stayed there three days,13and from there we sailed round the coast and arrived at Rhegium. After a day, a south wind came up and in two days we reached Puteoli.14There we found some brothers and were urged to stay with them for seven days. And thus we came to Rome.15The brothers from there heard about us and came as far as the Forum of Appius and Three Taverns to meet us. On seeing them, Paul gave thanks to God and took courage.16When he entered Rome, Paul was allowed to live by himself, with the soldier who was guarding him.17Three days later he called together the leaders of the Jews. When they had gathered he said to them, "My brothers, although I had done nothing against our people or our ancestral customs, I was handed over to the Romans as a prisoner from Jerusalem.18After trying my case the Romans wanted to release me, because they found nothing against me deserving the death penalty.19But when the Jews objected, I was obliged to appeal to Caesar, even though I had no accusation to make against my own nation.20This is the reason, then, I have requested to see you and to speak with you, for it is on account of the hope of Israel that I wear these chains."21They answered him, "We have received no letters from Judea about you, nor has any of the brothers arrived with a damaging report or rumor about you.22But we should like to hear you present your views, for we know that this sect is denounced everywhere."23So they arranged a day with him and came to his lodgings in great numbers. From early morning until evening, he expounded his position to them, bearing witness to the kingdom of God and trying to convince them about Jesus from the law of Moses and the prophets.24Some were convinced by what he had said, while others did not believe.25Without reaching any agreement among themselves they began to leave; then Paul made one final statement. "Well did the holy Spirit speak to your ancestors through the prophet Isaiah, saying:26'Go to this people and say: You shall indeed hear but not understand. You shall indeed look but never see.27Gross is the heart of this people; they will not hear with their ears, they have closed their eyes, so they may not see with their eyes and hear with their ears and understand with their heart and be converted, and I heal them.'28Let it be known to you that this salvation of God has been sent to the Gentiles; they will listen."29When he had said these words, the Jews departed, having a great dispute among themselves.30He remained for two full years in his lodgings. He received all who came to him,31and with complete assurance and without hindrance he proclaimed the kingdom of God and taught about the Lord Jesus Christ.

Letters of Paul (Pauline Epistles)

Romans

Romans Chapter 1

[1]Paul, a slave of Christ Jesus, called to be an apostle and set apart for the gospel of God,[2]which he promised previously through his prophets in the holy scriptures,[3]the gospel about his Son, descended from David according to the flesh,[4]but established as Son of God in power according to the spirit of holiness through resurrection from the dead, Jesus Christ our Lord.[5]Through him we have received the grace of apostleship, to bring about the obedience of faith, for the sake of his name, among all the Gentiles,[6]among whom are you also, who are called to belong to Jesus Christ;[7]to all the beloved of God in Rome, called to be holy. Grace to you and peace from God our Father and the Lord Jesus Christ.[8]First, I give thanks to my God through Jesus Christ for all of you, because your faith is heralded throughout the world.[9]God is my witness, whom I serve with my spirit in proclaiming the gospel of his Son, that I remember you constantly,[10]always asking in my prayers that somehow by God's will I may at last find my way clear to come to you.[11]For I long to see you, that I may share with you some spiritual gift so that you may be strengthened,[12]that is, that you and I may be mutually encouraged by one another's faith, yours and mine.[13]I do not want you to be unaware, brothers, that I often planned to come to you, though I was prevented until now, that I might harvest some fruit among you, too, as among the rest of the Gentiles.[14]To Greeks and non-Greeks alike, to the wise and the ignorant, I am under obligation;[15]that is why I am eager to preach the gospel also to you in Rome.[16]For I am not ashamed of the gospel. It is the power of God for the salvation of everyone who believes: for Jew first, and then Greek.[17]For in it is revealed the righteousness of God from faith to faith; as it is written, "The one who is righteous by faith will live."[18]The wrath of God is indeed being revealed from heaven against every impiety and wickedness of those who suppress the truth by their wickedness.[19]For what can be known about God is evident to them, because God made it evident to them.[20]Ever since the creation of the world, his invisible attributes of eternal power and divinity have been able to be understood and perceived in what he has made. As a result, they have no excuse;[21]for although they knew God they did not accord him glory as God or give him thanks. Instead, they became vain in their reasoning, and their senseless minds were darkened.[22]While claiming to be wise, they became fools[23]and exchanged the glory of the immortal God for the likeness of an image of mortal man or of birds or of four-legged animals or of snakes.[24]Therefore, God handed them over to impurity through the lusts of their hearts for the mutual degradation of their bodies.[25]They exchanged the truth of God for a lie and revered and worshiped the creature rather than the creator, who is blessed forever. Amen.[26]Therefore, God handed them over to degrading passions. Their females exchanged natural relations for unnatural,[27]and the males likewise gave up natural relations with females and burned with lust for one another. Males did shameful things with males and thus received in their own persons the due penalty for their perversity.[28]And since they did not see fit to acknowledge God, God handed them over to their undiscerning mind to do what is improper.[29]They are filled with every form of wickedness, evil, greed, and malice; full of envy, murder, rivalry, treachery, and spite. They are gossips[30]and scandalmongers and they hate God. They are insolent, haughty, boastful, ingenious in their wickedness, and rebellious toward their parents.[31]They are senseless, faithless, heartless, ruthless.[32]Although they know the just decree of God that all who practice such things deserve death, they not only do them but give approval to those who practice them.

Romans Chapter 2

[1]Therefore, you are without excuse, every one of you who passes judgment. For by the standard by which you judge another you condemn yourself, since you, the judge, do the very same things.[2]We know that the judgment of God on those who do such things is true.[3]Do you suppose, then, you who judge those who engage in such things and yet do them yourself, that you will escape the judgment of God?[4]Or do you hold his priceless kindness, forbearance, and patience in low esteem, unaware that the kindness of God would lead you to repentance?[5]By your stubbornness and impenitent heart, you are storing up wrath for yourself for the day of wrath and revelation of the just judgment of God,[6]who will repay everyone according to his works:[7]eternal life to those who seek glory, honor, and immortality through perseverance in good works,[8]but wrath and fury to those who selfishly disobey the truth and obey wickedness.[9]Yes, affliction and distress will come upon every human being who does evil, Jew first and then Greek.[10]But there will be glory, honor, and peace for everyone who does good, Jew first and then Greek.[11]There is no partiality with God.[12]All who sin outside the law will also perish without reference to it, and all who sin under the law will be judged in accordance with it.[13]For it is not those who hear the law who are just in the sight of God; rather, those who observe the law will be justified.[14]For when the Gentiles who do not have the law by nature observe the prescriptions of the law, they are a law for themselves even though they do not have the law.[15]They show that the demands of the law are written in their hearts, while their conscience also bears witness and their conflicting thoughts accuse or even defend them[16]on the day when, according to my gospel, God will judge people's hidden works through Christ Jesus.[17]Now if you call yourself a Jew and rely on the law and boast of God[18]and know his will and are able to discern what is important since you are instructed from the law,[19]and if you are confident that you are a guide for the blind and a light for those in darkness,[20]that you are a trainer of the foolish and teacher of the simple, because in the law you have the formulation of knowledge and truth—[21]then you who teach another, are you failing to teach yourself? You who preach against stealing, do you steal?[22]You who forbid adultery, do you commit adultery? You who detest idols, do you rob temples?[23]You who boast of the law, do you dishonor God by breaking the law?[24]For, as it is written, "Because of you the name of God is reviled among the Gentiles."[25]Circumcision, to be sure, has value if you observe the law; but if you break the law, your circumcision has become uncircumcision.[26]Again, if an uncircumcised man keeps the precepts of the law, will he not be considered circumcised?[27]Indeed, those who are physically uncircumcised but carry out the law will pass judgment on you, with your written law and circumcision, who break the law.[28]One is not a Jew outwardly. True circumcision is not outward, in the flesh.[29]Rather, one is a Jew inwardly, and circumcision is of the heart, in the spirit, not the letter; his praise is not from human beings but from God.

Romans Chapter 3

[1]What advantage is there then in being a Jew? Or what is the value of circumcision? [2]Much, in every respect. (For) in the first place, they were entrusted with the utterances of God. [3]What if some were unfaithful? Will their infidelity nullify the fidelity of God? [4]Of course not! God must be true, though every human being is a liar, as it is written: "That you may be justified in your words, and conquer when you are judged." [5]But if our wickedness provides proof of God's righteousness, what can we say? Is God unjust, humanly speaking, to inflict his wrath? [6]Of course not! For how else is God to judge the world? [7]But if God's truth redounds to his glory through my falsehood, why am I still being condemned as a sinner? [8]And why not say—as we are accused and as some claim we say—that we should do evil that good may come of it? Their penalty is what they deserve. [9]Well, then, are we better off? Not entirely, for we have already brought the charge against Jews and Greeks alike that they are all under the domination of sin, [10]as it is written: "There is no one just, not one, [11]there is no one who understands, there is no one who seeks God. [12]All have gone astray; all alike are worthless; there is not one who does good, (there is not) even one. [13]Their throats are open graves; they deceive with their tongues; the venom of asps is on their lips; [14]their mouths are full of bitter cursing. [15]Their feet are quick to shed blood; [16]ruin and misery are in their ways, [17]and the way of peace they know not. [18]There is no fear of God before their eyes." [19]Now we know that what the law says is addressed to those under the law, so that every mouth may be silenced and the whole world stand accountable to God, [20]since no human being will be justified in his sight by observing the law; for through the law comes consciousness of sin. [21]But now the righteousness of God has been manifested apart from the law, though testified to by the law and the prophets, [22]the righteousness of God through faith in Jesus Christ for all who believe. For there is no distinction; [23]all have sinned and are deprived of the glory of God. [24]They are justified freely by his grace through the redemption in Christ Jesus, [25]whom God set forth as an expiation, through faith, by his blood, to prove his righteousness because of the forgiveness of sins previously committed, [26]through the forbearance of God—to prove his righteousness in the present time, that he might be righteous and justify the one who has faith in Jesus. [27]What

occasion is there then for boasting? It is ruled out. On what principle, that of works? No, rather on the principle of faith. ²⁸For we consider that a person is justified by faith apart from works of the law. ²⁹Does God belong to Jews alone? Does he not belong to Gentiles, too? Yes, also to Gentiles, ³⁰for God is one and will justify the circumcised on the basis of faith and the uncircumcised through faith. ³¹Are we then annulling the law by this faith? Of course not! On the contrary, we are supporting the law.

Romans Chapter 4

¹What then can we say that Abraham found, our ancestor according to the flesh? ²Indeed, if Abraham was justified on the basis of his works, he has reason to boast; but this was not so in the sight of God. ³For what does the scripture say? "Abraham believed God, and it was credited to him as righteousness." ⁴A worker's wage is credited not as a gift, but as something due. ⁵But when one does not work, yet believes in the one who justifies the ungodly, his faith is credited as righteousness. ⁶So also David declares the blessedness of the person to whom God credits righteousness apart from works: ⁷"Blessed are they whose iniquities are forgiven and whose sins are covered. ⁸Blessed is the man whose sin the Lord does not record." ⁹Does this blessedness apply only to the circumcised, or to the uncircumcised as well? Now we assert that "faith was credited to Abraham as righteousness." ¹⁰Under what circumstances was it credited? Was he circumcised or not? He was not circumcised, but uncircumcised. ¹¹And he received the sign of circumcision as a seal on the righteousness received through faith while he was uncircumcised. Thus he was to be the father of all the uncircumcised who believe, so that to them (also) righteousness might be credited, ¹²as well as the father of the circumcised who not only are circumcised, but also follow the path of faith that our father Abraham walked while still uncircumcised. ¹³It was not through the law that the promise was made to Abraham and his descendants that he would inherit the world, but through the righteousness that comes from faith. ¹⁴For if those who adhere to the law are the heirs, faith is null and the promise is void. ¹⁵For the law produces wrath; but where there is no law, neither is there violation. ¹⁶For this reason, it depends on faith, so that it may be a gift, and the promise may be guaranteed to all his descendants, not to those who only adhere to the law but to those who follow the faith of Abraham, who is the father of all of us, ¹⁷as it is written, "I have made you father of many nations." He is our father in the sight of God, in whom he believed, who gives life to the dead and calls into being what does not exist. ¹⁸He believed, hoping against hope, that he would become "the father of many nations," according to what was said, "Thus shall your descendants be." ¹⁹He did not weaken in faith when he considered his own body as (already) dead (for he was almost a hundred years old) and the dead womb of Sarah. ²⁰He did not doubt God's promise in unbelief; rather, he was empowered by faith and gave glory to God ²¹and was fully convinced that what he had promised he was also able to do. ²²That is why "it was credited to him as righteousness." ²³But it was not for him alone that it was written that "it was credited to him"; ²⁴it was also for us, to whom it will be credited, who believe in the one who raised Jesus our Lord from the dead, ²⁵who was handed over for our transgressions and was raised for our justification.

Romans Chapter 5

¹Therefore, since we have been justified by faith, we have peace with God through our Lord Jesus Christ, ²through whom we have gained access (by faith) to this grace in which we stand, and we boast in hope of the glory of God. ³Not only that, but we even boast of our afflictions, knowing that affliction produces endurance, ⁴and endurance, proven character, and proven character, hope, ⁵and hope does not disappoint, because the love of God has been poured out into our hearts through the holy Spirit that has been given to us. ⁶For Christ, while we were still helpless, yet died at the appointed time for the ungodly. ⁷Indeed, only with difficulty does one die for a just person, though perhaps for a good person one might even find courage to die. ⁸But God proves his love for us in that while we were still sinners Christ died for us. ⁹How much more then, since we are now justified by his blood, will we be saved through him from the wrath. ¹⁰Indeed, if, while we were enemies, we were reconciled to God through the death of his Son, how much more, once reconciled, will we be saved by his life. ¹¹Not only that, but we also boast of God through our Lord Jesus Christ, through whom we have now received reconciliation. ¹²Therefore, just as through one person sin entered the world, and through sin, death, and thus death came to all, inasmuch as all sinned - ¹³for up to the time of the law, sin was in the world, though sin is not accounted when there is no law. ¹⁴But death reigned from Adam to Moses, even over those who did not sin after the pattern of the trespass of Adam, who is the type of the one who

was to come. ¹⁵But the gift is not like the transgression. For if by that one person's transgression the many died, how much more did the grace of God and the gracious gift of the one person Jesus Christ overflow for the many. ¹⁶And the gift is not like the result of the one person's sinning. For after one sin there was the judgment that brought condemnation; but the gift, after many transgressions, brought acquittal. ¹⁷For if, by the transgression of one person, death came to reign through that one, how much more will those who receive the abundance of grace and of the gift of justification come to reign in life through the one person Jesus Christ. ¹⁸In conclusion, just as through one transgression condemnation came upon all, so through one righteous act acquittal and life came to all. ¹⁹For just as through the disobedience of one person the many were made sinners, so through the obedience of one the many will be made righteous. ²⁰The law entered in so that transgression might increase but, where sin increased, grace overflowed all the more, ²¹so that, as sin reigned in death, grace also might reign through justification for eternal life through Jesus Christ our Lord.

Romans Chapter 6

¹What then shall we say? Shall we persist in sin that grace may abound? Of course not! ²How can we who died to sin yet live in it? ³Or are you unaware that we who were baptized into Christ Jesus were baptized into his death? ⁴We were indeed buried with him through baptism into death, so that, just as Christ was raised from the dead by the glory of the Father, we too might live in newness of life. ⁵For if we have grown into union with him through a death like his, we shall also be united with him in the resurrection. ⁶We know that our old self was crucified with him, so that our sinful body might be done away with, that we might no longer be in slavery to sin. ⁷For a dead person has been absolved from sin. ⁸If, then, we have died with Christ, we believe that we shall also live with him. ⁹We know that Christ, raised from the dead, dies no more; death no longer has power over him. ¹⁰As to his death, he died to sin once and for all; as to his life, he lives for God. ¹¹Consequently, you too must think of yourselves as (being) dead to sin and living for God in Christ Jesus. ¹²Therefore, sin must not reign over your mortal bodies so that you obey their desires. ¹³And do not present the parts of your bodies to sin as weapons for wickedness, but present yourselves to God as raised from the dead to life and the parts of your bodies to God as weapons for righteousness. ¹⁴For sin is not to have any power over you, since you are not under the law but under grace. ¹⁵What then? Shall we sin because we are not under the law but under grace? Of course not! ¹⁶Do you not know that if you present yourselves to someone as obedient slaves, you are slaves of the one you obey, either of sin, which leads to death, or of obedience, which leads to righteousness? ¹⁷But thanks be to God that, although you were once slaves of sin, you have become obedient from the heart to the pattern of teaching to which you were entrusted. ¹⁸Freed from sin, you have become slaves of righteousness. ¹⁹I am speaking in human terms because of the weakness of your nature. For just as you presented the parts of your bodies as slaves to impurity and to lawlessness for lawlessness, so now present them as slaves to righteousness for sanctification. ²⁰For when you were slaves of sin, you were free from righteousness. ²¹But what profit did you get then from the things of which you are now ashamed? For the end of those things is death. ²²But now that you have been freed from sin and have become slaves of God, the benefit that you have leads to sanctification, and its end is eternal life. ²³For the wages of sin is death, but the gift of God is eternal life in Christ Jesus our Lord.

Romans Chapter 7

1 Are you unaware, brothers (for I am speaking to people who know the law), that the law has jurisdiction over one as long as one lives? ²Thus a married woman is bound by law to her living husband; but if her husband dies, she is released from the law in respect to her husband. ³Consequently, while her husband is alive she will be called an adulteress if she consorts with another man. But if her husband dies she is free from that law, and she is not an adulteress if she consorts with another man. ⁴In the same way, my brothers, you also were put to death to the law through the body of Christ, so that you might belong to another, to the one who was raised from the dead in order that we might bear fruit for God. ⁵For when we were in the flesh, our sinful passions, awakened by the law, worked in our members to bear fruit for death. ⁶But now we are released from the law, dead to what held us captive, so that we may serve in the newness of the spirit and not under the obsolete letter. ⁷What then can we say? That the law is sin? Of course not! Yet I did not know sin except through the law, and I did not know what it is to covet except that the law said, "You shall not covet." ⁸But sin, finding an opportunity in the commandment, produced in me every

kind of covetousness. Apart from the law sin is dead. ⁹I once lived outside the law, but when the commandment came, sin became alive; ¹⁰then I died, and the commandment that was for life turned out to be death for me. ¹¹For sin, seizing an opportunity in the commandment, deceived me and through it put me to death. ¹²So then the law is holy, and the commandment is holy and righteous and good. ¹³Did the good, then, become death for me? Of course not! Sin, in order that it might be shown to be sin, worked death in me through the good, so that sin might become sinful beyond measure through the commandment. ¹⁴We know that the law is spiritual; but I am carnal, sold into slavery to sin. ¹⁵What I do, I do not understand. For I do not do what I want, but I do what I hate. ¹⁶Now if I do what I do not want, I concur that the law is good. ¹⁷So now it is no longer I who do it, but sin that dwells in me. ¹⁸For I know that good does not dwell in me, that is, in my flesh. The willing is ready at hand, but doing the good is not. ¹⁹For I do not do the good I want, but I do the evil I do not want. ²⁰Now if (I) do what I do not want, it is no longer I who do it, but sin that dwells in me. ²¹So, then, I discover the principle that when I want to do right, evil is at hand. ²²For I take delight in the law of God, in my inner self, ²³but I see in my members another principle at war with the law of my mind, taking me captive to the law of sin that dwells in my members. ²⁴Miserable one that I am! Who will deliver me from this mortal body? ²⁵Thanks be to God through Jesus Christ our Lord. Therefore, I myself, with my mind, serve the law of God but, with my flesh, the law of sin.

Romans Chapter 8

¹ Hence, now there is no condemnation for those who are in Christ Jesus. ² For the law of the spirit of life in Christ Jesus has freed you from the law of sin and death. ³ For what the law, weakened by the flesh, was powerless to do, this God has done: by sending his own Son in the likeness of sinful flesh and for the sake of sin, he condemned sin in the flesh, ⁴ so that the righteous decree of the law might be fulfilled in us, who live not according to the flesh but according to the spirit. ⁵ For those who live according to the flesh are concerned with the things of the flesh, but those who live according to the spirit with the things of the spirit. ⁶ The concern of the flesh is death, but the concern of the spirit is life and peace. ⁷ For the concern of the flesh is hostility toward God; it does not submit to the law of God, nor can it; ⁸ and those who are in the flesh cannot please God. ⁹ But you are not in the flesh; on the contrary, you are in the spirit, if only the Spirit of God dwells in you. Whoever does not have the Spirit of Christ does not belong to him. ¹⁰ But if Christ is in you, although the body is dead because of sin, the spirit is alive because of righteousness. ¹¹ If the Spirit of the one who raised Jesus from the dead dwells in you, the one who raised Christ from the dead will give life to your mortal bodies also, through his Spirit that dwells in you. ¹² Consequently, brothers, we are not debtors to the flesh, to live according to the flesh. ¹³ For if you live according to the flesh, you will die, but if by the spirit you put to death the deeds of the body, you will live. ¹⁴ For those who are led by the Spirit of God are children of God. ¹⁵ For you did not receive a spirit of slavery to fall back into fear, but you received a spirit of adoption, through which we cry, "Abba, Father!" ¹⁶ The Spirit itself bears witness with our spirit that we are children of God, ¹⁷ and if children, then heirs, heirs of God and joint heirs with Christ, if only we suffer with him so that we may also be glorified with him. ¹⁸ I consider that the sufferings of this present time are as nothing compared with the glory to be revealed for us. ¹⁹ For creation awaits with eager expectation the revelation of the children of God; ²⁰ for creation was made subject to futility, not of its own accord but because of the one who subjected it, in hope ²¹ that creation itself would be set free from slavery to corruption and share in the glorious freedom of the children of God. ²² We know that all creation is groaning in labor pains even until now; ²³ and not only that, but we ourselves, who have the firstfruits of the Spirit, we also groan within ourselves as we wait for adoption, the redemption of our bodies. ²⁴ For in hope we were saved. Now hope that sees for itself is not hope. For who hopes for what one sees? ²⁵ But if we hope for what we do not see, we wait with endurance. ²⁶ In the same way, the Spirit too comes to the aid of our weakness; for we do not know how to pray as we ought, but the Spirit itself intercedes with inexpressible groanings. ²⁷ And the one who searches hearts knows what is the intention of the Spirit, because it intercedes for the holy ones according to God's will. ²⁸ We know that all things work for good for those who love God, who are called according to his purpose. ²⁹ For those he foreknew he also predestined to be conformed to the image of his Son, so that he might be the firstborn among many brothers. ³⁰ And those he predestined he also called; and those he called he also justified; and those he justified he also glorified. ³¹ What then shall we say to this? If God is for us, who can be against us? ³² He who did not spare his own Son but handed him over for us all, how will he not also give us everything else along with him? ³³ Who

will bring a charge against God's chosen ones? It is God who acquits us. ³⁴ Who will condemn? It is Christ (Jesus) who died, rather, was raised, who also is at the right hand of God, who indeed intercedes for us. ³⁵ What will separate us from the love of Christ? Will anguish, or distress, or persecution, or famine, or nakedness, or peril, or the sword? ³⁶ As it is written: "For your sake we are being slain all the day; we are looked upon as sheep to be slaughtered." ³⁷ No, in all these things we conquer overwhelmingly through him who loved us. ³⁸ For I am convinced that neither death, nor life, nor angels, nor principalities, nor present things, nor future things, nor powers, ³⁹ nor height, nor depth, nor any other creature will be able to separate us from the love of God in Christ Jesus our Lord.

Romans Chapter 9

¹ I speak the truth in Christ, I do not lie; my conscience joins with the holy Spirit in bearing me witness ² that I have great sorrow and constant anguish in my heart. ³ For I could wish that I myself were accursed and separated from Christ for the sake of my brothers, my kin according to the flesh. ⁴ They are Israelites; theirs the adoption, the glory, the covenants, the giving of the law, the worship, and the promises; ⁵ theirs the patriarchs, and from them, according to the flesh, is the Messiah. God who is over all be blessed forever. Amen. ⁶ But it is not that the word of God has failed. For not all who are of Israel are Israel, ⁷ nor are they all children of Abraham because they are his descendants; but "It is through Isaac that descendants shall bear your name." ⁸ This means that it is not the children of the flesh who are the children of God, but the children of the promise are counted as descendants. ⁹ For this is the wording of the promise, "About this time I shall return and Sarah will have a son." ¹⁰ And not only that, but also when Rebecca had conceived children by one husband, our father Isaac - ¹¹ before they had yet been born or had done anything, good or bad, in order that God's elective plan might continue, ¹² not by works but by his call - she was told, "The older shall serve the younger." ¹³ As it is written: "I loved Jacob but hated Esau." ¹⁴ What then are we to say? Is there injustice on the part of God? Of course not! ¹⁵ For he says to Moses: "I will show mercy to whom I will, I will take pity on whom I will." ¹⁶ So it depends not upon a person's will or exertion, but upon God, who shows mercy. ¹⁷ For the scripture says to Pharaoh, "This is why I have raised you up, to show my power through you that my name may be proclaimed throughout the earth." ¹⁸ Consequently, he has mercy upon whom he wills, and he hardens whom he wills. ¹⁹ You will say to me then, "Why (then) does he still find fault? For who can oppose his will?" ²⁰ But who indeed are you, a human being, to talk back to God? Will what is made say to its maker, "Why have you created me so?" ²¹ Or does not the potter have a right over the clay, to make out of the same lump one vessel for a noble purpose and another for an ignoble one? ²² What if God, wishing to show his wrath and make known his power, has endured with much patience the vessels of wrath made for destruction? ²³ This was to make known the riches of his glory to the vessels of mercy, which he has prepared previously for glory, ²⁴ namely, us whom he has called, not only from the Jews but also from the Gentiles. ²⁵ As indeed he says in Hosea: "Those who were not my people I will call 'my people,' and her who was not beloved I will call 'beloved.' ²⁶ And in the very place where it was said to them, 'You are not my people,' there they shall be called children of the living God." ²⁷ And Isaiah cries out concerning Israel, "Though the number of the Israelites were like the sand of the sea, only a remnant will be saved; ²⁸ for decisively and quickly will the Lord execute sentence upon the earth." ²⁹ And as Isaiah predicted: "Unless the Lord of hosts had left us descendants, we would have become like Sodom and have been made like Gomorrah." ³⁰ What then shall we say? That Gentiles, who did not pursue righteousness, have achieved it, that is, righteousness that comes from faith; ³¹ but that Israel, who pursued the law of righteousness, did not attain to that law? ³² Why not? Because they did it not by faith, but as if it could be done by works. They stumbled over the stone that causes stumbling, ³³ as it is written: "Behold, I am laying a stone in Zion that will make people stumble and a rock that will make them fall, and whoever believes in him shall not be put to shame."

Romans Chapter 10

¹ Brothers, my heart's desire and prayer to God on their behalf is for salvation. ² I testify with regard to them that they have zeal for God, but it is not discerning. ³ For, in their unawareness of the righteousness that comes from God and their attempt to establish their own (righteousness), they did not submit to the righteousness of God. ⁴ For Christ is the end of the law for the justification of everyone who has faith. ⁵ Moses writes about the righteousness that comes from (the) law, "The one who does these things will live by them." ⁶ But the righteousness that comes from faith says, "Do not say in your heart,

'Who will go up into heaven?' (that is, to bring Christ down) 7 or 'Who will go down into the abyss?' (that is, to bring Christ up from the dead)." 8 But what does it say? "The word is near you, in your mouth and in your heart" (that is, the word of faith that we preach), 9 for, if you confess with your mouth that Jesus is Lord and believe in your heart that God raised him from the dead, you will be saved. 10 For one believes with the heart and so is justified, and one confesses with the mouth and so is saved. 11 For the scripture says, "No one who believes in him will be put to shame." 12 For there is no distinction between Jew and Greek; the same Lord is Lord of all, enriching all who call upon him. 13 For "everyone who calls on the name of the Lord will be saved." 14 But how can they call on him in whom they have not believed? And how can they believe in him of whom they have not heard? And how can they hear without someone to preach? 15 And how can people preach unless they are sent? As it is written, "How beautiful are the feet of those who bring (the) good news!" 16 But not everyone has heeded the good news; for Isaiah says, "Lord, who has believed what was heard from us?" 17 Thus faith comes from what is heard, and what is heard comes through the word of Christ. 18 But I ask, did they not hear? Certainly they did; for "Their voice has gone forth to all the earth, and their words to the ends of the world." 19 But I ask, did not Israel understand? First Moses says: "I will make you jealous of those who are not a nation; with a senseless nation I will make you angry." 20 Then Isaiah speaks boldly and says: "I was found (by) those who were not seeking me; I revealed myself to those who were not asking for me." 21 But regarding Israel he says, "All day long I stretched out my hands to a disobedient and contentious people."

Romans Chapter 11

1 I ask, then, has God rejected his people? Of course not! For I too am an Israelite, a descendant of Abraham, of the tribe of Benjamin. 2 God has not rejected his people whom he foreknew. Do you not know what the scripture says about Elijah, how he pleads with God against Israel? 3 "Lord, they have killed your prophets, they have torn down your altars, and I alone am left, and they are seeking my life." 4 But what is God's response to him? "I have left for myself seven thousand men who have not knelt to Baal." 5 So also at the present time there is a remnant, chosen by grace. 6 But if by grace, it is no longer because of works; otherwise grace would no longer be grace. 7 What then? What Israel was seeking it did not attain, but the elect attained it; the rest were hardened, 8 as it is written: "God gave them a spirit of deep sleep, eyes that should not see and ears that should not hear, down to this very day." 9 And David says: "Let their table become a snare and a trap, a stumbling block and a retribution for them; 10 let their eyes grow dim so that they may not see, and keep their backs bent forever." 11 Hence I ask, did they stumble so as to fall? Of course not! But through their transgression salvation has come to the Gentiles, so as to make them jealous. 12 Now if their transgression is enrichment for the world, and if their diminished number is enrichment for the Gentiles, how much more their full number. 13 Now I am speaking to you Gentiles. Inasmuch then as I am the apostle to the Gentiles, I glory in my ministry 14 in order to make my race jealous and thus save some of them. 15 For if their rejection is the reconciliation of the world, what will their acceptance be but life from the dead? 16 If the firstfruits are holy, so is the whole batch of dough; and if the root is holy, so are the branches. 17 But if some of the branches were broken off, and you, a wild olive shoot, were grafted in their place and have come to share in the rich root of the olive tree, 18 do not boast against the branches. If you do boast, consider that you do not support the root; the root supports you. 19 Indeed you will say, "Branches were broken off so that I might be grafted in." 20 That is so. They were broken off because of unbelief, but you are there because of faith. So do not become haughty, but stand in awe. 21 For if God did not spare the natural branches, (perhaps) he will not spare you either. 22 See, then, the kindness and severity of God: severity toward those who fell, but God's kindness to you, provided you remain in his kindness; otherwise you too will be cut off. 23 And they also, if they do not remain in unbelief, will be grafted in, for God is able to graft them in again. 24 For if you were cut from what is by nature a wild olive tree, and grafted, contrary to nature, into a cultivated one, how much more will they who belong to it by nature be grafted back into their own olive tree. 25 I do not want you to be unaware of this mystery, brothers, so that you will not become wise (in) your own estimation: a hardening has come upon Israel in part, until the full number of the Gentiles comes in, 26 and thus all Israel will be saved, as it is written: "The deliverer will come out of Zion, he will turn away godlessness from Jacob; 27 and this is my covenant with them when I take away their sins." 28 In respect to the gospel, they are enemies on your account; but in respect to election, they are beloved because of the patriarchs. 29 For the gifts and the call of God are irrevocable. 30 Just as you once disobeyed God but have now received mercy because of their disobedience, 31 so they have now disobeyed in order that, by virtue of the mercy shown to you, they too may (now) receive mercy. 32 For God delivered all to disobedience, that he might have mercy upon all. 33 Oh, the depth of the riches and wisdom and knowledge of God! How inscrutable are his judgments and how unsearchable his ways! 34 "For who has known the mind of the Lord or who has been his counselor?" 35 "Or who has given him anything that he may be repaid?" 36 For from him and through him and for him are all things. To him be glory forever. Amen.

Romans Chapter 12

1 I urge you therefore, brothers, by the mercies of God, to offer your bodies as a living sacrifice, holy and pleasing to God, your spiritual worship. 2 Do not conform yourselves to this age but be transformed by the renewal of your mind, that you may discern what is the will of God, what is good and pleasing and perfect. 3 For by the grace given to me I tell everyone among you not to think of himself more highly than one ought to think, but to think soberly, each according to the measure of faith that God has apportioned. 4 For as in one body we have many parts, and all the parts do not have the same function, 5 so we, though many, are one body in Christ and individually parts of one another. 6 Since we have gifts that differ according to the grace given to us, let us exercise them: if prophecy, in proportion to the faith; 7 if ministry, in ministering; if one is a teacher, in teaching; 8 if one exhorts, in exhortation; if one contributes, in generosity; if one is over others, with diligence; if one does acts of mercy, with cheerfulness. 9 Let love be sincere; hate what is evil, hold on to what is good; 10 love one another with mutual affection; anticipate one another in showing honor. 11 Do not grow slack in zeal, be fervent in spirit, serve the Lord. 12 Rejoice in hope, endure in affliction, persevere in prayer. 13 Contribute to the needs of the holy ones, exercise hospitality. 14 Bless those who persecute (you), bless and do not curse them. 15 Rejoice with those who rejoice, weep with those who weep. 16 Have the same regard for one another; do not be haughty but associate with the lowly; do not be wise in your own estimation. 17 Do not repay anyone evil for evil; be concerned for what is noble in the sight of all. 18 If possible, on your part, live at peace with all. 19 Beloved, do not look for revenge but leave room for the wrath; for it is written, "Vengeance is mine, I will repay, says the Lord." 20 Rather, "if your enemy is hungry, feed him; if he is thirsty, give him something to drink; for by so doing you will heap burning coals upon his head." 21 Do not be conquered by evil but conquer evil with good.

Romans Chapter 13

1 Let every person be subordinate to the higher authorities, for there is no authority except from God, and those that exist have been established by God. 2 Therefore, whoever resists authority opposes what God has appointed, and those who oppose it will bring judgment upon themselves. 3 For rulers are not a cause of fear to good conduct, but to evil. Do you wish to have no fear of authority? Then do what is good and you will receive approval from it, 4 for it is a servant of God for your good. But if you do evil, be afraid, for it does not bear the sword without purpose; it is the servant of God to inflict wrath on the evildoer. 5 Therefore, it is necessary to be subject not only because of the wrath but also because of conscience. 6 This is why you also pay taxes, for the authorities are ministers of God, devoting themselves to this very thing. 7 Pay to all their dues, taxes to whom taxes are due, toll to whom toll is due, respect to whom respect is due, honor to whom honor is due. 8 Owe nothing to anyone, except to love one another; for the one who loves another has fulfilled the law. 9 The commandments, "You shall not commit adultery; you shall not kill; you shall not steal; you shall not covet," and whatever other commandment there may be, are summed up in this saying, (namely) "You shall love your neighbor as yourself." 10 Love does no evil to the neighbor; hence, love is the fulfillment of the law. 11 And do this because you know the time; it is the hour now for you to awake from sleep. For our salvation is nearer now than when we first believed; 12 the night is advanced, the day is at hand. Let us then throw off the works of darkness (and) put on the armor of light; 13 let us conduct ourselves properly as in the day, not in orgies and drunkenness, not in promiscuity and licentiousness, not in rivalry and jealousy. 14 But put on the Lord Jesus Christ, and make no provision for the desires of the flesh.

Romans Chapter 14

1 Welcome anyone who is weak in faith, but not for disputes over opinions. 2 One person believes that one may eat anything, while the weak person eats only vegetables. 3 The one who eats must not despise the one who abstains, and the one who abstains must not pass judgment on the one who eats; for God has welcomed him. 4 Who are you to pass

judgment on someone else's servant? Before his own master he stands or falls. And he will be upheld, for the Lord is able to make him stand. 5 (For) one person considers one day more important than another, while another person considers all days alike. Let everyone be fully persuaded in his own mind. 6 Whoever observes the day, observes it for the Lord. Also whoever eats, eats for the Lord, since he gives thanks to God; while whoever abstains, abstains for the Lord and gives thanks to God. 7 None of us lives for oneself, and no one dies for oneself. 8 For if we live, we live for the Lord, and if we die, we die for the Lord; so then, whether we live or die, we are the Lord's. 9 For this is why Christ died and came to life, that he might be Lord of both the dead and the living. 10 Why then do you judge your brother? Or you, why do you look down on your brother? For we shall all stand before the judgment seat of God; 11 for it is written: "As I live, says the Lord, every knee shall bend before me, and every tongue shall give praise to God." 12 So (then) each of us shall give an account of himself (to God). 13 Then let us no longer judge one another, but rather resolve never to put a stumbling block or hindrance in the way of a brother. 14 I know and am convinced in the Lord Jesus that nothing is unclean in itself; still, it is unclean for someone who thinks it unclean. 15 If your brother is being hurt by what you eat, your conduct is no longer in accord with love. Do not because of your food destroy him for whom Christ died. 16 So do not let your good be reviled. 17 For the kingdom of God is not a matter of food and drink, but of righteousness, peace, and joy in the holy Spirit; 18 whoever serves Christ in this way is pleasing to God and approved by others. 19 Let us then pursue what leads to peace and to building up one another. 20 For the sake of food, do not destroy the work of God. Everything is indeed clean, but it is wrong for anyone to become a stumbling block by eating; 21 it is good not to eat meat or drink wine or do anything that causes your brother to stumble. 22 Keep the faith (that) you have to yourself in the presence of God; blessed is the one who does not condemn himself for what he approves. 23 But whoever has doubts is condemned if he eats, because this is not from faith; for whatever is not from faith is sin.

Romans Chapter 15

1 We who are strong ought to put up with the failings of the weak and not to please ourselves; 2 let each of us please our neighbor for the good, for building up. 3 For Christ did not please himself; but, as it is written, "The insults of those who insult you fall upon me." 4 For whatever was written previously was written for our instruction, that by endurance and by the encouragement of the scriptures we might have hope. 5 May the God of endurance and encouragement grant you to think in harmony with one another, in keeping with Christ Jesus, 6 that with one accord you may with one voice glorify the God and Father of our Lord Jesus Christ. 7 Welcome one another, then, as Christ welcomed you, for the glory of God. 8 For I say that Christ became a minister of the circumcised to show God's truthfulness, to confirm the promises to the patriarchs, 9 but so that the Gentiles might glorify God for his mercy. As it is written: "Therefore, I will praise you among the Gentiles and sing praises to your name." 10 And again it says: "Rejoice, O Gentiles, with his people." 11 And again: "Praise the Lord, all you Gentiles, and let all the peoples praise him." 12 And again Isaiah says: "The root of Jesse shall come, raised up to rule the Gentiles; in him shall the Gentiles hope." 13 May the God of hope fill you with all joy and peace in believing, so that you may abound in hope by the power of the holy Spirit. 14 I myself am convinced about you, my brothers, that you yourselves are full of goodness, filled with all knowledge, and able to admonish one another. 15 But I have written to you rather boldly in some respects to remind you, because of the grace given me by God 16 to be a minister of Christ Jesus to the Gentiles in performing the priestly service of the gospel of God, so that the offering up of the Gentiles may be acceptable, sanctified by the holy Spirit. 17 In Christ Jesus, then, I have reason to boast in what pertains to God. 18 For I will not dare to speak of anything except what Christ has accomplished through me to lead the Gentiles to obedience by word and deed, 19 by the power of signs and wonders, by the power of the Spirit (of God), so that from Jerusalem all the way around to Illyricum I have finished preaching the gospel of Christ. 20 Thus I aspire to proclaim the gospel not where Christ has already been named, so that I do not build on another's foundation, 21 but as it is written: "Those who have never been told of him shall see, and those who have never heard of him shall understand." 22 That is why I have so often been prevented from coming to you. 23 But now, since I no longer have any opportunity in these regions and since I have desired to come to you for many years, 24 I hope to see you in passing as I go to Spain and to be sent on my way there by you, after I have enjoyed being with you for a time. 25 Now, however, I am going to Jerusalem to minister to the holy ones. 26 For Macedonia and Achaia have decided to make some contribution for the poor among the holy ones in Jerusalem; 27 they decided to do it, and in fact they are indebted to them, for if the Gentiles have come to share in their spiritual blessings, they ought also to serve them in material blessings. 28 So when I have completed this and safely handed over this contribution to them, I shall set out by way of you to Spain; 29 and I know that in coming to you I shall come in the fullness of Christ's blessing. 30 I urge you, (brothers,) by our Lord Jesus Christ and by the love of the Spirit, to join me in the struggle by your prayers to God on my behalf, 31 that I may be delivered from the disobedient in Judea, and that my ministry for Jerusalem may be acceptable to the holy ones, 32 so that I may come to you with joy by the will of God and be refreshed together with you. 33 The God of peace be with all of you. Amen.

Romans Chapter 16

1 I commend to you Phoebe our sister, who is (also) a minister of the church at Cenchreae, 2 that you may receive her in the Lord in a manner worthy of the holy ones, and help her in whatever she may need from you, for she has been a benefactor to many and to me as well. 3 Greet Prisca and Aquila, my co-workers in Christ Jesus, 4 who risked their necks for my life, to whom not only I am grateful but also all the churches of the Gentiles; 5 greet also the church at their house. Greet my beloved Epaenetus, who was the firstfruits in Asia for Christ. 6 Greet Mary, who has worked hard for you. 7 Greet Andronicus and Junia, my relatives and my fellow prisoners; they are prominent among the apostles and they were in Christ before me. 8 Greet Ampliatus, my beloved in the Lord. 9 Greet Urbanus, our co-worker in Christ, and my beloved Stachys. 10 Greet Apelles, who is approved in Christ. Greet those who belong to the family of Aristobulus. 11 Greet my relative Herodion. Greet those in the Lord who belong to the family of Narcissus. 12 Greet those workers in the Lord, Tryphaena and Tryphosa. Greet the beloved Persis, who has worked hard in the Lord. 13 Greet Rufus, chosen in the Lord, and his mother and mine. 14 Greet Asyncritus, Phlegon, Hermes, Patrobas, Hermas, and the brothers who are with them. 15 Greet Philologus, Julia, Nereus and his sister, and Olympas, and all the holy ones who are with them. 16 Greet one another with a holy kiss. All the churches of Christ greet you. 17 I urge you, brothers, to watch out for those who create dissensions and obstacles, in opposition to the teaching that you learned; avoid them. 18 For such people do not serve our Lord Christ but their own appetites, and by fair and flattering speech they deceive the hearts of the innocent. 19 For while your obedience is known to all, so that I rejoice over you, I want you to be wise as to what is good, and simple as to what is evil; 20 then the God of peace will quickly crush Satan under your feet. The grace of our Lord Jesus be with you. 21 Timothy, my co-worker, greets you; so do Lucius and Jason and Sosipater, my relatives. 22 I, Tertius, the writer of this letter, greet you in the Lord. 23 Gaius, who is host to me and to the whole church, greets you. Erastus, the city treasurer, and our brother Quartus greet you. 24 The grace of our Lord Jesus Christ be with you all! Amen. 25 Now to him who can strengthen you, according to my gospel and the proclamation of Jesus Christ, according to the revelation of the mystery kept secret for long ages 26 but now manifested through the prophetic writings and, according to the command of the eternal God, made known to all nations to bring about the obedience of faith, 27 to the only wise God, through Jesus Christ be glory forever and ever. Amen.

I Corinthians

1 Corinthians Chapter 1

1 Paul, called to be an apostle of Christ Jesus by the will of God, and Sosthenes our brother, 2 to the church of God that is in Corinth, to you who have been sanctified in Christ Jesus, called to be holy, with all those everywhere who call upon the name of our Lord Jesus Christ, their Lord and ours. 3 Grace to you and peace from God our Father and the Lord Jesus Christ. 4 I give thanks to my God always on your account for the grace of God bestowed on you in Christ Jesus, 5 that in him you were enriched in every way, with all discourse and all knowledge, 6 as the testimony to Christ was confirmed among you, 7 so that you are not lacking in any spiritual gift as you wait for the revelation of our Lord Jesus Christ. 8 He will keep you firm to the end, irreproachable on the day of our Lord Jesus (Christ). 9 God is faithful, and by him you were called to fellowship with his Son, Jesus Christ our Lord. 10 I urge you, brothers, in the name of our Lord Jesus Christ, that all of you agree in what you say, and that there be no divisions among you, but that you be united in the same mind and in the same purpose. 11 For it has been reported to me about you, my brothers, by Chloe's people, that there are rivalries among you. 12 I mean that each of you is saying, "I belong to Paul," or "I belong to Apollos," or "I belong to Kephas," or "I belong to Christ." 13 Is Christ divided? Was Paul crucified for you? Or were you

baptized in the name of Paul? [14]I give thanks (to God) that I baptized none of you except Crispus and Gaius, [15]so that no one can say you were baptized in my name. [16](I baptized the household of Stephanas also; beyond that I do not know whether I baptized anyone else.) [17]For Christ did not send me to baptize but to preach the gospel, and not with the wisdom of human eloquence, so that the cross of Christ might not be emptied of its meaning. [18]The message of the cross is foolishness to those who are perishing, but to us who are being saved it is the power of God. [19]For it is written: "I will destroy the wisdom of the wise, and the learning of the learned I will set aside." [20]Where is the wise one? Where is the scribe? Where is the debater of this age? Has not God made the wisdom of the world foolish? [21]For since in the wisdom of God the world did not come to know God through wisdom, it was the will of God through the foolishness of the proclamation to save those who have faith. [22]For Jews demand signs and Greeks look for wisdom, [23]but we proclaim Christ crucified, a stumbling block to Jews and foolishness to Gentiles, [24]but to those who are called, Jews and Greeks alike, Christ the power of God and the wisdom of God. [25]For the foolishness of God is wiser than human wisdom, and the weakness of God is stronger than human strength. [26]Consider your own calling, brothers. Not many of you were wise by human standards, not many were powerful, not many were of noble birth. [27]Rather, God chose the foolish of the world to shame the wise, and God chose the weak of the world to shame the strong, [28]and God chose the lowly and despised of the world, those who count for nothing, to reduce to nothing those who are something, [29]so that no human being might boast before God. [30]It is due to him that you are in Christ Jesus, who became for us wisdom from God, as well as righteousness, sanctification, and redemption, [31]so that, as it is written, "Whoever boasts, should boast in the Lord."

1 Corinthians Chapter 2

[1]When I came to you, brothers, proclaiming the mystery of God, I did not come with sublimity of words or of wisdom. [2]For I resolved to know nothing while I was with you except Jesus Christ, and him crucified. [3]I came to you in weakness and fear and much trembling, [4]and my message and my proclamation were not with persuasive (words of) wisdom, but with a demonstration of spirit and power, [5]so that your faith might rest not on human wisdom but on the power of God. [6]Yet we do speak a wisdom to those who are mature, but not a wisdom of this age, nor of the rulers of this age who are passing away. [7]Rather, we speak God's wisdom, mysterious, hidden, which God predetermined before the ages for our glory, [8]and which none of the rulers of this age knew; for if they had known it, they would not have crucified the Lord of glory. [9]But as it is written: "What eye has not seen, and ear has not heard, and what has not entered the human heart, what God has prepared for those who love him," [10]this God has revealed to us through the Spirit.For the Spirit scrutinizes everything, even the depths of God. [11]Among human beings, who knows what pertains to a person except the spirit of the person that is within? Similarly, no one knows what pertains to God except the Spirit of God. [12]We have not received the spirit of the world but the Spirit that is from God, so that we may understand the things freely given us by God. [13]And we speak about them not with words taught by human wisdom, but with words taught by the Spirit, describing spiritual realities in spiritual terms. [14]Now the natural person does not accept what pertains to the Spirit of God, for to him it is foolishness, and he cannot understand it, because it is judged spiritually. [15]The spiritual person, however, can judge everything but is not subject to judgment by anyone. [16]For "who has known the mind of the Lord, so as to counsel him?" But we have the mind of Christ.

1 Corinthians Chapter 3

[1]Brothers, I could not talk to you as spiritual people, but as fleshly people, as infants in Christ. [2]I fed you milk, not solid food, because you were unable to take it. Indeed, you are still not able, even now, [3]for you are still of the flesh. While there is jealousy and rivalry among you, are you not of the flesh, and behaving in an ordinary human way? [4]Whenever someone says, "I belong to Paul," and another, "I belong to Apollos," are you not merely human? [5]What is Apollos, after all, and what is Paul? Ministers through whom you became believers, just as the Lord assigned each one. [6]I planted, Apollos watered, but God caused the growth. [7]Therefore, neither the one who plants nor the one who waters is anything, but only God, who causes the growth. [8]The one who plants and the one who waters are equal, and each will receive wages in proportion to his labor. [9]For we are God's co-workers; you are God's field, God's building. [10]According to the grace of God given to me, like a wise master builder I laid a foundation, and another is building upon it. But each one must be careful how he builds upon it, [11]for no one can lay a foundation other than the one that is there, namely, Jesus Christ. [12]If anyone builds on this foundation with gold, silver, precious stones,

wood, hay, or straw, [13]the work of each will come to light, for the Day will disclose it. It will be revealed with fire, and the fire (itself) will test the quality of each one's work. [14]If the work stands that someone built upon the foundation, that person will receive a wage. [15]But if someone's work is burned up, that one will suffer loss; the person will be saved, but only as through fire. [16]Do you not know that you are the temple of God, and that the Spirit of God dwells in you? [17]If anyone destroys God's temple, God will destroy that person; for the temple of God, which you are, is holy. [18]Let no one deceive himself. If any one among you considers himself wise in this age, let him become a fool so as to become wise. [19]For the wisdom of this world is foolishness in the eyes of God, for it is written: "He catches the wise in their own ruses," [20]and again: "The Lord knows the thoughts of the wise, that they are vain." [21]So let no one boast about human beings, for everything belongs to you, [22]Paul or Apollos or Kephas, or the world or life or death, or the present or the future: all belong to you, [23]and you to Christ, and Christ to God.

1 Corinthians Chapter 4

[1]Thus should one regard us: as servants of Christ and stewards of the mysteries of God. [2]Now it is of course required of stewards that they be found trustworthy. [3]It does not concern me in the least that I be judged by you or any human tribunal; I do not even pass judgment on myself; [4]I am not conscious of anything against me, but I do not thereby stand acquitted; the one who judges me is the Lord. [5]Therefore, do not make any judgment before the appointed time, until the Lord comes, for he will bring to light what is hidden in darkness and will manifest the motives of our hearts, and then everyone will receive praise from God. [6]I have applied these things to myself and Apollos for your benefit, brothers, so that you may learn from us not to go beyond what is written, so that none of you will be inflated with pride in favor of one person over against another. [7]Who confers distinction upon you? What do you possess that you have not received? But if you have received it, why are you boasting as if you did not receive it? [8]You are already satisfied; you have already grown rich; you have become kings without us! Indeed, I wish that you had become kings, so that we also might become kings with you. [9]For as I see it, God has exhibited us apostles as the last of all, like people sentenced to death, since we have become a spectacle to the world, to angels and human beings alike. [10]We are fools on Christ's account, but you are wise in Christ; we are weak, but you are strong; you are held in honor, but we in disrepute. [11]To this very hour we go hungry and thirsty, we are poorly clad and roughly treated, we wander about homeless [12]and we toil, working with our own hands. When ridiculed, we bless; when persecuted, we endure; [13]when slandered, we respond gently. We have become like the world's rubbish, the scum of all, to this very moment. [14]I am writing you this not to shame you, but to admonish you as my beloved children. [15]Even if you should have countless guides to Christ, yet you do not have many fathers, for I became your father in Christ Jesus through the gospel. [16]Therefore, I urge you, be imitators of me. [17]For this reason I am sending you Timothy, who is my beloved and faithful son in the Lord; he will remind you of my ways in Christ (Jesus), just as I teach them everywhere in every church. [18]Some have become inflated with pride, as if I were not coming to you. [19]But I will come to you soon, if the Lord is willing, and I shall ascertain not the talk of these inflated people but their power. [20]For the kingdom of God is not a matter of talk but of power. [21]Which do you prefer? Shall I come to you with a rod, or with love and a gentle spirit?

1 Corinthians Chapter 5

[1]It is widely reported that there is immorality among you, and immorality of a kind not found even among pagans - a man living with his father's wife. [2]And you are inflated with pride. Should you not rather have been sorrowful? The one who did this deed should be expelled from your midst. [3]I, for my part, although absent in body but present in spirit, have already, as if present, pronounced judgment on the one who has committed this deed, [4]in the name of (our) Lord Jesus: when you have gathered together and I am with you in spirit with the power of the Lord Jesus, [5]you are to deliver this man to Satan for the destruction of his flesh, so that his spirit may be saved on the day of the Lord. [6]Your boasting is not appropriate. Do you not know that a little yeast leavens all the dough? [7]Clear out the old yeast, so that you may become a fresh batch of dough, inasmuch as you are unleavened. For our paschal lamb, Christ, has been sacrificed. [8]Therefore let us celebrate the feast, not with the old yeast, the yeast of malice and wickedness, but with the unleavened bread of sincerity and truth. [9]I wrote you in my letter not to associate with immoral people, [10]not at all referring to the immoral of this world or the greedy and robbers or idolaters; for you would then have to leave the world. [11]But I now write

to you not to associate with anyone named a brother, if he is immoral, greedy, an idolater, a slanderer, a drunkard, or a robber, not even to eat with such a person. [12]For why should I be judging outsiders? Is it not your business to judge those within? [13]God will judge those outside. "Purge the evil person from your midst."

1 Corinthians Chapter 6

[1]How can any one of you with a case against another dare to bring it to the unjust for judgment instead of to the holy ones? [2]Do you not know that the holy ones will judge the world? If the world is to be judged by you, are you unqualified for the lowest law courts? [3]Do you not know that we will judge angels? Then why not everyday matters? [4]If, therefore, you have courts for everyday matters, do you seat as judges people of no standing in the church? [5]I say this to shame you. Can it be that there is not one among you wise enough to be able to settle a case between brothers? [6]But rather brother goes to court against brother, and that before unbelievers? [7]Now indeed (then) it is, in any case, a failure on your part that you have lawsuits against one another. Why not rather put up with injustice? Why not rather let yourselves be cheated? [8]Instead, you inflict injustice and cheat, and this to brothers. [9]Do you not know that the unjust will not inherit the kingdom of God? Do not be deceived; neither fornicators nor idolaters nor adulterers nor boy prostitutes nor practicing homosexuals [10]nor thieves nor the greedy nor drunkards nor slanderers nor robbers will inherit the kingdom of God. [11]That is what some of you used to be; but now you have had yourselves washed, you were sanctified, you were justified in the name of the Lord Jesus Christ and in the Spirit of our God. [12]"Everything is lawful for me," but not everything is beneficial. "Everything is lawful for me," but I will not let myself be dominated by anything. [13]"Food for the stomach and the stomach for food," but God will do away with both the one and the other. The body, however, is not for immorality, but for the Lord, and the Lord is for the body; [14]God raised the Lord and will also raise us by his power. [15]Do you not know that your bodies are members of Christ? Shall I then take Christ's members and make them the members of a prostitute? Of course not! [16](Or) do you not know that anyone who joins himself to a prostitute becomes one body with her? For "the two," it says, "will become one flesh." [17]But whoever is joined to the Lord becomes one spirit with him. [18]Avoid immorality. Every other sin a person commits is outside the body, but the immoral person sins against his own body. [19]Do you not know that your body is a temple of the holy Spirit within you, whom you have from God, and that you are not your own? [20]For you have been purchased at a price. Therefore, glorify God in your body.

1 Corinthians Chapter 7

[1]Now in regard to the matters about which you wrote: "It is a good thing for a man not to touch a woman," [2]but because of cases of immorality every man should have his own wife, and every woman her own husband. [3]The husband should fulfill his duty toward his wife, and likewise the wife toward her husband. [4]A wife does not have authority over her own body, but rather her husband, and similarly a husband does not have authority over his own body, but rather his wife. [5]Do not deprive each other, except perhaps by mutual consent for a time, to be free for prayer, but then return to one another, so that Satan may not tempt you through your lack of self-control. [6]This I say by way of concession, however, not as a command. [7]Indeed, I wish everyone to be as I am, but each has a particular gift from God, one of one kind and one of another. [8]Now to the unmarried and to widows, I say: it is a good thing for them to remain as they are, as I do, [9]but if they cannot exercise self-control they should marry, for it is better to marry than to be on fire. [10]To the married, however, I give this instruction (not I, but the Lord): a wife should not separate from her husband [11]- and if she does separate she must either remain single or become reconciled to her husband - and a husband should not divorce his wife. [12]To the rest I say (not the Lord): if any brother has a wife who is an unbeliever, and she is willing to go on living with him, he should not divorce her; [13]and if any woman has a husband who is an unbeliever, and he is willing to go on living with her, she should not divorce her husband. [14]For the unbelieving husband is made holy through his wife, and the unbelieving wife is made holy through the brother. Otherwise your children would be unclean, whereas in fact they are holy. [15]If the unbeliever separates, however, let him separate. The brother or sister is not bound in such cases; God has called you to peace. [16]For how do you know, wife, whether you will save your husband; or how do you know, husband, whether you will save your wife? [17]Only, everyone should live as the Lord has assigned, just as God called each one. I give this order in all the churches. [18]Was someone called after he had been circumcised? He should not try to undo his circumcision. Was an uncircumcised person called? He should not be circumcised. [19]Circumcision means nothing, and uncircumcision means nothing; what matters is keeping God's commandments. [20]Everyone should remain in the state in which he was called. [21]Were you a slave when you were called? Do not be concerned but, even if you can gain your freedom, make the most of it. [22]For the slave called in the Lord is a freed person in the Lord, just as the free person who has been called is a slave of Christ. [23]You have been purchased at a price. Do not become slaves to human beings. [24]Brothers, everyone should continue before God in the state in which he was called. [25]Now in regard to virgins, I have no commandment from the Lord, but I give my opinion as one who by the Lord's mercy is trustworthy. [26]So this is what I think best because of the present distress: that it is a good thing for a person to remain as he is. [27]Are you bound to a wife? Do not seek a separation. Are you free of a wife? Then do not look for a wife. [28]If you marry, however, you do not sin, nor does an unmarried woman sin if she marries; but such people will experience affliction in their earthly life, and I would like to spare you that. [29]I tell you, brothers, the time is running out. From now on, let those having wives act as not having them, [30]those weeping as not weeping, those rejoicing as not rejoicing, those buying as not owning, [31]those using the world as not using it fully. For the world in its present form is passing away. [32]I should like you to be free of anxieties. An unmarried man is anxious about the things of the Lord, how he may please the Lord. [33]But a married man is anxious about the things of the world, how he may please his wife, [34]and he is divided. An unmarried woman or a virgin is anxious about the things of the Lord, so that she may be holy in both body and spirit. A married woman, on the other hand, is anxious about the things of the world, how she may please her husband. [35]I am telling you this for your own benefit, not to impose a restraint upon you, but for the sake of propriety and adherence to the Lord without distraction. [36]If anyone thinks he is behaving improperly toward his virgin, and if a critical moment has come and so it has to be, let him do as he wishes. He is committing no sin; let them get married. [37]The one who stands firm in his resolve, however, who is not under compulsion but has power over his own will, and has made up his mind to keep his virgin, will be doing well. [38]So then, the one who marries his virgin does well; the one who does not marry her will do better. [39]A wife is bound to her husband as long as he lives. But if her husband dies, she is free to be married to whomever she wishes, provided that it be in the Lord. [40]She is more blessed, though, in my opinion, if she remains as she is, and I think that I too have the Spirit of God.

1 Corinthians Chapter 8

[1]Now in regard to meat sacrificed to idols: we realize that "all of us have knowledge"; knowledge inflates with pride, but love builds up. [2]If anyone supposes he knows something, he does not yet know as he ought to know. [3]But if one loves God, one is known by him. [4]So about the eating of meat sacrificed to idols: we know that "there is no idol in the world," and that "there is no God but one." [5]Indeed, even though there are so-called gods in heaven and on earth (there are, to be sure, many "gods" and many "lords"), [6]yet for us there is one God, the Father, from whom all things are and for whom we exist, and one Lord, Jesus Christ, through whom all things are and through whom we exist. [7]But not all have this knowledge. There are some who have been so used to idolatry up until now that, when they eat meat sacrificed to idols, their conscience, which is weak, is defiled. [8]Now food will not bring us closer to God. We are no worse off if we do not eat, nor are we better off if we do. [9]But make sure that this liberty of yours in no way becomes a stumbling block to the weak. [10]If someone sees you, with your knowledge, reclining at table in the temple of an idol, may not his conscience too, weak as it is, be "built up" to eat the meat sacrificed to idols? [11]Thus through your knowledge, the weak person is brought to destruction, the brother for whom Christ died. [12]When you sin in this way against your brothers and wound their consciences, weak as they are, you are sinning against Christ. [13]Therefore, if food causes my brother to sin, I will never eat meat again, so that I may not cause my brother to sin.

1 Corinthians Chapter 9

[1]Am I not free? Am I not an apostle? Have I not seen Jesus our Lord? Are you not my work in the Lord? [2]Although I may not be an apostle for others, certainly I am for you, for you are the seal of my apostleship in the Lord. [3]My defense against those who would pass judgment on me is this. [4]Do we not have the right to eat and drink? [5]Do we not have the right to take along a Christian wife, as do the rest of the apostles, and the brothers of the Lord, and Kephas? [6]Or is it only myself and Barnabas who do not have the right not to work? [7]Who ever serves as a soldier at his own expense? Who plants a vineyard without eating its produce? Or who shepherds a flock without using some of the milk from the flock? [8]Am I saying this on human authority, or does not the law

also speak of these things? 9It is written in the law of Moses, "You shall not muzzle an ox while it is treading out the grain." Is God concerned about oxen, 10or is he not really speaking for our sake? It was written for our sake, because the plowman should plow in hope, and the thresher in hope of receiving a share. 11If we have sown spiritual seed for you, is it a great thing that we reap a material harvest from you? 12If others share this rightful claim on you, do not we still more? Yet we have not used this right. On the contrary, we endure everything so as not to place an obstacle to the gospel of Christ. 13Do you not know that those who perform the temple services eat (what) belongs to the temple, and those who minister at the altar share in the sacrificial offerings? 14In the same way, the Lord ordered that those who preach the gospel should live by the gospel. 15I have not used any of these rights, however, nor do I write this that it be done so in my case. I would rather die. Certainly no one is going to nullify my boast. 16If I preach the gospel, this is no reason for me to boast, for an obligation has been imposed on me, and woe to me if I do not preach it! 17If I do so willingly, I have a recompense, but if unwillingly, then I have been entrusted with a stewardship. 18What then is my recompense? That, when I preach, I offer the gospel free of charge so as not to make full use of my right in the gospel. 19Although I am free in regard to all, I have made myself a slave to all so as to win over as many as possible. 20To the Jews I became like a Jew to win over Jews; to those under the law I became like one under the law - though I myself am not under the law - to win over those under the law. 21To those outside the law I became like one outside the law - though I am not outside God's law but within the law of Christ - to win over those outside the law. 22To the weak I became weak, to win over the weak. I have become all things to all, to save at least some. 23All this I do for the sake of the gospel, so that I too may have a share in it. 24Do you not know that the runners in the stadium all run in the race, but only one wins the prize? Run so as to win. 25Every athlete exercises discipline in every way. They do it to win a perishable crown, but we an imperishable one. 26Thus I do not run aimlessly; I do not fight as if I were shadowboxing. 27No, I drive my body and train it, for fear that, after having preached to others, I myself should be disqualified.

1 Corinthians Chapter 10

1I do not want you to be unaware, brothers, that our ancestors were all under the cloud and all passed through the sea, 2and all of them were baptized into Moses in the cloud and in the sea. 3All ate the same spiritual food, 4and all drank the same spiritual drink, for they drank from a spiritual rock that followed them, and the rock was the Christ. 5Yet God was not pleased with most of them, for they were struck down in the desert. 6These things happened as examples for us, so that we might not desire evil things, as they did. 7And do not become idolaters, as some of them did, as it is written, "The people sat down to eat and drink, and rose up to revel." 8Let us not indulge in immorality as some of them did, and twenty-three thousand fell within a single day. 9Let us not test Christ as some of them did, and suffered death by serpents. 10Do not grumble as some of them did, and suffered death by the destroyer. 11These things happened to them as an example, and they have been written down as a warning to us, upon whom the end of the ages has come. 12Therefore, whoever thinks he is standing secure should take care not to fall. 13No trial has come to you but what is human. God is faithful and will not let you be tried beyond your strength; but with the trial he will also provide a way out, so that you may be able to bear it. 14Therefore, my beloved, avoid idolatry. 15I am speaking as to sensible people; judge for yourselves what I am saying. 16The cup of blessing that we bless, is it not a participation in the blood of Christ? The bread that we break, is it not a participation in the body of Christ? 17Because the loaf of bread is one, we, though many, are one body, for we all partake of the one loaf. 18Look at Israel according to the flesh; are not those who eat the sacrifices participants in the altar? 19So what am I saying? That meat sacrificed to idols is anything? Or that an idol is anything? 20No, I mean that what they sacrifice, (they sacrifice) to demons, not to God, and I do not want you to become participants with demons. 21You cannot drink the cup of the Lord and also the cup of demons. You cannot partake of the table of the Lord and of the table of demons. 22Or are we provoking the Lord to jealous anger? Are we stronger than he? 23"Everything is lawful," but not everything is beneficial."Everything is lawful," but not everything builds up. 24No one should seek his own advantage, but that of his neighbor. 25Eat anything sold in the market, without raising questions on grounds of conscience, 26for "the earth and its fullness are the Lord's." 27If an unbeliever invites you and you want to go, eat whatever is placed before you, without raising questions on grounds of conscience. 28But if someone says to you, "This was offered in sacrifice," do not eat it on account of the one who called attention to it and on account of conscience; 29I mean not your own conscience, but

the other's. For why should my freedom be determined by someone else's conscience? 30If I partake thankfully, why am I reviled for that over which I give thanks? 31So whether you eat or drink, or whatever you do, do everything for the glory of God. 32Avoid giving offense, whether to Jews or Greeks or the church of God, 33just as I try to please everyone in every way, not seeking my own benefit but that of the many, that they may be saved.

1 Corinthians Chapter 11

1Be imitators of me, as I am of Christ. 2I praise you because you remember me in everything and hold fast to the traditions, just as I handed them on to you. 3But I want you to know that Christ is the head of every man, and a husband the head of his wife, and God the head of Christ. 4Any man who prays or prophesies with his head covered brings shame upon his head. 5But any woman who prays or prophesies with her head unveiled brings shame upon her head, for it is one and the same thing as if she had had her head shaved. 6For if a woman does not have her head veiled, she may as well have her hair cut off. But if it is shameful for a woman to have her hair cut off or her head shaved, then she should wear a veil. 7A man, on the other hand, should not cover his head, because he is the image and glory of God, but woman is the glory of man. 8For man did not come from woman, but woman from man; 9nor was man created for woman, but woman for man; 10for this reason a woman should have a sign of authority on her head, because of the angels. 11Woman is not independent of man or man of woman in the Lord. 12For just as woman came from man, so man is born of woman; but all things are from God. 13Judge for yourselves: is it proper for a woman to pray to God with her head unveiled? 14Does not nature itself teach you that if a man wears his hair long it is a disgrace to him, 15whereas if a woman has long hair it is her glory, because long hair has been given (her) for a covering? 16But if anyone is inclined to be argumentative, we do not have such a custom, nor do the churches of God. 17In giving this instruction, I do not praise the fact that your meetings are doing more harm than good. 18First of all, I hear that when you meet as a church there are divisions among you, and to a degree I believe it; 19there have to be factions among you in order that (also) those who are approved among you may become known. 20When you meet in one place, then, it is not to eat the Lord's supper, 21for in eating, each one goes ahead with his own supper, and one goes hungry while another gets drunk. 22Do you not have houses in which you can eat and drink? Or do you show contempt for the church of God and make those who have nothing feel ashamed? What can I say to you? Shall I praise you? In this matter I do not praise you. 23For I received from the Lord what I also handed on to you, that the Lord Jesus, on the night he was handed over, took bread, 24and, after he had given thanks, broke it and said, "This is my body that is for you. Do this in remembrance of me." 25In the same way also the cup, after supper, saying, "This cup is the new covenant in my blood. Do this, as often as you drink it, in remembrance of me." 26For as often as you eat this bread and drink the cup, you proclaim the death of the Lord until he comes. 27Therefore whoever eats the bread or drinks the cup of the Lord unworthily will have to answer for the body and blood of the Lord. 28A person should examine himself, and so eat the bread and drink the cup. 29For anyone who eats and drinks without discerning the body, eats and drinks judgment on himself. 30That is why many among you are ill and infirm, and a considerable number are dying. 31If we discerned ourselves, we would not be under judgment; 32but since we are judged by (the) Lord, we are being disciplined so that we may not be condemned along with the world. 33Therefore, my brothers, when you come together to eat, wait for one another. 34If anyone is hungry, he should eat at home, so that your meetings may not result in judgment. The other matters I shall set in order when I come.

1 Corinthians Chapter 12

1Now in regard to spiritual gifts, brothers, I do not want you to be unaware. 2You know how, when you were pagans, you were constantly attracted and led away to mute idols. 3Therefore, I tell you that nobody speaking by the spirit of God says, "Jesus be accursed." And no one can say, "Jesus is Lord," except by the holy Spirit. 4There are different kinds of spiritual gifts but the same Spirit; 5there are different forms of service but the same Lord; 6there are different workings but the same God who produces all of them in everyone. 7To each individual the manifestation of the Spirit is given for some benefit. 8To one is given through the Spirit the expression of wisdom; to another the expression of knowledge according to the same Spirit; 9to another faith by the same Spirit; to another gifts of healing by the one Spirit; 10to another mighty deeds; to another prophecy; to another discernment of spirits; to another varieties of tongues; to another interpretation of tongues. 11But one and the same Spirit produces all of these, distributing them individually to each person as he wishes. 12As a body is one though it has many parts, and all the parts of the body, though many, are one body, so also Christ. 13For in one Spirit we were all baptized into one body, whether Jews or Greeks, slaves or free persons, and we were all given to drink of one Spirit. 14Now the body is not a single part, but many. 15If a foot should say, "Because I am not a hand I do not belong to the body," it does not for this reason belong any less to the body. 16Or if an ear should say, "Because I am not an eye I do not belong to the body," it does not for this reason belong any less to the body. 17If the whole body were an eye, where would the hearing be? If the whole body were hearing, where would the sense of smell be? 18But as it is, God placed the parts, each one of them, in the body as he intended. 19If they were all one part, where would the body be? 20But as it is, there are many parts, yet one body. 21The eye cannot say to the hand, "I do not need you," nor again the head to the feet, "I do not need you." 22Indeed, the parts of the body that seem to be weaker are all the more necessary, 23and those parts of the body that we consider less honorable we surround with greater honor, and our less presentable parts are treated with greater propriety, 24whereas our more presentable parts do not need this. But God has so constructed the body as to give greater honor to a part that is without it, 25so that there may be no division in the body, but that the parts may have the same concern for one another. 26If (one) part suffers, all the parts suffer with it; if one part is honored, all the parts share its joy. 27Now you are Christ's body, and individually parts of it. 28Some people God has designated in the church to be, first, apostles; second, prophets; third, teachers; then, mighty deeds; then, gifts of healing, assistance, administration, and varieties of tongues. 29Are all apostles? Are all prophets? Are all teachers? Do all work mighty deeds? 30Do all have gifts of healing? Do all speak in tongues? Do all interpret? 31Strive eagerly for the greatest spiritual gifts. But I shall show you a still more excellent way.

1 Corinthians Chapter 13

1If I speak in human and angelic tongues but do not have love, I am a resounding gong or a clashing cymbal. 2And if I have the gift of prophecy and comprehend all mysteries and all knowledge; if I have all faith so as to move mountains but do not have love, I am nothing. 3If I give away everything I own, and if I hand my body over so that I may boast but do not have love, I gain nothing. 4Love is patient, love is kind. It is not jealous, (love) is not pompous, it is not inflated, 5it is not rude, it does not seek its own interests, it is not quick-tempered, it does not brood over injury, 6it does not rejoice over wrongdoing but rejoices with the truth. 7It bears all things, believes all things, hopes all things, endures all things. 8Love never fails. If there are prophecies, they will be brought to nothing; if tongues, they will cease; if knowledge, it will be brought to nothing. 9For we know partially and we prophesy partially, 10but when the perfect comes, the partial will pass away. 11When I was a child, I used to talk as a child, think as a child, reason as a child; when I became a man, I put aside childish things. 12At present we see indistinctly, as in a mirror, but then face to face. At present I know partially; then I shall know fully, as I am fully known. 13So faith, hope, love remain, these three; but the greatest of these is love.

1 Corinthians Chapter 14

1Pursue love, but strive eagerly for the spiritual gifts, above all that you may prophesy. 2For one who speaks in a tongue does not speak to human beings but to God, for no one listens; he utters mysteries in spirit. 3On the other hand, one who prophesies does speak to human beings, for their building up, encouragement, and solace. 4Whoever speaks in a tongue builds himself up, but whoever prophesies builds up the church. 5Now I should like all of you to speak in tongues, but even more to prophesy. One who prophesies is greater than one who speaks in tongues, unless he interprets, so that the church may be built up. 6Now, brothers, if I should come to you speaking in tongues, what good will I do you if I do not speak to you by way of revelation, or knowledge, or prophecy, or instruction? 7Likewise, if inanimate things that produce sound, such as flute or harp, do not give out the tones distinctly, how will what is being played on flute or harp be recognized? 8And if the bugle gives an indistinct sound, who will get ready for battle? 9Similarly, if you, because of speaking in tongues, do not utter intelligible speech, how will anyone know what is being said? For you will be talking to the air. 10It happens that there are many different languages in the world, and none is meaningless; 11but if I do not know the meaning of a language, I shall be a foreigner to one who speaks it, and one who speaks it a foreigner to me. 12So with yourselves: since you strive eagerly for spirits, seek to have an abundance of them for building up the church. 13Therefore, one who speaks in a tongue should pray to be able to interpret. 14(For) if I pray in a tongue, my spirit is at

prayer but my mind is unproductive. 15So what is to be done? I will pray with the spirit, but I will also pray with the mind. I will sing praise with the spirit, but I will also sing praise with the mind. 16Otherwise, if you pronounce a blessing (with) the spirit, how shall one who holds the place of the uninstructed say the "Amen" to your thanksgiving, since he does not know what you are saying? 17For you may be giving thanks very well, but the other is not built up. 18I give thanks to God that I speak in tongues more than any of you, 19but in the church I would rather speak five words with my mind, so as to instruct others also, than ten thousand words in a tongue. 20Brothers, stop being childish in your thinking. In respect to evil be like infants, but in your thinking be mature. 21It is written in the law: "By people speaking strange tongues and by the lips of foreigners I will speak to this people, and even so they will not listen to me, says the Lord." 22Thus, tongues are a sign not for those who believe but for unbelievers, whereas prophecy is not for unbelievers but for those who believe. 23So if the whole church meets in one place and everyone speaks in tongues, and then uninstructed people or unbelievers should come in, will they not say that you are out of your minds? 24But if everyone is prophesying, and an unbeliever or uninstructed person should come in, he will be convinced by everyone and judged by everyone, 25and the secrets of his heart will be disclosed, and so he will fall down and worship God, declaring, "God is really in your midst." 26So what is to be done, brothers? When you assemble, one has a psalm, another an instruction, a revelation, a tongue, or an interpretation. Everything should be done for building up. 27If anyone speaks in a tongue, let it be two or at most three, and each in turn, and one should interpret. 28But if there is no interpreter, the person should keep silent in the church and speak to himself and to God. 29Two or three prophets should speak, and the others discern. 30But if a revelation is given to another person sitting there, the first one should be silent. 31For you can all prophesy one by one, so that all may learn and all be encouraged. 32Indeed, the spirits of prophets are under the prophets' control, 33since he is not the God of disorder but of peace. As in all the churches of the holy ones, 34women should keep silent in the churches, for they are not allowed to speak, but should be subordinate, as even the law says. 35But if they want to learn anything, they should ask their husbands at home. For it is improper for a woman to speak in the church. 36Did the word of God go forth from you? Or has it come to you alone? 37If anyone thinks that he is a prophet or a spiritual person, he should recognize that what I am writing to you is a commandment of the Lord. 38If anyone does not acknowledge this, he is not acknowledged. 39So, (my) brothers, strive eagerly to prophesy, and do not forbid speaking in tongues, 40but everything must be done properly and in order.

1 Corinthians Chapter 15

1Now I am reminding you, brothers, of the gospel I preached to you, which you indeed received and in which you also stand. 2Through it you are also being saved, if you hold fast to the word I preached to you, unless you believed in vain. 3For I handed on to you as of first importance what I also received: that Christ died for our sins in accordance with the scriptures; 4that he was buried; that he was raised on the third day in accordance with the scriptures; 5that he appeared to Kephas, then to the Twelve. 6After that, he appeared to more than five hundred brothers at once, most of whom are still living, though some have fallen asleep. 7After that he appeared to James, then to all the apostles. 8Last of all, as to one born abnormally, he appeared to me. 9For I am the least of the apostles, not fit to be called an apostle, because I persecuted the church of God. 10But by the grace of God I am what I am, and his grace to me has not been ineffective. Indeed, I have toiled harder than all of them; not I, however, but the grace of God (that is) with me. 11Therefore, whether it be I or they, so we preach and so you believed. 12But if Christ is preached as raised from the dead, how can some among you say there is no resurrection of the dead? 13If there is no resurrection of the dead, then neither has Christ been raised. 14And if Christ has not been raised, then empty (too) is our preaching; empty, too, your faith. 15Then we are also false witnesses to God, because we testified against God that he raised Christ, whom he did not raise if in fact the dead are not raised. 16For if the dead are not raised, neither has Christ been raised, 17and if Christ has not been raised, your faith is vain; you are still in your sins. 18Then those who have fallen asleep in Christ have perished. 19If for this life only we have hoped in Christ, we are the most pitiable people of all. 20But now Christ has been raised from the dead, the firstfruits of those who have fallen asleep. 21For since death came through a human being, the resurrection of the dead came also through a human being. 22For just as in Adam all die, so too in Christ shall all be brought to life, 23but each one in proper order: Christ the firstfruits; then, at his coming, those who belong to Christ; 24then comes the end, when he hands over the kingdom to his God and

Father, when he has destroyed every sovereignty and every authority and power. 25For he must reign until he has put all his enemies under his feet. 26The last enemy to be destroyed is death, 27for "he subjected everything under his feet." But when it says that everything has been subjected, it is clear that it excludes the one who subjected everything to him. 28When everything is subjected to him, then the Son himself will (also) be subjected to the one who subjected everything to him, so that God may be all in all. 29Otherwise, what will people accomplish by having themselves baptized for the dead? If the dead are not raised at all, then why are they having themselves baptized for them? 30Moreover, why are we endangering ourselves all the time? 31Every day I face death; I swear it by the pride in you (brothers) that I have in Christ Jesus our Lord. 32If at Ephesus I fought with beasts, so to speak, what benefit was it to me? If the dead are not raised: "Let us eat and drink, for tomorrow we die." 33Do not be led astray: "Bad company corrupts good morals." 34Become sober as you ought and stop sinning. For some have no knowledge of God; I say this to your shame. 35But someone may say, "How are the dead raised? With what kind of body will they come back?" 36You fool! What you sow is not brought to life unless it dies. 37And what you sow is not the body that is to be but a bare kernel of wheat, perhaps, or of some other kind; 38but God gives it a body as he chooses, and to each of the seeds its own body. 39Not all flesh is the same, but there is one kind for human beings, another kind of flesh for animals, another kind of flesh for birds, and another for fish. 40There are both heavenly bodies and earthly bodies, but the brightness of the heavenly is one kind and that of the earthly another. 41The brightness of the sun is one kind, the brightness of the moon another, and the brightness of the stars another. For star differs from star in brightness. 42So also is the resurrection of the dead. It is sown corruptible; it is raised incorruptible. 43It is sown dishonorable; it is raised glorious. It is sown weak; it is raised powerful. 44It is sown a natural body; it is raised a spiritual body. If there is a natural body, there is also a spiritual one. 45So, too, it is written, "The first man, Adam, became a living being," the last Adam a life-giving spirit. 46But the spiritual was not first; rather the natural and then the spiritual. 47The first man was from the earth, earthly; the second man, from heaven. 48As was the earthly one, so also are the earthly, and as is the heavenly one, so also are the heavenly. 49Just as we have borne the image of the earthly one, we shall also bear the image of the heavenly one. 50This I declare, brothers: flesh and blood cannot inherit the kingdom of God, nor does corruption inherit incorruption. 51Behold, I tell you a mystery. We shall not all fall asleep, but we will all be changed, 52in an instant, in the blink of an eye, at the last trumpet. For the trumpet will sound, the dead will be raised incorruptible, and we shall be changed. 53For that which is corruptible must clothe itself with incorruptibility, and that which is mortal must clothe itself with immortality. 54And when this which is corruptible clothes itself with incorruptibility and this which is mortal clothes itself with immortality, then the word that is written shall come about: "Death is swallowed up in victory. 55Where, O death, is your victory? Where, O death, is your sting?" 56The sting of death is sin, and the power of sin is the law. 57But thanks be to God who gives us the victory through our Lord Jesus Christ. 58Therefore, my beloved brothers, be firm, steadfast, always fully devoted to the work of the Lord, knowing that in the Lord your labor is not in vain.

1 Corinthians Chapter 16

1Now in regard to the collection for the holy ones, you also should do as I ordered the churches of Galatia. 2On the first day of the week each of you should set aside and save whatever one can afford, so that collections will not be going on when I come. 3And when I arrive, I shall send those whom you have approved with letters of recommendation to take your gracious gift to Jerusalem. 4If it seems fitting that I should go also, they will go with me. 5I shall come to you after I pass through Macedonia (for I am going to pass through Macedonia), 6and perhaps I shall stay or even spend the winter with you, so that you may send me on my way wherever I may go. 7For I do not wish to see you now just in passing, but I hope to spend some time with you, if the Lord permits. 8I shall stay in Ephesus until Pentecost, 9because a door has opened for me wide and productive for work, but there are many opponents. 10If Timothy comes, see that he is without fear in your company, for he is doing the work of the Lord just as I am. 11Therefore no one should disdain him. Rather, send him on his way in peace that he may come to me, for I am expecting him with the brothers. 12Now in regard to our brother Apollos, I urged him strongly to go to you with the brothers, but it was not at all his will that he go now. He will go when he has an opportunity. 13Be on your guard, stand firm in the faith, be courageous, be strong. 14Your every act should be done with love. 15I urge you, brothers - you know that the household of Stephanas is the firstfruits of Achaia and that they have devoted themselves to the service of the holy ones - 16be subordinate to such people and to everyone who works and toils with them. 17I rejoice in the arrival of Stephanas, Fortunatus, and Achaicus, because they made up for your absence, 18for they refreshed my spirit as well as yours. So give recognition to such people. 19The churches of Asia send you greetings. Aquila and Prisca together with the church at their house send you many greetings in the Lord. 20All the brothers greet you. Greet one another with a holy kiss. 21I, Paul, write you this greeting in my own hand. 22If anyone does not love the Lord, let him be accursed. Marana tha. 23The grace of the Lord Jesus be with you. 24My love to all of you in Christ Jesus.

II Corinthians

2 Corinthians Chapter 1

1Paul, an apostle of Christ Jesus by the will of God, and Timothy our brother, to the church of God that is in Corinth, with all the holy ones throughout Achaia: 2grace to you and peace from God our Father and the Lord Jesus Christ. 3Blessed be the God and Father of our Lord Jesus Christ, the Father of compassion and God of all encouragement, 4who encourages us in our every affliction, so that we may be able to encourage those who are in any affliction with the encouragement with which we ourselves are encouraged by God. 5For as Christ's sufferings overflow to us, so through Christ does our encouragement also overflow. 6If we are afflicted, it is for your encouragement and salvation; if we are encouraged, it is for your encouragement, which enables you to endure the same sufferings that we suffer. 7Our hope for you is firm, for we know that as you share in the sufferings, you also share in the encouragement. 8We do not want you to be unaware, brothers, of the affliction that came to us in the province of Asia; we were utterly weighed down beyond our strength, so that we despaired even of life. 9Indeed, we had accepted within ourselves the sentence of death, that we might trust not in ourselves but in God who raises the dead. 10He rescued us from such great danger of death, and he will continue to rescue us; in him we have put our hope (that) he will also rescue us again, 11as you help us with prayer, so that thanks may be given by many on our behalf for the gift granted us through the prayers of many. 12For our boast is this, the testimony of our conscience that we have conducted ourselves in the world, and especially toward you, with the simplicity and sincerity of God, (and) not by human wisdom but by the grace of God. 13For we write you nothing but what you can read and understand, and I hope that you will understand completely, 14as you have come to understand us partially, that we are your boast as you also are ours, on the day of (our) Lord Jesus. 15With this confidence I formerly intended to come to you so that you might receive a double favor, 16namely, to go by way of you to Macedonia, and then to come to you again on my return from Macedonia, and have you send me on my way to Judea. 17So when I intended this, did I act lightly? Or do I make my plans according to human considerations, so that with me it is "yes, yes" and "no, no"? 18As God is faithful, our word to you is not "yes" and "no." 19For the Son of God, Jesus Christ, who was proclaimed to you by us, by Silvanus and Timothy and me, was not "yes" and "no," but "yes" has been in him. 20For however many are the promises of God, their Yes is in him; therefore, the Amen from us also goes through him to God for glory. 21But the one who gives us security with you in Christ and who anointed us is God; 22he has also put his seal upon us and given the Spirit in our hearts as a first installment. 23But I call upon God as witness, on my life, that it is to spare you that I have not yet gone to Corinth. 24Not that we lord it over your faith; rather, we work together for your joy, for you stand firm in the faith.

2 Corinthians Chapter 2

1For I decided not to come to you again in painful circumstances. 2For if I inflict pain upon you, then who is there to cheer me except the one pained by me? 3And I wrote as I did so that when I came I might not be pained by those in whom I should have rejoiced, confident about all of you that my joy is that of all of you. 4For out of much affliction and anguish of heart I wrote to you with many tears, not that you might be pained but that you might know the abundant love I have for you. 5If anyone has caused pain, he has caused it not to me, but in some measure (not to exaggerate) to all of you. 6This punishment by the majority is enough for such a person, 7so that on the contrary you should forgive and encourage him instead, or else the person may be overwhelmed by excessive pain. 8Therefore, I urge you to reaffirm your love for him. 9For this is why I wrote, to know your proven character, whether you were obedient in everything. 10Whomever you forgive anything, so do I. For indeed what I have forgiven, if I have forgiven anything, has been for you in the presence of Christ, 11so that we might not be taken advantage of by Satan, for we are not unaware of his purposes. 12When I went to Troas for the gospel of Christ, although a door was opened for me in the Lord, [13]I had no relief in my spirit because I did not find my brother Titus. So I took leave of them and went on to Macedonia. [14]But thanks be to God, who always leads us in triumph in Christ and manifests through us the odor of the knowledge of him in every place. [15]For we are the aroma of Christ for God among those who are being saved and among those who are perishing, [16]to the latter odor of death that leads to death, to the former an odor of life that leads to life. Who is qualified for this? [17]For we are not like the many who trade on the word of God; but as out of sincerity, indeed as from God and in the presence of God, we speak in Christ.

2 Corinthians Chapter 3

[1]Are we beginning to commend ourselves again? Or do we need, as some do, letters of recommendation to you or from you? [2]You are our letter, written on our hearts, known and read by all, [3]shown to be a letter of Christ administered by us, written not in ink but by the Spirit of the living God, not on tablets of stone but on tablets that are hearts of flesh. [4]Such confidence we have through Christ toward God. [5]Not that of ourselves we are qualified to take credit for anything as coming from us; rather, our qualification comes from God, [6]who has indeed qualified us as ministers of a new covenant, not of letter but of spirit; for the letter brings death, but the Spirit gives life. [7]Now if the ministry of death, carved in letters on stone, was so glorious that the Israelites could not look intently at the face of Moses because of its glory that was going to fade, [8]how much more will the ministry of the Spirit be glorious? [9]For if the ministry of condemnation was glorious, the ministry of righteousness will abound much more in glory. [10]Indeed, what was endowed with glory has come to have no glory in this respect because of the glory that surpasses it. [11]For if what was going to fade was glorious, how much more will what endures be glorious. [12]Therefore, since we have such hope, we act very boldly [13]and not like Moses, who put a veil over his face so that the Israelites could not look intently at the cessation of what was fading. [14]Rather, their thoughts were rendered dull, for to this present day the same veil remains unlifted when they read the old covenant, because through Christ it is taken away. [15]To this day, in fact, whenever Moses is read, a veil lies over their hearts, [16]but whenever a person turns to the Lord the veil is removed. [17]Now the Lord is the Spirit, and where the Spirit of the Lord is, there is freedom. [18]All of us, gazing with unveiled face on the glory of the Lord, are being transformed into the same image from glory to glory, as from the Lord who is the Spirit.

2 Corinthians Chapter 4

[1]Therefore, since we have this ministry through the mercy shown us, we are not discouraged. [2]Rather, we have renounced shameful, hidden things; not acting deceitfully or falsifying the word of God, but by the open declaration of the truth we commend ourselves to everyone's conscience in the sight of God. [3]And even though our gospel is veiled, it is veiled for those who are perishing, [4]in whose case the god of this age has blinded the minds of the unbelievers, so that they may not see the light of the gospel of the glory of Christ, who is the image of God. [5]For we do not preach ourselves but Jesus Christ as Lord, and ourselves as your slaves for the sake of Jesus. [6]For God who said, "Let light shine out of darkness," has shone in our hearts to bring to light the knowledge of the glory of God on the face of (Jesus) Christ. [7]But we hold this treasure in earthen vessels, that the surpassing power may be of God and not from us. [8]We are afflicted in every way, but not constrained; perplexed, but not driven to despair; [9]persecuted, but not abandoned; struck down, but not destroyed; [10]always carrying about in the body the dying of Jesus, so that the life of Jesus may also be manifested in our body. [11]For we who live are constantly being given up to death for the sake of Jesus, so that the life of Jesus may be manifested in our mortal flesh. [12]So death is at work in us, but life in you. [13]Since, then, we have the same spirit of faith, according to what is written, "I believed, therefore I spoke," we too believe and therefore speak, [14]knowing that the one who raised the Lord Jesus will raise us also with Jesus and place us with you in his presence. [15]Everything indeed is for you, so that the grace bestowed in abundance on more and more people may cause the thanksgiving to overflow for the glory of God. [16]Therefore, we are not discouraged; rather, although our outer self is wasting away, our inner self is being renewed day by day. [17]For this momentary light affliction is producing for us an eternal weight of glory beyond all comparison, [18]as we look not to what is seen but to what is unseen; for what is seen is transitory, but what is unseen is eternal.

2 Corinthians Chapter 5

[1]For we know that if our earthly dwelling, a tent, should be destroyed, we have a building from God, a dwelling not made with hands, eternal in heaven. [2]For in this tent we groan, longing to be further clothed with our heavenly habitation [3]if indeed, when we have taken it off, we shall not be found naked. [4]For while we are in this tent we groan and are weighed down, because we do not wish to be unclothed but to be further clothed, so that what is mortal may be swallowed up by life. [5]Now the one who has prepared us for this very thing is God, who has given us the Spirit as a first installment. [6]So we are always courageous, although we know that while we are at home in the body we are away from the Lord, [7]for we walk by faith, not by sight. [8]Yet we are courageous, and we would rather leave the body and go home to the Lord. [9]Therefore, we aspire to please him, whether we are at home or away. [10]For we must all appear before the judgment seat of Christ, so that each one may receive recompense, according to what he did in the body, whether good or evil. [11]Therefore, since we know the fear of the Lord, we try to persuade others; but we are clearly apparent to God, and I hope we are also apparent to your consciousness. [12]We are not commending ourselves to you again but giving you an opportunity to boast of us, so that you may have something to say to those who boast of external appearance rather than of the heart. [13]For if we are out of our minds, it is for God; if we are rational, it is for you. [14]For the love of Christ impels us, once we have come to the conviction that one died for all; therefore, all have died. [15]He indeed died for all, so that those who live might no longer live for themselves but for him who for their sake died and was raised. [16]Consequently, from now on we regard no one according to the flesh; even if we once knew Christ according to the flesh, yet now we know him so no longer. [17]So whoever is in Christ is a new creation: the old things have passed away; behold, new things have come. [18]And all this is from God, who has reconciled us to himself through Christ and given us the ministry of reconciliation, [19]namely, God was reconciling the world to himself in Christ, not counting their trespasses against them and entrusting to us the message of reconciliation. [20]So we are ambassadors for Christ, as if God were appealing through us. We implore you on behalf of Christ, be reconciled to God. [21]For our sake he made him to be sin who did not know sin, so that we might become the righteousness of God in him.

2 Corinthians Chapter 6

[1]Working together, then, we appeal to you not to receive the grace of God in vain.[2]For he says: "In an acceptable time I heard you, and on the day of salvation I helped you." Behold, now is a very acceptable time; behold, now is the day of salvation.[3]We cause no one to stumble in anything, in order that no fault may be found with our ministry;[4]on the contrary, in everything we commend ourselves as ministers of God, through much endurance, in afflictions, hardships, constraints,[5]beatings, imprisonments, riots, labors, vigils, fasts;[6]by purity, knowledge, patience, kindness, in a holy spirit, in unfeigned love,[7]in truthful speech, in the power of God; with weapons of righteousness at the right and at the left;[8]through glory and dishonor, insult and praise. We are treated as deceivers and yet are truthful;[9]as unrecognized and yet acknowledged; as dying and behold we live; as chastised and yet not put to death;[10]as sorrowful yet always rejoicing; as poor yet enriching many; as having nothing and yet possessing all things.[11]We have spoken frankly to you, Corinthians; our heart is open wide.[12]You are not constrained by us; you are constrained by your own affections.[13]As recompense in kind (I speak as to my children), be open yourselves.[14]Do not be yoked with those who are different, with unbelievers. For what partnership do righteousness and lawlessness have? Or what fellowship does light have with darkness?[15]What accord has Christ with Beliar? Or what has a believer in common with an unbeliever?[16]What agreement has the temple of God with idols? For we are the temple of the living God; as God said: "I will live with them and move among them, and I will be their God and they shall be my people.[17]Therefore, come forth from them and be separate," says the Lord, "and touch nothing unclean; then I will receive you[18]and I will be a father to you, and you shall be sons and daughters to me, says the Lord Almighty."

2 Corinthians Chapter 7

[1]Since we have these promises, beloved, let us cleanse ourselves from every defilement of flesh and spirit, making holiness perfect in the fear of God.[2]Make room for us; we have not wronged anyone, or ruined anyone, or taken advantage of anyone.[3]I do not say this in condemnation, for I have already said that you are in our hearts, that we may die together and live together.[4]I have great confidence in you, I have great pride in you; I am filled with encouragement, I am overflowing with joy all the more because of all our affliction.[5]For even when we came into Macedonia, our flesh had no rest, but we were afflicted in every way - external conflicts, internal fears.[6]But God, who encourages the downcast, encouraged us by the arrival of Titus,[7]and not only by his arrival but also by the encouragement with which he was encouraged in regard to you, as he told us of your yearning, your

lament, your zeal for me, so that I rejoiced even more.⁸For even if I saddened you by my letter, I do not regret it; and if I did regret it ((for) I see that that letter saddened you, if only for a while),⁹I rejoice now, not because you were saddened, but because you were saddened into repentance; for you were saddened in a godly way, so that you did not suffer loss in anything because of us.¹⁰For godly sorrow produces a salutary repentance without regret, but worldly sorrow produces death.¹¹For behold what earnestness this godly sorrow has produced for you, as well as readiness for a defense, and indignation, and fear, and yearning, and zeal, and punishment. In every way you have shown yourselves to be innocent in the matter.¹²So then even though I wrote to you, it was not on account of the one who did the wrong, or on account of the one who suffered the wrong, but in order that your concern for us might be made plain to you in the sight of God.¹³For this reason we are encouraged. And besides our encouragement, we rejoice even more because of the joy of Titus, since his spirit has been refreshed by all of you.¹⁴For if I have boasted to him about you, I was not put to shame. No, just as everything we said to you was true, so our boasting before Titus proved to be the truth.¹⁵And his heart goes out to you all the more, as he remembers the obedience of all of you, when you received him with fear and trembling.¹⁶I rejoice, because I have confidence in you in every respect.

2 Corinthians Chapter 8

1We want you to know, brothers, of the grace of God that has been given to the churches of Macedonia,²for in a severe test of affliction, the abundance of their joy and their profound poverty overflowed in a wealth of generosity on their part.³For according to their means, I can testify, and beyond their means, spontaneously,⁴they begged us insistently for the favor of taking part in the service to the holy ones,⁵and this, not as we expected, but they gave themselves first to the Lord and to us through the will of God,⁶so that we urged Titus that, as he had already begun, he should also complete for you this gracious act also.⁷Now as you excel in every respect, in faith, discourse, knowledge, all earnestness, and in the love we have for you, may you excel in this gracious act also.⁸I say this not by way of command, but to test the genuineness of your love by your concern for others.⁹For you know the gracious act of our Lord Jesus Christ, that for your sake he became poor although he was rich, so that by his poverty you might become rich.¹⁰And I am giving counsel in this matter, for it is appropriate for you who began not only to act but to act willingly last year:¹¹complete it now, so that your eager willingness may be matched by your completion of it out of what you have.¹²For if the eagerness is there, it is acceptable according to what one has, not according to what one does not have;¹³not that others should have relief while you are burdened, but that as a matter of equality¹⁴your surplus at the present time should supply their needs, so that their surplus may also supply your needs, that there may be equality.¹⁵As it is written: "Whoever had much did not have more, and whoever had little did not have less."¹⁶But thanks be to God who put the same concern for you into the heart of Titus,¹⁷for he not only welcomed our appeal but, since he is very concerned, he has gone to you of his own accord.¹⁸With him we have sent the brother who is praised in all the churches for his preaching of the gospel.¹⁹And not only that, but he has also been appointed our traveling companion by the churches in this gracious work administered by us for the glory of the Lord (himself) and for the expression of our eagerness.²⁰This we desire to avoid, that anyone blame us about this lavish gift administered by us,²¹for we are concerned for what is honorable not only in the sight of the Lord but also in the sight of others.²²And with them we have sent our brother whom we often tested in many ways and found earnest, but who is now much more earnest because of his great confidence in you.²³As for Titus, he is my partner and co-worker for you; as for our brothers, they are apostles of the churches, the glory of Christ.²⁴So give proof before the churches of your love and of our boasting about you to them.

2 Corinthians Chapter 9

1Now about the service to the holy ones, it is superfluous for me to write to you,²for I know your eagerness, about which I boast of you to the Macedonians, that Achaia has been ready since last year; and your zeal has stirred up most of them.³Nonetheless, I sent the brothers so that our boast about you might not prove empty in this case, so that you might be ready, as I said,⁴for fear that if any Macedonians come with me and find you not ready we might be put to shame (to say nothing of you) in this conviction.⁵So I thought it necessary to encourage the brothers to go on ahead to you and arrange in advance for your promised gift, so that in this way it might be ready as a bountiful gift and not as an exaction.⁶Consider this: whoever sows sparingly will also reap sparingly, and whoever sows bountifully will also reap

bountifully.⁷Each must do as already determined, without sadness or compulsion, for God loves a cheerful giver.⁸Moreover, God is able to make every grace abundant for you, so that in all things, always having all you need, you may have an abundance for every good work.⁹As it is written: "He scatters abroad, he gives to the poor; his righteousness endures forever."¹⁰The one who supplies seed to the sower and bread for food will supply and multiply your seed and increase the harvest of your righteousness.¹¹You are being enriched in every way for all generosity, which through us produces thanksgiving to God,¹²for the administration of this public service is not only supplying the needs of the holy ones but is also overflowing in many acts of thanksgiving to God.¹³Through the evidence of this service, you are glorifying God for your obedient confession of the gospel of Christ and the generosity of your contribution to them and to all others,¹⁴while in prayer on your behalf they long for you, because of the surpassing grace of God upon you.¹⁵Thanks be to God for his indescribable gift!

2 Corinthians Chapter 10

1Now I myself, Paul, urge you through the gentleness and clemency of Christ, I who am humble when face to face with you, but brave toward you when absent,²I beg you that, when present, I may not have to be brave with that confidence with which I intend to act boldly against some who consider us as acting according to the flesh.³For, although we are in the flesh, we do not battle according to the flesh,⁴for the weapons of our battle are not of flesh but are enormously powerful, capable of destroying fortresses. We destroy arguments⁵and every pretension raising itself against the knowledge of God, and take every thought captive in obedience to Christ,⁶and we are ready to punish every disobedience, once your obedience is complete.⁷Look at what confronts you. Whoever is confident of belonging to Christ should consider that as he belongs to Christ, so do we.⁸And even if I should boast a little too much of our authority, which the Lord gave for building you up and not for tearing you down, I shall not be put to shame.⁹May I not seem as one frightening you through letters.¹⁰For someone will say, "His letters are severe and forceful, but his bodily presence is weak, and his speech contemptible."¹¹Such a person must understand that what we are in word through letters when absent, that we also are in action when present.¹²Not that we dare to class or compare ourselves with some of those who recommend themselves. But when they measure themselves by one another and compare themselves with one another, they are without understanding.¹³But we will not boast beyond measure but will keep to the limits God has apportioned us, namely, to reach even to you.¹⁴For we are not overreaching ourselves, as though we did not reach you; we indeed first came to you with the gospel of Christ.¹⁵We are not boasting beyond measure, in other people's labors; yet our hope is that, as your faith increases, our influence among you may be greatly enlarged, within our proper limits,¹⁶so that we may preach the gospel even beyond you, not boasting of work already done in another's sphere.¹⁷"Whoever boasts, should boast in the Lord."¹⁸For it is not the one who recommends himself who is approved, but the one whom the Lord recommends.

2 Corinthians Chapter 11

1If only you would put up with a little foolishness from me! Please put up with me.²For I am jealous of you with the jealousy of God, since I betrothed you to one husband to present you as a chaste virgin to Christ.³But I am afraid that, as the serpent deceived Eve by his cunning, your thoughts may be corrupted from a sincere (and pure) commitment to Christ.⁴For if someone comes and preaches another Jesus than the one we preached, or if you receive a different spirit from the one you received or a different gospel from the one you accepted, you put up with it well enough.⁵For I think that I am not in any way inferior to these "superapostles."⁶Even if I am untrained in speaking, I am not so in knowledge; in every way we have made this plain to you in all things.⁷Did I make a mistake when I humbled myself so that you might be exalted, because I preached the gospel of God to you without charge?⁸I plundered other churches by accepting from them in order to minister to you.⁹And when I was with you and in need, I did not burden anyone, for the brothers who came from Macedonia supplied my needs. So I refrained and will refrain from burdening you in any way.¹⁰By the truth of Christ in me, this boast of mine shall not be silenced in the regions of Achaia.¹¹And why? Because I do not love you? God knows I do!¹²And what I do I will continue to do, in order to end this pretext of those who seek a pretext for being regarded as we are in the mission of which they boast.¹³For such people are false apostles, deceitful workers, who masquerade as apostles of Christ.¹⁴And no wonder, for even Satan masquerades as an angel of light.¹⁵So it is not strange that his ministers also masquerade as ministers of righteousness. Their end will correspond to their deeds.¹⁶I repeat, no one should consider me foolish; but if you do, accept me as a fool, so that I too may boast a little.[17]What I am saying I am not saying according to the Lord but as in foolishness, in this boastful state.[18]Since many boast according to the flesh, I too will boast.[19]For you gladly put up with fools, since you are wise yourselves.[20]For you put up with it if someone enslaves you, or devours you, or gets the better of you, or puts on airs, or slaps you in the face.[21]To my shame I say that we were too weak! But what anyone dares to boast of (I am speaking in foolishness) I also dare.[22]Are they Hebrews? So am I. Are they Israelites? So am I. Are they descendants of Abraham? So am I.[23]Are they ministers of Christ? (I am talking like an insane person.) I am still more, with far greater labors, far more imprisonments, far worse beatings, and numerous brushes with death.[24]Five times at the hands of the Jews I received forty lashes minus one.[25]Three times I was beaten with rods, once I was stoned, three times I was shipwrecked, I passed a night and a day on the deep;[26]on frequent journeys, in dangers from rivers, dangers from robbers, dangers from my own race, dangers from Gentiles, dangers in the city, dangers in the wilderness, dangers at sea, dangers among false brothers;[27]in toil and hardship, through many sleepless nights, through hunger and thirst, through frequent fastings, through cold and exposure.[28]And apart from these things, there is the daily pressure upon me of my anxiety for all the churches.[29]Who is weak, and I am not weak? Who is led to sin, and I am not indignant?[30]If I must boast, I will boast of the things that show my weakness.[31]The God and Father of the Lord Jesus knows, he who is blessed forever, that I do not lie.[32]At Damascus, the governor under King Aretas guarded the city of Damascus, in order to seize me,[33]but I was lowered in a basket through a window in the wall and escaped his hands.

2 Corinthians Chapter 12

[1]I must boast; not that it is profitable, but I will go on to visions and revelations of the Lord.[2]I know someone in Christ who, fourteen years ago (whether in the body or out of the body I do not know, God knows), was caught up to the third heaven.[3]And I know that this person (whether in the body or out of the body I do not know, God knows)[4]was caught up into Paradise and heard ineffable things, which no one may utter.[5]About this person I will boast, but about myself I will not boast, except about my weaknesses.[6]Although if I should wish to boast, I would not be foolish, for I would be telling the truth. But I refrain, so that no one may think more of me than what he sees in me or hears from me[7]because of the abundance of the revelations. Therefore, that I might not become too elated, a thorn in the flesh was given to me, an angel of Satan, to beat me, to keep me from being too elated.[8]Three times I begged the Lord about this, that it might leave me,[9]but he said to me, "My grace is sufficient for you, for power is made perfect in weakness." I will rather boast most gladly of my weaknesses, in order that the power of Christ may dwell with me.[10]Therefore, I am content with weaknesses, insults, hardships, persecutions, and constraints, for the sake of Christ; for when I am weak, then I am strong.[11]I have been foolish. You compelled me, for I ought to have been commended by you. For I am in no way inferior to these "superapostles," even though I am nothing.[12]The signs of an apostle were performed among you with all endurance, signs and wonders, and mighty deeds.[13]In what way were you less privileged than the rest of the churches, except that on my part I did not burden you? Forgive me this wrong![14]Now I am ready to come to you this third time. And I will not be a burden, for I want not what is yours, but you. Children ought not to save for their parents, but parents for their children.[15]I will most gladly spend and be utterly spent for your sakes. If I love you more, am I to be loved less?[16]But granted that I myself did not burden you, yet I was crafty and got the better of you by deceit.[17]Did I take advantage of you through any of those I sent to you?[18]I urged Titus to go and sent the brother with him. Did Titus take advantage of you? Did we not walk in the same spirit? And in the same steps?[19]Have you been thinking all along that we are defending ourselves before you? In the sight of God we are speaking in Christ, and all for building you up, beloved.[20]For I fear that when I come I may find you not such as I wish, and that you may find me not as you wish; that there may be rivalry, jealousy, fury, selfishness, slander, gossip, conceit, and disorder.[21]I fear that when I come again my God may humiliate me before you, and I may have to mourn over many of those who sinned earlier and have not repented of the impurity, immorality, and licentiousness they practiced.

2 Corinthians Chapter 13

[1]This third time I am coming to you. "On the testimony of two or three witnesses a fact shall be established."[2]I warned those who sinned earlier and all the others, and I warn them now while absent, as I did when present on my second visit, that if I come again I will not be lenient,[3]since you are looking for proof of Christ speaking in me. He is not weak toward you but powerful in you.[4]For indeed he was crucified out of weakness, but he lives by the power of God. So also we are weak in him, but toward you we shall live with him by the power of God.[5]Examine yourselves to see whether you are living in faith. Test yourselves. Do you not realize that Jesus Christ is in you? - unless, of course, you fail the test.[6]I hope you will discover that we have not failed.[7]But we pray to God that you may not do evil, not that we may appear to have passed the test but that you may do what is right, even though we may seem to have failed.[8]For we cannot do anything against the truth, but only for the truth.[9]For we rejoice when we are weak but you are strong. What we pray for is your improvement.[10]I am writing this while I am away, so that when I come I may not have to be severe in virtue of the authority that the Lord has given me to build up and not to tear down.[11]Finally, brothers, rejoice. Mend your ways, encourage one another, agree with one another, live in peace, and the God of love and peace will be with you.[12]Greet one another with a holy kiss. All the holy ones greet you.[13]The grace of the Lord Jesus Christ and the love of God and the fellowship of the holy Spirit be with all of you.

Galatians

Galatians Chapter 1

[1]Paul, an apostle not from human beings nor through a human being but through Jesus Christ and God the Father who raised him from the dead,[2]and all the brothers who are with me, to the churches of Galatia:[3]grace to you and peace from God our Father and the Lord Jesus Christ,[4]who gave himself for our sins that he might rescue us from the present evil age in accord with the will of our God and Father,[5]to whom be glory forever and ever. Amen.[6]I am amazed that you are so quickly forsaking the one who called you by (the) grace (of Christ) for a different gospel[7](not that there is another). But there are some who are disturbing you and wish to pervert the gospel of Christ.[8]But even if we or an angel from heaven should preach (to you) a gospel other than the one that we preached to you, let that one be accursed![9]As we have said before, and now I say again, if anyone preaches to you a gospel other than the one that you received, let that one be accursed![10]Am I now currying favor with human beings or God? Or am I seeking to please people? If I were still trying to please people, I would not be a slave of Christ.[11]Now I want you to know, brothers, that the gospel preached by me is not of human origin.[12]For I did not receive it from a human being, nor was I taught it, but it came through a revelation of Jesus Christ.[13]For you heard of my former way of life in Judaism, how I persecuted the church of God beyond measure and tried to destroy it,[14]and progressed in Judaism beyond many of my contemporaries among my race, since I was even more a zealot for my ancestral traditions.[15]But when (God), who from my mother's womb had set me apart and called me through his grace, was pleased[16]to reveal his Son to me, so that I might proclaim him to the Gentiles, I did not immediately consult flesh and blood,[17]nor did I go up to Jerusalem to those who were apostles before me; rather, I went into Arabia and then returned to Damascus.[18]Then after three years I went up to Jerusalem to confer with Kephas and remained with him for fifteen days.[19]But I did not see any other of the apostles, only James the brother of the Lord.[20](As to what I am writing to you, behold, before God, I am not lying.)[21]Then I went into the regions of Syria and Cilicia.[22]And I was unknown personally to the churches of Judea that are in Christ;[23]they only kept hearing that "the one who once was persecuting us is now preaching the faith he once tried to destroy."[24]So they glorified God because of me.

Galatians Chapter 2

[1]Then after fourteen years I again went up to Jerusalem with Barnabas, taking Titus along also.[2]I went up in accord with a revelation, and I presented to them the gospel that I preach to the Gentiles - but privately to those of repute - so that I might not be running, or have run, in vain.[3]Moreover, not even Titus, who was with me, although he was a Greek, was compelled to be circumcised,[4]but because of the false brothers secretly brought in, who slipped in to spy on our freedom that we have in Christ Jesus, that they might enslave us -[5]to them we did not submit even for a moment, so that the truth of the gospel might remain intact for you.[6]But from those who were reputed to be important (what they once were makes no difference to me; God shows no partiality) - those of repute made me add nothing.[7]On the contrary, when they saw that I had been entrusted with the gospel to the uncircumcised, just as Peter to the circumcised,[8]for the one who worked in Peter for an apostolate to the circumcised worked also in me for the Gentiles,[9]and when they recognized the grace bestowed upon me, James and Kephas and John, who were reputed to be pillars, gave me and Barnabas their right hands in partnership, that we should go to

the Gentiles and they to the circumcised.10Only, we were to be mindful of the poor, which is the very thing I was eager to do.11And when Kephas came to Antioch, I opposed him to his face because he clearly was wrong.12For, until some people came from James, he used to eat with the Gentiles; but when they came, he began to draw back and separated himself, because he was afraid of the circumcised.13And the rest of the Jews (also) acted hypocritically along with him, with the result that even Barnabas was carried away by their hypocrisy.14But when I saw that they were not on the right road in line with the truth of the gospel, I said to Kephas in front of all, "If you, though a Jew, are living like a Gentile and not like a Jew, how can you compel the Gentiles to live like Jews?" 15We, who are Jews by nature and not sinners from among the Gentiles,16(yet) who know that a person is not justified by works of the law but through faith in Jesus Christ, even we have believed in Christ Jesus that we may be justified by faith in Christ and not by works of the law, because by works of the law no one will be justified. 17But if, in seeking to be justified in Christ, we ourselves are found to be sinners, is Christ then a minister of sin? Of course not!18But if I am building up again those things that I tore down, then I show myself to be a transgressor. 19For through the law I died to the law, that I might live for God. I have been crucified with Christ;20yet I live, no longer I, but Christ lives in me; insofar as I now live in the flesh, I live by faith in the Son of God who has loved me and given himself up for me.21I do not nullify the grace of God; for if justification comes through the law, then Christ died for nothing.

Galatians Chapter 3

1 O stupid Galatians! Who has bewitched you, before whose eyes Jesus Christ was publicly portrayed as crucified? 2I want to learn only this from you: did you receive the Spirit from works of the law, or from faith in what you heard? 3Are you so stupid? After beginning with the Spirit, are you now ending with the flesh? 4Did you experience so many things in vain? - if indeed it was in vain. 5Does, then, the one who supplies the Spirit to you and works mighty deeds among you do so from works of the law or from faith in what you heard? 6Thus Abraham "believed God, and it was credited to him as righteousness." 7Realize then that it is those who have faith who are children of Abraham. 8Scripture, which saw in advance that God would justify the Gentiles by faith, foretold the good news to Abraham, saying, "Through you shall all the nations be blessed." 9Consequently, those who have faith are blessed along with Abraham who had faith. 10For all who depend on works of the law are under a curse; for it is written, "Cursed be everyone who does not persevere in doing all the things written in the book of the law." 11And that no one is justified before God by the law is clear, for "the one who is righteous by faith will live." 12But the law does not depend on faith; rather, "the one who does these things will live by them." 13Christ ransomed us from the curse of the law by becoming a curse for us, for it is written, "Cursed be everyone who hangs on a tree," 14that the blessing of Abraham might be extended to the Gentiles through Christ Jesus, so that we might receive the promise of the Spirit through faith. 15Brothers, in human terms I say that no one can annul or amend even a human will once ratified. 16Now the promises were made to Abraham and to his descendant. It does not say, "And to descendants," as referring to many, but as referring to one, "And to your descendant," who is Christ. 17This is what I mean: the law, which came four hundred and thirty years afterward, does not annul a covenant previously ratified by God, so as to cancel the promise. 18For if the inheritance comes from the law, it is no longer from a promise; but God bestowed it on Abraham through a promise. 19Why, then, the law? It was added for transgressions, until the descendant came to whom the promise had been made; it was promulgated by angels at the hand of a mediator. 20Now there is no mediator when only one party is involved, and God is one. 21Is the law then opposed to the promises (of God)? Of course not! For if a law had been given that could bring life, then righteousness would in reality come from the law. 22But scripture confined all things under the power of sin, that through faith in Jesus Christ the promise might be given to those who believe. 23Before faith came, we were held in custody under law, confined for the faith that was to be revealed. 24Consequently, the law was our disciplinarian for Christ, that we might be justified by faith. 25But now that faith has come, we are no longer under a disciplinarian. 26For through faith you are all children of God in Christ Jesus. 27For all of you who were baptized into Christ have clothed yourselves with Christ. 28There is neither Jew nor Greek, there is neither slave nor free person, there is not male and female; for you are all one in Christ Jesus. 29And if you belong to Christ, then you are Abraham's descendant, heirs according to the promise.

Galatians Chapter 4

1I mean that as long as the heir is not of age, he is no different from a slave, although he is the owner of everything, 2but he is under the supervision of guardians and administrators until the date set by his father. 3In the same way we also, when we were not of age, were enslaved to the elemental powers of the world. 4But when the fullness of time had come, God sent his Son, born of a woman, born under the law, 5to ransom those under the law, so that we might receive adoption. 6As proof that you are children, God sent the spirit of his Son into our hearts, crying out, "Abba, Father!" 7So you are no longer a slave but a child, and if a child then also an heir, through God. 8At a time when you did not know God, you became slaves to things that by nature are not gods; 9but now that you have come to know God, or rather to be known by God, how can you turn back again to the weak and destitute elemental powers? Do you want to be slaves to them all over again? 10You are observing days, months, seasons, and years. 11I am afraid on your account that perhaps I have labored for you in vain. 12I implore you, brothers, be as I am, because I have also become as you are. You did me no wrong; 13you know that it was because of a physical illness that I originally preached the gospel to you, 14and you did not show disdain or contempt because of the trial caused you by my physical condition, but rather you received me as an angel of God, as Christ Jesus. 15Where now is that blessedness of yours? Indeed, I can testify to you that, if it had been possible, you would have torn out your eyes and given them to me. 16So now have I become your enemy by telling you the truth? 17They show interest in you, but not in a good way; they want to isolate you, so that you may show interest in them. 18Now it is good to be shown interest for good reason at all times, and not only when I am with you. 19My children, for whom I am again in labor until Christ be formed in you! 20I would like to be with you now and to change my tone, for I am perplexed because of you. 21Tell me, you who want to be under the law, do you not listen to the law? 22For it is written that Abraham had two sons, one by the slave woman and the other by the freeborn woman. 23The son of the slave woman was born naturally, the son of the freeborn through a promise. 24Now this is an allegory. These women represent two covenants. One was from Mount Sinai, bearing children for slavery; this is Hagar. 25Hagar represents Sinai, a mountain in Arabia; it corresponds to the present Jerusalem, for she is in slavery along with her children. 26But the Jerusalem above is freeborn, and she is our mother. 27For it is written: "Rejoice, you barren one who bore no children; break forth and shout, you who were not in labor; for more numerous are the children of the deserted one than of her who has a husband." 28Now you, brothers, like Isaac, are children of the promise. 29But just as then the child of the flesh persecuted the child of the spirit, it is the same now. 30But what does the scripture say? "Drive out the slave woman and her son! For the son of the slave woman shall not share the inheritance with the son" of the freeborn. 31Therefore, brothers, we are children not of the slave woman but of the freeborn woman.

Galatians Chapter 5

1For freedom Christ set us free; so stand firm and do not submit again to the yoke of slavery. 2It is I, Paul, who am telling you that if you have yourselves circumcised, Christ will be of no benefit to you. 3Once again I declare to every man who has himself circumcised that he is bound to observe the entire law. 4You are separated from Christ, you who are trying to be justified by law; you have fallen from grace. 5For through the Spirit, by faith, we await the hope of righteousness. 6For in Christ Jesus, neither circumcision nor uncircumcision counts for anything, but only faith working through love. 7You were running well; who hindered you from following (the) truth? 8That enticement does not come from the one who called you. 9A little yeast leavens the whole batch of dough. 10I am confident of you in the Lord that you will not take a different view, and that the one who is troubling you will bear the condemnation, whoever he may be. 11As for me, brothers, if I am still preaching circumcision, why am I still being persecuted? In that case, the stumbling block of the cross has been abolished. 12Would that those who are upsetting you might also castrate themselves! 13For you were called for freedom, brothers. But do not use this freedom as an opportunity for the flesh; rather, serve one another through love. 14For the whole law is fulfilled in one statement, namely, "You shall love your neighbor as yourself." 15But if you go on biting and devouring one another, beware that you are not consumed by one another. 16I say, then: live by the Spirit and you will certainly not gratify the desire of the flesh. 17For the flesh has desires against the Spirit, and the Spirit against the flesh; these are opposed to each other, so that you may not do what you want. 18But if you are guided by the Spirit, you are not under the law. 19Now the works of the flesh are obvious: immorality, impurity, licentiousness, 20idolatry, sorcery, hatreds, rivalry, jealousy, outbursts of fury, acts of selfishness, dissensions, factions, 21occasions of envy, drinking bouts, orgies, and the like. I warn you, as I warned you before, that those who do such things will not inherit the kingdom of God. ²²In contrast, the fruit of the Spirit is love, joy, peace, patience, kindness, generosity, faithfulness, ²³gentleness, self-control. Against such there is no law. ²⁴Now those who belong to Christ (Jesus) have crucified their flesh with its passions and desires. ²⁵If we live in the Spirit, let us also follow the Spirit. ²⁶Let us not be conceited, provoking one another, envious of one another.

Galatians Chapter 6

1Brothers, even if a person is caught in some transgression, you who are spiritual should correct that one in a gentle spirit, looking to yourself, so that you also may not be tempted. ²Bear one another's burdens, and so you will fulfill the law of Christ. ³For if anyone thinks he is something when he is nothing, he is deluding himself. ⁴Each one must examine his own work, and then he will have reason to boast with regard to himself alone, and not with regard to someone else; ⁵for each will bear his own load. ⁶One who is being instructed in the word should share all good things with his instructor. ⁷Make no mistake: God is not mocked, for a person will reap only what he sows, ⁸because the one who sows for his flesh will reap corruption from the flesh, but the one who sows for the spirit will reap eternal life from the spirit. ⁹Let us not grow tired of doing good, for in due time we shall reap our harvest, if we do not give up. ¹⁰So then, while we have the opportunity, let us do good to all, but especially to those who belong to the family of the faith. ¹¹See with what large letters I am writing to you in my own hand! ¹²It is those who want to make a good appearance in the flesh who are trying to compel you to have yourselves circumcised, only that they may not be persecuted for the cross of Christ. ¹³Not even those having themselves circumcised observe the law themselves; they only want you to be circumcised so that they may boast of your flesh. ¹⁴But may I never boast except in the cross of our Lord Jesus Christ, through which the world has been crucified to me, and I to the world. ¹⁵For neither does circumcision mean anything, nor does uncircumcision, but only a new creation. ¹⁶Peace and mercy be to all who follow this rule and to the Israel of God. ¹⁷From now on, let no one make troubles for me; for I bear the marks of Jesus on my body. ¹⁸The grace of our Lord Jesus Christ be with your spirit, brothers. Amen.

Ephesians

Ephesians Chapter 1

1Paul, an apostle of Christ Jesus by the will of God, to the holy ones who are (in Ephesus) faithful in Christ Jesus: ²grace to you and peace from God our Father and the Lord Jesus Christ. ³Blessed be the God and Father of our Lord Jesus Christ, who has blessed us in Christ with every spiritual blessing in the heavens, ⁴as he chose us in him, before the foundation of the world, to be holy and without blemish before him. In love ⁵he destined us for adoption to himself through Jesus Christ, in accord with the favor of his will, ⁶for the praise of the glory of his grace that he granted us in the beloved. ⁷In him we have redemption by his blood, the forgiveness of transgressions, in accord with the riches of his grace ⁸that he lavished upon us. In all wisdom and insight, ⁹he has made known to us the mystery of his will in accord with his favor that he set forth in him ¹⁰as a plan for the fullness of times, to sum up all things in Christ, in heaven and on earth. ¹¹In him we were also chosen, destined in accord with the purpose of the one who accomplishes all things according to the intention of his will, ¹²so that we might exist for the praise of his glory, we who first hoped in Christ. ¹³In him you also, who have heard the word of truth, the gospel of your salvation, and have believed in him, were sealed with the promised holy Spirit, ¹⁴which is the first installment of our inheritance toward redemption as God's possession, to the praise of his glory. ¹⁵Therefore, I, too, hearing of your faith in the Lord Jesus and of your love for all the holy ones, ¹⁶do not cease giving thanks for you, remembering you in my prayers, ¹⁷that the God of our Lord Jesus Christ, the Father of glory, may give you a spirit of wisdom and revelation resulting in knowledge of him. ¹⁸May the eyes of (your) hearts be enlightened, that you may know what is the hope that belongs to his call, what are the riches of glory in his inheritance among the holy ones, ¹⁹and what is the surpassing greatness of his power for us who believe, in accord with the exercise of his great might, ²⁰which he worked in Christ, raising him from the dead and seating him at his right hand in the heavens, ²¹far above every principality, authority, power, and dominion, and every name that is named not only in this age but also in the one to come. ²²And he put all things beneath his feet and gave him as head over all things to the church, ²³which is his body, the fullness of the one who fills all things in every way.

Ephesians Chapter 2

1You were dead in your transgressions and sins ²in which you once lived following the age of this world, following the ruler of the power of the air, the spirit that is now at work in the disobedient. ³All of us once lived among them in the desires of our flesh, following the wishes of the flesh and the impulses, and we were by nature children of wrath, like the rest. ⁴But God, who is rich in mercy, because of the great love he had for us, ⁵even when we were dead in our transgressions, brought us to life with Christ (by grace you have been saved), ⁶raised us up with him, and seated us with him in the heavens in Christ Jesus, ⁷that in the ages to come he might show the immeasurable riches of his grace in his kindness to us in Christ Jesus. ⁸For by grace you have been saved through faith, and this is not from you; it is the gift of God; ⁹it is not from works, so no one may boast. ¹⁰For we are his handiwork, created in Christ Jesus for the good works that God has prepared in advance, that we should live in them. ¹¹Therefore, remember that at one time you, Gentiles in the flesh, called the uncircumcision by those called the circumcision, which is done in the flesh by human hands, ¹²were at that time without Christ, alienated from the community of Israel and strangers to the covenants of promise, without hope and without God in the world. ¹³But now in Christ Jesus you who once were far off have become near by the blood of Christ. ¹⁴For he is our peace, he who made both one and broke down the dividing wall of enmity, through his flesh, ¹⁵abolishing the law with its commandments and legal claims, that he might create in himself one new person in place of the two, thus establishing peace, ¹⁶and might reconcile both with God, in one body, through the cross, putting that enmity to death by it. ¹⁷He came and preached peace to you who were far off and peace to those who were near, ¹⁸for through him we both have access in one Spirit to the Father. ¹⁹So then you are no longer strangers and sojourners, but you are fellow citizens with the holy ones and members of the household of God, ²⁰built upon the foundation of the apostles and prophets, with Christ Jesus himself as the capstone. ²¹Through him the whole structure is held together and grows into a temple sacred in the Lord; ²²in him you also are being built together into a dwelling place of God in the Spirit.

Ephesians Chapter 3

1Because of this, I, Paul, a prisoner of Christ (Jesus) for you Gentiles - ²if, as I suppose, you have heard of the stewardship of God's grace that was given to me for your benefit, ³(namely, that) the mystery was made known to me by revelation, as I have written briefly earlier. ⁴When you read this you can understand my insight into the mystery of Christ, ⁵which was not made known to human beings in other generations as it has now been revealed to his holy apostles and prophets by the Spirit, ⁶that the Gentiles are coheirs, members of the same body, and copartners in the promise in Christ Jesus through the gospel. ⁷Of this I became a minister by the gift of God's grace that was granted me in accord with the exercise of his power. ⁸To me, the very least of all the holy ones, this grace was given, to preach to the Gentiles the inscrutable riches of Christ, ⁹and to bring to light [for all] what is the plan of the mystery hidden from ages past in God who created all things, ¹⁰so that the manifold wisdom of God might now be made known through the church to the principalities and authorities in the heavens. ¹¹This was according to the eternal purpose that he accomplished in Christ Jesus our Lord, ¹²in whom we have boldness of speech and confidence of access through faith in him. ¹³So I ask you not to lose heart over my afflictions for you; this is your glory. ¹⁴For this reason I kneel before the Father, ¹⁵from whom every family in heaven and on earth is named, ¹⁶that he may grant you in accord with the riches of his glory to be strengthened with power through his Spirit in the inner self, ¹⁷and that Christ may dwell in your hearts through faith; that you, rooted and grounded in love, ¹⁸may have strength to comprehend with all the holy ones what is the breadth and length and height and depth, ¹⁹and to know the love of Christ that surpasses knowledge, so that you may be filled with all the fullness of God. ²⁰Now to him who is able to accomplish far more than all we ask or imagine, by the power at work within us, ²¹to him be glory in the church and in Christ Jesus to all generations, forever and ever. Amen.

Ephesians Chapter 4

1I, then, a prisoner for the Lord, urge you to live in a manner worthy of the call you have received, ²with all humility and gentleness, with patience, bearing with one another through love, ³striving to preserve the unity of the spirit through the bond of peace: ⁴one body and one Spirit, as you were also called to the one hope of your call; ⁵one Lord, one faith, one baptism; ⁶one God and Father of all, who is over all and through all and in all. ⁷But grace was given to each of us according to the measure of Christ's gift. ⁸Therefore, it says: "He ascended on high and took prisoners captive; he gave gifts to men." ⁹What does "he ascended" mean except that he also descended into the lower (regions) of the earth? ¹⁰The one who descended is also the one who ascended far above all the heavens, that he might fill all things. ¹¹And he gave some as apostles, others as prophets, others as evangelists, others as pastors and teachers, [12]to equip the holy ones for the work of ministry, for building up the body of Christ, [13]until we all attain to the unity of faith and knowledge of the Son of God, to mature manhood, to the extent of the full stature of Christ, [14]so that we may no longer be infants, tossed by waves and swept along by every wind of teaching arising from human trickery, from their cunning in the interests of deceitful scheming. [15]Rather, living the truth in love, we should grow in every way into him who is the head, Christ, [16]from whom the whole body, joined and held together by every supporting ligament, with the proper functioning of each part, brings about the body's growth and builds itself up in love. [17]So I declare and testify in the Lord that you must no longer live as the Gentiles do, in the futility of their minds; [18]darkened in understanding, alienated from the life of God because of their ignorance, because of their hardness of heart, [19]they have become callous and have handed themselves over to licentiousness for the practice of every kind of impurity to excess. [20]That is not how you learned Christ, [21]assuming that you have heard of him and were taught in him, as truth is in Jesus, [22]that you should put away the old self of your former way of life, corrupted through deceitful desires, [23]and be renewed in the spirit of your minds, [24]and put on the new self, created in God's way in righteousness and holiness of truth. [25]Therefore, putting away falsehood, speak the truth, each one to his neighbor, for we are members one of another. [26]Be angry but do not sin; do not let the sun set on your anger, [27]and do not leave room for the devil. [28]The thief must no longer steal, but rather labor, doing honest work with his (own) hands, so that he may have something to share with one in need. [29]No foul language should come out of your mouths, but only such as is good for needed edification, that it may impart grace to those who hear. [30]And do not grieve the holy Spirit of God, with which you were sealed for the day of redemption. [31]All bitterness, fury, anger, shouting, and reviling must be removed from you, along with all malice. [32](And) be kind to one another, compassionate, forgiving one another as God has forgiven you in Christ.

Ephesians Chapter 5

[1]So be imitators of God, as beloved children, [2]and live in love, as Christ loved us and handed himself over for us as a sacrificial offering to God for a fragrant aroma. [3]Immorality or any impurity or greed must not even be mentioned among you, as is fitting among holy ones, [4]no obscenity or silly or suggestive talk, which is out of place, but instead, thanksgiving. [5]Be sure of this, that no immoral or impure or greedy person, that is, an idolater, has any inheritance in the kingdom of Christ and of God. [6]Let no one deceive you with empty arguments, for because of these things the wrath of God is coming upon the disobedient. [7]So do not be associated with them. [8]For you were once darkness, but now you are light in the Lord. Live as children of light, [9]for light produces every kind of goodness and righteousness and truth. [10]Try to learn what is pleasing to the Lord. [11]Take no part in the fruitless works of darkness; rather expose them, [12]for it is shameful even to mention the things done by them in secret; [13]but everything exposed by the light becomes visible, [14]for everything that becomes visible is light. Therefore, it says: "Awake, O sleeper, and arise from the dead, and Christ will give you light." [15]Watch carefully then how you live, not as foolish persons but as wise, [16]making the most of the opportunity, because the days are evil. [17]Therefore, do not continue in ignorance, but try to understand what is the will of the Lord. [18]And do not get drunk on wine, in which lies debauchery, but be filled with the Spirit, [19]addressing one another (in) psalms and hymns and spiritual songs, singing and playing to the Lord in your hearts, [20]giving thanks always and for everything in the name of our Lord Jesus Christ to God the Father. [21]Be subordinate to one another out of reverence for Christ. [22]Wives should be subordinate to their husbands as to the Lord. [23]For the husband is head of his wife just as Christ is head of the church, he himself the savior of the body. [24]As the church is subordinate to Christ, so wives should be subordinate to their husbands in everything. [25]Husbands, love your wives, even as Christ loved the church and handed himself over for her [26]to sanctify her, cleansing her by the bath of water with the word, [27]that he might present to himself the church in splendor, without spot or wrinkle or any such thing, that she might be holy and without blemish. [28]So (also) husbands should love their wives as their own bodies. He who loves his wife loves himself. [29]For no one hates his own flesh but rather nourishes and cherishes it, even as Christ does the church, [30]because we are members of his body. [31]"For this reason a man shall leave (his) father and (his) mother and be joined to his wife, and the two shall become one flesh." [32]This is a great mystery, but I speak in reference to Christ and the church. [33]In any case, each one of you should love his wife as himself, and the wife should respect her husband.

Ephesians Chapter 6

[1]Children, obey your parents (in the Lord), for this is right. [2]"Honor your father and mother." This is the first commandment with a promise, [3]"that it may go well with you and that you may have a long life on earth." [4]Fathers, do not provoke your children to anger, but bring them up with the training and instruction of the Lord. [5]Slaves, be obedient to your human masters with fear and trembling, in sincerity of heart, as to Christ, [6]not only when being watched, as currying favor, but as slaves of Christ, doing the will of God from the heart, [7]willingly serving the Lord and not human beings, [8]knowing that each will be requited from the Lord for whatever good he does, whether he is slave or free. [9]Masters, act in the same way toward them, and stop bullying, knowing that both they and you have a Master in heaven and that with him there is no partiality. [10]Finally, draw your strength from the Lord and from his mighty power. [11]Put on the armor of God so that you may be able to stand firm against the tactics of the devil. [12]For our struggle is not with flesh and blood but with the principalities, with the powers, with the world rulers of this present darkness, with the evil spirits in the heavens. [13]Therefore, put on the armor of God, that you may be able to resist on the evil day and, having done everything, to hold your ground. [14]So stand fast with your loins girded in truth, clothed with righteousness as a breastplate, [15]and your feet shod in readiness for the gospel of peace. [16]In all circumstances, hold faith as a shield, to quench all (the) flaming arrows of the evil one. [17]And take the helmet of salvation and the sword of the Spirit, which is the word of God. [18]With all prayer and supplication, pray at every opportunity in the Spirit. To that end, be watchful with all perseverance and supplication for all the holy ones [19]and also for me, that speech may be given me to open my mouth, to make known with boldness the mystery of the gospel [20]for which I am an ambassador in chains, so that I may have the courage to speak as I must. [21]So that you also may have news of me and of what I am doing, Tychicus, my beloved brother and trustworthy minister in the Lord, will tell you everything. [22]I am sending him to you for this very purpose, so that you may know about us and that he may encourage your hearts. [23]Peace be to the brothers, and love with faith, from God the Father and the Lord Jesus Christ. [24]Grace be with all who love our Lord Jesus Christ in immortality.

Philippians

Philippians Chapter 1

[1]Paul and Timothy, slaves of Christ Jesus, to all the holy ones in Christ Jesus who are in Philippi, with the overseers and ministers: [2]grace to you and peace from God our Father and the Lord Jesus Christ. [3]I give thanks to my God at every remembrance of you, [4]praying always with joy in my every prayer for all of you, [5]because of your partnership for the gospel from the first day until now. [6]I am confident of this, that the one who began a good work in you will continue to complete it until the day of Christ Jesus. [7]It is right that I should think this way about all of you, because I hold you in my heart, you who are all partners with me in grace, both in my imprisonment and in the defense and confirmation of the gospel. [8]For God is my witness, how I long for all of you with the affection of Christ Jesus. [9]And this is my prayer: that your love may increase ever more and more in knowledge and every kind of perception, [10]to discern what is of value, so that you may be pure and blameless for the day of Christ, [11]filled with the fruit of righteousness that comes through Jesus Christ for the glory and praise of God. [12]I want you to know, brothers, that my situation has turned out rather to advance the gospel, [13]so that my imprisonment has become well known in Christ throughout the whole praetorium and to all the rest, [14]and so that the majority of the brothers, having taken encouragement in the Lord from my imprisonment, dare more than ever to proclaim the word fearlessly. [15]Of course, some preach Christ from envy and rivalry, others from good will. [16]The latter act out of love, aware that I am here for the defense of the gospel; [17]the former proclaim Christ out of selfish ambition, not from pure motives, thinking that they will cause me trouble in my imprisonment. [18]What difference does it make, as long as in every way, whether in pretense or in truth, Christ is being proclaimed? And in that I rejoice. Indeed I shall continue to rejoice, [19]for I know that this will result in deliverance for me through your prayers and support from the Spirit of Jesus Christ. [20]My eager expectation and hope is that I shall not be put to shame in any way, but that with all boldness, now as always, Christ will be magnified in my body, whether by life or by death. [21]For to me life is Christ, and death is gain. [22]If I go on living in the flesh, that means fruitful labor for me. And I do not know which I shall choose. [23]I am caught between the two. I long to depart this life and be with Christ, (for) that is far better. [24]Yet that I remain (in) the flesh is more necessary for your benefit. [25]And

this I know with confidence, that I shall remain and continue in the service of all of you for your progress and joy in the faith, 26so that your boasting in Christ Jesus may abound on account of me when I come to you again. 27Only, conduct yourselves in a way worthy of the gospel of Christ, so that, whether I come and see you or am absent, I may hear news of you, that you are standing firm in one spirit, with one mind struggling together for the faith of the gospel, 28not intimidated in any way by your opponents. This is proof to them of destruction, but of your salvation. And this is God's doing. 29For to you has been granted, for the sake of Christ, not only to believe in him but also to suffer for him. 30Yours is the same struggle as you saw in me and now hear about me.

Philippians Chapter 2

1If there is any encouragement in Christ, any solace in love, any participation in the Spirit, any compassion and mercy, 2complete my joy by being of the same mind, with the same love, united in heart, thinking one thing. 3Do nothing out of selfishness or out of vainglory; rather, humbly regard others as more important than yourselves, 4each looking out for his own interests, but (also) everyone for those of others. 5Have among yourselves the same attitude that is also yours in Christ Jesus, 6Who, though he was in the form of God, did not regard equality with God something to be grasped. 7Rather, he emptied himself, taking the form of a slave, coming in human likeness; and found human in appearance, 8he humbled himself, becoming obedient to death, even death on a cross. 9Because of this, God greatly exalted him and bestowed on him the name that is above every name, 10that at the name of Jesus every knee should bend, of those in heaven and on earth and under the earth, 11and every tongue confess that Jesus Christ is Lord, to the glory of God the Father. 12So then, my beloved, obedient as you have always been, not only when I am present but all the more now when I am absent, work out your salvation with fear and trembling. 13For God is the one who, for his good purpose, works in you both to desire and to work. 14Do everything without grumbling or questioning, 15that you may be blameless and innocent, children of God without blemish in the midst of a crooked and perverse generation, among whom you shine like lights in the world, 16as you hold on to the word of life, so that my boast for the day of Christ may be that I did not run in vain or labor in vain. 17But, even if I am poured out as a libation upon the sacrificial service of your faith, I rejoice and share my joy with all of you. 18In the same way you also should rejoice and share your joy with me. 19I hope, in the Lord Jesus, to send Timothy to you soon, so that I too may be heartened by hearing news of you. 20For I have no one comparable to him for genuine interest in whatever concerns you. 21For they all seek their own interests, not those of Jesus Christ. 22But you know his worth, how as a child with a father he served along with me in the cause of the gospel. 23He it is, then, whom I hope to send as soon as I see how things go with me, 24but I am confident in the Lord that I myself will also come soon. 25With regard to Epaphroditus, my brother and co-worker and fellow soldier, your messenger and minister in my need, I consider it necessary to send him to you. 26For he has been longing for all of you and was distressed because you heard that he was ill. 27He was indeed ill, close to death; but God had mercy on him, not just on him but also on me, so that I might not have sorrow upon sorrow. 28I send him therefore with the greater eagerness, so that, on seeing him, you may rejoice again, and I may have less anxiety. 29Welcome him then in the Lord with all joy and hold such people in esteem, 30because for the sake of the work of Christ he came close to death, risking his life to make up for those services to me that you could not perform.

Philippians Chapter 3

1 Finally, my brothers, rejoice in the Lord. Writing the same things to you is no burden for me but is a safeguard for you. 2 Beware of the dogs! Beware of the evil workers! Beware of the mutilation! 3 For we are the circumcision, we who worship through the Spirit of God, who boast in Christ Jesus and do not put our confidence in flesh, 4 although I myself have grounds for confidence even in the flesh. If anyone else thinks he can be confident in flesh, all the more can I. 5 Circumcised on the eighth day, of the race of Israel, of the tribe of Benjamin, a Hebrew of Hebrew parentage, in observance of the law a Pharisee, 6 in zeal I persecuted the church, in righteousness based on the law I was blameless. 7 (But) whatever gains I had, these I have come to consider a loss because of Christ. 8 More than that, I even consider everything as a loss because of the supreme good of knowing Christ Jesus my Lord. For his sake I have accepted the loss of all things and I consider them so much rubbish, that I may gain Christ 9 and be found in him, not having any righteousness of my own based on the law but that which comes through faith in Christ, the righteousness from God, depending on faith 10 to know him and the power of his resurrection and (the) sharing of his sufferings by

being conformed to his death, 11 if somehow I may attain the resurrection from the dead. 12 It is not that I have already taken hold of it or have already attained perfect maturity, but I continue my pursuit in hope that I may possess it, since I have indeed been taken possession of by Christ (Jesus). 13 Brothers, I for my part do not consider myself to have taken possession. Just one thing: forgetting what lies behind but straining forward to what lies ahead, 14 I continue my pursuit toward the goal, the prize of God's upward calling, in Christ Jesus. 15 Let us, then, who are "perfectly mature" adopt this attitude. And if you have a different attitude, this too God will reveal to you. 16 Only, with regard to what we have attained, continue on the same course. 17 Join with others in being imitators of me, brothers, and observe those who thus conduct themselves according to the model you have in us. 18 For many, as I have often told you and now tell you even in tears, conduct themselves as enemies of the cross of Christ. 19 Their end is destruction. Their God is their stomach; their glory is in their "shame." Their minds are occupied with earthly things. 20 But our citizenship is in heaven, and from it we also await a savior, the Lord Jesus Christ. 21 He will change our lowly body to conform with his glorified body by the power that enables him also to bring all things into subjection to himself.

Philippians Chapter 4

1 Therefore, my brothers, whom I love and long for, my joy and crown, in this way stand firm in the Lord, beloved. 2 I urge Euodia and I urge Syntyche to come to a mutual understanding in the Lord. 3 Yes, and I ask you also, my true yokemate, to help them, for they have struggled at my side in promoting the gospel, along with Clement and my other co-workers, whose names are in the book of life. 4 Rejoice in the Lord always. I shall say it again: rejoice! 5 Your kindness should be known to all. The Lord is near. 6 Have no anxiety at all, but in everything, by prayer and petition, with thanksgiving, make your requests known to God. 7 Then the peace of God that surpasses all understanding will guard your hearts and minds in Christ Jesus. 8 Finally, brothers, whatever is true, whatever is honorable, whatever is just, whatever is pure, whatever is lovely, whatever is gracious, if there is any excellence and if there is anything worthy of praise, think about these things. 9 Keep on doing what you have learned and received and heard and seen in me. Then the God of peace will be with you. 10 I rejoice greatly in the Lord that now at last you revived your concern for me. You were, of course, concerned about me but lacked an opportunity. 11 Not that I say this because of need, for I have learned, in whatever situation I find myself, to be self-sufficient. 12 I know indeed how to live in humble circumstances; I know also how to live with abundance. In every circumstance and in all things I have learned the secret of being well fed and of going hungry, of living in abundance and of being in need. 13 I have the strength for everything through him who empowers me. 14 Still, it was kind of you to share in my distress. 15 You Philippians indeed know that at the beginning of the gospel, when I left Macedonia, not a single church shared with me in an account of giving and receiving, except you alone. 16 For even when I was at Thessalonica you sent me something for my needs, not only once but more than once. 17 It is not that I am eager for the gift; rather, I am eager for the profit that accrues to your account. 18 I have received full payment and I abound. I am very well supplied because of what I received from you through Epaphroditus, "a fragrant aroma," an acceptable sacrifice, pleasing to God. 19 My God will fully supply whatever you need, in accord with his glorious riches in Christ Jesus. 20 To our God and Father, glory forever and ever. Amen. 21 Give my greetings to every holy one in Christ Jesus. The brothers who are with me send you their greetings; 22 all the holy ones send you their greetings, especially those of Caesar's household. 23 The grace of the Lord Jesus Christ be with your spirit.

Colossians

Colossians Chapter 1

1Paul, an apostle of Christ Jesus by the will of God, and Timothy our brother, 2to the holy ones and faithful brothers in Christ in Colossae: grace to you and peace from God our Father. 3We always give thanks to God, the Father of our Lord Jesus Christ, when we pray for you, 4for we have heard of your faith in Christ Jesus and the love that you have for all the holy ones 5because of the hope reserved for you in heaven. Of this you have already heard through the word of truth, the gospel, 6that has come to you. Just as in the whole world it is bearing fruit and growing, so also among you, from the day you heard it and came to know the grace of God in truth, 7as you learned it from Epaphras our beloved fellow slave, who is a trustworthy minister of Christ on your behalf 8and who also told us of your love in the Spirit. 9Therefore, from the day we heard this, we do not cease praying for you and asking that you may be filled with the knowledge of his will through all spiritual wisdom and understanding ¹⁰to live in a manner worthy of the Lord, so as to be fully pleasing, in every good work bearing fruit and growing in the knowledge of God, ¹¹strengthened with every power, in accord with his glorious might, for all endurance and patience, with joy ¹²giving thanks to the Father, who has made you fit to share in the inheritance of the holy ones in light. ¹³He delivered us from the power of darkness and transferred us to the kingdom of his beloved Son, ¹⁴in whom we have redemption, the forgiveness of sins. ¹⁵He is the image of the invisible God, the firstborn of all creation. ¹⁶For in him were created all things in heaven and on earth, the visible and the invisible, whether thrones or dominions or principalities or powers; all things were created through him and for him. ¹⁷He is before all things, and in him all things hold together. ¹⁸He is the head of the body, the church. He is the beginning, the firstborn from the dead, that in all things he himself might be preeminent. ¹⁹For in him all the fullness was pleased to dwell, ²⁰and through him to reconcile all things for him, making peace by the blood of his cross (through him), whether those on earth or those in heaven. ²¹And you who once were alienated and hostile in mind because of evil deeds ²²he has now reconciled in his fleshly body through his death, to present you holy, without blemish, and irreproachable before him, ²³provided that you persevere in the faith, firmly grounded, stable, and not shifting from the hope of the gospel that you heard, which has been preached to every creature under heaven, of which I, Paul, am a minister. ²⁴Now I rejoice in my sufferings for your sake, and in my flesh I am filling up what is lacking in the afflictions of Christ on behalf of his body, which is the church, ²⁵of which I am a minister in accordance with God's stewardship given to me to bring to completion for you the word of God, ²⁶the mystery hidden from ages and from generations past. But now it has been manifested to his holy ones, ²⁷to whom God chose to make known the riches of the glory of this mystery among the Gentiles; it is Christ in you, the hope for glory. ²⁸It is he whom we proclaim, admonishing everyone and teaching everyone with all wisdom, that we may present everyone perfect in Christ. ²⁹For this I labor and struggle, in accord with the exercise of his power working within me.

Colossians Chapter 2

¹For I want you to know how great a struggle I am having for you and for those in Laodicea and all who have not seen me face to face, ²that their hearts may be encouraged as they are brought together in love, to have all the richness of fully assured understanding, for the knowledge of the mystery of God, Christ, ³in whom are hidden all the treasures of wisdom and knowledge. ⁴I say this so that no one may deceive you by specious arguments. ⁵For even if I am absent in the flesh, yet I am with you in spirit, rejoicing as I observe your good order and the firmness of your faith in Christ. ⁶So, as you received Christ Jesus the Lord, walk in him, ⁷rooted in him and built upon him and established in the faith as you were taught, abounding in thanksgiving. ⁸See to it that no one captivate you with an empty, seductive philosophy according to human tradition, according to the elemental powers of the world and not according to Christ. ⁹For in him dwells the whole fullness of the deity bodily, ¹⁰and you share in this fullness in him, who is the head of every principality and power. ¹¹In him you were also circumcised with a circumcision not administered by hand, by stripping off the carnal body, with the circumcision of Christ. ¹²You were buried with him in baptism, in which you were also raised with him through faith in the power of God, who raised him from the dead. ¹³And even when you were dead in transgressions and the uncircumcision of your flesh, he brought you to life along with him, having forgiven us all our transgressions; ¹⁴obliterating the bond against us, with its legal claims, which was opposed to us, he also removed it from our midst, nailing it to the cross; ¹⁵despoiling the principalities and the powers, he made a public spectacle of them, leading them away in triumph by it. ¹⁶Let no one, then, pass judgment on you in matters of food and drink or with regard to a festival or new moon or sabbath. ¹⁷These are shadows of things to come; the reality belongs to Christ. ¹⁸Let no one disqualify you, delighting in self-abasement and worship of angels, taking his stand on visions, inflated without reason by his fleshly mind, ¹⁹and not holding closely to the head, from whom the whole body, supported and held together by its ligaments and bonds, achieves the growth that comes from God. ²⁰If you died with Christ to the elemental powers of the world, why do you submit to regulations as if you were still living in the world? ²¹"Do not handle! Do not taste! Do not touch!" ²²These are all things destined to perish with use; they accord with human precepts and teachings. ²³While they have a semblance of wisdom in rigor of devotion and self-abasement and severity to the body, they are of no value against gratification of the flesh.

Colossians Chapter 3

¹If then you were raised with Christ, seek what is above, where Christ is seated at the right hand of God. ²Think of what is above, not of what is on earth. ³For you have died, and your life is hidden with Christ in God. ⁴When Christ your life appears, then you too will appear with him in glory. ⁵Put to death, then, the parts of you that are earthly: immorality, impurity, passion, evil desire, and the greed that is idolatry. ⁶Because of these the wrath of God is coming upon the disobedient. ⁷By these you too once conducted yourselves, when you lived in that way. ⁸But now you must put them all away: anger, fury, malice, slander, and obscene language out of your mouths. ⁹Stop lying to one another, since you have taken off the old self with its practices ¹⁰and have put on the new self, which is being renewed, for knowledge, in the image of its creator. ¹¹Here there is not Greek and Jew, circumcision and uncircumcision, barbarian, Scythian, slave, free; but Christ is all and in all. ¹²Put on then, as God's chosen ones, holy and beloved, heartfelt compassion, kindness, humility, gentleness, and patience, ¹³bearing with one another and forgiving one another, if one has a grievance against another; as the Lord has forgiven you, so must you also do. ¹⁴And over all these put on love, that is, the bond of perfection. ¹⁵And let the peace of Christ control your hearts, the peace into which you were also called in one body. And be thankful. ¹⁶Let the word of Christ dwell in you richly, as in all wisdom you teach and admonish one another, singing psalms, hymns, and spiritual songs with gratitude in your hearts to God. ¹⁷And whatever you do, in word or in deed, do everything in the name of the Lord Jesus, giving thanks to God the Father through him. ¹⁸Wives, be subordinate to your husbands, as is proper in the Lord. ¹⁹Husbands, love your wives, and avoid any bitterness toward them. ²⁰Children, obey your parents in everything, for this is pleasing to the Lord. ²¹Fathers, do not provoke your children, so they may not become discouraged. ²²Slaves, obey your human masters in everything, not only when being watched, as currying favor, but in simplicity of heart, fearing the Lord. ²³Whatever you do, do from the heart, as for the Lord and not for others, ²⁴knowing that you will receive from the Lord the due payment of the inheritance; be slaves of the Lord Christ. ²⁵For the wrongdoer will receive recompense for the wrong he committed, and there is no partiality.

Colossians Chapter 4

¹Masters, treat your slaves justly and fairly, realizing that you too have a Master in heaven. ²Persevere in prayer, being watchful in it with thanksgiving; ³at the same time, pray for us, too, that God may open a door to us for the word, to speak of the mystery of Christ, for which I am in prison, ⁴that I may make it clear, as I must speak. ⁵Conduct yourselves wisely toward outsiders, making the most of the opportunity. ⁶Let your speech always be gracious, seasoned with salt, so that you know how you should respond to each one. ⁷Tychicus, my beloved brother, trustworthy minister, and fellow slave in the Lord, will tell you all the news of me. ⁸I am sending him to you for this very purpose, so that you may know about us and that he may encourage your hearts, ⁹together with Onesimus, a trustworthy and beloved brother, who is one of you. They will tell you about everything here. ¹⁰Aristarchus, my fellow prisoner, sends you greetings, as does Mark the cousin of Barnabas (concerning whom you have received instructions; if he comes to you, receive him), ¹¹and Jesus, who is called Justus, who are of the circumcision; these alone are my co-workers for the kingdom of God, and they have been a comfort to me. ¹²Epaphras sends you greetings; he is one of you, a slave of Christ (Jesus), always striving for you in his prayers so that you may be perfect and fully assured in all the will of God. ¹³For I can testify that he works very hard for you and for those in Laodicea and those in Hierapolis. ¹⁴Luke the beloved physician sends greetings, as does Demas. ¹⁵Give greetings to the brothers in Laodicea and to Nympha and to the church in her house. ¹⁶And when this letter is read before you, have it read also in the church of the Laodiceans, and you yourselves read the one from Laodicea. ¹⁷And tell Archippus, "See that you fulfill the ministry that you received in the Lord." ¹⁸The greeting is in my own hand, Paul's. Remember my chains. Grace be with you.

I Thessalonians

1 Thessalonians Chapter 1

¹Paul, Silvanus, and Timothy to the church of the Thessalonians in God the Father and the Lord Jesus Christ: grace to you and peace. ²We give thanks to God always for all of you, remembering you in our prayers, unceasingly ³calling to mind your work of faith and labor of love and endurance in hope of our Lord Jesus Christ, before our God and Father, ⁴knowing, brothers loved by God, how you were chosen. ⁵For our gospel did not come to you in word alone, but also in power and in the

holy Spirit and with much conviction. You know what sort of people we were among you for your sake. [6]And you became imitators of us and of the Lord, receiving the word in great affliction, with joy from the holy Spirit, [7]so that you became a model for all the believers in Macedonia and in Achaia. [8]For from you the word of the Lord has sounded forth not only in Macedonia and in Achaia, but in every place your faith in God has gone forth, so that we have no need to say anything. [9]For they themselves openly declare about us what sort of reception we had among you, and how you turned to God from idols to serve the living and true God [10]and to await his Son from heaven, whom he raised from the dead, Jesus, who delivers us from the coming wrath.

1 Thessalonians Chapter 2

[1]For you yourselves know, brothers, that our reception among you was not without effect. [2]Rather, after we had suffered and been insolently treated, as you know, in Philippi, we drew courage through our God to speak to you the gospel of God with much struggle. [3]Our exhortation was not from delusion or impure motives, nor did it work through deception. [4]But as we were judged worthy by God to be entrusted with the gospel, that is how we speak, not as trying to please human beings, but rather God, who judges our hearts. [5]Nor, indeed, did we ever appear with flattering speech, as you know, or with a pretext for greed—God is witness— [6]nor did we seek praise from human beings, either from you or from others, [7]although we were able to impose our weight as apostles of Christ. Rather, we were gentle among you, as a nursing mother cares for her children. [8]With such affection for you, we were determined to share with you not only the gospel of God but our very selves as well, so dearly beloved had you become to us. [9]You recall, brothers, our toil and drudgery. Working night and day in order not to burden any of you, we proclaimed to you the gospel of God. [10]You are witnesses, and so is God, how devoutly and justly and blamelessly we behaved toward you believers. [11]As you know, we treated each one of you as a father treats his children, [12]exhorting and encouraging you and insisting that you conduct yourselves as worthy of the God who calls you into his kingdom and glory. [13]And for this reason we too give thanks to God unceasingly, that, in receiving the word of God from hearing us, you received not a human word but, as it truly is, the word of God, which is now at work in you who believe. [14]For you, brothers, have become imitators of the churches of God that are in Judea in Christ Jesus. For you suffer the same things from your compatriots as they did from the Jews, [15]who killed both the Lord Jesus and the prophets and persecuted us; they do not please God, and are opposed to everyone, [16]trying to prevent us from speaking to the Gentiles that they may be saved, thus constantly filling up the measure of their sins. But the wrath of God has finally begun to come upon them. [17]Brothers, when we were bereft of you for a short time, in person, not in heart, we were all the more eager in our great desire to see you in person. [18]We decided to go to you—I, Paul, not only once but more than once—yet Satan thwarted us. [19]For what is our hope or joy or crown to boast of in the presence of our Lord Jesus at his coming if not you yourselves? [20]For you are our glory and joy.

1 Thessalonians Chapter 3

[1]That is why, when we could bear it no longer, we decided to remain alone in Athens [2]and sent Timothy, our brother and co-worker for God in the gospel of Christ, to strengthen and encourage you in your faith, [3]so that no one be disturbed in these afflictions. For you yourselves know that we are destined for this. [4]For even when we were among you, we used to warn you in advance that we would undergo affliction, just as has happened, as you know. [5]For this reason, when I too could bear it no longer, I sent to learn about your faith, for fear that somehow the tempter had put you to the test and our toil might come to nothing. [6]But just now Timothy has returned to us from you, bringing us the good news of your faith and love, and that you always think kindly of us and long to see us as we long to see you. [7]Because of this, we have been reassured about you, brothers, in our every distress and affliction, through your faith. [8]For we now live, if you stand firm in the Lord. [9]What thanksgiving, then, can we render to God for you, for all the joy we feel on your account before our God? [10]Night and day we pray beyond measure to see you in person and to remedy the deficiencies of your faith. [11]Now may God himself, our Father, and our Lord Jesus direct our way to you, [12]and may the Lord make you increase and abound in love for one another and for all, just as we have for you, [13]so as to strengthen your hearts, to be blameless in holiness before our God and Father at the coming of our Lord Jesus with all his holy ones. (Amen.)

1 Thessalonians Chapter 4

[1]Finally, brothers, we earnestly ask and exhort you in the Lord Jesus that, as you received from us how you should conduct yourselves to please God—and as you are conducting yourselves—you do so even

more. [2]For you know what instructions we gave you through the Lord Jesus. [3]This is the will of God, your holiness: that you refrain from immorality, [4]that each of you know how to acquire a wife for himself in holiness and honor, [5]not in lustful passion as do the Gentiles who do not know God; [6]not to take advantage of or exploit a brother in this matter, for the Lord is an avenger in all these things, as we told you before and solemnly affirmed. [7]For God did not call us to impurity but to holiness. [8]Therefore, whoever disregards this, disregards not a human being but God, who (also) gives his holy Spirit to you. [9]On the subject of mutual charity you have no need for anyone to write you, for you yourselves have been taught by God to love one another. [10]Indeed, you do this for all the brothers throughout Macedonia. Nevertheless, we urge you, brothers, to progress even more, [11]and to aspire to live a tranquil life, to mind your own affairs, and to work with your (own) hands, as we instructed you, [12]that you may conduct yourselves properly toward outsiders and not depend on anyone. [13]We do not want you to be unaware, brothers, about those who have fallen asleep, so that you may not grieve like the rest, who have no hope. [14]For if we believe that Jesus died and rose, so too will God, through Jesus, bring with him those who have fallen asleep. [15]Indeed, we tell you this, on the word of the Lord, that we who are alive, who are left until the coming of the Lord, will surely not precede those who have fallen asleep. [16]For the Lord himself, with a word of command, with the voice of an archangel and with the trumpet of God, will come down from heaven, and the dead in Christ will rise first. [17]Then we who are alive, who are left, will be caught up together with them in the clouds to meet the Lord in the air. Thus we shall always be with the Lord. [18]Therefore, console one another with these words.

1 Thessalonians Chapter 5

[1]Concerning times and seasons, brothers, you have no need for anything to be written to you. [2]For you yourselves know very well that the day of the Lord will come like a thief at night. [3]When people are saying, "Peace and security," then sudden disaster comes upon them, like labor pains upon a pregnant woman, and they will not escape. [4]But you, brothers, are not in darkness, for that day to overtake you like a thief. [5]For all of you are children of the light and children of the day. We are not of the night or of darkness. [6]Therefore, let us not sleep as the rest do, but let us stay alert and sober. [7]Those who sleep go to sleep at night, and those who are drunk get drunk at night. [8]But since we are of the day, let us be sober, putting on the breastplate of faith and love and the helmet that is hope for salvation. [9]For God did not destine us for wrath, but to gain salvation through our Lord Jesus Christ, [10]who died for us, so that whether we are awake or asleep we may live together with him. [11]Therefore, encourage one another and build one another up, as indeed you do. [12]We ask you, brothers, to respect those who are laboring among you and who are over you in the Lord and who admonish you, [13]and to show esteem for them with special love on account of their work. Be at peace among yourselves. [14]We urge you, brothers, admonish the idle, cheer the fainthearted, support the weak, be patient with all. [15]See that no one returns evil for evil; rather, always seek what is good (both) for each other and for all. [16]Rejoice always. [17]Pray without ceasing. [18]In all circumstances give thanks, for this is the will of God for you in Christ Jesus. [19]Do not quench the Spirit. [20]Do not despise prophetic utterances. [21]Test everything; retain what is good. [22]Refrain from every kind of evil. [23]May the God of peace himself make you perfectly holy and may you entirely, spirit, soul, and body, be preserved blameless for the coming of our Lord Jesus Christ. [24]The one who calls you is faithful, and he will also accomplish it. [25]Brothers, pray for us (too). [26]Greet all the brothers with a holy kiss. [27]I adjure you by the Lord that this letter be read to all the brothers. [28]The grace of our Lord Jesus Christ be with you.

II Thessalonians

2 Thessalonians Chapter 1

[1]Paul, Silvanus, and Timothy to the church of the Thessalonians in God our Father and the Lord Jesus Christ: [2]grace to you and peace from God (our) Father and the Lord Jesus Christ. [3]We ought to thank God always for you, brothers, as is fitting, because your faith flourishes ever more, and the love of every one of you for one another grows ever greater. [4]Accordingly, we ourselves boast of you in the churches of God regarding your endurance and faith in all your persecutions and the afflictions you endure. [5]This is evidence of the just judgment of God, so that you may be considered worthy of the kingdom of God for which you are suffering. [6]For it is surely just on God's part to repay with afflictions those who are afflicting you, [7]and to grant rest along with us to you who are undergoing afflictions, at the revelation of the Lord Jesus from heaven with his mighty angels, [8]in blazing fire, inflicting

punishment on those who do not acknowledge God and on those who do not obey the gospel of our Lord Jesus. 9These will pay the penalty of eternal ruin, separated from the presence of the Lord and from the glory of his power, 10when he comes to be glorified among his holy ones and to be marveled at on that day among all who have believed, for our testimony to you was believed. 11To this end, we always pray for you, that our God may make you worthy of his calling and powerfully bring to fulfillment every good purpose and every effort of faith, 12that the name of our Lord Jesus may be glorified in you, and you in him, in accord with the grace of our God and Lord Jesus Christ.

2 Thessalonians Chapter 2

1We ask you, brothers, with regard to the coming of our Lord Jesus Christ and our assembling with him, 2not to be shaken out of your minds suddenly, or to be alarmed either by a "spirit," or by an oral statement, or by a letter allegedly from us to the effect that the day of the Lord is at hand. 3Let no one deceive you in any way. For unless the apostasy comes first and the lawless one is revealed, the one doomed to perdition, 4who opposes and exalts himself above every so-called god and object of worship, so as to seat himself in the temple of God, claiming that he is a god - 5do you not recall that while I was still with you I told you these things? 6And now you know what is restraining, that he may be revealed in his time. 7For the mystery of lawlessness is already at work. But the one who restrains is to do so only for the present, until he is removed from the scene. 8And then the lawless one will be revealed, whom the Lord (Jesus) will kill with the breath of his mouth and render powerless by the manifestation of his coming, 9the one whose coming springs from the power of Satan in every mighty deed and in signs and wonders that lie, 10and in every wicked deceit for those who are perishing because they have not accepted the love of truth so that they may be saved. 11Therefore, God is sending them a deceiving power so that they may believe the lie, 12that all who have not believed the truth but have approved wrongdoing may be condemned. 13But we ought to give thanks to God for you always, brothers loved by the Lord, because God chose you as the firstfruits for salvation through sanctification by the Spirit and belief in truth. 14To this end he has (also) called you through our gospel to possess the glory of our Lord Jesus Christ. 15Therefore, brothers, stand firm and hold fast to the traditions that you were taught, either by an oral statement or by a letter of ours. 16May our Lord Jesus Christ himself and God our Father, who has loved us and given us everlasting encouragement and good hope through his grace, 17encourage your hearts and strengthen them in every good deed and word.

2 Thessalonians Chapter 3

1Finally, brothers, pray for us, so that the word of the Lord may speed forward and be glorified, as it did among you, 2and that we may be delivered from perverse and wicked people, for not all have faith. 3But the Lord is faithful; he will strengthen you and guard you from the evil one. 4We are confident of you in the Lord that what we instruct you, you (both) are doing and will continue to do. 5May the Lord direct your hearts to the love of God and to the endurance of Christ. 6We instruct you, brothers, in the name of (our) Lord Jesus Christ, to shun any brother who conducts himself in a disorderly way and not according to the tradition they received from us. 7For you know how one must imitate us. For we did not act in a disorderly way among you, 8nor did we eat food received free from anyone. On the contrary, in toil and drudgery, night and day we worked, so as not to burden any of you. 9Not that we do not have the right. Rather, we wanted to present ourselves as a model for you, so that you might imitate us. 10In fact, when we were with you, we instructed you that if anyone was unwilling to work, neither should that one eat. 11We hear that some are conducting themselves among you in a disorderly way, by not keeping busy but minding the business of others. 12Such people we instruct and urge in the Lord Jesus Christ to work quietly and to eat their own food. 13But you, brothers, do not be remiss in doing good. 14If anyone does not obey our word as expressed in this letter, take note of this person not to associate with him, that he may be put to shame. 15Do not regard him as an enemy but admonish him as a brother. 16May the Lord of peace himself give you peace at all times and in every way. The Lord be with all of you. 17This greeting is in my own hand, Paul's. This is the sign in every letter; this is how I write. 18The grace of our Lord Jesus Christ be with all of you.

I Timothy

1 Timothy Chapter 1

1Paul, an apostle of Christ Jesus by command of God our savior and of Christ Jesus our hope, 2to Timothy, my true child in faith: grace, mercy, and peace from God the Father and Christ Jesus our Lord. 3I repeat the

request I made of you when I was on my way to Macedonia, that you stay in Ephesus to instruct certain people not to teach false doctrines 4or to concern themselves with myths and endless genealogies, which promote speculations rather than the plan of God that is to be received by faith. 5The aim of this instruction is love from a pure heart, a good conscience, and a sincere faith. 6Some people have deviated from these and turned to meaningless talk, 7wanting to be teachers of the law, but without understanding either what they are saying or what they assert with such assurance. 8We know that the law is good, provided that one uses it as law, 9with the understanding that law is meant not for a righteous person but for the lawless and unruly, the godless and sinful, the unholy and profane, those who kill their fathers or mothers, murderers, 10the unchaste, practicing homosexuals, kidnappers, liars, perjurers, and whatever else is opposed to sound teaching, 11according to the glorious gospel of the blessed God, with which I have been entrusted. 12I am grateful to him who has strengthened me, Christ Jesus our Lord, because he considered me trustworthy in appointing me to the ministry. 13I was once a blasphemer and a persecutor and an arrogant man, but I have been mercifully treated because I acted out of ignorance in my unbelief. 14Indeed, the grace of our Lord has been abundant, along with the faith and love that are in Christ Jesus. 15This saying is trustworthy and deserves full acceptance: Christ Jesus came into the world to save sinners. Of these I am the foremost. 16But for that reason I was mercifully treated, so that in me, as the foremost, Christ Jesus might display all his patience as an example for those who would come to believe in him for everlasting life. 17To the king of ages, incorruptible, invisible, the only God, honor and glory forever and ever. Amen. 18I entrust this charge to you, Timothy, my child, in accordance with the prophetic words once spoken about you. Through them may you fight a good fight 19by having faith and a good conscience. Some, by rejecting conscience, have made a shipwreck of their faith, 20among them Hymenaeus and Alexander, whom I have handed over to Satan to be taught not to blaspheme.

1 Timothy Chapter 2

1First of all, then, I ask that supplications, prayers, petitions, and thanksgivings be offered for everyone, 2for kings and for all in authority, that we may lead a quiet and tranquil life in all devotion and dignity. 3This is good and pleasing to God our savior, 4who wills everyone to be saved and to come to knowledge of the truth. 5For there is one God. There is also one mediator between God and the human race, Christ Jesus, himself human, 6who gave himself as ransom for all. This was the testimony at the proper time. 7For this I was appointed preacher and apostle (I am speaking the truth, I am not lying), teacher of the Gentiles in faith and truth. 8It is my wish, then, that in every place the men should pray, lifting up holy hands, without anger or argument. 9Similarly, (too,) women should adorn themselves with proper conduct, with modesty and self-control, not with braided hairstyles and gold ornaments, or pearls, or expensive clothes, 10but rather, as befits women who profess reverence for God, with good deeds. 11A woman must receive instruction silently and under complete control. 12I do not permit a woman to teach or to have authority over a man. She must be quiet. 13For Adam was formed first, then Eve. 14Further, Adam was not deceived, but the woman was deceived and transgressed. 15But she will be saved through motherhood, provided women persevere in faith and love and holiness, with self-control.

1 Timothy Chapter 3

1This saying is trustworthy: whoever aspires to the office of bishop desires a noble task. 2Therefore, a bishop must be irreproachable, married only once, temperate, self-controlled, decent, hospitable, able to teach, 3not a drunkard, not aggressive, but gentle, not contentious, not a lover of money. 4He must manage his own household well, keeping his children under control with perfect dignity; 5for if a man does not know how to manage his own household, how can he take care of the church of God? 6He should not be a recent convert, so that he may not become conceited and thus incur the devil's punishment. 7He must also have a good reputation among outsiders, so that he may not fall into disgrace, the devil's trap. 8Similarly, deacons must be dignified, not deceitful, not addicted to drink, not greedy for sordid gain, 9holding fast to the mystery of the faith with a clear conscience. 10Moreover, they should be tested first; then, if there is nothing against them, let them serve as deacons. 11Women, similarly, should be dignified, not slanderers, but temperate and faithful in everything. 12Deacons may be married only once and must manage their children and their households well. 13Thus those who serve well as deacons gain good standing and much confidence in their faith in Christ Jesus. 14I am writing you about these matters, although I hope to visit you soon. 15But if I should be delayed, you should know how to behave in the household of God, which is the church of the living God, the pillar and foundation of truth. [16]Undeniably great is the mystery of devotion, Who was manifested in the flesh, vindicated in the spirit, seen by angels, proclaimed to the Gentiles, believed in throughout the world, taken up in glory.

1 Timothy Chapter 4

[1]Now the Spirit explicitly says that in the last times some will turn away from the faith by paying attention to deceitful spirits and demonic instructions [2]through the hypocrisy of liars with branded consciences. [3]They forbid marriage and require abstinence from foods that God created to be received with thanksgiving by those who believe and know the truth. [4]For everything created by God is good, and nothing is to be rejected when received with thanksgiving, [5]for it is made holy by the invocation of God in prayer. [6]If you will give these instructions to the brothers, you will be a good minister of Christ Jesus, nourished on the words of the faith and of the sound teaching you have followed. [7]Avoid profane and silly myths. Train yourself for devotion, [8]for, while physical training is of limited value, devotion is valuable in every respect, since it holds a promise of life both for the present and for the future. [9]This saying is trustworthy and deserves full acceptance. [10]For this we toil and struggle, because we have set our hope on the living God, who is the savior of all, especially of those who believe. [11]Command and teach these things. [12]Let no one have contempt for your youth, but set an example for those who believe, in speech, conduct, love, faith, and purity. [13]Until I arrive, attend to the reading, exhortation, and teaching. [14]Do not neglect the gift you have, which was conferred on you through the prophetic word with the imposition of hands of the presbyterate. [15]Be diligent in these matters, be absorbed in them, so that your progress may be evident to everyone. [16]Attend to yourself and to your teaching; persevere in both tasks, for by doing so you will save both yourself and those who listen to you.

1 Timothy Chapter 5

[1]Do not rebuke an older man, but appeal to him as a father. Treat younger men as brothers, [2]older women as mothers, and younger women as sisters with complete purity. [3]Honor widows who are truly widows. [4]But if a widow has children or grandchildren, let these first learn to perform their religious duty to their own family and to make recompense to their parents, for this is pleasing to God. [5]The real widow, who is all alone, has set her hope on God and continues in supplications and prayers night and day. [6]But the one who is self-indulgent is dead while she lives. [7]Command this, so that they may be irreproachable. [8]And whoever does not provide for relatives and especially family members has denied the faith and is worse than an unbeliever. [9]Let a widow be enrolled if she is not less than sixty years old, married only once, [10]with a reputation for good works, namely, that she has raised children, practiced hospitality, washed the feet of the holy ones, helped those in distress, involved herself in every good work. [11]But exclude younger widows, for when their sensuality estranges them from Christ, they want to marry [12]and will incur condemnation for breaking their first pledge. [13]And furthermore, they learn to be idlers, going about from house to house, and not only idlers but gossips and busybodies as well, talking about things that ought not to be mentioned. [14]So I would like younger widows to marry, have children, and manage a home, so as to give the adversary no pretext for maligning us. [15]For some have already turned away to follow Satan. [16]If any woman believer has widowed relatives, she must assist them; the church is not to be burdened, so that it will be able to help those who are truly widows. [17]Presbyters who preside well deserve double honor, especially those who toil in preaching and teaching. [18]For the scripture says, "You shall not muzzle an ox when it is threshing," and, "A worker deserves his pay." [19]Do not accept an accusation against a presbyter unless it is supported by two or three witnesses. [20]Reprimand publicly those who do sin, so that the rest also will be afraid. [21]I charge you before God and Christ Jesus and the elect angels to keep these rules without prejudice, doing nothing out of favoritism. [22]Do not lay hands too readily on anyone, and do not share in another's sins. Keep yourself pure. [23]Stop drinking only water, but have a little wine for the sake of your stomach and your frequent illnesses. [24]Some people's sins are public, preceding them to judgment; but other people are followed by their sins. [25]Similarly, good works are also public; and even those that are not cannot remain hidden.

1 Timothy Chapter 6

[1]Those who are under the yoke of slavery must regard their masters as worthy of full respect, so that the name of God and our teaching may not suffer abuse. [2]Those whose masters are believers must not take advantage of them because they are brothers but must give better service because those who will profit from their work are believers and are beloved. [3]Whoever teaches something different and does not agree with the sound words of our Lord Jesus Christ and the religious teaching [4]is conceited, understanding nothing, and has a morbid disposition for arguments and verbal disputes. From these come envy, rivalry, insults, evil suspicions, [5]and mutual friction among people with corrupted minds, who are deprived of the truth, supposing religion to be a means of gain. [6]Indeed, religion with contentment is a great gain. [7]For we brought nothing into the world, just as we shall not be able to take anything out of it. [8]If we have food and clothing, we shall be content with that. [9]Those who want to be rich are falling into temptation and into a trap and into many foolish and harmful desires, which plunge them into ruin and destruction. [10]For the love of money is the root of all evils, and some people in their desire for it have strayed from the faith and have pierced themselves with many pains. [11]But you, man of God, avoid all this. Instead, pursue righteousness, devotion, faith, love, patience, and gentleness. [12]Compete well for the faith. Lay hold of eternal life, to which you were called when you made the noble confession in the presence of many witnesses. [13]I charge (you) before God, who gives life to all things, and before Christ Jesus, who gave testimony under Pontius Pilate for the noble confession, [14]to keep the commandment without stain or reproach until the appearance of our Lord Jesus Christ [15]that the blessed and only ruler will make manifest at the proper time, the King of kings and Lord of lords, [16]who alone has immortality, who dwells in unapproachable light, and whom no human being has seen or can see. To him be honor and eternal power. Amen. [17]Tell the rich in the present age not to be proud and not to rely on so uncertain a thing as wealth but rather on God, who richly provides us with all things for our enjoyment. [18]Tell them to do good, to be rich in good works, to be generous, ready to share, [19]thus accumulating as treasure a good foundation for the future, so as to win the life that is true life. [20]O Timothy, guard what has been entrusted to you. Avoid profane babbling and the absurdities of so-called knowledge. [21]By professing it, some people have deviated from the faith. Grace be with all of you.

II Timothy

2 Timothy Chapter 1

[1]Paul, an apostle of Christ Jesus by the will of God for the promise of life in Christ Jesus, [2]to Timothy, my dear child: grace, mercy, and peace from God the Father and Christ Jesus our Lord. [3]I am grateful to God, whom I worship with a clear conscience as my ancestors did, as I remember you constantly in my prayers, night and day. [4]I yearn to see you again, recalling your tears, so that I may be filled with joy, [5]as I recall your sincere faith that first lived in your grandmother Lois and in your mother Eunice and that I am confident lives also in you. [6]For this reason, I remind you to stir into flame the gift of God that you have through the imposition of my hands. [7]For God did not give us a spirit of cowardice but rather of power and love and self-control. [8]So do not be ashamed of your testimony to our Lord, nor of me, a prisoner for his sake; but bear your share of hardship for the gospel with the strength that comes from God. [9]He saved us and called us to a holy life, not according to our works but according to his own design and the grace bestowed on us in Christ Jesus before time began, [10]but now made manifest through the appearance of our savior Christ Jesus, who destroyed death and brought life and immortality to light through the gospel, [11]for which I was appointed preacher and apostle and teacher. [12]On this account I am suffering these things; but I am not ashamed, for I know him in whom I have believed and am confident that he is able to guard what has been entrusted to me until that day. [13]Take as your norm the sound words that you heard from me, in the faith and love that are in Christ Jesus. [14]Guard this rich trust with the help of the holy Spirit that dwells within us. [15]You know that everyone in Asia deserted me, including Phygelus and Hermogenes. [16]May the Lord grant mercy to the family of Onesiphorus because he often gave me new heart and was not ashamed of my chains. [17]But when he came to Rome, he promptly searched for me and found me. [18]May the Lord grant him to find mercy from the Lord on that day. And you know very well the services he rendered in Ephesus.

2 Timothy Chapter 2

[1]So you, my child, be strong in the grace that is in Christ Jesus. [2]And what you heard from me through many witnesses entrust to faithful people who will have the ability to teach others as well. [3]Bear your share of hardship along with me like a good soldier of Christ Jesus. [4]To satisfy the one who recruited him, a soldier does not become entangled in the business affairs of life. [5]Similarly, an athlete cannot receive the winner's crown except by competing according to the rules. [6]The hardworking farmer ought to have the first share of the crop. [7]Reflect on what I am

saying, for the Lord will give you understanding in everything. [8]Remember Jesus Christ, raised from the dead, a descendant of David: such is my gospel, [9]for which I am suffering, even to the point of chains, like a criminal. But the word of God is not chained. [10]Therefore, I bear with everything for the sake of those who are chosen, so that they too may obtain the salvation that is in Christ Jesus, together with eternal glory. [11]This saying is trustworthy: If we have died with him we shall also live with him; [12]if we persevere we shall also reign with him. But if we deny him he will deny us. [13]If we are unfaithful he remains faithful, for he cannot deny himself. [14]Remind people of these things and charge them before God to stop disputing about words. This serves no useful purpose since it harms those who listen. [15]Be eager to present yourself as acceptable to God, a workman who causes no disgrace, imparting the word of truth without deviation. [16]Avoid profane, idle talk, for such people will become more and more godless, [17]and their teaching will spread like gangrene. Among them are Hymenaeus and Philetus, [18]who have deviated from the truth by saying that (the) resurrection has already taken place and are upsetting the faith of some. [19]Nevertheless, God's solid foundation stands, bearing this inscription, "The Lord knows those who are his"; and, "Let everyone who calls upon the name of the Lord avoid evil." [20]In a large household there are vessels not only of gold and silver but also of wood and clay, some for lofty and others for humble use. [21]If anyone cleanses himself of these things, he will be a vessel for lofty use, dedicated, beneficial to the master of the house, ready for every good work. [22]So turn from youthful desires and pursue righteousness, faith, love, and peace, along with those who call on the Lord with purity of heart. [23]Avoid foolish and ignorant debates, for you know that they breed quarrels. [24]A slave of the Lord should not quarrel, but should be gentle with everyone, able to teach, tolerant, [25]correcting opponents with kindness. It may be that God will grant them repentance that leads to knowledge of the truth, [26]and that they may return to their senses out of the devil's snare, where they are entrapped by him, for his will.

2 Timothy Chapter 3

[1]But understand this: there will be terrifying times in the last days. [2]People will be self-centered and lovers of money, proud, haughty, abusive, disobedient to their parents, ungrateful, irreligious, [3]callous, implacable, slanderous, licentious, brutal, hating what is good, [4]traitors, reckless, conceited, lovers of pleasure rather than lovers of God, [5]as they make a pretense of religion but deny its power. Reject them. [6]For some of these slip into homes and make captives of women weighed down by sins, led by various desires, [7]always trying to learn but never able to reach a knowledge of the truth. [8]Just as Jannes and Jambres opposed Moses, so they also oppose the truth - people of depraved mind, unqualified in the faith. [9]But they will not make further progress, for their foolishness will be plain to all, as it was with those two. [10]You have followed my teaching, way of life, purpose, faith, patience, love, endurance, [11]persecutions, and sufferings, such as happened to me in Antioch, Iconium, and Lystra, persecutions that I endured. Yet from all these things the Lord delivered me. [12]In fact, all who want to live religiously in Christ Jesus will be persecuted. [13]But wicked people and charlatans will go from bad to worse, deceivers and deceived. [14]But you, remain faithful to what you have learned and believed, because you know from whom you learned it, [15]and that from infancy you have known (the) sacred scriptures, which are capable of giving you wisdom for salvation through faith in Christ Jesus. [16]All scripture is inspired by God and is useful for teaching, for refutation, for correction, and for training in righteousness, [17]so that one who belongs to God may be competent, equipped for every good work.

2 Timothy Chapter 4

[1]I charge you in the presence of God and of Christ Jesus, who will judge the living and the dead, and by his appearing and his kingly power: [2]proclaim the word; be persistent whether it is convenient or inconvenient; convince, reprimand, encourage through all patience and teaching. [3]For the time will come when people will not tolerate sound doctrine but, following their own desires and insatiable curiosity, will accumulate teachers [4]and will stop listening to the truth and will be diverted to myths. [5]But you, be self-possessed in all circumstances; put up with hardship; perform the work of an evangelist; fulfill your ministry. [6]For I am already being poured out like a libation, and the time of my departure is at hand. [7]I have competed well; I have finished the race; I have kept the faith. [8]From now on the crown of righteousness awaits me, which the Lord, the just judge, will award to me on that day, and not only to me, but to all who have longed for his appearance. [9]Try to join me soon, [10]for Demas, enamored of the present world, deserted me and went to Thessalonica, Crescens to Galatia, and Titus to Dalmatia. [11]Luke is the only one with me. Get Mark and bring him with

you, for he is helpful to me in the ministry. [12]I have sent Tychicus to Ephesus. [13]When you come, bring the cloak I left with Carpus in Troas, the papyrus rolls, and especially the parchments. [14]Alexander the coppersmith did me a great deal of harm; the Lord will repay him according to his deeds. [15]You too be on guard against him, for he has strongly resisted our preaching. [16]At my first defense no one appeared on my behalf, but everyone deserted me. May it not be held against them! [17]But the Lord stood by me and gave me strength, so that through me the proclamation might be completed and all the Gentiles might hear it. And I was rescued from the lion's mouth. [18]The Lord will rescue me from every evil threat and will bring me safe to his heavenly kingdom. To him be glory forever and ever. Amen. [19]Greet Prisca and Aquila and the family of Onesiphorus. [20]Erastus remained in Corinth, while I left Trophimus sick at Miletus. [21]Try to get here before winter. Eubulus, Pudens, Linus, Claudia, and all the brothers send greetings. [22]The Lord be with your spirit. Grace be with all of you.

Titus

Titus Chapter 1

[1]Paul, a slave of God and apostle of Jesus Christ for the sake of the faith of God's chosen ones and the recognition of religious truth, [2]in the hope of eternal life that God, who does not lie, promised before time began, [3]who indeed at the proper time revealed his word in the proclamation with which I was entrusted by the command of God our savior, [4]to Titus, my true child in our common faith: grace and peace from God the Father and Christ Jesus our savior. [5]For this reason I left you in Crete so that you might set right what remains to be done and appoint presbyters in every town, as I directed you, [6]on condition that a man be blameless, married only once, with believing children who are not accused of licentiousness or rebellious. [7]For a bishop as God's steward must be blameless, not arrogant, not irritable, not a drunkard, not aggressive, not greedy for sordid gain, [8]but hospitable, a lover of goodness, temperate, just, holy, and self-controlled, [9]holding fast to the true message as taught so that he will be able both to exhort with sound doctrine and to refute opponents. [10]For there are also many rebels, idle talkers and deceivers, especially the Jewish Christians. [11]It is imperative to silence them, as they are upsetting whole families by teaching for sordid gain what they should not. [12]One of them, a prophet of their own, once said, "Cretans have always been liars, vicious beasts, and lazy gluttons." [13]That testimony is true. Therefore, admonish them sharply, so that they may be sound in the faith, [14]instead of paying attention to Jewish myths and regulations of people who have repudiated the truth. [15]To the clean all things are clean, but to those who are defiled and unbelieving nothing is clean; in fact, both their minds and their consciences are tainted. [16]They claim to know God, but by their deeds they deny him. They are vile and disobedient and unqualified for any good deed.

Titus Chapter 2

[1]As for yourself, you must say what is consistent with sound doctrine, namely, [2]that older men should be temperate, dignified, self-controlled, sound in faith, love, and endurance. [3]Similarly, older women should be reverent in their behavior, not slanderers, not addicted to drink, teaching what is good, [4]so that they may train younger women to love their husbands and children, [5]to be self-controlled, chaste, good homemakers, under the control of their husbands, so that the word of God may not be discredited. [6]Urge the younger men, similarly, to control themselves, [7]showing yourself as a model of good deeds in every respect, with integrity in your teaching, dignity, [8]and sound speech that cannot be criticized, so that the opponent will be put to shame without anything bad to say about us. [9]Slaves are to be under the control of their masters in all respects, giving them satisfaction, not talking back to them [10]or stealing from them, but exhibiting complete good faith, so as to adorn the doctrine of God our savior in every way. [11]For the grace of God has appeared, saving all [12]and training us to reject godless ways and worldly desires and to live temperately, justly, and devoutly in this age, [13]as we await the blessed hope, the appearance of the glory of the great God and of our savior Jesus Christ, [14]who gave himself for us to deliver us from all lawlessness and to cleanse for himself a people as his own, eager to do what is good. [15]Say these things. Exhort and correct with all authority. Let no one look down on you.

Titus Chapter 3

[1]Remind them to be under the control of magistrates and authorities, to be obedient, to be open to every good enterprise. [2]They are to slander no one, to be peaceable, considerate, exercising all graciousness toward everyone. [3]For we ourselves were once foolish, disobedient, deluded, slaves to various desires and pleasures, living in malice and envy,

hateful ourselves and hating one another. ⁴But when the kindness and generous love of God our savior appeared, ⁵not because of any righteous deeds we had done but because of his mercy, he saved us through the bath of rebirth and renewal by the holy Spirit, ⁶whom he richly poured out on us through Jesus Christ our savior, ⁷so that we might be justified by his grace and become heirs in hope of eternal life. ⁸This saying is trustworthy. I want you to insist on these points, that those who have believed in God be careful to devote themselves to good works; these are excellent and beneficial to others. ⁹Avoid foolish arguments, genealogies, rivalries, and quarrels about the law, for they are useless and futile. ¹⁰After a first and second warning, break off contact with a heretic, ¹¹realizing that such a person is perverted and sinful and stands self-condemned. ¹²When I send Artemas to you, or Tychicus, try to join me at Nicopolis, where I have decided to spend the winter. ¹³Send Zenas the lawyer and Apollos on their journey soon, and see to it that they have everything they need. ¹⁴But let our people, too, learn to devote themselves to good works to supply urgent needs, so that they may not be unproductive. ¹⁵All who are with me send you greetings. Greet those who love us in the faith. Grace be with all of you.

Philemon

Philemon Chapter 1

¹Paul, a prisoner for Christ Jesus, and Timothy our brother, to Philemon, our beloved and our co-worker, ²to Apphia our sister, to Archippus our fellow soldier, and to the church at your house. ³Grace to you and peace from God our Father and the Lord Jesus Christ. ⁴I give thanks to my God always, remembering you in my prayers, ⁵as I hear of the love and the faith you have in the Lord Jesus and for all the holy ones, ⁶so that your partnership in the faith may become effective in recognizing every good there is in us that leads to Christ. ⁷For I have experienced much joy and encouragement from your love, because the hearts of the holy ones have been refreshed by you, brother. ⁸Therefore, although I have the full right in Christ to order you to do what is proper, ⁹I rather urge you out of love, being as I am, Paul, an old man, and now also a prisoner for Christ Jesus. ¹⁰I urge you on behalf of my child Onesimus, whose father I have become in my imprisonment, ¹¹who was once useless to you but is now useful to (both) you and me. ¹²I am sending him, that is, my own heart, back to you. ¹³I should have liked to retain him for myself, so that he might serve me on your behalf in my imprisonment for the gospel, ¹⁴but I did not want to do anything without your consent, so that the good you do might not be forced but voluntary. ¹⁵Perhaps this is why he was away from you for a while, that you might have him back forever, ¹⁶no longer as a slave but more than a slave, a brother, beloved especially to me, but even more so to you, as a man and in the Lord. ¹⁷So if you regard me as a partner, welcome him as you would me. ¹⁸And if he has done you any injustice or owes you anything, charge it to me. ¹⁹I, Paul, write this in my own hand: I will pay. May I not tell you that you owe me your very self. ²⁰Yes, brother, may I profit from you in the Lord. Refresh my heart in Christ. ²¹With trust in your compliance I write to you, knowing that you will do even more than I say. ²²At the same time prepare a guest room for me, for I hope to be granted to you through your prayers. ²³Epaphras, my fellow prisoner in Christ Jesus, greets you, ²⁴as well as Mark, Aristarchus, Demas, and Luke, my co-workers. ²⁵The grace of the Lord Jesus Christ be with your spirit.

General Letters (Catholic Epistles)

Hebrews

Hebrews Chapter 1

¹In times past, God spoke in partial and various ways to our ancestors through the prophets; ²in these last days, he spoke to us through a son, whom he made heir of all things and through whom he created the universe, ³who is the refulgence of his glory, the very imprint of his being, and who sustains all things by his mighty word. When he had accomplished purification from sins, he took his seat at the right hand of the Majesty on high, ⁴as far superior to the angels as the name he has inherited is more excellent than theirs. ⁵For to which of the angels did God ever say: "You are my son; this day I have begotten you"? Or again: "I will be a father to him, and he shall be a son to me"? ⁶And again, when he leads the first-born into the world, he says: "Let all the angels of God worship him." ⁷Of the angels he says: "He makes his angels winds and his ministers a fiery flame"; ⁸but of the Son: "Your throne, O God, stands forever and ever; and a righteous scepter is the scepter of your kingdom. ⁹You loved justice and hated wickedness; therefore God, your God, anointed you with the oil of gladness above your

companions"; ¹⁰and: "At the beginning, O Lord, you established the earth, and the heavens are the works of your hands. ¹¹They will perish, but you remain; and they will all grow old like a garment. ¹²You will roll them up like a cloak, and like a garment they will be changed. But you are the same, and your years will have no end." ¹³But to which of the angels has he ever said: "Sit at my right hand until I make your enemies your footstool"? ¹⁴Are they not all ministering spirits sent to serve, for the sake of those who are to inherit salvation?

Hebrews Chapter 2

¹Therefore, we must attend all the more to what we have heard, so that we may not be carried away. ²For if the word announced through angels proved firm, and every transgression and disobedience received its just recompense, ³how shall we escape if we ignore so great a salvation? Announced originally through the Lord, it was confirmed for us by those who had heard. ⁴God added his testimony by signs, wonders, various acts of power, and distribution of the gifts of the Holy Spirit according to his will. ⁵For it was not to angels that he subjected the world to come, of which we are speaking. ⁶Instead, someone has testified somewhere: "What is man that you are mindful of him, or the son of man that you care for him? ⁷You made him for a little while lower than the angels; you crowned him with glory and honor, ⁸subjecting all things under his feet." In "subjecting" all things (to him), he left nothing not "subject to him." Yet at present we do not see "all things subject to him," ⁹but we do see Jesus "crowned with glory and honor" because he suffered death, he who "for a little while" was made "lower than the angels," that by the grace of God he might taste death for everyone. ¹⁰For it was fitting that he, for whom and through whom all things exist, in bringing many children to glory, should make the leader to their salvation perfect through suffering. ¹¹He who consecrates and those who are being consecrated all have one origin. Therefore, he is not ashamed to call them "brothers," ¹²saying: "I will proclaim your name to my brothers, in the midst of the assembly I will praise you"; ¹³and again: "I will put my trust in him"; and again: "Behold, I and the children God has given me." ¹⁴Now since the children share in blood and flesh, he likewise shared in them, that through death he might destroy the one who has the power of death, that is, the devil, ¹⁵and free those who through fear of death had been subject to slavery all their life. ¹⁶Surely he did not help angels but rather the descendants of Abraham; ¹⁷therefore, he had to become like his brothers in every way, that he might be a merciful and faithful high priest before God to expiate the sins of the people. ¹⁸Because he himself was tested through what he suffered, he is able to help those who are being tested.

Hebrews Chapter 3

¹Therefore, holy "brothers," sharing in a heavenly calling, reflect on Jesus, the apostle and high priest of our confession, ²who was faithful to the one who appointed him, just as Moses was "faithful in (all) his house." ³But he is worthy of more "glory" than Moses, as the founder of a house has more "honor" than the house itself. ⁴Every house is founded by someone, but the founder of all is God. ⁵Moses was "faithful in all his house" as a "servant" to testify to what would be spoken, ⁶but Christ was faithful as a son placed over his house. We are his house, if (only) we hold fast to our confidence and pride in our hope. ⁷Therefore, as the holy Spirit says: "Oh, that today you would hear his voice, ⁸'Harden not your hearts as at the rebellion in the day of testing in the desert, ⁹where your ancestors tested and tried me and saw my works ¹⁰for forty years. Because of this I was provoked with that generation and I said, "They have always been of erring heart, and they do not know my ways." ¹¹As I swore in my wrath, "They shall not enter into my rest."'" ¹²Take care, brothers, that none of you may have an evil and unfaithful heart, so as to forsake the living God. ¹³Encourage yourselves daily while it is still "today," so that none of you may grow hardened by the deceit of sin. ¹⁴We have become partners of Christ if only we hold the beginning of the reality firm until the end, ¹⁵for it is said: "Oh, that today you would hear his voice: 'Harden not your hearts as at the rebellion.'" ¹⁶Who were those who rebelled when they heard? Was it not all those who came out of Egypt under Moses? ¹⁷With whom was he "provoked for forty years"? Was it not those who had sinned, whose corpses fell in the desert? ¹⁸And to whom did he "swear that they should not enter into his rest," if not to those who were disobedient? ¹⁹And we see that they could not enter for lack of faith.

Hebrews Chapter 4

¹Therefore, let us be on our guard while the promise of entering into his rest remains, that none of you seem to have failed. ²For in fact we have received the good news just as they did. But the word that they heard did not profit them, for they were not united in faith with those who listened. ³For we who believed enter into (that) rest, just as he has said: "As I swore in my wrath, 'They shall not enter into my rest,'" and yet his

works were accomplished at the foundation of the world. 4For he has spoken somewhere about the seventh day in this manner, "And God rested on the seventh day from all his works"; 5and again, in the previously mentioned place, "They shall not enter into my rest." 6Therefore, since it remains that some will enter into it, and those who formerly received the good news did not enter because of disobedience, 7he once more set a day, "today," when long afterwards he spoke through David, as already quoted: "Oh, that today you would hear his voice: 'Harden not your hearts.'" 8Now if Joshua had given them rest, he would not have spoken afterwards of another day. 9Therefore, a sabbath rest still remains for the people of God. 10And whoever enters into God's rest, rests from his own works as God did from his. 11Therefore, let us strive to enter into that rest, so that no one may fall after the same example of disobedience. 12Indeed, the word of God is living and effective, sharper than any two-edged sword, penetrating even between soul and spirit, joints and marrow, and able to discern reflections and thoughts of the heart. 13No creature is concealed from him, but everything is naked and exposed to the eyes of him to whom we must render an account. 14Therefore, since we have a great high priest who has passed through the heavens, Jesus, the Son of God, let us hold fast to our confession. 15For we do not have a high priest who is unable to sympathize with our weaknesses, but one who has similarly been tested in every way, yet without sin. 16So let us confidently approach the throne of grace to receive mercy and to find grace for timely help.

Hebrews Chapter 5

1Every high priest is taken from among men and made their representative before God, to offer gifts and sacrifices for sins. 2He is able to deal patiently with the ignorant and erring, for he himself is beset by weakness 3and so, for this reason, must make sin offerings for himself as well as for the people. 4No one takes this honor upon himself but only when called by God, just as Aaron was. 5In the same way, it was not Christ who glorified himself in becoming high priest, but rather the one who said to him: "You are my son; this day I have begotten you"; 6just as he says in another place: "You are a priest forever according to the order of Melchizedek." 7In the days when he was in the flesh, he offered prayers and supplications with loud cries and tears to the one who was able to save him from death, and he was heard because of his reverence. 8Son though he was, he learned obedience from what he suffered; 9and when he was made perfect, he became the source of eternal salvation for all who obey him, 10declared by God high priest according to the order of Melchizedek. 11About this we have much to say, and it is difficult to explain, for you have become sluggish in hearing. 12Although you should be teachers by this time, you need to have someone teach you again the basic elements of the utterances of God. You need milk, (and) not solid food. 13Everyone who lives on milk lacks experience of the word of righteousness, for he is a child. 14But solid food is for the mature, for those whose faculties are trained by practice to discern good and evil.

Hebrews Chapter 6

1Therefore, let us leave behind the basic teaching about Christ and advance to maturity, without laying the foundation all over again: repentance from dead works and faith in God, 2instruction about baptisms and laying on of hands, resurrection of the dead and eternal judgment. 3And we shall do this, if only God permits. 4For it is impossible in the case of those who have once been enlightened and tasted the heavenly gift and shared in the holy Spirit 5and tasted the good word of God and the powers of the age to come, 6and then have fallen away, to bring them to repentance again, since they are recrucifying the Son of God for themselves and holding him up to contempt. 7Ground that has absorbed the rain falling upon it repeatedly and brings forth crops useful to those for whom it is cultivated receives a blessing from God. 8But if it produces thorns and thistles, it is rejected; it will soon be cursed and finally burned. 9But we are sure in your regard, beloved, of better things related to salvation, even though we speak in this way. 10For God is not unjust so as to overlook your work and the love you have demonstrated for his name by having served and continuing to serve the holy ones. 11We earnestly desire each of you to demonstrate the same eagerness for the fulfillment of hope until the end, 12so that you may not become sluggish, but imitators of those who, through faith and patience, are inheriting the promises. 13When God made the promise to Abraham, since he had no one greater by whom to swear, "he swore by himself," 14and said, "I will indeed bless you and multiply you." 15And so, after patient waiting, he obtained the promise. 16Human beings swear by someone greater than themselves; for them an oath serves as a guarantee and puts an end to all argument. 17So when God wanted to give the heirs of his promise an even clearer demonstration of the immutability of his purpose, he intervened with an oath, 18so that by two immutable things, in which it was impossible for God to lie, we who have taken refuge might be strongly encouraged to hold fast to the hope that lies before us. 19This we have as an anchor of the soul, sure and firm, which reaches into the interior behind the veil, 20where Jesus has entered on our behalf as forerunner, becoming high priest forever according to the order of Melchizedek.

Hebrews Chapter 7

1This "Melchizedek, king of Salem and priest of God Most High, met Abraham as he returned from his defeat of the kings" and "blessed him." 2And Abraham apportioned to him "a tenth of everything." His name first means righteous king, and he was also "king of Salem," that is, king of peace. 3Without father, mother, or ancestry, without beginning of days or end of life, thus made to resemble the Son of God, he remains a priest forever. 4See how great he is to whom the patriarch "Abraham (indeed) gave a tenth" of his spoils. 5The descendants of Levi who receive the office of priesthood have a commandment according to the law to exact tithes from the people, that is, from their brothers, although they also have come from the loins of Abraham. 6But he who was not of their ancestry received tithes from Abraham and blessed him who had received the promises. 7Unquestionably, a lesser person is blessed by a greater. 8In the one case, mortal men receive tithes; in the other, a man of whom it is testified that he lives on. 9One might even say that Levi himself, who receives tithes, was tithed through Abraham, 10for he was still in his father's loins when Melchizedek met him. 11If, then, perfection came through the levitical priesthood, on the basis of which the people received the law, what need would there still have been for another priest to arise according to the order of Melchizedek, and not reckoned according to the order of Aaron? 12When there is a change of priesthood, there is necessarily a change of law as well. 13Now he of whom these things are said belonged to a different tribe, of which no member ever officiated at the altar. 14It is clear that our Lord arose from Judah, and in regard to that tribe Moses said nothing about priests. 15It is even more obvious if another priest is raised up after the likeness of Melchizedek, 16who has become so, not by a law expressed in a commandment concerning physical descent but by the power of a life that cannot be destroyed. 17For it is testified: "You are a priest forever according to the order of Melchizedek." 18On the one hand, a former commandment is annulled because of its weakness and uselessness, 19for the law brought nothing to perfection; on the other hand, a better hope is introduced, through which we draw near to God. 20And to the degree that this happened not without the taking of an oath—for others became priests without an oath, 21but he with an oath, through the one who said to him: "The Lord has sworn, and he will not repent: 'You are a priest forever'"— 22to that same degree has Jesus (also) become the guarantee of an (even) better covenant. 23Those priests were many because they were prevented by death from remaining in office, 24but he, because he remains forever, has a priesthood that does not pass away. 25Therefore, he is always able to save those who approach God through him, since he lives forever to make intercession for them. 26It was fitting that we should have such a high priest: holy, innocent, undefiled, separated from sinners, higher than the heavens. 27He has no need, as did the high priests, to offer sacrifice day after day, first for his own sins and then for those of the people; he did that once for all when he offered himself. 28For the law appoints men subject to weakness to be high priests, but the word of the oath, which was taken after the law, appoints a son, who has been made perfect forever.

Hebrews Chapter 8

1The main point of what has been said is this: we have such a high priest, who has taken his seat at the right hand of the throne of the Majesty in heaven, 2a minister of the sanctuary and of the true tabernacle that the Lord, not man, set up. 3Now every high priest is appointed to offer gifts and sacrifices; thus the necessity for this one also to have something to offer. 4If then he were on earth, he would not be a priest, since there are those who offer gifts according to the law. 5They worship in a copy and shadow of the heavenly sanctuary, as Moses was warned when he was about to erect the tabernacle. For he says, "See that you make everything according to the pattern shown you on the mountain." 6Now he has obtained so much more excellent a ministry as he is mediator of a better covenant, enacted on better promises. 7For if that first covenant had been faultless, no place would have been sought for a second one. 8But he finds fault with them and says: "Behold, the days are coming, says the Lord, when I will conclude a new covenant with the house of Israel and the house of Judah. 9It will not be like the covenant I made with their fathers the day I took them by the hand to lead them forth from the land of Egypt; for they did not stand by my covenant and I ignored them, says the Lord. ¹⁰But this is the covenant I will establish with the house of Israel after those days, says the Lord: I will put my laws in their minds and I will write them upon their hearts. I will be their God, and they shall be my people. ¹¹And they shall not teach, each one his fellow citizen and kinsman, saying, 'Know the Lord,' for all shall know me, from least to greatest. ¹²For I will forgive their evildoing and remember their sins no more." ¹³When he speaks of a "new" covenant, he declares the first one obsolete. And what has become obsolete and has grown old is close to disappearing.

Hebrews Chapter 9

¹Now (even) the first covenant had regulations for worship and an earthly sanctuary. ²For a tabernacle was constructed, the outer one, in which were the lampstand, the table, and the bread of offering; this is called the Holy Place. ³Behind the second veil was the tabernacle called the Holy of Holies, ⁴in which were the gold altar of incense and the ark of the covenant entirely covered with gold. In it were the gold jar containing the manna, the staff of Aaron that had sprouted, and the tablets of the covenant. ⁵Above it were the cherubim of glory overshadowing the place of expiation. Now is not the time to speak of these in detail. ⁶With these arrangements for worship, the priests, in performing their service, go into the outer tabernacle repeatedly, ⁷but the high priest alone goes into the inner one once a year, not without blood that he offers for himself and for the sins of the people. ⁸In this way the holy Spirit shows that the way into the sanctuary had not yet been revealed while the outer tabernacle still had its place. ⁹This is a symbol of the present time, in which gifts and sacrifices are offered that cannot perfect the worshiper in conscience ¹⁰but only in matters of food and drink and various ritual washings: regulations concerning the flesh, imposed until the time of the new order. ¹¹But when Christ came as high priest of the good things that have come to be, passing through the greater and more perfect tabernacle not made by hands, that is, not belonging to this creation, ¹²he entered once for all into the sanctuary, not with the blood of goats and calves but with his own blood, thus obtaining eternal redemption. ¹³For if the blood of goats and bulls and the sprinkling of a heifer's ashes can sanctify those who are defiled so that their flesh is cleansed, ¹⁴how much more will the blood of Christ, who through the eternal spirit offered himself unblemished to God, cleanse our consciences from dead works to worship the living God. ¹⁵For this reason he is mediator of a new covenant: since a death has taken place for deliverance from transgressions under the first covenant, those who are called may receive the promised eternal inheritance. ¹⁶Now where there is a will, the death of the testator must be established. ¹⁷For a will takes effect only at death; it has no force while the testator is alive. ¹⁸Thus not even the first covenant was inaugurated without blood. ¹⁹When every commandment had been proclaimed by Moses to all the people according to the law, he took the blood of calves (and goats), together with water and crimson wool and hyssop, and sprinkled both the book itself and all the people, ²⁰saying, "This is 'the blood of the covenant which God has enjoined upon you.'" ²¹In the same way, he sprinkled also the tabernacle and all the vessels of worship with blood. ²²According to the law almost everything is purified by blood, and without the shedding of blood there is no forgiveness. ²³Therefore, it was necessary for the copies of the heavenly things to be purified by these rites, but the heavenly things themselves by better sacrifices than these. ²⁴For Christ did not enter into a sanctuary made by hands, a copy of the true one, but heaven itself, that he might now appear before God on our behalf. ²⁵Not that he might offer himself repeatedly, as the high priest enters each year into the sanctuary with blood that is not his own; ²⁶if that were so, he would have had to suffer repeatedly from the foundation of the world. But now once for all he has appeared at the end of the ages to take away sin by his sacrifice. ²⁷Just as it is appointed that human beings die once, and after this the judgment, ²⁸so also Christ, offered once to take away the sins of many, will appear a second time, not to take away sin but to bring salvation to those who eagerly await him.

Hebrews Chapter 10

¹Since the law has only a shadow of the good things to come, and not the very image of them, it can never make perfect those who come to worship by the same sacrifices that they offer continually each year. ²Otherwise, would not the sacrifices have ceased to be offered, since the worshipers, once cleansed, would no longer have had any consciousness of sins? ³But in those sacrifices there is only a yearly remembrance of sins, ⁴for it is impossible that the blood of bulls and goats take away sins. ⁵For this reason, when he came into the world, he said: "Sacrifice and offering you did not desire, but a body you prepared for me; ⁶holocausts and sin offerings you took no delight in. ⁷Then I

said, 'As is written of me in the scroll, Behold, I come to do your will, O God.'" ⁸First he says, "Sacrifices and offerings, holocausts and sin offerings, you neither desired nor delighted in." These are offered according to the law. ⁹Then he says, "Behold, I come to do your will." He takes away the first to establish the second. ¹⁰By this "will," we have been consecrated through the offering of the body of Jesus Christ once for all. ¹¹Every priest stands daily at his ministry, offering frequently those same sacrifices that can never take away sins. ¹²But this one offered one sacrifice for sins, and took his seat forever at the right hand of God; ¹³now he waits until his enemies are made his footstool. ¹⁴For by one offering he has made perfect forever those who are being consecrated. ¹⁵The holy Spirit also testifies to us, for after saying: ¹⁶"This is the covenant I will establish with them after those days, says the Lord: 'I will put my laws in their hearts, and I will write them upon their minds,'" ¹⁷he also says: "Their sins and their evildoing I will remember no more." ¹⁸Where there is forgiveness of these, there is no longer offering for sin. ¹⁹Therefore, brothers, since through the blood of Jesus we have confidence of entrance into the sanctuary ²⁰by the new and living way he opened for us through the veil, that is, his flesh, ²¹and since we have "a great priest over the house of God," ²²let us approach with a sincere heart and in absolute trust, with our hearts sprinkled clean from an evil conscience and our bodies washed in pure water. ²³Let us hold unwaveringly to our confession that gives us hope, for he who made the promise is trustworthy. ²⁴We must consider how to rouse one another to love and good works. ²⁵We should not stay away from our assembly, as is the custom of some, but encourage one another, and this all the more as you see the day drawing near. ²⁶If we sin deliberately after receiving knowledge of the truth, there no longer remains sacrifice for sins ²⁷but a fearful prospect of judgment and a flaming fire that is going to consume the adversaries. ²⁸Anyone who rejects the law of Moses is put to death without pity on the testimony of two or three witnesses. ²⁹Do you not think that a much worse punishment is due the one who has contempt for the Son of God, considers unclean the covenant-blood by which he was consecrated, and insults the spirit of grace? ³⁰We know the one who said: "Vengeance is mine; I will repay," and again: "The Lord will judge his people." ³¹It is a fearful thing to fall into the hands of the living God. ³²Remember the days past when, after you had been enlightened, you endured a great contest of suffering. ³³At times you were publicly exposed to abuse and affliction; at other times you associated yourselves with those so treated. ³⁴You even joined in the sufferings of those in prison and joyfully accepted the confiscation of your property, knowing that you had a better and lasting possession. ³⁵Therefore, do not throw away your confidence; it will have great recompense. ³⁶You need endurance to do the will of God and receive what he has promised. ³⁷"For, after just a brief moment, he who is to come shall come; he shall not delay. ³⁸But my just one shall live by faith, and if he draws back I take no pleasure in him." ³⁹We are not among those who draw back and perish, but among those who have faith and will possess life.

Hebrews Chapter 11

¹Faith is the realization of what is hoped for and evidence of things not seen.²Because of it the ancients were well attested.³By faith we understand that the universe was ordered by the word of God, so that what is visible came into being through the invisible.⁴By faith Abel offered to God a sacrifice greater than Cain's. Through this he was attested to be righteous, God bearing witness to his gifts, and through this, though dead, he still speaks.⁵By faith Enoch was taken up so that he should not see death, and "he was found no more because God had taken him." Before he was taken up, he was attested to have pleased God.⁶But without faith it is impossible to please him, for anyone who approaches God must believe that he exists and that he rewards those who seek him.⁷By faith Noah, warned about what was not yet seen, with reverence built an ark for the salvation of his household. Through this he condemned the world and inherited the righteousness that comes through faith.⁸By faith Abraham obeyed when he was called to go out to a place that he was to receive as an inheritance; he went out, not knowing where he was to go.⁹By faith he sojourned in the promised land as in a foreign country, dwelling in tents with Isaac and Jacob, heirs of the same promise;¹⁰for he was looking forward to the city with foundations, whose architect and maker is God.¹¹By faith he received power to generate, even though he was past the normal age - and Sarah herself was sterile - for he thought that the one who had made the promise was trustworthy.¹²So it was that there came forth from one man, himself as good as dead, descendants as numerous as the stars in the sky and as countless as the sands on the seashore.¹³All these died in faith. They did not receive what had been promised but saw it and greeted it from afar and acknowledged themselves to be strangers and aliens on earth,¹⁴for those who speak thus show that they are seeking a

homeland.[15]If they had been thinking of the land from which they had come, they would have had opportunity to return.[16]But now they desire a better homeland, a heavenly one. Therefore, God is not ashamed to be called their God, for he has prepared a city for them.[17]By faith Abraham, when put to the test, offered up Isaac, and he who had received the promises was ready to offer his only son,[18]of whom it was said, "Through Isaac descendants shall bear your name."[19]He reasoned that God was able to raise even from the dead, and he received Isaac back as a symbol.[20]By faith regarding things still to come Isaac blessed Jacob and Esau.[21]By faith Jacob, when dying, blessed each of the sons of Joseph and "bowed in worship, leaning on the top of his staff."[22]By faith Joseph, near the end of his life, spoke of the Exodus of the Israelites and gave instructions about his bones.[23]By faith Moses was hidden by his parents for three months after his birth, because they saw that he was a beautiful child, and they were not afraid of the king's edict.[24]By faith Moses, when he had grown up, refused to be known as the son of Pharaoh's daughter;[25]he chose to be ill-treated along with the people of God rather than enjoy the fleeting pleasure of sin.[26]He considered the reproach of the Anointed greater wealth than the treasures of Egypt, for he was looking to the recompense.[27]By faith he left Egypt, not fearing the king's fury, for he persevered as if seeing the one who is invisible.[28]By faith he kept the Passover and sprinkled the blood, that the Destroyer of the firstborn might not touch them.[29]By faith they crossed the Red Sea as if it were dry land, but when the Egyptians attempted it they were drowned.[30]By faith the walls of Jericho fell after being encircled for seven days.[31]By faith Rahab the harlot did not perish with the disobedient, for she had received the spies in peace.[32]What more shall I say? I have not time to tell of Gideon, Barak, Samson, Jephthah, of David and Samuel and the prophets,[33]who by faith conquered kingdoms, did what was righteous, obtained the promises; they closed the mouths of lions,[34]put out raging fires, escaped the devouring sword; out of weakness they were made powerful, became strong in battle, and turned back foreign invaders.[35]Women received back their dead through resurrection. Some were tortured and would not accept deliverance, in order to obtain a better resurrection.[36]Others endured mockery, scourging, even chains and imprisonment.[37]They were stoned, sawed in two, put to death at sword's point; they went about in skins of sheep or goats, needy, afflicted, tormented.[38]The world was not worthy of them. They wandered about in deserts and on mountains, in caves and in crevices in the earth.[39]Yet all these, though approved because of their faith, did not receive what had been promised.[40]God had foreseen something better for us, so that without us they should not be made perfect.

Hebrews Chapter 12

[1]Therefore, since we are surrounded by so great a cloud of witnesses, let us rid ourselves of every burden and sin that clings to us and persevere in running the race that lies before us[2]while keeping our eyes fixed on Jesus, the leader and perfecter of faith. For the sake of the joy that lay before him he endured the cross, despising its shame, and has taken his seat at the right of the throne of God.[3]Consider how he endured such opposition from sinners, in order that you may not grow weary and lose heart.[4]In your struggle against sin you have not yet resisted to the point of shedding blood.[5]You have also forgotten the exhortation addressed to you as sons: "My son, do not disdain the discipline of the Lord or lose heart when reproved by him;[6]for whom the Lord loves, he disciplines; he scourges every son he acknowledges."[7]Endure your trials as "discipline"; God treats you as sons. For what "son" is there whom his father does not discipline?[8]If you are without discipline, in which all have shared, you are not sons but bastards.[9]Besides this, we have had our earthly fathers to discipline us, and we respected them. Should we not (then) submit all the more to the Father of spirits and live?[10]They disciplined us for a short time as seemed right to them, but he does so for our benefit, in order that we may share his holiness.[11]At the time, all discipline seems a cause not for joy but for pain, yet later it brings the peaceful fruit of righteousness to those who are trained by it.[12]So strengthen your drooping hands and your weak knees.[13]Make straight paths for your feet, that what is lame may not be dislocated but healed.[14]Strive for peace with everyone, and for that holiness without which no one will see the Lord.[15]See to it that no one be deprived of the grace of God, that no bitter root spring up and cause trouble, through which many may become defiled,[16]that no one be an immoral or profane person like Esau, who sold his birthright for a single meal.[17]For you know that later, when he wanted to inherit his father's blessing, he was rejected because he found no opportunity to change his mind, even though he sought the blessing with tears.[18]You have not approached that which could be touched and a blazing fire and gloomy darkness and storm[19]and a trumpet blast and a voice speaking words such that those who heard begged that no message be further addressed to them,[20]for they could not bear to hear the command: "If even an animal touches the mountain, it shall be stoned."[21]Indeed, so fearful was the spectacle that Moses said, "I am terrified and trembling."[22]No, you have approached Mount Zion and the city of the living God, the heavenly Jerusalem, and countless angels in festal gathering,[23]and the assembly of the firstborn enrolled in heaven, and God the judge of all, and the spirits of the just made perfect,[24]and Jesus, the mediator of a new covenant, and the sprinkled blood that speaks more eloquently than that of Abel.[25]See that you do not reject the one who speaks. For if they did not escape when they refused the one who warned them on earth, how much more in our case if we turn away from the one who warns from heaven.[26]His voice shook the earth at that time, but now he has promised, "I will once more shake not only earth but heaven."[27]That phrase, "once more," points to (the) removal of shaken, created things, so that what is unshaken may remain.[28]Therefore, we who are receiving the unshakable kingdom should have gratitude, with which we should offer worship pleasing to God in reverence and awe.[29]For our God is a consuming fire.

Hebrews Chapter 13

[1]Let mutual love continue.[2]Do not neglect hospitality, for through it some have unknowingly entertained angels.[3]Be mindful of prisoners as if sharing their imprisonment, and of the ill-treated as of yourselves, for you also are in the body.[4]Let marriage be honored among all and the marriage bed be kept undefiled, for God will judge the immoral and adulterers.[5]Let your life be free from love of money but be content with what you have, for he has said, "I will never forsake you or abandon you."[6]Thus we may say with confidence: "The Lord is my helper, (and) I will not be afraid. What can anyone do to me?"[7]Remember your leaders who spoke the word of God to you. Consider the outcome of their way of life and imitate their faith.[8]Jesus Christ is the same yesterday, today, and forever.[9]Do not be carried away by all kinds of strange teaching. It is good to have our hearts strengthened by grace and not by foods, which do not benefit those who live by them.[10]We have an altar from which those who serve the tabernacle have no right to eat.[11]The bodies of the animals whose blood the high priest brings into the sanctuary as a sin offering are burned outside the camp.[12]Therefore, Jesus also suffered outside the gate, to consecrate the people by his own blood.[13]Let us then go to him outside the camp, bearing the reproach that he bore.[14]For here we have no lasting city, but we seek the one that is to come.[15]Through him (then) let us continually offer God a sacrifice of praise, that is, the fruit of lips that confess his name.[16]Do not neglect to do good and to share what you have; God is pleased by sacrifices of that kind.[17]Obey your leaders and defer to them, for they keep watch over you and will have to give an account, that they may fulfill their task with joy and not with sorrow, for that would be of no advantage to you.[18]Pray for us, for we are confident that we have a clear conscience, wishing to act rightly in every respect.[19]I especially ask for your prayers that I may be restored to you very soon.[20]May the God of peace, who brought up from the dead the great shepherd of the sheep by the blood of the eternal covenant, Jesus our Lord,[21]furnish you with all that is good, that you may do his will. May he carry out in you what is pleasing to him through Jesus Christ, to whom be glory forever (and ever). Amen.[22]Brothers, I ask you to bear with this message of encouragement, for I have written to you rather briefly.[23]I must let you know that our brother Timothy has been set free. If he comes soon, I shall see you together with him.[24]Greetings to all your leaders and to all the holy ones. Those from Italy send you greetings.[25]Grace be with all of you.

James

James Chapter 1

[1]James, a slave of God and of the Lord Jesus Christ, to the twelve tribes in the dispersion, greetings.[2]Consider it all joy, my brothers, when you encounter various trials,[3]for you know that the testing of your faith produces perseverance.[4]And let perseverance be perfect, so that you may be perfect and complete, lacking in nothing.[5]But if any of you lacks wisdom, he should ask God who gives to all generously and ungrudgingly, and he will be given it.[6]But he should ask in faith, not doubting, for the one who doubts is like a wave of the sea that is driven and tossed about by the wind.[7]For that person must not suppose that he will receive anything from the Lord,[8]since he is a man of two minds, unstable in all his ways.[9]The brother in lowly circumstances should take pride in his high standing,[10]and the rich one in his lowliness, for he will pass away "like the flower of the field."[11]For the sun comes up with its scorching heat and dries up the grass, its flower droops, and the beauty of its appearance vanishes. So will the rich person fade away in the midst of his pursuits.[12]Blessed is the man who perseveres in

temptation, for when he has been proved he will receive the crown of life that he promised to those who love him.¹³No one experiencing temptation should say, "I am being tempted by God"; for God is not subject to temptation to evil, and he himself tempts no one.¹⁴Rather, each person is tempted when he is lured and enticed by his own desire.¹⁵Then desire conceives and brings forth sin, and when sin reaches maturity it gives birth to death.¹⁶Do not be deceived, my beloved brothers:¹⁷all good giving and every perfect gift is from above, coming down from the Father of lights, with whom there is no alteration or shadow caused by change.¹⁸He willed to give us birth by the word of truth that we may be a kind of firstfruits of his creatures.¹⁹Know this, my dear brothers: everyone should be quick to hear, slow to speak, slow to wrath,²⁰for the wrath of a man does not accomplish the righteousness of God.²¹Therefore, put away all filth and evil excess and humbly welcome the word that has been planted in you and is able to save your souls.²²Be doers of the word and not hearers only, deluding yourselves.²³For if anyone is a hearer of the word and not a doer, he is like a man who looks at his own face in a mirror.²⁴He sees himself, then goes off and promptly forgets what he looked like.²⁵But the one who peers into the perfect law of freedom and perseveres, and is not a hearer who forgets but a doer who acts, such a one shall be blessed in what he does.²⁶If anyone thinks he is religious and does not bridle his tongue but deceives his heart, his religion is vain.²⁷Religion that is pure and undefiled before God and the Father is this: to care for orphans and widows in their affliction and to keep oneself unstained by the world.

James Chapter 2

¹My brothers, show no partiality as you adhere to the faith in our glorious Lord Jesus Christ.²For if a man with gold rings on his fingers and in fine clothes comes into your assembly, and a poor person in shabby clothes also comes in,³and you pay attention to the one wearing the fine clothes and say, "Sit here, please," while you say to the poor one, "Stand there," or "Sit at my feet,"⁴have you not made distinctions among yourselves and become judges with evil designs?⁵Listen, my beloved brothers. Did not God choose those who are poor in the world to be rich in faith and heirs of the kingdom that he promised to those who love him?⁶But you dishonored the poor person. Are not the rich oppressing you? And do they themselves not haul you off to court?⁷Is it not they who blaspheme the noble name that was invoked over you?⁸However, if you fulfill the royal law according to the scripture, "You shall love your neighbor as yourself," you are doing well.⁹But if you show partiality, you commit sin, and are convicted by the law as transgressors.¹⁰For whoever keeps the whole law, but falls short in one particular, has become guilty in respect to all of it.¹¹For he who said, "You shall not commit adultery," also said, "You shall not kill." Even if you do not commit adultery but kill, you have become a transgressor of the law.¹²So speak and so act as people who will be judged by the law of freedom.¹³For the judgment is merciless to one who has not shown mercy; mercy triumphs over judgment.¹⁴What good is it, my brothers, if someone says he has faith but does not have works? Can that faith save him?¹⁵If a brother or sister has nothing to wear and has no food for the day,¹⁶and one of you says to them, "Go in peace, keep warm, and eat well," but you do not give them the necessities of the body, what good is it?¹⁷So also faith of itself, if it does not have works, is dead.¹⁸Indeed someone might say, "You have faith and I have works." Demonstrate your faith to me without works, and I will demonstrate my faith to you from my works.¹⁹You believe that God is one. You do well. Even the demons believe that and tremble.²⁰Do you want proof, you ignoramus, that faith without works is useless?²¹Was not Abraham our father justified by works when he offered his son Isaac upon the altar?²²You see that faith was active along with his works, and faith was completed by the works.²³Thus the scripture was fulfilled that says, "Abraham believed God, and it was credited to him as righteousness," and he was called "the friend of God."²⁴See how a person is justified by works and not by faith alone.²⁵And in the same way, was not Rahab the harlot also justified by works when she welcomed the messengers and sent them out by a different route?²⁶For just as a body without a spirit is dead, so also faith without works is dead.

James Chapter 3

¹Not many of you should become teachers, my brothers, for you realize that we will be judged more strictly,²for we all fall short in many respects. If anyone does not fall short in speech, he is a perfect man, able to bridle his whole body also.³If we put bits into the mouths of horses to make them obey us, we also guide their whole bodies.⁴It is the same with ships: even though they are so large and driven by fierce winds, they are steered by a very small rudder wherever the pilot's inclination wishes.⁵In the same way the tongue is a small member and yet has great pretensions. Consider how small a fire can set a huge forest ablaze.⁶The tongue is also a fire. It exists among our members as a world of malice, defiling the whole body and setting the entire course of our lives on fire, itself set on fire by Gehenna.⁷For every kind of beast and bird, of reptile and sea creature, can be tamed and has been tamed by the human species,⁸but no human being can tame the tongue. It is a restless evil, full of deadly poison.⁹With it we bless the Lord and Father, and with it we curse human beings who are made in the likeness of God.¹⁰From the same mouth come blessing and cursing. This need not be so, my brothers.¹¹Does a spring gush forth from the same opening both pure and brackish water?¹²Can a fig tree, my brothers, produce olives, or a grapevine figs? Neither can salt water yield fresh.¹³Who among you is wise and understanding? Let him show his works by a good life in the humility that comes from wisdom.¹⁴But if you have bitter jealousy and selfish ambition in your hearts, do not boast and be false to the truth.¹⁵Wisdom of this kind does not come down from above but is earthly, unspiritual, demonic.¹⁶For where jealousy and selfish ambition exist, there is disorder and every foul practice.¹⁷But the wisdom from above is first of all pure, then peaceable, gentle, compliant, full of mercy and good fruits, without inconstancy or insincerity.¹⁸And the fruit of righteousness is sown in peace for those who cultivate peace.

James Chapter 4

¹Where do the wars and where do the conflicts among you come from? Is it not from your passions that make war within your members?²You covet but do not possess. You kill and envy but you cannot obtain; you fight and wage war. You do not possess because you do not ask.³You ask but do not receive, because you ask wrongly, to spend it on your passions.⁴Adulterers! Do you not know that to be a lover of the world means enmity with God? Therefore, whoever wants to be a lover of the world makes himself an enemy of God.⁵Or do you suppose that the scripture speaks without meaning when it says, "The spirit that he has made to dwell in us tends toward jealousy"?⁶But he bestows a greater grace; therefore, it says: "God resists the proud, but gives grace to the humble."⁷So submit yourselves to God. Resist the devil, and he will flee from you.⁸Draw near to God, and he will draw near to you. Cleanse your hands, you sinners, and purify your hearts, you of two minds.⁹Begin to lament, to mourn, to weep. Let your laughter be turned into mourning and your joy into dejection.¹⁰Humble yourselves before the Lord and he will exalt you.¹¹Do not speak evil of one another, brothers. Whoever speaks evil of a brother or judges his brother speaks evil of the law and judges the law. If you judge the law, you are not a doer of the law but a judge.¹²There is one lawgiver and judge who is able to save or to destroy. Who then are you to judge your neighbor?¹³Come now, you who say, "Today or tomorrow we shall go into such and such a town, spend a year there doing business, and make a profit"—¹⁴you have no idea what your life will be like tomorrow. You are a puff of smoke that appears briefly and then disappears.¹⁵Instead you should say, "If the Lord wills it, we shall live to do this or that."¹⁶But now you are boasting in your arrogance. All such boasting is evil.¹⁷So for one who knows the right thing to do and does not do it, it is a sin.

James Chapter 5

¹Come now, you rich, weep and wail over your impending miseries. ²Your wealth has rotted away, your clothes have become moth-eaten, ³your gold and silver have corroded, and that corrosion will be a testimony against you; it will devour your flesh like a fire. You have stored up treasure for the last days. ⁴Behold, the wages you withheld from the workers who harvested your fields are crying aloud, and the cries of the harvesters have reached the ears of the Lord of hosts. ⁵You have lived on earth in luxury and pleasure; you have fattened your hearts for the day of slaughter. ⁶You have condemned; you have murdered the righteous one; he offers you no resistance. ⁷Be patient, therefore, brothers, until the coming of the Lord. See how the farmer waits for the precious fruit of the earth, being patient with it until it receives the early and the late rains. ⁸You too must be patient. Make your hearts firm, because the coming of the Lord is at hand. ⁹Do not complain, brothers, about one another, that you may not be judged. Behold, the Judge is standing before the gates. ¹⁰Take as an example of hardship and patience, brothers, the prophets who spoke in the name of the Lord. ¹¹Indeed we call blessed those who have persevered. You have heard of the perseverance of Job, and you have seen the purpose of the Lord, because "the Lord is compassionate and merciful." ¹²But above all, my brothers, do not swear, either by heaven or by earth or with any other oath, but let your "Yes" mean "Yes" and your "No" mean "No," that you may not incur condemnation. ¹³Is anyone among you suffering? He should pray. Is anyone in good spirits? He should sing praise. ¹⁴Is anyone among you sick? He should summon the presbyters of the church, and they should pray over him and anoint him with oil in

the name of the Lord, [15]and the prayer of faith will save the sick person, and the Lord will raise him up. If he has committed any sins, he will be forgiven. [16]Therefore, confess your sins to one another and pray for one another, that you may be healed. The fervent prayer of a righteous person is very powerful. [17]Elijah was a human being like us; yet he prayed earnestly that it might not rain, and for three years and six months it did not rain upon the land. [18]Then he prayed again, and the sky gave rain and the earth produced its fruit. [19]My brothers, if anyone among you should stray from the truth and someone bring him back, [20]he should know that whoever brings back a sinner from the error of his way will save his soul from death and will cover a multitude of sins.

I Peter

1 Peter Chapter 1

[1]Peter, an apostle of Jesus Christ, to the chosen sojourners of the dispersion in Pontus, Galatia, Cappadocia, Asia, and Bithynia, [2]in the foreknowledge of God the Father, through sanctification by the Spirit, for obedience and sprinkling with the blood of Jesus Christ: may grace and peace be yours in abundance. [3]Blessed be the God and Father of our Lord Jesus Christ, who in his great mercy gave us a new birth to a living hope through the resurrection of Jesus Christ from the dead, [4]to an inheritance that is imperishable, undefiled, and unfading, kept in heaven for you [5]who by the power of God are safeguarded through faith, to a salvation that is ready to be revealed in the final time. [6]In this you rejoice, although now for a little while you may have to suffer through various trials, [7]so that the genuineness of your faith, more precious than gold that is perishable even though tested by fire, may prove to be for praise, glory, and honor at the revelation of Jesus Christ. [8]Although you have not seen him you love him; even though you do not see him now yet believe in him, you rejoice with an indescribable and glorious joy, [9]as you attain the goal of your faith, the salvation of your souls. [10]Concerning this salvation, prophets who prophesied about the grace that was to be yours searched and investigated it, [11]investigating the time and circumstances that the Spirit of Christ within them indicated when it testified in advance to the sufferings destined for Christ and the glories to follow them. [12]It was revealed to them that they were serving not themselves but you with regard to the things that have now been announced to you by those who preached the good news to you through the Holy Spirit sent from heaven, things into which angels longed to look. [13]Therefore, gird up the loins of your mind, live soberly, and set your hopes completely on the grace to be brought to you at the revelation of Jesus Christ. [14]Like obedient children, do not act in compliance with the desires of your former ignorance [15]but, as he who called you is holy, be holy yourselves in every aspect of your conduct, [16]for it is written, "Be holy because I am holy." [17]Now if you invoke as Father him who judges impartially according to each one's works, conduct yourselves with reverence during the time of your sojourning, [18]realizing that you were ransomed from your futile conduct, handed on by your ancestors, not with perishable things like silver or gold [19]but with the precious blood of Christ as of a spotless unblemished lamb. [20]He was known before the foundation of the world but revealed in the final time for you, [21]who through him believe in God who raised him from the dead and gave him glory, so that your faith and hope are in God. [22]Since you have purified yourselves by obedience to the truth for sincere mutual love, love one another intensely from a pure heart. [23]You have been born anew, not from perishable but from imperishable seed, through the living and abiding word of God, [24]for: "All flesh is like grass, and all its glory like the flower of the field; the grass withers, and the flower wilts; [25]but the word of the Lord remains forever." This is the word that has been proclaimed to you.

1 Peter Chapter 2

[1]Rid yourselves of all malice and all deceit, insincerity, envy, and all slander; [2]like newborn infants, long for pure spiritual milk so that through it you may grow into salvation, [3]for you have tasted that the Lord is good. [4]Come to him, a living stone, rejected by human beings but chosen and precious in the sight of God, [5]and, like living stones, let yourselves be built into a spiritual house to be a holy priesthood to offer spiritual sacrifices acceptable to God through Jesus Christ. [6]For it says in scripture: "Behold, I am laying a stone in Zion, a cornerstone, chosen and precious, and whoever believes in it shall not be put to shame." [7]Therefore, its value is for you who have faith, but for those without faith: "The stone which the builders rejected has become the cornerstone," [8]and "A stone that will make people stumble, and a rock that will make them fall." They stumble by disobeying the word, as is their destiny. [9]But you are "a chosen race, a royal priesthood, a holy nation, a people of his own, so that you may announce the praises" of him who called you out of darkness into his wonderful light. [10]Once you

were "no people" but now you are God's people; you "had not received mercy" but now you have received mercy. [11]Beloved, I urge you as aliens and sojourners to keep away from worldly desires that wage war against the soul. [12]Maintain good conduct among the Gentiles, so that if they speak of you as evildoers, they may observe your good works and glorify God on the day of visitation. [13]Be subject to every human institution for the Lord's sake, whether it be to the king as supreme [14]or to governors as sent by him for the punishment of evildoers and the approval of those who do good. [15]For it is the will of God that by doing good you may silence the ignorance of foolish people. [16]Be free, yet without using freedom as a pretext for evil, but as slaves of God. [17]Give honor to all, love the community, fear God, honor the king. [18]Slaves, be subject to your masters with all reverence, not only to those who are good and equitable but also to those who are perverse. [19]For whenever anyone bears the pain of unjust suffering because of consciousness of God, that is a grace. [20]But what credit is there if you are patient when beaten for doing wrong? But if you are patient when you suffer for doing what is good, this is a grace before God. [21]For to this you have been called, because Christ also suffered for you, leaving you an example that you should follow in his footsteps. [22]"He committed no sin, and no deceit was found in his mouth." [23]When he was insulted, he returned no insult; when he suffered, he did not threaten; instead, he handed himself over to the one who judges justly. [24]He himself bore our sins in his body upon the cross, so that, free from sin, we might live for righteousness. By his wounds you have been healed. [25]For you had gone astray like sheep, but you have now returned to the shepherd and guardian of your souls.

1 Peter Chapter 3

[1]Likewise, you wives should be subordinate to your husbands so that, even if some disobey the word, they may be won over without a word by their wives' conduct [2]when they observe your reverent and chaste behavior. [3]Your adornment should not be an external one: braiding the hair, wearing gold jewelry, or dressing in fine clothes, [4]but rather the hidden character of the heart, expressed in the imperishable beauty of a gentle and calm disposition, which is precious in the sight of God. [5]For this is also how the holy women who hoped in God once used to adorn themselves and were subordinate to their husbands; [6]thus Sarah obeyed Abraham, calling him "lord." You are her children when you do what is good and fear no intimidation. [7]Likewise, you husbands should live with your wives in understanding, showing honor to the weaker female sex, since we are joint heirs of the gift of life, so that your prayers may not be hindered. [8]Finally, all of you, be of one mind, sympathetic, loving toward one another, compassionate, humble; [9]do not return evil for evil, or insult for insult; but, on the contrary, a blessing, because to this you were called, that you might inherit a blessing. [10]For: "Whoever would love life and see good days must keep the tongue from evil and the lips from speaking deceit, [11]must turn from evil and do good, seek peace and follow after it. [12]For the eyes of the Lord are on the righteous and his ears turned to their prayer, but the face of the Lord is against evildoers." [13]Now who is going to harm you if you are enthusiastic for what is good? [14]But even if you should suffer because of righteousness, blessed are you. Do not be afraid or terrified with fear of them, [15]but sanctify Christ as Lord in your hearts. Always be ready to give an explanation to anyone who asks you for a reason for your hope, [16]but do it with gentleness and reverence, keeping your conscience clear, so that, when you are maligned, those who defame your good conduct in Christ may themselves be put to shame. [17]For it is better to suffer for doing good, if that be the will of God, than for doing evil. [18]For Christ also suffered for sins once, the righteous for the sake of the unrighteous, that he might lead you to God. Put to death in the flesh, he was brought to life in the spirit. [19]In it he also went to preach to the spirits in prison, [20]who had once been disobedient while God patiently waited in the days of Noah during the building of the ark, in which a few persons, eight in all, were saved through water. [21]This prefigured baptism, which saves you now. It is not a removal of dirt from the body but an appeal to God for a clear conscience, through the resurrection of Jesus Christ, [22]who has gone into heaven and is at the right hand of God, with angels, authorities, and powers subject to him.

1 Peter Chapter 4

[1]Therefore, since Christ suffered in the flesh, arm yourselves also with the same attitude (for whoever suffers in the flesh has broken with sin), [2]so as not to spend what remains of one's life in the flesh on human desires, but on the will of God. [3]For the time that has passed is sufficient for doing what the Gentiles like to do: living in debauchery, evil desires, drunkenness, orgies, carousing, and wanton idolatry. [4]They are surprised that you do not plunge into the same swamp of profligacy, and they vilify you; [5]but they will give an account to him who stands

ready to judge the living and the dead. ⁶For this is why the gospel was preached even to the dead that, though condemned in the flesh in human estimation, they might live in the spirit in the estimation of God. ⁷The end of all things is at hand. Therefore, be serious and sober for prayers. ⁸Above all, let your love for one another be intense, because love covers a multitude of sins. ⁹Be hospitable to one another without complaining. ¹⁰As each one has received a gift, use it to serve one another as good stewards of God's varied grace. ¹¹Whoever preaches, let it be with the words of God; whoever serves, let it be with the strength that God supplies, so that in all things God may be glorified through Jesus Christ, to whom belong glory and dominion forever and ever. Amen. ¹²Beloved, do not be surprised that a trial by fire is occurring among you, as if something strange were happening to you. ¹³But rejoice to the extent that you share in the sufferings of Christ, so that when his glory is revealed you may also rejoice exultantly. ¹⁴If you are insulted for the name of Christ, blessed are you, for the Spirit of glory and of God rests upon you. ¹⁵But let no one among you be made to suffer as a murderer, a thief, an evildoer, or as an intriguer. ¹⁶But whoever is made to suffer as a Christian should not be ashamed but glorify God because of the name. ¹⁷For it is time for the judgment to begin with the household of God; if it begins with us, how will it end for those who fail to obey the gospel of God? ¹⁸"And if the righteous one is barely saved, where will the godless and the sinner appear?" ¹⁹As a result, those who suffer in accord with God's will hand their souls over to a faithful creator as they do good.

1 Peter Chapter 5

¹So I exhort the presbyters among you, as a fellow presbyter and witness to the sufferings of Christ and one who has a share in the glory to be revealed. ²Tend the flock of God in your midst, overseeing not by constraint but willingly, as God would have it, not for shameful profit but eagerly. ³Do not lord it over those assigned to you, but be examples to the flock. ⁴And when the chief Shepherd is revealed, you will receive the unfading crown of glory. ⁵Likewise, you younger members, be subject to the presbyters. And all of you, clothe yourselves with humility in your dealings with one another, for: "God opposes the proud but bestows favor on the humble." ⁶So humble yourselves under the mighty hand of God, that he may exalt you in due time. ⁷Cast all your worries upon him because he cares for you. ⁸Be sober and vigilant. Your opponent the devil is prowling around like a roaring lion looking for someone to devour. ⁹Resist him, steadfast in faith, knowing that your fellow believers throughout the world undergo the same sufferings. ¹⁰The God of all grace who called you to his eternal glory through Christ Jesus will himself restore, confirm, strengthen, and establish you after you have suffered a little. ¹¹To him be dominion forever. Amen. ¹²I write you this briefly through Silvanus, whom I consider a faithful brother, exhorting you and testifying that this is the true grace of God. Remain firm in it. ¹³The chosen one at Babylon sends you greeting, as does Mark, my son. ¹⁴Greet one another with a loving kiss. Peace to all of you who are in Christ.

II Peter

2 PeterChapter 1

¹Symeon Peter, a slave and apostle of Jesus Christ, to those who have received a faith of equal value to ours through the righteousness of our God and savior Jesus Christ: ²may grace and peace be yours in abundance through knowledge of God and of Jesus our Lord. ³His divine power has bestowed on us everything that makes for life and devotion, through the knowledge of him who called us by his own glory and power. ⁴Through these, he has bestowed on us the precious and very great promises, so that through them you may come to share in the divine nature, after escaping from the corruption that is in the world because of evil desire. ⁵For this very reason, make every effort to supplement your faith with virtue, virtue with knowledge, ⁶knowledge with self-control, self-control with endurance, endurance with devotion, ⁷devotion with mutual affection, mutual affection with love. ⁸If these are yours and increase in abundance, they will keep you from being idle or unfruitful in the knowledge of our Lord Jesus Christ. ⁹Anyone who lacks them is blind and shortsighted, forgetful of the cleansing of his past sins. ¹⁰Therefore, brothers, be all the more eager to make your call and election firm, for, in doing so, you will never stumble. ¹¹For, in this way, entry into the eternal kingdom of our Lord and savior Jesus Christ will be richly provided for you. ¹²Therefore, I will always remind you of these things, even though you already know them and are established in the truth you have. ¹³I think it right, as long as I am in this "tent," to stir you up by a reminder, ¹⁴since I know that I will soon have to put it aside, as indeed our Lord Jesus Christ has shown me. ¹⁵I shall also make every effort to enable you always to remember these things after my departure. ¹⁶We did not follow cleverly devised myths when we made known to you the power and coming of our Lord Jesus Christ, but we had been eyewitnesses of his majesty. ¹⁷For he received honor and glory from God the Father when that unique declaration came to him from the majestic glory, "This is my Son, my beloved, with whom I am well pleased." ¹⁸We ourselves heard this voice come from heaven while we were with him on the holy mountain. ¹⁹Moreover, we possess the prophetic message that is altogether reliable. You will do well to be attentive to it, as to a lamp shining in a dark place, until day dawns and the morning star rises in your hearts. ²⁰Know this first of all, that there is no prophecy of scripture that is a matter of personal interpretation, ²¹for no prophecy ever came through human will; but rather human beings moved by the holy Spirit spoke under the influence of God.

2 PeterChapter 2

¹There were also false prophets among the people, just as there will be false teachers among you, who will introduce destructive heresies and even deny the Master who ransomed them, bringing swift destruction on themselves. ²Many will follow their licentious ways, and because of them the way of truth will be reviled. ³In their greed they will exploit you with fabrications, but from of old their condemnation has not been idle and their destruction does not sleep. ⁴For if God did not spare the angels when they sinned, but condemned them to the chains of Tartarus and handed them over to be kept for judgment; ⁵and if he did not spare the ancient world, even though he preserved Noah, a herald of righteousness, together with seven others, when he brought a flood upon the godless world; ⁶and if he condemned the cities of Sodom and Gomorrah (to destruction), reducing them to ashes, making them an example for the godless (people) of what is coming; ⁷and if he rescued Lot, a righteous man oppressed by the licentious conduct of unprincipled people ⁸(for day after day that righteous man living among them was tormented in his righteous soul at the lawless deeds that he saw and heard), ⁹then the Lord knows how to rescue the devout from trial and to keep the unrighteous under punishment for the day of judgment, ¹⁰and especially those who follow the flesh with its depraved desire and show contempt for lordship. Bold and arrogant, they are not afraid to revile glorious beings, ¹¹whereas angels, despite their superior strength and power, do not bring a reviling judgment against them from the Lord. ¹²But these people, like irrational animals born by nature for capture and destruction, revile things that they do not understand, and in their destruction they will also be destroyed, ¹³suffering wrong as payment for wrongdoing. Thinking daytime revelry a delight, they are stains and defilements as they revel in their deceits while carousing with you. ¹⁴Their eyes are full of adultery and insatiable for sin. They seduce unstable people, and their hearts are trained in greed. Accursed children! ¹⁵Abandoning the straight road, they have gone astray, following the road of Balaam, the son of Bosor, who loved payment for wrongdoing, ¹⁶but he received a rebuke for his own crime: a mute beast spoke with a human voice and restrained the prophet's madness. ¹⁷These people are waterless springs and mists driven by a gale; for them the gloom of darkness has been reserved. ¹⁸For, talking empty bombast, they seduce with licentious desires of the flesh those who have barely escaped from people who live in error. ¹⁹They promise them freedom, though they themselves are slaves of corruption, for a person is a slave of whatever overcomes him. ²⁰For if they, having escaped the defilements of the world through the knowledge of (our) Lord and savior Jesus Christ, again become entangled and overcome by them, their last condition is worse than their first. ²¹For it would have been better for them not to have known the way of righteousness than after knowing it to turn back from the holy commandment handed down to them. ²²What is expressed in the true proverb has happened to them, "The dog returns to its own vomit," and "A bathed sow returns to wallowing in the mire."

2 PeterChapter 3

¹This is now, beloved, the second letter I am writing to you; through them by way of reminder I am trying to stir up your sincere disposition, ²to recall the words previously spoken by the holy prophets and the commandment of the Lord and savior through your apostles. ³Know this first of all, that in the last days scoffers will come (to) scoff, living according to their own desires ⁴and saying, "Where is the promise of his coming? From the time when our ancestors fell asleep, everything has remained as it was from the beginning of creation." ⁵They deliberately ignore the fact that the heavens existed of old and earth was formed out of water and through water by the word of God; ⁶through these the world that then existed was destroyed, deluged with water. ⁷The present heavens and earth have been reserved by the same word for fire, kept for the day of judgment and of destruction of the godless.

8But do not ignore this one fact, beloved, that with the Lord one day is like a thousand years and a thousand years like one day. 9The Lord does not delay his promise, as some regard "delay," but he is patient with you, not wishing that any should perish but that all should come to repentance. 10But the day of the Lord will come like a thief, and then the heavens will pass away with a mighty roar and the elements will be dissolved by fire, and the earth and everything done on it will be found out. 11Since everything is to be dissolved in this way, what sort of persons ought (you) to be, conducting yourselves in holiness and devotion, 12waiting for and hastening the coming of the day of God, because of which the heavens will be dissolved in flames and the elements melted by fire. 13But according to his promise we await new heavens and a new earth in which righteousness dwells. 14Therefore, beloved, since you await these things, be eager to be found without spot or blemish before him, at peace. 15And consider the patience of our Lord as salvation, as our beloved brother Paul, according to the wisdom given to him, also wrote to you, 16speaking of these things as he does in all his letters. In them there are some things hard to understand that the ignorant and unstable distort to their own destruction, just as they do the other scriptures. 17Therefore, beloved, since you are forewarned, be on your guard not to be led into the error of the unprincipled and to fall from your own stability. 18But grow in grace and in the knowledge of our Lord and savior Jesus Christ. To him be glory now and to the day of eternity. (Amen.).

I John

1 John Chapter 1

1What was from the beginning, what we have heard, what we have seen with our eyes, what we looked upon and touched with our hands concerns the Word of life—2for the life was made visible; we have seen it and testify to it and proclaim to you the eternal life that was with the Father and was made visible to us—3what we have seen and heard we proclaim now to you, so that you too may have fellowship with us; for our fellowship is with the Father and with his Son, Jesus Christ. 4We are writing this so that our joy may be complete. 5Now this is the message that we have heard from him and proclaim to you: God is light, and in him there is no darkness at all. 6If we say, "We have fellowship with him," while we continue to walk in darkness, we lie and do not act in truth. 7But if we walk in the light as he is in the light, then we have fellowship with one another, and the blood of his Son Jesus cleanses us from all sin. 8If we say, "We are without sin," we deceive ourselves, and the truth is not in us. 9If we acknowledge our sins, he is faithful and just and will forgive our sins and cleanse us from every wrongdoing. 10If we say, "We have not sinned," we make him a liar, and his word is not in us.

1 John Chapter 2

1My children, I am writing this to you so that you may not commit sin. But if anyone does sin, we have an Advocate with the Father, Jesus Christ the righteous one. 2He is expiation for our sins, and not for our sins only but for those of the whole world. 3The way we may be sure that we know him is to keep his commandments. 4Whoever says, "I know him," but does not keep his commandments is a liar, and the truth is not in him. 5But whoever keeps his word, the love of God is truly perfected in him. This is the way we may know that we are in union with him: 6whoever claims to abide in him ought to live (just) as he lived. 7Beloved, I am writing no new commandment to you but an old commandment that you had from the beginning. The old commandment is the word that you have heard. 8And yet I do write a new commandment to you, which holds true in him and among you, for the darkness is passing away, and the true light is already shining. 9Whoever says he is in the light, yet hates his brother, is still in the darkness. 10Whoever loves his brother remains in the light, and there is nothing in him to cause a fall. 11Whoever hates his brother is in darkness; he walks in darkness and does not know where he is going because the darkness has blinded his eyes. 12I am writing to you, children, because your sins have been forgiven for his name's sake. 13I am writing to you, fathers, because you know him who is from the beginning. I am writing to you, young men, because you have conquered the evil one. 14I write to you, children, because you know the Father. I write to you, fathers, because you know him who is from the beginning. I write to you, young men, because you are strong and the word of God remains in you, and you have conquered the evil one. 15Do not love the world or the things of the world. If anyone loves the world, the love of the Father is not in him. 16For all that is in the world, sensual lust, enticement for the eyes, and a pretentious life, is not from the Father but is from the world. 17Yet the world and its enticement are passing away. But whoever does the will of God remains forever.

18Children, it is the last hour; and just as you heard that the antichrist was coming, so now many antichrists have appeared. Thus we know this is the last hour. 19They went out from us, but they were not really of our number; if they had been, they would have remained with us. Their desertion shows that none of them was of our number. 20But you have the anointing that comes from the holy one, and you all have knowledge. 21I write to you not because you do not know the truth but because you do, and because every lie is alien to the truth. 22Who is the liar? Whoever denies that Jesus is the Christ. Whoever denies the Father and the Son, this is the antichrist. 23No one who denies the Son has the Father, but whoever confesses the Son has the Father as well. 24Let what you heard from the beginning remain in you. If what you heard from the beginning remains in you, then you will remain in the Son and in the Father. 25And this is the promise that he made us: eternal life. 26I write you these things about those who would deceive you. 27As for you, the anointing that you received from him remains in you, so that you do not need anyone to teach you. But his anointing teaches you about everything and is true and not false; just as it taught you, remain in him. 28And now, children, remain in him, so that when he appears we may have confidence and not be put to shame by him at his coming. 29If you consider that he is righteous, you also know that everyone who acts in righteousness is begotten by him.

1 John Chapter 3

1See what love the Father has bestowed on us that we may be called the children of God. Yet so we are. The reason the world does not know us is that it did not know him. 2Beloved, we are God's children now; what we shall be has not yet been revealed. We do know that when it is revealed we shall be like him, for we shall see him as he is. 3Everyone who has this hope based on him makes himself pure, as he is pure. 4Everyone who commits sin commits lawlessness, for sin is lawlessness. 5You know that he was revealed to take away sins, and in him there is no sin. 6No one who remains in him sins; no one who sins has seen him or known him. 7Children, let no one deceive you. The person who acts in righteousness is righteous, just as he is righteous. 8Whoever sins belongs to the devil, because the devil has sinned from the beginning. Indeed, the Son of God was revealed to destroy the works of the devil. 9No one who is begotten by God commits sin, because God's seed remains in him; he cannot sin because he is begotten by God. 10In this way, the children of God and the children of the devil are made plain; no one who fails to act in righteousness belongs to God, nor anyone who does not love his brother. 11For this is the message you have heard from the beginning: we should love one another, 12unlike Cain who belonged to the evil one and slaughtered his brother. Why did he slaughter him? Because his own works were evil, and those of his brother righteous. 13Do not be amazed, (then,) brothers, if the world hates you. 14We know that we have passed from death to life because we love our brothers. Whoever does not love remains in death. 15Everyone who hates his brother is a murderer, and you know that no murderer has eternal life remaining in him. 16The way we came to know love was that he laid down his life for us; so we ought to lay down our lives for our brothers. 17If someone who has worldly means sees a brother in need and refuses him compassion, how can the love of God remain in him? 18Children, let us love not in word or speech but in deed and truth. 19(Now) this is how we shall know that we belong to the truth and reassure our hearts before him 20in whatever our hearts condemn, for God is greater than our hearts and knows everything. 21Beloved, if (our) hearts do not condemn us, we have confidence in God 22and receive from him whatever we ask, because we keep his commandments and do what pleases him. 23And his commandment is this: we should believe in the name of his Son, Jesus Christ, and love one another just as he commanded us. 24Those who keep his commandments remain in him, and he in them, and the way we know that he remains in us is from the Spirit that he gave us.

1 John Chapter 4

1Beloved, do not trust every spirit but test the spirits to see whether they belong to God, because many false prophets have gone out into the world. 2This is how you can know the Spirit of God: every spirit that acknowledges Jesus Christ come in the flesh belongs to God, 3and every spirit that does not acknowledge Jesus does not belong to God. This is the spirit of the antichrist that, as you heard, is to come, but in fact is already in the world. 4You belong to God, children, and you have conquered them, for the one who is in you is greater than the one who is in the world. 5They belong to the world; accordingly, their teaching belongs to the world, and the world listens to them. 6We belong to God, and anyone who knows God listens to us, while anyone who does not belong to God refuses to hear us. This is how we know the spirit of truth and the spirit of deceit. 7Beloved, let us love one another, because love is of God; everyone who loves is begotten by God and knows God. [8]Whoever is without love does not know God, for God is love. [9]In this way the love of God was revealed to us: God sent his only Son into the world so that we might have life through him. [10]In this is love: not that we have loved God, but that he loved us and sent his Son as expiation for our sins. [11]Beloved, if God so loved us, we also must love one another. [12]No one has ever seen God. Yet, if we love one another, God remains in us, and his love is brought to perfection in us. [13]This is how we know that we remain in him and he in us, that he has given us of his Spirit. [14]Moreover, we have seen and testify that the Father sent his Son as savior of the world. [15]Whoever acknowledges that Jesus is the Son of God, God remains in him and he in God. [16]We have come to know and to believe in the love God has for us. God is love, and whoever remains in love remains in God and God in him. [17]In this is love brought to perfection among us, that we have confidence on the day of judgment because as he is, so are we in this world. [18]There is no fear in love, but perfect love drives out fear because fear has to do with punishment, and so one who fears is not yet perfect in love. [19]We love because he first loved us. [20]If anyone says, "I love God," but hates his brother, he is a liar; for whoever does not love a brother whom he has seen cannot love God whom he has not seen. [21]This is the commandment we have from him: whoever loves God must also love his brother.

1 John Chapter 5

[1]Everyone who believes that Jesus is the Christ is begotten by God, and everyone who loves the father loves also the one begotten by him. [2]In this way we know that we love the children of God when we love God and obey his commandments. [3]For the love of God is this, that we keep his commandments. And his commandments are not burdensome, [4]for whoever is begotten by God conquers the world. And the victory that conquers the world is our faith. [5]Who indeed is the victor over the world but the one who believes that Jesus is the Son of God? [6]This is the one who came through water and blood, Jesus Christ, not by water alone, but by water and blood. The Spirit is the one that testifies, and the Spirit is truth. [7]So there are three that testify, [8]the Spirit, the water, and the blood, and the three are of one accord. [9]If we accept human testimony, the testimony of God is surely greater. Now the testimony of God is this, that he has testified on behalf of his Son. [10]Whoever believes in the Son of God has this testimony within himself. Whoever does not believe God has made him a liar by not believing the testimony God has given about his Son. [11]And this is the testimony: God gave us eternal life, and this life is in his Son. [12]Whoever possesses the Son has life; whoever does not possess the Son of God does not have life. [13]I write these things to you so that you may know that you have eternal life, you who believe in the name of the Son of God. [14]And we have this confidence in him, that if we ask anything according to his will, he hears us. [15]And if we know that he hears us in regard to whatever we ask, we know that what we have asked him for is ours. [16]If anyone sees his brother sinning, if the sin is not deadly, he should pray to God and he will give him life. This is only for those whose sin is not deadly. There is such a thing as deadly sin, about which I do not say that you should pray. [17]All wrongdoing is sin, but there is sin that is not deadly. [18]We know that no one begotten by God sins; but the one begotten by God he protects, and the evil one cannot touch him. [19]We know that we belong to God, and the whole world is under the power of the evil one. [20]We also know that the Son of God has come and has given us discernment to know the one who is true. And we are in the one who is true, in his Son Jesus Christ. He is the true God and eternal life. [21]Children, be on your guard against idols.

II John

2 John Chapter 1

[1]The Presbyter to the chosen Lady and to her children whom I love in truth—and not only I but also all who know the truth—[2]because of the truth that dwells in us and will be with us forever. [3]Grace, mercy, and peace will be with us from God the Father and from Jesus Christ the Father's Son in truth and love. [4]I rejoiced greatly to find some of your children walking in the truth just as we were commanded by the Father. [5]But now, Lady, I ask you, not as though I were writing a new commandment but the one we have had from the beginning: let us love one another. [6]For this is love, that we walk according to his commandments; this is the commandment, as you heard from the beginning, in which you should walk. [7]Many deceivers have gone out into the world, those who do not acknowledge Jesus Christ as coming in the flesh; such is the deceitful one and the antichrist. [8]Look to yourselves that you do not lose what we worked for but may receive a full recompense. [9]Anyone who is so "progressive" as not to remain in the teaching of the Christ does not have God; whoever remains in the teaching has the Father and the Son. [10]If anyone comes to you and does not bring this doctrine, do not receive him in your house or even greet him; [11]for whoever greets him shares in his evil works. [12]Although I have much to write to you, I do not intend to use paper and ink. Instead, I hope to visit you and to speak face to face so that our joy may be complete. [13]The children of your chosen sister send you greetings.

III John

3 John Chapter 1

[1]The Presbyter to the beloved Gaius whom I love in truth. [2]Beloved, I hope you are prospering in every respect and are in good health, just as your soul is prospering. [3]I rejoiced greatly when some of the brothers came and testified to how truly you walk in the truth. [4]Nothing gives me greater joy than to hear that my children are walking in the truth. [5]Beloved, you are faithful in all you do for the brothers, especially for strangers; [6]they have testified to your love before the church. Please help them in a way worthy of God to continue their journey. [7]For they have set out for the sake of the Name and are accepting nothing from the pagans. [8]Therefore, we ought to support such persons, so that we may be co-workers in the truth. [9]I wrote to the church, but Diotrephes, who loves to dominate, does not acknowledge us. [10]Therefore, if I come, I will draw attention to what he is doing, spreading evil nonsense about us. And not content with that, he will not receive the brothers, hindering those who wish to do so and expelling them from the church. [11]Beloved, do not imitate evil but imitate good. Whoever does what is good is of God; whoever does what is evil has never seen God. [12]Demetrius receives a good report from all, even from the truth itself. We give our testimonial as well, and you know our testimony is true. [13]I have much to write to you, but I do not wish to write with pen and ink. [14]Instead, I hope to see you soon, when we can talk face to face. [15]Peace be with you. The friends greet you; greet the friends there each by name.

Jude

Jude Chapter 1

[1]Jude, a slave of Jesus Christ and brother of James, to those who are called, beloved in God the Father and kept safe for Jesus Christ: [2]may mercy, peace, and love be yours in abundance. [3]Beloved, although I was making every effort to write to you about our common salvation, I now feel a need to write to encourage you to contend for the faith that was once for all handed down to the holy ones. [4]For there have been some intruders, who long ago were designated for this condemnation, godless persons, who pervert the grace of our God into licentiousness and who deny our only Master and Lord, Jesus Christ. [5]I wish to remind you, although you know all things, that (the) Lord who once saved a people from the land of Egypt later destroyed those who did not believe. [6]The angels too, who did not keep to their own domain but deserted their proper dwelling, he has kept in eternal chains, in gloom, for the judgment of the great day. [7]Likewise, Sodom, Gomorrah, and the surrounding towns, which, in the same manner as they, indulged in sexual promiscuity and practiced unnatural vice, serve as an example by undergoing a punishment of eternal fire. [8]Similarly, these dreamers nevertheless also defile the flesh, scorn lordship, and revile glorious beings. [9]Yet the archangel Michael, when he argued with the devil in a dispute over the body of Moses, did not venture to pronounce a reviling judgment upon him but said, "May the Lord rebuke you!" [10]But these people revile what they do not understand and are destroyed by what they know by nature like irrational animals. [11]Woe to them! They followed the way of Cain, abandoned themselves to Balaam's error for the sake of gain, and perished in the rebellion of Korah. [12]These are blemishes on your love feasts, as they carouse fearlessly and look after themselves. They are waterless clouds blown about by winds, fruitless trees in late autumn, twice dead and uprooted. [13]They are like wild waves of the sea, foaming up their shameless deeds, wandering stars for whom the gloom of darkness has been reserved forever. [14]Enoch, of the seventh generation from Adam, prophesied also about them when he said, "Behold, the Lord has come with his countless holy ones [15]to execute judgment on all and to convict everyone for all the godless deeds that they committed and for all the harsh words godless sinners have uttered against him." [16]These people are complainers, disgruntled ones who live by their desires; their mouths utter bombast as they fawn over people to gain advantage. [17]But you, beloved, remember the words spoken beforehand by the apostles of our Lord Jesus Christ, [18]for they told you, "In (the) last time there will be scoffers who will live according to their own godless desires." [19]These are the ones who cause divisions; they live on the natural plane, devoid of the Spirit. [20]But you, beloved, build yourselves up in your most holy faith; pray in the holy Spirit.

²¹Keep yourselves in the love of God and wait for the mercy of our Lord Jesus Christ that leads to eternal life. ²²On those who waver, have mercy; ²³save others by snatching them out of the fire; on others have mercy with fear, abhorring even the outer garment stained by the flesh. ²⁴To the one who is able to keep you from stumbling and to present you unblemished and exultant, in the presence of his glory, ²⁵to the only God, our savior, through Jesus Christ our Lord be glory, majesty, power, and authority from ages past, now, and for ages to come. Amen.

Clement I

Clement I Chapter 1

¹By reason of the sudden and repeated calamities and reverses which are befalling us, brethren, we consider that we have been somewhat tardy in giving heed to the matters of dispute that have arisen among you, dearly beloved, and to the detestable and unholy sedition, so alien and strange to the elect of God, which a few headstrong and self-willed persons have kindled to such a pitch of madness that your name, once revered and renowned and lovely in the sight of all men, hath been greatly reviled. ²For who that had sojourned among you did not approve your most virtuous and steadfast faith? Who did not admire your sober and forbearing piety in Christ? Who did not publish abroad your magnificent disposition of hospitality? Who did not congratulate you on your perfect and sound knowledge? ³For ye did all things without respect of persons, and ye walked after the ordinances of God, submitting yourselves to your rulers and rendering to the older men among you the honor which is their due. On the young too ye enjoined modest and seemly thoughts; and the women ye charged to perform all their duties in a blameless and seemly and pure conscience, cherishing their own husbands, as is meet; and ye taught them to keep in the rule of obedience, and to manage the affairs of their household in seemliness, with all discretion.

Clement I Chapter 2

¹And ye were all lowly in mind and free from arrogance, yielding rather than claiming submission, more glad to give than to receive, and content with the provisions which God supplieth. And giving heed unto His words, ye laid them up diligently in your hearts, and His sufferings were before your eyes. ²Thus a profound and rich peace was given to all, and an insatiable desire of doing good. An abundant outpouring also of the Holy Spirit fell upon all; ³and, being full of holy counsel, in excellent zeal and with a pious confidence ye stretched out your hands to Almighty God, supplicating Him to be propitious, if unwillingly ye had committed any sin. ⁴Ye had conflict day and night for all the brotherhood, that the number of His elect might be saved with fearfulness and intentness of mind. ⁵Ye were sincere and simple and free from malice one towards another. ⁶Every sedition and every schism was abominable to you. Ye mourned over the transgressions of your neighbors: ye judged their shortcomings to be your own. ⁷Ye repented not of any well-doing, but were ready unto every good work. ⁸Being adorned with a most virtuous and honorable life, ye performed all your duties in the fear of Him. The commandments and the ordinances of the Lord were written on the tablets of your hearts.

Clement I Chapter 3

¹All glory and enlargement was given unto you, and that was fulfilled which is written My beloved ate and drank and was enlarged and waxed fat and kicked. ²Hence come jealousy and envy, strife and sedition, persecution and tumult, war and captivity. ³So men were stirred up, the mean against the honorable, the ill reputed against the highly reputed, the foolish against the wise, the young against the elder. ⁴For this cause righteousness and peace stand aloof, while each man hath forsaken the fear of the Lord and become purblind in the faith of Him, neither walketh in the ordinances of His commandments nor liveth according to that which becometh Christ, but each goeth after the lusts of his evil heart, seeing that they have conceived an unrighteous and ungodly jealousy, through which also death entered into the world.

Clement I Chapter 4

¹For so it is written, And it came to pass after certain days that Cain brought of the fruits of the earth a sacrifice unto God, and Abel he also brought of the firstlings of the sheep and of their fatness. ²And God looked upon Abel and upon his gifts, but unto Cain and unto his sacrifices He gave no heed. ³And Cain sorrowed exceedingly, and his countenance fell. ⁴And God said unto Cain, Wherefore art thou very sorrowful and wherefore did thy countenance fall? If thou hast offered aright and hast not divided aright, didst thou not sin? Hold thy peace. ⁵Unto thee shall he turn, and thou shalt rule over him. {This last phrase has also been translated: Be at peace: thine offering returns to thyself, and thou shalt again possess it.} ⁶And Cain said unto Abel his brother,

Let us go over unto the plain. And it came to pass, while they were in the plain, that Cain rose up against Abel his brother and slew him. ⁷Ye see, brethren, jealousy and envy wrought a brother's murder. ⁸By reason of jealousy our father Jacob ran away from the face of Esau his brother. ⁹Jealousy caused Joseph to be persecuted even unto death, and to come even unto bondage. ¹⁰Jealousy compelled Moses to flee from the face of Pharaoh king of Egypt while it was said to him by his own countryman, Who made thee a judge or a decider over us, Wouldest thou slay me, even as yesterday thou slewest the Egyptian? ¹¹By reason of jealousy Aaron and Miriam were lodged outside the camp. ¹²Jealousy brought Dathan and Abiram down alive to hades, because they made sedition against Moses the servant of God. ¹³By reason of jealousy David was envied not only by the Philistines, but was persecuted also by Saul [king of Israel].

Clement I Chapter 5

¹But, to pass from the examples of ancient days, let us come to those champions who lived nearest to our time. Let us set before us the noble examples which belong to our generation. ²By reason of jealousy and envy the greatest and most righteous pillars of the Church were persecuted, and contended even unto death. ³Let us set before our eyes the good Apostles. ⁴There was Peter who by reason of unrighteous jealousy endured not one not one but many labors, and thus having borne his testimony went to his appointed place of glory. ⁵By reason of jealousy and strife Paul by his example pointed out the prize of patient endurance. After that he had been seven times in bonds, had been driven into exile, had been stoned, had preached in the East and in the West, he won the noble renown which was the reward of his faith, ⁶having taught righteousness unto the whole world and having reached the farthest bounds of the West; and when he had borne his testimony before the rulers, so he departed from the world and went unto the holy place, having been found a notable pattern of patient endurance.

Clement I Chapter 6

¹Unto these men of holy lives was gathered a vast multitude of the elect, who through many indignities and tortures, being the victims of jealousy, set a brave example among ourselves. ²By reason of jealousy women being persecuted, after that they had suffered cruel and unholy insults as Danaids and Dircae, safely reached the goal in the race of faith, and received a noble reward, feeble though they were in body. ³Jealousy hath estranged wives from their husbands and changed the saying of our father Adam, This now is bone of my bones and flesh of my flesh. ⁴Jealousy and strife have overthrown great cities and uprooted great nations.

Clement I Chapter 7

¹These things, dearly beloved, we write, not only as admonishing you, but also as putting ourselves in remembrance. For we are in the same lists, and the same contest awaiteth us. ²Wherefore let us forsake idle and vain thoughts; and let us conform to the glorious and venerable rule which hath been handed down to us; ³and let us see what is good and what is pleasant and what is acceptable in the sight of Him that made us. ⁴Let us fix our eyes on the blood of Christ and understand how precious it is unto His Father, because being shed for our salvation it won for the whole world the grace of repentance. ⁵Let us review all the generations in turn, and learn how from generation to generation the Master hath given a place for repentance unto them that desire to turn to Him. ⁶Noah preached repentance, and they that obeyed were saved. ⁷Jonah preached destruction unto the men of Nineveh; but they, repenting of their sins, obtained pardon of God by their supplications and received salvation, albeit they were aliens from God.

Clement I Chapter 8

¹The ministers of the grace of God through the Holy Spirit spake concerning repentance. ²Yea and the Master of the universe Himself spake concerning repentance with an oath: ³for, as I live saith the Lord, I desire not the death of the sinner, so much as his repentance, ⁴and He added also a merciful judgment: Repent ye, O house of Israel, of your iniquity; say unto the sons of My people, Though your sins reach from the earth even unto the heaven, and though they be redder than scarlet and blacker than sackcloth, and ye turn unto Me with your whole heart and say Father, I will give ear unto you as unto a holy people. ⁵And in another place He saith on this wise, Wash, be ye clean. Put away your iniquities from your souls out of My sight. Cease from your iniquities; learn to do good; seek out judgment; defend him that is wronged: give judgment for the orphan, and execute righteousness for the widow; and come and let us reason together, saith He; and though your sins be as crimson, I will make them white as snow; and though they be as scarlet, I will make them white as wool. And if ye be willing and will hearken unto Me, ye shall eat the good things of the earth; but if ye be not willing, neither hearken unto Me, a sword shall devour you; for the mouth of

the Lord hath spoken these things. 6Seeing then that He desireth all His beloved to be partakers of repentance, He confirmed it by an act of His almighty will.

Clement I Chapter 9

1Wherefore let us be obedient unto His excellent and glorious will; and presenting ourselves as suppliants of His mercy and goodness, let us fall down before Him and betake ourselves unto His compassions, forsaking the vain toil and the strife and the jealousy which leadeth unto death. 2Let us fix our eyes on them that ministered perfectly unto His excellent glory. 3Let us set before us Enoch, who being found righteous in obedience was translated, and his death was not found. 4Noah, being found faithful, by his ministration preached regeneration unto the world, and through him the Master saved the living creatures that entered into the ark in concord.

Clement I Chapter 10

1Abraham, who was called the 'friend,' was found faithful in that he rendered obedience unto the words of God. 2He through obedience went forth from his land and from his kindred and from his father's house, that leaving a scanty land and a feeble kindred and a mean house he might inherit the promises of God. 3For He saith unto him Go forth from thy land and from thy kindred and from thy father's house unto the land which I shall show thee, and I will make thee into a great nation, and I will bless thee and will magnify thy name, and thou shalt be blessed. And I will bless them that bless thee, and I will curse them that curse thee; and in thee shall all the tribes of the earth be blessed. 4And again, when he was parted from Lot, God said unto him Look up with thine eyes, and behold from the place where thou now art, unto the north and the south and the sunrise and the sea; for all the land which thou seest, I will give it unto thee and to thy seed for ever; 5and I will make thy seed as the dust of the earth. If any man can count the dust of the earth, then shall thy seed also be counted. 6And again He saith; God led Abraham forth and said unto him, Look up unto the heaven and count the stars, and see whether thou canst number them. So shall thy seed be. And Abraham believed God, and it was reckoned unto him for righteousness. 7For his faith and hospitality a son was given unto him in old age, and by obedience he offered him a sacrifice unto God on one of the mountains which He showed him.

Clement I Chapter 11

1For his hospitality and godliness Lot was saved from Sodom, when all the country round about was judged by fire and brimstone; the Master having thus fore shown that He forsaketh not them which set their hope on Him, but appointeth unto punishment and torment them which swerve aside. 2For when his wife had gone forth with him, being otherwise minded and not in accord, she was appointed for a sign hereunto, so that she became a pillar of salt unto this day, that it might be known unto all men that they which are double-minded and they which doubt concerning the power of God are set for a judgment and for a token unto all the generations.

Clement I Chapter 12

1For her faith and hospitality Rahab the harlot was saved. 2For when the spies were sent forth unto Jericho by Joshua the son of Nun, the king of the land perceived that they were come to spy out his country, and sent forth men to seize them, that being seized they might be put to death. 3So the hospitable Rahab received them and hid them in the upper chamber under the flax stalks. 4And when the messengers of the king came near and said, "The spies of our land entered in unto thee: bring them forth, for the king so ordereth," then she answered, "The men truly, whom ye seek, entered in unto me, but they departed forthwith and are sojourning on the way;" and she pointed out to them the opposite road. 5And she said unto the men, "Of a surety I perceive that the Lord your God delivereth this city unto you; for the fear and the dread of you is fallen upon the inhabitants thereof. When therefore it shall come to pass that ye take it, save me and the house of my father." 6And they said unto her, "It shall be even so as thou hast spoken unto us. Whensoever therefore thou perceivest that we are coming, thou shalt gather all thy folk beneath thy roof and they shall be saved; for as many as shall be found without the house shall perish." 7And moreover they gave her a sign, that she should hang out from her house a scarlet thread, thereby showing beforehand that through the blood of the Lord there shall be redemption unto all them that believe and hope on God. 8Ye see, dearly beloved, not only faith, but prophecy, is found in the woman.

Clement I Chapter 13

1Let us therefore be lowly minded, brethren, laying aside all arrogance and conceit and folly and anger, and let us do that which is written. For the Holy Ghost saith, "Let not the wise man boast in his wisdom, nor the strong in his strength, neither the rich in his riches; but he that boasteth let him boast in the Lord, that he may seek Him out, and do judgment and righteousness" most of all remembering the words of the Lord Jesus which He spake, teaching forbearance and long-suffering: 2for thus He spake, "Have mercy, that ye may receive mercy: forgive, that it may be forgiven to you. As ye do, so shall it be done to you. As ye give, so shall it be given unto you. As ye judge, so shall ye be judged. As ye show kindness, so shall kindness be showed unto you. With what measure ye mete, it shall be measured withal to you." 3With this commandment and these precepts let us confirm ourselves, that we may walk in obedience to His hallowed words, with lowliness of mind. 4For the holy word saith, "Upon whom shall I look, save upon him that is gentle and quiet and feareth Mine oracles?"

Clement I Chapter 14

1Therefore it is right and proper, brethren, that we should be obedient unto God, rather than follow those who in arrogance and unruliness have set themselves up as leaders in abominable jealousy. 2For we shall bring upon us no common harm, but rather great peril, if we surrender ourselves recklessly unto the purposes of men who launch out into strife and seditions, so as to estrange us from that which is right. 3Let us be good one towards another according to the compassion and sweetness of Him that made us. For it is written: 4"The good shall be dwellers in the land, and the innocent shall be left on it but they that transgress shall be destroyed utterly from it." 5And again He saith, "I saw the ungodly lifted up on high and exalted as the cedars of Lebanon. And I passed by, and behold he was not; and sought out his place, and I found it not. Keep innocence and behold uprightness; for there is a remnant for the peaceful man."

Clement I Chapter 15

1Therefore let us cleave unto them that practice peace with godliness, and not unto them that desire peace with dissimulation. 2For He saith in a certain place, "This people honoreth Me with their lips, but their heart is far from Me," 3and again, "they blessed with their mouth, but they cursed with their heart." 4And again He saith, "They loved Him with their mouth, and with their tongue they lied unto Him; and their heart was not upright with Him, neither were they steadfast in His covenant." 5For this cause let the deceitful lips be made dumb which speak iniquity against the righteous. And again, "May the Lord utterly destroy all the deceitful lips, the tongue that speaketh proud things, even them that say, Let us magnify our tongue; our lips are our own; who is lord over us?" 6"For the misery of the needy and for the groaning of the poor I will now arise, saith the Lord. I will set him in safety; I will deal boldly by him."

Clement I Chapter 16

1For Christ is with them that are lowly of mind, not with them that exalt themselves over the flock. 2The scepter of the majesty of God, even our Lord Jesus Christ, came not in the pomp of arrogance or of pride, though He might have done so, but in lowliness of mind, according as the Holy Spirit spake concerning Him. 3For He saith, "Lord, who believed our report? and to whom was the arm of the Lord revealed? We announced Him in His presence. As a child was He, as a root in a thirsty ground. There is no form in Him, neither glory. And we beheld Him, and He had no form nor comeliness, but His form was mean, lacking more than the form of men. He was a man of stripes and of toil, and knowing how to bear infirmity: for His face is turned away. He was dishonored and held of no account." 4He beareth our sins and suffereth pain for our sakes: and we accounted Him to be in toil and in stripes and in affliction. 5And He was wounded for our sins and hath been afflicted for our iniquities. The chastisement of our peace is upon Him. With His bruises we were healed. 6We all went astray like sheep, each man went astray in his own path: 7and the Lord delivered Him over for our sins. And He openeth not His mouth, because He is afflicted. As a sheep He was led to slaughter; and as a lamb before his shearer is dumb, so openeth He not His mouth. In His humiliation His judgment was taken away. 8His generation who shall declare? For His life is taken away from the earth. 9For the iniquities of my people He is come to death. 10And I will give the wicked for His burial, and the rich for His death; for He wrought no iniquity, neither was guile found in His mouth. And the Lord desireth to cleanse Him from His stripes. 11If ye offer for sin, your soul shall see along lived seed. 12And the Lord desireth to take away from the toil of His soul, to show Him light and to mould Him with understanding, to justify a Just One that is a good servant unto many. And He shall bear their sins. 13Therefore He shall inherit many, and shall divide the spoils of the strong; because His soul was delivered unto death, and He was reckoned unto the transgressors; 14and He bare the sins of many, and for their sins was He delivered up. 15And again He Himself saith; "But I am a worm and no man, a reproach of men and an outcast of the people." 16"All they that beheld me mocked at me; they spake with their lips; they wagged their heads, saying, He hoped on the Lord; let Him deliver him, or let Him save him, for He desireth him." [17]Ye see, dearly beloved, what is the pattern that hath been given unto us; for, if the Lord was thus lowly of mind, what should we do, who through Him have been brought under the yoke of His grace?

Clement I Chapter 17

[1]Let us be imitators also of them which went about in goatskins and sheepskins, preaching the coming of Christ. We mean Elijah and Elisha and likewise Ezekiel, the prophets, and, besides them those men also that obtained a good report. [2]Abraham obtained an exceeding good report and was called the friend of God; and looking steadfastly on the glory of God, he saith in lowliness of mind, "But I am dust and ashes." [3]Moreover concerning Job also it is thus written; "And Job was righteous and unblamable, one that was true and honored God and abstained from all evil." [4]Yet he himself accuseth himself saying, "No man from filth; no, not though his life be but for a day." [5]Moses was called faithful in all His house, and through his ministration God judged Egypt with the plagues and the torments which befell them. Howbeit he also, though greatly glorified, yet spake no proud words, but said, when an oracle was given to him at the bush, "Who am I, that Thou sendest me?" [6]"Nay, I am feeble of speech and slow of tongue." And again he saith, "But I am smoke from the pot."

Clement I Chapter 18

[1]But what must we say of David that obtained a good report? of whom God said, "I have found a man after My heart, David the son of Jesse: with eternal mercy have I anointed him." [2]Yet he too saith unto God, "Have mercy upon me, O God, according to Thy great mercy; and according to the multitude of Thy compassions, blot out mine iniquity." [3]"Wash me yet more from mine iniquity, and cleanse me from my sin. For I acknowledge mine iniquity, and my sin is ever before me. Against Thee only did I sin, and I wrought evil in Thy sight; that Thou mayest be justified in Thy words, and mayest conquer in Thy pleading." [4]"For behold, in iniquities was I conceived, and in sins did my mother bear me. For behold Thou hast loved truth: the dark and hidden things of Thy wisdom hast Thou showed unto me." [5]"Thou shalt sprinkle me with hyssop, and I shall be made clean. Thou shalt wash me, and I shall become whiter than snow." [6]"Thou shalt make me to hear of joy and gladness. The bones which have been humbled shall rejoice." [7]"Turn away Thy face from my sins, and blot out all mine iniquities." [8]"Make a clean heart within me, O God, and renew a right spirit in mine inmost parts. Cast me not away from Thy presence, and take not Thy Holy Spirit from me." [9]"Restore unto me the joy of Thy salvation, and strengthen me with a princely spirit." [10]"I will teach sinners Thy ways, and godless men shall be converted unto Thee." [11]"Deliver me from blood guiltiness, O God, the God of my salvation. My tongue shall rejoice in Thy righteousness." [12]"Lord, Thou shalt open my mouth, and my lips shall declare Thy praise." [13]"For, if Thou hadst desired sacrifice, I would have given it: in whole burnt offerings Thou wilt have no pleasure." [14]"A sacrifice unto God is a contrite spirit; a contrite and humbled heart God will not despise."

Clement I Chapter 19

[1]The humility therefore and the submissiveness of so many and so great men, who have thus obtained a good report, hath through obedience made better not only us but also the generations which were before us, even them that received His oracles in fear and truth. [2]Seeing then that we have been partakers of many great and glorious doings, let us hasten to return unto the goal of peace which hath been handed down to us from the beginning, and let us look steadfastly unto the Father and Maker of the whole world, and cleave unto His splendid and excellent gifts of peace and benefits. [3]Let us behold Him in our mind, and let us look with the eyes of our soul unto His long-suffering will. Let us note how free from anger He is towards all His creatures.

Clement I Chapter 20

[1]The heavens are moved by His direction and obey Him in peace. [2]Day and night accomplish the course assigned to them by Him, without hindrance one to another. [3]The sun and the moon and the dancing stars according to His appointment circle in harmony within the bounds assigned to them, without any swerving aside. [4]The earth, bearing fruit in fulfillment of His will at her proper seasons, putteth forth the food that supplieth abundantly both men and beasts and all living things which are thereupon, making no dissension, neither altering anything which He hath decreed. [5]Moreover, the inscrutable depths of the abysses and the unutterable statutes of the nether regions are constrained by the same ordinances. [6]The basin of the boundless sea, gathered together by His workmanship into its reservoirs, passeth not the barriers wherewith it is surrounded; but even as He ordered it, so it doeth. [7]For He said, "So far shalt thou come, and thy waves shall be broken within thee." [8]The ocean which is impassable for men, and the worlds beyond it, are directed by the same ordinances of the Master. [9]The seasons of spring and summer and autumn and winter give way in succession one to another in peace. [10]The winds in their several quarters at their proper season fulfill their ministry without disturbance; and the ever flowing fountains, created for enjoyment and health, without fail give their breasts which sustain the life for men. Yea, the smallest of living things come together in concord and peace. [11]All these things the great Creator and Master of the universe ordered to be in peace and concord, doing good unto all things, but far beyond the rest unto us who have taken refuge in His compassionate mercies through our Lord Jesus Christ, [12]to whom be the glory and the majesty for ever and ever. Amen.

Clement I Chapter 21

[1]Look ye, brethren, lest His benefits, which are many, turn unto judgment to all of us, if we walk not worthily of Him, and do those things which are good and well pleasing in His sight with concord. [2]For He saith in a certain place, "The Spirit of the Lord is a lamp searching the closets of the belly." [3]Let us see how near He is, and how that nothing escapeth Him of our thoughts or our devices which we make. [4]It is right therefore that we should not be deserters from His will. [5]Let us rather give offense to foolish and senseless men who exalt themselves and boast in the arrogance of their words, than to God. [6]Let us fear the Lord Jesus [Christ], whose blood was given for us. Let us reverence our rulers; let us honor our elders; let us instruct our young men in the lesson of the fear of God. Let us guide our women toward that which is good: [7]let them show forth their lovely disposition of purity; let them prove their sincere affection of gentleness; let them make manifest the moderation of their tongue through their silence; let them show their love, not in factious preferences but without partiality towards all them that fear God, in holiness. Let our children be partakers of the instruction which is in Christ: [8]let them learn how lowliness of mind prevaileth with God, what power chaste love hath with God, how the fear of Him is good and great and saveth all them that walk therein in a pure mind with holiness. [9]For He is the searcher out of the intents and desires; whose breath is in us, and when He listeth, He shall take it away.

Clement I Chapter 22

[1]Now all these things the faith which is in Christ confirmeth: for He Himself through the Holy Spirit thus invite thus: "Come, my children, hearken unto Me, I will teach you the fear of the Lord." [2]"What man is he that desireth life and loveth to see good days?" [3]"Make thy tongue to cease from evil, and thy lips that they speak no guile." [4]"Turn aside from evil and do good." [5]"Seek peace and ensue it." [6]"The eyes of the Lord are over the righteous, and His ears are turned to their prayers. But the face of the Lord is upon them that do evil, to destroy their memorial from the earth." [7]"The righteous cried out, and the Lord heard him, and delivered him from all his troubles. Many are the troubles of the righteous, and the Lord shall deliver him from them all." [8]And again "Many are the stripes of the sinner, but them that set their hope on the Lord mercy shall compass about."

Clement I Chapter 23

[1]The Father, who is pitiful in all things, and ready to do good, hath compassion on them that fear Him, and kindly and lovingly bestoweth His favors on them that draw nigh unto Him with a single mind. [2]Therefore let us not be double-minded, neither let our soul indulge in idle humors respecting His exceeding and glorious gifts. [3]Let this scripture be far from us where He saith, "Wretched are the double-minded, which doubt in their soul and say, These things we did hear in the days of our fathers also, and behold we have grown old, and none of these things hath befallen us." [4]Ye fools, compare yourselves unto a tree; take a vine. First it sheddeth its leaves, then a shoot cometh, then a leaf, then a flower, and after these a sour berry, then a full ripe grape. Ye see that in a little time the fruit of the tree attaineth unto mellowness. [5]Of a truth quickly and suddenly shall His will be accomplished, the scripture also bearing witness to it, saying, "He shall come quickly and shall not tarry; and the Lord shall come suddenly into His temple, even the Holy One, whom ye expect."

Clement I Chapter 24

[1]Let us understand, dearly beloved, how the Master continually showeth unto us the resurrection that shall be hereafter; whereof He made the Lord Jesus Christ the firstfruit, when He raised Him from the dead. [2]Let us behold, dearly beloved, the resurrection which happeneth at its proper season. [3]Day and night show unto us the resurrection. The night falleth asleep, and day ariseth; the day departeth, and night cometh on. [4]Let us mark the fruits, how and in what manner the sowing

taketh place. 5The sower goeth forth and casteth into the earth each of the seeds; and these falling into the earth dry and bare decay: then out of their decay the mightiness of the Master's providence raiseth them up, and from being one they increase manifold and bear fruit.

Clement I Chapter 25

1Let us consider the marvelous sign which is seen in the regions of the east, that is, in the parts about Arabia. 2There is a bird, which is named the phoenix. This, being the only one of its kind, liveth for five hundred years; and when it hath now reached the time of its dissolution that it should die, it maketh for itself a coffin of frankincense and myrrh and the other spices, into the which in the fullness of time it entereth, and so it dieth. 3But, as the flesh rotteth, a certain worm is engendered, which is nurtured from the moisture of the dead creature and putteth forth wings. Then, when it is grown lusty, it taketh up that coffin where are the bones of its parent, and carrying them journeyeth from the country of Arabia even unto Egypt, to the place called the City of the Sun; 4and in the daytime in the sight of all, flying to the altar of the Sun, it layeth them thereupon; and this done, it setteth forth to return. 5So the priests examine the registers of the times, and they find that it hath come when the five hundredth year is completed.

Clement I Chapter 26

1Do we then think it to be a great and marvelous thing, if the Creator of the universe shall bring about the resurrection of them that have served Him with holiness in the assurance of a good faith, seeing that He showeth to us even by a bird the magnificence of His promise? 2For He saith in a certain place, "And Thou shalt raise me up, and I will praise Thee;" and; "I went to rest and slept, I was awaked, for Thou art with me." 3And again Job saith, "And Thou shall raise this my flesh which hath endured all these things."

Clement I Chapter 27

1With this hope therefore let our souls be bound unto Him that is faithful in His promises and that is righteous in His judgments. 2He that commanded not to lie, much more shall He Himself not lie: for nothing is impossible with God save to lie. 3Therefore let our faith in Him be kindled within us, and let us understand that all things are nigh unto Him. 4By a word of His majesty He compacted the universe; and by a word He can destroy it. 5Who shall say unto Him, "What hast thou done?" or who shall resist the might of His strength? When He listeth, and as He listeth, He will do all things; and nothing shall pass away of those things that He hath decreed. 6All things are in His sight, and nothing escapeth His counsel, 7seeing that "The heavens declare the glory of God, and the firmament proclaimeth His handiwork. Day uttereth word unto day, and night proclaimeth knowledge unto night; and there are neither words nor speeches, whose voices are not heard."

Clement I Chapter 28

1Since therefore all things are seen and heard, let us fear Him and forsake the abominable lusts of evil works, that we may be shielded by His mercy from the coming judgments. 2For where can any of us escape from His strong hand? And what world will receive any of them that desert from His service? 3For the holy writing saith in a certain place, "Where shall I go, and where shall I be hidden from Thy face? If I ascend into the heaven, Thou art there; if I depart into the farthest parts of the earth, there is Thy right hand; if I make my bed in the depths, there is Thy Spirit." 4Whither then shall one depart, or where shall one flee, from Him that embraceth the universe?

Clement I Chapter 29

1Let us therefore approach Him in holiness of soul, lifting up pure and undefiled hands unto Him, with love towards our gentle and compassionate Father who made us an elect portion unto Himself. 2For thus it is written: "When the Most High divided the nations, when He dispersed the sons of Adam, He fixed the boundaries of the nations according to the number of the angels of God. His people Jacob became the portion of the Lord, and Israel the measurement of His inheritance." 3And in another place He saith, "Behold, the Lord taketh for Himself a nation out of the midst of the nations, as a man taketh the first fruits of his threshing floor; and the holy of holies shall come forth from that nation."

Clement I Chapter 30

1Seeing then that we are the special portion of a Holy God, let us do all things that pertain unto holiness, forsaking evil speakings, abominable and impure embraces, drunkennesses and tumults and hateful lusts, abominable adultery, hateful pride. 2For God, He saith, "resisteth the proud, but giveth grace to the lowly." 3Let us therefore cleave unto those to whom grace is given from God. Let us clothe ourselves in concord, being lowly minded and temperate, holding ourselves aloof from all back biting and evil speaking, being justified by works and not by words. 4For He saith, "He that saith much shall hear also again. Doth

the ready talker think to be righteous?" 5"Blessed is the offspring of a woman that liveth but a short time. Be not thou abundant in words." 6Let our praise be with God, and not of ourselves: for God hateth them that praise themselves. 7Let the testimony to our well doing be given by others, as it was given unto our fathers who were righteous. 8Boldness and arrogance and daring are for them that are accursed of God; but forbearance and humility and gentleness are with them that are blessed of God.

Clement I Chapter 31

1Let us therefore cleave unto His blessing, and let us see what are the ways of blessing. Let us study the records of the things that have happened from the beginning. 2Wherefore was our father Abraham blessed? Was it not because he wrought righteousness and truth through faith? 3Isaac with confidence, as knowing the future, was led a willing sacrifice. 4Jacob with humility departed from his land because of his brother, and went unto Laban and served; and the twelve tribes of Israel were given unto him.

Clement I Chapter 32

1If any man will consider them one by one in sincerity, he shall understand the magnificence of the gifts that are given by Him. 2For of Jacob are all the priests and levites who minister unto the altar of God; of him is the Lord Jesus as concerning the flesh; of him are kings and rulers and governors in the line of Judah; yea and the rest of his tribes are held in no small honor, seeing that God promised saying, "Thy seed shall be as the stars of heaven." 3They all therefore were glorified and magnified, not through themselves or their own works or the righteous doing which they wrought, but through His will. 4And so we, having been called through His will in Christ Jesus, are not justified through ourselves or through our own wisdom or understanding or piety or works which we wrought in holiness of heart, but through faith, whereby the Almighty God justified all men that have been from the beginning; to whom be the glory for ever and ever. Amen.

Clement I Chapter 33

1What then must we do, brethren? Must we idly abstain from doing good, and forsake love? May the Master never allow this to befall us at least; but let us hasten with instancy and zeal to accomplish every good work. 2For the Creator and Master of the universe Himself rejoiceth in His works. 3For by His exceeding great might He established the heavens, and in His incomprehensible wisdom He set them in order. And the earth He separated from the water that surroundeth it, and He set it firm on the sure foundation of His own will; and the living creatures which walk upon it He commanded to exist by His ordinance. Having before created the sea and the living creatures therein, He enclosed it by His own power. 4Above all, as the most excellent and exceeding great work of His intelligence, with His sacred and faultless hands He formed man in the impress of His own image. 5For thus saith God "Let us make man after our image and after our likeness." And God made man; male and female made He them. 6So having finished all these things, He praised them and blessed them and said, "Increase and multiply." 7We have seen that all the righteous were adorned in good works. Yea, and the Lord Himself having adorned Himself with worlds rejoiced. 8Seeing then that we have this pattern, let us conform ourselves with all diligence to His will; let us with all our strength work the work of righteousness.

Clement I Chapter 34

1The good workman receiveth the bread of his work with boldness, but the slothful and careless dareth not look his employer in the face. 2It is therefore needful that we should be zealous unto well doing, for of Him are all things: 3since He forewarneth us saying, "Behold, the Lord, and His reward is before His face, to recompense each man according to his work." 4He exhorteth us therefore to believe on Him with our whole heart, and to be not idle nor careless unto every good work. 5Let our boast and our confidence be in Him: let us submit ourselves to His will; let us mark the whole host of His angels, how they stand by and minister unto His will. 6For the scripture saith, "Ten thousands of ten thousands stood by Him, and thousands of thousands ministered unto Him: and they cried aloud, Holy, holy, holy is the Lord of Sabaoth; all creation is full of His glory." 7Yea, and let us ourselves then, being gathered together in concord with intentness of heart, cry unto Him as from one mouth earnestly that we may be made partakers of His great and glorious promises. 8For He saith, "Eye hath not seen and ear hath not heard, and it hath not entered into the heart of man what great things He hath prepared for them that patiently await Him."

Clement I Chapter 35

1How blessed and marvelous are the gifts of God, dearly beloved!! 2Life in immortality, splendor in righteousness, truth in boldness, faith in confidence, temperance in sanctification! And all these things fall under our apprehension. ³What then, think ye, are the things preparing for them that patiently await Him? The Creator and Father of the ages, the All holy One Himself knoweth their number and their beauty. ⁴Let us therefore contend, that we may be found in the number of those that patiently await Him, to the end that we may be partakers of His promised gifts. ⁵But how shall this be, dearly beloved? If our mind be fixed through faith towards God; if we seek out those things which are well pleasing and acceptable unto Him; if we accomplish such things as beseem His faultless will, and follow the way of truth, casting off from ourselves all unrighteousness and iniquity, covetousness, strifes, malignities and deceits, whisperings and backbitings, hatred of God, pride and arrogance, vainglory and inhospitality. ⁶For they that do these things are hateful to God; and not only they that do them, but they also that consent unto them. ⁷For the scripture saith, "But unto the sinner said God, Wherefore dost thou declare Mine ordinances, and takest My covenant upon thy lips?" ⁸"Yet Thou didst hate instruction and didst cast away My words behind thee. If thou sawest a thief thou didst keep company with him, and with the adulterers thou didst set thy portion. Thy mouth multiplied wickedness and thy tongue wove deceit. Thou sattest and spakest against thy brother, and against the son of thy mother thou didst lay a stumbling block." ⁹"These things Thou hast done, and I kept silence. Thou thoughtest, unrighteous man, that I should be like unto thee." ¹⁰"I will convict thee and will set thee face to face with thyself." ¹¹"Now understand ye these things, ye that forget God, lest at any time He seize you as a lion, and there be none to deliver." ¹²"The sacrifice of praise shall glorify Me, and there is the way wherein I will show him the salvation of God."

Clement I Chapter 36

¹This is the way, dearly beloved, wherein we found our salvation, even Jesus Christ the High priest of our offerings, the Guardian and Helper of our weakness. ²Through Him let us look steadfastly unto the heights of the heavens; through Him we behold as in a mirror His faultless and most excellent visage; through Him the eyes of our hearts were opened; through Him our foolish and darkened mind springeth up unto the light; through Him the Master willed that we should taste of the immortal knowledge Who being the brightness of His majesty is so much greater than angels, as He hath inherited a more excellent name. ³For so it is written, "Who maketh His angels spirits and His ministers aflame of fire." ⁴But of His Son the Master said thus, "Thou art My Son, I this day have begotten thee. Ask of Me, and I will give Thee the Gentiles for Thine inheritance, and the ends of the earth for Thy possession." ⁵And again He saith unto Him, "Sit Thou on My right hand, until I make Thine enemies a footstool for Thy feet." ⁶Who then are these enemies? They that are wicked and resist His will.

Clement I Chapter 37

¹Let us therefore enlist ourselves, brethren, with all earnestness in His faultless ordinances. ²Let us mark the soldiers that are enlisted under our rulers, how exactly, how readily, how submissively, they execute the orders given them. ³All are not prefects, nor rulers of thousands, nor rulers of hundreds, nor rulers of fifties, and so forth; but each man in his own rank executeth the orders given by the king and the governors. ⁴The great without the small cannot exist, neither the small without the great. There is a certain mixture in all things, and therein is utility. ⁵Let us take our body as an example. The head without the feet is nothing; so likewise the feet without the head are nothing: even the smallest limbs of our body are necessary and useful for the whole body: but all the members conspire and unite in subjection, that the whole body maybe saved.

Clement I Chapter 38

¹So in our case let the whole body be saved in Christ Jesus, and let each man be subject unto his neighbor, according as also he was appointed with his special grace. ²Let not the strong neglect the weak; and let the weak respect the strong. Let the rich minister aid to the poor; and let the poor give thanks to God, because He hath given him one through whom his wants may be supplied. Let the wise display his wisdom, not in words, but in good works. He that is lowly in mind, let him not bear testimony to himself, but leave testimony to be borne to him by his neighbor. He that is pure in the flesh, let him be so, and not boast, knowing that it is Another who bestoweth his continence upon him. ³Let us consider, brethren, of what matter we were made; who and what manner of beings we were, when we came into the world; from what a sepulchre and what darkness He that molded and created us brought us into His world, having prepared His benefits aforehand ere ever we were born. ⁴Seeing therefore that we have all these things from Him, we ought in all things to give thanks to Him, to whom be the glory for ever and ever. Amen.

Clement I Chapter 39

¹Senseless and stupid and foolish and ignorant men jeer and mock at us, desiring that they themselves should be exalted in their imaginations. ²For what power hath a mortal? or what strength hath a child of earth? ³For it is written; "There was no form before mine eyes; only I heard a breath and a voice." ⁴What then? Shall a mortal be clean in the sight of the Lord; or shall a man be unblamable for his works? seeing that He is distrustful against His servants and noteth some perversity against His angels. ⁵Nay, the heaven is not clean in His sight. Away then, ye that dwell in houses of clay, whereof, even of the same clay, we ourselves are made. He smote them like a moth, and from morn to even they are no more. Because they could not succor themselves, they perished. ⁶He breathed on them and they died, because they had no wisdom. ⁷But call thou, if perchance one shall obey thee, or if thou shalt see one of the holy angels. For wrath killeth the foolish man, and envy slayeth him that has gone astray. ⁸And I have seen fools throwing out roots, but forthwith their habitation was eaten up. ⁹Far be their sons from safety. May they be mocked at the gates of inferiors, and there shall be none to deliver them. For the things which are prepared for them, the righteous shall eat; but they themselves shall not be delivered from evils.

Clement I Chapter 40

¹Forasmuch then as these things are manifest beforehand, and we have searched into the depths of the Divine knowledge, we ought to do all things in order, as many as the Master hath commanded us to perform at their appointed seasons. ²Now the offerings and ministrations He commanded to be performed with care, and not to be done rashly or in disorder, but at fixed times and seasons. ³And where and by whom He would have them performed, He Himself fixed by His supreme will: that all things being done with piety according to His good pleasure might be acceptable to His will. ⁴They therefore that make their offerings at the appointed seasons are acceptable and blessed: for while they follow the institutions of the Master they cannot go wrong. ⁵For unto the high priest his proper services have been assigned, and to the priests their proper office is appointed, and upon the levites their proper ministrations are laid. The layman is bound by the layman's ordinances.

Clement I Chapter 41

¹Let each of you, brethren, in his own order give thanks unto God, maintaining a good conscience and not transgressing the appointed rule of his service, but acting with all seemliness. ²Not in every place, brethren, are the continual daily sacrifices offered, or the freewill offerings, or the sin offerings and the trespass offerings, but in Jerusalem alone. And even there the offering is not made in every place, but before the sanctuary in the court of the altar; and this too through the high priest and the aforesaid ministers, after that the victim to be offered hath been inspected for blemishes. ³They therefore who do anything contrary to the seemly ordinance of His will receive death as the penalty. ⁴Ye see, brethren, in proportion as greater knowledge hath been vouchsafed unto us, so much the more are we exposed to danger.

Clement I Chapter 42

¹The Apostles received the Gospel for us from the Lord Jesus Christ; Jesus Christ was sent forth from God. ²So then Christ is from God, and the Apostles are from Christ. Both therefore came of the will of God in the appointed order. ³Having therefore received a charge, and having been fully assured through the resurrection of our Lord Jesus Christ and confirmed in the word of God with full assurance of the Holy Ghost, they went forth with the glad tidings that the kingdom of God should come. ⁴So preaching everywhere in country and town, they appointed their firstfruits, when they had proved them by the Spirit, to be bishops and deacons unto them that should believe. ⁵And this they did in no new fashion; for indeed it had been written concerning bishops and deacons from very ancient times; for thus saith the scripture in a certain place, "I will appoint their bishops in righteousness and their deacons in faith."

Clement I Chapter 43

¹And what marvel, if they which were entrusted in Christ with such a work by God appointed the aforesaid persons? seeing that even the blessed Moses who was a "faithful servant in all His house" recorded for a sign in the sacred books all things that were enjoined upon him. ²For he, when jealousy arose concerning the priesthood, and there was dissension among the tribes which of them was adorned with the glorious name, commanded the twelve chiefs of the tribes to bring to him rods inscribed with the name of each tribe. And he took them and tied them and sealed them with the signet rings of the chiefs of the tribes, and put them away in the tabernacle of the testimony on the table of God. ³And having shut the tabernacle he sealed the keys and likewise also the doors. ⁴And he said unto them, "Brethren, the tribe

whose rod shall bud, this hath God chosen to be priests and ministers unto Him." 5Now when morning came, he called together all Israel, even the six hundred thousand men, and showed the seals to the chiefs of the tribes and opened the tabernacle of the testimony and drew forth the rods. And the rod of Aaron was found not only with buds, but also bearing fruit. 6What think ye, dearly beloved? Did not Moses know beforehand that this would come to pass? Assuredly he knew it. But that disorder might not arise in Israel, he did thus, to the end that the Name of the true and only God might be glorified: to whom be the glory for ever and ever. Amen.

Clement I Chapter 44

1And our Apostles knew through our Lord Jesus Christ that there would be strife over the name of the bishop's office. 2For this cause therefore, having received complete foreknowledge, they appointed the aforesaid persons, and afterwards they provided a continuance, that if these should fall asleep, other approved men should succeed to their ministration. Those therefore who were appointed by them, or afterward by other men of repute with the consent of the whole Church, and have ministered unblamably to the flock of Christ in lowliness of mind, peacefully and with all modesty, and for long time have borne a good report with all these men we consider to be unjustly thrust out from their ministration. 3For it will be no light sin for us, if we thrust out those who have offered the gifts of the bishop's office unblamably and holily. 4Blessed are those presbyters who have gone before, seeing that their departure was fruitful and ripe: for they have no fear lest any one should remove them from their appointed place. 5For we see that ye have displaced certain persons, though they were living honorably, from the ministration which had been respected by them blamelessly.

Clement I Chapter 45

1Be ye contentious, brethren, and jealous about the things that pertain unto salvation. 2Ye have searched the scriptures, which are true, which were given through the Holy Ghost; 3and ye know that nothing unrighteous or counterfeit is written in them. Ye will not find that righteous persons have been thrust out by holy men. 4Righteous men were persecuted, but it was by the lawless; they were imprisoned, but it was by the unholy. They were stoned by transgressors: they were slain by those who had conceived a detestable and unrighteous jealousy. 5Suffering these things, they endured nobly. 6For what must we say, brethren? Was Daniel cast into the lions' den by them that feared God? 7Or were Ananias and Azarias and Misael shut up in the furnace of fire by them that professed the excellent and glorious worship of the Most High? Far be this from our thoughts. Who then were they that did these things? Abominable men and full of all wickedness were stirred up to such a pitch of wrath, as to bring cruel suffering upon them that served God in a holy and blameless purpose, not knowing that the Most High is the champion and protector of them that in a pure conscience serve His excellent Name: unto whom be the glory for ever and ever. Amen. 8But they that endured patiently in confidence inherited glory and honor; they were exalted, and had their names recorded by God in their memorial for ever and ever. Amen.

Clement I Chapter46

1To such examples as these therefore, brethren, we also ought to cleave. 2For it is written; "Cleave unto the saints, for they that cleave unto them shall be sanctified." 3And again He saith in another place; "With the guiltless man thou shalt be guiltless, and with the elect thou shalt be elect, and with the crooked thou shalt deal crookedly." 4Let us therefore cleave to the guiltless and righteous: and these are the elect of God. 5Wherefore are there strifes and wraths and factions and divisions and war among you? 6Have we not one God and one Christ and one Spirit of grace that was shed upon us? And is there not one calling in Christ? 7Wherefore do we tear and rend asunder the members of Christ, and stir up factions against our own body, and reach such a pitch of folly, as to forget that we are members one of another? 8Remember the words of Jesus our Lord: for He said, "Woe unto that man; it were good for him if he had not been born, rather than that at he should offend one of Mine elect. It were better for him that a millstone were hanged about him, and be cast into the sea, than that he should pervert one of Mine elect." 9Your division hath perverted many; it hath brought many to despair, many to doubting, and all of us to sorrow. And your sedition still continueth.

Clement I Chapter 47

1Take up the epistle of the blessed Paul the Apostle. 2What wrote he first unto you in the beginning of the Gospel? 3Of a truth he charged you in the Spirit concerning himself and Cephas and Apollos, because that even then ye had made parties. 4Yet that making of parties brought less sin upon you; for ye were partisans of Apostles that were highly reputed, and of a man approved in their sight. 5But now mark ye, who they are that have perverted you and diminished the glory of your renowned love for the brotherhood. 6It is shameful, dearly beloved, yes, utterly shameful and unworthy of your conduct in Christ, that it should be reported that the very steadfast and ancient Church of the Corinthians, for the sake of one or two persons, maketh sedition against its presbyters. 7And this report hath reached not only us, but them also which differ from us, so that ye even heap blasphemies on the Name of the Lord by reason of your folly, and moreover create peril for yourselves.

Clement I Chapter 48

1Let us therefore root this out quickly, and let us fall down before the Master and entreat Him with tears, that He may show Himself propitious and be reconciled unto us, and may restore us to the seemly and pure conduct which belongeth to our love of the brethren. 2For this is a gate of righteousness opened unto life, as it is written; "Open me the gates of righteousness, that I may enter in thereby and preach the Lord." 3This is the gate of the Lord; the righteous shall enter in thereby. 4Seeing then that many gates are opened, this is that gate which is in righteousness, even that which is in Christ, whereby all are blessed that have entered in and direct their path in holiness and righteousness, performing all things without confusion. 5Let a man be faithful, let him be able to expound a deep saying, let him be wise in the discernment of words, let him be strenuous in deeds, let him be pure; 6for so much the more ought he to be lowly in mind, in proportion as he seemeth to be the greater; and he ought to seek the common advantage of all, and not his own.

Clement I Chapter 49

1Let him that hath love in Christ fulfill the commandments of Christ. 2Who can declare the bond of the love of God? 3Who is sufficient to tell the majesty of its beauty? 4The height, whereunto love exalteth, is unspeakable. 5Love joineth us unto God; love covereth a multitude of sins; love endureth all things, is long-suffering in all things. There is nothing coarse, nothing arrogant in love. Love hath no divisions, love maketh no seditions, love doeth all things in concord. In love were all the elect of God made perfect; without love nothing is well pleasing to God: 6in love the Master took us unto Himself; for the love which He had toward us, Jesus Christ our Lord hath given His blood for us by the will of God, and His flesh for our flesh and His life for our lives.

Clement I Chapter 50

1Ye see, dearly beloved, how great and marvelous a thing is love, and there is no declaring its perfection. 2Who is sufficient to be found therein, save those to whom God shall vouchsafe it? Let us therefore entreat and ask of His mercy, that we may be found blameless in love, standing apart from the factiousness of men. All the generations from Adam unto this day have passed away: but they that by God's grace were perfected in love dwell in the abode of the pious; and they shall be made manifest in the visitation of the Kingdom of God. 3For it is written; "Enter into the closet for a very little while until Mine anger and Mine wrath shall pass away, and I will remember a good day and will raise you from your tombs." 4Blessed were we, dearly beloved, if we should be doing the commandments of God in concord of love, to the end that our sins may through love be forgiven us. 5For it is written; "Blessed are they whose iniquities are forgiven, and whose sins are covered. Blessed is the man to whom the Lord shall impute no sin, neither is guile in his mouth." 6This declaration of blessedness was pronounced upon them that have been elected by God through Jesus Christ our Lord, to whom be the glory for ever and ever. Amen.

Clement I Chapter 51

1For all our transgressions which we have committed through any of the wiles of the adversary, let us entreat that we may obtain forgiveness. Yea and they also, who set themselves up as leaders of faction and division, ought to look to the common ground of hope. 2For such as walk in fear and love desire that they themselves should fall into suffering rather than their neighbors; and they pronounce condemnation against themselves rather than against the harmony which hath been handed down to us nobly and righteously. 3For it is good for a man to make confession of his trespasses rather than to harden his heart, as the heart of those was hardened who made sedition against Moses the servant of God; whose condemnation was clearly manifest, 4for they went down to hades alive, and "Death shall be their shepherd." 5Pharaoh and his host and all the rulers of Egypt, their chariots and their horsemen, were overwhelmed in the depths of the Red Sea, and perished for none other reason but because their foolish hearts were hardened after that the signs and the wonders had been wrought in the land of Egypt by the hand of Moses the servant of God.

Clement I Chapter 52

1The Master, brethren, hath need of nothing at all. He desireth not anything of any man, save to confess unto Him. [2]For the elect David saith; "I will confess unto the Lord, and it shall please Him more than a young calf that groweth horns and hoofs. Let the poor see it, and rejoice." [3]For a sacrifice unto God is a broken spirit. [4]And again He saith; "Sacrifice to God a sacrifice of praise, and pay thy vows to the Most High: and call upon Me in the day of thine affliction, and I will deliver thee, and thou shalt glorify Me."

Clement I Chapter 53

[1]For ye know, and know well, the sacred scriptures, dearly beloved, and ye have searched into the oracles of God. We write these things therefore to put you in remembrance. [2]When Moses went up into the mountain and had spent forty days and forty nights in fasting and humiliation, God said unto him; "Moses, Moses, come down, quickly hence, for My people whom thou leadest forth from the land of Egypt have wrought iniquity: they have transgressed quickly out of the way which thou didst command unto them: they have made for themselves molten images." [3]And the Lord said unto him; "I have spoken unto thee once and twice, saying, I have seen this people, and behold it is stiff-necked. Let Me destroy them utterly, and I will blot out their name from under heaven, and I will make of thee a nation great and wonderful and numerous more than this." [4]And Moses said; "Nay, not so, Lord Forgive this people their sin, or blot me also out of the book of the living." [5]O mighty love! O unsurpassable perfection! The servant is bold with his Master; he asketh forgiveness for the multitude, or he demandeth that himself also be blotted out with them.

Clement I Chapter 54

[1]Who therefore is noble among you? Who is compassionate? Who is fulfilled with love? [2]Let him say; "If by reason of me there be faction and strife and divisions, I retire, I depart, whither ye will, and I do that which is ordered by the people: only let the flock of Christ be at peace with its duly appointed presbyters." [3]He that shall have done this, shall win for himself great renown in Christ, and every place will receive him: for "the earth is the Lord's and the fullness thereof." [4]Thus have they done and will do, that live as citizens of that kingdom of God which bringeth no regrets.

Clement I Chapter 55

[1]But, to bring forward examples of Gentiles also; many kings and rulers, when some season of pestilence pressed upon them, being taught by oracles have delivered themselves over to death, that they might rescue their fellow citizens through their own blood. Many have retired from their own cities, that they might have no more seditions. [2]We know that many among ourselves have delivered themselves to bondage, that they might ransom others. Many have sold themselves to slavery, and receiving the price paid for themselves have fed others. [3]Many women being strengthened through the grace of God have performed many manly deeds. [4]The blessed Judith, when the city was beleaguered, asked of the elders that she might be suffered to go forth into the camp of the aliens. [5]So she exposed herself to peril and went forth for love of her country and of her people which were beleaguered; and the Lord delivered Holophernes into the hand of a woman. [6]To no less peril did Esther also, who was perfect in faith, expose herself, that she might deliver the twelve tribes of Israel, when they were on the point to perish. For through her fasting and her humiliation she entreated the all-seeing Master, the God of the ages; and He, seeing the humility of her soul, delivered the people for whose sake she encountered the peril.

Clement I Chapter 56

[1]Therefore let us also make intercession for them that are in any transgression, that forbearance and humility may be given them, to the end that they may yield not unto us, but unto the will of God. For so shall the compassionate remembrance of them with God and the saints be fruitful unto them, and perfect. [2]Let us accept chastisement, whereat no man ought to be vexed, dearly beloved. The admonition which we give one to another is good and exceeding useful; for it joineth us unto the will of God. [3]For thus saith the holy word; "The Lord hath indeed chastened me, and hath not delivered me over unto death." [4]For whom the Lord loveth He chasteneth, and scourgeth every son whom He receiveth." [5]For the righteous, it is said, shall chasten me in mercy and shall reprove me, but let not the mercy of sinners anoint my head." [6]And again He saith; "Blessed is the man whom the Lord hath reproved, and refuse not thou the admonition of the Almighty. For He causeth pain, and He restoreth again: [7]He hath smitten, and His hands have healed."

Clement I Chapter 57

[1]Ye therefore that laid the foundation of the sedition, submit yourselves unto the presbyters and receive chastisement unto repentance, bending the knees of your heart. [2]Learn to submit yourselves, laying aside the arrogant and proud stubbornness of your tongue. For it is better for you to be found little in the flock of Christ and to have your name on God's roll, than to be had in exceeding honor and yet be cast out from the hope of Him. [3]For thus saith the All virtuous Wisdom; "Behold I will pour out for you a saying of My breath, and I will teach you My word." [4]Because I called and ye obeyed not, and I held out words and ye heeded not, but made My councils of none effect, and were disobedient unto My reproofs; therefore I also will laugh at your destruction."

Clement I Chapter 58

[1]Let us therefore be obedient unto His most holy and glorious Name, thereby escaping the threatenings which were spoken of old by the mouth of Wisdom against them which disobey, that we may dwell safely, trusting in the most holy Name of His majesty. [2]Receive our counsel, and ye shall have no occasion of regret. For as God liveth, and the Lord Jesus Christ liveth, and the Holy Spirit, who are the faith and the hope of the elect, so surely shall he, who with lowliness of mind and instant in gentleness hath without regretfulness performed the ordinances and commandments that are given by God, be enrolled and have a name among the number of them that are saved through Jesus Christ, through whom is the glory unto Him for ever and ever. Amen.

Clement I Chapter 59

[1]But if certain persons should be disobedient unto the words spoken by Him through us, let them understand that they will entangle themselves in no slight transgression and danger; [2]but we shall be guiltless of this sin. And we will ask, with instancy of prayer and supplication, that the Creator of the universe may guard intact unto the end the number that hath been numbered of His elect throughout the whole world, through His beloved Son Jesus Christ, through whom He called us from darkness to light, from ignorance to the full knowledge of the glory of His Name.

Clement I Chapter 60

[1]Thou through Thine operations didst make manifest the everlasting fabric of the world. Thou, Lord, didst create the earth. Thou that art faithful throughout all generations, righteous in Thy judgments, marvelous in strength and excellence, Thou that art wise in creating and prudent in establishing that which Thou hast made, that art good in the things which are seen and faithful with them that trust on Thee, pitiful and compassionate, forgive us our iniquities and our unrighteousnesses and our transgressions and shortcomings. [2]Lay not to our account every sin of Thy servants and Thine handmaids, but cleanse us with the cleansing of Thy truth, and guide our steps to walk in holiness and righteousness and singleness of heart and to do such things as are good and well pleasing in Thy sight and in the sight of our rulers. [3]Yea, Lord, make Thy face to shine upon us in peace for our good, that we may be sheltered by Thy mighty hand and delivered from every sin by Thine uplifted arm. And deliver us from them that hate us wrongfully. [4]Give concord and peace to us and to all that dwell on the earth, as Thou gavest to our fathers, when they called on Thee in faith and truth with holiness, [that we may be saved,] while we render obedience to Thine almighty and most excellent Name, and to our rulers and governors upon the earth.

Clement I Chapter 61

[1]Thou, Lord and Master, hast given them the power of sovereignty through Thine excellent and unspeakable might, that we knowing the glory and honor which Thou hast given them may submit ourselves unto them, in nothing resisting Thy will. Grant unto them therefore, O Lord, health peace, concord, stability, that they may administer the government which Thou hast given them without failure. [2]For Thou, O heavenly Master, King of the ages, givest to the sons of men glory and honor and power over all things that are upon the earth. Do Thou, Lord, direct their counsel according to that which is good and well pleasing in Thy sight, that, administering in peace and gentleness with Godliness the power which Thou hast given them, they may obtain Thy favor. [3]O Thou, who alone art able to do these things and things far more exceeding good than these for us, we praise Thee through the High priest and Guardian of our souls, Jesus Christ, through whom be the glory and the majesty unto Thee both now and for all generations and for ever and ever. Amen.

Clement I Chapter 62

[1]As touching those things which befit our religion and are most useful for a virtuous life to such as would guide [their steps] in holiness and righteousness, we have written fully unto you, brethren. [2]For concerning faith and repentance and genuine love and temperance and sobriety and patience we have handled every argument, putting you in remembrance, that ye ought to please Almighty God in righteousness and truth and long suffering with holiness, laying aside malice and pursuing concord in love and peace, being instant in gentleness; even

as our fathers, of whom we spake before, pleased Him, being lowly minded toward their Father and God and Creator and towards all men. ³And we have put you in mind of these things the more gladly, since we knew well that we were writing to men who are faithful and highly accounted and have diligently searched into the oracles of the teaching of God.

Clement I Chapter 63

¹Therefore it is right for us to give heed to so great and so many examples and to submit the neck and occupying the place of obedience to take our side with them that are the leaders of our souls, that ceasing from this foolish dissension we may attain unto the goal which lieth before us in truthfulness, keeping aloof from every fault. ²For ye will give us great joy and gladness, if ye render obedience unto the things written by us through the Holy Spirit, and root out the unrighteous anger of your jealousy, according to the entreaty which we have made for peace and concord in this letter. ³And we have also sent faithful and prudent men that have walked among us from youth unto old age unblamably, who shall also be witnesses between you and us. ⁴And this we have done that ye might know that we have had, and still have, every solicitude that ye should be speedily at peace.

Clement I Chapter 64

¹Finally may the All-seeing God and Master of spirits and Lord of all flesh, who chose the Lord Jesus Christ, and us through Him for a peculiar people, grant unto every soul that is called after His excellent and holy Name faith, fear, peace, patience, long-suffering, temperance, chastity and soberness, that they may be well pleasing unto His Name through our High priest and Guardian Jesus Christ, through whom unto Him be glory and majesty, might and honor, both now and for ever and ever. Amen.

Clement I Chapter 65

¹Now send ye back speedily unto us our messengers Claudius Ephebus and Valerius Bito, together with Fortunatus also, in peace and with joy, to the end that they may the more quickly report the peace and concord which is prayed for and earnestly desired by us, that we also may the more speedily rejoice over your good order. ²The grace of our Lord Jesus Christ be with you and with all men in all places who have been called by God and through Him, through whom be glory and honor, power and greatness and eternal dominion, unto Him, from the ages past and forever and ever. Amen.

Apocalyptic Book

Revelation

Revelation Chapter 1

¹The revelation of Jesus Christ, which God gave to him, to show his servants what must happen soon. He made it known by sending his angel to his servant John, ²who gives witness to the word of God and to the testimony of Jesus Christ by reporting what he saw. ³Blessed is the one who reads aloud and blessed are those who listen to this prophetic message and heed what is written in it, for the appointed time is near. ⁴John, to the seven churches in Asia: grace to you and peace from him who is and who was and who is to come, and from the seven spirits before his throne, ⁵and from Jesus Christ, the faithful witness, the firstborn of the dead and ruler of the kings of the earth. To him who loves us and has freed us from our sins by his blood, ⁶who has made us into a kingdom, priests for his God and Father, to him be glory and power forever (and ever). Amen. ⁷Behold, he is coming amid the clouds, and every eye will see him, even those who pierced him. All the peoples of the earth will lament him. Yes. Amen. ⁸"I am the Alpha and the Omega," says the Lord God, "the one who is and who was and who is to come, the almighty." ⁹I, John, your brother, who share with you the distress, the kingdom, and the endurance we have in Jesus, found myself on the island called Patmos because I proclaimed God's word and gave testimony to Jesus. ¹⁰I was caught up in spirit on the Lord's day and heard behind me a voice as loud as a trumpet, ¹¹which said, "Write on a scroll what you see and send it to the seven churches: to

Ephesus, Smyrna, Pergamum, Thyatira, Sardis, Philadelphia, and Laodicea." ¹²Then I turned to see whose voice it was that spoke to me, and when I turned, I saw seven gold lampstands ¹³and in the midst of the lampstands one like a son of man, wearing an ankle-length robe, with a gold sash around his chest. ¹⁴The hair of his head was as white as white wool or as snow, and his eyes were like a fiery flame. ¹⁵His feet were like polished brass refined in a furnace, and his voice was like the sound of rushing water. ¹⁶In his right hand he held seven stars. A sharp two-edged sword came out of his mouth, and his face shone like the sun at its brightest. ¹⁷When I caught sight of him, I fell down at his feet as though dead. He touched me with his right hand and said, "Do not be afraid. I am the first and the last, ¹⁸the one who lives. Once I was dead, but now I am alive forever and ever. I hold the keys to death and the netherworld. ¹⁹Write down, therefore, what you have seen, and what is happening, and what will happen afterwards. ²⁰This is the secret meaning of the seven stars you saw in my right hand, and of the seven gold lampstands: the seven stars are the angels of the seven churches, and the seven lampstands are the seven churches."

Revelation Chapter 2

¹"To the angel of the church in Ephesus, write this: 'The one who holds the seven stars in his right hand and walks in the midst of the seven gold lampstands says this:²"I know your works, your labor, and your endurance, and that you cannot tolerate the wicked; you have tested those who call themselves apostles but are not, and discovered that they are impostors.³Moreover, you have endurance and have suffered for my name, and you have not grown weary.⁴Yet I hold this against you: you have lost the love you had at first.⁵Realize how far you have fallen. Repent, and do the works you did at first. Otherwise, I will come to you and remove your lampstand from its place, unless you repent.⁶But you have this in your favor: you hate the works of the Nicolaitans, which I also hate.⁷"'Whoever has ears ought to hear what the Spirit says to the churches. To the victor I will give the right to eat from the tree of life that is in the garden of God.'"⁸"To the angel of the church in Smyrna, write this: 'The first and the last, who once died but came to life, says this:⁹"I know your tribulation and poverty, but you are rich. I know the slander of those who claim to be Jews and are not, but rather are members of the assembly of Satan.¹⁰Do not be afraid of anything that you are going to suffer. Indeed, the devil will throw some of you into prison, that you may be tested, and you will face an ordeal for ten days. Remain faithful until death, and I will give you the crown of life.¹¹"'Whoever has ears ought to hear what the Spirit says to the churches. The victor shall not be harmed by the second death.'"¹²"To the angel of the church in Pergamum, write this: 'The one with the sharp two-edged sword says this:¹³"I know that you live where Satan's throne is, and yet you hold fast to my name and have not denied your faith in me, not even in the days of Antipas, my faithful witness, who was martyred among you, where Satan lives.¹⁴Yet I have a few things against you. You have some people there who hold to the teaching of Balaam, who instructed Balak to put a stumbling block before the Israelites: to eat food sacrificed to idols and to play the harlot.¹⁵Likewise, you also have some people who hold to the teaching of the Nicolaitans.¹⁶Therefore, repent. Otherwise, I will come to you quickly and wage war against them with the sword of my mouth.¹⁷"'Whoever has ears ought to hear what the Spirit says to the churches. To the victor I shall give some of the hidden manna; I shall also give a white amulet upon which is inscribed a new name, which no one knows except the one who receives it.'"¹⁸"To the angel of the church in Thyatira, write this: 'The Son of God, whose eyes are like a fiery flame and whose feet are like polished brass, says this:¹⁹"I know your works, your love, faith, service, and endurance, and that your last works are greater than the first.²⁰Yet I hold this against you, that you tolerate the woman Jezebel, who calls herself a prophetess, who teaches and misleads my servants to play the harlot and to eat food sacrificed to idols.²¹I have given her time to repent, but she refuses to repent of her harlotry.²²So I will cast her on a sickbed and plunge those who commit adultery with her into intense suffering unless they repent of her works.²³I will also put her children to death. Thus shall all the churches come to know that I am the searcher of hearts and minds and that I will give each of you what your works deserve.²⁴But I say to the rest of you in Thyatira, who do not uphold this teaching and know nothing of the so-called deep secrets of Satan: on you I will place no further burden,²⁵except that you must hold fast to what you have until I come.²⁶"'To the victor, who keeps to my ways until the end, I will give authority over the nations.²⁷He will rule them with an iron rod. Like clay vessels will they be smashed,²⁸just as I received authority from my Father. And to him I will give the morning star.²⁹"'Whoever has ears ought to hear what the Spirit says to the churches.'"

Revelation Chapter 3

1"To the angel of the church in Sardis, write this: 'The one who has the seven spirits of God and the seven stars says this: "I know your works, that you have the reputation of being alive, but you are dead.2Be watchful and strengthen what is left, which is going to die, for I have not found your works complete in the sight of my God.3Remember then how you accepted and heard; keep it, and repent. If you are not watchful, I will come like a thief, and you will never know at what hour I will come upon you.4However, you have a few people in Sardis who have not soiled their garments; they will walk with me dressed in white, because they are worthy.5""The victor will thus be dressed in white, and I will never erase his name from the book of life but will acknowledge his name in the presence of my Father and of his angels.6"""Whoever has ears ought to hear what the Spirit says to the churches."'7"To the angel of the church in Philadelphia, write this: 'The holy one, the true, who holds the key of David, who opens and no one shall close, who closes and no one shall open, says this:8"""I know your works (behold, I have left an open door before you, which no one can close). You have limited strength, and yet you have kept my word and have not denied my name.9Behold, I will make those of the assembly of Satan who claim to be Jews and are not, but are lying, behold I will make them come and fall prostrate at your feet, and they will realize that I love you.10Because you have kept my message of endurance, I will keep you safe in the time of trial that is going to come to the whole world to test the inhabitants of the earth.11I am coming quickly. Hold fast to what you have, so that no one may take your crown.12"""The victor I will make into a pillar in the temple of my God, and he will never leave it again. On him I will inscribe the name of my God and the name of the city of my God, the new Jerusalem, which comes down out of heaven from my God, as well as my new name.13"""Whoever has ears ought to hear what the Spirit says to the churches."'14"To the angel of the church in Laodicea, write this: 'The Amen, the faithful and true witness, the source of God's creation, says this:15"I know your works; I know that you are neither cold nor hot. I wish you were either cold or hot.16So, because you are lukewarm, neither hot nor cold, I will spit you out of my mouth.17For you say, 'I am rich and affluent and have no need of anything,' and yet do not realize that you are wretched, pitiable, poor, blind, and naked.18I advise you to buy from me gold refined by fire so that you may be rich, and white garments to put on so that your shameful nakedness may not be exposed, and buy ointment to smear on your eyes so that you may see.19Those whom I love, I reprove and chastise. Be earnest, therefore, and repent.20"""Behold, I stand at the door and knock. If anyone hears my voice and opens the door, (then) I will enter his house and dine with him, and he with me.21I will give the victor the right to sit with me on my throne, as I myself first won the victory and sit with my Father on his throne.22"""Whoever has ears ought to hear what the Spirit says to the churches."'"

Revelation Chapter 4

1After this I had a vision of an open door to heaven, and I heard the trumpetlike voice that had spoken to me before, saying, "Come up here and I will show you what must happen afterwards." 2At once I was caught up in spirit. A throne was there in heaven, and on the throne sat 3one whose appearance sparkled like jasper and carnelian. Around the throne was a halo as brilliant as an emerald. 4Surrounding the throne I saw twenty-four other thrones on which twenty-four elders sat, dressed in white garments and with gold crowns on their heads. 5From the throne came flashes of lightning, rumblings, and peals of thunder. Seven flaming torches burned in front of the throne, which are the seven spirits of God. 6In front of the throne was something that resembled a sea of glass like crystal. In the center and around the throne, there were four living creatures covered with eyes in front and in back. 7The first creature resembled a lion, the second was like a calf, the third had a face like that of a human being, and the fourth looked like an eagle in flight. 8The four living creatures, each of them with six wings, were covered with eyes inside and out. Day and night they do not stop exclaiming: "Holy, holy, holy is the Lord God almighty, who was, and who is, and who is to come." 9Whenever the living creatures give glory and honor and thanks to the one who sits on the throne, who lives forever and ever, 10the twenty-four elders fall down before the one who sits on the throne and worship him, who lives forever and ever. They throw down their crowns before the throne, exclaiming: 11"Worthy are you, Lord our God, to receive glory and honor and power, for you created all things; because of your will they came to be and were created."

Revelation Chapter 5

1I saw a scroll in the right hand of the one who sat on the throne. It had writing on both sides and was sealed with seven seals. 2Then I saw a mighty angel who proclaimed in a loud voice, "Who is worthy to open the scroll and break its seals?" 3But no one in heaven or on earth or under the earth was able to open the scroll or to examine it. 4I shed many tears because no one was found worthy to open the scroll or to examine it. 5One of the elders said to me, "Do not weep. The lion of the tribe of Judah, the root of David, has triumphed, enabling him to open the scroll with its seven seals." 6Then I saw standing in the midst of the throne and the four living creatures and the elders, a Lamb that seemed to have been slain. He had seven horns and seven eyes; these are the (seven) spirits of God sent out into the whole world. 7He came and received the scroll from the right hand of the one who sat on the throne. 8When he took it, the four living creatures and the twenty-four elders fell down before the Lamb. Each of the elders held a harp and gold bowls filled with incense, which are the prayers of the holy ones. 9They sang a new hymn: "Worthy are you to receive the scroll and to break open its seals, for you were slain and with your blood you purchased for God those from every tribe and tongue, people and nation. 10You made them a kingdom and priests for our God, and they will reign on earth." 11I looked again and heard the voices of many angels who surrounded the throne and the living creatures and the elders. They were countless in number, 12and they cried out in a loud voice: "Worthy is the Lamb that was slain to receive power and riches, wisdom and strength, honor and glory and blessing." 13Then I heard every creature in heaven and on earth and under the earth and in the sea, everything in the universe, cry out: "To the one who sits on the throne and to the Lamb be blessing and honor, glory and might, forever and ever." 14The four living creatures answered, "Amen," and the elders fell down and worshiped.

Revelation Chapter 6

1Then I watched while the Lamb broke open the first of the seven seals, and I heard one of the four living creatures cry out in a voice like thunder, "Come forward." 2I looked, and there was a white horse, and its rider had a bow. He was given a crown, and he rode forth victorious to further his victories. 3When he broke open the second seal, I heard the second living creature cry out, "Come forward." 4Another horse came out, a red one. Its rider was given power to take peace away from the earth, so that people would slaughter one another. And he was given a huge sword. 5When he broke open the third seal, I heard the third living creature cry out, "Come forward." I looked, and there was a black horse, and its rider held a scale in his hand. 6I heard what seemed to be a voice in the midst of the four living creatures. It said, "A ration of wheat costs a day's pay, and three rations of barley cost a day's pay. But do not damage the olive oil or the wine." 7When he broke open the fourth seal, I heard the voice of the fourth living creature cry out, "Come forward." 8I looked, and there was a pale green horse. Its rider was named Death, and Hades accompanied him. They were given authority over a quarter of the earth, to kill with sword, famine, and plague, and by means of the beasts of the earth. 9When he broke open the fifth seal, I saw underneath the altar the souls of those who had been slaughtered because of the witness they bore to the word of God. 10They cried out in a loud voice, "How long will it be, holy and true master, before you sit in judgment and avenge our blood on the inhabitants of the earth?" 11Each of them was given a white robe, and they were told to be patient a little while longer until the number was filled of their fellow servants and brothers who were going to be killed as they had been. 12Then I watched while he broke open the sixth seal, and there was a great earthquake; the sun turned as black as dark sackcloth and the whole moon became like blood. 13The stars in the sky fell to the earth like unripe figs shaken loose from the tree in a strong wind. 14Then the sky was divided like a torn scroll curling up, and every mountain and island was moved from its place. 15The kings of the earth, the nobles, the military officers, the rich, the powerful, and every slave and free person hid themselves in caves and among mountain crags. 16They cried out to the mountains and the rocks, "Fall on us and hide us from the face of the one who sits on the throne and from the wrath of the Lamb, 17because the great day of their wrath has come and who can withstand it?"

Revelation Chapter 7

1After this I saw four angels standing at the four corners of the earth, holding back the four winds of the earth so that no wind could blow on land or sea or against any tree. 2Then I saw another angel come up from the East, holding the seal of the living God. He cried out in a loud voice to the four angels who were given power to damage the land and the sea, 3"Do not damage the land or the sea or the trees until we put the seal on the foreheads of the servants of our God." 4I heard the number of those who had been marked with the seal, one hundred and forty-four thousand marked from every tribe of the Israelites: 5twelve thousand were marked from the tribe of Judah, twelve thousand from the tribe of Reuben, twelve thousand from the tribe of Gad, ⁶twelve thousand from the tribe of Asher, twelve thousand from the tribe of Naphtali, twelve thousand from the tribe of Manasseh, ⁷twelve thousand from the tribe of Simeon, twelve thousand from the tribe of Levi, twelve thousand from the tribe of Issachar, ⁸twelve thousand from the tribe of Zebulun, twelve thousand from the tribe of Joseph, and twelve thousand were marked from the tribe of Benjamin. ⁹After this I had a vision of a great multitude, which no one could count, from every nation, race, people, and tongue. They stood before the throne and before the Lamb, wearing white robes and holding palm branches in their hands. ¹⁰They cried out in a loud voice: "Salvation comes from our God, who is seated on the throne, and from the Lamb." ¹¹All the angels stood around the throne and around the elders and the four living creatures. They prostrated themselves before the throne, worshiped God, ¹²and exclaimed: "Amen. Blessing and glory, wisdom and thanksgiving, honor, power, and might be to our God forever and ever. Amen." ¹³Then one of the elders spoke up and said to me, "Who are these wearing white robes, and where did they come from?" ¹⁴I said to him, "My lord, you are the one who knows." He said to me, "These are the ones who have survived the time of great distress; they have washed their robes and made them white in the blood of the Lamb. ¹⁵For this reason they stand before God's throne and worship him day and night in his temple. The one who sits on the throne will shelter them. ¹⁶They will not hunger or thirst anymore, nor will the sun or any heat strike them. ¹⁷For the Lamb who is in the center of the throne will shepherd them and lead them to springs of life-giving water, and God will wipe away every tear from their eyes."

Revelation Chapter 8

¹When he broke open the seventh seal, there was silence in heaven for about half an hour. ²And I saw that the seven angels who stood before God were given seven trumpets. ³Another angel came and stood at the altar, holding a gold censer. He was given a great quantity of incense to offer, along with the prayers of all the holy ones, on the gold altar that was before the throne. ⁴The smoke of the incense along with the prayers of the holy ones went up before God from the hand of the angel. ⁵Then the angel took the censer, filled it with burning coals from the altar, and hurled it down to the earth. There were peals of thunder, rumblings, flashes of lightning, and an earthquake. ⁶The seven angels who were holding the seven trumpets prepared to blow them. ⁷When the first one blew his trumpet, there came hail and fire mixed with blood, which was hurled down to the earth. A third of the land was burned up, along with a third of the trees and all green grass. ⁸When the second angel blew his trumpet, something like a large burning mountain was hurled into the sea. A third of the sea turned to blood, ⁹a third of the creatures living in the sea died, and a third of the ships were wrecked. ¹⁰When the third angel blew his trumpet, a large star burning like a torch fell from the sky. It fell on a third of the rivers and on the springs of water. ¹¹The star was called "Wormwood," and a third of all the water turned to wormwood. Many people died from this water, because it was made bitter. ¹²When the fourth angel blew his trumpet, a third of the sun, a third of the moon, and a third of the stars were struck, so that a third of them became dark. The day lost its light for a third of the time, as did the night. ¹³Then I looked again and heard an eagle flying high overhead cry out in a loud voice, "Woe! Woe! Woe to the inhabitants of the earth from the rest of the trumpet blasts that the three angels are about to blow!"

Revelation Chapter 9

¹Then the fifth angel blew his trumpet, and I saw a star that had fallen from the sky to the earth. It was given the key for the passage to the abyss. ²It opened the passage to the abyss, and smoke came up out of the passage like smoke from a huge furnace. The sun and the air were darkened by the smoke from the passage. ³Locusts came out of the smoke onto the land, and they were given the same power as scorpions of the earth. ⁴They were told not to harm the grass of the earth or any plant or any tree, but only those people who did not have the seal of God on their foreheads. ⁵They were not allowed to kill them but only to torment them for five months; the torment they inflicted was like that of a scorpion when it stings a person. ⁶During that time these people will seek death but will not find it, and they will long to die but death will escape them. ⁷The appearance of the locusts was like that of horses ready for battle. On their heads they wore what looked like crowns of gold; their faces were like human faces, ⁸and they had hair like women's hair. Their teeth were like lions' teeth, ⁹and they had chests like iron breastplates. The sound of their wings was like the sound of many horse-drawn chariots racing into battle. ¹⁰They had tails like scorpions, with stingers; with their tails they had power to harm people for five months. ¹¹They had as their king the angel of the abyss, whose name in Hebrew is Abaddon and in Greek Apollyon. ¹²The first woe has passed, but there are two more to come. ¹³Then the sixth angel blew his trumpet, and I heard a voice coming from the four horns of the gold altar before God, ¹⁴telling the sixth angel who held the trumpet, "Release the four angels who are bound at the banks of the great river Euphrates." ¹⁵So the four angels were released, who were prepared for this hour, day, month, and year to kill a third of the human race. ¹⁶The number of cavalry troops was two hundred million; I heard their number. ¹⁷Now in my vision this is how I saw the horses and their riders. They wore red, blue, and yellow breastplates, and the horses' heads were like heads of lions, and out of their mouths came fire, smoke, and sulfur. ¹⁸By these three plagues of fire, smoke, and sulfur that came out of their mouths a third of the human race was killed. ¹⁹For the power of the horses is in their mouths and in their tails; for their tails are like snakes, with heads that inflict harm. ²⁰The rest of the human race, who were not killed by these plagues, did not repent of the works of their hands, to give up the worship of demons and idols made from gold, silver, bronze, stone, and wood, which cannot see or hear or walk. ²¹Nor did they repent of their murders, their magic potions, their unchastity, or their robberies.

Revelation Chapter 10

¹Then I saw another mighty angel come down from heaven wrapped in a cloud, with a halo around his head; his face was like the sun and his feet were like pillars of fire. ²In his hand he held a small scroll that had been opened. He placed his right foot on the sea and his left foot on the land, ³and then he cried out in a loud voice as a lion roars. When he cried out, the seven thunders raised their voices, too. ⁴When the seven thunders had spoken, I was about to write it down; but I heard a voice from heaven say, "Seal up what the seven thunders have spoken, but do not write it down." ⁵Then the angel I saw standing on the sea and on the land raised his right hand to heaven ⁶and swore by the one who lives forever and ever, who created heaven and earth and sea and all that is in them, "There shall be no more delay. ⁷At the time when you hear the seventh angel blow his trumpet, the mysterious plan of God shall be fulfilled, as he promised to his servants the prophets." ⁸Then the voice that I had heard from heaven spoke to me again and said, "Go, take the scroll that lies open in the hand of the angel who is standing on the sea and on the land." ⁹So I went up to the angel and told him to give me the small scroll. He said to me, "Take and swallow it. It will turn your stomach sour, but in your mouth it will taste as sweet as honey." ¹⁰I took the small scroll from the angel's hand and swallowed it. In my mouth it was like sweet honey, but when I had eaten it, my stomach turned sour. ¹¹Then someone said to me, "You must prophesy again about many peoples, nations, tongues, and kings."

Revelation Chapter 11

¹Then I was given a measuring rod like a staff and I was told, "Come and measure the temple of God and the altar, and count those who are worshiping in it. ²But exclude the outer court of the temple; do not measure it, for it has been handed over to the Gentiles, who will trample the holy city for forty-two months. ³I will commission my two witnesses to prophesy for those twelve hundred and sixty days, wearing sackcloth." ⁴These are the two olive trees and the two lampstands that stand before the Lord of the earth. ⁵If anyone wants to harm them, fire comes out of their mouths and devours their enemies. In this way, anyone wanting to harm them is sure to be slain. ⁶They have the power to close up the sky so that no rain can fall during the time of their prophesying. They also have power to turn water into blood and to afflict the earth with any plague as often as they wish. ⁷When they have finished their testimony, the beast that comes up from the abyss will wage war against them and conquer them and kill them. ⁸Their corpses will lie in the main street of the great city, which has the symbolic names "Sodom" and "Egypt," where indeed their Lord was crucified. ⁹Those from every people, tribe, tongue, and nation will gaze on their corpses for three and a half days, and they will not allow their corpses to be buried. ¹⁰The inhabitants of the earth will gloat over them and be glad and exchange gifts because these two prophets tormented the inhabitants of the earth. ¹¹But after the three and a half days, a breath of life from God entered them. When they stood on their feet, great fear fell on those who saw them. ¹²Then they heard a loud voice from heaven say to them, "Come up here." So they went up to heaven in a cloud as their enemies looked on. ¹³At that moment there was a great earthquake, and a tenth of the city fell in ruins. Seven thousand people were killed during the earthquake; the rest were terrified and gave glory to the God of heaven. ¹⁴The second woe has passed, but the third is coming soon. ¹⁵Then the seventh angel blew his trumpet. There were loud voices in heaven, saying, "The kingdom of the world now belongs to our Lord and to his Anointed, and he will reign forever and ever."

16The twenty-four elders who sat on their thrones before God prostrated themselves and worshiped God 17and said: "We give thanks to you, Lord God almighty, who are and who were. For you have assumed your great power and have established your reign. 18The nations raged, but your wrath has come, and the time for the dead to be judged, and to recompense your servants, the prophets, and the holy ones and those who fear your name, the small and the great alike, and to destroy those who destroy the earth." 19Then God's temple in heaven was opened, and the ark of his covenant could be seen in the temple. There were flashes of lightning, rumblings, and peals of thunder, an earthquake, and a violent hailstorm.

Revelation Chapter 12

1A great sign appeared in the sky, a woman clothed with the sun, with the moon under her feet, and on her head a crown of twelve stars. 2She was with child and wailed aloud in pain as she labored to give birth. 3Then another sign appeared in the sky; it was a huge red dragon, with seven heads and ten horns, and on its heads were seven diadems. 4Its tail swept away a third of the stars in the sky and hurled them down to the earth. Then the dragon stood before the woman about to give birth, to devour her child when she gave birth. 5She gave birth to a son, a male child, destined to rule all the nations with an iron rod. Her child was caught up to God and his throne. 6The woman herself fled into the desert where she had a place prepared by God, that there she might be taken care of for twelve hundred and sixty days. 7Then war broke out in heaven; Michael and his angels battled against the dragon. The dragon and its angels fought back, 8but they did not prevail and there was no longer any place for them in heaven. 9The huge dragon, the ancient serpent, who is called the Devil and Satan, who deceived the whole world, was thrown down to earth, and its angels were thrown down with it. 10Then I heard a loud voice in heaven say: "Now have salvation and power come, and the kingdom of our God and the authority of his Anointed. For the accuser of our brothers is cast out, who accuses them before our God day and night. 11They conquered him by the blood of the Lamb and by the word of their testimony; love for life did not deter them from death. 12Therefore, rejoice, you heavens, and you who dwell in them. But woe to you, earth and sea, for the Devil has come down to you in great fury, for he knows he has but a short time." 13When the dragon saw that it had been thrown down to the earth, it pursued the woman who had given birth to the male child. 14But the woman was given the two wings of the great eagle, so that she could fly to her place in the desert, where, far from the serpent, she was taken care of for a year, two years, and a half-year. 15The serpent, however, spewed a torrent of water out of his mouth after the woman to sweep her away with the current. 16But the earth helped the woman and opened its mouth and swallowed the flood that the dragon spewed out of its mouth. 17Then the dragon became angry with the woman and went off to wage war against the rest of her offspring, those who keep God's commandments and bear witness to Jesus. It took its position on the sand of the sea.

Revelation Chapter 13

1Then I saw a beast come out of the sea with ten horns and seven heads; on its horns were ten diadems, and on its heads blasphemous names. 2The beast I saw was like a leopard, but it had feet like a bear's, and its mouth was like the mouth of a lion. To it the dragon gave its own power and throne, along with great authority. 3I saw that one of its heads seemed to have been mortally wounded, but this mortal wound was healed. Fascinated, the whole world followed after the beast. 4They worshiped the dragon because it gave its authority to the beast; they also worshiped the beast and said, "Who can compare with the beast or who can fight against it?" 5The beast was given a mouth uttering proud boasts and blasphemies, and it was given authority to act for forty-two months. 6It opened its mouth to utter blasphemies against God, blaspheming his name and his dwelling and those who dwell in heaven. 7It was also allowed to wage war against the holy ones and conquer them, and it was granted authority over every tribe, people, tongue, and nation. 8All the inhabitants of the earth will worship it, all whose names were not written from the foundation of the world in the book of life, which belongs to the Lamb who was slain. 9Whoever has ears ought to hear these words. 10Anyone destined for captivity goes into captivity. Anyone destined to be slain by the sword shall be slain by the sword. Such is the faithful endurance of the holy ones. 11Then I saw another beast come up out of the earth; it had two horns like a lamb's but spoke like a dragon. 12It wielded all the authority of the first beast in its sight and made the earth and its inhabitants worship the first beast, whose mortal wound had been healed. 13It performed great signs, even making fire come down from heaven to earth in the sight of everyone. 14It deceived the inhabitants of the earth with the signs it was allowed to perform in the sight of the first beast, telling them to make an image for the beast who had been wounded by the sword and revived. 15It was then permitted to breathe life into the beast's image, so that the beast's image could speak and could have anyone who did not worship it put to death. 16It forced all the people, small and great, rich and poor, free and slave, to be given a stamped image on their right hands or their foreheads, 17so that no one could buy or sell except one who had the stamped image of the beast's name or the number that stood for its name. 18Wisdom is needed here; one who understands can calculate the number of the beast, for it is a number that stands for a person. His number is six hundred and sixty-six.

Revelation Chapter 14

1Then I looked and there was the Lamb standing on Mount Zion, and with him a hundred and forty-four thousand who had his name and his Father's name written on their foreheads. 2I heard a sound from heaven like the sound of rushing water or a loud peal of thunder. The sound I heard was like that of harpists playing their harps. 3They were singing (what seemed to be) a new hymn before the throne, before the four living creatures and the elders. No one could learn this hymn except the hundred and forty-four thousand who had been ransomed from the earth. 4These are they who were not defiled with women; they are virgins and these are the ones who follow the Lamb wherever he goes. They have been ransomed as the firstfruits of the human race for God and the Lamb. 5On their lips no deceit has been found; they are unblemished. 6Then I saw another angel flying high overhead, with everlasting good news to announce to those who dwell on earth, to every nation, tribe, tongue, and people. 7He said in a loud voice, "Fear God and give him glory, for his time has come to sit in judgment. Worship him who made heaven and earth and sea and springs of water." 8A second angel followed, saying: "Fallen, fallen is Babylon the great, that made all the nations drink the wine of her licentious passion." 9A third angel followed them and said in a loud voice, "Anyone who worships the beast or its image, or accepts its mark on forehead or hand, 10will also drink the wine of God's fury, poured full strength into the cup of his wrath, and will be tormented in burning sulfur before the holy angels and before the Lamb. 11The smoke of the fire that torments them will rise forever and ever, and there will be no relief day or night for those who worship the beast or its image or accept the mark of its name." 12Here is what sustains the holy ones who keep God's commandments and their faith in Jesus. 13I heard a voice from heaven say, "Write this: Blessed are the dead who die in the Lord from now on." "Yes," said the Spirit, "let them find rest from their labors, for their works accompany them." 14Then I looked and there was a white cloud, and sitting on the cloud one who looked like a son of man, with a gold crown on his head and a sharp sickle in his hand. 15Another angel came out of the temple, crying out in a loud voice to the one sitting on the cloud, "Use your sickle and reap the harvest, for the time to reap has come, because the earth's harvest is fully ripe." 16So the one who was sitting on the cloud swung his sickle over the earth, and the earth was harvested. 17Then another angel came out of the temple in heaven who also had a sharp sickle. 18Then another angel (came) from the altar, (who) was in charge of the fire, and cried out in a loud voice to the one who had the sharp sickle, "Use your sharp sickle and cut the clusters from the earth's vines, for its grapes are ripe." 19So the angel swung his sickle over the earth and cut the earth's vintage. He threw it into the great wine press of God's fury. 20The wine press was trodden outside the city and blood poured out of the wine press to the height of a horse's bridle for two hundred miles.

Revelation Chapter 15

1Then I saw in heaven another sign, great and awe-inspiring: seven angels with the seven last plagues, for through them God's fury is accomplished. 2Then I saw something like a sea of glass mingled with fire. On the sea of glass were standing those who had won the victory over the beast and its image and the number that signified its name. They were holding God's harps, 3and they sang the song of Moses, the servant of God, and the song of the Lamb: "Great and wonderful are your works, Lord God almighty. Just and true are your ways, O king of the nations. 4Who will not fear you, Lord, or glorify your name? For you alone are holy. All the nations will come and worship before you, for your righteous acts have been revealed." 5After this I had another vision. The temple that is the heavenly tent of testimony opened, 6and the seven angels with the seven plagues came out of the temple. They were dressed in clean white linen, with a gold sash around their chests. 7One of the four living creatures gave the seven angels seven gold bowls filled with the fury of God, who lives forever and ever. 8Then the temple became so filled with the smoke from God's glory and might that no one could enter it until the seven plagues of the seven angels had been accomplished.

Revelation Chapter 16

[1]I heard a loud voice speaking from the temple to the seven angels, "Go and pour out the seven bowls of God's fury upon the earth." [2]The first angel went and poured out his bowl on the earth. Festering and ugly sores broke out on those who had the mark of the beast or worshiped its image. [3]The second angel poured out his bowl on the sea. The sea turned to blood like that from a corpse; every creature living in the sea died. [4]The third angel poured out his bowl on the rivers and springs of water. These also turned to blood. [5]Then I heard the angel in charge of the waters say: "You are just, O Holy One, who are and who were, in passing this sentence. [6]For they have shed the blood of the holy ones and the prophets, and you (have) given them blood to drink; it is what they deserve." [7]Then I heard the altar cry out, "Yes, Lord God almighty, your judgments are true and just." [8]The fourth angel poured out his bowl on the sun. It was given the power to burn people with fire. [9]People were burned by the scorching heat and blasphemed the name of God who had power over these plagues, but they did not repent or give him glory. [10]The fifth angel poured out his bowl on the throne of the beast. Its kingdom was plunged into darkness, and people bit their tongues in pain [11]and blasphemed the God of heaven because of their pains and sores. But they did not repent of their works. [12]The sixth angel emptied his bowl on the great river Euphrates. Its water was dried up to prepare the way for the kings of the East. [13]I saw three unclean spirits like frogs come from the mouth of the dragon, from the mouth of the beast, and from the mouth of the false prophet. [14]These were demonic spirits who performed signs. They went out to the kings of the whole world to assemble them for the battle on the great day of God the almighty. [15]("Behold, I am coming like a thief." Blessed is the one who watches and keeps his clothes ready, so that he may not go naked and people see him exposed.) [16]They then assembled the kings in the place that is named Armageddon in Hebrew. [17]The seventh angel poured out his bowl into the air. A loud voice came out of the temple from the throne, saying, "It is done." [18]Then there were lightning flashes, rumblings, and peals of thunder, and a great earthquake. It was such a violent earthquake that there has never been one like it since the human race began on earth. [19]The great city was split into three parts, and the gentile cities fell. But God remembered great Babylon, giving it the cup filled with the wine of his fury and wrath. [20]Every island fled, and mountains disappeared. [21]Large hailstones like huge weights came down from the sky on people, and they blasphemed God for the plague of hail because this plague was so severe.

Revelation Chapter 17

[1]Then one of the seven angels who were holding the seven bowls came and said to me, "Come here. I will show you the judgment on the great harlot who lives near the many waters. [2]The kings of the earth have had intercourse with her, and the inhabitants of the earth became drunk on the wine of her harlotry." [3]Then he carried me away in spirit to a deserted place where I saw a woman seated on a scarlet beast that was covered with blasphemous names, with seven heads and ten horns. [4]The woman was wearing purple and scarlet and adorned with gold, precious stones, and pearls. She held in her hand a gold cup that was filled with the abominable and sordid deeds of her harlotry. [5]On her forehead was written a name, which is a mystery, "Babylon the great, the mother of harlots and of the abominations of the earth." [6]I saw that the woman was drunk on the blood of the holy ones and on the blood of the witnesses to Jesus. When I saw her I was greatly amazed. [7]The angel said to me, "Why are you amazed? I will explain to you the mystery of the woman and of the beast that carries her, the beast with the seven heads and the ten horns. [8]The beast that you saw existed once but now exists no longer. It will come up from the abyss and is headed for destruction. The inhabitants of the earth whose names have not been written in the book of life from the foundation of the world shall be amazed when they see the beast, because it existed once but exists no longer, and yet it will come again. [9]Here is a clue for one who has wisdom. The seven heads represent seven hills upon which the woman sits. They also represent seven kings: [10]five have already fallen, one still lives, and the last has not yet come, and when he comes he must remain only a short while. [11]The beast that existed once but exists no longer is an eighth king, but really belongs to the seven and is headed for destruction. [12]The ten horns that you saw represent ten kings who have not yet been crowned; they will receive royal authority along with the beast for one hour. [13]They are of one mind and will give their power and authority to the beast. [14]They will fight with the Lamb, but the Lamb will conquer them, for he is Lord of lords and king of kings, and those with him are called, chosen, and faithful." [15]Then he said to me, "The waters that you saw where the harlot lives represent large numbers of peoples, nations, and tongues. [16]The ten horns that you saw and the beast will hate the harlot; they will leave her desolate and naked; they will eat her flesh and consume her with fire. [17]For God has put it into their minds to carry out his purpose and to make them come to an agreement to give their kingdom to the beast until the words of God are accomplished. [18]The woman whom you saw represents the great city that has sovereignty over the kings of the earth."

Revelation Chapter 18

[1]After this I saw another angel coming down from heaven, having great authority, and the earth became illumined by his splendor. [2]He cried out in a mighty voice: "Fallen, fallen is Babylon the great. She has become a haunt for demons. She is a cage for every unclean spirit, a cage for every unclean bird, (a cage for every unclean) and disgusting (beast). [3]For all the nations have drunk the wine of her licentious passion. The kings of the earth had intercourse with her, and the merchants of the earth grew rich from her drive for luxury." [4]Then I heard another voice from heaven say: "Depart from her, my people, so as not to take part in her sins and receive a share in her plagues, [5]for her sins are piled up to the sky, and God remembers her crimes. [6]Pay her back as she has paid others. Pay her back double for her deeds. Into her cup pour double what she poured. [7]To the measure of her boasting and wantonness repay her in torment and grief; for she said to herself, 'I sit enthroned as queen; I am no widow, and I will never know grief.' [8]Therefore, her plagues will come in one day, pestilence, grief, and famine; she will be consumed by fire. For mighty is the Lord God who judges her." [9]The kings of the earth who had intercourse with her in their wantonness will weep and mourn over her when they see the smoke of her pyre. [10]They will keep their distance for fear of the torment inflicted on her, and they will say: "Alas, alas, great city, Babylon, mighty city. In one hour your judgment has come." [11]The merchants of the earth will weep and mourn for her, because there will be no more markets for their cargo: [12]their cargo of gold, silver, precious stones, and pearls; fine linen, purple silk, and scarlet cloth; fragrant wood of every kind, all articles of ivory and all articles of the most expensive wood, bronze, iron, and marble; [13]cinnamon, spice, incense, myrrh, and frankincense; wine, olive oil, fine flour, and wheat; cattle and sheep, horses and chariots, and slaves, that is, human beings. [14]"The fruit you craved has left you. All your luxury and splendor are gone, never again will one find them." [15]The merchants who deal in these goods, who grew rich from her, will keep their distance for fear of the torment inflicted on her. Weeping and mourning, [16]they cry out: "Alas, alas, great city, wearing fine linen, purple and scarlet, adorned (in) gold, precious stones, and pearls. [17]In one hour this great wealth has been ruined." Every captain of a ship, every traveler at sea, sailors, and seafaring merchants stood at a distance [18]and cried out when they saw the smoke of her pyre, "What city could compare with the great city?" [19]They threw dust on their heads and cried out, weeping and mourning: "Alas, alas, great city, in which all who had ships at sea grew rich from her wealth. In one hour she has been ruined. [20]Rejoice over her, heaven, you holy ones, apostles, and prophets. For God has judged your case against her." [21]A mighty angel picked up a stone like a huge millstone and threw it into the sea and said: "With such force will Babylon the great city be thrown down, and will never be found again. [22]No melodies of harpists and musicians, flutists and trumpeters, will ever be heard in you again. No craftsmen in any trade will ever be found in you again. No sound of the millstone will ever be heard in you again. [23]No light from a lamp will ever be seen in you again. No voices of bride and groom will ever be heard in you again. Because your merchants were the great ones of the world, all nations were led astray by your magic potion. [24]In her was found the blood of prophets and holy ones and all who have been slain on the earth."

Revelation Chapter 19

[1]After this I heard what sounded like the loud voice of a great multitude in heaven, saying: "Alleluia! Salvation, glory, and might belong to our God, [2]for true and just are his judgments. He has condemned the great harlot who corrupted the earth with her harlotry. He has avenged on her the blood of his servants." [3]They said a second time: "Alleluia! Smoke will rise from her forever and ever." [4]The twenty-four elders and the four living creatures fell down and worshiped God who sat on the throne, saying, "Amen. Alleluia." [5]A voice coming from the throne said: "Praise our God, all you his servants, (and) you who revere him, small and great." [6]Then I heard something like the sound of a great multitude or the sound of rushing water or mighty peals of thunder, as they said: "Alleluia! The Lord has established his reign, (our) God, the almighty. [7]Let us rejoice and be glad and give him glory. For the wedding day of the Lamb has come, his bride has made herself ready. [8]She was allowed to wear a bright, clean linen garment." (The linen represents the

righteous deeds of the holy ones.) ⁹Then the angel said to me, "Write this: Blessed are those who have been called to the wedding feast of the Lamb." And he said to me, "These words are true; they come from God." ¹⁰I fell at his feet to worship him. But he said to me, "Don't! I am a fellow servant of yours and of your brothers who bear witness to Jesus. Worship God. Witness to Jesus is the spirit of prophecy." ¹¹Then I saw the heavens opened, and there was a white horse; its rider was (called) "Faithful and True." He judges and wages war in righteousness. ¹²His eyes were (like) a fiery flame, and on his head were many diadems. He had a name inscribed that no one knows except himself. ¹³He wore a cloak that had been dipped in blood, and his name was called the Word of God. ¹⁴The armies of heaven followed him, mounted on white horses and wearing clean white linen. ¹⁵Out of his mouth came a sharp sword to strike the nations. He will rule them with an iron rod, and he himself will tread out in the wine press the wine of the fury and wrath of God the almighty. ¹⁶He has a name written on his cloak and on his thigh, "King of kings and Lord of lords." ¹⁷Then I saw an angel standing on the sun. He cried out (in) a loud voice to all the birds flying high overhead, "Come here. Gather for God's great feast, ¹⁸to eat the flesh of kings, the flesh of military officers, and the flesh of warriors, the flesh of horses and of their riders, and the flesh of all, free and slave, small and great." ¹⁹Then I saw the beast and the kings of the earth and their armies gathered to fight against the one riding the horse and against his army. ²⁰The beast was caught and with it the false prophet who had performed in its sight the signs by which he led astray those who had accepted the mark of the beast and those who had worshiped its image. The two were thrown alive into the fiery pool burning with sulfur. ²¹The rest were killed by the sword that came out of the mouth of the one riding the horse, and all the birds gorged themselves on their flesh.

Revelation Chapter 20

¹Then I saw an angel come down from heaven, holding in his hand the key to the abyss and a heavy chain. ²He seized the dragon, the ancient serpent, which is the Devil or Satan, and tied it up for a thousand years ³and threw it into the abyss, which he locked over it and sealed, so that it could no longer lead the nations astray until the thousand years are completed. After this, it is to be released for a short time. ⁴Then I saw thrones; those who sat on them were entrusted with judgment. I also saw the souls of those who had been beheaded for their witness to Jesus and for the word of God, and who had not worshiped the beast or its image nor had accepted its mark on their foreheads or hands. They came to life and they reigned with Christ for a thousand years. ⁵The rest of the dead did not come to life until the thousand years were over. This is the first resurrection. ⁶Blessed and holy is the one who shares in the first resurrection. The second death has no power over these; they will be priests of God and of Christ, and they will reign with him for (the) thousand years. ⁷When the thousand years are completed, Satan will be released from his prison. ⁸He will go out to deceive the nations at the four corners of the earth, Gog and Magog, to gather them for battle; their number is like the sand of the sea. ⁹They invaded the breadth of the earth and surrounded the camp of the holy ones and the beloved city. But fire came down from heaven and consumed them. ¹⁰The Devil who had led them astray was thrown into the pool of fire and sulfur, where the beast and the false prophet were. There they will be tormented day and night forever and ever. ¹¹Next I saw a large white throne and the one who was sitting on it. The earth and the sky fled from his presence and there was no place for them. ¹²I saw the dead, the great and the lowly, standing before the throne, and scrolls were opened. Then another scroll was opened, the book of life. The dead were judged according to their deeds, by what was written in the scrolls. ¹³The sea gave up its dead; then Death and Hades gave up their dead. All the dead were judged according to their deeds. ¹⁴Then Death and Hades were thrown into the pool of fire. (This pool of fire is the second death.) ¹⁵Anyone whose name was not found written in the book of life was thrown into the pool of fire.

Revelation Chapter 21

¹Then I saw a new heaven and a new earth. The former heaven and the former earth had passed away, and the sea was no more. ²I also saw the holy city, a new Jerusalem, coming down out of heaven from God, prepared as a bride adorned for her husband. ³I heard a loud voice from the throne saying, "Behold, God's dwelling is with the human race. He will dwell with them and they will be his people and God himself will always be with them (as their God). ⁴He will wipe every tear from their eyes, and there shall be no more death or mourning, wailing or pain, (for) the old order has passed away." ⁵The one who sat on the throne said, "Behold, I make all things new." Then he said, "Write these words down, for they are trustworthy and true." ⁶He said to me, "They are accomplished. I (am) the Alpha and the Omega, the beginning and the

end. To the thirsty I will give a gift from the spring of life-giving water. ⁷The victor will inherit these gifts, and I shall be his God, and he will be my son. ⁸But as for cowards, the unfaithful, the depraved, murderers, the unchaste, sorcerers, idol-worshipers, and deceivers of every sort, their lot is in the burning pool of fire and sulfur, which is the second death." ⁹One of the seven angels who held the seven bowls filled with the seven last plagues came and said to me, "Come here. I will show you the bride, the wife of the Lamb." ¹⁰He took me in spirit to a great, high mountain and showed me the holy city Jerusalem coming down out of heaven from God. ¹¹It gleamed with the splendor of God. Its radiance was like that of a precious stone, like jasper, clear as crystal. ¹²It had a massive, high wall, with twelve gates where twelve angels were stationed and on which names were inscribed, (the names) of the twelve tribes of the Israelites. ¹³There were three gates facing east, three north, three south, and three west. ¹⁴The wall of the city had twelve courses of stones as its foundation, on which were inscribed the twelve names of the twelve apostles of the Lamb. ¹⁵The one who spoke to me held a gold measuring rod to measure the city, its gates, and its wall. ¹⁶The city was square, its length the same as (also) its width. He measured the city with the rod and found it fifteen hundred miles in length and width and height. ¹⁷He also measured its wall: one hundred and forty-four cubits according to the standard unit of measurement the angel used. ¹⁸The wall was constructed of jasper, while the city was pure gold, clear as glass. ¹⁹The foundations of the city wall were decorated with every precious stone; the first course of stones was jasper, the second sapphire, the third chalcedony, the fourth emerald, ²⁰the fifth sardonyx, the sixth carnelian, the seventh chrysolite, the eighth beryl, the ninth topaz, the tenth chrysoprase, the eleventh hyacinth, and the twelfth amethyst. ²¹The twelve gates were twelve pearls, each of the gates made from a single pearl; and the street of the city was of pure gold, transparent as glass. ²²I saw no temple in the city, for its temple is the Lord God almighty and the Lamb. ²³The city had no need of sun or moon to shine on it, for the glory of God gave it light, and its lamp was the Lamb. ²⁴The nations will walk by its light, and to it the kings of the earth will bring their treasure. ²⁵During the day its gates will never be shut, and there will be no night there. ²⁶The treasure and wealth of the nations will be brought there, ²⁷but nothing unclean will enter it, nor any (one) who does abominable things or tells lies. Only those will enter whose names are written in the Lamb's book of life.

Revelation Chapter 22

¹Then the angel showed me the river of life-giving water, sparkling like crystal, flowing from the throne of God and of the Lamb ²down the middle of its street. On either side of the river grew the tree of life that produces fruit twelve times a year, once each month; the leaves of the trees serve as medicine for the nations. ³Nothing accursed will be found there anymore. The throne of God and of the Lamb will be in it, and his servants will worship him. ⁴They will look upon his face, and his name will be on their foreheads. ⁵Night will be no more, nor will they need light from lamp or sun, for the Lord God shall give them light, and they shall reign forever and ever. ⁶And he said to me, "These words are trustworthy and true, and the Lord, the God of prophetic spirits, sent his angel to show his servants what must happen soon." ⁷"Behold, I am coming soon." Blessed is the one who keeps the prophetic message of this book. ⁸It is I, John, who heard and saw these things, and when I heard and saw them I fell down to worship at the feet of the angel who showed them to me. ⁹But he said to me, "Don't! I am a fellow servant of yours and of your brothers the prophets and of those who keep the message of this book. Worship God." ¹⁰Then he said to me, "Do not seal up the prophetic words of this book, for the appointed time is near. ¹¹Let the wicked still act wickedly, and the filthy still be filthy. The righteous must still do right, and the holy still be holy." ¹²"Behold, I am coming soon. I bring with me the recompense I will give to each according to his deeds. ¹³I am the Alpha and the Omega, the first and the last, the beginning and the end." ¹⁴Blessed are they who wash their robes so as to have the right to the tree of life and enter the city through its gates. ¹⁵Outside are the dogs, the sorcerers, the unchaste, the murderers, the idol-worshipers, and all who love and practice deceit. ¹⁶"I, Jesus, sent my angel to give you this testimony for the churches. I am the root and offspring of David, the bright morning star." ¹⁷The Spirit and the bride say, "Come." Let the hearer say, "Come." Let the one who thirsts come forward, and the one who wants it receive the gift of life-giving water. ¹⁸I warn everyone who hears the prophetic words in this book: if anyone adds to them, God will add to him the plagues described in this book, ¹⁹and if anyone takes away from the words in this prophetic book, God will take away his share in the tree of life and in the holy city described in this book. ²⁰The one who gives this testimony says, "Yes, I am coming soon." Amen! Come, Lord Jesus! ²¹The grace of the Lord Jesus be with all.

Enoch I

Abbreviations, Brackets, and Symbols

[ ] - These brackets mean that the words inside are found in the Greek version (Gg) but not in the Ethiopic version (E). [[ ]] - These brackets mean that the words inside are found in the Ethiopic version (E), but not in the Greek versions (Gg or Gs). < > - These brackets mean that the words inside are restored because they were missing from the original text. [ ] - These brackets mean that the words inside are interpolations, meaning they were added and are not part of the original text. ( ) - These brackets mean that the words inside were supplied by the editor for clarity or to complete the text. † † - This symbol shows that there is a corruption in the text, meaning a part of the text is damaged or has errors. . . . . - This indicates that some words have been lost. **Abbreviations for the versions of the Book of Enoch: E:** The Ethiopic version. **G:** The large fragment of the Greek version discovered at Akhmîm, currently kept in the Giza Museum, Cairo. **I-XXXVI, I-V** - Parable of Enoch on the future fate of the wicked and the righteous, with references to chapters.

Enoch 1 Chapter 1

¹The words of the blessing of Enoch, wherewith he blessed the elect [[and]] righteous, who will be living in the day of tribulation, when all the wicked [[and godless]] are to be removed. ²And he took up his parable and said–Enoch a righteous man, whose eyes were opened by God, saw the vision of the Holy One in the heavens, [which] the angels showed me, and from them I heard everything, and from them I understood as I saw, but not for this generation, but for a remote one which is for to come. ³Concerning the elect I said, and took up my parable concerning them: The Holy Great One will come forth from His dwelling, ⁴And the eternal God will tread upon the earth, (even) on Mount Sinai, [And appear from His camp] And appear in the strength of His might from the heaven of heavens. ⁵And all shall be smitten with fear And the Watchers shall quake, And great fear and trembling shall seize them unto the ends of the earth. ⁶And the high mountains shall be shaken, And the high hills shall be made low, And shall melt like wax before the flame. ⁷And the earth shall be [wholly] rent in sunder, And all that is upon the earth shall perish, And there shall be a judgement upon all (men). ⁸But with the righteous He will make peace. And will protect the elect, And mercy shall be upon them. And they shall all belong to God, And they shall be prospered, And they shall [all] be blessed. [And He will help them all], And light shall appear unto them, [And He will make peace with them]. ⁹And behold! He cometh with ten thousands of [His] holy ones To execute judgement upon all, And to destroy [all] the ungodly: And to convict all flesh Of all the works [of their ungodliness] which they have ungodly committed, And of all the hard things which ungodly sinners [have spoken] against Him.

Enoch 1 Chapter 2

¹Observe ye everything that takes place in the heaven, how they do not change their orbits, [and] the luminaries which are in the heaven, how they all rise and set in order each in its season, and transgress not against their appointed order. ²Behold ye the earth, and give heed to the things which take place upon it from first to last, [how steadfast they are], how [none of the things upon earth] change, [but] all the works of God appear [to you]. ³Behold the summer and the winter, [[how the whole earth is filled with water, and clouds and dew and rain lie upon it]].

Enoch 1 Chapter 3

¹Observe and see how (in the winter) all the trees [[seem as though they had withered and shed all their leaves, except fourteen trees, which do not lose their foliage but retain the old foliage from two to three years till the new comes.

Enoch 1 Chapter 4

¹And again, observe ye the days of summer how the sun is above the earth over against it. And you seek shade and shelter by reason of the heat of the sun, and the earth also burns with growing heat, and so you cannot tread on the earth, or on a rock by reason of its heat.

Enoch 1 Chapter 5

¹Observe [[ye]] how the trees cover themselves with green leaves and bear fruit: wherefore give ye heed [and know] with regard to all [His works], and recognize how He that liveth for ever hath made them so. ²And [all] His works go on [thus] from year to year for ever, and the tasks [which] they accomplish for Him, and [their tasks] change not, but according as [[God]] hath ordained so is it done. ³And behold how the sea and the rivers in like manner accomplish and [change not] their tasks [from His commandments]. ⁴But ye–ye have not been steadfast, nor done the commandments of the Lord, But ye have turned away and

spoken proud and hard words With your impure mouths against His greatness. Oh, ye hard-hearted, ye shall find no peace. ⁵Therefore shall ye execrate your days, And the years of your life shall perish, And [the years of your destruction] shall be multiplied in eternal execration, And ye shall find no mercy. ⁶a In those days ye shall make your names an eternal execration unto all the righteous, b And by you shall [all] who curse, curse, And all the sinners [and godless] shall imprecate by you, c And for you the godless there shall be a curse. d And all the . . . shall rejoice, e And there shall be forgiveness of sins, f And every mercy and peace and forbearance: g There shall be salvation unto them, a goodly light. i And for all of you sinners there shall be no salvation, j But on you all shall abide a curse. ⁷a But for the elect there shall be light and joy and peace, b And they shall inherit the earth. ⁸And then there shall be bestowed upon the elect wisdom, And they shall all live and never again sin, Either through ungodliness or through pride: But they who are wise shall be humble. ⁹And they shall not again transgress, Nor shall they sin all the days of their life, Nor shall they die of (the divine) anger or wrath, But they shall complete the number of the days of their life. And their lives shall be increased in peace, And the years of their joy shall be multiplied, In eternal gladness and peace, All the days of their life.

Enoch 1 Chapter 6

¹And it came to pass when the children of men had multiplied that in those days were born unto them beautiful and comely daughters. ²And the angels, the children of the heaven, saw and lusted after them, and said to one another: 'Come, let us choose us wives from among the children of men and beget us children.' ³And Semjâzâ, who was their leader, said unto them: 'I fear ye will not indeed agree to do this deed, and I alone shall have to pay the penalty of a great sin.' ⁴And they all answered him and said: 'Let us all swear an oath, and all bind ourselves by mutual imprecations not to abandon this plan but to do this thing.' ⁵Then sware they all together and bound themselves by mutual imprecations upon it. ⁶And they were in all two hundred; who descended [in the days] of Jared on the summit of Mount Hermon, and they called it Mount Hermon, because they had sworn and bound themselves by mutual imprecations upon it. ⁷And these are the names of their leaders: Sêmîazâz, their leader, Arâkîba, Râmêêl, Kôkabîêl, Tâmîêl, Râmîêl, Dânêl, Êzêqêêl, Barâqîjâl, Asâêl, Armârôs, Batârêl, Anânêl, Zaqîêl, Samsâpêêl, Satarêl, Tûrêl, Jômjâêl, Sariêl. ⁸These are their chiefs of tens.

Enoch 1 Chapter 7

¹And all the others together with them took unto themselves wives, and each chose for himself one, and they began to go in unto them and to defile themselves with them, and they taught them charms and enchantments, and the cutting of roots, and made them acquainted with plants. ²And they became pregnant, and they bare great giants, whose height was three thousand ells: ³Who consumed all the acquisitions of men. And when men could no longer sustain them, ⁴the giants turned against them and devoured mankind. ⁵And they began to sin against birds, and beasts, and reptiles, and fish, and to devour one another's flesh, and drink the blood. ⁶Then the earth laid accusation against the lawless ones.

Enoch 1 Chapter 8

¹And Azâzêl taught men to make swords, and knives, and shields, and breastplates, and made known to them the metals <of the earth> and the art of working them, and bracelets, and ornaments, and the use of antimony, and the beautifying of the eyelids, and all kinds of costly stones, and all colouring tinctures. ²And there arose much godlessness, and they committed fornication, and they were led astray, and became corrupt in all their ways. Semjâzâ taught enchantments, and root-cuttings, Armârôs the resolving of enchantments, Barâqîjâl, (taught) astrology, Kôkabêl the constellations, Ezêqêêl the knowledge of the clouds, <Araqiêl the signs of the earth, Shamsiêl the signs of the sun>, and Sariêl the course of the moon. And as men perished, they cried, and their cry went up to heaven . . .

Enoch 1 Chapter 9

¹And then Michael, Uriel, Raphael, and Gabriel looked down from heaven and saw much blood being shed upon the earth, and all lawlessness being wrought upon the earth. ²And they said one to another: 'The earth made †without inhabitant cries the voice of their crying† up to the gates of heaven. ³[[And now to you, the holy ones of heaven]], the souls of men make their suit, saying, "Bring our cause before the Most High."' ⁴And they said to the Lord of the ages: 'Lord of lords, God of gods, King of kings, <and God of the ages>, the throne of Thy glory (standeth) unto all the generations of the ages, and Thy name holy and glorious and blessed unto all the ages! ⁵Thou hast made all things, and power over all things hast Thou: and all things are naked and open in Thy sight, and Thou seest all things, and nothing can hide

itself from Thee. 6Thou seest what Azâzêl hath done, who hath taught all unrighteousness on earth and revealed the eternal secrets which were (preserved) in heaven, which men were striving to learn: 7And Semjâzâ, to whom Thou hast given authority to bear rule over his associates. 8And they have gone to the daughters of men upon the earth, and have slept with the women, and have defiled themselves, and revealed to them all kinds of sins. 9And the women have borne giants, and the whole earth has thereby been filled with blood and unrighteousness. 10And now, behold, the souls of those who have died are crying and making their suit to the gates of heaven, and their lamentations have ascended: and cannot cease because of the lawless deeds which are wrought on the earth. 11And Thou knowest all things before they come to pass, and Thou seest these things and Thou dost suffer them, and Thou dost not say to us what we are to do to them in regard to these.'

Enoch 1 Chapter 10

1Then said the Most High, the Holy and Great One spake, and sent Uriel to the son of Lamech, and said to him: 2'Go to Noah> and tell him in my name "Hide thyself!" and reveal to him the end that is approaching: that the whole earth will be destroyed, and a deluge is about to come upon the whole earth, and will destroy all that is on it. 3And now instruct him that he may escape and his seed may be preserved for all the generations of the world.' 4And again the Lord said to Raphael: 'Bind Azâzêl hand and foot, and cast him into the darkness: and make an opening in the desert, which is in Dûdâêl, and cast him therein. 5And place upon him rough and jagged rocks, and cover him with darkness, and let him abide there for ever, and cover his face that he may not see light. 6And on the day of the great judgement he shall be cast into the fire. 7And heal the earth which the angels have corrupted, and proclaim the healing of the earth, that they may heal the plague, and that all the children of men may not perish through all the secret things that the Watchers have disclosed and have taught their sons. 8And the whole earth has been corrupted through the works that were taught by Azâzêl: to him ascribe all sin.' 9And to Gabriel said the Lord: 'Proceed against the bastards and the reprobates, and against the children of fornication: and destroy [the children of fornication and] the children of the Watchers from amongst men [and cause them to go forth]: send them one against the other that they may destroy each other in battle: for length of days shall they not have. 10And no request that they (i.e. their fathers) make of thee shall be granted unto their fathers on their behalf; for they hope to live an eternal life, and that each one of them will live five hundred years.' 11And the Lord said unto Michael: 'Go, bind Semjâzâ and his associates who have united themselves with women so as to have defiled themselves with them in all their uncleanness. 12And when their sons have slain one another, and they have seen the destruction of their beloved ones, bind them fast for seventy generations in the valleys of the earth, till the day of their judgement and of their consummation, till the judgement that is for ever and ever is consummated. 13In those days they shall be led off to the abyss of fire: <and> to the torment and the prison in which they shall be confined for ever. 14And whosoever shall be condemned and destroyed will from thenceforth be bound together with them to the end of all generations. 15And destroy all the spirits of the reprobate and the children of the Watchers, because they have wronged mankind. 16Destroy all wrong from the face of the earth and let every evil work come to an end: and let the plant of righteousness and truth appear: [and it shall prove a blessing; the works of righteousness and truth] shall be planted in truth and joy for evermore. 17And then shall all the righteous escape, And shall live till they beget thousands of children, And all the days of their youth and their old age Shall they complete in peace. 18And then shall the whole earth be tilled in righteousness, and shall all be planted with trees and be full of blessing. 19And all desirable trees shall be planted on it, and they shall plant vines on it: and the vine which they plant thereon shall yield wine in abundance, and as for all the seed which is sown thereon each measure (of it) shall bear a thousand, and each measure of olives shall yield ten presses of oil. 20And cleanse thou the earth from all oppression, and from all unrighteousness, and from all sin, and from all godlessness: and all the uncleanness that is wrought upon the earth destroy from off the earth. 21[And all the children of men shall become righteous], and all nations shall offer adoration and shall praise Me, and all shall worship Me. And the earth shall be cleansed from all defilement, and from all sin, and from all punishment, and from all torment, and I will never again send (them) upon it from generation to generation and for ever.

Enoch 1 Chapter 11

1And in those days I will open the store chambers of blessing which are in the heaven, so as to send them down [upon the earth] over the work and labour of the children of men. 2And truth and peace shall be associated together throughout all the days of the world and throughout all the generations of men.**XII-XVI.** Dream Vision of Enoch: his intercession for Azâzêl and the fallen Angels: and his announcement to them of their first and final doom.

Enoch 1 Chapter 12

1Before these things Enoch was hidden, and no one of the children of men knew where he was hidden, and where he abode, and what had become of him. 2And his activities had to do with the Watchers, and his days were with the holy ones. 3And I, Enoch, was blessing the Lord of majesty and the King of the ages, and lo! the Watchers called me–Enoch the scribe–and said to me: 4'Enoch, thou scribe of righteousness, go, †declare† to the Watchers of the heaven who have left the high heaven, the holy eternal place, and have defiled themselves with women, and have done as the children of earth do, and have taken unto themselves wives: "Ye have wrought great destruction on the earth: 5And ye shall have no peace nor forgiveness of sin: and inasmuch as †they† delight themselves in †their† children, 6The murder of †their† beloved ones shall †they† see, and over the destruction of †their† children shall †they† lament, and shall make supplication unto eternity, but mercy and peace shall ye not attain."'

Enoch 1 Chapter 13

1And Enoch went and said: 'Azâzêl, thou shalt have no peace: a severe sentence has gone forth against thee to put thee in bonds: 2And thou shalt not have toleration nor †request† granted to thee, because of the unrighteousness which thou hast taught, and because of all the works of godlessness and unrighteousness and sin which thou hast shown to men.' 3Then I went and spoke to them all together, and they were all afraid, and fear and trembling seized them. 4And they besought me to draw up a petition for them that they might find forgiveness, and to read their petition in the presence of the Lord of heaven. 5For from thenceforward they could not speak (with Him) nor lift up their eyes to heaven for shame of their sins for which they had been condemned. 6Then I wrote out their petition, and the prayer in regard to their spirits and their deeds individually and in regard to their requests that they should have forgiveness and length <of days>. 7And I went off and sat down at the waters of Dan, in the land of Dan, to the south of the west of Hermon: I read their petition till I fell asleep. 8And behold a dream came to me, and visions fell down upon me, and I saw visions of chastisement, [and a voice came bidding (me)] I to tell it to the sons of heaven, and reprimand them. 9And when I awaked, I came unto them, and they were all sitting gathered together, weeping in 'Abelsjâîl, which is between Lebanon and Sênêsêr, with their faces covered. 10And I recounted before them all the visions which I had seen in sleep, and I began to speak the words of righteousness, and to reprimand the heavenly Watchers.

Enoch 1 Chapter 14

1The book of the words of righteousness, and of the reprimand of the eternal Watchers in accordance with the command of the Holy Great One in that vision. 2I saw in my sleep what I will now say with a tongue of flesh and with the breath of my mouth: which the Great One has given to men to converse therewith and understand with the heart. 3As He has created and given [[to man the power of understanding the word of wisdom, so hath He created me also and given]] me the power of reprimanding the Watchers, the children of heaven. 4I wrote out your petition, and in my vision it appeared thus, that your petition will not be granted unto you [[throughout all the days of eternity, and that judgement has been finally passed upon you: yea (your petition) will not be granted unto you]]. 5And from henceforth you shall not ascend into heaven unto all eternity, and [in bonds] of the earth the decree has gone forth to bind you for all the days of the world. 6And (that) previously you shall have seen the destruction of your beloved sons and ye shall have no pleasure in them, but they shall fall before you by the sword. 7And your petition on their behalf shall not be granted, nor yet on your own: even though you weep and pray and speak all the words contained in the writing which I have written. 8And the vision was shown to me thus: Behold, in the vision clouds invited me and a mist summoned me, and the course of the stars and the lightnings sped and hastened me, and the winds in the vision caused me to fly and lifted me upward, and bore me into heaven. 9And I went in till I drew nigh to a wall which is built of crystals and surrounded by tongues of fire: and it began to affright me. 10And I went into the tongues of fire and drew nigh to a large house which was built of crystals: and the walls of the house were like a tesselated floor (made) of crystals, and its groundwork was of crystal. 11Its ceiling was like the path of the stars and the lightnings, and between them were fiery cherubim, and their heaven was (clear as) water. ¹²A flaming fire surrounded the walls, and its portals blazed with fire. ¹³And I entered into that house, and it was hot as fire and cold as ice: there were no delights of life therein: fear covered me, and trembling got hold upon me. ¹⁴And as I quaked and trembled, I fell upon my face. ¹⁵And I beheld a vision, And lo! there was a second house, greater than the former, and the entire portal stood open before me, and it was built of flames of fire. ¹⁶And in every respect it so excelled in splendour and magnificence and extent that I cannot describe to you its splendour and its extent. ¹⁷And its floor was of fire, and above it were lightnings and the path of the stars, and its ceiling also was flaming fire. ¹⁸And I looked and saw [[therein]] a lofty throne: its appearance was as crystal, and the wheels thereof as the shining sun, and there was the vision of cherubim. ¹⁹And from underneath the throne came streams of flaming fire so that I could not look thereon. ²⁰And the Great Glory sat thereon, and His raiment shone more brightly than the sun and was whiter than any snow. ²¹None of the angels could enter and could behold His face by reason of the magnificence and glory and no flesh could behold Him. ²²The flaming fire was round about Him, and a great fire stood before Him, and none around could draw nigh Him: ten thousand times ten thousand (stood) before Him, yet He needed no counselor. ²³And the most holy ones who were nigh to Him did not leave by night nor depart from Him. ²⁴And until then I had been prostrate on my face, trembling: and the Lord called me with His own mouth, and said to me: 'Come hither, Enoch, and hear my word.' ²⁵ [And one of the holy ones came to me and waked me], and He made me rise up and approach the door: and I bowed my face downwards.

Enoch 1 Chapter 15

¹And He answered and said to me, and I heard His voice: 'Fear not, Enoch, thou righteous man and scribe of righteousness: approach hither and hear my voice. ²And go, say to [[the Watchers of heaven]], who have sent thee to intercede [[for them: "You should intercede"]] for men, and not men for you: ³Wherefore have ye left the high, holy, and eternal heaven, and lain with women, and defiled yourselves with the daughters of men and taken to yourselves wives, and done like the children of earth, and begotten giants (as your) sons? ⁴And though ye were holy, spiritual, living the eternal life, you have defiled yourselves with the blood of women, and have begotten (children) with the blood of flesh, and, as the children of men, have lusted after flesh and blood as those [also] do who die and perish. ⁵Therefore have I given them wives also that they might impregnate them, and beget children by them, that thus nothing might be wanting to them on earth. ⁶But you were [formerly] spiritual, living the eternal life, and immortal for all generations of the world. ⁷And therefore I have not appointed wives for you; for as for the spiritual ones of the heaven, in heaven is their dwelling. ⁸And now, the giants, who are produced from the spirits and flesh, shall be called evil spirits upon the earth, and on the earth shall be their dwelling. ⁹Evil spirits have proceeded from their bodies; because they are born from men, [[and]] from the holy Watchers is their beginning and primal origin; [they shall be evil spirits on earth, and] evil spirits shall they be called. ¹⁰[As for the spirits of heaven, in heaven shall be their dwelling, but as for the spirits of the earth which were born upon the earth, on the earth shall be their dwelling.] ¹¹And the spirits of the giants afflict, oppress, destroy, attack, do battle, and work destruction on the earth, and cause trouble: they take no food, [but nevertheless hunger] and thirst, and cause offences. And these spirits shall rise up against the children of men and against the women, because they have proceeded [from them].'

Enoch 1 Chapter 16

¹From the days of the slaughter and destruction and death [of the giants], from the souls of whose flesh the spirits, having gone forth, shall destroy without incurring judgement–thus shall they destroy until the day of the consummation, the great [judgement] in which the age shall be consummated, over the Watchers and the godless, yea, shall be wholly consummated." ²And now as to the Watchers who have sent thee to intercede for them, who had been [[aforetime]] in heaven, (say to them): ³"You have been in heaven, but [all] the mysteries had not yet been revealed to you, and you knew worthless ones, and these in the hardness of your hearts you have made known to the women, and through these mysteries women and men work much evil on earth." ⁴Say to them therefore: "You have no peace."**XVII-XXXVII.** Enoch's Journeys through the Earth and Sheol. XVII-XIX. The First Journey.

Enoch 1 Chapter 17

¹And they took [and] brought me to a place in which those who were there were like flaming fire, and, when they wished, they appeared as men. ²And they brought me to the place of darkness, and to a mountain the point of whose summit reached to heaven. ³And I saw the places of the luminaries [and the treasuries of the stars] and of the thunder [and] in the uttermost depths, where were a fiery bow and arrows and their quiver, and [[a fiery sword]] and all the lightnings. ⁴And they took me to the living waters, and to the fire of the west, which receives every setting of the sun. ⁵And I came to a river of fire in which the fire flows like water and discharges itself into the great sea towards the west. ⁶I saw the great rivers and came to the great [river and to the great] darkness, and went to the place where no flesh walks. ⁷I saw the mountains of the darkness of winter and the place whence all the waters of the deep flow. ⁸I saw the mouths of all the rivers of the earth and the mouth of the deep.

Enoch 1 Chapter 18

¹I saw the treasuries of all the winds: I saw how He had furnished with them the whole creation and the firm foundations of the earth. ²And I saw the corner-stone of the earth: I saw the four winds which bear [the earth and] the firmament of the heaven. ³[[And I saw how the winds stretch out the vaults of heaven]], and have their station between heaven and earth: [[these are the pillars of the heaven]]. ⁴I saw the winds of heaven which turn and bring the circumference of the sun and all the stars to their setting. ⁵I saw the winds on the earth carrying the clouds: I saw [[the paths of the angels. I saw]] at the end of the earth the firmament of the heaven above. ⁶And I proceeded and saw a place which burns day and night, where there are seven mountains of magnificent stones, three towards the east, and three towards the south. ⁷And as for those towards the east, <one> was of coloured stone, and one of pearl, and one of jacinth, and those towards the south of red stone. ⁸But the middle one reached to heaven like the throne of God, of alabaster, and the summit of the throne was of sapphire. ⁹And I saw a flaming fire. And beyond these mountains ¹⁰is a region the end of the great earth: there the heavens were completed. ¹¹And I saw a deep abyss, with columns [[of heavenly fire, and among them I saw columns]] of fire fall, which were beyond measure alike towards the height and towards the depth. ¹²And beyond that abyss I saw a place which had no firmament of the heaven above, and no firmly founded earth beneath it: there was no water upon it, and no birds, but it was a waste and horrible place. ¹³I saw there seven stars like great burning mountains, and to me, when I inquired regarding them, ¹⁴The angel said: 'This place is the end of heaven and earth: this has become a prison for the stars and the host of heaven. ¹⁵And the stars which roll over the fire are they which have transgressed the commandment of the Lord in the beginning of their rising, because they did not come forth at their appointed times. ¹⁶And He was wroth with them, and bound them till the time when their guilt should be consummated (even) [for ten thousand years].'

Enoch 1 Chapter 19

¹And Uriel said to me: 'Here shall stand the angels who have connected themselves with women, and their spirits assuming many different forms are defiling mankind and shall lead them astray into sacrificing to demons [[as gods]], (here shall they stand,) till [[the day of]] the great judgement in which they shall be judged till they are made an end of. ²And the women also of the angels who went astray shall become sirens.' ³And I, Enoch, alone saw the vision, the ends of all things: and no man shall see as I have seen.**XX.** Name and Functions of the Seven Archangels.

Enoch 1 Chapter 20

¹And these are the names of the holy angels who watch. ²Uriel, one of the holy angels, who is over the world and over Tartarus. ³Raphael, one of the holy angels, who is over the spirits of men. ⁴Raguel, one of the holy angels who †takes vengeance on† the world of the luminaries. ⁵Michael, one of the holy angels, to wit, he that is set over the best part of mankind [[and]] over chaos. ⁶Saraqâêl, one of the holy angels, who is set over the spirits, who sin in the spirit. ⁷Gabriel, one of the holy angels, who is over Paradise and the serpents and the Cherubim. ⁸Remiel, one of the holy angels, whom God set over those who rise.

Enoch 1 Chapter 21

¹And I proceeded to where things were chaotic. ²And I saw there something horrible: I saw neither a heaven above nor a firmly founded earth, but a place chaotic and horrible. ³And there I saw seven stars of the heaven bound together in it, like great mountains and burning with fire. ⁴Then I said: 'For what sin are they bound, and on what account have they been cast in hither?' ⁵Then said Uriel, one of the holy angels, who was with me, and was chief over them, and said: 'Enoch, why dost thou ask, and why art thou eager for the truth? ⁶These are of the number of the stars [of heaven], which have transgressed the commandment of the Lord, and are bound here till ten thousand years, the time entailed by their sins, are consummated.' ⁷And from thence I went to another place, which was still more horrible than the former,

and I saw a horrible thing: a great fire there which burnt and blazed, and the place was cleft as far as the abyss, being full of great descending columns of fire: neither its extent or magnitude could I see, nor could I conjecture. ⁸Then I said: 'How fearful is the place and how terrible to look upon!' ⁹Then Uriel answered me, one of the holy angels who was with me, and said unto me: 'Enoch, why hast thou such fear and affright?' And I answered: 'Because of this fearful place, and because of the spectacle of the pain.' ¹⁰And he said [[unto me]]: 'This place is the prison of the angels, and here they will be imprisoned for ever.'**XXII. Sheol, or the Underworld**

Enoch 1 Chapter 22

¹And thence I went to another place, and he showed me in the west [another] great and high mountain [and] of hard rock. ²And there was in it †four† hollow places, deep and wide and very smooth. †How† smooth are the hollow places and deep and dark to look at. ²And there were †four† hollow places in it, deep and very smooth: †three† of them were dark and one bright; and there was a fountain of water in its midst. And I said: '†How† smooth are these hollow places, and deep and dark to view.' ³Then Raphael answered, one of the holy angels who was with me, and said unto me: 'These hollow places have been created for this very purpose, that the spirits of the souls of the dead should assemble therein, yea that all the souls of the children of men should assemble here. ⁴And these places have been made to receive them till the day of their judgement and till their appointed period [till the period appointed], till the great judgement (comes) upon them.' ⁵I saw the spirits of the children of men who were dead, and their voice went forth to heaven and made suit. ⁶Then I asked Raphael the angel who was with me, and I said unto him: 'This spirit–whose is it whose voice goeth forth and maketh suit?' ⁷And he answered me saying: 'This is the spirit which went forth from Abel, whom his brother Cain slew, and he makes his suit against him till his seed is destroyed from the face of the earth, and his seed is annihilated from amongst the seed of men.' ⁸Then I asked regarding it, and regarding all the hollow places: 'Why are one separated from the other?' ⁹And he answered me and said unto me: 'These three have been made that the spirits of the dead might be separated. And such a division has been made <for> the spirits of the righteous, in which there is the bright spring of water. ¹⁰And such has been made for sinners when they die and are buried in the earth and judgement has not been executed on them in their lifetime. ¹¹Here their spirits shall be set apart in this great pain till the great day of judgement and punishment and torment of those who †curse† for ever, and retribution for their spirits. There He shall bind them for ever. ¹²And such a division has been made for the spirits of those who make their suit, who make disclosures concerning their destruction, when they were slain in the days of the sinners. ¹³Such has been made for the spirits of men who were not righteous but sinners, who were complete in transgression, and of the transgressors. They shall be companions: but their spirits shall not be slain in the day of judgement nor shall they be raised from thence. ¹⁴Then I blessed the Lord of glory and said: 'Blessed be my Lord, the Lord of righteousness, who ruleth for ever.'**XXIII. The Fire that deals with the Luminaries of Heaven**

Enoch 1 Chapter 23

¹From thence I went to another place to the west of the ends of the earth. ²And I saw a [[burning]] fire which ran without resting, and paused not from its course day or night but [ran] regularly. ³And I asked saying: 'What is this which rests not?' ⁴Then Raguel, one of the holy angels who was with me, answered me [[and said unto me]]: 'This course [of fire] [[which thou hast seen]] is the fire in the west which †persecutes† all the luminaries of heaven.'**XXIV-XXV. The Seven Mountains in the North-West and the Tree of Life**

Enoch 1 Chapter 24

¹[[And from thence I went to another place of the earth]], and he showed me a mountain range of fire which burnt [[day and night]]. ²And I went beyond it and saw seven magnificent mountains all differing each from the other, and the stones (thereof) were magnificent and beautiful, magnificent as a whole, of glorious appearance and fair exterior: [[three towards]] the east, [[one]] founded on the other, and three towards the south, one upon the other, and deep rough ravines, no one of which joined with any other. ³And the seventh mountain was in the midst of these, and it excelled them in height, resembling the seat of a throne: and fragrant trees encircled the throne. ⁴And amongst them was a tree such as I had never yet smelt, neither was any amongst them nor were others like it: it had a fragrance beyond all fragrance, and its leaves and blooms and wood wither not for ever: and its fruit [[is beautiful, and its fruit]] resembles the dates of a palm. ⁵Then I said: '[How] beautiful is this tree, and fragrant, and its leaves are fair, and its blooms [[very]] delightful in appearance.' ⁶Then answered Michael,

one of the holy [[and honoured]] angels who was with me, and was their leader.

Enoch 1 Chapter 25

¹And he said unto me: 'Enoch, why dost thou ask me regarding the fragrance of the tree, and [why] dost thou wish to learn the truth?' ²Then I answered him [[saying]]: 'I wish to know about everything, but especially about this tree.' ³And he answered saying: 'This high mountain [[which thou hast seen]], whose summit is like the throne of God, is His throne, where the Holy Great One, the Lord of Glory, the Eternal King, will sit, when He shall come down to visit the earth with goodness. ⁴And as for this fragrant tree no mortal is permitted to touch it till the great judgement, when He shall take vengeance on all and bring (everything) to its consummation for ever. It shall then be given to the righteous and holy. ⁵Its fruit shall be for food to the elect: it shall be transplanted to the holy place, to the temple of the Lord, the Eternal King. ⁶Then shall they rejoice with joy and be glad, And into the holy place shall they enter; And its fragrance shall be in their bones, And they shall live a long life on earth, Such as thy fathers lived: And in their days shall no [[sorrow or]] plague Or torment or calamity touch them.' ⁷Then blessed I the God of Glory, the Eternal King, who hath prepared such things for the righteous, and hath created them and promised to give to them.**XXVI. Jerusalem and the Mountains, Ravines and Streams**

Enoch 1 Chapter 26

¹And I went from thence to the middle of the earth, and I saw a blessed place [in which there were trees] with branches abiding and blooming [of a dismembered tree]. ²And there I saw a holy mountain, [[and]] underneath the mountain to the east there was a stream and it flowed towards the south. ³And I saw towards the east another mountain higher than this, and between them a deep and narrow ravine: in it also ran a stream [underneath] the mountain. ⁴And to the west thereof there was another mountain, lower than the former and of small elevation, and a ravine [deep and dry] between them: and another deep and dry ravine was at the extremities of the three [mountains]. ⁵And all the ravines were deep [[and narrow]], (being formed) of hard rock, and trees were not planted upon them. ⁶And I marveled [[at the rocks, and I marveled]] at the ravine, yea, I marveled very much.**XXVII. The Purpose of the Accursed Valley**

Enoch 1 Chapter 27

¹Then said I: 'For what object is this blessed land, which is entirely filled with trees, and this accursed valley [[between]]?' ²[[Then Uriel, one of the holy angels who was with me, answered and said: 'This]] accursed valley is for those who are accursed for ever: Here shall all [the accursed] be gathered together who utter with their lips against the Lord unseemly words and of His glory speak hard things. ³Here shall they be gathered together, and here shall be their place of judgement. In the last days there shall be upon them the spectacle of righteous judgement in the presence of the righteous for ever: here shall the merciful bless the Lord of glory, the Eternal King. ⁴In the days of judgement over the former, they shall bless Him for the mercy in accordance with which He has assigned them (their lot).' ⁵Then I blessed the Lord of Glory and set forth His [glory] and lauded Him gloriously.**XXVIII-XXXIII. Further Journey to the East**

Enoch 1 Chapter 28

¹And thence I went [[towards the east]], into the midst [[of the mountain range of the desert]], and I saw a wilderness and it was solitary, full of trees and plants. ²[[And]] water gushed forth from above. ³Rushing like a copious watercourse [which flowed] towards the north-west it caused clouds and dew to ascend on every side.

Enoch 1 Chapter 29

¹And thence I went to another place in the desert, and approached to the east of this mountain range. ²And [[there]] I saw aromatic trees exhaling the fragrance of frankincense and myrrh, and the trees also were similar to the almond tree.

Enoch 1 Chapter 30

¹And beyond these, I went afar to the east, and I saw another place, a valley (full) of water. ²And [therein there was] a tree, the colour (?) of fragrant trees such as the mastic. ³And on the sides of those valleys I saw fragrant cinnamon. And beyond these I proceeded to the east.

Enoch 1 Chapter 31

¹And I saw other mountains, and amongst them were [groves of] trees, and there flowed forth from them nectar, which is named sarara and galbanum. ²And beyond these mountains I saw another mountain [to the east of the ends of the earth], [[whereon were aloe trees]], and all the trees were full of stacte, being like almond-trees. ³And when one burnt it, it smelt sweeter than any fragrant odour.

Enoch 1 Chapter 32

¹ E 1 And after these fragrant odours, as I looked towards the north over the mountains I saw seven mountains full of choice nard and fragrant trees and cinnamon and pepper. G 1 To the north-east I beheld seven mountains full of choice nard and mastic and cinnamon and pepper. ² And thence I went over the summits of [all] these mountains, far towards the east [of the earth], and passed above the Erythraean sea and went far from it, and passed over [[the angel]] Zotiêl. E ³ And I came to the Garden of Righteousness, and saw beyond those trees many large trees growing there and of goodly fragrance, large, very beautiful and glorious, and the tree of wisdom whereof they eat and know great wisdom. G ³ And I came to the Garden of Righteousness, and from afar off trees more numerous than these trees and great–†two† trees there, very great, beautiful, and glorious, and magnificent, and the tree of knowledge, whose holy fruit they eat and know great wisdom. ⁴ [That tree is in height like the fir, and its leaves are] like (those of) the Carob tree: and its fruit is like the clusters of the vine, very beautiful: and the fragrance of the tree penetrates afar. ⁵ Then I said: '[How] beautiful is the tree, and how attractive is its look!' ⁶ Then Raphael the holy angel, who was with me, answered me [[and said]]: 'This is the tree of wisdom, of which thy father old (in years) and thy aged mother, who were before thee, have eaten, and they learnt wisdom and their eyes were opened, and they knew that they were naked and they were driven out of the garden.'

Enoch 1 Chapter 33

¹ And from thence I went to the ends of the earth and saw there great beasts, and each differed from the other; and (I saw) birds also differing in appearance and beauty and voice, the one differing from the other. ² And to the east of those beasts I saw the ends of the earth whereon the heaven rests, and the portals of the heaven open. ³ And I saw how the stars of heaven come forth, and I counted the portals out of which they proceed, and wrote down all their outlets, of each individual star by itself, according to their number and their names, their courses and their positions, and their times and their months, as Uriel the holy angel who was with me showed me. ⁴ He showed all things to me and wrote them down for me: also their names he wrote for me, and their laws and their companies.

Enoch 1 Chapter 34

¹ And from thence I went towards the north to the ends of the earth, and there I saw a great and glorious device at the ends of the whole earth. ² And here I saw three portals of heaven open in the heaven: through each of them proceed north winds: when they blow there is cold, hail, frost, snow, dew, and rain. ³ And out of one portal they blow for good: but when they blow through the other two portals, it is with violence and affliction on the earth, and they blow with violence.

Enoch 1 Chapter 35

¹ And from thence I went towards the west to the ends of the earth, and saw there three portals of the heaven open such as I had seen in the †east†, the same number of portals, and the same number of outlets.

Enoch 1 Chapter 36

¹ And from thence I went to the south to the ends of the earth, and saw there three open portals of the heaven: and thence there come dew, rain, †and wind†. ² And from thence I went to the east to the ends of the heaven, and saw here the three eastern portals of heaven open and small portals above them. ³ Through each of these small portals pass the stars of heaven and run their course to the west on the path which is shown to them. ⁴ And as often as I saw I blessed always the Lord of Glory, and I continued to bless the Lord of Glory who has wrought great and glorious wonders, to show the greatness of His work to the angels and to spirits and to men, that they might praise His work and all His creation: that they might see the work of His might and praise the great work of His hands and bless Him for ever.

Enoch 1 Chapter 37

¹ The second vision which he saw, the vision of wisdom–which Enoch the son of Jared, the son of Mahalalel, the son of Cainan, the son of Enos, the son of Seth, the son of Adam, saw. ² And this is the beginning of the words of wisdom which I lifted up my voice to speak and say to those which dwell on earth: Hear, ye men of old time, and see, ye that come after, the words of the Holy One which I will speak before the Lord of Spirits. ³ It were better to declare (them only) to the men of old time, but even from those that come after we will not withhold the beginning of wisdom. ⁴ Till the present day such wisdom has never been given by the Lord of Spirits as I have received according to my insight, according to the good pleasure of the Lord of Spirits by whom the lot of eternal life has been given to me. ⁵ Now three parables were imparted to me, and I lifted up my voice and recounted them to those that dwell on the earth.

Enoch 1 Chapter 38

¹ The First Parable. When the congregation of the righteous shall appear, And sinners shall be judged for their sins, And shall be driven from the face of the earth: ² And when the Righteous One shall appear before the eyes of the righteous, Whose elect works hang upon the Lord of Spirits, And light shall appear to the righteous and the elect who dwell on the earth, Where then will be the dwelling of the sinners, And where the resting-place of those who have denied the Lord of Spirits? It had been good for them if they had not been born. ³ When the secrets of the righteous shall be revealed and the sinners judged, And the godless driven from the presence of the righteous and elect, ⁴ From that time those that possess the earth shall no longer be powerful and exalted: And they shall not be able to behold the face of the holy, For the Lord of Spirits has caused His light to appear On the face of the holy, righteous, and elect. ⁵ Then shall the kings and the mighty perish And be given into the hands of the righteous and holy. ⁶ And thenceforward none shall seek for themselves mercy from the Lord of Spirits For their life is at an end.

Enoch 1 Chapter 39

¹ [And it †shall come to pass in those days that elect and holy children †will descend from the high heaven, and their seed will become one with the children of men. ² And in those days Enoch received books of zeal and wrath, and books of disquiet and expulsion.] And mercy shall not be accorded to them, saith the Lord of Spirits. ³ And in those days a whirlwind carried me off from the earth, And set me down at the end of the heavens. ⁴ And there I saw another vision, the dwelling-places of the holy, And the resting-places of the righteous. ⁵ Here mine eyes saw their dwellings with His righteous angels, And their resting-places with the holy. And they petitioned and interceded and prayed for the children of men, And righteousness flowed before them as water, And mercy like dew upon the earth: Thus it is amongst them for ever and ever. ⁶ a. And in that place mine eyes saw the Elect One of righteousness and of faith, ⁶ b. And I saw his dwelling-place under the wings of the Lord of Spirits. ⁷ a. And righteousness shall prevail in his days, And the righteous and elect shall be without number before Him for ever and ever. ⁷ b. And all the righteous and elect before Him shall be †strong† as fiery lights, And their mouth shall be full of blessing, And their lips extol the name of the Lord of Spirits, And righteousness before Him shall never fail, [And uprightness shall never fail before Him.] ⁸ There I wished to dwell, And my spirit longed for that dwelling-place: And there heretofore hath been my portion, For so has it been established concerning me before the Lord of Spirits. ⁹ In those days I praised and extolled the name of the Lord of Spirits with blessings and praises, because He hath destined me for blessing and glory according to the good pleasure of the Lord of Spirits. ¹⁰ For a long time my eyes regarded that place, and I blessed Him and praised Him, saying: 'Blessed is He, and may He be blessed from the beginning and for evermore. ¹¹ And before Him there is no ceasing. He knows before the world was created what is for ever and what will be from generation unto generation. ¹² Those who sleep not bless Thee: they stand before Thy glory and bless, praise, and extol, saying: "Holy, holy, holy, is the Lord of Spirits: He filleth the earth with spirits."' ¹³ And here my eyes saw all those who sleep not: they stand before Him and bless and say: 'Blessed be Thou, and blessed be the name of the Lord for ever and ever.' ¹⁴ And my face was changed; for I could no longer behold.

Enoch 1 Chapter 40

¹ And after that I saw thousands of thousands and ten thousand times ten thousand, I saw a multitude beyond number and reckoning, who stood before the Lord of Spirits. ² And on the four sides of the Lord of Spirits I saw four presences, different from those that sleep not, and I learnt their names: for the angel that went with me made known to me their names, and showed me all the hidden things. ³ And I heard the voices of those four presences as they uttered praises before the Lord of glory. ⁴ The first voice blesses the Lord of Spirits for ever and ever. ⁵ And the second voice I heard blessing the Elect One and the elect ones who hang upon the Lord of Spirits. ⁶ And the third voice I heard pray and intercede for those who dwell on the earth and supplicate in the name of the Lord of Spirits. ⁷ And I heard the fourth voice fending off the Satans and forbidding them to come before the Lord of Spirits to accuse them who dwell on the earth. ⁸ After that I asked the angel of peace who went with me, who showed me everything that is hidden: 'Who are these four presences which I have seen and whose words I have heard and written down?' ⁹ And he said to me: 'This first is Michael, the merciful and long-suffering: and the second, who is set over all the diseases and all the wounds of the children of men, is Raphael: and the third, who is set over all the powers, is Gabriel: and the fourth, who is set over the repentance unto hope of those who

inherit eternal life, is named Phanuel.' ¹⁰ And these are the four angels of the Lord of Spirits and the four voices I heard in those days.

Enoch 1 Chapter 41

¹ And after that I saw all the secrets of the heavens, and how the kingdom is divided, and how the actions of men are weighed in the balance. ² And there I saw the mansions of the elect and the mansions of the holy, and mine eyes saw there all the sinners being driven from thence which deny the name of the Lord of Spirits, and being dragged off: and they could not abide because of the punishment which proceeds from the Lord of Spirits.

Enoch 1 Chapter 42

¹Wisdom found no place where she might dwell; Then a dwelling-place was assigned her in the heavens. ²Wisdom went forth to make her dwelling among the children of men, And found no dwelling-place: Wisdom returned to her place, And took her seat among the angels. ³And unrighteousness went forth from her chambers: Whom she sought not she found, And dwelt with them, As rain in a desert And dew on a thirsty land. **XLIII. XLIV.** Astronomical Secrets.

Enoch 1 Chapter 43

¹And I saw other lightnings and the stars of heaven, and I saw how He called them all by their names and they hearkened unto Him. ²And I saw how they are weighed in a righteous balance according to their proportions of light: (I saw) the width of their spaces and the day of their appearing, and how their revolution produces lightning: and (I saw) their revolution according to the number of the angels, and (how) they keep faith with each other. ³And I asked the angel who went with me who showed me what was hidden: 'What are these?' ⁴And he said to me: 'The Lord of Spirits hath showed thee their parabolic meaning (lit. "their parable"): these are the names of the holy who dwell on the earth and believe in the name of the Lord of Spirits for ever and ever.'

Enoch 1 Chapter 44

¹Also another phenomenon I saw in regard to the lightnings: how some of the stars arise and become lightnings and cannot part with their new form. **XLV-LVII.** The Second Parable. The Lot of the Apostates: the New Heaven and the New Earth.

Enoch 1 Chapter 45

¹And this is the Second Parable concerning those who deny the name of the dwelling of the holy ones and the Lord of Spirits. ²And into the heaven they shall not ascend, And on the earth they shall not come: Such shall be the lot of the sinners Who have denied the name of the Lord of Spirits, Who are thus preserved for the day of suffering and tribulation. ³On that day Mine Elect One shall sit on the throne of glory And shall try their works, And their places of rest shall be innumerable. And their souls shall grow strong within them when they see Mine Elect Ones, And those who have called upon My glorious name: ⁴Then will I cause Mine Elect One to dwell among them. And I will transform the heaven and make it an eternal blessing and light. ⁵And I will transform the earth and make it a blessing: And I will cause Mine elect ones to dwell upon it: But the sinners and evil-doers shall not set foot thereon. ⁶For I have provided and satisfied with peace My righteous ones And have caused them to dwell before Me: But for the sinners there is judgement impending with Me, So that I shall destroy them from the face of the earth. **XLVI.** The Head of Days and the Son of Man.

Enoch 1 Chapter 46

¹And there I saw One who had a head of days, And His head was white like wool, And with Him was another being whose countenance had the appearance of a man, And his face was full of graciousness, like one of the holy angels. ²And I asked the angel who went with me and showed me all the hidden things, concerning that Son of Man who, who he was, and whence he was, (and) why he went with the Head of Days? And he answered and said unto me: This is the Son of Man who hath righteousness, With whom dwelleth righteousness, And who revealeth all the treasures of that which is hidden, Because the Lord of Spirits hath chosen him, And whose lot hath the pre-eminence before the Lord of Spirits in uprightness for ever. ⁴And this Son of Man whom thou hast seen Shall †raise up† the kings and the mighty from their seats, [And the strong from their thrones] And shall loosen the reins of the strong, And break the teeth of the sinners. ⁵[And he shall put down the kings from their thrones and kingdoms] Because they do not extol and praise Him, Nor humbly acknowledge whence the kingdom was bestowed upon them. ⁶And he shall put down the countenance of the strong, And shall fill them with shame. And darkness shall be their dwelling, And worms shall be their bed, And they shall have no hope of rising from their beds, Because they do not extol the name of the Lord of Spirits. ⁷And these are they who †judge† the stars of heaven, [And raise their hands against the Most High], †And tread upon the earth and dwell

upon it†. And all their deeds manifest unrighteousness, And their power rests upon their riches, And their faith is in the †gods† which they have made with their hands, And they deny the name of the Lord of Spirits, ⁸And they persecute the houses of His congregations, And the faithful who hang upon the name of the Lord of Spirits.**XLVII.** The Prayer of the Righteous for Vengeance and their Joy at its Coming.

Enoch 1 Chapter 47

¹And in those days shall have ascended the prayer of the righteous, And the blood of the righteous from the earth before the Lord of Spirits. ²In those days the holy ones who dwell above in the heavens Shall unite with one voice And supplicate and pray [and praise, And give thanks and bless the name of the Lord of Spirits] On behalf of the blood of the righteous which has been shed, And that the prayer of the righteous may not be in vain before the Lord of Spirits, That judgement may be done unto them, And that they may not have to suffer for ever. ³In those days I saw the Head of Days when He seated himself upon the throne of His glory, And the books of the living were opened before Him: And all His host which is in heaven above and His counselors stood before Him, ⁴And the hearts of the holy were filled with joy; Because the number of the righteous had been offered, And the prayer of the righteous had been heard, And the blood of the righteous been required before the Lord of Spirits.**XLVIII.** The Fount of Righteousness; the Son of Man–the Stay of the Righteous: Judgement of the Kings and the Mighty.

Enoch 1 Chapter 48

¹And in that place I saw the fountain of righteousness Which was inexhaustible: And around it were many fountains of wisdom; And all the thirsty drank of them, And were filled with wisdom, And their dwellings were with the righteous and holy and elect. ²And at that hour that Son of Man was named In the presence of the Lord of Spirits, And his name before the Head of Days. ³Yea, before the sun and the signs were created, Before the stars of the heaven were made, His name was named before the Lord of Spirits. ⁴He shall be a staff to the righteous whereon to stay themselves and not fall, And he shall be the light of the Gentiles, And the hope of those who are troubled of heart. ⁵All who dwell on earth shall fall down and worship before him, And will praise and bless and celebrate with song the Lord of Spirits. ⁶And for this reason hath he been chosen and hidden before Him, Before the creation of the world and for evermore. ⁷And the wisdom of the Lord of Spirits hath revealed him to the holy and righteous; For he hath preserved the lot of the righteous, Because they have hated and despised this world of unrighteousness, And have hated all its works and ways in the name of the Lord of Spirits: For in his name they are saved, And according to his good pleasure hath it been in regard to their life. ⁸In these days downcast in countenance shall the kings of the earth have become, And the strong who possess the land because of the works of their hands; For on the day of their anguish and affliction they shall not (be able to) save themselves. ⁹And I will give them over into the hands of Mine elect: As straw in the fire so shall they burn before the face of the holy: As lead in the water shall they sink before the face of the righteous, And no trace of them shall any more be found. ¹⁰And on the day of their affliction there shall be rest on the earth, And before them they shall fall and not rise again: And there shall be no one to take them with his hands and raise them: For they have denied the Lord of Spirits and His Anointed. The name of the Lord of Spirits be blessed. **XLIX.** The Power and Wisdom of the Elect One.

Enoch 1 Chapter 49

¹For wisdom is poured out like water, And glory faileth not before him for evermore. ²For he is mighty in all the secrets of righteousness, And unrighteousness shall disappear as a shadow, And have no continuance; Because the Elect One standeth before the Lord of Spirits, And his glory is for ever and ever, And his might unto all generations. ³And in him dwells the spirit of wisdom, And the spirit which gives insight, And the spirit of understanding and of might, And the spirit of those who have fallen asleep in righteousness. ⁴And he shall judge the secret things, And none shall be able to utter a lying word before him; For he is the Elect One before the Lord of Spirits according to His good pleasure. **L.** The Glorification and Victory of the Righteous: the Repentance of the Gentiles.

Enoch 1 Chapter 50

¹And in those days a change shall take place for the holy and elect, And the light of days shall abide upon them, And glory and honour shall turn to the holy, ²On the day of affliction on which evil shall have been treasured up against the sinners. And the righteous shall be victorious in the name of the Lord of Spirits: And He will cause the others to witness (this) That they may repent And forgo the works of their hands. ³They shall have no honour through the name of the Lord of Spirits, Yet

through His name shall they be saved, And the Lord of Spirits will have compassion on them, For His compassion is great. ⁴And He is righteous also in His judgement, And in the presence of His glory unrighteousness also shall not maintain itself: At His judgement the unrepentant shall perish before Him. ⁵And from henceforth I will have no mercy on them, saith the Lord of Spirits.**LI.** The Resurrection of the Dead, and the Separation by the Judge of the Righteous and the Wicked.

Enoch 1 Chapter 51

¹And in those days shall the earth also give back that which has been entrusted to it, And Sheol also shall give back that which it has received, And hell shall give back that which it owes. ²And he shall choose the righteous and holy from among them: For the day has drawn nigh that they should be saved. ³And the Elect One shall in those days sit on My throne, And his mouth shall pour forth all the secrets of wisdom and counsel: For the Lord of Spirits hath given (them) to him and hath glorified him. ⁴And in those days shall the mountains leap like rams, And the hills also shall skip like lambs satisfied with milk, And the faces of [all] the angels in heaven shall be lighted up with joy. ⁵a. For in those days shall the Elect One arise, ⁵b. And the earth shall rejoice, ⁵c. And the righteous shall dwell upon it, ⁵d. And the elect shall walk thereon. **LII.** The Seven Metal Mountains and the Elect One.

Enoch 1 Chapter 52

¹And after those days in that place where I had seen all the visions of that which is hidden—for I had been carried off in a whirlwind and they had borne me towards the west—²There mine eyes saw all the secret things of heaven that shall be, a mountain of iron, and a mountain of copper, and a mountain of silver, And a mountain of gold, and a mountain of soft metal, and a mountain of lead. ³And I asked the angel who went with me, saying, 'What things are these which I have seen in secret?' ⁴And he said unto me: 'All these things which thou hast seen shall serve the dominion of His Anointed that he may be potent and mighty on the earth.' ⁵And that angel of peace answered, saying unto me: 'Wait a little, and there shall be revealed unto thee all the secret things which surround the Lord of Spirits. ⁶And these mountains which thine eyes have seen, The mountain of iron, and the mountain of copper, the mountain of silver, And the mountain of gold, and the mountain of soft metal, and the mountain of lead, All these shall be in the presence of the Elect One As wax: before the fire, And like the water which streams down from above [upon those mountains], And they shall become powerless before his feet. ⁷And it shall come to pass in those days that none shall be saved, Either by gold or by silver, And none be able to escape. ⁸And there shall be no iron for war, Nor shall one clothe oneself with a breastplate. Bronze shall be of no service, And tin [shall be of no service and] shall not be esteemed, And lead shall not be desired. ⁹And all these things shall be [denied and] destroyed from the surface of the earth, When the Elect One shall appear before the face of the Lord of Spirits.'**LIII. LVI. 6.** The Valley of Judgement: the Angels of Punishment: the Communities of the Elect One.

Enoch 1 Chapter 53

¹There mine eyes saw a deep valley with open mouths, and all who dwell on the earth and sea and islands shall bring to him gifts and presents and tokens of homage, but that deep valley shall not become full. ²And their hands commit lawless deeds, And the sinners devour all whom they lawlessly oppress: Yet the sinners shall be destroyed before the face of the Lord of Spirits, And they shall be banished from off the face of His earth, And they shall perish for ever and ever. ³For I saw all the angels of punishment abiding (there) and preparing all the instruments of Satan. ⁴And I asked the angel of peace who went with me: 'For whom are they preparing these instruments?' ⁵And he said unto me: 'They prepare these for the kings and the mighty of this earth, that they may thereby be destroyed. ⁶And after this the Righteous and Elect One shall cause the house of his congregation to appear: henceforth they shall be no more hindered in the name of the Lord of Spirits. ⁷And these mountains shall not stand as the earth before his righteousness, But the hills shall be as a fountain of water, And the righteous shall have rest from the oppression of sinners.'**LIV.** The Deep Valley and the Punishment of Kings and Hosts of Azâzêl.

Enoch 1 Chapter 54

¹And I looked and turned to another part of the earth, and saw there a deep valley with burning fire. ²And they brought the kings and the mighty, and began to cast them into this deep valley. ³And there mine eyes saw how they made these their instruments, iron chains of immeasurable weight. ⁴And I asked the angel of peace who went with me, saying: 'For whom are these chains being prepared?' ⁵And he said unto me: 'These are being prepared for the hosts of Azâzêl, so that they may take them and cast them into the abyss of complete condemnation, and they shall cover their jaws with rough stones as the Lord of Spirits

commanded. ⁶And Michael, and Gabriel, and Raphael, and Phanuel shall take hold of them on that great day, and cast them on that day into the burning furnace, that the Lord of Spirits may take vengeance on them for their unrighteousness in becoming subject to Satan and leading astray those who dwell on the earth.'**LV.** Noachic Fragment on the First World Judgement.⁷And in those days shall punishment come from the Lord of Spirits, and he will open all the chambers of waters which are above the heavens, and of the fountains which are beneath the earth. ⁸And all the waters shall be joined with the waters: that which is above the heavens is the masculine, and the water which is beneath the earth is the feminine. ⁹And they shall destroy all who dwell on the earth and those who dwell under the ends of the heaven. ¹⁰And when they have recognized their unrighteousness which they have wrought on the earth, then by these shall they perish. **LV. 3-LVI. 4.** Final Judgement of Azâzêl, the Watchers, and their Children.

Enoch 1 Chapter 55

¹And after that the Head of Days repented and said: 'In vain have I destroyed all who dwell on the earth.' ²And He sware by His great name: 'Henceforth I will not do so to all who dwell on the earth, and I will set a sign in the heaven: and this shall be a pledge of good faith between Me and them for ever, so long as heaven is above the earth. And this is in accordance with My command.' **LV. 3-LVI. 4. Final Judgement of Azâzêl, the Watchers and their children.**³When I have desired to take hold of them by the hand of the angels on the day of tribulation and pain because of this, I will cause My chastisement and My wrath to abide upon them, saith God, the Lord of Spirits. ⁴Ye †mighty kings† who dwell on the earth, ye shall have to behold Mine Elect One, how he sits on the throne of glory and judges Azâzêl, and all his associates, and all his hosts in the name of the Lord of Spirits.'

Enoch 1 Chapter 56

¹ And I saw there the hosts of the angels of punishment going, and they held scourges and chains of iron and bronze. ² And I asked the angel of peace who went with me, saying: "To whom are these who hold the scourges going?' ³ And he said unto me: 'To their elect and beloved ones, that they may be cast into the chasm of the abyss of the valley. ⁴ And then that valley shall be filled with their elect and beloved, And the days of their lives shall be at an end, And the days of their leading astray shall not thenceforward be reckoned. **LVI. 5-8. Last struggle of heathen Powers against Israel.**⁵And in those days the angels shall return And hurl themselves to the east upon the Parthians and Medes: They shall stir up the kings, so that a spirit of unrest shall come upon them, And they shall rouse them from their thrones, That they may break forth as lions from their lairs, And as hungry wolves among their flocks. ⁶And they shall go up and tread under foot the land of His elect ones. [And the land of His elect ones shall be before them a threshing-floor and a highway:] ⁷But the city of my righteous shall be a hindrance to their horses. And they shall begin to fight among themselves, And their right hand shall be strong against themselves, And a man shall not know his brother, Nor a son his father or his mother, Till there be no number of the corpses through their slaughter, And their punishment be not in vain. ⁸In those days Sheol shall open its jaws, And they shall be swallowed up therein And their destruction shall be at an end; Sheol shall devour the sinners in the presence of the elect.'**LVII.** The Return from the Dispersion.

Enoch 1 Chapter 57

¹And it came to pass after this that I saw another host of wagons, and men riding thereon, and coming on the winds from the east, and from the west to the south. ²And the noise of their wagons was heard, and when this turmoil took place the holy ones from heaven remarked it, and the pillars of the earth were moved from their place, and the sound thereof was heard from the one end of heaven to the other, in one day. ³And they shall all fall down and worship the Lord of Spirits. And this is the end of the second Parable.**LVIII.** The Blessedness of the Saints.

Enoch 1 Chapter 58

¹And I began to speak the third Parable concerning the righteous and elect. ²Blessed are ye, ye righteous and elect, For glorious shall be your lot. ³And the righteous shall be in the light of the sun. And the elect in the light of eternal life: The days of their life shall be unending, And the days of the holy without number. ⁴And they shall seek the light and find righteousness with the Lord of Spirits: There shall be peace to the righteous in the name of the Eternal Lord. ⁵And after this it shall be said to the holy in heaven That they should seek out the secrets of righteousness, the heritage of faith: For it has become bright as the sun upon earth, And the darkness is past. ⁶And there shall be a light that never endeth, And to a limit (lit. 'number') of days they shall not come, For the darkness shall first have been destroyed, [And the light established before the Lord of Spirits] And the light of uprightness

established for ever before the Lord of Spirits.**LIX.** The Lights and the Thunder.

Enoch 1 Chapter 59

¹[In those days mine eyes saw the secrets of the lightnings, and of the lights, and the judgements they execute (lit. 'their judgement'): and they lighten for a blessing or a curse as the Lord of Spirits willeth. ²And there I saw the secrets of the thunder, and how when it resounds above in the heaven, the sound thereof is heard, and he caused me to see the judgements executed on the earth, whether they be for well-being and blessing, or for a curse according to the word of the Lord of Spirits. ³And after that all the secrets of the lights and lightnings were shown to me, and they lighten for blessing and for satisfying.]**LX.** Book of Noah–a Fragment. Quaking of Heaven: Behemoth and Leviathan: the Elements.

Enoch 1 Chapter 60

¹In the year five hundred, in the seventh month, on the fourteenth day of the month in the life of †Enoch†. In that Parable I saw how a mighty quaking made the heaven of heavens to quake, and the host of the Most High, and the angels, a thousand thousands and ten thousand times ten thousand, were disquieted with a great disquiet. ²And the Head of Days sat on the throne of His glory, and the angels and the righteous stood around Him. ³And a great trembling seized me, And fear took hold of me, And my loins gave way, And dissolved were my reins, And I fell upon my face. ⁴And Michael sent another angel from among the holy ones and he raised me up, and when he had raised me up my spirit returned; for I had not been able to endure the look of this host, and the commotion and the quaking of the heaven. ⁵And Michael said unto me: 'Why art thou disquieted with such a vision? Until this day lasted the day of His mercy; and He hath been merciful and long-suffering towards those who dwell on the earth. ⁶And when the day, and the power, and the punishment, and the judgement come, which the Lord of Spirits hath prepared for those who worship not the righteous law, and for those who deny the righteous judgement, and for those who take His name in vain–that day is prepared, for the elect a covenant, but for sinners an inquisition. ⁷And on that day were two monsters parted, a female monster named Leviathan, to dwell in the abysses of the ocean over the fountains of the waters. ⁸But the male is named Behemoth, who occupied with his breast a waste wilderness named †Dûidâin†, on the east of the garden where the elect and righteous dwell, where my grandfather was taken up, the seventh from Adam, the first man whom the Lord of Spirits created. ⁹And I besought the other angel that he should show me the might of those monsters, how they were parted on one day and cast, the one into the abysses of the sea, and the other unto the dry land of the wilderness. ¹⁰And he said to me: 'Thou son of man, herein thou dost seek to know what is hidden.' ¹¹ And the other angel who went with me and showed me what was hidden told me what is first and last in the heaven in the height, and beneath the earth in the depth, and at the ends of the heaven, and on the foundation of the heaven. ¹² And the chambers of the winds, and how the winds are divided, and how they are weighed, and (how) the portals of the winds are reckoned, each according to the power of the wind, and the power of the lights of the moon, and according to the power that is fitting: and the divisions of the stars according to their names, and how all the divisions are divided. ¹³ And the thunders according to the places where they fall, and all the divisions that are made among the lightnings that it may lighten, and their host that they may at once obey. ¹⁴ For the thunder has †places of rest† (which) are assigned (to it) while it is waiting for its peal; and the thunder and lightning are inseparable, and although not one and undivided, they both go together through the spirit and separate not. ¹⁵ For when the lightning lightens, the thunder utters its voice, and the spirit enforces a pause during the peal, and divides equally between them; for the treasury of their peals is like the sand, and each one of them as it peals is held in with a bridle, and turned back by the power of the spirit, and pushed forward according to the many quarters of the earth. ¹⁶ And the spirit of the sea is masculine and strong, and according to the might of his strength he draws it back with a rein, and in like manner it is driven forward and disperses amid all the mountains of the earth. ¹⁷ And the spirit of the hoar-frost is his own angel, and the spirit of the hail is a good angel. ¹⁸ And the spirit of the snow has forsaken his chambers on account of his strength–There is a special spirit therein, and that which ascends from it is like smoke, and its name is frost. ¹⁹ And the spirit of the mist is not united with them in their chambers, but it has a special chamber; for its course is †glorious† both in light and in darkness, and in winter and in summer, and in its chamber is an angel. ²⁰ And the spirit of the dew has its dwelling at the ends of the heaven, and is connected with the chambers of the rain, and its course is in winter and summer: and its clouds and the clouds of the mist are connected, and

the one gives to the other. ²¹ And when the spirit of the rain goes forth from its chamber, the angels come and open the chamber and lead it out, and when it is diffused over the whole earth it unites with the water on the earth. And whensoever it unites with the water on the earth . . . ²² For the waters are for those who dwell on the earth; for they are nourishment for the earth from the Most High who is in heaven: therefore there is a measure for the rain, and the angels take it in charge. ²³ And these things I saw towards the Garden of the Righteous. ²⁴ And the angel of peace who was with me said to me: 'These two monsters, prepared conformably to the greatness of God, shall feed . . . ²⁵ When the punishment of the Lord of Spirits shall rest upon them, it shall rest in order that the punishment of the Lord of Spirits may not come, in vain, and it shall slay the children with their mothers and the children with their fathers. Afterwards the judgement shall take place according to His mercy and His patience.'**LXI.** Angels go off to measure Paradise: the Judgement of the Righteous by the Elect One: the Praise of the Elect One and of God.

Enoch 1 Chapter 61

¹ And I saw in those days how long cords were given to those angels, and they took to themselves wings and flew, and they went towards the north. ² And I asked the angel, saying unto him: 'Why have those (angels) taken these cords and gone off?' And he said unto me: 'They have gone to measure.' ³ And the angel who went with me said unto me: 'These shall bring the measures of the righteous, And the ropes of the righteous to the righteous, That they may stay themselves on the name of the Lord of Spirits for ever and ever. ⁴ The elect shall begin to dwell with the elect, And those are the measures which shall be given to faith And which shall strengthen righteousness. ⁵ And these measures shall reveal all the secrets of the depths of the earth, And those who have been destroyed by the desert, And those who have been devoured by the beasts, And those who have been devoured by the fish of the sea, That they may return and stay themselves On the day of the Elect One; For none shall be destroyed before the Lord of Spirits, And none can be destroyed. ⁶ And all who dwell above in the heaven received a command and power and one voice and one light like unto fire. ⁷ And that One (with) their first words they blessed, And extolled and lauded with wisdom, And they were wise in utterance and in the spirit of life. ⁸ And the Lord of Spirits placed the Elect one on the throne of glory. And he shall judge all the works of the holy above in the heaven, And in the balance shall their deeds be weighed. ⁹ And when he shall lift up his countenance To judge their secret ways according to the word of the name of the Lord of Spirits, And their path according to the way of the righteous judgement of the Lord of Spirits, Then shall they all with one voice speak and bless, And glorify and extol and sanctify the name of the Lord of Spirits. ¹⁰ And He will summon all the host of the heavens, and all the holy ones above, and the host of God, the Cherubic, Seraphin and Ophannin, and all the angels of power, and all the angels of principalities, and the Elect One, and the other powers on the earth (and) over the water. ¹¹ On that day shall raise one voice, and bless and glorify and exalt in the spirit of faith, and in the spirit of wisdom, and in the spirit of patience, and in the spirit of mercy, and in the spirit of judgement and of peace, and in the spirit of goodness, and shall all say with one voice: "Blessed is He, and may the name of the Lord of Spirits be blessed for ever and ever." ¹² All who sleep not above in heaven shall bless Him: All the holy ones who are in heaven shall bless Him, And all the elect who dwell in the garden of life: And every spirit of light who is able to bless, and glorify, and extol, and hallow Thy blessed name, And all flesh shall beyond measure glorify and bless Thy name for ever and ever. ¹³ For great is the mercy of the Lord of Spirits, and He is long-suffering, And all His works and all that He has created He has revealed to the righteous and elect In the name of the Lord of Spirits.**LXII.** Judgement of the Kings and the Mighty: Blessedness of the Righteous.

Enoch 1 Chapter 62

¹ And thus the Lord commanded the kings and the mighty and the exalted, and those who dwell on the earth, and said: 'Open your eyes and lift up your horns if ye are able to recognize the Elect One.' ² And the Lord of Spirits seated him on the throne of His glory, And the spirit of righteousness was poured out upon him, And the word of his mouth slays all the sinners, And all the unrighteous are destroyed from before his face. ³ And there shall stand up in that day all the kings and the mighty, And the exalted and those who hold the earth, And they shall see and recognize How he sits on the throne of his glory, And righteousness is judged before him, And no lying word is spoken before him. ⁴ Then shall pain come upon them as on a woman in travail, [And she has pain in bringing forth] When her child enters the mouth of the womb, And she has pain in bringing forth. ⁵ And one portion of them shall look on the other, And they shall be terrified, And they shall be

downcast of countenance, And pain shall seize them, When they see that Son of Man Sitting on the throne of his glory. 6 And the kings and the mighty and all who possess the earth shall bless and glorify and extol him who rules over all, who was hidden. 7 For from the beginning the Son of Man was hidden, And the Most High preserved him in the presence of His might, And revealed him to the elect. 8 And the congregation of the elect and holy shall be sown, And all the elect shall stand before him on that day. 9 And all the kings and the mighty and the exalted and those who rule the earth Shall fall down before him on their faces, And worship and set their hope upon that Son of Man, And petition him and supplicate for mercy at his hands. 10 Nevertheless that Lord of Spirits will so press them That they shall hastily go forth from His presence, And their faces shall be filled with shame, And the darkness grow deeper on their faces. 11 And He will deliver them to the angels for punishment, To execute vengeance on them because they have oppressed His children and His elect. 12 And they shall be a spectacle for the righteous and for His elect: They shall rejoice over them, Because the wrath of the Lord of Spirits resteth upon them, And His sword is drunk with their blood. 13 And the righteous and elect shall be saved on that day, And they shall never thenceforward see the face of the sinners and unrighteous. 14 And the Lord of Spirits will abide over them, And with that Son of Man shall they eat And lie down and rise up for ever and ever. 15 And the righteous and elect shall have risen from the earth, And ceased to be of downcast countenance. And they shall have been clothed with garments of glory, 16 And these shall be the garments of life from the Lord of Spirits: And your garments shall not grow old, Nor your glory pass away before the Lord of Spirits.**LXIII.** The Unavailing Repentance of the Kings and the Mighty.

Enoch 1 Chapter 63

1 In those days shall the mighty and the kings who possess the earth implore (Him) to grant them a little respite from His angels of punishment to whom they were delivered, that they might fall down and worship before the Lord of Spirits, and confess their sins before Him. 2 And they shall bless and glorify the Lord of Spirits, and say: 'Blessed is the Lord of Spirits and the Lord of kings, And the Lord of the mighty and the Lord of the rich, And the Lord of glory and the Lord of wisdom, 3 And splendid in every secret thing is Thy power from generation to generation, And Thy glory for ever and ever: Deep are all Thy secrets and innumerable, And Thy righteousness is beyond reckoning. 4 We have now learnt that we should glorify the Lord of kings and Him who is king over all kings.' 5 And they shall say: 'Would that we had rest to glorify and give thanks And confess our faith before His glory! 6 And now we long for a little rest but find it not: We follow hard upon and obtain (it) not: And light has vanished from before us, And darkness is our dwelling-place for ever and ever: 7 For we have not believed before Him Nor glorified the name of the Lord of Spirits, [nor glorified our Lord] But our hope was in the sceptre of our kingdom, And in our glory. 8 And in the day of our suffering and tribulation He saves us not, And we find no respite for confession That our Lord is true in all His works, and in His judgements and His justice, And His judgements have no respect of persons. 9 And we pass away from before His face on account of our works, And all our sins are reckoned up in righteousness.' 10 Now they shall say unto themselves: 'Our souls are full of unrighteous gain, but it does not prevent us from descending from the midst thereof into the †burden† of Sheol.' 11 And after that their faces shall be filled with darkness And shame before that Son of Man, And they shall be driven from his presence, And the sword shall abide before his face in their midst. 12 Thus spake the Lord of Spirits: 'This is the ordinance and judgement with respect to the mighty and the kings and the exalted and those who possess the earth before the Lord of Spirits.'**LXIV.** Vision of the Fallen Angels in the Place of Punishment.

Enoch 1 Chapter 64

1 And other forms I saw hidden in that place. 2 I heard the voice of the angel saying: 'These are the angels who descended to the earth, and revealed what was hidden to the children of men and seduced the children of men into committing sin.'**LXV.** Enoch Foretells to Noah the Deluge and His Own Preservation.

Enoch 1 Chapter 65

1 And in those days Noah saw the earth that it had sunk down and its destruction was nigh. 2 And he arose from thence and went to the ends of the earth, and cried aloud to his grandfather Enoch: and Noah said three times with an embittered voice: 'Hear me, hear me, hear me.' 3 And I said unto him: 'Tell me what it is that is falling out on the earth that the earth is in such evil plight and shaken, lest perchance I shall perish with it?' 4 And thereupon there was a great commotion, on the earth, and a voice was heard from heaven, and I fell on my face. 5 And Enoch my grandfather came and stood by me, and said unto me: 'Why hast thou cried unto me with a bitter cry and weeping? 6 And a command has gone forth from the presence of the Lord concerning those who dwell on the earth that their ruin is accomplished because they have learnt all the secrets of the angels, and all the violence of the Satans, and all their powers–the most secret ones–and all the power of those who practice sorcery, and the power of witchcraft, and the power of those who make molten images for the whole earth: 7 And how silver is produced from the dust of the earth, and how soft metal originates in the earth. 8 For lead and tin are not produced from the earth like the first: it is a fountain that produces them, and an angel stands therein, and that angel is pre-eminent.' 9 And after that my grandfather Enoch took hold of me by my hand and raised me up, and said unto me: 'Go, for I have asked the Lord of Spirits as touching this commotion on the earth. 10 And He said unto me: "Because of their unrighteousness their judgement has been determined upon and shall not be withheld by Me for ever. Because of the sorceries which they have searched out and learnt, the earth and those who dwell upon it shall be destroyed." 11 And these–they have no place of repentance for ever, because they have shown them what was hidden, and they are the damned: but as for thee, my son, the Lord of Spirits knows that thou art pure, and guiltless of this reproach concerning the secrets. 12 And He has destined thy name to be among the holy, And will preserve thee amongst those who dwell on the earth, And has destined thy righteous seed both for kingship and for great honours, And from thy seed shall proceed a fountain of the righteous and holy without number for ever.**LXVI.** The Angels of the Waters Bidden to Hold Them in Check.

Enoch 1 Chapter 66

1 And after that he showed me the angels of punishment who are prepared to come and let loose all the powers of the waters which are beneath in the earth in order to bring judgement and destruction on all who [abide and] dwell on the earth. 2 And the Lord of Spirits gave commandment to the angels who were going forth, that they should not cause the waters to rise but should hold them in check; for those angels were over the powers of the waters. 3 And I went away from the presence of Enoch.**LXVII.** God's Promise to Noah: Places of Punishment of the Angels and of the Kings.

Enoch 1 Chapter 67

1 And in those days the word of God came unto me, and He said unto me: 'Noah, thy lot has come up before Me, a lot without blame, a lot of love and uprightness. 2 And now the angels are making a wooden (building), and when they have completed that task I will place My hand upon it and preserve it, and there shall come forth from it the seed of life, and a change shall set in so that the earth will not remain without inhabitant. 3 And I will make fast thy seed before me for ever and ever, and I will spread abroad those who dwell with thee: it shall not be unfruitful on the face of the earth, but it shall be blessed and multiply on the earth in the name of the Lord.' 4 And He will imprison those angels, who have shown unrighteousness, in that burning valley which my grandfather Enoch had formerly shown to me in the west among the mountains of gold and silver and iron and soft metal and tin. 5 And I saw that valley in which there was a great convulsion and a convulsion of the waters. 6 And when all this took place, from that fiery molten metal and from the convulsion thereof in that place, there was produced a smell of sulphur, and it was connected with those waters, and that valley of the angels who had led astray (mankind) burned beneath that land. 7 And through its valleys proceed streams of fire, where these angels are punished who had led astray those who dwell upon the earth. 8 But those waters shall in those days serve for the kings and the mighty and the exalted, and those who dwell on the earth, for the healing of the body, but for the punishment of the spirit; now their spirit is full of lust, that they may be punished in their body, for they have denied the Lord of Spirits and see their punishment daily, and yet believe not in His name. 9 And in proportion as the burning of their bodies becomes severe, a corresponding change shall take place in their spirit for ever and ever; for before the Lord of Spirits none shall utter an idle word. 10 For the judgement shall come upon them, because they believe in the lust of their body and deny the Spirit of the Lord. 11 And those same waters will undergo a change in those days; for when those angels are punished in these waters, these water-springs shall change their temperature, and when the angels ascend, this water of the springs shall change and become cold. 12 And I heard Michael answering and saying: 'This judgement wherewith the angels are judged is a testimony for the kings and the mighty who possess the earth.' 13 Because these waters of judgement minister to the healing of the body of the kings and the lust of their body; therefore they will not see and will not believe that those waters will change and become a fire which burns for ever.**LXVIII.**

Michael and Raphael Astonished at the Severity of the Judgement.

Enoch 1 Chapter 68

1 And after that my grandfather Enoch gave me the teaching of all the secrets in the book in the Parables which had been given to him, and he put them together for me in the words of the book of the Parables. 2 And on that day Michael answered Raphael and said: 'The power of the spirit transports and makes me to tremble because of the severity of the judgement of the secrets, the judgement of the angels: who can endure the severe judgement which has been executed, and before which they melt away?' 3 And Michael answered again, and said to Raphael: 'Who is he whose heart is not softened concerning it, and whose reins are not troubled by this word of judgement (that) has gone forth upon them because of those who have thus led them out?' 4 And it came to pass when he stood before the Lord of Spirits, Michael said thus to Raphael: 'I will not take their part under the eye of the Lord; for the Lord of Spirits has been angry with them because they do as if they were the Lord. 5 Therefore all that is hidden shall come upon them for ever and ever; for neither angel nor man shall have his portion (in it), but alone they have received their judgement for ever and ever.'**LXIX.** The Names and Functions of the Fallen Angels and Satans: the Secret Oath.

Enoch 1 Chapter 69

1 And after this judgement they shall terrify and make them to tremble because they have shown this to those who dwell on the earth. 2 And behold the names of those angels [and these are their names: the first of them is Samjâzâ, the second Artâqîfâ, and the third Armên, the fourth Kôkabêl, the fifth †Tûrâêl†, the sixth Rûmjâl, the seventh Dânjâl, the eighth †Nêqâêl†, the ninth Barâqêl, the tenth Azâzêl, the eleventh Armârôs, the twelfth Batarjâl, the thirteenth †Busasêjal†, the fourteenth Hanânêl, the fifteenth †Tûrêl†, and the sixteenth Sîmâpêsîêl, the seventeenth Jetrêl, the eighteenth Tûmâêl, the nineteenth Tûrêl, the twentieth †Rumâêl†, the twenty-first †Azâzêl†. 3 And these are the chiefs of their angels and their names, and their chief ones over hundreds and over fifties and over tens]. 4 The name of the first Jeqôn: that is, the one who led astray [all] the sons of God, and brought them down to the earth, and led them astray through the daughters of men. 5 And the second was named Asbeêl: he imparted to the holy sons of God evil counsel, and led them astray so that they defiled their bodies with the daughters of men. 6 And the third was named Gâdreêl: he it is who showed the children of men all the blows of death, and he led astray Eve, and showed [the weapons of death to the sons of men] the shield and the coat of mail, and the sword for battle, and all the weapons of death to the children of men. 7 And from his hand they have proceeded against those who dwell on the earth from that day and for evermore. 8 And the fourth was named Pênêmûe: he taught the children of men the bitter and the sweet, and he taught them all the secrets of their wisdom. 9 And he instructed mankind in writing with ink and paper, and thereby many sinned from eternity to eternity and until this day. 10 For men were not created for such a purpose, to give confirmation to their good faith with pen and ink. 11 For men were created exactly like the angels, to the intent that they should continue pure and righteous, and death, which destroys everything, could not have taken hold of them, but through this their knowledge they are perishing, and through this power it is consuming me†. 12 And the fifth was named Kâsdejâ: this is he who showed the children of men all the wicked smitings of spirits and demons, and the smitings of the embryo in the womb, that it may pass away, and [the smitings of the soul] the bites of the serpent, and the smitings which befall through the noontide heat, the son of the serpent named Tabââ'ĕt. 13 And this is the task of Kâsbeêl, the chief of the oath which he showed to the holy ones when he dwelt high above in glory, and its name is Bîqâ. 14 This (angel) requested Michael to show him the hidden name, that he might enunciate it in the oath, so that those might quake before that name and oath who revealed all that was in secret to the children of men. 15 And this is the power of this oath, for it is powerful and strong, and he placed this oath Akâe in the hand of Michael. 16 And these are the secrets of this oath . . . And they are strong through his oath: And the heaven was suspended before the world was created, And for ever. 17 And through it the earth was founded upon the water, And from the secret recesses of the mountains come beautiful waters, From the creation of the world and unto eternity. 18 And through that oath the sea was created, And †as its foundation† He set for it the sand against the time of (its) anger, And it dare not pass beyond it from the creation of the world unto eternity. 19 And through that oath are the depths made fast, And abide and stir not from their place from eternity to eternity. 20 And through that oath the sun and moon complete their course, And deviate not from their ordinance from eternity to eternity. 21 And through that oath the stars complete their course, And He calls them by their names, And they

answer Him from eternity to eternity. 22 [And in like manner the spirits of the water, and of the winds, and of all zephyrs, and (their) paths from all the quarters of the winds. 23 And there are preserved the voices of the thunder and the light of the lightnings: and there are preserved the chambers of the hail and the chambers of the hoarfrost, and the chambers of the mist, and the chambers of the rain and the dew. 24 And all these believe and give thanks before the Lord of Spirits, and glorify (Him) with all their power, and their food is in every act of thanksgiving: they thank and glorify and extol the name of the Lord of Spirits for ever and ever.] 25 And this oath is mighty over them And through it [they are preserved and] their paths are preserved, And their course is not destroyed.**Close of the Third Parable.**26 And there was great joy amongst them, And they blessed and glorified and extolled Because the name of that Son of Man had been revealed unto them. 27 And he sat on the throne of his glory, And the sum of judgement was given unto the Son of Man, And he caused the sinners to pass away and be destroyed from off the face of the earth, And those who have led the world astray. 28 With chains shall they be bound, And in their assemblage-place of destruction shall they be imprisoned, And all their works vanish from the face of the earth. 29 And from henceforth there shall be nothing corruptible; For that Son of Man has appeared, And has seated himself on the throne of his glory, And all evil shall pass away before his face, And the word of that Son of Man shall go forth And be strong before the Lord of Spirits.**This is the Third Parable of Enoch.LXX.** The Final Translation of Enoch.

Enoch 1 Chapter 70

1 And it came to pass after this that his name during his lifetime was raised aloft to that Son of Man and to the Lord of Spirits from amongst those who dwell on the earth. 2 And he was raised aloft on the chariots of the spirit and his name vanished among them. 3 And from that day I was no longer numbered amongst them: and he set me between the two winds, between the North and the West, where the angels took the cords to measure for me the place for the elect and righteous. 4 And there I saw the first fathers and the righteous who from the beginning dwell in that place.**LXXI.** Two Earlier Visions of Enoch.

Enoch 1 Chapter 71

1 And it came to pass after this that my spirit was translated And it ascended into the heavens: And I saw the holy sons of God. They were stepping on flames of fire: Their garments were white [and their raiment], And their faces shone like snow. 2 And I saw two streams of fire, And the light of that fire shone like hyacinth, And I fell on my face before the Lord of Spirits. 3 And the angel Michael [one of the archangels] seized me by my right hand, And lifted me up and led me forth into all the secrets, And he showed me all the secrets of righteousness. 4 And he showed me all the secrets of the ends of the heaven, And all the chambers of all the stars, and all the luminaries, Whence they proceed before the face of the holy ones. 5 And he translated my spirit into the heaven of heavens, And I saw there as it were a structure built of crystals, And between those crystals tongues of living fire. 6 And my spirit saw the girdle which girt that house of fire, And on its four sides were streams full of living fire, And they girt that house. 7 And round about were Seraphin, Cherubic, and Ophannin: And these are they who sleep not And guard the throne of His glory. 8 And I saw angels who could not be counted, A thousand thousands, and ten thousand times ten thousand, Encircling that house. And Michael, and Raphael, and Gabriel, and Phanuel, And the holy angels who are above the heavens, Go in and out of that house. 9 And they came forth from that house, And Michael and Gabriel, Raphael and Phanuel, And many holy angels without number. 10 And with them the Head of Days, His head white and pure as wool, And His raiment indescribable. 11 And I fell on my face, And my whole body became relaxed, And my spirit was transfigured; And I cried with a loud voice, . . .with the spirit of power, And blessed and glorified and extolled. 12 And these blessings which went forth out of my mouth were well pleasing before that Head of Days. 13 And that Head of Days came with Michael and Gabriel, Raphael and Phanuel, thousands and ten thousands of angels without number. [Lost passage wherein the Son of Man was described as accompanying the Head of Days, and Enoch asked one of the angels (as in 46) concerning the Son of Man as to who he was.] 14 And he (i.e. the angel) came to me and greeted me with His voice, and said unto me: 'This is the Son of Man who is born unto righteousness; And righteousness abides over him, And the righteousness of the Head of Days forsakes him not.' 15 And he said unto me: 'He proclaims unto thee peace in the name of the world to come; For from hence has proceeded peace since the creation of the world, And so shall it be unto thee for ever and for ever and ever. 16 And all shall walk in his ways since righteousness never forsaketh him: With him will be their

dwelling-places, and with him their heritage, And they shall not be separated from him for ever and ever and ever. 17 And so there shall be length of days with that Son of Man, And the righteous shall have peace and an upright way In the name of the Lord of Spirits for ever and ever.'LXXII. The Book of the Courses of the Heavenly Luminaries.

Enoch 1 Chapter 72

1 The book of the courses of the luminaries of the heaven, the relations of each, according to their classes, their dominion and their seasons, according to their names and places of origin, and according to their months, which Uriel, the holy angel, who was with me, who is their guide, showed me; and he showed me all their laws exactly as they are, and how it is with regard to all the years of the world and unto eternity, till the new creation is accomplished which dureth till eternity. 2 And this is the first law of the luminaries: the luminary the Sun has its rising in the eastern portals of the heaven, and its setting in the western portals of the heaven. 3 And I saw six portals in which the sun rises, six portals in which the sun sets and the moon rises and sets in these portals, and the leaders of the stars and those whom they lead: six in the east and six in the west, and all following each other in accurately corresponding order: also many windows to the right and left of these portals. 4 And first there goes forth the great luminary, named the Sun, and his circumference is like the circumference of the heaven, and he is quite filled with illuminating and heating fire. 5 The chariot on which he ascends, the wind drives, and the sun goes down from the heaven and returns through the north in order to reach the east, and is so guided that he comes to the appropriate (lit. 'that') portal and shines in the face of the heaven. 6 In this way he rises in the first month in the great portal, which is the fourth [of those six portals in the east]. 7 And in that fourth portal from which the sun rises in the first month are twelve window-openings, from which proceed a flame when they are opened in their season. 8 When the sun rises in the heaven, he comes forth through that fourth portal thirty mornings in succession, and sets accurately in the fourth portal in the west of the heaven. 9 And during this period the day becomes daily longer and the night nightly shorter to the thirtieth morning. 10 On that day the day is longer than the night by a ninth part, and the day amounts exactly to ten parts and the night to eight parts. 11 And the sun rises from that fourth portal, and sets in the fourth and returns to the fifth portal of the east thirty mornings, and rises from it and sets in the fifth portal. 12 And then the day becomes longer by †two† parts and amounts to eleven parts, and the night becomes shorter and amounts to seven parts. 13 And it returns to the east and enters into the sixth portal, and rises and sets in the sixth portal one-and-thirty mornings on account of its sign. 14 On that day the day becomes longer than the night, and the day becomes double the night, and the day becomes twelve parts, and the night is shortened and becomes six parts. 15 And the sun mounts up to make the day shorter and the night longer, and the sun returns to the east and enters into the sixth portal, and rises from it and sets thirty mornings. 16 And when thirty mornings are accomplished, the day decreases by exactly one part, and becomes eleven parts, and the night seven. 17 And the sun goes forth from that sixth portal in the west, and goes to the east and rises in the fifth portal for thirty mornings, and sets in the west again in the fifth western portal. 18 On that day the day decreases by †two† parts, and amounts to ten parts and the night to eight parts. 19 And the sun goes forth from that fifth portal and sets in the fifth portal of the west, and rises in the fourth portal for one-and-thirty mornings on account of its sign, and sets in the west. 20 On that day the day is equalized with the night, [and becomes of equal length], and the night amounts to nine parts and the day to nine parts. 21 And the sun rises from that portal and sets in the west, and returns to the east and rises thirty mornings in the third portal and sets in the west in the third portal. 22 And on that day the night becomes longer than the day, and night becomes longer than night, and day shorter than day till the thirtieth morning, and the night amounts exactly to ten parts and the day to eight parts. 23 And the sun rises from that third portal and sets in the third portal in the west and returns to the east, and for thirty mornings rises in the second portal in the east, and in like manner sets in the second portal in the west of the heaven. 24 And on that day the night amounts to eleven parts and the day to seven parts. 25 And the sun rises on that day from that second portal and sets in the west in the second portal, and returns to the east into the first portal for one-and-thirty mornings, and sets in the first portal in the west of the heaven. 26 And on that day the night becomes longer and amounts to the double of the day: and the night amounts exactly to twelve parts and the day to six. 27 And the sun has (therewith) traversed the divisions of his orbit and turns again on those divisions of his orbit, and enters that portal thirty mornings and sets also in the west opposite to it. 28 And on that night has the night

decreased in length by a †ninth† part, and the night has become eleven parts and the day seven parts. 29 And the sun has returned and entered into the second portal in the east, and returns on those his divisions of his orbit for thirty mornings, rising and setting. 30 And on that day the night decreases in length, and the night amounts to ten parts and the day to eight. 31 And on that day the sun rises from that portal, and sets in the west, and returns to the east, and rises in the third portal for one-and-thirty mornings, and sets in the west of the heaven. 32 On that day the night decreases and amounts to nine parts, and the day to nine parts, and the night is equal to the day and the year is exactly as to its days three hundred and sixty-four. 33 And the length of the day and of the night, and the shortness of the day and of the night arise–through the course of the sun these distinctions are made (lit. 'they are separated'). 34 So it comes that its course becomes daily longer, and its course nightly shorter. 35 And this is the law and the course of the sun, and his return as often as he returns sixty times and sixty, i.e. the great luminary which is named the sun, for ever and ever. 36 And that which (thus) rises is the great luminary, and is so named according to its appearance, according as the Lord commanded. 37 As he rises, so he sets and decreases not, and rests not, but runs day and night, and his light is sevenfold brighter than that of the moon; but as regards size they are both equal.LXXIII. The Course of the Moon.

Enoch 1 Chapter 73

1 And after this law I saw another law dealing with the smaller luminary, which is named the Moon. 2 And her circumference is like the circumference of the heaven, and her chariot in which she rides is driven by the wind, and light is given to her in (definite) measure. 3 And her rising and setting change every month: and her days are like the days of the sun, and when her light is uniform (i.e. full) it amounts to the seventh part of the light of the sun. 4 And thus she rises. And her first phase in the east comes forth on the thirtieth morning: and on that day she becomes visible, and constitutes for you the first phase of the moon on the thirtieth day together with the sun in the portal where the sun rises. 5 And the one half of her goes forth by a seventh part, and her whole circumference is empty, without light, with the exception of one-seventh part of it, (and) the fourteenth part of her light. 6 And when she receives one-seventh part of the half of her light, her light amounts to one-seventh part and the half thereof. 7 And she sets with the sun, and when the sun rises the moon rises with him and receives the half of one part of light, and in that night in the beginning of her morning [in the commencement of the lunar day] the moon sets with the sun, and is invisible that night with the fourteen parts and the half of one of them. 8 And she rises on that day with exactly a seventh part, and comes forth and recedes from the rising of the sun, and in her remaining days she becomes bright in the (remaining) thirteen parts.LXXIV. The Monthly Revolutions of the Moon.

Enoch 1 Chapter 74

1 And I saw another course, a law for her, (and) how according to that law she performs her monthly revolution. 2 And all these Uriel, the holy angel who is the leader of them all, showed to me, and their positions, and I wrote down their positions as he showed them to me, and I wrote down their months as they were, and the appearance of their lights till fifteen days were accomplished. 3 In single seventh parts she accomplishes all her light in the east, and in single seventh parts accomplishes all her darkness in the west. 4 And in certain months she alters her settings, and in certain months she pursues her own peculiar course. 5 In two months the moon sets with the sun: in those two middle portals the third and the fourth. 6 She goes forth for seven days, and turns about and returns again through the portal where the sun rises, and accomplishes all her light: and she recedes from the sun, and in eight days enters the sixth portal from which the sun goes forth. 7 And when the sun goes forth from the fourth portal she goes forth seven days, until she goes forth from the fifth and turns back again in seven days into the fourth portal and accomplishes all her light: and she recedes and enters into the first portal in eight days. 8 And she returns again in seven days into the fourth portal from which the sun goes forth. 9 Thus I saw their position–how the moons rose and the sun set in those days. 10 And if five years are added together the sun has an overplus of thirty days, and all the days which accrue to it for one of those five years, when they are full, amount to 364 days. 11 And the overplus of the sun and of the stars amounts to six days: in 5 years 6 days every year come to 30 days: and the moon falls behind the sun and stars to the number of 30 days. 12 And the sun and the stars bring in all the years exactly, so that they do not advance or delay their position by a single day unto eternity; but complete the years with perfect justice in 364 days. 13 In 3 years there are 1092 days, and in 5 years 1820 days, so that in 8 years there are 2912 days. 14 For the moon alone the days amount in 3 years

to 1062 days, and in 5 years she falls 50 days behind: [i.e. to the sum (of 1770) there is to be added (1000 and) 62 days.] ¹⁵ And in 5 years there are 1770 days, so that for the moon the days in 8 years amount to 2832 days. ¹⁶ [For in 8 years she falls behind to the amount of 80 days], all the days she falls behind in 8 years are 80. ¹⁷ And the year is accurately completed in conformity with their world-stations and the stations of the sun, which rise from the portals through which it (the sun) rises and sets 30 days.**LXXV.** The Leaders of the Heads of the Thousands.

Enoch 1 Chapter 75

¹ And the leaders of the heads of the thousands, who are placed over the whole creation and over all the stars, have also to do with the four intercalary days, being inseparable from their office, according to the reckoning of the year, and these render service on the four days which are not reckoned in the reckoning of the year. ² And owing to them men go wrong therein, for those luminaries truly render service on the world-stations, one in the first portal, one in the third portal of the heaven, one in the fourth portal, and one in the sixth portal, and the exactness of the year is accomplished through its separate three hundred and sixty-four stations. ³ For the signs and the times and the years and the days the angel Uriel showed to me, whom the Lord of glory hath set for ever over all the luminaries of the heaven, in the heaven and in the world, that they should rule on the face of the heaven and be seen on the earth, and be leaders for the day and the night, i.e. the sun, moon, and stars, and all the ministering creatures which make their revolution in all the chariots of the heaven. ⁴ In like manner twelve doors Uriel showed me, open in the circumference of the sun's chariot in the heaven, through which the rays of the sun break forth: and from them is warmth diffused over the earth, when they are opened at their appointed seasons. ⁵ [And for the winds and the spirit of the dew when they are opened, standing open in the heavens at the ends.] ⁶ As for the twelve portals in the heaven, at the ends of the earth, out of which go forth the sun, moon, and stars, and all the works of heaven in the east and in the west. ⁷ There are many windows open to the left and right of them, and one window at its (appointed) season produces warmth, corresponding (as these do) to those doors from which the stars come forth according as He has commanded them, and wherein they set corresponding to their number. ⁸ And I saw chariots in the heaven, running in the world, above those portals in which revolve the stars that never set. ⁹ And one is larger than all the rest, and it is that that makes its course through the entire world.**LXXVI.** The Twelve Windows and their Portals.

Enoch 1 Chapter 76

¹ And at the ends of the earth I saw twelve portals open to all the quarters (of the heaven), from which the winds go forth and blow over the earth. ² Three of them are open on the face (i.e. the east) of the heavens, and three in the west, and three on the right (i.e. the south) of the heaven, and three on the left (i.e. the north). ³ And the three first are those of the east, and three are of †the north, and three [after those on the left] of the south†, and three of the west. ⁴ Through four of these come winds of blessing and prosperity, and from those eight come hurtful winds: when they are sent, they bring destruction on all the earth and on the water upon it, and on all who dwell thereon, and on everything which is in the water and on the land. ⁵ And the first wind from those portals, called the east wind, comes forth through the first portal which is in the east, inclining towards the south: from it come forth desolation, drought, heat, and destruction. ⁶ And through the second portal in the middle comes what is fitting, and from it there come rain and fruitfulness and prosperity and dew; and through the third portal which lies toward the north come cold and drought. ⁷ And after these come forth the south winds through three portals: through the first portal of them inclining to the east comes forth a hot wind. ⁸ And through the middle portal next to it there come forth fragrant smells, and dew and rain, and prosperity and health. ⁹ And through the third portal lying to the west come forth dew and rain, locusts and desolation. ¹⁰ And after these the north winds: from the seventh portal in the east come dew and rain, locusts and desolation. ¹¹ And from the middle portal come in a direct direction health and rain and dew and prosperity; and through the third portal in the west come cloud and hoar-frost, and snow and rain, and dew and locusts. ¹² And after these [four] are the west winds: through the first portal adjoining the north come forth dew and hoar-frost, and cold and snow and frost. ¹³ And from the middle portal come forth dew and rain, and prosperity and blessing; and through the last portal which adjoins the south come forth drought and desolation, and burning and destruction. ¹⁴ And the twelve portals of the four quarters of the heaven are therewith completed, and all their laws and all their plagues and all their benefactions have I shown to thee, my son Methuselah.**LXXVII.** The Four Quarters of the World; the Seven Mountains, the Seven Rivers, etc.

Enoch 1 Chapter 77

¹ And the first quarter is called the east, because it is the first: and the second, the south, because the Most High will descend there, yea, there in quite a special sense will He who is blessed for ever descend. ² And the west quarter is named the diminished, because there all the luminaries of the heaven wane and go down. ³ And the fourth quarter, named the north, is divided into three parts: the first of them is for the dwelling of men: and the second contains seas of water, and the abysses and forests and rivers, and darkness and clouds; and the third part contains the garden of righteousness. ⁴ I saw seven high mountains, higher than all the mountains which are on the earth: and thence comes forth hoar-frost, and days, seasons, and years pass away. ⁵ I saw seven rivers on the earth larger than all the rivers: one of them coming from the west pours its waters into the Great Sea. ⁶ And these two come from the north to the sea and pour their waters into the Erythraean Sea in the east. ⁷ And the remaining four come forth on the side of the north to their own sea, <two of them> to the Erythraean Sea, and two into the Great Sea and discharge themselves there [and some say: into the desert]. ⁸ Seven great islands I saw in the sea and in the mainland: two in the mainland and five in the Great Sea.**LXXVIII.** The Sun and Moon; the Waxing and Waning of the Moon.

Enoch 1 Chapter 78

¹ And the names of the sun are the following: the first Orjârês, and the second Tômâs. ² And the moon has four names: the first name is Asônjâ, the second Eblâ, the third Benâsê, and the fourth Erâe. ³ These are the two great luminaries: their circumference is like the circumference of the heaven, and the size of the circumference of both is alike. ⁴ In the circumference of the sun there are seven portions of light which are added to it more than to the moon, and in definite measures it is transferred till the seventh portion of the sun is exhausted. ⁵ And they set and enter the portals of the west, and make their revolution by the north, and come forth through the eastern portals on the face of the heaven. ⁶ And when the moon rises one-fourteenth part appears in the heaven: [the light becomes full in her]: on the fourteenth day she accomplishes her light. ⁷ And fifteen parts of light are transferred to her till the fifteenth day (when) her light is accomplished, according to the sign of the year, and she becomes fifteen parts, and the moon grows by (the addition of) fourteen parts. ⁸ And in her waning (the moon) decreases on the first day to fourteen parts of her light, on the second to thirteen parts of light, on the third to twelve, on the fourth to eleven, on the fifth to ten, on the sixth to nine, on the seventh to eight, on the eighth to seven, on the ninth to six, on the tenth to five, on the eleventh to four, on the twelfth to three, on the thirteenth to two, on the fourteenth to the half of a seventh, and all her remaining light disappears wholly on the fifteenth. ⁹ And in certain months the month has twenty-nine days and once twenty-eight. ¹⁰ And Uriel showed me another law: when light is transferred to the moon, and on which side it is transferred to her by the sun. ¹¹ During all the period during which the moon is growing in her light, she is transferring it to herself when opposite to the sun during fourteen days [her light is accomplished in the heaven], and when she is illumined throughout, her light is accomplished full in the heaven. ¹² And on the first day she is called the new moon, for on that day the light rises upon her. ¹³ She becomes full moon exactly on the day when the sun sets in the west, and from the east she rises at night, and the moon shines the whole night through till the sun rises over against her and the moon is seen over against the sun. ¹⁴ On the side whence the light of the moon comes forth, there again she wanes till all the light vanishes and all the days of the month are at an end, and her circumference is empty, void of light. ¹⁵ And three months she makes of thirty days, and at her time she makes three months of twenty-nine days each, in which she accomplishes her waning in the first period of time, and in the first portal for one hundred and seventy-seven days. ¹⁶ And in the time of her going out she appears for three months (of) thirty days each, and for three months she appears (of) twenty-nine each. ¹⁷ At night she appears like a man for twenty days each time, and by day she appears like the heaven, and there is nothing else in her save her light.**LXXIX.** Recapitulation of several of the Laws.

Enoch 1 Chapter 79

¹ And now, my son, I have shown thee everything, and the law of all the stars of the heaven is completed. ² And he showed me all the laws of these for every day, and for every season of bearing rule, and for every year, and for its going forth, and for the order prescribed to it every month and every week: ³ And the waning of the moon which takes place in the sixth portal: for in this sixth portal her light is accomplished, and

after that there is the beginning of the waning: 4 <And the waning> which takes place in the first portal in its season, till one hundred and seventy-seven days are accomplished: reckoned according to weeks, twenty-five (weeks) and two days. 5 She falls behind the sun and the order of the stars exactly five days in the course of one period, and when this place which thou seest has been traversed. 6 Such is the picture and sketch of every luminary which Uriel the archangel, who is their leader, showed unto me.LXXX• Perversion of Nature and the Heavenly Bodies Owing to the Sin of Men.

Enoch 1 Chapter 80

1 And in those days the angel Uriel answered and said to me: 'Behold, I have shown thee everything, Enoch, and I have revealed everything to thee that thou shouldst see this sun and this moon, and the leaders of the stars of the heaven and all those who turn them, their tasks and times and departures. **LXXX. 2-8**. Perversion of Nature and the heavenly Bodies owning to the Sin of Men.2 And in the days of the sinners the years shall be shortened, And their seed shall be tardy on their lands and fields, And all things on the earth shall alter, And shall not appear in their time: And the rain shall be kept back And the heaven shall withhold (it). 3 And in those times the fruits of the earth shall be backward, And shall not grow in their time, And the fruits of the trees shall be withheld in their time. 4 And the moon shall alter her order, And not appear at her time. 5 [And in those days the sun shall be seen and he shall journey in the evening †on the extremity of the great chariot† in the west] And shall shine more brightly than accords with the order of light. 6 And many chiefs of the stars shall transgress the order (prescribed). And these shall alter their orbits and tasks, And not appear at the seasons prescribed to them. 7 And the whole order of the stars shall be concealed from the sinners, And the thoughts of those on the earth shall err concerning them, [And they shall be altered from all their ways], Yea, they shall err and take them to be gods. 8 And evil shall be multiplied upon them, And punishment shall come upon them So as to destroy all.LXXXI. The Heavenly Tablets and the Mission of Enoch.

Enoch 1 Chapter 81

1 And he said unto me: 'Observe, Enoch, these heavenly tablets, And read what is written thereon, And mark every individual fact.' 2 And I observed the heavenly tablets, and read everything which was written (thereon) and understood everything, and read the book of all the deeds of mankind, and of all the children of flesh that shall be upon the earth to the remotest generations. 3 And forthwith I blessed the great Lord the King of glory for ever, in that He has made all the works of the world, And I extolled the Lord because of His patience, And blessed Him because of the children of men. 4 And after that I said: 'Blessed is the man who dies in righteousness and goodness, Concerning whom there is no book of unrighteousness written, And against whom no day of judgement shall be found.' 5 And those seven holy ones brought me and placed me on the earth before the door of my house, and said to me: 'Declare everything to thy son Methuselah, and show to all thy children that no flesh is righteous in the sight of the Lord, for He is their Creator. 6 One year we will leave thee with thy son, till thou givest thy (last) commands, that thou mayest teach thy children and record (it) for them, and testify to all thy children; and in the second year they shall take thee from their midst. 7 Let thy heart be strong, For the good shall announce righteousness to the good; The righteous with the righteous shall rejoice, And shall offer congratulation to one another. 8 But the sinners shall die with the sinners, And the apostate go down with the apostate. 9 And those who practice righteousness shall die on account of the deeds of men, And be taken away on account of the doings of the godless.' 10 And in those days they ceased to speak to me, and I came to my people, blessing the Lord of the world.LXXXII. Charge given to Enoch; the Four Intercalary Days; the Stars which lead the Seasons and the Months.

Enoch 1 Chapter 82

1 And now, my son Methuselah, all these things I am recounting to thee and writing down for thee, and I have revealed to thee everything, and given thee books concerning all these: so preserve, my son Methuselah, the books from thy father's hand, and (see) that thou deliver them to the generations of the world. 2 I have given Wisdom to thee and to thy children, [And thy children that shall be to thee], That they may give it to their children for generations, This wisdom (namely) that passeth their thought. 3 And those who understand it shall not sleep, But shall listen with the ear that they may learn this wisdom, And it shall please those that eat thereof better than good food. 4 Blessed are all the righteous, blessed are all those who walk in the way of righteousness and sin not as the sinners, in the reckoning of all their days in which the sun traverses the heaven, entering into and departing from the portals

for thirty days with the heads of thousands of the order of the stars, together with the four which are intercalated which divide the four portions of the year, which lead them and enter with them four days. 5 Owing to them men shall be at fault and not reckon them in the whole reckoning of the year: yea, men shall be at fault, and not recognize them accurately. 6 For they belong to the reckoning of the year and are truly recorded (thereon) for ever, one in the first portal and one in the third, and one in the fourth and one in the sixth, and the year is completed in three hundred and sixty-four days. 7 And the account thereof is accurate and the recorded reckoning thereof exact; for the luminaries, and months and festivals, and years and days, has Uriel shown and revealed to me, to whom the Lord of the whole creation of the world hath subjected the host of heaven. 8 And he has power over night and day in the heaven to cause the light to give light to men–sun, moon, and stars, and all the powers of the heaven which revolve in their circular chariots. 9 And these are the orders of the stars, which set in their places, and in their seasons and festivals and months. 10 And these are the names of those who lead them, who watch that they enter at their times, in their orders, in their seasons, in their months, in their periods of dominion, and in their positions. 11 Their four leaders who divide the four parts of the year enter first; and after them the twelve leaders of the orders who divide the months; and for the three hundred and sixty (days) there are heads over thousands who divide the days; and for the four intercalary days there are the leaders which sunder the four parts of the year. 12 And these heads over thousands are intercalated between leader and leader, each behind a station, but their leaders make the division. 13 And these are the names of the leaders who divide the four parts of the year which are ordained: Mîlkî'êl, Hel'emmêlêk, and Mêl'êjal, and Nârêl. 14 And the names of those who lead them: Adnâr'êl, and Îjâsûsa'êl, and 'Elômê'êl–these three follow the leaders of the orders, and there is one that follows the three leaders of the orders which follow those leaders of stations that divide the four parts of the year. 15 In the beginning of the year Melkejâl rises first and rules, who is named †Tam'âinî† and sun, and all the days of his dominion whilst he bears rule are ninety-one days. 16 And these are the signs of the days which are to be seen on earth in the days of his dominion: sweat, and heat, and calms; and all the trees bear fruit, and leaves are produced on all the trees, and the harvest of wheat, and the rose-flowers, and all the flowers which come forth in the field, but the trees of the winter season become withered. 17 And these are the names of the leaders which are under them: Berka'êl, Zêlebs'êl, and another who is added a head of a thousand, called Hîlûjâsĕph: and the days of the dominion of this (leader) are at an end. 18 The next leader after him is Hêl'emmêlêk, whom one names the shining sun, and all the days of his light are ninety-one days. 19 And these are the signs of (his) days on the earth: glowing heat and dryness, and the trees ripen their fruits and produce all their fruits ripe and ready, and the sheep pair and become pregnant, and all the fruits of the earth are gathered in, and everything that is in the fields, and the winepress: these things take place in the days of his dominion. 20 These are the names, and the orders, and the leaders of those heads of thousands: Gîdâ'ijal, Kê'êl, and Hê'êl, and the name of the head of a thousand which is added to them, Asfâ'êl': and the days of his dominion are at an end.LXXXIII-XC. The Dream-Visions. LXXXIII. LXXXIV. First Dream-Vision on the Deluge.

Enoch 1 Chapter 83

1 And now, my son Methuselah, I will show thee all my visions which I have seen, recounting them before thee. 2 Two visions I saw before I took a wife, and the one was quite unlike the other: the first when I was learning to write: the second before I took thy mother, (when) I saw a terrible vision. And regarding them I prayed to the Lord. 3 I had laid me down in the house of my grandfather Mahalalel, (when) I saw in a vision how the heaven collapsed and was borne off and fell to the earth. 4 And when it fell to the earth I saw how the earth was swallowed up in a great abyss, and mountains were suspended on mountains, and hills sank down on hills, and high trees were rent from their stems, and hurled down and sunk in the abyss. 5 And thereupon a word fell into my mouth, and I lifted up (my voice) to cry aloud, and said: 'The earth is destroyed.' 6 And my grandfather Mahalalel waked me as I lay near him, and said unto me: 'Why dost thou cry so, my son, and why dost thou make such lamentation?' 7 And I recounted to him the whole vision which I had seen, and he said unto me: 'A terrible thing hast thou seen, my son, and of grave moment is thy dream-vision as to the secrets of all the sin of the earth: it must sink into the abyss and be destroyed with a great destruction. 8 And now, my son, arise and make petition to the Lord of glory, since thou art a believer, that a remnant may remain on the earth, and that He may not destroy the whole earth. 9 My son, from heaven all this will come upon the earth, and upon the earth there will be great destruction. 10 After that I arose and prayed and implored and besought,

and wrote down my prayer for the generations of the world, and I will show everything to thee, my son Methuselah. 11 And when I had gone forth below and seen the heaven, and the sun rising in the east, and the moon setting in the west, and a few stars, and the whole earth, and everything as †He had known† it in the beginning, then I blessed the Lord of judgement and extolled Him because He had made the sun to go forth from the windows of the east, and he ascended and rose on the face of the heaven, and set out and kept traversing the path shown unto him.

Enoch 1 Chapter 84

1 And I lifted up my hands in righteousness and blessed the Holy and Great One, and spake with the breath of my mouth, and with the tongue of flesh, which God has made for the children of the flesh of men, that they should speak therewith, and He gave them breath and a tongue and a mouth that they should speak therewith: 2 'Blessed be Thou, O Lord, King, Great and mighty in Thy greatness, Lord of the whole creation of the heaven, King of kings and God of the whole world. And Thy power and kingship and greatness abide for ever and ever, And throughout all generations Thy dominion; And all the heavens are Thy throne for ever, And the whole earth Thy footstool for ever and ever. 3 For Thou hast made and Thou rulest all things, And nothing is too hard for Thee, Wisdom departs not from the place of Thy throne, Nor turns away from Thy presence. And Thou knowest and seest and hearest everything, And there is nothing hidden from Thee [for Thou seest everything]. 4 And now the angels of Thy heavens are guilty of trespass, And upon the flesh of men abideth Thy wrath until the great day of judgement. 5 And now, O God and Lord and Great King, I implore and beseech Thee to fulfil my prayer, To leave me a posterity on earth, And not destroy all the flesh of man, And make the earth without inhabitant, So that there should be an eternal destruction. 6 And now, my Lord, destroy from the earth the flesh which has aroused Thy wrath, But the flesh of righteousness and uprightness establish as a plant of the eternal seed, And hide not Thy face from the prayer of Thy servant, O Lord.' LXXXV-XC. The Second Dream-Vision of Enoch: the History of the World to the Founding of the Messianic Kingdom.

Enoch 1 Chapter 85

1 And after this I saw another dream, and I will show the whole dream to thee, my son. 2 And Enoch lifted up (his voice) and spake to his son Methuselah: 'To thee, my son, will I speak: hear my words–incline thine ear to the dream-vision of thy father. 3 Before I took thy mother Edna, I saw in a vision on my bed, and behold a bull came forth from the earth, and that bull was white; and after it came forth a heifer, and along with this (latter) came forth two bulls, one of them black and the other red. 4 And that black bull gored the red one and pursued him over the earth, and thereupon I could no longer see that red bull. 5 But that black bull grew and that heifer went with him, and I saw that many oxen proceeded from him which resembled and followed him. 6 And that cow, that first one, went from the presence of that first bull in order to seek that red one, but found him not, and lamented with a great lamentation over him and sought him. 7 And I looked till that first bull came to her and quieted her, and from that time onward she cried no more. 8 And after that she bore another white bull, and after him she bore many bulls and black cows. 9 And I saw in my sleep that white bull likewise grow and become a great white bull, and from Him proceeded many white bulls, and they resembled him. And they began to beget many white bulls, which resembled them, one following the other, (even) many. LXXXVI. The Fall of the Angels and the Demoralization of Mankind.

Enoch 1 Chapter 86

1 And again I saw with mine eyes as I slept, and I saw the heaven above, and behold a star fell from heaven, and it arose and eat and pastured amongst those oxen. 2 And after that I saw the large and the black oxen, and behold they all changed their stalls and pastures and their cattle, and began to live with each other. 3 And again I saw in the vision, and looked towards the heaven, and behold I saw many stars descend and cast themselves down from heaven to that first star, and they became bulls amongst those cattle and pastured with them [amongst them]. 4 And I looked at them and saw, and behold they all let out their privy members, like horses, and began to cover the cows of the oxen, and they all became pregnant and bare elephants, camels, and asses. 5 And all the oxen feared them and were affrighted at them, and began to bite with their teeth and to devour, and to gore with their horns. 6 And they began, moreover, to devour those oxen; and behold all the children of the earth began to tremble and quake before them and to flee from them. LXXXVII. The Advent of the Seven Archangels.

Enoch 1 Chapter 87

1 And again I saw how they began to gore each other and to devour each other, and the earth began to cry aloud. 2 And I raised mine eyes again to heaven, and I saw in the vision, and behold there came forth from heaven beings who were like white men: and four went forth from that place and three with them. 3 And those three that had last come forth grasped me by my hand and took me up, away from the generations of the earth, and raised me up to a lofty place, and showed me a tower raised high above the earth, and all the hills were lower. 4 And one said unto me: 'Remain here till thou seest everything that befalls those elephants, camels, and asses, and the stars and the oxen, and all of them.' LXXXVIII. The Punishment of the Fallen Angels by the Archangels.

Enoch 1 Chapter 88

1 And I saw one of those four who had come forth first, and he seized that first star which had fallen from the heaven, and bound it hand and foot and cast it into an abyss: now that abyss was narrow and deep, and horrible and dark. 2 And one of them drew a sword, and gave it to those elephants and camels and asses: then they began to smite each other, and the whole earth quaked because of them. 3 And as I was beholding in the vision, lo, one of those four who had come forth stoned (them) from heaven, and gathered and took all the great stars whose privy members were like those of horses, and bound them all hand and foot, and cast them in an abyss of the earth. LXXXIX. 1-9. The Deluge and the Deliverance of Noah.

Enoch 1 Chapter 89

1 And one of those four went to that white bull and instructed him in a secret, without his being terrified: he was born a bull and became a man, and built for himself a great vessel and dwelt thereon; and three bulls dwelt with him in that vessel and they were covered in. 2 And again I raised mine eyes towards heaven and saw a lofty roof, with seven water torrents thereon, and those torrents flowed with much water into an enclosure. 3 And I saw again, and behold fountains were opened on the surface of that great enclosure, and that water began to swell and rise upon the surface, and I saw that enclosure till all its surface was covered with water. 4 And the water, the darkness, and mist increased upon it; and as I looked at the height of that water, that water had risen above the height of that enclosure, and was streaming over that enclosure, and it stood upon the earth. 5 And all the cattle of that enclosure were gathered together until I saw how they sank and were swallowed up and perished in that water. 6 But that vessel floated on the water, while all the oxen and elephants and camels and asses sank to the bottom with all the animals, so that I could no longer see them, and they were not able to escape, (but) perished and sank into the depths. 7 And again I saw in the vision till those water torrents were removed from that high roof, and the chasms of the earth were levelled up and other abysses were opened. 8 Then the water began to run down into these, till the earth became visible; but that vessel settled on the earth, and the darkness retired and light appeared. 9 But that white bull which had become a man came out of that vessel, and the three bulls with him, and one of those three was white like that bull, and one of them was red as blood, and one black: and that white bull departed from them. LXXXIX. 10-27. From the Death of Noah to the Exodus. 10 And they began to bring forth beasts of the field and birds, so that there arose different genera: lions, tigers, wolves, dogs, hyenas, wild boars, foxes, squirrels, swine, falcons, vultures, kites, eagles, and ravens; and among them was born a white bull. 11 And they began to bite one another; but that white bull which was born amongst them begat a wild ass and a white bull with it, and the wild asses multiplied. 12 But that bull which was born from him begat a black wild boar and a white sheep; and the former begat many boars, but that sheep begat twelve sheep. 13 And when those twelve sheep had grown, they gave up one of them to the asses, and those asses again gave up that sheep to the wolves, and that sheep grew up among the wolves. 14 And the Lord brought the eleven sheep to live with it and to pasture with it among the wolves: and they multiplied and became many flocks of sheep. 15 And the wolves began to fear them, and they oppressed them until they destroyed their little ones, and they cast their young into a river of much water: but those sheep began to cry aloud on account of their little ones, and to complain unto their Lord. 16 And a sheep which had been saved from the wolves fled and escaped to the wild asses; and I saw the sheep how they lamented and cried, and besought their Lord with all their might, till that Lord of the sheep descended at the voice of the sheep from a lofty abode, and came to them and pastured them. 17 And He called that sheep which had escaped the wolves, and spake with it concerning the wolves that it should admonish them not to touch the sheep. 18 And the sheep went to the wolves according to the word of the Lord, and another sheep met it and went with it, and the two went and entered together into the assembly of those wolves, and spake with them and admonished them

not to touch the sheep from henceforth. ¹⁹ And thereupon I saw the wolves, and how they oppressed the sheep exceedingly with all their power; and the sheep cried aloud. ²⁰ And the Lord came to the sheep and they began to smite those wolves: and the wolves began to make lamentation; but the sheep became quiet and forthwith ceased to cry out. ²¹ And I saw the sheep till they departed from amongst the wolves; but the eyes of the wolves were blinded, and those wolves departed in pursuit of the sheep with all their power. ²² And the Lord of the sheep went with them, as their leader, and all His sheep followed Him: and his face was dazzling and glorious and terrible to behold. ²³ But the wolves began to pursue those sheep till they reached a sea of water. ²⁴ And that sea was divided, and the water stood on this side and on that before their face, and their Lord led them and placed Himself between them and the wolves. ²⁵ And as those wolves did not yet see the sheep, they proceeded into the midst of that sea, and the wolves followed the sheep, and [those wolves] ran after them into that sea. ²⁶ And when they saw the Lord of the sheep, they turned to flee before His face, but that sea gathered itself together, and became as it had been created, and the water swelled and rose till it covered those wolves. ²⁷ And I saw till all the wolves who pursued those sheep perished and were drowned. **LXXXIX. 28-40.** Israel in the Desert, the Giving of the Law, the Entrance into Palestine. ²⁸ But the sheep escaped from that water and went forth into a wilderness, where there was no water and no grass; and they began to open their eyes and to see; and I saw the Lord of the sheep pasturing them and giving them water and grass, and that sheep going and leading them. ²⁹ And that sheep ascended to the summit of that lofty rock, and the Lord of the sheep sent it to them. ³⁰ And after that I saw the Lord of the sheep who stood before them, and His appearance was great and terrible and majestic, and all those sheep saw Him and were afraid before His face. ³¹ And they all feared and trembled because of Him, and they cried to that sheep with them [which was amongst them]: "We are not able to stand before our Lord or to behold Him." ³² And that sheep which led them again ascended to the summit of that rock, but the sheep began to be blinded and to wander from the way which he had showed them, but that sheep wot not thereof. ³³ And the Lord of the sheep was wrathful exceedingly against them, and that sheep discovered it, and went down from the summit of the rock, and came to the sheep, and found the greatest part of them blinded and fallen away. ³⁴ And when they saw it they feared and trembled at its presence, and desired to return to their folds. ³⁵ And that sheep took other sheep with it, and came to those sheep which had fallen away, and began to slay them; and the sheep feared its presence, and thus that sheep brought back those sheep that had fallen away, and they returned to their folds. ³⁶ And I saw in this vision till that sheep became a man and built a house for the Lord of the sheep, and placed all the sheep in that house. ³⁷ And I saw till this sheep which had met that sheep which led them fell asleep: and I saw till all the great sheep perished and little ones arose in their place, and they came to a pasture, and approached a stream of water. ³⁸ Then that sheep, their leader which had become a man, withdrew from them and fell asleep, and all the sheep sought it and cried over it with a great crying. ³⁹ And I saw till they left off crying for that sheep and crossed that stream of water, and there arose the two sheep as leaders in the place of those which had led them and fallen asleep (lit. "had fallen asleep and led them"). ⁴⁰ And I saw till the sheep came to a goodly place, and a pleasant and glorious land, and I saw till those sheep were satisfied; and that house stood amongst them in the pleasant land. **LXXXIX. 41-50.** From the Time of the Judges till the Building of the Temple. ⁴¹ And sometimes their eyes were opened, and sometimes blinded, till another sheep arose and led them and brought them all back, and their eyes were opened. ⁴² And the dogs and the foxes and the wild boars began to devour those sheep till the Lord of the sheep raised up [another sheep] a ram from their midst, which led them. ⁴³ And that ram began to butt on either side those dogs, foxes, and wild boars till he had destroyed them †all†. ⁴⁴ And that sheep whose eyes were opened saw that ram, which was amongst the sheep, till it †forsook its glory† and began to butt those sheep, and trampled upon them, and behaved itself unseemly. ⁴⁵ And the Lord of the sheep sent the lamb to another lamb and raised it to being a ram and leader of the sheep instead of that ram which had †forsaken its glory†. ⁴⁶ And it went to it and spake to it alone, and raised it to being a ram, and made it the prince and leader of the sheep; but during all these things those dogs oppressed the sheep. ⁴⁷ And the first ram pursued that second ram, and that second ram arose and fled before it; and I saw till those dogs pulled down the first ram. ⁴⁸ And that second ram arose and led the [little] sheep. ⁴⁸ᵇAnd that ram begat many sheep and fell asleep; and a little sheep became ram in its stead, and became prince and leader of those sheep. ⁴⁹And those sheep grew and multiplied; but all the dogs, and foxes, and wild boars feared and fled before it, and that ram butted and killed the wild beasts, and those wild beasts had no longer any power among the sheep and robbed them no more of ought ⁵⁰ And that house became great and broad, and it was built for those sheep: (and) a tower lofty and great was built on the house for the Lord of the sheep, and that house was low, but the tower was elevated and lofty, and the Lord of the sheep stood on that tower and they offered a full table before Him. **LXXXIX. 51-67.** The Two Kingdoms of Israel and Judah, to the Destruction of Jerusalem. ⁵¹ And again I saw those sheep that they again erred and went many ways, and forsook that their house, and the Lord of the sheep called some from amongst the sheep and sent them to the sheep, but the sheep began to slay them. ⁵² And one of them was saved and was not slain, and it sped away and cried aloud over the sheep; and they sought to slay it, but the Lord of the sheep saved it from the sheep, and brought it up to me, and caused it to dwell there. ⁵³ And many other sheep He sent to those sheep to testify unto them and lament over them. ⁵⁴ And after that I saw that when they forsook the house of the Lord and His tower they fell away entirely, and their eyes were blinded; and I saw the Lord of the sheep how He wrought much slaughter amongst them in their herds until those sheep invited that slaughter and betrayed His place. ⁵⁵ And He gave them over into the hands of the lions and tigers, and wolves and hyenas, and into the hand of the foxes, and to all the wild beasts, and those wild beasts began to tear in pieces those sheep. ⁵⁶ And I saw that He forsook that their house and their tower and gave them all into the hand of the lions, to tear and devour them, into the hand of all the wild beasts. ⁵⁷ And I began to cry aloud with all my power, and to appeal to the Lord of the sheep, and to represent to Him in regard to the sheep that they were devoured by all the wild beasts. ⁵⁸ But He remained unmoved, though He saw it, and rejoiced that they were devoured and swallowed and robbed, and left them to be devoured in the hand of all the beasts. ⁵⁹ And He called seventy shepherds, and cast those sheep to them that they might pasture them, and He spake to the shepherds and their companions: "Let each individual of you pasture the sheep henceforward, and everything that I shall command you that do ye. ⁶⁰ And I will deliver them over unto you duly numbered, and tell you which of them are to be destroyed—and them destroy ye." And He gave over unto them those sheep. ⁶¹ And He called another and spake unto him: "Observe and mark everything that the shepherds will do to those sheep; for they will destroy more of them than I have commanded them. ⁶² And every excess and the destruction which will be wrought through the shepherds, record (namely) how many they destroy according to my command, and how many according to their own caprice: record against every individual shepherd all the destruction he effects. ⁶³ And read out before me by number how many they destroy, and how many they deliver over for destruction, that I may have this as a testimony against them, and know every deed of the shepherds, that I may comprehend and see what they do, whether or not they abide by my command which I have commanded them. ⁶⁴ But they shall not know it, and thou shalt not declare it to them, nor admonish them, but only record against each individual all the destruction which the shepherds effect each in his time and lay it all before me." ⁶⁵ And I saw till those shepherds pastured in their season, and they began to slay and to destroy more than they were bidden, and they delivered those sheep into the hand of the lions. ⁶⁶ And the lions and tigers eat and devoured the greater part of those sheep, and the wild boars eat along with them; and they burnt that tower and demolished that house. ⁶⁷ And I became exceedingly sorrowful over that tower because that house of the sheep was demolished, and afterwards I was unable to see if those sheep entered that house. **LXXXIX. 68-71.** First Period of the Angelic Rulers—from the Destruction of Jerusalem to the Return from the Captivity. ⁶⁸ And the shepherds and their associates delivered over those sheep to all the wild beasts, to devour them, and each one of them received in his time a definite number: it was written by the other in a book how many each one of them destroyed of them. ⁶⁹ And each one slew and destroyed many more than was prescribed; and I began to weep and lament on account of those sheep. ⁷⁰ And thus in the vision I saw that one who wrote, how he wrote down every one that was destroyed by those shepherds, day by day, and carried up and laid down and showed actually the whole book to the Lord of the sheep—(even) everything that they had done, and all that each one of them had made away with, and all that they had given over to destruction. ⁷¹ And the book was read before the Lord of the sheep, and He took the book from his hand and read it and sealed it and laid it down. **LXXXIX. 72-77.** Second Period—from the time of Cyrus to that of Alexander the Great. ⁷² And forthwith I saw how the shepherds pastured for twelve hours, and behold three of those sheep turned back and came and entered and began to build up all that had fallen down of that house; but the wild boars tried to hinder them, but they were not able. ⁷³ And they began again to build as before, and they reared up that tower, and it was named the high tower; and they began again to place a table before the tower, but all the bread on it was polluted and not pure. 74 And as touching all this the eyes of those sheep were blinded so that they saw not, and (the eyes of) their shepherds likewise; and they delivered them in large numbers to their shepherds for destruction, and they trampled the sheep with their feet and devoured them. 75 And the Lord of the sheep remained unmoved till all the sheep were dispersed over the field and mingled with them (i.e. the beasts), and they (i.e. the shepherds) did not save them out of the hand of the beasts. 76 And this one who wrote the book carried it up, and showed it and read it before the Lord of the sheep, and implored Him on their account, and besought Him on their account as he showed Him all the doings of the shepherds, and gave testimony before Him against all the shepherds. And he took the actual book and laid it down beside Him and departed. **XC. 1-5.** Third Period–from Alexander the Great to the Graeco-Syrian Domination.

Enoch 1 Chapter 90

1 And I saw till that in this manner thirty-five shepherds undertook the pasturing (of the sheep), and they severally completed their periods as did the first; and others received them into their hands, to pasture them for their period, each shepherd in his own period. 2 And after that I saw in my vision all the birds of heaven coming, the eagles, the vultures, the kites, the ravens; but the eagles led all the birds; and they began to devour those sheep, and to pick out their eyes and to devour their flesh. 3 And the sheep cried out because their flesh was being devoured by the birds, and as for me I looked and lamented in my sleep over that shepherd who pastured the sheep. 4 And I saw until those sheep were devoured by the dogs and eagles and kites, and they left neither flesh nor skin nor sinew remaining on them till only their bones stood there: and their bones too fell to the earth and the sheep became few. 5 And I saw until that twenty-three had undertaken the pasturing and completed in their several periods fifty-eight times. **XC. 6-12.** Fourth Period–from the Graeco-Syrian Domination to the Maccabæan Revolt. 6 But behold lambs were borne by those white sheep, and they began to open their eyes and to see, and to cry to the sheep. 7 Yea, they cried to them, but they did not hearken to what they said to them, but were exceedingly deaf, and their eyes were very exceedingly blinded. 8 And I saw in the vision how the ravens flew upon those lambs and took one of those lambs, and dashed the sheep in pieces and devoured them. 9 And I saw till horns grew upon those lambs, and the ravens cast down their horns; and I saw till there sprouted a great horn of one of those sheep, and their eyes were opened. 10 And it †looked at† them [and their eyes opened], and it cried to the sheep, and the rams saw it and all ran to it. 11 And notwithstanding all this those eagles and vultures and ravens and kites still kept tearing the sheep and swooping down upon them and devouring them: still the sheep remained silent, but the rams lamented and cried out. 12 And those ravens fought and battled with it and sought to lay low its horn, but they had no power over it. **XC. 13-19.** The Last Assault of the Gentiles on the Jews (where vv. 13-15 and 16-18 are doublets). 13 And I saw till the †shepherds and† eagles and those vultures and kites came, and †they cried to the ravens† that they should break the horn of that ram, and they battled and fought with it, and it battled with them and cried that its help might come. 16 All the eagles and vultures and ravens and kites were gathered together, and there came with them all the sheep of the field, yea, they all came together, and helped each other to break that horn of the ram. 14 And I saw till that man, who wrote down the names of the shepherds [and] carried up into the presence of the Lord of the sheep [came and helped it and showed it everything: he had come down for the help of that ram]. 17 And I saw that man, who wrote the book according to the command of the Lord, till he opened that book concerning the destruction which those twelve last shepherds had wrought, and showed that they had destroyed much more than their predecessors, before the Lord of the sheep. 15 And I saw till the Lord of the sheep came unto them in wrath, and all who saw Him fled, and they all fell †into His shadow† from before His face. 18 And I saw till a great sword was given to the sheep, and the sheep proceeded against all the beasts of the field to slay them, and all the beasts and the birds of the heaven fled before their face. 19 And I saw till the Lord of the sheep came unto them and took in His hand the staff of His wrath, and smote the earth, and the earth clave asunder, and all the beasts and all the birds of the heaven fell from among those sheep, and were swallowed up in the earth and it covered them. **XC. 20-27.** Judgement of the Fallen Angels, the Shepherds, and the Apostates. 20 And I saw till a throne was erected in the pleasant land, and the Lord of the sheep sat Himself thereon, and the other took the sealed books and opened those books before the Lord of the sheep. 21 And the Lord called those men the seven first white ones, and commanded that they should bring before Him, beginning with the first star which led the way, all the stars whose privy members were like those of horses, and they brought them all before Him. 22 And He said to that man who wrote before Him, being one of those seven white ones, and said unto him: "Take those seventy shepherds to whom I delivered the sheep, and who taking them on their own authority slew more than I commanded them." 23 And behold they were all bound, I saw, and they all stood before Him. 24 And the judgement was held first over the stars, and they were judged and found guilty, and went to the place of condemnation, and they were cast into an abyss, full of fire and flaming, and full of pillars of fire. 25 And those seventy shepherds were judged and found guilty, and they were cast into that fiery abyss. 26 And I saw at that time how a like abyss was opened in the midst of the earth, full of fire, and they brought those blinded sheep, and they were all judged and found guilty and cast into this fiery abyss, and they burned; now this abyss was to the right of that house. 27 And I saw those sheep burning †and their bones burning†. **XC. 28-38.** The New Jerusalem, the Conversion of the surviving Gentiles, the Resurrection of the Righteous, the Messiah. 28 And I stood up to see till they folded up that old house; and carried off all the pillars, and all the beams and ornaments of the house were at the same time folded up with it, and they carried it off and laid it in a place in the south of the land. 29 And I saw till the Lord of the sheep brought a new house greater and loftier than that first, and set it up in the place of the first which had been folded up: all its pillars were new, and its ornaments were new and larger than those of the first, the old one which He had taken away, and all the sheep were within it. 30 And I saw all the sheep which had been left, and all the beasts on the earth, and all the birds of the heaven, falling down and doing homage to those sheep and making petition to and obeying them in every thing. 31 And thereafter those three who were clothed in white and had seized me by my hand [who had taken me up before], and the hand of that ram also seizing hold of me, they took me up and set me down in the midst of those sheep before the judgement took place. 32 And those sheep were all white, and their wool was abundant and clean. 33 And all that had been destroyed and dispersed, and all the beasts of the field, and all the birds of the heaven, assembled in that house, and the Lord of the sheep rejoiced with great joy because they were all good and had returned to His house. 34 And I saw till they laid down that sword, which had been given to the sheep, and they brought it back into the house, and it was sealed before the presence of the Lord, and all the sheep were invited into that house, but it held them not. 35 And the eyes of them all were opened, and they saw the good, and there was not one among them that did not see. 36 And I saw that that house was large and broad and very full. 37 And I saw that a white bull was born, with large horns and all the beasts of the field and all the birds of the air feared him and made petition to him all the time. 38 And I saw till all their generations were transformed, and they all became white bulls; and the first among them became a lamb, and that lamb became a great animal and had great black horns on its head; and the Lord of the sheep rejoiced over it and over all the oxen. 39 And I slept in their midst: and I awoke and saw everything. 40 This is the vision which I saw while I slept, and I awoke and blessed the Lord of righteousness and gave Him glory. 41 Then I wept with a great weeping and my tears stayed not till I could no longer endure it: when I saw, they flowed on account of what I had seen; for everything shall come and be fulfilled, and all the deeds of men in their order were shown to me. 42 On that night I remembered the first dream, and because of it I wept and was troubled– because I had seen that vision.' **XCI. 1-11.** Enoch's Admonition to his Children.

Enoch 1 Chapter 91

1 'And now, my son Methuselah, call to me all thy brothers And gather together to me all the sons of thy mother; For the word calls me, And the spirit is poured out upon me, That I may show you everything That shall befall you for ever.' 2 And there upon Methuselah went and summoned to him all his brothers and assembled his relatives. 3 And he spake unto all the children of righteousness and said: 'Hear, ye sons of Enoch, all the words of your father, And hearken aright to the voice of my mouth; For I exhort you and say unto you, beloved: Love uprightness and walk therein. 4 And draw not nigh to uprightness with a double heart, And associate not with those of a double heart, But walk in righteousness, my sons. And it shall guide you on good paths, And righteousness shall be your companion. 5 For I know that violence must increase on the earth, And a great chastisement be executed on the earth, And all unrighteousness come to an end: Yea, it shall be cut off from its roots, And its whole structure be destroyed. 6 And unrighteousness shall again be consummated on the earth, And all the deeds of unrighteousness and of violence And transgression shall prevail in a twofold degree. 7 And when sin and unrighteousness and blasphemy And violence in all kinds of deeds increase, And apostasy and transgression and uncleanness increase, A great chastisement shall

come from heaven upon all these, And the holy Lord will come forth with wrath and chastisement To execute judgement on earth. 8 In those days violence shall be cut off from its roots, And the roots of unrighteousness together with deceit, And they shall be destroyed from under heaven. 9 And all the idols of the heathen shall be abandoned, And the temples burned with fire, And they shall remove them from the whole earth, And they (i.e. the heathen) shall be cast into the judgement of fire, And shall perish in wrath and in grievous judgement for ever. 10 And the righteous shall arise from their sleep, And wisdom shall arise and be given unto them. 11 [And after that the roots of unrighteousness shall be cut off, and the sinners shall be destroyed by the sword . . . shall be cut off from the blasphemers in every place, and those who plan violence and those who commit blasphemy shall perish by the sword.] **XCI. 12.- 17** The Last Three Weeks. 12 And after that there shall be another, the eighth week, that of righteousness, And a sword shall be given to it that a righteous judgement may be executed on the oppressors, And sinners shall be delivered into the hands of the righteous. 13 And at its close they shall acquire houses through their righteousness, And a house shall be built for the Great King in glory for evermore, 14 a And after that, in the ninth week, the righteous judgement shall be revealed to the whole world, b And all the works of the godless shall vanish from all the earth, c And the world shall be written down for destruction. d. And all mankind shall look to the path of uprightness· 15 And after this, in the tenth week in the seventh part, There shall be the great eternal judgement, In which He will execute vengeance amongst the angels. 16 And the first heaven shall depart and pass away, And a new heaven shall appear, And all the powers of the heavens shall give sevenfold light. 17 And after that there will be many weeks without number for ever, And all shall be in goodness and righteousness, And sin shall no more be mentioned for ever. **XCI. 18- 19.** Enoch's Admonition to his Children (continuation). 18 And now I tell you, my sons, and show you The paths of righteousness and the paths of violence. Yea, I will show them to you again That ye may know what will come to pass. 19 And now, hearken unto me, my sons, And walk in the paths of righteousness, And walk not in the paths of violence; For all who walk in the paths of unrighteousness shall perish for ever.' **XCII-CV.** The Epistle of Enoch. XCII. Enoch's Book of Admonition for his Children (continuation).

Enoch 1 Chapter 92

1 The book written by Enoch–[Enoch indeed wrote this complete doctrine of wisdom, (which is) praised of all men and a judge of all the earth] for all my children who shall dwell on the earth. And for the future generations who shall observe uprightness and peace. 2 Let not your spirit be troubled on account of the times; For the Holy and Great One has appointed days for all things. 3 And the righteous one shall arise from sleep, [Shall arise] and walk in the paths of righteousness, And all his path and conversation shall be in eternal goodness and grace. 4 He will be gracious to the righteous and give him eternal uprightness, And He will give him power so that he shall be (endowed) with goodness and righteousness. And he shall walk in eternal light. 5 And sin shall perish in darkness for ever, And shall no more be seen from that day for evermore. **XCIII.** The Apocalypse of Weeks.

Enoch 1 Chapter 93

1 And after that Enoch both †gave† and began to recount from the books. 2 And Enoch said: 'Concerning the children of righteousness and concerning the elect of the world, And concerning the plant of uprightness, I will speak these things, Yea, I Enoch will declare (them) unto you, my sons: According to that which appeared to me in the heavenly vision, And which I have known through the word of the holy angels, And have learnt from the heavenly tablets.' 3 And Enoch began to recount from the books and said: 'I was born the seventh in the first week, While judgement and righteousness still endured. 4 And after me there shall arise in the second week great wickedness, And deceit shall have sprung up; And in it there shall be the first end. And in it a man shall be saved; And after it is ended unrighteousness shall grow up, And a law shall be made for the sinners. 5 And after that in the third week at its close A man shall be elected as the plant of righteous judgement, And his posterity shall become the plant of righteousness for evermore. 6 And after that in the fourth week, at its close, Visions of the holy and righteous shall be seen, And a law for all generations and an enclosure shall be made for them. 7 And after that in the fifth week, at its close, The house of glory and dominion shall be built for ever. 8 And after that in the sixth week all who live in it shall be blinded, And the hearts of all of them shall godlessly forsake wisdom. And in it a man shall ascend; And at its close the house of dominion shall be burnt with fire, And the whole race of the chosen root shall be dispersed. 9 And after that in the seventh week shall an apostate generation arise, And many shall be its

deeds, And all its deeds shall be apostate. 10 And at its close shall be elected The elect righteous of the eternal plant of righteousness, To receive sevenfold instruction concerning all His creation. 11 [For who is there of all the children of men that is able to hear the voice of the Holy One without being troubled? And who can think His thoughts? and who is there that can behold all the works of heaven? 12 And how should there be one who could behold the heaven, and who is there that could understand the things of heaven and see a soul or a spirit and could tell thereof, or ascend and see all their ends and think them or do like them? 13 And who is there of all men that could know what is the breadth and the length of the earth, and to whom has been shown the measure of all of them? 14 Or is there any one who could discern the length of the heaven and how great is its height, and upon what it is founded, and how great is the number of the stars, and where all the luminaries rest?] **XCIV. 1-5.** Admonitions to the Righteous.

Enoch 1 Chapter 94

1 And now I say unto you, my sons, love righteousness and walk therein; For the paths of righteousness are worthy of acceptation, But the paths of unrighteousness shall suddenly be destroyed and vanish. 2 And to certain men of a generation shall the paths of violence and of death be revealed, And they shall hold themselves afar from them, And shall not follow them. 3 And now I say unto you the righteous: Walk not in the paths of wickedness, nor in the paths of death, And draw not nigh to them, lest ye be destroyed. 4 But seek and choose for yourselves righteousness and an elect life, And walk in the paths of peace, And ye shall live and prosper. 5 And hold fast my words in the thoughts of your hearts, And suffer them not to be effaced from your hearts; For I know that sinners will tempt men to evilly-entreat wisdom, So that no place may be found for her, And no manner of temptation may minish. **XCIV. 6-11.** Woes for the Sinners. 6 Woe to those who build unrighteousness and oppression And lay deceit as a foundation; For they shall be suddenly overthrown, And they shall have no peace. 7 Woe to those who build their houses with sin; For from all their foundations shall they be overthrown, And by the sword shall they fall. [And those who acquire gold and silver in judgement suddenly shall perish.] 8 Woe to you, ye rich, for ye have trusted in your riches, And from your riches shall ye depart, Because ye have not remembered the Most High in the days of your riches. 9 Ye have committed blasphemy and unrighteousness, And have become ready for the day of slaughter, And the day of darkness and the day of the great judgement. 10 Thus I speak and declare unto you: He who hath created you will overthrow you, And for your fall there shall be no compassion, And your Creator will rejoice at your destruction. 11 And your righteous ones in those days shall be A reproach to the sinners and the godless. **XCV.** Enoch's Grief: fresh Woes against the Sinners.

Enoch 1 Chapter 95

1 Oh that mine eyes were [a cloud of] waters That I might weep over you, And pour down my tears as a cloud †of† waters: That so I might rest from my trouble of heart! 2 †Who has permitted you to practice reproaches and wickedness? And so judgement shall overtake you, sinners. † 3 Fear not the sinners, ye righteous; For again will the Lord deliver them into your hands, That ye may execute judgement upon them according to your desires. 4 Woe to you who fulminate anathemas which cannot be reversed: Healing shall therefore be far from you because of your sins. 5 Woe to you who requite your neighbour with evil; For ye shall be requited according to your works. 6 Woe to you, lying witnesses, And to those who weigh out injustice, For suddenly shall ye perish. 7 Woe to you, sinners, for ye persecute the righteous; For ye shall be delivered up and persecuted because of injustice, And heavy shall its yoke be upon you. **XCVI.** Grounds of Hopefulness for the Righteous: Woes for the Wicked.

Enoch 1 Chapter 96

1 Be hopeful, ye righteous; for suddenly shall the sinners perish before you, And ye shall have lordship over them according to your desires. 2 [And in the day of the tribulation of the sinners, Your children shall mount and rise as eagles, And higher than the vultures will be your nest, And ye shall ascend and enter the crevices of the earth, And the clefts of the rock for ever as coneys before the unrighteous, And the sirens shall sigh because of you-and weep.] 3 Wherefore fear not, ye that have suffered; For healing shall be your portion, And a bright light shall enlighten you, And the voice of rest ye shall hear from heaven. 4 Woe unto you, ye sinners, for your riches make you appear like the righteous, But your hearts convict you of being sinners, And this fact shall be a testimony against you for a memorial of (your) evil deeds. 5 Woe to you who devour the finest of the wheat, And drink wine in large bowls, And tread under foot the lowly with your might. 6 Woe to you who drink water from every fountain, For suddenly shall ye be consumed and

wither away, Because ye have forsaken the fountain of life. 7 Woe to you who work unrighteousness And deceit and blasphemy: It shall be a memorial against you for evil. 8 Woe to you, ye mighty, Who with might oppress the righteous; For the day of your destruction is coming. In those days many and good days shall come to the righteous–in the day of your judgement. XCVII. The Evils in Store for Sinners and the Possessors of unrighteous Wealth.

Enoch 1 Chapter 97

1 Believe, ye righteous, that the sinners will become a shame And perish in the day of unrighteousness. 2 Be it known unto you (ye sinners) that the Most High is mindful of your destruction, And the angels of heaven rejoice over your destruction. 3 What will ye do, ye sinners, And whither will ye flee on that day of judgement, When ye hear the voice of the prayer of the righteous? 4 Yea, ye shall fare like unto them, Against whom this word shall be a testimony: "Ye have been companions of sinners." 5 And in those days the prayer of the righteous shall reach unto the Lord, And for you the days of your judgement shall come. 6 And all the words of your unrighteousness shall be read out before the Great Holy One, And your faces shall be covered with shame, And He will reject every work which is grounded on unrighteousness. 7 Woe to you, ye sinners, who live on the mid ocean and on the dry land, Whose remembrance is evil against you. 8 Woe to you who acquire silver and gold in unrighteousness and say: "We have become rich with riches and have possessions; And have acquired everything we have desired. 9 And now let us do what we purposed: For we have gathered silver, 9 d And many are the husbandmen in our houses." 9 e And our granaries are (brim) full as with water, 10 Yea and like water your lies shall flow away; For your riches shall not abide But speedily ascend from you;For ye have acquired it all in unrighteousness, And ye shall be given over to a great curse. XCVIII. Self-indulgence of Sinners; Sin originated by Man; all Sin recorded in Heaven; Woes for the Sinners.

Enoch 1 Chapter 98

1 And now I swear unto you, to the wise and to the foolish, For ye shall have manifold experiences on the earth. 2 For ye men shall put on more adornments than a woman, And coloured garments more than a virgin: In royalty and in grandeur and in power, And in silver and in gold and in purple, And in splendour and in food they shall be poured out as water. 3 Therefore they shall be wanting in doctrine and wisdom, And they shall perish thereby together with their possessions; And with all their glory and their splendour, And in shame and in slaughter and in great destitution, Their spirits shall be cast into the furnace of fire. 4 I have sworn unto you, ye sinners, as a mountain has not become a slave, And a hill does not become the handmaid of a woman, Even so sin has not been sent upon the earth, But man of himself has created it, And under a great curse shall they fall who commit it. 5 And barrenness has not been given to the woman, But on account of the deeds of her own hands she dies without children. 6 I have sworn unto you, ye sinners, by the Holy Great One, That all your evil deeds are revealed in the heavens, And that none of your deeds of oppression are covered and hidden. 7 And do not think in your spirit nor say in your heart that ye do not know and that ye do not see that every sin is every day recorded in heaven in the presence of the Most High. 8 From henceforth ye know that all your oppression wherewith ye oppress is written down every day till the day of your judgement. 9 Woe to you, ye fools, for through your folly shall ye perish: and ye transgress against the wise, and so good hap shall not be your portion. 10 And now, know ye that ye are prepared for the day of destruction: wherefore do not hope to live, ye sinners, but ye shall depart and die; for ye know no ransom; for ye are prepared for the day of the great judgement, for the day of tribulation and great shame for your spirits. 11 Woe to you, ye obstinate of heart, who work wickedness and eat blood: Whence have ye good things to eat and to drink and to be filled?From all the good things which the Lord the Most High has placed in abundance on the earth; therefore ye shall have no peace. 12 Woe to you who love the deeds of unrighteousness: wherefore do ye hope for good hap unto yourselves? know that ye shall be delivered into the hands of the righteous, and they shall cut off your necks and slay you, and have no mercy upon you. 13 Woe to you who rejoice in the tribulation of the righteous; for no grave shall be dug for you. 14 Woe to you who set at nought the words of the righteous; for ye shall have no hope of life. 15 Woe to you who write down lying and godless words; for they write down their lies that men may hear them and act godlessly towards (their) neighbour. 16 Therefore they shall have no peace but die a sudden death. XCIX. Woes pronounced on the Godless, the Lawbreakers; evil Plight of Sinners in the last Days; further Woes.

Enoch 1 Chapter 99

1 Woe to you who work godlessness, And glory in lying and extol them: Ye shall perish, and no happy life shall be yours. 2 Woe to them who pervert the words of uprightness, And transgress the eternal law, And transform themselves into what they were not [into sinners]: They shall be trodden under foot upon the earth. 3 In those days make ready, ye righteous, to raise your prayers as a memorial, And place them as a testimony before the angels, That they may place the sin of the sinners for a memorial before the Most High. 4 In those days the nations shall be stirred up, And the families of the nations shall arise on the day of destruction. 5 And in those days the destitute shall go forth and carry off their children, And they shall abandon them, so that their children shall perish through them: Yea, they shall abandon their children (that are still) sucklings, and not return to them, And shall have no pity on their beloved ones. 6 And again I swear to you, ye sinners, that sin is prepared for a day of unceasing bloodshed. 7 And they who worship stones, and grave images of gold and silver and wood <and stone> and clay, and those who worship impure spirits and demons, and all kinds of idols not according to knowledge, shall get no manner of help from them. 8 And they shall become godless by reason of the folly of their hearts, And their eyes shall be blinded through the fear of their hearts And through visions in their dreams. 9 Through these they shall become godless and fearful; For they shall have wrought all their work in a lie, And shall have worshiped a stone: Therefore in an instant shall they perish. 10 But in those days blessed are all they who accept the words of wisdom, and understand them, And observe the paths of the Most High, and walk in the path of His righteousness, And become not godless with the godless; For they shall be saved. 11 Woe to you who spread evil to your neighbours; For you shall be slain in Sheol. 12 Woe to you who make deceitful and false measures, And (to them) who cause bitterness on the earth; For they shall thereby be utterly consumed. 13 Woe to you who build your houses through the grievous toil of others, And all their building materials are the bricks and stones of sin; I tell you ye shall have no peace. 14 Woe to them who reject the measure and eternal heritage of their fathers And whose souls follow after idols; For they shall have no rest. 15 Woe to them who work unrighteousness and help oppression, And slay their neighbours until the day of the great judgement. 16 For He shall cast down your glory, And bring affliction on your hearts, And shall arouse His fierce indignation, And destroy you all with the sword; And all the holy and righteous shall remember your sins. C. The Sinners destroy each other; Judgement of the fallen Angels; the Safety of the Righteous; further Woes for the Sinners.

Enoch 1 Chapter 100

1 And in those days in one place the fathers together with their sons shall be smitten And brothers one with another shall fall in death Till the streams flow with their blood. 2 .For a man shall not withhold his hand from slaying his sons and his sons' sons, And the sinner shall not withhold his hand from his honoured brother: From dawn till sunset they shall slay one another. 3 And the horse shall walk up to the breast in the blood of sinners, And the chariot shall be submerged to its height. 4 In those days the angels shall descend into the secret places And gather together into one place all those who brought down sin And the Most High will arise on that day of judgement To execute great judgement amongst sinners. 5 And over all the righteous and holy He will appoint guardians from amongst the holy angels To guard them as the apple of an eye, Until He makes an end of all wickedness and all sin, And though the righteous sleep a long sleep, they have nought to fear. 6 And (then) the children of the earth shall see the wise in security, And shall understand all the words of this book, And recognize that their riches shall not be able to save them In the overthrow of their sins. 7 Woe to you, Sinners, on the day of strong anguish, Ye who afflict the righteous and burn them with fire: Ye shall be requited according to your works. 8 Woe to you, ye obstinate of heart, Who watch in order to devise wickedness: Therefore shall fear come upon you And there shall be none to help you. 9 Woe to you, ye sinners, on account of the words of your mouth, And on account of the deeds of your hands which your godlessness as wrought, In blazing flames burning worse than fire shall ye burn. 10 And now, know ye that from the angels He will inquire as to your deeds in heaven, from the sun and from the moon and from the stars in reference to your sins because upon the earth ye execute judgement on the righteous. 11 And He will summon to testify against you every cloud and mist and dew and rain; for they shall all be withheld because of you from descending upon you, and they shall be mindful of your sins. 12 And now give presents to the rain that it be not withheld from descending upon you, nor yet the dew, when it has received gold and silver from you that it may descend 13 When the hoar-frost and snow with their chilliness, and all the snow-storms with all their plagues fall upon you, in those days ye shall not be able to stand before them. CI. Exhortation to the Fear of God: all Nature fears Him, but not the Sinners.

Enoch 1 Chapter 101

1 Observe the heaven, ye children of heaven, and every work of the Most High, and fear ye Him and work no evil in His presence. 2 If He closes the windows of heaven, and withholds the rain and the dew from descending on the earth on your account, what will ye do then? 3 And if He sends His anger upon you because of your deeds, ye cannot petition Him; for ye spake proud and insolent words against His righteousness: therefore ye shall have no peace. 4 And see ye not the sailors of the ships, how their ships are tossed to and fro by the waves, and are shaken by the winds, and are in sore trouble? 5 And therefore do they fear because all their goodly possessions go upon the sea with them, and they have evil forebodings of heart that the sea will swallow them and they will perish therein. 6 Are not the entire sea and all its waters, and all its movements, the work of the Most High, and has He not set limits to its doings, and confined it throughout by the sand? 7 And at His reproof it is afraid and dries up, and all its fish die and all that is in it; But ye sinners that are on the earth fear Him not. 8 Has He not made the heaven and the earth, and all that is therein? Who has given understanding and wisdom to everything that moves on the earth and in the sea. 9 Do not the sailors of the ships fear the sea? Yet sinners fear not the Most High. **CII.** Terrors of the Day of Judgement: the adverse Fortunes of the Righteous on the Earth.

Enoch 1 Chapter 102

1 In those days when He hath brought a grievous fire upon you, Whither will ye flee, and where will ye find deliverance? And when He launches forth His Word against you Will you not be affrighted and fear? 2 And all the luminaries shall be affrighted with great fear, And all the earth shall be affrighted and tremble and be alarmed. 3 And all the †angels shall execute their commands† And shall seek to hide themselves from the presence of the Great Glory, And the children of earth shall tremble and quake; And ye sinners shall be cursed for ever, And ye shall have no peace. 4 Fear ye not, ye souls of the righteous, And be hopeful ye that have died in righteousness. 5 And grieve not if your soul into Sheol has descended in grief, And that in your life your body fared not according to your goodness, But wait for the day of the judgement of sinners And for the day of cursing and chastisement. 6 And yet when ye die the sinners speak over you: "As we die, so die the righteous, And what benefit do they reap for their deeds? 7 Behold, even as we, so do they die in grief and darkness, And what have they more than we? From henceforth we are equal. 8 And what will they receive and what will they see for ever? Behold, they too have died, And henceforth for ever shall they see no light." 9 I tell you, ye sinners, ye are content to eat and drink, and rob and sin, and strip men naked, and acquire wealth and see good days. 10 Have ye seen the righteous how their end falls out, that no manner of violence is found in them till their death? 11 "Nevertheless they perished and became as though they had not been, and their spirits descended into Sheol in tribulation." **CIII.** Different Destinies of the Righteous and the Sinners: fresh Objections of the Sinners.

Enoch 1 Chapter 103

1 Now, therefore, I swear to you, the righteous, by the glory of the Great and Honoured and Mighty One in dominion, and by His greatness I swear to you: 2 I know a mystery And have read the heavenly tablets, And have seen the holy books, And have found written therein and inscribed regarding them: 3 That all goodness and joy and glory are prepared for them, And written down for the spirits of those who have died in righteousness, And that manifold good shall be given to you in recompense for your labours, And that your lot is abundantly beyond the lot of the living. 4 And the spirits of you who have died in righteousness shall live and rejoice, And their spirits shall not perish, nor their memorial from before the face of the Great One Unto all the generations of the world: wherefore no longer fear their contumely. 5 Woe to you, ye sinners, when ye have died, If ye die in the wealth of your sins, And those who are like you say regarding you: 'Blessed are the sinners: they have seen all their days. 6 And how they have died in prosperity and in wealth, And have not seen tribulation or murder in their life; And they have died in honour, And judgement has not been executed on them during their life." 7 Know ye, that their souls will be made to descend into Sheol And they shall be wretched in their great tribulation. 8 And into darkness and chains and a burning flame where there is grievous judgement shall your spirits enter; And the great judgement shall be for all the generations of the world. Woe to you, for ye shall have no peace. 9 Say not in regard to the righteous and good who are in life: "In our troubled days we have toiled laboriously and experienced every trouble, And met with much evil and been consumed, And have become few and our spirit small. 10 And we have been destroyed and have not found any to help us even with a word: We have been tortured [and destroyed], and not hoped to see life from day to day. 11 We hoped to be the head and have become the tail: We have toiled laboriously and had no satisfaction in our toil; And we have become the food of the sinners and the unrighteous, And they have laid their yoke heavily upon us. 12 They have had dominion over us that hated us †and smote us; And to those that hated us† we have bowed our necks But they pitied us not. 13 We desired to get away from them that we might escape and be at rest, But found no place whereunto we should flee and be safe from them. 14 And are complained to the rulers in our tribulation, And cried out against those who devoured us, But they did not attend to our cries And would not hearken to our voice. 15 And they helped those who robbed us and devoured us and those who made us few; and they concealed their oppression, and they did not remove from us the yoke of those that devoured us and dispersed us and murdered us, and they concealed their murder, and remembered not that they had lifted up their hands against us. **CIV.** Assurances given to the Righteous; Admonitions to Sinners and the Falsifiers of the Words of Uprightness.

Enoch 1 Chapter 104

1 I swear unto you, that in heaven the angels remember you for good before the glory of the Great One: and your names are written before the glory of the Great One. 2 Be hopeful; for aforetime ye were put to shame through ill and affliction; but now ye shall shine as the lights of heaven, ye shall shine and ye shall be seen, and the portals of heaven shall be opened to you. 3 And in your cry, cry for judgement, and it shall appear to you; for all your tribulation shall be visited on the rulers, and on all who helped those who plundered you. 4 Be hopeful, and cast not away your hopes for ye shall have great joy as the angels of heaven. 5 What shall ye be obliged to do? Ye shall not have to hide on the day of the great judgement and ye shall not be found as sinners, and the eternal judgement shall be far from you for all the generations of the world. 6 And now fear not, ye righteous, when ye see the sinners growing strong and prospering in their ways: be not companions with them, but keep afar from their violence; for ye shall become companions of the hosts of heaven. 7 And, although ye sinners say: "All our sins shall not be searched out and be written down," nevertheless they shall write down all your sins every day. 8 And now I show unto you that light and darkness, day and night, see all your sins. 9 Be not godless in your hearts, and lie not and alter not the words of uprightness, nor charge with lying the words of the Holy Great One, nor take account of your idols; for all your lying and all your godlessness issue not in righteousness but in great sin. 10 And now I know this mystery, that sinners will alter and pervert the words of righteousness in many ways, and will speak wicked words, and lie, and practice great deceits, and write books concerning their words. 11 But when they write down truthfully all my words in their languages, and do not change or minish ought from my words but write them all down truthfully–all that I first testified concerning them. 12 Then, I know another mystery, that books will be given to the righteous and the wise to become a cause of joy and uprightness and much wisdom. 13 And to them shall the books be given, and they shall believe in them and rejoice over them, and then shall all the righteous who have learnt therefrom all the paths of uprightness be recompensed.' **XCV.** God and the Messiah to dwell with Man.

Enoch 1 Chapter 105

1 In those days the Lord bade (them) to summon and testify to the children of earth concerning their wisdom: Show (it) unto them; for ye are their guides, and a recompense over the whole earth. 2 For I and My son will be united with them for ever in the paths of uprightness in their lives; and ye shall have peace: rejoice, ye children of uprightness. Amen. **CVI-CVII.** Fragment of the Book of Noah.

Enoch 1 Chapter 106

1 And after some days my son Methuselah took a wife for his son Lamech, and she became pregnant by him and bore a son. 2 And his body was white as snow and red as the blooming of a rose, and the hair of his head †and his long locks were white as wool, and his eyes beautiful†. And when he opened his eyes, he lighted up the whole house like the sun, and the whole house was very bright. 3 And thereupon he arose in the hands of the midwife, opened his mouth, and †conversed with† the Lord of righteousness. 4 And his father Lamech was afraid of him and fled, and came to his father Methuselah. 5 And he said unto him: 'I have begotten a strange son, diverse from and unlike man, and resembling the sons of the God of heaven; and his nature is different and he is not like us, and his eyes are as the rays of the sun, and his countenance is glorious. 6 And it seems to me that he is not sprung from me but from the angels, and I fear that in his days a wonder may be wrought on the earth. 7 And now, my father, I am here to petition thee and implore thee that thou mayest go to Enoch, our father, and learn from him the truth, for his dwelling-place is amongst the angels.' 8 And when Methuselah heard the words of his son, he came to me to the ends of the earth; for

he had heard that I was there, and he cried aloud, and I heard his voice and I came to him. And 1 said unto him: 'Behold, here am I, my son, wherefore hast thou come to me?' 9 And he answered and said: 'Because of a great cause of anxiety have I come to thee, and because of a disturbing vision have I approached. 10 And now, my father, hear me: unto Lamech my son there hath been born a son, the like of whom there is none, and his nature is not like man's nature, and the colour of his body is whiter than snow and redder than the bloom of a rose, and the hair of his head is whiter than white wool, and his eyes are like the rays of the sun, and he opened his eyes and thereupon lighted up the whole house. 11 And he arose in the hands of the midwife, and opened his mouth and blessed the Lord of heaven. 12 And his father Lamech became afraid and fled to me, and did not believe that he was sprung from him, but that he was in the likeness of the angels of heaven; and behold I have come to thee that thou mayest make known to me the truth.' 13 And I, Enoch, answered and said unto him: 'The Lord will do a new thing on the earth, and this I have already seen in a vision, and make known to thee that in the generation of my father Jared some of the angels of heaven transgressed the word of the Lord. 14 And behold they commit sin and transgress the law, and have united themselves with women and commit sin with them, and have married some of them, and have begot children by them. 15 Yea, there shall come a great destruction over the whole earth, and there shall be a deluge and a great destruction for one year. 16 And this son who has been born unto you shall be left on the earth, and his three children shall be saved with him: when all mankind that are on the earth shall die [he and his sons shall be saved]. 17 And they shall produce on the earth giants not according to the spirit, but according to the flesh, and there shall be a great punishment on the earth, and the earth shall be cleansed from all impurity. 18 And now make known to thy son Lamech that he who has been born is in truth his son, and call his name Noah; for he shall be left to you, and he and his sons shall be saved from the destruction, which shall come upon the earth on account of all the sin and all the unrighteousness, which shall be consummated on the earth in his days. 19 And after that there shall be still more unrighteousness than that which was first consummated on the earth; for I know the mysteries of the holy ones; for He, the Lord, has showed me and informed me, and I have read (them) in the heavenly tablets.

Enoch 1 Chapter 107

1 And I saw written on them that generation upon generation shall transgress, till a generation of righteousness arises, and transgression is destroyed and sin passes away from the earth, and all manner of good comes upon it. 2 And now, my son, go and make known to thy son Lamech that this son, which has been born, is in truth his son, and that (this) is no lie.' 3 And when Methuselah had heard the words of his father Enoch—for he had shown to him everything in secret—he returned and showed (them) to him and called the name of that son Noah; for he will comfort the earth after all the destruction. **CVIII.** An Appendix to the Book of Enoch

Enoch 1 Chapter 108

1 Another book which Enoch wrote for his son Methuselah and for those who will come after him, and keep the law in the last days. 2 Ye who have done good shall wait for those days till an end is made of those who work evil; and an end of the might of the transgressors. 3 And wait ye indeed till sin has passed away, for their names shall be blotted out of the book of life and out of the holy books, and their seed shall be destroyed for ever, and their spirits shall be slain, and they shall cry and make lamentation in a place that is a chaotic wilderness, and in the fire shall they burn; for there is no earth there. 4 And I saw there something like an invisible cloud; for by reason of its depth I could not look over, and I saw a flame of fire blazing brightly, and things like shining mountains circling and sweeping to and fro. 5 And I asked one of the holy angels who was with me and said unto him: 'What is this shining thing? for it is not a heaven but only the flame of a blazing fire, and the voice of weeping and crying and lamentation and strong pain.' 6 And he said unto me: 'This place which thou seest—here are cast the spirits of sinners and blasphemers, and of those who work wickedness, and of those who pervert everything that the Lord hath spoken through the mouth of the prophets—(even) the things that shall be. 7 For some of them are written and inscribed above in the heaven, in order that the angels may read them and know that which shall befall the sinners, and the spirits of the humble, and of those who have afflicted their bodies, and been recompensed by God; and of those who have been put to shame by wicked men: 8 Who love God and loved neither gold nor silver nor any of the good things which are in the world, but gave over their bodies to torture. 9 Who, since they came into being, longed not after earthly food, but regarded everything as a passing breath, and lived

accordingly, and the Lord tried them much, and their spirits were found pure so that they should bless His name. 10 And all the blessings destined for them I have recounted in the books. And he hath assigned them their recompense, because they have been found to be such as loved heaven more than their life in the world, and though they were trodden under foot of wicked men, and experienced abuse and reviling from them and were put to shame, yet they blessed Me. 11 And now I will summon the spirits of the good who belong to the generation of light, and I will transform those who were born in darkness, who in the flesh were not recompensed with such honour as their faithfulness deserved. 12 And I will bring forth in shining light those who have loved My holy name, and I will seat each on the throne of his honour. 13 And they shall be resplendent for times without number; for righteousness is the judgement of God; for to the faithful He will give faithfulness in the habitation of upright paths. 14 And they shall see those who were, born in darkness led into darkness, while the righteous shall be resplendent. 15 And the sinners shall cry aloud and see them resplendent, and they indeed will go where days and seasons are prescribed for them.'

Enoch II

Enoch II Chapter 1

1 There was a wise man, a great artificer, and the Lord conceived love for him and received him, that he should behold the uppermost dwellings and be an eye-witness of the wise and great and inconceivable and immutable realm of God Almighty, of the very wonderful and glorious and bright and many-eyed station of the Lord's servants, and of the inaccessible throne of the Lord, and of the degrees and manifestations of the incorporeal hosts, and of the ineffable ministration of the multitude of the elements, and of the various apparition and inexpressible singing of the host of Cherubim, and of the boundless light. 2 At that time, he said, when my one hundred and sixty-fifth year was completed, I begat my son Mathusal (Methuselah). 3 After this too I lived two hundred years and completed of all the years of my life three hundred and sixty-five years. 4 On the first day of the month I was in my house alone and was resting on my bed and slept. 5 And when I was asleep, great distress came up into my heart, and I was weeping with my eyes in sleep, and I could not understand what this distress was, or what would happen to me. 6 And there appeared to me two men, exceeding big, so that I never saw such on earth; their faces were shining like the sun, their eyes too (were) like a burning light, and from their lips was fire coming forth with clothing and singing of various kinds in appearance purple, their wings (were) brighter than gold, their hands whiter than snow. 7 They were standing at the head of my bed and began to call me by name. 8 And I arose from my sleep and saw clearly those two men standing in front of me. 9 And I saluted them and was seized with fear and the appearance of my face was changed from terror, and those men said to me: 10 Have courage, Enoch, do not fear; the eternal God sent us to you, and lo! You shalt to-day ascend with us into heaven, and you shall tell your sons and all your household all that they shall do without you on earth in your house, and let no one seek you till the Lord return you to them. 11 And I made haste to obey them and went out from my house, and made to the doors, as it was ordered me, and summoned my sons Mathusal (Methuselah) and Regim and Gaidad and made known to them all the marvels those (men) had told me.

Enoch II Chapter 2

1 Listen to me, my children, I know not whither I go, or what will befall me; now therefore, my children, I tell you: turn not from God before the face of the vain, who made not Heaven and earth, for these shall perish and those who worship them, and may the Lord make confident your hearts in the fear of him. And now, my children, let no one think to seek me, until the Lord return me to you.

Enoch II Chapter 3

1 It came to pass, when Enoch had told his sons, that the angels took him on to their wings and bore him up on to the first heaven and placed him on the clouds. And there I looked, and again I looked higher, and saw the ether, and they placed me on the first heaven and showed me a very great Sea, greater than the earthly sea.

Enoch II Chapter 4

1 They brought before my face the elders and rulers of the stellar orders, and showed me two hundred angels, who rule the stars and (their) services to the heavens, and fly with their wings and come round all those who sail.

Enoch II Chapter 5

1 And here I looked down and saw the treasure-houses of the snow, and the angels who keep their terrible store-houses, and the clouds whence

they come out and into which they go.

Enoch II Chapter 6

1 They showed me the treasure-house of the dew, like oil of the olive, and the appearance of its form, as of all the flowers of the earth; further many angels guarding the treasure-houses of these (things), and how they are made to shut and open.

Enoch II Chapter 7

1 And those men took me and led me up on to the second heaven, and showed me darkness, greater than earthly darkness, and there I saw prisoners hanging, watched, awaiting the great and boundless judgment, and these angels (spirits) were dark-looking, more than earthly darkness, and incessantly making weeping through all hours. 2 And I said to the men who were with me: Wherefore are these incessantly tortured? They answered me: These are God's apostates, who obeyed not God's commands, but took counsel with their own will, and turned away with their prince, who also (is) fastened on the fifth heaven. 3 And I felt great pity for them, and they saluted me, and said to me: Man of God, pray for us to the Lord; and I answered to them: Who am I, a mortal man, that I should pray for angels (spirits)? Who knows whither I go, or what will befall me? Or who will pray for me?

Enoch II Chapter 8

1 And those men took me thence, and led me up on to the third heaven, and placed me there; and I looked downwards, and saw the produce of these places, such as has never been known for goodness. 2 And I saw all the sweet-flowering trees and beheld their fruits, which were sweet-smelling, and all the foods borne (by them) bubbling with fragrant exhalation. 3 And in the midst of the trees that of life, in that place whereon the Lord rests, when he goes up into paradise; and this tree is of ineffable goodness and fragrance, and adorned more than every existing thing; and on all sides (it is) in form gold-looking and vermilion and fire-like and covers all, and it has produce from all fruits. 4 Its root is in the garden at the earth's end. 5 And paradise is between corruptibility and incorruptibility. 6 And two springs come out which send forth honey and milk, and their springs send forth oil and wine, and they separate into four parts, and go round with quiet course, and go down into the PARADISE OF EDEN, between corruptibility and incorruptibility. 7 And thence they go forth along the earth, and have a revolution to their circle even as other elements. 8 And here there is no unfruitful tree, and every place is blessed. 9 And (there are) three hundred angels very bright, who keep the garden, and with incessant sweet singing and never-silent voices serve the Lord throughout all days and hours. 10 And I said: How very sweet is this place, and those men said to me:

Enoch II Chapter 9

1 This place, O Enoch, is prepared for the righteous, who endure all manner of offence from those that exasperate their souls, who avert their eyes from iniquity, and make righteous judgment, and give bread to the hungering, and cover the naked with clothing, and raise up the fallen, and help injured orphans, and who walk without fault before the face of the Lord, and serve him alone, and for them is prepared this place for eternal inheritance.

Enoch II Chapter 10

1 And those two men led me up on to the Northern side, and showed me there a very terrible place, and (there were) all manner of tortures in that place: cruel darkness and unillumined gloom, and there is no light there, but murky fire constantly flaming aloft, and (there is) a fiery river coming forth, and that whole place is everywhere fire, and everywhere (there is) frost and ice, thirst and shivering, while the bonds are very cruel, and the angels (spirits) fearful and merciless, bearing angry weapons, merciless torture, and I said: 2 Woe, woe, how very terrible is this place. 3 And those men said to me: This place, O Enoch, is prepared for those who dishonour God, who on earth practice sin against nature, which is child-corruption after the sodomitic fashion, magic-making, enchantments and devilish witchcrafts, and who boast of their wicked deeds, stealing, lies, calumnies, envy, rancour, fornication, murder, and who, accursed, steal the souls of men, who, seeing the poor take away their goods and themselves wax rich, injuring them for other men's goods; who being able to satisfy the empty, made the hungering to die; being able to clothe, stripped the naked; and who knew not their creator, and bowed to the soulless (and lifeless) gods, who cannot see nor hear, vain gods, (who also) built hewn images and bow down to unclean handiwork, for all these is prepared this place among these, for eternal inheritance.

Enoch II Chapter 11

1 Those men took me, and led me up on to the fourth heaven, and showed me all the successive goings, and all the rays of the light of sun and moon. 2 And I measure their goings, and compared their light, and saw that the sun's light is greater than the moon's. 3 Its circle and the wheels on which it goes always, like the wind going past with very marvellous speed, and day and night it has no rest. 4 Its passage and return (are accompanied by) four great stars, (and) each star has under it a thousand stars, to the right of the sun's wheel, (and by) four to the left, each having under it a thousand stars, altogether eight thousand, issuing with the sun continually. 5 And by day fifteen myriads of angels attend it, and by night A thousand. 6 And six-winged ones issue with the angels before the sun's wheel into the fiery flames, and a hundred angels kindle the sun and set it alight.

Enoch II Chapter 12

1 And I looked and saw other flying elements of the sun, whose names (are) Phoenixes and Chalkydri, marvellous and wonderful, with feet and tails in the form of a lion, and a crocodile's head, their appearance (is) empurpled, like the rainbow; their size (is) nine hundred measures, their wings (are like) those of angels, each (has) twelve, and they attend and accompany the sun, bearing heat and dew, as it is ordered them from God. 2 Thus (the sun) revolves and goes, and rises under the heaven, and its course goes under the earth with the light of its rays incessantly.

Enoch II Chapter 13

1 Those men bore me away to the east, and placed me at the sun's gates, where the sun goes forth according to the regulation of the seasons and the circuit of the months of the whole year, and the number of the hours day and night. 2 And I saw six gates open, each gate having sixty-one stadia and A quarter of one stadium, and I measured (them) truly, and understood their size (to be) so much, through which the sun goes forth, and goes to the west, and is made even, and rises throughout all the months, and turns back again from the six gates according to the succession of the seasons; thus (the period) of the whole year is finished after the returns of the four seasons.

Enoch II Chapter 14

1 And again those men led me away to the western parts, and showed me six great gates open corresponding to the eastern gates, opposite to where the sun sets, according to the number of the days three hundred and sixty-five and A quarter. 2 Thus again it goes down to the western gates, (and) draws away its light, the greatness of its brightness, under the earth; for since the crown of its shining is in heaven with the Lord, and guarded by four hundred angels, while the sun goes round on wheel under the earth, and stands seven great hours in night, and spends half (its course) under the earth, when it comes to the eastern approach in the eighth hour of the night, it brings its lights, and the crown of shining, and the sun flames forth more than fire.

Enoch II Chapter 15

1 Then the elements of the sun, called Phoenixes and Chalkydri break into song, therefore every bird flutters with its wings, rejoicing at the giver of light, and they broke into song at the command of the Lord. 2 The giver of light comes to give brightness to the whole world, and the morning guard takes shape, which is the rays of the sun, and the sun of the earth goes out, and receives its brightness to light up the whole face of the earth, and they showed me this calculation of the sun's going. 3 And the gates which it enters, these are the great gates of the calculation of the hours of the year; for this reason the sun is a great creation, whose circuit (lasts) twenty-eight years, and begins again from the beginning.

Enoch II Chapter 16

1 Those men showed me the other course, that of the moon, twelve great gates, crowned from west to east, by which the moon goes in and out of the customary times. 2 It goes in at the first gate to the western places of the sun, by the first gates with (thirty)-one (days) exactly, by the second gates with thirty-one days exactly, by the third with thirty days exactly, by the fourth with thirty days exactly, by the fifth with thirty-one days exactly, by the sixth with thirty-one days exactly, by the seventh with thirty days exactly, by the eighth with thirty-one days perfectly, by the ninth with thirty-one days exactly, by the tenth with thirty days perfectly, by the eleventh with thirty-one days exactly, by the twelfth with twenty-eight days exactly. 3 And it goes through the western gates in the order and number of the eastern, and accomplishes the three hundred and sixty-five and a quarter days of the solar year, while the lunar year has three hundred fifty-four, and there are wanting (to it) twelve days of the solar circle, which are the lunar epacts of the whole year. 4 Thus, too, the great circle contains five hundred and thirty-two years. 5 The quarter (of a day) is omitted for three years, the fourth fulfills it exactly. 6 Therefore they are taken outside of heaven for three years and are not added to the number of days, because they change the time of the years to two new months towards completion, to two others towards diminution. 7 And when the western gates are finished, it returns and goes to the eastern to the lights, and goes thus

day and night about the heavenly circles, lower than all circles, swifter than the heavenly winds, and spirits and elements and angels flying; each angel has six wings. [8] It has a sevenfold course in nineteen years.

Enoch II Chapter 17

[1] In the midst of the heavens I saw armed soldiers, serving the Lord, with tympana and organs, with incessant voice, with sweet voice, with sweet and incessant (voice) and various singing, which it is impossible to describe, and (which) astonishes every mind, so wonderful and marvellous is the singing of those angels, and I was delighted listening to it.

Enoch II Chapter 18

[1] The men took me on to the fifth heaven and placed me, and there I saw many and countless soldiers, called Grigori, of human appearance, and their size (was) greater than that of great giants and their faces withered, and the silence of their mouths perpetual, and their was no service on the fifth heaven, and I said to the men who were with me: [2] Wherefore are these very withered and their faces melancholy, and their mouths silent, and (wherefore) is there no service on this heaven? [3] And they said to me: These are the Grigori, who with their prince Satanail (Satan) rejected the Lord of light, and after them are those who are held in great darkness on the second heaven, and three of them went down on to earth from the Lord's throne, to the place Ermon, and broke through their vows on the shoulder of the hill Ermon and saw the daughters of men how good they are, and took to themselves wives, and befouled the earth with their deeds, who in all times of their age made lawlessness and mixing, and giants are born and marvellous big men and great enmity. [4] And therefore God judged them with great judgment, and they weep for their brethren and they will be punished on the Lord's great day. [5] And I said to the Grigori: I saw your brethren and their works, and their great torments, and I prayed for them, but the Lord has condemned them (to be) under earth till (the existing) heaven and earth shall end for ever. [6] And I said: Wherefore do you wait, brethren, and do not serve before the Lord's face, and have not put your services before the Lord's face, lest you anger your Lord utterly? [7] And they listened to my admonition, and spoke to the four ranks in heaven, and lo! As I stood with those two men four trumpets trumpeted together with great voice, and the Grigori broke into song with one voice, and their voice went up before the Lord pitifully and affectingly.

Enoch II Chapter 19

[1] And thence those men took me and bore me up on to the sixth heaven, and there I saw seven bands of angels, very bright and very glorious, and their faces shining more than the sun's shining, glistening, and there is no difference in their faces, or behaviour, or manner of dress; and these make the orders, and learn the goings of the stars, and the alteration of the moon, or revolution of the sun, and the good government of the world. [2] And when they see evildoing they make commandments and instruction, and sweet and loud singing, and all (songs) of praise. [3] These are the archangels who are above angels, measure all life in heaven and on earth, and the angels who are (appointed) over seasons and years, the angels who are over rivers and sea, and who are over the fruits of the earth, and the angels who are over every grass, giving food to all, to every living thing, and the angels who write all the souls of men, and all their deeds, and their lives before the Lord's face; in their midst are six Phoenixes and six Cherubim and six six-winged ones continually with one voice singing one voice, and it is not possible to describe their singing, and they rejoice before the Lord at his footstool.

Enoch II Chapter 20

[1] And those two men lifted me up thence on to the seventh heaven, and I saw there a very great light, and fiery troops of great archangels, incorporeal forces, and dominions, orders and governments, Cherubim and seraphim, thrones and many-eyed ones, nine regiments, the Ioanit stations of light, and I became afraid, and began to tremble with great terror, and those men took me, and led me after them, and said to me: [2] Have courage, Enoch, do not fear, and showed me the Lord from afar, sitting on His very high throne. For what is there on the tenth heaven, since the Lord dwells there? [3] On the tenth heaven is God, in the Hebrew tongue he is called Aravat. [4] And all the heavenly troops would come and stand on the ten steps according to their rank, and would bow down to the Lord, and would again go to their places in joy and felicity, singing songs in the boundless light with small and tender voices, gloriously serving him.

Enoch II Chapter 21

[1] And the Cherubim and seraphim standing about the throne, the six-winged and many-eyed ones do not depart, standing before the Lord's face doing his will, and cover his whole throne, singing with gentle voice before the Lord's face: Holy, holy, holy, Lord Ruler of Sabaoth, heavens and earth are full of Your glory. [2] When I saw all these things, those men said to me: Enoch, thus far is it commanded us to journey with you, and those men went away from me and thereupon I saw them not. [3] And I remained alone at the end of the seventh heaven and became afraid, and fell on my face and said to myself: Woe is me, what has befallen me? [4] And the Lord sent one of his glorious ones, the archangel Gabriel, and (he) said to me: Have courage, Enoch, do not fear, arise before the Lord's face into eternity, arise, come with me. [5] And I answered him, and said in myself: My Lord, my soul is departed from me, from terror and trembling, and I called to the men who led me up to this place, on them I relied, and (it is) with them I go before the Lord's face. [6] And Gabriel caught me up, as a leaf caught up by the wind, and placed me before the Lord's face. [7] And I saw the eighth heaven, which is called in the Hebrew tongue Muzaloth, changer of the seasons, of drought, and of wet, and of the twelve constellations of the circle of the firmament, which are above the seventh heaven. [8] And I saw the ninth heaven, which is called in Hebrew Kuchavim, where are the heavenly homes of the twelve constellations of the circle of the firmament.

Enoch II Chapter 22

[1] On the tenth heaven, (which is called) Aravoth, I saw the appearance of the Lord's face, like iron made to glow in fire, and brought out, emitting sparks, and it burns. [2] Thus (in a moment of eternity) I saw the Lord's face, but the Lord's face is ineffable, marvellous and very awful, and very, very terrible. [3] And who am I to tell of the Lord's unspeakable being, and of his very wonderful face? And I cannot tell the quantity of his many instructions, and various voices, the Lord's throne (is) very great and not made with hands, nor the quantity of those standing round him, troops of Cherubim and seraphim, nor their incessant singing, nor his immutable beauty, and who shall tell of the ineffable greatness of his glory. [4] And I fell prone and bowed down to the Lord, and the Lord with his lips said to me: [5] Have courage, Enoch, do not fear, arise and stand before my face into eternity. [6] And the archistratege Michael lifted me up, and led me to before the Lord's face. [7] And the Lord said to his servants tempting them: Let Enoch stand before my face into eternity, and the glorious ones bowed down to the Lord, and said: Let Enoch go according to Your word. [8] And the Lord said to Michael: Go and take Enoch from out (of) his earthly garments, and anoint him with my sweet ointment, and put him into the garments of My glory. [9] And Michael did thus, as the Lord told him. He anointed me, and dressed me, and the appearance of that ointment is more than the great light, and his ointment is like sweet dew, and its smell mild, shining like the sun's ray, and I looked at myself, and (I) was like (transfigured) one of his glorious ones. [10] And the Lord summoned one of his archangels by name Pravuil, whose knowledge was quicker in wisdom than the other archangels, who wrote all the deeds of the Lord; and the Lord said to Pravuil: Bring out the books from my store-houses, and a reed of quick-writing, and give (it) to Enoch, and deliver to him the choice and comforting books out of your hand.

Enoch II Chapter 23

[1] And he was telling me all the works of heaven, earth and sea, and all the elements, their passages and goings, and the thunderings of the thunders, the sun and moon, the goings and changes of the stars, the seasons, years, days, and hours, the risings of the wind, the numbers of the angels, and the formation of their songs, and all human things, the tongue of every human song and life, the commandments, instructions, and sweet-voiced singings, and all things that it is fitting to learn. [2] And Pravuil told me: All the things that I have told you, we have written. Sit and write all the souls of mankind, however many of them are born, and the places prepared for them to eternity; for all souls are prepared to eternity, before the formation of the world. [3] And all double thirty days and thirty nights, and I wrote out all things exactly, and wrote three hundred and sixty-six books.

Enoch II Chapter 24

[1] And the Lord summoned me, and said to me: Enoch, sit down on my left with Gabriel. [2] And I bowed down to the Lord, and the Lord spoke to me: Enoch, beloved, all (that) you see, all things that are standing finished I tell to you even before the very beginning, all that I created from non-being, and visible (physical) things from invisible (spiritual). [3] Hear, Enoch, and take in these my words, for not to My angels have I told my secret, and I have not told them their rise, nor my endless realm, nor have they understood my creating, which I tell you to-day. [4] For before all things were visible (physical), I alone used to go about in the invisible (spiritual) things, like the sun from east to west, and from west to east. [5] But even the sun has peace in itself, while I found no peace, because I was creating all things, and I conceived the thought of placing foundations, and of creating visible (physical) creation.

Enoch II Chapter 25

[1] I commanded in the very lowest (parts), that visible (physical) things should come down from invisible (spiritual), and Adoil came down very great, and I beheld him, and lo! He had a belly of great light. [2] And I said to him: Become undone, Adoil, and let the visible (physical) (come) out of you. [3] And he came undone, and a great light came out. And I (was) in the midst of the great light, and as there is born light from light, there came forth a great age, and showed all creation, which I had thought to create. [4] And I saw that (it was) good. [5] And I placed for myself a throne, and took my seat on it, and said to the light: Go thence up higher and fix yourself high above the throne, and be A foundation to the highest things. [6] And above the light there is nothing else, and then I bent up and looked up from my throne.

Enoch II Chapter 26

[1] And I summoned the very lowest a second time, and said: Let Archas come forth hard, and he came forth hard from the invisible (spiritual). [2] And Archas came forth, hard, heavy, and very red. [3] And I said: Be opened, Archas, and let there be born from you, and he came undone, an age came forth, very great and very dark, bearing the creation of all lower things, and I saw that (it was) good and said to him: [4] Go thence down below, and make yourself firm, and be a foundation for the lower things, and it happened and he went down and fixed himself, and became the foundation for the lower things, and below the darkness there is nothing else.

Enoch II Chapter 27

[1] And I commanded that there should be taken from light and darkness, and I said: Be thick, and it became thus, and I spread it out with the light, and it became water, and I spread it out over the darkness, below the light, and then I made firm the waters, that is to say the bottom less, and I made foundation of light around the water, and created seven circles from inside, and imaged (the water) like crystal wet and dry, that is to say like glass, (and) the circumcession of the waters and the other elements, and I showed each one of them its road, and the seven stars each one of them in its heaven, that they go thus, and I saw that it was good. [2] And I separated between light and between darkness, that is to say in the midst of the water hither and thither, and I said to the light, that it should be the day, and to the darkness, that it should be the night, and there was evening and there was morning the first day.

Enoch II Chapter 28

[1] And then I made firm the heavenly circle, and (made) that the lower water which is under heaven collect itself together, into one whole, and that the chaos become dry, and it became so. [2] Out of the waves I created rock hard and big, and from the rock I piled up the dry, and the dry I called earth, and the midst of the earth I called abyss, that is to say the bottomless, I collected the sea in one place and bound it together with a yoke. [3] And I said to the sea: Behold I give you (your) eternal limits, and you shalt not break loose from your component parts. [4] Thus I made fast the firmament. This day I called me the first-created [Sunday].

Enoch II Chapter 29

[1] And for all the heavenly troops I imaged the image and essence of fire, and my eye looked at the very hard, firm rock, and from the gleam of my eye the lightning received its wonderful nature, (which) is both fire in water and water in fire, and one does not put out the other, nor does the one dry up the other, therefore the lightning is brighter than the sun, softer than water and firmer than hard rock. [2] And from the rock I cut off a great fire, and from the fire I created the orders of the incorporeal ten troops of angels, and their weapons are fiery and their raiment a burning flame, and I commanded that each one should stand in his order. [3] And one from out the order of angels, having turned away with the order that was under him, conceived an impossible thought, to place his throne higher than the clouds above the earth, that he might become equal in rank to my power. [4] And I threw him out from the height with his angels, and he was flying in the air continuously above the bottomless.

Enoch II Chapter 30

[1] On the third day I commanded the earth to make grow great and fruitful trees, and hills, and seed to sow, and I planted Paradise, and enclosed it, and placed as armed (guardians) flaming angels, and thus I created renewal. [2] Then came evening, and came morning the fourth day. [3] [Wednesday]. On the fourth day I commanded that there should be great lights on the heavenly circles. [4] On the first uppermost circle I placed the stars, Kruno, and on the second Aphrodit, on the third Aris, on the fifth Zoues, on the sixth Ermis, on the seventh lesser the moon, and adorned it with the lesser stars. [5] And on the lower I placed the sun for the illumination of day, and the moon and stars for the illumination of night. [6] The sun that it should go according to each constellation,

twelve, and I appointed the succession of the months and their names and lives, their thunderings, and their hour-markings, how they should succeed. [7] Then evening came and morning came the fifth day.[1] [Thursday]. On the fifth day I commanded the sea, that it should bring forth fishes, and feathered birds of many varieties, and all animals creeping over the earth, going forth over the earth on four legs, and soaring in the air, male sex and female, and every soul breathing the spirit of life. [2] And there came evening, and there came morning the sixth day. [3] [Friday]. On the sixth day I commanded my wisdom to create man from seven consistencies: one, his flesh from the earth; two, his blood from the dew; three, his eyes from the sun; four, his bones from stone; five, his intelligence from the swiftness of the angels and from cloud; six, his veins and his hair from the grass of the earth; seven, his soul from my breath and from the wind. [4] And I gave him seven natures: to the flesh hearing, the eyes for sight, to the soul smell, the veins for touch, the blood for taste, the bones for endurance, to the intelligence sweetness [enjoyment]. [5] I conceived a cunning saying to say, I created man from invisible (spiritual) and from visible (physical) nature, of both are his death and life and image, he knows speech like some created thing, small in greatness and again great in smallness, and I placed him on earth, a second angel, honourable, great and glorious, and I appointed him as ruler to rule on earth and to have my wisdom, and there was none like him of earth of all my existing creatures. [6] And I appointed him a name, from the four component parts, from east, from west, from south, from north, and I appointed for him four special stars, and I called his name Adam, and showed him the two ways, the light and the darkness, and I told him: [7] This is good, and that bad, that I should learn whether he has love towards me, or hatred, that it be clear which in his race love me. [8] For I have seen his nature, but he has not seen his own nature, therefore (through) not seeing he will sin worse, and I said After sin (what is there) but death? [9] And I put sleep into him and he fell asleep. And I took from him A rib, and created him a wife, that death should come to him by his wife, and I took his last word and called her name mother, that is to say, Eva (Eve).

Enoch II Chapter 31

[1] Adam has life on earth, and I created a garden in Eden in the east, that he should observe the testament and keep the command. [2] I made the heavens open to him, that he should see the angels singing the song of victory, and the gloomless light. [3] And he was continuously in paradise, and the devil understood that I wanted to create another world, because Adam was lord on earth, to rule and control it. [4] The devil is the evil spirit of the lower places, as a fugitive he made Sotona from the heavens as his name was Satanail (Satan), thus he became different from the angels, (but his nature) did not change (his) intelligence as far as (his) understanding of righteous and sinful (things). [5] And he understood his condemnation and the sin which he had sinned before, therefore he conceived thought against Adam, in such form he entered and seduced Eva (Eve), but did not touch Adam. [6] But I cursed ignorance, but what I had blessed previously, those I did not curse, I cursed not man, nor the earth, nor other creatures, but man's evil fruit, and his works.

Enoch II Chapter 32

[1] I said to him: Earth you are, and into the earth whence I took you you shalt go, and I will not ruin you, but send you whence I took you. [2] Then I can again receive you at My second presence. [3] And I blessed all my creatures visible (physical) and invisible (spiritual). And Adam was five and half hours in paradise. [4] And I blessed the seventh day, which is the Sabbath, on which he rested from all his works.

Enoch II Chapter 33

[1] And I appointed the eighth day also, that the eighth day should be the first-created after my work, and that (the first seven) revolve in the form of the seventh thousand, and that at the beginning of the eighth thousand there should be a time of not-counting, endless, with neither years nor months nor weeks nor days nor hours. [2] And now, Enoch, all that I have told you, all that you have understood, all that you have seen of heavenly things, all that you have seen on earth, and all that I have written in books by my great wisdom, all these things I have devised and created from the uppermost foundation to the lower and to the end, and there is no counsellor nor inheritor to my creations. [3] I am self-eternal, not made with hands, and without change. [4] My thought is my counsellor, my wisdom and my word are made, and my eyes observe all things how they stand here and tremble with terror. [5] If I turn away my face, then all things will be destroyed. [6] And apply your mind, Enoch, and know him who is speaking to you, and take thence the books which you yourself have written. [7] And I give you Samuil and Raguil, who led you up, and the books, and go down to earth, and tell your sons all that I have told you, and all that you have seen, from the lower heaven up to my throne, and all the troops. [8] For I created all forces, and there is

none that resists me or that does not subject himself to me. For all subject themselves to my monarchy, and labour for my sole rule. 9 Give them the books of the handwriting, and they will read (them) and will know me for the creator of all things, and will understand how there is no other God but me. 10 And let them distribute the books of your handwriting–children to children, generation to generation, nations to nations. 11 And I will give you, Enoch, my intercessor, the archistratege Michael, for the handwritings of your fathers Adam, Seth, Enos, Cainan, Mahaleleel, and Jared your father.

Enoch II Chapter 34

1 They have rejected my commandments and my yoke, worthless seed has come up, not fearing God, and they would not bow down to me, but have begun to bow down to vain gods, and denied my unity, and have laden the whole earth with untruths, offences, abominable lecheries, namely one with another, and all manner of other unclean wickedness, which are disgusting to relate. 2 And therefore I will bring down a deluge upon the earth and will destroy all men, and the whole earth will crumble together into great darkness.

Enoch II Chapter 35

1 Behold from their seed shall arise another generation, much afterwards, but of them many will be very insatiate. 2 He who raises that generation, (shall) reveal to them the books of your handwriting, of your fathers, (to them) to whom he must point out the guardianship of the world, to the faithful men and workers of my pleasure, who do not acknowledge my name in vain. 3 And they shall tell another generation, and those (others) having read shall be glorified thereafter, more than the first.

Enoch II Chapter 36

1 Now, Enoch, I give you the term of thirty days to spend in your house, and tell your sons and all your household, that all may hear from my face what is told them by you, that they may read and understand, how there is no other God but me. 2 And that they may always keep my commandments, and begin to read and take in the books of your handwriting. 3 And after thirty days I shall send my angel for you, and he will take you from earth and from your sons to me.

Enoch II Chapter 37

1 And the Lord called upon one of the older angels, terrible and menacing, and placed him by me, in appearance white as snow, and his hands like ice, having the appearance of great frost, and he froze my face, because I could not endure the terror of the Lord, just as it is not possible to endure A stove's fire and the sun's heat, and the frost of the air. 2 And the Lord said to me: Enoch, if your face be not frozen here, no man will be able to behold your face.

Enoch II Chapter 38

1 And the Lord said to those men who first led me up: Let Enoch go down on to earth with you, and await him till the determined day. 2 And they placed me by night on my bed. 3 And Mathusal (Methuselah) expecting my coming, keeping watch by day and by night at my bed, was filled with awe when he heard my coming, and I told him, Let all my household come together, that I tell them everything.

Enoch II Chapter 39

1 Oh my children, my beloved ones, hear the admonition of your father, as much as is according to the Lord's will. 2 I have been let come to you to-day, and announce to you, not from my lips, but from the Lord's lips, all that is and was and all that is now, and all that will be till judgment-day. 3 For the Lord has let me come to you, you hear therefore the words of my lips, of a man made big for you, but I am one who has seen the Lord's face, like iron made to glow from fire it sends forth sparks and burns. 4 You look now upon my eyes, (the eyes) of a man big with meaning for you, but I have seen the Lord's eyes, shining like the sun's rays and filling the eyes of man with awe. 5 You see now, my children, the right hand of a man that helps you, but I have seen the Lord's right hand filling heaven as he helped me. 6 You see the compass of my work like your own, but I have seen the Lord's limitless and perfect compass, which has no end. 7 You hear the words of my lips, as I heard the words of the Lord, like great thunder incessantly with hurling of clouds.

Enoch II Chapter 40

1 And now, my children, hear the discourses of the father of the earth, how fearful and awful it is to come before the face of the ruler of the earth, how much more terrible and awful it is to come before the face of the ruler of heaven, the controller (judge) of quick and dead, and of the heavenly troops. Who can endure that endless pain?1 And now, my children, I know all things, for this (is) from the Lord's lips, and this my eyes have seen, from beginning to end. 2 I know all things, and have written all things into books, the heavens and their end, and their plenitude, and all the armies and their marchings. 3 I have measured

and described the stars, the great countless multitude (of them). 4 What man has seen their revolutions, and their entrances? For not even the angels see their number, while I have written all their names. 5 And I measured the sun's circle, and measured its rays, counted the hours, I wrote down too all things that go over the earth, I have written the things that are nourished, and all seed sown and unsown, which the earth produces and all plants, and every grass and every flower, and their sweet smells, and their names, and the dwelling-places of the clouds, and their composition, and their wings, and how they bear rain and raindrops. 6 And I investigated all things, and wrote the road of the thunder and of the lightning, and they showed me the keys and their guardians, their rise, the way they go; it is let out (gently) in measure by a chain, lest by A heavy chain and violence it hurl down the angry clouds and destroy all things on earth. 7 I wrote the treasure-houses of the snow, and the store-houses of the cold and the frosty airs, and I observed their season's key-holder, he fills the clouds with them, and does not exhaust the treasure-houses. 8 And I wrote the resting-places of the winds and observed and saw how their key-holders bear weighing-scales and measures; first, they put them in (one) weighing-scale, then in the other the weights and let them out according to measure cunningly over the whole earth, lest by heavy breathing they make the earth to rock. 9 And I measured out the whole earth, its mountains, and all hills, fields, trees, stones, rivers, all existing things I wrote down, the height from earth to the seventh heaven, and downwards to the very lowest hell, and the judgment-place, and the very great, open and weeping hell. 10 And I saw how the prisoners are in pain, expecting the limitless judgment. 11 And I wrote down all those being judged by the judge, and all their judgment (and sentences) and all their works.

Enoch II Chapter 41

1 And I saw all forefathers from (all) time with Adam and Eva (Eve), and I sighed and broke into tears and said of the ruin of their dishonour: 2 Woe is me for my infirmity and (for that) of my forefathers, and thought in my heart and said: 3 Blessed (is) the man who has not been born or who has been born and shall not sin before the Lord's face, that he come not into this place, nor bring the yoke of this place.

Enoch II Chapter 42

1 I saw the key-holders and guards of the gates of hell standing, like great serpents, and their faces like extinguishing lamps, and their eyes of fire, their sharp teeth, and I saw all the Lord's works, how they are right, while the works of man are some (good), and others bad, and in their works are known those who lie evilly.

Enoch II Chapter 43

1 I, my children, measured and wrote out every work and every measure and every righteous judgment. 2 As (one) year is more honourable than another, so is (one) man more honourable than another, some for great possessions, some for wisdom of heart, some for particular intellect, some for cunning, one for silence of lip, another for cleanliness, one for strength, another for comeliness, one for youth, another for sharp wit, one for shape of body, another for sensibility, let it be heard everywhere, but there is none better than he who fears God, he shall be more glorious in time to come.

Enoch II Chapter 44

1 The Lord with his hands having created man, in the likeness of his own face, the Lord made him small and great. 2 Whoever reviles the ruler's face, and abhors the Lord's face, has despised the Lord's face, and he who vents anger on any man without injury, the Lord's great anger will cut him down, he who spits on the face of man reproachfully, will be cut down at the Lord's great judgment. 3 Blessed is the man who does not direct his heart with malice against any man, and helps the injured and condemned, and raises the broken down, and shall do charity to the needy, because on the day of the great judgment every weight, every measure and every makeweight (will be) as in the market, that is to say (they are) hung on scales and stand in the market, (and every one) shall learn his own measure, and according to his measure shall take his reward.

Enoch II Chapter 45

1 Whoever hastens to make offerings before the Lord's face, the Lord for his part will hasten that offering by granting of his work. 2 But whoever increases his lamp before the Lord's face and make not true judgment, the Lord will (not) increase his treasure in the realm of the highest. 3 When the Lord demands bread, or candles, or (the) flesh (of beasts), or any other sacrifice, then that is nothing; but God demands pure hearts, and with all that (only) tests the heart of man.

Enoch II Chapter 46

1 Hear, my people, and take in the words of my lips. 2 If any one bring any gifts to an earthly ruler, and have disloyal thoughts in his heart, and

the ruler know this, will he not be angry with him, and not refuse his gifts, and not give him over to judgment? ³ Or (if) one man make himself appear good to another by deceit of tongue, but (have) evil in his heart, then will not (the other) understand the treachery of his heart, and himself be condemned, since his untruth was plain to all? ⁴ And when the Lord shall send a great light, then there will be judgment for the just and the unjust, and there no one shall escape notice.

Enoch II Chapter 47

¹ And now, my children, lay thought on your hearts, mark well the words of your father, which are all (come) to you from the Lord's lips. ² Take these books of your father's handwriting and read them. ³ For the books are many, and in them you will learn all the Lord's works, all that has been from the beginning of creation, and will be till the end of time. ⁴ And if you will observe my handwriting, you will not sin against the Lord; because there is no other except the Lord, neither in heaven, nor in earth, nor in the very lowest (places), nor in the (one) foundation. ⁵ The Lord has placed the foundations in the unknown, and has spread forth heavens visible (physical) and invisible (spiritual); he fixed the earth on the waters, and created countless creatures, and who has counted the water and the foundation of the unfixed, or the dust of the earth, or the sand of the sea, or the drops of the rain, or the morning dew, or the wind's breathings? ⁶ I cut the stars out of fire, and decorated heaven, and put it in their midst.

Enoch II Chapter 48

¹ That the sun go along the seven heavenly circles, which are the appointment of one hundred and eighty-two thrones, that it go down on a short day, and again one hundred and eighty-two, that it go down on a big day, and he has two thrones on which he rests, revolving hither and thither above the thrones of the months, from the seventeenth day of the month Tsivan it goes down to the month Thevan, from the seventeenth of Thevan it goes up. ² And thus it goes close to the earth, then the earth is glad and makes grow its fruits, and when it goes away, then the earth is sad, and trees and all fruits have no florescence. ³ All this he measured, with good measurement of hours, and fixed A measure by his wisdom, of the visible (physical) and the invisible (spiritual). ⁴ From the invisible (spiritual) he made all things visible (physical), himself being invisible (spiritual). ⁵ Thus I make known to you, my children, and distribute the books to your children, into all your generations, and amongst the nations who shall have the sense to fear God, let them receive them, and may they come to love them more than any food or earthly sweets, and read them and apply themselves to them. ⁶ And those who understand not the Lord, who fear not God, who accept not, but reject, who do not receive the (books), a terrible judgment awaits these. ⁷ Blessed is the man who shall bear their yoke and shall drag them along, for he shall be released on the day of the great judgment.

Enoch II Chapter 49

¹ I swear to you, my children, but I swear not by any oath, neither by heaven nor by earth, nor by any other creature which God created. ² The Lord said: There is no oath in me, nor injustice, but truth. ³ If there is no truth in men, let them swear by the words, Yea, yea, or else, Nay, nay. ⁴ And I swear to you, yea, yea, that there has been no man in his mother's womb, (but that) already before, even to each one there is a place prepared for the repose of that soul, and a measure fixed how much it is intended that a man be tried in this world. ⁵ Yea, children, deceive not yourselves, for there has been previously prepared a place for every soul of man.

Enoch II Chapter 50

¹ I have put every man's work in writing and none born on earth can remain hidden nor his works remain concealed. ² I see all things. ³ Now therefore, my children, in patience and meekness spend the number of your days, that you inherit endless life. ⁴ Endure for the sake of the Lord every wound, every injury, every evil word and attack. ⁵ If ill-requitals befall you, return (them) not either to neighbour or enemy, because the Lord will return (them) for you and be your avenger on the day of great judgment, that there be no avenging here among men. ⁶ Whoever of you spends gold or silver for his brother's sake, he will receive ample treasure in the world to come. ⁷ Injure not widows nor orphans nor strangers, lest God's wrath come upon you.

Enoch II Chapter 51

¹ Stretch out your hands to the poor according to your strength. ² Hide not your silver in the earth. ³ Help the faithful man in affliction, and affliction will not find you in the time of your trouble. ⁴ And every grievous and cruel yoke that come upon you bear all for the sake of the Lord, and thus you will find your reward in the day of judgment. ⁵ It is good to go morning, midday, and evening into the Lord's dwelling, for the glory of your creator. ⁶ Because every breathing (thing) glorifies

him, and every creature visible (physical) and invisible (spiritual) returns him praise.

Enoch II Chapter 52

¹ Blessed is the man who opens his lips in praise of God of Sabaoth and praises the Lord with his heart. ² Cursed every man who opens his lips for the bringing into contempt and calumny of his neighbour, because he brings God into contempt. ³ Blessed is he who opens his lips blessing and praising God. ⁴ Cursed is he before the Lord all the days of his life, who opens his lips to curse and abuse. ⁵ Blessed is he who blesses all the Lord's works. ⁶ Cursed is he who brings the Lord's creation into contempt. ⁷ Blessed is he who looks down and raises the fallen. ⁸ Cursed is he who looks to and is eager for the destruction of what is not his. ⁹ Blessed is he who keeps the foundations of his fathers made firm from the beginning. ¹⁰ Cursed is he who perverts the decrees of his forefathers. ¹¹ Blessed is he who imparts peace and love. ¹² Cursed is he who disturbs those that love their neighbours. ¹³ Blessed is he who speaks with humble tongue and heart to all. ¹⁴ Cursed is he who speaks peace with his tongue, while in his heart there is no peace but a sword. ¹⁵ For all these things will be laid bare in the weighing-scales and in the books, on the day of the great judgment.

Enoch II Chapter 53

¹ And now, my children, do not say: Our father is standing before God, and is praying for our sins, for there is there no helper of any man who has sinned. ² You see how I wrote all works of every man, before his creation, (all) that is done amongst all men for all time, and none can tell or relate my handwriting, because the Lord see all imaginings of man, how they are vain, where they lie in the treasure-houses of the heart. ³ And now, my children, mark well all the words of your father, that I tell you, lest you regret, saying: Why did our father not tell us?

Enoch II Chapter 54

¹ At that time, not understanding this let these books which I have given you be for an inheritance of your peace. ² Hand them to all who want them, and instruct them, that they may see the Lord's very great and marvellous works.

Enoch II Chapter 55

¹ My children, behold, the day of my term and time have approached. ² For the angels who shall go with me are standing before me and urge me to my departure from you; they are standing here on earth, awaiting what has been told them. ³ For to-morrow I shall go up on to heaven, to the uppermost Jerusalem to my eternal inheritance. ⁴ Therefore I bid you do before the Lord's face all (his) good pleasure.

Enoch II Chapter 56

¹ Mathosalam having answered his father Enoch, said: What is agreeable to your eyes, father, that I may make before your face, that you may bless our dwellings, and your sons, and that your people may be made glorious through you, and then (that) you may depart thus, as the Lord said? ² Enoch answered to his son Mathosalam (and) said: Hear, child, from the time when the Lord anointed me with the ointment of his glory, (there has been no) food in me, and my soul remembers not earthly enjoyment, neither do I want anything earthly.

Enoch II Chapter 57

¹ My child Methosalam, summon all your brethren and all your household and the elders of the people, that I may talk to them and depart, as is planned for me. ² And Methosalam made haste, and summoned his brethren, Regim, Riman, Uchan, Chermion, Gaidad, and all the elders of the people before the face of his father Enoch; and he blessed them, (and) said to them:

Enoch II Chapter 58

¹ Listen to me, my children, to-day. ² In those days when the Lord came down on to earth for Adam's sake, and visited all his creatures, which he created himself, after all these he created Adam, and the Lord called all the beasts of the earth, all the reptiles, and all the birds that soar in the air, and brought them all before the face of our father Adam. ³ And Adam gave the names to all things living on earth. ⁴ And the Lord appointed him ruler over all, and subjected to him all things under his hands, and made them dumb and made them dull that they be commanded of man, and be in subjection and obedience to him. ⁵ Thus also the Lord created every man lord over all his possessions. ⁶ The Lord will not judge a single soul of beast for man's sake, but adjudges the souls of men to their beasts in this world; for men have a special place. ⁷ And as every soul of man is according to number, similarly beasts will not perish, nor all souls of beasts which the Lord created, till the great judgment, and they will accuse man, if he feed them ill.

Enoch II Chapter 59

¹ Whoever defiles the soul of beasts, defiles his own soul. ² For man brings clean animals to make sacrifice for sin, that he may have cure of his soul. ³ And if they bring for sacrifice clean animals, and birds, man

has cure, he cures his soul. 4 All is given you for food, bind it by the four feet, that is to make good the cure, he cures his soul. 5 But whoever kills beast without wounds, kills his own souls and defiles his own flesh. 6 And he who does any beast any injury whatsoever, in secret, it is evil practice, and he defiles his own soul.

Enoch II Chapter 60

1 He who works the killing of a man's soul, kills his own soul, and kills his own body, and there is no cure for him for all time. 2 He who puts a man in any snare, shall stick in it himself, and there is no cure for him for all time. 3 He who puts a man in any vessel, his retribution will not be wanting at the great judgment for all time. 4 He who works crookedly or speaks evil against any soul, will not make justice for himself for all time.

Enoch II Chapter 61

1 And now, my children, keep your hearts from every injustice, which the Lord hates. Just as a man asks something for his own soul from God, so let him do to every living soul, because I know all things, how in the great time to come there is much inheritance prepared for men, good for the good, and bad for the bad, without number many. 2 Blessed are those who enter the good houses, for in the bad houses there is no peace nor return from them. 3 Hear, my children, small and great! When man puts a good thought in his heart, brings gifts from his labours before the Lord's face and his hands made them not, then the Lord will turn away his face from the labour of his hand, and (that) man cannot find the labour of his hands. 4 And if his hands made it, but his heart murmur, and his heart cease not making murmur incessantly, he has not any advantage.

Enoch II Chapter 62

1 Blessed is the man who in his patience brings his gifts with faith before the Lord's face, because he will find forgiveness of sins. 2 But if he take back his words before the time, there is no repentance for him; and if the time pass and he do not of his own will what is promised, there is no repentance after death. 3 Because every work which man does before the time, is all deceit before men, and sin before God.

Enoch II Chapter 63

1 When man clothes the naked and fills the hungry, he will find reward from God. 2 But if his heart murmur, he commits a double evil; ruin of himself and of that which he gives; and for him there will be no finding of reward on account of that. 3 And if his own heart is filled with his food and his own flesh, clothed with his own clothing, he commits contempt, and will forfeit all his endurance of poverty, and will not find reward of his good deeds. 4 Every proud and magniloquent man is hateful to the Lord, and every false speech, clothed in untruth; it will be cut with the blade of the sword of death, and thrown into the fire, and shall burn for all time.

Enoch II Chapter 64

1 When Enoch had spoken these words to his sons, all people far and near heard how the Lord was calling Enoch. They took counsel together: 2 Let us go and kiss Enoch, and two thousand men came together and came to the place Achuzan where Enoch was, and his sons. 3 And the elders of the people, the whole assembly, came and bowed down and began to kiss Enoch and said to him: 4 Our father Enoch, (may) you (be) blessed of the Lord, the eternal ruler, and now bless your sons and all the people, that we may be glorified to-day before your face. 5 For you shalt be glorified before the Lord's face for all time, since the Lord chose you, rather than all men on earth, and designated you writer of all his creation, visible (physical) and invisible (spiritual), and redeemed of the sins of man, and helper of your household.

Enoch II Chapter 65

1 And Enoch answered all his people saying: Hear, my children, before that all creatures were created, the Lord created the visible (physical) and invisible (spiritual) things. 2 And as much time as there was and went past, understand that after all that he created man in the likeness of his own form, and put into him eyes to see, and ears to hear, and heart to reflect, and intellect wherewith to deliberate. 3 And the Lord saw all man's works, and created all his creatures, and divided time, from time he fixed the years, and from the years he appointed the months, and from the months he appointed the days, and of days he appointed seven. 4 And in those he appointed the hours, measured them out exactly, that man might reflect on time and count years, months, and hours, (their) alternation, beginning, and end, and that he might count his own life, from the beginning until death, and reflect on his sin and write his work bad and good; because no work is hidden before the Lord, that every man might know his works and never transgress all his commandments, and keep my handwriting from generation to generation. 5 When all creation visible (physical) and invisible (spiritual), as the Lord created it, shall end, then every man

goes to the great judgment, and then all time shall perish, and the years, and thenceforward there will be neither months nor days nor hours, they will be adhered together and will not be counted. 6 There will be one aeon, and all the righteous who shall escape the Lord's great judgment, shall be collected in the great aeon, for the righteous the great aeon will begin, and they will live eternally, and then too there will be amongst them neither labour, nor sickness, nor humiliation, nor anxiety, nor need, nor brutality, nor night, nor darkness, but great light. 7 And they shall have a great indestructible wall, and a paradise bright and incorruptible (eternal), for all corruptible (mortal) things shall pass away, and there will be eternal life.

Enoch II Chapter 66

1 And now, my children, keep your souls from all injustice, such as the Lord hates. 2 Walk before his face with terror and trembling and serve him alone. 3 Bow down to the true God, not to dumb idols, but bow down to his similitude, and bring all just offerings before the Lord's face. The Lord hates what is unjust. 4 For the Lord sees all things; when man takes thought in his heart, then he counsels the intellects, and every thought is always before the Lord, who made firm the earth and put all creatures on it. 5 If you look to heaven, the Lord is there; if you take thought of the sea's deep and all the under-earth, the Lord is there. 6 For the Lord created all things. Bow not down to things made by man, leaving the Lord of all creation, because no work can remain hidden before the Lord's face. 6 Walk, my children, in long-suffering, in meekness, honesty, in provocation, in grief, in faith and in truth, in (reliance on) promises, in illness, in abuse, in wounds, in temptation, in nakedness, in privation, loving one another, till you go out from this age of ills, that you become inheritors of endless time. 7 Blessed are the just who shall escape the great judgment, for they shall shine forth more than the sun sevenfold, for in this world the seventh part is taken off from all, light, darkness, food, enjoyment, sorrow, paradise, torture, fire, frost, and other things; he put all down in writing, that you might read and understand.

Enoch II Chapter 67

1 When Enoch had talked to the people, the Lord sent out darkness on to the earth, and there was darkness, and it covered those men standing with Enoch, and they took Enoch up on to the highest heaven, where the Lord (is); and he received him and placed him before his face, and the darkness went off from the earth, and light came again. 2 And the people saw and understood not how Enoch had been taken, and glorified God, and found a roll in which was traced The Invisible (spiritual) God; and all went to their dwelling places.

Enoch II Chapter 68

1 Enoch was born on the sixth day of the month Tsivan, and lived three hundred and sixty-five years. 2 He was taken up to heaven on the first day of the month Tsivan and remained in heaven sixty days. 3 He wrote all these signs of all creation, which the Lord created, and wrote three hundred and sixty-six books, and handed them over to his sons and remained on earth thirty days, and was again taken up to heaven on the sixth day of the month Tsivan, on the very day and hour when he was born. 4 As every man's nature in this life is dark, so are also his conception, birth, and departure from this life. 5 At what hour he was conceived, at that hour he was born, and at that hour too he died. 6 Methosalam and his brethren, all the sons of Enoch, made haste, and erected an altar at that place called Achuzan, whence and where Enoch had been taken up to heaven. 7 And they took sacrificial oxen and summoned all people and sacrificed the sacrifice before the Lord's face. 8 All people, the elders of the people and the whole assembly came to the feast and brought gifts to the sons of Enoch. 9 And they made a great feast, rejoicing and making merry three days, praising God, who had given them such a sign through Enoch, who had found favour with him, and that they should hand it on to their sons from generation to generation, from age to age. 10 Amen.

Jubilees

Moses receives the tablets of the law and instructions about past and future history, which he is commanded to write down in a book (verses 1-4). This is followed by a warning about Israel's future apostasy, where the people will turn away from God (verses 5-9). The captivity of Israel and Judah is then foretold (verses 10-13), followed by Judah's return and the rebuilding of the temple (verses 15-18). Moses prays to God on behalf of the people of Israel (verses 19-21), and God promises to redeem them and dwell among them (verses 22-25, 28) Moses is instructed to write down the future history of the world, likely referring to the "Book of Jubilees" (verse 26), while an angel is tasked with writing down the law (verse 27). This angel brings the heavenly chronological tablets to dictate them to Moses (verse 29). Prologue:

This is the account of the division of the days of the law and the testimony, of the events of the years, of their weeks, and of their Jubilees throughout all the years of the world, as the Lord spoke to Moses on Mount Sinai when he went up to receive the tablets of the law and the commandment, according to the voice of God who said to him, 'Go up to the top of the mount.'**God's Revelation to Moses on Mount Sinai** (chapter i, verses 1-26; cf. Exodus xxiv, verses 15-18).

Jubilees Chapter 1

1 And it came to pass in the first year of the exodus of the children of Israel out of Egypt, in the third month, on the sixteenth day of the month, [2450 Anno Mundi] that God spake to Moses, saying: 'Come up to Me on the Mount, and I will give thee two tables of stone of the law and of the commandment, which I have written, that thou mayst teach them.' 2 And Moses went up into the mount of God, and the glory of the Lord abode on Mount Sinai, and a cloud overshadowed it six days. 3 And He called to Moses on the seventh day out of the midst of the cloud, and the appearance of the glory of the Lord was like a flaming fire on the top of the mount. 4 And Moses was on the Mount forty days and forty nights, and God taught him the earlier and the later history of the division of all the days of the law and of the testimony. 5 And He said: 'Incline thine heart to every word which I shall speak to thee on this mount, and write them in a book in order that their generations may see how I have not forsaken them for all the evil which they have wrought in transgressing the covenant which I establish between Me and thee for their generations this day on Mount Sinai. 6 And thus it will come to pass when all these things come upon them, that they will recognise that I am more righteous than they in all their judgments and in all their actions, and they will recognise that I have been truly with them. 7 And do thou write for thyself all these words which I declare unto, thee this day, for I know their rebellion and their stiff neck, before I bring them into the land of which I sware to their fathers, to Abraham and to Isaac and to Jacob, saying: 'Unto your seed will I give a land flowing with milk and honey. 8 And they will eat and be satisfied, and they will turn to strange gods, to (gods) which cannot deliver them from aught of their tribulation: and this witness shall be heard for a witness against them. 9 For they will forget all My commandments, (even) all that I command them, and they will walk after the Gentiles, and after their uncleanness, and after their shame, and will serve their gods, and these will prove unto them an offence and a tribulation and an affliction and a snare. 10 And many will perish and they will be taken captive, and will fall into the hands of the enemy, because they have forsaken My ordinances and My commandments, and the festivals of My covenant, and My sabbaths, and My holy place which I have hallowed for Myself in their midst, and My tabernacle, and My sanctuary, which I have hallowed for Myself in the midst of the land, that I should set my name upon it, and that it should dwell (there). 11 And they will make to themselves high places and groves and graven images, and they will worship, each his own (graven image), so as to go astray, and they will sacrifice their children to demons, and to all the works of the error of their hearts. 12 And I will send witnesses unto them, that I may witness against them, but they will not hear, and will slay the witnesses also, and they will persecute those who seek the law, and they will abrogate and change everything so as to work evil before My eyes. 13 And I will hide My face from them, and I will deliver them into the hand of the Gentiles for captivity, and for a prey, and for devouring, and I will remove them from the midst of the land, and I will scatter them amongst the Gentiles. 14 And they will forget all My law and all My commandments and all My judgments, and will go astray as to new moons, and sabbaths, and festivals, and jubilees, and ordinances. 15 And after this they will turn to Me from amongst the Gentiles with all their heart and with all their soul and with all their strength, and I will gather them from amongst all the Gentiles, and they will seek me, so that I shall be found of them, when they seek me with all their heart and with all their soul. 16 And I will disclose to them abounding peace with righteousness, and I will remove them the plant of uprightness, with all My heart and with all My soul, and they shall be for a blessing and not for a curse, and they shall be the head and not the tail. 17 And I will build My sanctuary in their midst, and I will dwell with them, and I will be their God and they shall be My people in truth and righteousness. 18 And I will not forsake them nor fail them; for I am the Lord their God.' 19 And Moses fell on his face and prayed and said, 'O Lord my God, do not forsake Thy people and Thy inheritance, so that they should wander in the error of their hearts, and do not deliver them into the hands of their enemies, the Gentiles, lest they should rule over them and cause them to sin against Thee. 20 Let thy mercy, O Lord, be lifted up upon Thy people, and create in them an upright spirit, and let not the spirit of Beliar rule over them to accuse them before Thee, and to ensnare them from all the paths of righteousness, so that they may perish from before Thy face. 21 But they are Thy people and Thy inheritance, which thou hast delivered with thy great power from the hands of the Egyptians: create in them a clean heart and a holy spirit, and let them not be ensnared in their sins from henceforth until eternity.' 22 And the Lord said unto Moses: 'I know their contrariness and their thoughts and their stiffneckedness, and they will not be obedient till they confess their own sin and the sin of their fathers. 23 And after this they will turn to Me in all uprightness and with all (their) heart and with all (their) soul, and I will circumcise the foreskin of their heart and the foreskin of the heart of their seed, and I will create in them a holy spirit, and I will cleanse them so that they shall not turn away from Me from that day unto eternity. 24 And their souls will cleave to Me and to all My commandments, and they will fulfil My commandments, and I will be their Father and they shall be My children. 25 And they all shall be called children of the living God, and every angel and every spirit shall know, yea, they shall know that these are My children, and that I am their Father in uprightness and righteousness, and that I love them. 26 And do thou write down for thyself all these words which I declare unto thee on this mountain, the first and the last, which shall come to pass in all the divisions of the days in the law and in the testimony and in the weeks and the jubilees unto eternity, until I descend and dwell with them throughout eternity.'**God commands the Angel to write (i. 27-29).**27 And He said to the angel of the presence: Write for Moses from the beginning of creation till My sanctuary has been built among them for all eternity. 28 And the Lord will appear to the eyes of all, and all shall know that I am the God of Israel and the Father of all the children of Jacob, and King on Mount Zion for all eternity. And Zion and Jerusalem shall be holy.' 29 And the angel of the presence who went before the camp of Israel took the tables of the divisions of the years - from the time of the creation- of the law and of the testimony of the weeks of the jubilees, according to the individual years, according to all the number of the jubilees [according, to the individual years], from the day of the [new] creation when the heavens and the earth shall be renewed and all their creation according to the powers of the heaven, and according to all the creation of the earth, until the sanctuary of the Lord shall be made in Jerusalem on Mount Zion, and all the luminaries be renewed for healing and for peace and for blessing for all the elect of Israel, and that thus it may be from that day and unto all the days of the earth.**The Angel dictates to Moses the Primeval History: the Creation of the World and Institution of the Sabbath (ii. 1-33; cf. Gen. i.-ii. 3).**

Jubilees Chapter 2

1 And the angel of the presence spake to Moses according to the word of the Lord, saying: Write the complete history of the creation, how in six days the Lord God finished all His works and all that He created, and kept Sabbath on the seventh day and hallowed it for all ages, and appointed it as a sign for all His works. 2 For on the first day He created the heavens which are above and the earth and the waters and all the spirits which serve before him -the angels of the presence, and the angels of sanctification, and the angels [of the spirit of fire and the angels] of the spirit of the winds, and the angels of the spirit of the clouds, and of darkness, and of snow and of hail and of hoar frost, and the angels of the voices and of the thunder and of the lightning, and the angels of the spirits of cold and of heat, and of winter and of spring and of autumn and of summer and of all the spirits of his creatures which are in the heavens and on the earth, (He created) the abysses and the darkness, eventide <and night>, and the light, dawn and day, which He hath prepared in the knowledge of his heart. 3 And thereupon we saw His works, and praised Him, and lauded before Him on account of all His works; for seven great works did He create on the first day. 4 And on the second day He created the firmament in the midst of the waters, and the waters were divided on that day -half of them went up above and half of them went down below the firmament (that was) in the midst over the face of the whole earth. And this was the only work (God) created on the second day. 5 And on the third day He commanded the waters to pass from off the face of the whole earth into one place, and the dry land to appear. 6 And the waters did so as He commanded them, and they retired from off the face of the earth into one place outside of this firmament, and the dry land appeared. 7 And on that day He created for them all the seas according to their separate gathering-places, and all the rivers, and the gatherings of the waters in the mountains and on all the earth, and all the lakes, and all the dew of the earth, and the seed which is sown, and all sprouting things, and fruit-bearing trees, and trees of the wood, and the garden of Eden, in Eden and all plants after their kind. 8 These four great works God created on the third day. And on the fourth day He created the sun and the moon and the stars, and set them in the firmament of the heaven, to give light upon all the earth, and to rule over the day and the night, and divide the

light from the darkness. 9 And God appointed the sun to be a great sign on the earth for days and for sabbaths and for months and for feasts and for years and for sabbaths of years and for jubilees and for all seasons of the years. 10 And it divideth the light from the darkness [and] for prosperity, that all things may prosper which shoot and grow on the earth. 11 These three kinds He made on the fourth day. And on the fifth day He created great sea monsters in the depths of the waters, for these were the first things of flesh that were created by his hands, the fish and everything that moves in the waters, and everything that flies, the birds and all their kind. 12 And the sun rose above them to prosper (them), and above everything that was on the earth, everything that shoots out of the earth, and all fruit-bearing trees, and all flesh. 13 These three kinds He created on the fifth day. And on the sixth day He created all the animals of the earth, and all cattle, and everything that moves on the earth. 14 And after all this He created man, a man and a woman created He them, and gave him dominion over all that is upon the earth, and in the seas, and over everything that flies, and over beasts and over cattle, and over everything that moves on the earth, and over the whole earth, and over all this He gave him dominion. 15 And these four kinds He created on the sixth day. And there were altogether two and twenty kinds. 16 And He finished all his work on the sixth day -all that is in the heavens and on the earth, and in the seas and in the abysses, and in the light and in the darkness, and in everything. 17 And He gave us a great sign, the Sabbath day, that we should work six days, but keep Sabbath on the seventh day from all work. 18 And all the angels of the presence, and all the angels of sanctification, these two great classes -He hath bidden us to keep the Sabbath with Him in heaven and on earth. 19 And He said unto us: 'Behold, I will separate unto Myself a people from among all the peoples, and these shall keep the Sabbath day, and I will sanctify them unto Myself as My people, and will bless them; as I have sanctified the Sabbath day and do sanctify (it) unto Myself, even so will I bless them, and they shall be My people and I will be their God. 20 And I have chosen the seed of Jacob from amongst all that I have seen, and have written him down as My first-born son, and have sanctified him unto Myself for ever and ever; and I will teach them the Sabbath day, that they may keep Sabbath thereon from all work.' 21 And thus He created therein a sign in accordance with which they should keep Sabbath with us on the seventh day, to eat and to drink, and to bless Him who has created all things as He has blessed and sanctified unto Himself a peculiar people above all peoples, and that they should keep Sabbath together with us. 22 And He caused His commands to ascend as a sweet savour acceptable before Him all the days . . . 23 There (were) two and twenty heads of mankind from Adam to Jacob, and two and twenty kinds of work were made until the seventh day; this is blessed and holy; and the former also is blessed and holy; and this one serves with that one for sanctification and blessing. 24 And to this (Jacob and his seed) it was granted that they should always be the blessed and holy ones of the first testimony and law, even as He had sanctified and blessed the Sabbath day on the seventh day. 25 He created heaven and earth and everything that He created in six days, and God made the seventh day holy, for all His works; therefore He commanded on its behalf that, whoever does any work thereon shall die, and that he who defiles it shall surely die. 26 Wherefore do thou command the children of Israel to observe this day that they may keep it holy and not do thereon any work, and not to defile it, as it is holier than all other days. 27 And whoever profanes it shall surely die, and whoever does thereon any work shall surely die eternally, that the children of Israel may observe this day throughout their generations, and not be rooted out of the land; for it is a holy day and a blessed day. 28 And every one who observes it and keeps Sabbath thereon from all his work, will be holy and blessed throughout all days like unto us. 29 Declare and say to the children of Israel the law of this day both that they should keep Sabbath thereon, and that they should not forsake it in the error of their hearts; (and) that it is not lawful to do any work thereon which is unseemly, to do thereon their own pleasure, and that they should not prepare thereon anything to be eaten or drunk, and (that it is not lawful) to draw water, or bring in or take out thereon through their gates any burden, which they had not prepared for themselves on the sixth day in their dwellings. 30 And they shall not bring in nor take out from house to house on that day; for that day is more holy and blessed than any jubilee day of the jubilees; on this we kept Sabbath in the heavens before it was made known to any flesh to keep Sabbath thereon on the earth. 31 And the Creator of all things blessed it, but he did not sanctify all peoples and nations to keep Sabbath thereon, but Israel alone: them alone he permitted to eat and drink and to keep Sabbath thereon on the earth. 32 And the Creator of all things blessed this day which He had created for blessing and holiness and glory above all days. 33 This law and testimony was given to the children of Israel as a law for ever unto their generations.**Paradise and the Fall (iii. 1-35; cf. Gen. ii. 4-iii.).**

Jubilees Chapter 3

1 And on the six days of the second week we brought, according to the word of God, unto Adam all the beasts, and all the cattle, and all the birds, and everything that moves on the earth, and everything that moves in the water, according to their kinds, and according to their types: the beasts on the first day; the cattle on the second day; the birds on the third day; and all that which moves on the earth on the fourth day; and that which moves in the water on the fifth day. 2 And Adam named them all by their respective names, and as he called them, so was their name. 3 And on these five days Adam saw all these, male and female, according to every kind that was on the earth, but he was alone and found no helpmeet for him. 4 And the Lord said unto us: 'It is not good that the man should be alone: let us make a helpmeet for him.' 5 And the Lord our God caused a deep sleep to fall upon him, and he slept, and He took for the woman one rib from amongst his ribs, and this rib was the origin of the woman from amongst his ribs, and He built up the flesh in its stead, and built the woman. 6 And He awaked Adam out of his sleep and on awaking he rose on the sixth day, and He brought her to him, and he knew her, and said unto her: 'This is now bone of my bones and flesh of my flesh; she shall be called [my] wife; because she was taken from her husband.' 7 Therefore shall man and wife be one and therefore shall a man leave his father and his mother, and cleave unto his wife, and they shall be one flesh. 8 In the first week was Adam created, and the rib -his wife: in the second week He showed her unto him: and for this reason the commandment was given to keep in their defilement, for a male seven days, and for a female twice seven days. 9 And after Adam had completed forty days in the land where he had been created, we brought him into the garden of Eden to till and keep it, but his wife they brought in on the eightieth day, and after this she entered into the garden of Eden. 10 And for this reason the commandment is written on the heavenly tablets in regard to her that gives birth: 'if she bears a male, she shall remain in her uncleanness seven days according to the first week of days, and thirty and three days shall she remain in the blood of her purifying, and she shall not touch any hallowed thing, nor enter into the sanctuary, until she accomplishes these days which (are enjoined) in the case of a male child. 11 But in the case of a female child she shall remain in her uncleanness two weeks of days, according to the first two weeks, and sixty-six days in the blood of her purification, and they will be in all eighty days.' 12 And when she had completed these eighty days we brought her into the garden of Eden, for it is holier than all the earth besides and every tree that is planted in it is holy. 13 Therefore, there was ordained regarding her who bears a male or a female child the statute of those days that she should touch no hallowed thing, nor enter into the sanctuary until these days for the male or female child are accomplished. 14 This is the law and testimony which was written down for Israel, in order that they should observe (it) all the days. 15 And in the first week of the first jubilee, [1-7 A.M.] Adam and his wife were in the garden of Eden for seven years tilling and keeping it, and we gave him work and we instructed him to do everything that is suitable for tillage. 16 And he tilled (the garden), and was naked and knew it not, and was not ashamed, and he protected the garden from the birds and beasts and cattle, and gathered its fruit, and eat, and put aside the residue for himself and for his wife [and put aside that which was being kept]. 17 And after the completion of the seven years, which he had completed there, seven years exactly, [8 A.M.] and in the second month, on the seventeenth day (of the month), the serpent came and approached the woman, and the serpent said to the woman, 'Hath God commanded you, saying, Ye shall not eat of every tree of the garden?' 18 And she said to it, 'Of all the fruit of the trees of the garden God hath said unto us, Eat; but of the fruit of the tree which is in the midst of the garden God hath said unto us, Ye shall not eat thereof, neither shall ye touch it, lest ye die.' 19 And the serpent said unto the woman, 'Ye shall not surely die: for God doth know that on the day ye shall eat thereof, your eyes will be opened, and ye will be as gods, and ye will know good and evil. 20 And the woman saw the tree that it was agreeable and pleasant to the eye, and that its fruit was good for food, and she took thereof and eat. 21 And when she had first covered her shame with figleaves, she gave thereof to Adam and he eat, and his eyes were opened, and he saw that he was naked. 22 And he took figleaves and sewed (them) together, and made an apron for himself, and, covered his shame. 23 And God cursed the serpent, and was wroth with it for ever . . . 24 And He was wroth with the woman, because she harkened to the voice of the serpent, and did eat; and He said unto her: 'I will greatly multiply thy sorrow and thy pains: in sorrow thou shalt bring forth children, and thy return shall be unto thy husband, and he will rule over thee.' 25 And to Adam also he said, 'Because thou hast harkened unto the voice of thy wife, and hast eaten of the tree of which

I commanded thee that thou shouldst not eat thereof, cursed be the ground for thy sake: thorns and thistles shall it bring forth to thee, and thou shalt eat thy bread in the sweat of thy face, till thou returnest to the earth from whence thou wast taken; for earth thou art, and unto earth shalt thou return.' 26 And He made for them coats of skin, and clothed them, and sent them forth from the Garden of Eden. 27 And on that day on which Adam went forth from the Garden, he offered as a sweet savour an offering, frankincense, galbanum, and stacte, and spices in the morning with the rising of the sun from the day when he covered his shame. 28 And on that day was closed the mouth of all beasts, and of cattle, and of birds, and of whatever walks, and of whatever moves, so that they could no longer speak: for they had all spoken one with another with one lip and with one tongue. 29 And He sent out of the Garden of Eden all flesh that was in the Garden of Eden, and all flesh was scattered according to its kinds, and according to its types unto the places which had been created for them. 30 And to Adam alone did He give (the wherewithal) to cover his shame, of all the beasts and cattle. 31 On this account, it is prescribed on the heavenly tablets as touching all those who know the judgment of the law, that they should cover their shame, and should not uncover themselves as the Gentiles uncover themselves. 32 And on the new moon of the fourth month, Adam and his wife went forth from the Garden of Eden, and they dwelt in the land of Elda in the land of their creation. 33 And Adam called the name of his wife Eve. 34 And they had no son till the first jubilee, [8 A.M.] and after this he knew her. 35 Now he tilled the land as he had been instructed in the Garden of Eden.**Cain and Abel (iv. 1-12; cf. Gen. iv.).**

Jubilees Chapter 4

1 And in the third week in the second jubilee [64-70 A.M.] she gave birth to Cain, and in the fourth [71-77 A.M.] she gave birth to Abel, and in the fifth [78-84 A.M.] she gave birth to her daughter Âwân. 2 And in the first (year) of the third jubilee [99-105 A.M.], Cain slew Abel because (God) accepted the sacrifice of Abel, and did not accept the offering of Cain. 3 And he slew him in the field: and his blood cried from the ground to heaven, complaining because he had slain him. 4 And the Lord reproved Cain because of Abel, because he had slain him, and he made him a fugitive on the earth because of the blood of his brother, and he cursed him upon the earth. 5 And on this account it is written on the heavenly tables, 'Cursed is he who smites his neighbour treacherously, and let all who have seen and heard say, So be it; and the man who has seen and not declared (it), let him be accursed as the other.' 6 And for this reason we announce when we come before the Lord our God all the sin which is committed in heaven and on earth, and in light and in darkness, and everywhere. 7 And Adam and his wife mourned for Abel four weeks of years, [99-127 A.M] and in the fourth year of the fifth week [130 A.M.] they became joyful, and Adam knew his wife again, and she bare him a son, and he called his name Seth; for he said 'GOD has raised up a second seed unto us on the earth instead of Abel; for Cain slew him.' 8 And in the sixth week [134-40 A.M.] he begat his daughter Azûrâ. 9 And Cain took Âwân his sister to be his wife and she bare him Enoch at the close of the fourth jubilee. [190-196 A.M.] And in the first year of the first week of the fifth jubilee, [197 A.M.] houses were built on the earth, and Cain built a city, and called its name after the name of his son Enoch. 10 And Adam knew Eve his wife and she bare yet nine sons. 11 And in the fifth week of the fifth jubilee [225-31 A.M.] Seth took Azûrâ his sister to be his wife, and in the fourth (year of the sixth week) [235 A.M.] she bare him Enos. 12 He began to call on the name of the Lord on the earth.**The Patriarchs from Adam to Noah (cf. Gen. v.); Life of Enoch; Death of Adam and Gain (iv. 13-33).**13 And in the seventh jubilee in the third week [309-15 A.M.] Enos took Nôâm his sister to be his wife, and she bare him a son in the third year of the fifth week, and he called his name Kenan. 14 And at the close of the eighth jubilee [325,386-3992 A.M.] Kenan took Mûalêlêth his sister to be his wife, and she bare him a son in the ninth jubilee, in the first week in the third year of this week, [395 A.M] and he called his name Mahalalel. 15 And in the second week of the tenth jubilee [449-55 A.M.] Mahalalel took unto him to wife DinaH, the daughter of Barakiel the daughter of his father's brother, and she bare him a son in the third week in the sixth year, [461 A.M.] and he called his name Jared, for in his days the angels of the Lord descended on the earth, those who are named the Watchers, that they should instruct the children of men, and that they should do judgment and uprightness on the earth. 16 And in the eleventh jubilee [512-18 A.M.] Jared took to himself a wife, and her name was Baraka, the daughter of Râsûjâl, a daughter of his father's brother, in the fourth week of this jubilee, [522 A.M.] and she bare him a son in the fifth week, in the fourth year of the jubilee, and he called his name Enoch. 17 And he was the first among men that are born on earth who learnt writing and knowledge and wisdom and who wrote down the signs of heaven

according to the order of their months in a book, that men might know the seasons of the years according to the order of their separate months. 18 And he was the first to write a testimony and he testified to the sons of men among the generations of the earth, and recounted the weeks of the jubilees, and made known to them the days of the years, and set in order the months and recounted the Sabbaths of the years as we made (them), known to him. 19 And what was and what will be he saw in a vision of his sleep, as it will happen to the children of men throughout their generations until the day of judgment; he saw and understood everything, and wrote his testimony, and placed the testimony on earth for all the children of men and for their generations. 20 And in the twelfth jubilee, [582-88] in the seventh week thereof, he took to himself a wife, and her name was Edna, the daughter of Danel, the daughter of his father's brother, and in the sixth year in this week [587 A.M.] she bare him a son and he called his name Methuselah. 21 And he was moreover with the angels of God these six jubilees of years, and they showed him everything which is on earth and in the heavens, the rule of the sun, and he wrote down everything. 22 And he testified to the Watchers, who had sinned with the daughters of men; for these had begun to unite themselves, so as to be defiled, with the daughters of men, and Enoch testified against (them) all. 23 And he was taken from amongst the children of men, and we conducted him into the Garden of Eden in majesty and honour, and behold there he writes down the condemnation and judgment of the world, and all the wickedness of the children of men. 24 And on account of it (God) brought the waters of the flood upon all the land of Eden; for there he was set as a sign and that he should testify against all the children of men, that he should recount all the deeds of the generations until the day of condemnation. 25 And he burnt the incense of the sanctuary, (even) sweet spices acceptable before the Lord on the Mount. 26 For the Lord has four places on the earth, the Garden of Eden, and the Mount of the East, and this mountain on which thou art this day, Mount Sinai, and Mount Zion (which) will be sanctified in the new creation for a sanctification of the earth; through it will the earth be sanctified from all (its) guilt and its uncleanness through- out the generations of the world. 27 And in the fourteenth jubilee [652 A.M.] Methuselah took unto himself a wife, Edna the daughter of Azrial, the daughter of his father's brother, in the third week, in the first year of this week, [701-7 A.M.] and he begat a son and called his name Lamech. 28 And in the fifteenth jubilee in the third week Lamech took to himself a wife, and her name was Betenos the daughter of Baraki'il, the daughter of his father's brother, and in this week she bare him a son and he called his name Noah, saying, 'This one will comfort me for my trouble and all my work, and for the ground which the Lord hath cursed.' 29 And at the close of the nineteenth jubilee, in the seventh week in the sixth year [930 A.M.] thereof, Adam died, and all his sons buried him in the land of his creation, and he was the first to be buried in the earth. 30 And he lacked seventy years of one thousand years; for one thousand years are as one day in the testimony of the heavens and therefore was it written concerning the tree of knowledge: 'On the day that ye eat thereof ye shall die.' For this reason he did not complete the years of this day; for he died during it. 31 At the close of this jubilee Cain was killed after him in the same year; for his house fell upon him and he died in the midst of his house, and he was killed by its stones; for with a stone he had killed Abel, and by a stone was he killed in righteous judgment. 32 For this reason it was ordained on the heavenly tablets: With the instrument with which a man kills his neighbour with the same shall he be killed; after the manner that he wounded him, in like manner shall they deal with him.' 33 And in the twenty-fifth [1205 A.M.] jubilee Noah took to himself a wife, and her name was `Emzârâ, the daughter of Râkê'êl, the daughter of his father's brother, in the first year in the fifth week [1207 A.M.]: and in the third year thereof she bare him Shem, in the fifth year thereof [1209 A.M.] she bare him Ham, and in the first year in the sixth week [1212 A.M.] she bare him Japheth.**The Fall of the Angels and their Punishment; the Deluge foretold (v. 1-20; cf. Gen. vi. 1-12).**

Jubilees Chapter 5

1 And it came to pass when the children of men began to multiply on the face of the earth and daughters were born unto them, that the angels of God saw them on a certain year of this jubilee, that they were beautiful to look upon; and they took themselves wives of all whom they chose, and they bare unto them sons and they were giants. 2 And lawlessness increased on the earth and all flesh corrupted its way, alike men and cattle and beasts and birds and everything that walks on the earth -all of them corrupted their ways and their orders, and they began to devour each other, and lawlessness increased on the earth and every imagination of the thoughts of all men (was) thus evil continually. 3 And God looked upon the earth, and behold it was corrupt, and all flesh had corrupted its orders, and all that were upon the earth had wrought all

manner of evil before His eyes. 4 And He said that He would destroy man and all flesh upon the face of the earth which He had created. 5 But Noah found grace before the eyes of the Lord. 6 And against the angels whom He had sent upon the earth, He was exceedingly wroth, and He gave commandment to root them out of all their dominion, and He bade us to bind them in the depths of the earth, and behold they are bound in the midst of them, and are (kept) separate. 7 And against their sons went forth a command from before His face that they should be smitten with the sword, and be removed from under heaven. 8 And He said 'My spirit shall not always abide on man; for they also are flesh and their days shall be one hundred and twenty years'. 9 And He sent His sword into their midst that each should slay his neighbour, and they began to slay each other till they all fell by the sword and were destroyed from the earth. 10 And their fathers were witnesses (of their destruction), and after this they were bound in the depths of the earth for ever, until the day of the great condemnation, when judgment is executed on all those who have corrupted their ways and their works before the Lord. 11 And He destroyed all from their places, and there was not left one of them whom He judged not according to all their wickedness. 12 And he made for all his works a new and righteous nature, so that they should not sin in their whole nature for ever, but should be all righteous each in his kind alway. 13 And the judgment of all is ordained and written on the heavenly tablets in righteousness -even (the judgment of) all who depart from the path which is ordained for them to walk in; and if they walk not therein, judgment is written down for every creature and for every kind. 14 And there is nothing in heaven or on earth, or in light or in darkness, or in Sheol or in the depth, or in the place of darkness (which is not judged); and all their judgments are ordained and written and engraved. 15 In regard to all He will judge, the great according to his greatness, and the small according to his smallness, and each according to his way. 16 And He is not one who will regard the person (of any), nor is He one who will receive gifts, if He says that He will execute judgment on each: if one gave everything that is on the earth, He will not regard the gifts or the person (of any), nor accept anything at his hands, for He is a righteous judge. 17 [And of the children of Israel it has been written and ordained: If they turn to him in righteousness He will forgive all their transgressions and pardon all their sins. 18 It is written and ordained that He will show mercy to all who turn from all their guilt once each year.] 19 And as for all those who corrupted their ways and their thoughts before the flood, no man's person was accepted save that of Noah alone; for his person was accepted in behalf of his sons, whom (God) saved from the waters of the flood on his account; for his heart was righteous in all his ways, according as it was commanded regarding him, and he had not departed from aught that was ordained for him. 20 And the Lord said that he would destroy everything which was upon the earth, both men and cattle, and **The Building of the Ark; the Flood (v. 21-32; cf. Gen. vi. 13-viii. 19).** 21 beasts, and fowls of the air, and that which moveth on the earth. And He commanded Noah to make him an ark, that he might save himself from the waters of the flood. 22 And Noah made the ark in all respects as He commanded him, in the twenty-seventh jubilee of years, in the fifth week in the fifth year (on the new moon of the first month). [1307 A.M.] 23 And he entered in the sixth (year) thereof, [1308 A.M.] in the second month, on the new moon of the second month, till the sixteenth; and he entered, and all that we brought to him, into the ark, and the Lord closed it from without on the seventeenth evening. 24 And the Lord opened seven flood-gates of heaven, And the mouths of the fountains of the great deep, seven mouths in number. 25 And the flood-gates began to pour down water from the heaven forty days and forty nights, And the fountains of the deep also sent up waters, until the whole world was full of water. 26 And the waters increased upon the earth: Fifteen cubits did the waters rise above all the high mountains, And the ark was lift up above the earth, And it moved upon the face of the waters. 27 And the water prevailed on the face of the earth five months -one hundred and fifty days. 28 And the ark went and rested on the top of Lubar, one of the mountains of Ararat. 29 And (on the new moon) in the fourth month the fountains of the great deep were closed and the flood-gates of heaven were restrained; and on the new moon of the seventh month all the mouths of the abysses of the earth were opened, and the water began to descend into the deep below. 30 And on the new moon of the tenth month the tops of the mountains were seen, and on the new moon of the first month the earth became visible. 31 And the waters disappeared from above the earth in the fifth week in the seventh year [1309 A.M.] thereof, and on the seventeenth day in the second month the earth was dry. 32 And on the twenty-seventh thereof he opened the ark, and sent forth from it beasts, and cattle, and birds, and every moving thing. **Noah's Sacrifice; God's Covenant with him (cf. Gen. viii. 20-ix. 17). Instructions to Moses about**

eating of Blood, the Feast of Weeks, etc., and Division of the Year (vi. 1-38).

Jubilees Chapter 6

1 And on the new moon of the third month he went forth from the ark, and built an altar on that mountain. 2 And he made atonement for the earth, and took a kid and made atonement by its blood for all the guilt of the earth; for everything that had been on it had been destroyed, save those that were in the ark with Noah. 3 And he placed the fat thereof on the altar, and he took an ox, and a goat, and a sheep and kids, and salt, and a turtle-dove, and the young of a dove, and placed a burnt sacrifice on the altar, and poured thereon an offering mingled with oil, and sprinkled wine and strewed frankincense over everything, and caused a goodly savour to arise, acceptable before the Lord. 4 And the Lord smelt the goodly savour, and He made a covenant with him that there should not be any more a flood to destroy the earth; that all the days of the earth seed-time and harvest should never cease; cold and heat, and summer and winter, and day and night should not change their order, nor cease for ever. 5 'And you, increase ye and multiply upon the earth, and become many upon it, and be a blessing upon it. The fear of you and the dread of you I will inspire in everything that is on earth and in the sea. 6 And behold I have given unto you all beasts, and all winged things, and everything that moves on the earth, and the fish in the waters, and all things for food; as the green herbs, I have given you all things to eat. 7 But flesh, with the life thereof, with the blood, ye shall not eat; for the life of all flesh is in the blood, lest your blood of your lives be required. At the hand of every man, at the hand of every (beast) will I require the blood of man. 8 Whoso sheddeth man's blood by man shall his blood be shed, for in the image of God made He man. 9 And you, increase ye, and multiply on the earth.' 10 And Noah and his sons swore that they would not eat any blood that was in any flesh, and he made a covenant before the Lord God for ever throughout all the generations of the earth in this month. 11 On this account He spake to thee that thou shouldst make a covenant with the children of Israel in this month upon the mountain with an oath, and that thou shouldst sprinkle blood upon them because of all the words of the covenant, which the Lord made with them for ever. 12 And this testimony is written concerning you that you should observe it continually, so that you should not eat on any day any blood of beasts or birds or cattle during all the days of the earth, and the man who eats the blood of beast or of cattle or of birds during all the days of the earth, he and his seed shall be rooted out of the land. 13 And do thou command the children of Israel to eat no blood, so that their names and their seed may be before the Lord our God continually. 14 And for this law there is no limit of days, for it is for ever. They shall observe it throughout their generations, so that they may continue supplicating on your behalf with blood before the altar; every day and at the time of morning and evening they shall seek forgiveness on your behalf perpetually before the Lord that they may keep it and not be rooted out. 15 And He gave to Noah and his sons a sign that there should not again be a flood on the earth. 16 He set His bow in the cloud for a sign of the eternal covenant that there should not again be a flood on the earth to destroy it all the days of the earth. 17 For this reason it is ordained and written on the heavenly tablets, that they should celebrate the feast of weeks in this month once a year, to renew the covenant every year. 18 And this whole festival was celebrated in heaven from the day of creation till the days of Noah -twenty-six jubilees and five weeks of years [1309-1659 A.M.]: and Noah and his sons observed it for seven jubilees and one week of years, till the day of Noah's death, and from the day of Noah's death his sons did away with (it) until the days of Abraham, and they eat blood. 19 But Abraham observed it, and Isaac and Jacob and his children observed it up to thy days, and in thy days the children of Israel forgot it until ye celebrated it anew on this mountain. 20 And do thou command the children of Israel to observe this festival in all their generations for a commandment unto them: one day in the year in this month they shall celebrate the festival. 21 For it is the feast of weeks and the feast of first fruits: this feast is twofold and of a double nature: according to what is written and engraven concerning it, celebrate it. 22 For I have written in the book of the first law, in that which I have written for thee, that thou shouldst celebrate it in its season, one day in the year, and I explained to thee its sacrifices that the children of Israel should remember and should celebrate it throughout their generations in this month, one day in every year. 23 And on the new moon of the first month, and on the new moon of the fourth month, and on the new moon of the seventh month, and on the new moon of the tenth month are the days of remembrance, and the days of the seasons in the four divisions of the year. These are written and ordained as a testimony for ever. 24 And Noah ordained them for himself as feasts for the generations for ever, so that they have become thereby a memorial unto

him. 25 And on the new moon of the first month he was bidden to make for himself an ark, and on that (day) the earth became dry and he opened (the ark) and saw the earth. 26 And on the new moon of the fourth month the mouths of the depths of the abyss beneath were closed. And on the new moon of the seventh month all the mouths of the abysses of the earth were opened, and the waters began to descend into them. 27 And on the new moon of the tenth month the tops of the mountains were seen, and Noah was glad. 28 And on this account he ordained them for himself as feasts for a memorial for ever, and thus are they ordained. 29 And they placed them on the heavenly tablets, each had thirteen weeks; from one to another (passed) their memorial, from the first to the second, and from the second to the third, and from the third to the fourth. 30 And all the days of the commandment will be two and fifty weeks of days, and (these will make) the entire year complete. Thus it is engraven and ordained on the heavenly tablets. 31 And there is no neglecting (this commandment) for a single year or from year to year. 32 And command thou the children of Israel that they observe the years according to this reckoning- three hundred and sixty-four days, and (these) will constitute a complete year, and they will not disturb its time from its days and from its feasts; for everything will fall out in them according to their testimony, and they will not leave out any day nor disturb any feasts. 33 But if they do neglect and do not observe them according to His commandment, then they will disturb all their seasons and the years will be dislodged from this (order), [and they will disturb the seasons and the years will be dislodged] and they will neglect their ordinances. 34 And all the children of Israel will forget and will not find the path of the years, and will forget the new moons, and seasons, and sabbaths and they will go wrong as to all the order of the years. 35 For I know and from henceforth will I declare it unto thee, and it is not of my own devising; for the book (lies) written before me, and on the heavenly tablets the division of days is ordained, lest they forget the feasts of the covenant and walk according to the feasts of the Gentiles after their error and after their ignorance. 36 For there will be those who will assuredly make observations of the moon -how (it) disturbs the seasons and comes in from year to year ten days too soon. 37 For this reason the years will come upon them when they will disturb (the order), and make an abominable (day) the day of testimony, and an unclean day a feast day, and they will confound all the days, the holy with the unclean, and the unclean day with the holy; for they will go wrong as to the months and sabbaths and feasts and jubilees. 38 For this reason I command and testify to thee that thou mayst testify to them; for after thy death thy children will disturb (them), so that they will not make the year three hundred and sixty-four days only, and for this reason they will go wrong as to the new moons and seasons and sabbaths and festivals, and they will eat all kinds of blood with all kinds of flesh.**Noah offers Sacrifice; the Cursing of Canaan (cf. Gen. ix. 20-28): Noah's Sons and Grandsons (cf. Gen. x.) and their Cities. Noah's Admonitions (vii. 1-39).**

Jubilees Chapter 7

1 And in the seventh week in the first year [1317 A.M.] thereof, in this jubilee, Noah planted vines on the mountain on which the ark had rested, named Lubar, one of the Ararat Mountains, and they produced fruit in the fourth year, [1320 A.M.] and he guarded their fruit, and gathered it in this year in the seventh month. 2 And he made wine therefrom and put it into a vessel, and kept it until the fifth year, [1321 A.M.] until the first day, on the new moon of the first month. 3 And he celebrated with joy the day of this feast, and he made a burnt sacrifice unto the Lord, one young ox and one ram, and seven sheep, each a year old, and a kid of the goats, that he might make atonement thereby for himself and his sons. 4 And he prepared the kid first, and placed some of its blood on the flesh that was on the altar which he had made, and all the fat he laid on the altar where he made the burnt sacrifice, and the ox and the ram and the sheep, and he laid all their flesh upon the altar. 5 And he placed all their offerings mingled with oil upon it, and afterwards he sprinkled wine on the fire which he had previously made on the altar, and he placed incense on the altar and caused a sweet savour to ascend acceptable before the Lord his God. 6 And he rejoiced and drank of this wine, he and his children with joy. 7 And it was evening, and he went into his tent, and being drunken he lay down and slept, and was uncovered in his tent as he slept. 8 And Ham saw Noah his father naked, and went forth and told his two brethren without. 9 And Shem took his garment and arose, he and Japheth, and they placed the garment on their shoulders and went backward and covered the shame of their father, and their faces were backward. 10 And Noah awoke from his sleep and knew all that his younger son had done unto him, and he cursed his son and said: 'Cursed be Canaan; an enslaved servant shall he be unto his brethren.' 11 And he blessed Shem, and said: 'Blessed be the Lord God of Shem, and Canaan shall be his servant.

12 God shall enlarge Japheth, and God shall dwell in the dwelling of Shem, and Canaan shall be his servant.' 13 And Ham knew that his father had cursed his younger son, and he was displeased that he had cursed his son. and he parted from his father, he and his sons with him, Cush and Mizraim and Put and Canaan. 14 And he built for himself a city and called its name after the name of his wife Ne'elatama'uk. 15 And Japheth saw it, and became envious of his brother, and he too built for himself a city, and he called its name after the name of his wife 'Adataneses. 16 And Shem dwelt with his father Noah, and he built a city close to his father on the mountain, and he too called its name after the name of his wife Sedeqetelebab. 17 And behold these three cities are near Mount Lubar; Sedeqetelebab fronting the mountain on its east; and Na'eltama'uk on the south; 'Adatan'eses towards the west. 18 And these are the sons of Shem: Elam, and Asshur, and Arpachshad -this (son) was born two years after the flood- and Lud, and Aram. 19 The sons of Japheth: Gomer and Magog and Madai and Javan, Tubal and Meshech and Tiras: these are the sons of Noah. 20 And in the twenty-eighth jubilee [1324-1372 A.M.] Noah began to enjoin upon his sons' sons the ordinances and commandments, and all the judgments that he knew, and he exhorted his sons to observe righteousness, and to cover the shame of their flesh, and to bless their Creator, and honour father and mother, and love their neighbour, and guard their souls from fornication and uncleanness and all iniquity. 21 For owing to these three things came the flood upon the earth, namely, owing to the fornication wherein the Watchers against the law of their ordinances went a whoring after the daughters of men, and took themselves wives of all which they chose: and they made the beginning of uncleanness. 22 And they begat sons the Naphidim, and they were all unlike, and they devoured one another: and the Giants slew the Naphil, and the Naphil slew the Eljo, and the Eljo mankind, and one man another. 23 And every one sold himself to work iniquity and to shed much blood, and the earth was filled with iniquity. 24 And after this they sinned against the beasts and birds, and all that moves and walks on the earth: and much blood was shed on the earth, and every imagination and desire of men imagined vanity and evil continually. 25 And the Lord destroyed everything from off the face of the earth; because of the wickedness of their deeds, and because of the blood which they had shed in the midst of the earth He destroyed everything. 26 'And we were left, I and you, my sons, and everything that entered with us into the ark, and behold I see your works before me that ye do not walk in righteousness: for in the path of destruction ye have begun to walk, and ye are parting one from another, and are envious one of another, and (so it comes) that ye are not in harmony, my sons, each with his brother. 27 For I see, and behold the demons have begun (their) seductions against you and against your children and now I fear on your behalf, that after my death ye will shed the blood of men upon the earth, and that ye, too, will be destroyed from the face of the earth. 28 For whoso sheddeth man's blood, and whoso eateth the blood of any flesh, shall all be destroyed from the earth. 29 And there shall not be left any man that eateth blood, or that sheddeth the blood of man on the earth, Nor shall there be left to him any seed or descendants living under heaven; For into Sheol shall they go, And into the place of condemnation shall they descend, And into the darkness of the deep shall they all be removed by a violent death. 30 There shall be no blood seen upon you of all the blood there shall be all the days in which ye have killed any beasts or cattle or whatever flies upon the earth, and work ye a good work to your souls by covering that which has been shed on the face of the earth. 31 And ye shall not be like him who eats with blood, but guard yourselves that none may eat blood before you: cover the blood, for thus have I been commanded to testify to you and your children, together with all flesh. 32 And suffer not the soul to be eaten with the flesh, that your blood, which is your life, may not be required at the hand of any flesh that sheds (it) on the earth. 33 For the earth will not be clean from the blood which has been shed upon it; for (only) through the blood of him that shed it will the earth be purified throughout all its generations. 34 And now, my children, harken: work judgment and righteousness that ye maybe planted in righteousness over the face of the whole earth, and your glory lifted up before my God, who saved me from the waters of the flood. 35 And behold, ye will go and build for yourselves cities, and plant in them all the plants that are upon the earth, and moreover all fruit-bearing trees. 36 For three years the fruit of everything that is eaten will not be gathered: and in the fourth year its fruit will be accounted holy [and they will offer the first-fruits], acceptable before the Most High God, who created heaven and earth and all things. Let them offer in abundance the first of the wine and oil (as) first-fruits on the altar of the Lord, who receives it, and what is left let the servants of the house of the Lord eat before the altar which receives (it). 37 And in the fifth year make ye the release so that ye release it in righteousness

and uprightness, and ye shall be righteous, and all that you plant shall prosper. ³⁸ For thus did Enoch, the father of your father command Methuselah, his son, and Methuselah his son Lamech, and Lamech commanded me all the things which his fathers commanded him. ³⁹ And I also will give you commandment, my sons, as Enoch commanded his son in the first jubilees: whilst still living, the seventh in his generation, he commanded and testified to his son and to his son's sons until the day of his death.'**Genealogy of the Descendants of Shem: Noah and his Sons divide the Earth (viii. 1-30; cf. Gen. x.).**

Jubilees Chapter 8

¹ In the twenty-ninth jubilee, in the first week, [1373 A.M.] in the beginning thereof Arpachshad took to himself a wife and her name was Rasu'eja, the daughter of Susan, the daughter of Elam, and she bare him a son in the third year in this week, [1375 A.M.] and he called his name Kainam. ² And the son grew, and his father taught him writing, and he went to seek for himself a place where he might seize for himself a city. ³ And he found a writing which former (generations) had carved on the rock, and he read what was thereon, and he transcribed it and sinned owing to it; for it contained the teaching of the Watchers in accordance with which they used to observe the omens of the sun and moon and stars in all the signs of heaven. ⁴ And he wrote it down and said nothing regarding it; for he was afraid to speak to Noah about it lest he should be angry with him on account of it. ⁵ And in the thirtieth jubilee, [1429 A.M.] in the second week, in the first year thereof, he took to himself a wife, and her name was Melka, the daughter of Madai, the son of Japheth, and in the fourth year [1432 A.M.] he begat a son, and called his name Shelah; for he said: 'Truly I have been sent.' ⁶ [And in the fourth year he was born], and Shelah grew up and took to himself a wife, and her name was Mu'ak, the daughter of Kesed, his father's brother, in the one and thirtieth jubilee, in the fifth week, in the first year [1499 A.M.] thereof. ⁷ And she bare him a son in the fifth year [1503 A.M.] thereof, and he called his name Eber: and he took unto himself a wife, and her name was 'Azûrâd, the daughter of Nebrod, in the thirty-second jubilee, in the seventh week, in the third year thereof. [1564 A.M.] ⁸ And in the sixth year [1567 A.M.] thereof, she bare him son, and he called his name Peleg; for in the days when he was born the children of Noah began to divide the earth amongst themselves: for this reason he called his name Peleg. ⁹ And they divided (it) secretly amongst themselves, and told it to Noah. ¹⁰ And it came to pass in the beginning of the thirty-third jubilee [1569 A.M.] that they divided the earth into three parts, for Shem and Ham and Japheth, according to the inheritance of each, in the first year in the first week, when one of us who had been sent, was with them. ¹¹ And he called his sons, and they drew nigh to him, they and their children, and he divided the earth into the lots, which his three sons were to take in possession, and they reached forth their hands, and took the writing out of the bosom of Noah, their father. ¹² And there came forth on the writing as Shem's lot the middle of the earth which he should take as an inheritance for himself and for his sons for the generations of eternity, from the middle of the mountain range of Rafa, from the mouth of the water from the river Tina, and his portion goes towards the west through the midst of this river, and it extends till it reaches the water of the abysses, out of which this river goes forth and pours its waters into the sea Me'at, and this river flows into the great sea. And all that is towards the north is Japheth's, and all that is towards the south belongs to Shem. ¹³ And it extends till it reaches Karaso: this is in the bosom of the tongue which looks towards the south. ¹⁴ And his portion extends along the great sea, and it extends in a straight line till it reaches the west of the tongue which looks towards the south: for this sea is named the tongue of the Egyptian Sea. ¹⁵ And it turns from here towards the south towards the mouth of the great sea on the shore of (its) waters, and it extends to the west to 'Afra, and it extends till it reaches the waters of the river Gihon, and to the south of the waters of Gihon, to the banks of this river. ¹⁶ And it extends towards the east, till it reaches the Garden of Eden, to the south thereof, [to the south] and from the east of the whole land of Eden and of the whole east, it turns to the east and proceeds till it reaches the east of the mountain named Rafa, and it descends to the bank of the mouth of the river Tina. ¹⁷ This portion came forth by lot for Shem and his sons, that they should possess it for ever unto his generations for evermore. ¹⁸ And Noah rejoiced that this portion came forth for Shem and for his sons, and he remembered all that he had spoken with his mouth in prophecy; for he had said: 'Blessed be the Lord God of Shem And may the Lord dwell in the dwelling of Shem.' ¹⁹ And he knew that the Garden of Eden is the holy of holies, and the dwelling of the Lord, and Mount Sinai the centre of the desert, and Mount Zion -the centre of the navel of the earth: these three were created as holy places facing each other. ²⁰ And he blessed the God of gods, who had put the word of the Lord into his mouth, and the Lord for evermore. ²¹ And he knew that a blessed portion and a

blessing had come to Shem and his sons unto the generations for ever - the whole land of Eden and the whole land of the Red Sea, and the whole land of the east and India, and on the Red Sea and the mountains thereof, and all the land of Bashan, and all the land of Lebanon and the islands of Kaftur, and all the mountains of Sanir and 'Amana, and the mountains of Asshur in the north, and all the land of Elam, Asshur, and Babel, and Susan and Ma'edai, and all the mountains of Ararat and all the region beyond the sea, which is beyond the mountains of Asshur towards the north, a blessed and spacious land, and all that is in it is very good. ²² And for Ham came forth the second portion, beyond the Gihon towards the south to the right of the Garden, and it extends towards the south and it extends to all the mountains of fire, and it extends towards the west to the sea of 'Atel and it extends towards the west till it reaches the sea of Ma'uk -that (sea) into which everything which is not destroyed descends. ²³ And it goes forth towards the north to the limits of Gadir, and it goes forth to the coast of the waters of the sea to the waters of the great sea till it draws near to the river Gihon, and goes along the river Gihon till it reaches the right of the Garden of Eden. ²⁴ And this is the land which came forth for Ham as the portion which he was to occupy for ever for himself and his sons unto their generations for ever. ²⁵ And for Japheth came forth the third portion beyond the river Tina to the north of the outflow of its waters, and it extends north- easterly to the whole region of Gog, and to all the country east thereof. ²⁶ And it extends northerly to the north, and it extends to the mountains of Qelt towards the north, and towards the sea of Ma'uk, and it goes forth to the east of Gadir as far as the region of the waters of the sea. ²⁷ And it extends until it approaches the west of Fara and it returns towards 'Aferag, and it extends easterly to the waters of the sea of Me'at. ²⁸ And it extends to the region of the river Tina in a north-easterly direction until it approaches the boundary of its waters towards the mountain Rafa, and it turns round towards the north. ²⁹ This is the land which came forth for Japheth and his sons as the portion of his inheritance which he should possess for himself and his sons, for their generations for ever; five great islands, and a great land in the north. ³⁰ But it is cold, and the land of Ham is hot, and the land of Shem is neither hot nor cold, but it is of blended cold and heat.**Subdivision of the Three Portions amongst the Grandchildren: Oath taken by Noah's Sons (ix. 1-15; cf. Gen. x. partly).**

Jubilees Chapter 9

¹ And Ham divided amongst his sons, and the first portion came forth for Cush towards the east, and to the west of him for Mizraim, and to the west of him for Put, and to the west of him [and to the west thereof] on the sea for Canaan. ² And Shem also divided amongst his sons, and the first portion came forth for Ham and his sons, to the east of the river Tigris till it approaches the east, the whole land of India, and on the Red Sea on its coast, and the waters of Dedan, and all the mountains of Mebri and Ela, and all the land of Susan and all that is on the side of Pharnak to the Red Sea and the river Tina. ³ And for Asshur came forth the second Portion, all the land of Asshur and Nineveh and Shinar and to the border of India, and it ascends and skirts the river. ⁴ And for Arpachshad came forth the third portion, all the land of the region of the Chaldees to the east of the Euphrates, bordering on the Red Sea, and all the waters of the desert close to the tongue of the sea which looks towards Egypt, all the land of Lebanon and Sanir and 'Amana to the border of the Euphrates. ⁵ And for Aram there came forth the fourth portion, all the land of Mesopotamia between the Tigris and the Euphrates to the north of the Chaldees to the border of the mountains of Asshur and the land of 'Arara. ⁶ And there came forth for Lud the fifth portion, the mountains of Asshur and all appertaining to them till it reaches the Great Sea, and till it reaches the east of Asshur his brother. ⁷ And Japheth also divided the land of his inheritance amongst his sons. ⁸ And the first portion came forth for Gomer to the east from the north side to the river Tina; and in the north there came forth for Magog all the inner portions of the north until it reaches to the sea of Me'at. ⁹ And for Madai came forth as his portion that he should posses from the west of his two brothers to the islands, and to the coasts of the islands. ¹⁰ And for Javan came forth the fourth portion every island and the islands which are towards the border of Lud. ¹¹ And for Tubal there came forth the fifth portion in the midst of the tongue which approaches towards the border of the portion of Lud to the second tongue, to the region beyond the second tongue unto the third tongue. ¹² And for Meshech came forth the sixth portion, all the region beyond the third tongue till it approaches the east of Gadir. ¹³ And for Tiras there came forth the seventh portion, four great islands in the midst of the sea, which reach to the portion of Ham [and the islands of Kamaturi came out by lot for the sons of Arpachshad as his inheritance]. ¹⁴ And thus the sons of Noah divided unto their sons in the presence of Noah their father, and

he bound them all by an oath, imprecating a curse on every one that sought to seize the portion which had not fallen (to him) by his lot. 15 And they all said, 'So be it; so be it ' for themselves and their sons for ever throughout their generations till the day of judgment, on which the Lord God shall judge them with a sword and with fire for all the unclean wickedness of their errors, wherewith they have filled the earth with transgression and uncleanness and fornication and sin.**Noah's Sons led astray by Evil Spirits; Noah's Prayer; Mastêmâ; Death of Noah (x. 1-17; cf. Gen. ix. 28).**

Jubilees Chapter 10

1 And in the third week of this jubilee the unclean demons began to lead astray the children of the sons of Noah, and to make to err and destroy them. 2 And the sons of Noah came to Noah their father, and they told him concerning the demons which were leading astray and blinding and slaying his sons' sons. 3 And he prayed before the Lord his God, and said: 'God of the spirits of all flesh, who hast shown mercy unto me And hast saved me and my sons from the waters of the flood, And hast not caused me to perish as Thou didst the sons of perdition; For Thy grace has been great towards me, And great has been Thy mercy to my soul; Let Thy grace be lift up upon my sons, And let not wicked spirits rule over them Lest they should destroy them from the earth. 4 But do Thou bless me and my sons, that we may increase and Multiply and replenish the earth. 5 And Thou knowest how Thy Watchers, the fathers of these spirits, acted in my day: and as for these spirits which are living, imprison them and hold them fast in the place of condemnation, and let them not bring destruction on the sons of thy servant, my God; for these are malignant, and created in order to destroy. 6 And let them not rule over the spirits of the living; for Thou alone canst exercise dominion over them. And let them not have power over the sons of the righteous from henceforth and for evermore.' 7 And the Lord our God bade us to bind all. 8 And the chief of the spirits, Mastêmâ, came and said: 'Lord, Creator, let some of them remain before me, and let them harken to my voice, and do all that I shall say unto them; for if some of them are not left to me, I shall not be able to execute the power of my will on the sons of men; for these are for corruption and leading astray before my judgment, for great is the wickedness of the sons of men.' 9 And He said: Let the tenth part of them remain before him, and let nine parts descend into the place of condemnation.' 10 And one of us He commanded that we should teach Noah all their medicines; for He knew that they would not walk in uprightness, nor strive in righteousness. 11 And we did according to all His words: all the malignant evil ones we bound in the place of condemnation and a tenth part of them we left that they might be subject before Satan on the earth. 12 And we explained to Noah all the medicines of their diseases, together with their seductions, how he might heal them with herbs of the earth. 13 And Noah wrote down all things in a book as we instructed him concerning every kind of medicine. Thus the evil spirits were precluded from (hurting) the sons of Noah. 14 And he gave all that he had written to Shem, his eldest son; for he loved him exceedingly above all his sons. 15 And Noah slept with his fathers, and was buried on Mount Lubar in the land of Ararat. 16 Nine hundred and fifty years he completed in his life, nineteen jubilees and two weeks and five years. [1659 A.M.] 17 And in his life on earth he excelled the children of men save Enoch because of the righteousness, wherein he was perfect. For Enoch's office was ordained for a testimony to the generations of the world, so that he should recount all the deeds of generation unto generation, till the day of judgment. 18 And in the three and thirtieth jubilee, in the first year in the second week, Peleg took to himself a wife, whose name was Lomna the daughter of Sina'ar, and she bare him a son in the fourth year of this week, and he called his name Reu; for he said: 'Behold the children of men have become evil through the wicked purpose of building for themselves a city and a tower in the land of Shinar.' 19 For they departed from the land of Ararat eastward to Shinar; for in his days they built the city and the tower, saying, 'Go to, let us ascend thereby into heaven.' 20 And they began to build, and in the fourth week they made brick with fire, and the bricks served them for stone, and the clay with which they cemented them together was asphalt which comes out of the sea, and out of the fountains of water in the land of Shinar. 21 And they built it: forty and three years [1645-1688 A.M.] were they building it; its breadth was 203 bricks, and the height (of a brick) was the third of one; its height amounted to 5433 cubits and 2 palms, and (the extent of one wall was) thirteen stades (and of the other thirty stades). 22 And the Lord our God said unto us: Behold, they are one people, and (this) they begin to do, and now nothing will be withholden from them. Go to, let us go down and confound their language, that they may not understand one another's speech, and they may be dispersed into cities and nations, and one purpose will no longer abide with them till the day of judgment.' 23 And the Lord descended, and we descended with him to see the city and the tower which the children of men had built. 24 And he confounded their language, and they no longer understood one another's speech, and they ceased then to build the city and the tower. 25 For this reason the whole land of Shinar is called Babel, because the Lord did there confound all the language of the children of men, and from thence they were dispersed into their cities, each according to his language and his nation. 26 And the Lord sent a mighty wind against the tower and overthrew it upon the earth, and behold it was between Asshur and Babylon in the land of Shinar, and they called its name 'Overthrow'. 27 In the fourth week in the first year [1688 A.M.] in the beginning thereof in the four and thirtieth jubilee, were they dispersed from the land of Shinar. **The Children of Noah enter their Districts Canaan seizes Palestine wrongfully; Madai receives Media (x. 28-36)**28 And Ham and his sons went into the land which he was to occupy, which he acquired as his portion in the land of the south. 29 And Canaan saw the land of Lebanon to the river of Egypt, that it was very good, and he went not into the land of his inheritance to the west (that is to) the sea, and he dwelt in the land of Lebanon, eastward and westward from the border of Jordan and from the border of the sea. 30 And Ham, his father, and Cush and Mizraim his brothers said unto him: 'Thou hast settled in a land which is not thine, and which did not fall to us by lot: do not do so; for if thou dost do so, thou and thy sons will fall in the land and (be) accursed through sedition; for by sedition ye have settled, and by sedition will thy children fall, and thou shalt be rooted out for ever. 31 Dwell not in the dwelling of Shem; for to Shem and to his sons did it come by their lot. 32 Cursed art thou, and cursed shalt thou be beyond all the sons of Noah, by the curse by which we bound ourselves by an oath in the presence of the holy judge, and in the presence of Noah our father.' 33 But he did not harken unto them, and dwelt in the land of Lebanon from Hamath to the entering of Egypt, he and his sons until this day. 34 And for this reason that land is named Canaan. 35 And Japheth and his sons went towards the sea and dwelt in the land of their portion, and Madai saw the land of the sea and it did not please him, and he begged a (portion) from Ham and Asshur and Arpachshad, his wife's brother, and he dwelt in the land of Media, near to his wife's brother until this day. 36 And he called his dwelling-place, and the dwelling-place of his sons, Media, after the name of their father Madai.**The History of the Patriarchs from Reu to Abraham (cf. Gen. xi, 20-30); the Corruption of the Human Race (xi. 1-15).**

Jubilees Chapter 11

1 And in the thirty-fifth jubilee, in the third week, in the first year [1681 A.M.] thereof, Reu took to himself a wife, and her name was 'Ôrâ, the daughter of 'Ûr, the son of Kesed, and she bare him a son, and he called his name Sêrôh, in the seventh year of this week in this jubilee. [1687 A.M.] 2 And the sons of Noah began to war on each other, to take captive and to slay each other, and to shed the blood of men on the earth, and to eat blood, and to build strong cities, and walls, and towers, and individuals (began) to exalt themselves above the nation, and to found the beginnings of kingdoms, and to go to war people against people, and nation against nation, and city against city, and all (began) to do evil, and to acquire arms, and to teach their sons war, and they began to capture cities, and to sell male and female slaves. 3 And 'Ûr, the son of Kesed, built the city of 'Ara of the Chaldees, and called its name after his own name and the name of his father. 4 And they made for themselves molten images, and they worshipped each the idol, the molten image which they had made for themselves, and they began to make graven images and unclean simulacra, and malignant spirits assisted and seduced (them) into committing transgression and uncleanness. 5 And the prince Mastêmâ exerted himself to do all this, and he sent forth other spirits, those which were put under his hand, to do all manner of wrong and sin, and all manner of transgression, to corrupt and destroy, and to shed blood upon the earth. 6 For this reason he called the name of Sêrôh, Serug, for every one turned to do all manner of sin and transgression. 7 And he grew up, and dwelt in Ur of the Chaldees, near to the father of his wife's mother, and he worshipped idols, and he took to himself a wife in the thirty-sixth jubilee, in the fifth week, in the first year thereof, [1744 A.M.] and her name was Melka, the daughter of Kaber, the daughter of his father's brother. 8 And she bare him Nahor, in the first year of this week, and he grew and dwelt in Ur of the Chaldees, and his father taught him the researches of the Chaldees to divine and augur, according to the signs of heaven. 9 And in the thirty-seventh jubilee in the sixth week, in the first year thereof, [1800 A.M.] he took to himself a wife, and her name was 'Ijaska, the daughter of Nestag of the Chaldees. 10 And she bare him Terah in the seventh year of this week. [1806 A.M.] 11 And the prince Mastêmâ sent ravens and birds to devour the seed which was sown in the land, in order to destroy the land, and rob the children of men of their labours.

Before they could plough in the seed, the ravens picked (it) from the surface of the ground. 12 And for this reason he called his name Terah because the ravens and the birds reduced them to destitution and devoured their seed. 13 And the years began to be barren, owing to the birds, and they devoured all the fruit of the trees from the trees: it was only with great effort that they could save a little of all the fruit of the earth in their days. 14 And in this thirty-ninth jubilee, in the second week in the first year, [1870 A.M.] Terah took to a wife, and her name was 'Edna, the daughter of 'Abram, the daughter of his father's sister. 15 And in the seventh year of this week [1876 A.M.] she bare him a son, and he called his name Abram, by the name of the father of his mother; for he had died before his daughter had conceived a son. **Abram's Knowledge of God and wonderful Deeds (xi. 16-24).** 16 And the child began to understand the errors of the earth that all went astray after graven images and after uncleanness, and his father taught him writing, and he was two weeks of years old, [1890 A.M.] and he separated himself from his father, that he might not worship idols with him. 17 And he began to pray to the Creator of all things that He might save him from the errors of the children of men, and that his portion should not fall into error after uncleanness and vileness. 18 And the seed time came for the sowing of seed upon the land, and they all went forth together to protect their seed against the ravens, and Abram went forth with those that went, and the child was a lad of fourteen years. 19 And a cloud of ravens came to devour the seed, and Abram ran to meet them before they settled on the ground, and cried to them before they settled on the ground to devour the seed, and said, ' Descend not: return to the place whence ye came,' and they proceeded to turn back. 20 And he caused the clouds of ravens to turn back that day seventy times, and of all the ravens throughout all the land where Abram was there settled there not so much as one. 21 And all who were with him throughout all the land saw him cry out, and all the ravens turn back, and his name became great in all the land of the Chaldees. 22 And there came to him this year all those that wished to sow, and he went with them until the time of sowing ceased: and they sowed their land, and that year they brought enough grain home and eat and were satisfied. 23 And in the first year of the fifth week [1891 A.M.] Abram taught those who made implements for oxen, the artificers in wood, and they made a vessel above the ground, facing the frame of the plough, in order to put the seed thereon, and the seed fell down therefrom upon the share of the plough, and was hidden in the earth, and they no longer feared the ravens. 24 And after this manner they made (vessels) above the ground on all the frames of the ploughs, and they sowed and tilled all the land, according as Abram commanded them, and they no longer feared the birds. **Abram seeks to convert Terah from Idolatry; the Family of Terah (cf. Gen. xi. 27-30). Abram burns the Idols. Death of Haran (cf. Gen. xi. 28) (xii. 1-14).**

Jubilees Chapter 12

1 And it came to pass in the sixth week, in the seventh year thereof, [1904 A.M.] that Abram said to Terah his father, saying, 'Father!' 2 And he said, 'Behold, here am I, my son.' And he said, 'What help and profit have we from those idols which thou dost worship, And before which thou dost bow thyself? 3 For there is no spirit in them, For they are dumb forms, and a misleading of the heart. Worship them not: 4 Worship the God of heaven, Who causes the rain and the dew to descend on the earth And does everything upon the earth, And has created everything by His word, And all life is from before His face. 5 Why do ye worship things that have no spirit in them? For they are the work of (men's) hands, And on your shoulders do ye bear them, And ye have no help from them, But they are a great cause of shame to those who make them, And a misleading of the heart to those who worship them: Worship them not.' 6 And his father said unto him, I also know it, my son, but what shall I do with a people who have made me to serve before them? 7 And if I tell them the truth, they will slay me; for their soul cleaves to them to worship them and honour them. 8 Keep silent, my son, lest they slay thee.' And these words he spake to his two brothers, and they were angry with him and he kept silent. 9 And in the fortieth jubilee, in the second week, in the seventh year thereof, [1925 A.M.] Abram took to himself a wife, and her name was Sarai, the daughter of his father, and she became his wife. 10 And Haran, his brother, took to himself a wife in the third year of the third week, [1928 A.M.] and she bare him a son in the seventh year of this week, [1932 A.M.] and he called his name Lot. 11 And Nahor, his brother, took to himself a wife. 12 And in the sixtieth year of the life of Abram, that is, in the fourth week, in the fourth year thereof, [1936 A.M.] Abram arose by night, and burned the house of the idols, and he burned all that was in the house and no man knew it. 13 And they arose in the night and sought to save their gods from the midst of the fire. 14 And Haran hasted to save them, but the fire flamed over him, and he was burnt in the fire,

and he died in Ur of the Chaldees before Terah his father, and they buried him in Ur of the Chaldees. **The Family of Terah in Haran; Abram's Experiences there; his Journey to Canaan (xii. 15-31; cf. Gen. xi, 31-xii. 3).** 15 And Terah went forth from Ur of the Chaldees, he and his sons, to go into the land of Lebanon and into the land of Canaan, and he dwelt in the land of Haran, and Abram dwelt with Terah his father in Haran two weeks of years. 16 And in the sixth week, in the fifth year thereof, [1951 A.M.] Abram sat up throughout the night on the new moon of the seventh month to observe the stars from the evening to the morning, in order to see what would be the character of the year with regard to the rains, and he was alone as he sat and observed. 17 And a word came into his heart and he said: All the signs of the stars, and the signs of the moon and of the sun are all in the hand of the Lord. Why do I search (them) out? 18 If He desires, He causes it to rain, morning and evening; And if He desires, He withholds it, And all things are in his hand.' 19 And he prayed that night and said, 'My God, God Most High, Thou alone art my God, And Thee and Thy dominion have I chosen. And Thou hast created all things, And all things are the work of thy hands. 20 Deliver me from the hands of evil spirits who have dominion over the thoughts of men's hearts, And let them not lead me astray from Thee, my God. And stablish Thou me and my seed for ever That we go not astray from henceforth and for evermore.' 21 And he said, 'Shall I return unto Ur of the Chaldees who seek my face that I may return to them, am I to remain here in this place? The right path before Thee prosper it in the hands of Thy servant that he may fulfil (it) and that I may not walk in the deceitfulness of my heart, O my God.' 22 And he made an end of speaking and praying, and behold the word of the Lord was sent to him through me, saying: 'Get thee up from thy country, and from thy kindred and from the house of thy father unto a land which I will show thee, and I shall make thee a great and numerous nation. 23 And I will bless thee And I will make thy name great, And thou shalt be blessed in the earth, And in Thee shall all families of the earth be blessed, And I will bless them that bless thee, And curse them that curse thee. 24 And I will be a God to thee and thy son, and to thy son's son, and to all thy seed: fear not, from henceforth and unto all generations of the earth I am thy God.' 25 And the Lord God said: 'Open his mouth and his ears, that he may hear and speak with his mouth, with the language which has been revealed'; for it had ceased from the mouths of all the children of men from the day of the overthrow (of Babel). 26 And I opened his mouth, and his ears and his lips, and I began to speak with him in Hebrew in the tongue of the creation. 27 And he took the books of his fathers, and these were written in Hebrew, and he transcribed them, and he began from henceforth to study them, and I made known to him that which he could not (understand), and he studied them during the six rainy months. 28 And it came to pass in the seventh year of the sixth week [1953 A.M.] that he spoke to his father and informed him, that he would leave Haran to go into the land of Canaan to see it and return to him. 29 And Terah his father said unto him; Go in peace: May the eternal God make thy path straight. And the Lord [(be) with thee, and] protect thee from all evil, And grant unto thee grace, mercy and favour before those who see thee, And may none of the children of men have power over thee to harm thee; Go in peace. 30 And if thou seest a land pleasant to thy eyes to dwell in, then arise and take me to thee and take Lot with thee, the son of Haran thy brother as thine own son: the Lord be with thee. 31 And Nahor thy brother leave with me till thou returnest in peace, and we go with thee all together.' **Abram with Lot in Canaan and Egypt (cf. Gen. xii. 4-20). Abram separates from Lot (cf. Gen. xiii. 11-18) (xiii. 1-21).**

Jubilees Chapter 13

1 And Abram journeyed from Haran, and he took Sarai, his wife, and Lot, his brother Haran's son, to the land of Canaan, and he came into Asshur, and proceeded to Shechem, and dwelt near a lofty oak. 2 And he saw, and, behold, the land was very pleasant from the entering of Hamath to the lofty oak. 3 And the Lord said to him: 'To thee and to thy seed will I give this land.' 4 And he built an altar there, and he offered thereon a burnt sacrifice to the Lord, who had appeared to him. 5 And he removed from thence unto the mountain . . . Bethel on the west and Ai on the east, and pitched his tent there. 6 And he saw and behold, the land was very wide and good, and everything grew thereon -vines and figs and pomegranates, oaks and ilexes, and terebinths and oil trees, and cedars and cypresses and date trees, and all trees of the field, and there was water on the mountains. 7 And he blessed the Lord who had led him out of Ur of the Chaldees, and had brought him to this land. 8 And it came to pass in the first year, in the seventh week, on the new moon of the first month, [1954 A.M.] that he built an altar on this mountain, and called on the name of the Lord: 'Thou, the eternal God, art my God.' 9 And he offered on the altar a burnt sacrifice unto the Lord

that He should be with him and not forsake him all the days of his life. 10 And he removed from thence and went towards the south, and he came to Hebron and Hebron was built at that time, and he dwelt there two years, and he went (thence) into the land of the south, to Bealoth, and there was a famine in the land. 11 And Abram went into Egypt in the third year of the week, and he dwelt in Egypt five years before his wife was torn away from him. 12 Now Tanais in Egypt was at that time built- seven years after Hebron. 13 And it came to pass when Pharaoh seized Sarai, the wife of Abram that the Lord plagued Pharaoh and his house with great plagues because of Sarai, Abram's wife. 14 And Abram was very glorious by reason of possessions in sheep, and cattle, and asses, and horses, and camels, and menservants, and maidservants, and in silver and gold exceedingly. And Lot also his brother's son, was wealthy. 15 And Pharaoh gave back Sarai, the wife of Abram, and he sent him out of the land of Egypt, and he journeyed to the place where he had pitched his tent at the beginning, to the place of the altar, with Ai on the east, and Bethel on the west, and he blessed the Lord his God who had brought him back in peace. 16 And it came to pass in the forty-first jubilee in the third year of the first week, [1963 A.M.] that he returned to this place and offered thereon a burnt sacrifice, and called on the name of the Lord, and said: 'Thou, the most high God, art my God for ever and ever.' 17 And in the fourth year of this week [1964 A.M.] Lot parted from him, and Lot dwelt in Sodom, and the men of Sodom were sinners exceedingly. 18 And it grieved him in his heart that his brother's son had parted from him; for he had no children. 19 In that year when Lot was taken captive, the Lord said unto Abram, after that Lot had parted from him, in the fourth year of this week: 'Lift up thine eyes from the place where thou art dwelling, northward and southward, and westward and eastward. 20 For all the land which thou seest I will give to thee and to thy seed for ever, and I will make thy seed as the sand of the sea: though a man may number the dust of the earth, yet thy seed shall not be numbered. 21 Arise, walk (through the land) in the length of it and the breadth of it, and see it all; for to thy seed will I give it.' And Abram went to Hebron, and dwelt there. **The Campaign of Chedorlaomer (xiii. 22-29; cf. Gen. xiv.).**22 And in this year came Chedorlaomer, king of Elam, and Amraphel, king of Shinar, and Arioch king of Sellasar, and Tergal, king of nations, and slew the king of Gomorrah, and the king of Sodom fled, and many fell through wounds in the vale of Siddim, by the Salt Sea. 23 And they took captive Sodom and Adam and Zeboim, and they took captive Lot also, the son of Abram's brother, and all his possessions, and they went to Dan. 24 And one who had escaped came and told Abram that his brother's son had been taken captive and (Abram) armed his household servants . . . 25 . . . . for Abram, and for his seed, a tenth of the first fruits to the Lord, and the Lord ordained it as an ordinance for ever that they should give it to the priests who served before Him, that they should possess it for ever. 26 And to this law there is no limit of days; for He hath ordained it for the generations for ever that they should give to the Lord the tenth of everything, of the seed and of the wine and of the oil and of the cattle and of the sheep. 27 And He gave (it) unto His priests to eat and to drink with joy before Him. 28 And the king of Sodom came to him and bowed himself before him, and said: 'Our Lord Abram, give unto us the souls which thou hast rescued, but let the booty be thine.' 29 And Abram said unto him: 'I lift up my hands to the Most High God, that from a thread to a shoe-latchet I shall not take aught that is thine lest thou shouldst say, I have made Abram rich; save only what the young men have eaten, and the portion of the men who went with me -Aner, Eschol, and Mamre. These shall take their portion.' **God's Covenant with Abram (xiv. 1-20; cf. Gen. xv.).**

Jubilees Chapter 14

1 After these things, in the fourth year of this week, on the new moon of the third month, the word of the Lord came to Abram in a dream, saying: 'Fear not, Abram; I am thy defender, and thy reward will be exceeding great.' 2 And he said: 'Lord, Lord, what wilt thou give me, seeing I go hence childless, and the son of Maseq, the son of my handmaid, is the Dammasek Eliezer: he will be my heir, and to me thou hast given no seed.' 3 And he said unto him: 'This (man) will not be thy heir, but one that will come out of thine own bowels; he will be thine heir.' 4 And He brought him forth abroad, and said unto him: 'Look toward heaven and number the stars if thou art able to number them.' 5 And he looked toward heaven, and beheld the stars. And He said unto him: 'So shall thy seed be.' 6 And he believed in the Lord, and it was counted to him for righteousness. 7 And He said unto him: 'I am the Lord that brought thee out of Ur of the Chaldees, to give thee the land of the Canaanites to possess it for ever; and I will be God unto thee and to thy seed after thee.' 8 And he said: 'Lord, Lord, whereby shall I know that I shall inherit (it)?' 9 And He said unto him: 'Take Me an heifer of three years, and a goat of three years, and a sheep of three years, and a

turtle-dove, and a pigeon.' 10 And he took all these in the middle of the month and he dwelt at the oak of Mamre, which is near Hebron. 11 And he built there an altar, and sacrificed all these; and he poured their blood upon the altar, and divided them in the midst, and laid them over against each other; but the birds divided he not. 12 And birds came down upon the pieces, and Abram drove them away, and did not suffer the birds to touch them. 13 And it came to pass, when the sun had set, that an ecstasy fell upon Abram, and lo! an horror of great darkness fell upon him, and it was said unto Abram: 'Know of a surety that thy seed shall be a stranger in a land (that is) not theirs, and they shall bring them into bondage, and afflict them four hundred years. 14 And the nation also to whom they will be in bondage will I judge, and after that they shall come forth thence with much substance. 15 And thou shalt go to thy fathers in peace, and be buried in a good old age. 16 But in the fourth generation they shall return hither; for the iniquity of the Amorites is not yet full.' 17 And he awoke from his sleep, and he arose, and the sun had set; and there was a flame, and behold! a furnace was smoking, and a flame of fire passed between the pieces. 18 And on that day the Lord made a covenant with Abram, saying: 'To thy seed will I give this land, from the river of Egypt unto the great river, the river Euphrates, the Kenites, the Kenizzites, the Kadmonites, the Perizzites, and the Rephaim, the Phakorites, and the Hivites, and the Amorites, and the Canaanites, and the Girgashites, and the Jebusites. 19 And the day passed, and Abram offered the pieces, and the birds, and their fruit offerings, and their drink offerings, and the fire devoured them. 20 And on that day we made a covenant with Abram, according as we had covenanted with Noah in this month; and Abram renewed the festival and ordinance for himself for ever. **The Birth of Ishmael (xiv. 21-24; cf. Gen. xvi. 1-4.11).**21 And Abram rejoiced, and made all these things known to Sarai his wife; and he believed that he would have seed, but she did not bear. 22 And Sarai advised her husband Abram, and said unto him: 'Go in unto Hagar, my Egyptian maid: it may be that I shall build up seed unto thee by her.' 23 And Abram harkened unto the voice of Sarai his wife, and said unto her, 'Do (so).' And Sarai took Hagar, her maid, the Egyptian, and gave her to Abram, her husband, to be his wife. 24 And he went in unto her, and she conceived and bare him a son, and he called his name Ishmael, in the fifth year of this week [1965 A.M.]; and this was the eighty-sixth year in the life of Abram. **The Feast of First-fruits Circumcision instituted. The Promise of Isaac's Birth. Circumcision ordained for all Israel (xv. 1-34; cf. Gen. xvii.).**

Jubilees Chapter 15

1 And in the fifth year of the fourth week of this jubilee, [1979 A.M.] in the third month, in the middle of the month, Abram celebrated the feast of the first-fruits of the grain harvest. 2 And he offered new offerings on the altar, the first-fruits of the produce, unto the Lord, an heifer and a goat and a sheep on the altar as a burnt sacrifice unto the Lord; their fruit offerings and their drink offerings he offered upon the altar with frankincense. 3 And the Lord appeared to Abram, and said unto him: 'I am God Almighty; approve thyself before me and be thou perfect. 4 And I will make My covenant between Me and thee, and I will multiply thee exceedingly.' 5 And Abram fell on his face, and God talked with him, and said: 6 'Behold my ordinance is with thee, And thou shalt be the father of many nations. 7 Neither shall thy name any more be called Abram, But thy name from henceforth, even for ever, shall be Abraham. For the father of many nations have I made thee. 8 And I will make thee very great, And I will make thee into nations, And kings shall come forth from thee. 9 And I shall establish My covenant between Me and thee, and thy seed after thee, throughout their generations, for an eternal covenant, so that I may be a God unto thee, and to thy seed after thee. 10 <And I will give to thee and to thy seed after thee> the land where thou hast been a sojourner, the land of Canaan, that thou mayst possess it for ever, and I will be their God.' 11 And the Lord said unto Abraham: 'And as for thee, do thou keep my covenant, thou and thy seed after thee: and circumcise ye every male among you, and circumcise your foreskins, and it shall be a token of an eternal covenant between Me and you. 12 And the child on the eighth day ye shall circumcise, every male throughout your generations, him that is born in the house, or whom ye have bought with money from any stranger, whom ye have acquired who is not of thy seed. 13 He that is born in thy house shall surely be circumcised, and those whom thou hast bought with money shall be circumcised, and My covenant shall be in your flesh for an eternal ordinance. 14 And the uncircumcised male who is not circumcised in the flesh of his foreskin on the eighth day, that soul shall be cut off from his people, for he has broken My covenant.' 15 And God said unto Abraham: 'As for Sarai thy wife, her name shall no more be called Sarai, but Sarah shall be her name. 16 And I will bless her, and give thee a son by her, and I will bless him, and he shall become a nation, and kings of

nations shall proceed from him.' 17 And Abraham fell on his face, and rejoiced, and said in his heart: 'Shall a son be born to him that is a hundred years old, and shall Sarah, who is ninety years old, bring forth?' 18 And Abraham said unto God: 'O that Ishmael might live before thee!' 19 And God said: 'Yea, and Sarah also shall bear thee a son, and thou shalt call his name Isaac, and I will establish My covenant with him, an everlasting covenant, and for his seed after him. 20 And as for Ishmael also have I heard thee, and behold I will bless him, and make him great, and multiply him exceedingly, and he shall beget twelve princes, and I will make him a great nation. 21 But My covenant will I establish with Isaac, whom Sarah shall bear to thee, in these days, in the next year.' 22 And He left off speaking with him, and God went up from Abraham. 23 And Abraham did according as God had said unto him, and he took Ishmael his son, and all that were born in his house, and whom he had bought with his money, every male in his house, and circumcised the flesh of their foreskin. 24 And on the selfsame day was Abraham circumcised, and all the men of his house, <and those born in the house>, and all those, whom he had bought with money from the children of the stranger, were circumcised with him. 25 This law is for all the generations for ever, and there is no circumcision of the days, and no omission of one day out of the eight days; for it is an eternal ordinance, ordained and written on the heavenly tablets. 26 And every one that is born, the flesh of whose foreskin is not circumcised on the eighth day, belongs not to the children of the covenant which the Lord made with Abraham, but to the children of destruction; nor is there, moreover, any sign on him that he is the Lord's, but (he is destined) to be destroyed and slain from the earth, and to be rooted out of the earth, for he has broken the covenant of the Lord our God. 27 For all the angels of the presence and all the angels of sanctification have been so created from the day of their creation, and before the angels of the presence and the angels of sanctification He hath sanctified Israel, that they should be with Him and with His holy angels. 28 And do thou command the children of Israel and let them observe the sign of this covenant for their generations as an eternal ordinance, and they will not be rooted out of the land. 29 For the command is ordained for a covenant, that they should observe it for ever among all the children of Israel. 30 For Ishmael and his sons and his brothers and Esau, the Lord did not cause to approach Him, and he chose them not because they are the children of Abraham, because He knew them, but He chose Israel to be His people. 31 And He sanctified it, and gathered it from amongst all the children of men; for there are many nations and many peoples, and all are His, and over all hath He placed spirits in authority to lead them astray from Him. 32 But over Israel He did not appoint any angel or spirit, for He alone is their ruler, and He will preserve them and require them at the hand of His angels and His spirits, and at the hand of all His powers in order that He may preserve them and bless them, and that they may be His and He may be theirs from henceforth for ever. 33 And now I announce unto thee that the children of Israel will not keep true to this ordinance, and they will not circumcise their sons according to all this law; for in the flesh of their circumcision they will omit this circumcision of their sons, and all of them, sons of Beliar, will leave their sons uncircumcised as they were born. 34 And there will be great wrath from the Lord against the children of Israel. because they have forsaken His covenant and turned aside from His word, and provoked and blasphemed, inasmuch as they do not observe the ordinance of this law; for they have treated their members like the Gentiles, so that they may be removed and rooted out of the land. And there will no more be pardon or forgiveness unto them [so that there should be forgiveness and pardon] for all the sin of this eternal error.**Angelic Visitation of Abraham in Hebron; Promise of Isaac's Birth repeated. The Destruction of Sodom and Lot's Deliverance (xvi. 1-9; cf. Gen. xviii.-xix.).**

Jubilees Chapter 16

1 And on the new moon of the fourth month we appeared unto Abraham, at the oak of Mamre, and we talked with him, and we announced to him that a son would be given to him by Sarah his wife. 2 And Sarah laughed, for she heard that we had spoken these words with Abraham, and we admonished her, and she became afraid, and denied that she had laughed on account of the words. 3 And we told her the name of her son, as his name is ordained and written in the heavenly tablets (i.e.) Isaac, 4 And (that) when we returned to her at a set time, she would have conceived a son. 5 And in this month the Lord executed his judgments on Sodom, and Gomorrah, and Zeboim, and all the region of the Jordan, and He burned them with fire and brimstone, and destroyed them until this day, even as [lo] I have declared unto thee all their works, that they are wicked and sinners exceedingly, and that they defile themselves and commit fornication in their flesh, and work uncleanness on the earth. 6 And, in like manner, God will execute

judgment on the places where they have done according to the uncleanness of the Sodomites, like unto the judgment of Sodom. 7 But Lot we saved; for God remembered Abraham, and sent him out from the midst of the overthrow. 8 And he and his daughters committed sin upon the earth, such as had not been on the earth since the days of Adam till his time; for the man lay with his daughters. 9 And, behold, it was commanded and engraven concerning all his seed, on the heavenly tablets, to remove them and root them out, and to execute judgment upon them like the judgment of Sodom, and to leave no seed of the man on earth on the day of condemnation. **Abraham at Beersheba. Birth and Circumcision of Isaac (cf. Gen. xxi. 1-4). Institution of the Feast of Tabernacles (xvi. 10-31).**10 And in this month Abraham moved from Hebron, and departed and dwelt between Kadesh and Shur in the mountains of Gerar. 11 And in the middle of the fifth month he moved from thence, and dwelt at the Well of the Oath. 12 And in the middle of the sixth month the Lord visited Sarah and did unto her as He had spoken and she conceived. 13 And she bare a son in the third month, and in the middle of the month, at the time of which the Lord had spoken to Abraham, on the festival of the first fruits of the harvest, Isaac was born. 14 And Abraham circumcised his son on the eighth day: he was the first that was circumcised according to the covenant which is ordained for ever. 15 And in the sixth year of the fourth week we came to Abraham, to the Well of the Oath, and we appeared unto him [as we had told Sarah that we should return to her, and she would have conceived a son. 16 And we returned in the seventh month, and found Sarah with child before us] and we blessed him, and we announced to him all the things which had been decreed concerning him, that he should not die till he should beget six sons more, and should see (them) before he died; but (that) in Isaac should his name and seed be called: 17 And (that) all the seed of his sons should be Gentiles, and be reckoned with the Gentiles; but from the sons of Isaac one should become a holy seed, and should not be reckoned among the Gentiles. 18 For he should become the portion of the Most High, and all his seed had fallen into the possession of God, that it should be unto the Lord a people for (His) possession above all nations and that it should become a kingdom and priests and a holy nation. 19 And we went our way, and we announced to Sarah all that we had told him, and they both rejoiced with exceeding great joy. 20 And he built there an altar to the Lord who had delivered him, and who was making him rejoice in the land of his sojourning, and he celebrated a festival of joy in this month seven days, near the altar which he had built at the Well of the Oath. 21 And he built booths for himself and for his servants on this festival, and he was the first to celebrate the feast of tabernacles on the earth. 22 And during these seven days he brought each day to the altar a burnt offering to the Lord, two oxen, two rams, seven sheep, one he-goat, for a sin offering, that he might atone thereby for himself and for his seed. 23 And, as a thank-offering, seven rams, seven kids, seven sheep, and seven he-goats, and their fruit offerings and their drink offerings; and he burnt all the fat thereof on the altar, a chosen offering unto the Lord for a sweet smelling savour. 24 And morning and evening he burnt fragrant substances, frankincense and galbanum, and stackte, and nard, and myrrh, and spice, and costum; all these seven he offered, crushed, mixed together in equal parts (and) pure. 25 And he celebrated this feast during seven days, rejoicing with all his heart and with all his soul, he and all those who were in his house, and there was no stranger with him, nor any that was uncircumcised. 26 And he blessed his Creator who had created him in his generation, for He had created him according to His good pleasure; for He knew and perceived that from him would arise the plant of righteousness for the eternal generations, and from him a holy seed, so that it should become like Him who had made all things. 27 And he blessed and rejoiced, and he called the name of this festival the festival of the Lord, a joy acceptable to the Most High God. 28 And we blessed him for ever, and all his seed after him throughout all the generations of the earth, because he celebrated this festival in its season, according to the testimony of the heavenly tablets. 29 For this reason it is ordained on the heavenly tablets concerning Israel, that they shall celebrate the feast of tabernacles seven days with joy, in the seventh month, acceptable before the Lord -a statute for ever throughout their generations every year. 30 And to this there is no limit of days; for it is ordained for ever regarding Israel that they should celebrate it and dwell in booths, and set wreaths upon their heads, and take leafy boughs, and willows from the brook. 31 And Abraham took branches of palm trees, and the fruit of goodly trees, and every day going round the altar with the branches seven times [a day] in the morning, he praised and gave thanks to his God for all things in joy. **The Expulsion of Hagar and Ishmael (xvii. 1-14; cf. Gen. xxi. 8-21).**

Jubilees Chapter 17

[1] And in the first year of the fifth week Isaac was weaned in this jubilee, [1982 A.M.] and Abraham made a great banquet in the third month, on the day his son Isaac was weaned. [2] And Ishmael, the son of Hagar, the Egyptian, was before the face of Abraham, his father, in his place, and Abraham rejoiced and blessed God because he had seen his sons and had not died childless. [3] And he remembered the words which He had spoken to him on the day on which Lot had parted from him, and he rejoiced because the Lord had given him seed upon the earth to inherit the earth, and he blessed with all his mouth the Creator of all things. [4] And Sarah saw Ishmael playing and dancing, and Abraham rejoicing with great joy, and she became jealous of Ishmael and said to Abraham, 'Cast out this bondwoman and her son; for the son of this bondwoman will not be heir with my son, Isaac.' [5] And the thing was grievous in Abraham's sight, because of his maidservant and because of his son, that he should drive them from him. [6] And God said to Abraham 'Let it not be grievous in thy sight, because of the child and because of the bondwoman; in all that Sarah hath said unto thee, harken to her words and do (them); for in Isaac shall thy name and seed be called. [7] But as for the son of this bondwoman I will make him a great nation, because he is of thy seed.' [8] And Abraham rose up early in the morning, and took bread and a bottle of water, and placed them on the shoulders of Hagar and the child, and sent her away. [9] And she departed and wandered in the wilderness of Beersheba, and the water in the bottle was spent, and the child thirsted, and was not able to go on, and fell down. [10] And his mother took him and cast him under an olive tree, and went and sat her down over against him, at the distance of a bow-shot; for she said, 'Let me not see the death of my child,' and as she sat she wept. [11] And an angel of God, one of the holy ones, said unto her, 'Why weepest thou, Hagar? Arise take the child, and hold him in thine hand; for God hath heard thy voice, and hath seen the child.' [12] And she opened her eyes, and she saw a well of water, and she went and filled her bottle with water, and she gave her child to drink, and she arose and went towards the wilderness of Paran. [13] And the child grew and became an archer, and God was with him, and his mother took him a wife from among the daughters of Egypt. [14] And she bare him a son, and he called his name Nebaioth; for she said, 'The Lord was nigh to me when I called upon him.' **Mastêmâ proposes to God that Abraham shall be put to the Proof (xvi. 15-18).** [15] And it came to pass in the seventh week, in the first year thereof, [2003 A.M.] in the first month in this jubilee, on the twelfth of this month, there were voices in heaven regarding Abraham, that he was faithful in all that He told him, and that he loved the Lord, and that in every affliction he was faithful. [16] And the prince Mastêmâ came and said before God, 'Behold, Abraham loves Isaac his son, and he delights in him above all things else; bid him offer him as a burnt-offering on the altar, and Thou wilt see if he will do this command, and Thou wilt know if he is faithful in everything wherein Thou dost try him.' [17] And the Lord knew that Abraham was faithful in all his afflictions; for He had tried him through his country and with famine, and had tried him with the wealth of kings, and had tried him again through his wife, when she was torn (from him), and with circumcision; and had tried him through Ishmael and Hagar, his maidservant, when he sent them away. [18] And in everything wherein He had tried him, he was found faithful, and his soul was not impatient, and he was not slow to act; for he was faithful and a lover of the Lord. **The Sacrifice of Isaac: Abraham returns to Beersheba (xviii. 1-19; Cf. Gen. xxii. 1-19).**

Jubilees Chapter 18

[1] And God said to him, 'Abraham, Abraham'; and he said, Behold, (here) am I.' [2] And he said, Take thy beloved son whom thou lovest, (even) Isaac, and go unto the high country, and offer him on one of the mountains which I will point out unto thee.' [3] And he rose early in the morning and saddled his ass, and took his two young men with him, and Isaac his son, and clave the wood of the burnt offering, and he went to the place on the third day, and he saw the place afar off. [4] And he came to a well of water, and he said to his young men, 'Abide ye here with the ass, and I and the lad shall go (yonder), and when we have worshipped we shall come again to you.' [5] And he took the wood of the burnt-offering and laid it on Isaac his son, and he took in his hand the fire and the knife, and they went both of them together to that place. [6] And Isaac said to his father, 'Father;' and he said, 'Here am I, my son.' And he said unto him, 'Behold the fire, and the knife, and the wood; but where is the sheep for the burnt-offering, father?' [7] And he said, 'God will provide for himself a sheep for a burnt-offering, my son.' And he drew near to the place of the mount of God. [8] And he built an altar, and he placed the wood on the altar, and bound Isaac his son, and placed him on the wood which was upon the altar, and stretched forth his hand to take the knife to slay Isaac his son. [9] And I stood before him, and before the prince Mastêmâ, and the Lord said, 'Bid him not to lay his hand on the lad, nor to do anything to him, for I have shown that he fears the Lord.' [10] And I called to him from heaven, and said unto him: 'Abraham, Abraham;' and he was terrified and said: 'Behold, (here) am I.' [11] And I said unto him: 'Lay not thy hand upon the lad, neither do thou anything to him; for now I have shown that thou fearest the Lord, and hast not withheld thy son, thy first-born son, from me.' [12] And the prince Mastêmâ was put to shame; and Abraham lifted up his eyes and looked, and, behold a ram caught . . . by his horns, and Abraham went and took the ram and offered it for a burnt-offering in the stead of his son. [13] And Abraham called that place 'The Lord hath seen', so that it is said in the mount the Lord hath seen: that is Mount Sion. [14] And the Lord called Abraham by his name a second time from heaven, as he caused us to appear to speak to him in the name of the Lord. [15] And he said: 'By Myself have I sworn, saith the Lord, Because thou hast done this thing, And hast not withheld thy son, thy beloved son, from Me, That in blessing I will bless thee, And in multiplying I will multiply thy seed As the stars of heaven, And as the sand which is on the seashore. And thy seed shall inherit the cities of its enemies, [16] And in thy seed shall all nations of the earth be blessed; Because thou hast obeyed My voice, And I have shown to all that thou art faithful unto Me in all that I have said unto thee: Go in peace.' [17] And Abraham went to his young men, and they arose and went together to Beersheba, and Abraham [2010 A.M.] dwelt by the Well of the Oath. [18] And he celebrated this festival every year, seven days with joy, and he called it the festival of the Lord according to the seven days during which he went and returned in peace. [19] And accordingly has it been ordained and written on the heavenly tablets regarding Israel and its seed that they should observe this festival seven days with the joy of festival. **The Death and Burial of Sarah (xix. 1-9; cf. Gen. xxiii.).**

Jubilees Chapter 19

[1] And in the first year of the first week in the forty-second jubilee, Abraham returned and dwelt opposite Hebron, that is Kirjath Arba, two weeks of years. [2] And in the first year of the third week of this jubilee the days of the life of Sarah were accomplished, and she died in Hebron. [3] And Abraham went to mourn over her and bury her, and we tried him [to see] if his spirit were patient and he were not indignant in the words of his mouth; and he was found patient in this, and was not disturbed. [4] For in patience of spirit he conversed with the children of Heth, to the intent that they should give him a place in which to bury his dead. [5] And the Lord gave him grace before all who saw him, and he besought in gentleness the sons of Heth, and they gave him the land of the double cave over against Mamre, that is Hebron, for four hundred pieces of silver. [6] And they besought him saying, We shall give it to thee for nothing; but he would not take it from their hands for nothing, for he gave the price of the place, the money in full, and he bowed down before them twice, and after this he buried his dead in the double cave. [7] And all the days of the life of Sarah were one hundred and twenty-seven years, that is, two jubilees and four weeks and one year: these are the days of the years of the life of Sarah. [8] This is the tenth trial wherewith Abraham was tried, and he was found faithful, patient in spirit. [9] And he said not a single word regarding the rumour in the land how that God had said that He would give it to him and to his seed after him, and he begged a place there to bury his dead; for he was found faithful, and was recorded on the heavenly tablets as the friend of God. **Marriage of Isaac and second Marriage of Abraham (cf. Gen. xxiv. 15, xxv. 1-4); the Birth of Esau and Jacob (cf. Gen. xxv. 19 ff.) (xix. 10-14).** [10] And in the fourth year thereof he took a wife for his son Isaac and her name was Rebecca [2020 A.M.] [the daughter of Bethuel, the son of Nahor, the brother of Abraham] the sister of Laban and daughter of Bethuel; and Bethuel was the son of Melca, who was the wife of Nahor, the brother of Abraham. [11] And Abraham took to himself a third wife, and her name was Keturah, from among the daughters of his household servants, for Hagar had died before Sarah. And she bare him six sons, Zimram, and Jokshan, and Medan, and Midian, and Ishbak, and Shuah, in the two weeks of years. [12] And in the sixth week, in the second year thereof, Rebecca bare to Isaac two sons, Jacob and Esau, [13] and [2046 A.M.] Jacob was a smooth and upright man, and Esau was fierce, a man of the field, and hairy, and Jacob dwelt in tents. [14] And the youths grew, and Jacob learned to write; but Esau did not learn, for he was a man of the field and a hunter, and he learnt war, and all his deeds were fierce. **Abraham loves Jacob and blesses him (xix. 15-31).** [15] And Abraham loved Jacob, but Isaac loved Esau. [16] And Abraham saw the deeds of Esau, and he knew that in Jacob should his name and seed be called; and he called Rebecca and gave commandment regarding Jacob, for he knew that she (too) loved Jacob much more than Esau. [17] And he said unto her: My daughter, watch

over my son Jacob, For he shall be in my stead on the earth, And for a blessing in the midst of the children of men, And for the glory of the whole seed of Shem. 18 For I know that the Lord will choose him to be a people for possession unto Himself, above all peoples that are upon the face of the earth. 19 And behold, Isaac my son loves Esau more than Jacob, but I see that thou truly lovest Jacob. 20 Add still further to thy kindness to him, And let thine eyes be upon him in love; For he shall be a blessing unto us on the earth from henceforth unto all generations of the earth. 21 Let thy hands be strong And let thy heart rejoice in thy son Jacob; For I have loved him far beyond all my sons. He shall be blessed for ever, And his seed shall fill the whole earth. 22 If a man can number the sand of the earth, His seed also shall be numbered. 23 And all the blessings wherewith the Lord hath blessed me and my seed shall belong to Jacob and his seed alway. 24 And in his seed shall my name be blessed, and the name of my fathers, Shem, and Noab, and Enoch, and Mahalalel, and Enos, and Seth, and Adam. 25 And these shall serve To lay the foundations of the heaven, And to strengthen the earth, And to renew all the luminaries which are in the firmament. 26 And he called Jacob before the eyes of Rebecca his mother, and kissed him, and blessed him, and said: 27 'Jacob, my beloved son, whom my soul loveth, may God bless thee from above the firmament, and may He give thee all the blessings wherewith He blessed Adam, and Enoch, and Noah, and Shem; and all the things of which He told me, and all the things which He promised to give me, may He cause to cleave to thee and to thy seed for ever, according to the days of heaven above the earth. 28 And the Spirits of Mastêmâ shall not rule over thee or over thy seed to turn thee from the Lord, who is thy God from henceforth for ever. 29 And may the Lord God be a father to thee and thou the first-born son, and to the people alway. 30 Go in peace, my son.' And they both went forth together from Abraham. 31 And Rebecca loved Jacob, with all her heart and with all her soul, very much more than Esau; but Isaac loved Esau much more than Jacob. **Abraham's Last Words to his Children and Grandchildren (xx. i-ii).**

Jubilees Chapter 20

1 And in the forty-second jubilee, in the first year of the seventh week, Abraham called Ishmael, [2052 (2045?) A.M.] and his twelve sons, and Isaac and his two sons, and the six sons of Keturah, and their sons. 2 And he commanded them that they should observe the way of the Lord; that they should work righteousness, and love each his neighbour, and act on this manner amongst all men; that they should each so walk with regard to them as to do judgment and righteousness on the earth. 3 That they should circumcise their sons, according to the covenant which He had made with them, and not deviate to the right hand or the left of all the paths which the Lord had commanded us; and that we should keep ourselves from all fornication and uncleanness, [and renounce from amongst us all fornication and uncleanness]. 4 And if any woman or maid commit fornication amongst you, burn her with fire and let them not commit fornication with her after their eyes and their heart; and let them not take to themselves wives from the daughters of Canaan; for the seed of Canaan will be rooted out of the land. 5 And he told them of the judgment of the giants, and the judgment of the Sodomites, how they had been judged on account of their wickedness, and had died on account of their fornication, and uncleanness, and mutual corruption through fornication. 6 'And guard yourselves from all fornication and uncleanness, And from all pollution of sin, Lest ye make our name a curse, And your whole life a hissing, And all your sons to be destroyed by the sword, And ye become accursed like Sodom, And all your remnant as the sons of Gomorrah. 7 I implore you, my sons, love the God of heaven And cleave ye to all His commandments. And walk not after their idols, and after their uncleannesses, 8 And make not for yourselves molten or graven gods; For they are vanity, And there is no spirit in them; For they are work of (men's) hands, And all who trust in them, trust in nothing. 9 Serve them not, nor worship them, But serve ye the most high God, and worship Him continually: And hope for His countenance always, And work uprightness and righteousness before Him, That He may have pleasure in you and grant you His mercy, And send rain upon you morning and evening, And bless all your works which ye have wrought upon the earth, And bless thy bread and thy water, And bless the fruit of thy womb and the fruit of thy land, And the herds of thy cattle, and the flocks of thy sheep. 10 And ye will be for a blessing on the earth, And all nations of the earth will desire you, And bless your sons in my name, That they may be blessed as I am. 11 And he gave to Ishmael and to his sons, and to the sons of Keturah, gifts, and sent them away from Isaac his son, and he gave everything to Isaac his son. **The Dwelling-places of the Ishmaelites and of the Sons of Keturah (xx. 12-13).** 12 And Ishmael and his sons, and the sons of Keturah and their sons, went together and dwelt from Paran to the entering in of Babylon in all the land which is towards the East facing

the desert. 13 And these mingled with each other, and their name was called Arabs, and Ishmaelites. **Abraham's Last Words to Isaac (xxi. 1-25).**

Jubilees Chapter 21

1 And in the sixth year of the seventh week of this jubilee Abraham called Isaac his son, and [2057 (2050?) A.M.] commanded him: saying, 'I am become old, and know not the day of my death, and am full of my days. 2 And behold, I am one hundred and seventy-five years old, and throughout all the days of my life I have remembered the Lord, and sought with all my heart to do His will, and to walk uprightly in all His ways. 3 My soul has hated idols, <and I have despised those that served them, and I have given my heart and spirit> that I might observe to do the will of Him who created me. 4 For He is the living God, and He is holy and faithful, and He is righteous beyond all, and there is with Him no accepting of (men's) persons and no accepting of gifts; for God is righteous, and executeth judgment on all those who transgress His commandments and despise His covenant. 5 And do thou, my son, observe His commandments and His ordinances and His judgments, and walk not after the abominations and after the graven images and after the molten images. 6 And eat no blood at all of animals or cattle, or of any bird which flies in the heaven. 7 And if thou dost slay a victim as an acceptable peace offering, slay ye it, and pour out its blood upon the altar, and all the fat of the offering offer on the altar with fine flour and the meat offering mingled with oil, with its drink offering -offer them all together on the altar of burnt offering; it is a sweet savour before the Lord. 8 And thou wilt offer the fat of the sacrifice of thank offerings on the fire which is upon the altar, and the fat which is on the belly, and all the fat on the inwards and the two kidneys, and all the fat that is upon them, and upon the loins and liver thou shalt remove, together with the kidneys. 9 And offer all these for a sweet savour acceptable before the Lord, with its meat-offering and with its drink-offering, for a sweet savour, the bread of the offering unto the Lord. 10 And eat its meat on that day and on the second day, and let not the sun on the second day go down upon it till it is eaten, and let nothing be left over for the third day; for it is not acceptable [for it is not approved] and let it no longer be eaten, and all who eat thereof will bring sin upon themselves; for thus I have found it written in the books of my forefathers, and in the words of Enoch, and in the words of Noah. 11 And on all thy oblations thou shalt strew salt, and let not the salt of the covenant be lacking in all thy oblations before the Lord. 12 And as regards the wood of the sacrifices, beware lest thou bring (other) wood for the altar in addition to these: cypress, bay, almond, fir, pine, cedar, savin, fig, olive, myrrh, laurel, aspalathus. 13 And of these kinds of wood lay upon the altar under the sacrifice, such as have been tested as to their appearance, and do not lay (thereon) any split or dark wood, (but) hard and clean, without fault, a sound and new growth; and do not lay (thereon) old wood, [for its fragrance is gone] for there is no longer fragrance in it as before. 14 Besides these kinds of wood there is none other that thou shalt place (on the altar), for the fragrance is dispersed, and the smell of its fragrance goes not up to heaven. 15 Observe this commandment and do it, my son, that thou mayst be upright in all thy deeds. 16 And at all times be clean in thy body, and wash thyself with water before thou approachest to offer on the altar, and wash thy hands and thy feet before thou drawest near to the altar; and when thou art done sacrificing, wash again thy hands and thy feet. 17 And let no blood appear upon you nor upon your clothes; be on thy guard, my son, against blood, be on thy guard exceedingly; cover it with dust. 18 And do not eat any blood for it is the soul; eat no blood whatever. 19 And take no gifts for the blood of man, lest it be shed with impunity, without judgment; for it is the blood that is shed that causes the earth to sin, and the earth cannot be cleansed from the blood of man save by the blood of him who shed it. 20 And take no present or gift for the blood of man: blood for blood, that thou mayest be accepted before the Lord, the Most High God; for He is the defence of the good: and that thou mayest be preserved from all evil, and that He may save thee from every kind of death. 21 I see, my son, That all the works of the children of men are sin and wickedness, And all their deeds are uncleanness and an abomination and a pollution, And there is no righteousness with them. 22 Beware, lest thou shouldest walk in their ways And tread in their paths, And sin a sin unto death before the Most High God. Else He will [hide His face from thee And] give thee back into the hands of thy transgression, And root thee out of the land, and thy seed likewise from under heaven, And thy name and thy seed shall perish from the whole earth. 23 Turn away from all their deeds and all their uncleanness, And observe the ordinance of the Most High God, And do His will and be upright in all things. 24 And He will bless thee in all thy deeds, And will raise up from thee a plant of righteousness through all the earth, throughout all generations of the earth, And my name and thy name

shall not be forgotten under heaven for ever. ²⁵ Go, my son in peace. May the Most High God, my God and thy God, strengthen thee to do His will, And may He bless all thy seed and the residue of thy seed for the generations for ever, with all righteous blessings, That thou mayest be a blessing on all the earth.' ²⁶ And he went out from him rejoicing.**Isaac, Ishmael and Jacob join in Festival with Abraham for the Last Time. Abraham's Prayer (xxii. 1-9).**

Jubilees Chapter 22

¹ And it came to pass in the first week in the forty-fourth jubilee, in the second year, that is, the year in which Abraham died, that Isaac and Ishmael came from the Well of the Oath to celebrate the feast of weeks -that is, the feast of the first fruits of the harvest-to Abraham, their father, and Abraham rejoiced because his two sons had come. ² For Isaac had many possessions in Beersheba, and Isaac was wont to go and see his possessions and to return to his father. ³ And in those days Ishmael came to see his father, and they both came together, and Isaac offered a sacrifice for a burnt offering, and presented it on the altar of his father which he had made in Hebron. ⁴ And he offered a thank offering and made a feast of joy before Ishmael, his brother: and Rebecca made new cakes from the new grain, and gave them to Jacob, her son, to take them to Abraham, his father, from the first fruits of the land, that he might eat and bless the Creator of all things before he died. ⁵ And Isaac, too, sent by the hand of Jacob to Abraham a best thank offering, that he might eat and drink. ⁶ And he eat and drank, and blessed the Most High God, Who hath created heaven and earth, Who hath made all the fat things of the earth, And given them to the children of men That they might eat and drink and bless their Creator. ⁷ 'And now I give thanks unto Thee, my God, because thou hast caused me to see this day: behold, I am one hundred three score and fifteen years, an old man and full of days, and all my days have been unto me peace. ⁸ The sword of the adversary has not overcome me in all that Thou hast given me and my children all the days of my life until this day. ⁹ My God, may Thy mercy and Thy peace be upon Thy servant, and upon the seed of his sons, that they may be to Thee a chosen nation and an inheritance from amongst all the nations of the earth from henceforth unto all the days of the generations of the earth, unto all the ages.' **Abraham's Last Words to and Blessings of Jacob (xxii. 10-30).**¹⁰ And he called Jacob and said: 'My son Jacob, may the God of all bless thee and strengthen thee to do righteousness, and His will before Him, and may He choose thee and thy seed that ye may become a people for His inheritance according to His will alway. ¹¹ And do thou, my son, Jacob, draw near and kiss me.' And he drew near and kissed him, and he said: 'Blessed be my son Jacob And all the sons of God Most High, unto all the ages: May God give unto thee a seed of righteousness; And some of thy sons may He sanctify in the midst of the whole earth; May nations serve thee, And all the nations bow themselves before thy seed. ¹² Be strong in the presence of men, And exercise authority over all the seed of Seth. Then thy ways and the ways of thy sons will be justified, So that they shall become a holy nation. ¹³ May the Most High God give thee all the blessings Wherewith He has blessed me And wherewith He blessed Noah and Adam; May they rest on the sacred head of thy seed from generation to generation for ever. ¹⁴ And may He cleanse thee from all unrighteousness and impurity, That thou mayest be forgiven all the transgressions; which thou hast committed ignorantly. And may He strengthen thee, And bless thee. And mayest thou inherit the whole earth, ¹⁵ And may He renew His covenant with thee. That thou mayest be to Him a nation for His inheritance for all the ages, And that He may be to thee and to thy seed a God in truth and righteousness throughout all the days of the earth. ¹⁶ And do thou, my son Jacob, remember my words, And observe the commandments of Abraham, thy father: Separate thyself from the nations, And eat not with them: And do not according to their works, And become not their associate; For their works are unclean, And all their ways are a Pollution and an abomination and uncleanness. ¹⁷ They offer their sacrifices to the dead And they worship evil spirits, And they eat over the graves, And all their works are vanity and nothingness. ¹⁸ They have no heart to understand And their eyes do not see what their works are, And how they err in saying to a piece of wood: 'Thou art my God,' And to a stone: 'Thou art my Lord and thou art my deliverer.' [And they have no heart.] ¹⁹ And as for thee, my son Jacob, May the Most High God help thee And the God of heaven bless thee And remove thee from their uncleanness and from all their error. ²⁰ Be thou ware, my son Jacob, of taking a wife from any seed of the daughters of Canaan; For all his seed is to be rooted out of the earth. ²¹ For, owing to the transgression of Ham, Canaan erred, And all his seed shall be destroyed from off the earth and all the residue thereof, And none springing from him shall be saved on the day of judgment. ²² And as for all the worshippers of idols and the profane (b) There shall be no hope for them in the land of the living; (c) And

there shall be no remembrance of them on the earth; (c) For they shall descend into Sheol, (d) And into the place of condemnation shall they go, ²³ As the children of Sodom were taken away from the earth So will all those who worship idols be taken away. Fear not, my son Jacob, And be not dismayed, O son of Abraham: May the Most High God preserve thee from destruction, And from all the paths of error may he deliver thee. ²⁴ This house have I built for myself that I might put my name upon it in the earth: [it is given to thee and to thy seed for ever], and it will be named the house of Abraham; it is given to thee and to thy seed for ever; for thou wilt build my house and establish my name before God for ever: thy seed and thy name will stand throughout all generations of the earth.' ²⁵ And he ceased commanding him and blessing him. ²⁶ And the two lay together on one bed, and Jacob slept in the bosom of Abraham, his father's father and he kissed him seven times, and his affection and his heart rejoiced over him. ²⁷ And he blessed him with all his heart and said: 'The Most High God, the God of all, and Creator of all, who brought me forth from Ur of the Chaldees that he might give me this land to inherit it for ever, and that I might establish a holy seed-blessed be the Most High for ever.' ²⁸ And he blessed Jacob and said: 'My son, over whom with all my heart and my affection I rejoice, may Thy grace and Thy mercy be lift up upon him and upon his seed alway. ²⁹ And do not forsake him, nor set him at nought from henceforth unto the days of eternity, and may Thine eyes be opened upon him and upon his seed, that Thou mayst preserve him, and bless him, and mayest sanctify him as a nation for Thine inheritance; ³⁰ And bless him with all Thy blessings from henceforth unto all the days of eternity, and renew Thy covenant and Thy grace with him and with his seed according to all Thy good pleasure unto all the generations of the earth.'**The Death and Burial of Abraham (xxiii. 1-8; cf. Gen. xxv. 7-10).**

Jubilees Chapter 23

¹ And he placed two fingers of Jacob on his eyes, and he blessed the God of gods, and he covered his face and stretched out his feet and slept the sleep of eternity, and was gathered to his fathers. ² And notwithstanding all this Jacob was lying in his bosom, and knew not that Abraham, his father's father, was dead. ³ And Jacob awoke from his sleep, and behold Abraham was cold as ice, and he said 'Father, father'; but there was none that spake, and he knew that he was dead. ⁴ And he arose from his bosom and ran and told Rebecca, his mother; and Rebecca went to Isaac in the night, and told him; and they went together, and Jacob with them, and a lamp was in his hand, and when they had gone in they found Abraham lying dead. ⁵ And Isaac fell on the face of his father and wept and kissed him. ⁶ And the voices were heard in the house of Abraham, and Ishmael his son arose, and went to Abraham his father, and wept over Abraham his father, he and all the house of Abraham, and they wept with a great weeping. ⁷ And his sons Isaac and Ishmael buried him in the double cave, near Sarah his wife, and they wept for him forty days, all the men of his house, and Isaac and Ishmael, and all their sons, and all the sons of Keturah in their places; and the days of weeping for Abraham were ended. ⁸ And he lived three jubilees and four weeks of years, one hundred and seventy-five years, and completed the days of his life, being old and full of days. **The decreasing Years and increasing Corruption of Mankind (xxiii. 9-17).**⁹ For the days of the forefathers, of their life, were nineteen jubilees; and after the Flood they began to grow less than nineteen jubilees, and to decrease in jubilees, and to grow old quickly, and to be full of their days by reason of manifold tribulation and the wickedness of their ways, with the exception of Abraham. ¹⁰ For Abraham was perfect in all his deeds with the Lord, and well-pleasing in righteousness all the days of his life; and behold, he did not complete four jubilees in his life, when he had grown old by reason of the wickedness, and was full of his days. ¹¹ And all the generations which shall arise from this time until the day of the great judgment shall grow old quickly, before they complete two jubilees, and their knowledge shall forsake them by reason of their old age Land all their knowledge shall vanish away]. ¹² And in those days, if a man live a jubilee and a-half of years, they shall say regarding him: 'He has lived long, and the greater part of his days are pain and sorrow and tribulation, and there is no peace: ¹³ For calamity follows on calamity, and wound on wound, and tribulation on tribulation, and evil tidings on evil tidings, and illness on illness, and all evil judgments such as these, one with another, illness and overthrow, and snow and frost and ice, and fever, and chills, and torpor, and famine, and death, and sword, and captivity, and all kinds of calamities and pains.' ¹⁴ And all these shall come on an evil generation, which transgresses on the earth: their works are uncleanness and fornication, and pollution and abominations. ¹⁵ Then they shall say: 'The days of the forefathers were many (even), unto a thousand years, and were good; but behold, the days of our life, if a man

has lived many, are three score years and ten, and, if he is strong, four score years, and those evil, and there is no peace in the days of this evil generation.' 16 And in that generation the sons shall convict their fathers and their elders of sin and unrighteousness, and of the words of their mouth and the great wickednesses which they perpetrate, and concerning their forsaking the covenant which the Lord made between them and Him, that they should observe and do all His commandments and His ordinances and all His laws, without departing either to the right hand or the left. 17 For all have done evil, and every mouth speaks iniquity and all their works are an uncleanness and an abomination, and all their ways are pollution, uncleanness and destruction. **The Messianic Woes (xxiii. 18-25). [Eschatological partly.]**18 Behold the earth shall be destroyed on account of all their works, and there shall be no seed of the vine, and no oil; for their works are altogether faithless, and they shall all perish together, beasts and cattle and birds, and all the fish of the sea, on account of the children of men. 19 And they shall strive one with another, the young with the old, and the old with the young, the poor with the rich, the lowly with the great, and the beggar with the prince, on account of the law and the covenant; for they have forgotten commandment, and covenant, and feasts, and months, and Sabbaths, and jubilees, and all judgments. 20 And they shall stand <with bows and> swords and war to turn them back into the way; but they shall not return until much blood has been shed on the earth, one by another. 21 And those who have escaped shall not return from their wickedness to the way of righteousness, but they shall all exalt themselves to deceit and wealth, that they may each take all that is his neighbour's, and they shall name the great name, but not in truth and not in righteousness, and they shall defile the holy of holies with their uncleanness and the corruption of their pollution. 22 And a great punishment shall befall the deeds of this generation from the Lord, and He will give them over to the sword and to judgment and to captivity, and to be plundered and devoured. 23 And He will wake up against them the sinners of the Gentiles, who have neither mercy nor compassion, and who shall respect the person of none, neither old nor young, nor any one, for they are more wicked and strong to do evil than all the children of men. And they shall use violence against Israel and transgression against Jacob, And much blood shall be shed upon the earth, And there shall be none to gather and none to bury. 24 In those days they shall cry aloud, And call and pray that they may be saved from the hand of the sinners, the Gentiles; But none shall be saved. 25 And the heads of the children shall be white with grey hair, And a child of three weeks shall appear old like a man of one hundred years, And their stature shall be destroyed by tribulation and oppression. **Renewed Study of the Law followed by a Renewal of Mankind. The Messianic Kingdom and the Blessedness of the Righteous (xxiii. 26-32; cf. Isa. lxv. 17 ff. [Eschatological.]**26 And in those days the children shall begin to study the laws, And to seek the commandments, And to return to the path of righteousness. 27 And the days shall begin to grow many and increase amongst those children of men Till their days draw nigh to one thousand years. And to a greater number of years than (before) was the number of the days. 28 And there shall be no old man Nor one who is <not> satisfied with his days, For all shall be (as) children and youths. 29 And all their days they shall complete and live in peace and in joy, And there shall be no Satan nor any evil destroyer; For all their days shall be days of blessing and healing. 30 And at that time the Lord will heal His servants, And they shall rise up and see great peace, And drive out their adversaries. And the righteous shall see and be thankful, And rejoice with joy for ever and ever, And shall see all their judgments and all their curses on their enemies. 31 And their bones shall rest in the earth, And their spirits shall have much joy, And they shall know that it is the Lord who executes judgment, And shows mercy to hundreds and thousands and to all that love Him. 32 And do thou, Moses, write down these words; for thus are they written, and they record (them) on the heavenly tablets for a testimony for the generations for ever.**Isaac at the Well of Vision: Esau sells his Birthright (xxiv. 1-7; cf. Gen. xxv. 11,29-34).**

Jubilees Chapter 24

1 And it came to pass after the death of Abraham, that the Lord blessed Isaac his son, and he arose from Hebron and went and dwelt at the Well of the Vision in the first year of the third week [2073 A.M.] of this jubilee, seven years. 2 And in the first year of the fourth week a famine began in the land, [2080 A.M.] besides the first famine, which had been in the days of Abraham. 3 And Jacob sod lentil pottage, and Esau came from the field hungry. And he said to Jacob his brother: 'Give me of this red pottage.' 4 And Jacob said to him: 'Sell to me thy birthright and I will give thee bread, and also some of this lentil pottage.' 5 And Esau said in his heart: 'I shall die; of what profit to me is this birthright?' 6

And he said to Jacob: 'I give it to thee.' And Jacob said: 'Swear to me, this day,' and he sware unto him. 7 And Jacob gave his brother Esau bread and pottage, and he ate till he was satisfied, and Esau despised his birthright; for this reason was Esau's name called Edom, on account of the red pottage which Jacob gave him for his birthright. **Isaac's Sojourn in Gerar and Dealings with Abimelech (xxiv. 8-27; cf. Gen. xxvi.).**8 And Jacob became the elder, and Esau was brought down from his dignity. 9 And the famine was over the land, and Isaac departed to go down into Egypt in the second year of this week, and went to the king of the Philistines to Gerar, unto Abimelech. 10 And the Lord appeared unto him and said unto him: 'Go not down into Egypt; dwell in the land that I shall tell thee of, and sojourn in this land, and I will be with thee and bless thee. 11 For to thee and to thy seed will I give all this land, and I will establish My oath which I sware unto Abraham thy father, and I will multiply thy seed as the stars of heaven, and will give unto thy seed all this land. 12 And in thy seed shall all the nations of the earth be blessed, because thy father obeyed My voice, and kept My charge and My commandments, and My laws, and My ordinances, and My covenant; and now obey My voice and dwell in this land.' 13 And he dwelt in Gerar three weeks of years. 14 And Abimelech charged concerning him, [2080-2101 A.M.] and concerning all that was his, saying: 'Any man that shall touch him or aught that is his shall surely die.' 15 And Isaac waxed strong among the Philistines, and he got many possessions, oxen and sheep and camels and asses and a great household. 16 And he sowed in the land of the Philistines and brought in a hundred-fold, and Isaac became exceedingly great, and the Philistines envied him. 17 Now all the wells which the servants of Abraham had dug during the life of Abraham, the Philistines had stopped them after the death of Abraham, and filled them with earth. 18 And Abimelech said unto Isaac: 'Go from us, for thou art much mightier than we', and Isaac departed thence in the first year of the seventh week, and sojourned in the valleys of Gerar. 19 And they digged again the wells of water which the servants of Abraham, his father, had digged, and which the Philistines had closed after the death of Abraham his father, and he called their names as Abraham his father had named them. 20 And the servants of Isaac dug a well in the valley, and found living water, and the shepherds of Gerar strove with the shepherds of Isaac, saying: 'The water is ours'; and Isaac called the name of the well 'Perversity', because they had been perverse with us. 21 And they dug a second well, and they strove for that also, and he called its name 'Enmity'. And he arose from thence and they digged another well, and for that they strove not, and he called the name of it 'Room', and Isaac said: 'Now the Lord hath made room for us, and we have increased in the land.' 22 And he went up from thence to the Well of the Oath in the first year of the first week in the [2108 A.M.] forty-fourth jubilee. 23 And the Lord appeared to him that night, on the new moon of the first month, and said unto him: 'I am the God of Abraham thy father; fear not, for I am with thee, and shall bless thee and shall surely multiply thy seed as the sand of the earth, for the sake of Abraham my servant.' 24 And he built an altar there, which Abraham his father had first built, and he called upon the name of the Lord, and he offered sacrifice to the God of Abraham his father. 25 And they digged a well and they found living water. 26 And the servants of Isaac digged another well and did not find water, and they went and told Isaac that they had not found water, and Isaac said: 'I have sworn this day to the Philistines and this thing has been announced to us.' 27 And he called the name of that place the Well of the Oath; for there he had sworn to Abimelech and Ahuzzath his friend and Phicol the prefect of his host. **Isaac curses the Philistines (xxiv. 28-33).**28 And Isaac knew that day that under constraint he had sworn to them to make peace with them. 29 And Isaac on that day cursed the Philistines and said: 'Cursed be the Philistines unto the day of wrath and indignation from the midst of all nations; may God make them a derision and a curse and an object of wrath and indignation in the hands of the sinners the Gentiles and in the hands of the Kittim. 30 And whoever escapes the sword of the enemy and the Kittim, may the righteous nation root out in judgment from under heaven; for they shall be the enemies and foes of my children throughout their generations upon the earth. 31 And no remnant shall be left to them, Nor one that shall be saved on the day of the wrath of judgment; For destruction and rooting out and expulsion from the earth is the whole seed of the Philistines (reserved), And there shall no longer be left for these Caphtorim a name or a seed on the earth. 32 For though he ascend unto heaven, Thence shall he be brought down, And though he make himself strong on earth, Thence shall he be dragged forth, And though he hide himself amongst the nations, Even from thence shall he be rooted out; And though he descend into Sheol, There also shall his condemnation be great, And there also he shall have no peace. 33 And if he go into captivity, By the hands of those that seek his life shall they slay him on the way, And neither name nor seed shall be left to him on all the earth; For into eternal malediction shall he depart.' 34 And thus is it written and engraved concerning him on the heavenly tablets, to do unto him on the day of judgment, so that he may be rooted out of the earth.**Rebecca admonishes Jacob not to marry a Canaanitish Woman. Rebecca's Blessing (xxv. 1-23; cf. Gen. xxviii. 1-4).**

Jubilees Chapter 25

1 And in the second year of this week in this jubilee, Rebecca called Jacob her son, and spake unto him, saying: 'My son, do not take thee a wife of the daughters of Canaan, as Esau, thy brother, who took him two wives of the daughters of Canaan, and they have embittered my soul with all their unclean deeds: for all their deeds are fornication and lust, and there is no righteousness with them, for (their deeds) are evil. 2 And I, my son, love thee exceedingly, and my heart and my affection bless thee every hour of the day and watch of the night. 3 And now, my son, hearken to my voice, and do the will of thy mother, and do not take thee a wife of the daughters of this land, but only of the house of my father, and of my father's kindred. Thou shalt take thee a wife of the house of my father, and the Most High God will bless thee, and thy children shall be a righteous generation and a holy seed.' 4 And then spake Jacob to Rebecca, his mother, and said unto her: 'Behold, mother, I am nine weeks of years old, and I neither know nor have I touched any woman, nor have I betrothed myself to any, nor even think of taking me a wife of the daughters of Canaan. 5 For I remember, mother, the words of Abraham, our father, for he commanded me not to take a wife of the daughters of Canaan, but to take me a wife from the seed of my father's house and from my kindred. 6 I have heard before that daughters have been born to Laban, thy brother, and I have set my heart on them to take a wife from amongst them. 7 And for this reason I have guarded myself in my spirit against sinning or being corrupted in all my ways throughout all the days of my life; for with regard to lust and fornication, Abraham, my father, gave me many commands. 8 And, despite all that he has commanded me, these two and twenty years my brother has striven with me, and spoken frequently to me and said: 'My brother, take to wife a sister of my two wives'; but I refuse to do as he has done. 9 I swear before thee, mother, that all the days of my life I will not take me a wife from the daughters of the seed of Canaan, and I will not act wickedly as my brother has done. 10 Fear not, mother; be assured that I shall do thy will and walk in uprightness, and not corrupt my ways for ever.' 11 And thereupon she lifted up her face to heaven and extended the fingers of her hands, opened her mouth and blessed the Most High God, who had created the heaven and the earth, and she gave Him thanks and praise. 12 And she said: 'Blessed be the Lord God, and may His holy name be blessed for ever and ever, who has given me Jacob as a pure son and a holy seed; for he is Thine, and Thine shall his seed be continually and throughout all the generations for evermore. 13 Bless him, O Lord, and place in my mouth the blessing of righteousness, that I may bless him.' 14 And at that hour, when the spirit of righteousness descended into her mouth, she placed both her hands on the head of Jacob, and said: 15 Blessed art thou, Lord of righteousness and God of the ages And may He bless thee beyond all the generations of men. May He give thee, my Son, the path of righteousness, And reveal righteousness to thy seed. 16 And may He make thy sons many during thy life, And may they arise according to the number of the months of the year. And may their sons become many and great beyond the stars of heaven, And their numbers be more than the sand of the sea. 17 And may He give them this goodly land -as He said He would give it to Abraham and to his seed after him alway- And may they hold it as a possession for ever. 18 And may I see (born) unto thee, my son, blessed children during my life, And a blessed and holy seed may all thy seed be. 19 And as thou hast refreshed thy mother's spirit during her life, The womb of her that bare thee blesses thee thus, [My affection] and my breasts bless thee And my mouth and my tongue praise thee greatly. 20 Increase and spread over the earth, And may thy seed be perfect in the joy of heaven and earth for ever; And may thy seed rejoice, And on the great day of peace may it have peace. 21 And may thy name and thy seed endure to all the ages, And may the Most High God be their God, And may the God of righteousness dwell with them, And by them may His sanctuary be built unto all the ages. 22 Blessed be he that blesseth thee, And all flesh that curseth thee falsely, may it be cursed.' 23 And she kissed him, and said to him; 'May the Lord of the world love thee As the heart of thy mother and her affection rejoice in thee and bless thee.' And she ceased from blessing.**Jacob obtains the Blessing of the Firstborn (xxvi. 1-35; cf. Gen. xxvii.).**

Jubilees Chapter 26

1 And in the seventh year of this week Isaac called Esau, his elder Son,

and said unto him: 'I am old, my son, and behold my eyes are dim in seeing, and I know not the day of my death. 2 And now take thy hunting weapons thy quiver and thy bow, and go out to the field, and hunt and catch me (venison), my son, and make me savoury meat, such as my soul loveth, and bring it to me that I may eat, and that my soul may bless thee before I die.' 3 But Rebecca heard Isaac speaking to Esau. 4 And Esau went forth early to the field to hunt and catch and bring home to his father. 5 And Rebecca called Jacob, her son, and said unto him: 'Behold, I heard Isaac, thy father, speak unto Esau, thy brother, saying: "Hunt for me, and make me savoury meat, and bring (it) to me that I may eat and bless thee before the Lord before I die." 6 And now, my son, obey my voice in that which I command thee: Go to thy flock and fetch me two good kids of the goats, and I will make them savoury meat for thy father, such as he loves, and thou shalt bring (it) to thy father that he may eat and bless thee before the Lord before he die, and that thou mayst be blessed.' 7 And Jacob said to Rebecca his mother: 'Mother, I shall not withhold anything which my father would eat, and which would please him: only I fear, my mother, that he will recognise my voice and wish to touch me. 8 And thou knowest that I am smooth, and Esau, my brother, is hairy, and I shall appear before his eyes as an evildoer, and shall do a deed which he had not commanded me, and he will be wroth with me, and I shall bring upon myself a curse, and not a blessing.' 9 And Rebecca, his mother, said unto him: 'Upon me be thy curse, my son, only obey my voice.' 10 And Jacob obeyed the voice of Rebecca, his mother, and went and fetched two good and fat kids of the goats, and brought them to his mother, and his mother made them savoury meat such as he loved. 11 And Rebecca took the goodly raiment of Esau, her elder son, which was with her in the house, and she clothed Jacob, her younger son, (with them), and she put the skins of the kids upon his hands and on the exposed parts of his neck. 12 And she gave the meat and the bread which she had prepared into the hand of her son Jacob. 13 And Jacob went in to his father and said: 'I am thy son: I have done according as thou badest me: arise and sit and eat of that which I have caught, father, that thy soul may bless me.' 14 And Isaac said to his son: 'How hast thou found so quickly, my son?' 15 And Jacob said: 'Because the Lord thy God caused me to find.' 16 And Isaac said unto him: Come near, that I may feel thee, my son, if thou art my son Esau or not.' 17 And Jacob went near to Isaac, his father, and he felt him and said: 'The voice is Jacob's voice, but the hands are the hands of Esau,' 18 and he discerned him not, because it was a dispensation from heaven to remove his power of perception and Isaac discerned not, for his hands were hairy as his brother Esau's, so that he blessed him. 19 And he said: 'Art thou my son Esau?' and he said: 'I am thy son': and he said, 'Bring near to me that I may eat of that which thou hast caught, my son, that my soul may bless thee.' 20 And he brought near to him, and he did eat, and he brought him wine and he drank. 21 And Isaac, his father, said unto him: 'Come near and kiss me, my son.' 22 And he came near and kissed him. And he smelled the smell of his raiment, and he blessed him and said: 'Behold, the smell of my son is as the smell of a full field which the Lord hath blessed. 23 And may the Lord give thee of the dew of heaven And of the dew of the earth, and plenty of corn and oil: Let nations serve thee, And peoples bow down to thee. 24 Be lord over thy brethren, And let thy mother's sons bow down to thee; And may all the blessings wherewith the Lord hath blessed me and blessed Abraham, my father; Be imparted to thee and to thy seed for ever: Cursed be he that curseth thee, And blessed be he that blesseth thee.' 25 And it came to pass as soon as Isaac had made an end of blessing his son Jacob, and Jacob had gone forth from Isaac his father he hid himself and Esau, his brother, came in from his hunting. 26 And he also made savoury meat, and brought it to his father, and said unto his father: 'Let my father arise, and eat of my venison that thy soul may bless me.' 27 And Isaac, his father, said unto him: 'Who art thou?' And he said unto him: 'I am thy first born, thy son Esau: I have done as thou hast commanded me.' 28 And Isaac was very greatly astonished, and said: 'Who is he that hath hunted and caught and brought it to me, and I have eaten of all before thou camest, and have blessed him: (and) he shall be blessed, and all his seed for ever.' 29 And it came to pass when Esau heard the words of his father Isaac that he cried with an exceeding great and bitter cry, and said unto his father: 'Bless me, (even) me also, father.' 30 And he said unto him: 'Thy brother came with guile, and hath taken away thy blessing.' And he said: 'Now I know why his name is named Jacob: behold, he hath supplanted me these two times: he took away my birthright, and now he hath taken away my blessing.' 31 And he said: 'Hast thou not reserved a blessing for me, father?' and Isaac answered and said unto Esau: 'Behold, I have made him thy lord, And all his brethren have I given to him for servants, And with plenty of corn and wine and oil have I strengthened him: And what now shall I do for thee, my son?' 32 And Esau said to Isaac, his father: 'Hast thou but one blessing, O father? Bless me, (even) me also, father:' 33 And Esau lifted up his voice and wept. And Isaac answered and said unto him: 'Behold, far from the dew of the earth shall be thy dwelling, And far from the dew of heaven from above. 34 And by thy sword wilt thou live, And thou wilt serve thy brother. And it shall come to pass when thou becomest great, And dost shake his yoke from off thy neck, Thou shalt sin a complete sin unto death, And thy seed shall be rooted out from under heaven.' 35 And Esau kept threatening Jacob because of the blessing wherewith his father blessed him, and he said in his heart: 'May the days of mourning for my father now come, so that I may slay my brother Jacob.'**Rebecca induces Isaac to send Jacob to Mesopotamia. Jacob's Dream and View at Bethel (xxvii. 1-27; cf. Gen. xxviii.).**

Jubilees Chapter 27

1 And the words of Esau, her elder son, were told to Rebecca in a dream, and Rebecca sent and called Jacob her younger son, 2 and said unto him: 'Behold Esau thy brother will take vengeance on thee so as to kill thee. 3 Now, therefore, my son, obey my voice, and arise and flee thou to Laban, my brother, to Haran, and tarry with him a few days until thy brother's anger turns away, and he remove his anger from thee, and forget all that thou hast done; then I will send and fetch thee from thence.' 4 And Jacob said: 'I am not afraid; if he wishes to kill me, I will kill him.' 5 But she said unto him: 'Let me not be bereft of both my sons on one day.' 6 And Jacob said to Rebecca his mother: 'Behold, thou knowest that my father has become old, and does not see because his eyes are dull, and if I leave him it will be evil in his eyes, because I leave him and go away from you, and my father will be angry, and will curse me. I will not go; when he sends me, then only will I go.' 7 And Rebecca said to Jacob: 'I will go in and speak to him, and he will send thee away.' 8 And Rebecca went in and said to Isaac: 'I loathe my life because of the two daughters of Heth, whom Esau has taken him as wives; and if Jacob take a wife from among the daughters of the land such as these, for what purpose do I further live, for the daughters of Canaan are evil.' 9 And Isaac called Jacob and blessed him, and admonished him and said unto him: 'Do not take thee a wife of any of the daughters of Canaan; 10 arise and go to Mesopotamia, to the house of Bethuel, thy mother's father, and take thee a wife from thence of the daughters of Laban, thy mother's brother. 11 And God Almighty bless thee and increase and multiply thee that thou mayest become a company of nations, and give thee the blessings of my father Abraham, to thee and to thy seed after thee, that thou mayest inherit the land of thy sojournings and all the land which God gave to Abraham: go, my son, in peace.' 12 And Isaac sent Jacob away, and he went to Mesopotamia, to Laban the son of Bethuel the Syrian, the brother of Rebecca, Jacob's mother. 13 And it came to pass after Jacob had arisen to go to Mesopotamia that the spirit of Rebecca was grieved after her son, and she wept. 14 And Isaac said to Rebecca: 'My sister, weep not on account of Jacob, my son; for he goeth in peace, and in peace will he return. 15 The Most High God will preserve him from all evil, and will be with him; for He will not forsake him all his days; 16 For I know that his ways will be prospered in all things wherever he goes, until he return in peace to us, and we see him in peace. 17 Fear not on his account, my sister, for he is on the upright path and he is a perfect man: and he is faithful and will not perish. Weep not.' 18 And Isaac comforted Rebecca on account of her son Jacob, and blessed him. 19 And Jacob went from the Well of the Oath to go to Haran on the first year of the second week in the forty-fourth jubilee, and he came to Luz on the mountains, that is, Bethel, on the new moon of the first month of this week, [2115 A.M.] and he came to the place at even and turned from the way to the west of the road that night: and he slept there; for the sun had set. 20 And he took one of the stones of that place and laid it at his head under the tree, and he was journeying alone, and he slept. 21 And he dreamt that night, and behold a ladder set up on the earth, and the top of it reached to heaven, and behold, the angels of the Lord ascended and descended on it: and behold, the Lord stood upon it. 22 And he spake to Jacob and said: 'I am the Lord God of Abraham, thy father, and the God of Isaac; the land whereon thou art sleeping, to thee will I give it, and to thy seed after thee. 23 And thy seed shall be as the dust of the earth, and thou shalt increase to the west and to the east, to the north and the south, and in thee and in thy seed shall all the families of the nations be blessed. 24 And behold, I will be with thee, and will keep thee whithersoever thou goest, and I will bring thee again into this land in peace; for I will not leave thee until I do everything that I told thee of.' 25 And Jacob awoke from his sleep, and said, 'Truly this place is the house of the Lord, and I knew it not.' And he was afraid and said: 'Dreadful is this place which is none other than the house of God, and this is the gate of heaven.' 26 And Jacob arose early in the morning, and took the stone which he had put under his head and set it up as a pillar for a sign, and he poured oil upon the top of it. And he called the name of that place Bethel; but the name of the

place was Luz at the first. 27 And Jacob vowed a vow unto the Lord, saying: 'If the Lord will be with me, and will keep me in this way that I go, and give me bread to eat and raiment to put on, so that I come again to my father's house in peace, then shall the Lord be my God, and this stone which I have set up as a pillar for a sign in this place, shall be the Lord's house, and of all that thou givest me, I shall give the tenth to thee, my God.'**Jacob's Marriage to Leah and Rachel; his Children and Riches (xxviii. i- 30; cf. Gen. xxix., xxx., xxxi. 1-2).**

Jubilees Chapter 28

1 And he went on his journey, and came to the land of the east, to Laban, the brother of Rebecca, and he was with him, and served him for Rachel his daughter one week. 2 And in the first year of the third week he said unto him: 'Give me my wife, for whom I have served thee seven years'; and Laban said unto Jacob: 'I will give thee thy wife.' 3 And Laban made a feast, and took Leah his elder daughter, and gave her to Jacob as a wife, and gave her Zilpah his handmaid for an handmaid; and Jacob did not know, for he thought that she was Rachel. 4 And he went in unto her, and behold, she was Leah; and Jacob was wroth with Laban, and said unto him: 'Why hast thou dealt thus with me? Did not I serve thee for Rachel and not for Leah? Why hast thou wronged me? Take thy daughter, and I will go; for thou hast done evil to me.' 5 For Jacob loved Rachel more than Leah; for Leah's eyes were weak, but her form was very handsome; but Rachel had beautiful eyes and a beautiful and very handsome form. 6 And Laban said to Jacob: 'It is not so done in our country, to give the younger before the elder.' And it is not right to do this; for thus it is ordained and written in the heavenly tablets, that no one should give his younger daughter before the elder; but the elder one gives first and after her the younger-and the man who doeth so, they set down guilt against him in heaven, and none is righteous that doeth this thing, for this deed is evil before the Lord. 7 And command thou the children of Israel that they do not this thing; let them neither take nor give the younger before they have given the elder, for it is very wicked. 8 And Laban said to Jacob: 'Let the seven days of the feast of this one pass by, and I shall give thee Rachel, that thou mayest serve me another seven years, that thou mayest pasture my sheep as thou didst in the former week.' 9 And on the day when the seven days of the feast of Leah had passed, Laban gave Rachel to Jacob, that he might serve him another seven years, and he gave to Rachel Bilhah, the sister of Zilpah, as a handmaid. 10 And he served yet other seven years for Rachel, for Leah had been given to him for nothing. 11 And the Lord opened the womb of Leah, and she conceived and bare Jacob a son, and he called his name Reuben, on the fourteenth day of the ninth month, in the first year of the third week. 12 But the womb of Rachel was closed, for the Lord saw that Leah was hated and Rachel loved. 13 And again Jacob went in unto Leah, and she conceived, and bare Jacob a second son, and he called his name Simeon, on the twenty-first of the tenth month, and in the third year of this week. 14 And again Jacob went in unto Leah, and she conceived, and bare him a third son, and he called his name Levi, in the new moon of the first month in the sixth year of this week. 15 And again Jacob went in unto her, and she conceived, and bare him a fourth son, and he called his name Judah, on the fifteenth of the third month, in the first year of the fourth week. 16 And on account of all this Rachel envied Leah, for she did not bear, and she said to Jacob: 'Give me children'; and Jacob said: 'Have I withheld from thee the fruits of thy womb? Have I forsaken thee?' 17 And when Rachel saw that Leah had borne four sons to Jacob, Reuben, and Simeon, and Levi, and Judah, she said unto him: 'Go in unto Bilhah, my handmaid, and she will conceive, and bear a son unto me.' 18 (And she gave (him) Bilhah her handmaid to wife.) And he went in unto her, and she conceived, and bare him a son, and he called his name Dan, on the ninth of the sixth month, in the sixth year of the third week. 19 And Jacob went in again unto Bilhah a second time, and she conceived, and bare Jacob another son, and Rachel called his name Naphtali, on the fifth of the seventh month, in the second year of the fourth week. 20 And when Leah saw that she had become sterile and did not bear, she envied Rachel, and she also gave her handmaid Zilpah to Jacob to wife, and she conceived and bare him a son, and Leah called his name Gad, on the twelfth of the eighth month, in the third year of the fourth week. 21 And he went in again unto her, and she conceived and bare him a second son, and Leah called his name Asher, on the second of the eleventh month, in the fifth year of the fourth week. 22 And Jacob went in unto Leah, and she conceived and bare a son, and she called his name Issachar, on the fourth of the fifth month, in the fourth year of the fourth week, and she gave him to a nurse. 23 And Jacob went in again unto her, and she conceived and bare two children, a son and a daughter, and she called the name of the son Zebulun, and the name of the daughter Dinah, in the seventh of the seventh month, in the sixth year of the fourth week. 24 And the Lord was gracious to Rachel, and opened her womb, and she

conceived, and bare a son, and she called his name Joseph, on the new moon of the fourth month, in the sixth year in this fourth week. 25 And in the days when Joseph was born, Jacob said to Laban: 'Give me my wives and sons, and let me go to my father Isaac, and let me make me an house, for I have completed the years in which I have served thee for thy two daughters, and I will go to the house of my father.' 26 And Laban said to Jacob: 'Tarry with me for thy wages, and pasture my flock for me again, and take thy wages.' 27 And they agreed with one another that he should give him as his wages those of the lambs and kids which were born black and spotted and white, these were to be his wages. 28 And all the sheep brought forth spotted and speckled and black, variously marked, and they brought forth again lambs like themselves, and all that were spotted were Jacob's and those which were not were Laban's. 29 And the possessions of Jacob multiplied exceedingly, and he possessed oxen and sheep and asses and camels, and menservants and maidservants. 30 And Laban and his sons envied Jacob, and Laban took back his sheep from him, and he observed him with evil intent.**Jacob's Flight with his Family: his Covenant with Laban (xxix. 1-12; cf. Gen, xxxi.).**

Jubilees Chapter 29

1 And it came to pass when Rachel had borne Joseph, that Laban went to shear his sheep; for they were distant from him a three days' journey. 2 And Jacob saw that Laban was going to shear his sheep, and Jacob called Leah and Rachel, and spake kindly unto them that they should come with him to the land of Canaan. 3 For he told them how he had seen everything in a dream, even all that he had spoken unto him that he should return to his father's house; and they said: 'To every place whither thou goest we will go with thee.' 4 And Jacob blessed the God of Isaac his father, and the God of Abraham his father's father, and he arose and mounted his wives and his children, and took all his possessions and crossed the river and came to the land of Gilead, and Jacob hid his intention from Laban and told him not. 5 And in the seventh year of the fourth week Jacob turned his face toward Gilead in the first month on the twenty-first thereof, and Laban pursued after him and overtook Jacob in the mountain of Gilead in the third month, on the thirteenth thereof. 6 And the Lord did not suffer him to injure Jacob; for he appeared to him in a dream by night. And Laban spake to Jacob. 7 And on the fifteenth of those days Jacob made a feast for Laban, and for all who came with him, and Jacob sware to Laban that day, and Laban also to Jacob, that neither should cross the mountain of Gilead to the other with evil purpose. 8 And he made there a heap for a witness; wherefore the name of that place is called: 'The Heap of Witness,' after this heap. 9 But before they used to call the land of Gilead the land of the Rephaim; for it was the land of the Rephaim, and the Rephaim were born there, giants whose height was ten, nine, eight down to seven cubits. 10 And their habitation was from the land of the children of Ammon to Mount Hermon, and the seats of their kingdom were Karnaim and Ashtaroth, and Edrei, and Misur, and Beon. 11 And the Lord destroyed them because of the evil of their deeds; for they were very malignant, and the Amorites dwelt in their stead, wicked and sinful, and there is no people today which has wrought to the full all their sins, and they have no longer length of life on the earth. 12 And Jacob sent away Laban, and he departed into Mesopotamia, the land of the east, and Jacob returned to the land of Gilead. **Jacob, reconciled with Esau, dwells in Canaan and supports his Parents (xxix. 13-20; Cf. Gen. xxxii., xxxiii.).** 13 And he passed over the Jabbok in the ninth month, on the eleventh thereof, and on that day Esau, his brother, came to him, and he was reconciled to him, and departed from him unto the land of Seir, but Jacob dwelt in tents. 14 And in the first year of the fifth week in this jubilee he crossed the Jordan, and dwelt beyond the Jordan, and he pastured his sheep from the sea of the heap unto Bethshan and unto Dothan and unto the forest of Akrabbim. 15 And he sent to his father Isaac of all his substance, clothing and food and meat, and drink, and milk, and butter, and cheese, and some dates of the valley. 16 And to his mother Rebecca also four times a year, between the times of the months, between ploughing and reaping, and between autumn and the rain season and between winter and spring, to the tower of Abraham. 17 For Isaac had returned from the Well of the Oath and gone up to the tower of his father Abraham, and he dwelt there apart from his son Esau. 18 For in the days when Jacob went to Mesopotamia, Esau took to himself a wife Mahalath, the daughter of Ishmael, and he gathered together all the flocks of his father and his wives, and went up and dwelt on Mount Seir, and left Isaac, his father, at the Well of the Oath alone. 19 And Isaac went up from the Well of the Oath and dwelt in the tower of Abraham his father on the mountains of Hebron, 20 and thither Jacob sent all that he did send to his father and his mother from time to time, all they needed, and they blessed Jacob with all their heart and with all their soul.**Dinah ravished.**

Slaughter of the Shechemites. Laws against Intermarriage between Israel and the Heathen. The Choice of Levi (xxx. 1-26; cf. Gen. xxxiv.).

Jubilees Chapter 30

1 And in the first year of the sixth week [2143 A.M.] he went up to Salem, to the east of Shechem, in peace, in the fourth month. 2 And there they carried off Dinah, the daughter of Jacob, into the house of Shechem, the son of Hamor, the Hivite, the prince of the land, and he lay with her and defiled her, and she was a little girl, a child of twelve years. 3 And he besought his father and her brothers that she might be given to him to wife. And Jacob and his sons were wroth because of the men of Shechem; for they had defiled Dinah, their sister, and they spake to them with evil intent and dealt deceitfully with them and beguiled them. 4 And Simeon and Levi came unexpectedly to Shechem and executed judgment on all the men of Shechem, and slew all the men whom they found in it, and left not a single one remaining in it: they slew all in torments because they had dishonoured their sister Dinah. 5 And thus let it not again be done from henceforth that a daughter of Israel be defiled; for judgment is ordained in heaven against them that they should destroy with the sword all the men of the Shechemites because they had wrought shame in Israel. 6 And the Lord delivered them into the hands of the sons of Jacob that they might exterminate them with the sword and execute judgment upon them, and that it might not thus again be done in Israel that a virgin of Israel should be defiled. 7 And if there is any man who wishes in Israel to give his daughter or his sister to any man who is of the seed of the Gentiles he shall surely die, and they shall stone him with stones; for he hath wrought shame in Israel; and they shall burn the woman with fire, because she has dishonoured the name of the house of her father, and she shall be rooted out of Israel. 8 And let not an adulteress and no uncleanness be found in Israel throughout all the days of the generations of the earth; for Israel is holy unto the Lord, and every man who has defiled (it) shall surely die: they shall stone him with stones. 9 For thus has it been ordained and written in the heavenly tablets regarding all the seed of Israel: he who defileth (it) shall surely die, and he shall be stoned with stones. 10 And to this law there is no limit of days, nor remission, nor any atonement: but the man who has defiled his daughter shall be rooted out in the midst of all Israel, because he has given of his seed to Moloch, and wrought impiously so as to defile it. 11 And do thou, Moses, command the children of Israel and exhort them not to give their daughters to the Gentiles, and not to take for their sons any of the daughters of the Gentiles, for this is abominable before the Lord. 12 For this reason I have written for thee in the words of the Law all the deeds of the Shechemites, which they wrought against Dinah, and how the sons of Jacob spake, saying: 'We will not give our daughter to a man who is uncircumcised; for that were a reproach unto us.' 13 And it is a reproach to Israel, to those who live, and to those that take the daughters of the Gentiles; for this is unclean and abominable to Israel. 14 And Israel will not be free from this uncleanness if it has a wife of the daughters of the Gentiles, or has given any of its daughters to a man who is of any of the Gentiles. 15 For there will be plague upon plague, and curse upon curse, and every judgment and plague and curse will come upon him: if he do this thing, or hide his eyes from those who commit uncleanness, or those who defile the sanctuary of the Lord, or those who profane His holy name, (then) will the whole nation together be judged for all the uncleanness and profanation of this man. 16 And there will be no respect of persons [and no consideration of persons] and no receiving at his hands of fruits and offerings and burnt-offerings and fat, nor the fragrance of sweet savour, so as to accept it: and so fare every man or woman in Israel who defiles the sanctuary. 17 For this reason I have commanded thee, saying: 'Testify this testimony to Israel: see how the Shechemites fared and their sons: how they were delivered into the hands of two sons of Jacob, and they slew them under tortures, and it was (reckoned) unto them for righteousness, and it is written down to them for righteousness. 18 And the seed of Levi was chosen for the priesthood, and to be Levites, that they might minister before the Lord, as we, continually, and that Levi and his sons may be blessed for ever; for he was zealous to execute righteousness and judgment and vengeance on all those who arose against Israel. 19 And so they inscribe as a testimony in his favour on the heavenly tablets blessing and righteousness before the God of all: 20 And we remember the righteousness which the man fulfilled during his life, at all periods of the year; until a thousand generations they will record it, and it will come to him and to his descendants after him, and he has been recorded on the heavenly tablets as a friend and a righteous man. 21 All this account I have written for thee, and have commanded thee to say to the children of Israel, that they should not commit sin nor transgress the ordinances nor break the covenant which has been

ordained for them, (but) that they should fulfil it and be recorded as friends. 22 But if they transgress and work uncleanness in every way, they will be recorded on the heavenly tablets as adversaries, and they will be destroyed out of the book of life, and they will be recorded in the book of those who will be destroyed and with those who will be rooted out of the earth· 23 And on the day when the sons of Jacob slew Shechem a writing was recorded in their favour in heaven that they had executed righteousness and uprightness and vengeance on the sinners, and it was written for a blessing. 24 And they brought Dinah, their sister, out of the house of Shechem, and they took captive everything that was in Shechem, their sheep and their oxen and their asses, and all their wealth, and all their flocks, and brought them all to Jacob their father. 25 And he reproached them because they had put the city to the sword for he feared those who dwelt in the land, the Canaanites and the Perizzites. 26 And the dread of the Lord was upon all the cities which are around about Shechem, and they did not rise to pursue after the sons of Jacob; for terror had fallen upon them. Jacob's Journey to Bethel and Hebron. **Isaac blesses Levi and Judah (xxxi. 1-25; cf. Gen. xxxv.).**

Jubilees Chapter 31

1 And on the new moon of the month Jacob spake to all the people of his house. saying: 'Purify yourselves and change your garments, and let us arise and go up to Bethel, where I vowed a vow to Him on the day when I fled from the face of Esau my brother, because he has been with me and brought me into this land in peace, and put ye away the strange gods that arc among you.' 2 And they gave up the strange gods and that which was in their ears and which was on their necks and the idols which Rachel stole from Laban her father she gave wholly to Jacob. And he burnt and brake them to pieces and destroyed them, and hid them under an oak which is in the land of Shechem. 3 And he went up on the new moon of the seventh month to Bethel. And he built an altar at the place where he had slept, and he set up a pillar there, and he sent word to his father Isaac to come to him to his sacrifice, and to his mother Rebecca. 4 And Isaac said: 'Let my son Jacob come, and let me see him before I die.' 5 And Jacob went to his father Isaac and to his mother Rebecca, to the house of his father Abraham, and he took two of his sons with him, Levi and Judah, and he came to his father Isaac and to his mother Rebecca. 6 And Rebecca came forth from the tower to the front of it to kiss Jacob and embrace him; for her spirit had revived when she heard: 'Behold Jacob thy son has come'; and she kissed him. 7 And she saw his two sons, and she recognised them, and said unto him: 'Are these thy sons, my son?' and she embraced them and kissed them, and blessed them, saying: 'In you shall the seed of Abraham become illustrious, and ye shall prove a blessing on the earth.' 8 And Jacob went in to Isaac his father, to the chamber where he lay, and his two sons were with him, and he took the hand of his father, and stooping down he kissed him, and Isaac clung to the neck of Jacob his son, and wept upon his neck. 9 And the darkness left the eyes of Isaac, and he saw the two sons of Jacob, Levi, and Judah, and he said: 'Are these thy sons, my son? for they are like thee.' 10 And he said unto him that they were truly his sons: 'And thou hast truly seen that they are truly my sons'. 11 And they came near to him, and he turned and kissed them and embraced them both together. 12 And the spirit of prophecy came down into his mouth, and he took Levi by his right hand and Judah by his left. 13 And he turned to Levi first, and began to bless him first, and said unto him: May the God of all, the very Lord of all the ages, bless thee and thy children throughout all the ages· 14 And may the Lord give to thee and to thy seed greatness and great glory, and cause thee and thy seed, from among all flesh, to approach Him to serve in His sanctuary as the angels of the presence and as the holy ones. (Even) as they, shall the seed of thy sons be for glory and greatness and holiness, and may He make them great unto all the ages. 15 And they shall be judges and princes, and chiefs of all the seed of the sons of Jacob; They shall speak the word of the Lord in righteousness, And they shall judge all His judgments in righteousness. And they shall declare My ways to Jacob And My paths to Israel. The blessing of the Lord shall be given in their mouths To bless all the seed of the beloved. 16 Thy mother has called thy name Levi, And justly has she called thy name; Thou shalt be joined to the Lord And be the companion of all the sons of Jacob; Let His table be thine, And do thou and thy sons eat thereof; And may thy table be full unto all generations, And thy food fail not unto all the ages. 17 And let all who hate thee fall down before thee, And let all thy adversaries be rooted out and perish; And blessed be he that blesses thee, And cursed be every nation that curses thee.' 18 And to Judah he said: 'May the Lord give thee strength and power To tread down all that hate thee; A prince shalt thou be, thou and one of thy sons, over the sons of Jacob; May thy name and the name of thy sons go forth and traverse every land and region. Then shall the Gentiles fear before thy face, And all the nations shall quake

[And all the peoples shall quake]. 19 In thee shall be the help of Jacob, And in thee be found the salvation of Israel. 20 And when thou sittest on the throne of honour of thy righteousness There shall be great peace for all the seed of the sons of the beloved; Blessed be he that blesseth thee, And all that hate thee and afflict thee and curse thee Shall be rooted out and destroyed from the earth and be accursed.' 21 And turning he kissed him again and embraced him, and rejoiced greatly; for he had seen the sons of Jacob his son in very truth. 22 And he went forth from between his feet and fell down and bowed down to him, and he blessed them and rested there with Isaac his father that night, and they eat and drank with joy. 23 And he made the two sons of Jacob sleep, the one on his right hand and the other on his left, and it was counted to him for righteousness. 24 And Jacob told his father everything during the night, how the Lord had shown him great mercy, and how he had prospered (him in) all his ways, and protected him from all evil. 25 And Isaac blessed the God of his father Abraham, who had not withdrawn his mercy and his righteousness from the sons of his servant Isaac. **Rebecca journeys with Jacob to Bethel (xxxi. 26-32).** 26 And in the morning Jacob told his father Isaac the vow which he had vowed to the Lord, and the vision which he had seen, and that he had built an altar, and that everything was ready for the sacrifice to be made before the Lord as he had vowed, and that he had come to set him on an ass. 27 And Isaac said unto Jacob his son: 'I am not able to go with thee; for I am old and not able to bear the way: go, my son, in peace; for I am one hundred and sixty-five years this day; I am no longer able to journey; set thy mother (on an ass) and let her go with thee. 28 And I know, my son, that thou hast come on my account, and may this day be blessed on which thou hast seen me alive, and I also have seen thee, my son. 29 Mayest thou prosper and fulfil the vow which thou hast vowed; and put not off thy vow; for thou shalt be called to account as touching the vow; now therefore make haste to perform it, and may He be pleased who has made all things, to whom thou hast vowed the vow.' 30 And he said to Rebecca: 'Go with Jacob thy son'; and Rebecca went with Jacob her son, and Deborah with her, and they came to Bethel. 31 And Jacob remembered the prayer with which his father had blessed him and his two sons, Levi and Judah, and he rejoiced and blessed the God of his fathers, Abraham and Isaac. 32 And he said: 'Now I know that I have an eternal hope, and my sons also, before the God of all'; and thus is it ordained concerning the two; and they record it as an eternal testimony unto them on the heavenly tablets how Isaac blessed them. **Levi's Dream at Bethel; he is appointed to the Priesthood. Jacob celebrates the Feast of Tabernacles and offers Tithes. The Institution of Tithes (xxxii. 1-15; cf. Gen. xxxv.).**

Jubilees Chapter 32

1 And he abode that night at Bethel, and Levi dreamed that they had ordained and made him the priest of the Most High God, him and his sons for ever; and he awoke from his sleep and blessed the Lord. 2 And Jacob rose early in the morning, on the fourteenth of this month, and he gave a tithe of all that came with him, both of men and cattle, both of gold and every vessel and garment, yea, he gave tithes of all. 3 And in those days Rachel became pregnant with her son Benjamin. And Jacob counted his sons from him upwards and Levi fell to the portion of the Lord, and his father clothed him in the garments of the priesthood and filled his hands. 4 And on the fifteenth of this month, he brought to the altar fourteen oxen from amongst the cattle, and twenty-eight rams, and forty-nine sheep, and seven lambs, and twenty-one kids of the goats as a burnt-offering on the altar of sacrifice, well pleasing for a sweet savour before God. 5 This was his offering, in consequence of the vow which he had vowed that he would give a tenth, with their fruit-offerings and their drink- offerings. 6 And when the fire had consumed it, he burnt incense on the fire over the fire, and for a thank-offering two oxen and four rams and four sheep, four he-goats, and two sheep of a year old, and two kids of the goats; and thus he did daily for seven days. 7 And he and all his sons and his men were eating (this) with joy there during seven days and blessing and thanking the Lord, who had delivered him out of all his tribulation and had given him his vow. 8 And he tithed all the clean animals, and made a burnt sacrifice, but the unclean animals he gave (not) to Levi his son, and he gave him all the souls of the men. 9 And Levi discharged the priestly office at Bethel before Jacob his father in preference to his ten brothers, and he was a priest there, and Jacob gave his vow: thus he tithed again the tithe to the Lord and sanctified it, and it became holy unto Him. 10 And for this reason it is ordained on the heavenly tablets as a law for the tithing again the tithe to eat before the Lord from year to year, in the place where it is chosen that His name should dwell, and to this law there is no limit of days for ever. 11 This ordinance is written that it may be fulfilled from year to year in eating the second tithe before the Lord in the place where it has been chosen, and nothing shall remain over from

it from this year to the year following. 12 For in its year shall the seed be eaten till the days of the gathering of the seed of the year, and the wine till the days of the wine, and the oil till the days of its season. 13 And all that is left thereof and becomes old, let it be regarded as polluted: let it be burnt with fire, for it is unclean. 14 And thus let them eat it together in the sanctuary, and let them not suffer it to become old. 15 And all the tithes of the oxen and sheep shall be holy unto the Lord, and shall belong to his priests, which they will eat before Him from year to year; for thus is it ordained and engraven regarding the tithe on the heavenly tablets. **Jacob's Visions. He celebrates the eighth day of Tabernacles. The Birth of Benjamin and Death of Rachel (xxxii. 16-34; cf. Gen. xxxv.).** 16 And on the following night, on the twenty-second day of this month, Jacob resolved to build that place, and to surround the court with a wall, and to sanctify it and make it holy for ever, for himself and his children after him. 17 And the Lord appeared to him by night and blessed him and said unto him: 'Thy name shall not be called Jacob, but Israel shall they name thy name.' 18 And He said unto him again: 'I am the Lord who created the heaven and the earth, and I will increase thee and multiply thee exceedingly, and kings shall come forth from thee, and they shall judge everywhere wherever the foot of the sons of men has trodden. 19 And I will give to thy seed all the earth which is under heaven, and they shall judge all the nations according to their desires, and after that they shall get possession of the whole earth and inherit it for ever.' 20 And He finished speaking with him, and He went up from him. and Jacob looked till He had ascended into heaven. 21 And he saw in a vision of the night, and behold an angel descended from heaven with seven tablets in his hands, and he gave them to Jacob, and he read them and knew all that was written therein which would befall him and his sons throughout all the ages. 22 And he showed him all that was written on the tablets, and said unto him: 'Do not build this place, and do not make it an eternal sanctuary, and do not dwell here; for this is not the place. Go to the house of Abraham thy father and dwell with Isaac thy father until the day of the death of thy father. 23 For in Egypt thou shalt die in peace, and in this land thou shalt be buried with honour in the sepulchre of thy fathers, with Abraham and Isaac. 24 Fear not, for as thou hast seen and read it, thus shall it all be; and do thou write down everything as thou hast seen and read.' 25 And Jacob said: 'Lord, how can I remember all that I have read and seen? 'And he said unto him: 'I will bring all things to thy remembrance.' 26 And he went up from him, and he awoke from his sleep, and he remembered everything which he had read and seen, and he wrote down all the words which he had read and seen. 27 And he celebrated there yet another day, and he sacrificed thereon according to all that he sacrificed on the former days, and called its name 'Addition,' for this day was added and the former days he called 'The Feast '. 28 And thus it was manifested that it should be, and it is written on the heavenly tablets: wherefore it was revealed to him that he should celebrate it, and add it to the seven days of the feast. 29 And its name was called 'Addition,' because that it was recorded amongst the days of the feast days, according to the number of the days of the year. 30 And in the night, on the twenty-third of this month, Deborah Rebecca's nurse died, and they buried her beneath the city under the oak of the river, and he called the name of this place, 'The river of Deborah,' and the oak, 'The oak of the mourning of Deborah.' 31 And Rebecca went and returned to her house to his father Isaac, and Jacob sent by her hand rams and sheep and he-goats that she should prepare a meal for his father such as he desired. 32 And he went after his mother till he came to the land of Kabratan, and he dwelt there. 33 And Rachel bare a son in the night, and called his name 'Son of my sorrow '; for she suffered in giving him birth: but his father called his name Benjamin, on the eleventh of the eighth month in the first of the sixth week of this jubilee. [2143 A.M.] 34 And Rachel died there and she was buried in the land of Ephrath, the same is Bethlehem, and Jacob built a pillar on the grave of Rachel, on the road above her grave. **Reuben's Sin with Bilhah. Laws regarding Incest. Jacob's Children (xxxiii. 1-23; Cf. Gen. xxxv. 21-27).**

Jubilees Chapter 33

1 And Jacob went and dwelt to the south of Magdal90dra'ef. And he went to his father Isaac, he and Leah his wife, on the new moon of the tenth month. 2 And Reuben saw Bilhah, Rachel's maid, the concubine of his father, bathing in water in a secret place, and he loved her. 3 And he hid himself at night, and he entered the house of Bilhah [at night], and he found her sleeping alone on a bed in her house. 4 And he lay with her, and she awoke and saw, and behold Reuben was lying with her in the bed, and she uncovered the border of her covering and seized him, and cried out, and discovered that it was Reuben. 5 And she was ashamed because of him, and released her hand from him, and he fled. 6 And she lamented because of this thing exceedingly, and did not tell it to any one. 7 And when Jacob returned and sought her, she said unto him: 'I

am not clean for thee, for I have been defiled as regards thee; for Reuben has defiled me, and has lain with me in the night, and I was asleep, and did not discover until he uncovered my skirt and slept with me.' 8 And Jacob was exceedingly wroth with Reuben because he had lain with Bilhah, because he had uncovered his father's skirt. 9 And Jacob did not approach her again because Reuben had defiled her. And as for any man who uncovers his father's skirt his deed is wicked exceedingly, for he is abominable before the Lord. 10 For this reason it is written and ordained on the heavenly tablets that a man should not lie with his father's wife, and should not uncover his father's skirt, for this is unclean: they shall surely die together, the man who lies with his father's wife and the woman also, for they have wrought uncleanness on the earth. 11 And there shall be nothing unclean before our God in the nation which He has chosen for Himself as a possession. 12 And again, it is written a second time: 'Cursed be he who lieth with the wife of his father, for he hath uncovered his father's shame'; and all the holy ones of the Lord said 'So be it; so be it.' 13 And do thou, Moses, command the children of Israel that they observe this word; for it (entails) a punishment of death; and it is unclean, and there is no atonement for ever to atone for the man who has committed this, but he is to be put to death and slain, and stoned with stones, and rooted out from the midst of the people of our God. 14 For to no man who does so in Israel is it permitted to remain alive a single day on the earth, for he is abominable and unclean. 15 And let them not say: to Reuben was granted life and forgiveness after he had lain with his father's concubine, and to her also though she had a husband, and her husband Jacob, his father, was still alive. 16 For until that time there had not been revealed the ordinance and judgment and law in its completeness for all, but in thy days (it has been revealed) as a law of seasons and of days, and an everlasting law for the everlasting generations. 17 And for this law there is no consummation of days, and no atonement for it, but they must both be rooted out in the midst of the nation: on the day whereon they committed it they shall slay them. 18 And do thou, Moses, write (it) down for Israel that they may observe it, and do according to these words, and not commit a sin unto death; for the Lord our God is judge, who respects not persons and accepts not gifts. 19 And tell them these words of the covenant, that they may hear and observe, and be on their guard with respect to them, and not be destroyed and rooted out of the land; for an uncleanness, and an abomination, and a contamination, and a pollution are all they who commit it on the earth before our God. 20 And there is no greater sin than the fornication which they commit on earth; for Israel is a holy nation unto the Lord its God, and a nation of inheritance, and a priestly and royal nation and for (His own) possession; and there shall no such uncleanness appear in the midst of the holy nation. 21 And in the third year of this sixth week [2145 A.M.] Jacob and all his sons went and dwelt in the house of Abraham, near Isaac his father and Rebecca his mother. 22 And these were the names of the sons of Jacob: the first-born Reuben, Simeon, Levi, Judah, Issachar, Zebulon, the sons of Leah; and the sons of Rachel, Joseph and Benjamin; and the sons of Bilhah, Dan and Naphtali; and the sons of Zilpah, Gad and Asher; and Dinah, the daughter of Leah, the only daughter of Jacob. 23 And they came and bowed themselves to Isaac and Rebecca, and when they saw them they blessed Jacob and all his sons, and Isaac rejoiced exceedingly, for he saw the sons of Jacob, his younger son and he blessed them. **War of the Amorite Kings against Jacob and his Sons. Joseph sold into Egypt (cf. Gen. xxxvii.). The Death of Bilhah and Dinah (xxxiv. 1-19).**

Jubilees Chapter 34

1 And in the sixth year of this week of this forty-fourth jubilee [2148 A.M.] Jacob sent his sons to pasture their sheep, and his servants with them to the pastures of Shechem. 2 And the seven kings of the Amorites assembled themselves together against them, to slay them, hiding themselves under the trees, and to take their cattle as a prey. 3 And Jacob and Levi and Judah and Joseph were in the house with Isaac their father; for his spirit was sorrowful, and they could not leave him: and Benjamin was the youngest, and for this reason remained with his father. 4 And there came the king[s] of Taphu and the king[s] of 'Aresa, and the king[s] of Seragan, and the king[s] of Selo, and the king[s] of Ga'as, and the king of Bethoron, and the king of Ma'anisakir, and all those who dwell in these mountains (and) who dwell in the woods in the land of Canaan. 5 And they announced this to Jacob saying: 'Behold, the kings of the Amorites have surrounded thy sons, and plundered their herds.' 6 And he arose from his house, he and his three sons and all the servants of his father, and his own servants, and he went against them with six thousand men, who carried swords. 7 And he slew them in the pastures of Shechem, and pursued those who fled, and he slew them with the edge of the sword, and he slew 'Aresa and Taphu and Saregan and Selo and 'Amani- sakir and Ga[ga]'as, and he recovered his

herds. 8 And he prevailed over them, and imposed tribute on them that they should pay him tribute, five fruit products of their land, and he built Robel and Tamnatares. 9 And he returned in peace, and made peace with them, and they became his servants, until the day that he and his sons went down into Egypt. 10 And in the seventh year of this week [2149 A.M.] he sent Joseph to learn about the welfare of his brothers from his house to the land of Shechem, and he found them in the land of Dothan. 11 And they dealt treacherously with him, and formed a plot against him to slay him, but changing their minds, they sold him to Ishmaelite merchants, and they brought him down into Egypt, and they sold him to Potiphar, the eunuch of Pharaoh, the chief of the cooks, priest of the city of 'Elew. 12 And the sons of Jacob slaughtered a kid, and dipped the coat of Joseph in the blood, and sent (it) to Jacob their father on the tenth of the seventh month. 13 And he mourned all that night, for they had brought it to him in the evening, and he became feverish with mourning for his death, and he said: 'An evil beast hath devoured Joseph'; and all the members of his house [mourned with him that day, and they] were grieving and mourning with him all that day. 14 And his sons and his daughter rose up to comfort him, but he refused to be comforted for his son. 15 And on that day Bilhah heard that Joseph had perished, and she died mourning him, and she was living in Qafratef, and Dinah also, his daughter, died after Joseph had perished. 16 And there came these three mournings upon Israel in one month. And they buried Bilhah over against the tomb of Rachel, and Dinah also. his daughter, they buried there. 17 And he mourned for Joseph one year, and did not cease, for he said 'Let me go down to the grave mourning for my son'. 18 For this reason it is ordained for the children of Israel that they should afflict themselves on the tenth of the seventh month -on the day that the news which made him weep for Joseph came to Jacob his father- that they should make atonement for themselves thereon with a young goat on the tenth of the seventh month, once a year, for their sins; for they had grieved the affection of their father regarding Joseph his son. 19 And this day has been ordained that they should grieve thereon for their sins, and for all their transgressions and for all their errors, so that they might cleanse themselves on that day once a year. **The Wives of Jacob's Sons (xxxiv. 20-21).** 20 And after Joseph perished, the sons of Jacob took unto themselves wives. The name of Reuben's wife is 'Ada; and the name of Simeon's wife is 'Adlba'a, a Canaanite; and the name of Levi's wife is Melka, of the daughters of Aram, of the seed of the sons of Terah; and the name of Judah's wife, Betasu'el, a Canaanite; and the name of Issachar's wife, Hezaqa: and the name of Zabulon's wife, Ni'iman; and the name of Dan's wife, 'Egla; and the name of Naphtali's wife, Rasu'u, of Mesopotamia; and the name of Gad's wife, Maka; and the name of Asher's wife, 'Ijona; and the name of Joseph's wife, Asenath, the Egyptian; and the name of Benjamin's wife, 'Ijasaka. 21 And Simeon repented, and took a second wife from Mesopotamia as his brothers. **Rebecca's Last Admonitions and Death (xxxv. 1-27).**

Jubilees Chapter 35

1 And in the first year of the first week of the forty-fifth jubilee [2157 A.M.] Rebecca called Jacob, her son, and commanded him regarding his father and regarding his brother, that he should honour them all the days of his life. 2 And Jacob said: 'I will do everything as thou hast commanded me; for this thing will be honour and greatness to me, and righteousness before the Lord, that I should honour them. 3 And thou too, mother, knowest from the time I was born until this day, all my deeds and all that is in my heart, that I always think good concerning all. 4 And how should I not do this thing which thou hast commanded me, that I should honour my father and my brother! 5 Tell me, mother, what perversity hast thou seen in me and I shall turn away from it, and mercy will be upon me.' 6 And she said unto him: 'My son, I have not seen in thee all my days any perverse but (only) upright deeds. And yet I will tell thee the truth, my son: I shall die this year, and I shall not survive this year in my life; for I have seen in a dream the day of my death, that I should not live beyond a hundred and fifty-five years: and behold I have completed all the days of my life which I am to live.' 7 And Jacob laughed at the words of his mother. because his mother had said unto him that she should die; and she was sitting opposite to him in possession of her strength, and she was not infirm in her strength; for she went in and out and saw, and her teeth were strong, and no ailment had touched her all the days of her life. 8 And Jacob said unto her: 'Blessed am I, mother, if my days approach the days of thy life, and my strength remain with me thus as thy strength: and thou wilt not die, for thou art jesting idly with me regarding thy death.' 9 And she went in to Isaac and said unto him: 'One petition I make unto thee: make Esau swear that he will not injure Jacob, nor pursue him with enmity; for thou knowest Esau's thoughts that they are perverse from his youth, and there is no goodness in him; for he desires after thy death to kill

him. 10 And thou knowest all that he has done since the day Jacob his brother went to Haran until this day: how he has forsaken us with his whole heart, and has done evil to us; thy flocks he has taken to himself, and carried off all thy possessions from before thy face. 11 And when we implored and besought him for what was our own, he did as a man who was taking pity on us. 12 And he is bitter against thee because thou didst bless Jacob thy perfect and upright son; for there is no evil but only goodness in him, and since he came from Haran unto this day he has not robbed us of aught, for he brings us everything in its season always, and rejoices with all his heart when we take at his hands and he blesses us, and has not parted from us since he came from Haran until this day, and he remains with us continually at home honouring us.' 13 And Isaac said unto her: 'I, too, know and see the deeds of Jacob who is with us, how that with all his heart he honours us; but I loved Esau formerly more than Jacob, because he was the firstborn; but now I love Jacob more than Esau, for he has done manifold evil deeds, and there is no righteousness in him, for all his ways are unrighteousness and violence, [and there is no righteousness around him.] 14 And now my heart is troubled because of all his deeds, and neither he nor his seed is to be saved, for they are those who will be destroyed from the earth and who will be rooted out from under heaven, for he has forsaken the God of Abraham and gone after his wives and after their uncleanness and after their error, he and his children. 15 And thou dost bid me make him swear that he will not slay Jacob his brother; even if he swear he will not abide by his oath, and he will not do good but evil only. 16 But if he desires to slay Jacob, his brother, into Jacob's hands will he be given, and he will not escape from his hands, [for he will descend into his hands.] 17 And fear thou not on account of Jacob; for the guardian of Jacob is great and powerful and honoured, and praised more than the guardian of Esau.' 18 And Rebecca sent and called Esau and he came to her, and she said unto him: 'I have a petition, my son, to make unto thee, and do thou promise to do it, my son.' 19 And he said: 'I will do everything that thou sayest unto me, and I will not refuse thy petition.' 20 And she said unto him: 'I ask you that the day I die, thou wilt take me in and bury me near Sarah, thy father's mother, and that thou and Jacob will love each other and that neither will desire evil against the other, but mutual love only, and (so) ye will prosper, my sons, and be honoured in the midst of the land, and no enemy will rejoice over you, and ye will be a blessing and a mercy in the eyes of all those that love you.' 21 And he said: 'I will do all that thou hast told me, and I shall bury thee on the day thou diest near Sarah, my father's mother, as thou hast desired that her bones may be near thy bones. 22 And Jacob, my brother, also, I shall love above all flesh; for I have not a brother in all the earth but him only: and this is no great merit for me if I love him; for he is my brother, and we were sown together in thy body, and together came we forth from thy womb, and if I do not love my brother, whom shall I love? 23 And I, myself, beg thee to exhort Jacob concerning me and concerning my sons, for I know that he will assuredly be king over me and my sons, for on the day my father blessed him he made him the higher and me the lower. 24 And I swear unto thee that I shall love him, and not desire evil against him all the days of my life but good only.' 25 And he sware unto her regarding all this matter. And she called Jacob before the eyes of Esau, and gave him commandment according to the words which she had spoken to Esau. 26 And he said: 'I shall do thy pleasure; believe me that no evil will proceed from me or from my sons against Esau, and I shall be first in naught save in love only.' 27 And they eat and drank, she and her sons that night, and she died, three jubilees and one week and one year old, on that night, and her two sons, Esau and Jacob, buried her in the double cave near Sarah, their father's mother. **Isaac's Last Words and Admonitions: his Death. The Death of Leah (xxxvi. 1-24).**

Jubilees Chapter 36

1 And in the sixth year of this week [2162 A.M.] Isaac called his two sons Esau and Jacob, and they came to him, and he said unto them: 'My sons, I am going the way of my fathers, to the eternal house where my fathers are. 2 Wherefore bury me near Abraham my father, in the double cave in the field of Ephron the Hittite, where Abraham purchased a sepulchre to bury in; in the sepulchre which I digged for myself, there bury me. 3 And this I command you, my sons, that ye practise righteousness and uprightness on the earth, so that the Lord may bring upon you all that the Lord said that he would do to Abraham and to his seed. 4 And love one another, my sons, your brothers as a man who loves his own soul, and let each seek in what he may benefit his brother, and act together on the earth; and let them love each other as their own souls. 5 And concerning the question of idols, I command and admonish you to reject them and hate them, and love them not, for they are full of deception for those that worship them and for those that bow down to them. 6 Remember ye, my sons, the Lord God of Abraham your father,

and how I too worshipped Him and served Him in righteousness and in joy, that He might multiply you and increase your seed as the stars of heaven in multitude, and establish you on the earth as the plant of righteousness which will not be rooted out unto all the generations for ever. 7 And now I shall make you swear a great oath -for there is no oath which is greater than it by the name glorious and honoured and great and splendid and wonderful and mighty, which created the heavens and the earth and all things together- that ye will fear Him and worship Him. 8 And that each will love his brother with affection and righteousness, and that neither will desire evil against his brother from henceforth for ever all the days of your life so that ye may prosper in all your deeds and not be destroyed. 9 And if either of you devises evil against his brother, know that from henceforth everyone that devises evil against his brother shall fall into his hand, and shall be rooted out of the land of the living, and his seed shall be destroyed from under heaven. 10 But on the day of turbulence and execration and indignation and anger, with flaming devouring fire as He burnt Sodom, so likewise will He burn his land and his city and all that is his, and he shall be blotted out of the book of the discipline of the children of men, and not be recorded in the book of life, but in that which is appointed to destruction, and he shall depart into eternal execration; so that their condemnation may be always renewed in hate and in execration and in wrath and in torment and in indignation and in plagues and in disease for ever. 11 I say and testify to you, my sons, according to the judgment which shall come upon the man who wishes to injure his brother. 12 And he divided all his possessions between the two on that day and he gave the larger portion to him that was the first-born, and the tower and all that was about it, and all that Abraham possessed at the Well of the Oath. 13 And he said: 'This larger portion I will give to the firstborn.' 14 And Esau said, 'I have sold to Jacob and given my birthright to Jacob; to him let it be given, and I have not a single word to say regarding it, for it is his.' 15 And Isaac said, May a blessing rest upon you, my sons, and upon your seed this day, for ye have given me rest, and my heart is not pained concerning the birthright, lest thou shouldest work wickedness on account of it. 16 May the Most High God bless the man that worketh righteousness, him and his seed for ever.' 17 And he ended commanding them and blessing them, and they eat and drank together before him, and he rejoiced because there was one mind between them, and they went forth from him and rested that day and slept. 18 And Isaac slept on his bed that day rejoicing; and he slept the eternal sleep, and died one hundred and eighty years old. He completed twenty-five weeks and five years; and his two sons Esau and Jacob buried him. 19 And Esau went to the land of Edom, to the mountains of Seir, and dwelt there. 20 And Jacob dwelt in the mountains of Hebron, in the tower of the land of the sojournings of his father Abraham, and he worshipped the Lord with all his heart and according to the visible commands according as He had divided the days of his generations. 21 And Leah his wife died in the fourth year of the second week of the forty-fifth jubilee, [2167 A.M.] and he buried her in the double cave near Rebecca his mother to the left of the grave of Sarah, his father's mother 22 and all her sons and his sons came to mourn over Leah his wife with him and to comfort him regarding her, for he was lamenting her for he loved her exceedingly after Rachel her sister died; 23 for she was perfect and upright in all her ways and honoured Jacob, and all the days that she lived with him he did not hear from her mouth a harsh word, for she was gentle and peaceable and upright and honourable. 24 And he remembered all her deeds which she had done during her life and he lamented her exceedingly; for he loved her with all his heart and with all his soul.**Esau and his Sons wage War with Jacob (xxxvii. 1-25).**

Jubilees Chapter 37

1 And on the day that Isaac the father of Jacob and Esau died, [2162 A.M.] the sons of Esau heard that Isaac had given the portion of the elder to his younger son Jacob and they were very angry. 2 And they strove with their father, saying 'Why has thy father given Jacob the portion of the elder and passed over thee, although thou art the elder and Jacob the younger?' 3 And he said unto them 'Because I sold my birthright to Jacob for a small mess of lentils, and on the day my father sent me to hunt and catch and bring him something that he should eat and bless me, he came with guile and brought my father food and drink, and my father blessed him and put me under his hand. 4 And now our father has caused us to swear, me and him, that we shall not mutually devise evil, either against his brother, and that we shall continue in love and in peace each with his brother and not make our ways corrupt.' 5 And they said unto him, 'We shall not hearken unto thee to make peace with him; for our strength is greater than his strength, and we are more powerful than he; we shall go against him and slay him, and destroy him and his sons. And if thou wilt not go with us, we shall do hurt to

thee also. 6 And now hearken unto us: Let us send to Aram and Philistia and Moab and Ammon, and let us choose for ourselves chosen men who are ardent for battle, and let us go against him and do battle with him, and let us exterminate him from the earth before he grows strong.' 7 And their father said unto them, 'Do not go and do not make war with him lest ye fall before him.' 8 And they said unto him, 'This too, is exactly thy mode of action from thy youth until this day, and thou art putting thy neck under his yoke. 9 We shall not hearken to these words.' And they sent to Aram, and to 'Aduram to the friend of their father, and they hired along with them one thousand fighting men, chosen men of war. 10 And there came to them from Moab and from the children of Ammon, those who were hired, one thousand chosen men, and from Philistia, one thousand chosen men of war, and from Edom and from the Horites one thousand chosen fighting men, and from the Kittim mighty men of war. 11 And they said unto their father: Go forth with them and lead them, else we shall slay thee.' 12 And he was filled with wrath and indignation on seeing that his sons were forcing him to go before (them) to lead them against Jacob his brother. 13 But afterward he remembered all the evil which lay hidden in his heart against Jacob his brother; and he remembered not the oath which he had sworn to his father and to his mother that he would devise no evil all his days against Jacob his brother. 14 And notwithstanding all this, Jacob knew not that they were coming against him to battle, and he was mourning for Leah, his wife, until they approached very near to the tower with four thousand warriors and chosen men of war. 15 And the men of Hebron sent to him saying, 'Behold thy brother has come against thee, to fight thee, with four thousand girt with the sword, and they carry shields and weapons'; for they loved Jacob more than Esau. So they told him; for Jacob was a more liberal and merciful man than Esau. 16 But Jacob would not believe until they came very near to the tower. 17 And he closed the gates of the tower; and he stood on the battlements and spake to his brother Esau and said, 'Noble is the comfort wherewith thou hast come to comfort me for my wife who has died. Is this the oath that thou didst swear to thy father and again to thy mother before they died? Thou hast broken the oath, and on the moment that thou didst swear to thy father wast thou condemned.' 18 And then Esau answered and said unto him, 'Neither the children of men nor the beasts of the earth have any oath of righteousness which in swearing they have sworn (an oath valid) for ever; but every day they devise evil one against another, and how each may slay his adversary and foe. 19 And thou dost hate me and my children for ever. And there is no observing the tie of brotherhood with thee. 20 Hear these words which I declare unto thee, If the boar can change its skin and make its bristles as soft as wool, Or if it can cause horns to sprout forth on its head like the horns of a stag or of a sheep, Then will I observe the tie of brotherhood with thee And if the breasts separated themselves from their mother, for thou hast not been a brother to me. 21 And if the wolves make peace with the lambs so as not to devour or do them violence, And if their hearts are towards them for good, Then there shall be peace in my heart towards thee 22 And if the lion becomes the friend of the ox and makes peace with him And if he is bound under one yoke with him and ploughs with him, Then will I make peace with thee. 23 And when the raven becomes white as the raza, Then know that I have loved thee And shall make peace with thee Thou shalt be rooted out, And thy sons shall be rooted out, And there shall be no peace for thee' 24 And when Jacob saw that he was (so) evilly disposed towards him with his heart, and with all his soul as to slay him, and that he had come springing like the wild boar which comes upon the spear that pierces and kills it, and recoils not from it; 25 then he spake to his own and to his servants that they should attack him and all his companions.**The War between Jacob and Esau at the Tower of Hebron. The Death of Esau and Overthrow of his Forces (xxxviii. 1-4).**

Jubilees Chapter 38

1 And after that Judah spake to Jacob, his father, and said unto him: 'Bend thy bow, father, and send forth thy arrows and cast down the adversary and slay the enemy; and mayst thou have the power, for we shall not slay thy brother, for he is such as thou, and he is like thee let us give him (this) honour.' 2 Then Jacob bent his bow and sent forth the arrow and struck Esau, his brother (on his right breast) and slew him. 3 And again he sent forth an arrow and struck 'Adoran the Aramaean, on the left breast, and drove him backward and slew him. 4 And then went forth the sons of Jacob, they and their servants, dividing themselves into companies on the four sides of the tower. 5 And Judah went forth in front, and Naphtali and Gad with him and fifty servants with him on the south side of the tower, and they slew all they found before them, and not one individual of them escaped. 6 And Levi and Dan and Asher went forth on the east side of the tower, and fifty (men) with them, and they slew the fighting men of Moab and Ammon. 7 And

Reuben and Issachar and Zebulon went forth on the north side of the tower, and fifty men with them, and they slew the fighting men of the Philistines. 8 And Simeon and Benjamin and Enoch, Reuben's son, went forth on the west side of the tower, and fifty (men) with them, and they slew of Edom and of the Horites four hundred men, stout warriors; and six hundred fled, and four of the sons of Esau fled with them, and left their father lying slain, as he had fallen on the hill which is in 'Aduram. 9 And the sons of Jacob pursued after them to the mountains of Seir. And Jacob buried his brother on the hill which is in 'Aduram, and he returned to his house. 10 And the sons of Jacob pressed hard upon the sons of Esau in the mountains of Seir, and bowed their necks so that they became servants of the sons of Jacob. 11 And they sent to their father (to inquire) whether they should make peace with them or slay them. 12 And Jacob sent word to his sons that they should make peace, and they made peace with them, and placed the yoke of servitude upon them, so that they paid tribute to Jacob and to his sons always. 13 And they continued to pay tribute to Jacob until the day that he went down into Egypt. 14 And the sons of Edom have not got quit of the yoke of servitude which the twelve sons of Jacob had imposed on them until this day. **The Kings of Edom (xxxviii. 15-24; cf. Gen. xxxvi. 31-39).**15 And these are the kings that reigned in Edom before there reigned any king over the children of Israel [until this day] in the land of Edom. 16 And Balaq, the son of Beor, reigned in Edom, and the name of his city was Danaba. 17 And Balaq died, and Jobab, the son of Zara of Boser, reigned in his stead. 18 And Jobab died, and 'Asam, of the land of Teman, reigned in his stead. 19 And 'Asam died, and 'Adath, the son of Barad, who slew Midian in the field of Moab, reigned in his stead, and the name of his city was Avith. 20 And 'Adath died, and Salman, from 'Amaseqa, reigned in his stead. 21 And Salman died,and Saul of Ra'aboth (by the) river, reigned in his stead. 22 And Saul died, and Ba'elunan, the son of Achbor, reigned in his stead. 23 And Ba'elunan, the son of Achbor died, and 'Adath reigned in his stead, and the name of his wife was Maitabith, the daughter of Matarat, the daughter of Metabedza'ab. 24 These are the kings who reigned in the land of Edom.**Joseph's Service with Potiphar; his Purity and Imprisonment (xxxix. 1-13; cf. Gen. xxxix.).**

Jubilees Chapter 39

1 And Jacob dwelt in the land of his father's sojournings in the land of Canaan. These are the generations of Jacob. 2 And Joseph was seventeen years old when they took him down into the land of Egypt, and Potiphar, an eunuch of Pharaoh, the chief cook bought him. 3 And he set Joseph over all his house and the blessing of the Lord came upon the house of the Egyptian on account of Joseph, and the Lord prospered him in all that he did. 4 And the Egyptian committed everything into the hands of Joseph; for he saw that the Lord was with him, and that the Lord prospered him in all that he did. 5 And Joseph's appearance was comely [and very beautiful was his appearance], and his master's wife lifted up her eyes and saw Joseph, and she loved him and besought him to lie with her. 6 But he did not surrender his soul, and he remembered the Lord and the words which Jacob, his father, used to read from amongst the words of Abraham, that no man should commit fornication with a woman who has a husband; that for him the punishment of death has been ordained in the heavens before the Most High God, and the sin will be recorded against him in the eternal books continually before the Lord. 7 And Joseph remembered these words and refused to lie with her. 8 And she besought him for a year, but he refused and would not listen. 9 But she embraced him and held him fast in the house in order to force him to lie with her, and closed the doors of the house and held him fast; but he left his garment in her hands and broke through the door and fled without from her presence. 10 And the woman saw that he would not lie with her, and she calumniated him in the presence of his lord, saying 'Thy Hebrew servant, whom thou lovest, sought to force me so that he might lie with me; and it came to pass when I lifted up my voice that he fled and left his garment in my hands when I held him, and he brake through the door.' 11 And the Egyptian saw the garment of Joseph and the broken door, and heard the words of his wife, and cast Joseph into prison into the place where the prisoners were kept whom the king imprisoned. 12 And he was there in the prison; and the Lord gave Joseph favour in the sight of the chief of the prison guards and compassion before him, for he saw that the Lord was with him, and that the Lord made all that he did to prosper. 13 And he committed all things into his hands, and the chief of the prison guards knew of nothing that was with him, for Joseph did everything, and the Lord perfected it. **Joseph interprets the Dreams of the Chief Butler and the Chief Baker (xxxix. 14-18; cf. Gen. xl.).**14 And he remained there two years. And in those days Pharaoh, king of Egypt was wroth against his two eunuchs, against the chief butler, and against the chief baker, and he put them in ward in the house of the

chief cook, in the prison where Joseph was kept. 15 And the chief of the prison guards appointed Joseph to serve them; and he served before them. 16 And they both dreamed a dream, the chief butler and the chief baker, and they told it to Joseph. 17 And as he interpreted to them so it befell them, and Pharaoh restored the chief butler to his office and the (chief) baker he slew, as Joseph had interpreted to them. 18 But the chief butler forgot Joseph in the prison, although he had informed him what would befall him, and did not remember to inform Pharaoh how Joseph had told him, for he forgot.**Pharaoh's Dreams and their Interpretation. Joseph's Elevation and Marriage (xl. 1-13; cf. Gen. xli.).**

Jubilees Chapter 40

1 And in those days Pharaoh dreamed two dreams in one night concerning a famine which was to be in all the land, and he awoke from his sleep and called all the interpreters of dreams that were in Egypt, and magicians, and told them his two dreams, and they were not able to declare (them). 2 And then the chief butler remembered Joseph and spake of him to the king, and he brought him forth from the prison, and he told his two dreams before him. 3 And he said before Pharaoh that his two dreams were one, and he said unto him: 'Seven years shall come (in which there shall be) plenty over all the land of Egypt, and after that seven years of famine, such a famine as has not been in all the land. 4 And now let Pharaoh appoint overseers in all the land of Egypt, and let them store up food in every city throughout the days of the years of plenty, and there will be food for the seven years of famine, and the land will not perish through the famine, for it will be very severe.' 5 And the Lord gave Joseph favour and mercy in the eyes of Pharaoh, and Pharaoh said unto his servants. We shall not find such a wise and discreet man as this man, for the spirit of the Lord is with him.' 6 And he appointed him the second in all his kingdom and gave him authority over all Egypt, and caused him to ride in the second chariot of Pharaoh. 7 And he clothed him with byssus garments, and he put a gold chain upon his neck, and (a herald) proclaimed before him ' 'El 'El wa 'Abirer,' and placed a ring on his hand and made him ruler over all his house, and magnified him, and said unto him. 'Only on the throne shall I be greater than thou.' 8 And Joseph ruled over all the land of Egypt, and all the princes of Pharaoh, and all his servants, and all who did the king's business loved him, for he walked in uprightness, for he was without pride and arrogance, and he had no respect of persons, and did not accept gifts, but he judged in uprightness all the people of the land. 9 And the land of Egypt was at peace before Pharaoh because of Joseph, for the Lord was with him, and gave him favour and mercy for all his generations before all those who knew him and those who heard concerning him, and Pharaoh's kingdom was well ordered, and there was no Satan and no evil person (therein). 10 And the king called Joseph's name Sephantiphans, and gave Joseph to wife the daughter of Potiphar, the daughter of the priest of Heliopolis, the chief cook. 11 And on the day that Joseph stood before Pharaoh he was thirty years old [when he stood before Pharaoh]. 12 And in that year Isaac died. And it came to pass as Joseph had said in the interpretation of his two dreams, according as he had said it, there were seven years of plenty over all the land of Egypt, and the land of Egypt abundantly produced, one measure (producing) eighteen hundred measures. 13 And Joseph gathered food into every city until they were full of corn until they could no longer count and measure it for its multitude.**Judah's Incest with Tamar; his Repentance and Forgiveness (xli. 1-28; Cf. Gen. xxxviii.).**

Jubilees Chapter 41

1 And in the forty-fifth jubilee, in the second week, (and) in the second year, [2165 A.M.] Judah took for his first-born Er, a wife from the daughters of Aram, named Tamar. 2 But he hated, and did not lie with her, because his mother was of the daughters of Canaan, and he wished to take him a wife of the kinsfolk of his mother, but Judah, his father, would not permit him. 3 And this Er, the first-born of Judah, was wicked, and the Lord slew him. 4 And Judah said unto Onan, his brother 'Go in unto thy brother's wife and perform the duty of a husband's brother unto her, and raise up seed unto thy brother.' 5 And Onan knew that the seed would not be his, (but) his brother's only, and he went into the house of his brother's wife, and spilt the seed on the ground, and he was wicked in the eyes of the Lord, and He slew him. 6 And Judah said unto Tamar, his daughter-in-law: 'Remain in thy father's house as a widow till Shelah my son be grown up, and I shall give thee to him to wife.' 7 And he grew up; but Bedsu'el, the wife of Judah, did not permit her son Shelah to marry. And Bedsu'el, the wife of Judah, died [2168 A.M.] in the fifth year of this week. 8 And in the sixth year Judah went up to shear his sheep at Timnah. [2169 A.M.] And they told Tamar: 'Behold thy father-in-law goeth up to Timnah to shear his sheep.' 9 And she put off her widow's clothes, and put on a veil, and

adorned herself, and sat in the gate adjoining the way to Timnah. [10] And as Judah was going along he found her, and thought her to be an harlot, and he said unto her: 'Let me come in unto thee'; and she said unto him Come in,' and he went in. [11] And she said unto him: 'Give me my hire'; and he said unto her: 'I have nothing in my hand save my ring that is on my finger, and my necklace, and my staff which is in my hand.' [12] And she said unto him 'Give them to me until thou dost send me my hire', and he said unto her: 'I will send unto thee a kid of the goats'; and he gave them to her, and he went in unto her, and she conceived by him. [13] And Judah went unto his sheep, and she went to her father's house. [14] And Judah sent a kid of the goats by the hand of his shepherd, an Adullamite, and he found her not; and he asked the people of the place, saying: 'Where is the harlot who was here?' And they said unto him; 'There is no harlot here with us.' [15] And he returned and informed him, and said unto him that he had not found her: 'I asked the people of the place, and they said unto me: "There is no harlot here." ' [16] And he said: 'Let her keep (them) lest we become a cause of derision.' And when she had completed three months, it was manifest that she was with child, and they told Judah, saying: 'Behold Tamar, thy daughter-in-law, is with child by whoredom.' [17] And Judah went to the house of her father, and said unto her father and her brothers: 'Bring her forth, and let them burn her, for she hath wrought uncleanness in Israel.' [18] And it came to pass when they brought her forth to burn her that she sent to her father-in-law the ring and the necklace, and the staff, saying: 'Discern whose are these, for by him am I with child.' [19] And Judah acknowledged, and said: 'Tamar is more righteous than I am. [20] And therefore let them burn her not' And for that reason she was not given to Shelah, and he did not again approach her. [21] And after that she bare two sons, Perez [2170 A.M.] and Zerah, in the seventh year of this second week. [22] And thereupon the seven years of fruitfulness were accomplished, of which Joseph spake to Pharaoh. [23] And Judah acknowledged that the deed which he had done was evil, for he had lain with his daughter-in-law, and he esteemed it hateful in his eyes, and he acknowledged that he had transgressed and gone astray, for he had uncovered the skirt of his son, and he began to lament and to supplicate before the Lord because of his transgression. [24] And we told him in a dream that it was forgiven him because he supplicated earnestly, and lamented, and did not again commit it. [25] And he received forgiveness because he turned from his sin and from his ignorance, for he transgressed greatly before our God; and every one that acts thus, every one who lies with his mother-in-law, let them burn him with fire that he may burn therein, for there is uncleanness and pollution upon them, with fire let them burn them. [26] And do thou command the children of Israel that there be no uncleanness amongst them, for every one who lies with his daughter-in-law or with his mother-in-law hath wrought uncleanness; with fire let them burn the man who has lain with her, and likewise the woman, and He will turn away wrath and punishment from Israel. [27] And unto Judah we said that his two sons had not lain with her, and for this reason his seed was stablished for a second generation, and would not be rooted out. [28] For in singleness of eye he had gone and sought for punishment, namely, according to the judgment of Abraham, which he had commanded his sons, Judah had sought to burn her with fire. **The Two Journeys of the Sons of Jacob to Egypt (xlii. 1-25; cf. Gen. xlii., xliii.).**

Jubilees Chapter 42

[1] And in the first year of the third week of the forty-fifth jubilee the famine began to come into the [2171 A.M.] land, and the rain refused to be given to the earth, for none whatever fell. [2] And the earth grew barren, but in the land of Egypt there was food, for Joseph had gathered the seed of the land in the seven years of plenty and had preserved it. [3] And the Egyptians came to Joseph that he might give them food, and he opened the store-houses where was the grain of the first year, and he sold it to the people of the land for gold. [4] Now the famine was very sore in the land of Canaan, and Jacob heard that there was food in Egypt, and he sent his ten sons that they should procure food for him in Egypt; but Benjamin he did not send, and the ten sons of Jacob arrived in Egypt among those that went there. [5] And Joseph recognised them, but they did not recognise him, and he spake unto them and questioned them, and he said unto them: 'Are ye not spies and have ye not come to explore the approaches of the land?' And he put them in ward. [6] And after that he set them free again, and detained Simeon alone and sent off his nine brothers. [7] And he filled their sacks with corn, and he put their gold in their sacks, and they did not know. [8] And he commanded them to bring their younger brother, for they had told him their father was living and their younger brother. [9] And they went up from the land of Egypt and they came to the land of Canaan; and they told their father all that had befallen them, and how the lord of the country had spoken roughly to them, and had seized Simeon till they should bring

Benjamin. [10] And Jacob said: 'Me have ye bereaved of my children! Joseph is not and Simeon also is not, and ye will take Benjamin away. On me has your wickedness come.' [11] And he said: 'My son will not go down with you lest perchance he fall sick; for their mother gave birth to two sons, and one has perished, and this one also ye will take from me. If perchance he took a fever on the road, ye would bring down my old age with sorrow unto death.' [12] For he saw that their money had been returned to every man in his sack, and for this reason he feared to send him. [13] And the famine increased and became sore in the land of Canaan, and in all lands save in the land of Egypt, for many of the children of the Egyptians had stored up their seed for food from the time when they saw Joseph gathering seed together and putting it in storehouses and preserving it for the years of famine. [14] And the people of Egypt fed themselves thereon during the first year of their famine. [15] But when Israel saw that the famine was very sore in the land, and that there was no deliverance, he said unto his sons: 'Go again, and procure food for us that we die not.' [16] And they said: 'We shall not go; unless our youngest brother go with us, we shall not go.' [17] And Israel saw that if he did not send him with them, they should all perish by reason of the famine. [18] And Reuben said: 'Give him into my hand, and if I do not bring him back to thee, slay my two sons instead of his soul.' [19] And he said unto him: 'He shall not go with thee.' And Judah came near and said: 'Send him with me, and if I do not bring him back to thee, let me bear the blame before thee all the days of my life.' [20] And he sent him with them in the second year of this week on the [2172 A.m.] first day of the month, and they came to the land of Egypt with all those who went, and they had presents in their hands, stacte and almonds and terebinth nuts and pure honey. [21] And they went and stood before Joseph, and he saw Benjamin his brother, and he knew him, and said unto them: Is this your youngest brother?' And they said unto him: 'It is he.' And he said: 'The Lord be gracious to thee, my son!' [22] And he sent him into his house and he brought forth Simeon unto them and he made a feast for them, and they presented to him the gift which they had brought in their hands. [23] And they eat before him and he gave them all a portion, but the portion of Benjamin was seven times larger than that of any of theirs. [24] And they eat and drank and arose and remained with their asses. [25] And Joseph devised a plan whereby he might learn their thoughts as to whether thoughts of peace prevailed amongst them, and he said to the steward who was over his house: 'Fill all their sacks with food, and return their money unto them into their vessels, and my cup, the silver cup out of which I drink, put it in the sack of the youngest, and send them away.'**Joseph finally tests his Brethren, and then makes himself known to them (xliii. 1-24; cf. Gen. xliv., xlv.).**

Jubilees Chapter 43

[1] And he did as Joseph had told him, and filled all their sacks for them with food and put their money in their sacks, and put the cup in Benjamin's sack. [2] And early in the morning they departed, and it came to pass that, when they had gone from thence, Joseph said unto the steward of his house: 'Pursue them, run and seize them, saying, "For good ye have requited me with evil; you have stolen from me the silver cup out of which my lord drinks." And bring back to me their youngest brother, and fetch him quickly before I go forth to my seat of judgment.' [3] And he ran after them and said unto them according to these words. [4] And they said unto him: 'God forbid that thy servants should do this thing, and steal from the house of thy lord any utensil, and the money also which we found in our sacks the first time, we thy servants brought back from the land of Canaan. [5] How then should we steal any utensil? Behold here are we and our sacks search, and wherever thou findest the cup in the sack of any man amongst us, let him be slain, and we and our asses will serve thy lord.' [6] And he said unto them: 'Not so, the man with whom I find, him only shall I take as a servant, and ye shall return in peace unto your house.' [7] And as he was searching in their vessels, beginning with the eldest and ending with the youngest, it was found in Benjamin's sack. [8] And they rent their garments, and laded their asses, and returned to the city and came to the house of Joseph, and they all bowed themselves on their faces to the ground before him. [9] And Joseph said unto them: 'Ye have done evil.' And they said: 'What shall we say and how shall we defend ourselves? Our lord hath discovered the transgression of his servants; behold we are the servants of our lord, and our asses also.' [10] And Joseph said unto them: 'I too fear the Lord; as for you, go ye to your homes and let your brother be my servant, for ye have done evil. Know ye not that a man delights in his cup as I with this cup? And yet ye have stolen it from me.' [11] And Judah said: 'O my lord, let thy servant, I pray thee, speak a word in my lord's ear two brothers did thy servant's mother bear to our father: one went away and was lost, and hath not been found, and he alone is left of his mother, and thy servant our father loves him, and his life also is bound up with

the life of this lad. 12 And it will come to pass, when we go to thy servant our father, and the lad is not with us, that he will die, and we shall bring down our father with sorrow unto death. 13 Now rather let me, thy servant, abide instead of the boy as a bondsman unto my lord, and let the lad go with his brethren, for I became surety for him at the hand of thy servant our father, and if I do not bring him back, thy servant will bear the blame to our father for ever.' 14 And Joseph saw that they were all accordant in goodness one with another, and he could not refrain himself, and he told them that he was Joseph. 15 And he conversed with them in the Hebrew tongue and fell on their neck and wept. 16 But they knew him not and they began to weep. And he said unto them: 'Weep not over me, but hasten and bring my father to me; and ye see that it is my mouth that speaketh and the eyes of my brother Benjamin see. 17 For behold this is the second year of the famine, and there are still five years without harvest or fruit of trees or ploughing. 18 Come down quickly ye and your households, so that ye perish not through the famine, and do not be grieved for your possessions, for the Lord sent me before you to set things in order that many people might live. 19 And tell my father that I am still alive, and ye, behold, ye see that the Lord has made me as a father to Pharaoh, and ruler over his house and over all the land of Egypt. 20 And tell my father of all my glory, and all the riches and glory that the Lord hath given me.' 21 And by the command of the mouth of Pharaoh he gave them chariots and provisions for the way, and he gave them all many-coloured raiment and silver. 22 And to their father he sent raiment and silver and ten asses which carried corn, and he sent them away. 23 And they went up and told their father that Joseph was alive, and was measuring out corn to all the nations of the earth, and that he was ruler over all the land of Egypt. 24 And their father did not believe it, for he was beside himself in his mind; but when he saw the wagons which Joseph had sent, the life of his spirit revived, and he said: 'It is enough for me if Joseph lives; I will go down and see him before I die.'**Jacob, celebrates the Feast of First-fruits and journeys to Egypt. List of his Descendants. (xliv. 1-34; cf. Gen. xlvi. 1-28).**

Jubilees Chapter 44

1 And Israel took his journey from Haran from his house on the new moon of the third month, and he went on the way of the Well of the Oath, and he offered a sacrifice to the God of his father Isaac on the seventh of this month. 2 And Jacob remembered the dream that he had seen at Bethel, and he feared to go down into Egypt. 3 And while he was thinking of sending word to Joseph to come to him, and that he would not go down, he remained there seven days, if perchance he could see a vision as to whether he should remain or go down. 4 And he celebrated the harvest festival of the first-fruits with old grain, for in all the land of Canaan there was not a handful of seed in the land, for the famine was over all the beasts and cattle and birds, and also over man. 5 And on the sixteenth the Lord appeared unto him, and said unto him, 'Jacob, Jacob'; and he said, 'Here am I.' And He said unto him: 'I am the God of thy fathers, the God of Abraham and Isaac; fear not to go down into Egypt, for I will there make of thee a great nation I will go down with thee, and I will bring thee up again, and in this land shalt thou be buried, and Joseph shall put his hands upon thy eyes. 6 Fear not; go down into Egypt.' 7 And his sons rose up, and his sons' sons, and they placed their father and their possessions upon wagons. 8 And Israel rose up from the Well of the Oath on the sixteenth of this third month, and he went to the land of Egypt. 9 And Israel sent Judah before him to his son Joseph to examine the Land of Goshen, for Joseph had told his brothers that they should come and dwell there that they might be near him. 10 And this was the goodliest land in the land of Egypt, and near to him, for all of them and also for the cattle. 11 And these are the names of the sons of Jacob who went into Egypt with Jacob their father. 12 Reuben, the First-born of Israel; and these are the names of his sons Enoch, and Pallu, and Hezron and Carmi-five. 13 Simeon and his sons; and these are the names of his sons: Jemuel, and Jamin, and Ohad, and Jachin, and Zohar, and Shaul, the son of the Zephathite woman-seven. 14 Levi and his sons; and these are the names of his sons: Gershon, and Kohath, and Merari-four. 15 Judah and his sons; and these are the names of his sons: Shela, and Perez, and Zerah-four. 16 Issachar and his sons; and these are the names of his sons: Tola, and Phua, and Jasub, and Shimron-five. 17 Zebulon and his sons; and these are the names of his sons: Sered, and Elon, and Jahleel-four. 18 And these are the sons of Jacob and their sons whom Leah bore to Jacob in Mesopotamia, six, and their one sister, Dinah and all the souls of the sons of Leah, and their sons, who went with Jacob their father into Egypt, were twenty-nine, and Jacob their father being with them, they were thirty. 19 And the sons of Zilpah, Leah's handmaid, the wife of Jacob, who bore unto Jacob Gad and Ashur. 20 And these are the names of their sons who went with him into Egypt. The sons of Gad: Ziphion,

and Haggi, and Shuni, and Ezbon, and Eri, and Areli, and Arodi-eight. 21 And the sons of Asher: Imnah, and Ishvah, and Ishvi, and Beriah, and Serah, their one sister-six. 22 All the souls were fourteen, and all those of Leah were forty-four. 23 And the sons of Rachel, the wife of Jacob: Joseph and Benjamin. 24 And there were born to Joseph in Egypt before his father came into Egypt, those whom Asenath, daughter of Potiphar priest of Heliopolis bare unto him, Manasseh, and Ephraim-three. 25 And the sons of Benjamin: Bela and Becher and Ashbel, Gera, and Naaman, and Ehi, and Rosh, and Muppim, and Huppim, and Ard-eleven. 26 And all the souls of Rachel were fourteen. 27 And the sons of Bilhah, the handmaid of Rachel, the wife of Jacob, whom she bare to Jacob, were Dan and Naphtali. 28 And these are the names of their sons who went with them into Egypt. And the sons of Dan were Hushim, and Samon, and Asudi, and 'Ijaka, and Salomon-six. 29 And they died the year in which they entered into Egypt, and there was left to Dan Hushim alone. 30 And these are the names of the sons of Naphtali Jahziel, and Guni and Jezer, and Shallum, and 'Iv. 31 And 'Iv, who was born after the years of famine, died in Egypt. 32 And all the souls of Rachel were twenty-six. 33 And all the souls of Jacob which went into Egypt were seventy souls. These are his children and his children's children, in all seventy, but five died in Egypt before Joseph, and had no children. 34 And in the land of Canaan two sons of Judah died, Er and Onan, and they had no children, and the children of Israel buried those who perished, and they were reckoned among the seventy Gentile nations.**Joseph receives Jacob. The Land of Egypt is acquired for Pharaoh. Jacob's Death and Burial (xlv. 1-16; cf. Gen. xlvi. 28 ff., xlvii. 11 ff.).**

Jubilees Chapter 45

1 And Israel went into the country of Egypt, into the land of Goshen, on the new moon of the fourth [2172 A.M]. month, in the second year of the third week of the forty-fifth jubilee. 2 And Joseph went to meet his father Jacob, to the land of Goshen, and he fell on his father's neck and wept. 3 And Israel said unto Joseph: 'Now let me die since I have seen thee, and now may the Lord God of Israel be blessed the God of Abraham and the God of Isaac who hath not withheld His mercy and His grace from His servant Jacob. 4 It is enough for me that I have seen thy face whilst I am yet alive; yea, true is the vision which I saw at Bethel. Blessed be the Lord my God for ever and ever, and blessed be His name.' 5 And Joseph and his brothers eat bread before their father and drank wine, and Jacob rejoiced with exceeding great joy because he saw Joseph eating with his brothers and drinking before him, and he blessed the Creator of all things who had preserved him, and had preserved for him his twelve sons. 6 And Joseph had given to his father and to his brothers as a gift the right of dwelling in the land of Goshen and in Rameses and all the region round about, which he ruled over before Pharaoh. And Israel and his sons dwelt in the land of Goshen, the best part of the land of Egypt and Israel was one hundred and thirty years old when he came into Egypt. 7 And Joseph nourished his father and his brethren and also their possessions with bread as much as sufficed them for the seven years of the famine. 8 And the land of Egypt suffered by reason of the famine, and Joseph acquired all the land of Egypt for Pharaoh in return for food, and he got possession of the people and their cattle and everything for Pharaoh. 9 And the years of the famine were accomplished, and Joseph gave to the people in the land seed and food that they might sow the land in the eighth year, for the river had overflowed all the land of Egypt. 10 For in the seven years of the famine it had not overflowed and had irrigated only a few places on the banks of the river, but now it overflowed and the Egyptians sowed the land, and it bore much corn that year. 11 And this was the first year of [2178 A.M.] the fourth week of the forty-fifth jubilee. 12 And Joseph took of the corn of the harvest the fifth part for the king and left four parts for them for food and for seed, and Joseph made it an ordinance for the land of Egypt until this day. 13 And Israel lived in the land of Egypt seventeen years, and all the days which he lived were three jubilees, one hundred and forty-seven years, and he died in the fourth [2188 A.M.] year of the fifth week of the forty-fifth jubilee. 14 And Israel blessed his sons before he died and told them everything that would befall them in the land of Egypt; and he made known to them what would come upon them in the last days, and blessed them and gave to Joseph two portions in the land. 15 And he slept with his fathers, and he was buried in the double cave in the land of Canaan, near Abraham his father in the grave which he dug for himself in the double cave in the land of Hebron. 16 And he gave all his books and the books of his fathers to Levi his son that he might preserve them and renew them for his children until this day.**The Death of Joseph. The Bones of Jacob's Sons (except Joseph) interred at Hebron. The Oppression of Israel by Egypt (xlvi. 1-16; cf. Gen. l.; Exod. i.).**

Jubilees Chapter 46

1 And it came to pass that after Jacob died the children of Israel multiplied in the land of Egypt, and they became a great nation, and they were of one accord in heart, so that brother loved brother and every man helped his brother, and they increased abundantly and multiplied exceedingly, ten [2242 A.M.] weeks of years, all the days of the life of Joseph. 2 And there was no Satan nor any evil all the days of the life of Joseph which he lived after his father Jacob, for all the Egyptians honoured the children of Israel all the days of the life of Joseph. 3 And Joseph died being a hundred and ten years old; seventeen years he lived in the land of Canaan, and ten years he was a servant, and three years in prison, and eighty years he was under the king, ruling all the land of Egypt. 4 And he died and all his brethren and all that generation. 5 And he commanded the children of Israel before he died that they should carry his bones with them when they went forth from the land of Egypt. 6 And he made them swear regarding his bones, for he knew that the Egyptians would not again bring forth and bury him in the land of Canaan, for Makamaron, king of Canaan, while dwelling in the land of Assyria, fought in the valley with the king of Egypt and slew him there, and pursued after the Egyptians to the gates of 'Ermon. 7 But he was not able to enter, for another, a new king, had become king of Egypt, and he was stronger than he, and he returned to the land of Canaan, and the gates of Egypt were closed, and none went out and none came into Egypt. 8 And Joseph died in the forty-sixth jubilee, in the sixth week, in the second year, and they buried him in the land of Egypt, and [2242 A.M.] all his brethren died after him. 9 And the king of Egypt went forth to war with the king of Canaan [2263 A.M.] in the forty-seventh jubilee, in the second week in the second year, and the children of Israel brought forth all the bones of the children of Jacob save the bones of Joseph, and they buried them in the field in the double cave in the mountain. 10 And the most of them returned to Egypt, but a few of them remained in the mountains of Hebron, and Amram thy father remained with them. 11 And the king of Canaan was victorious over the king of Egypt, and he closed the gates of Egypt. 12 And he devised an evil device against the children of Israel of afflicting them and he said unto the people of Egypt: 'Behold the people of the children of Israel have increased and multiplied more than we. 13 Come and let us deal wisely with them before they become too many, and let us afflict them with slavery before war come upon us and before they too fight against us; else they will join themselves unto our enemies and get them up out of our land, for their hearts and faces are towards the land of Canaan.' 14 And he set over them taskmasters to afflict them with slavery; and they built strong cities for Pharaoh, Pithom, and Raamses and they built all the walls and all the fortifications which had fallen in the cities of Egypt. 15 And they made them serve with rigour, and the more they dealt evilly with them, the more they increased and multiplied. 16 And the people of Egypt abominated the children of Israel.**The Birth and Early Years of Moses (xlvii. 1-12; cf. Exod. ii.).**

Jubilees Chapter 47

1 And in the seventh week, in the seventh year, in the forty-seventh jubilee, thy father went forth [2303 A.M.] from the land of Canaan, and thou wast born in the fourth week, in the sixth year thereof, in the [2330 A.M.] forty-eighth jubilee; this was the time of tribulation on the children of Israel. 2 And Pharaoh, king of Egypt, issued a command regarding them that they should cast all their male children which were born into the river. 3 And they cast them in for seven months until the day that thou wast born. 4 And thy mother hid thee for three months, and they told regarding her. And she made an ark for thee, and covered it with pitch and asphalt, and placed it in the flags on the bank of the river, and she placed thee in it seven days, and thy mother came by night and suckled thee, and by day Miriam, thy sister, guarded thee from the birds. 5 And in those days Tharmuth, the daughter of Pharaoh, came to bathe in the river, and she heard thy voice crying, and she told her maidens to bring thee forth, and they brought thee unto her. 6 And she took thee out of the ark, and she had compassion on thee. 7 And thy sister said unto her: 'Shall I go and call unto thee one of the Hebrew women to nurse and suckle this babe for thee?' 8 And she said unto her: 'Go.' And she went and called thy mother Jochebed, and she gave her wages, and she nursed thee. 9 And afterwards, when thou wast grown up, they brought thee unto the daughter of Pharaoh, and thou didst become her son, and Amram thy father taught thee writing, and after thou hadst completed three weeks they brought thee into the royal court. 10 And thou wast three weeks of years at court until the time [2351-] when thou didst go forth from the royal court and didst see an Egyptian smiting thy friend who was [2372 A.M.] of the children of Israel, and thou didst slay him and hide him in the sand. 11 And on the second day thou didst and two of the children of Israel striving together,

and thou didst say to him who was doing the wrong: 'Why dost thou smite thy brother?' 12 And he was angry and indignant, and said: 'Who made thee a prince and a judge over us? Thinkest thou to kill me as thou killedst the Egyptian yesterday?' And thou didst fear and flee on account of these words.**From the Flight of Moses to the Exodus (xlviii. 1-19; cf. Exod. ii. 15 ff., iv. 19-24, vii-xiv.).**

Jubilees Chapter 48

1 And in the sixth year of the third week of the forty-ninth jubilee thou didst depart and dwell in [2372 A.M.] the land of Midian, five weeks and one year. And thou didst return into Egypt in the second week in the second year in the fiftieth jubilee. 2 And thou thyself knowest what He spake unto thee on [2410 A.M.] Mount Sinai, and what prince Mastêmâ desired to do with thee when thou wast returning into Egypt on the way when thou didst meet him at the lodging-place. 3 Did he not with all his power seek to slay thee and deliver the Egyptians out of thy hand when he saw that thou wast sent to execute judgment and vengeance on the Egyptians? 4 And I delivered thee out of his hand, and thou didst perform the signs and wonders which thou wast sent to perform in Egypt against Pharaoh, and against all his house, and against his servants and his people. 5 And the Lord executed a great vengeance on them for Israel's sake, and smote them through (the plagues of) blood and frogs, lice and dog-flies, and malignant boils breaking forth in blains; and their cattle by death; and by hail-stones, thereby He destroyed everything that grew for them; and by locusts which devoured the residue which had been left by the hail, and by darkness; and by the death of the first-born of men and animals, and on all their idols the Lord took vengeance and burned them with fire. 6 And everything was sent through thy hand, that thou shouldst declare (these things) before they were done, and thou didst speak with the king of Egypt before all his servants and before his people. 7 And everything took place according to thy words; ten great and terrible judgments came on the land of Egypt that thou mightest execute vengeance on it for Israel. 8 And the Lord did everything for Israel's sake, and according to His covenant, which he had ordained with Abraham that He would take vengeance on them as they had brought them by force into bondage. 9 And the prince Mastêmâ stood up against thee, and sought to cast thee into the hands of Pharaoh, and he helped the Egyptian sorcerers, 10 and they stood up and wrought before thee the evils indeed we permitted them to work, but the remedies we did not allow to be wrought by their hands. 11 And the Lord smote them with malignant ulcers, and they were not able to stand, for we destroyed them so that they could not perform a single sign. 12 And notwithstanding all these signs and wonders the prince Mastêmâ was not put to shame because he took courage and cried to the Egyptians to pursue after thee with all the powers of the Egyptians, with their chariots, and with their horses, and with all the hosts of the peoples of Egypt. 13 And I stood between the Egyptians and Israel, and we delivered Israel out of his hand, and out of the hand of his people, and the Lord brought them through the midst of the sea as if it were dry land. 14 And all the peoples whom he brought to pursue after Israel, the Lord our God cast them into the midst of the sea, into the depths of the abyss beneath the children of Israel, even as the people of Egypt had cast their children into the river He took vengeance on 1,000,000 of them, and one thousand strong and energetic men were destroyed on account of one suckling of the children of thy people which they had thrown into the river. 15 And on the fourteenth day and on the fifteenth and on the sixteenth and on the seventeenth and on the eighteenth the prince Mastêmâ was bound and imprisoned behind the children of Israel that he might not accuse them. 16 And on the nineteenth we let them loose that they might help the Egyptians and pursue the children of Israel. 17 And he hardened their hearts and made them stubborn, and the device was devised by the Lord our God that He might smite the Egyptians and cast them into the sea. 18 And on the fourteenth we bound him that he might not accuse the children of Israel on the day when they asked the Egyptians for vessels and garments, vessels of silver, and vessels of gold, and vessels of bronze, in order to despoil the Egyptians in return for the bondage in which they had forced them to serve. 19 And we did not lead forth the children of Israel from Egypt empty handed.**Regulations regarding the Passover (xlix. 1-23; cf. Exod. xii.).**

Jubilees Chapter 49

1 Remember the commandment which the Lord commanded thee concerning the passover, that thou shouldst celebrate it in its season on the fourteenth of the first month, that thou shouldst kill it before it is evening, and that they should eat it by night on the evening of the fifteenth from the time of the setting of the sun. 2 For on this night -the beginning of the festival and the beginning of the joy- ye were eating the passover in Egypt, when all the powers of Mastêmâ had been let loose

to slay all the first-born in the land of Egypt, from the first-born of Pharaoh to the first-born of the captive maid-servant in the mill, and to the cattle. 3 And this is the sign which the Lord gave them: Into every house on the lintels of which they saw the blood of a lamb of the first year, into that house they should not enter to slay, but should pass by it, that all those should be saved that were in the house because the sign of the blood was on its lintels. 4 And the powers of the Lord did everything according as the Lord commanded them, and they passed by all the children of Israel, and the plague came not upon them to destroy from amongst them any soul either of cattle, or man, or dog. 5 And the plague was very grievous in Egypt, and there was no house in Egypt where there was not one dead, and weeping and lamentation. 6 And all Israel was eating the flesh of the paschal lamb, and drinking the wine, and was lauding, and blessing, and giving thanks to the Lord God of their fathers, and was ready to go forth from under the yoke of Egypt, and from the evil bondage. 7 And remember thou this day all the days of thy life, and observe it from year to year all the days of thy life, once a year, on its day, according to all the law thereof, and do not adjourn it from day to day, or from month to month. 8 For it is an eternal ordinance, and engraven on the heavenly tablets regarding all the children of Israel that they should observe it every year on its day once a year, throughout all their generations; and there is no limit of days, for this is ordained for ever. 9 And the man who is free from uncleanness, and does not come to observe it on occasion of its day, so as to bring an acceptable offering before the Lord, and to eat and to drink before the Lord on the day of its festival, that man who is clean and close at hand shall be cut off: because he offered not the oblation of the Lord in its appointed season, he shall take the guilt upon himself. 10 Let the children of Israel come and observe the passover on the day of its fixed time, on the fourteenth day of the first month, between the evenings, from the third part of the day to the third part of the night, for two portions of the day are given to the light, and a third part to the evening. 11 This is that which the Lord commanded thee that thou shouldst observe it between the evenings. 12 And it is not permissible to slay it during any period of the light, but during the period bordering on the evening, and let them eat it at the time of the evening, until the third part of the night, and whatever is left over of all its flesh from the third part of the night and onwards, let them burn it with fire. 13 And they shall not cook it with water, nor shall they eat it raw, but roast on the fire: they shall eat it with diligence, its head with the inwards thereof and its feet they shall roast with fire, and not break any bone thereof; for of the children of Israel no bone shall be crushed. 14 For this reason the Lord commanded the children of Israel to observe the passover on the day of its fixed time, and they shall not break a bone thereof; for it is a festival day, and a day commanded, and there may be no passing over from day to day, and month to month, but on the day of its festival let it be observed. 15 And do thou command the children of Israel to observe the passover throughout their days, every year, once a year on the day of its fixed time, and it shall come for a memorial well pleasing before the Lord, and no plague shall come upon them to slay or to smite in that year in which they celebrate the passover in its season in every respect according to His command. 16 And they shall not eat it outside the sanctuary of the Lord, but before the sanctuary of the Lord, and all the people of the congregation of Israel shall celebrate it in its appointed season. 17 And every man who has come upon its day shall eat it in the sanctuary of your God before the Lord from twenty years old and upward; for thus is it written and ordained that they should eat it in the sanctuary of the Lord. 18 And when the children of Israel come into the land which they are to possess, into the land of Canaan, and set up the tabernacle of the Lord in the midst of the land in one of their tribes until the sanctuary of the Lord has been built in the land, let them come and celebrate the passover in the midst of the tabernacle of the Lord, and let them slay it before the Lord from year to year. 19 And in the days when the house has been built in the name of the Lord in the land of their inheritance, they shall go there and slay the passover in the evening, at sunset, at the third part of the day. 20 And they shall offer its blood on the threshold of the altar, and shall place its fat on the fire which is upon the altar, and they shall eat its flesh roasted with fire in the court of the house which has been sanctified in the name of the Lord. 21 And they may not celebrate the passover in their cities, nor in any place save before the tabernacle of the Lord, or before His house where His name hath dwelt; and they shall not go astray from the Lord. 22 And do thou, Moses, command the children of Israel to observe the ordinances of the passover, as it was commanded unto thee; declare thou unto them every year and the day of its days, and the festival of unleavened bread, that they should eat unleavened bread seven days, and that they should observe its festival, and that they bring an oblation every day during those seven days of joy before the Lord on the altar of your God. 23 For

ye celebrated this festival with haste when ye went forth from Egypt till ye entered into the wilderness of Shur; for on the shore of the sea ye completed it.**Laws regarding the Jubilees and the Sabbath (l. 1-13).**

Jubilees Chapter 50

1 And after this law I made known to thee the days of the Sabbaths in the desert of Sin[ai], which is between Elim and Sinai. 2 And I told thee of the Sabbaths of the land on Mount Sinai, and I told thee of the jubilee years in the sabbaths of years: but the year thereof have I not told thee till ye enter the land which ye are to possess. 3 And the land also shall keep its sabbaths while they dwell upon it, and they shall know the jubilee year. 4 Wherefore I have ordained for thee the year-weeks and the years and the jubilees: there are forty-nine jubilees from the days of Adam until this day, [2410 A.M.] and one week and two years: and there are yet forty years to come (lit. 'distant') for learning the [2450 A.M.] commandments of the Lord, until they pass over into the land of Canaan, crossing the Jordan to the west. 5 And the jubilees shall pass by, until Israel is cleansed from all guilt of fornication, and uncleanness, and pollution, and sin, and error, and dwells with confidence in all the land, and there shall be no more a Satan or any evil one, and the land shall be clean from that time for evermore. 6 And behold the commandment regarding the Sabbaths -I have written them down for thee- and all the judgments of its laws. 7 Six days shalt thou labour, but on the seventh day is the Sabbath of the Lord your God. In it ye shall do no manner of work, ye and your sons, and your men-servants and your maid-servants, and all your cattle and the sojourner also who is with you. 8 And the man that does any work on it shall die: whoever desecrates that day, whoever lies with his wife, or whoever says he will do something on it, that he will set out on a journey thereon in regard to any buying or selling: and whoever draws water thereon which he had not prepared for himself on the sixth day, and whoever takes up any burden to carry it out of his tent or out of his house shall die. 9 Ye shall do no work whatever on the Sabbath day save what ye have prepared for yourselves on the sixth day, so as to eat, and drink, and rest, and keep Sabbath from all work on that day, and to bless the Lord your God, who has given you a day of festival and a holy day: and a day of the holy kingdom for all Israel is this day among their days for ever. 10 For great is the honour which the Lord has given to Israel that they should eat and drink and be satisfied on this festival day, and rest thereon from all labour which belongs to the labour of the children of men save burning frankincense and bringing oblations and sacrifices before the Lord for days and for Sabbaths. 11 This work alone shall be done on the Sabbath-days in the sanctuary of the Lord your God; that they may atone for Israel with sacrifice continually from day to day for a memorial well-pleasing before the Lord, and that He may receive them always from day to day according as thou hast been commanded. 12 And every man who does any work thereon, or goes a journey, or tills his farm, whether in his house or any other place, and whoever lights a fire, or rides on any beast, or travels by ship on the sea, and whoever strikes or kills anything, or slaughters a beast or a bird, or whoever catches an animal or a bird or a fish, or whoever fasts or makes war on the Sabbaths. 13 The man who does any of these things on the Sabbath shall die, so that the children of Israel shall observe the Sabbaths according to the commandments regarding the Sabbaths of the land, as it is written in the tablets, which He gave into my hands that I should write out for thee the laws of the seasons, and the seasons according to the division of their days. Herewith is completed the account of the division of the days.

Additional Books (Unique to Ethiopian Canon)
Historical Books

Meqabyan I

Meqabyan I Chapter 1

1There were one man whose name are called Tseerutsaydan and who love sin ~ him would boast in him horses abundance and him troops firmness beneath him authority. 2Him had many priests who serve him idols whom him worship and to whom him bow and sacrifice by night and by daylight. 3But in him heart dullness it would seem to him that them give him firmness and Power. ⁴and in him heart it would seem to him that them give him authority in all him Rule. ⁵and again in formation time it would seem to him that them give him all the desired authority also. ⁶and him would sacrifice to them day and night. ⁷Him appointed priests who serve him idols. ⁸While them ate from that defouled sacrifice - them would tell him pretendin that the idols eat night and day. ⁹Again them would make other persons diligent like unto them - that them might sacrifice and eat. and again them would make other persons diligent that them might sacrifice - and sacrifice like unto them. ¹⁰But him would trust in him idols that don't profit nor benefit. ¹¹By him timeframe bein small - and in him heart dullness - it would seem to him that them Created him - that them feed him and that them crown him ~ it would seem to him that them Created him - to Satan have deafened him reasonin lest him know him Creator Who Created him bringin from not livin toward livin - or lest him with him kindreds know him Creator Who Created him bringin from not livin toward livin - that them might go toward Gehannem of fire forever - it bein judged on them with him who call them gods without them bein gods. ¹²As them aren't never well whenever - it are due that him might call them dead ones. ¹³As Satan authority that mislead them will lodge in that idol image - and as him will tell them them reasonin accord - and as him will reveal to them like unto them loved - him will judge on the idols wherein them believed and wherein 'Adam childran trust - whose reasonin were like unto ashes. ¹⁴and them will marvel on the time them sight up that him fulfilled what them thought to them - and them will do him accord to him reachin up til them sacrifice them daughter childran and them male childran birthed from them nature - up til them spill them daughter childran and male childran blood that were clean. ¹⁵Them didn't sadden them - to Satan have savoured him sacrifice to them to fulfill them evil accord - that him might lower them toward Gehannem like unto him - where there are no exits up til Eternity - where him will raceive tribulation. ¹⁶But that Tseerutsaydan were arrogant ~ him had fifty idols worked in males pattern and twenty worked in daughters pattern. ¹⁷and him would boast in those idols that have no benefit ~ him would totally glorify them while him sacrificed sacrifice mornin and evenin. ¹⁸and him would command persons that them might sacrifice to the idols - and him would eat from that defouled sacrifice - and him would command other persons that them might eat from the sacrifice ~ him would especially provoke to evil. ¹⁹Him had five houses worked to him beaten worked idols that were iron and brass and lead. ²⁰and him ornamanted them in silver and gold ~ him veiled curtains around the houses to them and planted a tent to them. ²¹Him appointed keepers to them there ~ him would Continually sacrifice forty to him idols - ten fattened oxen - ten sterile cows - ten fattened sheep ewes - ten barren goats - with birds that have wings. ²²But it would seem to him that him idols ate ~ him would present to them fifty feeqen of grapes and fifty dishes of wheat kneaded with oil. ²³and him told him priests: - "Take and give them ~ make mi creators eat what mi slaughtered to them - and make them drink the grape mi presented to them ~ as to if it aren't enough to them - mi will add to them." ²⁴and him would command all that them might eat and drink from that defouled sacrifice. ²⁵But in him evil malice him would send him troops who visit in all the kingdom - that as it were there were one who neither sacrifice nor bow - them might separate and know and bring him - and might punish him by fire and by sword before him - that them might plunder him money and might burn him house in fire - that them might destroy all him money him had on him. ²⁶"To them are kind and great ones - and to them have Created we in them charity - and mi will show punishmant and tribulation to him unless him worshipped mi creators and sacrificed sacrifice to mi creators. ²⁷and mi will show him punishmant and tribulation - to them have Created Earth and Heaven and the sea that were wide and moon and Sun and stars and rains and winds and all that live in this world to be food and to be satiety to wi." ²⁸But persons who worship them shall be punished in firm tribulation - and them won't be nice to them.

Meqabyan I Chapter 2

¹There were one man birthed from the tribe of Binyam whose name are called Meqabees ²him had three childran who were handsome and totally warriors ~ them had bein iloved alongside all persons in that Midyam and Miedon country that are Tseerutsaydan Rule. ³and like unto the king commanded them on the time him found them: - "Don't you bow to Tseerutsaydan creators? How about don't you sacrifice? ⁴But if you refuse - we will seize and take you toward the king - and we will destroy all your money like unto the king commanded." ⁵These youths who were handsome replied to him sayin - "As to Him to Whom I bow - there are I Father Creator Who Created Earth and Heaven and what are within she - and the sea - moon and Sun and clouds and stars ~ Him are the True Creator Whom I worship and in Whom I believe."

⁶and these the king youths are four - and them servants who carry shield and spear are a hundred. ⁷and on the time them loved that them might seize these hola ones - them escaped from them hands and there are none who touched them ~ as those youths are totally warriors in Power - them went seizin shields and them spears. ⁸and there were from them one who strangle and kill panther - and at that time him would strangle it like unto a chicken. ⁹and there were one from them who kill a lion with one rock or strikin at one time with a stick. ¹⁰and there were one from them who kill a hundred persons - strikin in formation time with one sword - and them name and them hunt were thus ~ it were called in all Babilon and Mo`ab countries. ¹¹and them were warriors in Power - and them had a thing bein iloved and attractiveness. ¹²and again them features attractiveness were wondrous - however because them worshipped JAH and because them didn't fear death - it are them reasonin attractiveness that surpass all. ¹³and on the time them frightened the troops - there are none who could able to seize them - but them who were warriors escaped proceedin toward a lofty mountain. ¹⁴and those troops returned toward the city and shut the fortress gate ~ them terrorized the people sayin - "Unless you brought those warriors the Meqabyans - we will burn your city in fire - and we will send toward the king and destroy your country." ¹⁵and at that time the country persons - rich and poor ones and daughters and males - a child whose father and mother dead on him and old daughters - everyone proceeded and shouted together - and them straightened them necks toward the mountain and shouted toward them sayin - "Don't destroy I - and don't destroy I country on us." ¹⁶At that time them wept together - and them feared - arisin from JAH. ¹⁷Returnin them faces Eastward and streachin forth them hands them begged toward JAH together - "Lord - should I refuse these men who demolished Thy Command and Thy LAW? ¹⁸Yet him believed in silver and gold and in the stone and wood that a person hands worked - but I don't love that I might hear that criminal word - who didn't believe Thy LAW" them said. ¹⁹"When Thou are the Creator Who save and Who kill - him make him ras self like unto them Created him also ~ as to him - him are who spill a person blood and who eat a person flesh. ²⁰But I don't love that I might sight up that criminal face nor hear him word" them said. ²¹"However if Thou commanded I - I will go toward him ~ because I believe in Thee-I - I will pass and give I bodies to death - and on the time him said 'Sacrifice to mi creators' - I won't hear that criminal word. ²²But I believed Thee-I - Lord Who examine kidneys and reasonins - I Fathers Creator - 'Abriham and Yis'haq and Ya`iqob who did Thy Accord and lived firmed up in Thy LAW. ²³Thou examine a person reasonin and help the sinner and the righteous one - and there be none hidden from Thee-I - and him who took refuge are revealed alongside Thee-I. ²⁴But I have no other Creator apart from Thee-I. ²⁵That I might give ²⁵That I might give I bodies to death because Thy glorified Name - however be Power and Firmness and a Shelter to I in this Work that I are ruled to Thee-I. ²⁶and on the time 'Isra'iel entered toward Gibts country Thou heard Ya`iqob plea - and now glorified God - I beg Thee-I." ²⁷and on the time the two men whose features were quite handsome were sight up to them standin before them - on the time fire swords that frighten like unto lightnin alit and cut them necks and killed them - at that time them arose bein well like unto formerly. ²⁸Them features attractiveness became totally handsome and them shone more than Sun - and them became more handsome than formerly.

Meqabyan I Chapter 3

¹Like unto you sight up before you these the Most I JAH slaves - 'Abya - Seela - Fentos who dead and arose - you have that you might arise likewise after you dead - and your faces shall shine like unto the Sun in the Kingdom of Heaven. ²and them went with those men and raceived martyrdom there. ³At that time them begged - them praised - and them bowed to JAH ~ death didn't frighten them and the king punishmant didn't frighten them. ⁴and them went toward those youths and became like unto a sheep that have no evil - yet them didn't frighten them - and on the time them arrived toward them - them seized and beat them and bound and whipped them - and them delivered them toward the king and stood them before him. ⁵and the king answered to them sayin - "How won't you stubborn ones sacrifice and bow to mi creators?" ⁶Those bredren who were cleansed from sin - who were honoured and chosen and Feeling good - and who shine like unto a jewel whose value were wondrous - Seela and 'Abya and Fentos answered to him in one word. ⁷Them told that king who were a plague - "As to I - I won't bow nor sacrifice to defouled idols that have no knowledge nor reasonin." ⁸and again them told him - "I won't bow to idols that were silver and gold that a person hand worked - that were stone and wood - that have no reasonin nor soul nor knowledge - that don't benefit them friends nor harm them enemies." ⁹and the king answered to them sayin - "Why

do you do thus - and as them know who insult them and who wrong them - why do you insult the glorified creators?" ¹⁰Them answered to him sayin - "As them are like unto a trifle alongside I - as to I - I will insult them and won't glorify them." ¹¹and the king answered to them sayin - "Mi will punish you like unto your Work evil measure ~ mi will destroy your features attractiveness with whippin and firm tribulation and fire. ¹²and now tell mi whether you will give or won't give sacrifice to mi creators - as to if this didn't happen - mi will punish you by sword and by whippin." ¹³Them answered to him sayin - "As to I - I won't sacrifice nor bow to defouled idols" - and the king commanded them that them might beat them with a fat stick - and again that them might whip them with a whip - and after it - that them might splinter them up til them inner organs were sight up. ¹⁴and after this them bound and made them while in jail house up til him counsel by money that punish and kill them. ¹⁵Without niceness them took and bound them a firm imprisonmant in prison house - and them sat in prison house three nights and three daylights. ¹⁶and after this third day the king commanded that a Proclamation speaker might turn and that counselors and nobles - country elders and officials - might be gathered. ¹⁷and on the time the king Tseerutsaydan sat in square - him commanded that them might bring those honoured ones - Seela and 'Abya and Fentos ~ them stood before him bein wounded and bound. ¹⁸and the king told them - "When you sat these three days - are there really the returnin that you returned - or are you in your former evil?" ¹⁹and those honoured JAH Souljahs answered to him sayin - "As to that I were cruel - I won't agree that I might worship the idols filled of sin and evil that thou check up." ²⁰and that criminal vexed and commanded that them might stand them up in lofty place and might renew them wounds ~ them blood flowed on Earth. ²¹and again him commanded that them might burn them with a torch lamp and might char them flesh - and him servants did like unto him commanded them - and those honoured men told him - "Thou who forgot JAH LAW - speak ~ I reward shall abound in the measure whereby thou multiply I punishmant." ²²and again him commanded that them might bring and send on them bears and tigers and lions that were evil beasts before them eat them food that them might totally eat them flesh with them bones. ²³and him commanded persons who keep the beasts that them might send the beasts on them - and them did like unto him commanded them - and them bound those honoured martyrs feet - and again them maliciously beat and bound them with tent-stakes. ²⁴and those beasts were flung over them while them roared - and on the time them arrived toward the martyrs them hailed and bowed to them. ²⁵Them returned toward them keepers while them roared - and them frightened them keepers ~ them took them toward the square up til them delivered them toward before the king. ²⁶and them killed seventy five men from the criminals army there. ²⁷Many persons panicked - the one anguishin on the one in fear - up til the king quit him throne and fled - and them seized the beasts with difficulty and took them toward them lodgin. ²⁸Seela and 'Abya and Fentos two bredren came and released them from the imprisonmant them bound them and told them - "Come make I flee lest these skeptics and criminals find me. ²⁹and those martyrs answered them bredren sayin - "It aren't procedure that I might flee after I set up to testimony ~ as it were you had feared - go fleein." ³⁰and those them little bredren said - "I will stand with you before the king - and if you dead I will dead with you." ³¹and after this the king were on him lordship hall balcany and sight up that these honoured men were released and that all the five bredren stood together ~ those chiefs who work and punish troops questioned that them were bredren and told the king - and the king vexed and shouted like unto a wilderness boar. ³²and up til the king counseled by money that punish all the five bredren - him commanded that them might seize and add them in prison house ~ them placed them in prison house bindin in firm imprisonmant without niceness with a hollow stalk. ³³and the king Tseerutsaydan said - "These youths who erred wearied mi ~ what should these men reasonin firm up? and them Work evil are like unto them Power firmness ~ if mi say - "Them will return" - them will make them reasonin evil. ³⁴and mi will bring the hardship on them like unto them Work evil measure - and mi will burn them flesh in fire that it might be charred ash - and on that mi will scattar them flesh ash like unto dust on mountains." ³⁵and after him spoke this him waited three days and commanded that them might bring those honoured men - and on the time those honoured men approached him commanded that them might burn a fire within the great pit oven - and that them might add within it a malice Work that flame the fire and whereby them boil a yat - the fat and soapberries - sea foam and resin and the sulfur. ³⁶and on the time fire flamed in the pit them messengers went toward the king when them said - "We did what thou commanded we - send the men who will be added." ³⁷and him commanded that them might

receive and cast them in the fire pit - and the youths did like unto the king commanded them - and on the time those honoured men entered toward the fire them gave them souls to JAH. ³⁸and when the persons who cast them sight up - Angels raceived and took them souls toward the Garden where Yis'haq and 'Abriham and Ya`iqob are - where Feeling good joy are found.

Meqabyan I Chapter 4

¹and on the time that criminal sight up that them dead - him commanded that them might burn them flesh in fire up til it are ash and that them might scattar them in wind - but the fire couldn't able to burn the corpse hair from them corpses side - and them sent them forth from the pit. ²and again them flamed fire over them beginnin from mornin up til evenin ~ it didn't burn them ~ them said - "An now come make we cast them corpses seaward." ³and them did like unto the king commanded them ~ them cast them on the sea ~ even if them cast them seaward addin great stones and iron hearthstones and a millstone whereby a donkey grind by turnin - there are no sinkin that the sea sank them ~ as JAH Spirit of Support have lodged in them - them floated on the sea yet them didn't sink ~ it failed him to destroy them by all the malice that were provoked on them. ⁴"As this them death have made weary more than them Life - make mi cast them corpses to beasts that them might eat them - yet what will mi do?" him said. ⁵and the youths did like unto him commanded them ~ vultures and beasts didn't touch them corpses ~ birds and vultures veiled them with them wings from burnin in Sun and the five martyrs corpses sat fourteen days. ⁶and on the time them sight them up - them bodies shone up like unto Sun - and Angels incircled them corpses like unto light incircle the Tent. ⁷Him counseled counsel ~ him lacked what him do - and after this him dug a grave and buried the five martyrs corpses. ⁸and when that king who forgot JAH LAW had reclined on a bed at night the five martyrs were sight up to him standin before him at night vexin and seizin swords. ⁹As it have seemed to him that them entered toward him house at night in crime - on the time him awoke from him slumber him feared and loved that him might flee from the bedchamber toward the hall - and as it have seemed to him that them kill him seemin that them committed crime on him - him feared and him knees trembled. ¹⁰Because this thing him said - "Mi lords - what do you love? as to mi - what should mi do to you?" ¹¹Them answered to him sayin - "Aren't I whom thou killed burnin in fire and I whom you commanded that them might cast on the sea? As JAH have kept I bodies because I believed in Him - it failed thee to destroy I ~ as a person who believed in Him won't perish - make glory and praise due to JAH - and I also who believed in Him didn't shame in the tribulation. ¹²"As mi didn't know that a punishmant like unto this will find mi - what reward should mi give you because the stead wherefore mi did a evil thing on you? ¹³and now separate to mi the reward mi give you - lest you take mi body in death and lest you lower mi body toward See'ol when mi are in Life. ¹⁴As mi have wronged you - forgive mi mi sin - because it were your Father JAH LAW Niceness" him told them. ¹⁵and those honoured martyrs answered to him sayin - "Because the stead wherefore thou did a evil thing on I - as to I - I won't pay thee a evil thing ~ as JAH are Who bring hardship on a soul - as to Him Who will pay thee hardship - there are JAH. ¹⁶However I were sight up to thee bein revealed that I were well to thy timeframe bein small and because thy reasonin deafness ~ as to it seemin to thee that thou killed I - thou prepared welfare to me. ¹⁷But thy idols priests and thou will descend toward Gehannem where are no exits forever. ¹⁸Woe to thy idols to whom thou bow havin quit bowin to JAH Who Created you when you were scorned like unto spit - and to you who worship them - and you don't know JAH Who Created you bringin from not livin toward livin ~ aren't you who are sight up today like unto smoke and tomorrow who perish?" ¹⁹and the king answered to them sayin - "What will you command mi that mi might do to you all that you loved?" ²⁰"It are to save thy ras self lest thou enter toward the Gehannem of fire - yet it aren't to save I ras selves who teach thee. ²¹to your idols are silver and gold - stone and wood - that have no reasonin nor soul knowledge - that a person hand worked. ²²But them don't kill ~ them don't save ~ them don't benefit them friend ~ them don't harm them enemy ~ them don't downbase ~ them don't honour ~ them don't make wealthy ~ them don't impoverish ~ them mislead you by demons authority - who don't love that the one from persons might be saved - yet them don't uproot nor plant. ²³Them especially don't love that the persons like unto you might be saved from death - you dull-hearted ones to whom them seem that them Created you - when you are who worked them. ²⁴As Satans and demons authority have lodged in them - them shall return a thing to you like unto you loved - that it might drown you within the sea of Gehannem. ²⁵But thou - quit this thy error and make this also be I reward because I dead stead - that I might benefit I souls worshippin I Creator JAH" them told him. ²⁶But him

were alarmed and would totally astony - and as all five have been sight up to him drawin them swords - him feared - and because this thing him bowed to them. 27"Hence mi knew that after dead ones who were dust dead them will really arise ~ as to mi - only a little had remained to mi to dead." 28After this them were hidden from before that king face ~ from that day onward that Tseerutsaydan who are totally arrogant quit burnin them corpses. 29As them have misled them many eras - him would be Feeling good in him idols and him reasonin error - and him misled many persons like unto him up til them quit followin in Worship JAH Who Created them - yet it aren't only him who erred. 30Them would sacrifice them daughter childran and them male childran to demons - yet them work a seducin and disturbance that are them reasonin accord - that them father Satan taught them that him might make the seducin and disturbance that JAH don't love. 31Them marry them mothers - and them abuse them aunts and them sistren ~ them abuse them bodies while them worked all that resemble this filthy Work ~ as Satan have firmed up those crooked persons reasonin - them said - "We won't return." 32But that Tseerutsaydan - who don't know him Creator - were totally arrogant - and him would boast in him idols. 33If them say - "How will JAH give the Kingdom to the persons who don't know Him in LAW and in Worship?" - them will totally return toward Him in repentance ~ as Him test them thus - it are because this. 34But if them totally return in repentance Him would love them - and Him would keep them Kingdom - but if them refuse a fire will punish them in fire of Gehannem forever. 35But it would be due a king to fear him Creator JAH like unto him lordship fame - and it would be due a judge to be ruled to him Creator while him judged goodly judgemant like unto him Rule fame. 36and it would be due elders and chiefs and envoys and petty kings to be commanded to them Creator like unto them lordship abundance measure. 37As Him are Heaven and Earth Lord Who Created all the Creation - because there are no other Creator in Heavan nor Earth who impoverish and make rich - Him are Who honour and downbase.

Meqabyan I Chapter 5

1"The one warrior from the sixty warriors were proud ~ JAH made him body Beginnin from him foot up til him head to swell with one spoon of sulphur ~ him dead in one plague. 2and again Keeram who built a iron bed were proud arisin from him powerfulness abundance - and JAH hid him in death. 3and again Nabukedenetsor were proud sayin - 'There are no other king without mi - and mi are Creator who make the Sun rise in this world' - and him said thus arisin from him arrogance abundance. 4and JAH separated from persons and sent him toward a wilderness seven years - and him made him fortune with Heaven birds and wilderness beasts up til him knew that JAH were Who Created him. 5and on the time him knew Him in worship - Him again returned him toward him kingdom ~ who are it who weren't of Earth - bein boldly proud on JAH Who Created him? 6How about who are it who demolished HIM LAW and Him Order and whom Earth didn't swallow? 7and thou Tseerutsaydan love that thou might be proud on thy Creator - and again thou have that Him might destroy thee like unto them - and might lower thee toward a grave arisin from thy arrogance. 8and again after them entered toward See'ol where are tooth grindin and mournin - that were darkness fulfillmant - thou have that Him might lower thee toward the deep pit Gehannem where are no exits forever. 9As to thou - thou are a man who will dead and be demolished tomorrow like unto arrogant kings who were like unto thee - who quit this world livin. 10As to I - I say - 'Thou are demolished ruins - but thou aren't JAH - to JAH are Who Created Earth and Heaven and thee.' 11Him downbase arrogant ones ~ Him honour them who were downbased ~ Him give firmness to persons who wearied. 12Him kill well ones ~ Him raise up the persons who were Earth - who dead buried in grave. 13and Him send slaves forth free in Life from sin rulership. 14O king Tseerutsaydan - why do thou boast in thy defouled idols who have no benefit? 15But JAH Created Earth and Heaven and great seas ~ Him Created moon and Sun - and Him prepared eras. 16Man graze toward him field - and him while when him plough up til it dusk – and Heaven stars live firmed up by Him Word. 17and Him call all in Heaven ~ there are nothing done without JAH knowin it. 18Him commanded Heaven Angels that them might serve Him and might praise Him glorified Name - and Angels are sent toward all persons who inherit Life. 19Rufa'iel who were a servant were sent toward Thobeet - and him saved Thobya from death in Ragu'iel country. 20Hola Meeka'iel were sent toward Giediewon that him might draw him attention by money that him destroy 'Iloflee persons and him were sent toward the prophet Mussie on the time him made 'Isra'iel cross 'Eritra sea. 21As only JAH have said him led them - there were no different idol with them. 22and Him sent them forth toward crops on Earth. 23and Him fed them Him plantation grain ~ as Him have totally loved them - Him cherished them feedin the honey

that firmed up like unto a rock. 24and that thou might totally keep Him kindreds by what are due - and that thou might do JAH Accord Who Created thee - Him crowned thee givin Authority on the four kingdoms. 25to Him have crowned thee makin loftier than all - and thy Creator totally crowned thee that thou might love JAH. 26and it are procedure that thou might love thy Creator JAH like unto Him loved thee - like unto Him trusted thee on all the people - and thou - do JAH Accord that thy era might abound in this world and that Him might live with thee in Support. 27and do JAH Accord that Him might stand to thee bein a Guardian on thy enemies - and that Him might seat thee on thy throne - and that Him might hide thee in him Wing of Support. 28As to if thou don't know - JAH chose and crowned thee on 'Isra'iel like unto Him chose Sa'ol fron 'Isra'iel childran when him kept him father donkeys - and Him crowned him on him kindreds 'Isra'iel - and him sat with 'Isra'iel on him throne. 29and Him gave him a lofty fortune separatin from him kindreds ~ JAH crowned thee on Him kindreds ~ as to henceforth onward - check - keep Him kindreds. 30As JAH have Ipointed thee over them that thou might kill and might save - keep them in evil thing - them who work a goodly thing and them who work a evil thing on a goodly thing" him told him. 31"An as JAH have Ipointed thee on all that thou might do Him Accord be it while thou whipped or while thou saved - pay them evil Work - them who work goodly Work and them who work goodly Work and evil Work. 32to thou are a slave of JAH Who rule all in Heaven - and thou - do JAH Accord that Him might do thy accord to thee in all thou thought and in all thou begged while thou wheedled before Him. 33There are none who rule Him - but Him rule all. 34There are none who Ipoint Him - but Him Ipoint all. 35There are none who dismiss Him - but Him dismiss all. 36There are none who reproach Him - but Him reproach all. 37There are none who make Him diligent - but Him make all diligent ~ as Heaven and Earth rulership are to Him - there are none who escape from Him Authority all are revealed alongside Him - yet there are none hidden from Him Face. 38Him sight up all - but there are none who sight Him up ~ Him hear the person prayer who pray toward Him sayin 'Save I' - to Him have Created man in Him Pattern - and Him accept him plea. 39As Him are a King Who live up til the Eternity - Him feed all from Him unchangin Nature.

Meqabyan I Chapter 6

1As Him crown to true the kings who do Him Accord - the kings wrote a straight thing because Him. 2As them have done JAH Accord - Him shall shine up in Light that aren't examined Yis'haq and 'Abriham and Ya`iqob - Selomon and Daweet and Hiziqyas lodgins in the Garden where are all beautiful kings whose lodgin were Light. 3Heaven Hall are what totally shone - yet Earth halls aren't like unto Heaven Hall ~ it floor - whose features are silver and gold and jewel features - are clean. 4and it features that totally shine are unexamined by a person reasonin ~ Heaven Hall are what shine like unto jewels. 5Like unto JAH knew - Who were a Nature Knower - the Heaven Hall that Him Created are what a person reasonin don't examine and what shine in total Light ~ it floor - that were worked in silver and gold - in jewels - in white silk and in blue silk - are clean. 6It are quite totally beautiful like unto this. 7Righteous ones who firmed up in religion and virtue are who shall inherit it in JAH Charity and to Pardon. 8and there are welfare Water that flow from it - and it totally shine like unto Sun - and there are a Light tent within it - and it are incircled by grace perfume. 9A Garden fruit that were beautiful and Iloved - whose features and taste were different - are around the house - and there are a oil and grape place there - and it are totally beautiful - and it fruit fragrance are sweet. 10When a fleshly bloodly person enter toward it - him soul would have separated from him flesh from the Feeling good joy abundance that are in it arisin from it fragrance flavour. 11Beautiful kings who did JAH Accord shall be Feeling good there ~ them honour and them place are known in the Kingdom of Heaven that live firmed up forever - where welfare are found. 12Him showed that them lordship on Earth were famed and honoured - and that them lordship in Heaven were famed and honoured; them shall be honoured and lofty in Heaven like unto them honour them and bow to them in this world ~ if them work goodly Work in this world them shall be Feeling good. 13But kings who were evil in them Rule and them kingdoms that JAH gave them - them don't judge to true by what are due ~ as them have ignored the destitute and poor ones cries - them don't judge Truth and save the refugee and the wronged child whose father and mother dead on him. 14Them don't save destitute and poor ones from the wealthy hand that rob them ~ them don't divide and give from them food and satta them who hungered - and them don't divide and give from them drink and give to drink the persons who thirsted - and them didn't return them ears toward the poor one cry. 15and Him shall take them toward Gehannem that were a dark endin ~ on the time that lofty Day arrived on them when JAH shall come - and on the time Him wrath were done on them like unto Daweet spoke in him Praises 'Lord - don't chastise I in Thy Judgemant and don't admonish I in Thy chastisement' - them problems and them downbasement shall abound like unto them fame abundance measure. ¹⁶When nobles and kings are who rule this world in this world - there are persons who didn't keep thy law. ¹⁷But JAH Who rule all are there in Heaven ~ all persons souls and all persons welfare have been seized by Him Authority ~ Him are Who give honour to persons who glorify Him - to Him totally rule all - and Him love the persons who love Him. ¹⁸As Him are Earth and Heaven Lord - Him examine and know what kidneys transported and what a reasonin thought - and to a person who begged toward Him with a pure reasonin - Him shall give him him plea reward. ¹⁹Him shall destroy powerful ones arrogance - who work evil Work on the child whose mother and father dead on him - and on old daughters. ²⁰It aren't by thy Power that thou seized this kingdom ~ it aren't by thy bein able that thou sat on this throne ~ Him loved to test thee thus that it be possible to thee to rule like unto Sa'ol who ruled him kindreds in that season - and Him seated thee on a kingdom throne - yet it aren't by thy Power that thou seized this kingdom ~ it are when Him test thee like unto Sa'ol who ignored the prophet Samu'iel word and JAH Word and didn't serve him army nor 'Amalieq king - yet it aren't by thy bein able that thou seized this kingdom. ²¹and JAH told the prophet Samu'iel - Go - and as them have saddened I by demolishin LAW and worshippin the idols and bowin to the idol and by them mosques and by all them hated Works without benefit - tell Sa'ol - 'Go toward 'Amalieq country and destroy them hosts and all the kings Beginnin from persons up til livestock.' ²²on them who saddened JAH - because this thing Him sent Sa'ol that him might destroy them. ²³But him saved them king from death - and him saved many livestock and beauties and daughters and handsome youths from death ~ As him have scorned I thing and as him didn't hear I Command - because this thing - JAH told the prophet Samu'iel - Go and divide him kingdom. ²⁴Because him stead - Inoint `Issiey child Daweet that him might reign on 'Isra'iel. ²⁵But on him adjourn a demon who will strangle and cast him. ²⁶As him have refused if I-man gave him a kingdom that him might do I Accord - on the time him refused I to do I Accord I-man dismissed him from him kingdom that are due him - but thou - go and tell him sayin - 'Will thou thus ignore JAH Who crowned thee on Him kindreds 'Isra'iel - Who seated thee on Him Lordship Throne?' ²⁷But thou - tell him - 'Thou didn't know JAH Who gave around this much honour and famousness' Him told him. ²⁸and the prophet Samu'iel went toward the king Sa'ol and entered him sittin at a dinnertable - and when 'Amalieq king 'Agag had sat on him left. ²⁹'Why did thou totally ignore JAH Who commanded thee that thou might destroy the livestock and persons?' him told him. ³⁰and at that time the king feared and arose from him throne and tellin Samu'iel 'Return to wi' him seized him clothes - and Samu'iel refused to return ~ Samu'iel clothes were torn. ³¹and Samu'iel told Sa'ol - 'JAH divided thy kingdom.' ³²and again Sa'ol told Samu'iel before the people - 'Honour mi and atone mi sin to mi before JAH that Him might forgive mi' ~ and as him have feared JAH Word Who Created him - but as him didn't fear the king who dead - Samu'iel refused to return in him word. ³³Because this thing him pierced 'Amalieq king 'Agag before him swallowed what him chewed. ³⁴and a demon seized that Sa'ol who demolished the LAW of JAH - and because Him were the King of Kings Who rule all - JAH struck on him head a king who worked sin - to it don't shame him. ³⁵to Him are all the Creation Lord Who dismiss all the nobles and kings Authority who don't fear Him - but there are none who rule Him. ³⁶Like unto Him spoke sayin - **Daweet kindred shall go while it were famed and honoured - but Sa'ol kindred shall go while it were downbased** - Him destroyed kingdom from him child and from Sa'ol. ³⁷Because it saddened Him - and because Him destroyed the criminals who saddened Him by them evil Work - JAH revenged and destroyed Sa'ol kindred childran - to a person who don't revenge JAH enemy - him are JAH enemy. ³⁸When it are possible to him to revenge and destroy - and when him have Authority - a person who don't revenge and destroy the sinner and don't revenge and destroy a person who don't keep JAH LAW - as him are JAH enemy - Him destroyed Sa'ol kindred childran.

Meqabyan I Chapter 7

¹and whether thou be a king or a ruler - what important thing are thou? ²Aren't it JAH Who Created thee bringin from not livin toward livin - that thou might do Him Accord and might live firmed up by Him Command and might fear Him Judgemant? Like unto thou vex on thy slaves and governed over them - all likewise there are also JAH Who vex on thee and govern over thee. ³Like unto thou beat without niceness persons who worked sin - all likewise there are also JAH Who will strike thee and lower thee toward Gehannem where are no exits up til Eternity. ⁴Like unto thou whip him who weren't ruled to thee and didn't bring a tribute to thee - to what are it that thou don't introduce a tribute to JAH? ⁵As Him are Who Created thee in order that thou love that them might fear thee - and Who crowned thee on all the Creation that thou might keep Him kindreds to true - to what are it that thou don't fear thy Creator JAH? ⁶Judge by what are due and to true like unto JAH Ipointed thee - yet don't sight up a face and favour to small nor great ~ whom will thou fear without Him? keep Him Worship and the Nine Commands. ⁷Like unto Mussie commanded 'Isra'iel childran sayin - 'I-man presented Water and fire to thee-I ~ add thy hand toward what thou loved' - don't go neither rightward nor leftward. ⁸Hear Him Word that I-man tell thee - that thou might hear Him Word and might do Him Command - lest thou say - 'She are beyond the sea or beyond the deep or beyond the river - who will bring to mi that mi might sight she up and might hear Him Word and might do Him Command?' ⁹Lest thou say - 'Who will proceed toward Heaven again and lower that JAH Word to mi that mi might hear and do she?' - JAH Word are what approached - check - to thou to teach she with thy mouth and give alms by she with thy hand. ¹⁰and thou didn't hear thy Creator JAH unless thou heard Him Book - and thou didn't love Him nor keep Him Command unless thou kept Him LAW. ¹¹and thou have that thou might enter toward Gehannem forever - and unless thou loved Him Command - and unless thou did Him Accord - Who honoured and famed thee separatin from all thy kindreds that thou might keep them to true - thou have that thou might enter toward Gehannem forever. ¹²Him made thee above all - and Him crowned thee on all Him kindreds that thou might rule Him kindreds to true by what are due while thou thought of thy Creator Name Who Created thee and gave thee a kingdom. ¹³There are them whom thou whip from persons who wronged thee - and there are him whom thou pardon while thou thought of JAH Work - and there are him to whom thou judge by what are due straightenin up thy reasonin. ¹⁴and don't favour havin sight up a face on the time them argued before thee ~ as Earth physique are thy money - don't accept a bribe that thou might pardon the sinner person and wrong the clean person. ¹⁵If thou did Him Accord - JAH shall multiply thy era in this world to thee - but if thou sadden Him - Him will diminish thy era. ¹⁶Think that thou will rise after thou dead - and that thou will be examined standin before Him on all the Work thou worked whether it be goodly or evil. ¹⁷If thou work goodly Work - thou will live in Garden in the Kingdom of Heaven - in houses where kind kings live and where Light filled. to JAH don't shame thy lordship authority - but if thou work evil Work - thou will live in See'ol Gehannem where evil kings live. ¹⁸But on the time thou sight up thy bein feared famousness - thy warriors award - thy hangin shield and spear - and on the time thou sight up thy horses and thy troops beneath thy authority and them who beat drum and persons who play on a harp before thee... ¹⁹But on the time thou sight up all this - thou make thy reasonin lofty - and thou firm up thy collar of reasonin - and thou don't think of JAH Who gave thee all this honour - however on the time Him told thee - Quit all this - thou aren't who quit it. ²⁰to thou have totally neglected the Ipointment Him Ipointed thee - and Him shall give thy lordship to another. ²¹As death shall suddenly come on thee - and as Judgemant shall be done in Resurrection time - and as all man Work shall be examined - Him shall totally investigate and judge on thee. ²²There are none who will honour this world kings - to because Him were Truth Judge - in Judgemant time poor and wealthy will stand together. This world nobles crowns wherein them boast shall fall. ²³Judgemant are prepared - and a soul shall quake ~ at that time sinners and righteous ones Work shall be examined. ²⁴and there are none who shall be hidden. on the time a daughter arrived to birthin - and on the time the fetus in she belly arrived to bein birthed - like unto she cyaan prevent she womb - Earth also cyaan prevent she lodgers that are on she ~ she will return. ²⁵and like unto clouds cyaan prevent rain lest them take and rain toward the place JAH commanded them - to JAH Word have Created all bringin from not livin toward livin - and to JAH Word again have introduced all toward a grave and all likewise - after Resurrection time arrived - it aren't possible to be that dead persons won't rise. ²⁶Like unto Mussie spoke sayin - 'It are by Words that proceed from JAH Tongue - yet it aren't only by grain that a person are saved'; and JAH Word again shall arouse all persons from graves. ²⁷Check - it were known that dead persons shall arise by JAH Word. ²⁸and again JAH said thus in Repeatin Law because persons who were nobles and kings who do Him Accord - **As the day have arrived when them are counted to destruction - I-man shall revenge and destroy them on the day when Judgemant are judged and at the time when them feet stumble Him said.** ²⁹and again JAH told persons who know Him Judgemant - **Know know that I-man**

were your Creator JAH - and that I-man kill and I-man save. ³⁰I-man chastise in the tribulation and I-man pardon ~ I-man lower toward See'ol and again I-man send forth toward the **Garden - and there are none who shall escape from I Authority** Him told them. ³¹JAH said thus because nobles and kings who didn't keep Him LAW - **As Earthly kingdoms are a passin - and as them pass from mornin up til evenin - keep I Order and I LAW that you might enter toward the Kingdom of Heaven that live firmed up forever** Him said. ³²to JAH callin Righteous ones are to glory - and sinners to tribulation ~ Him will make the sinner wretched but will honour righteous ones. ³³Him will dismiss the person who didn't do Him Accord - but Him will Ipoint the person who did Him Accord.

Meqabyan I Chapter 8

¹Hear I - make I tell thee the thing whereby dead persons shall arise ~ them shall plant a plant and be fertile and grapes shall send forth vines ~ as JAH shall bring the fruit *imhibe 'albo* ~ them shall cast wine from it. ²Overstand that that plant thou planted were small - but that she sent forth tips fruit and leaves today. ³JAH give she root to drink from Earth and Water - from both. ⁴But Him feed she wood from fire and wind ~ roots give leaves Water to drink - and Earth give firmness to woods. ⁵But the soul that JAH Created make them bear fruit amidst them - and dead persons arisin are likewise. ⁶on the time soul were separated from flesh - as each of them ras selves have gone - Him said - **'Gather souls from the four natures - from Earth and Water - wind and fire.'** ⁷But Earth nature lived firmed up in she nature and became Earth - and Water nature lived firmed up in she nature and became Water. ⁸and wind nature lived firmed up in she nature and became wind - and fire nature lived firmed up in she nature and became a hot fire. ⁹But a soul that JAH separated from flesh returned toward she Creator ~ up til Him raise she up inited with flesh on the time Him loved - Him place she in Garden in the place Him loved. ¹⁰Him place righteous souls in Light house in Garden - but that Him might send way sinners souls - Him also place them in darkness house in See'ol up til the time when Him loved. ¹¹JAH told the prophet Hiziq'iel - **'Call souls from the four corners'** - that them might be gathered and be one limb. ¹²on the time Him spoke in one Word sayin thus - the souls were gathered from the four corners. ¹³and Water nature brought verdure - and again fire nature brought fire. ¹⁴and again Earth nature brought Earth - and wind nature brought wind. ¹⁵and JAH brought a soul from the Garden place where Him placed it ~ them were gathered by one Word - and a Resurrection were made. ¹⁶and again I-man shall show thee the example that are alongside thee ~ the day dusk ~ thou sleep ~ the night dawn - and thou rise from thy beddin - but on the time thou slept it are thy death example. ¹⁷and on the time thou awoke it are thy arisin example - but the night when all persons sleep whose physiques were dark - to darkness have covered them - are this world example. ¹⁸But the mornin light - when darkness are eliminated and when light are in all the world and when persons arise and graze toward the field - are dead persons example. ¹⁹and this Kingdom of Heaven where man are renewed are like unto this ~ dead persons Resurrection are like unto this ~ as this world are passin - it are the night example. ²⁰and like unto Daweet spoke sayin - 'Him placed Him example in Sun' - as Sun shine on the time it rose - it are a Kingdom of Heaven example. ²¹and like unto Sun shine in this world today - on the time Kristos come Him shall shine like unto Sun in Kingdom of Heaven that are new ~ as Him have said - **'I-man am a Sun that don't set and a Torch that aren't extinguished'** - Him JAH are she Light. ²²and Him shall quickly arouse the dead persons again ~ I-man shall bring one example to thee again from thy food that thou sow and whereby thou are saved - and whether it be a wheat kernel or a barley kernel or a lentil kernel or all man seeds sown on Earth - there are none that grow unless it were demolished and rotten. ²³and like unto the person flesh thou sight up - on the time it were demolished and rotten - Earth eat stoutness with the hide. ²⁴and on the time Earth ate it stoutness it grow bein around a kernel seventh ~ JAH give a cloud that seized rain like unto Him loved - and roots grow on Earth and send forth leaves. ²⁵and if she were demolished and rotten she cyaan grow - but after she grew she send forth many buds. ²⁶and by JAH Accord fruit are given to those buds that grew - and Him clothe it stoutness in straw. ²⁷Sight up like unto the measure that the seed kernel thou sowed abounded - yet the silver and the leaf - the ear and the straw aren't counted to thee. ²⁸Don't be a dull one who don't know - and sight up thy seed that it abounded - and all likewise - think that dead persons shall raceive the arisin that them will arise - and them hardship like unto them Work. ²⁹Hear I - that if thou sow wheat - it won't grow bein barley - nor bein wheat if thou sow barley - and make I tell thee again that it won't grow ~ if thou sow wheat will thou gather barley? If thou sow watercress will thou gather linseed?

³⁰How about from plants kind - if thou plant figs will it really grow to thee bein nuts? How about if thou plant almonds - will it grow to thee bein grapes? ³¹If thou plant the sweet fruit will it grow to thee bein bitter? How about if thou plant the bitter fruit - are it possible to it to be sweet? ³²How about all likewise - if a sinner dead are it possible to arise bein righteous in Resurrection time? How about if a righteous person dead - are it possible to arise bein a sinner in Resurrection time? Every one shall raceive him hardship like unto him Work - yet him will raceive him hardship like unto him sin and him hand Work - yet there are none who will be canvicted by him companion sin. ³³A highland tree are planted and it send forth long branches ~ it will totally dry up ~ yet unless Heaven rained rain it leaves won't be verdant. ³⁴and the cedar will be uprooted from it roots unless summer rain alit on it. ³⁵and all likewise - dead persons won't arise unless welfare dew alit to them bein commanded from JAH.

Meqabyan I Chapter 9

¹Unless highland mountains and Gielabuhie regions rained a pardon rain to them bein commanded from JAH - them won't grow grass to beasts and animals. ²and 'Elam mountains and Gele`ad mountains won't give verdant leaves to sheeps and goats - nor to oribi and animals in wilderness - nor to ibexes and hartebeest. ³and likewise - pardon and dew bein commanded from JAH didn't alight to doubters and criminals who made error and crime a money beforehand ~ dead persons won't arise ~ and Deemas and Qophros who worship idols and dig roots and work and instigate a thing... ⁴and them who dig roots and practice sorcery and make persons battle - ⁵and them who lust havin departed from LAW - and Miedon and 'Atiena persons who believe in them idols - and them who play and sing to them while them beat violins and drums and strummed harps - them won't arise unless pardon dew alit to them bein commanded from JAH. ⁶These are who will be canvicted on the day when dead persons arise and when Definite Judgemant are done - yet persons who save them ras selves and who lust in them hands Work - them err by them idols. ⁷Thou wasteful of heart dull one - do it seem to thee that dead persons won't arise? ⁸on the time a trumpet were blown by the Angels Chief Hola Meeka'iel tongue - that dead ones arise then - as thou won't remain in grave without arisin - don't think a thing that are thus. ⁹Hills and mountains shall be level and shall be a cleared path. ¹⁰and Resurrection shall be done to all fleshly ones.

Meqabyan I Chapter 10

¹However if it weren't thus - it are that former persons might be buried in them fathers grave Beginnin from 'Adam - Beginnin from Siet and 'Abiel - Siem and Noh - Yis'haq and 'Abriham - Yosief and Ya`iqob - and 'Aron and Mussie - yet to what are it that them didn't love that them might be buried in another place? ²Aren't it to them to arise together with them cousins in Resurrection time? How about aren't it lest them bones be counted with evil ones and pagans bones - them who worship idols? to what are it that them didn't love that them might be buried in another place? ³But thou - don't mislead thy reasonin while thou said - 'How will dead persons arise after them dead - them who were buried in one grave bein tens of thousands and whose bodies were demolished and rotten?' ⁴and on the time thou sight up toward a grave - thou speak this in thy reasonin dullness while thou said - 'A whole fistful of Earth won't be found ~ how will dead persons arise?' ⁵Will thou say the seed thou sowed won't grow? Even the seed thou sowed shall grow. ⁶and all likewise - the souls JAH sowed shall quickly arise - as Him have Created man in Him Truth bringin from not livin toward livin - Him shall arouse them quickly by Him Word that save ~ Him won't delay Him arousin. ⁷and as Him have again returned him from livin - toward a grave in death - what about aren't it possible to Him again to return from death toward Life? ⁸Savin and liftin up are possible to JAH.

Meqabyan I Chapter 11

¹'Armon perished and she fortress were demolished ~ as JAH have brought the hardship on them like unto them evil and the Work them worked by them hands - persons who worship the idols in 'Edomyas and Zablon shall be downbased at that time ~ as JAH have approached - Who shall canvict them who worked in them infancy and didn't quit up til them aged - because them idols and them evil - Seedona and Theeros shall weep. ²Because them worked sin and seducin fornication and worshipped idols - because this thing JAH shall revenge and destroy them ~ to them didn't live firmed up in them Creator JAH Command - and Yihuda daughter childran shall be wretched. ³She lived firmed up in killin prophets and in Feeling good joy - yet as she didn't live firmed up in the Nine Laws and the Worship - on the time when dead ones arise - 'Iyerusaliem sin shall be revealed. ⁴At that time JAH shall examine she in Him Nature Wisdom ~ Him will revenge and destroy she on all she sin that she worked in she infancy era ~ she didn't quit workin she sin Beginnin from she beauty era up til she age. ⁵She

entered toward a grave and became dust like unto she former fathers who lived firmed up in them sin - and in Resurrection time Him shall revenge and destroy persons who demolished JAH LAW. ⁶It shall be judged on them - to Mussie have spoken because them sayin - 'Them LAW lodgin - them reasonins - became Sedom law lodgin.' ⁷and them kindred are Gemorra kindred - and them law are what destroy - and them Work are evil. ⁸and them law are snake poison that destroy - and viper poison that destroy from alongside that.

Meqabyan I Chapter 12

¹'Iyerusaliem child - as this thy sin are like unto Gemorra and Sedom sin - 'Iyerusaliem child - this are thy tribulation that were spoken by a prophet. ²and thy tribulation are like unto Gemorra and Sedom tribulation - and them law lodgin reasonin firmed up in adultery and arrogance. ³Aside from adultery and arrogance rain - pardon and humility rain didn't rain from them reasonins by money that them Law reasonin lodgin are fertile - apart from spillin man blood and robbin and forgettin them Creator JAH. ⁴and them didn't know them Creator JAH - apart from them evil Work and them idols - and them are Feeling good in them hands Work - and them lust on males and on livestock. ⁵As them eye of reasonin have been blinded lest them sight up secrets - and as them ears have deafened lest them hear or do JAH Accord that Him love - them didn't know JAH in them Work - and them reasonins are like unto Sedom law lodgin. and them kindred - Gemorra grapes kindred that bear sweet fruit. ⁶and if them examine them Work - it are poison that kill - to it have firmed up in curse Beginnin from the day when it were worked - and to it grounation have been in destruction era. ⁷As them Law lodgin - them reasonins - have firmed up in sin Work - as them bodies have firmed up in Satan burnin Work to build sin - them Law lodgin - them reasonins - have no goodly Work everytime. ⁸and on the time him shame and were baptise (by one who is led) it were to chastisemant and destruction - and him will firm up the persons who drank and them reasonins - and him will make them who destroy I - disgustin persons who distanced from JAH. ⁹to them have lived firmed up in them Work that were evil - and him will make them Deeyablos lodgin - and eatin what were sacrificed to the idols have been begun in the House of 'Isra'iel - and she proceed toward the mountains and the trees. ¹⁰and she worship the idols that peoples in she area worship - and she daughter childran and she male childran to demons who don't know goodly Work separatin from evil. ¹¹and them spill clean blood ~ them gush and spill grapes from Sedom to the idols forever. ¹²and she glorify and worship the Dagwon that the 'Iloflans worship - and she sacrifice to him from she flocks and she fattened cows - that she might be Feeling good in demons laziness that them taught she to sacrifice to them - and in them gushin and spillin the grapes - and that she might do them accord. ¹³She sacrifice to him that she might be Feeling good in demons laziness that them taught she lest she know she Creator JAH Who feed she at each time and Who cherished and raised she Beginnin from she infancy up til she beauty - and again up til she age - and again up til she age day when she dead. ¹⁴and again **I-man shall revenge and canvict him in Resurrection time - and as she didn't return toward I LAW - and as she didn't live firmed up in I Command - she time when she live in Gehannem shall be up til Eternity.** ¹⁵If them were Creators to true - make she idols arise with she and descend toward Gehannem and save she on the time I-man vexed and destroyed she - and on the time I-man distanced all the priests of the idols who lust with she. ¹⁶Like unto she made sin and insult on the Hola Items and on I Lodgin the Temple - I-man made she wretched by all this. ¹⁷When them told she - 'Check - this are JAH kindred - and she are 'Isra'iel Creator JAH Lodgin - and the famous King country 'Iyerusaliem who were separate from them who were separate - she are the Most I JAH Name Lodgin' - I-man made she wretched like unto she saddened I Name that were called in she. ¹⁸She boast in I that she were I slave and that I-man were she Lord ~ she wink on I like unto a criminal - yet she aren't who fear I and do I Accord like unto I bein she Lord. ¹⁹Them became a obstacle on she to mislead that them might distance she from I - yet she are ruled to other idols who don't feed she nor clothe she. ²⁰She sacrifice to them - and she eat the sacrifice - and she spill blood to them - and she gush and drink from the grapes to them ~ she smoke up ishence to them - and she make the ishence fragrance smell to them ~ she idols command she - and she are commanded to them. ²¹and again she sacrifice she daughter childran and she male childran to them - and as she present praises to them because them Love - she are Feeling good in the thing she spoke by she tongue and in she hands Work. ²²Woe to she on the day when Definite Judgemant are done - and woe to she idols whom she love and inite; and she shall descend with them toward Gehannem beneath See'ol - where the worm don't slumber and the fire aren't extinguished. ²³Woe to thee wretched 'Iyerusaliem child - to thou have quit I Who Created thee and have worshipped different idols. ²⁴and I-man shall bring the hardship on thee like unto thy Work ~ as thou have saddened I - and as thou have ignored I Word - and as thou didn't work goodly Work - I-man shall canvict thee toward thy pretensions. ²⁵to thou have saddened I Word - and to thou didn't live firmed up in I LAW whereby thou swore with I - that thou might keep I LAW and that I-man might live with thee in Support and might save thee from all who fight thee - and also that thou might keep I Order that I-man commanded thee - and I-man shall ignore thee and won't quickly save thee from the tribulation. ²⁶Thou didn't keep all this - and I-man ignored thee ~ as I-man have created thee - and as thou didn't keep I Command nor I Word - I-man shall canvict thee in Judgement time - and I-man honoured thee that thou might be I kin. ²⁷and like unto Gemorra and Sedom were separated from I - thou were separated from I. ²⁸and I-man judged and destroyed them - and like unto Sedom and Gemorra were separated from I - thou separated from I - and now like unto I-man vexed and destroyed them - I-man vexed and destroyed thee ~ as thou are from Sedom and Gemorra kindred whom I-man destroyed - I-man destroyed thee ~ as them whom I-man Created have saddened I by goin toward a youtmon wife and by lustin without LAW - with animals and males like unto arrivin with daughters - I-man destroyed them name invocation from this world lest them live in them Feeling good joy. ²⁹There are no fearin JAH in them faces Beginnin from a infant up til a elder ~ them help him in all them evil Work - yet Him don't vex on each one that them might quit workin the evil ~ as them Work are evil - them are sated of sin and iniquity. ³⁰All evil Work - robbery and arrogance and greed - are prepared in them reasonins. ³¹and because this thing JAH ignored them and destroyed them countries - and them are there that Him might burn them with fire up til them root grounation perish ~ them totally perished up til the Eternity - yet Him didn't make even one from them remain. ³²As them have firmed up in sin - them shall wait in destruction forever up til the Day of Advent when Definite Judgemant are done - to them have saddened I with them evil Work - and I-man won't pardon them nor forgive them. ³³and I-man ignored them ~ to thou won't find a reason on the time I-man vexed and seized thee because all thy Work were robbery and sin - adultery and greed and speakin lies - all error Work and the obstacle that I-man don't love - and thou 'Iyerusaliem child who were wretched - on the day when Judgemant are done thou will be seized in Judgemant like unto them. ³⁴I-man had made thee to honour - but thou downbased thy ras self ~ I-man had called thee I money - but thou became to another. ³⁵I-man had betrothed thee to honour - but thou became to Deeyablos - and I-man shall revenge and destroy thee like unto thy evil Work. ³⁶Because thou didn't hear all I Word - and because thou didn't keep the Command I-man commanded thee on the time I-man loved thee - I-man shall multiply and bring firm vengeance on thee - to I-man am JAH Who Created thee - and I-man shall judge on all sinners like unto thee - and on the day when Judgemant are done I-man shall bring the hardship on them like unto them evil Work. ³⁷As thou didn't keep I Word - and as thou have ignored I Judgemant - I-man shall canvict thee with them. ³⁸Woe to you - Gemorra and Sedom - who have no fearin JAH in your reasonin. ³⁹All likewise - woe to thy sista 'Iyerusaliem child on whom it shall be judged together with thee in fire of Gehannem - to you will descend together toward Gehannem that were prepared to you - where are no exits forever - and woe to all sinners who worked thy sin. ⁴⁰As you didn't keep I Command nor I Word - thou and she who didn't keep I Command nor I Word shall descend toward See'ol together on the day when Judgemant are judged. ⁴¹But kind persons who kept I Command and I Word shall eat the money that sinner persons accumulated - and like unto JAH commanded - kind persons shall share the loot that evil persons captured - and kind persons shall be totally Feeling good. ⁴²But wrongdoers and sinner persons shall weep - and them shall be sad because all them sin that them wronged havin departed from I Command. ⁴³Him who keep I Word and live firmed up in I Command - him are who find I blessin and are honoured alongside I. ⁴⁴All person who

keep I Word and live firmed up in I Command shall eat the fatness found from Earth - and shall live havin entered toward the Garden where enter kind kings who have straight reasonins.

Meqabyan I Chapter 13

¹As them shall be wretched and perish by I wrath on the time I-man seized them - woe to Theeros and Seedona and all Yihuda country regions who make them ras selves arrogant today. ²Conquerin JAH said thus ~ Him have said - **Deeyablos child who are totally arrogant shall be birthed from them - the False Messeeh who to a Truth thing are she enemy - who firm up him collar of reasonin - who boast and don't know him Creator** - and Him said - Woe to them - and JAH Who rule all said - I-man made him to I anger pattern that I-man might be revealed in him Power. ³and this Qifirnahom Semarya and Geleela and Demasqo and Sorya and 'Akeya and Qophros and all Yordanos region are kindreds who firmed up them collars of reasonin - who live firmed up in them sin - and whom death shadow and darkness covered - to Deeyablos have covered them reasonins in sin - and to them are commanded to that arrogant Deeyablos - and them didn't return toward fearin JAH. ⁴At that time woe to persons who are commanded to demons and who sacrifice in them name to them ~ as them have denied JAH Who Created them - them resemble animals without minds - to the False Messeeh who forgot JAH LAW and are Deeyablos child shall set up him image in all the places (to him have said 'Mi are a god') - and him shall be Feeling good in him reasonin accord - in him hand Work and in robbery and all the sins and perfidy and iniquity - in robbery and all the adulteries that a person work. ⁵to because it were counted alongside JAH that him work this - the era are known that them work sin. ⁶Sun shall darken and moon shall be blood - and stars shall be shaken from Heaven - all the Work shall pass by the miracles that JAH shall bring in Fulfillmant Era that Him might make Earth pass - and that Him might make all pass who live in sin of persons who live within she. ⁷As JAH have been proud on the Creation Him Created - and as Him have quickly made all Him loved in one hour - the Lord death shall destroy a small enemy Deeyablos. ⁸to JAH Who rule all have said - **I-man shall judge and destroy** - but after Advent - Deeyablos have no authority. ⁹and **on the day when him were seized by I anger - him shall descend toward Gehannem - to which him make application and where firm tribulation are ~ as him will take all who are with him toward chastisemant and destruction and perfidy - because I-man were Who send forth from Gehannem and Who introduce toward Gehannem - him will descend toward Gehannem.** ¹⁰As Him give firmness and Power to weak persons - and again as Him give weakness to powerful and firm persons - make a powerful one not boast in him Power. ¹¹As Him are a Ruler - and as Him judge and save the wronged persons from the persons hands who wrong them - Him will return the grudge of the widows and the child whose father and mother dead on him. ¹²**Woe to thee who boast and firm up thy collar of reasonin - to whom it seem that I-man won't rule thee nor judge and destroy thee - to in him boastin and him arrogance him have said - 'Mi will streach mi throne in stars and Heaven - and mi will be like unto JAH Who are lofty.'** ¹³and like unto Him spoke sayin - How Deeyablos fell from Heaven - him who shine like unto a mornin star that were Created precedin all - woe to thee. ¹⁴and thou dared and spoke this in thy arrogance - and thou didn't think of JAH Who totally Created thee by Him Authority ~ why did thou boast thy ras self that thou descend toward Gehannem in thy reasonin firmness? ¹⁵Thou were downbased separate from all Angels like unto thee - to them praise them Creator with a humbled reasonin because them knew that Him were Who Created them from fire and wind - and to them don't depart from Him Command - and to them keep them reasonins from perfidy lest them totally depart from Him Command. ¹⁶But thou did a firm perfidy in thy reasonin arrogance ~ thou became a wretched man separate from thy companions - to thou have cherished all the sin and iniquity - robbery and perfidy whereby persons who forgot JAH LAW and sinners like unto thee live firmed up - them who are from thy kindred and commit crime like unto thee - and who live firmed up by thy command and thy accord whereby thou teach sin. ¹⁷Woe to thee - to the demons thou misled in thy malice and thou will descend toward Gehannem together. ¹⁸O you JAH childran who erred by that misleadin criminal Deeyablos - woe to you ~ as you have erred like unto him by the money that him taught you and that him hosts taught you - you will descend toward Gehannem together - where are no exits forever. ¹⁹and formerly when JAH slave Mussie were there - you saddened JAH by the Water where argumant were made and on Korieb - and by 'Amalieq and on Mount Seena. ²⁰and moreover on the time you sent scouts toward Kene`an -

on the time them told you this sayin 'The path are far - and them ramparts and them fortresses that reach up til Heaven are firm - and warriors live there' - you vexed that you might return towad Gibts country where you work worrisome Work - and you saddened JAH Word. ²¹You didn't think of JAH Who firmed you up from the tribulation - and Who did great miracles in Gibts - and Who led you by Him Angel Authority. Him would veil you in cloud by day lest the Sun burn you and Him would shine a column of fire to you by night lest your feet stumble in darkness. ²²and on the time the army and Fer`on frightened you - you totally cried toward Mussie - and Mussie totally cried toward JAH - and Him lodged in Him Angel and kept you lest you meet with Fer`on. ²³But Him introduced them toward 'Eritra in tribulation ~ JAH led only 'Isra'iel - to Him have said - and **there were no different idol with them** - but Him buried them enemies in sea at one time - and Him didn't preserve none who flee from them. ²⁴and Him made 'Isra'iel cross amidst the sea by foot ~ there are no tribulation that found them arisin from the Gibtsans ~ Him delivered them toward Mount Seena - and there Him fed them menna forty eras. ²⁵As 'Isra'iel childran sadden JAH everytime - Him did all this goodly thing to them and them neglected to worship JAH. ²⁶Them placed evil in them reasonins Beginnin from them childhood up til them age - to JAH Mouth have spoken thus in 'Oreet where the fathers birth were written ~ as Him have spoken sayin - **'Adam childran reasonin are ash - and all them Work are toward robbery and them run toward evil ~ there are none from them who love straight Work - apart from gatherin a person money in violence and swearin in lie and wrongin companions and robbin and stealin** - them placed evil in them reasonins. ²⁷and all go toward evil Work in the era when them live in Life ~ 'Isra'iel childran who demolished JAH LAW totally saddened JAH Beginnin from Antiquity up til fufillmant era.

Meqabyan I Chapter 14

¹and on the time JAH destroyed Qayen childran - kindreds who preceded - in destruction Water because them sin - Him baptised Earth in Water of Destruction - and Him cleansed she from all Qayel childran sin. ²As Him have said - **I-man were sad because I-man Created man** - Him destroyed all wrongdoers ~ Him didn't preserve apart from eight persons ~ Him destroyed all ~ after this Him multiplied them and them filled Earth ~ them shared them father 'Adam inheritance. ³But Noh swore with JAH a oath ~ them swore a oath with JAH lest JAH again destroy Earth in Destruction Water - and lest Noh childran eat what deceased nor what lodged dead - lest them worship different idols apart from JAH Who Created them - and that Him might be a Love Father to them - and lest Him destroy them at one time in them vain sin - and lest Him prevent them the first and the spring rain - and that Him might give to livestock and persons them food at each time - that Him might give them the grass and the grain fruit and plants - and that them might work goodly Work in all that JAH love. ⁴and after Him gave them this Order - 'Isra'iel childran saddened JAH by them sin ~ them didn't live firmed up in Him LAW like unto them fathers Yis'haq and 'Abriham and Ya`iqob who didn't demolish them Creator JAH LAW. ⁵and Beginnin from the small up til the great - those 'Isra'iel childran who didn't keep JAH LAW are crooked in them Work. ⁶and whether them be them priests or them chiefs or them scribes - everyone demolish JAH LAW. ⁷Them don't live firmed up in JAH Order and Him LAW that Mussie commanded them in Repeatin Law sayin - **Love thy Creator JAH in thy complete body and thy complete reasonin.** ⁸Them don't firm up in JAH Order and Him LAW that Mussie commanded them in book where LAW were written sayin - **Love thy companion like unto thy body - and don't worship him idols that were different - and don't go toward a youtmon wife ~ don't kill a soul ~ don't steal. ⁹and don't witness in lie - and be it him donkey or be it him ox - don't love thy companion money nor all that thy bredda bought.** ¹⁰However after him commanded them all this - 'Isra'iel childran who were evil return toward treachery and sin - robbery and iniquity - toward a youtmon wife and toward lies and stealin and worshippin idols. ¹¹'Isra'iel childran saddened JAH on Korieb by workin a cow that graze toward grass ~ them bowed sayin - 'Check - these are we creators who sent we forth from Gibts.' ¹²and them were Feeling good in them hand Work ~ if them ate and drank and satta - them arose to sing. ¹³**As JAH have told him sayin - Thy kindreds whom thou sent forth from Gibts country where rulership are - them have proceeded from LAW and wronged - and them worked a cow image and bowed to the idol** - because this thing Mussie vexed and alit from Seena mountain. ¹⁴While Mussie vexed on him kindreds - him alit with him canfidante 'Iyasu - and on the time 'Iyasu heard - him said - 'Check - I-man hear warriors voice in 'Isra'iel camp.' ¹⁵and Mussie told 'Iyasu

503

- 'It are when 'Isra'iel play havin drunk the unboiled wine - yet as to a warrior voice - it aren't' - and him alit and broke them image and totally crushed it up til it were like unto dust ~ him mixed it within the Water that 'Isra'iel childran drink beside the mountain. ¹⁶and after this him commanded the priests that them might slay one another because the sin them worked before JAH. ¹⁷Them knew that defyin JAH surpass killin them and killin them fathers - and them did like unto him commanded them. ¹⁸and Mussie told them - 'Because you saddened JAH Who fed you and cherished you and Who sent you forth from a rulership house and Who bequeathed to you the inheritance that Him swore to your fathers that Him might give to them and to them childran after them - because this thing you made JAH Feeling good.' ¹⁹to them go toward sin and a evil thing - and them didn't quit saddenin JAH there. ²⁰Them aren't like unto them fathers Yis'haq and 'Abriham and Ya`iqob who made JAH Feeling good with them goodly Work that Him might give them what are on Earth and what Him prepared to persons who love Him in Heaven Beginnin from them infancy up til them youthood and up til them age ~ them aren't like unto 'Abriham and Yis'haq and Ya`iqob who made Him Feeling good with them Work that Him might give them a Earth of inheritance where Feeling good joy are found in this world - and a garden that make Feeling good - prepared to kind persons in hereafter world - what Him prepared to 'Abriham and Yis'haq and Ya`iqob who made JAH Feeling good when them were in Life and who love Him - Whom a eye didn't sight up nor a ear hear and Who aren't thought of in reasonin. ²¹and them childran who denied JAH and were evil and who live firmed up in them reasonin accord - them didn't hear JAH Command - Him Who fed them and cherished them and kept them Beginnin from them infancy. ²²Them didn't think of JAH - Who sent them forth from Gibts land and saved them from brick Work and a firm rulership. ²³But them totally saddened Him - and Him would arouse peoples in them area on them - and them would arise on them in enmity and also tax them like unto them loved.

Meqabyan I Chapter 15

¹and at that time Midyam persons arose on them in enmity - and them aroused them armies on 'Isra'iel that them might fight them - and them king name are called 'Akrandis ~ him quickly gathered many armies in Keeliqyas and Sorya and Demasqo. ²and campin beyond Yordanos him sent messengers sayin - 'An that mi might capture your money - pay tax toward 'Isra'iel to mi' ~ him told them - 'But if you don't pay tax - mi came that mi might punish and might capture your livestocks and take your mares and capture your childran.' ³'Mi will capture and take you toward the country you don't know - and there mi will make you Water pourers and wood pickers' him told them. ⁴'Don't boast while you said - "I are JAH kindreds and there are nothing able to I" - aren't JAH Who sent mi that mi might destroy you and plunder your money? and aren't mi whom JAH sent that mi might gather all your kindreds? ⁵Are there really a savin that them different idols saved the other kins that mi destroyed? Mi captured them mares and them horses and mi killed them and captured them childran. ⁶and unless you introduced the tax that mi commanded you - mi will destroy you like unto them' him said - and him crossed Yordanos that him might plunder them livestocks and them money and capture them wives. ⁷and after this 'Isra'iel childran wept a firm mournin toward JAH - and them totally cried - however them lacked one who help them. ⁸and because this thing JAH gave firmness to the three bredren - and them names are like unto this: - and them are Yihuda and Mebikyas and Meqabees - whose features were handsome and who were warriors in them Power. ⁹and 'Isra'iel childran totally wept there ~ on the time them heard - it saddened them in them heart arisin from all 'Isra'iel childran shout ~ the child whose mother and father dead on him - and widows - and them officials and them priests - all 'Isra'iel kindred - both daughters and males - and all childran - would weep sprinklin ash on them heads - and them nobles had worn sackcloth. ¹⁰But those bredren - who were attractive and comely - went and agreed that them might save them ~ them counseled sayin - 'Make I go and give I bodies to death because these persons.' ¹¹Tellin one another - 'Take heart - take heart' - them went girdin them swords on them waists and seizin them spears in them hands - and them went prepared that them might incriminate the warrior. ¹²and them arrived toward them camp ~ Mebikyas attacked the warrior (the king) when him had sat at a dinnertable ~ him cut him neck in one blow when food were in him mouth; and Meqabyus and Yihuda struck him armies on the king left and right by sword and killed them. ¹³and on the time them king were defeated - them entered toward them spears in them companions hearts - and them all totally fled and them bows were broken and them were defeated. ¹⁴But those bredren who are attractive and comely were saved from death ~ there are no evil thing that found them - but as JAH have returned chastisement toward them - them sliced up one another and were depleted. ¹⁵Them were defeated and dead and them crossed Yordanos - and up til them crossed them cast way all them money - and all them money remained - and pom the time 'Isra'iel childran sight up that them enemies fled - them went toward them camp and took both what them plundered and them money to them ras selves. ¹⁶JAH saved 'Isra'iel doin thus by the bredren and Mebikyu hand. ¹⁷'Isra'iel sat a few days while them made JAH Feeling good. ¹⁸But after that them again returned toward them sin ~ 'Isra'iel childran neglected worshippin JAH by what are due. ¹⁹and Him shall again sadden them by kins who don't know them and who will gather them field crops and destroy them grape places and plunder them flocks and slaughter and feed them them livestocks before them... ²⁰and who will capture them wives and them daughter childran and them male childran ~ because it were that them sadden JAH everytime; as them are kindreds who demolished the LAW - them will hammer them childran before them on each of them heads ~ them won't save them.

Meqabyan I Chapter 16

¹Them who do this are Theeros and Seedona and them who live beyond Yordanos river and on the sea edge - Keran and Gele`ad - 'Iyabuseewon and Kenaniewon - 'Edom and Giegiesiewon and 'Amalieq persons. ²All peoples do thus - who live firmed up in each of them tribes and countries and regions and in each of them Works and country languages - and all live firmed up like unto JAH worked them. ³and there are persons from them who know JAH - and whose Work were beautiful. ⁴and there are persons from them whose Work were evil and who don't know JAH Who Created them - and like unto them worked sin - Him ruled them in Sorya king Silminasor hand. ⁵As him plunder and take Demasqo money - and as him share Semarya loot that are before Gibts king - Him ruled them in Silminasor hand. ⁶Gielabuhie region and also persons in Fars and Miedon - Qephedoqya and Sewseegya - who live in the West mountains - in Gele`ad fortress and Phasthos that are part of Yihuda land... ⁷and these are who live in them region - and them are kindreds who don't know JAH nor keep Him Command - and whose collar of reasonin were firm. ⁸and Him shall pay them them hardship like unto them Work evil and them hands Work. ⁹to Gele`ad kindreds and Qeesarya region and 'Amalieq have become one there - that them might destroy JAH country that were filled of a Truth thing - and within which 'Isra'iel Creator are praised - Him Who are Most Glorified and Conquerin - and Whom Angels who are many many in Keerubiel chariots - them who stand before Him - serve fearin and tremblin - and Him shall pay them them hardship like unto them Work evil and them hands Work.

Meqabyan I Chapter 17

¹'Amalieq and 'Edomyas persons don't worship JAH by Whose Authority Earth and Heaven rulership were seized ~ as them are criminals who don't live firmed up in Truth Work - them don't fear to demolish Him Lodgin - the Temple. ²and there are no fearin JAH before them - apart from sheddin blood and adultery and eatin what were beaten and sacrificed to a idol and all that resemble what lodged dead - and these are scorned sinners. ³Them have no virtue nor religion ~ as them are who hated goodly Work - and as them don't know JAH - and as them don't know Love Work - apart from robbin a person money and from sin - and apart from disturbin a person and all hated Work - apart from games and song like unto them father Deeyablos taught them - them have no virtue nor religion. ⁴As him have ruled them with him host - demons - him teach them all evil Work that were to each of them ras selves - all robbery and sin - theft and falsehood - robbin money and eatin what were beaten and what lodged dead - and adultery Work. ⁵and him teach them all that resemble this - and goin toward a youtmon wife - and sheddin blood - eatin what were sacrificed to idol and what lodged dead - and killin a person soul in violence - and envy and winkin and greed and all evil Work that JAH don't love ~ Deeyablos who were them enemy teach them this teachin that him might distance them from JAH LAW Who rule all the world. ⁶But JAH Work are innocence and humility - not annoyin a bredren and lovin a companion - harmonisin and lovin with all persons. ⁷Don't be hypocrites to favour to a person face - and don't be wrongdoers nor totally robbers nor persons who go toward a youtmon wife - nor persons who work iniquity and evil Work on them companion - nor who cajole that them might wrong them companion in violence. ⁸Them wink and shake them heads and provoke to evil ~ them discourage to mislead that them might lower them toward Eternity Definite Judgemant.

Meqabyan I Chapter 18

¹Think that thou will go in death toward JAH in Whose Hand all are - and thou will stand before Him that Him might canvict thee before Him on all the sin thou Worked. ²As them who are arrogant and evil - and powerful ones childran who aren't strengthenin more than them - were

likewise formerly - because them sight up them stature and them Power and them firm authority - them didn't make JAH before them - and them didn't know that Him were them Creator Who Created them bringin from not livin toward livin. ³and when them fathers bein like unto "Angels" praised on Mount Hola with Angels - on the time them accord misled them - them alit toward this world where Definite Judgemant shall be done forever. ⁴As JAH in the Antiquity have Created human flesh to them - that it might mislead them because them reasonin arrogance and might test them as it were them kept Him LAW and Him Command - them married wives from Qayel childran. ⁵But them didn't keep Him LAW ~ Him lowered them toward Gehannem fire with them father Deeyablos; to JAH have vexed on the offspring of Siet who wronged like unto persons - and persons era diminished because them sin. ⁶and them took 'Adam childran toward sin with them ~ Him lowered them toward See'ol where them shall raceive a verdict. ⁷As persons era have been divided because Siet childran erred by Qayel childran - when a person eras were nine hundred in the Antiquity - them returned toward livin a hundred twenty eras. ⁸and as them are flesh and blood - JAH said - I Spirit of Support won't live firmed up on them. ⁹and because this thing I era were divided - to because I sin and I iniquity - I era have been divided from I fathers who preceded - and when them are in them infancy again - them are dyin. ¹⁰But I fathers era had abounded - because them kept Him LAW and because them didn't sadden JAH. ¹¹But I fathers era had abounded - because them vexed on them daughter childran that them might teach them - and because them vexed on them male childran lest them demolish JAH LAW. ¹²Because them didn't demolish JAH LAW with them daughter childran and them male childran - because this thing them era had abounded to true.

Meqabyan I Chapter 19

¹on the time Qayen childran abounded them worked drums and harps - santee and violins - and them made songs and all the games. ²Children who are attractive and comely were birthed to Qayen from the wife of the kind man 'Abiel - whom him killed because she - to she were attractive - and after him killed him bredda him took that and she who were him money. ³and separatin from him father - him seized them and went toward Qiefaz region that are toward the West - and that attractive one childran were attractive like unto them mother. ⁴and because this thing Siet childran descended toward Qayen childran - and after them sight them up them didn't wait one hour - and them made the daughters whom them chose wives to them ras selves. ⁵As them have taken I toward error together with them because them error - because this thing JAH vexed on I and vexed on them. ⁶and Deeyablos havin cajoled sayin - 'You will become creators like unto your Creator JAH' - him took I mother Hiewan and I father 'Adam toward him error. ⁷But it seemin Truth to them in them dullness - them demolished JAH LAW - Him Who Created them bringin from not-livin toward livin that them might bow and praise Him glorified Name. ⁸But Him - them Creator - downbased those 'Adam and Hiewan who made godhood to them ras selves - and Him downbased him who are arrogant. ⁹Like unto Daweet spoke sayin - ''Adam perish by the sinner Deeyablos arrogance' - Him abused them - to I father 'Adam have been canvicted on Deeyablos arrogance by Him true Judgemant. ¹⁰and Siet childran who erred by Qayel childran took I toward them sin thus ~ because this thing I era that JAH gave I were less than I fathers eras. ¹¹But them had worked goodly Work - to them had firmed up them reasonin in JAH - to them had taught them daughter childran and them male childran lest them depart from JAH LAW that them taught them - and there were no evil enemy who approach them. ¹²But if them worked goodly Work - there are nothing that benefit them if them didn't tell nor teach to them children. ¹³Like unto Daweet spoke sayin - 'Them didn't hide from them childran to another child - and teach JAH praise - the wondrous miracles Him did - and Him Power' - there are nothing that benefit them if them didn't teach to them childran that them might teach to them childran to make heart like unto them knew - and that them might know and do Him Accord - and that them might tell them JAH LAW Trust - and that them might keep Him LAW like unto them fathers who made JAH Feeling good with them beautiful Work. ¹⁴and them who told them Trust from them fathers in them infancy didn't demolish Him Command - like unto them fathers learned JAH Worship and the Nine Laws from them fathers. ¹⁵Them childran learned from them fathers that them might work goodly Work and might present praise to them Creator - to them have kept Him LAW - and to them have loved Him. ¹⁶and Him shall hear them in them prayer - and Him won't ignore them plea - but Him are a Forgiver. ¹⁷Havin multiplied Him wrath - Him shall return it to them - and Him wouldn't destroy all in Him chastisemant.

Meqabyan I Chapter 20

¹I bredren - think - don't forget what them told you formerly - that JAH keep the true Work of persons who work goodly Work. ²and Him multiply them childran in this world - and them name invocation shall live firmed up to a goodly thing up til the Eternity - and them childran won't be troubled to grain in this world. ³As Him shall dispute to them because them - and as Him won't cast them in them enemy hand - Him shall save them from them enemies hand who hate them. ⁴and to persons who love Him Name - Him shall be them Helper in them tribulation time ~ Him shall guard them and pardon them all them sin.

Meqabyan I Chapter 21

¹Daweet believed in JAH - to Him have believed in him - and Him saved him bein a Refuge from the king Sa'ol hand. ²and as him have believed in Him and kept Him LAW on the time when him child 'Abiesielom arose - and on the time when the 'Iloflans arose - and on the time when the 'Edomyans and the 'Amalieqans arose - on the time when the one from the four Rafayn arose - JAH saved Daweet from all this tribulation that enemies who disputed him brought on him. ³As prevailin are by JAH Accord - them were defeated by them enemies hand - yet but JAH didn't save the evil kings who didn't believe in Him. ⁴and Hiziqyas believed in JAH ~ Him saved him from Senakriem hand who were arrogant. ⁵But him child Minassie were defeated by him enemy hand - to him didn't make him trustin in JAH ~ as him didn't make him trustin in JAH and as him didn't fear JAH Who totally honoured and famed him - them bound and took him toward them country - yet but those enemies who defeated Minassie weren't like unto him. ⁶At that time Him denied him the kingdom Him gave him - to him didn't work goodly Work before him Creator JAH - that him era might abound and that Him might dispute him enemy to him and that him might have Power and firmness behind and in front. ⁷to it are better to believe in JAH than in many armies - than believin in horses and bows and shields. ⁸Believin in JAH surpass ~ a person who believed in Him shall firm up and be honoured and totally lofty. ⁹to JAH don't favour to a face - but persons who didn't believe in JAH - who believed in them money abundance - became them who departed from the grace and honour that Him gave them. ¹⁰Him shall guard the persons who believe in Him - but Him shall make the persons ignorant who call Him ignorant - and as them didn't discipline them reasonins to follow JAH nor keep Him LAW - Him won't quickly help them in them tribulation time nor in the time them enemies disputed with them. ¹¹But to a person who were disciplined in worshippin JAH and to keep Him LAW - Him shall be a Refuge in him tribulation time. ¹²By destroyin him enemy - and by plunderin him enemy livestock - and by capturin him enemy country persons - and by rainin eras rain - and by growin sprouts - and by introducin the grain pile - in the plant fruit... ¹³and by rainin the first and the spring rains - and by makin the grass verdant - and by givin the rain that rain at each time that thy kindreds beneath thy Authority might be Feeling good - Him shall make him Feeling good. ¹⁴Him shall make him Feeling good - that them might eat the other one money - that them might satta havin eaten the money them plundered from them enemy - that them might plunder animals and sheeps and cows - and that them might eat the other one dinnertable - and that them might take them enemies childran captive. ¹⁵JAH shall do all this to the person whom Him love - but Him will make the person who hate Him to him enemy ransackery. ¹⁶and Him shall bind him feet and him hands and shall cast him in him enemy hand - and Him shall make him to him enemies derision - and as him have become a blood shedder who demolished JAH LAW - Him won't make him Feeling good in him house seed. ¹⁷and him won't firm up in Judgemant time - and that Him might bring the hardship to persons who work sin - Him will also give persons who work evil Work them sin hardship. ¹⁸But it were commanded from alongside JAH to give persons who work goodly Work them reward - that Him might keep them in Him Authority. ¹⁹to Him are empowered on all the Creation Him Created that Him might do goodly Work and might give them Iternal welfare and that them might praise JAH Who Created them - and Him commanded that him might keep Him LAW ~ apart from only man there are none from all the Creations Him Created that departed from Him Command. ²⁰Like unto JAH commanded all who live firmed up in each of them Works - them all know and are kept in Him LAW. ²¹But man are emboldened on JAH Who crowned all on each of them inventions - on animal and beasts and on Heaven birds. ²²Be it what are in sea or all on land - JAH gave all the Creation Him Created to them father 'Adam ~ JAH gave them that him might do what him loved - and that them might eat them like unto grain that grew on Earth - and that them might rule and tax them - and that be them beasts or animals them might be commanded to man - and Him Ipointed them on all Him Created that persons who

reigned might be commanded to JAH Who gave them honour and that them might favour Him. 23But if them depart from Him LAW Him will separate them from the lordship Him gave them ~ as Him are Who rule Earth and Heaven - Him will give it to him who do Him Accord. 24Him Ipoint whom Him loved to Ipoint - but Him dismiss whom Him loved to dismiss ~ Him kill ~ Him save ~ Him whip in tribulation ~ Him forgive. 25There are no other Creator like unto Him ~ as Him are Ruler to all the Creation Him Created - as there are no other without Him - the Creator - in Heaven above Earth nor on Earth beneath Heaven - there are none who shall criticise Him. 26Him Ipoint ~ Him dismiss ~ Him kill ~ Him save ~ Him whip in tribulation ~ Him forgive ~ Him impoverish ~ Him honour. 27Him hear persons who beg Him in them plea ~ Him accept a person plea who do Him Accord with a clean reasonin; and Him hear them in them prayer - and Him do them accord to them in all that them begged Him. 28and Him make the great and the small to be commanded to them ~ all this are them money on hills and mountains and at trees roots and in caves and Earth wells and all them kindreds on both dry and sea. 29and to persons who do them Creator Accord all this are them money - and Him won't trouble them from them plenty - and Him shall give them them praise reward. 30and Him shall give them the honour Him prepared in Heaven to them fathers Yis'haq and 'Abriham and Ya`iqob ~ Him shall give them what Him prepared to Hiziqyas and Daweet and Samu'iel who didn't depart from Him LAW and Him Command. 31That them might be Feeling good in Him Lordship - Him shall give them who served Him Beginnin from Antiquity the honour Him prepared to them fathers Yis'haq and 'Abriham and Ya`iqob - to whom Him swore to give them a inheritance.

Meqabyan I Chapter 22

1Please - think of persons name who work goodly Work - and don't forget them Work. 2Straighten up that thy name be called like unto them name - that thou might be Feeling good with them in the Kingdom of Heaven - that were Light Lodgin that Him prepared to nobles and kings who did JAH Accord and were kind persons. 3and again - know and be canvinced of evil nobles and kings names - that Him shall canvict them and revile them alongside man after them dead. 4to them didn't line up them Work while them sight up and heard - and know and be canvinced that unless them did JAH Accord - Him shall judge on them in the Kingdom of Heaven more than criminals and persons who forgot JAH LAW. 5Be kindly - innocent - honest - yet don't thou also go on persons path who forgot JAH LAW - on whom JAH vexed because them evil Work. 6Judge Truth and save the child whose mother and father dead on him - and the widow from sinner persons hand who rob them. 7Be a guardian like unto him father to the child whose mother and father dead on him - that thou might save him from the wealthy one hand who rob him - and stand to him - and be alarmed on the time the child - whose mother and father dead on him - tears flowed before thee - I - lest thou be alarmed in fire sea where sinner persons who didn't enter repentance are punished. 8and straighten up thy feet toward Love and Inity path ~ as JAH Eyes check up Him friends - and as Him Ears hear them plea - seek Love and follow she. 9But JAH Face of Him Wrath are toward persons who work evil Work - that Him might destroy them name invocation from this world - and Him won't preserve a person who near on ramparts nor mountains. 10As I-man am JAH Who am jealous on I Godhood - as I-man am a Creator who revenge and destroy persons who hate I and don't keep I Word - I-man won't return I Face of Support reachin up til I-man destroy the person who don't keep I Word. 11and I-man shall honour persons who honour I and keep I Word.

Meqabyan I Chapter 23

1Don't live firmed up in Qayel order - who killed him bredda who followed him in innocence - it seemin to him that him bredda love him. 2and him killed him bredda envyin on a daughter ~ persons who make envy and iniquity and betrayal on them companion are like unto him. 3But as 'Abiel are innocent like unto a sheep - and as him blood are like unto the clean sheep blood that them sacrificed to JAH by a clean reasonin - them went on Qayel path that aren't on 'Abiel path. 4to because all the persons who live in innocence were persons whom JAH love - like unto a kind man 'Abiel - them have been innocent ones like unto 'Abiel - but those persons who live firmed up in 'Abiel Work love JAH. 5But JAH neglect evil ones - and them Definite Judgemant make application to them on them bodies - and it are written on the record of them reasonins - and on the time when Judgemant are judged - them shall read she before man and Angels and before all the Creation. 6At that time them shall shame ~ wrongdoers and refusers who didn't do JAH Accord shall shame. 7and a alarmin Word shall be given them that say - **Place them in Gehannem where are no exit up til Eternity.**

Meqabyan I Chapter 24

1But on the time Giediewon trusted JAH - him defeated uncircumcise peoples armies who were many many in army of a few tens of thousands and without number like unto locusts. 2**As there are no Creator without I - o nobles and kings - don't believe in the different idols.** 3**As I-man am your Creator JAH Who sent you forth from your mothers wombs and raised you and fed you and clothed you - why do you pretext? How about why do you worship other idols without I?** 4**I-man did all this to you ~ what did you give I? It are that you might live firmed up in I LAW and I Order and I Command and that I-man might give you your bodies welfare - yet what will I-man want from you?** 5JAH Who rule all said thus ~ Him said - **Save your ras selves from worshippin idols and practisin sorcery and discouragin pessimism.** 6As JAH chastisemant shall come on these who do this - and on them who hear them and do them accord and are them friends and who live firmed up in them command - save your ras selves from worshippin idols. 7As peoples - who don't know you and aren't nice to you - shall arise on you - unless you who feared did JAH Accord - them will eat the money wherefor you wearied ~ like unto Him servants the prophets spoke and like unto Hienok spoke and like unto 'Asaf spoke - unless you did JAH Accord - them will eat the money wherefor you wearied. 8**Evil persons will come havin changed them clothes** Him said ~ there are no other law alongside them apart from eatin and drinkin and adornin in silver and gold - and livin havin firmed up in sin all the Work JAH don't love. 9But them are prepared to go toward drink and food ~ after them were aroused from them slumber Beginnin from mornin up til evenin them go toward evil Work; there are misery and tribulation in them path - yet them feet have no Love path. 10and them don't know Love and Inity Work - and there are no fearin JAH in them faces ~ them are crooked evil ones without religion nor virtue ~ them are greedy ones who eat and drink alone ~ them are drunkards - and them sin are without LAW and without measure ~ them are who go toward seducin - sheddin blood - theft and perfidy and violently robbin him money who don't have it. 11and them are who criticise without Love and without LAW - to them don't fear JAH Who Created them - and there are no fear in them faces. 12Them don't shame in the person face that them sight up - and them don't shame a grey-hair nor a elder face ~ on the time them heard when them said - 'An there are money in this world' - them make it them ras self money before them sight it up with them eyes - to there are no fearin JAH in them faces - and on the time them sight it up with them eyes it seem to them that them ate it. 13and them nobles eat trust money ~ them are who eat ~ as them are negativists and as there are no straight thing in them tongues - them don't repeat in evenin what them spoke in mornin. 14to them ignore sufferahs and poor ones cries - and them kings hasten to evil - them who disturb a person - him havin saved refugees from wealthy ones hands who rob them. 15make them save him who were wronged and the refugee - yet make the kings not be them who begrudge justice because this thing. 16But them are who exact tribute ~ them are who rob a person money - and them are criminals - and as them Work are evil - them aren't nice when them eat the newborn calf with she mother and a bird with she egg ~ them make all them sight up and heard them ras self money. 17Them love that them might gather to them ras selves - yet them aren't nice to sick and poor ones - and them violently rob the money of a person who don't have it - and them gather all them found that them might be fattened and be Feeling good in it. 18to them shall perish quickly like unto a scarab that proceeded from it pit and whose track aren't found and that don't return toward it house - and because them don't work goodly Work when them are in they Life - woe to them bodies on the time JAH vexed and seized them. 19on the time JAH neglected them - them will perish at one time like unto them are in one chastisemant - to Him indure them meanin as it were them returned toward repentance - yet Him don't quickly destroy them - and them shall perish on the time when them shall perish. 20But if them don't return toward repentance - Him will quickly destroy them like unto former persons who were precedin them - who didn't keep JAH LAW by what are due. 21Them are who eat a person flesh and drink a person blood ~ as them gird and work violence to go toward sin - there are no fearin JAH in them faces everytime - and after them arose from them beddin they don't rest to work sin. 22and them Work are drink and food - goin toward destruction and sin - that them might destroy many persons bodies in this world.

Meqabyan I Chapter 25

1As them Work are crooked - and as all are who live firmed up in Satan Work that mislead - JAH Who rule all said - **Woe to your body on the time I-man vexed and seized she.** 2**But to them don't know**

JAH Work - to them have returned it toward them rear - and to them have neglected I LAW. ³and later in fulfillment era I-man shall bring the hardship on them like unto them evil measure ~ like unto them sin were written alongside I - I-man shall revenge and destroy them on the day when Judgemant are judged. ⁴As I-man JAH am full from horizon up til horizon - and as all the Creation have been seized in I Authority - there are none who escape from I Authority in Heaven nor Earth nor depth nor sea. ⁵I-man command a snake that are beneath Earth - and I-man command a fish that are within sea - and I-man command birds in Heaven - and I-man command the desert donkey in wilderness - to it are I money Beginnin from horizon up til horizon. ⁶As I-man am Who work wondrous Work and do miracles before I - there are none who escape from I Authority on Earth nor in Heaven ~ there are none who tell I - 'Where do Thou go? How about what do thou Work?' ⁷and I-man command on Angels chiefs and hosts ~ all Creations whose name are called are I money - and beasts in wilderness and all birds in Heaven and livestocks are I moneys. ⁸It arise from 'Azieb wind and firm up in drought in Mesi` ~ later in fulfillmant era 'Eritra sea shall perish bein heard - arisin from JAH - Who shall come toward she - bein feared and famousness. ⁹to Him rule them who dead and persons who are there - and she shall perish bein heard with Saba and Noba and Hindekie and 'Ityopphya limits and all them regions. ¹⁰and Him watch all in lofty Authority and innocence - to Him Authority surpass all the authority - and Him keep cangregations in Him Authority. ¹¹and to Him Authority firm up more than all the authority - and to Him Kingdom surpass all the kingdoms - and to Him Authority are what rule all the world - to Him able to all - and to there are nothing that fail Him. ¹²Him rule all clouds in Heaven ~ Him grow grass to livestocks on Earth - and Him give fruit on the buds. ¹³Him feed to all in each of the kinds like unto Him loved ~ Him feed all that Him Created by each of the fruits and each of the foods - and Him feed ants and locusts beneath Earth and livestocks on Earth and beasts - and to a person who prayed Him give him him prayer - and Him don't ignore the plea of the child whose mother and father dead on him - nor widows. ¹⁴As evil persons rebellion are like unto a swirlin wind and wrongdoers council like unto misty urine - Him shall rather accept the plea of them who beg toward Him at each time and clean ones. ¹⁵and as them body are like unto a flyin bird - and as them features attractiveness that are silver and gold are perishable in this world - examination will benefit persons who forgot JAH LAW yet not them gold - and moths shall eat them clothes. ¹⁶and weevils shall totally eat the wheat and the barley fatness - and all shall pass like unto the day that passed yesterday - and like unto a word that proceeded from a mouth don't return - sinner persons money also are like unto it - and them 'beautiful lifestyle' are like unto a passin shadow ~ sinner persons money before JAH are like unto a lie clothes. ¹⁷But if kind persons are honoured JAH won't ignore them - to them have been honoured while them were nice to poor ones - and them hear justice of sufferahs and a child whose mother and father dead on him ~ JAH won't ignore them - to without neglectin them house childran - them honour Him while them clothe the naked from the clothes JAH gave them that them might give to the refugee sufferah. ¹⁸Them don't favour loyal persons judgemant - and them don't make a hireling salary lodge ~ as JAH thing are Truth and honoured like unto a sword whose mouths were two - them won't do iniquity in them seasons number and in them balance measuremant.

Meqabyan I Chapter 26

¹But poor ones will think again on them beddin - but if wealthy ones don't accept them - them will be like unto dry wood that have no verdure - and a root won't be fertile from alongside where no moisture are - and the leaf won't be fertile if there are no root. ²As a leaf serve a flower to be a ornamant to fruit - unless the leaf were fertile it won't bear fruit ~ as man fulfillmant are religion - a person without religion have no virtue. ³If him firmed up religion him worked virtue - and JAH are Feeling good by a person who work Truth and straight Work. ⁴and to the person who begged Him - Him shall give him him plea and him tongue reward - and Him won't wrong the true person because him true Work that him worked. ⁵As JAH are true - and as Him have loved a Truth thing - Him won't justify the sinner person without repentance because the Work evil him worked - and as all persons souls have been seized in Him Authority because Him were Who ruled Earth and Heaven - as Him won't favour for the wealthy more than the poor in Judgemant time - Him won't justify him without repentance.

Meqabyan I Chapter 27

¹Him Created havin brought all the world from not livin toward livin - and Him totally prepared hills and mountains - and Him firmed up Earth on Water - and lest sea be shaken Him delineated she by sand - to in Him first Word JAH have said make **Light be Created**. ²Light were Created when this world had been covered in darkness ~ JAH Created all the Creation - and Him prepared this world - and Him firmed up this world by what are due and by money that are straight ~ Him said - make **evenin be dark**. ³and again JAH said make **Light be Created** ~ it dawned and there were Light - and Him Ilivated the upper Water toward Heaven. ⁴and Him streached it forth like unto a tent - and Him firmed it up by a wind - and Him placed the lower Water within a pit. ⁵and Him shut the sea lock in sand - and Him firmed them up in Him Authority lest them drown in Water - and Him placed animals and beasts within she - and Him placed within she Liewatan and Biehiemot who were great beasts - and Him placed within she the beasts without number - sight up and not sight up. ⁶on the third day JAH Created on Earth plants - all the roots and woods and fruits that bear forth in each of them kinds - and a welfare wood beautiful to them to sight it up. ⁷and Him Created a welfare wood that were both beautiful to them to sight it up and sweet to them to eat it - and Him Created grass - and all plants whose seeds are found from within them - to be food to birds and livestocks and beasts. ⁸It dusked ~ it dawned - and on the fourth day Him said - make **Light be Created in Heaven called cosmos** ~ JAH havin Created moon and Sun and stars - Him placed them in Heaven called cosmos that them might shine in this world and that them might feed them daylight and night. ⁹and after this moon and Sun and stars alternated in night and daylight. ¹⁰and on the fifth day JAH Created all animals and beasts that live within Water and all birds that fly on Heaven - all that are sight up and not sight up - all this. ¹¹and on the sixth day Him Created livestocks and beasts and others - and havin Created and prepared all - Him Created 'Adam in Him Example and Him Appearance. ¹²Him gave him all animals and beasts Him Created that him might reign on them - and again - all animals and beasts and all fishes - and Liewatan and Biehiemot that are in sea. ¹³and Him gave him all cows that live in this world and sheeps - the animals not sight up and them that are sight up. ¹⁴and Him placed in Garden 'Adam whom Him Created in Him Example and Him Appearance - that him might eat and might cultivate plants and might praise JAH there. ¹⁵and to lest him demolish Him Command - Him have said - on the time when you ate from this Herb of Fig you will dead death. ¹⁶and Him commanded him lest him eat from the Herb of Fig that bring death - that draw attention to evil and good - that bring death. ¹⁷I mother Hiewan were cajoled by a snake misleadin and she ate from that Herb of Fig and gave it to I father 'Adam. ¹⁸and 'Adam havin eaten from that Herb of Fig brought death on him childran and on him ras self. ¹⁹As him have demolished Him Command - and as him have eaten from that Herb of Fig that JAH commanded sayin - Don't eat from she - JAH vexed on I father 'Adam and expelled and sent him way from the Garden - and Him gave him that Earth that grow thistle and thorn - that Him cursed because him on the time him demolished Him Command - that him might eat him weariness reward havin toiled and laboured that him might plow she. ²⁰and on the time JAH sent him forth toward this land - 'Adam returned toward complete sadness - and havin toiled and laboured that him might plow Earth - him began to eat in weariness and also in struggles.

Meqabyan I Chapter 28

¹and after him childran lived havin abounded - there were from them ones who praise and honour JAH and don't demolish Him Command. ²There were prophets who spoke what were done and what will be done henceforth - and from him childran there were sinners who speak lies and who wrong persons ~ 'Adam firstborn child Qayel became evil and killed him bredda 'Abiel. ³JAH judged Judgemant on Qayel because him killed him bredda 'Abiel - and JAH vexed on Earth because she drank him blood. ⁴and JAH told Qayel - **Where are thy bredda 'Abiel?** - and Qayel in him heart arrogance said - 'Are mi mi bredda 'Abiel keeper?' ⁵'Abiel became a clean man - but Qayel became a sinner man by killin a kind man - him bredda 'Abiel. ⁶Again a kind child Siet were birthed ~ 'Adam birthed sixty childran ~ there are kind persons and evil persons from them. ⁷and there are kind persons from them ~ and there are persons who were prophets and them who were traitors and sinners. ⁸There are blessed persons who were kind persons - who fulfill them father 'Adam accord and all him told to him child Siet - Beginnin from 'Adam up til Noh who are a kind man who kept JAH LAW. ⁹and him sanctioned JAH LAW to him childran ~ him told them - 'Guard' - lest them demolish JAH LAW - and that them might tell to them childran like unto them father Noh told them - and that them might keep JAH LAW. ¹⁰and them lived while them taught them childran - persons birthed after them. ¹¹But Satan lived when him spoke to them fathers - havin lodged in idols that reached to a grave and

that have vows on them - and havin defeated the persons who told him alright - and when them did all that Satan - who are sin teacher - commanded them. 12and them lived when them worshipped the idols like unto them order - up til a kind man 'Abriham who fulfill JAH Accord. 13to him have lived firmed up in the LAW beforehand separate from him cousins - and JAH swore a oath with him - havin lodged in wind and fire. 14JAH swore to him that Him might give him a land of inheritance and that Him might give to him childran up til the Eternity. 15and Him swore to Yis'haq like unto him that Him might give him him father 'Abriham inheritance - and Him swore to Ya`iqob that Him might give him him father Yis'haq inheritance ~ Him swore to him like into Yis'haq. 16and Him separated them childran - who were birthed after them from Ya`iqob - from the twelve tribes of 'Isra'iel - and made them priests and kings ~ Him blessed them sayin - **Abound and totally be many many**. 17and Him gave them them father inheritance - however while Him fed them and loved them - them didn't quit saddenin JAH in all. 18and on the time Him destroyed them - at that time them will seek Him in worship - and them will return from sin and go toward JAH - to Him love them - and JAH shall pardon them. 19to bein nice to all Him Created - Him shall pardon them - and it are because them fathers Work that Him love them - yet it aren't because them ras selves Work. 20and Him streach forth Him Right Hand in plenty that Him might satta a hungry body - and Him reveal Him Eye to pardonin that Him might multiply grain to food. 21Him give food to crows chicks and to beasts that beg Him ~ on the time them cried toward Him - Him will save 'Isra'iel childran from them enemies hands who delayed from the time. 22and them will return toward sin again that them might sadden Him - and Him will arouse them enemies peoples in them area on them ~ them will destroy them and kill them and capture them. 23and again them will shout toward JAH in mournin and sadness - and there are the time when Him sent help and saved them by prophets hands. 24and there are the time when Him saved them by princes hands - and on the time them saddened JAH them enemies taxed them and captured them. 25and Daweet arose and saved them from the 'Iloflans hands; and again them saddened JAH - and JAH aroused on them peoples who worry them. 26and there are the time when Him saved them by Yoftahie hand - and again them forgot JAH Who saved them in them tribulation time. As JAH have brought the hardship on them - Him will arouse on them enemies who were evil who will firm up tribulation on them and totally capture them. 27and on the time them were worried by tribulation them were seized and again cried toward Him - and Him saved them by Giediewon hand - and again them saddened JAH by them hands Work. 28and again Him aroused on them peoples who firm up tribulation on them - and them returned and wept and cried toward JAH. 29and again Him saved them from peoples by Somson hand - and them rested a little from the tribulation. and them arose that them might sadden JAH by them former sin. 30and again Him aroused on them other peoples who worry them - and again them cried and wept toward JAH that Him might send help to them and that Him might save them from peoples hand who firm up tribulation on them. 31and again Him saved them by Bariq and Deebora hands. Again them lived a little season while them worshipped JAH - and again them forgot JAH in them former sin and saddened Him. 32and Him aroused on them other peoples who worry them - and again Him saved them by Yodeet hand and havin sat again a little season them arose that them might sadden JAH by them sin like unto formerly. 33and Him aroused on them peoples who rule them - and them cried and wept toward JAH to Him have struck on him head 'Abiemieliek who were a warrior who came that him might fight Yihuda country. 34and Him saved them by the childran in the area and by Matatyu hand - and on the time that warrior dead him army fled and were scattared - and 'Isra'iel childran followed and fought them up til 'Iyabboq - and them didn't preserve even one person from them. 35After this them waited a little and arose that them might sadden JAH - and Him aroused on them peoples who rule them - and again them totally cried toward JAH and JAH ignored them cryin and them mournin - to them have saddened JAH everytime - and to them have demolished Him LAW. 36and them captured and took them with them priests toward Babilon persons country. 37and then 'Isra'iel childran who were traitors didn't quit saddenin JAH while them worked sin and worshipped idols. 38JAH vexed that Him might destroy them one time in them sin ~ Hama havin introduced ten thousand gold in the king box - on the day when it were known - him lodged anger in the king 'Arthieksis reasonin - lest him preserve them childran in Fars country Beginnin from Hindekie and up til 'Ityopphya on the time him told him that him might destroy them. 39Him did thus - and him wrote a letter where a message were written by the king authority - and him gave him a seal in him hand that him might deliver toward Fars country. 40Him gave him a seal that him might destroy them on one day when him loved them to destroy them like unto the king commanded - but him commanded that him might introduce them money - the gold and the silver - toward the king box. 41and on the time 'Isra'iel childran heard this thing them totally cried and wept toward JAH - and them told it to Merdokyos - and Merdokyos told to 'Astier. 42and 'Astier said - 'Fast - beg - and all 'Isra'iel childran kindreds - cry toward JAH in the place where you are.' 43and Merdokyos wore sackcloth and sprinkled dust on him ras self - and 'Isra'iel childran fasted - begged - and entered repentance in the country where them were. 44and 'Astier were totally sad - and bein a queen she wore sackcloth ~ she sprinkled dust and shaved she head - and she didn't anoint perfume like unto Fars queens anoint perfume - and in she deep reasonin she cried and wept toward she fathers Creator JAH. 45and because this thing Him gave she bein loved alongside Fars king 'Arthieksis - and she made a kind lunch to she fathers Creator. 46and Hama and the king entered toward the lunch that 'Astier prepared - and like unto him loved that him might do on Merdokyos - JAH paid the hardship on that Hama - and them hanged him on a tall wood. 47The king letter were commanded that them might quit 'Isra'iel like unto them were in all them accord - and lest them tax them nor rob them nor wrong them nor take them money on them. 48As JAH shall pardon 'Isra'iel doin thus on the time them cried enterin repentance - it are that them might love them and honour them in Fars country where them lived - yet a king letter were commanded lest them destroy them country nor plunder them livestocks. 49and on them time them saddened Him - Him will arouse on them peoples who worry them ~ at that time them will totally weep and cry that Him might send them help to them and that Him might save them from peoples hand who firm up tribulation on them.

Meqabyan I Chapter 29

1and on the time Gibts persons also made 'Isra'iel childran work by makin them work bricks in difficulty - and on the time them worried them all the Work by kickin mud without straw and heatin bricks. 2and on the time them made them work havin appointed chiefs on them who rush workers - them cried toward JAH that Him might save them from workin all Gibts bricks. 3At that time Him sent to them 'Aron and Mussie who help them - to JAH have sent them that them might send forth Him kindreds from Fer`on rulership house - and Him saved them from brick Work ~ because in him arrogance him refused to adjourn 'Isra'iel lest them be ruled and sacrifice to JAH in wilderness - JAH have sent them that them might send forth Him kindreds 'Isra'iel from Gibts king Fer`on rulership house - and them saved them. 4to JAH neglect arrogant ones - and Him drowned Fer`on in 'Eritra sea with him army because him arrogance. 5and like unto him - Him shall destroy them who didn't work goodly Work in all the kingdoms that Him I-pointed and crowned them - that them who ignore JAH Word when them are nobles and kings might fulfill Him Accord to Him - and that them might give persons who serve in goodly thing them wage - and that them might honour Him famous Name. 6JAH Who rule all said - **But if them will straighten up I Kingdom - I-man will straighten up them kingdom to them. 7Work goodly Work to I - and I-man shall work goodly Work to you ~ keep I LAW - and I-man shall keep you your bodies ~ live firmed up in I LAW - and I-man shall live lodgin honesty in you like unto your reasonin. 8Love I - and I-man shall love your welfare ~ near toward I - and I-man shall heal you.** 9JAH Who rule all said - **Believe in I - and I-man shall save you from the tribulation.** 10Don't live side by side ~ as JAH Who rule all love straight Work - Him said - **You - approach toward I - and I-man shall approach toward you ~ you persons who are sinners and traitors - cleanse your hands from sin - and distance your reasonins from evil. 11and I-man shall distance I anger from you - and I-man shall return to you in Charity and Forgiveness. 12I-man shall distance criminals and enemies who work iniquity from you - like unto I-man saved I slave Daweet from him enemies who met him - from them much malice - and from Gwolyad hand who were a warrior - and also from Sa'ol hand who sought that him might kill him - and from him child 'Abiesielom hand who loved that him might take him kingdom. 13I-man shall save persons who keep I LAW and fulfill I Accord like unto him ~ I-man shall bequeath them honour - and them shall be Feeling good in the present world and yonder in the world that shall come ~ I-man shall crown them on all that them might be Feeling good.** 14Them shall be one with kings who served JAH and were honoured in them beautiful way of Life - like unto the prophet Samu'iel served Him in him beautiful way of Life Beginnin from him infancy - whom JAH - Him bein LAW - chose. 15Him told him that him 15 Him told him that him might tell 'Elee who were a servant elder - and when him served in JAH Lodgin the Temple - Samu'iel Work also were merciful and I-loved. ¹⁶ and on the time him grew when him served in JAH Lodgin the Temple - Him made him to be Ipointed and Inointed - that him might Ipoint him people and that kings might be Inointed by JAH Accord. As JAH have loved him that the kindred him chose from 'Isra'iel childran might be Ipointed - on the time him fulfilled JAH Accord Who Created him - Him gave him the Inointin of the Kingdom in him hand. ¹⁷ and when Sa'ol were in him kingdom JAH told Him prophet Samu'iel - **Go - and as I-man have loved `Issiey child Daweet who were birthed from Yihuda kin - Inoint him.**

Meqabyan I Chapter 30

¹ **I-man have hated Sa'ol kin - to him have saddened I because him violated I Word.** ² **and I-man neglected him - to him didn't keep I LAW - and I-man won't crown from him kin again.** ³ **and persons who didn't keep I LAW and I Word and I Order like unto him - I-man shall destroy I Kingdom and I gift from them childran up til the Eternity.** ⁴ **and as them didn't make I famous on the time I-man made them famous - I-man shall destroy them - yet I-man won't again return to lift them up ~ though I-man honour them - as them didn't honour I - I-man won't make them famous.** ⁵ **to them didn't do a goodly thing to I on the time I-man did a goodly thing to them - and to them didn't forgive I on the time I-man forgave them.** ⁶ **and as them didn't make I a Ruler on the time I-man made them rulers on all - as them didn't honour I on the time I-man honoured them more than all - I-man won't make them famous again nor honour them - and to them didn't keep I LAW.** ⁷ **and I-man withheld the gift I-man gave them - and I-man won't return the money I-man withheld from them like unto the measure I-man vexed and swore ~** JAH Who rule all said thus ~ Him said - **I-man shall honour them who honoured I - and love them who loved I.** ⁸ **I-man shall separate them who didn't honour I nor keep I LAW from the gift I-man gave them.** ⁹ JAH Who rule all said; **I-man love them who loved I - and make famous him who made I famous -** Him said. ¹⁰ **As I-man JAH am Who rule all - there are none who escape I Authority in Earth nor Heaven - to I-man am JAH Who kill and Who save and Who sadden and Who forgive.** ¹¹ **As famousness and honour are I money - I-man honour him whom I-man loved - to I-man am Who judge and Who revenge and destroy - and I-man make wretched him whom I-man hated.** ¹² **to I-man am Who forgive them who love I and call I Name everytime - to I-man am Who feed food to the wealthy and to the poor.** ¹³ and I-man feed birds and animals - fishes in sea and beasts and flowers - yet I-man aren't Who feed only man. ¹⁴ I-man feed crocodiles and whales - gophers and hippos - and badgers. ¹⁵ and all that live within Water - all that fly on wind - yet I-man aren't Who feed only man ~ all this are I money. ¹⁶ I-man am Who feed all that seek I by all that are due and I-loved.

Meqabyan I Chapter 31

¹ and **the kings don't reign without I Accord - and sufferahs are by I Command - yet them aren't poor without I Command - and powerful ones are by I Accord - yet them aren't strong without I Accord.** ² **I-man gave bein I-loved to Daweet and Wisdom to Selomon -** and **I-man added eras to Hiziqyas.** ³ **I-man diminished Gwolyad era - and I-man gave Power to Somson -** and **again I-man weakened him Power.** ⁴ and **I-man saved I slave Daweet from Gwolyad hand who were a warrior.** ⁵ and **again I-man saved him from the king Sa'ol hand and from the secand warrior who disputed him -** and **to him have kept I Command - and I-man saved him from the persons hand who dispute him and fight him.** ⁶ and **I-man loved him -** and **I-man love all the nobles and the kings who keep I LAW ~ as them have made I Feeling good - I-man shall give them prevailin and Power on them enemies.** ⁷ and **again that them might inherit them fathers land - I-man shall give them the cleansed and shinin land of inheritance that I-man swore to them fathers.**

Meqabyan I Chapter 32

¹ JAH Who rule all said - and **you the nobles and also the kings - hear I in I Word - and keep I Command ~ lest you sadden I and worship like unto 'Isra'iel childran saddened I and worshipped different idols - them whom I-man kept and saved when I-man JAH am them Creator -** JAH Who rule all said - **Hear I in I Word; and all whom I-man raised and loved and fed Beginnin that them were birthed from them mother and father.** ² and **whom I-man sent forth toward Earth crops - and** whom I-man fed the fatness found from Earth makin like unto are due - and whom I-man gave the grape vine and the oil-tree fruit that them didn't plant and the clear Water well that them didn't dig. ³ Hear I in I Word lest you sadden I like unto 'Isra'iel childran saddened I worshippin other idols when I-man JAH am them Creator - Him told them - Who fed them the sheep milk and the honey comb with the hulled wheat - and Who clothed them clothes where ornamant are - and Who gave them all them love. ⁴ and without it livin that I-man deprived them all them begged I.

Meqabyan I Chapter 33

¹ **Like unto Daweet spoke sayin - "Isra'iel childran were fed the menna that Angels lowered' - and again hear I in I Word lest you sadden I like unto 'Isra'iel childran saddened I worshippin the idols when I-man am them Creator JAH Who fed them sweet menna in wilderness -** Him said ~ **I-man did all this to them that them might worship I by what are due and to true.** ² JAH Who rule all said - **But them didn't worship I - and I-man neglected them ~ them saddened I and lived firmed up in law of idols that weren't I LAW.** ³ **and I-man shall bring the hardship on them like unto them sin ~ as them have neglected I Worship and as them didn't firm up in I counsel and I Order - I-man neglected them in the sin measure that them worked by them hands - and I-man shall lower them toward Gehannem in Definite Judgemant that are done in Heaven.** ⁴ **to them didn't keep I LAW - and to I-man vex on them - and I-man shall diminish them era in this world.** ⁵ **If thou be a king - aren't thou a man who shall dead and be demolished and tomorrow who shall be worms and dust?** ⁶ **But today thou boast and are proud like unto a man who won't dead forever.** ⁷ JAH Who rule all said - **But thou who are sight up bein well today are a man who will dead tomorrow.** ⁸ **But if you keep I Command and I Word - I-man shall bequeath thee-I a honoured country with honoured kings who did I Accord - whose lodgin were Light and whose crowns were beautiful - and whose thrones were silver and gold and whom persons who sit on them adorned -** Him said. ⁹ and them shall be Feeling good within Him country that are a place that approached to persons who worked goodly Work. ¹⁰ **But to persons who work sin - as them didn't keep I LAW - said** JAH Who rule all. ¹¹ it aren't due **them that them might enter toward that country where honoured kings shall enter.**

Meqabyan I Chapter 34

¹ Miedon kingdom shall perish - but Rom kingdom shall totally firm up on Meqiedonya kingdom - and Nenewie kingdom shall firm up on Fars kingdom. ² and 'Ityopphya kingdom shall firm up on 'Iskindriya kingdom ~ as peoples shall arise - Mo`ab kingdom shall firm up on 'Amalieq kingdom. ³ and bredda shall arise on him bredda - and JAH shall revenge and destroy like unto Him spoke that it might perish. ⁴ **Kingdom shall arise on kingdom - and the people on the people and country on country -** Him said. ⁵ and argumants shall be done and there shall be formations - famine - plague - earthquake - drought ~ as Love have perished from this world - JAH chastisemant descended on she. ⁶ to the day have arrived suddenly when JAH shall come - Who frighten like unto lightnin that are sight up from East up til West. ⁷ on the day when HIM JAH judge Judgemant - at that time everyone shall raceive him hardship like unto him hand weakness and him sin firmness - to Him have said **I-man shall revenge them on** the day when HIM JAH judge Judgemant and on the day when them feet are hindered - to the day when them are counted to destruction have arrived. ⁸ At that time JAH shall destroy in Gehannem forever persons who won't live firmed up in Him LAW - who work sin. ⁹ and **them who live in the West ilands and Noba and Hindekie - Saba and 'Ityopphya and Gibts persons - all persons who live in them.** ¹⁰ at that time shall know I that **I-man were JAH Who rule Earth and Heaven - and Who give bein I-loved and honour - and Who save and Who kill.** ¹¹ **I-man am Who send forth Sun - Who send it toward it settin - Who bring the evil and the good.** ¹² **I-man am Who bring peoples whom you don't know - who slaughter and eat the money whereby you wearied - your sheeps and your cows flocks.** ¹³ **and them shall capture your childran while them hammer them before you - and you cyaan save them.** Because JAH Spirit of Support didn't lodge in you - as you didn't fear JAH Command that you heard - Him shall destroy your lavishmants and your assignmants. ¹⁴ But a person in whom JAH Spirit of Support lodged will know all - like unto Nabukedenetsor told Dan'iel sayin - 'Mi sight up JAH Spirit of Support

that lodged in thee-I.' ¹⁵ and a person in whom JAH Spirit of Support lodged will know all - and what were hidden will be revealed to him - and him will know all that were revealed and that were hidden - yet there are nothing hidden from a person in whom JAH Spirit of Support lodged. ¹⁶ But as I are persons who will dead tomorrow - I sins that I hid and worked shall be revealed. ¹⁷ and like unto them test silver and gold in fire - like unto there are sinners - later on the Day of Advent them shall be examined - to them didn't keep JAH Command. ¹⁸ At that time all peoples and all 'Isra'iel childran Works shall be examined.

Meqabyan I Chapter 35

¹ As JAH vex on you because you didn't judge a Truth Judgemant to the child whose mother and father dead on him - woe to you 'Isra'iel nobles. ² Woe to you persons who go toward a drinkin house mornin and evenin and get drunk - who are partial in judgemant - and who don't hear the widow justice nor the child whose mother and father dead on him - who live in sin and seducin. ³ JAH told 'Isra'iel nobles sayin thus: - **Unless you lived firmed up in I Command and kept I LAW and loved what I-man love - woe to you - Him told them. ⁴ and I-man shall bring destruction and chastisemant and tribulation on you - and you will perish like unto what weevils and moths ate - and your tracks and your region won't be found** - Him told them. ⁵ and your country will be a wilderness - and all persons who sight she up formerly shall clap them hands ~ them shall marvel on she while them said - 'Weren't this country filled of she plenty and all who love it?; JAH made she thus by persons sin who live in she.' ⁶ Them shall say - 'As she have made she heart proud - and as she have ilivated she ras self - and as she have firmed up she collar of reasonin up til JAH make she wretched on Earth - and as she shall be a desert by persons arrogance who live in she - and as thorns have grown on she with thistles - woe to she.' ⁷ and she grow weeds and nettles - and she became a wilderness and a desert - and beasts shall live within she. ⁸ to JAH Judgemant have firmed up on she - and to she shall raceive JAH Judgemant Chalice because she reasonin arrogance by persons sin who live in she - and she became frightenin to persons who go toward she.

Meqabyan I Chapter 36

¹ Meqiedon persons - don't boast ~ as JAH are there Who shall destroy you - 'Amalieqans - don't firm up your collar of reasonin. ² to you will be lofty up til Heaven and you will descend up til Gehannem. ³ on the time 'Isra'iel formerly entered toward Gibts country in Mo`ab and Miedon kingdom Him said - Don't boast - to it aren't due to pretend on JAH that you might pretend on Him. ⁴ Thou Yisma'iel kindred - slave child - why do thou firm up thy collar of reasonin by what weren't thy money? How about don't thou think that JAH shall judge on thee on the time Him arose that it might be judged on Earth - on the day when it are judged on thee? ⁵ JAH Who rule all said - **At that time thou will raceive thy hardship like unto thy hand Work - how about why do thou ilivate thy reasonin? How about why do thou firm up thy collar of reasonin? ⁶ and I-man shall pretend on thee like unto thou pretended on persons who weren't thy kindreds - to thou do what thou love that thou might work sin - and I-man shall neglect thee in the place where them sent thee. ⁷ JAH Who rule all said - and I-man shall do thus on thee ~ Him said - But if thou worked goodly Work and if thou love what I-man love - I-man also shall hear thee-I in all that thou begged. ⁸ and if thou fulfill I Accord to I - I-man shall fulfill thy accord to thee-I - and I-man shall dispute thy enemies to thee-I - and I-man shall bless thy childran and thy seed to thee-I. ⁹ and I-man shall multiply thy sheeps and thy cows flocks to thee-I - and if thou lived firmed up in I Command and also if thou did what I-man love** - JAH Who rule all said - **I-man shall bless to thee-I all thou seized in thy hand. ¹⁰ But if thou don't do I Accord - if thou don't live firmed up in I LAW and I Command - all this tribulation that were told formerly shall find thee - to thou didn't indure tribulation firmed up in I Command - and to thou didn't live firmed up in I LAW - and thou cyaan escape from I anger that will come on thee everytime. ¹¹ and as thou didn't love what I-man loved - when I-man am Who Created thee bringin from not livin toward livin. ¹² all this were thy money - that thou might kill and heal to do all that thou loved - that thou might work and demolish - that thou might honour and abuse - that thou might ilivate and downbase - and as thou have neglected I Worship and I praise when I-man am Who gave thee lordship and also honour alongside persons who are beneath thy authority - thou cyaan escape from I anger that will come on thee.** ¹³ and if thou did JAH Accord and if thou lived firmed up in Him Command - Him will love thee-I that thou might be Feeling good with Him in Him

Lordship - and that thou might be a partaker with persons who inherited a honoured country. ¹⁴ to Him have said - **If them indure I - I-man will bequeath them bein I-loved and honour - to I-man shall make them Feeling good in the Temple where prayer are prayed** - to JAH Who rule all have said - and **them shall be I-loved and chosen like unto a sacrifice.** ¹⁵ Don't neglect to do Work whereby welfare are done and a goodly thing that you might cross from death toward Life. ¹⁶ But persons who work goodly Work - JAH shall keep them in all Him goodly Work - that them might be Him slaves like unto 'Iyob whom JAH kept from all the tribulation. ¹⁷ JAH shall keep them in all goodly Work - that them might be Him slaves to Him like unto 'Abriham whom Him saved on the time him killed the kings - and like unto Mussie whom Him saved from Kenaniewon hand and Fer`on hand - in whom 'Abriham lived - and who were also disturbin him body evenin and mornin night and day that them might make him worship idols. ¹⁸ But when them took him toward the idols that were them money - him would indure the tribulation while him refused. ¹⁹ to 'Abriham who believed Him Beginnin from him childhood were to JAH Him trusted friend - and while him refused him would worship JAH Who Created him. ²⁰ As him totally love JAH - him didn't quit worshippin JAH up til him dead - and him didn't depart from Him LAW up til when him dead - and him taught him childran that them might keep JAH LAW. ²¹ and like unto him father 'Abriham kept JAH LAW - them didn't depart from JAH LAW ~ like unto Him told to Angels sayin - **I-man have a friend in this world called 'Abriham - 'Abriham childran Ya`iqob and Yis'haq - who are Him slaves because whom JAH spoke - didn't depart from JAH LAW.** ²² JAH Who were praised alongside them and Who rule all said - **'Abriham are I friend ~ Yis'haq are I canfidante - and Ya`iqob are I friend whom I Reasonin loved.** ²³ But when Him totally loved 'Isra'iel childran - them lived when them Continually saddened Him - and Him lived when Him indured them and when Him fed them menna in wilderness. ²⁴ Them clothes didn't age- to them have been fed menna that are knowledge injera - and them feet didn't awaken. ²⁵ But them reasonins would distance from JAH everytime ~ as them were who work sin Beginnin from Antiquity - them had no hope to be saved. ²⁶ Them became like unto a crooked bow - yet them didn't become like unto them fathers Yis'haq and 'Abriham and Ya`iqob who served JAH in them beautiful way of Life ~ them would sadden Him everytime by them idols on the mountains and the hills ~ them would eat on the mountain and at the caves and the trees roots. ²⁷ Them would slaughter a steer ~ them would sacrifice a sacrifice - and them would be Feeling good in them hands Work ~ them would eat the rest of the sacrifice ~ them would drink of them sacrifice - and them would play with demons while them sang. ²⁸ and demons would admire all them games and them songs to them - and them would work drunkenness and adultery without measure - and them would do the robbery and greed that JAH don't love. ²⁹ to Kene`an idols - and to Midyam idols and to Be`al - and to 'Aphlon and Dagon and Seraphyon and 'Arthiemadies who are 'Eloflee idols. ³⁰ and to all peoples idols in them area - them would sacrifice; and all 'Isra'iel would worship idols like unto peoples worship idols by money that them sight up and heard ~ them would make them games and them songs and them bluster that peoples make. ³¹ All 'Isra'iel kindreds do likewise - who say 'We will worship JAH' - without keepin Him Command and Him LAW that Mussie told them in 'Oreet that them might keep JAH LAW and might distance from worshippin idols. ³² Lest them worship separated idols - apart from them fathers Creator Who fed them the honey found from Maga who fed them the plantation grain and sent them forth toward the Earth crops - and Who fed them the menna. ³³ Mussie commanded them sayin 'Don't worship' - to Him are them Creator - and to Him feed them who loved Him - and Him won't deprive them who loved Him and desired Him. ³⁴ But them didn't quit saddenin JAH - and them would sadden JAH on the time Him made them Feeling good. ³⁵ and on the time Him saddened them - them would cry toward Him - and Him would save them from the tribulation that found them - and them would again be totally Feeling good and would live many eras. ³⁶ and at that time them would totally return them heart toward sin that them might sadden JAH like unto formerly - and Him would arouse on them peoples in them area that them might destroy them - and them would worry and tax them. ³⁷ and again them would totally return and cry toward them Creator JAH. ³⁸ and Him would forgive them ~ it are because them fathers - Noh - Yis'haq and 'Abriham and Ya`iqob - who served JAH in them beautiful way of Life Beginnin from Antiquity - to whom Him firmed up Him Oath - yet it aren't because them ras selves Work that Him forgive them. ³⁹ and Him loved persons who kept Him LAW lovin that them might multiply them childran like unto Heaven stars and sea sand. ⁴⁰ But on the time dead ones arose that them have like unto sea sand - them are sinner persons souls that will separate from 'Isra'iel childran and enter toward Gehannem. 41 As JAH have told 'Abriham - **Sight up toward Heaven at night and count Heaven stars as it were thou could count** - likewise as Him have told him - **Thy childran and righteous ones shall shine in Heaven like unto Heaven stars** - them are like unto stars that shine in Heaven - but what them have are kind persons souls birthed from 'Isra'iel. 42 and again as Him have told him - **Overstand toward the river edge and the sea - and sight up what are amidst the sand ~ count as it were thou could count - and thy sinner childran are likewise** - who will descend toward Gehannem on the time dead ones arose - them are sinner persons souls. 43 and 'Abriham believed in JAH ~ because this thing it were counted to him bein Truth ~ him found him morale in this world - and after him wife Sora aged she birthed a child called Yis'haq. 44 to him have believed that persons who worked goodly Work shall arise and go toward the Kingdom of Heaven that live firmed up forever - and again him shall find a Kingdom in Heaven. 45 But to him have believed that persons who worked sin shall go toward Gehannem that live firmed up forever on the time dead ones arose - but that righteous ones who worked goodly Work shall reign with Him forever. 46 But to him have believed that it shall be judged forever to true without falsehood on persons who worked sin - to him shall find Life Kingdom in Heaven." Make glory and praise enter to JAH to true without falsehood - and the first book that speak the Meqabyans thing were filled and fulfilled.

Meqabian II

Meqabian II Chapter 1

1 This are a book that speak that Meqabees found 'Isra'iel in Mesphiethomya that are Sorya part and killed them in them region beginnin from 'Iyabboq up til 'Iyerusaliem square - and that him destroyed the country. 2 Because Sorya and 'Edomyas persons and the 'Amalieqans were one with the Mo`ab man Meqabees who destroyed 'Iyerusaliem country - as them have camped beginnin from Semarya up til 'Iyerusaliem square and up til all she region - them killed in war without preservin persons who fled apart from a few persons. 3 and on the time 'Isra'iel childran wronged - Him aroused Mo`ab man Meqabees on them - and him killed them by a sword. 4 And because this thing JAH enemies the peoples bragged on Him honoured country - and them swore in them crime. 5 And 'Iloflee and 'Idomyas persons camped - as Him have sent them because them pretended JAH Word - them began to revenge and destroy JAH country. 6 And that Meqabees country are Riemat that are Mo`ab part - and him arose from him country in Power and them swore also with persons with him. 7 And them camped in Gielabuhie region that are Mesphiethomya lot up til Sorya that them might destroy JAH country - and there him begged the 'Amalieqans and 'Iloflans ~ him gave them much silver and gold and chariots and horses that them might be one with him in crime. 8 Them came together and crushed the fortress ~ persons who lived in she shed blood like unto Water. 9 And them made 'Iyerusaliem like unto a plant keepin hut - and him made a voice heard within she ~ him worked all the sin Work that JAH don't love - and them also defouled JAH country that were filled of praise and honour. 10 Them made thy friends flesh and thy slaves corpses food to wilderness beasts and Heaven birds. 11 And them robbed childran whose mother and father dead on them and widows - to without fearin JAH them have done like unto Satan taught them - and up til JAH Who examine kidneys and reasonins vexed - them took out the fetus in pregnant daughters belly. 12 Them returned toward them country while them were Feeling good because them worked evil Work on JAH kindreds - and them took the plunder that them captured from a honoured country. 13 On the time them returned and entered toward them houses them made joy and song and clappin.

Meqabian II Chapter 2

1 The prophet whom them call Re`ay told him thus: - "Today be Feeling good a little on the time when Feeling good joy were made ~ JAH Whom 'Isra'iel glorified have that Him might revenge and destroy thee in the chastisemant thou didn't doubt. 2 Will thou say - 'Mi horses are swift ~ because this mi will escape by runnin'? 3 As to I - I-man tell thee - Persons who will follow thee are swifter than vultures ~ thou won't escape from JAH Judgemant and destruction that shall come on thee. 4 Will thou say - 'Mi wear iron clothes - and spear flingin and bow stingin aren't able to mi'?; JAH Who honour 'Isra'iel said - **It aren't by spear flingin that I-man will revenge and destroy thee"** Him told him ~ **"I-man shall bring on thee heart sickness and itch and rheumatism sickness that were worse and firmer than spear flingin and bow stingin - yet it aren't by this that I-man shall revenge and destroy thee. 5 Thou have aroused I anger**

~ **I-man shall bring heart sickness on thee - and thou will lack one who help thee - and thou won't escape from I Authority up til I-man destroy thy name invocation from this world. 6 As thou have firmed up thy collar of reasonin - and as thou have ilivated thy ras self on I country - on the time I-man quickly did this thing like unto a eye wink - thou will know I that I-man were thy Creator ~ as thou are before I like unto grass before the wind that fire eat - and as thou are like unto the dust that winds spill and scattar from Earth - thou are like unto them alongside I. 7 to thou have aroused I anger - and to thou didn't know thy Creator - and I-man shall neglect all thy kindred - and neither will I-man preserve him who neared on thy fortress. 8 and now return from all thy sin that thou worked ~ if thou return from thy sin and totally appease in mournin and sadness before JAH - and if thou beg toward him in clean reasonin - JAH will forgive thee all thy sin that thou worked before Him"** - him told him. 9 At that time Meqabees wore dust and mourned before JAH because him sin - to JAH have vexed on him. 10 to Him eyes are revealed - to Him don't withhold - and to Him ears are opened - to Him don't neglect - and to Him don't make the word Him spoke false - and to Him quickly do she at one time - to JAH knew lest Him preserve the chastisemant Him spoke by the prophet Word. 11 Him cast him clothes and wore sackcloth and sprinkled dust on him head and cried and wept before him Creator JAH because him sin that him worked.

Meqabian II Chapter 3

1 And the prophet came from Riemat and told him - to Riemat that are Mo`ab part are near to Sorya. 2 Him dug a pit and entered up til him neck and wept firm tears - and him entered repentance because him sin that him worked before JAH. 3 And JAH told the prophet thus: - **Return from Yihuda country Riemat toward the Mo`ab official Meqabees Him told him. Tell him - "JAH told thee thus"** - Tell him - **"Him told thee - I-man JAH Who am thy Creator sent thee by I Accord that thou might destroy I country - lest thou say - 'Mi destroyed the honoured country 'Iyerusaliem by mi Power firmness and mi army abundance' - yet it aren't thou who did this thing. 4 to she have saddened I by all she greed and she perfidy and she lustfulness. 5 and I-man neglected and cast she by thy hand - and now JAH forgave thee thy sin because thy childran whom thou birthed ~ it aren't because thou who firmed up thy collar of reasonin and say 'Mi incircled the country 'Iyerusaliem by mi authority firmness.' 6 As persons who doubt aren't disciplined to enter repentance - don't be a doubter - and now enter repentance bein disciplined in thy complete reasonin."** 7 However persons are admired who enter repentance in them complete reasonins and who don't again return toward thirst and sin by all that entered toward repentance because them sin. 8 Persons are admired who return toward them Creator JAH bein disciplined in mournin and sadness - in bowin and many pleas. Persons are admired who are disciplined and enter repentance - to Him have told them - **You are I moneys who entered repentance after you misled persons who entered repentance.** 9 Him told arrogant Meqabees on the time him returned toward Him in repentance after him misled - I-man forgive thee thy sin because thy fright and thy alarm; **to I-man am JAH thy Creator Who bring hardship on childran by a father sin up til seven generations if the child work the sin that the father worked - and Who do Charity up til ten thousand generations to persons who love I and keep I LAW.** 10 and now I-man will firm up I Oath with thee because these thy childran whom thou birthed - and JAH Who rule all and Who honoured 'Isra'iel said - **I-man will accept the repentance thou made because thy sin that thou worked.** 11 At that time him proceeded from the pit and bowed to the prophet ~ him swore sayin - "As mi have saddened JAH - make mi what thou loved - yet make JAH do mi thus thus lest mi separate from thee-I ~ as we have no Law - mi didn't live firmed up in Him Command like unto mi fathers ~ thou know that we fathers taught we and that we worship idols. 12 to mi are a sinner who lived firmed up in mi sin - who firmed up in mi collar of reasonin firmness and mi reasonin arrogance whereby mi saddened JAH Command - but up til now mi hadn't heard JAH servants the prophets Word - and mi didn't live firmed up in Him LAW and Him Command that Him commanded mi." 13 Him told him sayin - "As there are none from your kindred precedin you who trusted him sin - mi knew that the prophet raceived repentance today." 14 "But now quit thy worshippin idols and return toward knowin JAH that thou might have true repentance" him told him ~ him fell and bowed at the prophet feet - and the prophet lifted up and commanded him all the goodly Work that are due him. 15 and him returned toward him house doin also like unto JAH commanded him.

16 and that Meqabees returned him body toward worshippin JAH - and him destroyed from him house the idols and also the sorcery - persons who worship idols and pessimists and magicians. 17 and morn in and evenin like unto them fathers do - him would examine the childran him captured and brought from 'Iyerusaliem in all JAH Commands and Him Order and Him LAW. 18 and from the childran him captured - him appointed knowin ones on him house. 19 and again from the infants him appointed knowin childran who keep levelled childran who were small - who enter toward the beddin that them might teach them JAH LAW that 'Isra'iel childran do ~ him would hear from captured 'Isra'iel childran the Order and the LAW and the Nine Laws - that Mo`ab persons order and them mosques that them make were vain. 20 Him destroyed them mosques - them idols and them sorcery - and the sacrifice and the grapes sacrificed to the idols mornin and evenin from the goat kids and fattened sheeps flocks. 21 And him destroyed him idols whom him worship and beg and believe in all him Work while him sacrificed sacrifice afternoon and at noon - and to all priests told him - and him idols to whom him do them accord. 22 As it would seem to him that them save him in all that them told - him wouldn't scorn all the thing them told him. 23 But that Meqabees quit them Work. 24 After him heard the Ra`ay thing - whom them call a prophet - him accomplished him Work in repentance ~ as 'Isra'iel childran would sadden Him at one time - and on the time Him chastised them in the tribulation - as them know and also cry toward JAH - all Him kindreds worked goodly Work more than 'Isra'iel childran in that season. 25 On the time Him heard that them were seized and abused by peoples hand who firm up tribulation on them and that them cried toward Him - Him thought of them fathers oath and at that time Him would forgive them because them fathers Yis'haq - 'Abriham - and Ya`iqob. 26 And on the time Him saved them - them would forget JAH Who saved them from tribulation - and them would return toward worshippin the idols. 27 And at that time Him would arouse on them peoples who firm up tribulation on them - and on the time them firmed up on them and taxed them and ruled them - JAH would arouse princes to them that Him might save them on the time Him loved. 28 And on the time Him kept them - them again returned toward sin that them might sadden Him by them hands Work that were firm and by worshippin idols in them councils. 29 But Him would arouse on them Mo`ab and 'Iloflee - Sorya - Midyam and Gibts persons; and on the time them enemies defeated them - them would cry and weep ~ on the time them firmed up on them and taxed them and ruled them - JAH would arouse princes to them that Him might save them on the time Him loved.

Meqabian II Chapter 4

1 And in 'Iyasu time are a day when Him saved them. 2 And in Giediewon time are a day when Him saved them. 3 And in Somson time and in Deebora and Bariq and Yodeet time are a day when Him saved them - and lodgin whether on male or on daughter - Him would arouse princes to them that them might save them from them enemies hands who firm up tribulation on them. 4 And like unto JAH loved - Him would save them from persons who firm up tribulation on them. 5 And them would be totally Feeling good in all the Work that Him accomplished to them ~ them would be Feeling good in them land seed and in multiplyin all them flocks in wilderness and them livestock. 6 And Him would bless them plants and them livestock to them - to Him sight them up in Eye of Mercy - and to Him wouldn't diminish them livestock on them - to them are kind persons childran and Him would totally love them. 7 But on the time them were evil in them Work - Him would cast them in them enemies hands. 8 And on the time Him destroyed them - them would seek Him in worship - and them would return from sin and march toward JAH in repentance. 9 And on the time them returned in them complete reasonin - Him would atone them sin to them ~ Him wouldn't think of them former sin on them - to Him know them that them were flesh and blood - to them have this world misleadin thoughts on them - and to them have demons in them. 10 But on the time that Meqabees heard this Order that JAH worked in Him worshippin place the Temple - him were slain in repentance. 11 After him sight up and heard this - him didn't scorn workin goodly Work; him didn't scorn workin all the goodly Work that 'Isra'iel childran work on the time JAH forgave them - and after them trespassed from Him LAW - them weep and would cry on the time JAH whipped them - and again Him would forgive them - and them would keep Him LAW. 12 And Meqabees likewise would straighten up him Work - and him would keep Him LAW - and him would live firmed up in 'Isra'iel Creator JAH Command. 13 At that time after him heard all the Work whereby 'Isra'iel childran boast - Him would boast like unto them in keepin JAH LAW. 14 Him would urge him kindred and childran that them might live firmed up in JAH Command and all Him LAW. 15 And him would forbid the order that 'Isra'iel forbid - and him would hear and keep the Law that 'Isra'iel keep - and when him kindred are another Mo`ab man - him would forbid the food that 'Isra'iel forbid. 16 And him would send forth tithes ~ him would give all that were first birthed and that him owned from him cows and him sheeps and him donkeys - and returnin him face toward 'Iyerusaliem him would sacrifice the sacrifice that 'Isra'iel sacrifice. 17 Him would sacrifice sin and vow sacrifice - a sacrifice whereby welfare are done and a accord sacrifice - and the Itinual sacrifice. 18 And him would give him first crops - and him would gush and pour the grapes that 'Isra'iel pour - and him would give this to him priest whom him I-pointed - and likewise him would do all that 'Isra'iel do - and him would sweeten him ishence. 19 Him built a candlestick and a bowl and a seat and a tent and the four links of rings - and diluted oil to the Hola of Holas lamps - and the curtain that 'Isra'iel make in the Hola of Holas on the time them served JAH. 20 And like unto them worked goodly Work on the time them lived firmed up in Him Order and Him LAW and on the time JAH didn't neglect and cast them in them enemies hands - Meqabees also would work goodly Work like unto them. 21 Him would beg toward 'Isra'iel Creator JAH everytime that Him might be him Teacher and lest Him separate him from 'Isra'iel childran whom Him chose and who did Him Accord. 22 And again him would beg Him that Him might give him childran in Tsiyon and a house in 'Iyerusaliem - that Him might give them Heavenly Seed of Virtue in Tsiyon and a Heavenly House of Soul in 'Iyerusaliem - and that Him might save him from the destruction spoken by the prophet tongue - that Him might accept him repentance in all the mournin him wept before JAH bein sad and enterin repentance... 23 And lest Him destroy childran in this world on him - and that Him might keep him in him proceedin and enterin. 24 Kindreds from Mo`ab peoples beneath Meqabees Authority were Feeling good that them might believe - to them chief live firmed up in straight Work - and them would check up him judgemant and fulfill him accord - and them would scorn them country language and them country justice ~ them would overstand that Meqabees Work surpassed and were straight. 25 And them would come and hear Meqabees charity and Truth judgemants. 26 Him had much money ~ him had daughter slaves and male slaves and camels and donkeys - and him had five hundred horses that wear breastplates ~ him would totally defeat the 'Amalieqans and 'Iloflans and Sorya persons - but formerly when him worshipped idols him lived when them defeated him. 27 Him prevailed - yet but from him worshippin JAH onward - when him went toward battle there are none who defeated him. 28 But them would come in them idols Power that them might fight him - and them would call them idols names and curse him - however there were none who defeat him - to him have made him faith on him Creator JAH. 29 And when him did thus and when him defeated him enemies - him lived when him ruled peoples in him Authority. 30 Him would revenge and destroy wronged persons enemy to them ~ him would judge Truth to a child whose mother and father dead on him. 31 And him would raceive widows in them trouble time - and him would give from him food and satta them who hungered - and him would clothe the naked from him clothes. 32 And him would be Feeling good in him hands Work - and him would give from the money him had without begrudgin - and him would give tithes to the Temple ~ Meqabees dead havin lived in Feeling good joy when him did this.

Meqabian II Chapter 5

1 And him dead quittin him childran who were small - and them grew up like unto them father taught them ~ them kept them house Order - and them would keep all them kindred - and them wouldn't make poor ones cry - nor widows nor a child whose mother and father dead on him. 2 Them would fear JAH - and them would give them money alms to poor ones - and them would keep all the trust them father told them - and them would calm the child whose mother and father dead on them and widows in them trouble time - and them would be them mother and father ~ them would make them cast from persons hand who wrong them - and calm them from all the disturbance and sadness that found them. 3 Them lived five years while them did thus. 4 After this the Keledans king Tseerutsaydan came ~ him destroyed all them country - and him captured Meqabees childran and destroyed all them villages. 5 And him plundered all them money ~ them lived firmed up in all evil Work and sin - in adultery - insult and greed and not thinkin of them Creator - yet persons who don't live firmed up in JAH LAW and Him Command and who worship idols seized them also and took them toward them country. 6 Them eat what a beast bit and the blood and the carcass - and what a scavenger beat and cast - all that JAH don't love - yet them have no order from all the true Commands written in 'Oreet. 7 Them don't know JAH them Creator - Who sent them forth from them mothers wombs and fed them by what are due - were them Medicine. 8 Them marry from them aunt and them father wife - them step mother

- and them go toward robbery and evil thing and sin and adultery - yet them have no order in Judgemant time - and them work all evil Work and them marry them aunts and them sistren and them have no LAW. ⁹ And all them roads are dark and slippery - and them Work are sin and adultery. ¹⁰ But those Meqabees childran would keep in all them Order ~ them wouldn't eat what a scavenger beat nor what dead and lodged ~ them wouldn't work all the Work that the Keledans childran work - to them many Works are evil that weren't written in this book - that sinners work - and doubters and criminals - betrayers totally filled of robbery and sin and pagans childran. ¹¹ All the Work them Creator JAH love aren't there alongside them. ¹² And again them would worship a idol called Bi'iel Fiegor ~ them would trust it like unto them Creator JAH when it were deaf and dumb. to it are the idol that a person hand worked - to it are the person hand Work that a smith worked who work silver and gold - that have no breath nor knowledge - and it had nothing that it sight up nor hear. ¹³ It don't eat nor drink. ¹⁴ It don't kill nor save. ¹⁵ It don't plant nor uproot. ¹⁶ It don't harm it enemy nor benefit it friend. ¹⁷ It don't impoverish nor honour. ¹⁸ It will be a hindrance to mislead the Keledans persons who were lazy - yet it don't chastise nor forgive.

Meqabian II Chapter 6

¹ JAH enemy Tseerutsaydan who were arrogant appointed them who veil and falsehood priests to him idols. ² Him would sacrifice to them and him would pour the grapes to them. ³ and it would seem to him that them eat and drink. ⁴ and while it dawned him would give them cows and donkeys and heifers - and him would sacrifice mornin and evenin - and him would eat from that defouled sacrifice. ⁵ and again him would disturb and obligate other persons that them might sacrifice to him idols - yet it weren't that only them do it. ⁶ on the time them sight up Meqabees childran that them were handsome and that them worship them Creator JAH - the idols priests loved that them might mislead them to sacrifice and to eat from that hated sacrifice - but these honoured Meqabees childran refused them. ⁷ As them keep them father command - and as them have firmed up in workin goodly Work - and as them totally fear JAH - it failed them to agree... ⁸ on the time them bound them and insulted them and robbed them. ⁹ Them told to the king Tseerutsaydan that them refused sacrifice and bowin to him idols. ¹⁰ and because this thing the king vexed ~ him were sad and commanded that them might bring them - and them brought and stood them before him - and the king told them to him idols - "Sacrifice a sacrifice to mi idols." ¹¹ and them spoke and told him - "An I won't answer thee in this thing - and I won't sacrifice to thy defouled idols." ¹² Him frightened them by Works that abounded - yet him couldn't able to them - to them have disciplined them reasonins believin in JAH. ¹³ Him flamed a fire and cast them in fire - and them gave them bodies to JAH. ¹⁴ After them dead them arose and were sight up to him at night drawin them swords when him had reclined on him lordship throne - and him totally feared. ¹⁵ "Mi sirs - tell mi alright - what should mi do to you? Don't take mi body in death - that mi might do all thou commanded mi." ¹⁶ Them told him all that are due to him while them said - "Think that JAH were thy Creator - and JAH are there Who shall dismiss from this thy kingdom where thou are arrogant - and Who shall lower thee toward Gehannem of fire with thy father Deeyablos ~ when I worshipped I Creator JAH without a iniquity livin that I wronged thee - and when I bowed to Him in fearin Him JAH-ness - like unto thou burned I in fire - thou will finish all thy hardship by that also. ¹⁷ to Him are Who Created all - Earth and Heaven and sea and all that are within she. ¹⁸ and to Him are Who Created moon and Sun and stars - and to Him Who Created all the Creation are JAH. ¹⁹ to there are no other creator withou Him in Earth nor Heaven - to Him are Who able to all - and to there are nothing that fail Him. As Him are Who kill and Who save - Who whip in tribulation and Who forgive - when I bowed to Him in fearin JAH - like unto thou burned I in fire - thou will finish all thy hardship by that" them told him. ²⁰ "As Him are Who rule Earth and Heaven - there are none who escape from Him Authority. ²¹ There are none from the Creation Him Created who departed from Him Command - apart from thou who are a criminal - and criminals like unto thee whose reasonins thy father Satan hid - and thou and those thy priests and thy idols will descend together toward Gehannem where are no exits up til Eternity. ²² Thy teacher are Satan who taught thee this evil Work that thou might do a evil thing on I - yet as it aren't only thou who do this - you will descend toward Gehannem together. ²³ to thou make thy ras self like unto thy Creator JAH - yet thou didn't know JAH Who Created thee. ²⁴ and thou are arrogant in thy idols and thy hand Work up til JAH make thee wretched ~ Him shall canvict thee on all thy sin and iniquity that thou worked in this world.

Meqabian II Chapter 7

¹ Woe to you who don't know JAH Who Created you - to thy idols who are like unto thee - and to thee - and to you have that you might regret a regrets that won't profit on the time you were sad bein seized in See'ol difficulty - and woe to thee - to you who don't keep Him Word and Him LAW. ² You will have no exit from she up til Eternity - thy priests and thou who sacrifice to them like unto your Creator JAH - to thy idols who have no breath nor soul - who won't revenge and destroy him who did a evil thing on them - nor do a goodly thing to him who did a goodly thing to them. ³ Woe to you who sacrifice to them - to them are a person hands Work where Satan live - lodgin there to mislead lazy ones reasonin like unto thee - that him might lower you toward Gehannem of fire - and the priests who serve demons commanded to you and your idols. ⁴ As you don't know that there are nothing that will profit you - you wrong and err. ⁵ As to the animals that JAH Created to be food to you - and dogs and beasts - them are better than you - to besides one death there are no more candemnation on them. ⁶ But as you will dead and raceive hardship in Gehannem fire where are no exits up til Eternity - animals are better. ⁷ Havin spoken this - them went and were hidden from him. ⁸ But that Tseerutsaydan lodged when him trembled - seized by a firm fright - and fright didn't quit him up til it dawned.

Meqabian II Chapter 8

¹ and him lived firmed up in reasonin malice and arrogance. ² and as iron have been called firm - like unto Dan'iel sight it up on him kingdom - him turned in peoples countries in him area. ³ Him lived firmed up in evil and all him laziness and in disturbin persons. ⁴ and him totally destroy what I spoke formerly - and him eat a person money. ⁵ to him are diligent to evil like unto him father Deeyablos who firmed up him collar of reasonin - and him destroy what remained with him army. ⁶ Him say - "Mi era became like unto the Sun era" ~ yet him don't know JAH that Him were him Creator. ⁷ and in him reasonin him think that the Sun are found from him. ⁸ Him arise in Power - him camp in Tribe of Zablon lot and begin a formation in Meqiedonya - and him receive him food from Semarya - and them give him presents from Semarya. ⁹ Him camp in nomads region - and him reach up til Seedona - and him cast a tax on 'Akayya - and him elevate him collar of reasonin up til the flowin sea - and him return and send messengers up til Hindekie sea. ¹⁰ and likewise him elevate him collar of reasonin up til Heaven. ¹¹ Him live firmed up in bein arrogant and in evil - yet him don't have humblin him ras self. ¹² and him path are toward darkness and slipperiness - and toward crime and bein arrogant - and toward sheddin blood and tribulation. ¹³ and all him Work are what JAH hate ~ him do like unto robbery and evil and sin teacher Deeyablos taught him ~ him make a child cry whose mother and father dead on him - and him aren't nice to a poor one. ¹⁴ and him defeated and destroyed peoples kings by him authority. ¹⁵ and him ruled enemies chiefs - and him ruled many peoples - and him taxed them like unto him loved. ¹⁶ Even if him destroyed - him didn't quit ~ there are no person whom him didn't snatch Beginnin from Tersies sea up til 'Iyareeko sea. ¹⁷ Him would bow to idols ~ him would eat what dead and lodged - the blood - what a sword bloated and cut - and what were sacrificed to idols ~ all him Work are without justice - yet him have no justice ~ as him have been who alarm peoples beneath him authority - him would tax them tax like unto him loved. ¹⁸ As him do all that him loved before him - there are no fearin JAH before him - and him live in malice before JAH Who Created him. ¹⁹ Him didn't do it like unto him Creator - and like unto him did a evil thing on him companion on the time him vexed and seized him - JAH shall also pay him him hardship. ²⁰ As JAH have said **- I-man shall revenge and destroy sinner persons who don't live by I Command - that I-man might destroy them name invocation from this world** - like unto Him destroyed peoples who were precedin him - Him shall revenge and destroy him on the time when Him destroy. ²¹ and like unto evil persons did evil things - them shall raceive them hardship. ²² But bein commanded from JAH - goodly Work shall follow persons who work goodly Work. ²³ to like unto 'Iyasu destroyed the five Kene`an kings in cave in one day - and like unto him made Sun stand in Geba`on by him prayer that him might destroy them armies - Sun have stood amidst Heaven up til him destroyed 'Ewiewon and Kenaniewon - Fierziewon and Kiethiewon and 'Iyabusiewon armies - and like unto him killed around twenty thousand persons at one time - and like unto him killed them - and like unto him bound them makin foot from neck - and like unto him killed them in cave by spear - and like unto him fitted a stone on them... ²⁴ Tribulation like unto this shall find all persons who sadden JAH in them evil Work.

Meqabian II Chapter 9

¹ "O thou weak man who aren't JAH - why are thou proud? thou who are sight up today bein a man are Earth ashes tomorrow - and thou will

totally be worms in thy grave. ² to thy teacher are Deeyablos who return all persons sin hardship toward him ras self because him misled I father 'Adam - and See'ol will find thee again - and she will find persons who work thy sin. ³ to in firmin up him collar of reasonin and makin him ras self proud - like unto him refused to bow to 'Adam whom the Creator Created... ⁴ thou also have refused to bow to thy Creator JAH like unto thy teacher Deeyablos did. ⁵ Like unto thy precedin fathers - who don't know them Creator JAH in worship - will go toward Gehannem - thou also will go toward Gehannem. ⁶ Like unto Him revenged and destroyed them because them evil Work that them worked in this world - and like unto them descended toward Gehannem... ⁷ thou also will descend toward Gehannem like unto them. ⁸ As thou have aroused Him anger - and as thou have neglected to worship JAH Who gave thee Authority on the five kingdoms - do it seem to thee that thou will escape from JAH Authority? ⁹ Thou don't do thus that thou do Him Accord - thus Him examined thee - but if thou work goodly Work in this world - JAH will accomplish all thy Work to thee-I - and Him will accomplish and bless all the Work thou seized in thy hand to thee-I - and Him will subject thy Antiquity of enemies and thy day enemies to thee-I. ¹⁰ Thou will be Feeling good in thy enterins and thy proceedins and in thy child birthed from thy nature - and in thy flocks and thy fatnesses - and in all Work where thou placed thy hand - and in all that thou thought in thy heart ~ as Authority have been given thee-I from alongside JAH that thou might do thus and might work and plant and demolish - all will be commanded to thee-I. ¹¹ However if thou won't hear JAH Word nor live firmed up in Him LAW - like unto criminals who were precedin thee - and who don't worship JAH by what are due - and who didn't believe firmed up in HIM straight LAW - there are nothing whereby thou will escape from JAH Authority - to JAH Judgemant are Truth. ¹² All are totally revealed before Him - yet there are nothing hidden from before Him. ¹³ Him are Who seize the kings Authority and Who overturn powerful ones thrones. ¹⁴ Him are Who Ilivate them who were downbased and Who lift up them who fell. ¹⁵ Him are Who loose them who were bound and Who arouse them who dead ~ as pardon dew are found from alongside Him - on the time Him loved Him shall arouse persons whose flesh were demolished and rotten and were like unto dust. ¹⁶ and havin aroused and judged persons who worked evil Work - Him will take them toward Gehannem - to them have saddened Him. ¹⁷ to them are who demolished JAH Order and Him LAW - and Him will destroy them child from this world. ¹⁸ As kind persons Work are more difficult than sinner persons Work - sinner persons don't love that them might live in kind persons counsel. ¹⁹ Like unto Heavens were distanced from Earth - likewise kind persons Work were distanced from evil persons Work. ²⁰ But sinner persons Work are robbery and sin - adultery and iniquity - greed and perfidy Work ~ it are bein drunk in iniquity and robbin a person money. ²¹ It are quickly goin toward sheddin a person blood - and it are goin toward destruction that don't benefit - and it are makin a child weep whose mother and father dead on him ~ it are eatin blood and what dead and lodged - and it are eatin camel and boar flesh - and it are goin toward a daughter in she blood before she are cleansed - and toward a daughter in childbirth. ²² All this are sinner persons Work ~ she are Satan trap that were a wide and prepared path - and that take toward Gehannem that live firmed up forever - and toward See'ol. ²³ But righteous ones path that were totally narrow are what take toward welfare - and innocence and humbleness - and Inity and Love - and prayer and fast - and flesh purity - toward keepin from what don't benefit - from eatin what a sword bloated and cut and what dead and lodged - and from goin toward a youtmon wife and from adultery. ²⁴ Them keep from what weren't commanded by LAW - from eatin disgustin food and from all hated Work - and from all the Work that JAH don't love - to sinner persons do all this. ²⁵ As to kind persons - them distance from all the Work that JAH don't love. ²⁶ Him love them and shall keep them from all them tribulation like unto Trust money. ²⁷ to them keep Him Order and Him LAW and all that Him love - but Satan rule sinner persons.

Meqabian II Chapter 10

¹ Fear JAH Who Created you and kept you up til today - yet you the nobles and the kings - don't go on Satan path. ² Live in the LAW and Command of JAH Who rule all - yet don't go on Satan path. ³ As on the time 'Isra'iel childran came toward 'Amalieq that them might inherit Kiethiewon and Kenaniewon and Fierziewon country - Siefor child Balaq and Bele`am... ⁴ whom thou cursed are cursed - and him whom thou blessed blessed ~ don't go on Satan road - to him have said - "An mi will give thee much silver and gold that honour thee - that thou might curse to mi and - and havin cursed - that thou might destroy to mi." ⁵ and to Bele`am have come makin him sorcery reward a morale - and to Siefor child Balaq have shown him the place where 'Isra'iel childran camped. ⁶ to him have done him pessimism - and to him have

sacrificed him sacrifice - and to him have slaughtered from him fattened cows and sheeps - and to him have loved that him might curse and destroy 'Isra'iel childran. ⁷ Him returned a curse toward a bless - yet but as JAH didn't love that him might curse them by Him Word - don't go on Satan road. ⁸ "As thou are the kindred that JAH chose - as thou are JAH Lodgin that shall come from Heaven - make persons be cursed who curse thee-I - and make persons who bless thee-I be blessed" him said. ⁹ on the time him blessed them before him - after this Siefor child Balaq were sad - and him totally vexed and commanded that him might curse them. ¹⁰ to the kindred that JAH blessed have come toward this country - and Bele`am told him - "Mi won't curse 'Isra'iel whom JAH blessed." ¹¹ and Siefor child Balaq told Bele`am - "As to mi - mi had loved that thou might curse to mi ~ thou blessed them before mi - yet but thou didn't curse them ~ if thou had cursed to mi and told mi 'Give mi' - as to mi - mi would have given thee a house full of silver and gold - but thou totally blessed them - and thou didn't do a goodly thing to mi - and mi won't do a goodly thing to thee." ¹² Bele`am said - "What JAH told mi Speak with mi tongue - mi will speak it - yet as to mi - mi cyaan dare to ignore JAH thing. ¹³ Lest mi curse a blessed kindred - as JAH shall vex on mi if mi love money - as to mi - mi don't love money more than mi soul. ¹⁴ As JAH have told them father Ya`iqob - make persons who bless thee-I be blessed and make **persons who curse thee-I be cursed** - lest mi curse blessed Ya`iqob - as to mi - mi don't love money more than mi soul" him said - and as JAH have told him - **Him who bless thee-I are blessed**... ¹⁵ and **a person who curse thee**-I unjustly are cursed - accomplish thy path and thy Work that JAH might love thee. ¹⁶ and don't be like unto former persons who saddened JAH in them sin and whom Him neglected - and there are them whom Him destroyed in Destruction Water. ¹⁷ and there are them whom Him destroyed by them haters hands ~ there are them whom Him destroyed by them enemies hands - bringin enemies who were evil persons who firmed up tribulation on them - and them captured them lords with them priests and them prophets. ¹⁸ and them delivered them toward the foreign country them don't know ~ them totally captured them - and them plundered them livestocks on them and destroyed them country. ¹⁹ to them have demolished the honoured country 'Iyerusaliem fences and ramparts - and them made 'Iyerusaliem like unto a field. ²⁰ and the priests were capture - and the LAW were demolished - and warriors fought in war and fell. ²¹ and widows were capture ~ as them have been capture - them wept to them ras selves - yet them didn't weep to them husbands who dead. ²² and the childran wept - and elders shamed - and them weren't nice to neither a grey haired person nor a elder. ²³ Them destroyed all them found in the country - yet them weren't nice to beauties nor to them in LAW ~ as JAH have vexed on Him kindreds on the time Him loved that Him might beforehand destroy Him Lodgin the Temple - them captured and took them toward the country them don't know and toward peoples. ²⁴ As them sadden them Creator everytime - because this thing on the time JAH neglected 'Isra'iel childran - JAH made 'Iyerusaliem to be ploughed like unto a field. ²⁵ to Him are nice to them because them fathers - but Him didn't destroy them at one time ~ as Him love them fathers Yis'haq and 'Abriham and Ya`iqob who reigned to true and lived firmed up in straight LAW before them Creator - it are because them fathers kindness - yet it aren't because them ras selves kindness that him forgive them. ²⁶ and Him I-pointed them on honours that were twofold - and them found two Kingdoms - on Earth and in Heaven. ²⁷ and you the kings and the nobles who live in this passin world - like unto your fathers who lived firmed up in Work that are due and who were precedin you likewise inherited the Kingdom of Heaven - and like unto them names were beautiful to a child childran - think of them. ²⁸ and thou - straighten up thy Work - that Him might straighten up thy Kingdom to thee - and that thy name might be called in goodly invocation like unto the kind kings who were precedin thee who served JAH in them beautiful lifestyle.

Meqabian II Chapter 11

¹ Think of JAH slave Mussie who weren't annoyed when him kept around this kindred in him humbleness and him prayer and whom not even one person destroyed - and him begged toward JAH in him innocence to him sista and bredda who backbit him and loved that JAH might destroy them while him said - "As them have wronged Thee-I - Lord - pardon and don't neglect thy kindreds" - and him atoned them sin to them - yet Him thought of JAH servant Mussie who weren't annoyed. ² "To I-man have wronged Thee-I - and forgive I Thy slave who am a sinner - to Thou are Merciful - and to Thou are a Pardoner - and forgive them them sin." ³ and Mussie likewise atoned them sin to him sista and bredda who backbit him. ⁴ and because this thing him were called innocent. ⁵ and JAH totally loved him more than all the priests childran who were him bredren - to Him I-point the priests - and JAH made him like unto Him Ras Self alongside them. ⁶ But Him also

sank beneath Earth Qorie childran who challenged ~ Him lowered them toward See'ol with them livestocks and them tents when them said "We are there - we are there in flesh and soul" ~ as him Creator JAH have loved him - and as him didn't depart from Him Command - all the word him spoke would be done to him like unto JAH Word. 7 and unless thou demolished JAH Command likewise - JAH will do thy accord to thee-I and will love thy thing to thee-I - and Him will keep thy Kingdom to thee-I. 8 and 'Asaf and Qorie childran who departed from Mussie command grumbled on him because him told them - "Straighten up your reasonins to be ruled to JAH." 9 Them grumbled sayin "How about aren't we Liewee childran who work priesthood Work in Tent that were special?" 10 Them went and smoked up ishence seizin them censers that them might smoke up - but JAH didn't accept them plea - and them were burnt by the fire in them censers - and them melted like unto the wax that fire melt - and not even one person remained from them ~ as Him have said - **"Them censers were honoured by them bodies bein burnt"** - apart from them censers that entered toward JAH Lodgin to JAH Command - neither them clothes nor them bones remained. 11 Because this thing JAH told 'Aron and Mussie - **"Gather them censers toward the Tent ~ make it be a instrumant to I Lodgin wherefor I-man prepared all I-ginnin from outside up til within."** 12 and him prepared the honoured Tent instrumants ~ him prepared the rings and the joiners - Keerubiel picture sea. 13 Him worked the cups - the curtains - the Tent area grounds to the mobilisation - the altar and the jugs whereby them sacrifice in the Tent that were special. 14 Them sacrificed the sacrifice that them sacrifice by them accord - the sacrifice whereby welfare are made - the sacrifice whereby Him atone sin - and the vow sacrifice and the mornin and the evenin sacrifice. 15 All that Him commanded to Mussie - him commanded them in the Tent that were special - that them might work Work in she. 16 Them didn't scorn bein ruled to them Creator JAH - that Him Name might be praised by them in the LAW Lodgin Tent of them Creator JAH Who gave them a promise that Him might give to them to give them them fathers inheritance that produce honey and milk that Him swore to 'Abriham. 17 Them didn't scorn bein ruled to them Creator JAH - Who swore to Yis'haq and firmed up Him Worship to Ya`iqob... 18 and Who firmed up to 'Aron and Mussie the Tent where Him Worship are kept... 19 and Who firmed up Him Worship to both 'Elyas and Samu'iel in the Temple and Tent that Selomon worked up til it became JAH Lodgin in 'Iyerusaliem - and up til JAH Name Lodgin became JAH Lodgin that honoured 'Isra'iel. 20 to she are a supplication - and to she are a sin atonemant where it are overturned to them who live in innocence and to the priests. 21 and to she are a place to persons who do Him Accord where Him will hear them pleas... 22 and JAH LAW Canstruction that honoured 'Isra'iel. 23 to she are where sacrifice are sacrificed and where Ishence are smoked up that JAH Who honoured 'Isra'iel be in goodly Fragrance. 24 and Him would speak bein on the joiner where Him forgive in the Tent that were special ~ JAH Light would be revealed to Ya`iqob childran whom Him chose and to friends who live firmed up in Him LAW and Him Command. 25 But persons who ignored JAH LAW will be like unto Qorie childran whom Earth sank - and likewise sinner persons have that them might enter toward Gehannem that have no exits up til Eternity.

Meqabian II Chapter 12

1 You who didn't keep the LAW Him commanded you in Tent - woe to you 'Isra'iel nobles who also didn't do Him Accord - yet you did your ras selves accord - and this are bein arrogant and pride - greed and adultery - drink and bein drunk - and swearin in lie. 2 and **because this thing I anger - like unto chaff are burnt before a fire - and like unto fire burn the mountain - and like unto a whirl wind spill the crushed chaff from Earth and scattar it toward Heaven - lest it trace be found in it place - I anger will destroy you like unto that.** 3 JAH Who honoured 'Isra'iel said - **"I-man shall likewise destroy all persons who work sin"** - and think of JAH Who rule all and to Whom nothing fail. 4 Him love persons who love Him - and to persons who live firmed up in Him Command - Him will atone them iniquity and them sin to them ~ don't be dull and stingy of heart by not believin. 5 and make your reasonins straight to be ruled to JAH - and believe in Him that you might firm up your bodies - and **I-man shall save you from your enemy hand in your tribulation day.** 6 and **in your plea time I-man tell you - Check - I-man am there with you in Support ~ I-man shall save you from your enemy hand ~ as you have believed in I** - and **as you have done I Command - and as you didn't depart from I LAW** - and **as you have loved what I-man love** - JAH Who rule all said - **I-man won't neglect you on your tribulation day.** 7 Him love them who love Him - to Him are a Pardoner - and to Him are nice - and Him keep persons who keep Him LAW - like unto a trust money. 8 Him return Him anger to

them many times ~ because Him were who know them that them are flesh and blood - as Him are a Pardoner - Him didn't destroy all in Him chastisemant - and on the time them souls were separated from them flesh - them will return toward them Earthliness. 9 As Him have Created them bringin from not livin toward livin - them won't know the place where them live up til JAH love that Him might bring them from not livin toward livin ~ again Him separated them souls from them flesh - and Earth nature returned toward it Earthliness. 10 and again Him Accord shall bring them from not livin toward livin." 11 But Tseerutsaydan who denied JAH multiplied bein arrogant before JAH ~ him made him ras self lofty up til the day that him loved on the time him quit Him. 12 "An mi era became like unto Heaven era - and mi are who send forth Sun - and mi won't dead up til Eternity" him said. 13 and before him finished speakin this thing the Angel of Death whose name are called Thilimyakos alit and struck him heart ~ him dead in that hour ~ as him didn't praise him Creator - him were separated from him beautiful lifestyle and perished arisin from him arrogance abundance and him Work evil. 14 But when the Keledans king army had camped in the city and the country squares lovin to fight him - on the time him dead - them proceeded and destroyed him country ~ them plundered all him livestock - and them didn't preserve a elder who near and sight up ramparts. 15 Them plundered all him money - and them took him tiny money - and them burned him country in fire and returned toward them country.

Meqabian II Chapter 13

1 But these five Meqabees childran who believed gave them bodies to death refusin to eat the sacrifice to idols. 2 to them have known that pretendin with JAH surpass from pretendin with persons - and JAH anger from the king anger. 3 Havin known that this world will totally pass and that the Feeling good joy won't live firmed up forever - them gave them bodies to fire that them might be saved from fire in Heaven. 4 and as them have known that bein made Feeling good in Garden one day are better than livin many eras in this world - and that findin Thy Pardon one hour Lord - are better than many eras - them gave them bodies to fire. 5 What are I era? Like unto a shadow - like unto pass in wax melt and perish on a fire edge - aren't it like unto that? 6 But Thou Lord live forever - and Thy Era aren't fulfilled - and Thy Name invocation are to a child childran. 7 and Meqabees childran thought that it seemed all this ~ refusin to eat a disgustin sacrifice them chose believin in JAH. 8 Knowin that them will arise with persons who dead - and meanin because JAH - knowin that Judgemant shall be judged after Resurrection of Council - because this thing them gave them bodies to martyrdom. 9 You persons who don't know nor believe persons who dead risin - knowin that the Life them find later will surpass from this them passin Earthly Life - arisin from these five Meqabees childran who gave them bodies together to the death and whose appearance were handsome - after this them knew Resurrection. 10 Because them believed in Him knowin that all shall pass - and because them didn't bow to idols - because them didn't eat a disgustin sacrifice that don't give Support - them gave them bodies to death that them might find thanks from JAH. 11 to because this thing knowin that Him will make them Feeling good in flesh and soul in later era - them didn't know this world flavour and death tribulation a serious thing to them who have child and wife - and knowin that Resurrection be made in flesh and soul on the Day of Advent - them gave them bodies to death. 12 and knowin that persons who kept JAH LAW - with the nobles and the kings who believed JAH Word and were nice... 13 shall live reignin to a child childran many eras in Kingdom of Heaven where are no sadness and tribulation nor death - and knowin in them reasonins what will be done later - like unto wax melt amidst a fire - because this thing them gave them bodies to death. 14 Believin that them faces will shine seven hands more than the Sun - and that them will be Feeling good in Him Love on the time all arose in flesh and soul - them gave them bodies to death.

Meqabian II Chapter 14

1 But the Samrans and 'Ayhuds thing - the Seduqans who don't believe persons who dead risin - and the Fereesans thing quite totally sadden I - and it help I to I reasonin ~ "We will dead tomorrow" 'Ayhuds say - "Make we eat and drink ~ we will dead tomorrow ~ there are no Feeling good joy we will sight up in grave." 2 But the Samrans say - "As we flesh will be dust - it won't arise. 3 Because she were invisible like unto wind and like unto iyunder voice - check - she are here - and because she were what them don't call and invisible - as soul won't arise if flesh dead - on the time Resurrection are done we will believe we souls arisin. 4 But as beasts will eat she and as worms will eat she in the grave - we flesh are sight up alongside all ~ she will become dust and ashes. 5 and those beasts who ate she will become dust - to them have been like unto grass - and to them have become dust like unto them weren't Created - and

to them trace won't be found - but we flesh won't arise." 6 and the Fereesans say - "We believe as to persons who dead arisin - however Him will bring and Inite souls with another flesh that are in Heaven - that aren't on Earth ~ where will demolished and rotten fleshes be found?" 7 But the Seduqans say - "After we soul proceeded from we flesh - we won't arise with persons who dead - and flesh and soul have no arisin after them dead - and after we dead we won't arise." 8 and because this thing them totally err - and as them speak insult on JAH Lordship - them thing sadden I. 9 As them didn't believe JAH Who honour them - them have no hope to be saved - however them have no hope to dead and arise and be saved. 10 O 'Ayhudan who are blind of reasonin - when thou are whom Him Created bringin from not livin toward livin - and scorned like unto spit - will thou make JAH ignorant - Who made thee a person? Will it fail JAH Who Created thee in Him Example and Him Appearance to arouse Initin thy flesh and thy soul? 11 As thou won't escape from JAH Authority - don't think a thing that are thus ~ thou will arise without thou lovin - to there are the hardship thou will raceive in See'ol where thou were seized on the time thou dead - and it shall be judged on thee without thou lovin. 12 to the sin found from demons that demons place in thy reasonin are worked alongside thee after thou were birthed from thy mother womb - and to she are worked abundantly on the time thou grew up. 13 Them place she in thy body on the time thou dead - and she will bring hardship on them on the time them worked she. 14 Like unto there are sin in them collar of reasonin - as there are persons who work sin bein seized by she - she kindreds will present demons. 15 All sinner persons souls shall come from Heaven edge where them are - and thy sin likewise shall introduce thee toward Gehannem pullin and bringin thy soul from where thou are. 16 and after thy flesh lived separate from thy soul - JAH Charity dew shall arouse thee bein seven fold like unto I father 'Adam flesh. 17 Thou who live in grave - thou also err in thy error - yet make it not seem to thee that thou only mislead the others ~ thou say - "The arisin that persons who dead shall arise aren't there" - that them might depart from JAH Command and err. 18 Him shall arouse thee that Him might give thee thy hardship like unto thy Work that thou worked - yet who shall quit thee that thou might remain bein dust? 19 But at that time - whether wind in wind be thy nature - or if Water in Water be thy nature - or if Earth in Earth be thy nature - or if fire in fire be thy nature - it shall come. 20 and if a soul that lodged in thee be what lived in See'ol - she shall come. 21 and righteous ones souls that live in Garden in joy shall come. 22 But thou 'Ayhudan - Samran - Fereesan - Seduqan - will live in See'ol up til it are judged on thee. 23 At that time thou will sight up that JAH shall pay thee the hardship like unto thy sin because thou misled persons. 24 "Persons who dead won't arise ~ as we will dead - make we eat and drink" - and because thou sat in Mussie chair and misled by thy words while thou said - "Persons who dead won't arise" - thou will sight up that Him shall pay thee thy hardship. 25 and without thy knowin Oreet Book - and when thou teach the books word - because this thing thou erred ~ it would be better had thou remained without learnin from thy misleadin a person. 26 It would have been better if thou didn't know the books word - when thou promulgate JAH kindreds in thy evil teachin and thy worthless words. 27 to JAH don't favour havin sight up a face - and to Him shall give the grace and glory Him prepared to Him friends - persons who teach goodly Work - but thou have that thou might raceive thy reward like unto thy Work and the things that thou spoke. 28 But there are nothing whereby thou will escape from JAH Authority Who shall judge on thee - and Him have that Him might pay thee like unto thy Work - to them whom thou taught and thou together will raceive a sentance. 29 Know that persons who dead shall arise - and if them are persons who kept Him LAW them shall arise - and like unto Earth send forth grass on the time rain rained - as Him Command shall send them forth from a grave - it aren't possible to it to remain demolished and rotten. 30 Like unto moist wood drink dew and send forth leaves on the time Him satta she rain to Earth - like unto wheat bear forth fruit - and like unto grain produce buds - like unto it aren't possible to she to withhold that she might prevent she fruit if JAH loved... 31 and like unto it aren't possible to a daughter who canceived to close and prevent she womb on the time labour seized she - like unto it aren't possible to she to escape without birthin... 32 as dew have alit toward she bein commanded from JAH - at that time she shall produce them at one time - yet after she heard JAH Word - a grave also likewise cyaan prevent the persons gathered alongside she from arisin. 33 and fleshes shall be gathered in the place where them corpses fell - and them places where souls live shall be opened - and souls shall return toward the flesh where them were formerly separated. 34 and on the time a drum were beaten - persons who dead shall quickly arise like unto a eye wink - and havin arisen them shall stand before JAH - and Him shall give them them reward like unto them hand Work. 35 At that time thou will sight up that thou arise with dead ones - and thou will marvel at all the Work thou worked in this world - and on the time thou sight up all thy sins written before thee - at that time thou will regret a useless regret. 36 Thou know that thou will arise with dead ones and that thou will raceive thy hardship like unto the Work that thou worked.

Meqabian II Chapter 15

1 But persons who found them reward by them goodly Work shall be Feeling good at that time ~ persons who ignored while them said - "Persons who dead won't arise" shall be sad at that time on the time them sight up that persons who dead arose with them evil Work that don't benefit. 2 That - them Work that worked shall canvict them - and them ras selves shall know that it canvict them without one livin who will dispute them. 3 on the day when Judgemant and mournin are done - on the day when JAH shall come - on the day when Definite Judgemant are judged - persons who forgot JAH LAW shall stand in the place where them stand. 4 on the day when there shall be total darkness - and on the day when mist are pulled - on the day when flashes are sight up and when lightnin are heard... 5 and on the day when quakes and fright and heatwave and sleet frost are made... 6 on the day when a evil person who worked evil Work raceive hardship - and on the day when a clean person raceive him reward like unto him worked clean Work - and on the day when persons who forgot JAH LAW raceive the hardship like unto a sinner person worked sin - them shall stand in the place where them stand. 7 to on the day when a master aren't more honoured than him slave - and on the time when a mistress aren't more honoured than she slave... 8 and on the time when the king aren't more honoured than a poor one - and on the time when a elder aren't more honoured than a infant - on the time when a father aren't more honoured than him child - and on the time when a mother aren't more honoured than she child... 9 on the time when a wealthy one aren't more honoured than a poor one - and on the time when a arrogant one aren't more honoured than a downbased one - and on the time when the great aren't more honoured than the small - she are the day when Judgemant are judged - to she are the day when them raceive sentance and hardship - and to she are the day when all will raceive hardship like unto them worked sin. 10 and to she are the day when persons who worked goodly Work raceive them reward - and to she are the day when persons who worked sin raceive hardship. 11 and as she are the day when persons who found them reward are made Feeling good - persons who forgot JAH LAW shall stand in the place where them stand. Persons who make liars - who digest books while them said - "Persons who dead won't arise" - them shall sight up Resurrection. 12 At that time this world sinners - who didn't work goodly Work in this world - shall weep on them sin that them worked - because sadness found them without calmin. 13 and all likewise - kind persons who worked goodly Work - them Feeling good joy won't be fulfilled up til Eternity - to them have worked goodly Work when them were in this world. 14 to them have known that them will arise after them dead - and them didn't depart from them Creator LAW. 15 Because them didn't depart from Him LAW - them shall inherit two welfares ~ Him multiplied them seed in this world - and Him honoured them childran. 16 Him bequeathed them the Kingdom of Heaven where shall be found the welfare him swore to them fathers on the time when persons who dead arise - and on the time when rich ones become poor. 17 Persons shall weep who worked sin - who don't believe persons who dead arisin - who don't keep JAH LAW - and who don't think of Arisin Day. 18 At that time them will sight up the tribulation that shall find them and shall have no endin - and where are no calmin nor welfare - and it have the sadness that have no rest nor calmin in them reasonin. 19 and a fire that don't perish and worms that don't sleep shall find them. 20 and in the place where are them flesh are fire - sulphur - whirl wind - frost - hail - sleet ~ all this shall rain over them. 21 to persons who don't believe persons who dead arisin - there are fire of Gehannem on them.

Meqabian II Chapter 16

1 Thou - please think of what are on thy flesh - and thy feet and thy hands nails - and thy head hair - to them proceed quickly on the time thou cut them ~ know Resurrection by this - that thou have a reasonin - and that thou have religion and knowledge. 2 Thy feet and thy hands nails and thy head hair - thou say - "Where do these come from?" ~ aren't it JAH Who prepared it that them might proceed - that thou know arisin that shall be done on thy flesh that aren't on another flesh - that thou might know that thou will arise after thou dead? 3 Because thou misled persons while thou said - "There are no Resurrection of the dead ones" - on the time when dead ones arise thou will raceive thy hardship like unto thou worked sin and iniquity. 4 and as even what thou planted now won't remain refusin that it might grow - whether it be wheat or barley - thou will sight she up on the time the day arrived when thou

raceive thy hardship. 5 and again - the plant thou planted won't say - "I-man won't grow" - and be it a fig wood or a grape vine - it fruit and it leaf won't be changed. 6 If thou plant grapes - it won't be changed that it might be a fig - and if thou plant figs - it won't be changed that it might be grapes - and if thou sow wheat it won't be changed that it might be barley. 7 All - in each of the seeds - in each of it kinds - each of the fruits - each of the woods - each of the leaves - each of the roots - send forth fruit havin raceived Pardon Dew blessin by what are found from JAH - yet if thou sow barley also it won't be changed that it might be wheat. 8 and all likewise - that a grave might produce flesh and soul - she shall produce persons like unto JAH sowed on she ~ the flesh and soul that JAH sowed shall arise bein Inited - yet persons who worked goodly Work won't be changed in persons who worked evil Work - and persons who worked evil Work also won't be changed in persons who worked goodly Work. 9 on the time the hour arrived when a drum are beaten - persons who dead shall arise by the Pardon Dew found from JAH ~ persons who worked goodly Work shall arise in Life Resurrection - and them reward are the Garden where are Feeling good joy that JAH prepared to kind persons - where are no tribulation nor disease - and that are clean ones lodgin where them won't again dead after this. 10 But persons who worked evil Work shall arise a Definite Judgemant arisin - and with Deeyablos who misled them... 11 and with him armies - demons who don't love that even one person might be saved from all 'Adam childran... 12 them shall descend toward Gehannem that were darkness edge - where are tooth grindin and mournin - where are no charity nor pardon - and where are no exits up til Eternity - that are beneath See'ol forever. to them didn't work goodly Work in them Life in this world when them were in them flesh. 13 Because this thing it shall be judged on them on the time when flesh and soul arise bein Inited. 14 Woe to persons who don't believe the flesh and soul arisin whereby JAH show Him miracles abundance together. 15 and all and each one shall raceive him reward like unto him Work and him hands weariness.

Meqabian II Chapter 17

1 A wheat kernel won't grow nor bear fruit unless she were demolished. But if a wheat kernel are demolished she will send roots toward Earth ~ she will send forth leaves ~ there will be buds ~ it will bear fruit. 2 You know that the one wheat kernel will become many kernels. 3 and all likewise - this kernel grow risin up from Water and wind and Earth dew - to wheat cyaan bear fruit without Sun - but Sun are because fire stead. 4 and wind are because a soul stead - and wheat cyaan bear fruit without wind - and the Water give Earth to drink and satta she. 5 and after Earth that are ashes drank Water - she produce roots - and she tips are lofty upward ~ she bear fruit around what JAH blessed she. 6 But a wheat kernel are 'Adam example - in whom lodged a resonatin soul that JAH Created - and likewise a grape wood drink Water and send forth roots - and the thin root kinds drink Water. 7 to Pardon Dew found from JAH give to drink vines tips that were long - and it send the Water upward toward the leaf tips ~ it bud up from the Sun heat - and by JAH Accord it bear fruit. 8 It shall be a goodly fragrance that make a reasonin Feeling good - and on the time them ate it - it shall satta like unto Water that don't make thirsty and grain that don't make hungry - and on the time them immersed it - it will be the cluster blood. 9 and like unto it were told in Psalm sayin - "Grapes make a person reasonin Feeling good" - on the time them drank it - it make a person heart Feeling good - and on the time a person who came loose opened him mouth and drank it - him are drunk ~ him drink and fill in him lungs - and the blood flow toward him heart. 10 As grapes drunkenness totally mislead - and as it deprive him him mind - it make the pit and the cliff like unto a wide meadow - and him don't know obstacles and thorns on him feet and hands. 11 JAH did thus on she fruit and grape wood that Him Name might be praised by persons who believe dead persons arisin and who do Him Accord. 12 in the Kingdom of Heaven Him shall make persons Feeling good who believe persons who dead arisin.

Meqabian II Chapter 18

1 You persons who don't believe persons who dead arisin - around what error you err! and on the time them took you toward the place you don't know - you will regret a useless regrets - and because you didn't believe the arisin that persons who dead shall arise Inited in soul and flesh - and on the time persons cast you toward Gehannem... 2 if you work whether the good or the evil - you will raceive your reward like unto your Work - to you have misled them companions reasonin while you said - "We know that persons who dead - who were dust and ashes - won't arise." 3 As them death have no exit - and as them have no Power to them chastisemant that shall come on them - and as them weren't firm in them tribulation - because this thing them mislead them companions ~ to them have that them might stand in JAH Square. 4 on

the time Him vexed on them in Him wrath them will totally fear ~ because them didn't know that them were Created bringin from not livin toward livin - as them speak JAH LAW without knowin - it shall be judged on them all because them worked evil. 5 Them don't know Gehannem where them will go - to because them were angry and because them were crooked in them Work - them teach to them companions like unto them reasonin thirst measure - and to them are evil ones who teach a crooked thing while them said - "There are no Resurrection of dead ones." 6 At that time them shall know that persons who dead shall arise - and them shall know that it shall be judged on them because them didn't believe the persons who dead arisin that are to all 'Adam childran. 7 to all I are 'Adam childran - and to I have dead because 'Adam - and to death judgemant have found I all from alongside JAH because I father 'Adam error. 8 I will again arise there with I father 'Adam that I might raceive I hardship by I Work that I worked - to the world have been ruled to death by I father 'Adam ignorance. 9 By 'Adam infringin JAH Command - because this thing I raceived hardship ~ I flesh in grave melted like unto wax - and I bodies perished. 10 and Earth drank I marrow ~ I perished and I attractiveness perished in grave - and I flesh were buried in grave - and I beautiful words were buried in Earth. 11 and worms proceeded from I shinin eyes - and I features perished in grave and became dust. 12 Where are youtmons features attractiveness - who were attractive - whose stance were handsome and whose word thing succeeded? How about where are warriors firmness? 13 Where are the kings armies - or how about the nobles lordship? Where are adornin in horses and adornin in silver and gold and adornin in shinin weapons? Didn't it perish? 14 Where are sweet grape drink - and how about food flavour?

Meqabian II Chapter 19

1 O Earth who gathered the nobles and the kings and rich ones and elders and daughters who were attractive and beauties who were attractive - woe arisin from thee-I. 2 O Earth who gathered persons who were warriors - them who have attractiveness - and them who were fine of leg - and them who have reasonin and knowledge - and them whose words have words that were beautiful like unto a hummin harp and like unto a lyre and a violin beat... 3 and them who have a tune that make Feeling good like unto grape drink make Feeling good - and them whose eyes shine like unto a mornin star... 4 and them who sketch what were firm like unto them right hands lift up what are given and withheld and like unto them were - and them whose feet were beautiful to sight up - and them who run like unto rushin wheels - woe arisin from thee-I. 5 O death who separated attractive persons souls from them flesh - woe arisin from thee-I - to thou have been sent by JAH Accord. 6 As thou have gathered many persons whom JAH produced from thee-I and returned toward thee-I - thou Earth - woe arisin from thee-I ~ I were found from thee-I ~ I returned toward thee-I by Accord of JAH ~ I were Feeling good over thee-I by JAH Accord. 7 Thou became a carpet to I corpses ~ I recurred over thee-I - and I were buried within thee-I ~ I ate thy fruit - and thou ate I flesh. 8 and I drank the Water found from thy springs - and thou drank I blood springs ~ I ate the fruit found from thy Earthliness - and thou ate I body flesh. 9 Like unto JAH commanded thee-I to be I food - I ate grain from thy Earthliness that have beautiful dew - and thou raceived I fleh attractiveness and made it dust to thy food like unto JAH commanded thee-I. 10 O death who gathered the nobles and the kings who were powerful - woe arisin from thee-I ~ thou didn't fear arisin from them famousness and them frightenin - like unto JAH Who Created them commanded thee-I ~ o death - woe arisin from thee-I - and thou didn't scorn the sufferah. 11 and thou weren't nice to persons whose features are beautiful - and thou didn't quit powerful ones and warriors ~ thou didn't quit poor nor rich ones - neither kind nor evil ones - neither childran nor elders - neither daughters nor males. 12 Thou didn't quit persons who think a goodly thing and who didn't depart from the LAW - and thou didn't quit them who were like unto animals in them Work - who think a evil thing - who were totally beautiful in them features attractiveness - in them thing flavour and in them words ~ o death - woe arisin from thee-I. 13 Thou didn't quit persons whose words were angry and whose mouths were full of curses ~ thou gathered persons who live in darkness and in light and them souls in thy places ~ o death - woe arisin from thee-I. 14 and Earth gathered the persons flesh who live whether in cave or in Earth - up til a drum are beaten and persons who dead arise. 15 As persons who dead shall arise quickly like unto a eye wink by JAH Command and on a drum bein beaten - persons who worked evil Work shall raceive them hardship in them sin abundance measure that them worked it - and persons who worked goodly Work shall be Feeling good.

Meqabian II Chapter 20

1 and believe I that all I Work that I worked in this world won't remain

nor be hidden on the time I stood before Him fearin and tremblin. 2 and on the time I didn't seize provisions to I path - and on the time I won't have clothes to I bodies... 3 on the time I won't have a staff to I hands nor shoes to I feet... 4 and on the time I won't know the paths where demons take I - whether it be slippery or smooth - or be it dark - and whether it be thorns or nettles - or whether it be a Water depth or a pit depth - believe I that I Work that I worked in this world won't remain nor be hidden. 5 I won't know the demons who take I - and I won't hear them thing. 6 As them are black ones - and as them lead I toward darkness - I don't sight up them faces. 7 and like unto the prophet spoke sayin - "On the time I soul were separated from I flesh - Lord I Lord - Thou know I path - and them hid a trap on that path where I-man went - and I-man sight up returnin toward the right ~ I-man lacked one who know I - and I-man have nothing there whereby I-man will escape" - as them take I toward darkness - I won't sight up them faces. 8 As him know that demons ridicule on him - and as them will lead him toward the path him don't know - him speakin this are because this - and if him return leftward and rightward - there are no person who know him. 9 Him are alone amidst demons - and yet there are none who know him. 10 Angels of Light who are subtle are who are sent toward kind persons that them might raceive righteous ones souls - and might take toward a Light place - toward the Garden - where welfare are found. 11 Demons and Angels of darkness are who are sent that them might raceive them and might take them toward Gehannem that were prepared to him that them might raceive him hardship by them sin that them worked. 12 Woe to sinner persons souls who take them toward destruction - who have no welfare nor rest - nor escapin from the tribulation that found them - nor proceedin from Gehannem up til Eternity. 13 As them have lived firmed up in Qayel Work - and as them have perished by Bele`am iniquity price - and as them have lacked what them will do - woe to sinner persons - to them pretext to raceive interest and presents that in downgression them might take a foreigner money that weren't them money. 14 Them shall raceive them hardship in Gehannem by them sin that them worked.

Meqabian II Chapter 21
1 Where are persons who gather a foreigner money that weren't them hands Work nor them money? 2 to them take a person money for free - and to them shall be gathered without knowin the day when them dead that shall arrive on them - however them quit them money for a foreigner. 3 to like unto them fathers - them are sinners kindreds who worry and seize sinners like unto them whether it be by theft or by robbery - and them childran won't be Feeling good by them fathers money. 4 As them have gathered to them in downgression - and as it are like unto misty urine and like unto the smoke that wind scattar and like unto wiltin grass - and like unto wax that melt arisin from before a fire - as sinners glory shall perish like unto that - there are none whom them fathers money will benefit ~ like unto Daweet spoke sayin - "I-man sight up a sinner man... 5 bein honoured and famed like unto a cordia and like unto a cypress - but on the time I-man returned I-man lacked him ~ I-man searched and didn't find him place" - there are none whom them fathers money will profit nor benefit. 6 Because them gathered a person money in downgression - it seemin to them that them won't dead - like unto persons who wrong them companions won't boast - sinner persons destruction are likewise at one time. 7 You lazy ones - think that you will perish and that your money will perish with you - and if your silver and your gold abound it shall be rusted. 8 and if you birth many childran them shall be to many graves - and if you work many houses them shall be demolished. 9 to you didn't fulfill your Creator JAH Accord - and if you multiply livestock them shall be for your enemies capture - and all the money you seized in your hands won't be found - to it have been what weren't blessed. 10 Whether it be in house or in forest - and be it in wilderness or a pasture place - and be it in grape threshingfloor or in grain threshingfloor - it won't be found. 11 Because you didn't keep JAH Command - as JAH won't save you with all your household from the tribulation - there shall be sadness on you arisin from all your enemies - yet you won't be Feeling good in your childran birthed from your nature. 12 But from Him plenty - Him won't trouble persons who kept Him Order and Him LAW ~ Him give all who begged Him - yet Him bless them childran birthed from them nature and also them land fruit to them. 13 and Him make them rulers on all peoples in them area that them might rule lest them be who are ruled - and Him give them all Him plenty in them pasture place. 14 Him bless to them all them seized in them hand - all them field fruit - and all them livestocks places - and Him make them Feeling good in them childran birthed from them nature. 15 and Him don't diminish them livestocks on them ~ Him save them from all them tribulation and from weariness and illness and destruction - and from them enemy them don't know and from him them know. 16 and Him will dispute to them in Judgemant time - and Him shall save them from a evil thing and from tribulation and from all who dispute them ~ in the first era if a priest lived who work the Tent Work - who keep the LAW and keep the Tent Order and live firmed up in JAH Accord - by the first Order and all the LAW as them would give him the tithe and what were birthed first Beginnin from man up til livestock - Him would save them from all the tribulation. 17 Like unto Mussie commanded Newie child 'Iyasu - there was a country of sanctuary in all them country ~ by not knowin and by knowin up til them judged judgemant on whom them canvicted and to whom them acquitted... 18 if a person lived who killed a soul - him would be measured there that him might be saved. 19 Him told them - "Examine in your reasonins that him have a quarrel with him formerly - and be it by axe or be it by a stone or be it by wood - as it have fallen from him hand by not knowin - if him say "That person on whom it fell dead on mi" - examine and save him ~ if him did it in not knowin make him be saved. 20 But if him do it knowin - him will raceive him hardship like unto him sin - and there are none who will pardon him; but if him kill him in not knowin - as him have done it in not knowin - examine and save him lest him dead. 21 Him worked to them that them might distance from all the sin - yet Mussie would work like unto this to 'Isra'iel childran lest them depart from JAH LAW. 22 Him commanded them that 'Adam childran - who live firmed up in JAH Command from worshippin idols and eatin what dead and lodged and what a sword bloated and cut - and who distance from all evil work like unto him worked to them - that them might work it and might totally distance from all that aren't due. 23 Him commanded them lest them depart from the Command Him worked to them in the Tent example in Heaven - that them might save them bodies and might find them lodgin with them fathers. 24 As them have been birthed from Siet and 'Adam who did JAH Accord - persons who believed in JAH Word and lived firmed up in Him Command will be called kind persons childran. 25 As I are 'Adam childran - as Him have Created I in Him Example and Him Appearance that I might work all goodly Work that make JAH Feeling good - Him won't scorn it. 26 As Him totally won't separate Him friends - if I work goodly Work - I shall inherit the Kingdom of Heaven where are welfare with persons who work goodly Work. 27 Him totally love persons who beg him cleanly - and Him hear them in them prayer - and Him accept the repentance of persons who are disciplined and enter repentance ~ Him give firmness and Power to persons who keep Him Order and Him LAW and Him Command. 28 Persons who did Him Accord shall be Feeling good with Him in Him Kingdom forever - and whether them be persons who preceded or who arose later - them will present praise to Him Beginnin from today up til Eternity. Make glory due to JAH forever - and the secand Meqabyan arrived and were fulfilled.

Meqabyan III

Meqabyan III Chapter 1
1 Kristos shall rejoice Gibts persons - because Him shall come toward them in later era that Him will revenge and destroy Deeyablos - who wronged them who were kindly and innocent - and who misled persons - and who hate him Creator Work. 2 Him shall revenge and destroy him ~ Him shall return him lordship toward wretchedness and bein downbased - to him have been arrogant in him reasonin. 3 Him shall return him lordship toward bein downbased - to him have said - "As mi will enter toward the sea midst - and as mi will proceed toward Heaven - and as mi will sight up depths - and as mi will grasp and seize 'Adam childran like unto bird chicks - who are it who are loftier than mi? 4 Because mi became by them reason that mi might distance them from the straight LAW of JAH - as mi will strengthen on persons who live in this world unless them did JAH Accord - there are none who will depose mi from mi authority" him said. 5 "To mi will be a reason to return them toward a path that were smooth to go toward Gehannem with mi. 6 Persons who loved Him and kept Him LAW hate mi because this thing - but persons who departed from them Lord LAW and who erred will come toward mi and love mi and keep mi oath ~ as mi will make them reasonin evil and change them thoughts lest them return toward them Creator JAH - them will do mi command like unto mi commanded them. 7 and on the time mi showed them this world money - mi will mislead them reasonin from straight LAW - and on the time mi showed them beautiful and attractive daughters - mi will distance them by these from straight LAW. 8 and on the time mi showed them shinin Hindekie jewels and silver and gold - mi will distance them by this also from straight LAW that them might return toward mi Work. 9 and on the time mi showed them thin clothes and red silk and white silk - and linens and white silk - mi will distance them by this also from straight LAW - and mi will return them toward mi thoughts ~ on the time mi

multiplied money and livestocks like unto sand and showed them - by this also mi will return them toward mi Work. ¹⁰ and on the time mi showed them jealousy done in arrogance because daughters and because anger and quarrels - by all this mi will return them toward mi Work. ¹¹ and on the time mi showed them signs - mi will lodge in them companions reasonin - and mi will lodge a sign thing that were to each of the ras selves in them reasonin - and mi showed them words signs and misled them. ¹² and to persons in whom mi lodged mi lodgin - mi will show them signs - and be it in stars gait - or be it in cloud proceedin or in fire flickerin - or be it in beasts and birds cries - as them are mi lodgins - mi will lodge signs in them reasonin on them by all this. ¹³ Them will speak and give signs to them companions - and like unto those them naysayers told them - mi will precede and be a sign to them. ¹⁴ Mi will do them words signs to them - that persons who examined them might be misled - and that them might give a wage to magicians - and that them might tell to them companions sayin - 'There are no savants like unto so-an-so and so-an-so to whom it are done like unto them spoke - and who know prophecy - and who separate good and evil - and to whom all are like unto them spoke - and to whom it are done like unto them word.' ¹⁵ Mi will be Feeling good on the time them spoke this - that persons who perish and err by mi might totally abound and that 'Adam childran might perish - to JAH have downbased mi from mi rank because them father 'Adam - on mi sayin 'Mi won't bow to 'Adam who are downbased to mi.' ¹⁶ and mi will take toward destruction all him childran who live firmed up in mi command ~ mi have a Oath from JAH Who Created mi - that all persons whom mi misled might descend toward Gehannem with mi. ¹⁷ and on the time Him multiplied Him anger on mi - and on the time Him commanded that them might bind and cast mi toward Gehannem - on the time mi Creator commanded sayin thus - mi interceded with mi Lord ~ mi interceded before Him while mi said - 'As Thou have vexed on mi - and as Thou have admonished mi by Thy chastisemant - and as Thou have chastised mi by Thy wrath - Lord mi Lord - adjourn mi that mi might speak one thing before Thee-I.' ¹⁸ and mi Lord answered to mi sayin - Speak - I-man will hear thee ~ at that time mi began mi plea toward Him sayin - 'After mi were downbased from mi rank - make the persons whom mi misled be like unto mi in Gehannem where mi will raceive tribulation. ¹⁹ and make them be to Thy Lordship who refused mi - who didn't err by mi - who didn't keep mi command - that them might do Thy Command and might fulfill Thy Accord and might keep Thy Word - on the time them didn't err by mi like unto mi misled them havin refused like unto mi taught them - and on the time Thou loved mi - make them take the crown Thou gave to mi. ²⁰ Give them the crown of the authorities called Satans who were sent with mi ~ seat them on mi throne on Thy Right that were a wilderness from mi and mi hosts. ²¹ and make them praise Thee-I like unto Thou loved - and make them be like unto mi hosts and like unto mi ~ because Thou hated mi and loved them who were Created from ashes and Earth - as mi authority have perished - and as them authority have been lofty - make them praise Thee-I like unto Thou loved.' ²² Mi Lord answered to mi sayin - As thou have misled them while them sight up and while them heard - if thou misled them without them lovin I Order - make them be to thee like unto thy accord and like unto thy word. ²³ If them quit the Books Word and I Command and came toward thee - and if thou misled them while them destruction also saddened mi - make them raceive tribulation in Gehannem like unto thee Him told mi. ²⁴ You will raceive tribulation in Gehannem up til the Eternity - yet you will have no exits from Gehannem up til the Eternity - to them whom thou misled nor to thee.

Meqabyan III Chapter 2

¹ But I-man shall bequeath thy throne in lordship to them whom it failed thee to mislead - like unto I slave 'Iyob ~ JAH Who rule all said - I-man will give the Kingdom of Heaven to persons whom it failed thee to mislead. ² and mi provoke on 'Adam childran in all ~ if it were possible to mi to mislead them - mi won't quit them that them might firm up in goodly Work ~ to mi provoke on all 'Adam childran - and mi sweeten this world Feeling good joy to them. ³ Be it by lovin drink and food and clothes - or by lovin things - or by withholdin and givin... ⁴ or be it by lovin to hear and sight up - or be it by lovin to caress and go - or be it by multiplyin arrogance and things - or be it by lovin dreams and slumber... ⁵ or be it by multiplyin drunkenness and drink - or be it by multiplyin insults and anger - be it by speakin games and useless things... ⁶ or be it by quarrels and by backbitin them companion - or be it by sightin up this world daughters who were attractive - be it by smellin perfumes fragrance that mislead them... ⁷ mi hate them by all this lest them able to be saved ~ mi distance them from JAH LAW that them might enter with mi toward the destruction whereby mi were downbased from mi rank." ⁸ and the prophet told him - "Thou who destroy persons - perish ~ on the time thou departed from JAH LAW

and committed crime in thy reasonin firmness and thy arrogance - and by saddenin thy Creator and not worshippin thy Creator in thy reasonin firmness - will thou thus be arrogant on JAH Creation? ⁹ on the time thy Creator vexed on thee - Him downbased thee from thy rank because thy evil Work ~ why do thou take 'Adam toward sin - him whom him Creator Created from Earth - whom Him made like unto Him loved - and whom Him placed to Him praise?" him told him. ¹⁰ "On the time thou - who are subtle and were Created from wind and fire - were arrogant in sayin 'Mi are the Creator'... ¹¹ on the time thou boasted - as JAH have sight up thy evil Work and thou have denied JAH with thy hosts - Him Created 'Adam who will praise because thy stead - that him might praise Him Name without diminishin. ¹² As thou have made thy ras self prouder than all Angels hosts who are like unto thee - because thy arrogance JAH Created 'Adam with him childran that them might praise JAH Name because the praise that thou praise with thy hosts whom Him scorned. ¹³ and because this thing JAH destroyed thee separatin from all Angels chiefs like unto thee - and thy hosts Created in one counsel with thee - and thou - you proceeded and erred from JAH praise because your reasonin arrogance and because your reasonin firmness - and you were arrogant on your Creator - that aren't on another. ¹⁴ Because this thing Him Created 'Adam from Earth that Him might be praised by downbased persons - and Him gave him a Command and Law sayin Don't eat lest him eat from fig fruit. ¹⁵ and Him I-pointed him on all the Creation Him Created ~ Him notified him sayin - Don't eat from one fig fruit that bring death - lest thou bring death on thy ras self - yet eat fruit from all the woods amidst the Garden. ¹⁶ and on the time thou heard this Word - thou lodged perfidy in him arisin from the thing thou spoke in thy tongue to Hiewan who were found from 'Adam side bone. ¹⁷ Thou misled 'Adam who were clean - in firm perfidy that thou might make him a Law demolisher like unto thee. ¹⁸ on the time thou misled Hiewan - who were Created bein like unto a innocent dove and who don't know thy malice - thou made she betray by by thing that succeeded and thy crooked word - and after thou misled that Hiewan who were Created beforehand - she also went and misled JAH Creation 'Adam who were Created from Earth beforehand. ¹⁹ and thou made him betray a disturbance that aren't by thy arrogance - and thou made him to deny that him might deny him Creator Word - and thou destroyed 'Adam in thy arrogance. ²⁰ and in thy malice thou distanced him from him Creator Love - and by thy reason thou sent him way from the Garden where Feeling good joy are - and by thy hindrance thou made him quit the Garden food. ²¹ to Beginnin from Antiquity thou have quarreled with the innocent Creation 'Adam that thou might lower him toward See'ol where thou will raceive hardship - and that thou might send him way from the Love that brought him and Created him from not livin toward true livin - and by thy false thing thou made him thirst a drink from the Garden. ²² and when him are Earthly - Him made him a subtle Angel who totally praise him Creator in him flesh and him soul and him reasonin. ²³ and Him Created many thoughts to him - like unto harps praise in each of them styles.

Meqabyan III Chapter 3

¹ But Him Created one thought to thee - that thou might totally praise while thou were sent toward where thy Creator sent thee. ² But to 'Adam were given five thoughts that were evil and five thoughts that were goodly - ten thoughts. ³ and again him have many thoughts like unto sea waves - and like unto a whirl wind that scattar dust liftin up from Earth - and like unto the sea waves that shake - and arisin from him unnumbered thoughts abundance in him heart like unto unnumbered rain drops - 'Adam thoughts are like unto that. ⁴ But thy thought are one ~ as thou aren't fleshly - thou have no other thought. ⁵ But thou lodged in snake reasonin ~ in evil perfidy thou destroyed 'Adam who were one limb - and Hiewan heard the snake thing - and havin heard - she did like unto she commanded she. ⁶ After she ate a fig fruit - she came and misled JAH first Creation 'Adam - and she brought death on him and on she childran because she infringed she Creator Command. ⁷ Them proceeded from the Garden to JAH by Him true Judgemant ~ Him calmed them in the land where them were sent by them childran birthed from them nature and by them crops found from Earth - yet Him didn't distance them from the Garden quarrelin. ⁸ and on the time thou expelled them straight from the Garden - that them might plant plants and childran to be calmed and to renew them reasonin in the Earth fruit that Earth prepared from she Earthliness - and that them might be calmed by Earth fruit and the Garden fruit that JAH gave them... ⁹ JAH gave them woods more verdant than the Garden woods - and Hiewan and 'Adam - whom thou sent way from the Garden on them eatin it - were totally calmed from sadness. ¹⁰ As JAH know to calm Him Creation - them reasonins are calmed because them childran and because the crops found from Earth. ¹¹ As them have been sent toward

this world that grow nettles and thorns - them firm up them reasonins in Water and grain.

Meqabyan III Chapter 4

¹ The Lord have that Him might ransom 'Adam - and Him shall shame thee ~ Him will save a sheep from a wolf mouth ('Adam from Deeyablos). ² However thou will go toward Gehannem seizin with thee the persons whom thou ruled. ³ Persons who kept them Creator JAH LAW shall be Feeling good with them Creator JAH Who hid them from evil Work that Him might make them Him fortune - and that them might praise Him with honoured Angels who didn't infringe them Creator JAH LAW like unto thee. ⁴ But JAH - Who chose and gave thee more than all Angels like unto thee that thou might praise Him with Him servant Angels - withheld from thee a lofty throne in thy arrogance. ⁵ But thou became famous and were called one who love godhood - and thy hosts were called demons. ⁶ But persons who loved JAH shall be Him kindreds like unto honoured Angels - and the Surafiel and Keerubiel who praise Him streach forth wings and praise without slackness. ⁷ But in thy arrogance and thy laziness thou destroyed thy praise that thou might praise Him everytime with thy host and thy kindreds Created in thy features. ⁸ Lest the praise of JAH - Who Created thee makin a tenth tribe - be diminished on the time thou forgot the praise of JAH Who Created thee - it havin seemed to thee that it aren't posssible to Him to Create a Creation like unto thee - and lest the praise of JAH - Who Created thee - be diminished on the time thou were separated from thy bredren Inity - Him Created 'Adam because thy stead. ⁹ But in thy reasonin arrogance thou neglected the praise of JAH Who Created thee - and Him vexed on thee ~ Him ridiculed thee - and Him bound and banished thee in Gehannem with thy hosts also. ¹⁰ Him brought Soil from Earth with Him glorified Hands - and addin fire and Water and wind - Him Created 'Adam in Him Example and Him Features. ¹¹ Him I-pointed him on all the Creation Him Created in Him Authority - that Him praise might be filled by the praise thou would praise Him ~ 'Adam praise became one with Angels praise - and them praise were level. ¹² But in thy collar of reasonin firmness and thy arrogance thou were downbased from thy rank - and havin departed from JAH Lordship - Who Created thee - thou destroyed thy ras self. ¹³ Know that Him praise weren't diminished - to JAH have Created 'Adam who praised Him in him reasonin counsel lest Him JAH-ness praise be diminished. ¹⁴ to Him know all before it are done - and Him knew thee before Him Created thee that thou will demolish Him Command ~ as there are a counsel hidden alongside Him before Him Created the world - on the time thou denied Him - Him Created Him slave 'Adam in Him Features and Him Example. ¹⁵ Like unto Selomon spoke sayin - 'Before hills were Created and before the world succeeded bein Created - and before winds that are Earth grounations were Created... ¹⁶ and before Him firmed up hills and mountains grounations - and before this world Work firmed up - and before moon and Sun light shone - before eras and stars caretakin were known... ¹⁷ and before daylight and night alternated - and before the sea were delineated by sand - before all the Created Creation were Created... ¹⁸ and before all sight up today were sight up - before all the names called today were called - Him Created I Selomon' - Angels like unto you and thou and Him slave 'Adam were in JAH Reasonin. ¹⁹ Him Created 'Adam that Him glorified Name might be praised on the time thou mutinied - and that Him might be praised by Him downbased slave 'Adam who were Created from Earth on the time thou were arrogant. ²⁰ to bein in Heaven JAH hear poor ones plea - and Him love downbased persons praise. ²¹ Him love to save havin lodged in persons who fear Him - yet as Him don't love horse Power - and as Him don't step meanin to the lap of a concubine - JAH shall ignore arrogant ones thing. ²² and them shall weep while them cried because them sin that them worked. ²³ It failed them to plead in repentance. ²⁴ But 'Adam who were Created from Earth returned in repentance while him totally wept before JAH because him sin. ²⁵ But in thy collar of reasonin firmness and thy heart arrogance thou didn't know Love Work and thou didn't know repentance ~ it failed thee to plead before thy Creator JAH in repentance and mournin and sadness. ²⁶ But that 'Adam who are ashes and Earth returned toward repentance in mournin and sadness - and him returned toward humbleness and Love Work. ²⁷ But thou didn't downbase thy reasonin and thy ras self to JAH Who Created thee. ²⁸ As to 'Adam - him downbased him ras self and pleaded on the iniquity him wronged ~ him weren't proud. ²⁹ As thou have totally produced crime - it were found from thee - yet it aren't him who produced that error ~ in thy arrogance thou took him with thee toward thy destruction. ³⁰ Before him Created you both - as Him have known you that you were sinners - and as Him have known your Works - Him know that this that were done were in thy heart arrogance. ³¹ But Him returned that 'Adam - who were without arrogance or malice - in repentance mournin and sadness. ³² to a person who wrong

and don't plead in repentance have multiplied him iniquity more than him earlier iniquity - but in thy heart arrogance it failed thee to plead in repentance - but a person who plead and weep enterin repentance before Him Creator JAH... ³³ him entered repentance to true - and him found Work whereby him will be saved that him might fear him Lord Heart - and him pleaded before him Creator - to him have pleaded before Him in bowin and much repentance - and arisin from the earlier tribulation the Lord shall lighten him sin to him lest Him vex on Him slave - and Him will forgive him him former sin. ³⁴ If him didn't return toward him former sin and if him did this - this are perfect repentance ~ 'Adam didn't forget to think of him Creator nor to implore him Creator JAH in repentance. ³⁵ and thou - plea in repentance toward thy Creator JAH - and don't wrong them because them were flesh and blood - to JAH Who Created them know them weakness - and don't wrong the persons Him Created by Him Authority. ³⁶ and after them soul were separated from them flesh - them flesh shall be dust up til the day that JAH love.

Meqabyan III Chapter 5

¹ Know JAH WHo Created thee-I ~ as JAH have Created thee-I in Him Features and Him Example when thou are Earth - don't forget JAH Who firmed thee-I up and saved thee-I and Whom 'Isra'iel glorified ~ Him placed thee-I in Garden that thou might be Feeling good and might dig Earth. ² on the time thou demolished Him Command - Him sent thee way from the Garden toward this world that Him cursed because thee - that grow nettles and thorns. ³ to thou are Earth - and to she are Earth - to thou are dust - and to she are dust - to thou are Soil - and to she are Soil - to thou are fed the grain found from she - and to thou will return toward she - to thou will be Soil up til Him love that Him might raise thee - and to Him shall examine thee the sin thou worked and all the iniquity. ⁴ Know what thou will answer Him at that time ~ think of the good and evil thou worked in this world ~ examine whether the evil would abound or whether the good would abound ~ try. ⁵ If thou work a goodly thing - it are a goodly thing to thee-I that thou might be Feeling good on the day when persons who dead will arise. ⁶ But if thou work evil Work - woe to thee - to thou will raceive thy hardship like unto thy hands Work and like unto thy reasonin evil ~ to if thou work a evil thing on thy companion and if thou didn't fear JAH - thou will raceive thy hardship. ⁷ and if thou betray thy companion and if thou call JAH Name and swear in lie - as thou will raceive thy hardship like unto thy Work - woe to thee. ⁸ and thou tell thy false thing to thy companion simulatin Truth - but thou know that thou spoke a lie. ⁹ and thou persuade the persons with thee thy false thing simulatin Truth - and thou multiply false things that weren't Truth - and thou will raceive thy hardship like unto thy sin ~ thou deny thy companion while thou tell thy companion 'mi will give thee' what thou won't give him. ¹⁰ and on the time thou said 'Mi will give' in thy pure reasonin - demons make application to thee like unto dogs - and them make thee forget all - and if thou withhold or if thou love that thou might give - them don't know the person to whom them gather - yet as Him have said - Them shall fatten - this world money appetise thee that thou might fatten the money that won't benefit thee and that thou won't eat. ¹¹ and again - as Him have said - 'Adam liar childran make a balance false ~ as to them - them go from robbery toward robbery - this world money appetise thee. ¹² O persons - don't make hope in distortin scales and balances - and in stealin a person money - and in makin a person money one in downgression - and in infringin your companions money - and in stealin him field - in all the lies you do to your ras selves profit that aren't to your companions. ¹³ If you do this you will raceive your hardship like unto your Work. ¹⁴ O persons - be fed by your hands Work that were straight - yet don't desire robbery ~ don't love that you might totally rob and eat a person money without justice by what aren't due. ¹⁵ and if you eat it - it won't satta you ~ on the time you dead you will quit it to another - yet even if you fatten - it won't benefit you. ¹⁶ and if your money abound - don't distort your reasonins ~ as sinner persons money are like unto the smoke that proceed from a griddle and the wind take it - better than sinner persons money are the little money them accumulated in Truth.

Meqabyan III Chapter 6

¹ Think of the day when you will dead ~ on the time your souls were separated from your flesh - and on the time you quit your money to another - and on the time you went on the path you don't know - think of the tribulation that shall come on you. ² and the demons that will raceive you are evil - and them features are ugly - and them are frightenin in them splendour - and them won't hear your words - and you won't hear them words. ³ and because you didn't do your Creator JAH Accord - them won't hear you in your plea on the time you begged them ~ because this thing them will totally frighten you. ⁴ But persons

who fulfilled JAH Accord have no fear - to demons fear them. But demons shall ridicule sinner persons souls on them. 5 But kind persons souls shall be Feeling good on Angels in Feeling good joy - to them shall totally make them Feeling good because them scorned this world - but angels who are evil shall raceive sinner persons souls. 6 Pardon Angels shall raceive kind persons and righteous ones souls - to them are sent from JAH that them might calm righteous ones souls ~ as Angels that were evil are sent from Deeyablos that them might ridicule on sinner persons souls - demons shall raceive sinner persons souls. 7 Sinner persons - woe to you ~ weep to your ras selves before the day when you dead arrive on you ~ on the time you reach toward JAH... 8 enter repentance in your era that are there before your era pass - that you might live in Feeling goodness and joy without tribulation nor disease - yet as after you dead your era won't return that passed - weep. 9 Lest it be on you toward a vain accord that distance from JAH - in your firm criticism make lovin to be lavished and food and Feeling good joy not be found in you ~ as a body that are sated without measure won't think of JAH Name - Deeyablos wealth shall lodge on it - yet as the Hola Spirit won't lodge in it - make lovin the Feeling good joy not be found in you. 10 Like unto Mussie spoke - Mussie havin said - "Ya`iqob ate and were sated and fattened and tall and wide - and JAH Who Created him were separated from him. 11 and him lifestyle distanced from JAH" - as a body that were sated without measure nor moderation won't think of JAH Name - make lovin Feeling good joy not be found alongside you ~ as belly satiety without measure are bein like unto a boar and like unto a wanderin horse - make drinkin and eatin without measure and adultery not be found in you. 12 But a person who eat in measure shall live firmed up in JAH Support - and him shall live firmed up like unto the horizon and like unto a tower that have a stone fence; a person who forgot JAH LAW shall flee without one livin who chase him. 13 A kind person shall live in bein raspected like unto a lion. 14 But persons who don't love JAH won't keep Him LAW - and them reasonins aren't straight. 15 and JAH shall bring sadness and alarm on them when them are in this world - and bein seized in tremblin and fright - and bein seized in the tribulations without number by them money bein snatched - bein bound by them hands in chains from them masters hands... 16 lest them be who rested from the tribulation - and lest them lifestyle be in Feeling good joy - lest them rest when them are in alarmin tribulations that are on each of them ras selves - Him shall bring sadness and alarm on them.

Meqabyan III Chapter 7

1 But like unto Daweet spoke sayin - "I-man believed in JAH ~ I-man won't fear havin said - 'What would a person make I?'" - there are no fright and alarm on persons who believed in JAH. 2 and again like unto him spoke sayin - "If warriors surround I - I-man believed in Him ~ I-man begged JAH one thing ~ I-man seek that" - persons who believed in Him have no fright on them ~ a person who believed in Him shall live in Life forever - and him won't fear arisin from a evil thing. 3 Who are a person who shamed believin in JAH? how about who ignored Him to a desire? 4 As Him have said - I-man love him who loved I - and I-man shall honour him who glorified I ~ I-man shall keep him who returned toward I in repentance - who are a person who shamed believin in Him? 5 Judge Truth and save the widow body ~ save them that JAH might save you from all that oppose you in evil thing ~ keep them ~ as kind persons childran are honoured - them are given makin a profit - and yet Him shall save your childran after you - to them won't be troubled to grain.

Meqabyan III Chapter 8

1 'Iyob believed in JAH ~ as him didn't neglect to praise him Creator JAH - JAH saved him from all the tribulation that 'Adam childran enemy Deeyablos brought on him ~ him said - "JAH gave ~ JAH withheld ~ it happened like unto JAH loved on I - and make JAH Name be praised by all on Earth and in Heaven" - yet as him didn't sadden him reasonin - JAH saved him. 2 and on the time JAH sight up 'Iyob that him heart were cleansed from sin - Him raceived him in much honour. 3 and Him gave him money that abounded more than him money that preceded ~ to him have totally indured him tribulation - and Him cured him from him wounds because him indurin all the tribulation that arrived on him. 4 and if you like unto him indure the tribulation arisin from demons sent toward you - you will be admired. 5 Indure the tribulation ~ that JAH might be to you a fortress Refuge from persons who hate you - and that Him might be a fortress Refuge to your childran childran and to your childran after you - don't sadden your reasonins arisin from the tribulation that came on you ~ believe in Him - and Him shall be a fortress Refuge to you. 6 Beg Him ~ Him will hear you ~ make hope - and Him will forgive you ~ beg Him - and Him will be a Father to you; 7 Think of Merdokyos and 'Astier - Yodeet and

Giediewon and Deebora and Bariq and Yoftahie and Somson... 8 and other persons like unto them who were disciplined to believe in JAH and whose enemies didn't defeat them. 9 to JAH are True - and to Him don't favour havin sight up a face - but persons raceived hardship who love that them might work sin on them ras selves ~ all persons who fear Him and keep Him LAW shall keep bodies - and Him shall give them bein I-loved and honour. 10 Him shall make them Feeling good in them proceedin and them enterin - in them Life and them death - and in them arisin and sittin ~ to Him save - and Him seclude. 11 to Him sadden - and Him pardon. 12 to Him make poor - and Him honour ~ Him make wretched - and as Him honour - Him make them Feeling good.

Meqabyan III Chapter 9

1 and whether it be what are in Heaven - or whether it be what are on Earth - and be it either subtle or stout - everything n all Him money live bein firmed up in Him Order. 2 There are nothing that departed from JAH LAW and Him Order - Who Created all the world ~ be it a vulture track that fly in Heaven - Him command toward it destination where Him loved. 3 and Him command a Earth snake path that live in cave toward where Him loved - and a boat path that go on sea - apart from only JAH there are none who know it path. 4 and apart from only JAH - there are none who know the path where a soul go on the time it were separated from it flesh - be it a righteous or a sinner soul. 5 Who know where it will turn - that it would turn in wilderness or on a mountain? or that it would fly like unto a bird - that it would be like unto Heaven dew that alight on a mountain... 6 or that it would be like unto deep wind - or that it would be like unto lightnin that straighten up it path... 7 or that it would be like unto stars that shine amidst the deep - or that it would be like unto sand on a sea shore that are piled amidst the deep... 8 or that it would be like unto a horizon stone that firmed up on the sea deep edge - or like unto a wood that give she beautiful fruit that grew by a Water spout... 9 or that it would be that I likened unto the reed that heat of the Sun burnt - and that wind lift and take toward another place where it didn't grow - and whose trace aren't found... 10 or that it would be like unto misty urine whose trace aren't found - who know JAH Work? who are Him counsellors? how about with whom did Him counsel? 11 As JAH Thoughts are hidden from persons - who will examine and know Him Work? 12 As Him have Created Earth on Water - and as Him have firmed she up without stakes - there are none who examine and know JAH Counsel or Him Wisdom - and Him Created Heaven in Him perfect Wisdom and firmed it up in winds - and Him streached forth a lofty cosmos like unto a tent. 13 Him commanded clouds that them might rain rain on Earth - and Him grow grass - and Him grow fruits without number to be food to persons - that I might believe in JAH and be Feeling good in Inity. 14 JAH are Who give 'Adam childran the Feeling good joy and all the fatness and all the satiety ~ JAH are Who give that them might satta and praise JAH Who gave them fruit from Earth... 15 and Who dressed them in beautiful robes - Who gave them all the I-loved plenty - the Feeling goodness and the joy that are given to persons who fulfill JAH Accord. 16 Him give bein I-loved and honour in the house Him prepared and in the Kingdom of Heaven to them fathers who keep JAH LAW. 17 Him give bein I-loved and honour in the place Him prepared and in the Kingdom of Heaven to them fathers who lived firmed up in Him Worship and Him LAW - and who didn't depart from Him LAW - whom Him famed and raised that them might keep Him Order and Him LAW - and I-man sight up what JAH do to Him friends in this world by weakenin them enemies and by keepin them bodies. 18 I-man sight up that Him give them all them begged Him and that Him fulfill them accord to them ~ don't depart from JAH - and fulfill JAH Accord. 19 Don't depart from Him Command and Him LAW - lest Him vex on you and lest Him destroy you at one time - and lest Him vex and whip you in the tribulation from where you lived formerly - lest you depart from your fathers Order where you were formerly - and lest your lodgin be in Gehannem where are no exits up til the Eternity. 20 Keep your Creator JAH LAW when your soul are separated from your flesh that Him might do goodly Work to you on the time you stood before JAH. 21 to Earth and Heaven Kingdoms are to Him - and to Kingdom and capability are to Him - and to bein nice and pardonin are only to Him. 22 As Him make rich and Him make poor - as Him make wretched and Him honour - keep JAH LAW. 23 and Daweet spoke because Him while him said - "Man seem vain - and him era pass like unto a shadow." 24 Him spoke because Him sayin - "But Lord - Thou live forever - and Thy Name Invocation are to a child childran." 25 and again him said - "Thy Kingdom are all the world Kingdom - and Thy Rulership are to a child childran" ~ Thou returned a kingdom to Daweet bringin from Sa'ol. 26 But there are none who will I-point Thee-I ~ there are none who can dismiss ~ Thou sight up all - yet there are none who can sight up Thee-I. 27 and Thy kingdom won't perish forever to a child childran ~ there are none who will rule

Him - but Him rule all ~ Him sight up all - but there are none who sight Him up. 28 As Him have Created man in Him Features and in Him example that them might praise Him and might know Him Worship in straight reasonin without doubt - Him examine and know what kidneys smoked up and what a reasonin transported. 29 Yet them bow to stone - to wood - and to silver and gold that a person hand worked. 30 and them sacrifice to them up til them sacrifice smoke proceed toward Heaven - that them sin might live firmed up before JAH - but yet them refused to worship JAH Who Created them ~ Him shall downcuse them because all them sin that them worked in worshippin them idols. 31 Them learned bowin to idols and all stained Work that aren't due - naysayin by stars - sorcery - worshippin idols - evil accord - and all the Work that JAH don't love - yet them didn't keep JAH Command that them learned. 32 As them didn't love to worship JAH that them might save them bodies from sin and iniquity by Him servants the Angels and by money that them praise before JAH - them work all this in lackin goodly Work. 33 and on the time them all arose together from the graves where them were buried and where them bodies perished - them souls shall stand empty before JAH - and them souls lived in the Kingdom of Heaven prepared to kind persons. 34 But sinner persons souls shall live in Gehannem - and on the time graves were opened - persons who dead shall arise - and souls shall return toward the flesh that them were separated formerly. 35 Like unto them were bithed in them nakedness from them mother belly - them shall stand in them nakedness before JAH - and them sins that them worked Beginnin from them infancy up til that time shall be revealed. 36 Them shall raceive them sin hardship on them bodies - and whether them little or much sin - them shall raceive them hardship like unto them sin.

Meqabyan III Chapter 10

1 to the blood of soul found from JAH shall lodge in them like unto it lodged in them formerly - and if you didn't believe persons who dead arisin - hear that Creations shall arise in rainy season without bein birthed from them mother nor father. 2 and Him command them formerly by Him Word that them dead. 3 and them flesh bein demolished and rotten and again renewed - them shall arise like unto Him loved. 4 and again on the time rain alit and on the time it sated Earth - them shall live havin arisin like unto them were Created formerly. 5 As them who are everlivin in bloodly soul and who live in this world and them whom Water produce have been Created - Him havin said make them be Created - and as JAH Authority lodge on the Water - she give them a bloodly soul by Him Authority and by Him Word. 6 As them are Created by Him Authority and by Him Word without a father nor mother - thou blind of reasonin who say "Persons who dead won't arise" - if thou have knowledge or Wisdom - how will thou say persons who dead won't arise by them Creator JAH Word? 7 As persons who dead - who were ashes and dust in grave - shall arise by JAH Word - as to thou - enter repentance and return toward thy religion. 8 Like unto Him Word spoke formerly - them shall arise by the Pardon Dew found from JAH - and that Word shall turn all the world and arouse the persons who dead like unto Him loved. 9 and know that thou will arise and stand before Him - and make it not seem to thee in thy reasonin dullness that thou will remain in grave. 10 It aren't thus ~ thou will arise and raceive thy hardship like unto the Work measure that thou worked - whether it be goodly or evil - yet make it not seem to thee that thou will remain - to this Day are the day when them will raceive hardship. 11 and in Resurrection time thou will raceive thy hardship by all thy sin that thou worked ~ thou will finish thy sin hardship that were written Beginnin from thy infancy up til that time - and thou have no reason that thou will pretext on thy sin like unto this world Work that thou might deny thy sin. 12 Like unto thou make thy false word truth before thee - and like unto thou make the lie thing that thou spoke truth - thou have no reason that thou will pretext like unto this world Work. 13 Because it were that she know on thee all thy evil Work thou worked - and because it were that she will reveal on thee before she Creator JAH - as JAH Word shall lodge on thee and speak on thee - thou have no reason on what thou pretext. 14 Thou will shame there because thy sin that thou worked ~ it are that thou might be thanked with persons who are thanke on them beautiful Work - yet lest thou shame before man and Angels on the day when Judgemant are judged - quickly enter repentance in this world before thou arrive toward there. 15 Persons who praise JAH with Angels shall raceive them reward from them Creator without shamin - and them shall be Feeling good in the Kingdom of Heaven - however unless thou worked goodly Work when thou are in thy flesh in Life - thou have no fortune with righteous ones. 16 As thou weren't prepared when thou have knowledge and when thou have this world where thou enter repentance - there shall be a useless regret on thee - and to thou didn't give a morsel to the hungry when thou have money. 17 and to thou didn't clothe the naked when thou have clothes - and to thou didn't save the wronged when thou have Authority. 18 to thou didn't teach the sinner person when thou have knowledge - that him might return and enter repentance - and that JAH might forgive him him sin that him formerly worked in ignorance - and to thou didn't fight with demons who quarrel with thee when thou have Power that thou able to prevail. 19 and to thou didn't fast nor pray when thou have firmness that thou might weaken thy infancy Power that are on flesh - and that thou might subject thy ras self to Rightness that aren't favorin on flesh... 20 that aren't favorin Feeling good joy when it are in this world in beautiful drink and sweet food - and that aren't adornin in thin clothes and silver and gold... 21 and as thou didn't fast nor pray when thou have firmness that thou might subject thy ras self to Rightness that aren't adornin in honoured Hindekie jewels called emerald and phazyon - there shall be a useless regret on thee ~ this aren't a person ornamant that are due. 22 As to a person ornamant - it are purity - Wisdom - knowledge - lovin one another by what are due without envyin nor jealousy nor doubtin nor quarrels ~ while thou loved thy companion like unto thy ras self... 23 and without thy doin a evil thing on a person who did a evil thing on thee-I - it are lovin one another by what are due - that thou might enter toward the Kingdom of Heaven that are given to person who indured the tribulation - that Him might give thee the honoured Kingdom of Heaven and thy reward on makin hope in the Kingdom of Heaven in Resurrection time with honoured persons in knowledge and Wisdom. 24 and don't say "After we dead we won't arise" - to Deeyablos cut off hope of persons who speak and think this lest them be saved in Resurrection time ~ them will know that them have hardship on them on the time Advent arrived on them ~ in Resurrection time persons will be totally sad who worked sin in not knowin that Him might think of them sin on them - to them didn't believe in Him that them will arise on that Day. 25 Because this thing them shall be reproached like unto them Work evil measure that them worked in this world - and them shall sight up the Resurrection that them denied whereby them will arise together in flesh. 26 Them shall weep at that time because them didn't work goodly Work ~ it would have been better to them if them wept in this world if it are possible to them lest them be who weep in Gehannem. 27 If I didn't weep in this world by I accord - demons will make I weep without I accord in Gehannem ~ if I didn't enter repentance in this world - I prepare worthless and useless cries and mournin in Gehannem. 28 Prepare goodly Work - that you might cross from death toward Life - and that you might go from this passin world toward the Kingdom of Heaven - and that you might sight up the Kingdom of Heaven Light that surpass light in this world. 29 Refuse Feeling good joy that are in this world - that thou might be Feeling good without measure in the Kingdom of Heaven in Feeling good joy that aren't fulfilled Beginnin from today up til the Eternity with believe persons who dead arisin. Make Glory and praise due JAH forever - and the third book that speak the Meqabyans thing were fulfilled.

Prayer Books

Prayer of Manasses

The Greek and Russian Orthodox Churches accept the Prayer of Manasseh as Deuterocanonical Scripture. It is included as an appendix to the Latin Vulgate Bible. King of Judah when imprisoned in Babylon. **King of Judah, When He Was Held Captive in Babylon**

Prayer of Manasses Chapter 1

1 O LORD Almighty in heaven, God of our fathers Abraham, Isaac, and Jacob, and of their righteous offspring, 2 you who have made heaven and earth, with all their order, 3 who have bound the sea by the word of your commandment, who have shut up the deep, and sealed it by your terrible and glorious name, 4 whom all things fear, yes, tremble before your power, 5 for the majesty of your glory can't be borne, and the anger of your threatening toward sinners is unbearable. 6 Your merciful promise is unmeasurable and unsearchable, 7 for you are the Lord Most High, of great compassion, patient and abundant in mercy, and relent at human suffering. 8 You, O Lord, according to your great goodness have promised repentance and forgiveness to those who have sinned against you. Of your infinite mercies, you have appointed repentance to sinners, that they may be saved. You therefore, O Lord, who are the God of the just, have not appointed repentance to the just, to Abraham, Isaac, and Jacob, which have not sinned against you, but you have appointed repentance to me, a sinner. 9 For I have sinned more than the number of the sands of the sea. My transgressions are multiplied, O Lord, my transgressions are multiplied, and I am not worthy to behold

and see the height of heaven for the multitude of my iniquities. ¹⁰ I am bowed down with many iron bands, so that I can't lift up my head by reason of my sins, neither have I any relief; for I have provoked your wrath, and done that which is evil before you: I didn't do your will, neither did I keep your commandments. I have set up abominations and have multiplied detestable things. ¹¹ Now therefore I bow the knee of my heart, asking you for grace. ¹² I have sinned, O Lord, I have sinned, and I acknowledge my iniquities; ¹³ but, I humbly ask you, forgive me, O Lord, forgive me, and please don't destroy me with my iniquities. Don't be angry with me forever, by reserving evil for me. Don't condemn me into the lower parts of the earth. For you, O Lord, are the God of those who repent. ¹⁴ In me you will show all your goodness, for you will save me, even though I am unworthy, according to your great mercy. ¹⁵ Then I will praise you forever all the days of my life; for all the army of heaven sings your praise, and yours is the glory forever and ever. Amen.

SCAN THE QR CODE

AND ACCESS YOUR

PRIVATE AREA

Conclusion

Throughout this journey into the Ethiopian Bible, I have had the opportunity to explore one of the oldest and most complete spiritual heritages of Christianity. The Ethiopian Bible, with its 88 books, including canonical, deuterocanonical, and apocryphal texts, offers a perspective on the Christian faith that is both unique and vibrant. Translated into Ge'ez and preserved through centuries of tradition, it represents not just a collection of sacred scriptures, but also a reflection of the identity and spirituality of the Ethiopian people.

I chose to include texts such as the Books of Enoch, Jubilees, and Meqabyan, which are not found in Western biblical canons, because they deeply enrich the understanding of the biblical message. These texts show us how Ethiopia, one of the first nations to adopt Christianity, developed a unique tradition that deserves to be known and appreciated. Their inclusion in this Bible is a testament to the Ethiopian people's living and dynamic relationship with the Word of God, passing it down through the centuries with dedication and faith.

The Ethiopian Bible is not just a collection of books, but a symbol of strength, resilience, and unity. It has offered hope and support to Ethiopians during adversity, serving as a spiritual and cultural guide in moments of great challenge. It is tangible proof that faith sustains the soul and can also shape a nation, strengthening it through the trials of history.

By reading this Bible, I hope believers and curious minds alike may discover the beauty and depth of a Christian tradition that extends beyond Western boundaries, revealing new dimensions of faith and revelation. The Ethiopian Bible invites us to reflect not only on the past but also on how the Word of God continues to speak to each of us today through the many traditions that preserve it.

Edward Jones

If you have problems accessing the restricted area contact email support:
edwardjona2@gmail.com

Made in the USA
Monee, IL
28 March 2025

c99ee695-230f-4154-975d-82b0393c0f19R01